Encyclopedia of the

Consumer Movement

Encyclopedia of the
Consumer Movement

Stephen Brobeck
Editor

Robert N. Mayer
Robert O. Herrmann
Associate Editors

ABC-CLIO
Santa Barbara, California
Denver, Colorado
Oxford, England

Library of Congress Cataloging-in-Publication Data

Encyclopedia of the consumer movement / Stephen Brobeck, editor : Robert N. Mayer, Robert O. Herrmann, associate editors
p. cm.
Includes bibliographical references and index.
1. Consumer protection—Encyclopedias. I. Brobeck, Stephen. II. Mayer, Robert N. III. Herrmann, Robert O.
HC79.C63E53 1997 381.3'2'03—dc21 97-41345

ISBN 0-87436-987-8 (alk. paper)

03 02 01 00 99 10 9 8 7 6 5 4 3 2 (cloth)

ABC-CLIO, Inc.
130 Cremona Drive, P.O. Box 1911
Santa Barbara, California 93116-1911

This book is printed on acid-free paper ♾.
Manufactured in the United States of America

Contents

List of Entries, Alphabetical

List of Entries, by Subject

Advisory Board

Contributors

Madeleine Adamson
National Representative
Association of Community Organizations for Reform Now
Association of Community Organizations for Reform Now

Jason B. Adkins
Executive Director
Center for Insurance Research
Energy Cooperatives

Alan R. Andreasen
Professor, School of Business
Georgetown University
Low-Income Consumers

Erma B. Angevine
Board Member
National Consumers League
Consumer Leagues; Federal Consumer Advisory Bodies; National Consumers League; Rural Electric Cooperatives

Allan Asher
Deputy Chairperson
Australian Competition and Consumer Commission
Australian Consumer Movement

Alexander Auzan
President
Inter-Republican Confederation of Consumer Societies
Russia and the Commonwealth of Independent States, Consumer Movement in

Rosella Bannister
Director, National Institute for Consumer Education
Eastern Michigan University
Consumer Education; U.S. Office of Consumers' Education

Larry H. Blanchard
Vice President, Communications and Public Relations
CUNA Mutual Group
Credit Unions

Doug Blanke
Director of Consumer Policy
Minnesota Attorney General's Office
State Attorneys General

Michele Bloch
Chair, Tobacco Control and Prevention Subcommittee
American Medical Women's Association
Tobacco Control and Prevention

Kai Blomqvist
Swedish Society for Cooperative Studies
Swedish Consumer Movement

David Bollier
Independent Journalist
Nader, Ralph; Public Citizen

Thierry Bourgoignie
Professor, Centre de Droit de la Consommation
Université Catholique de Louvain
Belgian Consumer Movement

Stephen Brobeck
Executive Director
Consumer Federation of America
Action for Children's Television; Advocacy, Consumer; Coalitions; Consumer Federation of America; Consumer Interest; Consumers International; Ethnic Minorities as Consumers; Fund-Raising; Labor Movement; Peterson, Esther; Regulators, Consumer Advocates as; Research on the Consumer Movement; State and Local Consumer Organizations; Warne, Colston E.

James L. Brown
Associate Professor, Consumer Affairs
University of Wisconsin–Milwaukee
Electronic Funds Transfer Protections; Lemon Laws

W. Keith Bryant
Professor, Department of Consumer Economics and Housing
Cornell University
Consumer Economics/Studies

Mark E. Budnitz
Professor, School of Law
Georgia State University
Checking Account Protections

John R. Burton
Associate Professor, Family and Consumer Studies
University of Utah
Warranty Protections

Holly Cherico
Director of Public Relations and Communications
Council of Better Business Bureaus, Inc.
Better Business Bureaus

Judith Cohart
Director of Education
National Foundation for Consumer Credit
National Coalition for Consumer Education

Rebecca Arnold Cohen
Executive Vice President
Citizen Advocacy Center
Corporate Consumer Advisory Panels

Jean Constantine-Davis
Legal Counsel for the Elderly
American Association of Retired Persons
Mortgage Loan Protections

Kevin Cook
Former Global Publications Officer
Consumers International
Latin American Consumer Movement

Mark N. Cooper
Director of Research
Consumer Federation of America
Telephone Regulation

Theodore O. Cron
Adjunct Professor, National Center for Communication Studies
The George Washington University
Journalism, Consumer

Brenda Cude
Professor, Department of Agricultural and Consumer Economics
University of Illinois at Urbana-Champaign
Packaging Protections

Gerri Detweiler
Former Executive Director
Bankcard Holders of America
Bankcard Holders of America

Tom Devine
Legal Director
Government Accountability Project
Whistleblowers

Clarence M. Ditlow
Executive Director
Center for Auto Safety
Center for Auto Safety

Stanley W. Dreyer
Vice President, Business Development
National Cooperative Bank
National Cooperative Bank

Sandra Eberle
Former Chief, Implementation Branch, Indoor Air Division
Environmental Protection Agency
Indoor Air Quality Protections

Herschel T. Elkins
Senior Assistant Attorney General
State of California Department of Justice
Auto Repair and Service Protections

Maureen P. English
Assistant Director, Division of Consumer and Community Affairs
Board of Governors of the Federal Reserve System
Federal Reserve's Consumer and Community Affairs Programs

Sandra B. Eskin
Public Policy Consultant
Center for Science in the Public Interest
Medical Devices

Lesley Anne Fair
Attorney, Division of Advertising Practices
Federal Trade Commission
Infomercial Regulation

Josie Fernandez
Director, Regional Office for Asia and the Pacific
Consumers International
Asian-Pacific Consumer Movement

Steven Ferrey
Professor of Law
Suffolk University School of Law
Energy Conservation

Mary Ellen R. Fise
General Counsel
Consumer Federation of America
Consumer Product Safety Commission; Cosmetic Safety; Product Hazards

Allen J. Fishbein
General Counsel
Center for Community Change
Community Reinvestment

Carol Tucker Foreman
President
Foreman & Heidepriem, Inc.
U.S. Department of Agriculture

Melia Franklin
Former Editor/Media Coordinator
Toward Utility Rate Normalization
Toward Utility Rate Normalization (TURN)

Monroe Friedman
Professor, Psychology Department
Eastern Michigan University
Boycotts, Consumer

Marlene Futterman
Executive Director
Direct Selling Education Foundation
Direct Selling Protections

Louis Garcia
Executive Director
Society of Consumer Affairs Professionals in Business
Society of Consumer Affairs Professionals in Business

E. Thomas Garman
Professor, Department of Housing, Interior Design, and Resource Management
Virginia Polytechnic Institute and State University
Antitrust Protections; Presidents and the Consumer Movement; Self-Regulation

Loren V. Geistfeld
Professor, College of Human Ecology
The Ohio State University
Research on Consumer Issues

Robert Gellman
Privacy and Information Policy Consultant
Privacy Protections

Jacqueline S. Gillan
Vice President
Advocates for Highway and Auto Safety
National Highway Traffic Safety Administration

Carole Glade
Executive Director
National Coalition for Consumer Education
National Coalition for Consumer Education

Alexander Grant
Former Associate Commissioner, Office of Consumer Affairs
U.S. Food and Drug Administration
Food and Drug Administration

Barbara B. Gregg
Former Director
Montgomery County Office of Consumer Affairs
National Association of Consumer Agency Administrators; State and Local Consumer Affairs Offices

Suzanne Grunert-Beckmann
Professor, Department of Marketing
Copenhagen Business School
Women as Consumers

Pedro-José Bueso Guillén
Lecturer of Consumer Law
University of Zaragoza
Spanish Consumer Movement

Joshua C. Gwitira (deceased)
Former Director, Regional Office for Africa
Consumers International
African Consumer Movement

Lawrence E. Haller, Ph.D.
Food Cooperatives

Jean M. Halloran
Director, Consumer Policy Institute
Consumers Union
United Nations Consumer Protections

Visa Heinonen
Researcher
Finnish National Consumer Research Center
Finnish Consumer Movement

Robert O. Herrmann
Professor, Department of Agricultural Economics and Rural Sociology
The Pennsylvania State University
Public Opinion; Research on Consumer Issues; U.S. Consumer Movement: History and Dynamics

Cornish F. Hitchcock
Attorney at Law
Aviation Safety

Larry Hobart
Former Executive Director
American Public Power Association
Public Power

Ann Hoyt
Professor, College of Agricultural and Life Sciences
University of Wisconsin-Madison
Cooperatives, Consumer

H. Keith Hunt
Professor, Graduate School of Management
Brigham Young University
Consumer Satisfaction/Dissatisfaction

J. Robert Hunter
Director of Insurance
Consumer Federation of America
Insurance Regulation; National Insurance Consumer Organization

Cathy Hurwit
Legislative Director
Citizen Action
Citizen Action

Drew Hyman
Professor, Department of Agricultural Economics and Rural Sociology
The Pennsylvania State University
Citizen Utility Boards

Mitsuaki Imai
Professor of Economics
Kinjo Gakuin University
Japanese Consumer Movement

Michael F. Jacobson
Executive Director
Center for Science in the Public Interest
Center for Science in the Public Interest

Arthur Jaeger
Vice President for Communications
Public Voice for Food and Health Policy
Public Voice for Food and Health Policy

Jørgen Juul Jensen
Lecturer, College of Nutrition and Home Economics
Suhr's Seminarium
Danish Consumer Movement

Katherine O'Doherty Jensen
Lecturer, College of Nutrition and Home Economics
Suhr's Seminarium
Danish Consumer Movement

Robert W. Johnson
Senior Research Associate, Credit Research Center
Purdue University
Credit Protections

Rhoda H. Karpatkin
President
Consumers Union
Consumers Union

Robert R. Kerton
Professor, Department of Economics
University of Waterloo
Canadian Consumer Movement

Jean D. Kinsey
Professor, Department of Applied Economics
University of Minnesota
Food Purchase Protections

Joop Koopman
Former Director, Consumer and Market Policy
Ministry of Economic Affairs
Dutch Consumer Movement

Kenneth S. Kovack
Former Legislative Representative
United Steelworkers of America
Labor Movement

Robert M. Krughoff
President
Center for the Study of Services
Center for the Study of Services

Eberhard Kuhlmann
Professor of Marketing
Technical University of Berlin
German Consumer Movement

John E. Kushman
Professor, Consumer Economics
University of Delaware
Licensure

Anne-Christine Lacoste
Centre de Droit de la Consommation
Université Catholique de Louvain
Belgian Consumer Movement

Jinkook Lee
Assistant Professor, Retail and Consumer Science
University of Tennessee
South Korean Consumer Movement

Stewart M. Lee
Professor Emeritus, Business, Accounting and Management Department
Geneva College
American Council on Consumer Interests

Hans Peter Lehofer
Department Head
Federal Ministry of Health and Consumer Protection
Austrian Consumer Movement

Rodney E. Leonard
Executive Director
Community Nutrition Institute
Community Nutrition Institute

Mary Levy
Director, Publications and Media Division
Consumer Information Center
Consumer Information Center

Kathy Li
Director
National Consumer Resource Center
Immigrants as Consumers

Erich Linke
Principal Administrator
OECD Competition and Consumer Policy Division
OECD Committee on Consumer Policy

Lila Lomeli
Co-Founder
Asociacion Mexicana de Estudios Para La Defensa del Consumidor
Mexican Consumer Movement

Ann K. Lower
Associate Director
Consumer Federation of America
Natural Gas Regulation

Milton D. Lower, Ph.D.
Natural Gas Regulation

Joan Lucco, Ph.D.
U.S. Office of Consumer Affairs

Robert J. McEwen (deceased)
Former Professor Emeritus, Department of Economics
Boston College
Conference of Consumer Organizations (COCO); Resale Price Maintenance

Alastair Macgeorge
Consumer Consultant, London
Albanian Consumer Movement; Baltic Republics, Consumer Movement in the; Bulgarian Consumer Movement; Central and Eastern Europe, Consumer Movements in; Czech Consumer Movement; Hungarian Consumer Movement; Polish Consumer Movement; Romanian Consumer Movement; Slovakian Consumer Movement; Slovenian Consumer Movement; Yugoslavian Consumer Movement

Leta M. Mach
Director of Communications
National Cooperative Business Association
National Cooperative Business Association

M. Carole Macklin
Associate Professor, Department of Marketing
University of Cincinnati
Children as a Vulnerable Market

Lothar Maier
Professor of Home Economics
Technical University of Hamburg
European Union, Consumer Policy in

Robert N. Mayer
Professor, Family and Consumer Studies
The University of Utah
Coalitions; Consumer Interest; Initiatives and Referenda; U.S. Consumer Movement: History and Dynamics

E. Scott Maynes
Professor Emeritus, Department of Consumer Economics and Housing
Cornell University
Consumer Problems in Market Economies

Carol B. Meeks
Professor, Department of Housing and Consumer Economics
The University of Georgia
Housing Cooperatives

Edmund Mierzwinski
Consumer Program Director
U.S. PIRG
Public Interest Research Groups

Jeremy Mitchell
Director
International Consumer Policy Bureau
United Kingdom's Consumer Movement

Robin E. Mockenhaupt
State Operations Consultant
American Association of Retired Persons
Health Care Protections

Marilyn Moon
Senior Fellow, Health Policy Center
The Urban Institute
Older Consumers

Anne Morin
Legal Counsel
Institut National de la Consommation
French Consumer Movement

Steven A. Morrison
Professor, Department of Economics
Northeastern University
Airline Deregulation

Richard L. D. Morse
Professor Emeritus, Family Economics
Kansas State University
Savings Protections

James F. Mosher
Research Fellow
Marin Institute for the Prevention of Alcohol and Other Drug Problems
Alcohol Problems and the Consumer Movement

Jim Murray
Director
Bureau Européen des Unions de Consommateurs
Bureau Européen des Unions de Consommateurs

Dina Musante
Regional Office for Latin America and the Caribbean
Consumers International
Latin American Consumer Movement

Mark V. Nadel
Associate Director, Income Security
U.S. General Accounting Office
Congress and Consumer Protection

Diana Neidle
Health and Safety Coordinator
Consumer Federation of America
Drinking Water Safety

Lee Norrgard
Investigative Analyst, Consumer Affairs
American Association of Retired Persons
Funeral Protections

Willard P. Ogburn
Executive Director
National Consumer Law Center
Legal Aid; National Consumer Law Center

Brian O'Neill
President
Insurance Institute for Highway Safety
Highway Safety

Ed Perkins
Editor
Consumer Reports Travel Letter
Travelers' Rights

Michael Pertschuk
Director
The Advocacy Institute
The Advocacy Institute

Esther Peterson
Former Special Assistant to the President for Consumer Affairs
United Nations Consumer Protections

R. David Pittle
Technical Director
Consumers Union
Product Testing

Irwin A. Popowsky
Consumer Advocate
Pennsylvania Office of Consumer Advocate
Electricity Regulation

Ivan L. Preston
Professor, School of Journalism and Mass Communication
University of Wisconsin-Madison
Advertising Regulation

Kee-Choon Rhee
Professor of Consumer and Child Studies
Seoul National University
South Korean Consumer Movement

Lee Richardson
Professor, Department of Marketing
University of Baltimore
Postal Regulation; Telemarketing Regulation

Paul Roark
Former Attorney
Federal Trade Commission
Real Estate Brokerage Protections

Shirley L. Rooker
President
Call For Action
Call For Action

Barbara Roper
Director of Investor Protection
Consumer Federation of America
Investor Protections

Jerome G. Rose
Professor Emeritus, Department of Urban Planning
Rutgers University
Tenant Protections

Edwin S. Rothschild
Public Affairs Director
Citizen Action
Citizen Action

David Russell
Chief Executive
Consumers' Institute of New Zealand
New Zealand Consumer Movement

Tim Saasta
Director of Communication
Center for Community Change
Center for Community Change

Manuel-Angel López Sánchez
Professor of Commercial Law
University of Burgos
Spanish Consumer Movement

Ernest L. Sarason, Jr.
Assistant Attorney General
Massachusetts Office of the Attorney General
Home Improvement Protections

Jane Schuchardt
National Program Leader, Family Economics
Cooperative State Research, Education, and Extension Service
Cooperative Extension System

George Schwartz (deceased)
Former Associate Professor, Department of Marketing
University of Massachusetts
U.S. Consumer Protection Agency

Peter Schwartz
Professor, Department of Textiles and Apparel
Cornell University
Textile Product Flammability

Teresa M. Schwartz
Former Professor of Law
The George Washington University
Products Liability Law

Andrew Jay Schwartzman
Executive Director
Media Access Project
Broadcast Protections

Ben Senauer
Professor, Department of Agricultural and Applied Economics
University of Minnesota
Food Safety

Jonathan Sheldon
Staff Attorney
National Consumer Law Center
Deceptive, Unfair, and Unconscionable Sales Practices

Linda Sherry
Editorial Director
Consumer Action
Consumer Action

Pamela Chan Wong Shui
Chief Executive
Hong Kong Consumer Council
Hong Kong Consumer Movement

Norman I. Silber
Associate Professor, School of Law
Hofstra University
Law, Consumer

Mark Silbergeld
Co-Director
Consumers Union-Washington Office
Federal Trade Commission

Nina F. Simon
Legal Counsel for the Elderly
American Association of Retired Persons
Mortgage Loan Protections

Samuel A. Simon
President
Issue Dynamics Inc.
Telecommunications Research and Action Center

Gurjeet Singh
Senior Lecturer in Laws
Guru Nanak Dev University Regional Center
Indian Consumer Movement

Katrinka Smith Sloan
Manager, Consumer Affairs
American Association of Retired Persons
American Association of Retired Persons; Older Consumers

Peter L. Spencer
Editor
Consumers' Research
Consumers' Research

William A. Spratley
William A. Spratley & Associates
State Utility Consumer Advocates

Michael E. Staten
Director, Credit Research Center
Purdue University
National Foundation for Consumer Credit

Bradley C. Stillman
Former Telecommunications Policy Director
Consumer Federation of America
Cable Television Regulation

Eivind Stø
Director of Social Science Research
National Institute for Consumer Research
Norwegian Consumer Movement

Karen Peltz Strauss
Former Supervising Attorney
The National Center for Law and Deafness
Disabilities, Consumers with

A. Charlene Sullivan
Associate Professor, Krannert Graduate School of Management
Purdue University
Bankruptcy

Roger Swagler
Professor, Department of Housing and Consumer Economics
The University of Georgia
Consumer Rights; Consumerism, Modern; Rent-to-Own Protections

David A. Swankin
Director
Consumer H-E-L-P
Product Standards; Public Representation

Louise G. Trubek
University of Wisconsin Law School
Center for Public Representation
Center for Public Representation; Public Interest Law Practice; Transnational Consumer Protection

James S. Turner
Consumer Attorney
Swankin and Turner
Food and Drug Administration

W. Kip Viscusi
John F. Cogan Jr. Professor of Law and Economics
Harvard University
Economic Criticisms of the Consumer Movement

Michael L. Walden
Professor, Department of Agricultural and Resource Economics
North Carolina State University
Price Controls

David Walls
Professor, Department of Sociology
Sonoma State University
Community Organizations

Richard W. Waterman
Professor, Department of Political Science
University of New Mexico
Presidents and the Consumer Movement

Besse S. Weiner and **Judy Canahuati Weiner**
Consumers Education and Protective Association

Elizabeth M. Whelan
President
American Council on Science and Health
American Council on Science and Health

Richard Widdows
Professor, Consumer Sciences and Textiles
University of North Carolina-Greensboro
Disputes and Dispute Resolution

William L. Wilkie
Nathe Professor of Marketing
University of Notre Dame
Information Dissemination

Clifford Winston
Senior Fellow, Economic Studies Program
The Brookings Institution
Airline Deregulation

Jing Jian Xiao
Assistant Professor, College of Human Science and Service
University of Rhode Island
Chinese Consumer Movement

Cathleen D. Zick
Professor, Department of Family and Consumer Studies
University of Utah
Deregulation, Economic

Preface

The consumer movement has been a powerful force both in the United States and around the world. Particularly in the past several decades, consumer activists and others seeking to advance consumer interests have created stable institutions, successfully advocated numerous consumer protections, and strongly influenced public opinion. In regard to the last, perhaps no impact of the movement has been greater than fostering the development of what some have called "consumer consciousness"—an awareness among buyers that they have interests distinct from sellers and have enforceable rights in transactions with these vendors. In brief, the consumer movement has influenced both institutions and culture in ways that are likely to endure for many years to come.

This reference work summarizes what we know about the consumer movement. In a historical framework, it treats movement-related institutions, leaders, activities, and impacts, with particular attention to the laws and regulations that purport to protect consumers. The work focuses disproportionately on the United States because the movement there has been much larger and more active than those in other countries. Nevertheless, about one-fifth of the encyclopedia's entries treat consumer movements in nations or regions outside the United States.

The following process was used to select entries and authors. The three editors recruited several dozen advisors who, as academics or practitioners, have researched or participated in the movement for many years. We then compiled an initial list of topics for entries, which we asked the advisors to review. Based on their comments, we revised the list and, with their assistance and that of other experts, identified possible authors for each topic.

There are seven types of topics—general, consumer populations, consumer movement activities, government and consumer organizations, consumer leaders, consumer protections, and consumer movements in other countries and regions. Most of the nine entries of a general nature—such as Consumer Problems in Market Economies, Economic Deregulation, Consumer Satisfaction/Dissatisfaction, Public Opinion, and Economic Criticisms of the Consumer Movement—help define the economic and psychological context in which the consumer movement has operated. Other entries of this type—such as U.S. Consumer Movement: History and Dynamics, Consumerism, and Consumer Rights—consider general characteristics of the movement and its history.

The seven entries on consumer populations treat subsets of the population with special consumer needs or problems. The groups include children, women, ethnic minorities, immigrants, the elderly, and the poor. These entries focus most attention on the unique problems faced by each group and on efforts to mitigate these problems.

Twenty entries supply information about consumer activities or functions. Most of these activities—such as advocacy, litigation, education, information dissemination, research, product testing, journalism, licensing, dispute resolution, standard setting, and self-regulation—are each associated with different types of consumer institutions.

Sixty-six entries treat a specific institution or type of institution. Some of these institutions are governmental bodies—ranging from the U.S. Congress to state and local protection agencies. But most are nonprofit agencies. The latter include national, state, and local advocacy organizations; research or education organizations; consumer cooperative groups; and business or labor organizations. All of these groups achieved some degree of influence and visibility over a period of at least ten years.

Nearly all consumer leaders are discussed in the entries on those organizations with which these individuals are most closely associated. However, additional coverage of three individuals was deemed necessary. There are separate entries on Ralph Nader, Esther Peterson, and Colston Warne because of their great influence within the consumer movement. Although their influence was exercised initially within the United States, each of these individuals affected movement developments in other parts of the world as well. There is also an entry on consumer advocates who became government regulators.

Fifty-one entries treat consumer protections related to different types of products and sales practices. In almost all cases, the consumer movement played a role in the development of these protections. Some of these entries focus on the safety of products such as motor vehicles, food, cosmetics, medical devices, drugs, alcohol, and cigarettes. Other entries review financial protections associated with a broad array of goods (such as automobiles and food) and services. In relation to the latter, for example, there are several entries each on banking, insurance, and utility services. There are also entries on protections against deceptive and unfair marketing practices associated with packaging, advertising, infomercials, door-to-door sales, telemarketing, and direct mail. In addition, there are entries on protections related to post-purchase experiences of purchasers (e.g., warranties and consumer bankruptcy).

Many of the forty-one entries that treat different aspects of the global consumer movement, especially movements in countries or regions outside the United States, provide unique and previously unavailable information. The entries on Latin America, Africa, Eastern and Central Europe, and the Asian-Pacific region in particular contain information found in no published sources easily accessible to those outside these areas. Other related entries treat transnational consumer protections, United Nations' consumer protections, and the only international consumer group, Consumers International.

The 198 entries are arranged alphabetically. To facilitate their location, alternative titles for some entries are also listed alphabetically with a cross-reference. For example, for two titles without entries—Motor Vehicle Safety and Automobile Safety—there is a cross-reference to the entry on Highway Safety. A detailed index can also be used to locate not only entries but also specific information within entries.

Most entries consist of between 1,000 and 5,000 words. Most entries exceeding 1,500 words carry subheadings. At the end of most entries, there are cross-references to other entries that contain related information. There are also one to three readings that supply not only additional information about the topic but also, in many cases, extensive bibliographic information.

The chief limitation of the encyclopedia is related to the limitations of the literature on the consumer movement. The purpose of most scholarly sourcebooks of this type is to summarize existing research on a general subject. While many topics related to the consumer movement have been thoroughly researched, many others have not. Organizations in particular have been inadequately studied. For many of these groups, someone closely associated with the organization was recruited to prepare the related entry. This practice raises the question of bias. Most importantly, would authors who worked for organizations be tempted to emphasize the positive and omit the negative?

While many of the entries on individual organizations undoubtedly contain some bias, the editors took several steps to minimize it. In the first place, we tried to select authors who had been extensively educated and therefore might be expected to adhere to scholarly norms of objectivity and balance. Second, we developed criteria for development of the entries on organizations that specified what types of information should be included. Third, each of the editors carefully reviewed the content of each of these entries; and in many cases, other experts also evaluated these pieces. Fourth, most of the additional readings for these entries were selected by the editors. We took great pains to select sources, even when only newspaper or magazine articles were available, that wrote objectively of the organizations.

Even though the bias of self-interested authors can only be minimized, and never entirely eliminated, there is also a significant related benefit: most of these contributors prepared entries that contain important information and analysis that has never before been published. As a result, several dozen entries represent the most authoritative treatment of their topics. Accordingly, this encyclopedia not only summarizes existing knowledge; it also significantly advances our understanding of the consumer movement in the United States and throughout the world.

Acknowledgments

Many persons made important contributions to this book. It is a pleasure to acknowledge them.

My most fortunate decision was to invite Robert N. Mayer and Robert O. Herrmann to serve as associate editors. Happily they accepted, and the three of us worked closely at each stage of the planning and preparation of the reference work. Together we selected the topics and authors, recruited these authors, edited all manuscripts, and dealt with many other issues. Rob deserves special recognition for recruiting the authors of all entries on consumer movements outside the United States, then undertaking the first editing of manuscripts by authors for whom English was frequently not a first language.

The editors are most grateful to authors who, for no monetary compensation, conscientiously prepared manuscripts and worked constructively with us on revisions. We also appreciate the time spent by members of the Advisory Board in helping guide our selection of topics and authors.

I am greatly indebted to Consumer Federation of America staffers who provided essential assistance in the preparation of the encyclopedia. Miguel Carpio deserves a special commendation for creating and maintaining virtually all related computer databases as well as preparing correspondence to contributors. He received able assistance from Matt Gordon. Milena Carpio handled the copying of several manuscript drafts and their mailing to authors. My longtime executive assistant, Lydia Grogan, facilitated communications to authors and among editors. CFA Associate Director Ann Lower not only supervised the performance of these administrative tasks but also worked with the publisher on the format of the manuscript.

I am grateful to Stewart M. Lee for passing my name on to the publisher and to Rolf Janke, editorial director of ABC-CLIO, for agreeing to publish the encyclopedia. It was an especially great pleasure to work with Richard Bass, whose skillful and conscientious editing significantly improved the quality of the manuscript.

Finally, I wish to thank my wife, Susan, for her understanding and support.

— Stephen Brobeck

A

ACORN

See Association of Community Organizations for Reform Now.

Action for Children's Television

Action for Children's Television (ACT) was a national nonprofit advocacy organization operating between 1968 and 1992 that worked to encourage diversity in children's television and to eliminate commercial abuses targeted to children. Founded and led by Peggy Charren, the organization increased public awareness of these issues and initiated several related reforms.

ACT was organized by Charren in her living room in suburban Boston. Distressed by the commercialism in children's programming, she and three other mothers of preschoolers decided to form an organization to improve the quality and variety of this programming. Quickly, the group expanded to about thirty concerned parents. Its first target was sales pitches on "Romper Room" programs for related products.

These activists created a 501(c)(3) nonprofit organization controlled by a board of directors. During ACT's existence, its budget ranged from about $150,000 to $450,000 annually. These funds supported a paid staff that ranged between four and twenty persons. Hundreds of college interns, more than 100 volunteers, 25,000 contributing members, and 150 national associations also supported the organization.

ACT owed its success mainly to Charren. Her background as a staffer at an independent New York television station, manager of a print and frame shop in Providence, and director of a local creative arts council in Newton, Massachusetts, did not prepare her in obvious ways to lead a highly visible national organization, yet she was largely responsible for ACT's prominence and influence. By the early 1990s, she had written several books and had received several honorary degrees and other major awards. She serves as a visiting scholar in education at Harvard University's Graduate School of Education and is on a first-name basis with many of the nation's political and media leaders.

ACT based its efforts to improve children's television on its interpretation of the Communications Act of 1934's public service requirement. The group understood this requirement to mean that broadcasters bear a legal responsibility to provide programming for youngsters that enlightens as well as entertains and to maintain practices that do not exploit the child audience. The organization opposed censorship, preferring instead to increase choice and diversity in programming. But it considered the overcommercialization of children's media "particularly offensive." Not surprisingly, then, it strongly supported the children's programming on public broadcasting stations, including such shows as "Mister Rogers' Neighborhood," "Sesame Street," and "Wonderworks."

The organization's chief strategies were petitioning federal regulatory agencies, advocating congressional legislation, and filing lawsuits. In 1970, for example, ACT petitioned the

Federal Communications Commission (FCC) to require daily programming for children. Four years later, in response to ACT's petition, the FCC established minimum guidelines on the amount of children's programming and set forth specific advertising policies. That same year, the National Association of Broadcasters incorporated into its television code guidelines to reduce the amount of commercial time on children's programs.

In 1984, the FCC reversed itself by eliminating all quantitative commercial guidelines for television broadcasting. Two years later, ACT petitioned the U.S. Court of Appeals, District of Columbia Circuit, for a judgment to determine whether the FCC acted arbitrarily and without adequate explanation in eliminating its policy on commercialization of children's television programming. In 1987, the court ruled in favor of ACT, ordering the FCC to review its 1984 decision.

The lengthiest campaign conducted by ACT, however, was persuading Congress to pass legislation increasing choices in children's programming. In 1985, Representative Timothy Wirth (D-CO) and Senator Frank Lautenberg (D-NJ) introduced legislation known as the Children's Television Education Act. This legislation, and similar bills introduced in the next Congress, failed to pass. In 1988, both the House and the Senate passed similar legislation, but it was pocket-vetoed by President Ronald Reagan. Finally, after leadership by Representative Edward Markey (D-MA), in 1990 the Children's Television Act was approved by both the House and Senate, becoming law without President George Bush's signature. This act requires each television station to air programs specifically designed to serve the educational needs of children and to limit commercials on children's shows. Less than a year later, the FCC released guidelines for the implementation of this law.

With the passage of this act, the leaders of ACT decided that the organization had served its function and should be disbanded. When ACT ceased to exist in early 1992, it left behind a legacy of congressional, regulatory, and court decisions that had improved the quality of television watched by children. Perhaps just as significantly, by generating frequent news coverage of children's television issues, it had raised public awareness of the quality and effects of children's programs and their commercials.

— Stephen Brobeck

See also

Broadcast Protections; Children as a Vulnerable Market; Telecommunications Research and Action Center.

Readings

Cole, Barry, and Mal Oettinger (1978). *Reluctant Regulators: The FCC and the Broadcast Audience.* Reading, MA: Addison-Wesley Publishing Co.

"A Harsh Critic of Kids' TV" (1978). *Business Week.* (May 29): 52.

Advertising Regulation

Much but not all deceptive advertising is illegal. This characteristic of the law reflects the fact that, as regulators eliminate deceptions, advertisers create new ones. Thus, while the field has changed rapidly, the degree to which consumers may safely rely on sellers' claims has, over time, changed less.

The earliest American law of selling derived from the English concept of caveat emptor (let the buyer beware), which made buyer-seller interactions virtually lawless. False claims were allowed, and reliance on them was disallowed; consumers could rely only on their own independent determinations of truth. Failure to do such examining constituted negligence that left buyers wholly responsible for their losses.

Ignored by caveat emptor were such factors as speakers' deliberate falsities and listeners' difficulties in determining facts while lacking equivalent knowledge and experience. The only condition permitting reliance was when the object of sale was out of sight, in a distant location, or in transit. But when the item was available, consumers' only recourse was to examine it despite obvious impediments in their ability to do so successfully, such as their inability to evaluate technically complex products.

Eventually, society and government realized that buyers were unequal to sellers in transactions that the law had long insisted were made by parties negotiating on equal terms. The solution was to create remedies, such as the prohibiting of false selling claims, to try to eliminate instances where justifiable buyer reliance resulted in harm.

Creation of the Federal Trade Commission (FTC) in 1914 stands as the first major regulatory act to provide such remedies. The FTC and its counterpart agencies in the states, most of which follow its procedures, continue today as the principal sources of advertising regulation. The commission's first advertising case was in 1916 under its original jurisdiction to prohibit "unfair competition." Additional statutory power now enables it to prohibit "unfair or deceptive acts or practices in or affecting commerce."

The FTC defines deceptive acts as those having a potential to deceive, whether or not they have actually deceived. Intent by advertisers to create the potential is irrelevant; they may create it unknowingly and still be in violation. However, to be deceptive, a claim must be material regarding the object of sale, that is, capable of affecting consumers' purchasing decisions about it. And the claim must be factual, that is, capable of being true or false.

The basic evidence of deceptiveness, then, is a finding that consumers acting reasonably in their encounter with an advertisement, other promotional communication, or other selling activity view it as conveying a factual claim about the object of sale that is false, and that they are likely to be misled by that claim and so potentially to be harmed by it. That formulation has greatly improved consumer protection. Instead of consumers having to rely solely on their own experience to detect deceptiveness, regulators possessing far more knowledge are able to remove false claims from the market and, in some cases, to return money or otherwise restore losses.

This power has proved to be a significant deterrent. Blatantly false claims, such as quackery touting patent medicines as curing many ailments, became easy to prosecute and are now made only infrequently. By World War II, regulatory disapproval of such gross and explicit falsities had persuaded most advertisers to avoid making such claims.

A small but ever-present number of recalcitrant advertisers continue to test the system, usually losing. These stubborn users of explicit falsities make regulatory vigilance an ongoing necessity. However, such challenges do not fundamentally weaken regulation; rather, they confirm the law's continuing strength because such challenges typically fail.

Also problematic is the fact that, over the years, many advertisers have learned to use a true explicit claim in such a way as to imply an additional false claim. An automobile ad showed a crane lifting a car by cables attached to the guard rails embedded in its doors, which truthfully proved the doors' strength for that task. The FTC, however, saw a false claim that the doors would be equally strong when struck from the side as in a typical collision. Thus, while the ad truthfully showed a quality that consumers usually do not need, it also falsely implied a real quality that was absent.

In this way the steps regulators have taken have been matched by the steps advertisers have taken. When the regulators have closed the gap by prohibiting a type of falsity, the advertisers have widened it again by identifying and using what the law still permits. In time, the regulators usually have caught the new practice, yet there has usually been a period when the falsity is permitted to flourish.

That gap appears to be of considerable width today, although not because false implications have been ignored. Many years ago, a series of FTC cases established recognition of them through conclusions such as, "The ultimate impression upon the mind of the reader arises from the sum total of not only what is said but also of all that is reasonably implied."

Such decisions largely ended a period during which advertisers successfully used explicit truth as a defense. The rule is now clear that an ad's falsity depends on what consumers view it as saying. Even now that the general concept of false implications has been established, some advertisers persist in using implied falsities, forcing regulators to address each false claim.

The regulatory process permits these falsities through its inability to deter general types of claims before they occur; it can prohibit specific ones only after they have been used. Such prohibitions have been invoked in great number, with each slightly narrowing the gap. At least fifteen general types of implications have been identified. Nonetheless, advertisers have persisted in creating new types, most recently, the false implication made by thirty-minute advertisements that they are news programs independent of commercial interests. That falsity is now prohibited unless the commercial nature of the program is disclosed.

Despite the many successful actions of regulators, their overall ability to stop implied falsities has been compromised by a long-used working assumption that severely constrains their definition of deceptiveness. Regulators consider a claim capable of being deceptive only if it is a factual claim about the advertised item (usually a product or service). That designation appears to provide good coverage of the protection consumers need, yet, in fact, provides two loopholes, which advertisers have exploited.

The loopholes involve the types of claims left undesignated by the working assumption—factual claims that are not about the brands and nonfactual claims about the brand. These claims are permitted by regulators who apparently believe that they are not material—they cannot affect purchasing decisions because consumers will recognize their lack of relevance. Yet, advertisers continue to make use of these claims frequently.

The nonfactual claims they make are usually opinions, in particular, those known in the trade as "puffery." Recent examples include BMW's "the ultimate driving machine," Colombian Coffee's "the richest coffee in the world," Gillette's "the best a man can get," and Visa's "It's everywhere you want to be."

Claims that are factual, though not about the brand, tend to be claims about the nature of the consumer or of the societal context within which consumers encounter products. Recent examples include Heileman's PowerMaster malt liquor addressed to the urban ghetto poor, Kodak's "It's the one film to use for your family's biggest moments," and Diet Coke's women on the street ogling a shirtless male construction worker. As a trade journal story said: "Chevrolet television advertising has never been about cars. It has always been about us."

Emphasizing an attraction apart from the brand's actual features is not necessarily harmful, but it can be so when the features, such as the enhanced amount of alcohol in PowerMaster, have a harmful potential. Although in some cases the individual consumer's loss is only a modest amount of money, over millions of consumers, the aggregate amount can be very large.

The advertisers' use of many such nonfactual claims and nonbrand facts illustrates their strategy of flanking a barrier rather than attacking it directly. While false claims about a brand, even when only implied, are likely today to be deemed deceptive, advertisers have exploited to the maximum the two loopholes left open by the regulators' narrow designation of deceptiveness. Through the advertisers' inventiveness and the regulators' lag in keeping up, the proportion of deceptive claims in advertising remains high, and the opportunity for consumers to obtain useful truths on which they may rely remains low. Thus, regulation cannot be considered to have achieved all of its goals.

In addition to banning deceptiveness, which is the most important aspect of advertising regulation, the FTC and most states are also authorized to prohibit "unfair" acts or practices. This term has suffered from difficulties of definition; its use declined in the 1980s after the FTC failed to apply it to nondeceptive advertising directed to children. However, federal legislation of 1994 that has specifically defined unfairness may lead to new uses of the concept.

By the new definition, an act may be unfair when it "causes or is likely to cause substantial injury to consumers which is not reasonably avoidable by consumers themselves and not outweighed by countervailing benefits to consumers or to competition." The legislation states further that, "In determining whether an act or practice is unfair, the Commission may consider established public policies as evidence . . . [but] Such public policy considerations may not serve as a primary basis for such determination." Thus, the FTC will often have to show directly, rather than as an inference from policy, that an action causes substantial injury.

Unfairness is also potentially controllable by the Supreme Court's limitation on regulation of commercial speech. Whereas any restraint, up to and including a complete ban, is constitutional for deceptive commercial advertising (or for illegal products), the regulation of other ad content must meet several requirements. The government must prove that there is a substantial interest to be addressed, and the regulation must directly advance that interest while also having a reasonable fit with what is required; that is, a restraint must not be more than, or otherwise different from, what is needed to achieve the goal. (The rule also applies to commercial speech alleged to be neither deceptive nor unfair.)

In the case of cigarette advertising, the FTC's burden would be to prove that consumers could be injured, not by smoking itself, but by the presumably nondeceptive representations made in the ads. To determine whether such claims are in themselves injurious, which would mean that people smoke as a result of reliance on them, is a challenging task. Further, should the injury potential be found, the commission would next have to show that the injury is not reasonably avoidable by consumers' own actions, which is another challenging issue. For regulators considering a total ban of cigarette advertising, the issue of whether that might constitute overkill would have to be addressed. Together, these burdens are arduous.

Any such analysis of unfairness reflects an important underlying feature of governmental protection of consumers against the promotional speech of sellers. What is subject to control is the speech itself and not the response of consumers to the speech's topic. Products or services may be declared illegal by other regulation, but the use of legal products cannot be controlled through regulation, such as the 1914 Federal Trade Commission Act, that pertains solely to speech about them.

The enforcers of such regulation are authorized to ensure that commercial speech may be relied upon by consumers without harm; thus, they may prohibit any speech that is deceptive or that unavoidably injures. Such regulation, however, does not control consumers' use of the remaining speech, and so does not control consumers' choice nor guarantee that consumers will make decisions that serve their welfare. Thus, by controlling only information, the law of advertising promotes consumer welfare only indirectly. Information is only one of many factors that consumers use in pursuing their own welfare.

— Ivan L. Preston

See also

Better Business Bureaus; Deceptive, Unfair, and Unconscionable Sales Practices; Federal Trade Commission.

Readings

Petty, Ross (1992). *The Impact of Advertising Law on Business and Public Policy.* Westport, CT: Quorum Books.

Preston, Ivan L. (1994). *The Tangled Web They Weave: Truth, Falsity, and Advertisers.* Madison, WI: The University of Wisconsin Press.

Advocacy, Consumer

The consumer movement is known to the public largely for its advocacy. The most recognizable consumerist, Ralph Nader, is an advocate. Those consumer stories reported most widely by the media usually involve the initiatives or reactions of consumer advocates. And it is advocates who push, and often claim credit, for consumer protections established by legislation or regulation.

Consumer advocates seek to improve consumer welfare by influencing government decisions related to the consumer marketplace or by directly changing corporate policies and practices. The government decisions include those made by legislators, regulators, other executive branch leaders, and judges. These decisions involve the making and implementation of public policy, broadly defined. The business practices concern the characteristics of consumer goods and services—availability, price, quality, safety, guarantees—the way these products are marketed and sold, and the way related problems are resolved. (Advocacy on behalf of individual consumers is discussed in the entry Disputes and Dispute Resolution.)

Advocates

Except for a few individuals such as Nader and Esther Peterson, consumer advocacy is most closely identified with, and extensively practiced by, advocacy organizations. Since the early 1970s, there have been several hundred active groups. About twenty have been active in Washington, D.C., working on federal legislative, regulatory, and judicial issues. The most important of these organizations—Action for Children's Television, The Advocacy Institute, American Association of Retired Persons (AARP), Association of Community Organizations for Reform Now (ACORN), Bankcard Holders of America, Center for Auto Safety, Center for Science in the Public Interest, Citizen Action, Community Nutrition Institute, Consumer Federation of America, Consumers Union, National Consumer Law Center, National Consumers League, Public Citizen, Public Voice for Food and Health Policy, and U.S. PIRG (see Public Interest Research Groups)—have their own encyclopedia entries.

Most of the remaining organizations work at the state or local level. More than half of these groups are affiliated with ACORN, Citizen Action, Consumer Federation of America, or U.S. PIRG. Other national groups such as Consumers Union and Public Citizen maintain at least one advocacy office outside Washington, D.C. This encyclopedia devotes entries to a few of these state and local organizations and categories of organization: Center for Public Representation, Citizen Utility Boards (CUBs), Consumer Action, Consumers Education and Protective Association, Public Interest Research Groups (PIRGs), State Utility Consumer Advocates, and Toward Utility Rate Normalization (TURN). The entry on State and Local Consumer Organizations offers general discussion of advocacy at these levels.

It should be noted that many of these organizations work on both consumer and nonconsumer issues. For example, Public Citizen, U.S. PIRG, and individual PIRGs address environmental issues; National Consumers League and Citizen Action treat worker issues; and AARP views its top priority as promoting the general welfare of older persons. It should also be pointed out that Consumers Union is, first and foremost, an organization that conducts and publicizes the results of product testing.

Strategies

To achieve their goals, advocates employ various strategies. The most direct is personal communication with government or corporate decision-makers. Such efforts directed toward members of the legislative and executive branches of government are called lobbying. These communications can be with political leaders or their staffers. They can take written, oral, or even audio-video form. Written communications include testimony, letters, and regulatory petitions and comments. Verbal communications range from public comments such as oral testimony to telephone and face-to-face conversations. Sending audio-video communications to government officials is rarely done because these materials are relatively expensive to send and relatively inconvenient to listen to or to watch.

Advocacy includes pursuing other strategies for communicating with legislative and executive branch members. In general, for consumer advocates the most effective of these strategies has been seeking to influence press coverage. Such coverage can affect the views of citizens, to whom elected officials are accountable. It also can reach these officials directly. For a variety of reasons that include their expertise on consumer issues and their willingness to criticize government and business, advocates have enjoyed good access to the press.

Advocate communications with the press can be responsive or proactive. Advocates are often called by reporters seeking a response to a consumer issue that may involve a consumer problem or a government action related to a problem. Advocates also initiate communications with the press, not only to comment on problems and government actions, but also to identify new problems and their proposed solutions. Communications of the second type usually take the form of a news release, which is often mailed, faxed, or distributed at a press conference, where advocates have the opportunity to speak face-to-face with reporters.

An important subset of press communications is the efforts to persuade newspaper editorial page writers to publish information and opinion that serve the consumer interest. These efforts seek to publish one's own writing or to influence the writing of editorial page writers. Advocates submit to newspapers letters-to-the-editor or op-ed essays that react to some other editorial page piece or, for some op-ed essays, introduce a new issue to the editorial pages. Advocates also communicate with editorial editors and columnists in an effort to influence their choice of topics or how they treat these issues.

One of the most effective means of persuading the press to cover consumer issues, especially advocate perspectives on these issues, is to release policy-related research. This research also serves as the basis for many of the most effective arguments that advocates make while lobbying.

There are several types of this research. The most important type analyzes the impact of existing or proposed policies on consumers. Because most consumer advocacy is directed mainly at government decision-makers, most of this research assesses the effects of government policies. These policies may be viewed by consumer advocates as either pro- or anti-consumer.

Advocacy research can also evaluate corporate policies and practices ranging from prices charged to the safety of products marketed. In part, this research is intended to influence the marketplace directly—by documenting anti-consumer practices and persuading corporations to adopt more pro-consumer policies. While this research may initially be communicated only to affected companies, usually it is released to the press in the hope that related press coverage will influence consumer views of the targeted corporations. This coverage also can serve the purpose of creating or building public support for new or existing consumer protections.

Research that assesses consumer impacts is most effective when it credibly documents substantial financial or health/safety costs or benefits to consumers. Carefully constructed estimates of an industry overcharge of more than $1 billion or of product-related deaths of at least several hundred persons often will be reported by the press and taken seriously by policymakers.

Another type of policy-related research surveys consumers about their concerns, problems, and opinions. This research usually involves using an opinion research firm to survey a representative sample of adult Americans. Questions may relate to opinions not only about existing or proposed public policies, but also about corporate policies and practices. Survey research can be particularly effective for advocates if the questions are clear-cut and neutrally worded, and the results are unequivocal.

Two other advocacy strategies—coalition-building and grassroots mobilization—seek to broaden support for, or opposition against, public or corporate policies. Coalitions are important to advocates because there is strength in numbers and because allies may have access to policymakers with whom advocates have little or no influence. Through pooling of human and material resources, including expertise, coalitions have the potential to increase advocate influence on policy decisions. Coalitions with corporate members, for example, may have the resources to run newspaper and television ads advancing a policy position. Also, these coalitions may have broader access to policymakers than do its individual members.

Coalitions may be based on shared or complementary interests. Both consumer advocates and an industry may desire that government establishes minimum standards for that industry. On the other hand, advocates may exchange their support for one regulation desired by industry in return for industry support of another regulation that they have proposed. In regard to policy-related goals, coalitions can range in scope from exclusive focus on one policy decision to the promotion of shared and complementary interests in a broad area, such as consumer health and safety. This breadth of interest strongly influences the permanence of a coalition. When coalitions are organized to influence one policy decision, they usually disband after that decision is made. On the other hand, coalitions established to promote broader interests may last for many years. The most permanent coalitions are those incorporated as separate organizations with their own staff and budget.

Grassroots mobilization usually seeks to influence public policy decisions by encouraging communications to elected officials from their constituents. Letters, phone calls, and visits from consumers who reside in the district of an elected representative are usually taken more seriously by legislators than are communications from national consumer groups. Advocates sometimes seek to mobilize consumers at the grass roots by generating local press coverage. They can also activate citizens who are part of a network far more effectively. There are several types of grassroots networks that can be mobilized. One is a nonprofit "trade association," such as the Consumer Federation of America or U.S. PIRG, that is made up of state or local groups. Another is an organization with members who typically have been recruited through direct mail solicitations. A third is a network that was created specifically to work on a limited issue. Typically, network members are activated through personal communications by mail, phone, fax, or computer.

Other advocacy strategies seek to change a corporate policy or practice solely through publicity generated by picketing, leafletting, and other tactics. The Consumers Education and Protective Association, and other groups that it inspired, built sometimes powerful organizations that utilized such publicity to resolve individual problems (and even influence public policies). The most radical of such direct actions is the conducting of a consumer boycott, which is treated in a separate entry (see Boycotts, Consumer). A boycott is an explicit attempt to persuade consumers not to purchase products from a target company.

The strategies discussed above are intended mainly to influence directly the decisions of corporations, legislators, and, to a lesser extent, regulators and other executive branch leaders. Litigation differs from these strategies in that it intends to influence judicial decisions. There are two main types of litigation. Advocates may sue a corporation for a practice that they consider anti-consumer. They do so usually on behalf of the class of all individuals who have been harmed by the corporate practice. When this class is large, and there is a reasonable possibility of winning a substantial punitive damages award, advocates may gain significant leverage over a company. It should be noted, however, that most class action lawsuits on behalf of consumers are filed by private attorneys, not by consumer groups.

Advocates also sue government agencies for failing to implement or enforce adequately consumer laws. Lawsuits may target agencies that have issued regulations that advocates believe disregard legislative intent; they may also seek to compel adequate enforcement of existing regulations. This litigation is almost always initiated by consumer advocates, most often by the Public Citizen Litigation Group.

Another type of judicial intervention is the filing of amicus briefs in a lawsuit the outcome of which a consumer group considers will have a substantial effect on the consumer interest. While these briefs most often are filed on behalf of a plaintiff or defendant that is a nonprofit group, they sometimes support the position of a government or business organization. Because these filings require much less work than lawsuits, they are undertaken more frequently than litigation.

Impacts

The most visible effects of consumer advocacy are the hundreds, perhaps thousands, of laws and regulations established by federal, state, and local governments to protect consumers. Many of these laws have created agencies to enforce regulations that limit corporate decisions affecting consumers. Some of the major federal consumer laws are noted in the entry U.S. Consumer Movement: History and Dynamics. Many others are referred to in the several dozen entries that concern product protections.

Sometimes neglected, however, are the enormous impacts of consumer advocacy on American culture. Advocates have played a critically important role, for example, in the redefinition of the consumer role from that of passive consumer to that of active agent in the marketplace. In large measure because of the news coverage generated by advocates, in the 1990s most consumers see themselves as a class with interests separate and distinct from business, with rights that protect these interests, and with the ability to enforce these rights. This "consumer consciousness" has helped equalize the relationship between buyers and sellers in the marketplace.

— Stephen Brobeck

See also

Boycotts, Consumer; Coalitions; U.S. Consumer Movement: History and Dynamics.

Readings

Caplan, Marc (1983). *A Citizen's Guide to Lobbying.* New York: Dembner Books.

Ross, Donald (1973). *A Public Citizen's Action Manual: Tools for Change.* New York: Grossman.

The Advocacy Institute

David Cohen and Michael Pertschuk launched the Institute for Public Policy Advocacy, now called The Advocacy Institute, in 1986. From its first day, the goal of the institute was to show citizen groups how to alter public policy by building movements.

Cohen had always worked outside of government, in the public interest sector, exhorting policymakers to "do better." His base of operation from 1971 to 1981 was Common Cause, an organization he served first as chief lobbyist then as president.

Pertschuk had always worked inside government: first as general counsel to the Senate Commerce Committee, and later as chair of the Federal Trade Commission (FTC). His career was centered on consumer protection issues such as a broadcast ban on cigarette advertising, the establishment of safety standards for motor vehicles, and restraint of harmful advertising and marketing practices in a variety of industries.

In 1992, Cohen and Pertschuk were joined by Kathleen Sheekey, who became the organization's third co-chair. Earlier, Sheekey directed congressional liaison for the FTC, then served as legislative director of Common Cause.

The Advocacy Institute has chronicled successful campaigns, taught advocacy skills, mentored advocates, counseled public interest leaders, developed multimedia teaching materials, managed infrastructure-building programs, and provided a supportive environment for the advocacy community. Since its founding, the institute has worked with more than 2,000 nonprofit organizations. It has provided training in such advocacy skills as long-range strategy planning, organizing and sustaining alliances and coalitions, framing public arguments, strategic approaches to the mass media, application of interactive communications technologies to policy development and grassroots mobilization, access to and persuasion of decision-makers, and uncovering and countering special interest opposition.

Pertschuk's entire career has been grounded in issues of consumer protection. While serving on the FTC, he became the nation's most quoted critic of the advertising and marketing practices of the tobacco conglomerates. When he started The Advocacy Institute, he took with him an interest in protecting the consumer—particularly the youthful consumer—from the effects of tobacco. Soon, with initial funding from the Henry J. Kaiser Family Foundation, the institute initiated the Smoking Control Advocacy Resource Center (SCARC) to build an infrastructure to support movement activists. This infrastructure includes SCARCNet, an interactive computer network devoted to information and strategy exchange for the entire smoking control community. Today, SCARC is the communications hub of the movement worldwide.

SCARC was a laboratory in which to develop, test, and hone the elements necessary for building and sustaining a movement. It has a strong adversary with deep pockets; it has the potential to build a diverse and large alliance; and its issue affects people of all ages, races, geographic areas, and economic conditions (though not equally).

The strategies and skills acquired by SCARC were utilized in developing an alcohol control project, which was housed initially at the institute and, more recently, at the Center for Science in the Public Interest. The institute also developed a project to help build an infrastructure to support a movement against gun violence.

The advocacy skills training and materials, first developed for smoking control advocates, have been molded into a generic program for community-based activists. Institute staff have developed both advocacy and training skills that have been sought by leaders in many issue areas in the United States and in developing countries throughout the world. In 1993 and 1994, the institute conducted many training sessions around the country for the Community-Based Health Care Project, which was managed by the American Nurses Association and the National Consumers League. The institute has developed a Leadership Fellows Training Program, which brings together a diverse group of emerging community leaders for an intensive two-week program. Recent International Fellows have come from South Africa, India, and Bangladesh.

Another project of the institute, the Network for Efficient, Safe and Sustainable Transportation (NESST), concentrates on broadening the coalition of groups working on the issue of sustainable transportation and on bringing grassroots groups to the table where strategy decisions are made.

The Advocacy Institute is a nonprofit 501(c)(3) organization. For the past few years, its budget has been in the neighborhood of $2 million, and the staff (including interns) has ranged from twenty-five to thirty-five persons. Two years ago the institute, which is based in Washington, D.C., opened a two-person office in San Francisco, which applies advocacy counseling, training, and writing to statewide issues. In the future, this office could serve as a model for Advocacy Institute offices in other states.

— Michael Pertschuk

See also

Tobacco Control and Prevention.

Readings

Oldenburg, Don (1990). "Advocates for Activism." *Washington Post.* (January 9): D5.

Shepard, Scott (1992). "Gadflies Learn to Lobby from Expert Advocates." *Atlanta Constitution.* (December 28): A3.

African Americans as Consumers

See Ethnic Minorities as Consumers.

African Consumer Movement

The context within which African consumer associations operate is global. What has been globalized, however, is not just markets, with their systems of production, distribution, and consumption, but Western civilization in general.

African economies have become an integral part of a global economy dominated by transnational corporations (TNCs) and powerful lending institutions like the World Bank and International Monetary Fund (IMF). To survive in this context, African countries have pursued strategies of export-led growth and opened up African markets to international trade and investment. Governments of African countries, now under enormous pressure to make their countries conducive and attractive to foreign investment, have rendered themselves open to abuses by TNCs. Some of the abuses are: price fixing and anticompetitive behavior; variable product standards, especially lower standards for exports than those for domestic markets; dubious marketing practices; consumer information issues (e.g., misleading claims); and environmental/health problems (e.g., dumping of hazardous waste). Thus, amid the globalization of the world economy, African consumers are increasingly concerned about the need for competitive business practices and ethical business conduct.

The problems of African consumers are themselves part-and-parcel of broader social problems. These problems include the abject poverty of more than 1 billion people in the world, particularly women; the continuing deterioration of the global environment due to unsustainable consumption and production patterns, particularly in industrialized countries; continued population growth; the refugee crisis; and unemployment and underemployment of more than 120 million people worldwide.

In the case of Africa and many other developing countries, the globalization of Western civilization has also meant the development among a minority sector of the population of a consumer culture that emulates the unsustainable consumption patterns of the West, all in the name of being "sophisticated" or "civilized." The consumer culture is a way of thinking, a type of lifestyle generated by advertisements, cinema, music, magazines, comics, and other channels of the mass media whose objective is to persuade the consumer to buy products regardless of whether the products are good, bad, or needed. The consumer is made insecure unless he smokes a cigarette, unless he buys a certain brand of hair cream, unless she uses a certain brand of lipstick, unless in the home the color of the curtains matches the color of the carpet. As a result, a large part of the already meager income of African people is being siphoned off on worthless goods and activities, leaving little money for food, health, and recreation. For Africa the consumer culture is often dangerous (e.g., smoking causes cancer), and it generates egoism, individualism, and rivalry among people as well as corruption and nepotism.

The globalization of markets has been accompanied by the creation and reinforcement of regional economic blocs. The European Union is expanding and consolidating itself, the North American Free Trade Agreement has been concretized and is being implemented, and the Association of South East Asian Nations will soon become a trading bloc. It is even conceivable that there will be a bloc of Pacific countries covering North and South America.

Despite rhetorical commitment to Africa-wide economic integration, a multiplicity of small and often overlapping subregional entities exists, sometimes with conflicting mandates and duplicative institutions. Most of the eleven countries of the Southern African Development Community (SADC) are members of the Common Market for Eastern and Southern Africa (formerly the Preferential Trade Area). Sixteen West African countries are members of the Economic Community of West African States (ECOWAS). Notwithstanding the 1993 attempt to reaffirm the importance of this regional integration institution, seven of these countries had within six months formed (at the instigation of France) a rival organization, the Economic and Monetary Union of West Africa (UEMOA). This fragmentation, duplication, and destructive competition among subregional blocs is continuing despite the fact that in 1991 in Abuja, Nigeria, the Organization of African Unity established an African Economic Community comprised of Africa's five regions—North Africa, West Africa, Central Africa, East Africa, and Southern Africa.

Failure to rationalize and streamline the integration of institutions, along with inadequate infrastructure and other barriers to the flow of goods and factors of production, has inhibited intraregional trade in Africa, with adverse effects on consumers. In their lobbyist role, consumer organizations throughout Africa have thus called for increased economic integration and consumption of African goods and services. The organization of the world into economic blocs will exacerbate commercial, financial, and cultural competition as well as scientific and technical rivalry on an unprecedented scale.

Regional Context

African consumer associations are concerned about the continent's handicaps, failures, and relative marginalization. Although from 1960 to the present Africa has made more progress in education, science, culture, and communications than the progress made during a much longer period of the colonial era, these achievements cannot obscure the continent's innumerable failures over the past thirty years.

The African continent is still seriously handicapped by four centuries of slave trading and the ever-present weight of colonial and neocolonial domination. The benefits of contemporary civilization, such as they are, have not touched Africa, except for perhaps 5 percent of its population. Africa reports the highest general mortality and infant mortality rates, the lowest life expectancy, the lowest rates of economic growth, the lowest income per capita, the highest population growth, and the highest illiteracy levels. All these indicators are concrete manifestations and measures of Africa's poverty.

In sub-Saharan Africa (SSA), education, training, culture, information, and health budgets are constantly being cut while defense, security, and arms budgets are constantly being expanded. Administrations are often blighted by ethnic preference, a partisan approach, cronyism, nepotism, corruption, absenteeism, laxness, and generally low rates of return and efficiency. Misappropriation of public funds, waste, and chaos are not sufficiently discouraged in several African countries.

Africa's marginalization is well evidenced and documented by the statistics. In Africa, foreign debt in 1980 equaled 29.1 percent of the gross national product (GNP) ($56.2 billion out of a GNP of $192.8 billion), but today the entire GNP of SSA ($168.5 billion) is insufficient to meet the debt ($183.4 billion). For Africa as a whole, foreign debt constitutes 108 percent of the GNP, compared to 37.6 percent in Latin America and the Caribbean, 36.3 percent in Southeast Asia, and 27.9 percent in Asia and the Pacific. From being self-sufficient in food ten years ago, Africa has now become a net importer.

In order to address all these problems, more than two-thirds of African countries are implementing World Bank/IMF–inspired structural adjustment programs (SAPs). These programs have as their goal preparing a country for participation in the international system of free trade. They generally involve deregulating domestic markets and eliminating subsidies to domestic enterprises; removing barriers to imports from other countries;

and reducing inflation and pursuing other policies that promote monetary stability, including the reduction of government spending. The 5 percent of Africa's population that stands to benefit from the process of modernization continues to espouse the neoliberal route to Africa's development and see SAPs as the answer to the present quagmire. SAPs are designed to enable African economies to compete in the world export markets, but there have been no signs of improvement. Even countries like Ghana that have had SAPs for over a decade are beginning to ask whether SAPs really provide answers to their beleaguered economies.

Consumer associations are nevertheless wary of taking a one-sided, populist view of SAPs. The pre-SAP economies were not healthy. In effect, African governments had mismanaged and plundered their economies, as manifested by high unemployment levels, inflation, high domestic and international debt, declining real incomes, and the general poverty of their people. Yet, critics contend, the basic strategy behind SAPs is flawed. It is premised on African countries' outperforming one another (as well as countries in Asia and Latin America) in the export market. This orientation only intensifies competition among them and further cheapens their raw materials and products of their labor. Besides, an export market is too fragile and undependable a market on which to base any country's development. All developed countries have, first and foremost, built a solid home market on which an export market has been added. Thus, there is a need for most African economies to adjust, but whether the adjustment model imposed by the World Bank/IMF and its time phasing-in requirements are appropriate for Africa is what consumer organizations throughout the continent are questioning.

The situation implies that for the consumer movement to be relevant it must address Africa's greatest development challenge—how to eradicate poverty. It also means that the consumer movement must strive to influence official policy to restructure economies in ways that are appropriate to local realities.

Emergence of the Movement

The globalization of markets and Western civilization, the growing tendency for nations to combine into economic blocs, Africa's economic crisis, SAPs, and the new trend toward market economies suggest that Africa needs a strong and effective consumer movement. In addition to these background factors, three forces account for the emergence of the consumer movement in Africa.

First, the fall of the Soviet Union and the end of the Cold War have given way to greater human freedom and more democratic forms of government in many African countries. More people than ever before have a political choice—the right to vote, the right to choose among political parties, the right to assemble, the right to make their voices heard and their interests known, and an increased opportunity to hold their political representatives accountable. In short, there is rising tolerance on the part of several African governments that is allowing the emergence of consumer organizations and other groups in civil society.

Second, the impact of economic SAPs on consumers has contributed toward the emergence and growth of consumer organizations in Africa. Over two-thirds of sub-Saharan Africa countries are implementing SAPs. As noted earlier, these SAPs are characterized by the retreat of governments from the marketplace and from the provision of essential goods and services. Elimination of price, trade, and wage controls and devaluation of currencies by governments have led to a drop in purchasing power and price increases in essential goods and services. Privatization and the elimination of government subsidies for food, health, education, and shelter have made access to these basic services more difficult. Trade and market liberalization have their intended effect of providing consumers with more access to foreign goods and services, but these new options also increase consumer vulnerability and insecurity. Consequently, consumers are feeling the need to organize themselves in order to fill the void created by governments on the retreat.

Third, the work of Consumers International in Africa in recent years has stimulated the rapid growth of the consumer movement in many countries. This aspect is explained in the sections below on the state of the movement and the role of Consumers International.

Functions of the Movement

The consumer movement in Africa performs a number of broad functions, starting with the stimulation of a more efficient and equitable marketplace. The movement is also connected to the processes of democratization, economic development, nation building, and the advancement of women.

Economic theory states that in perfectly competitive markets, the consumer has sovereignty over what the producer offers, and the economic rewards go to those suppliers who most effectively provide consumers with what they want at the lowest possible cost. The reality of the situation is often far from this textbook ideal; consumer markets are highly imperfect, particularly in Africa, where poverty, monopolistic suppliers, inadequate information, fraudulent activities, and corruption are commonplace. All of these tendencies and practices inhibit economic democracy in the marketplace and the efficient allocation of resources, both of which are prerequisites for the economic development of a country. In the absence of effective government regulation, only a strong and effective consumer movement can act as a vanguard against imperfect and inefficient market conditions.

The consumer movement introduces fairness as well as efficiency into the marketplace. The movement constitutes a countervailing force, wedged between the providers of goods and services (private, local, and multinational companies as well as state-run industries) on the one hand, and government ministries and departments on the other hand.

Business is usually well organized and represented by such associations as chambers of commerce and confederations of industries. Even commercial farmers and small-scale producers in African countries are organized into national commercial farmers' unions and small-scale business units, respectively. The more organized the vested interests are, the more influence they have on government bureaucrats and policymakers. It is therefore necessary for consumers to form organizations dedicated to the protection and promotion of consumer rights and responsibilities.

It was noted earlier that African governments are now concerned about creating a favorable climate for attracting new foreign investment. This emphasis has often meant a general increase in unchecked, abusive practices such as shortweighting in the absence of effective weights and measures departments in many countries; adulteration of foodstuffs and beverages; false and misleading advertisements; sale of dangerous and inferior products (e.g., food and drinks containing toxic dyes, additives, chemicals, and bacteria); chemicals and drugs banned in source countries sold over-the-counter and on the streets; and the depletion and pollution of land, water, timber, and air resources due to commercial and industrial exploitation. Given these threats to the lives of consumers, the consumer movement in Africa seeks to create a fair marketplace through lobbying for adoption of policies that protect and empower consumers.

There is also an important nexus between the consumer movement and democracy in Africa. The consumer movement is both a product and an integral part of the democratization process in Africa. On the one hand, the movement is a product in the sense that without increased tolerance on the part of governments allowing for the emergence of civil society, consumer movements would not have emerged. One can observe that countries that have had political and civil strife—such as Mozambique, Somalia, Angola, and Rwanda—have no active consumer organizations. In these countries, survival issues dominate the agenda of the population. Peace and stability are a prerequisite for a thriving civil society. Countries that have had an emergent consumer movement and have subsequently plunged into political strife—such as Liberia,

Sierra Leone, and to a lesser extent Zaire—have witnessed suspension of the activities of the emergent consumer organizations.

On the other hand, the consumer movement is an integral component of the democratization process in Africa. Along with other organizations in civil society such as trade unions, women's and youth organizations, the free and independent press, and other nongovernmental groupings and associations, consumer organizations act as watchdogs, providing checks and balances against the excesses of politicians and administrators. Democracy is not just about having multiple political parties, national elections, and parliaments formulating laws that are enforced by separate judiciaries. Democracy is a culture in which citizens become involved in all decisions and issues affecting their lives. For democracy to exist and be sustainable, a vast array of organizations in civil society should be in existence. In many countries where new democratic freedoms have now been conferred on the population, the consumer movement has become the rallying point for social mobilization at the local and grassroots level.

There is also a nexus between the consumer movement and economic development. Development is about improving the quality of life of all people in a country. The main objective of the movement is to empower consumers in order to improve access to quality goods and services, and thereby improve the quality of life of people. Unlike their organizational counterparts in the developed world, which are preoccupied with such consumer issues as balancing prices and quality, consumer organizations in Africa have a different perception of their mission; they have put developmental issues high on their agendas.

Two shifts in outlook account for this emphasis on raising general standards of living by way of economic development. One is that there is now a more democratic perception of consumption in Africa. Consumption is not something that only the middle and upper classes have a right to enjoy. The poor, too, consume, even if they individually consume too little, in many cases barely enough even to survive. Given that the poor constitute over 80 percent of Africa's population, the relevance of Africa's consumer organizations rests on their ability to focus on the consumption and developmental needs of the poor.

The second change is that the concept of "quality" itself is increasingly being questioned by African groups. It is not just the question of whether there is more genuine meat in the sausage but also the question of whether people should eat sausages at all. In this particular instance, in order to produce one kilocalorie of energy from meat, cattle have to be fed with eight kilocalories of energy from green vegetation, a highly wasteful form of consumption. Indeed, the whole meat industry has undertaken to satisfy the consumption habits of a very small percentage of the local population and the overly fed population of the European Union, which imports the choicest meat. There are many examples of countries producing export crops at the expense of local consumption needs to earn foreign currency. Consumer organizations throughout Africa are now calling for increased production and consumption of local products.

As with democracy and economic development, the consumer movement plays a positive role in fostering national unity in many countries. Colonialism aggregated several tribes and nations into one territory in some countries and split other tribes into several countries in other cases. Nigeria alone has more than 400 different tribes, each speaking a different language. Tribalism and ethnicity have been at the root of much of the civil strife and wars in Africa. For example, the struggle and wars of the Hutus and Tutsis in Rwanda and Burundi have often erupted into violence and killing of massive proportion. The evidence from all over the world is that when people are not content, when their basic needs are not met, and when their lives are not in harmony with nature, it is difficult to achieve national unity. In its efforts to improve living conditions, the consumer movement diminishes ethnic tension.

A final function of the consumer movement is to strengthen the position of an often marginalized group of consumers, namely, women. As a group, women and children play a critical role both as producers (especially informal sector producers) and consumers of goods and services. Women are generally responsible for buying for their families and managing household disposable incomes, and yet they are still the poorest, most vulnerable, and most discriminated-against group of people.

Women experience directly in the marketplace the effects of inflation and unscrupulous marketing practices. They suffer more than men from lack of access to basic goods and services. This marginalization explains why nearly all of the older and more mature consumer organizations in Africa, including the Kenya Consumers' Organization, the Consumer Council of Zimbabwe (CCZ), the Housewives League in South Africa, and the Institute for Consumer Protection in Mauritius, were formed by women. The consumer movement thus provides a vehicle for women's social mobilization and for the strengthening of their position in society.

There is the additional trend now, particularly in West Africa, involving women as consumers. Women are forming consumer cooperatives in reaction to price increases resulting, in large part, from economic SAPs. The women-led consumer cooperatives are spreading rapidly in, for example, Senegal and Mali.

In other countries such as Kenya and Uganda, the consumer movement has forged important alliances with the traditional women's organizations, using the latter's existing networks in order to provide consumer education to the women living in rural areas. Consumer education is thus imparted through adult literacy programs, drama and theater, sports, traditional dancing, and other nonformal means.

State of the Movement

The consumer movement now exists in most African countries. Moreover, the movement is probably the fastest-growing social movement in Africa today. One indicator of this growth is the membership of African consumer organizations in Consumers International (CI), the umbrella organization of the world consumer movement. In 1991, forty African countries had no member organization or contact group with CI; in 1995, there were only fifteen such countries. Conversely, the number of member countries with full, associate members of CI went from six in 1991 to more than twenty in 1995. These trends reflect, of course, the expanded efforts of CI to establish consumer organizations in Africa as well as the increased receptivity of these countries.

An analysis by CI of sixty-six consumer organizations for which age information is available shows that most of the organizations (64 percent) are less than four years old and 82 percent of them are no more than eight years old. The median age of all African consumer organizations is three years. The strongest organizations are also the oldest—national consumer organizations of Kenya, Mauritius (two), South Africa, and Zimbabwe—all of which are at least twenty years old.

African consumer organizations are not only young; they are also weak. They lack the human and financial resources required to meet the challenges they face in their countries. These organizations function under exceedingly difficult circumstances: in most cases they lack an office from which to operate; if an office exists, it usually lacks basic office furniture and equipment such as computers, typewriters, telephones, photocopiers, and fax machines. All the organizations need information on consumer and related issues, and there is a general lack of technical expertise in the movement as a whole.

An analysis by CI's Regional Office for Africa (ROAF) of seventy African organizations for which staffing data were available showed that only thirteen (18 percent) of the organizations have at least one permanent staff employee; six of these have ten or more staff members and their own office. The remaining 82 percent of organizations are manned by volunteers working on a part-time basis, usually without a permanent office. This lack of staff and space is particularly characteristic of West and Central African organizations. It is therefore necessary for ROAF to undertake development programs that assist in making these associations more effective players in the marketplace and in all areas where decisions impacting consumers are made.

The biggest asset of most of these organizations is the dedication and devotion of their membership, particularly the association leaders, most of whom have devoted their personal resources to keep the associations alive. Many of the organizations also have among their members people with diverse academic and professional backgrounds, such as doctors, teachers, agricultural economists, and lawyers, who are often called upon to render specialized expertise according to their backgrounds. Thus, many associations are now being invited by governments to provide their input before important decisions are made, and in many countries consumer representatives now sit on policy-making boards and committees.

African countries can be classified into three categories according to the level of development of their consumer movement. The first group consists of those seventeen countries where no consumer associations are known to exist. It is ROAF's goal to ensure that at least an embryonic consumer movement is present in all African countries within the next three years.

The second, and by far the largest group, is composed of countries where consumer associations have emerged in the last few years. These countries are in need of support and assistance from CI in order for them to be able to stand on their own feet. ROAF strives to raise these organizations to a level where they have attained the critical mass required to be self-sustaining.

Finally, there is the category made up of those countries—Kenya, Mauritius, South Africa, Tunisia, and Zimbabwe—where the consumer organizations are relatively developed and well established. The groups in these countries need above all information and expertise on key consumer issues, including the challenges consumers face in a world of fast-changing technology. There is also a need in these countries to reorient the movement toward the needs of disadvantaged consumers, many of whom are located in rural areas.

The Role of Consumers International

Prior to 1994, the work of CI in Africa was conducted by the Africa Transitional Team based in The Hague through collaboration with the development agency Environment and Development Action (ENDA) in Senegal and Zimbabwe. The dawn of a new era in Africa's consumer affairs came with the official opening of ROAF in March 1994. Much has been achieved in the few years that CI's work has been extended to Africa.

CI has played an important development role in the formation and establishment of new consumer organizations in several African countries. It has made progress through identifying contact individuals and nongovernmental organizations in targeted countries; field visits by ROAF staff; and dissemination of publications, often produced by ROAF and CI, that describe what consumer organizations are and do, and how to start one. In some countries, such as Ethiopia, ROAF has organized feasibility studies on the need and niche for a consumer organization, and the potential scope of the organization once it is formed. In other nations—such as Zambia, Uganda, Burkina Faso, and Senegal—ROAF has extended seed grants to emerging groups to assist them in setting up small offices with basic equipment such as a telephone and fax machine.

Second, ROAF's work has enhanced the visibility and recognition of consumer organizations in various countries by governments, private sector organizations, and consumers themselves. Many governments now consult with their local consumer organization prior to making important policy decisions. In Mali, for example, the consumer organization ASCOMA (Association des

Consommateurs du Mali) has been invited to provide members for eight government boards and committees and even to chair some of them. In Senegal, ADEETelS (Association de Défense des Usagers de l'Eau, l'Électricité, les Télécommunications et les Services) has demanded and obtained representation on the quasi-governmental bodies mandated as providers of water, telephone service, electricity, and household waste disposal. Similar cases of consumer organizations with representation on governmental and quasi-governmental boards can be cited in Zimbabwe, Zambia, and Uganda.

Third, ROAF has facilitated exchange of experiences and ideas among consumer organizations through newsletters and the sponsorship of workshops and conferences. Several of these workshops have exposed the new groups to key consumer issues such as consumer protection legislation and consumer education. Three workshops in Dakar, Senegal (1992); Kadoma, Harare (1993); and Cotonou, Benin (1993), were held on the theme "Legislation and UN Guidelines for Consumer Protection." Seminars and conferences have also exposed consumer leaders to the global dimension of their work and the linkages between their own struggles at the local level and the global agenda. Participation at CI's 1994 World Congress was beneficial to the fifty African delegates who attended. With CI's assistance, African consumer activists have also started to participate in global debates on food and food standards (Codex Alimentarius) as well as trade and commercial policies (GATT and World Trade Organization issues).

Fourth, a start has been made to build and boost the capabilities and effectiveness of consumer organizations on the African continent. ROAF and the more experienced consumer organizations have jointly prepared organizational development and capacity-building training materials and modules. These items are produced using participatory approaches and a process of consultation with member organizations, thus making them directly relevant to the needs of consumer organizations. The manuals commissioned by ROAF and produced by CI's members in the region address subjects such as running a consumer organization, conducting a survey, managing a complaint-handling service, conducting consumer education in schools, and lobbying.

Fifth, ROAF has assisted consumer organizations in their local campaigns and programs. The two main areas into which this support has been directed are consumer protection legislation and consumer education. For example, ASDEC (Association Sénégalaise pour la Défense de l'Environnement et des Consommateurs) in Senegal and CCZ in Zimbabwe received technical and financial assistance to undertake programs on consumer education for their rural population.

Finally, ROAF has also engaged member organizations and consulting lawyers to produce a publication on the state of consumer protection legislation in Africa, which compares existing legislation to legislation consistent with the United Nations Consumer Protection Guidelines. This document, together with the Model Law for Africa, which is also being developed, will act as a tool for pressuring national governments and regional bodies into enacting appropriate consumer protection legislation and enforcement mechanisms.

All in all, impressive strides have been made during the last few years, but the consumer movement in Africa faces formidable challenges. With the exception of a few countries, consumer organizations remain small and face a constant struggle for financial resources. ROAF, which provides financial and technical assistance, is itself dependent on its ability to obtain further grants from international organizations. Despite the challenges and barriers, the consumer movement is intricately linked to broader processes of democratization, national unification, development, and the advancement of women. As a result, the movement is likely to retain, and perhaps solidify, its tenuous grip on African soil.

— Joshua C. Gwitira

See also
Consumers International.

Readings

"Back to Africa" (1996). *World Consumer.* 222 (September): 1–3.

Sim, Foo Gaik (1991). *IOCU on Record: A Documentary History of the International Organization of Consumers Unions, 1960–1990.* Yonkers, NY: Consumers Union. Chapter 4.

World Consumer (1994). 213 (May): 1–13.

Airline Deregulation

Airline deregulation is one of the most controversial public policies of our time—not among economic researchers, almost all of whom support it, but among the traveling public, the airline industry, and policymakers. The controversy is frequently framed in anecdotes. One traveler pays $150 to fly coast to coast while another pays $600 to fly 400 miles. One waits two hours to make a connection to complete a short flight while another chooses among several convenient nonstop flights.

Over the years, government and industry officials have amassed databases that represent the collective experience of the traveling public. Both exhaustive and relatively easy to interpret, the data can explain the disparate views of researchers and the public. Used with a few important caveats, they provide an empirical profile of industry concentration, fares, service quality, safety, and profits as they have evolved both before and since deregulation.

The first caveat concerns dating the beginning of deregulation. Regulation of domestic airlines began in the 1930s under the Interstate Commerce Commission, the same body that was then regulating railroads and trucks, and subsidization largely took the form of government airmail contracts. In 1938, airline regulation passed to a new agency, the Civil Aeronautics Board (CAB). The motivation for more closely regulating the airlines was their precarious financial condition at the time. Competition, it was feared, would only result in the disruption and perhaps destruction of the domestic airline industry. This, in turn, would be damaging to the military, the postal service, and the economic development of the country as a whole. Moreover, intense competition might lead airlines to compromise safety in their efforts to save money. All these reasons justified a system under which the routes and prices of airlines would be controlled by government to limit the market to the "right" number of competitors.

Officially, airline deregulation began on October 28, 1978, when President Jimmy Carter signed the Airline Deregulation Act. But the CAB had begun loosening the constraints of regulation as early as 1976, when it gave airlines greater freedom to set fares, especially discount fares, and began to relax the standards applied to applications for new routes. Thus, comparisons of the regulated and deregulated airline industry that use 1978 as deregulation's starting date are really comparing current performance not to regulated performance, but to partially deregulated performance, and thus will understate the changes caused by deregulation.

Second, simply comparing industry performance "before" and "after" deregulation assumes that all changes are the result of deregulation. Although changes in regulatory policy can, for example, raise or lower fares, fares can go up or down for other reasons. Developments quite independent of regulation—the ups and downs of the business cycle, technological change, changes in fuel prices—can dramatically affect fares. Rather than simply comparing deregulation with regulation, it is necessary to make a "counterfactual" comparison of what is with what would have been. To evaluate the effect of deregulation on fares, for example, it is necessary to compare actual deregulated fares with an estimate of what fares would have been had regulation continued. For example, a reasonable prediction of what regulated fares would be today is an updated version of the fare formula (the Standard Industry Fare Level, or SIFL) that the CAB used during the last few years of regulation.

Industry Structure

A fundamental premise of airline deregulation was that competition, rather than the government, would "regulate" the airlines. How has deregulation affected competition? Before the industry was deregulated, the largest eight airlines accounted for about 82 percent of domestic passenger miles. (A passenger mile is one passenger flying one mile.) That figure fell to a low of about 72 percent in 1985, before the 1986 merger wave began, and then rose to about 91 percent in 1995.

Airline competition flourishes at the route level. When the Airline Deregulation Act was signed in 1978, the average domestic airline route had slightly more than 1.5 effective competitors. That figure climbed steadily until mid-1986, declined for the next few years because of mergers, then reversed itself in mid-1989 and rose through the third quarter of 1990. The decline over the next two quarters reflected the liquidation of Eastern Airlines and the effect of the economic recession.

Even without adjusting for such events, airline competition at the route level is nearly as great today as it has ever been and clearly greater than it was under regulation. Today, only 3 percent of passengers fly on routes served by only one airline, down from 9 percent in 1978. Eighteen percent of passengers fly on carriers whose route market share is less than 20 percent, up from 7 percent in 1978. Under deregulation, fewer airlines compete nationally, but they compete against each other at the route level more often. The effects of deregulation on fares, service quality, safety, and profitability largely follow from this change in industry competition.

Fares

Has competition been effective in "regulating" fares? Industry revenue per passenger mile—referred to by airline analysts as "yield"—has been trending downward for two decades. After 14 years of deregulation, real yield (yield adjusted for inflation) in 1991 was roughly two-thirds what it was in 1976. But fares began falling before 1976. Would they have fallen further had the industry remained regulated?

Here is an issue that a counterfactual comparison can resolve. Actual yield has consistently been lower than regulated yield would have been, though the size of the gap has fluctuated greatly. The 1981–1982 recession produced the biggest disparity: because airline costs were increasing due to rising fuel costs, regulated fares would have increased. But because of the recession, carriers lowered fares to attract what business was available. Deregulation has led, on average, to fares 20 percent lower than they would have been if regulation had continued. The annual saving to the public is about $8 billion in 1990 dollars.

While deregulation lowered average fares, it also led to a proliferation of individual fares ranging from relatively high unrestricted coach fares to deeply discounted fares with a host of restrictions. In the fourth quarter of 1978, 60 percent of passengers paid fares that were below the average fare, while only 2 percent paid more than 1.5 times the average. By the end of 1990, 67 percent were paying fares below the average, and 12 percent were paying more than 1.5 times the average.

The increased variation reflects benefits to travelers who can obtain deeply discounted fares. For those travelers who pay well above the average, the increased variation does not simply reflect price gouging, though there has been some of that. Some variation reflects cost-based price differences, such as peak versus off-peak fares. Cost differences also arise because business travelers place a higher value on the convenience of booking a seat at the last minute than do pleasure travelers.

Another change in fare policy relates to the length of trips. Under regulation, the CAB intentionally set long-haul fares above cost and short-haul fares below cost. Now, competition has replaced the CAB's policy, and short trips cost more, and long trips less, than they did before deregulation.

A more controversial source of fare differences has been the hub-and-spoke route system—where passengers are routed by a carrier through one of its hub airports—whose use has been accelerated by deregulation. Developed by carriers to increase traffic density and lower unit costs, the system also seems to have enabled carriers to charge higher fares on routes connected to their hubs because other carriers are either unable to enter these routes or simply see no percentage in flying them. In a 1990 study, the U.S. General Accounting Office (GAO) reported that, in 1988, yield at fifteen concentrated hub airports (dominated by one or two carriers) was 27 percent higher than yield at 38 unconcentrated airports. The GAO study, however, effectively treated the unconcentrated and concentrated airports as identical in all respects other than concentration. When the hub premium is adjusted for such factors as trip distance, the relative number of connecting versus direct flights, the number of frequent-flier tickets used, the proportion of business and pleasure traffic, and the characteristics of the airlines that use the airports, the premium does exist, but only at about 5 percent, much lower than the GAO figure.

It should be noted that people do pay vastly different fares for similar and even identical trips. Travelers flying short distances do occasionally pay more than travelers flying longer distances. But these changes are only part of the effect of greater competition that has replaced CAB legislation. To be sure, not all travelers pay less than they would have if regulation had continued: three out of ten pay more.

Service Quality

By accelerating the development of hub-and-spoke route systems and by allowing fare competition, deregulation had a dramatic impact on airline service quality. One complaint about service under the hub-and-spoke system is that passengers now must take connecting flights to reach their destination. About 28 percent of all passengers changed planes on their trips in 1978; about 38 percent do so today. What has changed dramatically is the nature of these connections. In 1978, about half of passengers changing planes changed airlines. But because deregulation allowed airlines to nationalize their route systems, today fewer than 2 percent of passengers change airlines when making connections.

Travelers also complain that the hub-and-spoke system means they are forced to take circuitous routes to their destinations. However, the increase in excess air mileage since 1978 has been less than one percentage point.

One clear benefit of the hub-and-spoke system is that it offers increased frequency of service that makes flying more convenient. The annual benefits to passengers from the increased service frequency have, however, been partly offset by the rise in travel time since deregulation. Flight time for nonstop flights has increased between three and sixteen minutes, depending on distance. The increases stem partly from increased airport and airway congestion in the wake of deregulation. In addition, newer aircraft have slower cruising speeds, and older, faster planes are flying at slower speeds to conserve fuel. Because all of these influences are arguably independent of deregulation—in particular, congestion could be alleviated by appropriate airport pricing and investment policy—the rise in travel time should not be entirely attributed to deregulation.

In certain ways, fare deregulation has reduced service convenience. First and foremost, it has made the airlines work to fill planes. By increasing fare competition, it has driven up carriers' break-even point in terms of the percentage of seats filled, which industry analysts call load factor. The need to increase load factor has benefited the public by encouraging the widespread adoption of discount fares. But travelers now have a harder time getting seats on the flights of their choice. Also, since deregulation short flights have had more empty seats while longer flights have had fewer seats. The change is in keeping with the change in fares: in general, the fewer the seats filled, the higher the fares.

Safety

Safety itself was not deregulated. Safety standards continue to be enforced by the Federal Aviation Administration. Nonetheless, some people believe that increased competition in a deregulated marketplace will tempt airlines to skimp on maintenance, hire less-experienced pilots, or use older aircraft. Others counter that an airline that is unsafe (or even perceived to be unsafe) could not survive in the deregulated marketplace because other carriers are free to enter any route they desire.

The U.S. air carrier fleet is now nearly two years older on average than the non–U.S. fleet. But is deregulation the cause? The U.S. fleet has been aging faster than the non–U.S. fleet since 1967, when the U.S. fleet was newer than the non–U.S. fleet. Thus, the aging of the fleet is most likely related not to deregulation, but to factors such as high U.S. interest rates, low U.S. fuel prices, and the more recent development of aviation outside the United States.

But the question still remains: what has happened to the safety record of airlines since deregulation? Arguably the best measure of airline safety is the probability of an airline passenger dying in an airline accident. That probability has trended downward for some time and continues to fall. Although it cannot be ruled out that the accident rate would have improved even more if airlines were still regulated, the fact is that air safety continues to improve.

Airline Profits

Until recently, the financial performance of the airlines under deregulation has received relatively little attention. Of late, the bankruptcy of several carriers and the liquidation of Eastern and Pan American have raised concerns that the industry cannot satisfy investors and raise needed capital.

The industry's rate of return is cyclical, but since deregulation, it has rarely been as high as 12 percent. Yet, because the industry has been savaged by several economic shocks during the 1980s and 1990s, its profits have actually been higher than they would have been had the industry still been regulated.

According to a counterfactual study, although the 1980–1982 recession and the 1979 energy shock depressed industry earnings, the flexibility of the deregulated airlines in adjusting fares and operations kept losses lower during the early 1980s than they would have been had the carriers been regulated. The same line of reasoning applies to what happened during the early 1990s. A recession, the travel decline related to the Persian Gulf War, and fuel price rises combined to depress earnings, but these earnings would probably have been even lower if the industry were still regulated.

Finally, airlines are still adapting to deregulation. The industry nearly doubled the size of its aircraft fleet from 1985 to 1990 in response both to the long 1980s economic expansion and to its newly granted freedoms. The result was tremendous excess capacity and downward pressure on fares, even before the economy went into recession in 1990. When the industry has completed its shakeout, it should adapt more efficiently to the business cycle.

Since the airline industry was deregulated in 1978, service quality, safety, fares, and profits have all enjoyed net improvements. This progress does not mean that complaints of disgruntled air travelers are baseless. In fact, the data support many of the anecdotes—short trips are more expensive, trips to and from concentrated airline hubs command a small "hub premium," flight times are a little longer, and getting reservations on the flight of one's choice is a little harder. But the evidence suggests that, on balance, the industry is performing better today than it would if it were still regulated.

— Steven A. Morrison, Clifford Winston

See also

Aviation Safety; Deregulation, Economic; Travelers' Rights.

Readings

Morrison, Steven A., and Clifford Winston (1986). *The Economic Effects of Airline Deregulation.* Washington, DC: The Brookings Institution.

——— (1988). "Air Safety, Deregulation, and Public Policy." *Brookings Review.* (Winter): 10–15.

Airline Passenger Rights

See Travelers' Rights.

Airline Safety

See Aviation Safety.

Albanian Consumer Movement

In September 1991, Islam Cani, a retired family doctor and environmental health specialist, and his friend Shefqet Daka, a chemist, formally registered the Albanian Consumers' Association as "a voluntary union of the buyers of mass consumer goods and services from different organizations in Albania and abroad." Its declared aim is "to defend the buyer from individuals or particular groups that sell, produce, process and serve to the detriment of the consumer's interest, making unfair, dishonest and unworthy profits. The Association defends consumers' interests in problems of hygiene and ecology." In less than two years, it built up a registered paying membership of more than 12,600, with active branches in many areas of Albania.

Albania suffers from desperate poverty, little infrastructure, and high unemployment (estimates vary between 40 and 70 percent), with all the problems one would expect of a country whose production has collapsed and whose economy is based largely on "selling-on" (i.e., goods passing through multiple layers of distribution). The goals of the Consumers' Association are both the most basic and the most lofty: to establish consumer rights according to the United Nations Consumer Protection Guidelines; to eradicate the environmental problems created by garbage and untreated sewage; to campaign for a safe and adequate supply of drinking water, for health controls on food sold in the shops, for health education, and for improvements in children's health; and to attack unacceptable levels of unemployment and exploitation in the workplace.

Association representatives sit on management committees within five government ministries—Health, Metrology, Standards and Quality, Environment (where they have voting rights), and Food and Agriculture. Yet the government is prevented by statute from giving the association (or any other nongovernmental organization) financial support. This law was introduced to ensure that, by contrast with the Hoxha era, nongovernmental organizations would be truly independent.

On the legislative front, an Unfair Competition Act (1991), as is the norm in Central and Eastern Europe, preceded a general law on consumer protection, which was enacted in 1996. The latter recognizes the right of consumers to associate in their own interest, but it does not provide for their support. The law proposes the formation of a National Consumer Council composed of four consumer representatives, three representatives of suppliers, and a member of the Ministry of Industry and Trade. Its functions would include research, policy-making, advising the government on consumer issues, and collaboration with consumer organizations in Albania and abroad. It remains to be seen whether this body will strengthen or threaten the independent movement.

The most important development in the offing is a project—to be funded jointly by the PHARE program, the United Kingdom Know-How Fund, and the Westminster Foundation for Democracy—to establish a consumer advice center in the capital, Tirana. This project, in which specialists from Consumers International will be working with the Albanian

Consumers' Association, was getting under way at the beginning of 1996.

— Alastair Macgeorge

See also

Central and Eastern Europe, Consumer Movements in.

Reading

Kozminski, Andrzej K. (1992). "Consumers in Transition from the Centrally Planned Economy to the Market Economy." *Journal of Consumer Policy.* 14: 351–369.

Alcohol Problems and the Consumer Movement

Michael Jacobson was relaxing with a colleague early one evening in 1972 at the offices of the Center for Science in the Public Interest, drinking a beer after a long day of consumer advocacy. Jacobson, the center's executive director and a leader in the effort to require ingredient labeling on food products, idly perused the beer bottle's label. He and his colleague were immediately struck by what was missing. The label listed no ingredients. It did not even include a statement regarding the beer's alcohol content. Why not? Was the beer industry exempt from government requirements, even though the alcohol in the beer is a powerful psychoactive drug? Jacobson's quest for answers resulted in the center's mounting a major alcohol policy initiative.

Cari Lightner, a thirteen-year-old junior high school student, was walking along a bicycle path one May 1980 afternoon after a typical school day in Fair Oaks, California. Meanwhile, in another part of town, Clarence William Busch, a three-time convicted drunk driver, was just finishing another drinking bout. He climbed into his car in a drunken haze and weaved his way across town. Suddenly, tragedy struck. Busch's car swerved into the bicycle lane and struck Cari, throwing her 125 feet and fatally injuring her. Busch left the scene, never slowing down. Cari's mother, Candy Lightner, at first only felt the tragedy and grief. But as Busch's case meandered through the criminal courts, her anger rose. The legal system treated the case with extraordinary leniency. Policymakers were indifferent. Lightner channeled her anger and grief into political action, organizing victims of drinking-driving crashes to form Mothers Against Drunk Drivers (now called Mothers Against Drunk Driving), or MADD.

Alberta Tinsley-Williams was taking her daughter to a Detroit school on a cold January morning in 1988 when she saw a billboard for Top Rolling Papers. The slogan read: "Reach for the Top." Tinsley-Williams suddenly felt a deep anger. What did her child and her child's friends think of this message for drug paraphernalia? Why was her predominantly African-American community inundated with billboards promoting illegal drugs as well as the legal drugs—alcohol and tobacco? Unlike more affluent regions of the city, the inner-city neighborhoods had the billboards everywhere, even adjacent to schools and playgrounds. Tinsley-Williams decided to take action, organizing the Coalition against Billboard Advertising of Alcohol and Tobacco to address the alcohol industry's targeting of African-American communities.

These three incidents, occurring in eight-year intervals, signal the origins of three separate strands of the modern consumer movement to address alcohol problems in the United States. Each strand involves a distinct constituency, and each constituency operates with a distinct experience of alcohol problems. While the goals for the three constituencies have always overlapped, only recently have the groups begun to forge a common agenda for public policy reform.

Alcohol Problems

Alcohol-related problems constitute a consumer health and safety crisis in the United States. The federal government estimates that alcohol is a direct or indirect cause of approximately 105,000 deaths per year. Alcohol-related traffic fatalities and digestive diseases (including alcoholic cirrhosis of the liver) each total approximately 20,000 deaths per year each. Alcohol is also a major contributor to traumatic injury and violence. Alcohol-related motor vehicle crashes alone cause approximately 500,000 serious injuries annually. Of increasing concern is alcohol's contribution to violence—gun-related homicides and injuries, domestic violence, violence against women, and other forms of violent crime.

Alcohol-related injuries and deaths impact young people disproportionately. Alcohol-related motor vehicle crashes constitute the leading cause of death for those between the ages of four and thirty-four. Those dying from alcohol-related causes lose an average of twenty-six years from their normal life expectancy, far higher than other major causes of death in the United States. Teenagers and young adults are more likely to be heavy drinkers and to engage in high-risk drinking. More than one-third of high school seniors report frequent binge drinking.

Alcohol contains ethanol, a psychoactive, addictive drug. Its adverse health and safety impact is far greater than the impact of all illegal drugs combined. The federal government estimates that alcohol problems cause nearly $100 billion each year in economic costs to society. Yet, today alcohol is widely available in an expanding array of consumer outlets; it is one of the most heavily advertised and marketed consumer products in the media and in sporting and community events; the types of alcohol products available are constantly expanding; and alcohol prices continue to drop, to the point that beer is now price-competitive with soft drinks, and wine coolers are not much more expensive.

The powerful alcohol industry, particularly at the producer level, has orchestrated this massive consumer marketing campaign to normalize alcohol as an ordinary consumer product. Its success reflects its political and economic clout. With revenues now approaching $100 billion a year, it can easily fund massive marketing and lobbying campaigns that dwarf the financial resources of those representing consumer interests.

Of particular concern to activists are the marketing tactics used by the industry to target young drinkers. Alcohol advertisements frequently use youth-oriented appeals and images. The newest products in the market—such as wine coolers, Zima, and other sweet, soft-drink–style beverages—appeal to youthful tastes. Their relatively cheap prices and ready availability are an essential element in reaching the youth market.

National Consumer Group Activism

Alcohol was not treated seriously as a consumer issue between the end of Prohibition in 1933 and the early 1980s. This lack of consumer concern represents an anomaly in American history. Throughout the nineteenth century, alcohol constituted a major social issue. In the middle of that century, temperance was closely associated with both the anti-slavery and the women's suffrage movements. Following Prohibition, however, there was a general consensus that alcohol problems should be treated strictly as problems of alcoholic individuals unrelated to the consumer marketplace. This approach suited the alcohol industry's plans to dominate the structure and regulations of a rapidly growing alcohol market.

The expansion of the alcohol market in the 1960s and 1970s coincided with dramatic increases in per capita consumption and alcohol problems. Consumer attention to alcohol reawoke as the problems associated with its use increased. The national dialogue and debate brought the problems out from behind closed doors, breaking traditional ideological, social, and cultural barriers. Alcohol problems affect all parts of society—rich and poor, all races and ethnic groups, conservatives and liberals, young and old, males and females. The consumer coalitions that emerged are among the most diverse of those within the broader consumer movement.

The Center for Science in the Public Interest (CSPI) has played a pivotal role in organizing consumers for action at the national level. It has sought four major consumer protection measures, all of which have had strong support according to popular opinion polls.

In 1972, the same year that Michael Jacobson noticed the lack of ingredient labeling on alcohol containers, CSPI petitioned the Food and Drug Administration (FDA) and the Bureau of Alcohol, Tobacco, and Firearms to require ingredient disclosure. The FDA ordered such labeling in 1975, but a federal district court ruled that the Bureau of Alcohol, Tobacco and Firearms had jurisdiction over the matter. A bureau order requiring ingredient labels was partially rescinded by the Reagan administration in 1981. After many more court appeals, a compromise was reached that required disclosure of any ingredients found by the FDA to pose definite health risks. Full ingredient labeling is still not required, although the partial consumer victory has led to industry disclosures of saccharin, yellow dye #5, and sulfites. In a related struggle in 1986, CSPI petitioned the FDA to test and set limits on the levels of the cancer-causing chemical urethane in wine and distilled products. In the mid-1990s, the government and the industry reached a voluntary agreement to conduct tests and to reduce levels.

In the early 1980s, CSPI shifted its focus from ingredient labeling to alcohol-related problems, which was the result, according to Jacobson, of his shock at discovering the immense health damage that alcohol was causing to society. Joined by the National Council on Alcoholism and Drug Dependency (NCADD), which was formerly the National Council on Alcoholism, the center organized a broad-based coalition of over 100 consumer, public health, parent, children's advocacy, religious, and medical groups. The coalition sought federal legislation either to ban alcohol advertising on electronic media or to require equal time for health messages. The coalition was responding to massive advertising campaigns of the alcohol industry (over $1 billion worth in the measured media in 1994), the lack of any health messages in the ads, and the impact of the ads on young children and teenagers.

To initiate the campaign, CSPI and NCADD coordinated Project SMART (Stop Marketing Alcohol on Radio and Television), a drive to collect 1 million signatures in support of the federal legislation. Jacobson delivered the signatures to the House of Representatives Telecommunications Subcommittee on May 21, 1985. The hearing signaled the beginning of an extended battle for federal regulation of alcohol advertising in the electronic media, a struggle that continues to this date.

Despite broad-based support, Project SMART was derailed by a powerful coalition of special interests—the alcohol, broadcast, and advertising industries. These industries have succeeded in defeating every federal legislative effort to date. Most recently, in 1994 the industries successfully opposed the Sensible Advertising and Family Education Act (requiring that health warning statements be broadcast at the end of each alcohol advertisement, among other requirements). The measure failed without a vote in a Senate committee. Broadcasters have played a key role in the defeat of this consumer effort; they led opposition to legislation and, as an alternative, promoted voluntary public service announcements produced by the alcohol and advertising industries and the broadcasters themselves.

The campaign for health warning labels on alcohol containers began in 1977, when federal legislation was introduced to require disclosure on alcohol containers to warn pregnant women of the risk of fetal alcohol syndrome. The proposal died quietly, and the issue was not revisited until 1986. Senator Strom Thurmond, the congressional champion for health warnings, introduced a comprehensive bill in that year that would have required a rotating label providing five different warning messages. A two-year struggle ensued. NCADD and CSPI again organized a broad-based coalition to mount an effort to convince Congress to take action. In late 1988, Congress passed the Alcohol Beverage Container Warning Labeling Act.

This legislation compromised the consumers' proposal to a considerable degree. The warning label has a single, lengthy message rather than one selection from five short messages, and the required size of the message is so small that advocates handed out magnifying glasses at press conferences announcing the act's passage. These shortcomings, the result of industry pressure, greatly diminish the effectiveness of the label. In addition, the act preempts state action and precludes consumer tort claims against the industry based on a legal theory that the industry failed to disclose potential risks of using the product.

Alcohol taxes represent a consumer issue for three reasons: raising the price of alcohol reduces alcohol problems, including long-term health problems and alcohol-related motor vehicle crashes; higher prices have their greatest deterrent impact on young people, who have limited discretionary income; and increased revenues from alcohol taxes offset the monetary costs to government of alcohol problems and provide possible new revenues for health care and other consumer protection measures. Alcohol taxes at the state and federal level are levied on a per-volume basis (as an excise tax). Thus, as inflation erodes the value of the dollar, the value of the tax decreases. The federal government's failure to raise alcohol taxes to keep pace with inflation has resulted in a loss of approximately $100 billion in alcohol tax revenues since 1951.

CSPI has led a decade-long campaign to raise state and federal taxes. It has organized a third coalition, called the National Alcohol Tax Coalition, which seeks a three-part reform: double (or at least raise substantially) the excise tax rate on distilled spirits; equalize wine and beer taxes to those of distilled spirits, based on alcohol content; and index the tax rates to inflation.

In the past decade, Congress and state governments have imposed modest alcohol tax increases. At the state level, however, the national coalition and its sister groups can take only partial credit for these increases since they were largely the result of the need for new revenues. In fact, given these revenue needs, strong public support for alcohol taxes, and the continued erosion of the value of the tax due to inflation, it is surprising that state taxes have not been increased more substantially. But these factors have been largely offset by the efforts of the alcohol industry. Recently, for example, it convinced the Clinton administration to drop alcohol taxes as part of its health care reform proposal. Also, the industry spent over $30 million to defeat a voter initiative proposal in California that would have substantially increased alcohol taxes in that state, earmarking revenue for a variety of health and safety causes.

The Anti–Drunk Driving Movement

The anti–drunk driving movement represents a parallel, independent force addressing consumer concerns. Candy Lightner's decision in 1980 to organize a political movement of drunk driving victims produced an enthusiastic response. By 1985, Mothers Against Drunk Driving (MADD) had over 600,000 members, 360 chapters in all fifty states, and a budget approaching $10 million. Other groups, including Remove Intoxicated Drivers (RID), which predated MADD, and Students Against Driving Drunk (SADD), also formed. MADD received widespread media coverage and rapidly became the dominant group. The stories of its members brought widespread public support and demand for legislative action.

MADD has always maintained a primary focus on criminal justice reform, seeking increased penalties for convicted drunk drivers and increased enforcement efforts. Until recently, the organization has sought to accommodate, or at least avoid criticisms of, the alcohol industry and its marketing practices. Its early experiences with the industry helped to dictate this course. One of its first campaigns was to seek an increase in alcohol taxes in California. MADD had won a series of impressive legislative victories in its first two years, but the tax proposal was soundly defeated by industry lobbyists. Shortly after this defeat, MADD reorganized its board, reducing the number of consumer advocates and increasing representation from various industry groups (not including the alcohol industry itself). It then moved to Texas and accepted a grant from the Anheuser-Busch Company, the nation's largest brewer.

For the rest of the 1980s and the early 1990s, MADD continued its primary focus on criminal justice reform, acting cautiously on legislation addressing alcohol marketing issues. The organization joined the campaign for health warning labels and led a successful national campaign to increase the states' minimum legal drinking age to twenty-one, which led to federal legislation in 1984. But it refused to support Project SMART, causing a major rift between it and other consumer groups seeking alcohol policy reform. Instead, MADD called for voluntary advertising reform. This position was embraced by the National Association of Broadcasters, which has long been a supporter of MADD and has assisted the organization in gaining wide media exposure.

In the early 1990s, MADD faced serious internal dissension that led to an upheaval in leadership, including Candy Lightner's resignation, and investigations of its fund-raising policies. The new leadership reexamined the organization's positions on advertising, alcohol industry marketing, and alcohol taxes and decided to join other consumer and health advocates in the national coalitions formed by CSPI and NCADD. While the shift came only after MADD had lost much of its political clout, it and other anti–drunk driving groups had focused considerable public attention on alcohol problems, which influenced how Americans view and consume alcohol.

Consumer Advocacy at the Local Level

A third, parallel constituency for consumer-oriented alcohol policy reform has emerged at the grassroots level. Alberta Tinsley-Williams's campaign against billboard advertisements for alcohol spread rapidly in African-American communities across the country. The groups that formed began to address other pressing neighborhood and community issues, and encouraged the development of local coalitions in diverse communities across the country.

Supported by the national coalitions described above, these grassroots groups successfully advocated many legislative reforms. Baltimore recently enacted an ordinance that greatly reduced the number of alcohol and tobacco billboards. Los Angeles has reduced the number of liquor stores in inner-city communities following the civil unrest in 1992. A coalition in Gallup, New Mexico, has succeeded in enacting a higher alcohol tax for its county to help pay for alcohol treatment services. Activists in San Diego have challenged Anheuser-Busch's efforts to market beer at Marine World, a family-oriented theme park owned by the beer company. In the 1990s, hundreds of reforms have been approved by local governments.

Conclusion

During the past two decades, the consumer movement has achieved great success in reducing the toll of alcohol problems. There is a new awareness of alcohol-related problems that has made possible real social change. Drinking-driving crashes have declined steadily, and consumption rates have been either static or declined somewhat. The choice not to drink is not nearly as stigmatized as it was a decade ago, and heavy drinking is much less tolerated, particularly when combined with driving an automobile. The alcohol industry can no longer anticipate an ever-expanding market. The three strands of the alcohol-consumer movement share credit for these changes.

Yet, this success is mixed with considerable frustration at what still must be accomplished. Most of the legislative agenda has yet to be enacted. Alcohol marketing continues to be pervasive, using deceptive and misleading images and messages that target young people. Alcohol prices continue to drop. Alcohol availability is expanding to new consumer outlets. And the deaths, disability, and serious trauma associated with alcohol are at high levels. In addition, the alcohol industry has demonstrated its legislative prowess at the state and federal level, shrewdly using its economic clout and political access to block or compromise major policy reforms.

Nevertheless, a subtle change has occurred. The industry no longer can act with impunity in the halls of government and is increasingly on the defensive. The emergence of effective grassroots action to develop and implement alcohol policy reforms has provided a base for effective political responses to the industry at the national level.

— James F. Mosher

See also

Center for Science in the Public Interest; Highway Safety.

Readings

Cowan, Richard, and James F. Mosher (1985). "Public Health Implications of Beverage Marketing: Alcohol as an Ordinary Consumer Product." *Contemporary Drug Problems.* 12 (Winter): 621–657.

Holder, Harold D., and Griffith Edwards, eds. (1995). *Alcohol and Public Policy: Evidence and Issues.* Oxford: Oxford University Press.

Office of the Surgeon General (1989). *Surgeon General's Workshop on Drunk Driving: Proceedings.* Rockville, MD: U.S. Department of Health and Human Services, Public Health Service, Office of the Surgeon General.

American Association of Retired Persons

American Association of Retired Persons (AARP) is a nonprofit, nonpartisan organization dedicated to helping older Americans achieve lives of independence, dignity, and purpose. AARP is the nation's oldest and largest organization of older Americans, with a membership of over 33 million. Membership is open to anyone age fifty or older, both working and retired. Over one-third of the association's membership is in the work force.

AARP's motto is "To Serve, Not to be Served." The association's vision statement, "AARP excels as a dynamic presence in every community, shaping and enriching the experience of aging for each member and society," is supported by activities of members and staff who are involved in community, state, and national affairs.

In 1947, Ethel Percy Andrus, a retired school principal, founded the National Retired Teachers Association (NRTA). Andrus, a crusader, was concerned about the inadequacy of teacher pensions. The NRTA, then a department of the National Education Association, initially fought in state legislatures for pension reform for retired teachers, and in Congress for tax benefits for retired teachers. Andrus also addressed another social problem—that no insurance company would provide health insurance to a person over sixty-five. Through Leonard Davis, an insurance consultant, Andrus identified an insurer willing to support a trial program. After the launch with teachers, thousands of retired people who were not teachers asked to obtain the insurance as well.

In 1958, Andrus founded AARP as an entity parallel to but independent of the NRTA. Membership dues were $2 per year. AARP's two goals were "to aid the aged in their needs—social, physical, economic and intellectual" and "to make available to its members concrete, tangible answers to as many pressing everyday needs as possible." In the early 1980s, the two organizations merged.

AARP leaders include a chairman, a president, a president-elect, and an executive director, who runs the organization on a day-to-day basis. Since 1988, Horace B. Deets has served as executive director. From 1975 to 1988, he held a variety of management positions at AARP and, before then, worked at the U.S. Equal Employment Opportunity Commission.

In 1994, AARP's annual budget was $455,920,000. The primary source of revenues for the association is membership dues, currently $8 per year (including spouse). Other important sources of revenue are royalties and administrative fees paid by service providers who offer products to AARP members. The organization also generates substantial income by selling advertising in its magazine *Modern Maturity.*

The four primary functions of the organization are advocacy, education, community service, and member service. As an advocate, AARP represents a population that includes workers and retirees, women re-entering the work force, and frail older people living alone. The association seeks to promote their needs and interests at both the federal and state levels in legislative and regulatory arenas. AARP was instrumental, for example, in persuading Congress to approve the Medicare program, the Age Discrimination in Employment Act, and Medigap insurance reform.

The association's educational efforts are broad in scope. AARP/VOTE is designed to educate and involve voters on issues of concern to older Americans and the community at large. AARP also provides a wide range of consumer education materials on issues including nursing homes, driver safety, pensions and other financial issues, health care, caregiving, and housing. Each year, it distributes more than a million copies of brochures, booklets, self-help guides, and videos covering a range of issues that affect people as they age.

AARP also evaluates products and services that older people need or desire, thereby improving product standards and consumer knowledge. The products it has assessed include wheelchairs, electric scooters, hearing aids, living trusts, and life insurance.

In addition, AARP has created volunteer opportunities for thousands of older persons. AARP members help older people fill out tax forms each year, teach safe driving courses, provide bereavement counseling for widowed persons, and educate voters on key policy issues. AARP also works with the federal government to administer the Senior Community Service Employment Program, which provides temporary employment across the country for 12,000 low-income older persons while they hone their job skills and seek permanent employment.

AARP uses its strength in the marketplace to develop and offer a number of services to its members. Services include: group health insurance, automobile/homeowners/life insurance, mobile home insurance, an annuity program, an investment program, VISA and Mastercard programs, a motoring plan, and a mail-order pharmacy service.

Many of AARP's objectives are carried out in collaboration with other agencies and organizations. Each year, the Women's Financial Information Program (WFIP), implemented in partnership with community-based nonprofit organizations, provides over 21,000 women with objective financial information. Similarly, workshops on consumer fraud conducted with attorneys general around the country benefit thousands of people. Workshops are also conducted on legal instruments, such as durable health care powers of attorney and living wills, to help ensure that medical decisions are based on values, goals for treatment, and finances. Outreach efforts to provide low-income older persons with information about applying for public benefits are conducted with the Social Security Administration and local welfare offices.

Strategic directions for the association throughout the 1990s have included creating an enhanced presence in communities across the country, building and strengthening its relationship with members, crafting and implementing a coordinated communications strategy, increasing operational efficiency, positioning the association as an advocate to improve policies and practices that impact people as they age, and providing expert knowledge of aging issues.

— Katrinka Smith Sloan

See also
Older Consumers.

Readings

Schurenberg, Eric, and Lani Luciano (1988). "The Empire Called AARP." *Money*. 17 (October): 128–146.

"The Story of AARP." Reprinted from August/September 1976 issue of *Modern Maturity*. Available from the American Association of Retired Persons, Washington, D.C.

American Council on Consumer Interests

The American Council on Consumer Interests (ACCI) exists to provide a forum for the exchange of ideas and presentation of information about individuals and families as consumers. This mission includes the production, synthesis, and dissemination of information in the consumer interest. The organization's goals are twofold: to promote the well-being of individuals and families as consumers, nationally and internationally, by identifying issues, stimulating research, promoting education, and informing policy; and to provide for the professional development of the membership by creating, maintaining, and stimulating interactive communication among advocates, business representatives, educators, policymakers, and researchers through publications, educational programs, and networking opportunities.

In 1952, Colston Warne, president of the board of directors of Consumers Union and economics professor at Amherst College, saw the need for a consumer education association. With Warne were two other key persons who helped lay the foundation for this new consumer education organization—Henry Harap of the George Peabody College for Teachers and Ray Price of the University of Minnesota. Twenty-one persons accepted their invitation to attend a planning session at the University of Minnesota. At this session, plans were begun that resulted, in 1953, in the establishment of the Council on Consumer Information. In 1969, to emphasize that the organization had become national in scope, it changed its name to the American Council on Consumer Interests.

From the very beginning, ACCI was an interprofessional organization. The twenty-one charter members included nine from education, six from economics, three from home economics, and three from public policy.

With a $7,000 grant from Consumers Union, the planning group was able to begin recruiting members, publishing a newsletter and pamphlets, and organizing an annual conference. For almost two decades, ACCI depended on subsidies from Consumers Union, which came with no strings attached. By 1969, ACCI was able to support itself.

In the early years, ACCI was a loosely organized association with decisions made by a self-perpetuating board of directors. As the organization grew in membership, it decided that the board should be elected by the members. At the start, any person who became a member could vote. Then, after a vigorous debate at the 1975 conference, a bylaw was passed that denied voting rights to those employed by business by limiting this right to those affiliated with academic institutions, governmental organizations, and nonprofit groups. But in 1994, the bylaws were changed to give voting rights to all of ACCI's individual members, including employees of business groups.

Early in its existence, ACCI became the national organization for those interested in both consumer education and consumer rights in the marketplace. Members included college professors, public school teachers, government employees concerned about consumer protection, persons involved in public interest activities, and laypersons with a consumer interest. But the issue of whether the organization should be politically active divided members. In 1964, ACCI decided to be nonpolitical, taking no stand on issues of public policy. Nevertheless, because many ACCI members were personally committed to this activism, they helped establish groups such as the Consumer Federation of America, the Conference of Consumer Organizations, the National Association of Consumer Agency Administrators, the Consumer Protection Committee of the National Association of Attorneys General, and the National Coalition for Consumer Education. Today, ACCI holds memberships in Consumers International, the Consumer Federation of America, the United States Mission to the United Nations, and the Consortium of Social Science Association.

Perhaps the most significant contribution of ACCI to the consumer movement has been the organization's publications. For decades, the *ACCI Newsletter* has been an important source of information about publications, government consumer actions, organization activities, and other items of consumer interest. This publication was developed and, for three decades, edited by Stewart Lee.

In its early years, the organization published a series of educational pamphlets with titles such as: "Consumers Look at Farm Price Policies," "Consumers Look at Fair Trade," "Consumers Look at Discount Houses," and "What You Should Know about the Law." The publication of the pamphlets "The Consumer Looks at Deceptive Packaging" and "Truth-in-Lending Act" supported passage of the Fair Packaging and Labeling Act (1967) and the Truth in Lending Act (1969).

In 1966, under the editorship of Gordon Bivens, ACCI launched the *Journal of Consumer Affairs,* which has become the principal outlet for peer-reviewed articles on consumer topics. In 1970, the publication of the *Consumer Education Forum* represented an effort to recruit ACCI members from the public schools, but a lack of interest led, in 1982, to the publication's discontinuation. In 1987, ACCI began publishing another journal, *Advancing the Consumer Interest,* which is oriented to applied and practical aspects of the consumer in the marketplace. The *Consumer Interests Annual* is the published collection of the papers and speeches presented at the annual conference.

There have been three special ACCI publications: *The American Council on Consumer Interests: An Oral History, 1954–1984* (1987), directed by Marjorie Merchant and conducted by Norman Silber; *The Frontier of Research in the Consumer Interest* (1988), edited by E. Scott Maynes; and *Enhancing Consumer Choice* (1991), edited by Robert N. Mayer. The latter two publications contain papers presented at two special ACCI research conferences. *ACCI International* newsletter is published periodically with news on international consumer education activities.

Over the years, there have been only a few disputes among ACCI members. Those involving voting rights for business members and political activism have already been mentioned. Two others are worth noting. One centered on whether to publish a pamphlet on trading stamps. This pamphlet had been written by the executive secretary, who at the time had accepted a position with Sperry and Hutchinson, the issuer of Green Stamps. Because of this conflict of interest, the board ruled that the pamphlet should not be published. The other dispute concerned whether the ACCI headquarters should be relocated from the University of Missouri–Columbia to Texas Technological University. The ACCI president and board of directors voted for a move to Texas. But in a vote of the members at the annual business meeting, this decision was overturned. The national headquarters remained in Missouri.

A major event in the life of ACCI is the annual conferences. The first one was held in 1955 in Dayton, Ohio. The forty-first conference was held in Washington, D.C., in conjunction with the Consumer Federation of America's Consumer Assembly. At the ACCI conferences, two special, sponsored sessions are presented: the Colston Warne Lectureship and the Esther Peterson Consumer Policy Forum. Special awards presented at the annual conference include the Russell A. Dixon Award, Stewart M. Lee Consumer Education Award, Applied Consumer Economics Award, Dissertation Award, and Thesis Awards. Individuals who have served ACCI for years, making special contributions, are honored by being named ACCI Distinguished Fellows. Since 1973, twenty-six members have received this special honor.

Memberships and subscriptions represent the major sources of ACCI income. The annual report for 1994 showed total revenue of $169,009 and expenses of $166,972.

As of 1996, membership was 1,261, which included 489 individual, 82 student, and 690 institutional members. Eighty percent of the members reside in the United States, 4 percent in Canada and Mexico, and 16 percent overseas. Thirty-eight foreign countries are represented in the membership. ACCI is managed by a part-time executive director (seven-tenths time) who is assisted by a full-time administrative assistant and by graduate assistants.

The scope of ACCI activities is suggested by its committees: Applied Consumer Economics Award; Career Opportunities; Conference Exhibits; Consumer Education; Development; Distinguished Fellows Award; Finance; Future Directions; International Consumer Affairs; Membership; Nominations and Elections; Research; Stewart M. Lee Consumer Education Award; and Student Research Awards. In addition, ACCI selects representatives to the following organizations: Consumer Federation of America; Consumers International; National Coalition for Consumer Education; and the United States Mission to the United Nations.

In the future, ACCI faces several challenges. The cutback in funding of consumer education and consumer affairs at all levels of government has hurt the consumer movement, including ACCI. In addition, a number of colleges and universities have either curtailed or eliminated their consumer programs both at the undergraduate and graduate levels. Recently, the ACCI board created a Future Directions Committee. The deliberations of this committee are likely to shape the upcoming priorities and activities of the organization.

— Stewart M. Lee

See also

Consumer Economics/Studies; Research on Consumer Issues.

Readings

Merchant, M. M., ed. (1987). *The American Council on Consumer Interests: An Oral History*. Columbia, MO: American Council on Consumer Interests.

Morse, Richard L. D., ed. (1993). *The Consumer Movement: Lectures by Colston E. Warne*. Manhattan, KS: Family Economics Trust Press.

American Council on Science and Health

The American Council on Science and Health (ACSH) is an independent, nonprofit, nonpartisan consumer education organization that is supported by the unrestricted contributions of concerned individuals, foundations, corporations, and trade associations. It was founded in 1978 by a group of concerned scientists and policy advisers who felt that scientific information about America's health and environment was being misrepresented and distorted, biasing public health policy decisions.

ACSH's mission is to research and assess the risks and hyperbole associated with America's food supply, pharmaceuticals, chemicals, lifestyle options, and environment, and to report its findings through press releases, media appearances, consumer publications and reports, public forums, and seminars. Its goal is to ensure that peer-reviewed, mainstream science is communicated on a wider basis to the nation's health and environmental regulatory and legislative policymakers, and to the American people.

ACSH is led by president and founder, Elizabeth M. Whelan (Sc.D.), who manages a staff of around twelve persons. The organization is directed and advised by a scientific advisory board comprised of over 300 scientists and policy advisers. These directors and advisers are experts from different disciplines who help assure that ACSH's public health positions represent the most current scientific consensus. These scientists and policy advisers serve ACSH without compensation. In 1995, the organization's budget was about $1.1 million.

ACSH frequently opposes environmental groups who are calling for new government regulations on business. It believes that these environmentalists often advocate the removal of useful products and support burdensome regulations to "protect" the public from trivial or imagined risks associated with science and modern technology. ACSH maintains, to the contrary, that the nation's high standard of living can be directly attributed to scientific research and technological developments.

In controversies over the safe use of pharmaceuticals, pesticides, chemicals, and other modern technologies, ACSH has often been alone in defending these products and their scientist supporters. The organization led the defense of the safety of pesticides and chemicals such as Alar, ethylene dibromide (EDB), bovine somatotropin (BST), low-calorie sweetener agents, and various food additives and preservatives. ACSH also has argued for a balanced view of the environmental dangers of polychlorinated biphenyls (PCBs), asbestos, and dioxin. Moreover, the group supports developing new technologies such as biotechnology, food irradiation, and nuclear power.

To educate and inform the public about pertinent health and environmental issues, ACSH undertakes several activities. First, it prepares and releases scientific reports on controversial health issues. All of these reports are peer-reviewed by experts to ensure that they reflect mainstream scientific opinion. Second, it publishes a quarterly magazine, *PRIORITIES: For Long Life and Good Health,* that addresses what it considers to be the real issues that affect public health, not the fads and phobias it believes some consumer-oriented health magazines cover. Third, it provides counsel, comments, and expert testimony at congressional hearings, and to other regulatory and public health agencies. ACSH's board of scientific advisers often develops these communications.

Fourth, ACSH advances its positions aggressively through articles and interviews in the media, and through national press conferences and forums. ACSH representatives have been quoted and referenced by the press on public health issues. Its leaders have appeared on all the major networks' news programs including "60 Minutes" and "Larry King Live." Full-length columns produced by ACSH appear regularly in hundreds of national and local newspapers.

Fifth, although based in New York City, the organization maintains a Washington, D.C., liaison representative to counter liberal public interest groups by communicating with federal policymakers and national opinion leaders. This liaison tries to acquaint members of Congress, regulatory agencies, other executive branches, and the media with the positions developed by ACSH and disseminated in its publications.

Sixth, ACSH hosts educational roundtable forums to make its scientific advisers available to the public, key business leaders, and policy leaders. Seventh, the organization produces and distributes educational public health films and books. Whelan has written more than twenty-three books. ACSH produced and distributed nationally a documentary film, *Big Fears, Little Risks,* the first in a series of educational public health films.

Throughout its history, ACSH has tried to help the public distinguish between hypothetical and real health hazards. The organization's research—advanced through press conferences, television and radio interviews, reports targeted to specific audiences, newsletters, and press releases—has provided millions of Americans with information about the leading causes of premature, preventable disease and death in the United States and how to avoid them. At the same time, ACSH has worked to relieve what it believes to be unnecessary anxieties about hypothetical risks and controversies associated with the products of technology.

— Elizabeth M. Whelan

See also

Economic Criticisms of the Consumer Movement.

Readings

Dolan, Maura (1989). "Scientific Group Wages Crusade to Ease Food Safety Concerns." *Los Angeles Times*. (April 6): 133.

Kurtz, Howard (1990). "Dr. Whelan's Media Operation." *Columbia Journalism Review*. 28 (March/April): 43–47.

Antitrust Protections

Antitrust laws are aimed at protecting and preserving competition. Their roots can be traced to early British common law court decisions encouraging freer access to certain trades and occupations. U.S. antitrust laws are designed to allow consumers to choose among a variety of goods and services at a variety of prices. Free and open competition benefits consumers by ensuring lower prices and new and improved products. In a freely competitive market, each competing business tries to attract customers by cutting prices and/or increasing the quality of its product or service.

The reality concerning markets, however, is that pure or perfect competition does not exist. Economies of scale and technology often give the advantage to the largest and most efficient firms. When only a few firms dominate an industry, they are likely to set higher prices than would exist if more competition obtained. In addition, the firms may impose barriers to entry by other firms.

The federal government promotes fair competition with antitrust laws. These statutes concern government regulation of anticompetitive business practices. Anticompetitive abuses can result from trusts, cartels, monopolies, price discrimination, collusion, and deceptive or unfair business practices. The word *trust* comes from a business practice in the late 1800s in which several companies combined their assets into a common legal entity and then attempted to minimize or eliminate competition. A cartel is a combination of independent firms formed to regulate production, pricing, and marketing of goods by members in an effort to maintain or increase prices and profits.

The antitrust laws are aimed at preventing giant corporations from acting unfairly to dominate smaller rivals and to prevent firms from fixing prices, carving up markets, or engaging in other anticompetitive acts. Predatory pricing is defined by the U.S. Supreme Court as "pricing below an appropriate measure of cost for the purpose of eliminating competitors in the short run and reducing competition in the long run." It occurs when a price-cutting firm is willing to hold its new low prices for perhaps three to five years in an effort to drive out competition.

Congress and the courts have exempted a number of businesses from antitrust laws. Examples include natural monopolies such as electric and gas distribution companies, fishing organizations, agricultural cooperatives, labor unions, insurance companies (which are regulated by states), newspaper joint operating arrangements, professional baseball, and the joint export activities of American companies. Other industries have been granted partial exemptions.

Antitrust Laws

There are several major federal antitrust laws: the Sherman Antitrust Act, the Clayton Act, the Federal Trade Commission Act, the Robinson-Patman Act, the Cellar-Kefauver Act, and the Hart-Scott-Rodino Act. Antitrust lawsuits can be brought by the Department of Justice, the Federal Trade Commission (FTC), and state attorneys general, as well as by private persons and companies. The U.S. Supreme Court's *Illinois Brick Company v. Illinois* decision, however, prohibits consumers from suing price fixers in federal court unless they are directly affected. Only the direct purchaser affected by a manufacturer's price fixing, such as the middleman or wholesaler, can sue. But in 1989, the U.S. Supreme Court upheld state antitrust laws allowing those indirectly injured by illegal price fixing, such as consumers, to sue for damages.

The Sherman Antitrust Act, passed in 1890, declared illegal "every contract, combination in the form of trust or otherwise, or conspiracy, in restraint of trade or commerce among the several States, or with foreign nations." In 1911, the U.S. Supreme Court inserted the word *unreasonable* before *contract*. Thus, the law prohibits monopolization and other joint or concerted actions that attempt to restrain unreasonably trade and commerce, and threatens civil fines and criminal penalties for violations of this law.

A pure monopoly is a market condition in which there is one seller for a product for which there are no close substitutes. A monopolist has the ability to set the price by altering supply. But in modern economies, since there is almost always some competition, pure monopolies are more an abstraction than a reality. Thus, in practice, a monopoly is considered to be a firm that has the power to raise prices above competitive levels. Typically, this influence is gained when a business has exclusive control over a commercial activity. Monopolies may arise from a number of sources, including economies of scale, control of raw materials, and exclusive patent or copyright ownership. When a monopoly exists, the forces of supply and demand cannot determine production and price. Instead, the monopoly decides on the supply and the price for its own gain.

An oligopoly is a market condition in which the bulk of production is accounted for by a few dominant firms whose actions materially affect price and hence restrict competition. Because of the limited number of firms, each one must consider the reaction of rivals in matters relating to output and price. Price competition in oligopolistic industries is often minimal.

Monopolistic competition is a related noncompetitive market condition in which a number of firms produce similar, but somewhat differentiated, goods. Product differentiation usually gives each firm a limited degree of control over prices.

The U.S. Supreme Court has held that violations of the Sherman Antitrust Act occur when the behavior of firms "unreasonably restrains competition." Two approaches are used to assess such behavior. Per se actions are those that are intrinsically illegal because they always have a negative effect on competition and can never be justified or excused. The government has a number of per se rules. Rule of reason, on the other hand, is behavior not classified as illegal, per se, but as "unreasonable." It requires an inquiry into the actual competitive effects of the defendant's actions, as well as any justifications that the defendant may advance. In recent years, the trend in court decisions has been away from per se rules in favor of rule of reason analysis of alleged violations.

Violations of the Sherman Antitrust Act may give rise to both criminal and civil penalties. Individuals judged to have demonstrated criminal intent may be fined up to $100,000 per violation and/or be imprisoned for up to three years. Corporations may be fined up to $1 million per violation.

Dissatisfaction with the adequacy of the Sherman Antitrust Act led Congress, in 1914, to pass the Clayton Act. Its intention was to prevent monopolies by prohibiting anticompetitive corporate mergers and acquisitions, price discrimination, tying agreements, and interlocking directorships. The Clayton Act was designed to discourage businesses from substantially lessening competition or creating monopolies in any line of commerce. It is a statute with only civil penalties, although private plaintiffs can sue for treble damages or injunctive relief.

The Clayton Act prohibited mergers or acquisitions that are likely to lessen competition. A merger is the acquisition of one company by another company. A vertical merger results from bringing under one control a number of companies that have, or could have, a supplier-customer relationship, because they have engaged in different steps in manufacturing or marketing a product. These mergers are examined and sometimes challenged by government. A conglomerate merger results from bringing under one control a number of companies belonging to unrelated industries. Such mergers are rarely challenged.

In general, the judgment of the court is that a restraint of trade occurring through a merger must be undue and unreasonable in order to be considered illegal. Mere bigness is not proof of a violation. From time to time, the Justice Department and the FTC jointly issue guidelines and criteria that they use in evaluating individual mergers. The 1992 guidelines use the Herfindahl Index, a measure of market share, to test whether a merger will reduce competitiveness in a particular market.

In 1914, Congress also passed the Federal Trade Commission Act to combat unfair methods of competition because it believed that failures of the Sherman Antitrust Act were partially the fault of the institutions entrusted with its enforcement: the Justice Department and the courts. The law created a new government agency, the FTC, a bipartisan commission of five presidential appointees, confirmed by the Senate for staggered terms, to examine and prevent those practices that led to monopolies. The law declared that unfair competition should be unlawful. In 1938, Congress passed the Wheeler-Lea amendment to add a ban on "unfair or deceptive practices."

The Federal Trade Commission Act prohibits unfair methods, acts, and practices that lessen competition in interstate commerce. The law provides that the prohibitions can be interpreted and enforced through administrative proceedings by the FTC, subject to review by the courts. As amended, section five of the act uses sweeping language that empowers the FTC to "prevent unfair methods of competition and unfair or deceptive acts or practices in or affecting commerce." This section permits the FTC to prohibit existing, incipient, and potential practices.

The 1936 Robinson-Patman Act is commonly referred to as the "chain store act" because it prohibits price cutting of commodities by large firms in order to eliminate competition from small firms. It is illegal for companies engaged in interstate commerce to grant discounts for the same commodities to large firms, such as chain stores, without granting similar discounts to smaller independent stores when the selling costs do not vary between the two. The law does permit selling at different prices when costs are based on different methods of quantities or involved in the manufacture, sale, or delivery of the products.

The 1950 Cellar-Kefauver Act amended Section 7 of the Clayton Act to prohibit the acquisition of one firm's stock by another when the end results would lessen competition or create a monopoly. The 1976 Hart-Scott-Rodino Act requires premerger notifications. It mandates that all persons and businesses considering a merger of significant size notify the Antitrust Division of the Justice Department, as well as the FTC. *Parens patriae* (protector of those needing protection) is a legal concept permitted under this law that allows a state attorney general to bring civil actions in federal court on behalf of the people of his or her state to secure monetary relief for price fixing and anticompetitive business practices. A unanimous Supreme Court ruled in 1990 that state attorneys general can obtain court orders to undo illegal corporate mergers.

Antitrust Tools

The government uses four primary antitrust tools to promote fair competition. One tool is providing an incentive for private individuals to enforce the laws. Section 4 of the Clayton Act gives individuals the right to enforce the antitrust provisions of the Sherman Antitrust Act and the Clayton Act. Persons injured may recover treble damages plus costs and attorney's fees from the defendants. The damages can include lost profits and increased costs of doing business resulting from the violation.

A second antitrust tool is breaking up firms that dominate an industry. The government uses three types of orders in this situation: divestiture, which requires a defendant to sell the stock or assets of acquired companies; divorcement, which requires a defendant to sever a relationship by disposing of a functional level of operations, refraining from particular conduct, and canceling existing contracts; and dissolution, which requires a defendant to liquidate assets and go out of business.

A third antitrust tool is preventing mergers that would have an adverse effect on competition. The Clayton Act defines such mergers.

Government action against price fixing is a fourth antitrust tool. There are different types of such fixing. Horizontal price fixing occurs when competitors make direct agreements about the quantity of goods that will be produced, offered for sale, or bought. Vertical price fixing occurs when manufacturers make express or implied agreements with customers obligating them to resell at a price dictated by the manufacturer. However, manufacturers can lawfully state a "suggested retail price."

To stop price fixing and other unfair or deceptive trade practices, the government conducts an investigation. If this investigation shows that a violation exists, the FTC frequently settles the case with a consent agreement in which the respondents agree to refrain from engaging in the particular practice to which the commission objects. When a business signs a consent agreement, it is not an admission of prior wrongdoing. Most often such an agreement includes a cease and desist order, which is an order that requires the business to stop some particular practice.

A consent agreement, together with a cease and desist order, is called a consent decree. In this agreement, the defendant does not admit guilt but agrees to measures aimed at remedying the competitive harm from its actions. Should the illegal practice continue, the FTC can file a lawsuit charging the perpetrators with unfair trade practices. If the government wins, the business is subject to fines and criminal sanctions.

The federal government initiates the majority of antitrust cases. Most are settled in out-of-court agreements or in decrees between the parties. Judges must approve of all settlements, and in each case, a consent decree is filed with the court indicating that the firm agrees to its terms. In a relatively few instances, one firm sues another for an antitrust violation.

— E. Thomas Garman

See also

Federal Trade Commission; State Attorneys General.

Readings

Meier, Kenneth J., and E. Thomas Garman, eds. (1995). *Regulation and Consumer Protection.* Houston: DAME Publications, Inc. Chapter 4.

Shenefield, John H., and Irwin M. Stelzer (1996). *The Antitrust Laws: A Primer.* Washington, DC: AEI Press.

Asian-Pacific Consumer Movement

Prior to 1974, in many countries of the Asian-Pacific region, groups of socially conscious individuals worked independently on consumer issues. After the International Organization of Consumers Unions Regional Office for Asia and the Pacific (IOCU-ROAP) was established in 1974, it began to link up these disparate groups. Today, the office remains the key coordinator of the Asian-Pacific consumer movement.

IOCU's Regional Office

In IOCU's early years, its leaders believed that there should be regional bases to deal with special regional interests and needs. At IOCU's Seventh World Congress, held in Stockholm in 1972, the organization decided to give special attention to the Asian-Pacific region, where several consumer groups had already been organized. To do so, IOCU established in The Hague a provisional regional office, called the Consumer Center for Asia and the Pacific (CCAP).

Following an Asia/Pacific Seminar in 1974, IOCU's first regional office was set up in Singapore. The purpose of the IOCU-ROAP was to facilitate the exchange of information and materials among consumer groups in the region and to provide technical assistance to them. Anwar Fazal, a Malaysian, was appointed as IOCU-ROAP's first regional director. In 1975, to cut costs, the regional office moved to Penang, Malaysia, where it remains today. After IOCU changed its name to Consumers International (CI) in 1995, the regional office was referred to as CI-ROAP.

ROAP's first task was to link up established consumer groups, mobilizing their collective power. This was attempted through building membership in IOCU-ROAP and creating networks of organizations working on single issues such as pharmaceuticals, pesticides, breastfeeding, and smoking. The networks made possible worldwide efforts to promote and protect consumer rights.

To strengthen its campaigns, IOCU-ROAP initiated several research projects. Members collected data in selected countries. These data, supplemented by information from published reports, were presented at regional seminars and workshops. The first objective of these meetings was the sharing of information. Then action plans were developed for advocacy on individual issues.

National groups followed these regional meetings with grassroots advocacy and lobbying in their own countries. For example, the Citizens Alliance for Consumer Protection in the Philippines organized a People's Summit on Water to draw attention to water quality issues. The Federation of Malaysian Consumers Association campaigned successfully against increased charges by a private company that took over the public sewerage system. Also in Malaysia, the Education and Research Association for Consumers implemented a Food Security project that sought integrated pest management for rice farmers and education for consumers. Consumer representatives in Malaysia, Thailand, the Philippines, Bangladesh, South Korea, Pakistan, and Sri Lanka have succeeded in removing harmful drugs from the market in their countries. And, the South Pacific Consumer Protection Program has worked closely with consumer groups in the Pacific Islands to campaign against nuclear weapons testing and destructive mining and logging practices.

In 1991, IOCU-ROAP conducted a major management review of its structure and programs. Significant changes resulted: ROAP's programs on health care, tobacco, and pharmaceuticals were merged; a new Japan Desk was established in the office; dialogue with consumer organizations in other Asian and Pacific countries was expanded; and networks of consumer organizations that IOCU-ROAP had spawned to address pesticide and infant milk formula threats became autonomous organizations.

Recent Consumer Challenges

Many countries in the Asian-Pacific region recorded high economic growth rates during the 1990s, often 6 to 10 percent annually. This rapid growth, however, has not closed the gap between the rich and the poor. For example, a 1995 World Bank report found that the top 20 percent of Malaysian households earn and consume more than the remaining 80 percent. Development today in the region has two faces: high-rise buildings and huge shopping complexes amidst squatter areas without access to basic services; private hospitals sprouting while public health care facilities languish; streets choked with automobiles and their pollution combined with an absence of good public transport. To compete in the global market, liberalization, deregulation, and privatization have become the key words of the region's governments. Meanwhile, participation in the world economy is changing the lifestyles of the people in this region. Fast food, branded clothing, and electronic goods are replacing traditional consumption patterns. Wider consumer choice, however, has not been accompanied by pro-consumer regulations and policies governing the quality and safety of goods and services.

Given these conditions, ROAP's role in the region has remained important. Under the current leadership of Josie Fernandez, ROAP is a voice for consumers, particularly those who are especially vulnerable in the rapidly changing environment. ROAP has also strengthened the consumer organizations of the region and promoted the United Nations Consumer Protection Guidelines. As a result, the consumer movement in the Asian-Pacific region has grown rapidly in the last twenty-five years. Today, consumer groups are active participants not only in narrow issues of consumer protection but also in the broader arena of development in all of its economic, social, and environmental dimensions.

Indonesia

Indonesia's oldest consumer group is Yayasan Lembaga Konsumen Indonesia (YLKI), the Indonesian Consumers Organization. It was founded in 1973 through the initiative of fifteen citizens engaged in various development issues, including Erna Witoelar (CI's president from 1991 until 1997). YLKI has branches in some provinces and maintains links with other groups like the Institute for Consumer Protection and Development in Semarang. YLKI is active in research including surveys, in education and training, and in the dissemination of consumer information through *Warta Konsumen*, a consumer magazine. It participates in parliamentary hearings, policy dialogues, public forums, and interagency working committees to articulate and safeguard consumer interests. YLKI's policy interventions have led to the promulgation of regulations pertaining to food additives, condensed milk used as baby food, pesticide sale and marketing, and several commodity standards. It has worked closely with the Indonesian Environmental Forum on many environmental concerns.

Malaysia

In 1973, at approximately the same time that YLKI was being founded in Indonesia, the Federation of Malaysian Consumers Associations (FOMCA) was established. Today FOMCA's membership consists of twelve state consumer organizations. Among its affiliates is Malaysia's first consumer group, the Selangor and Federal Territory Consumers Association (SCA), founded in 1965. FOMCA's affiliates are autonomous bodies. FOMCA serves as a coordinating agency that provides consumer information and education, participates in the development of consumer protection policies, and represents consumers before government. Recently, FOMCA's concerns have broadened to include privatization, the environment, and women as consumers.

Predating FOMCA in Malaysia is the Consumers Association of Penang (CAP), which was founded in 1969. It has become an influential nongovernmental organization, championing the cause of consumers in the process of economic development. It has been involved in a broad array of issues that include the fulfillment of basic needs, food and product safety, the rational use of environmental resources, unfair business practices, and the specific problems of women. CAP has an effective complaints bureau. It publishes, in four languages, a popular bimonthly newspaper called *Utusan Konsumer* that has a circulation of over 80,000 and a much higher readership. It also produces a monthly version for schoolchildren that has a circulation of some 20,000.

Founded in 1985, the Education and Research Association for Consumers (ERA) has focused on disadvantaged consumers through its development projects with Malaysian farmers, workers, and indigenous communities. ERA's efforts in the areas of integrated pest management for rice production and occupational safety and health training and research have been widely acknowledged. For ten years, ERA was led by its founding president Josie Fernandez until she became director of CI-ROAP.

Private efforts to promote consumer protection in Malaysia have been complemented by government action. In 1991, the Malaysian government set up the Ministry of Domestic Trade and Consumer Affairs. Through its efforts, state and district consumer councils have been established throughout the country. In addition, laws pertaining to trade practices have been amended to include consumer protections. Since 1993, Malaysia has celebrated World Consumer Day, with the prime minister launching the event. The government has provided financial support to FOMCA and to several of its state affiliates. Also, a government-appointed council has advised the minister of domestic trade and consumer affairs on consumer needs, issues, and policies.

Philippines

The consumer movement also has deep roots in the Philippines. In 1963, the Consumers Federated Groups of the Philippines was formed under the auspices of the National Federation of Women's Clubs of the Philippines (NFWCP). In 1971, KMPI (Philippine Consumer Movement, Inc.) was established. The year 1978 saw the establishment of three more groups as a result of consumer dissatisfaction with oil price increases and other economic problems affecting ordinary consumers. These three groups were the Church-Based Consumers Movement, Konsumo Dabaw, and the Citizens' Alliance for Consumer Protection (CACP). The common purpose of Philippine consumer groups is to promote consumer rights and responsibilities through education, research, information, and advocacy activities. Konsumo Dabaw's goals go further: the organization envisions a "non-consumerist, non-materialist, non-violent society." It promotes alternative lifestyle and consumption patterns through campaigns against junk food and for healthy food, and by setting up community-based consumer cooperatives. CACP is committed to joining "the Filipino people in their efforts to realize a transformed society that upholds just, equitable, sovereign, gender-fair, culturally-adapted and ecologically sustainable development goals and processes."

In 1993, as provided for in the 1992 Consumer Protection Act, a National Consumer Affairs Council was set up with representatives from the government, business, and consumer sectors to improve the management, coordination, and effectiveness of consumer programs. The Philippine consumer movement has enjoyed the participation of well-known women, including newspaper columnist and certified public accountant Julie Amargo, educator and city council member Pilar Braga, school administrator Mary John Mananzan, and lawyer Zenaida Reyes.

Other Countries

In Singapore, the Consumer Association of Singapore (CASE) was established in 1971 by the National Trade Union Congress. CASE has striven to inform and educate consumers and protect them against unscrupulous traders. As well as organizing seminars, workshops, and exhibitions, CASE assists consumers in resolving complaints. Since 1971, CASE has handled over 16,000 written complaints and obtained refunds for consumers amounting to almost $500,000. CASE has also undertaken legislative lobbying, including working for enactment of Singapore's Fair Trading Act. In addition, CASE has represented consumer interests in bodies such as the Advertising Authority of Singapore, Insurance Ombudsman Committee, National Safety Council, and Public Utilities Board.

Thailand's consumer movement is trying to keep pace with its rapidly developing economy. Existing groups are seeking to strengthen their capacity to serve Thai consumers more effectively. Some of the groups that carry out consumer education and information activities, albeit on a limited scale, are the Voluntary Group for Consumers of Thailand, Consumer Protection Association, Consumers Group of Siam, National Council of Women of Thailand, and the Thai Association of University Women.

Vietnam's consumer movement is one of the youngest in the region. The Vietnam Standards and Consumer Organization (VINASTAS) was founded in 1988 and is based in Hanoi. Its primary activities are consumer information and education, complaint handling and redress, lobbying, product testing, and publication of a consumer magazine. In recent years, VINASTAS has cooperated with CI-ROAP to organize seminars on conducting simple product tests and promoting consumer protection measures. Ho Chi Minh City Consumers Association is active in the south of Vietnam.

—Josie Fernandez (with assistance from K. Balasubramaniam, Shila Rani Kaur, Loh Cheng Kooi, Manny Calonzo)

Readings

Newman, Barry (1980). "Watchdogs Abroad." *Wall Street Journal*. (April 8): 1ff.

Rachagan, S. Sothi (1992). "Protection against Unfair Trade Practices in Malaysia." *Journal of Consumer Policy*. 15: 255–274.

Wood, John T. D. (1991). "Consumer Protection in the Asian-Pacific Region." *Journal of Consumer Policy*. 14: 99–106.

Association of Community Organizations for Reform Now

With over 100,000 member families in thirty cities, the Association of Community Organizations for Reform Now (ACORN) is one of the nation's largest grassroots membership organizations of low- and moderate-income people. It was founded in June 1970 in Little Rock, Arkansas, as an offshoot of the National Welfare Rights Organization (NWRO).

An organization of mothers receiving Aid to Families with Dependent Children, NWRO used protest tactics in the mid-1960s to secure millions of dollars in special benefits for poor families. In reaction, states began instituting more restrictive public welfare programs. NWRO did not have sufficient political strength to block these decisions.

Some NWRO organizers decided that a new type of organization was needed that would bridge the gap between welfare recipients and other low- and moderate-income Americans, many of whom felt that their own problems had been ignored while national attention was focused on poverty and racial discrimination. With NWRO's support, the head organizer of the Massachusetts Welfare Rights Organization, Wade Rathke, moved to Little Rock, Arkansas, to develop a new approach. Born in Wyoming and raised in New Orleans, Rathke had dropped out of Williams College to become a welfare rights organizer. He arrived in Little Rock with plans to build a multiracial organization that would address a wide range of issues affecting low- and moderate-income Arkansans who, in 1970, earned less than $7,000 a year.

The first ACORN campaign was similar to earlier welfare rights efforts. Citing a state regulation providing for emergency assistance of $40 a year for each public assistance recipient, ACORN pressured the state welfare commissioner to make the funds available to families who needed furniture. After a series of demonstrations, the governor established a new state agency to collect, repair, and distribute furniture and appliances to welfare recipients.

Following this initial victory, ACORN organized both "welfare poor" and working poor people through campaigns for free lunches in the schools, tenant rights in public housing, jobs for Vietnam veterans, and improved emergency care at hospitals. By 1972, ACORN was building membership among moderate-income homeowners in the older neighborhoods of central Little Rock. They joined forces in a "Save the City" campaign, which opposed racial blockbusting by unscrupulous real estate brokers and demanded improved parks, streets, and drainage.

In 1973–1974, ACORN expanded beyond Little Rock, opening six regional offices across the state. The unifying issue for all of the chapters was utility rates, which had skyrocketed since the energy crisis. When Arkansas Power and Light announced plans to build a giant coal-fired generating plant, ACORN organized farmers whose crops would be affected by its emissions and pressured Harvard University, the largest stockholder in the utility's parent company, to conduct an environmental impact study. The state Public Service Commission (PSC) was convinced to cut the size of the plant in half, and the utility finally dropped the plan.

ACORN protests also convinced the PSC to give utilities significantly smaller rate increases than they had requested, but the PSC would not accede to ACORN's demands to change the rate structure. In 1976, ACORN took its proposal for "Lifeline" rates to the voters through the initiative process. Lifeline, a special low rate for the amount of electricity and gas needed for basic residential needs, won approval at the polls in Little Rock but was later struck down by the courts.

By this time, ACORN had begun organizing outside of Arkansas: in 1975, in South Dakota and Texas; and the following year, in Louisiana, Missouri, and Tennessee. Just as they had in Little Rock and as they still do, ACORN organizers recruited members by knocking on doors in low- and moderate-income neighborhoods and by bringing interested people together to form a neighborhood-based ACORN chapter.

Each ACORN chapter elects its own leadership and chooses its own issues and strategies. Each chapter has a representative on the citywide board, and if there are members in more than one city, the statewide ACORN board. Each state elects two delegates to the national association board, which sets policy for the organization as a whole.

Because most ACORN leaders are new to community activism when they join the organization, leadership development is a priority. Several week-long Leadership Schools are held each year, including one in Spanish. Weekend workshops are conducted in different cities throughout the year.

Principal leaders of the organization have included Maude Hurd, Elena Hanggi, and Gloria Wilson. Hurd was elected national president of ACORN in 1990. Left with five children to support when her husband died in the 1970s, she helped create an alcoholism treatment program at the Boston housing project where she lived, was trained to be a counselor, and continues to work in community substance abuse prevention. She joined ACORN in 1981, was elected to chair the Dorchester chapter then to serve as Massachusetts delegate, and finally was elected national president.

Hanggi, who previously served as the national president of ACORN, is now director of The Institute for Social Justice, a training organization associated with ACORN. She describes herself as a traditional Southern wife and mother who was not involved in anything before an ACORN organizer knocked on her door in Arkansas in 1974. While rising through the leadership ranks of the organization, Hanggi also went to college and law school. She was the first community activist to serve as president of a Federal Home Loan Bank board.

Wilson, ACORN's vice president, is also from Arkansas and has been active in the organization since its start in 1970. She is co-chair of her neighborhood group, host of a talk show on the community radio station affiliated with ACORN, state ACORN treasurer, and as of November 1994, an elected member of Little Rock's City Board of Directors (the City Council).

ACORN distinguishes between staff and leaders. There are about 200 dozen paid staff who perform tasks that include organizing, research, lobbying, and administration. They do not serve on the policy-making boards of the organization. Wade Rathke, who was the founding organizer, continues to serve as chief organizer of ACORN, working out of the Organizing and Support Center in New Orleans. There are also national offices in Washington, D.C., Brooklyn, Chicago, and Little Rock. ACORN's annual budget in 1995 was about $6 million. The majority of its funds come from internal sources, including annual membership dues of $60 per family and grassroots fund-raising events. Foundation and church grants help support special projects.

ACORN employs a wide array of tactics including research, lobbying, litigation, and voter registration. It is best known for its direct action organizing, using marches, pickets, sit-ins, and other forms of protest to confront decision-makers face-to-face.

Since the 1980s, ACORN's most significant achievements have been in the areas of housing and community reinvestment. Starting in Philadelphia, where there were 30,000 abandoned houses, ACORN adopted squatting as a tactic to force city officials to turn over properties to low-income families willing to fix them up. The campaign spread and resulted in new or improved homesteading programs in cities including St. Louis, Detroit, Chicago, and New York. Finding that sweat equity was insufficient to make badly deteriorated buildings livable, ACORN established the ACORN Housing Corporation to acquire and rehabilitate properties that are then sold at minimal cost to low-income families. The title for the land remains with the ACORN Community Land Association to help ensure neighborhood stability.

ACORN was the first community organization to challenge a bank's expansion plans under the federal Community Reinvestment Act (CRA). Through protests, formal challenges, and negotiations, it has secured agreements with more than forty banks, including many of the nation's largest, to provide mortgages to low- and moderate-income borrowers. The agreements significantly alter traditional underwriting standards to accommodate lower-income borrowers: for example, by counting welfare, Social Security, or food stamp benefits as income and by using records of regular rent and utility payments in lieu of a credit record for people who have not borrowed before. To help people qualify for mortgages, the ACORN Housing Corporation provides individual counseling, budget, and credit classes. The corporation aggressively recruits potential home buyers through community events.

Building on its experience and reputation for battling redlining by banks, ACORN has targeted insurance companies that provide substandard or overpriced coverage, or no coverage at all, in low-income and minority neighborhoods. Its research has prompted congressional hearings and the introduction of legislation requiring insurers to disclose in what geographic areas they have written, canceled, or refused to write policies. Following a series of demonstrations and negotiations, Allstate signed an agreement to invest in an ACORN partnership providing below market–interest rate mortgages, and Travelers Insurance agreed to a pilot program providing discount rates to ACORN members who participate in community safety programs.

Although best known at the national level for its achievements in housing and community reinvestment, ACORN has also won significant victories in local campaigns aimed at improving public schools, securing jobs for unemployed residents, cleaning up hazardous waste, improving neighborhood safety, and removing barriers to voter registration. Despite growing in size and sophistication, ACORN has remained committed to its original purpose of organizing the poor and powerless.

— Madeleine Adamson

See also

Community Organizations; Community Reinvestment.

Reading

Delgado, Gary (1986). *Organizing the Movement: The Roots and Growth of ACORN.* Philadelphia: Temple University Press.

Australian Consumer Movement

The Australian consumer movement can be traced to the ground-breaking work of Ruby Hutchison—a feminist, political activist, and first woman member of the West Australian Legislative Council. After experiencing frustration with a number of shoddily manufactured goods, Hutchison in 1957 began researching ways to establish a consumer protection organization. Her efforts led to a public meeting at the Sydney Town Hall in 1959, attended by fifty people, which launched the Australian Consumers' Association.

The association set out to establish product testing procedures and a magazine to publish the results. From these beginnings, the consumer movement in Australia has grown to the extent that consumer lobbyists are given a hearing by Australian governments, where every jurisdiction has consumer protection legislation, where reputable businesses take consumer concerns seriously, and where Australia influences the international consumer debate.

In Australia today, consumerism is advocated and advanced through a number of bodies and mechanisms: formal and informal, government and nongovernment. From constant confrontation and opposition in the "Naderist" 1960s and 1970s, the consumer movement has evolved to where it frequently finds itself working side-by-side with the business sector toward higher-quality (and more competitively priced) goods and services and toward the adoption of higher standards of business behavior.

The Australian consumer movement has been strongly influenced by two key factors: an inclusivist approach in which consumer policy is consciously linked to environmental, trade, and competition policies; and the adoption of responsive regulatory approaches by Australian authorities. Putting these factors into practice has required that there be effective consumer organizations that appreciate complex interactions among policies and the need to provide regulatory agencies with the authority and resources necessary to respond flexibly. The presence of these ingredients has allowed Australia's consumer movement to make contributions to both domestic and international consumer policy, especially in the Third World.

Inclusivism: Linkages with Consumer Policy

While the achievement of some of the eight consumer rights described in the United Nations Consumer Protection Guidelines has depended on the development of laws that confer such rights (e.g., the right to redress), the courtroom may not be the appropriate arena for gaining other consumer rights. For example, the right to satisfaction of basic needs may demand initiatives in agriculture and/or labor policy, and securing the right to choice requires a competitive marketplace.

The consumer movement in Australia has increasingly recognized the linkages between consumer policy and other policy domains, including instances in which consumerism can contribute to other policy goals. Australia has been a world leader in the use of consumer-led strategies to achieve environmental goals: it was the consumer movement that first advocated the use of recycling to reduce waste, and that advocated the introduction of energy-use labeling. Consumer protection authorities have also used laws prohibiting misleading conduct to act against deceptive environmental marketing claims on labels and in advertisements.

Perhaps the most important linkage has been between consumer policy and competition policy. At the level of the Australian Commonwealth, the linkage has been achieved through the Trade Practices Act. In practice, the competition laws have been administered by the Trade Practices Commission (TPC) so as to maximize consumer welfare. The laws have prevented restrictive trade practices such as price fixing and monopolization, while the consumer protection provisions have been frequently used by business to ensure fair competition.

At present, the linkage between consumer protection and competition policy is restricted by the fact that the Trade Practices Act does not apply to sole traders, partnerships, state government enterprises, the professions, and certain other bodies. The consumer protection provisions can sometimes be applied by virtue of fair trading acts passed in each state and territory that largely mirror the provisions of Part V of the Trade Practices Act; but no such mirror legislation concerning competition exists. This situation may change in the near future, however, given a recent agreement among all state and territory governments that a national competition policy should be established and that many of the present regulations and laws that protect business from competition should be reviewed and removed where appropriate. Apart from extending the Trade Practices Act to all forms of business activity, this reform will give the TPC additional responsibilities in areas involving the restructuring and reform of government business enterprises such as the gas, water, and electricity industries.

Responsive Regulation

It is difficult to generalize about the way consumer protection laws are administered in Australia because the agencies of six states, two territories, and the Commonwealth are involved. Nonetheless, it is clear that at the Commonwealth level (in the TPC), and to a greater or lesser extent in each of the states, the Australian approach is characterized by its use of "responsive regulation."

Responsive regulation, as described by Ian Ayres and John Braithwaite in a 1992 book with the same name, considers industry structure and industry conduct in an effort to find appropriate and innovative forms of regulatory intervention. The essence of responsiveness is flexibility: no single solution is mandated for every instance of particular conduct. To the greatest extent possible, regulatory policy mobilizes the resources and self-interest of the regulated to achieve a mutually beneficial result.

One element of the regulatory mix is self-regulation through codes of conduct. These codes are an increasingly popular method of encouraging good corporate behavior without government supervision in industries with the capacity to regulate their own affairs (e.g., with an effective trade association that claims a majority of the industry as members). Another option, one step higher on the regulatory scale, is co-regulation, which mixes voluntary and involuntary measures. One variant of co-regulation exists at the state level in Australia, where the government has the power to enforce codes as if they were law or to impose a code of conduct on an industry.

Another important component of responsive regulation, at the Commonwealth level, is the power of the TPC to negotiate binding agreements with companies that have allegedly contravened the law, without the need to initiate court action. The TPC has used this power in a number of ways, from requiring an insurance company to refund over $50 million (Australian) to policyholders it had misled, while funding a television program to educate consumers about insurance, to forcing battery manufacturers to live up to their claims of recyclability, even if it meant exporting used batteries to countries where recycling facilities exist.

Creative approaches to regulation have been underpinned by tough legal sanctions for unacceptable behavior. The Trade Practices Act allows for substantial financial penalties against corporations for restrictive trade practices and consumer protection violations. These penalties, coupled with the TPC's proven willingness to litigate when no other solution is appropriate or negotiable, provide the foundation for the kinds of regulatory responsiveness discussed above.

Consumer Organizations

The two major consumer organizations in Australia are the Australian Consumers' Association (ACA) and the Australian Federation of Consumer Organizations (AFCO). The ACA was founded in 1959 as a nonprofit, nonpartisan organization with the aim of promoting the interests of all consumers. With nearly 200,000 members, it is financed by subscriptions and sales of publications. The ACA assists consumers with their problems and works toward ensuring consumer protection by researching problem areas and lobbying government and other agencies. It also plays a role in improving the quality of products and services by conducting tests of a variety of products, conducting research, and publishing the results in one of its magazines, *Choice*. The current chief executive officer of the ACA is Louise Sylvan, who is also a member of the Executive Council of Consumers International.

AFCO was founded in 1974 to provide a forum for the discussion of matters that are of common interest to consumer organizations, focus attention on consumer problems and consumer affairs, and represent consumer views to the government. It has about fifty organizations as members. Its funding comes from a Commonwealth government grant, membership subscriptions, and research and employment grants. The current chair of AFCO is Dennis Nelthorpe, and its executive director is Jenni Mack. As well as acting as a focal point for existing organizations, AFCO has initiated the development of special-purpose organizations including: Consumer Health Forum, which researches and lobbies in relation to health issues; and Consumer Transport Network, which plays a similar role in relation to public transportation issues.

Not all consumer activism has taken such an organized form; nor has it always involved dialogue with government and business. For example, the unconventional group BUGA-UP (Billboards Utilizing Graffiti Against Unsafe Products) has campaigned directly against the tobacco industry and against sexism in advertising by defacing billboards throughout the nation. Activists worldwide have adopted BUGA-UP's conspicuous, though illegal, strategies.

A different type of consumerist effort is the Australian Broadcasting Corporation's television program "The Investigators." The program has developed a wide audience by focusing attention on cases of misleading, deceptive, and fraudulent behavior by business. In addition to helping individual consumers avoid and solve problems, it has raised general consumer awareness in Australia. The success of the "The Investigators" has even spawned similar segments on current affairs programs on advertising-supported networks.

International Role

In Sydney, during the 1975 International Organization of Consumers Unions World Congress, the United Nations Consumer Protection Guidelines were formally proposed. From that symbolic beginning, Australia has continued to champion consumer rights worldwide, especially in the Third World. This international and service orientation reflects both the geographic position and political commitment of the nation. Development assistance for nations in areas such as primary health care and product safety has flowed from both government (the Australian Development Assistance Bureau) and nongovernment (ACA, Community Aid Abroad) sources. Australia's legislation and regulatory approaches have been used as models by countries in the Asian-Pacific region, such as Indonesia, Malaysia, Thailand, Vietnam, and Fiji. Australia has sponsored, through the Federal Bureau of Consumer Affairs, the South Pacific Consumer Protection Forum; and it has contributed to other regional forums that explore and debate consumer protection and linked policies.

Australia has also tried to act as both champion and model for global market and regulatory reform. Its *Guide on Codes,* a how-to manual for co-regulation adopted by Australia's Ministerial Council on Consumer Affairs, has recently been presented to the Consumer Policy Committee of the Organization for Economic Cooperation and Development (OECD), with a view to its publication and adoption into international co-regulatory mechanisms. Allan Asher, a full-time commissioner with the TPC, is chairman of the OECD committee; while the chairman of the TPC, Professor Allan Fels, is deputy chairman of the OECD Competition Policy Committee.

Current and Future Issues

Four issues arising from Australia's geographic, demographic, and economic position constitute the key challenges for consumer policymakers, regulators, and activists in the foreseeable future: oligopolies, the Asian-Pacific region, financial services, and reform of government-owned businesses.

Australia is a sparsely populated nation, with markets that are smaller than those in many other industrialized nations. Competition is often less intense in these small markets, resulting in a tendency toward concentration, which in turn reduces price and quality competition. Because trade liberalization helps ensure that imported products impose competitive discipline on an otherwise oligopolistic marketplace, the consumer movement has a great interest in trade and foreign policy.

Linked to the previous point is Australia's location on the doorstep of the "Asian Tiger" economies. For the consumer movement, the challenge is to harness the competitive pressures that integration with this region must necessarily impose while ensuring that Australia's effective regulatory regimes for product safety and labor conditions not be compromised in the quest for productivity.

In recent years, many consumer problems have arisen from the purchase of investment products such as annuities and life insurance. There has been some improvement in the conduct of the industry following an extensive research project by the TPC, agitation from the consumer movement, and a number of high-profile enforcement actions. Both the banking and insurance industries have adopted codes of conduct that require, among other measures, the use of plain language in contracts and other documents related to these complex products. The banking industry has also provided funds for an ombudsman and an independent dispute resolution system. Providing protection for consumers in the area of financial services will remain a major challenge, however, given that the Australian economy is heavily dependent on foreign investment and the international commodities markets, both of which have been highly volatile in recent years.

Over 15 percent of Australia's gross domestic product is accounted for by government-owned business enterprises, principally utilities such as electricity and gas companies, and the postal services. Such bodies have sometimes been unresponsive to consumer interests: the lack of price competition has allowed inefficiencies to be subsidized, while the lack of any genuine alternatives has permitted lackluster performance in relation to service delivery and complaints handling. While reform of this sector appears imminent, the experience of other nations shows that corporatization, privatization, and the introduction of competition bring new risks. A challenge facing the consumer movement is to ensure that the promised benefits materialize.

— Allan Asher

Readings

Brown, Jane (1996). *A History of the Australian Consumer Movement.* Braddon, ACT: Consumers' Federation of Australia.

Halpin, David (1984). *Consumers' Choice: 25 Years of the Australian Consumers' Association.* Marrickville, NSW: Australian Consumers' Association.

Austrian Consumer Movement

The consumer movement in Austria can be traced back to the second half of the nineteenth century, when the first consumer cooperatives were formed. The cooperatives supplied their members with good quality foodstuffs and household goods at a cheap price, thereby supplementing the trade unions' struggle for better working conditions and higher pay.

It was not the idea of the consumer cooperative, however, that stimulated the development of Austria's present-day consumer movement. The cooperative movement, disrupted by the periods of the authoritarian state (1934–1938) and Nazi occupation (1938–1945), recuperated to become an important commercial force in post–World War II Austria, but did not rise again to act as a "consumer voice." The task of representing consumer interests, both in the political arena and in giving individual advice and support to consumers, was taken up by labor organizations.

It is an Austrian peculiarity that labor is represented not only by trade unions, based on voluntary membership, but also by institutions established by law and encompassing almost all employees (except public servants and employees in the agrarian sector) as mandatory members. These "Arbeiterkammern" (literally translated as "Chambers of Labor") were created in 1920 as a counterpart to the Chambers of Commerce, institutions that—also on the basis of mandatory membership—

represent the interests of business and industry. Reestablished after the end of World War II, the Arbeiterkammern became today's brain-trust of the labor movement. While the unions engage in collective bargaining and industrial action, the Arbeiterkammern focus more on research, training, and general policy issues in connection with workers' interests. In this division of work between the two types of labor organizations, consumer issues were addressed mainly by the Arbeiterkammern, which soon after World War II began to provide information for their members on key consumer questions.

The reason behind labor's strong interest in consumer issues was the same that had inspired labor activists a hundred years earlier to form consumer cooperatives: what is gained in collective bargaining on wages must not be lost in spending too much on overpriced and/or low-quality goods. This concept of consumer policy is still crucial for understanding consumer policy and the consumer movement in Austria today.

In 1955, the Viennese Arbeiterkammer began to fund the "Association for Advice on Shopping" (Verein für Einkaufsberatung), which established the first Austrian consumer advice center. In 1961, these efforts in consumer information were put on a broader basis. Together with the Austrian Trade Union Federation, the Federal Chamber of Commerce, and the main agricultural interest group, the Arbeiterkammern founded the "Association for Consumer Information" (Verein für Konsumenteninformation or VKI), which took over the consumer advice center and developed it into Europe's largest information center for consumers.

While the VKI started its magazine *Konsument* (Consumer) and its activities in comparative testing in 1961, in the 1970s it became an organization of nationwide prominence and importance. The 1970s in Austria was a decade of change and reform, and the social democratic government, newly elected to office in 1970, pursued an active policy in consumer issues that also raised public awareness and led to better funding of consumer organizations. For example, in 1974, the federal government agreed to double the funds the VKI received from its four founding members, thus giving a new boost to the association's activities.

Association for Consumer Information (VKI)

The VKI still consists of just four regular voting members: two organizations representing labor, one representing business, and one representing farmers. The Republic of Austria, represented by the Federal Minister of Health and Consumer Protection, is a member without voting rights (except on budgetary matters).

To anyone not familiar with the Austrian political system of the so-called second republic (after World War II), the logic behind this membership structure is hard to comprehend. It is a result of the special relationship between labor, industry, and agriculture known as *Sozialpartnerschaft,* characterized by high involvement of the four major interest groups in government policy and by the lack of serious industrial relations conflicts.

Sozialpartnerschaft builds on consensus: the bylaws of the VKI, for instance, require a four-fifths majority for any decision—which for a four-member association is unanimity. Nevertheless, although formally the regular members hold equal rights in the association, it is generally understood that the VKI is considered the domain of the labor side, with the president traditionally coming from the trade union movement. As a result, even though the membership structure is unusual, the VKI is generally accepted as Austria's leading consumer organization.

The VKI is a member of the two most important international consumer bodies—Consumers International and BEUC (Bureau Européen des Unions de Consommateurs). In addition, the president of the VKI is a member of the European Union's Economic and Social Council; the executive director represents Austria's consumers in international standardization bodies; and the head of the legal affairs department is Austria's only member in the European Consumer Law Group. The VKI cooperates with other European consumer organizations in comparative testing and, more recently, has started to build a special relationship with new consumer organizations in neighboring countries such as the Czech Republic, Slovakia, and Slovenia.

The VKI operates advice centers in the capitals of five out of nine Austrian provinces, does extensive comparative testing, and publishes the monthly magazine *Konsument*, as well as a series of brochures and books. It also acts as a "consumer voice" in public policy decision-making by using strategies such as press conferences or press releases to communicate opinions on planned legislation or demands for appropriate action by the authorities. The VKI is also empowered to file class actions against unfair standard contract terms, but it has regularly used this instrument only since 1992.

In 1994, the circulation of *Konsument* reached 120,000 copies (approximately 100,000 going to subscribers). Research shows that *Konsument* is read by far more people than its subscribers, eventually reaching about 20 percent of the population.

In the past few years, the earnings from the magazine and the other publications rose to 35 percent of the organization's total budget, while membership dues declined to 40 percent, with half of that paid by the Federal Ministry of Health and Consumer Protection. Fifteen percent of the budget is earned by fulfilling contracts, mainly with public institutions, for working out criteria for environmental labeling, or for developing a comprehensive report on the status of consumer protection in Austria, for example.

Labor Organizations

While Austria's homogenous and comparatively strong trade union movement does not take much initiative in consumer policy (beyond contributing membership dues to the VKI), the Arbeiterkammern remain very active in this field. The local Arbeiterkammern in every province, as well as the central organization in Vienna, have units specializing in consumer issues; these units work as a consumer lobby, engaging in the political process (especially in the preparation of new legislative or other measures by parliament or government), doing research, and also giving advice to individual consumers.

Independent Consumer Organizations

In Austria, there is no consumer movement that is independent from labor organizations. However, specialized organizations of nationwide importance have developed in two areas: housing (there are two large and a number of smaller tenant organizations) and cars. As well as these special interest groups, there are smaller "one-issue" consumer groups, for instance, on data protection or on specific environmental concerns. Finally, the Österreichische Gesellschaft für Verbraucherrecht (Austrian Consumer Law Group) is a small organization, composed mainly of professionals working in the consumer policy field, that deals with legal aspects of consumer protection.

Political Parties and Public Authorities

The Social Democratic Party has played an important role in consumer policy, especially between 1970 and 1983 when it formed a single-party government and gave consumer issues a prominent place on its political agenda. During the 1970s, Josef Staribacher, a popular Minister of Trade and Industry, institutionalized consumer policy at the government level by appointing a state secretary for consumer protection. Typically, the minister himself had come from a labor organization; his one-time press secretary, Fritz Koppe, went on to become the best-known consumer leader in present-day Austria, heading the Viennese Arbeiterkammer's consumer policy unit and, at the same time, serving as executive director of the VKI. (He retired from both jobs at the end of 1994.)

In government, the Federal Ministry of Health and Consumer Protection has the task of coordinating consumer policy. In that capacity, it works closely with the consumer organizations, especially the VKI (which it partly funds) and Arbeiterkammern. In addition, the ministry works as a consumer voice within government and supports consumer organizations (for instance, by offering training for employees of consumer organizations).

Recent Developments and Future Outlook

Austria is situated in the middle of Europe, has a highly export-oriented economy, and is increasingly interdependent with the economies of other European countries. A longstanding member of the European Free Trade Association, Austria became a member of the European Union in 1995. Thus, the problems facing Austrian consumers do not differ much from those encountered by consumers in other countries of the European Union, and their rights are similar as well.

The major developments currently affecting Austrian consumers are the shift in importance from products to services and from questions of price to questions of quality; deregulation and the gradual withdrawal of the state from business regulation; and the internationalization, even globalization, of markets. All of these developments can be seen, for instance, in the domain of financial services, where Austrian consumers have recently experienced an array of accentuated information problems in markets that are increasingly deregulated and international in scope.

Austria's successes in consumer policy are, to a large extent, a result of the culture of compromise in the so-called Sozialpartnerschaft. Even when the country was ruled by single-party governments, major reforms were mostly undertaken only when the four major interest groups (who are also the regular members of the VKI) agreed or at least did not find their vital interests endangered. Thus, advances in consumer policy have often been slow, but eventually have been supported by all parties concerned. Another manifestation of this tradition of compromise and collaboration is participation of consumer representatives on numerous committees or advisory councils, where they establish working contacts on an equal level with business representatives.

Recently, the close cooperation between the major interest groups and their influence on government policy—the very core of the Sozialpartnerschaft—has come under attack. For various reasons, none directly related to consumer policy, the problem-solving capacity of the Sozialpartnerschaft and its institutions has suffered greatly. In the future, it is likely that the major interest groups will focus more on issues of immediate importance to their membership, paying less attention to the consumer interest. As an illustration, in 1994 the Chambers of Agriculture drastically cut their contribution to the VKI (to about a third of previous years), thus creating the need to restructure this leading consumer organization and potentially endangering its existence.

Aside from the financial problems of the VKI, the readiness of business and consumer organizations to work collaboratively is decreasing markedly. This decline may be due partly to the mounting membership pressure not to be "too soft." Yet, it is also a consequence of the internationalization of commerce. The traditional strong allegiance of Austrian entrepreneurs to their business organization has grown weaker as they have increasingly had to compete with foreign firms that are relatively unconcerned about their reputation among Austrian business and consumer organizations.

— Hans Peter Lehofer

Readings

Kollmann, Karl (1986). *Konsumentenschutzpolitik in Österreich*. Vienna: Verlag des Österreichischen Gewekschaftsbundes.

Lehofer, Hans Peter (1994). "Minimum Implementation of Minimum Directives? Consumer Protection in Austria in the Context of European Integration." *Journal of Consumer Policy*. 17 (1): 3–22.

Auto Repair and Service Protections

Although automobiles are expensive to purchase and repair, most consumers know substantially less about their car than does the least capable mechanic; even worse, they do not have sufficient knowledge to determine the mechanical ability or experience of repairpersons. Moreover, consumers who can least afford it seem to pay the most for automobile repair. In 1977, the National Highway Traffic Safety Administration estimated consumer loss from unnecessary, incompetent, and fraudulent auto repair practices to be $20 billion per year.

A number of basic problems confront consumers needing auto repairs: first, escalation of the original estimate after the car has been taken apart; second, the unnecessary replacement or repair of parts or systems; third, bait and switch advertisements in which a price is advertised for parts and service although the repair dealer informs the consumer who responds to the ad that, to guarantee the service, additional work is needed because of the condition of the auto; fourth, inept performance, often caused by a shortage in the repair industry of well-trained mechanics; fifth, charges for parts or services that have not been supplied; sixth, meaningless warranties such as "50 percent off labor and parts when the work is done in our garage" when the price for parts and for labor are wholly within the control of the garage, and emergency repairs by other facilities are not covered by the warranty; and seventh, imposition of mechanics' liens or garage owners' liens by repair dealers to enforce their charges even when these charges are arbitrary. The consumer's legal remedies to remove the lien and prevent a lien sale by the repair dealer are expensive and cumbersome; the consumer who is not an experienced mechanic often finds proof of fault difficult to obtain; and normally the consumer would have to pay the disputed bill and then sue to recover the amount paid.

In its 1995 *Auto Repair Task Force Report*, the National Association of Attorneys General identified factors that often contribute to unnecessary repairs. These factors are: incentive compensation systems for service managers; lack of technician competence; repair dealer recommendations for service that exceed manufacturer recommendations; and inadequate consumer disclosures.

During the past thirty years, many remedies to these problems have been suggested. Governmental and nongovernmental remedies have been instituted in various jurisdictions with mixed results. But some of these remedies have shown promise.

Some states and local jurisdictions have established registration or licensing of repair dealers or of certain categories of repair dealers. The most important feature of this remedy is that it provides a central depository of complaints to enable the agency to spot patterns of abuse. The fees obtained allow undercover investigations using doctored vehicles to corroborate those complaints. The major problems are the cost of the program, particularly in smaller jurisdictions, and the growing reluctance to establish new bureaucracies. In addition, too often consumers do not realize that they have been victimized.

Some states require repair dealers to provide estimates before the work is done, obtain consent to perform new work not previously agreed upon, return most replaced parts upon request, and state on the invoice what work has been agreed upon. While these protections encourage repair dealers to treat consumers fairly, they can be circumvented by dishonest dealers who are clever. For example, it is difficult if not impossible for most consumers to determine whether work that is part of the initial estimate or that is communicated in a subsequent phone call is necessary.

Some nonprofit organizations have established diagnostic centers that do not make repairs, thus assuring objectivity and providing consumers with valuable information. The major problem is the viability of such programs. Companies organized for profit have almost always found that diagnostic centers that do not also offer repair services cannot sustain themselves economically. Yet, the joining of the two services compromises the objectivity of the diagnosis.

Governmental and nongovernmental auto repair arbitration programs allow disputes to be handled efficiently and with minimum cost. The major problem is the consumer's lack of mechanical expertise. To remedy this deficiency, some of the programs utilize the services of an expert. While these services can be helpful, employing them after the fact is often of limited value.

The 1990 Clean Air Act requires that new cars beginning with the 1996 model year have on-board diagnostics (OBD), which enable repair shops to diagnose electronically the condition of important systems; auto manufacturers are already required to provide independent shops with access to OBD diagnostic information. Both improve the quality of diagnosis, but they may be expensive and fail to cover all systems.

Private associations certify repair shops or technicians. However, there is as yet no statistical proof that certification of these repair shops or technicians decreases fraud, incompetence, or unnecessary repairs.

Several factors are helping alleviate repair problems. Recent model automobiles tend to need less maintenance; also, warranties are often longer. In addition, these automobiles often have warning systems that protect against the development of major problems.

Some state statutes have increased requirements for consumer disclosure, and some auto-related associations have encouraged repair shop members to provide greater disclosures. These disclosures have included signs indicating the hourly labor rate or listing governmental telephone numbers to call if the consumer experiences problems. These two trends have improved repair-related disclosures.

The Coordinating Committee for Automotive Repair—a group created by auto and parts manufacturers, distributors, repair shops, and educators—has organized to improve industry training efforts. Training is particularly important because of the growing sophistication of computer-based systems.

— Herschel T. Elkins

See also

Lemon Laws.

Readings

National Association of Attorneys General (1976). *Legislation Regulating Auto Repair.* Raleigh, NC: The Committee.

U.S. Congress; Senate Committee on Commerce, Science, and Transportation; Consumer Subcommittee (1993). *Auto Repair Fraud.* Washington, DC: U.S. Government Printing Office.

Automobile Lemon Laws

See Lemon Laws.

Automobile Safety

See Highway Safety.

Aviation Safety

By any measure, a commercial airline flight is the safest form of passenger transportation. The accident rate for large air carriers each year ranges between two and four accidents per one million departures. The fatal accident rate for scheduled airlines has been zero in some years, and no more than one in a million departures in others.

The major reason that air travel is so safe compared to other modes is that the flying public insists on an extremely high level of safety. Some speculate that this insistence reflects mainly the fact that passengers have no control over the way an airplane is operated. Whatever the reason, the federal government regulates virtually every aspect of airline operations to assure public safety.

Air transportation was tightly regulated even before Lindbergh's historic trans-Atlantic crossing in 1927. The U.S. Post Office issued the nation's first air safety standards in the mid-1920s when it began delivering mail by air. In 1935, the federal government undertook to operate an air traffic control system, and three years later, Congress began regulating airline economics. A 1938 law reflected Congress's judgment that the then-fledgling airline industry should be treated as a public utility, with a federal agency controlling which companies could enter the industry, what routes they could serve, and what fares they had to charge. That regime continued until 1978, when Congress deregulated airline economics by removing federal controls over airline routes and rates, leaving them largely free to fly where they wanted and at whatever rate they saw fit to charge.

Both before and after economic deregulation, however, air safety has continued to be the subject of strict federal controls. The current system for regulating air safety was created in 1958, at the dawn of the jet age, when Congress established what is now the Federal Aviation Administration (FAA) and gave it the mission of regulating air safety and upgrading the nation's air traffic control system.

The FAA controls virtually every aspect of air safety. For example, before a manufacturer can build a new aircraft "type" (e.g., a B-777, MD-11, or A-340), it must prove to the FAA that the new model fully complies with airworthiness standards set by the FAA. Similarly, every airline must obtain a license and must comply with FAA standards designed to assure safe operations. In addition, every pilot must pass examinations given by the FAA to assure that he or she is competent to fly aircraft.

Apart from setting and enforcing all of these safety standards, the FAA is responsible for operating the nation's air traffic control system. The agency also administers federal programs that give grants to local airport operators to improve the safety and capacity of the airport and airways systems.

When accidents do occur, the job of investigating them falls to a separate agency, the National Transportation Safety Board (NTSB). The NTSB is an independent agency headed by five presidential appointees. Its investigators are promptly dispatched to the scene of every aviation accident, and the safety board is responsible for determining the probable cause of each crash. The NTSB also makes recommendations to the FAA about what should be done to prevent similar accidents from occurring in the future.

In recent years, public and regulatory attention has focused on commuter airline safety, safety of the air traffic control system, and post-crash survivability. Commuter airlines are smaller airlines that operate smaller aircraft, often with fewer than thirty seats. They operate primarily on routes under 200 miles between a small community and a large city that serves as the "hub" of at least one major carrier. Commuter airlines have historically been subject to less stringent safety standards than have larger jet airlines: for example, commuter pilots are allowed to fly more hours on a daily, monthly, and yearly basis than are jet pilots. Commuter airline accident and fatality rates have also been higher than those of larger jets. The principal reason for this disparity has been the FAA's concern over the years that imposing more stringent safety standards would be too costly for smaller commuter companies. As the commuter industry grows and matures, however, standards are gradually being increased, and the accident rate is declining.

As more people fly more often, there is an increased focus on the ability of the air traffic control system to keep up with this growing demand. To some extent, this concern relates more to the capacity of the system than to its safety because, if air traffic controllers cannot handle a given flight safely, their practice is to keep that flight on the ground until the system can handle it.

In the 1980s, the FAA announced an ambitious program to modernize its air traffic control system by replacing aging technology with state-of-the-art equipment. This program, however, has been stalled for over a decade, prompting proposals to reform the FAA's procurement practices and perhaps even splitting off the air traffic control system from the FAA's regulatory duties and turning air traffic control operations into a quasi-governmental corporation, such as AMTRAK or COMSAT.

Despite the airlines' safety record, accidents have occurred. In some accidents, passengers survived the crash forces but were killed by the smoke and toxic fumes emitted when a fire broke out. When fires occur, they can block emergency exits, and the presence of smoke and poisonous gases can sharply reduce the time passengers have to evacuate safely. In recent years, with the encouragement of the FAA, the industry has sought to prevent fires from breaking out by using cabin materials that are less combustible. In addition, they have taken measures, such as installing emergency track lighting along the cabin floor, to guide passengers to the nearest exit. Work to achieve further improvements continues.

— Cornish F. Hitchcock

See also

Airline Deregulation.

Readings

Burton, John R., Cathleen D. Zick, and Robert N. Mayer (1993). "Consumer Views of the Need for Government Intervention in the Airline Market." *Journal of Consumer Affairs.* 27 (Summer): 1–22.

Nader, Ralph, and Wesley J. Smith (1994). *Collision Course: The Truth about Airline Safety.* Blue Ridge Summit, PA: Tab Books.

B

Baltic Republics, Consumer Movement in the

Life would be simpler for the three Baltic republics—Estonia, Latvia, and Lithuania—if they could operate as a single economic entity in the post-Soviet era. Alone, each is too small, and has too few natural and industrial resources, to find a smooth path toward self-sufficiency. All three countries turned their backs on the East in their search for new markets, and all three signed Association Agreements with the European Union in 1995. But linguistic, religious, cultural, and historic differences make closer integration among them difficult if not impossible.

The Association Agreements commit the Baltic countries to harmonizing their legislation with that of Western Europe. Latvia was the first to introduce a general consumer protection law in 1992; Estonia and Lithuania followed suit in 1994. Estonia has set up a State Board for the Protection of Consumers, incorporating the State Competition Office, accountable to the Ministry of Economy. Helle Aruniit, who has been involved in the development of consumer policy in Estonia, has recently been appointed director-general. Lithuania has extended the functions of the State Office of Price and Competition to cover consumer protection. A similar office is likely to be set up in Latvia, but for the moment, the consumer protection function in the Latvian government resides with the Trade Policy Section of the Ministry of Economy.

Voluntary consumer groups have struggled to make their mark in the Baltic republics. The Lithuanian Consumers' Association was the first to be formed, in 1989, under the presidency of a prominent trade unionist, Algirdas Kvedaravicius. Like the Bulgarian organization, it is prohibited by its constitution from carrying out any activities that would generate income. It receives no financial support from the government, nor does it choose to charge membership fees. Thus, it is heavily dependent on the enthusiasm of volunteers and practical backing from the trade union center that the president leads.

The Latvian Consumers' Club was founded in 1990 (originally as the Riga Consumers' Club) but has only recently begun to operate on a national scale. Staffed entirely by volunteers and led by Zinta Kovaleska, it operates as a complaint-handling and advocacy organization. It has been particularly active in promoting informed use of drugs in the Baltic states, in association with Health Action International, an international network of health advocacy organizations. Over the past year, it has developed contacts with city and municipal authorities to encourage them to develop consumer protection initiatives, and it is working with the government's Anti-Monopoly Committee on producing a newsletter for Latvian consumers.

Estonia was the last of the three republics to create a national organization: the Estonian Consumers' Union, which grew out of the Tallinn Consumer Club, was registered in June 1994 under the chairmanship of Jiri Raus. Like the Latvian Consumers' Club, it is staffed entirely by volunteers. Independent Estonia has not been slow to take advantage of the physical and linguistic proximity of Finland in developing its economic and social systems. A collaboration has been developing between Finnish consumer groups and the Estonian Consumers' Union, leading in June 1995 to a two-part seminar in Helsinki and Pori on consumer protection legislation and organization. The next major initiative planned is a consumer advice center in Tallinn, which will receive financial and practical support from the German consumer organization, AgV. The State Consumer Protection Board will also be involved in this development, which may in time lead to similar ventures in the other Baltic states.

There is also a privately produced consumer newspaper in Estonia, *Kulutaja*, edited and compiled by a young team of journalists led by Mart Luik. *Kulutaja* consists of a two- or three-page insert in the most important newspaper in Estonia, with a circulation of 37,000. Forced to accept advertising, *Kulutaja* cannot be regarded to be in the mainstream of consumer publications despite its lively championship of consumer causes.

— Alastair Macgeorge

See also

Central and Eastern Europe, Consumer Movements in.

Readings

Kozminski, Andrzej K. (1992). "Consumers in Transition from the Centrally Planned Economy to the Market Economy." *Journal of Consumer Policy*. 14 (4): 351–370.

Nehf, James P. "Consumer Policy in Latvia." *Journal of Consumer Policy*. 18 (4): 317–344.

Bank Deposit Protections

See Checking Account Protections.

Bankcard Holders of America

Bankcard Holders of America (BHA) was established in 1980 by former Congressman Mark Hannaford and Gary Serota as a non-profit, tax-deductible organization to help consumers make informed credit decisions. At a time of accelerating change in consumer credit markets, the founders saw a need for information that would help consumers sort through numerous offers of banking and credit products.

BHA is funded almost entirely by membership dues and paid requests for credit card lists and other publications. It does not seek or receive corporate or government funding.

BHA members are individual consumers who pay an annual membership fee to receive a newsletter, publications on credit topics, and consumer "best deal" lists of various types of credit cards. The organization's membership services staff, which is located in Salem, Virginia, handles fulfillment of member and non-member requests for all credit education materials.

BHA's executive director manages the organization out of executive offices located in McLean, Virginia. Former Congressman Pete Kostmayer and then Elgie Holstein served as executive directors for most of the organization's first decade. Since 1992, Gerri Detweiler and then Ruth Susswein have held this position.

BHA's primary focus is education. Toward that end, the organization has published over twenty credit education pamphlets and guidebooks, plus four credit card lists (Low-Interest/No-Fee; Secured; Rebate/Frequent Flyer; and Gold) to help cardholders choose the best cards for their needs. BHA also offers "Debt Zapper," a unique service that helps cardholders reduce their credit card debt through a computerized analysis. The Debt Zapper report prioritizes a consumer's credit card debt; it then shows consumers how much of the debt on each card to pay to reduce this indebtedness quickly and with the least expense. BHA also serves as an advocate for credit card holders by alerting consumers and the media to unfair or deceptive industry practices. It researches issues of potential interest to cardholders and disseminates findings through its newsletter and/or press releases.

In 1985, BHA was the first organization to compile and distribute a list of low-rate and no-fee credit cards. The following year, it published a list of legitimate secured credit cards. That same year, BHA released a national survey alerting consumers and the media to deceptive credit card advertising practices. The attention that this survey focused on the issue led, in part, to the passage of the Fair Credit and Charge Card Disclosure Act of 1989. Also in 1989, BHA revealed merchants' unfair credit card and check acceptance practices. This exposure helped persuade credit card companies to adopt stricter rules and convince twenty-one states to pass laws prohibiting these practices.

BHA represents the only independent, nonprofit consumer organization dedicated exclusively to credit education and advocacy. BHA's members provide an "early warning system," alerting the organization to unfair or deceptive credit practices, which enables BHA to alert the public through the distribution of educational materials and programs.

— Gerri Detweiler

See also

Credit Protections.

Reading

"Bankcard Holders: What's Up with Its Fringe Benefit" (1991). *Changing Times*. 45 (June): 76.

Banking Protections

See Checking Account Protections; Community Reinvestment; Credit Protections; Electronic Funds Transfer Protections; Mortgage Loan Protections; Savings Protections.

Bankruptcy

The Bankruptcy Reform Act of 1978 defines the bankruptcy code in the United States. The code was amended by the Bankruptcy Amendments and Federal Judgeship Act of 1984; the Bankruptcy Judges, United States Trustees, and Family Farmer Bankruptcy Act of 1986; and the Bankruptcy Reform Act of 1994.

A consumer debtor may voluntarily seek relief from creditors. There is no requirement that the debtor has difficulty paying creditors, that liabilities exceed assets, or that future income be insufficient to repay some or all of existing debts.

The bankruptcy code that became effective on October 1, 1979, offers consumer debtors two choices for seeking relief from creditors. The debtor may file a petition with the U.S. Bankruptcy Court under Chapter 7. In Chapter 7, called a liquidation bankruptcy, debtors forfeit all assets not legally exempted from creditors' seizure. The sale of nonexempt assets is the basis for calling Chapter 7 a liquidation. The proceeds from the sale are distributed to creditors. Debtors then receive a discharge or legal release from most preexisting, unsecured debts that do not have priority status. Debts that have priority status and are not dischargeable are alimony, child support, and taxes. Some other debts are also not dischargeable in Chapter 7. These debts include student loans that have not gone into repayment status, loans fraudulently incurred, and "load-up"—debt or debts incurred for luxury goods and services or cash advances above $1,000 in the sixty days before filing.

The debtor also has the choice to file under Chapter 13, which allows the debtor to keep all property in exchange for a promise to pay all or part of debts outstanding over a three-to-five year repayment plan approved by the court. Debtors with unsecured and secured debt in amounts up to $250,000 and $750,000 respectively are eligible to file under Chapter 13. In Chapter 13, the debtor's repayment obligation on secured debts may be "crammed down," or reduced, to the market value of the asset, which serves as security on the debt. Furthermore, some debts that are not dischargeable under Chapter 7 are dischargeable under Chapter 13. Consumers with regular income may choose Chapter 13 rather than Chapter 7 to benefit from the broader definition of debts that are dischargeable, to protect assets from liquidation, or to reduce any personal anguish that may be associated with bankruptcy since creditors may judge a Chapter 13 more favorably than a Chapter 7. The code stipulates that a debtor's repayment plan in Chapter 13 must provide as much of a recovery for unsecured creditors as they would have recovered with a liquidation under Chapter 7.

The act of seeking relief from debts, and the code that specifies legal conditions for that action, pits the interest of consumers against those of creditors. Bankruptcy law in the United States has traditionally been viewed as consumer-oriented. The Bankruptcy Act of 1898, which stood relatively unchanged until the Bankruptcy Reform Act of 1978, contained five consumer-oriented features: the availability of voluntary relief, the allowability of property exemptions, the availability of discharge, the limited exceptions to discharge, and the exemption of bankrupts from civil process to collect dischargeable debts. The Bankruptcy Reform Act of 1978 strengthened the consumer orientation of the code by providing a federal definition of property exemptions, reducing the availability of debtor reaffirmation of debts, reducing restrictions on the availability of Chapter 13, and changing the language of the code to remove the disgrace or social stigma associated with bankruptcy. The 1978 law provided that consumers filing under Chapter 7 are to be called "debtors" instead of "bankrupts."

The bankruptcy code allows a consumer to petition voluntarily for liquidation bankruptcy with no particular consideration given to the debtor's ability to repay debts out of future income. The code intended to allow any debtor who had not filed Chapter 7 in the prior seven years to gain a "fresh start." A sharp increase in the number of nonbusiness bankruptcy cases, following enactment of the 1978 act, generated calls for reform from creditors. Creditors wanted the code to restrict a debtor's access to Chapter 7 if the debtor had some ability to repay unsecured debts out of future income.

Creditors argued that the 1978 act made the discharge of unsecured debts in Chapter 7 too easy, thus resulting in a dramatic increase in bankruptcy, especially among persons who were not financially distressed. Consumer advocates argued that most of those filing bankruptcy either were poor or had suffered serious financial problems from income loss, and that restrictions on access to a "fresh start" in bankruptcy would significantly harm these individuals. In their debate, policymakers considered the possibility that creditors had become irresponsible in their granting of consumer credit, especially mass-marketed unsecured lines of credit. Consumer advocates argued against tests of debtors' ability to repay in bankruptcy, pointing out that the issue arose only because of creditors' failure to establish realistic credit limits.

Amendments to the Bankruptcy Code of 1978 addressed the issue without explicitly restricting the choice of those with the ability to repay debts out of future income to Chapter 13. The 1984 amendments allowed the courts to dismiss an individual debtor's Chapter 7 petition if the debts included on the petition were primarily consumer debts and the debtor was judged as "substantially abusing" the provisions of Chapter 7. The amendments did not specifically define this abuse. They also required debtors to contribute all projected disposable income to a Chapter 13 plan if creditors were not paid in full and also objected to the proposed plan.

The 1986 amendments provided that a U.S. trustee, typically an attorney appointed to represent the interests of unsecured creditors, could alert the court to the possibility that a debtor's petition represented a substantial abuse of the provisions of Chapter 7. Furthermore, a debtor had to be informed of his choices of Chapter 7 and Chapter 13 by his attorney.

The Bankruptcy Reform Act of 1994 increased the availability of Chapter 13 for persons having large amounts of secured and unsecured debt. And, the 1994 law requires Chapter 7 trustees to orally examine the debtor to ensure that he/she understands the effects of bankruptcy regarding reaffirmation and the effect of bankruptcy relative to the debtor's choice of Chapter 7 versus Chapter 13.

Critics maintain that the bankruptcy code creates incentives for abuse. Debtors can realize a benefit by taking on credit but not suffer a proportional loss when they declare bankruptcy. One cost of this abuse is higher interest rates on consumer credit.

Creditors have responded to a more lenient bankruptcy law by using credit information and credit use behavior to restrict or deny credit to likely bankrupts. Creditors have also developed methodologies for using risk to adjust the price of credit extended. Finally, they have developed credit products that are designed for those prone to bankruptcy.

— A. Charlene Sullivan

See also

National Foundation for Consumer Credit.

Reading

Sullivan, A. Charlene, and Debra Drecnik Worden (1992). *Personal Bankruptcy: Causes and Consequences*. Madison, WI: Filene Research Institute.

Belgian Consumer Movement

The Belgian consumer movement began at the end of the 1950s when individual consumers first organized to defend their collective interest. The movement's origin was exclusively private in nature; the public authorities hardly provided any subsidy to this initiative, and governmental action on behalf of consumers developed much later.

Key Actors

The growth of the Belgian consumer movement involved the creation of new associations exclusively dedicated to promoting consumers' interests as well as the enlargement of the activities of already existing associations—such as women's and family organizations, labor organizations, and consumer cooperatives—to include consumer protection.

The Association des Consommateurs/Verbruikersunie (AC/V) was set up in 1957. It was patterned after Consumers Union in the United States and Consumers' Association in the United Kingdom. The objective of the association was to study, in an independent and nonpartisan fashion, the quality of products and services found by its members in the market, and to inform members of the results of the investigations. The new association consisted of two legal entities: a cooperative responsible for providing consumer information through the publication of magazines, and a nonprofit organization entrusted with individual assistance to members, contacts with media, external relations, and defense of consumers' interests. The association has achieved financial independence as a result of income from subscriptions of its members and the sale of numerous publications. The association had 325,000 members in 1993. It is the only organization in Belgium exclusively devoted to the defense of consumers' interests.

The Union Féminine pour l'Information et la Défense des Consommateurs (UFIDEC) was created in 1959 through the joint initiative of women's, cooperative, and labor organizations sharing a socialist ideology. The objective of the association was to promote the interests of consumers of products and services. Subscriptions by members (around 120,000 in the early 1980s) to the association's publication represented its main source of financing. The association ended in 1984 because of the decision of socialist authorities to withdraw their financial support. Yet, cooperatives, labor organizations, and women's organizations continue to play a role in the Belgian consumer movement.

Two main federations of cooperatives are involved in the consumer movement: the Fédération Belge des Coopératives/Koöperatieve Verbruikersbeweging (FEBECOOP) and the Fédération Nationale des Coopératives Chrétiennes (FNCC), now dissolved and replaced by Arco group. The cooperatives contribute to the protection of consumers, mainly through providing consumer information and education at a local level. At one time, FNCC intervened to try to influence the legislative process. But at the present, Arco group confines itself to providing legal advice to its members.

On the basis of investigations and research, the consumer unit of FEBECOOP, the Centre Coopératif de la Consommation, identifies problems faced by consumers and then addresses the general public, companies, and public authorities. It publishes magazines in which the actions of public authorities related to consumer problems are analyzed, and it offers its members a legal advice service. It also manages a documentation center accessible to the public. Recent actions have been conducted by FEBECOOP in the fields of overindebtedness, the correct use of medicines, and the prevention of accidents in everyday life.

Since the 1960s, women's organizations have typically included consumer problems in their programs. Organizations such as Vie Féminine, Kristelijke Arbeider Vrouwengilden, and Mouvement Coopératif Féminin–Association des Consommatrices are engaged in informing and educating consumers, carrying out consumer surveys, and discussing the evolution of legislation related to consumer problems. Much like the women's organizations, the three traditional trade unions—the Confédération des Syndicats Chrétiens, the Fédération Générale du Travail de Belgique, and the Centrale Générale des Syndicats Libéraux de Belgique—have included consumer protection in their programs of action.

In addition to the diverse private organizations involved in the consumer movement, the Centre de Droit de la Consommation plays an important role. Created in 1978 within the Law School of the Université Catholique de Louvain, the center's objectives are to conduct research and training programs on topics related to the promotion of consumer interests and to contribute to the introduction of consumer law within the concerns of professional education. Its approach is interdisciplinary, treating not only the legal aspects of consumption, but its economic and sociological aspects as well. In addition to its research and training programs, the center pursues its objectives through compiling legal documentation, organizing scientific meetings, and assuming editorial responsibilities for consumer law periodicals. The center's work focuses on Belgium (at the regional and national levels) as well as European and international developments. In 1995, it included about twenty collaborators, project leaders, researchers, information officers, and administrative personnel.

Role of Public Authorities

Public authorities in Belgium have not directly subsidized consumer organizations. For example, there is no publicly funded consumer institution similar to the Institut National de la Consommation in France. One indirect government subsidy to the consumer movement was the creation, in 1975, of the Centre de Recherches et d'Information des Organizations de Consommateurs (CRIOC). The center is subsidized by the Ministry of Economics in order to provide technical assistance to consumer organizations through information, documentation, and investigation of sociological, technical, and legal matters. In 1994, the activities of the center were oriented especially toward unfair contract terms, access to justice, homeopathic and generic medicine, and the protection of young consumers. CRIOC is, as a general rule, not accessible to individuals. In 1994, the executive of CRIOC included representatives of the fourteen consumer organizations, including trade unions. With a budget of just under $2 million, recently it experienced financial difficulties.

The participation of consumers in public decision-making has been carried out by the Conseil de la Consommation, a consultative body set up in 1964 by the Ministry of Economic Affairs to discuss consumer matters. All organizations considered to be representatives of the consumer interest are eligible to sit on the council—"pure" consumer organizations as well as cooperatives, women's organizations, and worker organizations. The council has an advisory role in the government regarding all consumer problems. It consists of fourteen consumer organizations plus fourteen representatives of other, potentially opposing, interest groups from the production, distribution, agriculture, and service sectors.

Unlike other European countries such as France, the Netherlands, and the United Kingdom, in Belgium the participation of consumers in government decision-making is confined to this consultation system; there is no institution with executive power that could seek to influence final legal decisions. At present in Belgium, no specific department or secretariat of state is responsible for consumer matters. The responsibility is shared by numerous offices within several departments—Economic Affairs, Agriculture, Public Health, and Justice. Several administrative offices are also responsible for consumer matters. The diffusion of responsibility and absence of coordination among these offices often result in conflicts that impede major consumer initiatives.

The first important consumer laws, passed in 1964, concerned the protection of health, especially that related to food and medicines. In 1971, the law on trade practices promoted recognition of consumer organizations by granting them the right, under specific conditions and on a few matters only (e.g., misleading advertising), to ask for a cease and desist order.

The establishment of a consumer protection policy is, however, more recent. Most of the laws on consumer protection have been passed in the 1990s: consumer credit, financial services, trade practices, and product liability were regulated in 1991, mortgage credit in 1992, and product safety and travel packages in 1994.

Between 1987 and 1995, the Commission d'Étude pour la Réforme du Droit de la Consommation (CERDC) sought to codify Belgian consumer legislation and develop an overarching law on consumer protection. The members of the commission were academics, civil servants, and judges. The final report, presented in June 1995, proposes a model Consumer Protection Act for Belgium.

Characteristics and Concerns

The main characteristic of the consumer movement in Belgium is its multiplicity and pluralism, which reflects the traditional political, ideological, and linguistic divisions of the country. This diversity has had positive aspects, such as stronger local representation and an enlarged audience, but it has also weakened the consumer movement: internal conflicts and weak collective interests have made it difficult to agree on proposed reforms, lessening the movement's political influence.

After a first "crusade phase" mostly devoted to the dissemination of information to consumers through publication of comparative test results on the characteristics and qualities of consumer products, the consumer movement has treated consumer issues as legal matters. In the 1980s, it undertook the formation of legal departments in the consumer associations, the establishment of legal advice services, the preparation of publications dealing essentially with information of a legal type, the popularization of books on consumer law, and lobbying for the adoption of new consumer laws.

One important concern for consumer associations at present relates to access to justice in consumer matters, both for individuals and for consumer groups. Since the early 1970s, consumer groups have been entitled—particularly by the 1971 law on trade practices, which was repealed and replaced by a 1991 law—to seek cease and desist orders to protect the collective consumer interest. However, Belgian procedural law does not allow consumer groups to claim compensation, nor does it provide for class action lawsuits.

Although the Belgian consumer movement has emphasized legal remedies to consumer problems, it has recently addressed broader concerns. These concerns include protection of the environment, health care, new technologies, the global divide between rich and poor countries, and international trade.

Role within European and Global Consumer Movements

The problems addressed by the consumer movement in Belgium are usually of concern to consumer organizations all over Europe. Within the European Community, members of the Bureau Européen des Unions de

Consommateurs (BEUC) seek a consensus about the problems. But differences among these groups nevertheless exist. For example, the Belgian organization, AC/V, places more importance on financial services and insurance problems than do other organizations in Europe. FEBECOOP and the Centre de Droit de la Consommation also address issues related to financial services, especially the problem of indebtedness.

The AC/V has significant relations with international consumer bodies. It not only is a founding member of BEUC, but also helped to establish the umbrella organization for the global consumer movement, Consumers International. The association is also a founding member of International Consumer Research and Testing Limited (IT), an organization whose goal is to promote joint comparative testing activities.

Since 1987, the AC/V has established links with organizations in southern European countries: the Comitato Difesa Consumatori (CDC) in Italy, the Organización de Consumidores y Usuarios (OCU) in Spain, and the Associaçáo Portuguesa para a Defesa do Consumidor (DECO) in Portugal. With each of these organizations, it has formed a joint venture, creating an editorial company in each country to be responsible for the publication of comparative test information, and also a supra-national body for coordination of comparative tests in the four nations. Whenever possible, common tests are conducted, usually in conjunction with the activities of IT. The Belgian organization provides financial assistance and technical know-how to develop the comparative testing capabilities of these southern European organizations.

The Centre de Droit de la Consommation has concluded several cooperative agreements at the national and international levels. The Med Campus program provides for interuniversity cooperation with Mediterranean Third World countries (Egypt, Jordan, Lebanon). Since 1994, within the PHARE and TACIS programs of the European Union, the center has engaged in technical and scientific cooperation with eleven central European countries in the field of consumer law; it has also consulted on consumer protection legislation with the Study Committee on Monopolies and Consumer Protection of the Federation of Russia. In addition to the agreements linked to the Med Campus and PHARE and TACIS programs, the center has signed agreements that call for close cooperation and numerous common actions between the center and the Basque, Egyptian, and Hungarian signatory authorities.

In sum, in relation to the size of the country and level of government funding for consumer activities, Belgium has had a significant impact on the European and international consumer movements.

— Thierry Bourgoignie
and Anne-Christine Lacoste

Reading

Roberts, Eirlys (1966). *Consumers*. New York: International Publications.

Better Business Bureaus

A Better Business Bureau (BBB) is a private, nonprofit organization that provides services to assist consumers and businesses. Funded primarily by dues from business members, the mission of the BBB is to promote and foster the highest ethical relationship between businesses and the public through voluntary self-regulation, consumer and business education, and service excellence. In 1996, 166 BBBs and branches served every major metropolitan marketplace in the United States; another 16 BBBs are in Canada. The Council of Better Business Bureaus, the umbrella organization for the BBB system, is located in Arlington, Virginia, and administers programs to assist individual BBBs.

BBBs operate under the assumptions that fair business practices are good for both buyer and seller and that a large majority of buyers and sellers are honest and responsible. They collect and report information to help prospective buyers make informed purchasing decisions, develop programs to encourage businesses to regulate their advertising and selling practices, and serve as a neutral third party to help resolve marketplace disputes.

BBBs help consumers by providing reliability reports about a company, noting unanswered or unresolved complaints; by providing information about charities and other nonprofit organizations that are seeking donations; by helping consumers to resolve buyer/seller complaints against a company; and by disseminating accurate consumer information so that wise buying decisions can be made. They also assist consumers by fostering ethical advertising and selling practices; by alerting consumers to fraudulent and deceptive practices in the marketplace and cooperating with appropriate law enforcement agencies; by providing consumer information to broadcast, print, and online news media; and by publishing and distributing educational pamphlets and books on topics of interest to consumers and businesses.

BBB members are companies that meet the bureau's standards for membership, agree to support the BBB's principles of ethical business practices and voluntary self-regulation, and have accepted the bureau's invitation to join. Bureau members provide most of the funding to support its programs, staff, and activities. Approximately one-quarter of a million companies, ranging in size from a single employee to the largest of America's corporations, are BBB members.

History

BBBs were established more than eighty years ago as an effort by the business community to improve the truthfulness of advertising through voluntary self-regulation. Led by Samuel Dobbs, who later became president of Coca-Cola and one of the first presidents of the Associated Advertising Clubs of America, certain leaders of the business community believed that an honest marketplace, in the long run, would benefit both customers and merchants. They spread this message to their peers, and eventually, in cities across the country, businessmen organized "Advertising Vigilance Committees."

From the very beginning, the Vigilance Committees established the practice of educating the public and curbing marketplace abuses through voluntary efforts. These efforts attracted the attention of George W. Coleman, a Boston advertising executive, who in 1912 decided to form a National Vigilance Committee to extend the effort to regional and national advertising. This group became the National Better Business Bureau of the Associated Advertising Clubs of the World in 1921. Later it became known simply as the National Better Business Bureau.

In 1914, the previously all-volunteer Vigilance Committees began hiring professionals, with the Minnesota Vigilance Committee taking the lead by soliciting memberships from business firms and hiring the first full-time Better Business Bureau manager, H. J. Kenner. In 1936, Kenner, a leader of Better Business Bureau endeavors, published *The Fight for Truth in Advertising*, which influenced other institutions as well as BBBs.

In 1916, Vigilance Committees became known as Better Business Bureaus, and an effort was soon made to create a federation of BBBs. Incorporated in 1921, the federal organization evolved through several name changes to become, in 1946, the Association of Better Business Bureaus, Inc. Headquartered in New York City, the association functioned as a full-time organization with an executive staff until 1970, when it merged with the National Better Business Bureau to become the Council of Better Business Bureaus, Inc. (CBBB).

In 1928, with the founding of the first Canadian Better Business Bureau, the BBB movement became international. In the 1960s and 1970s, BBBs served local marketplaces in Mexico City, Venezuela, and Israel. Business communities in Latin and South America, Eastern Europe, the former Soviet Union, and other countries are currently exploring how to establish BBBs to serve their marketplaces.

Following World War I, BBBs rapidly expanded their consumer protection efforts. Questionable advertising of stocks and other investment offers flourished during this period. BBBs mounted public information efforts to alert consumers to swindlers and con artists and continued to campaign for truth in advertising.

To encourage truth in advertising, some business leaders believed that ground rules in this area had to be established. In 1912, the National Vigilance Committee first established "standards of practice." BBBs have since helped to prepare voluntary trade practices for many industries, including pharmaceuticals, retail, automobile dealers, commercial banks, savings banks, and federal savings and loans.

As the years progressed, BBBs not only continued efforts against fraudulent schemes and unethical advertising practices, but also created new programs to help consumers and businesses. Bureaus tried to persuade business to take formal steps to help educate consumers and be responsive to their needs. The Association of Better Business Bureaus sponsored business-consumer conferences in 1939 and 1940, bringing together representatives of business, education, government, and the public in an effort to increase public understanding of and confidence in advertising.

During World War II, the greatest demands on BBBs came from business and government investigations of charitable appeals made on behalf of servicemen. The War Charities Act was passed, requiring all appeals on behalf of servicemen to be cleared by the government. Unable to cope with the task, the government called on the BBBs for assistance because of their experience in the field of charity review. After peace was announced, BBBs began a War Savings Protection Program aimed at keeping the millions of dollars earned by servicemen and war industry workers out of the hands of waiting shysters. In various parts of the country, bureaus issued warnings under the slogan, "Before You Invest, Investigate," first coined in 1920.

Following World War II, BBBs began expanding the services they offered to assist American consumers who were eager to purchase homes, automobiles, appliances, and other goods. Through the 1950s, BBBs led the fight against kickbacks to doctors for prescription drugs and successfully pursued campaigns against home repair and improvement schemes, installment financing irregularities, and overcharges for automobile insurance.

In the 1960s, BBBs sought to emphasize their twin commitments to business and consumers. Inquiries to bureaus far outpaced complaints, underscoring the bureaus' increasingly important role as providers of information, services, and assistance to prevent complaints. BBBs were active in helping consumers with nondelivery of merchandise problems, warranty issues, and land speculation and contest/puzzle scams.

The emergence of franchises, holding companies, and conglomerates changed the way of doing business in America. The consumer movement intensified throughout the 1960s as the relationship between consumer and business became increasingly strained. Virginia Knauer, then President Nixon's adviser for consumer affairs, directly appealed to the BBBs in 1969 to assist in rebuilding positive relationships between sellers and buyers.

Council of Better Business Bureaus

Bureau system leaders responded by forming the Council of Better Business Bureaus in 1970, created by the merger of the National Better Business Bureau and the Association of Better Business Bureaus. The council's immediate goal was to help large corporations regain credibility with the American public by being responsive to the valid concerns of consumers.

Today, through the national memberships of more than 350 companies and the network of BBBs, the council provides programs and services on behalf of the nation's 166 BBBs and branches in the United States, operates a self-regulation forum on behalf of the national advertising community designed to sustain truthful and accurate advertising claims, issues reports on national charitable organizations, provides educational materials and publications with purchasing advice on more than eighty different products and services, and administers the BBB alternative dispute resolution (ADR) program. These services are provided by 141 staffers who operate on an annual budget of $14 million.

The council's national advertising industry self-regulation forum was established in 1971 as a response to consumer activists who were pushing for increased government regulation. At that time, the advertising industry formed a partnership, the National Advertising Review Council (NARC), which consisted of leaders from the American Advertising Federation, the American Association of Advertising Agencies, the Association of National Advertisers, and the Council of Better Business Bureaus. NARC designed a process to enable the industry to police itself. To ensure credibility and impartiality, the forum was placed under the purview of the Council of Better Business Bureaus.

The council's National Advertising Division (NAD) and the Children's Advertising Review Unit (CARU) constitute the investigative arm of the self-regulation program, reviewing and investigating inquiries from businesses, consumers, BBBs, trade associations, and other groups about the truthfulness and accuracy of national advertising claims. The National Advertising Review Board (NARB), composed of a peer review group of eighty-five advertising professionals and prominent public interest members, functions as an appeals process for those few cases that cannot be resolved through the NAD or CARU.

In its twenty-six-year history, this self-regulation mechanism has resolved more than 3,300 advertising inquiries and disputes. NARC is currently expanding the capabilities of the self-regulation program to online and other new interactive advertising media.

The council's Philanthropic Advisory Service (PAS) promotes ethical standards within the charitable community, provides information to the public on the thousands of national charitable organizations, and educates individual and corporate donors on wise giving. PAS encourages charitable organizations to accept the responsibility of self-regulation and adhere to the ethical practices outlined in the council's Standards of Charitable Solicitations. PAS works closely with BBBs, which distribute PAS charity reports and other educational materials, and report on local organizations engaged in fund-raising efforts.

The council's ADR programs assist businesses and their customers to resolve marketplace disputes. Its largest ADR program, BBB Autoline, serves 35 major car manufacturers and their customers. The council offers similar programs to national corporations who wish to precommit to ADR programs as an adjunct to their customer services efforts, and currently provides impartial third-party dispute resolution to 60,000 U.S. companies that participate in local BBB dispute resolution programs.

Consumers continue to rely on BBBs for prepurchase information and assistance in resolving marketplace disputes. In 1995, consumers contacted BBBs more than 11 million times to obtain information or to file a complaint.

The development in 1995 of a BBB home page on the World Wide Web demonstrated the BBB system's commitment to utilizing leading-edge technology to serve consumers and the business community in the newest marketplace, "cyberspace." The BBB World Wide Web server provides information on the BBB system's programs, publications, and services, while providing hyperlinks to council members, individual bureaus, and other appropriate organizations. Consumers can access the BBB home page to learn about the latest marketplace scams, utilize the nationwide directory of BBB offices, access recent press releases and consumer publications, and file complaints against businesses or charities. Consumers can use the BBB online complaint form to obtain assistance in resolving disputes that arise in the online marketplace or the more traditional marketplace. The complaint information is automatically forwarded to the appropriate BBB or CBBB staff, who try to help the consumer and the company reach a satisfactory settlement.

In the summer of 1996, the BBB system voted to permit BBBs the option of charging consumers for inquiry and complaint services. The bylaws change permits BBBs to charge a fee only for enhanced services and only with the express permission and supervision of the council's board of directors. Those BBBs electing to charge a fee will be required to offer consumers a "satisfaction guaranteed" policy and provide some reasonable alternate means of free access to BBB information and services.

— Holly Cherico

See also

Advertising Regulation; Disputes and Dispute Resolution.

Readings

Davis, Kristin (1990). "Beat Up on the BBB." *Changing Times.* (November): 51ff.

Davis, Tom E. (1987). *An Idea Becomes an Institution: The History of the Better Business Bureau, 1912–1987.* Arlington, VA: Council of Better Business Bureaus.

Munns, Joyce Matthews (1978). "Consumer Complaints as Pre-Purchase Information: An Evaluation of Better Business Bureau Reports to Consumers." *Journal of Consumer Affairs.* 12 (1): 76–87.

Blacks as Consumers

See Ethnic Minorities as Consumers.

Boycotts, Consumer

A consumer boycott may be viewed as an attempt by one or more parties to achieve certain objectives by urging individual consumers to refrain from making selected purchases in the marketplace. These objectives may include not only traditional marketplace goals of consumers such as lower prices and higher quality goods, but also goals external to the marketplace. These nonmarketplace goals have been the focus of organizations representing such diverse interests as animal welfare, environmental protection, the peace movement, various labor groups, women's rights, and the rights of minorities, including homosexuals, Native Americans, African Americans, Mexican Americans, Chinese Americans, and Jewish Americans.

While firm figures are not available, it appears that the number of boycotts has increased significantly in the past few decades. Hundreds of boycotts have been called at local, state, regional, and national levels, with most having taken place at local and national levels.

Over time, boycott strategy has shifted from an emphasis on reducing consumer purchases in the marketplace to one of generating media coverage for the boycott campaign. Instead of establishing picket lines and distributing handouts at the entrances to retail stores in an effort to convince shoppers to refrain from buying the targeted goods, boycott organizers have staged dramatic events in an attempt to draw the attention of the news media to the boycotters' cause. In the hopes of embarrassing targeted companies through negative depictions of their actions in the news media, they have undertaken such initiatives as marches, hunger strikes, guerrilla theater, and counteradvertising campaigns.

Those boycotts of special interest to the consumer movement focus on consumers not receiving adequate value for their expenditures in the marketplace. These actions, called consumer economic boycotts, have tended to be undertaken by ad hoc groups rather than by established consumer organizations. The actions have often resulted from an abrupt and seemingly unjustified drop in economic value secured from commonly made consumer purchases. The precipitating change sometimes has been a decrease in product or service quality but more typically has been an increase in the price of a consumer product or service. Moreover, most consumer economic boycotts have focused not on a single brand of product or service, but on a whole class of commodities, which often are food staples such as coffee, meat, milk, and sugar.

The organizers and many supporters of consumer economic boycotts have tended to be homemakers who work as volunteers. Their strategy for combating price increases has been both media-oriented and marketplace-oriented. The boycotters have often blamed various middlemen (e.g., wholesalers, distributors), rather than farmers or retailers, for the price increases. In the short run, the boycott efforts have sometimes been successful in that sales and/or prices for the boycotted items have declined. Yet, these decreases have rarely been sustained beyond the immediate post-boycott period.

Consumer economic boycotts were common during the early and mid-1970s when prices were rising relatively rapidly. But since then they have nearly disappeared. A principal reason may be the moderation of price increases by the early 1980s. Other factors may include the declining number of homemakers available to organize and participate in boycotts, the decreasing importance of food staples in the American family diet, and the increasing appeal of other, more dramatic issues, such as animal rights and environmentalism.

To sum up, during the last quarter century, American consumers have sometimes looked to boycotts as a vehicle for influencing consumer policy relating to the prices of essential goods consumed by themselves and their families. Through such direct action techniques as demonstrations, picketing, and leafletting, they have made their voices heard in the marketplace and in the halls of government.

These boycotts, however, have rarely succeeded in lowering prices beyond the short term. They have typically consumed many hours of volunteer time and energy without achieving permanent changes. Nonetheless, these boycotts have served an expressive function and have been a vehicle for recruiting activists into the consumer movement. Some state consumer organizations, such as the Maryland Citizens Consumer Council, evolved out of grassroots protests against rising food prices.

— Monroe Friedman

Readings

Friedman, Monroe (1995). "American Consumer Boycotts in Response to Rising Food Prices: Housewives' Protests at the Grassroots Level." *Journal of Consumer Policy*. 18 (2): 55–72.

——— (1996). "Grassroots Groups Confront the Corporation: Contemporary Strategies in Historical Perspective." *Journal of Social Issues*. 52 (1): 153–167.

British Consumer Movement

See United Kingdom's Consumer Movement.

Broadcast Protections

The American public's right to receive access to diverse entertainment and issue programming on television and radio is rooted in the First Amendment. As the U.S. Supreme Court ruled in the landmark *Red Lion Broadcasting Co. v. FCC* decision in 1969: "The people as a whole retain their interest in free speech by radio and their collective right to have the medium function consistently with the ends and purposes of the First Amendment. It is the right of the viewers and listeners, not the right of the broadcasters, which is paramount."

The *Red Lion* decision draws upon the historical analysis of Professor Alexander Meiklejohn. Although his work is not well known outside of the world of legal scholars and political scientists, Meiklejohn's influence on First Amendment jurisprudence has been profound. Meiklejohn emphasized that the Founding Fathers, particularly James Madison, perceived the First Amendment as a tool to insure deliberative democratic processes. Following this model, Justice White's *Red Lion* opinion, written for a unanimous Court, emphasized that: "It is the purpose of the First Amendment to preserve an uninhibited marketplace of ideas in which truth will ultimately prevail, rather than to countenance monopolization of that market, whether it be by the Government itself or a private licensee. . . . It is the right of the public to receive suitable access to social, political, esthetic, moral and other ideas and experiences which is crucial here. That right may not constitutionally be abridged either by Congress or by the FCC."

Broadcast Regulation

Despite tremendous technological changes, the underlying premises of broadcast regulation have remained essentially unchanged since Congress enacted the Communications Act of 1934. Under it, the right to broadcast using the publicly owned electromagnetic spectrum is awarded under licenses of limited terms (currently five years for television and seven for radio). These licenses are obtained without charge; the public is repaid in the form of the broadcasters' commitment to provide service "in the public interest." Broadcasters, then, are trustees for the public in their operation of these stations.

The trusteeship model is not the only available option. A government owned and operated system—the model originally employed in most countries—is incompatible with the First Amendment. But temporary licenses or outright ownership of the right to broadcast could have been auctioned or given away by means of lottery (as is the case with some low-power television licenses). A "common carriage" system (strongly advocated in the 1920s by AT&T) might have been adopted under which the operator of a broadcast transmitter would have sold time to all comers but retained no editorial control over the content. Instead, Congress chose the trusteeship system so as to promote the widest diversity of viewpoint and opinion while minimizing the governmental role in deciding content.

The effectiveness of this system has depended on insuring that broadcasters fulfill the commitments they make when they volunteer to serve as trustees of the publicly owned spectrum. However, until the 1960s, the Federal Communications Commission (FCC) refused to recognize that the public had any direct right to participate in enforcing the law. It claimed to be willing to consider complaints from the public about broadcasters' performance, but insisted that the commission was the only arbiter of what constituted adequate service under the Communications Act. Citizens were adequately represented, it said, by the agency's staff and commissioners.

In practice, FCC decisions had long since been influenced by the very industry it was charged to regulate. Licenses were renewed as a matter of course, and there was no meaningful effort to insure that broadcasters provided adequate service.

One of the most serious shortcomings of broadcasters was their insensitivity and, at times, hostility to the needs of racial and ethnic minorities. In 1964, the Office of Communication of the United Church of Christ assisted civil rights leaders in Mississippi in mounting a legal challenge to the FCC's refusal to afford legal "standing" to members of the listening public. Their petition charged the NBC affiliate in Jackson with blatant racial and religious discrimination: the station excluded blacks from local programming and refused to carry any desegregationist opinions in its news and public affairs programming. (Testimony established that the station interrupted network news coverage of the civil rights movement with graphics falsely stating, "Sorry, cable trouble.")

While acknowledging the charges as serious, the FCC nonetheless renewed the station's license on a probationary basis. The petitioners challenged the renewal in the U.S. Court of Appeals for the District of Columbia. To prevail, however, they first had to establish their "standing" to participate. In 1966, a three-judge panel ruled that citizens have the right to participate in broadcast renewal proceedings. In an opinion by Judge (later Chief Justice) Warren E. Burger, the court directed the FCC to give citizens the right to present their own case.

For purposes of convenience, this entry refers to television, even though many of its observations and suggestions apply equally to radio. In an age when public debate emphasizes the Internet and 500-plus channels of digital color television, radio retains its power and importance. Radio broadcasts are available to all, at any time and at any location. For many parts of the day, at work or in transit, radio is accessible when television is impractical. But until the rise of right-wing talk show hosts in the early 1990s, radio was given much less attention than television by many consumer groups.

Nonlegal Tactics

As in other industries subject to regulation, broadcasters have attempted to preempt legal obligations by creating the appearance of a self-regulating system through voluntary "codes" and other methods. Until it was declared to be a violation of the antitrust laws in 1982, the National Association of Broadcasters maintained a purposely obtuse and unenforceable "NAB Code of Good Practice." Since then, broadcasters and cable programmers have continued on their own to proclaim their social responsibility in purporting to meet community needs, to program for children's and other special needs, and to avoid content offensive to many.

For decades, a number of citizens and consumer groups have attempted, with varying degrees of success, to influence broadcasters' conduct by use of moral suasion. In recent years, an organization called Viewers for Quality TV has mounted letter-writing campaigns to induce networks not to cancel high-quality programs with marginal ratings. At the local level, many community groups have found that responsible broadcast managers welcome constructive program suggestions and are willing to address oversights in their news and public affairs coverage. At the national level, network programmers have come to welcome relationships with activists on how to make their programming more relevant. Civil rights, civil liberties, gay, environmental, children's, animal rights, and other groups have Hollywood-based representatives who regularly consult with programmers.

Such cooperation generally stops when disputes relate to financial, political, or regulatory affairs of the mass media industry or of their sponsors. The reason was succinctly summarized by former FCC Commissioner Nicholas Johnson in his 1970 book, *How to Talk Back to Your Television Set:* advertisers are the customer to whom viewers are sold at rates calculated in terms of the number of viewers reached.

Because of the critical role that advertisers play, consumer groups have on many occasions attempted to employ sponsor boycotts to influence broadcasters. In the early 1950s, the NAACP boycotted Blatz Beer advertisers to protest CBS's "Amos 'n' Andy" program. Shortly afterward, however, advertisers generally stopped the practice of being the sole sponsor (and often the owner) of a program and instead started purchasing commercials on a "spot" basis throughout the broadcast day. This practice has made it much more difficult to mount a boycott.

In the 1970s, the National Citizens Committee for Broadcasting and the National PTA devised methodology to identify advertisers who placed commercials in programming they considered to have excessively violent content. This methodology is expensive to implement and has had relatively minimal direct impact. Its primary practitioners today are groups that have the goal of censoring or penalizing the broadcast of certain kinds of content, typically matters involving material they consider offensive because of its sexual themes or content, or because of its depiction of graphic violence. While there is little dispute about the fact that the First Amendment protects the right to boycott, the primarily negative nature of these boycotts has also generated criticism from many consumer and civil liberties groups.

Recent Policy Issues and Legal Tactics

Perhaps the most important tool for insuring broadcasters' accountability is the fairness doctrine, which requires broadcasters to afford a reasonable opportunity for opposing viewpoints in their overall programming. Relying upon an opinion issued by Judge Robert Bork in 1987, the FCC stopped enforcing most aspects of the doctrine and extended its repeal to advertising on ballot issues in 1992. Although efforts to restore the fairness doctrine by legislation failed in 1992 and 1993, consumer groups hope that the fairness doctrine can be restored through litigation.

Despite massive deregulation during the Reagan era, many legal tools remain available to consumers. At the national level, consumer and civil rights groups seek to influence FCC policy to promote diversity by limiting the number of media properties any one entity can own, and by promoting ownership and employment of minorities and women in the mass media. They also advocate enforcing the children's television law enacted in 1991—which required stations to air educational children's programs and limit commercials on children's shows—by persuading the FCC to adopt aggressive interpretations of the requirements that broadcasters and cable programmers carry educational and informational programming for children. The utility of the 1991 children's television law is yet to be known, but prospects are promising.

Broadcasters must receive approval of the FCC to buy or renew their licenses. While it is now virtually impossible to succeed in challenging renewal based on broadcasters' community-based programming, license renewal challenges have been particularly valuable as a forum to raise questions about licensees' equal employment practices. In many cases, broadcasters seeking to buy new stations must obtain special waivers of the FCC's rules that limit the number of media properties any one entity can own. Challenges to those waiver requests can also be effective in promoting program diversity.

— Andrew Jay Schwartzman

See also

Action for Children's Television; Cable Television Regulation; Telecommunications Research and Action Center.

Readings

Aufderheide, Patricia (1990). "After the Fairness Doctrine: Controversial Broadcast Programming and Public Interest." *Journal of Communication*. 40 (Summer): 47–72.

Cole, Barry, and Mal Oettinger (1978). *Reluctant Regulators: The FCC and the Broadcast Audience.* Reading, MA: Addison-Wesley Publishing Co.

McChesney, Robert W. (1993). *Telecommunications, Mass Media, and Democracy: The Battle for U.S. Broadcasting, 1928–1935.* New York: Oxford University Press.

Bulgarian Consumer Movement

Consumer affairs in both the public and the private sectors has been slow to develop in Bulgaria. As in Albania, an Unfair Competition Act was introduced in 1991, and a draft law on protection of consumers' rights is under discussion. This draft asserts the right of consumer associations to obtain assistance and information necessary for their work from state and municipal bodies, companies, and other enterprises, and requires these bodies to respond to their proposals and complaints within not less than twenty days.

The current reality is, however, very different. The Bulgarian approach to the free market has been to deregulate rather than to privatize, to eliminate virtually all the controls that protected consumers—for instance, against unsafe and poor-quality products—and to put nothing in their place. The machinery of enforcement has been dismantled, and, with frequent changes of government, only the most basic of new laws have been introduced.

The Federation of Consumers in Bulgaria was formed in 1991 to fight for consumer rights. Its members are regional or product-oriented clubs or unions. The member organizations elect a federal council, which in turn appoints an executive council and president. The president is Iovtcho Topalov, an eminent cardiac surgeon, and the executive secretary is Pavel Kurlev, an engineer previously connected with a state product testing laboratory.

The federation charges no membership fees and is thought to be precluded by its legal constitution from charging for services. Before 1994, this restriction had not been considered to be a problem since the government had provided an office in the center of Sofia and covered all the federation's running costs. But this funding ($170,000 in 1993) ceased abruptly in April 1994. Since then, the federation's principal objective has been to identify ways of surviving in both the short and longer term. These means could include obtaining funds from international agencies for particular projects; persuading the government to make consumer protection a higher priority; strengthening the voluntary, independent concept by charging for membership and training volunteers to put their professional skills to work for the consumer; and, in the longer term, looking for acceptable means of generating income.

There are some signs that this approach is bearing fruit. Local consumer groups in some areas have been handling consumer complaints, on behalf of overloaded local authorities, to the benefit of consumers. At the national level, the relationship between the federation and relevant ministries has become more constructive and conciliatory.

Despite this progress, the underlying situation remains unchanged and, at present, consumers in Bulgaria face bleak prospects. Their independent champions lack resources, and their government seems in no hurry to provide them with even the most basic of legal rights.

— Alastair Macgeorge

See also

Central and Eastern Europe, Consumer Movements in.

Reading

Kozminski, Andrzej K. (1992). "Consumers in Transition from the Centrally Planned Economy to the Market Economy." *Journal of Consumer Policy.* 14 (4): 351–370.

Bureau Européen des Unions de Consommateurs

The Bureau Européen des Unions de Consommateurs (BEUC) is a federation of independent national consumer organizations from Western and Central Europe. The task of BEUC is to influence, in the consumer interest, the evolution of European Union (EU) policy.

BEUC was founded in 1962 by the independent consumer organizations in the (then) six member states of the European Economic Community (EEC). The founders had two main aims: to provide a framework for cooperation on product testing and to work together to influence the development of EEC policy. For about the first ten years, the member organizations met together regularly to discuss matters of mutual interest, to formulate joint positions on current topics, and to develop contacts with consumer organizations in other European countries that were not then members of the EEC. In the early days, the member organizations administered the BEUC secretariat; it was not until 1972 that Eirlys Roberts was appointed as its first director. Under her leadership, BEUC made an important contribution to the development, in 1975, of the first program for a Consumer Protection and Information Policy, agreed upon by the Council of Ministers.

With the inclusion of additional countries in the EEC and the growing strength of the national consumer organizations, support for BEUC grew. In 1980, while Tony Venables was director, BEUC scored a major success in organizing a consumer boycott to press for a ban on the use of hormones in beef production. Toward the end of the 1980s, again under the directorship of Venables, BEUC played a leading role in the successful campaign for lead-free gasoline in Europe.

Membership

Membership in BEUC is restricted to independent national consumer organizations in Europe working for consumers on a broad range of issues. Some of its best-known members are relatively large organizations that publish comparative test magazines and other publications, containing no advertising, that are sold directly to consumers.

While the activities of many member organizations are financed in large part by the sale of test magazines and other consumer publications, the work of others is subsidized by government. No member organizations, however, derive any income from advertising in their magazines or from other business sources.

Over 70 percent of BEUC's income is contributed by its member organizations (in the form of a levy on their total income). Much of the remainder represents a subsidy coming from the European Commission.

During the 1990s, the membership of BEUC has expanded greatly. Before 1990, membership was confined to national organizations from the member states of the European Community. Now, BEUC has member organizations in the fifteen EU member states (Austria, Belgium, Denmark, Finland, France, Germany, Greece, Ireland, Italy, Luxembourg, the Netherlands, Portugal, Spain, Sweden, and the UK) plus Norway and Iceland (members of the European Economic Area), Switzerland, and Slovenia.

The expansion of BEUC membership results from the fact that BEUC was established to try to influence the evolution of EU policy. EU laws now directly affect not only the member states but also countries, such as Norway and Iceland, that have signed the European Economic Area Agreement and countries in Central and Eastern Europe that have signed Association Agreements with the EU. These agreements require signatory countries, to a greater or lesser degree, to transpose certain EU directives and regulations into their own national law. Consumer organizations from the countries concerned wanted to join BEUC in order to participate in the process of trying to influence laws that would be adopted in their own country.

The BEUC General Assembly, consisting of representatives of all BEUC member organizations, meets twice a year and is the ultimate decision-making body. An executive committee of eight members meets about six times a year and is responsible for the overall direction of BEUC between general assemblies. As a campaigning organization, since there is frequent direct consultation between the secretariat and the member organizations, BEUC has the ability to act quickly and flexibly. Most actions are carried out by the full-time secretariat of fifteen people that is based in Brussels.

Activities

The lawmaking process in the EU is a highly complex one primarily involving three institutions—the European Commission, the European Parliament, and the Council of Ministers. The commission is sometimes called the "permanent bureaucracy" of the EU and has the sole right of initiative to propose new legal measures. In most cases, the final decision on laws rests with the Council of Ministers, representing the governments of the fifteen member states, and with the European Parliament, which now has a right to co-decision with the council in many but not all cases. As might be expected from this arrangement, the lawmaking procedures are lengthy and complicated. BEUC has to monitor the progress of relevant proposals through the legislative process, intervening at different times to try to influence the decisions taken in the commission, parliament, and council.

BEUC exerts influence by bringing its expertise and that of its member organizations to bear on decision-makers and by generating political pressure in support of its aims. BEUC's campaigning is based on a series of position papers that are developed by the secretariat in close consultation with the BEUC member organizations.

BEUC member organizations carry out extensive research and are in close touch with the concerns and experiences of consumers in their own countries. It is this base of expertise and experience that gives BEUC a unique authority to speak on behalf of consumers at the European level.

As a measure of the scale of BEUC activities, in 1994 the organization produced thirty-seven position papers, issued twenty-six press releases, and organized four press conferences. BEUC's activities are detailed in its annual reports and four-page quarterly, entitled *BEUC in Brief.*

There have been several major developments in the EU during the past five years that have been particularly relevant to BEUC's work. These were the 1992 deadline for the completion of the Single Market, the Treaty of European Union (the Maastricht Treaty), the enlargement of the EU, and the forthcoming Intergovernmental Conference.

The deadline for the completion of the European Single Market was December 31, 1992. This deadline, which had more political than legal significance, greatly accelerated progress toward the removal of barriers to the creation of a single market, but BEUC was quick to point out that many measures still had to be taken to create a single market for consumers. For BEUC, a single market for consumers is one in which consumers can be confident and active participants, not merely passive beneficiaries of economies of scale on the production and distribution side. It is still not easy for consumers to be active participants in the single market because there are too many sectors where it is difficult for consumers to buy cross-border (the car market being one of the best examples). It is also difficult for consumers to feel confident buying cross-border because of uncertainties about guarantees, after-sales services, and redress. The key problem here is that the process of creating a single market does not in itself imply any particular level of consumer protection; the level depends on political choices. BEUC has argued consistently for a single market based on a high level of consumer protection and has also campaigned to ensure that this objective is given firm expression in the treaties which are, in effect, the constitution of the EU.

The enlargement of the EU has had, and continues to have, an important impact on BEUC. Consumer organizations from new member states (or potentially new member states) have found that affiliation with BEUC can help greatly to increase their knowledge and understanding of EU policy. During the most recent expansion in EU membership, BEUC benefited from the admission of strong consumer organizations from Austria, Finland, Sweden, and Norway. (Norway eventually voted against the EU membership but remains a member of the European Economic Area and therefore subject to many EU rules.)

In 1990, the governments of the then member states began discussions on a new Treaty of European Union to build on the work of prior treaties such as the Treaty of Rome, which had established the EEC. BEUC pointed out that the previous treaties did not provide any legal basis for a consumer policy at the European level. It campaigned vigorously for the inclusion in the new treaty of a new article on consumer policy. These efforts were successful with the inclusion in the new Treaty of European Union (the Maastricht Treaty) of a new article, 129a, which for the first time provides a clear legal or constitutional basis for a consumer policy at the EU level. The new treaty article has already had positive effects, particularly in raising the profile of consumer policy within the European institutions. When the governments of the member states have convened in the context of the new treaty, BEUC has pressed them to use the Maastricht Treaty to make consumer protection an important objective of the EU.

In addition to the new article on consumer policy, the Maastricht Treaty contains other provisions of importance for consumers. The treaty strengthens the powers of the European Parliament, including giving it the power of co-decision with the council on a wide range of legislative measures. Before Maastricht, the parliament's power to amend legislation was limited; now, subject to the co-decision procedure, it effectively has the right to veto proposals. Given that the parliament is often the most consumer-friendly of the three main institutions, consumers have benefited from its increased power. BEUC works closely with members of the parliament and its relevant committees.

The Maastricht Treaty also introduced the principle of subsidiarity under which, in areas in which the Community does not have exclusive authority, it can act only if a proposed objective can be better achieved by EU action than by that of its member states. BEUC believes that this principle has been misused for undesirable political ends: it has served as a catch-all argument against action at the Community level while doing nothing to increase the freedom of action of the member states at the national level. The subsidiarity issue illustrates one of the dilemmas facing consumers in the future development of the EU—how to ensure the development of a high standard of consumer protection throughout the EU.

While many of its activities have been concerned with the EU legislative process, BEUC has also tried to influence the evolution of EU policy in other ways, for example, by intervening in administrative proceedings, or by intervening in or instituting legal actions. In 1994, the Court of First Instance of the European Communities upheld a complaint by BEUC against the commission's refusal to investigate an earlier BEUC complaint against an agreement between the British and Japanese motor industry associations to limit the number of Japanese cars on the UK market.

Most BEUC member organizations are also members of Consumers International (CI). The two organizations work closely together, particularly on trade, food, and health issues.

In the future, BEUC will continue to campaign for the consumer interest in the evolution of EU policy, but probably in somewhat different ways. Factors such as economic liberalization, political change, possible enlargement of the EU to include Eastern and Central European countries, technological changes, and changes in the consumer movement all are altering the context in which BEUC operates. The organization has begun to consider the implications of these changes for its work.

— Jim Murray

See also

European Union, Consumer Policy in the.

Readings

European Commission (1994). *European Consumer Guide to the Single Market*. Brussels: Office of Official Publications of the European Communities.

Micklitz, Hans W., and Stephen Weatherill (1993). "Consumer Policy in the European Community: Before and after Maastricht." *Journal of Consumer Policy*. 16 (3–4): 285–322.

C

Cable Television Regulation

Cable television began in the late 1950s and early 1960s as a service called Community Antenna Television. It was designed to deliver local broadcast television signals via wires to rural communities that were unable to receive over-the-air signals clearly.

During the late 1960s and throughout the 1970s and 1980s, the cable television industry began to produce its own programming, which was available only to those subscribing to cable television. With the creation of such services as advertising-free pay movie channels such as Home Box Office (HBO), Cable News Network (CNN), and Music Television (MTV), among scores of others, program offerings expanded well beyond local broadcast television. At the same time, cable television expanded from mostly rural areas to suburban and urban communities. By the early 1990s, cable television service was available to nearly every home in the United States. By 1995, 60 percent of households across the country subscribed to the service.

To operate in a community, a cable operator must first obtain a franchise from the relevant state or local authority (the franchising authority). In some cases, a single authority will negotiate and grant all cable franchises for an entire state. Most often, however, the franchising authority exists at the county or city level in the form of a cable television office. The franchising authority is charged with negotiating the terms under which a cable system must operate.

In most communities, there is an opportunity for public comment during the negotiation period. In the past, most communities granted exclusive franchises to a single cable television operator. Such agreements were made illegal by the 1992 Cable Act.

Franchise agreements typically run from five to twenty years. These agreements nearly always provide for a franchise fee, which cannot exceed 5 percent of the cable system's gross revenues and can be used at the discretion of the community to offset the expense of cable oversight or for unrelated purposes. Most cable systems also include a certain number of public access, educational, and governmental channels for local community use. Many franchise agreements also call for studios, equipment, and training to be provided to the public. Local franchising authorities are free to include many other requirements as part of the agreement with the cable operator. These authorities also handle complaints about a cable operator's service or selection of offerings.

Prior to 1984, virtually all cable television policy, including rate regulation, was made exclusively on the state or local level. As a result, the rules and regulations differed across communities. In 1984, Congress passed legislation that preempted state authority over cable rates and led to rate deregulation for 97 percent of all cable systems, effective in 1986.

This deregulation policy resulted in substantial rate increases and more complaints about service. Between 1986 and 1992, cable rates increased at three times the rate of inflation. By 1992, rates in those few markets where there was cable competition were nearly 30 percent lower than in the more than 11,000 monopoly cable markets across the country. There was also widespread dissatisfaction with customer service. Consumers complained about telephones not being answered by the companies, service calls being missed, and poor signal quality.

At the same time, by controlling the most popular cable television programming, the cable companies maintained their local monopolies. Cable operators prevented competing delivery systems, such as satellite and microwave wireless services, from having access to popular cable programming at reasonable rates.

In response to widespread consumer dissatisfaction, the Consumer Federation of America and local government officials helped persuade Senators Albert Gore (D-TN) and John Danforth (R-MO) and Representatives Edward Markey (D-MA) and Christopher Shays (R-CT) to introduce the 1992 Cable Act. Congress passed this legislation and overrode a veto by President George Bush. The 1992 Cable Act represented a comprehensive reregulation of the cable industry, covering rate regulation for cable service and equipment, customer service, competitors' access to cable programming, franchising terms, and guaranteed carriage for free over-the-air broadcast signals, among other issues. It provided for split jurisdiction between local franchising authorities and the Federal Communications Commission (FCC).

The 1992 Cable Act provided that cable rates only be regulated until effective competition develops in a market. Effective competition is defined as a comparable multichannel video service or services that are available to at least 50 percent of households in a franchise area and are subscribed to by at least 15 percent of those households. Between 1992 and 1995, there were no communities that met this definition of competition. In virtually every community across the country, cable television remained a local monopoly.

The FCC had the primary regulatory responsibility under the 1992 law. For most issues, it set the rules, and local franchising authorities helped to implement them. With respect to rate regulation, the 1992 Cable Act provided that the "basic tier" of services was to be regulated by the local franchising authority, according to rules established by the FCC, while the cable programming service tier was to be regulated directly by federal authorities. À la carte offerings, such as premium movie channels and pay-per-view services, were left unregulated.

Every cable system had to have at least a "basic tier" of service. By law, this tier had to be the lowest-priced package of services. Local free over-the-air broadcast channels—as well as public access, educational, and governmental channels—had to be carried on this tier of service. Aside from these specific services, the cable operator was free to choose what other services, if any, were included in the basic package.

The basic tier was regulated only if the local franchising authority was certified with the FCC to do so. To certify, the local authority had to show that it was legally authorized to regulate the service and that it had sufficient resources.

In many communities, there was an additional tier of service known as the "cable programming service" tier or "enhanced basic." This tier often included the most popular cable programming channels. It had to be purchased in addition to the basic package.

Regulation of this service was triggered by a complaint filed by a customer—the local franchising authority on behalf of affected consumers—who believed the cable system's rates for equipment and services were higher than permitted under the FCC's rate rules. A complaint had to be filed on a specific form provided by the FCC. Cable complaint forms were also available from most local franchising authorities and consumer organizations.

Local franchising authorities retained the right to negotiate franchise agreements with cable companies. Local authorities were also permitted to augment the minimum customer service standards established by the FCC to deal with specific service problems that a community might face.

The 1992 Cable Act, according to FCC estimates, lowered consumer costs on cable service and equipment by more than $2 billion annually. Yet it was highly unpopular with the cable industry and came under increasing fire from leaders in Congress, which had turned Republican in 1994. Thus, it was no surprise that the cable provisions of comprehensive telecommunications legislation passed in 1996—the Telecommunications Act of 1996—weakened cable television regulation significantly.

By the provisions of this act, as soon as a telephone company began offering a multichannel video service, the cable company's cable programming service rates would be deregulated. Also, individual consumers could no longer complain about their cable rates directly to the FCC. The new law mandated that only the local franchising authority, after receiving a number of complaints from consumers, could choose to challenge a cable operator's lease.

Perhaps most importantly, the new law provided that, instead of the market-based test for eliminating rate regulation once a competitor is in place, cable programming service rates for small cable operators—those companies serving in the aggregate less than 1 percent of all cable subscribers nationwide that do not have aggregate revenues in excess of $250 million annually—would be deregulated immediately. For larger cable operators, the law provided that rate deregulation take place no later than March 1999, regardless of whether there is a competitor in the market.

The new law left regulation of the basic tier in place. However, many cable operators had already removed most of the popular programming from the basic tier. With deregulation of the upper tier coming by 1999, cable operators are expected to move as much programming as they can to the more expensive, and unregulated, cable programming service tier.

— Bradley C. Stillman

Readings

Crandall, Robert W., and Harold Furchtgott-Roth (1996). *Cable TV: Regulation or Competition?* Washington, DC: Brookings Institution.

Ferris, Charles D., et al. (1996). *Cable Television Law: A Video Communications Practice Guide.* Matthew Bender & Co., Inc.

Call For Action

Ellen Sulzberger Straus founded Call For Action in 1963 at New York City radio station WMCA. After researching New York City housing problems, she established a citywide telephone referral system to handle housing complaints. Her efforts resulted in revisions in the code enforcement procedures of the Department of Rent and Housing Maintenance and four federal grand jury indictments against slumlords. In addition, together with the National Council of Negro Women, Straus conducted a voter registration campaign, which led to Call For Action's expansion into a central telephone information and referral service to handle all kinds of problems.

Straus's idea was simple: combine an ombudsman approach with the power of the media to provide free and confidential mediation services to individual consumers. Call For Action is a central telephone system located at a broadcast station. The station tells its audience about the service and provides the phone number. The phones are staffed by volunteers who are trained mediators and who help consumers resolve complaints.

The success of Straus's concept led to Call For Action becoming a national organization in 1969. That year, four additional radio stations became hosts to Call For Action, and the first consumer hotline network was born. The network now has twenty-six offices across the country, two in other nations, and the ability to handle complaints anywhere through the Network Hotline Office.

In 1975, Call For Action was incorporated. In the next year, the "Ask the Expert" program, in which experts such as lawyers, accountants, and doctors answer questions from callers, was established.

In 1989, Call For Action expanded its mission to include educating consumers as well as resolving their problems. In 1991, in partnership with the Federal Trade Commission, Call For Action wrote a brochure on advance-fee loan scams and, soon after, prepared two other brochures on phony prize offers and double-scamming frauds. In 1992, the organization produced and distributed "Scams, Schemes, and Deceptive Offers," a brochure to educate small businesses about frauds to which they are susceptible. This publication and its information was publicized in a national media tour. In 1993, Call For Action wrote a brochure on electronic transfers that was requested by many consumers. In the same year, it completed a video on consumer credit for the Hispanic community that aired on Univision and was widely distributed. Recently, the organization released another video in Spanish—this one on phone slamming (unauthorized switch of one's long-distance phone company).

Each year, Call For Action volunteers open about 150,000 new cases and recover more than $30 million for consumers. In addition, the network receives another 130,000 calls annually for information and advice. In 1990, Call For Action expanded its audience to include the deaf and speech impaired by installing telecommunications devices for the deaf (TDDs) in each affiliate office.

Call For Action functions as a consumer mediation and education service for both individual consumers and small businesses. The network has mediated disputes ranging from thousands of dollars lost in a double-scamming scheme to dissatisfaction with a product purchased at a neighborhood store.

Call For Action is governed by a board of directors who are elected by member affiliates. The board is comprised of leaders in business and broadcasting and Call For Action affiliate directors. Members of the board are elected to serve three-year terms and may be reelected. The officers are elected by the board of directors and include a chairman, president, vice president, secretary, and treasurer. The president functions as the chief executive officer of the corporation. A steering committee, made up of directors or individuals from affiliate offices, acts as liaison between the affiliates and the board.

Each affiliate office has a director (and sometimes a co-director), who manages the affiliate office and its staff of volunteers and also acts as a liaison with the broadcast station. The Call For Action offices are staffed by 950 volunteer mediators.

The Network Office, located in Washington, D.C., handles administrative tasks, coordinates national projects, develops new affiliates, and provides leadership and guidance to individual Call For Action directors. The small staff of the Network Office are the only salaried employees in the organization.

Shirley L. Rooker, current president of Call For Action, has been associated with the organization for more than twenty years. Since 1976, her reports on consumer issues and fraud directed against small businesses have been heard on WTOP in Washington, D.C. She became president of Call For Action in 1989. Rooker is a frequent guest on local and network radio and television programs across the country and is often cited in the national press as an authority on scams and fraud. She frequently speaks before national and local consumer and business groups throughout the country.

Call For Action operates with an annual budget of approximately $250,000. Funding is derived from the annual broadcaster assessment fee that each affiliate broadcaster pays, from individual and corporate donations, from corporate consumer education projects, from development fees for new affiliates, and from projects in partnership with government agencies.

— Shirley L. Rooker

See also
Disputes and Dispute Resolution.

Reading
Wnek, Madilee C. (1994). "Shirley Rooker's Consuming Passion: Radio Volunteers Respond to Calls for Action from Here and Abroad." *The Washington Times*. (August 2): 8.

Canadian Consumer Movement

Consumer organization in Canada differs sharply from that in the United States. The economies of both nations have been closely linked, and Canadians have read about or seen media reports on many U.S. consumer problems, starting with Upton Sinclair's exposé of meat-packing plants. But there are two differences between the countries that help explain the way their respective consumer movements have developed.

First, Canada is a confederation in which important powers are exercised at the provincial level. These powers include policy-making related to health care, trucking, and most other aspects of transportation. In Canada, for example, there is not even a national Securities and Exchange Commission.

The second major difference stems from the fact that there is a natural monopoly in North America for consumer testing. Since many of the same products are sold in U.S. and Canadian markets, *Consumer Reports* can meet most of the consumer information needs in both countries. As a result, no organization like Consumers Union that can help support a vibrant consumer movement has emerged in Canada. Nevertheless, during the past century thousands of volunteers have spurred grassroots consumer activism.

Roots of the Consumers Association of Canada

Canada, like other countries, developed a market economy without the institutions required to ensure that exchanges were fair. As early as 1897, a confederation of Canadian women's groups founded the National Council of Women to urge weighing standards and truthful grading of foods and other consumer goods. Some cities had consumers leagues or household leagues to monitor the quality of foods in shops. A breakthrough came in December 1941 after Canada had been at war for two years. The Wartime Prices and Trade Board (WPTB) faced a crisis of shortages and sharp price increases. The Minister of Finance and the chairman of the WPTB called together many women's organizations to establish a consumer branch of the WPTB. Thousands of women volunteered, founding groups known as Women's Regional Advisory Committees (WRACs) in each province and in many cities.

A year after the war ended, the WRACs were officially terminated, although some units, upset by post-war price rises, refused to disband. In early 1947, Harriet Parsons, the economic convener of the National Council of Women, and its president, Blanche Marshall, formed a committee to study the creation of a national consumer organization. On September 29, 1947, seventy voting delegates from over twenty women's organizations created the Canadian Association of Consumers. Their goal was to create a not-for-profit organization, independent of government and industry, that was controlled by 100,000 women members each paying fifty cents per year. In 1961, men were permitted to join, and the next year, the name of the organization was changed to the Consumers Association of Canada (CAC). At its peak during the 1970s, membership exceeded 150,000.

Collective Consumer Action

While some of the early battles were small, they signaled a major change from seller control of the marketplace. The first victory for the CAC came in 1948 when it fought successfully to have the ban on margarine lifted, which resulted in lower butter prices. In the early 1950s, the CAC protested the deceptive packaging of bacon. On the small window on the cardboard package, bacon marketers had printed red stripes to resemble lean meat. CAC protests ended this deceptive practice.

Consumer activism led to hundreds of other improvements at the provincial and national levels. In 1961, consumers in central Canada learned that they had been eating meat from animals that were already dead when brought to meat-packers. With the assistance of Thérèse Casgrain and others, Helen Morningstar led a campaign against this abuse. By 1962, they had succeeded in establishing food safety standards. CAC also helped persuade policymakers to create a list of safe food additives, require textile labeling (1949), pass the Hazardous Products Act (1970), mandate standardized packaging (1971), and in some provinces require elements of truth in lending.

Two long-standing CAC committees were especially influential. One, focusing on research and economics, was run for nearly twenty years by the "Two Helens" (Morningstar and Anderson). The other was the food committee, run by the "Two Ruths" (Jackson and Titheridge). These volunteer committees, working outside of Ottawa, succeeded in recruiting those with expertise and influence to advocate needed protections.

One of the CAC's greatest successes was Canada's Competition Act, passed in two stages: 1976 for services, and 1986 for mergers. Since 1889, Canada has had antimonopoly prohibitions, but until 1986, the government had never won a contested court case. For 16 years, the CAC campaigned for a more effective law promoting competition and discouraging monopoly.

One defeat suffered by the CAC was a successful industry campaign to overturn the 1969 pharmaceutical patent arrangement, which paid compulsory royalties to drug patent holders. While the CAC did win the creation of a Patented Medicines Prices Review Board, the loss of the patent arrangement cost millions of dollars in increased health costs per year.

The CAC also campaigned successfully for freer trade. After working for two decades, the organization played a role in removing trade barriers against lower-priced shoes and clothing for children. It failed, however, to block a restriction system that was introduced in 1974 for milk, eggs, chicken, and turkey products. The milk quota alone costs consumers $1 billion per year.

Most leaders of the national CAC first led provincial CAC organizations. During its half-century of existence, the national CAC has been controlled by a board of directors of which provincial presidents make up a majority. In addition, there is a Provincial President's Council (PPC), which operates to share information. But the strength of the CAC lies at the grass roots. A limited survey conducted in 1993 found dedicated volunteers working on issues that included food quality, energy, environmental quality, telephone and cable rates and service, retirement plans, warrantees and redress, bus safety, personal finance, and education. One such volunteer, E. J. Stansfield from a local in Manitoba, single-handedly answered over 35,000 calls for assistance. After 5,385 calls, she apologized that she "never had the physical strength to be active."

Consumer Information Activities

The CAC and some of its provincial affiliates have always used informal newsletters to communicate among volunteers. By 1963, the CAC began to publish, six times per year, a magazine: *Canadian Consumer/Consommateur Canadien.* As a result, the number of employees in the Ottawa office increased from three or four to forty-five persons. The magazine has been successful during those periods when it cooperated with Consumers Union. The first joint promotion took place in 1971. Canadians could, with one payment, acquire the product test results from *Consumer Reports* plus reports on Canadian services and collective action from *Canadian Consumer.* Sales of the Canadian publication rose to a peak of nearly 160,000 in 1982.

In 1980, the CAC's board of directors decided to expand the laboratories, publish monthly, and increase subscription fees. Despite rosy forecasts, the higher price resulted in a decline in subscriptions from which the magazine never recovered. By 1993, subscriptions had fallen to 63,000, and the magazine ceased publication. Since then, Consumers Union has published a CAC newsletter on Canadian activities that it delivers to its 200,000 Canadian subscribers.

Recent Activism

Over the last five decades, the main source of CAC activity has been grassroots activism by volunteers. These volunteers, who work in ten provinces and two territories, are motivated by public service and sometimes by outrage. In 1994, for example, in response to a large cable television company using a negative option technique to increase rates, consumer protests forced the company to cease this abusive practice.

Each province has its own consumer legislation, allowing experimentation. While no one province has led on every issue, Saskatchewan has often been early with improvements.

Funding for consumer organizations has always been a problem. Until about 1990, governments at several levels provided grants to the CAC, which subsidized travel expenses and some public interest work. But these grants rarely funded research, the preparation of position papers, or the staffing of local advice services. Some governments still make funds available for small projects. In Quebec, the government has been willing to fund Quebec-based consumer groups (and a high-quality publication, *Protégez-vous*) separate from those affiliated with the CAC.

At many universities, students fund Ralph Nader–inspired Public Interest Research Groups. More precarious is funding for groups like the Public Interest Advocacy Center, which depends on government grants.

From 1973 to 1990, the CAC operated a publicly funded Regulated Industries Program (RIP). Securely funded, RIP had a small secretariat and a couple of dedicated lawyers working out of an office in Ottawa. The group was highly visible and often successful in its interventions, especially on telephone rates and airline regulation. Moreover, the office was able to cooperate with provincial CAC organizations on interventions before regulatory boards that addressed issues involving electricity, cable, and natural gas heating.

The consumer movement in Canada helped spawn a number of important public interest groups. In some provinces, CAC leaders participated in the formation of environmental groups. Ruth Lotzkar, a former national president of CAC, helped found the Environmentally Sensitive Packaging organization. Several CAC leaders (and some of its experts) helped establish an umbrella coalition working on health issues.

The Canadian consumer movement has made progress in the areas of food safety, monopoly, and trade. Because Canada is a confederation with important powers resting at the provincial level, progress with consumer rights and with economic power has required activism in provincial capitals. Lacking financial support from a successful product testing magazine, this activism has depended largely on volunteers.

— Robert R. Kerton

Readings

Goldstein, Jonah (1979). "Public Interest Groups and Public Policy: The Case of the Consumers Association of Canada." *Canadian Journal of Sociology*. 12 (March): 137–155.

Trebilcock, Michael J. (1991). "Taking Stock: Consumerism in the 1990s." *Canadian Business Law Journal*. 19: 412–436.

Center for Auto Safety

The Center for Auto Safety (CAS) was founded by Ralph Nader and Consumers Union to give consumers a voice in Washington for auto safety, efficiency, and reliability. Nader, who was a board member of Consumers Union at the time, provided the inspiration, and Consumers Union provided the initial funding. In

1973, the CAS became independent of its founders.

The CAS is controlled by a five-member board of directors that is self-perpetuating. It has approximately 15,000 members, who are surveyed annually to determine their interests. Each year, the CAS has a meeting of members to hear their views and concerns. The center has a staff of ten to twelve full-time employees and three interns.

Clarence M. Ditlow is the center's executive director. He holds a degree in chemical engineering from Lehigh University and law degrees from Georgetown and Harvard. Before becoming the executive director of the CAS, Ditlow was a patent examiner in the U.S. Patent Office from 1965 to 1970. From 1971 to 1975, he was an attorney and director with Ralph Nader's Public Interest Research Group.

The annual budget is about $700,000. Approximately half of the budget comes from contributions of individual members, which average about $25 each. An additional 25 percent comes from sales of publications such as the *Lemon Book, Car Book,* and *IMPACT* newsletter. About 15 percent comes from foundation grants with the remaining 10 percent coming from miscellaneous sources such as interest and royalties.

The CAS advances consumer rights in many ways. It petitions and participates in rule-making before the different federal agencies that regulate the auto industry, including the National Highway Traffic Safety Administration, the Federal Trade Commission, and the Environmental Protection Agency. It testifies before congressional committees on issues affecting the consumer and transportation. It publishes a wide range of self-help information for consumers, ranging from packets on defects in individual cars to books on lemon rights and auto warranties. And it seeks redress for groups of consumers with the same problem through actions such as public pressure on auto manufacturers and organizing class action lawsuits.

The first director of the CAS was Lowell Dodge, who earlier had participated in the civil rights movement and graduated from Yale Law School. Under his direction, the center's first action (in 1970) was to publish a book on auto problems, titled *What To Do with Your Bad Car.* Based on 5,000 consumer complaints received by Ralph Nader, the book developed strategies for lemon purchasers and called for creation of new legal rights for lemon owners. Because the book had a big lemon on the cover, consumers called it the *Lemon Book,* and the name stuck for subsequent editions in 1980 and 1990. The *Lemon Book* provided the foundation for lemon laws in all fifty states.

In 1970, the CAS also began what became a twenty-year campaign to install airbags in all motor vehicles. The center fought for airbags in the federal agencies, courts, Congress, and halls of public opinion because airbag installation represented the most important strategy for advancing auto safety. The turning point in the fight for airbags came in 1983 when the U.S. Supreme Court overturned the Reagan administration's effort to revoke the rule.

In its early days, the CAS poured out a steady stream of books, reports, and studies that prompted administrative and legislative reform. It set up project task forces to focus on safety and consumer issues related to automobiles and transportation. Building on Nader's success in using the Chevrolet Corvair to focus attention on auto safety in *Unsafe at Any Speed,* the CAS organized an investigation of the Volkswagen Beetle, which served as the basis for *Small on Safety—The Designed In Hazards of the VW Beetle.*

Some early projects focused on topics other than the automobile. For example, the Mobile Home Task Force was created to examine mobile homes (now called manufactured houses), because the same companies that built motor homes also built mobile homes. The Mobile Home Task Force wrote *Mobile Homes—The Low Cost Housing Hoax,* which led to passage of the National Mobile Home Construction and Safety Standards Act in 1974 and the creation of a division within the Department of Housing and Urban Development to oversee mobile home safety and construction. Other projects focused on the inadequacies of voluntary industry standards, snowmobiles, and bicycles.

With support from the State Farm Foundation, the CAS set up a Highway Safety Project in 1973 to focus on design and construction hazards in highways. The Highway Safety Project wrote *The Yellow Brick Road,* which became a landmark in exposing roadside hazards and formed the basis for project action over the next ten years. Because the Federal Highway Administration refused to address safety hazards in a timely fashion, the CAS was forced to sue the agency numerous times to upgrade highway safety and comply with federal law. The center combined interventions such as lawsuits with such consumer actions as posting Highway Hazard Signs (with skull and crossbones) on roadside hazards on Rock Creek Parkway, which runs through the heart of Washington, D.C., and is traveled by many legislators and regulators. Another successful CAS tactic was to link up with labor unions, whose workers were exposed to hazards in highway construction projects.

During the 1970s, the CAS set up several branch offices and independent centers. Among the most successful were the Auto Safety Centers, headed up in Cleveland by Tom Vacar, who later became a consumer reporter, and in Hartford by Toby Moffett, who was later elected to Congress. Although these and other offices were successful, they never established an independent financial basis and withered once their initial leaders moved on.

In the 1970s and 1980s, the CAS helped start a number of independent consumer groups concerned with auto issues. One of these groups was Motor Voters (now known as Consumers for Auto Safety and Reliability, or CARS), which was launched in San Diego by Rosemary Pooler (now Shahan) to push for a state lemon law. Another was the Automobile Protection Association (APA) in Canada, which was started by Phil Edmonston, who earlier had worked at the CAS for a year to gain experience in running an auto consumer organization. Throughout its early years, the APA sent interns to the center for several months each.

The CAS was also instrumental in helping single-issue consumer action groups or campaigns, which usually addressed a particular auto problem for several years. Some of the most successful campaigns were organized around 1978–1985 General Motors (GM) cars with 350-cubic-inch diesel engines that suffered from numerous defects because GM had converted a gasoline engine to diesel. These groups included Lemon on Wheels in New York, Consumers Against General Motors in the West, and Disgruntled Owners of GM Diesels (DOGMAD) in Virginia. Other campaigns have been built around Pontiac Fieros that catch fire, GM pickups with exploding side-saddle gas tanks, Ford Cortinas lacking replacement parts, and Winnebagos with Renault diesel engines.

In 1978, the CAS became a membership organization, which helped provide long-term financial stability. In the same year, it exposed the hazards of the Ford Pinto with exploding gas tanks, forcing a recall. In 1979, the CAS successfully called for the recall of 15 million Firestone 500 steel-belted radials for tread separation, the largest tire recall ever.

In 1980, the CAS published the second edition of its *Lemon Book* with Ralph Nader and called for passage of state lemon laws. Beginning in 1981, first with Connecticut and then with California, every state passed a lemon law. In 1992, Arkansas was the fiftieth state to do so.

Litigation against federal agencies has always been a tool of the CAS, but it was used most frequently in the 1980s, when the Reagan administration tried to roll back many of the auto safety measures adopted during the 1970s. The CAS participated in and won lawsuits overturning the revocation of tire quality grading standards in 1982 and of the airbag rule in 1983. Other lawsuits restored the Environmental Protection Agency's emission recall program in 1984, prohibited oversize trucks from operating on highways unless specific safety criteria were met in 1985, required the installation of gasoline vapor recovery canisters on cars in 1991, and required mandatory bridge inspections in 1992.

The CAS has played a major role in establishing federal fuel economy standards for motor vehicles from their adoption in 1978 to their implementation through the 1990s. Its testimony was crucial to passage of gas guzzler taxes in 1980 and to blocking the Reagan administration's effort to repeal the fuel economy law in the mid-1980s. In 1991, the CAS published *The Safer Road to Fuel Economy,* which demonstrated how technology could be used to improve both safety and fuel efficiency.

The CAS has played a unique role in finding neglected safety areas and focusing the spotlight of public attention on them until they are corrected. In early 1990, the CAS published *Children at Risk,* the results of a year-long study of the National Highway Traffic Safety Administration's child seat standards and recall program that found that less than 7 percent of defective child seats were ever fixed under a recall. After Senate and House committee hearings on the CAS study, the agency adopted a child seat registration system so that owners of defective child seats could be notified of recalls. As a result of the CAS study, the agency also recalled 3.7 million Evenflo child seats for defective latches, the largest child seat recall ever.

The center's most recent campaign has been to expose secret warranties of auto companies, in which they adopt an internal policy to repair defects for free beyond the terms of the written warranty but fail to tell owners. In 1994, the CAS wrote a book on the practice called *Little Secrets of the Auto Industry,* which revealed that, at any one time, there were over 500 secret warranties covering more than $10 billion in defects. By 1995, four states—California, Connecticut, Virginia, and Wisconsin—had passed secret warranty disclosure laws to protect consumers from this abuse.

— Clarence M. Ditlow

See also

Highway Safety; Lemon Laws; National Highway Traffic Safety Administration.

Readings

Jensen, Christopher (1988). "This Man Gives the Auto Industry Nightmares." *Plain Dealer.* (July 24): D, 1ff.

Logan, Gary J. (1989). "Steering Toward Safety." *Everyday Law.* (February): 43-48.

Schorr, Burt, and Christopher Conte (1984). "Coming of Age: Public-Interest Groups Achieve Higher Status and Some Permanence." *Wall Street Journal.* (August 27): 1ff.

Center for Community Change

The Center for Community Change (CCC) has worked for more than twenty-seven years to strengthen the grassroots movement of independent, low-income, community-based organizations that sought to meet community needs. It has worked with hundreds of these organizations in both urban and rural areas in every state, helping the movement grow from a handful of groups to thousands of organizations, many of which have had significant impacts on their low-income communities.

The center grew out of the ideas and work of a broad range of people and institutions involved in battling poverty in the 1960s, including unions, the U.S. Office of Economic Opportunity (OEO), and the Ford Foundation. Each of these institutions had come to accept the idea that is at the heart of the center's work: that poor people themselves, through organizations they control, need to be involved in efforts to eliminate poverty. This idea had grown, in part, out of disenchantment with the federal government's "urban renewal" program, which many believed was aggravating the problems of inner cities by displacing people and destroying communities. As a result, one emphasis of the Johnson administration's War on Poverty was "community action," which involved supporting local organizations of low-income people who could advocate for their community's needs. While this emphasis did not last long, many people saw a continued need for this type of organization. Some of them helped create and fund the center as a way to support these organizations.

A few progressive unions, especially the United Auto Workers and its leader Walter Reuther, also saw a need for organizations of low-income people—what they began to call "community unions." The union helped establish a handful of such organizations, and the center was seen as a way to assist these groups. In 1969, the Ford Foundation, which had begun supporting community-based organizations in a few cities several years earlier, provided the center's initial grant.

For more than twenty years, the center's staff has been led by Pablo Eisenberg. Educated at Princeton and Oxford universities, Eisenberg earlier served as OEO's deputy director of research and demonstration programs. At the center, he has helped its budget grow from a little over $700,000 in 1975 to more than $4 million in 1995, with an additional $2 million going to several independent special projects that it sponsors. He has helped raise money for many of these projects as well as for many other national and local organizations, including a dozen on whose boards he serves. The center has nearly fifty staff people, most of whom are based at its offices in Washington, D.C., and San Francisco. A few staff work out of other cities, including Toledo, Boise, and Los Angeles.

The center's assistance to community-based organizations falls into two broad categories. First, it helps groups develop themselves as organizations and raise the money they need to run their programs. Center staff might help a group understand how to develop an effective board and run constructive meetings, develop a realistic three-year plan, write a good proposal or develop an effective accounting system, or involve more community residents in the organization.

Second, the center helps groups change their communities, either by changing the policies of a local institution or public agency, or by developing specific projects, such as building an affordable apartment building. CCC staff might help a group convince the city to provide more police services in its neighborhood or a bank to invest more money in its community. Or center staff might help the group put together the financing for a renovation project.

The center supports community-based organizations because it believes they are crucial to revitalizing poor neighborhoods. By involving residents, these groups tap their community's capacity for self-help and give individuals a sense that they have the power to change their lives and neighborhoods. They also develop community leaders. And because they involve residents who know their communities—and their problems—these organizations increase the effectiveness of efforts to overcome these problems.

Over the years, the center has also worked to make public policies more responsive to the needs of low-income communities. For nearly 20 years, it has helped pass, strengthen, implement, and preserve the Community Reinvestment Act, which has resulted in tens of billions of dollars of bank loans being made in low-income communities. It has worked to ensure that Community Development Block Grant (CDBG) money is used more effectively in these communities. It has successfully pushed for rules that require state and local governments to involve low-income people in the making of decisions about how to use CDBG money and other federal resources. It has helped create dozens of state and local Housing Trust Funds, which have invested hundreds of millions of dollars in affordable housing projects.

In late 1994, CCC hired staff to focus exclusively on public policy. They have worked on a series of issues, including opposition to the Balanced Budget Amendment, to cutbacks in housing programs, to welfare reform, and to efforts to restrict advocacy by nonprofits that receive federal grants or on-the-job gifts from federal employees. The center publishes a weekly update on national issues impacting low-income communities that helps community-based organizations across the country keep aware of, and try to influence, policy developments. Even more recently, the center has begun efforts to study what types of economic development initiatives work in low-income communities and to examine the economic impact of publicly-funded jobs.

The center has also been a base for more than 160 special projects that focus on issues related to low-income people and communities. Friends of VISTA, for example, helped save the VISTA volunteer program during the 1980s. The now independent National Committee for Responsive Philanthropy was begun at the center; it has opened up workplace fundraising drives to hundreds of low-income groups and other less traditional charities, as well as helped create dozens of "alternative funds." CCC's Eisenberg is co-chair of the committee and is widely regarded as one of the foremost critics of private philanthropy.

The center publishes a variety of newsletters, public policy updates, and "action guides." Its most recent publication focuses on how community-based organizations and others can effectively fight public policy battles.

— Tim Saasta

See also

Community Organizations; Community Reinvestment.

Reading

Williams, Roger (1987). "Centering on the Underdog." *Foundation News*. (September/October): 18–24.

Center for Public Representation

The Center for Public Representation (CPR) was founded in Madison, Wisconsin, in January 1974 by a group of citizens, law professors, and lawyers. The concept for the organization originated with George Bunn, the dean of the Wisconsin Law School. Observing the growth of public interest law firms representing citizen groups in Washington, D.C., in the 1960s, Bunn recognized the need for such groups in Madison, the state capital of Wisconsin. He also noted that representing clients before state and local agencies would provide an opportunity for law students to learn advocacy skills while providing legal services to groups and individuals unable to afford them. He obtained a small grant to employ Louise G. Trubek, an experienced lawyer, to create a public interest law firm.

CPR is a nonprofit, tax-deductible organization. Its articles of incorporation describe CPR's purpose to "provide representation in the public interest and to train law students and citizens to advocate on behalf of the unrepresented." The organization is directed by a board of directors selected from citizen leaders, members of the State Bar, and law professors from the University of Wisconsin Law School and Marquette University School of Law. The executive director, the chief executive position, is appointed by the board of directors. Since one of the purposes of the center is the training of law students, a position of clinical director was created in the bylaws. The staff includes attorneys, publication and education specialists, paralegals, and financial and administrative positions. Each semester, about twenty law students work at the center for academic credit.

Trubek was the first executive director and remained in that position until 1992. She currently serves as clinical director at the center as well as clinical professor of law at the University of Wisconsin Law School. She is a graduate of the Yale University School of Law. Prior to her move to Wisconsin, she practiced law in several public interest law firms in Connecticut. Trubek was succeeded as executive director by Michael Pritchard. After graduating from Yale University School of Law in 1975, he worked as a staff attorney at CPR. In 1995, the center's president of the board of directors was Professor Jay Grenig of the Marquette School of Law, a well-known arbitrator and an advocate for disabled children.

CPR's funding has come from citizen contributions, grants from charitable foundations, law school support, government contracts, revenue from sales of publications, conference fees, and attorney fees. In recent years, federal government grants to assist clinical programs for law students have been a major source of revenue. The size of the budget has varied dramatically, ranging from under $100,000 in the first year to $1,500,000 in the late 1980s to $500,000 in 1995.

CPR is a multi-issue public interest law firm; its charitable purpose is legal representation and education. Over the years, the board of directors and staff have selected the client groups and issues based on an assessment of need. The client groups have included the elderly, persons with disabilities, and ex-offenders. In 1995, CPR provided advocacy and education on behalf of health care clients, consumers, low-income persons, and children and families. The projects include improvement of the guardian ad litem system in family and juvenile courts, telecommunication access for all citizens, health care coverage for the uninsured, welfare reform to assist low-income persons, and community economic development in Madison.

Each project includes attorneys and law students who provide administrative agency representation at the state, local, and national levels, legislative advocacy, and representation in federal and state courts. Several projects include collaboration with community organizations in Madison and in Milwaukee. Private attorneys contribute pro bono services to assist in the guardian ad litem project by serving as mentors for students who observe and assist in their cases.

CPR has disseminated information through publications. The staff has written, produced, and distributed a series of pamphlets, brochures, manuals, and guides that explain the law, legal institutions, and public and private programs. Several of the guides include forms for do-it-yourself guides, for example, *The Basic Wills Handbook* and *Planning for Future Health Care Decisions*. Manuals explaining complex areas of the law, such as Medicare and guardianship, have also been written and distributed to attorneys and professionals. CPR has produced a quarterly newsletter which is distributed on a subscription basis.

CPR has also performed an education function through a series of conferences, training programs, and workshops that serve lawyers, professionals, and citizens. Each year CPR hosts a Consumer Forum where citizens learn about current consumer concerns: topics have included understanding telecommunications and filing an insurance complaint. CPR staff have provided continuing legal education programs for attorneys on subjects such as health care regulation and administrative procedure.

CPR has maintained a research program that has produced studies of legal institutions and administrative regulation. For example, an analysis of the Wisconsin used car administrative rule researched and written by CPR staff was submitted to the Federal Trade Commission as part of their proposed rulemaking for a national regulation. A study of the Wisconsin guardianship proceedings was undertaken by CPR staff and a University of Wisconsin professor with funding from the State Justice Institute.

CPR has functioned, in part, as an incubator for legal services for the unrepresented. Its history is notable for the many programs that it has developed, funded, and "spun off" into the community. The Elderly Benefit Specialist legal services program for Wisconsin seniors was initiated by CPR in the late 1970s to provide cost-effective legal services for the elderly. The project utilizes laypeople who are trained and supervised by full-time attorneys. The program is now a project of the Coalition of Wisconsin Aging Groups, a membership nonprofit organization that serves the elderly throughout the state. Another example is the Medigap Hotline, a toll-free service to assist the elderly in shopping for insurance policies. This project was funded initially through grants obtained by CPR; now it is part of the State Board of Aging and Long Term Care.

As issues and clients have changed, so has CPR. In 1995, it focused on telecommunications and low-income concerns such as community development, access to credit, and the preservation of a safety net for those unable to work. Since children are increasingly a group in need of legal services, CPR is providing assistance to the lawyers serving the interests of children in court.

Another CPR function is the provision of training for law students in public interest law and consumer law. In addition to teaching students at the law firm, CPR staff teach courses at the law school on subjects such as poverty law, consumer law, and guardian ad litem. In recent years, at the Marquette University School of Law, CPR staff have taught classes, assisted in the development of a clinic program, and with professors and students, have provided advocacy on behalf of disabled children.

CPR has been one of the most effective public interest law firms in the nation. Its staff have trained hundreds of law students to represent consumers in courts, the legislature, and administrative agencies. CPR's advocacy has resulted in improved consumer services at administrative agencies such as the Insurance Commissioners Office. CPR's litigation has led to court decisions providing compensation to consumers denied insurance and public benefits. CPR's legislative lobbying has contributed to increased health care coverage for the uninsured, and to the maintenance of records and meetings open to Wisconsin citizens. CPR's publications have provided thousands of consumers with information that helps them shop in the market and monitor businesses. Finally, CPR has created programs and mechanisms to meet consumer legal needs that have been institutionalized in Wisconsin public life.

— Louise G. Trubek

See also

Public Interest Law Practice.

Readings

Lautenschlager, Scott (1989). "Louise Trubek." *Wisconsin State Journal*. (July 23): G, 2.

Stockinger, Jacob (1989). "Legal Center Looks Upscale after Its Move." *Capital Times*. (October 4): 27.

Center for Science in the Public Interest

The Center for Science in the Public Interest (CSPI) was founded in Washington, D.C., in 1971 by three Ph.D. scientists who had met a year earlier, while all three were working at Ralph Nader's Center for the Study of Responsive Law. The scientists—chemist Albert J. Fritsch, microbiologist Michael F. Jacobson, and meteorologist James B. Sullivan—shared the vision of a public interest advocacy organization run by scientists. (A fourth founder and trustee, Kenneth Lasson, was an attorney who did not work at CSPI.) Part of that vision was to serve as a role model for other scientists. CSPI's founders believed that many scientists, if given the encouragement and opportunity, would devote their careers to public interest activism.

Unlike many organizations that are launched with the aid of a blue-ribbon board of directors and major foundation funding, CSPI had a homespun beginning. The founders lived off savings or small stipends (Fritsch was a Jesuit priest living in his Capitol Hill church) and worked in borrowed office space.

CSPI's early work was eclectic. In keeping with their respective disciplines, Fritsch's projects focused on toxic chemicals, strip mining, nuclear power, and oil. Jacobson's work focused on food additives and nutrition. Sullivan focused on highways and air pollution. The three co-directors wrote CSPI's newsletter and met frequently to discuss the emerging center's policies and activities.

Leadership

Initially, CSPI was run jointly by the three founding scientists. The departure of Fritsch and Sullivan in 1977 had two major impacts: first, CSPI focused almost exclusively on food issues, and second, Jacobson became the organization's executive director. Since then, CSPI's staff has gradually increased from fifteen to fifty, and its annual budget from less than $1 million to more than $11 million.

Five veteran CSPI staffers have played especially vital roles in the organization's growth and evolution. Executive director Michael Jacobson, who earned a Ph.D. in microbiology from the Massachusetts Institute of Technology, has worked at CSPI for almost his entire career. He has authored or coauthored more than a dozen major books and reports, including, most recently, *What Are We Feeding Our Kids?* and *Marketing Madness*. Jacobson appears frequently in the news media and has testified at numerous congressional hearings. He has also helped found the Center for the Study of Commercialism, as well as the Latino Council on Alcohol and Tobacco.

Dennis Bass, an attorney, has been CSPI's deputy director since 1981, before which he worked at Environmental Action and the National League of Cities. Bass directs CSPI's administrative staff and donor programs and has overseen a successful effort to increase the circulation of the *Nutrition Action Healthletter.*

Bonnie Liebman, CSPI's director of nutrition, has been with the organization since 1977. She holds an M.S. in nutritional sciences from Cornell University. Liebman has been the key link in formulating CSPI's policies on diet and health. She provides the scientific input on many of the organization's administrative petitions and legislative proposals, as well as writing many of the major articles for *Nutrition Action Healthletter.*

Bruce Silverglade has been CSPI's director of legal affairs since 1981, after having worked as an attorney at the Federal Trade Commission (FTC). He could well be called the "father of nutrition labeling" because of his leadership role in the passage of the landmark Nutrition Labeling and Education Act. Silverglade was also the driving force behind CSPI's efforts to halt deceptive food advertising, a concern dating from his days at the FTC.

George Hacker, an attorney, joined CSPI in 1982 to head its newly created Alcohol Policies Project. He has organized and directed broad national coalitions in support of higher alcohol taxes, restrictions on alcohol advertising, and warning notices on product labels. Hacker has authored and coauthored numerous reports and studies on alcohol issues. Between 1989 and 1992, he directed alcohol programs at the Advocacy Institute. He returned to CSPI in January 1993.

CSPI is ultimately overseen by its board of trustees, whose size has varied between six and ten people. Trustees have included scientists, attorneys, celebrities, and activists.

Funding and Publications

Financially, CSPI has traditionally depended upon several sources of income: foundation grants, the sale of publications and other products, and subscription fees and donations. In the early 1970s, those three sources provided roughly equal amounts of income. Work on nutrition and food safety was especially dependent upon book and poster sales, while the other projects enjoyed greater foundation support.

Beginning in the early 1980s, however, CSPI began earning an increasing portion of its funding from subscriptions and donations. Between 1980 and 1994, the circulation of *Nutrition Action Healthletter,* CSPI's flagship publication, increased from 30,000 to 800,000. Many of those subscribers provide donations in addition to their annual subscription fee.

By 1994, subscription revenue from *Nutrition Action Healthletter* provided roughly 75 percent of CSPI's annual budget of $11 million. Donations from subscribers provided 12 percent, sales of products and publications 9 percent, royalties 3 percent, and foundation grants 1 percent.

From its earliest days, CSPI has recognized the value of producing educational materials. For example, CSPI's Alcohol Policies Project has produced several publications that have generated much discussion. Those groundbreaking reports helped expand the national alcohol agenda from the treatment of alcoholism to include preventing alcohol abuse and alcoholism. *The Booze Merchants, Marketing Booze to Blacks, Marketing Disease to Hispanics,* and a report on federal alcohol taxes provided the public and journalists with analyses of alcohol advertising and taxes. Those reports helped generate reforms on these issues.

In addition to *Nutrition Action Healthletter*—the largest-circulation health newsletter in the United States—CSPI has produced a wide range of other publications concerning food. The book that first brought CSPI to public attention was *Nutrition Scoreboard,* which was published in 1973 and focused attention on the fat and sugar content in foods. A simple scoring system devised by Michael Jacobson was one of the first efforts to make nutrition more understandable to the public.

CSPI has also distributed millions of copies of colorful, fact-filled posters on nutrition and food additives. *The Fast-Food Guide*—in book and poster versions—helped focus public attention on nutritional drawbacks of the most popular foods offered by fast-food restaurants. Books for children (*Kitchen Fun for Kids*) and parents and teachers (*Creative Food Experiences for Children* and *Eat, Think, and Be Healthy*) reflected the center's concern that good nutrition begin at a young age.

Campaigns

CSPI's major projects typically feature a mix of research, education, and advocacy. The staff sees a symbiosis between those approaches: research provides the basis for education, education a backdrop for advocacy, and advocacy a means for educating the public through publications and media coverage.

Since 1980, CSPI's scientists, writers, and organizers have been bolstered by an in-house legal staff. CSPI's scientists and policy specialists actively encourage the agricultural, food processing, and restaurant industries to improve their products and market them honestly. When necessary, the organization's legal staff seeks solutions through enforcement of existing laws or adoption of new regulations or legislation.

One of CSPI's first major national undertakings was Food Day. The center sponsored this annual event from 1975 to 1977, spawning thousands of activities around the country concerning nutrition, hunger, and agribusiness. These activities included newspaper articles and television programs, rallies in city parks, a book, and even a healthy White House buffet dinner.

Food Day turned out to be one of the pivotal events that helped persuade the public and policymakers that nutrition had extremely important health effects. Until the mid-1970s, most nutrition experts had focused on obtaining adequate levels of vitamins and minerals. The "new" nutrition focused on the disease-promoting effect of a modern diet high in fat, cholesterol, and sodium, and low in dietary fiber. (By 1993, the federal government would estimate that diet and a sedentary lifestyle contributed to 310,000 to 580,000 deaths a year, about as many as were caused by tobacco.)

Beginning in the early 1980s, in response to the increased public demand for healthier food, many food manufacturers began promoting the supposed nutritional virtues of their products much more aggressively. CSPI began to identify numerous product labels and advertising campaigns that were clearly deceptive, if not fraudulent. After first seeking a halt to individual deceptions on a case-by-case basis, the organization began to advocate legislation to protect all consumers. That effort culminated almost a decade later with passage of the Nutrition Labeling and Education Act of 1990, which mandated clear and useful nutrition information on practically all food labels.

Some companies responded by moving deceptive statements from labels to ads. Yet, again as a result of CSPI's advocacy efforts, in 1994 the FTC responded by adopting a policy that called on companies to have their advertisements comply as fully as possible with the nutrition-labeling law.

CSPI has long been concerned about the healthfulness of restaurant foods. Prodded by the crackdown on deceptive advertising and its attendant publicity, by the late 1980s most large fast-food chains for the first time disclosed the ingredients of which their foods were made. The chains also provided more nutrition information and added lower-fat and lower-sodium products.

CSPI's work in this area involved several years of research, advocacy efforts, litigation, and negotiations with industry, as well as the publication of *The Fast Food Guide*. This publication provided the public, for the first time, with detailed nutritional information on the entire menu lines of the major national and regional fast-food chains.

Beginning in 1993, CSPI's nutritionists began a series of studies on the nutritional values of foods eaten in the most popular types of sit-down restaurants. The resulting studies of Chinese, Italian, Mexican, seafood, and other types of restaurants generated worldwide publicity. The enormous media coverage, in turn, prompted declines in sales at many restaurants, resulting in decisions by a number of major chains and independent restauranteurs both to lower the fat or sodium content of their dishes and to add a "health" section to their menus.

CSPI's related study of movie-theater popcorn found extraordinarily high levels of fat in typical bags of popcorn. Again, extensive publicity caused sales declines, which, in turn, prompted thousands of theaters to change the way they popped corn, switching from coconut oil and hydrogenated shortening, which promote heart disease, to air popping or canola or soybean oil, which do not promote this disease.

Even before it focused on nutrition, CSPI served as a watchdog group on food additives. In addition to publishing a book and poster on additives, CSPI sought to reduce consumer exposure to potentially risky additives. As a result of CSPI's work, the Food and Drug Administration (FDA) advised pregnant women to minimize or avoid the consumption of caffeine. The FDA also banned most uses of sulfite—a widely used preservative that caused numerous serious reactions and deaths of sensitive (usually asthmatic) individuals—in fresh vegetables and required better labeling of other foods. The U.S. Department of Agriculture (USDA) set tighter limits on the use of sodium nitrite, a preservative used in bacon, hot dogs, and most other processed meats. Nitrite inhibits bacterial growth and provides a "cured meat" color and flavor, but leads to the formation of cancer-causing nitrosamines.

Recognizing that pesticide use on farms endangers farmers, consumers, and the environment, CSPI has long urged reduced use of potentially dangerous agricultural chemicals. In the late 1980s, CSPI's Americans for Safe Food project concentrated its efforts on winning passage of a federal law that defined, for the first time, the meaning of "organic food." The USDA was expected to issue a final regulation in 1997.

In 1982, CSPI created a new program to focus on alcoholic beverages because those products kill an estimated 100,000 Americans a year and cause a wide range of health and social problems, ranging from drunk driving to suicide to ruined careers. Also, few other organizations were examining how federal policies on the labeling, advertising, and taxation of alcoholic beverages could be modified to reduce alcohol problems.

Despite massive resistance from the alcoholic-beverage industry and its allies in the broadcasting, publishing, tavern, and liquor-store industries, CSPI's goals have been partially achieved. Twice—in 1984 and 1990—federal taxes on distilled spirits, beer, or wine were increased, thereby raising the cost of the product and reducing youth drinking. Congress passed a law requiring a warning notice on all alcoholic beverages; the warning focused on drinking and driving and drinking during pregnancy.

Since the publishing of *The Booze Merchants* in 1983, CSPI has been a vocal critic of alcohol advertising targeted at youth, women, or minorities; ads linking sexual or business success with drinking; and ads showing drinking by people engaged in risky activities. CSPI's publications, petitions, and press statements have led to several congressional hearings and greatly increased concern about alcohol advertising. In 1993–1994, CSPI led a coalition seeking to win passage of legislation, introduced by Senator Strom Thurmond (D-SC) and Joseph Kennedy (D-MA), that would require health information in alcohol advertising, but the bill was stalled by brewers and broadcasters.

— Michael F. Jacobson

See also

Alcohol Problems and the Consumer Movement; Food Safety.

Readings

Baum, Geraldine (1995). "Do They Really Enjoy Being Dinner Party Don't-Invite-Ems?" *Los Angeles Times Magazine.* (August 6): 14.

Jacqueney, Theodore (1974). "Public Interest Groups Challenge Government, Industry." *National Journal Reports.* 6 (February 23): 267–277.

Marter, Marilyn (1988). "A Hungry Watchdog." *Philadelphia Inquirer.* (May 11): F, 1ff.

Center for the Study of Services

The Center for the Study of Services was founded in April 1974 by Robert Krughoff (president) and Gillian Rudd (vice president). Its purpose is to provide consumers information and education to help them choose and effectively use service firms and stores.

Krughoff has always been the leader and driving force of the organization. With a law degree from the University of Chicago, he held several positions, including director of research and evaluation planning for the U.S. Department of Health, Education, and Welfare, before founding the center. Krughoff reports to a board of directors made up mainly of leaders from public interest organizations. The board elects its own members.

The organization's annual budget is approximately $2 million. Revenues come primarily from sales of publications and information services. Important support is also received from individual consumer members/subscribers in the form of voluntary donations.

The functions of the center include publication of locally based magazines that offer service ratings of local service firms and stores, publication of books on various consumer information subjects, provision of consumer information services on automobile purchasing and leasing, and other consumer information and education activities.

In 1976, the organization published the first issue of *Washington Consumers' CHECKBOOK* magazine. The magazine rates auto repair shops, plumbers, hospitals, banks, and other types of service firms and stores in the Washington, D.C., metropolitan area. Ratings are based on surveys of consumers, counts of complaints on file at consumer agencies, surveys of "experts" (for example, auto body shop owners' ratings of auto insurance companies), analysis of publicly available databases (for example, hospital discharge records), "shopping" by researchers, and various other methods. The magazine has been published semiannually.

In 1979, the center published the first edition of *CHECKBOOK's Guide to Health Insurance Plans for Federal Employees.* This guide compares health plans in terms of premiums, benefits, and actuarially estimated out-of-pocket costs. Recent editions also have compared the quality of plans on the basis of member satisfaction surveys, staffing, and disenrollment rates. The guide has been published annually.

In 1982, the center published the first issue of *Bay Area Consumers' CHECKBOOK* magazine. This magazine parallels its Washington, D.C., sister publication, with the same or similar artwork and text but its own evaluations of San Francisco–area firms. This magazine has also been published semiannually.

In 1984, the year AT&T was broken up, the center published the *Complete Guide to Lower Phone Costs.* This book evaluated consumer options for long-distance services, local phone service, and telephone equipment. The same year, the organization launched a long-distance cost comparison service. This nationwide service compared the costs of various available long-distance service providers for consumers and small businesses, based on each customer's recent months' phone bills. Comparisons were done using a computer program developed by the center that incorporated the pricing formulas of each of more than fifty long-distance phone companies. Several years later, this service was discontinued when the differences in long-distance carriers' prices were judged by the center to be too small to justify the required fee for the analysis.

In 1985, the center published the first issue of *BARGAINS* in Washington, D.C. This periodical lists low-priced local stores for relatively expensive products such as appliances and home entertainment equipment. To compile it, a list of more than 3,000 products is sent to any local retailer interested in participating. Retailers can quote prices on as few or as many items as they wish but must sign an agreement to honor those prices until a specified date. The center's staff then sorts the prices and publishes in *BARGAINS* the lowest prices and the names of the stores offering them. The magazine is currently published semiannually, as is a San Francisco Bay Area edition.

In 1988, the organization published *Consumers' Guide to Hospitals.* This book, based on the center's adaptation of data released by the U.S. government's Health Care Financing Administration, reported on mortality rates at each of the nation's acute care hospitals. It also included information on hospitals' teaching programs, percentages of board-certified physicians, and other matters. Subsequent editions were published in 1992 and 1994.

Also in 1988, the center published *CHECKBOOK's Guide to Washington Area Restaurants.* This guide reported ratings of restaurants based on surveys of consumers. It also included summaries of comments by professional magazine and newspaper reviewers, price information, brief descriptive text, and other details. Subsequent editions were published in 1992 and 1995. San Francisco Bay Area editions were published in 1993 and 1995.

In 1991, the organization published the first issue of *CarDeals* newsletter. This nationwide newsletter reports on factory-to-customer rebates, factory-to-dealer incentive payments, and special financing plans offered by automobile manufacturers. It is currently published biweekly. At the same time, the center launched a syndicated newspaper feature, reporting the same information, that has been carried by several major metropolitan newspapers. It also is published biweekly.

Also in 1991, the center began offering a service called CarBargains. This nationwide service helps consumers get the best available new car purchase price. A consumer tells the CarBargains staff the make, model, and style of car that the consumer wishes to purchase. The staff then persuades at least five dealers in a consumer's local area to bid competitively to sell this make, model, and style. The consumer is then given a report that shows each dealer's bid and the name of the sales manager. CarBargains continues to serve new car purchase and lease customers through the present.

In 1994, the center conducted a survey of 150,000 members of 250 health plans. This nationwide survey of health maintenance organization members was the largest one conducted to provide information for public release. A year later, the center published *Consumers' Guide to Health Plans.* This guide contains plan-by-plan ratings based on the center's 1994 member survey and includes information on accreditation status, disenrollment rates, and other matters.

In 1995, the center launched a site for the Washington, D.C., area on America Online. This site includes articles and ratings from *CHECKBOOK* magazine, listings from *CHECKBOOK's Restaurant Guide,* product features and price information from *BARGAINS* (but updated monthly and including more products than can be included in the printed version), message boards where consumers and a group of experts selected by the center can exchange questions and answers, and questionnaires for users to rate services they have used.

A major contribution of the center has been to demonstrate the feasibility of evaluating various types of local service firms and stores. In many fields, this kind of evaluation was initially met with strong industry resistance. The center's work has provided legitimacy for such evaluations, and in many fields—most notably health care—there is now broad acceptance of the concept of publicly disclosed firm-by-firm evaluations.

The center's reports have assisted many consumers in making purchase decisions. For example, current paid circulation for *Washington Consumers' CHECKBOOK* magazine and *BARGAINS* is approximately 50,000, and for *Bay Area Consumers' CHECKBOOK,* approximately 30,000. The center's books have sold in quantities ranging from several thousand to more than 40,000.

There are several indications that the center has had substantial impact. First, its magazine reports receive broad television, radio, and newspaper coverage. Second, all local public libraries carry subscriptions to its publications. Third, in a 1981 study, a West German consumer institute interviewed a sample of *CHECKBOOK* subscribers and learned that their purchase decisions had been based on or supported by *CHECKBOOK*'s recommendations in 64 percent of the cases in which they had purchased types of services covered in recently published *CHECKBOOK* issues. Fourth, federal government records show that, in the first year that the center published *CHECKBOOK's Guide to Health Insurance Plans for Federal Employees,* enrollment in the highest-rated plan increased by more than 120 percent in the Washington area.

— Robert M. Krughoff

See also

Information Dissemination.

Readings

Hartjens, Peter, and Elizabeth Hartjens (1983). *Das Washington Consumer Checkbook: Modell Einez Lokelen Dienstleistungsbewertungssystems.* Hohenheim, Germany: University of Hohenheim.

Krughoff, Robert (1977). "*Checkbook,* a *Consumer Reports* for the Services." *Social Policy.* 8 (3): 36–38.

Central and Eastern Europe, Consumer Movements in

Totalitarian regimes and command economies are infertile ground for traditional consumer organizations. Before the collapse of the Soviet empire in 1988–1989, only three had emerged in the countries of Central and Eastern Europe: the Federacja Konsumentow in Poland, a byproduct of the Solidarity movement there; the National Consumer Council in Hungary; and the Association of Consumers of Yugoslavia.

Few observers of the "velvet revolution" would have predicted that, within a year, local and national consumer groups would have sprung up in almost every country in the region, ready to do battle with the new inequities arising from the switch to a market economy. It would have seemed bizarre that consumer champions should emerge at a time when there was so little to consume, and no choices to make. But unbeknownst to most Westerners, journalists and academics had for many years been aware of, and writing about, consumer ideas and activities. There was no shortage of causes to be espoused by the pioneering consumer leaders, including high prices, shortages, unsafe food and drugs, polluted air and water, and the absence of consumer rights and means of redress.

Some consumer groups were grassroots movements structured like trade unions with a federal office and local branches. Others grew out of state institutions such as standards and metrology departments. Still others were started by groups of activists with academic backgrounds in economics, law, and sociology. What is remarkable, though, is that some of these early leaders were quite unaware of the existence of consumer organizations elsewhere in the world. They were not copying a well-established model: they literally started from scratch, creatively, often angrily, out of a sense of social justice and community need.

The rate and depth of change since those pioneering efforts has been so great that it is hard to believe that only five years have elapsed. Social, economic, and legal systems have been transformed; shareholding democracies have been created; shops are full of goods, even if only a minority of the populace can afford them. Yet many people, particularly the elderly and the industrial work forces, cannot accept these changes as progress. They have not begun to feel the benefits personally. And it is certainly true that it is in the production sector, both industrial and agricultural, that the largest reforms still need to be made.

All these countries are now entering the second, or even third, phase of political, social, and economic reform. "New era" Communist regimes have been elected in many countries by voters disenchanted with the policies of the reformers and may come to power in others. Programs of reform have been slowed down, even halted in some instances. More seriously, perhaps, the process of building new social and economic structures is threatened by political in-fighting and the return, or persistence, of "old" thinking and systems.

It is, however, unsafe to apply broad generalizations of this kind to the progress of consumer protection in the region. It is in fact difficult to perceive a single regional pattern in the development of consumer institutions in either the public or the private sector.

It will surprise nobody to learn that, in the independent sector, the key factor in the growth of organizations has been the quality of the leadership, especially their professional skills and management and their influence in the community. In the public sector, the determining factors have probably been the political will and priorities of the party in power. Where consumer interests are low on the agenda and power changes hands frequently—as, for instance, in Poland—consumer protection legislation tends to lag behind. Yet, even where governments are keen to promote consumer interests—for example, to demonstrate interest in joining the European Union (EU)—the framework of consumer legislation is not being put in place as quickly as one might expect, sometimes because of excessive veneration for competition.

For all that, the majority of countries have introduced general consumer protection laws during the 1990s. Some are looking further, for instance, at advertising controls and curbs on the burgeoning financial sector, or even product liability protections. Those countries with their sights set on joining the EU are planning over time to bring their consumer legislation into line with that of Western Europe.

The EU is financing support to both governments and independent organizations under its technical assistance programs (PHARE and TACIS). Up until now, the focus of the public sector work has been on the framework of legislation, regulation, and enforcement necessary to ensure that consumers are properly protected against abuses of the free market. In general, enforcement is lagging considerably behind the legislative program. In the independent sector, the emphasis is on training programs involving all the countries of the region, on organizational development, and on setting up consumer advice centers in particular countries (in which the German consumer organization AgV is playing a vital role).

Consumers International, through its Program for Economies in Transition (PROECT), is also providing extensive practical support for voluntary groups throughout the region. By means of regular visits, workshops, training programs, newsletters, assistance with fund-raising, and project proposals, it is raising awareness of the region's consumer concerns among consumer groups, nongovernmental organizations (NGOs), and funding bodies worldwide, as well as helping to build up the skills and strengths of the individual organizations. Individual consumer organizations in the West, through their charitable foundations—notably Consumers Union's Colston Warne Fund and the Dutch Consumentenbond's Anne Fransensfond—have also played a valuable role in providing funds for essential equipment and key projects.

Two major problems face all the independent organizations in the region: how to gain public support for their work, and how to secure continuing funding. In most of the countries of Central and Eastern Europe, consumer organizations have had considerable success in communicating their messages through the media; but with few exceptions, ordinary people have not responded by queuing up to join the organizations or by paying for membership or services. In Soviet times, belonging to an organization meant being a member of the Party, paying your union dues, or getting preferential treatment in work or politics. The idea of joining an organization either for societal benefit or in support of a cause still appeals only to a tiny minority of the population. The prevailing view in most countries is that consumer advice and information should come free, like water out of the tap. It is all part of the old "dependency culture" in which the individual was powerless, and it was always somebody else's job to put wrongs to right. As a result, consumer organizations are finding it hard to persuade people to pay more than token membership fees or pay realistic prices for magazines and other services. As in other parts of the world, a self-aware middle class with money to spend on consumer goods may have to develop before consumer organizations can begin to reduce their dependence on government or international funding and reinforce their pioneering volunteers with paid professionals.

While private individuals have been slow to offer their support, in most countries there have been equal problems with public funding. Some governments have never given financial aid to their independent movements; and some others have provided grants for a year or two, then reduced or stopped them altogether. Only a few governments have been more consistently, but selectively, supportive. As a result, organizations have struggled to sustain their programs and have been forced to seek project funding abroad to retain or build up their professional services. Some have understandably been tempted to raise money through product certification schemes or have launched magazines or newspapers that could survive only by accepting advertising. Nevertheless, despite all the difficulties, not one of the national organizations established in the region since 1989 has closed its doors—a tribute to the integrity, dedication, and persistence of their founders and of those who have subsequently built on their pioneering foundations.

Whether the value systems laid down by the consumer organizations of the West, and enshrined in the constitution of Consumers International, can and should be applied with traditional rigor to the independent movements in Central and Eastern Europe is an issue that is likely to be debated fiercely over the next decade. There is little understanding in these countries of the nonprofit motive or of charitable institutions. There is anecdotal evidence from both Russia (where the consumer magazine *SPROS* carries no advertising) and Hungary (where 25 percent of the pages in *TESZT* are taken up by advertisements for consumer goods and services) that reader faith in the magazines' advice and recommendations is unaffected by whether or not they take advertising. It has even been suggested in Russia that consumers would welcome advertisements as an additional source of information about products and services.

All the consumer organizations of Central and Eastern Europe face enormous difficulties—sheer survival, securing reliable funding, replacing the original enthusiasts with a new generation of activists, developing professional skills and services, and increasing their impact on politicians and the public. Up until now, they have resisted the temptations of "easy money," choosing to remain independent of for-profit commercial enterprises.

— Alastair Macgeorge

See also

Albanian Consumer Movement; Baltic Republics, Consumer Movement in the; Bulgarian Consumer Movement; Czech Consumer Movement; Hungarian Consumer Movement; Polish Consumer Movement; Romanian Consumer Movement; Slovakian Consumer Movement; Slovenian Consumer Movement; Yugoslavian Consumer Movement.

Reading

Kozminski, Andrzej K. (1992). "Consumers in Transition from the Centrally Planned Economy to the Market Economy." *Journal of Consumer Policy.* 14 (4): 351–370.

Checking Account Protections

State and federal laws provide consumers using checking accounts a wide range of protections; those laws, however, also impose responsibilities on consumers. Moreover, checking accounts pose definite risks to consumers.

Until the late 1980s and early 1990s, many bank deposits were not insured by agencies of the federal government. During the solvency crises of that period, many depositors found that private deposit insurance was inadequate. Today, most bank accounts are insured by the Federal Deposit Insurance Corporation or the National Credit Union Administration. The insurance covers up to $100,000 of funds a consumer has on deposit in each financial institution. For the purpose of calculating this coverage, amounts in all deposit accounts—including checking, savings, and certificates of deposit—are aggregated.

When banks pay interest on consumer checking accounts, the federal Truth in Savings Act (TISA), passed by Congress in 1991, requires institutions to compute an annual percentage yield (APY) based on the daily principal balance. Previously, banks had used several methods of computation, one of which treated as principal only the 83 percent of the consumer's deposit that the institution was not required to keep on reserve. In addition, the TISA requires banks to make certain consumer disclosures in advertising and in other communications with customers: interest rates in terms of a uniform APY; minimum balances and withdrawal policies when accounts are opened; and thirty-day advance notice of decreases in APY or increases in fees on periodic statements.

The federal Expedited Funds Availability Act was passed by Congress in 1987 to prevent banks from unduly delaying consumers' ability to use funds from checks deposited in their accounts. How soon the funds must be made available depends on the type of check or other funds deposited and where the check came from. For example, banks must make funds from cash and government, cashier's, certified, and teller's checks available by the next business day after the day of deposit. Funds from checks written on local banks must be made available by the third business day, but funds from checks written on nonlocal institutions need not be made available until the seventh business day. Banks may delay availability beyond these deadlines in special cases such as newly opened accounts, a repeatedly overdrawn account, or when the bank has reason to believe the deposited check will not be paid.

Many checking account problems are governed by a state law known as the Uniform Commercial Code. In the early 1990s, most states enacted a revised version of this law, and some passed variations providing consumers with greater protection than the version adopted by most states. Consumers face possible liability for lost or stolen checks that a thief uses to obtain funds from the consumer's account. If the consumer fails to exercise ordinary care and that failure substantially contributes to the thief's forging the consumer's signature or altering the check, the consumer may be liable for any loss. An example of such conduct would be a consumer leaving blank checks unsupervised on a table in a public place. The consumer also faces liability for not promptly reviewing the bank's periodic statement of checking account activity and notifying the bank of checks containing unauthorized signatures and alterations. There is no upper limit on the consumer's maximum liability as there is with credit cards that are lost or stolen.

Balancing the consumer's responsibilities in regard to the theft and alteration of checks, the bank is liable if it does not exercise "ordinary care" in its handling of the consumer's checks. The law, however, defines ordinary care narrowly. For example, many consumers believe that, because they sign signature cards when they open checking accounts, the bank must examine the signatures on their checks and is liable for forgeries even if the consumer was careless. The law, however, provides that the ordinary care standard authorizes the bank to use automated methods to process checks even though this practice results in the examination of few signatures.

Consumers can use checks to protect themselves. For example, they can stop payment of the check. Consumers must act promptly, however, to notify the bank before it has taken certain actions in regard to the check. But on these stop payments, the bank usually imposes a substantial fee and can require the consumer to describe the check precisely, such as the exact amount of the check. Consumers have no right to stop teller's or cashier's checks.

Consumers sometimes write postdated checks because they lack sufficient funds in their account or do not want a seller to be able to cash the check until the goods arrive or the work is completed. Under the law now in effect in most states, the bank can ignore the date on the check and honor it immediately unless the consumer notifies the bank that the check is postdated and should not be paid before the date on the check.

Consumers have had limited success in protecting themselves against various types of abusive practices. Yet, some courts have found certain bank fees to be excessive; some state laws regulate the amount of certain fees; and a few states require banks to offer low-fee checking accounts, known as "lifeline" accounts, to low-income consumers.

Advances in technology are having an impact on checking accounts. Technology has facilitated banks' ability to "truncate" checks: banks or others store the checks and electronically transmit the information on the check to the bank, so that consumers do not receive any canceled checks with their statements. Banks have persuaded many customers to agree to truncation by lowering or eliminating fees on accounts. Consumers with truncated accounts must be especially diligent in keeping a record of checks written because it may be difficult for them to spot irregularities on a statement that is not accompanied by canceled checks.

While consumers have the right to demand return of individual checks or copies, banks can charge a fee for this service and are not required to return the checks within any specific time. A few states require banks to provide a certain number of canceled checks or copies at no charge. Technology also has enabled banks to process checks more quickly, giving consumers less time to stop payment on their checks.

Some banks offer "check cards" which look like credit cards. Banks advertise them as working like checks. Yet, unlike checks, the consumer cannot postdate a payment made with a check card and may lose the ability to stop payment. Consumers who forget to record the transaction in their check registers may have difficulty balancing their checkbooks and identifying irregularities.

Technology has presented thieves with new ways in which to steal. After learning consumer account numbers, they can use computers to produce counterfeit checks. Telemarketers can trick consumers into revealing their account numbers and check routing numbers, then use computers to issue what is called a preauthorized draft. Through this device, the telemarketer can withdraw money from the consumer's account even though the consumer has refused to agree to purchase the product or service. Banks honor these drafts even though they do not contain the consumer's signature because they appear authentic and the bank assumes the telemarketer's possession of the account information means the consumer authorized the draft.

The Telemarketing and Consumer Fraud and Abuse Prevention Act, passed in 1995, is designed to discourage this tactic. The Uniform Commercial Code also protects consumers if they can show that they, in fact, did not authorize the withdrawal. If consumers merely change their mind about purchasing the product or become dissatisfied with its quality, however, they cannot recover the amounts withdrawn from their accounts. By contrast, when consumers wish to withhold payment on a purchase made with a credit card, the law provides them with greater protection.

— Mark E. Budnitz

See also

Electronic Funds Transfer Protections; Savings Protections; Telemarketing Regulation.

Readings

Clark, Barkley, and Barbara Clark (1995). *The Law of Bank Deposits, Collections and Credit Cards.* Boston: Warren, Gorham & Lamont.

U.S. Congress, House Committee on Banking, Finance and Urban Affairs, Subcommittee on Consumer Credit and Insurance (1994). *Bank Fees Associated with Maintaining Depository, Checking, and Credit Card Accounts.* Washington, DC: U.S. Government Printing Office.

Children as a Vulnerable Market

Before World War II, children were not thought of as consumers but as future customers. Children were expected to save their allowances rather than spend them. Two developments after the war changed these perceptions: the baby boom and the spread of television. Today, marketers view children as a viable target, but many people worry that children are also a vulnerable market.

Concerns about marketing to children are diverse. Some worry about the safety of toys. Others are troubled by children's underdeveloped shopping skills that might result in poor product selection. Many are uneasy about the effects of advertising on children. Indeed, considerable attention has been directed to this last concern.

The range of advertising fears is broad. Some allege that children's heavy exposure to sugar cereal and unnutritious snack-food commercials has detrimental effects on their diets. Toy commercials with their special effects may create unreasonable expectations of performance and satisfaction. Consumption requests may create tensions between parents and children. Moreover, ads may encourage children to develop stereotypic views of gender and race roles. In sum, various critics claim that children's advertising results not only in undesirable behavior, such as unhealthy food consumption, but also in the creation of undesirable social values, such as close-mindedness and materialism.

Underlying these various concerns is the charge that marketing, and in particular advertising, is inherently unfair because children lack both the life experience and the cognitive abilities to understand selling efforts directed at them. Moreover, their limited life experience and cognitive deficits cause children to learn social norms and beliefs without benefit of more developed critical thinking skills.

Several theories have been advanced to understand children's reactions to marketing efforts. During the 1970s, Piaget's theory of cognitive development was used to explain age differences in terms of stages. Cognitive structures characterize each stage and explain how children perceive and use information obtained from their environment. Children in the preoperational stage (two to seven years) focus only on the dominant features. Children aged seven to eleven or twelve are in the concrete-operational stage marked by an increasing ability to consider multiple dimensions. Older children in the stage of formal operations gain the ability to think abstractly about ideas and to consider all possible information relayed by a commercial or other marketing effort.

Although Piaget's stage theory appeared useful in describing age-related patterns, dissatisfaction grew with its inadequacy to explain children's cognitive activity. During the 1980s, information processing theory was advanced as an alternative theory to understand age differences in children's responses to advertising. Information processing theory, with its emphasis on cognitive abilities to store and retrieve information, provided insight into age differences in children's reactions to advertising.

Information processing theory pinpoints two types of deficiencies: mediational deficiencies and production deficiencies. Children with mediational deficits cannot use storage and retrieval strategies to improve remembering. Children with production deficiencies have the capacity to use storage and retrieval strategies, but only when they are prompted to use them. Three types of processors reflect these processing deficiencies: limited, cued, and strategic. Very young children (below six years of age), who are limited processors, exhibit mediational deficiencies. Cued processors (ages six to nine/ten years) exhibit production deficiencies. Strategic processors (ages ten/eleven years and older) usually possess and use the skills necessary to store and retrieve information.

Different kinds of public policy interventions have been proposed as appropriate for the three types of processors. Special regulatory efforts may not be required for the oldest children, strategic processors. Education may help cued processors learn how to store and retrieve information. On the other hand, information directed to the youngest children (limited processors) may need to be scrutinized or even restricted.

Governments throughout the world have responded in diverse ways to these concerns. France does not allow children to appear in ads without adults. Both Spain and Germany do not allow commercials for war-related toys. Sweden bans advertising during children's television programs, while Austria forbids direct appeals to children. The European Community has enacted a more general set of rules that includes a ban on showing children in danger, exploiting their ignorance, or encouraging them to persuade adults to buy. The United States has also adopted a number of regulations and considered other proposed interventions.

In the United States, the issue of children's vulnerability to commercial persuasion gained attention during the 1960s when the three major television networks scheduled most of their children's programs together on Saturday mornings. In addition, the content of commercials aimed at children became more aggressive, prompting public concern. In 1974, the Federal Communications Commission (FCC) established two policy principles to govern television advertising for the children's audience. First, the FCC required stations to place limits on the maximum amount of advertising presented during children's programming. The limits were nine-and-one-half minutes per hour on weekends and twelve minutes per hour on weekdays. Second, stations must clearly separate programs from commercial content during children's shows.

Throughout the 1970s, interest in the topic of children and television advertising continued to surge. In 1978, the Federal Trade Commission (FTC) began proceedings to consider the possible regulation of children's television, including the banning of some types of advertising directed to children. In response to petitions from Action for Children's Television (ACT) and Consumers Union, the FTC issued a report declaring that advertising any product to young children is unfair and deceptive, within the meaning of Section 5 of the FTC Act. Children were described as being too young to understand the selling purpose of, or otherwise comprehend or evaluate, commercial messages.

The FTC opened a rulemaking proceeding and conducted hearings. A battle between children's television advertising supporters and opponents ensued. Supporters argued that opponents understated the extent to which children can recognize and understand advertising. Moreover, advertising provides information that helps children make good product choices. Supporters noted that advertising contributes to beneficial socialization by generating revenues that help fund children's programming. Supporters also argued that many self-regulation mechanisms were already in place, that the proper responsibility for the restriction of viewing rested with parents, and that a ban on ads would violate First Amendment rights.

After much debate, Congress passed the FTC Improvement Act of 1980, which prohibited the FTC from adopting a rule based on unfairness issues. While this action forced the FTC to close its rulemaking proceeding, it did not prevent them from examining children's advertising for deception and unfairness.

Television networks have established highly restrictive guidelines for children's advertising. For example, only ten seconds of a toy ad may contain animation and other special effects. Network censors particularly scrutinize ads submitted for Saturday morning programs.

The Council of Better Business Bureaus polices advertising directed to children. The National Advertising Review Council (NARC) was established in 1971 by the council, the American Association of Advertising Agencies, the American Advertising Federation, and the Association of National Advertisers. The NARC is regarded by many as a comprehensive and effective mechanism for the regulation of American advertising. It has two operating arms: the National Advertising Division (NAD) and the National Advertising Review Board (NARB). In 1974, the NAD established the Children's Advertising Review Unit (CARU).

CARU's revised guidelines (1993) outline six basic principles for advertising directed to children: first, advertisers should always take into account the level of knowledge, sophistication, and maturity of the audience to which their message is primarily directed; second, realizing that children are imaginative and that make-believe play constitutes an important part of the growing up process, advertisers should exercise care not to exploit unfairly the imaginative quality of children; third, recognizing that advertising may play an important part in educating the child, advertisers should communicate information in a truthful and accurate manner with full recognition that the child may learn practices from advertising that can affect his or her health and well-being; fourth, advertisers are urged to capitalize on the potential of advertising to influence behavior by developing advertising that, wherever possible, addresses itself to positive and beneficial social behavior, such as friendship, kindness, honesty, justice, generosity, and respect for others; fifth, care should be taken to incorporate minority and other groups in advertisements in order to present positive and pro-social roles and role models wherever possible; and sixth, although many influences affect a child's personal and social development, parents are primarily responsible for providing guidance to their children.

Despite this stringent self-regulation, concern for children's advertising again emerged as an issue in the late 1980s as marketers increasingly recognized and targeted the lucrative and growing children's market. The Children's Television Act of 1990 imposed new restrictions on the number of commercial minutes that networks and television stations can program to children (ten-and-one-half minutes per hour on weekdays and twelve minutes per hour on weekends). The act also restored rules requiring that commercial breaks be clearly distinguished from programming, and barring selling by on-air hosts. In addition, the FTC enacted a new rule for 900-number services (pay-per-call services). Under the 1993 rule, companies cannot advertise or direct pay-per-call services to children under twelve unless these services are educational and dedicated to areas of school study. If the ad is directed to consumers under the age of eighteen, it must state that parental permission is required to make the call.

Consumer interest in children's advertising appears to be increasing. Although Peggy Charren suspended operations of Action for Children's Television at the end of 1992 after twenty-three years of advocacy, a new group emerged that may encourage enforcement of the new rule. The Center for Media Education (CME), which was founded by Kathryn Montgomery and Jeff Chester, defined as priorities the improvement of children's programming and the limiting of commercialization directed at children. As the next century approaches, one can expect that CME or some other consumer group will continue to advocate on issues protecting this vulnerable audience.

— M. Carole Macklin

See also

Action for Children's Television; Better Business Bureaus; Federal Trade Commission.

Readings

Ratner, Ellis (1978). *FTC Staff Report on Television Advertising to Children.* Washington, DC: U.S. Government Printing Office.

Roedder, Deborah L. (1981). "Age Differences in Children's Responses to Television Advertising: An Information-Processing Perspective." *The Journal of Consumer Research.* 8 (2): 144–153.

Self-Regulatory Guidelines for Children's Advertising (1993). 4th ed. New York: Council of Better Business Bureaus, Inc., Children's Advertising Review Unit.

Chinese Consumer Movement

The consumer movement in China has largely resulted from the economic reform that started in the late 1970s. Before the reform, the term *consumer* was rarely used. Essentially, consumers—people with discretionary income to spend in markets with abundant supply—did not exist until the late 1970s. Since the reform and open-door policies started, the traditional centrally planned economy has begun transforming into a market economy. The Chinese people are experiencing an increasing abundance of consumer goods and services in the market. Their disposable incomes and expectations for consumption are also rising rapidly. At the same time, consumer problems and issues are also increasing, and a need for consumer protection is perceived by both government bodies and the general public.

One of the major reactions to the increasing consumer problems and issues is the formation of government-supported consumer associations at national, provincial, and local levels. In 1983, the first consumer association was founded in a county near Beijing. One year later, another consumer association, the first one in an urban area, was founded in Guangzhou in Guangdong Province, which was among the cities given some economic privileges by the central government. In December 1984, a national consumer protection agency, the China Consumer Association, was founded in Beijing. As of 1994, the China Consumer Association had more than 26,000 county and city branches, including the two that were founded before the national association.

All the provincial and city consumer councils have functions similar to the consumer protection agencies in some states and cities in the United States, but the China Consumer Association has no American counterpart. In September 1987, the China Consumer Association became an organizational member of Consumers International. The national association and its branches operate in the following ways. The staff members are always from other regulatory agencies—the China National Administration of Industry and Commerce (which has functions similar to the U.S. Federal Trade Commission), the China Commodity Inspection Bureau, and the China Standards Bureau (which resembles somewhat the U.S. Consumer Product Safety Commission). The China Consumer Association and its branches always invite high-ranking officials to serve as their honorary presidents. Well-known experts or scholars are invited to be advisers, and these 130 advisers serve on a volunteer basis.

The operating funds of consumer associations at national and local levels are provided by the government. The national association received about $20,000 from the government in 1989. The funds for associations at provincial, city, or county levels are provided by the governments at corresponding levels, and they are usually inadequate. Complaint handling and market inspections are the major functions of the consumer associations. In 1992, the associations handled 340,000 complaint cases and helped consumers get refunds amounting to nearly $30 million.

A special feature of China's consumer movement is that government is the sole sponsor of consumer protection activities. Almost no private consumer groups exist in China because the Chinese government tends to associate these groups with antigovernment activities. However, with the growth of privately owned properties in the national economy, some quasi-official organizations are forming. For example, a recently founded consumer foundation claims to be a private organization, although its president is a government official and the former president of the China Consumer Association.

The ideology of protecting consumers' interests is consistent with traditional Chinese values. China is an agricultural country with a history spanning more than 2,000 years. Compared to agriculture, trades and related professions are often considered as unproductive and dishonorable. The Chinese saying "wu shang bu jian" (no merchants are not liars) reflects a common belief among Chinese people. Protecting consumers is also consistent with the long-term reform plan promoted by the leaders of the Chinese government. The final goal of the economic reform is to move the national economy to a market economy, including fundamental reforms involving prices, housing, banking, and employment. These reforms will affect consumer well-being both positively and negatively, and the effects will be distributed unevenly by occupation, income level, and geographical area. To facilitate the transition to a market economy and reduce possible political consequences of consumer dissatisfaction, the government took the safe route of initiating consumer protection activities rather than leaving these activities to private parties.

Consumer Problems

Consumer problems in modern China can be placed into three categories. First, there are problems related to the economic transition. Price reform, for example, is one of the most important components of the economic reform. Before the reform, prices of most consumer goods and services were strictly controlled by the government and rarely changed. Consequently, Chinese people became used to stable prices. Under price reform, the government has loosened control over the prices of some consumer goods.

During the economic transition period, three types of prices exist: prices controlled and determined by the government; prices controlled by businesses, but within a certain range and under a government-specified ceiling; and prices controlled entirely by the market. The ultimate goal of the price reform is to achieve a market economy, which lets the "invisible hand" decide prices. This temporary price system has caused many administrative and regulatory problems and resulted in many consumer complaints. Very often, prices are unreasonably raised. Apart from prices regulated by the government, some businesses ask for surcharges and additional charges. Consumers are confused about the three kinds of prices. In different cities, the colors of tags for three prices may vary. While this arrangement is helpful for government agencies inspecting the market, it confuses most consumers.

A second set of problems is related to the early developmental stage of the market economy. These problems involve safety, quality, information, and redress. Many consumer goods with inferior quality are packaged beautifully. Unsafe drugs and cosmetics are common in the marketplace. Some domestically produced, low-quality goods are labeled in a manner to imply that they are made in foreign countries, such as Japan or the United States, because foreign goods sell better. Most packages do not give information regarding production date, expiration date, or warranty terms. Some do not provide names and addresses of manufacturers, or lists of ingredients. Spoiled food is often found in the marketplace. Food adulteration, such as adding water and industrial alcohol into alcoholic beverages and processing diseased pig meat into sausage, has occurred many times. Inferior goods, such as powdered milk diluted with sugar and flour, are common in grocery stores. Some famous brand foods are illegally reproduced at lower quality levels. Some "health" food actually has no nutritional value. Deaths resulting from unsafe household electronic equipment occur often. Many appliances have no warranty. It is very difficult for consumers to return goods to stores or manufacturers to obtain refunds or replacements.

Third, some problems are similar to ones in other countries, including more developed ones. Deceptive advertisements can be found anywhere. In China, some advertisements have promoted phony consumer goods with imaginary functions, such as "Super Memory Machine" and "Study Aid with Multiple Functions." Other advertisements contain nonexistent "facts" such as "high quality" or "award winning." Some drug advertisements carry dubious boasts regarding the effectiveness of their products. Some businesses and mass media institutions conspire to produce advertisements that appear to be news articles. Counterfeit trademarks are rampant in the marketplace, especially for cars, tractors, bicycles, watches, drugs, appliances, wine, cosmetics, clothing, and food.

Consumer Policies

In China's consumer movement, the government plays an important and irreplaceable role. It is the initiator, promoter, and implementer of consumer protection mechanisms and policies. The government has created a nationwide network of consumer protection organizations, headed by the China Consumer Association. Several other agencies also have responsibilities in terms of consumer protection. Campaigns have been initiated to reduce marketplace fraud, and the government is creating a better legal environment for consumers' redress and safety.

Besides the China Consumer Association and its branches across the country, two other major agencies with responsibilities for consumer protection are the China National Administration of Industry and Commerce and the China Standards Bureau. The chief responsibility of the China National Administration of Industry and Commerce and its local branches is regulating markets, trademarks, and advertisements. Staff members of consumer associations are mainly from this administration, and these associations in most cases are in the same buildings. That is why the consumer associations look powerful even though they have little authority to enforce laws.

The China Standards Bureau is responsible for inspecting the quality of industrial and consumer goods, publishing the results, and setting national standards. In 1985, the bureau formulated over 1,500 national standards, about 200 of which related directly to the consumer's well-being. It also created some basic standards, such as "The General Instruction of the Use of Consumer Products." According to this standard, producers of consumer products should provide warnings, specifications, and information about product maintenance.

Several consumer protection campaigns were initiated and implemented by these and other government regulatory agencies. The following case illustrates the process of agenda setting and implementation of these campaigns. In November 1984, a letter published in a paper exposed the fact that some of the suits and clothes on sale in Wuhan, a central southern industrial city, were previously used. The letter writer was angry because he found many clothes were dirty and harmful to the wearer's health. In the summer of 1985, a textile and clothing association in Beijing examined these imported suits and found that many were taken from patients or diseased people in foreign countries. Some underwear was even collected from garbage dumps. Health agencies tested some clothes and found a lot of pathogenic bacteria, such as syphilis. In October of 1985, the National Administration of Industry and Commerce and the Department of Health issued an emergency order to prohibit imports and sales of this kind of clothing. In November, the commissioner of the National Administration of Industry and Commerce delivered a public speech to call for destroying all imported used clothes. In more than twenty cities and counties, the administration's local branches conducted surprise searches for unsafe clothes, then confiscated and burned those they found.

Many laws and regulations dealing with trademarks, foods, drugs, prices, income taxes, stock markets, and unfair competition were created during the reform period. In 1987, the first local consumer protection regulation was formulated in Shengyang, an industrial city in northeastern China. As of 1994, thirty-five provinces or cities have enacted their own consumer protection regulations. A national consumer protection law was passed in 1993 and took effect in January 1994.

The courts have opened doors for consumers. In 1986, the spokesperson for the Shanghai Supreme Court announced that it would accept consumer lawsuits. An individual consumer won the first lawsuit against a department store for a defective color television set in the Nanjing Intermediate Court in 1987. Unethical business people whose activities caused serious consequences have received severe legal punishments. To illustrate, in Sichuan, four men were sentenced to death after they produced poisoned beverages that killed twenty-five people.

Consumer Information and Education

In China, consumer information and education activities are mainly performed by mass media institutions. One consumer magazine and several consumer newspapers were first issued during the 1984 to 1986 period. Three consumer newspapers—*China Consumer News, Consumer News,* and *Fujian Consumer News*—were sponsored by official consumer associations. *Consumption News,* a paper originally published by the Shanghai Institute of Social Science and later cosponsored by the Shanghai Consumer Association, has a larger circulation. These papers cover activities of consumer associations and report on consumer movements in other countries.

Consumer, a consumer magazine begun in the mid-1980s, is sponsored by the Beijing Institute of Finance and Trade. It is relatively independent and aggressive in representing consumer interests. In each issue, it uses large amounts of space to describe consumer movements and consumer protection activities in other countries. The main goal of this magazine is to promote awareness of consumer rights. In June 1986, the magazine solicited nominations for a "Black Sheep Cup" to encourage consumers to provide information about the worst goods or services they purchased in the marketplace. Names of providers of worst goods and services were published in the magazine. This activity resulted in tremendous pressure from some government agencies and offending businesses, which included a lawsuit against the magazine for publishing a complaint letter about the defective products made by a company.

Consumer news in the media is a major source of consumer information. National and local newspapers, radios, and television networks are offering an increasing number of consumer-oriented programs. Consumer protection stories often are on the front page or in the prime-time news. The media's extensive coverage educates and informs consumers about market frauds and prevention measures. The press also disciplines abusive businesses. The Jingjiang Phony Drug case was a major consumer issue during 1984 to 1986. All the national newspapers, radio stations, and television networks widely reported on this case. They were able to do so because the media are mainly controlled by the government.

At Chinese universities, consumer protection has been incorporated, to a limited degree, into teaching and research. Professor Shijie Yin at Hunan Normal University has achieved several "firsts" in the consumption economics field. He first proposed consumption economics as an independent field, published a textbook (*Socialist Consumption Economics*), sponsored a journal specifically devoted to consumption economics, created a consumption economics institute, and admitted graduate students for study in consumption economics. In 1993, he was the only academic to receive the Consumer Protection Award issued by the China Consumer Foundation.

The earliest research on consumer protection in China was a master's thesis in 1986 by Jing Jian Xiao at Zhongnan University of Economics and Finance, and several journal papers based on the thesis. Xiao documented China's consumer movement and attempted to develop a conceptual framework to address causes and remedies of Chinese consumer issues with a systematic approach. The earliest research on Chinese consumer satisfaction and dissatisfaction was conducted in the early 1980s by Hans B. Thorelli, an American marketing professor at Indiana University. Consumer research in China now focuses on methods of educating consumers and improving the effectiveness of official consumer associations.

International and Future Roles

China's consumer movement has been influenced by the global consumer movement. Officials of the consumer associations have learned about the organization and activities of consumer groups in other countries through visiting these countries and attending international meetings, such as Consumers International meetings. Increasingly frequent academic exchanges between China and other countries have allowed Chinese scholars to adapt concepts and approaches developed by their foreign counterparts to study and conceptualize consumer issues and remedies in China.

Conversely, the consumer protection activities in China have had some impact on the global consumer movement. The consumer movement in China provides a unique case of how a 1.2 billion population experiences consumer re-socialization in a short period of time, and how problems faced by these inexperienced consumers and corresponding remedies are developed. The consumer protection policies in China sometimes have influenced the consumer movements in other countries or areas, especially in Asia. For example, the passage of the national consumer protection law in mainland China gave a final push to a similar law in Taiwan in early 1994.

If the United States is a model of consumerism, China has a long way to go. In the United States, consumer protection has become a social norm that is pervasive in every sector of the society. Consumer protection activities and consumer information facilities are offered by a variety of government agencies, business-sponsored institutions, and nonprofit groups. Even though the American consumer movement is not currently at high tide, it exists independently of government support. In China, this type of private social movement does not exist. It may develop gradually, along with the evolution of the market economy, and go through several phases (as was the case in the United States). If economic reform continues in China, private consumer groups can be expected to grow for two reasons. With rapid economic growth, concerned consumers will have greater access to resources to form their own groups. Continuing economic reform will create a "middle class" of consumers in China, which will increase demand for consumer education and information, thus stimulating the supply of consumer information publications, consumer education in schools, and product testing and information dissemination facilities. In addition, the government is likely to be more tolerant of private consumer groups if it believes these groups will assist economic reform.

— Jing Jian Xiao

Readings

China Consumer Association (1991). *China Consumer Association.* Beijing: China Consumer Association.

Xiao, Jing Jian, Shijie Yin, Joan Gray Anderson, and Franziska E. Noring (1994). *Consumer Movement in a Transitional Economy: A Case of China.* Paper presented at the 9th Annual Conference of Chinese Economists Society, Chicago.

King, D. B., and Tong Gao (1991). *Consumer Protection in China: Transitions, Development and Recommendations*. Littleton, CO: Rothman.

Citizen Action

Citizen Action is a national consumer and environmental watchdog organization. It is a federation of statewide citizen groups that, since 1979, has built a large membership and organized broad coalitions while working on issues such as health care reform, the prevention of toxic pollution, restrictions on the use of cancer-causing pesticides, campaign finance reform, the protection of consumer rights in the civil justice system, fair energy pricing, and sustainable economics. Operating in thirty-two states, together these citizen organizations have several million members, thousands of activists, hundreds of full-time staffers, and combined budgets of more than $30 million a year. Citizen Action bases its strategy on its ability to build strong state and local organizations that use more than 90 percent of the organization's revenues.

Citizen Action is governed by a board of directors composed of forty-seven representatives elected by their member state organizations. Every state organization is represented on the board. The board, now chaired by Ellen Kennedy from Citizen Action of New York, meets three times a year while the executive committee meets monthly. Since 1979, Ira Arlook has been executive director of the national federation, which has a staff of twenty-five.

Origins

Citizen Action was founded in Chicago in December 1979 by the directors of five state organizations—the Connecticut Citizen Action Group, the Illinois Public Action Council (now Illinois Public Action), Massachusetts Fair Share (now Massachusetts Citizen Action), the Ohio Public Interest Campaign (now Ohio Citizen Action), and Oregon Fair Share—and the director of the Midwest Academy, Heather Booth. The Midwest Academy is a training institute modeled on the community organizing principles of Saul Alinsky. The Citizen/Labor Energy Coalition (C/LEC) also played an important role in the founding and development of Citizen Action.

C/LEC was founded in 1978 by a coalition of organizations, including the abovementioned state organizations and labor, consumer, senior, farm, and religious organizations that addressed the issues of fair energy prices and renewable energy. C/LEC set up a network of regional coalitions around the country, many of which then developed multiissue agendas and became part of Citizen Action. C/LEC's executive director, Robert Brandon, became Citizen Action's legislative and political director. The Midwest Academy, directed by Jackie Kendall since the mid-1980s, has worked closely with Citizen Action and its leaders on training staff, developing issues, and assisting state organizations.

Since 1975, most state Citizen Action affiliates have employed door-to-door canvassing for membership recruitment, public education, grassroots lobbying, electoral participation, and fund-raising. The development of this strategy in the late 1970s and early 1980s enabled Citizen Action to have between 500 and 1,000 staff members talking with 20,000 to 40,000 families per night. As *The Washington Post's* senior political reporter, David Broder, observed, "The [Citizen Action] groups use the most basic of organizing techniques: they send people . . . door to door to collect money and membership cards from residents, on a promise the proceeds will be used to fight for a clean environment, health and safety measures, lower utility rates or similar goals." These canvassers also provide citizens with information and solutions to problems that have motivated many of these individuals to send letters, make phone calls, or become volunteers with the organization.

National Campaign against Toxic Hazards

In 1984, in partnership with Clean Water Action, Citizen Action launched the National

Campaign against Toxic Hazards, a coalition of local, state, and national organizations working to protect people against increasing exposure to toxic chemical pollution. Previously, this campaign had developed for several years at the state and local levels where Citizen Action organizations and their local allies waged "right-to-know" campaigns. These efforts often succeeded in passing state laws and local ordinances that gave workers and communities right-to-know protections.

The most significant accomplishment of the national campaign was the establishment by federal law of a community's "right to know" about the releases by manufacturers of toxic pollution into the community's air, water, and soil. This was accomplished by requiring manufacturers to report their toxic emissions to the Environmental Protection Agency (EPA), which in turn published the data in its Toxic Release Inventory, or TRI. Through organizing and mobilization, this campaign was able to expand beyond those who traditionally support the environmental movement to people mainly concerned about the health risks associated with exposure to toxic chemicals. This "community-right-to-know" legislation has not only enabled the public to learn about the toxic chemicals that are released into their communities but also made it possible for local organizations, including Citizen Action, to demand that corporations reduce their emissions.

To assist those efforts, Citizens Fund, Citizen Action's research affiliate, issued annual state-by-state reports specifying which industries and which local companies were responsible for the release of toxic chemicals into the environment. These reports helped local activists and organizations demand that the companies reduce their toxic emissions.

Besides right-to-know legislation, the campaign sought to renew and strengthen Superfund, the law that requires cleanup of the nation's worst hazardous dump sites. In order to accomplish this goal, the campaign engaged in grassroots lobbying, held public events at local toxic waste sites, and exposed inadequate EPA cleanups. As a result of these efforts, federal legislation was passed that increased toxic waste cleanup resources and established standards for EPA cleanups at a time when all other programs were being cut.

Health Care Reform

During the 1980s and early 1990s, Citizen Action focused much of its efforts on health care reform. By using canvassing as a method of research, the organization was able to learn what health issues most concerned citizens. Based on this information, local health coalitions were formed with the goals of informing the public, policymakers, and the media at the local, state, and national levels about the causes of the health care crisis and proposing solutions through local and state reforms. Citizens Fund also produced and released many reports critical of the health care industry.

Citizen Action engaged in a wide range of activities with the intent of putting health care reform on the national agenda. Much of the strategy focused on state-level change in an effort to accomplish concrete goals, educate the public, and build support for more sweeping national reform. The work emphasized the need for comprehensive and universal health care coverage to hold down costs and solve the problem of inadequate or no coverage.

Through its campaign efforts, Citizen Action contributed to the reduction of inequities in health coverage for millions of uninsured or poor Americans. Due in part to Citizen Action's efforts, Medicaid was expanded to provide health services to a wider range of individuals, including children, pregnant women, persons with disabilities, and senior citizens. Programs were established that provided discounted prescription drugs to low-income senior citizens and families. Through state measures and, ultimately, reform of Medicare, senior citizens and persons with disabilities were protected from physician overcharges. During the 1980s, Citizen Action was also responsible for initiating the first insurance reform laws that provided continuity of health coverage to persons who changed jobs.

In the late 1980s, Citizen Action sought to implement the model of the Canadian national health insurance system in the United States. The organization began educating and mobilizing consumers and providers behind "single-payer" legislation in several states and developed national legislation that was introduced by Representative Marty Russo (D-IL) and more than fifty other House members.

In 1991, to help publicize the campaign, Citizen Action worked with the labor/community coalition Jobs with Justice, and the Washington, D.C.–based health care organization Families USA, to organize a cross-country "Emergency Drive for Health Care." Over a period of six weeks, five ambulance caravans traveled from different parts of the country to Washington, D.C., to dramatize the crisis in health care. With national leaders and celebrities riding in the ambulances, at each stop the caravans sought to engage the media and to educate local leaders and citizens. All the ambulances converged on Washington at a rally attended by hundreds in Lafayette Park across from the White House.

With public and media attention heavily focused on the health care crisis, the election of President Clinton in 1992 set the stage for a full-fledged debate on health care reform for the first time since the late 1940s. In 1993, Citizen Action organized the Campaign for Health Security, a coalition comprised of consumer, religious, senior, disability, provider, farm, and labor organizations. The focus of this campaign was to continue to educate and mobilize the public around the congressional debate surrounding the single-payer health system and the need for comprehensive health care reform. Analyses of legislative proposals, fact sheets, and a series of booklets on how health care reform would affect various constituencies were distributed throughout the country.

Citizen Action also helped lead a nationwide campaign to collect over one million postcards addressed to President Clinton. These postcards were delivered to Vice President Al Gore in January 1993 by twenty-five citizens who considered themselves victims of the health care system. Although Congress refused to pass major legislation, Citizen Action–led health care coalitions continued to push for reforms in two dozen states and nationally.

Citizen Action's current efforts to make health care accessible and affordable to consumers are taking place within the context of the debate surrounding the reconfiguration of the U.S. health care system into managed care. Citizen Action is focusing on building grassroots education, mobilization, lobbying, and media campaigns in the fight to protect consumers in both private coverage and the public Medicare/Medicaid programs.

In 1995, Citizen Action conducted a local, state, and national campaign to inform the press, public, and opinion leaders about the impact of proposed cuts in Medicare and Medicaid on consumers, providers, and delivery systems. The combination of this campaign and corresponding on-site training provided the resources necessary for full and effective consumer participation in the ongoing debate. In that same year, Citizens Fund worked with the Public Policy and Education Fund of New York in order to educate consumers on private managed care through their publication of *The Managed Care Consumer's Bill of Rights*, which explains managed care, analyzes current trends, and outlines ten rights essential to protecting the interests of consumers enrolled in managed care plans.

Civil Justice and State Campaigns

From its beginning, Citizen Action has worked to protect consumer rights and promote consumer safety. At the state and federal levels, Citizen Action has fought against proposals that would lessen the accountability of those whose actions cause injury or death: manufacturers of dangerous products, medically negligent doctors and hospitals, and unsafe drivers. Through its efforts, Citizen Action has been able to block anti-consumer product liability and medical malpractice legislation at the federal and state levels.

Citizen Action has supported efforts to give consumers critical information on products and practices, such as opening up the National Practitioners Data Bank, which lists information on physicians. But, believing that information alone is not a sufficient protection, the organization has worked to preserve consumers' legal rights and access. In the health care area, Citizen Action has concentrated on expanding the legal rights and remedies of millions of Americans enrolled in managed care plans, especially those in employer-based plans. Citizen Action has also opposed proposals to shift costs from parties responsible for causing injury to those who are injured, to impose caps on damages, to restrict noneconomic payments, and to eliminate joint and several liability.

Beyond Citizen Action's national campaigns on energy prices, member state organizations have made their marks at the state level on a wide range of consumer and environmental issues. The following examples indicate the scope of the organizations' efforts: Alabama Citizen Action, after a three-year campaign, won creation of the first public, nonmedical consumer representative on the state's Medical Licensure Commission; Citizen Action Coalition of Indiana forced the rollback of hundreds of millions of dollars in electric utility rates; New Jersey Citizen Action won a major court victory to prevent banks from discriminating in making housing loans; Citizen Action of New York was instrumental in winning legislative support for improvements in managed care; Ohio Citizen Action helped force two investor-owned utilities to scrap the uneconomic Perry II nuclear power plant; and Tennessee Citizen Action led the successful fight for legislation to improve workplace safety conditions and workers' compensation.

Mobilizing the Electorate

Initially, Citizen Action organized around issues but did not engage in electoral politics. In 1980, however, recognizing the need to help legislators who supported the organization's issue agenda, Citizen Action decided to participate in elections. Citizen Action organizations established three basic criteria for deciding whether to get involved in a particular election: the issues at stake in the outcome of the race had to be part of Citizen Action's agenda, there had to be a significant difference between the candidates, and the candidates had to be capable of running competitive campaigns. The key to Citizen Action's approach to electoral politics was the organization's ability to connect issues of importance to its members to a particular candidate. This strategy resulted in significant support for pro-consumer candidates like Senator Howard Metzenbaum (D-OH) and Senator Paul Simon (D-IL). Citizen Action members have also participated in state and local electoral coalitions that provide a program of training and consultation on electoral skills for a wide variety of citizen groups, staff, and leaders. This forum has provided the background education necessary for organizations to work toward electing progressive candidates. These efforts have led to the election of Citizen Action leaders and allies to state and local offices. The former executive director of the Connecticut Citizen Action Group, Miles Rapoport, is Connecticut's secretary of state; David Grubb, former director of West Virginia Citizen Action, is a state senator in West Virginia; Dwight Pelz, former director of Washington Fair Share (now Washington Citizen Action), is a state senator in Washington; Jay Westbrook, former director of Ohio Citizen Action's Cleveland office, was elected the chairman of the Cleveland City Council; and Roxanne Qualls, the former director of the Cincinnati office of Ohio Citizen Action, was elected mayor of Cincinnati.

Citizen Action is also concerned about the corrupting role of private, special interest money in the electoral and legislative processes. Private money in politics not only has strongly influenced public policy but also has diminished the trust and confidence of Americans in the value and relevance of public life. Citizen Action has spent the last decade exposing the influence of money in politics through a series of reports called *Unhealthy Money,* which examine the ties between campaign contributions and votes by members of Congress. These reports were featured in news stories in major national media outlets and in issue advocacy television and radio ads throughout 1996. Most of Citizen Action's state affiliates support the public financing of elections and are elevating the intensity of their efforts to rid state and local legislative and executive bodies of private money influence. The national federation has also made the issue a top priority.

In the late 1970s, Citizen Action's five founding groups set out to build a set of large membership organizations and broad coalitions of allied organizations that wage grassroots campaigns at the local, state, and national levels to connect individual problems with public issues. By any measure, they accomplished their purpose.

— Cathy Hurwit, Edwin S. Rothschild

Readings

Boyte, Harry C., Heather Booth, and Steve Max (1986). *Citizen Action and the New American Populism.* Philadelphia: Temple University Press.

Kelsey, Janet, and Don Wiener (1983). "The Citizen/Labor Energy Coalition." *Social Policy.* (Spring): 15–18.

Citizen Utility Boards

Citizen Utility Boards (CUBs) are private consumer organizations that provide class and proxy advocacy, oversight, and policy intervention for consumers of regulated public utilities (typically electric, gas, and telephone). CUBs are "class advocates" in that they make general demands on regulators and utility companies and articulate these demands in policy and decision-making arenas. (By contrast, "case advocates" address problems of specific individuals.) CUBs can also be considered "proxy advocates" since they act not on their own behalf, but on behalf of a group of citizens. CUBs seek to remedy existing problems and prevent future ones from occurring.

CUBs are typically organized as nonprofit organizations and are staffed by professionals. They intervene in rate cases, provide testimony in legislative hearings, present consumer views before state public service commissions, promote consumer participation, and provide education regarding utility price, quality, reliability, safety, and adequacy. Electric, gas, and telephone utilities come under the scrutiny of CUBs in states where these boards have been established.

CUBs were promoted by Ralph Nader and by organizations that Nader created or inspired, especially Public Interest Research Groups (PIRGs); however, all existing CUBs were established as independent, freestanding organizations. State CUBs have been established in Illinois, New York, Oregon, and Wisconsin. There is also a regional CUB called the Utility Consumers Action Network (UCAN) in the San Diego area, and a CUB-like private organization called Toward Utility Rate Normalization (TURN) in the San Francisco Bay Area.

CUBs are funded almost exclusively by member dues, generally a minimum of about \$5 to \$10. Initially, CUBs relied heavily on gaining access to utility bills for inserts informing consumers of their programs and soliciting memberships and contributions. This unique approach to funding depended on legislative action requiring utility companies to include the materials in customers' bills. This approach was declared unconstitutional by the U.S. Supreme Court in 1986. Today, all CUBs use other means to distribute information and solicit memberships.

Founded in 1979, the Wisconsin CUB is the oldest of the CUBs. It was established by an act of the legislature as a quasi-governmental organization. No funding was provided at that time. In 1984, the Wisconsin CUB became an independent, nonprofit organization. Funding was generated through solicitations included in utility bills. When the Supreme Court handed down its 1986 decision, these utility inserts were discontinued. At present, the organization raises funds using methods employed by other nonprofit organizations and receives "intervenor funding" from the state.

The Oregon CUB was formed in 1984 by initiative (statewide vote) of all citizens in response to public backlash against rapidly increasing utility rates and against perceived unresponsiveness to citizens by the single public utility commissioner. The original initiative allowed the CUB to put inserts in utility bills. After the Supreme Court's 1986 decision, this practice was discontinued. Today, the Oregon CUB uses typical nonprofit organization fund-raising practices. In 1995, the organization had about 10,000 dues-paying members.

The New York State CUB was incorporated in 1984. At that time, the N.Y. Public Service Commission (PSC) required CUB membership forms to be included in utility bills. After the Supreme Court decision, the group did not function until 1991, when Governor Mario Cuomo signed an executive order requiring state agencies to distribute membership materials with their mailings. The first mailings by state agencies, which were sent in 1994, led to the enrollment of more than 21,000 members. Governor Pataki halted the mailings in 1995.

CUBs have saved consumers millions of dollars. For example, the Oregon CUB claims to have saved consumers more than $350 million. Its specific interventions include: in 1987, a request to revoke an interim rate hike, resulting in a refund of $11 million to U.S. West customers; in 1989, a case to have Yellow Pages revenue returned to the rate base, which led to consumer refunds of $56 million; in 1986, a challenge of Northwest Natural Gas's rate increase request that saved ratepayers $29 million; and in 1993, an Oregon Supreme Court decision that U.S. West refund $15.5 million. Other CUBs and CUB-like organizations also claim to have saved residential ratepayers substantial monies through similar interventions.

As well as CUBs, state-funded consumer utility advocate offices and utility-created consumer advisory panels have been regarded as mechanisms for providing consumer representation in utility-related matters. In fact, the advocacy offices in some states were established as an alternative to CUBs. Because of their dependence on utilities, consumer advisory panels were viewed by most advocates as providing opportunities for consumer input, but not for effective consumer representation. By contrast, after their establishment, CUBs came to depend neither on state governments nor on utilities. Yet, the Supreme Court's decision curbing CUB access to utility mailings forced them to rely more heavily on access to state government mailings and to traditional nonprofit fund-raising methods. This new dependence has clouded their future somewhat.

— Drew Hyman

See also

State Utility Consumer Advocates.

Readings

Gormley, William T. (1981). "Public Advocacy in Public Utility Commission Proceedings." *Journal of Applied Behavioral Science.* 17 (4): 446–462.

Hyman, Drew (1979). "Toward a Theory of Citizens' Advocacy: The Role of Ombudsmen and Consumer Advocates in the Political Process." In S. Langton, ed. *Citizen Participation Perspectives.* Medford, MA: Lincoln Filene Center for Citizenship and Public Affairs. 148–155.

——— (1990). "Utility Consumer Dispute Settlement: A Regulatory Model for Mediation, Arbitration, and Class Advocacy." In M. K. Mills, ed. *Conflict Resolution and Public Policy.* Westport, CT: Greenwood Press. 63–76.

Clothing Flammability

See Textile Product Flammability.

Coalitions

Coalitions are temporary alliances among groups for the purpose of pursuing a common goal. Most coalitions with consumer participation seek to advance the consumer interest by influencing government decisions, especially those made by legislators. Other alliances attempt to influence directly either consumer or corporate behavior. The Consumer Literacy Consortium, for instance, is a working group of representatives from twenty-five government, corporate, and consumer organizations that developed and now disseminates money-saving tips to consumers. In the 1980s, consumer groups from many nations joined together to boycott the products of companies marketing infant formula in Third World countries. But because coalitions seeking to influence public policy constitute the majority of coalitions, are often highly visible, and sometimes wield great influence, this article will focus attention on them, especially those involving business groups.

Partners and Opponents

Consumer advocates join coalitions because they believe that their influence over public policy will be enhanced. They most often link up with other consumer advocates with whom they share interests. At one extreme, consumer and labor groups have created national and state consumer federations that are so well established that they no longer qualify as coalitions. At the other extreme, consumer advocates have formed ad hoc coalitions simply to work on one piece of legislation that they desire to pass or block.

Consumer advocates also join with advocates from other nonprofit groups with whom they partially share interests. Typically, these other nonprofits seek to represent the interest of a subset of the population, such as the elderly, the poor, or members of an ethnic group. These groups may also advocate another widely held general interest, such as a healthy environment, good government, or a humane workplace.

Consumer advocates have joined with different minority advocates to oppose racial discrimination in areas such as credit, housing, and telecommunications. Advocates have worked with environmentalists to oppose the construction of nuclear power plants and promote energy conservation. And they have linked up with political reform organizations, such as Common Cause, to promote campaign finance reform and reduce state legislator conflicts of interest. Beyond shared interests, these coalitions with other nonprofits are encouraged by the fact that the advocates who work in each interest group tend to share the same values and politics.

Less frequent, but of increasing significance, are advocate alliances with business groups with interests that complement those of consumers. Consumer groups may form coalitions with a single firm or subset of firms within an industry, or with an entire industry. In the former case, political divisions among producers of the same good or service may arise from competitive differentials created by economic factors or by government action. In the late 1980s, for instance, many large property/casualty insurers broke from the rest of their industry to support substantial modification of an antitrust exemption granted to insurers by Congress in the late 1940s. These companies were increasingly frustrated by a growing number of activist state regulators and sought more uniform federal regulation. Total repeal of this antitrust exemption had been a high priority for consumer groups such as the Consumer Federation of America and Consumers Union for many years.

There are many situations in which an entire industry may link up with consumer advocates. A common situation involves consumers and retailers joining together to resist the efforts of manufacturers or wholesalers to gain market power. For example, food retailers worked with consumer advocates throughout most of the 1980s to defeat the effort of beer wholesalers to obtain an antitrust exemption that would not only have raised beer prices but also have encouraged other food and beverage producers and wholesalers to seek similar exemptions.

Another common situation that can give rise to a consumer coalition with an entire industry occurs when a government policy transfers resources among consumers in a way that allows firms to serve needy but uneconomical markets. During the 1980s and early 1990s, for instance, electric and gas utilities fought alongside consumer advocates to preserve and strengthen federal weatherization and energy assistance subsidies to low-income households. These subsidies were supported by consumer groups on grounds of social justice and energy conservation, while utilities viewed them as a way of reducing uncollectible bills and dampening peak load demands.

The most extensive consumer-business alliances have involved property/casualty insurers, especially large auto insurers. During the 1980s and 1990s, insurers worked with consumer advocates to promote improved motor vehicle and highway safety. Advocates were primarily interested in reducing accident-related injuries and fatalities while insurers were mainly concerned about restraining economic losses associated with these accidents. In 1978, consumer groups and auto insurers formalized their partnership by creating Advocates for Auto and Highway Safety, which has taken the lead in coordinating motor vehicle safety advocacy before Congress, the National Highway Traffic Safety Administration, and state governments.

More recently, consumer advocates have also worked with insurers to restrain economic losses resulting from accidents by holding down the price of repair parts. Both groups participate in the Certified Automotive Parts Association, organized in 1988, which works to insure that after-market parts meet certain quality standards. Restraining economic losses is also the principal goal of the Coalition Against Insurance Fraud, which includes some twenty consumer, insurer, regulator, and law enforcement organizations. This coalition works to reduce both insurer and insuree fraud related to all types of property/casualty insurance.

The two insurer groups that have most actively promoted these alliances are State Farm Insurance and, under the leadership of Robert Vagley, the American Insurance Association. Within the consumer community, Consumer Federation of America has taken the lead in organizing alliances including the auto safety coalition, the fraud coalition, and the Coalition for Consumer Health and Safety, an umbrella coalition of some forty insurer, consumer, and health groups that has promoted improved health and safety on a broad range of consumer issues.

The most frequent opposition to the efforts of consumer coalitions has come from business groups. Automobile manufacturers, for example, usually led the opposition to motor vehicle–related safety initiatives. But resistance has come from other quarters as well. Conservative groups opposing government regulation, such as the Cato Institute and Capitol Legal Foundation, have supported businesses that were the target of proposed consumer regulations. Some government leaders concerned about budget deficits have also taken the lead against programs advanced by consumer-business coalitions that require public subsidies, such as low-income energy assistance.

In a few instances, consumer advocates working with business have been opposed by other advocates. Trade issues have been particularly divisive. Consumers Union (CU) has taken the lead in promoting free trade, in part because Consumers International, the one international consumer group, has strongly advocated this position. The U.S. group worked in concert with some corporations who are large exporters or importers. In the 1990s, CU has often found itself in opposition to Ralph Nader and his network of organizations, who fear that international trade agreements will weaken U.S. consumer and environmental protections. These latter consumer groups ally themselves with both environmental advocates and trade unions on trade issues.

Scope and Trends

The scope of consumer coalitions ranges on a continuum from one regulatory or legislative goal, to one issue area, to many related issue areas. In the area of motor vehicle safety, for instance, alliances have ranged from an ad hoc coalition to promote airbags, to Advocates for Auto and Highway Safety, to the Coalition for Consumer Health and Safety. The permanence of these coalitions is closely related to the scope of their issue interest. The informal coalition to promote airbags was disbanded after car manufacturers agreed to install these safety devices. Advocates and the Coalition for Consumer Health and Safety have now been active for eight years. When motor vehicle safety and insurer loss control are not congruent, consumer-insurer coalitions may undergo stress.

The extent to which coalitions are institutionalized relates closely to their permanence. Ad hoc coalitions rarely are independently staffed, often do not have their own letterhead, and practically never are incorporated. The more permanent coalitions, however, are separately incorporated and staffed.

In the past three decades, consumer advocates have increasingly been willing to form coalitions with business groups. The formal consumer-insurer alliances, for example, all were established in the past decade. In the 1960s and early 1970s, advocates were often reluctant to work closely with business for philosophical and political reasons. In this period, many advocates considered business groups to be untrustworthy partners who were usually opposed to the consumer interest. Moreover, in this heyday of consumerism, consumer groups often could successfully advocate new consumer protections without assistance from business groups. Such advocacy, however, grew increasingly difficult in the 1970s and early 1980s, first because business learned how to organize effective opposition, then because conservative Republicans gained control of the executive branch of the federal government. Increased isolation encouraged advocates to consider seriously alliances with business groups who could contribute resources and access to pro-business policymakers. At the same time, advocates developed a more sophisticated view of business, increasingly recognizing the diversity of business interests and their not infrequent congruence with consumer interests.

Benefits and Risks

Coalitions have the potential to expand advocate influence over government decisions because they increase access to resources and to a broader range of policymakers, and because they can impress opinion leaders and policymakers. Consumer groups, for example, rarely can afford newspaper ads, let alone those that run on radio and television. In 1995, several advocacy organizations collaborated with long-distance phone companies to produce and extensively air television ads opposing congressional legislation favored by local phone companies. This alliance also gave consumer advocates access to a broader range of legislators, which was especially important since Republicans controlled Congress. In addition, this consumer-business coalition made it more difficult for opinion leaders and policymakers who favored broad telecommunications deregulation to dismiss criticisms of this deregulation.

Coalitions, especially those with business groups, also carry the risks of weakening a consumer position and jeopardizing the integrity of consumer advocates. Since consumer and business interests are rarely perfectly congruent, the development of joint positions usually involves compromise. As the price for support from the American Insurance Association, consumer advocates were forced to accept substantial modification of the insurance industry's antitrust exemption, rather than its outright repeal. In addition, as a coalition advocates its position, additional compromises may be made on the insistence of business groups who may want immediate legislative relief or may not wish to take a confrontational stand with legislators. At times, the coalition of consumer groups and long-distance phone companies ceased to function as the long-distance carriers tried to negotiate their own deal with Congress and other interest groups within the telecommunications industry. What held this coalition together, in large measure, was the unwillingness of the opposition, local phone companies, to compromise their positions.

Consumer alliances with interest groups may also threaten the integrity, or at least the perceived integrity, of consumer advocates. The financial support by trial lawyers of some consumer groups, with whom they work in legislative coalitions, has received much press attention. Whether or not this support has biased the positions of advocates, it has certainly called into question the independence of these groups on issues affecting the trial bar. Such questions have also arisen when consumer groups allied with labor unions favored protectionist measures or even when these groups abstained from involvement in trade issues.

Some critics have suggested that partnerships with business may moderate advocates' criticisms of corporate positions or of capitalism itself. But consumer advocates have rarely criticized the nature of the free enterprise system. They have striven, rather, to enhance consumer sovereignty within a private marketplace through the promotion of consumer information, protections against deceptive and unconscionable sales practices, health and safety safeguards, competition, and when competition fails, economic regulation. Their most radical goal has been promotion of nonprofit consumer cooperatives, which for nearly a century, have coexisted with private firms in free markets.

Coalitions have clearly enhanced the political influence of consumer advocates. Moreover, they have become an increasingly important strategy for advocates as the political environment has grown less supportive of new consumer protections. On the other hand, consumer participants in these coalitions must remain continuously aware of the risks involved. The greatest asset of the consumer movement is the widespread perception that it represents only the consumer interest. To the extent that this perception is compromised, the overall influence of consumer advocates will lessen and be difficult to recover.

— Stephen Brobeck, Robert N. Mayer

Readings

Mayer, Robert N. (1988). "When Businesses Oppose Businesses in Support of Consumerist Goals." *Journal of Consumer Policy.* 11: 375–394.

Vogel, David, and Mark V. Nadel (1976). "The Consumer Coalition: Dimensions of Political Conflict." In R. N. Katz, ed. *Protecting the Consumer Interest: Private Initiative and Public Response.* Cambridge, MA: Ballinger Publishing Co. 7–28.

Community Nutrition Institute

The Community Nutrition Institute (CNI) began in the fall of 1969 with the publication of *CNI Weekly News,* later renamed *Nutrition Week.* The newsletter, published continuously for the past twenty-seven years, is the intellectual and financial heart of CNI. Its mission is to inform members and a newly emerging profession of managers of food and nutrition programs about nutritional issues.

Rodney E. Leonard started and was the first editor of *Nutrition Week.* When CNI was organized as a nonprofit 501(c)(3) organization in 1970, he became its executive director and has held that position until the present. Before organizing CNI, Leonard worked in the federal government, including serving as deputy director of the U.S. Office of Consumer Affairs.

Subscriptions to *Nutrition Week* are paid, and the newsletter generates a consistent income base around which other programs and activities arise that enable CNI to extend its educational and advocacy goals. Those goals include the development of the concept of community nutrition and support for public policies that carry forward the concept, especially programs to insure access to an adequate diet for groups at nutritional risk, regulatory programs in food safety and their implementation at federal and state levels, development of and funding for research programs in human nutrition and health, provision of nutrition education resources based on human genetics, and securing international agreements on procedures establishing product standards to enable American citizens to decide levels of acceptable risk from chemicals and substances in the foods they eat and the environment of their community. Projects related to educational and advocacy goals are funded through government contracts, foundation grants, and individual contributions.

The annual budget for CNI fluctuates yearly but has hovered recently around $400,000. About one-third of CNI income is from publications, and the remainder from foundation grants and contributions.

CNI is not a membership organization, although the needs of subscribers and readers of *Nutrition Week* guide the activities and direction of the organization. CNI develops projects with discrete objectives that generate their own funding, such as litigation to improve safety in meat and poultry inspection or advocacy for citizen participation in developing global standards, which are collected in Codex Alimentarius. While the executive director is the final authority on questions of policy and program activity, the staff has broad discretion in directing and guiding individual projects.

From an organizational perspective, the most notable accomplishment is the twenty-seven-year history of *Nutrition Week* as the publication of record in nutrition policy and management. In addition, CNI conceived and lobbied for the WIC program (Special Supplemental Nutrition Program for Women, Infants and Children) in 1970 to provide government-subsidized nutritional supplements to a key group at nutrition risk in America. CNI was responsible for designing the training program for the Older American Nutrition program, writing the training manuals, and training the first program managers in hundreds of communities in some twenty-five states during the mid- and late 1970s. CNI sponsored the first graduate intern program for nutritionists to become managers of local school food programs. The first nutrition labeling system implemented by the Food and Drug Administration (FDA) was developed by CNI in the 1970s, and CNI created the format still used by the FDA to select and train individuals who participate as citizen advisers in agency activities. Litigation initiated by CNI on food safety rules and on citizen participation in rulemaking initiated by CNI reached the U.S. Supreme Court several times and has become part of case law cited today. CNI helped launch World Food Day, a national educational effort to organize community activities, and organized a coalition of some 400 community-based organizations with CARE to support and promote the House Select Committee on Hunger.

CNI's focus is to link the local community and its residents with policies and programs of the national government, and to make government more open and responsive to people in the communities where they live. When food programs were new and hunger was prevalent, few people realized that there was neither staff nor local structure to manage and deliver nutrition services, other than those responsible for meals for schoolchildren. Food stamps had to be managed locally through the welfare agency, child nutrition through the education department, and WIC through the public health department. A management structure for meals for the elderly had to be created as a totally new community service. One result is that today, for example, WIC is the largest single employer of newly graduated nutritionists in the United States.

CNI, through *Nutrition Week* and through its advocacy and training activities, has helped create the field of community nutrition and nurture a professional managerial group in community nutrition programs. In the process, CNI has been the training ground for persons who occupy key leadership positions in federal programs in or related to nutrition. Bob Greenstein came to Washington as associate editor of *Nutrition Week,* learned food policy at CNI, became administrator of food programs under President Carter, and now directs a major public policy organization. Geoff Becker came to Washington also as associate editor, learned food policy, moved on to the Congressional Research Service, and now is director of the section analyzing food and agriculture policies and programs. Ellen Haas, formerly undersecretary of agriculture for food programs, and several key assistants started their Washington careers at CNI.

CNI has played a reformist role as a national consumer organization. This role is largely limited to focusing public attention through press relations, nagging Congress in public hearings, and proposing rules for action by government agencies.

— Rodney E. Leonard

Reading

Jeffs, Angela (1991). "Agitating for Consumer Awareness: Is the Food You're Eating Fit for Consumption?" *Agricultural Times of Japan.* (October): 1ff.

Community Organizations

Community organizers have accomplished much over the past three decades. They have built four influential national networks of grassroots groups, have nurtured a dozen training centers, and have greatly increased the tactical tools of citizen action. Moreover, community organizing has been celebrated as embodying visions of public philosophy ranging from civic republicanism to progressive populism to the cooperative commonwealth.

The label "community organizing" has been attached to a variety of activities drawing on disparate traditions and historical periods. The turn-of-the century settlement house movement, exemplified by Jane Addams's Hull House in Chicago, continues to influence social workers with its example of neighborhood improvement and social uplift. Saul Alinsky was more attracted to the militant alternative modeled by the Congress of Industrial Organizations (CIO) union drives and the radical neighborhood organizing of unemployed councils in the late 1930s.

Tactics of nonviolent direct action were refined from the mid-1950s through the 1960s by the civil rights movement in the South, which mobilized networks of local black churches, the National Association for the Advancement of Colored People (NAACP) chapters, and black colleges, with assistance from such movement catalysts as the Highlander Center and the Fellowship for Reconciliation. Activism by civil rights workers inspired New Left community organizing projects under the banners of "power to the people" and "let the people decide." Even the federal War on Poverty's Community Action Program sporadically encouraged organizing to achieve its mandate of the "maximum feasible participation" of the poor.

Around 1970, four national networks began to coalesce and develop systematic and distinctive approaches to community organizing: Industrial Areas Foundation (IAF), ACORN (Association of Community Organizations for Reform Now), Citizen Action, and National People's Action. Each was indebted, in greater or lesser degree, to Alinsky and his early organizing programs in Chicago through IAF.

Many influential organizers, including Tom Gaudette and Fred Ross, Sr., developed their characteristic approaches based on experiences with Alinsky's projects. With IAF support, Ross founded the Community Service Organization in California in 1949, enlisting talented young organizers Cesar Chavez and Dolores Huerta to develop a network of organizations in Mexican-American communities, and later worked with them in the United Farm Workers union. Although Alinsky and many others have argued that community organizing is a discipline distinct from wider social movements, his early projects drew energy and inspiration from such movements: Chicago's Back of the Yard Neighborhood Council was established in 1939 during the Packinghouse Workers organizing drive, and civil rights activities energized such 1960s projects as The Woodlawn Organization in Chicago and FIGHT in Rochester.

Methodical training of community organizers can be dated from 1969, when Midas Muffler founder Gordon Sherman gave Alinsky a sizable grant through IAF. Following Alinsky's death in 1972, Ed Chambers continued the program, making training the heart of IAF's expanded organizing activity, which was centered on federations of religious parishes and congregations. IAF's most successful projects have been based in Texas, where Communities Organized for Public Service (COPS) in San Antonio helped elect Henry Cisneros as the city's first Hispanic mayor. IAF state director Ernesto Cortes has built a powerful network of six affiliates, collectively known as Texas Interfaith. IAF's East Brooklyn Congregations set up Nehemiah Homes to build 21,000 low-cost houses and become a model for federal housing assistance. Baltimore's BUILD has tackled education, jobs, and housing.

ACORN began in 1970 as a spin-off from the National Welfare Rights Organization, founded by George Wiley, who enlisted civil rights workers and trained them in an Alinsky-influenced program at Syracuse University. From a base in Arkansas, Wade Rathke and Gary Delgado developed a replicable model of forming membership organizations and developing leaders in low-income neighborhoods, which relied heavily on young middle-class staff working for subsistence wages. ACORN has established local housing corporations to rehabilitate homes, and has successfully pressured banks to provide mortgages and home improvement loans in low-income communities. The Institute for Social Justice serves as ACORN's training arm.

Also focused on housing, former IAF organizer Shel Trapp and community activist Gale Cincotta founded National People's Action (NPA) and its associated National Training and Information Center in Chicago in 1972 to coordinate a loose network of neighborhood, church, union, farm, and seniors' organizations. Emphasizing campaigns against insurance and bank "redlining," NPA helped pass the Home Mortgage Disclosure Act of 1975, the Community Reinvestment Act of 1977, and the National Affordable Housing Act of 1990.

Inspired by their experience with the civil rights, women's, New Left, and labor movements, Heather Booth and Steve Max founded the Midwest Academy in Chicago in 1973 and later the associated Citizen Action network. Citizen Action affiliates include both statewide membership organizations with local chapters (like Massachusetts Fair Share) and statewide coalitions of labor, citizen, farm, and senior organizations (like Ohio Public Interest Campaign). All have used door-to-door canvassing to recruit members and raise money. Citizen Action has done extensive electoral work in support of Democratic candidates.

Grassroots organizations outside the national networks have often found it difficult to move beyond an initial period of enthusiasm and success to acquire disciplined approaches for sustaining and developing their organizations. The need to nurture independent groups has led to the growing importance of training and technical assistance centers—what Gary Delgado calls "training intermediaries." The Highlander Center near Knoxville, Tennessee, an early example founded in the 1930s by Myles Horton, represented a unique educational approach to grassroots leadership development. Mike Miller's Organize Training Center in San Francisco draws on his background as a civil rights worker and as an IAF organizer. Si Kahn's Grassroots Leadership in the Carolinas has initiated an innovative "barriers and bridges" project to deal with such diversity issues as racism, sexism, and homophobia.

The Center for Third World Organizing, founded by ACORN veteran Delgado, works with a network of organizations in communities of color. The Western States Center in Portland serves groups in eight Rocky Mountain and Pacific Northwest states, providing training conferences for activists and progressive public officials. The Center for Community Change, headquartered in Washington, D.C., provides technical assistance to community groups across the country. Lois Gibbs's Citizens Clearinghouse for Hazardous Wastes serves a similar function for grassroots groups in the environmental justice movement.

Populism has proved to be a double-edged sword: during the 1980s, the religious and populist right borrowed many techniques from progressive community organizers. In a parallel to the IAF model, fundamentalist church networks were mobilized by Beverly LaHaye's Concerned Women for America, Pat Robertson's Christian Coalition, and Donald Wildmon's American Family Association to combat abortion rights, pornography, gay and lesbian rights, secularism in the public schools, and other manifestations of liberalism.

On a state level, groups such as Lon Mabon's Oregon Citizens Alliance built campaigns against gay and lesbian rights on a network of fundamentalist congregations. Also, Alan Gottlieb and Ron Arnold adapted their Center for the Defense of Free Enterprise in Bellevue, Washington, as a right-wing "training intermediary" to coordinate the Wise Use Movement, a counterenvironmentalist network of ranching, mining, timber, and property owner associations, as well as hunting, motorcycling, and off-road vehicle clubs.

Community organizing entered the 1990s with no single guru, no vanguard organization, and no hegemonic model. Instead, a multiplicity of networks followed a variety of approaches in diverse situations with distinctive objectives. Grassroots organizations explored new partnerships, alliances, and relationships—with universities, with business, and with other nonprofit groups—including legal service providers and advocacy think tanks. Community activists faced the most friendly federal executive branch in years, yet one facing severe budgetary constraints that limited financial support to community organizations.

Although the field of community organization has tactical sophistication, it still lacks a strategic understanding of how significant reforms are won in American society. Grassroots organizers still fail to understand the importance of forging alliances with potential allies, including labor unions, other social movements, and the state and local chapters of national activist organizations with middle- and upper-middle-class members.

— David Walls

See also

Association of Community Organizations for Reform Now (ACORN); Center for Community Change; Citizen Action.

Readings

Betten, Neil, and Michael J. Austin (1990). *The Roots of Community Organizing, 1917–1939*. Philadelphia: Temple University Press.

Boyte, Harry C. (1980). *The Backyard Revolution: Understanding the New Citizen Movement*. Philadelphia: Temple University Press.

Community Reinvestment

The Community Reinvestment Act (CRA) was adopted in 1977 to curb "redlining," the discriminatory mortgage lending practice whereby lenders refuse to make loans to certain geographic areas based on the racial or ethnic composition of those areas or the age of their housing stock. The law reflected the congressional judgment that lending institutions were overlooking important credit needs within their local communities and that bank regulators were not adequately addressing these unmet needs.

The CRA is premised on the view that, although they are privately capitalized, banks and savings institutions are subject to an underlying charter obligation to serve the banking needs of their local communities. These public obligations are part of the quid pro quo for the extensive government backing that is provided to these types of financial institutions—federal backing for deposit insurance and access to the Federal Reserve System's lender of last resort facility. The CRA's enactment also represented a rebuke to federal banking supervisors for their lack of interest in policing the industry's lending practices. The CRA appears to have been aimed as much at modifying the behavior, norms, and attitudes of the regulators as it was at changing the practices of lenders.

The CRA clarifies the public responsibilities of federally insured financial institutions to their local communities. The law does this in three ways. First, it affirms the obligation of banks and savings institutions to help meet the credit needs (both housing and nonhousing) of the entire communities in which they are chartered, including low- and moderate-income areas. Second, the CRA directs banking and thrift regulators to evaluate, as part of their regular on-site examination, the extent to which lenders are meeting local credit needs. Regulations issued jointly by the four agencies that implement the law require them to rate these institutions on the basis of their community reinvestment records. Third, the CRA permits regulators to impose sanctions on lenders with weak records. The law directs the appropriate federal banking agency to "take [an institution's community reinvestment record] into account in its evaluation of an application for a deposit facility by such institution."

Regulations for the CRA generally focus on assessing the lender's community reinvestment record in serving underserved credit needs. Bank examiners are directed to look at thirteen assessment factors, which are grouped into five performance categories. Lenders are rated for their record within each performance category and then given one of four possible composite ratings to reflect their overall CRA performance: outstanding, satisfactory, needs improvement, and substantial noncompliance.

The CRA exam cycles vary by agency and by the size of the lending institutions. The most recent CRA ratings affect the frequency of the exam cycle—ranging from six months for lenders with poor performance ratings on their last exams, to twenty-four months for large national banks, to as long as six or seven years for small community banks. To a large extent, examiners rely on information provided by the lending institutions themselves. Procedures permit examiners to talk to community groups and public agencies about the community reinvestment records of local lenders. These procedures, however, are used with varying frequency, depending on the particular agency and the proclivities of the individual examiner.

Almost from the outset, community advocates criticized the way in which regulators enforced the CRA. The agencies were viewed as being too cozy and too protective of the institutions they supervise to enforce the new requirements effectively. In 1988, this laxity in enforcement was severely criticized in hearings initiated by Senator William Proxmire, then chairman of the Senate Banking Committee and the law's original sponsor. Although Proxmire's committee made no formal recommendations, the hearings appear to have had an impact on regulatory enforcement. Within twelve months, the four agencies issued new CRA policy guidelines in which they emphasized that deeds and not merely promises would receive greater weight in future CRA examinations. In the following year, Congress amended the CRA to require that federal regulators disclose their written CRA evaluations and ratings for individual lenders. The disclosure requirement was intended to spur reforms in the CRA evaluation process.

From the standpoint of grassroots citizens' organizations, the most important feature of the CRA has been that it provides implicit standing for these groups to intervene in lender expansion application proceedings. Banking law, either by statute or regulation, routinely provides opportunities for public comment on pending financial institution expansion requests (mergers, acquisitions, branch openings, and relocations of existing facilities). To reach a final decision, regulators have broad discretion in weighing an applicant's record, but evidence presented through the public comment process must be reviewed. While the CRA itself is vague and the regulatory process complex, the law has provided community groups with substantial leverage to end disinvestment practices and to obtain commitments from lenders to undertake new community reinvestment initiatives.

When an expansion application is submitted by a lender with a weak CRA record, the regulators have the option to deny the request or approve the request conditioned upon the applicant undertaking specific actions to improve its record. The Center for Community Change, a national nonprofit organization that advises community groups involved in CRA activities, estimates that, since the CRA's inception in 1978, federal regulators have denied approximately fifteen expansion requests on CRA grounds and granted conditional approval imposing CRA requirements in roughly fifteen to sixty cases.

Despite its popularity with local groups, the CRA challenge has rarely worked the way its drafters originally envisioned it would. During the law's initial ten years, only eight of an estimated 40,000 expansion applications acted upon by federal regulators were denied on CRA grounds. Instead, the effectiveness of the CRA challenge process usually rests with the ability of the community group leaders to use the law to negotiate an agreement under which applicants make specific commitments to improve their community reinvestment records. If such an agreement is reached, the community group protester withdraws its challenge, and the application continues to be processed by the regulator.

It is estimated that, from the CRA's enactment to 1992, community groups negotiated more than $7.5 billion in commitments from lenders. Moreover, in this period lenders made an additional $23 billion worth of unilateral commitments to community development lending while their expansion requests were pending before federal bodies. Thus, the CRA has contributed to total commitments in excess of $30 billion to low- and moderate-income communities throughout the country.

Public disclosure of the CRA ratings and evaluations appears to have stimulated new approaches for encouraging improvements in lender performance. One strategy centers on using the placement of deposits and investments in banking institutions with demonstrated commitments to community reinvestment. "Greenlining" strategies were employed to deter redlining even prior to the CRA's enactment, and state and local units of government have experimented with the placement of public funds based on social criteria. However, in the past these strategies were greatly handicapped by the lack of uniform criteria for rating individual lenders.

Seventeen state governments and nine large cities have instituted some type of linked deposit program that ties the placement of public funds to some specific lending activity requirements. Cincinnati, Los Angeles, Newark, New York, Pittsburgh, and St. Paul are among the municipalities whose linked deposit ordinances use the CRA evaluations as part of their weighting criteria. Moreover, the public disclosure requirements have opened up the opportunities for churches, labor unions, professional associations, and charitable organizations to use the CRA performance ratings to guide them on the placement of their funds.

— Allen J. Fishbein

See also

Center for Community Change.

Readings

Fishbein, Allen J. (1993). "The Community Reinvestment Act after Fifteen Years: It Works, But Strengthened Federal Enforcement Is Needed." *Fordham Urban Law Journal*. 20 (2): 293–310.

Scharfenberg, Kirk (1980). "The Community as Bank Examiner." *Working Papers for a New Society.* (September/October): 30–35.

Competition

See Antitrust Protections; Deregulation, Economic.

Complaints, Consumer

See Disputes and Dispute Resolution.

Conference of Consumer Organizations

The Conference of Consumer Organizations (COCO) is a national umbrella consumer organization that was a spin-off from the Consumer Federation of America. It included state and local groups that were often led by academics.

In the mid-1960s, a planning committee of state and local consumer leaders and educators met over a two-year period in an effort to form a national, unifying consumer body. In 1967, concluding that they were not able to mobilize sufficient resources to launch this organization, they joined with a national committee of Washington, D.C.–based consumer and union leaders who had already been planning Consumer Assembly, the first national consumer conference. Encouraged and sponsored by the president's special assistant for consumer affairs, Esther Peterson, this assembly was held in late 1967. Its success helped persuade planners to create the Consumer Federation of America (CFA), an association of pro-consumer organizations. CFA held its first annual meeting in April of 1968. Father Robert McEwen from the Massachusetts Consumer Association, who had chaired the planning committee, was elected the organization's first president.

After a few years, some state and local leaders became dissatisfied with CFA's concentration on national issues and legislation to the neglect of state and local organization needs. They were also unhappy with the domination of the organization by large national groups, especially labor unions.

In 1973, a group of the state leaders, gathered under the leadership of Currin Shields, the head of the Arizona Consumer Council, met twice—in Wisconsin and in Arizona. At a national symposium, organized by Shields and held in Tucson, they voted to establish a new consumer umbrella organization to be called the Conference of Consumer Organizations. The founding members were representatives from consumer groups in Arizona, Massachusetts, Nevada, Missouri, Virginia, New York, Pittsburgh, and Texas.

COCO was organized as a nonprofit, educational corporation "to encourage and assist in the formation and development of community and state consumer associations and agencies." The organization also defined as goals the fostering of dialogue with other segments of business and the public, and the promotion of educational programs to strengthen grassroots organizations. The original incorporators and members of the steering committee were Lynn Jordan of Virginia, McEwen of Massachusetts, and Shields of Arizona.

COCO has never had a paid, full-time staff. The dialogue and communication is accomplished by a monthly newsletter called *COCO intercom*. Shields, a professor at the University of Arizona, was chairman from 1973 to 1976; Louis Meyer, a professor at Edinboro State College, was chairman from 1977 to 1985; and McEwen, a professor at Boston College, was chairman from 1985 to 1996. Dues and subscription prices for the newsletter have always been $10 for individuals and $30 for organizations. The number of members and subscribers has usually ranged between 300 and 350.

The new group pledged to do three things that they felt other consumer organizations had refused or failed to do. They were to engage in dialogues with industry, including participation in joint consumer-industry advisory panels; to include government consumer agency officials in its membership; and to allow participation by consumer affairs officers of companies in COCO meetings and discussions.

In its early years, COCO sponsored joint meetings with the Direct Selling Association, the Outdoor Power Equipment Association, the American Petroleum Institute, the natural gas industry, the Electronic Industries Association, the Pennsylvania Power and Light Co., and AT&T. Meetings with the Electronic Industries, the gas industry, and AT&T have lasted until the present.

The first dialogue with AT&T was held in December 1975. It led to regular meetings with AT&T, typically five or six a year. Before divestiture broke up the phone company, the meetings were often held in different areas of the country, sponsored by a host local operating company in conjunction with the consumer affairs staff of AT&T. Soon, at the urging of central AT&T headquarters, almost every operating company had a consumer advisory panel of its own and a vice president of consumer affairs, who met regularly with counterparts from other companies in a Consumer Affairs Committee. In the late 1980s, the name of this COCO panel was changed to the AT&T Consumer Advisory Panel.

During the 1970s, COCO sponsored annual national meetings as well as numerous workshops and regional conferences. The annual meetings in 1976 and 1977 were both held in Tucson and cosponsored by the Arizona Consumer Council. COCO leaders raised funds for these events that permitted most consumer representatives to attend the conferences for free. But during the 1980s, shrinking funds and escalating costs made it impossible to continue the conferences. Since then, the principal vehicle for information and support has been the newsletter, *COCO intercom*, which has increasingly emphasized consumer advice and opinion.

— Robert J. McEwen

See also

Consumer Federation of America; State and Local Consumer Organizations.

Reading

Swanston, Walterene (1972). "Consumer Federation Waging Spirited Battle for Survival." *National Journal*. 4 (July 8): 1126–1136.

Congress and Consumer Protection

Periods of consumer activism in Congress have been cyclical, coming and going with shifting public mood and political fortune. While these changes tend to make consumer protection seem like a new issue at certain times, this protection has been a governmental responsibility and a subject of congressional interest since the earliest days of the Republic. Consumer protection in Congress has always reflected congressional philosophy about the appropriate role of government in the economy.

Origins

The Constitution explicitly empowers Congress to "fix the Standard of Weights and Measures." However, the primary purpose of such measures was to assure the orderly flow of commerce. The first manifestation of an explicit consumer interest was in the Progressive era. During that time, stretching roughly from the 1880s to 1910, Congress protected consumers against monopoly power in transportation with the Interstate Commerce Act and against monopolies more generally with the Sherman and Clayton antitrust laws.

Yet, it is in the food and drug controversies of the early part of the century that consumer politics and policy resemble controversies from the late 1960s to the present. For several years prior to the passage of the Pure Food and Drug Act in 1906, Dr. Harvey Wiley, chief chemist of the U.S. Department of Agriculture, relentlessly campaigned for legislation in Congress and before the public. Wiley gained considerable fame by establishing a "poison squad," a group of volunteers who tested the effects of preservatives by ingesting them. Legislation was also pushed by labor groups, "good government" groups, and the American Medical Association. Despite the blue-ribbon backing, pure food and drug legislation, which was passed twice in the House of Representatives, languished in the Senate. Ultimately, a much weakened bill passed the Senate, only then to be stalled in the House. The matter appeared deadlocked until the publication of Upton Sinclair's *The Jungle*, a 1906 novel that shocked the nation with its revelations of filth in the meat-packing industry. The book was quickly followed by a presidential study, which confirmed Sinclair's account. The scandal, and carefully applied pressure by President Theodore Roosevelt, pressured a still deadlocked Congress to pass first the Meat Inspection Act of 1906 and then the Pure Food and Drug Act. The pattern was set: scandal and anger at large corporations, skillfully manipulated by a president and the press, forced Congress to pass consumer legislation.

A similar pattern emerged during the next episode of important congressional action on a consumer issue—the passage of the Federal Food, Drug, and Cosmetic Act in 1938. Five years of congressional attention to problems of false advertising and dangerous drugs and cosmetics still had not led to legislation when 107 persons died as a result of taking a medicine called elixir sulfanilamide, which contained a toxic solvent. Once again, a weak bill was beefed up in the wake of a scandal, and a different President Roosevelt, Franklin, signed the bill into law on June 25, 1938. Together with amendments to the Federal Trade Act in the same year, Congress firmly established federal regulation of advertising and regulation of a broad category of consumer products. As with the original food and drug legislation during the Progressive period, the 1938 legislation should be seen as a product of a time of activist government—the New Deal.

The Ralph Nader Era

In the late 1960s and early 1970s, Congress was the locus of action not only in passing legislation but also in initiating it. From 1962 through 1972, Congress perceived a need and responded to public pressure for consumer protection measures in three ways. First, the legislature passed a wide array of regulatory measures intended to improve consumer health and safety as well as to provide better information and economic protection. The major measures included the Automobile Safety Act, Kefauver-Harris Drug Amendments, Wholesome Poultry Act, Fair Packaging and Labeling Act, and the Consumer Credit Protection Act.

Second, Congress created a new agency, the Consumer Product Safety Commission (CPSC), and significantly increased the power and role of existing agencies, particularly the Food and Drug Administration (FDA) and the Federal Trade Commission (FTC). The FDA was given the power to regulate not only the safety of drugs, but their effectiveness as well—a substantial increase in the agency's scope. The FTC, under the Magnuson-Moss Act, was empowered to promulgate regulations applicable to trade practices in an entire industry, rather than just case by case. There were also attempts in Congress in the 1970s to create a "Department of Consumers," but those efforts never succeeded.

Third, Congress acted as a "bully pulpit" through holding well-publicized hearings on a variety of consumer issues. Those hearings increased public support for the theory that businesses could and should be held more accountable for the safety of products and for business practices such as advertising. Probably the most profound shift was the public acceptance of the notion that injuries and deaths in automobile accidents were due in part to design features of cars, and that manufacturers have a responsibility, which could be mandated by government, to make their products safer.

These measures were connected not only by being generally considered as consumer protection laws, but also by having a common group of supporters in Congress. This group of supporters, all Democrats, voted consistently, and as a coherent block, for consumerist measures. During this period, the most pro-consumer and active senators were Paul

Douglas (D-IL), Lee Metcalf (D-MT), Warren Magnuson (D-WA), Gaylord Nelson (D-WI), Abraham Ribicoff (D-CT), and Thomas Dodd (D-CT). In the House of Representatives, the consumer champions were Benjamin Rosenthal (D-NY), Leonor Sullivan (D-MO), Harley Staggers (D-WV), Neal Smith (D-IA), Richard Ottinger (D-NY), and Thomas Foley (D-WA).

During this time, consumer protection was considered good politics. While the activists no doubt believed that the laws they enacted were sound and necessary policy, they also perceived that their pro-consumer stance was popular with the electorate. Preceding one election, Senator Magnuson had billboards around Seattle proclaiming "Magnuson's Law—Auto Safety," "Magnuson's Law—No Flammable Fabrics," and other messages. His slogan during his 1968 reelection campaign was "Keep the Big Boys Honest."

Groups such as Consumers Union, the Consumer Federation of America, and others were important as sources of information and legitimacy despite their limited resources and political power. It is a curious facet of American politics that a lone crusader such as Ralph Nader could have defeated far better financed industry lobbyists on so many fronts. In fact, Nader and other consumer advocates were not only lobbyists from the outside but also key parts of coalitions supporting the consumer-oriented members of Congress. These congressmen and senators were themselves key consumer activists bringing to bear their own considerable prestige and staff resources. These members of Congress gained recognition and public stature by becoming "policy entrepreneurs" on behalf of a new and popular issue. Indeed, unlike most other areas of public policy, consumer protection measures were usually initiated by Congress rather than by the president.

Business Counterattack

Passing consumer legislation that was usually opposed by business interests was difficult in the first place; it proved equally difficult to maintain pro-consumer policies in Congress. For example, the CPSC was created under legislation that required it to be periodically reauthorized by Congress. By the time it was up for reauthorization in 1981, a concerted effort was made to abolish the agency, an effort supported by the Reagan administration. The agency survived, but its new authorizing legislation called on the CPSC to rely more on voluntary standards and less on regulation.

An even more dramatic turnabout took place with regard to the FTC. Having been granted new powers in 1974, the FTC entered into a period of activism. It began investigations and proposed consumer protection regulations affecting some of the most powerful industries in the country—insurance, the legal and medical professions, automobiles, and pharmaceuticals. After the FTC began an inquiry into television commercials aimed at children, industry opposition coalesced. A lobbying coalition of more than three dozen companies and trade associations was arrayed against the commission in Congress on this proceeding alone, and soon thereafter, just about every industry affected by the commission furiously and successfully sought relief in Congress. Congress responded by passing legislation ending certain FTC investigations, including children's television advertising, and by establishing closer congressional control over all commission activities. In short, after a period of great consumer protection activism, Congress retreated significantly.

The retreat occurred for several reasons. First, Congress gave mixed signals to the consumer protection agencies. It was the Appropriations Committees that requested the FTC to undertake the children's advertising initiative and other committees that sought to shut it down. Secondly, leadership of key congressional committees changed, and consumer "entrepreneurs" left the scene. Finally, industry pressure on Congress increased. While business interests opposed creation of the CPSC and the expansion of the FTC's powers, the threat was still somewhat abstract. Once particular products and businesses became the target of specific regulation, they had much greater reason to enter the political fray—and did so with great success. The period of increased consumer protection regulation as an active and successful issue in Congress slowed down by the late 1970s, and largely evaporated during the Reagan administration in the 1980s. During the latter period, the principal role of congressional consumer advocates—notably, Senator Howard Metzenbaum (D-OH), Representative Henry Waxman (D-CA), and Representative Edward Markey (D-MA)—was to defend existing consumer protections from attack.

Redefinition and Confusion

Consumer protection reemerged as an issue in the late 1980s. Congress sought to protect consumers from certain adverse effects of deregulated industries, especially telecommunications and banking. It also sought to respond to growing consumer concerns about certain health and safety threats. On the other hand, it became more aware of the difficulty of defining a consumer interest when there were often trade-offs (e.g., cost versus safety) and one consumer's benefit might be another consumer's cost (e.g., low-income subsidies paid largely by the middle class).

Growing dissatisfaction by consumers against cable television monopolies persuaded Congress to reregulate cable rates in 1992 over a presidential veto. Increasing irritation by consumers against recently deregulated banks for pursuing profit-maximization strategies (e.g., raising fees, increasing check holds) encouraged the legislature to pass several new consumer banking protections—limits on check holds, curbs on home equity loan practices, and required savings disclosures. All of these new protections were approved by Democratic Congresses. While the Republican Congress that was elected in 1994 largely deregulated cable television rates (as part of comprehensive telecommunications legislation), despite vigorous bank lobbying, to date it has not weakened the consumer banking protections.

Growing public concern about health and safety, especially among the influential upper-middle class, also persuaded Congress to approve new protections targeted at types of products. In 1989, the legislature banned smoking on all domestic airline flights; in 1990, it mandated new disclosures of the nutritional contents of food. And in 1996, it approved safe drinking water legislation.

On the other hand, members of Congress were always aware that new health and safety protections often imposed costs not only on businesses but also on certain consumers. Many in Congress argued, for example, that regulation of pharmaceuticals and medical devices actually ended up harming consumers because such regulation stifled innovation by slowing the introduction of valuable drugs and medical devices. Such drugs and devices, it was alleged, had life-saving potential. Hearings were held in both houses of Congress around that theme. Moreover, there was a concerted public advertising campaign mounted by conservative public interest groups explicitly charging the FDA with killing consumers through bureaucratic inaction. For the first time since the original legislation in 1906, Congress seriously considered legislation to reduce the FDA's regulatory authority over drugs and devices.

Another controversial consumer issue that received renewed attention after 1994 was tort reform—proposed changes in laws allowing consumers to sue in order to receive compensation from damages caused by defective products, medical malpractice, and fraudulent business practices. Proponents of curbs on the ability of consumers to sue argued that excessive and unjustified litigation was discouraging manufacturers from making new products and raising the price of all consumer products. Against the opposition of most consumer advocates, in 1996 Congress passed legislation that would have curbed consumers' ability to bring product liability lawsuits. Although President Clinton vetoed this legislation, earlier he had signed into law legislation to limit the ability of consumers to sue and recover damages in cases of securities fraud.

While consumer protection in Congress has not been entirely a partisan issue, major consumer legislation has been usually caught up in the conflict between the parties. Moreover, because consumer protection laws establish rights and remedies that, by themselves, consumers cannot obtain in the marketplace, consumer protection in Congress follows the general contours of federal regulation of business. In periods when Congress regulates in order to correct perceived inadequacies in the marketplace, the consumer interest is also advanced. When Congress is more sympathetic to the view that the marketplace requires little if any government intervention, laws advancing the claims and interests of consumers are less likely to pass and are sometimes rolled back.

— Mark V. Nadel

See also

U.S. Consumer Movement: History and Dynamics; Presidents and the Consumer Movement.

Readings

Nadel, Mark V. (1971). *The Politics of Consumer Protection*. Indianapolis: Bobbs-Merrill Co.

Pertschuk, Michael (1982). *Revolt against Regulation*. Berkeley: University of California Press.

Conservation

See Energy Conservation.

Consumer Action

In June 1971, a few volunteers set up Consumer Action's first office in a nook donated by a San Francisco church. Kay Pachtner, student activist and homemaker, organized the fledgling group around the consumer complaints that began to pour in on Consumer Action's first hotline. The individual problems she listened to revealed widespread seller abuses of consumers. Pachtner and crew added a mobile complaint unit in an old van and irreverent public protests to their arsenal. The group found an eager partner in the press.

Consumer Action's ability to focus on both the little and the big pictures is a key element of its evolution, staying power, and growth. Twenty-six years after its inception, Consumer Action still operates a hotline to receive individual complaints, then uses that information to try to change the system through education, legislation, and legal action.

It was an individual complaint that brought Consumer Action to the public's attention a short time after the group's founding. Supporting a woman who had bought a used Jaguar that kept breaking down, Consumer Action set up a picket line in front of San Francisco's British Motors. The car dealership responded by suing the group for $6 million. Consumer Action won the case and the right of aggrieved consumers to picket businesses.

In 1973, after assisting the group as a volunteer, Neil Gendel joined Consumer Action full-time. Gendel, a young lawyer who had worked as a California assistant attorney general, developed a strategy that has been utilized by the group for more than two decades—conducting and publicizing surveys that compare services and prices. One of the most successful surveys, *Break the Banks: A Shoppers Guide to Banking Services*, was published in 1973, bringing the group nationwide recognition and even some revenue. Another report, *Deceptive Packaging*, which was released in 1974, indicted the California Consumer Affairs Department for maintaining a board that was made up of state-licensed tradespeople. Consumer Action continued to publish surveys on topics such as the prices of prescription drugs, bank accounts, credit cards, gasoline, and parking garages. *Consumer Action News*, the group's newsletter, which has been published almost since Consumer Action's founding, has helped publicize the results of this research.

In the mid-1970s, Consumer Action's work expanded beyond complaint handling, protests, and surveys to reform through legislation, regulation, and litigation. It continued to organize high-profile protests such as the 1976 "Lemonstration"—a parade of defective new cars that brought publicity to consumer concerns. But the group also spearheaded a false advertising complaint against Bank of America, resulting in a penalty for the bank, and helped the Federal Trade Commission draft related consumer protection regulations.

Pachtner and Gendel left Consumer Action in the late 1970s (though in the early 1990s, Gendel returned as director of the group's Lead Poisoning Prevention Project). Ken McEldowney, an early staff member, returned as executive director in 1980. McEldowney, a former consumer reporter and a founder of the San Francisco group Media Alliance, expanded the organization's focus to groups with special consumer needs.

These constituencies included low-income residents, who often did not have access to the advice of lawyers and accountants; older persons, who increasingly were the target of unscrupulous marketing tactics; the disabled, whose consumer needs were often ignored; and new citizens arriving from all over the world. Many of the immigrants lived on low incomes, did not speak English well, and were unfamiliar with the United States, making them vulnerable to exploitation by sellers. Consumer Action began to provide these consumers with free, easy-to-read surveys, guides, and fact sheets in English and seven other languages. By the early 1990s, Consumer Action was distributing annually, at no charge, more than one million pieces of information in California.

A key element of the plan to reach communities of color and persons with limited English-speaking ability is Consumer Action's use of multilingual employees who handle consumer complaints in Spanish and Chinese as well as in English. Bilingual outreach staff, based at Consumer Action's Los Angeles and San Francisco offices, work with an expanding network of about 1,900 community-based organizations around California to educate consumers and to identify emerging problems and trends.

Deregulation of the telephone and banking industries created additional problems and concerns for all consumers. For Consumer Action, the need to help consumers deal with these complex issues led to a new focus on the fields of banking, finance, and telecommunications.

In 1989, Consumer Action's Telephone Information Project was set up to provide community agencies and individual consumers with free information about telecommunications services. The project was funded through the Telecommunications Education Trust that had been established by the California Public Utilities Commission with a $16.5 million penalty paid by Pacific Bell for marketing abuses that occurred in the mid-1980s. Like other Telecommunications Education Trust grantees, Consumer Action sought to inform clients about the increasingly complex, changing world of telephone services. In its first four years, the project distributed more than 3 million free publications.

The Telephone Information Project produced a number of fact sheets and guides to phone services, including the *Telephone Users Guide,* a compendium that was updated four times in the early 1990s. The 300-page guide, written by Consumer Action's longtime staff member Michael Heffer, covers phone usage, from telemarketing fraud to privacy protections to technological developments. All of the materials created by Telecommunications Education Trust grantees are housed and distributed by a consumer resource center at Consumer Action's San Francisco offices.

In July 1993, Consumer Action launched a Credit & Finance Project to identify and address credit and finance problems in California. The project places its main focus on the concerns of low-income, minority, immigrant, and senior consumers. The project is funded by court-assessed penalties against Wells Fargo Bank for charging customers excessive credit card fees.

The emphasis of the Credit & Finance Project is on advocacy. It operates Consumer Action's free consumer hotline and produces and distributes fact sheets and statewide pricing surveys. *The Advocacy Report*, a quarterly newsletter intended to inspire action to promote change, debuted in the winter of 1993. The project also coordinates action through its Advocacy Network of community-based organizations and through its regular Advocacy Alerts. Members of the network are encouraged to present a unified voice for consumers on legislative and regulatory matters.

Under McEldowney's direction, Consumer Action moved beyond the barricades and into the boardrooms. Although the group's relationships with business and industry had been completely adversarial in the 1970s, McEldowney concluded that, during the Reagan-Bush years, it made more sense to work with selected corporations rather than to depend entirely on regulatory solutions. Many business groups responded favorably to Consumer Action's emphasis on consumer education; corporate-funded national educational contracts became a new source of funding for the group.

In the 1990s, Consumer Action's focus and influence expanded beyond California to the nation as a whole. The group's network of community-based organizations had grown to include 400 groups around the country, which distributed 500,000 publications annually. Consumer Action's expertise in the areas of banking, finance, and telecommunications, born during the federal deregulation of the 1980s, gave the group an authority recognized by government agencies such as the Federal Communications Commission and the Federal Trade Commission, as well as by the national media. Several times, McEldowney was elected president of the Consumer Federation of America. At present, Consumer Action is developing an online computer service with consumer information in English and other languages, and a national consumer education resource center.

During its first two decades, Consumer Action established itself as an effective advocacy and education group. In its second decade it also grew considerably, from a staff of four with a yearly budget of $80,000 in 1984, to a staff of seventeen and a budget of more than $800,000 in 1996. Two Consumer Action models—bilingual consumer education disseminated through community-based organizations, and comparative pricing surveys—have been widely imitated. By the end of 1995, Consumer Action's longtime focus on banking, finance, and telecommunications had expanded to include issues such as insurance discrimination, vehicle safety, electric deregulation, and the dangers of secondhand smoke, among other topics.

— Linda Sherry

See also

Immigrants as Consumers; State and Local Consumer Organizations.

Readings

Navarro, Mireya (1986). "Consumer Action: Grass Roots to Big Time." *San Francisco Examiner.* (June 18): B, 1ff.

Weinstein, Henry (1975). "Inside a Consumer Group." *New York Times.* (February 1975): III, 7.

Wilson, Gregory, and Elizabeth Brydoff (1980). "Grass Roots Solutions: San Francisco Consumer Action." In Laura Nader, ed. *No Access to Law: Alternatives to the American Judicial System.* New York: Academic Press. 417–459.

Consumer Cooperatives

See Cooperatives, Consumer.

Consumer Credit Counseling Services

See National Foundation for Consumer Credit.

Consumer Economics/Studies

Consumer economics/studies is an academic field in colleges and universities throughout the United States and other countries. It has always been both multidisciplinary and interdisciplinary. The field is multidisciplinary in that it is peopled by scholars trained in a variety of root disciplines as well as those whose formal training is in consumer economics/studies itself. It is multidisciplinary, also, in that research on consumer behavior, consumer markets, and policy is spawned within several disciplines from economics to psychology and law as well as by consumer economics/studies scholars. The field is interdisciplinary in that the content of consumer economics/studies curricula, extension programs, and research draws upon all of the social sciences, as well as law and the natural sciences, in an attempt at integrated understandings and explanations of consumer behavior, consumer markets, and the forces that have an impact on both. Because consumer markets are economic institutions within which consumer behavior occurs, economics is the primary root discipline for the field. Because the consumer is based in the family or constitutes one, consumer behavior can be considered to be one aspect of family behavior. As a result, many consumer economics/studies programs have, for a long time, been closely aligned with, or contained within, family economics and management programs.

Institutionally, the field of consumer economics/studies is organized as departments or programs in universities in the United States and Canada, although there are a few programs in other countries, principally in northern Europe and Southeast Asia. In the United States, most are located within colleges of human ecology (home economics) or colleges of agriculture in land grant and state universities. There are also a few departments and programs in private colleges and universities. Historically, the field has two origins: family economics and management programs within home economics, and consumer education programs within colleges of education and business and a few economics departments. These two roots intertwined and increasingly became one with the formation of the Council on Consumer Information, later renamed the American Council on Consumer Interests (ACCI).

The creation of this council in 1954 was simultaneously a spur to and a result of the field's growth. Because of the intimate connection between the field and ACCI in the last forty years, both the state of the field and the relationship between the field and the consumer movement can partly be analyzed by examining the history of ACCI and its relationships with the consumer movement.

The Field as Reflected by ACCI

The twenty-one charter members of ACCI reflect the heterogeneity of the field. They were mostly consumer educators in colleges of education, business schools, and economics departments along with a few home economists from state and land grant universities, agricultural economists in departments of agricultural economics, consumer researchers in federal research agencies, and leaders of the consumer movement. As disparate as their backgrounds and foci were, however, all were interested in consumer education. The charter members were brought together in 1953 to form ACCI at the instigation of Colston Warne, president of Consumers Union (CU) and "patron saint" of the consumer movement. Expenses for the organizing meeting were paid for by CU. Furthermore, CU underwrote ACCI with annual grants until the late 1960s. ACCI, therefore, was begun as a professional organization serving consumer educators and a few consumer researchers, and was directly subsidized for the first ten to fifteen years of its life by CU. The organizational link between the consumer movement and the field was clear from the beginning.

Not only was there an organizational link between ACCI (and, therefore, the field) and the consumer movement, the early leaders of the consumer movement were also important leaders in the field of consumer economics/studies. Mention has already been made of Colston Warne's pioneering leadership in both the field and the movement. In addition, Father Robert McEwen served ACCI in a number of capacities in the 1960s, including president, but also was a leader in the creation of the Consumer Federation of America (CFA) and became its first president in 1968. ACCI became a member of CFA and remains one. Nearly every charter member of ACCI, plus most of the presidents of ACCI until the mid-1970s, served on the board of directors of CU. The institutional links do not stop there, however. In 1964, ACCI joined the International Organization of Consumers Unions (IOCU), now Consumers International, and continues to send representatives to its meetings. Furthermore, ACCI has been an accredited member of the U.S. Mission to the United Nations at least since 1964 and has been represented by the same individual for the entire time.

Beyond the formal, institutional linkages between the field of consumer economics/studies and the consumer movement, there are the links forged by individual members of the field. People like Persia Campbell, Lillian Mohr, Richard Morse, Stewart Lee, Robert McEwen, and Helen Canoyer, to mention but a few, have all played important parts in the consumer movement. They have advised presidents on consumer policies, served in state government or at the federal level in consumer offices, championed particular consumer protection legislation—such as truth in lending and the abolition of fair trade laws—or served on various national and state consumer complaint organizations established for automobiles and consumer durables. These people have been simultaneously academicians, ACCI members, and consumer advocates or representatives in their own right.

Members of the field and of ACCI, however, maintain that the movement is about education as well as advocacy. That is, not only do consumer markets work better when optimally regulated by legislative law and constrained by civil law and the courts; consumer markets also work better when the consumer is fully informed and educated. Hence, in pursuing its goal of consumer education, the field of consumer economics/studies forms the "education wing" of the consumer movement. In this view, the field is a part of the consumer movement.

As clear as the links among the field, ACCI, and the consumer movement have been and are, the goals of the field, and therefore of ACCI as the professional organization serving it, were and are different from those occupying the core of the consumer movement. Political activism and information (in the case of CU) have been the primary goals of the core organizations within the consumer movement. Historically, education has been the primary goal of both the field of consumer economics/studies and ACCI. The goal of research on consumers and consumer markets has gained in importance in the field over the past forty years. The field and ACCI have fought hard to remain neutral politically and to protect their reputations as sources of objective consumer education and research materials. The fight has had to be refought periodically and, as times and conditions have changed, the resolutions of the conflicts have taken different forms.

The first conflict arose during ACCI's first few years. Initially, the organization had two primary goals: to stimulate scholarly and personal communication among consumer educators and researchers, and to produce consumer information pamphlets on aspects of consumer markets and behavior of use to consumers and consumer educators. The author of a manuscript, intended to be one of the first pamphlets, resigned his academic appointment for a position in business. Believing this constituted a conflict of interest, ACCI scuttled its publication. Publication of consumer pamphlets continued until the mid-1960s, after which the organization focused on its first goal.

This desire for "distance" from consumer professionals employed by business, and of business itself, carries through to this day. Businesses form "the other side of the market" from that occupied by consumers. To many in the field and in the consumer movement, there is and needs to be, if not an adversarial, at least an arm's-length relationship between the two sides of the market; consumers need a strong, separate voice to counteract the power of business. As a direct result of these views and a concern over the potential power within the organization of the growing number of ACCI members employed by corporations, ACCI disenfranchised consumer members employed by corporations at its annual meeting in 1975. This voting rights policy was reversed only in 1994.

The other result of ACCI's arm's-length view with respect to business has been stronger restrictions on accepting financial support from businesses than other professional and scholarly organizations impose. In an important and controversial annual meeting in 1977, ACCI established a policy of not associating "with any commercial or profit-making organization either in name or financially." While the injunction was subsequently relaxed, the association remains a reluctant and fiercely independent recipient of corporate funds and cosponsorships.

The arm's-length relationship with corporate sponsors maintained by ACCI is not necessarily maintained by individual consumer scholars in the field. As consumer affairs in business has come of age, some consumer economists have become members of the Society of Consumer Affairs Professionals in Business (SOCAP), some college programs have begun to train students explicitly for careers in corporate consumer affairs, and some programs have formed student clubs aligned with SOCAP, not ACCI. This movement is an important reason for the decline in student membership in ACCI since the late 1970s. It is also the case that consumer scholars are constrained by the policies of the academic institutions to which they belong. As governmental grant and contract funds have become harder to attract in recent years, consumer economists and educators have increasingly turned to the corporate sector for support of their programs.

The field of consumer economics/studies and ACCI have been equally guarded in stance with respect to adopting and supporting public policy positions. In the early days of the association and periodically thereafter, ACCI was asked to pass resolutions supporting the policy positions of advocacy groups or individual members of ACCI. While ACCI did pass a few such resolutions in its early days, a committee made up of Stewart Lee, Arch Troelstrup, and Robert McEwen was formed by the association in 1964 to consider whether it should remain a professional organization or become a political action committee. The committee returned a recommendation that ACCI "continue as a strictly professional organization without taking a political stand on issues." The recommendation was accepted and reflects the views of most in the field. In order to protect the currency of their educational and research materials, consumer educators and researchers maintain a similar policy. As individual citizens, however, they can and do take political positions.

Because ACCI is a creature of the field of consumer economics/studies, the stresses and strains that have affected ACCI are the same as those that have affected the field. One set of stresses arises from the two different scholarly emphases of the faculty within the field: consumer research and consumer education. The stress arises out of the fact that the membership in ACCI and the faculty in the field are roughly divided between consumer educators and consumer researchers. Consumer educators occupy positions as extension educators in state extension services and at the federal level. Those who emphasize consumer education also have their appointments in departments and programs in which their primary or sole responsibility is teaching. Most consumer researchers occupy positions in universities and federal agencies where their primary responsibility is research, or their research responsibility is at least co-equal with their teaching responsibility. The tensions between these two emphases are reflected in the struggle that has taken place historically within ACCI over the emphasis on research versus education in the association's conferences, programs, and publications.

The field and ACCI were both dominated by consumer educators initially. Indeed, without consumer educators, there would not have been a field of consumer economics/studies distinct from other fields nor would ACCI have been created as its professional association. Just as research became increasingly important as a scholarly activity in universities and colleges in the 1960s, 1970s, and 1980s, research became more important within the field of consumer economics/studies. In the process, it claimed a larger role on the conference programs and a larger fraction of the publications of ACCI. The switch, in the late 1960s, from publishing consumer information pamphlets to publishing a scholarly journal, the *Journal of Consumer Affairs,* is one index of the increasing role of consumer researchers in the field and in the association. Another index is the two research conferences, held separately from the annual conferences of ACCI, the first in 1986 and the second in 1990. The publication since 1990 by ACCI of *Advancing the Consumer Interest,* a journal devoted to consumer education, has been an attempt to regain a balance in the array of services ACCI provides its researcher and educator constituencies.

State of the Field

Since ACCI is the professional association serving the field, the fortunes of both the field and the organization are closely tied. The state of the field of consumer economics/studies can be assessed in several ways. One way is to examine statistics on the membership of ACCI.

Twenty-one charter members formed the organization in 1954. Three years later, there were 754 total members (including institutions like libraries and corporations), of which 369 were regular members and 271 were student members. This explosion of membership in the first three years of ACCI's existence represents not so much growth in the field as the initial enlisting of those already in the field. While only two of the charter members of ACCI had academic appointments in home economics, ACCI very quickly attracted many home economists concerned with consumer education. Indeed, despite the fact that most of the charter members of ACCI were economists in business education and economics programs, the faculties and students in consumer and family economics departments in home economics schools, and their successors, have constituted the bulk of ACCI's academic membership during most of the forty-four–year life of the organization. Raymon Heimerl, in his contribution to the oral history of ACCI edited by Merchant, mused that after the Vocational Education Act of 1963 assigned consumer education to home economics, interest in consumer education among business teachers in secondary schools and academics in college business education programs faded and, along with it, their interest in the field of consumer economics/studies and in ACCI.

Membership in ACCI reached its peak in the early 1970s at about the same time SOCAP was incorporated. In 1975, when there were 3,044 total members, 2,381 were regular members. 1975 was the year in which ACCI created nonvoting associate memberships for people employed by for-profit organizations. Annual breakdowns of the membership rolls in ACCI files do not begin until 1977. In that year, there were 1,233 regular members, 270 student members, and 806 institutional members. Membership has fallen consistently in all categories at rates of 3 to 5 percent per year since the mid-1970s. In 1995, regular and student memberships totaled 512 and 75 respectively. Institutional membership stood at 629.

Another way of assessing the state of the field is to examine statistics on the programs and departments of consumer economics/studies and of the students in them. Data on consumer economics/studies programs in the United States do not exist prior to the late 1970s. Cathleen Zick and Richard Widdows have, however, documented programs, enrollments, and graduates since 1977. On the basis of national data, Zick and Widdows document forty programs in existence in the United States in 1977/1978, forty-seven in 1984/1985 and thirty-eight in 1991/1992. Because of the source of the data, the programs documented include some general home economics programs as well as consumer and family economics programs. Widdows lists thirty-one undergraduate programs in consumer economics/studies in 1994. All but four also offer M.S. degrees, and twelve offer Ph.D. programs.

Zick and Widdows find that, between the late 1970s and the early 1990s, the number of graduates per program fell by 38 percent. On the basis of a subsequent survey of consumer and family economics departments in 1993, Zick and Widdows estimate the average size of these departments' undergraduate programs, in 1992, to be about 226 students, down 33 from 1989, a decline consistent with the fall in ACCI student membership over the 1980s.

Whether measured by membership in ACCI or by the number and sizes of college- and university-based programs, the field of consumer economics/studies has shrunk in the last fifteen years. Prior to the mid-1970s, the field grew. One cannot help correlating the rise and fall of ACCI membership, and by extension the field of consumer economics/studies, with what Robert Mayer, in *The Consumer Movement: Guardians of the Marketplace* (1989), has called the "third era of the consumer movement." Mayer dates the beginnings of this era of consumer activism and federal consumer legislation with the publication of Vance Packard's *The Hidden Persuaders* in 1957 and J. Kenneth Galbraith's *The Affluent Society* in 1958. The drumbeat of federal legislation began in 1962 with the Kefauver-Harris Amendments to the Federal Food, Drug, and Cosmetic Act, the same year that John F. Kennedy introduced his Consumer Bill of Rights. The passage of consumer legislation reached a crescendo in 1966–1968, and the era ended in 1975–1976 with the Magnuson-Moss Federal Trade Commission and Warranty Act and the Toxic Substances Control Act.

These successes put in place most of the agenda fought for by the consumer movement. The issues that came to dominate the nation's political agenda beginning in the late 1970s fragmented the movement or were irrelevant to it. These included: deregulation introduced by President Carter and expanded under Presidents Reagan and Bush, environmental protection, congressional reform, abortion rights, cost containment and efficiency in government, and free trade. None of these issues engaged the scholarly attention of more than a few consumer researchers or educators. Students who were interested by these issues went elsewhere in the university.

Another force contributing to the growth and subsequent decline of the field of consumer economics/studies was the baby boom and subsequent bust. Prior to the establishment of ACCI in 1954, scholars, programs, and departments of consumer economics/studies were few, small, and widely scattered. In addition to the individual consumer economists in a few business education and economics departments around the country, family economists in home economics schools devoted some of their efforts to consumer education and research. The programs and departments, especially in home economics, grew and multiplied as the baby boom generation entered college and as academia as a whole grew. The number of public high school graduates grew from 1.6 million in 1960, peaked at 2.8 million in the mid-1970s, and declined after 1980. Increasing numbers of older students enrolling in college and some increase in college matriculation rates by high school graduates kept college enrollments up. Since the late-1980s, however, college applicant pools have shrunk and are not expected to turn around until the late 1990s. Therefore, the movement of the baby boom through college, with only a slight lag, coincided with the third era of the consumer movement, helping to swell college student ranks, populate the field, and increase the demand for consumer economics/studies faculty. Likewise, as the third era of the consumer movement subsided in the 1980s and political activism turned to other issues, the field of consumer economics/studies ceased growing and began to contract. The contraction has been exacerbated by the passing of the baby boom.

A third important set of forces influencing the decline of ACCI membership and of the field has been the state of the economy combined with the rising cost of higher education in the 1980s and 1990s. Academic cost-cutting in Midwest and Great Plains universities and colleges, as a result of economic hardships in agriculture and manufacturing in the early and mid-1980s, began to trim consumer economics/studies budgets, shrink faculties, and merge consumer departments with departments in adjacent fields. Similar shrinkage has been and is occurring countrywide as a result of the joint effects of the recession of the early 1990s and the fight by universities to contain the continued increases in college costs.

Consumer welfare can be improved by increasing real incomes, by reducing consumer prices, or by increasing the quality of consumer goods. The successes of the consumer movement in the 1960s and 1970s in making consumer products safer and consumer information more available did increase the quality of consumer goods and services and did help hold consumer prices down. Technical change, more aggressive marketing, and the rise of consumer affairs professionals in business over the same period also contributed to increases in consumer product quality and after-sale service. With real family income stagnant or declining since the mid-1970s, policy interest has increasingly moved from consumer goods' prices and qualities to wages, employment, and taxes. Furthermore, the globalization of consumer goods manufacturing has greatly complicated consumer policy by linking it with international trade policy. Consequently, students of the 1990s are focused on other issues than consumer policy. All of these changes have shifted the focus of students and faculty away from consumer economics/studies.

Mayer refers to the consumer movement as "fragile but enduring." So is the field. It grew with the third era of the consumer movement and has contracted with its passing. Those in the field are bound together by membership in ACCI and by the services ACCI offers: the *Journal of Consumer Affairs* for consumer researchers, *Advancing the Consumer Interest* for consumer educators, and the *ACCI Newsletter* and the annual conferences of the association for both constituencies. During the next few years of budget stringency in colleges and universities, consumer departments and curricular programs will continue to contract and to merge with adjacent departments and curricula. During this period, the role of ACCI as the focal point for consumer scholars and the sustaining institution for the academic field is crucial.

— W. Keith Bryant

See also

American Council on Consumer Interests; Research on Consumer Issues.

Readings

Merchant, M. M., ed. (1987). *The American Council on Consumer Interests: An Oral History*. Columbia, MO: American Council on Consumer Interests.

Zick, Cathleen D., and Richard Widdows (1992). "Turning the Ebbing Tide of Consumer Studies Enrollments." *Advancing the Consumer Interest*. 4 (2): 19–23.

——— (1994). "Assessing the Health of Consumer and Family Economics Programs." *Advancing the Consumer Interest*. 6 (1): 26–30.

Consumer Education

Consumer education shares with the rest of the consumer movement the vision of improving the material standards of living and quality of life for all citizens. This education occurs in classrooms, workplaces, communities, and homes. Its practitioners include parents, teachers, consumer advocates, community leaders, government, business consumer representatives, academics, and the media.

Multidisciplinary by design, consumer education melds principles of economics, political science, mathematics, sociology, psychology, and law. It uses plain language to simplify complex issues and decisions faced by individuals and households. While consumer education has enjoyed broad support from the public for nearly 100 years, it has yet to demonstrate a significant and lasting impact on the nation's educational system and on consumer behavior in American society.

Definition and Concepts

A national study that developed a conceptual framework for consumer education provides a benchmark for reflecting on the historical developments of the field. The study, funded in 1978 by the U.S. Office of Consumers' Education and coordinated by the Michigan Consumer Education Center at Eastern Michigan University, was part of a larger Consumer Education Development Program. The resulting publication, *Classification of Concepts in Consumer Education,* has received broad acceptance as the conceptual framework for curriculum development and program design.

This study defined consumer education as the process of gaining knowledge and skills to manage personal resources and to participate in social, political, and economic decisions that affect individual well-being and the public good. It grouped the concepts of consumer education into three major categories: consumer choice and decision-making; personal resource management; and citizen participation.

For consumer choice and decision-making, the most important concepts are: personal and societal needs and wants, values, and goals; economic, social/cultural, and political environment; impact of technology on consumer choice; the consumer decision-making process; information availability, reliability, cost, and use; ethical marketplace behavior of producers, workers, and consumers; economic problems such as poverty, unemployment, and welfare costs; and consumer issues such as health and safety.

For personal resource management, the most significant concepts are: earning, spending, saving, and investing money; buying and using goods and services; budgeting and record keeping; using consumer credit and avoiding credit problems; insurance—life, health, property, and casualty; taxes—costs, benefits, problems, and policies; education, employability skills, and income; and environmental resources—conservation, use, and disposal.

For citizen participation in the marketplace, the most important concepts are: consumer protection laws; agencies and sources of assistance; rights and responsibilities of consumers, producers, and government; consumer redress—assertiveness and action strategies; and consumer organization—from individual to group action.

Historically, a primary focus of consumer education has been teaching individuals to become more skilled buyers. The classification study was designed to expand the range of consumer problem-solving skills from learning to cope with marketplace conditions to participation as citizens to influence change in the political, economic, and social arenas. Specific skills include coping, questioning, planning, purchasing, conserving, participating as citizens, and influencing change.

Coping includes applying basic consumer survival skills to everyday situations. The ability to cope with current circumstances is an important need for all consumers, but it is not the final goal of consumer education, especially where the existing conditions should be changed.

Questioning is an important analytical skill that encourages independent thinking. It teaches people to ask questions before purchasing and to challenge misinformation and fraud. Questioning may result in a decision not to buy.

Planning includes the process of managing financial resources after considering goals, needs, and available resources. It includes obtaining income as well as spending, saving, investing, borrowing, protecting, and paying taxes on this income.

Purchasing is the application of the decision-making process to buying goods and services. It involves seeking and using information, considering alternatives and consequences, and selecting the product or service by using appropriate criteria.

Conserving encourages consumer actions that preserve or use resources efficiently rather than wastefully.

Participating as citizens supports consumer involvement in business, government, and community policy decisions. The process includes questioning, analyzing, and suggesting alternative solutions to consumer issues and problems.

Influencing change promotes an awareness that consumers, through active participation, can exercise power to modify those policies, institutions, and systems within society that affect consumer interests.

History

While consumer education in the United States evolved largely during the twentieth century, a recognition of the need for consumer knowledge can be traced to the early years of the new republic. Thomas Jefferson, the chief spokesman for public education in the late 1700s, preached against all ignorance. He also stressed the need for household economics. The word *economics* comes from the Greek *oikonoma,* which was defined as the management of household and private affairs. When Jefferson addressed the need for what he called "household economy," he said, "We all know its value and that diligence and dexterity in all its processes are inestimable treasures."

The Morrill Act of 1862 paved the way for education for daily living, the learning of practical skills to help people function in the emerging consumer marketplace. This act established the land grant college system, which gave land to the states for a new kind of education in which agriculture, engineering, and other applied sciences were to be taught.

Between 1899 and 1908, a group of scientists concerned about consumer problems met each year at librarian Melvil Dewey's Lake Placid Club in upstate New York. This group was chiefly concerned about problems brought about by rapid industrialization, urbanization, and immigration. Ellen Richards, a chemist, was concerned about food and water purity and about unsanitary housing. Caroline Hunt, trained in philosophy and the classics, spoke of the need for a simple lifestyle rather than materialism, gadgets, and fashion. Wilbur Atwater, a biochemist, was concerned about the nutritional adequacy of people's diets. And Benjamin Andrews, an economist, focused on the long-range economic well-being of families.

This interdisciplinary band of scientists shared ideas and carried new enthusiasm back to their workplaces—the Massachusetts Institute of Technology, Cornell University, the University of Chicago, the University of California, and the University of Wisconsin. In 1909, the American Home Economics Association began as an organized continuation of the Lake Placid conferences.

In 1912, University of Chicago economist Wesley Mitchell wrote "The Backward Art of Spending Money," an influential essay that first appeared in the *American Economic Review.* Mitchell stressed the importance of the management by individuals of their consumption. He also emphasized the importance of schools in preparing individuals for consumption.

Beginning in the 1920s, college textbooks played an important role in the increased attention given to consumer education. In 1924, Henry Harap, professor of education at George Peabody College for Teachers in Nashville, and Ray Price wrote the influential book, *The Education of the Consumer,* with James Mendenhall. He was soon joined by other authors who made major contributions to the field. Other noteworthy consumer education textbooks published between the 1920s and 1950s were: *Economics for Consumers* (1939) by Leland Gordon and later by Stewart Lee; *Consumer Education: Background, Present Status and Future Directions* (1943) by James Mendenhall and Henry Harap; *Consumer Economic Problems* (1951) by Harmon Wilson and Elvin Eyster and, later, with other coauthors; *General Business for Everyday Living* (1951) by Ray Price and Vernon Musselman; *The Consumer in American Society: Personal and Family Finance* (1952) by Arch W. Troelstrup; and *Consumer Economics: Principles and Problems* (1959) by Fred Wilhelms and Raymon Heimerl.

In 1935, the Sloan Foundation funded a six-year consumer education program at Stephens College, a women's college in Columbia, Missouri. James Mendenhall was the program's associate director. This first consumer education department in a college existed for more than thirty years. Arch W. Troelstrup served as its chairman from 1941 through 1969. His book, *The Consumer in American Society,* incorporated research from the actual experiences of 400 Stephens College graduates who married and later described their most important household consumer problems.

In 1938, Henry Harap found that consumer courses in the high schools were most frequently offered by business education departments, although nearly as many of these courses were taught by home economics and social studies departments. A 1941 study concluded that the content of a particular course depended on the department offering the course. Home economics departments emphasized buymanship along with information use and budgeting. Business education stressed money management along with general buying procedures. Social studies emphasized governmental protection, economic problems, transportation, and taxes.

Ray Price served as an adviser to the *Consumer Education Study* of the National Association of Secondary School Principals, a five-year research project begun in 1942 to strengthen consumer education in the secondary schools. For twenty-four years, from 1948 to 1972, Price was professor of business education at the University of Minnesota. In 1953, with funding from Colston Warne of Consumers Union, Price and Henry Harap organized the first meeting of twenty-one charter members of the Council of Consumer Information, which later became known as the American Council on Consumer Interests. Price served as the first president of the organization, which consisted almost exclusively of college professors who were authors of books related to consumer affairs.

While domestic science (later called home economics) had a strong commitment to consumer education during the first half of the twentieth century, strong advocates for this education emerged from other fields as well. But the lack of a single disciplinary home may have discouraged the maturation and acceptance of consumer education within the academic community.

From the Great Depression of the 1930s through the end of World War II, consumer education was often described as antiadvertising, antibusiness, and pro-frugality. The "use it up, make it do, or do without" philosophy encouraged people to buy as little as possible. This image probably discouraged the growth of consumer education in the 1950s since many households with wartime savings and expanding incomes embraced the new "earn, spend, consume, and throw away" philosophy. Because many people were more interested in spending than in learning how to spend wisely, consumer education in the schools lacked support and too often became a dumping ground for low-motivated, low-achieving students. In some instances, this lack of support persisted well beyond the 1950s, negatively influencing consumer education's acceptance as a legitimate academic subject for all students in the nation's schools.

In the 1960s, the consumer movement experienced a renaissance that filtered down to consumer education. The tone was set in President John F. Kennedy's famous consumer message in 1962 when he proclaimed the four consumer rights—the right to be heard, the right to know, the right to safety, and the right to choose. The consumer was openly recognized as important to the effective functioning of the economic system. Education was measured by its "relevance," and consumer education rode a new wave of popularity.

Continuing the tone set by Kennedy, President Lyndon Johnson charged the government to stimulate consumer education as part of his vision of the Great Society. President Richard Nixon also spoke on behalf of consumer education. In his consumer message of February 1971, he stressed the importance of consumer education: "Consumer education is an integral part of consumer protection. It is vital if the consumer is to be able to make wise judgments in the marketplace. To enable him or her to do this will require a true educational process beginning in childhood and continuing on." Nixon directed the secretary of Health, Education, and Welfare to work with the nation's education system to promote the establishment of consumer education as a national education concern, provide technical assistance in the development of programs, encourage teacher training in consumer education, and solicit the use of all school and public libraries as consumer information centers.

The next president, Gerald Ford, recognized consumer education as a basic right for all consumers. In a consumer proclamation in 1975, he said: "The time has now come to recognize a fifth right—one without which consumers cannot gain the full benefit of the other four. This is the right to consumer education. . . . It is my earnest hope that consumer education will become an integral part of regular school instruction, community services and educational programs for people out of school."

Consumer Education in the Schools

Recent surveys in the United States suggest that consumer education has not kept up with rapid changes in the marketplace. Students have not yet reached a desirable level of knowledge and skill in managing personal financial resources. In 1991, the Consumer Federation of America and the American Express Company conducted a study of the consumer knowledge levels of high school seniors. This research revealed that many students lack the basic knowledge and skills needed to make important personal financial decisions they will face as adults. On this multiple-choice test, high school students answered only 42 percent of the questions correctly. Scores were especially low in the areas of credit, bank accounts, landlord-tenant obligations, and automobiles. For example, only 18 percent of the students understood the importance of the annual percentage rate (APR) when considering a loan.

In 1990, the National Coalition for Consumer Education surveyed chief state school administrators to gather data on the status of consumer education in grades K–12. The study, titled *Status of Consumer Education in U.S. Schools, Grades K–12,* revealed the condition of school-based consumer education. Thirty states and the District of Columbia had statewide consumer education policies. But great variations existed as to whether the subject was optional or mandatory, and how concepts were presented. Personal financial management was the topic most frequently mentioned in state responses as one that should be included in consumer education. Other topics cited, in descending order of frequency, included: economic system, purchasing decisions, personal factors such as values and lifestyle, and consumer protection. Nearly two-thirds of the states reported that consumer topics were more likely to be discussed in schools in 1990 than in 1985.

In 1967, Illinois was the first state to enact a law requiring that public school students "shall be required to study courses which include instruction in consumer education, including but not limited to installment purchasing, budgeting and comparison of prices." Cecil A. Partee, a freshman state senator, had submitted the consumer education bill to the Illinois General Assembly. Partee had worked for the Consumer Affairs Office of Cook County where he had observed that citizens experienced many consumer problems because of a lack of knowledge and information. The law was supported by business groups, consumer groups, and educators.

Throughout the history of consumer education in the schools, strategies for incorporating the concepts into the curriculum have been diverse. Some schools offer a special course; others infuse concepts into one or more courses; and still others use a combination of these strategies and provide a capstone course. In a 1993 publication, *Consumer Education in the States: A Blueprint for Action*, the National Institute for Consumer Education evaluated several approaches.

Creating a separate course has the advantage of a unified approach to consumer education and can give the subject a status equal to other areas of study. The major disadvantage to this approach is that school schedules are already overcrowded and a new subject increases time pressures. The lack of trained consumer teachers is another constraint.

In many schools, consumer education concepts are "infused" into other courses such as economics, math, business education, or life management. Practical from a scheduling viewpoint, this approach can strengthen existing courses by making them more relevant and by increasing student interest. A disadvantage of the curriculum infusion method is that consumer concepts that do not fit into the assigned courses are neglected or omitted entirely. Other concepts may be covered by more than one course. Moreover, when consumer concepts are integrated into existing courses that have other learning priorities, it is difficult to document student learning of these concepts.

Integration of consumer education into existing courses is sometimes combined with a senior year capstone course that ties consumer concepts together. If the course is required for graduation, all students benefit. But a capstone course may be difficult to add to a school's already crowded schedule. Also, it is difficult to train and motivate teachers.

Still another approach is the use of a team of teachers from various disciplines to teach a group of students during the same class hour. Each teacher brings a different perspective and knowledge to the program. The students rotate from teacher to teacher. Disadvantages of this approach include difficulty coordinating the team of teachers and scheduling the time of both teachers and students.

In 1970, David Schoenfeld, a social studies teacher, and Arthur Natella, principal of Lincoln High School in Yonkers, New York, wrote the high school textbook, *The Consumer and His Dollars*. Yonkers faculty had pioneered the interdisciplinary approach to consumer education in New York. At a regional consumer education conference in 1968, Natella gave the challenge: "Education in America has concentrated on . . . producer-type education . . . and cultural education. . . . But there is a third area that has been neglected. That is consumer education—the preparation of an individual as a consumer. We teach how to earn a living but we fall short of showing students how to best use the income they spend and save."

In 1968, Public Law 90-576 was passed with a program titled "Consumer and Homemaking Education." The Vocational Education Amendments of 1968 provided categorical funds to the fifty states in support of home economics education, including a number of innovative consumer education programs. The New Jersey Center for Consumer Education and the Michigan Consumer Education Center were initially funded by consumer and homemaking funds. Both of these programs promoted the multidisciplinary approach to consumer education. But eventually, turf problems prevented the use of consumer and homemaking funds for continuing support of these programs. The New Jersey Center was discontinued in the 1970s; the Michigan Center survived only with partnership funding from Eastern Michigan University, corporations, and foundations. (In 1991, the Michigan Center became the National Institute for Consumer Education at Eastern Michigan University. It manages a resource clearinghouse, develops educational materials, and conducts seminars, workshops, and courses for educators in classrooms, workplaces, and the community.)

Concern that consumer education was not reaching all students and that it did not adequately address consumer-citizen participation issues spurred the enactment of Public Law 92-318, Section 505 in the 1972 amendments to the Elementary and Secondary Education Act. While the law authorized spending of $80 million for consumer education curriculum and federal leadership, this section was never funded.

In retrospect, the fact that consumer educators and consumer interest groups did not lobby Congress to appropriate the authorized funds for consumer education has no clear explanation. While it is possible that most consumer educators in the nation's colleges and K–12 classrooms were not aware that the law existed, it is difficult to assume that the same was true for consumer advocates and the U.S. Office of Consumer Affairs.

A rare second chance for consumer education came in 1974 when Public Law 93-380 was passed. Its consumer education provisions were similar to those of the 1972 law. The original legislation was amended to authorize the establishment of a U.S. Office of Consumers' Education with a director and a grants and contracts program. Funds for the new federal consumer education program were first appropriated in 1976. Only $3.1 million of a $15 million authorization was appropriated during its first year of operation. A total of less than $19 million was appropriated during the six years of the program's existence.

A 1978 publication of the Consumer Education Resource Network, *Education of the Consumer: A Review of Historical Developments*, explored the relationships among the consumer movement, consumer education, and economic education. The authors concluded: "Consumer education shares a philosophy with the consumer movement and a base discipline with economic education. The future of consumer education would seem to be most securely based on a close cooperative relationship of shared philosophy, research and methodology with both the consumer movement and economic education." In reality, tensions between consumer and economic education have surfaced repeatedly throughout the history of both areas of study.

A recurring question in any analysis of consumer and economic education is whether the more theoretical approach of economics is preferable to the more utilitarian approach of consumer education at the K–12 level. The Joint Council on Economic Education (later named the National Council on Economic Education) was formed in 1949 to create a network of state councils and centers for teacher training and curriculum development in economic education. Major funding was provided by the business community.

A 1966 publication of the council, *Economics and the Consumer,* addressed the principles of economics needed for wise consumer decision-making and confronted the issues of the balance between theoretical economic analysis and applied personal economics in high schools. The publication reported the results of a 1966 New York University survey of a group of high school economics teachers and of a group of professional economists. The professional economists opposed the inclusion of topics usually emphasized in the development of consumer economics. In contrast, high school teachers insisted that personal economics should be emphasized.

Consumer Education beyond the Classroom

In a presentation at an International Organization of Consumers Unions conference in Ottawa, Canada, in 1982, Hayden Green observed that the schools are primary purveyors of education in most academic subjects, but "not so in consumer education where consumer organizations, business, government agencies, trade associations, and professional organizations all have roles in developing educational materials or activities." Consumer organizations such as the Consumer Federation of America, the National Consumers League, and the American Association of Retired Persons contribute significantly to the education of consumers, combining relevant information with action-oriented participation to effect change.

Professional organizations that support the disciplines involved in consumer education include: American Association of Family and Consumer Sciences, American Association of Financial Counseling and Planning Education, American Council on Consumer Interests, National Association of Consumer Agency Administrators, National Business Education Association, National Coalition for Consumer Education, National Council for the Social Studies, and National Council on Economic Education. Examples of state organizations that promote consumer education are the Illinois Consumer Education Association and Consumer Educators of Michigan.

These organizations, state and national, often sponsor professional journals, newsletters, conferences and workshops, special publications, and other activities. They serve as facilitators for the exchange of ideas, methods, and materials. For example, the National Coalition for Consumer Education sponsors a LifeSmarts contest for high school students, and the National Association for Consumer Agency Administrators sponsors an annual consumer education awards program.

The issue of whether business-sponsored materials are a threat to classroom integrity was raised publicly in 1979 when Sheila Harty's book, *Hucksters in the Classroom,* was published. This report stressed that corporations were inappropriate sponsors of educational materials because they subject students to blatant advertising and political or economic indoctrination. At the same time, many teachers lacking resources to purchase consumer education publications eagerly accepted business-sponsored materials as supplementary teaching tools. All agree, however, that consumers need increased sophistication in evaluating the validity of information.

An example of government-sponsored consumer education was the publication, by the President's Committee on Consumer Interests in 1970, of *Suggested Guidelines for Consumer Education, K–12.* This publication, which was widely distributed, became a highly respected work on the nature, content, and implementation of consumer education in the schools. To classroom educators, the publication was strong evidence that the federal government recognized the importance of consumer education to the economic well-being of American households.

Most government consumer education activities have been aimed primarily at information dissemination. The Consumer Information Center and the Federal Trade Commission are among federal agencies that provide numerous free and inexpensive materials that are suitable for educational use. For decades, the U.S. Department of Agriculture's Cooperative Extension System has operated consumer education programs in all fifty states and most counties in the United States. These and other state and local agencies offer workshops, seminars, press releases, and media appearances on current consumer issues.

While much lip service has been paid to consumer education, it has never been adequately supported by society. Almost everyone believes that consumer education should be a required subject in the schools, yet it is not an integral part of the curriculum in most schools. Presidents Jefferson, Kennedy, Johnson, Nixon, and Ford have delivered strong praise for consumer education, yet as the year 2000 draws near, the U.S. Department of Education provides no leadership or funding for this education. Personal finance education language was included in the 1972 revisions of the Elementary and Secondary Education Act, yet no funds have been appropriated to carry out the authorized activities.

— Rosella Bannister

See also

National Coalition for Consumer Education; U.S. Office of Consumers' Education.

Readings

Bannister, Rosella, and Charles Monsma (1982). *Classification of Concepts in Consumer*

Education. Cincinnati: South-Western Publishing Company. Monograph 137.

Green, Hayden (1988). "The Role of Secondary Schools." In E. Scott Maynes, ed. *The Frontier of Research in the Consumer Interest*. Columbia, MO: American Council on Consumer Interests. 819–829.

Royer, Gayle L., and Nancy E. Nolt (1980). *Education of the Consumer: A Review of Historical Developments*. Rosslyn, VA: Consumer Education Resource Network.

Consumer Federation of America

The Consumer Federation of America (CFA) was established in 1967 by national, state, and local pro-consumer groups to advocate the consumer interest before the U.S. Congress and federal regulatory agencies. By the early 1990s, it was not only representing the consumer interest before federal policymakers, but also advocating this interest in many states, providing product-related information directly to consumers, assisting other consumer groups, and helping unify the consumer movement.

Origins

CFA was organized by reform-minded advocates during a period of change and social protest. Most of these advocates came from organizations established earlier in the century—Consumers Union, industrial labor unions, and rural electric cooperatives, among others—who viewed the late 1960s as a time when political conditions permitted the establishment of new consumer protections and agencies.

In 1964, representatives of several of these groups in Washington, D.C., began meeting informally and planning strategy to advance consumer legislation. A year later, these activists began organizing a national consumer forum. Held in April 1966, this Consumer Assembly was cosponsored by thirty national organizations representing workers, small farmers, consumer cooperatives, and women as well as other consumers. At the meeting, White House Consumer Adviser Esther Peterson urged the creation of a federation of national, state, and local groups to press for consumer legislation.

To further this goal, later in the year Peterson convened a meeting of state and local consumer groups that was attended by twenty-eight of their representatives. Well into the night, many of these participants debated the character of such a federation. A decision was finally made to include not only consumer advocacy and education organizations, but also cooperatives, trade unions, and other supporting nonprofit groups. Many of these national groups had belonged to the Electric Consumer Information Committee.

These organizations formed a steering committee to plan the new federation. By the next assembly, held in November 1967, the foundation for the organization had been laid. With the assistance of attorney Rhoda Karpatkin, who later served as chief executive officer of Consumers Union, the organization's charter and bylaws were prepared and temporary officers selected. Father Robert McEwen from the Association of Massachusetts Consumers, Bob Smith of Consumers Union, Sarah Newman of the National Consumers League, Evelyn Dubrow of the International Ladies Garment Workers Union, Jacob Clayman of the AFL-CIO's Industrial Union Department, John J. Sheehan of the Steelworkers Union, George Myers of the Credit Union National Association, Shelby Southard of the Cooperative League of the U.S.A., and Erma Angevine of the National Rural Electric Cooperative Association were among those who worked the hardest to create CFA. During the federation's first annual meeting, held in April 1968, fifty-six charter members elected officers and directors, and appointed Angevine as executive director.

Organizational Structure

In developing a structure for the new organization, its founders faced a unique challenge. CFA's primary function was consumer advocacy, but at the time, few consumer advocacy groups existed, and most of these were run by volunteers. Moreover, the federation's income depended on contributions from trade unions and consumer cooperatives.

The charter that representatives of the three major CFA constituencies negotiated tried to accommodate each. Regardless of the level of their contributions, trade unions and groups such as the National Farmers Union were defined as supporting members with a limit of two votes at the annual meeting. Consumer groups, including co-ops, would each cast as many as twenty votes if they contributed at least $200 annually. But trade unions were given substantial representation on the 40-to-43-person board of directors, which included an eleven-person executive committee.

Representatives of CFA member organizations had the authority to elect officers and other board members and to determine the consumer policies of the organization. They were to exercise this authority at annual meetings of the organization. To facilitate policy setting, an elaborate policy resolutions committee and process were created. Subcommittees for individual issue areas, such as food and housing, were formed to which representatives of any member group could belong. Chairs of the subcommittee made up the full committee, which reviewed recommendations submitted by the subcommittees before these proposed changes were submitted to all members. By the 1990s, seventeen different subcommittees were part of this process.

Between annual meetings, the board of directors exercises authority over the federation. They in turn delegate authority to the executive committee and its officers. In the late 1960s, this committee consisted of a president, secretary-treasurer, five vice presidents, and four directors. In the 1970s, it was limited to ten members—a president, secretary-treasurer, and eight vice presidents—with the understanding that these officers would include representatives of both national and grassroots organizations.

Member participation and control is one of the greatest strengths of CFA. It helps ensure that policies reflect a broad grassroots consensus, and it provides the organization with credibility. Nevertheless, the CFA board has allowed executive directors to exercise much discretion in running the organization, including selecting personnel, recommending annual legislative and regulatory priorities, and interpreting policy resolutions. Accordingly, the history of the organization can be best understood by reviewing the terms of the four executive directors.

1968 to 1973: The Angevine Years

Erma Angevine served as executive director in a period when there was an upsurge of consumer activism. "Nader's Raiders" developed and published critiques of federal agencies and business. Hundreds of other reform-minded activists organized consumers at the grass roots.

Before joining CFA, Angevine had worked for major cooperative organizations. After teaching English at the University of Kansas, she held positions with the Consumer Cooperative Association, the Cooperative League of the U.S.A., and the National Rural Electric Cooperative Association, where her work included directing women's activities and serving as consumer lobbyist.

Angevine's great challenge was to take the lead on numerous consumer issues at a time when she had to build the organization from scratch. She had few resources with which to work. In this period, nearly all the organization's income came from dues contributions from member cooperatives, trade unions, and a few other well-established groups, notably Consumers Union. Thus, recruiting new member organizations represented the most important method of raising funds. By 1969, with the help of key board members, Angevine had persuaded 140 groups to affiliate with the federation. They contributed nearly $100,000 a year, which allowed her to hire two staffers.

At the time, there were tensions between grassroots consumer organizations and the trade unions and cooperatives. Because the unions and co-ops represented about three-quarters of the federation's membership, contributed most of its income, and were based in Washington, D.C., they could effectively control the organization. But some grassroots groups believed that their character as consumer advocacy organizations entitled them to run the federation. Also, certain grassroots leaders felt that, as CFA officers, they should make many of the organization's day-to-day decisions. This disagreement culminated in the establishment of the Conference on Consumer Organizations (COCO) by eight state consumer groups.

At the same time that Angevine had to build an organization and contend with divisions among members, she was expected to take the lead on numerous issues. She did so with great energy and effectiveness. Angevine involved CFA in dozens of congressional issues, developing position papers and fact sheets, mobilizing CFA members, and communicating with members of Congress and their staffers. Working closely with other consumer advocates, with cooperative and union lobbyists, and with congressional leaders such as Senators Philip Hart (D-MI), Warren Magnuson (D-WA), and Paul Douglas (D-IL) and Representative Leonor Sullivan (D-MO), she helped ensure passage of key consumer legislation such as truth in lending and truth in packaging.

At the state level, CFA coordinated opposition to the Uniform Consumer Credit Code. Angevine recruited volunteer attorneys to analyze the provisions of the code and circulated these analyses widely throughout the country. She also kept track of the actions of individual states on the code.

As well as organization-building and advocacy, Angevine was responsible for organizing annual consumer assemblies, which quickly became the annual meetings for most of the nation's consumerists. When she retired from CFA in 1973, Angevine left behind a federation with a solid organizational foundation and much credibility.

1973 to 1980: The Foreman/O'Reilly Years

In the mid- and late 1970s, the political environment for consumer advocates grew more challenging. During the Gerald Ford presidency, there was still much congressional interest in establishing new consumer protections on issues ranging from billing to warranties. Yet, after Jimmy Carter was elected president and appointed several leading advocates to top posts, consumer groups had to address questions about their role and relation to these administration appointees. Also, during the Carter presidency, business organized effectively against consumer initiatives.

Carol Tucker Foreman succeeded Angevine as executive director. The daughter and granddaughter of Arkansas politicians, Foreman had worked on Capitol Hill, in the executive branch, and in the advocacy community (Planned Parenthood) before joining CFA.

This experience and her own personal skills allowed Foreman to heighten the influence and credibility of the federation. She was highly regarded by many members of Congress and was the subject of articles in the *Wall Street Journal*, *New York Times*, and *Washington Star*. Foreman recruited a small but outstanding staff that included lobbyists Kathleen O'Reilly, who succeeded her as executive director, and Kathleen Sheekey, who later served as legislative director of Common Cause and co-director of the Advocacy Institute.

Foreman continued Angevine's recruitment of new member groups. By 1977, there were 225—about one-third of whom were consumer advocacy and education groups. Most of the state and local consumer organizations established during the early 1970s affiliated with CFA. During Foreman's tenure as executive director, tensions between these grassroots groups and the large cooperatives and labor unions were much less than during the Angevine years. In part, this was because of greatly expanded membership services to state and local groups, which included organizing national and regional meetings, and publishing a newsletter and organizing guides.

In this period, CFA's annual income available to support advocacy ranged from about $150,000 to $200,000. Consequently, the organization could afford only five core staffers. Despite their limited numbers, these staffers were active on the Hill and widely quoted by the press. A high priority was fighting inflation in the energy and food areas. Also important was seeking to establish a federal consumer protection agency and consumer cooperative bank. But there was hardly a consumer issue in Washington in which CFA was not involved. To encourage the election of a proconsumer Congress member, CFA established a Political Action Committee that endorsed, but did not make financial contributions to, congressional candidates.

In 1977, Foreman was appointed assistant secretary in the U.S. Department of Agriculture and was succeeded as CFA executive director by legislative director Kathleen O'Reilly. Before joining CFA in 1975, O'Reilly had practiced law in the District of Columbia. Her corporate and insurance industry defense litigation work included drafting the first federal nofault auto insurance legislation. At CFA, O'Reilly was known for her forceful consumer advocacy. She organized numerous coalitions, testified more than 200 times before congressional and state legislative bodies, and was frequently interviewed by national media. During her tenure as executive director, federal agencies established far more new consumer protections than did Congress, which finally killed the proposal for a federal consumer protection agency. But O'Reilly led a successful congressional effort to reduce sugar price supports and to expand protections against credit discrimination.

1980 to the Present: The Brobeck Years

In early 1980, O'Reilly left CFA to run for Congress—she later headed the Wisconsin Citizens Utility Board (CUB) for many years—and was replaced by Stephen Brobeck. Brobeck became executive director just before the election of Ronald Reagan as president. During Reagan's first term, consumer advocates in Washington were almost continuously on the defensive trying to protect agencies such as the Federal Trade Commission's Bureau of Competition and the Consumer Product Safety Commission (CPSC) from elimination, and to defend existing consumer protections, such as state usury ceilings, that were under attack.

By Reagan's second term, however, much of the force of the conservative offensive had been spent, so that consumer advocates were able to advance new initiatives. During the George Bush administration, a number of these proposals were approved by Congress and became law.

The election of Bill Clinton as president raised the hopes of consumer advocates even higher. Yet, these expectations were largely disappointed by an increasingly partisan and gridlocked Congress. Consumer activists, however, were unprepared for the overwhelming Republican victory in the 1994 elections.

In some respects, Brobeck was highly qualified to lead CFA, but in others he was unprepared. Academic training in social history and American studies, which he taught during the 1970s at Case Western Reserve University in Cleveland, provided him with broad understandings about social problems and social change. Cofounding and leading a grassroots consumer organization, Cleveland Consumer Action, in the same period informed him about consumer problems and remedies. And his service on the CFA board and executive committee from 1976 to 1979 familiarized him with the federation and its member groups. On the other hand, when he joined the CFA staff, Brobeck had never worked in Washington and was not well informed about legislative processes or lobbying.

Brobeck's greatest personal contributions to CFA have been as a builder. Under his leadership, annual income increased from about $200,000 to nearly $2 million; a reserve fund was created and built up to more than $600,000; and membership services expanded. Most notably, a state and local grants fund was created. By 1993, this fund was disbursing more than $100,000 a year contributed by Consumers Union.

Brobeck was also instrumental in building permanent coalitions to influence public policy or educate consumers. With Robert Vagley of the American Insurance Association, he spearheaded efforts to create new organizations to improve motor vehicle safety (Advocates for Auto and Highway Safety) and to fight insurance fraud (Coalition Against Insurance Fraud). With Samuel Simon, he founded the Tele-Consumer Hotline. And, with other CFA staffers, he organized the Coalition for Consumer Health and Safety and the Consumer Literacy Consortium.

Brobeck recruited talented staffers from other public interest organizations who remained with CFA for many years. Legislative director Gene Kimmelman, who came from Congress Watch, was considered one of the best lobbyists in Washington and played a critical role in passage of cable reregulation legislation over Bush's veto. Product safety director Mary Ellen Fise, who had worked for the National Consumers League, emerged as a leading product safety advocate and, on two occasions, was interviewed for vacant CPSC commission slots. Research director Mark Cooper, who had directed research for the Consumer Energy Council of America, produced such sophisticated economic analyses that he was invited to serve as an expert witness before dozens of state public service commissions. Public information director Jack Gillis, who had produced *The Car Book* with the Center for Auto Safety, helped prepare several commercially published books and, in 1994, began serving as CFA's consumer correspondent to *The Today Show.*

Associate director Ann Lower, who had run a congressional office, provided capable administrative and financial management of the growing organization. Other longtime staffers who made significant contributions were Barbara Roper, editor and director of investor protections; Edith Furst, grassroots and product safety coordinator; and secretary and executive assistant Lydia Grogan, who had been with CFA almost continuously from 1979.

As CFA grew in size and stability, the board increasingly deferred to the staff's judgment about programs, policies, and even board composition. But the board and member groups continued to make all important decisions and, in the case of large institutional members, provide financial support. Key board members supporting the federation were Kenneth Kovack of the Steelworkers, Arnold Mayer of the United Food and Commercial Workers, Alex Radin and Larry Hobart of the American Public Power Association, Robert Partridge and Robert Bergland of the National Rural Electric Cooperative Association, and Warren Braren and Mark Silbergeld of Consumers Union. From 1976 to the present, Silbergeld has chaired the important Policy Resolutions Committee.

In the 1980s, the proportion of CFA members who were state or local consumer groups increased. So too did their representation on the board, and the early practice of selecting the CFA president from among these grassroots leaders was reaffirmed. From 1986 until the present, Ken McEldowney from Consumer Action and Jean Ann Fox from the Virginia Citizens Consumer Council have alternated serving two-year terms as president.

While these state and local leaders and their groups increased the credibility of CFA, they could not contribute significant resources to the organization. Moreover, many of the larger organizations within the federation were forced to curtail their financial support. In fact, in 1980 and 1981 labor unions and Consumers Union cut back their funding by nearly $50,000 a year.

Brobeck responded to this challenge by developing a more diversified financial base that consisted of service and project-related income. During the 1980s, CFA staff established annual single-issue conferences on energy/utilities and financial services, prepared a half-dozen books and more than a dozen pamphlets, built toll-free hotlines on telephone services and radon, and conducted consumer literacy tests that served as the basis for a new organization, the Consumer Literacy Consortium, which developed and disseminated money-saving tips. These and other projects were funded by a diverse group of institutions including government agencies, publishers, corporations, trade associations, and CFA members.

Despite its expansion of consumer education activities and trade association functions, CFA's highest priority remained advocacy to influence public policy and corporate behavior. This advocacy was concentrated in the areas of financial services (banking, insurance, securities, real estate), energy and utilities (telecommunications, gas, electricity), and product safety (especially household safety and indoor air quality). In the early 1980s, most of this advocacy involved congressional lobbying, chiefly against anti-consumer measures proposed by the Reagan administration and by business groups.

During the second Reagan administration, CFA's advocates began to propose and advance new initiatives. In the banking area, they were instrumental in convincing the public of the need for new protections and successfully lobbied for legislation on check holds, home equity loans, credit cards, and savings disclosures. In the insurance area, with the National Insurance Consumer Organization (NICO), they mounted a successful campaign to lower credit life insurance rates; with NICO, Esther Peterson, and insurance agents, they undertook research and advocacy to increase the effectiveness and consumer responsiveness of state insurance departments; and with insurers, they organized a new group to fight insurance fraud. In the area of residential real estate brokerage, they used a series of widely publicized reports to help reform agent representation.

CFA's product safety advocacy sought mainly to influence Congress and the CPSC. Progress included a consent decree on all-terrain vehicles, a ban on lawn darts, a restriction on the use of methylene chloride in consumer products, and two CPSC reauthorizations. Outside the policy area, CFA conducted a successful campaign to improve the safety of playgrounds.

In the energy and utility areas, CFA lobbied successfully against accelerated deregulation of gas prices and, as part of Public Utility Holding Company reform, for increased transmission access. But the organization had its greatest impact in the area of telecommunications. CFA was the leading public interest group that contested Bell company expansion into long-distance, manufacturing, and information services without adequate consumer protections. Its most dramatic success was its lobbying of cable reregulation legislation, which Congress passed over a presidential veto.

In early 1995, two new developments promised to enhance the effectiveness of CFA's advocacy. Retiring Senator Howard Metzenbaum (D-OH) joined the federation as chairman. And NICO—led by recent Texas Insurance Commissioner J. Robert Hunter, former Vermont Banking and Insurance Commissioner James H. Hunt, and Kathleen O'Reilly—was incorporated into CFA.

— Stephen Brobeck

See also

Labor Movement; Rural Electric Cooperatives; State and Local Consumer Organizations.

Readings

Angevine, Erma (1982). "Lobbying and Consumer Federation of America." In Erma Angevine, ed. *Consumer Activists: They Made a Difference.* Mount Vernon, NY: Consumers Union Foundation. 331–342.

Logan, Gary J. (1988). "Profile: The Consumer Federation of America." *Everyday Law.* (May): 48–52.

Swanston, Walterene (1972). "Consumer Federation Waging Spirited Battle for Survival." *National Journal.* 4 (July 8): 1126–1136.

Consumer Information Center

The Consumer Information Center (CIC) was established in 1970 as a separately funded operation within the U.S. General Services Administration to be the central source of federal consumer information. CIC helps federal agencies and departments develop, promote, and distribute consumer information to the public. The agency fills consumer requests for publications through the U.S. Government Printing Office facility in Pueblo, Colorado. Each year through CIC, Americans order millions of booklets published by forty federal agencies.

To serve agencies and the public, the CIC staff of twenty-two provides a variety of services. The *Consumer Information Catalog* is published four times a year and distributed to millions of consumers. Each issue has descriptive listings of more than 200 free or low-cost booklets. Topics include health, federal benefits, money management, housing, child care, employment, small business, education, food and nutrition, cars, travel, and consumer protection. The *Catalog* is available through many schools, libraries, consumer groups, federal offices, and congressional offices; it is also sent by CIC in response to individual requests.

CIC pays close attention to emerging consumer issues and topics, and regularly reviews the booklets in the *Consumer Information Catalog*. When new issues need to be addressed, or old information updated, CIC assists the appropriate federal agency in developing and offering new publications to the public. As part of developing a publication, CIC works with the writers to keep out government jargon and legalese. Publication suggestions from consumers are also welcomed.

Although the majority of booklets listed in the *Consumer Information Catalog* are developed by federal agencies alone, the *Catalog* also includes consumer information produced jointly by government and private groups. CIC's criteria for cooperative publications were written in cooperation with the Society of Consumer Affairs Professionals in Business, the American Council on Consumer Interests, and the National Coalition for Consumer Education. The criteria require the publication to: receive the endorsement of the appropriate federal agency; clearly indicate that it is a joint government/industry effort; be an unbiased, objective presentation with clear labeling of industry or government positions whenever present; be free of advertising or promotional messages; and give permission for reprinting by educational and nonprofit groups.

CIC frequently uses television, radio, and print public service announcements to inform the public about the *Consumer Information Catalog*. These public service messages generate many of the individual requests for the *Catalog*. In addition, CIC regularly sends "New for Consumers" releases to more than 4,000 newspapers and magazines, consumer organizations, and state and local consumer agencies that have requested them. These releases highlight information from booklets listed in the *Catalog*, and provide ordering information for the booklets mentioned.

Members of the CIC media staff help reporters research consumer stories. Because the staff works closely with most federal agencies, they can put reporters in touch with contacts who will answer questions directly.

In addition, CIC sends out "Federal Consumer Focus" live copy scripts to more than 3,000 radio and television broadcasters. The scripts are written in varying lengths and highlight either information from publications or selected consumer news items. Both "New for Consumers" and "Federal Consumer Focus" are available in Spanish and English versions.

Finally, CIC works with magazines such as *Family Circle* and *Parade* to develop special media promotions on current consumer topics. In some cases, these promotions are for single booklets, while in others, the magazine mentions a number of publications as part of a larger feature story.

CIC is accessible electronically via its bulletin board system or the World Wide Web. The current *Catalog*, the full text of all publications listed, more than 250 other publications, and a library of "New for Consumers" press releases and "Federal Consumer Focus" broadcast scripts are available on the bulletin board. Additional bulletin board features include weekly updates of consumer news and notes from various federal agencies, selected *Federal Register* notices, and a calendar of consumer-related meetings, seminars, and conferences.

With an Internet connection, a consumer can reach CIC's World Wide Web home page, a more graphical electronic outlet. The home page allows access to the *Catalog;* a library of publications; CIC's television, radio, and print advertisements; and many other files.

CIC has a small staff of consumer information specialists available to speak at or participate in national conferences. CIC's exhibit, which includes free *Catalogs,* is shown at many major conferences.

— Mary Levy

Reading

Comptroller General of the United States. (1978). *The General Service Administration's Consumer Information Center: A Report.* Washington, D.C.: General Accounting Office.

Consumer Interest

The term *consumer interest* is, more than anything else, a rhetorical tool. Declaring that something is "in the consumer interest" is a way to bolster the case for a particular action or policy. Consumer advocates, by virtue of their work in representing consumers, believe that they can legitimately define what is (and what is not) in the consumer interest. Unfortunately, their efforts to define this interest are often met with competing definitions as well as assertions that there are so many consumer interests that it makes no sense to speak of "the" consumer interest. These conflicts are illustrated by the disagreements between two consumer magazines, *Consumer Reports* and *Consumers' Research,* which take diametrically opposed positions on most consumer issues.

To come up with a single definition of the consumer interest, one must first grapple with at least three issues: objective versus subjective definitions; differences among consumers; and tradeoffs for individual consumers.

Most uses of the term *consumer interest* imply an objective definition. This usage suggests implicitly that a consumer interest exists "out there"; it just takes an impartial and well-informed person to interpret it. For example, a judge ruling on the constitutionality of a ballot proposition rolling back automobile insurance rates in California declared the need to balance "the insurer's legitimate interest in financial integrity and the insured's interest in freedom from exploitation." The tone of this statement, especially the use of the word "legitimate," suggests that the judge, rather than the parties involved, defined the interests of insurance companies and insurance consumers.

The main problem with an objective definition of the consumer interest is that it is, ultimately, subjective. Whether the consumer interest is being interpreted by a judge, legislator, regulator, consumer advocate, or consumer researcher, the values and assumptions of the interpreter inevitably influence the definition. No one is omniscient and completely neutral.

If an objective definition of the consumer interest presents major problems, so does an explicitly subjective one. A subjective definition would allow each consumer to decide what is in his or her best interests. A subjective definition reduces consumer interests to consumer preferences. These preferences are best seen in individual behavior, especially purchases. The problem then arises of people doing things that are "bad" for them. If a person eats to the point of becoming obese, smokes three packages of cigarettes a day, and shoots up heroin, does it make sense to describe this person as acting in his "consumer interest"? From a purely subjective point of view, it does; from a common sense point of view, it does not.

A second part of the conundrum of defining the consumer interest stems from the fact that differences exist among consumers. This fact holds regardless of whether one defines the consumer interest objectively or subjectively. These differences are most obvious when they occur along lines of income, age, race, and geographical region.

Consider, for example, the consumer interest with respect to a minimal energy efficiency standard for air conditioners. The standard will eliminate low-efficiency, low-price models from the market. Such a standard is likely to be in the interest of consumers living in Houston, where air conditioners are used for more than half of the year, but not in the interest of consumers living in foggy Seattle. There are differences of consumer interest among Houston consumers too. The energy efficiency standard is in the interest of affluent consumers who will quickly recoup the high purchase price in terms of lower energy bills, but it may not be in the interest of poor consumers who cannot afford a more expensive purchase price.

Many other examples can be cited in which consumers might have different interests. Airline deregulation is in the interest of consumers living in large cities served by multiple carriers but not in the interest of consumers living in small cities and rural communities. Lifeline rates for electricity, telephone service, and banking serve the interests of low-income consumers but often at the expense of their more affluent counterparts. Rent control is in the interest of older people who already live in rent-controlled units, but it works against younger consumers who are first-time renters looking for space.

Apart from differing consumer interests with regard to specific policy interventions, consumers also have varying needs or "demand" for the objectives of consumer policy, such as risk reduction and information. For example, older persons have a greater need for information about health care while younger adults are more likely to need information about buying a home and obtaining a mortgage. To the extent that the "supply" of consumer policies is limited by societal resources, the interests of different groups of consumers inevitably compete with one another.

Even if consumers did not differ in terms of their income, age, race, and geographic location, further difficulties in defining the consumer interest would arise from the fact that a single consumer may have multiple and often competing interests. A bill introduced in the early 1970s described "the interests of consumers" as involving "the cost, quality, purity, safety, durability, performance, effectiveness, dependability and availability and adequacy of choice of goods and services offered or furnished to consumers." The problem with this definition of consumer interests is that many of these desirable qualities conflict with each other. The cost of an item is often in conflict with its safety and quality, as in the case of automobiles where bigger, more expensive cars are also safer. To cite another example, consumers want pharmaceutical products to be safe, effective, inexpensive, and quickly available after their discovery. The problem is that the process of ensuring safety and effectiveness raises prices and delays availability.

Despite these problems of defining the consumer interest, this term still has some value. There are at least four situations in which it can be useful to refer to a single, objective consumer interest.

First, and most obvious, consumers have an objective interest in obtaining the basic goods and services necessary for survival. Fortunately, relatively few items are needed for sheer survival, but depending on a society's standard of living, there may be many "perceived necessities." In more developed nations, these "necessities" might include a minimum level of access to health care, local telephone service, and simple banking services. All consumers have an interest in acquiring whatever goods and services are generally considered necessities in their society.

Second, even when a completely subjective definition of the consumer interest is used in which each individual determines his or her consumer interest, all consumers have an objective interest in getting the most "value," that is, obtaining a particular level of quality at the lowest possible price. Not all consumers will want the same level of quality, but all consumers will want to obtain their desired level of quality at the lowest possible price.

Third, consumers may share relatively few objective interests beyond access to basic necessities and obtaining value in the outcomes of market transactions. Nevertheless, consumers may share several additional interests in market processes, that is, in aspects of the opportunity to obtain goods and services. These interests refer to competition, information, representation, and redress. You cannot eat "competition," wear "information," drive "representation," or recline in "redress," but these processes affect the quality and price of the food, clothing, cars, and furniture consumers buy. Thus, all consumers have an interest in a competitive marketplace marked by accurate information, feasible avenues of redress, and opportunities for consumers to express their views to businesses and government agencies.

All of these uses of the term *consumer interest* are objective in the sense that an individual consumer may not perceive them. A starving consumer might choose to buy a cigarette rather than a glass of milk and a loaf of bread, but he or she would still have an objective consumer interest in purchasing the food. Similarly, a person might not know that opportunities exist to pay less for a given item, but the objective interest in maximizing the value of one's purchases still exists. Finally, the interest in opportunity factors such as competition, information, representation, and redress may not be readily perceived by consumers. As opposed to outcomes, these interests are abstract. People may not realize the importance of these opportunity factors until they experience a serious consumer problem.

Fourth, thinking of a single, objective consumer interest may be useful in situations where the consumer interest is pitted against other interests such as the business interest, the labor interest, or the environmental interest. Recognizing that none of these other interests is monolithic, it may still be important to distinguish what is at stake for consumers in a given situation and how this may differ from or conflict with the interests of another group. In the case of automobile safety features, it may be difficult to identify a single consumer interest because of the impact of safety features on new car prices and fuel economy. Still, it is important to distinguish the interests of consumers generally from those of automobile manufacturers, automobile workers, and environmental groups.

The term *consumer interest,* which is highly politicized, resists a single definition. There are pros and cons of using an objective versus a subjective definition, and one must recognize that there are many consumer interests—both between individuals and for a single person. Nevertheless, it is still possible to think of "the consumer interest" in objective terms and to use it in promoting consumer access to basic necessities; value in purchases; processes of competition, representation, information, and redress; and awareness of the relationship between the consumer interest and other societal interests.

— Robert N. Mayer, Stephen Brobeck

See also

Research on Consumer Issues.

Readings

Forbes, James D. (1987). *The Consumer Interest: Dimensions and Policy Implications.* London: Croom Helm.

Kroll, Robert J. (1991). "Advancing the Consumer Interest: Traditional Ideology versus a Generic View." *Advancing the Consumer Interest.* 3 (1): 22–26.

Consumer Leagues

The consumer league concept originated in England, spreading from there to the United States and to several European nations. In the United States, the leagues developed along with other social justice groups as part of the Progressive reform movement of the late nineteenth century.

In 1891, Josephine Shaw Lowell founded the New York City Consumers League to improve working conditions in the city's retail stores. League members believed that consumers had the ability and responsibility to eliminate child labor, reduce excessive hours of work, increase low wages, and improve working conditions.

The New York league initiated a Consumer White Label granted to manufacturers of cotton garments who met specified labor standards; it urged consumers to buy only White Label goods. After the Massachusetts Consumers League persuaded Boston's Filene's store to sell White Label cotton, conditions in factories improved.

Other consumer leagues soon were organized in Chicago and in Philadelphia. These two leagues, along with the New York City and Massachusetts leagues as well as others committed to social justice, organized and chartered the National Consumers League (NCL) in 1899 and hired Florence Kelley as its chief executive officer. Kelley, recognizing the need for a constituency, crisscrossed the nation organizing leagues among college students and in church, women's, and community groups. In five years, she had inspired the creation of sixty-four branches in twenty states. The number of branches in the United States peaked later at ninety.

The first international conference of consumer leagues was held in Geneva, Switzerland, in 1908. The NCL sent a delegation. By 1913, consumer leagues had been organized in England, France, Holland, Germany, Belgium, Switzerland, and the United States. Only those in the United States and Switzerland survived World War I.

Kelley depended on leagues around the country for assistance in persuading congressmen to vote for consumer legislation. She, in turn, helped the leagues draft state legislation and work for better state consumer and worker laws. She drafted a model minimum wage law for the Massachusetts Consumers League. In 1912, Massachusetts enacted the first U.S. minimum wage law.

The Oregon Consumers League persuaded its state legislature to limit the workday for women to ten hours. When the law was challenged and was appealed to the U.S. Supreme Court, Kelley secured Louis D. Brandeis of Boston to defend its constitutionality. Brandeis prepared a defense based on facts drawn from ninety reports from special committees in Europe and the United States concerning squalid working conditions. This defense was the first of the "Brandeis Briefs" for which he became famous. The Supreme Court voted unanimously that Oregon's law was constitutional.

Other leagues called on the NCL for help in resolving state issues. Brandeis continued to represent the league in many of these battles, always donating his time, until he was named to the Supreme Court.

The New Jersey Consumers League is best known for its investigation, in the early 1920s, of working conditions of girls who painted watch dials at the U.S. Radium Corporation. They visited homes of the girls, finding that eight were seriously ill and others had died. Death was caused by anemia and necrosis of the jaw. They visited the dentist who had treated the girls and learned they had symptoms resembling "phossy jaw," a disease caused by the use of phosphorus in manufacturing matches.

The league asked Kelley for assistance. She and Dr. Alice Hamilton secured a doctor's report that "conclusively established the fact that the deaths and illnesses among the employees . . . were due to the fact that the employees had been handling radioactive substances without proper protection." With this information, the NCL and the New Jersey Consumers League initiated a campaign to get radium mesothorium necrosis included in the list of compensable diseases under workman's compensation. New Jersey's governor signed the new provision into law in March 1926.

In the early 1930s, Elizabeth Magee, an Ohio Consumers League official, served as executive secretary of the state's Commission on Unemployment Insurance. She directed hearings and investigations, then wrote a report that led to passage of Ohio's 1935 law creating an unemployment insurance system to which both employers and employees contributed.

League members included both men and women who were dedicated to social reform. Many of them lived and worked in Hull House and the Henry Street Settlement. Hull House, under Jane Addams's leadership, became the Chicago focus of men such as Gerard Swope, Charles A. Beard, and Sidney Hillman and women such as Frances Perkins, Julia Lathrop, Grace Abbott, and Florence Kelley. Among the workers in Henry Street Settlement in New York City were Henry Morgenthau, Jr., Herbert Lehman, Adolph A. Berle, Jr., Eleanor Roosevelt, Lillian Wald, Josephine Goldmark, and also Kelley.

After Kelley's death in February 1932, NCL board leaders John R. Commons, a University of Wisconsin economics professor, and Nicholas Kelley, an economist who was Kelley's son, selected Lucy Randolph Mason to run the organization.

President Franklin Roosevelt's 1933 National Recovery Administration (NRA) was welcomed by consumer leagues. The NRA would establish codes prescribing maximum hours, minimum wages, and collective bargaining, and abolishing child labor. The NRA included a Consumer Advisory Board to review industrywide codes before they were adopted. But the NRA refused to accept the recommendations of this board. In response, board chairman Mary Harriman Rumsey, an official of the New York Consumers League, asked member Paul Douglas to organize a chain of local consumers' councils throughout the country to serve as the board's constituency. Douglas organized nearly 100 of these councils. When the Supreme Court declared the NRA unconstitutional, some councils that were former consumer leagues continued. Those without strong local leadership disappeared.

Despite the role played by league leaders in the New Deal, during this period many leagues were shut down. Some fell victim to lack of money or effective leadership. But the underlying reason that most of these leagues ceased to exist is that an expanding labor movement had taken over their central mission of fighting for improved working conditions for women and child workers.

Several state leagues and the NCL survived and were revived in the 1960s and 1970s, but with more of a traditional consumer than worker focus. Most of the issues they addressed were the same ones treated by dozens of other local, state, and national consumer organizations that were established during this period. Today, state leagues continue to operate in New Jersey, Oregon, and Wisconsin, and the NCL itself remains one of the most active national consumer organizations.

— Erma B. Angevine

See also

Labor Movement; National Consumers League; State and Local Consumer Organizations.

Readings

Athey, Louis Lee (1965). *The Consumers' Leagues and Social Reform, 1890–1923*. Ph.D. dissertation, University of Delaware.

Harrison, Dennis Irven (1975). *The Consumers' League of Ohio: Women and Reform, 1909–1937*. Ph.D. dissertation, Case Western Reserve University.

Keyserling, Mary Dublin (1982). "The First National Consumers Organization: The National Consumers League." In Erma Angevine, ed. *Consumer Activists: They Made a Difference*. Mount Vernon, NY: Consumers Union Foundation. 343–360.

Consumer Movement: History and Dynamics

See U.S. Consumer Movement: History and Dynamics.

Consumer Problems in Market Economies

Ever since Adam Smith, consumer sovereignty has been the universally accepted goal of economic activity. Consumer sovereignty means that each consumer obtains what he or she truly wants, limited only by the extent of personal income. If markets worked perfectly and consumers were fully informed and fully understanding, consumer sovereignty would prevail. There would be no need for "consumerism," consumer organizations, and consumer representation.

In reality, consumer sovereignty is far from realized in most market economies. There is an asymmetry of resources that favors business over consumers and permeates all aspects of our market economy. This asymmetry contributes to many problems that bedevil consumers: complex products and services that make quality assessment difficult; information on the existence of product variants and retailers, price, and quality that is often false, biased, or incomplete; in some markets for some goods, too few sellers and hence too little competition; unscrupulous sellers and uncaring civil servants; too little time, especially for two-earner families; the underrepresentation of the consumer interest in politics; and laws, regulations, and regulatory agencies that are ineffective or serve producers more than consumers. Also, certain consumers are disadvantaged by traits such as low intelligence, physical and mental disabilities, naivete, and insufficient education to master language, computational, and conceptual skills.

Asymmetric Power: Businesses versus Consumers

At every juncture, consumer problems are exacerbated by the vast asymmetry in resources for information-persuasion, complaint resolution, and influence between businesses and consumers. Evidence of this asymmetry abounds. For example, business employs more than 12 million persons with major responsibilities for information-persuasion (i.e., selling and advertising), while the two largest consumer information organizations, Consumers Union and the American Association of Retired Persons (AARP) employ about 1,000. Moreover, business spends more than $150 billion on advertising compared to total revenues of Consumers Union and AARP of less than $600 million.

In essence, American businesses collect a variable sales tax to finance their information-persuasion activities by setting prices high enough to cover these "necessary" costs. This practice arose so innocently and gradually that it is accepted without question. In the eighteenth century, there was no need for business to devote many resources to information-persuasion. Products were simple. Quality and price were readily discerned by inspection. In the rural, small town markets of that time, the existence of stores was common knowledge. There were no "brands." Consumers knew shopkeepers personally. Markets were relatively transparent.

During the past two centuries, products have become more complex, markets have grown larger, and consumers have made increasing numbers of purchases. Consequently, sellers felt the need to advertise and marketing grew more complex. Ultimately, information-persuasion was professionalized into marketing, advertising, and sales. Understandably, the sellers who paid for "messages" exerted control over their content.

In their dealings with businesses, consumers face three handicaps. The first is the fact that a person's interest as a consumer is always secondary to one's producer interest in a job-profession-business, at least until retirement. Both systematic research and casual observation confirm this conclusion. As a result, many individuals devote far more attention to work-related activities than to consumption-related ones.

A second consumer handicap is the dispersed nature of consumer activities compared to the focused nature of producer activities. As producer, a person is concerned with a single job, product, or industry. As consumer, by contrast, one's interest is spread thinly across thousands of transactions and the management of hundreds of possessions. Each product has its own informational requirements, terms, and associated grievances. This diversity of consumer problems precludes specialization and the expertise that it confers. The result is that, most of the time, the consumer is an amateur-generalist, frequently making choices in situations where he cannot possibly be expert. There is no clearer example of the knowledge gap between consumers and providers than in the area of health care services. Physicians tell patients what they need; patients cannot be knowledgeable about medical matters, and are often too sick to shop.

A third consumer handicap consists of the nonrecognition of the purchasing agent role of the consumer. Within households, the person who does most of the buying can achieve the same payoffs as purchasing agents in firms: lower prices; better value for money; appropriate products, features, and accessories. Unfortunately for households, this role has been little recognized and neither professionalized nor honored. Most often, this role has been neglected or even denigrated as "women's work."

Worse, few consumers are aware of an immense boon to the purchasing agent role: these earnings (in the form of money saved by wise purchasing) are untaxed and thus provide more purchasing power than ordinary income. For middle-income families, it is roughly correct that "a dollar saved is $1.75 earned." Yet, few seek these earnings aggressively.

Disadvantaged Consumers

Disadvantaged consumers, in some degree, are unable to perform well in local consumer markets. They may lack the understanding of markets, knowledge of products and their properties, mobility and time for shopping, or the ability to bargain. Some are disadvantaged by personal characteristics such as low intelligence; illiteracy with respect to language, culture, arithmetic, or computers; naivete; mental illness or instability; poor health or specific physical disabilities; or old age and the physical, mental, and psychological disabilities it sometimes brings on. Consumers may also suffer from disadvantages related to their economic or social status. If they are poor and less mobile, they are often forced to live in impoverished neighborhoods and shop in its inferior stores. In general, disadvantaged consumers tend to be poor, African-American, and Hispanic; to live in single-parent households; and to be aged, less-educated, dwellers in urban slums or rural poverty, and unable to afford a car.

A different disadvantaged group is the ideologically captured and the economically naive who believe, incorrectly, that local consumer markets work well. They embrace and follow such slogans as "price is an indicator of quality," or "you get what you pay for." They tend to trust sellers. The consequence of these misbeliefs is clear: these consumers lose out.

There are some products whose excessive use can render otherwise normal consumers "vulnerable" and disadvantaged: undesirable, addictive products, such as alcoholic beverages, cigarettes, cocaine, or other drugs; and hazardous products whose danger is underestimated or even unknown, such as thalidomide, asbestos, cigarettes, or motorcycles.

Disadvantaged consumers tend to be inefficient in their consumer choices: they pay more for a given quality, receive less quality while holding price constant, incur more consumer grievances than others, and are more often victims of unsafe products. One implication of this fact is that the conventional measure of poverty, the income/needs ratio, badly underestimates the true deprivation of the disadvantaged poor.

Informationally Imperfect Consumer Markets

A daunting consumer problem, unrecognized by most, is that, for almost all products in almost all local consumer markets, the correlation between price and true quality is near zero. In these informationally imperfect markets, consumers can lose substantial portions of their purchasing power and suffer serious losses as well.

One of the clearest examples of an informationally imperfect market is that for term life insurance. Here, quality varies little. Every company's policy pays the insured person's beneficiaries the face value of the policy. Yet, as reported many times in *Consumer Reports*, the highest price exceeds the lowest price by ratios of two to one or three to one. For most products, however, quality varies substantially, thus complicating the consumer's task.

In informationally imperfect markets, consumers lose in four ways: they may pay too much for a given level of quality; they may receive too little quality for a given price; they may choose a less-than-optimal trade-off between price and quality; and for more complex products such as automobiles, they may choose features and accessories that meet neither their needs nor their wants.

What sources of information do shoppers use? Information on retailers, locally available varieties, and prices usually comes from shopping. Its accuracy depends on the competence and diligence of the shopper.

Information on quality and on what varieties are available nationally comes mostly from Consumers Union through its magazine, *Consumer Reports*. This organization began product testing in 1936 and, in collaboration with thirty-five other consumer product testing organizations worldwide, has been improving its methods ever since. The magazine has about 5 million subscribers and fifteen to 20 million readers, and publishes eighty or so product evaluations annually.

There are many reasons for consumers to trust Consumers Union's quality ratings. First, the organization has developed, applied, and refined methods that are essentially scientific, i.e., replicable. Second, its ratings rest on laboratory tests, controlled use tests, expert judgments, and data from large-scale sample surveys that quantify subscribers' experiences. Third, Consumers Union uses surrogates to purchase its test samples anonymously. Fourth, its methods have been reviewed periodically in professional journals, yielding general approval along with particular criticisms. Finally, even though Consumers Union has been sued about twenty times by manufacturers of products rated as "unacceptable," none of these lawsuits has succeeded.

Why are most consumer markets informationally imperfect and opaque rather than informationally imperfect and transparent? The simple answer is that most consumers are unable and/or unwilling to obtain the information they need to make effective choices and thus discipline markets. A more detailed answer distinguishes between market-induced causes and seller-induced causes.

Market-induced causes of informationally imperfect markets are "innocent" in the sense that they derive from the character of affluent societies and modern markets, not from actions taken by sellers. One of these causes is the technical complexity and multicomponent nature of modern products, which make it difficult for consumers to gauge quality and price accurately. A second cause is price discrimination. This discrimination occurs when a single seller charges different buyers different prices for the same goods. Price discrimination is widely prevalent. It includes every genuine sale or "special," every instance of bargaining, coupons of all sorts, discounts to variegated groups (older persons and members of professional, fraternal, business, or church organizations), and loyalty awards (e.g., Frequent Flyers, special sales for long-standing customers). Price discrimination vastly multiplies the set of possible price offers among which a consumer must choose, thus complicating consumer choice.

The third cause of informationally imperfect markets is affluence. Affluence has increased both the number of choices possible and the amount of information required. Specifically, affluence has enlarged the number of purchases that an average family can make; increased the number of products, brands, models, and retailers among which they must choose; and increased the value of an individual's time and hence reduced the extent of his searching/shopping. Moreover, urbanization, the automobile, and shopping malls have further expanded the choice of products, brands, models, and retailers.

Seller-induced causes of informationally imperfect markets arise from the fact that manufacturers and retailers control most information-persuasion resources. To understand the consequences for consumers of this seller influence, it is useful to deal separately with two kinds of decision-makers, information seekers and delegators. Information seekers search themselves and then choose. In seeking information, these seekers follow the "marginal rule," seeking more information as long as the expected gain exceeds the expected cost of obtaining it.

By contrast, delegators let some other person, organization, or cue act as their "surrogates" in choosing. Their surrogates may be business-controlled sources such as salespersons, advertisements, or product-promotional literature from companies; neutral sources such as friends or relatives; someone they believe to be "expert"; articles in newspapers or magazines; publications of governments, universities, or nonprofit institutions; or "consumer" programs on television. Alternatively, delegators may rely on such extrinsic cues to value as brand names and store reputation, or such intrinsic cues as package design, warranty, or style.

Business control of information-persuasion resources contributes to informationally imperfect markets in two ways. First, in market economies individual sellers profit by selling their "own" varieties of products, whether or not they represent good value. This reality biases their efforts to obtain, disclose, or share relevant product information. Accordingly, business-controlled information sources are likely to be incomplete, biased, and misleading, thwarting the goals of both information seekers and delegators.

A second contribution of business control to informationally imperfect markets is information overload. Selling messages account for large proportions of television and radio time, magazine and newspaper pages, Yellow Pages, and conversations with salespersons. The volume of the incomplete, biased, and misleading nature of these messages overloads consumers with information, making it extremely costly and difficult for information seekers to cull the worthwhile from the worthless.

Together, market-induced and seller-induced factors account for the prevalence of undisciplined consumer markets in which prices and true quality are not correlated. Yet, both information seekers and delegators whose surrogates know of and rely heavily on good information sources are likely to fare well in these markets.

The limits of these sources should be noted, however. *Consumer Reports* publishes only eighty or so product reports a year. Further, since the magazine is national and prices are local, consumers must rely mainly on their own understanding of markets and their own shopping to obtain price information. Other neutral sources such as government, universities, and nonprofit institutions rarely make available brand-specific information.

The Classical Monopoly Problem

Since Adam Smith and even before, economists and consumers have known what to expect from "monopolists": higher prices (quality held constant), lower quality, and less output than competition would enforce. The sources of monopoly power are well known: economies of scale in production, financing, and marketing; enterprises that are "large" relative to the market they serve, their size arising from mergers, acquisitions, or natural growth; collusion, either overt or tacit among sellers; and barriers to entry into lines of activity arising from large capital requirements, lack of access to technology and finance, control of raw materials, or government regulation that seeks to conserve the competitors rather than competition.

Less recognized is the fact that consumers may be victimized by insufficient competition at the retail level as well as at the producer-distributor level. The extreme case is the small town, village, neighborhood, or airport that is served by only one food store, dentist, restaurant, hardware store, or other type of merchant.

Even though much of the world is populated by enormous transnational corporations, the monopoly problem has been lessened in recent years by increased international competition. This competition, from which not even the largest corporations are immune, has enlarged consumer choice. There is no better example than increased competition, during the past three decades, in the new car market.

Consumer Grievances

Given the unequal relationship between businesses and consumers generally, it is not surprising that there are many consumer grievances. Research suggests that consumers experience dissatisfaction with about 20 percent of their purchases. Grievances include: delivery failures, where the product or service is delivered or performed tardily, not at all, or not as specified; performance failures in design, production, or service, where the product underperforms or, worse, fails to work at all; inadvertent failures in communication, where the seller and buyer have different interpretations of what was promised with respect to attributes or performance, ancillary services (e.g., free delivery), prices, or other purchase terms; misrepresentation, deception, or fraud; unsafe products, an extreme form of performance failure; failure to correct an initial problem; and billing-payment problems ranging from errors in bills to difficulty resolving any problems.

The causes of consumer grievances are similar to those giving rise to informationally imperfect markets. As products become more technically complex, they are more likely to contain defects and more likely to be difficult to repair. But complexity is not confined to products; it also embraces contracts, laws, financing arrangements, and regulations.

A second source of grievances is the character of retail establishments. Increasingly, products are sold by individual stores that are branches of multiestablishment, geographically dispersed firms, which do not make the goods they sell and are often staffed by short-term employees. The result is often ambiguous placement of responsibility for problems, and impersonal and bureaucratic treatment of complainants.

Consumers are not blameless when it comes to consumer problems. They fail to read and follow instructions or misuse the product. In addition, the consumer's "amateur" status when it comes to a do-it-yourself project or to assembling a toy or piece of furniture may give rise to perceived product problems. Also, some consumers engage in fraud, concocting phony purchases and phony grievances for which they seek "redress."

Underrepresentation of the Consumer Interest

As long as an economy is effectively competitive with numerous sellers and well-informed consumers, there is no need for consumer representation. Consumers are protected by competition's "invisible hand." But in an economy where markets are informationally imperfect, and consumers experience other types of problems, they need representation that seeks to advance their interests. Even though everyone is a consumer, the consumer interest commands few resources. There are several reasons.

As indicated above, the consumer interest of individuals is spread thinly across the informational requirements, the terms of purchase, and the grievances arising from thousands of transactions and the management of hundreds of possessions, few with elements that repeat. By contrast, the seller's interest and the producer interest of the income-earning individual are highly focused, and centered on a particular job, a particular business, or a particular establishment-product-industry set.

The dispersion of the consumer interest has three consequences, all subversive to its representation. First, this interest lacks an obvious, cohesive political constituency.

Though most countries have "conservative," "liberal," and sometimes "labor" parties, none has a "Consumer Party." A second consequence is the difficulty of representing the consumer interest. A consumer representative is inevitably spread thin. In dealing with a particular issue, he or she often "starts from scratch" in mastering the subject. Third, the specialization of producer representatives and their resulting expertness, as contrasted with the nonspecialized background of many consumer representatives, results in more effective representation of producer than consumer interests before regulatory agencies. In addition, the actions of regulators may be influenced by the possibility of post-regulatory employment with the producers they are charged with regulating.

A second major reason for the underrepresentation of the consumer interest is lack of financing. Sellers finance their representation from the same "sales tax" that finances their information-persuasion activities. The consumer interest relies for its financing largely on revenues from the sale of consumer information, government appropriations to consumer-oriented agencies, targeted campaigns soliciting contributions for specific projects, membership dues from individuals or organizations, grants from foundations and other organizations, and awards from successful lawsuits. In addition, trial lawyers will often fund product liability, malpractice, and class action lawsuits that usually serve the interest of consumer plaintiffs.

Nevertheless, compared to producer interests (business, labor, farmers), the consumer interest is woefully underfinanced. This lack of financing has contributed to the slow growth of "consumer affairs professionals" in nonprofit and government consumer organizations.

A third major cause of the underrepresentation of consumers is the "public good" nature of the consumer interest: all consumers benefit from a successful reform achieved by a small number. This general dispersion of benefits provides the individual consumer with a negligible incentive to participate in or support the representation of consumers. He or she can be a "free rider" on the efforts of others.

Finally, "business" is hardly neutral with respect to the consumer interest, often viewing the competition for influence as zero-sum in nature, with business losing whenever consumers gain. By this interpretation, it is no accident that it was business lobbying that thwarted, in the 1970s, the establishment of a federal consumer protection agency. Nor is business neutral when consumer or public-oriented regulatory agencies are established. Business has often sought to "capture" these agencies, enlisting them for its own ends. That is why, for example, import restrictions on "unsanitary food" and "unsafe products" are often designed to forestall foreign competition.

One other factor that disadvantages many consumers today is severe time pressure. In a recent survey, 40 percent of women and 24 percent of men aged twenty-four to sixty-four say "they feel rushed to do the things they have to do." This should come as no surprise; 85 percent of men and 70 to 75 percent of women in the prime ages are in the formal labor force. In addition, as consumers they are "the keepers of their durables": one-third have children; nearly two-thirds own their home; and most own two or more cars, a color television, refrigerator, clothes dryer, microwave, electric oven, electric range, and other appliances. All of these things need to be managed in a 168-hour week. Not surprisingly, many consumers cannot find the time to manage effectively consumption that has grown more complex and dynamic.

— E. Scott Maynes

See also

Antitrust Protections; Consumers Union; Disputes and Dispute Resolution; Information Dissemination; Low-Income Consumers.

Readings

Andreasen, Alan R. (1988). "Consumer Complaints and Redress: What We Know and

What We Don't Know." In E. Scott Maynes, ed. *The Frontier of Research in the Consumer Interest.* Columbia, MO: American Council on Consumer Interests. 675–722.

——— (1975). *The Disadvantaged Consumer.* New York: The Free Press.

Maynes, E. Scott (1990). "An Information Desiderata Evaluation of Sources of Consumer Information." In Robert N. Mayer, ed. *Enhancing Consumer Choice: Proceedings of the Second International Conference in the Consumer Interest.* Columbia, MO: American Council on Consumer Interests. 491–514.

Consumer Product Hazards

See Product Hazards.

Consumer Product Safety Commission

The Consumer Product Safety Commission (CPSC) is an independent regulatory agency charged with protecting consumers from hazards associated with an estimated 15,000 different consumer products. These products include items used in and around the house, at schools, or in recreational areas, but exclude products regulated by other federal agencies, such as food, drugs, cars, and boats.

The use of consumer products in the home accounts for a significant number of injuries and deaths, resulting in billions of dollars of health care costs and property damage. In 1995, for example, there were an estimated 26,400 deaths that occurred in the home unintentionally and 19.6 million injuries, 7.3 million of which were disabling. The cost of these injuries was estimated to be $95.1 billion.

Congressional Mandate

Congress established the CPSC in 1972 "to protect the public against unreasonable risks of injury associated with consumer products." The CPSC has the authority to set mandatory standards, ban products, order recalls of unsafe products, or institute labeling requirements. The agency also provides information to the public about hazardous products. The CPSC learns about product-related injuries and deaths through a variety of sources, including the National Electronic Injury Surveillance System, consumer complaints, in-depth investigations by CPSC staff, and other databases and sources.

The CPSC is charged with carrying out six statutes. The most important, the Consumer Product Safety Act, was signed into law on October 27, 1972. This broad statute sets out the commission's jurisdiction and powers (bans, mandatory standards, and recalls) as well as its structure and organization. The act contains restrictive information disclosure provisions, such as one that limits the release of information that identifies a manufacturer's name. The CPSC must rely on voluntary consumer product safety standards, rather than promulgating mandatory standards, whenever compliance with the voluntary standard would eliminate or adequately reduce the risk of injury and there is likely to be substantial compliance with the voluntary standard. Although they are not technically part of the Consumer Product Safety Act, amendments addressing some product-specific hazards have been adopted.

The Federal Hazardous Substances Act was passed in 1960. Its original intent was to require precautionary or warning labels on hazardous household chemical products. Included under the act are substances that are toxic, corrosive, an irritant, a strong sensitizer, flammable, or combustible or that generate pressure through decomposition, heat, or other means. Through amendments, the act's jurisdiction expanded to include toys and other products intended for children that present an electrical, mechanical, or thermal hazard. The CPSC has regulated toys, cribs, rattles, pacifiers, walkers, and other products for children under this act.

The Poison Prevention Packaging Act was signed into law in 1970 to address the risk to children from ingestion of hazardous household substances. The act establishes child resistant packaging standards for certain household products. Any product subject to the standards must be contained in child resistant packaging unless the manufacturer also packages the substance in a package that is not child resistant and this package contains a conspicuous label stating: "This package for households without young children."

The Flammable Fabrics Act was enacted in 1953 as a response to fires involving children who were wearing highly flammable clothing. Under this law, fabric, articles of apparel, and interior furnishings must comply with flammability standards promulgated by the CPSC. The act has been extremely effective in reducing deaths associated with children's sleepwear—from sixty per year (during the early 1970s) to less than five per year (in the 1990s).

Enacted in 1956, the Refrigerator Safety Act requires all household refrigerators manufactured after October 1958 to have safety devices enabling them to be opened from the inside in order to prevent entrapment and suffocation inside the refrigerator. The value of the act is evidenced by the lack of deaths in refrigerators with the safety devices and continuing deaths in pre-1958 refrigerators. Between 1980 and 1988, for example, fifty-nine children died when they became trapped in old-style latch-type refrigerators and freezers.

The Fire Safe Cigarette Act was passed in 1990 to address cigarette-ignited fires. It directs the CPSC and the National Institute for Standards and Technology to develop a standard to determine cigarette ignition propensity, compile performance data for cigarettes, and conduct studies to predict cigarette ignition. In addition, the act charged the CPSC with implementing a study to collect data about the characteristics of cigarettes, products they ignited, smokers involved in fires, and costs of cigarette-ignited fires.

Leadership and Program Areas

Leadership of the CPSC is vested in a chairman and commissioners. The Consumer Product Safety Act provides for presidential appointment of five commissioners. One commissioner is designated by the president as chairman while the commissioners elect a vice chairman. In order to foster independence, no more than three commissioners can be affiliated with the same political party. The CPSC is headquartered in Bethesda, Maryland, a suburb of Washington, D.C. The agency has regional offices in New York, Chicago, and San Francisco.

The CPSC has three key program areas: hazard identification and reduction, compliance and enforcement, and information and public affairs.

The Office of Hazard Identification and Reduction has two separate programs. The Hazard Identification and Analysis program collects consumer injury and death data and analyzes it to determine whether more investigation is needed and whether hazard reduction strategies would be appropriate. The Hazard Assessment and Reduction program takes the data developed by the Identification and Analysis program and develops solutions (such as a standard, ban, or labeling requirement) to address the hazards. Alternatively, the CPSC may pursue a nonregulatory solution, such as providing information about the hazard to the public.

The Office of Compliance and Enforcement staff supervises compliance and administrative enforcement activity under all administered acts and reviews proposed standards and rules with respect to their enforceability. This office is also responsible for identifying and acting on safety hazards in consumer products already in distribution, promoting industry compliance with existing rules, and conducting litigation before an administrative law judge. It also directs the enforcement efforts of the field offices, monitors corrective action plans, and enforces statutory provisions requiring firms to identify and report product defects that could present possible safety hazards.

The Office of Information and Public Affairs program is responsible for the development, implementation, and evaluation of a comprehensive national information and public affairs program designed to promote product safety. The office manages the CPSC's toll-free hotline, which accepts consumer complaint information and gives out information on product recalls and other safety issues.

Over the years, the actions of the CPSC have been influenced by three sources: the data it gathers on consumer product hazards, the priorities established by the commission, and petitions from outside parties.

Data on consumer product hazards are collected from a variety of sources and are used to identify trends. The agency uses information from death certificates, hospital injury reports, and consumer complaints. The agency's compliance staff also becomes aware of hazard trends through its own investigations or through manufacturer reports of substantial product hazards, which are required by law to be reported.

The agency also has instituted regulations for the establishment of priorities for commission action. Priorities are decided by majority vote of the commission. Votes on all requests for appropriations, an annual operating plan, and any revisions reflect these priorities. Each year, the CPSC also designates specific priority issues. The public is invited to submit comments or to appear at an annual hearing on priorities. The commission examines the following criteria in establishing specific priorities: frequency and severity of injuries, causality of injuries, chronic illness and future injuries, costs and benefits of CPSC action, unforeseen nature of the risk, vulnerability of the population at risk, and probability of exposure to hazard.

The agency agenda is also affected by petitions filed by outside parties. While the specific petition provision of the Consumer Product Safety Act was repealed in 1981, the right to petition the agency still exists by virtue of the right of petition found in the Administrative Procedures Act. Generally, several petitions are filed each year seeking promulgation of a standard or ban of a consumer product in order to address a product hazard.

Historical Challenges

The CPSC has faced stiff challenges during its existence. Because the regulation of consumer product hazards is often complex, the agency has had to struggle to develop technical expertise. That struggle has been complicated by the fact that the agency often has had to rely on industry for information. Simultaneously, it has experienced a turnover of chairmen and/or commissioners, severe budget and staff cuts, and congressional amendment of its procedures for promulgation of safety rules.

During the Reagan administration, the CPSC was subjected to massive budget and personnel cuts. In 1982, the budget was reduced by 30 percent with a 27 percent reduction in agency staff. This budget and staff drain continued throughout most of the 1980s. Conservative appointments of chairmen and commissioners contributed to serious staff morale problems. Promulgation of regulations fell to an all-time low.

During the agency's first two decades of operation, a number of public interest consumer organizations emerged as advocates of product safety issues. Chief among these have been Consumer Federation of America, Consumers Union, U.S. Public Interest Research Group, Public Citizen's Congress Watch and Litigation Group, and the National SAFE KIDS Campaign.

These groups have filed petitions with the agency seeking standards or bans of dangerous consumer products. They have conducted surveys examining the availability of dangerous consumer products. On Capitol Hill, these organizations have lobbied Congress for statutory changes in CPSC laws to improve its structure and the procedures by which it operates; they have sought enactment of product-specific legislation when the agency itself has refused to take action; and they have supported increased appropriations for the CPSC. Finally, these groups have challenged in court specific agency actions or failures to act.

Because CPSC authority is nationwide, the agency's area of activity encompasses almost the entire manufacturing sector. The relevant business coalition varies, therefore, from issue to issue. A flammable fabrics rule will see action by textile manufacturers, a toy safety rule by toy makers, and a lawnmower rule by lawnmower manufacturers. On a more general level, the U.S. Chamber of Commerce and the National Association of Manufacturers have opposed what they see as CPSC regulatory excess, often before Congress, where they have supported amendments to weaken the CPSC's statutes.

The CPSC has had a troubled budget and staffing history. It began operation in fiscal year 1974 (its first full year) with a budget of $34.7 million and a staff of 786. Its budget rose to a high of $43.9 million in 1979, and its staff reached a high of 978 employees in 1980. During the Reagan and Bush administrations, the CPSC budget was cut substantially, and then increased modestly. The largest reduction occurred in 1982, when the agency's budget was reduced from $42.1 million (1981) to $32.1 (1982). Between 1980 and 1984, the number of staff positions was cut from 978 to 595.

In the past seven years, the CPSC has managed to obtain $1 million to $3 million increases, but it has lost an additional forty employees. The agency's 1995 appropriation marked the first time in the agency's history that the number of staff fell below 500—to 487 employees. The consumer and health communities believe that the agency's budget and staffing levels are inadequate and, on numerous occasions, have provided Congress with related testimony and correspondence. For example, in a 1993 letter to congressional appropriations committee members, 28 consumer and health groups called upon Congress to begin increasing the agency's budget over the next few years toward a goal of $55 million.

Despite the recent budget increases, the CPSC has not been able to keep pace with the demand for resources that its broad consumer product jurisdiction requires. Without the necessary funds, the agency must often discontinue projects or restructure them over several years. Their testing laboratories lack proper equipment, and their computer capabilities have been limited. Enforcement staff are hampered in their negotiations for recalls because they do not have enough resources to conduct investigations in a manner that will foster successful court challenges.

In spite of these challenges, CPSC actions have saved lives and money. From 1977 to 1989, deaths associated with consumer products decreased by 13 percent—from 25,000 per year to 21,600 per year. From 1979 to 1991, injuries associated with consumer products decreased by 14 percent. Commission actions are estimated to save society about $2.5 billion each year. In 1992, the agency estimated that since 1973, it had issued fifty mandatory standards or special packaging requirements, forty product bans, and sixty requirements for product labels. Additionally, in 1990 and 1991, the CPSC recalled 59 million product units and stopped importation of 405 shipments of products in violation of safety standards.

— Mary Ellen R. Fise

See also

Product Hazards.

Readings

Adler, Robert S. (1989). "From Model Agency to Basket Case: Can the Consumer Product Safety Commission Be Redeemed?" *Administrative Law Review.* 41 (1): 61–129.

Fise, Mary Ellen R. (1995). "Consumer Product Safety Regulation." In Kenneth J. Meier and E. Thomas Garman, eds. *Regulation and Consumer Protection.* Houston: DAME Publications, Inc. 277–294.

Zick, Cathleen D., Robert N. Mayer, and Laverne Alves Snow (1986). "Does the U.S. Consumer Product Safety Commission Make a Difference? An Assessment of Its First Decade." *Journal of Consumer Policy.* 9 (March): 25–40.

Consumer Protection Agency

See U.S. Consumer Protection Agency.

Consumer Representation

See Public Representation.

Consumer Rights

Most lists of consumers' rights and responsibilities are derived from the four consumer rights identified in President John F. Kennedy's March 15, 1962, message to Congress on protecting the consumer interest. Although its immediate impact was limited, the message has had long-term consequences that have been substantial for at least three reasons: first, it represented one of the few times any president directly addressed the consumer interest, thus ensuring that the reviving consumer movement would be taken seriously; second, the four rights served as a working agenda for the reforms of the 1960s and 1970s; and third, to a considerable degree, the issues associated with the four rights continue to resonate today.

The president's message identified the following rights: to safety (protection from the marketing of hazardous products); to be informed (protection from misinformation through advertising, labeling, or other practices); to choose (assurance of access to a variety of products and services at competitive prices, with government regulation where competition fails); and to be heard (a full consideration of consumer interests in the formulation of public policy).

The influence of this message is suggested by the fact that the four rights hardly seem noteworthy today. They have become so much a part of social and economic policy that they are taken for granted. But that was not the case in 1962. The idea that businesses might be selling unsafe products was considered radical; most safety legislation lay in the future. Even the need for information-based disclosure requirements—the most typical consumer reform of the next two decades—was not widely recognized. It is quite possible that subsequent reforms would have been implemented without the president's articulation of the four rights, but the message clearly shaped the debate and defined an action agenda.

In the decade after the president's message, safety became a major issue. Most important, new federal automobile and product safety protections and agencies were established. Even today, new safety protections are being debated.

The right to information seems self-evident today, but in 1962 neither the theoretical nor empirical underpinnings of the information issue were in place. Establishing a right to be informed was therefore an innovative step that was to leave more of an imprint than any of the other rights. That mark is evident in disclosure programs—from truth in lending through nutrition labeling to automobile gasoline mileage ratings—implemented after 1970. While consumer protection legislation had been passed in earlier periods, information-based regulations are unique to the years after 1962.

The right to choose may be the most ambiguous of the items on the list. In today's climate of deregulation, "choice" is likely to be interpreted differently than it was in 1962. In the 1962 setting, the right to choose tended to focus on a fair price, which broadly speaking meant restraining collusive elements in business.

Ensuring a right to be heard may have been the most controversial part of the president's message. By including this right, the president may have been encouraging federal regulatory agencies, particularly the Federal Trade Commission, to be more sensitive to consumer concerns. In discussing this point, Kennedy's adviser, Robert Lampman, linked the right to be heard to the consumer's right to redress in the market. The 1962 message, however, spoke only of representation in the policy-making process. The idea of a right to redress came later with President Richard M. Nixon's 1969 "Buyer's Bill of Rights."

The issues identified through the administrations of Kennedy, Lyndon B. Johnson, and Nixon provided the underpinnings for efforts to create a federal consumer protection agency. These efforts nearly succeeded more than once, but after a long fight, a greatly weakened proposal died in Congress during the administration of President Jimmy Carter. President Carter's alternative—designating a consumer spokesperson within each agency—seemed to many to be little more than window dressing. But it did give expression to Kennedy's original "right to be heard."

Looking back over three decades, one is still struck by the continued relevance of the four consumer rights. In some form or another, the elements identified in 1962 inform many of today's policy discussions. However, there are also some notable changes, reflecting the insights gained in more than thirty years of research and experience. The first has to do with the perspective on consumers themselves. The four rights do not portray the consumer as an active agent in the economy. The right to be informed, for example, is discussed in terms of improved consumer decision-making but gives no attention to the impact that improved decisions have on the system as a whole. There is no acknowledgment that much of the potential efficiency of a market system is lost if markets are not transparent and consumers are not in a position to make decisions that reward efficient producers and punish inefficient ones. The same is true about the right to choose. The overall implication is one of power flowing out from government rather than a more decentralized system in which power rests with individual consumers who are empowered to claim their own rights in the market.

Beyond that, little attention is given to possible contradictions among the four rights. The right to safety, for example, may conflict with the right to choose, since ensuring safer products will drive some products, and possibly some producers, from the market. The safety issue contains its own contradictions. Everyone may favor safer products, but one has to face the question of when diminishing returns on safety improvements cannot be justified. The more general recognition of such subtleties today reflects the progress that has been made in the analysis of how consumers and markets interact.

The list of consumer rights proposed by President Kennedy in 1962 has been augmented by other U.S. presidents. In 1975, President Gerald Ford announced the right to consumer education. More recently, President Bill Clinton declared the right to service. Nevertheless, none of these additions has provided the same degree of impetus and direction to the consumer movement as the declaration of the four original consumer rights.

— Roger Swagler

See also

Presidents and the Consumer Movement.

Reading

Lampman, Robert J. (1988). "JFK's Four Consumer Rights: A Retrospective View." In E. Scott Maynes, ed. *The Frontier of Research in the Consumer Interest.* Columbia, MO: American Council on Consumer Interests. 19–33.

Consumer Satisfaction/Dissatisfaction

When consumers get what they expect from a product or service, they are satisfied; when they get less than they expect, they are dissatisfied. This simple idea is the foundation of research on consumer satisfaction/dissatisfaction (CS/D). This research seeks to understand the nature and determinants of CS/D as well as its consequences. The consumer movement, government, and businesses have a stake in this research because all of these parties seek to increase consumer satisfaction and decrease consumer dissatisfaction.

Early Interest

The triggering event for the continuing and extensive interest in CS/D was the 1973 budget process at the U.S. Federal Trade Commission (FTC). With a budget insufficient to pursue solutions in all problem areas, the question was posed: which problems, if solved or reduced, would result in the greatest reduction in consumer dissatisfaction? The common sense solution was to apply resources to those problems involving high monetary costs to consumers and high levels of dissatisfaction. The number of complaints to Better Business Bureaus (BBBs), categorized by product or service and compiled by the national office, was the surrogate measure of comparative levels of dissatisfaction. The FTC staff and most others recognized that BBB complaints were not necessarily representative of dissatisfaction levels across the total population, but this measure was the best available and its use was free. Nevertheless, the need for a measure of CS/D that went beyond the people who complain to the BBB and beyond the products and services mentioned in their complaints was evident.

Within a few months after the FTC's consideration of CS/D, the U.S. Office of Consumer Affairs (OCA) contracted with Technical Assistance Research Programs, Inc. (TARP), to conduct a nationwide study of consumer problems and complaint-handling practices. This 1976 study included a nationwide survey of the consumer problems experienced in the previous year by the members of a national sample of 2,500 households. This study and subsequent ones discovered that most dissatisfied customers do not complain formally to businesses or government agencies but readily share their dissatisfaction with other consumers through word of mouth. This study helped change the way in which businesses and government agencies treated complaints. Complaints were no longer viewed as a nuisance to be minimized but rather as a valuable source of information.

Also in 1976, Call For Action and Ralph Nader's Center for Study of Responsive Law conducted a similar study. Starting with the assumption that complaint data may provide a biased point of view on consumer problems, the study asked a nationally representative sample of urban households about purchasing experiences in thirty-four product and service categories. The study, under the direction of Arthur Best and Alan Andreasen, aimed to measure both consumer satisfaction and perceived problems. Its most startling finding was that one in five purchases resulted in consumer dissatisfaction over something other than price.

While the two national studies (and others) demonstrated that large-scale research on CS/D could be conducted and yield results relevant to public and corporate policy, the conceptualization and measurement of CS/D had not been explicitly addressed. In the early 1970s, Martin and Anita Pfaff developed an index of consumer satisfaction, primarily focused on food products. But a 1974 search at the Library of Congress turned up only three articles on the general topic of CS/D written prior to 1972.

Given the lack of a research base for studies of CS/D, H. Keith Hunt submitted a proposal to the National Science Foundation to organize a conference on the conceptualization and measurement of CS/D to start the knowledge development process. Funding was approved for a 1976 conference. Substantial networking across discipline lines resulted in seventeen papers that laid the foundation for the academic field of CS/D. Ralph Day hosted a second CS/D conference in 1977, and Day and Hunt cohosted seven more CS/D conferences in the following decade. By 1988, the field had matured enough to warrant a journal, the *Journal of Consumer Satisfaction, Dissatisfaction and Complaining Behavior.* Debra Perkins's 1993 bibliography of literature on CS/D and complaining behavior contained over 3,000 entries.

Research Issues

Despite considerable progress, numerous CS/D research questions remain to be answered. Conceptualization and measurement remain the key issues, just as they were at the first conference in 1976. Although the "expected minus actual" CS/D model remains the standard, several variations of the simple model have been developed to predict and explain CS/D better.

The *normative deficit* model is one variation on the basic model. It attributes dissatisfaction to a violation of cultural norms. For example, having opposite sex teenage siblings share a bedroom would result in dissatisfaction because the living arrangement violates cultural norms. Another alternative, the *equity* model, focuses on the comparison of gains to each party in the social exchange. If the gains are unequal, the party receiving less would be dissatisfied. The *procedural fairness* model is based on conflict resolution research, with satisfaction being at least partly a function of the consumer perceiving that he or she had been treated fairly. The *desires* model compares actual results with desired results, but conceptualizes "desired" quite differently than "expected." An *attributional* model focuses on whose fault the disconfirmation is, not just on the existence of the disconfirmation.

Recognition of a difference between expected and actual, by itself, seldom results in any CS/D-related behavior. If the consumer does not become emotionally upset about the negative disconfirmation, nothing happens. If the consumer is emotionally upset but knows no appropriate CS/D behaviors, the outcome is general frustration. Only when the emotional component combines with knowledge of behavioral options do we see CS/D-related behavior. It is also likely that emotion and behavior repertoires are the key to understanding consumer response to positive disconfirmation, that is, when things go better than expected.

Debates over how best to conceptualize CS/D are mirrored in efforts to measure it. Douglas Hausknecht has presented an overview of most CS/D scales that shows tremendous variety and creativity but no standardization or even uniformity. Since the late 1970s, researchers have recognized that emotion is the key to understanding CS/D, yet even in the mid-1990s, they were still measuring CS/D with respect to cognition and wondering why their measures explain so little.

Another measurement "discovery" was that satisfaction and dissatisfaction might not be polar extremes but instead be two related but different phenomena. It appears that some variables seem primarily associated with satisfaction, others with dissatisfaction, some with both, and many with neither. Thus, separate measures might be needed.

Future Directions

In recent years, there has been growing interest in finding the commonality between CS/D and Total Quality Management (TQM). After all, one of the primary objectives of TQM is customer satisfaction. To date, this effort has been fruitless. While there seem to be numerous connections between CS/D and TQM, few actual links have been established. This failure may result from the two sides' language and conceptualization being so different and from the lack of overlap between their primary activity domains (production and consumption).

There has always been considerable interest in consumer responses to dissatisfaction. In the mid-1970s, Rex Warland, Robert Herrmann, and Jane Willits found that dissatisfied consumers are more likely than satisfied ones to make political contributions, send money to Ralph Nader, sign petitions, and use *Consumer Reports* before making purchases, but it is unclear whether these actions are caused by dissatisfaction. In recent years, research has revealed an increasing range of apparent responses to dissatisfaction, from brand/store avoidance, to grudge holding, to retaliation, and to physical harm and even death to sellers. At the same time, researchers are starting to recognize theoretically, and in practice, consumer responses to positive disconfirmations.

Several broad, philosophical questions remain. Is consumer satisfaction always desirable? What if a doctor's actions toward a cancer patient involve unpleasant procedures with no guarantee of "satisfaction"? Conversely, if cigarette smoking is "satisfying," should it not be taught and encouraged even at early ages? If a scam operation does not leave anyone dissatisfied, should it be forced out of business? Should consumer organizations aim to satisfy consumers, or are dissatisfied consumers necessary to support consumer protection initiatives? Does consumer satisfaction lead to consumer contentment, or does it lead to rising expectations and thereby dissatisfaction? Questions such as these should keep the field of CS/D active for years to come.

— H. Keith Hunt

See also

Disputes and Dispute Resolution.

Readings

Hunt, H. Keith (1988). "Consumer Satisfaction/Dissatisfaction and the Consumer Interest." In E. Scott Maynes, ed. *The Frontier of Research in the Consumer Interest*. Columbia, MO: American Council on Consumer Interests. 731–748.

Spreng, Richard A., Scott B. MacKenzie, and Richard W. Olshavsky (1996). "A Reexamination of the Determinants of Consumer Satisfaction." *Journal of Marketing*. 60 (3): 15–26.

Consumer Utility Advocates

See State Utility Consumer Advocates.

Consumerism, Modern

Consumerism is a term that has been used widely only in the past three decades. To those associated with the consumer movement, it denotes efforts to protect the consumer's interest. To some outside the movement, however, the term signifies "excess materialism." It is unclear which of these two definitions, or still others, is most widely accepted by the public.

The earliest documented use of the term was in a 1944 article in *The New Republic*, which discussed cooperatives. But the term did not begin to be used frequently until the late 1960s. By 1965, *Printer's Ink*, an advertising publication of the period, was using the derivative form, consumerist, as a pejorative to describe federal consumer protection initiatives. Use of the word appeared in a headline of a March 13, 1967, *Advertising Age* article about Betty Furness's appointment as consumer adviser to President Lyndon B. Johnson. Yet, despite repeated references to "the consumer interest," the article itself did not use the term.

That was to change fairly quickly. In May 1967, *Advertising Age* began an eight-part series entitled "Consumerism and Marketing." The tone of the series was broadly conciliatory, urging businesses to develop a positive response to consumer initiatives and to stop equating consumerism with socialism. Many of those equating business and capitalism with the "American way of life" had denounced consumerism as sinister and foreign. The consumer movement's historic association with cooperative and other reformist efforts, as reflected in the original mention of consumerism in 1944, made a convenient target.

By the early 1970s, however, it was evident that efforts to make *consumerism* a disparaging term had failed. Although early use of the word was often qualified by quotation marks or other disclaimers, the term quickly became established as a positive description of the efforts of the consumer movement. Both in academic literature and in popular writing, this use of the word was frequent.

By the late 1970s, consumerism had been defined even more fully and variously. These specific definitions fell into three broad categories. The first two referred to the content of consumer activities. One definition limited consumerism to the means by which consumers can assume their rightful place as informed decision-makers directing the market. This narrow definition restricted consumerism's concerns to such issues as consumer protection laws, the availability of product and price information, fraudulent and deceptive business practices, and product safety.

A broader definition of consumerism, however, extended reform beyond the market to the economic system as a whole. Those using the term in this sense were especially concerned with economic justice or fairness in the system. One use of this broader definition maintained that consumerism seeks nothing less for every American than a secure physical environment and a just economic one.

These two definitions reflected two American reform traditions. The broader use is more closely associated with late nineteenth-century populism, which called for systemic change and reflected a general uneasiness with many elements of capitalism. As these ideas reached the mainstream in the early part of this century they were modified, and the emphasis shifted from fundamental changes in the system to reforms that would make the system work better.

The third definition had less to do with the content of activities than with which actors were to be included under the consumerism umbrella. While most using this definition equated consumerism with the broad consumer movement, some limited the application of the term to organized groups seeking to protect consumers. Either of the two previous positions would be consistent with this view.

More recently, some outside the consumer movement have used the term *consumerism* to refer to excess materialism. Using consumerism to mean "protecting the consumer interest" is based on the dictionary definition of *-ism* as "doctrine, theory, or system of principles." However, -ism may also be defined as a "state or condition resulting from an excess of something," which is the basis for using consumerism to mean "excess materialism." In this sense, consumer is to consumerism what alcohol is to alcoholism.

This definition is not really new. Indeed, consumerism was being used in this way before the term was used with reference to protecting the consumer's interests. Vance Packard equated consumerism with materialism in his 1960 best-seller, *The Waste Makers*. He was not alone, although early examples of this usage could also be taken to mean "high levels of consumption," which does not sound as negative as "excess materialism."

More recent usage, however, has been more extreme. Consumerism is used to designate selfish and frivolous accumulation, materialism as an end in itself. This usage can be traced to such diverse sources as Pope John Paul II and the characters in the comic strip Calvin and Hobbes. In a 1991 encyclical, the former represented a papal accommodation with market capitalism, but warned that "Consumerism . . . can be as soulless as communism." In the United Kingdom, the Anti-Consumerism League fights against advertiser-driven consumption in favor of a simpler, more environmentally sensitive lifestyle.

Critics also charge that the social landscape has been eroded by consumerism. As a purely private exercise, consumerism limits individuals' links with the community. Thus, one analyst saw consumerism as a force "eating away at family time, neighborhood cohesion and public solidarities." An unrelated source used remarkably similar language in arguing that "consumerism crowds out our participation in family, learning, neighborhood, community and democratic government." Such characterizations treat consumerism as a cancer eating away at American life.

Although the evidence is not conclusive, it appears that using consumerism to mean excess materialism has become more common in recent years, particularly in the United Kingdom and Europe. If so, one would expect to see increasing numbers of references to consumerism as a destructive force. It is not clear, however, whether publics in various countries have accepted this definition.

— Roger Swagler

Reading

Swagler, Roger (1994). "Evolution and Applications of the Term Consumerism: Theme and Variations." *Journal of Consumer Affairs*. 28 (2): 347–360.

Consumers Education and Protective Association

When Max Weiner and fifteen other people founded the Consumers Education and Protective Association (CEPA) in 1966, consumer protection was almost nonexistent. Though always based in Philadelphia, this unique grassroots organization influenced consumerism throughout the nation.

CEPA began its work at a time when there were few consumer protection mechanisms within state and local governments or legal services offices serving neighborhoods. In 1965, as Weiner—who had worked as teacher, labor organizer, accountant, and real estate agent—visited potential clients for debt consolidation, he was shocked by sellers' schemes that greatly increased the debts of his potential clients, who were people of modest means. He discussed the possibility of addressing this problem with Ambler Bailey, who was to become CEPA's first chairman. He also showed his friend and former client, Garland Dempsey (CEPA's first vice chairman), that credit from finance companies was costly for some consumers. However, it took almost a year, and two successful interventions, to convince a small group of people to form a community-based organization to try to solve consumer problems.

The organizers of CEPA, led by Weiner, developed the association's structure and program during that first year. At the first meeting in February 1966, they adopted an eight-point program that emphasized issues such as combating the rising cost of living; lowering interest rates on consumer credit and increasing access to this credit; creating a state- or city-owned insurance company to provide insurance at standard rates to low-income clients; establishing required interest rate disclosures and outlawing interest on interest and excessive late charges; obtaining refunds for consumers swindled by salesmen, dealers, and finance companies; enforcing existing consumer protection laws; and supporting legislation that would require truth in packaging and truth in selling. CEPA was one of the first groups to publicize consumer abuses widely and to persuade policymakers to remedy them.

During its first active year, CEPA developed a unique three-step grievance procedure for resolving complaints: investigate, negotiate, and demonstrate. It also began publishing *Consumers Voice,* the newsletter that, for twenty years, reported on CEPA's complaint actions and broader campaigns. In the course of this first year, CEPA recruited hundreds of members and saved consumers hundreds of thousands of dollars.

CEPA functions through branches that were originally founded by individuals with a grievance. These branches, which meet weekly, are run by elected volunteers. Membership is open to those willing to participate and pay a modest fee. To receive assistance, an aggrieved individual must work with the branch, not just treat it as a referral agency. Once a branch takes on a case, a delegation including the complainant visits the business involved in an effort to open a dialogue to hear both sides of the complaint. It is only when negotiation fails that a public demonstration, such as "educational picketing," is considered. Complaints are not referred to lawyers or a social agency. While both state agencies and professionals collaborate with CEPA, they are never considered substitutes for what people working together in an organized fashion can accomplish.

By 1968, CEPA's strategies and tactics had been established. Along with the three-step grievance process on individual consumer complaints, CEPA applied direct action tactics to address consumer issues. CEPA picketed abusive merchants and held "lemoncades" to protest badly made cars and the lack of consumer protection for the owners of "lemons." The organization also conducted petition drives and participated in public hearings.

During the organization's first two years, eight branches were founded, including a Spanish-speaking branch and several outside of Philadelphia. Branch members participated in the district council, whose meetings were discussions aimed at training volunteer leaders in the process of carrying out the three-step procedure.

In 1967, a much larger group founded the Consumer Party, whose goal was to bring consumer issues into the political arena. Although the Consumer Party did not win any elections, over the years it influenced local and state politics and became a springboard and training ground for many people who later were elected to office. In addition, CEPA set up the Consumer Foundation, which, with funding from foundation grants, conducted a School for Consumer Education annually for several years.

Under the leadership of Weiner, who died in 1989, CEPA enjoyed successes beyond the resolution of individual grievances. It played a key role in the prohibition of holder-in-due-course notes and confessions of judgment, which helped reduce sheriff sales and mortgage foreclosures. It persuaded utility regulatory agencies to fund interventions in rate hearings, which helped restrain gas, water, and electric rates. CEPA was instrumental in defeating several legislative pay increases and a realty transfer tax, and forced the Philadelphia City Council to hold meaningful public hearings on these types of bills. In addition, the organization successfully opposed increases in mass transit fares and won refunds for millions of consumers who were misled by the local phone company into thinking that they were buying, not leasing, their phones. Recently, under the direction of its current educational director, Lance Haver, the organization spearheaded a successful campaign to defeat radical changes in the Philadelphia City Charter.

CEPA, the oldest grassroots consumer organization in the United States, is basically a self-help organization. With simple principles and an almost totally volunteer staff, it has mobilized thousands of consumers to solve their own problems and reform corporate and government policies. In the process, it has inspired the establishment of similar organizations in cities such as Cleveland, Milwaukee, and Seattle. Through extensive press coverage, it became an important national symbol of effective, grassroots consumer action.

— Besse S. Weiner and
Judy Canahuati Weiner

See also

State and Local Consumer Organizations.

Readings

Haas, Al (1986). "Consumed with Consumerism." *Philadelphia Inquirer* (January 2): E1.

Ittig, Kathleen Browne (1973). "Consumer Collective Action: A Study of Consumers Education and Protective Association International, Inc." M.S. thesis, Cornell University.

Consumers International

Consumers International (CI) is the only international organization of consumer groups from all regions of the world. It was founded as the International Organization of Consumers Unions (IOCU) in 1960 by consumer groups from Western Europe, Australia, and the United States. Over time, it expanded its goals from serving member groups to promoting the organization of consumers in the Third World and advocating consumer interests internationally. Today, it maintains a central office in London and regional offices in Southeast Asia, Latin America, and Africa.

Origins

IOCU was conceived by Elizabeth Schadee, later board chair of the Dutch Consumentenbond, and Caspar Brook, first director of Britain's Consumers' Association. They believed that, if existing consumer product testing organizations worldwide worked closely together, they would not only save money but respond more effectively to challenges from business. To encourage such cooperation, they proposed an international conference of consumer groups. Colston Warne, president of Consumers Union, persuaded his organization to donate $10,000 to help cover conference expenses. Jan van Veen was hired to organize the conference.

The First International Conference on Consumer Testing was held in January 1960 in The Hague under the sponsorship of Consumers

Union, the Consumers' Association, and Consumentenbond. The conference was attended by thirty-four persons from seventeen organizations in fourteen countries. Their discussion focused mainly on joint testing projects and the formation of an international organization. By the conference's end, they had agreed to set up an international Technical Exchange Committee to supervise joint product testing and to found the International Organization of Consumers Unions.

The international organization was to serve as a clearinghouse for information on product testing, to regulate the use of ratings and reprints of materials from member organizations, and to organize international meetings. It was to be controlled by a council made up of representatives from the five founding organizations—in addition to the three conference sponsors, Belgium's Association des Consommateurs and the Australian Consumers' Association. The first year's budget was about $10,000, about two-fifths of which was contributed by Consumers Union. Jan van Veen was hired as administrator and organized a permanent office in The Hague.

During the organization's first year, it began publishing *IOCU Bulletin* and created a Regional Office for Consumer Organizations in the European Community, which later became the Bureau Européen des Unions de Consommateurs (BEUC). Also, Colston Warne recruited Florence Mason, Consumers Union's librarian, to communicate with groups around the world to establish an international network and to recruit organizations into IOCU.

The founding constitution required members to be independent of business. Founding members also preferred that participating organizations be independent of government as well. But in the early 1960s, nontesting consumer groups and those financed by government insisted, with increasing force, that they be permitted to join. At the fourth international conference (now called a congress) in 1966, members created a special committee to propose changes in the constitution. It was chaired by Peter Goldman, who had succeeded Brook as the Consumers' Association's director. By the 1968 Congress held in New York City, the committee had developed a compromise proposal for a new constitution.

This constitution changed the organization fundamentally in two ways. First, it broadened membership beyond product testing organizations to all groups that "are active exclusively on behalf of the interests of consumers." Second, it democratized IOCU by shifting final authority from the Council to the General Assembly, which included representatives from all members (called associates).

Also at the 1968 Congress, IOCU expanded its goals. Members agreed that the organization would promote the organization of consumer groups throughout the world, including those funded by government. Special attention would be paid to "underdeveloped areas." They also agreed that IOCU must represent the consumer interest internationally, principally at the United Nations (UN) and its agencies.

The expanding focus from product testing to social justice during the organization's first decade was stated perhaps most succinctly by Goldman, who was then IOCU president, at the 1972 UN Conference on the Human Environment. Goldman said that the consumer movement was a protest and action movement directed at alleviating poverty, eliminating commercial chicanery, and ending environmental damage. This broad emphasis was incorporated in the organization's 1978 *Charter for Consumer Action,* which emphasized critical awareness, personal involvement and action, social and ecological responsibility, and international solidarity. More than any other person, Anwar Fazal—who served as Asian regional director, then as president—promoted these principles of consumer action worldwide. Fazal also proposed World Consumer Rights Day, which has been celebrated since 1983 on March 15.

Worldwide Expansion

IOCU's growing commitment to serving consumers in the Third World was first expressed institutionally by the creation of the IOCU Aid Committee in 1964. As a member of this committee, Florence Mason, who by then had retired from Consumers Union, expanded her correspondence with groups around the world. By 1981, she had corresponded with consumer activists from nearly 140 nations.

At first, the aid committee was funded by voluntary contributions from IOCU members. But eventually, support for work in the Third World was integrated into the organization's budget. In 1966, IOCU held a seminar called Consumer Education in Developing Countries in Haifa, Israel, that attracted twenty-six delegates from Asia, Africa, and Latin America. Three years later, the organization held its first meeting in a developing country (Jamaica).

At the Stockholm Congress in 1972, Goldman asserted that establishing an IOCU office in Asia was the organization's highest priority. Two years later, the Regional Office for Asia and the Pacific opened in Singapore to facilitate the exchange of information and materials among consumer groups in the region. Most of the funding for this office came from Consumers Union and the Consumers' Association. To reduce costs, in 1975 this office was moved to Penang, Malaysia, where it remains today. During the past two decades, the office has coordinated worldwide campaigns on many issues, including hazardous product exports, infant formula, and costly pharmaceuticals. It also took leadership in forming alliances with other public interest organizations.

The next region of the Third World to receive IOCU's attention was Latin America and the Caribbean. At the 1981 Congress, the organization decided to publish a newsletter for the region. At the 1984 Congress, IOCU set as an important goal the establishment of an office in Latin America. In 1987, such an office was set up in Montevideo, Uruguay (later relocated to Santiago, Chile). As they had in Asia, Consumers Union and the Consumers' Association provided most of the funding for operations.

During this period, IOCU members also grew more interested in stimulating consumer activity in Africa. Their initiatives generated growing interest by Africans in consumer work and record participation by Africans in the 1987 Congress. During the next year, IOCU organized two conferences in Africa: one in Nairobi, Kenya, and the other in Dakar, Senegal. In 1994, the organization established a regional office in Zimbabwe and a subregional office in Dakar.

IOCU also began focusing attention on Eastern Europe. It was fortuitous that the first meeting in this region was held in 1989, the year of growing democratization. Delegates representing thirteen groups from six countries participated in this meeting. While IOCU has not established an office in this region, it has provided technical and financial support to these Eastern European organizations.

During the past two decades, no leader in IOCU has provided more moral and financial support to Third World consumer groups than Rhoda Karpatkin, president of Consumers Union, who also served two terms as IOCU's president. Other key supporters of assistance to Third World organizations were Peter Goldman, John Beishon (Consumers' Association), Dick Westendorp (Consumentenbond), and Willy van Rijckeghem (Association des Consommateurs).

International Advocacy

While continuing its support for member organizations, IOCU increased its international advocacy. One advocacy role was coming to the aid of distressed members. For example, in 1987 the Asian-Pacific office notified the IOCU executive committee that the Malaysian government had detained leading activists, including the legal adviser to the Consumers' Association of Penang, Meenakshi Raman, without charges. In response, IOCU president Karpatkin wrote to the Malaysian prime minister, asking him either to charge this activist or to release her unconditionally. Many IOCU members also wrote to the Malaysian government, the UN Secretary-General, and human rights organizations. The Malaysian authorities eventually released Raman.

Much of IOCU's advocacy was directed at the United Natins and its associated agencies in an effort to persuade them to promote consumer education, adopt standards for consumer goods and services, and support the consumer interest in general. IOCU's first advocate to the United Nations was Persia Campbell, a longtime New York State consumer advocate who also served on President Kennedy's Consumer Advisory Council. Campbell made contacts at the United Nations that won respect for IOCU.

The most significant victory by IOCU at the United Nations was persuading this international body to adopt the UN Consumer Protection Guidelines in 1985. The guidelines represented a model for consumer protection policies. Subsequently, the guidelines played an important role in persuading many Third World countries to establish consumer protections. Key to the adoption of the guidelines was the lobbying of Esther Peterson, consumer adviser to two U.S. presidents, who was appointed IOCU's UN representative in 1983.

The other critically important international advocacy effort by IOCU was the establishment of global networks to address particular types of problems. The organization played an important role, for example, in the establishment of the International Baby Food Action Network (IBFAN) in 1979. This group took leadership in advocating international control of the promotion and marketing of infant milk formulas. IOCU's Asian and Latin American regional offices were leaders of this effort.

The success of this network encouraged IOCU to establish two other global networks—Health Action International (HAI) in 1981 and the Pesticide Action Network (PAN) in 1982. In the early 1970s, a new disease called SMON that appeared in Asia was traced to the drug Clioquinol. Partly through the efforts of IOCU, Clioquinol was withdrawn in 1978 from the Japanese market, where it caused over 700 deaths, and its use on a worldwide basis was restricted. In 1981, many of the groups that had been working on this campaign participated in the International Nongovernmental Organization Seminar on Pharmaceuticals, which led to the formation of HAI. This network was particularly concerned about the many nonessential drugs on the market and the high prices of brand-name drugs.

At the 1981 World Congress, IOCU organized Consumer Interpol, a project to deal with the export of hazardous products banned or controlled in their countries of origin. One of Consumer Interpol's early concerns was the exporting of pesticide-laden foods. At a 1982 International Workshop on Pesticides, PAN was created. Soon after the formation of PAN, the UN Food and Agriculture Organization developed a Code of Conduct on pesticide marketing, which was adopted in 1985.

These networks not only served as effective advocates against various health and safety threats; they provided IOCU the opportunity to link up with health, environment, and development groups. The combined expertise and energy of all these organizations permitted far more effective advocacy worldwide, especially on behalf of Third World consumers.

Reinvention

By the 1990s, IOCU had grown significantly. The 1994 World Congress was attended by 250 organizations from eighty nations. More than 200 of these groups were members of IOCU. Moreover, the budget of the organization had grown to several million dollars a year. These funds permitted the organization to employ more than sixty staffers in its four offices.

But the organization suffered from growing pains. According to a 1991 report by a consultant, IOCU was undergoing an identity crisis, lacking a clear vision and a statement defining its mission. This report referred to a "dual philosophy" in the consumer movement: consumer organizations in the Third World often sought to take on broader functions and represent broader interests than those in the industrialized world.

Encouraged by the many new members from the Third World, longtime IOCU leader

Rhoda Karpatkin argued successfully to other executive council members that the organization needed to be reinvented. New president Erna Witoelar provided essential leadership as IOCU debated, approved, and implemented several major changes. (Witoelar had been active in the consumer movement since 1975, when she was appointed as head of the Testing and Research Department of the Indonesian Consumer Organization. Later, she served as chief editor of its magazine, then as president of the organization.)

For a start, IOCU expanded the executive council to increase representation from Third World groups. Later, in 1994, the organization changed its name to Consumers International. The former name had suggested that the group was principally made up of product testing organizations. It also could be confusing to those unfamiliar with the consumer movement.

The organization decided to replace its Regional Office for Europe and North America, which had been created in the late 1980s, with a more modest Program for Developed Economies. That action was further evidence that the organization was devoting less attention to issues of the industrialized world and greater emphasis on challenges facing the Third World.

In addition, the organization resolved to make two broad issues high priorities—sustainable consumption and the globalization of the world economy. These issues were considered to be extremely important both to the Third World and to the future of the planet.

Finally, the organization reversed a decades-long trend toward decentralization by increasingly centralizing the direction of global campaigns. The new Global Policy and Campaigns Unit coordinates member input into the organization's policy positions and manages global campaigns. As Consumers International approaches the twenty-first century, it has reaffirmed its commitment, as stated by Rhoda Karpatkin in 1994, to "the broader ideals of social and economic justice" as part of a "global struggle to advance human rights and humanistic relationships."

— Stephen Brobeck

See also

African Consumer Movement; Asian-Pacific Consumer Movement; Latin American Consumer Movement; United Nations Consumer Protections.

Reading

Sim, Foo Gaik (1991). *IOCU on Record: A Documentary History of the International Organization of Consumers Unions, 1960–1990.* Yonkers, NY: Consumers Union.

Consumers' Research

Founded in 1928, Consumers' Research (CR) is an independent, nonprofit educational organization that produces *Consumers' Research* magazine, a nationally circulated monthly based in Washington, D.C. The organization was the world's first in testing and reporting by brand names on products bought and used by individual consumers. It played an important role in raising public awareness of the consumer's role in the marketplace and influenced early food and drug safety standards.

At present, rather than testing products, CR focuses on the consumer aspect of issues such as health care, the environment, cable television, and communications. The magazine circulates to about 15,000 subscribers, including individuals, libraries, and other research institutions. The organization produces the bulk of its revenue through subscriptions, reprint sales, and royalties.

The organization grew out of ideas explored by Stuart Chase and F. J. Schlink in a series of articles beginning in the December 1925 issue of *The New Republic,* which were subsequently expanded into their best-selling 1927 book, *Your Money's Worth: A Study in the Waste of the Consumer's Dollar.* Chase, an economist and popular writer, and Schlink, a mechanical engineer and physicist, demonstrated the pseudoscientific, misleading, and sometimes fraudulent nature of many types of product advertising of the time. They made a novel proposal: to extend for use by the consumer "the principle of buying goods according to impartial scientific" testing that the federal government used to make its purchases. The National Bureau of Standards' chemists, physicists, and engineers conducted some 180,000 tests each year to assess government purchases. Making these taxpayer-funded tests usable for the consumer, Schlink and Chase wrote, would save the public at least a billion dollars annually.

Turning federal tests toward consumer needs did not prove workable, although Schlink—who had held top posts at the National Bureau of Standards and the American Standards Association (later named the American National Standards Institute)—tried to do so for several years. Eventually, Schlink decided that a White Plains, New York, consumers' club he had helped organize in March 1926 should be expanded to obtain more data on goods and to meet the increasing demand for reliable, noncommercial information. The club's first rating guide was released in October 1927; its offers to join the new organization began in January 1928.

The nascent New York City–based Consumers' Club quickly gained members. Publishing the *Consumer Club Commodity List* (briefly titled *Scientific Buying*), the club was incorporated as Consumers' Research in December 1929 and began to publish *Consumers' Research Bulletin*. Fearing financially debilitating legal attacks from hostile businesses, CR issued "confidentiality" provisions in its subscription agreements, which stated that information was solely for the private use of subscribers, i.e., not public enough to be deemed libelous. (This policy was relaxed after 1935, but CR's annual *Bulletin* was marked confidential until the early 1950s.) CR also established a noncommercialization policy, taking no product advertising and not allowing its results to be used for commercial purposes.

By 1932, CR had 42,000 subscribers and had gained considerable national exposure. Chase was the first president. Schlink was the technical director, in which capacity (among other roles) he served for the next fifty-four years.

CR's purposes were straightforward: "to provide a clearinghouse where information of importance to consumers may be assembled, edited, and promulgated," and to "conduct, promote, and generally encourage scientific, technical and economic investigations and research into the nature of commodities and services in use by consumers and of interest to them," as its original charter states. Early testing of products was conducted by laboratories or consultants hired by CR. After moving from New York City to Washington, New Jersey, in 1933, CR conducted much more of its own product testing, although it always relied on outside consultants for some of its work. (Some of these consultants worked as chemists and engineers in industry and so remained acknowledged but unnamed in CR's publications to protect their jobs.)

Over the next fifty years, CR produced hundreds of devices to conduct thousands of tests to examine, for example, how a product held up to stress, whether it was reliable, and whether advertised claims were true. Schlink sought neither commercial gain from, nor exclusive use of, CR's testing techniques. He believed it beneficial for industry to use them to create, maintain, and improve commercial standards of product quality.

For many years, CR tested and rated the full range of consumer products, publishing the results in its monthly magazine and compiling them each year in its annual *Bulletin* (eventually titled *Handbook of Buying*). Automobiles were first reported on in 1928. The organization tested, rated, and studied thousands of products—from toothbrushes to razor blades, kitchen appliances to men's underwear, cosmetics to radio receivers. Its reporting broke new ground. It exposed dangers of electrical shock from appliances due to poor insulation. It published the first instructions for converting radio receivers to stereo. The aim was not only to report on quality and safety to assist buying, but also to develop, in effect, an "art and a science of consumption," by which "consumers may defend themselves against the invasions and aggressions of advertising and salesmanship." CR produced a test manual in 1937, for example, for consumers and students to conduct testing and analysis on their own.

CR's reporting on food, nutrition, and food packaging also was a prominent feature. This was highlighted by Schlink and then CR board member Arthur Kallet's 1933 book *100,000,000 Guinea Pigs: Dangers in Everyday Food, Drugs and Cosmetics*, which relied on scientific data and product horror stories to become the most popular consumer book of its time and a significant influence on the passage of the Food, Drug and Cosmetic Act of 1938. Other notable "guinea pig" books written by CR staffers included: *Skin Deep—The Truth about Beauty Aids—Safe and Harmful* by M.C. Phillips, Schlink's wife and longtime editor of CR; *Eat, Drink, and Be Wary* by Schlink; and *Guinea Pigs No More* by J. B. Matthews. Schlink revisited nutrition in *Meat Three Times a Day* and sales practices in *Don't You Believe It*, written with his wife. The food writer Beatrice Trum Hunter, herself author of a number of books on nutrition, food safety, and cooking, became a contributor to *Consumers' Research* in the early 1970s and continues to serve as its food editor.

Among other publication efforts, CR produced from 1937 to 1941 a general interest sister publication to its *Bulletin*. The monthly *Consumers Digest* offered abridged CR test results along with a variety of articles, including those on social and economic issues, such as consumers and the labor movement, socialist (and Communist) influence in the consumer movement, and the anti-consumer effects of both price controls and trade restrictions. (CR helped set up a related but separate nonprofit organization to publish this magazine after 1939.)

Over the years, CR frequently published commentaries and criticisms about federal policies toward the consumer. It was particularly vocal during the New Deal, when it advocated a federal Department of the Consumer and criticized the National Recovery Administration's Consumer Advisory Board. Indeed, CR's "free market" economic point of view developed in this era. While always generally supportive of federal food and drug safety standards, its publications reveal an evolving skepticism of government interventions in the marketplace.

Despite occasional portrayal as the "Ralph Nader" of his day, throughout his long career Schlink was first and foremost an engineer. He was active in the private standards-setting community, serving on advisory councils for Underwriters Laboratories and the American National Standards Institute, among others; maintained active membership in a number of professional scientific societies; and contributed articles to various economic, scientific, technical, and trade journals in the United States and England.

A bitter strike at Consumers' Research in September 1935 led directly to the creation of Consumers Union by some CR strikers and marked the decline of CR's influence in the consumer movement proper. The facts about the cause and motives of the strike remain clouded. Schlink held that the strike was prompted and backed by Communist activists and fellow travelers. Through the 1950s, Schlink, Phillips, and Matthews continued to cite instances of what they believed to be Communist influence at Consumers Union. Consumers Union and its allies maintained that the strike was strictly a matter of wages, job security, and worker representation on the board.

The growth of *Consumers' Research* eventually leveled off around 100,000 subscribers after World War II and stayed there (with an occasional push to over 150,000) until April 1980, when M. Stanton Evans took over the daily operations of the organization, became the magazine's publisher, and moved the editorial offices to Washington, D.C. Evans, former editor of the *Indianapolis News* and a nationally syndicated conservative columnist, kept *Consumers' Research* product-oriented approach but broadened the scope of its coverage of consumer issues and cut back on its nonpaying circulation, which had been badly overextended through mass sub scription agencies. Schlink continued to oversee testing operations until 1983, when the remaining engineering facilities in Washington, New Jersey, were shut down.

In the 1980s, *Consumers' Research* shifted from a product-testing orientation to a general-interest monthly focused on scientific and policy issues that affect consumers. In recent years, it has published many articles calling into question traditional consumer policies or exploring issues ignored by the mainstream consumer movement.

— Peter L. Spencer

See also

Consumers Union; Information Dissemination; Product Testing.

Readings

Morse, Richard L. D., ed. (1993). *The Consumer Movement: Lectures by Colston E. Warne*. Manhattan, KS: Family Economics Trust Press.

Schlink, F. J. (1988). "Who Serves the Consumer?" *Consumers' Research*. 71 (January): 22–23.

Consumers Union

Consumers Union (CU) is widely regarded as the most influential nonprofit consumer organization in the world. For more than sixty years, its magazine *Consumer Reports* has served as the most popular objective source of consumer information in the United States. But the influence of this organization has extended well beyond the dissemination of consumer information. It has also helped establish and support other consumer groups, both in the United States and in other countries, and has influenced both federal and state public policies.

History

The stage was set for the modern consumer movement in the 1920s. Rapid business expansion and the movement toward industrial efficiency that came from standardization made it almost inevitable. Although the consumer movement owes much to the development of buyers' cooperatives, to home economics education, to economists like Thorstein Veblen, to muckrakers like Upton Sinclair, and to the engineer Herbert Hoover, this new social movement was virtually invented by Stuart Chase and F. J. Schlink.

When *Your Money's Worth* by Chase and Schlink appeared in 1927, it became a best-seller, and with good reason. It was a guide to fraud and manipulation—in foods, medicine, cosmetics, autos, and household equipment. It named names and provided explicit detail. It showed that consumers were victims of unchecked frauds that were rife in the marketplace.

Schlink had belonged to a men's club in a Methodist church in White Plains, New York. With his technical bent, he had prepared a series of mimeographed sheets that summarized the product experiences of members of that club and assembled them into the *Consumer Club Commodity List*. Schlink had access to much of the engineering material of the American Standards Association. Wherever the ratings reflected business or governmental tests, the list indicated that. Readers of *Your Money's Worth* were invited to send in a dollar for a copy of the listing. Many did. By 1929, Schlink founded Consumers' Research, which was incorporated by New York State as a nonprofit consumer testing organization. It was the first organization of its kind in the world.

The effort foundered, however, after Schlink transplanted the new organization from New York City to the small town of Washington, New Jersey. Many employees grew dissatisfied, a union was organized, and a long strike ensued. Eventually, the striking workers decided to create their own organization.

Consumers Union

On February 6, 1936, Consumers Union of the United States, Inc., was incorporated under the laws of the State of New York. It began its operations in two rooms on East Seventeenth Street in New York City. Engineers, journalists, academics, professionals, and others committed themselves not only to product testing but also to joining with others to help achieve a "decent standard of living" for all consumers.

Since its founding, Consumers Union has grown from this small band with a small and hopeful following to an organization with a variety of information products and nearly 5 million paid subscribers to its major magazine, *Consumer Reports*.

For Consumers Union, there have been major turning points that attest to both its growth and its accommodation to a changing world. One such point—the decision to expand and improve laboratory facilities—has occurred three times. This first took place in 1954, when Consumers Union moved from New York City to Mt. Vernon, New York. It occurred again in 1991, when the organization relocated to its present Testing and Research Center in Yonkers, New York. (By 1996, after further expansion of these facilities, the center contained offices and fifty laboratories in 250,000 square feet.) And it occurred yet a third time when Consumers Union acquired a drag strip in East Haddam, Connecticut, and in 1989 renovated it into a state-of-the-art auto test facility.

Another major turning point occurred in the 1980s when Consumers Union turned to its subscribers for some of the financial resources necessary to create its testing center. Notwithstanding a limit on the amount of donations—initially $1,000 and later $5,000—and a refusal to accept any commercial funds, successful fund-raising resulted in over 600,000 donations and provided the resources for half the cost of the building.

A significant turning point of a different sort, which also took place in the 1980s, was the decision to transform the organization from the publisher of *Consumer Reports* to the publisher of information in many forms and of many sorts. This diversification expanded the help the organization could provide to consumers, and the resources to cover the costs of this assistance.

Other turning points involved the expansion of Consumers Union's advocacy role. Although the organization had been a consumer advocate from the day of its founding, in 1972 it opened a Washington office to make federal officials more aware of its research and its implications for public policy. Later in the decade, it established regional offices in California (1975) and in Texas (1979) to accomplish the same general public policy purposes.

At the time of its fiftieth anniversary in 1986, Consumers Union also renewed its emphasis on advocacy on behalf of the poor as consumers, launching programs and projects that helped reconnect the organization to its roots. The Texas and California offices specifically targeted issues affecting low-income consumers such as food prices, utility rates, and auto insurance rates.

Governance and Leadership

Consumers Union is a membership organization. Each year, all paid subscribers are mailed a ballot to vote for members of the board of directors. The act of voting constitutes membership.

The bylaws require at least two nominees for each board position, so subscribers have a choice. These directors govern Consumers Union. They make overall organizational policy, approve the budget, and maintain broad oversight over operations. They also appoint a president, who is charged with the management of the organization. Members of the board bring a varied set of experiences: they include academics, physicians, homemakers, journalists, and leaders of nonprofit organizations.

Each year, subscribers also are given the opportunity to complete a detailed questionnaire about recent product experiences. The data they provide form the basis for the frequency of repair records that are essential to product evaluation and choice. In 1995, for example, Consumers Union reported on the frequency of repair records of automobiles, washing machines, clothes dryers, electric and gas ranges, refrigerators, dishwashers, microwave ovens, color televisions, VCRs, CD players, camcorders, room air conditioners, and lawnmowers.

Consumers Union experienced long-term, stable leadership on its board and staff. The founding president of the board, Colston E. Warne, an Amherst College economics professor, served from 1936 to 1980. He brought to the organization the conviction that the marketplace needed to be made fair to consumers and a consistent vision of how Consumers Union could help achieve that. His successor, James A. Guest, has served from 1980 to the present, with a new title of chairman of the board. He has maintained the continuity of vision and purpose started by his former professor.

The founding executive director, Arthur Kallet, served from 1936 to 1957. He was an engineer whose research and writing in the 1920s, with F. J. Schlink, helped lead to the founding of Consumers' Research. In 1935, he helped lead the strike that resulted in the founding of Consumers Union a year later. His leadership at CU provided the focus, shape, and identity that has marked the organization to the present. A comparison of that early work of Consumers Union with its present work shows clearly how much of the pioneering efforts of Kallet and his staff remains relevant to the present.

Kallet has been succeeded by four other executive directors. The most recent, Rhoda H. Karpatkin, whose title is now president, has served since 1974. Karpatkin is a graduate of Brooklyn College and Yale Law School. For sixteen years, before becoming CU's chief executive officer, she was an outside legal counsel to the organization. Under her leadership, CU greatly expanded its facilities, research, and advocacy. Also, the circulation of *Consumer Reports* grew from about 2 million to 5 million.

Over the last several decades, many CU staff members have made major contributions to the work of the organization. From 1946 to 1971, technical director Morris Kaplan greatly improved consumer testing methods. Since 1982, technical director R. David Pittle—who earlier served as a commissioner on the Consumer Product Safety Commission—has guided the construction of the new auto test facilities as well as serving as a respected product safety advocate. From 1973 to 1994, editorial director Irwin Landau oversaw the development of carefully researched investigative and policy articles, and shaped a precise and often elegant editorial style. Longtime advocacy directors Mark Silbergeld and Harry Snyder expanded the Washington, D.C., and California advocacy offices respectively into highly regarded and influential advocates for the consumer interest.

Resources and Functions

Since 1991, Consumers Union's annual revenue has exceeded $100 million. The major share of its revenue comes from subscriptions to *Consumer Reports* magazine. The balance comes from the sale of other publications and consumer information and from donations from subscribers. Consumers Union accepts no money, products, or gifts of any sort from any commercial source, and its publications take no outside advertising. The organization, therefore, is supported by and beholden to consumers only. Since the capital campaign initiated to build a new test facility, Consumers Union has received contributions to enhance its programs and activities.

In 1995, the organization's revenue supported a staff of 455. The largest division is the Technical Division, with 149 engineers, chemists, statisticians, technicians, analysts, and related workers. Next largest is the Editorial Department, with a staff of 51. The balance of the staff advocates for the consumer interest, produces other information products, markets these products, and engages in the many support functions necessary to maintain the work of the organization.

Consumers Union's mission can be summed up by the words that appear on a banner in the entrance hall of the organization's National Testing and Research Center in Yonkers, New York: TEST, INFORM, PROTECT. The primary work of the organization is information and education: comparative testing of consumer products, comparative evaluation of consumer services, and research and analysis of issues affecting consumers.

Just as Consumers Union's fifty laboratories are located in the physical core of its building, so the testing is at the core of its work. Products are purchased at retail with cash by anonymous shoppers around the country, then subjected to state-of-the-art laboratory tests and common sense use tests. Each year, thousands of products undergo stringent, months-long, comparative testing. In addition, dozens of cars are tested at Consumers Union's auto test track in East Haddam, Connecticut.

Since the service marketplace cannot be scrutinized in a laboratory, consumers' experiences are used for evaluation. The organization's Survey Research Department surveys readers for their evaluation of services such as restaurants, hotels, airlines, department stores, auto insurance, homeowner's insurance, mail-order companies, supermarkets, diet programs, eyeglass chains, muffler and brake shops, rental car companies, real estate brokers, lawyers, doctors, and health maintenance organziations. The results of those surveys are published in *Consumer Reports.* In addition, the magazine covers public policy issues affecting consumers.

The results of this testing and research appear not only in the pages of *Consumer Reports* magazine, but are relayed, as well, in Consumers Union's radio program, newspaper column, television programming, online services, CD-ROM products, and general press coverage. Other vehicles for information dissemination include *Zillions*, a version of *Consumer Reports* that is designed for young people ten to fourteen years of age; two newsletters, *Consumer Reports on Health* and *Consumer Reports Travel Letter;* Consumer Reports Books; and Consumers Union's Price Services for new and used cars, for auto insurance, and for home purchases. The new car service, for example, provides the specifications and dealer costs of any car model and accessories. The auto insurance service, now offered in six states, supplies individual price quotes for different policies.

Impact

The impact of Consumers Union can be measured in several different ways. Quantitatively, one can measure how many people are reached with its information. As of 1995, paid circulation of *Consumer Reports* was about 4.7 million, putting *Consumer Reports* among the top ten American magazines in paid circulation. The publishing industry estimates a pass-along factor of about four readers per copy, bringing the total number of readers to over 18 million. There are about 30,000 library subscribers, and many have reported that *Consumer Reports* is extremely popular in libraries.

Consumers Union's information is also far reaching. Five ninety-second radio reports per week are heard in about 100 markets around the United States. Consumers Union's TV News Feature Service appears in newscasts on over eighty local stations, including most of the major markets, with twelve ninety-second spots each month. From time to time, television specials for adults and kids are broadcast over Home Box Office or public television.

Consumers Union's syndicated news column appears twice weekly in about 350 papers across the country. The Office of Public Information issues monthly press releases on the highlights of each of our publications' issues to a list of hundreds of journalists. Responding to the importance of technology, Consumers Union's information is now available through electronic media, such as America Online, Compuserve, Prodigy, Knight-Ridder, and Lexis/Nexis, and also on CD-ROM.

Zillions' paid circulation is over 300,000 homes and schools, and the Consumer Reports Books list, with over 75 active titles, reaches many more readers. The *Travel Letter* and *Consumer Reports on Health* reach hundreds of thousands of readers.

The combination of a large circulation for its print publications, plus additional methods of dissemination, means that Consumers Union's information reaches a significant proportion of the country's population. Much of this information is used in making purchase decisions. A 1989 survey by *Better Homes & Gardens* reported that 42.8 percent of consumers surveyed identified *Consumer Reports'* ratings as an important factor in buying a range. A *Motor Trend* magazine poll found, in 1985, that *Consumer Reports* had more clout among new car buyers than any other information source.

While the number of people reached is a significant measure of the impact of Consumers Union, there are other measures. The magazine's testing and reporting has had a direct effect on sales volume for the products involved. For example, sales of one humidifier went up 15 percent after it was rated "first" in *Consumer Reports;* a men's suit, carrying a "best buy," showed a 50 percent increase in sales. This marketplace influence has helped many small producers of excellent products. For example, a favorable review in *Consumer Reports* contributed to the popularity of a new infant carrier, with sales climbing from 300 to 8,000 per month.

Negative ratings also tend to depress sales and, more significantly, can cause long-term changes in the marketplace. The disclosure of safety-related information by *Consumer Reports* had a dramatic impact on sales of the Suzuki Samurai, a light jeep-type vehicle. As a result of a *Consumer Reports* article calling the product "not acceptable" for reasons of safety, sales dropped from over 6,000 to 2,200 per month. A year later, sales were still 71 percent lower than the pre-article level.

As well as affecting sales, Consumers Union has stimulated product improvement. For example, the organization played a significant role in rejection of the 1973 versions of microwave ovens for reasons of radiation leakage. Its report and petition to the Federal Drug Administration led to improved design and improved standards. Also, Consumers Union sparked a furious marketing war in the soft-drink industry over the presence of caffeine in soft drinks. As a result, manufacturers began producing "no caffeine" soft drinks, which are now widely available. In addition, when Consumers Union published a scathing report on the safety of kerosene heaters, not only were sales of this product depressed, but the Consumer Product Safety Commission was persuaded to take action. It issued a report echoing Consumers Union's concerns that resulted in industry agreement to implement the recommended changes.

A third impact of Consumers Union is not as measurable. For nearly sixty years, the organization has promoted more informed and empowered consumers. It has done this by giving unbiased, accurate, and useful test information and other evaluations about particular products and services and how to shop for them. These informed and assertive consumers have helped establish a fairer marketplace. Their individual and collective attitudes and expectations about the marketplace now permeate both consumer and producer consciousness, helping raise standards for quality and performance of products and services. Consumers Union's unrelenting demand for ethics in business, safety in products, and respect for consumers started as a lonely voice but has become a norm for the marketplace.

A final impact of Consumers Union's work is its many contributions to the consumer movement. The organization has promoted, helped launch, and contributed to the support of new consumer organizations, such as the Center for Auto Safety, American Council on Consumer Interests, Center for the Study of Services, Consumer Federation of America, and the International Organization of Consumers Unions (now Consumers International). In addition, it has provided technical and financial support for state and local consumer organizations in the United States and for consumer organizations in other countries. But perhaps the greatest international impact of Consumers Union is that many consumer testing magazines published in other industrialized countries are modeled after *Consumer Reports.*

— Rhoda H. Karpatkin

See also

Consumer Problems in Market Economies; Consumers' Research; Information Dissemination; Product Testing; Warne, Colston E.

Readings

Morse, Richard L. D., ed. (1993). *The Consumer Movement: Lectures by Colston E. Warne.* Manhattan, KS: Family Economics Trust Press.

Silber, Norman I. (1983). *Test and Protest.* New York: Holmes & Meier.

Warne, Colston E. (1982). "Consumers Union's Contribution to the Consumer Movement." In Erma Angevine, ed. *Consumer Activists: They Made a Difference.* Mount Vernon, NY: Consumers Union Foundation. 85–110.

Cooperative Extension System

Since its creation in 1914, the Cooperative Extension System (CES) has sought to transfer knowledge from universities to consumers where they live and work. For decades, CES has assisted thousands of consumers in developing practical skills, including those related to consumption.

The origins of CES date from the Civil War. President Abraham Lincoln's 1862 signing of the Morrill Act, known as the Land-Grant Bill, endowed new state agriculture colleges with 11 million acres of public land "to promote the liberal and practical education of the industrial classes." The 1887 Hatch Act appropriated $15,000 to each state land-grant institution for experiment stations. In 1890, a second Morrill Act established historically black land-grant colleges in southern states. These three acts made higher education more available to the children of working-class Americans.

On May 8, 1914, President Woodrow Wilson signed the Smith-Lever Act to establish the CES. The program's purpose, as stated by Congress, was to "aid in diffusing among the people of the United States useful and practical information on subjects related to agriculture and home economics [now known as family and consumer sciences] and to encourage the application of the same." This legislation was a capstone for a series of late nineteenth–century congressional actions that transformed the American system of higher education.

CES linked the land-grant university and agricultural experiment station structures with federal and county governments to form a uniquely American tripartite arrangement that focuses on applied education. Seaman A. Knapp proved this concept effective with demonstration projects.

The CES federal partner is the Cooperative State Research, Education, and Extension Service, an agency within the U.S. Department of Agriculture. Federal staff identify consumer needs and trends, allocate federal funds, coordinate national initiatives, provide program leadership, help assure accountability, and maintain contacts with state and county partners, Congress, other federal agencies, and national organizations.

The CES state partners are located in America's 1862 land-grant universities in each state, territory, and the District of Columbia; and in Tuskegee University, sixteen 1890 land-grant universities, and twenty-nine Native-American institutions that gained land-grant status in 1994. There is no fixed pattern for the organization of state extension offices. All have staff members assigned to major program areas of extension—family and consumer sciences, community and rural development, youth and leadership development, and agriculture. Most specialists are members of academic departments. Many have research and/or resident teaching responsibilities in addition to providing leadership for extension's statewide programs.

With a few exceptions, at least one extension educator works in each of the nation's 3,150 counties. They are assisted by paraprofessional staff and by more than 2 million volunteers to bring educational programs to consumers. The county professional-level staff make up two-thirds of extension employees.

In 1914, the "home demonstration agent" may have visited homes to teach canning as a way to preserve food or to give a talk to a small group of homemakers on the connection between pellagra and diet. Today, the "extension educator" may work with the learner on issues related to food, nutrition, diet, and health; housing; personal and family financial management; dependent care; family relationships; stress management; home management; consumer purchases (e.g., clothing, furnishings, appliances, financial products); and community leadership. The method may be face-to-face communication, as in 1914, or it may be through the mass media, the Internet, video or audio tapes, publications, home study series, or satellite video conferences. Often, today's extension educators are knowledge brokers, teaching other professionals from public, nonprofit, and private sectors who work directly with consumers.

Funding for CES comes from all of its partners. Federal funds support less than 30 percent of extension's work. The remainder comes from local and state funds, with the state often being the major funding source. Increasingly, public dollars are being leveraged to obtain additional funds from the nonprofit and private sectors and from other departments and agencies within government.

Though the words of the CES mission have changed somewhat over time, the messages of practical education, skill-building, and improved consumer behavior have remained the same. Today, the mission is "to enable people to improve their lives and communities through learning partnerships that put knowledge to work." Extension educators do not tell consumers what to do. Rather, through education, they allow consumers to discover their strengths, identify needs, see alternative courses of action, gather information, and make their own decisions.

Extension took major roles in helping consumers survive two world wars, the Great Depression of the 1930s, the farm crisis of the 1980s, and natural disasters such as earthquakes, floods, droughts, and hurricanes. Though emphasizing preventive education, the system has developed the capacity, enhanced by electronic technology, to respond quickly in times of crisis.

— Jane Schuchardt

Readings

Rasmussen, Wayne D. (1989). *Taking the University to the People: Seventy-Five Years of Cooperative Extension.* Ames, IA: Iowa State University Press.

Turner, Josephine (1988). "The Role of Cooperative Extension." In E. Scott Maynes, ed. *The Frontier of Research in the Consumer Interest.* Columbia, MO: American Council on Consumer Interests. 849–856.

Cooperatives, Consumer

A consumer cooperative is a business jointly owned and democratically controlled by consumers to provide goods or services on a not-for-profit basis. Consumers organize and join cooperatives to reduce prices, increase quality, or increase availability. The cooperative is a community self-help response to marketplace inadequacies.

In 1994, nearly 120 million Americans were served by 47,000 cooperative businesses, most of which were owned, controlled, and patronized by consumers. These co-ops include credit unions, mutual insurance companies, retail food stores, health maintenance organizations, child care centers, housing complexes, gas stations, student bookstores, rural utilities, and telecommunications services, among others.

In the mid–nineteenth century, the Rochdale Society of Equitable Pioneers developed the cooperative model that strongly influenced the development of U.S. consumer co-ops. In 1844, many weavers in Rochdale, England, were fired and blacklisted by mill owners after an unsuccessful weavers' strike. They organized a cooperative in an attempt to reduce prices on staple food items. It took a year to accumulate the twenty-eight pounds sterling necessary to start the cooperative society. The Pioneers' first store opened on December 21,

1844, with an initial stock of flour, lard, sugar, and oatmeal. Membership was open to anyone.

By 1855, the store sold a wide variety of merchandise and offered shoemaking, tailoring, drapery, and butchering services. The Rochdale Society had established a wholesale division to supply themselves and other cooperatives in the area. They also formed a manufacturing society that owned its own cotton and wool mills.

Two principles were critical to the Pioneers' success. First, profits made by the cooperative were divided between the members in proportion to their purchases, not the amount they had invested. Accumulated profits in excess of necessary reserves were considered overcharges and returned to the consumer. Second, voting power was separated from capital investment. Each member had one vote regardless of the amount of investment in or purchases from the cooperative, so all decisions were made democratically. The principles of profit distribution based on use and democratic control continue to be the distinguishing characteristics of cooperative business.

U.S. cooperatives have experienced several periods of widespread enthusiasm and success, followed by disinterest and failure. Often arising in response to specific local needs, especially in times of economic difficulty, many cooperatives have had short and isolated histories. There are also many successful and enduring consumer cooperatives that have had an impact on the marketplace.

In 1756, Benjamin Franklin organized the first cooperative in the United States, a mutual fire insurance company. During the next century, other co-ops were established, but sparse records prevent historians from learning much about these organizations. Cooperatives were organized in large numbers during the post–Civil War agricultural depression of the 1860s and 1870s, when labor and agricultural organizations began to promote them.

As in Europe, retail cooperatives in the United States were first established by working people. An early U.S. retail cooperative was opened in Boston in 1844 by the Working Man's Protective Union. The first U.S. consumer cooperative based on the Rochdale Principles was a general store opened in Philadelphia in 1864 by the Union Cooperative Association No. 1. Between 1874 and 1879, the Sovereigns of Industry was the first labor organization to promote the idea by developing cooperative stores in the Northeast.

By 1920, the U.S. Bureau of Labor Statistics had located 728 consumer cooperatives, primarily in the eastern and north-central states. These cooperatives were spurred by socialist promotion of the cooperative idea and the influx of immigrant groups, particularly Scandinavians and Germans, who were familiar with cooperative business. Early cooperatives sold retail goods and provided financial services, housing, and rural utilities.

In 1882, working people organized the first cooperative apartment building in New York City. A few decades later, Finnish housing cooperatives were built in New York (1916) and Minneapolis (1909). During the 1920s, the federal government established cooperative houses for single working women in Washington, D.C. In 1925, the first large-scale housing cooperatives, 700 units erected in New York, were developed by the United Workers Cooperative Associated. These low-income units were distinctive because they left 50 percent of the available land open for gardening and ventilation. These homes spurred the development of cooperative housing in New York City, the country's strongest area of cooperative housing.

The country's first cooperative health care began in San Francisco when French gold miners organized a cooperative benevolent society to provide health care to members in 1849. The society later became the French Hospital, which is still in operation.

Religious and philosophical organizations have also been involved in the retail cooperative movement. Between 1868 and 1880, under the leadership of Brigham Young, the Mormon leader, the Zion's Cooperative Mercantile Institute opened 146 branch stores in Utah. A few decades later, the Right Relationship League (1905–1919) traveled throughout the Midwest, setting up over 300 cooperative general stores, most of which soon failed.

In 1909, the Cooperative League of the United States was formed in Chicago by a physician and cooperative leader, James Peter Warbasse (1866–1957). The league, now known as the National Cooperative Business Association, is the national trade association for all U.S. cooperatives.

In the early twentieth century, cooperative credit unions—financial institutions owned and controlled by consumers—began to grow. At that time banks were unwilling to lend to or provide savings facilities for many working people. In response, workers pooled what little financial resources they had (shares were sometimes purchased for as little as twenty-five cents) to have a source of funds they could borrow from in times of emergency. From 1909 to 1921, Edward Filene (1860–1937) worked tirelessly to establish state legislation permitting the existence of credit unions throughout the country. Filene, owner of Filene's Department Store in Boston, was originally drawn to credit unions as a method by which his employees could develop economic security.

Late in this period, the Ohio Farm Bureau began selling auto insurance to its farmer members. The operation was organized as a cooperative whose member-owners were the consumers who purchased insurance. From its humble beginnings, the cooperative, the Nationwide Insurance Enterprise, has grown to be the country's fourth largest auto insurer, the fifth largest property casualty insurer, and the fifth largest homeowner's insurer.

Prior to World War I, cooperatives received no government support and ran the risk of violating federal antitrust laws. Yet during and after the war, the federal government not only began providing cooperatives with credit and technical assistance but also ensured their legal status. The Clayton Act of 1914, which established the legality of cooperatives, was followed by the Capper-Volstead Act of 1922. Capper-Volstead states that cooperatives would not be in violation of antitrust laws as long as they either followed the one member–one vote rule or restricted stock dividends. Capper-Volstead also established the principle that income earned by the cooperative, and returned to members based on amounts purchased from or marketed through the business (patronage refunds), would not be considered taxable income for the cooperative. These requirements for cooperatives remain in force today.

In the 1930s, consumer participation in cooperatives grew rapidly. Many people saw cooperatives as an alternative to a profit-making system that seemed to have failed. Previously, labor and farmers had been the mainstay of consumer cooperatives. Now middle-class interest in the idea grew, particularly in retail cooperatives and credit unions as a means to modest savings and wider distribution of private property.

The majority of supporters saw cooperatives as a road to social change without revolution and as a viable alternative to monopoly capitalism, fascism, and socialism. During this period, Toyohiko Kagawa (1888–1960), a Japanese Protestant clergyman, preached the "brotherhood economics" of consumer cooperation on college campuses throughout the United States. During these speaking tours, Kagawa influenced an entire generation of cooperative leaders and continued the religious influence on the movement. Kagawa was particularly inspirational to student cooperators. The 1930s were the first decade of the student cooperative movement, which is still strong today. By 1938, student housing, eating, and bookstore cooperatives had grown to 104,000 members.

Depression-era cooperatives tended to be stronger than those of earlier years. They had the benefit of drawing on the wisdom of older, more experienced cooperators who had already established board and management practices. They also received increased government support. The New Deal strongly promoted cooperatives, particularly self-help consumer and "swap" cooperatives for the unemployed and rural poor as well as rural electric and homestead cooperatives.

Although they received no direct aid, nonfarm distributive cooperatives were protected under the National Recovery Administration Codes of 1933 to 1934, which permitted cooperatives to offer members a year-end rebate on purchases. During this period, many consumer cooperatives were established, and important moves were made toward centralizing cooperative organizations so that consumers could control a larger portion of the distribution channel. In 1937, Cooperative Distributors, a successful mail-order business in the Northeast, reported 8,000 members and 150 affiliated nonprofit organizations. In California between 1934 and 1935, as part of Upton Sinclair's EPIC (End Poverty in California) movement, over fifty cooperatives were started.

In this period, a cooperative hospital, which would have a far-reaching impact on the entire organization of U.S. health care, was founded. In 1931 in Elk City, Oklahoma, withstanding efforts by the American Medical Association to destroy his career, a visionary doctor, Michael Shadid, started the first prepaid health care and hospital system. Shadid developed the idea in order to protect farmers from losing their land to bankers and doctors when they were unable to pay medical bills during the farm depression and the Oklahoma dust bowl. The Elk City hospital served as a model for the first health maintenance organization in the country and was adopted by the Group Health Cooperative of Puget Sound, which was established in Seattle in 1946 by a consortium of farm, labor, and local cooperatives. The Group Health Plan of Minneapolis (currently Health Partners), which was organized in 1948 out of a cooperative insurance organization, also followed the Shadid model.

Another New Deal program had tremendous impact on rural consumers. Under the Rural Electrification Program, rural electric cooperatives were started throughout the country. These consumer co-ops provided most rural Americans with the first electricity to their homes and farms. In 1949, Congress added to the Rural Electrification Program a Rural Telephone Program, which spurred formation of rural telephone cooperatives. By 1941, the Bureau of Labor Statistics counted 14,491 nonfarm cooperatives, of which 9,935 were credit unions with a total membership of 5 million.

World War II produced sweeping changes in the cooperative movement. Cooperatives of all types, particularly retail cooperatives, flourished but often failed quickly. At the same time, the federal government established retail cooperatives as a way of controlling retail prices in certain "transitory communities." A total of 109 retail cooperatives were organized in Japanese-American relocation camps. Conscientious objectors ran similar government-established cooperatives in wartime Civilian Public Service camps, and the Farm Security Administration established cooperative retail centers in farm migration camps in California.

Independent cooperatives, on the other hand, surged and failed with the fluctuating wartime and post-war economy. After a peak year in 1946, by 1949 the majority of petroleum and retail cooperatives had failed. Most of the food cooperatives that survived the post-war years differed little from their modern supermarket competitors. In this period, the first multistore cooperatives opened in urban centers such as Palo Alto, Berkeley, and the Washington, D.C., area. These cooperatives thrived until the 1980s when most were forced to close because of lack of adequate capitalization and tough competition from private sellers.

World War II had a negative effect on credit unions. Because of the shortage of high-priced consumer goods (which most workers would need a loan to purchase), credit union membership plummeted. Between 1942 and 1945, 1,200 credit unions were liquidated. For the credit unions that survived, however, the growth in consumer incomes, and the widespread availability of expensive consumer goods during the 1950s led to another period of growth in membership and assets.

Immediately following World War II, American consumers were introduced to larger, centralized shopping centers that competed with the older, smaller retail stores, both private and cooperative. In general, new cooperatives and those open to change succeeded, but those that resisted change went bankrupt. In nonretail sectors, meanwhile, health cooperatives, cooperative housing, and student cooperatives showed unprecedented growth.

Most post-war cooperative housing development occurred in New York City, where "war housing" was converted to cooperative ownership. During the 1950s, the federal government converted 35,000 units to cooperatives, while another 100,000 units were converted with private financing. The federal government also began to provide mortgage insurance for cooperatives through the Federal Housing Administration. This insurance encouraged private lenders to finance housing cooperatives, thus enabling increased cooperative housing development.

In the prosperous 1950s, there was little interest in forming or joining most consumer cooperatives. The savings offered by co-ops seemed modest compared to average wages. Also, conservative sentiment against anything "left-wing" discouraged interest in cooperatives. However, housing, credit unions, and insurance cooperatives continued to grow.

In the mid-1960s, as an outgrowth of the civil rights movement and the War on Poverty, hundreds of consumer cooperatives were started, often with federal government support. This co-op organizing was an attempt to help people with limited economic resources achieve economic independence. Most limited-resource cooperatives have needed large amounts of initial capital to start, and continuing financial assistance from outside sources to survive.

During this period, interest in consumer cooperatives, particularly food purchasing cooperatives, was not limited to the poor. News sources reported food cooperatives were "shooting up like mushrooms after a rain" all over the country. In contrast to previous periods, these new cooperatives were located in middle-class urban and suburban areas, often near universities. Inflation and rising unemployment had reduced the real income of middle-class consumers; the housewives' supermarket strikes of the period dramatized consumers' demands for lower food prices. In addition, the 1960s and 1970s saw a tremendous growth in the consumer rights movement. Citizens were protesting inferior products, exorbitant prices, health hazards in food and drugs, an impersonal and increasingly monopolistic marketplace, and fraudulent or grossly misleading consumer information. At the same time, the civil rights, student, and anti–Vietnam War movements were creating new political and economic awareness among young people. This was a period when consumers were not satisfied with products and services being provided by the market, nor with the general character of the economic system itself. Conditions were favorable for development of consumer-owned economic institutions whose bottom line is benefits to users rather than profits to investors.

Food cooperatives formed during this period came to be known as "new wave," as much for their specialization in natural foods as for their recent origins. The natural foods cooperatives enjoyed a near monopoly in natural foods for the first twenty years of their existence. Nearly 700 natural foods cooperative retail stores and thousands of informal cooperative buying groups operated during the 1970s.

Cooperative housing was fostered during this period by several major federal programs. One such program provided direct financing to cooperatives built for low- and moderate-income members at below-market interest rates (section 8 of the 1974 Housing Act). Another program involved purchase of cooperative mortgages from private lenders through the Federal National Mortgage Association.

During the 1960s and 1970s, as in the early part of the century, cooperatives represented a middle road to social change. Unlike radical organizations that advocated violent overthrow of the economic and political system, the cooperative movement offered a nonviolent way of altering the system. At the same time, cooperatives put into practice much of the New Left's emphasis on participatory democracy. Cooperative organizers stressed then, as they do now, the need for democratic processes as a way for communities to take control of their own futures.

Cooperatives have given consumers a voice in an increasingly concentrated and corporate marketplace. Food cooperatives, for example, have been active in supporting consumer demands for healthful and organic foods since the late 1960s. The now defunct Consumers Cooperative of Berkeley is a prominent example. As early as 1961, it issued an appeal to regulatory agencies and legislatures to set better food standards. Cooperatives lobbied extensively for the federal Fair Packaging and Labeling Law, passed in 1966. Food cooperatives have often led the way in carrying organic produce and natural foods, and in establishing recycling centers.

Federal support for any kind of cooperative development, with one major exception, was drastically reduced by Reagan administration budget cuts. Long-established federal programs that provided grants, loans, insurance, and technical assistance to housing cooperatives, energy projects, economic development and revitalization efforts, and community-based organizations were cut back or eliminated.

The only exception to this general rule was federal support of the National Cooperative Bank for consumer cooperatives. From its opening in 1980, the bank has grown to a $400 million institution with loans outstanding to consumer cooperatives throughout the country. These co-ops include several health maintenance organizations, a worker-owned cooperative that provides home health care services, a cable television network, a recreational equipment cooperative, numerous cooperative warehouses, and a wide variety of housing cooperatives.

In sum, consumer cooperative activity in the United States has been cyclical, often in response to outside economic and political conditions. Much of consumer cooperative development has been experimental and unorganized, with little evidence of a coherent local, regional, or national plan.

Although cooperatives enjoy some public support—a 1994 Gallup Poll found that two-thirds of Americans trust cooperatives more than other forms of business—most consumers do not have a clear idea of what a cooperative business is and how it can serve their needs. Consumers are not used to analyzing their status as a function of the ownership structure of the business that serves them, nor do most consumers identify themselves as business owners.

In the food area, only a handful of the cooperative retail supermarkets survive today. Yet, some of the survivors control as much as 25 percent of the retail food sales in their local market. Investor-owned food stores did not see the market potential of natural foods until the late 1980s. Since then, however, they have entered the market aggressively, often in trade areas originally developed by the cooperatives. The presence of effective competition, the absence of sufficient capital, and an inability to adapt to changing market conditions took a severe toll on natural foods cooperatives. Of the nearly 700 operating in the 1970s, only half survive today. The survivors, however, have grown stronger, larger, and more efficient. With eight stores and over $40 million in annual sales, Puget Consumers Co-op of Seattle is the country's largest natural foods cooperative. All of the wholesale distributors owned by consumer cooperatives between 1950 and 1980 have closed. In their place are nine natural foods distributors whose 1994 sales reached $167 million.

The largest consumer retail cooperative in the country is REI, Recreational Equipment, Inc. Started shortly before World War II by a husband and wife mountain climbing team, the cooperative owns forty retail outlets throughout the country and operates a catalogue business, a travel company, and several manufacturing subsidiaries. Total sales for REI in 1994 were nearly $400 million to 1.4 million consumer-owners.

There are currently twenty consumer-owned and -controlled health maintenance organizations, serving nearly 1 million people in the United States. Rural telephone cooperatives currently serve 1.2 million people in thirty-one states with sophisticated communications technology. New types of cooperatives developed in recent years include telecommunications and business purchasing and joint marketing cooperatives for small businesses.

The federal government is once again supporting cooperative development, albeit in a very limited way, by providing some funding for the National Rural Cooperative Development Task Force. The task force has established eight cooperative development centers throughout the country. At the same time, as part of the 1994 reorganization of the U.S. Department of Agriculture, the Agricultural Cooperative Service, which had provided a number of support services to agricultural cooperatives for many years, was reorganized into the Rural Business and Cooperative Development Service with a new focus on all kinds of cooperatives that could help revitalize rural areas. The new service has also been directed to focus specifically on solutions to rural poverty.

— Ann Hoyt

See also

Credit Unions; Energy Cooperatives; Food Cooperatives; Housing Cooperatives; National Cooperative Bank; Rural Electric Cooperatives.

Readings

Abrahamson, Martin A. (1976). *Cooperative Business Enterprise.* New York: McGraw-Hill.

Kress, Andrew J. (1941). *Introduction to the Cooperative Movement.* New York: Harper and Brothers.

Voorhis, Jerry (1961). *American Cooperatives.* New York: Harper and Brothers.

Corporate Consumer Advisory Panels

During the 1970s, forward-thinking businesses began to recognize that opening lines of communication to consumer organizations and consumer leaders could be beneficial. In the same period, many consumer leaders concluded that discussions with business groups could serve useful purposes. A number of companies and industries gave formal structure to this dialogue by creating consumer advisory panels.

Consumer advisory panels can take several forms. Long-term advisory panels have a permanent or rotating membership drawn from national and community consumer organizations. They hold regular meetings and usually make recommendations on a wide range of issues and corporate policies. In contrast, shoppers' panels consisting of regular patrons usually advise store management about more limited subjects, such as product selection, marketing, services, and store operations. Special forums or roundtables may be convened on a short-term basis to address one or more specific, often time-sensitive topics of interest to business and the consumer community.

Consumer advisory panels have been established in many different industries, including electric and gas utilities, telecommunications, and retail marketing. Companies give several reasons for sponsoring consumer advisory panels: to establish open communication between the company and both its customers and consumer leaders, to obtain information the company has no other way of learning in advance of making decisions, to help develop more competitive products and better customer service, to enhance the company's image, to understand consumer attitudes toward public policy issues, and to narrow differences and avoid costly conflicts.

Consumer and business leaders agree that several features tend to increase the likelihood that consumer advisory panels will be able to accomplish their intended purposes: the purposes and objectives are clear in advance, and the consumer members are sure they are not being "used"; the subjects to be addressed are considered to be important by both sides; there are well-understood and mutually acceptable ground rules; top management supports the existence of the panel and is accessible to it; the effective decision-makers within the company attend the meetings; the company provides backup support to the panel; background materials are circulated prior to meetings; and the activities of the panel are not publicized outside the company without the panel members' express consent.

Recommendations of consumer advisory panels have had an impact on company policy and practice in a variety of ways. Examples include: improvements in billing practices, revisions in credit policies, changes in operating hours to accommodate neighborhood needs, sensitivity training for customer service personnel, the addition of multilingual services, greater product variety and convenience, enhanced consumer education and information programs, narrowed differences on public policy issues, and the avoidance of damaging public debates.

Despite these and other benefits to businesses, enthusiasm for consumer advisory panels among some companies began to wane in the late 1980s and early 1990s. The management of these companies shifted their emphasis from structured advisory panels to less expensive alternatives, such as focus groups gathered to examine single issues or panels assembled once a year to be briefed on corporate plans. Some consumer leaders who had supported the development of consumer advisory panels and participated on them became disillusioned at what they viewed as business use of panels as focus groups to gather marketing data rather than to institutionalize consumer input into strategic planning or product design.

It is too soon to know whether consumer advisory panels will be enduring, influential institutions. The concept continues to have supporters among those in industry and in the consumer movement who believe that it is desirable to learn from one another and to solve differences through dialogue rather than confrontation.

— Rebecca Arnold Cohen

Readings

Cohen, Rebecca A. (1983). *Organizing a Company's Consumer Advisory Panel.* Washington, DC: American Association of Retired Persons.

Fernstrom, Meredith M. (1989). *Financial Institutions and the Public Interest: Forging Joint Ventures.* New York: American Express Company.

Cosmetic Safety

While some consumers might think of cosmetics as consisting simply of those products used on their face to enhance appearance, the federal government takes a broader view of cosmetics. The Federal Food, Drug and Cosmetic Act defines cosmetics as articles intended to be applied to the human body for cleansing, beautifying, promoting attractiveness, or altering the appearance without affecting the body's structure or functions. Thus, the term *cosmetics* includes skin creams, lotions, perfumes, lipsticks, fingernail polishes, eye and facial make-up preparations, shampoos, permanent waves, hair colors, toothpastes, deodorants, and any material intended for use as a component or ingredient of a cosmetic product.

Cosmetic products that are used to treat or prevent disease or that affect the structure or function of the human body are also considered drugs. These products must comply with both the cosmetic and drug requirements of the law. Many of these combined cosmetic/drug products are over-the-counter drugs, although some are prescription drugs that require government approval prior to marketing. Common examples of products that are both drugs and cosmetics include: fluoride toothpaste; suntan lotion intended to protect against sunburn; antiperspirants that are also deodorants; and antidandruff shampoos.

In the United States, cosmetic safety is a shared responsibility between government and the private sector.

Federal Law

Cosmetics marketed in the United States, whether manufactured here or imported from abroad, must comply with the provisions of the Federal Food, Drug and Cosmetic Act (1938, as amended), the Fair Packaging and Labeling Act (1966), and regulations promulgated under the authority of these laws. For the most part, the government's responsibility for cosmetic ingredient safety is carried out by the Food and Drug Administration (FDA).

It is important to note that cosmetic laws do not require that cosmetic manufacturers or marketers test their products for safety, although the FDA strongly urges that they do so. If the safety of a cosmetic is not adequately substantiated, the product must state on its label: "Warning—The safety of this product has not been determined." Failure to use this warning on products not substantiated for safety is a violation of law. With the exception of color additives and prohibited ingredients, a cosmetic manufacturer is free to use any raw material as a cosmetic ingredient and market the product without approval.

FDA law also requires that cosmetics not be "adulterated." According to the FDA, a cosmetic is adulterated if it contains a substance that may make the product harmful to consumers under customary conditions of use; if it contains a filthy, putrid, or decomposed substance; if its container is composed of a harmful substance; if it is manufactured or held under unsanitary conditions where it may become contaminated with filth or become harmful to consumers; or if it contains a nonpermitted color additive (hair dyes excluded).

The cosmetic product label must provide consumers with certain basic information about the product, such as: name of the product; a description or illustration of the use of the product; net quantity of contents; the name and place of business of the firm making the product; and name of the distributor, if different from the manufacturer.

In addition to this information, cosmetics produced for retail sale to consumers must include on their labels a listing of ingredients in descending order of predominance. Color additives and ingredients present at 1 percent or less do not have to be listed with regard to predominance. Cosmetics that are also drugs must first identify the drug ingredient as the "active ingredient" before listing any of the cosmetic ingredients. Ingredient labeling and warnings required by law must appear prominently and conspicuously so that they are likely to be read and understood by consumers under normal conditions of purchase. Tamper resistant packages are required for liquid oral hygiene products and for all cosmetic vaginal products when these goods are sold at retail.

The FDA also has issued specific regulations and prohibitions pertaining to several classes of cosmetic ingredients or products, and has begun investigations and studies of other issues affecting cosmetic safety. These products include aerosol products; bubble bath products; depilatories and hair straighteners; feminine deodorant sprays; hair shampoos, rinses, and conditioners; nail builders, hardeners, enamel, and preservation products; products containing hormones and vitamins; soap; and suntan products.

Hair dyes have also been the subject of concern and FDA requirements. The two major concerns regarding the use of hair dyes are skin irritation and cancer. Coal-tar hair dye products are not "adulterated" under FDA law if they have the following caution statement on their label: "Caution—This product contains ingredients which may cause skin irritation on certain individuals and a preliminary test according to accompanying directions should first be made. This product must not be used for dyeing the eyelashes or eyebrows; to do so may cause blindness." At least five hair dye ingredients have been reported to cause cancer in at least one species of animals.

Color additives are also addressed by FDA law. Cosmetics (as well as foods, drugs, and some medical devices) are "adulterated" if they contain color additives that have not been proved safe to the satisfaction of the FDA for the particular use. FDA regulations list the approved color additives and the conditions under which they may be safely used in cosmetics, including the amounts that may be used when limitations are necessary. Unless exempted by regulation, the FDA must test and certify each batch of color before it can be used. Consumer groups have been concerned that color additives that cause cancer in animals are still permitted by the FDA to be used in cosmetics and other consumer products.

Finally, the FDA has published regulations or interpretations stating its position regarding specific cosmetic ingredients and prohibiting their use in consumer products. In some cases, the ingredient is completely banned; in some cases, it may be limited to a certain amount; and in other cases, it may be limited to certain types of products.

Private Sector

In 1976, in an effort to establish a self-regulatory program, the Cosmetic, Toiletry and Fragrance Association (CTFA) created the Cosmetic Ingredient Review (CIR). A nonprofit organization, the CIR's chief purpose is to review the safety of cosmetic ingredients. The CIR's scientific evaluations of the cosmetic ingredients are performed by an expert panel consisting of seven physicians and scientists, including dermatologists and toxicologists. Three nonvoting members—consumer, industry, and FDA representatives—participate in the deliberations.

Ingredients specifically regulated by the FDA, such as color additives, are exempt from CIR review. Ingredients that are being evaluated by the FDA under the Over-the-Counter Drug Review or for use as a Direct Food Additive are also exempt from review until that evaluation is completed. Fragrance materials are not evaluated by the CIR because they are reviewed as part of the Research Institute for Fragrance Materials program.

The CIR review process entails the preparation and review of a report that reviews all scientific aspects and testing of the ingredients. A public comment period is provided, and meetings of the CIR expert panel are open to the public. After full review of a cosmetic ingredient, the CIR expert panel can essentially make one of four determinations: (1) the ingredient is safe, (2) it is unsafe, (3) it is safe at certain levels or for certain uses (a qualified conclusion), or (4) there are insufficient data to assess the ingredient's safety. These conclusions, as well as the scientific report on which the conclusion is based, are then published in the *Journal of the American College of Toxicology*. If additional data later become available, the CIR expert panel can reopen its review of an ingredient. Between 1976 and 1995, the CIR reviewed the safety of 438 cosmetic ingredients.

— Mary Ellen R. Fise

See also

U.S. Food and Drug Administration.

Readings

Congressional Research Service (1990). *Classification and Regulation of Cosmetics and Drugs: A Legal Overview and Alternatives for Legislative Change*. Washington, DC: The Library of Congress.

Stehlin, Dori (1991). "Cosmetic Safety: More Complex than at First Blush." *FDA Consumer*. 25 (9): 18–23.

U.S. Department of Health and Human Services (1995). *Cosmetics Handbook*. Washington, D.C.: U.S. Government Printing Office.

Credit Protections

The use of credit by consumers in the United States began in Colonial times, when retailers granted farmers open-book credit, with payments made when the crops were harvested.

Furniture was sold on installment credit as early as 1807, and sewing machines, pianos, and stoves were sold on credit later in the nineteenth century. However, it was not until the early 1900s that the growth of mass-produced and mass-marketed durable goods, such as automobiles, caused consumer credit to be widely used. Only then did sufficient concerns arise to demand protection for consumers in their use of this service.

Throughout most of the twentieth century, consumers sought protection from state legislatures. By 1965, there was a jerry-built system of laws and regulations that applied differently depending upon the state, the provider of credit, and the type of good or service financed. To bring order to the resulting morass, legislators followed two basic paths: the Uniform Consumer Credit Code (UCCC), which was enacted in whole or in part in a number of states beginning in the late 1970s, and federal statutes, which in several cases drew upon the UCCC.

These laws sought to address consumers' concerns with respect to five stages in arranging and paying for credit: information-seeking phase (provisions for uniform disclosure of credit terms in advertisements and credit agreements); negotiating phase (provisions to assure equal access to consumer credit and to limit the scope of the negotiations by restricting the price of credit and forbidding or requiring certain terms or practices); formalizing phase (provisions that codified the content and clarity of the legal documents obligating consumers); performing phase (provisions governing creditors' billing practices, collection efforts, and reporting of credit performance); and terminating phase (provisions specifying creditors' obligations upon consumers' payment of the obligation). The remainder of this discussion will concentrate on major developments in consumer protection in the consumer credit field.

Disclosure of Credit Terms

The major purpose of disclosure requirements is to provide a uniform way of disclosing the cost of all forms of credit to consumers in order to invigorate competition among credit grantors. In 1965, some credit grantors quoted the cost of credit as a monthly percentage rate, others as a dollar cost per initial $100 borrowed per year, and still others (credit unions) as an annual percentage rate. Nor was there agreement as to what charges comprised the "finance charge." While many state laws required that these charges be fully disclosed, there was no "common denominator" that consumers could use to identify which credit offer had the lowest cost.

The leader of the movement to require all grantors of consumer credit to quote only an annual percentage rate in advertising and credit agreements was Senator Paul H. Douglas (D-IL) and, later, Senator William Proxmire (D-WI). Many in the credit industry resisted their efforts on the grounds that it would be too complex to provide the information and that, for certain types of credit, disclosure could be deceptive. In spite of this opposition, Congress passed the Consumer Protection Act of 1968, which included the Truth in Lending Act. A later federal disclosure statute was the Consumer Leasing Act of 1976.

Truth in lending requires that consumer creditors conspicuously disclose key credit terms in uniform terminology. The finance charge must be expressed in dollars and as a yearly rate, known as the "annual percentage rate" (APR). Although the regulations needed to accommodate the many different types of credit and creditors were complex, the resulting APR provides all consumers with a standard yardstick for measuring the cost of credit.

Consumers did not benefit equally from having the information, however. Studies sponsored by the National Commission on Consumer Finance (which was created by the Consumer Protection Act) found that low-income, high-risk consumers were least aware of the APR, especially when shopping for used autos. Low-income consumers tended to focus instead on the size of the monthly payment. Moreover, credit sellers may bury a portion of the finance charge in the cash price of the goods or services sold.

Rate Ceilings

For many years, the negotiating phase has been subject to limits placed by state laws on the price that could be charged for credit. Ever since Colonial days, the most common "protection" in laws affecting consumer credit was rate ceilings. Initially, usury laws limiting rates to 6 percent to 8 percent were imported from England and continued to prevail in almost all states, even though England eliminated all rate ceilings on consumer credit in 1854. Vigorous battles were fought, led by the Russell Sage Foundation, to raise rate ceilings in order to permit the legitimate granting of credit to consumers. Opposition in many states came from a strange alliance between the clergy and loan sharks, but finally the states began passing laws to enable legal lenders to provide credit to consumers. The first small loan statute was enacted in New Jersey in 1914, allowing a rate of 36 percent on loans of $300.

Regulation of rates on consumer credit has remained with the states, which have gradually been eliminating various rate ceilings and allowing rates to be set by competition, fostered in part by truth in lending requirements. Today, most consumer advocates have recognized the age-old dilemma: the highest-risk consumers tend to be those who can least "afford" the price of their risk. The intuitive response to this dilemma is to protect these consumers by imposing strict rate ceilings on consumer credit. Yet much research has shown that rate ceilings hurt, rather than protect, consumers. When rate ceilings are imposed on cash credit, consumers who pose such a high risk that they cannot be served at the ceiling rate are rationed out of the legal cash credit market. These consumers must either do without cash credit or turn to such sources as loan sharks. When rate ceilings are imposed on sales credit, sellers can often push the cost of providing financing into higher cash prices. In these instances, cash buyers are forced to subsidize credit buyers.

Equal Access to Credit

Another limit on the negotiating phase is that creditors may not discriminate in granting of credit on the basis of such characteristics of the credit applicant as race, color, religion, national origin, sex, and marital status. Impetus for the Equal Credit Opportunity Act (ECOA), enacted in 1974, came in part from hearings held by the National Commission on Consumer Finance. The hearings demonstrated the difficulty that creditworthy married females faced in obtaining credit in their own names. While competition would eventually have forced the industry to correct their practices, the ECOA speeded the adjustment by forbidding creditors from requiring a cosigner or guarantor when an applicant applies for credit. Passage of the ECOA stimulated the usage of statistical credit evaluation systems in order to reduce the possibility that biases held by credit analysts would lead to discrimination.

Credit Reporting

Another antidote to discrimination in lending is the widespread availability of accurate information about consumers' credit performance. A record of prompt payment dominates credit decisions; for that reason, consumers need the opportunity to check the accuracy of their credit reports. That opportunity is mandated by the Fair Credit Reporting Act, which was enacted in 1970 with the support of many consumer advocates. Consumers who are denied credit on the basis of their credit report must be informed of their right to obtain a copy of their report and to have any inaccurate information corrected. Given the national scope of the act, consumers in all states have the same access to their reports, and credit grantors throughout the United States provide data on a uniform basis to credit reporting agencies. The resulting efficiency of credit markets is superior to that in all other nations.

Consumer-Creditor Relations

A number of other federal laws govern the relations between consumers and creditors during the negotiation phase and the performing phase. The Fair Credit Billing Act (1974) requires that creditors promptly settle disputes about consumer bills. An important element drawn from the UCCC is the provision that (within certain limits) a credit card issuer is subject to claims and defenses when the card is used as a method of payment. Thus, if a consumer pays with a credit card for an item that turns out to be defective, the card issuer may be held responsible. The remedy provides an incentive for card issuers to police the retailers that accept their cards. The Fair Debt Collection Practices Act of 1977 is designed to eliminate abusive and deceptive debt collection practices.

In summary, credit protections have been rationalized, to a considerable extent, by some states having adopted the UCCC, or portions thereof, and by the U.S. Congress's recognition that in many cases consumer protection is best provided by national laws that supersede disparate state laws. Consumer advocates, academic scholars, and industry representatives have all played a role in this improvement.

— Robert W. Johnson

See also

Community Reinvestment; Mortgage Loan Protections; National Consumer Law Center.

Readings

Canner, Glenn B., Arthur B. Kennickell, and Charles A. Luckett (1995). "Household Sector Borrowing and the Burden of Debt." *Federal Reserve Bulletin*. 81 (April): 323–338.

Hong, Gong-Soog, and Ramona K. Z. Heck (1995). "Credit Regulation." In Kenneth J. Meier and E. Thomas Garman, eds. *Regulation and Consumer Protection*. Houston: DAME Publications, Inc. 343–362.

Staten, Michael E., and Robert W. Johnson (1995). *The Case for Deregulating Interest Rates on Consumer Credit*. West Lafayette, IN: Credit Research Center, Purdue University.

Credit Unions

Credit unions are nonprofit, cooperative financial institutions that are owned and controlled by consumers who, when they join, become both members and owners. Credit union members pool their savings, on which they earn interest or dividends. These savings are the primary source of funds for loans that are made to members. Research has shown that credit unions tend to charge lower fees and loan rates, and pay higher savings rates, than other depository institutions.

U.S. credit unions are organized under federal or state law to allow people with a "common bond"—place of employment, community where they live, or regular association such as in churches and membership organizations—to join together to save and borrow for mutual benefit. The National Credit Union Administration (NCUA), an independent federal agency with a three-person board appointed by the president, regulates all federally chartered credit unions. NCUA also administers the National Credit Union Share Insurance Fund, which insures savings in credit unions up to $100,000 per member.

Members elect from among themselves a board of volunteer directors to establish credit union policies. The elections are held under a "one member–one vote" rule without regard to the size of individual savings accounts. Members also serve as volunteers on the credit committee, which approves loan requests, and the supervisory committee, which oversees the accuracy of the books and records. Volunteers may also serve on other committees, such as an education committee that develops programs to teach members about savings strategies and the wise use of credit.

The credit union's board of directors hires a chief executive officer to run the day-to-day operations. A few credit unions, usually small ones, operate without paid staff; in these institutions, a board member, typically the treasurer, serves as the chief executive officer.

U.S. credit unions trace their roots to Germany, India, and Canada. Credit unions were first organized in the mid-1800s in the Westerwald area of what is now Germany. Friedrich Wilhelm Raiffeisen, a local mayor, tried to solve the problems of a depression brought on by a famine known as the "hungry forties." He reasoned that if people mutually pooled their savings and loaned these savings to their fellow members, they would own and control the organization.

In 1908, with the help of Canadian credit union pioneer Alphonse Desjardins, the first U.S. credit union was organized in the largely French-speaking parish of St. Mary's in Manchester, New Hampshire. St. Mary's Cooperative Credit Association, also known as St. Mary's Bank, was formally chartered on April 6, 1909.

While on a world tour in 1907, Edward A. Filene, a Boston department store magnate and progressive thinker, came across credit and savings cooperatives. In India, he saw that in villages that had cooperatives, people were better housed, clothed, and fed than in those without them. He brought the idea home to the United States.

In 1915, Filene started the Massachusetts Credit Union Association as an "example" or "sample" credit union that others might replicate. But after five years and little success, he realized that credit unions would succeed only through the hard work of a centralized organizing effort. Accordingly, in 1921 Filene formed the Credit Union National Extension Bureau in Boston. Roy F. Bergengren, a Massachusetts attorney, was hired to head the bureau. Bergengren and Agnes Gartland, his chief assistant, organized hundreds of credit unions with the help of a handful of volunteers. They also organized state credit union leagues and lobbied to obtain state credit union legislation.

The Great Depression of the 1930s provided the stimulus for organizing more credit unions to serve larger numbers of people. In Washington, Bergengren lobbied long and hard for a national credit union act, which President Franklin D. Roosevelt signed into law in June 1934. Two Texas lawmakers, Senator Morris Sheppard (D-TX) and Representative Wright Patman (D-TX), championed the credit union idea of mutual self-help in their respective congressional chambers.

With a national law and many state credit union laws in place, and thirty state leagues organized, it became possible in 1934 to transform the Credit Union National Extension Bureau into a national organization, the Credit Union National Association (CUNA). In 1935, CUNA moved from Boston to Madison, Wisconsin. CUNA continues to be the primary trade association of U.S. credit unions, with a governmental affairs office in Washington, D.C., and with education, research, public relations, publications, marketing support, and other trade association activities based in Madison. (The National Association of Federal Credit Unions—NAFCU—was founded in 1967 to represent federally chartered credit unions before Congress and federal regulatory agencies.)

CUNA has organized other national organizations to serve credit unions and their members. One was CUNA Supply Cooperative, now CUNA Service Group, which provides credit unions with forms, promotional materials, IRA and credit card programs, and other services. Working with credit unions and state leagues, CUNA also organized corporate credit unions, which provide liquidity and investment services to credit unions, and process their checks, drafts, and credit card vouchers.

In 1935, Filene loaned CUNA $25,000 to form what is now known as the CUNA Mutual Group, owned by credit unions and their members. CUNA Mutual and affiliates, now with over $87 billion in life insurance policies in force, was created to provide affordable, quality insurance and related products and services to credit unions and their members. In addition to individual and group life and health insurance, CUNA Mutual provides low-cost credit insurance, annuities and investments, retirement and financial planning, and private mortgage insurance and auto coverage. CUNA Mutual also insures credit unions themselves, providing nearly all fidelity bond coverage, and most property and casualty coverage.

In late 1994, some 67 million consumers belonged to and owned the $300 billion in assets of 12,619 U.S. credit unions. Consumer savings in U.S. credit unions were $265 billion; and loans outstanding totaled $178 billion.

Through CUNA's membership in the World Council of Credit Unions, U.S. credit unions are affiliated with the worldwide movement of credit unions. In eighty-four countries, more than 100 million people belong to these cooperative organizations.

— Larry H. Blanchard

See also

Cooperatives, Consumer.

Readings

Moody, J. Carroll, and Gilbert C. Fite (1971). *The Credit Union Movement: Origins and Development, 1850–1970.* Lincoln: University of Nebraska Press.

Pugh, Olin S., and Jerry F. Ingram (1984). *Credit Unions: A Movement Becomes an Industry.* Reston, VA: Reston Publishing Corporation, Inc.

CUBs

See Citizen Utility Boards.

Czech Consumer Movement

Of all the countries in Central and Eastern Europe, the Czech Republic (along with Slovakia) is perhaps closest to joining the European Union. It has already become a member of Organization for Economic Cooperation and Development, and the present government is committed to a set of policies that are short on regulation and long on economic freedom. A general Consumer Protection Act has been in place since the end of 1992; it was introduced by the Federal Assembly shortly before the Czechs and Slovaks parted company. Over time, consumer legislation will be brought into line with Western European law.

The responsibility for consumer protection lies with a small department in the Ministry of Trade and Industry. In the spirit of minimum intervention in the market, no separate state consumer office has been set up or is contemplated.

As yet, there is no national organization representing consumers in the Czech Republic. An association founded in 1989 is moribund, but there is an active group based in Ostrava with national aspirations. This Consumers Defense Association was founded in February 1993, is staffed wholly by volunteers, and now has branches in twelve localities, including Brno. It publishes a monthly magazine *Stit Spotrebitele* (The Consumer's Shield). It aims to make consumers equal participants in the marketplace by informing consumers of their rights on the one hand, and by maintaining close contacts with government and municipal authorities with responsibility for consumer protection on the other. There is also a local group of dedicated activists based in the university area of Prague.

The most effective champion of the consumer cause in the Czech Republic, by far, is the monthly magazine, *d-TEST.* This remarkable venture is the creation of one person, Ida Rozova. It began in 1991 as a monthly free insert in the satirical weekly magazine *Dikebraz,* which enjoyed a circulation of 180,000 in the former Czechoslovakia. In September 1993, after Communism had receded and Czechoslovakia split, Rozova launched *d-TEST* as an independent monthly magazine.

This publication is a comparative testing magazine that carries no advertising and campaigns for safety and other consumer protections. At the start, some financial institutions whose services were not reviewed in the magazine provided support, but this funding has virtually ceased. Income now comes from subscription and sales revenue, from an annual government grant that covers the printing and paper costs, and from a central budget at the Office for Standardization, Metrology and

State Testing on which the magazine can draw for test projects. Despite a circulation of 30,000 (including 10,000 subscribers), sales income represents only about 20 percent of the total budget. But raising the cover price would put it out of the financial reach of most consumers. However, the Ministry of Trade, which has a high opinion of the integrity and usefulness of the magazine to Czech consumers, is prepared to subsidize its production so that it could reach a wide audience.

The magazine is unique in the annals of consumer publishing in one respect. From its first issue, it has had a paid staff of one—Ida Rozova herself. She has been publisher, editor, researcher in chief, "agony aunt" on the phone and by letter for all the problems that pour into her office, campaigner for the consumer cause on television and radio, subscription manager, and administrator for the magazine. In early 1996, she began receiving support from two assistants.

The principal challenges that lie ahead for the Czech consumer movement are to build a national organization (perhaps in association with the magazine), to strengthen the professional basis of research and testing on which *d-TEST*'s reputation rests, and to reduce its dependence on external funding.

— Alastair Macgeorge

See also

Central and Eastern Europe, Consumer Movements in.

Reading

Kozminski, Andrzej K. (1992). "Consumers in Transition from the Centrally Planned Economy to the Market Economy." *Journal of Consumer Policy.* 14 (4): 351–370.

D

Danish Consumer Movement

During the 1920s, local organizations concerned with issues such as nutrition, budgeting, financial planning, and hygiene were organized by Danish countrywomen. By the early 1930s, they advocated a central organization that would test products, coordinate activities, and prepare teaching materials.

In 1935, the Danish Government Home Economics Council was established to fulfill this need. The organization remains today a state institution that constitutes one part of the National Consumer Agency of Denmark. Its product testing and preparation of consumer information are still among the Council's central tasks. Research results are published in the bulletin *Technical Information,* while information in a more popular form is published in the magazine *Advice and Results.* The Home Economics Council also prepares teaching materials and conducts educational campaigns directed at selected target groups of consumers. In addition, it operates an extensive telephone advisory service. Consumer and women's organizations are represented on its board, as are specified educational institutions and government ministries.

An initiative in the 1940s, in which the interests of urban hoomemakers were more strongly represented, led to the foundation of the Danish Housewives Consumer Council as an independent organization in 1947. This effort was led by Bodil Begtrup, then chairperson of the National Women's Council. The main objective of the new organization was to secure women's influence on import restrictions and rationing of goods, issues raised by the end of World War II. The organization continues today as a thriving force in Danish consumer affairs, having shortened its name to the Danish Consumer Council. While it undertakes a wide variety of tasks, its most important function is to represent a coordinated consumer voice that is independent of political and business interests. Its most important publication is the consumer magazine *Think.*

Apart from local consumer groups, a variety of interest groups are represented in the Danish Consumer Council. These include national organizations for youth, pensioners, and tenants as well as organizations devoted to adult education and trade unions. A state subsidy provides a major part of the council's revenue.

The Danish Institute for Informative Labeling was established in 1956. The institute seeks to provide consumers with product information that enables them to compare quality and price. The greatest part of its work is being devoted to the preparation of informative labels in cooperation with producers and other interested parties. A significant proportion of the institute's revenue comes from a state subsidy.

The National Consumer Agency was established in 1988, incorporating three existing institutions. In addition to the Home Economics Council, they are the Consumer Complaints Board and the Consumer Ombudsman, both of which were originally established by legislative initiatives. The agency is located within the Ministry of Business and Industry, which requires the minister to maintain a balance between organized corporate and consumer interests. Both sets of interests are represented on the Consumer Complaints Board. The main task of the Consumer Ombudsman is to ensure that proper marketing standards are maintained. In practice, the ombudsman seeks to protect consumer interests related to market problems, especially those involving inaccurate, misleading, or insufficient marketing information.

In Denmark, private organizations receive a state subsidy and are represented within government bodies designed to promote cooperation among various sectors of the economy. Grassroots consumer organizations, less tied to the national government, also exist, although their character has changed in recent years.

Pressing Problems and Proposed Solutions

Several issues have received increased attention from the Danish consumer movement in recent years. One set of issues has been raised by the increasing economic polarization in Denmark. There is more awareness of the problems of vulnerable consumers, including the elderly, the unemployed, immigrant groups, and the so-called new poor. The traditional focus of consumer policies on providing information about product characteristics may not be especially relevant to these consumers.

Health issues are also increasingly salient in Denmark. It is recognized that poor nutrition, excessive alcohol consumption, and tobacco use give rise to a number of health problems affecting average life expectancy. For example, the fat content of the Danish diet constitutes 42 percent of energy intake, as opposed to the recommended level of 30 percent. Also, 44 percent of Danish adults smoke and, on any particular weekday, 37 percent drink alcohol, the number rising to 68 percent on weekends. Life expectancy has remained virtually unchanged for the last fifteen years, and mortality rates are significantly higher than in some other European countries.

The increasing pressure on the Danish "welfare state" has also raised some important consumer issues. Basic social, health, and educational services are financed by income taxes and are available to all citizens, for the most part, free of charge. At the same time, the relatively high level of income tax discourages the hiring of people to perform labor-intensive household services, thus reducing employment opportunities for people with relatively low levels of education. Two issues dominate the current debate about public services: first, the increase in the numbers of people receiving government financial assistance and the concurrent problems of financing this expenditure and of reducing these numbers; and second, how priorities within the health services can best be established and on what basis a rank ordering of services can be arrived at.

Each of these issues is influenced by Denmark's membership in the European Union. Consumer organizations fear that the harmonization of standards regarding goods and services within the European market, and the pressure to coordinate policies in a variety of fields, will require a "lowering" of Danish standards on several fronts, not least in the areas of food quality and environmental protection.

Consumer organizations in Denmark have recently devoted special attention to two areas of concern in preparing consumer information: household budgeting and the natural environment, especially the use of energy resources in households. The National Consumer Agency has developed a standard budget for families, differentiated according to the family structures that occur most frequently in Danish society. The standard budget can be employed by individual families as a frame of reference in their economic planning. It can also be used by banks, insurance companies, and others involved in making assessments of, or offering economic advisory services to, individual consumers and their families.

A number of public authorities and consumer organizations have undertaken campaigns to promote consciousness of energy consumption in the household and of behavior patterns that contribute to the goal of sustainable development. This type of cooperation is comparatively new in the Danish context. The Danish Consumer Council has played a leading role in this area. One recent example of such an initiative was an environmental campaign launched under the name "Our Common Future." The campaign aims to establish a national network of "green families," each of which would strive to reduce the negative effects of their household activities upon the environment.

The new European policy in regard to environmental labeling may aid consumer decision-making. This policy, influenced by the Danish point of view, requires mandatory labeling of energy use on household appliances. A Danish law that came into effect in March 1994 gives the Minister of Energy the right to establish norms regarding the energy efficiency of all electric household appliances sold in the domestic market.

As another example of action related to the consumer and the natural environment, in 1993 the Consumer Ombudsman issued a guide for businesses regarding the proper use of environmental marketing claims. The guide requires that environmental claims be accurate, precise, and well substantiated. General terms, such as *environmentally friendly,* may only be used in cases where a life-cycle analysis of the product has been conducted, using methods that are generally recognized for the type of product at issue.

Cooperation between consumers and environmental groups has also been evident in the preparation of an action program regarding nutrition and food policy. Three organizations—the Danish Consumer Council, Noah (an environmental organization), and the Danish Food and Allied Workers Union—have advocated greater influence by consumers and workers on the production, development, and marketing of food products. This effort led to the launching of projects in which consumers, environmentalists, and bakeries cooperated in the development, production, and marketing of high-quality organic bread.

International Cooperation

The main links among Denmark and other countries are: cooperation among the Nordic countries through the Nordic Committee of Senior Officials for Consumer Affairs (NEK), a subcommittee of the Nordic Council of Ministers; cooperation among representatives of the consumer movement in the member countries of the European Union (EU) through BEUC (Bureau Européen des Unions de Consommateurs) and through the Consumers Council under the Commission of the European Union; and membership in Consumers International.

Cooperation among Denmark, Sweden, and Norway was established in 1957, largely with a view to coordinating tasks within the areas of research and development as well as policy and education. The Danish Consumer Council and the National Consumer Agency of Denmark are both engaged in this work. One of the central current objectives of Nordic cooperation is advancing consumer interests within Europe as a whole.

The Danish Consumer Council has been represented in BEUC since Denmark joined the Common Market in 1973 and on its Executive Committee since 1977. The director of the Danish Consumer Council, Benedicte Federspiel, has been chairperson of BEUC and of the Consumers Council of the EU for several years. Danish representatives have worked hard to promote and strengthen the scope of consumer policy in the European market and EU. In part through their efforts, an article was included in the European Maastricht Treaty in 1993 (Article 129a) to the effect that the European Union will work toward the realization of a high level of consumer protection.

The Danish Consumer Council has actively participated in international cooperation on a more global level through its representation in Consumers International since that organization's inception in 1960. For many years, the council's representatives have been members of the Consumers International Governing Council and Executive Committee.

Current Prospects

In recent years, the public funding that has been made available to consumer organizations in the private and public sectors has been cut back. If this trend continues, it will give rise to the need for independent organizations to find new sources of revenue. The National Consumer Council has expressed the fear that the trend may lead to a situation in which limited resources are used to satisfy the perceived needs of relatively well-off consumers.

The Danish population, at approximately 5 million people, does not represent a sufficiently large market for the successful sale of a consumer magazine that could produce an income that could finance, for example, activities in the area of research and development. Membership fees, however, could be linked to the right to use a variety of services, such that any significant expansion of membership could provide a relatively stable source of future income.

Establishing cooperative links with corporate bodies in such areas as product development may represent an alternative source of future income. Although there is no tradition in Denmark of corporate sponsorship of consumer services, this possibility may well be considered in the future.

The consumer movement at the grassroots level has dwindled. There are fewer local consumer groups today than there were ten or twenty years ago. However, this movement appears to be merging with the environmental movement. Increasingly, consumer groups are expressing environmental concerns, and environmental groups are focusing on consumption. The same convergence of consumer and environmental issues can be found among nongovernmental organizations whose primary concern is social development on local and global levels.

Public funding has been made available to independent organizations for the purpose of establishing advisory services to consumers on environmental issues. One such initiative, in which the National Consumer Council and other organizations have been actively involved, was launched under the title "Green Information." Several county authorities have appointed environmental consultants, and the national network of Green Families has recently become a national organization. The latter initiative indicates the potential interest in a green consumer movement in which the focus of attention is not only upon the solution of individual consumer problems, but also upon the need for consumer cooperation in the solution of international and global problems.

Nevertheless, a green consumer movement does not represent all consumer concerns. It can be difficult for the green consumer movement to find a balance among household needs, collective activities on the local level, and the articulation of needs and solutions on the global level. It has also proven difficult to focus on the needs of the most vulnerable groups among Danish consumers while emphasizing environmental concerns.

— Jørgen Juul Jensen, Katherine O'Doherty Jensen

Readings

Bager, Torben (1988). "Identity Problems of Danish Consumer Cooperatives." *Journal of Consumer Policy*. 11: 223–233.

Jensen, Hans Rask (1986). "The Relevance of Alternative Paradigms as Guidelines for Consumer Policy and Organized Consumer Action." *Journal of Consumer Policy*. 9: 389–405.

Deceptive, Unfair, and Unconscionable Sales Practices

Federal and state law offer consumers important protections against deceptive, unfair, and unconscionable sales practices. The most important provisions prohibit any form of unfair or deceptive sales conduct. No matter how novel or ingenious a shady scheme, it can run afoul of statutory standards of unfairness and deception because these are broad and evolving concepts meant to adapt to any form of merchant abuse of consumers. For example, even though the concept of an Internet never existed when these laws were enacted, the standards apply effectively to Internet-related deceptive sales practices.

These standards were developed in response to consumer dissatisfaction with the concept of caveat emptor (let the buyer beware). No particular sales abuse was solely responsible for the death of caveat emptor. The consumer marketplace is filled with different types of sales leading to different potential forms of deception and unfairness. Practices also differ over time, in different geographic areas, and with different types of consumers.

Some problem areas that spurred reform can be identified, but the key notion was that the range of sales abuses was so wide, and the opportunities for new types of fraud so evident, that the emphasis was on broad protections that would apply to any sales abuse. Specific legislation had been enacted in certain states to cover discrete problem areas (for example, health spas, lemon cars, or automobile repair), but the thrust of the governmental response to unfair and deceptive sales practices has been to enact broad legislation prohibiting any such conduct.

Examples of specific areas of consumer abuse included: used car sales with hidden defects; unnecessary automobile repair or charges for repairs not performed; failure to correct defects in new cars; bogus trade schools; shoddy, unnecessary, or incomplete home repair work; high pressure door-to-door sales of vacuum cleaners, encyclopedias, and other products; late or nondelivery of mail orders; games, contests, and prize offers; bait and switch, deceptive price advertising and unavailability of advertised items; mobile home warranty problems; taking advantage of bereaved consumers in the sale of funerals; overreaching credit practices and abusive debt collection; sale of useless or almost useless insurance; and pyramid sales, referral sales, business opportunities, franchises, and related money-making offers. By and large, the legislative response was not to address each specific problem, but to enact laws that expansively outlawed unfair or deceptive merchant conduct and provided adequate federal, state, and private remedies to enforce merchant violations.

Historical Development

Medieval concepts of a just price, a fair bargain, and "a sound price warranting a sound commodity" persisted as late as 1800. Until this period, judges and juries in the United States and England would not enforce a one-sided bargain and would provide a remedy if a product did not live up to normal expectations.

This doctrine of an independent standard of fairness apart from the bargained contract conflicted with emerging nineteenth-century commercial notions of markets, speculation, and business bargains. Merchants did not want juries scrutinizing the fairness of a bargain. Eventually, notions developed of caveat emptor and of the sanctity of a written contract, whether it is fair or not. Actions seeking redress of fraud became more difficult, until finally in 1888 in the case of *Derry v. Peek*, an English court required the consumer to prove the merchant's intentional misrepresentation where the merchant sought for the consumer to rely on the misrepresentation.

Starting in the early 1900s, American courts and legislatures started moving slowly away from a pure caveat emptor approach. The Federal Trade Commission (FTC) was created in 1914 to deal, not with consumer fraud, but with monopolies. The FTC Act prohibited "unfair methods of competition." In 1938, this act was expanded with the Wheeler-Lea Amendment to prohibit not only "unfair methods of competition" but also "unfair and deceptive acts and practices." In other words, a federal standard was created that merchants should not engage in unfair or deceptive practices in trade or commerce.

The deception standard was applied by the courts and the FTC to be significantly broader than common law fraud. Only a capacity to deceive needed to be shown, with no proof of the merchant's intent or knowledge of the deception, or even that consumers were actually damaged or deceived. In addition, the concept of "unfairness" was even broader than "deception." For example, selling games of chance to children could be unfair even if not deceptive.

This federal standard prohibiting unfair or deceptive conduct ended on paper the doctrine of caveat emptor, because if there is confusion or unfairness as to what a product is or what is represented, then the merchant bears the risk, not the consumer. Nevertheless, while this standard was in place as early as 1934, it had only minimal impact on the consumer marketplace.

There were two reasons for this modest effect. First, FTC enforcement of the standard was minimal. The commission could only enjoin future conduct and not punish past conduct. Moreover, such orders only went into effect after all appeals had been exhausted. Accordingly, it might take a decade for the commission to order a merchant to stop using a particular deceptive technique.

In addition, there was no private or state enforcement of the FTC Act. The only remedy for a consumer who was a victim of deception or unfairness was to complain to the FTC, which might then initiate an investigation, and eventually a proceeding, to seek an order preventing other consumers from being similarly victimized.

In the 1960s and 1970s, steps were taken to strengthen consumer protections. With the Committee on Suggested State Legislation of the Council of State Governments, the FTC proposed state legislation, patterned after the FTC Act, that would be enforced by the state and by individual consumers. About the same time, the National Conference of Commissioners on Uniform State Laws (NCCUSL) and the American Bar Association (ABA) adopted the Consumer Sales Practices Act that provided private and state enforcement for deceptive and unconscionable practices, and a Uniform Deceptive Trade Practices Act that allowed one merchant to enjoin another merchant's deceptive conduct. NCCUSL and the ABA also adopted a Uniform Commercial Code that allowed courts to refuse to enforce unconscionable sales agreements or unconscionable provisions in sales agreements.

In response to these model laws and to a growing consumer movement, during the 1960s and 1970s every state enacted a general statute prohibiting deceptive and usually unfair or unconscionable practices and providing state enforcement (unfair and deceptive acts and practices, or UDAP, statutes). With the possible exceptions of Arkansas and Iowa (where case law only suggests a private right of action), injured consumers in all U.S. states now can also enforce the statutory standards.

The FTC model has predominated in most states: state UDAP statutes broadly prohibit deception and unfairness. Because these statutes have broad applicability, usually provide attorney fees and adequate remedies for prevailing consumers, and are also enforced by state attorneys general, UDAP statutes are frequently used today to challenge deceptive and unfair merchant conduct. They have effectively ended the concept of caveat emptor.

In the 1970s, the FTC's own enforcement power was expanded to allow it to promulgate trade regulation rules, obtain restitution for victimized consumers, obtain civil penalties for certain illegal conduct, and preliminarily to enjoin unfair or deceptive conduct. This increased authority has allowed certain national standards and expectations to be enforced as to proper merchant conduct.

As a result, the present standards of unfairness, deception, and unconscionability are not only federal but also state law. These standards are widely enforced and have real meaning in merchant-consumer transactions.

The Law of Unfairness and Deception

Federal law prohibits all unfair and deceptive conduct in trade or commerce. Unfairness and deception are broad standards developed by the FTC and the federal courts. Practices can be deceptive even if they do not meet the standards for common law fraud. The merchant need not intend to deceive the consumer, need not have to know that its representations are false, and can be acting in good faith. Nor is it a defense that the seller discontinued the practice when it became aware of the deception. A practice can be common in an industry and still deceptive. Proof of actual deception is unnecessary; only proof of the tendency and capacity to deceive is needed. Mere puffery may not be deceptive, but ambiguous, half-true, or literally true statements can be deceptive, as long as at least certain members of the intended audience could be misled. The failure to disclose important information can be deceptive, and oral statements can be deceptive even if the written agreement contains a true statement and even if the written agreement attempts to disclaim oral representations by sales personnel.

Even if a practice is not deceptive, it can still be unfair. For example, high pressure sales techniques, one-sided provisions in standard form contracts, illegal conduct, and sophisticated sellers taking advantage of vulnerable consumers can all be unfair even if not deceptive. The current definition of an unfair practice is one that causes substantial consumer injury, not outweighed by a countervailing business justification, which the consumer could not reasonably have avoided.

Merchants who violate these standards subject themselves to prosecution by the FTC or a state attorney general, and may be required to repay injured consumers, pay penalties, and not engage in similar conduct in the future. Private individuals in almost all states can also use state statutes, which are similar to the federal law enforced by the FTC, to sue for damages. In many states, a prevailing consumer's attorney fees are paid for by the merchant, and the merchant may also have to pay additional damages—for example, treble actual damages, punitive damages, or a minimum damage amount—no matter how small the injury.

Nevertheless, these broad standards and enforcement mechanisms have proved ineffective in at least one area. Sellers often attempt to separate the consumer's obligation to pay from the consumer's claims against the merchant. For example, a home improvement contractor might arrange for a home improvement loan from a finance company to the consumer, with the check signed over to the home improvement contractor. When the home improvement contractor skips town without doing any work, the contractor gets to keep the money and the finance company sues the consumer for repayment of the loan. The finance company will attempt to insulate itself from the home improvement contractor's fraud and tell the consumer to pay up and recover the money later from the contractor (if that party can ever be found).

In 1975, the FTC found this situation inherently unfair and enacted the "Holder Rule." This regulation requires that any consumer loan, originated by the seller or arranged by the seller, contain a notice allowing the consumer to defend on the loan based on the consumer's complaint against the seller. In the above example, the consumer could lawfully refuse to repay the finance company because the contractor arranged the loan and the contractor had defrauded the consumer.

Proposed Reforms

It is anomalous that, while federal law prohibits unfair and deceptive conduct in all trade or commerce, private consumers and state prosecutors cannot always remedy violations of that standard. There is no right for state agencies or individuals to use the federal law; they must instead rely on similar state laws. But in some states these laws do not prohibit unfair practices or do not apply to certain types of consumer transactions—such as utilities, insurance, credit, debt collection, real property, or regulated industries.

Consequently, federal law can prohibit conduct, but individuals and states may be helpless to remedy violations. The solution is either to create private remedies for the federal law or to expand state laws so that they have equal reach and scope as federal law.

— Jonathan Sheldon

See also

Federal Trade Commission; State Attorneys General.

Readings

Blumberg, Phillip I. (1986). "Consumer Protection in the United States: Control of Unfair or Unconscionable Practices." *The American Journal of Comparative Law.* 34 (supplement): 99–123.

National Consumer Law Center (1991). *Unfair and Deceptive Acts and Practices.* Boston: National Consumer Law Center.

Department of Agriculture

See U.S. Department of Agriculture.

Deregulation, Economic

Government influence on the functioning of the private sector has grown over this century to the point where many people would consider it pervasive. The government sets air and water emission standards for manufacturers, approves or denies requests for rate increases made by utility companies, and determines if an advertising claim has misled consumers—just to name a few forms of government intervention. Yet, in the past twenty years, there has also been a growing movement among policymakers to lessen or abolish selected areas of government regulation. Such actions are generally grouped under the title of "deregulation."

Deregulation is a very broad term. It is used to encompass retraction of regulations designed to insure that minimal social conditions are met, such as environmental quality standards and workplace safety rules; "privatization" of services that have been historically provided by government, such as garbage collection and police protection; and revocation of regulations that change markets by directly altering price, quality, and/or the number of firms competing. The focus here will be exclusively on this last type of deregulation—typically referred to as "economic deregulation" —because it has probably had the greatest impact on consumer welfare.

Arguments for Deregulation

The impetus behind economic deregulation has varied from industry to industry. Nevertheless, two primary arguments have been offered, each of which challenges the contemporary relevance of the original justification for regulation. First, technological or cost considerations may have once suggested that it is efficient for there to be only one seller in the market (i.e., the market is a natural monopoly). In such instances, the government has typically stepped in to regulate the seller's profits and/or the scope of its market. Over time, changes in technology or costs may facilitate new competition in a market that historically has been a government-regulated natural monopoly. As a consequence, the economic rationale for government intervention wanes, and support for deregulation grows. Such change has provided the primary impetus behind a number of deregulatory actions including the 1980 Depository Institutions Deregulation and Monetary Control Act, which phased out savings interest rate limits; the Justice Department's 1982 antitrust settlement with AT&T (implemented in January 1984), which led to divestiture of this phone company; the 1982 Garn-St. Germain Act, which allowed savings and loan companies to expand consumer products and investments; and the 1984 Cable Communications Policy Act, which phased out most cable television rate regulation.

Second, firms operating in certain industries need large capital investments and/or they must operate much of the time with large amounts of excess capacity (e.g., the airplane that flies with empty seats three out of every four times it travels from city A to city B). Policymakers have argued that economic regulation is needed in such industries to prevent the possibility of "destructive competition"—particularly when such industries are in their infancy. That is, high fixed capital investments and excess capacity induce firms operating in these industries to cut prices below costs periodically in the hope of increasing their market share. Such "price wars" lead firms to exit the market which, in turn, reduces competition in the long run. It has been argued that, as these industries mature, the need for government to prevent such destructive competition diminishes and, thus, support for deregulation grows. These arguments were the primary force behind deregulatory efforts such as the Airline Deregulation Act of 1978, the Staggers Rail Act of 1980, and the Motor Carrier Act of 1980, all of which curbed government restrictions on market entry and exit, and reduced or eliminated government price regulations.

Supporters of Deregulation

Economic deregulation has been championed by a wide range of economists and politicians who have typically argued that the government's imposition of entry restrictions and/or minimum price floors inhibits competition. Supporters have also suggested that the elimination of such regulations will promote competition by encouraging entry and innovation, reducing costs, and making firms more responsive to consumer preferences.

Consumer advocates have been more reserved in their support for deregulation. While they have generally supported deregulatory actions that have promised to expand consumer choice and foster greater price competition, consumer advocates have also expressed concerns about deregulation's possible negative consequences. These negative consequences include a weakening of the enforcement of antitrust and consumer protection provisions, growth in the informational burden on consumers, and the loss of services for certain groups of consumers.

Impact of Deregulation

To determine whether deregulation has helped or harmed consumers, scholars typically examine one or more of three dimensions of the deregulated market: concentration, price, and quality. Ultimately, researchers use information on these indicators to draw conclusions regarding the market's efficiency and/or distributional equity.

Consumers usually benefit when choice among sellers expands, and economic deregulation has typically precipitated the entry of new firms into previously restricted markets. For example, immediately after the final phase-out of airline regulation in 1983, seventeen new carriers entered the national market of this industry. Yet, the initial flurry of new entrants is sometimes followed by a swing back toward a more concentrated market. Again, the airline industry is a good example. By 1987, nine of those seventeen entrants had failed and four of the remaining eight had been acquired by other airlines.

It is important to note that after deregulation any movements toward re-concentration have typically stopped short of the concentration levels experienced under regulation. Nevertheless, the trend has become a concern for consumer advocates because a rise in the concentration level often signals a decline in the range of choices for consumers and/or an increase in some firms' ability to charge high prices. At an extreme, consumer choice may fall to zero. That is, subsets of consumers may discover that without government regulation, no firm finds it profitable to service them. Indeed, this has been the case for banking services in some poor, inner-city neighborhoods and for airline services in some smaller communities.

Observing a net increase in market concentration after deregulation should not automatically lead to the conclusion that consumer prices will increase, however. If the market remains contestable—that is, if credible threats of entry discipline pricing in a market—then a decline in the number of competitors need not translate into an increase in firms' prices.

To assess the degree of market pricing power that deregulated firms have, one should examine price rather than concentration.

There are three aspects of price that have been typically evaluated after deregulation: price trends, price discrimination, and predatory pricing. With respect to pricing trends, no clear pattern emerges. For example, the price levels for long-distance phone service declined by 45 percent in real terms between 1984 and 1991, and the expected profits in freight dropped by 8 to 19 percent between 1977 and 1981. In contrast, cable television subscription rates rose by more than 40 percent in the first three years following cable deregulation. Based on these pricing trends, it is tempting to conclude that deregulation's impact on prices depends on certain industry-specific characteristics.

Price discrimination occurs when a firm charges different prices to different consumers for the same product or service, and that price difference is not entirely a reflection of differences in the cost of servicing such consumers (e.g., it does not cost more to transport goods to two different local markets but different prices are charged). A firm's capacity to price discriminate is influenced by its market power and its ability to identify and separate consumers into subgroups who have different elasticities of demand.

Price discrimination has increased in several markets after deregulation. The airline industry provides one example of post-deregulation price discrimination. Airlines offer discounted fares to travelers who agree to purchase their tickets well in advance of their travel and who agree to travel at certain times and/or on certain days. Consumers who cannot meet these restrictions must pay full fares, which in the late 1980s, averaged 60 percent more than the full fares prior to deregulation. The railroads and telecommunications industries have also seen increases in post-deregulatory price discrimination.

Predatory pricing is a practice where a firm temporarily drops its price below costs in order to capture a larger fraction of the market and drive competitors out of business. If a firm is successful in the use of predatory pricing, it will be able to recoup short-run losses by raising its prices after its competitors have gone out of business. Predatory pricing is prohibited under the Clayton Antitrust Act of 1914; however, the practice is difficult to document. Thus, although allegations of predatory pricing in the deregulated trucking and airline markets have surfaced, they have remained unproven.

It has been frequently noted that, in markets where the government has regulated price, firms often have attempted to compete with one another on the basis of quality (e.g., banks giving away a new toaster when new checking accounts are opened, airlines offering passengers nonstop service between two small airports). Deregulation explicitly encourages price competition, and when such competition occurs, firms face pressures to cut production costs. One way of doing that is to lower product/service quality.

Surprisingly, forecasts of declines in quality have not come true in most deregulated markets. Instead, the combination of deregulation and technological innovation has usually enhanced quality. For example, when they are away from home, consumers may now use automatic teller machines to conduct financial transactions with their local bank. Likewise, cable companies have been able to expand the number of channels they offer to subscribers, and telephone sound quality has generally improved since deregulation because telephone companies invested in new, fiber-based transmission systems. The one exception to this trend is the airline market, where deregulation led both the new entrants and the established air carriers to offer fewer "frills."

Deregulation has also generally encouraged an expansion of the range of price-quality options within many markets. Today, consumers select among telephone plans that offer time or calling area–based discounts; they choose among checking account options that offer different service-fee combinations; and they weigh the tradeoffs between price and service (i.e., full-service versus no-frills airlines) when purchasing airline tickets. The greater range of price-quality combinations clearly benefits consumers to the extent that it enhances their choice. Yet, at the same time it can complicate consumer decision-making and increase the need for useful prepurchase information.

A final quality issue centers around consumer redress. When a consumer purchases a product/service where the quality is unacceptably low (e.g., lost baggage on a flight, poor sound quality for long-distance telephone calls), what are the options for redress? Historically, the government agency that was responsible for economic regulation often also had partial or complete responsibility for helping consumers obtain compensation for unacceptable purchasing outcomes (e.g., the Civil Aeronautics Board helped obtain compensation for lost baggage). With deregulation, oversight for consumer redress has sometimes been weakened or lost as regulatory agencies have been reorganized or dismantled altogether.

Impacts on Consumers

An efficient market is one where the products and services that consumers want are produced at the lowest possible cost. For economists, the overall assessment of whether a market has improved or worsened is typically evaluated in terms of changes in its relative efficiency. If market concentration or prices decline, or if quality-price combinations expand after deregulation, that is prima facie evidence that efficiency has improved.

Efficiency gains generally come about because the entry of new competitors forces existing firms to decrease their profit margins and/or identify new ways to reduce production costs. There is considerable evidence that firms in deregulated markets have sought ways to reduce their production costs. For example, development of hub-spoke transportation systems in the airlines and trucking industries have increased load factors (e.g., the number of occupied seats on a plane and the portion of a truck that is filled with cargo). Similarly, deregulation has induced many firms to take a harder stance on labor contract negotiations because they can no longer easily pass on increases in labor costs to consumers. As a consequence, labor costs have fallen in some deregulated markets (e.g., freight and airlines). Such shifts in load factors and labor costs reduce the average costs of production which, in turn, improve efficiency. On the whole, a fairly strong case can usually be made for deregulation-induced efficiency gains.

While economists typically assess deregulation's impact in terms of changes in market efficiency, consumer advocates have become increasingly concerned about deregulation's impact on distributional equity. Historically, regulated markets have often contained cross-subsidies to certain groups of consumers. For example, under regulation, rates for long-distance phone service were set above costs, and a portion of the revenues was used to subsidize the cost of basic phone service (to promote the goal of universal phone service). After deregulation, telecommunications companies quickly moved to a cost-based pricing structure that led to a decline in the price of long-distance calling (by an average of 33 percent over the first six years) and an increase in the price for basic phone service (by an average of 56 percent over the first six years). Thus, consumers with a fairly high demand for long-distance phone service enjoyed welfare gains while those consumers who had little need to make long-distance phone calls experienced welfare losses.

Concern over distributional equity is intensified when those who "lose" because of deregulation are low-income consumers while those who "win" are middle- or upper-income consumers. Banking deregulation provides the clearest example of this possibility. Deregulation-induced increases in bank fees and the closing of bank branches in inner-city areas have imposed the greatest financial cost on low-income consumers. At the same time, individuals with sizable bank deposits have begun to receive higher interest rates. If the product/service in question is generally viewed to be a consumer necessity, as in the case of basic banking services, then concern over pricing low-income consumers out of the market is heightened even more.

Has economic deregulation helped or harmed consumers? One's answer to this question is clearly influenced by the industry and market dimensions on which one chooses to focus. Supporters can point to selective figures on pre- and post-deregulation concentration levels, market contestability, declining prices, less price discrimination, and/or expansion in the range of products/services offered to consumers in the era of deregulation. Detractors of deregulation can cite selective evidence of trends in market concentration, rising prices, increased price discrimination, predatory pricing practices, and/or declines in product/service quality to support their position. The balance of research, however, suggests that economic deregulation has generally benefited consumers.

Government's Role in a Deregulated Market

Support for economic deregulation among politicians and policymakers is currently strong. Thus, from the consumer's perspective, an important question is the role of government after a market has undergone economic deregulation. From this perspective, there are four oversight dimensions that are critical to protecting consumer welfare in deregulated markets.

First, the government has a responsibility to take appropriate antitrust actions when evidence of rising concentration, declining market contestability, collusive behaviors, exclusionary strategies (including predatory pricing), and/or unfair or deceptive practices is brought forward.

Second, the government should play an active role in helping consumers deal with the informational complexities of newly deregulated markets. The government has historically been involved in regulating product/service standardization and information disclosure in a wide range of otherwise unregulated markets. Yet, there has been only limited recognition that the need to help consumers process information may be especially great in markets where deregulation has precipitated a new or expanded array of price-quality combinations. For example, in banking, with the passage of the Truth in Savings Act the government has made some effort to standardize consumer information about bank rates paid and prices charged on savings accounts. Consumerists believe, however, that government could do more to help consumers sort through, and make sense of, the extensive financial information they must now evaluate (e.g., requiring the standardizing of information on historical rates of return for investment alternatives). Furthermore, in other markets (e.g., telecommunications), deregulation has induced little or no action on the government's part to facilitate consumers' evaluation of increasingly complex information issues.

Third, economic deregulation should not be equated with the elimination of the government's consumer protection provisions. Consumers need access to appropriate channels of redress whenever promises regarding a firm's price and/or product/service quality are not fulfilled. The government needs to insure that, when the agencies that have administered economic regulations are reorganized or eliminated altogether, their consumer protection and consumer redress functions are not lost.

Finally, the government has a critical role to play in insuring distributional equity in the marketplace. That is, the government must insure that the welfare of potentially vulnerable consumers is not jeopardized by deregulation-induced changes in price and/or quality. In markets where a good/service is viewed as a necessity (e.g., basic banking and telephone services), this equity issue becomes a serious concern. At the extreme, increases in prices for basic services may force low-income consumers out of a market altogether. Furthermore, in those cases where the value of the service is partially dependent on the number of consumers who subscribe (e.g., local telephone service), the loss of low-income consumers from the market affects the welfare of all consumers.

The government has made some attempts to address deregulation-induced equity concerns in banking and telecommunications. Specifically, selected states have passed laws that require firms to offer low-cost options, typically referred to as "Lifeline" rates, to low-income consumers. How effective have these lifeline rates been? Most states have passed some sort of lifeline telephone rate law since the 1984 divestiture of AT&T. Trends in subscriptions to basic phone service—up from 91.4 percent of all households in 1983 to 93.6 percent of all households in 1991—suggest that phone lifeline rates have been successful. In contrast, fewer states have passed banking lifeline laws. The existence of such statutes may have moderated the trend, in the 1980s, for low- and moderate-income households to drop out of the traditional banking system.

In sum, economic deregulation has changed the character of markets in profound ways. In some instances, such as freight deregulation, virtually all consumers have benefited although not always in readily visible ways. In other instances (e.g., banking, telecommunications, airlines), the overall benefits have been positive, but some consumers have lost while others have gained.

Experiences in the United States during the past twenty years have reinforced support for economic deregulation both here and abroad. Nevertheless, government still has an active role to play in deregulated markets. Indeed, government must vigorously enforce antitrust laws, encourage the provision of accurate and easily understood prepurchase information, aggressively administer consumer protection provisions, and extend protection to potentially vulnerable consumer groups if society is to enjoy the maximum benefits of economic deregulation.

— Cathleen D. Zick

See also

Airline Deregulation; Electricity Regulation; Natural Gas Regulation; Price Controls; Telephone Regulation.

Readings

Greer, Douglas F. (1993). *Business, Government, and Society.* 3d ed. New York: Macmillan Publishing Company.

Kushman, John E. (1988). "Increasing Competition through Deregulation: Do Consumers Win or Lose?" In E. Scott Maynes, ed. *The Frontier of Research in the Consumer Interest.* Columbia, MO: American Council on Consumer Interests. 413–440.

Morrison, Steven A., and Clifford Winston (1986). *The Economic Effects of Airline Deregulation.* Washington, DC: The Brookings Institute.

Direct Selling Protections

Direct selling is an in-person channel of distribution of consumer goods and services away from a fixed retail location; sales are usually carried out by independent contractors dealing directly with consumers. It differs from sales contacts made solely by mail, by telephone, or in stores.

The Industry

In the United States in 1994, total direct retail sales amounted to $17 billion and were conducted by 6.3 million salespeople, nearly three-quarters of whom were women. Over 90 percent of all sellers worked part-time at direct sales, conducting their business largely through individual one-to-one selling or through the "party plan" or group sales approach. Approximately 12.5 percent of the salespeople were African Americans, while 4.7 percent were Hispanics, and 2 percent were Asians. Some 8 percent had a physical disability, and 4.5 percent were over sixty-five years of age. A 1992 survey found that 62 percent of direct salespeople earned less than $1,000 per year, and 90 percent earned under $5,000. Only 6 percent worked more than forty hours per week but, of these persons, more than half earned over $50,000 per year while about 10 percent earned more than $100,000 annually.

Direct selling is a pervasive marketing channel that is found in every region of the world. In more than forty reporting countries in 1995, over 17 million salespeople generated $67 billion in sales. The largest direct selling market in the world is Japan, followed by the United States, Germany, Taiwan, Brazil, Mexico, the United Kingdom, Korea, Italy, and Argentina. Products sold include those related to personal care (cosmetics, jewelry, skin care, vitamins), home and family care products (cleaning, cookware, cutlery), and leisure and educational products (books, encyclopedias, toys, and games). In Japan, even cars are sold door-to-door.

Many direct sales firms use a multilevel marketing approach with a compensation system in which one sells products and also can build and manage one's own sales force by recruiting, motivating, and training others to sell these products. As well as earnings from one's own sales, compensation often includes a percentage of the consumer sales of an entire sales group that one has recruited and advises.

Pyramid schemes are illegal frauds in which each participant pays for the chance to recruit others into the scheme and profit from payments of others who might join later. Usually, little or no effort is made to market products to consumers; money is made from new recruits who are often pushed to purchase large and costly amounts of inventory when they sign up.

Direct selling companies join together in national trade associations, and these, in turn, have formed a World Federation of Direct Selling Associations. The United States Direct Selling Association (DSA) traces its origins back to 1910. In 1968, it moved from Winona, Minnesota, to Washington, D.C.

Direct selling is as old as biblical times. Its roots in the United States are found in the Yankee peddler. Some of the current companies—such as The Southwestern Company, Golden Pride/Rawleigh, Watkins, and Avon—trace their beginnings to the nineteenth century. In the 1960s and 1970s, direct selling in the United States began to expand as a marketing channel, especially as many new companies formed and others grew. At the same time, the consumer movement was growing, voicing criticisms of marketplace abuses and demanding reforms.

Consumer Protection

One result of this consumer activism was an increase in legislative activity at the national, state, and local levels, some of which affected direct sellers. Many local communities adopted "Green River" ordinances, so called since the first such law was enacted in Green River, Wyoming. These laws prohibited salespeople from selling door-to-door unless they were invited to do so or had a prior appointment. Other municipal regulations required door-to-door sellers to obtain licenses and pay fees. Although intended to protect citizens from high-pressure and unethical tactics of itinerant salespeople, the laws also helped protect local businesses from outside competition.

Other legislative efforts to protect consumers were state "cooling-off" laws. They assured consumers of the ability to change their minds regarding purchases, enabling them to cancel contracts to purchase goods or services if the sale was made at a location other than a store. As early as March 1968, the Consumer Subcommittee of the Senate Committee on Commerce held hearings on a Senate bill that proposed a cooling-off period for contracts of $25 or more. While the bill was reported out of committee, no final action was taken. However, by mid-1969, fifteen states had adopted such laws, which varied from state to state in the length of time a consumer had to cancel a contract. In 1969, the Federal Trade Commission (FTC) issued its first cooling-off order aimed at a specific company, which required the company to allow buyers a three-day period to cancel its contracts.

Between 1969 and 1977, most states enacted cooling-off laws, and the FTC continued to promulgate cooling-off orders for specific direct selling companies. In 1974, the FTC promulgated a national cooling-off trade regulation rule aimed at products costing $25 or more sold by door-to-door sellers. The rule gave customers three working days to cancel contracts.

The DSA had, as early as 1940, adopted a Consumer Relations Code affirming "the principles of ethical business practice conducive to a high level of responsibility to the consumer." In addition, each DSA member company pledged to support a "Declaration of Principles" affirming that "salespeople must observe the highest standards of integrity, frankness and responsibility in dealing with consumers and in all selling" and endorsing the efforts of organizations such as the Better Business Bureau in establishing and maintaining high standards of truth and fair practices.

Nonetheless, responding to unresolved problems in the industry, in 1970 the DSA adopted an independently enforced Code of Ethics to protect the consumers of member company goods against deceptive or unlawful consumer practices. Enforcement of the code intended to assure accurate and truthful offers of products and services, terms of sales, and warranties and guarantees. Amendments in the 1970s and 1980s strengthened the code and its enforcement provisions by, among other things, providing increased powers for its independent code administrator, requiring all member companies to reaffirm annually their adherence to the code, providing for a formal hearing procedure if needed, and incorporating provisions to reimburse consumers who felt they had been wronged during hearing proceedings.

Throughout the remainder of the 1980s and into the 1990s, new marketplace challenges precipitated further amendments to the code. Earlier, the code had focused on the consumers of company products; now it also focused on protecting salespersons—the consumers of the industry's income-earning opportunities. 1992 amendments to the code protected salespeople against the misrepresentation of earnings or sales potentials and against having to overload on inventory by including a requirement that the company "buy back," at 90 percent of its net cost, inventory from distributors that they had purchased within the previous twelve months.

Following the lead of the United States, all national direct selling associations have adopted codes of ethics and, in 1995, the forty-three–nation World Federation of Direct Selling Associations adopted worldwide codes of ethics setting forth minimum requirements to which all national DSAs must subscribe. One code protects consumers, and the other protects salespeople and distributors.

— Marlene Futterman

Readings

Biggart, Nicole Woolsey (1989). *Charismatic Capitalism: Direct Selling Organizations in America.* Chicago: University of Chicago Press.

Keest, Kathleen (1992). "Spiking and Loan-Splitting in Home Improvement Financing: Artful Dodges." *Clearinghouse Review.* 26 (August): 415–421.

Disabilities, Consumers with

There are approximately 47 million Americans with physical or mental disabilities, making this group of individuals one of our largest minorities. Federal antidiscrimination statutes define an individual with a disability as one who has a physical or mental impairment that substantially limits one or more of his or her major life activities; has a record of such an impairment; or is regarded as having such an impairment. This definition has been interpreted broadly, encompassing individuals with permanent or temporary disabilities that affect mobility, hearing, vision, speech, and cognitive abilities, as well as physical or psychological health.

It is most common for consumers with disabilities to encounter both intentional and consequential discrimination in their daily lives. Attitudinal and physical barriers have long prevented these individuals from fully and meaningfully benefiting from the goods and services taken for granted by other members of society. Among other things, barriers have frequently prevented individuals with disabilities from receiving the same opportunities to benefit from employment, education, transportation, recreation, housing, health, and consumer services that are available to individuals without disabilities. For example, lack of effective communication between a vendor and a deaf individual can adversely affect the outcome of the transaction between these two parties, especially when the transaction involves the exchange of complicated or technical information, e.g., the purchase of a life insurance policy or an automobile. Similarly, a flight of stairs may prove to be an impassable barrier for an individual in a wheelchair who seeks access to a restaurant or a college building.

Passage of the Rehabilitation Act of 1973 was one of the first steps taken by Congress to end discrimination against individuals with disabilities. In that act, Congress prohibited discrimination on the basis of disability by all public and private entities that received federal financial assistance, including state and local governments, hospitals, and educational facilities. The Rehabilitation Act also banned job-related discrimination on the basis of disability by the federal government and its contractors.

The reach of the Rehabilitation Act, however, was limited by its restriction only to entities receiving federal funds. State statutes prohibiting disability discrimination in employment, housing, and transportation—often called human rights or human relations laws—closed this gap somewhat, but generally these statutes were severely limited in their scope and application.

In 1990, Congress passed the Americans with Disabilities Act (ADA). In an effort to accomplish the full integration of disabled consumers into the mainstream of society, the ADA set forth a series of mandates for both the public and private sectors. Specifically, the ADA prohibits discrimination against individuals with disabilities by all state and local governments and by the vast majority of private businesses, otherwise called "places of public accommodation." The latter include more than 5 million businesses and establishments in twelve different categories. For example, the ADA covers all retail establishments, places of lodging, theaters, insurance agencies, museums, banks, libraries, parks, exercise spas, day care centers, educational institutions, establishments serving food or drink, and professional offices. Exempt from the ADA's requirements are private clubs and entities that are operated and controlled by religious organizations.

Under the ADA, state and local governments and places of public accommodation must offer consumers with disabilities the same opportunities to participate in or benefit from their services and products as they offer to the general public. To accomplish this goal, covered entities must remove structural architectural and communication barriers (e.g., elevators without braille or raised-letter words and numbers) in their existing facilities when doing so is readily achievable. In addition, the ADA establishes strong and precise rules for constructing new and renovating old state and local buildings and places of public accommodation. The ADA also requires each entity covered by its provisions to provide auxiliary aids and services to ensure effective communication with individuals with hearing, speech, and visual disabilities, unless doing so would impose an undue financial or administrative burden on the covered entity. Auxiliary aids and services may include, but are not limited to, sign language interpreters, readers, text telephones, braille materials, open and closed captioning, assistive listening systems, and notetakers.

Another section of the ADA makes it unlawful for private businesses that employ at least fifteen individuals to discriminate in employment on the basis of disability. The ADA requires these businesses to make "reasonable accommodations" for otherwise qualified individuals with physical or mental disabilities in all terms and conditions of employment, including but not limited to interviews, training, rates of pay, promotions, job assignments, seniority, and social programs. "Reasonable accommodations" include modifications, such as the provision of structural access, the acquisition of equipment, or job reassignments and restructuring, that are necessary to enable the employee to perform essential job functions.

In most situations, providing access is simple, inexpensive, and easy to accomplish. Sometimes it may be as simple as reading a menu for a person who is blind or clearing a pathway to a bathroom for a customer with a mobility impairment. At other times, accommodating a disability may mean acquiring a sign language interpreter to assist in communication on a job or incorporating structural accessibility into the design plans for a new building. Whatever is needed, say advocates, providers of consumer goods and services should work with individuals with disabilities in eliminating existing barriers to access. Through their own experiences, individuals with disabilities have come to know the type of access best suited to their needs.

— Karen Peltz Strauss

Reading

Stephens, Debra Lynn, and Karyn Bergman (1995). "The Americans with Disabilities Act: A Mandate for Marketers." *Journal of Public Policy and Marketing*. 14 (Spring): 164–168.

Disputes and Dispute Resolution

To dispute something is to engage in argument or to struggle over something. In the consumer context, the "something" is a good or service that is perceived by the consumer to be substandard or unsatisfactory. That is, the consumer has a problem with a good or service. The dispute is with the seller, which could be the retailer of the item concerned or its producer.

Resolution is the act of solving a problem. The agency by which the problem is solved is termed a dispute resolution mechanism. The ultimate resolution mechanism is a court of law. In the consumer context, several additional mechanisms may be available. Sellers often have internal mechanisms in place such as complaint departments in stores or corporate 800 telephone numbers. Additional mechanisms could be available through a third party, often in a quasi-legal mediation or arbitration format. Thus, consumers have a range of mechanisms to choose from, should they wish to do so. An alternative always exists in the form of exit action—the decision to take one's custom elsewhere.

Consumer disputes do not necessarily involve an actual problem. What is important is that the consumer perceives there to be a problem and demands that the seller resolve it. Once these conditions are present, then whether or not a dispute arises depends on the response of the seller.

Genesis of Consumer Disputes

Empirical studies have shown that roughly one-third of consumers will perceive a problem with a good or service they purchase in any one year. More recent literature inspired by the Total Quality Management movement has termed consumer-seller interactions over consumer problems "moments of truth," to emphasize the notion that the seller is being called upon to perform. Moments of truth with high potential to spill over into disputes are sometimes termed "critical incidents," a concept used in psychological research. Critical incident analysis enables the features of the incident that triggered the dispute to be identified through narratives from the parties concerned. Analysis of these narratives shows that disputes are often accompanied by customer anger.

For a critical incident to turn into a dispute, the consumer must feel that the seller's response to a consumer problem is inadequate. An inadequate response may involve the seller's offering an acceptable remedy but in a discourteous manner. Other triggers are responses that come after a long interval of time, or that involve several layers of management. In some cases, the initial response is adequate, but the remedy is performed inadequately, e.g., the installation of a faulty replacement part.

Not everyone who has a problem complains, nor do all complaints end up in disputes. About 70 percent of those experiencing a problem do not complain. The probability of complaining is higher when the product involved is a "big ticket" item, when personal injury has occurred, and when the problem itself is severe. Sociodemographics also matter. The general consensus among researchers is that high-income, high education, and younger consumers are more likely to complain than are others. Rex Warland, Robert Herrmann, and Jane Willits identified an "upset-action" subgroup of the population, comprising persons who are angry that a consumer problem has arisen and are experienced in both political and consumer activities, as being the subgroup most likely to complain.

According to Technical Assistance Research Programs, Inc., the industries most subject to consumer complaints are automobiles, appliances, mail service, and clothing. The three most prevalent types of complaints in their study were stores not having products advertised for sale, unsatisfactory product performance, and unsatisfactory repairs. About 55 percent of people who complain are less than satisfied with the treatment they receive after complaining. It is from this group that most disputes arise.

Dispute Resolution

Several dispute resolution mechanisms are available to sellers. Whether or not these options are resorted to depends, for the most part, on the disputants. The seller often has a strong profit motive to settle a dispute quickly and completely: when disputes occur, customer loyalty declines and unfavorable "word of mouth" communications increase. The literature on customer service agrees that it is several times more costly to find new consumers than to retain existing ones, and that a loyal customer represents large volumes of repeat sales.

For these reasons, sellers often try to reduce the incidence of disputes. Their use of service centers accessible through toll-free 800 numbers is largely an attempt to resolve problems before they grow into disputes. Customer service representatives are often trained in anger diffusion techniques and empowered to offer remedies to customers. These preventive actions appear to reduce the incidence of disputes but not eliminate them entirely. To address these unresolved disputes, other mechanisms are available.

In some cases, once the dispute resolution mechanism is resorted to, mandatory procedures are set in motion. For example, the Magnuson-Moss Warranty Act mandates procedures to be followed in the resolution of warranty disputes. Where a dispute may be litigated, sellers often turn the problem over to their legal division, which follows internally mandated procedures. In most cases, however, there is considerable latitude on the selection of a dispute resolution procedure.

Most consumers take their problems first to the point of sale; that is, to the store, mail-order company, or other facility from which the product or service was purchased. If the frontline person contacted is not empowered to resolve the problem or, in the customer's opinion, responds inadequately, then a dispute may arise, and the matter is usually referred to a manager or to the aforementioned customer service center. In the vast majority of cases, over 90 percent for most companies, the dispute remains internal. Either the consumer is satisfied, or they go away unhappy and restrict further action to switching brands or unfavorable word of mouth. But in a minority of cases, customers request the intervention of a third party. The third party can be a mediator who offers suggestions to the original parties about how they might resolve the problem. This party can also be an arbitrator who makes a decision on how to resolve the problem after having listened to both sides. If either of these approaches is judged unsatisfactory, either party, or both, may seek a legal remedy.

Mediation and Arbitration

A mediator listens separately to the two parties with a view to assessing the merits of each side's case, defining the issues under dispute, and identifying ways of breaking the deadlock. He or she may engage in several rounds of one-on-one conversations with each side to explore ways to resolve the dispute. When the mediator perceives that an amicable settlement may be possible, the two parties can be brought together to settle the issue and exchange memoranda of agreement. The Better Business Bureaus (BBB) favor mediation as a first resort in dispute resolution and have their own system in place.

As a resolution technique, mediation has the advantage of flexibility. Its main limitation is that either party can opt out at any time. Persuading the parties to follow through on their promises can also be a problem. In BBB mediations, the reputation of sellers in the business community is at risk and serves as an incentive for them to agree to proposed solutions.

Consumer arbitration typically takes place through a hearing before a panel of arbitrators or arbitration board. Evidence from both sides is placed before the arbitrators, who then have the right to ask follow-up questions of either party. The panel deliberates on the issues raised and announces its decision, which may or may not be binding on either or both of the parties, depending on the rules of the particular board.

Consumer arbitration has been thought of generally as a cheaper, more timely, and less formal alternative to the courts. The expense and slowness of courts are regarded as barriers to their use by consumers, whose disputes often involve low-cost items that need to be fixed immediately. The formality of the courts is also seen as a barrier to their use by citizens who are not familiar with the ways of the law.

There are differences among arbitration boards in their procedures with respect to personal appearances of consumer and seller. For example, the BBB arbitration system requires that both parties appear, with dismissal in the opponent's favor as penalty for a no-show. Several of the so-called industry panels, arbitration boards sponsored by manufacturers, do not require personal appearances unless they are requested by either party; they rely instead on written testimony. If one party requests an appearance, the other will usually be invited to attend. Most systems permit, but do not encourage, representation of either party by an attorney.

In making its deliberations, the arbitration board is usually given parameters within which to work and must find the solution that it regards as a "fair" one. The parameters are set by the problem itself and what it would take to fix it. The panel usually faces two extremes. It can opt to do nothing, or it can replace or give a full refund for the product. Incidental or punitive damages are not a remedy available under consumer arbitration. Within the two extremes there are many options, such as instructing the seller to make certain repairs or replace specific components. Boards may choose to deduct from refunds a "user fee," an equivalent rental fee for use of the product by the consumer up to the time that the problem arose. In the event that arbitrators award full refunds for automobiles under warranty, such a fee is mandatory and is based on mileage.

Research shows that, in about 60 percent of hearings, the award gives at least some restitution to the consumer, but only about 15 percent of consumers come away from the process totally satisfied. Nevertheless, arbitration serves to end many disputes. Only a small percentage of consumers who go to arbitration continue with their dispute afterwards.

Litigation

To try to resolve a problem, consumers can always file a lawsuit; indeed, litigation is the only viable option where the dispute involves damages. Unlike arbitration and mediation, restitution through the courts is "win or lose": there are no creative compromises or partial remedies. On the other hand, awards with damages can be substantial where product liability is the issue. For sellers, the costs of litigation extend beyond monetary settlements to the negative publicity that usually surrounds consumer product court cases. Also, sellers face the risk of the case's outcome triggering a recall of their product.

As noted above, a major barrier to the use of litigation to resolve consumer disputes is its cost. Individual attorneys may be willing to take a case on contingency if there is a strong probability of a large settlement, as is the case in some product liability cases. Yet, for the majority of consumer cases, large awards are highly unlikely. For consumers with relatively small complaints, there is, however, the low-cost legal alternative of small claims courts. These courts are available in most large cities to hear cases involving sums of money below a set ceiling. The ceiling varies from state to state but is usually in the range of $1,000 to $5,000. The low filing fee—usually $30 or less—and the speed with which cases are heard often make small claims courts attractive as a consumer dispute resolution mechanism.

Small claims courts are "courts" in the sense that a judge hears the cases and announces a decision. But their hearings are less formal, and the cases dispatched more quickly, than in higher level courts. On the other hand, since the courts frequently hear landlord-tenant disputes and unpaid bill cases, for some people in low-income neighborhoods they have a pro-business reputation.

Small claims court procedure usually emphasizes the notion that the court is a last resort. The parties concerned may actually be encouraged to correspond to try to reach an agreement before the case is tried. A similar notion is prevalent in consumer arbitration mechanisms: to the extent that arbitration hearings may be suspended if a compromise appears to be in the making, the procedure will then switch to mediation or face-to-face negotiation. In both of these cases, the result should be a more amicable settlement of the issue.

Recent research suggests that obtaining the remedy after judgment may be a problem with small claims courts. Overall, the probability of receiving the full amount is about 50 percent. But this probability declines as the amount of the award increases and also if the defendant fails to show at the hearing.

Creative Resolution Mechanisms

Disputes can become so acrimonious that one party may refuse to participate in an available resolution mechanism. When a seller is so disposed, the likelihood that the consumer will take the matter to litigation increases. The consumer has other options, however. Seeking a new seller and spreading bad word-of-mouth information have already been mentioned. The anger or frustration of unresolved disputes can lead to creative action.

Creative actions usually involve the consumer's reaching out to others to express anger and frustration. In the past, consumers have resorted to techniques such as picketing seller facilities, or creating posters of their complaints and displaying them in prominent places. The purpose of these actions is to pressure the seller into responding to the complaint as well as to vent the consumer's anger. Some local consumer groups have found that these tactics are highly successful. But they also face the risk of the merchant's countering with a lawsuit alleging slander. For the seller, however, such litigation may generate negative publicity.

The success of individual consumer actions to resolve a dispute tend to increase as the audience expands. For this reason, some consumers have taken their dispute to the mass media. This strategy is potentially powerful in that seller reputation can be severely affected by bad press. One problem with the strategy, however, is persuading the mass media to report on the dispute. Also, once it has been covered, the complainant may lose leverage because it is unlikely that the press will report on it again. For this reason, the threat of media coverage is often more effective than the coverage itself in resolving grievances.

Media coverage of consumer problems has waxed and waned in recent years. It peaked in the 1970s, when many newspapers had regular consumer columns and local television stations used consumer reporters in their news segments. By the 1990s, consumer columns were less common, and consumer reporting on television was usually combined with more general human interest and personal finance reporting. The decline of media interest in consumer issues may reflect, in part, the inherent conflict between the media's need to obtain funding through advertising and the reporting of what may be interpreted by advertisers as anti-business stories. There is also the difficulty of obtaining fresh material over a long period.

In its 1979 study, Technical Assistance Research Programs, Inc., estimated that American households stood to lose some $2 billion if their most serious consumer problems were not resolved. They found that some 70 percent of the households who reported the most serious consumer problems did not have them satisfactorily resolved. Few invoked the third-party mechanisms described above. Given the potential costs of unresolved grievances to business and consumers, both could benefit by utilizing such third-party mechanisms.

— Richard Widdows

See also

Better Business Bureaus; Consumer Satisfaction/Dissatisfaction; State and Local Consumer Affairs Offices.

Readings

Goodman, John A., and Marc A. Grainer (1979). *Consumer Complaint Handling in America: Final Report.* Washington, DC: U.S. Office of Consumer Affairs.

Technical Assistance Research Programs, Inc. (1985). *Consumer Complaint Handling in America: An Update Study.* Washington, DC: U.S. Office of Consumer Affairs.

Warland, Rex H., Robert O. Herrmann, and Jane Willits (1975). "Dissatisfied Consumers: Who Gets Upset and Who Takes Action." *Journal of Consumer Affairs.* 9 (Winter): 148–163.

Door-to-Door Selling Protections

See Direct Selling Protections.

Drinking Water Safety

The federal government agency responsible for setting minimum standards for the quality of the nation's drinking water is the Environmental Protection Agency (EPA). Federal law requires that all public drinking water systems insure that this water not exceed maximum contaminant levels for certain potentially harmful bacteria and toxins as well as for certain toxic chemicals. Drinking water must meet other standards governing aspects such as acidity and odor. Although EPA sets these standards and requires all public water systems to report violations of standards and treatment methods, state governments (except in Wyoming) have been granted primary enforcement responsibility.

The purification of water for drinking consists of removal of suspended organic matter and particles such as bacteria and viruses (by mixing with a coagulant that binds together sediment in the water, followed by flocculation, sedimentation, and filtration) and disinfection (usually by treatment with chlorine). If the drinking water source is groundwater, the ground through which it passes may filter the water adequately. If the treatment plant draws water from surface water sources—such as rainwater collected in reservoirs, rivers, and lakes—the water usually requires filtering unless it can be demonstrated that the watershed has been adequately protected from pollution.

The EPA and its Science Advisory Board have ranked the contamination of this country's drinking water as one of the nation's four most critical environmental health risks. The chlorine disinfection of drinking water, which became common soon after its introduction in 1908, is no longer sufficient to protect against newly emerging disease-causing microbes. In addition, increasing quantities of toxic farm and industrial chemicals washed into the source waters from which drinking water is drawn also pose long-term health threats.

Scientists with the Centers for Disease Control and Prevention (CDC) have estimated that, each year, there are 940,000 cases of enteric (intestinal) illness, resulting in over 900 deaths from microbial contamination of the nation's drinking water. Microbial pathogens such as protozoa (e.g., giardia and cryptosporidium) as well as certain viruses (e.g., Hepatitis A) emerged in the 1980s as microbes newly implicated in waterborne illness outbreaks. These pathogens are of concern because they are infective at a much lower dose than are other waterborne pathogens; because no safe level of these microbes in water has yet been established; and because certain protozoa, such as cryptosporidium, are extremely resistant to chlorine.

Moreover, persons with weakened, underdeveloped, or seriously compromised immune systems—the elderly, the very young, the chronically ill—are at particular risk of severe illness and death from these pathogens. This vulnerable group is estimated to represent up to 25 percent of the U.S. population and is growing. AIDS patients, organ transplant recipients, and those undergoing chemotherapy are some of those at great risk from cryptosporidiosis. Although the 1993 cryptosporidiosis outbreak in Milwaukee, in which 400,000 were made ill and 100 died, was the first to receive wide publicity, since 1982 there have been many documented outbreaks across the country. Cryptosporidium is a microbial parasite that enters source waters through the runoff of animal feces—often from otherwise healthy cattle and, some believe, from deer.

The risks posed by metals and chemicals found in finished tap water are, in some cases, serious. It has been established that elevated lead levels in the blood of young children can cause lifelong learning impairment. In 1993, the EPA found that the tap water of 800 U.S. cities exceeded the maximum "action level" for lead set by the agency. Implementation of EPA controls for lead in tap water has reduced these levels in many of these cities since 1993.

Some chemical contaminants in drinking water are known to be carcinogens or harmful to the nervous system. Many different pesticides are present in drinking water at levels that pose serious health risks, yet their presence in tap water goes unregulated. Arsenic, radon, and trihalomethanes in water deserve special mention because they are inadequately regulated.

Arsenic is widely known to be a human carcinogen. However, the EPA's permissible level for arsenic in drinking water, set in 1942, has not been adjusted downward since then to reflect the discovery that drinking arsenic-contaminated water was associated with cancer of the skin, bladder, kidney, liver, and lungs as well as with vascular disease and diabetes. The EPA has estimated that arsenic is in the drinking water of 63 million Americans. Arsenic levels could be substantially reduced by several treatment methods, including simple modifications of existing coagulation and filtration systems.

Three of four trihalomethanes and some other disinfection by-products have been determined by the EPA to be probable human carcinogens. Trihalomethanes are formed when water is chlorinated and interacts with organic matter. To reduce trihalomethanes, drinking water can be treated with granulated activated carbon or other modern treatment technology at a modest cost for the large majority of consumers. Although this is done in Europe, very few American treatment plants do so.

Radon is a gas that occurs in drinking water derived from groundwater as a result of the decay of naturally occurring radioactive rock underground. Radon is considered by the National Academy of Sciences and by other health officials to be a known human carcinogen. Despite the fact that the removal of radon from water using aeration is simple and usually inexpensive, most tap water has not been so treated.

Today, major barriers to improving the quality of the nation's drinking water are an antiregulatory mood, aging water treatment plants, and decreasing dollars at all levels of government for health and safety measures. Of special concern to health advocates recently have been congressional efforts to weaken EPA regulations and budgets. To an extent, these attacks have succeeded: health advocates have found it difficult to establish health standards for new drinking water contaminants and to enforce existing contaminant standards.

At the same time, many politicians have opposed new federal regulations and supported shifting regulatory authority to states and localities. However, state governments, which have always had primary responsibility for enforcement of drinking water standards, were already finding it difficult to raise taxes or other funds either for such enforcement or for modernization of aging water treatment plants.

In the early 1900s, the American Public Health Association organized its association around a campaign to eradicate cholera and typhus by promoting chlorination of drinking water and, to this day, has continued to promote clean tap water. Environmental and consumer activism beginning in the 1960s has drawn public and governmental attention to new and increasing drinking water contaminants. Rachel Carson, in her 1964 book, *Silent Spring*, warned of the increasing environmental degradation of land and water by the heavy use of pesticides and industrial chemicals. Today, several national environmental groups—including the Natural Resources Defense Council, Clean Water Action, Friends of the Earth, and the Environmental Working Group—are very active advocates for clean water.

Ralph Nader, who began his consumer advocacy in the late 1960s with calls for the increased safety of automobiles, soon broadened the consumer movement's agenda to many more issues including the safety of drinking water and food. Consumer groups focusing on safe drinking water include the U.S. Public Interest Research Group and the National Consumers League.

— Diana Neidle

Readings

Craun, Gunther, ed. (1993). *The Safety of Water Disinfection: Balancing Chemical and Microbial Risk.* Conference Proceedings, International Life Sciences Institute.

U.S. Environmental Protection Agency, Drinking Water Committee (1995). *Safe Drinking Water: Future Trends and Challenges.* Washington, DC: The Board.

Drunk Driving

See Alcohol Problems and the Consumer Movement.

Dutch Consumer Movement

Today's consumer movement in the Netherlands can be traced back to two separate lines of development. The first branch consists of consumer cooperatives, which originated in many Western European countries in the late nineteenth century. In the early 1950s, about 10 percent of all households were still members of a cooperative. The co-ops were united in the federation of cooperatives (the "Centrale"), whose main goal was "to increase general welfare by organized self-help of consumers."

The activities of the cooperatives consisted of running stores, especially grocery shops. In the mid-1950s, the co-ops started to decline; by the 1970s, they had disappeared altogether.

The second branch of the consumer movement has its foundation in the Netherlands Union of Housewives (NVH), which came into existence in 1912. Its early activities were aimed at fighting abuses related to the hygiene of food. It was to a large extent because of the NVH's pressure that, in 1919, a law on food safety was enacted and a food inspection department created. In 1926, the NVH founded an institute (IVHA), charged with the task of providing information on the "economic management of the household," which later issued the still existing label trademark: "Approved by the NVH."

In the mid-1930s, at the peak of the Great Depression, two other organizations were founded that also focused on providing information and on helping families to meet ends: the Netherlands Federation for Household and Family Information, which was later transformed to the still-existing Netherlands Family Council (NGR); and the Foundation for Household Information in Rural Areas (HVP).

In 1953, the product testing organization Consumentenbond (CB) was established. At present, CB counts over 650,000 members, covering one out of every nine Dutch families (the largest penetration rate of any consumer organization in the world). CB joined with the NVH, NGR, HVP, and several trade unions to found the Consumer Contact Organ (CCO), a vehicle for applying joint pressure on the government. CCO collapsed in 1971 when CB opted out, not wanting any longer to play a subordinate role to CCO when dealing with the government. The remaining organizations then founded Konsumenten Kontakt (KK), consisting of a small but effective bureau that analyzed consumer problems. It used these findings to exert pressure on government, business, and local authorities to remedy ills. CB and KK, who were allies rather than rivals, dominated the Dutch consumer scene in the 1970s and 1980s.

Government Involvement

Spurred by the development of private consumer organizations, the Dutch government entered the field of consumer affairs. Its involvement was both direct and indirect, through the subsidization of new, "private" organizations.

The first consumer subsidy (about $15,000) was granted in 1961 by the Ministry of Economic Affairs (EZ) to CCO for comparative testing of products. Over the years this subsidy increased, as did the involvement of EZ with respect to consumer affairs.

In 1965, the Social Economic Council, an advisory body to the government composed mainly of leaders of labor and employer organizations, established a special committee for advising on consumer affairs (CCA). Members of the CCA were appointed from labor, employer, and consumer organizations, with representatives of the consumer and labor groups constituting a majority. The CCA was the first official body in which consumer organizations were represented. Its task was, and with certain modifications still is, twofold: advise government on consumer policy proposals and provide a platform for consultation and negotiations between consumer organizations and industry.

In 1974, the minister of EZ became the coordinating minister for consumer affairs. In the same ordinance, an interdepartmental coordinating committee (ICC) was established. A year later, a directorate for consumer affairs (DCB) was created around the already existing nucleus at EZ. Its functions were: general policy development, preparation of consumer policy at the ministry itself, and support of other ministries in integrating consumer policy considerations in their own policies.

In 1979, a major government consumer policy memorandum was published in which the position of the consumer and consumption vis à vis other phenomena, interests, and policies was set out in a fundamental manner. The objective of government consumer policy became: "the improvement of the opportunities to satisfy needs through consumption," with an emphasis on "strengthening the position of the consumer in the marketplace."

The CCA's first advice concerned the proposal by EZ to found an institute for comparative testing, SVWO, to be managed by CB and KK and to be subsidized by EZ. The advice laid down the conditions for conducting and publishing test results so as to safeguard reliability and the interests of the manufacturers concerned. The subsidy made it possible to publish results of some ten to fifteen more expensive tests annually.

In 1970, CB established, together with organizations representing specific industries, a Foundation for the Resolution of Disputes (SGC), set up to address consumer disputes involving stores affiliated with these industries. Among the first participating industries were the travel sector (agents as well as the tour operators) and the clothes cleaning industry (both wet and chemical cleaning sectors). Dispute resolution takes place in committees that have been set up for each of these industries. Generally speaking, these committees consist of an independent chairman (trained in law), a representative from the industry concerned, and a member designated by CB.

In 1975, government recognized SGC's charter, which made subsidization possible. This subsidy gradually declined and, by the mid-1990s, amounted to about 50 percent of total costs and a share for industry of about 40 percent. The number of these committees is still rising and stood at twenty in 1994.

In 1974, the Union for the Interests of Homeowners (VEH) was founded. VEH is the only important category-based consumer organization in the Netherlands, and it now counts more than 400,000 members. VEH and CB work well together in areas of common interest.

In 1979, CB and KK established a Foundation for Scientific Research on Consumer Affairs (SWOKA), which was subsidized entirely by government. It played a role in the determination of government policy in a number of instances. Also in 1979, the National Institute for Information on Household Budgeting (NIBUD) was established. NIBUD is being subsidized by government and the relevant financial industries. In 1983, the Consumer Safety Institute was established, fully subsidized by the Ministry of Health. The institute is charged with providing information on, and monitoring, product hazards.

International Activities

The international activities of the Dutch consumer movement occur at the European and global levels. In 1962, the Netherlands was one of six member countries in the European Community. Independent consumer organizations from these nations, including CB, participated in the foundation of the European Bureau of Consumer Unions (BEUC). CB has always played an active role in its operation and provided its president for many years.

The six member states of the European Community effectively commenced their common consumer policy with the drawing up and the implementation of the first program of consumer protection of 1975 on the basis of the five consumer rights they had promulgated in 1972. These rights differ from the four "Kennedy rights" insofar as they do not explicitly recognize the right to choose, but acknowledge, in contrast to the Kennedy rights, the right to protection of economic interests. The Dutch government, with its free trade mentality and interests, has always been a loyal supporter of the European policy directed at the completion of the single market and the new goals of the Maastricht Treaty of 1992. This orientation was also visible in its contribution toward European consumer policy.

At the global level, CB was one of the five founders of the International Organization of Consumers Unions (IOCU) in 1960, and CB's director has frequently served as a member of the governing board of IOCU (now named Consumers International). Moreover, IOCU's headquarters were located in The Hague until 1993. Both CB and the Directorate for Consumer Affairs have always supported IOCU and taken part in its operations, emphasizing the need and duty to assist Third World countries, and more recently to help the consumer organizations of the Eastern European countries in their transition from command economies to market-based ones.

In 1970, the governments of the Netherlands and the United States were instrumental in the establishment of Organization for Economic Coopoeration and Development's Committee on Consumer Policy. This Dutch support has always remained strong since this committee and its secretariat provides an excellent platform for the exchange of consumer policy intentions, discussions, and policy preparation. Its reports have always been of high quality.

Achievements

In the past twenty-five years or so, two phases of about equal length may be distinguished. The first phase was devoted to raising awareness of the consumer dimension in policy development and building institutions capable of adequately coping with consumer problems. This phase coincided with the then prevailing belief in the malleability of society and the role of government therein. The second phase should be viewed as one of reflection on the roles of various parties. This is the consequence of the general recognition that government had reached or even overstepped its limits, given the many negative side effects of its endeavors.

Achievements in the area of institution-building are conspicuous. First and foremost, the position of CB attracts attention. Its well-developed function of serving its members through its inexpensive monthly *Consumentengids*, additional publications, individually tailored advice, and support on legal questions has reduced the need for other general purpose consumer organizations. Membership dues (about $30 in 1994) yield a subscription to the monthly magazine, access to services (many of which are free), and publications at a considerable discount.

For many of CB's members, access to publications and services is sufficient, but CB is much more. It is a movement. It has a democratically elected council, consisting of 100 members, in which its highest authority is vested. This council elects the board, approves and defines the course of the organization, and creates commissions that advise the board. At the local or regional level, many working groups of its members exist that occupy themselves with themes of local or national importance. CB has gained societal recognition. The media take account of its views and so does business. Dick Westendorp, its director since 1982, appears regularly on television. CB's dominant position also explains why, in the Netherlands, no need was felt to develop ombudsman-type institutions as in Scandinavia.

Many institutions that were developed in the first phase, such as SGC and NIBUD, have acquired a solid place in society. Nevertheless, they will always feel the pressure of being dependent on subsidies, since their services can never be fully marketed. SWOKA underwent a transformation in order to meet the challenge of the marketplace. This was in reply to a decision by government that it would, after a transitional period, cease providing institute support. After that date, SWOKA would have to compete with other research institutes to carry out studies that matched the government's specific research needs.

Other institutions disappeared because they had become obsolete. The ICC was discontinued in 1987 because the departments had by then recognized the necessity of integrating the consumer perspective into policy planning. Moreover, the need for interdepartmental fine-tuning and coordination had diminished considerably. SVWO was terminated in 1992 because it was felt that the government should not subsidize the regular comparative testing of products any longer. DCB continued, however, to support innovative comparative testing. These activities were then transferred to CB.

There is still room for new institutions, if need be. In the mid-1980s, the Federation of Patient and Consumer Organizations (NPCF) was set up. NPCF consists of local, regional and national organizations of patients with a common illness. NPCF provides support to patients and participates in the discussion and transformation of the health care systems. As another example, a foundation for environmental labeling (SMK) was set up in 1992. SMK receives a government subsidy, but it must eventually become largely self-supporting.

Some achievements have also been made in representing the consumer viewpoint in policy-making. In general, Dutch political philosophy emphasizes not only involving participants in the process of decision-making, but also making them, to the extent possible, responsible for policies in which they participate. This philosophy underlies both the building of consumer protection policies as well as deregulation policies, which gained such prominence in the 1980s. With respect to consumer policy, deregulation did not put the goals of consumer protection at stake, but rather its instruments. The consumer organizations were urged to cover the "retreat" of government in areas in which they were thought to be able to exert sufficient influence on industry. DCB's budget for consumer affairs, of which the largest share accrued to the aforementioned foundations, was increased by one-third to about $10 million, enabling it to subsidize consumer organizations capable of carrying out tasks in the general interest, that is, in excess of the obligations of these organizations toward their members. This approach of widening the competence of consumer organizations has always been the cornerstone of DCB's subsidizing policy. In this instance, the additional funds were used mainly for more and better consumer information on radio and television and, to a lesser extent, for dispute resolution and support in negotiating better contract terms.

Overall, the level of consumer protection achieved by the Dutch consumer movement appears to be adequate. Judged by the incidence of reported complaints and the relative quiet in the marketplace, this conclusion cannot be easily refuted. The position of Dutch consumers is roughly comparable to consumers in the other northern member states of the European Union.

Recent Developments and Prospects

In view of the conviction that major consumer problems had disappeared and that the focus of its policy should be more strongly directed at the pursuit of the free, though balanced, functioning of markets, the need for a separate consumer policy directorate was no longer felt. Its activities merged in 1992 with those of competition and others related to the functioning of markets.

In 1992, the trade unions announced their withdrawal from KK, as they did not view these activities to coincide any longer with their core business. In 1994, KK was discontinued.

In the fall of 1994, influenced by continued budgetary pressures, EZ decided to gradually reduce DCB's consumer budget by nearly $4 million to the level of $3 million by 1997 and even less thereafter. Discussions have started with the Ministry of Justice for taking over its role in subsidizing the dispute resolution mechanism of SGC. On a project basis, subsidies may be granted, provided these projects contribute to the government's efforts to improve the functioning of markets.

Despite the government's recent retrenchment in the area of consumer protection, several major consumer issues will have to be addressed in the coming years. First, there is the further adaptation and harmonization of consumer policy resulting from the continued general integration of Europe. It is hoped that the Dutch "fabric" of consumer policy that has proved to be so effective in the Netherlands can be maintained. Second, the consumer movement needs a position with respect to environmental problems; these are especially crucial because of the high population density of the Netherlands. Many of these problems may require changes in consumer lifestyles.

Rapid technological change constitutes a third area of challenge. The further advance of technology will make possible new techniques of production, which may, at times, be questionable from the consumer point of view (e.g., biotechnology). The Internet and rapidly developing communications technologies may, because of their sophistication and expense, pose problems to weaker, less-educated groups in society, including new citizens from abroad. Since participation in society increasingly depends on the ability to cope with relatively advanced technologies, their design and introduction require great care.

Fourth, the much stronger market orientation of today will have many positive and negative effects. A number of long-trusted welfare state pillars may lose their solidity. The pursuit of individualism and competition will provide new opportunities for some, but uncertainty and possible marginalization for others. Without ignoring the benefits derivable from liberalizing markets, the consumer movement must focus on the empowerment of consumers who are not the primary beneficiaries of market deregulation. This is especially important in light of the decline in disposable income and the steep rise in the price of fixed outlays such as rents, local taxes, and insurance, all of which aggravate the position of the poor.

Finally, consumers must cope with quality and price issues involving monopolistic services such as health care and those of public authorities. Value for money is problematic since the consumer voice is insufficiently heard in markets for services. It is not clear to what extent government sees itself as being in the vanguard of these developments and helping to steer their course in desired directions. It also remains to be seen to what degree CB will be able to influence these developments since the required concern and attention will only be possible at the expense of other activities. It will be particularly difficult for CB to be involved in issues that do not involve the direct interests of its members and which were formerly partly subsidized.

— Joop Koopman

Readings

Consumers International (1995). *Balancing the Scales, Part 2: Consumer Protection in the Netherlands and Germany.* London: Consumers International.

Hollmann, Hermann H. (1981). "Consumer Protection Movement in Western Europe and Its Impact on Business." *International Contract.* 2 (June/July): 259–276.

E

Eastern European Consumer Movement

See Central and Eastern Europe, Consumer Movements in.

Economic Criticisms of the Consumer Movement

The U.S. consumer movement reached national prominence in the 1970s. Although there has been an apparent waning of the influence of this movement since the 1980s, it remains a well-established feature of the political landscape. Unfortunately, the consumer movement has not achieved its full potential because of a narrow interpretation of its advocacy role and a failure to understand fully the mechanisms by which the economy operates.

The starting point for this assessment will be to specify the criteria used to evaluate the consumer movement. The appropriate yardstick of success is not the amount of financial support the consumer movement has raised, the membership in consumer organizations, the prominence of the consumer movement in the national media, or even the number of pieces of legislation it has helped pass. Rather, the overall test should be how well the movement has succeeded in enhancing the welfare of American consumers. This task of enhancement is different from that facing society as a whole. The consumer movement need not be held responsible for advancing other societal objectives, such as the profitability of businesses, even though the shareholders of these businesses are individuals and also consumers. Rather, since the consumer movement is an advocacy group, the appropriate test of its efforts is whether they have advanced the well-being of consumers.

The consumer movement is not without successes. The existence of consumer representatives as a lobbying force is in and of itself an important role. Groups such as the Consumer Federation of America, Public Citizen, and Consumers Union, as well as individuals such as Ralph Nader, have put political issues pertaining to consumers on the national agenda.

Consumer advocates have called our attention to the fact that there is a legitimate inadequacy in the way in which the economy often treats consumers. These transgressions range from bumping policies that result from overbooked airlines to safety hazards in children's toys that are not apparent to prospective users.

These types of difficulties arise from a failure in the way in which markets operate. One reason that consumer interests might not be well protected is that a company may have no competitors who can offer consumers a choice of better or less expensive products. Another reason may be a lack of consumer information about the quality or riskiness of products. But these problems reflect market failures, not the profit motive. All companies, whether operating in imperfect markets or dealing with informed consumers in competitive markets, seek to make as much profit as possible.

The more radical consumer movement critiques of corporate decision-making that blame the failures on corporate greed may be effective means for arousing public support and personalizing transgressions against consumers. Yet, these radical views overlook the fact that, as a general rule, corporations are greedy in the sense that they do what is best for corporate interests. In adequately functioning markets, this greed is disciplined through competition and the expression of informed consumer preferences. Companies do not provide sound and desirable products because of altruism, but rather because they make more money by doing so. When markets function imperfectly, society should take appropriate action, which may take the form of regulating monopolies, controlling quality, or informing consumers of potential risks.

A primary mechanism the consumer movement has used to attempt to influence the economy is government regulations. Throughout this century, consumer protection efforts have led to a wide variety of governmental interventions ranging from the Food, Drug and Cosmetic Act in 1906 to numerous consumer protection statutes in the 1960s. By bringing national attention to issues such as occupational safety and nuclear safety, consumer advocates were also instrumental in the creation, in the early 1970s, of federal regulatory agencies to address these hazards.

Although putting these issues on the national agenda and creating government agencies to address them should be regarded as a success, the particular policy approaches selected did not recognize the important radeoffs involved. High levels of safety and other improvements in consumer products come at a price. Ultimately, any changes in product attributes that raise the costs of producing products will generate higher prices for consumers. Installing seatbelts or antilock brakes in cars will make these vehicles more expensive. Similarly, more extensive testing requirements for new pharmaceutical products will raise the cost of drugs and deprive consumers of potentially beneficial products while they are being tested.

The U.S. Department of Transportation estimates that each year more than 1,000 people are killed in car crashes because of the switch to smaller, more fuel-efficient vehicles, which have the offsetting disadvantage of being less crashworthy. Clearly, consumers could be made safer if cars were made to resemble tanks. Yet, doing so would not be in consumers' interests since the cost of the added safety would be higher purchase prices and operating costs. The test for whether we should convert all cars into tanks is whether, on balance, consumers will be made better off by these changes, taking into account the fact that changes in the characteristics of cars that affect purchase price or operating cost will be shifted to consumers.

Ultimately, consumers will pay most costs of the changes brought about by the consumer movement. The existence of such costs does not imply that all safety and other consumer-related efforts are misguided. There are competing effects. We should continue to pursue these efforts as long as the additional benefits to consumers outweigh the costs they must pay.

Unfortunately, consumer protection efforts often do not recognize the existence of these tradeoffs. Legislation enacted with the support of consumer advocates generally stipulates, as in the case of the safety and efficacy requirements for pharmaceuticals, that the product must be made safe. However, these laws do not formally recognize the legitimate tradeoffs that exist. The Food and Drug Administration places greater weight on risks created by new drugs than on risks averted by new drugs. No one wants to be held responsible for approving the next Thalidomide, but the thousands of patients who may die because a new heart medicine is not approved are not easily identifiable and do not comprise an effective lobbying group. Well-identified constituencies, such as AIDS victims, have commanded greater advocacy attention since their interests are better defined than other similarly situated groups at risk. Since consumer movements tend to respond to their funding and to well-identified groups, there is a tendency to place a greater weight on the interests of such constituencies rather than on broader groups who may face a very small statistical risk to their lives.

A more important shortcoming of consumer protection efforts is their stringent character. Consumers do not want absolute safety. Making products risk-free is not feasible. Nor is eliminating all hazards desirable, since almost all activities in life are inherently risky. Each time we fly in a plane, especially at high altitudes, we expose ourselves to hazardous radiation, and all forms of transportation pose hazards of various kinds. Our task is not to make life risk-free but to strike a sensible balance between the risks we choose to face and the costs of preventing these risks.

In their daily lives, consumers make such tradeoffs between risk and money. On average, workers in blue-collar jobs, for example, face an annual risk of death from work-related causes of 1 in 10,000 per year. Economists have estimated that workers receive an average amount of $500 per year in compensation for the risks they face. Consequently, for 10,000 workers facing an average risk of 1 in 10,000 of death, there will be one expected death and $5 million in compensation. These types of estimates have led economists to estimate that the implicit value of a statistical life is in the range of $5 million. Similar estimates have been made for product choices, such as the choice of safer cars. Although there is legitimate debate over whether the appropriate value that consumers place on a statistical life is $3 million, $5 million, $7 million, or some other figure, it is clear that we place a finite price on statistical lives.

If our objective is to reflect the interests of consumers who ultimately will pay for safety improvements, we should attempt to promote only those efforts that are commensurate with their valuations of safety. Unfortunately, government agencies pursue risk reduction objectives that fail to grapple with such tradeoffs. Policies often involve wildly extravagant expenditures of funds for little benefit. Regulations from the Environmental Protection Agency and Occupational Safety and Health Administration, for example, frequently impose costs from $50 million to $100 million per statistical life saved. By reallocating priorities, more lives could be saved for less money.

In some cases, the failure of consumer advocates to recognize tradeoffs or to make appropriate tradeoffs leads to policies that are not sufficiently ambitious. The U.S. Department of Transportation, for example, never pursues programs when the cost per life saved exceeds $3 million. If advocates could persuade the department to address safety hazards where lives lost cost $5 million or $7 million each, more ambitious consumer protection efforts would result. But for most other federal agencies, focusing on tradeoffs would result in less stringent policies. This reduced stringency, however, could allow these agencies to undertake more frequent initiatives if, as expected, more sensible policies reduced business resistance and the number of court challenges.

Another persistent failure of the consumer movement is its surprisingly strong reliance on engineering solutions. Many critiques by consumer groups emphasize the ways in which our technologies have failed us. They have called attention, for example, to defective consumer products and to risks from genetically engineered produce. Ironically, many policies espoused by consumer advocates also contain a technology-forcing bias. If cars are unsafe, we need only equip them with appropriate safety devices.

In contrast, consumer advocates devote relatively little attention to making consumers more responsible. They seldom view public education campaigns to alter safety-related behavior as the first policy option. Instead, their primary effort is to shift responsibility to the producing firm, thus allowing consumers to remain passive. Yet, safety is jointly produced through individual effort in conjunction with product characteristics. Properly engaging the consumer in the safety process, along with improving the safety of technologies, will promote safety more effectively than an exclusive focus on technologies.

The important role of individual precautions is emphasized by the disappointing performance of many consumer protections. When the automobile safety effort of the 1960s emerged, safety advocates confidently predicted that there would be dramatic and immediate declines in the automobile fatality rate. These bold predictions failed to materialize because safety advocates neglected the role of individual driver behavior, such as drunken driving. There is also the possibility that, if drivers feel better protected by seatbelts and other safety devices, they may drive less carefully.

An added dimension to individual safety behavior is present in the case of government-mandated safety caps for sealing products. Many officials suggested that these caps now made the products "childproof." But some research shows that the safety caps for products such as aspirin and prescription drugs produced no statistically significant effect on the protected products. Many parents left the caps off, and many other individuals were lulled into a false sense of security. After the introduction of safety caps, parents became less careful about allowing their children access to such products. The existence of this lulling effect, as well as other dampening of consumer precautions in response to safety regulations, tend to mute the beneficial effects of these interventions.

These limitations do not imply that consumer protection efforts have no benefits. Information provision policies, for example, have no doubt improved consumer decisions, and safety regulations have produced notable safety gains. This progress has been much less, however, than what could have been achieved had the role of consumer behavior been better recognized.

The remaining task for consumer advocates is to recognize that consumers should get what they pay for from new regulations. Safer, better products come at a price. Consumer advocates should promote sensible tradeoffs rather than focusing exclusively on only one component of a product. Moreover, advocates should stress that consumers have a major responsibility in making informed and safe choices. Imposing the entire burden on manufacturers, rather than dividing the burden between manufacturers and consumers, has produced fewer gains for consumers than could have been realized had consumers been more actively engaged in this effort.

Unless the mission of the consumer movement is broadened in this manner, its role is essentially over. We have now institutionalized most of the major consumer protection functions. No new consumer agencies or sweeping areas of safety reform are on the horizon. Absolute levels of safety and product quality are unachievable. The new policies that are needed to promote consumers' interests best must incorporate recognition of tradeoffs between the benefits consumers derive and the price that they ultimately pay.

— W. Kip Viscusi

See also

Consumer Interest.

Readings

Mayer, Robert N. (1989). *The Consumer Movement: Guardians of the Marketplace.* Boston: Twayne Publishers.

Viscusi, W. Kip (1992). *Fatal Tradeoffs: Public and Private Responsibilities for Risk.* New York: Oxford University Press.

Economics, Consumer

See Consumer Economics/Studies.

Education, Consumer

See Consumer Education.

Elderly as Consumers

See Older Consumers.

Electricity Regulation

The early days of the electric industry were marked not by regulation, but by raucous competition. In the late nineteenth century, many American cities had numerous electric generating companies striving to recruit customers street by street for their new service.

By the beginning of the twentieth century, a consensus had developed that regulation, rather than competition, was the preferred approach for the future of the burgeoning electric industry. In particular, it was recognized that it made little sense to build forests of competing electric distribution poles and lines in some districts of a city, while others went unserved.

Rather than continuing to compete, electric companies across the nation began to consolidate within each city and region. Some of these new utilities were municipally owned, but the majority remained in private hands. To the extent that these privately owned companies were no longer subject to competition, but were instead the recipients of government granted monopoly franchises, it was clear that the rates charged by these entities would have to be regulated. The burden of regulation fell primarily on the states, which created public utility commissions to regulate the rates and service of electric utilities and other monopoly service providers.

By the 1920s, the consolidation of electric utilities that had begun on a local and state basis was reaching national proportions. Giant public utility holding companies had been created. These holding companies consisted of layers of corporate subsidiaries in a vast web of interlocking ownership and control. By the mid-1920s, sixteen holding companies controlled 85 percent of the nation's electricity.

The elaborate multistate holding company structure gave rise to a number of abuses, including the "pyramiding" of corporate structures, excessive write-ups of utility assets, and excessive charges on intracorporate affiliated transactions. Many of these abuses were beyond the reach of state regulators, who could not regulate beyond their state boundaries. Another gap in state regulatory authority was exposed by the U.S. Supreme Court in 1927 when it held that state public utility commissions have no jurisdiction over interstate power transactions.

In 1935, Congress acted to correct these problems when it passed the Federal Power Act (FPA) and the Public Utility Holding Company Act (PUHCA). The FPA established jurisdiction within the Federal Power Commission (now the Federal Energy Regulatory Commission) to regulate the interstate transmission and wholesale sale of electricity. PUHCA effectively required the breakup of the multistate holding companies into smaller companies that were either confined to one state or, in the case of "registered" holding companies, permitted to operate integrated electric utility systems in contiguous states.

The mid-1930s also saw the expansion of efforts to spread the benefits of electricity to all areas of the nation. In 1935, President Roosevelt issued an executive order establishing the Rural Electrification Administration (REA). With financial assistance from the REA, in the next decade hundreds of cooperatively owned rural electric companies were organized in unserved or underserved parts of the nation. In addition, President Roosevelt launched the federal power agencies—the Tennessee Valley Authority and the Bonneville Power Administration.

The period from 1935 to the mid-1960s was an era of steady growth and strong financial health for the electric utility industry, which supplied relatively low rates and increasingly reliable service to most consumers. The first signs that all was not well in this industry appeared in 1965. In November of this year, a blackout plunged much of the northeastern United States into darkness. Public concern was expressed that utilities did not have adequate reserve margins to meet their capacity needs.

In the late 1960s and the 1970s, many utilities began significant construction programs. Some new power plants used nuclear power, which, some proponents claimed, would be "too cheap to meter." These construction programs occurred at a time when interest rates, and therefore the capital cost of these large construction programs, began to increase dramatically.

Meanwhile, the steady growth in electricity usage, which had given rise to forecasts showing the need for new plants, was halted. The critical event in that period was the Arab oil embargo of 1973 to 1974, which led to a severalfold increase in oil prices. These price hikes drove up electricity rates, which in turn led to a decline in the demand for electricity. In 1974, sales of electricity in the United States declined for the first time since 1946.

The utilities' financial outlook received a comparable jolt in April 1974 when a major New York utility, Consolidated Edison, failed to pay its common stock dividend. Con Ed's actions shattered the conventional financial wisdom of the time that electric utilities were an almost perfectly safe investment and that dividends were absolutely secure.

Perhaps the most critical blow to the structure of the modern electric utility industry occurred on March 28, 1979, when a cooling system malfunction forced the shutdown and threatened the meltdown of the Three Mile Island (TMI) Unit 2 nuclear reactor near Harrisburg, Pennsylvania. Although the physical damage resulting from that accident was generally contained within the reactor walls, the financial fallout spread to utilities throughout the nation. Nuclear plants, which were already facing construction delays and cost overruns, were subject to greater public and regulatory scrutiny as the inherent safety of nuclear power was called into question.

No nuclear plants were ordered in the United States after 1978, and more than seventy nuclear plants that had been ordered or were under construction at the time of the TMI accident were subsequently canceled. Those plants that were completed faced cost overruns amounting, in many cases, to billions of dollars. Moreover, the forecasted electricity demands that had been used to justify construction of many of those plants failed to materialize, thus leaving some utilities with extraordinarily expensive excess capacity.

The combination of these forces gave rise to a major advance in consumer advocacy, primarily at the state public utility commission level. Whereas electric utility proceedings had previously been quiet affairs between utilities and public utility commission staffs, with perhaps some representation of large industrial customers, the rate cases of the late 1970s and 1980s became heated and well-publicized political, economic, and financial debates.

Grassroots consumer groups, as well as state-authorized consumer advocate offices, were established to represent the interests of consumers in electric and other utility rate proceedings across the nation. Issues in the electric cases included whether ratepayers should have to pay the cost of canceled nuclear power plants as well as the cost of completed plants, which were unneeded and uneconomical by the time they came on line. Detailed investigations of the prudence of specific plant expenditures were also conducted before state public utility commissions. Consumer representatives in many states also spearheaded efforts to require utilities to reduce their reliance on huge new nuclear and fossil-fueled generating plants, and to turn instead to conservation, energy efficiency, and renewable energy resources.

While billions of dollars of nuclear power plant expenditures ultimately were disallowed from utility rates, many more billions of dollars of costs were included in rates. As a result, the rates charged to customers of heavily nuclear utilities increased dramatically and contributed to a major disparity in rates among utilities within states and across regions.

This great disparity in rate levels also helped give rise to the most significant issue facing electric utilities today—the potential growth in competition at both the wholesale and retail levels. It has become clear in recent years that the generation function in the electric utility industry is not a natural monopoly. That is, unlike the transmission and distribution functions, there is no strong economic basis to restrict electric generation to a single regulated entity in any given geographic area.

The move toward a competitive generation industry had already been given a major boost in 1978 by Congress in the Public Utility Regulatory Policies Act (PURPA). Under PURPA, electric utilities must purchase power from certain qualifying cogeneration and small power facilities at rates based on the utility's avoided cost—that is, the cost that a utility would incur if it built its own generating unit or purchased power elsewhere. Under PURPA, the nonutility generation industry began to flourish, and, by 1990, more than half of the new electric capacity in the United States was being built by nonutility generators.

Congress gave electricity competition another boost with the passage of the Energy Policy Act of 1992 (EPAct). EPAct created a new category of independent power producers, called exempt wholesale generators (EWGs). EWGs are generally exempt from restrictions imposed by PUHCA, do not have to meet the special qualification requirements of PURPA, and can be owned by electric utility affiliates. Perhaps more importantly, EPAct also greatly increased the ability of third-party buyers and sellers of electricity to gain access to utility-owned transmission facilities. With this increased access to transmission, the wholesale market for electricity was greatly expanded.

The fundamental question now facing the electric utility industry is whether competition should be extended to the retail sale of electricity through so-called retail wheeling. Advocates of retail competition contend that rates will be reduced and economic efficiency increased if customers can "shop" for electricity from a number of suppliers and require the local utility to transmit or "wheel" that power to the customers' premises. In legislative and regulatory decisions in many states, there is a clear trend toward bringing about greater retail generation competition, but, as of this writing, it is by no means clear what forms these competitive initiatives will ultimately take.

A number of significant questions arise whenever retail competition is discussed, such as who will pay the "stranded investment" from existing uneconomic facilities if customers are permitted to seek out lower-cost power from other sources. This question applies both to utility-owned facilities (particularly nuclear plants) and to contracts with nonutility generators where the projected "avoided costs" on which contracts were based have turned out to be greatly in excess of the value of such resources in an open market. There is also an issue of whether the benefits of retail competition will be received by all consumers, or only by large industrial customers who have the greatest access to competitive alternatives.

Whatever the answers to these questions, it is clear that the electric utility industry is in a state of transition to a more competitive structure. The critical task confronting consumer representatives today and in the future is to ensure that consumers are protected from excessive electricity rates either through continued regulation or through full and fair competition that benefits all consumers, not just a selected few.

— Irwin A. Popowsky

See also

Energy Conservation; Public Power; Rural Electric Cooperatives.

Readings

Hyman, Leonard S. (1988). *America's Electric Utilities: Past, Present and Future.* 3d ed. Arlington, VA: Public Utilities Reports, Inc.

Phillips, Charles F., Jr. (1993). *The Regulation of Public Utilities: Theory and Practice.* 3d ed. Arlington, VA: Public Utilities Reports, Inc.

Rudolph, Richard, and Scott Ridley (1986). *Power Struggle: The Hundred Year War over Electricity.* New York: Harper & Row Publishers.

Electronic Funds Transfer Protections

In the late 1960s, various technological developments occurred in the fields of electronic data processing and telecommunications that enabled the manipulation, processing, and transmission of huge amounts of routine data in a highly cost-effective manner. Noting that many conventional consumer financial transactions involve a few regular, relatively simple steps, bankers began developing systems to utilize these emerging technologies to deliver routine consumer financial services.

Consumers could be provided electronically encoded cards, insertable into specially equipped machines (automated teller machines, or ATMs). These machines were linked by telephone lines to computer systems that could then permit withdrawals or deposits by the consumer at the ATM with a corresponding debit or credit to the consumer's bank account. Systems using these technologies—electronic funds transfer (EFT) systems—began emerging in the early 1970s.

Some individual financial institutions developed their own proprietary networks of ATMs to serve only their own customers. In other cases, numerous institutions banded together to create shared networks, encompassing broader geographic areas. In either case, consumers could obtain cash, make deposits, and direct certain, simple account transfers at hundreds (and, quickly, thousands) of ATMs located far from their banks and generally at any time of day, wherever and whenever it was most convenient. Eventually, these regional networks were connected through various exchange arrangements, allowing such transactions across the country and even around the world.

The unique characteristics of this unfamiliar technology, however, raised many issues. For example, how could parties establish that a transfer of value had even occurred when there was no paper record (such as a canceled check) reflecting it? How might transaction disputes be resolved where there was no paper document generated to which to refer? Would consumers accept a system where there was nothing—not a coin, not a bill, not a check, literally nothing—to touch and, thereby, reassure? Who would bear responsibility for loss when transactions went awry?

Historically, banking has been a heavily regulated industry. Extensive laws and regulations establishing the various rights between parties to financial transactions in other payment systems existed for decades. Included among these were numerous consumer protection standards controlling various payment and financial transfer means. However, it was far from clear what, if any, existing legal structures governed rights and responsibilities when transactions were made via an EFT system.

The issue was further complicated in that consumers possessed widely varying rights depending on which particular payment medium they might be using, such as cash, checks, or credit cards, all of which were governed by different legal standards. Should parties have the same rights in EFT transactions as when using other funds transfer means? And, if so, which other means? Were EFT transactions more like cash transactions or check transactions? Considering the peculiarities of EFT technologies, were new rights necessary or desirable?

To attempt to identify the many issues raised by EFT, Congress created a national commission, which began meeting in 1976, to examine the many implications of EFT, specifically consumer protection needs. In the meantime, beginning with Wisconsin in December 1976, several states enacted consumer protection standards regarding EFT.

Given the obvious benefits in uniform standards in facilitating interstate transactions, Senator William Proxmire (D-WI), chairman of the Senate Banking Committee, introduced legislation in 1977 to establish consumer protection standards governing EFT systems. His bill was enacted as the Electronic Funds Transfer Act in 1978. The primary consumer protections enacted in the law were: mandated disclosures of account terms and conditions; required documentation to be given to consumers, both upon performing an EFT transaction and in periodic account statements; controls on how consumers might preauthorize certain transactions; limitations on consumer liability for unauthorized transactions; procedures for resolving disputes between consumers and banks and for correcting errors involving EFT transactions; limitations on the issuance of access cards used to participate in EFT systems; and restrictions on forced participation in EFT systems to obtain certain financial services.

The legislation was extensively lobbied by the financial services industry and by consumer advocates. Most of the banking industry opposed legislated establishment of consumer protection standards for EFT systems, arguing that the evolution of the technology—still in its infancy—would be unnecessarily stunted by "premature" regulation. Consumer groups, on the other hand, stressed the potential for consumer confusion and abuse, as well as the enormous financial losses consumers might suffer, given the untested and unfamiliar nature of EFT technologies generally. Their arguments were buttressed by specific instances in which consumers of limited sophistication had suffered substantial losses through involvement (often without anything approaching informed consent) in pioneer EFT systems.

Many subsequent technological developments in EFT technology and their application have raised additional questions about the adequacy of existing EFT consumer protection law to address such developments and their implications. Yet, the mushrooming growth of EFT systems across the country, and the widespread consumer acceptance of EFT that such growth reflects, suggests that early industry predictions regarding possible stultifying effects of appropriate consumer protection regulation were misplaced.

New methods of applying or combining emerging electronic technologies have recently been tested for delivering consumer financial services. One such method is stored value cards, where spendable value is electronically loaded onto and stored in a microchip contained in a card carried by a consumer who can then have some portion of that value debited from the card directly at the point of sale to obtain goods or services. Potential uses for frequent, low-value transactions abound, such as newsstands, vending machines, public telephones, mass transit, fast-food outlets, and laundromats. At the same time, the retention of various consumer-specific information in the microchip raises numerous concerns regarding the privacy of such information.

Another new delivery method, still in its infancy, is virtual banking. Here, value can be exchanged between buyer and seller in a variety of forms, as directed by a few keystrokes on a personal computer via emerging worldwide computer-based networks, primarily the Internet. One set of issues here involves establishing the accuracy and performance of intended transactions, including receipts, statements, and liability for unauthorized usage. A second set of issues concerns the credit worthiness of the institution to which the consumer entrusts his or her value for storage or transfer, and how the customer assesses that creditworthiness.

The ongoing challenge for consumerists is to anticipate and respond to such emerging EFT applications. The rapid (and seemingly accelerating) rate of change in the underlying technologies, coupled with the importance of the consumer needs they serve, make it especially important for consumerists to respond effectively.

— James L. Brown

See also

Checking Account Protections.

Readings

Baker, Donald I., and Roland E. Brandel (1996). *The Law of Electronic Fund Transfer Systems: Legal and Strategic Planning*. Boston: Warren Gorham & Lamont.

Solomon, E. (1986). *Electronic Funds Transfers and Payments: The Public Policy Issues*. Boston: Kluwer, Nijhoff Publishing.

Energy Conservation

In 1974, energy exports to the United States were partially embargoed by the Organization of Petroleum Exporting Countries (OPEC). All of a sudden, energy was the top domestic and foreign policy issue in the nation. Gasoline lines formed, President Jimmy Carter donned a cardigan sweater to give televised chats on the energy crisis, and citizens everywhere became conscious of their use of energy and its cost.

There was little that the average citizen could do about the supply of various energy sources by major multinational companies. But decisions about consumption of energy are made in a disaggregated manner by hundreds of millions of consumers. Energy conservation and energy efficiency are core tools for controlling unnecessary energy consumption and its attendant costs.

The consumer movement, through several organizations and individuals, focused on energy conservation as a fundamental consumer issue during the 1970s and 1980s. The consumer focus on energy conservation had as an ancillary goal to change the locus of energy decision-making. When large energy companies or utilities faced the energy crisis of the 1970s, they chose to develop additional energy supplies, often by way of tax or direct federal subsidy. Their first instinct with regard to the energy crisis was to endeavor to produce more energy, without addressing the efficiency with which that energy was being utilized. This response was only natural, since sellers of energy are paid for the gross quantity of energy sold, not for cutting their sales by encouraging more efficient use of lesser quantities of their product.

Consumer groups posed the key policy question: what is energy conservation? Energy conservation has been analogized to plugging the drain in the bathtub as a means to draw a warm bath efficiently. Energy conservation employs existing resources more efficiently and carefully to achieve the same level of comfort and function. By contrast, energy supply augmentation strategies have been characterized as leaving the bathtub drain unplugged and running the water taps more vigorously. The former option does more with less, while the latter does more with more. From the perspective of economics and equity, efficiency was superior to many energy supply options.

The thrust of the energy conservation efforts of the consumer movement were evident on federal, state, and local levels. At the federal level, national organizations—including the Consumer Federation of America, Consumers Union, Public Citizen, and the National Consumer Law Center—supported legislation to promote energy conservation.

In 1978, President Carter signed five pieces of landmark energy legislation known collectively as the National Energy Act. Three of these five statutes included energy conservation provisions. The Energy Tax Act provided tax credits for residential and commercial energy conservation investments. The National Energy Conservation Policy Act provided various grant programs for energy conservation and required minimum energy efficiency for major consumer appliances. The Public Utility Regulatory Policies Act promoted the efficient production of energy and the use of renewable resources. Today, this act is credited with having triggered the ongoing restructuring and deregulation of the electric utility industry.

In ensuing years, additional legislation was enacted at the direct behest of consumer groups to foster energy conservation. Noteworthy among these was the Solar Energy and Energy Conservation Bank Act, the funds for which President Ronald Reagan illegally impounded and refused to spend. This impoundment prompted a lawsuit against the president by the National Consumer Law Center, on behalf of a variety of consumer and environmental groups. During the 1980s, the Solar Energy and Energy Conservation Bank funded innovative programs for energy conservation throughout the states.

In the late 1970s and the 1980s, the consumer movement secured and maintained funding for programs to weatherize low-income homes; funding was often administered and delivered by local community action programs. Also in the 1980s, this movement steered unclaimed funds, restituted by oil companies that had violated price controls, to the benefit of energy conservation programs operated by the various states.

Consumer groups successfully challenged U.S. Housing and Urban Development (HUD) energy conservation policies. Rather than install energy efficiency improvements to public housing, HUD spent scarce program dollars to place individual meters on public housing, thereby allowing HUD to pass on to low-income tenants a larger portion of utility costs. This practice, in lieu of conservation improvements, was halted by litigation on behalf of consumer groups.

Consumer organizations also took action at the state and local levels. Across the nation, consumer groups became active in issues of electric utility supply planning and rate setting. Consumer groups contested a range of state utility regulatory matters, including the decision of utilities to build new generation facilities, the failure of utilities to compare electric supply decisions against energy conservation options (so-called least-cost planning), the design of utility rates that favored consumers of large amounts of electricity, and funding of utility energy conservation programs.

The consumer movement achieved significant victories in many states. In 1981, California pioneered utility-funded energy conservation programs for consumers. These programs served as models for similar conservation programs that, during the early 1980s, were established in many other states. By 1990, a majority of the nation's 206 investor-owned electric utilities were engaged in least-cost planning, which was supported by utility-funded energy conservation efforts.

At one level, energy conservation issues united consumer groups with environmental groups. Both groups favored energy conservation over additional energy development. However, the goals of the two movements differed somewhat. Environmental groups favored energy conservation for two reasons: conservation reduces the need to construct additional electric power plants, especially controversial nuclear-powered facilities; and reduced electricity generation lessens air and water pollution. While many consumers and their organizations supported these goals, the consumer movement sought mainly to control the cost of energy and to promote the decentralization of energy decision-making. Where environmental groups sometimes supported energy conservation at any cost, consumer groups often focused on cost-effective and decentralized energy conservation options. The energy industry never sufficiently perceived nor exploited these differences. These basic differences between consumer and environmental goals on energy planning and policy persist today.

In the 1990s, energy and its conservation remain prominent issues for the consumer movement and its constituents. The electric utility industry is the most capital-intensive industry in the nation. More dollars are invested in construction of electric power plants than in any other single industry, including automobiles, steel, or telecommunications. Because electricity cannot be stored efficiently, it must be produced efficiently and used immediately in an efficient manner. With large power plants now costing multiple billions of dollars each, on both the demand and supply sides, energy decisions remain of critical importance.

Today, in the dual names of deregulation and market-driven efficiency, the electric utility industry is on the brink of a fundamental deregulation. This change will be the most radical alteration to affect the electric utility industry in more than sixty years. Many observers believe that energy conservation initiatives, currently underwritten by utilities, will be a prime casualty of this reform. In a deregulated competitive environment, electric utilities may not want to underwrite any investments that do not translate directly to their bottom lines.

This deregulation portends a day when every consumer will have to choose his or her electricity supplier and negotiate for electric rates. For the energy industry, this new era offers a giddy chaos. For consumers, who are likely to have much less bargaining power than large industrial and commercial customers, there will be the need for consumer group vigilance and advocacy. Energy conservation and efficiency will likely remain a consumer issue in the forefront of national policy.

— Steven Ferrey

See also

Electricity Regulation; National Highway Traffic Safety Administration.

Readings

Ferrey, Steven (1991). "Shaping American Power: Federal Preemption and Technological Change." *Virginia Environmental Law Review.* 11 (1): 47–129.

——— (1996). *The Law of Independent Power: Development, Cogeneration, Utility Regulation.* Ch. 3. New York: Clark Boardman Callaghan.

Munson, Richard (1985). *The Power Makers: The Inside Story of America's Biggest Business—and Its Struggle to Control Tomorrow's Electricity.* Emmaus, PA: Rodale Press.

Energy Cooperatives

In the wake of the energy crises of the 1970s, many Americans resented the power of the oil industry. In 1983, to meet their own energy needs, consumers in Washington, D.C., began an experiment in market sovereignty by banding together to purchase home heating oil. Consumer advocate Ralph Nader and two associates helped jump-start the effort by negotiating the first of dozens of contracts with heating oil dealers who were willing to drop their prices in exchange for the group's volume of business. In the first winter, 400 low- and moderate-income families saved up to $250 each on their heating bills.

This group became Buyers Up, a member of Nader's umbrella group Public Citizen. By 1991, more than 18,000 Buyers Up member families had bought 39 million gallons of heating oil for $32 million at a savings of $6.2 million below market rates. Supported by five local offices, membership stretched from Richmond, Virginia, to Philadelphia. In 1995, the 9,500 participating Buyers Up members saved roughly $1.5 million on their heating oil bills.

Buyers Up owns no heating oil or trucks and makes no deliveries itself. It negotiates the cut-rate heating oil contracts with local dealers, who must agree to provide full delivery, credit, and furnace services at low rates. Buyers Up staffers monitor the companies' performance and publicize the program through the media and in talks to churches and neighborhood groups. Upon joining the program, a member is assigned to an oil dealer in his or her area who delivers the oil and provides furnace services at the negotiated rate. Over twenty-five such oil companies have subscribed to Buyers Up contracts.

Buyers Up is one of dozens of grassroots consumer energy cooperatives and other forms of nonprofit heating oil buying groups. Up and down the eastern seaboard, tens of thousands of consumers have banded together in neighborhood and citywide groups to purchase their heating oil, furnace cleaning services, and energy conservation supplies and installations. Discounts on these services range from 5 to 35 percent and can total hundreds of dollars of savings per family per year.

In the late 1970s and throughout the 1980s, energy co-ops emerged in cities such as greater Boston, New York, and Washington, D.C., where heating oil is a primary source of winter heating and utilities can consume 10 to 20 percent of household income. In Massachusetts, where most families heat with oil, five energy cooperatives covering most of the state provide heating oil to nearly 10,000 families. The New York Public Interest Research Group (NYPIRG), a student-run consumer advocacy organization, provides the 14,000 members of its Fuel Buyers Group with discounts on heating oil in greater New York City, Long Island, and metro Albany. Smaller groups operate in Philadelphia and Baltimore.

Although organized somewhat differently, the groups operate similarly to Buyers Up by contracting with existing dealers who trade lower prices for higher volume. All of the groups fund their operations through annual membership fees ranging from $10 in Boston to $25 in New York, and receipt of several cents per gallon of oil bought by members. Buyers Up has supported a full-time staff of twenty, published a newsletter containing energy saving and safety tips, and experimented with energy conservation installation and indoor air quality programs. In addition, other groups, such as the Boston Oil Consumers Alliance and Ecological Innovations, also in Boston, provide innovative energy conservation programs, which include discounts on products and installation.

These groups also give voice to their communities. Many groups advocate on behalf of their members before town meetings, state legislatures, and Congress. Through investigative reports, legislative testimony, and press conferences, Buyers Up has publicly exposed costly heating oil and gasoline pricing scams, opposed cuts in energy assistance for the poor, publicized the hazards of indoor air pollution, and encouraged the Environmental Protection Agency to improve oversight of the radon testing and mitigation industry. Its quarterly newsletter, *Buyers Up News*, informs about home safety, energy conservation, and current policy issues. The newsletter regularly includes directories to cooperatives, nonprofit service organizations, and other energy groups.

— Jason B. Adkins

See also

Cooperatives, Consumer; Public Citizen.

Readings

Giese, William, and Bertha Kainen (1988). "Your Home: Heating Bargains." *Changing Times*. 42 (5): 20–22.

Sinclair, Molly (1983). "Nader Forms Local Group To Sell Heating Oil at Bargain Prices." *Washington Post*. (December 8): C3.

Ethnic Minorities as Consumers

Ethnic minorities represent groups of consumers with several distinctive characteristics. For many, their skin color and other physical traits mark them as different. For many, their lack of fluency in conventional English may constrain their full participation in the marketplace and increase the risks of this participation. And for many, a lack of financial resources may limit their ability to purchase certain products and shop around for all goods and services.

While the entry Immigrants as Consumers addresses some of these issues, it focuses attention on Asian and Hispanic consumers. Yet, African-American consumers also deserve attention. Among ethnic minorities, they have a skin color that differs the most from that of the white majority. Also, most African Americans not only grew up in the United States but also come from families that have lived in this country for many generations. Accordingly, this entry will focus on African-American consumers, although many of their experiences and problems apply to other ethnic groups as well.

The major challenge in addressing the topic of African-American consumers is the difficulty in isolating the influence of their economic characteristics from that of race. This dilemma is complicated by the fact that, as a group, African Americans have always been less affluent than whites. While African-American–white earning ratios have narrowed over the past fifty years, these ratios still differ considerably. For all workers, this ratio was about 40 percent in 1939. By 1980, this ratio had grown to 85 percent and, over the next decade, remained at this general level.

Despite this difficulty in separating the effects of the economic and racial characteristics of African-American consumers, some research does so successfully. One of the most recent and convincing studies was prepared by Janet Wagner and Horacio Soberon-Ferrer. Their research attempted to isolate the influence of race from that of other variables possibly affecting consumption. After noting that African-American households have consistently spent a smaller proportion of their budgets on food and automobile transportation, and larger proportions on clothing, personal care, nonautomobile transportation, and alcoholic beverages than have whites, the analysis suggests that these differences may reflect nonracial socioeconomic or demographic variables.

This research cites other research indicating that the clothing consumption of African Americans may reflect values of their African ancestry such as affect, communalism, and expressive individualism. It also notes other research suggesting that African-American consumers may be less likely to spend more than other households for food at home, and less on food outside the home, because of lack of transportation and the existence of discrimination. It then tested these hypotheses and found that, while the effect of ethnicity was small, it was nevertheless significant.

Unique Consumer Problems

African Americans experience some consumer problems more frequently than do the rest of the U.S. population. They have more difficulty than whites in gaining access to many goods and services. When they do gain access, they are more likely than whites to face higher prices and lower quality.

The lack of access appears to reflect factors related both to sellers and to African-American consumers. Sellers may be reluctant to locate retail outlets in predominantly African-American neighborhoods because of their perception that these areas or individual consumers are associated with higher costs (e.g., crime or fraud) or because of a prejudiced desire to avoid physical contact with African Americans. Research has revealed that, in general, these communities are "underbanked," with some being served by no banking institutions, only by alternative financial service providers such as pawnshops and check-cashing outlets. Other research has found that, compared to more affluent areas, these communities are served by relatively few supermarkets.

An absence of important services not only makes shopping less convenient for residents but also increases their costs. Pawnshops charge relatively high loan rates while check-cashers assess fees that are usually much higher than those levied by banks and thrifts. Small grocers and convenience stores patronized by many inner-city residents usually charge higher prices than do supermarkets.

Similarly, sellers may be averse to selling housing to African Americans outside predominantly African-American neighborhoods. The most extensive research on this type of discrimination involves housing and mortgage loans. Many studies during the 1960s and early 1970s documented the reluctance of real estate agents to show African Americans properties in white communities. (In the same period, some whites complained about "blockbusting" real estate agents who sold one house on a block to an African-American buyer so that they could buy up other houses at low prices, then resell them to African Americans seeking to escape low-income neighborhoods.) While the research indicates that overt discrimination of this type has diminished, the segregated character of many communities suggests that it still persists.

Research also has revealed that mortgage lenders have discriminated against African Americans by denying them mortgages. In fact, it was alleged by many that some lenders have "redlined" whole areas, refusing to make mortgage loans available to all residents. A more subtle form of this discrimination involved lenders making it more difficult for blacks to obtain a mortgage by demanding high down payments, charging high interest rates, and restricting the length of the loan. To address this issue, Congress in 1977 passed the Community Reinvestment Act (CRA).

This law requires all lenders to demonstrate that they are pursuing affirmative actions to make available mortgage credit to low- and moderate-income communities. Subsequent research suggests that this law has reduced, but not eradicated, discrimination by mortgage lenders.

In addition to documented discrimination, there are perceptions of unequal treatment. In one survey, African Americans were far more likely than whites to think that they were unfairly overcharged for goods and that they were sold spoiled or inferior goods. Interestingly, however, the same survey indicated that African Americans were no more likely than whites to say that they were treated disrespectfully in stores.

The consumer problems of African-American consumers, however, sometimes reflect the characteristics of this population. The most important is their economic condition. If they have low incomes or unstable job histories, they are more likely than others to be denied credit. They also are more likely to live in inner-city areas where, according to studies such as David Caplovitz's *The Poor Pay More,* retailers may be more likely than in other areas to employ exploitive practices. The fact that low-income African Americans are less likely than others to own a car further limits their shopping opportunities.

Consumer Activism

One observation by many in the consumer movement is that relatively few African Americans have participated. That seems especially true of advocacy groups. Apart from consumer leaders such as Florence Rice of the Harlem Consumer Education Council, Regene Mitchell of the Consumer Federation of California, and Solomon Harge of Cleveland's Consumer Protection Association, there are few African Americans who have led well-established consumer organizations. But this observation does not hold for consumer leaders in government, especially federal agencies. From Alex Grant at the Food and Drug Administration, to Edith Barksdale Sloan at the Consumer Product Safety Commission, to Bonnie Guiton at the U.S. Office of Consumer Affairs, there have been dozens of African Americans who have held influential government consumer offices.

One can only speculate on the reasons for the lack of African-American consumer activism in the nonprofit sector. Some have suggested that, as a predominantly middle-class phenomenon, the consumer movement has held limited appeal historically to African Americans, who were more likely to have low to moderate incomes, or were committed to serving the needs of disadvantaged groups. Some have also observed that African-American activists were far more likely to be recruited to the civil rights movement than to the consumer movement. (It is significant that, in recent times, the civil rights movement preceded and helped inspire the consumer movement.)

Much of the African-American participation in the consumer movement has been in the Consumers Education and Protective Association (CEPA) and groups it inspired. Most members and leaders of this aggressive advocacy group have been African Americans from North Philadelphia. CEPA helped inspire other African-American activists such as Florence Rice. Rice founded the Harlem Consumer Education Council in 1967 for the purpose of disseminating consumer education information to "combat the economic exploitation suffered by Harlem consumers." For nearly thirty years, the council has organized conferences, boycotts, and pickets to protect unfair practices and educate consumers about how to protect themselves. For a time, Rice served on the board of CEPA.

CEPA also inspired Solomon Harge to organize Cleveland's Consumer Protection Association. In 1979, Harge established a complaint-handling organization that picketed a local car dealer. Over the years, it evolved into a low-income consumer assistance center—supported financially mainly by United Way—which employed counselors to help low-income citizens resolve problems including utility shut-offs. Cleveland also was the site of another predominantly African-American consumer organization, the East Side Chapter of Cleveland Consumer Action (CCA). Affiliated during its first year (1970–1971) with CEPA, for more than twenty-five years this CCA chapter has been meeting weekly in the East Cleveland Public Library to hear and work on individual consumer complaints. In Detroit, Alberta Tinsley-Williams founded and led the Coalition against Billboard Advertising of Alcohol and Tobacco.

Consumer activists have used the documentation of discrimination against African-American consumers to persuade Congress to pass legislation remedying these abuses, especially in the credit area. The Community Reinvestment Act and Equal Credit Opportunity Act are the most important statutes designed to reduce racial discrimination in the marketplace.

— Stephen Brobeck

See also

Community Reinvestment; Consumers Education and Protective Association; Low-Income Consumers; State and Local Consumer Organizations.

Readings

Simpson, George Eaton, and J. Milton Yinger (1985). *Racial and Cultural Minorities: An Analysis of Prejudice and Discrimination*. New York: Plenum Press.

Wagner, Janet, and Horacio Soberon-Ferrer (1990). "The Effect of Ethnicity on Selected Household Expenditures." *The Social Science Journal*. 27 (2): 181–198.

European Union, Consumer Policy in the

Consumer policy in the European Union (EU) developed later than in most of the EU's member states because it lacked a sufficient legal basis: the European Economic Community (EEC) Treaty of 1957 provided for almost no competence in this sector. This lack of attention reflected the facts that consumer organizations during the 1950s and 1960s were not strong enough to enforce their demands and that the six founding members of the original EEC—Belgium, France, Germany, Italy, Luxembourg, and the Netherlands—viewed consumer policy as of secondary importance.

Legal Basis

As a belated response to the 1962 declaration of consumer rights by President John F. Kennedy in the United States, in 1975 the Council of Ministers of the EEC adopted, following a proposal of the European Commission, a "Preliminary Program for Consumer Protection and Information." The program included a declaration of five fundamental consumer rights: protection of health and safety, protection of economic interests, redress, information and education, and representation.

After 1975, these five rights were considered the Consumer Charter of the Community. Although the declaration's direct effects on the Community's consumer policy should not be overestimated, it served as a guideline for several national consumer legislation projects, such as the Spanish consumer protection law of 1982. In the Community itself, a department dealing with consumer affairs was set up in one of the existing directorate generals.

In 1981, 1985, 1986, and 1987, additional consumer policy programs were adopted, and by 1989, the Community started the practice of three-year action plans in this field. In the meantime, the Single European Act of 1985, which paved the way for a unified market, provided clear authority for the European Commission (the "government" of what was then called the EC) to take actions in the field of consumer policy that were important for the completion of the Single Market.

The 1992 Maastricht Treaty, which transformed the Community into today's EU, included a provision in Article 129a that entitles the European Commission to legal and other activities to ensure a high level of consumer protection in the fields of health and safety, protection of economic interests, and information and education—three of the five fundamental consumer rights. Following the "principle of subsidiarity," EU consumer protection legislation is limited to cases where the agreed upon level of protection cannot be reached better by national measures. Consequently, since the signing of the treaty, the commission has been cautious in promoting new consumer legislation, concentrating its efforts only on the most important issues.

Consumer Institutions of the EU

Five institutions deal with consumer affairs. The first three are organs of the EU according to the Union Treaty. One is the European Parliament (EP), especially its Committee on Environment, Public Health and Consumer Affairs. The EP has always played an important role in consumer legislation, proposing many amendments to the commission's proposals for directives (to be transformed into national laws) or decrees (being immediately effective in all member states). Most of these amendments have been in the interest of consumers. Very important for the standing of consumer policy in the EU was also the continuous and successful struggle of the EP for the defense of the commission's consumer budget against repeated attempts by the Council of Ministers to reduce it.

A second body is the Economic and Social Committee (ECOSOC), a body of the EU established by Article 193 of the EEC Treaty. Its function is to give advice to the commission and the Council of Ministers on economic and social questions. It must be consulted whenever legislative measures in these fields are being planned by the commission (which has the exclusive right to propose such measures). A subcommittee of the ECOSOC deals with environment, health, and consumer affairs.

Although the ECOSOC as a specific EU body has received much attention in discussions of the EU's formal structure, its importance for consumer legislation is limited since it tends to take positions similar to those of the commission. After the establishment of the Consumers Consultative Council (CCC) in 1990, the importance of the ECOSOC as a voice for consumers decreased further.

A Commissioner for Consumer Affairs took a place at the commission's table for the first time in 1989, strengthening the importance of consumer questions by his or her mere presence. Fortunately, the first commissioner, Karel van Miert, a Belgian socialist, played a decisive role in giving direction to European consumer policy. He was followed from 1993 to 1994 by Christiane Scrivener, a French conservative, and in February 1995, by Emma Bonino, an Italian radical. The commissioners were not exclusively responsible for consumer affairs. Commissioner van Miert also dealt with traffic policy, Commissioner Scrivener with taxation, and Commissioner Bonino with fisheries policy.

Directorate General XXIV is the authority within the commission dealing with all questions of consumer policy. It developed out of the former Consumer Policy Service (CPS), which was established by Commissioner van Miert in 1989. In March 1995, the CPS was upgraded to a directorate general (DG), a measure that considerably improved the standing of consumer policy in the EU. The main tasks of the DG XXIV are to assess, from the consumer's point of view, all the measures of the commission that touch upon consumer interests; to formulate at least some of the measures that are designed to protect consumer interests; to administer the EU's consumer budget; and to organize consumer information campaigns. In 1997, the European Commission changed the name of DG XXIV from "Consumer Policy" to "Consumer Policy and Consumer Health Protection," thereby emphasizing the directorate general's role in protecting health in the European Union, especially with respect to food.

The Consumer Committee was established in June 1995 by the commission. It succeeded the CCC, which had been established by Commissioner van Miert in 1990. The council, in turn, was preceded by a committee with the same acronym (CCC), which had existed since 1973 and was charged with advising the commission. While the original transformation from a committee to a council increased its status considerably since there are hundreds of committees in the EU but only a few councils, the latest reform of this advisory body reduced its importance. This change resulted from dissatisfaction by CCC member organizations, especially the Bureau Européen des Unions de Consommateurs (BEUC), with the participation of unions and consumer cooperatives.

The committee has several main tasks. One is to elaborate and adopt, at the commission's request, opinions on draft directives. In 1992, the year of the CCC's greatest activity, it dealt with twenty-six cases. Much of the work of the committee is conducted by working groups, with up to twelve members, that prepare opinions.

The committee also has the right to take initiatives. The CCC used this right in order to make pronouncements on crucial topics in European consumer policy and to propose structural changes in consumer representation. For instance, it initiated the establishment of a consumer council on standardization (Association pour la Normalisation Européenne des Consommateurs, ANEC).

The committee also has the task of fostering information exchange among the member organizations and appoints consumer representatives to sectoral committees of the EU. Among the 200 such EU committees, about fifty deal with consumer matters. The committee nominates the delegates and supervises their work.

As a consequence of the 1995 "reform," the Consumer Committee was downsized from the CCC's forty-five members to only twenty. There is one national delegate from each of the fifteen member states, to be proposed by the leading national consumer organization, plus five additional members representing European-wide consumer organizations like BEUC.

While the future direction of the Consumer Committee is not clear, the importance of its predecessor, the CCC, lay in the fact that it was the only institution entitled to speak for all European consumers. Given that the commission has accepted approximately 30 percent of the committee's proposed amendments, its work has been relatively successful.

Independent European Consumer Organizations

The most important of the independent European consumer organizations that participate in EU affairs is BEUC, which is discussed in its own entry. There are several remaining organizations of importance. One is the European Trade Unions Council (ETUC) and its consumer policy department, Euro C. This department represents especially consumer organizations established and inspired by labor unions. Such organizations play an important role in Italy, France, Portugal, and some other countries, but in northern Europe they are ineffective or nonexistent.

The Confédération des Organisations Familiales auprès de la Communauté Européenne (COFACE) is an association of family organizations. These organizations are active in almost all member states of the EU and deal with many consumer issues.

Eurocoop represents the interests of Europe's consumer cooperatives. These consumer cooperatives are still strong in Italy (with 7 million member households), the United Kingdom, and the Scandinavian countries; in other European countries, co-ops have become nearly indistinguishable from corporations.

A final example of an independent, European-wide organization is the Institut Européen Interrégional de la Consommation (IEIC). This organization represents the regional consumer organizations and institutes, especially those involved in providing information and advice on trans-border shopping.

Consumer Policy Advances

With the appointment of a Commissioner for Consumer Affairs and the establishment of a directorate general, consumer policy gained considerable status in the EU. For example, the European Commission realized that the Single Market would be accepted by Europeans only if it were seen as useful to ordinary citizens. As a result, they added consumer rights to the four freedoms upon which the Single Market is based (freedom of movement for people, merchandise, capital, and services).

Apart from including three of the five fundamental consumer rights—protection of health and safety, protection of economic interests, and information and education—in the Union Treaty, the commission tried to enforce consumer rights through the three-year action plans for consumer policy. The first of these plans was presented by Commissioner van Miert for the period 1990 to 1992. For the most part, both the first and the second plans were adopted by the commission.

Most European citizens do not realize that most of the progress that has been made in consumer protection is a result of European initiatives. In some countries, especially in southern Europe, consumer legislation is entirely of European origin. Even in more advanced countries like France, Germany, and the Netherlands, almost all new initiatives for consumer legislation during the 1980s came from Brussels and not from the national capitals.

For the completion of the Single Market, more than 100 legislative projects were necessary. In most cases, the EU decided against establishing entirely new, communitarian law, preferring to harmonize existing national legislation. Nevertheless, where national legislation did not exist, European law was imposed. Some of the most important European consumer protection laws—actual or proposed—deal with product liability (eliminating the burdensome task of proving negligence or fault on the part of the producer), product safety (aimed especially at products from countries with relatively weak safety standards and quality control in production), technical standards, distance selling via telephone or catalog, unfair contract terms, trans-border payments, guarantees, and consumer redress and access to justice in trans-border purchases.

— Lothar Maier

See also

Bureau Européen des Unions de Consommateurs; Transnational Consumer Protections.

Readings

Micklitz, Hans W., and Stephen Weatherill (1993). "Consumer Policy in the European Community: Before and After Maastricht." *Journal of Consumer Policy.* 16 (3–4): 285–322.

Orsini, Marie Antoinette (1988). "Consumer Policy and the European Economic Community (EEC)." In E. Scott Maynes, ed. *The Frontier of Research in the Consumer Interest.* Columbia, MO: American Council on Consumer Interests. 510–521.

F

Fair Trade Laws

See Resale Price Maintenance.

Federal Consumer Advisory Bodies

The Consumer Advisory Council established by President John F. Kennedy in 1962 was not the first effort to bring the consumer interest into the federal government. In 1933, the National Recovery Administration (NRA) created the first federal consumer advisory agency, the Consumer's Advisory Board. President Franklin D. Roosevelt selected Mary Harriman Rumsey, a friend of the First Lady who was active in the National Consumers League, as chairperson. She was the daughter of railway magnate E. H. Harriman and sister of W. Averill Harriman.

Rumsey saw the board's job as representing the consumer on an equal basis with business, labor, and farmers. Gardiner C. Means, economic adviser to Secretary of Agriculture Henry Wallace, who had created a Consumers Counsel in the Agricultural Adjustment Administration (AAA), also served on the Consumer's Advisory Board. He prepared the two documents that spelled out the need to include consumers in setting economic policy: *NRA, AAA and the Making of Industrial Policy* and *The Consumer and the New Deal*. The latter addressed the difference between the consumer interest and the public interest. It attempted to "interpret for the public, in the context of an economy where market coordination had broken down and administrative decision-making was predominant, why and in what sense consumer representation was part of the structure of agencies trying to bring industry and agriculture back on track."

Consumer's Advisory Board members and staff, who had academic backgrounds, had a more sophisticated understanding of the economy than did representatives of either industry or labor. Leon Henderson, an economist at the Russell Sage Foundation, and Paul H. Douglas, economics professor at the University of Chicago, both served on the board.

Douglas, in his memoir *In the Fullness of Time* (1971), described some of the activities of the board. Rumsey asked him to set up a chain of local consumers' councils throughout the country. He remembers organizing nearly 100 of these bodies, which helped generate public interest in economic problems. But, when the NRA was declared unconstitutional in 1935, these local councils were shut down. So was the Consumer's Advisory Board.

The AAA's Consumer Counsel was more effective than the board. It functioned exclusively through its staff, which included the Bureau of Home Economics. Donald Montgomery and Mary Taylor developed public awareness of consumers' role and built a direct information service to the consuming public. After the Supreme Court declared the Agricultural Adjustment Act unconstitutional in 1935, the counsel continued within the department but with diminished support. Its activities included publishing a monthly *Consumers Guide* (until 1947) and developing a weekly radio program.

Congress created the Bituminous Coal Consumer Council in the Bituminous Coal Act of 1936. The act was to aid a sick industry by putting a floor under prices and limiting cutthroat competition. Congress created the consumer council to help ensure that this assistance to the industry did not harm consumers. It also made the council responsible to Congress and gave it a larger budget than other consumer agencies had had. The council functioned until the act expired during World War II.

The National Defense Advisory Commission established in May 1940 had commissioners representing business, industry, labor, agriculture, transportation, and consumers. With the other commissioners, Harriet Elliott, the consumer commissioner, advised the Defense Department on all aspects of the defense program. But according to a memo sent by President Roosevelt, she was to focus especially on health, child welfare, and nutrition. The Agriculture Department accepted her leadership and called a nutrition conference. The Children's Bureau and other welfare agencies considered her to be a coordinator of their activities. The surgeon general, however, said that the health field "would not accept coordination, leadership, or anything else from a lay civilian, least of all from a woman."

When the defense program converted into a war program, the Defense Advisory Commission was replaced by a series of administrative agencies for carrying on wartime production and distribution. The price and consumer offices were combined into the Office of Price Administration.

In 1943, Chester Bowles, Office of Price Administration administrator, established a Consumer Advisory Committee. Esther Cole Franklin, a leader of the American Association of University Women, was named staff adviser. The committee intervened in price-fixing decisions with varying degrees of success. It focused on preserving product quality and availability. The committee continued functioning through the reconversion from a war- to a peacetime economy, trying to prevent the removal of price controls that might cause sudden inflation. It failed in this attempt.

The Employment Act of 1946 created the Council of Economic Advisers, which had responsibility for consulting with business, labor, farmers, and consumers. Some of those who had served on the Office of Price Administration Consumer Advisory Committee asked the council to appoint a Consumer Advisory Committee. Their advice was not accepted. The group did form a committee representing national organizations that occasionally met with a Council of Economic Advisers staff member.

In a 1960 Bronx campaign speech, John F. Kennedy promised, if elected, to appoint a consumer counsel. Fourteen months after his inauguration, President Kennedy delivered the first presidential message to Congress relating to consumer affairs. In it he set forth consumers' rights to safety, to be informed, to choose, and to be heard; he also announced that he would establish a Consumer Advisory Council and that the head of each federal agency whose work affected consumers would name a liaison officer with the council. Kennedy directed the council to advise, monitor, and maintain relations with government agencies to assist them in serving consumers more effectively.

The president named Helen Canoyer, dean of Cornell's College of Home Economics, chair; others appointed were Helen Nelson and Persia Campbell, who served as Consumer Counsel for California and New York respectively; Walter Mondale, Minnesota's Attorney General and chair of the Association of States' Attorneys General Consumer Committee; Colston Warne, Consumers Union's president; Percy Lee, former League of Women Voters' president; David Angevine, Cooperative League of the USA's information director; Edward Lewis, of the Urban League; Caroline Ware, New Deal consumer activist; Richard Morse, Kansas State University family economics professor; Steven DeBrul, financier; and Sylvia Porter, newspaper columnist. She later resigned, feeling it inappropriate for a member of the press to serve in a government office.

While declaring the council independent of other federal agencies, Kennedy attached it to the Council of Economic Advisers. Somewhat confused, the Consumer Advisory Council and Council of Economic Advisers agreed that the consumer council would speak through the Council of Economic Advisers both to the president and to the public, and work directly with all federal agencies. Most of the council's work was with representatives of each of the ten departments and twelve independent agencies. The council listened, advised, encouraged, and criticized. It even faulted certain cabinet members for failing to include funds in their budget requests for projects that the council felt were important, and criticized the Food and Drug Administration for depending too much on industry self-regulation.

The council accomplished some of its work through subcommittees—standards, information, consumer representation, consumer credit, federal-state relations, coordination of federal consumer services, and economic expansion. Following enactment of truth in lending legislation, the council's credit subcommittee helped write regulations carrying congressional intent into effect.

The president sought the council's support of various pieces of legislation, including truth in lending and truth in packaging. He also asked the council's support of a tax cut, which was granted reluctantly by a vote of four to one, with one abstention and five absences.

Early on, the council recommended that the president appoint a consumer adviser who would report directly to him in the White House. In 1964, President Lyndon Johnson acted on this recommendation by naming Esther Peterson, then Assistant Secretary of Labor, as his special assistant for consumer affairs.

Soon after Kennedy's assassination, Johnson met with the council and renewed its mandate and its working relationships. Following his election in 1964, he appointed new council members, including two holdovers. At the end of his administration, the council was discontinued.

Among numerous suggestions, the council recommended that the president call a White House Consumer Conference. While this recommendation was not accepted, several national organizations recognized the need for such a conference and organized Consumer Assembly '66. From this conference, a year and one-half later, emerged the Consumer Federation of America.

— Erma B. Angevine

See also

Presidents and the Consumer Movement; U.S. Office of Consumer Affairs.

Readings

Campbell, Persia (1940). *Consumer Representation in the New Deal*. New York: Columbia University Press.

Executive Office of the President (1963). *Consumer Advisory Council: First Report*. Washington, DC: U.S. Government Printing Office.

Federal Reserve's Consumer and Community Affairs Programs

Since the late 1960s, the Federal Reserve has been involved in implementing a number of federal laws intended to protect consumers in credit and other financial transactions. Congress has assigned the Federal Reserve the duty of implementing these laws to ensure that consumers receive comprehensive information and fair treatment. Virtually all financial transactions involving consumers are covered by these consumer protection laws. Covered transactions include those involving charge and credit cards from financial institutions and retail establishments, automated teller machines, deposit accounts, automobile leases, and mortgages.

Section 18(f) of the Federal Trade Commission Act, 15 USC 57a(f), passed by Congress in early 1975, required that each of the federal banking agencies establish a separate division of consumer affairs to receive and take appropriate action on complaints dealing with unfair and deceptive acts and practices. At that time, the Federal Reserve established what is now known as the Division of Consumer and Community Affairs to handle its consumer affairs responsibilities. The Federal Reserve's responsibilities in this area include: writing and interpreting regulations to carry out the consumer protection laws; reviewing bank compliance with the regulations; responding to inquiries and complaints from the public; addressing issues of state and federal jurisdiction; testifying before Congress on consumer protection issues; and administering a community affairs program.

The first law—the Truth in Lending Act—was enacted almost thirty years ago. This legislation requires creditors to use a uniform way to reflect the cost of credit (the annual percentage rate, or APR) and to disclose credit terms to consumers. In addition, the law deals with rules on the issuance and unauthorized use of credit cards. The Federal Reserve also implements laws that: protect consumers against inaccurate credit reports (Fair Credit Reporting Act); establish rules on a consumer's liability for the unauthorized use of an ATM or other debit card (Electronic Funds Transfer Act); require institutions to disclose the cost and terms of lease transactions (Consumer Leasing Act); prohibit discrimination in credit transactions on such bases as gender, marital status, age, race, and religion (Equal Credit Opportunity Act); and encourage financial institutions to help meet the credit needs of their communities (Community Reinvestment Act).

The Federal Reserve writes regulations to implement these laws, which cover not only banks but also many businesses, including finance companies, mortgage brokers, retailers, and automobile dealers. The board also revises and updates its regulations to address new products, such as home equity lines of credit, adjustable-rate mortgages, and electronic banking; to implement legislative changes to existing laws; and to address problems encountered by consumers.

The Federal Reserve conducts a specialized examination program to ensure that financial institutions carry out the federal consumer protection laws. Its responsibilities for enforcement generally extend to state-chartered banks that are members of the Federal Reserve System. (Other federal regulators are responsible for examining bank and thrift institutions under their jurisdictions and for taking enforcement action.)

Each Federal Reserve Bank has specially trained examiners who regularly evaluate the performance of banks in its district. Examinations generally are conducted every eighteen months, but poorly rated banks are examined more frequently, and highly rated banks are examined every twenty-four months. The examiners review the bank's policies, procedures, consumer files, and other financial documents. They verify that disclosures are given in a timely and accurate fashion and that the bank has dedicated enough resources to ensure compliance.

The Federal Reserve operates a systemwide program to respond to inquiries and complaints from the public about consumer protection issues involving the policies and practices of financial institutions. Complaints involving state member banks are investigated, and complaints involving other institutions are referred to the appropriate regulatory agency. Special procedures are followed in investigating complaints alleging illegal lending discrimination.

Information on consumer inquiries and complaints is maintained in a database that alerts the Federal Reserve to potential problems at individual institutions and assists the division in carrying out its responsibilities, under the Federal Trade Commission Improvement Act, to identify potentially unfair or deceptive bank practices. Approximately 2,600 complaints are lodged annually with the Federal Reserve; about 1,200 of them are against state member banks.

In accordance with the Community Reinvestment Act (CRA), the Federal Reserve encourages banks to work with community organizations to promote local economic development. In the examination process, the Federal Reserve reviews a bank's efforts to meet the credit needs of its entire community, including low- and moderate-income neighborhoods, and gives it a separate rating for its compliance with the CRA. The Federal Reserve also takes an institution's performance under the CRA into account when deciding whether to approve an application for acquisition or merger. The public may protest the approval of an application on the basis of the institution's record in community reinvestment.

Each reserve bank has a community affairs officer who is familiar with the credit needs in the communities served by institutions in its district. The officer's responsibilities include fostering communication among banking institutions, government agencies, and community groups. Through newsletters and other publications, seminars, workshops, and conferences, the Federal Reserve provides information to financial institutions about economic initiatives in the private sector, public-private partnerships, and federal and state development programs. Staff members also work directly with individual bankers and community development representatives to promote community lending.

Since 1976, the Federal Reserve has been advised by a Consumer Advisory Council, whose members represent the interests of consumers, community groups, and creditors nationwide. Dozens of areas have been represented on the council over the years: state and local government offices responsible for consumer affairs matters; the credit union, banking, and retail industries; a wide range of academic disciplines from colleges and universities; and consumer and community organizations. The council is comprised of thirty members who serve three-year terms. The council meets three times a year at the Federal Reserve Board's central offices in Washington, D.C.; its meetings are open to the public.

— Maureen P. English

See also

Community Reinvestment; Credit Protections.

Readings

Board of Governors of the Federal Reserve System (1994). *The Federal Reserve System: Purposes and Functions.* Washington, DC: Board of Governors of the Federal Reserve System.

Eccles, George S. (1982). *The Politics of Banking.* Ch. 20. Salt Lake City: University of Utah Graduate School of Business.

Federal Trade Commission

Congress created the Federal Trade Commission (FTC) in 1915, by enacting the Federal Trade Commission Act at the urging of President Woodrow Wilson. The original law directed the agency to stop unfair methods of competition in commerce. Its purpose was to protect consumers, as well as honest competitors, from unscrupulous business practices. (In 1938, Congress passed the Wheeler-Lea Amendment to the FTC Act, which made explicit the agency's mandate to protect consumers from unfair or deceptive acts or practices.) Then as today, Congress wanted the agency to deal both with marketing practices and with the kinds of behavior that fall within the body of law known as antitrust. Antitrust laws and doctrines are meant to stop business behavior that can eliminate or reduce competition among businesses.

Structure and Leaders

The FTC is headed by a body of five commissioners who are appointed by the president and confirmed by the Senate. One commissioner is designated by the president as chair. The chairman acts as the administrative head of the agency. The president can at any time change the designation of chair among sitting commissioners, or designate a newly appointed commissioner as chair. (Until 1950, the chairpersonship rotated among commissioners, first approximately every six months, then on an annual basis.)

Commissioners hold office for a seven-year term (or the remaining portion of a seven-year term, if they are appointed to complete a partially served term). Although some commissioners serve a full term and more, it is not unusual for a commissioner to serve for less than seven years. By law, no more than three commissioners can be members of the same political party.

The chair appoints key staff members and makes important administrative decisions. The extent of consultation and the collegiality of decision-making with the other four commissioners about staff appointments and agency administration matters have varied among chairs. A majority vote among the sitting commissioners is required to make legal decisions, such as charging a business with having violated the law or deciding that a violation of the law has occurred.

Congress created the agency to be independent of political influence from either the executive or legislative branch. Federal case law, including a U.S. Supreme Court decision, confirms the intended insulation of the agency from politics. As a matter of law, this scheme has worked. However, as a practical matter, both the president and Congress significantly affect the agency's work. The executive branch sets the philosophical direction of the agency through the presidential power of commissioner appointments. And, through the congressional powers of annual budgetary appropriations and legislative oversight, Congress can set directions for and limit the agency's exercise of its statutory authority.

The agency is divided, in addition to the five commissioner's offices, into three operating bureaus, an executive director's office, and several other support-function offices. It also has ten regional offices, located in cities in different regions of the country, that conduct investigations and enforce the law.

The operating bureaus are the Bureau of Consumer Protection, the Bureau of Competition, and the Bureau of Economics. The bureaus are each headed by a bureau director appointed by the chair.

The more than seventy-five people who have served as Federal Trade Commissioners since 1915 have included many notable members of the private legal establishment, a distinguished federal appeals judge, and at least three who subsequently served in presidential cabinet positions. A number of commissioners have been appointed as a political reward.

The current chairman of the FTC is Robert Pitofsky. Pitofsky, a Democrat, previously served at the Federal Trade Commission as the Bureau of Consumer Protection's director under Chairman Miles W. Kirkpatrick in the 1970s. Later, he was a commissioner of the agency, under an appointment by President Carter, for almost three years from 1978 to 1981. After leaving the agency, he served as dean and a professor of law of the Georgetown University Law Center, Washington, D.C., and practiced antitrust law in Washington. The term of Pitofsky's commissionership expires in 2001.

The previous chair was Janet D. Steiger, a Republican appointed by President Bush in 1989. She had previously been chair of the U.S. Postal Rate Commission. She is a moderate who took the agency back toward the center of the "activism" spectrum, in comparison with her two immediate Republican predecessors. Her background is in business rather than law. This continued a pattern of nonlawyer chairs and commissioners that started in the early 1980s. Her term expired in 1995.

The FTC is funded primarily by an annual appropriation of Congress. Its fiscal year 1995 budget was about $100 million.

Functions

The three operating bureaus carry out the statutory directive of Congress to enforce the FTC Act and the various other consumer protection and antitrust laws that Congress has added to the agency's list of responsibilities since 1915. The agency can regulate business practices in several ways. It can issue informal guidelines. These guidelines describe certain circumstances under which the agency may charge that a company has violated the law.

The agency also can issue formal rules that define requirements of law. Rules must be established through a rulemaking procedure that is partly like an administrative trial and partly like a legislative hearing. Once a rule becomes final and is published, the agency can then charge a business with violating the law if the business violates the rule. Rules are used when the commission finds that a practice is widespread in an industry.

Most often, however, the agency challenges the practices of an individual business firm. The agency and the business involved can settle the agency's charges without a contest, or the company can fight the charges. When the company does not choose to contest the charges, it consents to an "order," which states both the commission's charges and the future course of conduct to which the company has agreed upon as a condition of settling the case.

If the company does not settle by consent, the FTC issues formal charges alleging that the company has broken the law. In this case, the matter is subjected to a trial-like proceeding that tries issues of fact and hears arguments about the law. The formal agency document that names the company and the practices challenged by the agency as unlawful is called a "complaint."

Under some of the statutes the agency enforces, the trial in contested cases takes place before one of the agency's administrative law judges. Under others, the proceeding takes place in an actual U.S. District Court trial. After an administrative law judge decides a case, either the business involved, the agency's own lawyers, or both may appeal all or any part of the decision to the commissioners, sitting as a body. When a business loses an appeal to the commissioners, the commissioners' decision may in turn be appealed by the company to a U.S. Court of Appeals.

Many agency decisions have been ruled on by the federal courts in this process of judicial review. Over the years, by their generally very broad reading of the agency's powers, the courts' rulings have played an important role in the development of FTC legal doctrine.

The Bureau of Consumer Protection has a wide variety of enforcement responsibilities under the FTC Act and various other acts. These include authority over the following business practices: advertising, marketing practices, credit practices (by creditors not regulated by bank-regulatory agencies), and service industry practices.

The list of business practices that the agency regulates to assure consumer protection is extensive and touches on many aspects of the marketplace. It is possible here only to provide a partial catalog. Its advertising regulation deals with such issues as general advertising claims, tobacco and alcohol ads, food and nutritional claims, product performance and energy-saving claims, environmental claims for products, "infomercials," and many other product advertising practices. Marketing practices that have come under the FTC's scrutiny include warranty practices (the agency enforces the Magnuson-Moss Act's warranty requirements), used car sales, door-to-door selling, book and record club sales, commercial funeral service practices, telemarketing, "900-number" services, mail and telephone orders, unordered merchandise, the labeling of various products, and deceptions involving defective products. The agency also enforces several federal consumer credit protection laws with respect to lenders not regulated by the bank-regulatory agencies: the Fair Credit Reporting Act, the Truth in Lending Act, the Fair Credit Billing Act, the Electronic Funds Transfer Act, the Consumer Leasing Act, and the Fair Debt Collection Practices Act. It also has issued its own credit practices rules to restrict creditors' unfair practices. And it can obtain financial restitution for defrauded consumers.

The Bureau of Competition is responsible for antitrust enforcement. Antitrust activities involve enforcement of the antitrust laws, including the nation's primary antitrust law, the Sherman Act. The agency shares this responsibility with other federal agencies, principally the U.S. Department of Justice, whose Antitrust Division is the other major antitrust enforcement arm of the federal government. The Justice Department handles all criminal antitrust cases, but divides with the FTC responsibility for potentially anticompetitive practices in which only civil sanctions are sought by the government. In recent times, the FTC's antitrust scrutiny has been mainly on the professions, especially health care service providers. The FTC also enforces the Clayton Act (another antitrust law) and the Robinson-Patman Act (designed to protect the competitive position of smaller businesses). And, under the Hart-Scott-Rodino Act, it receives required notification of and reviews mergers large enough that they may affect competition. This law gives the agency time to decide whether to challenge a large corporate merger before it takes place and becomes difficult or impossible to undo.

The FTC's jurisdiction over anticompetitive practices, however, is greater than the formal provisions of the Sherman Act and the other antitrust laws. Its authority under the original FTC Act to prevent "unfair methods of competition" has been broadly interpreted to cover anticompetitive acts or practices that technically do not violate specific antitrust provisions.

The Bureau of Economics evaluates economic issues related to the work of the other two bureaus, provides them with support in investigations and law enforcement activities, studies the effects of regulations, and makes independent studies of economic issues related to the agency's responsibilities. This bureau also can perform studies at the request of Congress.

History

The FTC has played a key and often controversial role in the history of U.S. consumer markets. Its approach to its statutory duties has fluctuated widely. During the 1960s, when it engaged in low-key, noncontroversial law enforcement, it was characterized as "the little old lady of Pennsylvania Avenue." Then, when it began aggressively to regulate the practices of large, national advertisers during the 1970s, it was generally characterized as rejuvenated. And by the late 1970s, when it began to address some social aspects of product marketing such as advertising during children's television programming hours, it was depicted as "the national nanny."

For several decades after it was established, the agency approached consumer protection on a case-by-case basis. It challenged blatant marketplace frauds and deceptive advertising practices. By the 1960s, however, the agency was addressing only small, trivial matters while ignoring the marketing practices of large, national business corporations. It also was not well managed. Much of this condition was attributable to the administration of Chairman Paul Rand Dixon. He had been a high-ranking congressional staffer who was appointed in 1961 by President Kennedy at the request of Kennedy's former political rival, Senator Estes Kefauver (D-TN). Another contributing factor was a lack of effective congressional oversight. A report issued by consumer activist Ralph Nader in 1970 charged the agency with sloth and neglect of consumers' interests. The report said that Dixon, who chaired the agency for almost nine years, ran the agency like a rural Tennessee courthouse, staffing it with political cronies and mediocre professional staff. A second report by a special committee of the American Bar Association essentially confirmed Nader's findings. Soon after, President Richard Nixon appointed the chair of that bar committee, Miles W. Kirkpatrick, a respected Philadelphia trade regulation lawyer, to chair the commission.

Kirkpatrick took office in late 1970 and ran the agency for almost two and one-half years. Under his leadership, the FTC entered into one of its most aggressive regulatory eras, challenging a broad spectrum of advertising and marketing practices by major national advertisers. No longer did it allocate resources primarily to small companies engaged in practices with little national impact.

In this period, the FTC developed two important new standards about advertising. One was the advertising substantiation doctrine. This standard makes it deceptive for a company to advertise a claim about a product's performance unless it has existing, reasonable proof that the claim is true. The other new standard was the corrective advertising doctrine. Under this doctrine, in cases where a false or deceptive ad claim is particularly memorable to consumers, the agency may require new ads paid for by the advertiser that state the truth about the illegal claim.

These developments resulted in high public visibility for the agency and political resistance from the business community. When Kirkpatrick retired, President Nixon appointed as Kirkpatrick's two immediate successors Lewis A. Engman and then Calvin J. Collier, who cooled the political fires by reducing somewhat the high profile of the agency's actions. But they continued to focus agency resources on significant issues.

The most controversial era in modern times, however, was during the late 1970s. In 1977, President Jimmy Carter appointed Michael Pertschuk as FTC chair. As a high-level U.S. Senate aide, he had been a driving force behind congressional enactment of many of the nation's new consumer protection laws during the 1960s and early 1970s. During Pertschuk's nearly four-year tenure as chair, the agency initiated a rulemaking proceeding aimed at regulating television advertising during programming for younger children. This proposal became a lightning rod for those who felt that the agency was increasingly expanding beyond questions of truth and consumer deception into issues of social values. The *Washington Post,* in criticizing this proposal, stated that the agency threatened to become "the national nanny." The political uproar over the children's television rule was amplified by business opposition to other agency-proposed rules. One of these proposals, which never became a final rule, sought to impose significant restrictions on food advertising claims. Another required that used car dealers post windshield stickers listing important information about the conditions of the automobiles they offered for sale to consumers.

The Pertschuk-led commission pursued these new rules in rapidly changing political circumstances. By 1980, Congress had become less tolerant of activist regulation of business practices. It killed the children's television rule and it pressured the agency to produce a scaled-down used car rule, which it then voted to eliminate through legislative action. This congressional veto eventually failed for constitutional reasons. But Congress had sent a clear message to the agency that aggressive regulation was dead.

There followed a period of agency focus on more traditional law enforcement against basic frauds by smaller businesses. For the following eight-year period, the agency was headed by two successive chairmen appointed by President Ronald Reagan: James C. Miller III and Daniel Oliver. Miller was an economist, the first nonlawyer to head the agency. He asked Congress for basic changes in the FTC Act. These alterations, intentionally, would have made it far more difficult for the agency to charge businesses with violating the law. Congress rejected most of Miller's proposals. But the Senate Commerce Committee, the more conservative of the agency's two congressional oversight committees, wrought a number of concessions from the agency. These changes limited its exercise of power without a need to amend the law. By the end of the Miller-Oliver era, the commission was considered by consumer activists, congressional critics, and several state attorneys general to be a do-nothing agency. The inactivism of the agency during this era fostered a hostile relationship between the agency and many of these state consumer protection officials. Some of them, acting under their own state consumer protection laws, brought charges against nationwide advertising and marketing practices by large national companies.

President George Bush's appointment of Janet D. Steiger as chair swung the pendulum back toward the middle. Steiger proved a shrewd diplomat. She made a point of repairing frayed relationships with state attorneys general. She worked to create an image of the agency as dedicated to its statutory responsibilities, without ever openly criticizing her two Republican predecessors for having failed to meet these responsibilities. And she increased the number of cases of national significance brought by the agency. At the same time, the era of her leadership was often characterized, by some critics, as insufficiently aggressive. They were particularly critical of the agency's decision not to challenge tobacco advertising practices that they claimed were directed at teenagers.

The FTC has had a significant impact on the American marketplace. It has played a major role in ending an era dominated by demonstrably phony advertising, quackery, and bunco marketing schemes from which consumers had little defense. While such practices still exist, they are now far from the norm. With the development of modern, electronic communications—first radio, then television, now the Internet—Americans increasingly have become exposed to advertising. And the social value and effects of modern advertising may be subject to serious debate. But relatively little of it contains objectively false representations. Perhaps the most persuasive evidence of the long-term effects of the FTC on business practices is that all fifty states now have "Little FTC Acts" as tools to deal with business practices in their own jurisdictions.

— Mark Silbergeld

See also

Advertising Regulation; Antitrust Protections; Deceptive, Unfair, and Unconscionable Sales Practices; Infomercial Regulation; State Attorneys General; Telemarketing Regulation; Warranty Protections.

Readings

Harris, Richard A., and Sidney M. Milkus (1989). *The Politics of Regulatory Change: A Tale of Two Agencies.* New York: Oxford University Press.

Wagner, Susan (1971). *The Federal Trade Commission.* New York: Praeger Publishers.

Finnish Consumer Movement

The Finnish consumer movement derives from three different sources: women's organizations, the cooperative movement, and home economics. From those sources emerged government bodies involved directly in consumer protection and a private, national consumer advocacy organization.

Origins

Finnish women's organizations are grassroots organizations, founded around the turn of the twentieth century, to promote the political interests of women. The first of these organizations, founded in 1884, was Suomen Naisyhdistys (Finnish Association for Women). The first chairpersons of Suomen Naisyhdistys were Elisabeth Löfgren and Alexandra Gripenberg, both members of the Finnish nationalist movement, Fennomania. Another women's organization, Naisasialiitto Unioni (Women's Union), was founded in 1892, and the Sivistystä Kodeille-yhdistys (Education for Homes Society, later called the Martha Organization) was established in 1899. The Martha Organization eventually developed into a mass organization. Lucina Hagman and Alli Nissinen were the most important figures in the organization's first decades.

The Martha Organization emphasized advising and educating women about domestic issues, whereas the other two organizations focused on gender issues. Nevertheless, the three groups cooperated in organizing domestic advising at the local level until just before the outbreak of the Finnish Civil War in 1918. The Martha Organization published the journal *Emäntälehti* (Housewife's Journal) beginning in 1902. Its activities during the first decades emphasized the importance of home, family, and full-time housewifery, as well as Christian values and practices.

The turn of the century was a time of numerous popular movements, including temperance societies and women's organizations. Based on an ideology of emancipation with the help of enlightenment, these popular movements were a reaction to efforts to "Russify" Finland and decrease its autonomy. Also, political parties formed around the turn of the century created special divisions for women. The Suomen Sosialidemokraattinen Naisliitto (Finnish Social Democratic Women's League), founded in 1900, was particularly active in addressing household issues relevant to women. Nevertheless, the number of the league's active members remained fairly low. Miina Sillanpää, a member of the Finnish Parliament and a Minister, was the strong leader of the Social Democratic women's movement.

Gradually during the 1920s and 1930s, the women's division of the Finnish agricultural societies became a women's mass organization, adopting the name Maatalousnaiset (Agricultural Women) in 1933 and competing with the Martha Organization. Maatalousnaiset was originally composed of female members of agricultural societies. The organization's membership increased from 19,500 in 1927 to 59,300 in 1937, while the membership of the Martha Organization rose from 24,200 in 1927 to 57,800 in 1937. Both organizations received state funding for providing advice to homemakers. Other popular organizations offering domestic advice were the Pienviljelijäin Liitto (Smallholders League), founded in 1910, and Pienviljelijäin Keskusliitto (Small Farmers Central League), founded in 1922.

The second source of the Finnish consumer movement is consumer cooperatives. The Finnish cooperative movement developed around the turn of the century with the organization of agricultural production cooperatives. Its spokesman and founder, Professor Hannes Gebhard, was an important figure in the organization of Finnish agricultural production. He was also the founder of the abovementioned Small Farmers Central League. Hannes Gebhard's wife, Hedvig Gebhard, was a member of Parliament. Her contribution to the development of household education and household issues was of great importance during the years between World Wars I and II. Hedvig Gebhard worked in close cooperation with Miina Sillanpää in the promotion of household issues. After a split within the cooperative movement in 1916 between left-wing and more bourgeois factions, the left-wing consumer cooperatives and their newly founded organization Kulutusosuuskuntien Keskusliitto (Central Union of Consumer Cooperatives) were the most prominent advocates of the consumers' interests until World War II.

During the 1920s and 1930s, the primary consumer activities of the cooperative movement were advising and educating wage earners, both men and women. The leader of Kulutusosuuskuntien Keskusliitto, Väinö Tanner, was a well-known Social Democratic politician and, later, Prime Minister of the Finnish government. He emphasized the importance of consumer education, and the organization published two consumer magazines: *Kuluttajain Lehti* (Consumers' Magazine), first published in 1916, and its Swedish version *Konsumentbladet,* begun in 1921. In the 1920s and 1930s, Kulutusosuuskuntien Keskusliitto organized household management courses, discussion meetings, and cooperative festivals; it also published booklets and disseminated the cooperative ideology.

During the 1920s and 1930s, Finnish society was still strongly influenced by its agricultural heritage. As late as 1940, 64 percent of the entire population earned its livelihood from agriculture or forestry. On a farm, the spheres of production and consumption are not clearly separated. Consumer interests, to the extent that they were perceived as distinct from producer interests, were seen as strongly subordinate to producer interests or were reduced to a private, household matter.

The third source of the consumer movement in Finland is the centralized, state-controlled domestic advising activity that originated after the Finnish Civil War, in 1921, to relieve the country's poor economic situation, including a lack of food. Suomen Kotitalouskeskus (the Finnish Household Center) was founded as a result of the work of Valtion Kotitaloustoimikunta (the State Domestic Economy Committee), which had existed since 1917.

The chairperson of the Finnish Household Center was Laura Harmaja. Harmaja's life's work was as an advocate and as a teacher of domestic and consumer subjects. She promoted a scientific approach to domestic issues and imported the study of home economics, mainly from Germany. Also, she wrote several articles and basic texts dealing with these subjects. Harmaja expressed the idea of establishing a special domestic policy. The first Household Center was short-lived; disagreement about its role put an end to its public funding. A new center was founded in 1941 by a number of citizens' organizations. The Household Centers, together with the founding of a professorship in home economics and nutrition in the late 1940s, eventually led to the establishment of the National Consumer Research Center.

Post–World War II Developments

The rise of interest in domestic science between the two world wars culminated when a professorship in home economics was established at the University of Helsinki in 1946, and Elli Saurio was appointed to the office. She was an active member of the Martha Organization in the 1930s and wrote her dissertation on the use of time by rural homemakers. Another important institution was founded in 1943: Työtehoseura (the Society for the Rationalization of Work). Its executive director, Maiju Gebhard, daughter of Hannes and Hedvig Gebhard, promoted the application of scientific principles to household work and use of household technology.

The World War II rationing system was abolished gradually at the end of the 1940s. After that, the structure of retail trade changed quite rapidly as Finnish society shifted from agrarian self-sufficiency toward a developed market economy. Urbanization, rapid economic growth, and the growth of market-based consumption culminated in the liberalization of import restrictions in 1957 and the free trade agreement between Finland and EFTA in 1961.

Today, four organizations play a leading role in dealing with consumer issues. Two are the long-standing Martha Organization and Maatalousnaiset (under the title Maa-ja Kotitalousnaiset [Agricultural and Home Economy Women]). A third is Kuluttajat r.y. (the Consumers' Society), an organization founded in 1965 as an independent consumer advocacy group. Finally, there is Suomen Kuluttajaliitto (the Finnish Consumers' Union), an outgrowth of the household section of the Finnish Social Democratic Women's League. The league received state financing for household advisory work, beginning in 1924. Household and child care advising became independent spheres of activities in 1957 when Kotineuvontaliitto (the Home Advisory Union) started its work. As a nonpolitical organization, the Home Advisory Union received public financing. In 1979, it changed its name to Kuluttajaneuvontaliitto (Consumer Advisory Union) and, in 1987, to the Finnish Consumers' Union.

Eventually, the demands of consumers resulted in direct government action. Kuluttajaneuvosto (the Finnish Consumer Council) was organized in 1965 as a state organ devoted to consumer affairs. This was the continuation of the trend toward state-controlled consumer action that had its modest beginning in the third source of the consumer movement—advising organized by the state in the beginning of the 1920s. The Finnish Consumer Council was patterned after a similar council in Sweden, with members representing research institutes, labor unions, home economists, consumer organizations, educators, and a variety of business interests. The vice chairman, the director of price control in the Ministry of Social Affairs, Olavi Väyrynen, was one of the main initiators of the Finnish Consumer Council. The council first published a periodical, *Kuluttajatietoa* (Consumer Information), in 1967.

Current Status

By the 1970s, most consumer protection laws had been enacted, and the system of communal consumer advisers had been established. In the 1990s, the government's consumer administration was reorganized under the leadership of the Ministry of Trade and Industry, and the national organization Kuluttajavirasto (the National Consumer Office) was established. Other national bodies are the National Food Office, Consumer Complaints Board, Office of the Consumer Ombudsman, and the above-mentioned National Consumer Research Center.

The deep economic recession at the beginning of the 1990s raised several economic and social problems in Finland, including mass unemployment, rapidly growing foreign debt, and a banking crisis. Most of these problems were relatively new to Finnish society, especially the overindebtedness of many households. Today, Finnish firms are doing better, and the future appears to be brighter for the Finnish economy as well.

The processes of market liberalization and widening international trade pose new challenges for the Finnish consumer movement. An additional force for change is Finland's 1995 entrance as a member of the European Union. Threats to the natural environment and the need to promote sustainable development are additional challenges. Many of the problems faced by consumers in the 1990s require international cooperation among consumer organizations. That is an important reason that Finnish consumer organizations participate in Consumers International, where they are a strong voice for ecologically and socially sustainable global development.

— Visa Heinonen

Reading

Wilhelmson, Thomas (1991). "Product Liability in Finland." *Journal of Consumer Policy.* 14: 15–28.

Food and Drug Administration

Among the many federal regulatory agencies, none touches the day-to-day lives of citizens more directly than the Food and Drug Administration (FDA). Although consumers spend nearly $1 trillion annually on FDA-regulated products, the FDA's fiscal year 1996 budget totaled only $966 million.

The FDA's mission is threefold. First, it ensures that foods are safe, wholesome, and sanitary; human and veterinary drugs, biological products, and medical devices are safe and effective; cosmetics are safe; and electronic products that emit radiation are safe. Second, regulated products must be honestly, accurately, and informatively represented. Third, these products must be in compliance with the law and FDA regulations, noncompliance must be identified and corrected, and any unsafe or unlawful products must be removed from the market. The FDA is also responsible for regulating such products as vaccines, serums, and blood, including blood banks; the sanitation of food, water, and sanitary facilities on interstate vessels, trains, planes, and buses; and color televisions, cellular phones, and microwaves.

Located in the Department of Health and Human Services (HHS), the FDA is one of eight agencies within the U.S. Public Health Service, but the FDA is the only regulatory agency. It functions autonomously under specific laws, regulations, and budgetary constraints. Although the commissioner of the FDA is a presidential appointment, he or she reports directly to the Secretary of Health and Human Services.

The FDA is influenced by laws established by Congress and the interpretation of those laws by the courts. The Senate's power to approve the agency's budget is especially significant. The public influences the FDA through Congress, but it also has the ability to communicate directly with the agency.

The FDA works cooperatively with many other federal agencies on a number of different issues and products. For example, the Federal

Trade Commission is responsible for regulating advertising for over-the-counter (OTC) drug products; the Environmental Protection Agency regulates pesticides that are acceptable for use on products for consumption; the Department of Agriculture is responsible for the regulation of meat and poultry; and all habit-forming drugs approved by the FDA must be registered with the Drug Enforcement Agency. In recent years, the FDA and other agencies have worked more closely to protect consumers from harmful products.

History

Prior to 1906, the regulation of food and drug products was the responsibility of individual states, and variations in these laws from state to state made it difficult to enforce regulations. Products deemed legal in one state were considered to be adulterated in other states, and a lack of consistency in labeling requirements made it impossible for consumers to know the contents of the products they purchased.

Three converging influences created the conditions for passage of the Pure Food and Drug Act of 1906, which was first introduced in Congress in 1889. First, crusading journalist Upton Sinclair wrote *The Jungle,* a muckraking novel exposing corruption in the Chicago stockyards. Second, a diphtheria epidemic killed a number of children. Third, Dr. Harvey Wiley, chief of the Department of Agriculture's Bureau of Chemistry, led a campaign against unsafe food additives, which peaked in 1906.

A struggle between pro- and anti-Wiley state regulators underlay these dramatic events. States such as Pennsylvania, home of Heinz 57, and Wisconsin enacted relatively stringent food safety laws.

Wiley, a professor from Purdue University, left academia in 1883 to become the chief chemist of the Division of Chemistry in the U.S. Department of Agriculture. He and his colleagues developed scientific methodology to test foods and determine their actual content. Wiley helped establish that many product labels failed to disclose ingredients or made unsubstantiated health claims. Twelve young male employees of the Department of Agriculture volunteered to test the safety of food additives such as borax, sulfites, and saccharin. They ate meals laced with these substances and were then tested for adverse effects. The volunteers became known as Dr. Wiley's "poison squad."

Wiley's experiments on food additives and preservatives brought him public attention. He led a campaign to expose the misleading information provided by many food and drug manufacturers and bring the regulation of food and drug products under the authority of the federal government.

The National Consumers League (NCL) advocated the passage of a federal law governing food and drug products. Other organizations such as the American Medical Association, the National Canners Association, and the American Pharmaceutical Association joined in the fight to raise consumer awareness of the need for a federal food and drug law. Several popular magazines, including *Good Housekeeping, Ladies' Home Journal,* and *Colliers Weekly,* helped bring the issue to the public. In 1903, Wiley and his consumer partners pressed for the passage of a federal law addressing public safety. He credited these partners with turning the tide of opinion in favor of the Pure Food and Drug Act, which was passed in 1906.

The act gave the federal government the authority to prevent the shipment of "adulterated" or "misbranded" foods and drugs across state lines. The law defined the terms *adulterated* and *misbranded,* but the burden of proof was placed on the government to prove that a drug company intended to mislead consumers. This loophole provided drug marketers with the defense that they had not intended to mislead consumers, which limited the FDA's authority to prevent unsafe drugs from entering the market. The law mandated that certain dangerous drugs (e.g., heroin, cocaine, and morphine) and alcohol be labeled and their amounts stated. It established the U.S. Pharmacopeia and National Formulary as the official compendia for drug standards. The law did little, however, to control the use of dangerous and fraudulent drugs and devices. In 1927, Congress created a related law enforcement agency, which in 1930 was renamed the Food and Drug Administration. This agency lacked the authority to regulate drugs adequately, and it took catastrophic incidents to propel further action.

In the early 1930s, dinitrophenol, widely used for weight reduction, resulted in deaths and hundreds of cases of blindness, agranulocytosis (a potentially fatal blood disorder), and other serious adverse reactions. In 1937, more than 100 people in fifteen states, most of them children, died as a result of taking a liquid form of the drug sulfanilamide. This new liquid formulation, Elixir Sulfanilamide, contained diethylene glycol (a chemical cousin of antifreeze) and was marketed without toxicity testing. New drugs were not yet required to be proven safe prior to marketing.

These tragedies prompted Congress to pass the Federal Food, Drug and Cosmetic (FD&C) Act of 1938, which considerably expanded consumer protection by requiring safety testing of new drugs prior to approval for marketing. The law also mandated that drug labeling include adequate directions for use. The FD&C Act provided consumers with an assurance that approved drug products were safe for use.

In the late 1950s and early 1960s, Senator Estes Kefauver, troubled by the large markups and profits of pharmaceutical manufacturers, held a series of congressional hearings. As these hearings on the economic aspects of the industry progressed, defects in the safety and efficacy of drugs were revealed. Additionally, drug advertisements were shown to be frequently misleading, and it was clear that many drugs had no clear advantages over their alternatives.

In 1961, Kefauver introduced a bill to amend the FD&C Act that would require drugs to be proven effective as well as safe before they could be marketed. Once again, a catastrophic event influenced legislative action. As this legislation was being debated in Congress, an application for approval of thalidomide, a sedative-hypnotic, was pending at the FDA. This drug was used extensively in Europe before it was determined to be a teratogen (a drug or substance causing birth defects in the fetus). Thousands of babies were born malformed as a result of their mothers taking the drug during pregnancy. Fortunately, a new medical officer at the FDA, Dr. Frances Kelsey, did not act on the application because she felt the data were insufficient to support a conclusion of safety.

The controversy surrounding thalidomide persuaded Congress to pass the 1962 amendments. In addition to requiring drug manufacturers to provide substantial evidence to support a drug's effectiveness and safety, the law eliminated the sixty-day review period (required under the 1938 law), thus allowing the FDA the opportunity to review applications more carefully and deliberately. The law also gave the FDA enhanced authority to inspect manufacturers' production and quality control records, and it transferred jurisdiction over prescription drug advertising from the Federal Trade Commission to the FDA, which permitted the latter agency to review prescription drug advertising for scientific content.

Public Participation and Consumer Affairs

Public participation in the process of product regulation has been enhanced by legislation and specific presidential actions. The authority given to the FDA to review and approve new products under the FD&C Act promotes public participation. The FDA relies heavily on public input through testimony at advisory committee meetings and public hearings, written comments, and citizen petitions. The importance of public participation in the government's decision-making process was legally recognized in 1946, when Congress passed the Administrative Practices and Procedures Act. In December 1952, the FDA hired sixteen consumer consultants to serve as liaisons between the agency and the public on a wide variety of consumer problems.

In 1962, President John F. Kennedy established the Consumer Bill of Rights, providing consumers with the rights to choice, information, safety, and to be heard. Kennedy believed that the right to be informed and the right to be heard would provide the foundation for two-way dialogue between consumers and government. The Freedom of Information (FOI) Act, passed in 1966, provided the public with another mechanism to access the federal government. The FOI Act provided access to government information, which improved the public participation process by allowing consumers to gather information on government decisions and actions.

Spurred by Kennedy's Consumer Bill of Rights, the FDA created three consumer-related branches in its new Bureau of Education and Voluntary Compliance: the Consumer Information Branch, which developed educational materials for consumers and answered queries to headquarters; the Consumer Consultant Branch, which planned programs for consumer education through consultants; and the Consumer Survey Branch, which evaluated consumer interests and attitudes. In the mid-1960s, the consumer education program focused on three target audiences: the elderly, primary and secondary schoolteachers, and workers. Consumer consultants now were expected to devote about half their time to conferences or workshops for these audiences.

By the late 1960s the nature of the resource materials used to educate consumers began to change. Consumer specialists prepared Spanish-language press releases, radio and television scripts, and pamphlets; they carried out mass distribution of reprints from *FDA Papers* and its successor, the *FDA Consumer;* and they used one-page fact sheets to inform consumers of particular issues. By the end of the decade, twenty consumer specialists and ten part-time consumer consultants were employed. The FDA currently has forty-three public affairs specialists and technicians who educate consumers on the FDA issues and encourage their input into agency policy.

In 1972, Congress established the Federal Advisory Committee Act. This law provided an opportunity for the general public to participate in the policy process by serving on advisory committees and panels to federal regulatory agencies, and was intended to balance input from industry with that from the public. The FDA used this opportunity to foster an open-door policy for consumers. It implemented changes to inform the public of proposed policies and improve consumer participation through public testimony and written comments. The FDA extended the minimum time for public comment on proposed FDA regulations and policy statements from thirty to sixty days. The extension was designed to provide consumers, whose resources are limited, with more time to research the issues under consideration and participate more effectively in the process. The FDA also required that all *Federal Register* proposals include a preamble, in lay language, explaining the background and reasons for the action to be taken. In addition, the FDA was required to publish a summary of all comments received during the public comment period, including the FDA's response, with any rule. With the establishment of the Federal Advisory Committee Act, the FDA began appointing consumer representatives to its advisory committees.

By the late 1980s, consumers were members of thirty-five FDA advisory committees. The process for recruiting and recommending consumer representatives for these committees is managed by the Office of Consumer Affairs (OCA). Currently, forty-six committees have consumer representatives, twenty-six of which have voting status.

In addition, when pending applications or current health issues are discussed before an advisory panel, consumers and patients can access the agency through public testimony or written comment. Potential beneficiaries of successful new drugs (consumers) can work with the FDA to effect changes in the approval process. In 1987, the OCA played a pivotal role in establishing lines of communications with the AIDS community through a series of meetings with activists. During this same period, the agency launched an initiative to expand access for seriously ill patients to promising experimental drugs before their approval. This procedure provides patients with life-threatening diseases such as cancer, Alzheimer's disease, advanced Parkinson's disease, advanced congestive heart failure, and AIDS with access to investigational drugs under a specific treatment protocol before the drugs have been approved.

Women's health issues continue to evolve as a focus of consumer activism, but the National Women's Health Network's (NWHN) history of activism in relation to the FDA is unique. NWHN has utilized every form of public participation—testifying at advisory committees, serving as consumer representatives on advisory committees, filing citizens' petitions, organizing write-in campaigns and public demonstrations, and meeting with FDA staff. Since 1969, NWHN has supported patient package inserts (PPI) for oral contraceptives, opposed Depo Provera as a contraceptive, requested safety review of drugs used in pregnancy, supported FDA regulation of breast implants, and supported female condoms and other new barrier contraceptives.

Recent Consumer Protections

Much recent congressional legislation to protect the public from unsafe, ineffective, and misleading products includes a role for the FDA. In 1970, in *Upjohn v. Finch,* the U.S. Court of Appeals upheld enforcement of the 1962 drug effectiveness amendments by ruling that commercial success alone does not constitute substantial evidence of drug safety and efficacy. Also, the Environmental Protection Agency was established and took over the FDA program for setting pesticide tolerance levels. In 1971, the Bureau of Radiological Health was transferred to the FDA; its mission was protection against unnecessary human exposure to radiation from electronic products in the home, industry, and the healing arts. In 1972, over-the-counter drug review was mandated to enhance the safety, effectiveness, and appropriate labeling of drugs sold without prescription. Also, regulation of biologics—including serums, vaccines, and blood products—was transferred to the FDA. In 1973, the Consumer Product Safety Commission was created by Congress. It took over programs pioneered by the FDA under the 1927 Caustic Poison Act, 1960 Hazardous Substances Labeling Act, 1966 Child Protection Act, and Public Health Service accident-prevention activities for safety of toys, home appliances, and other products.

In 1976, the Medical Device Amendment was passed to ensure the safety and effectiveness of medical devices, including diagnostic products. Some products must have premarket approval by the FDA; others must meet performance standards before marketing. Vitamins and minerals amendments stopped the FDA from establishing standards that limited the potency of vitamins and minerals in food supplements or regulated them as drugs solely on potency. In 1977, Congress passed the Saccharin Study and Labeling Act, lifting the FDA ban on the chemical sweetener, but requiring a label that the substance has been found to cause cancer in laboratory animals.

In 1980, the Infant Formula Act established special the FDA controls to ensure necessary nutritional content and safety. In 1982, the Tamper Resistant Packaging Regulations were issued by the FDA to prevent poisonings such as occurred from cyanide placed in Tylenol capsules. The Federal Anti-Tampering Act of 1983 made it a crime to tamper with packaged consumer products. In 1983, the Orphan Drug Act enabled the FDA to promote research, approval, and marketing of drugs needed for treating rare diseases that otherwise would not be profitable. In 1985, an AIDS test for blood was approved by the FDA.

In 1990, the Nutrition Labeling and Education Act mandated that all packaged foods carry nutrition labeling and required that all health claims for foods be consistent with terms defined by the Secretary of Health and Human Services. The law preempted state requirements as to food standards, nutrition labeling, and health claims. Also, the Safe Medical Devices Act required users of medical devices, such as hospitals and nursing homes, to report promptly to the FDA any incidents that suggest a medical device caused or contributed to the death, serious illness, or serious injury of a patient. In 1992, the Mammography Quality Standards Act required all mammography facilities in the United States to be accredited and federally certified as meeting quality standards. After initial certification, facilities must pass annual inspections by approved federal or state inspectors.

— Alexander Grant, James S. Turner
(with assistance from Marcia Treater)

See also

Cosmetic Safety; Food Purchase Protections; Food Safety; Health Care Protections; Medical Devices; Public Representation.

Readings

Friedman, Robert S. (1978). "Representation in Regulatory Decision Making: Scientific, Industrial, and Consumer Inputs to the F.D.A." *Public Administration Review.* (May/June): 205–214.

Grant, Alexander, and Sharon Olmstead (1995). "Regulating Drugs." In Kenneth J. Meier and E. Thomas Garman, eds. *Regulation and Consumer Protection.* Houston: DAME Publications, Inc. 235–256.

Kuntze, Patricia M. (1993). "Communicating with the FDA: The Office of Consumer Affairs." *Food and Drug Law Journal.* 48: 15–21.

Food Cooperatives

Food cooperatives have existed in the United States since the mid–nineteenth century. But the large majority of food co-ops in existence in the mid-1990s were founded in the 1970s and 1980s by consumers who wanted high-quality natural foods at reasonable prices but could not find them in traditional stores.

All of these cooperatives are organized around the six Rochdale principles (after the Rochdale Cooperative Society, see below): open membership, democratic control, limited return on equity, net surplus belonging to the user-owners, continuous education, and cooperation among cooperatives. Beyond these principles, the organization of food co-ops may vary greatly. Some co-ops operate stores that are open to the public and offer items identical to those sold in for-profit grocery stores, while other co-ops sell only organically produced products exclusively to members.

There are two main types of food co-ops: buying clubs, or preorders; and retail stores. A buying club is a group of individuals and families who pool their purchases to buy in bulk. Buying clubs are often organized within other organizations, such as churches, day care or school groups, or neighborhoods. Members of a buying club order food in advance of delivery, consolidate member orders into a group order, and, upon delivery, break down the bulk purchases into individual member orders. Beginning in the late 1980s, buying clubs have increasingly used personal computers to consolidate their orders and produce invoices for individual members. This practice has decreased time requirements while increasing the integrity of the billing and ordering systems. There is little equity capital required for this type of co-op. Buying clubs typically have no inventory and few assets. All work is generally done on a volunteer basis, and sales are only to members.

Retail co-ops are diverse in their organization and operation. Some retails sell only to members; others sell mainly to the general public. Some require that all members work in the store on a regular basis; others rely exclusively on paid staff. Some retail co-ops offer a limited variety of minimally processed bulk and natural foods; others sell a full line of groceries, plus many other services—from gasoline and oil to hardware and credit union membership. Members make their purchases from inventory stocked in the store. The need for inventory and store equipment make the capital needs of retail co-ops much greater than those of buying clubs.

The history of food cooperatives in the United States can be broken roughly into three periods. The first consumer food cooperatives were founded in the late nineteenth and early twentieth centuries. The second wave of co-op formation, now usually referred to as the "old wave," occurred during the 1930s. The third period, the "new wave," came in the late 1960s and continued into the early 1980s.

The origins of the first round of cooperative formation can be traced to the Rochdale Cooperative Society of Rochdale, England, and to the waves of Scandinavian immigrants who came to the New World at the end of the nineteenth century. While the first consumer cooperative based on the Rochdale principles was organized in 1862 in Philadelphia, it was not until the early twentieth century that cooperatives were formed in great numbers. It was during this time that the Cooperative League of the USA (now the National Cooperative Business Association) was organized. The consumer co-ops founded then were like the general stores of their day: they not only sold food, but also often carried hardware, furniture, coal, and home supplies, while some even ran restaurants and home dairy delivery. Scandinavian immigrants, primarily Finns, organized consumer goods co-ops in widely scattered parts of the country: New England, the North Central states, New York City, and northern California. Many of these co-ops operated for several decades, though none exist today. As the communities in which they were founded became more diverse, and later generations lost their ethnic identity, these co-ops failed to attract new members.

In the 1930s, spurred by the Great Depression and Franklin Roosevelt's New Deal, many new cooperatives were organized. While the New Deal mainly promoted cooperatives for agricultural producers and rural consumers, it created a climate of moral support and encouragement for the formation of cooperatives by other groups. Some of the oldest and largest food cooperatives were founded at this time. Among these are the Hanover Consumer Cooperative of Hanover, New Hampshire, and the Hyde Park Cooperative Society of Chicago. Others grew and prospered for a time, but eventually failed or left the food business. In this period, Greenbelt Cooperatives, near Washington, D.C., was founded. At one time it operated five supermarkets, ten furniture stores, seven auto service centers, and one pharmacy, with a total annual volume of $48 million. By the end of the 1980s, it had closed or sold all of its businesses except its retail furniture business.

Three forces strongly influenced cooperative formation in the 1960s and 1970s: the increasing recognition of the "politics of food," a desire for alternative economic systems, and the renaissance of consumerism. As the 1960s progressed, many people became concerned with the rise in use of petrochemicals, fossil fuels, and pesticides in food production and processing of food for domestic consumption. These concerns, coupled with an increasing awareness of the inequities of global food distribution, led many to see food as a political issue. These consumers developed an interest in natural foods, minimally processed and grown with few or no chemicals.

In addition, other consumers were especially concerned with food products' poor quality, high prices, and low nutritional content. These individuals were not concerned with the political aspects of the food they purchased, only with its value and safety.

At the time, there was also an increasing lack of respect for the business world. Members of the counterculture and increasing numbers of women in the workplace found the impersonal, profit-driven, male-dominated business environment alienating. They increasingly distrusted corporations that processed and marketed food, and wanted to organize a more equitable, alternative food distribution system. The consumer-owned cooperative business form presented the opportunity for shaping a nonalienating workplace where the consumer-owner could be assured of receiving high-quality, minimally processed food at fair prices. Cooperatives sprang up quickly, and by 1975 there were an estimated 700 retail cooperatives in existence. Individual cooperatives joined together to organize cooperatively owned federations and wholesalers to improve their sources of supply, provide trucking services, and hold joint training conferences.

As the co-ops grew, the disparate interests of their members came increasingly into conflict. Many retail co-ops began operations as buying clubs. As their sales grew, they decided to open a store. These retails frequently required members to work on a regular basis. Some cooperative organizers felt that a work requirement was essential for reinforcing the idea that the co-op is member-controlled. But many others with limited time questioned the necessity for member labor.

Also, those committed to minimally processed natural foods had conflicts with those who envisioned cooperatives as an alternative economic vehicle serving all groups in society, including those with standard diets. Conflicts also arose concerning cooperatives as businesses. Many of the founders of these cooperatives felt that any of the tools used by capitalist businesses, including standard management and financial skills, were suspect. These co-op leaders fought any attempt to make the co-ops more "businesslike." As a result, many co-ops failed during this period. By 1980, the number of retail food co-ops had declined to about 340.

At this time, there were also about 3,000 preorder buying clubs. While their annual sales increased, these sales totalled less than $100 million in a $345 billion food marketplace. There were also forty to fifty cooperative natural foods wholesalers serving many areas of the country.

During the 1980s, as co-op leaders saw many cooperatives fail, they began to realize that, while a co-op may be a vehicle for social change or an advocate for high-quality food, it must be run as a business to survive. As a result, the number of failing cooperatives fell sharply, and the remaining co-ops grew stronger. By the mid-1990s, there were about 350 retail cooperatives and 4,000 buying clubs with combined sales of $400 million. Consolidation or failure had reduced the number of wholesale cooperatives to ten, ranging in size from $5 million to $30 million in sales. In the mid-1990s, cooperatives continue to be leaders in the safe, healthy foods movement and are the nation's largest sellers of organically grown produce.

— Lawrence E. Haller

See also

Cooperatives, Consumer.

Readings

Hall, Bruce F., and Lana L. Hall (1982). "The Potential for Growth of Consumer Cooperatives: A Comparison with Producer Cooperatives." *Journal of Consumer Affairs.* 16 (1): 23–45.

Lee, Janet (1993). "Food Co-ops: What Hippies Did Right." *Business Week.* (November 29): 146.

Food Purchase Protections

Food purchase protection for consumers in the United States starts with regulations on the production and processing of raw commodities and follows with regulations about the handling and labeling of food. Protection takes two main forms: the protection of consumers' health and safety, and the protection of consumers' economic interests.

The protection of health and safety requires relatively restrictive forms of regulation about what foods, food additives, and manufactured food ingredients may be sold; what must be inspected, tested, labeled, banned, or recalled; and the physical and sanitary conditions under which food can be handled and sold. These types of regulations are considered to be appropriate when the consumer cannot know the nature of the product or its potential hazards through personal inspection or use. Since the consequences of eating food that is harmful to health, ranging from a temporary illness to death, are considered unacceptable risks for consumers to bear, government regulations try to prevent or reduce exposure to these risks. In addition, there are rules about the health and safety of the shopping environment. For example, food stores must be well lighted, be accessible to handicapped people, and control insect and rodent infestations.

The protection of consumer economic interests while purchasing food consists largely of providing information about the characteristics of what consumers are buying, its quantity, and its price. This form of protection tries to prevent consumers from making purchases inconsistent with their preferences by informing them about what to expect from a particular food. Most of this protection takes the form of rules about telling the truth about ingredient and nutritional contents, prices and price per unit, freshness of perishables, and advertising claims.

Private Sector Protections

Earning consumers' brand and store loyalty is a powerful incentive for those who produce and sell food to provide products that are safe and deliver the satisfaction expected at a competitive price. Repeat business is especially important in a mature economy with a slow-growing and well-fed population. Some grocers and food retailers have instituted their own food safety and quality assurance programs, including private testing and certification (organic or pesticide residue–free) programs. Some grocers voluntarily provide ingredient and nutritional labeling on foods where it is not required by law. Others provide cooking instructions, lessons, or samples to taste. In the case of a suspect product, some businesses readily make available recalls and refunds. The benefits to the seller from these programs include building a good public image, obtaining consumer confidence, and consequently, increasing sales volume and possibly market share. The benefits to the consumer are greater satisfaction and more informed choices.

Economic protections offered by the private sector primarily take the form of truth in advertising and labeling, and of monitoring prices charged against prices advertised/labeled. With more data available about who buys what, when, and where, consumers are more likely to experience target marketing. While this marketing can reward customer loyalty with discounts, it discriminates against the shopper who is unfamiliar to the store; it also means that advertised prices might not be the same for all shoppers. The voluntary use of coupons has always been by consumers seeking bargain prices.

Some third-party private firms scrutinize food and food sellers and publicize their findings. These groups include Consumers Union, which publishes *Consumer Reports;* various news media shows; and various advocacy groups such as Public Voice for Food and Health Policy and the Center for Science in the Public Interest. These watchdog groups have played an important role in advancing protections such as the improved inspection of meat, poultry, and seafood.

Government Protections

Several federal, state, and local governmental agencies regulate the safety of the country's food supply. Federal regulations apply mostly to production and processing standards that affect food sold across the country, if not around the world. They include testing of milk from dairy farms, the inspection and grading of grains and meats, the testing for accurate weights on scales throughout the food chain, and a whole host of rules about the use of pesticides and the sale of new ingredients or newly engineered food products. Federal regulations fall into five main categories: setting standards of safety through scientific research; protecting consumers from excessive exposure to unsafe and unhealthy food and food additives, ingredients, and chemical residues; protecting against fraud and deception from false and misleading labeling or advertising; setting standards of identity; and establishing food handling and service codes that can be adopted by local jurisdictions or voluntarily by food providers.

Scientific research on the effect of ingestible substances on human health provides the basis for regulations set by the Food and Drug Administration (FDA), the Environmental Protection Agency (EPA), the U.S. Department of Agriculture (USDA), and other agencies that have some responsibility for protecting consumers from harmful food. In general, those substances known to be harmful are banned altogether. Those substances that carry both substantial benefits and potential risks are regulated as to quantity that can be used (pesticides), information that must accompany the product (warning, ingredient, and nutritional labels), and advertising restrictions (health claims for particular foods). When substances in food or food products have been found to be generally harmless, the FDA puts them on a list called "generally recognized as safe" (GRAS), and they do not need to be retested for safety or efficacy unless some new problem arises.

Regulatory remedies for unsafe food take three major approaches. One is to ban a product or process. The second is to certify the food handling and manufacturing process, which is the case with the pasteurization of milk. A newer version of this approach is to establish a science-based analysis of potential hazards, to determine where hazards can occur in processing, and then institute preventive measures at critical hazard points. This newer system has been instituted by the FDA for seafood and fish; it is called Hazard Analysis and Critical Control Point (HACCP). A third approach is to set standards of quality and safety for the final product, then inspect the product to see that it meets those standards. An example of this approach is the testing of fruits and vegetables for pesticide residues or the testing of ground beef for microbes. The standards-based method is more expensive but allows food processors more flexibility in manufacturing. One area of controversy is whether foreign producers should be permitted to use their own processing methods as long as their products test "safe."

The main regulatory tools employed by the EPA are the setting of tolerances for pesticide residues, which are the upper limits for acceptable levels of chemical residues in fresh and processed food and animal feed, and food manufacturing process standards. Although the EPA sets the tolerances, the FDA is the inspecting and enforcing agency. The scientifically established links between pesticides and cancer in test animals have caused great public concern about the type of protection offered by this regulation. Yet, it should be noted that, as of 1995, there was no documented link between pesticide residues on or in food and any type of human cancer. Consequently, food scientists consider microbial contamination, whose effects are well documented and to which consumers are frequently exposed, to pose greater risks to consumers.

Food that has been found to be unsafe is usually banned. For example, sulfites cannot be used to preserve fresh produce in restaurants, and raw eggs are no longer served in most places. The FDA and the USDA (meat and poultry) inspect samples of food products for a variety of contamination, from pesticide residues to bacteria. When a sample is found to be unsafe, the food from which it came is pulled off the market for more intense inspection. Imported food is subject to the same regulation. In fact, U.S. inspectors are often located in the foreign country from which a product is shipped to ensure that the process of handling the food and the final quality meet U.S. standards. While fairly well designed, this regulatory system is underfunded and understaffed to monitor the volume of food products being sold.

The third major type of government protection is to ensure accurate information. The FDA regulates labeling of all foods, except meat and poultry, which is the jurisdiction of the USDA, and the Federal Trade Commission regulates truth in advertising. In 1994, two laws that regulate the information on food packages became effective. The American Technology Preeminence Act of 1991 requires food manufacturers to list the net contents of their products in both metric units and inch and pound units. The Nutrition Labeling and Education Act of 1990 requires that nearly all food sold have nutrition labels, and if the item contains more than two ingredients, all ingredients must be listed in an easy-to-read format. This law also established definitions for nutrient claims such as "low-fat" or "high-fiber," and limited the use of health claims to scientifically proven food-health links.

The act also requires food packages to list the net weight of the edible contents; the standardized serving size; nutritional content including information on fat, cholesterol, sodium, and some other nutrients; the name and location of the manufacturer or distributor; the pull date (last day it is recommended to be sold); the expiration date (last day it is recommended to be eaten); and any grades or standards that apply, such as AA grade eggs. All of this information applies to food sold by stores in packages that are large enough to carry this information. But these information regulations do not apply to food sold ready to eat from delicatessens or in a restaurant, to bulk food, or to food sold by small businesses that sell less than $50,000 worth of food a year. Some food service establishments make this information available upon request.

Setting standards of identity is a form of information provided by the FDA. These requirements are sometimes referred to as the recipe law since they regulate the proportions of ingredients that foods such as catsup, mayonnaise, and ice cream must contain. Among other things, mayonnaise must contain eggs and ice cream must be made from cow's milk. These regulations allow consumers quickly to identify common foods; they have also led to use of new terms such as *imitation ice cream* or *salad dressing*.

The fifth main type of protection is a set of standards established by the FDA in their Food Code. This code, first offered in 1933 and since periodically revised, is neither federal law nor regulation but is offered as model legislation to states and local regulatory departments that license and inspect food service establishments, from fine restaurants to nursing homes, from food stores to vending machines. The Food Code defines standards of safety and behavior such as washing of hands, controlling insects and bacteria in buildings and food, cooking temperatures for meat, and refrigerator temperatures of storage.

Other federal, state, and local government agencies are involved with other consumer food protections. The Consumer Product Safety Commission (CPSC) regulates the safety of equipment used in stores by employees or consumers, for example, that of grocery carts or automatic doors. State health departments typically are in charge of inspecting restaurants, hospitals, prisons, and schools where food is prepared and served. The Centers for Disease Control in Atlanta, Georgia, gathers and analyzes data on food-related illnesses and establishes networks for quick informational response to outbreaks of foodborne illness. Some states also maintain a similar service to track and analyze disease outbreaks. Information learned from monitoring such outbreaks is used to establish new safety standards and protections for food consumers.

The need for consumer food protections will continue in the future. With new food additives, preservatives, and ingredients being developed all the time, continued testing for efficacy and safety will be needed. With new ways to sell food—through home delivery, computer shopping, and vending schemes—yet to be discovered, continued regulation of truth in advertising, labeling, and pricing will also be important. As the speed of scientific discovery, of delivery and product turnover, and of shopping itself—notably, by way of computer—increases, the potential for unsafe products, fraud, and deception increases as well.

— Jean D. Kinsey

See also

Center for Science in the Public Interest; Community Nutrition Institute; Food and Drug Administration; Food Safety; Public Voice for Food and Health Policy; U.S. Department of Agriculture.

Reading

Senauer, Ben, Elaine Asp, and Jean Kinsey (1991). *Food Trends and the Changing Consumer.* St. Paul, MN: Eagan Press.

Food Safety

Food safety is a major area of consumer protection. There is a long history of government action to establish and enforce food safety laws and regulations to insure that the food supply is safe and wholesome. However, there remain a number of unresolved issues.

Food safety regulation, historically and to the present day, has been driven by crises that have aroused the public's concern. Before the turn of the century, the food industry was virtually unregulated. Upton Sinclair's classic book, *The Jungle,* was published in 1906. It described the appalling conditions that existed in the meat-packing industry. At about the same time, other problems were dramatically brought to the public's attention. A study by the New York City Health Commission found that over half the milk sampled in the city was adulterated with water, chalk, and plaster of paris.

In 1906, Congress reacted to the crisis by passing the Pure Food and Drug Act and the Meat Inspection Act, the first major food safety laws. The former stated that food moving in interstate commerce was to be safe. Although initially not very effective, the laws clearly established that the federal government has a responsibility to ensure the safety of the food supply. In 1931, the Food and Drug Administration (FDA) was created. In 1938, the Federal Food, Drug and Cosmetic Act was passed, empowering the FDA to fine and imprison violators.

In 1954, the Miller Pesticide Amendment was approved. In 1958, the Food Additives Amendment, with its Delaney clause, was passed. This clause states that "no additive shall be deemed safe if it is found to induce cancer when ingested by man or animal," thus establishing a zero-tolerance standard. In 1957, as the poultry industry began to grow rapidly, the Poultry Products Inspection Act was passed. The 1958 Food Additives Amendment required that manufacturers demonstrate that an additive is safe before it can be introduced. The 1972 Federal Insecticide, Fungicide, and Rodenticide Act (FIFRA) regulates pesticide residues on fresh produce. While the most influential, these major pieces of legislation are only some of the federal laws enacted to regulate food safety.

Food safety regulation just begins with the passage of laws by Congress. Specific executive branch agencies, principally the FDA and U.S. Department of Agriculture (USDA), are authorized to implement the legislation. Specific rules and regulations must be developed. Usually, preliminary regulations are published in the *Federal Register* with a period for public comment and hearings before final rules are established. The effectiveness of the food safety laws depends on their enforcement by the agencies responsible.

Many consumer and environmental groups argue that the government regulatory system is inadequate and that agricultural and food industries ignore substantial risks to consumers. On the other side of the issue, many in the food industry feel that they are overregulated. They argue that, for insignificant safety benefits, regulation has forced consumers to pay higher food prices, placing special burdens on those with low incomes.

General Issues

Food safety has recently become a major consumer concern because of several widely publicized incidents. In 1989, it was suggested that Alar (daminazide), a chemical used on apples, might be carcinogenic; after much controversy, its use was discontinued. The same year, a few grapes imported from Chile were found to have been injected with cyanide. In 1993, there was a major outbreak of illness in Washington State resulting from contamination of certain fast-food hamburgers by a foodborne pathogen, E. Coli 0157: H7. Each of these incidents received extensive media coverage and induced widespread public concern about the specific problem and food safety in general.

In recent Food Marketing Institute annual surveys of consumers, about three-fourths indicate they are completely or mostly confident of the safety of their food. However, when read a list of specific issues, a large proportion of the respondents answer that several pose a serious hazard. Of greatest concern are pesticide residues, followed by antibiotic and hormone use in poultry and livestock, nitrates, food irradiation, additives and preservatives, and artificial coloring. In general, the major concern of consumers relates to the use of possibly carcinogenic chemicals in food production and processing.

Consumers' concerns sharply diverge from the ranking of food safety risks by knowledgeable professionals. These experts rank microbiological pathogens as the most important food-related health hazard, followed by malnutrition and chronic diseases related to diet, environmental contaminants in food such as mercury in fish, naturally occurring toxins in food, and then pesticide residues and additives. Policymakers face the dilemma of whether to give priority to the major food safety concerns of consumers or to those health risks that scientific evidence indicates are most hazardous.

What many consumers do not realize is the seriousness of foodborne illness. Most cases go unreported. Nearly everyone has suffered the effects of some foodborne pathogen at some time, although many might simply have considered it a case of stomach flu. Estimates of the number of cases per year range from several million to over 100 million, with an estimated 9,000 to 12,000 deaths per year related to foodborne pathogens. The cost has been estimated to be some $5 billion per year.

Food safety decisions involve an estimate of the risk involved and a policy judgment concerning the acceptable level of risk. Animal tests, usually with mice or rats, are the primary method for establishing the toxicity or health risk of substances. However, there are many problems in extrapolating from animal tests to humans. The dose per unit of body weight given to the test animals is frequently many times greater than the potential human exposure. This protocol is necessary to check for very small risks with a limited number of test animals. On the other hand, great advances have been made in our ability to detect minute quantities of substances. Amounts as small as parts per trillion can now be detected in some cases.

The risk standards applied in food safety regulation vary enormously and relate to how the substance enters the food supply rather than to the actual health hazard posed. The current regulatory system has been criticized for this inconsistency. At one end of the spectrum is the Delaney standard of zero risk; at the other is the risk-benefit approach of FIFRA. The latter approach allows the environmental and health risks to be offset by the economic benefits resulting from increased agricultural production. In recent years, there has been movement toward a "de minimis," or negligible risk, standard in food safety regulation. This standard is typically interpreted as one in one million—the hazard should not cause more than one additional death per million people over their lifetimes.

An alternative to regulation of products is to require only that consumers be provided with relevant information about potential risks. An example of this approach is the new Nutrition Labeling Regulations that went into effect in 1993. They provide new information regarding levels of such components as fat, saturated fat, and dietary fiber. Another example is the safe handling labels introduced in 1994, which instruct consumers how to properly store, handle, and cook raw meat and poultry products. The chief limitations of an informational approach are that many consumers will not spend the time to become adequately informed and that even those who do may lack the expertise to understand the significance of the disclosures.

Unresolved Issues

At present, there are a number of unresolved issues in specific areas. There is a broad consensus that the current USDA system of meat and poultry inspection, which is primarily visual, is antiquated. The most serious health hazards are microbiological. Salmonella contamination is a particular problem with poultry. There is widespread agreement that a Hazard Analysis Critical Control Point (HACCP) system should form the basis of the reforms. The HACCP approach has already had a major impact on quality control in the food processing industry. A HACCP approach sets up a trace-back system, monitors critical control points, and focuses on high-risk problems. Advanced scientific techniques and monitoring equipment would be used to screen for microbial contamination.

Until very recently, there was no mandatory federal inspection program for fish and seafood. Yet, major health hazards with these food products, especially shellfish, have been identified. After many years of congressional debate and inaction, the FDA is moving forward with a proposed HACCP approach for seafood, although it will require several years to implement fully.

Various aspects of the current regulation of pesticides have been widely criticized. Old pesticides in use when FIFRA was enacted have not had to meet the same safety standards as new ones. In 1992, a federal court ruled that the Delaney clause and its zero-tolerance provision should be applied to pesticide residues in processed foods. The EPA would be required to ban a number of possibly carcinogenic pesticides. The major reform proposals would shift from the current risk-benefit approach to a negligible risk standard. Priority would be given to health concerns, not economic considerations, and the reduction of pesticides would be promoted.

Food imports, particularly fresh fruits and vegetables, have been increasing. The agricultural chemicals used in their production are regulated by each country's own laws. However, U.S. regulations apply to any chemical residues in the food. There are concerns that the imported foods may be less safe than those grown domestically, particularly in terms of pesticide residues. A major problem is the shortage of FDA personnel and other resources to inspect food imports. Under the new General Agreement on Tariffs and Trade (GATT), countries will still have control over their own food safety regulations. However, health and safety regulations cannot be used to restrict imports unless there is evidence that they legitimately protect domestic consumers.

Consumers are purchasing an increasing proportion of their food already prepared to eat at a multitude of different providers, from restaurants to grocery delis. The enforcement of sanitary standards in food service is not a responsibility of the federal government but is under the jurisdiction of local food inspectors and state health departments. The adequacy of this inspection in many locales has been criticized.

Many consumers are concerned about the use of genetically engineered products in food. A precedent was established with recombinant bovine growth hormone (rBGH), which the FDA approved for commercial use in dairy cows in 1994. The FDA intends to approve biotechnology products when it feels that the scientific evidence demonstrates their safety and effectiveness. There is the further question of the special labeling of biotechnology products. Milk produced with the new growth hormone need not be labeled. While milk produced without the hormone can be so labeled, the label must indicate that there is no significant difference in composition, nutrition, or safety between milk from rBGH-treated and nontreated cows.

A major constraint to action on unresolved issues is a lack of consensus. Many times, scientific evidence about hazards is not clear-cut: there is disagreement about the risk involved and the willingness to accept tradeoffs. Major food safety issues are resolved through the political policy process, which is often responsive to crises that are the focus of media attention, and the advocacy of various interest groups. Consequently, the protection of consumers is a major, but not the only, factor affecting food safety policies.

— Ben Senauer

See also

Center for Science in the Public Interest; Community Nutrition Institute; Food and Drug Administration; Food Purchase Protections; Public Voice for Food and Health Policy; U.S. Department of Agriculture.

Readings

Jones, Julie (1992). *Food Safety.* St. Paul, MN: Eagan Press.

Senauer, Ben, Elaine Asp, and Jean Kinsey (1991). *Food Trends and the Changing Consumer.* St. Paul, MN: Eagan Press.

French Consumer Movement

Following World War II, French families emerged from a long period of deprivation and regained their purchasing power. Mass consumption developed rapidly under the irresistible impulse of new production methods and advertising that filled up radio and then television.

France has had a criminal law against commercial fraud dating back to 1905, but the relationship between individuals and merchants or producers has been regulated primarily by the Napoleonic Code dating from the early nineteenth century. Based on a liberal concept under which individual freedom to engage in transactions was emphasized, the Civil Code made the contract "the law of the parties." With contracts supposedly negotiated on equal terms, there was no recourse once they were agreed upon.

Within a context of mass production and mass distribution, where standardized contracts were common and where there were multiple intermediaries between producers and consumers, such a totally private principle of consumer protection proved to be completely inappropriate to the reality of transactions. Moreover, the rules of civil and criminal procedure were essentially individualistic: the consumer is alone to enforce his or her rights and bears, in the vast majority of cases, burden of proof when bringing legal actions.

Development of Consumer Groups and Protections

It is in this context, and under pressure from the political unrest of May 1968, that the modern French consumer movement developed in the 1960s. By the end of that decade, the Institut National de la Consommation (INC) was created, and the first fundamental consumer protection laws began to operate.

Although family associations and consumer cooperatives had existed in France for a long time, there was not a genuine consumer movement until the end of the 1960s. At that time, consumer organizations were established and multiplied, buoyed by the dynamic example of the American consumer movement. The articulation of consumer rights by President John F. Kennedy and the considerable efforts of Ralph Nader played an important role in giving birth and inspiration to the French consumer movement. The movement was also stimulated by several tragedies, such as the death of thirty-six infants in 1972 due to adulterated talcum powder. Today, the 1960s and 1970s are considered to be the golden age of consumerism in France.

A number of basic laws were enacted by the French Parliament under the force of public pressure during the 1970s. The law on door-to-door sales (1972), the Royer law on deceptive advertising (1973), and the Scrivener laws of 1978 and 1979 on credit and unfair contract terms constitute the foundation for modern consumer law in France. These new consumer laws did not question the basic principle of contract as it existed in civil law, but they began to correct the obvious abuses associated with contractual freedom by reestablishing a certain balance between the parties in question (for example, by introducing the ideas of vulnerable consumers, cooling-off periods, and preformulated contracts).

Beginning in 1973, representative consumer organizations were authorized to defend the collective interests of consumers in front of tribunals. This role of "private prosecutor" recognized the new role of consumer organizations as economic actors; only the labor unions had a similar right, achieved at the beginning of the twentieth century. This collective interest action, which is not a matter of representing the aggregated interests of individual consumers (as in class actions), is nevertheless an effective instrument in reforming commercial practices. The consumer associations increased their activities on the basis of this new power, but limitations of strategies and resources reduced their impact.

Through the numerous schisms and regroupings that occurred between 1959 and 1982, the three great strands of the French consumer movement formed: strictly consumer associations, family-oriented organizations, and labor union–based organizations. Two magazines for the general public emerged: *Que choisir?* (What to Choose?), produced by the Union Fédéral des Consommateurs (UFC), and *50 millions de consommateurs* (50 Million Consumers), published by INC.

Role of the State

The INC, founded in 1966 by the public authorities, is not an association of consumers, but a technical center for research and information. Its status is unique: it is a public body but it enjoys independence of expression. It has a mission of public service (technical assistance to the consumer movement, information, training, comparative product tests) for which it receives a subsidy from the state, but it operates under certain commercial constraints and is financially self-supporting to a large extent.

During the 1970s and 1980s, the INC was involved in numerous controversies within the consumer movement. The INC was regarded as an incontestable and indispensable technical tool, but it was viewed by the most liberal elements of the movement as overly dependent on public authorities, especially in its function of conducting and publishing comparative product tests. The INC found itself most often in conflict with its direct competitor in the field of product testing and magazine publishing, the UFC.

The INC works today in collaboration with several of its counterparts in other European countries, especially in carrying out comparative product tests and studies. The INC also participates as an expert in many national and European Union–wide groups. Recently, the INC has reoriented itself toward the development of its research at the national and European level to promote the interest of consumers and to communicate its work to consumer associations who will, in turn, utilize these studies in their activities as pressure groups. Besides its monthly magazine, *50 Million Consumers,* the INC publishes a weekly technical magazine (INC-HEBDO).

The presence of the state in French consumer policy has been and remains strong. In 1960, the government created the National Committee of Consumers to promote dialogue between consumer associations and the public authorities. In addition to creating the INC in 1966, over the years the state has aided the growth of consumer associations through subsidies (to approximately twenty groups at present). In 1985, the state created a special administration, the Bureau of Competition, Consumption, and the Repression of Fraud (DGCCRF) under the authority of the Ministry of the Economy, whose task is to ensure the proper functioning of economic markets. The bureau participates in the enforcement of regulations regarding competition and consumer law by checking on enforcement and by distributing information.

Two specialized commissions created by the initiative of the state also play an important part in the protection of the consumer. The Unfair Contract Terms Commission (CCA), created in 1978, is charged with analyzing contract terms proposed by professionals to consumers and with making proposals to do away with unfair clauses as defined by the law of 1978 (recently revised by the law of February 1995). The commission may be required to act as an expert in court proceedings.

A second commission, the Commission for the Safety of Consumers (CSC), was created by the 1983 law on the safety of consumers. Its mission is to prevent and reduce risks to which consumers are exposed in their private lives. The commission has power to hold inquiries and to submit proposals. It informs consumers via electronic services on the Minitel online system and through its journal.

Over the years, public authorities have institutionalized consumer affairs at the highest levels of government. France was one of the first countries to establish a state Secretariat for Consumer Affairs in 1976 and then a Minister of Consumer Affairs in 1981. Since 1993, however, consumer affairs has been placed under the direct control of the Ministry of the Economy.

State support for private consumer organizations results partly from a French tradition of intervention by public authorities to protect the economic interests of the weakest citizens. Its enactment of consumer laws also illustrates this interventionism.

Current Status and Concerns

There are in France today twenty national organizations of consumers. Along with the three types of organizations mentioned previously (consumerist, family-oriented, and union-based), associations exist with a more specific focus (for example, housing, transportation, and users of public services).

Consumer organizations exist in all regions of the country. They play an important part in advising consumers and settling individual cases. These organizations are involved in public education through newspapers and television broadcasts, on a local level or through national networks. The licenses of public broadcasting networks require them to broadcast programs dealing with consumption. The production of these programs is the responsibility of the INC or regional technical centers for consumers.

The French organizations belong, according to their respective types, to European groups. Purely consumer organizations belong to the Bureau Européen des Unions de Consommateurs (BEUC); family-based organizations belong to the Confédération des Organisations Familiales auprès de la Communauté Européenne (COFACE); and labor-based organizations belong to the Confédération Européenne des Syndicats (CES).

Despite the impressive number of consumer organizations in France, the consumer movement is weak because it is divided. Furthermore, the period of big battles has passed. The involvement of the majority of these organizations in the processes of consultation and negotiation has given the movement credibility but, at the same time, muzzled it. With their resources scattered over many issues, the organizations tend to exhaust themselves in technical matters, battling well-prepared professionals.

The three main components of the movement in France—the governmental DGCCRF, the quasi-governmental INC, and the consumer organizations—have difficulty defining their respective roles. Among the latter, independence can be compromised, not by state funding, but by the broader agendas of family organizations and labor unions. For example, the consumer associations of union origin can be torn between two types of collective interests. How do you defend the consumer who is a victim of repeated strike without jeopardizing the right to strike? How do you demand complete compensation for damages suffered by consumers from a defective product without threatening the employees of the responsible firm? National economic difficulties resulting in unemployment, loss of purchasing power, and increasing poverty have also diverted the attention of some of the consumer movement's supporters and arrested the movement's development.

All of these factors make it impossible to imagine that the consumer movement will ever be a countervailing power in the marketplace sufficient to reduce the need for state intervention. It is clear that the protection of French consumers essentially rests on a body of public laws and, consequently, upon structures capable of controlling and applying such legislation.

Two current concerns of the French consumer movement are particularly important: advancing French consumer protection law while taking into account European integration, and addressing new issues linked to the internationalization of trade and the development of sophisticated new commercial technologies.

If one measures consumer protection legislation by the five fundamental rights defined by the European Council in 1975 (the rights to safety, protection of economic interests, redress, information and education, and representation), one must conclude that France is very advanced. Moreover, all the texts relating to consumer protection were combined into a single text in 1992. In doing so, the Reform Commission on Consumer Law, presided over by Jean Calais-Auloy, restructured the texts to give them cohesion and foresight. This codification also had symbolic value: it further legitimized the field of consumer law in France.

Despite efforts at codification, French consumer law remains complex and poorly known even to legal professionals. Moreover, consumer law texts have become more and more precise, making them more easily distorted by dishonest professionals and more difficult for consumers to understand.

Today, the problem is less one of adopting protective legislation than one of enforcing existing laws. To facilitate this enforcement, efforts are under way to establish reversal of the burden of proof, free access to justice, class action, and simplification of the rules of litigation settlement.

The creation of a single European market raises additional issues. The opening of borders and free circulation of products and services present an increased risk for consumers if these developments are not accompanied by adequate protective measures. Even though consumer protection was a separate part of the Maastricht Treaty, producer concerns are still predominant. The difficulties encountered by consumers on a national level in asserting their rights are increased by the inherent obstacles of transactions conducted under different languages and national laws. Harmonization of law across the European Union via directives can sometimes weaken strong consumer protections such as those in France. The role of consumer associations on a national level and in representing consumers at the European level is therefore fundamental.

Additional consumer concerns in the years to come are related to the development of new technologies. New transactions methods involving telephones, television, and online services raise issues of consumer protection and privacy. In addition, safety (e.g., product liability, medical responsibilities, dangerous products), service quality (e.g., malpractice, public services), credit and its corollary of household overindebtedness, and access to justice remain fundamental topics for the near future.

International Role

By virtue of its strategic position between the northern and southern European countries, countries of common law and countries of written law, countries of strict liberalism and countries of more administrative intervention, France could serve a pivotal role in the elaboration of European law. Its most active association at the European level, the UFC, is very influential within BEUC and Consumers International, themselves supporters of a market-oriented approach to consumer protection. Despite strong cultural links with Portugal, Spain, Italy, and Greece, France has not forged a common consumer policy with southern countries with their more state-dominated regimes. Finally, the predominance of the English language in the scientific and technical universe certainly reduces the power and influence of the French consumer movement.

The French consumer movement participates in virtually all European or global associations dealing with consumer issues. The INC increasingly plays the role of expert among research groups (e.g., the European Law Group and various technical commissions). The INC conducts certain comparative tests and inquiries in the framework of the Group of Five (Portugal, Italy, Spain, France, Germany), while the UFC belongs to an international testing group.

In the future, the movement will probably be more streamlined and more aggressive. Recent economic difficulties have influenced individual consumers to become more responsible, more aware, and more demanding. Constant budgetary restrictions imperil not only the private consumer associations but also the INC. The INC will certainly concentrate on its missions of technical expertise and public service to meet great needs for information and education.

— Anne Morin
(translated by Robert N. Mayer)

See also

Bureau Européen des Unions de Consommateurs; Consumers International.

Readings

Calais-Auloy, Jean (1990). *Propositions pour un code de la consommation.* La Documentation française, 2 trimester.

Chambraud, Agnès, Patricia Foucher, and Anne Morin (1994). "The Importance of Community Law for French Consumer Protection Legislation." *Journal of Consumer Policy.* 17: 23–38.

Institut National de la Consommation (1996). *Rapport d'activité: 1995.* Paris: Institut National de la Consommation.

Fund-Raising

Fund-raising strongly influences the extent and character of the consumer movement's advocacy, research, and education activities. Without significant funds, consumer groups usually cannot sustain meaningful activities over a period of years. Yet, the sources of funding can bias the goals, and even threaten the integrity, of these organizations.

Types of Funding

There are two important general characteristics of funding apart from its level. Funding can be provided by individuals or institutions, and it can represent contributions or payment for goods or services received. Accordingly, most funding can be grouped into one of four categories.

Contributions to consumer groups from individuals are usually solicited by mail, by phone, or by door-to-door canvassing. National groups such as Center for Science in the Public Interest and Public Citizen have relied heavily on mail solicitations. Although fund-raising costs can be high, both organizations receive millions of dollars a year in contributions. Grassroots organizations belonging to the U.S. Public Interest Research Group, Citizen Action, and ACORN networks have frequently used door-to-door canvassing to build membership and financial support.

A unique source of individual contributions that has been much criticized by conservative groups is the activity fees contributed to Public Interest Research Groups by students on college or university campuses. The focal point of attack was fees received from a negative check-off in which students could refuse to make a contribution only through an affirmative action.

Contributions to consumer groups from organizations often take the form of annual payments for group membership or donations to fund-raising events such as dinners or receptions. In the 1970s, the Consumer Federation of America (CFA) derived almost all of its income from annual dues payments and awards dinner contributions by sympathetic nonprofit organizations, including consumer cooperatives and trade unions. Similarly, state-based groups such as the Consumer Federation of California and the now defunct

Ohio Consumer Association also depended heavily on contributions from these more affluent institutions. Grants from foundations and relatively affluent groups such as Consumers Union and American Association of Retired Persons are, strictly speaking, neither contributions nor payment for services received, yet share characteristics of both of these sources of funding.

Consumer groups sell a variety of products such as publications and conference registrations to individuals and organizations. In recent years, Consumers Union has generated more than $100 million annually through the sale of its magazine *Consumer Reports* and other information services. In most years, these products have produced a surplus, a portion of which has been used to fund its nonrevenue-producing activities and to contribute to other groups, including Consumers International (formerly the International Organization of Consumers Unions), CFA, and state and local consumer organizations through a grants program administered by CFA. At the other extreme, grassroots groups, particularly those run by volunteers, have generated revenues through sale of baked goods, T-shirts, and the like.

Some consumer organizations also sell various "services" to organizations. Groups such as CFA and National Consumers League (NCL) organize conferences that corporate representatives are invited to attend and for which they pay a higher registration fee than do nonbusiness attendees. Several national consumer leaders each receive more than $10,000 a year in honoraria by speaking to corporate or student groups. Also, many consumer groups have been paid by government agencies or corporations for technical services. In the early 1990s, for instance, the Resolution Trust Corporation provided contracts to groups such as ACORN for assistance in promoting sale of houses to low-income consumers, and the Environmental Protection Agency made CFA a cooperative partner in its radon and indoor air consumer education programs. National groups such as Center for Auto Safety have also sold information and advice to professionals such as plaintiffs' attorneys.

Funding Constraints

Although funds available to the consumer movement have grown, they have imposed constraints on the types and character of movement activities. Ideally, these activities should not be influenced by funding sources, only by consumer needs. But for most groups, funding sources have influenced program activities.

The individual contributions received by many groups provide them with much, but not complete, autonomy in program development. These organizations are under some pressure to select highly visible issues that allow the group to maintain a high profile. In contrast, their selection of technical issues whose consumer impact is not obvious could well reduce the effectiveness of fund-raising appeals. Also, keeping a high profile may be easiest if a group takes relatively extreme positions or employs confrontational strategies. (On the other hand, such extremism may limit opportunities to raise funds from conservative institutional sources.)

Organizations that target fund-raising appeals at special groups in the population may face even greater constraints. Public Citizen and some state groups that solicit funds from individual trial attorneys may feel an obligation to address tort reform issues and ally themselves with the plaintiff's bar.

Contributions from certain organizations to consumer groups have the potential to bias activities because so much of this support is from organizations with interests somewhat different from those of consumers. In the past, questions have been raised about pro-labor positions taken by CFA and NCL, which both receive union contributions. Even more problematic are contributions from business or law firms that, at one time or another, have been accepted by many consumer organizations. Fortunately, no bonafide consumer group is heavily dependent on corporate funding.

Funding for services received imposes its own constraints. Consumer groups who are approached by funders may be tempted to shift program priorities. When consumer organizations search for program funding, their proposals may reflect the availability of funds more than consumer need.

Selling services also may limit a group from undertaking advocacy. In general, foundations and government agencies will not fund activities intended to influence public policy. Recently, congressional Republicans have even proposed severe limitations in the types of nonprofit groups that could receive government grants and contracts. Also, foundations and government agencies usually will not fund a program for more than a few years.

Selling services to corporations is even more problematic. Business funding of advocacy raises questions of credibility and conflict of interest. Corporate support of research and education is also troublesome, but activities can be structured to minimize corporate bias. Corporate funding of dialogues, conferences, and other meetings, where a central purpose is consumer-business interchange, may impose even fewer constraints on consumer groups that plan them.

While constraints imposed by particular types of funding may limit individual consumer groups, they do not impose similar limits on the entire consumer movement because of the variability of the movement's funding sources. Different groups receive different types of funding so are subject to varying constraints. As a result, there is usually a group (or groups) able to work on any pressing consumer issue. The principal limitation on consumer movement activity is not the type of funding but its level.

— Stephen Brobeck

Reading

Upshur, Carole C. (1982). *How To Set Up and Operate a Non-Profit Organization*. Englewood Cliffs, NJ: Prentice-Hall, Inc.

Funeral Protections

In 1994, approximately 2.3 million people died in the United States. This total was slightly higher than the number of deaths in 1993. While the death rate is now relatively stable, at about the year 2005, as baby boomers turn sixty, it will begin a steep climb upwards. Experts in the death services industry predict that between 2005 and 2050 there will be great demand for funeral services.

To honor the dead, we practice a ritual that is part social and part religious. Most older Americans prefer what is called a traditional funeral. This type of funeral includes some combination of the following: a casket (wood, metal, or in some instances, plastic); an outer burial container (vault or grave liner); care of the body, including embalming; use of the funeral home for a viewing or rosary; a religious service at a house of worship; an in-ground burial with some form of memorialization; transportation of the body; the services of a funeral director and cemeterian; and extras such as flowers, music, and newspaper obituaries.

The cost of a traditional funeral is more than $4,000, and the burial could add from $500 to $5,000. It is not uncommon for consumers to pay $10,000 or more for a traditional funeral, depending upon the location and the options chosen. The single most expensive item is the casket. It constitutes anywhere from 10 to 30 percent of the cost of the funeral and burial. Caskets range in price from hundreds of dollars for cloth-covered wood, to thousands of dollars for copper and bronze. The grave plot could cost hundreds or thousands of dollars, depending upon the location of the cemetery and grave site.

Cremations are increasing in popularity. By the year 2000, one-fourth of all final dispositions will be cremations. On the West Coast, more than 40 percent of the deceased are cremated.

While many consumers view cremation as a low-cost alternative, this perception is not always correct. A cremation is only a means of final disposition. One can conduct a full traditional funeral and then cremate the body in the newly purchased casket. The ashes, more properly called cremains, could then be interred in a burial plot. Such a cremation is as costly as a traditional funeral.

What is called an immediate cremation is a low-cost alternative. It usually costs less than $1,000. Here the body is cremated in an alternative container. There is no embalming or viewing, although a memorial service honoring the deceased could be held. In place of a burial or placing the cremains in a columbarium, a place for cremated remains, these remains are spread over the ocean or in some other favored spot.

Another low-cost alternative is what is called immediate burial. Here the body is interred without any embalming, often without a casket. The basic charges here are the services of the funeral director and the cost of the burial plot.

While most consumers do not distinguish between them, there are two separate sides to the death services industry: the funeral home and the cemetery. There are more than 22,000 funeral homes spread across the country. Many of these homes are small, performing fewer than 100 funerals a year. While most homes are independent operations, chains of funeral homes are growing. SCI of Houston, for example, owns 850 funeral homes and 230 cemeteries in the United States with additional facilities in France, Australia, and Great Britain. While chains own less than 6 percent of all U.S. funeral homes, these 1,300 facilities conduct 14 percent of the funerals.

Most states license funeral directors and regulate them through a state board of funeral directors and embalmers. On the federal level, in 1984 the Federal Trade Commission (FTC) implemented a sales rule called the Funeral Rule. It requires funeral directors to disclose prices, even over the phone. In addition, the rule prohibits funeral directors from making certain false claims (e.g., this casket will preserve the body indefinitely) and requires that they secure permission before embalming the body.

Cemeteries, on the other hand, are not covered by the Funeral Rule unless they sell both funeral goods and services. On the state level, about thirty-five states license or regulate the nation's approximately 10,000 cemeteries (most of which are municipal, religious, or private). In some states, state cemetery boards oversee cemeteries; in other states, bodies such as the real estate commission oversee these facilities.

In some states, such as California, combination operations have grown. Here the funeral home is located on cemetery grounds.

Competition in funeral pricing is increasing in many areas. Traditionally, consumers viewed funerals/burials as a fixed cost item. They selected a funeral home or cemetery based on religious or cultural traditions, not cost. Only now are consumers beginning to shop around. When they do, they often find that the large chains do not usually charge the lowest prices. Instead, enterprising storefront operations with limited overhead are the funeral homes most likely to compete on price.

Even though the death rate is relatively flat, funeral and burial sales have increased dramatically in the last ten years. That is because funeral homes and cemeteries are conducting advance sales. This practice is called preneed or the sale of funeral/burial services in advance. More than 14 million older adults already own their grave plot or space in a mausoleum. More than 7 million have prepaid their funeral, and almost 9 million have purchased cemetery products or services such as a headstone or opening and closing the grave. In most instances, these purchases will not be delivered for years.

Every state except Alabama has passed a preneed funeral law or regulations to protect consumers' funds. Thirty-five states have preneed cemetery laws. These statutes require that a percentage (ranging from 30 to 100 percent) of the preneed payment be held in trust until the time of need. That is, the consumer contracts for a certain funeral or burial with the funeral director or cemeterian. He/she pays the vendor an amount equal to the cost of the goods and services, and the contractor deposits the required percentage of funds in a trust account in a financial institution.

Along with preneed trusts, life insurance policies are used to fund preneed contracts. Here the life insurance policy is sold by the funeral director or cemeterian. The face amount of the policy is equal to the cost of the goods and services, and the benefits are assigned to the funeral home or cemetery.

While estimates vary, close to $20 billion in preneed funeral/burial funds are held in trust or in a life insurance policy. Depending upon the state, the funeral board, real estate commission, banking commission, or cemetery board oversees these funds. Scandals, conflicts of interest, and violations of fiduciary responsibility have plagued the administration of these funds. While most consumers have received the funeral or burial for which they paid, the real test will come when the death rate climbs.

— Lee Norrgard

See also

Older Consumers.

Reading

Sommer, Robert, Sandra Nelson, and Kathleen Hoyt (1985). "Funeral Price Disclosure in an Urban Market." *Journal of Consumer Affairs*. 19 (2): 241–254.

G

Gas Regulation

See Natural Gas Regulation.

German Consumer Movement

The consumer movement of a particular country reflects its political traditions, level of economic development, social conditions, and cultural values. Germany has had authoritarian governments for most of its history, with real democracy only existing between 1919 and 1933 and since 1949. As a result, the German population has had very little opportunity to learn democratic patterns of political participation, including organizing to deal with problems without the initiative and support of public authorities. Accordingly, most of the existing consumer organizations in Germany are state-run institutions or depend on government funding.

Until the 1950s, the German economy was characterized by scarcity. Until then, the biggest challenge for most private households was to buy goods and services in sufficient quantity and of sufficient quality as cheaply as possible. The foundation of consumer cooperatives, beginning in 1845, was one response to this problem of scarcity. For the same reason, consumer cooperatives declined during Germany's post–World War II "economic miracle." (The cooperatives first tried to turn themselves into normal retailing organizations and then finally disappeared because of mismanagement.)

Yet, consumer affluence brought problems as well. Most consumers did not have enough impartial information to judge the expanding array of goods and to buy them efficiently. To address this problem, Stiftung Warentest (SW) was established in 1964 as a product testing organization. The initiative for founding SW came partially from labor organizations but mostly from the government.

Affluence has also increased the concern of the German citizenry about pollution, destruction of the natural environment, and the resulting reduction in the quality of life. An ecological movement came into being and has greatly influenced the consumer movement and consumer policy.

In general, consumer organizations pursue some combination of protection, education, and information. These organizations seek to stimulate action on the part of government, businesses, and consumers themselves. Consumer organizations in Germany differ in their goals and methods but can be divided into those that are primarily state-subsidized and those that are largely private.

Stiftung Warentest

Stiftung Warentest is one of the most important state-subsidized consumer organizations. Located in Berlin, it was founded in 1964 as a testing institute. Its job is to inform the public about the quality and environmental acceptability of competing products and services. This, in turn, allows consumers to protect their health and environment as well as spend their income rationally.

SW is run by a board of managers, controlled by a board of supervisors, and advised by a body of experts. In 1995, SW had more than 200 employees and contracted with a large number of external testing professionals. Its budget totaled more than $70 million, including a fixed subsidy of nearly $10 million from the federal government.

SW's activities can be divided into information generation and information dissemination. Information generation consists of comparative testing and compilation of more general consumer information (e.g., on money management, consumer health, or environmental protection). Information dissemination occurs through regular and special publications. The monthly product testing magazine, *Test,* has a circulation of about 900,000, and the bimonthly magazine, *Finanztest,* has a circulation of 370,000.

A decision by the federal supreme court requires SW to carry out its tests and surveys in a well-informed, objective, and neutral manner. This emphasis on quality has led SW to elaborate and improve its procedures.

Ideas for new testing projects are suggested mainly by employees of SW or affiliated consumer organizations. The final decision about which projects to implement is made by a supervisory body consisting of officials of other consumer groups, representatives of companies and trade associations, and neutral experts from universities and other public research institutions. Projects are then handed over to consulting committees on which private sector industry experts participate. In this way, SW benefits from the expertise of these private sector specialists, but without any obligation to follow their recommendations. When a testing project is decided upon and initial consultations are made, companies know which products and services will be scrutinized, but the exact period during which the tests will be performed is not revealed.

The criteria to be applied in a test are extremely important and depend on the nature of the product or service in question. General categories such as safety, durability, economy, handling, and environmental compatibility have to be specified and adapted to each case. Among these criteria, environmental compatibility has gained increased prominence since the 1980s. As a result, procedures for measuring a product's environmental impact have been refined, and more weight has been given to environmental attributes in the overall test.

SW does not run a testing institute of its own, thus avoiding the pressure of high overhead expenses. For each project, a testing institute is chosen from a range of about 150 institutions located throughout Europe. To be eligible for a test, institutes must use state-of-the-art testing technology and offer their services at a reasonable cost. This outsourcing of test implementation, combined with highly elaborate testing procedures, is one of the key sources of SW's success.

To arrive at an overall recommendation for a particular brand being tested, objective, quantitative methods are applied. In a first step, the test criteria are projected on an interval scale, ranging from one (very good) to four (unsatisfactory). The subsequent steps resemble a standard scoring model: the various criteria receive weights and an overall score is computed from the sum of weighted scores. If a tested item fails to meet certain minimum levels of highly important criteria (e.g., safety or environmental compatibility), an overall score of "unsatisfactory" is given, regardless of how well the item might have performed on the remaining criteria.

Companies may use test results in their advertising. As a result, "good" and "very good" results are often displayed in the mass media, on product packages and labels, and on in-store displays. To avoid misuse of its test results, SW has issued a set of recommendations for companies wishing to use test results in their advertising. One such recommendation is that test results and other advertising messages be displayed separately. Another recommendation is that the overall scores must be included, not just positive aspects when the report also contains less positive aspects.

Many of these features of SW's operations distinguish it from the world's other large product testing organizations, Consumers Union (United States) and the Consumers' Association (Britain). The acceptance of government funding, high level of consultation with business representatives, use of environmental criteria, publication of quantitative scores, outsourcing of test work, and willingness to allow test results to be used in advertisements are all practices eschewed by some product testing organizations.

Other Government-Subsidized Consumer Organizations

The Stiftung Verbraucherinstitut was founded in 1978 and is based in Berlin. Its main task is to support professionals who communicate with consumers—teachers, social workers, journalists, and others who work in the fields of consumer advice, consumer education, and consumer information. With this aim, the employees of the institute carry out further training courses and develop teaching materials. In 1994, the organization had about twenty employees and relied primarily on the state for its funding.

In each of the sixteen states of the Federal Republic of Germany, there exists one organization in charge of providing consumers with advice, the Verbraucher-Zentrale. These organizations operate consumer advice centers in more than 200 German cities. Their highly qualified personnel give advice about budgeting, managing debt, buying various products, conserving energy, considering environmental impacts, buying and renting housing, and exercising legal rights of redress. The advice centers also devise and distribute booklets to inform consumers. In some states, databases have been established that enable the advisers to give computer-aided counseling. In the past, the consumer advice centers were financed by the federal government, but in the future they will have to be funded by the states and through their own earnings.

The Arbeitsgemeinschaft der Verbraucherbände (AgV) (Alliance of Consumer Associations) is the umbrella organization for almost all consumer organizations in Germany. It was founded in 1953 and has four main tasks. First, it is supposed to advocate the interests of consumers in the legislative and administrative activities of government. It is the only government institution that represents consumer interests in public policy-making. A second task is to coordinate and focus the activities of the various independent and loosely connected consumer organizations. A third AgV function is to collect information (e.g., by price surveys) and disseminate it to audiences who can influence consumer policy (e.g., politicians, journalists, educators, and managers of public and nonprofit organizations). Finally, AgV is charged with representing the German consumer movement on a European and international level.

As of 1995, AgV had thirty-seven organizational members, plus the sixteen state-level consumer offices. Its most important publication is the *Verbraucherpolitische Korrespondenz,* which publicizes economic, agricultural, legal, environmental, and health issues. As a member of the Bureau Européen des Unions de Consommateurs (BEUC) and Consumers International, AgV supports these organizations in many ways. It is especially involved in the formation of consumer organizations in Poland, Hungary, Slovenia, and Slovakia.

Private Consumer Organizations

There are also private consumer organizations in Germany. Some of these organizations are run solely by consumers, while others are supported by private sector firms or trade associations.

Private consumer organizations in Germany typically function at the local or regional level, and they do not have many members. The most important of these organizations are tenants' societies, groups to promote neighborly help, and food cooperatives.

There are several automobile clubs in Germany that are nearly 100 years old. These organizations were established to advance the interests of consumers as motorists. Since they have very large memberships, they must be run by professionals. As a result, these associations have taken on the character of businesses, with all the intensive marketing that implies. The associations publish magazines containing information relevant to car owners and tourists.

Privately published magazines also exist for people interested in audio, video, photographic, and computer equipment. Although these magazines conduct tests, their scientific quality and objectivity cannot compete with those of Stiftung Warentest.

The German Society for Consumer and Family Sciences is an association of scientists engaged in research on issues pertaining to private households. Along with publishing a magazine, *Hauswirtschaft und Wissenschaft*, the society promotes research on consumer education.

Several private companies have established consumer affairs departments. Their employees receive queries, handle complaints, and, when appropriate, forward suggestions for product or service improvement. Some trade associations have established conciliation boards for situations in which consumers are dissatisfied but firms are not prepared to take corrective action. Boards set up by automobile dealers and clothes cleaners are two examples.

Current Issues and Activities

After German reunification in 1990, acquainting the population of the former German Democratic Republic with the conditions of a market economy and a buyers' market was a great challenge. East German consumers were overwhelmed by the enormous variety of products and services available to them, by the variation in both prices and quality, and by the aggressive methods of advertising and distribution. Many of these consumers could not resist the temptations of the market and piled up large debts. Since then, Stiftung Warentest, Stiftung Verbraucherinstitut, and AgV have been active educating and informing East German consumers. The former West German consumer advice centers also helped establish advice centers in the new German states.

Germany is a densely populated, industrial nation in which destruction of the natural environment; pollution of the air, soil, and water; and pressure on both animals and human beings are increasing. These negative developments conflict with the strong affection that many Germans have for nature. As a result, German consumer policy has included laws and statutes to protect consumers from harmful substances in food and the pollution from sources such as smoke, noise, and gasoline. Germany was the first country in the world to adopt an environmental seal of approval, the Blue Angel, to help consumers select products that minimize environmental damage. Consumer organizations do their part by informing consumers about healthy and environmentally beneficial behavior.

Of German consumer organizations, Stiftung Warentest and AgV are the most involved in international consumer affairs. SW has been a major proponent of European cooperation in product testing. More recently, SW has been active in founding testing organizations in several Central and Eastern European countries that are changing from planned to market economies. Both SW and AgV are full members of Consumers International. AgV is also a member of BEUC and, like SW, is working to form effective consumer organizations in Central and Eastern Europe.

After 1960, the German consumer movement grew rapidly. But recently, this expansion has slowed. Consumer organizations, especially Stiftung Warentest, continue to work effectively. Nevertheless, their total impact on the economy and consumers is not substantial.

— Eberhard Kuhlmann

Readings

Consumers International (1995). *Balancing the Scales, Part 2: Consumer Protection in the Netherlands and Germany.* London: Consumers International.

Köhne, Anne-Lore (1991). "Empowering the Consumer Movement in Central and Eastern Europe: Experiences of a United

Germany." *Journal of Consumer Policy*. 14: 229–237.
Kuhlmann, Eberhard (1990). *Verbraucherpolitik*. Munich: Vahlen.

Grassroots Consumer Movement

See Community Organizations; State and Local Consumer Organizations.

H

Health Care Protections

Built into the U.S. health care system, as fragmented as it is, are some basic protections for health care consumers. These protections include consumer input into health care decisions; consumer involvement in health care structures and organizations, such as managed care organizations and licensing boards; state and local regulatory protections regarding health professional licensing and monitoring; and access to the court system. These protections vary depending on the setting, type of program, state of residence of the consumer, and health care provider.

An informed and empowered customer of health care is the basic consumer protection. Patients who are knowledgeable about their health care and participate in related decision-making experience better health outcomes, lower medical costs, and higher patient satisfaction.

As a consumer of health care, each individual has both rights and responsibilities. In January 1995, the board of directors of the National Health Council (NHC), a nonprofit association of 118 national health organizations, endorsed ten principles of patients' rights and responsibilities. These principles emphasize information disclosure, confidentiality protections, and active patient participation in health care decisions. Specifically, all patients have the right to: informed consent in treatment decisions, timely access to specialty care, and confidentiality protections; concise and easily understood information about their coverage; knowledge of how coverage payment decisions are made and how they can be fairly and openly appealed; complete and easily understood information about the costs of their coverage and care; reasonable choice of providers and useful information about provider options; and knowledge of what provider incentives or restrictions might influence practice patterns. At the same time, all patients have the responsibility to pursue healthy lifestyles; become knowledgeable about their health plans; actively participate in decisions about their health care; and cooperate fully on mutually accepted courses of treatments.

Most professional associations of health care providers regulate members through a code of professional ethics and disciplinary programs. These programs often include a consumer complaint mechanism and ongoing quality review procedures. Most associations include consumer or public members, but these members may not be representative of the typical consumer of the professional service and may be political appointees.

Because of the failure of these associations to discipline member conduct adequately, each state licenses certain health professionals and regulates the professional activities of practicing health professionals, usually through the state department of health or department of regulatory agencies. According to a Pew Task Force on Health Care Workforce Regulation, this regulation should promote effective health outcomes; protect the public from harm; be accountable to the public; respect consumers' right to choose from a range of safe options of competent providers; encourage a flexible, rational, and cost-effective health care system that allows effective working relationships among providers; and facilitate professional and geographic mobility among competent providers.

Consumer advocates have argued that state regulators should do more to increase the number of public members on boards, to inform consumers of their rights, to provide information on how to access the boards, and to install toll-free phone lines. For example, in 1995 the auditor general of Arizona released a report that recommended increasing public representation in board decisions, providing broad and open access to information on regulated professionals, and involving the complainant in the complaint process.

The U.S. health care system is being transformed by "managed care" methods of financing and delivery of health services. In the private sector, managed care is rapidly becoming the dominant health care delivery system. Even in Medicare, where currently only 10 percent of all beneficiaries receive care through managed care programs, and in Medicaid, where about 32 percent are enrolled in managed care, significant enrollment growth is occurring and will continue in the future. There is an accelerating trend to urge low-income older adults and persons with disabilities to enroll in Medicare health maintenance organizations (HMOs) as a way to cut Medicare and Medicaid costs. While proponents claim that enrolling more older persons and those with disabilities into HMOs will lead to higher quality health care at lower cost, many advocates question whether HMOs can achieve this ambitious goal.

Managed care programs—such as HMOs, preferred provider organizations (PPOs), point of service (POS) systems, and provider service networks (PSNs)—present new challenges to the traditional provider-patient relationship and to consumer protection. The rules of the old fee-for-service system were decided by professionals who determined who could practice and how they were to be educated. These changes, which include a consolidation of purchasers of health care and a consolidation of the provider community into networks, demand even greater consumer knowledge and participation. The National Committee for Quality Assurance (NCQA) is widely recognized as the accrediting body for managed care. NCQA physicians and health experts conduct examinations of managed care organizations before approval.

Consumer advocates maintain that these new and rapidly growing methods of health care delivery and financing should be required to meet specific standards that relate to the quality of care provided, fiscal solvency, and operational practices. These standards should ensure members that all covered services will be available and accessible, and that appropriate due process protections will be available if a member has been denied care. Insurance companies, HMOs, and PPOs are currently regulated by a web of federal and state laws that address these standards, but the newest entities, provider service networks, are not regulated by any federal or state regulations or laws. Even under these standards, however, in some states it has been easier to file a complaint against a barber or realtor than against a health plan such as an HMO.

Advocates also hold that, in addition to the regulatory protections, it is important for managed care enrollees to receive information that enables them to make informed choices about the health plan options that are offered through their employers or through government programs. Advocates also maintain that consumers should be represented on health plan decision-making bodies and that all health plans should have grievance procedures in place that provide for a timely, written response to a member's complaint.

When these complaints are not satisfactorily resolved by plan or professional organizations, or by government agencies, consumers can file lawsuits in the civil court system. Patient litigation against physicians has increased over the past forty years because medical practice has become more dependent on technologies, treatments have grown more intrusive, and third-party financing has made treatments available to more people. In this period, courts have begun to impose tort liability on all hospitals. A health care institution (a hospital, nursing home, or clinic) is liable to its patients for negligence in maintaining its facilities; providing and maintaining medical equipment; hiring, supervising, and retaining employees; and failing to have in place procedures to protect patients.

— Robin E. Mockenhaupt

See also

Insurance Regulation.

Reading

Rodwin, Marc A. (1996). "Managed Care and Consumer Protection: What Are the Issues?" *Seton Hall Law Review.* 26 (3): 1007–1054.

Highway Safety

Motor vehicle crashes are a public health concern of huge scope. Crashes are the leading cause of death among Americans one to thirty-five years old. Long-term trends are downward, from 53,543 total deaths and a per capita death rate of 27 per 100,000 people in 1969, to 40,115 deaths and a rate of 16 in 1993. But crashes still kill tens of thousands of Americans every year. They cause more than 3 million people to be injured. And, unlike most other leading causes of mortality, since crash deaths disproportionately involve young people, the lost years of life are relatively greater. Crashes also cause substantial property damage.

Strategies for reducing crash losses focus on countermeasures targeting the driver, the vehicle, and road-related factors that contribute to crashes and the losses they generate. Yet, these strategies can only reduce, never eliminate, the deaths, injuries, and property damage.

Emergence of a Scientific Approach

Until the mid-1960s, efforts to reduce motor vehicle crash deaths and injuries focused almost exclusively on trying to prevent crashes from occurring by changing driver behavior. These efforts were based not on science, but largely on myths and "solutions" that had not been validated by competent research.

In the late 1960s, a scientific approach began to be widely applied. The first characteristic of this approach is that a logical structure allows identification of the complete range of loss reduction options. The second feature is that potential countermeasures are carefully evaluated before wide implementation. Thus, a scientific approach does not rely on programs that merely appear to make sense. Indeed, solutions that sound intuitively on target have often been shown by good research to be ineffective, e.g., programs to improve drivers' skills in order to prevent crashes.

The man generally recognized as having pioneered a scientific approach was a physician, William Haddon, Jr., who developed the first logical framework for systematically considering options for reducing motor vehicle crash losses. In this framework, which is still used today, the events involved in a crash are divided into three separate time phases—those occurring before the crash (precrash), those occurring during the crash, and postcrash events. Each event presents opportunities for intervening to reduce potential losses. The precrash phase includes all of the events that determine whether a crash takes place (e.g., whether the driver is impaired by alcohol or the condition of the vehicle's brakes). The crash phase includes all factors that determine whether people are injured in crashes (e.g., the crashworthiness of the vehicle or whether a safety belt is used), while the postcrash phase includes everything that determines whether the results of the crash are aggravated (e.g., whether adequate medical care is available).

Interacting with each of these three phases of events are three sets of factors—human, vehicle, and environment. Combining the three crash phases and three sets of factors results in a nine-cell matrix, each cell of which offers opportunities for intervention to reduce deaths and injuries. This Haddon matrix supplies highway safety researchers with a paradigm that allows systematic and comprehensive identification of countermeasure options.

Limits of Consumer Education

Prior to the scientific approach, programs to reduce crash deaths and injuries were almost exclusively confined to trying to change driver behavior through education. The focus, in effect, was in only one cell of Haddon's nine-cell matrix. According to this line of thinking, driver error was involved in most crashes, so the focus should be on preventing the errors. This approach also implicitly assumed that, in the majority of crashes, driver error was the sole cause, so preventing the errors would be sufficient to prevent crashes.

While focusing almost all highway safety efforts on crash prevention might sound reasonable to people outside the field of highway safety, it ignores prevention possibilities elsewhere in the Haddon matrix. The key is recognizing the wide range of available options to prevent losses. Preventing crashes is but one of the many options.

Even when considering crash prevention options, assuming that most crashes have a single cause oversimplifies what are highly complex events. Few crashes have a single cause. For example, a crash involving a driver going too fast around a curve and losing control may involve not only driver error but, most likely, other factors too. The road surface coefficient of friction may play a role. So may the condition of the vehicle's tires and brakes.

Even now that a scientific approach has been accepted for more than twenty-five years, many people continue to believe that improving drivers is the key to reducing losses. They continue to claim that highway safety problems can be solved by educating drivers, specifically by improving their driving skills. Yet, many driver problems are caused by poor attitudes, not poor skills, and changing people's attitudes through education is, at best, a very difficult task. And, in many cases, it is impossible. Teenagers, for example, can be taught driving skills. But changing their attitudes is much more difficult because these attitudes so often are related to the need to rebel, to comply with peer pressure, to seek thrills, and generally to disregard adult influence. Given these realities, it is not surprising that short-term education efforts fail.

Even when it comes to simple behavior such as using safety belts, approaches based on education alone fail. Despite major efforts including expensive media campaigns, for example, high rates of belt use have never been achieved anywhere in the world through education alone. Nor has high school driver education succeeded in producing drivers who are involved in fewer crashes than young people who learn from parents or private driving schools.

Role of Regulation

The most effective approach to changing driver behavior in the short term involves the combination of publicity and vigorous enforcement of traffic laws: for example, laws intended to prevent crashes by making sure motorists do not drink and drive, speed, run red lights, and violate other statutes, and laws intended to reduce crash injuries by making occupants buckle up and motorcyclists wear helmets. This approach works better than emphasis on the possibility of death or injury in a crash because motorists can be convinced more easily of the likelihood of getting a ticket than of the likelihood of being involved in a crash. This fact points to one of the fundamental reasons the behavioral approach to highway safety usually fails: drivers overwhelmingly believe that they are at least average, or above average, and that safety problems involve other "bad" drivers. Thus, drivers are not motivated to change their driving behavior. Yet, they continue to believe that education is necessary to improve the "bad" drivers, a group to which virtually no drivers admit belonging.

Research has already demonstrated the kinds of driver behavior changes that can be accomplished with moderate traffic law enforcement plus publicity. The latest and most ambitious of these programs in the United

States is North Carolina's multiyear program, begun in 1993, to enforce highway safety laws beginning with belt use and child restraint laws. Virtually all local police departments and sheriffs' offices in the state are cooperating with the state highway patrol. In late 1993 and again in mid-1994, two periods of concentrated enforcement of the belt law were conducted and, in each case, the enforcement was accompanied by intensive publicity on television, on radio, and in newspapers. During the second of the two enforcement periods, a total of 2,938 safety belt checkpoints were conducted during a three-week period. The result is that belt use rose from 64 percent before the program to more than 80 percent.

Despite widespread claims that alcohol-impaired driving causes up to 50 percent of all fatal motor vehicle crashes, nobody knows how many crashes are caused by alcohol impairment. What is known is that alcohol impairment is a serious highway safety problem and that many serious crashes involve drivers with very high blood alcohol concentrations. The most effective approach to reducing this problem involves enacting, enforcing, and publicizing laws making it illegal to drive with a blood alcohol concentration at or above a specified threshold that is known to cause significant impairment—usually 0.08 or 0.10 percent.

Following the adoption of effective laws during the past 10 to 15 years, the proportion of fatal crashes involving drivers with high blood alcohol concentrations has decreased. Laws raising the legal purchasing age for alcohol to twenty-one years old have been especially effective, significantly reducing the problem of alcohol-impaired driving by young people.

Administrative license suspension laws are also effective. Requiring suspension of a driver's license upon failure or refusal to take a chemical test for alcohol, these laws work because penalties are imposed independently from criminal proceedings in which penalties may be avoided altogether or substantially delayed. But such laws are effective only if motorists believe that they are likely to be caught driving while impaired by alcohol. Sobriety checkpoints can help by increasing motorists' perceptions that arrest for alcohol-impaired driving is likely. Checkpoints are so visible and attract so much publicity that they remind potential offenders of the likelihood of arrest. Deterrence, not apprehension of huge numbers of offenders, is the purpose of checkpoints. The objective is to deter so many potential offenders that, ultimately, there are none left to apprehend.

Almost from the beginning of automobile use, state legislators drafted laws aimed at driver behavior. Yet, except for a few areas such as lighting, the vehicle itself was not regulated. Even as automobile registrations increased and public concern about crash deaths mounted, attention remained focused largely on driver issues.

For example, safety belts began to be used in race cars in the 1920s but, despite pleas by physicians and others that began in the 1930s, neither belts nor anchor points for fitting cars with belts were made standard in U.S. cars until the mid-1960s, and then only in response to state laws. In 1959, Volvo was the first manufacturer to install lap/shoulder belts as standard equipment on cars sold in the United States. Yet, it was not until the 1973 model year that all manufacturers installed such belts as standard equipment for front-seat occupants. Most rear seats were not equipped with lap/shoulder belts until the late 1980s.

At a 1962 conference convened by Consumers Union and the Association for the Aid of Crippled Children, Haddon and Dr. James L. Goddard noted that the safety establishment's preoccupation with crash causation was making it overlook possibilities for preventing deaths and injuries once crashes occur. The two public health physicians pointed out that steering wheels were crushing people's chests, radio knobs were penetrating skulls, and doors were springing open in crashes.

Three years later, General Motors (GM) president James Roche explained to a subcommittee of the U.S. Senate that, in 1964, his company spent only $1.25 million on safety while earning $1.7 billion in profits. But it was publicity surrounding the release of Ralph Nader's *Unsafe at Any Speed* (1965), and the exposure of a GM investigation of Nader, that raised wide public concerns about auto safety.

In the following year, President Lyndon Johnson signed the landmark highway safety laws that formed the cornerstone of the federal effort to reduce motor vehicle crash losses. The National Traffic and Motor Vehicle Safety Act authorized the federal government to set safety standards for new vehicles, while the Highway Safety Act authorized development of a national highway safety program. Both laws were important because, until they were enacted, motor vehicle safety laws and regulations were set by states and varied widely.

Haddon was the first head of the Federal Highway Safety Bureau created under the 1966 legislation. He established programs reflecting a scientific approach to highway loss reduction. For about two decades thereafter, most progress toward safer motor vehicles resulted from government regulation. It is because of government regulation, for example, that all new cars sold since the 1970s have safety features like lap/shoulder belts and not-so-noticeable features such as energy-absorbing steering columns and high-penetration-resistant windshields.

The best-known of all federal motor vehicle safety regulations is the one, issued in 1984, that requires automatic restraints. For years, Haddon and others had been championing airbags as an automatic, or passive, approach to cushioning occupants in the "second impact" of crashes that occur when people slam into vehicle interiors. A federal requirement that would have led to airbags was first proposed as early as 1969. But automakers fought this requirement in a battle so heated that the U.S. Supreme Court characterized it as the "regulatory equivalent of war."

By 1986, forty-nine federal motor vehicle safety standards were on the books. But not all cars offered the same level of safety. One reason for safety differences is that federal standards require only minimum levels of safety performance: manufacturers are free to choose different designs to meet these requirements, and some designs are better than others. Another reason is that some cars are larger than others, and the laws of physics dictate that large cars can offer occupants more crash protection than can small cars.

Marketplace Contributions

Henry Ford II conceded in 1977 that "we would not have the kinds of safety built into automobiles that we have had unless there had been a federal law." Ford was pointing to the cost any single automaker would have incurred to take the lead on safety improvements. Uniform federal standards were presumed to level the playing field for all manufacturers and, for two decades, spurred the design of safer vehicles.

For years, most automakers ignored safety as a marketing advantage, mistakenly believing that safety would not sell cars. This myth began when 1956 Chevrolets outsold Fords that were being marketed with a strong emphasis on safety features. Automakers assumed, from the Fords' poor showing, that consumers did not want safety. In fact, Ford officials estimated at the time that, without the safety features and the company's aggressive marketing of them, fewer Fords would have been sold—that sales would have been even more lopsided in favor of Chevrolet.

This myth remained firm despite clear signals of consumer interest in safety design. Adverse publicity about the safety of Chevrolet's Corvair, for example, contributed to its demise. Widespread negative publicity about problems with the fuel tanks of Ford Pintos was responsible for its significant decline in sales and eventual demise.

Although Volvo and Mercedes-Benz were exceptions—they have been advertising safety for years—it was not until 1987 that a Ford executive admitted that the myth about safety not selling was "yesterday's news. Times have changed. People are interested." Now virtually all automakers are moving faster on safety advancements than government regulations require. They are scrambling to design and install features, such as side-impact airbags, for which no federal requirement is even being considered. And they are using their safety advancements in advertising. These consumer-driven efforts by manufacturers to improve auto safety represent the most significant auto safety trend in recent years.

Consumer Information

Valuable safety-related information is available to consumers from many sources. The Highway Loss Data Institute, for example, publishes information on the likelihood of an insurance claim being filed for one passenger vehicle compared with another. The Insurance Institute for Highway Safety publishes lists of recent model cars with driver deaths per registered vehicle. These information sources are based on real-world crashes and thus reflect the complete spectrum of crashes. However, they are also influenced by the demographics of their drivers and other factors that do not involve the vehicles.

Information on front-into-barrier crash test results is also available from the U.S. Department of Transportation's New Car Assessment Program. The public release of these results has provided consumers with useful information since 1978 and has put pressure on automakers to design vehicles that perform well. Yet, as with safety information based on real-world crash experience, this information has limitations. The chief one is that the federal crash test results cannot be used to compare vehicles of different sizes. In addition, the federal New Car Assessment Program, which has remained essentially unchanged since it began in 1978, now needs to be overhauled.

Nevertheless, the New Car Assessment Program is still useful. Its full-width-barrier crash tests are the most demanding tests of restraint systems, and the tests have produced remarkable improvements. For example, cars with steering assemblies that rotated upward in a crash to meet the face of a belted occupant are no longer sold in the United States. Restraint systems have been improved so much that virtually all new cars now get good New Car Assessment Program scores. Now, however, the small differences among current test scores provide little in the way of useful information on which consumers can base choices among cars.

Researchers worldwide now are looking beyond full-width-barrier tests to frontal offset tests to assess vehicles' structural integrity and, in particular, how well they resist occupant compartment intrusion in serious frontal crashes. The Insurance Institute for Highway Safety, for example, is evaluating cars based on offsets that, unlike full-width-barrier tests, engage only part of a vehicle's front end.

Publishing more comprehensive vehicle safety information, including the results of frontal offset tests, is not limited to the United States. In Australia, a consortium of government agencies, insurers, and auto clubs is testing new cars and reporting offset and other crash test results. The German magazine *Auto Motor und Sport* and ADAC, the German equivalent of the American Automobile Association, publish reports of various crash tests.

Conclusion

Past auto safety improvements have relied heavily on consumer involvement, and so will future progress. In the future, it is important to remember two basic truths.

First, technological breakthroughs are not needed to save more lives in motor vehicle crashes. In most cases, the technology already exists. What is needed is public commitment and political support to implement known methods for improving drivers, vehicles, and highways. For example, vehicle interiors could be made less dangerous to the occupants who slam into them in crashes. Vehicles' front-end structures could be improved to resist intrusion in a crash and better protect occupants' legs. Such improvements are becoming especially important now that airbags and safety belts are doing such a good job of protecting occupants' upper bodies.

Also, many head restraint designs could be improved to do a better job of preventing neck injuries in rear-end collisions. At present, head restraints in too many new cars do not extend behind occupants' heads unless they are manually adjusted to do so and, even then, may not be high enough and may be too far behind an occupant's head to prevent injury.

When it comes to drivers, new ways are available to reduce crashes. For example, researchers know that teenage drivers account for far more than their share of motor vehicle crashes, including fatal crashes, and that the problem is worst among sixteen-year-old drivers. Researchers also know that graduated licensing programs reduce crash involvement among beginning teenage drivers by restricting when and with whom such drivers can operate motor vehicles. Such programs are already in place, and saving lives, in New Zealand and elsewhere, but they are just beginning to attract interest in the United States.

Second, there is no single solution to the problem of motor vehicle crash deaths and injuries. One program alone, no matter how important or effective, cannot solve this problem. A whole range of proven programs addressing drivers, vehicles, and roadways during the precrash, crash, and postcrash phases is needed to keep people alive and unharmed in their vehicles.

— Brian O'Neill

See also

Alcohol Problems and the Consumer Movement; Center for Auto Safety; National Highway Traffic Safety Administration.

Reading

Mashaw, Jerry L., and David L. Harfst (1990). *The Struggle for Auto Safety.* Cambridge, MA: Harvard University Press.

History of the Consumer Movement

See U.S. Consumer Movement: History and Dynamics.

Home Improvement Protections

Recently, Americans have spent more than $40 billion a year on additions and alterations to their homes. Complaints related to these home improvements represent one of the largest categories of consumer grievances voiced to protection agencies. Particularly serious is the targeting of vulnerable consumers—including the poor and the elderly—by home improvement contractors who use deceptive sales and financing techniques to persuade them to pay substantial sums for shoddy workmanship or even no workmanship at all.

Home improvement contractors have historically been regulated by piecemeal application of a variety of federal and state statutes, including state retail installment sales acts, the federal Truth in Lending Act, Federal Trade Commission (FTC) rules, and state consumer protection statutes prohibiting unfair and deceptive practices. New schemes by unscrupulous home improvement contractors, such as recent second mortgage scandals, have created the need for new ways to protect consumers and provide redress.

Until the 1960s, clever contractors sometimes charged high effective interest rates by characterizing their financed transactions as credit sales rather than as loans, thereby avoiding interest ceilings imposed by state usury laws. Since then, however, all states have enacted retail installment sales acts that set limits on charges in credit sales, including home improvement sales. These acts also impose obligations on sellers to disclose fully all contract terms clearly and conspicuously.

Many consumers were still unable to understand the real cost of home improvement contracts that often placed their homes at risk. Congressional attention—most notably by Senators Paul Douglas (D-IL) and William Proxmire (D-WI) and Representative Leonor Sullivan (D-MO)—to consumer abuse in the credit industry led to the enactment of the federal Truth in Lending Act in 1968. This law is primarily a credit disclosure statute that focuses on consumer need for complete, accurate, timely, and standardized information before entering into increasingly complex credit transactions. The act represented a compromise between increased federal regulation of the marketplace and state regulation of consumer credit terms.

The act also created a three-day right of rescission for consumers who allow home improvement contractors and other creditors to place liens on their homes as collateral for financing. During the rescission period, the consumer can evaluate the terms and the impact of the secured loan while the contractor is prohibited from starting work. Failure to give the required disclosures, or notice of the right of rescission, can extend the rescission period for up to three years.

Until the 1970s, consumers also suffered when their home improvement contractors became insolvent or disappeared before completing their projects satisfactorily but after assigning their credit contracts to banks and other financial institutions. Under the holder in due course doctrine, which insulated assignees from claims against sellers, the consumer's attempt to raise claims of shoddy workmanship against the bank seeking repayment often was not successful. The FTC's "Holder Rule," effective since 1976, has usually made assignees of home improvement contracts responsible for any claims or defenses the consumer could have raised against the contractor, even though the assignee was not a party to the original agreement. This change in law has compelled lending institutions to investigate more thoroughly the contractors with whom they do business. Many states have enacted similar "anti–holder in due course" rules.

Home improvement sales are frequently initiated by the sellers at the homes of consumers where they are a captive audience for high-pressure sales pitches. Home solicitation abuses in the home improvement industry led the FTC in 1973 to promulgate its Rule for Door-to-Door Sales. The rule gives consumers the right to cancel any home improvement solicitation made at his/her home within three days following the transaction. As in the case of the Truth in Lending right to rescission, the "cooling-off" period allows consumers an opportunity to reevaluate the sale without the salesperson present. The seller also must inform the consumer, in writing and orally, of the right and the procedures required to cancel the sale. As in the Truth in Lending context, a contractor is liable for any work performed during the three-day period if the consumer subsequently chooses to exercise the right to cancellation.

Beginning in the 1970s, states started to enact consumer protection statutes that regulated unfair and deceptive acts and practices, commonly referred to as UDAP statutes. These laws have been highly effective in allowing challenges of unacceptable practices, including high-pressure sales, bait and switch, and other deceptive pricing tactics, and misrepresentations relating to warranties, product characteristics, and cancellation rights. State UDAP statutes are helpful to consumers because these laws usually do not require a judicial finding of the contractor's intent to defraud but merely evidence that the contractor engaged in illegal conduct. UDAP statutes often provide for multiple damages and/or attorney's fees; consumers can also join together and pursue contractors with class action suits. Additionally, most states have special provisions for the state's attorney general to sue on behalf of injured consumers, to seek restitution for consumers, to collect penalties, and to obtain court orders preventing offensive behavior.

Consumer advocates may also pursue contractors for breaching warranties imposed by state and federal law. Warranties are implied or express promises of quality of materials and workmanship in the sale of goods. Every home improvement contract has an implied warranty that the goods sold will be fit for ordinary use. For example, the sale of siding for a house contains an implied warranty that the siding will keep rain and snow from entering the house. However, in most states and under the federal Magnuson-Moss Warranty Act, the implied warranty may be disclaimed. An express warranty is an oral or written promise by the seller; for example, a contractor's promise that the siding will last for twenty years.

The contractor's "breach" (that is, violation) of the warranty will ordinarily require the contractor to repair or replace the goods or give the consumer damages. To obtain relief for a breach of warranty, the consumer will have to prove that there was a warranty (which may be difficult with unwritten warranties) and that the warranty was violated (which may require the use of an expert).

The most recent and egregious attempts by unscrupulous contractors to evade the regulatory framework have been the home improvement/second mortgage scams of the 1980s. As housing market values appreciated faster than family income and as financial institutions became deregulated, home equity loans (or second mortgage loans) became more commonplace. "Equity skimmers" saw an opportunity to prey upon homeowners who had accumulated substantial equity in their homes, but were nonetheless "cash poor," by convincing them to take out high interest rate second mortgage loans to finance home improvement contracts. Contractors either would make the loans directly and then sell them to third-party lenders, or would encourage customers to enter into mortgage transactions directly with certain financial institutions. In both instances, contractors tried to distance themselves from financing arrangements.

The loans were based on the value of the consumers' homes, not on their ability to repay the loans. Because the terms of repayment were often as much as 70 percent of consumers' monthly incomes, borrowers frequently struggled to make the high payments to avoid foreclosure. Despite their efforts, even when the contractor's work was of such poor quality that it decreased the value of the home, many consumers lost their homes to foreclosure.

As these scams unfolded in the media, state legislators, regulators, and advocates moved quickly to try to prevent further harm to consumers. Advocates sought the imposition of moratoria on foreclosures springing from second mortgage transactions to provide time to seek more permanent relief. Attorneys general and private class action lawyers filed comprehensive litigation against contractors and lenders.

Several states enacted legislation intended to regulate the activities of previously unregulated contractors and mortgage companies. For example, in 1991 Massachusetts enacted a statute that required home improvement contractors to register with a state agency (with criminal penalties for failure to register) and to put all home improvement contracts over $1,000 in writing. The law also prohibited home improvement contractors from acting as brokers or agents for mortgage lenders. In addition, the new law established a consumer restitution fund to help consumers who could not recover damages directly from their contractors.

— Ernest L. Sarason, Jr.

See also

Deceptive, Unfair, and Unconscionable Sales Practices; Mortgage Loan Protections.

Readings

Cipparone, Joseph A. (1989). "The Home Improvement Act Defense." *Connecticut Bar Journal*. 63 (December): 329–359.

Keest, Kathleen (1992). "Spiking and Loan-Splitting in Home Improvement Financing: Artful Dodges." *Clearinghouse Review*. 26 (August): 415–421.

Home Repair Protections

See Home Improvement Protections.

Hong Kong Consumer Movement

At the end of 1973, Hong Kong was caught up in the effects of worldwide economic inflation and financial disorder. Prices of basic goods skyrocketed. The public demanded government intervention to check widespread profiteering.

In April 1974, the government responded by establishing the Consumer Council with a view to encouraging fair play in the marketplace and providing effective safeguards against the exploitation of consumers. In July 1977 under the Consumer Council Ordinance, the council became a statutory body. It was charged with the responsibility to protect and promote consumers' interests in goods, services, and immovable property.

The twenty-two council members appointed by the government are from all walks of life. As of 1994, most of the 101 staff members are stationed in the head office, and some work in the sixteen advice centers located throughout the territory. The Consumer Council has had six chairpersons. Together with the council's two executive directors, Ophelia Cheung (1974 to 1985) and Pamela Chang Wong Shui (1985 to the present), they have made significant contributions to the consumer movement.

A comparison of the nature and focus of the council's work over the years shows the growth of the consumer movement. In the area of price monitoring, what began in 1974 as the daily announcement of retail food prices on radio is now the quarterly price survey of products in supermarkets and the survey of petrol retail prices in comparison to import costs. The list of publications added to the monthly Chinese-language magazine, *Choice*, includes *Property Guide* and *Medical Digest*. These publications disseminate independent consumer information, thereby facilitating informed choice.

The nearly 10,000 consumer complaints lodged each year, combined with findings of independent product tests and surveys, reveal the lack of protection for consumers and their weak bargaining power. In addition to publicizing the pitfalls, the council advocates consumer protection legislation and encourages self-regulation of businesses. Legislation for which the council has lobbied over the years and is now being enforced includes the Trade Descriptions Ordinance, Gold and Platinum Marketing Orders, Control of Exemption Clauses Ordinance, Travel Agents Ordinance, Money Changers Ordinance, Small Claims Tribunal Ordinance, and Toys and Children's Products Safety Ordinance.

The council also engages in extensive discussion with industries in order to increase protection for consumers. Notable among these efforts are licensing and self-regulation of insurance intermediaries, disclosure of accurate information on properties, and regulation of real estate agents. The council's activities to enhance consumers' awareness and empowerment extend to the local community level, reaching out to students, homemakers, and senior citizens through a network of consumer advice centers.

Since the late 1980s, Hong Kong has evolved from a manufacturing-based to a service-based economy. While the manufacturing-based, export-oriented economy is more attuned to competition in the international market, a service-based economy is highly susceptible to domestic monopolization and high concentration of market power. Such a phenomenon is likely to be detrimental to consumer interests.

The Consumer Council was called upon by the governor in late 1992 to defend free markets and to give consumers full access to redress against unscrupulous business practices. This charge has provided the impetus for the council's two recent projects: studies of competition policy for Hong Kong, and the creation of a Consumer Legal Action Fund.

Release of the first report, *Are Hong Kong's Depositors Being Treated Fairly?*, challenged the interest rate cartel of banks, which has been in existence for over thirty years. This report drew overwhelming public support for its recommendations; as a first step, the government has agreed to discard the cap on time deposits. Other studies of competition have covered supermarkets, telecommunications, broadcasting, energy supplies, and the property market.

Besides industry-specific studies on the competitive environment, the Consumer Council will undertake a market structural analysis to examine whether there are indications of monopolization and concentration in markets. The analysis will serve as the basis for recommendations concerning a comprehensive competition policy for Hong Kong. At present, no competition laws exist, nor is there any government agency similar to the U.S. Federal Trade Commission or the U.K. Office of Fair Trading.

Markets that are not competitive are one source of consumer complaints. The Consumer Council has also received numerous complaint cases over the years about sellers who engage in malpractice or other unconscionable conduct. Empirical studies have shown the difficulty that consumers have experienced in attempting to obtain redress for their grievances.

In the past, the council has mediated disputed cases or advised consumers to take action in the Small Claims Tribunal or the higher courts with the assistance of Legal Aid. This limited assistance is, however, insufficient to assist the majority of consumers who fail to find satisfaction because of factors including: fear of the economic strength of the trader whose size, expertise, and access to sophisticated legal advice is much greater than the individual plaintiff's; ignorance of legal remedies; lack of skills in using existing redress procedures; lack of financial means to pursue legal action; and lack of an administrative procedure by which claims for damages arising from multiple wrongdoings can be collectively pursued. The need for a mechanism to obtain redress on a collective basis is especially needed. Recently, the council sought and received more than $1 million to establish the Consumer Legal Action Fund, which provides consumers with legal support to pursue their claims.

Consumers need to be aware of not only their rights but also their responsibilities. Particularly important is their contribution toward a better natural environment through sustainable consumption. The Consumer Council performs a key role in disseminating accurate information on the environmental impacts of products, through its test programs and research work, to make consumers more aware of the effect of their consumption patterns and lifestyles on the environment. As a further step, the Consumer Council supports the establishment of an eco-labeling scheme and cooperates with the government to work out the criteria for environmental assessment.

Since 1976, the Consumer Council has been a member of the council of Consumers International and has actively participated in its research, information, and education activities. In 1991, the council hosted the thirteenth International Organization of Consumers Unions World Congress.

The Consumer Council's commitment to consumer welfare in the last twenty years has enabled it to go beyond handling complaints against unscrupulous trade practices to shaping major government policies to safeguard consumer interests. In this latter regard, regional coordination is no less important than international liaison because similar consumer products are involved and regional consumer movements are at a similar level of development. Regional sharing of experience allows a wider perspective on consumer concerns and their possible solutions.

The transfer of sovereignty back to the People's Republic of China in 1997 signifies a new era in which Hong Kong will become a Special Administrative Region of China under the arrangement of "one country, two systems." Hong Kong sees a further strengthening of ties with a large number of consumer associations in China with whom the council has frequent contact. With increased traffic with China, the council will face new and larger challenges.

— Pamela Chan Wong Shui

See also

Chinese Consumer Movement.

Housing Cooperatives

Cooperative housing is a by-product of the general cooperative movement. Housing cooperatives were intended to reduce the cost of housing by emphasizing the benefits of occupancy and de-emphasizing speculation and profit. Cooperative organizations usually have a limited return, restore any surplus to members in proportion to their participation, and confer one vote on each member. In most housing cooperatives, a member owns a share in the development based on the value of the dwelling occupied; the dwelling itself is not owned. The most common form of cooperative housing is nonprofit. The cooperative is governed by rules, regulations, and a legal charter. Rules govern membership criteria, fees, equity accrual provisions, and governing structure. Cooperatives may have a sponsoring organization such as a church or labor union.

Cooperative housing, in contrast to other forms of ownership, is relatively recent. The first known housing cooperative was in France in 1720. By the twentieth century, many European countries, including Austria, Denmark, Germany, Norway, Sweden, and Switzerland, had strong cooperative housing organizations. Cooperative housing in the United States began in New York City in the nineteenth century. These New York City cooperatives were known as "home clubs"; their stockholders were entitled to long-term leases of apartments within the building owned by the company. These first cooperatives were designed to provide high-income consumers with the advantages of home ownership without the responsibilities. But cooperative housing did not flourish until the end of World War I.

In 1918, the Finnish Home Building Association established a cooperative housing development in Brooklyn, New York. These early stockholder-occupied cooperatives were often for upper–middle-income owners who were attracted, in part, by the exclusivity of membership. With the passage of the New York Housing Act of 1927, middle- and low-income cooperatives grew rapidly. The law granted tax exemptions to the developments as well as condemnation permits for obtaining adequate sites. Under this program, thirteen cooperatives were built. Labor unions often had a role in the development of cooperatives. One of the first in the Bronx was built by the Amalgamated Clothing Workers Union.

By 1926, cooperative developments had been built in sixteen U.S. cities, including Chicago, Detroit, Buffalo, San Francisco, and Philadelphia, but about half of all cooperatives were located in New York City. In the 1920s, many housing co-ops were experiencing financial problems, which worsened during the Great Depression. By 1934, over 75 percent of the cooperatives in Chicago and New York had gone bankrupt. Factors that contributed to this financial instability were lack of social cohesion in many of the developments, lack of knowledge about how to operate in cooperation, and especially lack of capital.

Between 1945 and 1950, cooperative housing revived. The Emergency Price Control Act of 1942 was a major impetus for co-op conversions. This act contained rent control provisions, which spurred apartment owners to convert buildings into cooperatives to obtain relief from the combination of fixed rents and increasing maintenance costs. Further incentives were provided by the federal government through Section 216 of the Internal Revenue Code as well as by some state governments through tax benefits to new nonprofit housing ventures. Trade union cooperatives made important progress, especially in the New York area under the leadership of Abraham Kazan, who had been a manager with the Amalgamated Clothing Workers Union. However, despite this progress, in 1950 there were only about 4,500 cooperative units nationwide.

By providing government insurance, Section 213 of the 1950 Housing Act stimulated investments in middle-income cooperatives. Section 221(d)(3) and Section 236 programs financed, with subsidized mortgages, 55,000 cooperative units. New York's Mitchell-Lama program of subsidized mortgages helped produce more than 50,000 co-op units.

Three housing cooperative organizations were formed during this time. The National Association of Housing Cooperatives was organized in 1950 as a nonprofit federation of housing cooperatives, professionals, nonprofits, government agencies, and individuals whose goal is to promote the interests of cooperative housing communities. The Cooperative Housing Foundation (CHF) was organized in 1951 as a national nonprofit institution dedicated to research and education related to housing cooperatives. In 1952, the foundation created a company to provide architectural, engineering, and other services to cooperative housing projects. The Federation of Section 213 Cooperatives (now the Federation of New York Housing Cooperatives) was organized during the 1950s to exchange information and education, to stimulate consumer activities, and to undertake joint projects. Approximately 100,000 people live in co-ops associated with the federation.

In the 1960s, spurred by large-scale developments by the CHF and the United Housing Foundation, housing co-ops grew. Most of the growth was concentrated in major metropolitan areas. By 1972, with cooperatives established in thirty cities, the CHF was the largest sponsor of nonprofit housing in the United States. Rising interest rates and the 1973 government moratorium on low- and moderate-income housing development stopped this momentum. Since then, there have been some for-profit conversions of upper-income housing in New York City, several major cooperatives built for senior citizens, and some cooperative development initiated by nonprofit developers. The Section 8 new construction program, which began in the late 1970s, assisted in the development of a few thousand cooperatives, primarily for senior citizens.

Financing for cooperative development, as well as for individual owners, has often been a problem. The creation of the National Cooperative Bank (NCB) in 1978 provided a national lender with a focus on loans to housing and business cooperatives. Since it went private in 1981, the NCB has serviced $1 billion in housing loans. In addition, a secondary market for loans is beginning to emerge. Both the Federal National Mortgage Association (Fannie Mae) and the Federal Home Loan Mortgage Cooperation (Freddie Mac) will purchase cooperative loans. These purchases, however, are primarily for resale to buyers rather than for the development of a new cooperative.

Further assistance to the development of housing cooperatives was provided by low-income housing tax credits, which were part of the Tax Reform Act of 1986. These tax credits have been used by limited partnerships that have developed cooperatives. Although they add to the complexity and difficulty of the development process, they represent the only viable source of financial assistance available today to lower-income housing cooperatives.

In 1991, the National Association of Housing Cooperatives created the Center for Cooperative Housing. The twofold purpose of the center was to provide technical assistance in developing housing cooperatives and to link potential local sponsors with the cooperative housing network and with federal programs designed to facilitate the creation of cooperative housing.

That same year, there were 742,000 cooperative housing units in the United States. Of these units 630,000 were occupied. Owners accounted for 63 percent of the occupants compared with 37 percent who were renters. Although less than 1 percent of the units were new construction, 9 percent were occupied by recent movers. Households with a head over age sixty-five occupied 30 percent of the units. Below-poverty households accounted for 8 percent of the occupants.

As the country once again explores alternatives to traditional ownership, new interest in housing cooperatives is emerging. Well-managed housing cooperatives often provide a low-cost solution to housing needs. Without adequate training, however, prospective occupants may not understand the concept or the commitment that they must make. The lack of financial infrastructure has also impeded development.

— Carol B. Meeks

See also

Cooperatives, Consumer; National Cooperative Bank.

Readings

Helm, John Paul, and Sanford Horvitz (1993). "Cooperative Homeownership: An Affordable Alternative." *Journal of Housing.* 50 (November/December): 238–240.

Siegler, Richard, and Herbert J. Levy (1986). "Brief History of Cooperative Housing." *Cooperative Housing Journal.* 12: 12–19.

Housing Protections

See Home Improvement Protections; Mortgage Loan Protections; Real Estate Brokerage Protections; Tenant Protections.

Hungarian Consumer Movement

Hungary was one of the three Central and Eastern European countries to give birth to a consumers' association during the Communist era. Prompted by a rise in consumer complaints and an awareness in academic circles of consumer groups in other countries, a number of activists came together in 1982 to form the National Consumer Council. Emerging from the Patriotic People's Front, an umbrella for various civil movements, it successfully fought off attempts by the government and the unions to absorb it; the council retained its strong regional structure and a measure of independence despite accepting substantial government funding, and despite the restraining hand of the Communist Party.

During most of the 1980s, Hungarian consumer organizations sought to uncover breaches of the law by local shopkeepers, especially with respect to food and drink. Members of consumer organizations would act as voluntary trade inspectors, reporting offenders to the authorities who would then prosecute (thereby extending the enforcement machinery). The central office helped the regional councils to identify and tackle local problems.

In 1989, the newly elected government made it clear that institutions and individuals associated with the old regime would be cut loose from official support and would have to prove themselves in the new climate. The council remodeled itself in 1991 as the National Association for Consumer Protection in Hungary (NACPH). In the same year, its grant was slashed by two-thirds and, in 1992, suspended altogether. The result has been a struggle for survival.

Also in 1992, one of its board members, Matyas Vince, who was editor of Hungary's leading economics journal in the 1980s, successfully launched a comparative testing magazine, *TESZT*, with financial contributions from government and from advertisers, without which it would not have been commercially viable. Circulation has stabilized at between 25,000 and 30,000 per month, of which about half subscribe on a regular basis and half purchase sporadically from newsagents and street stalls. Initially, under Vince's editorship, the magazine remained close to NACPH, although it was published by a separate company, the Media Foundation. Since Vince moved on to edit one of Hungary's major newspapers, *TESZT* has been more distant from NACPH, although it shares offices and continues to devote a half page per issue to the association's material. Advertisements are accepted from companies whose products are reviewed in the magazine, which disqualifies NACPH for membership in Consumers International.

At the beginning of 1994, Istvan Garai, who was the original secretary to the council in 1982 but left in 1991 to work for the Institute for Commercial Quality Control (KERMI), rejoined NACPH as its director. This was made possible by funding from the German consumer organization Arbeitsgemeinschaft der Verbraucherbände (AgV) (Alliance of Consumer Associations) to run a chain of twenty-three advice offices for consumers. This grant provided enough money up until the end of 1995 to pay for a lawyer and administrative staff as well as a secretary. All the advice centers are staffed by volunteers trained by NACPH and AgV.

The major challenge currently facing NACPH is continuing its work and building its organization when financial assistance from foreign organizations such as AgV ends. It is eager to become involved in consumer education in schools, to seek the cooperation of business in eradicating counterfeit branded goods from the market, to forge links with environmental and women's organizations, and to continue its general and legal advice service in the main centers of Hungary. Charging for membership, previously free, is a contentious issue (there are about 2,000 members in the regional branches). It remains to be seen whether the government is prepared to provide support. First indications are encouraging: as a result of the AgV project, the government promised $90,000 for 1996, which represented an increase of its funding by 600 percent.

Consumer protection has, up until now, not been a government priority. There are a variety of laws, some pre-1989 and some post-1989, that cover particular aspects of consumer protection, including, uniquely in the region, a product liability law. These laws are, however, weakly enforced, and there is as yet no general law on consumer protection. Draft versions have been rejected as insufficiently close to European Union legislation, with which Hungary seeks to harmonize its laws. The major initiative in 1995, however, was the creation of a new Consumer Protection Superintendence as a nationwide authority with more than 200 staff members. This agency combines the functions of the former Consumer Protection Inspectorate, parts of the State Trade Inspectorate, and a part of KERMI.

— Alastair Macgeorge

See also

Central and Eastern Europe, Consumer Movements in.

Reading

Kozminski, Andrzej K. (1992). "Consumers in Transition from the Centrally Planned Economy to the Market Economy." *Journal of Consumer Policy.* 14 (4): 351–370.

Immigrants as Consumers

In the 1980s, more than 9 million people immigrated to the United States. Many came as war refugees, relatives of American residents, skilled professionals, or special agricultural workers. The 1990 census shows that nearly 20 million people in the United States—8 percent of the total population—were not born in America. More than one-fifth of these foreign-born hold a bachelor's degree and a managerial or professional job. Their average household income is $28,314, compared to $30,176 for residents born in the United States. Most reside in California, New York, Texas, and Florida.

The more than 30 million American residents who speak a language other than English at home face daily challenges of understanding and adapting to a new social and economic structure, including the U.S. marketplace. These challenges mainly reflect unfamiliarity with English, cultural differences, and lack of knowledge of this marketplace.

Many newcomers have difficulty speaking and comprehending English, which restricts their ability to learn about their consumer rights and responsibilities and makes them vulnerable to consumer frauds. Language barriers also limit the access of many recent immigrants to potentially helpful consumer information. There are still few consumer educational materials, including price surveys and scam alerts, that have been translated into multiple languages or posted in media forms familiar to newcomers.

In the marketplace, Western culture is very different from other cultures, especially Eastern ones. For example, Asian immigrants prefer to have an informative advertisement from which they can learn facts, rather than the impressions conveyed by fancy visual images: to many, functionality is all that they value in a product; symbolism is not important. Asian immigrants value and trust transactions done in person. Because Asian societies tend to be less mobile, one can easily hold salespersons accountable there because they usually live in the same neighborhood. That is why this group of immigrants is victimized so often by affinity scams. A friend's "friend" may appear at parties and social events offering opportunities for high-profit investments that are fraudulent.

Countries also differ in how they govern their society and regulate their businesses. Consumers from China might expect to find just one centralized phone company because that is the case in China. Consumers from Korea or Japan might not realize that nonprofit consumer groups can fight government and corporations on their behalf because such groups are not common in their countries.

Some concepts sound strange to new arrivals. When Vietnamese need money, they often try to obtain it from relatives and friends, or even from an acquaintance met at school, rather than applying for a loan from a stranger who works at a bank. Some immigrants find it difficult to trust the "system." Their distrust of the banking system, for example, results in many Asian immigrants holding large sums of cash at home.

For those coming from a cash-only society, such as older generations of Vietnamese and Cambodians, credit card and electronic transactions may be incomprehensible and not trustworthy. While companies in the American market try to entice customers from competitors with new products, Asian Americans tend to develop lifelong relationships with particular brands.

To function effectively in the United States, newcomers need the most basic understanding of U.S. consumer rights—how American businesses are regulated, and where to obtain information and education on consumer issues. Such an introduction to the U.S. marketplace minimizes both immigrants' frustration at not knowing where to seek assistance and law enforcement's frustration with not having cooperation from newcomers who are the victims of fraud. Increasingly, the threat to "report you to the INS" is being used to stop immigrant consumers from complaining about unfair practices.

In general, the consumer movement has paid little attention to the consumer problems of recent immigrants. One exception has been Consumer Action's efforts that began in California and are spreading throughout the country. The organization's multicultural and multilingual consumer outreach specialists network with more than 2,000 community-based organizations. Through these groups, Consumer Action distributes hundreds of thousands of free, multilingual consumer education publications each year, and makes culturally appropriate presentations to newcomer groups. The organization also works closely with the ethnic media to encourage them to cover consumer issues. Finally, it works with government agencies, encouraging them to establish special multilingual information lines and serve the consumer needs of newcomers in other ways.

In the next fifty years, the U.S. Census Bureau projects a minimum of 350,000 immigrants annually. Helping ensure that these newcomers function effectively in the United States poses significant challenges for government, nonprofit consumer groups, businesses, and the immigrants themselves.

— Kathy Li

See also

Consumer Action.

Readings

Andreasen, Alan R. (1982). "Disadvantaged Hispanic Consumers: A Research Perspective and Agenda." *Journal of Consumer Affairs*. 16 (1): 46–61.

Peñaloza, Lisa (1995). "Immigrant Consumers: Marketing and Public Policy Considerations in the Global Economy." *Journal of Public Policy & Marketing*. 14 (1): 83–94.

Indian Consumer Movement

Although the consumer protection movement is relatively new to India, concern for the consumer is centuries old. Consideration of the Indian consumer dates back to the Vedic ages (5000 B.C. to 2500 B.C.). One can also find seeds of consumer protection during the Mughal times (A.D. 712 to 1765) and especially during the time of the Khaljis (A.D. 1296 to 1316). Some concern for the consumer was also visible during the British regime (1765 to 1947).

In 1904, the cooperative movement started in India and flourished in some parts (especially in the state of Maharashtra), but this movement primarily emphasized the distribution of consumer goods rather than consumer protection. The post-independence era, however, witnessed a series of measures, including the passing of at least forty-two pieces of legislation concerned directly or indirectly with consumer protection. Still, the average Indian consumer did not enjoy the benefits of these statutory enactments. More recently, the worldwide crusade of Consumers International against consumer exploitation as well as the passing of the United Nations Consumer Protection Guidelines have culminated in the enactment of a comprehensive statute for the protection of Indian consumers. Until the enactment of this statute, access to justice had been a luxury for most Indian citizens.

The enactment of the Consumer Protection Act of 1986 was a milestone in the history of socioeconomic legislation in India. It considerably consolidated the process of consumer protection and has given rise, during the past few years, to a new consumer jurisprudence. The act introduced three tiers (district, state, and national) of quasi-judicial consumer dispute redressal mechanisms for dispensing inexpensive and timely consumer justice. Though passed in 1986, its effective implementation started only in 1990 when the institutions envisaged under the act were established, by and large, throughout the country. This development enabled many consumers and consumer organizations to approach these forums for the redress of grievances. This has contributed, in turn, to the growth of consumer organizations, the emergence of specialized consumer law reports, and a much higher profile for consumer protection in India than ever before. As a result, during the 1990s the Indian consumer movement has grown stronger.

History

Historically, the modern consumer movement in India can be looked at from two perspectives: from that of business self-regulation and from that of consumer voluntarism and activism. In terms of business self-regulation, the movement primarily owes its origin to the Gandhian ideology, particularly to his theory of trusteeship. Nationalist leader Mahatma Gandhi, whom Ralph Nader has described as "the greatest consumer advocate the world has ever seen," attached great importance to moral and ethical values in the domain of economic and business management. The Gandhian principle of trusteeship expresses the inherent responsibilities of business enterprises to their customers, workers, shareholders, and the entire community. Gandhi's concern for the consumer, in particular, was reflected in his famous statement: "A customer is the most important visitor on our premises. He is not dependent upon us. We are dependent upon him. He is not an interruption in our work—he is the purpose of it. We are not doing him a favor by serving him. He is doing us a favor by giving us the opportunity to serve him."

Acharaya Vinobha Bhave and Jayaprakash Narayan—the two greatest exponents of the Gandhian philosophy—expressed similar views, thereby enjoining the business community to regulate itself responsibly in a true social and ethical spirit. Prime Minister Lal Bahadur Shastri and President V. V. Giri also encouraged the business community to be conscious of its social responsibilities.

The views of these public-spirited individuals did have some impact upon at least a few socially conscious leaders of trade and industry who decided to regulate themselves in the interests of consumers. The idea of establishing an organization to promote voluntary self-regulation by business first took root in the 1960s in Bombay among a few conscientious businessmen. After considerable deliberations, a code of ethics was finalized in July 1966, and a new organization called the Fair Trade Practices Association came into being, later named the Council for Fair Business Practices. The association was formally launched on October 2 (Gandhi's birthday) in 1966, and it heralded a movement for business self-regulation in India. Despite criticism from consumer activists, this pioneering organization is a sincere effort toward making the business community accountable to the society at large.

In terms of consumer voluntarism and activism, the Indian Association of Consumers was probably the first full-fledged Indian consumers' association in the post-independence era. Set up in Delhi in 1956 but devoted to protecting consumer interests nationwide, it did not make headway despite leadership from eminent persons and financial backing from the Planning Commission.

Many consumer organizations were established during the 1960s. One, the National Consumer Service, was set up in 1963 as a wing of Sevak Samaj, a social organization. Its main objectives were to collect market information, study the trend of rising prices, publish bulletins for consumers, and agitate against malpractices by sellers. Another consumer organization, popularly known as the Price Rise Resistance Movement, was started in Delhi in 1964. It used to hold meetings to protest against rising prices and formed special squads to keep a watch on price trends in different areas of the city. Gayatri Charitable Trust, Jyoti Sangh Grahak Suraksha Vibhag, and Bombay Civil Trust were other prominent consumer-oriented organizations established in India in the early 1960s. However, the foremost consumer association that surfaced during this period was the Consumer Guidance Society of India (CGSI). It was established by nine homemakers in Bombay in 1966 to inform, educate, and organize consumers in order to enable them to secure, protect, and preserve their interests and assert their rights. The Consumer Guidance Society of India is today one of India's most important consumer organizations.

During the 1970s, India witnessed a proliferation of consumer organizations in various parts of the country. These organizations included the All-Indian Bankers Association (1968), Surat Consumer Association (1969), Karnataka Consumer Services Society (1970), Visaka Consumers Council (1973), Akhil Bharatiya Grahak Panchayat (1974), and Trichy District Consumer Council (1976).

The birth of India's leading and most powerful consumer organization, the Consumer Education and Research Center (CERC), at Ahmedabad in the state of Gujarat in 1978, appears to have coincided with the emergence of the "Social Action Litigation Movement" in India. In this revolutionary era in the judicial history of India, the concept of legal standing was considerably liberalized and, for the first time, Indian courts started recognizing the rights of social workers and public interest groups to approach them in the event that the legal rights of an individual or a class of persons are violated. CERC, which is now among the most successful consumer groups in the entire Third World, has been instrumental in safeguarding consumers' interests by disseminating information, spreading consumer education and awareness, and above all, by litigating on behalf of consumers. The recent spurt in consumer-oriented social action litigation owes much to the tireless efforts of CERC. Even the enactment of the Consumer Protection Act of 1986 was largely a result of intensive lobbying by consumer organizations like CERC and CGSI.

In India, by rough estimates, there are now at least 2,000 consumer organizations. Typically, their functioning and impact have been local. It has only been since 1990 that an effective, nationwide movement articulating the voice of consumers has emerged. In addition to CERC and CGSI, some of the more prominent associations working at the national level are: Akhil Bharatiya Grahak Panchayat, Bombay Telephone Users' Association, Consumer Action Group, Common Cause, Consumer Unity and Trust Society, Jagrut Grahak, Mumbai Grahak Panchayat, and Voluntary Organization in the Interest of Consumer Education.

Recent Developments

After the enactment of the 1986 Consumer Protection Act, and more particularly since 1990, significant changes have taken place in the field of consumer protection in India. What began as a desultory effort has burgeoned into a large number of consumer organizations spread across the country, even rural areas, encouraging consumers to demand their rights.

Four significant developments are taking place in the Indian legal system and consumer movement: a spurt in consumer-oriented social action litigation, the emergence of environmental litigation as a part of consumer protection, an increase in business self-regulation, and the awarding of exemplary damages by the consumer tribunals.

Social action litigation is increasingly being used to seek consumer justice. Ever since the enactment of the 1986 act, numerous petitions have been filed by consumer organizations on behalf of consumers. The 1986 act itself encourages consumer groups to approach the consumer forums established under the act on behalf of consumers who may not be willing or in a position to approach these forums on their own. The language of the act is also flexible enough to allow consumer associations to file a complaint on a consumer's behalf, even if the consumer does not belong to the association. The principle of standing has been further liberalized by a 1993 amendment to the 1986 act, which enables one or more consumers having the same cause of action to file a complaint or representative petition on behalf of all such consumers. In accordance with the provisions of the 1986 act, the country's leading consumer associations have approached the consumer forums to seek relief for the victims of exploitation at the hands of both the private and public sectors. Besides taking on domestic traders and manufacturers, these associations have now also started a crusade against abuses by transnational corporations doing business in India.

Second, the distinction between environment protection and consumer protection is disappearing as consumer groups all over the world now deal with environmental issues, particularly those relating to health and safety, discouraging conspicuous consumption because of its adverse affects on the environment. The emergence of environmental litigation before the consumer forums has been an equally prominent development. Despite the Bhopal disaster (known popularly as "Bhoposhima"), the environmental movement in India has found it difficult to find appropriate legal mechanisms. In the area of consumer protection law, in contrast, comparatively smaller issues—ranging from inadequate banking services and delayed insurance claims to misleading advertisements and absence of after-sales services—argued before the consumer forums have now reached a more advanced stage of development. The consumer associations have, therefore, now started using consumer tribunals as forums for highlighting many environmental violations.

Third, there has been increasing business self-regulation in India in the last few years, particularly after the enactment of the 1986 act. The mounting pressure from consumer organizations and the growing number of cases filed by consumers before the consumer forums have persuaded businesses to become more socially accountable. Whereas the public sector has regulated itself by making institutional arrangements to redress consumer grievances (e.g. celebrating "consumer weeks" and opening consumer complaints offices), the private sector is increasingly developing and publicizing specific codes of ethics.

Fourth, consumer forums have increasingly awarded exemplary damages to aggrieved consumers. However, since the consumer forums have frequently used five terms—compensation, damages, exemplary damages, penal damages, and punitive damages—interchangeably, the law in this area is still uncertain and in transition.

Current Challenges

Even though consumers and consumer activists consider the 1986 Consumer Protection Act as a great weapon to fight against exploitation and to strengthen the emerging consumer movement in India, in the 1990s they face a variety of challenges. One is introducing consumer education in the schools and to illiterate portions of the population. Another is expanding the consumer movement to the grassroots level and to rural areas. Although India is predominantly a rural economy, the Indian consumer movement is still largely based in cities.

Perhaps the foremost challenge, however, has been extending the protections of the 1986 act to medical services. The only services not covered by this law are those rendered free of charge and those provided under a contract of personal service. Services including education, health, housing, postal service, and telecommunications not mentioned specifically by the act had been considered to be excluded from coverage by this law. But the consumer forums have succeeded in bringing all of these services within the ambit of the consumer protection law, except for services rendered by private medical practitioners, hospitals, and nursing homes. Despite the fact that consumer tribunals and even the National Commission—the highest institution in the hierarchy of consumers' forums—maintained that these private medical homes are covered by the 1986 act, at present the controversy remains unresolved.

Another change affecting all kinds of businesses that is likely to take place in India during the 1990s is the emergence of consumer product testing laboratories set up and run by leading consumer groups in the country. Their findings from comparative testing, ranking, and evaluation will be published as buyers' guides. These findings will expose those firms whose products are unsafe, substandard, or of poor quality.

Consumer groups in India have begun to realize that enthusiasm and sincerity, though necessary, are not sufficient to ensure the promotion and protection of consumer interests in the 1990s. Programs need to be organized by the government and nongovernmental organizations, some of them promoted by management schools, to equip consumer activists with skills and insight. Competition among consumer groups can also be anticipated as the number of consumer groups continues to grow across the country. There will be stiff competition among groups for funds and media coverage. Credibility will be essential for group survival, and some groups will inevitably have to close down.

— Gurjeet Singh

Readings

Pandit, Gyan (1992). *Fostering Consumer Activism.* New Delhi: Consumers' Forum.

Singh, Gurjeet (1995). "Group Actions and the Law: A Case Study of Social Action Litigation and Consumer Protection in India." *Journal of Consumer Policy.* 18: 25–54.

Indoor Air Quality Protections

The quality of air inside homes and offices was not an issue of concern until the early 1980s when consumer advocates and public health officials struggled to address the health problems experienced by residents of mobile homes and consumers who insulated their homes with urea formaldehyde foam insulation (UFFI). The presence of high levels of formaldehyde, an irritating and potentially cancer-causing gas inside these homes, focused the public's attention on the hazard of exposure to pollutants indoors.

The issue of formaldehyde also foretold how difficult and contentious it would be to address indoor air quality issues. The Consumer Product Safety Commission (CPSC) banned UFFI because of the hazardousness of formaldehyde, only to have that regulation overturned in the courts. Later findings by the Environmental Protection Agency (EPA), which confirmed the CPSC's health concerns, drew strong industry criticism and also did not result in regulation of formaldehyde. Fifteen years later, voluntary action by those industries that used urea formaldehyde resins in their products, along with regulation by the Occupational Safety and Health Administration (OSHA) and U.S. Department of Housing and Urban Development, have resulted in lowered formaldehyde exposures.

Studies demonstrated that levels of pollutants indoors were consistently higher than outdoor levels, even in industrialized cities. Since consumers spend almost 90 percent of their time indoors, including transportation, these exposures represent serious health concerns. Estimates of the annual costs in lost productivity and increased health care are in the tens of billions of dollars. Despite findings by the EPA that indoor air pollution is among the top-ranked environmental risks to public health, efforts to enact legislation increasing the EPA's authority to address indoor air hazards have not been successful. Recent legislation sought federal health advisories on the effects of various levels of exposure to common indoor air pollutants and technological solutions to mitigate those exposures. New indoor air legislation has not become law even with the consistent backing of organizations such as the Consumer Federation of America and the American Lung Association, and strong support from legislators such as Senators George Mitchell (D-ME) and Frank Lautenberg (D-NJ), and Congressmen Joseph Kennedy (D-MA) and Henry Waxman (D-CA).

As a result, indoor air quality is a shared responsibility among numerous federal agencies, with no one agency exerting consistent or authoritative leadership to address indoor pollution, its sources, or the technologies for its mitigation. This diffuse responsibility is reflected in the federal interagency coordinating committee on indoor air, the Council on Indoor Air Quality (CIAQ), which has met regularly for more than ten years. About twenty agencies participate in this body, with the chairmanship shared among five co-chair agencies: the CPSC, the EPA, OSHA, the U.S. Department of Energy, and the U.S. Department of Health and Human Services. The EPA assumes most of the administrative burden of coordinating the committee. The General Accounting Office has criticized the fact that the CIAQ does not exercise policy leadership on indoor air issues.

Over the years, these agencies have coordinated their research as well as their public information and education efforts as they addressed asbestos; lead; formaldehyde; radon; combustion pollutants such as carbon monoxide, nitrogen dioxide, and particulates; chlorinated solvents such as methylene chloride; environmental tobacco smoke; and more recently, biological pollutants such as infectious diseases and allergens. This coordination has resulted in uniform and consistent public policy approaches emphasizing source control and ventilation as primary solutions to indoor air quality problems. Federal regulation of indoor sources is largely limited to enforcement of traditional pesticide and consumer product labeling statutes.

Source control depends on consumers making wise purchasing decisions and using products in accordance with manufacturers' intentions, rather than on regulators removing potentially hazardous sources from the marketplace. For large buildings and schools, architects, building owners, facility managers, and purchasing agents should select building materials, furnishings, office equipment, cleaning products, and pesticides based in part on whether they could contribute to poor indoor air quality. They also must carefully plan the installation of products to dilute the frequently high emissions of new products, to provide for direct exhaust of some emitting equipment like photocopiers, and to make available separately ventilated smoking rooms in buildings where smoking is allowed. Providing good ventilation has usually meant meeting the ventilation guidelines of the professional engineering society (ASHRAE) that were in effect at the time the building was built, or the current standard if the design constraints of an older building's ventilation system permitted it.

This approach places responsibility for evaluating the adequacy of the building's ventilation system, and determining whether the occupants are being provided adequate fresh air, on the building owner or operator. The agencies, often led by the EPA, have produced guidance documents and training courses on procedures and practices for promoting good indoor air through source control and ventilation for consumers, building owners and operators, and school personnel. These agencies rely completely on individual initiative and acknowledge that prevention seldom occurs until after an indoor air quality crisis motivates concern. Especially for schools, media attention often contributes to public recognition of a problem.

The public policy choice of relying on informed action by consumers in their homes and by building owners and managers on behalf of their tenants has obvious limits. In 1994, OSHA, in response to petitions from labor organizations, attempted to address indoor air quality more directly by proposing regulations that would have required employers to carry out many of these generally agreed upon indoor air "good operations and maintenance" practices. As part of the same proposal, OSHA sought to restrict involuntary exposure to environmental tobacco smoke (ETS). The EPA had earlier found ETS to be a human carcinogen estimated to cause some 3,000 lung cancer deaths each year. Concurrently, the EPA attempted to organize a voluntary partnership program that would have provided public recognition and other incentives to building owners who implemented operations and maintenance practices designed to provide healthful indoor air. Both the OSHA regulation and the EPA voluntary program drew unusually strong opposition from a broad alliance of business interests, including the tobacco industry. While analysis of more than a year's worth of hearing testimony and comment on the OSHA proposal is likely to continue over several years, the EPA voluntary partnership program has been scrapped.

The continued opposition of some product manufacturers and business groups, augmented by support from the tobacco industry, represents a powerful barrier to effective governmental action to minimize most indoor air pollution problems. One exception to that trend may be action to address the health risks presented by exposure to biological pollutants, including infectious diseases, allergens, mycotoxins, and endotoxins. Several recent episodes of sick building syndrome have been associated with moisture problems in buildings resulting in severe biological contamination. The expensive repair and cleanup costs highlight the importance of indoor air quality. No manufacturer's product is involved when public health authorities condemn these opportunistic organisms that require only moisture to grow in most indoor environments. The health consequences of exposure can be serious—Legionnaires' disease, tuberculosis, respiratory allergies, asthma, infections, hypersensitivity pneumonitis, and the potential for central nervous system effects from toxic fungi. Asthma, closely linked to indoor allergens, alone causes 4,000 deaths each year and an estimated $62 million in medical costs. While regulatory initiatives to reduce product emissions are unlikely, as is any effective government oversight of indoor air quality in office buildings, the many indoor environmental problems will continue to provide opportunities for consumer advocates to improve public health.

— Sandra Eberle

See also

Tobacco Control and Prevention.

Readings

U.S. Environmental Protection Agency (1987). *Unfinished Business: A Comparative Assessment of Environmental Problems.* Washington, DC: U.S. Government Printing Office.

——— (1995). *The Inside Story: A Guide to Indoor Air Quality.* Washington, DC: U.S. Government Printing Office.

Infomercial Regulation

Until 1984, federal law limited the number of commercial minutes per hour that a television station could run. With the lifting of these restrictions, infomercials—program-length commercials devoted solely to the sale of a product or service—quickly became a fixture on independent stations and cable networks. But criticisms of these infomercials mounted and led to increased Federal Trade Commission (FTC) efforts to police this new marketplace.

According to critics, the most misleading and deceptive infomercials were those broadcast in the late 1980s. Ads for questionable products such as diet pills and get-rich-quick schemes proliferated. In 1988, Congress convened hearings to investigate the direction the industry appeared to be taking. The primary focus of the probe was an infomercial entitled "Money Money Money," which made allegedly false and unsubstantiated claims for a book about the supposed ready availability of "no strings attached" government grants and loans.

In 1992, a group of consumer organizations petitioned the Federal Communications Commission (FCC) for stricter infomercial disclosure requirements. Since deregulation, the FCC's role in this area has been limited to the enforcement of two remaining regulations related to program-length ads. The FCC still requires that, when program-length spots are broadcast, the licensee ensures that sponsorship is disclosed and the sponsoring party is named. In addition, the Children's Television Act of 1990 limits the number of commercial minutes during hours dedicated to children's programming.

To date, the FTC has taken an active role in challenging deceptive practices by infomercial marketers. The FTC's concerns have been twofold: First, do consumers understand that the program they are watching is a paid advertisement, rather than a newscast or entertainment programming? Second, are infomercial claims supported by the same level of substantiation required of any advertisement, whether thirty seconds or thirty minutes in length?

At the time the FTC brought its first action against an infomercial marketer, many infomercials mimicked the format of investigative programs such as *60 Minutes* or daytime talk shows. In 1989, the FTC alleged that the marketers of BluBlocker sunglasses, JS&A Group, Inc., deceptively misrepresented the commercial nature of what appeared to be a thirty-minute program, "Consumer Challenge." In reaching this conclusion, the FTC looked to both the format of the broadcast and express statements in the script. For example, the infomercial opened with the voice-over announcement: "Welcome to 'Consumer Challenge,' hosted by Jonathan Goldsmith, the show that examines popular new products for you, the consumer, with investigative reporters Don Hale and Catherine Grant." The "reporters" then spoke from what appeared to be a newscaster's anchor desk.

The FTC's primary concern was that "Consumer Challenge" could leave reasonable consumers with the impression that the broadcast was an independent news or investigative report, rather than a thirty-minute ad. Although the FTC has not found infomercials to be inherently deceptive, it has taken action when advertisers have misrepresented the commercial nature of the broadcast.

Infomercials were not the first instance of an allegedly deceptive advertising format. As early as 1968, the FTC declared that a print ad in the format of a news article was deceptive if it did not include a clear and conspicuous disclosure that it was an advertisement. Although the FTC has not promulgated regulations specific to infomercials, it has applied the same reasoning in cases such as JS&A to conclude that an advertisement that is falsely represented—either expressly or by implication—to be an independent program is deceptive under existing federal consumer protection law because it is likely to mislead consumers acting reasonably under the circumstances.

To remedy the deceptive nature of some infomercial formats, the FTC's consent orders with Twin Star Productions, Inc. (1990) and Synchronal Corp. (1993) mandated specific disclosures at the beginning of infomercials and whenever ordering instructions are given. Although these disclosure requirements are legally binding only on the specific companies who have been the subject of FTC action, other companies have voluntarily added them to their infomercials, and some television stations have made the disclosures a requirement for buying airtime.

To date, the FTC—often in conjunction with its state consumer protection counterparts—has brought over thirty infomercial cases. More than seventy-five corporate entities and individual infomercial marketers are now under order. Most of the cases have challenged the underlying substantiation for product claims, as well as the alleged deception in the format of the infomercial itself.

Infomercials making unsubstantiated health claims for products such as diet aids, impotence cures, baldness treatments, "pinhole" eyeglasses, and pain relief devices make up the bulk of these cases. In evaluating the accuracy of these product claims or the sufficiency of a marketer's substantiation, the FTC applies the same scientific standards that it uses to evaluate similar claims in traditional print or television ads. Applying well-settled principles of consumer protection law, the FTC has also brought a number of actions against companies marketing business or investment opportunities using infomercials.

Some infomercial cases have resulted in substantial redress for consumers. For example, in Synchronal, the FTC recovered $3.5 million in redress for purchasers of a baldness product and a cellulite treatment.

Although every infomercial is different, many rely on expert endorsements, consumer testimonials, or on-camera demonstrations to sell the product. Infomercials have generated a number of actions against health professionals who appeared as expert endorsers. In a 1993 consent order with James L. McElhaney, M.D., the FTC challenged claims for a pain relief device made by a physician who was also a corporate officer. In Synchronal and Patricia Wexler, M.D. (1992), the complaints alleged that two dermatologists who appeared on a baldness infomercial had deceptively endorsed the product. Questionable endorsements have been of particular concern when they come from learned professionals or when they relate to health claims that consumers may not be able to evaluate for themselves.

Consumer endorsements are another common feature of infomercials. According to FTC law, an advertisement reflecting the experience of an individual or a group of consumers on a key product attribute will be interpreted as representing that the endorser's experience portrays what consumers can expect to achieve in actual use. If that is not the case, the ad must either disclose what the generally expected performance will be or must disclose the limited applicability of the endorser's experience to what consumers can expect to achieve. The FTC has brought a number of infomercial cases challenging the consumer testimonials as deceptively atypical.

The FTC has also challenged deceptive on-camera demonstrations. For example, in a 1993 consent order with National Media, Inc., the commission alleged that, in a purported demonstration of a kitchen mixer "whipping" skim milk, frozen dessert topping had been substituted for milk. In the same infomercial, the mixer was shown to blend a fresh pineapple into juice when, according to the FTC's complaint, precrushed pineapple had actually been used on camera.

In less than seven years, infomercials have grown from a late-night novelty to a reported $1 billion industry. Although many infomercials still use the "operators are standing by" format of direct sales, more national companies are using infomercials to promote the retail availability of high-ticket items such as computers, cars, or vacation packages. In a *TV Guide* poll, 29 percent of consumers surveyed said they have purchased a product advertised on an infomercial. According to another recent survey, 91.5 percent of responding television stations air infomercials. Many have come to rely on them as a steady source of income; however, the level of prescreening for potentially deceptive formats or claims varies widely from station to station.

— Lesley Anne Fair

See also

Advertising Regulation; Deceptive, Unfair, and Unconscionable Sales Practices; Federal Trade Commission.

Readings

Hayes, Rader, and Herbert J. Rotfeld (1989). "Infomercials and Cable Network Programming." *Advancing the Consumer Interest.* 1 (2): 17–22.

Lewis, W. H. Ramsay (1992). "Infomercials, Deceptive Advertising and the Federal Trade Commission." *Fordham Urban Law Journal.* 19 (Spring): 853–874.

Information Dissemination

Information dissemination refers to providing consumers with data about individual markets and offerings, geared to consumers' specific purchase decisions. This topic has become more important over the past thirty years as markets have grown, new products and services have appeared, and consumers have become increasingly educated. Consumer advocates, marketers, public policymakers, and consumer researchers have all debated this topic. These debates have involved what information should be made available, who should make it available and in what form, and in some instances (such as tobacco or alcohol), whether restrictions on information dissemination are appropriate.

On the positive side, it is important to recognize that nearly everyone supports the basic concept of consumer information. Two distinct arguments are often made in favor of consumer information provision. One, essentially a philosophical position, is that consumers have a right to be informed. This position was articulated by President John F. Kennedy in his 1962 address, which defined four basic consumer rights. The second argument flows from the free-enterprise economic model: here, maximal social welfare is assumed to result when consumers have the greatest opportunity to exercise free choice in their purchases. Aggregate purchases then serve to direct the planning and resource allocation functions of the economy, and these purchases are assumed to be informed and rational choices on the part of consumers.

There are three basic reasons that there has been so much controversy in this area. First, there are dollar costs associated with providing information. This issue raises cost/benefit tradeoff questions (is this piece of information worth its costs of disclosure?), as well as the issue of who should pay these costs. A second basis for controversy lies in the fact that marketers are granted significant First Amendment (freedom of speech) rights in the United States. These rights allow an individual marketer broad freedoms in choosing what to say (and what not to say) and how to say it. These rights need to be respected by consumer advocates and public policymakers when considering what information consumers should receive, from whom, and in what form.

The third complicating factor involves consumers' imperfect use of information. Most consumers do not possess anything close to "full" information about their purchases. Based on this observation, critics of current advertising and marketing practices charge that much relevant information is not being made available to consumers, and that such "enforced ignorance" leads to higher prices, artificial brand differences, and the advertising of nonfunctional frills that provide no real benefits to consumers. Marketers and advertisers, on the other hand, generally do not accept these charges as valid. Instead, they point to many instances in which product promotions consisting of the provision of an unusual amount of factual information had little effect on sales. They also argue that, if consumers really wanted and would use more information, the competitive system would provide it.

Definition of Consumer Information

Consumer information is considered to be distinct from consumer education. Consumer education is similar to "consumer civics" in that it tries to teach people to be intelligent consumers through lessons on how market systems operate, instruction regarding consumer rights, and explanations of products and good purchasing strategies (e.g., how to gain the components of a balanced diet). Consumer information, on the other hand, refers to data about individual offerings that are oriented to a particular buying decision.

A scientifically precise meaning of the term *information* can be elusive. Within information theory, the field that formed the basis of the development of computers, an information "bit" (contraction of "binary digit") is defined as that amount of information required to determine which of two equally likely alternative states exists. Thus, information is useful in reducing our uncertainty about the state of the world. More recently, however, researchers in a number of disciplines have pointed out that there are different types of uncertainty, and that a given bit of information will not necessarily reduce all these types of uncertainty. For example, in consumer behavior the provision of information about two new brands, or some new product features, will help consumers know their options better, but it is also likely to increase a consumer's uncertainty about which purchase option to choose.

Thus, there are serious definitional issues related to the use a consumer might make of informational input. Because of these difficulties in definition, the Federal Trade Commission's Task Force on Consumer Information Remedies (1979) decided to define this term as referring to any factor that is potentially relevant to the decision to purchase goods or services. Under this definition, "consumer information" can possess several significantly different properties. One important distinction is that some consumer information is objective in nature (reflecting the use of a common standard of measurement) while other information is subjective in nature, reflecting the opinion or taste of the information provider. Another important distinction is that information is sometimes used to influence consumers' behavior, while at other times it is used merely to describe or communicate a piece of knowledge. Also, sometimes information is simple, while other times it is complex. Further, some consumer information is directed at prepurchase decisions (e.g., advertising), some comes during the consumer's purchasing event itself (e.g., credit terms), and some information is provided for use following purchase (e.g., instruction manuals). All types of consumer information can be provided by different parties at different times. In fact, because consumers often will use a specific piece of information solely for the purpose of making a single purchase decision, the timeliness of information dissemination is vital; information that is not easily accessible to a consumer at the right time will simply not be considered.

All of these issues are relevant to providers of consumer information. The following sections examine four types of information disseminators who provide meaningful information to consumers: other consumers, marketers, not-for-profit consumer rating organizations, and public policymakers. The consumer movement has influenced the nature of the information being disseminated by each source type through its various activities over time—research, education, litigation, and political action.

Consumers as Information Disseminators

One of the most influential forms of consumer information is that provided by consumers to each other, including exchanges among members of families or households, relatives, friends, and members of social groups. The power of these "word of mouth" recommendations stems from three factors. First, consumer communications usually have high source credibility. Most discussions with friends or family are carried out with a feeling of trust and openness: there is usually little suspicion of a manipulative intent. Second, consumer word of mouth employs a two-way flow of communication. In contrast to a broadcast ad, a magazine rating report, or many other forms of information disclosure, in a conversation the consumer has the opportunity to ask questions, obtain clarifications, follow up on issues of interest, and spend as much time as desired on the topic. Thus, word of mouth is extremely conducive to a successful learning situation. The third strength of word of mouth comes from its ability to offer vicarious (imagined) trial experience. For example, a consumer can gain some experience of having tried a restaurant or movie simply by asking a friend who has tried it already.

Consumer word-of-mouth information dissemination is extremely important in the diffusion of the innovation process, when new products and services begin to be offered in the marketplace. The study of the adoption process across the population shows something approximating a normal (bell-shaped) distribution, in which a small number of consumers (the innovators) are the first to try the new offering; they are followed by a larger set of early adopters, then by the bulk of the market, and finally by a group of laggards and nonadopters. Of these groups, researchers have found that the early adopters perform as "opinion leaders," who offer much advice and encouragement to other consumers to try the new offering. A special group of opinion leaders has recently been singled out for further research attention: these so-called market mavens are consumers who evidence high interest and knowledge about a particular sector of consumer purchases, and eagerly offer information and guidance to others of their acquaintance. Of all the forms of information dissemination, word of mouth is the sector having the strongest potential for social influences to be operating in conjunction with the information being passed. This is particularly true for social "reference groups" with which a consumer wishes to be identified. Recommendations from these sources can be very powerful in influencing purchase behaviors.

The other major sector in which consumers serve as information disseminators is within the household. Intergenerational influences are at work here, for example, as parents pass along to their children many opinions and preferences, such as favorite brands, styles, and stores. These effects can be very powerful and can persist over many years. One study of auto insurance, for example, found that 55 percent of families in their thirties held auto policies with the same company as that of the husband's parents.

In addition to long-term effects, households also provide many forms of information dissemination on a daily basis, as members perform different roles for the household unit. At various points, individuals provide information about their wants, needs, and preferences, to be factored into financial allocations and specific purchase decisions. Family members also provide inputs to stimulate a purchase; expertise about options, features, sources of supply, prices, and product quality; and reports of the experiences of others outside the household. At various points, moreover, individuals may play the role of shopper, purchaser, preparer, user, and/or caretaker of purchases, and any of these roles might involve either the delivery or receipt of information. The common occurrence of "joint decisions," in which spouses might work together to make large purchases (such as housing, automobiles, or appliances), often involves the sharing and receiving of much information.

In summary, consumers themselves serve as important disseminators of information in the marketplace. This information often deals with local market offerings, such as prices, sales, and store availability. It frequently meshes influence together with descriptions, and often reflects implicit social pressures as to the issue involved. Overall, consumer word of mouth is high in credibility, and moderate or high in empathy (that is, the similarity of the provider's perspectives to those of the receiver), but often low in expertise (that is, the technical knowledge of the information source).

Marketers as Information Disseminators

The strengths and weaknesses of marketer-provided information are almost the direct opposite of those for consumer word of mouth. Marketing information is high in expertise, in that sellers specialize in a certain range of goods or services and will know these products very well. Conversely, consumers recognize that marketers desire to win their purchases, so marketer-provided information is often rated low on grounds of credibility (possible presence of a manipulative intent on the part of the information provider) and low on empathy (the similarity of perspectives between provider and receiver). Further, each individual marketer is offering information intended to influence the consumer to prefer that marketer's brand (offering). From the consumer's perspective, then, he or she is receiving a set of marketer-controlled information that is in some sense contradictory: the marketing system is providing information that suggests that every product and brand should be purchased, and is thus not particularly helpful for a consumer's budget allocation decisions.

There are two types of marketers who offer large amounts of information to consumers—those who manufacture products and those who sell them at the retail level. Thus, some marketing information stresses the brand, and other information stresses stores and prices. Marketers have a wide range of tools through which to disseminate information, including advertising, salespersons, printed materials, and toll-free phone lines.

In consumers' minds, advertising is often considered to be synonymous with marketing. Advertising is a huge industry: it accounts for about 3 percent of the U.S. gross national product, or more than $150 billion per year in expenditures. There are many forms of advertising that are intended to accomplish different goals. Four types of goals are: persuasion, reinforcement, reminder, and purchase precipitation. In order to achieve its overall goal of increasing consumer purchases, advertising is designed to communicate effectively both information and influence to consumers. Any given ad might reflect a long-term or short-term time frame for its intended effects: that is, sales at some point in the future, or a sale immediately. Thus, advertising content might range from almost pure entertainment (as in the Super Bowl television commercials each year) to almost total information, as in classified ads or Yellow Page listings. A wide range of media is available to carry advertising to consumers, including television, radio, newspapers, magazines, billboards, direct mail, and the Internet.

In contrast to consumer word of mouth's two-way communication mode, advertising is usually restricted to a one-way mode of communication: messages must be designed, created, and transmitted to consumers, who then "decode" the message and take away whatever effects are felt. This limitation places great pressure on the advertising designer to ensure that all aspects of the desired message are successfully incorporated into the ad. Advertising is likely to be tightly crafted toward a particular market segment (or "target market") of consumers. There are many ways in which market segments can be defined: some of the most popular include gender, age group (e.g., teens, elderly), ethnic grouping, occupation, and lifestyle preferences, together with extent of usage of the particular product or service. Such a focus allows advertising to rate higher on the empathy dimension for information.

From the advertiser's perspective, successful communication is extremely challenging. The fact that numerous competitors are also advertising to offer information and influence makes the task much more difficult. Further, the fact that consumers frequently have little or no prior interest in receiving an ad communication means that their attention must be gained and maintained in order for an ad to work. William McGuire, a noted social psychologist, described a "hierarchy of advertising effects" system requiring that six stages of consumer impact be successfully achieved in order for an ad to be successful. These include: the ad be presented to a consumer; he or she then pay attention to it; it be comprehended; it lead to the consumer yielding (being persuaded as to the ad's recommendations); the persuasion or influence be retained over some time span; and the overt purchase action the ad recommends be actually taken by the consumer. The striking aspect of this system is seen when probabilities are applied to an ad's chances for success. For example, if there were a 50 percent chance for success at each stage, the overall level of success for the ad would be less than 2 percent.

The extent of the challenge facing advertisers is generally supported by reports in advertising research. In one study, for example, only 5 percent of viewers of a television commercial for tires recalled the key point of the commercial by the next day. In another study, only 16 percent of consumers were able to identify the sponsor of an ad they had seen two hours previously, while another 8 percent of consumers provided the wrong brand name. Thus, it is no surprise to marketers that a famous early advertiser is said to have complained: "I know that half the money I spend on advertising is wasted, but I cannot figure out exactly which half it is." This quote remains a classic even today because it captures two of the essential characteristics of advertising: businesses use advertising because it does work, but no one is yet quite sure how it works.

Despite these difficulties facing marketers, social critics have long complained about various aspects of consumer advertising, and defenders have arisen as well. For example, in economic debates on advertising, convincing points are made both that advertising is a barrier to entry (by raising the cost for small producers who are new to a market), and that it is just the opposite—that advertising serves to create a path for a new entry to become known and to be successful in a market. Similarly, debates exist on whether advertising serves to raise prices to consumers (as it is a cost of doing business which must be paid for through the price charged) or to lower prices (through increasing volume to lower costs per unit sold). In the social domain, the "seven sins of advertising" voiced by critics are: persuading people to do things they otherwise would not; propagandizing in favor of a materialistic life; lowering the values and ethical standards of society; employing bad taste and questionable morals; employing negative stereotypes; impacting the poor negatively; and exploiting the immaturity of children for financial gain.

In their influential 1968 study of advertising in America, Raymond Bauer and Stephen Greyser asked consumers about their views about this institution. When asked what they liked about advertising, a majority of consumers favorably mentioned the information that advertising provides to them. Consumers reported that ads helped them to understand products better, learn about new products and services, and stay current about prices and specials.

One in five persons also mentioned the economic contribution of advertising—the roles that advertising plays in providing employment to workers and contributing to lowering prices for mass-market products. Consumers also recognized the role of advertising in making available entertainment. First, some consumers mentioned that they liked some of the humorous, warm, and exciting ads. Second, some consumers expressed appreciation for the advertising subsidies to television, radios, newspapers, and magazines that lower the cost of these media. When asked what they disliked about advertising, consumers in this study also raised a number of criticisms. They most frequently mentioned the intrusiveness of ads: there are too many ads; some ads are repeated far too often; and some television ads seem to be recorded at higher volumes. Second, consumers complained about falsity and exaggeration; they expressed the opinion that some ads do not present a true picture of the product or service, and may be misleading.

Salespersons offer a different source of consumer information, one that is personal in nature, is marketer-controlled, and is available at the point of purchase. Salespersons perform the exchange function between marketers and consumers—they provide the means by which actual purchases are made, and in this capacity, can transmit considerable information and influence to consumers. As with advertising, personal selling is quite common within marketing. In the United States alone, more than 11 million salespersons meet with consumers on a daily basis. Their functions can range widely, from order-taking (cashiers), through customer consultation and assistance, to high-pressure creation of demand. In many cases, consumer salespersons represent a store that offers a number of brands. In other cases, such as direct selling or telephone solicitation, a salesperson may represent only a single brand offering.

As a marketer-controlled information source, salespersons would normally be seen as offering high expertise, but low credibility and empathy (similar to advertising). However, because selling involves a two-way communication flow, individual salespersons have the opportunity to raise their scores for both empathy and credibility during the sales interaction.

Research on personal selling confirms that this does take place during the normal sales process, as the salesperson attempts to find out more about a customer's background as well as desires and constraints, and as the salesperson searches for options that best fit the consumer's emerging needs. Thus, the salesperson performs several roles when dealing with consumers: he or she is an information provider and product/service consultant, as well as being an advocate for "closing the sale." Although influence and persuasion are certainly involved, and abuses sometimes occur, it is also the case that salespersons are often seen by consumers as useful information providers. This point is especially clear in the case of service providers such as real estate brokers, stockbrokers, and tax accountants. It is also true, however, for sellers of products. In one major study of recent purchasers of major household appliances, for example, when asked about "your most useful source of information for your purchase," a national sample of consumers answered, "my salesperson," by a three-to-one margin over the next most useful information source, friends and relatives.

While advertising and personal selling do provide consumers with vast amounts of information, this communication is normally done within a context of persuasion or influence. However, marketers also possess a number of other means of disseminating product information to consumers, frequently without a strong element of persuasion. For example, many products and services use explanatory brochures to introduce consumers to the range of features or options available. Similarly, while packaging and labels do perform some attention-getting and influencing functions, they also are used to convey much information, which can include the product's maker, unit quantity, ingredients or contents, pertinent use instructions, and any warnings that may be appropriate. Thus, when perusing the labels, consumers may gain some information prior to purchase, at point of purchase, or following purchase.

In recent years, astute marketers have increasingly recognized that their long-term success depends upon consumers who are satisfied after purchasing the product. Thus, the "post-purchase" stage has taken on increasing importance. Some firms have redesigned owners' manuals to communicate more clearly. Research by Technical Assistance Research Programs, Inc. (TARP), which shows that dissatisfied consumers frequently engage in negative word of mouth, has led marketers to encourage consumers to communicate their complaints. Many firms have introduced toll-free telephone lines for consumers to use in contacting the firm. General Electric's "GE Answer Center" receives some 60,000 calls per week: 15 percent of these calls are actual complaints, with about 75 percent being requests for further information or assistance. In each of these instances, the firm has an opportunity to customize any information it provides to the needs of that consumer who has taken the trouble to call. In this way, it improves the prospects of a satisfactory resolution and the chances for a long-term positive relationship between the firm and that customer.

Recent technological advances have created new opportunities for interactive information provision, custom-tailored to a consumer's interest. Much of this potential lies with the development of marketer-controlled sites on the Internet: here, a consumer will be able to search for substantial amounts of information, using as extensive a time period as he or she may wish.

Independent Organizations as Information Disseminators

Both consumers and marketers have shortcomings as sources of prepurchase information to assist a consumer in making a decision. Information from other consumers may be high in credibility, and moderate to high in empathy, but can be low in expertise. Information from marketer sources, on the other hand, is typically seen as being high in expertise, but low in credibility and empathy. Thus, there is a natural role for information from a third source that could be high in all three characteristics.

The best-known of the independent testing organizations in the United States is Consumers Union, which publishes *Consumer Reports* magazine. The magazine describes itself as a comprehensive source for unbiased advice about products and services, personal finance, health and nutrition, and other consumer concerns. In the last sixty years, its mission has been to test products, inform the public, and protect consumers. Consumers Union provides four related types of informational services. Most prominent is the extensive laboratory testing of consumer products, reporting detailed brand-by-brand ratings of quality, particularly with respect to performance, safety, features, and price. Opinions as to brands offering favorable value for the money ("Best Buys") are also provided. Second, Consumers Union surveys its members as to their experiences with various products after purchase, seeking to elicit information on frequency of repair and satisfaction with performance and with marketer service. Third, the organization publishes articles about topics of concern to consumers, offering suggestions on "how to buy" particular items, news of safety recalls, and discussions of relevant public policy issues, as well as offering books, newsletters, automobile pricing services, and other assists for consumer buying decisions. Fourth, as a representative of the consumer interest, Consumers Union will often seek to influence the development of public policy in the consumer arena. The total set of activities thus extends beyond consumer information, including both consumer education and political action.

Consumers Union has been scrupulous in protecting its reputation for providing consumer information that is unbiased by commercial interests. It refuses to accept any advertising in *Consumer Reports* and also refuses to allow any companies to use the ratings for commercial purposes. Thus, its information scores high in credibility, and likewise scores high in expertise. Further, as an independent rating organization, it offers exactly that form of information that is not usually offered by the marketing system—direct comparisons of brands on a large number of characteristics.

The organization's empathy score might best be judged as only moderate, however, since individual consumers may have different tastes or preference schedules than those adopted for the ratings. Further, the prices and styles reported in a national magazine publication may not be available to consumers in a local market. And the magazine does not contain information on local services ranging from plumbing to banking. Local newspapers and city magazines sometimes provide information on these services, but usually do so sporadically and incompletely. Consumers in metropolitan Washington, D.C., and the San Francisco Bay Area, however, do have available a *Checkbook* magazine, published by the Center for the Study of Services, that rates local services and identifies "best buys."

Thus, the independent consumer rating organization plays an important role in information dissemination by providing information that is high in credibility, high in expertise, and at least moderate in empathy. A number of studies have shown, however, that such information is used by a relatively small sector of the entire consumer population. Within the marketplace, this limited penetration still can have significant impacts since it affects the future decisions of marketers as to prices and quality of offerings. However, it has long been the case that the direct beneficiaries of such product information, those consumers who use it in their own purchasing, are precisely the people who would seem to need it the least. Studies by Hans Thorelli of product testing agency subscribers in Germany, Norway, and the United States, for example, found the same type of patrons in all three cultures—

those who have higher incomes, more education, and are greater readers of newspapers than the average consumer.

Public Policymakers as Information Disseminators

The general role for public policymakers in a marketplace economy is to create a consumer/marketer environment that is both efficient and fair. Consumer information programs are a popular alternative for policymakers because of their relatively nonrestrictive nature—marketers can still sell and consumers are free to buy when an information program is in effect. Further, since marketers are continually sending information to consumers, public policymakers frequently have the option of seeking to modify some aspect of that flow (i.e., having marketers disseminate the desired information) rather than having government create another dissemination flow.

Consumer information programs of this nature can be found in abundance. They exist at all levels of government and are sometimes supplemented by industry self-regulatory efforts. At the federal level, consumer information efforts are undertaken across a wide range of government departments, including the Environmental Protection Agency (automobile gas mileage), the U.S. Department of Transportation (tire performance ratings), the Consumer Product Safety Commission (hazard warnings and product recalls), the Securities and Exchange Commission (investment disclosures), the U.S. Department of Agriculture (food grades), and the Food and Drug Administration (drug interactions and side effects, nutrition labels). The General Services Administration (GSA) maintains the Consumer Information Center in Pueblo, Colorado, to centralize the distribution of many of the publications put out by some thirty federal agencies. The major center of government consumer information activity, however, is the Federal Trade Commission (FTC), which regulates most of the marketing activity in the U.S. system. In 1979, the FTC convened a Consumer Information Task Force to examine this area. Some key points from the task force findings follow.

There are four key principles to be followed with respect to a potential consumer information program in public policy. The first is the cost/benefit tradeoff, in which benefits should exceed costs. Three types of costs are commonly found in information dissemination programs: compliance costs (to marketers for supplying the information), enforcement costs (to government), and unintended side effects (for example, less effective ads because of too much disclosure). Three types of benefits, however, can flow from increased consumer information: improved consumer decisions, enhanced product quality, and/or lower prices through increased competition.

The other three principles reflect possible program designs. "Incentive compatibility" refers to an attempt to create regulations with which marketers will want to comply, rather than try to undercut. The next principle, First Amendment protection, reminds regulators to strive to maintain freedom of speech and not simply order marketers around by whim. This principle reflects a belief that consumers will benefit most when the marketing/consumer environment has a free flow of marketing information in it. The last principle, communication effectiveness, stresses that the dissemination should be designed to be successful for its target market. Consumers should be able to understand what is being said, and the disclosure should be interesting, noticeable, timely, and useful.

Public policymakers can take quite different approaches toward handling consumer problems. In some instances, policy programs involve the removal of restraints that have grown up within the marketplace. Such restraints sometimes ensure product quality but sometimes also protect existing sellers from price competition. In the late 1970s, for example, studies showed that consumers were paying 25 to 40 percent higher prices in states that restricted the advertising of eyeglasses than in states that allowed advertising of eyeglass prices. FTC policymakers decided that the states' ad bans were keeping marketers from informing consumers about prices and thus not allowing price to be used as a competitive tool. The FTC then moved against the bans, thus freeing marketers to advertise and compete on price in all states. Prices dropped substantially as the competitive market began to work more freely.

Following the eyeglass rule, regulators moved into cases involving the professions, including physicians, dentists, attorneys, and accountants whose societies had created codes that banned most forms of marketing to potential clients. Since these professions deal largely in intangible services, rather than more standardized products such as eyeglasses, the issues are more debatable and controversial. However, most professional societies have today changed their codes to allow advertising, at least in certain forms.

In contrast to restraint removal, public policymakers sometimes believe that it is necessary to restrict the flow of certain information to consumers. Because free speech is such an important right in the United States, any such restrictions must be approached with great care, and only when less restrictive options are not available. One of the few instances of a complete ban occurred in 1970, when the U.S. Congress banned cigarette advertising from television and radio. A variety of other options are also possible in this area. For example, the amount or style of advertising might be restricted rather than banned entirely (this has happened with advertising to children, and with advertising prescription drugs to consumers). Alternatively, consumer policy might restrict the timing of information disclosures. For example, in recent years public support for restricting telephone marketers from "cold calling" homes during dinner hours or late in the evening has grown. Increased consumer concerns about invasion of privacy and the distribution of personal information such as finances, medical histories, and memberships have also generated pressure for new restrictions on marketers in these areas.

Enhancing the flow of information is the most frequently used public policy option and includes a variety of approaches. The most basic form of public policy program that supports enhanced information dissemination lies in the area of standard setting. The creation of product standards (that is, establishing a common metric) allows all marketers to communicate using a similar basis: these standards also afford consumers the chance to compare different brands on comparable bases. In the area of food, for example, the calorie, pound, and U.S. RDA (recommended daily allowance) are all standards that have been decided in public policy. Tens of thousands of other standards also exist: current policy issues involve what new standards should be set, if any.

Additional programs are possible when policymakers determine that the existing information environment is somehow deficient and needs to be enhanced. A variety of options are available. For example, prior to the 1970 government ban on broadcast advertising for cigarettes, the Federal Communications Commission (FCC) had provided a novel information remedy called "countercommercials." From 1967 to 1970, the FCC required television and radio stations to provide free advertising to responsible critics of cigarette smoking, in the ratio of one counteradvertisement slot for every four brand cigarette commercials. The FCC's view relied on the "fairness doctrine": since the airways were owned by the public, balanced discussions covering both sides of significant public issues should be presented. Cigarette advertising alone did not allow such a balanced presentation; thus, counteradvertisements were appropriate. Given this history, the 1970 congressional ban restricting information flow can be seen as a reaction to the FCC's public policy remedy that had enhanced information flow.

Other types of programs can also support information dissemination goals. For example, a major concern is to prevent bad consumer purchases made through deception and/or high-pressure selling. One way to help is to give the consumer more time to make a decision: "cooling-off" laws, for example, often allow three days for a consumer to cancel sales agreements that may have been made under high-pressure sales conditions, as in door-to-door selling or telephone solicitations. A related policy option involves the separation of diagnosis from treatment: in the FTC's eyeglass regulations, for example, the eye examiner was required to inform a consumer, in writing, of his or her exact prescription: the consumer then could use this information to shop elsewhere for the best prices on lenses and frames, if he or she so desired.

The requirement for a marketer to disclose certain information to consumers reflects an "affirmative disclosure" program, the most common form of consumer information remedy used in public policy. Examples include those listed at the start of this section by various government agencies: these disclosures are usually required by all marketers in a product class, thus assisting the consumer in comparing the offerings of one seller to another, particularly on product performance bases. (But they require that relevant metrics and/or performance standards, such as nutritional RDAs, have already been determined by policymakers.)

Another form of affirmative disclosure pertains only to a particular marketer, who must then disclose certain information to consumers. This remedy is usually ordered in reaction to a deceptive or fraudulent program by that marketer. The FTC has used this type of remedy quite often in its cases, reflecting the belief that once consumers possess necessary information, they will be able to protect themselves against possible future deceptions by that marketer. A 1987 study by William Wilkie reports on more than 200 such affirmative disclosure orders by the FTC during a seven-year period and discusses a framework of information dissemination issues that arise in this area.

Consumer information plays a central role in a marketplace economy. Because the U.S. marketplace is so large, dynamic, and relatively uncontrolled, the topic of information dissemination cannot be understood without consideration of the many ways by which consumers come to gain information, as well as the fact that their use of information, typically in pursuit of a purchase decision, is imperfect. Four types of information disseminators were briefly examined: other consumers, marketers, independent rating organizations, and public policymakers. The consumer movement has played an important role in improving the character of consumer information available in our system through its impacts on each of these disseminator groups.

— William L. Wilkie

See also

Center for the Study of Services; Consumer Education; Consumer Problems in Market Economies; Consumers Union.

Readings

Federal Trade Commission (1979). *Consumer Information Remedies: Policy Review Session.* Washington, DC: U.S. Government Printing Office.

Mazis, Michael B., Richard Staelin, Howard Beales, and Steven Salop (1981). "A Framework for Evaluating Consumer Information Regulation." *Journal of Marketing.* 44 (Winter): 11–21.

Wilkie, William L. (1987). "Affirmative Disclosure at FTC: Communication Decisions." *Journal of Public Policy and Marketing.* 6: 33–42.

Initiatives and Referenda

One of the political tools that consumer advocates have at their disposal is the ballot initiative. Efforts to persuade legislators to vote in favor of consumer protection measures may be thwarted by the lobbying skills and resources of business interests, but ballot initiatives put power directly in the hands of voters. If people are convinced that an initiative is in their interests as consumers, they can enact it. Not all states allow the ballot initiative, but in those that do, consumer advocates have made increasingly effective use of this mechanism of social change.

In November 1992, for example, there were 232 statewide issues on ballots in the United States. While initiatives on congressional term limits and property tax reductions were most common, a small portion of these proposals did affect consumers. Several initiatives involved consumer issues such as automobile insurance (Michigan), labeling of toxic substances (Ohio), and recycling and reuse of product packaging (Massachusetts). Additional proposals had clear consumer aspects, even if they are not traditionally considered consumer issues: abortion (Arizona and Maryland), state vouchers for school choice (Colorado), increased cigarette taxes (Massachusetts), and mandatory health care coverage for employees (California). Clearly, ballot initiatives have the potential to set policy with respect to a wide variety of consumer issues.

The terms *initiative* and *referendum* are often used interchangeably, but there is a difference between them. Initiatives permit citizens to propose (or "initiate") a legislative measure by filing a petition bearing a minimum number of valid signatures. Referenda, in contrast, do not require the petition process; they occur when a government body, typically a legislature, "refers" a proposed or existing law to the citizenry for their approval or rejection. Constitutional amendments and bond issues exemplify referenda items. From the point of view of making consumer policy, initiatives are more important. The term *initiatives* will be used in this article to encompass both forms of citizen lawmaking.

The initiative process developed largely during the Progressive Era, a period that saw a number of efforts to make government more open, accountable, and honest. Whereas Progressivism was a national phenomenon, the initiative mechanism was established primarily in midwestern and western states. In these two sections of the country, Populism combined with Progressivism to accentuate the need for direct democratic involvement in government decision-making. In the Northeast, by contrast, the large number of immigrants may have discouraged the middle and upper classes from supporting the initiative process. In the South, the large number of blacks who had recently gained the vote made initiatives less attractive to the white majority. Today, the majority of states that allow their citizens to propose laws are located west of the Mississippi River, with Michigan and Massachusetts being the most notable exceptions.

The number of consumer initiatives can vary widely depending on how one defines a consumer issue. If one restricts these issues to privately purchased goods and the traditional consumer rights of safety, information, competition, representation, and redress, there are relatively few consumer initiatives. If one defines consumer issues more broadly to include the provision of public services, clean government concerns, and environmental quality, there is a larger number. This article construes consumer issues narrowly.

It is important to remember that initiatives involving consumer issues may involve limiting the rights of consumers or reducing their welfare. In recent years, for example, the insurance and tobacco industries have sponsored initiatives that purported to help consumers but, to most consumer groups, were really intended to benefit business groups. One might call these anti-consumer initiatives.

Even with pro-consumer initiatives, not all consumers stand an equal chance of benefiting from the initiative. Virtually all consumer policies benefit certain consumers more than others. For instance, an initiative that allows greater freedom in who may provide legal or medical services will usually benefit rural areas (where professionals are more scarce) more than urban areas. Moreover, some policies explicitly transfer wealth from one subset of consumers to another subset. A ballot initiative to establish lifeline utility rates, for example, essentially represents a subsidy by the class of higher-income utility consumers (and business consumers) to the class of lower-income consumers. Thus, not all consumers have viewed particular ballot initiatives as "good for consumers," which partially explains why some consumer initiatives have been defeated.

With these caveats and qualifications in mind, below are examples of pro-consumer and anti-consumer initiatives, including the consumer issue involved in the initiative, the state in which the vote took place, its year, and its outcome.

Consumer initiatives frequently are designed to reduce or restrain prices. A 1978 South Dakota initiative to institute lifeline utility rates was defeated. A 1982 Washington initiative to limit interest charges on retail credit was defeated. A 1986 Maine initiative to ban local measured telephone rates was approved. A 1988 California initiative to reduce auto insurance premiums was approved, but a 1996 effort to introduce no-fault automobile insurance in California was defeated, as was a 1992 Michigan initiative to reduce auto insurance benefits and redress.

Closely related to these initiatives are those intended to foster competition. A 1984 Montana initiative to allow denturist services by paraprofessionals was approved.

Initiatives also have addressed product safety and quality issues. A 1986 California initiative to provide warnings for carcinogens and teratogens was approved. A 1988 California initiative to fund cigarette counteradvertisements was approved. A 1990 Oregon initiative to require seatbelt use was approved. And a 1994 California initiative to reduce restrictions on tobacco sales was approved.

Finally, consumer initiatives have been designed to increase consumer representation or redress. A 1982 Ohio initiative to elect public utility commissioners was defeated. A 1984 Oregon initiative to establish a Citizen Utility Board was approved. And a 1990 Arizona no-fault auto insurance initiative was defeated.

While backers of pro-consumer initiatives have enjoyed some notable successes in recent years, a number of questions have been raised about the advisability of using the ballot box to make consumer policy. One is whether, given the complexity of so many issues, citizens are capable of making well-informed and farsighted decisions. A second question is whether, given the greater propensity of older, whiter, and more affluent people to vote, the initiative process discriminates against society's less advantaged citizens. A third question is whether, given the power of political advertising on television and radio to influence votes, consumer groups can successfully compete with well-financed business coalitions.

Defenders of the initiative process respond in kind: is the initiative process any less capable of making informed decisions, any less insensitive to disadvantaged citizens, and any less vulnerable to corporate campaign spending than other methods of making consumer policy? They argue that legislative and regulatory decision-making is often shortsighted, insufficiently concerned with disadvantaged groups, and overly influenced by business campaign contributions and lobbying.

Any evaluation of the initiative process must consider that initiatives can have wide-ranging effects. Even initiatives that are defeated can succeed in raising public awareness of an issue. Successful initiatives can set off a chain reaction in other states, thereby exerting influence on a national level.

— Robert N. Mayer

See also

Public Interest Research Groups.

Readings

Moore, John W. (1988). "Election Day Lawmakers." *National Journal.* 20 (September 17): 2296–2297.

Schmidt, David D. (1989). *Citizen Lawmakers: The Ballot Initiative Revolution.* Philadelphia: Temple University Press.

Insurance Regulation

Insurance has been regulated by the states since New Hampshire first created a Board of

Insurance Commissioners in 1851. One of the earliest proponents for strong insurance regulation, Elizur Wright, was a member of the Massachusetts Board of Insurance Commissioners. He not only sought to reform anti-consumer practices of insurers, but also was the first to call for federal regulation of the industry.

The first major case pertaining to insurance regulation in the U.S. Supreme Court was *Paul v. Virginia* (1869). Here, the court ruled that insurance was not interstate commerce and thus not subject to federal regulation. At the time, insurers desired federal regulation because they believed it would be more lenient than regulation by many states. But they changed their opinion about federal regulation after Theodore Roosevelt was elected president. The antitrust laws he championed convinced the industry that they were better off with state regulation.

In 1944, in deciding *United States v. Southeastern Underwriters Association* (dubbed the "SEUA case"), the Supreme Court reversed its earlier decision, declaring that insurance *was* interstate commerce. In response, the industry persuaded the states, who feared they would lose the power to collect premium taxes, to join it in lobbying Congress to establish the states as the regulatory locus and to confer on the industry an antitrust exemption. President Franklin Roosevelt supported the former but not the latter. Each house of Congress passed a bill, the McCarran-Ferguson Act, that delegated regulation of insurance to the states but, after a two-year moratorium, would impose the federal antitrust laws on insurance. Heavily lobbied by the industry, the conference committee, however, conferred a permanent moratorium.

Insurance continues to be regulated by the states. Except when Congress enacts a special act to do so, such as Medicare or the Federal Flood Insurance Program, the federal government has no regulatory role. Every state has a regulatory authority in place. State insurance departments are headed by an insurance commissioner who is either elected (twelve states) or appointed, usually by the governor.

State legislatures write the laws to establish regulatory parameters, and the state courts interpret these laws. The insurance departments are executive branch offices that carry out the day-to-day administration of these regulatory responsibilities. Commissioners license companies and agents, examine companies as to solvency and market conduct, approve policies and other forms, may approve rates, control investments to a degree, and otherwise establish the regulatory enforcement mechanism for the state within the authorities granted by the legislature.

The insurance commissioners from the states make up the National Association of Insurance Commissioners (NAIC). The NAIC helps to assure some level of uniformity among the states in the regulation of insurance through promulgation of model laws and model regulations. In recent years, the NAIC went further in the area of insolvency regulation when it adopted an accreditation program where, if a state failed to meet certain requirements, the state's domestic insurers would be subject to extra examination by other states.

In 1990, to increase consumer participation in its meetings, the NAIC created a program that provided $50,000 annually to cover the expenses of participating advocates. The grants were made by a board of five regulators and two advocates. In a typical year, between fifteen and twenty advocates participate in NAIC meetings, providing an opportunity for regulators to hear consumer points of view in addition to those of the hundreds of insurer representatives who attend these meetings.

Over the years, there has been considerable debate about the appropriate role of the federal government in regulating the insurance industry. Since the SEUA case, several attempts have been made to subject the industry to federal antitrust laws. Advocates have seen this effort as a critical step to encourage the states to make resolute decisions either to regulate fully the business (to qualify for the state action doctrine protection) or to allow the forces of competition to operate fully and effectively (by assuring that the competitors operate in a noncollusive manner). Critics of the current regulatory system point out that the regimes in many states fall into the cracks by deregulating rates even when collusive activities continue. Since insurers jointly make rates, or parts of rates, with little or no meaningful state oversight, these rates are usually higher than they would be in a more competitive market.

Property/Casualty Insurance

Property/casualty insurance protects policyholders against loss of property. The two types of this insurance of greatest interest to consumers are auto and homeowners. The problems that individuals have that relate to auto and home insurance are similar. They relate to purchase of coverage and settlement of insurance claims.

When consumers seek auto or home insurance, they may experience problems related to underwriting or pricing. Underwriting is the insurance company's process of deciding whether to write the consumer's business or, if accepted, into which of their insurers to place the coverage. When an insurer decides these matters, it uses what are called "underwriting guidelines" to make the decision. Guidelines can include diverse factors such as the number of accidents, credit history, and residence. Except in Texas, states do not require approval of these guidelines; in fact, the majority do not even collect them. But community and consumer activists have charged that some insurers "redline" whole areas.

A second consumer problem related to underwriting is the placement of an applicant into a higher-priced affiliated insurance company. Many insurers have what is known as "running mates" or "pup" affiliates with different prices. Often an insurer will have a preferred company (with the lowest rates), a standard company (with the middle price), and a substandard company (with the highest rates). This differentiation is not understood by many consumers. As a result, many states seek to educate policyholders, often by preparing and making available price guides. In the future, insurance departments may provide computerized price and service information or facilitate the development of private information brokers to do so.

Consumer leaders have been pressing for reform of bad underwriting practices. These efforts include anti-redlining legislation, which has stalled in Congress, and "good driver" or "good house" legislation. The latter would enable people who are "good" under state criteria, such as number of accidents or meeting the building code, to be able to obtain insurance from the company of their choice. Several states have good driver protections, and Michigan has also approved good house protections.

The key problem with pricing is the weakness of state price review coupled with weak competitive forces in the industry, especially within certain market segments. The property/casualty business grew up as a cartelized form of price system. Since federal law still exempts insurance from the antitrust laws, insurers can cooperate in pricing through cartel-like structures, called "rating bureaus." These organizations either produce full rates, or a large portion of these rates, for participating companies. Other barriers to competition include poorly informed consumers, laws that forbid agents from competing against each other on price, and laws that prohibit groups from organizing to purchase auto and home insurance.

For more than a decade, consumer groups have sought repeal of the federal antitrust exemption as well as repeal of anticompetitive state laws. Their greatest victory was the passage, in 1988, of Proposition 103 in California and the successful defense, in 1994, of legal challenges to this measure. Among other reforms, it repealed the state antitrust exemption, rolled back prices of auto insurance 20 percent subject to administrative review for confiscation, strengthened regulation, mandated good driver protections, required computerized price information, and simplified the classification system to discourage insurer avoidance of other protections. This initiative sparked the passage of similar insurance reforms in many other states.

Several states have created an office to represent consumers before the insurance department at rate hearings and in other matters. The Office of Public Insurance Counsel in Texas and the Intervener Compensation Program of California provide the most effective representation of consumer interests among the states.

The other major consumer concern is the practices of insurers in paying off claims for auto and home insurance. Insurance departments receive far more complaints about problems related to claims settlement than about any other issue. Most states have unfair claims settlement acts and staff to handle complaints. About half of the complaints that states receive are justified. If the insurer persists in denying these claims or shaving offers, they often are sued by the policyholder. Arguably, the most effective protection to consumer interests in the area of claims settlement practice has been the development of "bad faith" law in which an insurer must pay punitive damages if it breaches the covenant of good faith it has with the policyholder.

Life Insurance

There are two basic forms of life insurance—term and cash value. The latter includes whole life, universal life, and variable life. Term insurance pays if the insured dies during the term of the policy. The term can be one year with the guaranteed availability of renewal (annual renewable term) or for a longer term such as five or ten years. Term policies insuring young individuals are extremely low in cost, but the price rises and becomes very high at older ages.

Cash value policies, which cost the same each year for as long as one holds them, can be confusing because the product marries a life insurance policy to an investment. Except for older persons, premiums on cash value policies are much higher than those of term policies (when the death benefits are the same). But the investment component of cash value policies can be cashed out or converted to an annuity.

There are many consumer problems in life insurance. Some relate to its purchase. While term policies are relatively easy to understand, cash value products are not. The disclosure required by the NAIC for the latter, the so-called illustration, is difficult to fathom and subject to manipulation by agents and other salespersons. In the 1990s, the commissioners promised reforms that have been delivered only in part. The new illustration model is still confusing to consumers, does not show the interest rate they will earn, and does not disclose the commission and other essential components of the price.

The industry has built economic incentives into the products to encourage the sale of cash value rather than term. An agent typically makes five to ten times as much selling cash value as term. Some salespersons have gone beyond taking advantage of consumer confusion about the value of a cash value product to misleading consumers into thinking that the product is not life insurance or to manipulating the illustrations. Some agents have promised that premiums would "disappear." And some agents have churned customers from one policy to another in order to capture the high first-year commissions (usually between 55 and 100 percent of the first-year premium).

Most companies have not made a determined effort to check these practices; in fact, some have illustrated impossibly high interest rate assumptions and have otherwise misled consumers into purchasing policies offering poor value. Recently, regulators have levied fines totaling tens of millions of dollars on several large companies that have failed to check abuses against their policyholders.

The influence of the life insurance industry with federal policymakers has thwarted efforts by Congress and regulatory agencies to address these problems. When the Federal Trade Commission (FTC) prepared a study in the late 1970s that showed cash value life insurance investments provided much lower yields than did many comparable investments, the industry persuaded Congress to take away the FTC's power even to study problems in the insurance industry. Today, the FTC can study insurance issues only if Congress specifically directs it to do so.

The other major problem in life insurance is insolvency resulting from poor investment policies. In the late 1980s, there was a rash of insolvencies, which revealed the lack of adequate state regulatory authority and resources to assure solvency, and a state guarantee fund system that did not pay off policyholders promptly, forcing them to wait as long as a decade for their funds.

Through its accreditation program, the NAIC has moved strongly to respond to the first problem. However, a portion of the industry, and several states, continue to oppose this program. The guarantee fund problems have not been resolved. Consumer advocates have called on the NAIC to work with the National Organization of Life and Health Guarantee Associations to limit the time that consumer monies can be tied up.

One type of life insurance that has been especially controversial is credit insurance, which pays off a loan in the event a borrower, for a specified reason, is unable to pay. The most common types of this insurance are credit life, which pays off a loan in the event of death, and accident and health, which pays off a loan in the event of disability. Credit life insurance in particular has been much criticized by consumer advocates who claim that it is overpriced in that a relatively small percentage of premiums are paid out in claims.

Because consumers rarely shop for credit insurance, its prices are regulated by all states. Yet, until recently, despite a suggested minimum loss ratio (ratio of claims' payments to premiums received) of 60 percent by the NAIC, most states allowed loss ratios of under 40 percent. Prodded by consumer groups, however, recently regulators in about twenty states lowered allowable prices. As a result, the average loss ratio nationwide climbed from 37 percent to around 45 percent.

— J. Robert Hunter

See also

Health Care Protections; National Insurance Consumer Organization.

Readings

Caddy, Douglas (1986). *Legislative Trends in Insurance Regulation.* College Station: Texas A&M University Press.

Kimball, Spencer L., and Herbert S. Denenberg (1969). *Insurance, Government, and Social Policy: Studies in Insurance Regulation.* Homewood, IL: R. D. Irwin.

McDowell, Banks (1994). *The Crisis in Insurance Regulation.* Westport, CT: Quorum.

International Organization of Consumers Unions

See Consumers International.

Investor Protections

Although the first stock exchange in America was formed in 1790, the securities markets were not regulated until the early twentieth century, when securities fraud and speculation had become a serious social problem. Responding to the calls for reform from victims of such schemes, in 1911 Kansas became the first state to adopt a "blue sky" law, so called because these state laws were designed to protect citizens from fraudulent schemes with no more basis "than so many feet of blue sky." Over approximately the next two decades, forty-six other states followed Kansas in passing such laws, which have been called the first consumer protection statutes.

In 1956, the National Conference of Commissioners on Uniform State Laws completed the initial draft of the Uniform Securities Act (USA). Designed to promote uniformity of state securities regulation, this model statute includes regulatory oversight and antifraud provisions related to security offerings, broker-dealers, and investment advisers. Regularly updated since its initial draft, the act has since been enacted in whole or in part in most states.

The stock market crash of 1929 prompted Congress to act, leading to passage of four major federal laws over the next decade. Congress adopted the Securities Act of 1933, regulating primary securities offerings; the Securities Exchange Act of 1934, creating the Securities and Exchange Commission (SEC) and regulating trading in the secondary markets; the Investment Adviser Act of 1940, regulating those firms that give advice about securities; and the Investment Company Act of 1940, governing mutual funds. These federal laws include provisions for regulatory oversight and antifraud language. They continue to provide the framework of federal regulation today.

The passage of the Securities Exchange Act of 1934 also formalized the system of self-regulation in the securities industry. The various national and regional stock exchanges, as well as the National Association of Securities Dealers, all acquired official self-policing authority under the oversight of the SEC. These responsibilities include conducting inspections, enforcement against unfair trade practices, and resolution of disputes through industry-run arbitration programs.

Beginning in the 1970s, a steadily increasing number of middle-income Americans became consumers of investment products. By the mid-1990s, investments in mutual funds alone exceeded consumer deposits in the entire banking system. Faced with a complex variety of investments to choose among, and often relatively unsophisticated about finances, many of these new investors found it difficult to assess the products available to them and became consumers of investment advice. They also became targets for scams and victims of self-dealing and incompetent advice. Thus, the large-scale entry of less sophisticated investors into the markets had, by the late 1980s, begun to raise fundamental questions about the adequacy of existing investor protections, particularly in the areas of regulatory oversight, disclosure, and redress.

Three factors primarily drove the consumer agenda in the area of investor protections during this period: a highly competitive financial press, which emphasized investigative reporting of emerging problems; an activist congressman, Representative Edward J. Markey (D-MA), who chaired the House Telecommunications and Finance Subcommittee from 1987 through 1994; and pro-investor state securities regulators, who often were the first to identify problems confronting small investors. Consumer groups played a largely secondary role, generally supporting initiatives developed by Markey with help from the state regulators.

A combination of factors worked against enactment of effective investor protections, including a powerful securities industry lobby and, during the Reagan and Bush years, an often antagonistic SEC. Also, then Senate Securities Subcommittee Chairman Christopher Dodd (D-CT) worked closely with Ranking Minority Member Phil Gramm (R-TX) to water down or defeat a series of bills that had won overwhelming, often unanimous, support in the House.

One investor protection issue on which consumer advocates did take the lead was financial planning regulation. A 1987 report by Consumer Federation of America outlined growing problems resulting from loose regulatory oversight and inadequate disclosure of conflicts of interest. An initial legislative proposal introduced in 1990 by Representative Rick Boucher (D-VA) would have brought all financial planners under the federal Investment Adviser Act, which covers those who give advice about investing in securities. It would have greatly increased the compensation disclosure that planners were required to provide when they both gave advice and sold products to implement their recommendations. Supported by consumer advocates, state securities regulators, and fee-only financial planners, this legislation could not overcome the combined opposition of the securities industry, insurance industry, accountants, and largest financial planning groups.

Later, compromise legislation by Representatives Boucher and Markey that improved disclosure and oversight for investment advisers (including most but not all those who call themselves financial planners) sailed through the House in both 1992 and 1993. Despite the fact that this legislation was endorsed by the Clinton administration, the Senate refused to consider the stronger House provisions to increase disclosure and improve the SEC's oversight program and passed only a bill to increase funding. When a deal was finally struck at the end of the 1994 congressional session that included a modest disclosure provision, Gramm killed the bill.

During the same period, however, a number of states did take steps to improve regulation of financial planners. Several states that did not have investment adviser laws adopted such laws, and a number of others updated their investment adviser laws to clarify their application to financial planners. Two states—Maryland and Georgia—passed laws covering the vast majority of those who hold themselves out to the public as financial planners. In addition, SEC Chairman Arthur Levitt promised to look into improving compensation disclosure through rulemaking, but no rules had been proposed by the end of 1994.

Limited partnerships were one of the hottest investments of the 1980s, sold aggressively by brokers and financial planners, often in violation of industry requirements that they sell only investments that are suitable for their clients. When many of these partnerships became all but worthless, general partners began combining several of the finite-life partnerships into single, infinite-life, exchange-traded investments. While these controversial reorganizations, known as roll-ups, generated lucrative fees for general partners, they almost always lost a great deal of money for limited partners.

In 1992 and 1993, the House passed strong bills to prevent abuses of limited partners by general partners. Senator Gramm, however, adamantly opposed the legislation, which he succeeded in stopping in 1992. Rather than risk a similar defeat the next year, and faced with the opposition of Senators Dodd and Gramm to the stronger House proposals, the House agreed to a scaled-back bill, which was enacted and signed into law in 1993. The bill limited the compensation general partners could receive and required more meaningful and understandable disclosure to limited partners assessing the roll-up transaction. As a result of the concessions made, however, the final bill was too weak for consumer advocates, who had endorsed the earlier House version, to support.

Another area that attracted congressional attention in the late 1980s was the growing problem of penny stock fraud, which state securities regulators estimated was costing consumers at least $2 billion a year. In 1990, Congress passed and the president signed legislation to clean up the penny stock market. After passing the House on a voice vote, the legislation was weakened in the Senate and then again in the rulemaking process at the SEC. The Penny Stock Reform Act of 1990, however, did give the commission greater authority to police the unregistered "consultants" and "promoters" who often worked behind the scenes to manipulate the market, required better disclosure to penny stock investors, and directly attacked some of the most abusive products sold through the penny stock market.

At the same time that investor fraud was growing, a series of Supreme Court decisions scaled back defrauded investors' right to redress. In 1986, the Court upheld the right of securities firms to apply pre-dispute binding arbitration clauses in customer contracts to disputes involving securities fraud. In 1991, the Court created a new, restrictive statute of limitations for federal securities fraud cases, requiring that such cases be filed within one year from discovery of the violation and no more than three years from the occurrence of the violation, long before many frauds can be uncovered. Furthermore, the Court applied its decision retroactively, throwing a number of pending cases out of court. In 1994, the Court eliminated liability for aiders and abetters of fraud on the grounds that it was not expressly provided for in the law.

Representative Markey, Energy and Commerce Committee Chairman John Dingell (D-MI), and others introduced legislation in 1988 to ban mandatory pre-dispute binding arbitration clauses in customer contracts and to reform the securities industry's arbitration process. Fiercely opposed by the industry, this legislation failed to garner the support needed to get it out of subcommittee. The legislative effort did have some effect, however, by encouraging the securities self-regulatory organizations, which run securities arbitration, to adopt some modest but important reforms on their own. These measures included making arbitration decisions public and limiting the industry ties of "public" arbitrators.

By the early 1990s, however, the increased use of mandatory arbitration clauses, and the refusal of most brokers to allow the use of an independent arbitration forum, had clogged the securities industry's arbitration system. In particular, an increasing number of large, highly complex cases ill-suited to the expedited procedures of arbitration were slowing the process. In response, the industry had begun to clamor for a new set of "reforms," including limits on nonattorney representation, restrictions on punitive damages, and new, coercive procedures to encourage settlements. These proposals, all of which would have limited investor rights in arbitration, were opposed by the Consumer Federation of America, the American Association of Retired Persons, and state securities regulators. In 1994, the SEC rejected the settlement offers proposal presented by the National Association of Securities Dealers and reaffirmed its support for the availability of punitive damages in arbitration.

Representative Markey and Senator Richard Bryan (D-NV) led the effort to extend the statute of limitations for securities fraud lawsuits. Their attempts were blocked, however, by congressional members intent on attaching drastic new litigation restrictions, such as "loser pays" provisions, to any such legislation. In the end, Congress included a provision overturning the retroactive application of the Court's statute of limitations ruling in the bank reform bill enacted in 1991.

A coalition of accountants, insurance companies, and high-tech firms that had been defendants in securities fraud cases continued to push aggressively for legislation to limit their liability. In response, Senator Dodd and Representative Billy Tauzin (D-LA) introduced two similar bills in 1993 that would restrict investor rights in securities fraud litigation. These bills were opposed by consumer advocates, state securities regulators, and the SEC, as well as by plaintiffs' attorneys. Although neither bill was voted on, they did attract a number of sponsors from both political parties. Furthermore, severe limits on securities fraud litigation were incorporated in the Republican Party's congressional agenda, the "Contract with America." In 1995, Congress passed such legislation over the president's veto.

Although Republican-controlled Congresses have been reluctant to approve new investor protections, the SEC has become far more receptive to investor concerns. Chairman Levitt has begun to question fundamental industry practices, such as the hiring and retention of brokers with poor disciplinary histories and the abusive nature of some industry compensation practices.

— Barbara Roper

Readings

Roper, Barbara L. N. (1993). *State and Federal Regulation of Financial Planners: A Policy Overview and Model for Reform.* Washington, DC: American Association of Retired Persons Public Policy Institute.

Seligman, Joel (1995). *The Transformation of Wall Street: A History of the Securities and Exchange Commission and Modern Corporate Finance.* Boston: Northeastern University Press.

J

Japanese Consumer Movement

In the late-nineteenth and early-twentieth centuries, consumer activism in Japan—including protests over rice prices and the formation of a coal miners' cooperative union in the 1880s—was isolated and sporadic. Immediately after World War II, the "kome-yokose undo" (Give-Us-Rice Movement) was organized by workers facing poverty who demanded a fair cost of living. In 1948, homemakers demanded the elimination of defective matches that did not light. They organized the Japan Housewives Association.

Beginning in the 1950s, Japan's current consumer movement began to take shape. In 1956, the National Federation of Consumer Organizations was founded. At its first convention in 1957, the organization adopted a "consumer declaration" stating that "sovereignty rests with the consuming public" and that "all price and quality decisions must be made by respecting the will of the consumers." In 1960, in response to the labeling of canned horse meat and whale meat as beef, consumer organizations started the "Movement To Purge False Labeling of Canned Goods," and the government began to consider labeling regulations.

In 1961, the Office of Consumer Education, a section of the Japan Productivity Center, was dissolved after it was criticized for being too pro-business, and the Japan Consumers Association was established. The association introduced its Declaration and its Six Consumer Movement Principles: ensure fair competition, select goods and services from a wide variety of choices, promote accurate knowledge, respect the consumer's will, organize a consumer section in the government administration, and promote the consumer's social responsibility. The association received support from the Ministry of International Trade and Industry, and its activities were centered around consumer education, comparative product tests, and consultation for consumers.

In 1964, the environmentally oriented New Life Association was established. Unlike previous consumerist activities that were led by centrally organized groups, the association's activities were organized primarily by small community groups to address such issues as the detection of toxins from plastic dishes. This emphasis on the health and environmental consequences of consumption has remained an important feature of Japanese consumerism through the present day.

In 1967, the Japan Consumer Federation was established. The consumer movement, which until then had been female-oriented, became male-oriented and more aggressive in nature. Three years later, the consumer movement reached its summit. Inspired by the example of Ralph Nader in the United States, the Consumers Union of Japan was established. At approximately the same time, the Japan Consumer Information Center began operation.

The most memorable mass consumer action during the 1970s was a successful boycott of a two-tier price structure for color television sets wherein domestic prices were higher than export prices. This boycott coincided with separate consumer agitation involving food additives, synthetic detergents, and pharmaceutical products. However, while the number of consumer organizations grew as groups split and organized new groups, the total membership decreased. One reason is that more women began to seek work outside of their homes, decreasing the number available for volunteer activism.

In the 1980s, as the economy matured, consumer issues became more service-related than product-related. Consumer groups worked toward revising the Door-to-Door Sales Law. In the 1990s, the consumer movement has focused on issues related to service providers (e.g., contractual issues involving health spas, telemarketing of training and certification programs, and fraudulent marketing of a "pot of happiness" to those who are psychologically vulnerable). Other consumer issues—recycling and other environmental concerns, price differences between domestic and overseas markets, and industry deregulation—have reflected the increasingly global nature of commerce and the interdependence of consumers. A particularly difficult issue is how to achieve domestic food security, minimize exposure to pesticides, and protect family farmers within an international trading system increasingly hostile to protectionist measures.

For twenty years, consumer groups advocated product liability protections. While a law was finally passed in 1994, these groups considered it to be inadequate. As a result, the consumer movement advocated, as a preventive measure, product safety warning labels and signs, and as a remedial measure, the ability to sue for damages.

Among the leaders of Japan's consumer movement in the early days were Toyohiko Kagawa, who embodied the Christian spirit in the cooperative movement; Mumeo Oku, Yuri Takada, and Kii Nakamura of Shufuren (Japan Housewives Association); economists Nobuo Noda and Susumu Yamazaki and home economist Hisako Ujiie, who were all associated with the Japan Consumers Association; and Naokazu Takeuchi, a Ministry of International Trade and Industry bureaucrat, who later worked with the Japan Consumer Federation.

— Mitsuaki Imai

Readings

Fumitoshi, Takahashi (1996). "Japan's Product Liability Law: Issues and Implications." *Journal of Japanese Studies*. 22 (1): 105–128.

Imai, Mitsuaki (1986). *Consumer Education in Japan*. Nagoya: Kinjo Gakuin University.

Vogel, David (1992). "Consumer Protection and Protectionism in Japan." *Journal of Japanese Studies*. 18 (1): 119–154.

Journalism, Consumer

Journalism is a field of great breadth. Residing within it is a kind of reporting and writing that is designed to serve the reader as "consumer." This journalism helps the reader (or listener or viewer) make a reasoned judgment—a choice—about a product or service in the marketplace or a course of conduct or action. That choice is then expressed in an exchange decision of some kind, a transaction that can enhance the consumer's social, economic, physical, or personal well-being.

Consumer journalism is an American invention. It springs from the goal of having a free marketplace for sellers, freedom of choice for consumers, and—particularly in recent years—the desire of individuals to achieve greater self-actualization. Consumer journalism, therefore, delivers appliance information to appliance buyers, university tuition information to students and parents, home inspection information to home buyers, sources of legal assistance to victims, fertilizer information to gardeners, and health information to everyone. It is journalism that readers want in order to cope and to succeed in America's dynamic social and economic environment.

Origins

Consumer journalism is not new. Its roots may be detected early in the nineteenth century, which was a time of great scientific, technological, and economic ferment. The Industrial Revolution was underway: steam-powered engines drove merchant ships and locomotives and ran textile and armament factories; the flatbed printing press appeared, as did photography and photographic platemaking; banks were chartered and a new national currency was in circulation; electromagnetism, electricity, and telegraphy appeared; and so did the sewing machine and the safety pin.

A new and thriving middle class built and ran the new factories, stores, and banks. When the Treaty of Ghent finally ended the War of 1812 and all further Anglo-American hostilities, this new middle class helped inaugurate a highly nationalistic "era of good feelings." But the president, Andrew Jackson, focused his attention on farmers and workers in burgeoning new industries, eulogizing "the common man." Many members of the new entrepreneurial middle class—mainly Whigs, Federalists, and some alarmed Democrats—feared that the rough-hewn Jacksonian democracy would overwhelm American culture, taste, and manners.

Into this cultural vacuum stepped newspaper and periodical writers who were "journalists of manners." They were forerunners of many succeeding generations of writers and editors who today are called "consumer" or "lifestyle" journalists. These early–nineteenth-century journalists reported on the mores of the new middle class, described how the best of them lived, and instructed the rest of them on the way they ought to live. Since most newspaper editors had neither the patience nor the interest for such material, over time these journalists of manners migrated to a new genre—the magazine.

One of the most influential and successful of America's earliest magazines of manners was *The Saturday Evening Post.* Founded in August 1821, *The Post* evolved from a weekly newspaper published on a large folded sheet. As a magazine, it concentrated less on the news of the day and more on shaping the ethos of the new society. Among its fiction and poetry, *The Post* carried regular columns instructing its readers on religion, morals, manners, and taste. Since most of *The Post's* readers tended to be women, a special column—and its most popular feature—was titled "The Ladies' Friend." The concept of *The Post* proved to be so popular that, in 1840, its publisher (George R. Graham) began a second magazine, *Graham's Lady's and Gentleman's Magazine,* featuring similar contents—a mix of culture (fiction, poetry) and personal service (fashion, homemaking).

In 1830, a strong competitor to *The Post* appeared: *Godey's Lady's Book,* the first magazine directed solely to women. In another innovative move, publisher Louis Antoine Godey chose Sara Josepha Hale to be the magazine's "editress." *Godey's Lady's Book* ignored politics, fiction, and poetry, concentrating instead on fashion and clothes, recipes and diet, homemaking and home decoration, hints for better health and beauty, sewing and embroidery patterns, and the requisite columns on manners, morals, and taste. One of *Godey's* most unusual features was the publication of a complete plan for a small house, plus a list of the materials needed to build it and its cost. A highly successful publication, *Godey's* influenced later service magazines such as *House Beautiful, Good Housekeeping,* and *Ladies' Home Journal.*

In the five decades prior to the Civil War, American magazines catered to readers proud of their new prosperity within a national domain that was not only expanding (south to Louisiana and west to Oregon) but shifting from an agricultural to a manufacturing base. In this era of rapid change, the popular women's and home magazines provided their readers with a stabilizing literature that focused on family and children, the comfort and safety of the home, and the basic social courtesies appropriate in the new American culture. Even though each publication was created for a specific urban audience (mainly in Boston, New York, or Philadelphia), the demand was enough to support as many as 2,500 magazines of one kind or another between 1850 and 1865.

Evolution of Muckraking

Just prior to the Civil War, a more thoughtful type of magazine appeared, carrying articles on science, technology, art, and international travel, as well as the obligatory pieces on manners and taste. Two of the most successful were *Harper's New Monthly Magazine* (1850) and *Frank Leslie's Illustrated Magazine* (1856). A special example of this new journalistic maturity was the campaign in 1858 by *Leslie's* to ban the sale of "swill milk"—milk produced by cows fed on the grain waste discharged by New York–area whiskey distillers. *Leslie's* campaign, bitterly fought in print and on the streets, was ultimately successful. It remains one of the best examples of what later came to be known as "muckraking," a branch of investigative journalism that was to become, a half century later, a major subset of the larger field of consumer journalism.

One boon to the magazines was the establishment of a national postal system serving farm communities as well as urban centers. In March 1879, Congress authorized second-class postal privileges for magazines, a special mailing rate that enabled these publications to serve old readers and find new readers—anywhere in the country.

The latter half of the nineteenth century was a great age of retailing. During these years R. H. Macy, Arnold Constable, Jordan Marsh, John Wanamaker, and Marshall Field invented the department store. It also was the era of the chain store: in 1869 George Gilman and George Huntington Hartford opened their first store with the inflated name, The Great Atlantic & Pacific Tea Company, and over the next thirty years the "A&P" appeared as a major food retailer in hundreds of American communities from coast to coast. In 1879, F. W. Woolworth opened his first "Five-and-Ten-Cent Store" in Utica, New York; by the turn of the century he had opened nearly sixty more. It was also the age of the great mail order houses: Sears, Roebuck and Montgomery Ward, whose catalogs broke open the field of consumer merchandising.

Consumer display advertising first appeared in the consumer magazines of the 1870s and 1880s, now familiar journals dedicated to home, health, and women's needs. More in the form of announcements than graphic creations, these early appeals were small, tightly written, single-column blocks of copy set in agate type. But the constricted advertising envelope was broken open in daily newspapers, where each city's major retailers used increasing page areas to announce the availability of their mass-produced goods at fixed, low, advertised prices. (Haggling was largely relegated to small stores around the corner.)

Advertising was a major source of support for consumer magazines and figured prominently in the growth and significance of one of America's most durable publications: *Good Housekeeping*. Founded in 1885 by Clark W. Bryan, *Good Housekeeping* contained not only a sprinkling of essays and stories by famous writers, but also many articles (most of them written by readers) about home, food, clothing, family, and household affairs. The articles were brief but instructive, presented in straightforward, plain English.

In the 1880s and 1890s, the genteel, instructive tone of the women's service magazines, like *Good Housekeeping,* could not always be sustained because of marketplace abuses and hazards. The *Good Housekeeping* editorial staff, in close touch with readers, soon became aware of questionable practices in the processing of food products. In an editorial in their September 18, 1886, issue, the editors warned readers to "Guard against Adulteration." This piece was the first of many *Good Housekeeping* warnings to consumers about potential dangers in the marketplace. These editorials, delivered in cautious, measured prose, differed from the more sensational prose of other journalists who examined the ethics of American business leaders.

In 1893, America slid into its first modern depression. For the next four years, government fumbled with ways to cope with industrial and financial excesses, establishing few laws to protect consumers. Among those crusaders who stepped into this vacuum of public confidence was a new generation of consumer journalists, writers who were deeply suspicious of what passed for progress.

At the head of their phalanx was a small but impressive group of journalists who hoped to bring about social and political reform. At the end of the nineteenth century, city political bosses tolerated, and even promoted, graft and corruption. Reform-minded journalists began to generate a popular literature of shame and disgust for which the reading public seemed especially ready.

Joseph Pulitzer was the newspaper publisher who invented a new type of tabloid journalism to reflect this public anger: "yellow journalism." Pulitzer bought the enfeebled *New York World* in 1883 and turned it into a "truly democratic" newspaper in the Jacksonian "common-man" tradition. Pulitzer said his paper was "dedicated to the cause of the people," and promised that it "will expose all fraud and sham, fight all public evils and abuses—[and] will battle for the people with earnest sincerity."

The sensational "yellow journalism" practiced by Pulitzer was extremely successful, and the *New York World* soon had one of the largest daily circulations of any newspaper in the world. Its reporters and editorial writers documented with angry clarity all kinds of evils. While their exposés enraged the rich and powerful, their readers loved them. Soon, the Pulitzer journalists were joined by colleagues writing for other newspapers, magazines, and books.

One of the most controversial and successful imitators of the *New York World* was the *Denver Evening Post*. Crusaders Henry H. Tammen and Frederick G. Bonfils bought the paper in 1895. In daily editorials, titled "So the People May Know," Tammen attacked the local water company (for charging exorbitant rates), the coal companies, purveyors of allegedly fresh food, and many other special interests. In a campaign unique to the *Post*, Tammen and Bonfils accused Denver's major department stores of being little more than "junk shops . . . filled with a confusion of the commonest and coarsest rubbish." The paper originally was concerned about alleged exploitation of child labor, but when the stores withdrew their advertising from the newspaper, the *Post's* writers broadened their attacks to the stores' shoddy merchandise and exorbitant pricing.

These angry investigative reporters and editors around the country came to be known as the "muckrakers," a sobriquet given them by President Theodore Roosevelt in a 1906 speech. By then, the muckrakers worked for many publications. The most impressive work was being published in *McClure's*, whose managing editor, Lincoln Steffens, serialized his *Shame of the Cities*, later publishing his articles in book form. *McClure's* also published Ida Tarbell's exposé of John D. Rockefeller, Sr., and the Standard Oil company; Burton J. Hendrick's enraged "Story of Life Insurance"; and Raymond Baker's series on America's rapacious railroads. Elsewhere, Charles E. Russell took on the Beef Trust in *Everybody's* magazine, and *Collier's* serialized "The Great American Fraud," Samuel Hopkins Adams's exposé of the patent medicine industry. Edward W. Bok, editor of *Ladies' Home Journal*, worked the same mine, running exposés of the patent medicine industry at every opportunity and refusing to carry their advertising. In 1906, Upton Sinclair, aided by a $500 advance from the socialist magazine *Appeal to Reason*, wrote *The Jungle*, a shocking fictional look inside the meat-packing industry (e.g., dead rats in the sausage, missing workers turning up in the lard).

Sinclair's journalistic *tour de force* is often cited as the most influential of the muckraking genre. It is certainly one of a line of seminal American books (e.g., Harriet Beecher Stowe's *Uncle Tom's Cabin*, Rachel Carson's *Silent Spring*, Arthur Kallet and F. J. Schlink's *100,000,000 Guinea Pigs*, Ralph Nader's *Unsafe at Any Speed*) that have helped change the course of American social and political history.

The general public read *The Jungle;* so did members of Congress. The year after its publication, 1906, Congress passed two pieces of landmark consumer legislation: the Meat Inspection Act and the Pure Food and Drug Act. The former said the government was responsible for insuring the quality of any meat shipped in interstate commerce; the latter did the same for grains, most processed foods, and all patent medicines in interstate commerce. (Congress waited another sixty years, however, before it passed similar laws regarding fish and poultry.)

Muckraking consumer journalists continued their print crusades, but the rising public outcry for action and the responses of Congress and the president took the steam out of the muckraking movement. One of the last magazines to pursue cleanup campaigns was *Hampton's Broadway,* founded in 1898, which published articles by John L. Matthews, Herbert N. Casson, and the ubiquitous Charles E. Russell.

Development of Product Testing

Less sensational but no less significant for the development of consumer journalism was the approach taken in 1900 by the editors of *Good Housekeeping.* Familiar with—and alarmed by—the extent of the "muck" being raked up in the marketplace, the editors set up an "experiment station" to test the items they planned to write about in subsequent issues. In this way, they could assure their readers that the consumer articles published in *Good Housekeeping* could be believed and trusted. The idea was enthusiastically received by readers. Two years later, the editors took the next step: they decided to accept advertisements only for products that they had themselves tested in their "experiment station." In 1909, *Good Housekeeping* upgraded its "experiment station" to an "institute," installed a modern laboratory, and settled upon an oval seal with the legend, "Tested and Approved by the *Good Housekeeping* Institute conducted by *Good Housekeeping* magazine." The oval seal was shown prominently in the advertising of those products that successfully came through the institute's testing program.

In another brilliant stroke, the editors of *Good Housekeeping* hired Harvey W. Wiley in 1912 to come to the institute to direct a new *Good Housekeeping* bureau of foods, sanitation, and health. Wiley had been a chemist at the U.S. Department of Agriculture in Washington, D.C., where he and a small staff had contributed much data to support the landmark Pure Food and Drug and Meat Inspection Acts of 1906. Wiley and his staff had earned themselves the name of "The Poison Squad" because they tested an array of suspicious foods and patent medicines by ingesting them themselves and writing up the results. For *Good Housekeeping,* Wiley wrote a monthly "Question Box," one of consumer journalism's most popular and longest-running columns. Wiley continued writing it until shortly before his death in 1930.

In the mid-1930s, Rexford G. Tugwell, assistant secretary of agriculture in President Franklin D. Roosevelt's New Deal administration, drafted a Food, Drug and Cosmetic Act. When finally enacted in 1938, the law established a new federal agency, the Food and Drug Administration, with the power to conduct a wide range of consumer protection activities, including the kind of testing purportedly being carried out by the nongovernmental *Good Housekeeping* Institute. A companion law, the Wheeler-Lea Act, gave the Federal Trade Commission (FTC) new authority to regulate food and drug advertising. Armed with the FD&C Act and Wheeler-Lea, Tugwell and the New Deal fought the *Good Housekeeping* seal on grounds that it was "misleading and deceptive." Finally, in 1941, the FTC ordered *Good Housekeeping* to "cease and desist" from saying that the sealed products were really "tested and approved." Reluctantly the magazine agreed. However, its table of contents contained a blanket endorsement that all products advertised in the magazine "are good ones."

In the 1920s, the government established the National Bureau of Standards to do for government purchasing agents what the *Good Housekeeping* Institute was supposed to have done for the readers of *Good Housekeeping:* test products to see if they lived up to expectations. One of the bureau's engineers, F. J. Schlink, thought the kind of objective, disinterested testing done by and for the government ought to be extended to the private consumer as well. In 1927, Schlink joined forces with economist-writer Stuart Chase, who two years before had published *The Tragedy of Waste,* an exposé of the consequences of America's rapid industrialization. Together Schlink and Chase published *Your Money's Worth: A Study in the Waste of the Consumer's Dollar,* a view of the American consumer's impotence in a marketplace shaped and degraded by shoddy goods and false advertising.

F. J. Schlink became one of the country's best-known consumer writers as a result of the success of *Your Money's Worth.* Impressed by the public's response, Schlink left government in 1929 and established Consumers' Research as a product testing organization. He wrote up his test results and published them in his new advertising-free journal, *Consumer Bulletin.*

One of the testing engineers hired by Schlink was Arthur Kallet. Using data generated at Consumers' Research, in 1932 Kallet and Schlink wrote *100,000,000 Guinea Pigs,* an account of government fumbling and inaction with regard to foods and drugs of doubtful integrity and safety being sold to unsuspecting consumers. The Kallet-Schlink book was a sensation and became required reading within the Tugwell circle of New Deal reformers.

In 1936, as a result of political and labor conflicts, Kallet left Schlink and Consumers' Research to start Consumers Union and its own magazine, *Consumer Reports.* After sixty years of publication, *Consumer Reports* remains the preeminent example of pure consumer journalism: factual, objective, advisory, and focused on what the consumer needs to know in order to make a reasoned judgment about a product or service in the marketplace.

By the time *Consumer Reports* appeared, consumer journalism had expanded the "five w's" of traditional newsgathering (who, what, where, when, and why) to include "how to." The result was and remains the formula for the success of the editorial program in *Consumer Reports* and similar consumer service periodicals: who (or whom) to see for it, what to look for, where to find it, when to buy it, why to ask for it, and how to use it.

During the Great Depression and World War II, virtually every newspaper and magazine carried articles to help consumers cope with adversity, scarcity, poverty, and fear. For the first time, the federal government began disseminating extensive consumer information: the Department of Agriculture mailed thousands of recipes, gardening tips, home repair hints, and other helpful items to local, regional, and national publications. During the 1930s and 1940s, the department's Extension Service and public information staffs helped develop a new generation of writers, editors, and illustrators to produce reliable, believable consumer journalism. Many of these professionals remained with the federal government, but others returned to hometown newspapers, state universities, state government offices, or the national media to continue providing consumer information to the public.

Rise of Business "Journalism"

After World War II, the U.S. economy began a long and sustained economic boom. Consumer writers of this era were enthusiastic about the new cornucopia of goods and services available: pharmaceuticals (especially antibiotics and sulfas, first used during the war); improved radio reception and the arrival of television; sleek, fast automobiles and high-speed intercontinental passenger planes; nylon, rayon, polyester, and dozens of fiber blends; instant coffee, powdered milk, and frozen dinners; and whole new suburban communities of prefabricated module-built, single-family homes. Every development was reported on and evaluated by journalists.

During this period, consumer journalism and consumer advertising developed a partnership. Newspapers and women's and service magazines circulating in expanding suburbs offered advertisers special pages, sections, or editions focusing on consumer needs, thus creating a selling-oriented, consumer-friendly "editorial environment" within which local or national advertisers could present their own messages. To help write and edit these new editorial environments, publishers began employing consumer public relations writers. This new, rising subset of consumer journalism included persons trained in journalism who worked directly for manufacturers and service and professional groups to write articles in which their products or services were presented to the public in a positive light.

With the help of public relations writers, government public information writers, and a few resident consumer journalists, newspaper and magazine editors developed seasonal issues with related editorial material. For example, a September issue might contain news to complement the advertising for Labor Day back-to-school sales and late-season clearance sales of sporting goods, gardening tools, camping and fishing gear, and sales of late summer vegetables (tomatoes, squash, eggplants, etc.).

Emergence of a New Consumer Journalism

During the 1960s and 1970s, the public insisted on new consumer protections. Along with political leaders like President John F. Kennedy and consumer leaders like Ralph Nader, journalists played an important role in the development of consumer awareness and expectations. During this time, consumer reporting as a distinct specialty within the journalism profession was accepted. One reason for this acceptance was the courage and intelligence of Morton Mintz, an investigative national affairs reporter for the *Washington Post.* Covering thalidomide and other drug-related stories in the 1960s, Mintz wrote in the best muckraking tradition of Tarbell, Steffens, and Sinclair. While continuing to cover the drug industry, Mintz soon branched out to report on other consumer issues. He also inspired other journalists, who increasingly worked closely with reformers in Congress and federal agencies.

Another major influence on consumer journalism in this period was Ralph Nader, whose investigative work on the Chevrolet Corvair drew the attention of its manufacturer, General Motors. The company tried and failed to stop Nader from proceeding. By 1965, Nader had published *Unsafe at Any Speed,* which concluded that America's annual toll of 51,000 highway deaths could be significantly reduced by industry improvements to motor vehicles. Several years later, he recruited hundreds of students—called "Nader's Raiders"—who researched and published reports on the failure of many government agencies and programs. Nader, an ascetic in a sybaritic city, not only became a favorite news source of Washington's journalists; he also encouraged them to do their own investigative consumer reporting. The industries targeted by consumer journalists included drug, food, automobile, tobacco, pesticide, flammable home furnishings and children's clothing, airline, and oil.

In response to increased media interest in consumer topics, university departments of journalism began adding a "consumer reporting" elective. Graduates with that training were hired not only by Washington-based publications and wire services but also by the national and regional media. Consumer reporters were given daily time slots for special television reports: among the leaders were Betty Furness for WNBC in New York, Roberta Baskin for WTTW in Chicago, Jean Carper for CNN in Atlanta, Lea Thompson for WRC in Washington, D.C., and Herbert Denenberg for WCAU in Philadelphia. The National Press Club in Washington, D.C., recognized the value of this kind of journalism by establishing an annual awards program for excellence in consumer reporting.

The 1960s and 1970s were the golden years of post–World War II consumer journalism. Even the Republican administrations of Presidents Nixon and Ford felt compelled by public pressure to support consumer reforms. But the impetus for reform weakened. A turning point came in the late 1970s when Michael Pertschuk, chairman of the FTC, established an agency priority for "doing something about" the violence and the heavy advertising of candy and toys on children's television. But many objected, including a number of editorial writers. The *Washington Post*, long a friend of the consumer movement, charged that the FTC was trying to become a "national nanny." The press then began to treat the consumer movement more objectively and critically.

The 1980s were aptly called the "Me Decade," since so much attention was given to earning more money in order to indulge one's self—to buy more clothes, another home, a second or third car, or an expensive vacation. The assignment to cover these trends and trendy people fell to consumer writers who already knew something about quality, prices, sources, taste, and manners. They now took on a larger territory that included popular health and medical news, physical fitness and noncompetitive sports, diet and weight control, alternative medicine (meditation, yoga, acupuncture), interpersonal relations, marriage and divorce, child-bearing and child-rearing, cults, and virtually every other aspect of personal, family, and social life. All became fair subject matter for the consumer writer, whose articles now appeared in newspaper sections titled "Life," "Style," "LifeStyle," "Today's Living," "Contemporary Life," and "Home" or in such new or redesigned magazines as *Self, Working Woman, Us, Metropolitan Home, Kiplinger's Personal Finance Magazine, Longevity, American Health, Connoisseur, Weight Watchers Magazine, Money, Escape, The Walking Magazine, Modern Maturity,* and *Backpacker.*

Independent of this trend was the development, since the late 1970s, of a separate branch of consumer journalism to serve businesses and business executives. Some publications, like *Home Office* and *Black Enterprise,* bridged both business and the traditional consumer/reader market. But others—such as *Business Week, U.S. News, Governing,* and a variety of periodicals serving business purchasing agents—all included a type of consumer reporting geared to help the corporate or business purchaser make informed decisions—to upgrade an office telephone system, purchase computers or uniforms, pick a health and life insurance program, or establish an employer-sponsored anti-smoking program. Those writing these stories needed the journalistic skills of investigative reporters as well as the consumer journalist's predisposition, at the end of the story, to make a personal judgment or evaluation about what has been learned.

By the 1990s, the new consumer journalism was still being practiced, but not as extensively as fifteen or twenty years earlier. Nevertheless, consumer activists who documented a widespread abuse could almost always find journalists to cover it, even if these reporters were not defined narrowly as consumer journalists. One type of consumer journalism that did flourish, however, was coverage of consumer issues by television news magazine shows. *60 Minutes* was the first program of this type. Yet, by the mid-1990s, one could find programs of this kind on most evenings. According to viewer surveys, hard-hitting consumer stories were among the most popular of these segments. They were often developed by broadcast journalists, such as Lea Thompson and Roberta Baskin, who had earlier done consumer reporting for local television stations.

The historical record indicates the value and popularity of consumer journalism, whatever the medium. In the future, it is likely that consumer journalism will be practiced in cyberspace, on digitized television, and in any other medium yet to be discovered.

— Theodore O. Cron

See also

Consumers' Research; Consumers Union; Information Dissemination; U.S. Consumer Movement: History and Dynamics.

Readings

Colburn, David R., and George E. Pozzetta (1983). *Reform and Reformers in the Progressive Era*. Westport, CT: Greenwood Press.

Endres, Kathleen L., and Theresa L. Lueck, eds. (1995). *Women's Periodicals in the United States: Consumer Magazines*. Westport, CT: Greenwood Press.

Lieberman, Trudy (1994). "What Ever Happened to Consumer Reporting?" *Columbia Journalism Review*. 33 (3): 34–40.

L

Labor Movement

For the past century, the labor movement and consumer movement have supported each other. From the 1890s through the 1920s, the top priority of middle-class consumer groups was to win improvements in the wages and conditions of workers, especially women and children. Recently, especially during the late 1960s and 1970s, labor provided critical financial and legislative support to the consumer movement. Today, the relationship between the two is still strong but more complex.

During the Progressive period, the only consumer groups in existence were consumers leagues and their national organization, the National Consumers League. The principle goal of these organizations was to improve the wages and working conditions of workers, especially those of women and children. In fact, during this period the leagues took the lead on many of these issues. Both the leagues and unions did join together to fight for passage of pure food and drug legislation. But food safety reforms had appeal to labor not just because they promised to improve consumer health, but also because they created an opportunity to improve dismal working conditions in the food industry, especially in the meatpacking plants exposed in Upton Sinclair's *The Jungle,* published in 1906.

The consumer leagues continued their support of workers into the 1930s and beyond, focusing special attention on such job security protections as unemployment compensation. Increasingly, these leagues were supported by labor groups. In 1942, for example, the Consumers' League of Ohio was supported by seven union locals. At the end of the war, thirteen other union groups were making contributions. By 1957, when the league worked with labor in support of minimum wage legislation, eighty-four unions participated in the consumer group. Three years later, when the league supported unions in opposition to "right-to-work" laws, forty-seven other union groups joined the consumer organization.

Also during the 1930s, because of a labor dispute, dissident staffers left Consumers' Research to establish a new product testing organization, Consumers Union. Leaders of Consumers Union were strongly pro-labor and created an organization whose labor union remains influential to this day.

In the 1950s, consumer groups continued their backing of trade union issues. In the early 1950s, the Amalgamated Meatcutters Union launched a campaign for poultry inspection in order to prevent the runaway of processing plants from northern states to the South. Supported by the National Consumers League and progressive women's groups, the union persuaded Congress to pass the nation's first poultry inspection law in 1957. During the next decade, the union lobbied Congress to strengthen this law, which it did in 1968. A year later, again with support from consumer advocates, the Amalgamated began a campaign to pass a fish inspection law. It did not succeed until the 1990s and then only because the Food and Drug Administration increased oversight of fish handling.

An important link between the labor movement and consumer movement was

Esther Peterson. Having worked for two unions and the American Federation of Labor-Congress of Industrial Organizations (AFL-CIO), and having served as assistant secretary of labor in the Kennedy administration, Peterson had great credibility and influence with labor. But she also was strongly committed to advancing the welfare of consumers. When she proposed the creation of a consumer federation that would include trade unions as well as consumer groups, Jacob Clayman of the AFL-CIO's Industrial Union Department, John J. Sheehan of the Steelworkers Union, and other labor leaders supported the effort, contributing both money and organizational skills. The Consumer Federation of America (CFA), created in 1967, included as members several dozen labor groups, chiefly international unions, several of which were represented on the federation's board of directors.

During the late 1960s and 1970s, labor groups contributed about 40 percent of CFA's budget and supported many of its legislative campaigns. In fact, the political skill and clout of labor lobbyists such as Arnold Mayer of the Meatcutters Union (later United Food and Commercial Workers Union) and Evelyn Dubrow of the International Ladies Garment Workers Union (now UNITE) were in no small measure responsible for the passage of consumer laws ranging from truth in lending to truth in packaging. Sheehan and Kenneth S. Kovack of the Steelworkers Union also provided critical support for these efforts and for the federation generally. For more than twenty years, Kovack served as secretary-treasurer of CFA.

During this period, labor gave much more to CFA than it requested. In part, this generosity reflected the fact that the industrial unions, the strongest union supporters of the federation, were relatively affluent and exercised considerable political influence with federal policymakers. In part, it resulted from the commitment of trade unions to serve the needs of their members not only as workers but also as consumers. In fact, unions such as the United Auto Workers (UAW) created extensive consumer programs to assist their members. The Community Services Department of the AFL-CIO encouraged member unions to provide consumer education and other consumer services, offering technical support. Moreover, for many years consumer journalist Sidney Margolius published a consumer column in numerous union publications.

Outside Washington in several states, trade unions supported consumer-labor coalitions that mirrored CFA. These groups included the Ohio Consumers Association, the Consumer Federation of California, and the Michigan Consumer Federation. As with CFA, labor supplied funding for these volunteer-based groups and also contributed political savvy and support to enhance their political effectiveness.

Labor support for CFA and for the National Consumers League continues until this day. Furthermore, labor activists serve on the boards of both organizations and participate in their policy-making process. But the bond between these consumer groups and labor is not as strong as it was in the late 1960s and 1970s. These consumer organizations have matured, depending far less on labor support than they did in their early years. The percentage of CFA's budget contributed by labor fell from 40 percent in the 1970s to about 2 percent by the mid-1990s.

Just as important, the labor movement found itself under increasing attack from market forces, employers, and even some government leaders. Most of the industrial unions lost membership and were forced to lay off staff and reduce contributions to allied groups. Trade unions also found it necessary to devote greater attention to narrow labor issues, leaving less time for consumer issues. Consumer and labor groups continued to work together on issues in which they had shared or complementary interests, such as improving meat, poultry, or fish inspection. And they still participated in coalitions focused on broader policy issues such as opposing a balanced budget amendment or severe cuts in social programs.

From time to time, conflicts between consumer and labor groups emerged. In a ten-year fight over rewriting the nation's telecommunications law, for example, communications workers allied themselves with regional phone companies while most consumer organizations worked in coalitions with their long-distance competitors. On several occasions, labor-related groups within CFA sought, without notable success, to moderate the federation's advocacy on this issue.

The most problematic issues for consumer and labor groups have related to international trade. As inexpensive products began to inundate the U.S. market in the 1970s, some trade unions called for increasing trade restrictions. The United Auto Workers was particularly active seeking quotas, which often took the form of U.S. content restrictions. These and other trade restrictions were opposed by the nation's largest consumer organization, Consumers Union, which argued that they hurt not only U.S. consumers but also workers in poorer nations. For many years, there was a tacit agreement within CFA that it would not take a position on these trade issues. But in the early 1980s, it deviated from this position by agreeing to support UAW-initiated legislation mandating content restrictions on automobiles. This decision, however, represented an exception to organizational tradition. Several years later, CFA refused to endorse UAW-backed legislation establishing import restrictions on cars.

In the 1990s, many national consumer groups including CFA joined with labor to oppose certain international trade agreements. From labor's perspective, these agreements encouraged imports into the U.S. market, replacing domestic manufactured goods produced by American workers. From the perspective of the consumer organizations, the agreements jeopardized U.S. health, safety, and environmental standards. But Consumers Union continued to support policies encouraging freer international trade.

One labor issue on which many unions and consumer groups cooperated without reservations was protest against poor working conditions of Third World workers who made products for the U.S. market. The National Consumers League coordinated a coalition of union, consumer, and progressive organizations—the Child Labor Coalition—that voiced concerns to Third World governments and to U.S. companies involved in the manufacture, distribution, and sale of these products.

Despite some differences, most members of the consumer movement and labor movement continue to view each other as allies. They are joined by their shared commitment to promoting social welfare, by their belief that government has a critical role to play in advancing this welfare, and by their historic partnership. During the attack by a Republican Congress in 1994 on many consumer and worker protections, the two movements found themselves working more closely together on issues than at any time in the previous two decades.

— Stephen Brobeck, Kenneth S. Kovack

See also

Coalitions; Consumer Federation of America; National Consumers League; Peterson, Esther.

Readings

Barkin, Solomon (1973). "Trade Unions and Consumerism." *Journal of Economic Issues.* 7 (June): 317–321.

Warne, Clinton L. (1973). "The Consumer Movement and the Labor Movement." *Journal of Economic Issues.* 7 (June 1973): 307–316.

Landlord-Tenant Law

See Tenant Protections.

Latin American Consumer Movement

The consumer movement in Latin America—South America, Central America, and the Caribbean—has undergone modest growth over the past two decades. It has also broadened to include governmental consumer protection bodies, formally recognized nongovernmental organizations (NGOs), research centers, development organizations, university departments, and citizens' groups throughout the region.

Many governments in the region have drawn on the advice and expertise of consumer groups, and some have set up official departments to enforce consumer legislation. Consumer groups have influenced the development of government policies, especially those regulating products and services. Consumer education programs have also been launched to encourage more informed consumer behavior and to increase the knowledge and buying power of the poor.

Regional Conditions

Throughout the 1980s, the region's economic crisis was manifested in soaring consumer prices—with annual inflation rates reaching 3,000 per cent in Argentina and Brazil—combined with falling wages and growing unemployment. Government servicing of huge foreign debts led to drastic cuts in social spending while the net transfer of resources out of the region averaged $30 billion annually for nine successive years.

By the middle of the 1990s, much of Latin America appeared to be recovering from its so-called Lost Decade. National economies recorded modest growth, as economic liberalization policies generated the privatization of hundreds of state-owned enterprises. The removal of import and investment barriers by governments led to renewed foreign direct investment and rapid growth in the operations of both transnational corporations and international financial markets, which have opened and transformed domestic trade.

These trends have signaled a major economic turnaround in a region where the 1980s left most people poorer, not richer. Yet, striking differences still remain in levels of wealth and development—both between and within countries—as numerous obstacles block the region's progress toward achieving stable and socially equitable domestic economies.

Most countries still fall far short of meeting the basic needs of their poor. About 40 per cent of all Latin Americans earn less than a minimum wage, their meager incomes eroded by high inflation. It is estimated that investments exceeding $50 billion are needed to provide consumers with efficiently run basic services such as potable water, electricity, sewers, and telephones.

Such problems are a main concern of many consumer organizations working on related issues like pricing, inflation, and consumer access to food, basic goods, housing, and education. Consumer protection is also of vital importance since the lack of effective legislation has left consumers vulnerable to disreputable services, faulty products, fraudulent sales practices, and other abuses. Most consumers do not have sufficient information and awareness to protect themselves in the marketplace, nor to make knowledgeable buying choices.

Regional governments and the mass media have shown much greater interest in consumer protection issues following the 1985 adoption of the United Nations Consumer Protection Guidelines. A number of countries—Brazil, Ecuador, Honduras, Peru, Uruguay, and Venezuela among them—have either proposed or enacted important legislation in this area within the last several years.

South America

The priorities of South American consumer organizations have reflected the significant challenges facing the region. A number have lobbied their governments for much-needed consumer protection laws, sometimes playing a strong role in the drafting of key legislation. Others have effectively focused their efforts on consumers' basic needs, addressing concerns like public services, prices, and abusive commercial practices, while also developing programs to help consumers protect themselves and make wise buying choices in their local markets.

Most South American consumer groups have limited resources, yet a number engage in regular comparative tests and research on goods and services. The movement encompasses government agencies, NGOs, research centers, development organizations, university departments, and citizens' groups working in the consumer interest. Almost all of the region's private, independent groups have been formed within the past ten years, fostered by the democratization of national governments and a wave of new consumer protection legislation.

National laws for consumer protection have been enacted in no less than six countries during the past eight years—Chile (1988), Brazil (1991), Peru (1991), Venezuela (1992), Ecuador (1992), and Argentina (1993). Colombia is currently debating a major reform of its 1981 national law. Three countries—Uruguay, Paraguay, and Bolivia—are still without any national law for consumer protection.

Consumer protection has also received increased recognition within regional integration processes. A Technical Commission on Quality and Regulation was recently created by MERCOSUR (the Common Market of Argentina, Brazil, Uruguay, and Paraguay), while ALADI (the Latin American Association of Integration) has welcomed the participation of consumer organizations in its development of a new technical committee. An agreement was signed recently between Consumers International (CI) and ALADI that has led to the formation of a technical committee to propose the harmonization of consumer protection laws within ALADI member states.

Consumer organizations are especially strong in Argentina, Brazil, and Chile. The Andean zone nations of Bolivia, Colombia, Ecuador, Peru, and Venezuela have lower levels of consumer protection, despite the existence of consumer legislation and organizations. Consumer groups are least developed in Paraguay and Bolivia.

Recent actions taken by consumer organizations in South America reveal the expanding scope of their activities. The League for Consumer Action in Argentina (ADELCO) has been a pioneer in the area of comparative testing. In 1992, ADELCO carried out a comparative test of potentially hazardous antidiarrheal medicines, revealing serious irregularities in the labeling, efficacy, and overall quality of drugs. The Brazilian Institute of Consumer Defense (IDEC) also publishes comparative test results. Following a 1992 report revealing that most condoms sold in Brazil were unreliable for AIDS prevention, IDEC campaigned for higher national standards for condom quality.

Even in the absence of comparative test results, consumer organizations are carrying out effective lobbying efforts. For example, the Guyana Consumers' Association joined the Public Utilities Commission in preventing the national electric company from increasing its utility charges by as much as 100 percent. The Uruguayan League for Consumers' Defense lobbied Parliament for new consumer protection legislation, now under consideration by lawmakers.

Consumer education remains an important activity as well, as the following examples suggest. The Coordinating Office of Uruguayan Consumer Groups launched a series of training workshops on food, food quality, prices, nutrition, and health for seventy-six food-purchasing cooperatives around the country. The Ecuadorian Center for the Promotion and Action of Women developed a program to help community food cooperatives educate people about good nutrition and their rights as consumers. Chile's National Consumer Service put on a play about consumers' rights and responsibilities at a downtown theater in Santiago before an audience of representatives from social organizations.

Central America

Until recently, the consumer movement has been slow to develop in Central America—a particularly troubled and violence-prone region where guerrilla insurgencies, civil wars, and military dictatorships have compounded the problems of widespread poverty and deteriorating living standards. In the 1990s, however, new consumer organizations and effective leaders have emerged in countries including El Salvador, Guatemala, Nicaragua, and Honduras, where no such groups existed previously. As in South America, the enactment of new consumer protection legislation has been a driving force behind the rapid development of consumer organizations.

Consumer protection was given formal recognition in El Salvador's historic Peace Agreement, signed in January 1992. In Guatemala, a law approved in the 1980s is currently being reformed. The government of Honduras is also in the process of reforming a national law that, if approved, will create a Federal Agency of Consumer Affairs with broad responsibilities for protecting, educating, and informing consumers. New national consumer protection laws have also been enacted in Nicaragua (September 1994) and Costa Rica (January 1995). Panama is now the only Central American country without a national consumer protection law.

Independent consumer organizations in El Salvador, Guatemala, and Nicaragua have been very much involved in the initiation and development of new laws for their countries. Although government consumer bodies still exceed private organizations in size and strength, an increasing number of small groups have been working effectively in the subregion. Two of the strongest are the Consumers' League (LIDECON) of Guatemala and the Consumer Defense Committee (CDC) of El Salvador.

LIDECON's experience is especially notable for its multifaceted approach to defending consumers' interests. Much of its work is concentrated in poor communities where it has set up small cooperatives that sell basic food products at reduced prices. It has also run a loan program for small farmers aimed at creating jobs and encouraging new food-producing initiatives.

Since its formation, the CDC has received good press coverage for its diverse campaigns and activities. It now produces two regular radio programs on consumer issues, has a regular column in the *Diario Latino,* and publishes its own consumer magazine.

Because of the tropical climate in which they operate, the consumer organizations of Central America are especially active in the control of pharmaceutical products and pesticides. For example, El Salvador's CDC launched a public campaign against the sale of antidiarrheal drugs that are restricted or prohibited in other countries. The Mexican Association for Consumer Defense drew attention to the problem of counterfeit pharmaceuticals, which are commonly sold to the poor after being tainted with sawdust, coffee, dirt, and other contaminants. LIDECON in Guatemala has launched campaigns against hazardous and unregistered drugs, adulterated and mislabeled food products, and environmental problems resulting from pesticide use.

Caribbean

The Caribbean subregion has not had a well-organized consumer movement until fairly recently, when new governmental consumer organizations in Guyana and Grenada were established, joining longer-established groups in Antigua, Aruba, Barbados, Jamaica, and Santa Lucia. One of these new groups is Guyana's Consumers Advisory Bureau (CAB), which promotes sustainable development and consumer education in the country. In Belize, the government is seeking ways to revitalize consumer education and protection. In Grenada, the National Consumers' Union (NCUG), although small in scope with very limited resources, has been working actively to advance the interests of consumers through media campaigns and the lobbying of relevant government ministries.

The National Consumers League of Jamaica is one of the oldest consumer organizations in the region. Recently, it lobbied successfully for a change in condominium laws, thus allowing owners to negotiate insurance below complete replacement value. It also has been working to reform laws on poverty insurance, motor vehicle insurance, and personal life insurance.

Consumer Protection Legislation in Latin America

A number of new consumer protection laws have been enacted in Latin America. In fact, nowhere in the developing world have governments showed a greater interest in consumer protection than in this region. This development was noted by UN Secretary-General Boutros Boutros-Ghali in June 1992, when he commended Latin American governments for progress made in consumer protection. Boutros-Ghali also pointed out the important role of the 1985 United Nations Consumer Protection Guidelines in stimulating government awareness and actions.

Despite this progress, some Latin American governments have not translated their concern for consumer rights into effective actions that protect consumers. A majority of the region's consumer laws—especially those of El Salvador and Chile—have relatively weak frameworks. Disreputable services, shoddy products, and fraudulent sales practices are still common in the marketplace. Consumer protection laws have also not succeeded in ensuring that basic, essential products are within reach of low-income and marginalized consumers.

Furthermore, large gaps exist in the coverage of several laws, which are weakened even more by the absence of corresponding monitoring and enforcement measures needed to give them "teeth." Opposition to consumer protection laws by businesses and other vested interests has led to their frequent misrepresentation as undesirable obstacles to foreign and local investment.

On the other hand, the national laws of countries like Brazil and Mexico have proved to be adequate for most tasks of consumer protection. Brazil's Consumer Defense Code mandates stiff penalties (including prison terms) for a wide range of serious abuses that were previously tolerated by government and endured by consumers. Under Mexico's law, a federal consumer agency is working in a number of areas to promote and protect consumers' rights.

Latin American consumer protection laws tend to be more general and wide-ranging in scope than those of more developed regions. Nevertheless, four key areas can be analyzed with respect to the adequacy and effectiveness of specific laws: the extent of government involvement in consumer protection; the regulation of advertising; the establishment of conflict-resolution mechanisms; and support for consumer organizations.

Government involvement in consumer protection reaches its highest level in Mexico, also the birthplace of the Latin American consumer movement. The country's Federal Consumer Attorney Office (PROFECO) advises consumers and provides them with legal representation for disputes requiring judicial settlement.

Brazil has established legal consumer defense offices, small claims courts, and a police force specialized in investigating consumer abuses. The governments of Costa Rica and Venezuela are strongly involved in regulating prices and setting quality standards for products. Government agencies have been set up in Honduras, El Salvador, and Peru to handle consumer complaints. El Salvador's consumer protection law authorizes the Ministry of Economy to regulate the prices of goods and services and, in some cases, those of imports and exports. A broad range of consumer services is provided by the National Consumer Service of Chile (SERNAC), whose offices throughout the country provide free information and advice to consumers.

Advertising regulation in Latin America ranges from Brazil's stringent penalties for offenses (a conviction for false advertising can bring a jail term of three months to one year), to Chile's voluntary "Advertising Ethics Code" (amounting to self-regulation by industry). Advertising regulation is hardly touched upon by Argentina's new consumer protection law, enacted in 1995. Peru's national law to regulate advertising, enacted in 1991, goes considerably further by penalizing false and abusive advertising and by establishing special standards for advertisements that target children or criticize rival products. The laws of Honduras and Mexico allow those governments to suspend advertisements as they deem necessary.

The lack of adequate advertising regulation in Chile's consumer protection reform bill is considered by many to be its most glaring weakness. Apart from elaborating a few minor penalties for certain offenses, the bill gives only superficial treatment to advertising problems that are rampant in Chilean society. CI's Regional Office for Latin America and the Caribbean (ROLAC) has called for the bill to incorporate stronger advertising regulations before it is enacted.

Argentina's consumer protection law provides consumers with greater access to courts and other bodies where they can seek redress for their grievances. Under their respective laws, the countries of Ecuador, El Salvador, Honduras, Mexico, and Venezuela use different administrative mechanisms to settle consumer complaints. In Colombia, consumer organizations are empowered to bring cases to trial courts, while Brazilian organizations can represent consumers in class action suits.

Finally, both the right and the need for consumer groups to organize are not recognized by many consumer protection laws. Those of Argentina, Brazil, Ecuador, and Venezuela acknowledge the role of consumer groups, while others—notably those of Chile, Costa Rica, El Salvador, Honduras, and Peru—have relatively little to say about consumer organizations and their role in consumer protection.

With or without the backing of their governments, however, Latin American consumer groups have proved to be strong and effective advocates for consumers' interests and needs. In fact, in some cases, the successes achieved by unrecognized groups have served as a catalyst for the enactment of new and supportive consumer protection laws.

Role of Consumers International

Founded in 1986 by the Worldwide Federation of Consumer Organizations, CI's Regional Office for Latin America and the Caribbean (ROLAC) is dedicated to building a strong consumer movement in Latin America and the Caribbean and to promoting the rights of consumers at the national and international levels. Both objectives are based on CI's mission of helping to establish more just and equitable markets and societies for all consumers.

The involvement of CI in regional consumer protection initiatives began in 1987, when a working group of legal experts was formed by ROLAC. The group's first task was to produce a "Model Law on Consumer Protection," inspired by the United Nations Consumer Protection Guidelines. The model law has aided the drafting of consumer protection legislation in several Latin American countries. The number of legal experts cooperating with ROLAC has also expanded steadily, representing a growing circle of international lawyers, government advisers, consumer representatives, and other professionals.

ROLAC seeks to address the challenges and needs of individual consumer organizations—many of which are young, inexperienced, and lacking resources and technical expertise. ROLAC's four subregional development programs and two suboffices allow its staff to meet, plan, and work directly with groups in Central America and the Spanish-speaking Caribbean, in the English-speaking Caribbean, and in the Andean and Southern Cone countries of South America.

ROLAC organizes national and regional conferences, workshops, and training sessions that provide support and expertise to consumer groups and many other public and private organizations. Research programs, reports, and publications are also aimed at stimulating awareness and action in areas linked to food, health, the environment, trade, consumer protection, education, and other issues.

The activities of ROLAC are predicated on the view that all consumers have eight basic rights that should be promoted by the consumer movement in Latin America and the Caribbean: the right to satisfaction of basic needs, to safety, to information, to choice, to representation, to redress, to consumer education, and to a healthy environment. While there is still a very long way to go before consumers' rights are adequately protected across the Latin American continent, governments have shown a clear willingness to move in that direction.

To promote the rights of consumers, ROLAC advises and lobbies national governments and regional bodies like the UN Economic Commission for Latin America and the Caribbean (ECLAC). ROLAC has established joint working agreements with United Nations Economic, Scientific, and Cultural Organization and the Latin American Council of Adult Education. ROLAC also seeks to influence regional policies and integration processes of the MERCOSUR Common Market, NAFTA, the Andean Pact, the Caribbean Community and Common Market (CARICOM), the Central American Common Market, and ALADI.

To develop its activities and to promote needed changes at a regional level, ROLAC draws upon the suggestions and support of consumer organizations in each country of the continent. These consumer organizations, with the support from CI, will continue playing an active part in promoting and evaluating national laws to protect all consumers in the region.

— Kevin Cook, Dina Musante

See also

Consumers International; Mexican Consumer Movement.

Readings

Arrighi, Jean Michel (1992). "Integration and Consumer Protection: The Case of Latin America." *Journal of Consumer Policy.* 15: 179–190.

Consumers International (1996). *World Consumer.* 220 (January). Entire issue.

Law, Consumer

Consumer law is the law that governs the conditions under which personal, household, and family purchases in the marketplace may take place. From such law flows opportunity for both the protection and exploitation of consumers. Broadly considered, consumer law affects nearly every aspect of the relationship between buyers and sellers. This entry outlines some of the major currents shaping this law in the United States.

Consumer law has been created and enforced by both private and public arrangement. Private rules, informal trade customs, and industry standards establish the context in which everyday consumer transactions take place—for example, the custom permitting us to take a bite out of an apple in the vegetable market before we buy a dozen of them. Sometimes private laws are embodied in codes or other methods for self-regulation that are developed by industry trade associations with little consumer input.

Public consumer laws often are embodied in statutes, administrative codes, and judicial interpretations. Many of the first consumer protection laws were enacted to alleviate problems connected with monopoly pricing, price controls, rationing under conditions of scarcity, short weighting, and adulteration, as well as laws that set the hours during which some goods could be bought. In some places, laws restricted the consumption of certain goods (for example, tobacco and alcohol) and services (for example, abortions) on public health and moral grounds.

Underlying almost all consumer law in the United States have been the court-fashioned or "common law" consumer rules that evolved from customary assumptions about purchase transactions. In cases without blatant fraud or deception, some early judicial rulings applied the maxim caveat emptor (let the buyer beware). That maxim presumed that buyers could and should inform themselves and bargain about the risks attached to purchasing decisions. It did not distinguish between consumer buyers and commercial buyers.

Accepting caveat emptor, however, never signified that fraud, misrepresentation, or negligent conduct was acceptable under American consumer law. Where outright fraud and misrepresentation could be demonstrated, the law of torts (nonconsensual injuries) might be employed to return victims of these injuries back to where they were before they were injured. The law of contractual obligations, including the common law interpretations of warranties, might entitle aggrieved consumers to compensation for the difference between the value they received and the value that had been represented and agreed on. A fraudulently induced contract, or one tainted by bad faith in its performance, might be rescinded (abrogated or repealed); or consumers might be excused from meeting further payment obligations; or they might recover, in addition to direct costs, those costs that were the foreseeable consequence of a seller's wrong or neglect.

Historically, the legal requirements that aggrieved consumers needed to meet in court often have involved presenting elusive elements of proof. For example, a consumer trying to rescind a contract might have to show much more than that she sustained an injury after she relied on the seller's misrepresentation. She also might be required to demonstrate that the reliance was justified and that the seller made an actual representation of a present fact that was material and false, known or recklessly assumed to be false, and made for the purpose of inducing the buyer to buy.

The law, furthermore, made a direct connection between individual sellers and buyers that proved nearly indispensable to recovery through the courts. Where consumers were injured by manufactured products, neither the law of contracts and warranties nor the law of torts would permit a consumer to recover from any contractor or supplier of a seller, except in rare instances. Requirements such as these might be relaxed under special circumstances, but they made elements of proof difficult for consumers to satisfy and deterred consumers from seeking redress.

The differences between ordinary household consumer transactions and typical commercial transactions (in which the buyers were typically companies) have grown more pronounced as products have become more complicated and selling techniques more sophisticated. Commercial entities retained specialized purchasing expertise, while most household consumption was undertaken individually without the benefit of effective laws that might disclose information in ways allowing meaningful analysis and comparison. Handcrafted goods generate occasional nonuniform product defects, but a defect in the design of a single mass-produced product might be multiplied into hundreds of thousands of defective products that are advertised and sold nationally.

Disparities in bargaining power, in the ability to estimate the risk of entering into a transaction, and in the costs associated with obtaining information about a product, became wider than ever. Doctrines of privity (connectedness between the parties) generally insulated remote manufacturers from suit by consumers when consumers bought from intermediary retailers. At the same time, sellers had many legal weapons to enforce the payment terms they had exacted. Rules governing the ability of creditors to enforce judgments against consumers for nonpayment of debts, for example, permitted creditors a wide variety of legal remedies, including wage garnishments, liens on the property of consumer debtors, and foreclosures on collateral such as houses, furniture, and vehicles.

Traditional common law legal standards of the nineteenth century seemed, to many Americans, to be patently antiquated or otherwise inadequate to the new consumer problems. In response, some higher courts and legislatures departed from traditional approaches. Legislatures proscribed monopolistic and other anticompetitive behavior. Courts developed doctrines, more realistic for the modern marketplace, that recognized that individual consumers often had neither the bargaining power nor the information they needed to give informed and meaningful consent to the terms of a bargain and to accept all of the risks attached to it. In a contract opinion written in 1873, for example, Chief Justice Charles Doe of New Hampshire determined that the boilerplate language of an insurance contract had worked a fraud on the payer of a premium. "It was printed in such small type, and in lines so long and so crowded, that the perusal of it was made physically difficult, painful and injurious," wrote the chief justice.

In a breakthrough case in the law of products liability, in 1916 Judge Benjamin Cardozo held that the Buick Motor Company was responsible for an injury to a driver that resulted from a defective wheel manufactured by one of Buick's suppliers. Buick "was not at liberty to put the finished product on the market without subjecting the component parts to ordinary and simple tests," the judge wrote. Doctrines of strict liability and implied warranty were broadened, in the law of products liability, to make manufacturers and some other remote producers responsible for the physical injury caused by the dangerous products that they had manufactured, regardless of the manufacturer's good intentions, reasonable care, or its remoteness from the seller.

Even as common law doctrines recognized important distinctions between consumer contracts and other types of doctrines, the court-fashioned remedies were proving to be inadequate to the task of providing legal regulation of consumer transactions. Judicial opinions, after all, were promulgated post hoc in a piecemeal fashion. They were uncodified, and not uniform among the states.

Statutes were adopted, and regulatory agencies were created, according to their political sponsors, to establish better rules and enforcement procedures than common law jurisprudence allowed. Major federal departments and agencies charged with consumer protection responsibilities were created by federal statutes. These laws established different types of legal standards—for minimum quality, minimum disclosure, or merchandising behavior—in connection with different consumer goods and services.

The first laws and amendments regulating consumer transactions include the Mail Fraud Act (1872), prohibiting the use of the mails to conduct fraudulent sales activities; the Meat Inspection Act (1904), establishing a system for government inspection of conditions under which meat was manufactured and sold; the Pure Food and Drug Act (1906), establishing an agency to enforce minimum food and drug advertising standards; the Federal Trade Commission Act (1914), prohibiting certain unfair and deceptive trade practices, which came to include advertising regulation; the Food, Drug and Cosmetic Act (1938), proscribing standards of disclosure for truth in pharmaceutical labeling; the Securities Act (1933), creating disclosure standards for certain investment instruments; the Flammable Fabrics Act (1953), mandating the use of fire-retardant fabrics in certain clothing; and the Food Additives Amendments to the FDA (1958), mandating that food additives generally be recognized as safe prior to their use.

In 1962, President John F. Kennedy reflected the emerging social concern for consumer legal rights by asserting that consumers had at least four of them: a right to safety, to be informed, to choose, and to be heard. As the consumer movement grew during the 1960s and 1970s, the laws legislated at every jurisdictional level to promote consumer welfare in the marketplace multiplied. Those who were injured by the unfair or deceptive practices of sellers no longer were burdened with proving a court action at common law: every state passed antifraud legislation relieving consumers from having to prove that sellers had an evil intent, or that consumers were justified in relying on a deceptive representation.

In the 1960s and 1970s, Congress passed much consumer legislation. The legislation included the Hazardous Substances Labeling Act (1960), concerning disclosure rules for dangerous household and other products; the Kefauver-Harris Drug Amendments (1962), promoting competition in the pharmaceutical industry; the Fair Packaging and Labeling Act (1965), providing standardized disclosure rules for many foods and other products; the National Traffic and Motor Vehicle Safety Act (1966), concerned with motor vehicle safety standards; the Cigarette Labeling Act (1966), mandating warnings to consumers about the perils of smoking; the Truth in Lending Act (1968), requiring the disclosure of information about the costs associated with consumer debt transactions; the Toy Safety Act (1969), permitting government to monitor the children's toy market; the Fair Credit Reporting Act (1970), controlling information contained in consumer credit reports and the conditions for their release; the Equal Credit Opportunity Act (1974), barring certain kinds of discrimination in the extension of credit by lenders; the Magnuson-Moss Warranty Act (1975), regulating disclosure and certain substantive aspects of warranties; and the Fair Debt Collection Practices Act (1978), designed to discourage excessive collection efforts. The newly created Consumer Product Safety Commission, and other government departments and agencies, issued legal standards for product safety. On occasion they insisted upon product recalls. The extent to which these governmental efforts were implemented and effectively enforced has been a matter of political and academic dispute. Also challenged by studies in law, economics, and history was the extent to which various regulations improved consumer welfare or diminished it.

After 1976, except for laws that deregulated the economy to encourage competition, few major consumer reform initiatives were approved at the federal level. The Airline Deregulation Act (1978) was designed to open the airline industry to greater competition over prices and routes, and the Consumer Cable Communications Law (1993) claimed to broaden the incentive of licensed cable communications monopolies to meet consumer needs at reasonable prices. Receiving new attention were areas of law not previously associated with consumer law, but integrally connected to it, particularly laws designed to protect consumer privacy, to restructure the health care industry, and to encourage consumers to behave in ways deemed environmentally responsible.

In many states and localities, federal laws were complemented by local counterparts. Whether state and local laws would be preempted or displaced by federal laws through the operation of the Supremacy Clause of the U.S. Constitution became an issue of importance in many consumer law disputes. State and local laws were enforced by state attorneys general, consumer affairs departments, and other bodies. Some state laws allowed consumers to act as private attorneys general by bringing actions individually, and to recover attorneys' fees, court costs, and punitive damages. Rules of evidence and procedure in several states permitted representative parties to file class action lawsuits. In cases involving serious injuries caused by defective mass-produced products and devices, or in cases involving collectively large but individually minor overcharges, common questions of law and fact made class actions a superior method for recovery.

Numerous uniform state laws, including the Uniform Commercial Code, the Uniform Consumer Credit Code, and others, established generalized rules for consumer transactions on the state and local levels. Together with professionally drafted restatements of law in such areas as torts, contracts, agency, and suretyship (guarantees of performance), broadly consistent standards of legal interpretation in consumer disputes developed. These standards helped to determine when agreements were so one-sided as to be unconscionable, whether sellers performed their part of a bargain in bad faith, or whether consumers were acting the way reasonably prudent persons would act.

Standards by which consumer laws are interpreted, and the laws themselves, are being transformed continually by public and private institutions. New topical statutes that deal with particular types of abuse are frequently proposed. Approaches to consumer dispute resolution, which encourage private resolution through mediation or arbitration instead of through the courts, have become more common.

Consumer law appears destined forever to be playing "catch-up" with changing methods of selling and changing products. It also appears that, in the United States, consumer interests routinely are underestimated in the normal process of lawmaking and rulemaking. Under these circumstances, attention by consumer groups to the representation of consumers in the making of consumer law and the litigation of consumer grievances assumes great importance.

— Norman I. Silber

See also

Congress and Consumer Protection; Products Liability Law; U.S. Consumer Movement: History and Dynamics.

Readings

Greenfield, Michael M. (1995). *Consumer Law: A Guide for Those Who Represent Sellers, Lenders, and Consumers.* Boston: Little, Brown.

Pridgen, Dee (1986 and supp.). *Consumer Protection and the Law.* New York: Boardman.

Spanogle, John A., Ralph J. Rohner, Dee Pridgen, and Paul Rasor (1991). *Consumer Law: Cases and Materials.* St. Paul, MN: West Publishing Co.

Leagues, Consumer

See Consumer Leagues.

Legal Aid

The terms *legal aid* and *legal services* generally refer to local community programs that provide civil legal representation to low-income individuals without charge. These free services are provided by lawyers and other legal workers who are usually full- or part-time employees of the legal aid program, although sometimes a panel of private lawyers is used.

Civil representation refers to cases and legal matters outside of the criminal justice system. In the criminal justice system, a person charged by the government with a criminal violation of the law will be entitled to the services of a public defender if the person is unable to afford a lawyer. If the legal matter is not criminal in nature, a person unable to afford a lawyer may sometimes be able to secure legal representation from a legal aid or legal services program. The civil matters most commonly handled by legal aid attorneys are divorce and other family matters, public benefits disputes, housing matters including evictions, and consumer cases. The number of legal aid offices and attorneys is insufficient to assure that representation is available to all qualified individuals who need it.

Legal services has played an important role in consumer law. A substantial portion of consumer law cases contested in the courts involves clients represented by legal aid attorneys. Legal services programs closed more than 250,000 consumer cases in 1994. Typical consumer cases involve car purchases and leases, debt collection harassment, home improvement contracts, credit and loan contracts and mortgages, various forms of credit insurance and related products, credit discrimination, and a wide variety of unfair and deceptive acts and practices. Most of the private attorneys specializing in consumer protection law today once practiced with a legal services program.

Many of the most important consumer cases have been litigated by legal services programs. These cases have helped define how a consumer protection law will be interpreted and applied, or have affected many consumers. Some of the U.S. Supreme Court cases establishing a consumer's constitutional right to notice of court proceedings initiated by a creditor and the right to be heard in court were argued and won by legal services attorneys.

Types of Programs

A community may host different kinds of legal aid offices. Every community is served by a legal services office funded in part by the federal government through the Legal Services Corporation. The corporation is a private, nonprofit organization, but it is funded by Congress and governed by a board appointed by the president. The corporation, in turn, funds local programs governed by a local board of directors, which sets the local programs' priorities. As a result, programs in many parts of the country handle consumer cases, while programs in other places do not. Each county in the country falls within the service area of a legal services program funded by the Legal Services Corporation. Nationwide, there are more than 300 such programs and 1,200 offices.

Many communities, especially cities, host other legal aid programs as well. Most are small, single office programs that serve a small community or a special group of clients or that specialize in a particular subject. For example, a neighborhood might have a church- or foundation-sponsored legal clinic serving the area; other legal aid offices might be established to assist elderly clients, disabled clients, or prisoners; or a legal services program might handle only housing cases or civil rights matters.

Nearly all legal aid offices are intended to serve individuals who otherwise would not have access to professional legal assistance. Most serve only low-income individuals. Offices receiving funds from the federal Legal Services Corporation have income eligibility guidelines tied to the poverty level. A few, such as those serving older Americans, have no income guidelines.

History

The first legal aid program was established in 1876 in New York City as a private charitable effort to assist recent German immigrants. Thereafter, the American Bar Association and Reginald Heber Smith promoted legal aid societies to serve the "deserving poor." Beginning in Boston in 1900, legal aid societies were formed in most major cities, usually with the support of lawyers, United Way organizations, and other local public and private funders. For the most part, these organizations handled only routine individual legal matters.

Today's legal services was profoundly shaped in the 1960s. At the beginning of the decade, legal aid societies employed only about 200 full-time attorneys nationwide. But as part of a growing antipoverty movement, national foundations began to experiment with full-service legal services programs focusing on chronic problems of poverty.

Under President Lyndon Johnson, and extending until 1974, the federal Office of Economic Opportunity established neighborhood legal services offices in many parts of the country as part of its "War on Poverty." These offices were established under local community control and outside the control of state and local governments. In addition, a few national organizations, such as the National Consumer Law Center, were funded to shape and support the local delivery of legal services. As a result, the first in a series of important poverty law cases began reaching the Supreme Court.

The legal rights of poor people, as newly voiced with legal services program assistance, generated political controversy at the local level and in Congress. In an effort to insulate federal financial support for legal aid from this controversy, responsibility for the legal services program was removed from the federal bureaucracy and transferred to a newly created, private nonprofit Legal Services Corporation. Proposed by President Richard Nixon, in 1974 the corporation was created by Congress with strong support from the American Bar Association. Funding is appropriated annually by Congress.

By the late 1970s, funding for legal services had increased to the point where there was one legal services attorney funded by the corporation for every 5,000 poor persons, and every county in the country was served. However, the larger and more active legal services became, the louder its critics grew. Many of these opponents were targets of legal services lawsuits, while other critics objected philosophically to the program's activist role. In the Reagan administration and again in the mid-1990s, these critics found many sympathetic ears, and these officials succeeded in curtailing both the authority and federal funding of legal services. Increases in local funding offset only a small part of the losses in federal monies. Today, legal services receives more funding than in the 1960s, but far less than in the 1970s.

— Willard P. Ogburn

See also

Low-Income Consumers; National Consumer Law Center.

Readings

Feldman, Marc (1995). "Political Lessons: Legal Services for the Poor." *The Georgetown Law Journal.* 83 (April): 1529–1632.

Katz, Jack (1982). *Poor People's Lawyers in Transition.* New Brunswick, NJ: Rutgers University Press.

Kessler, Mark (1987). *Legal Services for the Poor: A Comparative and Contemporary Analysis of Interorganizational Politics.* Westport, CT: Greenwood Press.

Legal Services

See Legal Aid.

Lemon Laws

Lemon laws are warranties, created by state laws, that protect purchasers of motor vehicles. They represent a type of protection that is usually not available to buyers of other products.

Consumer expectations for the performance of new vehicles are great, especially given the high cost involved in acquiring them. At the same time, as the pace of consumers' lives has accelerated dramatically, their dependence on the reliability of their vehicles has increased. Problems experienced in servicing or repairing vehicles can thus create enormous difficulties, inconvenience, and frustration for consumers. Reliable, accurate servicing of increasingly complex vehicles, done properly at the first attempt, has become critical.

In an attempt to address these growing expectations, and recognizing the competitive advantages to be gained in doing so, auto manufacturers have substantially expanded and lengthened the warranties to repair vehicles given in the contracts of sale. This broadening, in turn, has further raised consumer expectations. When these expectations are not met, consumers often become highly dissatisfied. For years, complaints to consumer protection agencies regarding automotive repair problems have been at (or near) the top of almost every consumer protection agency's list of problem areas.

A warranty is a promise, and like any promise, its value exists only when it is kept. Thus, the key question is whether the manufacturer/warrantor has kept its promise to repair. Like any unkept promise, an unfulfilled warranty can theoretically be enforced through court action. Unlike other promises, such as failure to deliver (which would allow a consumer to withhold payment), failure to perform under a warranty occurs only after a consumer has both accepted and paid (or incurred debt) for a vehicle. Traditional contract law addresses that unkept promise by undoing ("revoking" legally) that acceptance when the warrantor fails to perform. A critical threshold question is whether the warrantor has had a "reasonable" opportunity to repair the vehicle. The subjective, amorphous nature of this standard of "reasonableness" has rendered remedies under traditional contract law largely inadequate to resolve warranty concerns.

In response to heightened consumer expectations regarding their new vehicles, to the expanded associated warranty promises made by manufacturers, and to the complaints of consumers regarding inadequate performance under warranties, beginning in 1982 every state enacted a lemon law. A lemon law is a warranty created by state statute. It is intended to supplement preexisting contract law, other statutory laws, and various characteristics of the civil court system, which together had proven inadequate to address many new vehicle warranty problems.

Most importantly, lemon laws define quantitatively how many repair attempts are "reasonable," or what is a "reasonable" time that a warrantor can keep a vehicle out of service for repairs. In addition, lemon laws provide that a consumer's right to revoke a vehicle purchase is not defeated by ongoing use of a vehicle with problems, as it generally would be under previous laws.

Most lemon laws utilize legal presumptions. Once a consumer establishes that a problem (usually called a "nonconformity") exists and that the warrantor has had "reasonable" opportunity (as defined quantitatively in the statute) to repair it and has failed to do so, the lemon law presumes that the consumer is entitled to have the vehicle bought back by the manufacturer, and be provided with either a replacement vehicle or a refund of the purchase price paid. (These remedies are the same as under traditional contract law, namely, specific performance or damages.)

The legal burden of proof then shifts to the manufacturer to demonstrate any reasons that the consumer should not receive the specified relief, for example, because of any unauthorized vehicle modification or abuse by the consumer. Victorious consumers can also recover attorney fees and court costs associated with a lemon law action.

Auto manufacturers initially resisted lemon laws vehemently. However, the responsiveness of legislatures to consumer complaints in enacting lemon laws was overwhelming. The political appeal of such laws was undoubtedly enhanced by the demographic characteristics (and the resulting political attractiveness) of affected consumers, i.e., those acquiring new vehicles. Most (though not all) lemon laws include provisions encouraging manufacturers to create alternative dispute resolution mechanisms (ADRMs) to provide informal processes in which consumers can have their service complaints arbitrated without resorting to litigation. A few also created state-run ADRMs. Both these mechanisms provide means for consumers to seek lemon law relief without having to incur the costs and delays of formal litigation.

Manufacturer-offered ADRMs are encouraged by provisions in lemon laws involving certification of those mechanisms according to specific procedural and substantive rights enumerated in the lemon law. Once an ADRM has been determined by the relevant state agency to be in compliance with these requirements, the manufacturer usually is allowed to require a consumer with a warranty dispute first to submit the dispute to the ADRM. If the consumer is dissatisfied with the decision for any reason, he or she is then free to seek lemon law relief in a civil court action. The incentives to the manufacturer in offering an ADRM are not only the avoidance of potentially costly litigation and an increase in the likelihood of reaching a mutually acceptable resolution to the complaint, but also improvement in customer relations.

Lemon laws have proven to be extremely popular with legislators of all political parties. Since their first enactment, many states have promulgated various amendments expanding the scope of coverage, increasing the range of remedies available, providing for various notices to consumers regarding their rights under these statutes, and restricting subsequent disposition of reacquired vehicles.

Perhaps the most significant impact of lemon laws, however, has been to provide strong incentives for manufacturer/warrantors and their affiliated dealerships to be more accurate when first providing service, and to be more responsive to consumer complaints about that service. By putting "teeth"' into the remedies available to a consumer when a warranty promise is not kept, manufacturers have been compelled to improve their performance according to their promises. Ultimately, lemon laws work to ensure that promises made are more likely to be kept.

—James L. Brown

See also

Auto Repair and Service Protections; Center for Auto Safety; Disputes and Dispute Resolution; Warranty Protections.

Readings

"Automobile Lemon Laws" (1995–1996). *Loyola Consumer Law Reporter.* 8 (1).

Dahringer, Lee D., and Denise R. Johnson (1988). "Lemon Laws: Intent, Experience, and a Pro-Consumer Model." *Journal of Consumer Affairs.* 22 (1): 158–170.

Licensure

Licensure is the granting of formal authority to do something. A firm may license another company to sell their product or a manufacturer to use their brand name. The consumer movement is primarily concerned with occupational licensure—the government's granting of a license to practice an occupation. It is often helpful to define occupational licensure negatively; government prohibits unlicensed people from practicing an occupation.

Licensure is primarily a state function in which states exercise their constitutional power to regulate in the interest of public health and safety. Licensure is the strongest common form of occupational regulation, with registration and certification being weaker alternatives. Registration implies nothing about quality of service, but it may help a dissatisfied consumer identify the seller and seek redress. Certification requires practitioners to meet certain qualifications, which suggests that they have a certain expertise.

An important distinction between registration/certification and licensure is that sellers and consumers have an incentive and the power to create their own registration and certification. In medicine and dentistry, where the state imposes licensure, doctors and dentists also pay to register with private referral services. Likewise, there are certifying agencies funded by industry groups such as Underwriter's Laboratories. New health care organizations have sponsored new private agencies to inspect and certify them. The American Dental Association operates a process to approve dental products at the expense of manufacturers. Like registration, certification to serve the consumer interest can go on without government.

Licensure requires the police power of the state because it denies some people the right to engage in activities. Since capitalist culture and law have a general presumption that anyone can take up any occupation, denying this right takes a specific act of government. States license hundreds of occupations, from plumbers and cosmetologists to lawyers and physicians.

There is a standard "public interest" model of how licensure improves consumer welfare. Without licensure, consumers demand various levels of service quality. Some consumers mistake very low quality services for a higher quality. If they were better informed, these consumers would choose a higher quality (or safer) service, even if they had to pay more for it. Some consumers select what looks like a bargain but end up with too little quality at too high a price. Since adequately informing consumers is impractical, the state bans all services below some minimum quality. Licensing cuts off the lower levels of quality or safety available to consumers.

The public interest theory rests on several assertions: it is more cost-effective to stop some mistaken consumer choices than to educate consumers to avoid those mistakes, licensure removes lower levels of quality from the market, and state authorities can judge quality for consumers better than consumers can for themselves. The validity of these assertions varies among occupations. Each instance where consumers do not have good information about the quality of services offered by sellers requires separate examination. Nevertheless, each of the assertions has been questioned on general grounds.

First, it has been noted that there are instances in which consumers have or can get low-cost information about relative qualities. For example, most consumers have automobiles serviced, and many service centers work on many auto brands. A consumer can easily ask friends, relatives, and coworkers about their satisfaction with various auto shops. They can join an automobile club that certifies repair shops. Even if a consumer learns by trial and error, they are likely to find a reliable shop before running up catastrophic expenses on bad repairs. For some bad repairs, they have recourse.

Where consumer education or search is inexpensive and an error in consumption is minor or reversible, it is argued, there is little reason for licensing. If government needs to play any role, it is to help consumers obtain information on quality before purchase or to ease redress after purchase. For example, while many states license barbers, information on barbering is easy to obtain, and the consequences of a poor choice—a bad haircut and a few dollars wasted—are small.

Contrary to the second assertion, it has been suggested, licensing does not remove low-quality services from the market. Furthermore, it may reduce the average quality of service. Licensure does not ban low quality services. Licensure merely bans practitioners who do not pass the licensure test. The test shows that the practitioner at one time performed at a minimal level on a subset of knowledge and practical tasks. An applicant who tests poorly can obtain a license through persistence.

Once licensed, practitioners may produce various qualities, even within the same practice. Even the most competent licensed practitioner may find it profitable to supply consumer demands for low-quality services. The alternatives are refusing to render service or trying to educate consumers, a job that was too big for government.

Other reasons have been advanced that cast doubt on whether licensure assures a minimum level of quality or increases the average quality of service. Sellers who cannot qualify for licensure have an incentive to work just outside the legal boundaries of licensure. Thus, chiropractors, podiatrists, massage therapists, and "root doctors" offer services that compete with physicians'. The persistence of these practices demonstrates that consumers sometimes see them as substitutes for physicians. In some states, drawing up family trusts is practicing law. The licensing process theoretically reserves it for attorneys. Financial advisers, however, draw up trusts in those states. The financial advisers (who may themselves be licensed professionals) engage in a black market for trusts. Is the average quality of a trust higher or lower with a licensed market beside a black market than it would be without restricting the making of trusts to attorneys? Licensure encourages the development of parallel grey and black markets. The services licensure presumes to ban are available in these markets.

The extreme case where licensure may reduce the quality of services is when licensure is part of an overall scheme that reduces the supply of services. In this case, licensure raises the service price and drives some consumers away. Licensure tests alone are not likely to reduce the supply of services much. While there is a charge for taking these tests, these costs are not high enough to discourage many applicants. Moreover, licensure tests are porous; with persistence, an applicant has a good chance of passing them. Contents of the tests are predictable. In dentistry, for instance, an applicant knows what dental procedures will be required on the practical exam. Questions on the theoretical tests are similar from year to year.

The licensure mechanism specifies qualifications to take the test. Control over entry is at this qualifying stage. By setting standards for test eligibility, the licensing authority can exclude many potential practitioners. Some controversial qualifications for tests have required U.S. citizenship and no Communist affiliations.

The public interest theory of licensure contains an inherent conflict of interest. Only practitioners who qualify for licensure have the knowledge to design, develop, and administer the licensing procedure. Yet, these people have an economic interest in restricting the number of new entrants and the supply of services. From their self-interested perspective, the optimal number of entrants provides buyers for existing practices but does not lower service prices. Licensing entrusts the same licensed professionals who have this self-interest with the public interest, an inherent conflict.

In recent years, licensing boards have recruited an increasing number of consumer representatives. Still, boards remain dominated numerically and operationally by the licensed professionals. It appears that these professionals sometimes advance their narrow self-interest on licensing decisions. When the supply of licensed professionals becomes plentiful, qualifications for tests and test evaluations tighten. The result is higher prices for service from licensed practitioners.

A predictable result of higher service prices is less use of services by consumers. Consumers do not utilize the licensed practitioners as frequently as they would at lower prices. Less frequent use can result, for instance, in serious health problems when consumers do not use the health service at all. Licensing trades (e.g., plumbers and electricians) may encourage consumers to resort to do-it-yourself alternatives, thus possibly increasing injury and lowering service quality.

The last assertion of the public interest theory of licensure is that those controlling the licensure process can choose for consumers better than consumers can choose for themselves. This assumption contains some truth since professionals are comparatively good judges of quality. But these professionals do not always know the best combination of price and quality for each consumer. The result of licensure is a paternalistic choice by professionals acting for consumers. The self-interest of the professional makes it doubtful that the choice will even be purely paternalistic.

Capture theory provides a competing explanation of licensure. It emphasizes the self-interest of existing practitioners in controlling entry into the profession. According to capture theory, licensure is a tool serving the selfish interests of licensed professionals. Capture theory arises from the observation that practitioners of any trade or profession have a common interest in that occupation. It is the dominant, usually the only, source of their income. Consumers, in contrast, have only a minor interest in any one service. Their consumption spreads over many goods and services, providing little incentive to give attention to one.

Incentive to control the market for a service is more concentrated among sellers than among consumers. This is true for nearly all goods and services, but there is a general social and legal presumption against sellers controlling entry into a market. Occupational regulation requires justification for an exception to the presumption. Consumers being incompetent or uninformed, combined with relatively high risks from mistaken purchases, provides a rationale for sellers to regulate the market.

Licensure is a political act. Political acts result from balancing competing interests. Legislators balance the public interest against the interests of service sellers. Consumers and sellers represent votes and power. This balancing suggests that regulations will take different forms for different occupations.

Licensure is most likely to be created when the self-interest of the profession is large and concentrated, when sellers have a large information advantage, and when consequences of a mistaken purchase are severe. Where these conditions do not prevail, there is more likely to be no regulation, only registration, or only certification.

— John E. Kushman

See also

Product Standards.

Readings

Friedman, Milton (1962). *Capitalism and Freedom.* Chicago: University of Chicago Press.

Graddy, Elizabeth (1991). "Toward a General Theory of Occupational Regulation." *Social Science Quarterly.* 72 (December): 676–695.

Leland, Hayne E. (1979). "Quacks, Lemons, and Licensing: A Theory of Minimum Quality Standards." *Journal of Political Economy.* 87 (December): 1328–1346.

Low-Income Consumers

Low-income consumers have long been a special concern of public policymakers and consumer activists. Evidence abounds that such consumers obtain less value for their consumer dollars in marketplaces worldwide, a phenomenon that has existed through at least thirty-five years of investigation. These investigations have also shown that the marketplace problems of the poor have complex cause-and-effect relationships and interact with other dimensions of their lives. These relationships often serve to reinforce the plight of the low-income consumer.

The characteristics of the poor population in the United States have changed over the past three decades. The poverty rate itself has increased only slightly. In the late 1960s and early 1970s, about 12 percent of the population was officially classified as poor; today, the figure hovers around 13 percent. Yet, in this period the demographic traits of the poor changed significantly. The elderly, who constituted almost one-quarter of the poor in 1970, represented only 14 percent of the total in 1990. Much more often, poverty is now a problem of children and families with single mothers. In 1970, about 15 percent of all children were poor; in 1990, the figure was close to one in five. In 1970, families with single mothers represented 15.4 percent of all families in poverty; in 1990, they represented 25.1 percent. Poverty hits teenage black males particularly hard: about one in three is unemployed, compared to one in seven white teens.

Many factors help explain the persistence of poverty in the face of significant increases in government welfare expenditures. These factors include negative effects from soaring illegal immigration, absolute decline in government and military jobs, changes in the supply of low-paying jobs in poor communities, increases in teenage pregnancies, and the abandonment of ghettos by middle-class blacks.

Low-Income Consumers' Problems and Their Sources

Research published by Alan Andreasen in 1975 and 1993 reveals that, in the past two decades, the marketplace problems of the poor have not changed. First, the poor pay more. For food, furniture, housing, insurance, and many services, the prices paid by the poor are higher than those paid by comparable middle-class households. For example, recent studies in New York City showed the following: food prices of twenty-one products in sixty stores in low-income communities were at least 8.8 percent higher than in more affluent areas, costing a family of four $350 more per year; automobile drivers in low-income neighborhoods in Brooklyn and the Bronx could only purchase insurance policies that cost significantly more than those of other New York City residents; 81.6 percent of drivers in the southern half of the Bronx were placed in the high-risk (and high-cost) insurance pool compared to only 16.6 percent in more affluent neighborhoods in Staten Island, although 58 percent of the former had not had an accident or moving violation in three or more years; minority homeowners in neighborhoods in Brooklyn, Queens, and the Bronx had been subject to home improvement fraud with financing contracts charging interest rates as high as 21 percent.

Second, the poor have inadequate arrays of goods and services available to them. Studies in the 1970s and more recently make clear that poor areas have fewer supermarkets, discount outlets, and banking services, and have more small stores with limited assortments. In addition, the stores in which the poor shop are more often subject to sanitary code violations and less often have suburban amenities such as ATM machines. Also, there are fewer doctors in poor neighborhoods.

Third, goods and services are often not available to them. The poor often cannot obtain home insurance, bank loans to buy homes, or bank accounts. Redlining often denies them insurance.

Fourth, their treatment by sellers and service representatives is often patronizing, demeaning, prejudicial, and even fraudulent. As a consequence, many poor consumers become alienated from the marketplace and, by extension, from society as a whole.

There are three major sources of the marketplace problems experienced by low-income consumers: personal characteristics, an inadequate marketplace, and merchant behavior.

Low-income consumers have personal characteristics that put them at a disadvantage when trying to obtain maximum value from severely limited budgets. Small weekly paychecks affect their ability to stretch their resources by stocking up on sale items, buying large economy sizes, or getting the "discount for cash." They do not have sufficient savings to open bank accounts that require minimum deposits. Since they cannot afford a 20 percent down payment on a house to qualify them for a mortgage, they cannot escape rents that are often exorbitant.

The poor are also disadvantaged by their restricted access to consumer credit caused by their unsteady income. Because they frequently need credit to make unplanned or unexpected purchases that are necessary to tide them over between paychecks, they are forced to patronize outlets and service people who charge them high prices and exorbitant interest while often treating them poorly. Their need for credit also makes it less likely that they will speak up about unfair treatment, even at legitimate outlets, for fear of losing what little chance they have for the credit they need.

Among the poor, members of minority groups may be particularly disadvantaged. They may feel that they are captive to shopkeepers with whom they feel comfortable because, for example, they speak the same language. These shopkeepers have little pressure to be competitive in price and service.

Other groups also suffer disadvantages in the marketplace. Poor persons who are elderly may have hearing, eyesight, and mobility problems that can make them victims. If they are single mothers, they may have restricted time to shop around, often in distant markets, for bargains that would stretch their meager budgets.

The second major source of problems for low-income consumers is the marketplace in which they shop. Many poor people and members of minority groups live in inner-city areas with limited selections of goods and services. Operating costs for retailers are high, crime is prevalent, and working conditions discourage the best qualified workers from going there. These and other factors pressure sellers to charge high prices or even to relocate to more affluent areas. Such factors also dissuade low-cost competitors, such as Wal-Mart, from locating in low-income areas. For the same reasons, services are often not available in these areas. Banks sometimes close inner-city branches to concentrate on more profitable suburban locations. For many of the poor without health insurance, hospital emergency rooms provide the only health care service.

The poor often find it difficult to escape this environment. Only about half of low-income households have automobiles that allow them to travel to low-price stores in the suburbs. Public transit systems, which they could afford, are usually designed to bring suburbanites to downtown businesses, not inner-city residents to suburban stores. Also, low-income consumers who are ethnic or racial minorities often feel that they are not welcome in suburban stores.

Another problem in poor neighborhoods is that stores are increasingly owned by members of ethnic or racial groups different from the resident population. Inner-city blacks and Latinos may especially resent any high prices or limited selections offered by Korean, Indian, or Chinese merchants.

The combination of frustration about their own poor circumstances and about having to pay high prices to "foreigners" is an incendiary mixture that can generate ugly confrontations, even riots. Such feelings caused stores in East Los Angeles to be the targets of looting and arson during the summer riots of 1992.

The third major source of problems for the poor is closely related to the other two. Being poor and shopping in poor areas means that the poor are more often prey to disreputable merchants who take advantage of the fact that low-income consumers need credit and have limited shopping options. These sellers often charge high interest rates and sell shabby or defective merchandise. Any racial or ethnic hatreds they feel may help them rationalize this exploitation of vulnerable individuals.

Solutions to Problems

The types of solutions that have been proposed to ameliorate the problems of low-income consumers parallel the three sources of their marketplace problems. The most effective of these solutions are grounded in the assumption that one cannot repeal the basic workings of the free market system. That is, they recognize that one cannot reasonably urge rational business owners to take excessive risks or to accept profits that are below their cost of capital or rates of return for comparable businesses serving more affluent consumers. Of course, there will always be a few altruistic corporations and individuals who will make sacrifices to operate uneconomically to serve the poor. But these commitments are often short-lived and idiosyncratic. In many cases, they are responses to crisis situations or to pressures from government, religious, or community leaders to take action. But when the crisis ends or the pressure abates, these commitments often also wane.

The problem with solutions that rely on personal or corporate goodwill is that the resulting actions are not likely to be long-lasting because they are not grounded in market economics. Effective solutions must be grounded in these economics. They can involve removing personal characteristics that cause the problems, improving the marketplace in poor areas, and policing seller practices.

The simplest solution to the problems of the low-income consumer is to give the poor more money. This means that the consumer problem is really a problem of employment, discrimination, and education. But, until these problems are addressed, what can be done?

One answer is to make the poor smarter consumers. This means helping them find the lowest prices where they already shop. It means teaching them about interest rates and borrowing and the need for a good credit history. It means teaching them the need for budgeting and how to budget, so that they can take advantage of any bargains, thus helping them conserve funds needed to make loan payments on time and preserve an acceptable credit rating. It means persuading them to plan for those times when the breadwinner is laid off.

A second answer is to increase the mobility of the poor. If their problems stem from being stuck in a high-price neighborhood, they need to have the incentive and ability to shop elsewhere. Depending on the target group, this may mean teaching them about the bargains available at Home Depot and Wal-Mart and where to find those stores. In other cases, it may mean providing transportation to the outlet malls and the suburban discounters, a service now provided by many senior citizen centers and some poverty programs. For still others, it may mean making babysitting available to single mothers. For ethnic and racial minorities, increasing mobility may mean education and token trips to the suburbs to show them that the environment is not hostile and that stores may even have personnel who speak languages other than English and who belong to ethnic and racial minorities. Increasing the shopping skills and mobility of low-income consumers not only will widen their options but also will bring pressure to bear on the sellers in inner-city markets.

Proposals for reform of marketplaces in poor neighborhoods fall into two broad categories. A number of proposals are based on the conclusion that the economic reward structure for low-cost sellers must be changed in order to change the marketplace. This change could be effected by government agencies that reduced the costs of starting up businesses in poor neighborhoods by providing loans or loan guarantees, by offering free or low-cost amenities such as public parking facilities, by demolishing unsafe properties, and/or by installing road or traffic lights as needed. It could also be brought about by policies that increased the operating profits of the enterprises by providing greater police/security services, offering reduced taxes, charging low interest rates on guaranteed loans, providing free or subsidized municipal services (e.g., trash collection), and/or entering into fixed long-term contracts for the inner-city firm's products or services.

A second set of solutions is based on the assumption that the economics of operating in poor neighborhoods is not nearly as disadvantageous to operators in the area as are their poor decisions. One solution to this problem is training in basic managerial skills. One of these skills is knowledge of cooperative buying options to reduce costs of goods.

Teaching merchants how to deal with low-income consumers can also help these sellers be more profitable, in part, by reducing frictions with their customers. By acquainting sellers with the characteristics and preferences of African- or Mexican-American consumers, this education can make it possible for merchants to meet the needs and wants of these customers more effectively. Such education can also increase the empathy between racial and ethnic groups.

Sellers may also benefit by learning that poverty is not always a permanent condition and that long-term good customer relations is an important goal. This knowledge may encourage them to be more farsighted when transacting with customers temporarily down on their luck.

To police seller practices, two broad sets of solutions have been tried. The first is traditional external enforcement against sellers acting illegally or unethically. In the early 1970s, there was a flurry of research, and hearings held by the Federal Trade Commission and city consumer protection agencies, to discover the nature and extent of the problems faced by low-income consumers. There were cries for new laws and more enforcement of existing laws. Today, many analysts feel that better enforcement of existing laws, not additional laws, represents the most effective strategy. While some experts suggest that more enforcement staff are needed, others argue that the redirection of existing staff to protecting the poor, rather than policing such things as white-collar crime and inconsequential drug use, is the wisest course of action.

The other set of solutions involves helping low-income consumers police their own marketplace. Two options have been proposed. One involves making it easier for individual consumers to voice complaints and helping them to do so. The other involves educating consumers about complaint options, and training and motivating them to pursue these options. Simply telling the poor that most legitimate businesses want to avoid, not create, problems can help supply this motivation.

The final approach is to establish watchdog groups to police the market on behalf of poor consumers. This function has often been performed by poverty law centers in poor neighborhoods but can also be practiced by vigilant neighborhood groups who know how to bring the bright glare of publicity on errant sellers or service providers.

— Alan R. Andreasen

See also

Ethnic Minorities as Consumers; Legal Aid; National Consumer Law Center.

Readings

Alwitt, Linda F., and Thomas D. Donley (1996). *The Low-Income Consumer: Adjusting the Balance of Exchange.* Thousand Oaks, CA: Sage Publications.

Andreasen, Alan R. (1975). *The Disadvantaged Consumer.* New York: The Free Press.

——— (1993). "Revisiting the Disadvantaged." *Journal of Marketing and Public Policy.* 12 (2): 270–275.

M

Medical Devices

Medical devices include nearly everything used to diagnose, treat, or prevent illness, and support and sustain life. These products range from disposable items such as tongue depressors and bandages, to complex diagnostic machines such as magnetic resonance imagers, to implantable products including heart valves and pacemakers. Annual sales of medical devices, manufactured by an estimated 12,000 firms worldwide, total more than $31 billion.

Medical devices first became subject to federal regulation in 1938, with passage of the Federal Food, Drug and Cosmetic Act. The act gave the Food and Drug Administration (FDA) limited authority over medical devices. It granted the FDA only the authority to protect against "adulterated" or "misbranded" medical devices that had entered interstate commerce.

The medical devices used in the 1930s and 1940s were mainly simple instruments, such as stethoscopes and scalpels; fraudulent devices that offered "miracle" cures were of much greater concern. However, as technological advances produced more complex medical devices, such as heart-lung machines and dialysis equipment, the 1938 act proved inadequate. Prompted in large part by serious problems with the Dalkon Shield (an intrauterine contraceptive device), in 1976 Congress revised medical device regulation.

The Medical Device Amendments of 1976 addressed not only the safety of medical devices, but also their effectiveness (i.e., whether the device performs as is claimed). The amendments authorized the FDA to regulate medical devices during all phases of their development, testing, production, distribution, and use. The new law provided for premarket review, good manufacturing practice requirements, and postmarketing surveillance.

The 1976 amendments required that all devices be classified and regulated by degree of risk. "Class I" devices, which pose the least risk (e.g., tongue depressors, bandages, and bedpans), must conform only to the FDA's "general controls." These controls include prohibitions against adulteration and misbranding, as well as registration, notification, and good manufacturing practices requirements. "Class II" devices are medium-risk devices (e.g., cardiac monitors, anesthesia machines, syringes, and hearing aids) that are subject to both general controls and performance standards. "Class III" devices, those that pose the greatest risk of injury or that support or sustain life (e.g., cardiac pacemakers, artificial heart valves, and heart-lung machines), are subject to premarket approval. Device manufacturers must submit documentation (clinical studies) to the agency demonstrating that a Class III device is safe and effective.

Section 510(k) of the 1976 amendments also provided that, if a manufacturer claimed that a new device is "substantially equivalent" to a device that was on the market before 1976, then only premarket notification, and not premarket approval, would be required. Under the premarket notification process, a manufacturer must submit a report to the FDA, ninety days before marketing a new device, that includes a description of the device, its technical specifications, and information about test results supporting a finding of "substantial equivalence" to a pre-1976 device. Well over 98 percent of new devices that enter the market each year do so through section 510(k).

In 1984, Congress enacted the Drug Price Competition and Patent Term Restoration Act, which also applied to medical devices. This legislation granted patent term "extensions" to any medical device that has had its patent life significantly curtailed as a result of the regulatory review process. In addition, the 1984 act also allows federal financial assistance for the development of devices for rare conditions.

Studies conducted by the Government Accounting Office and testimony presented at congressional hearings during the 1980s criticized implementation of the 1976 Medical Device Amendments. The overwhelming majority of devices were apparently reaching the market after only a relatively cursory premarket review. The FDA had failed to develop performance standards for over 1,000 Class II devices. While the law required that Class II and III devices be inspected at least once every two years, inspections occurred in, at best, only 60 percent of domestic device manufacturing plants. The law also established a medical device reporting system for any deaths or serious injuries linked to devices. There was, however, serious underreporting of device-related deaths and injuries; less than 1 percent of medical device problems occurring in hospitals were being reported to the government.

As a result of congressional dissatisfaction with the implementation of the 1976 amendments, Congress passed the Safe Medical Devices Act of 1990, which gave the FDA greater authority over new devices and device monitoring. The 1990 act streamlined procedures for the FDA to establish performance standards, encouraged use of voluntary industry standards, and authorized special controls such as patient registries for Class II devices. It also directed the agency to establish "tracking" requirements for high-risk devices.

In addition, the 1990 act extended from 90 to 180 days the time period within which the FDA must respond to premarket notification filings under section 510(k). Further, it imposed new reporting requirements on hospitals and other "device-user facilities." Moreover, it gave the FDA clear authority to order the recall of problem devices.

Consumer groups, in particular the Public Citizen Health Research Group, continue to monitor medical device regulation. The group has criticized the FDA for approving devices, such as the Bjork-Shiley artificial heart valve and silicone-gel breast implants, the safety and effectiveness of which have been questioned. The Health Research Group has also faulted the FDA for failing to prosecute device firms that have violated the law.

Industry groups have criticized the agency for taking too long to approve potentially beneficial devices. During 1994, the agency did streamline the premarket approval process and cut down the substantial backlog in applications for new devices. Industry members have supported the imposition of user fees to speed up the review process, but legislation authorizing such fees did not pass in the 103rd Congress.

— Sandra B. Eskin

See also

Food and Drug Administration.

Readings

U.S. General Accounting Office (1989). *Medical Device Recalls: An Overview and Analysis, 1983–88*. Washington, DC: U.S. Government Printing Office.

——— (1989). *Medical Device Recalls: Examination of Selected Cases*. Washington, DC: U.S. Government Printing Office.

——— (1989). *Medical Devices: FDA's Implementation of the Medical Device Reporting Regulation*. Washington, DC: U.S. Government Printing Office.

Mexican Consumer Movement

The Asociación Mexicana de Estudios para la Defensa del Consumidor (AMEDC) was created in 1970, using as models the Consumers

Union of the United States and the Consumers Federation of France, organizations whose main objective is the comparative testing of products and services. AMEDC was the first consumer organization of its kind in Latin America. AMEDC's main founder, Arturo Lomeli, had researched consumer habits in Mexico and in Central America for fifteen years before the organization was formed.

The expertise that Lomeli brought to the group of nine professionals who created AMEDC's first constitution was important in identifying the serious problems confronted by consumers in diverse areas of sales and services. In 1971, Lomeli and his wife, Lila, visited Consumers Union and met with its president, Colston Warne. Florence Mason, who had worked at Consumers Union, provided AMEDC with both information and encouragement.

By March 1971, AMEDC was firmly established and able to publish the first issue of *Guia del Consumidor.* The issue contained the results of comparative tests on powdered "chicken soups," the flammability of fabrics used for children's sleepwear, and sunglasses, in addition to more general articles.

In 1975, AMEDC was accepted as a corresponding member of the International Organization of Consumers Unions (IOCU), now called Consumers International. Robert Ledogar visited Mexico to gather information for his book, *Hunger for Profits.* Lomeli and AMEDC were responsible for publishing the Spanish version of the book in 1978 after close collaboration with the author.

Meanwhile, *Guia del Consumidor* was attracting the attention of many businesses. The target audience of the magazine was middle-class consumers, but 70 percent of its subscribers were directors of industry and trade who wanted product information that was unavailable in the country at the time. The interest of these business groups was such that the specialized business magazine *Expansión* published an interview with Arturo Lomeli titled "La defensa del consumidor: Un muro de contención para los negocios?" (Consumers Defense: A Retaining Wall for Business?). This title reflected the curiosity business groups had about whether they should be worried about the consumer movement. Lomeli's answer was, "Yes, if you abuse consumers."

Despite many obstacles, the number of AMEDC's subscribers grew slowly. Consumers were unfamiliar with the idea of a private consumer organization; it was difficult to persuade them that they needed to buy information, especially since there was limited choice in the Mexican marketplace.

Arturo Lomeli, as the director of AMEDC, became the leader of Mexican consumers. His frequent comments to the press sparked improvements. For example, a research study on household paper products (e.g., toilet paper, paper towels, napkins) in which AMEDC found insufficient quality and quantity was used by officials of the Ministry of Commerce to force action on the part of business. Recently, an investigation of government-owned telephone services revealed serious problems. By governmental decision, AMEDC's results were widely reported by the media in order to prepare public opinion in favor of privatization of the telephone company.

As AMEDC's legitimacy grew, so did its impact. In 1974, AMEDC's services were hired by the government to produce a daily television program on consumer education. The program lasted three years and won a national television award. On another occasion, a task force including Lomeli was constituted for the purpose of creating the first draft of what later became, in 1976, the Federal Law for Consumer Protection, the first federal law of its kind in Latin America. Two official institutions were established as a result of the federal law: Instituto Nacional del Consumidor (INCO) and Procuraduria Federal del Consumidor (PROFECO). While INCO ceased to exist in 1993, for nearly fifteen years it was involved in almost the same activities as AMEDC. With substantial government funding, INCO assured the public that the government was their real and only defender. Its magazine, *Revista del Consumidor,* contained politically biased articles but also some useful consumer information.

AMEDC survived the "competition" from INCO and continues to reach consumers through radio and television programs, newspaper and magazine columns, and its own magazine. AMEDC is geared primarily toward the middle class, but its work has benefited all consumers. Studying and reporting problems related to prices, the quality of food and beverages, and abusive and misleading commercial practices has been helpful. So has promoting improvements in laws, standards, regulations, consumer awareness, and education. Representing AMEDC, Lomeli is a member of various national standardization committees and participates in the main private agencies of verification and certification of official standards.

In addition to several hundred issues of its monthly magazine, AMEDC has published seven books. Its office receives consumer complaints and guides consumers to better alternatives in their shopping. AMEDC is also a consultant to students and professionals. With a grant from the Inter-American Foundation, AMEDC conducted a broad study throughout Mexico entitled *La Industria Alimentaria y los Hábitos Alimenticios de los Mexicanos* (The Food Industry and Mexican Eating Habits). In this study, AMEDC researched fifty-two different segments of the food industry through comparative testing and surveys. The results of these studies stimulated improvements in food labeling and quality.

Lila Lomeli spearheaded AMEDC's consumer education efforts through regular programs on television and radio. She currently appears twice weekly on a radio program in which she promotes an ecological viewpoint on consumer practices.

AMEDC and Arturo Lomeli founded several international networks of consumer groups designed to control the sale in developing nations of infant milk formula, pesticides, drugs, irradiated food, and other dangerous substances. Most of these networks involved close collaboration with IOCU and its general director Anwar Fazal. Dr. and Mrs. Lomeli have been volunteer consultants to many private and governmental organizations in Latin America, and they have promoted the consumer movements in the region through *La Voz del Consumidor*, a publication sponsored by IOCU until 1994. From 1991 to 1994, Dr. Lomeli was a member of the executive committee of IOCU. AMEDC has been part of the governing council of IOCU since 1986.

The key governmental consumer protection body in Mexico is the PROFECO. It plays an important role by receiving an average of 800,000 consumer complaints yearly of which, according to official figures, 70 percent are resolved in favor of consumers.

The PROFECO has experienced changes in direction and policies reflecting differences among its six different directors. While consumer complaint handling has advanced, consumer education has not. The official magazine *Revista del Consumidor*, inherited by the PROFECO from INCO, conducts comparative testing in collaboration with industry. The magazine accepts advertising, including ads from brands reported in the "comparative tests."

From the Mexican perspective, national consumer problems tend to need global answers because of the transnationalization of business practices and regionalization of trade. This applies especially to problems involving drugs, pesticides, asbestos, junk products, outdated technologies, and misleading publicity. All these problems are common in Latin America and need regional or global responses.

— Lila Lomeli

See also

Latin American Consumer Movement.

Readings

Arrighi, Jean Michel (1992). "Integration and Consumer Protection: The Case of Latin America." *Journal of Consumer Policy*. 15: 179–190.

Moffett, Matt (1988). "Mexican Consumers Have a Stout Friend in Arturo Lomeli." *Wall Street Journal*. (January 18): 1ff.

Vargas, Jorge A. (1989). "An Overview of Consumer Transactions Law in Mexico." *New York Law School Journal of International and Comparative Law.* 10: 345–382.

Mortgage Loan Protections

Homeownership is, for many, the culmination of the American dream. For most prospective homeowners, this dream is not achievable without the availability of mortgage financing. Mortgage loans from banks, savings and loan associations, mortgage companies, and federally sponsored and insured programs are used by most consumers who finance the purchase of a home. These mortgage loans are installment loans, payable over a term of one to thirty years, in which the lender obtains a security interest—mortgage or deed of trust—in the consumer's home. The security interest is a high-priority lien that allows the lender to force a sale of the home through foreclosure if the homeowner fails to make required mortgage payments or otherwise violates the terms of the mortgage agreement.

Prior to the 1960s, unscrupulous mortgage lending practices were pervasive. Lenders used various methods to calculate interest that misled consumers about the true cost of their credit. For example, a 10 percent loan calculated by the "discount" method might be significantly more expensive than a 12 percent loan calculated by the "actuarial" method. Since lenders were not required to disclose their method of calculating interest and other loan costs, consumers were unable to comparison shop effectively for mortgage financing. In addition, some lenders charged exorbitant fees and made loans that they knew consumers would be unable to repay.

In the 1960s, consumer advocates worked with federal and state legislators to enact broad consumer protection legislation aimed at curtailing credit abuses. These statutes were intended to provide consumers with accurate information about the cost and other terms of their loans and to eliminate exploitive practices. Because of the importance of homeownership, the size and complexity of mortgage financing, and the risk that a home could be lost through foreclosure, policymakers established special consumer protections for mortgage-related financing.

The federal Truth in Lending Act (TILA), enacted in 1968, provided important protections for mortgage borrowers. Most importantly, the act required lenders to compute loan rates in a uniform manner and to disclose their annual percentage rate (APR) to borrowers. TILA required lenders to disclose their costs of credit to these borrowers, both as a total dollar amount and as a percentage amount, in a uniform way. Significantly, the act accorded special protections to homeowners who refinanced first mortgages or took out second or third mortgage loans. The most important protection was a three-day right of recission, or "cooling-off" period. During these three days, a homeowner can cancel the loan for any reason whatsoever without cost or penalty; in fact, a lender is required to return any money already paid by the homeowner. If any of the mandatory disclosures are not properly provided, the right to rescind expands from three days to three years, provided the consumer continues to own the home.

This extended right checks many abusive practices because a consumer who rescinds a mortgage loan is not liable for any interest or fees charged on the loan. Following rescission, the lender is required to deduct all fees originally charged in settling the loan and then return to, or credit, the consumer with all payments made on the loan. The borrower is liable only for those sums that actually benefited him or her, such as money paid to satisfy a prior mortgage or to pay a consumer's bills, reduced by payments made. For example, suppose that a consumer with a fifteen-year, $50,000 mortgage loan, at an interest rate of 15 percent with initial fees and charges of $3,500, is able to rescind the loan after two years. If the borrower had made twenty of twenty-four monthly payments of $704.75 owed on the loan, he or she would owe only

$32,405 after rescission. By contrast, the creditor would be forced to absorb a loss of approximately $22,600.

In the 1970s and 1980s, property values rose rapidly throughout most of the country, providing homeowners with equity that could be accessed through refinancing their homes or through second or third mortgage loans. Changes in the federal tax code, which removed the tax deduction for nonmortgage consumer interest, fueled a dramatic rise in the use of home equity borrowing for college loans, debt consolidation, car loans, and home improvement loans. In the same period, abusive lending practices increased as predatory lenders targeted "house rich, cash poor" homeowners and persuaded them to use their home to access funds that they could not afford to repay. It was not until the 1990s that consumer advocates helped persuade federal legislators to enact consumer protections for these homeowners.

Since 1994, Congress has passed legislation that altered TILA protections. The Home Ownership and Equity Protection Act of 1994 enhanced protections to homeowners with high-cost mortgages. Lenders who charge fees or interest rates that are considered "high cost" must provide consumers with new disclosures warning the homeowners about the risks of these loans. The law also provides consumers with an extended right to rescind "high-cost" loans containing certain prohibited practices, such as short-term balloons, negative amortization, or prepayment penalties. Moreover, the statute prohibits equity skimming—lending money based on the value of the home when the owner lacks sufficient income to repay the loan.

In contrast, the Truth in Lending Act Amendments of 1995 scaled back protections for homeowners. Yet, in response to lobbying by consumer advocates, the legislation preserved many of these protections for homeowners facing foreclosure.

In the 1980s, home equity loans grew rapidly in popularity and, with them, lender abuses. In 1988, Congress passed legislation to correct some of these abuses. Among other provisions, the legislation eliminated lenders' right to change unilaterally the terms of loans, prohibited lenders from calling in loans before the due date except under certain circumstances, required certain disclosures, and prohibited misleading sales practices, such as advertising short-term teaser rates without disclosing that these rates would increase significantly over time.

In addition to requiring credit disclosures, Congress established consumer protections related to the settlement costs of mortgage loans. The Real Estate Settlement Procedures Act (RESPA), enacted in 1974, requires lenders to provide potential mortgage borrowers with a good faith estimate of the costs of settlement, including such items as broker's fees, lender's points, attorney's fees, insurance, and title charges, within three days of application for a loan. Like TILA disclosures, which are intended to enable consumers to comparison shop for credit, the good faith estimate is designed to provide consumers with information that allows comparison shopping for settlement services. RESPA also mandates the use of a standardized settlement sheet, which itemizes both charges to the home purchaser, or refinancing homeowner, and disbursements of the loan proceeds. And, the act prohibits referral fees and kickbacks, with penalties to lenders of treble damages, subject to a one-year statute of limitations.

State unfair deceptive acts and practices (UDAP) laws protect consumers against a broad array of deceptive and unconscionable sales practices. These laws afford protection to homeowners who are victimized by misrepresentations, high-pressure sales tactics, loans made with no likelihood of repayment ("foreclosure loans"), and overpriced loans and practices that target or exploit vulnerable or disabled homeowners. They provide remedies including rescission of the loan, multiple damages, and recovery of attorney's fees.

Homeowners in default on mortgage loans can lose their homes through foreclosure. State laws provide varying degrees of protection to individuals facing foreclosure. Approximately one-half of the states require lenders to seek court permission to force the sale of a home through foreclosure. The remaining states allow lenders to force the sale of a home at auction under authority contained in the mortgage documents ("power of sale" clause) after providing some form of notice to the homeowner. In these nonjudicial foreclosure states, lenders are not required to go to court to foreclose on properties. Homeowners can try to stop a foreclosure only by attacking the lender's compliance with the state foreclosure process or by claiming violations of federal and state consumer protection statutes outlined above.

— Nina F. Simon, Jean Constantine-Davis

Readings

Barron, Paul (1992). *Federal Regulation of Real Estate and Mortgage Lending*. 3d ed. Boston: Warren, Gorham & Lamont.

Ornstein, Stephen F. J. (1996). "Examining the Effect of New Legislation on Consumer Protection for 'High Cost Mortgages.' " *Real Estate Law Journal*. 25 (Summer). 40–55.

Motor Vehicle Safety

See Highway Safety; National Highway Traffic Safety Administration.

N

Nader, Ralph

It is hard to imagine the rise of the modern consumer movement without the leadership, resourcefulness, and sheer persistence of Ralph Nader, a self-described "public citizen" who has been at the forefront of scores of progressive campaigns over the past thirty years.

Born in Winsted, Connecticut, and educated at Princeton and Harvard Law School, Nader first gained national attention in 1965 as the thirty-one-year-old author of *Unsafe at Any Speed*. The book indicted unsafe automobile design in general and General Motors' Corvair in particular. When it became publicly known that General Motors had hired private detectives in an attempt to dig up information that might discredit Nader, a Senate subcommittee looking into auto safety summoned the president of General Motors to explain his company's harassment and personally apologize to Nader.

This incident catapulted auto safety into the public spotlight, leading to a series of landmark laws that have prevented hundreds of thousands of motor vehicle–related deaths and injuries. The episode also certified Nader in the public mind as the fierce, incorruptible advocate for the "little guy," a reputation that he has parlayed into one of the most singular and enduring careers in American politics. Without ever holding public office, Nader has used his considerable talents as an organizer, activist, legal analyst, and pamphleteer to rally public opinion to push through dozens of reforms in business, government, and various professions.

The range of issues that Nader has addressed is broad: consumer protection, congressional reform, openness in government, nuclear power safety and renewable energy, food and drug safety, air and water pollution, fair taxation, product liability protection, union democracy, and consumer reforms in insurance, banking, pension law, and telecommunications. Nader has even sponsored consumer initiatives to reform university governance, educational testing, daily newspapers, women's health care, legal services, and professional sports.

More than anyone, Nader transformed "consumerism" into a movement that could effectively counter the power wielded by business in the marketplace and by government policymakers. Before 1965, most consumer reforms were prompted by tragedy and sporadic congressional leadership (Hubert Humphrey, Estes Kefauver, Philip Hart, Gaylord Nelson); they were rarely instigated by consumers themselves. Nader's leadership gave the consumer movement a proactive, visionary dimension. Through a process that he once described as "documenting your intuition," Nader spent the latter half of the 1960s investigating a host of abuses against individuals by American business and government. His reports spurred passage of new laws addressing unsanitary conditions in meatpacking and poultry production, the dangers of natural gas pipelines, radiation emissions from television sets and X rays, and hazardous working conditions in coal mines.

In 1968, to expand his efforts, Nader recruited a task force of law students to investigate the Federal Trade Commission (FTC), the agency charged by Congress with protecting consumers from shoddy products, fraudulent business practices, and deceptive advertising. The Nader team found the FTC "fat with cronyism, torpid through an inbreeding unusual even for Washington, manipulated by the agents of commercial predators, [and] impervious to governmental and citizen monitoring." The Nader report, released in 1968, sparked a congressional investigation and a major overhaul of the FTC. It also produced admiring publicity for the resourceful citizen-investigators, burnishing Nader's public image even further.

Flush with this success, Nader hired several dozen undergraduate and law students in the summer of 1969 to investigate a still-wider array of government and corporate abuses: incompetence and corruption at the now defunct Interstate Commerce Commission, the health hazards of air pollution, and the Food and Drug Administration's lax oversight of the food industry, among other abuses. It is a measure of Nader's cachet that in 1970 more than 30,000 students—and one-third of the Harvard Law School—applied for 200 summer jobs that Nader created from the proceeds of his publishing and paid appearances. Journalist William Greider, then a *Washington Post* reporter, dubbed the crusading students "Nader's Raiders," a tagline that stuck.

In subsequent summers, new "raids" were launched against the nation's worsening water pollution; the secrecy, conflicts of interest, and concentration of power at First National City Bank (now Citibank); the indignities and frauds practiced by nursing homes; the dangerous use of pesticides on agricultural crops; and the despoliation of land in California by developers and speculators. By 1972, seventeen Nader books had been published.

The early Nader investigations were influential primarily because of the deficiencies of mainstream journalism at the time. Investigative journalism was hardly practiced at most daily newspapers, and few legislators scrutinized federal agencies from the perspective of the average citizen. Nor did many journalists or legislators name names, assemble meticulous documentation, and propose ambitious yet practical remedies—an activist strategy that has since become commonplace.

Unlike muckrakers of the early 1900s who took satisfaction in unmasking scandal and then moving on, Nader wanted to experiment with new strategies of citizen action and to establish organizations that could empower ordinary consumers. In the marketplace, Nader's self-avowed agenda was "nothing less than the qualitative reform of the Industrial Revolution." In the civic sphere, Nader's ambition was to reinvigorate the possibilities of citizenship in a modern society dominated by institutional giants—multinational corporations, government bureaucracies, labor unions, bar associations, universities.

Nader argued that Thomas Jefferson did not envision how monied special interests, official secrecy, procedural complexities, and the sheer size of the nation would, by the mid–twentieth century, erode the sinews of government accountability. Nor, said Nader, could James Madison, author of the famous *Federalist No. 10* essay, have predicted how competing special interest factions might not yield the public good. In this sense, Nader's creation of a loose agglomeration of citizen groups to represent the people as a whole—"the public interest"—was a bold, innovative development in American politics. By demonstrating that an individual armed with facts, fortitude, and creative zeal could actually achieve important reforms, Nader sought to demonstrate the relevance of citizenship in modern mass society.

Nader's chief vehicle for advancing his reform agenda has been the citizen advocacy group—modestly funded organizations of a few researchers and sometimes an attorney who investigate a given field, publish reports, organize citizens and other allies, lobby Congress, petition regulatory agencies, and litigate in court. From his Washington, D.C., headquarters, the Center for Study of Responsive Law, Nader has provided the moral leadership, political and legal advice, and seed financial support for a sprawling network of more than four dozen groups that he has founded. While most of them are now formally independent of Nader, they frequently collaborate as the occasion arises. Perhaps the most significant of Nader's institutional creations is Public Citizen, a membership organization founded in 1972 that now consists of five quasi-autonomous groups: Congress Watch, the Health Research Group, the Litigation Group, Critical Mass Energy Project, and Buyers Up, a fuel-buying cooperative.

A few recurrent themes tend to animate most of Nader's campaigns. The first is challenging the "seller-sovereign" economy with a "consumer-side" vision. Nader has believed that a "seller-sovereign" marketplace, unchecked by meaningful mechanisms of accountability, naturally tends to generate anti-consumer abuses. Accordingly, much of Nader's activism has sought to document the many harms of a seller-sovereign economy: price-fixed products and services; "product fixing" to thwart innovation that could generate competition; deceptive packaging and false advertisements; wholly ineffective and hazardous drugs; product obsolescence; energy-wasting vehicles and appliances; unsafely designed cars and products; junk food; serious product side effects such as air pollution and poor land use; adulterated products; and overselling of credit, insurance, and health care.

"A seller-sovereign economy," Nader once wrote, "includes sellers who are monopolistic or oligopolistic without being confronted by the ultimate consumers who are organized in monopsonistic (a single buyer) or oligopsonistic (a few buyers) modes. It is an economy where enormous skill, artifice, and resources are used in getting consumers to buy what the sellers want to sell, notwithstanding the availability of more efficient, safe, economical, durable, and effective alternatives, including that of buying nothing at all."

These insights prompted Nader to launch a nine-member task force of law students in 1970 to document the concentration of corporate power in America and its anticompetitive effects. This research has been followed with campaigns against the legal profession's price fixing and ban on advertising, the anticompetitive effects of industry standard-setting groups, the territorial monopolies of beer brewers, and the special antitrust exemption that allows two newspapers in a single city to share facilities, among many other anticompetitive practices.

To help stimulate competition in the marketplace, Nader has also sought to generate greater quantities of reliable consumer information about products and services. Developing and publicizing such information—particularly when sponsored by the government—can transform markets and induce new, more socially beneficial forms of competition. This impact has in fact occurred after the consumer movement won mandatory disclosures of the crashworthiness of cars; the tar and nicotine levels of cigarettes; the energy efficiency of appliances; the levels of sodium, sulfites, vitamin, and additives in food products; the terms of consumer loans; and the health hazards of prescription drugs (thus required to be accompanied by warnings).

When economic regulation of markets has artificially limited competition, Nader has vigorously supported deregulation. His advocacy played a critical role in the deregulation of the trucking and airline industries in the late 1970s, for example. Nader has always, however, opposed deregulation of health, safety, and environmental protections; he has always contended that, in these areas, laissez-faire competition results in less protection for consumers, workers, and the public.

Because government subsidies can inflate prices and retard innovation in the marketplace, Nader has been a staunch critic of various government subsidy programs—for nuclear power, supersonic jets, agribusiness interests, synthetic fuels development, and dozens of obscure tax subsidies. "Ours is a system of corporate socialism," Nader has asserted, "where companies capitalize their profits and socialize their losses. . . . In effect, they tax you for their accidents, bunglings, boondoggles and mismanagement, just like a government. We should be able to dis-elect them."

To gain greater influence over corporate decision-making, in the 1970s Nader sought to secure formal consumer representation in corporate governance. "Project GM" agitated for three seats for public representatives on the company's board of directors. Although the effort failed, it did illustrate the value of mounting dissident shareholder campaigns, a tactic later adopted by dozens of other citizen advocates. It also prompted many major corporations to begin to take "social responsibility" more seriously. The 1976 book by Nader, Green, and Seligman, *The Taming of the Giant Corporation,* was Nader's most ambitious effort to achieve greater public accountability in corporate governance, through federal chartering of corporations.

A common thread in many Nader crusades has been a concern with empowering the "consumer side" of the economy. Adam Smith, the seminal economist of free market economics, declared, "Consumption is the sole end and purpose of all production; and the interest of the producer ought to be attended to, only so far as it may be necessary for promoting that of the consumer." Nader has taken this injunction to heart, promoting innovative vehicles by which consumers can express their common interests.

In the 1970s, Nader was one of the leading champions of consumer cooperatives as a way to assert greater consumer autonomy in the marketplace. When the co-op movement did not achieve the heights that Nader envisioned for it, he characteristically modified his tactics by promoting "group buying" experiments that aggregated consumer purchasing power without the organizational overhead of a co-op. One such Nader-launched innovations, Buyers Up, a purchasing organization for home heating oil, continues to serve consumers in several East Coast cities. Another consumer-side innovation promoted by Nader has been the "Time Dollars" barter-service model, which allows people with little money but much free time to exchange volunteer services using a "one hour, one time dollar" currency system.

In the 1990s, Nader applied the lessons of group buying to the nation's largest consumer, the federal government. If the purchasing powers of government procurement could be leveraged—so that markets could develop for environmentally benign products, for example—the ripple effects could be huge, Nader reasoned. This tactic, in fact, finally convinced automakers to offer airbags in automobiles: Nader had persuaded the U.S. General Services Administration to let a contract requiring airbags in part of the federal fleet of cars. By the mid-1990s, a Nader project was pressing the federal government to adopt "green" principles in its purchases of paper, cars, lighting, and other products.

A second theme in Nader's campaigns has been developing new mechanisms to foster government accountability. Nader's original campaigns against corporate abuses in the marketplace usually called on government to pass legislation or issue regulations. But Nader's groups found that corporate abuses were often ignored or even defended by legislators and regulators representing big business interests. Accordingly, Nader launched a series of initiatives to ensure that the procedures of the democratic process—in Congress, the executive branch, and the judiciary—were open to public scrutiny and not corrupted by influence-peddling and conflicts of interest.

The first major crusade to reform government was the Congress Project, a 1971 attempt by hundreds of college students to profile every member of Congress and six key congressional committees. The project exposed the little-known world of "protocol, alcohol and Geritol" to an American public that barely knew how Congress operated. A subsequent book based on the research, *Who Runs Congress?,* eventually went through four different editions and a print run of more than one million copies, making it the best-selling book ever written about Congress.

The Congress Project, soon institutionalized as Congress Watch, successfully advocated "sunshine laws" that opened up congressional committees to the public and new procedural reforms that weakened the power of entrenched committee chairpersons. Over the past two decades, Nader and Congress Watch have been leading advocates for campaign finance reform, ethics reforms, and bans on lobbyist-paid gifts and travel. Whenever members of Congress have sought to raise their own pay over the past twenty years, Nader has personally waged highly vocal campaigns seeking to shame them into freezing their compensation.

Within the executive branch, Nader has repeatedly sought to ensure the integrity of decision-making by prohibiting secret deliberations, the withholding of public documents, and the stacking of advisory panels with industry representatives. Nader forces played a critical role in winning passage of the landmark 1974 amendments to the Freedom of Information Act, which has been a significant tool for rooting out waste, abuse, and other wrongdoing in government and industry.

A widespread practice that Nader and his associates have fought is the private taking of what Nader calls "taxpayer assets"—federally owned forests, minerals, grazing lands, waterways, coastal lands, airwaves used for television and radio, and government-generated research and information. Even though these capital assets nominally belong to the public, in practice the government has often colluded with corporate interests to give them away at fire-sale prices. Over the years, Nader and his associates have documented these practices in the development of California lands, the exploitation of Alaska's natural wealth, the commercialization of basic drug research, the "privatization" of government databases, and the commercialization of the public's airwaves.

A third focus of Nader's campaigns has been to mobilize the energies of key constituencies to serve a public interest agenda. One example is Nader's influence on American journalism, whose watchdog capacities Nader has repeatedly sought to invigorate. His groups' research and reports have acted as agenda-setters for reporters, suggesting fruitful lines of inquiry and promising sources. His influence has also been felt, and absorbed into professional journalism, through the Nader-founded Capitol Hill News Service, which in the early 1970s pioneered investigative reporting about Congress. By founding the Freedom of Information Clearinghouse, Nader has also tried to educate journalists about how they can obtain government documents under the Freedom of Information Act, providing litigation support when necessary.

In the legal profession, Nader has mobilized plaintiffs' attorneys to form Trial Lawyers for Public Justice in order to advocate legal reforms. Recently, Nader has also been a leading champion of public interest law, securing various new funding mechanisms to support such advocacy and exhorting a generation of law students to pursue such jobs. To help spur the idealism of young people, over the years Nader has helped found a network of more than twenty student-run Public Interest Research Groups (PIRGs) on college campuses. Some PIRGs, such as New York PIRG, have been major forces in their states for consumer and environmental reforms. Within the past five years, Nader has also mobilized a number of Ivy League alumni organizations, starting with his own Princeton Class of 1955 and Harvard Law School Class of 1958, to help college students obtain internships and jobs with public advocacy organizations working for systemic change.

Nader's crusades for citizenship range from the local to the global. In Elmhurst, Illinois, and in his hometown of Winsted, Connecticut, a foundation he helped launch retained a "Community Lawyer" in 1990 to help citizens exercise their rights and participate in local government—a demonstration project that he hopes will be replicated elsewhere. Internationally, he has helped export many lessons of the U.S. consumer movement to foreign activists, particularly in less-developed nations. One vehicle has been the monthly magazine he founded in 1980, *The Multinational Monitor,* a singular source of investigative reporting about international corporate behavior. In 1990, Nader encouraged activists to oppose GATT (General Agreement on Tariffs and Trade) negotiations, which he felt would degrade health, safety, and environmental protections; undermine democratic processes; and give multinational corporations greater control over Third World markets and resources.

The legacy that Nader has achieved over thirty years of advocacy is considerable. It can be seen in entirely new bodies of legislation and case law, dozens of new governmental programs designed to protect the public, industries whose competition is more robust and performance more innovative than previously, and far more plentiful consumer-oriented information. He has also helped bring into being a national network of activists and supporters, whose careers, strategies, and ideals he has strongly influenced. Paradoxically, a large number of Nader's most significant triumphs—for new consumer rights, open government, and more humane business practices—have been so integrated into the culture that they are now taken for granted.

— David Bollier

See also

Public Citizen; Public Interest Research Groups; U.S. Consumer Movement: History and Dynamics.

Readings

Bollier, David (1991). *Citizen Action and Other Big Ideas*. Washington, DC: Center for Study of Responsive Law.

Gorey, Hays (1975). *Nader and the Power of Everyman*. New York: Grosset & Dunlap.

McCarry, Charles (1972). *Citizen Nader*. New York: Saturday Review Press.

National Association of Consumer Agency Administrators

The National Association of Consumer Agency Administrators (NACAA) is an association of state and local government consumer agencies. Its origins can be traced to the annual National Seminars for Directors of Consumer Agencies, sponsored by Helen Nelson, who was then director of the Center for Consumer Affairs at the University of Wisconsin; to a 1974 White House conference, sponsored by presidential consumer adviser Virginia Knauer; and to the Consumer Federation of America's (CFA) annual Consumer Assemblies, at which Helen Nelson provided encouragement and guidance.

NACAA's first board of directors was elected in Milwaukee in July 1976, at the fourth National Seminar for Directors of Consumer Agencies. That board reflected the nationwide character of the organization and its mix of jurisdictions—state, county, and city—representing Oregon, Delaware, and Minnesota; New Orleans, Louisiana, and Dallas, Texas; both the City and State of New York; and Suffolk County, Long Island.

The goals of the organization were, in the beginning, threefold: to assist state and local offices of consumers affairs, to help agency directors improve their performance as administrators and consumer advocates, and to comment on significant nationwide consumer issues.

In the early years, while some policy resolutions were adopted, the association concentrated on establishing credibility by building membership and providing membership services. In each succeeding year, progress was made toward the establishment of a viable organization. In 1977, NACAA was incorporated and began publishing *NACAANEWS*, which reported on member activities and other matters of consumer interest. In 1978, NACAA was granted status as a nonprofit corporation. It also began to sponsor annual conferences to give members and others the opportunity to share accomplishments and develop strategies to address emerging consumer issues.

During NACAA's early years, organization structure and governance procedures were established. They have largely remained in place down to the present time. Full NACAA membership is open to administrators of state, county, and municipal consumer agencies. These agencies typically mediate consumer complaints, conduct investigations, prosecute violators of consumer laws, license and regulate various professions, promote strong consumer protection legislation, conduct consumer education, and advocate the consumer interest. In 1992, NACAA recognized the increasingly global nature of the marketplace and consumer protection by making representatives of equivalent agencies in other countries eligible for full membership.

Associate membership in NACAA is open to staff of full member agencies and to officials of federal consumer protection offices in the United States and abroad. It is also open to students and faculty at institutions of higher learning, and to legislators and staff interested in consumer issues.

The NACAA executive board has twelve members who are elected by the membership at the annual conference. One is an associate member; the others represent full member agencies. The board appoints an executive director who, supported by a small staff and interns from Washington, D.C.–area universities, carries out the board's policies. In developing public policy positions and consumer educational materials, the executive director consults closely with board members and member agencies.

NACAA derives funding, which recently has been about $200,000 annually, from several sources: membership dues, conference revenues, consultant fees, corporate subscribers, public and private grants and donations, and sales of publications. In 1990, NACAA instituted the Corporate Subscriber Program to facilitate communication and cooperation between the private and public sectors. The program has resulted in increased dialogue and the implementation of joint consumer education projects.

Once its original organizational goals had been met, NACAA was ready to increase its membership services and expand its role as consumer educator and advocate. Information is provided to members through the *NACAANEWS*, published ten times a year and containing reports from member agencies and others about current enforcement, legislative, administrative, and educational activities; the *Roundtable*, which is compiled for the annual conference and highlights the major cases, issues, programs, and other activities of members; the *Health Fraud Information Exchange*, a comprehensive resource book detailing investigations, litigation, public policy initiatives, and educational programs related to health issues; and a membership directory that lists all NACAA contacts. Members and other attendees also exchange information and viewpoints at NACAA's annual conference and at regional conferences sponsored or cosponsored by the organization.

NACAA also promotes consumer education and public awareness of consumer issues, sometimes in concert with other organizations and businesses. Drawing on the knowledge of staff and members, NACAA has worked on: revisions to the U.S. Office of Consumers Affairs resource handbook; an American Express brochure on mail and telephone shopping rights; a pamphlet on 900 numbers and other pay-per-call services with MCI; a brochure, prepared jointly with CFA and Sprint, on how consumers can resolve complaints effectively; and radio announcements with AT&T Universal Card and television spots with VISA on the wise use of credit. Another example of a joint initiative is the annual survey of consumer agencies that NACAA conducts with CFA, which highlights the most frequent and worst consumer complaints and the protections that are needed to address them.

In the public policy arena, NACAA has provided comments to federal regulatory agencies, congressional committees, and others on a wide array of important consumer concerns, including auto repair, dietary supplement labeling, credit reporting, telemarketing fraud, consumer product safety priorities, poultry labeling, vocational schools, 900 numbers and other telecommunications issues, Federal Trade Commission reauthorization and its relation to state and local consumer enforcement agencies, and federal policies that will affect consumers' access to the "information superhighway." In addition, NACAA members have represented the organization on boards and in working groups dealing with consumer education, fraud prevention, and other consumer issues.

NACAA has played a role in bringing grassroots consumer perspectives to Washington. Its member agencies have knowledge of problems and remedies that can be useful to policymakers and to business. Through its many activities, NACAA has helped to heighten public awareness of consumer issues, increase the effectiveness of consumer agencies, and highlight the importance of direct consumer services provided to people in cities, counties, states, provinces, and other jurisdictions around the world.

— Barbara B. Gregg

See also

State and Local Consumer Affairs Offices; State Attorneys General.

Reading

Richardson, Lee (1995). "State and Local Consumer Protection." In Kenneth J. Meier and E. Thomas Garman, eds. *Regulation and Consumer Protection.* Houston: DAME Publications, Inc. 393–406.

National Coalition for Consumer Education

The National Coalition for Consumer Education, Inc. (NCCE), is a national nonprofit, 501(c)(3) organization that promotes consumer education in the nation's schools, communities, and workplaces. Formed in 1981, it was the first organization to establish a state-based national network to support consumer education at national, state, and local levels. In 1992, the coalition became a membership organization and now represents hundreds of individuals, organizations, companies, and international groups.

In the spring of 1981, the movement to reduce federal government regulation and funding threatened the Office of Consumer Education, a unit within the U.S. Department of Education. Under the leadership of James Boyle, the Consumer Federation of America brought together a diverse committee of consumer education leaders to try to preserve federal support for consumer education. While this effort was not successful, the committee saw a need to strengthen and encourage consumer education in classrooms, businesses, government, and communities. Accordingly, it established the Coalition for Consumer Education ("National" was added two years later), which incorporated and hired Judith Cohart as executive director. Initial funding came from a government subcontract. During the past fifteen years, most of its funding has come from government grants and corporate contributions.

At its inception, the coalition set the ambitious goal of persuading the nation to make consumer education a priority. One of its first projects was the recruitment of a network of fifty volunteer state coordinators. Coordinators from consumer, academic, business, and government organizations would represent the coalition and undertake activities in support of consumer education. At the coalition's first national conference in November 1981, the coordinators were urged to develop state networks to lobby for increased federal spending on consumer education. A month later, the coalition surveyed its coordinators and board members to learn what activities they considered most important and what was needed to support local and state consumer education. These coordinator surveys continue to the present.

In February 1982, the coalition began publishing a quarterly newsletter, the *Coalition Exchange,* to spotlight state activities, provide news on national initiatives, and review new consumer education materials. In 1983 and 1984, the state coordinators gathered in Washington, D.C., to discuss issues of mutual interest. Virginia Knauer, special assistant for consumer affairs to the president, was the keynote speaker in 1983. Representative Newt Gingrich (R-GA) was the keynote speaker in 1984.

During this period, the coalition sponsored a nationwide poster contest for students in elementary, junior, and senior high schools to celebrate National Consumers Week. In addition, the coalition published education materials on energy, individual retirement accounts, and health insurance.

When Cohart left the organization in 1985, it became less active. But in 1986, the coalition was revived under the leadership of Rosella Bannister and John Knapp, educators at Eastern Michigan University. Within a year, forty-four state coordinators had been recruited, and the *Coalition Exchange* was reactivated. With the Food and Drug Administration, the coalition sponsored the first National Consumer Education Materials Contest.

In 1988, Irene Williamson was appointed executive director and moved the coalition's headquarters to New York City. In 1990, Carole Glade was hired as executive director and relocated the organization's offices to New Jersey.

In both 1989 and 1990, the organization held state coordinators' conferences. In 1990, the coalition also conducted the National Survey on the Status of Consumer Education in U.S. Schools Grades K–12 to determine state educational policies, mandates, class levels, and concepts. In the same year, AT&T Universal Card Services joined forces with the coalition to establish the NCCE/AT&T Consumer Credit Education Fund. This four-year million-dollar project supported consumer credit projects through local nonprofit organizations and schools.

In the mid-1990s, the coalition continued to be active. State and regional coalitions were expanded. Membership in the coalition was opened to individuals and organizations who are committed to consumer education. In 1993, with support from federal agencies and business groups, the first International Conference on Consumer Literacy was held. In 1994, with support from MCI Telecommunications Corporation, LifeSmarts—a game show competition to test high school students' knowledge of consumer information—was established. In 1995, the first national championships took place. Throughout this period, one-day educational programs on issues, Academies for Consumer Education, were held.

Today, by bringing together key leaders from business, government, education, the media, and community and consumer groups, NCCE endorses and creates partnerships that sponsor research on consumer education and consumer skills, assists others in designing and implementing consumer education programs, seeks to influence public policy, and encourages local consumer education initiatives. It has also begun efforts to forge international partnerships.

— Carole Glade, Judith Cohart

See also

Consumer Education; U.S. Office of Consumers' Education.

Readings

Glade, Carole (1991). "The New National Coalition for Consumer Education." *Advancing the Consumer Interest*. 3 (1): 27.

Knapp, John (1989). "A New National Coalition for Consumer Education." *Advancing the Consumer Interest*. 1 (1): 35.

National Consumer Law Center

The National Consumer Law Center is a national expert on legal and policy issues concerning low-income consumers. The center is best known for its advocacy on behalf of low-income consumers; its research of public policy matters affecting the legal needs and rights of low-income consumers; and its publications and treatises on consumer, energy, and public utility law.

The center, or NCLC, is a nonprofit organization located in Boston, Massachusetts, with an office in Washington, D.C. Its work, however, is national in scope, and it is common for center staff to be engaged in projects with public agencies, community groups, and lawyers across the country. The board and staff of the center itself are drawn from around the country.

Consumer law is the broad jurisdiction of the center's work. Topics of focus have ranged from insurance and warranties to housing and access to markets. The primary emphasis over the years, however, has been consumer credit, debt, and finance problems, and the affordability of necessities of life such as home heat, utility services, and home repairs.

As experts in consumer law and policy, NCLC staff serve as a resource to lawyers representing low-income clients, to public agencies designing and administering laws and programs serving the poor, to legislators and other policymakers, and to private nonprofit and for-profit organizations and companies with special concerns for low-income consumers. The center does not offer services to individual consumers, although some center publications of interest to the general public may be purchased from the center.

The NCLC was founded during 1968 and 1969 at the Boston College School of Law. William Willier, commercial law professor and consumer advocate, was the moving force in getting the center started, with the support of the law school's dean, Father Robert Drinan. Willier served as the organization's first executive director. He was succeeded by Richard Hesse, formerly a legal services attorney in New Jersey. During his tenure, the center established itself as a national representative of the interests of low-income consumers. The next director, who began in 1975, was Mark Budnitz. Budnitz left the clinical program at Boston University School of Law to join the center, where he had previously served as the litigation director. During his tenure, the center expanded its advocacy into areas of energy law and policy. In 1979, Robert Sable became director. Sable was former civil director of the Cleveland Legal Aid Society and deputy director of the center. The current director, Willard P. Ogburn, began in 1987. Ogburn is a former Massachusetts deputy commissioner of banking and former deputy director of the center. During the terms of Sable and Ogburn, the center greatly expanded its publications and diversified its funding base. Throughout its history, the strength of the center has been its staff of expert legal and technical specialists.

Initial funding was provided by the federal Office of Economic Opportunity (OEO) as part of the nation's War on Poverty. OEO was then funding new legal services neighborhood organizations to assure that low-income Americans had access to lawyers and the ability to protect and assert their rights in court and in public affairs. To support and complement the work of local legal services offices, OEO funded a small number of national backup centers, beginning with the Center on Social Welfare Policy and Law at Columbia University School of Law, followed shortly by other centers including the National Housing Law Project (at Boalt Hall, Berkeley), the Center for Law and Education (at Harvard Law School), and the National Consumer Law Center (at Boston College School of Law). Ever since, the NCLC has worked closely with legal services programs, which now serve every part of the country.

In 1973, the center separated from Boston College for financial reasons, incorporated as a nonprofit, tax-exempt organization, and moved into space in downtown Boston. Funding for the center has greatly expanded to include donations; foundation support; grants and contracts from public and private national and local organizations; and sale of publications, conferences, and services, among other sources.

Following its founding, the center had an almost immediate impact on state consumer credit laws. The National Conference on Uniform State Laws, using funds provided by the retail credit and financial services industry, drafted and proposed a Uniform Consumer Credit Code for adoption by each state. The code contained many provisions detrimental to consumers. In response, the National Consumer Law Center drafted a National Consumer Act, and later a Model Consumer Credit Act, and joined with local advocates to oppose adoption of the code unless it was amended to be more favorable to consumers. Thereafter, the code was withdrawn and revised to reflect many improvements proposed by the center. At the same time, the National Consumer Act and the Model Consumer Credit Act have served as models for state law provisions in both so-called code states and non-code states.

Language and policies drafted by the NCLC have been adopted or have influenced consumer protection laws at both the state and federal levels. In addition to state credit codes, center work is reflected in laws and regulations on debt collection, prepaid service contracts, interest rate ceilings, credit insurance, warranties, and other matters. Similarly, national consumer protection laws have been influenced by the center. Many federal consumer protection statutes—including the Truth in Lending Act, the Fair Debt Collection Practices Act, and the Home Ownership and Equity Protection Act—reflect the testimony and draftsmanship of center staff. In addition, federal programs to help assure affordability of utility services, especially home heating, have been shaped by NCLC expertise.

Sometimes the rights of low-income consumers are the subject of government agency adjudication or rulemaking. Center staff have frequently testified before public utility commissions and worked with utility advocates to assure fair treatment for low-income households. The NCLC is especially well known for having created, fostered, and helped to implement "percentage of income plans" or PIPs, which seek to match the need for essential utility services with the ability of low-income households to pay. At the federal level, the center served as appointed public advocates for the Holder in Due Course and the Credit Practices Rules adopted by the Federal Trade Commission to require basic fairness in the consumer credit marketplace.

The NCLC also has undertaken litigation when important principles are at stake. Center attorneys have appeared and participated in groundbreaking cases before federal and state courts at all levels, including the U.S. Supreme Court. The cases have established constitutional due process rights of consumers, especially debtors; expanded standards of deception and unfairness; secured appropriate interpretations of consumer protection laws; caused hundreds of millions of dollars of illegal overcharges by oil companies to be set aside for the benefit of low-income households; and attacked illicit industry practices abusing low-income consumers. Frequently such litigation is handled in conjunction with local advocates.

In addition to advocacy, the NCLC undertakes research and public policy analyses addressing the circumstance of low-income households in the area of consumer and energy law. For example, the center has released a series of reports analyzing the adverse impacts of energy and utility costs on low-income households. Another report was the first to detail the impending crisis (and possible solutions) for low-income households caused by water and sewer bills rising as a result of clean water initiatives. Another study, on unfair home equity lending practices, led to federal reform legislation. Private entities also commission NCLC studies on particular industry practices, emerging consumer problems, or alternative public policy responses.

The center's twelve-volume Consumer Credit and Sales Legal Practice Series is a collection of practice manuals and treatises widely used by the legal profession. Each volume addresses a topic of consumer law, such as debt collection, credit reporting, unfair and deceptive acts and practices, utility customer service, bankruptcy, or sales of goods and services; is a guide to all major related state and federal statutes and judicial interpretations; and provides extensive analysis and legal practice resources. The center publishes two regular newsletters: *NCLC Reports* highlights new developments and consumer law trends; and *The Energy and Utility Update* reports on low-income energy policy developments. In addition, the NCLC has issued numerous monographs, books, and reports.

NCLC publications are primarily addressed to lawyers, advocates, and specialists, although many studies are of broader interest.

A few consumer education pieces are developed and distributed from time to time. The NCLC's *Surviving Debt: Counseling Consumers in Financial Distress* provides practical advice for consumers who find themselves overcome with debt. It is particularly appropriate for counselors, social workers, clergy, and organizers who work with financially distressed households.

The center also sponsors annual conferences in the area of consumer and energy law, and its staff participates regularly as presenters at conferences, training seminars, and continuing legal education sessions. Its first Consumer Law Specialist Training Conference was held in Kansas City, Missouri, in 1976. Today, its popular Consumer Rights Litigation Conference is held in a different city each year. Its first Annual Low Income Energy Conference was held in 1987 and is convened each year in Washington, D.C.

Once a year, the center awards the Vern Countryman Consumer Law Award to one of the nation's top consumer law attorneys. The award recognizes at least ten years of exceptional consumer law practice or an achievement that profoundly affects the rights of a large number of low-income consumers. The award was funded by friends of Professor Countryman, a founding trustee of the NCLC, upon his retirement from Harvard Law School.

— Willard P. Ogburn

See also

Credit Protections; Legal Aid; Low-Income Consumers.

Reading

Rothschild, Donald P., and David W. Carroll (1977). *Consumer Protection: Text and Materials.* 2d ed. Cincinnati: Anderson Publishing Co.

National Consumers League

The National Consumers League (NCL) is America's oldest national consumer organization. It was founded in 1899 by leaders of consumer leagues in New York City, Philadelphia, Boston, and Chicago who believed that consumers had the ability and responsibility to raise the living standards of the disadvantaged, especially women and child workers. NCL continues to be active today but focuses most of its attention not on worker issues, but on consumer issues such as telemarketing fraud. Headquartered in Washington, D.C., it has affiliated leagues in several states.

NCL is a nonprofit membership organization governed by an elected board of directors. Directors include citizens and representatives of corporations, trade associations, public interest organizations, and labor unions. They establish policies, approve the budget, and select a president who serves as the organization's chief executive officer. Resources include revenue from membership dues, conferences, grants, publication sales, and events.

1899–1932: The Kelley Years

Leaders of the four consumer leagues selected Florence Kelley, Illinois's chief factory inspector, as NCL's chief executive. Kelley, who had lived at Hull House in Chicago, moved to Henry Street Settlement in New York City and opened NCL's office in May 1899. Under Kelley's leadership, NCL researched industrial conditions and supported legislation to prohibit child labor, to limit working hours and night work, to abolish sweatshops, and to improve other working conditions.

NCL also campaigned to prevent the sale of impure milk and to pass state pure food laws. In 1905, it investigated conditions under which food products were prepared and the working conditions of employees who produced them. In 1906, it established a permanent food committee and played a major role in securing President Theodore Roosevelt's support for the Federal Food and Drug Act, which he signed into law in June 1906.

The league's plan of action was to investigate, educate, agitate, and legislate. It worked to secure child labor laws that would effectively safeguard working children in every state. It led the effort to create a federal Children's Bureau, which President William Howard Taft signed into law in April 1912.

NCL members in several states secured maximum labor hour laws. In 1908, Kelley asked Louis D. Brandeis of Boston to defend pro bono the constitutionality of Oregon's ten-hour workday for women before the U.S. Supreme Court. The league raised funds to print the brief and pay court expenses. The Supreme Court unanimously agreed that the law was constitutional. Before President Woodrow Wilson appointed him to the Supreme Court in 1916, Brandeis also orally defended nine women's labor laws or filed briefs prepared under his direction by his sister-in-law, Josephine Goldmark, the league's publications secretary from 1903 to 1917. In each instance, state or federal courts sustained the laws as constitutional.

After Brandeis joined the Supreme Court, Felix Frankfurter, who was then a Harvard Law School professor, continued NCL's legal work, also pro bono, working with Goldmark and later Mary Dewson, the league's research secretary. When Frankfurter also joined the Supreme Court, Dean Acheson, who after law school went to Washington to clerk for Brandeis, donated his time.

In 1924, at Kelley's invitation, Dr. Alice Hamilton, authority on industrial diseases and professor of industrial toxicology at Harvard's School of Public Health, agreed to consult with NCL's committee investigating dangers of fumes and dust to women and child workers, and to help draft model legislation to protect those workers. When the New Jersey Consumers League reported an alarming death rate of women engaged in painting luminous watch dials, with Dr. Hamilton's help, NCL and the New Jersey Consumers League helped the women's families sue U.S. Radium Corporation. Dr. Hamilton and Kelley then took their data to the federal government, urging the surgeon general and the U.S. Public Health Service to study industrial poisons and develop standards.

In 1928, the surgeon general called a conference of experts on radium, which prepared a report on the subject that helped persuade the U.S. Public Health Service to call for effective, continuous inspection of dial painting factories and to set standards for use of radioactive mixtures and for working conditions of those using such mixtures.

In 1920, NCL was a leader in establishing the Women's Bureau in the Labor Department. The league helped educate the public in support of national health insurance legislation, pioneered promotion of workers' compensation laws, supported compulsory state-administered employment insurance, supported federal infant and maternity programs, investigated migrant agricultural workers' living conditions, and helped organize the Southern Council for Legislation for Women and Children in Industry.

After the stock market crash of 1929, many of the state leagues reported that minimum wage, sweatshop, and child labor laws were being ignored. NCL called a conference in New York City, inviting labor department officials from eastern states. The group agreed that labor standards committees should be organized in as many states as possible and that model state minimum wage legislation should be drafted. A committee of Felix Frankfurter, Benjamin V. Cohen, Josephine Goldmark, and Mary Dewson drafted legislation basing wage rates on "reasonable value of services rendered" rather than "cost of living." New York was the first state to enact the law (1933).

1932–1976: The League in Transition

Kelley, who had guided NCL's activities for thirty-two years, died in February 1932. Directors named her son Nicholas, an economist, as board chairman. With the help of the league's president, University of Wisconsin economics professor John R. Commons, he selected Lucy Randolph Mason to run the organization. Mason had been serving NCL as its southern representative while on the staff of both the League of Women Voters and the

Young Women's Christian Association in Richmond, Virginia. Mason was an activist particularly concerned about low wages, poor working conditions, and racial discrimination in the South.

NCL board minutes of the time claimed about 2,500 members and twelve active branches. Before her death, Kelley had selected NCL representatives from some areas without state and local leagues. These representatives included Jeannette Rankin in the West, Caroline Ware in the District of Columbia, and Mason in the South.

In 1933, President Franklin D. Roosevelt urged governors of industrial states to enact minimum wage laws similar to those that NCL had drafted. Six states did. After the National Industrial Recovery Act (NRA) was adopted in 1933, the league focused its energies on improvement and enforcement of the laws.

Eleanor Roosevelt, along with other Junior League members, had joined NCL when she was a young girl. Her aunt, Mrs. Douglas Robinson, was an NCL vice president. Roosevelt was assigned to work at the Rivington Street settlement house, where she taught girls calisthenics and dancing. She also investigated sweatshops. Roosevelt later served as NCL vice president, an office she held while first lady and until her death in 1962.

Frances Perkins was vice president of the league until she assumed her official duties as secretary of labor and the first woman cabinet officer. Josephine Roche, another vice president, became assistant treasury secretary. Dewson, the league's research secretary, subsequently headed the Democratic Party's women's division and, in 1935, became a member of the Social Security Board. John G. Winant, NCL president, was named chairman of the Social Security Board in 1935.

During World War II, NCL lost membership and leadership. Its directors hired Elizabeth S. Magee, executive secretary of the Ohio Consumers League, to administer the league's affairs from her office in Cleveland. Under her leadership, NCL continued its support for social issues, but its identity as a national organization suffered.

After his election in 1948, President Harry Truman sought to amend the Fair Labor Standards Act to increase the minimum wage, to expand Social Security eligibility, and to increase benefits for retired workers. NCL worked for these liberalizing amendments, and their enactment helped the league celebrate its fiftieth birthday.

In 1958, NCL moved its headquarters to Washington, D.C. Under a succession of executive directors, it focused attention on migratory labor, licensing of private employment agencies, problems with consumer regulatory agencies, and protection of workers using radioactive materials.

1976–Present:
A National Consumer Leader

In 1976, NCL's board selected Sandra L. Willett, a Wellesley College graduate with a master's degree in public administration from Harvard, to head the organization. She moved the league into new consumer issues. The organization developed an Assertive Consumer Project, training leaders who in turn trained consumers in credit, warranty rights, and assertive behavior. To build consumer participation into government processes, the league contracted with the Consumer Product Safety Commission to involve industry, consumers, and technicians in standards setting. It also participated in Federal Trade Commission proceedings representing consumers on home insulation standards and certification. In 1979, along with two universities, NCL undertook improving consumer education materials.

From 1985 to the present, NCL has been led by Linda Golodner, who earlier had worked as a congressional staffer before running her own public affairs firm. In this period, NCL has participated in more than forty-six coalitions and advisory committees to provide consumer perspectives on issues ranging from clean air and water to health care reform. It has sponsored conferences, forums, workshops, and legislative briefings on consumer issues, including privacy, health care reform, medication safety, financial services, safe drinking water, and consumer fraud. It has published brochures, handbooks, and manuals on the environment, credit, fraud, insurance, health, and food and drug safety.

Many NCL publications are available in Spanish and other languages. It publishes four newsletters: *NCL Bulletin,* a bimonthly overview of consumer news; *Child Labor Monitor,* a quarterly for the Child Labor Coalition; *Community Health Link,* a quarterly for the Community-Based Health Care Project; and *Quarterly* for the Alliance Against Fraud in Telemarketing.

The National Fraud Information Center provides a data link for organizations and agencies fighting fraud. It includes an electronic message center, data exchange, and an information and referral service, available 24 hours a day. Complaints received at the center are linked directly with several federal regulatory and enforcement agencies and state attorneys general.

Since league founder Florence Kelley established the first state Child Labor Committee in 1902, protecting children from exploitative working conditions has been a top NCL priority. Today, the league co-chairs and administers the national Child Labor Coalition, a group of organizations dedicated to stopping the growing number of child labor violations and injuries worldwide. The coalition has developed a model state law that several states have incorporated into their state codes. NCL annually surveys state departments of labor about the status of children in the workplace, including information regarding safety issues and compliance efforts. Recently, it has agitated for improvement in Asian and Latin American sweatshops that employ children to produce products sold in U.S. markets.

In 1996, in anticipation of its hundredth birthday, the league organized a series of annual conferences held outside of Washington, D.C. The forums, each of which focused on a different product area, provided the league an opportunity to gather information to help the organization set priorities for its second century.

— Erma B. Angevine

See also

Consumer Leagues; Labor Movement.

Readings

Keyserling, Mary Dublin (1982). "The First National Consumers Organization: The National Consumers League." In Erma Angevine, ed. *Consumer Activists: They Made a Difference.* Mount Vernon, NY: Consumers Union Foundation. 343–360.

National Consumers League. *National Consumers League Bulletin* (bimonthly). Washington, DC.

National Cooperative Bank

The National Consumer Cooperative Bank was chartered by an act of Congress in 1978 as a mixed-ownership government corporation. It was created to close the gaps that existed in financing for cooperatives nationwide. The legislation evolved after a four-year effort by a broad coalition of supporters coordinated by the Cooperative League of the USA (now the National Cooperative Business Association). Since 1983, the bank has been doing business as the National Cooperative Bank (NCB). NCB began lending operations on March 21, 1980.

Initial funding was provided through purchase of the bank's Class A stock by the U.S. Treasury. In addition, capital was to be created by the sale of Class B stock to borrowers as a part of their loan package. The Bank Act provided for redemption of Treasury stock over a thirty-year period beginning in 1990.

In 1981, amendments to the Bank Act were approved to privatize the bank. The $184 million of stock owned by the U.S. government was converted to Class A notes to be repaid by the year 2020, and control was transferred to cooperative stockholders effective December 31, 1981. Borrower/stockholders elect twelve of the fifteen-member board of directors. Directors may be selected from among housing, consumer goods, consumer service, low-income, and other categories of eligible cooperatives, but no more than three directors may serve from any one category. The president of the United States can name three board members to represent, respectively, small business, government, and low-income cooperatives.

The bank is examined annually by the Farm Credit Administration, and the General Accounting Office is authorized to audit the bank. Reports of such examinations and audits are forwarded to Congress, which has the sole authority to amend or revoke the bank's charter.

NCB is headquartered in Washington, D.C., with offices in New York, Minneapolis, and San Francisco and satellite offices in Atlanta and Anchorage, Alaska. It is chartered to operate in all states, U.S. Territories, and the Commonwealth of Puerto Rico.

The board of directors establishes the business services and policies governing NCB's lending operations in compliance with the Bank Act. The policies adopted by the board are carried out by management. Management in turn adopts and implements guidelines and procedures consistent with stated board directives. Lending policies and guidelines are reviewed regularly by the board and management to make needed changes and amendments.

As a $535 million, cooperatively owned financial institution, NCB is the leading source of credit for the nation's consumer, worker, housing, and retailer-owned cooperatives as well as for other organizations operating on a cooperative basis. NCB operates as a cooperative and returns its earnings to its customers in relation to the amount of business they do with the bank.

Cooperatives and legally chartered entities that are primarily owned and controlled by their member users are eligible to utilize NCB services. They must be operated on a cooperative basis and be engaged in producing or furnishing goods, services, or facilities primarily for the benefit of their members or voting stockholders who are the ultimate users of those services.

NCB provides a full line of commercial lending, mortgage banking, development, member finance, depository, and investment banking services to customers in a broad range of cooperative-related industries including housing, consumer goods, natural foods, hardware and building supply, food, health care, retirement housing, employee ownership, credit and finance, telecommunications, child care, franchising, and manufacturing.

The Bank Act limits the amount of NCB's funds that can be held in residential real estate loans to 30 percent of total assets. As a result, NCB originates most of its high-quality affordable or market rate cooperative mortgage loans for sale into the secondary mortgage markets through its wholly owned subsidiary, NCB Mortgage Corporation. NCB also provides share loans to individual members of housing cooperatives.

NCB's major funding resources are its own member equity equal to 20 percent of assets, long-term government debt, borrowings from commercial banks, and member deposits in the NCB Savings Bank. NCB interest rates approximate market rates charged by other lending institutions for comparable types of financing. Loans are generally secured by specific collateral sufficient to protect NCB from loss.

NCB undertakes to fulfill its mission and statutory obligations by providing financing opportunities to cooperatives through several subsidiaries including NCB Savings Bank and two SEC-registered entities—Cooperative Funding Corporation, providing corporate financial services for eligible customers of NCB, and NCB Investment Advisers, supplying investment advisory services to cooperatives and related organizations.

The NCB Development Corporation (NCBDC) is the development finance affiliate of NCB. It is chartered under Title II of the Bank Act and was organized in 1982 as a 501(c)(3) nonprofit corporation. Six of its nine directors are directors of NCB. The NCBDC provides risk capital and other types of financing to start-up and newly established cooperatives. It works with developers, intermediary organizations, community development corporations, and others to finance existing cooperative businesses, as well as to develop new applications of cooperatives. Over 65 percent of its financing is devoted to organizations serving low-income persons. It is the only development bank dedicated to the creation and support of cooperative enterprises nationwide. With assets of $63 million, NCBDC's core lines of business include affordable housing, community health care, employee ownership, consumer-owned natural food cooperatives, and community economic development corporations.

Under the Bank Act, the board of directors must use its best effort to insure that at least 35 percent of its outstanding loans are to cooperatives whose members are predominantly low-income persons or to cooperatives that provide specialized goods, services, or facilities to serve the needs of predominantly low-income persons. NCB defines a "low-income person" as an individual whose family income does not exceed 80 percent of the median family income, adjusted for family size for the area where the cooperative is located.

— Stanley W. Dreyer

See also

Cooperatives, Consumer; Housing Cooperatives; National Cooperative Business Association.

Readings

Crock, Stan (1986). "The Bank Reagan 'Killed' Is Alive and Well." *Business Week.* (April 14): 83.

Nadeau, E. G., and David J. Thompson (1996). *Cooperation Works: How People Are Using Cooperative Action To Rebuild Communities and Revitalize the Economy.* Rochester, MN: Lone Oak Press.

Richter, Jay (1985). *Where Credit Was Due: The Creation of the National Consumer Cooperative Bank.* Washington, DC: Cooperative League Fund.

National Cooperative Business Association

The National Cooperative Business Association (NCBA) is a national cross-industry membership association that represents cooperatives—47,000 nonprofit businesses with more than 100 million members. These co-ops, which range in size from small buying clubs to Fortune 500 businesses, provide services such as housing, health care, insurance, child care, food, utilities, and financial services.

NCBA represents cooperatives before Congress and federal agencies. It also supports cooperatives in the United States and overseas through training, technical assistance, publications, and other programs. This work reflects NCBA's mission "to develop, advance, and protect cooperative enterprise."

The oldest national cooperative organization, NCBA was founded in 1916 as the Cooperative League of America. In 1922, the name was changed to the Cooperative League of the USA (CLUSA). The organization began doing business as the National Cooperative Business Association in 1985. Originally formed to promote and support consumer cooperatives, NCBA has expanded its membership to include all types of cooperatives as well as individuals and other businesses interested in cooperative enterprise.

The organization's founder and first president was James Peter Warbasse, who had been a surgeon in New York City and was author of a standard text in that field. Eugene Bowen served as executive secretary of the league from 1934 to 1946. His major contribution was to expand the league's membership to a broad array of producer and consumer cooperatives providing farm supply, insurance, health care, housing, credit, and electricity services.

In 1941, Murray Lincoln was elected league president, a position he held until 1965. Lincoln had worked as the executive secretary of the Ohio Farm Bureau Federation, where he was instrumental in the formation of Nationwide Insurance Company. At the league, he stimulated innovative thinking about the provision and expansion of cooperative services. Former California Congressman Jerry Voorhis became executive director in 1947 and held that position until 1965. Through writing and public speaking, Voorhis sought to educate America about the great potentials of cooperation. Under his leadership, the league sponsored numerous cooperative organizations such as the National Association of Housing Cooperatives and the Continental Association of Funeral and Memorial Societies.

NCBA has spearheaded many cooperative development efforts. At the end of World War II, the organization was one of the founders of the Cooperative for American Remittances to Europe, or CARE as it is more commonly known. Since the early 1950s, NCBA has been active in cooperative development overseas, working with organizations such as the U.S. Agency for International Development and the Peace Corps.

In 1978, NCBA's efforts were instrumental in the establishment of the National Cooperative Bank (NCB). A leader in the campaign to establish this bank was Stan Dreyer, who served as NCBA president from 1967 to 1978. After leaving NCBA, he served as a vice president of the newly formed NCB. Glenn Anderson, who succeeded Dreyer as NCBA president, also played a significant role in the launching of the consumer bank.

After Anderson's death, E. Morgan Williams was appointed president, serving from 1980 to 1986. He was succeeded by Robert Scherer, who had worked for many years with cooperatives in Ohio. During his administration, from 1987 to 1993, NCBA supported the merger of the agricultural banks for cooperatives, which resulted in the creation of CoBank.

The current NCBA president is Russell Notar, who assumed the position in 1993. He presided over the planning of the cooperative community's 150th anniversary, which included a Cooperative Economic Summit in Washington, D.C., and the completion of the documentary *The Spirit of Cooperation*, which was shown on more than 130 public television stations.

In January 1996, NCBA established the CLUSA Institute for Cooperative Development. The institute uses NCBA's knowledge of international cooperative development to promote cooperative solutions to economic and social problems.

Another NCBA role is to provide information about cooperatives to consumers, the media, and policymakers. To help people find information, NCBA provides an 800 number and a Web site. In 1995, more than 4,000 people asked for information about cooperatives. NCBA also has available general brochures, books, and videos.

As a membership organization, NCBA holds an annual meeting at which members elect representatives to the board of directors and adopt the Statement of Policy. The organization is funded by membership dues and fees for services as well as by grants and contracts from organizations such as the U.S. Agency for International Development. Just over thirty employees work in the organization's Washington, D.C., headquarters, while several contract employees work on cooperative development projects in more than a dozen countries.

Through the years, NCBA has worked closely with like-minded organizations to further cooperative enterprise. NCBA's support has been important for the establishment of many organizations, including the Consumer Federation of America, the Cooperative Development Foundation, the Cooperative Communicators Association, the North American Students of Cooperation, the National Association of Housing Cooperatives, the Continental Association of Funeral and Memorial Societies, and Cooperative Business International. In this way, NCBA's impact has spread far beyond the organization itself.

— Leta M. Mach

See also

Cooperatives, Consumer; National Cooperative Bank.

Readings

Knapp, Joseph G. (1973). *The Advance of American Cooperative Enterprise: 1920–1945.*

Danville, IL: The Interstate Printers and Publishers, Inc.

Kress, Andrew J. (1941). *Introduction to the Co-operative Movement*. New York: Harper & Brothers.

Voorhis, Jerry (1961). *American Cooperatives*. New York: Harper & Brothers.

National Foundation for Consumer Credit

The National Foundation for Consumer Credit (NFCC) is the umbrella organization for the nation's largest network of nonprofit consumer credit counseling agencies. Located in Silver Spring, Maryland, the NFCC promotes public awareness and access to credit counseling for consumers in financial trouble. It also sets and maintains standards for the quality of service delivered by member agencies. The foundation's stated mission is to "build and maintain a nonprofit, nationwide, integrated program that educates all segments of American society in the wise use of consumer credit and provides an impartial forum for managing and resolving debt problems."

The NFCC was formed in 1951 to promote the responsible use of consumer credit and educate a post-war public largely unfamiliar with the concept of using loans to finance the purchase of durable goods. An early project sponsored the creation of a secondary school textbook on the use of credit. As credit usage increased over the next decade, so did the number of consumers who fell behind in their loan payments. By the early 1960s, the foundation began supporting the development of credit counseling agencies to assist financially troubled consumers in major cities nationwide. These experiments demonstrated the value of a network of offices that could provide budgeting advice and assist consumers in setting up debt repayment plans with creditors. Major reorganization of the foundation in the late 1960s created a broad-based board of trustees bringing together representatives from major national creditors, labor groups, and social service agencies. Out of this partnership evolved today's network of credit counseling offices.

Market forces have driven a rapid expansion of the NFCC member network since 1985. As recently as 1984, 265 NFCC member agencies served consumer clients throughout the United States. However, the use of consumer credit exploded during the 1980s, and the annual volume of personal bankruptcies tripled from 280,000 in 1984 to more than one million in 1996. Both consumers and credit grantors sought an alternative to bankruptcy for handling overindebtedness. Many consumers wished to avoid the social and economic stigma associated with filing for bankruptcy and had sufficient income to repay their debts over a two- to four-year period. Creditors recognized that their collection efforts often drove desperate consumers to the bankruptcy court, where creditor recoveries of outstanding balances were minimal. Credit counseling agencies were uniquely situated to offer both parties an alternative to bankruptcy by brokering an agreement between a consumer client and creditor grantors to set up a voluntary, extended repayment plan. By the end of 1994 over 1,000 NFCC member offices served consumers nationwide.

NFCC member agencies offer a mix of educational programs, budget counseling, and formal debt management plans. According to NFCC data, member agencies conducted individual budget counseling sessions with 710,000 consumers during 1994. On average, about 35 percent of clients discovered that, with the budget instruction provided by the counselor, they could handle their debts on their own. Another 35 percent were referred elsewhere for legal or other assistance. About 30 percent of all clients were placed in debt management plans.

In setting up a debt management plan, the counseling agency works for the consumer to negotiate lower monthly payments as well as waivers or reductions in finance charges. The objective is to structure a repayment plan out of the client's available monthly income that repays all creditors within three to four years.

The average debt plan negotiated during 1994 involved nine creditors and $12,522 of debt to be repaid. The plan is strictly voluntary between the consumer and creditors: not all creditors need participate (though the successful negotiation of a plan hinges on convincing as many to participate as possible), and the consumer can back out at any time. Participating creditors agree to suspend collection efforts as long as plan payments continue. Nationwide, these debt plans facilitated the return of $1.3 billion to creditors during 1994.

In addition to providing budget counseling and setting up debt management plans, NFCC member agencies develop credit education materials and make presentations in their respective communities as a public service. According to NFCC data, member agencies conducted over 38,000 educational seminars that reached 3.5 million people during 1994. In recent years, many agencies have begun housing prepurchase counseling (9,400 sessions in 1994) as well as home-buying seminars (1,600 seminars with 47,000 attendees in 1994).

All NFCC members are nonprofit, community-based organizations with local boards of directors. As a condition of membership in the NFCC, each agency agrees to quality standards, set by the NFCC, that include accreditation, certification of counselors, audits, and core policies that ensure the delivery of quality service. On average, member agencies derive about 75 percent of their income from "fair share" contributions from creditors participating in debt management plans. Such contributions are typically calculated as a percentage (normally 10 to 15 percent) of the dollars paid to creditors through debt plans. Another 18 percent of agency income derives from client fees. In 1994, consumers paid, on average, $17.65 for the initial counseling session, and $11.81 per month if set up on a debt management plan. The remaining 7 to 8 percent of agency income derives from local charities, United Way, and miscellaneous contributions. It is important to note that creditor fair share contributions are indeed voluntary: by NFCC policy, agencies cannot refuse to deal with creditors who fail to make a fair share contribution. For their part, creditors recognize the value of collectively supporting credit counseling. The revenues that creditors provide agencies, based on the 30 percent of counseled consumers who enter into debt plans, pay for the large majority of the counseling operations and educational efforts.

The NFCC itself is governed by a board of trustees representing a broad spectrum of parties interested in the organization's mission. NFCC board members include executives and/or directors from member counseling agencies, as well as representatives from firms in the credit granting industry, consumer groups, and academic institutions. No more than 40 percent of all trustees may be affiliated with creditors and debt collectors. Trustees serve renewable, two-year terms. Trustees are elected by the membership at the annual meeting. Approximately 60 percent of NFCC revenues comes from member dues. An additional 25 percent represents grants and other contributions from charitable foundations, government agencies, and other sources.

— Michael E. Staten

See also

Bankruptcy.

Readings

Davis, Kristin (1994). "Credit Counseling Services: Debtors Find Relief." *Kiplinger's Personal Finance Magazine.* 48 (December): 36–37.

DiGiulio, Joan Ferry, and Gerald J. Janosik (1982). "Successful Partners: Credit Counseling and Family Services." *Social Casework.* 63 (October): 482–488.

National Highway Traffic Safety Administration

The National Highway Traffic Safety Administration (NHTSA), which is one of ten agencies constituting the U.S. Department of Transportation, is responsible for regulating the automobile manufacturing industry in three major areas: safety, damageability, and fuel economy. The NHTSA determines minimum safety standards that must be met by every manufacturer, foreign and domestic, selling cars and other related products in the United States, including tires, child safety seats, and motorcycle helmets. Additionally, the agency administers a grant program for the states to conduct various traffic safety programs, such as anti–drunk driving, safety belt use, speed control, motorcycle safety, and emergency medical services.

Origins

Automobile safety regulation and reform resulted from the American public's realization that cars were responsible for many injuries and fatalities. Beginning in the early 1950s, traffic fatalities across the country grew rapidly, from 35,586 in 1954 to 49,000 in 1965. Representative Kenneth A. Roberts (D-AL) was one of the first U.S. legislators concerned about auto safety. During his years of congressional service from 1954 to 1964, Roberts held a number of hearings on vehicle safety, including safety belts. His most significant legislative accomplishment in this area was the enactment of a bill in 1964 that required the General Services Administration, the procurement agency of the federal government, to set safety standards for new motor vehicles purchased by the federal government.

In the mid-1960s, the continued increase in the number of fatalities and injuries, Ralph Nader's exposé of the safety deficiencies of automobiles, and the efforts of General Motors to discredit Nader persuaded Congress to enact legislation that created a strong federal role in regulating automobile safety.

In 1965, Ralph Nader's *Unsafe at Any Speed*, a critical analysis of the safety defects of the Chevrolet Corvair, a popular car manufactured by General Motors, was published and immediately caught the attention of the press as well as such members of Congress as Senator Abraham Ribicoff (D-CT). That year, in his capacity as chairman of a Government Operations subcommittee, Ribicoff aggressively pursued the issue by scheduling hearings. Two revelations during these hearings aroused media and public interest. Senator Robert Kennedy (D-NY) disclosed that General Motors, with yearly profits in excess of $1.7 billion, spent only $1.5 million a year on safety research. Then it was revealed that this company had attempted to discredit Nader by using a private detective to investigate his private life. A public apology by a General Motors executive before a Senate hearing galvanized congressional support for motor vehicle safety legislation.

Since Ribicoff's subcommittee did not have jurisdiction over the legislation, it became the responsibility of Senator Warren Magnuson (D-WA), the powerful chairman of the Senate Commerce Committee. By the summer of 1966, legislation regulating the auto industry had been drafted, debated, and decided by both the Senate and the House. The National Traffic and Motor Vehicle Safety Act of 1966 and the Highway Safety Act of 1966 were both passed and signed into law by President Lyndon Johnson on September 9, 1966.

The National Traffic and Motor Vehicle Safety Act of 1966 empowered the National Highway Safety Bureau in the Department of Commerce to establish "reasonable, practicable, and appropriate" crashworthiness standards for automobiles and to create a system for reporting safety defects. The Highway Safety Act of 1966, a companion bill, provided grants for states to operate highway safety programs to improve highway safety designs and to address driver behavior issues. Both laws were administered by a new federal agency created within the Department of Commerce, the National Highway Safety Bureau. This arrangement only lasted, though, until Congress passed legislation to create a federal Department of Transportation. In 1967, the automobile safety functions were transferred to the National Highway Safety Bureau located within the Federal Highway Administration, the agency responsible for building highways within the Department of Transportation. In March 1970, motor vehicle and traffic safety functions were established in a separate agency within the U.S. Department of Transportation—the National Highway Traffic Safety Administration.

Since 1966, Congress has enacted other laws giving NHTSA additional regulatory responsibilities to improve the safety and fuel efficiency of motor vehicles as well as to encourage the creation of traffic safety programs to reduce impaired driving, increase occupant protection, and control excessive speed. These statutes include the 1972 Motor Vehicle Information and Cost Savings Act, which provides for the establishment of low-speed collision bumper standards, consumer information activities, and odometer regulations; 1975 amendments establishing the secretary of transportation's responsibility for issuing automotive fuel economy standards; and a 1975 law requiring states to establish and enforce a fifty-five miles per hour national speed limit (repealed in November 1995). Another statute, adopted in 1982, authorized grants to states that strengthened state alcohol safety programs and expanded the National Driver Register, which assists states in electronically exchanging information about the driving records of certain problem drivers. Still another law, enacted in 1984, established the National Minimum Drinking Age Law and imposed a sanction for states that did not have a law establishing a twenty-one-year-old minimum drinking age. In late 1995, Congress amended the National Minimum Drinking Age Law to require states also to enact a zero-tolerance blood alcohol content (BAC) for drivers under the age of twenty-one by October 1, 1998, or have a portion of their federal highway funds withheld. A 1992 law authorized NHTSA to issue regulations for reducing motor vehicle thefts. The Intermodal Surface Transportation Efficiency Act of 1991 created a new program authorizing incentive grants to states that enacted both safety belt and all-rider motorcycle helmet laws. States without both laws by October 1, 1994, would have a portion of their federal highway construction dollars redirected to highway safety programs. The National Highway System Designation Act, enacted in 1995, repealed the motorcycle helmet law requirement.

Funding and Structure

Motor vehicle crashes account for more than 90 percent of all transportation fatalities, yet the agency's budget accounts for only 1 percent of the Department of Transportation's budget. NHTSA's annual budget is approximately $275 million: about half of these funds support the agency's operations and research programs, and the remaining half are distributed to states as safety grants. These grants support state and community efforts to create and implement innovative highway safety programs. Funds supporting the research and operations functions of the agency come from general revenues, which are appropriated each year in the transportation spending bill approved by Congress. Traffic safety programs for states are funded from federal gas tax revenues in the Highway Trust Fund. Each year, Congress decides how much money will be spent from the Highway Trust Fund on these traffic safety activities. Funds are distributed to the states based on a legislatively determined formula at the beginning of each federal fiscal year.

NHTSA is directed by an administrator who is appointed by the president and subject to Senate confirmation. The deputy administrator of the agency is also an appointee of the president but does not require Senate approval. Reporting to the administrator are seven associate administrators who are career government employees. The associate administrators have responsibility for directing divisions of the agency responsible for rulemaking; traffic safety programs (occupant protection, alcohol, and emergency services); enforcement (defects investigations and vehicle safety compliance); research (crashworthiness and crash avoidance); policy (strategic planning, regulatory analysis, and budget);

and administration and regional operations. NHTSA has slightly more than 600 employees.

Agency Safety Initiatives

While Ralph Nader helped focus public debate on crash safety, much of the credit for developing the conceptual analysis of motor vehicle crashes must go to William Haddon, Jr., a medical doctor who was appointed the first administrator of NHTSA, and Robert Brenner, an engineer who served as his deputy. Under Haddon and Brenner, NHTSA shifted the emphasis of government traffic safety programs from accident prevention to injury prevention. One of NHTSA's first actions (in January 1967) was the issuance of thirty motor vehicle safety standards, including the mandatory installation of lap-shoulder belts by January 1, 1968. In issuing safety standards, NHTSA began its role as the pacesetter in technological innovations that would prevent death and injury on the road.

In 1971, NHTSA issued one of the most important standards requiring automatic crash protection. An upgrading of the original static safety belt standard, it required motor vehicles to be equipped with devices such as airbags or automatic belts to protect occupants in a thirty-miles-per-hour crash. In response, auto manufacturers resorted to administrative, legal, and legislative maneuvers to delay implementation of this standard.

After the standard was first issued, Henry Ford II and Lee Iaccoca, CEO of Chrysler, met with President Nixon and convinced him to delay the standard's effective date. Ford offered an alternative proposal, the "interlock" system, which required belts to be buckled before a car would start. While this measure increased safety belt usage, it failed because of intense public opposition that persuaded Congress to rescind the requirement in 1974.

On the recommendation of the newly appointed NHTSA administrator, Joan Claybrook, the standard was reissued in 1977 by Secretary of Transportation Brock Adams. It required the phased-in installation of either airbags or automatic seat belts over three years: model year 1982 for large cars, 1983 for midsized cars, and 1984 for small cars. The controversial decision withstood intense auto industry lobbying in support of a congressional veto resolution sponsored by Representatives Bud Shuster (R-PA) and John Dingell (D-MI). However, it did not survive the antiregulation emphasis of the Reagan administration, which withdrew the standard in 1981. State Farm Insurance challenged the withdrawal of the standard. The insurer succeeded when, in 1983, the U.S. Supreme Court overturned the administration's decision.

In July 1984, the U.S. Department of Transportation issued a new version of the automatic occupant restraint standard. It included a contingency that the new standard would be revoked if two-thirds of the population were covered by state seat belt use laws by April 1989. Mainly as a result of a major auto industry legislative campaign, many states enacted safety belt laws, though several populous states included provisions that did not allow the federal government to count them toward the recision of the standard. In any event, the car makers did not reach the two-thirds goal. Nevertheless, their campaign did play an important role in informing the public of the risks of driving and the need for safety measures.

Uncertain about the outcome of the safety belt issue, auto manufacturers began preparing for the eventual installation of airbags. In 1989, Iacocca announced that Chrysler would make airbags standard equipment for drivers of all models. Soon after, other manufacturers followed suit.

The standard was changed again in 1991 by Congress. Long frustrated about the delays in making airbag technology widely available to the public in all front seating positions, Congress passed legislation requiring that the front seat of all passenger vehicles, including light trucks and vans, be equipped with airbags beginning in model year 1998.

Agency Conservation Measures

In response to the 1973 oil crisis, Congress enacted the Energy Policy and Conservation Act of 1975. This law required passenger car manufacturers to achieve fleet-average fuel economy of 27.5 miles per gallon by the 1985 model year. As a result of this law as well as consumer demand, auto manufacturers succeeded in nearly doubling average fuel economy between the mid-1970s and 1984. Since then, this fuel economy has changed little.

Despite U.S. dependency on oil imports, there have been no additional advances in fuel efficiency in the auto fleet either on a voluntary basis by the auto industry or because of federal regulatory actions. All three of the major domestic auto companies resist efforts to improve fuel efficiency and have spent millions of dollars opposing federal legislative initiatives to make modest improvements in fuel economy. The insurance industry also opposes additional improvements because of concerns that the auto industry will achieve increased fuel efficiency by making cars smaller. Consumer and environmental advocates argue that existing technologies could improve both the fuel efficiency and the crashworthiness of vehicles. Some of these technologies have already been incorporated into research vehicles built and tested by the federal government. Yet, in the absence of an oil crisis that raises public concern, neither regulatory nor legislative action is expected.

In 1996 and 1997, however, controversy raged as the press reported the deaths of children and others from inflating airbags. In response, NHTSA considered short-term measures, which included allowing airbags to be switched off. In the long-term, though, technological improvements should greatly reduce the risks of using these protective devices.

— Jacqueline S. Gillan

See also

Center for Auto Safety; Energy Conservation; Highway Safety.

Readings

Mashaw, Jerry L., and David L. Harfst (1990). *The Struggle for Auto Safety*. Cambridge, MA: Harvard University Press.

Stone, Judith Lee (1995). "Automobile Safety Regulation." In Kenneth J. Meier and E. Thomas Garman, eds. *Regulation and Consumer Protection*. Houston: DAME Publications, Inc. 295–314.

National Insurance Consumer Organization

The National Insurance Consumer Organization (NICO) was established in 1980 by J. Robert Hunter and Ralph Nader. For fifteen years, it was the leading consumer group in the nation on issues pertaining to insurance. It advocated reforms before federal and state governments and sought to educate consumers about these reforms and about sensible purchase practices. In 1995, the organization was folded into the Consumer Federation of America (CFA) as its "Insurance Group."

Hunter and Nader established NICO because insurance is the fourth leading purchase that Americans make, but there was no organization in the country that was speaking out on behalf of consumers on insurance matters. In 1945, by passing the McCarran-Ferguson Act, Congress largely exempted the insurance industry from the application of the nation's antitrust laws, allowing insurers to collude with each other on pricing and other decisions exempted from federal review. Also in that year, it delegated authority to regulate insurance to the states but set no standards for the state's regulatory efforts nor routine oversight of these efforts by the federal government.

For several decades, the large majority of insurance commissions failed to protect insurance consumers adequately. One reason for this neglect was the close ties of most insurance commissioners to the industry: studies by the U.S. General Accounting Office and others revealed that about one-half of state commissioners came from the industry and that about one-half returned to the industry.

Hunter had been the Federal Insurance Administrator under Presidents Gerald Ford and Jimmy Carter. He wrote a paper outlining the need for an organization to redress the imbalance in power between the insurance industry and the consumer. Nader read the paper and suggested that Hunter undertake such an effort. He agreed to do so and established NICO with the assistance of funding contributed by Nader.

NICO's first board was made up of Hunter; Howard Clark, a former South Carolina insurance commissioner; and James Hunt, a former Vermont commissioner of banking and insurance. Hunter was a casualty actuary, Hunt a life actuary, and Clark an insurance lawyer. Between them, they had more than seventy-five years of insurance experience.

The first study published by NICO was a 1980 report on the then-prevalent practice of rates being set by insurance companies without giving consideration to their investment income, the time value of the money consumers paid in premiums in advance of claims being paid out. Using auto insurance as an example, NICO showed that rates could be reduced by about $5 billion if this factor was reflected. The NICO report led to a multiyear study of the issue by the National Association of Insurance Commissioners (NAIC) and, in 1984, eventual adoption by the NAIC of the methods proposed by NICO. Texas was the first state to adopt these methods. Afterwards, Texas rates fell by the NICO prediction of one-quarter of $1 billion.

NICO also campaigned for the creation of independent public advocates dealing with insurance in each state. It pointed out that the commissioner has a conflict when an insurer comes before him or her with a proposal. If the commissioner acts like a judge, only one side—the insurer's—is heard. If the commissioner acts like a consumer advocate in the proceeding, then the fairness of the commissioner's decision is in question. As a result of NICO's efforts, states such as Texas and Oregon have established consumer advocates.

During NICO's life as a separate entity, it led a campaign to repeal the federal antitrust exemption conferred by the McCarran-Ferguson Act. Under this exemption, states can choose to "deregulate" while collusive activities continue. Without the exemption, states who chose to deregulate would be able to do so and be certain to have the competing insurers operating at arm's length; states who chose to regulate would have to meet a tougher "state action" level of regulation. While the House Judiciary Committee has approved related legislation, this reform has not been approved by either house of Congress.

In addition to these and other advocacy efforts, NICO undertook efforts to educate consumers. It published information for buyers of different insurance products and obtained wide dissemination of this information both through direct order and, even more significantly, through the media. In the process, NICO—especially Hunt on life insurance issues and Hunter on all other insurance issues—became the leading consumer spokespersons to the media on consumer insurance matters. NICO also published a newsletter every other month for members. About 5,000 persons joined NICO while it had memberships available. When the organization merged with CFA, memberships ceased.

NICO also undertook to help establish other consumer groups and assist existing groups to advocate the consumer interest on insurance issues. On the national and state level, NICO worked with major consumer organizations, who considered Hunter especially as the leading consumer expert on insurance issues and related regulatory matters. The involvement of NICO with several groups in California led to the state legislature's assigning a study on insurance problems faced by consumers there. Although the legislature failed to act on the study's recommendations, their refusal triggered the organization of separate ballot initiatives by two groups. In 1988, California voters passed one of these initiatives—Proposition 103. NICO's general counsel, Jay Angoff, now insurance commissioner of Missouri, was a key campaigner for the reform.

The passage of Proposition 103 and related insurance reforms introduced in the following year in more than forty states put the insurance industry on notice that they were now receiving much closer public scrutiny. Before this passage, most of the industry just passed costs to policyholders, earning larger profits in the process. After passage, the insurance industry reached out to NICO and to other consumer groups to try to address mutual concerns. The National Association of Professional Insurance Agents, for example, persuaded Esther Peterson, NICO, CFA, and Public Citizen to work with them to study the quality and resources of state regulation to try to upgrade the quality of such regulation. Research by this Consumer Insurance Interest Group (CIIG) convinced many that state insurance departments needed additional resources and greater autonomy.

In this period, NICO and CFA began to work together closely. They prepared studies of auto insurance and credit life insurance. The latter research, which documented what was called the "worst consumer insurance rip-off" in the country, led to reform of credit insurance pricing in about twenty states.

In 1993, Hunter left NICO to become Texas insurance commissioner and was replaced as president by Kathleen O'Reilly, who earlier had served as CFA executive director, then as head of Wisconsin's Citizen Utility Board (CUB). During her tenure, the organization began to offer Hunt's service to evaluate the cash-value insurance policies held by individuals.

In 1995, when Hunter returned from Texas, the NICO board and that of CFA decided to merge NICO into the federation as its "Insurance Group." Hunter began serving CFA as its director of insurance, Hunt as life insurance actuary, and O'Reilly as insurance counsel. As NICO did in the past, the new Insurance Group serves as the nation's leading consumer insurance advocate.

— J. Robert Hunter

See also

Insurance Regulation.

Readings

Geisel, Jerry (1986). "Industry 'Gadfly' Draws Praise, Scorn." *Business Insurance.* 20 (February 17): 1ff.

Milligan, John W. (1987). "Insurance: The Holy War of J. Robert Hunter." *Institutional Investor.* 21 (October): 291–294.

Natural Gas Regulation

From the late 1930s until the early 1970s, the natural gas industry in the United States was a closely regulated, consumer-protected industry. Sparked by the oil price shocks of 1973 to 1974 and 1979 to 1980, however, the industry was transformed: first, by the deregulation of wellhead pricing; next, by the unbundling of pipeline transportation and marketing functions; and finally, by the repackaging of gas commodities with marketing and financial services.

Federal regulation began when Congress passed the Natural Gas Act of 1938, requiring the Federal Power Commission (later the Federal Energy Regulatory Commission [FERC]) to establish a "just and reasonable" price for pipeline transport in interstate commerce. This consumer standard was extended to interstate wellhead prices in the 1954 *Phillips v. Wisconsin* decision of the U.S. Supreme Court.

The act structured gas supply so as to stabilize the relationships among producers, pipelines, and consumers. The reserves of each natural gas field were dedicated under long-term contract to a given pipeline and specific end-users. Pipelines could not be abandoned nor contracts be renegotiated without regulatory approval. Pipelines took ownership of the gas as merchant carriers and were required to provide a secure, bundled package of services to consumers: gas acquisition, storage, and transport.

For years, this regulated interstate gas market coexisted with unregulated intrastate markets in producer states, with little divergence between the regulated and the free market price. However, by 1975, as the price of oil exploded in the wake of the Arab oil embargo, prices for gas in intrastate markets rose to nearly two-and-one-half times the prices in interstate markets. This disparity, in the severe winter of 1977, seriously disrupted supply in consumer states—while bumper stickers in producer states threatened, "Let Them Freeze in the Dark."

In the Natural Gas Policy Act of 1978 (NGPA), the price gap was addressed as a case of "underpricing" in the interstate market. Congress imposed phased deregulation in interstate markets for the period 1978 to 1984, with a mix of pricing incentives and fuel use guidelines. After 1984, when phased deregulation would presumably have brought most production to market clearing levels, the "just and reasonable" price of new gas was abandoned, and the price was released to market determination. However, "old gas" (gas then flowing) remained subject to a consumer "cost of production" standard.

Most consumer groups opposed the NGPA and contested its assumption that natural gas was underpriced. Between 1973 and 1977, the average delivered price to residential consumers had risen by 82 percent (in constant dollars, 36 percent, or 8 percent per year). Anticipating further price escalation, the Consumer Federation of America (CFA) and Energy Action argued that deregulation would transfer tens of billions of dollars from consumers to oil companies. But neither consumers nor Congress predicted the extent of energy inflation, and its redistribution of benefits and burdens, that was set off by the 1979 Iranian disruption of oil supply and the Carter administration's phased decontrol of oil.

In the renewed crisis atmosphere of 1979 to 1980, compromises embodied in the NGPA were challenged by many. Less than 24 months after passage, powerful producer and industrial groups began pushing the White House, Congress, and the FERC to deregulate both old and new gas quickly and totally. National and state consumer groups and their congressional allies sought to block attempts to deregulate old gas. The Consumer Energy Council of America testified that old gas deregulation would shift up to $100 billion to the natural gas industry. CFA released a special report and testified before Congress that the top twenty oil and gas producers stood to gain a $68.3 billion windfall from their sales of deregulated old gas for the period 1983 to 1990. On the state level, the Citizen Labor Energy Coalition mobilized more than 200 grassroots groups opposing further deregulation.

Despite these efforts, the 1973 to 1984 increase in the nominal wellhead price ballooned 1,109 percent (representing a 463 percent constant-dollar increase at the wellhead). From 1973 to 1984, residential gas bills nearly quintupled, rising by 121 percent even in constant dollars.

When the cartel oil shock ended, the gas industry and consumers faced residual problems. The crisis-induced run-up in gas prices had become embedded in those same long-term contracts between pipelines and producers that had assured stability under regulation. Worse, under take-or-pay provisions, pipelines had obligated themselves to pay for high-priced gas whether they were able to take delivery or not. Experiencing a 26 percent decline in total U.S. gas demand between 1973 and 1986, many pipelines could neither take nor pay. Residential and commercial users, who consumed 11 percent less gas in 1986, paid twice as much for gas as they had back in 1973.

While wellhead prices declined after 1985, they did not fall by nearly as much as they had risen. Residential prices declined even less. In real terms, after a 463 percent run-up during 1973 to 1984, wellhead prices declined only 58 percent between 1984 and 1995. By 1990, residential prices in constant dollars had declined only 23 percent, and by 1995, had declined only 9 percent more.

At the grassroots level, state commissions had stopped requiring utilities to seek the best price, arguing that the rapid price changes had made public review too costly and burdensome. Yet, automatic "fuel-cost adjustments" and "purchased gas charges" on monthly electric and gas bills continued.

Alarmed by the persistence of high prices, the insecurity of supply in unenforceable contracts, and the relaxation in state regulatory oversight, consumers organized to protect the interests of residential ratepayers. In the early

1980s, they forced utility issues onto state ballots, intervened in state cases, and initiated new consumer advocacy strategies. Michigan Citizens Lobby won a ballot proposal ending the automatic fuel cost adjustments. In California, after Toward Utility Rate Normalization contested costly Canadian gas purchases, the distribution company was fined $35 million for "buying imprudently." Richmond, Virginia, and other East Coast cities won suits against a pipeline for purchases constituting "fraud and abuse." In Wisconsin, a Citizens Utility Board (CUB) was the first consumer advocacy organization to be created by legislative mandate to represent ratepayers.

Wellhead decontrol and the collapse of regulated bundling did not by themselves create viable markets. Before new buyers and sellers could establish gas and service markets, existing long-term contracts, especially take-or-pay contracts, had to be abrogated, renegotiated, or otherwise ended. Pipelines, no longer merchant carriers as under regulation, had to offer open access transportation to the new market entrants.

This creation of markets was orchestrated by a series of FERC orders after 1985, though legal maneuvering by pipelines, consumer groups, and large end-users preceded and forced the issue. One pipeline escaped its high-cost obligations via the contract's *force majeure* (essentially "act of God") clause, a legal out formerly invoked only in natural disasters.

By the end of 1988, nearly all gas pipeline transport was on behalf of open access customers: marketers, distributors, end-users, and brokers. That same year, the spot sales share of the total gas market rose to 70 percent (from 4 percent in 1983). Under regulation, the production, transport, and marketing of natural gas were closely coordinated to the end of long-term delivery to users at stable prices. As price, contracts, and coordination (bundling) of essential services were removed from control by a central authority, natural gas was transformed into a stand-alone commodity, its price determined daily in separate markets. These gas markets quickly acquired two classic characteristics of commodity markets: the prevalence of cash (spot) trades, and price volatility (frequent swings in price).

Such price volatility, which has continued into the 1990s, poses make-or-break risks for those buying or selling large volumes of gas for delivery on fixed dates. Moreover, with the expanding number of players in markets, each faces the risk that other prices (of transportation, storage, credit, foreign exchange rate, for example) may move adversely.

For each such risk, whether to seller or buyer, there has evolved under commoditization a "hedge" against price or other changes in gas and associated markets. Strategies for hedging take complex forms, but increasingly, large marketers offer to repackage for producers bundles of physical and financial services. Some packages simply offer to place gas over a month or many years at conditionally guaranteed prices; other packages may bundle together most services—from gathering, to transmission, to storage, to marketing—previously supplied by pipelines under regulation.

As early as 1989, such repackaging had dramatically shifted natural gas sales away from the short-term, unhedged spot market. To hedge against the volatility of spot markets, after the opening of a futures market in 1990, additional gas began to be bought and sold through contracts for future delivery at a fixed price. From 70 percent in 1988, the share of spot market sales fell to 40 percent in 1994.

If the entire national pipeline grid allowed easy movement between regions, a futures market might alone smooth out the price volatility of natural gas markets. Apart from repackaging, this hope was the sole assurance held out to consumers against potential shortages and price run-ups in volatile markets.

Such market perfection has not yet been achieved. Indeed, in the winter of late 1995/early 1996, natural gas prices on the New York futures market exploded to record levels. This run-up was attributed to cold weather, transportation glitches, and, according to some analysts, a classic "short squeeze" in which traders scrambled to meet overextended obligations for future deliveries.

Rebundling, though it has restored some of the stability that existed under regulation, has not been without costs to consumers. This is because of growth in the number of middlemen who now collect a margin for physical or financial services between the wellhead and the residential consumer. The evidence for this is the "price spread."

In 1988, after wellhead prices were fully out from under long-term contracts at crisis-induced prices, the average wellhead price was $1.69 per mcf (thousand cubic feet). The average price of natural gas for residential delivery was $5.47, and the "price spread" was thus $3.78, or 2.24 times the wellhead price. In subsequent commoditization, repackaging, and expansion of middleman services, this spread had by 1995 gradually drifted up to $4.47 per mcf, or 2.81 times the wellhead price. The result for consumers is that the nominal price they pay has increased in most years and, as noted earlier, has never in real terms returned to 1973 levels.

Independent producers, who find and produce most natural gas from relatively small individual operations, have also taken note of the middleman spread. Many of them see the price spread as a squeeze on producers by giant marketers and financial speculators who have taken over the natural gas industry. In response, some independents launched a failed effort in Congress in 1995 to allow independents to form producer cooperatives, patterned after agricultural cooperatives. Under this scheme, independents could aggregate sufficient volumes to market gas directly to end-users, enabling volume discounts for some services and the ability to bypass other middlemen. Such an effort could clearly reduce price spreads between the wellhead and end-users, but the net impact on consumers is unclear.

As of 1996, local distribution companies, which take possession of gas at city gates and provide packaged services to end-users, remain the only major segment of the natural gas industry that is still regulated. The vision that some hold for this sector is the system now operating in Ontario, Canada, where homeowners can choose a gas supplier, much as they can select long-distance telephone carriers today.

In the regulated U.S. market, local distribution companies do of course bargain for supplies on behalf of their residential and other customers in increasingly volatile markets. While in some areas, pilot projects have permitted them to engage in financial hedging, consumers are protected by regulation from any losses incurred.

State and local consumer advocates across the nation are viewing any deregulation beyond the city gate with skepticism, in light of the very mixed experience with wellhead and pipeline deregulation. While the impacts of earlier deregulation would have been vastly less disruptive in a period of stable oil prices, a new round of unbundling beyond the city gate, once set in motion, could have unpredictable consequences for tens of millions of residential gas consumers.

— Ann K. Lower, Milton D. Lower

See also

Citizen Action.

Readings

DeVany, Arthur S., and W. David Walls (1995). *The Emerging New Order in Natural Gas.* Westport, CT: Quorum Books.

Lower, Ann K. (1983). "Natural Gas Pricing: Market Outcome or Industrial Policy?" *Journal of Economic Issues.* 17 (June): 423–432.

Pruner, David (1995). "U.S. Gas Market Adapting to Commoditization." *Oil and Gas Journal.* 93 (March 13): 66–70.

New Zealand Consumer Movement

The first attempt to start a consumer organization in New Zealand occurred in 1935. It was inspired by the formation of product testing organizations in the United States. A group of citizens in the university city of Dunedin tried to set up a formal consumer body in New Zealand. They renewed their efforts in 1939, but their enthusiasm was diverted by the outbreak of World War II. At the same time, through the initiative of the Manawatu Farmers Union, a consumers' league was formed, but it too was a wartime casualty.

It was not until 1959 that interest in a national consumer body revived. The National Council of Women, the Public Service Association, and other groups with an interest in the welfare of consumers persuaded the left-leaning Labor government of the day to sponsor a consumer organization. The Minister of Industries and Commerce (the Honorable P. N. Holloway) and the Secretary of the Department (Dr. W. B. Sutch) actively supported the idea.

Consumer Council and Consumer Service

In July 1959, the Consumer Council came into being and later was given statutory recognition under the Finance Act of 1959. At the inaugural meeting of the council, the minister noted that consumers now had a voice, which he hoped would be heard, not only by traders and manufacturers, but also by governments.

The fledgling Consumer Council was established as a division of the Department of Industries and Commerce. Its operating arm was the Consumer Service.

The founding objectives of the Consumer Council were numerous. The council was to determine consumers' preferences and make these known to producers and suppliers of goods and services. It was to publicize existing safeguards to consumers' interests and welfare, notably those concerning price, quality, health, safety, labeling, and contractual relationships. If necessary, it was supposed to initiate measures to ensure adherence to standards of quality and safety. Moreover, the council was to advise appropriate authorities of ways in which existing safeguards needed to be improved to serve consumers better.

For consumers in particular, the council was given the task of publishing reports (including results of tests), thus enabling comparative evaluation of goods and services, with particular reference to the correlation of price and quality. The council was also asked to form an association of subscribing members representing the consumer interest.

The council was given one final, broad assignment: to undertake any work relative or additional to the roles described above necessary to serve consumers' interests and welfare. Thus, the objectives and functions of the council have been altered and updated over the years, although the underlying principles have remained the same.

The Consumer Service's first magazine, *Consumer*, was published in late 1959. It carried reports on pain relievers, safety in dinghies, children's shoes, canned fruit, nylon stockings, and meat. The magazine also publicized the formation of four regional consumer committees.

The first chairman of the council was G. E. Wood, a recently retired government statistician. He was the inspirational leader of the organization during its formative years. He retired in 1975.

The Consumer Service and its magazine were initially heavily subsidized by their sponsoring government department. In 1967, however, ties with the Department of Industries and Commerce were severed, and the organization was restructured under its own act of Parliament, the Consumer Council Act. By this action, the Consumer Service (which by then was known as the Consumers' Institute) and its governing body, the Consumer Council, achieved a major degree of independence.

The new act specified: "The functions of the Council shall be to protect and promote the interests of consumers of goods and services by whatever lawful means appear to it expedient, and by so doing to encourage the improvement and development of industries and commerce." Along with organizational independence came a drop in government financial support—from 70 percent initially to 35 percent in 1967. Government funding ranged between 35 and 45 percent until 1989.

Between 1967 and 1989, Consumers' Institute flourished, to a large extent, because of the dedication and guidance of its director, R. J. Smithies. Membership rose from 55,000 in 1967 to a peak of 135,000 in 1975, which meant that one in ten households in New Zealand was receiving *Consumer* magazine. While the number of subscribers fell in the late 1970s, by comparison with consumer organizations in other countries, New Zealand numbers remained high in relation to the size of the population.

Until 1989, Consumers' Institute provided comprehensive coverage of comparative product tests, surveys of services, criticisms of marketplace malpractices, and commentaries on consumer issues of the day. In addition, it ran a consumer complaints service and a school-based consumer education program. It was also responsible for testing potentially unsafe products and lobbying Government for the development and reform of consumer legislation. As part of its statutory functions, the institute provided consumer representatives for a number of outside agencies.

In 1989, there was a further restructuring of the organization. The Consumer Council Act was repealed, and all government funding ceased. Functions such as the complaints service, consumer education, and responsibility for product safety were handed over to the Ministry of Consumer Affairs, which had been formed in 1986. Consumers' Institute became an incorporated society, owned and governed by its membership. The institute's main interest became providing information and advice to its subscribing members.

Role in Economic Restructuring

The Institute's change in status took place in a period of economic change. Until the mid-1970s, the country's economy had been highly regulated. Strict import controls meant that a few large companies had a virtual monopoly on the manufacture of household goods, particularly kitchen and laundry appliances; price controls were in place for some goods and services; there were, for a period, interest rate controls; virtually all utilities were publicly owned in some form or other; and an inspectorate-based government bureaucracy dominated the lives of consumers.

Then economic policy changed radically. State assets were sold, barriers to trade were removed, the tax system was reformed by lowering the income tax and introducing a consumption tax, and all subsidies were wiped out.

Today, New Zealand is one of the least regulated countries in the developed world: the market is open to virtually anyone. Theorists say that competition will grow and produce efficiencies that will provide consumers with goods and services of the best quality at the lowest prices. In some areas of the economy, these expectations have been realized. The price of cars has dropped dramatically. There is fierce competition among several large supermarket chains. There has been an appreciable drop in the price of telephone toll calls since a second telecommunications company started business.

In other areas, however, the outcome has not been to the benefit of consumers. A restructuring of the electricity industry has led to higher prices for residential consumers. Government charges for a range of services have increased. An all-consuming desire by the government through its Reserve Bank to hold inflation to less than 2 percent has caused home mortgage rates to rise.

As the only national broad-based consumer organization in New Zealand, Consumers' Institute has argued for a pragmatic approach to economic reforms to ensure that the theoretical benefits of restructuring and deregulation actually accrue to all sectors of society, not just to the most attractive and profitable customers.

In the immediate future, the institute intends to be not only an evaluator of goods and services but also an advocate of consumers on broader structural economic issues. To achieve this end, it sees great benefit in maintaining links with overseas consumer groups to draw upon their experiences and research.

— David Russell

Reading

Lysonski, Steve, and Michael F. Duffy (1992). "The New Zealand Fair Trading Act of 1986: Deceptive Advertising." *Journal of Consumer Affairs*. 26 (1): 177–199.

Norwegian Consumer Movement

Consumer cooperatives in Norway were first founded in 1860; unions composed of cooperatives were established in 1906; and for the next fifty to sixty years, consumer cooperatives played an important role in Nordic labor and consumer policy. Despite these precursors, consumer policy and consumer organizations are largely post–World War II phenomena.

History

In 1935, the first consumer organization on the governmental level was created. Since then, the goals and means of consumer organizations have developed in four phases. Yet, during the past sixty years, no general-purpose, private consumer organization has been established in Norway. The consumer movement has been linked to women's organizations, trade unions, consumer cooperatives, or other nationwide organizations, on the one hand, and to national or local government, on the other.

In the first phase, 1935 to 1945, consumer policy and consumer interests were defined in a narrow way. Consumer problems were linked solely to questions concerning home economics. In 1936, the Norwegian Advisory Service for Home Economics was established, with twenty local offices around the country.

A slight shift in consumer matters took place after World War II. During this second phase, 1945 to 1960, national consumer institutions were established, in particular, the Norwegian Consumer Council in 1953. The need for consumer information provided by consumer organizations was first recognized by various women's organizations, who were linked to labor and farmer movements or to consumer cooperatives. Nevertheless, all the new consumer institutions were established by the government, with total financial support from the Parliament. These organizations, however, were granted a high degree of political independence. This dualism between government support and political independence has been the main characteristic of Norwegian consumer policy for the last forty years. For example, representatives of women's, household, and labor organizations were members of the board of the Consumer Council, but they were appointed by the Ministry of Family Affairs.

The consumer magazine *Forbrukerrapporten* (Consumer Report) was started during this post-war period. Another innovation was the Declaration Committee for Consumer Goods, designed to obtain voluntary agreements with producers regarding labeling of consumer goods.

During the third period, 1968 to 1978, various changes in consumer matters took place in Norway. Important general consumer legislation passed Parliament. The right to redress was ensured by a general act covering the sales of goods act, a new door-to-door sales act, and a consumer credit act. Consumers were also protected against unfair and misleading advertising by the Marketing Control Act of 1972.

The consumer authorities were not content with merely adopting new laws. Both the Consumer Council and the National Institute for Consumer Research (a research and testing body) were reorganized. The Marketing Control Act in the early 1970s set up new and separate institutions: the Consumer Ombudsman (CO) to encourage compliance with the law and the Market Council to serve as an appeal body for CO decisions. Government-financed consumer complaint boards were also introduced to ensure consumers of their right to redress. As a result of this transition in Nordic consumer policy, although consumer information was still important, consumer protection received increasing emphasis.

The fourth phase in consumer policy, 1980 to the present, is complex. Although deregulation is the main trend in this period, new consumer laws have passed Parliament. There has been legislation dealing with product safety and product liability as well as consumer finances and credit. But consumer protection has not been stressed as heavily as earlier. Instead, there is a returning emphasis on consumer information. In addition, a governmental commission has been set up to evaluate consumer policy in Norway, with particular stress on its organizational structure.

Consumer Organizations

The main consumer institution in Norway is the Consumer Council. It was founded in 1953, and reorganized in 1972, becoming more independent of the government. Still, the Consumer Council receives most of its money (about 75 percent) from the government, and the government appoints the head of the Consumer Council. Every two years, there is a national meeting of the Consumer Council at which the other eight members of the council are elected. The two main delegate groups are sent by countrywide organizations representing women, single persons, youth, workers, the disabled, and other interest groups, and by local consumer authorities. The Consumer Council has local offices in every county and nearly 150 permanent employees, half of them on the local level.

The organizational structure of the Consumer Council makes it a semigovernmental body, but one that acts very much like an independent consumer organization. Every year the Consumer Council is contacted by approximately 120,000 households, most of them with complaints. Another major task of the council is providing consumer information. Its monthly magazine *Forbrukerrapporten*, founded in 1958, has 100,000 subscribers. Like other consumer magazines in Europe, it publishes test results and gives advice to consumers. Perhaps most important, the Consumer Council is active in formulating consumer policy and strengthening consumer influence in markets for goods and services, whether private or public.

The Marketing Control Act, which passed the Norwegian Parliament in 1972, established two new consumer institutions: the Consumer Ombudsman (CO) and the Market Council. The main task of the CO is to supervise and implement the act, designed to protect the interests of consumers. The council functions as a "court," an appeals body for ombudsman decisions.

The CO is appointed by, and receives money from, the government. Within this framework, the CO is an independent administrative body that seeks to keep a running account of business conduct and influence all actors engaged in trade and industry to conduct their operations in conformity with the provisions of the Marketing Control Act. The CO may lay down prohibitions against illegal marketing practices, and it deals with complaints as well as cases taken up on his/her own initiative. The CO's office has a staff of twenty-one. Local cases on marketing practices are dealt with by eight regional offices of the Competition Authority. More than 3,000 new cases are registered every year.

Established in 1939, the National Institute for Consumer Research (SIFO) is the oldest of the Norwegian consumer institutions, but it was reorganized in 1972. SIFO is an independent research institute, receiving approximately 60 percent of its money from the government, the other 40 percent coming from commissioned research projects. SIFO has a staff of fifty and conducts both consumer research and product testing.

Over the years, the main focus at SIFO has shifted from private consumer problems related to the kitchen and home economics to consumer problems in the market and society. The institute is divided into two research groups, one for social sciences and one for natural sciences. Within the social sciences the main topics have been household finances, distribution of goods and services, food and nutrition, and advertising. Within the natural sciences, the main activity has been testing products like toys, textiles, and household appliances, and research projects in the field of product safety.

Consumer Policy

Norwegian consumer policy is dualistic in the sense that independent consumer institutions are financed by the government. This model is found in all the five Nordic countries, with some differences. The Norwegian Consumer Council is among the most dualistic organizations. It is financed by the government, the chairperson is appointed by the government, and the Minister of Children and Family Affairs is politically responsible for the activity carried out by the Consumer Council. On the other hand, the Consumer Council is an independent consumer organization. It takes instructions from neither the government nor the Minister of Children and Family Affairs. In addition, the local offices, one in every county, are responsible to both the county administration and to the Consumer Council.

The Consumer Ombudsman (CO) and SIFO also reflect the dualism of Norwegian consumer policy. In the case of the CO, the government has established an official to act on behalf of the collective interests of individuals, not on behalf of government or ministries. The work of SIFO is carried out with governmental money "to the benefit of the consumer," yet SIFO is an independent institution whose employees answer to academic standards of research quality.

The CO is a governmental institution, which is appointed by the government, receives all its money from the government, and has been established by law: the Marketing Control Act. Its main task is to protect consumers against unreasonable and misleading advertising. For more than twenty years, the CO has accomplished this task while also becoming an important advocate for the consumer interest and a part of the consumer movement.

Recent Consumer Issues

Norwegian consumer institutions are well established and are strongly supported by consumers. Their main challenges for the future relate to the internationalization of world economy and policy, deregulation and growth of a market economy, and the relation between the environment and consumption.

In a November 1994 referendum, Norwegian voters decided, for the second time, not to join the European Union (EU). Still, Norway remains a member of the European Economic Area and is influenced by the decisions made in the EU. Norway has also signed the new GATT agreement.

The internationalization of economic activity creates new possibilities and opportunities for Norwegian consumers. The result of this process could be lower prices for many consumer goods and greater choice regarding what and where to buy goods and services. On the other hand, this internationalization represents a form of pressure on Norwegian consumer policy. The question is whether it is possible to pursue a national Norwegian consumer policy that is partly in conflict with the policy in the European Union.

Deregulation and growth of a market economy influences consumers in many of the same ways as internationalization. More products will find their way to the market, and at lower prices, increasing a consumer's right to choose. On the other hand, deregulation may threaten product safety.

Both these tendencies, internationalization and growth of a market-oriented economy, represent challenges to the Norwegian consumer movement. This movement is, to a large degree, dependent on consumer laws and public policy on a governmental level, but governmental means may not be effective in the future. In 1994, a governmental commission was set up to evaluate Norwegian consumer policy, with the main task of assessing organizational questions. One result of its evaluation could be reducing financial support to the Consumer Council and making it more independent of the government.

The linkage between consumption and the environment is becoming increasingly important to both the green movement and to the consumer movement. This interconnection of environmental and consumer concerns is a relatively new phenomenon. A number of terms are significant to this debate: zero growth, reduced consumption, environmental space, and sustainable consumption. It will be a challenge to consumer organizations and authorities in the 1990s to establish a theoretical understanding of the relation between consumption and environment, and to develop means to move consumption in the direction of sustainable consumption.

Role in Global Consumer Movement

The Norwegian Consumer Council is a member both of Consumers International (CI) and the Bureau Européen des Unions de Consommateurs (BEUC). Due to European integration, BEUC has recently become more important to the Norwegian consumer movement than Consumers International. This is also a result of the priorities set by CI, which focuses on building the consumer movement in the Third World. But because many consumer problems are global in nature, it is likely that Norway will remain an active participant in CI.

In the 1990s, Norwegian consumer organizations have worked hard to strengthen European contacts and cooperation. The single European market represents a challenge to the consumer movement in Europe, and the Norwegian institutions have taken part in the efforts to strengthen consumer influence in the new European Economic Area economically, politically, and legally. In that process BEUC has played an important part. The Consumer Council also takes part in International Testing, a European cooperative venture that gives the council access to consumer tests of goods and services. Both the Consumer Council and SIFO have, for the last several years, taken part in the European standardization bodies.

The Nordic Council of Ministers has, for more than twenty years, established and developed cooperation among the governments, consumer organizations, consumer ombudsmen, research institutes, and other consumer institutions of the five Nordic countries. Norwegian consumer organizations take part in this cooperation, financed by the Nordic governments. The cooperation covers consumer rights, education, information, influence, household financial management, technical equipment, and, more recently, the relation between consumption and environment. One specific outgrowth of this cooperation was the development of the Nordic Swan, a multinational environmental seal of approval.

After the breakdown of the Soviet Union, the Nordic Council of Ministers took initiatives to develop cooperation between the Nordic and Baltic states in the consumer field. In 1992, a Nordic-Baltic consumer conference took place in Pärnu, Estonia. The aim of this conference was to strengthen consumer influence, protection, and information in the new market economy in the Baltic states. This conference represented the starting point of further Baltic-Nordic consumer cooperation.

— Eivind Stø

Readings

Annual Report of the Consumer Ombudsman 1995 (1996). Lysaker: Forbrukerombudet.

Graver, Kjersti (1986). "A Study of the Consumer Ombudsman Institution in Norway with Some References to the Other Nordic Countries, Part I." *Journal of Consumer Policy*. 9: 1–23.

Rose, Lawrence L. (1981). "The Role of Interest Groups in Collective Interest Policy-Making: Consumer Protection in Norway and the United States." *European Journal of Political Research*. 9 (March): 17–45.

O

OECD Committee on Consumer Policy

The Organization for Economic Cooperation and Development (OECD) is an intergovernmental organization, located in Paris, encompassing twenty-five member countries. Generally characterized as industrial or developed, they are: Australia, Austria, Belgium, Canada, Denmark, Finland, France, Germany, Greece, Iceland, Ireland, Italy, Japan, Luxembourg, Mexico, the Netherlands, New Zealand, Norway, Portugal, Spain, Sweden, Switzerland, Turkey, the United Kingdom, and the United States. OECD's goals are to help countries achieve the highest sustainable levels of economic growth and employment and assist development of the world economy, especially through trade on a multilateral, nondiscriminatory basis. OECD's Committee on Consumer Policy plays a unique part in the pursuit of these overall goals.

Created in 1969, the Committee on Consumer Policy is composed of government officials representing policymakers and enforcement bodies in the field of consumer policy. It provides a forum for the regular exchange of specific consumer policy issues of common interest. This work includes the regular publication of reports on the development of consumer policies in member countries. Over nearly three decades, the committee has examined a variety of emerging consumer policy issues. Recent issues include cross-border shopping, environmental marketing claims, and electronic funds transfers. The committee has published reports on product safety, interactive on-line systems, life insurance, agricultural policy, and advertising directed at children. Despite the wide variety of issues the committee tackles, a constant theme is the impact of new business practices and government policies on economic efficiency, competition, and international trade. The conclusions of the committee's reports frequently are transformed into recommendations by OECD's highest body, the OECD Council, to member governments. Thus, the Committee on Consumer Policy both monitors and influences consumer policy developments.

The committee consults, when appropriate, with a variety of advisory bodies representing groups involved in consumer policy, including businesses, labor unions, and consumer organizations. As an indication of the importance of OECD and the Committee on Consumer Policy, Consumers International recently organized a campaign to establish full-time contact with the OECD.

Despite its considerable achievements, the committee faces an unsettled future. OECD is under budgetary pressure, and consumer policy constantly struggles to differentiate itself from competition policy on the one hand and environmental policy on the other.

— Erich Linke

Readings

Organization for Economic Cooperation and Development (1995). *Consumer Policy in OECD Countries, 1993–94.* Paris: OECD.

——— (1995). *A Global Marketplace for Consumers.* Paris: OECD.

Office of Consumers' Education

See U.S. Office of Consumers' Education.

Older Consumers

In the United States in 1993, there were 32.8 million persons age sixty-five and older, representing 12.7 percent of the U.S. population, and that number is growing more rapidly than the rest of the population. Between 1990 and 1993, the number of older Americans increased by 5 percent, compared to an increase of 3 percent for the under–sixty-five population.

Historically, the elderly have been viewed with sympathy and as a vulnerable group. Rates of poverty were high for those who could no longer participate in the paid labor force, often because of poor health or frailty. As a group, the elderly were termed the "deserving poor" and protected by numerous laws. But in the 1980s, just as society began to view consumerism more skeptically, it reevaluated its stereotypes of the elderly.

Economic Status and Related Needs

Perhaps the most important transition in attitudes toward the elderly occurred in the area of economic well-being. By almost any measure of financial status, the average person over the age of sixty-five gained during the 1980s. The rate of poverty declined from 15.7 percent in 1980 to 12.1 percent in 1988, and went down to 11.7 percent in 1994. Moreover, this increasing affluence occurred when income growth for younger adults was slowing. For example, between 1980 and 1993, median incomes of those over the age of sixty-five increased 18.2 percent in real terms, while an average person age thirty-five to forty-four experienced only a 3.9 percent increase. Older persons who were (and remain) largely outside the work force did not suffer from the severe recession in the early part of the decade. Moreover, cost-of-living adjustments have partially sheltered this group from inflation.

The rising affluence of the elderly as a group occurred at a time when society also became reluctant to expand the size of the government. A considerable share of the well-being of the elderly stems from government programs, a fact not lost on those who wish to shift support away from this group. In fact, the swing in the portrayal of older persons in the media has been dramatic, shifting from sympathy to antipathy toward those "greedy geezers." These stereotypes are no more subtle or accurate than were the old notions of all elderly as poor. Nevertheless, it has become more difficult to argue on income grounds alone that the elderly should be treated as a homogeneous group in need of special protections.

Despite the growth in average incomes for older Americans, their financial picture is not uniformly rosy. More than 3.7 million persons over age sixty-five remain below the poverty level, the highest rate among all adult Americans. Nearly as many older persons have incomes below or just above the poverty threshold. Thus, nearly one-fifth of older Americans, and over one-third of those who are widowed and living alone, have incomes below or just above the poverty threshold.

Older persons often face critical decisions regarding their finances. Investment of savings to supplement retirement income can make the difference between living well and just getting by. Often, retirement benefits are available in a lump sum payment that individuals must invest.

The death of a spouse creates major disruptions in the financial affairs of the survivor, and decisions must often be made while the individual is under great stress. Changing needs and circumstances may necessitate the sale of the family home, generating a major shift in resources. The consequences of making poor decisions can leave older persons with few options. Since they are usually out of the labor force, they cannot make up for mistakes by "working harder."

Health Condition and Related Needs

Older Americans use more health care services than younger persons by a factor of over three to one. They interact with the full array of health care providers and services, consuming more hospital care, nursing home care, drugs, home care, and physician services per capita than do the nonelderly. Thus, asking health care users to be more aggressive consumers places a disproportionate burden on older persons.

Layered on top of this service use is the necessity of dealing with a public program—Medicare—and generally either one or more private supplemental insurance plans or Medicaid. After those payers interact with providers, the elderly must still cope with substantial out-of-pocket costs, and with the associated complex forms and bills. For some, keeping track of health care expenditures can be a full-time job. Medigap policies (private plans to supplement Medicare) historically have been pushed aggressively, but do not always provide good value to policyholders. Among other problems, older consumers are often persuaded to overinsure.

Unfortunately, the greatest of these health-related burdens often results from serious illnesses. Being a prudent consumer becomes complicated by the diminished ability of individuals to manage decisions and associated stress.

The poor health of many elderly also complicates the meeting of other consumer needs. Frailty associated with chronic conditions or the aging process creates special needs in housing and everyday activities such as shopping. Consequently, older persons may rely more on hired services to meet needs ranging from remodeling their home to undertaking everyday chores. At the same time, because of frailty or ill health, they may become more isolated and have less access to friends and other sources of information and support.

Cognitive problems linked to mild or full cases of dementia also create special consumer needs, and intervention to protect persons of diminished capacity may be necessary. Such individuals are more vulnerable to abuse from unscrupulous salespersons or service providers.

On the other hand, it is easy to stereotype older persons and assume that any confusion on their part is due to senility. If so, older persons may become victims not only of those who seek to abuse them, but also of those who seek to be helpful. Although Alzheimer's and other cognitive dysfunctions constitute very real problems for older persons, it should not be forgotten that only one of every six persons over eighty suffers from dementia.

While the elderly experience health-related consumer problems more frequently than do other age groups, most of these experiences are not unique. Poverty and low incomes disproportionately affect female-headed families with young children. Important financial decisions, such as the purchase of housing, are made by adults at all ages. Disability and high medical costs can be suffered by anyone.

Vulnerability to Fraud

Older Americans are particularly vulnerable to fraud and deception because they are less familiar with basic consumer issues and more trusting of salespersons than are younger adults. The American Association of Retired Persons (AARP) constructed a consumer vulnerability index that measures consumer awareness of sources of consumer information, knowledge of consumer rights, openness to appeals from telemarketers, and wariness of misleading sales practices. In research using the index, AARP found that 34 percent of people age seventy-five and older had "high vulnerability," compared to 24 percent of persons age sixty-five to seventy-four and only 7 percent of younger adults.

Given the relative consumer vulnerability of older people, it is not surprising that they are disproportionately targeted by fraudulent businesses, especially telemarketers. Senior Sentinel, a 1995 FBI raid of illegal telemarketing operations, found that more than 78 percent of targeted victims were over age fifty-five.

Needed Consumer Protections

Many examples of age-based consumer protections exist, and others have been proposed. In some states, for instance, penalties for persons convicted of mugging older persons are more severe than for those who victimize younger adults. Private health insurance plans that supplement Medicare, and are marketed primarily to the elderly, are specifically regulated to prevent duplicate coverage. Federal tax returns offer favored treatment to those age sixty-five and older.

On the other hand, some regulations place restrictions only on older persons: For example, several states require that all individuals over a particular age take additional driver's license tests. Also, the price of insurance for automobiles and health may increase with age. Liability damages paid to injured individuals are generally lower for older persons than for working-age adults.

Do these age distinctions make sense? And are older persons, on balance, hurt or helped? At least some of the concerns for the elderly can be viewed as proxies for other concerns. For instance, the logical reason to seek higher penalties for individuals who rob older persons is the greater physical harm that can be caused. But another approach would be to devise laws that stipulate stiffer penalties when the robbery results in an injury to the victim, regardless of age. In such a case a proxy is not needed; a more direct link is possible.

In other cases, special needs for the elderly reflect their different bundles of consumption. Bunk bed safety is not an issue of great interest to most persons over the age of sixty-five, but standards for sales of hearing aids are likely to be disproportionately of concern.

Perhaps the greatest contribution that age-based policies can make is to sensitize those charged with protecting the public to the special needs and concerns of the elderly. As people age, their physiology also changes: Metabolic and other physiological changes have implications for all sorts of products. For example, the elderly are the largest per capita consumers of prescription drugs, yet when drugs are tested for efficacy and safety, the subjects tend to be middle-aged adults. Even for those drugs heavily consumed by older persons, drug tests are not routinely conducted on persons over the age of sixty-five. After the fact, and often after the harm, age-related problems with drugs show up in the literature. Requirements that the drugs be tested on samples weighted with the appropriate population could help avoid later problems. Even for those drugs primarily consumed by younger persons, special tests of sensitivity may be in order for older consumers.

Another example is related to food standards. Often, taste buds alert people to problems in foods: If it tastes or smells bad, they are likely to avoid the food. A decline in taste or smell in many older persons makes them especially susceptible to tainted food; if they are frail as well, they may suffer more from the ill effects. Should separate standards be established for seniors, or should standards be set that take such vulnerabilities into account? Should the overall standards be raised to reflect the special needs of one group?

Still another example relates to sleepwear flammability. Studies show that the two most vulnerable groups to apparel fires are the very young and the very old. Moreover, when older persons are burned, they are more likely to die from their injuries. Sleepwear for children is subject to flammability standards, but no such protections exist for older persons. Because it is difficult to identify sleepwear that would be used by persons over the age of sixty-five, any standards would have to apply to all adult sleepwear. If the costs of making sleepwear safer are very high, the benefits, when averaged across all adults, might not be high enough to justify requiring that nightwear be treated. Thus, it becomes difficult to argue for protection for a minority when the regulations would affect a much larger group. In this particular case, a request was made for improved labeling—a low-cost solution that would allow those concerned about sleepwear flammability to identify those products that offered better protection. Even this low-cost alternative was recently rejected by the Consumer Product Safety Commission.

As the elderly grow as a percentage of the population, policymakers and opinion leaders are increasingly confronted with pressures to adopt age-sensitive practices without fueling conflict among generations. The sheer size of the older population and its unprecedented influence are already shifting many carefully crafted balances, and offer new challenges to our society.

— Marilyn Moon, Katrinka Smith Sloan

See also

American Association of Retired Persons.

Readings

Friedman, Monroe (1992). "Confidence Swindles of Older Consumers." *Journal of Consumer Affairs.* 26 (1): 20–46.
Moon, Marilyn (1990). "Consumer Issues and the Elderly." *Journal of Consumer Affairs.* 24 (2): 235–244.

P

Packaging Protections

Until the early 1900s, most goods displayed in a typical store were not packaged. The consumer could see and touch them, and often could consult the seller personally to make a selection. However, with the advent of self-service retailing and impersonal merchandising, packaging became essential. Packaging performs important utilitarian functions: It ensures safe delivery of the product by protecting it in transport and throughout its shelf life, and it can be designed to increase consumer convenience in transport, storage, and use.

Packaging also is important to the marketer. Nabisco's Uneeda biscuit package is credited with pioneering the idea of the package as a marketing tool. To compete in today's marketplace, packaging must advertise its contents. It also reduces manufacturer and distributor losses from breakage and spoilage in transport. Both consumers and sellers are benefited by packaging designed to reduce shoplifting and prevent tampering. Packaging can also assist both parties by communicating information.

Despite its benefits to consumers, packaging is associated with problems that include deception, inadequate or misleading information, safety concerns, and environmental impacts. Deceptive package design takes many forms, including packages designed to appear to hold a larger quantity than they actually do, short-weighted packages (containing less than the labeled weight), reduced net weight but not package size, and multiple or odd package sizes that increase the difficulty of price comparisons. Other problems relating to product information on the package include obscure labeling, misleading art, and misleading information.

The Fair Packaging and Labeling Act of 1968 promotes uniformity and simplicity of language by requiring the label to identify the commodity and the name and place of business of the manufacturer or distributor; state the net quantity in a uniform and prominent location in ounces, pounds, pints, or quarts; and state the net quantity of a serving when relevant. The law also prohibits statements such as "jumbo quart" that exaggerate the net weight.

This act charges many federal agencies with developing regulations to enforce its provisions. Consumer advocates criticize the law for permitting sellers to misuse cents-off pricing; relying on voluntary industry limitations on the number of different package sizes, which has not reduced the number significantly; and insufficiently supporting regulatory agencies. Control of weights and measures in the United States is the primary domain of the states, and although model laws have been drafted, great variations in state regulations still exist.

Information continues to be an important consumer packaging issue. The Nutrition Labeling and Education Act of 1990 required the Food and Drug Administration to implement sweeping changes in regulations governing food labeling. The legislation made a nutrition label with expanded information mandatory on nearly all foods and standardized the definitions of some key terms related to nutrition claims and serving size.

Safety issues in packaging relate primarily to concerns about childproof packaging and product tampering. The Poison Prevention Packaging Act of 1970, which set standards for child-resistant closures, is credited with reducing accidental ingestions of poison by children. More recent incidents of product tampering in the marketplace have led industry to develop new designs that make undetected tampering more difficult. Consumer groups also advocate the need for ingredient labeling to protect individuals with food allergies and ensure that products with potentially hazardous ingredients are used and disposed of properly.

The environmental impacts of packaging are of concern to many consumers. Paradoxically, although packaging creates municipal waste, it also prevents it. An often-cited example is the food spoilage rate in the United States—less than 3 percent. This low rate is attributed in part to sophisticated packaging and distribution systems.

However, packaging imposes environmental costs. Discarded packaging makes up one-third of our garbage, although as much as 40 percent of that total is estimated to be shipping-related—pallets, crates, and cardboard cartons, for example. Consumer product packaging is conservatively estimated to be as little as 15 percent of the waste stream. Nearly one-half of all discarded packaging is paper and paperboard.

The Tellus Institute has estimated the hidden environmental costs, from air pollution to lung disease, of producing various packaging materials. The cost per package ranged from 11.52 cents for a half-gallon PET (polyethylene terephthalate) jug to 3.84 cents for a half-gallon paperboard carton to 0.6 cent for a recycled aluminum can. Recycled material production impacts ranged from 16 percent of the corresponding virgin material in aluminum to 97 percent for steel cans.

Industry can decrease the adverse environmental impacts of packaging in a number of ways: reduced use of raw materials, weight reduction for more energy-efficient transport, recycling and the use of recycled materials, and reduced use of toxic materials in packaging. Although industry has voluntarily made many changes in package design, in recent years state legislators have introduced over 2,000 bills per year concerning solid waste. Packaging and product bans, which often target toxic substances or materials difficult to recycle, are frequently the legislative goal. So-called rates-and-dates legislation typically requires packages to be smaller, recyclable or reusable, or to meet minimum standards for recycled content.

Recently, environmental labeling has been an important issue. Numerous states have passed legislation banning the use of certain environmental claims on product labels or at least defining the terms that may be used. In 1992 the Federal Trade Commission issued guidelines that define deception in environmental claims.

— Brenda Cude

Readings

Holmes, Hannah, and Patricia Poore (1993). "Packaging in the 90s." *Garbage.* 5 (December/January): 24ff.

Kelley, William T., and Etienne Gorse (1973). "The Fair Packaging and Labeling Act of 1966." In William T. Kelley, ed. *New Consumerism: Selected Readings.* Columbus, OH: Grid. 425–449

Sacharow, Stanley (1982). *The Package as Marketing Tool.* Radnor, PA: Chilton Book Co.

Peterson, Esther

Esther Peterson is known as the "grand dame of the consumer movement," but in a career spanning more than sixty years, she also effectively advocated the rights of workers, women, the elderly, and citizens of Third World countries.

Peterson was born in Provo, Utah, in 1906. Her father, Lars Eggertsen, was superintendent of schools in that city while her mother, Annie Nielson Eggertsen, raised a family of six children and helped run the family farm. Peterson's parents were Mormon and Republican.

Peterson earned a bachelor's degree from Brigham Young University in 1927 and a master's degree from Columbia Teacher's College in New York City. In 1930, while teaching at the Windsor School in Boston, she worked with the National Consumers League, which for years had advocated the interests of women and child workers. Two years later, she joined the staff of the Bryn Mawr School for Women. The purpose of this school was to teach factory workers about democracy and the role of workers in it.

Later that year Peterson married Oliver Peterson, a radical whom she had met earlier at Columbia. When he joined the Roosevelt administration, she moved with him to Washington, where she worked with the International Ladies Garment Workers Union, and later as assistant director of education for the Amalgamated Clothing Workers Union of America. Later in the 1930s, she and her husband, who worked for the foreign service, lived in Sweden and Belgium for several years.

Back in the United States during World War II, Peterson became interested in consumer education because of food shortages and rationing. After the war, as a labor lobbyist she helped persuade Congress to expand the coverage of the Fair Labor Standards Act to guarantee a minimum wage and maximum working hours for workers. In the mid-1950s, Peterson joined the staff of the AFL-CIO as its first woman lobbyist. Assigned to work with Senator John F. Kennedy, Peterson developed a relationship that led, in 1961, to her appointment as director of the Women's Bureau of the Department of Labor and later as an assistant secretary of labor, a post she held through 1968.

In 1963, after proposing the creation of a subcabinet-level consumer adviser to the president, Kennedy asked Peterson if she would take the job. Although Kennedy died before Peterson could accept, President Johnson renewed the offer, this time as special assistant to the president for consumer affairs. Peterson accepted, and served in that position through 1967. During this period, she also chaired the president's Committee on Consumer Interests.

As special assistant, Peterson saw her role as "coordinating government-consumer activities, locating the gaps, and stimulating local and private consumer groups." Her specific goals were to establish premarket testing for cosmetics; expand authority to require hazard warnings on rugs, cosmetics, and pressurized containers; require the Agriculture Department to certify the safety of pesticides before they were marketed; extend the federal government's authority to inspect meat and poultry that did not cross state lines; allow the Federal Trade Commission to issue temporary cease-and-desist orders while hearings were held on possibly hazardous products or misleading advertising; and enact truth in packaging and truth in lending bills.

Many of these goals were achieved. During Peterson's tenure as special assistant, legislation was enacted on truth in lending, truth in advertising, open dating, unit pricing, meat and poultry inspection, occupational safety, and truth in packaging. She also proposed the creation of a federation of consumer organizations and convened meetings that led to the founding of the Consumer Federation of America in 1967.

In 1970, Peterson worked as consumer adviser to Giant Food and persuaded them to adopt unit pricing and open dating policies. Giant's adoption of these policies was instrumental in the acceptance of improved consumer disclosures by other large food chains.

In 1977, President Carter reappointed Peterson as special assistant to the president for consumer affairs, a position she held through 1980. One of her chief goals was the establishment of a federal office of consumer protection. Widespread business opposition to this proposal, and the refusal of some consumer advocates to compromise, led to its congressional defeat.

In the 1980s, Peterson supported numerous progressive causes. She worked closely with the Older Women's League to fight for and enhance the rights of middle-aged women in society. She helped organize the United Seniors Health Cooperative, which uses group buying power to win discounts on an array of products. She also brought together consumer groups and insurance agents into a coalition called the Consumer Insurance Interest Group to persuade state governments to strengthen their regulation of the insurance industry.

Peterson's greatest contribution in this period, however, was leadership of the campaign to persuade the United Nations to adopt, in 1986, its Consumer Protection Guidelines. Working with the International Organization of Consumers Unions (now Consumers International), she was instrumental in convincing the General Assembly to approve minimum health and safety standards. Most importantly, these standards set goals for Third World nations to attain.

— Stephen Brobeck

See also

United Nations Consumer Protections; U.S. Office of Consumer Affairs.

Readings

Halamandaris, Val J. (1990). "Champion of the Underprivileged: A Tribute to Esther Peterson." *Caring People.* 3 (June/July): 2–13.

Peterson, Esther, with Winifred Conkling (1995). *Restless: The Memoirs of Labor and Consumer Activist Esther Peterson.* Washington, DC: Caring Publishing.

PIRGs

See Public Interest Research Groups.

Polish Consumer Movement

Founded in 1981, Federacja Konsumentow (FK) is the second oldest consumer organization in Central and Eastern Europe. It is a federation of more than fifty clubs, covering the main cities of Poland, with an elected council of about twenty. The total individual membership of the clubs is around 20,000. The central office in Warsaw has a staff of fourteen, and the regional offices have forty-seven, but most of the local and regional advice centers are now run by volunteers.

The key figure in FK is president and founder Malgorzata Niepokulczycka, who played a leading role in the development of consumer protection in Poland both within the Federacja and, for a brief period, as senior officer at the Ministry of Trade and Industry. Under her leadership, FK became the first Eastern European council member of Consumers International and also played a substantial part, in the late 1980s, in bringing together the groups emerging throughout Central and Eastern Europe.

FK's constitution permits no income-generating activities other than a consumer magazine; organizational memberships are free. Local clubs, which must have at least ten members to qualify for federation membership, must cover their own costs. During its fifteen-year history, FK has engaged in diverse activities that include policy-making, consumer and legal advice, publishing, information programs on issues of major concern to Polish consumers, work with the media, representation on certification, participation in standards and consumer committees, comparative testing (via a small Consumer Institute for Quality set up in 1991), promotion of informed drug use (with Health Action International), and consumer education. Yet, despite funding from many sources, including the Polish government, Western consumer organizations, the German government via AgV, and the European Union's PHARE Program, FK itself has long struggled to establish a secure financial foundation. With the recent provision of government funding (totaling about $121,500 in 1994 and $196,000 in 1995), the financial condition of the organization has improved.

FK's monthly magazine *ATUT,* which began in 1988 and was the first to be published in the region, lasted less than two years. The newsletter *KONSUMENT,* distributed free through the consumer clubs and shops, followed in 1992 but ceased publication a year later when the government refused to fund it. A major initiative in 1992 to set up consumer advice centers in nine major cities, based on the most active consumer clubs and undertaken with the assistance of AgV and the German government, petered out after two years when the financial aid came to an end. As a result, the clubs reverted to using volunteers to provide legal and general advice.

In 1995, Poland launched its first consumer education project for primary and secondary schools. The Federacja, aided by funds from the PHARE FIESTA program, developed the materials for students and teachers for this pilot project, which is coordinated by the Antimonopoly Office.

In general, FK has been pushed to its limits structurally and financially by the demands of the consumer agenda in Poland and by the ambitiousness of its own programs. It also faces competition: In 1993, the functions of the Anti-Monopoly Office were expanded to include creating consumer policy and coordinating consumer protection measures. The role of the office was expanded further in 1995 when it was given the task of bringing Poland's consumer policy more in line with that of the European Union, the Organization for Economic Cooperation and Development, and the World Trade Organization.

In the independent sector, Grazyna Rokicka, former general secretary of the Federacja and subsequently first director of the Consumer Protection Department at the Anti-Monopoly Office, in 1994 launched the monthly magazine *TEST,* which initially was an eight-page insert in a well-established women's magazine, *SUKCES*. The arrangement with *SUKCES* ended in 1995. A plan to publish *TEST* as a paid feature in regional newspapers with a combined circulation of 3 million fell through in 1996.

Stowarzyszenie Konzumentow Polskich (Association of Polish Consumers) started at the same time as *TEST.* At present, it has a core membership of fifty engaged in projects funded by the PHARE program that are complementary to the work of the Federacja.

In terms of consumer protections, Poland lags behind many of its neighbors. Frequent changes of government and political in-fighting have kept these protections a low priority. As of 1996, no general law was even in draft, let alone enacted. Even had such a law been passed, it would now be subject to major revision aas part of Poland's efforts to bring it consumer protection policies more in line with those of the European Union.

— Alastair Macgeorge

See also

Central and Eastern Europe, Consumer Movements in.

Reading

Kozminski, Andrzej K. (1992). "Consumers in Transition from the Centrally Planned Economy to the Market Economy." *Journal of Consumer Policy.* 14 (4): 351–370.

Poor People as Consumers

See Low-Income Consumers.

Postal Regulation

The United States Postal Service (USPS) is the world's largest postal system and is regulated by the federal government as authorized by the Constitution. The United States Postal Inspection Service (USPIS), a division of the USPS, is empowered by federal laws and regulations to enforce all federal statutes designed to preserve the safety, security, and integrity of the U.S. mail. The USPIS is also armed with investigative authority, manpower, and technical resources to carry out its objectives.

Currently, as the federal government's oldest law enforcement agency, the USPIS is authorized to enforce over 200 postal laws and regulations. This evolving body of law is primarily the result of the USPIS's response to crimes facilitated through, or directed at, the U.S. mail. Crimes involving the mail are federal offenses, and stiffer penalties are generally imposed than for similar crimes in which the mail is not used. These enhanced penalties, combined with aggressive enforcement and a conviction rate of over 90 percent, effectively keep postal crime in check.

History

The early colonial postal system bore little resemblance to the present-day postal network. Many areas were sparsely populated, yet the geographical boundaries of the growing frontier necessitated an ever-expanding network for postal delivery. The early system was rudimentary at best: Mail was transported by rider, stagecoach, or steamboat to its general destination. Such transportation methods often involved the use of contractors, rather than postal employees, who delivered the mail in bundles to innkeepers and others entrusted with the mail. Local citizens then sorted through the mail to retrieve their own. Unusual delays and loss of mail by theft were common. So insecure was the mail then that those wishing to mail money sometimes tore bills in half, mailed the first half, then waited for confirmation of receipt before mailing the other half.

In 1775 the colonial system became the American Postal Service, and the Continental Congress elected Benjamin Franklin to the position of Postmaster General. Franklin appointed inspection agents and set up methods of internal control, traceability, and accountability, which greatly improved the reliability of the mail. Congress enacted laws and regulations that made various violations against the U.S. postal system federal crimes. In 1830 the Office of Instructions and Mail Depredations was established to investigate and assist in the prosecution of postal crimes. After it successfully prosecuted several postal employees and contractors, losses of mail became less frequent and more isolated.

As the West was settled, the number of postal crimes increased. In 1853 the postal system was decentralized, and inspection agents were assigned responsibility for specific territories and diverse duties ranging from inspecting the conditions of railroads, steamboats, and other mail transport conveyances to investigating postal crimes. Eventually, additional agents were hired and assigned exclusive responsibility for specific duties. The group of agents assigned responsibility for investigating postal crimes became the Inspection Service, the forerunner of the current USPIS.

After the Civil War, lotteries and other mail-order swindles, which included the sale of "greenbacks" (counterfeit money) and various devices and potions of medical quackery, dramatically increased. Although local fraud statutes existed, state law enforcement against these schemes was generally ineffective because jurisdiction over out-of-state offenders could not be obtained. Because only federal legislation could overcome these jurisdictional problems, in 1872 Congress enacted the Mail Fraud Statute to combat fraudulent schemes involving the U.S. mail. Not only did the Mail Fraud Statute carry stiff penalties for fraudulent mail schemes, it authorized the postmaster general to issue mail-stop orders against known offenders. The number of inspection and enforcement agents was increased; by 1939 there were over 600 Inspection Service agents.

The economic expansion that followed World War II greatly increased the volume of mail. Regular air travel permitted the USPS to increase dramatically the speed with which mail could be transported over great distances. Because of technological advances, both criminal techniques and the methods of the Inspection Service grew more sophisticated. In 1946, crime laboratories were established in five major cities; they used forensic photography, chemical and handwriting analysis, and fingerprint identification to gather and analyze physical evidence of postal crimes.

During the 1950s, as passenger air transportation increased, the postal system became increasingly reliant on air transport of mail aboard passenger flights. A terrorist bomb exploded aboard an aircraft for the first time in 1955. Inspection Service agents were able to determine that the bomb had been contained in the mail on board. That revelation led to enhanced security measures designed to protect the safety of the mail as well as that of air passengers.

Over the years, the reliability of the U.S. mail increased to the point where government, individuals, and businesses regularly entrusted mail with valuable contents to the USPS for delivery. However, realizing that the mail often contained cash, checks, and merchandise, criminals targeted unsecured links in the postal network. Attacks on post offices increased, as did the theft of mail onboard planes and in transit to and from airports. By the late 1960s, assuring the security and safety of the mail required an increasing amount of manpower and technical resources. In the early 1970s, a uniformed security force was established to patrol major postal facilities and escort valuable mail shipments between postal terminals and airports. The number of inspectors increased from fewer than 1,000 in 1960 to more than 1,700 in 1975. Postal loss from burglary, which reached a record $3.2 million in 1970, was reduced 91 percent by 1975.

Postal Law and Enforcement

The USPS assumes responsibility for protecting the mail from the time the sender deposits the letter or parcel into a postal receptacle to the time the recipient removes it from a mailbox. The current body of postal law is consistent with the USPS's objectives of maintaining the safety, security, and integrity of the U.S. mail and is comprehensive in scope. Nearly all postal law is federal, and therefore enforced at the federal level. Although the USPS assumes responsibility for investigating postal crimes, it may also enlist the assistance of the Federal Bureau of Investigation (FBI) or other federal agencies. Depending on the nature and severity of the crime, the USPIS may enforce postal laws through its own administrative proceedings or forward cases to a U.S. Attorney for prosecution.

Preserving the safety of the mail is accomplished primarily through mailability requirements—laws that prohibit the mailing of certain classes of items. These requirements are designed to ensure the safety of the mail by prohibiting the mailing of items that have the potential of injuring postal customers, mail carriers, and others. Examples of items prohibited from the U.S. mail include fireworks, explosives, and many chemicals. Prosecution for violations, however, usually depends on complaints from recipients, unless the illegal nature of the parcel's contents is revealed during transit.

The security of the mail—the assurance to the sender that the parcel he or she deposits for delivery will actually reach its intended recipient—is maintained in several ways. The presence of security cameras and/or armed and uniformed guards at post offices and other points in the delivery network reduces the vulnerability of the mail to theft by either dishonest employees or outsiders. Particularly valuable mail shipments may even be escorted to their destinations by armed guards. Missing parcels can sometimes be traced to a specific point in the delivery network, which may identify a weak link. Mail theft is a federal offense and subjects violators to tougher penalties than those for ordinary theft. Because the USPS assumes jurisdiction over mail until it is actually received by its intended recipient, USPS jurisdiction and enhanced penalties also apply to theft from personal mail receptacles.

The integrity of the mail is preserved through a combination of mailability requirements and the many provisions of the Mail Fraud Statute. Mailability requirements prohibit the mailing of anything that is inherently illegal, such as illicit drugs, counterfeit money, and child pornography. Also, closely regulated items such as firearms and liquor cannot be mailed by the general public, only by law enforcement agencies in certain instances. The Mail Fraud Statute, originally enacted in 1872, has been enhanced numerous times to close loopholes and halt evolving swindles. Fraud by mail subjects violators to federal jurisdiction and more severe penalties than for ordinary fraud.

The Mail Fraud Statute was so effective that violators resorted to private delivery services to avoid USPIS jurisdiction. Fraudulent telemarketer operations often rely on delivery services to receive checks for purchases made by telephone or to deliver promotional materials, but their activities came under the jurisdiction of the USPIS only when the U.S. mail was used. Thus, when a private delivery service was used to facilitate a fraud, USPIS jurisdiction was effectively avoided. This loophole was closed with an amendment to the Mail Fraud Statute in 1994 that brought commercial delivery services under the scope of the statute.

When the USPS receives a complaint indicating that the mail is being used for commercial fraud or deception, the grievance is forwarded to the USPIS for investigation. If the resulting investigation reveals that the Mail Fraud Statute has been violated, the evidence is forwarded to the U.S. Attorney for a determination of whether to proceed with criminal prosecution. Either as an alternative or an addition to a criminal prosecution, the USPIS may initiate an administrative action. The USPIS may also seek a temporary restraining order, or injunction, through a civil action in the federal court, which may prevent the promoter from receiving orders by mail until the administrative hearing has been held and a decision reached.

The promoter is given proper notice of the administrative hearing and may participate in the proceeding, in which the USPS has the burden of proving evidence of the charges. The hearing is presided over by an administrative law judge whose decision may recommend that final action be taken by the USPS's judicial officer. If, after evaluating the evidence, the judicial officer determines that the evidence supports the complaint, a mail stop order and/or a cease-and-desist order is issued. If the judicial officer determines that the evidence is insufficient and refuses to grant an injunctive order, there is no appeal.

If a mail stop order is issued, the respondent may examine detained mail only in the presence of postal employees and accept only mail that bears no relationship to a fraud or misrepresentation. If either a mail stop or cease-and-desist order is issued, the respondent is entitled to seek judicial review in a U.S. District Court. Either side may seek an appeal through the U.S. Court of Appeals or, eventually, the U.S. Supreme Court.

As an alternative to either criminal prosecution or administrative action, the USPS may, in minor cases, contact the promoter directly to seek voluntary compliance. If this attempt at resolution is successful, the promoter may enter into a consent agreement with the USPS to cease and desist and/or mail out corrective advertising.

One serious shortcoming of the USPIS's efforts is that it lacks international jurisdiction. Fraudulent and deceptive advertisers from other countries, whose schemes or methods may be legal where they operate but illegal in the United States, may refuse to comply voluntarily with U.S. law. In these cases, the USPS cannot withhold incoming mail even when the return address of the violator is recognized, although the USPS can obtain mail stop orders against foreign violators to prevent them from receiving outgoing mail. But the service approaches each case of this kind on an individual basis and relies on complaints from U.S. postal customers of foreign-operated scams and lotteries.

Unlike many other law enforcement agencies, whose investigative and enforcement efforts are often divided and diverse, the USPIS's responsibilities are narrow and focused. Decentralized investigative authority and an efficient network of manpower and technological resources permit postal inspectors to develop a finely tuned expertise in the field of investigation and case-building against postal law violators. Well-focused and aggressive enforcement measures, combined with enhanced penalties for violators of postal laws, discourage violation of these statutes.

— Lee Richardson

Readings

Stone, Bob (1994). *Successful Direct Marketing Methods.* Lincolnwood, IL: NTC Business Books. Chs. 5–9.

U.S. Congress, Committee on Post Office and Civil Service, Subcommittee on Postal Operations and Services. 1994. *Mail Fraud.* Washington, DC: U.S. Government Printing Office.

Presidents and the Consumer Movement

Most presidential scholars identify the birth of the modern presidency with the inauguration of Franklin Delano Roosevelt in 1933. In recent years, however, several scholars have traced the roots of the modern presidency to the earlier administration of Theodore Roosevelt, who pursued an aggressive foreign policy and sought to influence the deliberations of Congress. One of his congressional "interventions" was in support of the first two major pieces of consumer legislation—the Meat Inspection Act of 1906 and the Pure Food and Drug Act of 1906.

The impetus for the Pure Food and Drug Act came not from President Roosevelt but from Dr. Harvey Wiley, the chief chemist for the U.S. Department of Agriculture, although Roosevelt played a critical role in the legislation's passage. The House of Representatives had twice passed a bill, but a recalcitrant Senate stalled the legislation. In 1905, Roosevelt entered the debate by actively urging the Senate to pass the legislation. Primarily because of his intervention, the bill was reintroduced in the Senate. Yet, had it not been for the publication of Upton Sinclair's muckraking novel *The Jungle* in 1906, the legislation might have stalled in the Senate once again. The book's graphic details of the poor sanitary and working conditions in meat slaughtering facilities brought a public outcry for reforms.

Roosevelt took advantage of the public's mood to promote aggressively a new meat inspection law. Roosevelt appointed Charles P. Neill and James B. Reynolds to investigate *The Jungle*'s charges. He then encouraged Congress to draft meat inspection legislation. When this bill bogged down, Roosevelt released the Neill-Reynolds report, which forestalled an attempt by the House Agriculture Committee to weaken the bill's provisions. The legislation passed and was signed into law; following on its coattails was the passage of the Pure Food and Drug Act of 1906.

As with the development of the consumer protection movement, the evolution of the modern presidency did not occur in a strictly linear fashion. Considerable periods of inactivity were punctuated by times of rapid change. The next president after Theodore Roosevelt to wield presidential power aggressively was also the next president to contribute significantly to the development of the consumer protection movement. On December 2, 1913, Woodrow Wilson called for the congressional enactment of a bill explicitly identifying unfair competitive practices. The following year, Wilson urged Congress to create the Interstate Trade Commission, an idea Theodore Roosevelt had proposed as early as 1908. Later that year, Congress established an agency with similar functions: the Federal Trade Commission (FTC), which subsequently played a major role in consumer protection.

U.S. participation in World War I diverted attention from consumer protection needs. Likewise, the pro-business mood of the country during the 1920s discouraged attention to consumer problems. In addition, the presidents of the 1920s left legislative matters largely to Congress. Thus, during the presidencies of Warren G. Harding, Calvin Coolidge, and Herbert Hoover, both the development of the modern presidency and progress in consumer protection were effectively stalled. Not until 1933, and the ascension of Franklin Roosevelt to the presidency, did both the modern presidency and the consumer protection movement again progress.

Shortly after his inauguration, Roosevelt instructed Rexford Tugwell, a close confidant and a member of his "brain trust," to revise the food and drug laws. In 1911 the Supreme Court had largely emasculated the labeling provisions of the 1906 act. At the urging of President William Howard Taft, Congress passed the Sherley amendment prohibiting "false and fraudulent" healing claims in 1911, but it was clear that the 1906 act needed to be strengthened. Because Roosevelt's attention was focused on restoring the nation's economic vitality, consumer protection was largely left to Assistant Secretary of Agriculture Tugwell, a man much distrusted on Capitol Hill. Tugwell supported comprehensive legislation, but the bill remained stalled throughout the first years of the New Deal. Not until June 25, 1938, was the Federal Food, Drug and Cosmetic Act finally signed into law. Tugwell, who by this time had left the Agriculture Department, considered the bill to be weak. Although a provision regulating false advertising had been stricken from the bill and assigned to the Federal Trade Commission through the Wheeler-Lea amendment to the FTC Act that same year, the new legislation gave the Food and Drug Administration additional authority to regulate drugs, cosmetics, and food products.

While these laws represented Roosevelt's major legislative achievement in the area of consumer protection, his presidency also witnessed the development of the first explicitly consumer agencies. Most importantly, a Consumer Advisory Board was established within the National Recovery Administration (NRA), but in this largely pro-business agency, the influence of the board was negligible, and the head of the NRA usually ignored the board's advice. The Consumer Advisory Board later disappeared when the Supreme Court ruled that the legislation enacting the NRA was unconstitutional. Consumer protection–related units were also created in a number of other federal agencies during Roosevelt's presidency, but none survived beyond the end of World War II.

Like World War I, World War II diverted attention from the need for consumer protection. Nor were the 1950s a fertile period for consumer initiatives. As in the 1920s, the country was largely pro-business, and the president, Dwight David Eisenhower, did not support a consumer protection agenda. In fact, he opposed a proposed truth in lending bill and took no position on several auto safety proposals.

John F. Kennedy, a more active legislative president than his predecessor, became the first president to deliver a consumer message to Congress. On March 15, 1962, Kennedy observed about consumers that: "Their voice is not always as loudly heard in Washington as the voices of smaller and better organized groups—nor is their point of view always defined and presented. But under our economic as well as our political form of democracy, we share an obligation to protect the common interest in every decision we make." Kennedy identified four basic consumers' rights: to safety, to be informed, to choose, and to be heard. The Kennedy message spurred interest in consumer concerns, both in the United States and around the world. The president also directed his Council of Economic Advisers to create a Consumer Advisory Council (CAC) to provide advice to the government, and he ordered relevant federal agencies to designate a special assistant to give attention to consumer interests. Esther Peterson, an assistant secretary of labor and well-known activist, was named consumer adviser to President Kennedy. CAC, which had little influence, requested that Peterson be designated as a consumer adviser on the White House staff, but the appointment was not granted until Lyndon Johnson became president.

The charismatic Kennedy provided strong rhetorical support for the consumer protection movement, but his support for a consumer legislative agenda was tepid. For example, he first refused to endorse Senator Estes Kefauver's amendments to the 1938 Food, Drug and Cosmetic Act, then attempted to water them down by proposing a weaker alternative. Only after Kefauver orchestrated media coverage of the thalidomide prescription drug crisis (a tranquilizer and sleep-inducing drug responsible for thousands of infants born with deformed limbs in twenty countries, although few in the United States) did the Kennedy administration reverse its position. Suddenly, it declared its own proposed legislation inadequate and called for passage of the Kefauver-Harris drug amendments.

Lyndon Johnson became not only the most active legislative president since FDR, but also the White House's first and, to date, greatest champion of consumer protection issues. As a savvy former majority leader in the Senate, President Johnson knew how to push and cajole the Congress into passing legislation, including many consumer bills. As with Kennedy's reluctant support for the Kefauver amendments, politics had much to do with Johnson's consumer advocacy.

By the mid-1960s a consumer protection movement had begun to influence Congress. Prior to the 1960s no organized consumer protection lobby existed, but by the end of the decade the consumer movement emerged as a genuine social movement. This movement was given a boost by consumer activist Ralph Nader, who captured the public's attention with a critical study of auto safety and the uncovering of a related investigation of his private life conducted by General Motors. For the first time, consumer protection issues were widely covered by the media.

President Johnson saw an opportunity to gain popularity by proposing and supporting consumer initiatives. These issues were not nearly as controversial as civil rights and Medicaid, which had dominated the legislative agenda in 1964 and 1965. For a president who was daily becoming more embroiled in the details of the Vietnam War, consumer protection had appeal.

Like his predecessor, Lyndon Johnson delivered a consumer protection message to Congress (in 1964). Johnson also created a new White House position—special assistant for consumer affairs—and appointed Esther Peterson to the post. That same year, by executive order Johnson established the President's Committee on Consumer Interests (PCCI). The organization was made up of members of the Consumer Advisory Council, which Kennedy had established in 1962, and officials of Johnson's administration. PCCI members rarely met, but Peterson, the head of the committee, used the PCCI staff to advance consumer protection reforms aggressively.

Johnson did not deliver a consumer protection message in 1965, his busiest legislative year, but he did in 1966, which was the same year he signed into law the National Traffic and Motor Vehicle Safety Act. In 1968, Johnson included several consumer reform proposals in his State of the Union address. He expanded the role of special assistant for consumer affairs to include advocacy. Betty Furness, a former television personality who succeeded Esther Peterson as Johnson's consumer spokesperson, used her media skills to promote the president's consumer protection agenda. During the Johnson years, laws were enacted requiring fair packaging and labeling of foods, licensing of drug manufacturing, new standards for flammable fabrics, minimum standards for the inspection of meat and poultry, and truth in lending.

By the late 1960s the consumer protection movement had become so effective that when Richard Milhous Nixon, a Republican, assumed the presidency in 1969, he continued to deliver annual consumer protection messages to Congress. The 1969 message enunciated a "Buyer's Bill of Rights," which added the right to redress to the list set out by John Kennedy. Like Johnson, Nixon also named an adviser for consumer affairs: Virginia H. Knauer, who had been director of the Pennsylvania Bureau of Consumer Protection. (Nixon's first choice was the woman who headed the Good Housekeeping seal operation, but her name was withdrawn when she indicated to the press that she would work in Washington part-time and retain her Good Housekeeping position.) Nixon also issued Executive Order 11583 to strengthen the U.S. Office of Consumer Affairs, which evolved from the PCCI.

Despite these outward demonstrations of support, Nixon was not a strong advocate of consumer protection. More concerned with business than consumer interests, the Nixon administration watered down or opposed a number of important consumer protection proposals. For example, President Nixon opposed the creation of a new agency to regulate product safety, instead preferring regulation by existing agencies. The fact that the Consumer Product Safety Commission (CPSC) and the National Highway Safety Traffic Association (NHTSA) were established during Nixon's presidency demonstrates how much clout the consumer protection movement still had. This influence, and the moderate character of Nixon's conservatism, helped lead to approval of other consumer laws establishing egg inspection standards, limitations on liability for unauthorized use of credit cards, procedures for correcting inaccurate information in credit reporting agency files, child-resistant packaging of hazardous substances, listing of prescription drug ingredients, specifications for motor vehicle cost information, improved powers for the Federal Trade Commission, national standards for manufacturers' warranties, protections against billing errors in credit card accounts, prohibitions against discrimination in consumer credit, and strengthened automobile recall and repair procedures.

Following Nixon's resignation, Vice President Gerald Ford assumed the presidency. Ford served as president for less than three years, but he had a major impact on the debate over the future of consumer protection regulation. Where Richard Nixon had been concerned about the costs of government regulation, Ford developed management strategies specifically designed to control regulatory bureaucracies. Of these strategies, the use of cost-benefit analysis (where the potential costs of a regulation are compared to its potential benefits) would have the greatest long-term impact on the formulation of consumer policy. Ford's successors, including Democrats Jimmy Carter and Bill Clinton, continued using cost-benefit analysis.

As a member of Congress, Ford supported the creation of a federal consumer protection agency (also called Agency for Consumer Advocacy). As president, however, he disappointed consumer advocates by opposing related legislation (which did not pass Congress). Nevertheless, during the Ford presidency, legislation was enacted that required energy-efficient labels on home appliances; established refund and replacement options for defective automobiles, tires, and vehicle replacement parts; repealed the so-called fair trade laws; institutionalized procedures to assist consumers in resolving credit billing disputes; and prohibited discrimination in consumer credit. At the prompting of Virginia H. Knauer, who continued to serve as special assistant for consumer affairs, the president added the "right to consumer education" to the presidential Consumer Bill of Rights first announced by Kennedy.

President Jimmy Carter continued the Democratic party's support of the consumer protection agenda. He appointed well-known consumer advocates—notably, Joan Claybrook, Carol Tucker Foreman, and Michael Pertschuk—to major executive-branch positions. Though Carter was displeased with the performance of the CPSC (in 1977 he considered abolishing the agency), Esther Peterson, his special assistant for consumer affairs, helped persuade the president to support its reauthorization in 1978. Consumer-protection accomplishments during the Carter administration include the passage of regulations to: eliminate abuses in debt collection, reduce exploitation in hearing-aid sales, require improved alcohol beverage labeling, provide consumer protections for electronic funds transfers, and establish a national bank to fund consumer cooperatives and self-help organizations. Despite Carter's support, the proposal for a federal consumer protection agency failed to pass Congress and died.

In his 1980 presidential campaign, Republican Ronald Reagan proposed abolishing the CPSC. Reagan's election marked a significant downturn in the political fortunes of the consumer protection movement, even though he failed to eliminate the CPSC. As with the environmental movement, consumer advocates found their access to the Reagan White House curtailed. In addition, the Reagan administration initiated antiregulatory actions that severely weakened the enforcement capabilities of environmental and consumer agencies. The budgets of such agencies as the Environmental Protection Agency, Food and Drug Administration, National Highway Traffic Safety Administration, and Consumer Product Safety Commission were cut severely, especially in the areas of enforcement and research and development.

Reagan also appointed officials who shared his antiregulatory views to lead these agencies. These appointees often used their positions to promote the interests of the business community rather than those of consumers. For example, Raymond Peck, Reagan's administrator of the National Highway Traffic Safety Administration, repealed a recently enacted rule, thus delaying the installation of airbags in U.S.-manufactured automobiles for almost a decade. Similarly, CPSC became less diligent in its oversight of defective products, and the Federal Trade Commission became less attentive in its regulation of advertising. At the Food and Drug Administration, a pilot project for testing prescription drug inserts to inform consumers was eliminated.

Virginia Knauer provided consumer advice to President Reagan, the third president she served in that capacity. However, Reagan downgraded Knauer's position by removing her from the White House, placing her in the Department of Health and Human Services, and retitling her job "special adviser to the president for consumer affairs." This demotion symbolized the lack of respect of the Reagan White House for traditional consumer education and protection functions and activities. Although the Reagan administration took actions that were claimed to serve the consumer interest—such as "fast-tracking" for breakthrough drugs and a refusal to increase duties on many imported products—these decisions were not influenced by any organized consumer advocacy.

Reagan's Republican successor, George Bush, was not virulently antiregulation, but he provided little support for, and some opposition to, consumer protection initiatives. Although the budgets for many consumer agencies increased slightly, support for environmental and consumer-protection regulation was undermined by the anti-consumer efforts of Vice President Dan Quayle's Council on Competitiveness. Bush's one veto was of congressional legislation to reregulate the cable television industry. (It was overridden.)

On the positive side for consumer protection, President Bush fashioned an agreement for government agencies to require greatly improved nutritional labeling of food products, and he signed legislation to create truth in savings, standardize medigap insurance policies, and place limits on advertising in television programming aimed at children. During the Bush administration two people served as special adviser to the president for consumer affairs—Bonnie Guiton, the first African American to hold the position, and Ann Windham Wallace, a Texas Republican activist.

In 1993, Democrat Bill Clinton entered the White House. Clinton had an ambitious agenda during his first two years in office, but it included only one major consumer issue—ambitious health care reform, which failed to pass Congress. Only later did the administration turn its attention to consumer issues such as stricter poultry and meat inspection standards. Despite Arkansas ties between Clinton and the poultry industry, the administration supported reforms whose need was demonstrated by an outbreak of E. coli bacteria infections from undercooked hamburger products. New consumer protections included not only improved meat inspection standards, but also a mandatory seafood inspection program, stronger telemarketing rules, and the addition of the "right to service" to the Consumer Bill of Rights.

Although Clinton restored the "special assistant" title for his consumer spokesperson, the position remained in the Department of Health and Human Services and was largely ignored by the White House. The president's first appointee to this position, Polly Baca, a Hispanic American, resigned after less than one year. She was replaced by former Congressman Leslie Byrne. In late 1996, however, Clinton appointed two consumer activists to important positions in his administration—Ann Brown to head the CPSC and Ellen Haas to manage Department of Agriculture food and nutrition programs.

U.S. presidents do not see themselves as consumer advocates; after all, they must serve diverse interests and constituencies. Yet, some presidents have been more sympathetic to consumer interests and the need for consumer protections than have others. In general, Democratic presidents are more supportive of the consumer movement's agenda than Republican leaders. Two underlying factors, however, influence the positions of all presidents on consumer issues. One is the extent to which the public demands new consumer protections. When this demand is evident, presidents almost always either take the lead in promoting new protections or accede to them. The second factor is general economic conditions. In the 1960s particularly, when Americans were optimistic about the economic future, relatively little concern was felt about the impacts of consumer protections on business efficiency. As growth slowed, businesses restructured, and foreign economic competition increased, the public grew more sympathetic to business arguments that consumer regulations hindered their competitiveness and financial health. Consequently, even in the fundamentally pro-consumer Clinton administration there was some support for the use of cost-benefit analysis to evaluate consumer protections. If economic forecasts are to be believed, future presidents must remain concerned about the economic impacts of any new protections.

— Richard W. Waterman, E. Thomas Garman

See also

Congress and Consumer Protection; U.S. Consumer Movement: History and Dynamics; U.S. Consumer Protection Agency; U.S. Office of Consumer Affairs.

Readings

Mayer, Robert N. (1989). *The Consumer Movement: Guardians of the Marketplace.* Boston: Twayne Publishers.

Meier, Kenneth J., and E. Thomas Garman, eds. (1995). *Regulation and Consumer Protection.* 2d ed. Houston: Dame Publications.

Nadel, Mark V. (1971). *The Politics of Consumer Protection.* Indianapolis: Bobbs-Merrill Co.

Price Controls

At first glance, price controls appear to serve the consumer interest. After all, if price controls prevent prices from being higher, then will not consumers benefit by paying lower prices and being able to afford more products? Also, are not price controls needed to protect consumers from the power that some businesses have to set prices at any level they want?

A key to the evaluation of price controls is the difference between their short-run and long-run impacts. Initially, price controls may help consumers by keeping prices lower. But over time, businesses react to price controls in such a way that some or all of the short-run benefits to consumers are eliminated.

Definition and Implementation

There are two types of controls: One simply establishes by law the price of a product and the second sets price ceilings. A price ceiling sets a limit above which prices cannot legally go. If market conditions establish a price below the ceiling, the price ceiling is said to be nonbinding. If market conditions would have established a price above the ceiling, the ceiling is said to be binding.

Numerous examples of price controls abound in American history. Economy-wide price controls have frequently been imposed during wartime, for example during World War II, the Korean War, and the latter part of the Vietnam War. Price controls have also been set—and in some cases continue to be set—for specific products and services, including airline fares, trucking rates, telephone service rates, energy rates, auto insurance rates, and housing rents.

Price controls cannot be imposed without costs. If they are to be effective, they must be enforced, and enforcement costs money. Staff must be hired to perform many functions associated with price controls. First, if price controls are to be set by other than educated guesses, staff must be hired to conduct studies to derive the "proper" price or price ceiling. Further, if the controls are to be allowed to change over time, staff must periodically update these analyses. Other staff must perform the enforcement duties associated with price controls; for example, detectives and lawyers must be hired to find and prosecute price control violators. Implementation costs of price controls are not insignificant. During World War II, thousands of persons were hired to manage the price controls. Businesses must also spend money to comply with the price control regulations.

Moreover, price controls rarely proceed smoothly. Businesses often find ways around them, and when they do, price control regulators must expend resources to deal with the situation. One widely cited example comes from the price controls of the Nixon administration in the early 1970s. Plywood producers were not happy with their regulated price in the booming economy of the early 1970s. To get around the controls, these producers simply created a "new" product by punching holes in, and adding grooves to, regular plywood. These holes and grooves served no useful purpose, but they allowed the producers to claim legally that the altered plywood was a new product and not subject to the price control on plywood. However, the resources expended to alter the plywood were wasted from the point of view of the overall efficiency of the economy.

Effects

Shortages are the fundamental problem of price controls, although it may take time for the shortage to occur. Initially, consumers purchase the same amount as they did before the controls, getting the same amounts at lower prices. But as consumers increase their desired purchases and businesses decrease their production, shortages occur.

The shortages resulting from price controls will be quickly obvious for nondurable, frequently purchased products. For example, if price controls are applied to supermarket products, within months (one production cycle) consumers will notice barer shelves and smaller amounts for sale.

In durable goods markets, especially housing rental markets, the shortages appear through both lower quantity and lower quality. Lower quantity occurs as fewer new rental dwellings are constructed. Lower quality results from landlords reducing their investment in the units by providing less maintenance and repair, which in turn leads to a deterioration in the quality of the units. Landlords may allow the units to deteriorate until the revenue they receive from the units, divided by the units' investment value, equals a market rate of return.

How will the shortage created by price controls be eliminated? One way is through longer waits and longer shopping time. Consumers soon realize that gasoline pumps quickly run dry and that supermarket shelves rapidly empty soon after new supplies arrive. Thus, when new supplies arrive, consumers line up at stores in an attempt to "get theirs" before the supply is depleted. Not only is additional time devoted to waiting in line, but time is also taken to plan shopping expeditions around the shipping schedules of suppliers.

Some consumers may try to use undue influence, and suppliers may accommodate them, to get priority on products. Consumers may offer money under the table in return for being moved to the front of the line. In New York City, finder's fees and key deposits of several thousand dollars sometimes are used to get around rent controls. Underground markets also develop as a means to eliminate the shortages caused by price controls.

Government may directly address the shortages induced by price controls through rationing. In this case, government uses a formula, usually based on household size, to issue ration coupons that give households the right to purchase a certain amount of the product or service. The problem, of course, is that government formulas can never replicate the complex factors that determine how much of a product a household desires to purchase.

Empirical Evidence

The most extensive price controls in U.S. history occurred during World War II. Careful analysis of these price controls shows that they worked in holding prices lower than would otherwise be the case. Paul Evans estimates that the general price level was 30 percent lower during World War II as a result of price controls. But this benefit came at a cost. Evans also calculates that the price controls caused economy-wide output to be 7 percent lower and employment to be 12 percent lower than they would have been without the controls.

Rent controls are one type of price control that continues in some communities. New York City, Santa Monica, Toronto, and other communities have restrictions on the rents that landlords can charge to tenants. A detailed analysis of the Toronto program by Lawrence Smith and Peter Tomlinson shows that the rent controls have caused lower rates of construction, less maintenance and repair on existing units, lower valued dwellings, and rental shortages. Thus, tenants who are able to hold onto rent-controlled units benefit by paying less, but they also receive less in terms of quality. Also, many who want to rent at the controlled rates simply cannot find space.

Last, the experience with the airline industry in the last decade and a half shows that the removal of price controls, when combined with the removal of barriers to entering the industry, can result in lower prices over time. Prior to 1978, the U.S. airline industry operated under stringent federal price and entry controls. Operators were not free to enter the industry or open new routes. Ticket prices were also regulated by a federal agency.

With federal legislation passed in 1978 and implemented in the 1980s, price and entry regulation of the airlines came to an end. Operators gained the freedom to enter and leave specific routes and the entire industry, and to set ticket prices wherever they want. As a result, consumers have benefited from lower airline fares. Numerous studies conclude that the real (inflation-adjusted) price per passenger mile has fallen as a result of deregulation. For example, William Evans and Joannis Kessides estimate that the average real price per passenger mile fell 16 percent between 1978 and 1988 as a result of deregulation.

Evaluation

Is there any situation where price controls are a good idea? Some form of price control is needed when an industry is dominated by one firm, that is, when there is a monopoly supplier rather than many competitive suppliers. It can be shown that prices will be higher and output lower with a monopoly supplier than with many competitors. The monopoly supplier will make "monopoly profits," and price controls are one way of limiting these profits and forcing the monopoly to lower prices and increase output. In most states, power utilities are considered monopoly suppliers, and their prices are controlled by a state agency.

Although the usefulness of price controls depends on the firm being a monopoly supplier, if technology and/or markets change, a one-time monopoly supplier is likely to find itself in competition with other firms. This situation is occurring in the power generation industry. Efficient, high-power transmission lines now make it possible for energy utilities in one region of the country to transfer power to another region and compete with the local utility. If this kind of competition becomes common (and legal), price controls on energy utilities will become unnecessary.

Despite this exception, the costs of price controls usually exceed their benefits. Price controls create a disparity between the amount of a product or service that consumers desire to buy and the amount that businesses want to provide. This disparity, called a shortage, must be made up in some nonprice way, such as increased waiting time to purchase the product, influencing the producer, or official rationing by the government. For products and services with a quality dimension, another result of price controls is a reduction in quality.

If prices are considered too high for particular products or services, there are alternatives to price controls. Most important, the product or service should be examined for any restrictions on the entry of competitors. For example, import restrictions and tariffs, local content regulations, and territory restrictions (e.g., car dealerships being assigned exclusive territory in a locality) are examples of entry restrictions that keep prices high.

Second, local, state, and federal regulations must be examined for their impact on prices. Policymakers should carefully study the benefits and costs of all regulations to ensure that any resulting increase in product price is justified by accompanying benefits.

Last, as an alternative to price controls on monopolies, consideration should be given to eliminating the monopoly status of such firms by introducing competitors. This has successfully been done for long-distance telephone service and airline service. On the horizon is the opening up of competition in cable television, local telephone, and local energy services.

— Michael L. Walden

See also

Deregulation, Economic.

Readings

Evans, Paul (1982). "The Effects of General Price Controls in the U.S." *Journal of Political Economy.* 90 (5): 944–966.

Evans, William, and Joannis Kessides (1993). "Structure, Conduct, and Performance in the Deregulated Airline Industry." *Southern Economic Journal.* 59 (3): 450–467.

Smith, Lawrence, and Peter Tomlinson (1981). "Rent Controls in Ontario: Roofs or Ceilings." *Journal of the American Real Estate and Urban Economics Association.* 9 (2): 93–114.

Privacy Protections

Privacy is an enduring American value with roots that predate the U.S. Constitution. Despite its history and importance, it has no generally accepted definition. Privacy is often cited as an element of the First Amendment right of association, the Fourth Amendment protection against unreasonable searches and seizures, and the Fifth Amendment right against self-incrimination. In *Griswold v. Connecticut* (1965), the U.S. Supreme Court observed that these and other guarantees in the Bill of Rights create zones of privacy. However, the word *privacy* does not appear in the Constitution, and there is no direct constitutional right of privacy.

The idea of a formal right to privacy originated in a famous 1890 *Harvard Law Review* article by Louis Brandeis and Samuel Warren in which privacy was described as "the right to be let alone." Others split privacy into two separate interests. The first is an interest in avoiding disclosure of personal matters. The second is an interest in independence for personal decisions involving marriage, procreation, contraception, family relationships, child rearing, and education.

Of these two interests, most recent privacy legislation relates to personal information. Another term often used, especially abroad, to refer to this subset of privacy issues is "data protection." This term is a more precise way of referring to privacy values that arise concerning the collection, use, and dissemination of personal data.

The right to privacy is rarely, if ever, an absolute value. Evaluating privacy in any situation requires a balancing of interests. The interests most commonly balanced against privacy are law enforcement, national security, efficiency, oversight of government activities, freedom of speech and press, and public health. Balancing the interests of an individual against broader societal interests is often difficult.

Federal Privacy Statutes

The first major modern information privacy statute was the Fair Credit Reporting Act

(FCRA) of 1970. The FCRA was a response to the growth of third-party record keeping about consumers and the resulting problems and unfairness. As consumer credit expanded in the last half of the twentieth century, the consumer reporting industry grew in size and importance. Consumer reporting agencies (credit bureaus) maintain files on millions of individuals, and problems with confidentiality, accuracy, relevance, and fair use grew along with the industry. Following media attention, consumer frustration, and congressional hearings, Congress passed the FCRA in 1970 to regulate the collection and use of consumer credit information.

Principal provisions of the FCRA include: limiting permissible uses of credit reports to credit transactions, employment purposes, insurance underwriting, governmental licensing, and legitimate business needs; restricting the reporting of obsolete information such as bankruptcy filings more than ten years old; limiting the use of investigatory consumer reports about a person's character, general reputation, and lifestyle; disclosing to consumers the nature and substance of credit reporting information, the sources of the information, and the recipients of credit reports; notifying consumers of adverse action taken based on credit reports; establishing procedures for resolving disputes about the accuracy of credit reports; assigning administrative enforcement activities to the Federal Trade Commission; and providing credit reporting agencies with qualified immunity from liability for reporting inaccurate information. The U.S. Public Interest Research Group is a leader among consumer organizations in advocacy work on recently proposed amendments to the FCRA.

In 1974, Congress enacted the Privacy Act of 1974. This law sets broad rules for the collection, maintenance, use, and disclosure of personal information by federal agencies. The act followed congressional hearings that focused on fears about the growth of computerized databanks. A 1988 amendment added procedural rules for computer matching (the computerized comparison of information about individuals to evaluate eligibility for federal benefit programs).

Although the concept dates to the early 1970s, the Privacy Act of 1974 is the first formal implementation of fair information practices, and now forms the basis for privacy laws throughout the industrialized world. Fair information practices offer a useful list of privacy concerns to be considered when developing or evaluating any privacy policy or law. Among American public interest groups, the Center for Democracy and Technology is an advocate for fair information practices.

Fair information practices include eight elements: openness (no secret data systems), individual participation (the right to see and correct records), collection limitation (data should be collected by lawful and fair means), data quality (data should be accurate, complete, and timely for its purpose), use limitation (data should be used only for a purpose specified at the time of collection), disclosure limitation (external disclosures are prohibited without consent or legal authority), security (data should be protected by reasonable security safeguards), and accountability (record keepers should be accountable for complying with the fair information practices).

Federal laws designed to address privacy concerns about other categories of records include: Family Educational Rights and Privacy Act (students and parents may inspect and correct student data, restricts disclosure of student data), Right to Financial Privacy Act (requires customer notice of federal government subpoenas for bank records in some circumstances), Cable Communications Policy Act of 1984 (subscribers must be notified about personal data collected, subscribers may inspect and correct personal data, and disclosure of personal data restricted), Electronic Communications Privacy Act (establishes privacy rules for stored wire and electronic communications and transactional records access), Video Privacy Protection Act of 1988 (restricts disclosure of information about specific selections of customers without consent and limits law enforcement access to identifiable customer information), Telephone Consumer Protection Act (requires the Federal Communications Commission to issue regulations permitting residential telephone subscribers to avoid receiving unwanted telephone solicitations), and Driver's Privacy Protection Act of 1994 (establishes rules governing the disclosure of individually identifiable information by state motor vehicle departments). Consumer information on many privacy laws is available from the Privacy Rights Clearinghouse in San Diego, California.

Other Privacy Protections

The American approach to privacy legislation is sometimes called sectoral. Frequently, laws covering specific types of records are passed in response to a specific highly publicized incident or court decision, resulting in a patchwork of inconsistent protections. Major categories of records, such as health, employment, and insurance, are not protected by federal privacy laws. A few states have privacy laws, but these statutes tend to be incomplete and inconsistent. Whether federal privacy laws should preempt state laws is in dispute; the disagreement is primarily between the need for uniformity in an interstate environment and the ability of interest groups to secure more favorable laws from the states.

In contrast, most European countries have omnibus laws that apply fair information practices to all personal records maintained by public and private sector organizations. European institutions such as the Council of Europe, Organization for Economic Cooperation and Development, and the European Union spent years developing and implementing common privacy principles. In 1995 the European Union adopted a data protection directive designed to increase harmonization of European data protection laws; it also may limit the disclosure of personal information to countries with inadequate privacy protections.

Another major difference between American and European approaches is in enforcement. Most American laws allow individuals to file lawsuits when rights have been violated, but because lawsuits are expensive and time-consuming, enforcement is occasional and beyond the reach of many consumers. Most European countries have formal government agencies that oversee privacy laws and provide a source of expertise, assistance, and enforcement. Proposals to establish a privacy agency in the United States have met with resistance from business.

Many states have tort remedies for some invasions of privacy. Four distinct privacy torts are commonly recognized: intrusion upon an individual's seclusion or solitude, public disclosure of private facts, placing an individual in a false light highly offensive to a reasonable person, and an unpermitted use for private commercial gain of a person's identity. Whether a tort lawsuit is an effective remedy for most people is an open question; it is also uncertain whether these torts are responsive to the ongoing creation of private databanks with detailed consumer profiles compiled from public and private records.

Records maintained by state and local governments are a major source of personal data about consumers. Examples include records about motor vehicles, property taxes, occupational and other licenses, voter registration, police activities, and land ownership. In many states these records are publicly available and sold by the state. Private companies can obtain the records, use them without restriction, and merge the data with private databases. The result is more detailed consumer profiles maintained by private companies.

Impacts of Technology

In many ways, the history of information privacy in the last hundred years is a response to technology, the most important of which is the computer. Public concerns about loss of privacy have risen sharply with the spread of computers. Private companies and governments now can collect and maintain unlimited amounts of personal information about individuals. Records of routine consumer activities result in the creation of permanent records showing the time, date, location, and nature of the activities. Such records are called transactional records because they are the by-product of consumer transactions.

Those who provide consumer services are necessarily in possession of detailed personal information, data that are of value for other uses. Those who compile the data may exploit that value in many ways, including selling or renting to others. It is a common practice for companies to collect, compile, and sell consumer profiles as mailing lists or similar databases. Few laws exist to regulate the collection, use, or sale of transaction records.

Some companies give consumers a choice by offering a notice of data resale and reuse practices and allowing the consumer to object, a procedure called opt-out (those who do not want their information released must take action to prevent it). Another approach is opt-in: Personal data cannot be used or disclosed without the affirmative consent of the customer. A few laws require opt-out before some uses or disclosures of consumer information are permitted. The business community strongly opposes any opt-in requirements.

Another point of view sometimes expressed is that consumers should have property rights in their personal information. Celebrities have legal grounds to prevent others from exploiting their names and images, and the argument is that ordinary consumers should have similar rights to exploit their own data. However, a property right in personal information is just a theory; no firm legal precedent exists, only many unresolved legal, policy, and administrative questions.

Another consequence of technology is that existing privacy laws are outdated. The authors of the Privacy Act of 1974 used paper records and mainframe computers as models for personal data systems. With the expanded use of personal computers, the act's provisions no longer offer meaningful guidance to record keepers or protections to record subjects. Other privacy laws have also become outdated by technology or by changes in government or private data practices. The widespread use of computer networks such as the Internet raises new issues not foreseen in existing laws.

Technology also offers ways to enhance the privacy of individuals. Cryptography is the technique of concealing the contents of a message by a code or cipher. The use of cryptographic techniques for storing and exchanging personal data can protect data against unauthorized access or use, a technology especially valuable for computer network activities. Another way to enhance privacy is anonymization. For example, proposals for using digital cash in consumer transactions are being pursued and implemented. Computers may also allow more effective consumer choice and avoid the need for opt-out or opt-in rules. Increased use of these technologies may hinge on greater acceptance in the marketplace and more standardization. The Electronic Privacy Information Clearinghouse is a leader among public interest organizations in monitoring and promoting technologies of privacy.

Privacy is a broad and complex issue, with no sharply defined boundaries. Privacy rules can affect anyone who maintains data about individuals, and that includes virtually every business and government. The result is that it can be difficult to adopt new rules. Pressures from consumers and privacy advocates for new protections are likely to continue to meet resistance from business and government. International regulatory actions will grow in importance and may provide an incentive for multinational businesses to support more standardization of privacy rules. In addition, computer networks create privacy concerns that may be beyond the scope of existing national governments to address, as network transactions and activities readily cross national borders. Future developments in technology, government, and business are certain to put added pressure on consumer privacy interests.

— Robert Gellman

Readings

Privacy Protection Study Commission (1977). *Personal Privacy in an Information Society.*

Washington, DC: U.S. Government Printing Office.
Regan, Priscilla M. (1995). *Legislating Privacy: Technology, Social Values, and Public Policy.* Chapel Hill: North Carolina Press.
Schwartz, Paul, and Joel M. Reidenberg (1996). *Data Protection Law: A Study of United States Data Protection.* Charlottesville, VA: Michie Law Publishers.

Product Hazards

Each year, millions of American consumers are injured or die in incidents associated with consumer products frequently used in and around the home. It is the responsibility of the U.S. Consumer Product Safety Commission (CPSC) to address most of these occurrences.

Reducing injuries and deaths from consumer products requires an understanding of the product's function and operation and the consumer's use of the product. In some cases, a product is designed improperly, and the design flaw causes consumers to be injured. In other cases, the design may be appropriate, but a manufacturing error renders the product unsafe. In still other cases, a product may contain some inherent hazard (e.g., a knife with a sharp blade) that requires safe use by the consumer and may cause injury if used improperly.

The five acts administered by the CPSC give it authority to set standards, ban products, require labeling, and provide for recalls of hazardous consumer products. For the most part, these acts are not product specific in that they set out procedures for agency actions with respect to products found by the commissioners to pose an unreasonable risk of injury. Over the years, the CPSC has used the authority of these acts to take action to protect consumers. In addition, Congress directs the CPSC to take action on specific products to protect the public from hazards about which Congress is concerned and for which the CPSC has not exercised its regulatory authority.

In its first twenty-three years, the CPSC enacted regulations addressing hazards associated with architectural glazing materials; matchbooks; citizen band antennas; power lawnmowers; swimming-pool slides; cellulose insulation; cigarette lighters; automatic residential garage-door openers; unstable refuse bins; contact adhesives; lead-containing paint; patching compounds; artificial emberizing materials; general-use garments containing asbestos; lawn darts; consumer products containing chlorofluorocarbons; coal- and wood-burning appliances; charcoal briquettes; benzene, turpentine, and other hazardous substances; fireworks; art materials; fire extinguishers; extremely flammable water-repellent treatments; liquid drain cleaners; toys with small parts, sharp edges, sharp points, or electrical hazards; caps for toy guns; baby walkers; pacifiers; bicycles; baby cribs; baby rattles; infant cushions; children's sleepwear; carpets and rugs; mattresses and mattress pads; refrigerators; and medicines and other substances that pose a risk of poisoning to children.

The products discussed below—all-terrain vehicles, bunk beds, toys, bicycle helmets, five-gallon buckets, upholstered furniture, walkers, window-blind cords, window falls, and flammable chiffon skirts—are more recent examples of how the agency responds to hazards. These products were the subject of petitions, judicial complaints, recall actions, education campaigns, rulemaking, and congressional mandates.

All-terrain vehicles (ATVs) are three- or four-wheeled vehicles designed for off-road, recreational, and other uses. ATVs are generally characterized by large, low-pressure tires; saddle seats; and handlebar steering. They typically weigh between 250 and 500 pounds, and many models are capable of speeds of over fifty miles per hour.

Between 1982 and September 1987, more than 900 deaths from the use of ATVs were reported to the CPSC. The commission attributed the fatalities primarily to the instability of ATVs. Because of these deaths and hundreds of thousands of injuries, CPSC started a rulemaking in 1985; in 1987 it filed suit against five ATV distributors to stop the sale of all three-wheel ATVS and require distributors to offer a refund for all four-wheel ATVs purchased for use by children under sixteen. On the same day as this filing, however, the lawsuit was settled by a preliminary consent decree that required that sales of three-wheel ATVs be stopped and that safety information be disseminated to the public.

Consumer and health groups, as well as Republican and Democratic members of Congress and one of the three sitting commissioners, strongly disagreed with the consent decree settlement. They argued that the decree failed to get the unsafe three-wheel and four-wheel ATVs purchased for children out of consumers' hands. Despite these objections, the CPSC finalized the decree and terminated its rulemaking in 1991. From 1991 through 1993, more than 173,000 injuries were associated with ATVs.

A Consumer Federation of America (CFA) petition in 1986 asked CPSC to set a mandatory standard to address strangulation deaths and injuries from bunk beds. Despite over 200,000 injuries and 72 deaths, in 1988 the commission denied the petition and asked the industry to set a voluntary standard. Deaths and injuries occur when children inadvertently are entrapped in, hang from, or fall from bunk beds. Although a standard was subsequently developed, in 1995 CFA reiterated its request for a mandatory standard because of the additional 45 deaths and 111,000 injuries occurring from 1990 to 1994. In addition, in 1994 and 1995 the CPSC recalled over 600,000 unsafe bunk beds.

In 1987, in response to a petition by a consumer group and a state attorney general, CPSC examined toys that pose a choking hazard to young children. It started, but later terminated, a rulemaking. Countering this termination, Congress enacted the Child Safety Protection Act in 1994. Addressing toys and bicycle helmets, this law required toys intended for children ages three through five that contain small parts to carry a prominent warning of the choking hazard these small parts pose to young children. The labels are also required on packages of marbles, small balls, and balloons. Also, balls intended for children under age three must be at least 1.75 inches in diameter so as not to pose a choking hazard. In response to a consumer-group petition, CPSC began, but terminated, a rulemaking addressing infant strangulation on crib toys.

The Child Safety Protection Act also requires that CPSC develop a uniform federal standard for bike helmets. The standard must address, among other things, the risk of bike helmets rolling off during a fall and the need for special protection of children's heads. While this standard is being developed, all manufacturers must comply with one of three voluntary standards (ANSI, Snell, or ASTM) or any other standard the commission deems appropriate. Between 1984 and 1988, 2,985 bicyclists in the United States died from head injuries. It is estimated that 85 percent of all head injuries suffered by bicyclists could be prevented by using bicycle helmets.

Infants of eight to fourteen months are at risk of falling into and drowning in five-gallon buckets. The increased popularity of these buckets—which come filled with paint, drywall compound, or other substances, or can be bought empty—has been accompanied by a rise in deaths. The agency estimates that 40 children drown in such buckets each year. In 1994 the commission voted to publish an Advance Notice of Proposed Rulemaking and examine regulatory options, including labeling and a performance standard for buckets. After the industry voluntarily labeled buckets about the risk of infant drowning and initiated a public education program to warn of this hazard, the CPSC terminated this rulemaking.

Fires involving upholstered furniture cause more deaths than any other product under the commission's jurisdiction, claiming an average of 1,000 victims, and cause more than 2,000 injuries and destroy $300 million of property annually. In 1994, CPSC published an Advance Notice of Proposed Rulemaking to address fires occurring when small open flames ignited upholstered furniture. Such fires were estimated in 1991 to result in approximately 150 deaths, 580 injuries, and $66 million in property losses. In 1996, CPSC staff developed an open-flame test method for consideration by the commission in 1997.

In 1994 the CPSC began a rulemaking to examine injuries and deaths associated with baby walkers. The commission targeted this rulemaking on the 18,500 injuries that occur each year from baby walkers falling down stairs. This issue was raised with CPSC in a petition filed by consumer groups and pediatricians. In 1997 the rulemaking was on hold pending the outcome of the development of a voluntary standard.

Alarmed about children who were strangling and dying when drawstrings on the hoods and necks of their clothing caught on playground equipment and other surfaces, CPSC persuaded children's clothing manufacturers and retailers voluntarily to modify or eliminate strings from children's clothes. At least 12 deaths and 27 near-strangulations occurred between 1985 and 1994. Almost 30 manufacturers and retailers joined the voluntary program.

Between 1981 and 1994, 140 children died when they strangled on window-blind and drapery cords. Typically the young victims, most under the age of two, were playing with cords hanging beside their crib or near the floor. CPSC warned parents of the danger and is working with window-covering manufacturers and retailers to provide consumers with free tassels for the cords that will allow the nooselike feature of window-blind cords to be eliminated.

To respond to the 70 deaths and 42,000 emergency room–treated injuries resulting from falls out of windows each year, in July 1994, CPSC convened a roundtable to examine risk-reduction strategies. Manufacturers, retailers, physicians, consumer advocates, and others participated. This meeting led to the development of a voluntary standard for window guards to prevent falls.

In August 1994, CPSC announced a stop sale and recall of a popular style of rayon/cotton-blend skirt that is dangerously flammable. The skirts, which fail the Flammable Fabrics Act and burn faster than newspaper, are long, full, and two-layered, with a sheer chiffon layer of fabric over a gauze lining. When the agency first announced the recall, it had received no reports of injuries associated with the skirts. However, within a week of the recall announcement, CPSC received several reports of past incidents of the skirts catching on fire and causing burn injuries. This recall illustrates the importance of media coverage in obtaining greater information from consumers about adverse product experience.

— Mary Ellen R. Fise

See also

Consumer Product Safety Commission; Textile Product Flammability.

Readings

Adler, Robert S. (1995). "Redesigning People versus Redesigning Products: The Consumer Product Safety Commission Addresses Product Misuse." *The Journal of Law & Politics*. 11 (Winter): 79–127.

Coalition for Consumer Health and Safety (1997). *The Nation's Health and Safety: A Status Report*. Washington, DC: Consumer Federation of America.

Fise, Mary Ellen R. (1995). "Consumer Product Safety Regulation." In Kenneth J. Meier and E. Thomas Garman, eds. *Regulation and Consumer Protection*. Houston: DAME Publications, Inc. 277–294.

Product Standards

Product standards play an important role in the nation's economy and produce significant societal benefits by aiding information flow, hastening technology transfer, and promoting efficiencies in production and distribution. Standards are technical prescriptions for material, production, design, installation, safety, or performance characteristics of products. They are developed through organizations that bring together committees of persons knowledgeable in discrete product areas. These committees make judgments about acceptable product characteristics, and their conclusions are condensed into the form of product standards.

Product standards often form the basis for buyer-seller transactions. With many products, purchasers can make rational decisions based solely on advertising, inspection, or knowledge acquired through prior experience with the product. But many products have attributes that cannot be efficiently evaluated by individual purchasers through inspection and sometimes even through experience. For these products, standards can be an important source of information for buyers.

Several types of standards are recognized. For instance, definitional standards establish precise, uniformly accepted meanings and nomenclature for materials, apparatus, processes, and the like. Standard specifications prescribe use of particular materials, designs, production processes, performance levels, and test methods. Interchangeability standards dictate product or equipment dimensions and thereby promote product uniformity, simplification, and compatibility. Standard classifications allow for comparison of competing products based on relative quality or performance gradings. Standard recommended practices describe installation, use, or maintenance instructions believed necessary for safe or satisfactory product performance. Standard test methods specify the apparatus, procedures, and test conditions to be used in determining whether a product meets the requirements of an applicable standard.

A variety of other terms are commonly used in reference to standards. For instance, standards that address product safety may be referred to simply as safety standards. A distinction is often drawn between design and performance standards. Design standards generally state requirements in terms of various input factors such as materials, production processes, and product dimensions. Performance standards, on the other hand, address output requirements relating to actual product use, such as strength, durability, conductivity, and flammability. Standards adopted by government authorities for regulatory purposes are called mandatory, while private-sector standards are referred to as voluntary standards.

The National Institute of Standards and Technology (NIST), an agency of the federal government, estimates that over 400 private organizations in the United States either write standards or sponsor standards development activities. These organizations produce roughly 20,000 nongovernment commercial standards.

On the positive side, standards promote efficient individual consumption decisions when they provide accurate information about the suitability of products for specific needs and the true costs of using certain products. Consumers of products with a "systems" character, such as computers or stereos, benefit from the reduced transaction costs achieved by standards that promote compatibility and interchangeability.

Standards also promote safety, thereby reducing risks of injury to health and property. When the use of a product is accompanied by significant risks or costs to others (negative externalities), standards and certification can promote an acceptable level of product safety that shifts the costs of the risk back to the creator of the risks (internalizing the costs). Standards thereby reduce the risk of injury to third parties.

Standards may have negative consequences as well: A market may perform in an inefficient manner upon evidence of deception problems; the poor quality of information conveyed by standards or certifications may cause inefficiency in resource allocation; product or process variations may be prohibited without countervailing competitive benefits; products of equivalent or superior quality may be excluded; requirements that reduce output may be unjustified or excessive, creating unnecessary costs or causing prices to remain above a competitive level; and product innovations and technological progress may be delayed or deterred without increasing productive economic activity.

An exhaustive Federal Trade Commission (FTC) rulemaking proceeding that took place between 1978 and 1983 concluded that private standards could be used to exclude competition or convey deceptive and misleading information, to the substantial detriment of consumers and the competitive process. Moreover, the standards-setting process provided opportunities for abusive and anticompetitive behavior.

Consumer Participation

To overcome the potential negative effects of private standards, the U.S. Supreme Court, U.S. Department of Justice, and some consumer advocates suggest that voluntary standard-writing organizations put in place basic due-process protections, including an assurance that all interests impacted by a standard have a voice in its development. The FTC rulemaking proceeding (which did not result in a final rule) would have required all standards developers to provide all persons equal opportunity to participate in all phases of standards development.

Today, in most standards development organizations, the actual work is performed by groups of individuals organized into several hierarchical levels variously designated as committees, subcommittees, task groups, and work groups in descending order of size and scope. The voluntary standards committees are composed of individuals considered at least knowledgeable, if not expert, in their respective fields of technology. These individuals determine the need for a standard and establish its scope and its specific requirements. These volunteers are usually not paid or otherwise compensated by the standards developer; thus, the demands that can be placed on them with respect to attendance, deadlines, subject matter of discussions, and general participation are limited. Costs of participation in standards development are commonly assumed by the companies by whom the individuals are employed or by interested groups such as trade associations.

Participation in standards development at the working level requires a substantial commitment of time and effort. It is thus understandable that industry members who are most concerned with the standard, whether from the standpoint of the user or the producer, are most likely to ensure that they are adequately represented in the process. Apart from industry interests, it often is difficult to identify those who would be both interested in a particular standard and willing to participate in its development. Supporters of increased consumer and public interest participation in standards development recognize that the restraints of inadequate funding and time are major impediments.

A suggestion to generate greater consumer interest and willingness to participate is to organize or pool selected consumer representatives so that the requisite technical abilities could be identified and used in appropriate cases. At the FTC rulemaking hearing, Esther Peterson, then President Carter's special assistant for consumer affairs, suggested that her office would be interested in helping in the selection of such representatives.

A few standards developers fund individual consumers and consumer organizations to participate directly in standards development. Perhaps the most significant activity of this sort is that of the American Society for the Testing of Materials (ASTM), the nation's largest developer of voluntary standards. In the early 1980s, ASTM allocated $40,000 a year for four years to fund consumer participation in certain ASTM committees under the auspices of the National Consumers League (NCL). Under the terms of the agreement, NCL provided technical and lay representatives to participate in committee, subcommittee, and working groups. This project was considered successful by both parties, and according to NCL, demonstrated the importance of allowing consumer representatives with technical expertise to participate directly at the working levels of standards development when consumer interests are at stake. NCL concluded that effective consumer representation should assure that conflicting, different, and perhaps unpopular and unfamiliar concepts are fully considered in the development process.

At the FTC rulemaking hearings, standards developers, as well as other participants and supporters of voluntary standards activities, strongly opposed the proposition that standards developers be required to fund consumer or other interest participation in standards development. However, one organization opposing such mandatory funding requirements, Underwriters Laboratories (UL), also stated that a number of standards developers appeared to be willing to pay for such participation and should be permitted to do so. UL also suggested that, if such funding proved to have merit, a government agency such as the Small Business Administration should provide it.

No database exists that indicates the number of consumer representatives who participate in the standard-setting activities of the more than 400 voluntary standards-writing bodies. Although many organizations have amended their procedures to allow direct consumer participation, only a tiny percentage of these groups have such participants, and even fewer underwrite any of the costs of such participation. Without funding, the level of consumer participation is likely to remain low.

— David A. Swankin

See also

Licensure; Product Testing; Public Representation.

Readings

U.S. Federal Trade Commission (1983). *Report of the Presiding Officer on Proposed Trade Regulation Rule: Standards and Certification.* 16 CFR Part 457; Public Record 215–61.

U.S. Federal Trade Commission, Bureau of Consumer Protection (1983). *Standards and Certification: Final Staff Report.* April.

Product Testing

Americans live in a society whose marketplace is filled with the latest applications of modern technology. They have the opportunity to eat better, work more efficiently, play harder, and explore more new vistas than many other peoples of the world. However, the breadth of choices presented to Americans can be both exciting and overwhelming. Many of the products promoted to consumers are beyond their understanding—either of what to expect from the product or what is expected from them as end-users. Moreover, even for a mature product whose function and features are generally understood, it is virtually impossible for the lay consumer to assess objectively that product's quality, safety, or value at the point of purchase.

It is important to note that a new product's access to the American marketplace is relatively unencumbered. Whenever the U.S. Congress is confronted with the question of whether to require premarket testing and clearance, it generally opts for free access, without premarket clearance. Prescription drugs and medical devices are among a relatively small class of products required by federal law to demonstrate effectiveness and safety before they may be offered for sale to consumers. Such a policy has its obvious virtues: Products can enter the market quickly, and their costs do not contain the expenses of obtaining premarket approval.

The downside, of course, is that consumers must fend for themselves in areas foreign to their experience and expertise. To approach rationally the myriad purchase decisions consumers encounter in the course of everyday living, they need the specialized skills of a chemist, engineer, statistician, auto mechanic, and nutritionist at their ready command. Advertisements provided by manufacturers and retailers are not helpful in this regard because they rarely contain the type or quantity of information consumers need to make rational choices. Fortunately, a number of ongoing activities at work in the marketplace help the consumer. Most of these involve testing, and each has a specific, unique purpose.

Product testing is any activity that seeks to measure the attributes of a product to determine its performance, safety, quality, and often its compliance with established standards. When a consumer tastes a new food product and decides whether or not he or she likes it, that consumer is testing the product for acceptance. Usually, such tests are not rigorous and ultimately measure only the consumer's personal preferences regarding that food. It is highly unlikely that any consumer will measure contamination or pesticide residues, although such attributes may be important to them. Likewise, consumers can assess, after purchase, how well they like an electric appliance by using it, but they are not able to measure energy efficiency or electrical leakage attributes that could have significant impact on its safety and use. Similarly, consumers can assess how well they like a garment with regard to style, fit, and finish, but they are not in a position to determine for themselves whether the label claims of fiber content are accurate, which in some situations could have a direct bearing on the price the consumer is willing to pay for the product.

It is clear that many dimensions of products are invisible to consumers but nevertheless play a vital role in their use experience and the value they receive. In essence, the consumer is in a weak position to make rational choices among competing products. To help balance the market against unfair competition from suppliers who take advantage of such vagueness and to provide confidence and objective data to the consumer, testing for performance, safety, and quality is conducted in varying degrees by the federal and state governments, industry trade groups, and consumer organizations. Individual companies perform a substantial part of the primary testing responsibilities for performance and safety, in part because they are best able to conduct such tests quickly and at the least cost. A unique activity, that of testing for the purpose of comparing competing products, offers special challenges in the laboratory and special benefits to the consumer.

The Industry Role

The questions of test protocol and pass/fail criteria are of great significance. Depending on how the standards are set and who participates in the decisions, the final standards adopted by an industry can be quite different from those initially proposed. Hundreds of adequate industry voluntary standards covering consumer products have been developed over the years and enjoy widespread compliance within the affected industries. Usually the standard is developed within a consensus process attended mostly by members of the industry, sometimes with one or more government and/or consumer representatives. As part of the system, the companies agree to either self-certify that their products comply with the standard or engage independent laboratories to test their products for compliance. The certification process involves testing samples of a production lot in accordance with the standard to establish the lot's compliance. Generally, the consumer is made aware of such compliance by a hang-tag or label on the product at the point of purchase.

Industry voluntary standards cover a broad array of consumer products ranging from lawnmowers to toys to gas heaters. Virtually every major consumer product industry has formed a national trade association, whose duties include developing standards or managing the standards-writing process. Organizations such as the Outdoor Power Equipment Institute (OPEI), Toy Manufacturers of America (TMA), American Gas Association (AGA), Chemical Manufacturers Association (CMA), National Paint and Coatings Association (NPCA), Association of Home Appliance Manufacturers (AHAM), and Juvenile Products Manufacturers Association (JPMA) are but a few. After the standards are set, compliance testing takes place much closer to the manufacturing site.

It is important to note that calling these industry standards "voluntary" stretches the imagination a bit. A manufacturer may choose to ignore the standard, but only at some risk to its sales volume and perhaps even to its defense posture in a product liability lawsuit. Once a standard is adopted by the industry, usually a great push to promote complying products occurs, and consumers are encouraged to look for products bearing the seal or hang-tag that denotes conformance with the industry standard. Such an approach can make it extremely difficult for a manufacturer to opt out. In fragmented industries comprised of many small manufacturers such pressure is easier to resist, but in large industries with relatively few producers, compliance is virtually guaranteed.

Underwriters Laboratories, with its hundreds of "UL Standards" addressing the safety aspects of consumer products, illustrates how successful this system can be. With UL standards adopted by reference into the National Electrical Code, which is often written into the building codes of local jurisdictions, an appliance manufacturer who wants to ship to a national market has no real choice but to meet the UL standard and label its products as such.

Since 1894, Underwriters Laboratories has been writing and certifying compliance with hundreds of safety standards, many of which have directly affected consumer safety. As of 1994, UL had developed some 665 safety standards, and in 1993, some 6.2 billion products bearing the UL mark entered the U.S. marketplace. The UL staff of engineers, scientists, investigators, and support staff number more than 4,100, operate more than 1 million square feet of laboratory space, and in 1993, conducted more than 76,000 product investigations.

UL and other voluntary standards organizations undoubtedly make a significant contribution to the overall safety of the American marketplace, but their strength is also their weakness. They can push an affected industry to make changes only so fast and so far, the speed and distance being limited primarily by technological and economic feasibility, and the willingness of the industry. They are not in a position, for example, to set a standard that would be prohibitively expensive or cause a significant number of manufacturers to go out of business. As background for the Final Report of the National Commission on Product Safety (NCPS) in 1970, several examples of hazardous products bearing the UL mark were presented at the commission's hearings. Industry self-regulation in general was criticized as being prone to lowest-common-denominatorism and subject to the whims of the strongest players. Moreover, the use of certification seals, especially when issued by an industry's own trade association, was viewed with skepticism. Although UL was not an industry trade association, the value of its unique contributions to product safety was called into question.

When successful, the adequacy of the standards and the testing that ensure compliance are appropriate to the need. However, when change is needed, the voluntary standards system can upgrade its standards only to the extent that the members of the industry are willing. When factors such as competitive jealousy or the cost of implementing improved standards arise, the system can grind to a virtual halt. Such a breakdown is especially likely to occur when the new standard appears to favor a small number of manufacturers or one segment of the industry.

The Government Role

When the industry's voluntary system will not or cannot solve a serious problem, the government agency with jurisdiction over that problem can set mandatory standards. These standards and test protocols are almost always more stringent and come closer to reducing the hazard than do the existing voluntary ones. Moreover, complying with the requirements of a mandatory standard is likely to be more difficult technologically and economically. The federal regulatory framework with respect to products is set up primarily to address safety issues, especially regarding food, consumer products, automobiles and highways, and drugs and medical devices.

As with voluntary standards, significant responsibility to test for compliance with the standard is placed on the manufacturer. Different from most voluntary standards, however, is the presence of test programs, conducted by the agency, which serve to monitor compliance in the marketplace. Manufacturers whose products are out of compliance may be subject to recalls and to civil and criminal penalties. The presence of these sanctions is another major difference between mandatory and voluntary standards.

An interesting and useful adjunct to product standards is the availability of comparative product information based on objective testing. For example, the National Highway Traffic Safety Administration (NHTSA) tested the crashworthiness of passenger-restraint systems by crashing new cars equipped with monitored dummies into a fixed barrier. The public was given full access to the test results, and it soon became clear that automobile manufacturers were designing their cars to perform well in those tests. Indeed, automobiles, and their restraint systems in particular, became more crashworthy in the process. While no standards had been set, the public's ready access to the test information served as a powerful incentive. Similarly, testing foods to determine nutritional components and making that information available at the point of purchase offers great benefit to consumers who wish to control certain aspects of their diets. The improvement of nutritional labels, following the passage of 1990 congressional legislation, permitted consumers to assess and compare fat content and other ingredients much more easily.

Although safety hazards are subject to mandatory and "voluntary" regulation, performance, convenience, quality, and durability are not. For example, Underwriters Laboratories has written and enforced hundreds of safety standards, but has established no quality standards. Such fundamental properties are left to consumers to sort out, and caveat emptor reigns. Most industry voluntary standards are devoid of any but the most minimal performance criteria, and no government agency has responsibility for setting quality standards for consumer products. Thus, a huge information gap exists, and for consumers to succeed as rational participants in a free-market economy, they need vast amounts of perfect information.

It is hard to imagine that any industry group could supply unbiased comparative product information covering the products manufactured by its members; after all, the group itself exists to serve its members' needs, and supplying consumers with information critical of any of its members' products would surely create conflicts within that group. Individual manufacturers, of course, flood the market with all forms of advertising, often masquerading as information, whose sole purpose is to create an image and feeling that inspires confidence. Such material is an integral part of the market system, but clearly cannot be considered balanced, objective, complete, or unbiased.

Consumer Group Testing

Comparative testing performed by an independent entity got its start within the consumer community. In the 1920s and early 1930s, within a marketplace flooded with products for which fantastic claims were often made, consumers were unable to judge if products' advertised claims were true, which products offered the best value, and which products were safe. To help meet these consumer needs, in 1928 a new product testing organization, Consumers' Research, was established. In 1936 this group split apart, and a new organization, Consumers Union (CU), was created. CU developed into the nation's largest nonprofit consumer group. Its major activity is product testing and the dissemination of test results in its flagship publication *Consumer Reports*. Consumers' Research continued its testing work until 1983, but never developed into a major supplier of consumer information.

By 1995, CU's National Research and Testing Center in Yonkers, New York, occupied over 250,000 square feet and housed its testing, research, and publishing operations. The organization's auto test facility, situated on 327 acres in rural Connecticut, is the largest consumer-owned auto test center in the world.

Including staff of advocacy offices in Washington, Austin, and San Francisco, more than 450 persons are employed by Consumers Union. In a typical year, the organization buys thousands of samples of 1,500 to 2,000 products, ranging from cameras to computers to cars, and publishes its findings in its magazines, *Consumer Reports* and *Zillions,* and in a broad array of books, newsletters, radio and television programs, and computer-based electronic publications. In addition to consumer products, CU has broadened its scope of evaluation to include health, finance, and travel services.

As mentioned earlier, testing for compliance with a commercial and regulatory standard focuses on pass/fail criteria that are limited to the specific attributes for which the standard was set. A safety standard setting maximum electrical leakage for a television set, for example, is blind to grossly inferior picture or sound quality. Accordingly, most regulatory standards perform the valuable but limited service of blocking serious safety defects from entering or staying on the market.

Comparative testing, on the other hand, has a much broader objective and carries unique responsibilities. To begin, the objective is to evaluate all those aspects of a group of competing products that are important to a consumer's decision process. Hence, deciding what to test for is crucial, and careful planning is required to determine both what is important to know about the product and what is important to consumers. To add to the challenge, the test protocols are generally not "on the shelf," and therefore considerable resources are devoted to test development.

The scope of the products to be compared has special significance. First, the testing must include only those models that are fair alternatives to one another; to choose otherwise would risk comparing "apples and oranges." For example, a sports car and a minivan can each be evaluated, but in many respects cannot be compared in any sensible way. Likewise, comparing high-end audio components with portable sound equipment can be grossly misleading. Second, products must be chosen that consumers are likely to encounter at retail. CU makes special efforts to learn from manufacturers which products will be for sale during a given period, and the test group is drawn up to include every major supplier, consistent with available time and test resources. To do otherwise would be a disservice to consumers and suppliers alike.

The cardinal element of an objective, comparative test program, however, is complete and total independence from the suppliers of consumer products and services. At CU, for example, all products are purchased at retail just as a consumer would. No samples or prototypes are accepted from anyone for any reason. No gifts of any kind are accepted from any business for any reason. No outside advertising is accepted for any of the organization's publications. Such a policy, which has been in effect since the organization began, minimizes any chance of compromise or bias and leaves the organization free to speak the truth as it believes the facts support. CU has no stake in whose product does best, and the organization need not worry that it is losing revenue from advertisers of products that do poorly, nor do consumers need fear that CU's findings and advice have been manipulated to curry favor with advertisers.

Performance, durability, safety, convenience, and value are all essential elements of products available in today's marketplace, but without help, consumers usually cannot assess these components, either singularly or in total. Only if the results of comprehensive, objective product testing are available can they begin to understand these attributes and make informed product choices.

— R. David Pittle

See also

Consumers' Research; Consumers Union; Product Standards.

Readings

Pittle, R. David (1984). "Product Quality: Who Decides It?" In Karen P. Goebel, ed. *Pro-*

ceedings, 30th Annual Conference of the American Council on Consumer Interests. Columbia, MO: American Council on Consumer Interests. 80–84.

Sieber, Peter (1996). "Behind the Ratings: The Reasons To Believe—A Review of Consumer Product Testing." In Karen Folk, d., *Consumer Interests Annual.* 42: 31–36.

Silber, Norman I. (1983). *Test and Protest.* New York: Holmes & Meier.

Products Liability Law

Products liability law encompasses a broad spectrum of liability rules based on both contract and tort law. The focus here is on the tort rules and, in particular, on the common law doctrines of negligence and strict liability, which serve as the primary bases for personal injury and property damage claims. Contract or warranty law, while providing another basis for such claims, plays its primary role in cases of commercial loss.

Products liability law continues to be a dynamic and controversial area of tort law, although it started out as a relatively insignificant area of law because traditional liability rules kept the courthouse doors closed to most product claims. By the early part of this century a handful of judicial decisions opened the doors a crack, but not until the mid-1960s did courts open their doors widely to product claims. Over the next twenty years, decisions by state and federal courts throughout the country brought about fundamental—some would say revolutionary—changes in the common law. These decisions expanded dramatically the obligations of manufacturers and sellers to protect consumers from product-related injuries. Although they fell far short of imposing absolute liability, the liability of product sellers was increased quite substantially.

A combination of factors—economic, political, and social—contributed to the willingness of courts to undertake such fundamental reform of the liability system. First, in this period the consumer movement was strong and product safety issues were high on the public agenda. Further, numerous federal statutes were enacted to protect consumers from hazards in the marketplace, and courts were encouraged to be activist and innovative in solving social problems. In this environment, it is not surprising that the judiciary, urged on by legal scholars, undertook an expansion of the role of the common law in addressing product injuries.

As the numbers and types of product claims increased, however, criticisms of the liability system also grew. At first, those most adversely affected by these common law developments—insurers and manufacturers—complained that the courts had gone too far. Later, other groups, including increasing numbers of scholars, joined in the criticism. They argued that the new liability standards were too open-ended, the costs of the system were too high, and the system needed to be brought under control. In response, many state legislatures enacted pro-defendant reform legislation to limit liability. In the mid-1980s, the changing political environment began to be reflected in judicial decisions, and the pro-plaintiff expansionary trends in the courts largely came to an end.

Products liability today remains a dynamic field of law. The courts continue to refine liability standards, and legislatures at the state and national level continue to consider tort reform measures. Under these circumstances, any description of products liability law, including the one provided below, runs the risk of becoming quickly outdated.

Early History

Originally, product claims were governed exclusively by contract law. Under contract law, a party's duty ran only to those with whom a person had dealt directly, i.e., those in privity with that person. Thus, a consumer injured by a product could sue the retailer from whom he or she had purchased the product, but not the party who designed, produced, and advertised the product, i.e., the manufacturer. The privity rule was a relic of horse-and-buggy days when product makers sold their goods in face-to-face transactions with buyers, but the courts continued to apply it well into the twentieth century. The seminal case to reject the rule was *MacPherson v. Buick Motor Company,* decided by the New York Court of Appeals in 1916. Recognizing that the privity rule was an anachronism in the modern marketplace, Judge Benjamin Cardozo ruled that a manufacturer's duty no longer would be governed solely by contract law but by tort law as well.

With the general demise of the privity rule that followed *MacPherson,* the courthouse doors theoretically were open to an array of product claims based on tort law. However, no great upsurge in claims occurred during the next five decades because traditional negligence doctrine created its own significant barriers to recovery. First, negligence requires proof of the manufacturer's or seller's fault, which is often difficult for plaintiffs to establish in products cases. Second, a number of rigid "no duty" rules barred or limited a wide array of claims. For example, the patent danger rule barred claims where product risks were obvious. The contributory negligence rule barred recovery where even the slightest negligence on the part of the plaintiff contributed to his injury. The intended-use rule barred claims where products were put to foreseeable but unintended uses. Collectively, these harsh rules prevented most consumers from seeking relief under tort law.

After *MacPherson,* contract law remained (as it does today) an alternative ground for product claims, but in addition to the privity requirement, it posed other obstacles to recovery. Contract terms, drafted by manufacturers and sellers, often disclaim liability, limit damages, or require prompt notice of a product defect. Such contract provisions, described as booby traps for unwary consumers, are generally given effect by the courts if they are drafted in compliance with state statutes such as the Uniform Commercial Code.

In cases where these obstacles can be overcome, however, consumers may have claims for breach of implied and express warranty that offer some real advantages over negligence. Warranty claims, like strict liability claims, do not require proof of negligence, nor is due care a defense. The implied warranty claim arises when the product proves to be unfit for the purposes for which it normally is used. The express warranty claim arises when the seller's representations about its product prove to be untrue. In many cases, however, the advantages of warranty law do not outweigh its disadvantages. Thus, before the advent of the liability revolution, consumers faced serious obstacles to recovery for product-related injuries under both negligence and contract law.

The Product Liability Revolution

Most scholars trace the birth of modern product liability law to two events in the mid-1960s. The first was the 1963 case of *Greenman v. Yuba Power Products, Inc.,* in which the California Supreme Court adopted an entirely new theory for product claims—strict liability in tort. The theory resembled implied warranty law but without the intricacies of contract law. *Greenman* required a plaintiff to show only that his injury was caused by a product that, unknown to him, was defective and dangerous when used as intended.

The second event, which occurred two years later and was motivated by the *Greenman* decision, was the American Law Institute's adoption of strict products liability in Section 402A of the Restatement (Second) of Torts. Like *Greenman* and like warranty law, Section 402A imposes a true strict liability that requires no proof of fault on the part of the seller or manufacturer. It makes all sellers in the distributive chain strictly liable for injuries caused by products that are in a defective condition or unreasonably dangerous to consumers or their property. Products are defective and unreasonably dangerous if their dangers exceed the expectations of ordinary consumers, a standard resembling the implied warranty requirement that goods be fit for their ordinary purpose.

The underlying rationale for strict liability—as articulated in *Greenman* and Section 402A—is fairness, deterrence, and loss distribution. Strict liability, even more than negligence, provides a strong incentive for manufacturers to reduce product risks, thereby benefiting consumers generally. It imposes the costs of product-related injuries on manufacturers, who can insure against such losses and distribute their costs among the buyers of their products, rather than on injured consumers for whom such costs can be an overwhelming misfortune. Strict liability serves to protect consumer expectations and requires sellers to stand behind their products. It also streamlines litigation by eliminating the evidentiary problems associated with proving negligence.

The drafters of Section 402A intended strict liability to apply only to the infrequent and random injuries caused by flawed products containing latent defects. They had little reason to expect that it would lead to a greatly expanded liability system. However, the judicial response to Section 402A and *Greenman* was dramatic. Not only did courts in almost every state adopt strict liability for flawed products, they extended its scope to cover claims involving product designs and warnings. These claims, unlike flawed product claims, challenged products that were designed and marketed as intended. They implicated entire lines of products and significantly increased the liability exposure of manufacturers.

The courts soon recognized that Section 402A's consumer expectation test often was not suitable for design and warning claims, and struggled to find new tests for strict liability in the context of these claims. They universally rejected any notion that strict liability should mean absolute liability, and eventually developed standards that bear a striking resemblance to negligence. This is especially true for warning claims where both theories require reasonable product warnings about risks that are known or should have been known to the manufacturer. For these claims, strict liability is not distinguishable from negligence.

In design cases, courts attempt to draw greater distinctions between strict liability and negligence, but many courts and commentators see little actual difference in the two doctrines. The predominant test for strict liability in design is the risk/utility or risk/benefit test, which, in general terms, requires plaintiffs to establish that the risks of the product design outweigh its benefits. The test calls for balancing a number of factors, such as the likelihood and seriousness of injury; the feasibility and costs of an alternative, safer design; and the user's awareness of the risk and ability to avoid it. These same factors and a similar risk/utility balancing test are at the core of negligence as well.

Still, many litigators as well as judges believe that, despite the similarities in the two doctrines, strict liability offers some advantages to plaintiffs. Courts often point out that under strict liability the focus is on the condition of the product, not the conduct of the manufacturer, and therefore the plaintiff's case is easier to prove. Also, some courts have devised strict liability standards that are somewhat more favorable to plaintiffs. They have simplified the plaintiff's prima facie case, for example, by shifting the burden of proof under the risk/utility test to defendants or by presuming defendants' knowledge of product risks. Although some courts use the consumer expectation test in design cases, these more favorable standards are in the minority. In the final analysis, design claims remain extremely difficult to prove under either theory.

Given the similarities of strict liability and negligence, how important a factor was strict liability in the great expansion of liability that occurred from the mid-1960s to the mid-1980s? Certainly Section 402A played a role in stimulating the judiciary to expand liability rules, but much of the expansion probably would have occurred anyway under negligence.

Under negligence, the courts made some of their most far-reaching decisions. Among the most significant were those rejecting two traditional "no duty" rules mentioned earlier—the intended-use rule and patent danger rule.

In doing away with the intended-use rule, for example, the courts greatly expanded the manufacturers' duty of care. Symbolic of this change was the judicial recognition that auto manufacturers have a duty to design cars to be reasonably crashworthy, i.e., to minimize injuries to passengers from second collisions during automobile accidents. Under the intended-use rule, courts had rejected the notion that auto makers had any duty to take measures to protect consumers against such injuries. Under the foreseeability test, however, a duty was virtually compelled by the statistical certainty that automobiles will be involved in accidents. Although the courts made clear that the new duty required only the exercise of reasonable care in auto design and not the design of crashproof cars, the ramifications of these crashworthiness rulings, as well as the general rejection of the intended-use rule, were far-reaching—not only for auto makers but for manufacturers of all products.

Doing away with the patent danger rule similarly enlarged the responsibility of manufacturers in designing their products. Previously, no matter how minimal the costs of correcting an obvious risk, there was no duty to do so. Under the new judicial approach, the obviousness of product risks continued to be relevant in deciding whether a product was reasonably safe (and on the facts, in some cases, might be determinative) but was no longer an absolute bar to a claim. Again, doing away with a rigid "no duty" rule in favor of a more flexible approach under negligence expanded liability for manufacturers across product lines.

Along with these more flexible approaches under negligence, courts also fashioned flexible rules on the issue of causation, where plaintiffs often face special problems of proof. Some courts created a presumption of causation in cases of inadequate warnings; others reduced plaintiffs' burden of showing the extent of their aggravated injuries in crashworthiness cases. Courts have devised innovative collective liability rules for cases like those involving the generic drug DES, where plaintiffs, through no fault of their own, are unable to identify which manufacturer's product caused their injuries. Such special rules, while reflective of the general pro-plaintiff trends in the courts, are far from universal, however.

Finally, as part of the judicial trend toward greater consumer protection, courts addressed perhaps the greatest barriers of all to consumer claims—the affirmative defenses of contributory negligence and assumption of risk. If the courts failed to modify these doctrines, the elimination of the no-duty rules described above would have been meaningless. For example, the assumption-of-risk defense, if left intact, would defeat claims where product risks were obvious, in effect reinstating the patent danger rule. Likewise, contributory negligence defense, if left unchanged, would bar recovery where plaintiffs foreseeably misused products, in effect reinstating the intended-use rule. Thus, to preserve the newly expanded duties of manufacturers, the courts also had to limit the availability of these traditional affirmative defenses. This occurred in two ways. First, comparative fault principles were adopted, through statute and common law developments, that limits the circumstances in which plaintiff's fault completely bars recovery. Under comparative fault, plaintiff's negligence might reduce recovery, but generally will not bar it, except in modified comparative fault jurisdictions where recovery can still be denied if plaintiff's fault is sufficiently great.

Second, affirmative defenses were severely restricted under strict liability doctrine. Courts interpreted Section 402A as largely eliminating the contributory negligence defense and greatly restricting the assumption of risk defense. The effect was to make a great many claims viable under strict liability that could not succeed under negligence. A case in point was the first, a groundbreaking case involving asbestos, *Borel v. Fiberboard Paper Products, Inc.* Borel lost his negligence claim because his failure to wear a protective mask was found to constitute contributory negligence, but he won his strict liability claim because contributory negligence was no bar to that claim. In recent years, it should be noted, courts increasingly are applying comparative fault principles to strict liability claims as well as to negligence claims. Thus, a distinction between the two theories, once considered significant, may become less so in the future.

Recent Trends

The developments described above reveal that, despite the enormous expansion in liability during the common law revolution, the courts have not created a system of absolute liability. Indeed, for warning and design claims, which constitute the vast bulk of product liability claims, strict liability remains a very close cousin to negligence. As a result, most product liability claims remain difficult to bring; they tend to involve complex, technical issues that are difficult to prove, and the costs of litigation are high. Numerous studies confirm that only a small percentage of injured victims with meritorious legal claims ever pursue them. Thus, while the tort system has become more friendly to injury claims over the past several decades, the courthouse doors remain closed to many victims.

By the mid-1980s, criticisms of the tort system escalated. Calls for reforming the system came from many quarters, including the Reagan administration's Justice Department, the business community, insurers, legislators at the state and national levels, and academics. The criticisms—many of which consumer groups and academics challenge as unfounded and exaggerated—nevertheless have had an impact. First, the impact on the judiciary ended the expansionary trend in the common law. Called a quiet revolution because it was not immediately noticed, the pro-defendant judicial trends across the country are now well documented. For the most part, courts have not overturned the common law developments described above, but they are resisting any further expansion of them.

Of course, tort law expansion could not continue forever. More troubling to consumer groups is the enactment of state statutes that overturn common law developments and place significant new limits on liability. Since the latter half of the 1980s, virtually every state, in response to extensive lobbying efforts by business interests, has enacted pro-defendant reform legislation. Among the most popular reforms are those that limit punitive damages, cap noneconomic damages, and limit joint and several liability.

The future may bring a continuation of—and perhaps even an escalation in—these pro-defendant trends. National product liability reform legislation was passed by the 104th Congress, although vetoed by President Clinton. Legislative activity continues in the states. In addition, a substantial revision of Section 402A is under consideration by the American Law Institute. The new Restatement (Third) would make little change in the common law with respect to flawed products and warning claims, but would make design cases more difficult to bring. It would eliminate the pro-plaintiff evidentiary rules that some jurisdictions have developed and impose a more onerous burden of proof on plaintiffs than many jurisdictions now require. The new restatement would single out prescription products for an even more demanding standard of proof in design cases and make them virtually impossible to bring. If history is any guide, the new restatement, like Section 402A, will have a significant impact on common law developments, and may even stimulate greater contraction of liability rules than its specific provisions require.

The total effect of the pro-defendant developments—the judicial trends, the proposed restatement, and the state and national legislative activity—is difficult to predict, but it appears to signal an era of reduced consumer protection in the years ahead.

— Teresa M. Schwartz*

---

*This article was prepared while the author was on the George Washington University Law School faculty. The views are the author's alone and do not reflect the views of the Federal Trade Commission or any individual commissioner.

See also
Law, Consumer.

Readings

Bernstein, Anita (1995). *Products Liability Anthology.* Cincinnati: Anderson Publishing Co.
Gerner, Jennifer L. (1988). "Product Safety: A Review." In E. Scott Maynes, ed. *The Frontier of Research in the Consumer Interest.* Columbia, MO: American Council on Consumer Interests. 37–60.
Shapo, Marshall S. (1990). *The Law of Products Liability.* Salem, NH: Butterworth Legal Publishers.

Public Citizen

One of the most influential organizations of the consumer movement is Public Citizen, founded in 1971 by Ralph Nader. An independent-minded group with talented leadership, Public Citizen has been at the vanguard of some of the key consumer issues of the past generation: congressional reform, government waste and abuse, freedom of information, nuclear power plant safety, tax justice, food and drug safety, and consumer empowerment. By 1994, Public Citizen had an annual budget of $9 million and a staff of seventy-nine. Funding comes primarily from its 100,000 members along with foundation grants and sales of publications; it refuses any government or corporate monies.

Much of Public Citizen's success stems from the leadership of Nader and several top Nader associates: Joan Claybrook, the longtime auto safety advocate who has been Public Citizen's president since 1980; Alan B. Morrison, the unofficial dean of the public interest bar; and Sidney M. Wolfe, M.D., the leading consumer activist on drug safety and other health policy concerns.

Public Citizen serves as the umbrella organization for a handful of semiautonomous groups, each with its director and focused advocacy agenda, including Congress Watch, Health Research Group, Litigation Group, Critical Mass, and Buyers Up, a fuel-buying group. Another influential Public Citizen group, which folded in 1987, was the Tax Reform Research Group.

Distinguishing Public Citizen from most other public interest lobbies founded in the 1970s is its simultaneous activism in multiple forums—Congress, federal agencies, the courts, the news media, and selected congressional districts. The federation structure of Public Citizen makes it possible to give each organization the freedom to respond aggressively and flexibly to changing political circumstances while enjoying a stable fundraising and administrative structure. Also, the technical experts, lobbyists, litigators, organizers, and journalists in each group can collaborate freely with one another, making it easier to follow an issue from its first stirrings in the press through legislation, agency rulemaking, and litigation in court.

Congress Watch

Congress Watch is an outgrowth of the Ralph Nader Congress Project/Citizens Look at Congress, a massive research effort mounted by Nader and nearly 1,000 young people to profile every member of Congress and six key congressional committees. Generating 14,000 pages of printed materials, the Congress Project was a milestone in providing information to the public about the little-reported byways of the U.S. Senate and House of Representatives. A resulting publication, *Who Runs Congress?*, published in 1972, sold more copies than any other book ever written about Congress.

To maintain the momentum of the project, Nader founded Congress Watch in 1972 to serve as an ongoing citizen watchdog of Congress, a novel concept at the time. Joan Claybrook, a former congressional aide who first worked with Nader during his 1966 auto safety lobbying crusade and was a leader of the Congress Project, became the first director.

The group was originally a kitchen table operation that relied on old mimeograph machines, volunteer typists, and creative lobbyists. Housed in an old nunnery near the Capitol Building, Congress Watch was one of the first public interest groups to bring citizen pressure on Congress to curb corporate abuses and government waste, secrecy, and conflicts of interest.

Congress Watch also became the launching pad for some noted careers in journalism and consumer advocacy. Joan Claybrook later became the director of the National Highway Safety Administration in the Carter administration (1977–1980) and president of Public Citizen throughout the 1980s and 1990s; Mark Green, Claybrook's successor at Congress Watch, later became the second-ranking public official in New York City, the Public Advocate; and James Fallows and David Ignatius became leading journalists. (Other prominent journalists who once worked at Nader groups include Michael Kinsley, Joseph Nocera, Raymond Bonner, David Corn, and Matthew Rothschild.) Dozens of Congress Watch researchers and lobbyists moved on to influential staff positions in Congress, the Carter administration, and various advocacy organizations.

One of Congress Watch's enduring priorities is congressional and governmental reform. The group helped push through the landmark Freedom of Information Act Amendments of 1974, which make government information more accessible to any citizen who requests it. It also helped enact numerous ethics bills such as the Civil Service Reform Act of 1978, which curbed the abuses of the "revolving door," in which former government officials lobby their old colleagues; "sunshine laws," which opened up government meetings and records to the public and protected whistleblowing by government employees; and strict limits on and disclosures of lobbyist-paid gifts and travel.

Another ongoing concern is campaign finance reform. Nader and Congress Watch were among the first to document the corrupting effects of big-money campaign contributions and to agitate for reform. The first result of this effort was the Federal Election Campaign Act of 1974, which closed many of the loopholes in the Corrupt Practices Act of 1925 and required disclosure of campaign receipts and expenditures. A year later, in the wake of the Watergate scandal and disclosures of the Nixon campaign's unethical fund-raising schemes, Congress Watch was able to help push through new amendments to the law.

Many of the issues pursued by Congress Watch reflect Ralph Nader's philosophical agenda for the consumer movement. The group played an important role in the passage of the Magnuson-Moss Warranty Act of 1975, which made it easier for consumers to force auto companies to repair or replace "lemon" automobiles; deregulation of airlines and trucking (finally enacted in 1978); creation of a bank to help finance consumer cooperatives (enacted in 1977); and development of a proposal to create a federal consumer protection agency (narrowly defeated in 1978). Congress Watch has also been a driving force behind new regulatory standards for pesticides and food safety (1988), auto safety (1974), auto fuel efficiency (1975), medical devices (1976), consumer product safety (1981), toxic chemical control (1976), and toxic-waste cleanup (the Superfund law, 1980 and 1986). On many occasions, Congress Watch has opposed government subsidies to assorted industries, government boondoggles, and corporate tax loopholes.

Health Research Group

The Public Citizen Health Research Group (HRG) has been directed by Sidney M. Wolfe since he founded it with Ralph Nader in 1971. A former researcher at the National Institutes of Health, Wolfe has created a distinctive niche by combining rigorous medical research with tenacious consumer advocacy and public education. With a staff of eight, Wolfe—the recipient of a MacArthur "genius" grant in 1990—aggressively seeks protections from unsafe food products and additives, unsafe drugs and medical devices, and occupational hazards. The Health Research Group also focuses on women's health issues, empowerment of health-care consumers, and structural reform of the health-care system.

HRG's first crusade was a November 1971 petition to the Food and Drug Administration (FDA) requesting a ban on Red Dye No. 2, a popular color dye that could cause cancer. The campaign attracted widespread attention, alerting consumers to the prevalence of potentially hazardous additions to the nation's food supply. Five years later, after a tortuous series of scientific and legal squabbles, HRG prevailed, and the FDA banned the dye.

The episode served as something of a prototype for many HRG initiatives: marshal the scientific evidence of a harm, petition the appropriate federal agency for a ban or limitation on it, litigate in court while publicizing the substance's risks, and lobby Congress, if necessary. HRG has used this basic strategy to help win dozens of similar consumer triumphs, including bans on cancer-causing drugs such as chloroform and DBCP; dangerous medications such as Oraflex, an arthritis drug; harmful food additives such as cyclamates; dangerous medical devices such as the Bjork-Shiley artificial heart valve; and toxic substances such as formaldehyde and benzene. HRG also played a key role in exposing the risks of silicon-gel breast implants.

HRG is not only vigilant in spotting dangerous new drugs, medical devices, and food additives, it aggressively seeks to educate the public through consumer guidebooks about the radiation dangers of X rays; drugs on the market whose safety and efficacy have not been proved; the fatal risks of aspirin to children with the flu or chicken pox; the special dangers that some drugs pose to elderly people; the addictive risks of Valium and related drugs; and the thousands of physicians in the nation who engage in unethical practices or provide substandard or negligent care.

The crux of HRG's work is the demystification of the practice of medicine in order to empower consumers to make more informed health-care decisions for themselves. At one level, HRG acts as the consumers' expert surrogate in Washington, representing an otherwise neglected viewpoint in agency rulemakings, enforcement actions, congressional hearings, and other policy-making arenas. On another level, the group acts as a bridge between assorted bodies of professional knowledge (e.g., pharmacology, physiology, epidemiology) and popular knowledge, enriching both the medical professions and consumers in the process.

Litigation Group

The Public Citizen Litigation Group has been one of the most influential public interest law practices in the nation since its founding in 1972 by Alan B. Morrison and Ralph Nader. Few law firms, corporate or public interest, can rival the Litigation Group's impact on so many different areas of law, including freedom of information, open government, union democracy, lawyers' ethics, food safety, occupational safety and health, and the constitutional separation of powers. Over the past twenty-five years, the group has taken more than thirty-three cases to the U.S. Supreme Court, winning twenty-two.

The Litigation Group's chief "clients" are the various Public Citizen and Nader-affiliated organizations that need legal expertise or litigation support, particularly in the appellate courts and the U.S. Supreme Court. The group's staff of nine attorneys also accept other cases that hold the promise of establishing valuable legal precedents on behalf of people not ordinarily represented in litigation: citizens and scholars seeking access to government documents, workers exposed to toxic substances on the job, union members deprived of their rights by labor unions, citizens victimized by anticompetitive business practices, and consumers recklessly exposed to cancer-causing drugs.

Morrison was a thirty-three-year-old attorney with the U.S. Attorney in the Southern District of New York City when he joined Nader in forming the Litigation Group. Its litigation in the early 1970s was unusual. Until then, the average citizen rarely had the inclination, imagination, or money to wage litigation in the federal courts on public policy questions other than traditional environmental or civil liberties issues. Morrison made the deliberate decision to pursue lawsuits for a novel array of clients rather than duplicate the litigation efforts of other public interest groups.

Some of the most important cases won by the Litigation Group involve the Constitution's separation-of-powers doctrine. Although it is an obscure issue for most politicians and lawyers, the doctrine is critical for ensuring a responsible exercise of power among the three branches of the federal government—the legislature, executive branch, and judiciary. Separation of powers prevents one part of the government from acquiring too much power, and also ensures that responsibility for decision-making can be clearly assigned so that voters can hold accountable the president or congressional leaders.

In 1972, when President Nixon refused to spend money that Congress had appropriated for specific highway programs, the Litigation Group represented the chair of every standing Senate committee in the case of *State Highway Commission of Missouri v. Volpe.* Morrison's victory now prevents any president from seizing the "power of the purse," which the Constitution clearly assigns to Congress. Perhaps the most significant separation-of-powers case brought by the Litigation Group was a challenge to the "legislative veto," a provision inserted by Congress into dozens of laws in an attempt to retain control over how laws are carried out, an executive branch responsibility. In the 1983 decision of *INS v. Chadha,* the Supreme Court invalidated the legislative veto provisions in nearly 200 federal statutes, one of the most sweeping rulings of unconstitutionality in Supreme Court history.

Over the years, the Litigation Group's advocacy was critical in overturning price-fixing by the legal profession (in the 1975 Supreme Court case of *Goldfarb v. Virginia State Bar*) and in legalizing advertising by the legal profession (enabled by the key 1976 precedent of *Consumer Council v. Virginia State Board of Pharmacy,* which gave rise in 1977 to *Bates v. State Bar of Arizona*). When state bars erect artificial barriers to competition within the profession, the Litigation Group often intervenes to help consumers.

Through its Freedom of Information Clearinghouse, the Litigation Group provides indispensable technical and legal assistance to individuals, public interest groups, and the media in obtaining information held by the government. The Litigation Group also sponsors the Supreme Court Assistance Project to help allies of the consumer movement argue their cases before the U.S. Supreme Court.

Alan Morrison stepped down as director of the Litigation Group in 1992, although he remains a litigator at the group. He was succeeded by a longtime colleague, David Vladeck.

Other Public Citizen Groups

Buyers Up, a nonprofit corporation founded in 1983 by Ralph Nader and Public Citizen, acts as an agent for consumers in negotiating group discounts on home heating oil. On behalf of its members, Buyers Up also negotiates group service agreements for furnace and home repairs, energy conservation services, and insurance and legal services. The Buyers Up strategy is part of a larger effort by Nader to develop the "consumer side" of the economy by aggregating individual consumer purchasing power. The group estimates that its typical member saves $100 a year on heating oil bills because of the discounts negotiated by Buyers Up.

Although Buyers Up provides a direct service to consumers—mostly in Washington, Baltimore, Philadelphia, Richmond, and Wilmington—the organization also acts as a policy advocate on energy issues at the national level. For example, it issues regular reports on the state of the oil industry and advocates energy conservation. It has also branched into health and safety issues affecting households, such as the dangers posed by lead in drinking water, radon, indoor air pollution from household chemicals, and chemicals spread by lawn services.

The Critical Mass Energy Project was one of the key organizers and advocates of the antinuclear safe-energy movement in the 1970s and early 1980s. In the late 1960s and early 1970s, citizen concern about nuclear power was diffused, with no national focal point. To propel and consolidate the movement, Nader, Claybrook, and Public Citizen convened the first national antinuclear conference, Critical Mass '74. In Nader's wry reformulation of nuclear lingo, the term *critical mass* (the amount of radioactive material needed to sustain a chain reaction at a constant rate) was now used to refer to the coming together of citizens in sufficient numbers to stop nuclear power. The conference attracted 1,200 activists and gave new energy and vision to a movement that had been fragmented and increasingly discouraged.

Nader's prediction that nuclear power would become the nation's "technological Vietnam" was borne out in succeeding years. Critical Mass, the new Public Citizen group founded to carry on the work of the 1974 conference, used the Freedom of Information Act to document a large number and variety of malfunctions at the nation's 100 nuclear reactors: accidents, near-accidents, emergency shutdowns, and assorted instances of mismanagement. Through congressional testimony, petitions to the Nuclear Regulatory Commission, and articles in the *Critical Mass Journal*, Critical Mass exposed the nuclear industry's reckless design and construction habits, routine secrecy, scientific arrogance, addiction to government subsidies, and antidemocratic zealotry. The 1978 near-catastrophe at the Three Mile Island nuclear plant—coming just days after the release of the Jane Fonda film *China Syndrome*—gave new credibility and clout to the safe energy movement among mainstream Americans.

In the 1980s, Critical Mass intensified its advocacy of safe, renewable energy alternatives (solar, wind, biomass, water) by documenting their superior safety and cost-efficiencies. It also focused on reforms of utility regulation and the perils of nuclear-waste disposal and nuclear-plant decommissioning. The director of Critical Mass is William J. Magavern.

The Tax Reform Research Project, now defunct, pioneered the advocacy of tax reform to benefit the average citizen. In the early 1970s, citizens had little influence over federal tax policy except through their elected representatives. To increase this influence, Nader founded the Tax Reform Research Project in 1972; Tom Stanton, an attorney, became the first director. Along with Robert Brandon and Jonathan Rowe, Stanton sought to demystify the tax system and explain how it was manipulated to win obscure subsidies for business and shift new burdens to the average citizen.

For example, the group helped expose the once-common practice by Wilbur Mills, the powerful chairman of the House Ways and Means Committee, of polling committee members to see what special-interest tax breaks they wanted for their favorite corporate friends and supporters. By shining a new spotlight on such tax patronage and challenging the secret legislative process for tax policy, the Tax Reform Research Project helped win important procedural reforms.

By 1976 the group had developed the field of citizen tax analysis sufficiently to publish *Tax Politics: How They Make You Pay and What You Can Do About It*, a major critique of the inequities of the tax code and a how-to guide for citizen-reformers. With a staff that never exceeded three, the group exposed biased tax analyses prepared by businesses or Congress, brought to light "tax expenditures" that benefit major corporations, and assailed the Internal Revenue Service's abuse of ordinary taxpayers and small businesses while favoring major corporations represented by former senior bureaucrats of the Internal Revenue Service.

Throughout the 1970s and 1980s, the group's newsletter, *People & Taxes*, offered some of the best independent critiques of the tax system, frequently digging up abuses that were then picked up by the mainstream press or investigated by congressional committees. The group had several noteworthy directors—Brandon, Robert McIntyre (now director of the labor-backed Citizens for Tax Justice), Tyler Bridges, and Jeff Drumtra—before it closed its doors in 1987.

— David Bollier

See also

Energy Cooperatives; Nader, Ralph.

Readings

Bollier, David (1989). *Citizen Action and Other Big Ideas: A History of Ralph Nader and the Modern Consumer Movement*. Washington, DC: Center for Study of Responsive Law.

Burt, Dan M. (1982). *Abuse of Trust: A Report on Ralph Nader's Network*. Chicago: Regnery Gateway.

Jacqueney, Theodore (1973). "Nader Network Switches Focus to Legal Action, Congressional Lobbying." *National Journal*. 5 (June 9): 840–849.

Public Interest Law Practice

Public interest law is the work done by lawyers on behalf of poor individuals, unrepresented interests, and the general good. Public interest law services are usually provided at no cost to the beneficiaries, who are either too poor to pay or are not organized in ways that would allow them to retain lawyers. Public interest lawyers work in the courts, government agencies, and legislatures, and also through mass media and community organizations.

History

The history of public interest law in the United States can be located in part in constitutionalism. An intimate relationship exists between public interest law and the Constitution. First, the governmental structure created by the Constitution makes public interest law both necessary and possible. Second, without public interest law, many constitutional protections might be ineffective. Finally, the broader American tradition of constitutionalism depends on institutions like public interest law. The governmental structure created by the Constitution makes legal advocacy important for the pursuit of many individual and collective interests. U.S. government is one by representation, not by direct participation. Although in theory citizens are supposed to be knowledgeable about public issues, and elected representatives are supposed to take into account the interests of all constituents, in fact most decisions are made in remote arenas and officials often are not aware of all affected interests. As a result, direct advocacy by professionals makes a difference in outcomes. If all such advocacy must be purchased in the marketplace, the system is skewed toward the interests of the "haves." The presence of public interest advocates, at least to some degree, offsets this bias.

Another source of the strength of public interest law in the United States, in addition to constitutionalism, is the importance of private lawyers in the enforcement of the law. Many laws are enforced by private lawsuits in which the lawyers are paid by a percentage of the award obtained for the client if the claim is successful. This system of payment, called contingency fees, allows lawyers to represent people who otherwise could not afford their fees, and contributes to the belief that lawyers can and should represent the disadvantaged.

In the late nineteenth and early twentieth centuries, despite the rapid growth of industry, the courts were reluctant to allow regulation of the use of industrial property. The Progressives, a group of elected officials in various states, and their allies successfully challenged this doctrine. They were responsible for the creation of federal agencies that could intervene to protect the public against the abuses of the market. Some Progressives, such as Louis Brandeis, also believed that lawyers had a social obligation to consider public consequences as part of their professional role.

Constitutionalism, the contingency fee, and the progressive tradition are essential to understanding public interest law. The growth in the number of practicing public interest lawyers and the current understandings of the concept, however, date to the 1960s. The social activism of that period—which included the creation of the Legal Services Program and the increasing willingness of the federal courts to fashion new procedural remedies—convinced many people that social change could be achieved through legal activity. Private foundations and the federal government assisted lawyers in establishing new nonprofit law firms called public interest law firms. At present, approximately 6,000 public interest lawyers are employed as staff attorneys in public interest law firms, including lawyers who work on behalf of the civil legal rights of the poor, law school clinical instructors, and lawyers in nonprofit law firms.

Consumerism and Public Interest Law

Consumerism was an aspect of the social activism of the 1960s. Ralph Nader's book *Unsafe at Any Speed* (1965) and the subsequent Senate hearings on General Motors (GM) created consumerism as a key aspect of citizen activism. Nader used the proceeds from the sale of his book and the settlement from GM to fund the establishment of a nonprofit public interest law firm, the Center for Study of Responsive Law. Other public interest firms working on behalf of consumers were initiated in that period, most with the active involvement of Ralph Nader: Public Interest Research Groups, Public Citizen, the Washington and state offices of Consumers Union, and the Center for Auto Safety. The Legal Services Corporation also created the National Consumer Law Center to serve as a backup center for local legal services centers representing poor people with consumer problems. Some local public interest law firms also provide representation for consumers, such as the Center for Public Representation in Madison, Wisconsin, which also provides clinical legal education for law students

The most distinctive aspect of public interest practice is the use of litigation, or the threat of litigation, on behalf of dispersed and unorganized consumers. Consumer public interest lawyers litigate in two general areas: enforcement of consumer-protection laws and access to information. A recent example of this public interest litigation is a successful class action in Wisconsin against a rent-to-own company that did not comply with the State Consumer Act and did not provide adequate information on interest rates. The Wisconsin lawyers who represented the consumers were public interest lawyers with the Center for Public Representation and Legal Aid.

Public interest legal practice on behalf of consumers extends beyond litigation. Public interest lawyers monitor regulatory agencies, represent individual clients with claims against businesses, educate consumers on their rights to redress, and write reports that expose abuses in the market. Often, lawyers also work with community groups in organizing activities where citizens express their concerns about consumer abuses. Recent examples of nonlitigative, consumer-protection activities include Consumers Union's monitoring of the activities of state insurance commissioners, and national and local public interest lawyers lobbying to preserve and enforce the Community Reinvestment Act.

In addition to nonprofit, tax-deductible law firms, attorneys practice public interest consumer protection in other areas. The role of some government-employed lawyers is to bring class actions on behalf of consumers; in many states, the attorney general brings class actions on behalf of consumers and refunds the monies directly to the aggrieved consumers. Several law schools provide law students with clinical legal placements in consumer representation, for example, the University of San Diego Law School's Center for Public Interest Law. Some private law firms practice consumer litigation in which statutory attorneys' fees can be awarded, for instance, in fair-lending class actions or automobile lemon-law cases.

Current Issues in Public Interest Law

In recent years, the institutions and practice of public interest law have changed. The 1960s vision is difficult to pursue in an increasingly conservative society. The federal judiciary is no longer the activist branch that 1960s lawyers anticipated, and legislators seek to reduce the ability of citizens to use the courts by restricting fee awards.

The willingness of many foundations and the federal government to fund public interest practice facilitated expansion of public interest law in the 1960s and early 1970s. However, since that time both foundations and the federal government have reduced their financial commitments. Other sources of funding for public interest law firms include direct mail, door-to-door canvassing, and sales of publications. Attorney-fee awards in class actions and statutory fees in areas such as lemon law continue to be a source of funds, but recent legislative efforts to reduce attorney awards may jeopardize this source as well.

Public interest law now spans the political spectrum. Some of the more notable liberal public interest law groups include the American Civil Liberties Union (ACLU) and the NAACP Legal Defense and Educational Fund. Public interest law groups of a conservative persuasion include the Pacific Legal Foundation, which brings suits against governmental regulation.

Interest in public interest law by law students, however, is increasing. Students have formed organizations that raise funds to support student fellowships in public interest law and student loan-forgiveness programs to allow students to work in public interest jobs after graduation. These local groups, envisioned and assisted by Ralph Nader, are part of a national network called the National Association for Public Interest Law, based in Washington, D.C. The bar associations at the state and national level also encourage pro bono work on behalf of poor and unorganized clients; over 100,000 lawyers donate their time as part of these pro bono programs.

Other societies show a significant interest in public interest law. In South Africa and Latin America, public interest law is flourishing, inspired and funded by U.S. lawyers and foundations.

The practice of public interest law is also shifting to new client groups such as gays and lesbians, new arenas such as community economic development, and new alliances such as the environmental justice movement. Many public interest lawyers consider individual client representation appropriate social-change activity.

Public interest law, as idea and institution, is a reflection of the faith in the redemptive power of law and legal institutions. To be sure, law does not always fulfill the expectations of many Americans. Public interest law is often weak and ineffective, and legal solutions may not lead to real gains. Nonetheless, public interest lawyers have won victories for their clients. The practice of public interest law helps ensure that market forces and the status quo do not run roughshod over democracy and constitutional values.

— Louise G. Trubek

See also

Center for Public Representation; Law, Consumer; Public Citizen.

Readings

Aron, Nan (1989). *Liberty and Justice for All: Public Interest Law in the 1980s and Beyond*. Boulder, CO: Westview Press.

Weisbrod, Burton A. (1978). *Public Interest Law: An Economic and Institutional Analysis*. Berkeley: University of California Press.

Public Interest Research Groups

The state Public Interest Research Groups (PIRGs) are nonprofit, nonpartisan consumer protection, government reform, and environmental advocacy groups that today form one of the nation's largest grassroots social change networks. Although originally inspired and given their initial push by Ralph Nader, from the start the PIRGs have been independent and self-sustaining.

The first PIRGs were founded in 1970 by college students in Oregon and Minnesota in response to Nader's challenge to students: "This country has more problems than it should tolerate and more solutions than it uses." Within several years, other PIRGs were formed on college campuses in some twenty states. Later, PIRGs were also organized in several Canadian provinces.

About half of the PIRGs' 1 million members, and many of its leaders, are college students. However, since the late 1970s, PIRG door-to-door canvasses have recruited citizen members as well. Today, staffed state PIRGs are active in twenty-two states. In addition, U.S. PIRG, the national lobbying office, has field offices in fourteen other states. In 1996 the PIRGs had a full-time professional staff of over 350 lawyers, scientists, and organizers. Year-round, part-time and full-time canvassers go door-to-door collecting signatures on petitions, educating the public, and seeking members for PIRGs.

In the 1960s and early 1970s, students conducted many successful campaigns, including civil rights organizing, campus protests against the Vietnam War, and the first Earth Day teach-ins. Others worked in Washington as Nader's Raiders, investigating government and corporate abuses. Taking ideas from all these sources, and following meetings on campuses and in Washington with numerous student activists, Ralph Nader and his associates proposed a model for institutionalizing student activism in stable, well-funded public interest organizations.

Organizing Model

The original PIRG organizing model was proposed by Ralph Nader and Donald K. Ross in the book *Action for a Change* (1971). Ross, who later became the first executive director (1973–1981) of New York PIRG, also wrote *A Public Citizens' Action Manual,* which described sample citizen projects for PIRGs and other advocacy groups to conduct. As outlined by Nader and Ross, interested students would petition student governments and college administrations for the right to establish a stable fee mechanism to fund PIRG activities. School chapters would pool resources into statewide organizations, governed by representatives from member campuses. The model linked the idealism and energy of students with the continuity and political acumen of staffed citizen action organizations.

Early efforts were widely supported by faculty and some administrators because PIRG provided excellent academic credit field-work opportunities and was run by students, who developed leadership skills. The model worked well. PIRG has trained thousands of student activists, some who started as student interns, others who served as members of campus boards of directors, and others who began as door-to-door canvassers. Some of these activists have made PIRG a career. Many PIRG student interns and student board members now serve as senior staff members of the PIRGs, including former MASSPIRG board chair Kenneth Ward, now executive director of NJPIRG; former Oregon PIRG chair Maureen Kirk, now its executive director; former CALPIRG board chair Andre DeLattre, now its organizing director; former ConnPIRG board chair and executive director Ed Mierzwinski, now U.S. PIRG consumer program director; and former NYPIRG intern and longtime MASSPIRG program director Mindy Lubber, now serving as president of Green Century Funds, a PIRG-founded mutual fund family promoting socially responsible investments.

The labor union checkoff served as an important basis of the organizing. Its premise was that a majority of students could vote to tax themselves to establish a citizenship organization. A PIRG chapter and campus fee would be established only following a majority petition drive of the student body and negotiations with campus administrators. Some PIRGs are funded through a student government contract, but most seek a separate, voluntary PIRG fee added to tuition bills, which provides students the choice of declining to pay. Fee contracts are renewable every two to three years based on ongoing student referenda.

In 1996 the fees at ninety-six campuses around the country ranged from a student government contract equal to 75¢ per student per semester at the University of Wisconsin–Madison to a $6.75-per-student waivable fee at Rutgers University. The largest PIRGs, Massachusetts and New York, each have over twenty campus chapters. Although some state PIRGs that were successful in the 1970s, such as North Carolina and Iowa, no longer exist,

PIRGs today have greatly expanded their geographic reach, overall membership, and political power.

The PIRG student fee mechanism achieved its goal of providing stable funding for student-based activism. Over the years, students have regularly won numerous campus referenda and petition drives to establish PIRGs. However, one sign of PIRGs' success is that opponents of its pro-consumer, pro-environmental platform have repeatedly challenged the idea that students can use student fees for so-called political purposes such as lobbying and other advocacy. These challenges to PIRGs attempt to focus attention on the fairness, or even constitutionality, of PIRG fees.

Ostensibly, these challenges are made to protect the rights of students, yet most are funded or supported by industry opponents of PIRG. In 1983 the Mid-Atlantic Legal Foundation, one of several corporate-funded, conservative "public interest" law firms established in the 1980s, brought a suit against Rutgers University on behalf of student Joe Galda, who was found through an advertisement. Although widely cited by PIRG opponents, *Galda v. Bloustein*'s result was narrow. Rutgers and New Jersey PIRG simply adopted a waivable checkoff fee, replacing a previous refundable fee. The checkoff, and other widely used PIRG fee mechanisms, have withstood all other legal challenges.

In 1994, following passage of several stringent environmental laws and initiatives supported by Massachusetts PIRG, the manufacturers' lobby, Associated Industries of Massachusetts, convinced Massachusetts to pass an anti-PIRG fee law, which MASSPIRG overturned in a successful 1994 ballot campaign. Similarly, in 1995 the New Jersey Business and Industry Association pushed through a law that attempts to restrict the use of student fees.

While some campus administrations oppose establishment of PIRGs, nearly all defend the university's right to decide the use of student fees. In August 1995, the PIRGs and the college community faced the first congressional curb on the use of student fees when Representative Gerald Solomon (R-NY) brought an anti-PIRG amendment to the House floor that would bar federal funds to any campus where student fees were used by groups "seeking to influence public policy." Opposed by every college trade association and hundreds of college presidents, it was defeated, 263–161.

National Networks

Recognizing not only the prudence of diversifying income but also the enhanced influence from a broader base, in the late 1970s the PIRGs began recruiting nonstudent members, primarily through door-to-door canvassing. Even before that effort, in 1977 the PIRGs created their first national association. The National PIRG Clearinghouse was first located in Ames, Iowa, at Iowa PIRG's offices, then moved to Washington, D.C., and became known as National PIRG. Dissolved in 1979, National PIRG conducted association and grant-seeking functions, but did not have sufficient resources to serve as a Washington lobbying office.

Building on that experience, in the early 1980s PIRGs established two successful national networks. The first, created in 1982, was the Fund for Public Interest Research, a joint technical assistance, fund-raising, and training arm. The fund coordinates fund-raising and other joint projects for most PIRGs, especially the smaller ones; a large PIRG may have adequate resources to recruit staff or prepare legislative campaign materials, but small PIRGs may not.

Douglas Phelps, who also chairs the U.S. PIRG board of directors, and associate director Margie Alt now direct the fund. Phelps was executive director of Massachusetts PIRG during its rapid growth from 1978 to 1989, when it emerged as one of the nation's most powerful and persistent state-based citizen groups. For example, MASSPIRG conducted a six-year bottle bill campaign, led by Lubber and Susan Birmingham, that finally succeeded in 1982. That campaign involved several legislative attempts, a successful veto override, and ultimately, defeat of an industry-sponsored repeal initiative.

Numerous campaigns first organized by the PIRGs through the fund have developed into successful affiliated or separate organizations, including the National Environmental Law Center (NELC), a public interest environmental law firm that conducts research and handles environmental litigation for the PIRGs and other environmental groups; the National Student Campaign against Hunger and Homelessness, jointly founded in 1985 by the PIRGs and USA for Africa, the hunger relief group organized by leading musicians; and the National Association for Public Interest Law (NAPIL), which assists law students in forming campus groups that raise money to fund summer law clerkships with nonprofit groups.

National Lobbying

In 1984 the PIRGs established U.S. PIRG, the national lobbying office for the state PIRGs. Directed since its inception by Gene Karpinski, who had been field director of Nader's Public Citizen's Congress Watch and Norman Lear's People for the American Way, U.S. PIRG is funded by dues contributions from PIRGs and individual memberships from its own canvass operations. It is affiliated with the U.S. PIRG Education Fund, a 501(c)(3) research and education nonprofit organization, which is funded mainly by foundation grants.

Although the progressive foundation community provides substantial resources for PIRG campaign finance reform and environmental preservation projects, it does not focus on consumer protection. Significant funding for expansion of U.S. PIRG and state PIRG consumer programs in the 1990s has come instead from the Consumer Federation of America's State and Local Grants Program and the Colston Warne Grants Program of Consumers Union.

U.S. PIRG lobbying focuses on taking innovative and successful state PIRG ideas to the national level. For example, following passage by MASSPIRG and NYPIRG of state legislation restricting bank check holds, U.S. PIRG successfully advocated passage of a federal check hold law (1987). PIRG played a key role in the passage of other financial legislation, including the 1991 Truth in Savings Act, the 1988 Home Equity Loan Disclosure Act, and the 1989 Fair Credit and Charge Card Act.

U.S. PIRG's product safety work emphasizes children's health. Since 1986, annual PIRG "Trouble in Toyland" reports have resulted in Consumer Product Safety Commission (CPSC) recalls of over thirty-five toys. When an effort by U.S. PIRG, Consumers Union, and Consumer Federation of America (CFA) to enact a federal toy safety label requirement failed, the PIRGs turned to the states. ConnPIRG succeeded, in 1992, in passing the nation's first toy safety labeling law, which was upheld in federal courts after the Toy Manufacturers of America filed suit to overturn it. Federal legislation finally passed in 1994.

PIRG has always fought against environmental degradation and has proposed innovative environmental solutions. U.S. PIRG's environmental advocacy builds on successful state campaigns, such as MASSPIRG and Oregon PIRG's pioneering toxics use-reduction laws and the returnable beverage container, or bottle bill, laws. U.S. PIRG also supports tough campaign finance reforms and publishes numerous reports on political action committee (PAC) contributions to Congress.

Many U.S. PIRG lobbyists have gone on to direct other organizations and projects. Former CALPIRG intern and U.S. PIRG consumer program director Pamela Gilbert became director of Public Citizen's Congress Watch and is now executive director of the CPSC; Rick Hind, environmental program director, now directs Greenpeace USA's toxics campaign; Bill Magavern, staff attorney, became director of Public Citizen's Congress Watch and Critical Mass Energy Project; and Kathleen Welch, former NYPIRG intern and U.S. PIRG energy lobbyist, became director of the National Association for Public Interest Law (NAPIL).

State Advocacy

PIRGs' real strength has always been the grassroots reach of the state PIRG campuses and canvasses. Regular activities include generating letters to public officials, holding district meetings, organizing national lobby days, and organizing state coalitions on issues.

PIRGs are pragmatic strategists who use a variety of methods to achieve diverse organizing goals. State PIRG advocacy tactics include legislative and ballot initiative campaigns, litigation, economic development projects, and publication of reports and consumer guides. PIRG legislative successes range from roles in passage of the nation's first new-car lemon laws (ConnPIRG and CALPIRG, 1982) to passage of the first state Superfund law for hazardous waste cleanup (NYPIRG, 1981).

PIRGs prepare hundreds of investigative reports and consumer guides on numerous topics, including hearing-aid sale rip-offs, small claims court, landlord-tenant relations, the Clean Water Act, escalating bank fees, credit bureau errors, playground safety, overpackaged products, toxic consumer products, nuclear waste transportation safety, campus consumer survival, meat grading and inspection, energy alternatives, unfair property tax assessments, and antienvironmental corporate welfare subsidies in the federal budget. PIRGs often collaborate with other organizations on these reports. For example, a successful 1993 national bank fee report was researched and written by PIRG and CFA staff and volunteers, then co-released at press conferences by PIRGs and CFA local groups in twenty-three states.

PIRGs successfully qualify more questions for state ballots than any other organization. Initiative campaigns are a leading strategy for achieving significant PIRG public policy goals, particularly because business money strongly influences many legislatures. Also, initiatives are a logical use of PIRG's grassroots capabilities.

Recent ballot initiatives proposed by state PIRGs focus on eliminating big money from the political system and on "green consumerism," or encouraging the use of recycled products. In November 1994, PIRGs helped lead successful ballot campaigns to limit campaign contributions to $100 in Montana, Oregon, and Missouri. A similar PIRG-supported referendum in Colorado was narrowly defeated when corporate opponents made large, last-minute donations, including $20,000 from the Tobacco Institute, days before the election. In 1994, MASSPIRG introduced an initiative, the first of its kind, to restrict corporate contributions to ballot campaigns. Corporations spent over $2.5 million, nearly 90 percent of it from out of state, to defeat it.

PIRG litigation currently focuses on violations of the federal Clean Water Act. The 1993 annual report of the U.S. Department of Justice commended the PIRGs and other groups for their actions as private attorneys general under the Clean Water Act's citizen suit provisions. Since their Clean Water Litigation program began in the early 1980s, the PIRGs have won over seventy-seven clean water lawsuits and recovered over $40 million in fines and penalties, which courts usually direct be used to fund environmental cleanup and research programs by state agencies, universities, and conservation groups. New Jersey PIRG established a foundation, endowed by penalties, that provides funds to groups conducting ongoing antipollution work in New Jersey watersheds.

In 1995, PIRG and NELC attorneys settled a case against Shell Oil, which had been illegally dumping selenium and other heavy metals into San Francisco Bay. The court ordered Shell to cease polluting and to pay a $2.2 million fine, which will fund the projects of twenty-four environmental groups.

NYPIRG lawsuits have been instrumental in ensuring that students on college campuses retain the right to vote at their school addresses. Minnesota PIRG's litigation program ranges from a successful case against Ford for misleading television advertising of the durability of pickup trucks driven off-road to an unsuccessful 1984 Supreme Court case challenging the constitutionality of the Solomon (R-NY) Amendment, which required draft-eligible students to sign a statement that they had registered for the draft to be eligible for student financial aid.

The PIRGs have established several economic development projects. Both NYPIRG and PennPIRG run heating-oil buying cooperatives. Thousands of members save up to twenty cents a gallon or more on their heating-oil purchases. In 1991 the PIRGs founded a socially responsible investment fund family, Green Century Funds, and a long-distance telephone company, Earth Tones. Green Century also lobbies corporations and files shareholder resolutions to force environmental compliance.

As grassroots organizations, PIRGs' primary strength is an ability to run field campaigns, mobilizing staff and volunteers to urge thousands of citizens to take action—whether to attend a rally, sign a petition, send a letter to Congress or the statehouse, or answer a survey. A description of some current and past campaigns is illustrative.

NYPIRG's ongoing "Straphangers Campaign" attacks unfair rate hikes and forced New York City's transit officials to clean up subway cars. In 1995 the Boston Metropolitan Transit Authority and MASSPIRG announced a joint newspaper recycling program on the "T" as part of MASSPIRG's "Reduce, Reuse, Recycle" campaign.

Florida PIRG's "Save Our Shores" campaign collects petition signatures on beaches, publishes reports, and conducts other activities in ongoing opposition to offshore oil drilling. Since 1972, students, staff, and citizen volunteers of NJPIRG's "Waterwatch" have stream-walked and monitored water quality at hundreds of rivers and streams, providing agencies with numerous reports of violations and NJPIRG with data to support passage of remedial legislation.

Between 1979 and 1991, NYPIRG conducted a campaign to establish a Citizen Utility Board (CUB), a nonprofit consumer group funded through inserts in state mailings to citizens. This effort finally resulted in an executive order by Governor Mario Cuomo requiring the state Public Service Commission to enact regulations to establish the organization, which began recruiting memberships in 1994.

In 1980 the PIRG Campaign for Safe Energy picketed against nuclear power at presidential candidate events around the country, resulting in the insertion of a safe energy plank in the Democratic platform. In 1990, PIRGs coordinated a national Clean Air Act campaign. Over 300 environmental groups generated more than 500,000 Clean Air postcards sent to Congress, ensuring passage of tough amendments to the law.

The April 1995 National Earth Day Rally, chaired by Karpinski and staffed primarily by the PIRGs, brought over 200,000 citizens to the Capitol Mall for Earth Day to send a message to Congress: "Don't turn back the clock on 25 years of environmental protection." The rally was part of a larger campaign. Following an emergency Free the Planet student conference attended by nearly 2,000 students in Philadelphia in February 1995, PIRG and other organizations announced the 1995 Environmental Bill of Rights petition drive. After successful completion of the million-signature petition drive in the fall of 1995, PIRG students planned to organize on campus to achieve its twenty-five-point platform of environmental protection and preservation strategies.

Since 1984 the National Student Campaign for Voter Registration has registered hundreds of thousands of students and others to vote. The kickoff conference brought nearly 2,000 students to a national conference in Boston.

Staff and Resources

The largest state PIRGs, by budget and membership, are NYPIRG and MASSPIRG, each with about 100,000 citizen and student members and budgets of over $1 million annually. These PIRGs are among the largest and most successful citizen groups in any state, yet smaller PIRGs with no more than five to ten staffers each also achieve legislative successes.

A strength of the PIRGs is dedicated staffers. In addition to the longtime staff mentioned above, many senior PIRG staff have been with the organization twelve years or more, including Janet Domenitz, MASSPIRG director; Rich McClintock, Colorado PIRG director; NYPIRG Director Jay Halfon; PIRG National Canvass Director Jon Scarlett; NYPIRG Legislative Director Blair Horner; and NYPIRG counsel Gene Russianoff.

Numerous PIRG alumni have moved to leadership positions in other organizations: Ed Lloyd, former NJPIRG director, directs the Rutgers University Public Interest Law Clinic; Indiana PIRG co-founder Jim Jontz served that state in Congress (1986–1992) and now directs the Endangered Species Coalition; ConnPIRG co-founder Mary Mushinsky and former board chair/legislative director Jim O'Rourke serve in that state's legislature; Tom Novick, NYPIRG board chair and Oregon PIRG director, served several terms in the latter's state legislature (as former student Mark Sorenson does today); and former Oregon PIRG director Joel Ario is now policy director for the state's Insurance Regulation Department. Many former PIRG staff serve the progressive foundation community, including Ross, former COPIRG and NYPIRG director Tom Wathen, former VPIRG director John Gilroy, and longtime NJPIRG program director Rob Stuart.

During their first twenty-five years, the PIRGs have demonstrated resiliency and adaptability in the face of repeated corporate attacks. The rapidly shifting political climate of the 1990s offers numerous challenges and opportunities for citizen organizing and movement building. The PIRGs plan to continue working to ensure the fundamental right of citizens to buy safe products, at fair prices, while living in an environment where the air is safe to breathe, the food is safe to eat, and the water is safe to drink.

— Edmund Mierzwinski

See also

State and Local Consumer Organizations.

Reading

Griffin, Kelley (1987). *More Action for Change.* New York: Dembner Books.

Public Opinion

Questions bearing on consumer issues have been included in public opinion polls since the early days of scientific polling in the 1930s and appear periodically in the polls of the major polling organizations, including Gallup, Roper, and Harris. The pollsters' choice of questions and the public's responses provide insights into what issues both the pollsters and the public thought were important over the past sixty years. Not surprisingly, questioning on consumer issues is more common in periods when consumer movement and legislative activity are high. A few specially commissioned studies also provide useful insights into public opinion on consumer issues. Two particularly important studies are *Consumerism at the Crossroads,* done for Sentry Insurance by Louis Harris in late 1976, and *Consumerism in the Eighties,* done for the Atlantic Richfield Company by Harris in late 1982.

Examination of past poll results provides only a limited basis for identifying changes in opinions on consumer issues over time because only a few questions have been used repeatedly. Even those repeated questions seldom have been used for more than a decade. Similar questions can be compared, however, and response patterns at particular points in time provide insights into the formation and structure of public attitudes.

Poll results serve several important functions. They legitimize consumer protection proposals put forward by sympathetic legislators and officials. They serve an important secondary function by motivating consumer movement activity and media coverage of consumer issues. Another important secondary effect in the 1970s and 1980s was persuading corporate executives to take the consumer movement and its concerns more seriously.

Product Safety

Over the years, two different approaches have been used to ensure product safety. One broad set of approaches promotes safety by limiting choices: banning unsafe products, requiring safety devices, and restricting use. An alternative set of approaches seeks to ensure informed choice and use through safety warning labels and user licensing.

Consumers' willingness to limit choices in order to ensure auto safety is revealed in the responses to polls dating to the mid-1930s. In one of the earliest such questions, 68 percent said that they favored the use of governors on cars to prevent speeds in excess of fifty miles per hour (Gallup 1936). Twenty years later, 70 percent favored the use of governors to limit speeds to a maximum of sixty miles per hour (Gallup 1956). Seat belt installation had widespread support well before Ralph Nader focused public attention on auto safety. In a 1955 poll, 49 percent favored requiring the installation of seat belts; over the next ten years, the percentage of supporters grew to 56 percent (Gallup 1955, 1965). In this period, most of the public as well as the auto industry believed that improving driver performance was the best way to reduce the number and severity of auto accidents. Relatively few respondents mentioned increasing safety features, reducing engine power, or controlling mechanical failures (Gallup 1966).

More recent questioning shows broad public support for requiring the installation of safety devices, but also suggests that the public does not favor requiring their use. In 1984 questioning, 60 percent favored requiring all new cars to have front-seat airbags, while 31 percent were opposed (Gallup). Fifty percent favored requiring the installation of passive-restraint seat belts, while 44 percent were opposed. However, when asked their position on fining drivers and front-seat passengers $50 if they did not wear seat belts, only 30 percent were in favor, while 65 percent were opposed.

The public also seems unwilling to ban products totally. Beginning in the mid-1930s, public support for forbidding the sale of beer, wine, and liquor clearly declined. In 1936, 38 percent favored such a ban, but by 1976 only 19 percent favored it (Gallup 1936, 1976), and in 1994, 21 percent favored a ban (Gallup). A similar pattern prevails for cigarettes. When asked in 1981 if cigarettes should be banned completely, only 20 percent of the respondents agreed, while 74 percent disagreed (Gallup). More recently, only 11 percent said smoking should be made totally illegal (Gallup 1994). In 1992, 92 percent of those questioned were aware of the controversy over the safety of silicone breast implants, but only 31 percent favored banning them entirely (Gallup). However, product bans may be more acceptable if alternatives are available. When asked if they favored banning the use of chlorofluorocarbons even if this meant higher prices for air conditioners, refrigerators, and other products, 79 percent favored such a move, while only 12 percent were opposed (Gallup 1991).

Many members of the public appear to think that consumers should be permitted to trade off safety in order to reduce product prices. When asked if they favored allowing consumers a choice between a very safe product at a higher price and the same product without safety equipment at a lower cost, 51 percent agreed that consumers should have the opportunity to buy the lower-priced product without the safety equipment, while 44 percent felt they should not (Harris 1980).

When presented with more general questions about product safety, the public appears to prefer measures that enhance or facilitate choice. When presented with the statement that the best way to solve product safety problems is not to ban products but to require health warnings on them, 73 percent said they tended to agree (Harris 1974). But, at the same time, most of the respondents recognized that "a lot of people do not read the directions, or misuse products"—88 percent of those questioned tended to agree (Harris 1974). The public does not appear to believe that those who ignore directions and are injured are entitled to damages. When asked if they felt those injured in such cases were entitled to damages, 60 percent disagreed (Harris 1976).

However, the public sees large damage awards to consumers injured by defective products as a way to focus corporate attention on product safety. In a 1980 survey, 77 percent of the public respondents questioned agreed that large awards were a useful device (Harris 1980).

The study *Consumerism in the Eighties* concluded that the public was much more favorable to health, safety, and other types of protective regulation (e.g., controls on misleading ads and dangerous products) than to economic regulation (controls on interest rates and consumer prices). Even those who preferred less regulation overall typically did not favor rollback of a variety of existing regulations (Harris 1982). Advocates of regulatory rollbacks in recent years have failed to take these public preferences into account and have been surprised by the public reaction to their proposals.

Regulation of Competition and Trade Practices

Those who examine public opinion on government regulation of business activity conclude that public attitudes are ambivalent. On the one hand, the public is concerned about controlling excessive corporate power, while on the other hand it is concerned about the growth of excessive government power. The interplay of these two concerns can be seen in survey results from the 1970s. After the early years of the decade, survey results indicated increased public confidence in big business (Gallup 1973 to 1979). At the same time, public confidence in government fell. The declining ability of the consumer movement to get new legislation in the late 1970s is perhaps explained by these two shifts. Confidence in big business remained high in the early 1980s, but declined sharply after 1986 (Gallup 1983–1994).

Changes in confidence in key institutions can be seen in the shifting responses to a question in which respondents were asked to indicate the biggest threat to the nation: business, labor, or government (Gallup). In 1959 labor was most frequently named—41 percent. In 1967 government was the most frequently named—49 percent. In 1979 government was named by 43 percent, while 28 percent named business. In 1983, with Ronald Reagan in the White House, 51 percent named government, while only 19 percent named business.

Over the years, encouraging business competition has had clear public support. Antitrust laws, which are seen as one way of promoting this competition, are widely favored. In the mid-1970s, the Harris poll asked respondents if they would favor or oppose eliminating antitrust laws if their elimination meant competition would be sharply reduced. Almost two-thirds indicated they would be opposed (1974, 1976, 1977). Many of the public also indicated that they would be willing to accept reduced efficiency in order to protect smaller companies. Almost three-fourths opposed eliminating antitrust laws even if this meant that smaller, less efficient companies would be replaced by bigger, more efficient ones (Harris 1974, 1976, 1977).

Support for breaking up the largest companies into smaller ones as a way to encourage competition was also substantial. The percentage favoring this idea rose from 38 percent in 1959 to 53 percent in 1981 (Opinion Research Corp.). Interest in government ownership of corporations, however, declined between the late 1930s and the late 1940s. In 1937, 59 percent favored government ownership of electric power companies, but by 1948 only 23 percent supported this idea (Roper).

Information and Education

Opinions about the information available for consumer decision-making appear contradictory. Many survey respondents indicate that adequate information is available, but many also express concern about inadequate and deceptive information. In the *Consumerism at the Crossroads* study, when consumer respondents were asked if they felt enough information was available to make sensible consumer decisions, 58 percent agreed (Harris 1976). Almost two-thirds also agreed that consumers do not use the information available to them. However, when asked how worried they were over each item of a list of consumer issues, 44 percent said that the failure of companies to live up to their advertising claims worried them a great deal, making this one of the most widespread concerns. In responding to another item on the same list, 26 percent said that the absence of reliable information about different products and services worried them a great deal. Misleading packaging or labeling also was a widespread concern, with 34 percent saying that it worried them a great deal.

A number of surveys document the low opinion in which the public holds advertising executives and the advertising they produce. During the 1960s and 1970s, one-third or more rated the honesty and ethical standards of advertising executives as low or very low (e.g., Gallup 1976). Attitudes toward television advertising tend to be more negative than those toward print ads. When asked how much of television advertising is seriously misleading, 46 percent said that some or all of it was, while 28 percent thought that some or all newspaper and magazine ads were seriously misleading (Harris 1976).

Surveys also suggest that the public has a low opinion of the honesty and ethical standards of another source of consumer information: sales agents with whom they have face-to-face contact. In the mid-1970s, car salesmen were the most widely distrusted, with about half of those questioned rating their honesty as low or very low. During the 1980s, this proportion increased and, by the mid-1990s, had grown to three-fifths. About one-third rated insurance salesmen as low or very low, a proportion that also increased during the 1980s; by the mid-1990s, it had risen to over two-fifths. A little under one-third rated real estate salesmen as low or very low, and by the mid-1990s, this rating had improved somewhat (Gallup 1976–1994).

Widespread support for maintaining and even increasing government controls on the honesty and accuracy of claims made by advertising is evident. When asked their opinion on needed changes in government regulation of advertising, 60 percent said that more regulation was needed (Roper 1974, 1980). Corrective advertising, in particular, found widespread support; 95 percent favored forcing companies to correct false statements in future advertising (Harris 1976). Another, harsher measure also found a good deal of support: Barring a company whose ads are proven misleading or false from advertising for a period of time was favored by 78 percent (Harris 1976).

Along with widespread support for making advertising more trustworthy, increased consumer education received broad support. Consumer respondents in the *Consumerism at the Crossroads* study were asked if requiring all high school students to study consumer affairs would be a good thing or a bad thing. An overwhelming 92 percent said this would be a good thing.

Redress

Public awareness of consumers' problems in obtaining redress increased during the 1970s. Both the specific mention of redress in President Nixon's Buyer's Bill of Rights message in 1969 and the efforts of the U.S. Office of Consumer Affairs played a role in this growing awareness. When questioned for the *Consumerism at the Crossroads* study, slightly less than half of the consumer respondents said that they thought warranties were written mainly for the protection of manufacturers. In the same study, slightly over half rated most warranties as not understandable, and a somewhat larger number rated them as not adequate (Harris 1976).

A comparison of 1976 and 1982 survey results indicates that redress problems became a more widespread concern over this period. When asked how much certain consumer problems worried them, 30 percent of the 1976 respondents said that inadequate guarantees and warranties worried them a great deal; in 1982, this number increased to 36 percent. When asked how much they worried about the failure of companies to handle complaints properly, 29 percent of the 1976 respondents said this worried them a great deal; by 1982, this concern was 39 percent (Harris 1976, 1982).

Consumer Movement

When questioned in 1976 and 1982 surveys, the overwhelming majority of the public felt that the consumer movement had done some good (Harris 1976, 1982). In 1976, 16 percent felt that the movement had done a great deal of good, while in 1982, 12 percent agreed. In 1976, 67 percent felt the movement had done some good, and in 1982, 71 percent agreed.

Approval of the movement was most common in the East and among those with more formal education. Although the percentage with negative views was small, it increased from 4 to 13 percent over the six-year period. Negative views were most common among those with less formal education. Opinions about the movement and its leadership crystallized over the period; the percentage indicating they were not sure about the impacts of the movement declined sharply.

However, comparison of 1976 and 1982 survey results shows a sharp increase in the numbers who felt that the leaders of the consumer movement were out of touch with consumers (Harris 1976, 1982). This percentage rose from 22 to 45 percent, while the number who felt movement leaders reflected consumers' feelings fell from 59 to 45 percent. The numbers who thought that the movement leadership did not consider the cost of what they were asking for also sharply increased, from 30 percent in 1976 to 49 percent in 1982. Along with these more critical views of the consumer movement came more critical views of Ralph Nader. The percentage of those who rated him positively declined from 54 percent in 1976 to 39 percent in 1982. Much of this decline in support was among those eighteen to twenty-nine year old, with many 1982 respondents indicating they knew too little to evaluate him. In both years, approval of Nader's efforts was particularly strong among those living in the East and among those with education beyond high school.

The *Consumerism in the 80s* study included several questions to assess the future potential of consumerism. In two separate questions, respondents were asked if they had ever taken an active part in a consumer group and if they had ever contributed money to such a group. In the combined responses that were reported, 16 percent indicated that they had been active in or contributed money to a consumer group (Harris 1982). The percentages reporting such support were highest among those in the East and those who were young, had more formal education, and had higher household incomes.

Public opinion's importance grows out of its interlinkages with media coverage and government policy-making. Many consumer problems receive little attention until government policymakers or the media focus public attention on them. Editors usually do not allocate space to consumer topics unless they perceive that the public has an ongoing interest in these issues. Legislators and regulatory officials, in turn, are guided by their perceptions of consumer and media support in deciding their positions and setting their priorities for action. Their proposals and efforts to build public support for consumer issues have the potential to generate a new round of media coverage, with resulting changes in public opinion.

— Robert O. Herrmann

Readings

Herrmann, Robert O., and Rex H. Warland (1976). "Nader's Support: Its Sources and Concerns." *Journal of Consumer Affairs.* 10 (1): 1–18.

Mayer, Robert N. (1991). "Gone Yesterday, Here Today: Consumer Issues in the Agenda-Setting Process." *Journal of Social Issues.* 47(1): 21–40.

Shapiro, Robert Y., and John M. Gilroy (1984). "The Polls: Regulation—Part I," and "The Polls: Regulation—Part II." *Public Opinion Quarterly.* 48(2): 531–542 and 48(3): 666–677.

Public Power

Public power is the oldest form of electric utility ownership in the United States. Butler, Missouri, turned on arc lamps atop its courthouse on December 6, 1881, and continues to operate its own municipal electric system today. Over 178 publicly owned electric systems have been in existence 100 years or more.

Today, more than 2,000 publicly owned electric utilities serve nearly 15 percent of all U.S. electric consumers. Twelve of the country's thirty largest cities are served in whole or in part by public power. Moreover, municipal utilities, utility districts, state authorities, joint action agencies, and other public entities own almost 12 percent of the nation's generating capacity. The annual total electric operating revenue of public power systems exceeds $24 billion.

Public power systems differ from investor-owned utilities in several respects. First, public power systems are nonprofit institutions that belong to the citizens they serve; the users and owners are one and the same, and all economic benefits are retained locally. Private power companies are organized for profit and owned by stockholders, who are paid dividends.

Second, public power systems are service-oriented, with no built-in economic bias toward a particular technique or technology. Private power companies are normally guaranteed a specified rate of return on plant investment, thus encouraging capital-intensive projects that increase the total number of dollars available for dividends.

Third, citizens of communities served by public power direct the activities of these systems through the selection of city councils and governing boards, and through participation in the formulation of policies and programs. Customers of private companies cannot fire private utility board members or executives who make policies deemed to be anti-consumer.

Fourth, cities and towns with municipal utilities are both distributors and users of electricity. Accordingly, they have a clear and unconstrained interest in the cost-effective delivery of this service for streetlighting, sewage treatment, and other electricity costs.

History

In the 1870s, inventors developed equipment to produce and harness electricity for lighting buildings and streets. In the late nineteenth and early twentieth centuries, public power systems and investor-owned utilities competed over local franchises. By 1900 there were some 800 municipal electric systems and about 2,200 private electric utilities. The largest concentration of these public power systems were in Great Lakes states and the central part of the nation. Most served small communities that could not obtain electric service from privately owned companies. However, by 1895 municipal systems served Anaheim, California; Jacksonville, Florida; Tacoma, Washington; and Austin, Texas.

The number of public power systems peaked at 3,066 in 1923, then declined because of an accelerating trend toward consolidation among private electric utilities. By the late 1920s, sixteen corporate empires controlled more than 85 percent of the nation's power supply (as well as railroads, coal companies, water companies, and other operations). These private companies waged a campaign to discredit "government in the power business" as a threat to democracy. Between 1924 and 1934, private power holding companies bought out more than 1,500 municipal systems.

Advocates for consumers fought back. In 1928, Congress ordered the Federal Trade Commission (FTC) to investigate political and financial practices in the private utility industry. After four years, the FTC issued a study that charged private companies with an abuse of the public trust and misleading attacks on public power. Led by reformers, an aroused public supported tighter regulation of private utilities and the encouragement of "consumer-owned systems," run by municipalities or cooperatives.

In the 1930s, Congress created three major federal power-related agencies affecting public power. The Tennessee Valley Authority was established in 1933 to develop resources in the Tennessee River valley. These resources included power production through dams and power plants to which municipal systems were given first purchase rights at cost-based rates. The Rural Electrification Administration was created in 1935 to promote the establishment of electric cooperatives serving rural consumers without access to electric service. In coming decades, these rural cooperatives served as important allies of public power systems when both were attacked by private utilities.

The Bonneville Power Administration was established in 1937 to market hydropower throughout the Pacific Northwest. Municipal systems were given first purchase rights to this power at cost-based rates. Subsequently, other federal power agencies were created. In 1995, five of these agencies marketed power from 132 hydropower projects in the West, Southwest, and South.

During this period, public power also began to expand the scope of its operations at the state and local levels, and several state power authorities were established in the 1930s. In the 1930s and 1940s, public or people's utility districts (PUDs) were created as areawide government entities to provide electric and water services. Today, most of the 100-plus PUDs are in Washington, Oregon, Nebraska, and California. In the 1940s, Nebraska became an all–public power state by public mandate.

Between 1950 and 1970, local public power systems focused on improving power supplies. An important strategy was to create joint-action agencies—groups of municipal systems that built facilities large enough to serve a number of cities and towns. By the late 1980s, more than fifty of these joint-action agencies were in existence.

American Public Power Association

American Public Power Association (APPA), the national service organization for publicly owned electric utilities, was formed in 1940 as a nonprofit corporation under the laws of the District of Columbia for the purpose of encouraging the cooperation and promoting the improvement of its members. By 1995, APPA represented more than 1,750 community-owned, locally controlled, nonprofit electric utilities located in forty-nine states (all but Hawaii). Through dues, the purchase of association publications, and conference registration fees, these members provide most of the organization's funding.

Activities of the association are determined by actions at an annual meeting of members, and by direction of a thirty-person board of directors and nine-person executive committee drawn from the board. Each board member is an official of a member system and is elected to serve a three-year term. The executive committee is composed of four APPA officers and five board members selected by the association's president. The president is an official of an APPA member system who has served on the board for at least one term, and is elected by the membership for a one-year term.

Guidance is also provided by a forty-member policy boards advisory council, an advisory committee, and a legislative and resolutions committee. Additional input is made by sections organized by function—e.g., engineering and operations, accounting and finance, energy services, and legal.

The staff are headed by an executive director chosen by the executive committee and responsible to the board. The executive director develops a work plan and budget, selects and supervises other staff, and acts as an APPA spokesperson. Typically, executive directors hold this position for many years. Alex Radin, trained as a journalist, served as APPA executive director from 1948 to 1985. He was succeeded by Larry Hobart, also trained as a journalist, who first joined APPA in 1960. In 1995, Alan Richardson was appointed executive director. Richardson joined APPA in 1977 as legislative counsel after serving as majority counsel to the Committee on Rules of the U.S. House of Representatives.

APPA supports members with advocacy and information and supplies representation before Congress, the courts, and federal agencies. It maintains a library and a database of industry facts and figures, and publishes *Public Power* magazine and *Public Power Weekly.* It carries out a program of educational courses and supports research and development efforts. It prepares or commissions studies and reports designed to assist in effective operation of a public power system and numerous other trade association functions.

During its life, APPA has sought to protect and preserve the public power option. It has been in the forefront of efforts to apply the antitrust laws to the electric utility industry, ensure that benefits of high-voltage electric transmission are available to all utilities on fair and equitable terms, and preserve cost-based rates as a measure of consumer protection.

The association is a strong supporter of energy conservation measures and the development of technologies that reduce air and water pollution. For example, it responded to profound energy changes of the 1970s by promoting the concept of energy services planning. The goal of this process is to increase utility efficiency and satisfy customer demand through cost-effective methods. It assumes that reliable service can be met most economically by embracing technologies and services, demand-side as well as supply-side, that best match utility and customer needs.

APPA participates in the traditional consumer movement chiefly through the Consumer Federation of America. APPA helped found the federation in 1968, and serves on the board and important policy committees of this organization. In the late 1980s, it persuaded more than twenty public power systems to join the federation, to which APPA provides expertise on electricity issues and representation for those tens of millions of consumers served by public power.

— Larry Hobart

See also

Electricity Regulation.

Readings

American Public Power Association (1987). *Public Power in America: A History.* Washington, DC: American Public Power Association.

Rudolph, Richard, and Scott Ridley (1986). *Power Struggle: The Hundred Year War over Electricity.* New York: Harper & Row Publishers.

Public Representation

Lack of organizational structure may be the key difference between the consumer interest and other special interests. People organize in almost every economic, social, and professional category, except as consumers. It is no wonder, therefore, that the consumer interest has been given only token recognition by the molders of public policy and that consumer (or public) representation on and before policy-making government institutions has been spotty at best. This fact is of more than passing significance because the consumer interest in public policy decisions is often different from that of other, better organized sectors.

Since the 1920s, professional consumer research organizations such as Consumer Union have attempted to make up for this deficiency. Alone, these organizations were not strong enough to counteract the power of other economic groups, but together with their allies—cooperatives, labor unions, and scattered professional, voluntary, service, and women's organizations—consumer organizations were responsible for promoting the idea of a legitimate consumer interest that deserves representation in governmental decision-making processes.

Federal Level

Efforts to bring about consumer or public representation on governmental decision-making bodies date to the New Deal in the 1930s. The National Recovery Administration (NRA) included a Consumer Advisory Board in its organizational structure. The Agricultural Adjustment Administration (AAA) had a Consumer Council. To provide a consumer viewpoint on the revitalization of the nation's coal industry, a Bituminous Coal Consumer Counsel was established. In 1940 the National Defense Administration's (NDA) seven-member advisory commission included one commissioner appointed to represent consumer concerns.

Virtually every evaluation of these early efforts to institutionalize consumer representation in government concluded that the impact of consumer representatives was at best marginal. They lacked political clout because they had no organized constituencies to back up their positions. Historian Arthur Schlesinger,

Jr., in his book *The Coming of the New Deal,* referred to consumer representatives on these 1930s agencies as "spearheads without shafts."

After World War II, the few existing consumer organizations continued to prevail upon government to recognize the consumer interest, even without agreement among themselves as to the nature of this interest. They achieved their first major success in 1962 when President John F. Kennedy sent the Congress a Message on Consumer Interests. That message contained a basic proclamation of consumer rights: the right to safety, the right to be informed, the right to choose, and the right to be heard.

In 1962 a Consumer Advisory Council (CAC) was appointed under the Council of Economic Advisers (CEA). Composed mainly of representatives of consumer organizations and their allies, the council's mandate was to "examine and provide advice to the Government on issues of broad economic policy, on Government programs protecting consumer needs, and on needed improvement in the flow of consumer research material to the public; this Consumer's Council will also give interested individuals and organizations a voice in these matters."

The Kennedy consumer council was the first such group appointed during relatively stable times. The council had not been in operation long, however, before it became obvious that CEA and CAC were not comfortable bedfellows. The old problem of consumer goals conflicting with overall economic policy arose again. For the most part, CEA considered the goals and legislative recommendations of CAC of minor importance. Others felt it an unnecessary irritant to the business community, whose support was necessary to achieve major legislative goals.

For its part, CAC felt hemmed in by CEA. CAC members complained that the consumer interest was not receiving sufficient exposure, and they requested a more independent status. Walter Heller, then chairman of CEA, agreed that the council could better serve its purpose if it were independent of CEA. Besides, Heller was anxious to divest himself of the responsibility for "servicing" a CAC whose liabilities seemed to him perhaps to outweigh its assets.

Thus, in February 1964, President Lyndon B. Johnson established by executive order the President's Committee on Consumer Interests, which was to be composed of two groups: representatives of the major federal agencies with responsibilities in consumer affairs and the Consumer Advisory Council. In addition, he established the Office of Special Assistant to the President for Consumer Affairs and appointed a special assistant, Esther Peterson, as chair of the committee.

The office still exists, although in a much less prominent place, having been relocated from the immediate office of the president to the Department of Health Education, and Welfare (now Health and Human Services). The office's major accomplishment is the increase of public awareness of consumer needs and responsibilities in a mass-consumption society. Its major problem has always been to find ways and means of carrying out a broad mandate with limited staff and resources. Like the consumer movement itself, the committee suffers because it operates in a system geared to respond to organized special interests that have a clear set of objectives.

By the 1970s, consumer organizations began to fight for direct consumer representation in governmental decision-making. Under the 1975 Magnuson-Moss Warranty–Federal Trade Commission Improvement Act, Congress substantially expanded consumer representation in government decision-making, at the same time greatly increasing the FTC's consumer protection responsibilities. Because FTC legal procedures were being upgraded, the lawmakers felt it necessary to improve opportunities for diverse, legitimate groups to participate in rulemaking. Therefore, Congress appropriated a modest sum (the original $500,000 was later increased to $750,000) for a public intervenor program to reimburse the expenses not only of consumer representatives but also of small business concerns whose participation was considered essential to fair and effective FTC proceedings. Congress recognized that very few consumer organizations or small businesses can absorb the expense of preparing expert testimony, presenting oral arguments, and cross-examining witnesses at hearings that last several months.

The FTC program became the precedent for more than ten public participation programs in different federal agencies. These agencies were guided by criteria set by Congress in awarding reimbursement: the group or individual contributes substantially to the record a viewpoint that would not otherwise be represented by agency staff or other witnesses; no financial interest in the outcome is involved; and the group or individual could not afford to participate without reimbursement. These agencies recognized that their ability to reach a consensus and the ultimate quality of their decisions depended on having specific evidence, broad-minded questions, and rational rebuttals from legitimate consumer and small-business representatives.

Also in the 1970s, the Food and Drug Administration (FDA) provided consumer participation on the technical advisory panels that make recommendations to the agency concerning the approval of new drugs and devices. This FDA program introduced a technique for identifying consumer representatives who are endorsed by the organized consumer community: A consortium of consumer organizations screens the résumés of candidates for the consumer representative positions.

In addition to the consumer consortium nomination process, the FDA program also cast in stark relief some of the issues associated with the contribution to government decisions that consumer representatives are expected to make. The FDA panels were created to provide the agency with technical advice, but the expectation of the consumer community is that their representatives will introduce a human dimension in the panel's deliberations, raising questions that the scientists might ignore.

In the 1980s federal public representation programs lost most of their funding because the Reagan administration did not support them. Without government funds, and given the time-consuming, complex issues (such as deregulation) facing government decision-makers, consumer participation had to be reshaped. Consumer activist organizations, now bearing the entire cost involved, found it impossible to participate; few groups were able to afford such contributions.

State Level

The history of public representation on decision-making bodies at the state government level differs from that at the federal level. Much state activity was generated by state laws requiring the appointment of citizen representatives on professional and occupational licensing boards. By the early 1990s, thousands of citizen representatives were appointed to these boards. In California, for example, laws were enacted that required all state licensing boards, except those that regulate health care professionals, to contain a majority of public members.

The impetus for appointing public members came in the late 1960s in the wake of criticism that professional licensing boards were using their powers to limit competition. Restrictions on entry limited the supply of practitioners, often resulting in higher costs to consumers. Also, restrictions on advertising deprived consumers of information that could enable them to make smarter purchase decisions. Lack of enforcement and failure to discipline incompetent or unethical practitioners indicated that some boards were failing to fulfill their public protection mandate. Therefore, some believed that the problem could be fixed by ending exclusive self-regulation and appointing public members to the boards to act as watchdogs and advocates of the public interest.

Supporters of public membership assumed, perhaps naively, that governors and their appointment secretaries would identify and place the "right" people. Very little attention was paid to questions such as how public members might be found, what qualifications or connections would be desirable, and exactly how the public member's role should be defined and his or her performance measured. The early laws defined public members solely in terms of conflict of interest. This well-intentioned effort tried to exclude individuals with a financial stake in board decisions from public membership.

Professional societies typically supply appointment authorities with lists of nominees who will bring the association's perspective to the regulatory table. However, consumer groups did not propose names of people to fill the new public member slots, so governors turned to patronage lists. Over the years, many public members have been conscientious and have played meaningful roles. Many others, however, never developed an interest in their boards and stopped attending. Some became involved, only to be overwhelmed and co-opted by the professional members. Still others never reached beyond their own social circles to ascertain the public stake in issues that came before their boards. Many had no relationship with any organized consumer, community, or citizen group.

Recent evaluations of the states' experience with public representation focus on three problem areas that may explain why public representation has not been as successful as some consumer activists would have wished: weakness in the identification and selection of candidates for appointment as consumer representatives, inadequate definition of roles and goals for public members, and insufficient training and ongoing support to help public members execute their responsibilities.

By the mid-1990s, consumer organizations began to recognize the need to overcome these three shortcomings if consumer representation in the next century is to have a chance to fulfill its promise. A growing dissatisfaction with government accountability and credibility seems to be inspiring a new acceptance of the idea of citizen representation. Accordingly, the twenty-first century may bring new opportunities for citizen and consumer groups to achieve their long-sought goal of direct representation.

— David A. Swankin

See also

Federal Consumer Advisory Bodies; Product Standards; U.S. Office of Consumer Affairs.

Readings

Barger, Debra, and Susan G. Hadden (1984). "Placing Citizen Members on Professional Licensing Boards." *Journal of Consumer Affairs.* 18 (1): 160–170.

Friedman, Robert S. (1978). "Representation in Regulatory Decision Making: Scientific, Industrial, and Consumer Inputs to the F.D.A." *Public Administration Review.* (May/June): 205–214.

Mayer, Robert N., and Debra L. Scammon (1983). "Intervenor Funding at the FTC: Biopsy or Autopsy." *Policy Studies Review.* 2 (February): 506–515.

Public Voice for Food and Health Policy

Public Voice for Food and Health Policy is a national nonprofit organization that uses research, education, and advocacy to promote a safer, healthier, and more affordable food supply for all Americans. It focuses on the full spectrum of food policy issues, including the way food is grown, how safely it is processed, how it is marketed, and its availability to low-income Americans. Public Voice is a leader in linking people and issues to create a climate for regulatory and policy changes in the areas of nutrition, food safety, sustainable agriculture, and food security. For example, it has helped organize the chef's community for action on food policy issues. The organization's agenda now concentrates on three areas: inner-city food access; agriculture, markets, and the environment; and nutrition and food safety.

Public Voice was founded in 1982 by Ellen Haas, recently undersecretary for food, nutrition, and consumer services at the U.S. Department of Agriculture. In the early 1970s, Haas was a leader in grassroots protests against rising beef prices, which led to the establishment of the Maryland Citizens Consumer Council. As a leader in that organization, she participated in the Consumer Federation of America and later served several terms as the federation's president. During the late 1970s and early 1980s, she also worked for the Community Nutrition Institute.

During its first decade, Public Voice was very much Haas's organization. She used her extensive political contacts and exceptional advocacy skills to influence legislative and regulatory policy-making. Along with staffers such as Allen Rosenfeld, she was assisted by a relatively small board of directors that included consumer leaders—Carol Tucker Foreman, Ann Brown, Stephen Brobeck–and political influentials such as the late commerce secretary Ron Brown, former congressman Mike Barnes, and political consultant John Deardourff, who now chairs the organization.

From 1993 to late 1996, the president of Public Voice was Mark S. Epstein, an attorney. Before joining the organization, Epstein served as executive director of the Oregon Natural Resources Council. He was succeeded by Arthur Jaegger, who had been serving as the organization's public affairs director.

In 1996, Public Voice had an annual budget of $1.3 million derived from foundation, government, and corporate grants; conference income; publication sales; membership fees; and individual contributions. This budget supported a full-time staff of seventeen, who had backgrounds in public health, law, communications, hunger advocacy, agricultural production, and economics.

Over the past decade, Public Voice has played a leading role in campaigns for improved nutrition labeling, healthier school food programs, stronger pesticide and food safety laws, "greener" and more consumer-friendly farm legislation, and tougher meat, poultry, and seafood inspection standards. It successfully petitioned the U.S. Department of Agriculture for an improved beef grading system, helped secure passage of legislation requiring more informative food nutrition labels, organized a national campaign to enact a mandatory federal seafood safety inspection program, and pressured the U.S. Department of Agriculture to improve nutritional standards for the school lunch program. Throughout its history, Public Voice has been the lead consumer organization in campaigns to reform anti-consumer federal sugar, peanut, and dairy programs.

Public Voice frequently presents testimony on food safety, agriculture, and nutrition issues to congressional committees, federal agencies, and scientific panels. Each year the staff are invited to speak before a broad spectrum of food industry, media, and advocacy audiences. Public Voice's annual conferences and workshops bring together diverse stakeholders to debate complex food policy issues. Its National Food Policy Conference represents the leading annual consumer forum for food policy stakeholders.

— Arthur Jaeger

See also

Food Purchase Protections; Food Safety.

Reading

Sinclair, Ward (1986). "Ellen Haas: Bringing a New Approach to the Consumer Movement." *Washington Post.* (August 18): A, 15.

R

Real Estate Brokerage Protections

The purchase and sale of a home is often the largest financial transaction of a consumer's life. Some experienced buyers and sellers opt to avoid any brokerage fees and undertake the transactions on their own. However, for about 80 percent of housing transactions, one or more brokers is involved.

Brokers are, in the most general sense, information intermediaries. They can assist consumers in a range of tasks associated with the housing transaction. Most fundamentally, they can lower the search costs for consumers and thus increase the likelihood of consumers maximizing their interests in either selling the home for the highest price in the shortest time, or purchasing a home that most meets a consumer's criteria and budget. The most important tool available to brokers, but not directly accessible by consumers, is the local Multiple Listing Service (MLS). The MLS is usually the brokers' primary source of information in determining the likely selling price for a home, and the primary tool in actually making a market in real estate.

Like any product or service a consumer purchases, the characteristics and prices of competing brokers vary. Perhaps the most basic objective variable in brokerage services involves the nature and extent of the brokers' agency/fiduciary duties to consumers. Brokers have traditionally been considered agents of their principals, and as such, they have legal duties to use their expertise to maximize the interests of these principals. These legal duties do not replace basic honesty and integrity nor make appropriate financial incentives unimportant, but they provide consumers with powerful legal remedies should there be problems. In negotiating problems, the courts, state agencies that license brokers, and the brokers themselves pay close attention to agency duties.

Consumer Problems

Confusion concerning the most basic aspect—who the principal is—is perhaps the industry's most important issue in recent years. First raised to national prominence by the Federal Trade Commission's 1983 *Staff Report on the Residential Real Estate Brokerage Industry*, the issue was highlighted by a consumer survey reporting that about three-quarters of both buyers and sellers felt that the broker working with the buyer in the typical "cooperative" (two-broker) transaction actually represented the buyer. In fact, under the rules and teachings of the industry, these brokers worked in the interests of sellers—selling houses for the highest price and passing perhaps confidential buyer information to sellers. In most instances, the buyers reported telling "their" brokers the highest price they were willing to pay. Most sellers reported that their brokers told them how high they thought the buyer would go. If a broker with integrity explicitly or implicitly agreed to work in the buyer's interest, that broker risked being considered an undisclosed dual agent, which is ground for rescision of the transaction and nonpayment of brokerage commissions, even if no damages result.

Most states have now passed laws requiring disclosures by brokers in an effort to deal with this issue. However, most do little to educate consumers about their options. Specifically, brokers can agree to be buyers' agents and can be paid in the traditional method—by splitting the commission with the seller's broker. While buyers can negotiate other forms of payment that might provide superior incentives for their agents to negotiate the lowest price possible, few forms are widely available for this purpose.

This issue continues to be contentious primarily because many brokers would like to work with both buyer and seller, but are reluctant to tell consumers that they cannot provide full agency representation when this occurs. Under the laws of most states, all brokers in the entire company that has the seller's listing must be the seller's agents. Thus, if buyers are aware of their options to have full agency representation, large firms with many listings are especially concerned that they will be unable to handle both ends of the transaction and avoid splitting the commission.

To side-step this issue and continue to work with both buyer and seller, brokers in many parts of the country are trying to be "dual agents" or even nonagent "transaction brokers." Thus, while the broker traditionally was considered an agent of the seller with fiduciary duties to that seller, today the agent may try to avoid duties to any party, while still attempting to be paid the full commission.

The sellers' major sources of loss are paying too high a brokerage commission rate/fee and selling the house for a price that is below market. Although about half of consumers appear to believe otherwise, brokerage fees are negotiable. Nonetheless, most transactions are at either 6 or 7 percent, depending on the area. Because of the nature of the MLSs, commission splits, and the "cooperative" form of brokerage that dominates most areas, commission rates tend to be uniform within geographic regions. Although new technology may replace the MLS at some point, today it makes the market in residential real estate in all significant market areas. To use the MLS effectively, the seller must make sure that the listing broker offers to pay the cooperative/buyer broker a competitive fee. Otherwise, other brokers may be reluctant to show the house to buyers. That effectively leaves sellers with only the option of negotiating a lower percentage on that portion of a commission (typically 50 percent) that their brokers receive.

Government Regulation

All states require brokers and salespeople to be licensed. Licensing statutes delineate licensure requirements, set forth prohibited practices and affirmative requirements, and establish state regulatory departments to administer the licensing process and enforce the statutes. As the primary regulatory bodies overseeing brokers, the state real estate departments or commissions could play an important role in educating consumers and protecting them from incompetent or dishonest brokers.

The Federal Trade Commission (FTC), as part of its 1983 staff report, and the Consumer Federation of America and American Association of Retired Persons, in a 1994 study, analyzed state real estate departments. Both studies noted, among other things, that dominance of the real estate commissions by industry practitioners and lack of funding for education may be significantly compromising the departments' consumer protection mission. State prohibitions on disparagement of competitors, deceptive advertising, and commission rebating, while presumably intended to protect consumers, were also occasionally used to suppress innovative forms of competition. The use of the real estate departments to suppress competition is probably related to the control of the governing commissions by the industry.

Regardless of the weaknesses of the state regulatory regimes, real estate departments and rules can provide consumers with some protection. For example, violations of the state rules can put a broker's license at risk. Thus, because most states now require disclosure of whom the broker represents, if a broker fails to make this disclosure, the potential risk to the broker's license may give the consumer some leverage to negotiate a remedy. Complaints to the state licensing departments may be most effective when a violation of fiduciary duty is alleged by the consumer.

The federal government also is involved in regulating brokerage practices through its law enforcement functions. Following its 1983 staff report, the FTC opened numerous investigations of MLSs for antitrust violations. A number of settlements were reached that significantly helped promote competition among brokers. In general, if two or more firms agree to restrict competition—including through their real estate board or MLS rules—this agreement may amount to an antitrust violation that can be dealt with by the FTC or through a private action. In private actions, treble damages may be available to a prevailing plaintiff.

Additionally, the U.S. Department of Housing and Urban Development (HUD) enforces the Real Estate Settlement and Procedures Act (RESPA). Among other things, RESPA requires the disclosure of settlement costs and prohibits kickbacks to brokers for referrals to ancillary services, including kickbacks from lenders and title insurance companies. However, the disclosure of settlement costs is too late in the process, and very little enforcement of the RESPA anti-kickback requirements takes place. Moreover, large brokerage firms are not prohibited from having affiliated (controlled) companies that provide ancillary services. Large companies tend to steer buyers to these affiliated providers.

A broker with a fiduciary-agency duty to work in the buyer's interest has a duty not to steer that consumer to an ancillary provider based on some undisclosed benefit that the broker may receive from the provider. On the other hand, under state law a nonagent or agent of the other party has no such duty.

— Paul Roark

Readings

Erxleben, William C. (1981). "In Search of Price and Service Competition in Residential Real Estate Brokerage: Breaking the Cartel." *Washington Law Review*. 56: 179–215.

Federal Trade Commission (1983). *The Residential Real Estate Brokerage Industry*. Washington, DC: U.S. Government Printing Office.

Referenda

See Initiatives and Referenda.

Regulators, Consumer Advocates as

A number of consumer leaders have been appointed to federal or state regulatory positions. President Carter, for example, selected Public Citizen's Congress Watch director Joan Claybrook to head the National Highway Traffic Safety Administration (NHTSA), Consumer Federation of America executive director Carol Tucker Foreman to run the U.S. Department of Agriculture's (USDA) food safety programs, and activist congressional staffer Michael Pertschuk to chair the Federal Trade Commission (FTC). He also reappointed Pittsburgh activist and professor R. David Pittle to a second term as a Consumer Product Safety Commission (CPSC) commissioner. More recently, President Clinton appointed longtime consumer advocate Ann Brown to head the CPSC and Public Voice president Ellen Haas to administer the USDA's food nutrition and welfare programs.

At the state level, governors have selected several consumer advocates as insurance commissioners—longtime industry critic Herb Denenberg in Pennsylvania, former Congress Watch lobbyist Jay Angoff in Missouri, and National Insurance Consumer Organization founder and president J. Robert Hunter in Texas. Although other activists were appointed to influential government positions—most notably Esther Peterson as White House consumer adviser to two presidents—these posts did not carry with them regulatory powers.

These and other appointments of consumer advocates to regulatory positions confronted most appointees with several dilemmas. The activists were forced to redefine their consumer roles, and in so doing were often compelled to deal with issues such as their relationship to advocacy groups, elected officials who appointed them, and career civil servants working in their agencies. These issues also included their priorities as regulators, particularly the time they spent on administrative matters versus policy issues, and their policy priorities.

Reasons for Appointments

The consumer activists who served as regulators not only were willing to work for the government, but in many instances actively sought regulatory appointments. Their interest reflected several factors, perhaps the most important of which is their belief that serving as a regulator represented the most effective way for them to protect the pocketbooks, or health and safety, of consumers. As Pittle frequently notes, it is far easier to protect consumers by requiring several manufacturers to improve product design than it is to persuade tens of millions of consumers to change their behavior.

Personal factors may also enter into the decisions of some activists to seek regulatory positions. As well as conferring influence usually greater than that of activists, the posts often enhance the income and status of the advocates. This author's own impression, however, is that these personal considerations are not nearly as important as the opportunity to serve consumers more effectively. After all, most worked on behalf of the consumer interest for many years for no or low monetary compensation, and for little conventional recognition.

In some instances, the activists were courted by an elected official. Hunter, for example, declined an offer to serve as New Jersey insurance commissioner before he agreed to serve as Texas commissioner. At the federal level, though, activists often had to mount campaigns to win regulatory appointments. These campaigns usually included not only cultivating the White House, but also building support within Congress, the nonprofit community, and business. Even a White House preference for an activist did not secure an actual appointment. Significant opposition from the Senate, or even other sources, could persuade the White House to shift preference to another candidate.

Consumer activists can be attractive to the White House as candidates for regulatory posts for several reasons. Such appointments help persuade voters that the president is committed to serving the public interest, and help convince activists that the president shares such a commitment and also rewards advocates who supported his candidacy. The president may also be genuinely committed to serving consumers.

Why governors or presidents select one advocate rather than another to serve in their administration is a complex question, but in most instances proven administrative ability and leadership on an issue are extremely important. Hunter, for example, had served as federal insurance administrator and was recognized throughout the consumer community as the most knowledgeable advocate on insurance issues. Similarly, Claybrook had led Public Citizen's Congress Watch and, with Ralph Nader, was considered to be the most effective advocate on auto safety issues.

Other factors sometimes influence the decision. Political support can be influential. Foreman and Haas had helped organize groups of consumer leaders supporting presidential candidacies. Brown was rewarded, to an extent, for her many years of service on behalf of the Democratic party and its candidates. Particularly in the Clinton White House, consumer appointments were used as one means of ensuring adequate representation of women and minorities in the administration.

Governors and presidents often face pressure not to appoint a consumer activist. This opposition most frequently comes from business interest groups and conservatives, who often portray the consumer candidate as a radical who would severely harm business interests. In the face of such opposition, the elected official might be forced to spend political capital and take on some political risk.

Dilemmas Faced by Regulators

A unique dilemma faced by activists is adapting to a regulatory role different from that of advocate. The principal function of an advocate is to promote aggressively the interest of consumers to the exclusion of other interests such as those of sellers. A regulator is also supposed to promote the consumer interest, but must do so within constraints imposed by congressional mandates and statutes. One constraint is the expectation, or even requirement, that the regulator consider the impact of any decisions on society, including business. That is the central purpose of cost-benefit analysis, which regulators have increasingly been required to employ over the past three decades before adopting regulations.

Typically, regulators also are burdened with far greater administrative responsibilities than advocates. When Foreman led CFA, she managed a staff of five persons; at USDA she supervised the work of thousands. As Pertschuk lamented: "You can get worn down by the day-to-day problems of hiring, firing, and fights over turf. You have to worry about having enough parking spaces in the garage, about lawyers getting file cabinets."

The accountability of regulators also differs from that of advocates. For all practical purposes, some activists are accountable to no one but themselves. Others are accountable only to their peers or to leaders of their organization, including members of a board of directors and funders (in consumer groups, boards typically give staff great discretion). On the other hand, regulators are accountable to many—a governor or president, other executive-branch officials (e.g., NHTSA is accountable to the secretary of transportation), and a legislative body that oversees their work and approves their funding. Because they are public officials, the work of regulators is scrutinized far more closely by the press than are the activities of activists.

Another major challenge faced by most advocates-turned-regulators is dealing with critics. Some of the toughest criticisms received by President Carter's consumer appointees were leveled by other advocates. Nader, for instance, criticized Claybrook for "a trail of averted or broken promises" and for failing to resign over delays in required installation of airbags. Activists faulted Pertschuk for not moving quickly enough to consider a ban on television ads for candy and sugar-coated cereals.

The opposition to regulators from business and conservatives was much fiercer and more sustained. Not just farm groups, but also one conservative columnist attacked Foreman, calling her the "dragon lady of USDA." Auto manufacturers found fault with most of Claybrook's decisions. Many industries organized a coalition to fend off initiatives from the Pertschuk-led FTC, and succeeded in persuading Congress to reduce the authority of the commission.

Businessmen and conservatives most often claimed that regulators imposed onerous, anticompetitive burdens on sellers. Given the opportunity, they also complained about the alleged favoritism of regulators. Because Foreman was married to a high-ranking labor official, and because her department let a contract to the Consumer Federation of America (which she had headed), Foreman was a prime subject of these attacks.

Regulators respond to business and conservative criticisms in different ways. In general, they try to accommodate these interests to a greater extent in the 1990s than in the late 1970s. Pertschuk in particular refused to try to mollify many congressional and business critics. On the other hand, in Texas, Hunter made a point of meeting with and accommodating any legitimate concerns of legislators and industry leaders. Brown sought not only to meet with congressional leaders and business groups, but also to develop appropriate partnerships with the latter.

Impacts of Regulators

In general, consumer advocates working as regulators significantly advance the consumer interest. They have opportunities to succeed because of their authority within their own agency, influence over the disposition of agency resources, regulatory authority, access to the president and Congress, and credibility with the press and general public.

Several regulators considerably strengthened their agencies through reorganization and morale-building. Because the Texas insurance department had been wracked by poor management and scandal, Hunter was compelled to devote most of his time as commissioner to rebuilding the agency. Even from skeptical legislators and industry leaders he received considerable praise for these efforts.

When Brown became chair of the CPSC, which had suffered severe budget cuts and much criticism for more than a decade, many agency staff were dispirited and demoralized. Brown acted quickly to infuse the agency with a sense of purpose and importance. Most staffers now work harder and more productively than at any time since the late 1970s.

Depending on the political climate, regulators have opportunities to issue regulations establishing new consumer protections and enforce old regulations more effectively. In Washington, the most favorable climate has been produced by a Democratic president and Congress. Pertschuk's FTC, for example, was able to promulgate and implement trade regulation rules governing funeral practices. It also had the opportunity to develop innovative penalties for deceptive advertising, such as mandatory counter ads correcting deceptive ads. At the CPSC, Pittle was instrumental in the development of safety standards for lawnmowers, chainsaws, toys, toxic chemicals, and other potentially hazardous products. At NHTSA, Claybrook was largely responsible for the issuance of standards for airbags and passive restraints, requiring auto manufacturers to install one or the other. Though revoked by President Reagan, the airbag/passenger restraint standard was reissued to comply with a 1983 U.S. Supreme Court decision.

Consumer advocates working as regulators also have the chance to identify new issues and put them on the public agenda. Through the completion of detailed, critical studies of complex products, Pertschuk's FTC laid the foundation for reform of several financial services products. FTC reports on life insurance and residential real estate brokerage services, for instance, remain today the most informative documents on these subjects. By initiating crash testing of cars at thirty-five miles per hour and releasing results of this testing (and other car information) in *The Car Book*, Claybrook pressured auto manufacturers to improve the crashworthiness of their vehicles. Today, Jack Gillis, who compiled *The Car Book* at NHTSA, continues to issue this publication privately on an annual basis.

As regulators, advocates sometimes have opportunities to lobby issues even more effectively than in their past role of consumer advocate. As a USDA assistant secretary, for example, Foreman helped persuade Congress to eliminate the requirement that recipients pay something for food stamps. As insurance commissioner, through research and lobbying of industry, Hunter and his department persuaded insurers voluntarily to hire more minority agents and write more policies in underserved areas.

Particularly in the late 1970s, regulators were able to build support for their initiatives by making funds available to advocacy groups to participate in regulatory proceedings. Pertschuk's FTC, for example, made available more than $1 million for this purpose.

Even when these regulators were not able to make or help shape pro-consumer policies, they sometimes succeeded in using the position as a bully pulpit to put issues on the national agenda. For example, efforts begun by Foreman at USDA to increase the usefulness of food labeling helped lead, more than a decade later, to the passage of congressional legislation and the issuing by FDA of effective nutritional labeling regulations. Claybrook's advocacy for and education on airbags contributed significantly to decisions made by government and industry over a decade later that ensured the installation of these safety devices.

As noted earlier, aggressive advocacy by these regulators carries risks. The business community might have targeted the Pertschuk-led

FTC even if the chairman had been more responsive to their criticisms voiced directly and through Congress. Yet, the fact that he was not sufficiently responsive to complaints (by his own admission) contributed to congressional decisions to weaken the agency.

Consumer advocates working as regulators must make difficult judgments about how aggressively to pursue stronger consumer protections. Overall, their decisions have been sound, making significant contributions to progress toward a more consumer-friendly marketplace.

— Stephen Brobeck

See also

Presidents and the Consumer Movement.

Readings

Mayer, Caroline E. (1978). "A Rude Awakening for Activists in Government." *U.S. News & World Report*. 84 (March 6): 52ff.

Pertschuk, Michael (1982). *Revolt against Regulation: The Rise and Pause of the Consumer Movement*. Berkeley: University of California Press.

Rosenbaum, David E. (1976). "Public Affairs Groups, Now on Outside, Expect Access to Power under Carter." *New York Times*. (1 December): II, 6.

Rent-To-Own Protections

Rent-to-own programs, or rental-purchase agreements, are common throughout the United States. Unlike traditional rental agencies, such programs offer both extended rentals and the possibility of ownership at the end of the rental agreement. As many as 7,500 stores nationwide offer merchandise through rental-purchase agreements, with a total annual volume approaching $4 billion, a sixfold increase over the past decade. Televisions and videotape recorders are the most commonly rented items, but larger stores offer a full range of electronics equipment, appliances, and furniture.

Rental-purchase plans have an inherent paradox. Fundamental conceptual and legal differences exist between rentals and purchases, yet in practice, renting-to-own is similar to buying on credit. In both cases, the consumer makes a periodic payment for the product, a point at the heart of the legal battle over regulating rent-to-own programs. The resulting confusion is compounded by advertisements that stress low periodic payments and treat ownership as a costless bonus to the consumer. Neither contention is warranted.

Acquiring ownership through a rent-to-own program requires customers to rent for twelve to eighteen months. Contracts are extended only on a weekly or monthly basis, with an automatic extension when the customer makes the next payment; otherwise, the merchandise is returned at the end of the week or month. Eventual ownership may always be an option, but it is never a requirement. The consumer has no long-term obligation, and the rental agent has no long-term responsibility.

Payments appear low only because billing periods are short. For example, a basic nineteen-inch color television typically rents for $12 to $15 a week for up to seventy-eight weeks. Such sets retail for around $300, which means the customer could end up paying over three times the price of the set, with an effective annual percentage rate (APR) of well over 300 percent. Rates could actually be higher because some outlets charge registration fees, and all assess late fees. Beyond that, an individual who quits renting after a year has nothing, because no equity accumulates unless the contract is renewed for the full twelve- or eighteen-month period. Studies show that most rent-to-own customers quit renting before they acquire title to the merchandise.

Although rent-to-own programs represent an expensive purchase option, they have some attractive points. The customer can obtain the merchandise immediately, with no long-term commitment. Also, no credit check is involved. Not surprisingly, studies show that rent-to-own patrons tend to have troubled credit histories and may have no access to less expensive credit.

The tremendous growth of the rent-to-own industry since the early 1980s corresponds to the deregulation of conventional financial institutions. Most banks no longer make small installment loans, and finance companies have moved away from the small, unsecured loans that were once their mainstay. Thus, rent-to-own programs are part of the larger pattern of growth in "fringe banking," which includes the revival of pawn shops and the growth of check-cashing services. In each case, those individuals who are least able to pay incur higher costs than more affluent consumers.

With rent-to-own programs, customers also forfeit much of the protection enjoyed by those using conventional credit sources. Legally, the case rests on the argument that because the customer is technically a renter, no credit is extended and no APR is involved. This critical point exempts rental agencies from federal and state legislation. The federal Consumer Leasing Act of 1976, which promotes "meaningful disclosure" of the terms of leases, applies only to leases of at least four months. With a single rental period of no longer than one month, rent-to-own programs are exempted.

Federal truth in lending legislation requires that a credit contract be used, but the rent-to-own industry has argued successfully that, since contracts can be canceled at any time, no contractual arrangement exists. This point is a source of ongoing contention, but at the federal level the industry's position has been maintained thus far. The regulation of rent-to-own programs is therefore left to state courts. As of 1993, twenty-nine states had laws specifically regulating rent-to-own, all of which had industry support. The industry has proved willing to accept disclosure requirements and related limitations in return for maintaining rental-purchase agreements as noncredit transactions. Thus, rent-to-own programs are not subject to state usury laws.

Nevertheless, the degree of protection afforded consumers varies significantly from state to state. Legislation in New York limits total payments to twice the retail price (which must be posted) and requires that a renter renewing a lapsed lease be given credit for prior payments. So far, Pennsylvania is the only state that specifically includes rent-to-own contracts under the definition of credit. The state-to-state record with respect to case law is confused. A Connecticut court found in favor of the consumer in a rental-purchase case (based on unequal bargaining power). In a nearly identical case, however, a Kansas court ruled against the consumer. In an odd twist, Kansas rent-to-own operators even went to court to contest state taxes on their inventory, claiming that the merchandise was the property of the renters. Claims that rent-to-own contacts are not credit, of course, rest on the opposite contention.

The ongoing contract-as-credit argument represents the most important rent-to-own issue at this time. Other issues include passing off used merchandise as new, aggressive marketing of expensive add-ons (such as insurance), providing poor service quality, and inflating purchase prices.

— Roger Swagler

See also

Credit Protections; Low-Income Consumers.

Reading

U.S. Congress, House Committee on Banking and Finance (1993). *Rent To Own: Providing Opportunities or Gouging Consumers?* Washington, DC: GPO. 3103–3124.

Resale Price Maintenance

Resale price maintenance is a practice, common to many parts of the world, by which a manufacturer or distributor of a branded product compels a reseller, whether wholesaler or retailer, to charge either a fixed price or a minimum price set by the manufacturer. Usually the practice is sanctioned by fair trade laws and is a form of what is called vertical price control or vertical price fixing.

The impetus for such practices comes from two sources. The first is a manufacturer or distributor who wants to prevent any price cutting on its product, including its use as a "loss leader," which might make other retailers refuse to stock this product. The second source is small, independent retail stores, often bound together in a trade association, who fear price competition from big chains.

In the United States, retail price maintenance would have been prohibited by antitrust laws such as the Sherman Act, but in 1937, Congress passed the Miller-Tydings Act, which granted an exemption from the antitrust laws to state laws permitting resale price fixing.

Sellers and their lobbyists then sought to pass state laws that manufacturers could agree by contract with the sellers of their branded products to sell the products only at the price set by the manufacturer. After an aggressive nationwide campaign, they succeeded in persuading forty-five states to pass such laws.

However, these sellers soon discovered a further obstacle: It was difficult for a manufacturer to obtain signed contracts with all sellers in all states. To remove this barrier, they conceived the idea of the "nonsigner clause," which said that, if a manufacturer obtained one signed contract in a state, all other sellers of that product in that state would be legally bound as if they had signed. When this practice was declared unconstitutional by the U.S. Supreme Court in 1951, Congress immediately passed a new law, the McGuire Act, to permit it.

This provision ultimately led to the fair trade laws being declared unconstitutional, in one state after another, as violations of state constitutions, but it took nearly twenty years for this to happen. Finally, in 1975, Congress repealed all federal laws supporting resale price fixing, and this practice again became a violation of the Sherman Act. As a practical matter, however, under business-friendly administrations no federal agency took steps to enforce the law against such price fixing. From 1973 to 1993, agencies such as the Federal Trade Commission brought no cases for violation of this law.

The U.S. proponents of resale price maintenance were clever to call their proposed laws "fair trade laws," a term they persuaded legislators to use in legislation and hearings, and for the most part the press accepted it. The Europeans, however, have always called the practice "resale price maintenance." Proponents of fair trade supported the fair trade price system with an economic argument that distinguished between "brand competition," which they supported, and "seller competition," which they opposed. Through years of debate, a minority of academics and lawyers have defended the elimination of seller competition.

Several important results flowed from the fair trade debate. Consumer advocates gained a potent rallying cry to win support for consumer action. It sparked the rise of the so-called discount houses—some of which rose from modest beginnings to become giant leaders of retail distribution. Some of these retailers gained notoriety and free advertising by openly boasting about how they were the consumer's friend by violating fixed fair trade prices and being frequently sued in court by manufacturers.

A remnant of the fair trade price system can be found today in the common practice of producers having a "suggested retail price" affixed to their products. Retailers are free to claim that they are selling below the suggested price.

For some U.S. consumer advocates, the fight against resale price maintenance laws has special significance. Many early leaders of the consumer movement, mainly professors from consumer and agricultural economics departments—Colston Warne, Stewart Lee, Robert McEwen, Richard Morse, and Leland Gordon—and lawyers from the U.S. Department of Justice, were drawn together by their common efforts to stop the passage of the fair trade laws. In Washington and in the states, they forged alliances with key legislators, which helped their subsequent efforts to persuade legislators to pass consumer protection laws.

— Robert J. McEwen

See also
Antitrust Protections.

Readings

Lee, Stewart Monroe (1959). "Enforcement of Resale Price Maintenance." *Yale Law Review.* 69: 172–177.

Shepard, Lawrence (1978). "The Economic Effects of Repealing Fair Trade Laws." *Journal of Consumer Affairs.* 12 (2): 220–236.

Research on Consumer Issues

Research on consumer issues is a multidisciplinary subset of consumer research, conducted by those trained in such diverse disciplines as sociology, political science, psychology, marketing, law, communications, and history. However, most of it has been undertaken by economists and consumer economists who focus on some aspect of the consumer interest. Much of this research falls into two broad categories. The first and most important relates to marketplace characteristics that affect consumers' well-being, and the second relates to consumer characteristics that affect consumers' economic well-being.

Recognizing that research on consumer issues is an applied field, researchers look to basic disciplines for theoretical guidance and models that can assist them in organizing their research. In recent years, this research has drawn on such important contributions to the discipline of economics as George Stigler's theory of the economics of information, Kelvin Lancaster's theory of the technology of consumption, and Gary Becker's theories of household production. Recent work on the consumer movement as a social movement has drawn on resource mobilization theory from sociology, which views movement leaders as entrepeneurs who select issues to gain support for the movement.

Marketplace Characteristics Affecting Consumers' Well-being

Economists consider the most important consumer problems to be those that restrict efficient operation of markets. This perspective is predicated on the belief that efficient markets allow consumers to make decisions that optimize well-being. Efficient markets ensure that competitive forces are sufficient to create an ideal relationship between sellers and consumers. Sellers who offer shoddy products and poor service at high prices will lose to competitors who are shrewd enough to offer consumers what they want. Accordingly, when markets are efficient, consumers are sovereign in the marketplace, and their needs and wants determine the products offered in the marketplace. In a market economy, this determination is made by consumer purchases.

Three elements can cause the market to function inefficiently: information deficiencies, noncompetitive markets, and externalities. Government intervention is often viewed as a strategy for reducing these inefficiencies.

For consumers' needs and wants to be reflected in their purchases, consumers must be adequately informed. Consumers need to know what is offered, the quality of these offerings, where goods and services are offered, and for how much they are being offered. For the auto market to operate efficiently, for example, consumers need easily locatable information on the type of automobile, all models consistent with this type, all the dealers in the relevant market, model and dealer quality, and the prices at which relevant models can be purchased.

Noncompetitive markets are associated with monopolies, oligopolies, and monopolistic competition. A major concern is the power of the seller to exercise control over prices and the quantities of goods offered for sale, typically resulting in prices that are significantly higher than would prevail in a competitive market.

Oligopolies often engage in nonprice competition. At its worst, nonprice competition is based on minor differences between product models. Examples include model changes in which the most significant difference between the old and new models is the model number, minor changes in trim and model name, and such inherently subjective attributes as sex appeal. The primary attraction for sellers is that it is more difficult for competitors to respond to these types of differences than to price differences.

Another problem with monopolies and oligopolies is the absence of viable alternatives when making a purchase. An example is the situation of a traveler in a remote area who has a blown tire. The only tire store for miles around will likely charge substantially more for a replacement tire than would a store in a more populated area.

Externalities arise from production and consumption activity, affecting others not directly involved in the activity. Externalities sometimes are labeled "spillovers" because of their effect on others beside the principals in an activity. Negative externalities result in levels of production or consumption that are higher than optimal from the standpoint of society, whereas positive externalities result in levels that are lower than optimal. An example is the manufacturer who decides not to treat the waste water from his plant in order to reduce his costs. He can then afford to sell for less, but he has shifted the cost of his plant's pollution onto others. Many consumer safety and health policies can be justified as efforts to reduce negative externalities, while policies related to information, representation, and redress are means to promote positive externalities.

Over the centuries, American society has developed a body of law, regulations, and customs to ensure that the marketplace operates efficiently and fairly. This body of regulation seeks to encourage competition, limit negative externalities, improve the information available to consumers for making decisions, and discourage marketing efforts that unduly distort consumers' preferences or encourage unwise or unsafe consumption.

In terms of regulation, the consumer movement focuses both on mandating and proscribing certain actions by sellers. Although consumer advocates work for bans and restrictions on unsafe products and on deceptive advertising, they also promote disclosure, for example of important information on labels. An important type of research on consumer issues is policy analysis, which assesses the effectiveness of programs, legislation, and regulations. Solutions to consumer problems are often conceived with good intentions, but implementation of solutions may not result in the expected outcomes.

Much policy analysis research is ex post evaluation—that is, evaluation of a policy after it is implemented—but it is also possible for this research to be conducted ex ante. Ex ante policy analyses focus on whether a proposed policy generates sufficient anticipated benefits to warrant the anticipated costs of implementation. Ex post consumer policy analyses can estimate either policy effectiveness alone (benefits) or determine efficiency as well (costs versus benefits or alternative ways of providing a given level of benefits).

Consumer Characteristics Affecting Consumers' Well-being

Consumers' well-being does not depend solely on the nature of the marketplace in which they buy, but also on the skills and resources they bring with them into the marketplace. Improving the performance of the marketplace has been the principal concern of the consumer movement in recent decades, but the improvement of consumers' skills and resources for dealing with the marketplace is a major priority for a number of consumer organizations.

The ability to consume has not been a major research focus, although some researchers have examined the general economic environment in which consumers operate and how consumers respond to it. Some studies look at the response to income changes, while others focus on the role of resources other than income, including time, production skills, and knowledge.

The consumer movement's efforts to ensure that product and service information are available for the consumers who want it are crucial. This information not only helps the consumers, it promotes better performance by sellers. If at least some consumers find the best product at the best price, other sellers are encouraged to improve their offerings in order to stay competitive. Research in this area focuses on the characteristics of consumers who seek and use information, the types of information consumers want, format preferences, and the effects of information on choices including the returns-to-search effort.

An understanding of how consumers make decisions is an essential prerequisite for improving the decision process. Research in this area focuses on the actual decision process and its outcomes, as distinguished from information acquisition, and deals with such economic elements as efficiency and optimality as well as the psychological and sociological elements in the decision-making process per se.

Marketing researchers have produced a substantial body of work on consumer satisfaction/dissatisfaction. Most of this work seeks to understand who complains and why, problems that are of concern to corporate managers who want to reduce complaints and deal with them as effectively as possible. A small portion of this research proceeds from a consumer perspective and considers the effectiveness of alternative complaining strategies.

While many externalities, or spillover costs, are the result of producer and retailer decisions, some are the result of consumer decisions. Consumers' energy use and conservation decisions are particularly likely to create spillover costs, and thus are the focus of a small group of studies.

Outlets for Research on Consumer Issues

The most fully developed, and carefully reviewed, research on consumer issues usually is published in scholarly journals. University faculty conduct most of it, though government researchers also make contributions.

Many journals contain articles reporting research on consumer issues, principally by academics trained in economics, consumer economics, agricultural economics, or marketing. These publications include: *Journal of Consumer Affairs, Journal of Consumer Policy, Advancing the Consumer Interest, Consumer Policy Review, Journal of Public Policy and Marketing, American Journal of Agricultural Economics, Journal of Law and Economics, Journal of Marketing Research, Journal of Marketing, Journal of Political Economy, Sociological Issues,* and *Journal of Consumer Research.* Several of these journals, and their editorial policies, deserve special note.

The premier journal in the area is the *Journal of Consumer Affairs.* The purpose of this scholarly journal of the American Council on Consumer Interests is to "foster and disseminate professional thought and scholarly research advancing the consumer interest. The *Journal* serves as a forum for communication, discourse, and debate on consumer affairs and consumer protection issues. The scope of the *Journal* includes consumer policy, consumer education, consumer economics, and consumer behavior. Acceptable manuscripts . . . should . . . have clear implications for government, household, or business policy."

The *Journal* typically takes more than a year to review and publish articles. Partly as a result, the American Council on Consumer Interests created another journal, *Advancing the Consumer Interest,* with briefer articles and shorter turnaround on submissions. This journal is "designed to appeal to professionals working in the consumer field. . . . Manuscripts may address significant trends in consumer affairs and education, innovative consumer education programs . . . reasoned essays on consumer policy, and applications of consumer research, theories, models and concepts."

The *Journal of Consumer Policy* is the leading European journal containing consumer issues research. This journal "is an international scholarly journal which encompasses a diverse range of issues in the field of consumer affairs. It analyzes the consumer's dependence upon existing social economic structures; it seeks to define the consumer's interest, and to discuss the ways in which this interest can be fostered—or restrained—through actions and policies of consumers, industry, organisations, government, educational institutions, and mass media."

A second European journal containing research on consumer issues is the *Consumer Policy Review.* Published by the (British) Consumers' Association, this journal "provides a forum for the publication of research and discussion articles on matters relevant to the consumer interest. The aim is to stimulate analysis and debate on matters such as competition policy, government regulation, consumer legislation, rights and redress—in the UK, the European Community and further afield. Contributors are encouraged to formulate proposals for public policy to strengthen the consumer interest in decision-making and develop systems of consumer protection."

Three of these journals use the words *consumer interest* in their policy statements, and it is the principal focus of the fourth, though the term is not used in its statement. Each journal indicates that policies related to consumers are an important focus.

Conference proceedings represent another outlet for research on consumer issues. The quality of the articles tends to be more variable than that in journals because of the limited review process; however, these articles are often timely. As with journals, contributions to these proceedings are dominated by university faculty, with government researchers a distant second.

Examples of conference proceedings include the *Consumer Interest Annual* (American Council on Consumer Interests) and *Advances in Consumer Research* (Association for Consumer Research). The most enduring proceedings tend to be associated with international conferences focusing on a particular topic. Two such proceedings stand out: *The Frontier of Research in the Consumer Interest* (1988), edited by E. Scott Maynes, and *Enhancing Consumer Choice* (1991), edited by Robert N. Mayer. Both conferences were sponsored by the American Council on Consumer Interests. Presenters at both meetings came from universities, government, consumer groups, and businesses, but the principal papers were presented by academic researchers.

The papers from the first conference represent the single best source of research on consumer issues. Within a conference structure reflecting the seven consumer rights, most of the papers treat consumer problems that adversely affect market efficiency.

— Loren V. Geistfeld, Robert O. Herrmann

See also

American Council on Consumer Interests; Consumer Economics/Studies; Consumer Problems in Market Economies; Research on the Consumer Movement.

Readings

Mayer, Robert N., ed. (1991). *Enhancing Consumer Choice: Proceedings of the Second International Conference on Research in the Consumer Interest.* Columbia, MO: American Council on Consumer Interests.

Maynes, E. Scott, ed. (1988). *The Frontier of Research in the Consumer Interest: Proceedings of the International Conference on Research in the Consumer Interest.* Columbia, MO: American Council on Consumer Interests.

Research on the Consumer Movement

Research on the consumer movement is diverse; it has been conducted by many types of researchers, published in a variety of sources, and addresses a broad range of topics.

In *The Modern Consumer Movement: References and Resources* (1990), Stephen Brobeck identified 786 secondary sources about the movement. Of these, 31 percent were written by academics, 49 percent by journalists, 17 percent by movement participants, and 3 percent by others, including government officials and business leaders. The academics were trained in diverse fields that include history, sociology, social psychology, political science, law, economics, consumer economics, marketing, and business administration. The breakdown of the sources are 51 percent, newspaper or magazine articles; 20 percent, journal articles; 12 percent, books; 6 percent, chapters in books; 4 percent, papers read at conferences; and 2 percent, dissertations.

Types of Sources

Most literature sources on the consumer movement can be categorized in ten types: general works by social scientists, dissertations by historians, historical accounts by movement participants, survey research by social scientists, analyses by movement participants and sympathizers, biographies of Ralph Nader by journalists, political analyses by social scientists, cost-benefit studies by economists, conservative critiques, and left-liberal critiques.

Academics have written more than a dozen general works on the consumer movement, past and present, and all the authors were trained as social scientists. Most of the sources are articles published in business or marketing journals. The large majority of works, especially those in journals, are primarily derivative, based solely or mainly on secondary sources.

Eight doctoral dissertations have been written by historians about the consumer movement. They were prepared by graduate students at major eastern or midwestern universities, including Yale and Chicago. Two of these studies treat Consumers Union; two, the National Consumers League; and the remaining four, the rise of consumerism and the consumer movement. Only two were published in revised form as books.

These dissertations share traits that reflect the training of their authors as historians. First, they focus on change over decades, usually twenty to thirty years. Second, the studies examine the relationship of the consumer movement, or parts of it, to the larger society, especially to broad reform movements such as Progressivism and the New Deal. Third, the dissertations incorporate exhaustive empirical research in primary sources. Fourth, the primary focus is on the consumer movement before 1960, the beginning of its modern era.

Given the incompleteness and inaccessibility of this historical research, accounts by movement participants, most of whom participated before 1960, assume great importance. The participants wrote about their experiences in the movement, and most commonly about the organization or organizations with which they were most closely affiliated.

In the past two decades, academics trained in the social sciences have published a number of articles on public attitudes toward consumerism and the consumer movement. Nearly all of these researchers were associated with business schools or schools of human ecology. Most of the eight articles were published in journals devoted to research on consumer topics, such as the *Journal of Consumer Affairs*, and address public opinion about two general subjects—marketplace practices and the consumer movement.

Movement activists and sympathizers have published more than twenty analyses of the modern consumer movement. Some of these sources treat individual organizations or organizational networks. Others examine grassroots consumer groups, still others focus attention on the consumer movement as a whole, and several discuss the relation of the consumer movement to groups including academics, the civil rights movement, and the labor movement. Most of these sources were published in the 1980s by national leaders or grassroots activists who held academic positions.

Journalists have written a half-dozen biographies of Ralph Nader. All were published between 1972 and 1976—at or just after the peak of Nader's prestige and power. Most were based largely on extensive interviews with Nader and his colleagues, opponents, and observers. Four are highly sympathetic, while two are sharply critical.

Social scientists have researched the participation of consumer advocates in the public policy-making process. Most of these academics were trained in political science or public policy, and all but one study were published after 1975. Most of the works focus on legislative processes—public interest lobbyists and their relation to business lobbyists, specific legislative issues, and consumer policy-making in general, as well as its impact on business. Two works examine public interest litigation, and another looks at consumer participation in the regulatory process.

Economists use cost-benefit analysis to assess the economic impacts of consumer laws and regulations, research that can be grouped into two categories. Major economic journals have published several articles highly critical of consumer regulations, and only two studies published in mainstream journals present data supportive of regulations. Those studies that are neutral or favorable to these regulations were published in journals of consumer economics, agricultural economics, marketing, or public policy.

A number of books or lengthy studies criticize the consumer movement from a conservative perspective. Most are one-sided, as their titles suggest—*Destroying Democracy, Abuse of Trust, The Disaster Lobby, Coercive Utopians,* and *The Consumer Advocate versus the Consumer.* Several of these studies were funded by conservative foundations, and their most frequent criticism is that the regulations advanced by the movement impose huge costs on business and limit consumer choices.

A smaller number of books and articles criticize the consumer movement from a leftist or liberal perspective. Most of these writers are academics, and they explicitly fault consumer advocates as weak and/or misguided. Specific critiques range from the Galbraithian to the environmentalist to the populist/New Left to the Marxist. Their most common theme is that the consumer movement is too "reformist," failing to challenge fundamental flaws in the political and economic system.

Other types of sources exist besides these ten, but none is as cohesive or as important. For example, academics and movement participants frequently write about the future of the consumer movement, but these works are usually highly speculative. Many collections of articles or conference papers can be found, but such anthologies most often address a variety of topics and contain reprinted articles.

Noteworthy Sources

A few secondary sources, most of which were published in the 1980s, are especially valuable for understanding the consumer movement. All treat the movement in general and its organizations, leaders, or activities. Mainly because the academic research on the movement is incomplete, works by movement participants or sympathizers are included. Although often biased in favor of their subjects, these sources are rich in detailed descriptions and explanatory hypotheses about the movement.

All but one of the most valuable general works are by academics. Robert Herrmann's *Journal of Marketing* article on consumerism (October 1970, pp. 55–60) represents the first well-researched study of the history of the consumer movement. It proposes a division of this history into three periods distinguished by widespread reform efforts.

Lucy Black Creighton's *Pretenders to the Throne: The Consumer Movement in the U.S.* (1976) was the first book by an academic on the modern consumer movement. Although its principal purpose is to criticize the movement for failing to understand the modern economy and address broad issues such as income distribution, it contains useful analyses of the history and then-current character of consumer advocacy.

Consumer Activists: They Made a Difference (1982), edited by Erma Angevine, is a unique collection of recollections and analyses by movement participants. The most useful chapters draw heavily from the personal experiences of the authors, who include Colston Warne, Caroline Ware, and Angevine. Just as valuable is *The Consumer Movement: Lectures by Colston E. Warne,* edited by Richard L. D. Morse and published in 1993. These lectures by the movement's most respected leader from the 1930s to the 1970s cover topics ranging from Consumers Union to the network of groups founded by Ralph Nader.

An article published by Herrmann, Edward Walsh, and Rex Warland in *The Frontier of Research in the Consumer Interest* (edited by E. Scott Maynes) in 1988 on "the organization of the consumer movement" is a well-researched treatment of four major consumer groups: the Nader network, Consumers Union, the American Council on Consumer Interests, and local boycott groups. However, the single most useful secondary source on the consumer movement is Robert Mayer's *Consumer Movement* (1989). Incorporating nearly all earlier research, a broad range of topics is covered, including the movement's history, organization, worldview, political success, and economic impacts.

Most important works on movement organizations were written by consumer leaders or sympathizers. Two deal with Consumers Union—*The Consumer Movement: Lectures by Colston E. Warne,* noted above, and Norman Silber's *Test and Protest* (1983), which contains a well-documented analysis of the emergence of consumerism, the origins of Consumers Union, and the societal impact of its advocacy.

The two most useful sources of information on the Nader network were written from different perspectives. David Bollier's *Citizen Action* (1989) is an authorized history of the network by a sympathetic journalist that identifies participating groups, their leaders, a chronology of events, and claimed accomplishments. Dan Burt's *Abuse of Trust* (1982) is an unsatisfactory exposé of Nader-related groups, but contains useful information about dozens of these organizations, including their finances and interrelationships.

Two books by sympathizers treat Citizen Action and the public interest research group network, respectively. *Citizen Action and the New American Populism* (1986) by Harry Boyte, Heather Booth, and Steve Max discusses the origins, leaders, member organizations, resources, and advocacy campaigns of this network. *More Action for Change* (1987) by Kelley Griffin contains useful information about the Public Interest Research Group (PIRG) network's history, advocacy, and impacts.

Several good sources on congressional lobbying by consumer activists can be found. Two were written by academics: Mark Nadel's *Politics of Consumer Protection* (1971) examines the making of federal consumer policies in the late 1960s, and Jeffrey Berry's *Lobbying for the People* (1977) uses survey responses from public interest lobbyists to understand how they lobby, their influence, and the organizations that support them. One other source on congressional lobbying was written by advocate and former regulator Michael Pertschuk. His *Revolt against Regulation* (1982) represents the most informative account of the role of consumer advocates in shaping federal legislation in the late 1960s and the 1970s.

The most useful analysis of consumer litigation is included in Joel Handler's *Social Movements and the American Legal System* (1978). The best research on consumer boycotts is by Monroe Friedman. His most recent publication on the topic is a March 1995 article in the *Journal of Consumer Policy* on food price boycotts.

The only recently published bibliography on the literature of the consumer movement is Brobeck's. As well as an introductory essay on this literature, it contains annotated sources grouped in the following categories: information sources, general works, early history, public opinion, national organizations, state and local organizations, movement relationships, movement leaders, movement perspectives, movement advocacy, political impacts, economic impacts, business responses, criticisms of the movement, and the international consumer movement.

This encyclopedia not only summarizes existing research but also creates new knowledge. Many of the entries, particularly on organizations and foreign consumer movements, contain important information that cannot be found in published sources. Until researchers use primary documents and interviews with participants to examine these topics carefully, related encyclopedia entries will represent their most authoritative treatment.

— Stephen Brobeck

See also

Research on Consumer Issues.

Reading

Brobeck, Stephen (1990). *The Modern Consumer Movement: References and Resources.* Boston: G. K. Hall & Co.

Rights, Consumer

See Consumer Rights.

Romanian Consumer Movement

In March 1995, according to Gheorghe Tiplica, secretary of state in the government's Office of Consumer Protection (OPC), Romania had eighty-three nongovernment consumer associations, with nearly 47,000 members among them, and 200 professional associations and "sectoral consumers associations," such as tenants' associations. Given that these groups include the national Association for the Protection of Consumers (APC), the Institute for Consumers and Competition Protection (IPCOC), and the Romanian Society of Consumer Protection (SOROPCO) as well as the state OPC, it is not surprising that ordinary Romanians are confused about those who purport to represent their consumer interests.

The consumer movement began in Romania in February 1990, two months after the revolution, with the formation of APC. Founded by professionals from the state inspection and quality assurance service, the group used the media and their official connections to help stem the flow of poor-quality goods (food and drink in particular) onto the Romanian market. Because consumers found it difficult to distinguish volunteer activists from state quality inspectors (they were by and large the same people), they did not flock to join the new association. The headquarters of APC was located in the central Inspectorate, with branches in the forty-one regional offices. Up until late 1992, most of the members were drawn from, or joined through, the Inspectorate, upon whose resources they drew heavily for their voluntary work.

This somewhat incestuous relationship was brought to an end in August 1992 by the Ordinance on Consumer Protection, introduced by the secretary of state for reform strategy and economic integration, Bujor Bogdan Teodoriu (now an opposition MP and founder-president of IPCOC, a small, unfunded consumer institute concerned with a broad range of policy and practical issues). This ordinance, which the next government formally ratified, created a problem for the officers of APC. The State Quality Inspectorate was replaced by the Office of Consumer Protection—the first of its kind to be established in the region—with wide powers and functions, including the responsibility to nurture the voluntary movement; metrology and standardization were sent off to separate institutions. The ordinance defined the terms under which consumer organizations were entitled to become "social partners" with the right to be represented in relevant consultative bodies, and forbade senior employees of public administration bodies to take leading roles in voluntary associations. The leaders of APC, at whom this prohibition was aimed, were thus forced to decide between their salaried jobs and their voluntary work.

Those who decided to remain with APC were moved elsewhere in the public sector. The rest were absorbed into OPC under its first director-general, Emil Bojin (now an active board member of APC). In 1995, although structurally flawed and weakened by the separation from its power base, APC reemerged as a serious, active consumers' association under new leadership. Recently, APC obtained funding from OPC for two projects: a comparative test of toys and an information leaflet. It has produced other leaflets with the help of Consumers Union's Colston Warne Fund, and the PHARE program has funded essential equipment. APC also hopes to obtain backing from PHARE to set up a consumer advice center in Bucharest that will also be supported by AgV.

Progress in advancing the consumer interest in Romania remains slow, however, for two reasons. First, the independent movement is still fragmented, with arms-length relations between its components, and it shows no sign of being ready to coalesce into one powerful national organization with local branches. Secondly, the movement suffers from the traditional thinking that is entrenched in society at all levels: If something seems to be wrong, it must be controlled, curbed, or eradicated by official action. This thinking is not always apparent in published intentions. The 1992 ordinance, a radical if imperfect piece of legislation, recognized that consumers should be provided with the necessary means of participating in the market economy on equal terms; in June 1994, Consultative Councils for Consumer Protection were established at national, regional, and municipal levels to coordinate consumer protection activities. These councils were given the tasks of suggesting improvements in the implementation of consumer protection, strengthening consumer education and information, and assessing the response of central and local authorities to the demands of the voluntary associations. But as yet, there are few signs that education and information are favored over centralized controls as strategies for assisting consumers in the marketplace.

In 1995, for the first time the state provided funds, administered by OPC, to enable independent organizations to carry out small projects such as the information leaflet and tests of toys mentioned earlier. If the government expands its commitment to a partnership between the public and voluntary sectors, with clearly defined roles and significant financial support for each, Romania could be a leader in consumer protection in Central and Eastern Europe.

— Alastair Macgeorge

See also

Central and Eastern Europe, Consumer Movements in.

Reading

Kozminski, Andrzej K. (1992). "Consumers in Transition from the Central Planned Economy to the Market Economy." *Journal of Consumer Policy*. 14 (4): 351–370.

Rural Electric Cooperatives

Today, about a thousand rural electric cooperatives provide electric service to consumers. Each co-op is an independent nonprofit organization, incorporated under the laws of the state in which it operates. Consumers who receive electric service are members of the cooperative and, as such, share responsibility for its success or failure. Each co-op member can vote on its board of directors and on any other decisions made at the co-op's annual meeting.

History

Cities had electricity shortly after Thomas Edison built the first central station electric system in lower Manhattan in 1882, but as late as the mid-1930s, nine out of ten rural homes were without electric service.

On May 11, 1935, under the Emergency Relief Appropriation Act, President Franklin D. Roosevelt signed Executive Order 7037 establishing the Rural Electrification Administration (REA) as part of a general program to relieve unemployment. A year later, Congress approved the act, giving the REA long-term lending authority.

In 1943, Congressman Stephen Pace of Georgia introduced a bill authorizing an interest rate of 2 percent and a loan repayment period of thirty-five years, and establishing the REA as a permanent agency. Roosevelt signed the Pace Act in September 1944, hailing it as "a great step forward in achieving the ultimate objective of the rural electrification program."

Farm people had long been familiar with cooperative organizations. Since pioneer days, farmers had been establishing cooperatives to buy feed and fertilizer, gin their cotton and market their grain, build irrigation systems, and provide themselves with telephone service. The co-op was the favored kind of voluntary effort for any task too big for the individual farm family to handle alone. Thus, when investor-owned utilities showed little interest in using REA loan funds to build electric lines in thinly populated rural territories, leaders of farm organizations proposed the formation of cooperatives to provide electric service on a nonprofit basis.

County agents from state and federal extension services, and farm leaders already familiar with other types of cooperatives, helped start the rural electric cooperatives. For its part, REA sent out field representatives to help the new enterprises organize and solve many of the technical problems they faced. In many states, legislatures passed special enabling laws to make it easier for people in rural counties to incorporate their cooperatives and borrow from REA.

The cost of building electric lines was generally estimated at between $1,500 and $2,000 per mile when rural electrification got under way. This cost, plus the expense of other components making up any electric system, was to be repaid from rates charged those who received electric service.

In cities, where customers generally live close together, a power company could expect adequate revenue from each mile of installed line because the line would serve twenty, thirty, or more customers. Rural systems, however, might serve only one customer in a mile. REA knew that construction costs would have to be cut if rural people were to be able to afford electric service.

REA engineering staff found new ways to build systems more economically. They established new standard specifications for various equipment, giving manufacturers and suppliers an opportunity to produce these items economically for this new market. Farmers and ranchers helped build the systems by digging holes and setting poles, thus furnishing some free labor.

The cooperative idea took hold and spread because it was a practical way for people to help themselves and keep costs down. One of many tasks faced by new cooperatives was obtaining easements from property owners across whose land power lines would run. Investor-owned utilities, as profit-making organizations, are expected to apply for easements. However, because of the feeling of shared responsibility and cooperation among co-op members, REA borrowers were able to acquire line easements free, saving their member consumers much expense.

In the 1930s and 1940s, virtually all those served by rural electric cooperatives were farmers, ranchers, and small-town residents who supported these producers, but today they represent less than half of all co-op members. Increasingly, populations have expanded into the service areas of rural electric co-ops.

National Rural Electric Cooperative Association

The National Rural Electric Cooperative Association (NRECA) is the service organization for the nation's consumer-owned rural electric systems. Member cooperatives coordinate activities, exchange information, solve problems, conduct research, and share service opportunities; they also advise Congress and government agencies.

The association is a nonprofit organization owned and controlled by the rural electric systems that make up its membership. Its operations are financed with annual dues from its members and income from its revenue-producing services. It works closely with the REA in the Department of Agriculture, but receives no funds from it.

Member cooperatives elect the NRECA board of directors, one from each state that has a distribution co-op, with each director serving a one-year term. The board directs the association's affairs, carries out policies adopted by the membership, sets policies between membership meetings, selects and counsels the chief executive officer, reviews operations, approves budgets, defines current problems, authorizes future activities, and elects its own officers.

The principles and policies that govern the association begin in the member co-ops, where each consumer member has one vote. Through their local co-ops, these individual members select persons who establish the association's policies at regional and national meetings. Each member co-op has one vote in selecting a state association director and one vote in its region in electing representatives to each of twelve standing committees, which develop policies in specific areas. Regional and annual meeting delegates then vote on these policies.

Policy development begins each May with directors appointing an issues committee, composed of ten members, one from each region, to identify areas of importance to rural electric co-ops and recommend new or amended policy resolutions. The committee presents these resolutions to directors and member co-ops prior to fall regional meetings, at which a resolutions committee reports on the issues committee's proposals, and delegates accept, modify, or reject them. Regional resolutions committee members then meet to achieve consensus where possible and to present their agreements and disagreements to the board-appointed resolutions committee at the association's annual spring meeting. Twelve to fifteen thousand consumer-elected delegates, co-op managers, directors, employees, and their families attend this meeting, thus representing the nation's largest assembly of rural people. Standing committees review the combined regional resolutions committee's proposals, and the resolutions committee takes its recommendations to the floor. The adopted resolutions guide the association's efforts during the coming year.

The association was established in March 1942 in the nation's capital. At its first meeting, directors invited several members of Congress to discuss rural electrification. Among them was Arkansas Congressman Clyde T. Ellis, who had won his seat in 1938 in a head-on battle with the president of his state's strongest power company. During his term of office he championed rural electrification, and the board offered him the job of general manager. In January 1943, Ellis became the association's chief executive officer, a job he held for twenty-five years.

In 1943 and 1944, NRECA led the successful fight for the Pace Act. In 1952 the association made presentations to the platform committees of both national parties and visited the candidates, but did little during the campaign. During the Eisenhower administration, it wished that it had. Although the Rural Electrification Act stated that there should be "no political test or qualification" for appointment of agency officials, in 1953 the REA administrator was asked to resign, career employees were demoted or fired, and others left in disgust. The association promptly launched a management division and began to help rural electric co-op members with technical problems.

The Congressional proposal for REA's 1957 budget doubled the interest rate for loans and sought to force the co-ops to seek financing on the open money market. In response, Ellis and Alex Radin, general manager of American Public Power Association, organized Electric Consumer Information Committee, a coalition of labor unions, cooperatives, farm organizations, regional co-ops, and consumer groups seeking congressional support for rural electrification and comprehensive resource development. This coalition proved influential in the power and resource battles that occurred during the next decade. As a consumer-oriented organization, NRECA's focus was narrow, centering on electric power and issues affecting the welfare of rural America. Working through the coalition, the association broadened its concern to national fiscal policy, high interest rates, unemployment, world trade, poverty, federal resource development, and the consumer movement.

In 1962 the association's board authorized adding a woman to the executive manager's staff to direct women's activities. Women attending the 1963 regional meetings agreed to lend their support to the legislative drive for truth in packaging and truth in lending. Esther Peterson made her first speech as President Johnson's special assistant for consumer affairs at the annual meeting in Dallas in March 1964. Association members adopted a resolution supporting this consumer legislation.

The NRECA's women's activities coordinator became its consumer lobbyist. Ellis testified in support of truth in lending, and the association supported the first Consumer Assembly in 1966, where Peterson called for a federation of consumer and consumer-oriented groups. Association directors attended and encouraged the women's coordinator to work closely with a coalition setting up a national federation. When efforts to raise the needed funds lagged, Robert Partridge, who succeeded Ellis as the association's general manager, joined Jacob Clayman of the Industrial Union Department (AFL-CIO) and Bob Smith of Consumers Union in finding the money.

The Electric Consumer Information Committee included in its membership many of the national organizations involved in the creation of Consumer Federation of America. Partridge and Clayman polled the committee's board, and Partridge talked with rural electric co-op officials who were members of the committee. Clayman talked with the unions and other organizations, who urged the committee to merge with the new federation and turn its assets over to it. There were no dissents.

Consumer Federation of America opened its office in May 1968 with the committee's furniture and its membership, helping guarantee the new federation's stability. Partridge, Radin, Smith, and Clayman were elected to the board. Erma Angevine, NRECA's women's coordinator, became the federation's first executive director. The association continues to support the federation and many consumer initiatives to the present.

One of NRECA's most important objectives is to secure favorable actions from Congress and REA on policies supported by rural electric cooperatives. To accomplish this goal, the association works directly with members of Congress and their staffs, encourages and supports statewide associations and local rural electric systems in lobbying their congressmen and senators, sponsors a spring legislative conference, helps rural electric systems with their "adopt an urban congressman" program, compiles background information, monitors government agencies, participates in rulemaking procedures, and coordinates and supports technical projects with other organizations involved in utility research. The association also created the Action Committee for Rural Electrification, a voluntary political action committee organized to assist candidates who support the association's legislative objectives.

In terms of budget and number of employees, the association's largest effort is its insurance, retirement, and safety program, to which member systems may subscribe. These services aim at improving the financial security of rural electric co-ops and their employees by providing selected insurance and pension contracts. The association also provides an array of conferences, management training, and consulting services for managers, directors, and employees of rural electric systems in this country and overseas.

— Erma B. Angevine

See also

Consumer Federation of America; Cooperatives, Consumer; Electricity Regulation.

Readings

Childs, Marquis William (1980). *Yesterday, Today and Tomorrow: The Farmer Takes a Hand.* Washington, DC: National Rural Electric Cooperative Association.

Colton, Roger D. (1993). *The Regulation of Rural Electric Cooperatives: The Common Law, Consumer Law and a Cornucopia of Consumer Protections.* Boston: National Consumer Law Center.

Russia and the Commonwealth of Independent States, Consumer Movement in

The consumer movement in Russia began in the last years of the Soviet Union while it was still a united federal state. This timing gave rise to a number of unusual if not unique features: a combination of national and supranational consumer organizations, a widening contrast in the "standard of living" of the various regional organizations after the collapse of the Soviet Union, and major shifts of activity within the movement during the 1990s.

In 1991, at the time of the break-up of the USSR and the beginning of the Commonwealth of Independent States (CIS), the consumer movement consisted of an all-union organization, the USSR Federation of Consumers' Unions (predecessor of the current Inter-Republican Confederation of Consumers' Societies), and national consumer societies in Russia, White Russia (Belarus), Ukraine, Lithuania, Kazakhstan, Turkmenistan, Uzbekistan, and Tadjikistan. Local consumer organizations existed in Moldavia, Georgia, and Latvia.

By the mid-1990s, the Baltic states were looking toward cultural and political integration with Western Europe rather than with the CIS, and a similar separation was experienced within the consumer movement. In other countries, such as Georgia, internal or external military conflicts brought consumer activity to a halt. As of 1995, an active consumer movement remained only in Russia, Belarus, Ukraine, Kazakhstan, and Turkmenistan.

The pattern of development of each of these countries differs both economically and politically. To some extent all are in crisis, but the living conditions and the extent to which a consumer market has been established differ significantly. The standard of living in Russia, for instance, is two or three times higher than in the Ukraine or Kazakhstan. Thus, the consumer movement in neighboring countries finds itself with widely differing priorities.

Government attitudes toward independent consumer organizations also vary. The Russian government, for instance, is obliged by statute to take into account the views of consumer organizations in working out its policies, and the Ukrainian, Belarussian, and Kazakhstani governments also look benignly on the consumer movement. By contrast, the government of Turkmenistan refuses to recognize the existence of independent civil movements, but tolerates the operation of a consumer union.

The activities of national and local consumer organizations in the CIS now derive to a considerable extent from the intellectual resources, high profile, and reputation of the supranational organization—the Inter-Republican Confederation of Consumers' Societies (KonfOP). KonfOP is both shield and spear: It coordinates the activities of the national, regional, and local consumer organizations who are its members; and it carries out its own consumer protection projects in CIS countries, above all in Russia. These latter initiatives will remain vital for all CIS countries while Russia retains its lead in economic and legal reform. In this context, Russia is a testing ground for consumer thinking, policy development, and activity throughout the region.

History

The idea of establishing consumer organizations within the USSR first surfaced in the 1960s, prompted by the achievements of the pioneering organizations in Western countries and the semiliberal economic reforms occurring in some socialist countries. For more than twenty years, some well-known Russian newspapers, notably *Literaturnaya Gazeta* (later *Nedelya*) carried consumer affairs columns. Journalists were the first to promote consumerist ideas, and Anatoly Rubinov, the correspondent of *Literaturnaya Gazeta*, was perhaps the most prominent. His articles on consumer problems excited interest and sometimes had significant social results. For instance, his critical analyses of postal and telephone services, published in newspapers with a circulation of millions, forced the communist government to introduce some changes. Nevertheless, during Brezhnev's regime it remained impossible to create independent consumer organizations.

When Gorbachev began perestroika (the process of economic liberalization), the situation changed radically. Vitaly Syrokomsky, the editor-in-chief of *Nedelya*, set up a Buyers' Club attached to the newspaper, which was joined by well-known Soviet intellectuals. The publicity thus generated for consumer ideas was the preliminary stage in the foundation of the consumer movement.

The first independent consumer organization was formed in the fall of 1988 in Leningrad (now St. Petersburg). Moscow followed, then Chelyabinsk, Novosibirsk, Sverdlovsk (now Ekaterinburg), Kiev, Alma-Ata (now Almaty), and other cities.

The history of the consumer movement from the late 1980s can be divided into three periods. The first, 1988 to 1990, marked the establishment of the movement's organizational structure. The main event of the second period, late 1990 to early 1992, was the introduction of legislation as a result of the lobbying and influence of the new movement. The third period, 1992 through the present, entailed strengthening the consumer movement against the backdrop of economic reforms.

In terms of organizational structure, the consumer movement in the CIS is based on the activities of local consumer groups in large cities. Almost all national consumer organizations and the supranational KonfOP are umbrella organizations that unite these local, legally independent, consumer societies. Membership in these urban consumer organizations is typically confined to a few hundred dues-paying members, of whom ten to fifteen constitute the core activists. In the early days, some local groups (in Odessa, for example) were substantially larger, with a membership of several thousand. Organizations of this kind were founded on the basis of so-called black queues—a self-regulating system of people who put their name on a list to buy consumer goods, such as furniture or a television set, and waited months or even years before getting the goods they ordered. The consumer movement thus brought together intellectuals who supported the idea of consumer sovereignty and frustrated consumers prepared to organize for the goods they wanted.

From the very beginning, there was an instinct to unite. It was reinforced by the publication of the first special consumer newspaper, *V Zaschitu Prav Potrebiteley* (For Consumer Rights Protection) in December 1988. A year later, leaders of local consumer groups joined with the newspaper to found the USSR Federation of Consumers' Societies, with the well-known independent deputy (later mayor of St. Petersburg) Anatoly Sobchak as its first president. At approximately the same time, national consumer organizations were founded in Ukraine and Belarus. Kazakhstan followed, and the Consumer Union of Russia was set up at the end of 1990.

The joining together of local consumer groups and the creation of a federation were necessary to establish a platform from which to campaign for consumer legislation. The federation's first victory in this sphere was the decision by the Constitutional Court in September 1990 to abolish the rules limiting consumer redress. In May 1991 the Soviet Parliament adopted the Consumer Rights Protection Act, and over the next ten months the governments of Ukraine, Kazakhstan, and Russia followed suit with similar national acts.

Since 1992 the main task of the consumer movement has been the implementation and enforcement of the new legislation. Using the law in the courts and giving legal information and advice to consumers have become important goals. To achieve them, groups of highly qualified professionals, such as lawyers and journalists, were formed to create a system of legal assistance for individual consumers and consumer organizations.

In February 1992 the USSR Federation of Consumers' Societies was transformed into the Interrepublican Confederation of Consumers' Societies (KonfOP). Alexander Auzan, professor of economics at Moscow State University, was elected president. In December 1994, Auzan was reelected at the second Congress of KonfOP, in which fifty-four consumer organizations from five countries participated. The Congress also declared that the consumer movement had succeeded in carrying out the tasks it had set at the beginning of the reform period. The organizations had not merely maintained themselves; they had brought many court actions, set important precedents, established good relations with the mass media, and carried out major campaigns on behalf of consumers.

Auzan was one of several consumer leaders who gained national prominence and influence. Peter Shelisch, a St. Petersburg sociologist, created the first consumer organization in the Soviet Union and later became chairman of the Consumer Union of Russia and a deputy in the Russian Parliament. Leonid Bochin, an economist who created the Moscow Consumer Union, became the head of the State Anti-monopoly Committee, a government body responsible for national consumer policy. Mikhail Polyachek, a journalist who founded the first consumer publication in the USSR, has been a permanent member of the governing body of the federation and KonfOP since 1989. Grigori Schevchenko, a retired colonel of the Red Army, created one of the largest local consumer organizations in Ukraine, and he served as president of the Ukrainian Consumer Association and senior vice president of KonfOP from 1992 until 1994. Sanitary specialist Ata Akiev, who founded the Consumer Union in Ashgabad, became the president of the Turkmenistan Consumers' Society and one of KonfOP's most authoritative leaders.

The consumer organizations of the CIS have made great strides in several areas: legislative consumer protection, consumer education and information, research and product testing, and coordination among organizations.

Lobbying for Consumer Legislation

Protecting consumers through legislation began only with the passage of laws. Many of the acts introduced by the young national parliaments failed to be implemented, and ordinary people had no faith in the courts. To establish effective consumer protection, systems of legal assistance for consumers had to be organized and cases won in order to set precedents.

The systems of legal assistance are in varying stages of development among the consumer organizations of the region. At first, all legal assistance offered by consumer organizations was free of charge; but that could not last, because the organizations had no money with which to pay their lawyers. When economic reforms got under way, fees were introduced, and the number of lawyers working in consumer organizations increased significantly.

The next stage was the creation of specialized consumer law "firms." The first of these, Advokat Potrebitelya (Consumer Lawyer), was set up by KonfOP, and the second, Zakhist, by the Ukrainian Consumers' Association in Kiev. These firms became the coordinating centers for lawyers specializing in consumer protection in the CIS and Ukraine. KonfOP publishes the special bulletin *Advokat Potrebitelya,* containing analyses of important court decisions, and it organizes annual seminars for lawyers of consumer organizations throughout the region.

The breakthrough came when young lawyers working for consumer organizations began to win precedent-setting cases. In January 1992, Diana Sork won the first case in which compensation was awarded for "moral damage" (i.e., distress, inconvenience), a concept that, although enshrined in the law, had never before been put to the test. Since then, compensation for moral damage has become common in Russian court decisions, and the practice has been taken up in other CIS countries.

In June 1992, Lada Orlova, together with the State Anti-monopoly Committee of Russia, won the first class-action case on behalf of a group of consumers who had been deceived into buying fake Levi's jeans. In January 1993, Svetlana Victorova won the first consumer case against a public utility. Other cases established important precedents in the fields of air transportation (Andrey Mikhalin), telephone connections (Oleg Samchishin), and financial services (Evgeny Belousov and Denis Galitsky). Widespread publicity for these and other legal victories radically changed consumer attitudes toward court procedures. By the mid-1990s, consumer lawyers had won more than 20,000 cases, the majority in Russia.

The legal victories had three notable consequences. First, the Russian Supreme Court affirmed a special decree on court practice on behalf of consumers. Second, the number of out-of-court settlements of consumer problems has grown rapidly. Third, the judicial successes have brought about legislative changes. In the Consumer Rights Protection Acts in Russia, Ukraine, and Kazakhstan, the enforcement machinery has been extended, and mechanisms for calculating compensation for damage have been created. Consumer organization experts now take an active part in drawing up new consumer regulations, especially in Russia. New proposals on regulating advertising, financial markets, consumer cooperatives, and natural monopolies bear witness to the high standing of consumer organizations in the formulation of consumer policy.

Consumer Education and Information

Whereas laws and judicial decisions bring about top-down change, consumer education creates change from the bottom up. Indeed, consumer education was one of the first priorities for the new consumer organizations in the CIS. In the beginning, explaining basic consumer rights (along the lines of the United Nations Consumer Protection Guidelines) and national consumer laws was important. In time, the main focus changed to publicity arising from court actions. Consumer organizations now regard protection through information and education as two of their most important activities.

The first consumer education programs were drawn up within organizations and used to train consumer activists and the staff of state consumer protection bodies. A number of educational centers were created in cities such as St. Petersburg, Odessa, and, most notably, Volgodonsk, where Anatoly Dolxhenko founded the well-known Center of Consumer Education.

During the 1990s, experts from consumer organizations lectured in universities. In 1993 education in consumer law became a compulsory curriculum subject in high schools. In response, KonfOP set up its own Department of Consumer Education to develop a core of expertise in education programs for both primary and secondary schools. These programs —involving topics such as basic consumer rights, product safety, and consumer buying habits—are already being implemented in some regions of Russia.

Consumer protection through information requires disseminating information about dangerous products, actual features of goods and services, misleading advertising, and dishonest market practices. Three sources of such information are consumer publications, telephone hotlines, and consumer information agencies. Television, radio, and the press are increasingly sympathetic to the consumer cause.

The first special consumer publications were newspapers. The USSR Federation's *V Zaschitu Prav Potrebiteley* (For Consumer Rights Protection) led the way between 1988 and 1992, with local consumer newspapers also appearing in Volgodonsk, Sverdlovsk (Ekaterinburg), Odessa, Minsk, Dnepropetrovsk, Kiev, and other cities. By the mid-1990s, almost all of these consumer publications had been forced to close down because of either financial difficulties or the fractionalization of consumers in the society.

The emergence of a significant number of Russian households with money to spend created the opportunity to introduce a consumer magazine of the traditional, product-testing variety. After a number of experiments, *SPROS* (Demand) was launched in October 1992, with Larisa Leonova as editor and Irina Vinogradova as director. It is an official publication of KonfOP and is distributed in Russia, Belarus, Ukraine, and Kazakhstan. Up until 1994 the magazine depended heavily on financial, technical, and practical support from the German product-testing organization Stiftung Warentest; without this support, the magazine would never have gotten beyond the drawing board. Additional help was provided by Consumers Union (United States) and European consumer organizations through the mediation of Consumers International. The magazine has been financially self-supporting since the end of 1994, with six issues per year and a circulation of about 200,000. It does not accept advertising and relies heavily on the expertise of KonfOP's professionals.

Telephone hotlines have been set up in local consumer organizations such as the Rostov Consumer Union in southern Russia to collect information from consumers about their problems and to advise them on their rights and means of redress. Hotline programs with consumer specialists are widely used by local television and radio stations. In the fall of 1993, KonfOP opened a hotline especially for dissatisfied consumers of financial services. It is well known in Russia and other CIS countries because of the publicity it receives in the major newspaper.

From the hotlines developed the concept of a consumer information agency, which was created within KonfOP by Michael Polyachek and Oleg Komarovsky at the end of 1993. The agency distributes information and, when possible, sells it, and it has established good relations with the most influential newspapers, television stations, and radio stations. Its work points the way for other CIS consumer organizations involved in publishing information, while also extending the reputation and effectiveness of the entire consumer movement.

Research and Testing

Even during the period of the Soviet Union, research projects on consumer topics were commissioned and funded by the government. Since 1992, KonfOP has operated an Institute for Consumer Policy, which develops research-based policy recommendations for local authorities and consumer organizations. One topic of research is how to calculate moral damages; another, how to assess the quality of financial services. KonfOP also has a service that conducts sociological research, such as surveys of the most important consumer issues of the day. Another KonfOP service studies food safety. Based in Turkmenistan, it analyzes food safety standards in CIS countries and makes recommendations to national and local consumer organizations on monitoring food safety.

KonfOP does not monopolize the field of consumer research. The Consumers Union of Russia carries out research on living standards, transportation services, and medical services. The Society of Automobile Consumers compares the safety of cars and reviews the consequences of traffic accidents. Consumer organizations of Ukraine and Bashkiria conduct ecological research.

Another important area of consumer movement activity is the creation of consumer cooperatives. With the support of KonfOP and other organizations, buying cooperatives and financial services cooperatives have been established. The most significant is the Russian League of Credit Unions, founded in 1994.

Comparative testing, the staple fare of the most powerful Western consumer organizations, is still in its infancy. At first, consumer organizations dreamed of creating or owning their own testing facilities. By the mid-1990s, though, it was clear that this dream was beyond their reach. All that has survived from these efforts are a few local laboratories specializing in food testing, the best being Zaporozhye in Ukraine. In its 1994 Congress, KonfOP changed its strategy on testing. Rather than conduct their own testing for the magazine *SPROS,* KonfOP has followed the lead of many Western product-testing organizations by contracting with private and public laboratories in CIS and conducting joint tests with foreign organizations.

Coordination among Consumer Organizations

Coordinating consumer organizations with widely differing philosophies and structures across the length and breadth of the CIS has proved to be a real test. This challenge has been addressed in three ways: bringing the organizations under one roof through membership in a federal-type body, exchanging information, and conducting mass campaigns based on common goals.

Virtually all of the national and supranational organizations are themselves composed of local consumer organizations and serve as a means of coordination through regular meetings and other forms of information exchange. (In the early years, primitive communications and office systems proved a formidable handicap, but slowly the introduction of fax and e-mail connections brought a much needed improvement.) Coordination is essentially nonauthoritarian—the umbrella organizations make recommendations; they do not issue orders. Nevertheless, tensions inevitably arise among local, national, and supranational bodies over issues such as the rules governing relations with political parties or trade and industry, and over the acceptance of funds from businesses. KonfOP's bylaws forbid the acceptance of money from businesses or alignment with particular political parties, but the practices of local organizations vary. As the movement develops and the countries of the CIS grow farther apart in their economic and social development, this "consumer brotherhood" is likely to prove increasingly difficult to hold together.

Even now, some consumer organizations belong to KonfOP but not to their national federations, and vice versa. Other organizations, mainly in Russia, are not affiliated with any umbrella group. These are often single-issue lobbies, such as unions of small investors or consumers of medical services. Some groups are made up of consumers, and others are not, strictly speaking, consumer groups at all. The Independent Buyers' Association, for example, has its own retail network and accepts advertising in its newspaper. A family spirit nonetheless prevails between the consumer movement and these types of organizations. The more powerful organizations offer advice and opportunities to participate in education and information programs.

Lobbying and mass campaigning remain a powerful binding force in a consumer movement that is no more nor less fractious and fragmented than that of other countries (or in the world as a whole). The secret of success in conducting joint campaigns is establishing good relations with the mass media; until that happened, most consumer campaigns were unsuccessful.

The first truly successful mass campaign involved counterfeit Levi's jeans. In addition to a victory in court, consumers were encouraged to ask for receipts, and businesses responded positively when provided with proof of purchase. In 1993, KonfOP, in collaboration with major newspapers, effectively campaigned for more openness in the operation of investment funds (which were the main financial institutions during the privatization period). The largest funds were forced to publish their financial reports, which in turn were analyzed critically by independent experts. Somewhat less successful was the 1993 attempt to pressure Aeroflot, the principal Russian air carrier, to compensate passengers for delays and remove restrictive clauses from its ticket contracts. This attack, launched by Gregory Tsekher, managed to establish the principle of compensation for delays, but restrictive contract clauses remain.

Government has also bowed to consumer pressure. As a result of a mass campaign, its own decree on increasing import taxes on food has been abolished. In March 1995, KonfOP and other organizations embarked on a campaign to force multinational corporations to bring their product guarantees in line with Russian consumer law. Sony is the focus of this action.

The success of mass campaigns is but one indicator that the consumer movement in the CIS since 1988 has developed the capability of influencing even the most powerful institutions in business and government as well as shifting consumer behavior in a period of economic flux. The principal sources of the movement's influence are ready access to the media, ability to raise funds for its work from legitimate sources, and creative thinking about increasing the scope and range of its work.

— Alexander Auzan

Readings

Auzan, Alexander A. (1995). "Changes in the Behavior of Russian Consumers under Recent Reforms." *Journal of Consumer Policy*. 18: 73–84.

Kozminski, Andrzej K. (1992). "Consumers in Transition from the Centrally Planned Economy to the Market Economy." *Journal of Consumer Policy*. 14 (4): 351–370.

S

Savings Protections

In the 1990s, consumers held trillions of dollars in savings. These savings served several purposes, including covering high unexpected expenses such as medical bills, unexpected loss of income from being laid off, high expected expenditures such as the payment of college tuition, and expected loss of income from retirement. Savings dollars are invested in a broad array of savings and investment vehicles ranging from bank accounts to real estate, insurance, and retirement programs.

Role of Savings

Savings and its counterpart, credit, usefully balance out variations in income and expenses since income and expenses are seldom equal. Young persons, for example, need credit to finance education, cars, homes, and furnishings. Those in middle age with higher incomes should be able not only to cover expenses but also to reduce indebtedness. Those approaching retirement with lower family expenses and higher incomes should be able not only to zero out accumulated debts, but also to build up savings and investments to achieve economic independence and be less dependent on government or family in later years.

Preretirement wealth accumulation, however, is imprudently low, reflecting gross neglect or a history of misfortune. Half of married persons have accumulated savings of less than two years' expenses, depending on retirement programs, social security, and pensions to sustain them. Home owners typically amass the greatest accumulation. Married couples are better prepared than those never married, divorced, widowed, or separated. White Americans fare better than African Americans and Hispanic Americans.

Savings programs are logically framed with references to an individual's personal situation (family orientation, personal insurance, and intergenerational expectations); sociocultural situation (i.e., community support agencies; in-kind services; insurance for health, disability, or unemployment); the regulatory framework for protections covering the individual's securities, savings, and pensions; and forces beyond a person's control, such as weather, inflation, war, and environmental hazards, which may adversely impact financial programs.

Good money management must recognize such factors and provide for them, if possible, through insurance, savings, and personal discipline. Success is greatly influenced by government's social and economic programs, full employment, and wise investments, as well as luck. Failure is greatly influenced by costly health experiences and lack of adequate health insurance, work interruptions and unemployment, care of dependent children and parents, longevity, and a history of unfortunate credit or savings decisions.

Consumer Protection Needs

Individuals must evaluate and choose between six conflicting considerations. The first is safety of principal. Consumers must avoid deceptive, misleading, and fraudulent schemes. They must also entrust funds with institutions insured by the Federal Deposit Insurance

Corporation (FDIC) or National Credit Union Association (NCUA), in pensions protected by ERISA and the Pension Benefit Guarantee Corp., and in government-issued Treasury bills, notes, and bonds. But even such safe investments risk changes in market value because a rise in market interest rates lowers the market value of fixed-rate obligations.

The second consideration is liquidity, as measured by the time and money cost of converting invested funds back to cash. The third is safety of purchasing power, which may be approximated by investing in indexed equity funds or the Treasury's inflation protection notes.

The fourth factor is growth in value of investments. This growth may be realized by investing in equities. High risks are more appropriate for younger than for older investors. The fifth consideration is taxes, which have varying impacts on ordinary income, capital gains, and estate transfers depending on the individual's taxable income level and stage in the life cycle.

The sixth factor is interest rate and rate of return, which rewards postponing consumption and encourages wealth accumulation. Until recently, however, rates lacked direct comparability because they were expressed in a myriad of confusing terms.

Protections for consumer savings may focus on consumer behavior, and range in philosophy from protecting fools from being foolish with their funds by prohibiting false, misleading, and deceptive practices to a laissez-faire posture that honors the rights of individuals to make mistakes and be so disciplined. A second form of protection is that of establishing "rules of the road" for the savings market—licensing public institutions, such as banks, to comply with regulations. A third form seeks to ensure that the public is well informed about the savings and investments options from which it can choose. That is the purpose of federal laws such as the Trust in Securities Act of 1934 and the Truth in Savings Act of 1991.

History of Truth in Savings

The roots for truth in savings were planted in 1961 and made public in the 1963 report of the Consumer Advisory Council to President John F. Kennedy. This document identified the periodic percentage rate (PPR) as the true rate that, multiplied by the number of periods in a year, defined the annual percentage rate (APR) for truth in lending. This simple rate, compounded for the year, is the annual percentage yield (APY) for truth in savings.

The idea of truth in savings was first expressed by Senator William Proxmire and Treasury Undersecretary Joe Barr in a colloquy over whether an 18 percent APR truthfully represented a 1.5 percent monthly percentage rate. Although the bankers and retailers claimed it did not, if they had been correct they would have been wrong to advertise 4 percent on a savings account paying 1 percent each quarter, as Barr observed.

Jackie Pinson, a graduate student of Richard Morse, a professor of family economics at Kansas State University and longtime critic of bank savings and credit disclosures, researched the ways banks paid interest on savings. Morse shared these findings with members of the consumer advisory committee of the American Bankers Association, which included Bob Harvey, the editor of *Changing Times.* Harvey's 1971 article "Maybe We Need 'Truth in Savings' Too" was read by Howard Marlowe, legislative aide to Senator Vance Hartke, who called Morse for guidance in drafting legislation. Within months, Hartke and Representative Bill Roy introduced legislation that standardized terminology and required it in savings disclosures.

In the next Congress, the 93rd, truth in savings bills were introduced. At the initiative of Hartke, Proxmire reluctantly held hearings at which considerable evidence of confusion in savings advertising and computations was introduced, revealing the need for clarifying standards. Conflicting views were presented about what rate or rates should be disclosed and how they should be computed. There was no committee report.

In late 1973, Deputy Secretary of the Treasury William E. Simon was persuaded of the logical need to include truth in savings with banking reform legislation the administration supported. With the encouragement of President Richard Nixon's consumer adviser, Virginia Knauer, Simon announced the introduction by Senators John Sparkman and John Tower of truth in savings as Title I of the Financial Institutions Act of 1973. This bill, which required disclosure of the annual percentage rate and the annual percentage yield, was stricken by Proxmire.

In the first days of the 94th Congress, Representative Leonor Sullivan reintroduced truth in savings, but there was no further action in the House. The Financial Institutions Act was reintroduced in the Senate with a truth in savings title. In late 1975, Senator Proxmire deleted this title in committee.

Concerns about savings disclosures reflected not only the cost of implementation and maintenance to financial institutions, but also purported "information overload" on consumers. During the late 1970s these reservations were increasingly offset by consumer concerns about bank practices costing them money in a high-interest-rate economy. As inflation and interest rates rose into double digits, regulations constrained banks from paying market rates on savings accounts. Through loopholes, however, they were able to offer a confusing array of new savings instruments that were brought to the attention of Congress by Morse and others. Representative Benjamin Rosenthal held hearings on these issues, to which Morse contributed 262 pages of testimony and exhibits.

Meanwhile, the need for action was recognized at the state level, first in Maryland, then in New York. In 1978 the New York State Assembly passed the Truth in Savings Act, which directed the State Banking Board to write regulations that became effective in late 1979. These regulations conform to the provisions of the *Model State Truth in Savings Act,* which was published by Morse in response to requests from many state legislators who had grown weary of waiting for federal legislation. New York also officially recognized Morse's rate tables and required banks to make tables available to customers to enable them to verify interest paid on accounts. In 1985, Massachusetts enacted a Truth in Savings Act, which also authorized Morse's proposed "cents per $100" disclosures.

In the 99th Congress, Representative Richard Lehman reintroduced a bill he had first introduced in the previous Congress. It was amended into broader legislation, which passed the House. Senator Christopher Dodd introduced similar legislation, which also was amended into a broader bill and passed the Senate. Unfortunately, the two houses were unable to reconcile differences between their bills. In the 101st Congress, truth in savings titles were incorporated in broader legislation that passed the House and the Senate, yet again could not be reconciled.

In the 102nd Congress, after a Consumer Federation of America bank survey revealed that some banks were failing to disclose that they were not paying interest on all savings, only on "investable balances," congressional interest in passing truth in savings reforms increased. Representatives Richard Lehman, Henry Gonzales, Esteban Torres, and Jim Slattery introduced separate truth in savings bills. The House Consumer and Monetary Affairs Subcommittee amended most of the Slattery provisions—a standardized 365-day year, computation of "APY Earned," and verification and use of the APR in disclosing the simple annual rate—into the Torres bill, then voted it out of subcommittee. It passed the full House. In conference committee consideration of the Federal Deposit Insurance Corporation Improvement Act of 1991, the House version of truth in savings was included and approved, and the act became law in December of that year. Morse and U.S. PIRG were especially active in supporting this legislation.

This Truth in Savings Act recognized the needs of depositors for comparable rates and to be informed about fees, charges, and specifics that affect the net return. The Federal Reserve Board wrote implementing regulations, known as Regulation DD. (NCUA drafted comparable regulations for credit unions, which became effective in January 1995.) The regulations require that advertised rates be expressed as the APY and that depositors receive account statements giving the activity, fees and charges, and the APY earned. Interest must be computed using a 365-day year based on the daily principal balance, thereby removing from banking practices some seven methods that paid depositors less interest.

Consumer advocates faulted the regulation, however, for allowing banks to pay on either the "collected" or "ledger" daily balances, leaving the computation process ambiguous and not "truthful." They also criticized the Fed for ignoring congressional recognition of the need for verification of the interest paid on deposit accounts.

— Richard L. D. Morse

Readings

Morse, Richard L. D. (1988). "Truth in Savings—A Consumer's Perspective." *Journal of Retail Banking*. 10 (3): 53–64.

——— (1992). *Truth in Savings*. Manhattan, KS: Family Economics Trust Press.

———, ed. (1993). *The Consumer Movement: Lectures by Colston E. Warne*. Manhattan, KS: Family Economics Trust Press. 280–290.

Self-Regulation

In an effort to avoid government regulation as well as to promote good business practices, businesses attempt to regulate themselves. They may create private codes of practice, which set standards for products and services in an industry, then publish these codes and enforce them. For example, the furniture industry has established flammability standards for upholstery fabrics to prevent fires caused by smokers. The mattress industry has approved similar standards. In another area, major television networks have set standards for substantiating the claims made in commercial advertisements.

From a business perspective, self-regulation can demonstrate the ability of business to respond to the needs of consumers without government intervention. Industries that are effectively self-regulated often succeed in warding off strict government regulations and maintaining a good public image. Also, self-regulation helps reputable businesses maintain minimum standards over which they retain control. From a consumer perspective, buyers gain from the speed, informality, and modest cost of a self-regulatory system. On the other hand, the industry standards may not adequately protect consumers or may be ignored by some members of that industry.

The most well-known example of self-regulation is the Better Business Bureaus (BBBs). Established early in the twentieth century, BBBs are local or regional organizations that promote ethical practices by businesses. BBBs promote businesses who conform to these practices and may publicize those businesses that act unethically. More specifically, they collect information, maintain files on businesses in their communities, and respond to requests from consumers to identify those businesses with unsatisfactory complaint records. Most also forward consumer complaints to businesses that are members. In the early 1990s, prepurchase inquiries to the BBBs totaled about 10 million per year, and complaints received exceeded 2 million per year. To raise revenue, BBBs sell memberships to area businesses.

Less well known than BBBs, but just as active in business self-regulation, are the more than 400 standards-setting organizations in the United States. The American Society for Testing Materials (ASTM) and the American National Standards Institute (ANSI) deal exclusively in developing standards for industry regarding materials, products, systems, and services. Voluntary standards are set by professional and technical associations such as the American Society of Mechanical Engineers and the Society of Automotive Engineers. Testing laboratories such as Underwriters Laboratories (UL) also establish voluntary uniform and quality standards for different products.

Trade associations often seek to regulate their industries. For example, the American Gas Association directs the development of standards for gas-related residential and industrial products. Perhaps the most widely publicized industry efforts are those of the advertising industry. The American Association of Advertising Agencies has established and published ethical standards, and its members are expected to adhere to these minimum standards, although they have the option of establishing tougher rules.

The advertising industry enforces its standards through its self-regulatory National Advertising Review Board (NARB), which is made up of representatives from the industry and the public. NARB works cooperatively with the National Advertising Division (NAD) of the National Council of Better Business Bureaus, the trade association of BBBs. NAD's professional staff typically investigates more than 100 complaints annually about possible breaches of truth and accuracy in national advertising, and attempts to determine the truth of the claims in question. If adequate substantiation cannot be found, NAD initiates investigations, determines the issues, collects and evaluates data, and negotiates settlements. If a resolution cannot be reached, appeals can be made to a five-member panel of NARB. Cases are kept confidential until resolved, and no fines are imposed. In a typical year, about 70 percent of advertising challenges are brought by competing advertisers, about 20 percent are initiated by NAD staff, and about 10 percent are submitted by local BBBs, consumers, and other sources. NARB's Children's Advertising Review Unit (CARU) handles about ninety inquiries each year.

NAD may ask the advertiser for advertising substantiation. If NAD finds the documentation inadequate, it first requests that the advertiser change the advertisement (it cannot order changes). If the advertiser refuses, NAD can ask NARB to review the facts and rule against the advertiser. Should the company still refuse to change the advertisement, the refusal is publicized by NARB, and the case information is forwarded to the appropriate government regulatory agency for action, typically the Federal Trade Commission.

Critics complain that, by the time NAD and NARB finally determine that an ad is deceptive, it has usually run for a number of months. Nonetheless, the broad consensus is that these self-regulatory efforts play an important role in discouraging deceptive or false advertising claims.

— E. Thomas Garman

See also

Better Business Bureaus; Product Standards.

Readings

Armstrong, Gary M., and Julie L. Ozanne (1983). "An Evaluation of NAD/NARB Purpose and Performance." *Journal of Advertising.* 12 (3): 15–26.

Boddewyn, Jean J. (1992). *Global Perspectives on Advertising Self-regulation: Principles and Practices in Thirty-eight Countries.* Westport, CT: Quorum Books.

Service Contract Protections

See Warranty Protections.

Slovakian Consumer Movement

Slovak consumers are among the best protected in the region, both legally and practically. Slovakia signed an Association Agreement with the European Union (EU) in October 1993, committing it to harmonize its consumer legislation with that of the EU, and applied for full membership in the union in June 1995. The Federal Assembly of Czecho-Slovakia passed a general Consumer Protection Act in December 1992, only a month before the disintegration of the federal republic, but the act was assimilated into Slovak legislation without change. A year later, the Ministry of Economic Affairs was given overall responsibility for enforcement and for the development of consumer policy and protection; the Slovak Commercial Inspection, under the jurisdiction of the Ministry of Economic Affairs, is responsible for supervising all business activity. The 1993 act also gives consumer associations the right to work with public authorities in creating and monitoring consumer policy, and in improving the effectiveness of its administration. Since 1994 a number of other directives regulating various aspects of the market have been in force. As of 1996, a product liability law in line with the 1985 directive of the European Community was still being prepared.

The first independent organization to emerge in Slovakia was the Bratislava Forum, a small, loose network of activists and journalists led by Marta Cerna, who joined in 1989 to campaign against consumer abuses, receiving much favorable media coverage. After Cerna was appointed director of commercial inspection in 1991—to which role she brought her consumer sympathies and campaigning energies—the forum grew less active. When Cerna retired from government service in 1995, many people expected him to try to revive the organization, and reports to that effect have circulated, but nothing more concrete could be reported by the end of 1996.

The Slovakian Consumers Association (Zdruzenie Slovenskych Spotrebitelov) (SCA) was founded in February 1990 by Pavel Hrasko, professor of market research on the economics faculty of Bratislava University, and others who had been working on consumer issues since the 1970s. The government provided initial funding of some $4,500, but this grant was not renewed, resulting in insufficient resources to capitalize on the initial interest aroused both in the media and among consumers. Although members are charged a small entry fee, the fees generate little income, so Hrasko uses his political and academic contacts to generate funds by carrying out small research projects on behalf of government departments and state agencies.

SCA acts as a federal umbrella for some twenty regional and local associations with a total membership of about 3,000. All the regional organizations are represented on its National Council; in 1994, the association introduced a rotating presidency, and the following year created the post of director.

In 1993 the association was strengthened at both the national and local levels by the introduction of a consumer advice project, with the professional and financial support of the German consumer organization AgV. Until that time, the association could afford only one part-time staff member; all other work was carried out both nationally and regionally by volunteers. With advice centers opened in Bratislava and three other towns, the number of staff increased to ten: four part-timers at headquarters and six in the regions. These centers are open eight hours a day, five days a week, and serve as models for centers in other areas that lack funding and are staffed only by volunteers.

Like the Poles and Hungarians, the Slovaks faced a serious dilemma when the two-year funding for this project ended in November 1995. It is an indication of the good relations between SCA and the government that the Ministry of Economic Affairs agreed to fund the four consumer advice centers, and to increase its funding of the association to at least $35,000 in 1996. The ministry also agreed to fund the development of the first Slovak consumer magazine. Called *TERC* (Target), it is published in Zilin, a town in southern Slovakia, by the Center for Consumer Protection and Advice (CCPA), a member of SCA. The pilot issue of this magazine was produced in October 1995 as a supplement to a local newspaper; subsequent issues are published monthly and sold at the modest price of seventeen cents.

— Alastair Macgeorge

See also

Central and Eastern Europe, Consumer Movements in.

Reading

Kozminski, Andrzej K. (1992). "Consumers in Transition from the Centrally Planned Economy to the Market Economy." *Journal of Consumer Policy*. 14 (4): 351–370.

Slovenian Consumer Movement

Slovenia enjoys a lively tourist industry, open trading borders with Austria and Italy, a relatively strong manufacturing base, and cultural and religious traditions strongly rooted in Austro-Hungaria. Achieving independence in 1991, it now has probably the highest standard of living among former communist countries.

Nevertheless, in a country of only 7,800 square miles and a population of 2 million, it is difficult for both a government and a consumers' association to achieve economic self-sufficiency. Slovenia has an exceptionally dynamic, ambitious, and effective association, yet after five years it remains heavily dependent on project funding from a variety of sources at home and abroad. Founded in June 1990 by Breda Kutin, an economist and former researcher at the home economics institute Domus, Zveza Potrosnikov Slovenije (ZPS) was modeled after Western consumer organizations, which have paying members, a test-based magazine, and involvement in consumer policy-making and campaigning.

From small beginnings, ZPS has grown organically, living dangerously but never overreaching itself, constantly in the news, listened to with respect by those in power, and feared by racketeers. Breda Kutin is responsible for getting the funds to sustain and expand the association's work and services; her persistence, thorough preparation, and professionalism are largely responsible for the organization's success.

The magazine *VIP*, started in 1991, published eight issues in 1995 and ten issues in 1996. Articles cover basic questions on such issues as food, diet, energy saving, health and social services, educational problems, and water supplies. With little money available for testing within Slovenia, most test reports are reprinted or adapted from other consumer magazines. However, ZPS, along with the Russian magazine *SPROS*, has joined the International Testing consortium in the hope of participating in joint test programs with Western consumer organizations. Despite financial help from the government in printing, distributing, and even promoting the magazine, *VIP* has yet to achieve the large circulation its quality and value deserve. Current sales are around 8,000—3,000 to members as part of their $36 annual subscription, and the remainder through retailers at $3.50 per copy. Beginning in 1996, the plan was for the magazine to be available only through subscription.

With funding from the PHARE Democracy Programs, ZPS has set up consumer advice centers with trained staff and legal support in four areas outside Ljubljana, the capital, and developed the software for an information database. At headquarters, ZPS provides a Consumer Advocacy Service, effectively offering free, expert legal advice to members by phone and in person; nonmembers are given general information, but must join to receive assistance on complex problems. Resources being strictly limited, ZPS brings cases to court only when an important legal precedent must be established or an epidemic of problems arises from one particular trader or trade practice. (Unlike some Eastern European countries, Slovenia does not allow class actions, though provision for them is made in the draft Consumer Protection Act.)

One of the strengths of the organization lies in its integrated approach. Lobbying grows out of research and legal work, media campaigns back up written and oral evidence to government, and invitations to join or chair official commissions and inquiries follow successful advocacy. ZPS enjoys constant exposure in the media (Breda Kutin is a national figure, recognized by shoppers and feared by shopkeepers) and works with all television channels on educational, news, and consumer programs. For two years, ZPS has had its own hour-long program on a national channel, shown live in prime time once a month.

ZPS also promotes sustainable and "green" consumerism; with government support, it publishes a series of practical leaflets on basic issues such as waste management, recycling, energy saving, water conservation, and sensible shopping.

To build a professional base to carry out research for consumers, the Slovenian government, and—in the longer term—the consumer movement in Central Europe, Kutin set up an International Consumer Research Institute in 1992 that now functions as the research unit for the magazine and also works on a number of government contracts. The institute works jointly with the United Kingdom International Consumer Policy Bureau on a project, funded by the PHARE program, to draw up guidelines on administering the consumer policy function in government and on the relationship between government and the independent consumer movement in Central and Eastern Europe.

With a total staff of twenty-five (nineteen in the head office and regional centers, plus six in the institute), ZPS is now one of the strongest consumer organizations in the region, with a reputation extending far beyond the borders of Slovenia. At Consumers International's 1994 World Congress, it was elected as the second Central European council member.

Despite constant pressure from ZPS, the government of Slovenia has yet to enact the general law on consumer protection that has been in draft since 1992, with a modified version adopted for debate by Parliament in February 1995. This new version is a significant improvement, and would be easier to harmonize with EU legislation as required under the Association Agreement recently signed by the Slovenian government.

Included in this agreement is an article that goes much further than the normal commitment to consumer protection: it declares that the Parties shall promote and provide active consumer protection policies—in line with Community legislation and, where appropriate, United Nations guidelines—and effective legal protection of consumers in order to improve quality and guarantee adequate safety standards for consumer goods. Cooperation in this field may include exchanges of information on dangerous products; training of government and nongovernmental organization experts in the field of consumer protection; assistance with the development of independent organizations whose goal is to make available information to consumers, particularly through awareness campaigns; the establishment of information and advice centers to settle disputes and provide legal and other advice to consumers; cooperation between Slovenian and Community centers; access to Community databases; and development of exchanges between representatives of consumers' interests. This clause appears to be unique in Association Agreements between the EU and Central and Eastern European countries.

For all this, the Slovenian consumer movement still faces challenges. Consumers apparently believe that the government should provide them with free information and advice, but the government is preoccupied with liberalizing the market, leaving little time for consumer protection. The good news is that the government has decided to sustain the advice center network after PHARE funding comes to an end and to continue providing financial support to ZPS and its services at the current level, possibly for more than one year.

— Alastair Macgeorge

See also

Central and Eastern Europe, Consumer Movements in.

Reading

Kozminski, Andrzej K. (1992). "Consumers in Transition from the Centrally Planned Economy to the Market Economy." *Journal of Consumer Policy.* 14 (4): 351–370.

Society of Consumer Affairs Professionals in Business

In the early 1970s many corporations responded to the challenge of consumerism by upgrading their complaint-handling mechanisms into consumer affairs departments that represented consumers to top management. The Society of Consumer Affairs Professionals in Business (SOCAP) was formed in 1973 as an association of professionals from these departments and other consumer functions within companies. Its purpose is not only to support and develop a fledgling profession, but also to help shape the business community's response to changing consumer attitudes.

One of SOCAP's key missions is to make the marketplace better for consumers by addressing their concerns within the corporate culture. The society's incorporation papers describe the organization as "a society of individuals whose purposes are to foster and maintain the integrity of business in dealings with consumers; to encourage and promote effective communication and understanding between business and government and consumers; and to define and advance the consumer affairs profession." Those purposes remain the same today.

The Council of Better Business Bureaus (CBBB) played a key role in the formation of SOCAP. Bruce Palmer, CBBB president in 1973, authorized CBBB aid for the creation of a consumer relations group. The CBBB sent a mailing to *Fortune* 500 companies asking for information on consumer affairs and the name of the person responsible for that function. Palmer offered funding and staffing to the small group of consumer affairs professionals who led the formation drive.

The new organization was born on May 24, 1973, at a CBBB assembly in Anaheim, California. Jack Scarcliff, director of consumer affairs for Firestone Tire and Rubber Company, was elected SOCAP's first president.

Membership in the new organization grew rapidly. In less than a year, 450 members were enrolled, and by the end of the 1980s, SOCAP membership exceeded 2,000. In 1995 more than 2,700 individual members, representing more than 1,500 companies, belonged to the organization.

SOCAP is structured as an individual membership organization. Although the society's membership rolls include students, government officials, and educators, the vast majority of members are vice presidents, directors, managers, and supervisors of consumer affairs/customer service for large national and multinational corporations.

These business professionals are usually involved in five basic functions—consumer communications, consumer information and education, consumer issue and trend analysis, consumer liaison, and consumer representation. They handle the traditional inquiry and complaint processing function, and also act as liaisons between consumers and top management. These professionals bring consumer feedback and insight into the corporation for strategic use in the development of new products and services as well as the revision of existing ones. They represent the company's views to consumers, and consumer views to the highest level of management.

The membership elects twenty-three members to the board of directors, the governing body of SOCAP; the board consists of a president, president-elect, vice president, first vice president, secretary, treasurer, two immediate past presidents, and fifteen directors. The chief elected officer of the society is the president. The board supervises, controls, and directs the affairs of the society; determines policies; and oversees the disbursement of funds.

In 1981 the SOCAP board appointed Louis Garcia as executive director, a position he continues to hold. Garcia has more than twenty-five years of experience in association management and is certified as an association executive by the American Society of Association Executives. As the society's chief administrative officer, Garcia is responsible for all management functions and the operations of the SOCAP national office.

The national office is located in Alexandria, Virginia, and is staffed by seven full-time employees. The SOCAP annual operating budget exceeds $1,300,000. Revenue sources include membership dues, conference and seminar registrations, advertising, sponsorship and exhibit fees, and resource center sales.

SOCAP is a member service organization. Members pay annual dues and, in return, receive benefits and services from the organization. The major service areas are networking opportunities, information, and education. The emphasis is on the professional development of the consumer affairs/customer service executive and the enhancement of the company's consumer response function. The society assists members with establishing and maintaining a personal network of professional contacts, keeping informed about pertinent issues and trends, and positioning the consumer affairs function within the corporation.

The organization's major achievements include its work with the Conference Board to produce a study of personal and job characteristics of consumer affairs professionals; the development and distribution of a handbook entitled *A Guide to Professional Management in Consumer Affairs;* assistance in planning and executing the first National Consumers' Week; the development of the society's *Guidelines for Business Sponsored Consumer Education Materials;* the introduction and publication of *Mobius*, the only professional journal for consumer affairs executives in business; studies on the business use of 800 telephone numbers for customer service activities; the cooperative effort with the American Association of Retired Persons to publish *Organizing a Company's Consumer Advisory Panel;* and the development and distribution of *Close to the Customers*, a joint research project with the American Management Association.

SOCAP's current plans are driven by the society's vision statement for the future, adopted by the board of directors in April 1994: provide leadership and services for achieving and sustaining value-based customer satisfaction for members and their organizations. SOCAP defines value-based customer satisfaction as the effective management of customer-retention processes that contribute to the success of an organization.

SOCAP is unusual among professional organizations. It does not lobby legislatures or advance one point of view above all others. As an organization of representatives from many industries, SOCAP does not try to protect some businesses from others; rather, it works to promote the mutual and complementary interests shared by all consumers and businesses.

— Louis Garcia

See also

Better Business Bureaus.

Readings

Fernstrom, Meredith (1988). "Consumer Affairs: A View from Business." In E. Scott Maynes, ed. *The Frontier of Research in the Consumer Interest*. Columbia, MO: American Council on Consumer Interests. 621–627.

Fornell, Claes (1988). "Corporate Consumer Affairs Departments: Retrospect and Prospect." In E. Scott Maynes, ed. *The Frontier of Research in the Consumer Interest*. Columbia, MO: American Council on Consumer Interests. 595–620.

South Korean Consumer Movement

The Korean consumer movement can be traced to the 1960s; by the 1990s, consumerism in South Korea was well received by the public because of increases in the country's level of affluence, the education of its people, and the complexity of choices faced by consumers.

Korean consumer activism can be divided into three periods: the 1960s, the 1970s, and the 1980s to the present. These periods of activism can be understood as expressions of two disparate impulses, nationalism and humanitarianism. Leadership for the movement came mainly from the female leaders of women's associations. The salient consumer problems of each era grew out of changes in the marketplace, the terms of international trade, and consumer autonomy. Furthermore, in each period the consumer movement has had to overcome the same problems: attracting public attention, generating organizational resources, and stimulating government action.

The first wave began as a nationalistic movement in 1965. In this era, Koreans experienced rapid industrialization directed by the government under the "First 5-Year Economic Development Plan." However, this industrialization was confined to basic industries such as railroads, highways, and steel. Also, economic development under the government's guidance resulted in highly concentrated markets dominated by government-subsidized firms. As a result, consumers did not enjoy the fruits of a competitive marketplace.

In 1965, Japan and Korea reinstituted political and economic relations for the first time since the end of World War II. Still, many Koreans resisted contacts with the Japanese and rejected trade with Japan; Korean consumers even organized a citizen's alliance to boycott Japanese products. Thus, from the beginning, Korean consumerism had a strong nationalist slant.

Along with the boycott of Japanese products, consumer organizations emerged in the 1960s. The Korean Women's Association opened an office handling consumer complaints, and in 1967 published the first issue of the general-interest magazine *Consumer Protection.* In 1968 the Korean YMCA established the Consumer Protection Committee within the Department of Social Problems, and the Korean Association of Consumer Protection registered with the government, only to be dissolved in 1969 when government subsidies were discontinued.

The consumer movement was directed by the leaders of women's associations such as the Korean Federation of Housewives Club, the National Housewives Association, and the Korean National Council of Women. As a result, consumerism was often confused with, or even overshadowed by, the feminist movement.

In 1969, Esther Peterson and Colston E. Warne visited Korea to help organize a "consumers union" capable of carrying out independent product tests, and their encouragement led to the formation of the Consumers Union of Korea in 1970. Its establishment was a landmark in the history of Korean consumerism because it separated the consumer movement from the feminist movement. The Consumers Union of Korea suffered from a lack of human and financial resources, but in the 1980s it became a full member of Consumers International and established branch offices in local communities.

The 1970s constituted the second era of Korean consumerism. By the completion of the second and third 5-Year Economic Development Plans, Korea's economy and exports had developed, improving material well-being but also increasing consumer problems.

In 1976 leaders of five women's associations held a conference to organize the Korean consumer movement more effectively, which resulted in the founding of the National Council of Consumer Protection Organizations. The council integrated existing consumer-interest organizations into a single entity, and after registering with the government, the council invigorated the consumer movement by focusing on legislation related to basic consumer rights. In 1979 the council began publishing a monthly magazine, *Consumer,* which reported market information and news from its associated member organizations. The magazine's contents were later broadened to include product testing and comparison pricing.

In 1979 the government established the Administration of Consumer Affairs under the Division of Consumer Pricing Policy in the Department of the Economic Planning. Although it lacked specific regulatory powers, the Administration of Consumer Affairs studied consumer protection issues, handled consumer complaints, and mediated buyer-seller disputes.

By the late 1970s, the importance of consumer protection was recognized by the Korean public. As a result, the Consumer

Protection Act was passed in 1979 and implemented in 1980. The law was the beginning of government involvement in protecting consumer interests, and its passage was the most notable achievement of the 1970s period of consumer activism.

In the 1970s, leaders of the women's associations played key roles in the consumer movement, and the organizers became more influential. However, the movement still lacked adequate human and financial resources, and groups found it difficult to involve consumers, in part because government suppressed free speech and banned formal political gatherings.

The third era of the Korean consumer movement runs from the 1980s to the present. In the 1980s consumers became more aware of health and safety issues as their economic well-being continued to improve. The consumer movement focused on food and drug safety problems, persuading the government to recognize the importance of regulating hazardous products.

In the 1980s consumer advocates became more active in the international consumer movement. In 1983 the Citizen's Alliance for Consumer Protection of Korea was founded, and the alliance became an associate member of Consumers International (CI). Within CI, the alliance seeks to abolish international trade in hazardous drugs and pesticides, encourage breast feeding in less-developed nations, and promote environmentally sustainable consumption. On the domestic front, the alliance is involved in consumer education, consumer research, product testing, and lobbying campaigns.

Supported by growing public interest in consumer well-being, the Consumer Protection Act was amended in 1986. The major features of this amendment include recognition of seven basic consumer rights, establishment of the Consumer Protection Board, and expansion of the National Council of Consumer Protection Organizations. The seven rights of consumers are: protection of health, safety, and economic interests; to be informed; to choose; to be heard; to redress; of education; and of representation.

The Consumer Protection Board was established to serve consumer interests by: redressing consumer complaints and losses, encouraging consumer education, disseminating consumer information including product and service testing, conducting research on ways to enhance consumer interests, and making consumer policy recommendations.

Institutions of higher learning also contributed to the growth of consumerism in Korea. In the 1980s, Seoul National University instituted a doctoral program in consumer science and taught consumer science at both the undergraduate and graduate levels. Consumer education was also added to the curriculum of many middle and high schools. In 1990 the Korean Society of Consumer Studies was established, focusing on developing a knowledge base that the consumer movement could use in the development and advocacy of consumer policy.

Current Challenges

Consumerism has risen in the 1990s as a result of new economic conditions that warrant a fresh examination of sellers' relationship to buyers. In the past, the Korean market has been a seller's market with few incentives for sellers (either private or public) to serve consumer interests. This seller orientation is changing as the consumer movement becomes more vocal and government policymakers take greater interest in consumer issues.

One challenge faced by the Korean consumer movement relates to international trade. Import restrictions impose high costs on consumers—not just higher prices, but also reduced consumer choice and reduced incentives for the domestic industry to meet consumer needs and wants. With the recent global trend toward freer trade, especially the Uruguay Round of GATT, the Korean sellers' domination of the domestic market is being challenged by importers.

Consumers may eventually benefit from reduced trade barriers, but increased trade brings new problems. For example, consumers are sometimes confused by the breadth of choices, which makes it even more important for the Korean consumer movement to provide accurate and relevant consumer information. Consumer concerns about the safety of imported products have also grown. In 1990 the lack of proper testing for imported food products became an issue, and in 1993 the hazards of pesticides in farm products were widely publicized.

Another issue of concern to Korean citizens is overconsumption stimulated by newly imported products. The argument is that these products encourage overspending and discourage savings, endangering the financial condition of individual consumers and the nation as a whole.

The possibility of Korean reunification also raises challenges for the consumer movement. Reunification with North Korea remains a goal for many Koreans, but its possible side-effects are of concern, and could lead to a number of consumer problems. Moreover, the inexperience of North Korean consumers could make them susceptible to exploitation. Conversely, South Korean consumers would want assurance that products from North Korea meet the levels of safety and quality to which they are accustomed.

A final challenge involves overcoming the centralization of the Korean consumer movement in Seoul. Currently one-quarter of the Korean population lives in the Greater Seoul area, where the nation's political, economic, and cultural activities are concentrated. However, the Korean government is planning to decentralize administration to encourage more balanced local development, which could encourage the development of local consumer groups to address the everyday problems of local consumers.

— Kee-Choon Rhee, Jinkook Lee

Readings

Rhee, Kee-Choon (1988). *Consumer Education.* Seoul: GyoMoonSa.

Song, Bo Kyung, and Jae Ok Kim (1987). *Consumer Movement.* Seoul: Citizens Alliance of Consumer Protection of Korea.

Spanish Consumer Movement

The Spanish consumer movement is relatively recent; its origins are found in the regime that preceded the 1976 democratic reforms. In 1962, under the auspices of the National Movement (an amalgamation of political forces that supported Franco's authoritarian regime), housewives' associations were created on a provincial level. The Spanish consumer movement as it is known today, however, began after Franco's death in 1975, when King Juan Carlos presided over the creation of democratic institutions of government.

History

A variety of political and economic circumstances—recognition of the right of free association, the State's new territorial organization, incorporation of Spain in what is today the European Union, improvements in living conditions and consumption patterns, and the appearance of new demands in Spanish society—spurred the movement's growth. In December 1975, the first consumer organization independent from the preexisting regime was constituted: the Organización de Consumidores y Usuarios. Its creator was Antonio García-Pablos, who abandoned Franco's Internal Commercial and Consumption Council both because of its ineffectiveness in protecting the consumer interest and because he wanted to establish an independent, privately financed consumer association.

The semigovernmental housewives' associations, in existence since 1968, modified their articles of association in 1977 to transform themselves into the Federación Española de Amas de Casa, Consumidores y Usuarios. Later, the Unión Cívica de Consumidores y Amas de Hogar was established by Margarita Font Melis and the current president, Margarita Fernández de Lis, as a unit of the federation. This evolution was apparently endorsed by the favorable attitude (at least formally) of the new Spanish legal system toward consumer organizations. Specifically, Section 2 of Article 51 of the 1978 Spanish Constitution essentially establishes that public authorities, both national (the State) and regional (the Autonomous Regions), must encourage consumer organizations and attend to them in matters affecting consumers. In 1979 the Asociación General de Consumidores, originating from the old Unión Nacional de Cooperativas, was created to serve as a collective of consumer cooperatives.

In the early 1980s, Spain witnessed an explosion of consumer organizations, fostered by the Autonomous Regions as well as by the political parties and trade unions. Consumer protection was discovered to attract voters, especially after the 1981 tragedy involving adulterated cooking oil in which the government's regulatory apparatus was shown to be a failure. Two years later, from eleven independent associations based in the Autonomous Regions the Confederación Estatal de Consumidores y Usuarios was created. In addition, the Unión de Consumidores de España was formed in 1984 under the auspices of the Spanish Workers Socialist party and the socialist trade union, the General Union of Workers.

Despite all this activity, the establishment of State regulations specific to consumer organizations did not occur until July 1984. As part of the General Consumer Protection Act, Chapter VI is dedicated to the right of consumers to be consulted and participate, through their organizations, in the development of consumer policy. In July 1990 this chapter was further developed by Royal Decree 825, in which the State's legal statute regarding consumer associations was established, the Census of Consumers and Users Associations and Consejo de Consumidores y Usuarios (Consumers and Users Council) were regulated, and the conditions enumerated under which consumer associations could access certain benefits granted by Spanish law (e.g., subsidies, membership in consultative bodies, and exemption from certain legal fees in case of litigation).

Organizational Features and Activities

The consumer organizations in Spain are diverse. Some are general, focusing on a broad range of consumer issues, or sectoral, devoted to a single issue such as banking services. Others are private associations, such as consumer cooperatives, subject to Private Law, or they may be governmental, operating at either the level of the State or the Autonomous Regions (this point was clarified by the Constitutional Court in its Decision 15 of January 25, 1989). Regardless of their private or public status, these organizations must operate in a democratic fashion.

The consumer associations are empowered to bring legal actions in the courts in matters such as misleading advertising and unfair methods of competition. Depending on the nature of the claim and the type of organization, they can take advantage of various benefits (e.g., exemption from court fees).

Currently, several consumer organizations are national in scope. In addition to those already mentioned, the Federación de Consumidores y Usuarios Independientes (Federation of Users and Independent Consumers) was established in 1986, emerging from fifteen independent associations in diverse Autonomous Regions.

These associations all participate, to a greater or lesser extent, in the global consumer movement and especially in the European Union, either maintaining collaborative relations with consumer associations in other EU member states or participating in several bodies that represent consumer interests (such as the European Office of Consumer Unions, Consumers Consultation Council, and Economic and Social Committee). The Spanish consumer organizations also participate in international bodies such as Consumers International.

Problems and Challenges

Spanish consumer associations are advancing, albeit slowly, on the road to consolidation. The absence of a unified, tightly coordinated movement is not explained entirely by the relatively late development of the Spanish consumer movement. The sheer number of organizations is a barrier; as of the end of 1993, there were 230. Although the total number of members is estimated to be about 1.7 million, many organizations have few members. To a great extent this low affiliation rate is due to the weak structure of Spanish civil society, especially the lack of a tradition of participation in private, voluntary associations. Further, the existence of some consumer associations links directly to the availability of government subsidies. In fact, it is possible that some associations—the so-called phantom associations—have been created for the main purpose of obtaining subsidies.

Nor is the prominent Consejo de Consumidores y Usuarios exempt from criticism. Established under public law, the council is the State's major body for the representation and consultation of Spanish consumers. It is accused of ineffectiveness because it excludes some of the largest consumer associations (e.g., Organización de Consumidores y Usuarios), which do not meet the requirements of the 1990 Royal Decree 825. Royal Decree 2211, issued December 1995, attempts to improve both the representative nature and structure of the council. Regarding representation, consumer associations and public bodies of the Autonomous Regions now have access to the council, and the requirements for membership by registered associations have been softened. In terms of structure, specialized commissions have been created within the council. Despite these changes, the main reason for the council's ineffectiveness as a representative body has not been faced.

Although Spain is a member of the European Union, the overall priority accorded to consumer protection policy at the national level is low compared to many other policies. This explains the late incorporation of European Community directives on consumer protection and the incomplete development of the 1984 act. The shortcomings of Spain's consumer protection legislation are manifest, especially in facing new problems (e.g., teleshopping and time-share ownership) or problems of specific groups (e.g., the elderly and children). The lack of protection for Spanish consumers is not solely due to deficiencies in the laws, but also to lack of enforcement of legislation. At the root of this problem is the generalized lack of information and education of Spanish consumers despite the efforts of administrations and consumer associations (the publication of the magazine *Ciudadano* comes to mind), insufficient government control and inspection (usually because of a lack of resources), and the scarcity of consumer association personnel trained in consumer protection matters.

Finally, steps are being taken to facilitate the resolution of consumer conflicts by means of an arbitration system whose procedures were finalized in 1993. Consumer associations take part by having representatives on some of the arbitration panels. Nevertheless, the effectiveness of the system is limited by the fact that sellers can choose not to submit to it.

— Manuel-Angel López Sánchez,
Pedro José Bueso Guillén

Readings

López Sánchez, Manuel-Angel (1994). "Implementation of EEC Consumer Protection Directives in Spain." *Journal of Consumer Policy.* 17: 83–100.

Rodriguez-Cano, Bercovitz, and R. y Salas Hernandez [ed.] (1992). *Comentarios a la Ley General para la Defensa de los Consumidores y Usuarios.* Madrid: Civitas. 485–640.

State and Local Consumer Affairs Offices

State and local government consumer offices first appeared in the late 1800s and early 1900s when some state legislatures passed laws guaranteeing the accuracy of weights and measures in the sale of goods. However, state, city, and county consumer protection offices with wide-ranging authority to prevent deceptive trade practices were not created until the late 1950s. Most were established during the 1970s, and by 1995 there were approximately 250 agencies.

This growth resulted in large part from a Federal Trade Commission (FTC) initiative that encouraged states and localities to enact laws to protect the public from deceptive and unfair trade practices. These laws mirror those enforced by the FTC and are frequently referred to as "Mini-FTC Acts." The FTC was motivated in part by a desire to give power and responsibility to the states and localities as a way to save money for the federal government, which at the time was engaged in the costly Vietnam War. Local officials were motivated by injustices they saw in the marketplace and a desire to redress the imbalance of power between businesses and consumers.

These agencies vary greatly in size and authority, ranging from single-person offices, whose responsibility is primarily mediation of complaints, to large departments with hundreds of employees responsible for enforcing many consumer protection laws and regulations. Some states have consumer protection divisions at both state and local levels; other states offer little, if any, assistance to consumers. Many of these divisions are located in the office of the state attorney general.

Although differences exist, these offices have many things in common. Most handle individual consumer complaints and implement consumer/merchant education programs. Many administer Mini-FTC Acts, license selected businesses, administer cable television franchises, and advocate the consumer interest before Congress and state and local legislatures.

Complaint Handling

Most state and local consumer agencies handle a large volume of consumer complaints. Automotive and home improvement complaints are typically the most numerous, although changing technologies are giving rise to new complaints against telemarketers and computer-generated and related businesses.

Complaints received by these government agencies range widely. For example, a homeowner complained that he was being evicted from his own home. An investigation showed that he had fallen prey to a dishonest refinancing scheme in which he unknowingly signed over the title to his house. In another case, a student who had enrolled in a vocational school offering technical medical training and had paid tuition of $5,000 in advance sought help when he was asked to leave the school for poor performance but was refused any tuition reimbursement. The agency found that the school had no screening procedure for admission and knew, or should have known, that this student was not equipped to benefit from training. A used-car purchaser complained after her car experienced numerous mechanical breakdowns. A certified automotive technician employed by the consumer protection agency found that, before its sale, the car had been seriously damaged. Another consumer was surprised when his request for mortgage financing was turned down on the basis of a bad credit rating. An investigation showed that another company had wrongly reported unsubstantiated debts, which adversely affected the consumer's credit. People who are especially vulnerable, such as the elderly and those not fluent in English, are frequently the targets of unscrupulous merchants.

Consumer agency staffers who handle complaints first attempt to persuade the parties to reach a mediated settlement. Should this prove impossible, agencies pursue a variety of alternatives, depending on the scope of their legal authority and their analysis of the particular case. Many agencies can issue subpoenas to uncooperative merchants and civil citations (tickets) when violations of law are clear and no further investigation is needed. Administrative adjudicative hearings and arbitration proceedings are sometimes available to bring cases to closure; the latter usually require that both parties agree to be bound by the decision rendered. Small claims court is often an option; some offices not only refer consumers to these courts but assist them in filing and presenting their cases.

Agencies with substantial enforcement powers are better able to mediate complaints successfully. Volunteer mediators and arbitrators are often used to resolve consumer-merchant disputes and augment professional staff resources. When patterns of deceptive trade practices are found, agencies move beyond individual complaint handling and use other means to prevent these marketplace problems (and resulting complaints).

Consumer and Merchant Education

Consumer education is the most frequently used preventive activity. Telephone advice lines, brochures, pamphlets, speeches, press releases, television and radio shows, and computer bulletin boards provide information and advice to the public on a wide range of topics such as leasing a car, buying a house, establishing credit, choosing a contractor, or filing an action in small claims court. This information is usually free, but some agencies with shrunken budgets are now charging for printed materials and telephone advice, the latter by use of a 900 number. Other agencies suffering budget cuts have been forced to discontinue services offered through 800 numbers.

One of the most popular information services is public disclosure of merchant complaint records. Not only are consumers supplied with useful information, but such records often lead to early settlement of disputes by businesses that value their reputation and seek to avoid establishing a bad record.

Merchant education is also an important function carried out by many agencies. These offices help merchants understand their legal responsibilities by issuing advisories about new legislation or organizing classes to explain existing laws.

Law Enforcement

Most strong agencies administer a Mini-FTC Act and use the many law enforcement tools provided by such consumer protection legislation. Often, these offices are executive-branch agencies that report to a governor, mayor, or county executive; others are located in the offices of state attorneys general or attached to the office of the local district attorney.

Mini-FTC Acts contain broad language prohibiting business practices that are misleading or deceptive. Examples include failure to honor warranties, failure to disclose important information, and false statements in advertising. To investigate allegations of law violations, agencies have subpoena power. To remedy violations, they can seek civil penalties (usually between $500 and $5000 per violation), restitution for injured consumers, and an agreement or court order to cease the offending practices.

These powers are illustrated in the following case, in which an office filed a lawsuit resulting in a $2.6 million settlement against a car dealer. The suit alleged that the dealer had engaged in a variety of deceptive trade practices, including selling damaged and used vehicles as new, requiring consumers to purchase a package of so-called dealer installed accessories at unconscionably high prices, and charging consumers for many accessories that were never installed or were installed by the manufacturer and therefore already included in the vehicle's sticker price. The lawsuit also charged that defendants violated the law by engaging in numerous false and deceptive advertising and financing practices. The settlement provided restitution for consumers and reimbursed the jurisdiction for its investigative expenses. In addition, the dealer agreed that he would not own, operate, manage, or be employed by any vehicle dealerships in the jurisdiction for a period of ten years.

State attorneys general sometimes bring multistate actions to enforce consumer protection laws. In one such case, twenty-six states joined in a lawsuit against a large mortgage lender that had overcharged homeowners' escrow accounts. The company settled the lawsuit, agreeing to refund approximately $150 million to nearly 1 million mortgage holders across the country. It also agreed to pay $520,000 in legal costs to the states and change its escrow account practices.

Advocacy

Many consumer protection offices identify potentially deceptive practices that are widespread. To address these abuses they develop corrective legislation, then actively support this legislation in their state and local legislatures. Other offices are more passive, but are frequently called upon to comment on legislation initiated by elected officials. Often such consumer protection legislation is developed to address problem industries. For example, high-pressure sales tactics by some members of the health spa industry caused states and localities to adopt legislation giving consumers a certain number of days within which to cancel contracts, auto repair complaints gave rise to laws requiring shops to make certain disclosures to consumers, and auto manufacturers' reluctance to honor warranties resulted in the passage of "lemon laws" requiring manufacturers to fix defective cars within a certain number of attempts or buy back the vehicle. The consumer protection agencies enforce these laws, which are helpful in solving complaints and preventing problems.

Some agencies testify before Congress on consumer issues and participate in federal rulemaking, especially those of the FTC and Consumer Product Safety Commission (CPSC). Because state and local agencies hear from many individuals with problems, they are valuable sources of information to federal elected and appointed officials. These agencies also sometimes challenge attempts to erode important federal consumer protections.

Licensing and Other Responsibilities

Some state and local consumer protection offices license businesses. Auto repair shops, towing companies, home improvement contractors, new-home builders, and landlords are examples of businesses often subject to these licensing requirements. Licensure sometimes requires proof of technical competency and financial ability, and often establishes certain rules under which the licensed business must operate. It also brings in revenue to pay for regulation and, through license revocation or suspension for continued violation of consumer laws, represents an effective enforcement tool.

Some offices oppose these licensing responsibilities as not related closely enough to their mission of law enforcement in the area of consumer protection. To others, it is an ongoing and accepted government function that complements and supports their consumer protection mission.

Weights and measures programs have been established in every state to ensure accuracy and fairness in the marketplace by testing devices, checking scanners for verification of pricing accuracy, and inspecting a variety of products, including petroleum derivatives and prepackaged goods. In some jurisdictions, these weights and measures programs exist within the consumer protection agency.

A few consumer offices are charged with representing the consumer's interest before utility commissions with regard to rates and other matters. These offices often hire or contract with technical staff to help them carry out these duties.

Consumer protection agencies may have responsibilities for franchising cable television providers and overseeing these franchises. A few are also assigned the task of producing programming on the government cable television station.

Not infrequently, consumer affairs offices enforce laws intended to address community problems unrelated to product purchases. For example, they may be required to regulate the involuntary towing of cars from private property.

Cooperation with Other Agencies

Cooperation between consumer agencies and other law enforcement authorities, and among consumer agencies, is common and becomes increasingly important as resources dwindle. For example, many offices work closely with the local police, Federal Bureau of Investigation, and postal authorities to combat serious white-collar crimes. The consumer agencies are often the first to hear from victims of a scam, while the law enforcement authorities can offer investigative resources and the threat of large fines and possible jail time for lawbreakers. Interagency cooperation is facilitated by the National Association of Consumer Agency Administrators (NACAA) and the National Association of Attorneys General (NAAG) through conferences, publications, and multistate law enforcement actions.

The future of consumer agencies is uncertain. On the one hand, they enjoy widespread support, according to a 1995 survey conducted by the Opinion Research Corporation for NACAA. Agency surveys report satisfaction rates between 85 and 90 percent for those filing complaints. Yet, despite this consumer support, some consumer agencies have recently been shut down, and others have experienced budgetary cutbacks. This weakening of some agencies reflects factors including the current anti-government and pro-business climate, diminishing financial resources for government, and the lack of an organized consumer constituency. If abuses against consumers increase substantially, however, the public may insist that elected officials strengthen these consumer offices.

— Barbara B. Gregg

See also

Deceptive, Unfair, and Unconscionable Sales Practices; Disputes and Dispute Resolution; Licensure; National Association of Consumer Agency Administrators; State Attorneys General.

Reading

Richardson, S. Lee (1995). "State and Local Consumer Protection." In Kenneth J. Meier and E. Thomas Garman, eds. *Regulation and Consumer Protection*. Houston: DAME Publications, Inc. 393–406.

State and Local Consumer Organizations

Before the 1960s, few state or local consumer organizations advocating the consumer interest were well established. In that decade and the succeeding one, however, hundreds of grassroots groups were organized to promote individual and collective consumer interests. Many of them, particularly those addressing mainly economic issues, are still active in the 1990s.

Historical Overview

During this country's first two centuries, individuals or small groups occasionally protested seller practices, but these spontaneous protests were neither organized nor continuous. Not until the late nineteenth century, when the expansion of cities and the development of national markets helped create the conditions for consumerism, did consumer advocates and consumer groups emerge.

Between 1891 and 1903, state-based consumer leagues were organized in twenty states. Their highest priority was to improve the working conditions of women and children. The leagues urged consumers to purchase products made only by producers with adequate working conditions. They lobbied for legislation that would curtail child labor, limit the workweek, and improve workplace conditions. These groups also supported the establishment of pure food laws to address problems identified by scientist Harvey Wiley and muckrakers such as Upton Sinclair. Their efforts culminated not only in the establishment of some state and local protections, but also in the passage by Congress of the Pure Food Act in 1906.

During the first half of the twentieth century, much grassroots consumer activism was undertaken by women's groups. Especially in the 1930s and 1940s, members of organizations such as the General Federation of Women's Clubs, National League of Women Voters, National Women's Trade Union League, American Association of University Women, American Home Economics Association, National Congress of Parents and Teachers, and League of Women Shoppers initiated most grassroots advocacy against business abuses and in support of consumer reforms. Their actions ranged from voicing complaints against individual sellers to lobbying for reforms such as accurate textile labeling.

Often this activism resulted from specific consumer concerns, and practical goals were sought and action carried out by individuals or ad hoc coalitions. A typical grassroots initiative was the District of Columbia protest against high milk prices in the late 1930s and early 1940s. To assist farmers, the Roosevelt administration proposed, and Congress approved, a variety of agricultural support programs. One created milk marketing orders to stabilize milk prices at a level that would provide producers with adequate incomes. However, these prices were too high for many low- and moderate-income households, and individuals belonging to a variety of women's groups in Boston, New York, and the District of Columbia organized milk committees to seek lower prices through reduced markups of wholesale prices.

The Consumer Milk Committee of the District of Columbia was established in 1938 by representatives of the Women's Trade Union League, League of Women Shoppers, League of Women Voters, Federation of Women's Clubs, and other groups. Individual members were charged modest dues to raise funds to print brochures and cover other expenses. One of the committee's first activities was comparing District milk prices with those in four other cities, then publicizing the finding that District prices were the highest. When in 1939 the U.S. Department of Agriculture organized a hearing on the District's Milk Marketing Agreement, the Milk Committee testified that wholesale and retail prices were too high and offered several proposals to increase milk affordability. As a result of related press coverage and additional committee efforts, a local dairy and grocery chain lowered their milk prices, and a milk relief program was established by District commissioners.

For the next several years, the Milk Committee sought to open up local markets to nonlocal milk, thus forcing lower prices, and to persuade the Department of Agriculture to lower wholesale prices. After World War II, the newly created Washington Committee for Consumer Protection continued to advocate consumer interests on milk issues.

Recent Activism

Only in the 1960s and 1970s, however, did grassroots consumer activism become a powerful force in our society. In this period, hundreds of state and local consumer groups were established to assist individuals and influence public policy. In 1969 a survey by Consumers Union found 38 state or local consumer groups. By 1983 a survey by the Consumer Federation of America (CFA) identified nearly 400 organizations. By 1992 another CFA survey reported that the number of groups exceeded 400.

These organizations were part of a larger social movement. Grassroots consumer leaders drew inspiration from various sources including the civil rights movement, the antiwar movement, the labor movement, and Ralph Nader. However, their principal impetus to action was concern about specific local and state consumer problems they often experienced, and a determination to solve them.

Most state and local groups performed at least one of three general functions: complaint resolution, consumer education and information dissemination, and lobbying and regulatory intervention to influence government decisions affecting consumers. Many of these groups concentrated their work in a single product area. In the 1983 survey by CFA, 391 state and local advocacy groups reported the following priority areas: utilities (175), health (106), housing (95), food (63), energy (38), banking (27), taxation (24), and transportation (15).

Grassroots consumer groups shared several important characteristics. First, all were completely or largely autonomous. If they were part of a national network with a national office, the state or local groups exercised more influence over the national office than it did over them. Second, nearly all grassroots leaders believed that government had a critically important role to play in consumer protection, including complaint resolution, enactment of consumer laws, issuing consumer regulations, and enforcement of these protections. Third, most groups concentrated on pocketbook concerns such as deceptive and abusive sales practices, price gouging, and defective products. The grassroots organizations usually deferred to national organizations on health and safety issues, which were more often national in scope and most effectively addressed by the federal government (the major exception to this rule was the organization of several groups by victims of unsafe products). Fourth, despite limited resources, most groups were highly visible because they received much press coverage. In fact, in the late 1960s and the 1970s, many local reporters saw themselves as consumer advocates championing the grievances of grassroots groups.

Grassroots activists and organizations also differed in many ways, including origins, goals, activities, resource levels, and degree of cooperation. An analysis of these differences suggests that several types of state and local organizations have existed.

State Advocacy Organizations

The oldest type of grassroots group is state advocacy organizations made up almost exclusively of volunteers. By the 1960s, consumers leagues—especially those in Oregon, Louisiana, Ohio, Nevada, Wisconsin, Iowa, and New Jersey—had evolved into this kind of organization. In that decade and the next they were joined by similar groups that often had the words *consumer council* in their name: Pennsylvania Citizens Consumer Council, Maryland Citizens Consumer Council, Virginia Citizens Consumer Council, North Carolina Citizens Consumer Council, Arizona Consumers Council, Rhode Island Consumers Council, Association of Massachusetts Consumers, and Idaho Consumer Association, all of which survived into the 1990s.

These organizations are usually run and supported by middle-class professionals. Many are academics, including Father Robert McEwen (Massachusetts), Lee Richardson (Louisiana, then Maryland), Currin Shields (Arizona), Helen Nelson and Jim Brown (Wisconsin), Louis Meyer (Pennsylvania), and Clinton Warne (Ohio). Others such as Dermot Shea (Massachusetts) and Phyllis Rowe (Arizona) were active for many years in state politics. The principal focus of these groups is persuading states to establish effective consumer protections. Their tactics emphasize communications with elected officials through letters, testimony, and personal conversations. They usually publish newsletters to keep their own members informed and encourage them to communicate with policymakers. To cover publication expenses and other activities, members pay annual dues and sometimes make additional contributions. Annual budgets of these groups rarely exceed a few thousand dollars.

Nearly all of these organizations joined CFA and participated in this federation for many years. Also, in the early 1970s a number of these groups organized the Conference of Consumer Organizations (COCO).

In the past three decades, one of the most effective of these organizations has been the Virginia Citizens Consumer Council (VCCC). This volunteer group was founded in 1966 by several northern Virginia housewives who banded together to protest rising meat prices. They picketed supermarkets, demanding an end to unnecessary services, such as trading stamps, that raised food prices. Since then, VCCC has served as the principal voice of Virginia consumers on a broad array of issues.

The period of greatest activity for VCCC was its first decade, when dozens of volunteers set up chapters in different areas of the state. Legal authority was vested in a board of directors, which included chapter presidents, but for practical purposes the chapters were given great autonomy to develop initiatives, which involved lobbying, regulatory intervention, litigation, complaint handling, and education. Major accomplishments include enactment of the Virginia Consumer Protection Act and the establishment of local consumer protection offices, a favorable U.S. Supreme Court decision allowing the advertising of prescription drugs, passage of a strong new-car "lemon law," successful challenges to laws restricting physician and attorney information to the public, and mandated public representation on health regulatory boards.

As a modestly funded organization dependent on volunteers, VCCC never institutionalized itself. As the volunteers of the 1970s took government consumer positions or moved on to other challenges, the group grew weaker. In 1986, VCCC was revived by Jean Ann Fox, a home economist who had served as a Pennsylvania consumer protection official. Fox quickly established herself as a presence in the statehouse, lobbying successfully for reforms ranging from lower credit life insurance prices to tougher regulation of home contractors to the strengthening of Virginia's consumer protection law. With a budget rarely exceeding $30,000, under Fox's leadership VCCC also conducted many consumer price surveys and published guides to various services. In recognition of her capability and contributions, both Consumers Union and Consumer Federation of America elected her to leadership positions within their respective organizations.

Local Consumer Action Groups

A second type of grassroots organization is local consumer action groups that seek to organize consumers to achieve social change. These organizations include Consumers Education and Protective Association (Philadelphia), Consumer Action (formerly San Francisco Consumer Action), Chicago Consumer Coalition, Consumer Protection Association (Cleveland), Cleveland Consumer Action, Concerned Consumers League of Milwaukee, Seattle Consumer Action Network, Ft. Wayne Consumer Center, Pittsburgh Alliance for Consumer Protection, Niagara Frontier Consumer Association, and Harlem Consumer Education Council.

Most were organized in the late 1960s or the 1970s by young, college-educated activists who saw the consumer movement as part of a larger progressive movement to create a more just, democratic society. For instance, Max Weiner, the founder of Consumers Education and Protection Association, participated in leftist groups in the 1940s and 1950s. Ken McEldowney of San Francisco Consumer Action and Stephen Brobeck of Cleveland Consumer Action were active in Students for a Democratic Society in the 1960s. Many of these organizations, especially those with self-help complaint-handling groups, recruited members from nearly all socioeconomic groups.

Many of these organizations were influenced by the complaint-organizing model first developed by Consumers Education and Protective Association (CEPA). CEPA organized consumers by requiring that those with complaints participate in the resolution of the grievances of others as a condition of receiving help with their own problem. The method of resolution included a complaint letter stating the consumer's grievance and requested settlement, followed by a delegation of CEPA members to discuss the grievance with the merchant, followed by the organizing of weekly "educational pickets" until the merchant agreed to resolve the problem. Cleveland Consumer Action has used this complaint resolution method for the past twenty-five years, and for at least one year, so did the Harlem Consumer Education Council, Seattle Consumer Action Network, Concerned Consumers League of Milwaukee, Ft. Wayne Consumer Center, Pittsburgh Alliance for Consumer Protection, and Consumer Action.

However, most local action groups undertake a broad range of advocacy and educational activities. For the past twenty-five years, for example, Consumer Action has sought to influence public policy decisions affecting consumers at the local and state levels. For most groups, consumer education is also a priority. As well as undertaking traditional educational activities—publishing a newsletter and pamphlets, organizing workshops, and establishing information hotlines—many of these organizations communicate with consumers through such nontraditional methods as picketing and making "news" to be reported by the media.

Most of these local organizations employ full-time staffers and are funded largely by membership dues, government grants, and foundation grants. With the exception of the budget of Consumer Action, which now exceeds $750,000 a year, the budgets of these groups rarely exceed $50,000 a year. Yet, the influence of these organizations is often far greater than their budgets suggest, because most involved volunteers regularly contribute more than twenty hours per week.

The history of Cleveland Consumer Action (CCA) illustrates many of these points and chronicles the development of perhaps the most socially and economically diverse of the local consumer groups. The idea for this organization was brought to Cleveland by Stephen Brobeck, who learned about CEPA as a graduate student in Philadelphia. In 1971, with wife Susan Williams Brobeck and VISTA volunteer Jay Seaton, he organized a CEPA chapter in the Near West Side, an ethnically diverse community. With the assistance of other VISTAs contributed by the Legal Aid Society of Cleveland, which also advised the group and protected its right to picket, within a year the Brobecks organized a second complaint group in the largely black East Side. A year later, that group involved Robert and Sue Weaver, who later set up a third group in Cleveland Heights. Two years later, seven complaint chapters met weekly to resolve consumer complaints.

The group structured itself democratically. Although it had a board of directors, important decisions were made by all members at periodic meetings. In its heyday, the group involved more than 100 volunteers, most of whom had had a complaint resolved. Although its leaders included professionals such as the Brobecks (teachers) and the Weavers (lawyers), most were from blue-collar families. Moreover, the group was ethnically diverse: About one-third of the members were black, and Latinos, Native Americans, and recent Eastern European immigrants were also active.

In 1972 the organization—now independent of CEPA and called Consumer Action Movement—expanded its activism beyond complaint resolution. It organized a successful initiative petition campaign to establish a Cleveland Office of Consumer Affairs, and it conducted price surveys, using the results to call for improved disclosures. In 1973 several members of the group—the Weavers, Seaton and his wife Susan, and Fran Suda—set up an educational group, Citizen Action, whose principal activity was the publication of *bait&switch*, a newsletter with information on local sellers, especially the prices they charged.

In 1976, Consumer Action Movement and Citizen Action merged to form Cleveland Consumer Action. That organization, which employed full-time staffers supported by contributions and foundation grants, expanded its activities to include the publication of book-length consumer guides to local banking services, primary care physicians, and consumer complaint agencies. In 1979 and 1980, activity diminished when the Brobecks, Weavers, and Seatons moved on to other challenges. Nevertheless, the East and West Side complaint chapters continue to function into the 1990s, largely because of the leadership of committed volunteers Elizabeth West, Ruth Williams, Robert Howard, Paul Armbruster, and Bob and Irene Schiffrik.

Other Types of Organizations

In terms of size and influence, the Public Interest Research Groups (PIRGs) are the most important group of state and local consumer organizations. In the 1970s and early 1980s, PIRGs were organized on college and university campuses in more than twenty states. At the outset they were inspired by Ralph Nader and organized under the direction of Donald Ross, but they were established as independent groups controlled by local boards of directors chiefly consisting of students. In the early years, virtually all funding came from student activity fees; later, to supplement these resources, PIRGs undertook nationwide door-to-door canvassing, raising millions of dollars annually. Most canvassers and the interns who performed much of the support and research work were students. Much of the money raised paid for full-time staffers, who often were recent graduates, and the program of the groups. This program emphasized statewide advocacy on consumer, environmental, good government, and student issues. Advocacy included not only lobbying, but also grassroots networking and the release of reports that generated considerable press coverage. In part to solidify their base on college campuses, the groups also developed student services such as providing information about local products.

In the 1980s, conservative groups mounted attacks on the ability of PIRGs to receive student activity fees, sometimes succeeding. By the 1990s, although some groups struggled to maintain budgets, PIRGs in twenty states were still active, supported by several national PIRG groups: in the 1970s, the National PIRG Clearinghouse (which became National PIRG); then, throughout most of the 1980s and 1990s, the Fund for Public Interest Research, which provided technical assistance; U.S. PIRG, the lobbying arm in Washington, D.C.; and the U.S. PIRG Board of Directors, which helped run these and other national efforts.

Another type of grassroots organization, inspired by Nader and organized largely by PIRGs, is Citizen Utility Boards (CUBs). These statewide consumer utility advocacy groups were funded through a requirement that private utilities allow CUBs to use bill mailings to solicit dues-paying members. The first CUB was established in Wisconsin, and others were set up in Illinois, California, Oregon, and New York. Their chief function was to intervene in utility rate filings on behalf of residential ratepayers. The CUBS have enjoyed some success in this endeavor, claiming savings of millions of dollars in a number of individual cases.

However, CUBs never realized the potential envisioned for them by Nader and PIRG organizers, in part because other utility advocacy groups that received state funding—consumer utility counsels—were established in most states. CUBs also were weakened by a U.S. Supreme Court decision that forbids states to require utilities to give the advocacy groups access to their mailings. Those CUBs still existing either have access to certain state mailings or raise funds using conventional methods employed by other nonprofit organizations.

Another type of state consumer organization is a consumer federation that includes allied groups from the cooperative and labor communities. These federations, which were usually set up in the 1960s or early 1970s, include the Consumer Federation of California, Illinois Consumer Federation, Ohio Consumers Association, Consumer Association of Michigan, and New York Consumer Assembly. These organizations coordinated the activities of member groups in lobbying state legislatures and undertaking other consumer advocacy. Most did not prosper, however, because their nonactivist member groups usually considered consumer issues to be of secondary importance and therefore rarely made substantial financial contributions. Only in California and New York have these groups survived to the present.

Other types of state or local organizations work on some consumer issues but do not call themselves consumer groups. The most important of these organizations were affiliated with ACORN or the Citizen/Labor Energy Coalition, which later became part of Citizen Action. One independent group of this type was the Michigan Citizens Lobby, led for many years by Joseph Tuchinsky, which campaigned on many populist consumer and economic issues. As the entry on community organizations indicates, these groups have progressive goals but a community base, and usually take on issues of concern to local communities for which corporations or government can be held responsible. The state offices of the American Association of Retired Persons also work on consumer issues.

One other type of group that deserves mention is consumer groups affiliated with university law schools. Legal clinics at law schools often provide students with the opportunity to work on small consumer cases, and at a few schools a related consumer organization has been established. At George Washington University Law School, for example, John Banzhaf set up a variety of litigation groups and Don Rothschild organized Consumer Help. But the largest and most long-lived organization of this type is the Center for Public Representation, organized by several persons associated with the University of Wisconsin Law School.

Consumer boycotts sometimes lead to the creation of an organizing committee, yet these groups rarely institutionalize themselves. One exception is the Chicago Consumer Coalition, which Dan McCurry and others organized in the early 1970s to protest rising food prices; they quickly broadened its focus to include banking, communications, transportation, and other issues.

Evaluation

In 1972, Philip Sorensen submitted a perceptive analysis of state and local organizations to Consumers Union, in which his conclusions suggested that most of these groups had far to go before institutionalizing themselves. He stressed that they were poor in money, weak in technical skills ranging from lobbying to fund-raising, and highly dependent on a few leaders.

Today, these grassroots organizations have matured to a great extent. Many, especially the PIRGs, developed a significant resource base, and most of the others figured out ways to cover basic expenses, in part through CFA grants. Moreover, skill levels are fairly high. Most state and local leaders have developed expertise through many years of experience and have been assisted by national networks such as PIRG and CFA, who (with significant financial assistance from Consumers Union) perform a training function. Although the groups are still highly dependent on a relatively small number of leaders, many of these individuals are choosing to make consumer advocacy and education their life's work. In brief, despite continuing internal and external challenges, many state and local consumer organizations have succeeded in institutionalizing themselves.

Sorensen also concluded that even as early as 1972, "through complaints handled, legislation enacted, information communicated, and other accomplishments, state and local consumer organizations have made significant contributions to the ultimate consumer." By 1996 these historical contributions had become far greater. Grassroots consumer groups played a critical role in the establishment not only of hundreds of state and local consumer protections, and agencies to enforce these safeguards, but also of many federal protections and agencies. They succeeded in communicating important consumer information to tens of millions of consumers, a wide reach made possible, in large measure, through the interest of local media in reporting on consumer initiatives. In the process, these groups involved thousands of citizens in efforts to make the marketplace friendlier and more responsive to consumers. Such involvement is consistent with two historic American traditions—citizen activism and citizen participation in volunteer organizations.

Perhaps most important of all, state and local consumer organizations play an important role in the development of what may well be the most enduring contribution of the consumer movement—the creation of "consumer consciousness," the awareness by consumers that their interests are distinct from those of sellers, that they have rights in their dealings with sellers, and that they have the ability to enforce these rights. Along with the advocacy of consumer groups, this consciousness plays an essential role in the institutionalization of consumer functions in such mainstream organizations as government, the media, and even corporations. The existence of this consciousness also means that the advancement of the consumer interest does not depend entirely on consumer advocates and other professional consumerists. Most Americans have become, to a greater or lesser extent, consumer activists.

— Stephen Brobeck

See also

Association of Community Organizations for Reform Now; Center for Public Representation; Citizen Utility Boards; Consumer Action; Consumer Federation of America;

Consumer Leagues; Consumers Education and Protective Association; Public Interest Research Groups; Toward Utility Rate Normalization.

Readings

Nelson, Helen E. (1977). *A Guide to Consumer Action*. Washington, DC: U.S. Office of Consumers' Education.

Herrmann, Robert O., Edward J. Walsh, and Rex H. Warland (1988). "The Organizations of the Consumer Movement: A Comparative Perspective." In E. Scott Maynes, ed. *The Frontier of Research in the Consumer Interest*. Columbia, MO: American Council on Consumer Interests.

State Attorneys General

In recent years, state attorneys general have assumed an increasingly prominent place in the American consumer movement. Indeed, in many communities, a state attorney general is today the most visible consumer advocate, public or private. This prominence is a relatively new phenomenon; thirty years ago, the consumer protection role of attorneys general was limited and unfocused. As recently as 1980, attorneys general were almost exclusively law enforcers, with their activities concentrated primarily on the prosecution of local cases of deliberate fraud.

Today, the evolving role of attorneys general finds them performing a far broader range of consumer protection functions, from mediating individual consumer complaints to designing innovative education and prevention campaigns to helping shape the course of consumer protection policy on emerging state and national issues. As law enforcers, their influence continues to expand as the states further refine the relatively new techniques of multistate law enforcement and bring them to bear against even the largest corporations, either in collaboration with or independent of federal consumer protection agencies. Ongoing changes in the global economy, technology, and the American political landscape suggest that the role of state attorneys general will continue to evolve and grow into the twenty-first century.

Evolving Role

Attorneys general are the chief legal officers of each of the fifty states, as well as the jurisdictions of the District of Columbia, American Samoa, Guam, the Northern Mariana Islands, Puerto Rico, and the Virgin Islands. Although the office of attorney general is rooted in 700 years of Anglo-American common law, the duties and authority of the office vary markedly among the jurisdictions. Broadly speaking, each of the attorneys general provides legal advice and counsel to his or her state and its agencies, and in most instances exercises broad control over the state's litigation.

Contrary to widespread public perception, most state attorneys general do not control criminal law enforcement and prosecution within their jurisdictions; in most states, legal authority to initiate criminal cases is vested primarily, if not exclusively, in local prosecutors. Nor were attorneys general historically responsible for the legal protection of the general public. The consumer protection function of attorneys general is instead an extension of their common law responsibilities, representing both a logical outgrowth of their representation of state agencies and an explicit expansion of their powers in response to a perceived need for enhanced consumer protection.

As counsel to state agencies, attorneys general play a consumer protection role as they help client agencies fulfill mandates intended to protect the consuming public. Consumer protection responsibilities pervade the functions of such state agencies as those that regulate the insurance and banking industries, oversee food safety and public health, regulate public utilities, or license professions and occupations, to mention only a few examples. Over time, experience in these and similar areas led most states to adopt piecemeal consumer protections meant to remedy specific abuses as they were encountered. Often, responsibility for enforcing these safeguards was delegated to the attorney general. In addition, the historic common law powers of the attorney general—dating from an era when the office represented the interests of the English crown with respect to corporations, trusts, and associations—included sweeping, if seldom exercised, powers of oversight with regard to corporations, partnerships, and other legal entities. This uneven foundation enabled state attorneys general, throughout much of this century, to act for the benefit of their states' consumers on an occasional, but inconsistent, basis.

The modern role of attorneys general in consumer protection dates from the tenure of New York Attorney General Louis Lefkowitz, who began a concerted campaign against consumer frauds in the late 1950s. He relied primarily on his inherent common law powers and his authority, under the corporation laws, to seek to enjoin the activities or annul the charter of a corporation, association, or partnership that conducted its business in a persistently fraudulent manner. From this beginning, Lefkowitz gradually fashioned a full-fledged consumer protection program, winning passage of legislation expanding his enforcement powers and creating a program for redress of individual consumer problems. Soon, many other attorneys general began fledgling consumer protection programs, often stretching their vague statutory authority until they were able to demonstrate the need for more explicit consumer protections. In Minnesota, for example, Attorney General Walter Mondale became celebrated for his aggressive use of ill-defined common law powers to investigate abuses by a national charity for victims of polio and for using the limited powers available under corporation laws to pursue dishonest home improvement and door-to-door sales schemes.

By 1970 the Council of State Governments had recommended that principal authority for enforcing state consumer protection laws should usually reside with the attorneys general, and most attorneys general had established consumer protection programs, although they varied greatly in size and quality. In 1975, for example, twelve of the fifty-four attorneys general had no attorneys assigned full time to consumer protection, while six had ten or more consumer protection attorneys.

By the end of the 1970s, almost every state had adopted a basic consumer protection act, sometimes referred to as a "Little FTC Act" or UDAP (unfair and deceptive acts and practices) statute. These civil statutes tend to follow one of three general models. The first parallels provisions of the Federal Trade Commission Act in prohibiting "unfair methods of competition and unfair or deceptive acts or practices" in trade or commerce. The second prohibits "false, misleading, or deceptive acts or practices in the conduct of any trade or commerce." The third prohibits an itemized list of specified deceptive trade practices, followed by a catch-all prohibition against "any other act or practice which is unfair or deceptive to the consumer."

Under any of these statutes, the effect is similar: The attorney general is given broad power to act against almost any deceptive practice harmful to consumers. In addition, as states gain experience with a wide range of consumer problems, attorneys general help develop and enact numerous supplemental statutes necessary to address abuses encountered in specific industries. Among the most common problem areas are auto repair, home improvement, pyramid schemes, odometer tampering, landlord-tenant relations, land sales, collection practices, charitable solicitations, door-to-door sales, hearing-aid sales, prearranged funeral sales, and health clubs.

In the 1980s, state attorneys general emerged as national consumer protection leaders. In large measure, this phenomenon was a spontaneous and unexpected reaction to developments at the national level where, through much of the decade, federal consumer protections were scaled back or abandoned. With federal agencies often unable or unwilling to act—whether through lack of staff, budget, or will—state attorneys general repeatedly found themselves drawn into issues that had long been the exclusive domain of the federal government. The result was the emergence of multistate consumer protection activities—a development that quickly catapulted attorneys general into the thick of national consumer law enforcement and policy-making.

In earlier years, states occasionally cooperated in pursuit of a common objective; a prominent example was the collaboration, in the late 1970s, of more than forty states in litigation against a major automaker for substituting engines from one of its divisions into more expensive cars sold by another division. In the 1980s, however, joint investigations, negotiations, and occasionally litigation became a standard operating procedure. By pooling staff and resources, states were able to address abuses by even the largest corporations, and take on other issues previously beyond their apparent capacity to address. For example, several dozen states collaborated in settling a case of alleged fraud at the nation's largest auto transmission repair chain, and another regarding alleged odometer tampering in connection with the sale of new vehicles by a major manufacturer.

Multistate collaboration quickly moved from joint investigation of a single case to the creation of working groups to investigate industrywide problems. Beginning in the 1980s, ad hoc multistate working groups formed to study problems of airline advertising, car rental practices, ambulance safety, all-terrain vehicle safety, deceptive price advertising, health claims in food advertising, deceptive energy-saving claims, abuses under new-car "lemon laws," environmental advertising claims, deceptive pay-per-call practices, telemarketing frauds, credit reporting abuses, frauds against older consumers, sweepstakes frauds, mortgage escrow overcharging, auto leasing, health quackery, pharmaceutical marketing, and tobacco sales to children. As states gained experience with this process, they began to use multistate working groups not only to investigate specific companies but also to develop voluntary guidelines, proposals for federal reforms, or model state legislation to address industrywide problems. This process continues in the 1990s, with multistate groups increasingly combining individual enforcement actions with systematic proposals for policy reform, often developed in public dialogue with the affected businesses and other interested parties.

Consumer Protection Functions

Although law enforcement remains at the center of an attorney general's consumer protection responsibilities, in most states those responsibilities now extend to an array of related functions that continue to grow in importance as the office evolves. Among them are the resolution of consumer disputes, public outreach and consumer education, and policy and legislative advocacy.

At the heart of the attorney general's role is the duty to enforce the state's consumer protection laws. As noted previously, the laws of every state include at least one grant of sweeping consumer protection authority, as well as a series of more narrowly drawn protections. In most jurisdictions, the attorney general is also invested with broad investigative powers, enabling him or her to demand the production of documents and to take depositions or pose interrogatories before filing a civil action. When an attorney general is successful in proving violation of the consumer protection laws, the remedies available in most states are equally broad, and typically include restitution to consumer victims, such injunctive relief as may be necessary to remedy the harm done and ensure that the misconduct does not recur, monetary civil penalties to the state, and reimbursement to the state for the costs of the investigation and litigation. Because the law enforcement responsibilities of the attorneys general cover the entire spectrum of consumer transactions, the cases brought under these statutes are diverse. Frequent areas of litigation, in addition to those previously mentioned, include fraudulent telemarketing schemes, often involving phony sweepstakes or prize offers; deceptive practices in connection with the advertising, sale, or repair of cars and trucks; home repair frauds; abuses in connection with credit practices and collections; and get-rich-quick business opportunity schemes.

Most attorneys general have no legal authority to bring litigation on behalf of individual consumers. Rather, they represent the state, and their litigation is brought in the interest of the state or the public in general, though it often results in restitution to individual victims. Moreover, as attorneys general become more prominent as consumer advocates, public requests for assistance increase; in response, most states gradually develop programs for informal assistance to individual consumers who encounter problems in the marketplace.

In many states this assistance includes information, referral services, and consumer tips on many consumer issues, often offered through toll-free telephone hotlines that, in some states, handle as many as several hundred thousand calls annually. Some states also offer assistance through storefront offices or even mobile "circuit-riding" representatives. Where permitted by a state's privacy laws, these services may include information about the complaint record of particular businesses.

In more than thirty states, the office of the attorney general also accepts individual consumer complaints for voluntary mediation. Although this process depends on the goodwill and cooperation of the parties, states have found that most complaints can be resolved to the satisfaction of everyone involved. In some states, mediation programs now resolve tens of thousands of complaints and recover several millions of dollars for consumers each year. As these alternative dispute resolution programs continue to develop, some states incorporate the use of volunteers as mediators, and a few experiment with the use of arbitration mechanisms for complaint resolution.

The third element of consumer protection for most attorneys general is consumer education and information. In most states, this function evolved only as an adjunct to the attorney general's law enforcement and complaint-handling functions, but today it represents one of the areas of greatest potential growth for many offices. Driven in part by budgetary and staffing constraints, and in part by the inability of litigation to achieve meaningful remedies for many types of consumer fraud, attorneys general are increasingly concluding that the most cost-effective approach to many consumer problems may be to prevent them by creating an informed public.

Although modest in size, the information programs of the attorneys general are increasing rapidly in sophistication and scope. Almost all include print information on the most common consumer problems, ranging from simple pamphlets in some states to comprehensive books in others. Most programs also include regular newspaper columns. Many run radio or television spots as well; in recent years, a number of states have experimented with the use of television public service announcements.

In addition, attorneys general are expanding their educational efforts into less traditional channels, including the distribution of specialized newsletters, the development of specialized school curricula and other classroom-based materials and programs, and the formation of broad coalitions to conduct outreach campaigns on particular issues such as fraud against senior citizens. In some states, consumer education programs now take the form of public-private partnerships in which corporations, trade associations, consumer organizations, and others combine efforts to help raise the consumer literacy of students and other consumers. Examples of such collaborations include a statewide campaign to protect older consumers in the state of Washington; establishment of an educational foundation in North Carolina, with an emphasis on preventing telemarketing frauds; and the convening of a national "consumer education summit conference" in Minnesota. The latest area of attention for these programs is the new frontier of cyberspace, as states explore ways to make consumer information available electronically through new sites on the World Wide Web.

Given their role as law enforcers, their experience in handling individual consumer problems, and their position as independently elected officials, it is not surprising that attorneys general are emerging as prominent advocates for policies and laws to protect consumers' interests better. This advocacy takes a variety of forms. In many states, the attorney general has long been a primary source of consumer legislation. For example, attorneys general helped develop not only the basic consumer protection statutes of most states, but also many of the industry-specific statutes written in response to particular problems, such as the new-car "lemon laws" now in place in every state.

In addition, through the National Association of Attorneys General and multistate working groups, the influence of state attorneys general now extends to federal legislation and rules. Recent federal legislation addressing problems of telemarketing fraud, for example, stems largely from the problems experienced by state attorneys general in protecting their states' citizens against these long-distance scams. Similarly, many federal consumer protection rules have been shaped in large measure by the advocacy of attorneys general. Examples include the U.S. Food and Drug Administration's rule on nutritional labeling for food, the Federal Communications Commission's rule on pay-per-call telephone services, and the Consumer Product Safety Commission's rule on child-safe packaging for potentially poisonous iron supplements.

Finally, several of the most successful policy initiatives of the attorneys general focus not on formal legislative mandates but rather on framing the public debate on emerging issues. These initiatives, sometimes undertaken in conjunction with enforcement cases, typically include public hearings, written reports, and recommendations for voluntary self-regulatory measures. Such projects shape public policy and business practices concerning the charging of mortgage escrow fees, the use of environmental claims in advertising, secondhand smoke in fast-food restaurants, the sale of tobacco to children, and the repair of motor vehicles.

State attorneys general play a critical role in the protection of American consumers. Their development of coordinated multistate initiatives as tools for both law enforcement and effective advocacy assures them a central place in the consumer protection movement. Given the current emphasis on a reduced federal role in national life, in the coming decade their influence is likely to increase.

— Doug Blanke

See also

Deceptive, Unfair, and Unconscionable Sales Practices; Federal Trade Commission; State and Local Consumer Affairs Offices; State Utility Consumer Advocates.

Readings

Clayton, Cornell W. (1994). "Law, Politics and the New Federalism: State Attorneys General as National Policymakers." *Review of Politics*. 56 (3): 525–553.

Green, Mark (1989). "Filling the Deregulatory Vacuum." *The Nation*. 249 (23 October): 441ff.

State Utility Consumer Advocates

State utility consumer advocates are empowered by state laws to protect public utility ratepayers from monopoly abuses and profiteering. Acting independently of each state's public utility commission (PUC), these advocates represent ratepayers in more than forty states and the District of Columbia.

In nineteen states, state attorneys general provide utility consumer advocate representation. In twenty other states, governors appoint consumer advocate office directors with names such as consumers' counsel, public counsel, and consumer advocate. Most of these agencies were created by state legislatures after natural gas and electric prices were driven up by the energy crises of the 1970s, fueled by Arab oil embargoes, gas deregulation, and costly nuclear power plants.

Since the 1970s these advocacy agencies have saved utility consumers billions of dollars through interventions in ratemaking proceedings and through court actions. The advocates have also established legal precedents for consumer rights relating to the quality and terms of public utility service.

During the late 1970s and early 1980s, the principal role of the state advocates was to challenge requests by electric, natural gas, telephone, and water monopolies for rate hikes. This role was carried out largely by intervening in formal, economic regulatory cases before public utility commissions. More recently, the role of these advocates has expanded to include protecting consumers in the transition from highly regulated markets dominated by monopolies to less regulated markets in which utilities and other firms increasingly compete with one another. As a result, traditional advocate concerns of avoiding unfair cost of service allocations to residential ratepayers or preventing monopoly profits are shifting to new concerns about PUC economic "re-regulation" focused on consumer price stability, monitored service performance, and relaxed (or unrestrained) utility profit-taking in newly competitive markets.

National Association of State Utility Consumer Advocates

In May 1979 at a meeting in Columbus, Ohio, the National Association of State Utility Consumer Advocates (NASUCA) was established as a national organization for agencies designated by state law to act as independent ratepayer advocates. Founded to exchange ideas and improve consumer representation at the state and federal levels, NASUCA encourages greater consumer participation in the regulatory process.

NASUCA membership now includes forty-one offices of utility consumer advocates in thirty-eight states and the District of Columbia. Each fall, the annual meetings of NASUCA are held coincident with the annual convention of the state utility regulators sponsored by the National Association of Regulatory Utility Commissioners (NARUC). NASUCA also convenes a midyear meeting and a special issues conference. Policy is made by member adoption of resolutions proposed by committees representative of various regions. The association also provides educational workshops, papers, and newsletters to its members. NASUCA's national policies and activities are coordinated by a national office in Washington, D.C.

NASUCA business is directed by a strong executive committee composed of utility consumer advocates from eleven states. The diverse representation of NASUCA's leadership is best exemplified by the list of its nine national presidents: Edward Petrini, Virginia Attorney General Insurance and Utilities Regulatory Section, 1994–1996; Martha Hogerty, Missouri Office of Public Counsel, 1992–1994; Ronald Binz, Colorado Office of Consumer Counsel, 1991–1992; Donna Sorgi, Massachusetts Department of Attorney General Utilities Division, 1989–1991; David Barasch, Pennsylvania Office of Consumer Advocate, 1987–1989; Felshaw King, Utah Department of Commerce Committee of Consumer Services, 1985–1987; Steven Hamm, South Carolina Department of Consumer Affairs Division of Consumer Advocacy, 1983–1985; Jack Shreve, Florida Office of Public Counsel, 1981–1983; and William Spratley, Office of the Ohio Consumers' Council, 1979–1981.

Advocacy Role

The role of state utility consumer advocates focuses primarily on legal representation of residential and sometimes small commercial consumers in formal cases before state public utility commissions where monopoly utilities seek approval of rate increases and other policy changes. Advancing consumer policy positions by means of lawyers and experts, advocates also create public awareness and policy options for state and federal regulators and legislators.

The effectiveness of state utility consumer advocates rests largely on the credibility of their professional staff and consulting experts on legal, economic, accounting, engineering, and related issues. Because of their superior financial resources, these advocates usually exercise greater influence than consumer activists (representing low-income, environmental, nuclear safety, and other, narrower ratepayer issues) who also participate in the regulatory process.

Some critics of state utility consumer advocates claim that these offices too often face political pressures from elected officials who are lobbied by the utility companies. Others point out that many state utility consumer advocates do not receive sufficient state funds to participate effectively in regulatory processes in which utilities often spend hundreds of thousands or even millions of dollars to litigate or negotiate one case. Still others note the inability of many advocates to organize grassroots consumer involvement in regulatory issues. Despite these limitations, critics also agree that state utility consumer advocates provide relatively effective representation for utility consumers.

Other Consumer Utility Advocacy

Instead of a utility consumer advocate agency fully independent of the PUC, California and other states maintain "intervenor compensation" programs to award after-the-fact fees to grassroots consumer advocacy groups for their participation in regulatory proceedings. The Public Utilities Regulatory Policy Act of 1978 (PURPA) provides that utilities must compensate intervenors who "substantially contribute to the approval, in whole or in part, of a position advocated by such consumer[s]," concerning enumerated electric utility topics set forth in the statute, where the state provides no "alternative means" for their representation. Under the law, consumer intervenors may recover their costs by reasonable state procedures or by a civil action in state court against the utility.

According to the National Consumer Law Center, in 1995 intervenor funding for some public utility proceedings was available in thirteen states. State statutes for some intervenor funding exist in California, Colorado, Idaho, Maine, Michigan, Minnesota, Oklahoma, and Wisconsin. The Indiana Supreme Court has held that intervenors who succeed in litigating a multimillion-dollar refund to ratepayers from a utility are entitled to reasonable attorney's fees on a "common fund" theory.

In California, two nonprofit groups—Toward Utility Rate Normalization (TURN) and Utility Consumers Action Network (UCAN)—are sustained by intervenor funding. In other states—Illinois, Wisconsin, Oregon, and New York—Citizen Utility Boards (CUBs) have sought access to utility mailings to solicit paid memberships. However, a 1986 U.S. Supreme Court decision denied this access, forcing them to seek access to state government mailings or rely on more traditional fund-raising methods. As a result, each CUB has faced stiff challenges adequately funding representation of consumers before public service commissions.

— William A. Spratley

See also

Broadcast Protections; Cable Television Regulation; Citizen Utility Boards; Electricity Regulation; Natural Gas Regulation; Telephone Regulation; Toward Utility Rate Normalization.

Reading

Mayer, Robert N., Cathleen D. Zick, and John R. Burton (1989). "Consumer Representation and Local Telephone Rates." *Journal of Consumer Affairs.* 23 (2): 267–284.

Swedish Consumer Movement

The Swedish consumer movement consists of several types of voluntary nongovernmental organizations. Independent consumer organizations have as their primary goal the defense of consumer interests. They may address a broad range of consumer issues, or focus on a specific product or service (e.g., home ownership, automobiles, or bank services). Historically, however, they have not played as prominent a role in Sweden as in other countries such as the United States. More important than the independent consumer organizations are consumer cooperatives and organizations like trade unions, for which consumer matters are secondary or even tertiary interests.

Consumer organizations are only one part of a tripartite system for determining consumer policy; the other two are representatives of business and representatives of government. This corporatist system of various commissions, boards, and agencies took shape during the 1970s.

Organizational Development

During the 1940s, the main actors in the field of consumer affairs were women's associations. These organizations focused on household economic issues, trying to make household work more efficient through research, product testing, and educational activities. From the 1950s through the 1970s, voluntary consumer organizations initiated various activities, which the government quickly took over and ran. Eventually, the two central trade union organizations—the Trade Union Confederation and the Confederation of Salaried Employees—became a voice for the consumer interests of their members. Together with the Cooperative Union, these labor organizations became the main countervailing force to organized business on the governing bodies set up to address consumer issues.

In 1967 voluntary organizations initiated local activities to provide consumers with information about the price and quality of goods, educate consumers, handle consumer complaints, and survey consumer opinion. These activities resulted in the establishment of municipal consumer advisory councils, supported by the national and local governments. Nevertheless, no formal confederation of consumer organizations existed until 1986, when the Cooperative Union established a Consumer Policy Council to serve as a common forum for the Cooperative Union, the two major labor confederations, and a few other consumer cooperatives. In 1992 the Consumer Policy Council was replaced by the Swedish Consumer Council, a body comprised of twelve national voluntary organizations involved in consumer policy activities.

On the governmental side, Sweden established in 1971 the world's first consumer ombudsman as well as a Market Court. Two years later, the National Board for Consumer Policies was created, and in 1976 the board and the ombudsman were merged.

Also during the mid-1980s, other nongovernmental organizations engaged in regional and local activities such as establishing advisory councils, offering training courses for consumer ombudsmen, developing educational materials on consumer policy, and recommending consumer legislation. Both the National Board for Consumer Policies and the municipal consumer advisory authorities supported these activities.

Consumer activities have also been undertaken by organizations whose primary goals lie outside the realm of consumer protection, such as the labor federations already mentioned. Organizations representing the disabled seek to ensure accessibility to public places as well as product health and safety. Housewives' organizations launch information campaigns on prices and household financial management. Pensioners have a national organization with local representatives trained to conduct price surveys and lobby on issues such as transportation and the care of the elderly. Environmental organizations educate and inform consumers about the effects of consumption on the environment. Even sports organizations conduct projects to improve the quality of leisure products.

Current Consumer Issues

The Swedish model of consumer protection in which governmental consumer bodies are combined with consumer voluntary associations is being reevaluated. For more than a decade, the government has provided financial support for voluntary consumer organizations, and has been especially generous in support of programs providing consumer education to children. Now, however, the budgets of public agencies such as the National Board for Consumer Policies and the municipal advisory councils are being curtailed. An important question is whether voluntary organizations can continue to play their traditional role and take on even wider responsibilities in the field of consumer policy. Although their activities are increasing, their financial and human resources are limited, and in some cases have decreased in recent years.

Certain broad economic developments pose pressing consumer problems. The 1990s have been marked by recession in Sweden and the Nordic countries as a whole, and difficult economic times create a greater need for household economic advice. Freer international trade expands consumer choices, but also makes it more difficult for consumers to inform themselves. Sweden's entry into the European Union requires that it develop a strong voice if its views are to be effectively shared. Public utilities are being reorganized, creating a need for better consumer information, protection of vulnerable groups, and improved complaint handling procedures. Finally, threats to the natural environment are of increasing concern to Swedes.

Innovative Policies

Sweden is a world leader in certain areas of consumer policy. Three examples are its consumer ombudsman, aggressive antismoking policies, and strong cooperative movement.

The world's first consumer ombudsman was established in Sweden in 1971. Although the ombudsman may impose penalties in a relatively small number of situations, its primary goal is to protect the interests of consumers by encouraging business compliance with existing laws. The Swedish ombudsman serves as a model for similar national positions in Norway, Denmark, and Finland, and the general concept has spread to specific industries and individual firms in non-Nordic countries (e.g., banking and insurance ombudsmen in the United Kingdom).

Swedish efforts to address the health effects of cigarette smoking are bold and broad. The centerpiece of these efforts is a 1975 agreement negotiated between the Swedish Tobacco Branch Association and the Consumer Ombudsman. This self-regulatory agreement includes a variety of limitations on the media in which tobacco products can be advertised as well as restrictions on the content of advertising. In 1975 the Swedish government was the first in the world to pass a law requiring a rotating set of warnings on cigarette packages, a policy now found in most developed nations.

A final example of Swedish leadership in the area of consumer affairs is provided by its consumer cooperatives. Until recently at least, these cooperatives played a significant and progressive role in Sweden. Whereas consumer cooperatives in most countries operate on the fringes of the marketplace, Swedish co-ops have achieved substantial market shares in industries such as food retailing, gasoline, insurance, travel services, burial services, and housing. The co-ops not only help increase competition and lower prices, they also help introduce pro-consumer practices such as unit pricing, full refunds, self-service discounts, and limitations on nonreturnable beverage containers.

International Role and Future Prospects

The Swedish Consumer Council is the primary representative of the Swedish voluntary organizations at the level of the Nordic countries, within the European Union, and within Consumers International. Representatives of the National Swedish Board for Consumer Policies are active in many of the same international bodies, plus a variety of standard-setting bodies and the Consumer Policy Committee of the Organization for Economic Cooperation and Development.

The tripartite constellation of Swedish consumer policy results in a relatively advanced consumer protection system. Even if funding for federal consumer protection efforts remains constant or is reduced, the decentralization of consumer policy activities, involving voluntary consumer organizations in collaboration with municipal consumer agencies, is a source of strength. The number of municipalities in which joint consumer initiatives are undertaken has increased considerably in the last few years. Moreover, local and voluntary consumer organizations represent a more holistic view on consumer policy issues, addressing cultural and social aspects of consumption to a degree not possible for public agencies.

— Kai Blomqvist

Readings

Consumers International (1995). *Balancing the Scales, Part I: Consumer Protection in Sweden and the United Kingdom.* London: Consumers International.

Eklund, Per (1994). "The Effect of the EEA Agreement on Consumer Protection Interests in Sweden." *Journal of Consumer Policy.* 17: 123–134.

Hetzler, A. (1984). "Sweden's Regulation of Consumer Affairs." *Journal of Consumer Policy.* 7: 167–169.

T

Telecommunications Regulation

See Cable Television Regulation; Telephone Regulation.

Telecommunications Research and Action Center

The Telecommunications Research and Action Center (TRAC) grew out of a movement to establish an independent citizens' voice on how the public airwaves are used. During the 1970s, the National Citizens Committee for Broadcasting (NCCB) was especially visible as a leader on broadcasting issues ranging from media concentration to cigarette advertising. In 1980, NCCB changed its name to TRAC.

In May 1967 the National Citizens Committee for Public Television was formed in response to a Carnegie Commission report recommending that an organization of concerned citizens be established to improve the quality of broadcasting through furthering public television. Thomas P. F. Hoving, then director of the New York Metropolitan Museum of Art, served as chair. The committee's founder-trustees included former Federal Communications Commission (FCC) chair Newton N. Minow, known for labeling commercial television a "vast wasteland," and author Ralph W. Ellison.

The trustees were joined by other prominent figures in public life, the arts, business, education, and television to form the original committee of fifty-two members. Supported by Carnegie, Danforth, Ford, and other leading foundations, the committee became the chief source of information concerning public television and its most vocal proponent.

Largely because of the committee's work, including a much publicized *Citizens Report on the State of Public Television,* Congress appropriated monies as authorized under the Public Broadcasting Act of 1967. These funds included $10.5 million for facilities and $9 million to get the Corporation for Public Broadcasting under way.

In early 1969 the committee's board (now numbering 120) recognized that reform was needed in many areas of broadcasting, and the name was changed to the National Citizens Committee for Broadcasting. The committee became a catalyst in such areas as freeing one hour of prime time television for news reporting and other use by local stations, decentralizing network control of program content, media cross-ownership challenges, program violence, overcommercialization, and long-range funding for public broadcasting.

In January 1971, NCCB moved from New York to Washington, D.C., in order to work more closely with other public interest groups and have firsthand access to the FCC, Federal Trade Commission (FTC), and Congress. Warren Braren, the former manager of the New York Television Code Office of the National Association of Broadcasters, became NCCB's executive director. His testimony before Congress, blowing the whistle on the industry's ineffective self-regulation of cigarette commercials, effectively supported legislation banning the advertising of cigarettes on radio and television.

With Hoving still as chair, Charles Benton, president of Films, Inc., a subsidiary of Encyclopedia Britannica, became president of NCCB. The committee conducted the first international study comparing children's television programs and schedules in the United States with those aired in other countries and submitted the results to the FCC. NCCB also submitted thousands of petitions to the FCC from groups and individuals in support of specific children's television guidelines.

With more than 16,000 citizen supporters, NCCB became a clearinghouse and resource center for the exchange of information among public interest groups focusing on broadcasting and telecommunications. With funding from foundations drying up, Braren moved on to become associate director of Consumers Union, and his position was assumed by Jane Goodman, who was affiliated with the Office of Communication, United Church of Christ, a group known for its activist work in representing the public interest through legal action and regulatory interventions.

In 1974, Commissioner Nicholas Johnson left the FCC to lead NCCB. At the FCC, he had been an ardent defender of the rights of listeners and viewers to diverse information sources; he also wrote a book, *How to Talk Back to Your Television,* that provided a consumer primer on how the public could exercise their legal rights to hold television station operators to their public interest obligations.

Under Johnson's leadership, NCCB expanded its national membership organization of television viewers. It published *Access,* a monthly magazine that served as a quasi-independent journal to provide various perspectives on communications issues. NCCB also issued *Media Watch,* a newsletter to inform members of its activities and alert them to needed actions.

In this period, NCCB worked closely with public interest law firms in the communications field, mainly Citizens Communications Center. Citizens was headed by Albert Kramer, a lawyer who later served as director of the Bureau of Consumer Protection at the FTC during the Carter administration. NCCB and its members helped set the agenda for Citizens, which represented NCCB in administrative and legal proceedings.

NCCB launched several campaigns: one would require the three major networks to air at least three hours of public affairs programming weekly; another would protect the Fairness Doctrine from repeated efforts to repeal it; still another would reduce television violence; and a fourth was meant to persuade the FCC to issue rules banning the ownership by newspapers of television stations in the same markets. The latter two efforts achieved measurable successes.

In the mid-1970s, NCCB, joined by the National PTA, initiated a nationwide effort to educate the public on the potential harm of the increasing amount of gratuitous violence on American television. A national rating system was created to inform the public about the least and most violent programs on television, and for several years the networks reduced the violence in their programming.

NCCB also worked for greater diversity of information sources available to the viewer. Based on an NCCB petition, the FCC adopted rules that prohibited cross-ownership by newspapers of television outlets in the same community. Further, the rules required that existing cross-ownership be divested. NCCB defended the FCC decision in the courts, and in *NCCB v. FCC,* the Supreme Court ruled that diversity of ownership sources was a primary purpose of the Communications Act of 1934.

In 1978, Ralph Nader became chair of the organization, with Johnson staying on as head of the organization's lobbying arm, National Citizens Communications Lobby (NCCL). Samuel A. Simon, a Nader activist and an original member of the 1970 Public Interest Research Group, was appointed executive director. Under Simon's leadership, the NCCB broadened its focus to include telephone and telecommunications issues. It petitioned the FCC for a $100 million refund from AT&T

based on overearnings in 1978. In a case that lasted nearly seven years, NCCB established several important precedents. After the organization sued the FCC for failing to act on its petition, the Court of Appeals ruled that, if the FCC failed to act on a petition within a reasonable time, it would treat this failure as a decision and would take up the case directly.

In the meantime, NCCB launched several new programs in the telephone and technology fields. In 1980 it sponsored the first meeting on the implications of new information technologies for consumers. Working with the White House Conference on Libraries, NCCB hosted a preconference seminar on the implications of new digital information services for consumers. NCCB also published several books, including *Reverse the Charges, How to Save $$$ on Your Telephone Bill,* which was later distributed by Book-of-the-Month Club. Simon became a national spokesman for consumer interests in telephone and technology.

NCCB continued working against television violence and promoting the rights of listeners and viewers. It helped launch a new organization, the National Coalition on Television Violence, which created a monitoring service of network programming based on violent content. As telephone industry changes accelerated, NCCB increasingly worked on telecommunications issues, and in recognition of this shift, the organization changed its name to the Telecommunications Research and Action Center (TRAC). TRAC board members included influential media activists such as Everett Parker, Albert Kramer, Nicholas Johnson, Michael Botein, Wilhemina Cooke, Andrew J. Schwartzman, and Kathy Bonk.

TRAC's program included advocacy, education, and legal intervention. The organization participated before Judge Harold Greene during the supervision of the breakup of AT&T and was the primary consumer witness before Congress in their oversight of the breakup. Later, TRAC led a campaign for legislation to protect consumers against abuses by Alternative Operator Services. After failing to persuade the FCC to abolish these abuses, TRAC helped Congress draft legislation that limited rates and required consumer notification of prices and practices.

TRAC maintains an active legal program. In addition to helping obtain the $100 million refund from AT&T, the organization established new rights for consumers when it sued Allnet, an upstart long-distance company, for rate discrimination. In a landmark decision, the U.S. Court of Appeals held, for the first time, that in some circumstances associations could represent their members in actions for damages.

TRAC also launched education initiatives with the publication of *TeleTips,* a rate comparison chart to help consumers select telephone companies during the growth of long-distance competition. It produced a video based on its book *Reverse the Charges,* and co-founded the Tele-Consumer Hotline with the Consumer Federation of America. From 1984 to the present, the hotline has advised individual consumers about telephone services.

When Simon set up his own consulting firm in 1986, he resigned as executive director of TRAC. He continued to oversee the organization, which was housed in the offices of his firm, but without his full-time attention, the organization reduced its level of activity considerably, emphasizing mainly consumer education.

— Samuel A. Simon

See also

Broadcast Protections; Telephone Regulation.

Readings

Cole, Barry, and Mal Oettinger (1978). *Reluctant Regulators: The FCC and the Broadcast Audience.* Reading, MA: Addison-Wesley Publishing Co.

Mayer, Caroline E. (1986). "Simon Says: Enough." *Channels of Communications.* 5 (March): 16.

Telemarketing Regulation

Telemarketing is not a new phenomenon, but it is increasing and is likely to expand well into the next century. Industry analysts estimate that approximately $500 billion worth of products and services are currently sold by telephone, and annual revenues from telemarketing sales operations are expected to reach $1 trillion by the year 2000. Nationwide, approximately 3.4 million people are presently employed in telemarketing, not just as salespeople but also as market researchers, solicitors for nonprofit organizations, and other workers.

Although the vast majority of telemarketers represent legitimate businesses, a small but significant number of telemarketing operations deceives or defrauds consumers. As the number of telemarketing operations increases, so does the number of fraudulent operators who conduct various scams by telephone against the public.

Consumer protection laws address two distinctly separate consumer issues in telemarketing: nuisance and fraud. The nuisance aspect of telemarketing regulation recognizes that consumers deserve protection from certain types and times of telephone solicitations. The fraud aspect of telemarketing, however, is more destructive, and therefore the primary focus of this entry.

Telemarketing has been practiced since the 1920s. Because of labor shortages during World War II, telemarketing was a popular replacement for door-to-door sales. During the 1970s, steeply rising fuel prices rendered widespread door-to-door solicitations impractical and led to a resurgence in telemarketing by retailers who saw it as a more cost-efficient means of marketing their products.

Over the years, the public has become more accustomed to telemarketing solicitors. Credit card and sight draft payment options—as well as technological advances such as facsimile communications, speed dialing, and automated dialing equipment—have contributed to the success of telemarketing as an efficient means of reaching potential customers and conducting transactions. Because of the low overhead costs associated with telemarketing, retailers are often able to offer products and services at discounted prices as well as provide busy working couples with the advantage of shopping from home. Low overhead cost, combined with the readiness of many consumers to buy by telephone, results in the growth of telemarketing operations.

Telemarketing Crime

"Boiler rooms," as they are commonly called, are usually just a crew of telemarketers, equipped with little more than desks and telephones, who sell inferior and overpriced—or nonexistent—products and services. Fraud in telemarketing is nothing new; in fact, the term *boiler room* stems from the earliest fraudulent telemarketing operations that worked from the boiler rooms of basements to avoid detection. Modern boiler room–type scam operations, however, usually work in rented office space that can be quickly vacated when state or federal authorities pursue related consumer complaints.

Victims of telemarketing fraud are typically contacted in one of two ways. The first method involves an initial telephone contact with the buyer. This is accomplished either by "cold" calling, where the telemarketer makes many indiscriminate calls to the public at large, hoping to sell to just a fraction, or by calling from lists of leads purchased from information brokers. These lists may include senior citizens exclusively, past customers of other telemarketing operations (legitimate or otherwise), or any one of many other target groups of an identified profile for a particular scam. The second method of initial contact involves using an advertisement or a mail offer to persuade the potential victim to make the call. Although more expensive per contact than cold calling, this method provides the telemarketer with a potentially more reliable revenue source because those who call already have some interest in making a purchase.

Anyone is a potential victim of telemarketing fraud. Even the most cautious consumers, who insist on checking references and various other assurances of legitimacy, can become victims. A truly disproportionate number, however, are senior citizens. Because they are generally more trusting than others, more easily persuaded, available during day-time hours, and more reluctant to appear rude by hanging up on solicitors, seniors are often specifically targeted by fraudulent telemarketers. Also, elderly people typically make the worst possible witnesses for state or federal investigators because they often cannot remember precisely what they were told or promised.

Law Enforcement Problems

By far the single most difficult obstacle in combating telemarketing fraud is that it so frequently goes unreported. Victims feel foolish for having misplaced their trust, often preferring to absorb their losses quietly instead of informing authorities. Yet, a small number of reported complaints is usually inadequate to invoke civil injunctions or criminal prosecutions. Although investigators may strongly suspect that the fraudulent operator has victimized many more individuals, a small number of reported complaints is usually insufficient to prove fraudulent intent. Wrongdoers will often explain that the complaints result from some misunderstanding on the part of the victims; particularly when they make a good-faith effort to resolve the known complaints, the investigation will end, allowing the fraudulent operation to continue without penalty.

Investigators have no way of identifying additional victims, so they must rely solely on those who come forward and file formal complaints. Only with a significant number of consumer complaints can investigators be granted injunctions and/or criminal indictments against the perpetrators. This often means that fraudulent telemarketing operations, even when identified and located, continue to victimize consumers. While investigators build their case, which may often take a year or more, the fraudulent operation continues to defraud others. The operation may even relocate and assume a new name, further frustrating enforcement efforts.

Telemarketing scams typically fall into one of two categories—low loss and high loss. The first category, low loss, generally consists of a large number of victims who each have lost a relatively small amount of money. These scams usually involve the sale of inferior and overpriced merchandise. Popular low-loss scams include the sale of office supplies, perfumes, and vitamins, the actual retail value of which may be difficult, if not impossible, to determine accurately. Although victims often recognize that they have been misled, they usually do not consider it worthwhile to file a formal complaint. Thus, low-loss scams are vastly underreported and may operate undetected in the same location for an extended period of time. Low-loss scams do not get a lot of repeat business, but there is no shortage of potential new customers.

High-loss scams involve a relatively small number of victims who are each defrauded of a substantial sum of money. Popular high-loss scams involve the sale of commodities, precious metals and gemstones, penny stocks, undeveloped real estate in "up-and-coming" but distant areas, and prepaid vacation packages. The high-loss scam, which is not an easy sell, is typically conducted by high-pressure telemarketers who are well schooled in the art of deception. Apprehensive buyers are provided with false references and testimonials for investments, promises of inside knowledge of the future performance of stocks, and certificates of authenticity of gemstone purchases as well as future buy-back guarantees. But typically the oil wells are dry, the stocks do not perform, and the gemstones cannot be appraised because of the plastic that encases them (which, if tampered with, invalidates the buy-back guarantee). Real estate acreage represented as valuable turns out to be swamp or desert, and prepaid vacations either provide accommodations at third-rate hotels far inferior to the fancy resorts promised in the promotional literature, or can never be scheduled during a time when the would-be traveler would like to go.

The key to the success of a high-loss scam operation is that a substantial period of time passes between the unsuspecting victims' tender of payment and their eventual realization of the fraud. These victims often purchase investments upon which they are told not to expect returns for a year or more. Even as customers become suspicious and call back to complain, smooth-talking scam operators provide the aggrieved customers with reassurances and explanations, thereby gaining additional time before the authorities will likely be alerted. Eventually, when verbal reassurances will not pacify the defrauded customers, the boiler room operators disconnect the telephone service, evacuate the rented space, and move quickly and quietly to a new location to begin again under a new company name.

Although the victims of high-loss scams are more vocal in their complaints to authorities than victims of low-loss scams, they often decide not to complain because of the embarrassment associated with having fallen for an offer that should have been recognized as too good to be true. Also, by the time most victims realize their losses, which may be several years later, the scam operation has likely relocated. Victims of telemarketing fraud are generally armed with little more than the first names (or aliases) of the offenders and could not provide visual identification even if authorities successfully located them.

To add insult to injury, after being defrauded once, some victims are telephoned again by someone promising to regain the lost money for a fee. These operations are sometimes referred to as "recovery rooms," and their scam is called "reloading" or "double slamming." The caller, who will require that the "collection fee" be paid in advance, is either the same scam artist who defrauded the victim in the first place or one who has obtained the victim's name from a sucker list purchased from an information broker. The victim is then defrauded for the second time.

Besides the lack of reporting by fraud victims, the mobility of scam operations, and the problem of identifying specific offenders if and when the relocated business is found, reporting and law enforcement efforts among state agencies and authorities are often fragmented and uncoordinated. Many, if not most, scam operations physically operate in one or more states but telemarket to other states, so they benefit from the lack of centralized complaint reporting. Consumer complaints are most often directed to local law enforcement and consumer agencies, which do not routinely or systematically share information with sister states or federal authorities. As mentioned previously, a small number of complaints, particularly when the losses are small, is often not sufficient evidence to prove the requisite intent to defraud that could lead to injunctions and prosecutions.

Enforcement may be a problem when the scam operator is not within the confines of the victim's state. Many states have long-arm statutes that permit them to enforce their state laws across state lines through the "minimum contact" of the telephone call that resulted in the committed fraud, but then either lack the resources to pursue the offender or lack the cooperation of the offender's state law enforcement agency, which may also be short of resources.

Telemarketing Losses

Telemarketing fraud costs consumers an estimated $40 billion per year. The obvious victims are, of course, the consumers themselves, with some losing moderate amounts of money while others lose large amounts. As mentioned previously, the elderly are often specifically targeted by scam operators because of their vulnerability; some lose their entire life's savings in phony investments. Legitimate telemarketing operations also lose because telemarketing fraud creates apprehension and distrust in the minds of consumers who might otherwise purchase products and services by telephone. However, individuals and honest sellers are not the only victims.

Because telemarketing purchases are generally not cash transactions, credit cards and sight drafts are frequently used. To accept credit card payments, a telemarketing operation needs a merchant account with a member bank. Scam operators either open their own merchant accounts or convince legitimate businesses to permit them access to their accounts. When scam operators open their own merchant accounts to process their credit card receipts, they generally provide the member banks with false information to make tracing difficult when problems later arise.

Some victims of telemarketing fraud realize early on that they have been pressured and/or cheated, then dispute the charges placed against their credit cards for their purchases. This complaint results in a charge-back to the member bank against the merchant account. Because charge-backs often take sixty to ninety days to reach member banks, the fraudulent telemarketing operation can disappear, leaving the member bank to absorb the losses. Sometimes scam operators gain access to another business's merchant account, through which they process their charge receipts, a process known as credit card laundering. Unsophisticated owners of small businesses are usually targeted and persuaded to be unsuspecting victims of the scheme. Again, by the time charge-backs start flooding in, the scam operator has disappeared. The holder of the legitimate merchant account—the small-business owner—must either absorb the loss or pass it back to the bank through bankruptcy. Visa and MasterCard estimate that their member banks lose $300 million each year as a result of telemarketing fraud involving credit card payments.

Another common method used to obtain funds illegally is the unauthorized use of the sight draft. This scheme involves soliciting the victim to provide his or her checking account number, then writing an unauthorized check against the victim's account. The unauthorized withdrawal is unknowingly processed by the victim's bank. Eventually the victim discovers the loss, reports it to the bank, and the bank becomes liable. Scam operators using this scheme usually transfer or withdraw their ill-gotten funds daily to frustrate future tracing efforts by victimized banks. Losses to banks are either absorbed or passed along to others through higher fees.

Law Enforcement Activities

Telemarketing fraud occurs so frequently that state and federal authorities are now directing much attention to the problem. A Louis Harris survey conducted in the spring of 1992 revealed that 3 percent of a national sample believed that, in the previous two years, they had bought something from fraudulent telemarketers. Fewer than one-third of these victims actually filed a formal complaint.

Many states are strengthening their laws against telemarketing fraud, and a few have begun licensing and bonding all telemarketers operating within their jurisdictions. Local consumer protection groups and Better Business Bureaus have improved their networking, and many now systematically report unresolved complaints to the Federal Trade Commission (FTC). The FTC is taking steps to establish and maintain a national database of consumer fraud complaints, which will help federal authorities establish patterns of conduct that tend to prove criminal intent. Although the FTC is without prosecutorial power, it can issue civil injunctions against individuals and businesses who frequently engage in deceptive business practices.

The FTC also informs and assists other federal agencies such as the Federal Bureau of Investigation (FBI) and, when the scheme also involves the use of mail, the U.S. Postal Inspection Service (USPIS). The FBI and USPIS, with the cooperation and support of the U.S. Department of Justice, have prosecutorial powers and, unlike state law enforcement efforts, have jurisdiction throughout the nation. Both the FBI and the USPIS aggressively pursue known offenders and have been successful not just in prosecuting fraudulent telemarketers, but also in seizing millions of dollars of scam operators' assets, much of which has been used to reimburse fraud victims.

In 1990 the FBI initiated a sophisticated and successful undercover operation called "Operation DISCONNECT," which specifically targeted fraudulent telemarketing operations. With the cooperation of eighteen field offices, the FBI identified approximately 540 suspects involved in fraudulent telemarketing at 123 locations. By May 1993 the FBI had arrested approximately 210 individuals and seized more than $4.5 million in cash and other assets from their operations.

Relatively recent amendments to federal law now provide consumers with additional protections. The Telephone Consumer Protection Act of 1991 led, in late 1992, to the implementation by the Federal Communications Commission (FCC) of strict regulations on the use of automatic dialing equipment and unrequested facsimile transmissions. The Senior Citizens against Marketing Scams Act of 1994 led to the creation of new laws imposing enhanced penalties on fraudulent operators who either target senior citizens specifically or are repeat offenders of any fraudulent act. The act also requires that restitution be paid to the victims of telemarketing schemes (in addition to any other penalties), and makes restitution compliance a condition of parole for offenders.

The most comprehensive piece of federal telemarketing legislation, the Telemarketing and Consumer Fraud and Abuse Prevention Act of 1994, directs the FTC to prescribe regulations restricting many identified deceptive and abusive telemarketing practices. The new regulations took effect on December 31, 1995; they prohibit telemarketers from making calls between the hours of 9:00 P.M. and 8:00 A.M., calling people who have previously asked not to be called, operating "recovery rooms" or charging a fee to regain customers' money lost in other frauds, debiting a customer's checking account without written or tape-recorded authorization, and misrepresenting certain specified facts (and risks) relevant to the goods or services they are selling.

This legislation also prohibits credit card laundering and requires that at the beginning of telemarketing calls various disclosures be given, including the fact that it is a sales call, what company the caller represents, and, if it is a prize promotion, that no purchase is necessary to enter the contest.

Perhaps the most significant aspect of the act is that it subjects violators to a $10,000 penalty for each violation. Until now, fraudulent telemarketers have been able to take advantage of the fact that a few violations of fraud statutes are generally insufficient to invoke civil and criminal penalties. Although it is still necessary to prove the violator's intent to defraud in order to invoke criminal sanctions, the fines prescribed by this legislation are assessed for each violation, independent of other applicable statutes where the standard of proof is often higher.

Many state and national nonprofit consumer advocacy groups deserve credit for assisting victims and keeping the issue of telemarketing fraud before legislative bodies. Among them are the National Fraud Information Center (NFIC), which maintains a toll-free hotline for victims of fraud and assists them in filing formal complaints that are passed on to appropriate law enforcement agencies. The National Consumers League, which took the lead in setting up the NFIC, targets telemarketing fraud; it led lobbying efforts in support of the Telemarketing and Consumer Fraud and Abuse Prevention Act of 1994.

The fight against fraud is not over, and probably never will be. Just as evolving technology and payment options expand the boundaries for people to buy and sell products by telephone, so do they permit criminals to find new ways to exploit the unsuspecting. For example, as more Americans access the Internet and shop from computer bulletin boards, they will be targeted by fraudulent operators. Consumer advocates, legislators, and law enforcement officials face the continuing challenge of anticipating and preventing new frauds made possible by evolving technology.

— Lee Richardson

See also

Federal Trade Commission.

Readings

Stone, Bob (1994). *Successful Direct Marketing Methods.* Lincolnwood, IL: NTC Business Books.

U.S. Congress, Senate Special Committee on Aging (1996). *Telescams Exposed: How Telemarketers Target the Elderly.* Washington, DC: U.S. Government Printin Office.

Telephone Regulation

Three characteristics set telephone service apart from the other industries regulated at the federal and state levels as utilities (electricity, natural gas, and water). Telephone service was once provided by a near-monopoly, the service is relatively young, and it is technologically dynamic. These characteristics provide the context for the profound changes that took place in the telecommunications industry and its form of regulation in the 1980s and 1990s.

Telephone service is the only utility that ever approached the status of a national monopoly. In 1970 the Bell system accounted for about 85 percent of total telephone industry revenues. In contrast, at the peak of concentration in the electric utility industry in the late 1920s, sixteen companies accounted for 85 percent of the output of that industry.

The breakup of the telephone company in 1984 (known as divestiture) mandated a massive industrial reorganization that created eight companies. The seven Regional Bell Operating Companies (RBOCs) were given local telephone services; AT&T retained interstate long distance and manufacturing. Each of these companies ranks among the top fifty of all U.S. corporations.

The economic and regulatory environment never settled. Divestiture tried to separate what was thought to be a monopoly—local telephone service—from more competitive segments of the industry such as long distance, information services, and the manufacturing of telephone equipment. However, within a few years regulators granted hundreds of waivers for entry into other businesses to the RBOCs, and the courts permitted the local companies to enter information services and the cable television business. Long distance and cable television companies responded by seeking entry into the local telephone business.

Telephone service is the youngest of the utilities. In the mid-1930s, when regulation of electricity and telecommunications at the federal level was reorganized as part of the New Deal, two-thirds of all residences had electricity, but less than one-third had telephone service. In the mid-1950s, when 99 percent of residences had electricity, less than 75 percent had phone service. Even in the 1990s, more than 7 million residences are without telephone service, and millions more lack single-party service.

As a result, "universal service" remains a hotly debated public policy issue sixty years after it was declared a national goal by the Communications Act of 1934. Soon after divestiture, the Federal Communications Commission (FCC) instituted a national lifeline program to help ensure that low-income households have access to telephone service. This program is in addition to a large, high-cost federal fund intended to keep rates affordable in low-density rural areas.

Telecommunications is more technologically dynamic than the other utilities. In the period between 1970 and the mid-1990s, productivity in telecommunications grew five times faster than the national average, and ten times more quickly than in the electric and natural gas utilities.

The telecommunications industry is one of the primary beneficiaries of the revolution in computer technology. At the heart of the modern telecommunications network are digital switches, which are essentially large computers that manage and direct electronic information (bits). The introduction of high-speed digital switching and high-capacity fiber-optic cables dramatically lowered operating costs.

Ultimately, the benefits of the computer revolution for the telecommunications industry may be larger on the demand side. Voice, data, fax, and video, which are indistinguishable from the point of view of a digital network, open up a wide range of potential new services to be sold by telecommunications companies over the information superhighway.

In the dozen years after divestiture, homes with personal computers (PCs) rose from virtually zero to almost half. Even controlling for income, households with PCs are twice as likely to have a second telephone line as those without these computers. The speed (baud rate) at which regular residential subscribers can send information increased a hundredfold, from 300 bits per second (bps) to 28,800 bps. As a result, services such as the Internet are expected to be the new marketplaces of the information age.

Regulatory Change

Until divestiture, the telecommunications industry was generally regulated much like other utilities at the federal and state levels. Like local electric and gas utilities, the local telephone company was granted a monopoly within its franchise territory, thereby assuming an obligation to serve all customers who requested service within that area.

Cost of service was the predominant form of regulation. The amount of money the company was allowed to charge in the aggregate (the revenue requirement) was set by estimating a fair rate of profit (rate of return) on the capital assets (rate base) the telephone company deployed to provide service. This return on investment was combined with depreciation and expenses to arrive at the revenue requirement.

After the revenue requirement was determined, rates for individual services were set with the goal of achieving universal service: keeping service affordable for residential ratepayers. Various economic justifications are used for these social pricing decisions—value of service pricing (in which businesses who use telephone service to generate commerce are charged more) and residual pricing (in which discretionary services are charged more). Whether the result is an outright subsidy to residential customers (i.e., at prices below costs) or merely a different markup above costs is a debate that has never been resolved. Only in the case of high-cost rural areas is there agreement that subsidies exist and should continue.

Reflecting the profound economic and technological changes of the 1980s, regulation of the telecommunications industry also experienced dramatic changes. Federal and state regulators experimented with different approaches to the two key elements of cost of service regulation: regulating profits and setting the rates. Telecommunications became the test bed for regulatory reform in other industries.

By 1996 the states were equally divided between traditional rate-of-return regulation, incentive regulation, and profit deregulation. About one-third of the states retained rate-of-return regulation, in which regulators set a specific allowed rate of return. Another third of the states ceased looking at the rate of return altogether. Profits are not analyzed or used to alter rates, and other mechanisms are presumed to keep rates at just and reasonable levels. This approach can be called profit deregulation.

The states were also equally divided between traditional rate setting and price indexing. In a traditional rate setting, no changes in rates are allowed without a hearing and order of the commission, regardless of profit levels. Under price indexing, after initial rates are set, an index is used to allow companies to change their rates automatically in subsequent years. The index is usually calculated by reference to the consumer price index, although in virtually all cases where an index is used, telecommunications prices go up less than the rate of inflation because of the superior productivity growth in the telecommunications industry.

In large measure, the impetus behind the move to alternative regulation was the emergence or desire for greater competition in telephone service. Almost from the day of divestiture, local exchange companies complained that their revenue streams were being eroded by competition. They argued that technology made it easy for certain large customers to bypass the local network and that social pricing policies (pricing business services and long-distance services high to keep residential prices low) gave these customers the incentive to do so. They demanded greater pricing flexibility to meet this threat and higher rates of return to reflect the increased risk they faced.

On the other side, long-distance companies complained that they were being overcharged for access to local networks, on which they relied to complete their interstate calls, and requested competitive alternatives to drive these costs down.

Regulators and then legislatures authorized more competition. Competition began with specific services like intrastate long distance and Centrex. Introducing full-fledged competition for local exchange service proved a more difficult task. If the telecommunications network is to achieve its full value, seamless interconnection between all service providers is necessary. Every telephone subscriber wants and needs to be able to reach every other telephone subscriber on an equal basis.

Most policymakers recognized that the local exchange companies had deployed a ubiquitous network of transportation and switching facilities under conditions of monopoly protection and that new entrants to the local business could not replicate this network. Policymakers sought to ensure that access to the network and its underlying bottleneck facilities would be made available to competitors on competitively neutral, nondiscriminatory terms. At the same time, policymakers were concerned that a competitive marketplace would retard progress toward the goal of universal service, which had been the focal point of public policy for over half a century.

The resulting regulatory and legislative struggles to introduce local competition lasted for years. Incumbent monopoly companies sought to defend their advantage, arguing that the network was private property that was not an essential facility and could not be "taken" by regulators. Potential competitors insisted that, if competition were to succeed, public policy required the network to be unbundled into its most basic functions, with each of its parts made available for lease at rates that were nondiscriminatory and would support the economic viability of competitive offerings. Federal policymakers—first the Department of Justice, which had won the case to break up the national monopoly, and then Congress—identified a series of conditions that were deemed necessary to support local competition, but they left the details to the states.

State and federal policymakers also grappled with the problem of universal service. In the states, the approach taken most often was to expand the lifeline program for low-income customers and create or expand state high-cost funds for rural areas. At the federal level, the FCC considered extending the lifeline concept to long-distance services.

The Future

As the turn of the century approaches, the uncertainty and turmoil ushered in by divestiture is shifting from the regulatory arena to the marketplace. The economic prospects of the industry are certainly bright, and the potential for continued cost reduction and increased utilization of the network continues to be excellent. The major players in the industry—the RBOCs and the larger long-distance companies—are earning record levels of profit, in part because much of the profit stream of the industry has been deregulated.

The prospects for competition, however, are less clear. Despite a decade of talk about competition for local telephone service being provided by cable companies, electric utilities, wireless services, or long-distance companies, few residential or small-business customers of the local telephone companies can select another, comparable local service option. The RBOCs still account for 98 percent of all minutes switched for long-distance companies. AT&T continues to dominate the long-distance market. A pattern of price leadership persists, in which AT&T sets a price and others follow suit. Joint ventures and mergers of telephone companies, cable companies, and computer companies call into question the likelihood that residential or small-business customers will have a choice of providers for any of these services.

Thus, consumers face an uncertain future in a key industry of the information age. Regulation has been weakened and consumer protection stripped away as the telecommunications industry sheds it utility label, but market forces have not rushed in to replace the discipline of regulation that has been removed. It is certainly possible that the telecommunications conglomerates forming at the end of the twentieth century will follow the path of the rail, steel, and oil conglomerates that formed at the end of the nineteenth—combining rapid economic growth with so much abuse of market power that public opinion and public policy once again will demand more regulation and greater consumer protection.

— Mark N. Cooper

See also

Deregulation, Economic; Telecommunications Research and Action Center.

Readings

Cooper, Mark (1996). *Universal Service: An Historical Perspective and Policies for the 21st Century*. Washington, DC: Benton Foundation and Consumer Federation of America.

Hyman, Leonard S.; Richard C. Toole, and Rosemary M. Avellis (1989). *The New Telecommunications Industry: Evolution and Organization*. Arlington, VA: Public Utilities Reports.

Television Regulation

See Broadcast Protections; Cable Television Regulation.

Tenant Protections

Beginning in the 1960s, the courts and state legislatures adapted landlord-tenant law to the needs of an urban democracy. Numerous programs and techniques were devised to improve tenants' rights and living conditions. Among the new tenant remedies were rent abatement, rent escrow, receivership, tenant right to repair and deduct, tenant unions, and protection against landlord retaliation.

Under common law, the obligation of tenants to pay rent was suspended only when they were evicted. Thus, tenants had no right to refuse to pay rent on the grounds that the premises were unhabitable or below minimum standards of decency. The right of tenants to refuse to pay rent for substandard premises, however, has been granted by many courts and by legislatures in many states. The judicial creation of a tenant right of rent abatement is based on such diverse legal principles as the implied warrant of habitability created by housing codes, constructive eviction, illegal contract, and partial failure of consideration. Also, the legislatures of some states have adopted programs of statutory rent abatement.

The difference between tenant remedies of rent abatement and rent escrow is that abatement suspends the tenant's obligation to pay, while escrow provides a procedure by which rent is paid into a fund to be used for the repair and improvement of the premises. The rent escrow program has not developed into an effective remedy for several reasons. First, the program is useful only when the defective condition affects the entire building. Second, the courts have had difficulty finding an administrator willing and capable of using the funds in a productive and efficient manner. Third, rental income has not been sufficient to pay for repairs and maintenance.

The ineffectiveness of rent escrow points up the need for a legal apparatus by which a court-appointed administrator can finance the long-term repayment of expenditures for substantial repairs. Housing receivership is designed to accomplish this objective by providing for the appointment of a receiver who is authorized to secure a long-term loan to be applied to the costs of repair by offering a mortgage that is superior to existing mortgages. Without such security, lenders are unwilling to make loans for repair.

In most states, landlords are required to keep the premises in repair but are not required to pay the costs of repair assumed by the tenant unless the lease or the law specifies otherwise. Although housing codes impose the obligation of repair on the landlord, the courts are divided on whether the codes give the tenant the right to make the repairs they require. When the lease contains an agreement by the landlord to keep the premises in repair and he or she fails to do so, the tenant may make the repairs and deduct their costs from the rent. However, landlords rarely consent to include such an agreement in the lease. Some states grant tenants legal authority to deduct the costs of repair from the rent, but such statutes are ineffective because the amount of expenditures authorized is usually limited to an insignificant sum.

The willingness of tenants to submit to substandard housing conditions and onerous lease provisions reflects the individual tenant's limited bargaining power against the landlord in a housing market characterized by a great demand for and limited supply of low-cost housing. Tenant unions are a device by which tenants can increase their limited economic power through collective bargaining. Despite the potential advantages of a tenant union, organization of tenants has been slow and difficult. Many people distrust organizations; others are unwilling to pay union dues, without which the organization cannot function effectively; and many fear landlord retaliation.

Landlords frequently respond to tenant organizing by threatening to terminate services or abandon the building. If the property is worth preserving, the landlord may undermine the support for a tenant union by improving the condition of the building. Once this concession is made, many tenants lose interest in the union and withdraw their support.

Tenants who arouse the antipathy of landlords place themselves in a vulnerable position. Most tenants of substandard apartments occupy them without a lease and without a fixed term of residence. With no lease to limit the amount of rent and assure a period of habitation, the landlord is free to raise the rent or terminate the tenancy upon thirty days' notice. Tenant remedies have only limited usefulness if the landlord can use his or her power to raise rent or evict in retaliation for a tenant's exercise of those remedies.

A few courts and some state legislatures have recognized the need to protect tenants against landlord retaliation. In one landmark decision, a U.S. Court of Appeals ruled that proof of a retaliatory motive is a good defense against eviction. But the court held that the tenant must prove that the landlord sought to evict him because he had reported violations of the housing code.

Tenants in government-funded units have greater rights than private tenants. Government-supported units include public housing, which is paid for by the federal or state government, and subsidized housing, which is owned by a private landlord who receives funding from a government.

Tenants in a few cities, including New York, may live in rent-controlled units. Most economists believe that, over the long term, rent control harms tenant interests by discouraging the creation of new rental units and the maintenance of existing units. Others, however, note that in high-rent cities, many tenants can afford to live only in rent-controlled housing.

— Jerome G. Rose

Readings

Bezdek, Barbara (1992). "Silence in the Court: Participation and Subordination of Poor Tenants' Voices in Legal Process." *Hofstra Law Review.* 20 (Spring): 533–608.

Glendon, Mary Ann (1982). "The Transformation of American Landlord-Tenant Law." *Boston College Law Review.* 23: 503ff.

Rose, Jerome G. (1973). *Landlords and Tenants: A Complete Guide to the Residential Rental Relationship.* New Brunswick, NJ: Transaction Books.

Textile Product Flammability

The most common hazard associated with textile products is related to their reaction when burned. Burn injuries are among the most life-threatening and most painful injuries, requiring extended healing times and often repeated reconstructive surgery. Even when textile materials do not completely ignite, they may produce gases that, in confined spaces, can lead to asphyxiation and death.

A textile material is said to be flame-resistant if it retains its shape and does not ignite below 315°C (600°F). Those that are flame-retardant may ignite but will not support combustion when the source is removed. Flammable materials ignite and continue to burn even when the source is removed. With the exception of a few modern fibers used in military and industrial applications that are inherently flame-resistant (FR), and mineral fibers such as glass and asbestos, fibers support combustion to varying degrees. Through the use of additives during fiber formation, the flammability of manufactured fibers can be varied over a wide range. For example, although acrylic fibers might ignite easily, modified acrylic fibers, or modacrylics, have fillers that make them much less likely to ignite and support combustion.

The flammability of textile products is not simply related to the properties of the constituent fibers; it is a more complex function of the total assembly. Generally, flammability of a textile product is controlled by three factors: fiber flammability; construction (e.g., weight, tightness, surface characteristics); and topical treatments or surface finishes.

In order for a textile material to burn, a combination of two factors must be present. First, the temperature of the material must be raised to that which will permit combustion, and second, sufficient oxygen must be present to support combustion. Thus, it is not surprising that light, airy fabrics burn more easily than those made from identical fibers in more dense constructions. Also, fabrics with surface texture, such as the napped surface of flannel, burn more easily and rapidly than those with a more plain surface. These features can threaten the safety of very young children and the elderly, who often wear flannel and lightweight fabrics.

Finally, the flammability of a textile product can be modified by applying a topical FR finish. In this way, naturally combustible fibers such as cotton, wool, rayon, nylon, and polyester can achieve flame resistance. In the mid-1970s, most children's sleepwear fabrics were chemically treated to meet flammability requirements. In response to consumer concern over the discovery that one popular topical treatment, tris (2,3 dibromopropylphosphate), was potentially a long-term carcinogen, most of these fabrics disappeared from the market by 1978. Spurred by consumer demand, manufacturers rushed to develop inherently FR fibers to fill the niche. Today, although some apparel fabrics are topically FR-treated, fabrics destined for protective clothing for firefighters, aircraft or automotive interiors, theater curtains, and carpeting may undergo this FR treatment. The only way natural fibers (e.g., cotton and wool) can be made flame resistant is by topical treatment. Topical FR treatments on apparel are said to be durable if they last the life of the garment, usually defined as fifty washings; if not, they are termed semidurable.

The pioneering legislation to develop standards for flammability was the Flammable Fabrics Act (FFA) of 1953. The intent of the FFA was "to regulate the manufacture for sale in interstate commerce of all highly flammable wearing apparel fabrics." In 1954 the Flammability of Clothing Textiles Standard, the first standard promulgated under the FFA, set standards only for the rate of burning, not for the elimination of burning. The 1953 act was amended in 1967, and responsibility for its enforcement was given to the Consumer Product Safety Commission. Currently, federal standards exist for children's sleepwear (sizes 0–6 and 7–14), large and small carpets and rugs, and mattresses and mattress pads. Standards have been proposed for upholstered furniture in response to injuries and deaths from cigarette ignition of upholstery. With an increasing number of elderly caring for themselves, standards for "dangerous categories" of adult apparel are being considered.

Because of the extensive use of textile products in transportation systems, both the U.S. Department of Transportation (DOT) and the Federal Aviation Agency (FAA) are interested in flammability standards. Automobile, truck, and bus interiors are covered under a DOT motor vehicle safety standard. Textile items in aircraft passenger cabins and crew compartments fall under the aegis of an FAA standard.

— Peter Schwartz

See also

Consumer Product Safety Commission; Product Hazards.

Readings

Grayson, Stephen J.; Vytenis Babrauskas, and Marcelo M. Hirschler (1994). "Testing: A New International Standard for Flammability Testing." *Plastics Engineering.* 50 (April): 29–31.

Mischutin, Vladimir (1987). "Review of U.S. and Foreign Flammability Standards." *American Dyestuff Reporter.* 76 (January): 33–45.

Norton, Marjorie J., Robert F. Johnson, and Kenneth A. Jordan (1984). "Assessment of Flammability Hazard and Its Relationship to Price for Women's Nightgowns." *Textile Research Journal.* 54 (11): 748–760.

Tobacco Control and Prevention

Tobacco products—including cigarettes, smokeless tobacco, pipes, and cigars—are a major cause of preventable, premature death in the United States. Cigarettes kill half of all long-term smokers, primarily from lung and other cancers, cardiovascular disease, and lung disease. Of these individuals, half die in old age, losing five to ten years of normal life expectancy, and half die in middle age, losing twenty to twenty-five years of normal life expectancy. Additionally, an estimated 50,000 nonsmokers die each year from exposure to environmental tobacco smoke (ETS). In total, nearly 500,000 American deaths are caused by tobacco products each year. Nonetheless, approximately one in four Americans smokes.

The central problems concerning tobacco products are that they cause nicotine addiction and that they were popularized around the world well before their risks were appreciated. Simultaneously, tobacco cultivation and manufacturing became entrenched in the economy and political structure of the United States. As a consequence, tobacco is the only dangerous consumer product that is not regulated by the U.S. government in ways that provide meaningful protection for consumers. Tobacco products are unique in that, when used as intended by the manufacturer, they are lethal and addictive. There is now broad consensus that reducing tobacco use is of paramount importance to the nation's public health.

Native to the New World, the tobacco plant has been used by indigenous peoples for social, medicinal, and religious purposes for thousands of years. European explorers initiated the spread of tobacco use around the world, and until the twentieth century, tobacco consumption was largely limited to products that did not require inhalation for normal use. In 1881, James Bonsack invented the cigarette-making machine; this device and an increasingly urbanized population were major factors in the rapid increase of cigarette use.

Prior to the turn of the century, the health hazards of tobacco products (including cancer) were widely suspected, though not proven. "Anti-tobacco" activity, most visible in the form of anti-cigarette leagues, flourished from the late 1800s to the 1920s, and the activity of these leagues roughly paralleled that of temperance organizations. These groups helped pass many state and local laws against cigarette sales or use, especially against use by children.

The extent of the health hazards of tobacco use became widely apparent only in the mid-twentieth century, decades after many individuals began smoking cigarettes in large quantities. Scientific studies linking tobacco to disease began to emerge in the 1920s, and the accumulated data became irrefutable by the mid-1950s. In 1957 the Study Group on Smoking and Health of the American Cancer Society, the American Heart Association, the National Cancer Institute, and the National Heart Institute agreed that smoking was causally related to the increasing incidence of lung cancer.

Public awareness of tobacco's health hazards was slow to develop. Physicians, many of whom smoked, resisted accepting that tobacco use was harmful. Additionally, newspapers and magazines, most of which accepted cigarette advertisements, did not adequately inform the public about the growing scientific consensus for fear of offending tobacco advertisers. *Reader's Digest* and *Consumer Reports* were notable exceptions. The first congressional hearings to investigate tobacco were convened by John Blatnik (D-MN) in 1957. After these hearings, the congressional leadership punished Blatnik by stripping him of his subcommittee chairmanship.

Development of a Movement

In 1964 the United States Public Health Service formally recognized the link between tobacco use and disease when the Surgeon General released the Report of the Advisory Committee on Smoking and Health. This document was instrumental in launching the modern tobacco control and prevention movement. For the next thirty years, government agencies, together with medical and voluntary health organizations, would play leading roles in decreasing tobacco use. These agencies not only funded important research, but also initiated and supported education and smoking cessation programs.

As suspicion about the health hazards of environmental tobacco smoke (ETS) grew in the 1970s, small grassroots citizen's organizations, commonly referred to as nonsmokers' rights groups, organized to limit their own exposure to ETS. These groups were formed by people who were annoyed, irritated, and/or believed they were being physically harmed by the then-commonplace exposure to smoke. In an era in which individual rights were stressed, nonsmokers' rights groups emphasized that nonsmokers had rights too. Invariably, groups were run from private homes, without the benefit of paid staff or significant budgets, and were primarily active at the local level. They adopted a public health approach to tobacco control, turning to legislative, regulatory, and advocacy activities to accomplish their aims. In doing so, nonsmokers' rights groups confronted tobacco companies' efforts to promote smoking. Early on, these activists identified the tobacco industry as the major obstacle to effective tobacco control and prevention policy.

Through much of the 1970s and early 1980s, medical and health organizations, which were dominated by medical professionals and nonsmokers' rights groups run by lay citizens, disagreed over tactics and strategies to reduce tobacco use. Health and medical organizations emphasized public education and smoking cessation; they were slow to appreciate the need for public policy solutions. These groups rejected the confrontational approach of the nonsmokers' rights groups as undignified, in poor taste, and likely to offend smokers, many of whom were their financial contributors. During the early part of this period, the American Medical Association actively cooperated with the tobacco industry's research program. For their part, nonsmokers' rights groups were impatient with the deliberate, scientific approach of the health and medical organizations. The inability of these two segments of the tobacco control movement to collaborate hindered progress for many years.

Nonetheless, beginning in 1975, nonsmokers' rights groups helped pass hundreds of local ordinances limiting public exposure to ETS in public places and workplaces. Their work accelerated in the 1980s when the scientific evidence linking ETS with disease in nonsmokers became irrefutable. Though unintended, their work contributed to the dramatic decrease in the social acceptability of smoking and a marked decline in smoking among adults, especially highly educated ones.

The Advocacy Institute, founded in 1985, helped unite the disparate members of the tobacco control and prevention movement. The institute's tobacco control project was directed by Michael Pertschuk, a former chair of the Federal Trade Commission. The project provided technical assistance, training, and strategic information to hundreds of organizations. In 1990, the institute developed the first national electronic network of tobacco control.

In 1985, Joe Tye founded Stop Teenage Addiction to Tobacco (STAT). STAT attracted hundreds of advocates to its annual conference, and was especially adept at uniting diverse organizations with an interest in youth tobacco issues. STAT was among the first groups to call attention to tobacco industry–targeted marketing to youth and to work directly with youth. Doctors Ought to Care (DOC), founded by Dr. Alan Blum, pioneered an activist, confrontational approach to controlling tobacco use.

By the late 1980s the various segments of the tobacco control movement began to form into coalitions at the federal, state, and local levels. The National Cancer Institute's COMMIT project, and its successor ASSIST, which specifically required coalition building, helped advance this process. Tobacco control coalitions sought to expand their base of support by encouraging diverse groups to join. Gradually, increasing numbers of health, scientific, consumer, and other groups became involved in tobacco control and prevention efforts. Then Surgeon General C. Everett Koop used the bully pulpit of his office to focus the public's attention on the tobacco industry's contribution to tobacco use. Policy and media advocacy began to surpass smoking cessation as the dominant effort of the tobacco control movement.

By 1993 the National Cancer Institute and the Centers for Disease Control and Prevention were providing funding for statewide tobacco control activities in forty-nine states and the District of Columbia. The fiftieth state, California, had its own exemplary tobacco control program, funded by a dedicated tobacco excise tax. The Robert Wood Johnson Foundation also began funding tobacco control and prevention research and activities, including coalition building and policy advocacy.

Equally important, after years of research and discussion, effective public policy solutions were demonstrated. Broad agreement was reached within the movement that its goals should include raising the price of tobacco products by increasing excise taxes, eliminating or restricting advertising and promotion of tobacco products, protecting the public from exposure to ETS, and reducing the provision of tobacco products to youth. As the 1990s progress, two types of activity are helping to advance this agenda: litigation against tobacco companies and increasing government oversight of tobacco manufacturers.

Tobacco product liability suits have long sought to establish the legal liability of tobacco manufacturers for tobacco-related illnesses of individual smokers, but had been unsuccessful for years. However, the once invincible tobacco industry appears to be increasingly vulnerable to legal challenge. During the 1990s several class-action lawsuits were filed, including a class-action suit of nonsmoking flight attendants who assert that they suffer adverse health effects from ETS (*Broin v. Philip Morris Companies, Inc.*), a class action on behalf of cigarette smokers who maintain that tobacco companies knew that nicotine was addictive despite their claims to the contrary (*Engle v. RJ Reynolds Tobacco Company*), and a class action alleging that tobacco companies intentionally manipulate nicotine in cigarettes despite knowing it to be hazardous and addictive (*Castano v. American Tobacco Company*).

In March 1996, in a surprising break with tradition, a cigarette company (Liggett Group) agreed to a settlement in the *Castano* case.

Liggett Group also agreed to a settlement with 22 state attorneys general. In doing so, the cigarette manufacturer acknowledged that tobacco is addictive and causes cancer, agreed that some tobacco marketing was directed toward children, and agreed to cooperate with the states in suits against other companies. Michigan Attorney General Frank J. Kelley characterized the company's action by saying, "We got the least important culprit to turn state's evidence and give testimony against the really bad guys."

National Advocacy

Despite the findings of the 1964 Surgeon General's Report, the federal government took little leadership on smoking issues until recently. For three and one-half years beginning in July 1967, anti-cigarette public service announcements (PSAs) were aired nationally. These PSAs had been mandated by the Federal Communications Commission under the fairness doctrine and were so effective that the tobacco industry agreed to withdraw from the airwaves. As a result, the Public Health Cigarette Smoking Act of 1969 was enacted, banning cigarette advertising on television and radio and preempting states or localities from regulating cigarette advertising and promotion for health reasons. The Comprehensive Smokeless Tobacco Health Education Act of 1986 required warning labels on smokeless tobacco and prohibited smokeless tobacco advertising on television and radio.

Further congressional action on tobacco issues has been limited to a ban on smoking in airplanes (1988), and more recently, a ban on smoking in agencies serving children and receiving federal funding (1994). The United States has one of the lowest cigarette excise taxes of any developed country, but Congress rejected efforts in 1993 to significantly raise the federal cigarette excise tax.

In a dramatic shift, Dr. David Kessler, commissioner of the Food and Drug Administration (FDA), determined after an eighteen-month investigation that the FDA could regulate nicotine as a drug and assert jurisdiction over tobacco products. In August 1996, with the support of President Bill Clinton, the FDA issued regulations restricting the sale and distribution of cigarettes and smokeless tobacco to children. The rule was immediately challenged in court by the tobacco industry. In a significant setback to the tobacco industry, a federal district judge in North Carolina upheld the FDA's power to regulate tobacco as a drug. This ruling holds out the promise that, for the first time, tobacco products will be subject to meaningful federal regulation.

The Coalition on Smoking OR Health—comprised of the American Cancer Society, American Heart Association, and American Lung Association—was formed in 1982. For many years the group devoted few resources to lobbying at the federal level, but in 1993 they increased their advocacy to support the campaign to raise the federal cigarette excise tax to $2 per carton, and in 1995 they expanded this advocacy to support the proposed FDA regulations.

In 1996 the Robert Wood Johnson Foundation, together with the American Cancer Society and other organizations, announced a major federal initiative to reduce smoking by children, entitled the National Center for Tobacco Free Kids. Since its formation, the center has worked vigorously with its more than 100 members to support the FDA rule and other initiatives designed to decrease youth smoking. The center has also conducted an unprecedented high-profile, hard-hitting advertising campaign, aimed at tobacco companies and their supporters in Congress and state legislators.

In May 1994, Mississippi Attorney General Michael Moore filed suit against the nation's tobacco companies to recover the state's Medicaid costs for treating tobacco-induced illnesses. In the ensuing years, more than three dozen additional states followed Mississippi's initiative. After extensive discussions between the state attorneys general and the tobacco companies, a proposal for a "global settlement" was put forth on June 20, 1997. The proposal would provide immunity from most lawsuits and provide some measure of predictability to the tobacco industry, in exchange for financial payments and some restrictions on the ability of companies to market tobacco products.

Because the "global settlement" does not simply resolve the cases between the states and tobacco industry, it would require passage of federal legislation for enactment. Critics have strongly criticized the settlement proposal, charging that it inappropriately limits the FDA's existing authority, does not apply meaningful financial penalties to the industry, takes no action on international tobacco marketing, and provides the industry with undeserved legal protections.

Tobacco Industry Activities

For more than forty years, the tobacco industry has maintained a united front in defense of their products. The industry's aggressive response to the "health scare" of the 1950s set the pattern for future efforts. Cigarette manufacturers moved quickly to reassure the public by developing filter-tip and king-size cigarettes, which according to industry advertising could eliminate or transform the irritating components of cigarette smoke. These products foreshadowed the later development of so-called low-tar, low-nicotine, or low-yield cigarettes. None of these products appreciably decrease the risk of smoking, in part because consumers compensate for the lower tar and nicotine levels by smoking harder.

In 1954 several major cigarette companies founded the Tobacco Industry Research Committee (TIRC), later renamed the Council for Tobacco Research (CTR). Full-page newspaper advertisements entitled "A Frank Statement to Cigarette Smokers" accompanied the founding of TIRC, stating that it would research "all phases of tobacco use and health." In actuality, CTR's mission was to cast doubt on the link between smoking and disease. One of its key strategies is to co-opt researchers by providing funds for basic science research. In 1996, CTR was being investigated by the U.S. Department of Justice.

Since the 1950s the tobacco companies' public posture on health issues has remained consistent. With minor cosmetic changes in the wording of their messages, the cigarette companies consistently deny the lethal and addictive nature of tobacco products. For decades, company spokespersons described the health hazards of tobacco use as "unproven" and called for more research to determine whether or not tobacco products were harmful. When, by the late 1980s, this public position became untenable, spokespersons began saying that the cigarette was a "risk factor" for disease, without ever conceding actual causation. The industry consistently denies the addictive nature of tobacco or nicotine.

Tobacco companies have a unique problem: Each year, 2.5 million customers either die or quit smoking. As a result, large expenditures on advertising and promotion (in 1993 more than $6 billion) are needed to recruit new customers. Since virtually all new smokers are children, much of the industry's marketing is aimed at children. Tobacco product advertising and promotion is intended to lull the public into thinking that tobacco products are not harmful. For instance, a popular cigarette brand has long used the slogan "Alive with Pleasure" in advertising copy. And, while cigarette sales stagnate in the United States, companies are increasingly looking abroad to increase sales.

One of the industry's many goals is to deflect attention from their efforts to promote tobacco use. As part of this strategy, the industry seeks to portray the smoking issue as a battle between nonsmokers and smokers that could be solved through simple common courtesy. The industry is also believed to provide substantial funding to smokers' rights organizations in an effort to build a grassroots constituency to oppose restrictions on smoking.

For many years the tobacco industry has provided financial support to community groups, including educational, artistic, political, and other organizations. These contributions are intended to engender goodwill, improve the reputation of the industry with the community, and deter anti-tobacco activities on the part of the recipient organizations. In the past, women's and ethnic organizations have been among the most frequent recipients of industry funds.

For decades the tobacco industry has utilized its considerable economic resources to oppose tobacco control and prevention legislation. At present, the tobacco industry is a major contributor to candidates at the federal and state levels. Partly as a consequence, the industry is especially powerful at these levels. To date, it has enjoyed significant success blocking or modifying reform proposals. It has also worked for federal legislation that preempts state and local governments from regulating tobacco products and their use.

— Michele Bloch

See also

Advocacy Institute, The; Indoor Air Quality Protections.

Readings

Kluger, Richard (1996). *Ashes to Ashes: America's Hundred-Year Cigarette War, the Public Health, and the Unabashed Triumph of Philip Morris.* New York: Alfred A. Knopf.

U.S. Department of Health and Human Services (1989). *Reducing the Health Consequences of Smoking: 25 Years of Progress. A Report of the Surgeon General.* Atlanta, GA: U.S. Department of Health and Human Services, et al.

——— (1994). *Preventing Tobacco Use among Young People: A Report of the Surgeon General.* Atlanta, GA: U.S. Department of Health and Human Services, et al.

Toward Utility Rate Normalization

Toward Utility Rate Normalization (TURN) was created in 1973 as a 501(c)(3) nonprofit organization to advocate fair rates and high-quality service for residential and small-business customers of California's large investor-owned utilities.

TURN was founded by consumer activist Sylvia Siegel after she organized a group of consumers to attend a hearing at the California Public Utilities Commission (CPUC), the state agency that regulates the utilities. The experience convinced her that consumer oversight of the regulatory processes governing the monopolies providing the essential services of heat, power, and telephone service was inadequate. To meet this need, Siegel founded TURN. Initially, the organization operated out of her home and subsisted on volunteers and occasional contributions.

TURN is governed by a volunteer board of directors that meets quarterly to provide fiscal oversight and governance. The organization's twelve-member staff now includes an executive director, a supervising senior attorney, a senior telecommunications attorney, two staff attorneys specializing in electric and natural gas regulation, an energy analyst, a telecommunications analyst, a media director, an outreach coordinator, a development director, and two administrative staffers. These staffers work out of offices in San Francisco and Los Angeles.

TURN is supported by approximately 30,000 dues-paying members. Although members do not elect the governing board or vote on policy issues, their activism plays a crucial role in increasing TURN's influence.

Siegel was born in Detroit and graduated from Wayne State University with a bachelor's degree in sociology. In 1944 she moved to San Francisco, where she worked as an analyst for the War Labor Board and later for the California Nurses Association. A grandmotherly figure with no formal legal training, Siegel was a master of media showmanship and legal strategy. Her sharp tongue and quick wit—along with her imposing knowledge of utility issues—made her a favorite source with the news media. Her near-constant presence in the media and in the hearing room helped establish TURN as an influential force. In 1984, Siegel was featured on the television program *60 Minutes.*

When she retired in 1989, Audrie C. Krause, a journalist trained at the University of Minnesota, was chosen to succeed her. During an assignment to cover the California Public Utilities Commission from 1984 to 1988 for the *Fresno Bee,* Krause became knowledgeable about utility issues.

Both Siegel and Krause relied heavily on the legal work of Michel P. Florio, who joined TURN in 1978. After receiving a law degree from New York University and a Masters of Public Policy from Princeton University, Florio joined TURN's staff as an unpaid volunteer. He has served as TURN's senior attorney since 1989, overseeing the organization's legal advocacy.

In 1995, Nettie Y. Hogue became executive director of the organization. She had previously worked for Consumers Union and the California Department of Insurance.

TURN currently operates on an annual budget of $1.9 million. Funding comes from three primary sources: membership contributions, attorney fee awards, and restricted grants from foundations. During the 1994–1995 fiscal year, 32 percent of TURN's revenues came from individual donors, 65 percent from legal fees, and 3 percent from restricted grants.

As California's only independent, statewide consumer utility advocate, TURN's core function is to represent the interests of residential and small-business utility consumers in rate and policy proceedings before the CPUC. In addition, TURN has sought to represent the consumer interest before the California legislature, the U.S. Congress, and the courts. For example, between 1983 and 1985, the organization waged a battle to allow consumer messages to be inserted into customers' utility bills in what became known as the "bill stuffer" case. TURN's appeal was eventually defeated by a 1986 U.S. Supreme Court decision.

TURN provides information and referral services to consumers seeking assistance in resolving billing disputes or other problems. In addition, it engages in public outreach and consumer education through a speaker's bureau, a full-time outreach coordinator, and a media education effort that includes publication of *Utility Watch,* a quarterly media advisory. TURN also publishes a quarterly newsletter, *The Consumer's Advocate,* and produces and circulates fact sheets and legislative alerts.

From 1989 through 1995, TURN received funding from the Telecommunications Education Trust, a fund established by the CPUC with monies from a fine levied against Pacific Bell for marketing abuse, to educate consumers and community agencies on the impact of telecommunications regulation. To this end, TURN publishes a bimonthly educational newsletter, *Inside Line;* conducts workshops; and provides technical assistance to numerous community-based organizations.

From 1980 through 1982, TURN was funded by the U.S. Department of Energy to establish and operate the Western Consumer Utility Energy Training Center. The Western Center provided research, education, and training for consumer representatives from the twelve western states on issues raised by the Public Utilities Regulatory Policies Act of 1978 (PURPA). In 1994, TURN was funded by the Richard and Rhoda Goldman Fund to train senior activists in the San Francisco Bay area to advocate on energy issues.

Since its founding in 1973, TURN has participated in over 200 energy and telecommunications proceedings before the CPUC, saving consumers billions of dollars. In 1975, for example, TURN won its first major consumer victory when it convinced the CPUC to adopt a conservation rate structure now commonly referred to as baseline rates, an approach widely replicated throughout the United States. In 1982, TURN and a coalition of environmentalists and gas producers defeated a plan to build a $3.9 billion liquefied natural gas receiving terminal that had been jointly advocated by Pacific Gas and Electric and Southern California Gas.

In the mid-1980s, TURN promoted safeguards for small gas consumers in the deregulation of the natural gas industry, winning the adoption of a crucial regulatory distinction between those customers who have no options about gas purchases and those who do. In 1992, TURN convinced the CPUC to adopt strong consumer privacy safeguards before allowing the telephone companies to offer controversial caller identification services. In 1993, TURN successfully litigated a complaint against Pacific Bell for systematically imposing late fees on customers who had actually paid their bills on time. As a result, Pacific Bell was forced to pay $49 million in customer refunds and fines.

— Melia Franklin

See also

State and Local Consumer Organizations; State Utility Consumer Advocates.

Readings

Escobedo, Duwayne (1991). "CPUC Gets Mixed Reviews for Intervenor Programs." *Public Utilities Fortnightly.* 128 (15 August): 9.

Keppel, Bruce (1989). "Turning Point." *Los Angeles Times.* (29 July): IV, 1.

Transnational Consumer Protection

Transnational consumer protection is advocacy that transcends borders, a response to the creation and growth of transnational governance and institutions operating on regional and international levels. Transnational arenas can both promote and hinder consumer protection. A binding regional agreement, for example, may force one nation to accept lower environmental protection standards than it had before the agreement, yet give consumers of all party nations recourse to an independent judicial process that was not available before the agreement. To protect consumers in the future, it may be necessary for consumer advocates to operate in the transnational arena while continuing to maintain strong national programs.

Generally, consumer advocates operate in two types of transnational arenas: regional and international. The European Union (EU) and the North American Free Trade Agreement (NAFTA) are two examples of regional arenas. The EU specifically recognizes that both an open internal market and positive consumer rights are essential to adequate consumer protection. The EU identifies five basic rights of consumers: redress, representation, protection of health and safety, protection of economic interests, and information and education. These rights are espoused in two consumer programs, and although they are not binding on EU's member states, they have had three effects. First, they have encouraged subsequent EU directives that do bind member states. Second, some EU members, such as Spain, have directly adopted these rights into their national constitutions. Third, these rights attained quasi-legal status in a case before the Court of Justice of the European Communities.

Positive consumer rights are only one-half of EU's consumer protections. The other half is the support of an open internal market that protects consumers by promoting competition between suppliers of goods and services. Without both consumer rights and the free flow of goods, consumer interests would become compromised.

NAFTA is a regional arrangement that creates consumer challenges and opportunities. Policy analysts and consumer advocates must consider both the immediate and long-term changes NAFTA may effect. One area of concern is the labor side accord, the North American Agreement on Labor Cooperation (NAALC). Although the NAALC neither changes any U.S. labor laws nor requires the United States, Mexico, and Canada to harmonize their labor laws at any time in the future, it may have more subtle effects. Currently, Mexico's laws are very different from U.S. laws: Minimum wages are relatively low; youth labor laws are more lenient; and unions are ineffective. If the means of production can easily move across borders and large differences remain between the labor standards of the member countries, those countries may enter a "race to the bottom" as employers move their operations in search of the lowest labor costs and weakest labor protections. (In a similar way, environmental standards could be compromised.)

The NAALC, however, also creates an enforcement mechanism whereby private persons or entities can bring a dispute to their country's enforcement official. The dispute may eventually move to a trilateral dispute-settlement program. Thus, although NAFTA may create new problems for consumers, it also creates new areas in which consumers can protect their rights.

The dynamics of consumer protection are evolving in new international areas as well, such as the United Nations Consumer Protection Guidelines, approved in 1985. Although the guidelines are not binding upon UN member states, they influence and foster basic consumer rights and protections, especially in developing countries.

The General Agreement on Tariffs and Trade (GATT) is another agreement that can affect transnational consumer protection in the international arena. Some GATT provisions may invalidate both domestic and international laws if these laws violate the GATT definition of free trade. However, no international agreement binds a country unless that country ratifies it. As the number of countries that ratify GATT increases, so does the effect of the agreement. Broad acceptance of a GATT or other international agreement also increases the power of that law as "customary international law." Thus, transnational consumer protection is carried out both through direct and indirect changes that treaties may make in domestic laws, and through the creation of transnational laws and enforcement institutions that operate independent of domestic law.

— Louise G. Trubek (with assistance from Shawn D. Guse)

See also

European Union, Consumer Policy in the; United Nations Consumer Protections.

Readings

Bejar, Alejandro Alvarez (1994). "Industrial Restructuring and the Role of Mexican Labor in NAFTA." *U.C. Davis Law Review.* 27: 897.

Reich, Norbert (1993). "From Contract to Trade Practices Law: Protection of Consumers' Economic Interests by the EC." In Thomas Wilhelmsson, ed. *Perspectives of Critical Contract Law.* Brookfield, VT: Dartmouth Publishing Co. 55ff.

Travelers' Rights

The only legally established traveler's rights apply to air travelers, who are entitled to compensation when they are bumped off a plane because of overbooking and to a seat in the nonsmoking section of a plane. Travelers on charter flights or tours have the additional right that their prepayments be deposited in an escrow account. Beyond those three instances, the only rights travelers have are those that suppliers choose to volunteer or those that consumers can assert under ordinary contract law.

Airline Overbooking

Many airlines deliberately overbook a flight (accept more reservations than the number of seats available) to compensate for no-shows (people who make reservations but fail to show up for the flight). The airlines are skillful at predicting the number of no-shows, and on most flights no one is bumped. Occasionally, however, more people show up than predicted, so the airline must bump one or more travelers with confirmed reservations.

Federal law specifies the compensation due travelers who are bumped due to overbooking. If the airline can get them to their destinations within an hour of the original schedule, it owes them nothing. If it gets them there one to two hours late (one to four hours for international flights), they are entitled to a cash payment of the amount of the one-way fare, with a cap of $200. If they are later still, the compensation increases to twice the fare, with a cap of $400. In either case, travelers also keep their original tickets. The bumping rule applies to all scheduled flights within the United States and from the United States to foreign countries. It does not apply to charter flights, flights on planes that hold sixty or fewer passengers, or international flights inbound to the United States.

This rule is one of the most effective consumer protections in any industry. To avoid the cash payments, most airlines entice volunteer bumpees with offers of free future trips or credit toward future ticket purchase. These offers are almost always attractive enough to free up the required seats so that the airlines are rarely forced to write checks.

Nonsmoking Seats

On U.S. lines, all travelers have the legal right to a nonsmoking seat, provided they have checked in on time and have a valid ticket. The rule is now moot on domestic flights, where smoking is totally forbidden.

The rule, however, does apply on those U.S. airlines that still permit smoking on some intercontinental flights. If, on such a flight, all the previously designated smoking seats are filled, the airlines are required to enlarge the nonsmoking section to accommodate all those who request a nonsmoking seat. Often, however, that right is a chimera. Typically, seats switched from smoking to nonsmoking are immediately adjacent to the smoking area, so that travelers seated in them are exposed to almost as much secondhand smoke as those in the official smoking section. Moreover, the law does not apply to flights to or from the United States on foreign lines.

The no-smoking requirement is gradually becoming unnecessary. All flights within the United States are totally nonsmoking, and the number of nonsmoking international flights increases every month. By the year 2000, travelers should be able to find nonsmoking flights on just about any route to and from the United States, and on many flights between two foreign countries as well.

Escrow Protection

Over the years, tour-operator financial failures have been the plague of travelers on charter flights or package tours that use charter flights. Such trips must typically be prepaid, often months in advance, and every year or so, one or two big tour operators fail before delivering on the promised trips. Usually, the travelers are simply left at home with neither their trips nor their prepayments. Occasionally, the operator pays an airline to take travelers to their destinations but cannot pay for the return trips, and travelers are stranded away from home.

Federal law requires that tour operators place charter travelers' prepayments into escrow accounts, with disbursement allowed only to airlines, hotels, and other suppliers. Despite the law, tour operators occasionally get their hands on those prepayments and use them for other purposes. Travelers' best protection against that risk is to buy trip-interruption insurance that covers operator failure. The fee is usually 5.5 percent of the trip cost.

Other Rights

The traveler protections described above are the only ones mandated by law. Yet, an airline may have many more reasons, beyond overbooking, to deny travelers seats for which they have valid tickets, and many other ways to fail to get travelers to their final destinations within two hours of the original schedules. For example, if an airline bumps a traveler because it switches the flight to a smaller plane, or promises a 7:00 A.M. departure but does not leave until 7:30 P.M., travelers are not protected by any law. The law requires only that airlines have a written policy on how they handle various problems, which is available to travelers.

At that, air passengers fare better than buyers of other travel services. Cruise passengers, hotel guests, and car renters have no specific rights at all. Moreover, none of the trade associations in those industries has any sort of consumer protection program.

As a practical matter, many suppliers are reasonably good about taking care of travelers who have been inconvenienced. When airlines are at fault for a long en route delay, travelers often receive meal vouchers and even overnight accommodations. Hotels traditionally walk overbooked travelers to another hotel of about the same quality and pay for the first night. However, travelers have no legal right to demand such treatment—it is given as a matter of business practice, not law.

Problem Resolution

Most large travel suppliers maintain at least a nominal in-house consumer relations function. If a supplier refuses to rectify a problem, outside assistance is available to some travelers. The Department of Transportation's Aviation Consumer Protection Agency occasionally follows up on a traveler's complaint about an airline, but has authority only to press for a solution, not to compel one. The American Society of Travel Agents operates an effective mediation program, but only for travelers who encounter problems with a member agency. The National Tour Association and the U.S. Tour Operators Association both offer mediation, but only for travelers who encounter problems with a member tour operator. Some publications, radio stations, and television stations operate consumer-assistance programs that can take up a consumer's battle, but these media choose only a few cases with broad public interest.

As a last resort, travelers can exercise their citizen's right to redress through the courts; for a typical travel problem, that usually means small claims court. Travelers who turn to small claims court should keep two facts in mind. First, they must be able to show an actual out-of-pocket loss or failure to live up to a specific contractual commitment, not just dissatisfaction or annoyance. Second a small-claims action is usually feasible only against a supplier with some kind of office in or near a traveler's home city. With an airline problem that is relatively easy, because an airline can be sued at a local ticket office or airport address. However, if the problem is with an out-of-town travel agency or tour operator, most travelers could not justify the expense and time of traveling to the supplier's base to pursue a small claim.

— Ed Perkins

See also

Airline Deregulation; Aviation Safety.

Readings

Dickerson, Thomas A. (1982). "Travel Law: Securing Travelers' Rights and Remedies." *Trial*. 18 (August): 44–47.

U.S. Department of Transportation (1994). *Fly-Rights: A Consumer Guide to Air Travel.* Washington, DC: GPO.

TURN

See Toward Utility Rate Normalization.

U

Unfair Sale Practices

See Deceptive, Unfair, and Unconscionable Sales Practices.

Unions

See Labor Movement.

United Kingdom's Consumer Movement

The consumer movement in the United Kingdom (UK) is best viewed as a function of a few highly influential organizations—notably Consumers' Association and the National Consumer Council. In addition, it is important to understand the roles of local advice bureaus and government enforcement authorities. Together, they constitute a consumer movement of unusual domestic effectiveness and international impact.

The consumer movement in the United Kingdom was born in 1957, when the country was still in the shadow of World War II. Wartime food rationing, which persisted into the 1950s, was still a recent memory, but for the first time consumers were emerging from an economic situation dominated by scarcity of goods and services to find themselves faced with problems of choice. These problems were thrown into sharp relief by the rapid development of branded products and intensified competition between brands, fueled by the launch of commercial advertising on television in 1955.

Many of the products themselves were new: washing machines, detergents, ballpoint pens, television sets, and clothes made from synthetic fibers. The benefits of technological innovation in products were counterbalanced by the consumer's inability to draw on purchasing knowledge and skills transmitted from the previous generation.

These changes took place at the same time that personal disposable incomes increased rapidly and consumers' expectations of higher living standards rose. Consumers' greatest need was for reliable, independent information to help them make rational decisions in a period when products, markets, incomes, and expectations were changing so quickly.

Consumers' Association and *Which?*

The consumer movement in the United States provided a specific and well-formed template for the UK. An Anglo-American couple living in London, Dorothy and Ray Goodman, were subscribers to *Consumer Reports*. They gathered together a group of friends and associates to launch a similar guide to goods and services, based on comparative testing. With Michael Young—now Lord Young of Dartington—as the first chair and driving force, Consumers' Association (CA) was set up; the first issue of *Which?* was launched in the fall of 1957.

Consumers Union (CU) was more than a model for the UK initiative. One of Colston Warne's imaginative actions was to make a grant (the equivalent of about $5,000) to the nascent CA, almost its only capital resource. Many of CU's principles were adopted by CA from the outset: freedom from business control, influence, and finance; prohibition on manufacturers using *Which?* test results or ratings in their own marketing; and purchase of test samples on the open market. One significant difference is that, unlike Consumer Reports, *Which?* is a subscription magazine, available only to members of CA.

Serious doubts arose at the launch of *Which?* as to whether it would survive the anticipated spate of libel actions by manufacturers whose named products were often criticized in a forthright manner—and sometimes even subjected to a "not recommended" verdict. However, accurate research and reasoned judgments ensured the organization's legal survival. Not only is comparative testing no longer a novelty in the UK, it is the established centerpiece of its consumer movement.

The initial success of *Which?* took the founding group by surprise: ten thousand members joined CA in the first week. A key factor in the rapid growth of membership was the insistence of the first editor, Eirlys Roberts, that the magazine's comparative test reports should be written clearly and simply, so that they could be understood without difficulty. Reliability and impartiality of test results were necessary, of course, but effective communication was vital.

By 1975 the membership of CA had risen to 700,000. In 1990 it exceeded 1 million, but as a result of the economic recession and subscription price increases, by the spring of 1995 fell to just over 800,000. Each copy of *Which?* is read by an estimated average of four people, and with an annual revenue of $80 million, CA holds its position as one of the largest consumer organizations in the world.

The organization has had problems of governance over the years. In its early days, considerable apprehension was felt that a fully democratic organization might be vulnerable to a takeover by business interests. Although the governing council was elected, the franchise was limited to a relatively small number of voting members. Today, all members are entitled to vote for the council, although the numbers entitled to propose candidates for election to this body are still limited.

Which? continues to be the focus of CA's activity and its public reputation, but a constellation of satellite periodicals includes (in descending order of subscription numbers) *Gardening Which?*, *Holiday Which?*, *Drug and Therapeutics Bulletin*, *Which? Way to Health*, *Legal Services*, *Which? Wine Monthly*, and *Consumer Policy Review*. A recent attempt to produce a consumer magazine for younger readers, *Check It Out!*, was abandoned after two years. A wide range of books is offered, many of which deal with health issues. CA also offers a subscription-based legal advice service and produces computer software to help consumers with tax problems.

Although CA's primary function is to provide consumers with the information needed to make informed decisions, it also engages in lobbying government and business on behalf of consumers' interests. It has achieved some notable successes, including playing a major part in getting the Unsolicited Goods and Services Act 1971 and the Unfair Contract Terms Act 1977 on the statute books, and more recently in reforming the sale of goods law. CA campaigns continuously and effectively on such issues as the lifting of controls on shop opening hours, automobile safety, and food hygiene.

CA's campaigning strategy faces the problem familiar to consumer organizations worldwide—how to manage slender resources of people, time, and money in dealing with a wide range of issues that affect the lives of consumers. Paradoxically, the more effective the campaigns, the worse the problem: Success in pressing for better representation of consumer interests leads to greater demands for a consumer view from government and business. CA responds to consultative documents on a wide range of issues and has representatives or nominees on no less than fifty-five other bodies, ranging from the British Dental Health Foundation to the Vehicle Crime Prevention Group. It also plays an active role in the standardization process through representation on British, European, and international standards committees.

National Consumer Council

The growth of the independent, self-financing Consumers' Association has been paralleled by the development of a publicly funded consumer body in the government sector. This development has occurred in many European countries and elsewhere in the world, but not in the United States. As early as 1962, a government-appointed Committee on Consumer Protection recommended that the government establish a Consumer Council, which would have the job of safeguarding the interests of consumers, especially in relation to their legal rights, but which would not compete with CA in testing goods and services. The Conservative government of the day created a Consumer Council, but eight years later another Conservative government abolished the agency.

Shortly thereafter, the Labour party in opposition announced that if it won the next general election, it would establish a National Consumers' Agency, funded by a tax on advertising, whose main job would be to act as a countervailing power to advertising pressures on consumers. When the Labour party won power in 1974, it went ahead with its plans, but in a considerably modified form. The proposed tax on advertising was dropped, and a National Consumer Council (NCC) was set up with a wide-ranging permit to represent consumers' interests to central and local government, other public bodies, and business. To redress the perceived middle-class bias of other consumer bodies, NCC was given special responsibility to represent the interests of "inarticulate and disadvantaged" consumers, especially low-income consumers, ethnic minorities, and disabled people.

A major characteristic of NCC's work is that it has broadened the interpretation of the consumer to include the consumer of public as well as private services. Much of its work focuses on the problems people have when dealing with public utilities, the health service, the social security system, the legal system, education, and a wide variety of local government services. Ranging even more widely, NCC has produced influential reports on how the Common Agricultural Policy of the European Union and international trade barriers affect consumers.

Like CA and the UK consumer movement generally, NCC is scrupulous in not aligning itself with any one political party on a continuing basis. Yet, many of the issues with which it concerns itself have a political context, so NCC forms issue-based alliances with political and other interests. One example is the long-running controversy over the reform of legislation restricting shop opening hours, in which NCC worked with CA and other consumer organizations, some larger retailers, and the majority of Conservative members of Parliament against an alliance of trade unions, religious bodies, and most Labour members of Parliament.

It is testimony to NCC's political and lobbying skills that, while it was originally set up by a Labour government in 1975, the Conservative governments that have been in power continuously since 1979 have kept it in existence, even though on many occasions NCC publicly criticized and lobbied against them on specific issues affecting consumers.

NCC also has a history of getting consumer protection laws on the statute book. It was primarily responsible for the Credit Unions Act of 1979 and the Consumer Safety Act of 1986, and works closely with Consumers' Association on the provisions of other draft legislation.

The structure of NCC differs sharply from that of CA. Because it has no individual consumer members, NCC faces repeated challenges from business as to its legitimacy as a consumer organization. The chair and members of its governing council are appointed by the government, and include people from the business community. Fortunately, the first two chairs were people of considerable vision—Michael Young, who eighteen years previously had brought Consumers' Association into the world, and the late Michael Shanks.

Another distinguishing feature of the National Consumer Council's structure is its associated "country" consumer councils for

Scotland, Wales, and Northern Ireland, which focus on the distinctive problems facing consumers in those countries. For example, recent studies carried out by the Scottish Consumer Council deal with problems faced by rural consumers and the special characteristics of poverty in Scotland.

Unlike CA, NCC's output is not aimed primarily at the individual consumer. Rather, it is a research-based policy body, carrying out studies and campaigning in the interests of consumers, and its reputation rests on the quality of its research. Although it has proved its ability to work with political interests across the ideological spectrum, NCC faces a new challenge presented by the government's decision, in line with its general approach to cutting public expenditure, to reduce its financial grant.

Broader Consumer Movement

One of the National Consumer Council's functions is to act as a facilitator for the development of the Consumer Congress, an independent association with its own constitution and more than 100 member organizations. The Consumer Congress meets annually and aims to develop policies on matters of concern to consumers and encourage joint action to promote these policies.

Membership of the Consumer Congress is extremely diverse, not only in terms of the size and resources of the member organizations but also in subject matter. Some are mainstream consumer bodies, such as the National Federation of Consumer Groups (NFCG). NFCG dates from 1963, and in the heyday of the UK's local consumer group movement had over fifty geographically based local consumer groups. The number has stabilized at sixteen, which includes groups in large population centers such as Birmingham, Edinburgh, Aberdeen, and Plymouth, but none in the major conurbations of Manchester, Liverpool, or Leeds. The continuing existence of any local group depends very much on a self-renewing nucleus of consumer activists. Most local consumer groups publish their own magazine, and inevitably the quality of these publications varies, but the best include systematic local surveys comparing retail prices and facilities as well as reports on public transport and local authority services.

Many member organizations of the Consumer Congress are highly focused or special interest groups, such as the British Standards Institution Consumer Policy Committee and the Legal Action Group. Others straddle the vague frontier between consumer and citizen issues, such as Shelter, the National Campaign for the Homeless. Another category includes observer membership for bodies that do not qualify as consumer organizations. Some, such as the Retail Credit Group, are firmly based in the business community. Given the diversity of the Consumer Congress's membership, its success should be measured primarily in terms of providing a networking facility for joint action rather than achieving policy goals itself.

Citizens' Advice Bureaus

Although not strictly part of the consumer movement, Citizens' Advice Bureaus make a major contribution to the lives of millions of consumers in the UK. The origins of the service date to 1939 when locally run advice bureaus, manned by volunteers, were set up to deal with information and inquiries arising out of the mass evacuation of people from large cities in anticipation of bombing raids and the onset of wartime regulations. The service continued after World War II, and has expanded to its present level of over 1,500 information and advice outlets throughout the country.

Each bureau is run by its own local management committee and is locally funded, predominantly by grants from local authorities. A staff of 27,000, 90 percent of whom are volunteers, deal with some 7.5 million requests for information and advice every year, with social security and debt being the two largest categories of interest. All information and advice is provided without charge. The frontline "generalist" staff are backed up by groups of specialist advisers in certain fields such as debt counseling and immigration.

The bureaus in England, Wales, and Northern Ireland are grouped together in the

National Association of Citizens' Advice Bureaus (NACAB) (and in Scotland, Citizens' Advice Scotland). The national organizations, funded mainly by government grants, provide a central databank of information for the individual bureaus as well as training for staff.

Increasingly, the national advice organizations are asked to draw on the vast reservoir of inquiries and problems handled by individual bureaus to assess the impact of legislation and the quality of public and private services. For example, NACAB has submitted evidence to the government on social security issues, consumer debt, rent distress, and industrial tribunal procedures.

The bureau movement provides a distinct and effective blend of public funding and private effort. Its importance to citizens is revealed by the statistic that over 25 percent of the adult population has used a bureau on at least one occasion.

International Context

From the start, the UK consumer movement played a leading role in the development of the international consumer movement. In 1960, with the support of Consumers Union from the United States and the Australian and Belgian consumer organizations, Consumers' Association joined with the Netherlands consumer organization Consumentenbond to form the International Organization of Consumers' Unions (now known as Consumers International).

CA continues to play an important part in the progress of the world consumer movement. However, the UK's membership in the European Union (EU) provides a more sharply etched focus for international activity because the EU provides a framework for consumer protection legislation that is binding on member states.

Both Consumers' Association and the National Consumer Council are vigorous members of Bureau Européen des Unions de Consommateurs, the coordinating body in Brussels that provides a platform for intensive lobbying for the consumer interest in EU policies. Previously, promotion of the consumer cause was hindered by the absence of any explicit reference to the consumer interest in the founding Treaty of Rome. This deficiency was rectified in the Treaty of Maastricht, which provided new impetus to the effort to convince EU policymakers to take consumer needs into account.

Within the UK, since 1978 the Consumers in Europe Group (CEG) has constituted a small but effective umbrella body of over thirty organizations with an interest in furthering the consumer interest in EU policies and legislation. CEG directly lobbies the institutions of the EU—for example, the European Commission and European Parliament—and makes representations to the UK government on European issues.

Government and the Consumer Interest

From the early 1960s to the mid-1970s, a wave of new consumer protection legislation was introduced by both Labour and Conservative governments. The new laws covered product safety, weights and measures, and trade practices, including advertising and other forms of promotion. Financial services were covered by statutes regulating rental purchases and consumer credit.

Institutional change paralleled legislative change. Consumer protection in the UK is based on a system of national legislation enforced by local (city and county) authorities. For many decades, local enforcement focused primarily on weights and measures and environmental health issues, but the new range of consumer protection legislation represents a radical change in the scope and size of local authority enforcement functions. The old local weights and measures offices emerged as trading standards departments, and in some areas, consumer advice centers were opened to complement the existing network of citizens' advice bureaus. Currently, 126 local trading standards departments employ some 1,500 trading standards officers.

At the national level, the 1973 Fair Trading Act established the statutory post of Director General of Fair Trading, supported by the

Office of Fair Trading. The powers and functions of the director general include monopoly, merger, and restrictive trade practices, as well as consumer affairs and consumer credit. Among the specific consumer protection functions of the Director General of Fair Trading are licensing of consumer credit firms and estate agents (realtors), requiring remedial action from manufacturers and traders who have persisted in a course of conduct that is detrimental and unfair to consumers, encouraging trade associations to draw up codes of practice that safeguard and promote the interests of consumers, and providing consumers with information.

Although the Director General of Fair Trading is appointed by the government of the day, it is not a political appointment. The first two holders of the post, the late Sir John Methven and Sir Gordon Borrie, exercised considerable political acumen in deploying their powers without coming into conflict with the government. More recently, the inherent contradictions in the UK's approach to competition (antitrust) policy were brought into the open by the third holder, Sir Bryan Carsberg; many of his recommendations on mergers and monopolies were rejected by the government, and he subsequently resigned.

Current Status and Future Prospects

The UK consumer movement can point to some notable successes. Consumers' Association has a substantial membership, beyond the wildest dreams of its progenitors. Its magazine, *Which?*, has an unchallenged reputation for publishing accurate, impartial, and informative test reports. Both CA and the National Consumer Council are responsible for getting consumer legislation on the statute book and for influencing a wide range of public policies. Indeed, so successful have they been in campaigning on behalf of consumers that now they can scarcely meet the flow of requests for a consumer perspective on various policy developments. The representation of consumer interests has made notable advances; for example, three board members of the new self-regulatory authority for the life insurance and retail investment industry come from the consumer movement. Perhaps the most notable achievement is that the consumer perspective has been introduced into policy areas far removed from traditional mainstream consumer issues such as access to justice, poverty and deprivation, social security, education, and public transport systems.

All of this has been achieved with a distinctive style. The UK consumer movement advances the consumer cause through issue-based alliances rather than permanent coalitions, and its work is characterized by rational persuasion and based on thorough research and fact-gathering, with little reliance on emotional appeals. In the words of Maurice Healy, "We are governed by the head, not the heart." This approach has its limitations; in particular, it lacks the ready attractions of the environmental movement, in which the visionary idealism of global goals (e.g., ecological balance) can be reinforced by specific, local action (e.g., protesting against the felling of woodland to make space for a new motorway).

Continuing commitment to the consumer cause is attractive, but only to a minority. The UK consumer movement shares a common problem with consumer movements throughout the world—the great majority of people think of themselves as consumers only when something goes wrong. Apart from a nucleus of consumer activists, most people's identification with the consumer movement is highly intermittent, and for this reason, the UK consumer movement is unlikely ever to become a mass movement. The high membership figures for Consumers' Association reflect the fact that *Which?* provides a money-saving consumer information service.

The recent political climate in the UK has not favored the advancement of consumer interests. In the 1970s, a Conservative government had a Minister for Consumer Affairs, and the succeeding Labour government had a Secretary of State for Prices and Consumer Protection, with a place in the cabinet. Now, consumer affairs is the political responsibility of a junior Minister for Consumer Affairs and

Small Firms, within the Department of Trade and Industry. Moreover, the government grant to the National Consumer Council has been cut back. Indeed, the government seems to find the very word *consumer* anathema, and much prefers to use either *citizen* (in relation to public services) or *customer* (in relation to private goods and services), with an emphasis on the contractual or quasi-contractual nature of the relationship. In the area of enforcing consumer protection legislation, severe financial pressures on local authorities cause their powers of prosecution to be used more infrequently, and most local authority consumer advice centers have been closed down.

— Jeremy Mitchell

Readings

Consumers International (1995). *Balancing the Scales, Part 1: Consumer Protection in Sweden and the United Kingdom.* London: Consumers International.

Martin, John, and George W. Smith (1968). *The Consumer Interest.* London: Pall Mall Press.

Smith, George W. (1982). *The Consumer Interest.* London: John Martin Publishing.

United Nations Consumer Protections

During the last several decades, technological advances in transportation and communications have gradually transformed the world into a global economy. During the 1960s and 1970s, consumers began to enjoy fresh fruits and vegetables imported from places with opposite seasons, and transnational corporations began to market products ranging from infant formula to pesticides worldwide. It soon became apparent to the consumer movement, however, that these products were spreading faster than knowledge about their potential hazards and that, in many parts of the world, systems to ensure global product safety and fairness in the marketplace did not exist. As a result, the consumer movement began to work with various arms of the United Nations (UN) to address these consumer protection needs.

One of the first efforts on a product safety and marketing problem dealt with aggressive and deceptive marketing practices of infant formula manufacturers. In a number of developing countries, consumer organizations documented how sales representatives would dress like health professionals, distribute free product samples, and advise women who had just given birth that infant formula was superior to breast milk. Infant formula has an important role for women who cannot or do not want to breast feed, but in developing countries it is often extremely difficult to obtain clean water to add to dry formula and to sterilize bottles. Formula is also expensive. Once a mother begins giving formula, her body stops producing breast milk, so she cannot stop using formula.

Concerned about unethical marketing, groups worldwide began to communicate and organize, forming the Infant Formula Action Coalition. In 1977 they called for a worldwide boycott of Nestlé products because Nestlé was one of the most aggressive marketers of formula in developing countries. They also lobbied the UN World Health Organization (WHO) for a code of conduct that would specify unethical marketing practices and recommend that member nations outlaw them.

In 1981, after many long and fierce battles, WHO adopted the International Code of Marketing of Breast-Milk Substitutes by a vote of 118–1, with the United States casting the only dissenting vote. Since then, more than 150 countries have taken action to put the code in effect. Problems have not disappeared, but consumers and governments now have a standard they can use to evaluate business behavior and take action.

Another early international effort by consumer groups was advocacy for the establishment of a UN directory of banned and restricted products. In 1977, after a flame retardant used on children's sleepwear was banned in the United States, U.S. companies shipped some 2 million pairs of treated pajamas and other garments abroad and sold them for more than a year. Consumer groups worldwide protested, expressing concern over the difficulty of one country learning of another's product bans and restrictions.

During the Carter administration, Esther Peterson, then special assistant to the president for consumer affairs, led an effort seeking approval for an executive order that would create a list of U.S. banned and restricted products, as well as a system of notification when any such products were shipped abroad. Despite intense industry protests, President Carter signed the order in the closing days of his administration. The order was revoked by President Ronald Reagan only thirty-four days later.

Objections to this revocation were voiced by consumer advocates and UN officials. A Venezuelan delegate sought out nongovernmental organizations (NGOs), the UN term for consumer and environmental groups, to urge them to support a UN version of the Carter executive order. Again, lobbying was intense worldwide. Eileen Nic and Esther Peterson, now representing the International Organization of Consumers Unions (IOCU) at the UN, worked hard to convince UN delegates in New York of the value of a directory of hazardous products, while consumer groups in dozens of countries took the case to their national governments. Although industry strongly opposed the measure, in 1982 the UN General Assembly voted, with only the United States dissenting, to establish the UN Consolidated List of Products Whose Consumption and/or Sale Have Been Banned, Withdrawn, Severely Restricted or Not Approved by Governments.

As of 1996, the UN list was in its fifth edition and included information on more than 700 pharmaceuticals, pesticides, chemicals, and consumer products that have been banned or restricted in one country or another. The list has been widely used; for example, the Korean Citizen's Alliance for Consumer Protection used it to convince their government to ban twenty-four hazardous drugs and restrict twenty-seven others that had been banned or restricted in the developed world.

These efforts by the consumer movement revealed to activists how greatly countries varied in the degree of consumer protection provided to their citizens. The IOCU therefore made it a priority to convince the UN General Assembly to adopt Consumer Protection Guidelines. At the UN, the IOCU has Category I status, which gives it the right to "sit at the table" and speak like a national delegation, but not to vote on issues.

The goal of the guidelines was to set out a comprehensive framework for consumer protection that governments could use as a blueprint for protecting their consumers in the global marketplace. The idea immediately triggered fierce opposition. Large transnational corporations and the U.S. delegation, serving under President Reagan, charged that the guidelines would make the UN a "global nanny," and claimed that a consumer's best protection is a free market. Esther Peterson and the IOCU countered by arguing that Americans had not depended on unfettered free enterprise "since the days of Teddy Roosevelt." After much effort and some compromise, the guidelines passed in 1985.

The guidelines have been likened to an international consumer bill of rights. In an eight-page document, they cover the fundamentals of consumer protection: Governments should adopt safety regulations, adopt policies to ensure that products are durable and reliable, take action against false and misleading claims and fraud, establish mechanisms for redress if consumers experience problems with products, and encourage competition. Separate paragraphs are devoted to the need for establishing standards that ensure the safety of food, water, and pharmaceuticals.

The Consumer Protection Guidelines have had an impact. The UN organized two international conferences to help countries understand and implement them. One was held in 1987 in Uruguay for the benefit of Latin America, and the second in 1990 in Bangkok for the benefit of Asia. The IOCU held follow-up workshops in Asia (Samoa, Hanoi, and Kuala Lampur) and Africa (Senegal, Zimbabwe, and Benin). At a 1992 meeting in Slovenia attended by 100 consumer activists from twenty-one Eastern European countries, the guidelines served as a benchmark in many discussions. An IOCU briefing kit on the guidelines has been translated into languages ranging from Turkish to Maori.

Increasingly, the guidelines are being translated into legislation. One of the earliest laws was India's Consumer Protection Act of 1986 (COPRA). Although certain basic standards were in place before this law went into effect, India suffered from lack of enforcement, and COPRA created an Indian version of small claims court. Consumer Dispute Forums were granted wide powers to deal with defective goods and services; they must act quickly (within ninety days), have no filing fees, and encourage consumers to argue their own cases.

In 1991 the Philippines passed a Consumer Act, which created a statutory ombudsman to deal with complaints against government agencies. In 1993, Japan passed its first product liability law.

In Africa, because of the guidelines, a number of countries established departments of consumer affairs. The Consumer Council of Zimbabwe launched a campaign for the establishment of a small claims court that achieved success in 1992. Nigeria created a drug registration system that same year.

IOCU's Regional Office for Latin America (ROLAC) created an Informal Legal Advice Group, which used the Consumer Protection Guidelines to prepare and publish a Model Law for Consumer Defense. The criteria and proposals in this document influenced national legislation that followed soon after in Brazil (1991 Consumer Defense Code), Ecuador (1990 and 1991 Consumer Defense Law and Regulations), Peru (1991 Legislative Decree on Norms for Advertising for Consumer Defense), and Mexico (1992 New Federal Law on Consumer Protection). The Model Law has also been discussed by lawmakers in half a dozen other countries. Because of its value, ROLAC published an updated version in 1994. It is expected to play an important role in an effort under way to harmonize regional consumer protection under trade agreements.

In the mid-1990s, IOCU, which changed its name to Consumers International, urged the UN to broaden the scope of the Consumer Protection Guidelines to address the question of sustainable consumption. In 1995 the UN Commission for Sustainable Development and the UN Economic and Social Council recommended expansion of the guidelines to include the promotion of sustainable consumption. This additional guideline would encourage governments to develop policies, such as environmental labeling of products, that make consumption more compatible with the health of the biosphere.

In the mid-1990s, the consumer movement faces new challenges and opportunities worldwide. Following adoption of the General Agreement on Tariffs and Trade (GATT), in 1993 the Codex Alimentarius Commission, part of the UN World Health Organization and the UN Food and Agriculture Organization, assumed new importance. Codex evaluates safety and establishes standards for pesticide and drug residues, additives, and food labeling. Many countries have adopted Codex standards, and its standards must be considered in any trade dispute. Consumers International monitors its proceedings closely. Elsewhere, this organization participated in negotiations under the UN Economic Commission for Europe on standards for child restraints in automobiles, and succeeded in making them stronger. As our world effectively shrinks, the role of the United Nations in consumer protection becomes increasingly pivotal.

— Esther Peterson, Jean M. Halloran

See also

Consumers International; Peterson, Esther.

Readings

Harland, David (1987). "The United Nations Guidelines for Consumer Protection." *Journal of Consumer Policy.* 10: 245–266.

Peterson, Esther (1985). "International Consumer Guidelines." In Karen P. Schnittgrund, ed., *Proceedings of the 31st Annual Conference, American Council on Consumer*

Interests. Columbia, MO: American Council on Consumer Interests. 305–309.

U.S. Congress and Consumer Protection

See Congress and Consumer Protection.

U.S. Consumer Information Center

See Consumer Information Center.

U.S. Consumer Movement: History and Dynamics

The consumer movement consists of the organized efforts of individual citizens and private, not-for-profit organizations to enhance the rights and collective welfare of consumers. The primary goal of the movement is to advance efficiency and equity in the marketplace. Although the consumer movement is a global phenomenon, this entry focuses primarily on the consumer movement in the United States. The U.S. consumer movement is itself highly diverse, with activity at the local, state, and national level. This entry focuses mainly on the movement at the national level. (Movement developments at the grassroots level are summarized in the entry on "State and Local Consumer Organizations" and treated in greater detail in entries on specific state and local groups.)

Within the United States, individuals such as Ralph Nader and Esther Peterson and organizations such as Consumers Union and the Consumer Federation of America exemplify the consumer movement. The consumerist philosophy of these activist individuals and organizations is often shared by parties outside the movement itself—consumer-oriented legislators and regulators, journalists, scientists, educators, and consumer affairs personnel working in businesses. While these parties have supported the movement and contributed to its achievements, their primary allegiance is typically to an entity or set of values separate from the consumer movement.

The U.S. consumer movement is diverse in the goals, levels of commitment, and social background of its participants. The movement contains people who are motivated by economic issues and seek benefits for themselves as well as those who are guided by moral concerns and pursue benefits for others. The movement is entrepreneurial in the sense that it relies heavily on the activity of full-time professionals who generate support and mobilize resources around particular issues, but it is also characterized by spontaneous, short-term, grassroots action. Whereas the consumer movement has largely attracted white, middle-class participants, it has also afforded leadership opportunities to women and racial minorities.

Diversity within the consumer movement is particularly pronounced with respect to preferred tactics and strategies. The movement is largely reformist in terms of its basic acceptance of existing economic and political institutions and its attempt to solve consumer problems, often in collaboration with business interests. Nevertheless, the movement also contains more radical elements who believe that existing institutions require fundamental change and who distance themselves from business interests.

Members of the movement also differ on other dimensions. One segment seeks policies that expand consumer alternatives and encourage informed choices among them, while another segment takes the more paternalistic view that choices that might prove harmful to consumers should be restricted (e.g., by limiting the availability of alcohol and tobacco or by punishing those who do not use seatbelts or motorcycle helmets). Finally, some consumer organizations (e.g., the American Council on Science and Health) define their role as advocacy against government interventions on behalf of consumers, even when these interventions are supported by the majority of consumer organizations.

In sum, the U.S. consumer movement consists of a broad and loosely coordinated set of individuals and private, not-for-profit organizations that consciously seek to advance the welfare of consumers. These movement participants share an equally broad and loosely constructed set of values and beliefs about the situation of consumers. This flexibility in the structure and goals of the consumer movement allows for diversity in the commitment, motives, preferred strategies, and geographical location of movement participants.

The First Era: The Early 1900s

In the early days of the nation, consumers' welfare depended in large part on their own skills and on the honesty and competence of local storekeepers. Both consumers and storekeepers were forced to depend on past experience in judging goods, since they had little in the way of technical information, trademarks, or grades to guide them. The laws governing trade focused on ensuring orderly commerce rather than on protecting consumers specifically. Fraud and adulteration were frequent and difficult to control since many items were in bulk form and moved through many hands on their way to the consumer.

The economic life of the country and the situation of consumers changed rapidly in the last four decades of the nineteenth century. Industrial output and employment increased fivefold. The population doubled and became increasingly urbanized. Nationwide markets developed as manufacturers of consumer goods began to trademark their wares, advertise them in the new mass-circulation magazines, and ship them via the growing rail system to remote areas.

About 1900 a new group of political reformers concerned with the problems of a more urban and industrialized society emerged in the urban middle and professional classes. These reformers of the Progressive movement were joined by the veterans of the Populist movement of the previous decade and sought to use the power of government to bring about the social and economic reforms they believed were needed.

A variety of reform organizations concerned with local social problems and political corruption appeared between 1890 and 1900. One such group, a voluntary organization of middle- and upper-class "do-gooders," sought to improve working conditions by education, research, and selective retail patronage. The first Consumers' League, formed in New York City in 1891, began its work by preparing an approved "white list" of shops that paid fair wages, had reasonable hours, and maintained sanitary conditions. They asked consumers to concentrate their patronage on these shops. In 1898, the local groups joined in a national federation, the National Consumers League (NCL), the first national consumers organization. By 1903, the national organization had branches in twenty states. While the Leagues's early investigations focused on working conditions, more recently NCL has worked mainly on consumer issues.

For three decades after the Civil War, workers' real incomes grew steadily. But beginning in 1897, these gains turned to losses as a long chain of increases in consumers' cost of living began. Between 1900 and 1914, with the help of unions, private sector workers were able again to increase their real annual incomes. But, the pressure of price increases was felt keenly by government employees and others on fixed incomes. Trusts, corporate schemes to eliminate competition and control prices, became a focus of blame for the new rise in prices. The muckraking journalistic exposés of the period both reflected and fed the suspicions of the public about the trusts.

McClure's magazine became a muckraking publication by accident when it commissioned a study of Standard Oil, the largest American trust, as a follow-up to a series it had run on great American business achievements. Beginning in 1902, the series by Ida Tarbell showed that Standard Oil had grown through bribery, graft, fraud, violence, and the destruction of competition. It created a sensation, encouraging several other new mass-circulation magazines to use exposés of corruption in business and government as a device to build circulation. Life insurance companies, railroads, trusts, and politicians all were scrutinized, and the demand for reform grew.

The nationwide rail network and the development of refrigerated rail cars opened a national market to food processors and meat packers. The packers' and canners' understanding of the principles of food safety and preservation was rudimentary, and preservatives were used liberally. Official attention to the problem in the Division of Chemistry of the U.S. Department of Agriculture began with the arrival of Dr. Harvey W. Wiley in 1883. In the course of their investigations, Wiley and his staff cataloged 1,400 pages of documented cases of adulteration, but they were unable to arouse much interest among the public or Congress. To dramatize the problem, Wiley created a "poison squad," a volunteer group of healthy young men whom he fed a diet of typical food adulterants in order to determine their effects. Although the tests proved little, they made excellent copy for the media.

Beginning in 1892, a series of unsuccessful attempts were made to obtain federal pure food legislation. Opposition to the bills came from three groups: business and regional interests affected by the proposed legislation, southern Democrats reluctant to grant increased powers to the federal government, and those who believed that other legislative matters were more pressing. Another attempt was made in 1902. This bill made little headway, but support for new legislation was gathering and included the General Federation of Women's Clubs, the National Consumers League, and state food and dairy chemists. The muckraker press aided with exposés on the dangers of adulterated food and the hazards of unlabeled patent medicines laced with opiates and alcohol. Despite this support, the efforts for new legislation failed.

In 1904, after Theodore Roosevelt was elected president in his own right, he was urged by consumer advocates to support pure food legislation. In his annual message to Congress the following year, Roosevelt urged the enactment of a pure food and drug law. After Senate passage, the proposed law stalled in the House. Then, in 1906, Upton Sinclair's *The Jungle* was published. This fictional exposé of the working conditions in the Chicago meat packing houses nauseated the public with its graphic descriptions of adulteration techniques and unsanitary conditions. The president's reaction was similar to the public's. He was, moreover, concerned about the deficiencies in federal inspection detailed in the book. When two independent investigations bore out Sinclair's charges, Roosevelt put his support behind the passage of meat inspection legislation.

After Senate passage of the bill, the groups opposing meat inspection legislation hoped to water it down in the House, but Roosevelt urged the House to action. To his message he appended the first portion of the report made by the federal officials who had checked conditions at his request. The report touched off a new wave of indignation. Sales of meat and meat products had dropped by half, and the loss of European markets was threatened. The packers then began to realize that a strengthened system of federal inspection was the only way to save their reputations. A bill, the Meat Inspection Act, quickly passed Congress and was signed by the president. The momentum created by the meat inspection issue also carried the Pure Food Bill to the floor of the House where it also was passed quickly. The fight for the pure food law finally had been won, but only after two decades of effort, the help of a full-scale scandal, and strong presidential support.

The Progressives' battle with the corporate trusts, the fight for pure food, rising prices, and the growing volume of advertising all helped to make the public aware of their interests as consumers as distinguished from their interests as workers or property-owners. This appearance of a consumer consciousness is perhaps the most important result of the first era of the consumer movement. In 1914, Walter Lippmann pointed out the growing political power of consumers as an interest group and noted that "we hear a great deal about the class-consciousness of labor; my own observation is that in America today consumers'-consciousness is growing very much faster."

There was little activity in the consumer movement during the next decade. The accelerated rise in prices between 1914 and mid-1920 created hardships for many. For others, especially businessmen and farmers, wartime income increases outran price increases. Patriotic fervor, wartime scarcities, and postwar readjustment diverted attention from consumer problems.

The Second Era: The 1930s

In the 1920s, consumer incomes rose gradually, while prices remained relatively stable. Times were good for all but the farmers. Consumers were inundated with advertising from billboards, electric signs, newspapers, magazines, and the new medium of radio. Not surprisingly, then, sales of autos, refrigerators, vacuum cleaners, radios, and phonographs were brisk.

Although the public was little concerned about consumer issues, educators began to recognize the need for more and better consumer education. Consumer problems had been a major concern of home economists from the formative years of their association at the turn of the century. In the mid-1920s, they became concerned about the "scanty amount of economics in our home economics" and began new research into consumer problems. About the same time, Henry Harap proposed a comprehensive curriculum for consumer education based on a comparison of actual consumption patterns and scientifically based standards in his book, *The Education of the Consumer.*

As the decade passed, vague discontent grew among consumers who were purchasing new and unfamiliar consumer durables, food items, and personal hygiene products with little solid information to guide them. This discontent found expression in 1927 in *Your Money's Worth,* a book by Stuart Chase and F. J. Schlink. The book, subtitled *A Study in the Waste of the Consumer's Dollar,* attacked advertising and high-pressure salesmanship and called for scientific testing and product standards to provide consumers with the technical information they needed to make purchase decisions. The book, which gave expression to widely felt concerns, became a best-seller and a Book-of-the-Month Club selection.

At the close of their book, Chase and Schlink proposed the formation of a consumer-sponsored organization to do product testing and described the testing activities of a local "Consumers' Club" in White Plains, New York. Inquiries from readers convinced Schlink that the local group should be expanded. In 1929, Consumers' Research was formed to perform this testing work on a larger scale. The new organization was only one of a number of new product testing laboratories that appeared in the late 1920s. The potential of scientific testing of consumer goods was accepted widely; several major department stores and trade associations also began testing laboratories about this time.

The Great Depression made the problems of consumers far more immediate and compelling than they had been in the 1920s. Reduced incomes and unemployment forced most consumers to consider how to spend more wisely. The problems of consumers were aggravated by a flood of shoddy merchandise at bargain prices. In the first years of the depression, real bargains in distress sale merchandise were offered and sold well. As these stocks were exhausted, they were replaced with inferior merchandise that played on consumers' belief that real bargains were still available. These false bargains created a widespread belief that the quality of clothing, shoes, and sheets had deteriorated. This feeling created further support for quality testing and grade labeling of consumer products, which continued to be major themes of the consumer movement throughout the 1930s.

Business and its excesses in the 1920s were blamed for the debacle of the 1930s, and much of the blame was focused on advertising. There were increasing concerns among consumers that advertising encouraged wasteful proliferation of brands, led to unwise spending, and added to the cost of consumer goods while providing little useful information.

These concerns were given new voice in *100,000,000 Guinea Pigs* by Arthur Kallet and F. J. Schlink of Consumers' Research, which appeared in 1933. This book was followed by several other "guinea pig" books—*Skin Deep; Counterfeit; Partners in Plunder; Eat, Drink and Be Wary;* and *Guinea Pigs No More*—all devoted to debunking (a favorite word of the time) nationally advertised products.

The development of the National Recovery Administration (NRA) program of codes regulating industrial competition led to the first formal representation of the consumer interest in the federal government. The National Industrial Recovery Act, passed in June 1933, provided for industrial, labor, and consumer advisory boards to participate in the code-making process. The Consumer Advisory Board experienced persistent difficulty in influencing the work of the NRA because, unlike the Industrial and Labor Advisory Boards, it lacked the backing of any organized pressure group. NRA administrators saw no need for special consumer representation. They were not persuaded by the argument that consumers, workers, and sellers each have separate interests and that the public interest is the resolution of conflicts among divergent groups for the good of all. They preferred equating the consumer interest with the public interest and firmly believed they represented the public interest.

During the early 1930s, Consumers' Research (CR) developed under the close control of Schlink, who insisted that CR concentrate on product testing and stay clear of broader social and economic issues. In 1935, CR was divided by a bitter strike over unionization of its employees. An association of CR subscribers originally formed to help settle the strike became the nucleus of a new organization, Consumers Union (CU).

From the beginning, CU tested products and disseminated the results in its magazine as well as concerned itself with a broad range of consumer and social problems. CU grew rapidly and, within three years, its membership passed CR's. In 1939 and 1940, CU and the consumer movement came under a cloud when alleged Communist influences in CU and thirteen other consumer organizations were investigated by the House Un-American Activities Committee. Although the Dies Committee was able to prove little beyond the fact that CU's director, Arthur Kallet, was highly critical of the capitalist system, CU's reputation was temporarily tarnished.

By the 1930s, the Pure Food and Drug Act of 1906 was badly in need of revision. Early in the 1930s, the New Deal administration did offer a new bill that would have extended the powers of the Food and Drug Administration (FDA) to include cosmetics as well as food and drugs and to cover both labeling and advertising. The FDA dramatized the need for new legislation with an exhibit of useless and dangerous patent medicines, unsafe cosmetics, and adulterated foods. The press dubbed the exhibit "The Chamber of Horrors." When hearings began on the bill in 1933, the American Home Economics Association and the National Congress of Parents and Teachers were the only groups actively supporting it. The opposition characterized the bill as an interference with consumer choice and "the right of self-medication." The newspapers, cowed by fear of lost advertising revenue, or for other reasons, gave little attention to the bill.

In 1935, President Franklin D. Roosevelt sent a message to Congress urging passage of new legislation to strengthen the FDA but never gave the measure full support. Historian Charles O. Jackson suggests that the legislation was considered to be a reform proposal rather than part of the crucial New Deal recovery program. Without either strong administration or public support, the measure failed. In 1936, Ruth De F. Lamb's *American Chamber of Horrors* documented the FDA's case in print and carried it to a wider audience. Other concerned groups joined in the fight.

A shocking tragedy finally provided the impetus for congressional action. In 1937, a liquid form of a sulfa drug for infections was placed on the market. Although the drug was safe in capsule form, the liquid form (elixir sulfanilamide) relied on a toxic solvent. It proved lethal, and over 100 people died, including several children. A new section was added to the proposed bill requiring that manufacturers prove the safety of new drugs to the satisfaction of the FDA before placing them on the market. In June 1938, a much modified version of the bill finally was passed.

By the late 1930s, some businesses that had become concerned about the impact of the consumer movement commissioned a survey to assess its effects on public attitudes. In 1940, public opinion researcher George Gallup reported that about one quarter of those questioned in his study had read one of the "guinea pig" books, and about half of this group said they had changed their buying habits as a result of what they had read. About one-fifth said they had read research reports of one of the product rating services. Gallup found that the movement had developed its greatest strength among teachers, well-educated groups, the wealthy, and the young. He concluded that the movement had made considerable headway and was likely to continue to grow because of its strength among influential groups.

The Third Era: The 1960s and 1970s

The tempo of activity in the consumer movement and its impact had increased throughout the 1930s. Consumerism undoubtedly would have gained even greater influence in the next few years if the coming of World War II had not diverted attention to the problem of national survival. As its contribution to the war effort, consumer education turned its attention to resource conservation, adjustment to scarcities and rationing, and the consumer's role in fighting inflation. Consumers Union membership fell by a third as a result of the Dies Committee investigation and declining interest in buying information in a period of wartime shortages.

With the end of the war, CU's circulation began a remarkable upward climb as consumers sought product information to guide them in spending their wartime savings. Circulation grew from 50,000 in 1944 to almost a 500,000 in 1950. There was, however, little activity among grassroots consumer organizations.

Although prices rose rapidly in the early years of the Korean War, so did wages, and memories of World War II shortages seem to have stilled consumer protests. A resurgence of interest in consumer education came in the early and middle 1950s as families struggled with the problems of meeting installment payments, financing new homes, choosing life insurance, and selecting television sets and other new durables. In the late 1950s, however, consumer education and other life adjustment courses in the secondary schools suffered setbacks when increased emphasis was given to basic disciplines after the USSR's launch of the first Sputnik satellite in late 1957.

In 1953, the Council on Consumer Information was formed by a group of consumer educators to encourage fact-finding on consumer problems and the dissemination of consumer information. The group instituted a newsletter, a pamphlet series with analyses of policy issues and self-help information aimed at the general public, and a program of annual conferences. The group, whose membership consisted chiefly of college and secondary school teachers and extension workers, grew steadily.

Despite the relative quiet of the 1950s, flare-ups of consumer concern did occur. One such incident came after the publication of Vance Packard's *The Hidden Persuaders* in 1957. Packard, accepting at face value the ad agencies' and market researchers' claims about their powers in influencing consumers, argued that the public was being manipulated without realizing it. The resulting round of charges and countercharges received extensive press coverage and showed that, given the right issues, there still was public interest in consumer problems.

The beginning of the third era of the consumer movement often is dated from John F. Kennedy's Consumer Message to the Congress in the spring of 1962. In fact, Kennedy's influence may have begun even earlier. Historian Arthur Schlesinger, Jr., has pointed out that in Kennedy's 1960 campaign, he "communicated, first of all, a deeply critical attitude toward the ideas and institutions which American society had come in the fifties to regard with such enormous self-satisfaction." Schlesinger argues that the widespread acceptance of these views released the nation's capacity for self-criticism, which had been checked by complacency and McCarthyism in the 1950s. This self-critical perspective was reflected in a succession of examinations of the nation's social and economic problems, many of which deeply involved consumers: Michael Harrington's *The Other America* (1962) on the problems of the poor; Rachel Carson's *The Silent Spring* (1962) on the hazardous effects of pesticides; Jessica Mitford's *The American Way of Death* (1963), an exposé of funeral industry practices; and David Caplovitz's *The Poor Pay More* (1963) on the problems of low-income consumers.

In the preamble to his Consumer Message to Congress in March 1962, President Kennedy enunciated the now famous Consumer Bill of Rights: the right to safety, the right to be informed, the right to choose, and the right to be heard in government decision-making. The main body of the message outlined the need to improve existing programs and to implement new ones. The regulation of food and drugs was one of the areas singled out by Kennedy for special attention.

The weaknesses of the existing laws in insuring that drugs on the market were both effective and safe had become clear in Senator Kefauver's hearings on the regulation of the drug industry. New drug legislation came only after a new tragedy forced action upon the Congress. Word of the thalidomide case reached the public in June 1962. The drug, a sedative and morning sickness drug for pregnant women, had resulted in severe birth defects in Europe. Fortunately, the drug had been kept off the market in the United States by deliberate delays within the FDA. By August, legislation expanding the powers of the FDA had been passed and signed into law.

To implement the fourth right of his Consumer Message, the right to be heard in government proceedings affecting consumers, Kennedy asked the Council of Economic Advisers to appoint a Consumer Advisory Council. Although the functions of the council were strictly advisory, the consumer interest never before had been represented at so high a level. The council undertook comprehensive studies of consumer needs but had limited impact on Congress and public consciousness.

About this same time, a new surge of interest in consumer education occurred. Educators and the public both came to recognize that consumer education was an important and useful subject for all students, college-bound and vocational, and boys and girls alike. New curricula continued to stress both buymanship techniques and money management, and gave new emphasis to the problems and uses of installment credit. Agricultural extension and adult education activity in consumer education also increased greatly during the 1960s. These efforts were supported by an active consumer publication program by the federal government.

As a result of its rapid growth during the 1950s, Consumers Union was publishing nearly 1 million copies of *Consumer Reports* at the time of its twenty-fifth anniversary in 1961. CU increasingly came to view itself as an organization to educate consumers, rather than just as a disseminator of product test results. It concerned itself with educating consumers about all phases of their relationship with the market: interest rates, guarantees and warranties, life insurance, product safety, and doctor selection. In addition, CU provided leadership and funding for the development of other consumer organizations, including an organization of consumer educators (formerly the Council on Consumer Information, now the American Council on Consumer Interests) and an international federation of consumer product testing agencies (formerly the International Organization of Consumers Unions, now Consumers International).

Early in his administration, President Lyndon Johnson recognized that public and congressional interest in consumer problems was growing and that consumer legislation could allow him to build a domestic legislative record with minimal budgetary outlays. In February 1964, he sent a consumer message to Congress urging passage of twelve new laws, including measures on truth in lending, meat inspection, drug inspection, and pesticide control.

In January 1964, Johnson created the new White House post of special assistant for consumer affairs and appointed Esther Peterson to fill it. She played several key roles—as a spokesperson for consumers before Congress, as a publicist for the administration's program of consumer legislation, and as a promoter of local consumer organizations.

By early 1969, there were state consumer organizations in twenty-nine states and nine major cities or counties supported organizations. These organizations provided support to the consumer representatives in state and local governments and became increasingly skilled at putting together temporary coalitions to advance the cause of consumers in the state legislatures.

After the liberal landslide in the election of 1964, the possibilities for new consumer legislation improved. In the spring and summer of 1965, hearings were held on tire and auto safety. The hearings revealed the lack of any deep concern over safety problems in either industry and ended inconclusively after the auto manufacturers argued that principal responsibility for auto safety lay with the driver.

The view that manufacturers bore little responsibility for automobile safety was challenged a few months later by Ralph Nader. His book *Unsafe at Any Speed* presented evidence that auto accidents and injuries were typically the result of faulty engineering, construction, and design. Public concern mounted and, in his State of the Union message in January 1966, President Johnson promised new legislation. During the hearings on the proposed legislation, the news broke of General Motors's investigation of Nader's background and activities. Congressional opinion was alienated by this interference with a key witness. The safety legislation that passed later that year was significantly stronger than the bill originally proposed by the White House, and two years later, the National Highway Traffic Safety Administration was established. In 1966, after five years of congressional inaction, Senator Phillip Hart's (D-MI) "Truth in Packaging" bill was passed and signed into law.

During the first years of the 1960s, consumer prices rose gradually. This made a sudden jump in food prices in 1966 a major cause for consumer concern. Suddenly, large groups of consumers were faced with a noticeable decline in purchasing power. Consumer discontent found open expression in October in a wave of consumer boycotts of food stores. Store contests and games, which had been used widely in the previous year, were the focus of blame, although the real problem was short supplies of meat and produce.

After Ralph Nader's successful efforts in promoting auto safety legislation, he developed a pattern of action. For each issue, he built a well-documented case with information that he and his "Raiders" had searched out or obtained from concerned insiders in industry and government. Then, he enlisted congressional interest and support. At the same time, he publicized his findings in the press and in his lectures. He institutionalized this exposé approach by founding the Center for Study of Responsive Law.

Government regulatory agencies were a major target of early Raider efforts. These agencies included the Federal Trade Commission, the Food and Drug Administration, and the Interstate Commerce Commission. The resulting reports argued that the agencies had not been aggressive enough or had become captives of the special interests they were supposed to regulate. As a result of his contacts in Congress, Nader had far more impact than the muckrakers of the early 1900s or the "guinea pig" authors of the 1930s.

One of Nader's early exposés was of the unsanitary conditions in meat packing plants that sold only intrastate and thus were not subject to federal regulation. This problem was remedied with the passage of the Wholesome Meat Act of 1967, which was signed in a White House ceremony that included Upton Sinclair, then nearly 90 years old.

In 1966, Esther Peterson proposed the creation of a federation of consumer organizations. In 1967, such an organization, the Consumer Federation of America, was organized by Consumers Union, state and local consumer organizations, consumer cooperative groups, and labor unions. Its principal purpose was the representation of the consumer interest before Congress and federal regulatory agencies. Its conference, Consumer Assembly, continues to be the largest annual gathering of consumer advocates from around the nation.

In 1968, the legislative pace quickened. In his State of the Union Message and his Consumer Affairs message in February, President Johnson called for passage of a long list of consumer bills. During the course of the year, a truth in lending bill finally was passed, eight years after the original bill was introduced by Senator Paul Douglas (D-IL). Other new legislation on poultry inspection, pipeline safety, fraudulent land sales, and hazardous appliance radiation also was approved.

Richard Nixon continued the tradition of delivering a consumer message to Congress. In his 1969 message, he offered a Buyer's Bill of Rights that made significant additions to the Consumer Bill of Rights enunciated by John Kennedy. Most importantly, Nixon added the right to register dissatisfaction and to have complaints heard and weighed. He also proposed to give the Office of Consumer Affairs more permanent status by seeking congressional authorization to replace the executive order by which it had been established.

In 1972, Congress created the Consumer Product Safety Commission (CPSC). The new agency combined some existing regulatory activities, such as regulation of flammable fabrics, with new ones, including toys, recreation equipment, and household cleaners and chemicals. In 1975, Congress passed another major piece of legislation, the Magnuson-Moss Warranty Act, which strengthened the consumer's right to redress.

During the 1970s, a variety of national consumer organizations with specialized interests sprang up. In contrast to the broader agendas of earlier organizations, these groups focused more narrowly on such issues as auto safety (Center for Auto Safety), food safety and nutrition (Center for Science in the Public Interest, Community Nutrition Institute), medical issues (Public Citizen's Health Research Group), and local marketplace information (Center for the Study of Services). Highly entrepreneurial, these organizations established themselves as visible, influential advocates for the consumer interest. Over time, they found innovative ways to finance their activities with a combination of grants, supporter contributions, and publication sales.

In his 1976 campaign, Jimmy Carter campaigned as an outsider, calling for better fiscal management by government and reductions in the bureaucracy. Carter's legislative efforts were hampered by the fragmentation of the Democratic majority and the need for fiscal restraint. The increasing public disillusionment with government, which Carter had played upon as a candidate, also proved a handicap when he proposed governmental solutions to social and economic problems.

A watershed in the third era of activity was the defeat, in 1978, of legislation to create an agency for consumer advocacy. The idea of a Department of Consumers to parallel the Departments of Commerce and Labor had been discussed for some time. In the 1970s, under the leadership of Ralph Nader, attention shifted to creating a consumer advocacy agency that would have no regulatory powers of its own but could monitor the activities of other government agencies and intervene in their regulatory decision-making. This structure was urged by Nader, who believed that regulatory responsibility is incompatible with advocacy activity.

The defeat of the consumer advocacy agency proposal came after nine years of effort by one of the largest and most active consumer coalitions in history. The Consumer Federation of America, many of its member organizations, Consumers Union, the Nader network, and about 100 corporations and trade groups were faced by a new, broad coalition of business interests. These business opponents of the proposal foresaw an agency with extensive powers and the ability to intervene in all aspects of government. They argued that the proposed agency would create a new bureaucracy, increase the complexity of regulatory hearings, and force the disclosure of trade secrets.

The bill's defeat appears to have had several causes. Because it focused on process rather than the control of specific risks or abuses, the bill did not arouse the level of public support that more specific protection proposals often do. Another problem was that for the first time, business had built a broad, powerful coalition to oppose a consumer proposal. In the face of this strong opposition, the consumerist camp became deeply divided on the questions of whether, when, and how to compromise.

After the congressional defeat of proposals for a consumer advocacy agency, the Carter administration tried another approach to representing the consumer interest in government. Using an executive order, Carter called for the creation of consumer affairs programs in major federal agencies. The plan, which created consumer advocates in each agency, drew praise from many consumer leaders but was criticized by Ralph Nader. He concluded that the advocates would have little real clout since they lacked subpoena power and the power of judicial review, and were unlikely to criticize their bosses. After the Carter administration, these consumer offices remained but functioned as information disseminators to those outside government, rather than as advocates.

Despite the defeat of the consumer advocacy agency bill, the Carter administration did succeed in moving the consumer interest forward on some fronts. Several leading consumer advocates were appointed to key regulatory posts, where they succeeded in reinvigorating their agencies. In addition, several deregulatory proposals designed to increase competition were put into effect, including the 1978 deregulation of the airline industry. Aggressive antitrust action against AT&T by the Justice Department eventually lead to the 1984 breakup agreement that separated long distance operations from local telephone operating companies. There were setbacks, however. No-fault auto insurance was defeated, and in 1979 Congress imposed restrictions on a number of major FTC investigations.

Recent Decades

The Ronald Reagan administration promoted both economic and social (especially health and safety) deregulation. To implement its program of deregulation, the Reagan administration reduced enforcement activities by cutting agency appropriations and appointing agency heads with a narrower view of their agency's mission. These changes were particularly visible at the FTC, where there were cutbacks in both antitrust and advertising regulatory activities, and at the CPSC. While the public supported many of the economic deregulation proposals, proposals for health, safety, and environmental deregulation met with resistance. The pressures of the Reagan cutbacks and the experience of lobbying together for the agency for consumer advocacy proposals brought the organizations of the consumer movement more closely together. In his early years, Ralph Nader had been dubbed "the Lone Ranger of the consumer movement" because of his unwillingness to collaborate with other segments of the movement. Beginning in the late 1970s, the Nader network, Consumers Union, and the Consumer Federation of America increasingly worked together in ad hoc issue coalitions.

During the 1980s, a top priority of the Nader network was to establish citizen groups funded by small contributions by many consumers at both the national and state levels. This funding approach had been successful in creating Public Interest Research Groups, or PIRGs, on college campuses. The principal result of these efforts was the formation of a few citizen utility boards (CUBs). These CUBs lost much of their ability to organize when they were denied access to utility mailings in a 1986 Supreme Court decision.

The activities of the consumer movement in the late 1970s and early 1980s were hampered by serious financial problems. During this period, "stagflation" and recession cut revenues from contributions and subscriptions. Movement revenues also suffered a major reduction when the Reagan administration eliminated most grants and contracts to consumer groups. Consumers Union, the Consumer Federation of America, and the Nader flagship organization Public Citizen all experienced financial problems. As economic conditions improved during the 1980s, and as consumer leaders devoted more attention to building stable funding bases, the movement recovered financially. The revenues of Consumers Union doubled during the 1980s. It used some of its substantial surpluses to fund state and local consumer groups and to increase aid for consumer organizations in the Third World.

The consumer movement lost much of its visibility during the 1980s. After some media coverage of the movement's protests of the Reagan administration's budget cuts and regulatory rollbacks, media attention shifted elsewhere. Despite this lack of coverage, the movement continued to push its agenda and was able to promote some narrowly focused but significant reforms. Mandatory seat belt use laws were passed in virtually every state, and a federal passive restraint standard was finally implemented after a decade-long battle. Important victories were also won in the area of financial services, with consumers gaining new rights with respect to cashing checks and taking out home equity loans.

The George Bush administration proved somewhat more receptive to consumer protection concerns than had the previous one. In particular, President Bush made several strong appointments to regulatory agencies. Important changes in nutritional labeling were instituted by the FDA at congressional request despite strong objections from livestock interests. The new labels added information on such problem constituents as sodium, saturated fat, and cholesterol, and also added information on fiber content.

During the Bush presidency, consumers also won the right for standardized disclosure of interest on savings accounts, and the FTC (spurred by aggressive actions from state attorneys general) issued guidelines for environmental marketing claims (e.g., "ozone friendly," "recyclable," "photodegradable"). The rapid proliferation of computers during the late 1980s and early 1990s led to increased concern about consumer privacy, especially with respect to credit and medical records. No new federal legislation was passed to safeguard consumer privacy, but several firms and industry groups addressed this concern through self-regulatory policies.

As a Democrat, President Bill Clinton might have been expected to be sympathetic to consumer issues. While Clinton's efforts to reform health care were applauded by the consumer movement, he never developed a concrete set of priorities regarding consumer issues before losing his Democratic majority in the Congress in the 1994 elections. Nevertheless, consumer protection efforts continued during Clinton's administration, mostly in the form of regulatory decisions. The FTC issued rules to discourage abusive practices involving 900-telephone numbers (1993) and fraudulent telemarketing efforts (1995). The CPSC also regained some of its vigor, especially in the area of protecting children. Thus, even in the absence of major, new legislation and without a president explicitly committed to traditional consumer issues, the consumer movement enjoyed successes both before and after the 1994 elections.

Overarching Patterns

Since the U.S. consumer movement's origins in the last decade of the nineteenth century, the movement has experienced several periods of especially intense activity, corresponding roughly to the Progressive era of the early twentieth century, the New Deal period of the 1930s, and the Great Society of the 1960s and early 1970s. While consumerist activity continued in between these three peaks, a striking feature of the American consumer movement remains its periodic (and some might argue its cyclical) character. One important feature of all three periods has been diminished public confidence in business and heightened confidence in government and, by implication, new regulatory controls. In addition to the movement's periodic character, five other general patterns can be seen in the movement's century-long history: institutionalization, specialization, professionalization, changing strategies, and internationalization.

Institutionalization. Social movements, by their very nature, challenge a society's existing arrangements and ways of thinking. When these movements first arise, they must struggle to be taken seriously by both the general public and policymakers. At the same time that an emerging social movement seeks support and legitimacy, opponents of the movement attempt to discredit and delegitimize it. Social movement leaders may be described by their opponents as naive do-gooders, self-appointed elitists seeking to impose their values on others, or as enemies of capitalism and democracy. This entry has already reviewed the allegations of Communist influence aimed at Consumers Union during the late 1930s. In the 1960s, consumer leader Ralph Nader was variously criticized as arrogant, uncompromising, authoritarian, paranoid, puritanical, and devoid of economic common sense. Another consumer leader, FTC Chairman Michael Pertschuk, was accused of turning the commission into a "national nanny."

Despite criticism leveled at the leaders, organizations, and basic ideology of the consumer movement, it has gradually grown in its public legitimacy. At the same time, the movement has become more institutionalized and permanent. The movement has established a set of ongoing organizations with a relatively reliable financial base and a pool of leaders who rely more on professional and organizational skills than on charisma to achieve movement goals. The institutionalization of the consumer movement has also brought forth institutionalized responses on the part of government and business. Consumer affairs departments have been created within government agencies and large corporations, and professional associations have been established for consumer agency administrators (National Association of Consumer Agency Administrators), state utility consumer advocates (National Association of State Utility Consumer Advocates), and consumer affairs professionals in business (Society of Consumer Affairs Professionals in Business).

A final aspect of the consumer movement's institutionalization is its growing self-reflexiveness and awareness of its history. Consumers Union has published several books and produced a film (*America at Risk: A History of Consumer Protest*) on the history of the consumer movement. Under the guidance of Professor Richard L. D. Morse, an archive of consumer movement documents was established at Kansas State University in the late 1980s. During the early 1990s, consumer leader Helen Nelson produced a film (*Change Makers: The Struggle for Consumer Rights*) and established an archive based on videotaped interviews with thirty-five prominent consumer activists. Stephen Brobeck, executive director of the Consumer Federation of America, published an annotated bibliography of resource materials on the consumer movement. This encyclopedia marks a further step in the institutionalization of the consumer movement.

Specialization. The number of national, state, and local consumer organizations has increased dramatically since the early days of the consumer movement. A 1992 study by the Consumer Federation of America counted more than 400 such organizations. More striking than the increase in the sheer number of consumer organizations has been the emergence of groups specializing in a particular domain or on a particular set of issues. Whereas organizations such as the National Consumers League, Consumers Union, Public Citizen, and the Consumer Federation of America remain "generalists" in the consumer field, a number of other organizations have established themselves as experts in particular areas such as food safety and nutrition, health care, automobile safety, credit cards, insurance, privacy, and telecommunications fraud.

The division of consumer organizations into generalist and specialist organizations has occurred largely on an unplanned basis. To the extent that there is coordination among these diverse organizations, it is sometimes accomplished through the Consumer Federation of America, the continuing personal influence of Ralph Nader, or the formation of temporary coalitions devoted to a particular action or issue.

Given the number and diversity of consumer organizations, it should not be surprising that competition and conflict sometimes exist. Differences in tactics are, however, more prevalent than differences in goals. Some organizations are comfortable working collaboratively with business organizations, while other organizations view contacts with business as compromising their integrity. Honest differences of opinion can also exist regarding when and how much to compromise in seeking legislative solutions to consumer problems. Still, overt conflict among consumer organizations is rare; and, given the need to stretch resources across a large number of issues, most organizations are only too pleased to let another group take the lead on a particular issue.

Professionalization. Consumer advocates have become increasingly professionalized over time. Many of the movement's first leaders were either volunteers (usually homemakers) or people who had careers in other domains (as chemists, economists, lawyers, or engineers). They had little formal training in consumer affairs and could not claim to be experts in more than one consumer area, if that. Today, consumer leaders are full-time professionals who can build a career in consumer affairs or public interest advocacy. To deal effectively with technical issues such as telecommunications policy, public utilities, pharmaceutical safety, and financial services, it is no longer possible for consumer leaders to rely on righteous indignation. They have become increasingly knowledgeable in specialized areas, and able to prepare and critique technical documents. Moreover, consumer leaders have gained considerable expertise in the methods of political action—from conducting direct mail solicitations and lobbying legislators to organizing ballot initiatives and taking cases to the U.S. Supreme Court. In sum, work in the area of consumer affairs has been transformed from a part-time, uncompensated, and transient task conducted primarily by homemakers to a full-time, compensated, career-oriented occupation capable of attracting talented men and women.

Changing Strategies. From its earliest days, the consumer movement has relied on a mix of political strategies, including seeking change directly from businesses and using governmental laws and regulations to alter business conduct. For example, consumerists at the turn of the twentieth century urged consumers to buy from a "white list" of companies whose labor practices stood above the suspect standards of the day, while at the same time pressing for federal legislation to ensure the safety of foods and pharmaceutical products.

A similar mix of political strategies can be seen today, only the mix is much broader. Along with boycotts are "buycotts," efforts to direct consumer spending and investing toward firms whose social performance is particularly laudatory. Efforts to educate consumers have expanded from classrooms and meetings organized by agricultural extension agents to the airwaves and the information superhighway. Consumer advocates have also gained skill in using the state initiative and referendum process to make consumer policy or give strong direction to state legislators. Similarly, consumerists have honed their skills in the judicial arena, learning how to use the courts to block undesirable actions and sustain past successes.

Still, the primary tactic of the consumer movement is lobbying governments for legislative and regulatory action. Some of the lobbying attempts to limit seller behavior by setting minimal standards for safety or performance or by outlawing certain goods and services. Automobile safety standards and the drug approval process fall in this category. Other efforts are directed at expanding consumer choice (e.g., airline, telecommunication, and banking deregulation) or making choices more informed (e.g., requiring disclosure data on product performance or price).

Overall, the general thrust of the U.S. consumer movement has been less an effort to influence consumer product choices and more an attempt to alter seller behavior directly through legislative and regulatory means. That is why the movement's strategies are somewhat centralized and focused on Washington, D.C., and capitals of the most populous states.

Internationalization. In its early years, the consumer movement in the United States developed in relative isolation from the consumer-oriented activities in other countries (e.g, consumer cooperatives and housewives' organizations). Since around 1960, the consumer movements of the world have become increasingly interlinked. In many instances, the U.S. consumer movement has set the pace for other nations, but in other cases, the U.S. has "imported" consumerist ideas from abroad.

The single most important event in the internationalization of the U.S. consumer movement was the formation in 1960 of the International Organization of Consumers Unions (IOCU). IOCU, whose name was changed to Consumers International in 1994, was initially intended to spread the practice of comparative product testing, pioneered in the United States by Consumers' Research and Consumers Union, to other industrialized nations. Over time, IOCU has become a vehicle for spreading consumer advocacy, protection, and education to both more and less developed nations.

By virtue of its size and influence, the U.S. consumer movement has been responsible for the diffusion of specific elements of consumer policy. These policies span the areas of safety (e.g., passive restraints in automobiles; smoking bans on airplanes; systematic, national collection of product-related injury data), information (e.g., permitting comparative advertising; requiring disclosure of energy efficiency data and nutritional information), competition (e.g., airline and telecommunications deregulation), and redress (e.g., lemon laws; cooling-off periods; and class action lawsuits). On the other hand, the United States has adopted consumer policies pioneered in other nations. These policies include mandatory seat belt use laws (Australia), rotating cigarette warnings (Sweden), environmental seals of approval (Germany), accelerated drug approval (United Kingdom), and consumer ombuds (the Nordic countries).

During the 1990s, the U.S. consumer movement has found itself increasingly drawn into a set of issues that are international by their very nature: free trade and environmental protection. Consumer groups in the United States, which once ignored issues related to trade liberalization and protectionism, confronted consumer issues raised by the North American Free Trade Agreement (NAFTA) and the latest round of the General Agreement on

Tariffs and Trade (GATT). In contrast to consumer groups in Europe, which were cautiously supportive of free trade agreements like the GATT, most U.S. consumer groups tended to take the position that the lower prices brought about by free trade were not worth the threat to strict consumer and environmental standards posed by free trade agreements. A notable exception was Consumers Union, which supported the trade agreement.

Environmental issues also are pushing the U.S. consumer movement to think more globally. In the United States, the consumer and environmental movements have developed largely in parallel, with relatively little interaction except over issues such as pesticides, energy conservation, and recycling. In the rest of the world, the relationship between the consumer and environmental movements is more intimate. The Dutch product testing magazine, for instance, considers a product's environmental impact as an integral part of its overall product rating, whereas Consumers Union in the United States does not. As consumer organizations in the United States increasingly come into contact with those of other nations, especially those of formerly socialist nations and the less developed world, environmental issues may occupy a more important position in the priorities of the U.S. movement.

Persisting Tensions within the Movement

If a social movement is to endure, it must solve, or at least manage, a number of problems. Some of these problems involve the movement's identity and internal relationships, including the problem of preserving a tough, combative spirit. Other problems involve the movement's relationship to its external environment, especially the problems of obtaining adequate financial and human resources and maintaining its legitimacy among the public and policymakers.

A set of persisting problems concerns the consumer movement's proper goals and scope. Should the movement focus on a narrow set of issues that arise from individual purchases of goods and services in the private market, or should it focus on a broader set of economic issues that includes the availability and quality of public services and the fairness of tax policy? Organizations within the U.S. consumer movement differ in how broadly they define consumer issues, but relative to the consumer movements of less developed countries with their heavy emphasis on providing basic necessities and obtaining redress from unresponsive, government-owned enterprises, the U.S. movement operates with a relatively narrow definition of consumer issues.

Closely related to the issue of scope is the problem of balancing the interests of middle-class and poor consumers. With a few notable exceptions, the U.S. consumer movement has primarily recruited its participants from the middle class and pursued issues relevant to middle-class consumers. Consumer advocates show little regard for the argument that mandating a consumer safety and performance feature will increase a product's price and therefore make it less affordable for low-income consumers. Nevertheless, there are several notable areas in which consumer advocates have devoted special attention to problems of low-income consumers: price increases that threaten access to electricity, natural gas, telecommunications, and banking services; discrimination in credit and insurance markets; and excessive price differences between inner-city and suburban stores. Still, most of the U.S. movement's activities are based on the assumption that consumers have more difficulty spending money wisely than earning it.

Consumer organizations are not only sensitive to the charge that they have a middle-class bias, but also to the charge that they are self-appointed and out of touch with the real desires of consumers. Critics of the U.S. consumer movement contend that it was consumer advocates, not consumers, who wanted the ineffective interlock seatbelt system on cars, mandatory motorcycle helmet laws, a ban on saccharin, and conservative rules for approving new drugs. Thus, a continuing challenge for the movement is to be accountable to the consuming public and to their financial contributors, while still being able to pursue consumer problems that may be only dimly perceived or imperfectly understood by these constituencies.

A further internal problem involves coordination of movement activities. As would be expected of organizations that were established at different times, in different locales, and for different purposes, the organizations of the consumer movement guard their autonomy. Efforts at coordination are further complicated by differences in preferred tactics, especially the question of whether consumer groups should work with, and even accept funds from, business groups. Consumers Union and the organizations founded by Ralph Nader are very cautious about contact with business interests, while groups like the National Consumers League and the Consumer Federation of America are more accommodating toward business interests.

The most basic external problem of any social movement is to "mobilize resources," that is, to obtain the financial and human resources necessary to support the movement's activities. Despite favorable tax treatment, the organizations of the consumer movement constantly face the problems of financial insecurity and personnel turnover. Even those organizations that have established a relatively firm financial base usually cannot match resources with business-financed opponents.

An additional external problem of the consumer movement is being able to operate credibly in dealing with increasingly complex issues. Issues may require knowledge of biology, chemistry, and physics (e.g., food irradiation and genetically engineered food); geology and transportation systems (e.g., natural gas and electricity regulation); economics (e.g., trade liberalization and telecommunications deregulation); and medicine (e.g., health care reform and pharmaceutical regulation). It is difficult for consumer organizations to develop the expertise and confidence to address such complex issues and then obtain the necessary expertise to lobby effectively.

The task of dealing with increasingly technical issues is often complicated by the uneasiness of many consumer advocates with scientists, even ones sympathetic to the consumerist perspective. The culture of the scientist and the activist are quite different. Whereas the activist sees issues in relatively black-and-white terms, the scientist tends to consider all sides of an argument. The activist needs research that directly addresses a particular policy proposal; the scientist is concerned with policy implications but also with more basic and enduring scientific questions. The activist needs the research results almost immediately; the scientist will be ready when he or she is satisfied that the work meets certain professional standards of quality. The activist wants research results that are clear-cut and dramatic, while the scientist wants to hedge and qualify findings. Unfortunately, consumer advocates have failed to form productive relationships with consumer-oriented academics in the natural and social sciences, although the blame for this appears to fall on both camps.

A final persisting tension in the consumer movement is the management of its relationships with other social movements, especially organized labor and the environmental movement. Historically, the ties between the consumer movement and organized labor have been very close, and labor unions continue to participate actively in the National Consumers League and the Consumer Federation of America. Labor unions have provided financial support, manpower, and their militant tradition of standing up to injustice to the U.S. consumer movement. At the same time, the consumer movement sometimes finds itself at odds with the position of organized labor, especially on issues relating to trade protection, where consumer benefits in terms of lower prices and greater choice may come at the expense of domestic jobs.

The consumer movement also must negotiate its relationship with the environmental movement. While the consumer and environmental movements have similar reformist ideologies, recruit resources from similar segments of society, and face similar problems as public interest movements, they also have areas of potential conflict. The efforts of environmentalists to protect the natural environment may require consumers to pay higher prices for goods (e.g., auto air conditioning coolants), face restricted choices (e.g., reduced access to ecologically sensitive areas), or endure inconveniences (e.g., product recycling). Conversely, environmentalists sometimes view consumerists as contributing to, rather than challenging, the materialism and "consumerism" of modern, industrialized societies. *Consumer Reports*, they might argue, should not even compare the relative merits of large, luxury cars; instead, the magazine should tell consumers to avoid all such gas-guzzlers. These tensions between the consumer and environmental movements are often overcome or submerged, but neither movement can take the other's support for granted.

Contributions

Despite the problems facing social movements in general and the consumer movement in particular, the U.S. consumer movement has a century-long history and a substantial record of achievement. The actions of the consumer movement have resulted in a long list of laws, regulations, and judicial decisions that have improved consumer welfare. The consumer movement's greatest accomplishments, however, may have relatively little to do with these specific, concrete accomplishments. The movement's most enduring effects may be sensitizing the mass media, businesses, and consumers themselves to consumer interests.

Individuals now recognize that they have distinct interests as consumers and that these interests must be continually guarded. Individuals are aware that they have certain rights as consumers regarding safety, information, competition, representation, redress, education, and privacy. Consumers who complain about shoddy products or poor service are no longer regarded as cranks and whiners, but rather as people who are taking the time to stand up for themselves and others. When citizens consider alternative candidates for public office, they not only want to know where a candidate stands on national defense, the economy, civil rights, and abortion, but also on consumer protection issues.

The mass media, too, have been strongly influenced by the consumer movement. While they were at first resistant to the idea of covering consumer issues for fear of alienating advertisers, the mass media have become an important force for educating consumers. While programs and articles are rare that explicitly and regularly cover consumer topics, many of the health, safety, and financial exposés carried by the mass media involve consumer topics. Similarly, media coverage of the legislative, administrative, and judicial actions of government contains a large share of consumer-relevant news. Furthermore, the media themselves have instituted "reader advocates" or other mechanisms to be responsive to their own customers.

Finally, the consumer movement has had an enduring effect on the business community. Progressive marketers no longer view themselves as trying to "sell" something to consumers, but rather as trying to meet consumer needs and build ongoing relationships with consumers. Many companies have special consumer affairs representatives, consumer advisory panels, or complaint-handling offices. Treating customers properly and listening to consumer leaders has been embraced as both a moral obligation (part of corporate social responsibility) and as a necessary part of maximizing long-term profitability.

The U.S. consumer movement has experienced three periods of intense activity in this century, One might ask whether there will be another such period. Certainly, the pace of legislative and regulatory action on behalf of consumers has slackened compared to its peak in the 1960s and the first half of the 1970s. Moreover, the issues that galvanized the movement in the past were relatively straightforward ones, involving dramatic problems of safety and fairness. Most of the consumer problems that remain or are likely to arise are more complex. They are less likely to lend themselves to dramatic exposés by "issue entrepreneurs" and spectacular media coverage.

Is a fourth era of consumer activism unlikely, then? Perhaps a more appropriate question might be: will a fourth era be necessary? The consumer movement is so thoroughly institutionalized, and the values of the movement are so fully embedded in society, that it may be accurate to say that the third era has never really ended. Even under Republican administrations, consumer organizations and their allies in government and corporation settings have remained remarkably focused on consumer welfare and effective in carrying out their missions. Future achievements will be more difficult, requiring careful study and preparation, skillful coalition building, and persistent political pressure. But the influence of the U.S. consumer movement is becoming permanent because its role has become indispensable.

— Robert O. Herrmann, Robert N. Mayer

See also

Congress and Consumer Protection; Consumer Education; Journalism, Consumer; Presidents and the Consumer Movement; State and Local Consumer Organizations.

Readings

Angevine, Erma, ed. (1982). *Consumer Activists: They Made a Difference.* Mount Vernon, NY: Consumers Union Foundation, Inc.

Herrmann, Robert O. (1991). "Participation and Leadership in Consumer Movement Organizations." *Journal of Social Issues.* 47 (1): 119–134.

Mayer, Robert N. (1989). *The Consumer Movement: Guardians of the Marketplace.* Boston: Twayne.

U.S. Consumer Product Safety Commission

See Consumer Product Safety Commission.

U.S. Consumer Protection Agency

In 1978 a fierce nine-year battle over the creation of a federal consumer protection agency ended with a victory for business opponents over consumer groups and sympathizers. During this period, the proposed agency was referred to variously as Consumer Protection Agency, Agency for Consumer Protection, Agency for Consumer Advocacy, and Office of Consumer Representation. This entry will refer to it as Consumer Protection Agency (CPA).

The effort to establish a federal CPA evolved out of an attempt by Senator Estes Kefauver (D-TN) Tennessee to create a cabinet-level department of consumer affairs in 1959. Under his proposal, the department would be the focal point in the federal government for matters pertaining to and promoting the interests of consumers.

Kefauver was unsuccessful, and after his death, Congressman Benjamin S. Rosenthal (D-NY) of New York took over. Rosenthal also was unsuccessful in creating a cabinet-level department, but the idea evolved into an attempt to create an independent consumer protection agency. Ralph Nader was instrumental in this shift because he believed strongly in a consumer advocacy agency that would monitor federal consumer protection activities and represent consumer interests before federal regulatory agencies and executive departments.

Nader's views were generally shared by other consumer advocates and organizations, including Esther Peterson, President Lyndon Johnson's first special assistant for consumer affairs; Consumers Union; and the Consumer Federation of America. As a result, Rosenthal dropped the department idea and, in association with leading consumerists, developed the proposal to establish a consumer protection agency.

Consumer advocacy had bipartisan support. Congresswomen Florence P. Dwyer of New Jersey, ranking Republican member of the House Committee on Government Operations, introduced a bill at about the same time Rosenthal did. Her proposal would not create an agency, but rather expand the function of the Office of Consumer Affairs in the executive office of the president. The Nixon administration also introduced a bill providing for consumer advocacy, among other functions, which would assign advocacy functions to a consumer protection division in the U.S. Department of Justice.

From 1969 to 1978 the proposals varied, but several provisions were common to most of the bills. First, a new, independent agency was to be created, headed by a director appointed by the president. This agency would have no regulatory functions and would be independent in the manner of the Federal Trade Commission.

Second, the major proposed function of the agency was to represent consumer interests before federal agencies and courts. In formal hearings the agency would be authorized to intervene as a party, if necessary, to represent the interests of consumers. With such authority, the agency could participate in formal proceedings, including shaping the issues, presenting and testing evidence, and arguing the significance of evidence and the meaning of precedents. The agency also was to be authorized to participate in informal proceedings.

Third, the proposed agency would have authority to represent consumer interests in federal civil court proceedings involving review or enforcement of federal agency actions that substantially affected consumer interests. Besides participating in suits brought by others, the proposed agency would be empowered to initiate lawsuits to review agency decisions if a substantial consumer interest was involved.

Fourth, the proposed agency would act as a clearinghouse for complaints of individual consumers against business enterprises. The agency would not be authorized to force business to respond to such complaints, but rather to inform the business enterprise and the relevant federal and state agencies.

Under the representation authority, the proposed agency would be able, for example, to appear before the Federal Communications Commission and argue against an increase in long-distance telephone rates. Moreover, if the agency was of the opinion that a decision affecting consumers by a federal regulatory body was legally in error, it could seek a review of that decision in federal courts.

Legislative History

The first serious effort to create a federal consumer protection agency, in 1969, came at the end of a decade during which the consumer movement gained more strength and power than ever before. This effort, begun in the 91st Congress, continued into succeeding sessions until it was defeated in February 1978. Its supporters decided to terminate the effort because they believed it could not succeed.

During much of this period, the bill enjoyed substantial bipartisan support. In both houses of Congress, leaders working for the CPA's creation came from both parties.

In the 91st Congress (1969–1970), the Senate passed a CPA bill by a vote of 74–4 and the House Government Operations Committee endorsed a CPA bill 31–4, but the House Rules Committee failed to clear a bill for House consideration by a 7–7 vote. In the 92nd Congress (1971–1972), the House passed a CPA bill by a vote of 344–14, but the effort in the Senate was thwarted by a filibuster, after a cloture motion failed to get sufficient votes (52–30). In the 93rd Congress (1973–1974), the House passed a CPA bill by a vote of 239–94, but again a Senate vote was prevented by a filibuster after a cloture motion received a 64–34 vote.

In the 94th Congress (1975–1976), the Senate voted 61–28 to create a CPA, and the House voted 208–199 for a CPA bill. The latter vote was not large enough to override an expected veto by President Ford, and the effort was abandoned during this session. At the inception of the 95th Congress (1977–1978), in the first year of President Carter's term, the White House sent a strong message to Congress supporting the establishment of a CPA, but for the first time, the House defeated the bill, 227–189, thus ending the nine-year effort.

During five of the nine years between 1969 and 1978, Richard Nixon was president. The Nixon administration's position on the bill was sometimes negative, sometimes positive, and at times divided. Whatever its philosophical position, the White House was very much aware of the political power of the consumer movement, and sought to court it or at least avoid antagonizing it.

President Ford took the position that consumer protection at the federal level should be enhanced by improving the operation of existing governmental bodies rather than creating a new agency. He directed the seventeen departments and agencies under his control to establish consumer representation offices if they had not already done so. His order specified the "direct and active" solicitation of consumer views at early stages in the development of policy and rules, and greater attention to consumer complaints in policy and program planning.

The CPA proposal did not receive strong support from the White House until the arrival of President Carter. Both as a candidate and as president he supported the bill, and his aides worked for its passage.

The Contending Forces

With relatively few exceptions, major U.S. corporations and business associations vigorously opposed the CPA proposal. The bill was favored by consumer organizations, organized labor, a variety of environmental and other organizations, and a handful of major corporations.

Ralph Nader was a leading strategist and spokesman in the campaign, and he was joined by Esther Peterson and officials from Consumers Union and the Consumer Federation of America. In addition, the bill's supporters assembled a coalition of senior citizen, religious, and community groups, and state and local officials.

In testimony before Congress, Nader presented the names of ninety-five companies that supported creation of the CPA. Among them were large firms such as Atlantic Richfield, Connecticut General Life Insurance, Gulf and Western, Levi-Strauss, Mobil Oil, and Montgomery Ward.

That U.S. business was substantially united against the CPA proposal was reflected by opposition from the three most prestigious national business organizations—the U.S. Chamber of Commerce, National Association of Manufacturers, and Business Roundtable. These groups were joined by others, including the Grocery Manufacturers of America, National Federation of Independent Business, and National Small Business Association. Many individual firms, such as Ford Motor, Sears-Roebuck, Armstrong Cork, General Foods, and Gulf Oil, contributed to the effort.

The campaign to defeat the bill was well organized and coordinated. Success was achieved through the formation of an ad hoc coalition ultimately named the Consumer Issues Working Group (CIWG). In the final stages of the opposition effort, it was chaired by Emmett Hines, the Washington lobbyist for Armstrong Cork.

The CIWG coalition had one of the longest lives of any such group in Washington, and was widely regarded as having been effective in orchestrating the defeat of the CPA proposal. It is now common for business representatives in Washington to consider organizing a similar coalition to influence the political process whenever an important issue arises.

An Evaluation

Considering the substantial pro-consumer sentiment that prevailed in the United States during much of the 1969–1978 period, and given the large majorities registered in both houses of Congress, the defeat of the consumer protection agency bill must be regarded as one of the largest victories ever won by business opponents of proposed legislation. The coalition's strategy of delaying congressional action until the bill could be defeated was a successful one. In the early 1970s, when there was much congressional support for the agency, they barely succeeded in keeping legislation off the floors of both houses of Congress. By the time of Ford and Carter, however, the mood of the country had changed. The United States had entered the post-Watergate era, lack of confidence in government was widespread, and antipathy toward big government and its massive bureaucracy was growing. In these circumstances, consumerists who wanted to use the power of government to reduce the ills of the marketplace suffered significant erosion of political support.

This mood was obvious in the substantial reduction in CPA support in the House of Representatives in 1975, when it passed by only nine votes. Moreover, President Ford could make known his opposition to the CPA concept even though he expected to contend with consumerists during a campaign for election. Although the CPA bill had previously been stymied in the Congress, during the Ford administration it stalled on its way to the White House because the majority in the House was not large enough to override an expected veto.

By the time Carter entered the White House, the lack of confidence in government and antipathy toward big government increased beyond the levels prevailing in the first two years of the post-Watergate era. In fact, candidate Carter himself promoted and strengthened these attitudes by running as a federal outsider who condemned big government and promised greater efficiency.

In the area of tactics, the consumer coalition appears to have had serious weaknesses. One CPA supporter, Representative Richard Bolling (D-MO), gave the consumer forces low marks and appraised the business effort as skillful. In his opinion, the consumer coalition badly overplayed its hand and tried to bully legislators into voting for poorly written bills.

The business coalition, however, was aided by superior resources and the manner in which they used them. Not only did this coalition organize broad business opposition to the bill, it employed relatively sophisticated lobbying, opinion surveys, and campaign contributions to persuade legislators. What business learned here was later applied to other legislative battles, including the effort to weaken the Federal Trade Commission.

— George Schwartz

See also

Presidents and the Consumer Movement; U.S. Office of Consumer Affairs.

Reading

Schwartz, George (1979). "The Successful Fight against a Federal Consumer Protection Agency." *MSU Business Topics*. Summer: 45–56.

U.S. Department of Agriculture

When President Abraham Lincoln created the U.S. Department of Agriculture in 1862, he referred to it as "the people's department." It was an appropriate nickname at the time—the population was largely rural, and farming was the leading industry—but today only 2 percent of Americans earn their living farming. The Department of Agriculture has not only survived this radical demographic shift, it may still make some claim to the Lincoln title. Consumer-oriented programs—food assistance, human nutrition research and education, and food safety—dominate the department's budget, occupy many of its staff, and serve virtually all Americans. By adding or reshaping programs, the department's leaders not only maintain the institution's relevance to an urban nation, but also preserve a voice in the president's cabinet for the small minority of Americans whose first interest remains producing, rather than consuming, agricultural products.

A department charged with serving both producers and consumers faces conflicting interests and intriguing anomalies. Although consumer programs absorb most of the budget, every secretary of agriculture has had political roots in the producer community, and some have not been comfortable with the department's consumer role. Many agricultural leaders and members of Congress opposed appointing consumer advocates to lead consumer programs or attempted to limit their power and jurisdiction. Department leaders justify consumer programs, not on their own merit, but because they increase sales of agricultural products.

The Department of Agriculture's primary consumer-oriented missions—meat and poultry inspection, food assistance, and nutrition research and education—were created to protect or increase markets. Most can be traced through each of the department's three major eras: the old department, 1862 to 1932; the New Deal department, 1933 to 1961; and the modern department, 1961 to the present. Even the newest mission, food assistance, has its roots in the Depression era of sixty years ago.

Two other consumer programs merit mention. Intended to help farmers and other rural Americans as both consumers and producers, the Rural Electrification Administration brought electricity and telephones to millions who lived in areas too sparsely populated to attract investor-owned companies. The Cooperative Home Extension taught rural Americans how to preserve food and feed their families safely, nutritiously, and cheaply.

Also worthy of note is a group of regulatory programs—including meat, milk, egg, and fruit and vegetable grading—that were begun to establish a uniform language of trade between farmers and distant customers, but came to serve consumers as well. Most Americans use the meat grades (prime, choice, and select) as shopping aids.

Food Safety

The first meat inspection law was passed in 1890 to persuade foreign purchasers that beef imported from the United States was free of animal disease organisms. In 1891 the law was extended to cover meat sold for domestic consumption. The Federal Meat Inspection Act of 1906 was spurred by filthy conditions described in Upton Sinclair's book *The Jungle.* The basic structure established in that act remains in place today. It required preinspection of each animal and postmortem inspection of every carcass sold in interstate commerce. Meat sold and consumed within one state was not covered by uniform federal safety standards until the Wholesome Meat Inspection Act passed in 1967.

The Wholesome Meat Inspection Act and its companion, the Poultry Products Inspection Act of 1968, provide the statutory basis for the inspection program of today. The laws incorporate adulteration and misbranding provisions (already applied to other food products by the Federal Food, Drug, and Cosmetic Act) and provide strong new enforcement tools.

The Department of Agriculture lags in adjusting inspection to meet the human health concerns of the last years of the twentieth century. New problems are arising from a food system characterized by mass production; worldwide distribution; changing consumer habits; widespread use of chemical pesticides, animal drugs, and growth hormones; and emerging and increasingly virulent pathogenic bacteria. The inspection program continues to emphasize animal health and relied primarily on sight, smell, and touch rather than microbial testing to detect threats. Until 1994, the department argued that pathogenic bacteria in raw meat and poultry were not adulterants.

In the 1985 report *Meat and Poultry Inspection: The Scientific Basis of the Nation's Program,* a National Academy of Sciences committee recommended redirecting inspection to achieve public health goals, requiring plants to identify potential health hazards and take effective prophylactic actions, and testing for and controlling pathogenic bacteria in meat and poultry products.

The recommendations languished until early 1993, when fast-food hamburger, contaminated with a relatively new and exceptionally virulent bacterium, E. coli O157:H7, sickened 300 West Coast children and killed four. Additional outbreaks and deaths followed across the country, and by 1995 the Centers for Disease Control reported that E. coli

O157:H7 caused an estimated 20,000 illnesses and 500 deaths each year. Contaminated, undercooked ground beef is the most common source of the disease. Victims, consumer activists, members of Congress, and editorial writers demanded that the department adopt more modern and effective methods to reduce bacterial food poisoning.

The Agriculture Department's allies in Congress responded to criticisms that inspection was outmoded and its leadership too close to industry. They established a new position, Undersecretary of Agriculture for Food Safety, to reorient inspection to meet human health goals. The department proposed adopting the hazard identification and control system recommended ten years earlier and requiring plants to meet human health-related performance standards. The new system was implemented in early 1997.

Food Assistance

Over half of the Department of Agriculture's budget is spent on social welfare programs. Beginning in the 1930s, government used food stamps, commodity distribution, and the school lunch program to remove surpluses from the market, funnel them to hungry Americans, and help drive up farm prices. Commodity distribution and the original food stamp program ended when World War II began and the demand for food increased.

After the war, farm and social welfare advocates sought to renew the programs. Commodity distribution resumed, and Congress made school lunch a permanent national program in 1946. Not until 1961 was Congress persuaded (by President Kennedy) to launch a pilot test of a new food stamp program. The program was expanded substantially by President Johnson in 1964 and President Nixon in 1971. Food stamps allowed low-income Americans to purchase coupons with a value greater than their cost and exchange them for food. The program was superior to surplus food distribution because it was easier to transport stamps than surplus food; recipients could purchase any food they desired, and stamps increased rather than replaced retail food sales. President Carter ended the purchase requirement for food stamps, making the program more accessible and simplifying its administration. The Clinton administration began to replace paper stamps with electronic benefit transfer cards.

Food stamps help ease the pain of fluctuating economic conditions. When unemployment rises, the number of people eligible for food stamps increases. Benefits are adjusted as food prices change. In 1994 an average of 27,468,779 people participated in the food stamp program at a cost of $24.5 billion. Because the size and cost of the food stamp program increase when the nation's economy is troubled, it is an inviting target for those who favor reducing the size of government. However, when Congress began to return social welfare programs to the states as block grants in the mid-1990s, food stamps survived as a federal program. The program survived at least in part because it benefited farmers, food processors, and retailers as well as low-income consumers.

The original school lunch program grew over the years to include a wide range of child nutrition efforts. These initiatives include the school breakfast program, the summer feeding program to replace school-based meals for lower income children during vacations, and—when mothers of young children flocked into the work force and expanded the demand for child care—the child care feeding program.

In 1974, Congress created a new type of food assistance program. The Special Supplemental Food Program for Women, Infants, and Children, known as WIC, provides a prescription food package that addresses the specific nutritional needs of women who are pregnant, postpartum, or nursing, and of young children. To qualify for the food package, participants must be enrolled in a prenatal or well-baby program and be at risk for nutritional problems. The chance to get extra food creates an extra incentive for women to remain in health care programs.

Nutrition Research and Education

In 1893 the department first received direct funds for human nutrition research. Over the years, that mandate was expanded and made more specific. Until the late 1970s, Department of Agriculture research and education efforts aimed to help consumers get enough calories and vital nutrients and avoid deficiency diseases. During the Depression, the department's Bureau of Home Economics developed and distributed menu guides and tips for buying adequate food at low cost. In 1941 the department published "The Basic Seven," a guide to good nutrition that gained widespread public acceptance. In the early 1970s, research indicated that Americans consumed too much food, especially fat, salt, and sugar. When the Department of Agriculture suggested that some agricultural products should be consumed less frequently or in smaller amounts, the affected producer groups were not pleased. In 1980 the Department of Agriculture joined with the Department of Health and Human Services to publish the first Dietary Guidelines for Americans.

The guidelines are seven suggestions for eating more healthfully. They recommend that Americans moderate their consumption of fat, salt, and sugar. Meat, dairy, and egg producers and presidential candidate Ronald Reagan attacked the guidelines initially, and when Reagan was elected, they were withdrawn. As research on the relationship between diet and health accumulated, the Reagan administration relented and republished the Dietary Guidelines. The guidelines and the more specific Food Pyramid, which portrays recommended proportions for different food groups, became mainstays of the department's nutrition education program, and in 1994 became the basis for menus used in child nutrition programs.

Efforts to provide more nutrition information on food labels grew out of the White House Conference on Hunger and Nutrition in 1972. In 1980 the Department of Agriculture joined the Food and Drug Administration and the Federal Trade Commission to propose food labels that would make it easier for consumers to follow the government's new dietary counsel. The effort failed, but in the late 1980s consumer groups persuaded Congress and the Bush administration to enact the Nutrition Labeling and Education Act. The law requires specific listing of calories and fat, and limits health claims on products. However, the law is limited to products regulated by the Food and Drug Administration, and does not cover meat and poultry products. The Department of Agriculture attempted to establish different and less rigorous requirements for labeling fat in meat and poultry than the Food and Drug Administration had developed for milk, butter, eggs, and vegetable fats. In 1992, President Bush had to resolve the disagreement between the departments of Agriculture and Health and Human Services. He directed Agriculture to follow the same labeling rules as the Food and Drug Administration.

Consumer Counsel and Consumer Advocacy

Beginning with Depression-era efforts to control crop prices and markets, some officials recognized that increasing income for producers also increased food prices for consumers. In 1933 the department established a Consumers' Counsel Division to inform and advocate for consumers, but it was disbanded a few years later. In an era of food price inflation, President Gerald Ford attempted to placate restless consumers and head off creation of a federal consumer protection agency by directing cabinet departments to create consumer offices. A consumer affairs office, directed by the undersecretary for food and consumer services and located in the Food and Nutrition Service, is still active today. However, the office has never influenced pricing decisions. The Department of Agriculture's consumer-related activities have evolved through programs that serve specific consumer needs for food assistance, food safety, and nutrition information; they do not include advocacy within the department to make production policies more responsive to consumer concerns.

At the end of the twentieth century, the U.S. Department of Agriculture is still attempting to work out an appropriate balance between producer and consumer concerns. Departmental leaders must navigate between trying to serve an expanded constituency, thereby running the risk of displeasing their core supporters, or remain faithful servants of a narrower group and risk becoming increasingly marginal in an urban society.

— Carol Tucker Foreman

See also

Food Purchase Protections; Food Safety.

Readings

Hurt, R. Douglas (1989). *The Department of Agriculture.* New York: Chelsea House Publishers.

Meier, Kenneth J. (1995). "Regulating Agriculture." In Kenneth J. Meier and E. Thomas Garman, eds., *Regulation and Consumer Protection.* Houston: DAME Publications, Inc. 125–146.

Rasmussen, Wayne D., and Gladys L. Baker (1972). *The Department of Agriculture.* New York: Praeger Publishers.

U.S. Federal Trade Commission

See Federal Trade Commission.

U.S. Food and Drug Administration

See Food and Drug Administration.

U.S. National Highway Traffic Safety Administration

See National Highway Traffic Safety Administration.

U.S. Office of Consumer Affairs

Efforts by consumer groups to institutionalize consumer representation in the White House culminated in the establishment of the Office of Consumer Affairs in 1971, and its successor, the U.S. Office of Consumer Affairs, in 1978. During the 1980s and 1990s, the latter office was downgraded in status and lost influence. The most important factors influencing the position and strength of these offices are popular support for consumer reforms, the influence of the consumer movement, and the views of the president.

In the administration of President Franklin Roosevelt, largely unsuccessful efforts were made to institutionalize consumer representation in New Deal agencies. Under President Harry Truman, a weak Consumer Advisory Council consulted with the White House Council of Economic Advisers. The offer of its members to provide advice or assist in organizing a successor unit in the administration of President Dwight Eisenhower was not even acknowledged.

Kennedy and Johnson Administrations

John Kennedy was the first president to place consumer representation in the White House. In 1962 he created a Consumer Advisory Council in response to pressures to keep a campaign promise for such representation. These pressures were brought to bear mainly by consumer advocates Persia Campbell, Colston Warne, and Richard Morse, as well as the senatorial offices of Estes Kefauver (D-TN), Maureen Neuberger (D-OR), Kenneth Keating (R-NY), and Hubert Humphrey (D-MN).

Although President Kennedy and his staff wanted to placate the consumer constituency, the White House's desire not to antagonize business groups influenced them to develop a less visible and influential form of consumer representation than that first suggested by Kennedy. A Consumer Advisory Council (CAC) was placed within the Council of Economic Advisers (CEA). Its establishment was announced in Kennedy's Consumer Message to Congress, in which he advanced four consumer rights.

Although the White House heeded little of CAC's advice, the council influenced consumer affairs developments during subsequent administrations. That influence extended to President Lyndon Johnson's appointment of a special assistant to the president for consumer affairs (SAPCA) and his selection of Esther Peterson to fill the position, and included the creation of the President's Committee on Consumer Interests (PCCI). When the term of office of Kennedy's CAC lapsed, Johnson reconstructed it as part of this committee.

In January 1964, by executive order, the president established the PCCI to be the voice of consumers in the White House. Its activities were to be fact-finding and advising the president and federal agencies on consumer issues. Johnson named Peterson as special assistant as well as chair of PCCI and CAC. The president wanted her to work in these positions on a half-time basis while retaining her position in the Labor Department as head of the Women's Bureau and later as assistant secretary. Before joining this department, Peterson worked in the labor movement as a volunteer and in positions at the International Ladies Garment Workers Union, Amalgamated Clothing Workers, and AFL-CIO.

PCCI's budget, which came from both discretionary presidential funds and contributions from the ten departments and agencies assigned to the committee, was around $300,000. Peterson was given a secretary, but was expected to borrow other staff if she needed help. She found it difficult to recruit appropriate experts to work in her operation. After three years her staff numbered nineteen.

PCCI rarely met, nor did it accomplish anything of substance. However, the special assistant and her staff, which was nominally the staff of PCCI, were active in promoting the consumer interest. Peterson's chief role was to build support for legislative measures by identifying problems and raising public awareness of their distinct interests as consumers. She also assisted consumers in their efforts to organize, and supported Johnson's legislative efforts.

To identify problems and enhance the quality of her recommendations, Peterson studied the 2,000 pieces of mail she received daily, talked with consumer leaders, organized conferences, and carried out investigations. She stayed in touch with the leaders of CAC and consumer groups throughout the nation. Additionally, she met once a month with consumer representatives having a Washington office. These meetings were characterized by an easy give-and-take on policy ideas and cooperative planning on mutually desired projects.

Peterson also engaged in many public activities, including numerous press conferences and releases, interviews with journalists, appearances in the electronic media, hundreds of speeches before organizations, and meetings with consumer, civic, and business groups. She and other members of her office testified before Congress five times and sent seven written comments for the record on consumer-related debates.

Peterson's office also worked to stimulate consumer education in schools and federal programs. Further, it issued sixteen publications to raise consumer awareness, help consumers with specific problems, and assist consumer leaders in carrying out programs. One of Peterson's most important achievements was her leadership in organizing a coalition of consumer-oriented groups—the Consumer Federation of America.

At times, Peterson sought to raise consumer awareness and support consumer assertiveness too vigorously to suit the administration. Her outspoken criticism of unfair practices in the food and used-car industries as well as support of consumer boycotts aroused the ire of White House staff members made uncomfortable by complaints from businesspeople.

Even though advising the White House was a primary function of the consumer unit, that advice was rarely heeded. One exception was SAPCA's writing of early drafts of presidential consumer messages to Congress in which Peterson told the president what she thought was best for consumers. She and her assistants also developed their own legislative proposals and commented on consumer-related legislation presented by other agencies. The fair packaging and labeling and truth in lending bills were two top priorities of her office. On these issues and many others, Peterson desired stronger legislation than Johnson proposed.

In May 1967, Betty Furness succeeded Peterson and served through 1968. Like Peterson, she was designated SAPCA, chair of the PCCI, and executive secretary of CAC. Furness was a well-known television actress and recently had worked to promote Volunteers in Service to America and Head Start. Furness's budget was $313,000, and her staff included ten professionals (four borrowed from other agencies, which paid their salaries) and fourteen clerical workers.

President Johnson wanted to pass thirteen consumer bills, and Furness's primary role was to publicize and mobilize support for this legislation. To carry out this mission, she addressed a variety of organizations, issued press releases, and was interviewed on radio and television. The special assistant requested that consumer leaders encourage their constituents to write letters to members of Congress. Furness presented testimony before Congress on eight bills and contacted members of Congress in less formal ways.

At first, because of her background, Furness was viewed skeptically by consumer leaders. However, her talents and increasing commitment to the consumer cause gained her increasing respect from these advocates. That she seemed able to speak for the administration on certain issues added to their hope that she could be effective. For example, Johnson allowed her to speak strongly for the administration on a meat safety bill even though the Department of Agriculture had a different opinion.

However, Furness was not as close to consumer leaders as her predecessor. Although she spoke with them at various times, she did not meet with them on a regular and frequent basis as Peterson had. Instead, one person in her office was responsible for working with groups to obtain support for the president's proposals and to learn what the groups wanted.

Furness's advisory activities centered on task forces in which the administration asked her to participate. These units studied issues and developed legislative suggestions to solve consumer problems. The first was a joint task force with the Federal Trade Commission and the Departments of Commerce and Labor on appliance repairs. The second was designed to prepare for the consumer legislative program of 1968. Its work provided the basis for Johnson's 1968 Consumer Message and the consumer portion of the State of the Union message. Of the eleven proposals submitted in its report, four were accepted (two in diluted form); some pending bills were also endorsed. One recommendation of special interest to consumer leaders was a proposal for advancing consumer representation in the executive and judicial branches of government.

Furness's greatest contribution was developing public support for consumer legislation. The favorable public reaction toward consumer bills stimulated by enormous positive publicity, much of it provided by SAPCA, made it more difficult for members of Congress to vote against the measures. Furness's work, like Peterson's, kept consumer issues on the agenda of the public and government. Moreover, after their terms were over, both of Johnson's special assistants persisted in efforts to establish a strong consumer presence.

Nixon and Ford Administrations

Although Nixon's philosophical and personal preferences did not predispose him to pursue consumer movement goals, the popularity of consumer issues persuaded him to appoint a credible representative of consumers to a White House post. He named Virginia Knauer to be his SAPCA, and continued PCCI to provide staff for Knauer's operation. Knauer became interested in consumer affairs during eight years on the Philadelphia City Council and had served most recently as head of the Pennsylvania Bureau of Consumer Protection.

In February 1971, to replace PCCI, Nixon created by executive order the Office of Consumer Affairs (OCA) in the executive office of the president and appointed Knauer as its first director. In January 1973, the president transferred OCA from the White House to the Department of Health, Education, and Welfare (HEW). In the transfer, OCA absorbed the existing Office of Consumer Services at HEW. Nixon reappointed Knauer as OCA director and ordered OCA to continue supplying staff support for her in her positions as SAPCA and member of cabinet-level committees. Appended to Knauer's office was a Consumer Advisory Council, for which she served as executive secretary.

In 1969, Knauer's office had a budget of $450,000. Its staff included eighteen professionals and nineteen clerical employees. By the end of Nixon's term, Knauer's staff had grown to fifty-five, and her budget reached $1.5 million.

Although Nixon desired positive publicity associating him with consumer welfare, he also wished to block the major proposals of consumer advocates, which he viewed as antibusiness. Knauer proceeded as best she could to serve both consumers and the president as she made recommendations, kept in contact with groups, undertook some educational activities, and provided publicity that was meant both to assist consumers and burnish the image of the president. However, the office's lack of formal authority and minimal discretionary ability hindered its capability to carry out these activities effectively.

Some of Knauer's recommendations were conveyed in face-to-face meetings with the president, but most were made through the office of Peter Flanigan, a top Nixon aide who was one of the major decision-makers on consumer affairs in the Nixon administration. No process was established through which the consumer units could know of or contribute regularly to policy formation relating to consumer interests. Knauer was able to convey her advocacy of some consumer group goals in writing early drafts of presidential consumer messages to Congress, memoranda with suggestions, and reports of activities and studies that revealed consumer problems. She also had the opportunity of offering pro-consumer viewpoints at meetings of the many White House committees to which she belonged.

Early in her term, Knauer vigorously advocated stronger measures for making class-action suits feasible. Her advocacy led to the incorporation of a class-action measure in the president's 1969 consumer message to Congress, though that version was much weaker than the one prepared by her office.

During the Nixon administration two types of proposals were made to strengthen consumer representation in the executive branch. One plan involved making the office of SAPCA statutory and giving it the functions of a counsel that would provide representation for consumers in agency and court proceedings. The other proposal, supported by congressional consumer advocates and consumer organizations, featured the establishment of a strong independent agency for consumer protection. Such an agency became the number one priority of the consumer movement, and remained so for a decade. Although Knauer's office and Representative Florence Dwyer (R-NJ) offered measures for strengthening the White House office, the final White House bill, strongly influenced by the Departments of Justice and Commerce, gave very few powers to the consumer office. No final action was taken on these bills.

Despite Nixon's opposition to an independent agency, he felt compelled to develop a legislative countermeasure to bills already under consideration on Capitol Hill. In 1971 and 1973, Knauer testified before the House of Representatives for Nixon's version of the proposals. However, in 1974, when Watergate preoccupied the White House, she endorsed the passage of a stronger variant of the bill being considered by the Senate. Despite the fact that Knauer exercised little influence over White House decisions, some of her recommendations made the president, White House staff, and agencies aware of consumer problems.

Knauer used consumer groups for developing proposals less than had the consumer office in the Johnson administration. She met with them monthly, but little give-and-take took place at these meetings.

Among the areas to which the consumer office made contributions were complaint handling by government and business, encouragement of local consumer offices, development of educational aids, and publicizing consumer problems. OCA surveyed government consumer offices at all levels to determine the top complaints, then disseminated the results to federal agencies and businesses. It let a contract to Technical Assistance Research Programs, Inc. (TARP), for a comprehensive investigation of these complaints.

In 1971, Nixon gave Knauer increased authority to handle complaints against industry. In addition to informing consumers where to send their complaints, she was authorized to send complaints to heads of industries with a request for information on their disposition.

The president valued positive publicity about White House support for consumer issues, so SAPCA was fairly free to engage in activities that attracted media coverage. It was clear from Knauer's copious mail, over 3,500 letters a month, and the demand for her as a speaker that many consumers knew of SAPCA's activities. Exposure to her communications no doubt increased public awareness of consumer issues and led to greater government and business awareness as well.

The educational efforts of OCA included publishing tips on particular categories of products, curriculum guides for schools, and directories of consumer offices and organizations. The office also issued a newsletter with a circulation of 25,000.

At the outset, consumer movement leaders were pleased by Knauer's consumer credentials and her early, strong testimony and other statements on credit investigation and reporting, and product safety. Leaders of private organizations and members of Congress praised her dedication to consumers. But over time, they lost confidence in her ability to influence the administration, and therefore pursued their own efforts to create stronger executive-branch representation in the form of an independent consumer agency.

In August 1974, President Gerald Ford made Virginia Knauer's office part of the White House Office of Public Liaison (OPL), which was enlarged to facilitate communication with the private sector. In the new organization, Knauer continued as SAPCA but reported to the head of OPL, William Baroody. OCA still provided staff support for her activities, and its budget and staff remained virtually the same.

In April 1975, Ford announced opposition to the consumer agency and made a counterproposal that each of seventeen executive departments and agencies appoint a single official to handle consumer complaints and comments and represent consumer interests in the departments' deliberations. Until that point, Knauer's office had continued for the most part to pursue the activities it had begun under Nixon. Now, promoting Ford's proposal, known as the Consumer Representation Plans (CRPs), became its principal assignment. Knauer coordinated individual agency plans in association with the director of the Office of Management and Budget and served as moderator for many nationwide consumer conferences, the purpose of which was to explain the CRPs to interested parties, receive comments on them, and provide positive publicity for the president. Knauer also prepared congressional testimony in favor of the CRPs. When OCA promoted a program that consumer leaders deemed virtually useless and failed to support the creation of an independent agency with strong powers, relations between OCA and the consumer movement deteriorated further.

Carter Administration

Jimmy Carter was the first president to include consumer groups in his basic coalition and make their priorities his own. In 1977 he appointed Esther Peterson (also the choice of many consumer leaders) as consumer representative on his White House staff. At the outset, the single major charge given to her was to do everything possible to see that legislation was enacted creating the proposed Consumer Protection Agency (CPA).

In contrast to her situation in the Johnson White House, Peterson reported directly to the president, and no obstacles prevented her from seeing him when she needed to. OCA in HEW was to remain organized as it was until the new consumer agency was set up; in the meantime, it would be used as staff for the SAPCA's office. OCA had fifty employees, and Peterson's immediate staff ranged from four to ten and was on the OCA payroll, as was Peterson herself. SAPCA also was able to detail people from other departments and agencies to work on White House consumer unit projects.

While the CPA legislation was pending, OCA had five consecutive acting directors. In August 1978, Peterson took over OCA in addition to her White House duties. In October the office was reorganized and renamed the U.S. Office of Consumer Affairs (USOCA). During the Carter period, the consumer office budget increased from $1.75 million to $2 million.

In late 1977 and early 1978, the White House consumer unit was totally preoccupied with the passage of CPA legislation. Lobbying and support-gathering strategies were planned, assigned, and carried out. Much of this activity involved working directly with consumer group representatives. Congressional testimony was prepared and delivered by Knauer, whose office helped redraft the measure. Speeches were written for Peterson, who spent about one-third of her time traveling and speaking to grassroots groups to build support for the agency.

After the agency bill was rejected by the House of Representatives, Esther Peterson's role as adviser became more central to her activities. President Carter told her she could work on any consumer area she considered important, and he directed heads of all executive-branch departments and agencies to cooperate with her. Peterson was now a regular participant in the institutionalized White House domestic legislative development system that centered on the Presidential Review Memoranda. Her choice of areas to target, enhanced ability to obtain agency support, and systematic participation in the principal advising operation in the White House, as well as significant support for working on consumer groups goals, signified unprecedented influence for her office. In addition, members of the consumer office could make recommendations in meetings with other White House aides and in assemblies of standing committees to which they belonged.

Peterson and her office searched for consumer-related aspects of broader legislation proposed by the administration, and sought to advance three long-standing priorities: public participation in agency proceedings, class-action suits, and enlarged standing to sue the government. Peterson also made recommendations, solicited by the president, on appointments to consumer-sensitive agencies. To enhance their advisory capacity, the White House consumer unit and OCA sought information through studies of agencies and issues.

To strengthen consumer representation in agency proceedings, Peterson's unit prepared formal comments and intervened as a formal party in a few cases; her staff interacted with Congress on behalf of consumers through both formal and informal contacts. Peterson and representatives of her office personally testified before Congress on seven occasions and sent fifty-two formal comments on legislation.

SAPCA and USOCA engaged in such educational efforts as speeches and publications. The office sponsored conferences, usually with universities or consumer groups as cosponsors, on specific consumer problems. Among its publications was a book, *People*

Power, describing examples of practical projects to help consumers fight inflation and giving detailed instructions for carrying them out. Another major publication was the *Consumers' Resource Handbook,* a manual to help consumers resolve complaints. OCA's newsletter became biweekly; it was renamed *Consumer Action Update* and expanded, with an emphasis on providing useful information to activists.

In 1980 the president issued an executive order directing each department to upgrade its consumer programs and appoint consumer advocates to high-level posts; hopefully, SAPCA's stronger oversight authority over agency plans would make them more effective than those developed by the previous administration.

Peterson maintained good working relationships with all major national consumer groups. In her projects, she enhanced the role of the consumer movement in policy-making. Her top staffers included former leaders of several major consumer groups. In addition to easy access to SAPCA, advocates had increased access to the president, with whom they met several times. (Nixon and Ford had never acceded to their requests for meetings.)

Recent Administrations

In 1981, President Reagan placed his SAPCA and director of USOCA, Virginia Knauer, in the White House Office of Public Liaison (OPL). She reported to an assistant to the director of OPL, who in turn reported to the president's chief of staff. After a year and a half, Reagan moved SAPCA to USOCA at HHS and changed Knauer's title from special assistant to special adviser to the president for consumer affairs. She then reported to the White House Office of the Chief of Staff. USOCA's budget fell from $2,256,000 in 1981 to $1,670,000 by 1988. Its staff dropped from sixty to twenty-two, with the greatest decline (sixty to thirty-nine) in the first year of the administration.

The central task given to USOCA and its director in the Reagan period was to contribute to achieving the president's basic goals for the economy: reduction of inflation and unnecessary government regulations. The president, who had strongly opposed enhanced consumer representation and disparaged the consumer movement during the 1980 campaign, declared that gaining these ends would be the best means for advancing the interests of consumers.

Practically, USOCA emphasized education and voluntary actions as solutions to consumer problems. The office's educational activities and projects included numerous speeches and interviews with the media, the distribution of a consumer information radio series, and press and video news releases. In 1982, USOCA organized an annual National Consumers Week during which educators, businesses, and government officials were encouraged to participate in projects to educate consumers. The office also served as a catalyst for business-government conferences on issues such as consumer complaints and mediation. It continued to publish *Consumers' Resource Handbook* and a consumer newsletter, which became a monthly publication, and published or requested the publication of several educational brochures. Other government agencies as well as businesses contributed significant funding for USOCA projects. The office had little interaction with consumer groups.

After 1982, USOCA testimony and comments to Congress and agencies on legislation and regulations greatly diminished. SAPCA headed the U.S. delegation to meetings of the Organization for Economic Cooperation and Development's Committee on Consumer Policy.

President George Bush named Bonnie Guiton to be director of USOCA in April 1989 and, following Reagan's precedent, gave her the title of special adviser to the president for consumer affairs. In November 1990 he designated Ann Windham Wallace to be Guiton's successor as director of USOCA. The president did not confer the title of special adviser upon his second USOCA head, although her job description included advising the president. Guiton had most recently served as assistant secretary for vocational and adult education at the U.S. Department of Education and as vice-chair of the U.S. Postal Rate Commission between 1984 and teachers, concerned about macroeconomic theory and student scores on college placement exams, were willing to leave consumer education to vocational programs, which they viewed as lacking in academic rigor. In the aggregate, these attitudes and behaviors had a negative impact on the success of OCE and its mission to strengthen and support the education of consumers in schools, communities, and workplaces.

In 1981, James Boyle, government affairs director of the Consumer Federation of America, organized a broad-based coalition to try to preserve the office. These efforts proved insufficient in the face of an administration determined to eliminate OCE along with other small Department of Education programs. The National Coalition for Consumer Education, however, survives to the present, increasing cooperation among various consumer education constituencies.

The Office of Consumers' Education provided increased visibility and legitimacy for the field of consumer education. It was directly responsible for creating the *Classification of Concepts in Consumer Education*, which became the generally accepted framework for curriculum, program development, and research in the United States and other countries. This classification documented the interdisciplinary nature of consumer education, integrating concepts from such disciplines as economics, mathematics, sociology, political science, psychology, and law. The conceptual framework included the broad categories of personal and external factors affecting consumer decision-making, personal financial management, environmental awareness, and citizen participation to influence economic, social, and political systems. This new consumer/citizenship role was to replace a passive and reactive role considered inadequate for the complex and rapidly changing economic marketplace.

In the years following the demise of OCE, the momentum for consumer education waned. Although the need for sophisticated consumer knowledge escalated, consumer education remained on the fringe of public education in K–12 classrooms, colleges, and adult and community education settings. The popularity of consumer education parallels the cycles of public commitment to the larger consumer movement in the United States.

— Rosella Bannister

See also

Consumer Education; National Coalition for Consumer Education.

Readings

Royer, Gayle L., and Nancy E. Nolt (1980). *Education of the Consumer: A Review of Historical Developments.* Rosslyn, VA: Consumer Education Resource Network.

Slagel, Michelle L. (1982). *The Implementation of a Discretionary Project Program: A Case Study of the Office of Consumers' Education.* Ph.D. dissertation. Washington, DC: George Washington University.

U.S. Presidents

See Presidents and the Consumer Movement.

Utilities Regulation

See Electricity Regulation; Natural Gas Regulation; Telephone Regulation.

1987. Ann Wallace's background included positions as executive director of the Governor's Commission for Women and head of Community Leadership and Volunteer Services in the office of the governor of Texas.

USOCA's budget increased from $1,678,000 to $2,103,000, and the agency had twenty-two staff members. It focused much attention on privacy, product safety recalls, telemarketing fraud prevention, and financial services. As in the Reagan administration, the office emphasized education and voluntary action. However, in the Bush administration, USOCA worked more often with consumer organizations as co-sponsors of conferences and other projects than it had under Reagan. Among the groups involved were Consumer Federation of America, National Consumers League, and National Coalition for Consumer Education.

In January 1994, President Bill Clinton appointed Polly Baca as director of USOCA, and restored to that position the title of special assistant to the president (last used in the Carter era). Baca, who had served for twelve years in the Colorado legislature, resigned in November of that year.

From then until 1996, when former Congressman Leslie Byrne was appointed director, the office was run by acting directors who received little support from the White House. In fact, in 1995 a Republican Congress tried to eliminate the office's funding. Only through aggressive advocacy by acting director Bernice Friedlander, supported by consumer and business groups, did the office survive. However, its funding was cut from $2,159,000 in 1994 to about $1 million in 1996. This recent experience illustrates the reality that, in a budget-cutting era, USOCA has no assurance of surviving, let alone prospering, without the strong support of the president.

— Joan Lucco

See also

Federal Consumer Advisory Bodies; Peterson, Esther; Presidents and the Consumer Movement; U.S. Consumer Protection Agency.

Readings

Peterson, Esther, with Winifred Conkling (1995). *Restless: The Memoirs of Labor and Consumer Activist Esther Peterson.* Washington, DC: Caring Publishing.

Petracca, Mark, ed. (1992). *The Politics of Interests: Interest Groups Transformed.* Boulder, CO: Westview Press.

U.S. Office of Consumers' Education

The federal Office of Consumers' Education (OCE) was created by the U.S. Congress in 1975 and abolished in early 1982. Housed within the U.S. Department of Education, the office received program funds during a six-year period of decreasing voter interest in consumer affairs.

Origins

Senator Allan Cranston (D-CA) was one of the first members of Congress to address the inadequacy of federal support for consumer education. Cranston believed that existing federal programs were totally insufficient. Federal aid was limited to providing consumer education within home economics courses, but only 35 percent of high school girls, and less than 1 percent of high school boys, took such courses. Moreover, in Cranston's view, the consumer education aspects of home economics were narrowly limited to such topics as nutrition and home budgeting.

Senator Lee Metcalf (D-MT) backed Cranston's legislation. The senator was particularly concerned that students understand powerful government-business relationships and the importance of citizen participation in regulatory issues.

Legislation creating the consumer education program was first included in amendments to the Elementary and Secondary Education Act of 1972. This legislation authorized funding levels at $20 million for 1973, $25 million for 1974, and $35 million for 1975. No dollars were actually appropriated until 1976, and from 1976 through 1981, annual appropriations exceeded $4 million in only one year. During its six years of operation, the office received less than $19 million for its grants and contracts program.

Following a brief period of management by Dean Bistline, Dustin Wilson was appointed director of OCE, a position he held for the next six years. Wilson was a former school superintendent with experience in various leadership roles within the U.S. Office of Education. During a period of decreasing support for consumer education, Wilson's commitment to the office, knowledge of school administration, and political savvy contributed significantly to the successes of the program.

Activities

The director of the new program was authorized to make grants and contracts with institutions of higher education, state and local education agencies, and other public and private agencies and institutions. The law specifically required that funds be available for activities such as the development of curricula, including interdisciplinary curricula, in consumer education; dissemination of information relating to such curricula; support of education programs at the elementary, secondary, and higher education levels; and preservice and in-service training programs and projects, including fellowship programs, institutes, workshops, symposiums, and seminars for educational personnel to prepare them to teach in subject matter areas associated with consumer education.

The director and staff of OCE were charged with developing the rules and criteria for awarding grants and contracts. A comparison of the enabling legislation and subsequent regulations reveals a shift of primary focus from elementary, secondary, and teacher education to adult and community education. The reasons for it are somewhat obscure, but one influential factor was the perception that significant funding was already being provided for "consumer and homemaking" education at the secondary level through the federal vocational education program. Another reason for the shift from elementary and secondary education to community education was the effectiveness of lobbying by activists and special interest groups.

Nonetheless, the OCE regulations provided a definition of consumer education and guidelines for subject matter useful to educational practitioners. Consumer education was defined as the process by which consumers develop skills to make informed decisions on the purchase of goods and services in light of personal values, maximum utilization of resources, available alternatives, ecological considerations, and changing economic conditions; become knowledgeable about the laws, rights, and methods of recourse in order to participate effectively and self-confidently in the marketplace, and take appropriate action to seek consumer redress; and develop an understanding of the consumer-citizen role in the economic, social, and governmental systems and how to influence those systems to make them responsive to consumers' needs.

The regulations also provided guidelines as to the subject matter that could be included in funded projects: basic economics of the marketplace; management of personal and financial resources; purchase of goods and services such as food, transportation, credit, insurance, housing, repairs, health care, and legal assistance; methods of consumer self-reliance and alternatives to the use of scarce or costly goods, services, or resources; consumer laws, rights, responsibilities, and redress; government assistance and services such as social security and education; the consumer role in determining energy conservation and ecological policies; individual or collective consumer participation in the economic and governmental systems, including the regulatory and legislative processes; special issues and problems such as advertising or product safety; and areas of critical importance in which consumer action can limit costs, such as energy, housing, food, and health care, including medical services and insurance.

OCE was authorized to distribute funds through both grants and contracts. Grants

placed responsibility for identifying problems and solutions with applicants, but contracts placed responsibility on the professional staff of OCE. With grants, little could be done for failure to perform; contracts, on the other hand, required deliverables for payment.

Between 1976 and 1980, OCE reviewed 2,976 grant applications and funded 300 projects. The types of projects funded included development of community consumer education materials and programs, classroom activities, teacher training, curriculum development, and media projects. In 1980, for example, $3.6 million was appropriated to OCE, of which 77 percent was distributed through grants. Nonprofit and public agencies received 71 percent of the grant funds, and local and state education agencies, community colleges, and universities received the remainder. Projects ranged from a $1,289 grant to the National Council on Aging to conduct educational programs focused on energy needs of the elderly to a $125,625 grant to the National Consumers League to prepare materials on effective consumer participation procedures for consumer affairs officers in government.

The office's evaluation of the early years of the program convinced it to shift some funds from grants to contracts. Over six years, OCE allocated about $4 million of nearly $19 million to contracts. Contract work included conferences for consumer educators, position papers on needs perceived by various consumer education stakeholders, and support for the development of print and audiovisual materials integrating consumer and economic education. The two largest contracts funded the Consumer Education Development Program (CEDP) and the Consumer Education Resource Network (CERN).

The CEDP was a two-year contract with the Michigan Consumer Education Center at Eastern Michigan University, the National Consumers League in Washington, D.C., and the City University of New York to conduct research to define the field of consumer education and identify its concepts. Among the documents produced by this study were a *Classification of Concepts in Consumer Education* and a statement of *Purposes and Objectives of Consumer Education.*

CERN was funded by a three-year agreement with InterAmerica Research Associates, Inc., of Rosslyn, Virginia. Its purpose was to establish a clearinghouse to collect, process, and disseminate information to consumer educators, and to provide a communications network among them. In addition to the resource database function, CERN also developed research papers and training materials, published a monthly newsletter, and responded to information requests.

Evaluation

The Office of Consumers' Education was abolished on February 12, 1981, during the first few weeks of the Reagan administration by executive order of the president. Several unique education programs within the Department of Education were folded into the Omnibus Budget Reconciliation Act of 1981, a block grant program providing discretionary money to the states.

Although OCE tried hard to meet the nation's consumer education needs during its six-year existence, it failed to become a strong catalyst for systemic change in policies affecting consumer education in the United States. A significant barrier to its success was a lack of unity within the consumer education community itself. Academics at universities often had little respect for consumer activists, and grassroots community groups, who were focused on immediate problems, had little patience for the long-term benefits of strengthened consumer education in the schools.

Home economics teachers, secure in their federal vocational consumer and homemaking funds, were not receptive to exploring interdisciplinary approaches with colleagues in business, mathematics, and economics. Business teachers were more comfortable teaching new keyboard technologies and the free enterprise system than in addressing the need fo[r] citizen participation and consumer protectio[n] against marketplace problems. Economi[sts]

W

Warne, Colston E.

From the 1930s to the 1970s, Colston Estey Warne was the most influential consumer leader in the country. He helped guide Consumers Union as it grew into the largest and most effective consumer organization in the world, and he was instrumental in the establishment of organizations ranging from the International Organization of Consumers Unions (now Consumers International) to the American Council on Consumer Interests. Perhaps most important of all, the combination of his ethical commitments and scientific rigor helped ensure that the consumer movement institutionalized itself as an important conscience and monitor of business practices in a free market economy.

Warne was born in 1900 in the Finger Lakes region of central New York State. His father was a farmer, country store operator, and pillar of the Presbyterian church. As a college student at nearby Cornell University, Warne was introduced to the writings of Thorstein Veblen and also to his future wife, Frances Lee Corbett, who was studying home economics. After his marriage, Warne studied money and banking at the University of Chicago, where his most important experience was studying with Paul H. Douglas, who introduced him to the field of labor relations and to the international cooperative movement. The subject of his doctoral dissertation was Illinois cooperatives.

Warne's teaching career began at the University of Denver and continued at the University of Pittsburgh (which he left in 1930 after a protest against infringement of academic freedom); he settled at Amherst College, where he worked as an economist for some forty years. Warne was not a conventional college professor solely interested in research and teaching. In the summer of 1933, for example, he assisted in the training of individuals who became key organizers of the Congress of Industrial Organizations (CIO). In 1935, when Consumers Union split from Consumers' Research over a labor dispute, Warne became president of the new organization.

Warne hoped that Consumers Union would represent a joint effort of consumers and workers to raise consumer living standards, chiefly through product testing, but the labor movement was too occupied with its own challenges. Teachers, technicians, scientists, engineers, and other professionals were the ones who recognized the potential importance of a product-testing consumer organization. Nevertheless, Warne insisted that Consumers Union not limit its activities to product-testing, but also serve as a spokesperson for consumers on a broad range of issues in numerous forums. This vision, as much as anything, strengthened the organization's commitment to lobbying policymakers, publishing books, subsidizing grassroots consumer advocacy, and promoting the international consumer movement in addition to its main work of product research disseminated in *Consumer Reports*.

Warne also played critically important roles in creating and advancing other consumer institutions. In 1953 he conceived the idea of educators organizing themselves into a group, which became the American Council on Consumer Interests. In the 1950s and 1960s, Warne actively promoted the spread of grassroots consumer organizations. He persuaded Consumers Union to assess the grassroots consumer movement and then figure out ways to support it. The funds Consumers Union contributed in the late 1980s and 1990s through the Consumer Federation of America to state and local groups were consistent with Warne's vision of the role of his organization. Today, a Consumers Union fund bearing his name helps support other consumer endeavors as well.

Of even greater significance was Warne's leadership in the establishment of an international consumer movement. His travels, his communications with activists in other countries, and Consumers Union's monitoring of consumer activities in other nations set the stage for the creation of such a movement. In 1960, Warne succeeded in establishing the International Organization of Consumers Unions and served as the group's president for the next decade. Consumers Union continues to provide significant support and leadership to this organization.

Warne contributed to the public interest in numerous other ways. In the mid-1930s, he was president of the People's Lobby. In the late 1940s, he served on the first Consumer Advisory Committee to the President's Council of Economic Advisers. In 1962 he served a two-year term as a member of the Consumer Advisory Council to the President. He also held positions on consumer advisory groups in New York and Massachusetts. Yet, more important than any formal position was his effective advocacy of a vision for a more ethical, consumer-friendly society.

— Stephen Brobeck

See also

American Council on Consumer Interests; Consumers International; Consumers Union.

Readings

Gordon, Leland J. (1970). "Colston Estey Warne: Mr. Consumer." *Journal of Consumer Affairs.* 4 (Winter): 89-92.

Morse, Richard L. D., ed. (1993). *The Consumer Movement: Lectures by Colston E. Warne.* Manhattan, KS: Family Economics Trust Press.

Newell, Barbara Warne (1980). "Tribute to Colston E. Warne." *Journal of Consumer Affairs.* 14 (Summer): 1-8.

Warranty Protections

A warranty, which is a promise by the seller (or manufacturer) that a product will perform to a certain standard, may be classified as either express or implied. In an express warranty, the standard is established by explicit action (typically in writing) by the seller. In an implied warranty, the standard has been established by law to mean that the product is of at least average quality and reasonably fit for ordinary purposes.

Warranties have a long and checkered history. From the emergence of the legal concept of caveat emptor in the sixteenth century, warranty protection for the consumer decreased steadily until the end of the nineteenth century. Not until the middle of the twentieth century did consumers regain significant warranty protection: The courts recognized implied warranties, and states passed the Uniform Commercial Code.

In the first three-quarters of the twentieth century, little action concerning warranty protection took place at the federal level. Consumer activists focused on antitrust, advertising, safety, and credit protection, and support for federal warranty legislation did not build until the late 1960s. Even then, warranty issues did not gain as much attention as other consumer legislation.

In 1974 the Magnuson-Moss Warranty and Federal Trade Improvement Act, simply called Magnuson-Moss, was passed by Congress. Factors that contributed to passage of this landmark legislation were broad public support for consumer protection; lack of sophistication by business interests in fighting consumer legislation; politicians, such as Warren Magnuson, who sought "apple pie" issues with broad voter support; support by major consumer groups and labor; and last, but not least, public dissatisfaction regarding warranties. As products became more complex and prone to malfunction, and repair costs increased, the demand grew for government solutions to protect the public from weak and confusing warranties.

After World War II, the marketing of many new, complicated products and the spread of a complex distribution system increased the need for effective warranties. Yet, manufacturers persisted in giving weak, short-term warranties and disclaimed any stronger implied warranties.

The specific product warranty that precipitated the eventual passage of Magnuson-Moss was the automobile warranty. By the early 1960s, auto companies used warranties as a competitive marketing tool. However, these manufacturers were making defect-prone vehicles and not meeting consumer expectations about warranty service. Household appliance manufacturers also were criticized for offering weak warranties. These automobile and appliance warranty problems were described in studies conducted in the late 1960s and early 1970s.

Federal Trade Commission (FTC), congressional, and other studies undertaken in the late 1960s and early 1970s revealed these flaws: Consumers had expectations of warranties that were not met by the warranty terms; a significant amount of warranty work was not performed to customer satisfaction; the performance of manufacturers and dealers under express warranties was not achieved to the levels implied; warranties were replete with limitations; warranties did not provide consumers with adequate information concerning their rights, duties, or remedies under contract; warranties contained unfair disclaimers couched in legal jargon; and warranties were frequently advertised in a deceptive manner. Other studies showed that, because manufacturers established the rules and the procedures, consumers were at a disadvantage in dispute resolution. In brief, this research on warranty problems revealed the wide gulf between consumer expectations and seller delivery, resulting in consumer disillusionment, frustration, anger, and a cry for action—an action that led to the passage of Magnuson-Moss.

The basic goals of Magnuson-Moss are to provide consumers with information through mandated disclosures and labeling, improve the quality of warranties by defining full warranties, and create redress procedures through informal dispute-resolution programs and private action, including class-action lawsuits. The underlying expectation was that warranties would be improved through competition, and disclosure requirements and standardization of terms and practices were intended to facilitate it.

Magnuson-Moss disclosure standards include information about parties covered, components of the product covered, specific periods of coverage, warrantor responses to consumer claims, procedures to obtain service and resolve disputes, and coverage limitations (which must be conspicuous). One part of the information section requires that warranty information be made available to the consumer before purchase.

Magnuson-Moss also creates a two-tier warranty coverage: full warranties and limited warranties. To be classified as a full warranty, certain standards must be met that include an anti-lemon clause and prohibitions against implied warranty limitations, unreasonable requirements to have a product repaired (e.g., send a piano back to the manufacturer), and excessive charges for repairs or diagnoses. Disclaimers against consequential damages are permitted.

Any warranty on products selling for $15 or more that does not meet the full warranty standards is categorized as a limited warranty. No performance standards are mandated for limited warranties, and manufacturers are encouraged to devise informal dispute resolution procedures. Automobile manufacturers were particularly encouraged to establish FTC-approved arbitration programs.

To what extent has Magnuson-Moss achieved its objectives in the areas of information, quality, and redress? Several studies conducted during the late 1970s and early 1980s could not agree. An early one by the FTC found positive changes in the content of automobile warranties that may have resulted from Magnuson-Moss. Some studies found warranties more readable, but the general consensus of researchers was that some consumers were still unable to comprehend the content of express warranties. Although researchers agreed that post–Magnuson-Moss warranties disclosed more information, some writers found that the act did little to minimize deception either in advertisements about warranties or in the warranties themselves.

Disclaimers, a critical issue for consumerists during the congressional hearings of the early 1970s, continue to be used in most warranties. A primary disclaimer problem, one often addressed in the literature and in the subcommittee hearing, is the implied warranty disclaimer. Consumer advocates cited it as a ploy to permit the manufacturer's express warranty to override any greater rights given under an implied warranty. Although prohibited by a few states, the implied warranty disclaimer is permitted by most.

Consumer advocates hoped that the "full warranty" classification would enhance warranty quality, but a large majority fall into the limited category. In many cases, full warranties apply only to part of a product, while limited warranties apply to other parts.

Studies of the impact of the informal dispute-resolution section are inconclusive. Although Magnuson-Moss encouraged manufacturer-run informal dispute-resolution programs that were recognized by most states, thirteen states established their own arbitration programs. *Consumer Reports* recounts higher consumer satisfaction from state-run arbitration programs than from those controlled by manufacturers or private arbitrators.

Although express warranties that come with the product at no additional charge have a number of problems, extended warranties (commonly known as service contracts) may pose greater economic risks to consumers. Sales of extended warranties are increasing steadily, and are now purchased by nearly half of auto buyers and about 15 percent of those buying appliances. These service contracts are highly profitable for the seller, with profits ranging from 100 percent to 600 percent.

High profitability and an asymmetry of information create conditions in which deception flourishes. Service contracts contain numerous exclusions; if a repair *is* covered, consumers often find it difficult, if not impossible, to obtain the promised service. Some service contract arrangements include extra disincentives for performance of covered repairs. One of the greatest problems with these service contracts is the high failure rate of nonmanufacturer-sponsored agreements. Also, the high profitability of service contracts is an incentive for manufacturers to minimize the importance of regular warranties and a disincentive for retailers to carry products with strong regular warranties that might discourage the sale of lucrative extended warranties.

Although Magnuson-Moss addresses extended warranties, the FTC has not promulgated regulations concerning disclosures of their terms and conditions. Some states strictly regulate extended warranties by classifying them as insurance, while others regulate them under consumer protection laws. Because the purchase of service contracts offers such poor economic value, consumer educators and activists strongly advise against it.

So-called secret warranties, sometimes known as warranty extensions or goodwill adjustments, are a form of warranty protection given only to those consumers who are aggressive in obtaining redress and/or knowledgeable about nonpublic information concerning a manufacturer's willingness to correct an inherent nonsafety problem in a product. Consumer activists label such warranties as unfair because they are discriminatory in application, but manufacturers defend them, claiming they result in savings that can be passed on to consumers. Although several states have considered legislation to extend the protection of secret warranties to all vehicle owners, only Virginia and Connecticut require manufacturers to notify consumers of postwarranty adjustments. The FTC has given minimal attention in recent years to secret warranties.

Several writers and consumer activists recommend improvements in warranty protections. During the congressional hearings prior to the passage of Magnuson-Moss, many consumerists testified that this legislation should mandate a higher level in protection than was included in the bill in its final compromise form. These same criticisms are still voiced today. Omitted items that would have strengthened the legislation include prohibitions against disclaimers of implied warranties, a rule that exclusions in warranties be limited to those items specifically named, and prohibitions of disclaimers for consequential damages. Consumerists advocate the creation of minimum standards for warranties as well as the establishment of a national standard for minimum warranty periods that would automatically cover most parts of products.

Consumer advocates also propose legislation to improve consumer protection in extended warranty sales. These protections might include financial reserve requirements for warrantors, mandated readability standards, inclusion of lemon clauses, mandated standards of coverage to preclude unfair contract exclusions, establishment of dispute-resolution procedures, required presale availability of extended service warranty contracts, mandated minimum disclosure standards, and transfer of liability to the seller in the event of failure of the original warrantor.

Some of these proposals do not require legislation; they could be initiated by FTC Trade Regulation Rules. However, the FTC has enacted few trade rules since the 1970s, so significant reform appears unlikely until there is dramatic change in the philosophy and leadership of the FTC and Congress.

Since 1975 substantive proposals for warranty legislation on the federal level have been limited. Other than some minimal effort at legislating protection in the areas of service contracts and secret warranties, any significant reform in federal warranty protection has little organized support. Considering the current pro-business and anti-regulation political environment, few prospects are in sight for any meaningful legislation.

—John R. Burton

See also

Center for Auto Safety; Federal Trade Commission.

Reading

Burton, John R. (1995). "Warranty Protection: A Consumerist Perspective." In W. Blichke and W. Murthy, eds, *Product Warranty Handbook*. New York: Marcel Dekker, Inc. 719–757.

Water Quality

See Drinking Water Safety.

Whistleblowers

Legally, whistleblowers are those who disclose information evidencing a reasonable belief of illegality, abuse of authority, gross mismanagement, gross waste, or a substantial and specific danger to public health or safety. Practically, they are individuals who bear witness to challenge dishonesty, cover-ups, or outdated conventional wisdom in the status quo.

Whistleblowers cannot be stereotyped by motives, which range from idealism to vengeance, or jobs, which range from maintenance workers to top executive personnel. What they have in common is knowing something that they believe should not be kept to themselves and choosing to act on that knowledge.

Deciding whether to blow the whistle means facing one of life's crossroads—making a choice between valid but conflicting values. The conflict raises personal issues of loyalty and livelihood. Loyalty to one's family, which involves meeting its income needs, and loyalty to colleagues often discourage whistleblowing. But whistleblowers often feel another loyalty—to the public trust, the law, and the communities in which they live.

When whistleblowers act strategically with the truth on their side, they can make a difference. That is why 90 percent of scientific whistleblowers in a Research Triangle Institute study said they probably would do it again, even though more than two-thirds reported suffering harassment or serious reprisal.

Whether as anonymous "deep throats" or public dissenters, for centuries whistleblowers have changed the course of history. The following illustrations, which involve consumer welfare, represent cases on which the Government Accountability Project (GAP) has worked since 1982. Whistleblowers provided the evidence that led to injunctions against two incinerators and the cancellation of three more that spewed toxic substances such as dioxin, arsenic, chromium, mercury, and other heavy metals into the environment in Arkansas, Indiana, Ohio, and South Carolina. They also helped persuade the Environmental Protection Agency to declare a moratorium against new incinerators and institute a national combustion policy establishing dioxin limits for all hazardous-waste incinerators.

In the 1980s, whistleblowers forced cancellation of proposals to replace federal meat inspection with industry honor systems for the U.S. Department of Agriculture seal of approval. They disclosed secret tobacco industry additives in cigarettes, creating a public backlash that helped blunt political pressures to ease government oversight of smoking.

Much GAP-assisted whistleblowing involves nuclear power plant safety. By revealing that a 97-percent-completed nuclear power plant had been built with metal from junkyards passed off as nuclear-grade steel, many X rays on safety welds were falsified, and portions of the plant were never inspected, whistleblowers forced its conversion to coal. They exposed and forced the conversion to gas of a nuclear plant being built next to a school and directly atop a large underground crater. They exposed illegalities that sparked an overhaul of the post-Three Mile Island power plant cleanup. They forced the shutdown of a nuclear weapons plant that had released over 500,000 pounds of radioactive emissions in the environment around Cincinnati.

Whistleblowers revealed that the Hanford nuclear weapons reservation had emitted over 400 times more radioactive waste than admitted by the government and its contractors. As one example, a whistleblower proved that more than 1 million gallons had leaked from a tank that, according to official records, had lost only 5,000 gallons. Whistleblowers thwarted plans to dump more than 7 million gallons of liquid radioactive waste into the water supply, stopped the restart of a plutonium reprocessing plant scheduled to pump out some 50 million tons of carcinogenic carbon tetrachloride, and triggered a commitment from that facility to cut radioactive emissions by 60 percent.

Whistleblowers pay a price to make a difference by "committing the truth," a term coined by Pentagon cost-control expert Ernie Fitzgerald. After his congressional testimony exposed Air Force lies about some $2 billion in cost overruns for the C5-A aircraft, he was treated as if he had committed a crime. Reprisals are not unique to the United States; a study from the University of Queensland in Australia found that 94 percent of whistleblowers reported direct or indirect harassment. Techniques to neutralize dissenters are numerous: use a spotlight to make whistleblowers, rather than their message, the issue; build a record as the foundation for later retaliation; threaten them into silence; attack them physically; isolate them; publicly humiliate them; destabilize their support base; make up ridiculous but damaging charges; leave them twisting in the wind; prosecute them; paralyze their careers; eliminate their job; and blacklist them.

None of these techniques is new. Defensiveness and the instinct to strike back when threatened seem part of human nature. The immediate challenge for consumers is to offer solidarity to whistleblowers, because it is unrealistic to expect workers to defend the public if the public does not defend them. Profiles in courage are the exception, not the rule.

— Tom Devine

Readings

Vinten, Gerald (1994). *Whistleblowing: Subversion or Corporate Citizenship?* New York: St. Martin's Press.

Westman, Daniel P. (1991). *Whistleblowing: The Law of Retaliatory Discharge.* Washington, DC: Bureau of National Affairs.

Women as Consumers

Women represent the largest group of consumers. They take part in the consumption cycle—choosing, buying, using, and disposing—both for themselves and for others. This second task is often the dominant one; because a woman is responsible for most of the shopping does not necessarily imply that she uses what is bought. On the contrary, as the family manager she often buys what suits her husband and children rather than herself. In this dual role, women are more exposed to various marketing practices than are men.

Women are poorer than men. Although many women participate in the labor force or deliver unpaid labor in the household, in all countries they still earn considerably less than men. Women perform two-thirds of the world's work but earn only one-tenth of the world's income. These relatively low incomes limit the autonomy of women as consumers, and they experience many other forms of discrimination in the marketplace. The multiple roles and fragile economic status of women make them especially vulnerable to unethical marketing practices such as discriminatory advertising, unfair pricing strategies, and fraudulent services. Food, housing, technology, health care and pharmaceutical products, hazardous products, financial and legal services, and transport are only a few of the areas in which women are treated disadvantageously.

Nevertheless, women have also taken leadership in the consumer movement and played leading roles in seeking to establish consumer rights: access to essential products and services, choice, safety, information, representation, redress, and education. Boycotting producers and retailers, organizing food cooperatives, and founding banks for female customers are examples of female empowerment aimed at redressing the power imbalance.

Multiple Roles

In their daily lives, women (and men as well) fulfill multiple roles that include being partners, parents, employees, and homemakers. But both qualitatively and quantitatively, women bear heavier burdens associated with these roles. Even in a country such as Norway, which has relatively little gender inequality, women spend considerably more hours on household tasks than do men. In most countries, women make up between 25 and 40 percent of the formal labor force, and they also perform a large majority of work in the informal sector. The consequences of these work burdens include limited time for leisure activities, health-related problems, and dissatisfaction with products and services.

A Canadian study found that women's working status was related to time-saving tendencies. Women employed outside the home spent more on household durables and purchased meals away from home more frequently than did homemakers. But the fact that the study found no differences in the frequency of buying convenience foods suggests that women were still trying to fulfill their role as "gatekeepers" in caring for and nurturing their families.

Women often cope by seeking to play the "superwomen" role. Superwomen are expected to exhibit traits of both the traditional masculine and feminine gender-role stereotypes. They do not prioritize their various roles, but rather consider successful performance in all roles to be important for their self-esteem. When new role expectations are added to old ones, considerable stress may result.

Women who try to play many roles are more likely to place greater importance on their own appearance, and report significantly more symptoms of eating disorders, than do women who consider only a few roles to be central. In the Western Hemisphere, eating disorders among women are dramatically increasing, associated mainly with continuous or near-continuous attempts to lose weight. In the United States, for example, each year an estimated 15,000 women die because of anorexia.

An experiment based on the hypothesis that "eating lightly" is gender-related demonstrated that women, but not men, "are what they eat." Both female and male judges regarded a woman who ate small meals as significantly more feminine, and significantly less masculine, than a woman who ate large meals. Furthermore, information about meal size influenced the judges' tendencies to attribute stereotypical feminine personality traits. Women who ate smaller portions were perceived to be considerably more expressive, kind, and understanding of others; more concerned about their appearance; and significantly better looking than the women who ate large meals. In contrast, the amount eaten by men was not used in judging their masculinity and femininity.

This social norm of equating thinness with attractiveness is responsible for dysfunctional eating patterns such as continuously going on and off diets, which often leads to disorders like anorexia or bulimia. This permanent restriction of food intake has become so common that it could be regarded now as "normal" eating, not deserving of therapeutic treatment. Even though beauty ideals have changed throughout the centuries, it seems plausible that a certain percentage of women have always suffered from eating disorders to keep pace with socially imposed body norms of either Twiggylike shapes or baroque proportions.

Weight loss is big business. In the United States, weight-loss companies' revenues approached $2 billion in 1993, and 90 percent of the clients were women. The large majority regain any lost weight within three years. Besides the physiological reasons for the failure of weight-loss programs, one other cause is clearly linked: the ambiguous messages women receive from mass media, especially women's magazines, which provide women with both cooking recipes and diet plans, thus perpetuating the paradox of the great cook and family caretaker who also must be slim to be attractive.

Another problem faced by women as consumers is a marketplace that does not meet their expectations. Polls, studies, and focus groups reveal that many women are dissatisfied with the selection, quality, service, retailing, and advertising of products, and experience limited enjoyment in shopping.

Mass media such as movies, television soap operas, magazines, and advertisements reinforce traditional stereotypes of gender roles. Instead of accurately reflecting the diversity of society, media are more likely to reflect male-dominated images of society and its consumers. A recent analysis of Norwegian printed food advertising illustrates this point: Only 7 percent of the advertisements appeared in men's magazines, while 63 percent were published in newspapers and magazines directed at a female audience. The most frequent subjects of these ads were meal preparation, health, and child care. Also, many soap operas and films reinforce the role of beautiful "superwomen" who are able to manage with little stress. Goods and services that are claimed to help fulfill this role are heavily advertised, thus perpetuating the consumption society's premise that a product always exists that can solve a given problem.

Economic Discrimination

In both poor and affluent societies, women face wage discrimination. They earn less than men for the same work. They have less chance than men to secure jobs with the highest incomes. They usually experience higher unemployment rates than men. They have less access than men to consumer credit even though evidence shows that women are more reliable in paying off debt. In poor nations, development projects have offered credit mainly to men, often enabling them to grow cash crops on land previously used by women for food production.

On the other hand, women often pay higher prices for goods and services than do men. The following recent examples from North America illustrate this point. In Chicago, a study revealed that car sellers charged white women 40 percent higher markups than white men; they charged African American men more than twice, and African American women more than three times, the markup paid by white men. According to a survey by the Department of Consumer Affairs, in New York City two out of three hair salons charged women an average of 25 percent more than men for the same basic shampoo, cut, and blow-dry. In Washington, D.C., according to a lawsuit filed by George Washington University law students, city dry cleaners charged women up to 200 percent more than men to launder a plain cotton shirt. Also in Washington, as reported by a newspaper, wool turtleneck sweaters in the men's section of a clothing store cost $97.50, while these sweaters in the women's section cost $145.00.

Given that women in the United States still make less than seventy-seven cents for every dollar earned by men, a double trap exists: Women cannot attain the same level of living as men when they are forced to spend more money, from lower earnings, for higher prices of identical consumer goods and services.

Not only the private sector but also the public sector is often inattentive to the needs and wants of women by failing to consult with them about preferences and experiences related to various government-sponsored services. A typical example is the case of cervical screening services in Britain, which are designed by mostly male professionals who control service delivery without taking into account their clients' preferences. These wishes include a preference for female staff, more skilled practitioners, protection of privacy and personal dignity, and clear instructions on the procedure and test results.

Activism

To combat gender discrimination, women have sought remedies ranging from self-help to boycotts to legal protection. In the United States, housewives in many local areas have spontaneously organized boycotts against rising food prices. Worldwide, women led a boycott of Nestlé products because of the company's aggressive marketing of baby milk products in the Third World. After the Chernobyl disaster, women organized food co-ops in Western European countries. Women also pursue consumerist goals through networking, both at the local level (e.g., local women's groups in England to secure better health care) and at the global level (e.g., the Women's Global Network on Reproductive Rights, based in the Netherlands).

Sometimes the goal of this activism and networking is legal protections. In the United States, women's groups have lobbied successfully for protections against credit discrimination, yet they have failed to win approval of equal rights constitutional protections that are part of the constitutions of several European nations.

Women's experiences in the marketplace are the basis for consumer activism and activism in other social movements. Those who have challenged anti-consumer business practices gain experience that helps equip them to confront other gender-related problems in their community. Moreover, women's concern for the quality of the environment in which they and their families live makes them more sympathetic to the concerns of the environmental movement.

— Suzanne Grunert-Beckmann

Reading

Douglas, Susan J. (1994). *Where the Girls Are: Growing Up Female with the Mass Media.* New York, NY: Times Books.

Wells, Troth, and Foo Gaik Sim (1987). *Till They Have Faces.* Penang: International Organization of Consumers Unions.

Whittelsey, Frances Cerra, and Marcia Carroll (1993). *Women Pay More and How To Put a Stop to It.* New York, NY: The New Press.

Y

Yugoslavian Consumer Movement

In 1995, while economic sanctions have been in place, the so-called Yugoslav Consumer Association in Belgrade has been isolated from the world movement. This association had its origins in the Federal Board of Family and Household that was founded in 1957 and renamed the Association of Consumers of Yugoslavia in 1969. It has always been funded entirely by the government. In 1991, the association was reborn, at least in part under the old leadership. It claims to be funded by membership fees, donations, and sponsorship but may also receive direct or indirect contributions from industry and government. It has published a number of issues of a magazine, *10 Million Consumers*, which contains advertising and seems written for an international audience rather than for the benefit of Serbian consumers.

Consumers International (CI) reports the emergence of grassroots consumer groups in both Croatia and Macedonia. The latter has been accepted for membership in CI. As of 1995, no groups existed in Bosnia.

— Alastair Macgeorge

Reading

Kozminski, Andrzej K. (1992). "Consumers in Transition from the Centrally Planned Economy to the Market Economy." *Journal of Consumer Policy*. 14: 351–370.

Index

Baker Commentary on the Bible

Walter A. Elwell
Editor

BakerBooks
A Division of Baker Book House Co
Grand Rapids, Michigan 49516

Published by Baker Books
a division of Baker Book House Company
P.O. Box 6287, Grand Rapids, MI 49516-6287

Previously published as *Evangelical Commentary on the Bible*
Published in 2000 as *Baker Commentary on the Bible*

Printed in the United States of America

ISBN 0-8010-2254-1

For current information about all releases from Baker Book House, visit our web site:
http://www.bakerbooks.com

CONTENTS

PREFACE

To the evangelical Christian the Bible is the very Word of God. Here one looks when comfort, strength, guidance, or instruction is needed; having looked, one is never disappointed. Each generation needs to look afresh there so that the truth of God's Word may be effectively applied to the specific needs that exist. To assist in this task commentaries are written. They are not designed to replace Scripture, but are to be used as an aid to understanding it. That is the purpose of this commentary. It was written to help the average reader understand what the biblical text says.

All of the writers are evangelical Christians who are technical scholars in their field. They all have a knowledge of the original language of the text and have studied it extensively; many have already written elsewhere on the same material that they address in this volume. The content of this commentary is, therefore, both accurate and reflective of a commitment to the full and final authority of the Bible as God's Word.

The writers were instructed to write in such a way that persons without technical training could understand the Bible. Many excellent books have been written by scholars for scholars, but that was not the design of this work. Certainly, if a scholar reads this commentary, he will see the scholarly effort that it entailed, but it was not written for that reason. Rather, it was written to assist the pastor, student, church school teacher, or interested layperson in grasping the meaning of Scripture and applying it to his or her life.

This commentary was not written just to answer difficult questions, but also to point out the spiritual and personal elements that can be found in the Bible. An attempt was certainly made to clarify existing difficulties, but that, in itself, was not deemed sufficient. That the Word be allowed to speak to our needs is also important.

Although this commentary is not a textbook on systematic theology, important points of biblical theology are brought out. The great doctrines of the faith, such as creation, redemption, sanctification, and resurrection, are discussed in the appropriate places.

The writers were encouraged to include material from their latest research when this would be helpful, so fresh material and ideas can be found here for the reader's interest and benefit.

The writers were chosen for their knowledge of the subject, not for their denominational point of view. Hence, writers from many points of view are included in this volume. It could well be that at certain points differences might exist, but no attempt was made to impose an artificial unity on what is here. Each writer was allowed to speak for himself; the reader may make the decision as to which point of view is ultimately to be preferred. The one thing that binds all the writers together is a common fidelity to the Bible as the Word of God.

The sincere desire of the writers of this commentary is that its use will make the Scriptures more intelligible and that by knowing them believers will come to know God better, for that in the end is the true purpose of life. As certainly as God exists we will someday stand in his presence utterly transparent in the pure light of his scrutiny. If this commentary can be of help as we make our slow but certain pilgrimage unto him who is the Source of life, the writers will be well compensated for their efforts.

Dates listed for some persons or events in the time lines are subjects of scholarly debate. Those given for rulers reflect the time of their reigns; for a chronology of some prophets, the time lines reflect the work of Leon J. Wood in *The Prophets of Israel* (Grand Rapids: Baker, 1979). Scripture references in boldface indicate subsections of larger passages that are listed in the subheads.

Special acknowledgment is due to Allan Fisher of Baker Book House for his guidance and encouragement, and to Vivian Youngberg for her cheerful, efficient secretarial work.

CONTRIBUTORS

Austel, Hermann J. Ph.D., University of California, Los Angeles. Dean and Professor of Old Testament, Northwest Baptist Seminary, Tacoma, Washington.

Baker, William H. Th.D., Dallas Theological Seminary. Professor of Bible and Theology, Moody Bible Institute, Chicago, Illinois.

Bowling, Andrew C. Ph.D., Brandeis University. Professor of Biblical Studies, John Brown University, Siloam Springs, Arkansas.

Burge, Gary M. Ph.D., King's College, University of Aberdeen. Chairman, Department of Biblical and Theological Studies, North Park College, Chicago, Illinois.

Chamblin, J. Knox. Th.D., Union Theological Seminary in Virginia. Professor of New Testament, Reformed Theological Seminary, Jackson, Mississippi.

Davis, James A. Ph.D., Nottingham University. Associate Professor of Biblical Studies, Trinity Episcopal School for Ministry, Ambridge, Pennsylvania.

De Young, James B. Th.D., Dallas Theological Seminary. Professor of New Testament Language and Literature, Western Conservative Baptist Seminary, Portland, Oregon.

Dillard, Raymond B. Ph.D., Dropsie College. Professor of Old Testament Language and Literature, Westminster Theological Seminary, Philadelphia, Pennsylvania.

Elwell, Walter A. Ph.D., University of Edinburgh. Professor of Biblical and Theological Studies, Wheaton College Graduate School, Wheaton, Illinois.

Erickson, Richard J. Ph.D., Fuller Theological Seminary. Assistant Professor of New Testament; Director, Seattle Extension, Fuller Theological Seminary, Seattle, Washington.

Ewert, David. Ph.D., McGill University. Emeritus Professor of Biblical Studies, Mennonite Bible College, Winnipeg, Manitoba, Canada.

Gilchrist, Paul R. Ph.D., Dropsie College. Stated Clerk of the General Assembly, the Presbyterian Church in America, Atlanta, Georgia.

Goldberg, Louis. Th.D., Grace Theological Seminary. Professor of Theology and Jewish Studies, Moody Bible Institute, Chicago, Illinois.

Gruenler, Royce Gordon. Ph.D., University of Aberdeen. Professor of New Testament, Gordon-Conwell Theological Seminary, South Hamilton, Massachusetts.

Hamilton, Victor P. Ph.D., Brandeis University. Professor of Religion, Asbury College, Wilmore, Kentucky.

Harrison, R. K. Ph.D., University of London. Emeritus Professor of Old Testament, Wycliffe College, University of Toronto.

Hill, Andrew E. Ph.D., University of Michigan. Associate Professor of Old Testament, Wheaton College, Wheaton, Illinois.

Hoffmeier, James K. Ph.D., University of Toronto. Associate Professor of Old Testament and Archaeology, Wheaton College, Wheaton, Illinois.

Knight, George W., III. Th.D., administrator and professor of New Testament, Knox Theological Seminary, Fort Lauderdale, Florida.

Livingston, G. Herbert. Ph.D., Drew University. Emeritus Professor of Old Testament, Asbury Theological Seminary, Wilmore, Kentucky.

Longman, Tremper, III. Ph.D., Yale University. Associate Professor of Old Testament, Westminster Theological Seminary, Philadelphia, Pennsylvania.

Luter, A. Boyd, Jr. Th.D., Dallas Theological Seminary. Chairman and Associate Professor of Bible Exposition, Talbot School of Theology, La Mirada, California.

Martens, Elmer A. Ph.D., Claremont Graduate School. Formerly President; Professor of Old

Testament, Mennonite Brethren Biblical Seminary, Fresno, California.

McClelland, Scott E. Ph.D., University of Edinburgh. Associate Professor of Religion, The King's College, Briarcliff Manor, New York.

McRay, John. Ph.D., University of Chicago. Professor of New Testament and Archaeology, Wheaton College Graduate School, Wheaton, Illinois.

Moo, Douglas. Ph.D., University of St. Andrews. Associate Professor of New Testament, Trinity Evangelical Divinity School, Deerfield, Illinois.

Motyer, Stephen. M.Litt., Bristol University. New Testament Lecturer, London Bible College.

Noll, Stephen F. Ph.D., University of Manchester. Academic Dean; Associate Professor of Biblical Studies, Trinity Episcopal School for Ministry, Ambridge, Pennsylvania.

Patterson, R. D. Ph.D., University of California, Los Angeles. Chairman, Department of Biblical Studies, Liberty University, Lynchburg, Virginia.

Rayburn, Robert S. Ph.D., University of Aberdeen. Pastor, Faith Presbyterian Church (Presbyterian Church in America), Tacoma, Washington.

Schrader, Stephen R. Th.D., Grace Theological Seminary. Professor of Religion, Liberty University, Lynchburg, Virginia.

Schreiner, Thomas R. Ph.D., Fuller Theological Seminary. Associate Professor of New Testament, Bethel Theological Seminary, St. Paul, Minnesota.

Schultz, Carl. Ph.D., Brandeis University. Professor of Old Testament; Chairman of the Division of Religion and Philosophy, Houghton College, Houghton, New York.

VanGemeren, Willem A. Ph.D., University of Wisconsin. Professor of Old Testament; Chairman of the Department of Old Testament, Reformed Theological Seminary, Jackson, Mississippi.

Van Groningen, Gerard. Ph.D., University of Melbourne. President Emeritus, Trinity Christian College, Palos Heights, Illinois. Adjunct Professor of Old Testament, Covenant Theological Seminary, St. Louis, Missouri.

Vos, Howard F. Th.D., Dallas Theological Seminary; Ph.D., Northwestern University. Professor of History; Chairman, Department of History, The King's College, Briarcliff Manor, New York.

White, R. E. O. B.D., London University; M.A., Liverpool University. Formerly Principal, Baptist Theological College of Scotland.

Wolf, Herbert M. Ph.D., Brandeis University. Associate Professor of Theological Studies, Wheaton College, Wheaton, Illinois.

ABBREVIATIONS

SCRIPTURE VERSIONS

AV	Authorized Version
JB	Jerusalem Bible
KJV	King James Version
NASB	New American Standard Bible
NEB	New English Bible
NIV	New International Version
NJB	New Jerusalem Bible
RSV	Revised Standard Version
TEV	Today's English Version

GENERAL

Arab.	Arabic
Aram.	Aramaic
ca.	about, approximately
CD	Damascus Document
cf.	compare
chap(s).	chapter(s)
compar.	comparative
DSS	Dead Sea Scrolls
esp.	especially
et al.	and others
f./ff.	and following
fn.	footnote
ft.	feet
Ger.	German
Gk.	Greek
Heb.	Hebrew
i.e.	that is
Lat.	Latin
lit.	literally
LXX	Septuagint
marg.	margin
Mish.	Mishnah
MS(S)	manuscript(s)
MT	Masoretic Text
n./nn.	note(s)
par.	parallel
pass.	passive
pl.	plural
sing.	singular
trans.	translated, translation
viz.	namely
vs.	versus
v./vv.	verse(s)

Old Testament Introduction

The Old Testament consists of thirty-nine books, written and collected over a period exceeding a thousand years. Sacred to both Jews and Christians, it was the Bible used by Jesus, Paul, and the early church. It was the Old Testament from which the first Christians drew their doctrine, upon which they grounded their lives, in which they found prophetic references to Jesus and themselves, and from which they derived comfort, strength, encouragement, and vision for the future.

The books are of unequal length (Obadiah being barely a page long, Psalms having 150 chapters), written mostly in Hebrew. (Small portions of Ezra, Jeremiah, and Daniel are written in Aramaic, a language similar to Hebrew.) These books exhibit great diversity of literary style, including narrative, poetry, sermons, dialogue, prayers, hymns, songs, letters, and prophecies. They also show great linguistic diversity.

While there were many other books written in antiquity, some of which are mentioned in the Old Testament (the book of Jashar, for example), these were not preserved and used as sacred literature by the Israelites. But under the guidance of God, those books that he had inspired were gathered together, until, at last, the collection of writings was complete. There the Word of God to his people was to be found.

The books, as found in the Protestant Bible (the Roman Catholic Bible adds another small collection called the Apocrypha), are arranged in the order of history–poetry–prophecy. The historical material (Genesis–Esther) begins with the creation of the world, continues through Israel's waxing and waning fortunes, and ends with Israel's return to its homeland after seventy years of exile in Babylon. Some overlap occurs in the accounts and the material does not run in strict chronological order, but it is history in the fullest sense of the word. Here are events of life, often broadly conceived on a national scale, where nations rise and fall, but also seen on a personal level where the courage or deceit of individuals is the focus of attention.

The poetic books (Job–Song of Solomon) were grouped together mainly because they are almost entirely in poetic form. These books deal with very personal issues, from devotion to God to human love.

The prophetic books contain the complex message of Israel's prophets. These messages are urgent, direct, contemporary, morally informed, and filled with warning, promise, or judgment. There is also a universality about them that reaches out to the nations surrounding Israel; indeed, they speak to any nation at any time.

In spite of the great diversity of the Old Testament books, a profound unity remains as well. What gives the Old Testament its focus is the doctrine of a personal God who created the world and, in spite of the world's defection from him because of sin, has not given up on it. God's fatherly concern was expressed in his selection of a nation to represent him to mankind, and through which he would offer salvation to anyone willing to accept it. The many theological themes to be found in the Old Testament are all part of this presentation of God as the Creator, Sustainer, and Redeemer of the world.

The writers of the New Testament look back upon the Old Testament as foreshadowing, indeed prophesying, their own day. God was preparing the world for a full and final revelation of himself in his Son, Jesus Christ, in the types and shadows that he used in earlier times. "In the past God spoke to our forefathers through the prophets at many times and in various ways, but in these last days he has spoken to us by his Son" is how the writer of Hebrews puts it (Heb. 1:1–2). Jesus is seen as the fulfillment of all that went before and as the summation of all of God's dealing with mankind. His life, death, and resurrection marked the end of the old and the beginning of the new. Because the Old Testament pointed directly to Jesus, the early Christians used it as their own Bible and structured their lives according to its spiritual teachings.

The Pentateuch

This is the Greek name for the "five books" of what the ancient Hebrews called the "Law" or "Torah." The Hebrew word, however, more properly means "instruction," because the Pentateuch contains the legal, doctrinal, and ritual basis upon which Hebrew covenantal life was established.

Genesis ("origin") deals with creation, primeval human history, and the patriarchal period of Israelite life, ending with the twelve tribes living in Egypt. Exodus tells how these tribes were delivered from enslavement by God's power and welded into a covenant nation during a four-decade wilderness experience. Leviticus contains the detailed prescriptions for sacrificial worship, along with regulations for community living. Numbers deals with events at the beginning and ending of the wilderness period to provide a representative description of the entire desert sojourn. Deuteronomy is a covenant-renewal document which furnishes a detailed description of what the Sinai covenant meant for the Israelites. The Torah shows God as the sole Creator and Sustainer of the universe. It teaches that humanity was created to worship God and have fellowship with him. In particular it describes how the Hebrews were chosen from all the nations to witness to God's existence and power in the world. Their way of life was to reflect his high moral and spiritual qualities, and they were commanded specifically to behave as a priestly kingdom and a holy nation. In a superstitious pagan world they were to be examples of obedience and faithfulness to the one true God's revealed will for mankind. If they behaved in this way they would be blessed richly, but if not they would be punished.

The Pentateuch forms the historical, religious, and theological basis for the entire course of Hebrew history. Its legal and moral implications laid the foundation for all prophetic teachings, which included the promise of a redeeming Messiah. In his ministry Jesus fulfilled all that the Law and the Prophets had spoken concerning him, and the new covenant that he instituted on Calvary became the basis of all Christian faith.

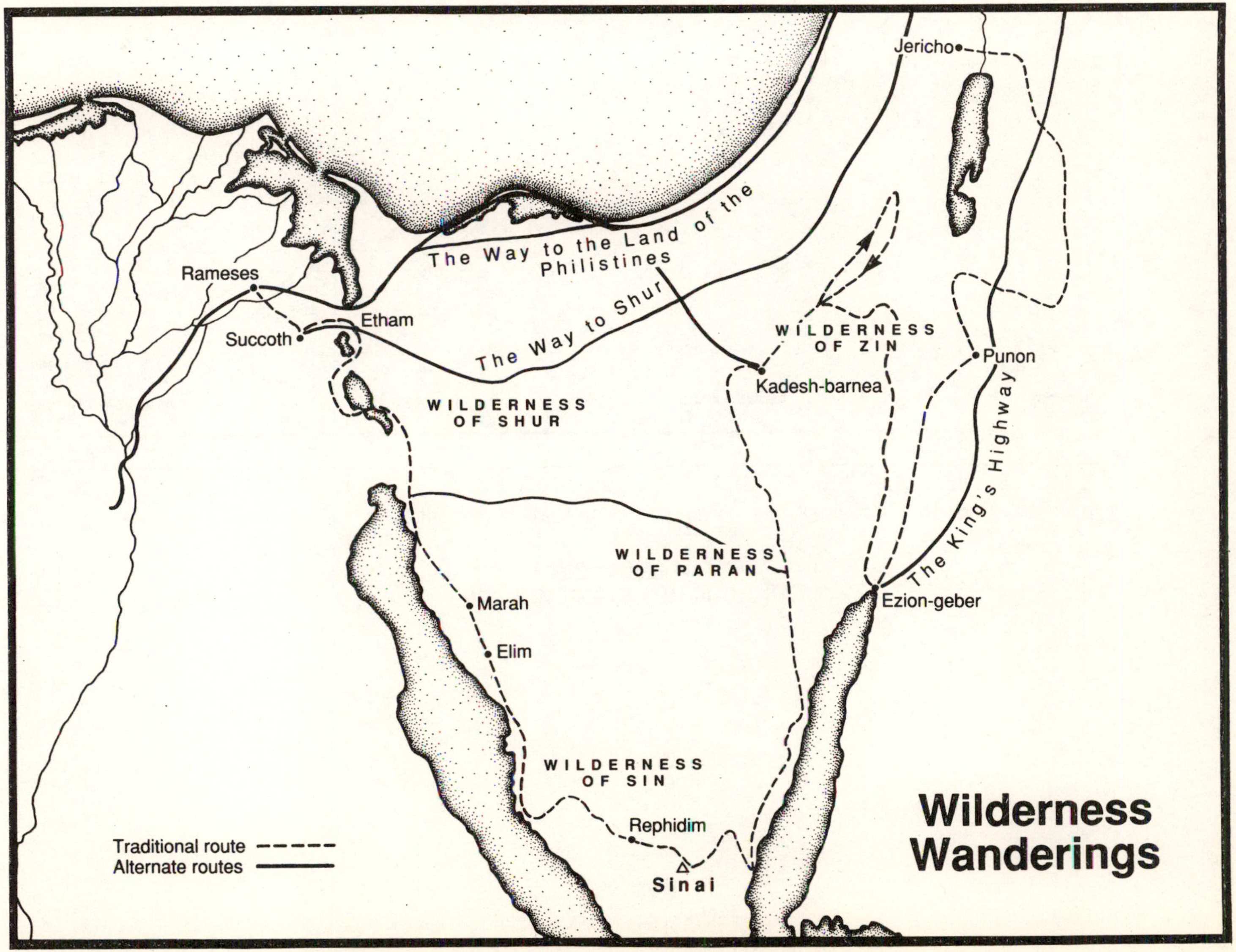
Wilderness Wanderings
Jericho
Punon
The King's Highway
Ezion-geber
The Way to the Land of the Philistines
The Way to Shur
Rameses
Succoth
Etham
WILDERNESS OF SHUR
WILDERNESS OF ZIN
Kadesh-barnea
WILDERNESS OF PARAN
Marah
Elim
WILDERNESS OF SIN
Rephidim
Sinai
Traditional route
Alternate routes

Old Testament Chronology
1450–1050 B.C.

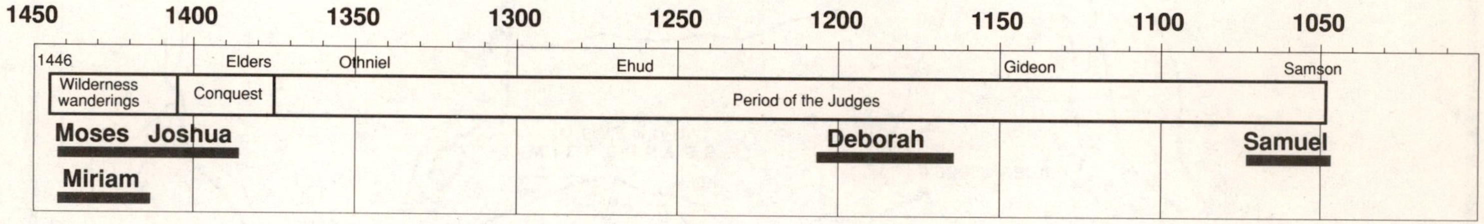

GENESIS

Victor P. Hamilton

INTRODUCTION

Moses' name does not appear in the Book of Genesis as it does in the other four books of the Pentateuch. For that reason, strictly speaking, Genesis is an anonymous book. There is no real problem with acknowledging this, for the majority of the books in the Old Testament are anonymous. Who wrote Kings? Who wrote Judges? We do not know.

Jewish and Christian tradition alike have attributed Genesis to Moses. This position is based more on inference, or the lack of a more appealing alternative, than on clear textual data in Genesis. When the New Testament uses phrases such as "Moses and all the Prophets" (Luke 24:27) or "Moses and the Prophets" (Luke 16:29), we know that Jesus is speaking of the first two sections of the three-sectioned Hebrew Bible (Law/Prophets/Writings). As "Prophets" stands for Joshua–Judges–Samuel–Kings–Isaiah–Jeremiah–Ezekiel–the Twelve Minor Prophets, "Moses" stands for the Torah, Genesis–Deuteronomy. Jesus thus marks Genesis as Mosaic.

Most critical biblical scholars outside the evangelical circle find the above conclusion both unconvincing and unacceptable. In its place they offer the documentary hypothesis, or the JEDP theory, which rejects both the Mosaic authorship of Genesis (and the rest of the Pentateuch) and its literary unity. It is alleged that multiple authors are indicated by: (1) the presence of doublets (two creation accounts, two flood stories, two banishments of Hagar and Ishmael, etc.) which contain contradictory and mutually exclusive information; (2) several distinctly different writing styles and theological perceptions; and (3) the use of multiple names for deity (Elohim, Yahweh, Yahweh-Elohim), often in a single story.

Specifically, four documents are posited. The first is *J* (for in it the name for deity is Yahweh/Jehovah), which was written in the time of David/Solomon in Jerusalem. The second is *E* (Elohim is the name for deity here), written about a century later somewhere in northern Israel. After these two documents were spliced, *D* (= Deuteronomy, or parts of Deuteronomy) was produced in the late eighth or seventh century B.C. Finally, around the time of the exile or shortly thereafter

(550–450 B.C.), the remaining *P* (= priestly) materials were added. Subsequently someone edited all of the documents to give us our Pentateuch.

There are two possible (evangelical) explanations for the origin of Genesis. First, Genesis 1–36 could have originally existed as tablets. Moses then arranged these tablets in chronological order and added the material about Joseph. This makes Moses the compiler (not author) of Genesis. Second, Genesis may have been composed around the time of the exodus from Egypt. Emphasizing as it does the promise of God to Israel's forefathers and the origins of the founding fathers, Genesis would be an appropriate composition to read to the tribes before they departed for Sinai. The most likely author of such a composition would be the person designated to lead them to Sinai—Moses.

Genesis can be divided into an introduction and ten sections, each of which is introduced by the formula *these are the generations of* (2:4; 5:1; 6:9; 10:1; 11:10; 11:27; 25:12; 25:19; 36:9; 37:2). Five times the formula is followed by narrative (2:4; 6:9; 11:27; 25:19; 37:2). In these verses the New International Version understandably translates "generations" as "account of." Five times the formula is followed by a genealogy: either a vertical genealogy (a genealogy that focuses on one line of descendants; 5:1; 11:10); or a horizontal genealogy (a genealogy that highlights subgroups; 10:1; 25:12; 36:1). Through both narrative and genealogy Genesis traces a specific line of descendants from Adam to Jacob as a reflection of God's will for one people.

It is debatable whether the phrase *these are the generations of* introduces what follows (a superscription) or whether it concludes what has just preceded (a subscription or colophon). In favor of the first interpretation is the fact that the phrase is always followed by the genitive of the progenitor, never of the progeny. In favor of the second interpretation is the fact that often (e.g., 5:1; 37:2) the preponderance of information given about the person named in the phrase comes before the phrase, not after it.

Additionally, we may note the fact that Genesis covers multiple generations in chapters 1–11, but only four generations in chapters 12–50. Patriarchal history is the more crucial segment, and hence receives a more extensive treatment. Similarly, note that while only two chapters are given to a rehearsal of creation (1–2), thirteen-and-a-half are devoted to Abraham (12:1–25:11). Why six times as much space for Abraham as for Adam and Eve? Or, why consign the narration of the fall to one chapter (3), while there are twelve chapters for Joseph (37; 39–48; 50), a marginal character not in the Abraham–Isaac–Jacob–Judah chain?

This does not mean that the creation story is less important than the Abraham story, or that the fall narrative is less significant than the Joseph narrative. Longer does not mean more crucial any more than shorter means less important. But it does say something about focus and emphasis. Presumably the creation story, confined to Genesis 1–2, could have been stretched over a dozen chapters or so, but it was not. Genesis does not address itself exhaustively to questions such as "Who is man?" or "What is man's origin?" as it does questions like "What does it mean for a person to follow God in faith?" (hence, the Abraham story) or, "How does God use the life of the one who will honor him?" (hence, the Joseph story).

Genesis, as the title suggests, is a book about beginnings, specifically the beginning of humankind (1–11) and the beginning of a single family (12–50). Genesis 1–11 begins with a world untouched by sin. That pristine situation will not reoccur until Revelation 21. The untarnished world of Genesis 1–2 is shattered by Adam and Eve's dissatisfaction with their creaturely status, and their coveting of a godlike stature. Sin puts a wedge between relationships established by God. There is alienation between humankind and God, between man and the animals, between man and woman, between man and land, between man and himself.

In chapters 4–11 sin snowballs. Genesis 3 may be read as the cause and 4–11 as the effects of sin. Cain, Lamech, the sons of God, the contemporaries of Noah, and the tower builders all follow in Adam's and Eve's footsteps. Fratricide, polygamy, lust, violence, and self-aggrandizement are the fruits of disobeying God.

Paul says that where sin increased, grace increased all the more (Rom. 5:20). Clearly we have abounding sin in Genesis 3–11. Do we also have abounding grace? May Paul's dictum be applied to Genesis 1–11 and beyond? True, God banishes Adam and Eve from the garden, and he makes Cain a refugee, but note that *before* God banishes Adam and Eve he clothes them; *before* he exiles Cain he places a protecting mark on him. *Before* God sends the flood he announces to Noah a covenant that will come on the heels of that flood. The God of 1–11 is a God of judgment *and* a God of grace.

Even the whole patriarchal section (chaps. 12–50) may be read as God's plan of redemption through one family (and eventually one person out of the family) for the sin-infested world of Genesis 3–11. Thus, Genesis 3–11 may be read as the problem, and Genesis 12–50 as the solution.

To that end, running throughout the patriarchal narratives is the theme of promise: (1) the promise of a son; (2) the promise of descendants; (3) the promise of land; (4) the promise of God's own presence; and (5) the promise of spiritual influence among the nations. At every major point the patriarchs are buoyed by the "I wills" of God. God's covenant with the patriarchs is primarily unilateral rather than reciprocal. He is the one who commits himself to the fulfillment of this covenant and these promises. Only secondarily is human behavior introduced as a contingency factor. "You will" is subordinated to "I will" in Genesis 12–50.

Genesis makes it clear that the greatest threats to the promises of God are seldom external ones. Generally, the most potentially damaging threat to the divine promises is the bearers of those promises. Note, for example, how frequent are deception scenes in 12–50: Abraham and the Pharaoh; Abraham and Abimelech; Isaac and Abimelech; Jacob and Esau; Jacob and Isaac; Jacob and Laban; Laban and

Jacob; Joseph's brothers and their father; Judah and Tamar; Joseph and his brothers. All of these produce strife and alienation, and many an anxious moment. Yet, an Abraham or a Jacob is never exiled from Canaan along the lines of the punishment meted out to Adam and Eve or to Cain. Nor are they reprimanded by God for their highly questionable behavior and tactics. Silence does not exonerate them. Silence does indicate, however, the primary focus of Genesis 12–50—God's election of and commitment to one family as the means for world redemption. God will no more lay aside the family of Abraham as his chosen vessel than he will scuttle the church and establish a surrogate institution.

OUTLINE

I. Primitive History (1:1–11:32)
  A. The Creation of the World (1:1–2:3)
  B. Adam and Eve (2:4–25)
  C. The Fall (3:1–24)
  D. Cain and Abel (4:1–26)
  E. From Adam to Noah (5:1–32)
  F. The Flood (6:1–8:22)
  G. Noah after the Flood (9:1–29)
  H. The Table of Nations (10:1–32)
  I. The Tower of Babel (11:1–9)
  J. The Shemites (11:10–32)
II. Abraham (12:1–25:18)
  A. The Call of Abram (12:1–9)
  B. Abram in Egypt (12:10–20)
  C. Abram and Lot Separate (13:1–18)
  D. Abram Rescues Lot (14:1–24)
  E. God's Covenant with Abram (15:1–21)
  F. Hagar and Ishmael (16:1–15)
  G. The Covenant of Circumcision (17:1–27)
  H. The Lord of Birth and Death (18:1–33)
  I. The Destruction of Sodom and Gomorrah (19:1–38)
  J. Abraham and Abimelech (20:1–18)
  K. Friction Inside and Outside the Family (21:1–34)
  L. Abraham's Test (22:1–24)
  M. The Death of Sarah (23:1–20)
  N. Isaac and Rebekah (24:1–67)
  O. Abraham and Ishmael (25:1–18)
III. Jacob (25:19–36:43)
  A. Esau and Jacob (25:19–34)
  B. Isaac and Abimelech (26:1–35)
  C. Jacob's Deceit (27:1–46)
  D. Jacob Flees to Haran (27:47–29:14)
  E. Jacob, Leah, and Rachel (29:15–30:24)
  F. Jacob and Laban (30:25–31:55)
  G. Jacob and Esau (32:1–33:20)
  H. The Rape of Dinah (34:1–31)
  I. Jacob Returns to Bethel (35:1–29)
  J. Esau's Descendants (36:1–43)

IV. Joseph (37:1–50:26)
  A. Joseph and His Brothers (37:1–36)
  B. Judah and Tamar (38:1–30)
  C. Joseph and Potiphar's Wife (39:1–23)
  D. Joseph's Interpretation of Dreams (40:1–41:57)
  E. Joseph's Brothers in Egypt (42:1–38)
  F. The Second Journey to Egypt (43:1–34)
  G. Judah's Plea (44:1–34)
  H. Joseph and His Brothers (45:1–28)
  I. Jacob in Egypt (46:1–50:14)
  J. Joseph's Reassurance (50:15–21)
  K. Joseph's Death (50:22–26)

COMMENTARY

I. Primitive History (1:1–11:32)

A. The creation of the world (1:1–2:3). The Bible does not begin by attempting to prove the existence of God. It simply assumes this fact. But it does begin by describing God's creation of the heavens and the earth (**1:1–2**). This phrase may be an illustration of what is known as merism, the expression of totality through the use of opposites. Thus, verse 1 is simply saying that God created everything. This he did in the beginning. John begins his Gospel with the same prepositional phrase (John 1:1), but surely means something different by it. The whole verse may be interpreted as a statement of the fact of an action which is described in detail in 1:2–2:3.

The earth is described as formless and empty. This pair of words occurs again only in Jeremiah 4:23 and Isaiah 34:11, both in the context of divine judgment. One may not conclude, however, that Genesis 1:2a refers to something that is the result of God's fury. The two words designate a state of material devoid of order, prior to God's meticulous work on it.

Some have connected the word *deep* with the Akkadian goddess of chaos, Tiamat. Not only is this linguistically suspicious, but Genesis 1 itself rules it out, for here the deep is the impersonal watery mass that covered the world before God brought about the created order. Over this deep hovers the Spirit of God. The verb here is employed elsewhere of birds (Deut. 32:11). The translation *Spirit of God* is preferable to *wind of God.* The traditional interpretation makes better sense of the "us" in verse 26. It is the Spirit who holds things together.

There are a number of elements common to the creation day units: (1) introduction—"and God said"; (2) the creative word—"let there be"; (3) fulfillment of the word—"and it was so"; (4) a name-giving/blessing—"God called"; (5) the divine commendation—"and God saw that it was good"; (6) the concluding formula—"and there was evening, and there was morning—the_____day."

Actually light is the only item created by fiat alone (**1:3–5**). Everything else in Genesis 1 is created by fiat plus some divinely instigated type of activity. Note that the darkness is not called "good," and that there are sources of light in the universe (day 1) besides sunlight (day 4).

One Hebrew word designates heaven both as the place where God dwells and the place where birds fly (**1:6–8**). It is the second sense that is used here. The Hebrew word may be translated "expanse, firmament, vault" and is that element that divides heavenly waters from terrestrial waters.

In a second work of separation, land is separated from seas, just as in verse 6 waters were separated from waters (**1:9–13**). Vegetation is created mediately—"Let the land produce vegetation." The productive power of the earth is a God-given gift.

For a specific reason the moon is called (only here) the lesser light, and the sun is called (also only here) the greater light (**1:14–19**). Among Israel's neighbors sun and moon were designations for deities. Not so in God's world! In fact, they are not light proper, but carriers of the light. They are lamps, and their duties are spelled out to show their status as servants. They are not arbiters of man's destiny.

Day 5 parallels day 2. On the second day the habitat was created (sky separating waters), and on the parallel day the creatures who live in that habitat (birds and fish) are created (**1:20–23**). The land can "produce" vegetation (v. 11) and animals (v. 24), but the sea does not "produce" fish and the sky does not "produce" birds. Only the earth/land (a feminine word in Hebrew) is life-producing. Here, however, for the first time we see the verb *create* (*bārâ*) applied to a specific creature. The choice of this verb is to emphasize a uniquely divine act.

Day 3 brought about the environment (land and vegetation); day 6 brings about those beings (animals/humankind) who inhabit that environment (**1:24–31**). Unlike the other days the sixth day is alone designated by the article: "*the* sixth day." And when it is completed God evaluates only this day's work as *very good*. These two facts indicate the climactic nature of the sixth day.

Humanity's creation is preceded by the phrase *let us make man* (v. 26). While we should hesitate to read this as a clear-cut trinitarian statement, a matter about which the Old Testament is essentially silent, neither should we interpret it mythologically ("God said to the other gods") or angelically ("God said to the angels"). It does suggest that there is a distinction of personalities in the Divine Being. God, so to speak, can step outside of himself and speak to himself. May it be that God is addressing his Spirit (1:2)?

God creates humankind in *his image, his likeness*. Man is animal, but he is more than animal. Man is godlike, but he is less than God. "Image" emphasizes man's close similarity to God, while "likeness" stresses that this similarity is not exact. God and man are not indistinguishable. Verse 27 clearly states that the distinction of the sexes (male and female) is also of divine origin. One's sexuality is far from a biological accident.

As the divine image bearer, man is to subdue and rule over the remainder of God's created order. This is not a license to rape and destroy everything in the environment. Even here he who would be lord of all must be servant of all. This is indicated, among other ways, by the fact that God created his image bearers as vegetarians (vv. 29–30).

Everything God created thus far is called "good" or "very good." The seventh day alone is called "holy" (**2:1–3**). It is significant that the word *holy* is applied in Scripture first to the concept of time, not to space. Pagan mentality would place a premium on space-holy places; time and history are viewed as cyclical.

The absence of the phrase *and there was evening, and there was morning—the______day* after the seventh day indicates that God is not resting because he is exhausted but is desisting from his work of creation. It is not so much a date as it is an atmosphere. The seventh day, like man and woman (1:28), is blessed. If "blesses" in 1:28 is meant to confer the power to beget new life, might "blessed" in 2:3 mean the same?

B. Adam and Eve (2:4–25). Genesis 1 says little about how God created humankind. It simply notes that God created male and female, adding a few remarks about their relationship to the rest of creation. Genesis 1 emphasizes man as one *created with* authority; Genesis 2 emphasizes man as one *under* authority.

This section (**2:4–7**) is introduced as "the account of the heavens and the earth"; this is the first of ten units in Genesis introduced with "account of" (or, "story of, descendants of"). In a sense man is viewed as the offspring of the heavens and the earth. But it is an earth without vegetation (v. 5a) and water (v. 5b), except for subterranean streams (v. 6).

God is pictured as a potter. He forms man from the dust. Perhaps we should translate dust as mud or clay, for potters do not work with dust. The idea of God creating man from the earth is mentioned elsewhere in the Old Testament (Job 4:19; 10:8; Pss. 90:3; 103:14; 104:29; 146:4). Not only is God potter, he is animator as well. God breathes the breath of life into man.

The garden of Eden (**2:8–14**) is located in the east, but an explicit location is not given. The word *Eden* may be connected with Sumerian-Akkadian *edinu* ("wilderness, flatland"). Three times (2:8, 10; 4:16) the word refers to the geographical location of the garden. That the garden is planted after man's creation indicates that the Lord God did not live there.

The trees in this garden produce edible fruit. But two trees are given special significance: the tree of life and the tree of the knowledge of good and evil. There are only a few references to the tree of life in the Old Testament (Prov. 3:18; 11:30; 13:12; 15:4) and a few in the New Testament (Rev. 2:7; 22:2, 14, 19). Man is not dependent for life upon this tree, for he already has life (man was "a living being" [v. 8] before the tree of life [v. 9]). What he is dependent upon is a proper relationship with God.

Work is not a result of the fall; manual labor is prefall. Adam is put into the garden to work it and to take care of it (**2:15–17**). God has been doing the work thus far, and now he shares that responsibility with his image bearer. Even before Genesis 3, then, a biblical work ethic is sounded.

With this assignment comes an additional word from God. In Genesis 2 God creates two institutions. The first is law, the purpose of which is to teach one to live under authority. The second is marriage, the purpose of which is to teach one to live for someone other than himself.

God reminds Adam of his ample provision for humankind: "You are free to eat from any tree." The Lord is not stingy. Then he follows that with a single prohibition: "You must not eat from the tree of the knowledge of good and evil." There is much debate about the meaning of the phrase *knowledge of good and evil.* One popular suggestion is that this knowledge is sexual knowledge, for when the couple eat from this tree they immediately realize they are naked (3:7). But why would God want to withhold sexual knowledge from those he just created male and female? A second popular interpretation of the phrase is that "good and evil" means everything (a merism), and what was forbidden was the acquisition of omniscience. But then 3:22 would teach that Adam and Eve, when they disobeyed, actually became omniscient. The serpent would be proved correct that disobedience to God brings only gains and advantages.

A third possibility, and the one accepted here, is that the knowledge of good and evil means the ability and power to determine what is good and what is evil. Of course, this is God's prerogative alone. He has never delegated moral autonomy to any of his creatures. This suggestion is lent credibility by the fact that the phrase *good and evil* is most often used in the Old Testament where some kind of a decision is demanded.

Interestingly, it is God who determines that it is not good for man to be alone (**2:18–25**). There is no indication that Adam himself was dissatisfied with his circumstances. After making his evaluation (v. 18a), God proposes a solution (v. 18b). God will provide a helper for Adam. God already is Adam's helper (but a superior helper). The animals are also Adam's helpers (but inferior helpers). This helper, then, must be one that will be equal to him. Furthermore, she is to be suitable for him. The Hebrew word for "suitable" suggests something that completes a polarity, as the north pole is "suitable" to the south pole. One without the other is incomplete.

To that end, God parades the animals before Adam (vv. 19–20). The force of this is to stress that Adam himself chooses who his partner will be. Rather than force a decision on Adam, God allows the man to make a free decision. Man is not free to choose what is right and wrong, but he is free to choose his life partner.

After the scene with the animals is over, God administers anesthesia to Adam; and while the man is in a deep sleep, God makes woman from one of his ribs (a Hebrew word, incidentally, that is translated "side" everywhere else it appears in the Old Testament). Actually the text says that the Lord "built" woman.

When Adam says that the woman is "bone of my bones and flesh of my flesh" (v. 23) he is giving the ancient equivalent of our "in weakness and in strength." One of the meanings of the verb behind the noun *bone* is "to be strong." Flesh, on the other hand, represents weakness in a person.

The man is to leave his father and mother (neither of which Adam has!) and cleave to his wife. Elsewhere in the Old Testament these are covenant terms. When Israel forsakes God's covenant she "leaves" him. And when Israel is obedient to God's covenant she "cleaves" to him. Already Genesis 2:24 is saying that marriage is a covenant simply through the use of covenant terminology.

The climax of creation is this: the man and his wife were both naked. How appropriate! Physical nudity? Yes. But there are other kinds of nakedness. The verse is claiming a total transparency between this primal couple.

C. The fall (3:1–24). There are only four chapters in the Bible where Satan is not present, the first two and the last two. The Bible begins and ends with him out of existence. But between Genesis 3 and Revelation 20 he is a factor to be reckoned with. The Hebrew word for "serpent" may be connected either with an adjective/noun meaning "bronze" (suggesting something that is shiny), or with a verb meaning "to practice divination." Two things are said about the serpent (**3:1–7**). First, a word about his character—he is crafty, subtle. This is a neutral word, and in the Old Testament may be either a commendable or a reprehensible trait. Second, there is a word about his origin—he was made by God. This point is stressed to make it plain that the serpent is not a divine being, not a co-equal with God.

The serpent's first tack is to suggest to Eve that God is sinister, that in fact God is abusing her. This is the force of his question in verse 1a. "Would God let you see and touch these trees (i.e., raise the desire), but not let you eat *any* of them? A God who would do something like that certainly does not love you." Eve responds with a little hyperbole of her own ("you must not touch it") in her defense of God.

The serpent's second tack is to deny the truthfulness of God's word (v. 4), and to suggest that disobedience, far from bringing any disadvantages, will in fact bring an advantage—"you will be like God" (v. 5).

No further conversation ensues between the two. Verse 6 tells us that the temptation appealed, in order, to (1) Eve's physical appetites, (2) what she could see, and (3) her imagination. Note the thrust in this temptation. The serpent does not ask homage from Eve. Rather, he indirectly suggests that she shift her commitment from doing God's will to doing her own will.

God does not track down this wayward couple. He simply walks in the garden in the cool of the day (**3:8–13**). Hearing his sound, they hide from him. This is as foolish as Jonah who thought he could actually run from the presence of the Lord.

The Lord begins with a question just as the serpent had—"Where are you?" This question does not mean that God is ignorant of Adam's whereabouts. Rather, it is God's way of drawing Adam out of hiding.

Adam does two wrong things. First, he hides rather than face the truth (v. 10). His fear drives him from God rather than to God. Second, he blames his spouse and God. Adam refuses to admit that even complicity is a way of being involved in wrongdoing. Eve is not any better than her husband. She, too, looks for a scapegoat (the serpent, v. 13b). What Adam and Eve have in common is their refusal to accept personal responsibility for their actions.

The consequences of sin are detailed in **3:14–19.** Only the serpent is cursed. God does not curse those he created in his image. Phrases like "crawl on your belly" and "eat dust" may be understood as metaphorical expressions denoting the serpent's submission. He is now himself a servant. True, snakes do "crawl on their belly" as a means of locomotion, but they do not eat dust.

Also, the serpent is told that he is to be on the losing side of a battle between the seed of the woman and himself. In this eventual showdown, his head will be crushed by the seed of the woman. Is the "seed" collective or singular? The Hebrew allows for either, but the Septuagint has "he." (The Latin Vulgate even has "she"!) Not without good reason many have referred to Genesis 3:15 as the protoevangelium, "the first good news." An as-yet-unidentified seed of the woman will engage the serpent in combat and emerge victorious. It is likely that Eve does not comprehend this word. But the snake is not left in the dark—he is to be cursed, a crawler, and crushed.

God speaks to Eve about her role as mother (v. 16a) and as wife (v. 16b). Here are the two points where, in biblical thought, a woman experiences her highest fulfillment. And at these two points there will be pain and servitude. It may well be that we should read these words in verses 16–19 not as prescriptions, but as descriptions by God himself of what it means to be separated from him. Note that in chapter 1 God created male and female to rule jointly. Now in chapter 3 male rules female (same Heb. verb). The word for desire in verse 16 is used again in 4:7 (sin's desire to have Cain). Is Eve's desire for Adam normal desire or is it a desire for domination as in 4:7?

God speaks to Adam about his role as a worker. Here is where the male experiences his highest fulfillment. And for him, too, there will be pain. If we read these words as divine mandates, then we should not see these speeches of God as his way of "getting even" or "teaching a lesson" to Adam and Eve. They may in fact be love gifts from God, his way of wooing the couple back to himself. Why should a person who once walked in perfect fellowship with God and is now separated from the garden want to get back to God if he sees no need for that, and his life is essentially problem-free? For Adam that involves trying to till a cursed ground. It is not labor, but the difficulty of that labor. Sin always puts a wedge between things or people in Genesis 3. It puts a wedge between God and humans, between man and woman, between man and himself, and now between man and the soil.

It is interesting that on the heels of this divine word (**3:20–24**) Adam names his wife "Eve," which is connected with the word for "life, living." It is a name of dignity and reflects the eventual joy of motherhood she will experience. Here is hope in the midst of judgment.

Adam gives a name, but the Lord clothes Adam and Eve with garments of skin. The important thing here is garments rather than skins. God provides a covering for this naked couple, but it is a divine covering, not a human covering (v. 7b). Throughout the Old Testament one of the meanings of "to atone" is "to cover." It is no wonder that God's righteousness is compared to clothing, as is unrighteousness ("filthy garments"). It is important to note that God covers the couple *before* he expels them. Here is grace before law.

The Lord banishes Adam and Eve from Eden, and restricts reentry to Eden via cherubim and a flaming sword. Adam has indeed become "like one of us" (v. 22) but not in the sense the serpent said he would. Anytime a person believes he can decide for himself what is right and wrong, he becomes god. He has usurped the divine prerogative.

D. Cain and Abel (4:1–26). Cain and Abel, Adam's sons, are born after the fall (**4:1–16**). Cain's birth is connected by Eve with the verb *to bring forth.* In Hebrew this verb sounds like "Cain." Eve has been allowed to share in the creative work of God. Unlike Cain's, Abel's name is not explained by Eve. "Abel" is the word *vanity* appearing in Ecclesiastes 1:2—"Abel of Abels, all is Abel"—unless "Abel" is to be connected with a cuneiform word meaning "son." Traditionally understood, his name reflects the transitory nature of his existence.

Abel is a shepherd and Cain is a farmer. Both brothers bring offerings to the Lord suitable to their vocations. There is no indication in the text that one offering is inferior to the other.

The Lord looks favorably on the presentation of Abel's fatty portions. We should not spend a lot of time trying to answer why God accepted Abel's offering and rejected Cain's. Genesis 4 does not supply an answer, but rather shifts its concerns to another matter: How does one respond when God says no?

Cain is very angry and his face is downcast. Cain is the first angry and depressed man in the Bible. He should be able, however, to overcome these feelings before they overcome him ("if you do what is right," v. 7). Cain still retains the power of decision. Sin is now crouching demonlike at Cain's door. A serpent in a garden and now sin at the door. What is Cain to do? The last portion of verse 8 may be read as a command ("you *must* master it"); an invitation ("you *may* master it"); or a promise ("you *will* master it").

Cain kills Abel in the field (Cain's?). First, man fell out of relationship with God. Now he falls out of relationship with his brother. How can Cain love God whom he cannot see, when he cannot love Abel whom he can see? God's question to Cain is followed by the famous question: "Am I my brother's keeper?" The answer to that question, incidentally, is no. "To keep" means to be responsible for, to control, to exercise authority over. That is why God is repeatedly called Israel's "keeper." We are not called to be our brother's keeper, but our brother's lover. Abel's blood cries out because the earth will not receive and cover over innocent blood.

As a consequence, Cain is to be driven from the land and become a wanderer. The ultimate penalty for a Hebrew is not death, but exile, a loss of roots.

Unlike his father and mother, Cain complains about the harshness of his sentence (v. 13). He will be forced to become a nomad; God will hide his face; he will become the object of blood revenge (v. 14). This last phrase assumes a populated earth, indicating the existence of others besides Adam, Eve, and Cain. To that end God places a mark on Cain before he expels him. This will protect Cain from recrimination. Here again is mercy before judgment. What clothing is to Adam and Eve, the mark is to Cain. Note that in neither Genesis 3 nor 4 do the disobedient repent of their sin. Cain dwells in Nod, which sounds like the verb *to wander.*

In light of the reference to Adam and Eve's "other sons and daughters" (5:4), does Cain marry an unnamed sister? Or are there women represented among "whoever finds me"?

Now Cain the wanderer has become Cain the city-builder (**4:17–24**). Does this indicate that the divine penalty has been mitigated? Or is this further proof of Cain's self-determination?

Although out of fellowship with God, Cain is still able to multiply and fill the earth. Several of his descendants are worthy of note. Lamech (v. 19) is both polygamous and given to titanic revenge (v. 23). Lamech fathers four children: Jabal ("to lead flocks"), Jubal ("Trumpet"), Tubal-cain ("Cain" = "forger"), and Naamah (close to Hebrew "pleasant," as in "Naomi"). The skills of shepherding, music, and metallurgy are attributed to the fallen line of the Cainites. Many of history's most significant cultural advances have come from people who stand outside the orbit of the God of Scripture.

Obviously **4:25–26** should not be understood as a sequel to verses 17–24. Cain's genealogy does not extend six generations before Adam fathers a child again. Adam and Eve's third child is called Seth, here connected with a verb meaning "he has granted." Eve has lost Abel to death and Cain to exile. Seth is a replacement for Abel, not for Cain.

In a chapter given over so much to names, how appropriate it is to read that at this time men begin to call on the name of the Lord (Yahweh). Long before God revealed himself fully as Yahweh to one people called Israel (Exod. 3:6), or even to the patriarchs, there is at least a small group of people who grasp the identity of the true God.

E. From Adam to Noah (5:1–32). In a genealogy stretching over ten generations, the lineage from Adam to Noah is traced. Only in the last section does this vertical genealogy become a horizontal one (v. 32).

In the description of each generation, the same literary structure is followed: (1) the age of the father at the birth of the firstborn; (2) the name of the firstborn; (3) how many years the father lived after the birth of this son; (4) a reference to the fathering of other children; (5) the father's total lifespan.

The names of Adam's progeny are: Seth, Enosh, Kenan, Mahale, Jared, Enoch, Methuselah, Lamech, and Noah. The genealogical data about Noah are only partially given in verse 32, and are not completed until 9:28–29.

Two things need to be said about these individuals. First, there is close or exact similarity between some of the names in the Sethite list (5:1–32) and some of the names in the Cainite list (4:17–24). There is, for example, a

Cainite Lamech (4:18–24) and a Sethite Lamech (5:25–28), a Cainite Enoch (4:17) and a Sethite Enoch (5:21). Also, names like Irad (4:18) and Jared (5:15), Methushael (4:18) and Methuselah (5:21) are very close to each other. These similarities do not force us, however, to assume that the respective genealogies are imaginary, or that both chapters 4 and 5 are dependent upon a stock genealogy. Two separate lines, with two names common to each, are traced.

The second item of interest in chapter 5 is the unusually long lifespans. Methuselah's is longest (969 years). Some would dismiss these figures as totally impossible. While they are indeed high, the numbers are quite ordinary when laid alongside another document from the ancient world known as the Sumerian King List (ca. 2000 B.C.). It begins with an introductory note about the origin of kingship. Then it gives a list of eight preflood kings who reigned a total of 241,200 years. One of these kings, Enmenluanna, reigned 43,200 years. The shortest reign is 18,600 years. Furthermore, it is difficult to distinguish whether some of the earlier entries in the king list are gods, mortal, or both. The farther one goes back, the less the distinction between deity and humanity is maintained. Not so in Genesis 5. Push humanity as far back as possible and one encounters only "earthling" (a literal translation of "Adam"). The chasm between the finite and the infinite is never blurred in the Bible. The long lifespans may also be a reflection of God's blessing upon the Sethites. Longevity in Old Testament thought is a sign of divine blessing upon the godly (see Deut. 4:25; 5:33; 30:20).

One of the names in this passage is well known—Enoch. It is not without significance that he is the seventh (the perfect position) in this genealogy. Unlike everyone else in the chapter whose death is recorded, Enoch is "taken away." Perhaps long life is not the greatest blessing one can experience. To be elevated into God's presence is better. It is ironic that the one man in Genesis who does not experience death (Enoch) fathers history's oldest individual (Methuselah). That Enoch walked with God is a virtue and a privilege he shares with Noah (6:9).

F. The flood (6:1–8:22). Few episodes in Scripture defy dogmatic interpretation as does this one. The sons of God marry the daughters of men; and Nephilim are said to be on the earth (**6:1–4**). Until this point Genesis has dealt only with the sins of individuals—Cain, Lamech, Eve, Adam. Now the emphasis is on the sin of a group, the sons of God. Who are these sons of God? The term *sons of God* elsewhere in the Old Testament designates angels (see Job 1:6; 38:7; Pss. 29:1; 89:7). The New Testament, however, teaches that angels do not marry (Matt. 22:29–30; Mark 12:24–25; Luke 20:34–35). Furthermore, if the angels are the villains, then why is God's anger directed against *man?*

The sons of God may be the Sethites (the godly line), while the daughters of men are the Cainites (the ungodly line). The trespass would be the unequal yoking together of believer and unbeliever. This interpretation is not without its problems, but it is quite entrenched in Christian tradition.

Whatever the correct interpretation, the union is illicit, for God is provoked. It is interesting that the reference to God's displeasure (v. 3) comes before the reference to the Nephilim (v. 4). This shows that God's annoyance is with the nuptial arrangement itself. More than likely, the 120 years does not refer to a shortened lifespan (for only Joseph lives less than 120 years in Genesis), but to a period of grace before the flood commences. As such it may be compared with Jonah 3:4, "forty more days and Nineveh will be overturned." The text does not say that the Nephilim ("those who were made to fall") are the offspring of this alliance. Rather, they are contemporaries of the other two parties (sons/daughters/Nephilim). According to Numbers 13:33, they form part of the pre-Israelite population of Palestine.

There is a clear-cut reason for the flood (**6:5–22**). The sons of God see how beautiful the daughters of men are. The Lord sees how terrible the earth has become (wickedness). The problem is not only what man *does;* even his *thoughts* are evil. Sin is both extensive and intensive. Verse 6 says God repents (KJV); the New International Version reads that he "was grieved." In the majority of cases when the Hebrew verb *to repent* is used, surprisingly the subject is God.

Noah stands out among his peers. He is righteous, blameless, and walks with God. Thus verse 9 supplies the answer to why Noah finds favor in the Lord's eyes (v. 8). Divine favor is not something Noah wins; it is something he finds.

God spoke his first intention to destroy the earth to himself (v. 7). Now he shares that information with Noah (v. 13), just as he later tells Abraham that he intends to destroy Sodom (18:17–21).

Noah is told to build an ark about 450 feet long, 75 feet wide, and 45 feet high. It is really a ship, but Genesis calls it an "ark." The only other place this Hebrew word is used is in Exodus 2, to refer to "the ark" into which baby

Moses is placed. In both instances an individual destined to be used by God is saved from drowning by being placed in an ark. Again, note the announcement of a covenant (v. 18) before the flood starts. Here again is grace before judgment.

God now repeats his earlier word to Noah (6:18–20) to enter the ark (**7:1–10**). What the narrator earlier observes about Noah's character (6:9), God confirms (7:1). This time Noah is told to take aboard, in addition to his family, seven of every kind of clean animal and two of every kind of unclean animal. In 6:19–20 and 7:15–16 we read that Noah is to take *two* of all living creatures. Is this a discrepancy, and thus evidence for the blending in Genesis 6–9 of two flood stories? One pair/seven pairs? Not necessarily so. Genesis 6:19–20 and 7:15–16 provide general information. Noah is to bring aboard pairs of animals. In Genesis 7:2, specific information is given about how many pairs—seven. It is not surprising that God desires salvation of the clean animals. But why spare the unclean animals? Does God's compassion extend to them too?

Noah is given a week's warning before the flood begins. The Hebrew word for "rain" in verse 4 is different than the word for "rain" in verse 12. That used in verse 12 designates a heavy downpour. The rain of verse 4 is no shower—it is to last forty days and forty nights. Noah does what God says (vv. 7–9) and God fulfills his word (v. 10).

As the flood starts (**7:11–16**), again we find the deliberate use of repetition and summarization. This is a characteristic of epic composition. Note: the flood (v. 6); entry into the ark (vv. 7–9); the flood (vv. 10–12); entry into the ark (vv. 13–16). Actually, there are two references to the flood's beginning: verse 10 and verse 11. The additional data given in verse 11 are about the two sources of the rain: the springs of the great deep and the floodgates of heaven. But the following verse refers only to the second of these.

Although Noah's wife, sons, and daughters-in-law are also saved, there is no reference to their character. Their salvation is due to their husband/father/father-in-law. Note also that while the sons are named no women are.

Interestingly, it is "God" who commands the group to enter the ark (v. 16a), but "the Lord" who shuts them in (16b). Perhaps this shift to God's more personal name suggests that God is the protector of the ark.

As the waters rise (**7:17–24**), verses 13–16 focus on the action inside the ark, while verses 17–24 focus outside the ark. To be outside the ark is akin to being outside the garden. Salvation inside the ark is total; destruction outside the ark is total.

The reference to 150 days (v. 24) includes the forty days of rainfall, plus the length of time before the flood waters begin to diminish (40 + 110 = 150; not 40 + 150 = 190). This is confirmed by 8:4, which states that the ark rested on a mountain peak five months later (second month to seventh month). This period of time represents five months of thirty days.

Suddenly the story shifts; God remembers Noah (**8:1–22**). Not Noah's righteousness, or blamelessness, or his walk with God. Just Noah. There are seventy-three instances in the Old Testament where God is said to "remember." This remembrance moves God to send a wind over the earth. One Hebrew word translates "wind" and "Spirit." In 1:2 it is the Spirit who hovers over the waters. Twice the divine *rûaḥ* encounters the waters, first restraining them, now evaporating them. The sun plays no role in the drying up of the waters. In pagan myths this is exactly what happens. The ark finally comes to rest on the mountains of Ararat (in modern Armenia and eastern Turkey).

Noah must now determine whether the waters have receded sufficiently for dry land to reappear (**8:6–14**). To find out, Noah sends out first a raven, then a dove (twice). God does not tell Noah when the ground has dried out even though he did tell him about when the flood would start and exactly how to build the ark. Here Noah moves from being the passive recipient of revelation to being the active investigator of what and when the next move is.

The raven does not return because, as a carrion-eater, it is able to feed on the animal corpses on the mountain tops. The dove, by contrast, is a valley bird that feeds off food in the lower areas, the last to dry out. This is why it returns to the ark.

In verses 13 and 14 we have two Hebrew words for "dry," just as we had two words for "rain" in chapter 7. The first (v. 13) means to be free of moisture. The second (v. 14) refers to the complete absence of waters. Thus the choice of verb and the progression from verse 13 to verse 14 is logical.

Twice God speaks in **8:15–22,** once to Noah (vv. 15–17), and once to himself (vv. 21–22). Between these two speeches is the departure of Noah from the ark (vv. 18–19) and his act of worship (v. 20). Even though the dove does not return, Noah does not leave the ark until God tells him. God, and only God, can give the green light.

The divine soliloquy is composed of a negative statement (v. 21) and a positive one (v. 22). In spite of man's congenital proclivity to sin, the God of mercy will not exterminate him (v. 21). There will be predictability in the natural world (v. 22). And all this will be a gracious gift from God. No rites associated with fertility cults will bring about this condition. Only grace will.

G. Noah after the flood (9:1–29). Genesis **9:1–17** spells out in more explicit detail what God revealed to Noah in 8:20–22 about the post-flood stage. That God talks to Noah as he does in verse 1 ("Be fruitful and increase in number and fill the earth") indicates that Noah is a second Adam. These are the same imperatives addressed to Adam in chapter 1. But the world of Genesis 9 is not exactly the same as the world of Genesis 1. For one thing, man is now allowed to kill animals for food and add meat to his diet (vv. 2–3). Just as Genesis 2 stated a permission followed by a prohibition, Genesis 9 provides the same sequel: permission (vv. 2–3)-prohibition (v. 4). Interestingly, even animals are now held accountable for crimes (vv. 5–6).

God now proceeds to establish his covenant with Noah (vv. 8–11) and with the animals. The covenant is unilateral. That is, it is one that lays all obligations on God and no obligations on man. It is a covenant in which the Almighty binds himself to a certain course of action—never again to destroy the earth by a deluge.

To cement that covenant God establishes a sign both with Noah and with unborn generations. He will put his rainbow in the clouds. The Hebrew language does not distinguish between a rainbow and a bow (weapon). One word covers both. In what is a radical reinterpretation of divine power, the bow ceases to function as a sign of God's militancy, and begins to function as a sign of God's grace.

We are perhaps surprised to read that the bow is in the sky for God's benefit—"Whenever . . . the rainbow appears . . . I will remember." Perhaps there is a play here on the verbs *see* and *remember.* The flood story began with God "seeing" (6:5, 12) the unrestrained evil in the world. It ends with God "seeing" the rainbow. The flood story reaches a turning point when God "remembers" Noah (8:1). It reaches a climactic point when he "remembers" his covenant.

The story of Noah in **9:18–27** focuses on Noah's nakedness and not on his drunkenness. Why Noah is nude we do not know. Is he in a drunken stupor, or is he preparing to have intercourse with his wife? One of his sons—Ham—sees his father's nakedness. To be sure, this phrase (see Lev. 18) may mean to have sexual relations with a relative (incest). More than likely, here it simply means that Ham sees Noah's genitalia. Shem and Japheth, on the other hand, cover their father's nakedness. (Note again the emphasis here on "seeing" and "not seeing.")

As a result of Ham's involvement, Noah curses not Ham, but his grandson Canaan. This may illustrate the talionic principle of justice. The youngest son of Noah sins, and as a result, a curse is placed on Ham's youngest son. Other interpretations are possible.

Noah also blesses the Lord of Shem, and Canaan is to be slave to both Shem (v. 26) and Japheth (v. 27). God has talked about the future (vv. 8–17). Now Noah talks about the future (vv. 25–27).

H. The table of nations (10:1–32). The account of Noah's descendants begins with a list of Noah's sons in this order (v. 1): Shem, Ham, Japheth; but in the verses that follow that order is reversed: Japheth, Ham, Shem. The Japhethites (**10:1–5**) are peoples (seven are identified) most remote from Palestine, and most of the nations/places mentioned here are in the Mediterranean islands and Asia Minor. We recognize names like Magog and Meshech from the Book of Ezekiel. Javan represents early Greeks (Ionians) in the Aegean area. Madai represents the Medes. Kittim is to be associated with Cyprus, and Rodanim reflects the island of Rhodes, by the southwest coast of Turkey.

Ham has four sons, the most surprising of them being Canaan. The fourth generation is traced only through Cush. Most of the peoples in this section (**10:6–20**) are Gentiles with whom Israel had unpleasant relationships. For example, Cush represents Ethiopia, Mizraim Egypt, and Put modern Somaliland.

Most interesting here is Nimrod (vv. 8–12). So well known is he that he has established a reputation as a mighty hunter. This refers probably to his martial prowess. The four cities he founds—Babylon, Erech, Akkad, and Calneh (?)—are all to the east of Canaan, not to the south/southwest as is Egypt. Does this indicate that Egyptian power extended at one point as far east as the Euphrates?

Shem fathers four sons. This section (**10:21–32**) is last in this list because it is the most crucial of the three. In this section we discover the name *Eber,* the connection of which with "Hebrew" should be obvious. "The earth was divided in Peleg's time" (v. 25). This may mean that the Semitic groups were divided into two branches. Or, because Peleg is related to an Akkadian word meaning "canal," it may mean that Peleg was involved in the construction of irrigation canals. Or, it may contain a hint of the tower of Babel story in which people were divided from each other.

Geographically, Genesis 10 ranges as far east as Persia (Elam), as far south as Ethiopia (Cush), as far north as the Aegean Sea (Caphtorim), and as far west as Egypt and Libya. Theologically, the list affirms God's blessing on Noah's progeny. Israel, or Eberites, have no monopoly on attributing their existence to God. It is not incidental that Jesus sends out seventy (or seventy-two) disciples (Luke 10:1). Jesus is reflecting the Genesis 10 list of the seventy nations in the then-known world, sending his disciples into every part of that world.

I. The tower of Babel (11:1–9). The whole world with which verse 1 begins has just been described at length in chapter 10. Further, we read, this world has one language and a common speech. This is puzzling, for already in Genesis 10 we have read, three times, about the descendants of Noah who were divided on the basis of their respective languages (vv. 5, 20, 31). There are three possible ways of handling this. One is to maintain that the two chapters are in contradiction to each other. A second way is to suggest that chapter 10 refers to local languages and dialects, while chapter 11 refers to an international language, a lingua franca. A third approach is to suggest that chapter 10, although actually falling after 11:1–9, is placed ahead of chapter 11, lest chapter 10 be read as a manifestation of God's judgment on the Noahites.

Shinar is the land of Babylonia. The tower the people want to build is probably a ziggurat, a seven-staged tower. In addition they want to build a city, and thus join Cain (4:17) in such an enterprise. In itself this is not sinful. Nor is it sinful to wish to build a tower that reaches to the heavens. The sin comes in the purpose: "so that we may make a name for ourselves and not be scattered." "Name" means reputation. They want to erect an edifice that will memorialize them.

It is difficult to miss the irony or humor in verse 5. The people want to build a skyscraper, but the Lord still comes down to see the city and the tower. Once again there is an emphasis on somebody seeing something.

Note that God does not halt the project while it is in process of construction. Nor does he destroy it once it is completed. What God does is to judge the language, not the tower or the city. The people's tongues, and not their hands, feel the wrath of God. This gives rise to the name *Babel,* which means in Hebrew "to confound, confuse." The Babylonians themselves call their city *bab-ili* or *bab-ilani,* "gate of the god(s)," which is reflected in the Greek *Babylon.*

J. The Shemites (11:10–32). Here is another ten-generation genealogy stretching from Shem to Terah/Abraham. The list is much like that in 10:21, 24–25. Four of the names are repeated—Arphaxad, Shelah, Eber, and Peleg. Additionally, some of the names are to be identified with place names in northwest Mesopotamia (e.g., Serug/Sarugi; Nahor/Nakhur). This lends historical credibility to the genealogy.

Abraham, however, comes from Ur of the Chaldeans (v. 28), which is in southern Mesopotamia. There is a great deal of evidence to support a movement of Terahites from Ur north to Haran, which provides support for linking Abraham with lower Mesopotamia and the patriarchs with northern Mesopotamia.

II. Abraham (12:1–25:18)

A. The call of Abram (12:1–9). God's first word to Abram is an imperative: *leave!* The three things he is to leave behind are arranged in ascending order: country, people, father's household. The imperative is followed by a series of promises relating to progeny, reputation, and blessing. There is quite a contrast between 11:4 ("we may make a name for ourselves") and 12:2 ("I will make your name great"). The climax of the divine "I wills" is that all peoples on earth (Gen. 10) will be blessed through Abram. Abram is to be not only a recipient of the blessing, but also a channel through which this blessing may flow to others.

This all happens when Abram is seventy-five years old. God gets involved for the first time in the life of this septuagenarian.

Abram's response is prompt: "so Abram left." First the Lord speaks to Abram (v. 1). Then God appears to him (v. 7). Now that Abram has moved into Canaan (Shechem, Bethel), God makes a further promise to him: "to your offspring I will give this land." Abram does not yet have even one child, and here is God talking about offspring. First God speaks (vv. 1–3), then Abram journeys (vv. 4–6). Next God appears (v. 7a), then Abram worships (v. 7). The chapter begins with the promise to make of Abram a great "name" and concludes with Abram calling on the Lord's "name."

B. Abram in Egypt (12:10–20). A famine sends Abram to Egypt. He is certain that, once there, the Egyptians will abduct Sarai and murder him. Why he thinks that or how he knows this is not clear. Since God is certain about Abram's future (vv. 1–9), why cannot Abram himself be as certain?

Abram asks Sarai to identify herself to Pharaoh as his sister (which is partially the truth). The logic of Abram's move is clear enough. As brother to the woman involved he can be ignored; as husband to the woman he would have to be eliminated.

There are two flaws in Abram's ruse. It is one laced with deception (not the first time we have met this in Genesis; it is as old as chap. 3). Second, it is a plan in which Sarai has to make herself vulnerable. Indeed, Genesis 12:10–20 describes actual adultery, rather than potential adultery, for Sarai is taken into Pharaoh's palace.

As a result Pharaoh falls under God's wrath, albeit he has sinned in ignorance. This is an immediate fulfillment of 12:3, "whoever curses you I will curse." Perhaps Abram did this for a good purpose, so he thought. If he is slain what will happen to God's promises? They will be aborted. Abram must do anything to prevent this. One of the great foibles of this man of God is in believing that now and then the Almighty is in need of a helping hand.

C. Abram and Lot separate (13:1–18). The Negeb is the desert region south of Palestine. It is through this region that Abram, his wife, and Lot (he also goes to Egypt) travel on their way back to Canaan. Abram is a wealthy man (v. 2), but his wealth is not necessarily an evidence of divine blessing for obedience. Back in his own backyard, Abram's first priority is to renew his life of worship (v. 4).

There is a problem, however. Not a problem with outsiders, but inside the family. Abram and Lot each have so much that the land cannot support them both. This leads to quarreling among their respective employees (v. 7).

Abram moves quickly to settle the strife. He foments strife in 12:10–20. Here he settles it. As the elder person, Abram would have been fully within his rights to decide who gets what portion of land. As the younger, Lot would have to accept passively what was left over or assigned to him.

It is not always propitious to exercise one's prerogatives. Abram believes that. Voluntarily he gives priority of choice to his nephew. Note the change between the Abram of 12:1–20 and the Abram of 13:1–12. In the first instance he is obsessed with himself, his safety, his future. He must become deceitful. In the second instance, Abram assigns himself position number two. He empties himself of patriarchal authority.

All of this action takes place north of Jerusalem in the area of Benjamin. From here the lush Jordan Valley can be seen (v. 10). Lot chooses the plain of the Jordan which is comparable to Eden and Egypt. A person is known by his choices. Lot's choice puts him in contact with Sodomites, people whose lives are contrary to God's way (v. 13).

Only after the difference is settled does God get involved. He has been watching two of his children hammering out their differences, allowing each to live with the consequences of his choice. God speaks to Abram now that Lot has departed. For a second time God gives Abram a series of promises. The first is land (v. 15) and the second is innumerable offspring (v. 16). Abram is to lift up his eyes (v. 14) and lift up his feet (v. 17). Twice in this chapter Abram builds an altar. He settles in Mamre, which is approximately twenty miles south of Jerusalem. Hebron is two miles south of Mamre.

D. Abram rescues Lot (14:1–24). Four powerful kings from the east head an assault against five minor Palestinian kings (**14:1–13**). It is impossible to identify the four kings with certainty. Amraphel means "the mouth of god has spoken," and he is the king of Shinar (i.e., Babylonia). Arioch matches the name *Arriyuk* and is a good Hurrian name. Kedorlaomer means "servant of Lagamar" (an Elamite god). Tidal is the Hebrew equivalent of the Hittite regnal name *Tudhalia,* borne by several Hittite kings.

These four kings engage the five petty kings in battle near the Valley of Siddim, where the Salt Sea now is. Verse 4 suggests that the battle is instigated by an attempt of the minor kings to establish independence. To quell the revolt, these kings march, according to place names in verses 5–7, from Syria to the Gulf of Aqaba, then north again to Kadesh.

In the midst of these hostilities Lot is captured (v. 12). He is now suffering one of the consequences of his choice. Abram is informed of this, and it is here that we find the interesting phrase *Abram the Hebrew.* In the one chapter where Abram engages in military activity he is spoken of as a "Hebrew." Some have suggested a possible relationship between "Hebrew" and "Habiru," the latter being those who in times of war hired themselves out as mercenaries.

Abram does not have to rescue Lot singlehandedly (**14:14–16**). He has 318 trained men. This indicates that Abram is anything but a nomadic shepherd who passes time counting sheep and stars. He is a powerful individual with a substantial number of troops on call.

How does one man with an army of 318 men go against four major kings and their armies? Certainly not head-to-head. It is a nocturnal battle (v. 15). Perhaps this story about the retrieval of Lot and the success of Abram anticipates the degree of success God pictures for his people Israel, even though they too will be a minority.

On his way home, Abram meets the king of Sodom in the Valley of Shaveh (**14:17–24**). Melchizedek is identified as king of Salem. This is most certainly an abbreviation for Jerusalem. Melchizedek means "my king is righteous/ justice." Further, he is described as priest of God Most High (v. 18). It was common in pagan cultures for the king to be both head of state and head of church. Not so in Israel, except for one who properly bears the function of prophet, priest, and king.

He blesses Abram (v. 19) and God (v. 20), and Abram responds with a tithe from the war booty (v. 20b). It is to Melchizedek's credit that he knows the real reason why Abram was victorious. It is God, and not Abram's military sagacity, that wins the battle. It is no wonder that Hebrews 7 relates Melchizedek and Christ typologically. The story concludes with Abram conversing with the king of Sodom (vv. 22–24). He insists that the king take the war spoils. One king already enriched him (12:10–20). He does not want that to happen again.

E. God's covenant with Abram (15:1–21). "After this" (v. 1) must refer to the harrowing experiences Abram encountered in chapter 14. He has reason to be afraid of the possible repercussions of his rescue mission. God's word to him, then, is most appropriate (**15:1–6**): "Do not be afraid, Abram." God is Abram's shield, not his 318 servants. And God himself is Abram's reward.

Abram has a major concern. He is still childless, and apparently resigned to that fact. For he is prepared to designate his servant Eliezer as the heir to his estate (v. 2). This procedure reflects Nuzi law, in which a childless father might adopt a servant and name him as heir.

God's first word to Abram is about himself. His second word (vv. 4–6) is about Abram. First, there is the promise of a natural heir (v. 4), and then there is the promise of legions of descendants (v. 5). This is the third time Abram receives promises (12:1–7; 13:14–17), and it is sufficient evidence for Abram. He believes the Lord. He is willing now to stake his life on the reliability of the promises of his Lord. The Hebrew verb *to believe* is the source of "amen." Whenever one believes, he is saying "amen." God's response to Abram's amen is to credit it to him as righteousness. This is, of course, the great text on which Paul builds the truth about justification by faith (Rom. 4:1ff.; Gal. 3:7ff.).

God's covenant with Abram is confirmed by a ritual (**15:7–21**). Abram is to bring a heifer, a goat, a ram, a dove, and a young pigeon. The heifer and the ram he is to cut in two and arrange in parallel rows. The most frequent way in Hebrew to say "make a covenant" is "cut a covenant." The only other reference in the Old Testament to this kind of covenant ritual is Jeremiah 34:18.

In a deep sleep Abram observes a smoking firepot and a blazing torch pass between the portions of animal flesh. These fiery elements can only be symbols of God himself, for in the Bible fire represents the presence of God. The ritual here is dramatic. It is as if God is placing himself under a potential curse: "Abram, if I do not prove faithful to my word, let the same thing happen to me as has to this heifer and ram." Abram thus believes the Lord.

Abram will not himself possess this land (vv. 13–16). Only when the sin of the Amorites (i.e., Canaanites) has reached its final stage of decay, will it pass to Israel. Although this is generations away, God already knows exactly the boundaries of the Promised Land (vv. 18–21).

F. Hagar and Ishmael (16:1–15). How does one handle the problem of childlessness, especially in a society that places a premium on having children? To the contemporary reader Abram's and Sarai's method appears quite strange and highly suspect. Sarai offers her maidservant Hagar to Abram. He cohabits with her, and he fathers a child—Ishmael. This child then becomes Sarai's child. Such a procedure, however illicit it may sound to us, is well documented in ancient literary sources such as the Code of Hammurabi and in the texts from Nuzi.

Still, one wonders to what degree Abram's belief in the Lord (15:6) informs his action in 16:1ff. If there is a vivid contrast between the Abram of the first half of chapter 12 and the second half of chapter 12, then we observe an equally vivid contrast between the Abram of chapter 15 and that of chapter 16.

Hagar does not help the situation. She despises her mistress, for she can bear a child while Sarai cannot. Sarai is, understandably, incensed (v. 5). Abram is of little help. He refuses active involvement with his lame "do with her whatever you think best." As a result, Hagar is banished from the premises.

God finds her at a spring on the road to Shur (a word meaning "wall") which runs from Egypt to Beersheba. He engages her in conversation by asking her questions (v. 8) to which he knows the answers.

It is the angel of the Lord who meets Hagar in the wilderness. But in verses 13ff. the text says that it is God who speaks with her. The angel of the Lord and the Lord—distinct, yet the same. All sorts of explanations, usually along the lines of form-critical concerns (what was the original form of the story?), have been offered to explain this "incongruity." Might we see here, as we saw in the "us" of 1:26 and 11:7, a hint of God's trinitarian nature?

The child born of this union between Hebrew patriarch and Egyptian servant girl is Ishmael. The name means "El [God] has heard," but the explanation given for the name is that the Lord has heard. This shows there is no real difference between El(ohim) and Yahweh as names of deity.

Ishmael is to be a wild donkey of a man (v. 12). He will live the life of a Bedouin, a nomad, and at the same time he will be warlike.

Now it is Hagar's turn to name somebody. And she names God. She calls him "You are the God who sees me" (and, again, note the emphasis on seeing as in previous chapters), or as the Hebrew has it, *El Roi.* And she names the well where this all takes place *Beer Lahai Roi,* "well of the Living One who sees me." Hagar ran away from Sarai and ran into God. These names do not stress the gift she has received (a child), but the Giver of that gift. A distraught, frightened, pregnant, non-Israelite slave girl encounters God in a desert, and is never the same again.

G. The covenant of circumcision (17:1–27). Nothing of real significance happens in Abram's life between the ages of eighty-six (16:16) and ninety-nine (17:1). God now appears to him as *El Shaddai,* meaning either "God Almighty" or "God of the Mountain." God's self-identification is followed by a moral imperative: "walk before me and be blameless" (**17:1–14**). We observed in chapter 15 that all of the obligations of the covenant fell upon God. Chapter 17 lends a bit of balance to that. Abram does not have license to live as he pleases. His behavior is to reflect the character of the One who called him.

In the course of conversation, God tells Abram that his name will be changed from *Abram* ("father is exalted") to *Abraham.* The only difference between the two is the syllable *ha* in the new name. The explanation "father of many nations" is arrived at on the basis of "Abraham" being assonant with Hebrew *ab hămôn,* "father of a multitude." Every one of the major characters in Genesis 11–50 undergoes a name change, except Isaac. A new name indicates a new destiny.

The name change is followed by another series of promises about progeny (vv. 6–7) and land (v. 8), and here the point is made that Abraham is to keep the covenant. He is not to play fast and loose with the word of the Lord.

There are four great imperatives addressed to Abraham: walk . . . be blameless . . . keep . . . circumcise. Verses 9–14 focus on the last of these. This is not something presented to Abraham as an option. It is mandatory. It is to be administered to every male after his eighth day of birth. It extends even to servants (v. 12), and thus is not an elitist ritual. Circumcision functions as a sign of the covenant. Earlier the rainbow was a sign of God's covenant with Noah. The sign here must be for the benefit of the recipient. By an ineradicable mark cut into his flesh, the believer is constantly reminded that he is God's special child. The sign speaks of God's mercies and his expectations.

Sarai is to become Sarah, not a significant name change; thus her new name is not explained as is Abraham's. Something more important than her name is to change. The condition of her womb is to change (v. 16). She is to give birth not only to children, but to kings (**17:15–27**).

Abraham laughs (v. 17). Here we have the first of three instances linking laughter with the name *Isaac* (see also 18:12; 21:6). It is unclear whether it is the laughter of joy or of unbelief. Verse 18 (Abraham's concern for Ishmael) and verse 17 (Abraham's realism) favor the latter interpretation. Both he and his wife are beyond child-producing and child-bearing years. Often God seems to insist on the impossible to increase dependence on him.

True, God will bless Ishmael (v. 20), but his covenant is with Isaac (v. 21). Ishmael is not lost, damned, or condemned, but he is clearly placed outside the covenant family.

Abraham's implementation of the divine directive (vv. 11–14) is not carried out until verses 23–27. Sandwiched between is the promised birth of Isaac. One wonders if Abraham ever questioned circumcising Ishmael since he was not to be a link in the covenant chain.

H. The Lord of birth and death (18:1–33). This chapter highlights the forthcoming birth of Isaac and the forthcoming death of Sodom. In this contrast between the beginning of life and the end of life, Abraham has opportunity first to be host, then to be intercessor. As host he entertains three men by his home at Mamre (**18:1–15**). One of these is obviously the Lord (v. 1). The other two must be angelic companions, both of whom essentially drop out of the story after verse 9. The number three should not be pressed for any trinitarian significance.

Abraham serves the three visitors a meal, and watches while they eat (v. 8b). The supernatural character of these visitors is evidenced by the fact that they know Abraham is married, and they also know his wife's name. This probably shocks Abraham. He does not recognize his visitors, but his visitors know all about him. There stands with Abraham One whom he does not know.

Sarah overhears the announcement about her forthcoming pregnancy. It is an incredible promise. Under her breath Sarah laughs—another play on the name *Isaac*—for she and Abraham are too old. Sarah, however, needs to see beyond her lord (Abraham) and see her Lord. Not only is she unbelieving, but she denies that she is (v. 15).

Even God has intimates to whom he bares his soul, and Abraham is one of these. God knows Abraham, and therefore is not hesitant to inform Abraham about his intentions for Sodom (**18:16–33**).

What God hears is the outcry against Sodom and Gomorrah. This word is used in the Old Testament normally to describe the cry of the oppressed who are brutalized by their taskmasters. Ezekiel 16:49–50 makes it clear that Sodom's sin was social as well as sexual immorality.

God himself conducts a personal inspection of the city (v. 21)—or at least he intends to. Abraham now stands before the Lord. (Some commentators feel that the original text may have been "The Lord stood before Abraham.")

Abraham is convinced that the Judge of all the earth will do right. He has no doubts about the integrity and consistency of God. Therefore, he speaks plainly with God. This is no place for cliches and shibboleths. He asks if God would refrain from judging Sodom if there were fifty righteous people in the city. Eventually he jumps not by fives but by tens, and finally asks if God would spare Sodom for the sake of ten righteous people. Abraham believes that the presence of a few who are godly has a saving influence on the many who are ungodly. It is interesting to reflect what this story has to say about petitionary prayer, prayer as dialogue, and an omniscient, sovereign God who is moved to action or inaction by the intercessions of the faithful.

I. The destruction of Sodom and Gomorrah (19:1–38). Like his uncle Abraham, Lot has opportunity to play host to two angels (**19:1–11**). Even before they can retire for the night, Lot's house is surrounded by the townspeople who demand that Lot hand over his guests so that the townspeople, as the New International Version puts it bluntly, might "have sex with them." This clearly points to the fact that part of the sin of the Sodomites is sexual depravity.

Lot offers to turn over his two daughters as surrogates for the two angels. Perhaps he considers this the lesser of two evils. As host he must allow no harm to come upon his guests while they are under his roof. That was an ancient Near Eastern law of hospitality. This does not mean that Lot was justified in his action. Here the daughters are used, but in verses 30–38 the tables are turned and they are the ones in charge.

Lot and his family are warned about God's judgment on Sodom and are given a chance to escape (**19:12–29**). Nothing has been said about Lot's righteousness as was the case with Noah. But in many ways the Noah story and the Lot story are parallel. A chosen family is spared the judgment of God.

Lot's sons-in-law ignore his warning, thinking he is joking. Lot is not taken seriously by his family. Even Lot himself hesitates (v. 16) when given the ultimatum. Lot is exempted from death because the Lord is merciful.

Lot turns down the suggestion that he flee to the mountains and asks instead for refuge in the village of Zoar. Zoar means "small," and is connected with Lot's reference in verse 20 to the place as a very small one. Lot will be saved.

Only verses 24 and 25 describe the actual catastrophe. The disaster is a combination of volcanic activity and earthquake. Lot's wife still longs for Sodom; she looks back, and that is the end of her. Verse 29 provides a second reason why God spares Lot: He remembers Abraham. This is the second time Lot owes his life to his uncle. He has been delivered from capture and now from death.

Lot ends up in the mountains, even after earlier stating that he would not go there. Lot gets drunk after the disaster, as did Noah. And while drunk, he is taken advantage of by a family member, as was Noah. His two daughters get him drunk, and then sleep with him (**19:30–38**). As a result, two sons are born: Moab ("by the father") and Ben-Ammi ("son of my parent"), from whom come the Moabites and Ammonites. The story says more about Lot than anything. He is shortsighted, insensitive, and unattractive. His relationship with God does not measure up to that of his uncle.

J. Abraham and Abimelech (20:1–18). For a second time Abraham finds himself an alien in a foreign land, with Sarah by his side (see chap. 12). And for a second time he resorts to deceit. He asks Sarah to identify herself as his sister. This time he is in Gerar, a city of the Philistines, and the king is Abimelech. On this occasion Abraham does not draw attention to Sarah's striking beauty as he did in 12:11. But this is almost twenty-five years later.

Unlike chapter 12 which presents a case of actual adultery, this chapter deals with potential adultery. Sarah is taken, but before Abimelech can cohabit with her God speaks to him in a dream. This part of the story is also unlike that of chapter 12. There the Pharaoh discovered Sarah's true identity only when plagues were unleashed on his kingdom. Here knowledge is communicated not through an act of God, but through a word of God.

Interestingly, God identifies Abimelech's near-adultery as a "sin against me" (v. 6). It is not a sin against people as much as it is a sin against God. For he is the one who created the marriage relationship, and his guideline was one man for one woman, one woman for one man.

Not only is Abraham a liar, he is a prophet (v. 7). One of the functions of a prophet is to represent someone before God. The prophet is an intercessor par excellence. Abraham is to pray for Abimelech.

Unlike in chapter 12, Abraham offers a lame excuse which he believes justifies his ruse: "there is surely no fear of God in this place" (v. 11). There is no Hebrew word for "religion." The expression *fear of God* is as close as it comes. Here specifically, "fear of God" means consideration for the rights and safety of outsiders.

Abimelech is more gracious than the Pharaoh. The latter expelled Abraham as a persona non grata. Abimelech, on the other hand, opens his territory to Abraham (v. 15); additionally, he earmarks an appreciable sum of money for Sarah to cover any ignominy she has had to endure (v. 16).

The irony in all this is that Abraham can pray for the salvation of the depraved Sodomites, and God responds. Abraham can pray for barren Philistine women, and God responds. Yet Sarah is still barren.

K. Friction inside and outside the family (21:1–34). One of the characteristics of Abraham's faith is his ability to wait and to be patient—at least most of the time. Twenty-five years earlier God had promised Abraham a son (chap. 12). Now that promise becomes reality (**21:1–7**) after some false hopes and false moves. Appropriately, and following an earlier directive, Abraham names the child Isaac, meaning "he laughs." Who laughs? God? Isaac? Abraham? Then Abraham circumcises Isaac (v. 4).

For a third time somebody laughs, and here it is Sarah (vv. 6–7). This is a joyful laughter, and her joy will be contagious.

How quickly festivities can turn into friction (**21:8–21**). Sarah sees Ishmael mocking Isaac after Isaac has been weaned (about three years). Actually the Hebrew word for "mocking" is "to laugh." Ishmael was "Isaac-ing" Isaac. Paul's choice of "persecuted" in Galatians 4:29 indicates that Isaac and Ishmael were not engaged in harmless play.

Sarah is enraged. Laughter turns to shouting: "get rid of that slave woman and her son." She is too angry to call either of them by name. Abraham is more impressive here than he was in the earlier situation involving Hagar and Sarah. He protests (v. 11) and makes sure that Hagar and Ishmael leave with ample provisions (v. 14).

This story has often been read as standing in bold contrast to that in chapter 16. For instance, it is maintained that the Ishmael of chapter 16 is a lad of sixteen years or so, while the Ishmael of chapter 21 is but an infant whom Hagar carries on her shoulders and "throws" under the tree to watch him die. A closer reading of chapter 21, however, shows that Ishmael is anything but an infant. Chapter 21 is not a second account of the same incident in chapter 16, but a sequel to it.

Sarah does not feel much compassion for this banished mother and son. But God does. Note again, as in an earlier chapter, the intermingling in verse 17 of God and angel of God. God opens his heart and he opens Hagar's eyes to a well of water.

The problem in **21:23–34** is not over two boys, but over a well belonging to Abraham that has been seized by Abimelech. To begin with, Abimelech requests honest, open dealings with Abraham, to which Abraham commits himself.

To attest that the well is indeed his, Abraham makes a treaty with Abimelech and presents animals to him, including seven live lambs. They are a witness to Abraham's honesty. As a result, the place is called Beersheba, which can be translated either as "well of seven" or "well of oath." In Hebrew "to swear an oath" is "to seven." It is to Abraham's credit that he is able to prevent what could have been a major altercation. Apparently he is better at keeping peace internationally than he is at home.

L. Abraham's test (22:1–24). Some time later God tests Abraham. It is not clear how much later, but Isaac is old enough to carry wood for a fire and carry on an intelligent conversation with his father. For the first time the verb (but not the idea) *test* occurs in the Bible. As early as chapter 12 God tested Abraham when he told him to leave Ur with his family, and Abraham went out "not knowing where he was going." As a matter of fact, Abraham's life begins and ends, as far as divine speech goes, with two imperatives: *Leave! Take!* And just as he is told to leave three things in chapter 12, here in chapter 22 he is told to take (1) his son, (2) his only son Isaac, (3) whom he loves. Each expression becomes more intense.

Abraham and Isaac leave Beersheba and travel three days to Mount Moriah. There is only one other reference to this site in the Old Testament, 2 Chronicles 3:1, and this passage tells us that Moriah is Jerusalem. Not one word is said about that emotion-filled three-day journey. What were Abraham's thoughts? Did he pray: "If it be possible, let this cup pass from me"?

Abraham does not expect this to be the last he would see his son ("we will come back to you," v. 5b). Yet this story is as much an illustration of Isaac's faith as it is of Abraham's. He willingly submits to his father (v. 9), when in point of fact he could have tied up his father, had he so decided.

Only when the knife is raised (v. 10) is Abraham stopped by the Lord's angel. This test has proved that Abraham "fears God." That was the expression used by Abraham back in 20:11. To fear God in chapter 22 means to believe his word fully and absolutely, and to be loyal to his directives.

In a nearby bush is a ram caught by its horns. Actually the Hebrew says "another ram." Ancient and modern versions have missed the point when they render "a ram" or "a ram behind him." Isaac was the first ram. Here is the second one.

Abraham calls the name of this place "The LORD will provide." The name he chooses does not draw attention to himself but to his Lord. He does not name the place "Abraham believed." He focuses on God's mercy and faithfulness, not on his own obedience.

This place-naming is followed by one of the few instances where God's promises flow out of Abraham's performance: "because you have done this . . . I will." These verses actually bring the story to its climax. The story would be without a proper conclusion had it stopped at verse 14. It is not difficult to see why the New Testament interprets the binding of Isaac as a forerunner of the binding of One greater than Isaac.

Verses 20–24 report the birth of children to Nahor, Abraham's brother. In the midst of this story is the name *Rebekah,* thus preparing us for the next generation of patriarchs. Most of the names in this genealogy are the ancestors of cities and tribes around Israel. They are precisely the peoples who are to be blessed through Abraham's offspring (v. 18).

M. The death of Sarah (23:1–20). Sarah dies at the age of 127, thirty-seven years after the birth of Isaac. The last city she lives in is Kiriath-arba, "city of the four," which is another name for Hebron. Abraham is not a man without emotion. He mourns and weeps for her.

For at least a third time in Genesis Abraham is an alien and a stranger. His hosts this time are the Hittites. "Hittites" may be a name for non-Semitic peoples living in Canaan, or it may be a synonym for "Canaanites." Most likely, it refers to the Hittites of Asia Minor, part of whom made their way into southern Canaan where they established an enclave. In favor of this interpretation are the many authentic Hittite elements in the story.

For example, Abraham wants to buy only the cave of Machpelah on the property of Ephron the Hittite (v. 9). Instead, Ephron insists that Abraham purchase the entire field, cave and all (v. 11). According to the Hittite law code one who bought a field from another had to assume feudal obligations for the field. By requesting only a part, Abraham is trying to avoid these obligations.

Abraham pays four hundred shekels of silver for the field. This seems a high price, given the fact that many generations later Jeremiah will pay seventeen shekels of silver for a field at Anathoth (Jer. 32:9). On more than one occasion, God had promised Abraham that he would "give" him this land. Here, however, Abraham buys land, and only a parcel of it at that. The transaction is carried out the usual way, at the gate of the city. Nowhere in this event is God involved. He never addresses Abraham after chapter 22.

N. Isaac and Rebekah (24:1–67). Abraham loses one family member (a wife), then gains another (a daughter-in-law). He is now old (somewhere between 137 and 175). Isaac is near forty (25:20) and still single. To remedy this situation Abraham sends a servant (Eliezer of chap. 15) to Aram-Naharaim ("Syria of the two rivers") to obtain a bride for Isaac.

Abraham makes two specific requests. The girl must not be a Canaanite. Isaac must not be unequally yoked. Second, Isaac and his bride must return to Canaan. Isaac is not to make Aram-Naharaim a home away from home, for God had said to Abraham "to you and to your descendants I will give this land." All this is sealed by an oath (v. 9).

The servant proposes a test to determine who Isaac's bride will be by suggesting to God that the girl who offers to water his camels be the one for Isaac (v. 14).

Rebekah is now introduced. She is a hard worker (v. 15), beautiful (v. 16a), chaste (v. 16b), courteous (v. 18), and thoughtful (v. 19). The gifts the servant gives Rebekah are not bridal gifts. These will come later (v. 53). They are, instead, an expression of appreciation for her kindness.

The girl is more than ready to give the servant a night's lodging in her family home.

All of this produces an outburst of praise to God by the servant.

That Rebekah tells her mother's household (v. 28) about the stranger must mean that her father Bethuel is dead. (The word *Bethuel* in v. 50 has no strong textual support, and probably should not be read there.)

It is noteworthy that Laban should greet the servant as "blessed by the Lord" (v. 31). Where would he have picked up either the name or the theology? If the God of Israel could reveal himself to Abimelech in a dream, could he not also have made himself known in some way to Laban?

Once settled in, the servant relates to Laban the purpose of his mission (vv. 34–41). It is most interesting that the servant relates the part about not staying in Aram-Naharaim, even if he has to return empty-handed, and that while he is in Laban's family room in Aram-Naharaim. Then he relates to Laban his first encounter with Rebekah (vv. 42–49).

Laban responds quickly and positively. In verse 57 Rebekah is consulted for her thoughts on the matter. She is not asked, however, if she wants to marry Isaac. That has already been settled by Laban. She is asked whether or not she desires to accompany the servant to his master's land. Assyrian law protected a woman's right to stay in her own homeland.

In verses 62–67 Isaac and Rebekah meet for the first time. He is out in the field meditating (v. 63)—the Hebrew word is uncertain. As Isaac draws nearer, she veils herself (v. 65). They are married, and only now does Isaac's grief at the death of his mother subside.

O. Abraham and Ishmael (25:1–18). Abraham remarries after Sarah's death, and his second wife's name is Keturah. Even though he himself felt he was past the age of fathering children before Isaac, he now produces six more children (v. 2). The places represented by these names are all Arabian. The best-known of them (from the books of Numbers and Judges) is Midian. These six children of Abraham do not supplant Isaac as the son of promise (v. 5).

Abraham lives until he is 175 years old (**25:7–11**). This means, according to 12:4, that he lived exactly one hundred years in the land of promise. Of interest is the fact that Ishmael and Isaac are both involved in the burial of their father. Ishmael, though exiled, returns for his father's funeral. Two other brothers (Esau and Jacob), long separated from each other, also meet for their father's funeral (35:29). That the text says Abraham is "gathered to his people" (v. 8b) indicates that death was never conceived of as extinction.

Ishmael fathers twelve children (**25:12–18**), more than his father did. Ishmaelites are located in the northwestern part of the Arabian peninsula. The text does not say, as it did of Abraham, that Ishmael lived a life "full of years."

III. Jacob (25:19–36:43)

A. Esau and Jacob (25:19–34). Like Sarah, Rebekah is unable to bear children. Isaac's prayers reverse this situation, however (v. 21). Rebekah conceives and gives birth to twins, Esau and Jacob.

It is Rebekah who is given the startling prophecy that of the two children she is carrying, the older (Esau) will serve the younger (Jacob). This is a departure from the normal procedure where priority went to the firstborn. That the prophecy is made before the birth of the children stresses that Jacob's elevation is due to God's grace and decree, and is not based on any merit in Jacob.

As they grow older, Esau becomes an excellent hunter, while Jacob remains a quiet man. Esau's strength is his weakness. Famished from a hunt, he is willing to abandon his birthright in return for some red stew. His stomach overrules his conscience. Jacob wants more than a gentleman's agreement. He insists on an oath from Esau, just in case Esau has second thoughts. Although Esau will later swear at Jacob, he is content here to swear to Jacob. No commentary is made about Jacob's exploitation of his brother, or of his modus operandi in getting the birthright. God had not said "the younger shall exploit the older."

B. Isaac and Abimelech (26:1–35). This is the one chapter in Genesis devoted exclusively to Isaac. And it does not show him at his best. He imitates his father in the wife-as-sister deception. The one difference is how Abimelech is informed about the woman's identity. Abimelech sees Isaac caressing Rebekah. This can only be sexual fondling, and Abimelech is able to draw the right conclusion. Abimelech shares some of the moral values of the patriarchs. He too believes adultery is wrong, and that it brings guilt upon people.

Isaac fares well (vv. 12–14), but there is a problem. The Philistines have filled in the wells Isaac's father had dug; Isaac proceeds to open them up again. He then digs his own wells, only to have the Gerarites claim ownership of them. The quarreling here is reminiscent of that between Abraham's servants and Lot's. Isaac gives the wells names that reflect this dispute: Esek ("contention"), Sitnah ("enmity"); but then he does better with Rehoboth ("wide places") and Shibah ("seven").

All of this concludes with a covenant between Isaac and Abimelech, solemnized by a covenant meal. The Philistines recognize a spiritual dimension in Isaac's life (vv. 28, 29b). Perhaps this is because of the mature way in which he handles the dispute. He does not lower himself to the level of the disputants. But Isaac, now at peace with neighbors, still has domestic problems. Esau marries outside the faith.

C. Jacob's deceit (27:1–46). Isaac, now advanced in age and gradually losing his eyesight, requests Esau to go out into the fields and hunt some wild game (**27:1–4**). It is paradoxical that Esau lost his birthright after he returned from a hunt, and he is about to lose the blessing after he leaves for a hunt.

It is Rebekah's suggestion that Jacob pretend to be Esau, and thus obtain the blessing through deceit (**27:5–17**). This includes presenting Isaac with some choice delicacies that she will prepare, plus covering Jacob with Esau's clothes and the exposed parts of his body with goatskins. At no point does Jacob question the propriety of this course of action. He does know that if his disguise fails, it will bring a curse on him (v. 12). Rebekah, however, accepts full responsibility if anything goes wrong.

This is no innocuous prank. It is deadly serious. Either way it will bring Jacob problems. If the plan is thwarted he will be cursed by his brother. Deception is bad enough. To deceive one's own father is even worse. To deceive a father who is senile and physically handicapped is reprehensible. Of course, Isaac was not above using deceit himself if circumstances warranted (chap. 26). Here Isaac has become Abimelech, and Jacob has become Isaac (**27:18–29**). Like father, like son! What makes Jacob's deception utterly dastardly is his reference to God's help in the allegedly quick capturing of the game (v. 20), when in fact his mother prepared it.

The truth comes out—plainly and painfully (**27:30–40**). It is Jacob, not Esau, whom Isaac has blessed. But a word once spoken cannot be recalled. This is the reason, by the way, for the many injunctions in the Old Testament against speaking too much, making rash vows, injudicious talk, and so forth. There is an irrevocable quality attached to words. One cannot "unsay" them.

For a second time, there is a play on Jacob's name, this time by Esau (v. 36). He is correctly called Jacob, says Esau, for twice now Jacob has supplanted him. The Hebrew word for "Jacob," "heel," and "supplant" are alike. Esau is blessed by Isaac (vv. 39–40), but it is hardly a positive word from the father.

D. Jacob flees to Haran (27:41–29:14). Rebekah now has a second problem on her hands. The first was to get the blessing away from Esau. The second is to get Jacob away from Esau. She accomplishes this by urging Jacob to go to Mesopotamia until Esau calms down (**27:41–46**). She also reminds her husband about Esau's two Hittite wives (v. 46). In effect, she says to Isaac: "You do not want another Hittite daughter-in-law, do you?"

For a second time, and with full awareness of whom he is blessing, Isaac gives Jacob a warning, some advice about marriage, and a blessing (**28:1–9**). Isaac nowhere rebukes his son for his earlier antics, any more than God rebuked Abraham or Isaac for similar ruses. Silence, however, should not be taken to mean approval. The purpose of the Genesis stories in chapters 11–50 is to illustrate the election of one family through whom nations will be blessed, the promises made to that family, and God's commitment to those promises. Esau, still holding on, tries to buy a little favor with his parents by marrying a non-Canaanite girl (vv. 6–9). Jacob imitated him. Now he will imitate Jacob.

Somewhere between Beersheba and Haran, at a site referred to nebulously as "a certain place" (v. 11), Jacob makes preparations to go to sleep. Here we have the third instance of God communicating via a dream (**28:10–22;** cf. Gen. 15:12; 20:3). Presumably all three of these revelations took place at night.

In his dream, Jacob sees a stairway stretching from heaven to earth, with angels ascending and descending on it. The King James Version has "ladder" and not "stairway" (NIV). The latter suggestion has gained wide acceptance for two reasons. First, it allows comparison with the Babylonian ziggurat and its stairways; and, second, two-way traffic on a ladder is inconceivable. However, this latter point is a moot one, and for that matter, why do angels even need anything on which to ascend and descend? The traditional "ladder" may be retained.

This is the first time God speaks to Jacob. And he does not rebuke Jacob for any previous indiscretions. On the contrary, he gives Jacob promises that include descendants, land, spiritual influence, and God's own presence (vv. 13–15).

Jacob's response to this is strange: he is afraid. Whenever God showed himself to Abraham, Abraham never trembled. Maybe the best parallel here is Adam who was afraid in the garden when the Lord's presence became apparent. In Jacob's case, is this fear born of awe of God's presence, of his own spiritual insensitivity, or of a guilty conscience?

Jacob calls this place "Bethel," which means "God's house/abode." No longer is it just a place, a site, but it is now *El*'s dwelling-place. Only later in the narrative are we informed that previously the shrine was called Luz (v. 19). To memorialize this encounter with God, Jacob takes the stone he had laid his head on and erects it as a pillar (a phenomenon that becomes illicit in later times, but is permissible in patriarchal times).

Jacob's vow is of interest in that it picks up on the promise of verse 15, but excludes verse 14. It is God's presence and a safe return to the land from which he has fled that concerns Jacob. The climax of the vow is that Jacob will commit himself to tithing (v. 22). This moves the Bethel encounter out of the realm of emotion exlusively, and into the realm of self-denial and stewardship.

"Eastern peoples" (29:1) is used as a general designation for anybody living east of Canaan. Jacob meets a number of shepherds milling around the well, which is covered by a large stone. Happily these shepherds know who Laban is and the state of his health. And even better, Laban's daughter Rachel comes to the well while Jacob is there. All of this is not fortuitous, but an indication of God's guidance (**29:1–14**).

Jacob urges the shepherds to water their flocks and return them to pasture. When they protest that this would be a breach of formalities, Jacob himself rolls away the stone. All this may be deliberately designed by Jacob to buy some time alone with Rachel. Jacob's kissing of Rachel should be seen as the custom of the day, and not as an act of indiscretion, or a good way to end a courtship before it begins.

E. Jacob, Leah, and Rachel (29:15–30:24). Laban has two daughters, Leah ("cow") and Rachel ("ewe lamb") (**29:15–30**). Rachel is the younger and the one Jacob finds more attractive. His suggestion that he work seven years in return for her hand in marriage is a magnanimous offer. Jacob goes to this extreme in hopes of guaranteeing his marriage with Rachel. Laban agrees to the proposal (v. 19).

On the night of the wedding feast, Laban manages to substitute Leah for Rachel. It is unlikely that a heavily veiled Leah could dupe Jacob. Probably Laban was able to succeed only because Jacob was drunk. We are not told about Leah. Was she drunk too? Did she have any say in the matter? Did she believe she was entitled to marry Jacob? Or does she passively submit to her father's orders? There can be no doubt that this scenario contrasts with the event of chapter 27. The perpetrator of deceit is now the victim of deceit. Jacob surely wondered why Laban did not offer the explanation found in verse 26 earlier. But no trickster can let the cat out of the bag prematurely.

Leah gives birth to four sons—Reuben, Simeon, Levi, and Judah (**29:31–35**). Jacob never names the children. Leah does, and the significance of each name is explained by a Hebrew phrase that contains a word or words that sound like the proper name.

Most intriguing here are the births of Levi and Judah. From these sons come two of the most crucial institutions of the Old Testament—priesthood and kingship. Both institutions have their origin in an unwanted marriage laced with deception and bitterness. Paul is correct; God does work in all things for good.

The competition between Leah and Rachel means more children for Jacob (**30:1–24**). Reflecting an allowable custom of her day, Rachel gives her maidservant Bilhah to Jacob as a surrogate wife, much as Sarah gave Hagar to Abraham. Bilhah gives birth to Dan and to Naphtali. As with the names in 29:31–35, the meaning of each name is explained by a Hebrew phrase reflecting the circumstances of the child's birth. In verse 7 "a great struggle" may be translated "wrestlings of God." In chapter 30 it is Rachel who wrestles with God. In chapter 32 it is Jacob who wrestles with God.

Zilpah, Leah's maid, also bears two children, Gad and Asher (vv. 9–12). This is more than Rachel can take. She believes, mistakenly, that if she can just get some mandrakes, now in Reuben's possession, she will be able to conceive. Mandrakes are herbs that give off a distinct odor and produce a fruit that is like a small orange. They were thought to aid in conception, an idea helped along no doubt by the fact that the Hebrew words for mandrake and love are from the same root word. Verses 22–24, however, make it clear that it is not mandrakes that bring fertility to Rachel. She gives birth to Joseph not because of magic, but because God remembers her and opens her womb.

F. Jacob and Laban (30:25–31:55). Earlier Rachel had said to Jacob, "give me children." Now Jacob says to Laban, "give me my wives and children." It is time for him to head back to Canaan. To that end, he asks that Laban give him the speckled and spotted sheep and goats as his wages (**30:25–43**).

Laban believes that Jacob is giving himself the short end of the deal (very few irregular animals will be bred from this), and so he quickly agrees to Jacob's proposal.

Jacob, however, knows more about cross-breeding and the laws of heredity than Laban knows—and more than Laban gives him credit for knowing. Through the use of a visual stimulus (branches of certain trees which Jacob marks with white stripes) the monochromes give birth to multicolored young. In the process, not only does Jacob get more flocks than Laban bargained for, but he gets healthier flocks as well. Now it is Laban's turn to be outwitted.

Jacob's rods may be compared with Rachel's mandrakes. It is God, not the mandrakes, who bestows fertility on Rachel. Similarly, it is a dream revelation from God (31:10–12), not the rods per se, that make it possible for Jacob to obtain a decent wage from his uncle. In both instances, success is due to the providence of God, rather than to magic.

All factors indicate that it is high time for Jacob to bid adieu to Laban (**31:1–21**). The attitude of Laban and his sons (vv. 1–2) and a direct revelation from God (v. 3) confirm this. Jacob is careful, however, to share this with his wives, not with his father-in-law. They concur immediately with Jacob, for Laban now considers them, in their judgment, only as foreigners. Jacob is careful to make his move while Laban is out shearing his sheep. Rachel takes only what she can carry—the clothes on her back and her father's household gods. It is unlikely she takes these gods as decorations for her new living quarters, or even for divine protection on their trip to Canaan. Some have suggested that she takes the gods in an attempt to establish Jacob as the legitimate heir of Laban's possessions. But there are problems with this explanation as well.

That Laban catches up with Jacob in seven days means either that Laban moved incredibly fast, or else his home was not as far from Canaan as Mesopotamia (**31:22–42**). He is enraged, and an enraged man is an irrational man. God comes to him in a dream at night (as with Abimelech in chap. 20), warning Laban to do no physical harm to Jacob. If Jacob is to get any hard knocks it will be from God, not Laban.

Laban seems to be most upset by the fact that he believes Jacob has stolen his gods. This is ironic. Can gods be stolen? Can deity be kidnaped? In nonbiblical thought, yes. If you make your gods or buy your gods, then they become vulnerable.

Rachel is as deceptive as her father and her husband. She is the one who has stolen the gods, without telling Jacob. Jacob did not tell Laban he was leaving, and Rachel did not tell Jacob she had taken Laban's gods. She pretends that she is having her menstrual period, and is thus unable to move as Laban conducts his search. Not only are the gods stolen, but now they suffer a further indignity—they are stained by Rachel's blood. Jacob has his chance to rebuke Laban. Note his interesting reference to the Lord as the "Fear of Isaac" (v. 42), a name for God that appears in the Old Testament only here and in verse 53.

Rather than part in bitterness, Jacob and Laban choose to part amiably, and this is to their credit. Accordingly they make a covenant. To memorialize this moment they raise a pillar of stones, which Laban names "Jegar Sahadutha" (Aram. the heap of witness), and which Jacob names "Galeed" (Heb. the heap of witness). Also, the site is called "Mizpah," meaning "watchpost." Both pledge not to intrude on the peace of the other, or to become belligerent toward the other. Laban seals this covenant interestingly, with a reference not to his own gods, but to the God of Abraham. Is this religious courtesy and ecumenism, or is Laban moving toward belief in the one true God?

G. Jacob and Esau (32:1–33:20). It has been at least twenty years since Jacob last saw Esau. Time heals all wounds, so the saying goes. Sometimes time intensifies wounds. Jacob is far from believing that with Esau all is forgotten and forgiven. To that end, he makes preparations to meet Esau, with fear and trepidation (**32:1–21**). The skeletons in Jacob's closet are now coming out. Jacob moves from crisis to crisis, from hot water to hot water. Laban confronted him in chapter 31, and now he is about to meet Esau.

Jacob is as diplomatic as possible. He identifies himself, through his messengers, as "your servant" (v. 4, not "your brother"). And he refers to Esau as "my lord" (v. 5).

Terrified to learn that Esau has four hundred men with him, Jacob divides his entourage into two, breathes a quick prayer, and prepares a lavish gift for Esau. Jacob reveals his purpose for these presents: "I will pacify him" (v. 20). Appeasement, then, is a must for Jacob. The Hebrew for "pacify" reads literally "cover his face." Note Jacob's position: his gifts go on ahead of him.

Jacob, in chapter 28, was interested only in getting away from Esau. But God met him unexpectedly. Here Jacob is thinking only of how to prepare for Esau. Again, unexpectedly, God meets him (**32:21–32**).

The action begins at night when a man(?) wrestles with Jacob. Incidentally, the verb for "wrestle" and the place where this match occurs, Jabbok, are from the same root, one of the many word plays in this story. This wrestling continues until daybreak. Jacob displays a few admirable characteristics. One of these is a confession of unworthiness: "What is your name?" "Jacob," he answers. "Jacob" is not only *who* he is, but *what* he is. Here is an explicit case where a name is descriptive of one's nature. Who am I? Trickster. Supplanter. Heel-grabber.

A second commendable virtue is Jacob's consuming hunger for God. "I will not let you go unless you bless me." One result of this meeting with God is that Jacob's name is changed to Israel, which in the explanation given is connected with a Hebrew verb meaning "to contend with, strive." As with Abraham in chapter 17, a new name indicates a new destiny. The first evidence of real spirtitual transformation in Jacob's life is that he receives a new name.

God first gives a name, and then Jacob gives a name. He calls the site "Peniel" (Penuel is a variant), meaning "the face of God." Jacob is doubly surprised. He has a new name, and he has seen God and lived to tell about it. But his hip is not healed. Jacob leaves, no, limps away from Peniel. That limp will be a constant reminder to him of this experience with God. Finally, Jacob's run-in with God carries influence well beyond his own lifetime (v. 32, though this particular dietary prohibition is not spoken of in later legislation).

Jacob is about to see Esau again (**33:1–20**). He lines up his family in order of least loved to most loved (v. 2). There is one difference. Before Jacob met God at Peniel he would stay "behind" (32:16, 18, 20). Now he goes "before" his entourage (v. 3). Not only did Jacob receive a new name at Peniel, but he received new courage as well.

The narrator refers to Esau as Jacob's "brother" (v. 3b) as does Esau of Jacob (v. 9). Jacob, however, still addresses Esau as "my lord" (vv. 8, 14, 15), and alludes to himself as "your servant" (v. 5).

Jacob insists that Esau accept the gifts he has brought, and Esau takes them only reluctantly. He who earlier took twice from Esau now demands that Esau take something from him.

When Esau suggests that Jacob follow him back home to Seir, Jacob offers an excuse why he cannot and promises to come to Seir later, a promise that Jacob likely has no intention of keeping. Apparently there is still a bit of Jacob in him. Jacob goes to Shechem, and there purchases a piece of land for a quarter of the amount his grandfather had paid for his land.

Even before going to Shechem he goes to Succoth ("huts, booths"). The altar he builds he calls *El Elohe Israel* ("God, the God of Israel [Jacob]"). Does not that bring to completion the word of the Lord to Jacob in 28:13, "I am the LORD, the God of your father Abraham and the God of Isaac"? Now he is the God of the third generation, too. Jacob is reconciled with God in chapter 32. He is reconciled with his brother in chapter 33. Anyone who does not love his brother cannot love God (1 John 4:20).

H. The rape of Dinah (34:1–31). Life has not treated Jacob well. As a young man he was forced to flee home. In the wilderness he met God and was afraid. Then he was tricked and embarrassed by Laban. He fled Laban. At Peniel he wrestled with God and limped away. Before and after that he agonized over meeting Esau. And now his one beloved daughter, Dinah, is violated.

The criminal is Shechem, son of Hamor. He is called a Hivite in verse 2. An ancient version of the Bible renders this as "Horite" (i.e., Hurrian), showing perhaps that the original settlers of Shechem were Hurrians.

Jacob's sons (but not Jacob himself) are understandably incensed. Hamor attempts to appease them with the offer of peaceful coexistence. One more time we encounter an instance of deception in Genesis. Jacob imitates his father, who imitated his father. And now Jacob's sons imitate their father. Simeon and Levi are the ringleaders. They let on that it is proper for Dinah to marry a Hamorite only if all the males are circumcised.

Three days later, when the pain from the operation would be greatest, Dinah's brothers strike with a vengeance. Holy war is declared against the Hamorites. Jacob protests the excesses of their retaliation, but his sons defend their action as noble. A vigilante mentality always insists that the answer to violence is more violence. Jacob himself has been set free from such a mindset.

I. Jacob returns to Bethel (35:1–29). Jacob continues to evidence spiritual maturity. He is, for instance, sensitive to anything that is at cross-purposes with the presence of God in his life. That is why he orders the removal of foreign gods (probably those brought by Rachel from Laban's house) and the change of clothes (symbolizing spiritual renewal). Even the rings in their ears are removed. Wherever Jacob goes the power of God is manifest (v. 5).

Jacob now renames Bethel *El Bethel* ("God of the House of God"). More important than Bethel as a site of cherished memory is the remembrance of the God who met him there. Lastly, God repeats Jacob's new name, Israel. This is not another tradition parallel to 32:28. Why, then, repeat it? May the repetition indicate that it is only when Jacob is reconciled to Esau that Jacob indeed becomes Israel? This reminder is then followed by a reiteration of the divine promises (vv. 11–13).

Still, there are a few more unpleasant, grief-producing incidents for Jacob. Rebekah's nurse dies. His beloved Rachel dies in giving birth to Benjamin ("son of the right [hand]"). Reuben, his firstborn, commits incest. Finally, his father Isaac dies. None of the other patriarchal figures ever had to endure the tragedies that Jacob did. From chapter 28 on, hardly a chapter passes without some unsettling or disturbing incident taking place.

J. Esau's descendants (36:1–43). Chapter 36 is not among the more exciting chapters of Genesis. It is given entirely to a listing of Esau's descendants. The structure is much like that of chapter 25, where the record of Abraham's death (vv. 7–11) is followed by Ishmael's genealogy (vv. 12–18). Here, the account of Isaac's death is followed by Esau's genealogy.

The names include Esau's immediate family (vv. 1–19), the sons of Seir (vv. 20–30), and a list of Edomite kings (vv. 31–39) who "reigned in Edom before any Israelite king reigned" (v. 31). This would suggest that they are all pre-Saul. A footnote in the New International Version suggests an alternate reading: "before an Israelite king ruled over them." That would mean they are all pre-David. Repeatedly these individuals are referred to as "chiefs" (vv. 15, 18, 19, 29, 30, 40). This term is used in the Old Testament for Edomite leaders.

It is interesting that one of the longest chapters in Genesis is devoted to a genealogy of a marginal person—Esau. For that fact, the rest of Genesis (chaps. 37–50) is mostly a narrative about Joseph, also a marginal nonpatriarchal individual, and not the son of promise through whom the covenant is perpetuated. Esau is not Jacob, but he is not a nobody either. God has been gracious to him, by his own admission (33:11).

IV. Joseph (37:1–50:26)

A. Joseph and his brothers (37:1–36). Joseph gives his brothers three reasons to dislike him. First, he "snitches" on them (v. 2). Second, their father openly loves Joseph more than any other of his children (vv. 3–4). Third, he has two dreams which his brothers interpret as arrogant and egotistical (vv. 5–11). The younger brother will have authority over the older brother, just as Jacob did over Esau. Even Jacob is jolted by Joseph's second dream. Will he, too, bow the knee to his son? Jacob's "will your mother and I" must be understood as a posthumous reference to Rachel, for she has already died.

The Bible makes no comment, other than the brothers' response, about the motivation for Joseph telling these dreams. Could he not anticipate that sharing them would inevitably produce antagonism? Probably Joseph, at the young age of seventeen, did not think it through that far. What he is doing is sharing the sense of destiny that God is opening up before him with anybody who will listen. God has a plan for Joseph's life, and that plan involves leadership and authority. For sharing this sense of excitement about God's will for his future, he is sold by his own flesh as a slave. That was not part of the dream! Where does this nightmare fit into God's glorious future for Joseph?

Joseph travels from Hebron to Shechem to Dothan in search of his brothers. This is no small trip by any means. Joseph would have traveled approximately one hundred miles. The brothers realize that this is their moment for getting even with their brother and his grandiose dreams (**37:12–36**). They will kill him by throwing him into a cistern, where he will surely die of starvation and exposure.

Reuben, desirous of avoiding bloodguilt, suggests an alternative, as does Judah (vv. 21–22, 26–27). In the end Joseph is sold as chattel to Midianites (i.e., Ishmaelites).

Meanwhile, the brothers put Joseph's coat into goat's blood to convince their father that Joseph has been attacked and killed by a wild animal. Once again we encounter deception. Jacob, the master deceiver, is deceived by his own sons.

He buys their ruse—hook, line, and sinker. Jacob's affirmation that he will "go down to the grave to my son" (v. 35) shows again belief in an afterlife. Joseph, meanwhile, is sold to an Egyptian officer, Potiphar. It is most likely that Joseph is not yet able to make the connection between his dreams of destiny and this devastating experience. Little does he know that this is but the first event God will use to implement his plan for Joseph's life.

B. Judah and Tamar (38:1–30). Momentarily Joseph drops out of the narrative to be replaced by his brother Judah. Judah marries a Canaanite girl by whom he has three children: Er, Onan, and Shelah. Er marries Tamar, but he is put to death by God for an unspecified sin. As a result, Tamar is left a childless widow.

It is then the responsibility of the next eldest son, Onan, to father a child by his sister-in-law to bear the name of the deceased. This custom is known as levirate marriage (Lat. *levir,* brother-in-law), and is spelled out in detail in Deuteronomy 25:5–10. The institution is reflected in the New Testament story about the woman who was married to seven husbands

(Matt. 22:23–28). In the resurrection, Jesus is asked, to whom will she belong?

Onan refuses to exercise his responsibility, and as a result dies. He who would in one sense keep his brother alive dies himself.

The third son, Shelah, is too young. Tamar is to return for a while to her father's home. When Shelah grows a bit older, Judah will send for her.

Like many promises, this is never carried out. Judah forgets his word to Tamar, intentionally or inadvertently. She takes matters into her own hands. Disguising herself as a prostitute (the normal Hebrew word for harlot is used in v. 15, but the Hebrew word for "sacred prostitute" occurs in vv. 21–22), she seduces her father-in-law. He impregnates her and she bears twins by him, Perez ("breaking out") and Zerah ("scarlet"). Judah is quick to condemn Tamar for her blatant immorality (v. 24b), but draws back and blushes when his own sin is exposed.

One more time we have a story built around deception. It is Judah this time who is deceived. There are a number of parallels between this story and the ones in chapters 37 and 39. Joseph's morality in the face of temptation may be contrasted with Judah's immorality. In chapter 37 Jacob is deceived; in chapter 38 Judah is deceived. In both instances the truthfulness of the situation is confirmed by the presentation of evidence. Jacob "knows" Joseph is dead because of the bloodied coat. Judah knows he is the father of Tamar's children when she produces his seal, cord, and staff.

C. Joseph and Potiphar's wife (39:1–23). Joseph finds himself in the employ of Potiphar, a high-ranking official of the Pharaoh. What goes through the mind of the bewildered teenager, who has been uprooted violently from his home, sold as a servant, made to live with strangers, was purchased off the trading block, and is dwelling in a foreign country?

Joseph has two things going for him. First, the Lord is with him. Joseph may not know this—at least not yet. In addition to the divine presence, Joseph is a diligent worker, one who impresses his master with his conscientious industriousness. Joseph is to Potiphar what Jacob was to Laban. Both of these non-Israelites experienced blessings because a child of Abraham was in their midst. Joseph oversees everything except Potiphar's food (v. 6).

Potiphar's wife finds herself romantically drawn to this young, handsome, unattached Hebrew. At a propitious moment she propositions him. Joseph adamantly refuses to become her lover for two reasons. First, it would be a disservice to his master who has trusted him. (vv. 8–9a). Second, it would be a sin against God (v. 9b). It is Joseph's commitment to high moral principle that keeps him free from an illicit affair. How different he is from David!

In a last-ditch attempt to get rid of Joseph for rejecting her, the wife grasps a section of his cloak, and then spreads the vicious lie that Joseph tried to rape her. That cloak is her incriminating evidence. She passes the same lie on to her husband. She cannot call Joseph by his name, but refers to him as "that Hebrew slave."

We do not know why Potiphar put Joseph into prison, rather than killing him. Did Potiphar have reason to be suspicious of his wife's story? Had she done something like this before? Maybe Potiphar trusts Joseph more than he trusts his wife. If that is the case, caution is called for. You can release an innocent man from incarceration, but you cannot resurrect him.

Many have observed the parallel between this story and the thirteenth-century B.C. Egyptian story, "The Tale of Two Brothers." The latter is about two brothers, one of whom is married. In the married brother's absence, the wife tries to seduce her brother-in-law, who refuses her. She then complains to her husband, when he returns, about the "initiative" taken by the younger brother. Eventually the truth emerges, and the wife is slain for bearing false witness.

Even in prison Joseph is productive, and is quickly given authority (vv. 21–23). The Lord is with him. Joseph shares a sense of destiny, and it gets him a pit and a ride to Egypt. He is committed to being morally pure, and it lands him in jail. What is to be made of these paradoxes?

D. Joseph's interpretation of dreams (40:1–41:57). Joseph finds himself in custody with two of Pharaoh's officers, the cupbearer and the chief baker (**40:1–23**). Potiphar's house would have to be in the capital city of the empire. That is the only way Joseph would end up in the same prison as Pharaoh's officials.

Both officials have dreams relating to their position. The cupbearer dreams of three blossoming branches on a grape vine. He squeezes the grapes into Pharaoh's cup and puts the cup in his hand (vv. 9–11). The baker dreams of three baskets of bread on his head, and of birds which eat the bread out of the basket (vv. 16–17).

Joseph is not a skilled dream interpreter by nature. He makes that plain when he says, "Do not interpretations belong to God?" (v. 8b). He knows who is to get the credit. It is not without significance that in an ancient world filled with guilds of dream interpreters (oneiromantics) with which every king surrounded himself, the Old Testament seldom mentions this. To be sure, dreams are common, but there are only two places in the Old Testament where *A* interprets *B*'s dreams. Those two incidents involve Joseph and Daniel, one at the beginning and one at the end of the Old Testament. And both times they interpret the dreams of a non-Israelite.

The cupbearer's dream anticipates a happy future. Jospeh tells him that within three days Pharaoh will take up his case. The verdict will be a good one. The cupbearer will be restored to his position.

The baker's dream does not bode well for his future. Birds in the flood story were a good omen, but here they are a threat. Within three days Pharaoh will literally lift up the baker's head—he will die.

Joseph has one little favor to ask. When the cupbearer is restored to his position Joseph requests that he use his influence to get Joseph released from jail, for he is there because of a false charge. The cupbearer, however, forgets him.

Here are the thorns in Joseph's flesh: his brothers, Potiphar's wife, and now the cupbearer. The first abused him. The second lied about him. The third forgets him. Joseph has more than sexual temptations to confront. There is the temptation to be resentful, to be angry, to be depressed, and even to be cynical. How will he rise above these?

For two years Joseph has been imprisoned for a crime he did not commit. For two years the cupbearer forgets about him completely. That is all about to change, for Pharaoh has two dreams, the interpretation of which elude the wise men of Egypt and his magicians (**41:1–57**).

In the first dream seven fat cows are eaten by seven lean cows. In the second dream seven healthy heads of grain are swallowed by seven thin heads of grain. One would think that the dreams should have been essentially self-explanatory. They both have to do with the number seven, and with something good and healthy being overcome by something unhealthy. At least the magicians might have guessed at it. Does God not only make the difficult discernable, but also the easy indiscernable?

It is ignorance that opens the door for Joseph. Suddenly the cupbearer recalls Joseph. Little notes such as the fact that Joseph shaves (v. 14) serve to authenticate the Egyptian milieu of the story. The Egyptians, unlike the Hebrews, were always clean-shaven. Only the Pharaoh wore a beard, and even that was an artificial one.

Joseph is able both to interpret the Pharaoh's dreams (vv. 25–31), and to explain why Pharaoh had dual dreams (v. 32). In addition to making known the future to Pharaoh (seven years of plenty followed by seven years of famine), Joseph suggests a future course of action in order to prepare for the lean years.

Such foresight commends Joseph to Pharaoh, who immediately gives Joseph a position of leadership and invests him with the symbols of authority that go with that office. Also, Joseph obtains a wife (Asenath, daughter of Potiphera) and a new Egyptian name—Zaphenath-paneah.

Joseph fathers two children, Manasseh and Ephraim (vv. 50–52). The first name is connected with the verb *to forget* (i.e., "he made me forget"), and the second is connected with the verb *to be fruitful* (i.e., "he made me fruitful"). No problem is seen with Joseph marrying an Egyptian, as there was with Esau marrying a Hittite.

For the first time something happens to Joseph in which he is not a victim. Only now do the silent workings of God begin to dawn on him. Joseph is beginning to discover that God is truly with him.

E. Joseph's brothers in Egypt (42:1–38). There must be at least seven years between the end of chapter 41 and the beginning of chapter 42, for there is now the reality of famine which Joseph had predicted.

It is interesting to observe Joseph's strategy in dealing with his brothers. First, he pretends to be a stranger. Second, he speaks harshly to them. Third, he accuses them of being spies. Fourth, he repeats that accusation. Fifth, he tests their integrity by insisting that one brother stay behind while the others return to Canaan and bring back their youngest brother. Finally, he slips the money they give him for the grain back into their sacks, creating the impression that they are thieves.

To say the least, Joseph has made it as difficult for the brothers as possible. Some would say that this is vindictiveness on the part of Joseph. Here is his chance to reciprocate, and he relishes the moment. A more likely suggestion is that Joseph is testing (see v. 15) his brothers. Are they any different than when he last saw them? Will the brothers really recognize the terrible nightmare through which they put Joseph if they have to endure some suffering of their own?

It is not difficult to see why the brothers would not recognize Joseph. It has been at least twenty years since they last saw him. Also, he is clean-shaven and uses an interpreter. Even his selection of Simeon (v. 24) as the one to stay behind may be an attempt not to give his hand away too soon. Had he chosen Reuben, as one would expect, then maybe the brothers would have started putting two and two together. For it was Reuben who spoke up in Joseph's defense (v. 22; 37:21–22).

All of this produces more turmoil for Jacob. His own unhappy experiences are not yet ended. They are still dogging him, and will continue to do so to the grave.

F. The second journey to Egypt (43:1–34). Because of the continuing famine, Joseph's brothers must return to Egypt to procure additional grain. This time it is Judah who comes to the fore. It is he who reminds Jacob of the terms Joseph set for any future purchase of food. Before he will release any supplies, they must bring Benjamin with them.

Judah says nothing about the charge that they were spies. Nor does anybody seem to have much to say about Simeon. He is miles away, incarcerated somewhere in Egypt. Judah, however, is willing to go surety for Benjamin (vv. 8–9), and this convinces Jacob to send Benjamin. Either Judah is using a bit of delightful hyperbole (v. 10), or else there was a protracted, heated debate on what was best for the family to do.

Reluctantly Jacob agrees. The brothers will return to Egypt, with Benjamin, and take some gifts to appease Joseph, much as Jacob brought a gift to Esau to appease him. Jacob also doubles the amount of silver that Joseph put back into their sacks (v. 12). Jacob may be without food, but he is not without money.

For the first time in many years Joseph sees his younger brother Benjamin, and his emotions get the better of him. After getting control of himself, he serves a sumptuous dinner, with extra portions for Benjamin. Why all this lavish attention on Benjamin?

G. Judah's plea (44:1–34). Joseph's final plan to "incriminate" his brothers is to send them back to Canaan again. But before they leave he slips his silver cup into Benjamin's grain sack. This is Pharaoh's cup, and the one with which he practices divination. Water divination was a common practice in Egypt, a method of determining the future. One might read the pattern of drops that fell from a cup, or one might throw something into the water in the cup which would form patterns that were omens.

The brothers maintain their innocence. Why do such a stupid thing, they ask? This incident reminds us of Rachel's theft of her father's gods. Laban hunted Jacob down and accused him of being a thief. Jacob protested, claiming innocence, and even pronounced a curse on any person who did take them.

Imagine the brothers' horror when the silver cup is found in Benjamin's sack. Until this point, the brothers do not have a clue that all this has been staged by Joseph. They believe that all this is happening because of divine retribution (v. 16).

One of the most moving speeches in all of Scripture is Judah's plea for Benjamin (vv. 18–34). This is quite a different Judah than the one we read about in chapter 38. He is the intercessor par excellence, and even offers himself as a substitute for Benjamin—"take me, but let him return." And Judah's concern is as much for his father as it is for his young brother.

Joseph's strategy, however wrenching, is producing positive changes in his formerly calloused brothers.

H. Joseph and his brothers (45:1–28). It is now two years into the famine. That means it has been twenty-two years since Joseph has seen his father. Unable to hide his identity any longer, Joseph weeps aloud and identifies himself to his brothers: "I am Joseph!" So astonished are they that they cannot respond (v. 3b). Doubtless they now expect the worst. However, Joseph is above vindictiveness and retaliation. An eye for an eye and a tooth for a tooth is not his procedure. Instead, he shares with his brothers a beautiful interpretation of what has happened to him. He affirms that it was to save lives that God sent him ahead. And quite possibly "to save lives" may refer to Hebrew lives and Egyptian lives. Not only are Jacob's relatives spared because of Joseph, but so are the Egyptians. It was not the brothers who sold him, but God who "sent" him. It is unlikely that Joseph saw it in exactly that light twenty-two years earlier. Now the truth of Romans 8:28, long before it was written, shapes Joseph's attitudes.

He becomes a bit more specific in verse 7 when he says "God sent me ahead of you to preserve for you a remnant." It now becomes clear that Joseph is the divine means for the salvation of his family. Even though he is not the son through whom the covenant promise is passed, he is the son that God uses to keep the flame alive.

Joseph promises them land if they move to Egypt. They will live in Goshen, a fertile area in the northeast Delta region. Unlike many immigrants who are consigned to desolate places, Jacob and his sons will move into lush land where harvests will be bountiful. Goshen is the perfect place for Jacob to settle his family. Here they can live without close contact with the native Egyptian people.

As the brothers head back to Canaan they do so with Egyptian carts, new clothes, food, and provisions, with something extra for Benjamin (vv. 21–23). Joseph's injunction that they not quarrel on the way (v. 24) shows that he has not forgotten what his brothers are capable of doing.

Jacob is stunned to learn that Joseph is still alive. And well he should be. Actually, he needs little convincing—only the Egyptian carts. In spite of advancing age, he is now most anxious to see his son. It is not clear why the father called "Jacob" in verses 25–27 is now called "Israel" in verse 28. Jacob, a name overladen with pejorative overtones, would be inappropriate at a moment of ecstasy and euphoria. Israel, the new name, the name of new direction, is the better one to use at this happy time.

I. Jacob in Egypt (46:1–50:14). Jacob prepares to head down to Egypt to see Joseph (**46:1–34**). On the way he stops at Beersheba and offers sacrifices to the Lord. Isaac, his father, had built an altar there (26:25). It is significant that the Lord speaks to Jacob after Jacob has worshiped.

The last time God had confronted Jacob was also at night (32:22). The first time God spoke to Jacob was through a dream (28:10–22). The last time God speaks to Jacob is through a vision. God's first word to Jacob was nothing but promises for his future (28:13–15). His last word to Jacob is similarly promissory (46:3–4). This is exactly the same with Abraham. God's first word (12:1ff.) and his last word (22:15–18) are promises. The lives of these two patriarchs are bracketed by the "I wills" of God. This structure underscores the cruciality of promise as the major theme of Genesis.

The number of those who go to Egypt, excluding Jacob's daughters-in-law, is sixty-six (v. 26). This number is obtained by the deletion of Er and Onan (v. 12) who are already dead, by the deletion of Joseph, Ephraim, and Manasseh who are already in Egypt, plus the inclusion of Jacob's daughter, Dinah (70 − 5 + 1 = 66).

Judah, always the go-between, is sent ahead to prepare for the meeting of father and son (v. 28). Few events in Scripture can match the emotion-filled intensity of this reunion. Tears are many. Words are few. Jacob's only reason for not wanting to die has been erased. He knows Joseph is alive, and he has seen him again.

Joseph urges his family to identify themselves as shepherds to Pharaoh. The reason for this is clear enough. Goshen, with its scrub-covered plains, was an excellent area for cattle. This fact would encourage the Pharaoh to allow the Jacobites to settle in Goshen.

The meeting between Jacob and his sons and the Pharaoh is carefully orchestrated by Joseph. Everything goes smoothly (**47:1–31**). The Pharaoh knows this territory well, and requests that the royal cattle be put under the supervision of one of Joseph's brothers (v. 6b). Goshen is identified in verse 11 as the district of Rameses. This must be an editorial note, for the area did not acquire this name until the thirteenth century B.C.

Jacob's autobiography is far from positive. He tells Pharaoh: "My years have been few and difficult" (v. 9). True, Jacob (147 years) does not live as long as his father (180 years) or his grandfather (175 years), but more than lifespan is in mind here. Looking back over his past, Jacob sees a few bright moments, but they have been eclipsed by a constant series of setbacks, family problems, tragedies, and nightmares.

Joseph must continue to oversee the country. He collects the money which the people use to purchase the grain. When the money is all gone, he accepts livestock as payment. When the livestock is all sold, he accepts land as payment. Only the priests are exempted from this administrative policy.

Life is not prosperous for the Egyptians, but at least they are alive, and for this they are grateful to Joseph. Their words, "you have saved our lives" (v. 25), confirms that the "save lives" of 45:5 includes Egyptians. Already the promise of God to Abraham about nations being blessed is being fulfilled. The Egyptians are blessed by Joseph's presence. They do not die. They survive a catastrophe, thanks to Joseph.

Just before he dies, Jacob summons Joseph to him. The phrase *put your hand under my thigh* (v. 29) lends solemnity to the occasion of the oath. (The same procedure is mentioned in 24:2.) Joseph binds himself by oath not to inter Jacob in Egypt. Jacob's "swear to me" directed to Joseph (v. 31) may be compared with his "swear to me" directed long ago to Esau (25:33). But there is a world of difference between the conniving Jacob of chapter 25 and the dying Jacob of chapter 47. Jacob wants no burial plot in Egypt. This is not, he knows, God's destiny for his people. He wants to leave when they leave.

Before Jacob blesses his own sons, he blesses the two sons of Joseph (**48:1–22**). Advanced age plus debilitating illness indicate that Jacob is near death. In a bedside conversation he reminds Joseph of God's earlier workings in his own life (vv. 3–4; cf. 35:11–12).

Jacob refers to Ephraim, then Manasseh (v. 5), reversing the order of verse 1. This anticipates the reversal of order that will be spelled out later in the chapter. Jacob will adopt these two sons, which explains why Manasseh and Ephraim are reckoned as sons of Jacob.

Jacob's eyes may be failing, but his spiritual insight is not. Joseph lines up Manasseh, the firstborn, opposite Jacob's right hand, and Ephraim, the younger son, opposite Jacob's left hand. In this way the right hand of blessing will be placed on the head of Manasseh. Joseph believes he has arranged everything correctly.

There are limits, however, to Joseph's knowledge. He may interpret dreams and predict famines, but he does not know the future of his own two sons. Jacob surprises Joseph by crossing his hands and placing his right hand on Ephraim, the younger. This is ironic. Jacob, the younger, usurped Esau; and now this same Jacob blesses the younger (grand)son. The way of God repeats itself two generations later. Joseph is still ignorant. He thinks his father's eyesight or else his mind is the problem. But Jacob knows exactly what he is doing. Ephraim will become a more prominent tribe than Manasseh. But both are to become a source of blessing for all Israel (v. 20). This quiets Joseph, and now he sees the rightness of his father's action.

Jacob is about to leave Joseph, but God will not (v. 21). The word for "ridge" in verse 22 is the word for Shechem which, we recall, after Joshua's day became part of the territory of Ephraim. But where did Jacob engage in militarism? To think, if Jacob had stayed in Canaan and chose not to visit Egypt, he never would have seen Joseph, Joseph's sons, or had this happy opportunity to be a prophet of God.

Most of Genesis **49:1–33** is poetry. The content is mostly concerned with Jacob's blessing of his twelve sons. We use the word *blessing* in a general sense, for there is little actual blessing in the chapter. Only Joseph is literally blessed (vv. 25–26). We retain the title *Jacob's blessing* primarily because of verse 28: "this is what their father said to them when he blessed them." Some of the sections read more like a curse than a blessing.

Verse 1 would suggest that the words that follow are Jacob's addressed to individuals—his twelve sons. Verse 28, however, extends the perspective: "all these are the twelve tribes of Israel."

One of the reasons this chapter is problematic is that it is so difficult to translate from the original. Indeed, it is probably the most difficult chapter in Genesis. Just a glance at the many footnotes in the New International Version, which suggest alternate readings, will bear this out.

Reuben, the firstborn, is disqualified from the rights of primogeniture because of his earlier incestuous behavior (35:22). Eventually the Reubenites settled in the Trans-Jordan as one of the minor tribes. Simeon and Levi lose out because of their violence against the Shechemites (chap. 34). Indeed, Simeon was absorbed into Judah, and Levi was dispersed among the other tribes. These are the only three sons whose fate in Genesis 49 is explicitly connected with earlier material in the Genesis narrative. They provide a further illustration of more pain in Jacob's life. Even on his deathbed, he is reminded of outrageous acts committed by members of his family.

Judah is not disqualified because of his immorality (chap. 38). Clearly Judah is cut out for a place of preeminence and royal leadership. Verses 11–12 confirm the messianic thrust of this section. Judah will usher in an age of abundance and prosperity.

Zebulun will live by the seashore. There is a maritime dimension to the Israelite way of life that is not always appreciated. Issachar will occupy fertile farmland, but will be too capitulatory. Dan will emerge as a power in the period of the judges—like a serpent, small but victorious. Gad will also settle in the Trans-Jordan and will be attacked by nomadic groups. Asher inhabits fertile land in western Galilee. Naphtali is also a northern tribe, but the thrust of verse 21 is by no means clear.

Joseph is to be a prosperous tribe, and is to be victorious over his enemies. But all this prosperity and victory is due to the presence of God. Six times in verses 25–26 some form of "bless" appears. Benjamin is to have warlike qualities and is compared to a wolf. (Note the frequent use of animal imagery in this chapter: oxen—v. 6; lion's cub, lion, lioness—v. 9; donkey—vv. 11, 14; serpent—v. 17; horse—v. 17; doe, fawns—v. 21; wolf—v. 27.)

Jacob now dies. The chapter returns to "sons" (and not tribes)—a parallel to its beginning (v. 1).

Both Jacob (v. 2) and Joseph (v. 26) are embalmed (i.e., mummified), a standard Egyptian practice (**50:1–26**). The seventy days of mourning for Jacob were also traditional in Egypt. Joseph has a little easier time leaving Egypt with the Pharaoh's permission than did Moses. Joseph is a man of his word. He does return to Egypt after he and his brothers have buried their father (v. 14). This is quite a different trip to Egypt for Joseph than the one recorded in chapter 37. Then he went to Egypt *because of* his brothers. Now he goes to Egypt *with* his brothers. Joseph is held in such high esteem that a large Egyptian entourage participates in Jacob's burial (v. 7). Even the Canaanites are impressed.

J. Joseph's reassurance (50:15–21). Now, however, the brothers feel that Joseph will retaliate since their father is out of the way. Nowhere is it recorded that Jacob gave to his other sons the directives which verse 16 claims he did. Either the brothers are fabricating this, or they are recalling a legitimate word that did not make it into the biblical record.

Their apprehension is all for naught. They fail to see that Joseph is different, that he is compassionate and forgiving, that he is unlike his brothers. "Am I in the place of God?" he asks. Then Joseph follows with a classic line: "You intended to harm me, but God intended it for good" (v. 20). The best evidence of spiritual maturity in Joseph's life is his ability to relate all the experiences of his life, good and bad, to the sovereign will of God.

K. Joseph's death (50:22–26). Joseph dies at the age of 110 years (v. 22), which in Egyptian literature is the ideal length of human life. Moreover, Joseph lives long enough to see his great-grandchildren (v. 23), a privilege shared by no other patriarchal figure. There is no question that one day Joseph's family will leave Egypt. "Take my bones with you when you leave," he says. Joseph, of course, is not aware of the titanic struggle that awaits God's people as they seek release from bondage. But having seen the reality and power of God in his own life, he has every reason to believe that God is quite capable of finishing what he started.

SELECT BIBLIOGRAPHY

Aalders, G. C. *Genesis.* Grand Rapids: Zondervan, 1981.

Kidner, D. *Genesis.* Downers Grove: Inter-Varsity, 1967.

Leupold, H. C. *Exposition of Genesis.* Grand Rapids: Baker, 1956.

Stigers, H. G. *A Commentary on Genesis.* Grand Rapids: Zondervan, 1976.

Vawter, B. *On Genesis: A New Reading.* Garden City, N.Y.: Doubleday, 1977.

EXODUS

James K. Hoffmeier

INTRODUCTION

The second book of the Pentateuch gets its English name from the Greek of the Septuagint, meaning "a going out" or "road" or "way out," referring to the event of Israel's departure from Egypt. In the Hebrew Bible, Exodus is called "these (are the) names" (1:1a).

Traditionally the early church, the rabbis, and the New Testament writers included Exodus in the five books of Moses or the Pentateuch. Josephus also mentioned the "Five Books of Moses." Thus it was the accepted view that Moses was the author of the Book of Exodus. Gnostic heretics of the second and third centuries A.D. questioned the divine inspiration of parts of the Pentateuch and Mosaic authorship. These views were not seriously considered by Christian or Jewish scholars, though Origen and Augustine wrote apologetic works which defended the canon. The Reformers, especially Calvin, upheld the traditional view.

Beginning in the seventeenth century, the traditional view became the target of literary critics. Their inquiry focused on the written or oral sources handed down (even to Moses) which were then recorded. This literary approach, usually called "higher" or "source" criticism, attached significance to the different ways of referring to God as indicative of various literary traditions.

The documentary hypothesis was fully developed by K. H. Graf, A. Kuenen, and J. Wellhausen. Known by the acronym *JEDP,* it suggested that various groups of writers composed different parts of the Pentateuch (see figure 1). By and large, evangelical scholars have not subscribed to this analysis of the Pentateuch. The primary reason is that this view denies the testimony of Scripture about itself.

Exodus 17:14 refers to Moses recording the events of the battle against the Amalekites. Furthermore, Exodus 24:4 informs us that Moses recorded the words of the covenant, and subsequently was directed to rewrite the words of the covenant after the first tablets were destroyed (cf. Exod. 34:28). Moses is said to have "finished writing in a book the words of this law from beginning to end" (Deut. 31:24). This most likely refers to the Book of Deuteronomy itself. In all there are twenty-six references to writing in the Pentateuch, virtually

Figure 1 The Documentary Hypothesis (JEDP)

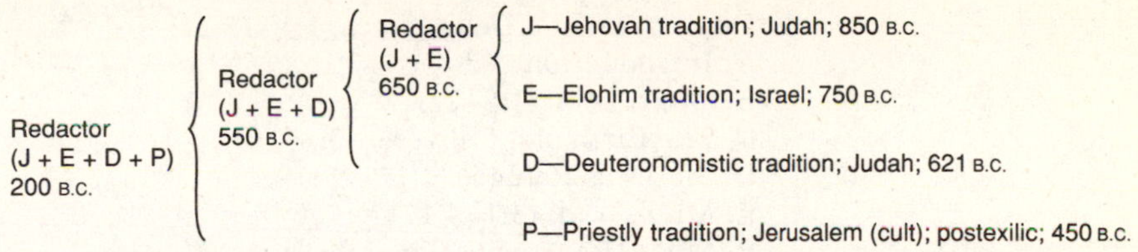

*Dates are approximate

all referring to the activity of Moses. There is also the witness of the balance of the Old Testament on the matter. (See, e.g., Josh. 8:31–32; 23:6; 1 Kings 2:3; 8:9; 2 Kings 14:6; 2 Chron. 5:10; 23:18; 25:4; 34:14; 35:6, 12; Ezra 3:2; 6:18; Dan. 9:11, 13.)

To accept Mosaic authorship of the Pentateuch is not a matter of faith. Both internal and external evidence support it. As a methodological principle, one should accept the testimony of a literary work about itself unless it can be proven otherwise. To date, that has not been done for Exodus.

No topic has fostered more debate in recent decades than the date of the exodus from Egypt. The Book of Exodus itself provides no date nor the name of the pharaoh under which it took place. However, 1 Kings 6:1 dates the fourth year of Solomon, when work on the temple commenced, as being 480 years after the exodus from Egypt. Since Solomon's fourth year is quite securely dated to 966/7 B.C., one need only add 480 to that figure to arrive at 1446/7 B.C. This would fall during the reign of the eighteenth-dynasty monarch, Amenhotep II (ca. 1450–1425 B.C.). There is some evidence which suggests that this pharaoh was the king of Egypt at the time of the exodus. However, a survey of the literature shows that the problem of the date of the exodus remains debated by scholars. Most would agree, however, that this takes nothing away from the importance of the event nor its place in salvation history. No position can be said to be *the* evangelical position. Until more evidence emerges, any position is tentative at best.

Three obvious themes are emphasized in the Book of Exodus: (1) deliverance, (2) the covenant, and (3) the land of promise. The deliverance theme is most evident in the exodus event and God's saving acts at the sea (Exod. 14:10–31; 15:1–21). The covenant at Sinai (Exod. 20–24) draws Israel into a unique relationship with God. God promised the patriarchs that he would give their descendants the land of Canaan after a period of sojourning in a foreign land (Gen. 15:13–21). This promise is repeated to Abraham (Gen. 17:8), then to Isaac (Gen. 26:3), and to Jacob (Gen. 28:13). The departure from Egypt is a necessary prerequisite to the fulfillment of this promise and so is a central theme in the Book of Exodus (Exod. 3:8; 6:5–9). The Sinai covenant, as we shall see, is a fulfillment of the Abrahamic covenant.

OUTLINE

- I. Oppression and Deliverance (1:1–15:21)
  - A. Introduction (1:1–7)
  - B. Oppression (1:8–22)
  - C. The Birth of a Deliverer (2:1–10)
  - D. Moses as Refugee (2:11–25)
  - E. Moses' Call (3:1–4:17)
  - F. Moses Returns to Egypt (4:18–31)
  - G. Increased Oppression (5:1–23)
  - H. God Encourages Moses (6:1–13)
  - I. Moses' Genealogy (6:14–30)
  - J. Moses and Aaron Warn Pharaoh (7:1–13)
  - K. The Nine Plagues (7:14–10:29)
  - L. The Tenth Plague Announced (11:1–10)
  - M. The Passover (12:1–27)
  - N. The Exodus (12:28–51)
  - O. Consecration of the Firstborn (13:1–16)
  - P. The Crossing of the Red Sea (13:17–14:31)
  - Q. Celebration of Salvation (15:1–21)
- II. The Journey to Mount Sinai (15:22–19:2)
  - A. From the Sea to Elim (15:22–27)
  - B. From Elim to the Wilderness of Sin (16:1–36)
  - C. From Sin to Rephadim (17:1–16)
  - D. Moses' Family (18:1–27)
  - E. From Rephadim to Sinai (19:1–2)
- III. The Sinaitic Covenant (19:3–24:18)
  - A. Preparations (19:3–25)
  - B. The Covenant (20:1–23:33)
  - C. The Covenant Ceremony (24:1–18)
- IV. Instructions for Israel's Sanctuary (25:1–31:18)
  - A. Preparations (25:1–9)
  - B. The Ark (25:10–22)
  - C. The Table (25:23–30)
  - D. The Lampstand (25:31–40)
  - E. The Tabernacle (26:1–37)
  - F. The Altar (27:1–8)
  - G. The Courtyard (27:9–19)
  - H. The Oil (27:20–21)
  - I. The Priestly Garments (28:1–43)
  - J. Consecration of the Priests (29:1–46)
  - K. The Altar of Incense (30:1–10)
  - L. The Offering (30:11–16)
  - M. The Laver (30:17–21)
  - N. The Anointing Oil and Incense (30:22–36)
  - O. Bezalel and Oholiab (31:1–10)
  - P. Sabbath Instructions (31:12–18)
- V. Apostasy and Intercession (32:1–33:23)
  - A. The Golden Calf (32:1–33:6)
  - B. The Tent of Meeting (33:7–23)
- VI. The New Tablets (34:1–35)
- VII. Execution of Sanctuary Instructions (35:1–40:38)

COMMENTARY

I. Oppression and Deliverance (1:1–15:21)

The first third of the Book of Exodus is devoted to the events surrounding the bondage of the Israelites in Egypt and how that grew increasingly repressive until God intervened. Moses is the central figure. His birth, his upbringing at the royal court, his exile in Midian, and his call by Yahweh, the God of his fathers, are reported. The deliverance from Egypt becomes a symbol in the rest of the Old Testament for spiritual salvation.

A. Introduction (1:1–7). These verses serve to connect Exodus to the patriarchal stories in Genesis. The names of the twelve sons of Jacob (who by now are twelve tribes) are listed. Seventy male members of Jacob's family had settled in Egypt with the aged patriarch (cf. Gen. 46:27) and Joseph. Exodus 1:6 mentions the death of Joseph and his brothers. Genesis 50:22–26 ends with the death of Joseph and his statement about God's plan to bring the Hebrews out of Egypt to the land promised to Abraham, Isaac, and Jacob.

In Genesis 1:28 God instructed Adam and Eve to "be fruitful and increase in number; fill the earth." These same three words are used in 1:7 in reference to the Israelites.

B. Oppression (1:8–22). The multiplication of the Hebrews, along with the mention of a new king (in all likelihood a new dynasty) are literary devices used to indicate the passage of a considerable amount of time. In order to keep the Hebrews from aligning with Egypt's enemies (lit. those who hate us, as in NASB), the Hebrews are pressed into hard labor (v. 11) which includes the building of two store cities. The names of these cities, Pithom and Rameses (v. 11), have been discussed in much detail. Pithom is the Hebrew transliteration for *pi-atum,* "house" or "temple of Atum." Atum was equated with Re the sun god. The name *Rameses* has led many scholars to identify it with Rameses II's capital, Pi-Rameses. But the capital city would hardly be called a "store city." Perhaps the Hebrews worked on storage facilities connected to the capital.

In verses 12–14 hardship for the Hebrews intensifies. But this servitude does not accomplish its purpose—reducing the population of the Hebrews. The king introduces a second plan (vv. 15–16): the Hebrew midwives are to destroy male babies at birth.

The mention of the delivery stool (v. 16) (lit. two stone bricks) reflects Egyptian birthing practice. The Hebrew women while in Egypt may have borrowed the practice of squatting on two bricks, one for each foot, while giving birth.

The midwives "fear" or "revere" God and so cannot carry out the king's order. When the king sees that his plan has failed, he summons the midwives to determine why Hebrew male babies are being born. They tell him that the Hebrew women deliver so quickly, unlike Egyptian women, that by the time the midwives arrive, the babies are already born. It would appear that the midwives deliberately twist the truth in the interest of preserving life. We may be inclined to question the ethics of these women, but clearly their action is approved by God who rewards them for reverencing him and preserving life rather than obeying Pharaoh and destroying life.

The midwives are rewarded with families (v. 21). Occasionally in the ancient Near East, barren women served as midwives. If this is the case here, these faithful women are rewarded with children which Scripture regards as a gift from God (Ps. 127:3–5). For barren women in particular giving birth is cause for great joy (Gen. 21:6–7; 1 Sam. 1:1–2:10; Luke 1:6–14, 57–58). Pharaoh turns next to a more diabolical scheme, ordering that Hebrew male babies be thrown into the Nile at birth (v. 22).

C. The birth of a deliverer (2:1–10). From verse 1 we learn that Moses' parents are from the tribe of Levi. For some reason, their names are not mentioned here, though they are disclosed in 6:20. His father is Amram and his mother is Jochebed. The child is described as being *ṭôb* (v. 26), which is often rendered "goodly" (KJV, RSV); but the word also means "beautiful" and some translations have so rendered it (NASB). The beauty of this child makes it even more difficult for Jochebed to comply with the pharaoh's edict, so she hides him for three months. But this can only last so long.

Jochebed places her baby in a papyrus basket waterproofed with bitumen, and casts it into the water, in a sense fulfilling the pharaoh's edict. Exactly what her reasons are for doing this are not stated. It is not certain whether the basket was placed so that it would be found by a member of the royal family or a wealthy Egyptian who might take the baby in, rear him, and use him as a servant. Semitic slaves worked as house servants and butlers and were valued by the Egyptians.

The daughter of Pharaoh sees the basket when she goes to the Nile to bathe. The text does not reveal if this was anticipated by Jochebed. No name is given to this princess, and the futility of trying to determine who she might have been must be stressed since there were many children in the royal court.

The princess immediately recognizes the baby as a Hebrew. The baby's sister, identified later as Miriam (15:20), who has been watching the unfolding drama, offers to obtain a Hebrew nurse for the baby because the princess in some way had taken pity (so RSV, NEB, NASB) on the child.

Apparently Moses is reared by his mother (v. 9) until weaning age, probably age two or three. When the baby is returned to the princess, she names him Moses, because "I drew him out of the water" (v. 10). This explains the meaning of the name.

Moses' upbringing in the royal court is passed over without comment. He is a young child in verse 10 and a grown man in verse 11. It is fair to assume that Moses was reared in the royal harem along with other princes. There he likely would have been trained in the use of weapons, chariotry, and writing. His training in writing would make him well suited to the task of recording God's law. From what is known of the education of Egyptian princes, the statements by Stephen (Acts 7:22) and Josephus (*Antiquities* 2.9.7–10.2) about Moses' training are well founded.

D. Moses as refugee (2:11–25). The time lapse between verses 10 and 11 is not recorded but Stephen in his sermon to the Sanhedrin states that Moses was forty (Acts 7:23). There is nothing in Exodus to substantiate this claim. Exodus 7:7 states that Moses was eighty when he returned from exile in Midian, and his age at death is recorded as 120 (Deut. 34:7). This has led some scholars to divide his life into three segments of forty years: forty in Egypt, forty in Midian, and forty in the wilderness with the Israelites. But Exodus does not disclose Moses' age when he fled to Midian, nor how long he was there. Stephen may have been reflecting a rabbinic tradition common in Christ's day.

Though Moses was an Egyptian by virtue of his upbringing, he knows that he is a Hebrew (v. 11). If Moses is thirty to forty years old at this point, it means that during the years he was growing up, the oppression of the Hebrews continued. Moses goes out to see their hard labor. Upon seeing an Egyptian (taskmaster undoubtedly) beating (apparently to death) a Hebrew, Moses intervenes. Even at this early stage in his career, Moses has a strong desire to see justice done. Thinking the coast is clear, Moses strikes the Egyptian and kills him. Later, news of the incident reaches Pharaoh, who is enraged and wants Moses put to death. So Moses flees to Midian, probably located on the east side of the Gulf of Aqaba, opposite the Sinai peninsula.

We might be inclined to regard Moses' sojourn in Midian as a wasted portion of his life. But a close look at Exodus 2:16–4:17 reveals quite the opposite. First, he meets Jethro, the priest of Midian, and marries one of his seven daughters, Zipporah (vv. 16–21). The Midianites, like Moses himself, were descendants of Abraham by his wife Keturah (Gen. 25:1–2). There is some justification in thinking that these people had preserved something of Abraham's faith and that Jethro might have been a priest of Elohim. It is possible, but by no means certain, that Moses may have learned something of Yahweh from his father-in-law.

Moses tends Jethro's flock in the Sinai area. In so doing, Moses gains valuable experience in the very terrain where later he will lead an even larger flock!

While all is well in Midian, the oppression in Egypt only grows worse even though the king from whom Moses fled has died. There is great urgency in the situation, and this is undoubtedly the reason why God chooses this moment in time to call Moses to liberate his people.

Verses 24 and 25 contain a series of anthropomorphisms: God hears, God remembers, God looks, and God is concerned. These expressions indicate God's intimate involvement with Israel though all outward appearances suggest that he has abandoned his people. God's remembering his covenant with Abraham does not mean that he has somehow forgotten it. To say that he remembers means that he is about to take a significant step toward fulfilling the covenant (cf. Gen. 8:1, where God remembers Noah and the others in the ark and takes steps toward abating the flood water). In this case, the next chapter shows what that step is: calling Moses to lead the people out of bondage.

E. Moses' call (3:1–4:17). God appears to Moses at Horeb, the mountain of God. No convincing explanation has been given for why this mountain should be called both Horeb and Sinai (see 19:11, 18, 20).

After centuries of silence, the God of the patriarchs breaks through. It is an awesome moment, and his sacred presence demands that Moses come no closer and that he remove his shoes because the ground is holy.

God indicates that the cries of his people have not gone unnoticed. He says, "I have come down to rescue them . . ." (v. 8). Of course, God did not need to "come down" to see what was going on. In Genesis 11:7 and 18:21, where this idiom is used, God is about to exercise judgment (on the world with the flood and on

Sodom with fire). This then hints that judgment on Egypt is about to take place.

"The hand of the Egyptians" (v. 8) means the power or control that the Egyptians have over Israel. Not only does God intend to free Israel from Egypt, but also he plans to give the land of promise to his people. The prosperity of the land is described by the phrase *a land flowing with milk and honey* (v. 8).

God informs Moses that he will represent Israel's cause before Pharaoh. Moses' objections are twofold (v. 11): Who am I that I should go to Pharaoh? Who am I that I should bring the Israelites out of Egypt? Knowing that the previous king had sought his life makes Moses fearful about returning to the Egyptian court. But his upbringing and court training make him the ideal candidate for this assignment.

God responds by reminding Moses that "I will be with you" (v. 12). In addition, God promises a sign to show "that I have sent you: When you have brought the people out of Egypt, you will worship God on this mountain." At first glance, it is difficult to identify the promise. What assurance of God's presence comes from being told that Israel will worship God *after* the flight from Egypt? Some think that in the statement *this will be the sign* God may be referring to the burning bush. In other words, the sign is God's appearance to Moses. Reflecting on that awesome experience would sustain him through difficult times ahead.

Somewhat encouraged (but not fully convinced) by that pledge, Moses asks, "Suppose I go to the Israelites and say to them, 'The God of your fathers has sent me to you,' and they ask me, 'What is his name?' Then what shall I tell them?" (v. 13). Moses is not demanding to know God's name per se, but the character behind that name. God's answer supports this, because he does not say "Yahweh" (v. 14) but interprets the name "I AM WHO I AM." This may appeal to his infinite existence: "the Lord God Almighty, *who was, and is, and is to come*" (Rev. 4:8b, emphasis added).

Moses is instructed to return to Egypt and to disclose God's plan to the elders of Israel who in turn will accompany Moses when he approaches Pharaoh. In his omniscience, God knew that Pharaoh would not allow the Israelites to depart unless compelled by a "mighty hand" (v. 19). This will be accomplished when God "stretches out his hand" (a gesture with militaristic overtones) and strikes Egypt with "wonders." When God is through flexing his arm, the Egyptians will give the Hebrews gold, silver, and clothing.

Moses is still reluctant, fearing that the Hebrews will not believe him (4:1). God causes Moses' staff to change into a serpent and back again. This is meant to demonstrate that God's power is with Moses. A second sign, the ability to make his hand leprous and then restore it, would be quite convincing since leprosy was considered to be incurable. A third sign to show the doubting Israelites is to take water from the Nile and turn it to blood on the ground. None of this sways Moses. In verse 10 he points to his limitations as a speaker. Though Moses may have suffered from some sort of speech impediment (see 6:12, 28–30), he probably is acknowledging his lack of oratorial experience (like the youthful Jeremiah), or that the task of communicating God's message is so onerous that he simply cannot do it clearly. By this point God is becoming annoyed with Moses, and argues that he is the one who made the mouth and can direct it to speak (vv. 11–12).

Having exhausted his excuses, Moses declares "Oh Lord, please send someone else to do it" (v. 13). God then expresses his anger and indicates that Aaron, Moses' brother, will serve as spokesman. And there the dialogue ends.

F. Moses returns to Egypt (4:18–31). Moses goes to Jethro to ask his permission to leave. This may not be simply an act of respect, for it is thought that Moses may have had a marriage arrangement involving a period of service, much like his ancestor Jacob had with Laban (Gen. 29:18–20). Perhaps because he was sensitive to God, Jethro complies with the request. Lest there be any hesitation on Moses' part, God commands him to "go back to Egypt" (v. 19). Accompanied by his wife and two sons, Moses begins the trek across the desert to Egypt.

Apparently while en route, God again appears to Moses and informs him that despite the signs Moses will show, Pharaoh will not comply with his request, for God will harden Pharaoh's heart. Why should God do this? The answer is not easy. Due to Pharaoh's intransigence, a greater judgment will result: both as retribution for Israel's enslavement, and as punishment for defying God.

God even tells Moses what to say to Pharaoh (vv. 22–23). Israel is God's firstborn (the heir of the father's estate and honored one) and God demands his release. If Pharaoh refuses, God will slay the heir to Egypt's throne!

A second incident that takes place on the return journey to Egypt is the bizarre attack on Moses or his son (vv. 24–26). This story is marked by several obscurities. The Lord meets and seeks to kill *him* (v. 24). There is no antecedent in the sentence to be certain whether it is

Moses or his son who is attacked. Apparently, Moses had failed to circumcise his sons as demanded by the Abrahamic covenant (Gen. 17:11–14). We would expect the attack to be directed at Moses who was responsible for carrying out the rite. Why he should have been attacked at this time at this place is odd. Zipporah, apparently sensitive to what is taking place, circumcises her son with a flint. The precise meaning of her statement "Surely you are a bridegroom of blood to me" (v. 25b) is also obscure. Zipporah's action brings an immediate end to the attack.

Meanwhile, God has spoken to Aaron, telling him to join his brother in the wilderness. They meet at "the mountain of God" (v. 27). There Moses recounts God's intentions for Israel and the two then hasten on to Egypt to meet with the elders, as God has instructed. The message, delivered by Aaron, is believed and the people bow their heads and worship.

G. Increased oppression (5:1–23). Moses and Aaron appear before Pharaoh, apparently proclaiming God's request together. Aaron's task is primarily to address the Hebrews, but Moses' knowledge of court protocol and his command of the Egyptian language make him the ideal spokesman to Pharaoh. The formula *thus says the Lord* is used by the Israelite prophets to show that it is Yahweh's word they are enunciating, not their own. The request to make a journey into the desert to offer sacrifices is not unreasonable.

Pharaoh's response is insulting. "Who is the Lord, that I should obey him and let Israel go? I do not know the Lord . . ." (v. 2). Moses and Aaron change their request. They specify that it will entail a three-day journey (one way) and they fear that if they do not meet their God's demand that Israel might be struck by pestilence. This latter point at least should have concerned the monarch if he wanted continued productivity from the Hebrews. But the king is unfazed and charges Moses and Aaron with "taking the people away from their labor" (v. 4). Pharaoh then defiantly orders Moses and Aaron to get to work. Now not even Moses with his court connections is exempt from hard labor.

Rather then help Israel's plight, the visit to Pharaoh only exacerbates matters as the monarch orders that the Hebrews now have to provide their own straw for making bricks. At the same time, the Israelites are expected to maintain their quota (v. 8).

This new directive, enforced by the taskmasters (v. 10), forces the Hebrews to go out and collect the straw. The taskmasters prod the poeple to meet their quotas and beat them when they fail.

The Hebrew foremen protest the unrealistic demands to Pharaoh, probably by way of the vizier or the "overseer of works." Again they are told to get back to work and to meet their quotas. Moses and Aaron wait to see if the foremen have received a reprieve. The angered foremen question whether Moses has in fact received a word from God about Israel's release. In fact, they blame Moses for the worsening situation (v. 21). Understandably, Moses is grieved and returns to God. "Why have you brought trouble upon this people? Is this why you sent me?" (v. 22). Things are getting worse, not better.

H. God encourages Moses (6:1–13). God's response to Moses follows immediately: "Now you will see what I will do to Pharaoh" (v. 1). What God is about to do will drive Pharaoh to force (i.e., "strong hand") Israel out of the country. There is some irony here, for it was by power and force that Israel had been enslaved. That same hand will drive them out. God then repeats his self-identification: "I am the Lord" (v. 2). It is important that Moses not forget who God is, the eternal, infinite God of the universe.

God's encouragement continues in verses 5–8, and, as in 2:24, mention is made of his "remembering" the covenant with Abraham which means that God is about to take action. This is followed by a series of promises to Israel: "I will bring you out . . . I will free you . . . I will redeem you with an outstretched arm . . . I will take you as my own people, and I will be your God . . . I will bring you to the land." In these statements the three major theological themes of Exodus—deliverance, the covenant, and the land of promise—are stressed.

Moses repeats these profound words to the Israelites, but they do not listen because their spirits are broken. Their depression is understandable. They had been promised liberation and now things are worse.

With the promises of verses 3–8 still in mind, God tells Moses to go to Pharaoh once again and to tell Pharaoh to let the Israelites go. Moses reasons that if the people did not pay heed to God's plan, how would Pharaoh listen? He blames Israel's response, and predicts a similar response from the king.

God counters by giving a "charge" to Aaron and Moses that they are to tell Pharaoh and the people about Israel's departure from Egypt. When God uses this strong language, Moses is silent. He has to carry out God's command; there is no option.

I. Moses' genealogy (6:14–30). Genealogies in Scripture are important for establishing the identity and importance of an individual. Why this genealogy should appear at this juncture is most puzzling. We already know quite a bit about Moses. We might expect the genealogy to appear at the outset of chapter 2, but that is not the case. In Hebrew literature it is quite common to explain an earlier point later in a literary work. That may be the case here. Furthermore, the genealogy may serve to legitimate Moses and Aaron since the Hebrews were refusing to listen to them and were questioning their divine call.

This genealogy is a limited one, beginning with Jacob's eldest son, Reuben, and his sons (v. 14), going on to Simeon and his sons (v. 15), and then on to Levi. Levi is clearly the important individual in this section because only his life span is given (137 years). Not only are his three sons mentioned, but the line extends two more generations: Levi–Kohath–Amram–Moses.

Verse 26 underscores the fact that it is the same Aaron and Moses whose genealogy is established here that God ordered to lead Israel out of Egypt. By repeating Moses' concern for his "faltering lips," verses 28–30 resume the flow of the narrative from verses 12–13, where the same expression is used.

J. Moses and Aaron warn Pharaoh (7:1–13). God continues to encourage Moses. God addresses Moses' concern about his speaking ability by reminding him that Aaron will be his spokesman: "I have made you like God to Pharaoh, and your brother Aaron will be your prophet" (v. 1). Just as a prophet proclaims God's Word, so Aaron will state what Moses has told him. That Moses will be God to Pharaoh is undoubtedly meant to contain an ironic twist. In Egyptian thought Pharaoh was the incarnation of the god Horus, the son of Re (head of the Egyptian pantheon). Therefore, Moses will have authority over Pharaoh. God will instruct Moses, who in turn will pass the message on to Aaron, who will then communicate with Pharaoh. It is not clear why on some occasions Moses speaks to Pharaoh (e.g., 8:29; 9:8), while on others Aaron addresses the king (5:1; 7:10, 20; 10:8). It seems unlikely that Moses was speaking Hebrew and Aaron translating, because Moses surely was more conversant in Egyptian than his brother.

Despite the authority God has entrusted to Moses and Aaron, the king will not be swayed because God will "harden Pharaoh's heart" (v. 3). In keeping with the Old Testament's view of the sovereignty of God, even an evil spirit is said to come from God (1 Sam. 16:14). When David took his infamous census in 2 Samuel 24:1ff., we are told that "the anger of the LORD burned against Israel, and he incited David . . ." to number the people. In 1 Chronicles 21:1, where the same event is recounted, the text states that Satan incited David. It appears that the writer of Samuel could not bring himself to say that this action took place outside of God's will. So with God's hardening of Pharaoh's heart: the monarch still was responsible for his action.

God plans to use Pharaoh's intransigence as an opportunity to display his power (v. 5). Egypt and Pharaoh in particular will no longer be able to say, "Who is Yahweh?" It will also lead to the exodus, the event that will bring Israel to faith.

In verses 8–9 God instructs his servants on the next step to take in dealing with Pharaoh. They are to demonstrate God's power using Aaron's staff. The purpose of this is to persuade the king to let Israel go; if this demonstration fails to convince him, the plagues will follow. Aaron's staff, when thrown to the ground, becomes a snake (v. 10). The Egyptian wise men, sorcerers, and magicians are summoned. Pharaoh may initially see something sporting in this act. His magicians are able to duplicate Aaron's act, but Aaron's staff swallows those of the magicians, thus showing superiority. The ability of the Egyptian magicians to turn their staffs into serpents is not due to miraculous powers.

Even though Aaron's staff has shown itself superior to the others, Pharaoh is not moved to change his mind. This leads God to declare that the next day Moses will warn the king of the plagues that are to strike the Nile.

K. The nine plagues (7:14–10:29). The plagues, or signs and wonders as they are often called, are regarded by later writers as indications of God's superiority over Pharaoh and Egypt (Num. 14:11; Deut. 4:34; Josh. 24:17; Pss. 78:43; 105:27; Jer. 32:21). Prior to the tenth plague God says, "I will pass through Egypt and strike down every firstborn—both men and animals—and I will bring judgment on all the gods of Egypt . . ." (Exod. 12:12). Some take this verse as an indication that each plague is directed against specific Egyptian deities. While this can be demonstrated in some cases (i.e., the Nile, the darkening of the sun, and the death of the firstborn, especially the crown prince), it is simply not convincing in the case of the third through the eighth plagues.

The first plague is the plague of blood (**7:14–24**). Moses is told to meet Pharaoh at the river's edge in the morning. This is an appropriate place, for the first plague directly affects the Nile and all the water in Egypt (v. 19). The text does not explain why Pharaoh was going to the river in the morning. Pharaoh may have been undergoing a ceremonial rite when confronted by Moses. Alternatively, since the Nile was the Egyptian counterpart to our present-day highways, Pharaoh may have been going to his boat for travel purposes.

At the command of God, Aaron raises his staff and changes all the water into blood. The Egyptian magicians, on a smaller scale, are able to duplicate this act. Since the act is repeated by his own magicians, at least superficially, Pharaoh is unimpressed by what he sees.

The second plague (**8:1–15**), like the first, is duplicated in some measure by the Egyptian magicians (v. 7), but they are unable to remove the hordes of frogs in the land.

The first two plagues appear when Aaron stretches out his hand (7:19; 8:6). But the third is introduced (**8:16–19**) when Aaron stretches out his rod and strikes the ground. Such actions, called parabolic or symbolic acts, are reminiscent of the Old Testament prophets. When a prophet performed such an act, it symbolized what was about to take place (cf. 2 Kings 13:15–19; Jer. 13:1–9; Ezek. 5:1–5). The magicians are unable to produce the "gnats." They tell Pharaoh (v. 19), "This is the finger of God." By this statement, they concede that they are up against a superior force. The magicians now recognize that they are being confronted by divine action, not human magic. But Pharaoh is not convinced (v. 19b); in fact, he becomes even more obstinate.

The fourth plague (**8:20–32**) prompts Pharaoh to offer a compromise: "Go, sacrifice to your God here in the land" (v. 25). Moses argues that it would be abominable to the Egyptians for the Israelites to perform sacrifices in Egypt. The meaning of this statement has spawned some discussion. Some think that Moses was afraid to sacrifice animals (especially the cow) which the Egyptians deemed sacred. Others think that the objection would have to do with sacrificing sheep; the Egyptians had an aversion to sheep because of their dislike of the Bedouin who raised them (cf. Gen. 46:34). A third suggestion is that Moses was more concerned that the specific rites involved in Israelite sacrifice would be abominable to the Egyptians. Whether or not one of these suggestions is what was in Moses' mind, we cannot tell. But implicit in his protest is that it would be inappropriate to offer Yahweh pure offerings in a pagan land.

Pharaoh's compromise is unacceptable to Moses, but just the same, Moses prays that the flies be removed, and the next day they disappear.

For the fifth time Moses is instructed to approach the king and announce that if he does not allow the Hebrews to go, a severe plague will strike the livestock of the Egyptians, but not that of the Israelites. The result is the death of all the cattle of the Egyptians (**9:1–7**). Even though none of the Israelites' cattle dies, Pharaoh is unmoved.

A symbolic act, throwing ashes into the sky, introduces the sixth plague (**9:8–12**). Most English translations identify the skin condition as "boils." The same Hebrew word is used to describe Job's sores (2:7) and Hezekiah's near-fatal condition (Isa. 38:21). The severity of these sores explains why the Egyptian magicians cannot make an appearance to vie with Moses (v. 11). But as before, Pharaoh refuses Moses' request.

This is the first time we read that God hardens Pharaoh's heart. In earlier cases, Pharaoh hardened his own heart (8:15, 32) or his heart was hard (7:13; 8:19; 9:7). Not until the beginning of the third cycle of plagues is God involved in the hardening process. This is similar to what God allows the sinner who rejects his revealed truth to do (Rom. 1:18–26).

The next day Moses appears before Pharaoh, this time disclosing more of God's purpose in the plagues (**9:13–17**). He wants Egypt to know that "there is no one like me in all the earth" (v. 14b). God could have obliterated Pharaoh and his people but he has allowed them to live "that I might show you my power and that my name might be proclaimed in all the earth" (v. 16).

After stating in more detail the reason for the plagues, Moses announces that hail (the seventh plague) will strike Egypt (**9:18–35**). Not only does Moses predict what will happen, but also he warns the Egyptians to get their cattle into shelters. Some "fear" the word of God and act accordingly. While some of the Egyptians now believe Moses, Pharaoh does not. Thunderstorms are not that common in Egypt, though they are known to occur occasionally and do damage. Hail is even less common. Therefore its presence would undoubtedly make quite an impression on Pharaoh. The severity of the hail storm is emphasized by the statement: "It was the worst storm in all the land of Egypt since it had become a nation" (v. 24; cf. v. 18).

The hail devastates fields and trees, as well as animals and people, but the land of Goshen is spared. The extent of the destruction has a softening effect on Pharaoh, who summons Moses and Aaron and makes a modest confession (v. 27). He declares that he has sinned but implies that guilt also rests with his people, as if to remove some of his own responsibility. Despite words that sound sincere, Moses knows better: "I know that you and your officials still do not fear the Lord God" (v. 30). Verse 31 describes the damage to Egypt's primary crops that were approaching harvest. This note on the crops, indicating that the wheat and spelt were not destroyed because they arrive later in the season, establishes the time of year (late January to early February). After leaving Pharaoh, Moses spreads his hands out to the Lord and the storm stops (v. 33). This expression is descriptive of a gesture associated with prayer (cf. Isa. 1:15). When Pharaoh sees the plague abate, his heart is hardened.

Moses and Aaron tell Pharaoh that God will send locusts to consume what the hail has missed (**10:1–20**). Pharaoh's advisors are annoyed by his intransigence: "How long will this man be a snare to us? Let the people go, so that they may worship the LORD their God. Do you not yet realize that Egypt is ruined?" (v. 7). Perhaps the king, cloistered within his palace, was not aware of the full extent of the damage done by the plagues which have now gone on for possibly five or six months.

The reality of Egypt's dilemma leads the monarch to make a new offer: the men can go and worship, but the women and children must stay (v. 11). This concession is not enough, so locusts are brought in by a powerful east wind. Once again Pharaoh declares, "I have sinned against the LORD your God and against you" (v. 16). This time he shares the blame with no one else, and it seems as though he is truly penitent. But no sooner are the locusts removed then Pharaoh refuses to let the Hebrews go; God hardens his heart (10:20). God has two more plagues he intends to unleash in order to demonstrate his power.

Darkness (**10:21–29**), the last plague of the third cycle, was probably a sand storm or *khamisin* (Arab. fifty; such storms usually occur during the fifty days of spring, with March being at the center of this period). This suggestion is further enhanced by the fact that the locusts were driven away by a "very strong west wind" (v. 19). This could well have established favorable meteorological conditions for a *khamisin*, which occurs when the wind shifts from its prevailing patterns and blows from the south.

The impact of this three-day darkness on Egypt would have been significant. Re, the sun god, would have been overshadowed, which would have been alarming, especially to the king, who was believed to be the incarnation of Horus, Re's son.

The darkness prompts Pharaoh to call for Moses. He declares that the people can all go, but they must leave their flocks and herds behind. Moses protests; they must take all their animals along for he does not know what God will require them to sacrifice. Once again God hardens Pharaoh's heart. He has one final judgment for Egypt. Moses is dismissed; his request is denied; and Pharaoh says that if he ever sees Moses again he will be put to death.

L. The tenth plague announced (11:1–10). A reading of 11:4–9 gives the impression that these words were spoken immediately after 10:29. Moses warns about God's visitation of Egypt, in which every firstborn son in Egypt, from the crown prince to the lowest servant, and the firstborn of the cattle, too, will be struck down. Moses then leaves the palace in anger, for even this warning is not accepted by the monarch.

What, then, is to be done with 11:1–3? It appears that God may have provided this revelation on the spot. There will be one more plague (v. 1a), and the Egyptians will readily give up their jewelry to the departing Hebrews (v. 2). Then verse 4 describes the plague. God had already told Moses about the jewelry and the "favor" in 3:21–22, when he called Moses. God had also spoken to him about the hardening of Pharaoh's heart which would lead to the slaying of the firstborn of Pharaoh (4:21–23). This suggests that Moses has not received a new revelation, but is being reminded of what he had been told earlier.

M. The Passover (12:1–27). The Passover is to commemorate God's deliverance of Israel from Egypt. Due to the importance of Passover, the month in which it occurred was to mark the beginning of the Hebrew calendar (v. 2). On the tenth day of Abib each family was to select a lamb that was a year old. It was to be male "without defect" (v. 5). On the fourteenth day the lamb was to be slain and its blood applied to the doorposts and lintel of the people's houses (vv. 6–7). By doing this the residents could prevent the death of their firstborn sons (v. 13). Unlike the previous plagues from which the Israelites were protected (cf. 9:7, 26; 10:23b), this occasion was different. Each family had to act on the warning, thus demonstrating their faith in God's provision.

The lamb was to be roasted and eaten with unleavened bread and bitter herbs (v. 8). The bitter herbs were to remind the people of the bitter experience of their slavery. Verse 17 indicates that in addition to observing Passover on this day, they were to celebrate the Feast of Unleavened Bread. The intent of this twofold observance might be to celebrate God's bringing them out of the land of Egypt and into the land of promise. This might parallel the salvation of the believer in Christ: "For he has rescued us from the dominion of darkness and brought us into the kingdom of the Son he loves" (Col. 1:13).

The union of Passover and the Feast of Unleavened Bread can be seen in the observance of the Last Supper. Christ breaks the bread and passes the cup of wine, the former being unleavened bread, the latter symbolizing the blood of the sacrificed lamb.

At the conclusion of these instructions, the people bow their heads and worship (v. 27). This is the same faith response they had exhibited when Moses first told them of God's plan for their redemption (4:31). They are apparently convinced that God will deliver them, for they do as they are instructed (v. 28).

N. The exodus (12:28–51). The dreaded passover event strikes as foretold. The firstborn sons of Egypt are killed, including "the firstborn of Pharaoh, who sat on the throne" (v. 29). The death of the crown prince (or co-regent) is significant. The death of a king in Egypt was traumatic because there was always the possibility of intrigue, where one faction of the royal house might try to place a prince on the throne over another.

Pharaoh is finally broken and tells Moses to leave—with no conditions attached (vv. 31–32). Perhaps because he now truly fears Moses and Yahweh, Pharaoh does not follow through on his earlier threat to kill Moses if he should see the Hebrew again (10:28). Pharaoh even asks that Moses bless him (presumably when the Israelites make their offerings to Yahweh). As predicted earlier (3:21–22; 11:2–3), the Egyptians are so desperate to get rid of the Hebrews that they gladly give them silver, gold, and clothing (v. 35).

The Israelites depart from Rameses (v. 37), which is probably the place mentioned in 1:11. No reason is given why they journey to Succoth. The number of men is given as six hundred thousand (v. 37). Adding the women, children, and the "other people" (v. 38—probably non-Israelites who were also enslaved and took advantage of this opportunity to leave), a figure in excess of two million results.

At issue is the meaning of the word *'eleph,* here translated as "thousand." It can also mean "clan" (cf. Judg. 6:15; 1 Sam. 10:19) or military unit (Num. 1). So the figure in 12:37 may mean six hundred clans.

Verses 40–41 provide information on the duration of Israel's stay in Egypt. English translations follow the Masoretic Text in citing 430 years as the length of time. However, the Septuagint and Syriac versions include the period from Abraham's sojourn to Jacob's descent to Egypt in that 430-year period.

Fortunately, no theological issue is at stake on the question of the number of people involved in the exodus, or how long the sojourn lasted. One's view on these matters should not be used as a test of orthodoxy; the issue is a hermeneutical one which still requires scholarly investigation.

Verses 43–50 provide an addendum to 12:1–27. Foreigners, temporary residents, and hired workmen must not participate in the meal, while "aliens" can, provided they are circumcised. The implication is that one who lives in Israel, though not an Israelite by birth, can become a member of the covenant community by living in the land and undergoing the rite of circumcision.

Without any explanation, the Hebrews are instructed to eat the Passover lamb indoors without breaking any of its bones (v. 46). John sees something messianic in this latter statement, for he points out that, unlike the two robbers with whom Jesus was crucified, Christ's legs were not broken (John 19:32–33). Then he observes, "These things happened so that the scripture would be fulfilled, 'Not one of his bones will be broken' " (19:36).

O. Consecration of the firstborn (13:1–16). Just as the Israelites are to present the firstfruits of the ground to the Lord (23:19), so they are to bring all male (clean) animals and male children which are the "first offspring of every womb" (v. 2).

Verses 3–10 depart from the "firstborn" theme and return to the topic of unleavened bread. This unit offers no new insights on the observance except to mention the name of the month (Abib) in which the feast is to be held (v. 4).

Verses 11–16 return to instructions concerning the firstborn. This order is perplexing indeed to the Western mind. However, the logic behind the sequence of these verses may be that the offering of the firstborn is connected with unleavened bread since the latter is an agricultural observance closely related to eating the new grain (see Josh. 5:10–12) and the former is associated with animals. The Passover lamb is never specified as the firstborn, but it certainly may have been. Thus a logical and theological connection between Passover, unleavened bread, and firstfruits is quite plausible. The dedication of the firstborn, like the other two observances, is tied directly to God's deliverance of Israel from Egypt (v. 14). In that deliverance, God took the firstborn of Egypt, a point mentioned in verse 15a. But as had been demonstrated to Abraham centuries earlier, God did not want the firstborn of humans to be sacrificed to him (cf. Gen. 22:10–14). Consecration (v. 2) means to set apart for God's service or worship. In actuality this meant a sacrifice was to be performed (v. 15). Since an unclean animal, like an ass, could not be sacrificed, a lamb was to take its place, that is, it was to be redeemed (v. 13). If for some reason the animal was not or could not be redeemed, its neck was to be broken, its life given back to God.

Male children were to be redeemed, not sacrificed (13). God had shown in the death of Egypt's firstborn that Israel's firstborn was to be preserved. The Canaanites practiced child sacrifice, but God did not want the Hebrews to follow that abominable rite.

These observances are to be "a sign on your hand and a symbol on your forehead" (v. 16). Later Judaism insisted that these signs and symbols were literal objects to be worn. The phylacteries referred to in Matthew 23:5 reflect that practice. While not specifically condemning the practice of wearing phylacteries, Jesus appears to be saying that the Jews had missed the point. The expression in 13:16 is likely meant to be taken symbolically.

P. The crossing of the Red Sea (13:17–14:31). God does not lead the Israelites through Philistine country. In 13:21–22 we are introduced to the method of God's leading: a pillar of cloud during the day and a pillar of fire at night. Exodus 14:19 indicates that the angel of the Lord is behind these phenomena.

God does not lead the Hebrews on the most direct route to Canaan, knowing that they might turn back "if they face war" (v. 17b). This may refer to the Egyptian military forts in the area guarding the border of Egypt. Moses may have been aware of these outposts from his flight years earlier.

There is another reason God does not lead the Hebrews by this route. God had specified that after leaving Egypt, the Israelites were to appear before him at Mount Sinai (3:12).

Reconstructing the route of the exodus is extremely difficult since the point of departure and many of the places along the way are uncertain. We know that the Israelites passed through Succoth (12:37; 13:20), and traveled toward the Red Sea (13:18). We are not helped by mention of the sea because even its location is not precisely known.

The manner of Israel's march (13:18b) likewise poses a problem for translators. The Revised Standard Version, the New American Standard Version, the New International Version, and the Jerusalem Bible say that the Israelites were armed; the King James Version says they were "harnessed"; the New English Bible says that the "fifth generation" of Israelites went up out of Egypt. It seems unlikely that the Egyptians would have allowed the Israelites to bear arms while in Egypt, and their response to the approaching Egyptian army (14:6–10) is not one that we would expect had they been armed. The Hebrew word *ḥămušîm* may have to do with the orderliness of the army, perhaps marching in groups of fifty.

Centuries before, Joseph had prophesied that God would one day lead the Israelites out of Egypt and back to the land of promise (Gen. 50:24–25). He requested that when the Hebrews left Egypt, they take his bones along. Exodus 13:19 informs us that his request is fulfilled. (Eventually he was reinterred at Shechem [Josh. 24:32]).

Etham is mentioned as a place where the Israelites camp (v. 20), but its location is not known. From the place names in 14:2, it appears that a turn toward the north has been made.

God tells Moses that the people are to "turn back and encamp near Pi-Hahiroth (House of [the goddess] Hathor), between Migdol and the sea . . . directly opposite Baal Zephon" (14:2). Of this list, only Migdol can be identified with any certainty, most likely being an Egyptian frontier town. "The sea" is probably the same one named in 13:18. This would mean that in turning back, the Israelites were retracing their steps from a more northerly route to a southeasterly direction.

In addition to telling them to "turn back," God directs Israel to camp "by the sea" (v. 2b). God deliberately leads the Israelites to this location, setting the stage for them to be trapped by the Egyptians on one side and the sea on the other. God also points out Pharaoh's next move. Because he thinks the Israelites are wandering around in confusion, he believes that he can easily recapture them.

Pharaoh dispatches a chariot force, horsemen, and troops to pursue the fleeing Hebrews. Six hundred of his best chariots, as well as others, are included, "with officers over them" (v. 7b).

The Israelites, who thought that they had seen the last of Pharaoh and his army, are understandably terrified when they see the Egyptians approaching (14:10). The people cry out to the Lord—not a prayer of faith, but a complaint. From the euphoria they must have felt as they left Rameses and Succoth, they begin to wish that they were serving back in Egypt rather than waiting to die in the desert.

Moses responds with the memorable words: "Do not be afraid. Stand firm and you will see the deliverance the LORD will bring you today. . . . The LORD will fight for you; you need only to be still" (vv. 13–14).

God announces his plan. The sea against which the Israelites are trapped will actually provide a way of escape (v. 16). The Egyptians will try to follow and be destroyed. This will be the final act by which God demonstrates his sovereignty over Egypt and Israel alike.

In order to protect the Israelites from the Egyptians during the night, the angel of the Lord moves the pillar of fire between the two camps (vv. 19–21). The crossing of the sea takes place early in the morning. When enough distance separates the Egyptian army from the Israelites, the wall of protection is removed and the Egyptians pursue Moses and the people. Once in the sea, the chariots get bogged down. God also throws the Egyptians into confusion. The Egyptians decide to turn back when they realize that Yahweh is fighting against them (v. 25).

God directs Moses to stretch his hand over the water once again to close the division (v. 26). The water returns to its normal state, drowning the pursuers. The text is careful not to say what happened to Pharaoh; he may well have stayed back from entering the sea.

God's deliverance here is once again described as "salvation" (v. 30). Understandably the Hebrews, seeing what has happened, are overwhelmed and "fear" Yahweh. More importantly, "they put their trust in him and in Moses his servant" (v. 31b).

Q. Celebration of salvation (15:1–21). A fitting response to God's saving acts is to praise him, and so the Israelites do, with Moses and Miriam taking the lead. It was a custom in the ancient Near East to commemorate military victories to national gods. The "Song of the Sea" might be regarded as Israel's hymn celebrating Yahweh's victory. It appropriately begins with "I will sing to the Lord, for he is highly exalted" (v. 1).

"The song" is poetic in form, with a strophic structure, evidenced by the threefold repetition of lines referring to God's victorious arm or hand (15:6, 12, 16).

Parallelism, the "rhyming" of ideas or thoughts, is also widely used throughout. The opening line is an example of synthetic parallelism in that the second line expands on the idea set forth in the first line of the couplet. Synonymous parallelism (the two parts of the couplet are synonymous) is widely used:

> He is my God, and I will praise him,
> my father's God, and I will exalt him. [15:2]
>
> Pharaoh's chariots and his army he has
> hurled into the sea.
> The best of Pharaoh's officers are drowned in
> the Red Sea. [15:4]

Additional examples of synomous parallelism are 15:6, 11, and 15.

The poem concludes, as do Canaanite hymns to their gods, with the mention of the victorious Warrior Yahweh building an abode for himself (v. 17). While this may anticipate the temple on Mount Zion, it more likely refers to Mount Sinai, known also as "the mountain of God" (3:1). From his abode, Yahweh will "reign for ever and ever" (v. 18).

Verse 19 provides the context of this song, namely, Israel's deliverance from the sea and Egypt. Miriam leads the women with timbrel and dance and sings the very same song (only the opening verse of the song is recorded since it would be redundant to repeat the whole thing). It was an ancient practice for women to meet the warriors returning from battle with timbrel, dance, and song.

Miriam is called a "prophetess." She is not the only woman in the Old Testament who bears this title: Deborah (Judg. 4:4–5), Isaiah's wife (Isa. 8:3), Huldah (2 Kings 22:14–20), and Noadiah (Neh. 6:14) are all called "prophetesses." The early prophet(ess) seems to be closely associated with worship, and musical instruments are occasionally mentioned (cf. Num. 11:24–29; 1 Sam. 10:5–6).

II. The Journey to Mount Sinai (15:22–19:2)

The exact route taken by the Israelites in their flight from Egypt to the Red Sea is uncertain. Equally uncertain is the route taken by the Hebrews after crossing the sea as they were led by the cloud toward Mount Sinai. Likewise, the precise identification of Mount Sinai has not been made, which complicates matters even further.

A more southern location seems plausible in light of Deuteronomy 1:2, which states that "it takes eleven days to go from Horeb to Kadesh Barnea by the Mount Seir road." A final problem associated with establishing the route to Mount Sinai is that many of the place names in the Pentateuch were given as a result of some action that took place at a particular camp site (e.g., "Marah" in Exod. 15:23; "Meribah" in 17:7). We would not expect a camp site of only several days or weeks to yield much archaeological data. Thus we will have to remain in the dark with regard to the geography and toponyms in the Sinai.

A. From the sea to Elim (15:22–27). Once across the sea, the Israelites enter the Desert of Shur (v. 22) in the northwestern part of Sinai. When the Israelites come to Marah, the water is undrinkable, which causes the people to grumble against Moses. He cries out to the Lord, interceding for the people. This is the first in a series of occasions where Moses is cast into the role of intercessor—a quality associated with a prophet (cf. Gen. 20:7). God's response is to show Moses a piece of wood which he throws into the water, and the water turns sweet.

The result of this event is God's introduction of an ordinance for Israel (vv. 25b–26). The purpose of this event is to "prove" or "test" Israel. After witnessing God's saving act at the sea, how would they respond to the dilemma of the bitter water? Would they look to God? No, they complain, or break faith with God. This is merely the first of many instances where this happens. Numbers 14 records that when the spies return with their reports of the land, the people fear the inhabitants of Canaan. God's anger is expressed in the statement, "How long will these people treat me with contempt? How long will they refuse to believe in me, in spite of all the miraculous signs I have performed among them?" (14:11). Numbers 14:22 notes that this is the tenth time Israel has tested God. Israel's unbelief, beginning at Marah and stretching out for the next couple of years, culminates with Numbers 14 which leads to a prolonged period of wandering in the wilderness. Israel is barred from entering the land of promise. So we are reminded in Hebrews 3:18 that just as the Hebrews of old were unable to enter the rest of God (the Promised Land), we too cannot experience spiritual rest if we are unfaithful to God.

The ordinance introduced by God is simple enough: "If you listen carefully to the voice of the LORD your God . . . I will not bring on you any of the diseases I brought on the Egyptians; for I am the LORD, who heals you" (v. 26). If Israel wants God's protection and blessing through this trek, obedience is imperative.

After leaving Marah, the Israelites next camp at Elim (v. 27), an oasis blessed with spring water and date palms.

B. From Elim to the wilderness of Sin (16:1–36). From Elim the journey continues to the Desert of Sin, located between Elim and Sinai (v. 1). The word *Sin*, a transliteration of the Hebrew and in no way sharing the meaning of the English homonym, is apparently etymologically related to "Sinai." The difference between the two terms is the *ai*. But verse 1 makes it clear that the Desert of Sin is not Sinai. So even if the words are related, they refer to different geographic areas. The name of the encampment in Sin, according to the log kept by Moses (Num. 33:1–49), is Dophkah. Far more important than the identification of Dophkah and Sin are the events that occur there, namely, the second murmuring of the people, this time directed at both Aaron and Moses (v. 2).

The people's complaint is legitimate enough—there is no food. The people conclude that they would be better off in Egypt (v. 3). God tells Moses that he will provide "bread from heaven" (v. 4). He then provides both manna and quails. God tells Moses that the people should gather the manna daily; on the sixth day, enough should be gathered for the Sabbath as well. Some find it curious that mention should be made of the Sabbath prior to revealing the Ten Commandments, the fourth of which lays down the laws for the Sabbath (Exod. 20:8–11). The rationale for "resting" on the seventh day (20:11) is that it conforms to the pattern established by God at creation (Gen. 2:2–3). The explanation given in 20:11 suggests that this concept was already known by the Israelites but required clarification, for in Egypt they probably were unable to observe the Sabbath.

God sends quail for the people to eat (v. 13). Quail was not a regular part of the Israelite diet, as the record suggests, but on a few occasions would be available during seasonal migrations. On the other hand, the provision of manna lasted the entirety of the wilderness period. The word *manna* derives from two Hebrew words, *mān hûʾ*, which mean "What is it?"—the very question posed by the people in verse 15. From the various descriptions of manna in the Pentateuch (Exod. 16:14–15, 31; Num. 11:7–8) we learn that manna was a flaky, granular substance that could be ground into flour and made into bread. Thus it served in place of wheat or barley. Attempts have been made to explain manna as a natural substance, but these explanations fit only certain times of the year and apply to restricted areas. The provision of manna occurs throughout the forty-year period in the wilderness (v. 35). It is noteworthy that when the people first eat the produce of the land of Canaan that the manna ceases the very next day (Josh. 5:11–12). God supplies the manna only when it is needed. This suggests that it is a supernatural provision (see John 6:30–34).

C. From Sin to Rephadim (17:1–16). At God's direction, the journey continues by stages (or encampments) to Rephadim. Apparently the Israelites move toward this site for water. But when they arrive, there is none. As expected, the people complain to Moses about the situation.

The similarity between this story and the one in Numbers 20:1–13 has led some scholars to conclude that these are simply different versions of the same event. In both instances, water is produced from a rock, the site is called Meribah, and the people contend with Moses.

However, more striking than the similarities between the two passages are the differences. Exodus 17 occurs en route to Sinai; Numbers comes clearly after Sinai. The locations of the two events are different. God's instructions to Moses on each occasion are different. In Exodus 17:6 Moses is to strike the rock, while in Numbers 20:8 he is to speak to the boulder. In Numbers 20 when Moses strikes the rock, he does so in violation of God's directive and is punished. When he strikes it in Exodus 17, it is in response to God's instruction and he is not condemned for his action. Thus it should be clear that the two stories are different.

Verse 6 records that the rock that produced the water is located at Horeb. This suggests that this incident takes place very close to the area of Mount Sinai, for the terms *Horeb* and *Sinai* are used interchangeably.

God is angered by the reaction of the people to this crisis. By virtue of their complaints they are asking, "Is the LORD among us or not?" (v. 7b). After witnessing the plagues, the crossing of the sea, the sweetening of the water at Marah, the provision of food, and the ever-present cloud, how could it be that God is not with them? "To whom much has been given, much is required." There is no excuse, from God's perspective, for this breach of faith.

While at Rephadim the Israelites battle the Amalekites, a seminomadic people who are descendants of Esau (Gen. 36:12). Verse 8 makes it clear that the Amalekites are the aggressors, a point confirmed in 1 Samuel 15:2.

Moses is instructed to hold up his staff which figured prominently in the plagues of Egypt and at the crossing of the sea. The significance of Moses' raising the rod over his head is not clear. As a man of advanced years (early eighties) he would not be able to lead the troops into the field of battle; that is left to Joshua (vv. 8–10), who is mentioned here for the first time in the Pentateuch. Hands in an upraised position is a gesture associated with prayer, and some scholars think that this may be involved here. But this does not account for the presence of Moses' staff. By this time the staff had become symbolic of God's saving acts, and holding it could remind the people of this fact and encourage them in battle.

The importance of Moses' hands upholding the staff is seen in the success of Israel's army when they are raised and its failure when they are lowered (v. 12). In order to sustain Moses, Aaron and Hur make him sit on a stone and prop up his tired arms (v. 2). Israel prevails.

God directs Moses to record this event in a book (probably a scroll) and to make sure that Joshua hears it. This statement is important for it shows that God wants his people to have a sense of history.

The victory is marked by erecting an altar to God and calling it, "The LORD is my Banner" (v. 15). God is Israel's banner, perhaps symbolized by the staff of Moses.

D. Moses' family (18:1–27). Word of Israel's triumph over Pharaoh reaches Jethro in Midian. So Jethro comes to join Moses, bringing with him Moses' wife (whom he had sent away) and two sons (v. 2). The expression *sent away* usually means divorce, but that is most certainly not the case here. Zipporah had at least begun the journey back to Egypt with Moses (4:24–25), but for some unknown reason he sent her back to Jethro with the two boys. Perhaps after the initial audience with Pharaoh proved fruitless and problems loomed ahead for Moses, he thought it best to send his family back to the safety of Midian. Once out of Egypt, the family could be reunited.

The meeting between Moses and Jethro displays the typical honor paid to a respected person (v. 7). Moses recounts how God has acted on Israel's behalf. Jethro pronounces a blessing on Yahweh for his saving acts. Whether Jethro was a believer in Yahweh before these events is uncertain, but his words in verse 11 indicate that he certainly is afterward: "Now I know that the LORD is greater than all other gods."

In verses 13–26 we are introduced to Moses the judge, who up to this point is Israel's only judicial leader, handling all disputes himself. Moses' activity is reminiscent of the later prophets to whom people inquire of God's direction in a matter. Jethro, a man of great insight, recognizes that the burden for one man is far too great and so he suggests that Moses select competent, trustworthy men to share the load. Moses will still handle the more difficult cases and those that require divine instruction. Moses responds positively to this recommendation. This demonstrates a number of his qualities. Even though he is without doubt the most important leader in Israel's history, he accepts counsel from others and does not cling to his prerogatives. This is a lesson which all leaders in church work need to learn (cf. Acts 6:1–6; Eph. 4:11–13; 1 Tim. 2:2).

After a short stay with Moses, Jethro returns to Midian taking with him the stories of God's saving acts for his own people to hear.

E. From Rephadim to Sinai (19:1–2). Rephadim was apparently a short distance from the Desert of Sinai, and Mount Sinai may have been visible in the distance from that point, as suggested by Exodus 18:5. At some point after leaving Rephadim, the Israelites arrive in the wilderness of Sinai, which coincides with the appearance of the third new moon since the departure from Egypt (vv. 1–2). Camp is set up near "the mountain of God."

III. The Sinaitic Covenant (19:3–24:18)

God had ordered Moses to come to Sinai to worship him (3:12). But this was not going to be just another worship experience. God was about to enter into a covenant relationship with Israel. The patriarchs had enjoyed a special relationship with God, but that covenant was analogous to the betrothal between God and his bride Israel (cf. Ezek. 16:8). The Sinai covenant is the actual marriage ceremony where the relationship will be consummated.

A. Preparations (19:3–25). The people of Israel are to prepare themselves to meet God. Three days are set aside so they might purify themselves for this divine encounter. These purification rites are necessary since God is holy and he cannot tolerate impurity, be it physical or spiritual. Furthermore, the mountain itself, where God will appear for the ceremony, is to be cordoned off, segregated from the people, because sinful man is unable to tolerate too close an encounter with the "Holy One of Israel."

Prior to the actual theophany, Israel is warned that this covenant will be conditional, linked to their obedience to God's commands which he is about to make known (v. 5). Only then will Israel be the "holy nation" and "kingdom of priests" God intends them to be. Israel is a nation just like any other nation. She is made holy only by virtue of her relationship with God, not because of any inherent good in her. Furthermore, Israel's unique relationship with Yahweh carries with it certain "missionary" responsibilities. This point can be traced back to the purpose of Abraham's call (Gen. 12:3).

The final instruction connected to the preparation is: "Abstain from sexual relations" (v. 15b). The principle behind this prohibition is that the preparation for the covenant ceremony is a solemn matter, requiring the complete attention (physical and spiritual) of the people; no diversions can be tolerated. It also illustrates that the preparations are essentially spiritual in nature (1 Cor. 7:5).

The theophany on Mount Sinai is an awesome event. In preparation for God's descent there is thunder and lightning; a thick cloud envelops the mountain and there is the sound of a very loud trumpet blast (v. 16). As God descends, fire and smoke are seen and the trumpet blast grows in intensity.

B. The covenant (20:1–23:33). The structure of the covenant (chaps. 20–24) follows the form or structure of ancient Near Eastern treaties, particularly the type made between a sovereign and his vassal. The structure of the Exodus covenant (and the Book of Deuteronomy, for that matter) reflects the pattern characteristic of treaties from 1600 to 1200 B.C. Not only does this help us establish a relative date for the writing of Exodus, it also provides us with a key for understanding this section. God in his revelation uses literary forms known to the Hebrews so that they might better understand the nature of their relationship with God. The following six-point structure of ancient treaties from the middle of the second millennium is aligned with passages in Exodus to demonstrate how the Sinaitic covenant/treaty fits this pattern.

1. *Title/Preamble.* The preamble introduces the maker of the treaty. Therefore, Exodus 20:1–2a reads, "God spoke all these words: 'I am the LORD your God.' "

2. *Historical Prologue.* Here the maker of the treaty would recount the history of his relationship with his vassal. Thus God says he is the one who brought Israel out of the land of Egypt, out of the house of bondage (Exod. 20:2b).

3. *Stipulations/Conditions.* The stipulations outline what is expected of the vassal and the conditions for the relationship between the two parties. Ancient kings expressed concern that their vassals not establish treaties with other kings which might lead them to rebel against their sovereign. The stipulations also spelled out responsibilities in the area of taxation, and restricted the size of armies and chariotry. The stipulations in Exodus are concerned with Israel's spiritual fidelity. There are to be no other gods (20:3); there must be no treaties with other peoples (23:32) for God will protect them (23:22). Israel is to bring regular offerings to God.

4. *Deposit of Text/Public Reading.* A copy of the treaty would be placed in the national shrine of each party. Israel's, of course, was to be placed in the ark (25:16). It was to be read to the people (24:7), and then periodically to be reread and the terms reaffirmed by the people (a covenant renewal). The Book of Deuteronomy is in fact a rereading of the law and a commentary by Moses (Deut. 1:5). Deuteronomy 31:9–11 specifies that the covenant renewal should take place every sabbatical year on the Feast of Booths when the nation is

gathered at the tabernacle (or temple). The purpose of this ceremony is clear. Israel needs to know what God expects of them and this demands a renewal of their commitment to him.

5. *Witnesses.* Since a treaty was a legal document, it required witnesses. The gods of ancient pagan kings usually served this purpose. Long lists of deities were recorded who might be called upon to judge the party who had violated the terms. In Exodus 24:4 Moses erects twelve pillars which serve the purpose (for the use of stones as witness to a covenant, see Gen. 31:46–49). In Deuteronomy the witnesses to the covenant renewal are heaven and earth (31:16–30; 32:1).

6. *Covenant Ceremony.* The ceremony finalized the covenant. Oaths of fidelity would be taken, animals would be sacrificed, and a meal would be eaten. Curses would be listed as warnings of what would befall the vassal if he violated the covenant. Blessings would be promised the obedient vassal. In the Sinai ceremony, mention is made of the people gathering to take the oath (24:3, 7), oxen are sacrificed, and a meal is shared (24:11). The reason for the sacrifice and meal is twofold. There is certainly fellowship between the king and the vassal, between God and Israel, but the death of the animal also serves as a warning. If the vassal does not fulfill the obligations, then the sovereign has the right to slay the vassal just as the animal has been slain (cf. Jer. 34:18).

Noticeably absent from Exodus are the curses and blessings. However, Leviticus 26:3–13 cites blessings and 26:14–33 records the curses. The Book of Leviticus itself is a continuation of the ceremonial stipulations of the covenant. Therefore this section of blessings and curses goes with the Exodus covenant material. Deuteronomy 28:1–14 and 15–68 contain the blessings and curses respectively that accompany the covenant renewal. So this part of the covenant formula is certainly present in the Pentateuch.

The Ten Commandments (lit. words) of 20:2–17 are spoken to the people, but they are overwhelmed by the theophany and fear for their lives. So they request that Moses personally receive the laws from God and then communicate them to the congregation. So from this point onward, Moses becomes the intermediary between God and the people (20:21ff.). Thus Moses ascends the mountain, still shrouded by clouds, to receive instructions from time to time.

The Ten Commandments (**20:1–21**) can be divided into two categories: those which pertain to man's relationship with God (1–4), and those dealing with man's relationship to his fellow man (5–10). All the rest of the laws in the Pentateuch fit into these two categories. For this reason, Jesus teaches that the greatest commandment is "Love the Lord your God" while the second is "Love your neighbor as yourself" (Matt. 22:37–39). Then he proceeds to say "All the Law and the Prophets hang on these two commandments" (22:40). In many respects the laws of the Pentateuch are guides to living out these two principles.

The first commandment (v. 3) is a clear prohibition against the worship of other deities. This is not an admission that other gods exist. There is only the One, as the credal statement in Deuteronomy 6:4 affirms: "Hear, O Israel: The LORD our God, the LORD is one." For this reason, he must be worshiped in the prescribed way. The people are not to make any idols. God cannot be identified with any beast or the likeness of one. The prohibition of the second commandment (v. 4) is not against crafting art objects per se. Objects of worship or veneration are prohibited (v. 5a). Those who obey God receive his covenant loyalty or faithfulness (v. 6).

The third commandment (v. 5) deals with taking the name of Yahweh in vain. This relates to evoking God's name in an oath and then not fulfilling the vow. It is clear that God expects Israel to use his name in oaths provided the people faithfully execute what has been promised (Jer. 4:2).

The observance of the Sabbath or seventh day is dealt with in the fourth commandment (vv. 8–11). Just as God in creation worked for six days and rested on the seventh, so too man is to continue this principle established at creation (Gen. 2:1–3). This injunction is directed to everyone, even servants, sojourners, and animals. God, our Creator, recognizes the need for man to have a respite.

The fifth commandment (v. 12) deals with the honor or respect due to a parent. The sixth through eighth commandments are common to most cultures. The prohibition against killing (v. 13) actually means murder, which is quite different than the sort of killing that goes on in the course of a battle. A distinction between murder and death in battle is apparent in David's statement in 1 Kings 2:5. A whole range of circumstances that lead to death will be dealt with in 21:12–27. These laws make it clear that the sixth commandment is a general statement that requires expansion.

Bearing false witness (v. 16) has to do with giving false testimony in a judicial setting. According to Old Testament legislation (see

Deut. 19:15–20), the witness of two or three was the basis for a conviction and the death penalty should the crime be a capital offense. Therefore, a law against perjury was needed to prevent false charges from being brought against an individual. Finally, coveting or desiring a neighbor's property is prohibited (v. 17).

Exodus **20:22–26** deals with laws pertaining to the types of altars that are permissible for Israel to make and use. Those made of beaten clay and unhewn stone are allowable. Clearly some altars were too similar to those used by the Canaanites and were not to be copied. The statement about the priest's nakedness in verse 26 is most curious. When this same word for "nakedness" occurs elsewhere in the Pentateuch (e.g., Lev. 20:17–21), it has to do with sexual impropriety. Therefore "nakedness" here probably refers to the type of Canaanite fertility rituals that included sexual acts such as those described in Amos 2:7–8.

Exodus **21:1–6** details laws that pertain to slavery. The type of slavery being dealt with here played an important role in Israelite society. If one were in debt and could not pay, the debtor would have to serve the creditor to pay off that debt. The story of the widow in 2 Kings 4:1–7 is an example of how this worked. Verse 2 indicates that the period of servitude could last a maximum of six years; on the sabbatical year, the slave was to be released. Of course, if someone were to come forward and pay the debt, thus redeeming the individual, he would be released. During the period of servitude, if the owner should give a wife to the slave and they should have children, the children and wife ultimately belong to the master. The slave could decide to stay with the master and thus keep his family. In this case the slave voluntarily attached himself to his master and the sign of this relationship was the boring of a hole in the ear of the slave (v. 6).

Exodus **21:7–11** deals with the legal protection of female slaves. A young woman was often given by a wealthy man to his daughter at marriage to be her maid, and in some cases, to serve as a surrogate mother (see Gen. 16:1–4; 29:24, 29). A man might purchase a slave woman to be his wife or concubine, or to give her to his son for the same purpose. If the man decided against marriage, he was to allow her to be redeemed by a near kinsman (as in Lev. 25:48–54). Further, such redeeming was to take place within the community, by her family or clan.

Exodus **21:12–17** deals with capital offenses while **21:18–32** deals with bodily injuries which in some cases require the death penalty. Verse 12 is a general statement: "Anyone who strikes a man and kills him shall surely be put to death." This is not a new law, but a reaffirmation of Genesis 9:6. God makes provision for different types of attacks on an individual based on motive and intent. Verse 13a indicates that if the act is not premeditated, the killer is to receive protection from family members who might seek vengeance. The altar was a place where one might find sanctuary. Joab, David's commander-in-chief, sought refuge at the altar when he fell out of favor with Solomon. In this case sanctuary was denied (1 Kings 2:28–34). The second possibility for protection is a place God would appoint for such purposes (v. 13b). This, of course, is clarified in Numbers 35:9–15 and Deuteronomy 19:4–10 with the provision of cities of refuge. But in cases of premeditated attacks, no refuge is to be provided (v. 14).

Verses 15 and 17 deal with children and parents. In verse 15 it appears that any action against a parent, regardless of intent, merits the death penalty. Verse 17 appears even harsher: "Anyone who curses his father or his mother must be put to death" (cf. Lev. 20:9). Dishonor in a general sense is implied. Obviously proper respect to parental authority is very important to God.

Kidnapping is the concern of verse 16, as well as taking a person in order to sell him into slavery. Here we recall the action of Joseph's brothers in selling him into slavery in Egypt (Gen. 37:27–28).

Verses 18–19 are a logical expansion of verse 12. One's intention when striking another might be revealed in the weapon used in the attack. A fist or a stick or stone that is picked up and used in the heat of a quarrel would not constitute a premeditated attack. In the case cited here, the victim lives proving the intention is not murder. If an injury results, leading to loss of work time, the attacker is to compensate the victim for time lost.

Ownership of slaves and rules regulating their tenure of service was dealt with in 21:1–11, while 21:20–21 deals specifically with injuries to slaves. If a slave is struck by his master and dies, the text states that master "must be punished." Genesis 9:6 would seem to indicate that the social status of a victim has nothing to do with the punishment of the offender; slave and master alike are made in the image of God. Therefore, we would naturally expect the same punishment here. Why the text does not explicitly state that the guilty slave master should be put to death is unclear. Regardless of how this verse is to be understood, it does signify that slaves have some protection under the law. This can be seen in more detail in verses 26–27 where bodily injuries occur to a slave that do not lead to death. The loss of a slave's eye means freedom for the slave, whereas other injuries follow the lex talionis.

Of special interest to many Christians are verses 22–25. Unfortunately, most translations leave the reader with a false impression, which has led in turn to the wrong application of this passage to the abortion issue. In short, this law deals with the results of a pregnant woman being struck (accidentally) by two men who are fighting. The result of this unfortunate attack is a "miscarriage" according to most English translations. The text continues: "[If] there is no serious injury, the offender must be fined. . . . if there is serious injury, you are to take life for life, eye for eye . . ." (v. 23). This has often been interpreted to mean that a miscarriage occurred. Then the issue becomes how the *mother* was affected—the implication being that the fetus really did not matter; it was not considered a human and the focus of attention was the mother. This passage is often conveniently used by advocates of abortion to say that since God did not demand punishment for the loss of the child, then the fetus did not have image-of-God status.

However, the Hebrew of 21:22 literally reads "and hit a pregnant woman so that her child(ren) come forth, and no harm follows, the one who hurt her shall be fined." Here the King James and New International translations are helpful. The Hebrew word for *miscarriage* is not used here. Our text portrays a woman being struck and then delivering prematurely.

The very passage used by some to support abortion, in fact, goes in the opposite direction. In this case the woman is accidentally struck, but if she or the child dies as a result, then the guilty party could be sentenced to death. This is the only instance in the Torah where involuntary manslaughter calls for the death penalty. Generally, the guilty party was to receive refuge from "the avenger of blood" and was not to be put to death (Deut. 19:4–10). Injury to the unborn is the only exception. The reason seems clear enough: God places high value on the unborn. The law always expresses concern for those least able to defend themselves.

Since Israel was an agrarian society, a number of the laws in the Torah deal directly with problems a farmer might face. Exodus **21:28–22:5** contains provisions that would fit into this category. The case of the goring ox is dealt with in verses 28–32. If an ox kills a man or woman, the ox is to be stoned to death. If the ox has a history of goring but has not killed anyone, the owner is warned. If the ox kills a man after this warning, then the owner is liable. In cases where an ox injures another ox, the "eye for eye, tooth for tooth" principle is applied (vv. 35–36).

One is responsible for injuries to another's animals, specifically if the animals fall into an open pit. Compensation for injury or loss of life is to be monetary or in kind (vv. 33–34).

Theft of livestock is the concern of 22:1–4. If the stolen animal is killed (butchered?) or sold, then restitution is to be made—fourfold for a sheep and fivefold for an ox. The difference has to do with the economic value placed on the respective beasts. If the thief is unable to make restitution (22:3), he is to be sold as a slave and the purchase price is then given to the person who suffered the loss. This difference suggests that man, who is to have dominion over the animals (Gen. 1:26), is of higher value in God's view.

Exodus **22:6–15** deals with responsibility for damage done to another's property and the loss of borrowed objects. Restitution is to be made to the party suffering the loss.

The next series of laws (**22:16–31**) are primarily related to social responsibilities. The seduction of an unbetrothed virgin requires that the man marry her. The father could always object to the marriage, in which case the seducer would still be required to pay the bridal price to the father (v. 17).

In the midst of this section of social laws is a segment that is concerned with pagan practices, all of which are capital offenses. Sorcery is not to be tolerated (v. 18; Deut. 18:9–14 contains an expanded list of such offenses). Bestiality (v. 19) was obviously a problem that would face Israel in Canaan, because this issue is mentioned several more times in the Pentateuch (Lev. 18:23; 20:16; Deut. 27:21). Verse 20 prohibits sacrificing to any other god. Apparently this is meant to make explicit a point not specifically mentioned in connection with the first two commandments (Exod. 20:3–5).

Verses 21–27 turn toward social-ethical issues. The law is concerned to protect everyone in the community of Israel, especially those whose rights might be ignored. The resident alien or sojourner could be easily exploited, not unlike migrant workers today. The Israelites should be especially sensitive about these people since they know all too well how sojourners could be mistreated after their experience in Egypt.

Loans are to be made without interest (v. 25), though one could hold a debtor's cloak as collateral, provided it was returned before sundown to keep him warm at night. During Amos's day the practice of returning the cloak was being ignored, which prompted a denunciation by the prophet (2:8).

The dishonoring of God is the subject of verse 28. The punishment for reviling or dishonoring God is spelled out in Leviticus 24:15–17. God's appointed ruler is not to be cursed either.

The second commandment prohibits the worship and service of other gods. "Service" includes the cultic aspects of worship: offerings and sacrifices. In **22:29–30** the Israelites are reminded of their "firstfruits" obligation, which is one aspect of "service."

Since Israel is a nation of priests (19:6) and priests are not to be defiled by or present impure offerings (including animals killed by predators; cf. Lev. 7:19–26; 17:15), the people are not to eat impure things, especially an animal killed by a predator.

Justice in Israel is the theme of **23:1–9.** Verses 1–3 appear to be a logical expansion of the eighth commandment. Conspiracy is certainly in mind in verse 1, while verses 2–3 are concerned with the general perversion of justice, especially against the poor who are easy victims of the rich. Later prophets note that this law was being violated (Isa. 33:15; Amos 5:12).

The Sabbath day observance is extended to the seventh year of rest or "sabbatical year" (**23:10–12**). During this year the land is not to be planted or harvested. The reason for this is twofold. The poor are to enjoy the produce of the land. This may mean that they were to harvest the wild crops or those that might naturally spring up due to the previous season's planting. Or perhaps on this year the poor could actually cultivate the land. This latter point seems less likely, because the second reason for the land lying fallow is that it might have rest (see Lev. 25:4). The advantages of this practice are clearly understood by modern farmers. The land is not continually deprived of nutrients (crop rotation and fertilization serve similar purposes).

The difference between 23:12 and 20:8–11 is that here an additional reason for observing the weekly Sabbath is made. It is for the "refreshment" of those upon whom the greatest work burden would fall: draught animals, slaves, and bondservants.

The third commandment forbids the misuse of God's name, while **23:13** prohibits any use or mention of pagan deities by name. An abuse of this law is seen in employing a pagan deity's name in personal names.

Every male Israelite is to appear before God (i.e., where the sanctuary is located) three times a year for special observances (**23:14–17**). The three occasions are Passover/Unleavened Bread; the Feast of Harvest (also called the Feast of Weeks/Pentecost; cf. Exod. 34:26; Lev. 23:10–22; Num. 28:26–31); and the Feast of Ingathering or the Feast of Tabernacles or Booths (cf. Lev. 23:33–36; Deut. 16:13–15). Put simply, Israel celebrated thanksgiving three times a year; and each person appearing before God was to bring some sort of thank offering. The types of acceptable offerings are briefly outlined in **23:18–19,** while much of Leviticus is devoted to a whole range of sacrifices and the various occasions and reasons for their presentations. The firstfruits principle, discussed already in 22:29–30, is reiterated in verse 19a.

Verse 19b reads, "Do not cook a young goat in its mother's milk." Traditionally in Judaism this verse was connected with dietary laws; hence it is not kosher to eat dairy and meat products at the same time. But the context of this passage—offerings—suggests otherwise. Most commentators maintain that this refers specifically to a Canaanite fertility ritual. This makes perfect sense. Verses 14–19 begin with the warning against appealing to pagan deities (23:13), and end with a mention of a specific pagan ritual. In the broader context of agricultural festivals, the connection with a Canaanite fertility practice is clearly what God is prohibiting.

Exodus **23:20–33** closes the stipulation section with promises and exhortations for Israel, especially as they relate to the conquest of Canaan. The location of this segment is puzzling, since the conquest would not begin for some time yet. In Numbers 10:11 the Hebrews depart from Sinai nearly a year later, heading for Canaan. The reason for mentioning the conquest at this point is because the land is the focus of the Abrahamic covenant, and God is now going to fulfill that promise. The Sinaitic covenant is quite naturally concerned about how God is going to achieve this and Israel's part in it.

If the Israelites obey the stipulations, they will enjoy God's protection. God's messenger will guard them (v. 20). He will instruct them and they should listen to him (v. 21). God's protection and guidance are provided by the messenger. Obedience to this messenger would apply to the movement of the cloud and Israel's following the divine directive (v. 23). Verse 23b mentions the occupants of the land at the time of the conquest. This same group of six nations was already introduced in 3:17, and the report of the spies in Numbers 13:29 informs us where some of these people lived. Israel is not to honor their deities in any way. It was common in the ancient Near East for the conqueror of a land to worship at the sanctuaries of his conquered people. But God alone is to be worshiped. Furthermore, Israel is to destroy the Canaanite sanctuaries. Covenants or treaties (probably the suzerainty-vassal type) are not to be made with the peoples of the land (v. 32).

God is going to overwhelm the residents of Canaan with terror and throw them into confusion (v. 27). The conquest of the Promised Land will not be instantaneous, but will take some time (v. 29). Otherwise the land will go wild and wild animals will occupy settled areas (cf. 2 Kings 17:25).

C. The covenant ceremony (24:1–18). Moses' part in the covenant ceremony is central. He alone is to "approach the LORD" (v. 2a), which implies an intercessory role. At the conclusion of the ceremony, Moses is ordered to return to the mountain to meet God and to receive "the tablets of stone" with the law and the commandments. With Joshua at his side (v. 13) Moses follows God's directive. This occasion is no different from the earlier appearance of Yahweh on Mount Sinai (19:16–20). The glory of God descends and the mountain is shrouded by a cloud. The glory of God is likened to a "consuming fire" (v. 17).

IV. Instructions for Israel's Sanctuary (25:1–31:18)

The fourth point of the covenant formula specified that the vassal had to have a copy of the treaty deposited in the national shrine. Now that the copy of the laws has been received, Israel quite naturally needs a repository. This explains the placement of the tabernacle instructions just after the conclusion of the covenant ceremony.

A. Preparations (25:1–9). The sanctuary was to be made from offerings brought by the people (vv. 1–2). These offerings were to be made voluntarily. God was and still is primarily concerned with the heart of the giver. From the list recorded in verses 3–7 it is clear that a wide variety of objects, ranging from gold and precious stones to animal skins and wool were needed for the construction. The sanctuary, a consecrated structure, was not just a repository for the law. It was also going to be God's dwelling-place. The structure is more specifically called "tabernacle."

B. The ark (25:10–22). Because the ark was the focal point of the sanctuary, God's glory would rest over it. Therefore it is dealt with first. It was to be a small rectangular chest made of acacia wood and overlaid with gold, measuring approximately three feet nine inches long and two feet three inches in height and width. It was to be carried by poles passing through rings affixed to the four bottom corners of the box. The lid (atonement cover) was to be made of solid gold. Over this cover were two winged figures or cherubim (the English transliteration of the Hebrew).

C. The table (25:23–30). In ancient temples, a table would be placed before the cult image of a deity and various food offerings would be presented to the god. So too with Yahweh. The table was to be furnished with food continually. Like the ark, this table was to be made of acacia wood overlaid with gold, and was to be carried by poles. The name *bread of Presence* (RSV) literally means "bread of face before me." It is clear that God does not need this food for nourishment, but that it symbolizes thankfulness for his provision of daily bread.

D. The lampstand (25:31–40). Candles would not have been used at this early date; rather small bowls held olive oil into which wicks were placed and lit. The lampstand had six branches, three on each side (v. 32).

E. The tabernacle (26:1–37). Essentially the tabernacle was a prefabricated structure that could be easily assembled and dismantled for travel. Tent-shrines were quite widely known in the ancient Near East. There has been considerable discussion by scholars on the configuration of the tabernacle; and many attempts have been made to execute models. But problems abound because the language is highly technical and the meaning of many words continues to elude us.

The structure was to be made of acacia poles or frames (v. 15) covered by various tapestries and animal-skin curtains. There were two parts to the main structure, the Holy Place and the Holy of Holies (where the ark was to be situated). These two areas were to be separated by a curtain. Judging from the dimensions of the materials which covered the tabernacle, it would have measured about forty-five feet long and fifteen feet wide, with the Holy of Holies measuring approximately fifteen feet square. Solomon's temple would utilize the pattern of the tabernacle, but he apparently doubled the size of the structure (2 Chron. 3:8, 15). The Holy Place housed the lampstand, table of the bread of Presence, and the incense altar. The ark of the covenant was in the Holy of Holies.

F. The altar (27:1–8). With the altar, we move outside of the tabernacle proper, for it was situated in the outer court. As with the ark, the altar was to be mobile. It was to be constructed of acacia wood covered with bronze, and was to measure roughly seven-and-one-half feet square and five feet in height. There may be some symbolic significance to the horns that were affixed to the corners of the altar. They probably served to secure animals on the altar. For ease of transport, the altar had carrying poles. Because the various sacrifices were presented and burnt on the altar, it was the most important cultic object in the court.

G. The courtyard (27:9–19). Surrounding the tabernacle was an enclosure or court. The court was made of linen curtains hanging over a series of poles. The court measured around 180 feet in length and seventy-five feet in width. Within the court most of the cultic activities took place. It is here that worshipers gathered, for only the priests could enter the tabernacle proper.

H. The oil (27:20–21). The Israelites are commanded to bring olive oil for the lamp in the tabernacle (v. 20). Since the oil was used within the Holy Place, verse 21 specifies that only Aaron's descendants will serve in this part of the sanctuary. When Uzziah enters the Holy Place to burn incense (2 Chron. 26:16–21), the priests confront him and have him removed from the temple.

In verse 21 the tabernacle is called the "tent of meeting." This expression is usually reserved for a different structure outside the camp so named by Moses (Exod. 33:7). The tabernacle, on the other hand, was at the center of the encampment. In the case of verse 21, the tabernacle is clearly in mind.

I. The priestly garments (28:1–43). The garb of the high priest was to be both holy and beautiful. The descriptions of the multicolored cloth and the precious stones that were used bear this out. Of special interest is the ephod (this is the actual Hebrew word, not a translation) or breastpiece (28:4, 15, 30). The breastpiece was inlaid with twelve stones, symbolizing the twelve tribes who would be represented whenever the priest carried out his duties.

Verse 30 informs us that the breastplate contained the Urim and Thummim. The text does not specify their function or purpose. These words apparently mean "curses" and "perfection," respectively. They functioned as lots. A question would be posed and God would answer "No" (Urim) or "Yes" (Thummim). The ephod or the Urim and Thummim could be consulted (cf. 1 Sam. 14:37; 23:9; 2 Sam. 2:1) and served as a means of ascertaining God's will.

J. Consecration of the priests (29:1–46). To qualify to serve as a priest in ancient Israel, one first had to be a member of the tribe of Levi, and specifically a son of Aaron, the brother of Moses. Second, the sons of Aaron had to undergo a specific initiation ritual that consecrated them for priestly service. This section lays down what is entailed in the rites of installation: washing, anointing, sacrifice, and ordination. A young bull and two rams are specified as the animals to be sacrificed.

The rites were to take place at the entrance to the "tent of meeting," involving ablutions (v. 4), the donning of the priestly regalia (v. 5), and anointing with oil. Later in Israelite history, kings would be anointed by prophets to show that they were designated by God for this office (1 Sam. 10:1; 16:13). Prior to the sacrifices being made, verse 9 states "Thus you shall ordain Aaron and his sons." The idiom rendered "ordain" (RSV, NASB, NIV) or "invest" (JB) is "fill the hand" and is known in cuneiform inscriptions from Mesopotamia related to the ordination of priests. It is not certain whether this expression is to be taken literally or figuratively. Gifts are placed in the priest's hand in verses 23–24; while in verses 27–28 and 34, "ordination" is mentioned in connection with the perpetual offerings of the priesthood.

The types of offerings are the sin offering (v. 14), whole burnt offerings (v. 18), the anointing of the priest's extremities with the blood of the rams (vv. 19–21), and the wave offering (vv. 22–28). Further information about these offerings and their signification is detailed in Leviticus 3–5 and 7–9.

A number of regulations are related to the consecration. Verse 29 notes that the priestly garb will be passed on to the successor of Aaron. The priest now considered "holy" can eat the edible parts of the sacrifice.

One of the daily duties of the priest was to preside over the morning and evening sacrifice of a lamb (v. 39). These daily, perpetual offerings are a constant reminder of man's need for atonement so that God might dwell among his people.

K. The altar of incense (30:1–10). Why the altar of incense was not dealt with earlier when instructions were given for the other objects in the Holy Place is uncertain. The function of this altar was solely for burning incense (30:1, 7–10). It might be recalled that Zechariah, father of John the Baptist, was burning incense at the altar in the temple when the angel appeared to him (Luke 1:8–9, 11). This altar was also where the seraphim picked up a burning coal to apply to Isaiah's lips (Isa. 6:6–7). The purpose of burning incense is never stated here. Incense may have purified cultic objects and people (vv. 23–29; Num. 16:46). Incense would also have a deodorizing influence on the sanctuary, which must have reeked with the smell of blood and burning animal flesh. Symbolically, burning incense was associated with prayer (Ps. 141:2; Luke 1:9–10; Rev. 5:8; 8:3–4).

L. The offering (30:11–16). It is unclear why this monetary offering or taxation should be dealt with here amid instructions concerning cult-related objects. In that the half shekel offering was for atonement purposes (v. 12), it may be thematically linked to the other sections.

The purpose of this offering is for the cost of upkeeping the tabernacle (v. 16). Since the preceding section deals with incense, one can only speculate as to the possibility that some of this money would have been used to purchase incense, which was costly and had to be imported from Arabia and Africa (cf. Jer. 6:20).

M. The laver (30:17–21). Located between the altar and the tabernacle was the laver, a round bronze vessel that was to hold water for the purification of the priests who were to wash their hands and feet before performing their duties.

N. The anointing oil and incense (30:22–36). A variety of exotic spices and aromatic substances were to be mixed together to consecrate objects in the sanctuary and the priests. Since these were for sacred purposes, they were not for common use by the people.

O. Bezalel and Oholiab (31:1–10). In order to make the artistic utensils for the tabernacle as well as the structure itself, great skill and craftsmanship were required. Bezalel of the tribe of Judah was to direct the work with assistance from Oholiab. It should not be assumed that these two men did all the work; rather, they were the skilled artisans who directed the work. Verse 3 indicates that Bezalel was specially gifted by God to do this work. His abilities are "wisdom," "understanding," and "knowledge" (KJV). These terms, well-known in Hebrew wisdom literature, demonstrate that the concepts bound up in these words are quite broad. "Wisdom" and "understanding" are better rendered "skill" or "skilful" (NIV, NEB) and "ability" or "perception."

P. Sabbath instructions (31:12–18). Sabbath regulations have been given already in 20:8–11 and 23:12–13. This exhortation comes just after God has instructed the people about the work on the tabernacle. This suggests that even work on God's tabernacle was under Sabbath regulations.

Verse 18 indicates that the forty-day period which Moses spent on the mountain (24:18) has come to an end. However, this does not mark the end of the revelations that Moses is to receive.

V. Apostasy and Intercession (32:1–33:23)

This section recounts Israel's greatest apostasy in Sinai, the making and worship of the golden calf. God naturally has to judge this sin and once again Moses emerges as Israel's intercessor.

A. The golden calf (32:1–33:6). The people want to get on with their trek to Canaan and grow impatient. They ask Aaron to make "gods" to lead them on their way since they do not know what has become of Moses (v. 1). Aaron makes a single image of gold, usually translated as "calf." Even though a single image is made, Aaron's cry is "These are your gods, O Israel, who brought you up out of Egypt!" (v. 4). Is Aaron introducing a new god or new gods? It is most likely that Aaron and the people envisioned this image as a physical representation of God.

God informs Moses of what is taking place at the foot of the mountain. In referring to the Israelites as "stiff-necked" (v. 9), he means that they are obstinate and stubborn. Justifiably, God is angry and ready to wipe out his people and make a nation of Moses' descendants.

Moses immediately begins to intercede as he has done several times before. Moses is concerned that God's reputation might be lessened in the eyes of the Egyptians if word comes of Israel's demise in the desert (v. 12). He also appeals to the patriarchal promise to give Israel the land (v. 13). How can this be fulfilled if Israel is obliterated? So God relents.

Moses goes down the mountain and at a lower level meets Joshua, who hears the noise and thinks that a battle is raging. Upon seeing what is taking place, Moses angrily throws down the two stones and breaks them. Perhaps Moses was hoping to nullify the covenant and thus avoid its curses. Even though God had decided against annihilating Israel, it did not mean that there would be no punitive action taken.

Aaron is chided for his part in the apostasy but his priesthood remains intact. Moses calls for those who are on Yahweh's side to join him. Moses' own tribe, the Levites, has stayed true to God and is called upon to execute the image worshipers; three thousand are cut down (v. 28). Since God sends a plague after this for additional judgment, it would appear that the action of the Levites was directed against the ringleaders of the rebellion while the plague afflicted all the participants. The fidelity of the Levites wins them a special place in the service of God in the tabernacle (v. 39).

Apparently Moses did not think that the three thousand who died were the only guilty ones, for he tries to further intercede, perhaps hoping to ward off the plague. Moses offers his own life in exchange for the salvation of his people. He offers that his name be blotted out of "your book" (v. 32). This might be the same book referred to in Isaiah 4:3 and Psalm 69:28. In Daniel 12:1 "the book" is clearly used for judgment of the just and unjust. This makes it appear that there is a heavenly record of the righteous and wicked. But this concept may have developed from the practice of recording the names of the people who had sworn their loyalty to the covenant, as in Nehemiah 9:38–10:1. In this case, Moses would be removing himself from the covenant community and God's blessings, not necessarily from God's salvation.

God will allow the people to go to Canaan and the promised angel will accompany them, but God himself will be distant from them, coming only to judge (v. 34).

Hearing this, the people mourn their fate and as a sign of their distress, take off their ornaments. The people recognize that their ornaments had been used to make the golden image, and so from this point they no longer wear their jewelry (v. 6), apparently fearing they might be misled again.

B. The tent of meeting (33:7–23). Earlier, "the tent of meeting" (e.g., 27:21; 30:18) refers to the tabernacle. Here we are introduced to another tent which Moses pitched outside the camp and called "the tent of meeting." This tent is not a place for offerings and sacrifices; its function is oracular and prophetic (Num. 11:24–25). Here Moses plays an intercessory role (vv. 8–9) just as Aaron does in cultic matters in the tabernacle. In this tent God speaks with Moses "face to face" (v. 11a).

Verses 12–16 contain Moses' response to God's statement in verses 1–3. He is apparently not satisfied with God's plan to distance himself from his people. Moses appeals to God on the basis of his relationship with God and the "favor" God has toward him, hoping that God will go with his people. God responds by saying, "My Presence will go with you [sing., i.e., Moses]" (v. 14). Verse 16 makes it clear that Moses cannot separate himself from his people. He wants God's blessing to be on them as well as him. Israel is distinct from other peoples only by virtue of God's presence.

God agrees to do as Moses requests. Seeing his success in interceding for his people, Moses now wants to experience more of God's presence, apparently building on God's earlier statement (v. 14). His request, "show me your glory" (v. 18), is somewhat odd since he had witnessed God's glory previously (24:9–11, 15–18) and in 33:11 we are informed that Moses and God communicated directly. It seems then that Moses desires to know more of God's character and person than he has experienced to this point.

God will only partially fulfill Moses' request; he will let his goodness pass before him (v. 19) for no man can see God's face and live. God further says that when his goodness passes before Moses, the name *Yahweh* will be proclaimed as part of the theophany. The proclamation of the divine name might hint that something of God's eternal qualities are revealed to Moses. But even in this manifestation Moses has to be protected (vv. 21–22). God's glory is to be more fully revealed in Jesus Christ: "we have seen his glory, the glory of the One and Only, who came from the Father" (John 1:14).

VI. The New Tablets (34)

Since Moses had broken the first set of tablets which contained the Ten Commandments (and presumably the laws of chaps. 20–23 and 25–31) and Israel had been pardoned, new tablets are needed.

Moses is directed to prepare two stone tablets to replace the first set. Moses is to ascend the mountain yet again. As with the previous theophany, the mountain is to be cordoned off to all for God will descend to the peak for this revelation (34:3, 5; cf. 19:12–13, 16–23).

The opening words of God's discourse (vv. 6–7) represent one of the lengthiest descriptions of the character of God in Scripture. It is similar to 20:5–6, but there is greater emphasis on the mercy and forgiveness of God. This he has just proven in pardoning Israel after the golden calf incident. At these words, Moses prostrates himself and worships.

God agrees once again to make a covenant with Israel, and a brief summary of the stipulations follow (presumably the laws of chaps. 20–23 derive from the new copies which are written at this time). The emphases in these stipulations are: (1) observe God's commandments (v. 11a); (2) follow conquest regulations (vv. 11b–16); (3) make no images (v. 17); and (4) obey worship regulations (vv. 18–26).

God instructs Moses to write "these words." Moses is God's scribe, just as Baruch records Jeremiah's dictations (Jer. 36:4) and Silas writes for Peter (1 Pet. 5:12). Like before, Moses spends forty days communing with God and recording the laws (v. 28a).

"And he wrote on the tablets . . ." (v. 28). Is God or Moses the writer? Perhaps this ambiguity is designed to show the cooperative nature of the recording process.

This meeting with God is obviously different than the previous one, because Moses now radiates God's glory when he returns to the camp (34:29), a phenomenon that has not occurred before. The radiance is too much for the people, so Moses veils himself. In fact, whenever he communicates new messages he receives while in the tent of meeting, he will put the veil back over his face.

VII. Execution of Sanctuary Instructions (35:1–40:38)

This section is a near duplication of chapters 25–31. The use of repetition in Semitic literature is a method of emphasizing the importance of something, and that may be the case here. Further, the fact that God orders the tabernacle built indicates that he would reside with his people in spite of their apostasy.

It should be noted that the form of this section is different than the earlier one, which records God's instructions to Moses. Exodus 35–40, on the other hand, begins with Moses' report of God's instructions to the people. As each part of the tabernacle and its utensils are mentioned, we are told that they are made in accordance with God's command.

Moses assembles the whole community and presents God's commandments concerning the sanctuary (**35:1–3**). The initial tabernacle instructions conclude with Sabbath laws (31:12–17); here Moses' instructions begin with this injunction.

Moses directs the people to make their contributions for the project (**35:4–29;** par. 25:1–9). The major differences here are that all who are skilled can participate in the work (v. 10) and we see the response of the people (vv. 20–29). Many are willing (lit. whose hearts were lifted up) and their contributions are recorded in verses 22–29.

Bezalel and Oholiab are once again designated as the head artisans (**35:30–36:7**). Unlike the earlier passage, we are told that every skilled individual was invited to work (36:2) and that Oholiab and Bezalel instructed other artisans (35:35).

The instructions for the tabernacle (**36:8–38**) are virtually identical to those in 26:1–37, with only minor changes in tenses of verbs and difference in person. A noticeable change in the order between the earlier instructions and the execution is that the tabernacle is discussed first whereas the ark was the beginning point in God's instructions to Moses. The reason for this variation is not certain, but different perspectives on the sanctuary may be the rationale. In chapters 25–31 the order moves from the ark (located in the Holy of Holies), to the objects in the Holy Place, and then to the tabernacle itself. The actual execution reverses this order, beginning with the tabernacle, and then going to the contents of the tabernacle in the same order as 25:10–40. However, the lampstand is included along with the objects of the Holy Place (25–29), not as it had been in the first section.

Three parts of the construction are outlined:

Curtains	36:8–19//26:1–14
Frames	36:20–34//26:15–32
Screen	36:35–38//26:33–35

Bezalel is said to have made the ark (**37:1–9**), whereas Moses says "so I made the ark" in Deuteronomy 10:3. Moses is not actually taking credit for making the ark; rather, he directed the work and made certain that it was executed according to the divine pattern.

Exodus **37:10–16** presupposes knowledge of God's instructions for the table of the bread of Presence in 25:23–30, for the function of this table is not mentioned here. It is simply called "the table."

The lampstand or menorah is made (**37:17–24**) in accordance with the instructions of 25:31–40. The lampstand and its accessories are molded out of one talent of gold, or about seventy-five pounds.

The altar for burning incense (**37:25–29**) is crafted as specified in 30:1–5. An additional note informs us that the sacred oils and incense are prepared as spelled out in 30:22–38.

Since the tabernacle and its contents have been completed, the work on the court follows. With only a few variations, **38:1–7** parallels 27:1–8. As before, the altar is the first item dealt with from the court.

The bronze laver receives only passing mention (**38:8**). We are told that it was made and, of course, would have conformed to the specifications of 30:17–21. A new piece of information provided is that the bronze for the laver came from the mirrors of the women who served or ministered at the entrance to the tent of meeting. The mirrors were undoubtedly brought along from Egypt. These would have been highly polished bronze or copper discs mounted on wooden or metal handles. What exactly these women did at the tent of meeting (here likely referring to the tent that Moses had pitched in 33:7) is not stated.

Finally the court which surrounded the tabernacle and the area of sacrifice is constructed (**38:9–20**) following the instructions of 27:9–19.

If our understanding of ancient Israelite measures are correct, then just over one ton of gold, four tons of silver, and three tons of copper are used (**38:21–31**). This is a clear indication of the richness and beauty of this structure. God alone is worthy of such tribute.

The garments of the priests receive considerable attention here (**39:1–31**) as they did when

God instructed Moses in 28:6–43. At the conclusion of making each piece of the priestly apparatus or clothing, the text emphatically states that it was done as God had commanded Moses (39:1b, 5, 7, 21, 26, 29, 31). This sevenfold repetition stresses the care taken to carry out God's instructions.

The completed work is brought to Moses for his assessment (**39:32–43**) for he had received the divine instructions and would logically be in the best position to approve the finished product. Note again that this section begins and ends with the statement of the faithful execution of the tabernacle and its furnishings: "just as the LORD commanded Moses" (39:32b, 42). Moses places his seal of approval upon the work by noting that it was done "just as the LORD had commanded" (39:43), so he blesses the workers for their efforts.

God orders Moses to erect the tent on the first day of the first month, or New Year's day (**40:1–16**). In so doing, Israel is entering a new era. Furthermore, it would be symbolically connected to God's creation which took place at the beginning of time. Also, the tabernacle would be ready for the observance of Passover two weeks later.

God explains to Moses where all the furnishings of the tabernacle are to be placed (vv. 3–8) and orders that the objects be consecrated with the sacred oil (vv. 9–11). Then Aaron and his sons are consecrated (in accordance with 29:1–46) and dressed in the noble garments.

Moses faithfully carries out God's directives (**40:17–33**) and once again a sevenfold "as the LORD commanded" is used to indicate the precision of execution (40:19, 21, 23, 25, 27, 29, 32). Verse 17 dates the erection of the tabernacle to New Year's day "in the second year," that is, the second year after the exodus, two weeks before the actual second anniversary of Passover.

The tabernacle is now ready for its divine occupant (**40:34–38**). The glory of God had taken up temporary residence in the tent of meeting (i.e., Moses' tent, 33:7–9) and could now relocate to the tabernacle (vv. 34–35). This represents the climax of the book. God's glory that had appeared on the mountain during the covenant ceremony (19:16–20; 24:15–18) some distance from the people, will now accompany Israel wherever she goes. God thereby fulfills an important aspect of the patriarchal promise, "I will be with you," and cements his relationship with Israel. God's glory would be transferred to the temple when it was built (2 Chron. 7:1–3). That same glory would depart when Judah's sins reached the point where God's sacred presence could no longer tolerate the situation (Ezek. 10:18; 11:22–23) and the temple would be destroyed. But after the exile when the temple would be rebuilt, God's glory once again would fill the Most Holy Place (Hag. 2:7–9). Ultimately that glory would be revealed in Jesus Christ: "The Word became flesh and made his dwelling [lit. tabernacled] among us. We have seen his glory, the glory of the One and Only, who came from the Father, full of grace and truth" (John 1:14).

SELECT BIBLIOGRAPHY

Bright, J. *A History of Israel.* 3d ed. Philadelphia: Westminster, 1981.

Childs, B. S. *The Book of Exodus.* Philadelphia: Westminster, 1974.

Cole, R. A. *Exodus: An Introduction and Commentary.* Downers Grove: Inter-Varsity, 1973.

Hyatt, J. P. *Exodus.* Grand Rapids: Eerdmans, 1980.

Noth, M. *Exodus.* Philadelphia: Westminster, 1962.

LEVITICUS

Louis Goldberg

INTRODUCTION

The Book of Leviticus is the third book of the Pentateuch. Its Hebrew title, from the first word of the book, is *wayyiqrā'*, "and he called." In the Septuagint, the book is called *Leuitikon* or *Leueitikon*, "pertaining to the Levites." The Latin Vulgate translated the Septuagint title as *Liber Leviticus*, "the book of Leviticus," which then became the book's title in the English Bible.

While Leviticus pertains to the duties of priests and Levites, it also concerns sacrifices, moral regulations, guidelines for observing holidays, tithes, and offerings, and in general, the call for obedience to God's covenant.

While in many places in Exodus, Numbers, and Deuteronomy mention is made of Moses recording what God has revealed to him, nowhere in Leviticus does it indicate that he wrote down what the Lord shared with him. However, there are at least three factors pointing to the Mosaic authorship of this book.

First, because God does speak to Moses in Leviticus (e.g., 1:1; 8:1; 11:1), we would presume that as an obedient servant, he wrote down whatever was revealed to him.

Second, a further proof for Mosaic authorship is the similarity of the covenant form of Leviticus 26 to the Sinaitic covenant of Exodus 20–23. It is only logical that Moses expanded what he had already recorded.

Third, the Pentateuch is a unit. Genesis relates how Israel begins as a family and settles in Egypt. Exodus carries the narrative further, describing how Israel as a nation departs from Egypt and is led by Moses to Sinai where the law is given. Leviticus is an expansion of this law, directing Israel to proper worship of the Lord and a life-style pleasing to him. Numbers describes the wilderness experiences and confirms that the people finally reach the banks of the Jordan. Deuteronomy details how God has led Israel to the Promised Land and describes how Moses repeats, expands, and reinterprets the law given at Sinai. The point is that the Pentateuch is a progressive whole with just enough overlap and repetition to reflect the work of one author, Moses.

While we have no question that Moses wrote Leviticus and the rest of the Pentateuch, we do need to consider briefly critical statements on the unity of this book, including how it was put together and who wrote it.

The documentary hypothesis of K. H. Graf (1815–1869) and J. Wellhausen (1844–1918) posited that four sources (documents) could be identified in the Pentateuch: J, passages from Genesis and Exodus that use the name *Jehovah* (ca. 850 B.C.); E, passages from Genesis and Exodus containing the name *Elohim* (ca. 750 B.C.); D or Deuteronomy (ca. 621 B.C.); and finally, P or Priestly source (ca. 450 B.C.), which includes the Book of Leviticus and other portions of the Pentateuch. Redactors along the way and at the end produced the Pentateuch as we have it by approximately 200 B.C. Graf and Wellhausen also maintained that the oral materials concerning the beginnings of Israel prior to the earliest documents were based on a confusing assortment of myths and legends, and that Moses was a legendary figure.

There are problems with the documentary hypothesis: (1) it is based on an evolutionary development of Israel's religion, implying that no well-developed concepts of sin and sacrifice were possible until after the Babylonian exile (ca. 500 B.C.); and (2) it is not supported by the best archaeological research of the twentieth century. The concepts of worship, sacrifice for sin, and the ritual involved with the sacrifice were not as primitive as the supporters of the documentary hypothesis maintained. Even though the ancient religions were idolatrous, they were extremely complicated. If this is true of the pagan worship system, it is reasonable to assume that Israel also had a highly developed worship system, given by the God of Israel. The evolutionary reconstruction of Israel's worship simply does not square with the claims of Exodus, Leviticus, and Deuteronomy.

A. Klostermann, in *Der Pentateuch* (1877), described Leviticus 17–26 as a separate law code, calling it the "holiness code" (H). He believed that these chapters represented a special unit within the Book of Leviticus, constituting a collection of laws written during the Babylonian exile possibly by Ezekiel, and then incorporated in Leviticus after the exile. Klostermann maintained that this H code had certain points of resemblance with the Book of the Covenant (Exod. 20–23), and especially Deuteronomy and Ezekiel. Klostermann did not consider Moses to be the author.

In reply to Klostermann's claim, we can point to the abundance of archaeological materials from 2000–1500 B.C. and maintain that the entire Book of Leviticus could very easily have been written by Moses during this period. For example, with the early presence of highly developed moral standards in Israel, a prophet would naturally use what had been in existence for a long period of time; it is not necessary to insist that Ezekiel composed Leviticus 17:1–26:46 as a moral standard for the remnant of Israel during the Babylonian exile.

Furthermore, in response to the claim that Ezekiel used materials from the Book of Deuteronomy (which supposedly appeared only in 621 B.C.) and incorporated them in a so-called H code, we can reply that current archaeological information does not support such a position. Furthermore, since the curses and blessings of Leviticus 26 and Deuteronomy 28 bear a resemblance to the Sinai covenant of Exodus, then Leviticus must be placed earlier in the second millennium B.C. By insisting that the H code appeared after the exile, we have a strange out-of-date sequence for the formulae of blessings and curses normally found in a suzerainty treaty.

The form-critical school gave up on the so-called written documents which Wellhausen proposed and declared instead that Israel had an original sacred oral tradition that was passed on and embellished by the people. The objective of form criticism is to attempt to discover what these original traditional materials were by examining parallel information from various cultures in the Middle East.

One basic problem with the form-critical concept is that if practically all of Israel's neighbors in the second millennium B.C., and some a thousand years earlier, were recording all kinds of literature in written form, why suggest that Israel began with a smaller body of tradition and not until a thousand years later produced a fully written form of their sacred books?

Much of what has been developed in reply to critical claims gives us a clue as to the date of the composition of Leviticus. The complicated worship systems of Israel's pagan neighbors of 2000–1500 B.C. suggest that Moses could have written down the complex worship system detailed by the God of Israel. Since these nations also possessed complicated law systems, Israel could also have developed a refined legal code. Finally, the suzerainty treaties of the second millennium B.C. are very similar to the Mosaic covenant. While Moses received the revelation of God, he also used and adapted the covenant form of his day, fashioning it for Israel's needs as a unique people of the Lord.

When we examine the internal evidence of the Pentateuch, some interesting facts emerge regarding the date of Leviticus. The Passover took place on the fourteenth day of the first month of the exodus (Exod. 12:2, 3, 6), and the tabernacle was set up one year later on the first day of the first month in the second year (Exod. 40:1). The Book of Numbers begins with the first day of the second month in the second year (Num. 1:1). Therefore, the information contained in Leviticus could only have been given sometime between the first Passover and the erection of the tabernacle. During the time of the wilderness experience, there would have been ample opportunity for Moses to prepare the final form of the Book of Leviticus.

The purpose of Leviticus is fourfold. First, Israel had to realize that because of God's revelation of his sacred character, the people also had to be holy. Israel was to live as a nation set apart to God in a special way.

Second, the Israelites were to separate themselves from the pagan nations around them. Because of the idolatry and immorality of these nations, Israel was not to have contact with them.

A third purpose was to teach Israel some important truths. God is gracious and merciful and makes it possible for his people to find atonement for their sins and to yield their lives in dedication to his will. Israel had indeed been called to be a blessing to all nations (Gen. 12:3). Through their witness, pagan peoples could also have an opportunity to respond to God's truths.

Fourth, Israel had received the Ten Commandments. However, these were not given so that the people could earn their salvation, but were to serve as a guide to a pious life-style. The commandments also functioned as a moral standard by which nations and individuals would be judged.

"Holy" (or "holiness") is a key word in Leviticus, occurring some eighty-seven times. At Mount Sinai Israel had been confronted by the holiness of God when he revealed himself amid thunder and lightning in a thick cloud (Exod. 19:16). His presence was so awesome that everyone trembled in the camp. That same God reveals himself in the Book of Leviticus.

Because God is holy, Israel was to acknowledge him as the one true God and was never to worship any other gods. To do so would be a terrible affront to God's holiness. Neither were the people of Israel to consult mediums and diviners. God could only interpret this involvement as an attack upon his sacred character.

There is a distinct connection between God's holiness and moral and ritual cleanness. Leviticus was to be Israel's guide to purity of life. Food was designated clean and unclean. Because life and blood are synonomous (17:11), there had to be a reverence for life and the blood which represents life; to ignore this was contrary to the holiness of God.

Instructions were also provided concerning what to do about temporary uncleanness. Persistent skin diseases required special attention. Specific rituals were necessary before healed individuals could be fully accepted back into society.

Those who broke Israel's moral laws were regarded as unclean; there was to be no atonement for these indiscretions. Such unnatural acts were considered contrary to God's holiness, and called for the death penalty.

One of the features of the law was to remind people that they were sinners. But when individual Israelites sinned, God mercifully provided sacrifices, making atonement possible to anyone who wanted it.

Leviticus provided Israel with an absolute moral which, in its application, made for the best possible relations in many areas of life. Chapter 18 is dedicated to the family, defending the marriage relationship and detailing the proper place of children within the family. All the commandments are further interpreted and applied in chapter 19 to a number of areas of life. In chapter 20, careful guidelines are then given to judge and remove offenders from among the holy people of God.

The covenant is expanded in Leviticus. Chapters 1–7 detail how worship should be observed; chapters 8–10 describe the priests and their office; and chapters 11–25 describe the model life-style. Chapter 26 is an actual covenant document, complete with both blessings and curses, spelling out the consequences of obedience and disobedience.

For many Christians, Leviticus is a closed book. However, it is an important one because it provides much of the background for the sacrifice of Jesus the Messiah as well as the life-style which Paul commends in the New Testament.

A word of caution, however, needs to be observed in studying Leviticus. Many Christians tend to ignore what the text meant to individual Israelites or to the community of Israel in Old Testament times and go immediately to a type study of Jesus and how he fulfilled many parts of Leviticus in the New Testament. We must first examine the text to see what it meant for Old Testament Israel. Only then can we proceed to a study of Jesus.

Finally, we note this book's relevance for today. Because the law has been written upon our hearts as believers, we can appreciate how the moral law in Leviticus sets forth the proper way to live a godly life in this world.

OUTLINE

- I. The Offerings (1:1–7:38)
  - A. General Regulations (1:1–6:7)
  - B. Priestly Regulations (6:8–7:38)
- II. The Priesthood (8:1–10:20)
  - A. Consecration (8:1–36)
  - B. Installation (9:1–24)
  - C. Consequences of Disobedience (10:1–20)
- III. Cleanness and Uncleanness (11:1–16:34)
  - A. Regulations (11:1–15:33)
  - B. The Day of Atonement (16:1–34)
- IV. The Holiness Code (17:1–26:46)
  - A. The Sanctity of Blood (17:1–16)
  - B. Moral Laws (18:1–20:27)
  - C. Priestly Regulations (21:1–22:33)
  - D. Worship Calendar (23:1–44)
  - E. Oil, Bread, and Blasphemy (24:1–33)
  - F. The Sabbath Year and Jubilee (25:1–55)
  - G. Rewards and Punishments (26:1–46)
  - H. Vows and Tithes (27:1–34)

COMMENTARY

I. The Offerings (1:1–7:38)

A. General regulations (1:1–6:7). While the sacrificial system had been mentioned briefly when the Mosaic covenant was introduced (see Exod. 23:14–19; 24:5–8), it needed to be spelled out in greater detail in order for the people to properly worship the Lord. Leviticus teaches Israel how to approach God through sacrifices.

After the fall, a barrier existed between God and man. Perhaps God explained to Adam and Eve how atonement for sin could be attained through sacrifice, but in succeeding generations this truth had either been lost or perverted by pagan idolatry, except for isolated witnesses here and there. Now, however, through Israel, God intends to provide the knowledge of atonement. In the sacrificial system with its sin and guilt offerings, the barrier between God and man could be removed: and once an individual entered the family of God, other offerings enhanced the fellowship a redeemed person could have with the Lord.

The sin offering (**4:1–5:13**) actually takes precedence over the burnt offering of chapter 1, at least in the procedural order of the sacrifices. In the three times in the Book of Exodus when God says, "I will meet with you" (25:22; 29:42; 30:36) the progression in the believer's relationship with God is pictured.

Atonement took place at the mercy seat above the ark of the covenant. The high priest could enter the Holy of Holies only on the Day of Atonement. On other occasions the blood from offerings was sprinkled on the curtain which hung in front of the mercy seat: its application was as if it had been applied on the mercy seat.

Dedication occurred at the altar of burnt offering in front of the tabernacle (later, the temple). After a person had received atonement from sin, he was then to yield himself to the Lord's will. Following dedication, *communion and fellowship* with the Lord were confirmed through the incense offered at the table standing in front of the curtain.

We will follow the progression of worship indicated in these passages from Exodus, recognizing, however, that Moses actually starts with the dedicatory and thanksgiving offerings in Leviticus (chaps. 1–3), primarily because everyone knew about these offerings. After presenting what the people know, he then proceeds to the truth of atonement, which, apart from God's revelation, is either perverted or forgotten.

Moses carefully explains the necessity of the sin offering: "when anyone sins unintentionally" (v. 2). But what does it mean to sin inadvertently? A person can sin and not even be aware of it. The sin offering reminds the Israelites that one is a sinner by virtue of his or her very nature.

Various sin offerings are to be presented depending on who has sinned: for the priest, a bull (4:3); for the entire Israelite community, a bull (4:13); for the leaders, a male goat (4:23); and for the common people, a female goat (4:28), a female lamb (4:32), a pair of turtle doves or pigeons (one for the sin offering; 5:7), or one-tenth of an ephah of fine flour (5:11). While God requires that everyone bring an offering, we also see his mercy at work, making it possible for each person to provide an offering according to his or her means.

The priest has to offer the most expensive offering, even though he might be poor, because his position is so important in the community. If he fails, the laypeople might also fail and be led astray.

In the case of the bull offered for the priest or the people, the fat and inner parts of the sacrifice, the best parts, are offered on the altar. The blood is sprinkled seven times on the curtain in front of the Holy of Holies and is placed on the horns of the altar of incense. The rest is poured out at the base of the altar of burnt offering standing at the entrance. What is left of the carcass is then taken outside the camp and burned. In the other cases, the priest can eat of the flesh while what is left is then burned outside the camp (see also 6:24–30).

Four major principles can be derived from this sacrifice:

1. *Substitution.* When the offerer brought his particular animal to the altar, it took the place of the offerer.
2. *Identification.* As the offerer placed his hands on the head of the animal, he confessed his sins. The sin of the offerer was thereby transferred to the substitute which then became sin.
3. *Death of the substitute.* The offerer now killed the animal because it had become sin. If no substitute had been provided, then every person would have had to die in his own sins (Ezek. 18:4). However, a merciful God provided one who was to die in place of the offerer.
4. *Exchange of life.* While this principle is difficult to derive from the text, nevertheless, it relates to the meaning of atonement. When the animal died as a substitute, bearing the sin life of the offerer through identification, it gave up *its own life* to the offerer, thereby effecting an exchange of life. The offerer could now have a new life.

The Israelites could respond in one of three ways to the sin offering: (1) *total unconcern*, becoming agnostics or turning to pagan deities; (2) *ritualism*, bringing sacrifices and going through the motions of offering them; (3) *belief*, accepting by faith the four principles and internalizing them.

It was not necessary that each Israelite look forward to the cross to see the Messiah dying for his or her sin. While some of the more spiritual Israelites recognized some fulfillment in the future (Isa. 53), most became believers simply by being obedient to what Moses had specified. From the human point of view, they found salvation from their sins, but from God's point of view, their sacrifices were ratified through the one supreme sacrifice of the coming Messiah (Heb. 10:12).

The definite type-antitype teaching of the Old Testament sin offering can be recognized in the person and ministry of Jesus the Messiah as he died for our sins. Even as the animal had to be perfect, without blemish, so Jesus himself was perfect (1 Pet. 3:18). Even as the substitute in the Old Testament became sin for the offerer through identification and had to die, so Jesus, when he identified with us, bore our sins in his body on the cross, thereby dying for our sins (1 Pet. 2:24). Just as the substitute animal died, giving its life to the offerer, so likewise, when Jesus died, he gave believers access to his life (John 17:2, 3; Rom. 5:10).

The principles of atonement in the sin offering do not change from the Old Testament to the New Testament. However, instead of an animal, Jesus is the sin offering. When a person receives Christ, he recognizes him as his substitute, placing his hands by faith upon Christ's head and confessing his sins. The believer acknowledges that Jesus has become sin, and reckons that Jesus died for him because the penalty of sin required death, but that God has provided a substitute who died on his behalf. Through the exchange of life, the new believer now has within him the life of Christ. Finally, in a special sense, even as the carcass of the sin offering was taken outside the camp and burned, so too we are reminded that Jesus suffered outside the city gate to make us holy (Heb. 13:11–14).

While the sin offering atones for the sin nature of an individual, the guilt offering is for specific acts of sin, intentional or inadvertent, against God or man (**5:14–6:7**). The two offerings are quite distinct.

The animal offered is a ram. The same four principles for the sin offering also apply to the guilt offering: (1) the ram served as a substitute; (2) the offerer had to identify with the animal, confessing his sins; (3) the offerer then killed the animal while the priest took its blood and applied it in the proper place; and (4) there was an exchange of life. Unlike the sin offering, the guilt offering also involved *restitution*. For example, when a tithe to God was withheld, it eventually had to be paid, plus one-fifth more as a fine. The Israelites had to learn that it was better to be consistently faithful to God. On the other hand, when no specific sin was mentioned or even known, the offerer then offered only the ram with no restitution.

If anyone stole, cheated, or extorted (6:1–7), restitution consisted of the value of whatever was taken, plus one-fifth of its value, paid to the person who was wronged. Next, the offerer provided a guilt offering to the Lord. The guilt offering, like the sin offering, also atones for sin.

The prophet Isaiah recognized the connection between the type and antitype: "the LORD makes his life a guilt offering" (Isa. 53:10). The Messiah was not only to atone for our sin nature, but also for every individual sin as well.

Just as the ram had to be perfect, so Jesus is without defect (1 Pet. 1:19). Just as the ram was the substitute for the offerer in the guilt offering, so Jesus is our substitute (1 Pet. 2:24). Just as each specific sin was placed on the ram, making it sin so that the offerer had to kill it, so likewise each sin placed on our Substitute called for his death (1 Cor. 15:3; Heb. 9:28). Because of his death, we receive his life.

We must continually look to Jesus and appropriate his death on the cross for our individual sins. We are not to continue in sin that grace may abound, but rather, when we do sin, we have an advocate with the Father, Jesus Christ the Righteous (1 John 2:1). The fact that he can plead for every one of our sins is because his death as a guilt offering atones for each sin, whether against God or our fellow man.

In addition, however, there is the restitution factor. What was true in the Old Testament remains true in the New Testament. Jesus says that if someone should be offering a gift at the altar but remembers that his brother has something against him, he first has to make restitution and then he can offer his sacrifice to God (Matt. 5:23–24). Jesus tells Zaccheus that he wants to stay at his house. One of the first promises Zaccheus makes is that he will restore "four times the amount" of what he has taken unlawfully (Luke 19:8). Once Zaccheus says this, Jesus proclaims that Zaccheus has received atonement (Luke 19:9–10). In our everyday contact with people as well as in fellowship with God we must constantly be aware of all that is questionable or sinful, first by appropriating the guilt offering of Jesus and then carefully making restitution whenever possible.

The sin and guilt offerings are mandatory, but the burnt offering (**1:1–17**) and the grain and thanksgiving offerings are voluntary. God does not demand them; when a believer really loves the Lord, he freely gives these offerings.

God makes it possible for the Israelites to choose a burnt offering in accordance with their economic status: (1) the rich, a bull (1:3); (2) the middle class, a male goat or sheep; and (3) the poor, a pair of pigeons or doves (5:7). If a priest, however, sees either rich or middle-class people bringing pigeons or turtle doves, he is to reject outright such offerings as totally detestable to God and a perversion of his mercy.

The burnt offering emphasizes dedication, occurring after the atonement of the sin and guilt offerings. Four principles also apply to the burnt offering:

1. *Substitution.* Each offering served as a substitute for the offerer.
2. *Identification.* The Israelite placed his hands upon the animal's head, not to confess his sins, but as a symbolic gesture that whatever happened to the animal was as if the offerer had experienced it himself.
3. *Death of the animal.* The offerer killed the animal and the priest caught the blood and applied it around about the altar of burnt offering. The symbolism of the death of the animal meant that the Israelite had no life of his own, but it was to be laid down and, in a sense, turned over completely to the Lord.
4. *Burning of the carcass.* This was a further reminder that the Israelite's life was not his own, but the Lord's.

Just as not every Israelite saw the Messiah in the sin and guilt offerings, so it was not necessary for genuine believers to see Jesus as the fulfillment of the dedication offering in order for them to dedicate their lives to God. But there were spiritually minded believers who did see the relationship of the burnt offering to the Antitype. David declares, "I desire to do your will, O my God; your Law is within my heart" (Ps. 40:8). Jesus came to accomplish perfectly, in total dedication, the will of God (Heb. 10:5–7).

Paul urges believers to present their bodies as living sacrifices (Rom. 12:1), and his appeal is nothing less than what the Israelite believer was asked to do when he completely yielded his life. The dedication of our lives is our only reasonable course as sons and daughters of God for spiritual worship. Furthermore, when we yield our lives to God, we must at the same time not be conformed or pressed into this world's patttern of thinking. The Lord has to be in complete control so that we can be transformed, continually testing and approving God's pleasing and perfect will for our lives (Rom. 12:2).

The grain offering (**2:1–16**) also has a dedicatory emphasis. An Israelite could bring a grain offering in a number of forms: (1) as fine flour; (2) baked in an oven; (3) prepared on the griddle; (4) cooked in a pan; and (5) as roasted heads of new grain (firstfruits). In each case, the priest offers a part on the altar while the remainder is used as food by the priests.

A great deal of hard work was involved in producing flour and therefore the lesson of the grain offering is the work of dedication. In the burnt offering, dedication was measured by giving up one's life; the grain offering represents work sanctified by God. No matter where God calls an Israelite, what he does is sanctified by the Lord.

Oil and incense are added to the flour placed upon the altar. The smell of the incense is another way of indicating God's favor upon the work involved in producing the flour. The oil is important. It gives some consistency to the flour placed upon the altar so it will not blow away, and it is a symbol of God's anointing on the labor required to produce the flour.

No leaven is to be added to the part presented to the Lord. Since leaven or yeast was a symbol for sin, it was never to be placed upon the altar. Neither was honey to be added because of the danger of fermentation. Salt was mixed into the grain offerings; because it was a preservative, it could arrest any undesirable feature that would be offensive to the Lord.

The grain offering also has its fulfillment in the ministry of Jesus Christ. Both his teaching and works were perfect. His work on the cross demonstrated that perfect work, which God sanctified.

Once we have been saved by God's grace, we are then asked to serve him; we are to be God's workmanship "created in Christ Jesus to do good works" (Eph. 2:10). "God is not unjust; he will not forget your *work* and the *love* you have shown him as you have *helped* his people and *continue to help* them. We want each of you to show this *same diligence* to the very end, in order to make your hope sure" (Heb. 6:10–11, emphasis added). Likewise, the testimony of the grain offering is an encouragement for us to serve God faithfully and with diligence, knowing that he sanctifies and blesses our work. One day we will hear his words of commendation for what we have done in his name.

The peace or thanksgiving offering (**3:1–17**) enables the Israelites to thank God for all of his blessings, beginning with salvation.

Only two offerings are suitable for the thanksgiving offering: (1) for the rich, a bull or a cow; and (2) for the middle class and poor, a male or female goat or sheep. Since a fellowship meal takes place in connection with this offering, turtle doves or pigeons would hardly be sufficient to feed such a large gathering!

Again, four major principles apply to the thanksgiving offering:

1. *Substitution.* The animal took the place of the offerer.

2. *Identification.* The Israelite placed his hands on the head of the animal which was to represent him.
3. *The death of the substitute.* The offerer killed the animal, not as a sin or guilt offering, but to prepare for the communal meal.
4. *The fellowship meal.* The Israelite shared a feast of thanksgiving with his family, eating the animal he had offered to the Lord.

When offering animals for thanksgiving, the fat and inner organs are to be removed and offered by the priest on the altar; their consumption by the fire leaves a pleasing aroma (vv. 5, 16). When the breast is removed, it is waved before the altar in a horizontal motion, and all the priests have it as their food (7:34). The right thigh is also taken from the carcass and provides a fellowship meal for the officiating priest and his family (7:32–33).

With the thanksgiving offering, the Israelite brings "cakes of bread made without yeast and mixed with oil, wafers made without yeast and spread with oil, and cakes of fine flour well-kneaded mixed with oil" as well as cakes of bread made with yeast (7:12–13). One of each of these breads is given to the officiating priest so he can eat them with his own fellowship meal; these are also offered before the Lord with an up and down motion.

The Israelite takes what is left of the carcass, and after preparing it for a meal, he, along with his family and friends, thanks God for his mercies and goodness. The table upon which the sacrifice rests is the Lord's table and around it sit thankful believers, praising God for his blessings.

This offering could also be a vow or freewill offering. Vows were usually made at the fellowship meal and were publicly confessed so that everyone knew the offerer's intention to serve God. Freewill offerings usually took place on special occasions, such as weddings. Usually, no meat of a vow or freewill offering was to be left over until the second day. However, if members of a family were not able to arrive on the particular day when the meal took place, a dinner from this offering would be permitted on the second day. But under no circumstances was such meat to be eaten on the third day. The people of Israel were protected from contaminating themselves with unclean or diseased food.

In his death, Jesus demonstrated that he is our peace or thanksgiving offering. "He himself is our peace . . . to create in himself one new man out of the two, thus making peace" (Eph. 2:14–15). He also reconciles "to himself all things . . . by making peace through his blood, shed on the cross" (Col. 1:20).

The application of the thanksgiving offering is the experience at the communion table. Even as the Israelite offerer and his family thanked God for his blessings, we also can be thankful, partaking of the bread and fruit of the vine, symbols of the body and blood of the Messiah and what he accomplished for us on the cross. We also thank and bless God for what he does for us day by day as we seek to serve him.

B. Priestly regulations (6:8–7:38). Having considered the offerings presented by believers, we now need to see how the priests carried out the ritual stipulations.

After a day of worship when carcasses and ashes had accumulated from the burnt offerings, the priests and Levites on duty dressed in linen clothes and removed everything that remained, placing it beside the altar (**6:8–13**). By keeping the hearth clean, the fire could burn well. They then changed to ordinary clothes and carried the refuse outside the camp while the tabernacle was still standing. Once the temple was built, the ashes and carcasses were taken out through the Dung Gate at the south wall and deposited in a clean place in the valley. In the early days, the area was called the Valley of Hinnom (Heb. *gê hinnōm*) but in time, the area took on symbolic significance; because of the continual smoke going up from this valley, it became the symbol for the ultimate destiny of unbelievers (Gehenna; Matt. 5:22).

The priests were also expected to ensure a continual fire at the altar of burnt offering in front of the tabernacle. One could make a gift of wood, so that a good supply of it was on hand at all times.

For each grain offering presentation, the officiating priest offered its memorial portion, with incense and oil, so that it burned on the altar as a pleasing aroma to the Lord (2:1–2; **6:14–23**). What was left over was food for the priests.

Further instructions pertained to the anointing of priests. Each one to be anointed had to bring one-tenth of an ephah of fine flour as a grain offering, half of it to be presented in the morning and the other half in the evening at the times of the national burnt offering (Exod. 29:38–42). The priest was thereby reminded that his service was on behalf of the people of Israel. The flour was to be mixed with oil, incense was placed upon it, and it was burned completely on the altar; none was used for food.

The blood of the sin offering on behalf of a priest who had sinned as well as that offered by the representatives of the nation was taken into the tabernacle (later the temple) and sprinkled on the curtain in front of the ark of the covenant (**6:24–30**). The flesh of these offerings was not to be eaten; after the fat and innards had been placed upon the altar and the blood had been offered, the carcasses were taken outside the camp (later to the Valley of Hinnom) and burned.

The flesh of the sin offerings of the civil authorities as well as the laypeople could be eaten by the priests in the courtyard. Eating any part of the flesh made a person holy. If any blood was spattered on a garment, it had to be washed within the courtyard. Care was even taken when cooking the sin offering: (1) if prepared in a clay pot, then the pot had to be destroyed as there was no way to remove the blood which had seeped into the clay crevices; (2) if in a bronze pot, then the pot could be scoured clean, rinsed, and reused. Care was taken with this offering because it was sacred.

The fat and inner organs of the ram of the guilt offering (**7:1–10**) were to be burned on the altar along with its fat tail. Since the blood of this animal was not taken within the tabernacle, the priests could eat its flesh. What remained of the carcass was then taken outside the camp and burned.

The regulations for the priests regarding the thanksgiving or peace offering (**7:11–36**) have already been discussed (3:1–16): the priests could have the breast of any thanksgiving offering, while the officiating priest shared in the cakes of the grain offering as well as the right thigh of the animal offered as a thanksgiving offering.

II. The Priesthood (8:1–10:20)

Once all instructions regarding the sacrifices have been given, Moses, as the representative of God, is ready to install Aaron and his sons as priests before God. Whenever a priest or Levite turned thirty years of age, he would go through the procedure outlined here (cf. Num. 4).

A. Consecration (8:1–36). In preparation for consecration, Aaron and his four sons bring their special garments, anointing oil, a bull for a sin offering, two rams (one for a burnt offering and the other for the ordination), and a basket of unleavened bread for the grain offering.

The clothing (vv. 1–9, 13). Aaron and his sons wash themselves thoroughly with water. Aaron then puts on a tunic (a linen undergarment) and a long, seamless robe of blue linen. Pomegranates made of blue, purple, and scarlet yarn are on the hem of the robe at certain intervals and between these are golden bells (Exod. 28:31–35). A woven waistband is then tied around the robe.

Next is the gold ephod, similar to a short jacket, made of blue, purple, and scarlet material, and of finely twisted linen (Exod. 28:6). On the shoulders of the ephod are two onyx stones set in gold; the names of six tribes are engraved on each stone (Exod. 28:7–12).

Moses next places the breastplate on Aaron. The Urim and Thummim are put in the breastplate. The high priest therefore bears up the tribes of Israel on his shoulder before God, while the names of the tribes on the breastplate over his heart signify how the high priest should intercede for Israel. In the same way, Jesus the Messiah bears us up as he intercedes for us (Heb. 7:25; 1 John 2:1).

A turban is placed on Aaron's head and on his forehead is a golden plate engraved with the words "HOLY TO THE LORD" (Exod. 28:36). The high priest is to constantly remember that he is set apart to God for service and that his life-style is to be consistent with his calling. Likewise, Jesus is our high priest, ministering for us in accordance with the holiness of God.

Aaron's sons are also brought forward, and they, too, put on their distinctive clothes and headbands (Lev. 8:13). However, their tunics are more plain (Exod. 39:27).

The anointing (vv. 10–13). Moses then anoints the tabernacle and furniture with oil, thereby preparing the sanctuary for service. The altar of burnt offering in front of the tabernacle is anointed with oil seven times (the perfect number), thereby preparing it in a unique way to receive the sacrifices of both priests and people. After the altar utensils and basin for purification are anointed, Moses sprinkles some of the anointing oil on Aaron and his sons, consecrating them for their office. In the same way, Jesus the Messiah is anointed for ministry with the oil of joy by God himself (Heb. 1:9).

The sacrifices (vv. 14–29). The first sacrifice is the bull for the sin offering. Moses himself slaughters the bull after Aaron and his sons identify with it, marking the institution of the Levitical priesthood as unique. Some of the blood of this offering is placed on the horns of the altar, whereby all offenses by Aaron and his sons against the altar are taken away, and in a very special sense, atonement is made for them. The rest of the blood of the sacrifice is poured out at the base of the altar, thereby consecrating it.

The next sacrifice is the ram for the burnt offering. Moses also slaughters this animal and cuts it into pieces. Aaron and his sons must realize that their dedication calls for total submission to God. On this occasion, a ram is offered instead of a bull because this experience marks the consecration of the priests.

Moses next takes the ram for the ordination and after Aaron and his sons place their hands on this animal, identifying it as their substitute, he slaughters it. Taking some of its blood, he places it on the lobes of the right ears of Aaron and his sons, the thumbs of their right hands, and the big toes of their right feet (8:23); the rest of the blood is sprinkled against the altar on all sides. By virtue of this special dedication offering, Aaron and his sons are to remember that what they hear with their ears, do with their hands, and where they go with their feet, is to be totally consecrated to God. Anything less is detestable to him and a bad example to the people.

Jesus the Messiah exemplified a perfect dedication in whatever he heard and did, and wherever he walked. We, too, are priests and the very anointing of the Old Testament priests relates to how we use our ears, hands, and feet for the Lord.

The rest of the ram of ordination is handled as a unique thanksgiving offering (vv. 25–32): the fat, fat tail, and inner organs along with some of the unleavened bread are placed on the right thigh, all of which is then placed in the hands of Aaron and his sons and waved before the Lord as a wave offering. All of it is placed on the altar of burnt offering as a pleasing aroma before the Lord. On all other occasions afterward, however, the officiating priest could have this thigh as food. The breast is also waved before the Lord, and is Moses' portion for his service. What is left of the ram carcass is then cooked and its flesh along with the unleavened bread is served as a meal of thanksgiving for Aaron and his sons. The leftovers are burned. After the meal, Moses tells the priests to remain within the tabernacle area for seven days and nights in anticipation of their ministry.

B. Installation (9:1–24). After the week has passed, Moses summons Aaron and his sons as well as the leaders of Israel. He tells Aaron to "take a bull calf for your sin offering and a ram for your burnt offering," and the leaders to "take a male goat for a sin offering, a calf and a lamb—both a year old and without defect—for a burnt offering, and an ox and a ram for a fellowship offering to sacrifice before the LORD, together with a grain offering mixed with oil" (9:3–4). Moses announces to the gathering that God is going to appear before them; the entire assembly comes and stands before the tent of meeting.

Aaron now offers sacrifices for himself and his sons (vv. 7–14). He first kills the bull as a sin offering for himself, signifying that he has begun his ministry. Aaron also slaughters the burnt offering, sprinkling the blood along the base of the altar. The carcass is then cut into pieces, washed, and placed on the altar, signifying the priests' dedication of their work.

Sacrifices are offered for the people (vv. 15–21). The goat for the sin offering is slaughtered. The burnt offering is presented in the prescribed way as well as the grain offering. Next, Aaron slaughters the ox and ram as the thanksgiving offering in the prescribed manner (3:1–11; 7:28–34); the exception on this occasion is in the waving side to side of the right shoulder instead of the usual vertical motion. Following these offerings, Aaron then turns to face the people and blesses them with the Aaronic blessing in the sincere desire that they too may enter into the peace God wants to share with them (Num. 6:24–26). Aaron and Moses next face God in the tent of meeting. After coming out, they again bless the people. At this point, the awesome glory of God ignites all of the portions on the altar, setting them ablaze. When the people see this special revelation of God, they shout for joy and worship him.

C. Consequences of disobedience (10:1–20). Once Aaron and his sons are installed, each one takes his turn ministering to the people. This chapter demonstrates what happens when God's servants do not pay careful attention to his instructions regarding worship.

Two of Aaron's sons, Nadab and Abihu, take their censers, put fire in them, and add incense. The text says that they offer "unauthorized fire" (v. 1). Whatever goes wrong, fire comes forth from the Lord, and they die. Sadly, Moses has to remind Aaron that unless the priests respect God's holiness and obey his instructions, they will suffer the penalty of death.

Some commentators think that Nadab and Abihu disobeyed God's instructions not to drink wine or any fermented drink and therefore died. However, we cannot be sure what strange fire provoked God's anger; it is enough to say that these two sons failed to follow the regulations God specified for worship.

Moses tells Aaron and his remaining sons, Eleazar and Ithamar, not to mourn in any way, or the Lord will be further provoked. Since the priests are in the sanctuary area, they are to keep themselves pure. Relatives remove the bodies and mourn for the dead.

Moses now teaches the priests how to handle offerings, telling the two remaining sons of Aaron to take the grain offering left over for the priests and to eat it before the Lord. Instructions concerning how to handle the thanksgiving offering are repeated (see 7:28–34).

Moses asks about the goat of the sin offering and finds it has been completely burned. He becomes angry because Eleazar and Ithamar failed to eat the sin offering in the sanctuary. Aaron comes to their defense, asking if the Lord would have been pleased if he had eaten of the sin offering after such a tragedy. God could, on this one occasion, overlook Aaron's serious error of burning the goat of the sin offering. How many times has God been gracious with us when under unusual circumstances, we too commit serious error!

III. Cleanness and Uncleanness (11:1–16:34)

Some people may find it odd that the very food one eats, the control of disease, and the birth of children can be classified as worship. Yet the instructions in Leviticus are a reminder that there is no dividing line between the sacred and the profane.

A. Regulations (11:1–15:33). Four kinds of food are considered (**11:1–47**): animals, marine life, fowl, and insects. Only those animals which chewed cud and had split hooves were permissible for food.

One basic consideration for "clean food" was hygienic. With no refrigeration and a hot climate, meat could not be kept for longer than a day. Contaminated meat posed a real health hazard. In addition, if not cooked properly, meat would be dangerous (e.g., trichinosis).

While hygiene was important for a people dedicated to God, the primary reason for dietary regulations in Leviticus was theological. The only flesh of animals Israelites could eat was of those which fed on various kinds of grasses. They could not eat carnivorous predators. Blood and life are synonymous (Lev. 17:11), and the Israelite had to be very careful of what he ate so that he exercised respect for life. Even acceptable animals had to be slaughtered in a specific manner so that their blood could be drained out in the proper way.

The only marine life permitted for food were creatures with fins and scales. Any other marine life was forbidden because they were carnivores, eating flesh and blood together.

The list of prohibited fowl in this chapter includes birds which prey on other forms of life (vv. 13–19); therefore, by implication, only chickens, ducks, and geese would be permissible for food. Of all flying insects, only the grasshopper and various kinds of locust were allowed for food since these creatures were also herbivorous.

A number of other guidelines apply to what may be eaten (vv. 26–45). No flesh was to be eaten of animals which died of natural causes (v. 24). Whoever touched their carcasses had to wash his clothes and was considered unclean until evening, that is, the next day. Even touching forbidden creatures (vv. 29–31) made one unclean until evening. Whenever any creature died and fell on wood, cloth, hide, or sackcloth, the article had to be washed and was considered unclean until evening. Any pot into which a dead animal had fallen had to be broken as there was no way to clean clay. If a carcass fell on an oven or cooking pot, then it must be broken up because there was no way to scour it. In general, when any carcass fell on any article, it was considered unclean. Even when an animal permissible for food died, anyone who touched the carcass or ate of it had to wash himself thoroughly and wait until the evening.

Purification also relates to the time required for a woman to stop bleeding after giving birth to a child (**12:1–8**). Again, blood was considered sacred and every care was taken to respect it.

For a boy, the mother was considered ceremonially unclean for seven days, just as during her monthly period (15:19). On the eighth day, the male child was circumcised, the earliest possible moment after the seven-day period. The mother then had to wait an additional thirty-three days, making sure that all bleeding had stopped (15:25), so that the total time required before a woman could enter the sanctuary was forty days. While any bleeding was present, the woman could not enter the sanctuary or touch anything dedicated to God.

With a female baby, the mother was regarded as unclean for two weeks and then had to wait an additional sixty-six days for final purification. While no specific reason is given for the difference between a boy and girl, there might be two possibilities: (1) the girl's future menstruation; or (2) a reminder that it was Eve who was tempted in the garden, and that she in turn tempted Adam to eat the forbidden fruit. The extra time of purification for a girl would then be another emphasis that sin first entered the human race through the woman.

When the days of purification were over, the woman then either had to bring a lamb for a burnt offering and a young pigeon or dove for a sin offering to the priests or, if she were poor, two doves or two young pigeons (5:7). The priest was to explain the meaning of the principles of atonement and dedication. In every aspect of life, the law acted as the schoolmaster in the attempt to reach God's people with the messages of atonement and dedication.

Careful attention was given to the treatment of various skin diseases (**13:1–59**). The King

James Version uses the word *leprosy* to define all skin diseases, but the Hebrew word does not refer only to leprosy. Doubtless certain strains of leprosy existed in ancient times, but the generally accepted position is that this chapter deals with infectious skin diseases and fungi.

The skin diseases mentioned in verses 1–19 include various kinds of infections, swellings, and rashes. Priests were trained to recognize if the course of a disease had stopped or if it was still spreading; in case of the latter, the priest had to pronounce the infected person unclean and quarantine him for seven days. After this period, the priest examined the infected person and if the condition remained unchanged, he was then quarantined for another seven days. When the priest examined the infection again and if the affected area had begun to fade and had not spread, he pronounced the person clean and restored him to society. But if the skin disease had spread, the priest could only pronounce such a person unclean; the infected individual then had to separate himself from family and society.

Verses 18–44 deal with boils, burns, sores on the head or chin, white spots on the skin, or when a man loses his hair, leaving a reddish-white sore on his head or forehead. The same procedure was followed for examining infected persons as already mentioned. When a person was pronounced unclean, he had to separate him or herself from society and "wear torn clothes, let his hair be unkempt, cover the lower part of his face, and cry out 'Unclean! Unclean!' " (vv. 45–46). These were the rites of mourning; such a person was considered dead by the community. People had no contact with unclean individuals so as to avoid any defilement, and the separation remained indefinite or until the symptoms of the disease disappeared.

Mildewed clothing appearing either green or red in color had to be brought to the priests for examination who then quarantined it for seven days. If the mildew had spread after seven days, then the clothing was burned; there was no way to control the spread of the fungus or rot. If the mildew had not spread, then the clothing was washed and set aside for another week. If the fungus or rot still persisted, the clothing had to be burned; but if the discoloration had begun to fade, then the contaminated part of the clothing was cut out and the rest could be used after it was washed. But if the discoloration should reappear, the rest of the clothing had to be burned.

Moses provided regulations for people when they were healed of their skin diseases, carefully prescribing how they could be restored to society (**14:1–57**).

If a person was healed of disease while still separate from society, he sent word to a priest who had to come and see if the person was actually cured. On being assured that healing had occurred, the priest then ordered that two live clean birds, some cedar wood, scarlet yarn, and hyssop be brought for the person to be cleansed. One of the birds was killed over fresh water in a clay pot (the Hebrew word for "fresh" here refers to actual running water, which was evidently obtained from a brook or river). The live bird was tied to the cedar wood and hyssop with the scarlet yarn and all were dipped into the pot containing the water and blood which in turn was sprinkled seven times on the person to be cleansed by the priest. The live bird was released to fly away, and the restored person was pronounced clean.

The principles behind this ritual are meaningful: (1) the bird which was put to death was considered identical to the uncleanness of the person; (2) when the live bird was dipped into the blood and water, the person received the life of the bird which had been killed; (3) the pungent odor of the hyssop and cedar wood was as if the uncleanness was driven away; (4) the live bird took away the uncleanness of the person being cleansed; (5) sprinkling seven times suggests that the person was considered completely clean of his disease.

Following this experience, the restored person washed his clothes, shaved off all his hair, and bathed. He was ceremonially clean and permitted to enter the camp, but could not yet have contact with his family or possessions; he still had to wait one more week to make absolutely sure he was completely clean. After this period, he again shaved off all his hair, his beard, his eyebrows, and the rest of his hair, washed his clothes, bathed, and was finally regarded as clean.

In spite of establishing a person's right to be a part of the community again, the priest himself could never heal. God did the healing, and the priest, as God's representative, had to recognize that healing took place as a result of divine intervention.

In Moses' day, the pagans believed that when a person had a disease, he was possessed by evil spirits and that exorcism was required for cleansing to occur. The restoration prescribed by God had nothing to do with driving away evil spirits. The symbolism instead taught the person being cleansed the meaning of the sin nature and how it has devastated mankind, even through disease. In the cleansing process, such a person was confronted with the truths of atonement and a personal knowledge of God.

On the eighth day, after the week of quarantine, offerings were presented before the Lord and a priest had to officiate for the person to be restored to the community. One of the male lambs was killed and presented as a guilt offering (see 5:15–6:7 for the principles associated with this offering), which was to make atonement for the particular uncleanness. The priest also took some of the blood of this offering and put it on the lobe of the right ear of the one to be cleansed, on the thumb of his right hand, and on the big toe of his right foot. He also took some of the oil from the log, sprinkling it seven times before the Lord, while the remaining oil was placed on the right ear lobe of the restored person, the thumb of his right hand, and on the big toe of his right foot; the remaining oil was then poured out on his head. Obviously, such a person could not help but be confronted by tremendous truths that reminded him of his need for atonement.

The priest next sacrificed either the ewe lamb or one of the pigeons or doves as the sin offering. The guilt offering was presented first, prior to the sin offering, thereby emphasizing the specific cleansing of the person being restored; then came the offering for the sin nature. The burnt offering was presented next, either one of the male lambs or the second of the pigeons or doves, and was a call for the person being cleansed to yield himself completely to the Lord; the grain offering pointed to the sacredness of the future work of the person.

Even as mildew, fungus, and rot can affect clothing, so likewise they can spread on houses, especially if the climate is damp and humid. Guidelines were provided to control such occurrences. If a house was affected, it was closed for a week. If after that time the mildew or fungus had spread, then the contaminated stones were torn out and replaced by new ones; in addition, the rest of the walls had to be scraped and replastered. If with the passage of another week the mildew or fungus had not reappeared, then the house was pronounced clean; if after that period the mildew or fungus was spreading once more, the house was torn down.

When a house was finally pronounced clean and free from contamination, the same procedure for restoration took place as for a person restored from his disease (vv. 4–7).

Personal cleanliness was largely left to individuals (**15:1–33**). Bodily discharges from sexual organs were not considered as serious as infectious skin diseases, but everyone was expected to practice good hygiene. Theologically, proper attention to normal male and female functions was related to holiness.

The instructions for the male were quite explicit (vv. 1–18). Any sexual discharge not only rendered a man unclean, but if the discharge made contact with any articles of furniture or clothing, they too were unclean. The individual involved had to wash himself and everything which was unclean; both person and article(s) remained unclean until evening. In addition, on the eighth day, the individual had to bring two doves or two young pigeons before the Lord, and the priest sacrificed them, one for a sin offering and the other for a burnt offering. Not only was personal hygiene involved; one's sacred standing was also affected.

Instructions also were given regarding the woman's monthly period (vv. 19–24). During this time she was regarded as ritually unclean and was not to enter the sanctuary area. Any person, article of clothing, or piece of furniture she contacted was also unclean until evening and until it was washed. If she and her husband had intercourse during this time, both were rendered unclean for a week.

If a woman had any unusual or exceptional discharge of blood, she was considered unclean as long as she had any bleeding; any person or object she touched was also unclean (vv. 25–30) until washed. After the woman's discharge had ceased, she then had to wait an additional seven days at which time she would be ceremonially clean. On the eighth day she then followed the procedure for offerings as for a normal period, after which she could resume her place within society.

In no way was the unfortunate woman to be maligned; rather, Israel had to have a healthy respect for blood as well as for the ovum which was passed during the time of her period. The rules of good hygiene combined with the theological dimension were designed to keep Israel as a special people before the Lord. If the Israelites disregarded these instructions, thereby defiling God's dwelling-place, then God would have to discipline them (v. 31).

B. The Day of Atonement (16:1–34). The phrase *the Day of Atonement* does not occur in this chapter, appearing only in 23:27–28. On this occasion, every Israelite had to face God and seek forgiveness for his sins. Every year, God wiped the slate clean for the nation, placing a special burden on each individual to face up to his or her need for atonement.

One basic lesson was how hard it was to approach a holy God: (1) the tribes of Israel encamped around the enclosure; (2) the men could enter the courtyard; (3) the priests could enter the Holy Place for ministry; (4) only the high priest could enter the Holy of Holies. Before doing so, he had to bathe himself and don special garments.

The offerings consisted of: (1) a young bull for the sin offering and a ram for the burnt offering for the high priest and his household; and (2) for Israel, two goats for the sin offering and a ram for the burnt offering. The high priest cast lots over the two goats; one was to be sacrificed, while the other was the scapegoat to be led out into the wilderness.

The high priest followed a specific ritual. First, he took a censer of burning coals and finely ground incense and proceeded into the Holy of Holies. There he placed the incense upon the coals before the Lord, and the Holy of Holies was filled with the cloud and odor of the incense. Next, he went out and slaughtered the bull for his own sin offering and for his household. He caught the blood with the help of other priests; he then returned to the Holy of Holies and offered the blood, sprinkling it seven times before the mercy seat.

Going outside again, the high priest slaughtered the goat of the sin offering for the people and then took its blood into the Holy of Holies, sprinkling it in the same way as that of the bull. He possibly also sprinkled blood in the Holy Place where the altar of incense stood. On this day, the high priest cleansed the Holy of Holies and the entire tabernacle, not only for himself but also for Israel.

He then exited from the tabernacle and, taking some of the blood of the bull and goat, he put it on the horns of the altar of burnt offering outside of the sanctuary and also sprinkled blood before the altar seven times so as to consecrate it from the sins of the people.

The scapegoat was next brought to the high priest. He prayed over it on behalf of Israel. The scapegoat was then driven out into the wilderness, symbolically taking away the sin of the nation.

The high priest then took off his linen garments, bathed in a holy place, and put on the regular garments of the priesthood. He sacrificed the rams of the burnt offering for himself as well as for the people, indicating symbolically that he and the people had dedicated themselves to the Lord.

The person who led the goat into the wilderness had to wash his clothes and bathe himself before he could reenter the camp. He too had become sin as he guided the goat into the wilderness; therefore he needed cleansing. Finally, the remaining carcasses of the bull and goat of the sin offerings were taken outside the camp and burned.

The Day of Atonement was a holy day. The people were not to work and were also to "deny themselves" (fast). As the high priest ministered before the Lord, every Israelite was reminded that he needed to be delivered from sin.

IV. The Holiness Code (17:1–26:46)

A. The sanctity of blood (17:1–16). This chapter is the very heart of Leviticus, emphasizing once more the importance of blood and life.

No Israelite was allowed to sacrifice outside the camp or apart from the sanctuary. If he did, he was held guilty of bloodshed and he was cut off from the community. Sacrificial animals had to be brought to the priest at the entrance to the tabernacle (later, the temple) and offered in the prescribed way. The point is that the blood of these animals had to be cared for at the prescribed altar and their fat had to be burned as an aroma pleasing to the Lord.

The penalty was severe to keep Israelites from straying from the worship of the Lord and offering sacrifices to pagan gods (v. 7), thereby prostituting themselves. The injunction is repeated again: no Israelite or alien in Israel was to offer a burnt offering except before the Lord at the tabernacle (or temple).

The very heart of Leviticus is the blood: "the life of a creature is in the blood. . . . it is the blood that makes atonement for one's life" (v. 11). Life is therefore synonymous with blood and is sacred in God's sight. No one was to eat blood with meat. This is why domestic animals used for food had to be brought to the sanctuary where the priests were careful to drain out their blood. Game animals did not have to be brought to the sanctuary, but the blood of such animals had to be drained out on the ground and covered up before the meat was cooked. No flesh or dead carcasses were to be eaten, no matter how these animals died, because the blood had not been properly drained from the meat. Anyone touching dead beasts was rendered unclean and had to wash and was not clean until evening. If he did not cleanse himself, then he was held responsible by God for insensitivity regarding blood and life.

B. Moral laws (18:1–20:27). There is a direct link between proper worship of God and a lifestyle of holiness. To guide Israel in this regard, the Ten Commandments receive special consideration in chapters 18 to 20, particularly the seventh commandment.

God warns Israel to avoid the family relations common to the Egyptians and Canaanites (**18:1–30**). In Canaan particularly, the fertility cult associated with the worship of pagan deities meant that temple priests and priestesses engaged in immoral relationships with the worshipers. Israel was to have nothing to do with this immorality.

Once God briefly mentions the unacceptable life-style of the families of Canaan, he provides Israel with guidelines for acceptable behavior. By using the formula of authority, "I am the LORD" (v. 6), God declares that no sexual relations must take place between close relatives within a family (vv. 7–17).

While polygamy existed in ancient Israel, measures to curb and in time to completely stamp out the practice are introduced (v. 18). Other sexual offenses are strictly prohibited: (1) relationships between a man and his wife during her monthly period (15:19); (2) relationships between a man and his neighbor's wife; (3) homosexuality; and (4) relationships with beasts, considered a gross perversion of moral law.

The list of injunctions in chapter 18 are repeated in **20:1–27**, and in each case God prescribes the death penalty for those who violate the moral standard. Israel is to walk righteously before him and to enjoy his love and blessings. Any perversion of the moral law means a deliberate defiance of the special status a holy God had accorded to his people. For this reason, his instructions are quite clear about what should be done to any offenders caught in immoral behavior.

Israel is further warned that if the moral breakdown should ever spread across the nation, then they stand in danger of being exiled. Even as the pagan nations in Canaan were thrown out of the land because of their moral perversion (vv. 22–23), so Israel must never pervert themselves in a similar manner or they too will be put out.

Furthermore, Israel is to distinguish between clean and unclean animals for food, related directly to the tie between what is holy and what is perverted (vv. 25–26). No one is to be involved in the occult, thereby mimicking pagan practices. Israel is to be a nation set apart to God.

While chapters 18 and 20 are an interpretation and expansion of the seventh commandment, **19:1–37** is an expansion of the remaining nine commandments. The entire message begins with an introductory statement of certification: "Be holy, because I, the LORD your God, am holy" (v. 2).

The first commandments mentioned call for children to respect their parents and for Israel to observe the Sabbath. Parents stand as God in relation to their children who will find it difficult to respect God if they do not respect their father and mother. The people are not to make idols of cast metal. Proper care is to be taken with fellowship or thanksgiving offerings so that no flesh is left over until the third day; the people must distinguish between what is clean and unclean, thereby being sensitive to God's holiness.

The farmer's care for the poor (vv. 5–8) refers to the eighth commandment (Exod. 20:15). Such concern is a blessing to God because he is the champion of the needy.

The Law demands respect for fellow human beings. There is to be no lying, stealing, or deceiving. Slander, which is a form of lying, is strictly forbidden because it ruins a person's reputation. No one is to hate or hold a grudge. Finally, God exhorts each of his people to love their neighbor as themselves (v. 18b).

A number of miscellaneous instructions in verses 19–37 relate in some way to each of the commandments. Two kinds of seed must not be sown in the same field, different animals are not to be mated, and clothing of two different kinds of materials must not be worn (v. 19). Israel is a nation separated to the Lord, and the principle of separation extends even to these areas of life.

The seventh commandment is further defined: no man is to sleep with a slave woman promised to another man. The man is required to bring the sin and guilt offerings as well as make restitution in the amount prescribed by the priest. No man is to sell his daughter as a prostitute, for example, by placing her as a priestess in a pagan temple.

Neither are the people to follow other pagan practices: cutting the hair at the sides of the head or clipping the edges of the beard (v. 27), cutting their bodies for the dead or putting tatoo marks on themselves (v. 28), or engaging in occult practices (vv. 26, 31).

Israel is also reminded to not eat any meat with the blood (v. 26), to observe the Sabbath, and to have reverence for the Lord's sanctuary. The aged are to be honored because God is their Lord in a special sense (v. 32). Aliens likewise are not to be mistreated. Israel should remember what it was like to be aliens when they were slaves in the land of Egypt. Honest scales and honest weights, and honest ephah and honest hin are to be used; no one is to defraud his neighbor. Even fruit trees are to be cared for in a God-honoring manner (vv. 23–25).

The commandments are given to Israel in order that they might demonstrate their allegiance to the Lord in conduct reflecting his holiness, justice, and righteousness. The nation is to be a testimony to other nations.

C. Priestly regulations (21:1–22:33). Ministering priests were not to make themselves ceremonially unclean by mourning for the dead;

only when not on duty at the sanctuary could they mourn for their dead relatives. If they did not listen to these guidelines, they would only defile themselves and cause others to stumble.

Neither were priests to mimic the life-style of the pagan cult religions: shaving their heads; shaving the edges of their beards or cutting their bodies; marrying women defiled by prostitution, particularly prostitutes in pagan temples; marrying those divorced from their husbands. If a priest's daughter became a temple prostitute, the most stringent of capital punishment must be exacted: she was to be burned by fire! The priests were Israel's moral guides. When they went astray, then the nation also went astray. The principle still applies today: when God's ministers live deplorable lives and preach a perverted Word, then they will be held responsible when people go astray in spiritual and moral matters.

The high priest in particular was to live an exemplary life. Because he had been anointed to serve in a special office, he, too, had to be careful not to mourn his loved ones who died or be in any place where there was a dead body. He was required to marry a virgin. The high priest represented Israel in a special way, particularly on the Day of Atonement when he stood in the Holy of Holies, offering sacrifices on behalf of the nation.

Unfortunately, some priests had physical defects. They could never present offerings to God, although they could enter the sanctuary to eat the food of the offerings. Israel was to be a sacred nation separated to God, and therefore no reminder of physical evil as a result of the fall could be allowed in the presence of God.

All gifts presented to God were sacred, and the priest had to treat each offering with the greatest of respect. People presented their offerings to God himself and the priests had to realize they were only the intermediaries, offering these gifts on behalf of the Israelites.

No diseased or contaminated priest could take part in offering any sacrifice in the sanctuary. If he attempted to do so, he was to be cut off from the presence of God, because he could not distinguish between what was clean and unclean. When a priest was ceremonially unclean, he had to bathe himself and wait until evening before serving at the sanctuary or eating of the sacred food.

No one outside a priest's family could eat of the sacred food; it was reserved for the priest, his family, and the servants in his household. When a priest's daughter married outside of her tribe, she was no longer eligible to eat of the sacred offerings; but if she ever became a widow with no children or was divorced, she could return to live in her father's house and eat of his food again.

Should anyone eat of this reserved food by mistake, he was required to offer the sin and guilt offerings, making restitution: the value of the offering he ate, plus one-fifth.

Regulations spelled out what kind of sacrifices were permissible: none were to be presented which were defective in any way. How could people offer to God their worst when he had showered Israel with every blessing? Furthermore, defective offerings as types within Israel only mocked the Antitype, Jesus the Messiah.

Further instructions reflect humane considerations. No newborn animals were to be used as sacrifices before they were eight days old, out of consideration for the mother, but after this time period, such young sacrifices were desirable. No female and its newborn young were to be slaughtered on the same day, again out of consideration for the female who had just given birth. The Israelites had to be careful with their sacrifices because the sacrificial system was designed to give glory to the Lord and also to be an attraction to visitors from surrounding nations whereby some would want to be converted.

Chapters 21 and 22 have a direct relationship to New Testament teaching. Even as it was necessary for the high priest to be perfect, so Jesus is perfect (Heb. 7:26). Even as the sacrifice had to be as perfect as possible, so our Savior also offered himself as a perfect sacrifice (Heb. 9:14). Just as the Old Testament priests were to be godly examples, so likewise, Christian leaders need to have a good testimony (1 Tim. 3).

D. Worship calendar (23:1–44). Israel had to appear three times a year before the Lord (Exod. 23:14–17), therefore, the religious calendar revolved around a cycle of three annual feasts. Later, as Israel's history unfolded, other festivals and fast days were added.

The religious calendar described in Leviticus 23 begins in the spring with the Passover during the first month (v. 5). Later, when Israel returned from exile in Babylon, they had a civil calendar which began in the fall, starting with the first day of the month of Tishri (the seventh month of the religious calendar). Possibly the fall observance of the civil calendar was influenced by the Babylonian calendar, which also began in the fall and was marked by the crowning of the king. Both calendars are reflected in Scripture: Jeremiah, a preexilic prophet, dates his prophecies in accordance with the religious calendar, while both Daniel and Ezekiel in the exile date their prophecies according to the civil calendar.

The first holiday was the Sabbath day (v. 3) in which no work was to be done. The Sabbath reflects the creation ordinance; God "rested" on the seventh day and blessed it, making it holy (Gen. 2:2–3). The fourth commandment enjoins Israel to observe this day (Exod. 20:8).

Passover began at twilight on the fourteenth day of the first month (March–April), while the Feast of Unleavened Bread commenced on the fifteenth day and was observed for seven days (vv. 4–14). On these occasions Israel remembered her deliverance from Egypt. The generation which left Egypt did not have time to bake leavened bread; one way to remember this holiday was to eat only unleavened bread. The first and the seventh day of the week were set aside as sacred assemblies before the Lord.

By the first century, Passover and the Feast of Weeks had coalesced into one major holiday. The Passover was sacrificed at "twilight," set during the mid-afternoon on the fourteenth of the first month while the Passover meal was eaten on the evening of the fifteenth. On the sixteenth, the day after the Sabbath or second day of the Feast of Unleavened Bread (all holidays were Sabbaths), a sheaf of barley was offered before the Lord as well as a burnt and grain offering on behalf of the nation. After the firstfruits of the barley were offered to God, the people were able to eat bread made from newly harvested barley.

The next holiday, the Feast of Weeks or Pentecost (May–June), was observed fifty days after the second day of the Feast of the Unleavened Bread when the firstfruits of the barley were presented (vv. 15–22). On the fiftieth day, the priests offered the firstfruits of the wheat harvest. A controversy arose in the first century between the Pharisees and the Sadducees as to what was meant by the phrase *the day after the Sabbath* (v. 15). The former insisted that the first day of the Sabbath was the first day of the Feast of Unleavened Bread and counted fifty days from the second day of the feast, or the sixteenth of the month. The latter understood the Sabbath as the first seventh day after the Feast of Unleavened Bread began, and counted therefore, from the day after the literal seventh day. After the temple was destroyed in A.D. 70, the Pharisees' interpretation prevailed.

Two loaves of bread were baked from two-tenths of fine flour from the newly harvested wheat, to which yeast was added, and on the day of the feast, the priests presented them before the altar. Because the bread had yeast in it, the loaves could not be placed on the altar, but instead were waved horizontally, back and forth. Two lambs were also offered as a wave offering which the officiating priest could have for his fellowship meal. Other sacrifices consisted of the sin and burnt offerings, grain offerings, and thanksgiving offerings. Wheat flour was a staple of life and this occasion called for a time of great festivity and thankfulness to God. No work was to be done on this day and people remembered the gracious abundance which the Lord provided.

The Jewish and church calendars are clearly interrelated. Even as the firstfruits of the barley harvest were offered in connection with Passover and the Feast of Unleavened Bread, so during this time Jesus died and rose again, becoming the firstfruit of New Testament believers. And, even as the firstfruits of the wheat harvest were offered fifty days later, so on this day, the Holy Spirit came upon three thousand new believers who were the firstfruits of the church.

The first day of the seventh month (September–October) was commemorated with trumpet blasts. No work was permitted on the Feast of Trumpets (vv. 23–25). As already explained, this day came to mark the beginning of the civil year. The only place in the Old Testament where "new year" is mentioned is Ezekiel 40:1, leaving us with a question as to whether it refers to the religious or civil calendar. Because the tenth day of the month is noted, some have thought this refers to the Day of Atonement in Tishri and therefore the prophet had in mind the civil calendar.

The tenth day is the Day of Atonement (vv. 26–32) and was the occasion for a sacred assembly. No work was permitted and each Israelite was to "deny himself" (fast) from the evening of the ninth day until the following evening. The Day of Atonement became the occasion for Israel to meet God and come to faith.

On the fifteenth day of the seventh month was the Feast of Tabernacles (vv. 33–44), lasting for seven days. This feast commemorated the general harvest of the land when all crops had been gathered in.

On the first day, choice fruits from the trees, palms, leafy branches, and poplars were to be waved before the Lord, and the people were to rejoice for seven days, blessing and thanking God for his abundant blessings. In time the religious leaders developed the practice whereby Jewish worshipers held "four species in their hands," the citron, similar to a lemon, in the left hand while branches of the palm, myrtle, and willow were held in the right hand. These were then waved before the Lord. Furthermore, the people were to live in booths for seven days, reminding themselves that they certainly could enjoy the good things which God provided in the general harvest, while at the same time remembering that even as the booth is transitory, so is life. The practice of living in booths was also a reminder to Israel that their ancestors had lived in tents and makeshift shelters on their way from Egypt to the Promised Land.

The eighth day was yet another sacred assembly (vv. 36, 39), designating the crowning day of the sacred season of holidays. Literally, the day was one "of restraint or closing up." So, after twenty-two days, worshipers could return to their homes, thanking God that they had completed one more year of their earthly pilgrimage.

E. Oil, bread, and blasphemy (24:1–33). Maintaining the Holy Place of the sanctuary was important (vv. 1–9). The priest had to care for the seven-branched golden candlestick, keeping it burning at all times. Its light was a symbol of God's presence in the midst of Israel. Jesus reflects some aspect of this menorah because just as it had to stay lit at all times, so the Messiah can declare that he indeed is "the light of the world" (John 8:12).

In addition, the priests set out twelve loaves of bread on the golden table of the presence in the Holy Place. Each loaf contained a prescribed amount of fine flour. The loaves were arranged in two rows, six per row; along each row some pure incense was placed as a memorial portion. Every Sabbath day, the bread was changed and what was removed served as food for the priests within the tabernacle courtyard.

The bread signified God's presence among his people. He sustains them, both in a physical and a spiritual sense. Jesus himself is the bread which came down from heaven (John 6:35), and he satisfies our deepest longings.

A specific instance of blasphemy occurs when the son of an Israelite mother and an Egyptian father picks a fight with another Israelite, and the former blasphemes the name of God (vv. 10–16). While it was common practice for pagans to curse their enemies using the names of their gods, the name of the Lord God of Israel was never to be taken in vain (Exod. 20:7; 22:28). God himself gives the word to Moses that the offender has to be put to death. Ever afterward this is the penalty for any alien or Israelite. God is holy and everything about him is holy.

A just law requires that the penalty for a crime must be commensurate with the offense (vv. 17–22). The law of "eye for eye and tooth for tooth" declares that, for example, if someone knocks out the tooth of his opponent, then the latter cannot turn around and kill the one who has attacked him. Penalties for crimes must be just, reflecting the holiness and righteousness of God.

F. The Sabbath Year and Jubilee (25:1–55). Based on the cycle of working six out of seven days, Israel was to work for six years and then rest during the seventh year, the Sabbatical, when no fields were to be sown and no full-scale reaping was to occur. Both people and animals were to eat of what grew in the fields. Everyone was to rest, Israelites and their servants as well as their livestock.

Later legislation also specified that all debts were to be remitted and debtors released during the Sabbatical (Deut. 15:1–3). Only non-Israelites who did not subscribe to the covenant had to pay their debts if they came due on the Sabbatical.

The second unique piece of legislation regulated the year of Jubilee, which occurred every fiftieth year; in a cycle of forty-nine years, it followed the Sabbatical year. People enjoyed a Sabbatical on the forty-ninth year of the Jubilee cycle and also had the fiftieth year for rest as well. When the trumpet blew, closing the Day of Atonement of the forty-ninth year, the year of Jubilee began when there was "liberty throughout the land" (v. 10).

At this time, all lands reverted to their original owners. If a family desperately needed money during the Jubilee cycle, it could "sell land" to a countryman. Land, however, was never sold because it actually belonged to God who was the Landlord. Only the *crop value* of the land was sold until the next year of Jubilee. Those with means were to buy the crop value and not take advantage of the family who desperately needed money. And yet, the family who had to sell the use of the land never lost it entirely, because in the next year of Jubilee, the land reverted to them.

Would food be available in sufficient quantities in the period from harvest time at the end of the forty-eighth year until the harvest following the first year after Jubilee? God promised Israel an abundant crop before the seventh Sabbatical or forty-ninth year to tide them over for three years until the next harvest time.

When God made his covenant with Israel, he demanded justice. While poverty could not be eliminated entirely, everyone could begin anew in the Year of Jubilee. Moses carefully prescribed procedures for helping others in need. When a farmer and his family were in need, the nearest relative able to help his kin was to redeem, or buy his crop value, until the next Jubilee. The family who prospered was to help others who were in desperate straits. When a poor family recovered sufficiently, they could redeem their land which meant paying back the crop value, but only for the period from the time of redemption until the next year of Jubilee. The person or family who had bought the original crop value had to release it. If a poor family was not able to redeem its property, they repossessed their land in the Jubilee, as already explained. Reclamation of land prevented the build-up of landed estates, whereby the few would become rich while the majority of people became increasingly poor.

A person in desperate need could also sell his house, but the purchaser did not have full title to the house until one full year had elapsed after its sale. Opportunity was given for the seller to redeem it if he could acquire sufficient money to do so. If the original owner could not buy back his house within the year, then the purchaser received full title to it.

The Levites lived in cities and on parcels of land surrounding those cities, scattered among the twelve tribes, but they did not own land as other tribes. If a Levite sold a house when he desperately needed money, he *always* had the right to redeem it; if he could not before the Jubilee year, the house reverted to him at that time. Pasture lands could never be sold because these possessions were all they had.

While the covenant law attempted to equalize everybody's economic standing, it could not prevent poverty in every case. When individuals fell upon hard times and were unable to support themselves even after selling the crop value of their land, special provisions were made. When poor people needed additional loans, interest was never to be taken from them, and no food was to be sold to them for profit. A poor person could hire himself out to a rich person who then had to care for him; the poor person, however, was not to be treated as a slave, but rather, as a hired worker or temporary resident until the next year of Jubilee. Normally, such individuals were to be freed in the seventh year of their service (Exod. 21:2; Deut. 15:12) but if the Jubilee came first, then their release came sooner. The poor and possibly their children could then regain the land of their fathers. Only non-Israelites could be treated as slaves, although the Law forbade harsh treatment.

Any member of a family with means was encouraged to redeem the land of a poor relative and thereby allow him to return to it and make his own living. The attempt was made, as much as possible, to alleviate the plight of the poor while giving them some sense of dignity.

G. Rewards and punishments (26:1–46). Before the covenant is formally defined, mention is made of the second and fourth commandments, reminding Israel not to worship pagan gods and to observe the Sabbath (vv. 1–2). The people must have reverence for the sanctuary, sanctified by the Lord's presence. God reminds the people that "I am the LORD"; Israel is to act responsibly before him.

The blessings of the covenant (vv. 3–13) are based on a conditional phrase: "if you follow my decrees and are careful to obey my commands" (v. 3). When Israel is obedient to the terms of the covenant, God's blessings will be theirs, both material as well as spiritual: the land will yield its fruit in abundance; Israel will have peace and should they be attacked by any enemy, the latter will suffer great defeat because the Lord will consider their battle as an attack upon himself; God will be pleased to live among his people, walk among them, and be their God. Israel will be a special, unique people, enjoying freedom in their land.

God also details the curses (vv. 14–39) that will befall Israel as a result of disobedience. Discipline, as harsh as it sounds, is designed to correct a rebellious people. Should they suffer enough, they might repent and then seek the Lord. If these efforts fail, God promises an even more severe discipline: Israel's cities will be wasted, their sanctuary destroyed, and the nation will have to go into exile where their hearts will become fearful and they will waste away in the land of their captors. While God has to judge sin, yet in his mercy he will remain faithful to his promise to Abraham (Gen. 17:7). When the people finally realize how far they have fallen and confess their sins, God will then remember the covenant he made with Abraham, Isaac, and Jacob, which included the promise of the land to the patriarchs and to their descendants.

H. Vows and tithes (27:1–34). A vow to the Lord was a promise of a special gift (Gen. 28:20–22) or a particular pious action (2 Sam. 15:8). Once a person made a vow to God, he or she had to keep that promise. Therefore, vows were usually made in public before witnesses as a safeguard from making rash promises which could not be kept.

A vow promised to God could be translated into a monetary payment made to the priests of a value equivalent to the person's service (v. 2). These monies were used by the priests for the general maintenance of the sanctuary.

The value of a vow was based on a person's status in society (vv. 3–8): (1) those in the prime of life were worth the most (a man twenty to sixty years old, fifty shekels, and a woman, thirty shekels); (2) those preparing for their place in society (five to twenty years of age: a male, twenty shekels, and a female, ten shekels); (3) those whose active life was almost over, but could still contribute to society because of their wisdom and experience (a man, fifteen shekels, and a woman, ten shekels); and (4) infants or children (a male, five shekels, and a female, three shekels). Should a person not be able to give the set amount, then the priest adjusted it to an affordable figure.

Clean animals vowed to the Lord belonged to him. If for any reason the offerer wanted to exchange an animal, he could provide a substitute, but then both the original and the substitute were considered sacred and were not returned to him. However, if an unclean animal was vowed, then the priest set the fair equivalent value for it. If the owner wanted to redeem his vow, he had to give an additional one-fifth of the set value to the priest, and the animal was returned to the offerer.

The Law also specified how special gifts could be given to the Lord (vv. 14–29). If a person dedicated his house to the Lord, then the priest assessed a fair value for the house. If the original owner wished to redeem it, he had to give an additional one-fifth of the set value to the priest. When a person vowed or dedicated a part of his family land, its value was determined by the seed needed for planting until the next Jubilee. The vow had greater value if made near the beginning of a Jubilee cycle and proportionately less if made later. If the farmer wished to redeem what was dedicated, he had to add one-fifth of the value already determined and present it to the priests. If an Israelite did not redeem land dedicated before the Jubilee, then it belonged to the priests and could never again be redeemed. Or an Israelite farmer could dedicate a plot of land to the sanctuary whereby the priests realized the value of the seed for planting while the owner kept the crops. If this farmer did not want to cultivate his field so as to pay on the vow and instead turned it over to someone else to work and keep the produce, he thereby forfeited the field in question to the priests who had been promised the vow.

An Israelite could also dedicate a field which he had bought for its crop value to the next year of Jubilee, and then give the value he determined to the priest. In the year of Jubilee, however, that portion of the land reverted to its original owner.

No one could dedicate the firstborn of clean animals to the Lord because they already belonged to him. However, the Israelite could redeem the firstborn of unclean animals at a set value, adding one-fifth to the original value. Whatever else was devoted was placed under the ban (Heb. *ḥērem*) and it belonged to the Lord. No one could redeem such articles or animals. Likewise any person placed under the ban could never be ransomed; he or she had to be put to death.

Tithes were to be given on all crops, fruits, and animals. In time, however, the traditional understanding of tithing included three tithes (Tob. 1:7; Josephus, *Antiquities of the Jews,* 4.8.22): (1) the general tithe, which was paid to the Levites (see also Num. 18:21); (2) the tithe used for the fellowship meal with both offerer and Levite sharing in the first, second, fourth, and fifth year of the Sabbatical cycle (Deut. 14:22–27); and (3) a tithe paid every third and sixth year and given to the poor (Deut. 14:28–29).

The tithe included everything the land produced: grain from the soil, fruit from the trees, and the produce of the vineyard. However, the farmer could redeem a part of his tithe, giving one-fifth of the value to the priests; the part that was taken back was used as seed for planting the new crops for the following year. Any tithe, however, of the herd or flocks belonged entirely to the Lord, whether it was a good or a bad animal; no redemption was allowed, but under certain situations, if the animal selected was sickly, the owner could substitute a better one for it but then both animals belonged to the Lord.

Moses emphasizes in a concluding statement that all the commands given by the Lord on Mount Sinai to Israel have now been recorded. These instructions had great meaning for the Israelites. Leviticus also affords Christians a better understanding of the ministry of Jesus the Messiah. The moral standard of the covenant is now written upon our hearts by the Holy Spirit and is the guide for our lives.

SELECT BIBLIOGRAPHY

Bonar, A. *Commentary on the Book of Leviticus.* London: Banner of Truth, 1966.

Eerdman, C. *The Book of Leviticus.* New York: Revell, 1951.

Goldberg, L. *Leviticus.* Grand Rapids: Zondervan, 1980.

Harrison, R. K. *Leviticus, An Introduction and Commentary.* Downers Grove: Inter-Varsity, 1980.

Wenham, G. J. *The Book of Leviticus.* Grand Rapids: Eerdmans, 1979.

NUMBERS

Gerard Van Groningen

INTRODUCTION

Various names have been given to the fourth book of the Pentateuch. The Hebrew Bible has the title *In the Desert,* which is the fourth word in the Hebrew text. The Latin Vulgate uses the word *Numbers;* this name was suggested by the censuses that are reported in the book. Neither title adequately summarizes the content. The censuses cover approximately four chapters, the desert wanderings less than twenty-one of the thirty-six chapters.

The content of the book includes: (1) instructions concerning Israel's organization while in camp and while traveling; (2) instructions concerning specific offices, roles, functions, and vows; (3) instructions concerning the Passover, the red heifer rite, tithes, and offerings; (4) instructions on how to maintain moral purity and physical sanctity; (5) descriptions of various experiences and the Lord's responses to these; (6) the reasons why Aaron and Moses do not enter the Promised Land and their deaths; (7) instructions concerning the division of the land; (8) a record of how some nations sought to impede or destroy Israel; (9) the establishment of cities of refuge; (10) the evaluation of Moses as leader and prophet; and (11) the appointment of men to succeed Moses and Aaron.

The basic theme of the Book of Numbers is that the Lord keeps his covenant with his people. This theme includes several aspects. First, Yahweh is the sovereign Lord of heaven, earth, nations, and creation. Second, having bound himself to his people with the covenant bond of love, he redeems his people and is ever with and for them. He will, however, maintain his holiness. He therefore demands that his redeemed people be sanctified in all dimensions of their lives. Third, the Lord is with his people in their varied circumstances and instructs, blesses, chides, chastises, and punishes them in the immediate context of their lives. Furthermore, he demands fellowship, worship, and work from his people at all times and in all circumstances. They have the great privilege of being the prized possession of the Lord, members of his kingdom, a priestly people among nations. These privileges, however, entail awesome responsibilities. When obediently met, covenant blessings follow; when disobedience is evident, the curse of the covenant is administered. Fourth, the Lord provides qualified leaders essential to the people's well-being; they are to be acknowledged and respected. Finally, the concept of the promised messiah pervades the book and is proclaimed, demonstrated by the Lord's servants, and symbolized and typified by persons, things, and events.

Moses wrote the Book of Numbers; this is the testimony of the Scriptures. There is a direct reference to Moses writing in Numbers 33:2. One hundred and forty times mention is made of the Lord speaking to or with Moses and that the Lord "commands" Moses or speaks through Moses. This testimony of the Book of Numbers concerning Moses' authorship is supported by numerous passages in the Bible which refer to Moses as the writer of the Pentateuch.[1]

Some statements in the book seem to oppose Mosaic authorship. However, it should be remembered that inspired writers, such as Joshua or Samuel, could have added a number of illuminating details once Moses' writings were copied and edited. These editors were careful to preserve Moses' writings as completely and correctly as possible. Reasons some scholars have denied that Moses wrote Numbers are: later insertions; third-person references; the belief that Numbers, as other books of the Pentateuch, was compiled from a number of sources, each of which were written after the division of the kingdom; the belief that the Old Testament books reflect what Israelites believed and hoped, rather than what God revealed in his interaction with his people; modern scientific historical scholarship questions the fact that Moses wrote and that various events he described actually could have taken place.

Moses wrote this book during the period while Israel was wandering in the wilderness. This period began a little more than a year after Israel's departure from Egypt. If, as various scholars calculate, the exodus took place about 1440 B.C. (see 1 Kings 6:1) and Solomon began to reign approximately 960 B.C., then Moses wrote this book in the years 1439–1400 B.C. Scholars have referred to Moses' journalistic style; by this they intend to convey the idea that Moses wrote as events occurred; he reported these and, in some instances, commented on them.

Smooth transitions from one part to the next are often lacking. This is probably because Moses was writing a series of accounts or reports at various times and places. These then, were collected and placed in an order that was not always strictly chronological. In addition, Moses also wrote on specific themes; he would finish a theme before referring to events that took place before or during the period the Lord gave instructions (e.g., 9:1–10:10).

OUTLINE

I. At Sinai (1:1–10:10)
  A. The First Census (1:1–54)
  B. The Arrangement of the Camp (2:1–4:49)

1. For further study, see R. K. Harrison, *Introduction to the Old Testament* (Grand Rapids: Eerdmans, 1979); E. J. Young, *Introduction to the Old Testament* (Grand Rapids: Eerdmans, 1949), especially 50–52; J. P. Lange, *Numbers and Deuteronomy* (Grand Rapids: Zondervan, n.d.), 1–15.

C. Legislation (5:1–8:26)
D. Final Events at Sinai (9:1–10:10)

II. From Sinai to Edom (10:11–20:21)
A. To Kadesh (10:11–12:16)
B. At Kadesh (13:1–20:21)

III. From Edom to the Jordan (20:22–36:13)
A. Aaron's Death (20:22–29)
B. The Destruction of Arad (21:1–4)
C. The Bronze Serpent (21:5–9)
D. The Journey to Moab (21:10–20)
E. Initial Victories (21:21–35)
F. The Plains of Moab (22:1–36:13)

COMMENTARY

I. At Sinai (1:1–10:10)

Numbers 1:1–10:10 relates what took place at Sinai during the final twenty days of Israel's stay there. The tabernacle had been erected on the first day of the second year at Sinai (Exod. 40:17); from this tent of meeting the Lord had given the legislation contained in the Book of Leviticus (Lev. 1:1). A month after the tabernacle had been completed, the Lord gave Moses the instructions recounted in the first part of Numbers. It is a matter of conjecture as to why this section is not included in the Book of Leviticus since the census and arrangement of the camp are related directly to the tabernacle and the legislative sections are similar to the material in Leviticus. No reason is stated; however, the mention of the census probably underscored the military strength necessary for the wilderness experiences and the arrangement of the tribes established the marching order of the Israelites.

A. The first census (1:1–54). The command to take the census (**1:1–16**) is given by God; it is not motivated by Moses' fears about what lies ahead in the wilderness. The census gives concrete evidence that the Lord has kept his covenant promise to Abraham concerning a numerous seed (Gen. 15:5), that Israel could indeed be a nation (Exod. 19:6), and that they could be a kingdom of priests (i.e., serve as the Lord's priestly representatives among the nations). The census inspires confidence in the people that they are strong enough, under the Lord's blessing, to face their enemies in the wilderness. Finally, the census bestows a heightened sense of God's miraculous deeds on their behalf; as he has delivered a great host of people, he will continue to provide for them in the face of seemingly insurmountable obstacles.

Every family group, every family, every male twenty years old and older is counted. There are no exceptions; all must know they are part of the Lord's redeemed body and that the privilege of belonging brings responsibilities to serve, particularly in the defense and protection of the Lord's people in a hostile environment.

Moses is charged to call for the census. Aaron and Moses are to number the people by divisions. Assisting Moses and Aaron are leaders, one from each tribe (except Levi's). The Lord appoints these men also. Most of their names refer to God (*el, Elohim* [God]; *Sha-i, Shaddai* [God Almighty]). Some names have particular references (Amminadab, generous; Ammihud, glorious; Enan, waterspring). These names witness to an awareness of God's presence and help in various ways.

The numbers of the tribes vary (**1:17–46**). The lowest number (32,200, Manasseh) is less than half of Judah's 74,600. Seven tribes have more than fifty thousand males twenty years old or older. No explanation is given for the vast differences in the numbers of some tribes. But it is stated clearly that Moses, Aaron, and their helpers register and number the people in obedience to the command of the Lord.

The total number of military-age males is 603,550 (1:46). This figure is also given in reference to Israel's departure from Egypt (Exod. 12:37); however, women and children are included as well as a mixed multitude of non-Israelites. Scholars have wondered about the accuracy of this number when considering the logistics involved in leading so many people from Egypt in one night and in the breaking and setting up of camp when on the march. In addition, they question how a barren desert could supply nourishment for the livestock and all the people before manna fell. W. F. Albright, however, notes that "in the time of Moses the peninsula of Sinai was not a complete desert. . . .The charcoal burners, goats and camels had not yet destroyed . . . vegetation . . . wherever there was some subsurface water. There was such water, which was preserved by vegetation cover."[2]

Some have suggested that the figure 603 comes from the sum of the Hebrew letters in the phrase *the children of Israel.* (The letters of the Hebrew alphabet were used to indicate numbers.) Others have suggested that the Hebrew word for thousand, *'eleph,* also means clans; thus there were 603 clans. However, the additional figure of 550 is extremely difficult to account for if *'eleph* means clans. That the approximate figure of six hundred thousand is given in Exodus 12:37 and in Numbers 26:51 supports the accuracy of the census. The Lord had fulfilled his promise to Abraham: he had multiplied his people, even under the oppression of the pharaohs in Egypt. This large number of people also demands the tribal arrangements and order prescribed in the chapters that follow.

The Levites are not counted in the first census (**1:47–53**). (They are numbered, however, soon afterward; 3:14.) This portion of chapter 1 provides a brief overview of the Levites' duties in regard to the tabernacle; the duties are detailed more extensively in chapters 3 and 4. The warning that no person other than a Levite should come near the tent of the Lord's dwelling is repeated twice (1:51, 53). The Lord is willing to dwell among his people, but will not tolerate lack of respect, indifference, or disobedience in regard to even the smallest detail. The Levites are appointed to ensure the sanctity of the Lord's dwelling and to prevent the outpouring of the Lord's wrath.

The concluding comment (**1:54**) records the obedience of the people to God. They express this by accepting Moses as the spokesman of the Lord and carrying out all God's commands regarding the census.

B. The arrangement of the camp (2:1–4:49). Each tribe is to have its place in camp, must show the banners or flags of various family groups, and have its place in the order of march. The Lord insists on good order. This calls for discipline, obedience, and cooperation on the part of all individuals and groups. No duty is to be omitted, no aspect of the camp is to be forgotten, and no person is to feel left out.

The position of each tribe is specified (**2:1–34**). The tent of the Lord's dwelling and meeting with his people is completely surrounded by the tribes. Verse 17 states that the place of the tabernacle in the order of march is to be between the camps (see chap. 3 for detailed instructions). Verse 34 repeats that Moses and Israel obey the Lord by carrying out all the instructions in detail.

The Levites are omitted during the census and are not given assigned places when the other tribes receive theirs. They are given separate and more specific treatment.

Aaron and his sons (**3:1–4**) are mentioned first. Although detailed instructions concerning them had already been given (Exod. 28–29; Lev. 8), brief mention is made here so that the record concerning the Levites and priests is complete. Eleazar and Ithamar had been anointed to serve as priests by assisting their father Aaron, the high priest.

Three important facts concerning the Levites are recorded: their ministry, their unique role, and their census (**3:5–39**).

The Lord again commands Moses to function as his official administrative representative. He is to station the Levites in the presence of Aaron. This positioning of the Levites indicates their relationship and duty; they are to assist Aaron and his sons. The Hebrew term used emphasizes ministry, not merely menial tasks. They are to perform official duties as they participate in the work of the priesthood at the tabernacle under Aaron's and his sons' supervision. Their ministry is for the entire congregation as well as for the priests. This passage makes it clear that there was a division of labor and a priestly organization with rank. Each Levite had his duty—whether as high priest, priest, or assisting minister. These duties were to be the only responsibilities the Levites had; if they functioned as demanded, no other Israelite had reason to come near the Lord's dwelling and thereby bring death upon himself. The intention of the Lord is clear: he will dwell among his people; he will maintain his majesty, glory, and holiness; he will be served and worshiped in such a manner that his people will be protected. The priests and ministering Levites are to serve as mediators, giving concrete and meaningful expression to the mediatorial office and work Jesus Christ would fulfill perfectly.

The Levites have a unique role (**3:11–13**). They are to be substitutes for all the firstborn in Israel. As God had taken the firstborn in Egypt, so he claims all the firstborn in Israel. He does not take the firstborn of every family, however; he claims the tribe of Levi as his specifically consecrated ones. They, including the domesticated animals, are to give realistic expression to the sparing of Israel's firstborn in Egypt. This substitutionary role is most fully expressed by Jesus Christ.

2. "Moses in Historical and Theological Perspective," in *Magnalia Dei,* ed. F. Cross (Garden City, N.Y.: Doubleday, 1977), 125. See also N. Glueck, *Rivers in the Desert* (Kampen: Kok, 1962).

Since there is to be one Levite for each firstborn, the Levites have to be counted (**3:14–39**) as well as the firstborn (3:40–51). Aaron's three sons and their sons are mentioned. The number of male descendants a month old or older is given for each of the three sons: (1) Gershon, 7500; (2) Kohath, 8600; and (3) Merari, 6200. As they are counted and registered, they are assigned their position in the camp: Gershon on the west, between the tabernacle and Ephraim; Kohath on the south, between the tabernacle and Reuben; Merari on the north, between the tabernacle and Dan. Moses and Aaron and his priest sons are to camp on the east, between the opening of the tabernacle and Judah. Each of the three clans is also given specific assignments for when the tabernacle is taken down, carried, and set up again.

The Lord commands Moses to count and register all the firstborn (**3:40–51**). As with the Levites, so also now, all males a month old and older are counted. The cattle, indicating the Lord's claim on possessions as well as on the possessors, are also counted. The census reveals that there are 273 more firstborn than Levites. Because there are no substitutes for them, money has to be given to the priests. This money is considered redemption money; the Levites, as substitutes, redeem the firstborn. The accuracy of either the number of firstborn, which would suggest the exact number of families, or the total census has been questioned. Perhaps only those born during the period of time from the exodus to the census were counted; or the firstborn were counted according to the rules by which the Levites were counted.

A second census of the Levites is taken to determine how many males between thirty and fifty years of age are present, for only these can minister and handle the various parts of the tabernacle (**4:1–49**). The Kohathites (2750, v. 36) are responsible for "the most holy things" (v. 4). Aaron and his sons must take every precaution that the Kohathites handle only "covered" sacred objects. Eleazar is placed in charge of the Kohathites. It is the Lord's intense desire to maintain his majesty and holiness as he dwells among his people. His appointed servants must minister to him; thus Moses must give detailed instructions to Aaron, his sons, and the Levites. The families of Gershon (2600) and Merari (3200) are given duties related to the tabernacle proper, the furniture in the courtyard, and the poles, ropes, and curtains used to enclose the court around the tabernacle. Each is assigned his task according to the command of the Lord through Moses. There are no options. God is a "consuming fire, a jealous God" (Deut. 4:24). Idolatry and the mishandling of the holy things of the tabernacle have tragic results.

C. Legislation (5:1–8:26). Impurity and lack of cleanliness (**5:1–4**) are not to be tolerated in the camp where the holy Lord has his dwelling among his people. Three types of impurity are mentioned: leprosy, discharges, and the touching of a dead body. There are hygienic reasons for requiring these people to live outside the camp; the spread of disease in a primitive camping situation had to be prevented. There are also religious reasons: the holiness of God, the holiness of Israel, and the symbolic significance of diseases (sin and its effects). Contaminated people are to be sent outside the camp. (It is not stated that they were driven into the desert away from the ministry the camp could offer; nor is it stated that all these persons were permanently banished.)

In the fluid environment of a camp, personal possessions are difficult to guard. Stealing and other offenses against neighbors are forbidden. A misdeed is first of all an act of unfaithfulness to the Lord. Confession of sin and restitution of the entire amount, plus one-fifth, must be made (**5:5–10**). The offender is to bring a ram for sacrifice so that atonement might be made. Specific instructions are given concerning who the recipient of the restitution must be—in this order: (1) the person wronged, (2) a close relative who is responsible to assist a relative in need; (3) the Lord; and (4) the priest. It is interesting to note that as the Lord demands political and religious order, good administration and unity, so he also makes various social demands. It is heartening to read that provision for confession, restitution, atonement, and full restoration is made. The Lord and his people know how to forgive and restore those who earnestly and obediently seek these according to covenant stipulations.

Numbers **5:11–31** has been entitled variously: the husband's jealousy, the ordeal of jealousy, the test of the unfaithful wife, the law of jealousy(ies). All are partially correct; none convey the entire message. The intent of this legislation is to warn the wife of illicit sexual relationships, to protect her from the unwarranted jealousies of her husband, and to promote sexual morality. The emphasis is on wives, who are the bearers of the covenant seed the Lord had promised and prized as a means for the continuity of the covenant. This passage provides a test for exposing unfaithfulness which could become a problem in the close interactions in camp life. A suspected wife did not have to fear the elaborate ordeal if she were innocent. It was the Lord's prescribed ordeal and the woman could trust the Lord to acquit her. Once she was acquitted, nothing could be held against her. Attempts to compare this ordeal with Hammurabi's law code and other passages in Scripture that deal with adultery and jealousy have failed to point up significant comparisons or relationships between them.

The Nazirite vow (**6:1–21**) involves separation to the Lord and from a number of normally legitimate aspects of life. No product of the vine in any form is to be used. To indicate his consecration to the Lord, the Nazirite's hair must not be cut (hair being an evidence of strength and endurance). He must not go near a dead body—not even that of a close relative. Death, reeking of defilement and corruption, is totally opposed to holiness. Should a Nazirite accidentally touch a dead body, it is a sin and provisions must be made for cleansing, atonement, and reinstatement; a sin offering, burnt offering, and guilt offerings are to be made. An elaborate rite is also prescribed for the person who completes the period of the vow. The person is to complete the vow in the presence of the Lord, bringing a series of sacrifices which the priest presents to the Lord. His head is to be shaved and his hair burned along with a peace offering. The Nazirite vow speaks of separation and consecration to the holiness of God. It is a personal intent to realize what God said Israel was—a kingdom of priests and a holy nation (Exod. 19:6) before God and in the midst of the world. There is no reason to consider the Rechabites as true Nazirites (Jer. 35). That the vow remained an option throughout Israel's history is evident from Amos 2:11–12. There is no evidence to suggest that John the Baptist was commanded to fulfill the entire Nazirite vow (Luke 1:15). The Nazirite vow has meaning for us: we are to surrender and consecrate ourselves entirely to the Lord (Rom. 12:1–2; 1 Pet. 2:9–10).

Aaron and his sons are commanded to bless the people (**6:22–27**). It is difficult to determine why this passage was placed in this context; it would more logically follow 3:1–4 or 3:38. Two reasons can be given for its present position: (1) the Nazirite vow did not give the Nazirites priestly prerogatives; (2) not just the Nazirites could expect the Lord's blessing; all Israelites were to consider themselves blessed of God and in close relationship with him. The various phrases of the priestly blessing explicate what it means to bless. When the Lord blesses, he gives himself to his people; he assures them he is their keeper; he is their light; he will bestow grace upon them; he will look upon them with love as a father and will give them wholeness and fullness of life and peace. To pronounce these assurances is to put God's name on them. To receive this benediction, then, is to be named God's children and as such to be and to receive all that God assures them he will make and give them.

An important factor in this passage must not be overlooked. Aaron and his sons are not to pray or call this blessing down upon the people. As anointed and ordained priests they stand in the place of God and speak authoritatively in his name. They put the name of God upon the people. Here we have a clear statement of the function of those specifically ordained to represent God in the assembly of the Lord.

The offerings at the dedication of the tabernacle are described in **7:1–88.** The leaders from each tribe bring gifts (offerings) so that the Levites might do their work. These gifts are of various sorts; note that oxen and wagons are given to Gershon and Merari who are to care for the outer parts of the tabernacle, some of which may have been too heavy to carry.

Offerings for the altar, once it is consecrated by anointing oil, are brought daily until each tribe has made its contribution. Gold and silver utensils, flour, and animals are offered. After twelve days, a large collection of wealth has been gathered. Many sacrifices are offered to express the unity and communion of the believing Israelites. The altar in the courtyard is consecrated to the Lord by the anointing oil poured on it and its dedication is completed by the people's offerings. The altar removes whatever separates God and his people (sin and guilt) and opens the way to fellowship by offerings of grain, oil, and other nonblood items.

The voice of God is heard from above the mercy seat (**7:89**). God had spoken to and with Moses previously at Mount Sinai. Once the altar is anointed and consecrated and the way is opened for man to approach God, he speaks from between the cherubim that are on the mercy seat of the ark. The Lord, dwelling in the tabernacle he had called for, communicates and fellowships with his people through the mediation of Moses. It is important for us to know and believe that the cross replaced the altar, the throne at the Father's right hand replaced the mercy seat, and thus for us the way to fellowship and communion with our covenant Father is through Jesus Christ.

The Lord calls for the light of the lampstand to shine in front of it (**8:1–4**). Aaron is to place it on the left side of the Holy Place so that Moses will stand in the light as God converses with him. Moses is to know and experience that God is light, and speaks and fellowships in the light (Ps. 27:1; John 1:5; 3:19; 8:12; 12:36: Eph. 5:14).

The account of the purification of the Levites (**8:5–26**) repeats a number of important facts discussed in 1:47–53; 3:1–13, 44–51. This purification rite is one of the last preparatory acts before Israel is to break camp. The Levites are to be separated from the other tribes. They must thoroughly shave, cleanse themselves, and wash their clothes. This signifies their separation. Then, with offerings, the Levites are to be placed before the tabernacle and thus before the Lord; the people are to place their hands on the heads of the Levites, thereby signifying their identification with the Levites. The Levites, placing their hands on the bulls to be sacrificed, indicate their acceptance of a substitute to carry away sin and guilt. In this way, the Levites become a dedicated offering to the Lord.

In verse 24 it is stated that Levites from the age of twenty-five and upward are to serve; in 3:15, when the Levites were counted as substitutes for the firstborn, all those from one month and upward were counted. When the Levites were counted for the work of setting up, taking down, and carrying the tabernacle, those thirty to fifty years of age were counted. This heavier work demanded those in the prime of life. Ministry at the tabernacle was less heavy work. Later, when the tabernacle and temple were permanently established in Jerusalem, David called for Levites twenty years old and older to serve (1 Chron. 23:24–25). The Lord cares for his people individually and gives them duties according to their age, strength, and abilities.

D. Final events at Sinai (9:1–10:10). The Lord gives a number of specific instructions concerning the celebration of the Passover (**9:1–14**). At the time of the institution of the Passover the Lord had said, "When you enter the land that the LORD will give you as he promised, observe this ceremony" (Exod. 12:25). But Israel is not to wait until then. Before they depart from Sinai, where the Lord has covenanted with his people, they are to commemorate their deliverance from Egypt. They are to give thanks to the Lord for delivering them from Egypt and the Lord will reassure them that as they journey through the desert, their sovereign covenant-keeping God will sustain them.

A few specific points must be mentioned. The Lord gives this command a month before his call for the census (cf. 1:1; 9:1). This indicates that Moses is not following a strict chronology; rather, he groups three events that pertain directly to the commencement of the journey. Second, the Lord demands that the keeping of the feast be a top priority. No one is excused. Failure to celebrate the Passover will result in excommunication. But the Lord allows for two exceptions: if a person is unclean because of contact with a dead body or is away on a journey at the time. Third, the feast is open to non-Israelites who identify themselves with the Lord's people and who are prepared to follow the Lord's requirements. The Lord thus reveals himself as a delivering and protecting Lord for all people; the biological bloodline of Abraham, Isaac, and Jacob is not the determining factor for inclusion in the covenant people of God.

The cloud (**9:15–23**) indicates the presence of the Lord (Exod. 13:21–22; Deut. 1:33). The Lord is Israel's guide; he is completely in charge of Israel's journey. Verse 15 gives the heart of the matter: by means of the cloud the Lord tells Israel when to travel and when to remain in camp. Here again the Lord's sovereign control of every dimension of life is revealed.

The silver trumpets (**10:1–10**) are to be used for calling the community together or having the camps set out. The two silver trumpets are to be made and used in conjunction with the rising and settling of the cloud. The trumpets, blown by the priests, are to be regarded as the voice of the Lord, calling the people to heed the Lord's directions as indicated by the cloud of his presence. In other passages of Scripture, the trumpet is also associated with the call to recognize the Lord's presence or to hear his voice (e.g., Isa. 18:3; 27:13; Jer. 6:17; Joel 2:1, 15; Zech. 9:14; Matt. 24:31; 1 Cor. 15:52; Rev. 1:10; 4:1; 8:2, 6, 13). In each instance a momentous event is the occasion for the blowing of the trumpet.

II. From Sinai to Edom (10:11–20:21)

A. To Kadesh (10:11–12:16). The Israelites break camp and depart from Sinai in the prescribed order (**10:11–28**). Israel has been at Sinai less than a year. During that short period of time, Israel is transformed from a large band of freed slaves into an organized nation; they have become a kingdom of priests to serve the Lord in the midst of the nations.

Hobab (**10:29–32**), Moses' brother-in-law, likely accompanied his father Jethro when he had come to visit Moses (Exod. 18:1). Jethro seems to have left alone (Exod. 18:27). So, before Israel's journey in the wilderness begins, Hobab is invited to remain with Israel and to serve as a guide. Well-acquainted with the area, Hobab knows the various passes, routes, watering places, pastures, and danger places; he could be Israel's "eyes." Hobab is believed to have stayed with Israel; his sons eventually settle in southern Judah (Judg.

1:16). Thus the Lord's guidance is supplemented and enriched by the skills of a knowledgeable man, who in turn shares in the blessings the Lord has in store for Israel.

The role of the ark is given special attention (**10:33–36**). Instructions for covering it in preparation for travel had already been given (4:5). As the cloud of the Lord's presence is above, the ark, the throne of the Lord, travels some distance (three-days walk) in front of the people. Moses' proclamation as the ark begins to move and when it stops is to remind Israel that the Lord is sovereign; he protects and gives his people victory. His abiding presence is their source of well-being and peace.

Dissatisfaction and lack of trust on the part of the people are expressed by their complaints (**11:1–9**) which are voiced very soon after the journey begins. The Lord, in his anger, warns the people with a fire that burns some of the outer parts of the camp. Moses' prayer on behalf of Israel gives evidence he is an effective, interceding, priestly mediator—he typifies Christ.

The warning by fire is not enough (**11:10–15**). The rabble (some Israelites, some people of mixed blood, and other non-Israelites who left Egypt with the Israelites) tire of manna. They recall the food in Egypt. The Israelites start wailing.

Moses is deeply troubled. He has to cope with the complaints of the mixed crowd, and with the weeping of all the people. And the Lord's blazing anger only adds to his burden. Moses, in a moment of weakness, finds fault with God (v. 11). He accuses the Lord of shifting responsibility upon him. Moses does not consider himself responsible for the origin of the people, for the land promised them, or for their daily nourishment. He would rather die than be crushed by too much responsibility. Moses is neither admonished nor complimented; the Lord responds to Moses with grace, understanding, and assistance.

God promises to provide seventy male helpers and meat for the people (**11:16–23**).

The helpers are to be leaders and officers from among the people. They are to bear the burden of decision-making, comforting and providing for the people (Moses elaborates on their responsibilities in Deut. 1:9–18). This they can do only with the presence and the sustaining power of the Spirit of the Lord. The Lord wants the people to consecrate themselves, and to repent for complaining against him. But the people nevertheless are to be chastised by an overabundance of the meat they craved because of their rejection of the Lord and their longing for Egypt. Moses misunderstands the Lord's intention and again expresses his frustration at the thought of having to do more than he humanly can. The Lord's rebuke to him is a word for all people of all times: wait and see; nothing is impossible with the Lord (v. 23).

Sixty-eight of the chosen helpers, having been placed around the tabernacle, having seen the Lord descend in the cloud, having heard the Lord speak to Moses, having received of the Spirit which Moses had, prophesy (**11:24–30**). Some interpreters think the sixty-eight men had a nonrepeating ecstatic experience. This must be questioned for a number of reasons: (1) The Spirit's presence was to equip them as servant helpers for Moses. Moses, however, with the Spirit upon him, did not display ecstatic behavior. (2) Moses was a prophet, a spokesman for God (cf. 12:1–8). He spoke the word of the Lord. This is the basic meaning of prophecy. (3) Moses expressed a wish for all the people to be prophets and to be equipped by the Spirit. Joshua, Moses' assistant and one of the seventy, took the prophesying of Eldad and Medad as a threat to Moses' leadership. Moses did not believe that at all. He knew that if the people were all equipped with the Spirit they would not be dissatisfied, but would accept and declare the word of the Lord and trust him to fulfill that word.

The conclusion that receives most warrant is that "prophecy" in this passage refers to the recitation and declaration of the words and deeds of the Lord. That is what Moses did as prophet. That is also what people did on Pentecost after Jesus had ascended: when the Spirit came upon them, they began to speak in various languages "declaring the wonders of God" (Acts 2:4, 11). These seventy men, only on this occasion, declared the word of God as Moses did. They are thus shown to be authentic helpers for Moses.

The two men who do not appear before the tent also receive the Spirit. Why they were absent is not stated; their absence is legitimate, we may conclude, for the Spirit is not withheld from them. Rather, the Spirit overcomes obstacles and is not dependent on organization or on the cooperative action of a group.

The Lord supplies meat (**11:31–35**). Moses could and should have remembered that the Lord had brought large flocks of quail before (Exod. 16:13–15). The abundant supply, instead of lessening greed and gluttony, intensifies them. The Lord shows his displeasure by causing a serious illness that kills those "who had craved other food" (v. 34). The exact cause and nature of the illness is not known; suffice it to say that it was a means in the hands of the Lord to warn, to chastise, and to punish an ungrateful people.

Moses' leadership is challenged by his sister Miriam and brother Aaron (**12:1–15**) on the journey to Paran. Moses' marriage to a non-Israelite (Cushite) woman is cited as a legitimate reason for disqualifying him as the Lord's sole spokesman (prophet). This challenge to Moses comes from a qualified woman (Exod. 15:20, a prophetess) and the ordained high priest. It also comes after the seventy elders have been appointed and equipped to help Moses. Moses, when attacked personally, will not defend himself because he is very meek (v. 3). But the Lord deals with sinful jealousy among family members and leaders. He declares his sovereign prerogative in choosing his spokesmen, prophets who receive his word by means of dreams and visions. He declares that Moses is unique because he, the Lord, has chosen Moses to be the trusted leader of Israel. He therefore speaks personally, directly, and clearly to him. The challenge against Moses is therefore a challenge against the Lord. He punishes Miriam with leprosy, making her an outcast. Moses' intercession, demonstrating a forgiving spirit, is heard. But Miriam has to experience being an outcast for seven days.

The Israelites continue their journey to Kadesh in Paran (**12:16**). A number of camping places are mentioned where specific incidents take place.

B. At Kadesh (13:1–20:21). Twelve spies are appointed and charged at the command of the Lord (**13:1–20**). The men chosen are not the top chiefs but recognized and trusted leaders believed to be equipped for the challenge. Each tribe is represented. Ephraim's representative is Hoshea, meaning "help"; Moses calls him Joshua, meaning "Yahweh helps." The name change indicates Moses' reliance on the Lord and his awareness of the spies' need to do so as they carry out their specific assignments.

The request to send out spies (Deut. 1:22) is not necessarily an evidence of lack of trust in the Lord. But the spies are employed by the Lord to test the people's confidence in his guidance and protection after their deliverance from Egypt, which was full of wonders. The people need to believe that what the Lord had done to a mighty nation he can also do to the scattered city fortresses of Canaan.

The spies spend forty days in the Promised Land (**13:21–23**). The first major place they spy out is Hebron. Just beyond Hebron is Eshcol, a fertile valley. The inhabitants are descendants of Anak, a tall and strong people, much larger than the average man. These large men, as also the Amalekites and other inhabitants (13:29), make a deeper impression on the spies than do the huge clusters of grapes and the "milk and honey" flowing in the land (13:27). The spies confirm that the Lord had promised them a fertile land where they could have an abundance of daily provisions. Their fear, however, overwhelms their gratitude; ten of the spies emphasize the evil rather than the good. Caleb is a man of courage; he asserts that they can certainly defeat their enemies.

The people's reaction is tragic (**14:1–4**). They not only disbelieve the Lord (believing the evil report of the ten spies instead) but they also weep, complain, and rebel. They doubt the promises of the Lord; they speak as if they have more concern for their children, the seed of the covenant, than does the Lord. They reveal their folly by expressing a preference for Egypt with its physical slavery, spiritual bondage, and terror of losing their male babies. They prefer the land where they had groaned and cried out to God in utmost misery (Exod. 1:14–16; 2:23–25). True, life in the wilderness would not be easy, but it would be a life blessed with provisions from the Lord and the opportunity to worship him according to his revealed will. The people would also have the opportunity to prepare their covenant children to walk in the way of the Lord. But they fear the sword of enemies and do not believe that Moses, the agent and servant of the Lord, will be able to lead them to the Promised Land.

Four men prove to be men of courage, faith, and conviction (**14:5–19**). Moses and Aaron prostrate themselves before the people. As they pray, Caleb and Joshua express their sorrow and deep regret before God by tearing their clothes. They attempt to convince the people of their wrong attitudes by mentioning several points: (1) It is a very good land; it will meet your every expectation (cf. how Moses described it later; Deut. 8:7–13; 11:8–15). (2) The Lord can and will bring us into the land if he is pleased with us (the implication being that the Lord will not delight in a complaining, weeping, and rebellious people). (3) The people of the land are soft and weak before us because they have no power or means to stand before or against the Lord who is with us. Our God who fights for us will destroy them. However, the prayers and well-grounded arguments fall on deaf ears, and the people think about stoning the four men.

The ever-present Lord, in the cloud of fire and glory, appears before the people at the tabernacle and speaks directly to Moses. He makes three accusations: (1) My people despise me; they have no mind to do otherwise. (2) My people do not believe in me. (3) My people do not remember what I have done for them. The questioning form of these accusations reveals the frustration and pain of the Lord who has revealed his covenant love repeatedly. The people, rejecting the blessings of the covenant, are now threatened with the full impact of the curse of the covenant—pestilence (death) and disinheritance. They will not receive the benefits of God's love and redeeming grace either in life or death. But the Lord will not declare his covenant null and void. He will continue it, not with the tribe of Judah (Gen. 49:8–12), but with Levi, specifically with Moses as the representative agent and head of the people. Moses thus could be both a type of Christ and an ancestor because the Messiah would come through his offspring.

Moses' meekness is demonstrated once again. He does not respond to the Lord's alternate plan which would give him an exalted name and position. Moses recognizes that the Egyptians will be quick to proclaim that the Lord of the Israelites was not able to keep his covenant with them by bringing them to the land of blessing and peace. Thus opportunity would be given to the vanquished Egyptians to proclaim the superiority of their gods and nation. Moses also displays an all-consuming passion for the Lord's name and honor. He pleads for a continued demonstration of the Lord's power—not by bringing death and destruction but by forgiving the sins and pardoning the guilt of the people. Moses knows that the Lord has the capacity to do this; he has done so before (Exod. 32–34). At that time the virtues of the Lord were proclaimed—patience, abiding love, grace to forgive, holiness, and justice. Indeed, the Lord demonstrated all of these in sparing and forgiving an iniquitous and rebellious people. Moses concludes his intercession on behalf of the people by asking God, in accordance with his great love, to forgive the people. Moses bases his intercession on the character of God, on the covenant promises God has given his people, on the wondrous deeds performed in the past on behalf of his people, on his own love for and devotion to the Lord, and on his deep concern for the people. Moses is a true type of the covenant mediator.

The Lord responds to Moses' intercession (**14:20–35**). First, he grants pardon. He forgives the people; the nation will not be destroyed as he has threatened. But forgiveness and pardon do not mean that the punishment will be revoked. "As surely as I live" (v. 28) refers to the Lord's eternal existence and abiding presence. He will exercise his sovereign power in his dealings with Israel and with other nations. As the glory of the Lord had been revealed in Egypt, in the exodus, and at Mount Sinai, so it will continue. This demonstration of his glory will assure the carrying out of the curse of the covenant upon a rebellious covenant people.

Those over twenty years of age are to die in the wilderness: (1) They had seen and benefited from God's glorious deeds of deliverance, protection, and providence in Egypt and the wilderness; they had experienced his grace, mercy, and power. (2) They had tested the Lord; ten times previous to this (ten could refer to specific occasions, which are not all recorded, or could be taken as a full number) and the Lord had proved true to his word each time. There is therefore no reason at all for doubt in this circumstance. (3) They had despised the Lord. They consciously and willfully turned away from him.

The judgment to be carried out is determined by the people's behavior. For each day spent in Canaan, a time when confidence in and gratitude to the Lord should have developed, they are to spend a year in the wilderness. Because the adults had spoken of dying in the wilderness (14:2–3), they will actually die there. A pardoned people needs to learn that the consequences of repeated sins against a holy and just God must be faced.

In the midst of judgment, the Lord demonstrates his mercy and justice toward those who had trusted in him and called for submission to the Lord. Caleb and Joshua are to experience the blessed truth that the Lord remembers and rewards those who wholeheartedly rely upon him and do not hesitate to follow him. In addition, the Lord shows his grace by continuing his covenant works with the children of the murmurers and complainers. The children, in a limited way, had to share in the judgment by remaining in the wilderness for forty years. But they, with Caleb and Joshua, will receive their inheritance.

The Lord provides an immediate demonstration (**14:36–38**) of the certainty of judgment. The original text says of the ten men who had spoken slander about the Promised Land, "they died, these men . . . by means of a plague before the face of Yahweh." The emphasis is on *they died*—then and there. That the Lord used an unexpected and unusual punishment on just the ten men is to impress the people with the sureness and severity of judgment upon willful unbelief and rebellion (15:30–31).

When Moses informs the people of the Lord's word they are deeply grieved—not because of their sins but because they have to face the consequences of their sins (**14:39–45**). They demonstrate their continued folly and rebellion by deciding to proceed to the Promised Land after all. When the door is open to them, they refuse to enter; when it is closed, they try to force it open. They are deaf to Moses' warning; they refuse to acknowledge they are transgressing against the Lord's word; they do not believe that the Amalekites and Canaanites can prevent them. They think they can proceed without Moses and the presence and leadership of the Lord. They are humiliated in their folly; they are defeated and flee before their opponents. The tragedies that result from unbelief, disobedience, rebellion, and self-will stand as a stark warning to people of all ages. The privileges of a covenantal relationship and covenantal promises are not realized when covenantal responsibilities are ignored or refused.

The Israelites had been commanded to go back into the desert (14:25). It is not expressly stated that they do so after their defeat, but it can be assumed they did (see 20:1; 33:36–37). Of the thirty-eight years spent in the wilderness, comparatively little is recorded. Aside from the rebellion reported in chapter 16, Moses records only some additional legislation that the Lord gives during this time.

After the judgment is announced, Israel is given assurance that they will enter the Promised Land by receiving instruction concerning sacrifices that are to be offered once they are there (**15:2**). This legislation has direct relevance to the events that take place at Kadesh.

In **15:1–10** the Lord tells the people how to offer supplementary burnt offerings. Cereals, wine, and/or oil are to be used in specified quantities with certain offerings.

In **15:11–16** the point is made that these specific supplemental offerings are to be brought in the same manner by either a native Israelite or by a non-Israelite who has identified himself with Israel.

In **15:17–21** Moses elaborates on the firstfruit offerings that had been prescribed earlier (Exod. 34:26; Lev. 23:9–14). Once Israel is in the Promised Land, and the grinding of the first grain is begun, a cake made from the coarsely ground flour is to be offered. The Lord presses his claim on all activities of the people.

Offerings for unintentional sins are detailed in **15:22–26.** A specific offering by fire is to be made by the priest on behalf of the person and the entire people and then forgiveness will be granted. The solidarity of the nation and corporate responsibility are clearly taught in this passage. The Lord also reveals his grace and mercy by providing a means to cover sins committed thoughtlessly or by unexpected error. Note again the emphasis on one law for native and stranger alike (v. 29).

Defiant sin (**15:30–31**) cannot be covered by a sacrifice. To sin premeditatively is to willfully rebel against the Lord and to bring shame and reproach upon him. This conscious "reviling" of the Lord will not be forgiven; the ultimate penalty has to be exacted (cf. Exod. 21:12–14).

An example of defiant sin is given in **15:32–36.** The command to keep the Sabbath day was known by the people (Exod. 20:8–11; 23:12). To keep the Sabbath was to acknowledge the Lord's sanctification of his people. To do any kind of work was to profane the Lord, to break his covenant, and to repudiate the sign of the Lord's work of creation (Exod. 31:12–17). When a man is found gathering firewood on the Sabbath, Moses is not sure how he must deal with this situation. The Lord reveals that his word and covenant must not be violated. The entire congregation is called to repudiate this willful sin by participating in the stoning of the guilty man.

The Lord insists that his people be holy (**15:37–40**). The people are commanded to place tassels on the hems of their clothes and a purple-blue cord on the tassels to help them remember the Lord's revealed covenantal will wherever they are and whatever they do.

Aaron and Miriam had rebelled against Moses and the Lord had dealt with them (chap. 12). Now, certain men either are not aware, forget, or reject the Lord's dealing with that rebellion. The rebels are named (**16:1**): Korah of the Levitical clan of Kohath; and Dathan, Abiram, and On of the tribe of Reuben. These Reubenites may have considered themselves eligible leaders because their father was Jacob's firstborn. On is not mentioned again.

The rebellion is well organized (**16:2–3**). The leaders persuade 250 well-known men who are influential representatives of their respective tribes to join them against Moses and Aaron. The rebels accuse the Lord's appointed agents of assuming too much authority and responsibility among a people who are holy and have the Lord in their midst. The conspirators refuse to submit to the Lord's ordained representatives. Moses and Aaron bear the brunt of the enmity and are, in a real sense, helpless because they are being personally attacked. To defend the Lord's revealed will calls for self-defense.

Moses first addresses Korah the Levite (**16:4–11**). The Lord will answer Korah. He will reveal who is holy, that is, separated unto the Lord. The Lord will make his choice known by his acceptance or rejection of incense offerings. Korah, a Levite, does not appreciate the role and responsibilities the Lord has given him in the tabernacle on behalf of the Lord in the midst of the congregation. His basic intention is to become a priest. However, to oppose Aaron and his sons is to oppose and defy God.

Moses tries to respond to Dathan and Abiram (**16:12–14**). But they defy Moses; they accuse him of bad leadership and of exalting himself over the people.

Moses becomes angry (**16:15**); it is a righteous anger. He has been falsely accused but more, the Lord's instructions and plan of action have been consciously rejected. Moses declares his innocence before the Lord and requests that the Lord reject the incense offering to be made on the following day. Moses has bold confidence in the Lord and in his position before the Lord and among the people.

Moses proceeds to challenge and to instruct Korah (**16:16–24**). Korah, with all his followers, is ordered to appear before the Lord at the entrance to the tabernacle; each person is to have a censer. The Lord honors Moses on the following day; he appears in his cloud of glory before Moses, Aaron, Korah, Korah's followers, and all the people who come to witness the outcome of the confrontation. Moses, the interceding mediator, again pleads for the people when the Lord threatens to destroy all those involved and those gathered to witness the confrontation. He addresses the Lord as the "God of the spirits of mankind." Moses thereby acknowledges that God is the Creator; he has given the breath of life and fully controls it. The Lord hears Moses' plea and tells him to have the people separate themselves from the rebel leaders.

Moses obeys the Lord (**16:25–30**). He speaks as directed. The people are warned that they will suffer the Lord's judgment if they do not separate themselves. When they do, Moses, in the presence of the rebel leaders, declares that the Lord will either vindicate him or support the rebel leaders. Moses demonstrates great courage and conviction as he describes the unusual action he wishes the Lord to take. In so doing, he expresses his faith in the Lord's sovereign power over the created world and the Lord's ability to bring judgment on those who despise him.

The Lord responds to Moses' words (**16:31–40**). He opens the earth and buries Korah, his associates, his family, and his possessions. He causes a fire to burn the 250 men who had listened to the rebel leaders and had lit their incense burners. He commands Moses to have Eleazar make bronze coverings for the altar from the censers that the 250 men had used. These sheets are to serve as a reminder that the Lord will accept incense offerings only as he has prescribed. The Lord's judgment on the rebels is a complete vindication of Moses and Aaron, but also confirms his authority. Personal ambition and qualifications are not valid reasons for challenging Lord's designated leaders.

The people, however, have not learned their lesson (**16:41–50**). They accuse Moses of killing the people. The Lord appears in his glory once more. He vindicates his appointed leaders and brings judgment upon the people by sending a plague which kills 14,700 people. Aaron, using an incense burner lit by fire from the altar, brings an atoning sacrifice which the Lord honors. The plague is stopped.

The vindication of Aaron takes place by means of a budding staff (**17:1–13**). The Lord provides a dramatic display in order to convince the people that he has appointed Aaron to the high priesthood and that he expects the people to accept Aaron as his servant. Moses is commanded to have a leader from each tribe bring a wooden staff. One of these will sprout. All the tribal representatives cooperate; twelve rods are placed in the tabernacle before the Lord. The next day Moses brings out the rods and all can see that Aaron's has not only sprouted, but bears ripe nuts as well. This is a remarkable display of the Lord's power over creation. Further, it is a complete vindication of Moses and Aaron before a people who doubted the word of the Lord, who murmured because they considered Moses and Aaron to be self-appointed, and who considered themselves eligible for the honor of holding the office. The rod of Aaron, with its almonds, is to be kept in the tabernacle as a sign for the people to keep them from doubting, expressing dissatisfaction, and murmuring complaints. Although it may be difficult to recognize leaders, the Lord expects this recognition and submission to them. To do so is to recognize and submit to the Lord himself (Rom. 13:1–4; 1 Tim. 2:1–3; Heb. 13:17).

In the context of reaffirming the Lord's will regarding the priesthood after the conspiracy by Korah and his followers, the Lord gives additional instructions on the responsibilities and privileges of the priests and Levites.[3]

First of all, the Lord details the duties of the priests and Levites (**18:1–7**). They are to be responsible for offenses against the sanctuary (tabernacle). If priests or holy things are desecrated, if the people defile any aspect of the tabernacle, or if a desecrating gift is brought (Exod. 28:38), the priests will be held responsible and must rectify matters. The prevention of any kind of desecration is the Lord's intent. The Levites are to assist the priests in all the duties of the tabernacle, but must not go near

3. For background material, see Exod. 40:12–15; Lev. 6:6, 16, 18; 7:6, 32; 10:2–15; Num. 3:6–10, 25, 31.

the furnishings of the sanctuary and the altar. Only the priests are to attend these. God sets the Levites and priests apart for service.

Offerings for the priests and Levites (**18:8–20**) are prescribed. The Lord gives what remains of the offerings to Aaron and his sons as a perpetual due (NIV your portion and regular share). The finest of the grains, fruits, oils, wines, and animals are not to be consumed by fire but by the people and their families who serve at the tabernacle. Detailed instruction is given concerning the place where the priests and their families are to eat the "holy things" given to the Lord. No unclean person may partake. The priests and their families are also to have every firstborn son and firstborn male of clean animals, the money used to redeem them, and the money derived from the redeeming of unclean animals. The flesh of firstborn clean animals is for the priests but the blood is to be sprinkled on the altar and the fat burned as a special thank offering to the Lord. This passage concludes with two important statements: (1) "It is an everlasting covenant of salt before the Lord and your offspring." Salt speaks of durability and preservation; thus the Lord makes an indissoluble or inviolable arrangement for and with the priests. (2) The priests are to have no inheritance of land. The Lord is their inheritance; he will supply in a direct and sufficient manner the priests' daily needs.

The Lord provides for the Levites in a manner similar to that of the priests (**18:21–32**). They are not to have an inheritance except the tithes which the other eleven tribes offer to the Lord. They receive eleven-tenths; with this arrangement the Levites are able to give the best one-tenth to the Lord and still have full provision. This tenth provides the materials to be used on the altar for a daily burnt offering and gifts for the priests and Levites to give to the widows, the poor, and the stranger (Deut. 14:28–29).

The red heifer rite is dealt with in detail. To understand this rite properly, a number of factors must be kept in mind. (1) The Lord is holy and is the source of life; nothing is to detract from or diminish these divine qualities. (2) Death is the result of sin. Sin is defiling; it renders the holy impure and by death brings corruption. (3) The red heifer is not a sacrifice; she is not slain on an altar but is brought outside the camp and completely burned there. (4) There is no symbolism, typology, or analogy of Jesus Christ's atoning sacrifice or of his blood which cleanses from sin. Rather, the red heifer rite functions as a means of sanctification for the Israelites.

A number of specific instructions should be noted (**19:1–10**). The animal is to be a heifer because the female conceives, brings forth, gives life, and provides nourishment. It is to be red, the color of blood in which is life (Lev. 17:11). It is to be without blemish, never used for other purposes (no yoke). Eleazar, the priest, is to supervise the killing; the high priest is never to involve himself in situations where he might become defiled. Yet a priest has to supervise the killing because the blood has to be collected and sprinkled seven times in the direction of the door of the tabernacle; thus the heifer is wholly dedicated to the Lord. Persons assisting Eleazar are also unclean. A clean person is to gather the ashes and put them in a storage place; he will then be unclean. This uncleanness is due to touching the heifer as it dies or when it is dead. The ashes are to be supplemented by cedar wood, which is durable; by hyssop which has purifying qualities; and by scarlet wool to add redness, the color of blood, to the ashes. The supplemented ashes are to be kept and mixed with water whenever someone requires purifying. The rite of the red heifer is to apply to all people in the assembly—Israelite and non-Israelite alike.

The cleansing rite is detailed in **19:11–22.** Anyone who touches a dead body, who is in or enters a tent where someone has died within the past seven days; who touches a soldier killed in battle, a dead body, a bone, or a grave is unclean. Any container without a covering in the tent of death is also unclean. If someone touches the dead and comes near the tabernacle, he defiles it. If water mixed with ashes is thrown on him, he is clean. To refuse this cleansing calls for excommunication from the people of God. The tent, contents, and containers can be cleansed only by a sprinkling of the water of cleansing on the third and seventh days after the defiling. A seven-day period is required for cleansing. The person sprinkling, however, is unclean until he washes his clothes and evening comes.

For the New Testament believer, the red heifer and cleansing rites are instructive because they point out the corruption of death, which is the result of sin and is contrary to the Lord's holiness. But Christ, having died, has taken the sting out of death (1 Cor. 15:52–55). He has sanctified the grave and removed the spiritual and moral defilement of death. Believers therefore do not have to fear touching the body of a dead person as it awaits its resurrection at the Lord's return.

The Israelites had been commanded to leave Kadesh after the spies' evil report (14:25). They had moved southward toward the Red Sea and spent thirty-seven years in the eastern part of the Sinai peninsula. Now, in the first month of the fortieth year in the wilderness, they return to Kadesh and from there proceed toward the east side of the Jordan (20:22).

The death of Miriam is reported briefly (**20:1**). Circumstances are not mentioned; there is no reference to mourning. She had been a leader among the women (Exod. 15:20) in spite of her problems (chap. 12).

The account of the water at Meribah includes Moses' dishonoring of the Lord (**20:2–13**). The people confront Moses and Aaron with complaints about the lack of water, grain, and fruits in the wilderness (cf. Exod. 17:1–7). Reference is again made to Egypt as a less evil place than the wilderness. Evidently the older people recall life in Egypt when they were children and teenagers and, comparing that memory, which was most likely embellished, with what they have, they complain and blame Moses and Aaron.

At the tabernacle, where Moses and Aaron humble themselves before the Lord, God, appearing in his glory, instructs Moses on how to provide water. He is to take a staff and speak to the rock (v. 8). Moses obeys—in part. He takes the rod—most likely the rod of Aaron which had bloomed and been placed before the Lord (17; 20:9); this rod should have reminded Moses, Aaron, and the people of the wonders the Lord could perform in the realm of nature. But Moses concentrates more on the sins of the people than on the Lord as the gracious and incomparable sovereign provider for his people. Instead of magnifying the Lord as the Shepherd of his people and as the source of living water, Moses in anger speaks of Aaron and himself as the providers. He also disobeys by striking the rock twice.

The Lord reveals his compassion, mercy, grace, and power by supplying an abundance of water in spite of Moses' sin and the people's lack of trust and gratitude for their deliverance from Egypt. Moses and Aaron, however, are severely chastised. They, with the older generation, are not to enter the land of promise and blessing. Their sin is twofold: (1) they did not believe the Lord would open the rock; and (2) they did not honor the Lord before the people. The Lord reveals his righteous character and demonstrates his justice by preventing Moses and Aaron from entering the Promised Land. They knew what the Lord had commanded and what he had done before but chose to ignore or disbelieve these facts in a time of tension and stress. The responsibilities of leadership are awesome and can have tragic consequences for those who fail to lead and for those who are hesitant or refuse to follow.

Moses continues to provide leadership (**20:14–21**). While at Kadesh he asks the king of Edom to give Israel permission to pass through the country of Edom. Moses calls Israel Edom's brother; this is true because as Israel descended from Jacob, Edom descended from Jacob's brother, Esau (Gen. 27; 32:3). The brief review of Israel's past experiences, which the king of Edom knows (vv. 14–16), a statement of Israel's need to travel through Edom, and the assurance that Edom will receive full payment for water and food fall on deaf ears in Edom's royal palace. The king of Edom prepares to engage Israel in battle. Edom refuses to assist his brother. The hatred spoken of in Genesis 27:41 is still alive and strong. In fact, it never died (Amos 1:11; Obad. v. 10). The last Edomites in Scripture are the Herods, one of whom attempts to kill Jesus. As Obadiah prophesied, the people who carried a deep hatred for generations against a brother are eventually removed as a people. Perpetual hatred brings death.

III. From Edom to the Jordan (20:22–36:13)

A. Aaron's death (20:22–29). The Israelites take a detour around the northwest side of Edom and come to Mount Hor, five months after arriving at Kadesh (33:38–39). Aaron is 123 years old. Moses, at the command of the Lord, takes Aaron and his son Eleazar to the top of the mountain. All the people witness the ascent. On the mountain, three specific events take place. (1) Before Aaron dies, the high priesthood is taken from him when Moses strips his garments from him. Thus the office of the high priest is not defiled by death. (2) Eleazar is made high priest when Moses dresses him in the high-priestly robes. (3) Aaron dies. Reference is made to the disobedience Aaron shared with Moses (20:1–13). The phrase *Aaron will be gathered to his people* suggests either: (1) that Aaron joined all those who were over twenty years of age at the time of the departure from Egypt, and was reckoned with the disobedient; or (2) Aaron was taken by the Lord to join the fellowship of the patriarchs and their obedient descendants. This suggests that life after death was assured by the Lord. The people mourned for Aaron thirty days. He had not been a strong leader, but he had been a compassionate representative of the people before the Lord and had ministered meaningfully to them.

B. The destruction of Arad (21:1–4). The king of Arad hears about Israel's northward movement. He attacks and captures some of the Israelites. Israel vows that if the people of Arad are delivered into their hands, they (Israel) will completely destroy the people and their cities. This, according to verse 3, happens. Discussion concerning when this destruction took place is not unanimous. Joshua 12 informs us that Joshua defeated the king of Arad and his neighbor, the king of Hormah. It was left to Judah, Simeon, and the Kenites to destroy the cities of the area (Judg. 1:16–17). It seems reasonable to conclude that what is stated in 21:3b was accomplished in time. In Moses' time, then, the people of Arad were defeated, the Israelite captives were retaken, and because Israel did not completely destroy the kingdom of Arad, the southern route into Canaan was not open; Israel therefore marches around Edom and goes eastward and then northward to the Trans-Jordan area.

C. The bronze serpent (21:5–9). The rough, slow journey causes impatience. True, Moses had attempted to travel a better route (20:14–21). The people again recall Egypt and its delicacies. The people speak out against God and against Moses. The Lord sends poisonous serpents into the Israelite camp and many people die. Moses again proves to be effective in his intercessory prayer to the Lord. Moses obeys the Lord in providing a remedy for those bitten; he makes a bronze serpent and puts it upon a pole. The serpents are not removed; they remain as a means to chastise but also to test the obedience and faith of the people. As people are bitten and look at the providential bronze serpent, they live. The bronze serpent is thus a symbol and type of Christ. Israel needs to learn that the Lord is sovereign. He uses the serpent to punish; he also uses it to heal in conjunction with obedience and faith. Israel thus is given a message to proclaim to all nations who used the serpent in a magical manner. But Israel follows the nations instead (2 Kings 18:4).

D. The journey to Moab (21:10–20). The journey to Moab is repeated in more detail in Numbers 33:41–49. Reference to the "Book of the Wars of the LORD" (v. 14) indicates that an account, other than Moses', was written. When Israel arrives in Beer (Heb. well) they sing as they did when they were delivered from Egypt (Exod. 15). The song speaks of the leaders of Israel digging a well. This water is a gift from the Lord (v. 16) but it cannot be enjoyed without the manual labor of the leaders.

E. Initial victories (21:21–35). The area on the east side of the Jordan River may not have been considered initially as part of the Promised Land. But once it was captured, and its fertility and other assets were recognized, it was included as part of the promised inheritance.[4]

Moses asks Sihon, king of the Amorites, to permit Israel to pass through his country (**21:21–31**). Moses assures Sihon that Israel will not live off the land. Sihon refuses; Israel defeats him and his army, and takes possession of the entire area under Sihon's rule. This includes the northern half of the land Moab once had (v. 26). Sihon's earlier victory over Moab proves to be advantageous, giving Israel a large area in which to camp and graze their cattle and sheep.

Moses continues the conquest of the east Jordan area (**21:32–35**). He captures the remainder of the Amorites' land and villages. He turns northward and captures all the land under Og's rule. This gives Israel the entire east Jordan area. The only territories Israel does not capture belong to the descendants of Lot's two grandsons, Moab and Ammon. The Ammonites lived to the east of the northern part of Sihon's area and the Moabites to the south. This invasion of Sihon's and Og's territories is in accordance with the Lord's will. The possession of the entire eastern area, often referred to as the Trans-Jordan, is an initial fulfillment of the Lord's promise that he would give the descendants of Abraham a land to possess, to dwell in, and from which they could be a blessing to all nations (Gen. 12:1–3; 15:7). It is also an initial execution of the Lord's judgment upon the Ammorites for their iniquity. The Lord gives specific instructions concerning the removal of the Canaanites west of the Jordan and explains why this removal is necessary.

F. The plains of Moab (22:1–36:13). Balak, king of Moab, is terrified (**22:1–6**). The reasons for his fear are understandable. Israel had completely conquered the entire region north of the Arnon River where the Amorites lived. Their numbers and needs were imposing. They had moved to the southwest area of the conquered region known as the Plains of Moab. The possibility of Israel marching south is real in the mind of Moab's leaders; Moab could easily be annihilated. Balak calls on the Midianites who live south of Edom and east of the Gulf of Aqaba, expressing his fears and implying that Midian could expect a similar invasion. Balak, having heard of Balaam, who lived a great distance to the northeast in Pethor near the

4. For a proper understanding of where the Israelites traveled and what they did, the reader should acquaint himself or herself with the nations on the east side of the Dead Sea, the Jordan River, and the Sea of Galilee.

Euphrates River, ascribes magical powers to Balaam: "those you bless are blessed, and those you curse are cursed" (v. 6). What only the Lord can do is attributed to a man. Balaam is not averse to being known as such.

Balaam receives his first invitation (**22:7–14**) from the leaders of Moab who are joined by those of Midian. Balak had evidently convinced them that they were also threatened. Balaam is known as a diviner who expects pay for his work (v. 7). This is clear evidence that he is not a prophet of the Lord. But in this specific circumstance the Lord does speak to Balaam. Balaam receives instruction which should have ended the matter: "Do not go with them. You must not put a curse on those people, because they are blessed." Balaam refuses this first invitation. The Lord reveals his sovereign control over his people and also over a foreign diviner.

Balak sends a second invitation (**22:15–20**). This time the messengers are princes, not elders. The reward offered is greater. Balaam replies in a pious manner. He hopes for a sign that will give him the freedom to go. He receives it from the Lord with the stipulation: "do only what I tell you." Balaam is informed that he will not be able to curse as a diviner; rather, he is to be the Lord's agent. This should have convinced Balaam that he will not be able to serve Balak, Moab, or Midian.

Balaam journeys with the delegation to Moab (**22:21–35**). The Lord is angry. The details of the confrontation between Balaam and the angel of the Lord are well known. The Lord demonstrates to Balaam that he is sovereign; he has power over Balaam's donkey, making it serve him by speaking to Balaam. Balaam admits he is going to Moab contrary to the Lord's will for he says, "I have sinned. . . . I shall go back." The Lord tells him to proceed, but only to bless Israel and curse Moab. Balaam proceeds, not as Balak's man, but as the sovereign Lord's servant.

Balak meets Balaam at the northeast boundary of Moab (**22:36–40**). Balak assumes he has Balaam in his service and speaks as an autocratic king. But Balaam admits that although he has come, his divination powers will be ineffective. He can only be a submissive mouthpiece of the Lord. Balak's disregard of Balaam's warning is evident. He attempts to persuade Balaam of his good intentions by sacrificing cattle and sheep. He gives some of these animals to Balaam and the messengers as evidence of his gratitude. Balak does his utmost to challenge the Lord and to bring Balaam into his service.

Balaam's first oracle (**22:41–23:12**) gives Balak evidence that Balaam is not in his service despite the efforts of both to draw the Lord's favor from Israel to Moab. Balaam, following Balak's example, calls for sacrifices. He wants to make sure that he does all he can to perform as the Lord expects of him. He asks for seven (the complete number) altars, seven bulls, and seven rams. Balak is ordered to stand by the altar of burnt offerings, thus indicating that he, by these offerings, seeks the blessing of the Lord for himself and Moab. Balaam goes off by himself, hoping to be assured that he, having set Balak in a favorable position, will be able to evoke a curse on Israel and a blessing on Moab. After all, should a man offering seven rams and seven bulls on seven altars not receive what he desires? This setting up of a sacrificial rite is part of the divination process; the Lord rejects it completely.

Balaam goes to a barren height to look for an omen. It is not related how the Lord meets and speaks to Balaam; that he did cannot be doubted. Balaam is commanded to speak as the Lord directs, not as Balak and he desire. So, from a vantage point at which an outlying part of Israel can be seen, Balaam speaks—not as a diviner, but as a man under the Lord's control. He states the case: "Balak brought me from Aram to curse and denounce the Israelites. But God has blessed them; I cannot curse them." He gives three reasons why he cannot curse Israel: (1) Israel is unique (v. 9); they are not as other nations. Israel is God's covenant people, a holy, royal priesthood. The Lord has given himself to them, and is related to them in a bond of compassion, love, and life. He has covenanted with them. (2) Israel is a numerous people (v. 10a). They cannot be wiped out or even reduced in number by evil words or magical powers. (3) Israel is righteous (v. 10b). They have the Law of the Lord and are called to live according to it. As they do so in submission, faith, and obedience, their covenantal relationship with the Lord is unbreakable. Balaam includes a self-condemnation in the form of a pious wish: as a diviner I am unrighteous, doomed to death; would I were with Israel, then I would live and die in a living relationship with the Lord. Balak fully realizes that Balaam has blessed Israel contrary to his request. Balaam fully realizes that as a diviner he is powerless.

Balaam's second oracle (**23:13–26**) expresses even more strongly the desire of the Lord to bless Israel. Balak takes Balaam to a higher vantage point from where he can see another part of Israel. The sacrificial ritual is followed once again. Balaam again goes apart, as a diviner, to look for an omen. Upon his return,

Balak is eager to know if the Lord has spoken. Balaam tells Balak the following: (1) God is truth. He is unchangeable and thus faithful to himself and his word of truth. He is not to be compared with man. (2) The word of the Lord will not be revoked according to any man's desire. In fact, man is totally incompetent to alter the word or work of God. (3) The people of Israel have been redeemed by the Lord from Egypt. He has made them a royal nation. He has made them strong and invincible. They have not done anything that would warrant the Lord's curse. (4) Israel as a nation was brought forth by a miracle performed by God himself. This makes Israel comparable to the lion and lioness, the regal creatures of the animal world. Israel is victorious and invincible. Balak's response to this message is for Balaam to say nothing; if he cannot curse them, he should at least refrain from blessing them. Balaam protests that he is not free to do as Balak orders.

Balaam's third oracle is Spirit-controlled (**23:27–24:11**). Balak takes Balaam to a still higher mountain peak from which the entire nation of Israel can be seen. Balak still tries to get a curse uttered with all the people in view. Possibly he thought this sight would affect Balaam. Only the sacrificial rite is performed; Balaam does not seek magical powers or insights. The Spirit of the Lord speaks through Balaam whereas previously Balaam merely repeated what the Lord told him to say. As a Spirit-led prophet, unwilling as he personally is, Balaam prophesies as follows: (1) I speak the word of the Lord; I have seen and heard that the Lord is Almighty; I submit to him. (2) Israel is beautiful in God's sight, to be compared with the richest scenes nature offers. (3) Israel is a fruitful people. Water, seeds of life, royalty, and dominion have given Israel an exalted position among the nations. (4) Israel is a victorious people. (5) Israel is a means of blessing to those who bless them, but a curse to those who curse them. Thus Balak and Moab are requesting a curse. Balak's response, in anger, is: (1) you have blessed, not cursed as I asked of you; (2) flee to your home (a threat to his life); (3) you will receive no reward because you quoted the Lord. In reply to Balak, Balaam prophesies against a number of nations; Moab is the first one to be cursed.

Balaam's fourth oracle (**24:12–25**) is, in effect, a continuation of his third oracle. After Balak expresses his anger, Balaam reminds him that all along he could speak only as the Lord of the Israelites permitted him to. He will now warn Balak what this people will do to Balak's people. Balaam repeats what he has said before but adds that he has received knowledge from the only exalted, enthroned God. Balaam first of all elaborates on what he only intimated before (23:21, the shout of the King is among them). He speaks of the star and the scepter who is to rise. Here is a prophecy of the Christ who is the light and guiding power of Israel. Thus, not Israel as a people, but the sovereign Christ, coming from Israel, is the conquering One. The Christ was not yet present, or near, but to see Israel was to see the Christ whom the Lord had promised. Balaam then speaks of the Christ as sovereign judge and executor. He, the offspring and ruler of Israel, will crush the forehead and/or temple of the Moabites. He will uproot Edom from its land. Amalek, who came out to fight Israel (Exod. 17:8–13), will be destroyed. The Midianites (Kenites) who joined Moab in requesting the curse on Israel will be captured by Assyria; and Assyria in turn will be destroyed.

Three remarkable factors stand out in these oracles of Balaam. First, he repeats in one form or another the covenant promises the Lord had made to Abraham, Isaac, and Jacob (Gen. 12:1–3, 15; 17; 22). Second, the kingship of God is absolute. He rules over all thoughts and actions of men. He holds total dominion over all nations. At the heart of his kingship is his rule over, protection of, provision for, and use of his covenant people whom he has redeemed for himself. Trust, obedience, and sanctity in all areas of life are required of the Lord's people. Third, the Lord will execute the curse of the covenant upon all those who refuse to assist the redeemed people of God, upon all those who oppose them or seek to have them cursed.

After Balaam proclaims the gospel of the kingdom of the Lord, he and Balak separate, each going his own way.

Soon after Balaam returns home the Israelites, by their actions (**25:1–5**), invoke the wrath and curse of the Lord. The men of Israel indulge in sexual immorality with young women of Moab and join them in orgiastic worship of Baal of Peor. There is open violation of the first, second, and seventh commandments of the Law. The Lord, in his righteous anger, commands Moses to execute the leaders of those people who have committed physical and spiritual adultery, and then to hang their dead bodies in the sun. Moses, in turn, commands the judges to carry out the Lord's command on the adulterous leaders under their jurisdiction.

While the whole assembly is weeping at the tent of meeting, a leader of the Simeonite family (Zimri) brings a Midianite woman (Cozbi) into his tent (**25:6**). This is open and full defiance of the Lord and of the leaders of Israel and constitutes a defilement of the entire congregation.

Phinehas (**25:7–9**), son of the high priest Eleazar, seeing this defiant moral act, enters Zimri's tent and kills the couple. The Lord's response to this act is twofold. He stops the plague and commends Phinehas.

Phinehas is commended (**25:10–13**) though he has defiled himself by killing and being in a tent with dead people. By his act Phinehas turns the Lord's anger away, is jealous with divine jealousy, makes atonement for the people, and receives the covenant of peace. This covenant is explained in verse 13 as the Lord assuring him and his descendants of a perpetual priesthood; they are to serve as the Lord's mediators on behalf of the people.

The Lord commands Israel to harass and smite the Midianites (**25:16–18**) because of their participation in Israel's adulterous acts with the Moabites and particularly on account of Cozbi. This is carried out and is related in Numbers 31.

The Lord commands that a second census be taken (26:1–27:11). Thirty-nine years have passed. All those twenty years and older when the exodus took place have died except Moses, Joshua, and Caleb. While they were in the wilderness battles had been fought. Plagues and judgments had taken others.

The Lord commands Moses and Eleazar to count the men, twenty years old and older, who are able to go to war (**26:1–4;** cf. 1:1–4). Detailed instructions on how the census is to be taken are not repeated.

The census is taken and reported (**26:5–51**). The reason for the census is given in 25:52–56. Some brief genealogies and references to the family clans are included. The total number of able-bodied men is 601,730. When compared with the 603,550 of the first census it is clear that the desert experience had not strengthened Israel numerically though their losses in the harsh circumstances were surprisingly small. The sovereign Lord has kept his covenant people in spite of wars and plagues.

The Lord gives Moses initial instructions concerning the division of the land (**26:52–56**). Since not all tribes are of equal size, not all portions of land are to be equal. The land is to be distributed by lot.

The Levites are numbered again (**26:57–62**). It is difficult to explain why five families are mentioned as descendants of Gershon, Kohath, and Merari, while eight are mentioned in Numbers 3:17–20. The reference to Jochebed as a daughter of Levi should be taken to mean a descendant who was born in Egypt, because at least four generations separate the patriarch Levi from those living at the time that Amram, Moses', Aaron's, and Miriam's father, is born. The number of Levites is one thousand more than in the former census (3:39). That the Levites did not join in the war may account for their increase, while the total number of the other tribes has decreased.

Not a person counted in the first census is counted this time with the exception of Joshua and Caleb (**26:63–65**). The Lord has carried out his word concerning the people who rebelled against him when the ten spies brought an evil report (14:26–35). The Lord keeps his promises of blessing; but he also carries out his word of judgment.

Zelophehad, of the tribe of Manasseh, had died as a result of personal sin. Since he had not taken part in the rebellion of Korah, he had not forfeited his family's inheritance (v. 3). He has no sons to whom his inheritance might be given. His five daughters, desiring to uphold the rights and privileges of their father's family, present their case to Moses as he ministers before the Lord at the tabernacle (**27:1–11**). The specific question they have is: Can we possess our father's inheritance? This question is important for three reasons: (1) To receive a portion of the Promised Land was to participate in the realization of the Lord's covenant promises. (2) The death of a father who had no sons could eliminate a family from its clan and tribe and totally destroy its identity as a part of the covenant people of God. (3) If no male representative was alive, could a daughter not serve as the family representative? The Lord gives an affirmative answer. A family is not to lose its inheritance; its rights, privileges, and responsibilities are to be assumed, if there are no sons, by daughters; if there are no daughters, a list of relatives is given in the order they are to receive the inheritance. A modification is added later (chap. 36).

Moses is informed of his impending death as instructions are given concerning the Promised Land (**27:12–23**). Miriam and Aaron are dead; Moses is already on part of the territory to be allotted. But he is to go no further.

The Lord instructs Moses to ascend a mountain in the Abarim range. From there he will see the land God has promised to his people. The reason Moses is not to enter is repeated (cf. Num. 20:2–13; Deut. 3:27). Before he ascends, he carries out various instructions and speaks the words recorded in Deuteronomy.

Moses' concern for the people is uppermost in his heart. Moses again addresses the Lord as the God of the spirits of all mankind, the Creator of man who has given him the breath of life. His plea is for a shepherd for the people to go ahead of them, to lead them, and to protect them. The people need someone to govern the daily affairs of their lives as well as administer national affairs. Joshua, who has been Moses' assistant (Exod. 17:9–14; 24:13; 32:17; 33:11; Num. 11:28; 14:6, 30–38) is chosen by the Lord. Joshua is a man who is submissive to and led by the Spirit of the Lord. Having Spirit-directed Moses as a mentor, he has developed spiritual capacity and abilities. Moses is to lay his hands on Joshua, thus indicating a transferral of authority. This is to take place in the presence of the high priest, who is to confirm the transferral, and in the presence of the people who are to witness it. Thus Joshua is to be respected and obeyed as Moses had been. Joshua, however, is not to have the Lord speak with him face to face. The priest is to consult the Urim, which, with the Thummim, is in the high priest's breastplate (Exod. 28:30; Lev. 8:8). Joshua—chosen, appointed, authorized, and equipped to be Moses' successor—is not made equal to Moses. Moses remains unique.

Preparation for entering, living, and worshiping in the Promised Land includes instructions concerning offerings for specific occasions. Once in the land, Israel would have all the provisions required to bring the offerings at the specified times as the Lord calls for them.

Each day two unblemished rams (one-year-old male sheep) are to be offered, one in the morning, the other at sundown (**28:1–8**). These are to constitute the continual burnt offering (signifying total dedication of those bringing the offerings). These rams are to be accompanied by specific measures of flour (cereal), oil, and fermented drink. These offerings are to be gifts to the Lord, and when brought in accordance with the Lord's directions, they are pleasant and delightful to him.

For each Sabbath (**28:9–10**), in addition to the daily offerings, two unblemished rams are to be brought, as well as flour, oil, and wine.

On the first day of each month (**28:11–15**) additional offerings are to consist of two young bulls, a mature ram, and seven young rams. Specified measures of cereal, oil, and wine are to accompany each animal. A sin offering is also to be brought as a sacrifice for sin; the people are "covered" (atoned) as the month begins.

For each annual feast of unleavened bread (**28:16–25**) beginning after the day of Passover, additional offerings are to be the same as those for the first day of the month. These are to be offered each day for seven days. On the first and seventh day of the festive week, no one is to work; the people are to give themselves completely to the worship of the Lord.

For the annual feast of weeks (**28:26–31**) beginning on the day of firstfruits (Pentecost), the additional offerings are to be as for the two previously mentioned occasions.

For the annual feast of trumpets (**29:1–6**) to be held on the first day of the seventh month, twice the number of offerings prescribed for the first day of the month are to be brought.

For the day of atonement (**29:7–11**) on the tenth day of the seventh month, additional instructions to those for other feast days are given. The people are not to work, but to fast and to gather in a holy assembly.

For the feast of tabernacles (**29:12–40**) specific instructions are given for each day of the week of the feast which is to begin on the fifteenth day of the seventh month. A holy assembly and no work are prescribed for the first and eighth days. The offerings are to consist of young bulls, mature rams, and young rams with accompanying offerings of flour, oil, and wine. The first day thirteen bulls are to be sacrificed, and each day one less; on the seventh day seven bulls; on the eighth only one. Each day a ram is also to be brought for a sin offering. These prescriptions for daily and feast day offerings are concluded by a reminder that votive and freewill offerings are to be in addition to these.

Special instruction is given on women's vows (**30:1–16**). These vows are in relation to the sacrifices referred to in chapter 29. A man's vow must always be kept because by a vow a man binds himself to God. To break a vow is to violate his honor and truthfulness (Lev. 27; Deut. 23:21–23). A woman can also make a vow, but it is void in certain situations: (1) if she is still in her father's house, and her father disapproves; (2) if she makes a vow before marriage, and her husband later disapproves; (3) if she is married and if her husband disapproves. Fathers and husbands have the right to void a vow only when they first hear of it. If they wait, the vow has to be fulfilled. Obedience to fathers and submission to husbands is the determining factor. A woman's vow not kept because of a father's or a husband's disapproval is forgiven. A widowed or divorced woman must keep her vow.

Immediately after Israel's adultery with the Moabites and Midianites, the Lord had instructed Moses that Israel was to harass the Midianites (25:16–18). Israel now takes vengeance on the Midianites.

Israel achieves a great victory over Midian (**31:1–20**). It is Moses' last military campaign. The war against the Midianites avenges Israel's honor and executes the Lord's covenantal curse upon the Midianites; they had sought to curse

Israel and thereby the Lord; they had seduced Israel. The Lord in his holiness, righteousness, and faithfulness to his promises, calls for vengeance. This is the Lord's holy war; this explains why Phinehas the priest, with tabernacle vessels and trumpets, is sent along. The victory is complete. The adult males are slain, including the king, princes, and Balaam. The women and children are taken as captives along with much booty. Moses is angry with the military leaders when he sees the Midianite women. They, on Balaam's advice, had turned Israel away from the Lord. He commands the officers to kill all the boys and every woman who has slept with a man. The virgins and little girls are spared; they will be assimilated into the congregation of Israel by marriage. Thus, in the midst of vengeance, there is compassion.

The men who had gone to battle have to be purified (**31:21–24**). The red heifer rite provides the means for this purification (chap. 19). But whatever can stand fire must be cleansed by fire as well. The demand for purification and sanctity, after dealing with licentious Midian, emphasizes the fact that the Lord is holy, and that his people must be holy also.

The division of the booty is carefully regulated (**31:25–54**). The booty is to be divided between the soldiers and the rest of the community. The congregation is to bring as a gift for the Lord, one of every fifty persons and animals to Eleazar the priest (the soldiers are to bring one of every five hundred). The part brought to the high priest is for the Levites.

The vengeance of the Lord on Midian is severe. Their idolatrous worship, including sexual aberrations, is an extreme abomination. The Midianites attempted to seduce, defile, and eliminate the people of the covenant, thereby bringing the full curse of the covenant upon themselves.

The division and allotment of the area east of the Jordan River takes place (**32:1–5**) when men from the tribes of Reuben and Gad request the lands of Jazer and Gilead. Their reason is simple: they have large herds and good pasture land is there. So they ask not to cross the Jordan (v. 5b). (This phrase has been wrongly spiritualized and applied to half-hearted Christians. The Reubenites and Gadites proved to be supportive members of the nation.)

Moses' initial response is harsh (**32:6–15**). He compares them with the people who believed the evil report of the spies and did not want to conquer the land. Their action, Moses believes, will discourage the other tribes and bring the wrath of God upon all the people. Moses, in his last days, does not want to see the people discouraged, disobedient, and rebellious.

The commitment of the Reubenites and Gadites is commendable (**32:16–42**). They express their desire to build pens for their livestock and cities for themselves. They also agree to lead Israel in the conquest of the western territories. Moses concurs, but warns them that if they fail in their commitment, it will be sin against the Lord and they will be punished. After the Reubenites and Gadites confirm their commitment, Moses speaks to Eleazar, Joshua, and the heads of the tribes. If Reuben and Gad do as they have promised, they are to be given their inheritance; if they fail to do their part, their inheritance is to be on the west side and they will not have their request fulfilled. The Reubenites, the Gadites, and the half-tribe of Manasseh are to demonstrate that they are a people who, living separated from the other tribes, will remain faithful to the Lord.

This section on the Trans-Jordanian tribes closes by relating how the land that had been Sihon's and Og's is divided (**32:33–42**). As cities are built or rebuilt, some are renamed (v. 38) because they originally had been named after the gods of the Amorites. Manasseh receives a double portion—one on the east side, another on the west side. The wise provision of the sovereign Lord for his people is clearly evident in this account. He provides for the needs of the cattlemen; he gives an enlarged inheritance to Israel (more than the west side of the Jordan); he provides warriors to lead Israel in its further conquests.

The stages in Israel's journey are summarized (**33:1–49**). The fact is stated plainly: Moses, obeying the command of the Lord, writes this record (v. 2) "by stages." The itinerary can be divided into four parts.

1. *From Egypt to Sinai* (vv. 3–15). This section is introduced by a striking contrast: Israel went out boldly, while the Egyptians buried their dead. The Lord gave Israel a great victory over Egypt. This truth sets the tone for the record of all the encampments. Israel left Rameses going southeast to the edge of the wilderness (v. 6), then turned north (v. 7). At this point, the Egyptians tried to recapture them but the Lord gave Pharaoh one more stroke of judgment and brought glory to his name.

2. *From Sinai to Kadesh* (vv. 16–18). Only three places are mentioned; Taberah is omitted (cf. 11:1–4). Hazeroth is believed to have been on the north end of the Gulf of Aqaba, near Ezion-geber.

3. *From Kadesh to Kadesh* (vv. 19–36). This section covers the thirty-nine years of wilderness wandering. Only seventeen places are mentioned, and these are encampments during

Israel's southward journey. As the forty years were just about finished, they moved from Ezion-geber, back to Kadesh, and on to Canaan. The comparatively low number of encampments suggests that Israel settled in various places for a few years and moved on only when grass and water supplies diminished. It should be remembered that the eastern part of the Sinai peninsula had sufficient rainfall most years for water storage and good pasture on the steppes and slopes. Most of the places mentioned cannot be located with certainty today.

4. *From Kadesh to the east bank of the Jordan* (vv. 37–49). Uncertainty about the exact route followed by the Israelites has not been eliminated by archaeological endeavors. Rather, three possible routes have been suggested. One route would be east of Edom; another route through Edom; and the third, to the west and north of Edom. The last represents the best solution.

Instructions for life in Canaan conclude the Book of Numbers. The command to exterminate the Canaanites is pointedly stated (**33:50–56**). God's admonition contains the following points: (1) Israel is to remove all people living west of the Jordan; (2) Israel is to completely destroy all idols and places of worship; (3) Israel is to take possession of the land given by lot; (4) God warns that if the Canaanites are not driven out they will become a threat and source of pain; and (5) the Lord will do to Israel what he plans to do to the Canaanites if Israel does not carry out his will. As Israel had done east of the Jordan (21:21–35) and to Midian (chap. 32) so Israel must do on the west side of the Jordan. The Canaanites' iniquity is complete and the time to fulfill the Lord's promises to Abraham has arrived.

The Lord lays out the boundaries of the land he is giving to the Israelites (**34:1–15**) west of the Jordan. The boundaries for two-and-a-half tribes had already been laid out (vv. 13–15). The southern border is to be in the wilderness south of Kadesh. The western boundary is to be the Mediterranean Sea (v. 6). The northern boundary is difficult to identify; very likely it stretched across what is known today as southern Lebanon. The Jordan River, Sea of Galilee, and a line north represents the eastern boundary. Note the emphatic statement in verse 12: "This will be your land." Israel receives assurance concerning the Lord's promises.

The Lord gives instructions concerning which men are to be in charge of the division of the land (**34:16–29**). Joshua and Eleazar the high priest are to supervise the division. A leader from each tribe is named. Equal representation eliminates suspicions of partiality.

Cities for the Levites and cities of refuge are to be provided by the twelve tribes. The Lord had given the Levites and priests special duties. He had also given instruction regarding their daily provisions and tithes. When instructions were given to divide the land by lot, the tribe of Levi was omitted. But the Lord does not forget that the priests and Levites need places to live. In the wilderness, the priests and Levites camped around the tabernacle. Once the tabernacle was permanently stationed, most of the Levites would no longer be needed near it. The Lord instructs Moses to tell the twelve tribes that each of them has to provide cities in which the Levites might live (**35:1–8**). Thus they will be spread throughout the nation and be available for conducting worship in local areas, the teaching of the people, and the gathering of tithes and offerings. The tribes with large portions of land are to provide more cities than those with small portions; the total number of cities is to be forty-eight. Grazing land around each city also has to be provided for the animals owned by the Levites.

Of the forty-eight Levitical cities, six are to be selected as cities of refuge for any person who has killed a human being (**35:9–15**). There are to be three on each side of the river. The reason for these cities is at least threefold (**35:16–34**). First, the holiness of the Lord is to be maintained. The shedding of blood defiles the land. The Lord dwells among his people and will not tolerate willful defilement of his holiness. Second, mercy has to be shown. Not every person who kills another does so intentionally. Such a person has to have a means to escape the avenger of blood by fleeing to the nearest city of refuge and remaining in it until the death of the high priest in office at the time of the killing. Third, justice has to be carried out for the unintentional as well as the intentional murder. All human life is precious in the sight of the Lord. Anyone who destroys it has to forfeit his life at the hand of a family's avenger of blood or give up a great measure of freedom by remaining in the city. If a murderer escapes to a city of refuge, and two or more witnesses testify to the intentional killing, by whatever means, the avenger has to destroy the murderer. Justice also requires that neither the unintentional nor intentional murder can be ransomed. Thus the rich and poor, as well as the native and stranger are dealt with impartially. The killing of an intentional murderer is just; it is an act that maintains the Lord's sanctity and sanctifies the people and the land.

The inheritance of married daughters is addressed (**36:1–12**). The issue is raised because the daughters of Zelophehad had been given the right to inherit their father's land (27:5–11). Since tribal leaders were jealous of their tribal inheritance, they did not wish to have daughters who inherited land to take that inheritance with them when they married men of other tribes. During the Year of Jubilee the husband's family would have his wife's land for his inheritance (Lev. 25:10). The Lord commands that daughters who receive an inheritance cannot marry outside their tribes. The women comply by marrying their cousins (vv. 10–12).

The final statement in the Book of Numbers (**36:13**) reiterates that the Lord is in command of his covenant people and that Moses is spokesman.

SELECT BIBLIOGRAPHY

Hirsch, S. R. *Numbers.* New York: Judaica, 1971.

Lange, J. P. *Commentary on the Holy Scriptures: Numbers–Deuteronomy.* Grand Rapids: Zondervan, 1956.

Noordtzij, A. *Numbers.* Grand Rapids: Zondervan, 1983.

Wenham, G. J. *Numbers.* Downers Grove: Inter-Varsity, 1981.

DEUTERONOMY

Paul R. Gilchrist

INTRODUCTION

The Book of Deuteronomy is the keystone of the Old Testament. Jesus Christ cherished Deuteronomy, as is evidenced by his many quotations from it. In fact, there are extensive quotations and allusions throughout the Scriptures to this book. Its centrality arises no doubt from the fact that the book epitomizes the covenantal relation between God and his people. The whole Book of Deuteronomy is, in fact, an expanded covenant expression.

The Book of Deuteronomy is essentially a covenant renewal document couched in the language and structure of ancient Near Eastern treaties. The basic idea of covenant is a relationship binding a suzerain king to his vassals. In the Scriptures, the suzerain King is Yahweh, the Lord God. There is a bond between this great King and Shepherd and his people or flock (cf. Pss. 95–100). This bond is established on the initiative of the great King himself and calls for a response of faith and obedience.

The main focus in Deuteronomy is the heart relationship between God and his people, just as between shepherd and sheep, father and son. Significantly, these titles for the great King of the covenant are labels by which God reveals himself in relationship to his people. The theme of the book amplifies these titles. As the great Shepherd of the sheep, the Lord leads, protects, and provides for his people. As a Father, he cares for his children and instructs them in the way in which they should walk. In all these relationships, he not only corrects and disciplines his wayward people, but also heals and restores the contrite in heart.

The basic covenant relationship and requirement is expressed cogently in two passages: "Hear, O Israel: The LORD our God, the LORD is one. Love the LORD your God with all your heart and with all your soul and with all your strength. These commandments that I give you today are to be upon your hearts" (6:4–6). "And now, O Israel, what does the LORD your God ask of you but to fear the LORD your God, to walk in all his ways, to love him, to serve the LORD your God with all your heart and with all your soul, and to observe the LORD's commandments and decrees that I am giving you today for your own good?" (10:12–13).

The Hebrew title of Deuteronomy is "These are the words" from the first two words of the book. The Hebrew idea of "word" emphasizes the graciousness of God's divine revelation. From 17:18, a second title is "a copy of this law" (unfortunately translated into Greek as "a second law.") Hebrew *torah* emphasizes primarily the idea of authoritative instruction, more so than law in the sense of legislation or regulation. To be sure, there is a repetition of the "ten words" (cf. Deut. 5 and Exod. 20). But even there the stipulations are part of the covenant, as gracious instruction from a father to his son.

Deuteronomy is not simply a repetition of previously revealed laws. Rather, it is addressed to laypeople, in simple and yet profound language, with repetitive phrases to emphasize the importance of a heart relationship to the great King of the covenant. It aims at proclaiming Yahweh as the sovereign King of his people and to exhort his people to continual heartfelt allegiance.

The traditional view that Moses is the author of Deuteronomy along with the other four books of the Pentateuch has been maintained from ancient times. This tradition is based on the claims of the book itself. In 1:1 and 5, Moses is said to have spoken all these words (cf. 5:1; 27:1, 9; 29:2; 31:1; 33:1). Deuteronomy 31:9 and 24 claim that Moses wrote "this law" in a book until it was complete, and then gave it to the priests to place beside the ark of the covenant (31:26). The whole Pentateuch (including Deuteronomy) is attributed to Moses throughout the Old Testament (Josh. 22:5, 9; 23:6; 1 Kings 2:3; 2 Kings 14:6; 23:25; 2 Chron. 23:18; 25:4; 35:6, 12; Ezra 6:18; Neh. 8:1, 14). The ancient Jewish and Samaritan traditions maintain this view as well. The New Testament witness is also replete with claims to Mosaic authorship (see Matt. 19:8; Mark 12:26; Luke 24:27, 44; John 7:19, 23; Acts 13:39; 15:5; 1 Cor. 9:9; 2 Cor. 3:15; Heb. 9:19; 10:28).

The traditional view further maintains that Moses first presented the message of Deuteronomy on the plains of Moab shortly before his death and the conquest of the Promised Land. This would have taken place at the end of the forty years of wilderness wanderings, and after the general conquest of the eastern side of the Jordan (Moab, Ammon, Gilead, and Bashan [1:4]).

Other authors have been suggested, including Samuel, priests, prophets, or wise men. One view maintains that much of the material dates back to Moses, but was not put into final written form until the time of the united monarchy.

A commonly held view today dates the book to the time of Josiah. Deuteronomy is identified as the book of the law discovered during the refurbishing of the temple in 621 B.C. (2 Kings 22–23). The book is said to contain a considerable strata of Mosaic material which had been preserved in religious circles, but which was put down in writing during a time of terrible apostasy (possibly during the days of Manasseh). This material is presented as Mosaic sermons, thereby lending it greater authority.

Another view of the authorship of Deuteronomy suggests that it was not a program for reform but part of an exilic or postexilic document (written possibly in Babylon) aimed at giving encouragement and a sense of direction to a people who had lost everything—their king, their temple, and even their land. In this view, Deuteronomy is the first book of the so-called Deuteronomic history which extends through 2 Kings.

All of the views which deny the traditional Mosaic authorship and date of Deuteronomy fail to take seriously the claims of the book itself as having been written by Moses, as well as the claims of the rest of the Scripture.

The historical narrative is written by an eyewitness who had experienced the wanderings in the wilderness. Many incidental geographical notes betray the author's familiarity with the history and topography of the fourteenth century B.C. Personal reminiscences of thoughts, prayers, and activities in earlier days point to the same Moses of the earlier narratives (see 9:22 and 24:9, among others). This suggests another bit of evidence—the character of Moses. His weaknesses are never minimized, towering figure though he was. Here is not a highly idealized portrait painted by a much later Judaism. Rather, Deuteronomy presents a view of Moses which is consistent with what is revealed of him in the earlier historical narratives. There is no reason to doubt Mosaic authorship.

Earlier commentators recognized that Deuteronomy was composed of a series of farewell sermons given by Moses just before his death. Consequently, they simply organized their outlines indicating first sermon, second sermon, and so on. Liberal scholars suggested that the book was a cultic celebration, Gerhard von Rad (1932) identifying it as a feast of covenant renewal with component parts coming from various literary strata. Martin Noth (1948) saw Deuteronomy as an introduction to Deuteronomic history down through 2 Kings.

With the seminal study by G. E. Mendenhall (1955), who pointed out the amazing parallels between the covenant in the Pentateuch and ancient Hittite treaties, a renewed understanding of Deuteronomy has taken place. The analogy between the ancient international political treaties and the biblical covenant between the Lord and his people was generally well received by liberal and conservative scholars alike, though with certain variations.

Suzerainty or vassal treaties were imposed by powerful nations upon weaker or defenseless nations. The king of a powerful nation was recognized as the suzerain or sovereign, while the king of the conquered or smaller nation had to submit himself as a vassal. Such a treaty was solemnly imposed upon a king or people in the presence of divine witnesses. In such cases, the vassal king and people had no option but to accept the terms of the treaty.

A number of elements were common to these suzerainty treaties:

The *preamble* identified the suzerain king, often referred to as the "great king."

The *historical prologue* summarized the suzerain's previous relations with the vassal, particularly his benevolent activities on behalf of the vassal.

The *treaty stipulations* expressed the requirements imposed upon the vassal for continued benefits from the suzerain. The core requisite was uncompromising allegiance to the great king to the exclusion of any other alliance. The gods of the suzerain and of the vassal were called as *divine witnesses.* If there ever would be a breach of the treaty, the suzerain could call on the gods to bring down judgment on the rebelling vassal.

Blessings and curses related to the maintenance or the breaking of the treaty.

There were other elements found in some treaties, not in others. These were a *ratification ceremony* where the oath of allegiance was taken, *deposition of documents* in the temple of the great king and the temple of the vassal, and the *periodic public reading* of the document as a reminder of treaty responsibilities.

Deuteronomy, then, is a covenant renewal document enlarging on the earlier Abrahamic and Sinaitic covenants, with appropriate repetitions and modifications. Some modifications may be seen in the Decalogue (Deut. 5:6–21), especially the reasons for the Sabbath and the Passover feast (Deut. 16:5–8; cf. Exod. 12:7, 46). Deuteronomy's covenant renewal is built on the foundation of the older covenants.

Theologically, Deuteronomy presents Yahweh as the great King who sovereignly imposes his covenant on Israel. The Lord is revealed through his various names and titles, both as the supreme God of the universe and of all the nations of the world, and as the great King of his people, providing for their needs and guiding and protecting them. He reveals himself as the Shepherd of his flock and as a tender and loving Father to his children. In various ways he reveals himself as a gracious and loving God, forgiving sin and rebellion when there is repentance and faith. This is explicit in the blessings. Through warnings and curses he reveals himself as a God of justice and wrath toward those who do not put their trust in him. Yet his justice is never executed in any arbitrary fashion; judgment always is in keeping with the crime.

The people of Israel are especially chosen by God to be his people, yet not because of any greatness in themselves, but only because of the love of God. Deuteronomy reveals that left to themselves, the people of God will tend toward rebellion and apostasy.

Deuteronomy is not so concerned to show how God's people are to be saved. That had already been revealed in their redemption from Egypt. Rather, it is concerned with sanctification, that is, how the people are to live before the Lord in a covenant relationship. Faith, repentance, and obedience from the heart are presented as the only way to covenantal life. Anything short of this heart consecration and devotion to the great King will lead to difficulties, and ultimately to apostasy and rebellion.

Finally, the covenant extends to every aspect of life, not only the spiritual and religious. This is because God is sovereign over all of life.

OUTLINE

I. Prologue (1:1–5)
II. The Great King's Faithfulness (1:6–4:43)
   A. From Sinai to Kadesh-barnea (1:6–2:1)
   B. From Edom to the Plains of Moab (2:2–3:29)
   C. Exhortation to Obedience (4:1–40)
   D. Cities of Refuge (4:41–43)
III. The Covenant Way of Life (4:44–26:19)
   A. Introduction (4:44–49)
   B. The Great Commandment (5:1–11:32)
   C. Ancillary Stipulations (12:1–26:19)
IV. Covenant Sanctions (27:1–30:20)
   A. Ratification Ceremony (27:1–26)
   B. Blessings and Curses (28:1–68)
   C. The Covenant Oath (29:1–30:14)
   D. Call to Decision (30:15–20)
V. Provisions for the Future (31:1–34:12)
   A. Leadership and the Law (31:1–29)
   B. The Song of Moses (31:30–32:47)
   C. The Testament of Moses (32:48–33:29)
   D. The Death of Moses (34:1–12)

COMMENTARY

I. Prologue (1:1–5)

The first element in ancient treaties was the preamble, which identified the suzerain king. He was often referred to as the great king, the shepherd of the vassal nation, the father of the people, the king of the land, the valiant one, the favorite of the gods. In the Abrahamic covenant, Yahweh identified himself simply as "God Almighty" (Gen. 17:1). In the Sinaitic covenant, he identified himself as "the LORD your God" (Exod. 20:2a). In Deuteronomy, God identifies himself through his mediator.

Moses is the mediator of the covenant on behalf of Yahweh. He serves here as God's spokesman, a function assigned to the Old Testament prophets (see 18:14–22). He speaks to Israel for God.

The location of this great assembly of the people of Israel is in the desert east of the Jordan (v. 1). The time is specifically designated as winter–spring of the fortieth year since the exodus from Egypt (v. 3). The eleventh month of the sacred calendar would fall in January–February. On the plains of Moab by the Dead Sea, this would have been a very pleasant time of year conducive to a conference or camp meeting. This time reference dovetails beautifully with the Israelites' crossing of the Jordan at "flood stage during the harvest" (Josh. 3:15), that is, during the spring of the year. Verse 4 specifically mentions that this takes place after the conquest of Sihon, king of Heshbon, and Og, king of Bashan, on the east side of the Jordan.

Moses begins to expound the Law to the people. He delivers a hortatory exhortation designed to move the hearts and minds of his hearers to "choose life" (30:19). This final conference is intended by Moses to give Israel instruction in the faith and to press home the requirements of the covenant relationship. Moses' address is the authoritative instruction of a father to his son, of a shepherd to his flock, of a wise man to his disciple, rather than a judicial rehearsal of legal requirements. Here is Moses at his finest, as a faithful pastor expounding on the life of faith and obedience which demands single-minded devotion and allegiance to the Lord of the covenant. Moses is a type of "the great Shepherd of the sheep," Christ (Heb. 13:20). The same spirit, the same love and concerns, the same kind of warnings pervade, because it is the same Holy Spirit revealing the great King.

II. The Great King's Faithfulness (1:6–4:43)

The historical prologue of ancient treaties reviewed the activities of the suzerain, underscoring his faithful care of the vassal. It often justified actions being taken, and was designed to inspire confidence so that the vassal would respond with gratitude to the treaty stipulations which followed.

A. From Sinai to Kadesh-barnea (1:6–2:1). In this first section, Yahweh's providential care for his people during the wilderness wanderings is briefly detailed. As a summary of Numbers 10:1–20:13, what is omitted is significant.

Moses begins with the breaking up of the encampment at Sinai after a stay of a little over a year (**1:6–8**; cf. Num. 9:1, 5; 10:11). The description of the land possessed by the Canaanites (v. 7) is an accurate rehearsal of the topographical features of the Promised Land. The divine initiative at this point is prompted by the promises made to the patriarchs and confirmed by oath. Moses reminds the people that God's love for them comes only because of grace and through the promises, not because of any intrinsic merit.

By the time of the exodus, the descendants of Abraham had become a vast multitude, not to mention the many Gentile aliens. The enormous responsibility given to Moses could only be handled by the appointment of leaders **(1:9–18).** Though Moses was the leader ordained by God, he needed help. The leaders appointed by Moses included the leading men of the tribes (lit. the heads of the tribes), commanders (lit. clerks/scribes who served as officers or quartermasters), and judges who were to hear legal disputes or problem cases. In dealing with judicial cases, they were to show impartiality, a quality characteristic of Yahweh their God.

The land was God's gift to Israel (v. 21). The Lord urged the Israelites to send spies to check out this land (**1:19–25;** cf. Num. 13:1). They penetrated to the Valley of Eshcol, probably two miles north of Hebron, from where they brought a great cluster of grapes on a pole. All twelve spies agreed that the land was good.

However, Israel's response was rebellious and faithless **(1:26–33).** Their unwillingness to take up the challenge of conquest was tantamount to rebellion against their great King. Their unbelief turned into grumbling against the Lord. Contrary to all the evidence of the Lord's faithfulness, they complained that he hated them and intended to destroy them. They put their misguided faith in the ten spies, who convinced them of the danger posed by the stronger and taller people, walled cities, and the Anakites (lit. sons of the Anakim). The descendants of Anak, one of the early inhabitants of Hebron (Josh. 15:13), had a reputation for being tall and strong ("Who can stand up against the Anakites?" 9:2; cf. 2:10, 21; Num. 13:33).

Moses recounts the evidence revealing the mighty power of God in face of impossible situations, both in the exodus from Egypt and in the deserts of Sinai and the Negeb. The account is extremely abbreviated compared to the material written earlier (see Exod. 1–19; Num. 10:1–20:13). Moses does not dwell on the numerous occasions of murmuring and rebellion. He is satisfied to note the turning point in that generation's spiritual commitment. How like God, who so tenderly deals with his people in spite of their many transgressions. God carries Israel as a father carries his son (v. 31).

Yet God's judgment **(1:34–40)** stands side by side with his steadfast love, mercy, and compassion. This judgment is temporal, designed to bring his children to repentance and faith (cf. the increasing degree of severity in the curse passages, all of which are designed to lead to repentance: Lev. 26:14–39; Deut. 28:15–68; and Solomon's prayer in 1 Kings 8:28–53). This redemptive judgment must be seen in light of the promises for the generation which Moses is currently addressing (vv. 38–39). Their fathers' unbelief is recalled primarily as a means of challenging this generation to faith and commitment.

Disobedience and unbelief go hand in glove, just as the graces of faith and repentance **(1:41–2:1).** God's presence in the midst of his people is a sine qua non for victory and success. For their presumption, Israel was defeated at Hormah. For thirty-eight years the Israelites wandered in the desert regions between the Negeb and the gulf of Eilat (1:40, 44, 46; 2:1), skirting around the hill country of Seir (lit. Mount Seir).

B. From Edom to the Plains of Moab (2:2–3:29). At the end of the wilderness wanderings, the Lord again took the initiative with commands and promises to lead the people into the Promised Land. His gracious care preceded the command for conquest. This second generation responded in faith and obedience, resulting in victory over the Canaanites.

With most of the first generation gone, the command to prepare for the conquest of the land was reiterated. Israel was prohibited from provoking the Edomites to war **(2:2–8).** They were to go around Edom on the east side of the Jordan. The Edomites were Israel's brothers (descendants of Esau; Num. 20:14–21). God as universal Sovereign had given that territory to Esau for his descendants (v. 5; Gen. 36:8). The fact that God would not allow Israel to touch the land of Edom was further evidence that his solemn word must not be violated. What God had given, he would not take away, unless extreme rebellion called for it. This prohibition did not preclude the Israelites from getting provisions from the Edomites (vv. 28–29). The matter-of-fact way in which verse 8 states how that part of the journey went underscores the fact that the word of the great King can be trusted. Moses is magnanimous not to remind Israel of their rebellion which brought God's judgment (see Num. 21:4–9).

The Moabites were not to be harassed or provoked into warfare **(2:9–15).** They were descendants of Lot, Abraham's nephew (cf. Gen. 19:37–38; Num. 21:10–20). Their land had also been given to them by the Lord (v. 9). Verses 10–12 parenthetically review the former inhabitants of Moab and Edom, again suggesting that however powerful they might have been, the great Suzerain of the covenant was able to dispossess them. This is further evidence that God is a powerful God, able to back up his word of promise with mighty deeds. The crossing of the Zered Valley (marking the boundary between Edom and Moab) concluded the thirty-eight years of wilderness wanderings. The evidence is clear that God does not speak lightly, but fulfills his promise of blessing or curse.

The Ammonites **(2:16–23)** were also descendants of Lot (Gen. 19:37–38) and were to be bypassed.

The crossing of the Arnon River would mark the first territory to be possessed. The command to cross it (**2:24–25**) had been given with the assurance that God would give the Israelites the land of the Amorite king, Sihon of Heshbon. The earlier discouragement (cf. Num. 21:4) was dispelled by new confidence based on the evidence that God's word could be counted on.

Sihon's refusal of the peace treaty was evidence that God had hardened his heart (**2:26–37**). Moses goes out of his way to emphasize that the victory was due to the Lord's benevolent activity. Note the marvelous balance between God's sovereign power and man's active participation. The captured territory was from the Arnon Gorge north to the Jabbok River.

The victory over Sihon encouraged Israel to press on against Og, king of Bashan (**3:1–11**). Moses repeats the encouraging words, "Do not be afraid of him, for I have handed [given] him over to you . . . " (v. 2). The victory sufficed to encourage the people that God's word could be trusted.

Verses 8–10 summarize what had been conquered up to that time, from the Arnon as far as Mount Hermon. How much territory north of Edrei might have been captured and controlled is not clear. The iron bed (v. 11) might better be considered a sarcophagus, but the reference underscores the huge size of Og.

Moses gives a summary description of the land granted to the two-and-half tribes on the east side of the Jordan (**3:12–17**; given in more detail in Num. 32:33–42). No specific boundaries are given to distinguish between Reuben and Gad. This territory was excellent grazing land (cf. Num. 32:1).

Moses next reviews the lecture given in Numbers 32:1–32 to Reuben, Gad, and the half-tribe of Manasseh (**3:18–20**). In light of the reticence expressed then, the thrust of that message was to show the necessity for solidarity in the corporate body. Fragmentation and independence could lead only to disaster. Rest (v. 20) includes freedom from attacks by the enemy, alluding to peace from oppression.

Moses was forbidden to cross the Jordan (**3:21–28**). Joshua had already been selected to succeed Moses as leader of the nation. Encouragement for the future had its foundation in God's mighty acts in the past. "The Lord your God himself will fight for you" (v. 22) was not just a motto, it was a historical reality. When Moses pleaded for the privilege of leading the people across the Jordan, God's response was an angry rejection. The specific reason is not mentioned here, but Numbers 20:12 and 27:14 point to rebellious unbelief. Moses claimed credit for himself, rather than giving God the glory.

However, evidence of God's grace and pardon to Moses was that he was permitted to see the Promised Land from Pisgah. Moses also had the privilege of commissioning Joshua for his new responsibilities.

Verse 29 concludes the historical section of Moses' address. It forms an inclusio with 1:5. Israel is here now because of the good hand of the Lord who has guided them all the way.

C. Exhortation to obedience (4:1–40). Moses now gives the theological basis for obedience to the covenant way of life.

"Hear, O Israel" is a definitive call to give heed to the gracious revelation of God (**4:1–8**). It carries the notion of hearing or listening with the intent to obey. This is repeated frequently throughout the Book of Deuteronomy (see, e.g., 5:1; 6:3, 4; 9:1).

Verse 2 explicitly prohibits adding to or taking away from the revelation God has given (cf. Rev. 22:18–19). In short, Moses says: "Do not change the law which reflects the attributes, character, and nature of God. Otherwise, you may have a god who reflects what *you* imagine a god to be. Let God reveal himself through his Word." Following after other gods is idolatry. Idolatry questions the sufficiency of God's work of redemption.

A nation is not great because of the number

of its people or the extent of its territory, but because its foundation is the very Word of God (vv. 6–8). The wisdom of the people is not so much their intellectual acumen as the skill with which they apply God's Word to every area of life and in relationship to him.

Finally, verse 8 points to the Law as the foundation for a great nation. Law here may refer to the material in Deuteronomy, or more broadly to the whole Pentateuch. It is righteous because it reflects the very attributes of Yahweh.

Moses enjoins personal and family responsibility (**4:9–14**): "Only be careful and watch yourselves closely so that you do not forget the things your eyes have seen or let them slip from your heart as long as you live. Teach them to your children and to their children after them" (v. 9).

The experience at Horeb (v. 10) was the historical climax of the first stage of Israel's salvation. In that historical event there was a great theological lesson: the Lord God is spiritual and unique in his essence. The people heard his voice, but he was invisible. This revelation served as the basis for the second commandment. This was no abstract doctrine, but a revelation of God who established a personal relationship with his people. This relationship is a covenant (v. 13), which God graciously wrote not only on stones but intended to be inscribed on the believer's heart.

Moses gives a most solemn warning to all Israel against idolatry (**4:15–24**). If the Lord was angry with Moses, how much more will his judgment fall on Israel if they forget the covenant and make idols which will corrupt them spiritually and morally? God demands exclusive worship because he is "a consuming fire, a jealous God" (v. 24).

Moses lists the consequences of idolatry (**4:25–31**), appealing for faithfulness to God's covenant. Heaven and earth will be called as witnesses to any deviation from fidelity. Moses introduces the specter of a lawsuit, in which these silent witnesses as representatives of all creation serve as a jury. The possibility of judgment is an awesome threat. The people will perish from the land and will be scattered among the nations (a threat carried out with the deportation by the Assyrians in 722 B.C. and by the Babylonians in 586 B.C.). Their deliberate rebellion against God will result in their slavery to gods of wood and stone.

Nonetheless, God's drastic judgments are "redemptive" because he intends through them to recall his people to the covenant. The theological ground for redemptive judgment is the compassion and mercy of God (v. 31). God has revealed himself as such (Exod. 34:6–7; Deut. 7:9). He will not forget his covenant promises to Abraham. Yet God will require the people to seek him with all their heart (v. 29), with a genuine sense of repentance, in obedience to his voice.

God is unique and incomparable, as evidenced by his mighty acts in history (**4:32–40**). Moses appeals to history to justify his claims, going back to the day God created man (v. 32). More specifically, he appeals to the mighty wonders at the time of the exodus. Verses 32–34 serve as rhetorical questions to show the incomparability of Yahweh. God is unique. All the gods of Egypt and Canaan are not really gods; there is only One. All these things happen that Israel might know God. To know the Lord experientially is different from knowing *about* God. The Old Testament is not satisfied with theologizing about God, but ever presses for a personal relationship with the Lord. The covenant is given to reveal this unique and incomparable God.

God's love (v. 37) is an electing love. It is not based on merit, but solely on his everlasting mercy and grace (7:7–8; 10:15; 23:5). The appeal to respond is given repeatedly (5:10; 6:5; 7:9; 10:12; 11:1; 13:3; 19:9; 30:6). "So that it may go well with you" (v. 40) is another recurring theme of the exhortations (5:16, 33; 6:3, 18; 12:25–28; 22:7).

D. Cities of refuge (4:41–43). In Numbers 35:1–8, provision for cities of refuge was made in principle. Now that the Trans-Jordan has been conquered, Moses specifically identifies three cities to serve this purpose. The reasons for these refuge cities are enumerated in Numbers 35:10–34 and amplified in Deuteronomy 19:1–13, where an additional three cities are designated for the western territory of the Promised Land. In tribal cultures, the nearest of kin was responsible for carrying out the punishment against a criminal. In cases of unintentional murder, the murderer could seek asylum in one of these cities of refuge. This appendix serves as a token of God's gracious dealings with his people; he mercifully provides even for criminals.

III. The Covenant Way of Life (4:44–26:19)

The third major section of ancient Near Eastern treaties outlined stipulations which the great king demanded of his vassal. This section expressed the requirements imposed upon the vassal, the basic one being uncompromising allegiance to the great king to the exclusion of all foreign allegiances. The stipulations included both basic principles and specific requirements.

The general stipulations of the covenant at Sinai begin with the apodictic word: "You shall have no other gods before me. You shall not make for yourself an idol . . ." (Exod. 20:3–4). Then, beginning at verse 18, the more specific covenant requirements are given, some couched in casuistic (case) form; others in apodictic (imperative) style. As a constitutional document, the covenant was intended to guide and instruct the people of God in the way of life demanded by their gracious Sovereign.

As covenant renewal, Deuteronomy follows this pattern. Certain stipulations given earlier suited the unsettled conditions of the people of God. With the anticipation of entering the land of promise, some stipulations are enlarged or changed to meet the needs of a settled community. Chapters 5–11 are primarily an extended explication of the first and second commandments, thus expressing the major concern that is on Moses' heart. Chapters 12–26 are essentially ancillary to these commandments and flow from them. The more specific stipulations are couched at times as case laws (if . . . , then . . .) but should not be construed as covering all possible cases which might emerge in the new land. They are given as examples of the outworking of the basic principles enunciated in the first and second commandments, which together might be called "the great commandment" and is succinctly stated in 6:4–5.

A. Introduction (4:44–49). The introduction repeats the setting briefly (cf. 1:1–5). The stipulations which follow are designated as "decrees and laws" (v. 45) and are specifically attributed to Moses (v. 44).

B. The great commandment (5:1–11:32). Chapters 5–11 set forth the primary requirement of the covenant relationship, namely, complete consecration to Yahweh in one's innermost spirit. God's demand for exclusive lordship is based on the covenant relationship established at Sinai. Deuteronomy repeats the basic features of the Sinai covenant.

"Hear, O Israel" is a summons to listen with the intention of obedience (**5:1–5**). Moses will repeat what had been given at Horeb (v. 2), but will enlarge upon it by explicating the principles of covenant life. God's covenant was made not only with the patriarchs or the first generation out of Egypt, but "with all of us who are alive here today" (v. 3b). Note the solidarity of succeeding generations. This solidarity places certain responsibilities on all succeeding generations. Moses acknowledges his mediatorial work (v. 5), especially needful because of the people's fear incurred by the fiery theophany.

Moses reaffirms the Sinai covenant (**5:6–21**). Three major components of that covenant are reiterated: the preamble; the historical prologue; and the covenant stipulations. The fourth covenant word is repeated but with a different rationale. Otherwise, this passage is essentially the same as Exodus 20:1–17.

The stress in the first four covenant words are on the sovereign rights of the great King whose identity (vv. 6–7), nature (vv. 8–10), name (v. 11), and day (vv. 12–15) are to be fully acknowledged. The first three words call for holiness in worship, while the fourth calls for holiness in work and serves as a transition to the last six commandments. The redemption from Egypt is a significant basis for keeping the Sabbath holy. The creation ordinance is not abrogated, nor is the creation model set aside. Rather, both creation and redemption serve as the basis for this work and rest principle. The last six covenant stipulations call for holiness in life, and stress obligations of covenant believers to each other (vv. 16–21).

Moses recalls the resplendent glory and majesty of Yahweh on Sinai and Israel's reaction (**5:22–27**). The mountain itself had been ablaze with fire (5:23; cf. Exod. 24:17; Heb. 12:29). The fear of the people at hearing God speak stood in stark contrast to Adam and Eve's delight in the presence and fellowship of the Lord in the garden of Eden. Instead of taking God's gracious work as beneficial, their fallenness made them perceive it as a threat to life. Nevertheless, in faith they acknowledged the Lord as their God and committed themselves to obedience, asking only that Moses serve as their mediator before the awesome King.

God honored Israel's response (**5:28–33**). Everything they said was good and God yearned for their heartfelt obedience. Deuteronomy is an exposition of God's way of life (5:33) which is rewarded with prosperity and longevity.

Deuteronomy 6:1–25 stands as the centerpiece of the book as it expresses the principle of total heart commitment to the exclusive lordship of the great King.

God's way of life is prescribed for this and following generations (**6:1–3**). Once again prosperity and longevity are promised as the reward for faithfulness to the Lord.

The great confession (**6:4**) is expressed in the indicative, as a statement of fact. It declares who Yahweh is. It is very personal: The Lord *our* God. Furthermore, *The Lord is one;* he is unique. This great confession is to be constantly on the hearts and lips of God's people.

Only after the great confession is the great commandment given and it is in the imperative (**6:5**). Note the sequence in Exodus: the great redemption from Egypt (indicative), then the covenant with its stipulations (imperative). Israel must submit exclusively to the Lord with totality of being *(heart)* and intensity of devotion *(love)*. Jesus called this exclusive demand for total commitment and intense love "the first and greatest commandment" (Matt. 22:37–38; Mark 12:29–30; Luke 10:27). It is this total heart devotion that bonds the covenant relationship. Past mercies already mentioned in the historical prologue together with the revelation of who the Lord is, prompts love and reverent obedience to all the instructions which follow.

Not only is the individual to make this confession and to keep this commandment, but the family ("impress them on your children" and "write them on the doorframes of your houses," vv. **7–9a**) and the community ("write them . . . on your gates," v. **9b**) are also to come under the governance of the covenant stipulations. Moses is not advocating the inordinate externalism of later Judaism with its philacteries and mezuzahs.

The immediate application is that Israel is strictly prohibited from any allegiance to other gods (**6:10–15**). When the covenant promises of Yahweh are fulfilled, Israel is not to forget the Lord, their Redeemer from Egyptian bondage. The danger of forgetting the past mercies of the Lord is of paramount concern to Moses (cf. 4:9, 23; 8:11, 14, 19; 9:7; 25:19). Forgetfulness naturally leaves a vacuum leading to idolatry (cf. 7:4; 17:3; 28:36, 64; 29:26; 30:17; 31:20). The Lord who is ever present is as jealous as a husband toward any impropriety of a wayward wife.

The implication is a warning against imposing conditions on Yahweh (**6:16–19**). Massah was the place where Israel tested the Lord (Exod. 17:1–7). The test was in the form of a question of unbelief: "Is the Lord among us or not?" Such presumption demands proof of God's presence (v. 15) and power (v. 19). Rather, Israel is responsible for diligence and faithfulness to the covenant. Christ used this warning to ward off Satan's temptation (Matt. 4:7).

The promulgation is for the covenantal nurture of succeeding generations (**6:20–25**). This enlarges on verses 7–9 (cf. Ps. 78:1–8). It is also crucial for the welfare of the nation as a people of God. Children will ask questions. Fathers are to respond with the basic element of faith, namely, the story of the bondage in Egypt and the redemption by the mighty acts of God. "Our righteousness" (v. 25b) does not mean salvation by the works of the Law but stresses the Law's function of revealing the standard of conduct expected of a believer, a righteousness which is from God himself. The purpose of God's presence is "to bring us in and give us the land" (v. 23), not "to make us and our children and our livestock die" (Exod. 17:3).

The policy of destruction of the Canaanites is dictated by the *ḥērem* principle (**7:1–5**). Seven nations or peoples are listed, but elsewhere the number varies from three to ten (cf. Josh. 3:10; 24:11). The ancient curse on Canaan by Noah (Gen. 9:25–26) had been reiterated at Sinai (Exod. 23:20–33; 34:11–16). Moses now states it as a program of conquest and extermination, especially because of the degenerate nature of Canaanite religion. Their hatred of the Lord whose witness they had heard since the patriarchal period is now under the everlasting ban of extermination; as reprobates they are devoted to the wrath of God (cf. Rom. 9:22; 1 Pet. 2:8; Rev. 16:1–14). Intermarriage is prohibited not for social reasons but for religious reasons as 7:4 makes clear: "for they will turn your sons away from following me to serve other gods." Positive consecration to the Lord demanded in chapter 6 calls for total destruction of pagan religious cults.

The reason for the conquest is Israel's character by virtue of covenantal relation (**7:6–11**). There is no room for compromise, for Israel is in covenant relationship with the great King as a holy people, a treasured possession. Israel's special status is by virtue of election—chosen by God, not because of any inherent greatness but solely because of God's love and the oath-bound promise made to Abraham. God's sovereignty is also expressed in his faithfulness (v. 9), whereby he keeps his "covenant of love to a thousand generations of those who love him and keep his commands." Love (Heb. *ḥesed*, mercy, steadfast love, loyalty, covenant love) is the epoxy that binds people and God together. Note the amazing grace of God expressed in the Decalogue where the *thousand generations* to whom God's covenant love is applied is placed in contrast to God's punishing the iniquity of the fathers on the children to the *third* and *fourth generation* of those who hate him (Exod. 20:5–6; Deut. 5:9–10). Such a high calling is often accompanied by pride and boastfulness (problems which Moses deals with in chaps. 8–10). Israel is not to presume on God's covenant love and grace, for carelessness only leads to destruction as a further exhibit of God's justice.

The result of obedience is prosperity, health, and success (**7:12–16**). If the covenant curses are no idle threat for those who despise the grace of the covenant, neither are the blessings of the covenant idle promises. It is not Baal, but Yahweh who freely bestows fertility and blessings on crops, family, and flocks. The diseases in Egypt were God's judgment on a rebellious nation, but the same God will turn the curse into a blessing.

The difficulties of conquest demand faith (**7:17–26**). If Israel's special status tempted them to become proud and boastful, the awesome responsibility of conquest would tempt them to become timid (Num. 13:31–33). Faith to overcome such temptation can only be attained through first recalling the miraculous signs and wonders, the mighty hand and outstretched arm of God in Egypt (vv. 18–19). God's presence is assured. The same all-powerful God will be with the people. He is a great and awesome God who will drive out the Canaanites before them. Finally, faith is strengthened by taking the warnings and the program of conquest seriously. Israel's participation in the thing banned would only weaken allegiance to the Lord, making them partake of the character of the Canaanites and become liable to extermination themselves (see Josh. 7).

God's people may not declare themselves independent, but are to submit to the lordship of Yahweh (**8:1–20**).

Verse 1 reiterates the summons to obedience along with God's benevolent aim. Obedience is the fruit of redemption, not the cause of it. As a corollary to faith, it results in well-being. The purpose of the forty years in the wilderness was to humble the Israelites and to test their heart motive. The humbling experience was designed to teach them that man does not live by bread alone. Far more importantly, they were to subsist on every word that comes from the mouth of the Lord (v. 3). Would they really trust the Lord who proved sufficient for every need in the past? Was his word of promise and instruction to be relied upon to meet their every need? In fact, their clothes did not wear out and their feet did not swell during that time, a testimony to Yahweh's gracious providence. To discipline (v. 5) is to train and instruct (an educational word), not so much to punish (a judicial word). This could be accomplished through a rigorous course of training, such as the wilderness experience. The reason for remembering the wilderness experience is to prepare Israel for settlement in the land (vv. 7–10).

Moses warns Israel against pride and forgetfulness (vv. **11–20**). Israel has a solemn obligation to remember her covenant Lord and his stipulations. Verses 12–17 are a stern warning against the self-sufficiency which easily emerges from wealth and abundance. The sin of pride emerges from the heart. From there it translates into overt forgetfulness (Prov. 30:8–9). Israel must never forget God's protection and care in the wilderness. To claim success by virtue of one's own power is to deny the true source of wealth and abundance. Moses reiterates the solemn warning about forgetting the Lord and serving other gods (vv. 19–20). Such disobedience will only lead to destruction.

Israel's victory in conquest is not because of her intrinsic righteousness (**9:1–6**). Only God's omnipotence will overcome the Canaanites' overwhelming strength and defensive walls. The moral anger of God in destroying the Canaanites is described as a "devouring fire" (v. 3).

The gift of the land is not because Israel has merited it, but because of the righteousness of God, expressed in judgment on sinful Canaan (v. 4). God's righteousness is also exhibited in the fulfillment of the prophecies made to the patriarchs (v. 5). Israel is far from righteous—they are a stiff-necked people (v. 6).

Moses provides evidence of Israel's stubbornness (**9:7–10:11**). The golden calf incident is a classic example of Israel's rebellion (vv. 7–17). The golden calf was an outright denial of the covenant. It contradicted the principle of exclusive consecration to the Lord. Israel's lapse of faith was reversed only through the intercessory prayer of Moses, the servant of the Lord.

The second evidence of Israel's stubborn unbelief is constant rebellion (vv. 22–24). The incidents at Taberah (Num. 11:1–3), Massah (Exod. 17:1–7), and Kibroth Hattaavah (Num. 11) are recalled as provocations against the Lord. Verse 23 details the unbelief and rebellion at Kadesh-barnea (Num. 14:1–12). Unbelief ("you did not trust Him") is at the heart of sin and rebellion.

Again, Moses reminds Israel of his mediatorial ministry (vv. 25–29). His appeal is to the God who made covenant promises to the patriarchs, and to the possible abuse that the heathen might make of any disaster attending Israel.

In contrast to Israel's tendency to apostasy, Moses proclaims the sovereign grace of God exhibited in the preparation of two new tablets of stone following the golden calf episode (10:1–5). One has to review Exodus 34:1–9 to fully appreciate the marvel of God's graciousness, love, and mercy.

Parenthetically, Moses points out that God provided the tribe of Levi as priestly intercessors on account of Israel's tendency to rebellion (vv. 6–9). On the journey to Moserah, Aaron died and was replaced by his son Eleazar as high priest (Num. 20:25–28). Then, on the journey to Jotbathah, the tribe of Levi was set apart for blessing in Israel. Their task was specifically to carry the ark of the covenant and to attend to the details of that work, to stand before the Lord in the service of the tabernacle, and to pronounce blessings in the name of the Lord.

Finally, Moses summarizes his mediatorial intercession and its benevolent result, followed by a renewed command to proceed to the conquest of the land. This new command is evidence of the pardoning grace of God.

The basic requirements for covenant relationship between the great King and his people are repeated (**10:12–22**). These requirements are expressed in a series of five infinitives: *to fear the Lord, to walk in all his ways, to love him, to serve the Lord,* and *to observe the Lord's commands* (vv. 12–13). In a chiastic scheme, the emphasis falls on the middle element, *to love him.* Love is the epoxy that bonds the covenant relationship between Yahweh and his people.

The covenant Giver is more completely revealed (vv. 14–22). He is not a local deity who cannot act or be trusted. Instead, he is the Lord of the universe, the Lord of redemption and covenant, the supreme and transcendent God, the righteous Judge, and the sovereign Lord of history and nature. The Israelites, in response, are to *circumcise their hearts* (v. 16; lit. circumcise the foreskin of your heart). God expects of the redeemed a true heart response to his majesty and goodness. True fear and true love produce wholehearted service and obedience to God.

The basis of the covenant is the goodness of God as exhibited in his mighty acts in the past (**11:1–7**). Yahweh was the sovereign Judge of Israel's enemies, particularly the Egyptians. He revealed himself as a sovereign Father who provided for his children in the wilderness. He showed Israel not to presume their election by judging Dathan and Abiram. In sum, God has been good to Israel. How can they do anything less than yield wholehearted devotion and love to their Lord?

Moses also appeals to God's acts in the future (**11:8–25**). He particularly speaks to the younger generation who will see the mighty acts of God on their behalf. Yahweh will show himself sovereign over the land, bringing blessing on his obedient people. Moses includes a solemn warning against idolatry (vv. 16–17). Canaanite religion will have all kinds of enticements and allurements.

Yahweh will show himself as sovereign over the Canaanites by dispossessing them from the land. Moses exhorts Israel to impress these gracious words upon their minds, to teach them to their children, and to write them on their hearts and the doorposts of their houses. Covenant loyalty will result in perpetual tenure of the land. Fulfilling the spiritual requirements of the covenant will result in the possession of the land and the displacement of the Canaanites from it.

The sanctions of the covenant (**11:26–32**) are now squarely placed before Israel for her response. Note how the idolatry of the Canaanites weighs heavy on Moses' heart. When Israel completes the renewal of the covenant, Moses instructs them to place the blessings on Mount Gerizim and the curses on Mount Ebal.

C. Ancillary stipulations (12:1–26:19). The preceding section emphasized the spiritual requirements of the covenant; this section emphasizes the outward expression of covenant life. It begins with the worship requirements of the covenant community (12:1–16:17), then goes on to the requirements for governmental leadership (16:18–21:23), followed by various ordinances exhibiting the sanctity of the divine order (22:1–25:19), concluding with the covenant community's confession of Yahweh as their Redeemer-King (26:1–19). These more specific stipulations are the practical application of the principles presented in chapters 5–11, and cannot be interpreted in isolation from them.

The law of the sanctuary demands one place of worship (**12:1–7**). "Destroy completely all the places" (v. 2) is a command in keeping with the program of conquest. All forms and places of idolatry (often accompanied by depraved practices) are to be "devoted to the Lord" and annihilated. Canaanite methods of worship are not to be adopted for the worship of Yahweh. Israelites are to seek the Lord and worship him as he prescribes and in places which he has designated. "The place the LORD your God will choose" (v. 5) should not be taken to refer to a single place. It is not urging centralization of worship. Rather, it refers to wherever the tabernacle was to be located and the name of the Lord was to be worshiped, whether in Shiloh, Bethel, Gilgal, Shechem, or Jerusalem (see Exod. 20:24; lit. in every place where I cause my name to be remembered).

New regulations for sacrifices and worship are given (**12:8–14**). The implications of the law of the sanctuary are elaborated. The twelve tribes had lived around the tabernacle during the wilderness years, everyone having immediate access to it. But as they were soon to possess the land, they would be living two or three days distant. "Everyone as he sees fit" (v. 8) expresses traditional practice since patriarchal times. That is changing. Now Israel is to be regulated in their worship as a covenant community. They are to bring everything to whatever place the Lord has designated and share with others, including the Levites. The Levites were given no territory but lived in cities throughout the land (Num. 35:1–8). As sojourners and pilgrims without land, they were to be the object of tender care and concern to all of Israel.

Whereas strict attention is to be given official sacrifices according to the regulations and Levitical rules, the Israelites are allowed to eat all kinds of meats at home in normal society (**12:15–28**). The only exception is that special attention should be given not to eat blood (cf. Lev. 17:11), the symbol of life. This Old Testament reverence for blood (Gen. 9:4–6) serves as a foreshadow of the covenant blood and sacrifice of Christ's atonement (see Lev. 16; Heb. 9:12–14; 13:20; 1 Pet. 1:18–19; 1 John 1:7).

In the expanded territory of Israel provision is made for sacrifices and meals if the distance to a designated place of worship is too far. Moses carefully urges upon those so far away to be careful to obey, repeating the exhortations given earlier.

The main danger presented by foreign religion is the sin of idolatry (**12:29–32**). Canaanite idolatry is paramount in Moses' mind. These verses serve as a transition from the law of the sanctuary to the ever-present danger of apostasy through idolatry. Israel must beware of potential entrapment. Minor things may eventually lead to heinous practices, such as burning their sons and daughters in the fire as sacrifices (v. 31; cf. 2 Chron. 28:3; 33:6). The following sections teach Israel what to do when there is the temptation to idolatry.

A prophet or other religious leaders may come claiming to bring God's message (**13:1–5**). The people may legitimately expect authentication. For credentials, a prophet may perform a miraculous sign or wonder. However, no matter what credentials he may have, if he teaches something contrary to previous revelation, he proves himself a false prophet and is not to be accepted. The primary test of a true prophet of the Lord is whether his message is in harmony with previous revelation (cf. Isa. 8:20). The Lord permits even religious leaders with miraculous credentials as a test, "to find out whether you love him with all your heart" (v. 3). Allegiance to Yahweh must be uppermost in the people's hearts. For encouraging rebellion (lit. apostasy, defection, turning aside, withdrawal) against the Lord, which is tantamount to treason, a false prophet deserves the death penalty.

If a close relative or friend secretly entices (lit. incites, allures, instigates, seduces) a believer to idolatrous practices, that person is liable to the death penalty (**13:6–11**). Stoning was a common means of executing the offender. The accuser cast the first stone, thereby showing there was sufficient evidence and that the charge was serious. Verse 11 suggests there is a deterrent effect for the rest of Israel when this is taken seriously.

If a whole town has defected and has been seduced into idolatry, the same principles apply (**13:12–18**). Wicked men (v. 13; lit. sons of Belial) might be considered urban revolutionaries. A thorough investigation must be made. Anything gained through such procedures must be put under the ban and devoted to the Lord; this requirement prohibits undue seizure of goods for the gain of the town, tribe, or nation.

Pagan mourning rites are forbidden (**14:1–2**). "Cut" (v. 1; lit. lacerate) may be a reference to seasonal rites in the Canaanite fertility cult (cf. 1 Kings 18:28). Because of their new relation as sons of God by creation and redemption, the Israelites may not deface their bodies which are created in his image.

The section on clean and unclean foods (**14:3–21**) parallels Leviticus 11:2–23. Clean and unclean animals, fish, and birds are listed. What is not clear is whether the reasons for such distinctions are religious or hygienic, or possibly both. Dead creatures are prohibited because of the toxins in the carcasses. The religious reason for this prohibition is that the blood has not been drained according to Levitical regulations (Lev. 17:10–12). The kid cooked in the milk of its mother seems to have been a heinous Canaanite religious practice.

The tithe (**14:22–29**) is an act of gratitude or devotion (cf. Gen. 14:20; 28:22), not so much a legal demand. It is a recognition that all possessions are gifts of God (8:18). Every third year, the Israelites are to bring a second tithe to the storehouses of the Levitical cities (v. 28). As an expression of love to God and to neighbor, this tithe supplies the needs of the Levites themselves, as well as the resident aliens, the poor, the widows, and the orphans. God promises rich blessings to those who give bountifully and cheerfully.

Every seventh year is to be a year to cancel debts (**15:1–6**). It is not a time for simply lengthening the term of payments or of not pressing for payment, but as verse 9 suggests, it is a time for remission of debts. The exception is with respect to the foreigner who borrows as part of a commercial transaction (v. 3). As an expression of love toward a fellow Israelite in dire straits, this principle reflects God's love for him too, since it is called "the LORD's time for canceling debts" (v. 2).

Love for one's neighbor has tremendous social implications (**15:7–11**). The poor man is a brother. Moses strongly exhorts the Israelites not to be hardhearted or tightfisted toward him. Charity must come from the heart. To withhold assistance because the year of remission will force cancellation of the debt is to harbor a wicked thought (v. 9). The people are to give generously and without a grudging heart.

God provides for the emancipation of indentured Hebrew servants (**15:12–18**). Slavery was not condoned in the Old Testament, any more than polygamy. Slaves procured as spoils of war were permitted, but this was carefully regulated (see 21:10–14; 23:15–16). An Israelite might indenture himself for economic reverses. In such cases, he was to serve no more than six years from the time he became indentured, and then was to be released in the seventh year. The person released was to be given a generous bonus (v. 14) to enable him to get a good start in life. The reason for such a gracious law is Israel's experience of release by the Lord from Egyptian slavery. God's nature and redemptive action become a model for ethics.

All of life belongs to God as the Source and Giver of life. As an acknowledgment of this truth, the firstborn of the flock are dedicated to the Lord (**15:19–23**). Sacrifices must be without defect as are all other gifts.

Moses next discusses the three major feasts (**16:1–17**). Passover celebrates Israel's deliverance from Egypt (vv. 1–8; for the original celebration, see Exod. 12:1–31). The month of Abib (later called Nisan) is equivalent to March–April. This was the time of the barley harvest, hence the name *firstfruits* and the seven additional days of eating unleavened bread (v. 3). Both Passover and the Feast of Unleavened Bread serve as a memorial of the great redemption accomplished through the exodus. There are changes from previous regulations; the slaying and eating are to take place at the assembly rather than in private homes (vv. 7–8).

The Feast of Weeks (vv. 9–12) is also called the Feast of Harvest (Exod. 23:16), the day of the firstfruits (Num. 28:26), and the day of Pentecost (Acts 2, based on the Septuagint of Lev. 23:16, "fifty days"). It was to be celebrated fifty days (seven weeks) after Passover. This places it sometime in May or June, at the time of the wheat harvest. It is an occasion for joy as worshipers share a common meal before the Lord. Not only family members participate, but also servants, Levites, resident aliens, the fatherless, and the widows. The people are to remember the years of slavery and the kindness expressed by the Lord to them—hence the concern for the poor and destitute. This feast again expresses delight in the Lord and total dedication to him.

The Feast of Tabernacles (vv. 13–15) is to be celebrated at the end of the grape and fruit harvest and when all the threshing of the grain is completed (September–October). The Israelites are to gather in their temporary branch-covered booths. The Feast of Tabernacles is also called the Feast of Ingathering (Exod. 23:16b), the feast to the Lord (Lev. 23:29), or simply the Feast (Ezek. 45:25; John 7–8). Again, the occasion is for joy and love as marks of the covenant life and worship of the people of God. It is a time for thanksgiving. Although the exodus took place in the spring of the year, here it is memorialized in the fall.

Since each annual feast is to be celebrated in conjunction with some harvest season (barley, wheat, grapes), Israelite men are to bring tithes of their produce to the Lord, each according to his ability in recognition of the bountiful blessings from the Lord (vv. 16–17).

Israel's leadership in the political realm, no less than in ecclesiastical and judicial, is to reflect the righteousness of the great King. This is a further exposition of the fifth commandment, specifically explicating the responsibilities of those in authority.

Moses expands the principles of judicial justice (**16:18–20**) given in 1:13–18. There the qualifications and method of appointment for leaders were discussed in relation to the wilderness experience. Moses now prepares the way for the settled life. Every town is to have judges and officials. Note well the plural which strongly argues against the potential tyranny of an autocratic judge (cf. also 19:17). Judges are more than officers of justice, but are also leaders of the local council of elders. Officers are more than mere scribes but possibly court clerks attached to judges.

The basic concern is that judicial administration be carried out with justice. The emphasis is not on organizational structure (which has changed from the patriarchal period through the commonwealth period), but that true justice be done, "righteous judgment." Righteous(ness) is more a religious term than an ethical term, the demand being primarily the establishment of God's will in the land, secondarily justice. It is what God establishes as the proper standard—firm, straight, steady, and immovable. This standard is necessary because of God's regard for the helpless and poor who need protection from exploitation. Hence, there is an equivalence between righteousness and salvation (cf. 1 Sam. 12:7–8; Mic. 6:5). The principle underlying justice does not originate in man, but in the very nature of God. The only sure and authoritative basis for law is the justice of God.

Moses provides regulative principles for judicial procedures (**16:21–17:7**). Moses first states three apodictic laws concretizing the regulative religious principles of the first three words of the Decalogue. The authority of Yahweh alone must be consulted, not an Asherah pole or a sacred stone.

Moses then states four rules of evidence and judgment (17:2–7) using a case of apostasy as an example requiring the maximum punishment. The selection of a case of apostasy (cf. also Exod. 22:20; Deut. 13) underscores the emphasis throughout this book on the exclusive lordship of Yahweh, particularly in the judicial process.

Whatever the source of an accusation, justice demands a thorough investigation. There must be adequate evidence, such as the testimony of two or three witnesses (v. 6). This rules out the possibility of someone using the system for his own vengeful purposes. The accused has a right to face and to know his accuser, and the accuser has a responsibility to confront the accused in court.

The purpose of such safeguards of justice is in order to purge and purify the covenant community, especially from breaches of the covenant. But another clear purpose expressed in Scripture is the repentance and restoration of the criminal, a principle based on the very nature of God, who abounds in mercy and forgives rebellion and sin (Exod. 34:6–7). Provision is made for an appropriate ransom or sacrifice upon true repentance, with the possible exception of premeditated murder (see Num. 35:30–32).

Previously, Moses served as the final arbiter in cases (Exod. 18:13–22). Now, lower courts are to be decentralized, while the higher tribunal is to be at the sanctuary, wherever it may be located (**17:8–3**). This serves as a reminder that the Lord who dwells there is the supreme Judge in Israel (cf. Gen. 18:25; Deut. 32:36; Ps. 94:2–3; 2 Tim. 4:1, 8; Heb. 12:23). This central judicatory is not to serve as an appellate court, but very difficult cases (perhaps those which have some unusual feature or where there is no explicit regulation or precedent) are to be judged there (cf. 19:16–18; Job 42:3). The higher tribunal is to be composed of a plurality of priests and judges, each having as its presiding officer the high priest and the chief justice (v. 12). Verdicts are to be scrupulously followed. "The law they teach you" (v. 11) clearly expresses the instructional purpose of the decisions as well as the punitive and purifying influence.

Moses does not deny Israel the right to have a king, but warns against autocratic and tyrannical rule as opposed to a theocratic kingship (**17:14–20**). There are specific requirements for Israel's king. Israel must make sure that any future king is a man whom Yahweh chooses. "Let us set a king over us" (v. 14) is echoed in the demand of the people in the days of Samuel (1 Sam. 8:5, 19–20), where in unbelief the people reject the Lord. "Like all the nations around us" (v. 14) is the precise point of the prohibition, for the Canaanites and other ancient Near Eastern nations had despotic monarchs. The theocratic monarchy would reflect the rule of God, not the capriciousness of autocratic Near Eastern despots. The basic requisite is that such a king be "from among your own brothers" (v. 15), a member of the covenant community.

Restrictions are placed on the Israelite monarchy. Since Yahweh is the great King, no human monarch may have absolute power, much less declare himself to be a god as in Egypt. Limitations will cause him to acknowledge his dependence upon the sovereign Lord. The monarch is limited in his military and economic aggrandizement. He must not acquire large numbers of horses and chariots. Instead of trusting Yahweh, he will then trust military might (cf. 20:1; Pss. 20:7; 118:8). The monarch is also to limit the number of wives he has. The concern is not social (the number of wives per se) but religious ("his heart will be led astray," v. 17). The potential danger of syncretism and idolatry is exhibited in the effect Solomon's wives had on him (1 Kings 11:1–4). And finally, the monarch is limited in amassing personal wealth (v. 17b).

The king is to have a duplicate copy of the covenant (vv. 18–20). He is to write for himself a copy of the law. The purpose of reading the covenant is that he may fear the Lord and remain humble. He is to devote himself to reading from it daily, to govern his own life by it as well as the nation. The promise for obedience is longevity and dynastic continuity. Note the conditional element here, whereas in the Davidic covenant, the messianic promise will remain unconditional (2 Sam. 7:12–16).

Moses discusses offerings for the priests and Levites (**18:1–8**). Israel is responsible for supporting all Levites. The reason is that Levites were not given land as an inheritance (see 10:6–9). They have an administrative role in the care of the tabernacle (vv. 6–8) as well as some judicial responsibilities (4:41–43; 19:2–13; Num. 35:6; Josh. 20:7–9).

The priests are to serve as ministers of the altar, wherever the sanctuary might be located. They are accorded supreme honor because of their mediatorial work. They also have teaching responsibilities together with the Levites. Levitical rights are guaranteed. Since the other Levites serve as functional subordinates and are social dependents, they are protected from encroaching restrictions because of the vested interests of the priests. Together, priests and Levites share the commission of instructing Israel in the covenant law (33:10; Lev. 10:11; 2 Chron. 17:8–9). Possibly during the coregency of David and Solomon, the Levites were organized to oversee the construction of the temple, to serve as officers and judges in the land, and as gatekeepers and musicians (1 Chron. 23:4–5, 25–32). Levites are to enjoy equally the provisions from their work.

As Moses recognizes the realities of life, he prepares the people for any future revelation which the Lord will make (**18:9–22**). The immediate source of guidance was the priestly use of the Urim and Thummim (33:8; Ezra 2:63; Neh. 7:65). The danger now is that Canaanite practices might prove tempting for determining the future. Hence, Moses starts negatively, prohibiting the practices of the Canaanites (vv. 9–14), then presents the positive, requiring the people to wait on God's initiative in revelation through a prophet (vv. 15–22).

Pagan magic was identified with pagan religion. So any practice of the occult was an expression of rebellion against the basic demand of Yahweh for Israel's loyalty to the covenant. Canaanite oracular and occult practices were particularly detestable to the Lord. Nine such superstitions are identified: (1) februation, the custom of sacrificing one's son or daughter in the fire (especially identified with the Ammonite and Moabite god Molech); (2) divination, or obtaining oracles; (3) sorcery, more specifically, the practice of witchcraft; (4) interpretation of omens, such as reading animal or fowl livers and entrails; (5) witchcraft; (6) casting spells; (7) consultation of a medium; (8) spiritism; and (9) necromancy. For such abominable practices the Canaanite nations would be dispossessed of their homeland. God's revelation through Moses and the prophets is vested with authority. If Israel resorts to these methods, they will reject God himself. Assuming such unbelief, not even a voice from the dead will help.

God will take the initiative in revelation, revealing himself through a prophet. God will raise up a prophet like Moses (v. 15). The singular is used to designate the establishment of the prophetic institution. This prophetic institution has divine authorization. Its purpose is to guard Israel from the superstitious practices of her neighbors.

Moses gives the distinctive marks of a true prophet. Beyond the most important test stated in 13:1–2, that a true prophet must render a message in harmony with previous revelation, Moses gives additional guidelines, with the caveat that even false prophets may be able to fulfill some of them. Is he a member of the covenant community? Is the source of his message a revelation from the Lord, or does it come through sorcery or divination? By what authority does the prophet speak? Does the prophet claim to be a spokesman on behalf of Yahweh? Or does he speak for Baal or Asherah? Does the prophet give an authenticating sign or prediction? If any of these prove negative, the prophet has spoken presumptuously and is liable to the death penalty (v. 20). These questions may be put today to anyone who claims to have a prophetic message from the Lord.

Moses expounds the sixth, eighth, and ninth words of the covenant (**19:1–21**; cf. Deut. 5:17, 19, 20). These stipulations are designed to secure a fair trial and a true verdict.

Moses lays down basic regulations for blood revenge by requiring at least three additional cities of refuge (see 4:41–43 for those on the east side of the Jordan). The purpose of these cities is to limit the rule of blood revenge, especially as it applies to the manslayer. Such cases are unintentional and without malice and thus not deserving of death. Hence the restraint placed on the indiscriminate execution of the right of blood revenge. In case of further territorial expansion, three additional cities of refuge must be provided (vv. 8–10). One could presume that upon even further territorial expansion, the principle of additional cities would apply. In cases of premeditated murder (vv. 11–13), even though such a deliberate murderer should seek refuge, the elders are to extradite him and place him in the hand of the kinsmen of the victim for blood revenge.

Moses also discusses the sanctity of inherited property. To move boundary stones is to encroach on and steal another man's property (cf. Prov. 23:10; Isa. 5:8; Hos. 5:10). These stones may be a pile of stones which serve as a landmark. In 27:17, Moses pronounces a curse on those who would commit such a crime against God-given inheritance.

Moses cautions against false witnesses. First, there must be protection from insufficient evidence (v. 15). One witness is not sufficient to convict a man. Assuming that there is only one witness and a crime has been committed, Israel must trust in the providence of God to bring about justice. At least two or three witnesses are required to establish the evidence. Also, there must be protection from malicious witnesses (vv. 16–19). The accused and the accuser must stand before a panel of justices made up of priests and judges when a thorough investigation is called for. When the testimony is found to be perjured, the malicious witness is liable according to the lex talionis, that is, the malicious witness deserves the punishment he intended for the accused. The principle of penalty based on the law of retaliation, far from encouraging vengeance, limits vengeance and establishes guidelines for verdicts and penalties. Essentially, it is the principle of "let the punishment suit the crime" (cf. Exod. 21:23–25; Lev. 24:17–22).

Moses now gives instruction for future wars (**20:1–20**). War, when necessary, is an expression of theocratic justice, of the judgment of the nations, especially in the case of Israel's conquest of the Canaanites. But even in war, there must be a humanitarian expression of love.

"Do not be afraid" (v. 1) is a command aimed at encouragement to trust and confidence in the great King. The memory of Yahweh's past exploits are an assurance of his presence. The priest functions as a representative of the Lord, consecrating the battle to God's glory.

Three groups of people are exempt from military service on humanitarian grounds: (1) the man who has built a house and has not yet dedicated it (v. 5); (2) the one who has planted a vineyard and has not yet enjoyed its fruit (v. 6—only in the fifth year were Israelites permitted to enjoy the fruit [Lev. 19:23–25]); and (3) the newly engaged or married man (v. 7). Nothing should distract attention from the priority of victory in battle. Related to the humanitarian reasons, the faint-hearted is also exempt, so as not to weaken general morale.

Moses makes clear that war is to be waged as a last resort. A peace treaty is to be offered at the outset (cf. Josh. 9:15; 1 Kings 5:12; Isa. 27:5). If the enemy accepts, they become vassals under the treaty; otherwise Israel must lay siege and make war. Women, children, and livestock are to be regarded as general booty or plunder (but note the rights of women taken captive [21:10–14]).

Anything that may undermine Israel's total allegiance to the great King is to be destroyed or put under the ban (see 7:1–5; cf. Josh. 7:21–26; 11:10–15). This does not contradict loving one's enemies, for Israel is serving as God's instrument of judgment on the Canaanites (9:4).

Not only the earlier humanitarian principle, but now environmental concerns are stated. The total destruction of property is ultimately God's prerogative. In contrast to the Egyptian scorched-earth policy and their practice of cutting down trees, Israel is to conserve trees, especially fruit trees, for future use.

The fifth and sixth commandments are further amplified (**21:1–23**). In a case where homicide has gone undetected (not even one witness), there is a religious implication: the whole community must take responsibility. The elders and judges from the nearest town are to take a young heifer and make atonement for the unsolved crime. Only in this manner can guilt be expiated.

Moses outlines three areas of responsibility for heads of households. Husbands of war brides are limited in their authority. The conditions for taking a war bride (vv. 12–13) indicate her transfer from her pagan nation to the family of Israel and her mourning for her own family. Since war brides are people, not slaves or chattels, they may be let go but may not be sold as slaves or as merchandise. The rights of the firstborn are to be maintained (vv. 15–17). Finally, the elders at the gate (where judicial cases are brought) are to strengthen and support parental authority in the case of a rebellious son as a means of reinforcing the security and continuity of the covenant community.

There are to be limits to the practice of execution by hanging on a tree—a body must not hang overnight. This is because the criminal is under God's curse; his body desecrates the land. Hanging was the worst possible penalty, signifying one's final separation from the people of God as a covenant community.

At the heart of the ordinances of stewardship of God's world (**22:1–12**) is the principle that man is God's steward of everything he uses. The Israelite is to seek his neighbor's welfare by returning that which he has lost, making every effort to find the rightful owner. "Do not ignore" (v. 1; lit. do not hide yourself) carries the meaning of shouldering responsibility toward others in the community. Direct assistance must be given to a neighbor even in the most difficult of circumstances.

Transvestism is prohibited because of its association with homosexual practices or the cults of certain deities, or in other cases possibly because of its use in magical practices to cure infertility. Sparing the mother bird (vv. 6–7) may reflect the sanctity of the parental relationship or even a concern for endangered species. Making a parapet (v. 8) expands on the sixth commandment by emphasizing safety precautions in buildings as opposed to carelessness and negligence. The reasons for the prohibition of planting two kinds of seeds, of yoking a donkey with an ox, and of mixing wool and linen are not quite so easy to discern. It may be for religious and theological reasons, such as distinctions in created order, or opposition to certain Canaanite or Egyptian practices, or for pragmatic and humanitarian concerns. Knots and tassels on garments (v. 12) may serve as a special reminder of the great King's suzerainty over Israel so that the people might walk in faithfulness to his gracious stipulations.

A further explication of the seventh covenant word stresses the divine institution of marriage and the family (**22:13–30**). If there are false allegations by a man, provisions are made to prove a virgin's innocence. But if there are just allegations, she is liable to the death penalty. Unfaithfulness in the marriage relationship is the same as unfaithfulness in the covenantal relationship. Marriage ought to be and is a reflection of the covenant relationship (cf. Hos. 2–3; Eph. 5:21–33). In the case of adultery, both must die. A pledged (betrothed or engaged) woman was considered a "wife." In the case of the seduction of a young girl, the solution may be to pay the bride price. This provision may be taken as descriptive rather than prescriptive, since it is possible the man may be precluded from marrying the girl. Incestuous relations are forbidden.

The congregation of the Lord is holy (**23:1–18**). The covenant community is both inclusive and exclusive. The following are to be excluded from the assembly: the eunuch (because of the religious cultic practices in the Near Eastern nations); those born of forbidden marriages; Ammonites and Moabites (because they did not assist Israel before the conquest even though they were cousins); and Edomites and Egyptians.

Uncleanness must not be tolerated in the camp. Nocturnal emission, like various discharges of blood (cf. Lev. 12:4–5; 15:19–30), very likely represents the loss of "life liquids" and hence is viewed as polluting the land. The principle of holiness applies to proper sanitation facilities and equipment.

Various social and cultic laws are detailed in verses 15–18. The assembly of Israel is to grant asylum to the refugee slave who flees his master. He is not to be extradited or returned. He is an image-bearer of God, not lost merchandise (cf. Exod. 22:21; Lev. 19:33). Israel is forbidden to have temple prostitutes, who figure so prominently in the heinous Canaanite cultic practices.

Moses details a number of property laws (**23:19–25**). Money loaned at usury-interest is forbidden to a fellow Israelite but not to a foreigner. The reason for the prohibition is concern for the poor. Vows are words of promise to be kept as sacred, especially since they reflect on the Name of the holy God (cf. 5:11; Lev. 27; Num. 30; Ps. 15:4; Prov. 20:25). Provision is to be made for hospitality to travelers and the poor, yet they are not to take advantage of such hospitality and generosity.

Family laws are given (**24:1–5**). Moses does not institute divorce (a mistaken view of the Pharisees corrected by Christ [Matt. 19:7–8]). Rather, he assumes the problem of divorce in the ancient Near East and seeks to guard family life after a divorce. After divorce and remarriage, there cannot be another divorce in order to remarry the first party (v. 4). This may serve to protect the second marriage. That Moses "permits" (or tolerates) divorce is clearly explained by Christ as the result of "the hardness of Israel's heart" (Mark 10:5). However, the original standard was given in the creation ordinance (Gen. 2:23–24) and is not abrogated (Matt. 19:9). Verse 5 makes an exemption from military service for the newly married man (cf. 20:5–8).

Various specific regulations are given as expositions of the covenant stipulations (**26:6–15**). The concern is for things essential to the preservation of God's people. A millstone is not to be taken in pledge (as security or collateral) because this would deprive a man of his livelihood. Kidnaping is not only theft, but maltreatment of an image-bearer as though he were a slave or merchandise. This is social murder, a cutting off from the covenant family of the Lord. The lesson of Miriam's leprosy is to be a constant reminder of God's purposes (Num. 12:10–15). Collateral is permitted, as a right to the lender (but see limitations in 23:19–20). But the borrower has rights. His dignity as God's image-bearer is to be maintained. In keeping with concern for the poor, wages are not to be withheld. This rule seeks to uphold the integrity of the covenant community.

Laws of justice are rehearsed in **24:16–22.** Even though corporate responsibility is emphasized in the Old Testament, there is also a clear statement of personal responsibility for one's own sins. "To the third and fourth generation" (Deut. 5:9) is descriptive of the effects and consequences of sin, rather than prescriptive of who is to pay the penalty. The law of loving one's neighbor is exhibited in the social concern for the alien, the fatherless, and the widow. The motive for the care of the destitute and helpless is the gracious redemption experienced at the exodus. In the same spirit, the law of love is exemplified by leaving what is not harvested for the sake of the orphan and widow (cf. Lev. 19:9–10; 23:22; Ruth 2). The governing principle in the theocratic life of the people of God must be a love for the Lord exhibited in love for others.

The sanctity of God's image-bearer (**25:1–19**) has been treated before, but is now brought to the fore. There are limits to corporal punishment. After deciding a case, appropriate punishment is to be meted out, but with proper precautions to maintain the criminal's dignity.

The laboring ox is not to be muzzled (v. 4); the laborer is worthy of his hire (cf. 1 Cor. 9:9–10; 1 Tim. 5:18). This proverbial statement may serve as a counterpart to the law that man ought to receive all due honor for his good deeds.

God's image-bearer is an immortal servant of the Lord whose eternal blessedness is an inheritance in God's kingdom. Levirate marriage witnessed to the dignity of that immortal servant by the perpetuation of his name. There are conditions and limitations to the law. The law applies only if the brother shares the same estate. It was not compulsory, since verses 7–10 give procedures when not followed. However, if the practice is not followed, the surviving brother is stigmatized for his failure (v. 10). The Book of Ruth is an excellent illustration of the application of this law.

The dastardly way for stopping a fight described in verses 11–12 is a deliberate expression of contempt for the sign of the covenant (circumcision). Commercial enterprises are to be controlled by equity in standards. The golden rule and the love for neighbor as self are the requirements of economic relationships. The Amalekites are to be exterminated; the law of love for neighbor does not abrogate the requirement for conquest. Those who identify themselves as intransigent enemies of God and his people have allied themselves with the kingdom of Satan which is doomed to destruction. This is a struggle between life and death. Hence the laws of love and hate are mutually expressive of God's nature. Believers are to love those whom God loves and hate those whom God hates. Love must not degenerate into indifference toward godlessness.

Chapter 26 concludes the whole section on the stipulations of the covenant renewal document by requiring two rituals and providing a concluding exhortation (**26:1–19**).

The presentation of the firstfruits (vv. 1–11) seems to refer to all the firstfruits suggested for the various annual pilgrimage feasts in Deuteronomy 16. It surely does not refer to a new religious institution in Israel. The declaration (v. 3) is a personal testimony that the individual has entered the land. The baskets (v. 4) represent his acknowledgment of the blessings received from the Lord, the Giver and Sustainer of life. The recital of the creed (vv. 5–9) serves as a testimony acknowleding his family roots, the history of God's redemptive work, and his present inheritance as a gift of God's grace in redemption—all in fulfillment of God's oath verifying the covenant promises.

"In the third year" refers to a special tithe received every third year (vv. 12–15). It does not replace or set aside other tithes (cf. 14:28–29). The accompanying statement affirms the integrity of the giver, who then looks to God for continual blessings and provisions on the basis of his covenant promises.

The basic demand of the covenant is repeated again (vv. 16–19): to love the Lord with all their hearts. In turn, the great King acknowledges them as his people, his treasured possession, and that he will continue to set them above all nations. This must not be taken for granted, but is conditioned on their own faithfulness.

IV. Covenant Sanctions (27:1–30:20)

A. Ratification ceremony (27:1–26). A ratification ceremony is to serve as the renewal of the covenant after Israel enters the land of Canaan.

Instructions are given for the final ratification ceremony (**27:1–8**). The people are to set up large stones coated with plaster (lime or cement), perhaps following Egyptian custom. The whole Book of Deuteronomy is to be written on them. This suggests that all the words were already written so that they could be copied onto the stone. The reason for this written record is that Israel's faith must be an intelligent and informed act of consecration to the great King. It further emphasizes the permanence of the covenant. Mount Ebal (v. 4) is the place where the curses are to be pronounced. The script is to be written very clearly, probably large and clear enough so that the people could read it for their edification.

With the reading of the book of the covenant, Moses and the priests charge the people with the obligations imposed by the renewal of the covenant (**27:9–10**).

The people of Israel are to divide evenly with six tribes on Mount Gerizim and six on Mount Ebal, facing each other for a ceremony (**27:11–26**). The ancient sacred site of Shechem lay in the saddle between the two mountains. The tribes on Mount Gerizim are the descendants of Leah and Rachel; they are to recite the blessings of the covenant. The six tribes on

Mount Ebal are to recite the curses of the covenant. The Levites in each of these groups are to pronounce the curses and the blessings antiphonally, the people responding "Amen," a solemn affirmation of the statements recited.

The actual ratification of the covenant will take place when the people respond by saying "Amen" to these self-maledictory oaths (**27:15–26**). The substance of these are taken from the commandments.

B. Blessings and curses (28:1–68). The blessings express the numerous benefits the faithful vassal may expect to receive. Conversely, the curses pronounce the judgment he may expect for unfaithfulness. This is not a matter of legal merit in which the vassal can force the suzerain to submit to his own whims. The righteousness which Israel enjoys is that which is given by the grace of God. This is far from a religion of works salvation. God-given righteousness is to be worked out in the life of the people, or it is not true righteousness. In the Sinaitic covenant, blessings and curses are interspersed with the stipulations. The curse is expressed in God's "punishing the children for the sin of the fathers to the third and fourth generation of those who hate me" (Exod. 20:5). Blessings are expressed in God's "showing love to a thousand generations of those who love me and keep my commandments" (Exod. 20:6).

The great King will bless the people corporately and individually (**28:1–14**). These blessings encompass all areas of life: in foreign lands, in the city and country, in the family, in war and peace, and their spiritual relationship with the Lord. This last point is what gives witness to the world that Yahweh is truly sovereign over the universe. Not legal obedience but exclusive and singlehearted devotion to the Lord is required.

In the Sinaitic covenant, the blessings predominate (Exod. 23:20–33). After forty years in which recidivism reared its head, the emphasis falls on the curses (**28:15–68**; cf. Lev. 26). From the relatively mild malediction on the Israelite in town and country (v. 16) to the extreme curse of banishment to foreign lands (vv. 49–68), the curses increase in intensity to serve both as a reminder of Israel's having broken the covenant as well as a call to repentance and renewed allegiance to the great King.

The introductory curse formula (vv. 15–19) parallels the areas of life which the blessings cover (vv. 3–6). God's covenant vengeance will be poured out on violators, even within the sanctuary of their own land. "Forsaking him" (v. 20; Heb. because you have forsaken me) is at the heart of covenant breaking, namely, the violation of the first commandment. This is the essence of sin and rebellion. It is of the nature of holiness not only to show love and mercy (the blessings) but also just retribution for sin (the curses). Hence diseases, drought, and war all aim at disciplining Israel in order to reclaim her to covenantal relationship. Instead of man exercising dominion over the creation and feasting upon it, covenant-breaking man will be devoured by the birds and beasts (v. 26). Instead of protection from the diseases of Egypt (7:15), Israel will be afflicted with diseases in which their powerlessness and frustration will be manifest. Their families and produce will be violated or destroyed, becoming objects of scorn and ridicule.

Failure and frustration (vv. 38–48) in areas over which man exercises dominion are the direct result of failure to serve God joyfully and gladly. The ultimate curse will be the scattering among the nations (vv. 48–57). To avoid these curses, Israel must remember the conditional character of the sanctions and obey the covenant stipulations from true heart devotion to the Lord of glory. Should they reject and repudiate their election and covenant relationship, they will be liable to a worse slavery than Egypt, namely, bondage to sin and Satan, and eventually to death and hell.

C. The covenant oath (29:1–30:14). Israel is exhorted to take the covenant oath (**29:1–15**). A historical review (vv. 1–9) serves as the basis for the exhortation which follows. The miracles in Egypt exhibited the omnipotence of God and his faithfulness to his covenant promises. Yet apart from the redeeming and gracious work of the Lord the people do not have a mind that understands the meaning of the mighty acts of God. The marvelous provisions during the exodus and the wilderness experience can be discerned only through insight granted by the Spirit of God. On the evidence of past history, not on mere myth or blind faith, Moses exhorts the people to carefully follow the terms of the covenant.

The central purpose of the ceremony is to enter into a covenant with the Lord and to seal it with an oath. The covenant community corporately (no mere observers) is involved in this ceremony: leaders and chief men, elders and officials, men, women, and children, as well as resident aliens or servants. A reference to "those who are not here today" (v. 15) expresses God's promise to show his covenant faithfulness down to a thousand generations of those who love him (5:10; 7:9).

Serious penalties are in store for hypocrisy and rebellion (**29:16–28**). The root that produces bitter poison (v. 18) is the heart which turns away from the Lord to serve idols. Sin does its work imperceptibly. A professing believer may take the oath and boast that he is safe even though he persists in going his own way. Such hypocrisy can only bring the wrath of God and the curses of the covenant on the individual and on the rest of the covenant community.

The root of hypocrisy will produce a bitter poison in later generations to come. The calamities warned against in the curses will be viewed by posterity and by foreigners as acts of Yahweh's wrath on Israel. They will recognize and proclaim that these calamities have come upon Israel because they abandoned the covenant and worshiped other gods.

Israel is not held accountable for the secret things, the decretive will of God from eternity, but the things revealed in the words of the covenant (**29:29**).

When all the calamities of the curses are executed on a rebellious people, the Lord promises to remain faithful to his oath. Not only curses but ultimately blessings will be showered upon them (**30:1–14**). "Take them to heart" (lit. cause them to return to your heart, v. 1) and "return to the LORD. . . with all your heart" (v. 2) express the sovereign and gracious design of the great King to woo his people back to himself. Through God's help, they will return to him from apostasy. This prospect of restoration forms the basis for the remnant theology which the prophets proclaim. Renewal and restoration take place only because of God's compassion and steadfast love. Apart from the divine initiative, there is no way they can respond with the wholehearted devotion required by the covenant. All the blessings and provisions of the covenant will be experienced when they obey the Lord and return to him. The revealed Word of God is not secret or mysterious. Israel may not plead ignorance, for they are held responsible for the written revelation.

D. Call to decision (30:15–20). The ratification of the covenant closes with a call to radical decision. The people must decide between life and prosperity or death and destruction. Faith, love, and obedience are all instruments for receiving the blessings. Rejection and disobedience are tantamount to accepting a substitute suzerain, which leads to death.

V. Provisions for the Future (31:1–34:12)

A. Leadership and the law (31:1–29). These two subjects are interwoven here although they are treated separately in other Near Eastern treaties.

At almost 120 years of age, Moses admits that he is unable to lead the people (**31:1–8**). Most likely Moses acknowledges that God is not permitting him to cross over the Jordan (31:2b). The transition of leadership from Moses to Joshua is parallel to the dynastic succession in the ancient treaties. Joshua had served under Moses (Exod. 17:9) and received a great measure of authority (Num. 27:18–23; Deut. 1:38). Now he receives the commission for leadership directly from Yahweh. Past experience in Trans-Jordan serves as the basis for encouragement in the future conquest. The presence of Yahweh going before them and granting victory is the important ingredient: "he will never leave you nor forsake you" (v. 6b).

The book of the law is to be read completely every seventh year, the year of release, at the time of the Feast of Tabernacles (**31:9–13**). The priests are responsible for the care of the documents and for the regular teaching of the authoritative revelation of God. It is to be placed beside the ark of the covenant which already contained the Sinaitic covenant. The whole community, including women, children, and resident aliens, is to be instructed from this document, so that they may learn to fear the Lord, the basic covenantal requirement.

Moses and Joshua appear at the entrance of the tabernacle, where all the people can witness that it is God who is commissioning Joshua, not Moses alone (**31:14–23**). The glory cloud that had been their guide and protector, symbolic of the visible presence of the Lord God (v. 15; Exod. 13:21; 33:9–11; Num. 9:15–23), appears. God uses this occasion to confirm the dreaded prophecies of the curses. As a constant reminder to Israel in the generations to come, Moses is told to write a song of witness.

On completing the song of witness and the book of the law, Moses charges the Levites to properly care for the written documents (**31:24–29**). They are to store them beside the ark of the covenant which is in the tabernacle.

B. The song of Moses (31:30–32:47). With a few changes from the treaty structure, the suzerainty treaties provided for judicial proceedings to be instituted against a rebel vassal. Likewise, the biblical covenant uses the covenant lawsuit whereby the Suzerain declares his intention of enforcing the sanctions of the covenant. Moses' song of witness follows the same pattern.

Heaven and earth are called as witnesses (**32:1–2**). Scripture identifies the heavenly witnesses as "heaven and earth" (Deut. 30:19; Isa. 1:2a) or the mountains and the foundations of the earth (Mic. 6:2). "The words of my mouth" and "my teaching" integrate the way of the covenant with the way of wisdom as words of grace in the midst of a judicial lawsuit.

Moses serves as prosecuting attorney on behalf of the divine Plaintiff, proclaiming the name of the Lord (**32:3–4**). God is a Rock, a reliable place of refuge for his covenant people; he is just, faithful, and upright in contrast to the fickleness of the people.

Moses briefly summarizes Israel's rebellion (**32:5–6**). The people have rejected their position as God's children, and failed to follow the pattern set for them by him (lit. Father who bought you; a reference to God as Redeemer from the bondage of Egypt). Such is the warping effect of sin and corruption.

The theological relationship has already been introduced in verse 6, where God has a prior claim on Israel as Father, Creator, and Redeemer. This relationship is now amplified by the mighty acts of the great King on behalf of his elect people (**32:7–14**). The boundaries of the nations were outlined with Israel in mind. The Lord superintended Israel's travels in the wilderness, protecting them and providing for all their needs. The Lord alone led Israel, making their later apostasy that much more inexcusable.

Moses provides a record of rebellion (**32:15–18**). Jeshurun (v. 15), a poetic name for Israel, means "upright, law-keeping, upholding justice. But instead of living up to its name, the nation grew fat and kicked. Their sinful rebellion is expressed in the verbs *abandoned, rejected, made him jealous, angered, deserted.* At the heart of their rebellion is their failure to keep the basic requirement of the covenant, namely, exclusive heart devotion to Yahweh. They transferred their allegiance to foreign gods, detestable idols, and demons. The loving relationship of Father and son was abandoned (v. 18a), and that of mother and child was forsaken (v. 18b).

God pronounces curses on the covenant breakers (**32:19–27**). God had revealed himself as a jealous God, allowing no rival deities (5:9; Exod. 20:5). If marital adultery called for the death penalty, much more would spiritual adultery incur the wrath of the jealous Husband (v. 21). While pronouncing the sentence as an expression of divine jealousy, God always aims at recalling his people to himself. The curses of the covenant are pronounced as the sentence for such sin. But the Lord also considers the awful taunts of the enemy nations.

In contrast to the suzerainty treaties which made no provision for repentance, the biblical covenant is unique in that the covenant blessings are fulfilled through a judgment that is redemptive in nature (**32:28–43**). Enemy nations are without sense or discernment. Divine vengeance and retribution against the enemy nations amount to a stay of execution of God's curses on Israel. This stay of execution is rooted in the very nature of God, his jealousy for his own glory. Even the ultimate preservation of Israel through a remnant is rooted in the very nature of God, his compassion and steadfast covenant love for them. The covenant lawsuit majestically asserts the absolute and universal sovereignty of Yahweh. He rules over death and life. The lawsuit concludes with a call to all nations to celebrate the victory of the Lord on behalf of all his people (v. 43).

Moses makes a final appeal to fidelity (**32:44–47**). Joshua stands beside Moses. They appeal to the covenant community to continue cultivating a heart relationship with God in succeeding generations.

C. The testament of Moses (32:48–33:29). After Moses is told to go up to Mount Nebo to die, he gives his last will and testament. In the tradition of the ancient Near East, such a testament was legal and irrevocable. In the case of the patriarchs, the final testamentary blessings carry the authority of the prophetic Spirit of God. It is significant that covenant and testament are here brought together, particularly because in the biblical concept of covenant the promise of redemption can be inherited only after the death of the testator. This adds further significance to the covenantal relationship of Father and children, the principle of adoption into the family of God.

God tells Moses to prepare for his death on Mount Nebo (**32:48–52**). The Abarim range is the craggy mountains above the Moabite plains by the Dead Sea, among which the summit of Mount Nebo is located.

Before his death, Moses blesses the tribes (**33:1–29**). "Man of God" (v. 1) is the first time this prophetic title appears in the Scriptures. It denotes Moses' closeness to the Lord and his intimate knowledge of the will of God. Moses describes the glory of the Lord as he first announced his covenant kingship at Sinai. This resplendent glory was like a glorious sunrise on the mountains of Sinai or in the desert east of the Arabah. Attending the great King were his heavenly armies, his holy ones. The last part of verse 2 might better be translated, "from his right hand came a fiery law for them," which well describes the Sinai covenant.

The blessings on the tribes are in the form of prayers, praises, commands, and prophecies, in the tradition of Jacob's testamentary blessings (see Gen. 49:1–27). If the song of witness (chap. 32) foreshadowed a bleak future, the blessings of Moses look forward to prosperity and glory. Moses begins by blessing the tribes descended from the first four sons of Leah. The omission of Simeon may be to maintain the number twelve since Joseph is represented by his two sons, Ephraim and Manasseh. Simeon seems to have been absorbed early on into the tribe of Judah (Josh. 19:1–9), so it may be assumed they are included in the blessings on Judah. Moses prays that Reuben not become extinct, possibly as a reference to their near extinction because of the rebellion of Dathan and Abiram (Num. 16:1–30). For Judah, the prayer is that Jacob's blessing be fulfilled in the kingly office of Judah, conquering the enemies of God and his people. Moses invests Levi with special tasks because of his faithfulness in observing the Word and covenant. They have been given the privilege of receiving special revelation through the Thummim and the Urim; they are to be teachers of the Law; they are responsible for the cultic worship in the tabernacle of the Lord. This blessing then closes with a prayer that Levi's priestly ministry on behalf of Israel will prove successful.

Moses prays for Benjamin's security. Benjamin is beloved of the Lord, possibly a reference to the pride that Jacob had in him and, further, because the Lord would include in his territory the city of Jerusalem. For Joseph, whose double portion of the patriarchal inheritance is represented by his two sons, Moses prays that God will bless them with the best produce of the land and with military success.

For Zebulun and Issachar, the last two sons of Leah, Moses prays for success in their commercial enterprises on the seas and in the sands (whether beaches or deserts is unclear). They inherited the productive Valley of Jezreel down to the Jordan River. They will lead people in thankful acknowledgment of the Lord's blessings. Moses sings a doxology to him who enlarges Gad's domain. The tribe already had inherited a large portion of the Trans-Jordanian territory. But they also carried out the Lord's righteous will by crossing over the Jordan in the conquest of the Promised Land.

Next are Dan and Naphtali, the sons of Bilhah, Rachel's handmaid. Moses compares Dan's adventurous spirit with a lion cub from Bashan. He seems to anticipate the Danite migration from the Philistine territory originally given them to the northern boundaries in Bashan at the foot of Mount Hermon (Judg. 18). Moses issues a command (not a promise) to Naphtali to inherit ("possess!") the land southward to the lake, meaning from the northern extremities down to the sea of Chinnereth on the western side of the Jordan. For Asher, the younger son of Zilpah, Moses prays that his feet may be bathed in oil, a reference to the productive olive groves in Upper Galilee. He further prays that they may be given strong protection from their enemies. The promise appended in verse 25b is beautifully translated: "your strength will equal your days," a precious promise all the more real for believers today.

In the conclusion to his testamentary blessings, Moses extols Israel's God. There is none like him; he really is the Giver of all the blessings bequeathed. Yahweh is the only true God who gives rain from above. God promises to drive out the enemy from the land as Israel proceeds to conquer and to dwell in safety. Finally, the blessings that Israel enjoys and will enjoy originate in the unique covenant Redeemer. Even their enemies will eventually acknowledge his supremacy.

D. The death of Moses (34:1–12). Moses climbs Mount Nebo alone, from the plains of Moab by the Dead Sea to the top of Pisgah, a jagged ridge to the west, from where he will be able to view the Promised Land. The panoramic view turns counterclockwise, beginning with a look northward toward Gilead (which is already conquered), to Dan (at the headwaters of the Jordan River), across to Naphtali with its mountains on the western side of the Upper Jordan, down through Ephraim and Manasseh (south of the Valley of Jezreel), to Judah, possibly seeing the western sea (the Mediterranean) in the distance beyond Judah, the Negeb in the southern part of Judah, and the whole Arabah, in the immediate foreground below him, to the north and south of the Dead Sea. Moses is permitted to see the land, but not enter it. Later, Moses will stand with Elijah and with Christ on one of these mountain peaks (cf. Matt. 17:3; Mark 9:4; Luke 9:30–31). God buries him (v. 6) in some unknown valley or depression on Mount Nebo, so that greater glory might be ascribed to God. A hundred and twenty years old (v. 7) is not an unreasonable age, even though in Egypt "a hundred and ten" was an accolade of highest honor to someone who had done an outstanding work in his life, no matter what his actual age at death may have been.

Joshua succeeds Moses. Filled with the spirit of wisdom, Joshua assumes leadership as dynastic heir. Verses 10–12 are a summary epitaph of Moses. Whatever prophet has risen after him, none was like Moses, to whom the Lord spoke face to face (cf. Exod. 33:11; Num. 12:8).

This whole chapter seems to have been given by revelation from God to a succeeding prophet. Two things suggest this. Since no one was with him, how could anyone know the nature of the conversation between God and Moses in 34:4? Why would his burial site have remained unknown? Furthermore, since Joshua explicitly added his book to the "book of the law of God" (Josh. 24:26), and his introduction in many ways is similar to this concluding chapter, it is reasonable to assume that Joshua wrote this appendix on the death of Moses.

SELECT BIBLIOGRAPHY

Craigie, P. C. *The Book of Deuteronomy.* Grand Rapids: Eerdmans, 1976.

Kline, M. G. *Treaty of the Great King.* Grand Rapids: Eerdmans, 1963.

Manley, G. T. *The Book of the Law: Studies in the Date of Deuteronomy.* Grand Rapids: Eerdmans, 1957.

The Historical Writings

These compositions describe the life and growth of the Israelite nation once the Promised Land had been occupied. Beginning with the Book of Joshua, they trace the people's history through the turbulent period of the judges and explain how the monarchy came to be formed. The events leading to the existence of two separate kingdoms, Israel and Judah, are described, including their devastation at the hands of foreign nations and the events that followed this catastrophe.

The ancient Hebrews were excellent writers of history, and hence their records are reliable and objective accounts of what transpired. But because the Israelites were by nature a religious community, the historical books always contain theological overtones. Some, indeed, such as Chronicles, are actually compiled from this special standpoint. The narratives of Israel's history demonstrate covenant theology by showing how God blessed his people when they obeyed his will, and the punishments that followed when they dallied with Canaanite idolatry. Despite periodic revivals of covenantal faith, the Israelites proved unable to resist the attractions of false gods, and were exiled as a result, after many warnings.

The return of Judah from captivity in Babylonia marked a new beginning for Hebrew national life. The idea of a kingdom was abandoned in favor of a religious community governed by a priesthood which mediated God's will directly. While the teachings of the Law were emphasized under this system, its impact was modified somewhat by the rise of political groups such as the Sadducees and Pharisees. These brought divisiveness to what should have been a unified Jewish community, and many people began to look for the Messiah to rule the nation.

Roman rulers in Palestine restricted these ambitions, and when

Jesus came to fulfil the messianic promises he was careful not to associate himself with an earthly kingdom. Some four decades after his ascension the Jewish kingdom was dispersed and the Jerusalem temple destroyed. This was God's final pronouncement upon a people that had strayed from covenant spirituality and rejected the Messiah sent for their salavation. From that point the Christian church replaced Judaism as God's witnesses in the world. The Old Testament historical records as such end in the middle of the fifth century B.C.

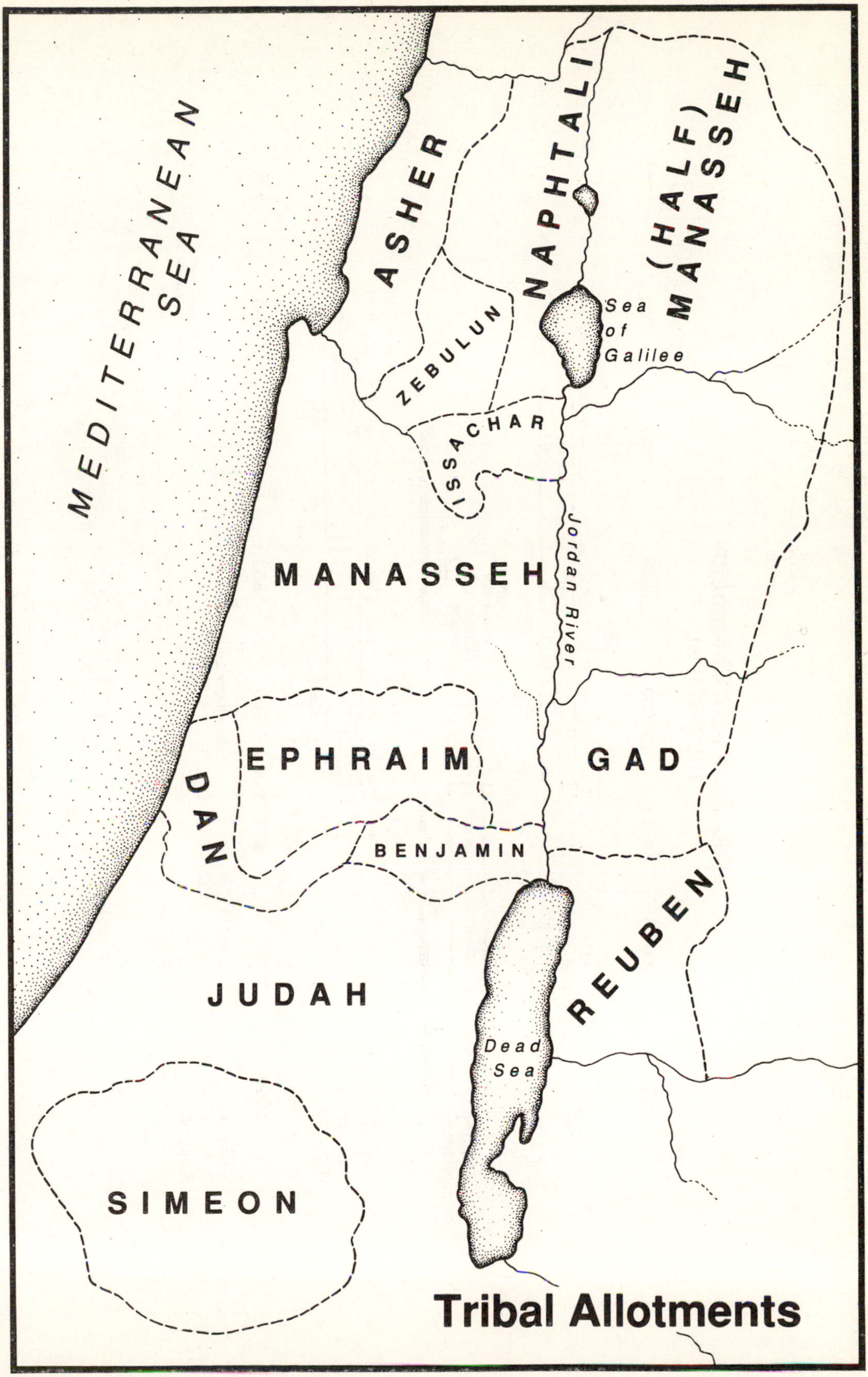

Tribal Allotments

Old Testament Chronology
1050–700 B.C.

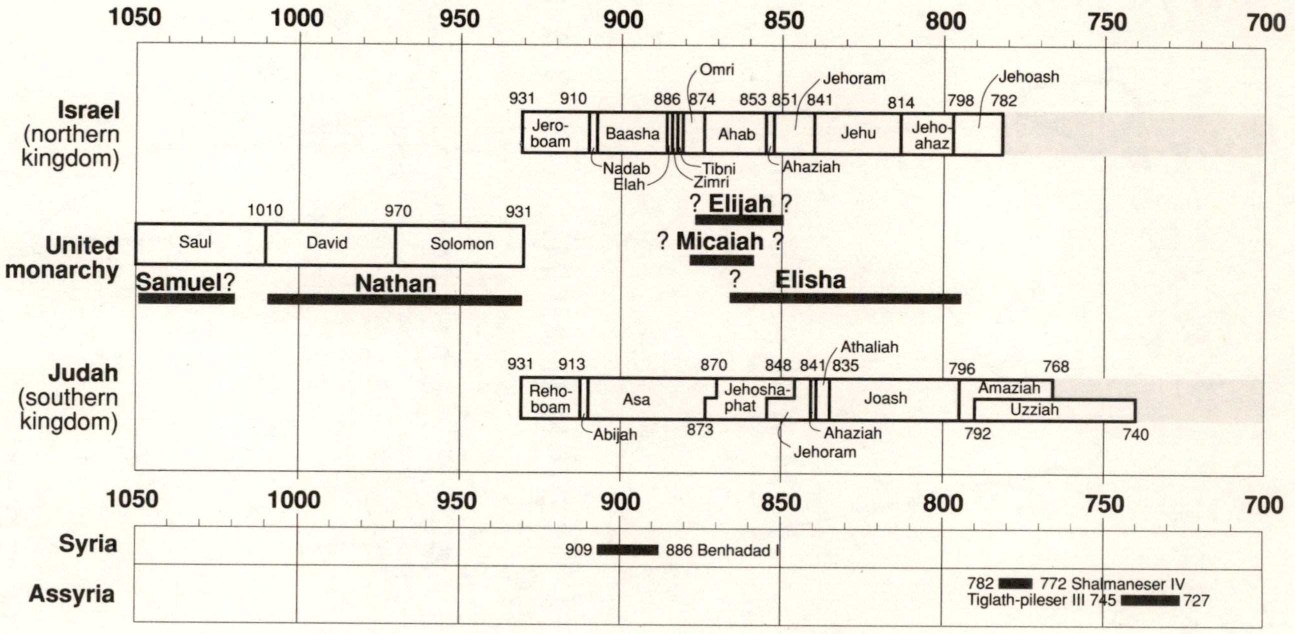

JOSHUA

Andrew C. Bowling

INTRODUCTION

The date of Joshua's composition is difficult to discern since some of the evidence is ambiguous. Both the first-person, eyewitness references to events (e.g., 5:1) and the fact that Rahab lived at the time the book was written (6:25) may indicate an early date of composition. However, this evidence is compromised by the ancient concept of national solidarity. "We" and "us" may refer to the identity of the nation, not a given group of individuals, and Rahab may have lived on centuries after her death in her clansmen.

References to Canaanites living in Gezer (16:10) and to Jebusites in Jebus (15:8, 63) seem to date the book before Israel gained control of these centers. However, at least in the case of Jebus, indigenous inhabitants remained there after Israelite control was established (1 Chron. 21:18).

References that seem to underscore the preeminence of Sidon (11:8; 19:28) might indicate a date before Tyre's ascendance (ca. 1200 B.C.). On the other hand, another context in which Sidonians are mentioned uses "Gebalites" as representative of the Phoenicians (13:4–5). The writer may have used terminology that represented past historical situations. If so, Sidon could have been cited as the representative Phoenician city even after Tyrian supremacy.

The sole reference to Philistines (13:3) is ambiguous. The fact that Philistines played a minor role—even being referred to as "Canaanite"—indicates composition before the large-scale arrival of Philistine settlers. On the other hand, referring to the Philistines in terms of their traditional five cities would indicate a date after the founding of the Philistine Pentapolis.

The book refers to events that happened later in the time of the judges, such as the Danite migration north (19:47).

Allowing for all the uncertainties in the evidence, the book was probably written by an unknown author during the period of the judges or the early monarchy.

The Book of Joshua is made up of different types of materials working together to develop a single theme and promote a single point of view. The writer of Joshua is quite opportunistic in taking materials at hand and incorporating them with minimal change as long as they develop his theme.

The territorial descriptions probably represent the least degree of adaptation. On the other extreme are the episodes in which the overt topic is subordinated to the development of a covenant theme. The account of the spying out of Jericho, which is used to develop the theme of the conversion of Canaanites, serves as an example.

As in most of the Old Testament, the underlying presupposition is God's covenant relationship with his people. Every event in the book represents a working out of God's covenant relationship with Israel.

The unifying theme of Joshua is that God is giving the land, promised by the covenant, to the Israelites. The conquest accounts (chaps. 1–12) describe the historical process by which the land is given. Israel's right to the land is confirmed by sacred assignment of the land to the various tribes (chaps. 13–21). The last three chapters (22–24) deal with covenant faithfulness in the land.

However, the book also develops lesser covenant themes: the character of the ideal covenant leader (chap. 1); the conversion of Canaanites to Yahweh (chaps. 2, 9); God's presence with the covenant people (chaps. 3–4); giving the land in response to obedience (chap. 6); and the withdrawal of blessing because of disobedience (7:1–8:29). The narratives of the southern and northern campaigns illustrate God's marvelous working in giving the land (chaps. 10–11). Several chapters record affirmations of the covenant relationship (8:30–35; 23; 24).

Of these, the theme of the conversion of Canaanites may be the most significant. Two major episodes deal with this theme. In addition, other episodes touch on this theme in a secondary fashion. The first covenant renewal at Shechem makes specific mention of "aliens" (8:33, 35), and Joshua's challenge to discard "foreign gods" (24:23) best fits a setting with converted Canaanites.

A pressing issue is God's harshness in commanding the slaughter of the Canaanites. The Canaanites basically had two options. They had witnessed God's great deeds on behalf of Israel. Those, like Rahab and the Gibeonites, who responded to this witness in faith, lived as part of the covenant people. Those who were hardened by their willful rejection of this witness faced mortal destruction. This was no particular harshness to the Canaanites; all men, even in the present age, face a similar choice: acceptance of God's witness and life or rejection of God's witness and death.

The many references to the peoples of Canaan present a special problem in that these names reflect the ambiguities typical of popular geographical terminology. Scholars generally agree that two names are used to represent all of Canaan, "Amorites" (Gen. 15:16) and "Canaan" (Num. 33:51). These terms also had more restricted usages. "Amorite" referred to the peoples in the mountains and hill country, and "Canaanite" was used for the mercantile peoples in the coastal plain and valleys (5:1). "Jebusites," "Girgashites," and "Perizzites" seem to have been Amorite subgroups. "Hittites" are regularly included in the peoples of Canaan (Exod. 3:8; Num. 13:29; Deut. 20:17). Used in this way, the term does not imply domination by the Hittite Empire. Rather, it merely recalls the general dispersion of the "Sons of Heth" (i.e., "Hittites") among the population of the land. This situation made it possible for the term *Hittite* to refer to all Palestine (1:4). "Hivvites" were best known from the Gibeonite league (chap. 9) though they were also found in other locations (see 11:3). Association with the Rephaim suggests that the "Anakites" were among the aboriginal "mighty" inhabitants of Palestine (Deut. 2:10–11).

OUTLINE

- I. The Conquest of the Land (1–12)
  - A. Preparations (1–5)
  - B. The Central Campaign (6–9)
  - C. The Southern Campaign (10)
  - D. The Northern Campaign (11:1–15)
  - E. The Continued Conquest (11:16–23)
  - F. The Conquered Kings (12)
- II. The Division of the Land (13–21)
  - A. Unconquered Peoples (13:1–7)
  - B. The Trans-Jordanian Inheritances (13:8–33)
  - C. The Canaanite Inheritances (14–19)
  - D. The Sacred Inheritances (20–21)
- III. Life in the Land (22–24)
  - A. Covenant Faithfulness (22)
  - B. Reaffirmation of the Covenant (23:1–24:27)
  - C. Three Burials (24:28–33)

COMMENTARY

I. The Conquest of the Land (1–12)

A. Preparations (1–5). The explicit topic of chapter 1 is the confirmation of God's chosen leader for the conquest of the land. The chapter also describes the character of the ideal covenant leader as illustrated in the person of Joshua.

Joshua had already been selected as Moses' successor (Deut. 31:1–8). Israel is camped east of the Jordan River at Shittim (cf. 3:1), awaiting God's command to enter the land. Great leadership is needed for the tremendous task before them.

God commands Joshua to assume active leadership (**1:1–9**). He is to lead the people across the Jordan into the land. The land will be given to Joshua in accordance with the covenant promised to Moses. The bounds of the land are described in very general terms. Toward the east and south, the cultivated land of Palestine was bordered by a belt of "wilderness" (NIV desert) of the Negeb and the Jordan Valley. This wilderness, or desert (Heb. *midbār*), could refer to semidesert pasturage as well as to deep, sandy desert. In the north the land extended as far as Mount Lebanon, although the phrase *this Lebanon* (exact translation) might indicate a white limestone range closer to the Israelite camp. Toward the northeast the land extended as far as the Euphrates. Since the term *Hittites* routinely occurs in the lists of people living in Canaan, "all the Hittite country" in this context is best taken as another way of describing the land of Canaan. The Mediterranean marked the western boundary. God's presence and the resulting victory are prerequisites for possessing the land.

Finally, Joshua is challenged to perpetual faithfulness to the covenant. The preeminent duty of the ideal leader is to exemplify perfect obedience to the covenant demands of the law. He is to be "strong and courageous" (vv. 6–7), a recurrent covenant challenge. This phrase embraces such overtones as strength in conflict, firmness in resolution, and victory over enemies. The covenant law is to color the leader's speech, fill his mind, and govern his entire life, thus producing prosperity. The ideal leader can be strong, brave, and unafraid because God is always with him. Normally, God's presence with the leader also implies his presence with the people.

Joshua immediately obeys God's commands (**1:10–11**). He orders the people to prepare to take the land promised by the covenant, though his intention to cross in three days turns out to be overly optimistic.

The Trans-Jordanian tribesmen demonstrate the proper reaction of God's people to his chosen leader (**1:12–18**). Their faithfulness is all the more impressive in that they are the ones who stand to realize the least personal gain from obedience; they already have their inheritances. Their obedience demonstrates faith since their own families and goods will be vulnerable to attack while the men are away.

First, they affirm that they will obey Joshua with the same obedience they gave to Moses, the first and greatest of the theocratic leaders. Second, they wish for God's presence with Joshua (v. 17b); this is significant since God's presence with his people is one of the great theological themes of the book. Third, they vow to support Joshua's leadership by imposing the death penalty on those who are disobedient. And, finally, they add their weight to the recurrent covenant challenge to "be strong and courageous" (v. 18b).

Chapter 2 illustrates the twofold role played by many of the episodes recorded in Joshua—the historical role and the theological role. From the historical perspective, this account records a spy expedition, a natural step in an invasion. But the high point and theme of this account is the conversion of a Canaanite clan to Yahwism.

Events quickly lead up to a dramatic decision on Rahab's part (**2:1–2**). Joshua sends out the spies, and they try to make themselves inconspicuous in Rahab's establishment. Rahab's profession is not completely clearcut. She may have been a cultic religious prostitute, an honorable status in most of the world at that time. Under that title she could have operated a public establishment of some other sort, such as an inn. On the other hand, she could have been a professional courtesan. In either case, her house would have been a place where strangers might try to blend anonymously into a crowd and where they would be recognized as suspicious by the king's agents.

Circumstances force Rahab to choose between loyalty to her own people and commitment to the God of the Hebrews (**2:3–7**). Having hidden the spies, Rahab lies to her own people. The account seems to presuppose that it is proper to lie to God's enemies in advancing his purposes. Some argue that truth is obligatory only to those who have a right to it; conversely, lying to those who have no just claim on the truth is morally acceptable. However, this view risks opening the way to a casuistic justification of any and all lying. Rahab's lie advances God's purposes by misdirecting the king's agents.

This brings us to the climax of the passage: Rahab's statement of faith (**2:8–11**). Her faith is tied in with God's great deeds. God's great deeds are highly significant in the Old Testament. These great, miraculous deeds showed that God was present with and working for his people. There were two reactions to hearing of these deeds. First, the nations could fall into demoralization as the Canaanites did, or they could hear, praise God, and accept him in faith as Rahab did (v. 11). As always in the Old Testament the content of faith is not the full New Testament knowledge of redemption. Rahab's confession expresses the faith appropriate for the knowledge available to her.

Rahab and the spies confirm their agreements for the preservation of her clan (**2:12–21**). Their agreement depends upon Rahab's continued silence (v. 14). Rahab offers helpful advice for eluding their pursuers, and then receives the word that leaving a cord in the window is to be the sign that will guarantee her family's safety.

Is it possible to harmonize the preservation of Rahab's family with the command to exterminate the Canaanites? God's purpose in such commands was to forbid the continued existence of Canaanites as Canaanites. But it was within God's purposes that those Canaanites who would give up their Canaanite identity in order to become Israelites, culturally and religiously, should be absorbed into the Hebrew nation and be allowed to survive. This conclusion is supported by many evidences of openness to Gentile converts in the Old Testament.

The spies, hidden in the opposite direction from where they are being sought, wait until the search is finished and then return to Joshua (**2:22–24**). The fear and demoralization of the Canaanites, as reported to Joshua, is one of the expected results of hearing of God's great deeds.

The crossing of the Jordan is a powerful, miraculous example of God's presence with his people. The central focus of the account is not the fact of crossing the Jordan. Even at flood stage, the Jordan is fordable—with difficulty—provided the right locations are sought out. The focus of the account is that the crossing occurs in a miraculous way, demonstrating God's presence with his people.

The unity and coherence of this account are frequently criticized, and the alleged difficulties in structure are taken as evidence that two or more source documents have been combined, somewhat carelessly and mechanically, to produce the account before us. However, it is possible to view the text more sympathetically in light of two complementary literary devices: (1) the usage of fragmentary literary anticipations in which purposefully incomplete references to topics anticipate later, fuller treatments of those same topics; and (2) the usage of literary retrospections that fill out details omitted in earlier fragmentary anticipations.

Viewed in these terms, the following analysis gives a plausible structure for the account:

1. Preparations for crossing (3:1)
2. The place of the ark in the crossing (3:2–6)
3. The crossing as a miraculous work of God (3:7–13)
4. The crossing executed (3:14–17)

The crossing is more or less described three times, twice in preparatory commands (vv. 2–6; 7–13) and once in the actual historical narrative (vv. 14–17).

The Israelites are ready to leave Shittim (**3:1**). They travel about nine miles through rough, barren country to the Jordan, where their progress is doubtless noted by the spies of the fearful Canaanite rulers. Perhaps the easier fords were guarded by military detachments. It is naive scholarship to find a factual discrepancy between Joshua's overly optimistic hope to cross the Jordan in three days (1:11) and the fact that the actual time elapsed was closer to eight days (cf. 2:22; 3:2). A disparity between human hopes and unfolding realities is not a factual error in the text.

The first series of commands emphasizes the dominant place of the ark in the events (**3:2–6**). The ark is to lead the line of march. The people are told to maintain a distance between themselves and the ark, thus emphasizing its sanctity. God's presence, as represented by the ark, demands a sanctified people. The ark is placed at the head of the people.

This miracle demonstrates, to both the Israelites and the Canaanites, that God is present with his people to work on their behalf, particularly in giving victory over the peoples mentioned (**3:7–13**). The twelve men (v. 12) tie into the theme since they are to build a memorial for this great deed; but for the moment, this verse is another fragmentary anticipation of an idea to be more fully explained later (see 4:2–3). When the symbol of God's presence is in the river, the waters will miraculously cease to flow.

The crossing is executed (**3:14–17**). There may be a natural explanation for this miracle, possibly a landslide at Adam. There are several instances in recorded history when the rugged cliff banks have fallen and blocked the Jordan. However, even if that were the case, the timing of the event still points to God's miraculous power.

The impact of the miracle is considerable. The waters cease while the nation crosses the dry river bed and continue to hold back until other tasks are completed. All the participants and all the watchers are impressed with God's power and his presence with his people.

Chapter 4 is taken up with the altar commemorating this great event. It is always incumbent upon God's people to remember the great works which God has done for them, and various kinds of reminders—ritual ceremonies, monuments, recitations—help them remember. In this passage, an altar (possibly two) is to be built which will remind the people of this great deed.

This account is structured around three increasingly lengthier repetitions of the incident's content: (1) God's command concerning the memorial; (2) Joshua's command to the people; and (3) the execution of the commands. This pattern or motif of expanded repetition gives a structural basis for a sympathetic analysis of the unity of this chapter.

After the entire nation has crossed the Jordan, the commands for the memorial are given. Joshua is to "take" (not "choose"; the men had been chosen earlier [3:12]) twelve men, who represent all the people, and build an altar at their encampment at Gilgal (**4:1–3**).

Joshua's command to the people (**4:4–7**) adds more details, thus giving a fuller restatement of the content of God's command. This principle of expanded repetition seems to be a deliberate literary device in the Book of Joshua. The men are commanded to get stones from the middle of the Jordan. Joshua tells the people, no doubt passing on what God had told him earlier, that the altar will be a sign to remind them of God's wondrous deeds.

The Israelites obey, taking twelve stones with them to their camp (**4:8–24**). Verse 9 seems to suggest the construction of a second altar in the middle of the Jordan where the priests stood with the ark. However, it probably simply indicates the source of the stones used for the altar at Gilgal, not the building of a second altar.

The total obedience of the priests in waiting

until the people cross is again described (vv. 10–13; cf. 3:17). This does not represent an alternate, parallel source somewhat clumsily redacted into a composite text. Rather it is a literary retrospection that introduces the next major event in the narrative: the exiting of the ark from the Jordan. As God had promised, the ideal leader is exalted in this event (v. 14). Obedience is reemphasized in that everything is done by specific command.

The central theme of the entire crossing account is taken up again when the ark leaves the water. When the symbol of God's presence is taken from the river bed, the waters immediately flow again. The miraculous power of God's presence with his people has been dramatically shown.

The date emphasizes a new beginning: it is in the first month of the sacred calendar, a new year for a new land (v. 19). The significance and remembrance of the memorial altar and the sign are reemphasized. The altar firmly points the Israelites to their historical ties with God. Further, God's great signs are testimonies, not just to Israel, but also to the whole world.

This passage may also demonstrate the nature of official worship at Gilgal. In light of the ancient custom of associating holy places with sacred stories, it is quite possible that the official worship activity at Gilgal was intended to be the recitation of this particular example of God's great works.

The great sign has an expected result: the kings of Canaan are thrown into fear and demoralization (**5:1**). On the other hand, the full impact of God's great deeds also should have included leading some to faith. "Amorite" is a general term for the dwellers in the hill country and "Canaanite" for the inhabitants of the coast—and presumably of the valleys as well.

Several features mark the new status of the Israelites after entering the covenant land: circumcision, a Passover celebration, eating the produce of the land, and another manifestation of God's presence.

On a practical level, circumcision (**5:2–9**) was the principal sign of the covenant. Even on Old Testament terms, the sign of covenant membership implied inner holiness (Deut. 10:16–20). Though there is no purely literary feature that identifies the account as etiological, the nature of the historical content indicates that the "Hill of Foreskins" (i.e., "Gibeath Haaraloth") gained its name from this occasion (v. 3). The reason for Israel's forty-year neglect of circumcision is not clear. The content of the biblical explanation could indicate as simple a reason as the difficulty of circumcising while "on the move."

The "reproach of Egypt" (v. 9) has been understood in different ways: (1) that the Egyptians practiced circumcision and the lack of the rite was disgraceful in Egyptian eyes; (2) that Israel's failure to circumcise was an Egyptian reproach since the failure began in Egypt; or (3) that it marked the end of Egyptian bondage. Since "Gilgal" is a common name, seemingly applied to several locations, it is better to regard the mention of that name as a pun on the appropriateness of a name already existing ("Gilgal" = "rolling" or "wheel") rather than the original assignment of a new name.

What better time to begin life in the land than at Passover near the beginning of a new sacred year (**5:10–12**)? Three important events are recorded here: the celebration of Passover, the halting of the manna, and eating the produce of the land. All three can be thematically linked to the appropriation of the land and its benefits. The celebration of Passover indicates the presence, perhaps even the renewal, of the covenant. The land is Israel's because of, and only because of, the covenant promise. Eating the produce of the land marks the first step in appropriating the land. The ceasing of the manna marks the end of a provision necessary only during the wanderings outside the land.

At this critical time God encourages Joshua with another special vision (**5:13–15**). Joshua's question is probably less a request for information than a request for reassurance. The response indicates that it is more a matter of God's people being "for" God than God being for his people. Another issue in God's promise of victory is his holiness. God's people must properly revere his holiness for God to be present and to give victory.

B. The central campaign (6–9). It is possible that the social structure in Canaan influenced the conquest. Both archaeology and extrabiblical literature reveal that the population of cities of Palestine were generally divided into two classes: the militaristic ruling aristocracies and the common people. At that time, the common people were not completely loyal to the ruling aristocracies of Palestine. This early conquest could have focused on the ruling classes of Palestine, leaving the "masses" to be dealt with in the later campaigns of tribal conquest.

Militarily, the initial conquest consists of three campaigns: the central campaign, which effectively divides Canaan into two parts (chaps. 6–9); the southern campaign, which destroys the united resistance of the kings of southern Canaan (chap. 10); and the northern campaign, which accomplishes the same objective in the north (chap. 11). The first step in the central campaign is the conquest of Jericho, in order to open a direct route into the central hill country near the northern end of the Dead Sea.

The theological principle embodied in this account is victory in response to obedience. This principle gives meaning to God's commands. The very structure of the account relates the victory of the Israelites not to their military skills or brilliant strategy but to obedience to militarily irrelevant instructions.

In the face of invasion, Jericho is shut up under siege waiting for the Israelites to strike (**6:1**). Following the normal factionalism of Canaan, the other cities protect themselves and leave Jericho to its fate. The kings of Canaan do not undertake united military action until it is too late.

The basic structural motif of this account is carefully constructed repetitions. In effect, the general pattern of events is related three times, once here as God commands Joshua (**6:2–5**), a second time when Joshua passes the commands on to the people (vv. 6–7), and third, when the execution of the commands is described (vv. 8–16). Although the second presentation is briefer than the first, the general pattern is still from shorter, less detailed presentation to longer, more detailed presentation. This expanded repetition gives a structural basis for the unity of this account. God deals with the problem of Jericho with a promise of victory and militarily irrelevant commands concerning Israel's line of march.

The destruction of Jericho is detailed (**6:8–27**). The line of march begins with an armed guard. This is followed by seven priests with trumpets and then the ark itself. The ark, as in other settings, symbolizes God's presence with his people. Then the armed rear guard closes up the order of march. This entourage marches around the city once each day for six days with the trumpets sounding continuously. On the seventh day they circle the city seven times. After the seventh circuit and a particularly noteworthy trumpet blast, the shout, often used as a sign of going into battle, is given (vv. 16, 20). Then the walls fall and the city is taken.

The spoils of the city are put under the ban, that is, they are dedicated to God. The normal way to dedicate destructible goods to God was to destroy them or abandon them. This dedication of the goods of Jericho could be likened to the firstfruits principle. Like the firstfruits of the fields and livestock, the firstfruits of the spoils of Canaan belonged to God. Only Rahab and her clan are allowed to live. The people are warned that violation of the ban will bring quick destruction. Nondestructible items are "banned" by placing them in the tabernacle treasuries.

The fall of the walls of Jericho is best seen as a divinely executed miracle. Such naturalistic explanations as that the vibrations of the marching hosts weakened the walls are somewhat fanciful.

Rahab and her family are exiled from the camp, perhaps for a period of purification. The reference to Rahab living among the Hebrews "to this day" (v. 25) is most easily taken as referring to Rahab's own life-span. However, from the ancient perspective, in which the individual and his or her family were identified with each other, this statement would not be falsified if the significance was that Rahab's family survived among the Hebrews "to this day." The underlying principle is that Canaanites who were properly converted to Yahwism and who accepted Hebrew identity were exempted from the general destruction of the Canaanites.

The dedication to Yahweh, or the ban of the site, is to be permanent, but it is often taken as referring to Jericho as a fortified settlement. There are several references to Jericho's being inhabited (Josh. 18:21; 2 Sam. 10:5) before the curse upon rebuilding the city's fortifications was executed (1 Kings 16:34). This victory helps, once more, to exalt Joshua, the ideal leader (v. 27).

The next step in the central campaign is to move west from Jericho and seize control of the central mountain country. A natural target was Ai near the major route going up into the highlands beyond Michmash. The identification of Ai is uncertain since the archaeology of the possible site does not completely fit the literary evidence.

At this point, Israel's relationship with God is broken. Achan takes some of the goods devoted to Yahweh (**7:1**). This sin may be viewed from several perspectives. First, it is disobedience to the covenant, and obedience is prerequisite for God's presence and blessings. Then the sin might be viewed as especially significant because this is a critical time in the history of Israel. Just as the sin of Ananias and Sapphira (Acts 5) in its critical setting demands a particularly pointed judgment, so this sin, in its setting, warrants especially strong attention. Finally, the sin violates God's rights to the firstfruits of Canaan.

Joshua sends men to spy out Ai. There is nothing wrong with prudent military operations as long as they do not contradict some clearly specified divine purpose. In view of later events, the Israelites are somewhat overconfident.

The Israelites send a relatively small force and are defeated. The small number of casualties for such a disastrous defeat discloses something of the scope of this campaign. The defeat produces demoralization. The theological principle of the incident is clear; sin removes God's presence, and, when God's presence is removed, defeat and disaster follow.

In contrast with the promised pleasures and benefits, sin really produces grief (**7:6–9**). Tearing one's clothing is a formal sign of grief. The leaders correctly bring their sorrow to God. They complain to God about the unexpected turn of events. Instead of victory as in the capture of Jericho, the people have experienced defeat. Not only that, God's great name will suffer if his people are destroyed.

The leaders of the people presented themselves to God to seek a solution to their problem, and God responds to them (**7:10–15**). God's answer has been taken as a rebuke to Joshua for praying instead of acting (v. 10). It is true that, after God's clear answer, there was no need to continue in prayer. But the gist of the statement is for Joshua to act after God has spoken rather than to rebuke him for not acting earlier.

God then informs Joshua that the people have sinned. Several expressions are used to describe their sin, but the most powerful one, in this context, is that they have violated the covenant with God. The theology is clearly stated: sin hinders God's presence with his people. Therefore, their efforts have failed. The people must purge themselves from sin if they are to return to a course of victory.

Instructions are then given on how to purge the sin. Possibly using the sacred lots, the Urim and Thummim, as a way of selection, first the tribe, then the clan, then the extended family, then the individual family is to be chosen. Utter destruction of the guilty family is the penalty for the crime. This passage illustrates the relationship between personal forgiveness and the need for punishment within the corporate setting. The issue is the corporate well-being of the nation. Even though Achan may have been completely repentant in respect to personal moral guilt, the long-range welfare of the nation demands the punishment of his sin. Personal forgiveness of the individual does not automatically invalidate the penalty required by society or by the church.

The guilty family is discovered according to God's instructions. Joshua is tender and sorrowful, addressing Achan as "my son" (v. 19). Achan confesses his guilt. He had seen objects of wealth and luxury and had taken them for himself. The goods are retrieved and his guilt is established. Today it seems strange that Achan's sin should have affected others so drastically. The sense of the corporate unity of God's people was much stronger in biblical times than in modern, individualistic society.

Achan, his family, and all his property are destroyed. The crime was impossible without the complicity and agreement of the family; therefore they share the penalty. The drastic punishment communicates a powerful lesson to the nation at this early, critical period of their history.

The mention of the Valley of Achor (i.e., "Valley of Disaster") may use the similarity between "Achor" and "Achan" for a derisive pun on Achan's name (v. 24). This same pun may also underlie the later substitution of "Achar" for "Achan" (1 Chron. 2:7).

With the evil purged from the nation, fellowship with God is restored and victory could again come to Israel. This time, the spoils will be available to the people (**8:1–2**).

There are two factors in this victory. As in earlier successes, obedience to God's commands is indispensable for success. This time human strategy is also a factor (**8:3–9**). Although he is obeying God's command, Joshua conducts a prudent, well-planned operation in contrast to the overconfidence of the earlier attack. The ambush force alone is numbered at thirty thousand (v. 3). The men of Ai must have been recklessly overconfident to overlook such a large force. The plan is to lure the men of Ai out with a frontal attack whereupon the ambush force will destroy the city by burning. The ambush force hides just west of Ai.

The next day Joshua leads the main body of his troops to a camp north of Ai, giving the appearance of preparing for battle the following day (**8:10–29**). The plan works perfectly. The next morning the men of Ai come out to battle. Joshua retreats before the men of Ai and their allies from Bethel. Joshua's outstretched javelin (v. 18), which remains outstretched until the battle is completed, symbolizes God's power in a way reminiscent of Moses' rod. The ambush force then takes the city and burns it. Although nothing is said specifically, it is likely that Bethel is also eventually destroyed. At this point Joshua's army reverses its direction and the men of Ai are caught between Israel's main army and the ambush force. The slaughter is complete. The king of Ai is brought to Joshua alive. No contradiction is demanded by the return of the Israelites to Ai to complete the slaughter and destruction.

Had the people of Ai, like Rahab, reacted to God's great signs with faith leading to conversion they also could have become a part of the

Hebrew nation. Instead, they reacted to God's great deeds with stubborn resistance, and, for this reason, are destroyed.

The ruins of Ai become a permanent memorial of God's great deeds. The king of Ai is executed, disgraced by the public display of his corpse, and his body is incorporated into the memorial ruins. Since the king represented his people and their gods, his personal defeat and disgrace hold special meaning.

The next event recorded is a ceremony of covenant renewal at Shechem (**8:30–35**). Since the basic structural framework of the Bible is topical rather than chronological, it is not certain that this event is next in chronological sequence. "Then" (v. 30) could mean "sometime afterward" rather than "immediately next." However, if, as most commentators seem to do, one assumes immediate temporal sequence, this event is full of significance. Israel has not yet subdued the territory near Shechem. Thus, their unopposed passage to Shechem indicates that most of the population in this region were people who would be naturally tolerant of the Israelites. Perhaps related settlers in the region of Shechem were willing allies for the newly arrived Israelites.

Both the days immediately preceding this book and the end of this book are marked with great covenant renewals. Covenant renewal at this time, when the Israelites have barely established a foothold in the land, is appropriate for two reasons: (1) it reaffirms the loyalty of Israel to Yahweh in the early stages of the conquest; and (2) it gives interested "aliens" (i.e., non-Hebrews) who are already in the land an opportunity to become formally identified with the covenant people. Part of the population around Shechem could have been among the "aliens" involved in this ceremony.

At this time, then, the people obey the command of Moses to reaffirm the covenant from Mount Ebal (Deut. 27). As commanded earlier, Joshua builds an altar of undressed stone. The offering of whole burnt offerings expresses the nation's total commitment to God in worship and service, and the fellowship offerings represent the bond of fellowship among the people and between the people and God. Then Joshua carves the provisions of the law onto a prepared surface on the altar on Mount Ebal.

The two references to aliens (vv. 33, 35) indicate that converted Canaanites were already being brought into the covenant. The terminology used to describe the law here (v. 34) recalls the three major parts of the covenant: the laws which were to be obeyed, the blessings given for keeping the law, and the curses for disobeying the law.

Chapter 9 is a complex chapter that develops several themes. First, the account relates another step in the subjugation of Canaan, the alliance with the Gibeonite league. Second, the theme of the conversion of the Canaanites is advanced with the record of the conversion of the Gibeonites, however questionable or insincere it may have been. Third, the danger of trusting in human wisdom without God's supernatural direction is illustrated.

The land is viewed in three major divisions: the hill country, the western foothills (i.e., Shephelah), and the Mediterranean coast. The great valleys, controlled by the Canaanite merchant aristocracies, were probably linked with the coastal areas. Israel's success to this point brings an unusual reaction, a general, unified concern on the part of some of the kings of Canaan (**9:1–2**).

The Gibeonites and their allies also react to what they have seen, but the Gibeonites choose a different strategy (**9:3–15**). They seek a way to make peace with the invaders. The issue at stake should be clarified. There are numerous indications that Canaanites who were willing to give up their Canaanite identity, religion, and immorality by becoming Yahwists could be accepted into the Hebrew nation. However, national identity, especially explicit identification with one's own ancestors in one's own land, was precious to people of the ancient biblical world. The Gibeonite league was interested not only in preserving their lives, but also in preserving their lives in such a way that their historic identity could also be preserved, even if under a new religious umbrella. This is the real issue of the Gibeonite deception. Their strategy is to gain a treaty with Israel by pretending that they have come from a great distance even though this implies acceptance of Israelite lordship and, at least formally, religion.

The Gibeonites prepare stale food and worn-out clothing and go to Gilgal where they present their deceptive request. The Israelites are suspicious, but not suspicious enough. Several points are clear in the negotiations. The Gibeonites assume the subordinate role in the discussions. The term *servants* in this context implies a position of vassalage. In the ancient world, the subordinate role implied not only political submission but also acceptance of the sovereignty of the ruler's gods. Thus, in this context, the Gibeonite acknowledgment of God's great deeds amounts to a formal acceptance of Yahweh as their God.

The Gibeonites' false report of their preparations and journey, while duplicating material presented earlier, represents a high level of narrative technique and a skillful use of repetition. The failure to depend upon God rather than human wisdom is dramatically presented in Israel's testing of the fabricated evidence without seeking God's direction. A treaty is made, and, from general historical practice, includes at least three provisions: (1) Gibeon's acceptance of the God of Israel; (2) Gibeon's observance of the duties of a vassal; and (3) Israel's acceptance of the duties of a lord, mainly that of defending their vassals.

Three days later the Israelites discover that they have guaranteed the existence of Canaanites within the nation (v. 16). The passage of centuries would bring so much corrupting contact with Canaanite communities that the role of the Gibeonites in that corruption might seem relatively trivial. However, at this time the continued existence of the Gibeonites appears to be a unique threat to Israel's religious purity (**9:16–26**).

Here we learn that the Gibeonite league consists of four cities, at least two of which, Gibeon and Kiriath-jearim, would be heard from repeatedly throughout the history of Israel. To their fellow Canaanites the Gibeonite league represents a formidable military force (see Josh 10:2).

The place of an anomalous Canaanite group in Israel has to be defined. The treaty demands that they be exempt from execution. They are to be woodcutters and drawers of water for the community and the central shrine. They are not state slaves. They retain sufficient status that seven of Saul's descendants are executed for violating their historical rights (2 Sam. 21:1–5). Finally, their chief city, Gibeon, becomes one of the most influential sites of the tabernacle (1 Chron. 16:39; 2 Chron. 1:5).

Careful attention to the language permits an alternate interpretation, more in line with the general course of subsequent events. The continued existence of the Gibeonites as a recognized societal unit, as worshipers of Yahweh, and as free allies is guaranteed by treaty. Granting that the Gibeonites were not dispersed throughout the nation to serve as menial laborers for the "community" (NIV), the original Hebrew permits the interpretation that they are given a symbolic, demeaning role in the religious festivities as menial servants to the "congregation" but only as it is gathered for worship wherever the tabernacle is (v. 27).

The Gibeonites manage to preserve their identity according to treaty and become Yahwists, at least formally, by the same treaty. But the demeaning nature of their formal service to the centralized shrine is to be a perpetual reminder that their status is not the desired ideal and that they had gained their questionable status by trickery.

Once again, the real gist of this chapter is not that the Gibeonites manage to survive within the Israelite community; other Canaanites and foreigners also achieve this goal. The irregularity is that they accomplish their conversion and survival in such a way that they also maintain their historic Canaanite identity.

C. The southern campaign (10). Chapter 10 is noteworthy in that it is the first episode in the book as long as a chapter in length in which the internal structure of the account is not overtly influenced by its theological theme. For example, the internal structure of Joshua 2 is clearly manipulated to indicate that Rahab's conversion, rather than the espionage adventure, is the climax of the account. In this chapter, the theological theme is certainly present; the passage illustrates God's fulfilling his covenant promise by giving the land. But the narrative content of the account makes the point without internal restructuring.

The kings of the south are described as "Amorite." This term had its origins in a historically defined group of invaders who established a chain of dynasties throughout the Fertile Crescent. These people subjugated Palestine from 2200–1700 B.C. At least some of these biblical Amorites were descendants of the historical Amorites, but several centuries of history resulted in the blending of several ethnic waves of invaders into one more or less homogeneous mix. Perhaps the military aristocracies of this mix that lived in the foothills and mountains could be called "Amorites" whatever their predominant ethnic background may have been. This campaign may have had its greatest impact on the Amorite military classes of the south rather than upon the population in general.

The conquest of Jericho and Ai together with the alliance with the Gibeonite league divides the central ridge of Canaan into two parts separated by the Israelites and their vassals. By any standards, the Israelites appear as a formidable enemy against whom united action is necessary. Thus, Adoni-Zedek of Jerusalem attempts to gather united opposition to them, although the immediate target of the opposition is Israel's Canaanite allies, the Gibeonite league (**10:1–5**).

The geographic range of the alliance is quite extensive. Looking from Jerusalem south, the alliance includes Hebron; looking to the southwest into the Shephelah along the road toward Gaza, the alliance includes Jarmuth, Lachish, and Eglon in that order. Perhaps the influence of these kings as leaders over other kings justifies the reference to "all the Amorite kings" (cf.

v. 6). However, many cities within the geographic bounds of that territory either do not respond or respond too late as does Gezer (cf. v. 33).

The five kings marshal their armies against Gibeon, apparently hoping to destroy Israel's allies before engaging the Israelites themselves.

The Gibeonites appeal to Israel for help. A typical treaty of submission required that the lord be ready to defend his loyal vassals. Two quite different factors, one human and one supernatural, are seen in Israel's victory. One of the consequences of a generation of marching through the wilderness is Israel's surprising mobility and stamina. To this is added the divinely aroused panic and miraculous events in nature hostile to the enemies of God's people (**10:6–28**).

The Amorites first flee to the east from Gibeon to Beth-horon (probably passing through both Upper and Lower Beth-horon) and then down the Valley of Ajalon to the southern road through the region of Zorah and Eshtaol. From there they flee to Azekah and Makkedah north of Lachish. The great hailstones, which kill more of the enemy than does Israel, deserve to be recorded among God's great deeds.

Another miracle happens that day, the supernatural extending of the effects of daylight (vv. 12–14). This miracle is first related in poetry and is then repeated in prose. This is one of the greatest of God's Old Testament sign deeds. The exact mechanics of how an omnipotent God could accomplish this deed are best left to God's miraculous power. God is capable of physically lengthening the time between sunrise and sunset, and of doing it in such a way that other potential cataclysmic consequences of such a drastic change could be negated. Or God could have merely manipulated the path of the sun's light so that daylight was extended and nighttime shortened during an otherwise ordinary day. The popular allegation that some great astronomer or a NASA computer has discovered mathematical evidences of this great event is unsubstantiated.

Starting with verse 16, the text gives a retrospective, full account of one detail of the pursuit. During the course of the pursuit, the five enemy kings take refuge in a cave at Makkedah where Joshua leaves them under guard until the pursuit is completed. Then, after the pursuit, but before the Israelites return to Gilgal, Joshua deals with the kings.

The killing of the kings is full of symbolic meaning. The kings represent, at least, a significant portion of the aristocratic military might of southern Palestine. Placing feet upon their necks (v. 24) symbolizes the military suppression of these aristocracies. The humiliation of the kings both strengthens the morale of the Israelites and proclaims to the watching fugitives of southern Canaan that a new power, a new movement which rejects the might and authority of the old aristocracies, has appeared in Canaan. Joshua kills the kings, exposes their bodies until sunset as an act of contempt, and places their bodies in the cave where they had hidden. The stones heaped over their corpses serve as a memorial or reminder to later Israelites of this great victory.

Although Makkedah had not answered the original call for an offensive alliance, it is clearly in sympathy with the Amorite kings, and Joshua treats the city as an enemy.

The Israelites at this point are neither numerous enough nor strong enough to subdue and occupy all of southern Canaan. This is clear from the overall circumstances present in the Book of Judges. However, it is prudent for Israel to deal as decisively as possible with the established military classes of southern Canaan. This is the purpose of the campaign of devastation related in **10:29–43.**

The defeat of the Amorite alliance had virtually given Joshua a free hand along the route from Makkedah northeast to Jerusalem on past Jericho to Gilgal. Apparently, after returning to Gilgal after their great day of victory, the Israelites then return to Makkedah as their jumping-off point for the devastation of southern Palestine. If the names given are intended to be complete, it is a selective campaign, perhaps aimed at the more threatening cities. The campaign, first, devastates some major cities of the Shephelah west of the hill country. Libnah, near Azekah, is destroyed. From there, the Israelites proceed roughly in the direction of Gaza to Lachish, one of the original allies. This city is also completely ruined. Gezer comes to help Lachish and their army is destroyed. A few miles further in the same direction brings Israel to Eglon, another of the five, which is likewise totally destroyed.

From there, with the Shephelah relatively secured, the line of march goes eastward to Hebron and then back to Debir. Both of these are totally destroyed. This conquest of Hebron seems to be described more fully in Joshua 11:21–22. The results of these campaigns are summarized (vv. 40–42).

Other historical evidences, both biblical and extrabiblical, demonstrate unequivocally that Israel did not conduct a universal massacre of the entire population of southern Canaan. How, then, are the universal-sounding assertions to be taken? A valid suggestion is that the focus of these statements was the militaristic ruling classes of southern Canaan. The subject classes may have, more or less, taken refuge and removed themselves from this conflict so that after the Israelites had completed their devastating conquest and massacre of the aristocratic ruling classes, the survivors, from the subject classes of the Judean hill country, emerged from hiding, rebuilt their homes and cities, and were there to harass Israel as described in the Book of Judges.

D. The northern campaign (11:1–15). The northern coalition (**11:1–5**), at least for the region north of the Valley of Jezreel, seems to have been more inclusive than the southern coalition. The leader of the effort is the king of Hazor, the greatest of the cities of Canaan in the second millennium B.C. The cities listed are significant international trade centers: Hazor, and probably Madon, on the great north-south trade route through Palestine; Shimron and Achshaph near the Valley of Jezreel; and Dor on the Canaanite coast. In addition, two general regions are identified; the kings in the Jordan Valley in the fertile regions just south of the Sea of Galilee (NIV the Arabah south of Kinnereth) and the Hivites south of Mount Hermon. The remaining listings are quite general and probably describe vassals and allies of the Canaanites. Some of these allies were from the hill country and foothills. The most distinctive feature of this coalition is the presence of Canaanite chariotry. These all mobilize at the Waters of Merom north of the Sea of Galilee.

The lack of specific reference to the hill country south of Jezreel may be significant. Two facts indicate a different status for this region: (1) the unhindered Israelite march to Shechem (8:30–35); and (2) the mention of only two cities, Tappuah (12:17) and Tirzah (12:24) from this region in the catalog of conquered kings. These facts indicate that this region, despite Ephraim's difficulties with this "hill country," did not present the level of opposition either of the southern hill country or of the Canaanites from Jezreel north.

This campaign differs from the southern campaign in two important respects. First, it is aimed primarily at the Canaanite aristocracies of the great valleys and the plains rather than the Amorites in the hill country. Second, it does not result in the occupation of the Canaanite plains or valleys though it severely weakens those enemies.

The narrative omits Joshua's march northward to a place within a day's journey of the Canaanite army. Joshua is promised victory and commanded to neutralize the military capacities of the chariotry (**11:6–9**). There may have been two reasons for this destruction of valuable military goods: (1) chariots symbolized the corrupting wealth of the Canaanite cities; and (2) the Israelites lacked the urbanized wealth necessary to support such a military machine.

Once again, on the human side, Israel's mobility apparently is a decisive factor. Quick movement makes a surprise attack possible near the Waters of Merom, and the enemy is defeated. Pursuit of the fleeing Canaanites goes in several directions, toward Sidon to the northwest, toward Misrephoth-maim more directly west on the coast, and to the northeast toward Mizpah, south of Mount Hermon. The disintegration of the Canaanite army shows the thoroughness of the victory.

As in the southern campaign, the defeat of the main enemy army is followed by the devastation of the enemies' cities (**11:10–15**). First, Hazor is totally destroyed and the resident population is killed. This marks an eclipse, at least temporarily, of the most significant Canaanite city during most of the previous second millennium B.C.

The identities of "all these royal cities" (v. 12) are not clear. They may be all the cities, named and unnamed, which are part of the northern coalition. Perhaps they are the northern cities listed in chapter 12. These cities are taken, and all the population which has not gone into hiding is killed. But the cities, though plundered, are not destroyed. This slaughter of Canaanite opposition is in harmony with God's commands. Later history shows that substantial numbers of Canaanites escaped the killing by going into hiding and presented continued opposition to Israel (cf. Judg. 4; 5).

E. The continued conquest (11:16–23). Up to this point the biblical narrative has dealt only with the rapid initial conquest of the land. Now the text describes the slower, long-range task of subjugation. This struggle of "a long time" (v. 18) is summarized. The general regions and bounds of the land are described, though not all the regions mentioned are clearly definable. The omission of the coastal plain is significant. The north-south extent ranges from Mount Halak to Baal Gad near Mount Hermon. "All their kings" (v. 17) must be taken in a general rather than an absolute sense. Some local dynasties survived the conquest. Only one people, the Hivites of Gibeon, make peace. This hostility is attributed to God's sovereign working.

The last notice of the chapter shows the importance of the Anakites by singling them out for specific mention in a retrospective description of the events of Joshua 10:36–39. The

Anakites, like the Rephaites, were a powerful military class with ties to Philistine territories. Joshua completely drives them from the region of Hebron; they take refuge in cities which will later belong to the Philistines. We learn from the Book of Judges that they eventually make their way back into Hebron from which Caleb once again drives them out (1:10). Apparently there is a brief respite from war (v. 23b) before tribal efforts at subjugation begin.

F. The conquered kings (12). Kings represented virtually all aspects of corporate life in the ancient Near East. Therefore, to talk of defeating a king was to boast of defeating the people in a particularly pointed way.

The boundaries of the Trans-Jordanian conquest are described (**12:1–6**). They extend from the Arnon Gorge as far north as the foothills of Mount Hermon and include the entire eastern side of the Jordan Valley (i.e., the eastern Arabah). The sometimes indefinite boundary toward the east is left undescribed (v. 1).

Then the holdings of two conquered kings are described. A sense of legitimacy is implied in these descriptions. Israel's holdings in Trans-Jordan are legitimate because they were properly taken in military conquest (cf. Judg. 11:14–27).

The area conquered from Sihon, one of the many Amorite kings, extends from the Arnon Gorge as far north as the point at which the Jabbok becomes the western boundary of Ammon. The phrase *eastern Arabah from the Sea of Kinnereth* (v. 3) implies that Sihon ruled the eastern Jordan Valley as far north as the Sea of Galilee, thus shutting off the kingdom of Og from the Jordan Valley.

The area conquered from Og extends from the territory of Sihon as far north as the foothills of Mount Hermon. "Over Mount Hermon" (v. 5) probably refers to only part of the foothills of that range. It includes half of Gilead (though that term, like the modern term *Ozarks,* is not always used with precision) as well as Bashan, except for the Jordan Valley as already noted. At this point, Geshur and Maacah may not have been specific geographic regions since the two peoples, like the Israelites, may have still been seminomadic.

The description of the western conquests (**12:7–24**) roughly coincides with that of the preceding chapter (11:16–17). The north-south extent is from Mount Halak to Baal Gad in the Bekaa Valley. Several regions are defined: the hill country or Shephelah (NIV western foothills), the Jordan Valley (i.e., the Arabah), and the Negeb in the extreme south of Judah. The regions referred to as "mountain slopes" and "desert" (v. 8) cannot be precisely defined.

The list of thirty-one conquered Caananite kings seems to be quite straightforward except that not all important kings are included. In very general terms, the list matches the sequence of conquest in chapters 9–11. Two conquered cities of the central campaign are listed first (v. 9), though the third related conquest, Bethel, is not mentioned until verse 16. The five kings of the southern alliance are listed next (vv. 10–12), followed immediately by their obvious ally, Gezer (v. 12). Makkedah (v. 16) is also associated with the southern alliance, but the remainder of the southern names (vv. 13–16) mixes kings listed in chapter 10 with those not included there with no clear rationale.

The northern kings (vv. 17–24) also show no clear pattern. Tappuah, in the hills of Ephraim north of Bethel, and Aphek, on the western edge of the hill country, show a shift of perspective to the north. Hepher (v. 17) may be unusual in representing a successful conquest far into the coastal plain. The location of Lasharon (v. 18) is unclear. Madon, Hazor, Shimron Meron, and Acshaph are cities specifically mentioned in the northern coalition. The cities of verses 20 and 21 as well as Jokneam of verse 22, control the Valley of Jezreel and the trade flowing through it. Dor is on the Mediterranean coast, Kedesh and Goyim in Galilee, and Tirzah probably in the hills of Ephraim. The list is remarkable for the limited number of names from the hill country of Joseph south of the Valley of Jezreel.

II. The Division of the Land (13–21)

This section must be seen in light of covenant theology. The land was the major blessing of the covenant; it had been promised and "conquered" (at least the major organized opposition had been destroyed). Therefore, it is time to divide the land among the tribes. Affirming the right of each tribe to a particular section of land also confirms that God has completed his covenant promise of "giving" the land to Israel. This chapter begins a nine-chapter description of the distribution of the land among the tribes of Israel. The underlying theological presupposition of this section is that faith and obedience will bring full possession of the land; failure to possess the land is always a matter of doubt and disobedience.

A. Unconquered peoples (13:1–7). The allocation of the land occurs near the end of Joshua's life. The record begins with the description of several peoples which remain to be conquered. This description presents a major difficulty in that it expands the borders of the covenant land from the Nile to Byblos, an extent not found elsewhere. A possible resolution may be the fact that this description deals with peoples instead of territories per se. For example, though Philistine territory is here said to extend to the Nile (vv. 2–3), the portion included in the covenant land extended only to the Wadi Arish.

The Philistine lands are counted as Canaanite (v. 3), perhaps acknowledging their similar mercantile policies. Also included with this region are the Geshurites and the remnants of the Avvites, the aboriginal inhabitants killed or suppressed by the Philistines. Though the allotment occurs about a century and a half before the Philistines arrive in large numbers, the region is, nevertheless, partly defined by the cities that will later make up the Philistine Pentapolis.

The next phrase (v. 4a) refers to the largely unconquered holdings of the historic Canaanite mercantile cities along the coastal plain from Aphek, not far north of Ekron, up to the holdings of Sidon. The great valleys of Jezreel and Beth-shean, between Ephraim and Galilee, are also controlled by Canaanite cities.

"The region of the Amorites" (v. 4b) refers to those areas in the foothills and mountains controlled by the remnants of the Amorite peoples.

"The area of the Gebalites" (v. 5) uses "Gebal" (i.e., "Byblos") to represent all the Phoenician territory from Sidon north to Byblos, since Byblos had been the chief Phoenician city from time to time during the early second millennium B.C. To this is attached the inland region east of Phoenicia from Baal Gad, just west or northwest of Mount Hermon, northward through the Bekaa Valley toward Hamath. Like the Philistine area, only part of this territory, the Phoenician regions assigned to Asher (19:24–31), is allotted to Israel.

There seems to have been a Sidonian incursion inland toward the southern end of the Lebanon which God, in this passage, promises to destroy. At least part of this promise is fulfilled in the Danite massacre of the Sidonian colony at Laish (Judg. 18:27). The closing reiteration of the command to allocate the land emphasizes the importance of this subject.

B. The Trans-Jordanian inheritances (13:8–33). Chapter 13 reiterates that Reuben, Gad, and half-Manasseh have already received their inheritances on the east of the Jordan. The bounds of those Trans-Jordanian conquests are then described. The special inheritance of Levi is mentioned once again.

The tribe of Reuben holds the southernmost territories east of the Jordan (**13:15–23**). Their territory extends from the Wadi Arnon northward as far as Heshbon about even with the northern tip of the Dead Sea. The identity of the "town in the middle of the gorge" (v. 16) is obscure. The northern border likely ran down the middle of the valley extending roughly from Heshbon toward the Dead Sea. The major cities of the area are listed though some of their locations are uncertain. Reuben's holdings, apart from the Jordan Valley, coincide with the realm of Sihon the Amorite.

As the text presently stands, there seems to be a discrepancy between the bounds of Sihon as described elsewhere (e.g., Num. 21:24; Josh. 12:2–3) and in the present passage. In the other passages the bounds of Sihon extend north "to the Jabbok." Here the bounds of Reuben, which are said to include "all" the territory of Sihon, extend only as far north as Heshbon. If one understands that Sihon's territory reached as far north as that part of the Jabbok marking the west border of Ammon, this problem is resolved. There remains the difficulty that Reuben did not inherit Sihon's holdings in the Jordan Valley. Perhaps the biblical writer's perspective in referring to "all" the realm of Sihon focuses only upon Sihon's highland holdings.

Gad is located immediately north of Reuben, extending from Heshbon north to the Jabbok so that it includes part of Gilead (**13:24–28**). "All the towns of Gilead" (v. 25) would seem to be a textual corruption since it clearly conflicts with the notice that half of Gilead is allotted to Manasseh (cf. v. 31). Further, the text indicates that the eastern Jordan Valley as far north as the Sea of Galilee is assigned to Gad.

The territory of Manasseh includes the territories of Og, from the Jabbok north (**13:29–33**). Two details here merit further discussion. The historic personality, Jair (v. 30), was either an illegitimate descendant of Hezron of Judah or was descended from an unusual marriage arrangement involving Hezron and a Manassite woman (1 Chron. 2:21). This union occurred some time before the wanderings in the wilderness. Apparently because of these unusual circumstances, Jair and the clan which bore his name was reckoned as Manassite after Jair's mother rather than as Judean after Hezron, Jair's father. At the time of the conquest, either Jair or the clan bearing his name conquered the region known as the "settlements of Jair."

The name *Makir* (v. 31) deserves some attention. Since all the traditional clans of Manasseh were descended from Manasseh through Makir (Num. 26:29–32), half of Manasseh could be referred to as half of Makir, as in the present setting. However, in other contexts, the name was conventionally applied to the west

Manassites (Judg. 5:14) despite the fact that the west Manassite clans also were descended from Gilead.

C. The Canaanite inheritances (14–19). It is convenient to distinguish between those tribes whose holdings were more centrally located, more secure, and more firmly held and those whose holdings were on the periphery of Israel's territory, less secure and less firmly held. They can be called the "heartland" tribes and the "peripheral" tribes, respectively.

The religious authority represented by Eleazar, the theocratic military authority in the person of Joshua, and the traditional tribal authorities represented by the tribal elders, all have their part in the allotment of the land (**14:1–5**). The land is distributed "by lot," a methodology which, presumably, left the matter more in God's hands than did any other method of allotment. The sacred Urim and Thummim may have been used as lots. Once again, the text relates that the Levites do not receive tribal inheritances among the other tribes.

The heritage of Caleb is described (**14:6–15**). Various views have been expressed concerning Caleb's Kenizzite background (v. 6). Some have concluded that Caleb was a foreigner from an Edomite clan named "Kenaz" (Gen. 36:11). Even if Caleb were foreign, there are two possibilities concerning his status. First, by the general kinship standards of the ancient world—and there is no unequivocal evidence that Israelite customs differed on this issue—conversion followed by adoption would have made Caleb no less an Israelite than any native-born Hebrew. If so, the truth of Scripture is not compromised by the notion that Caleb's family may have been a foreign family, adopted into Israel. Second, Caleb's Judean character may have come from a foreign father marrying a Judean woman. Alternatively, Kenaz may be treated as a good Judean name and could refer only to Caleb's family ties within Judah.

Caleb's claim is based upon his faithfulness in the historic apostasy at Kadesh-barnea. Caleb is a powerful illustration of the human side of covenant faithfulness. The man who is faithful to the covenant merits God's blessings. The illustration is rendered even more powerful in that the blessing involved is the land itself, the most precious and central of the covenant blessings. Caleb's faithfulness has already been rewarded by another covenant blessing, good health (vv. 10–11; cf. Deut. 7:15).

Caleb's readiness to go against a formidable enemy is the kind of faith which should characterize all the Israelites. His allotment centers upon Hebron which is possessed by the mighty Anakites. These were apparently either a powerful warrior class or a warrior race. They may have been endowed with great size and strength by heredity. However, their military prowess and physical size may have been enhanced both by their favorable living conditions as a military ruling class and by their status as professional warriors trained for warfare from youth. Their stature is shown by the fact that they typify the general military prowess of Canaan (Deut. 9:1–2). There is an affinity between the Anakites and the Rephaites; perhaps the Rephaites were a more general group of which the Anakites were a particular example.

Since the major point here is simply the fact that Caleb holds Hebron as a covenant blessing, details of this conquest are completely omitted. The "rest from war" (v. 15b) may refer only to the fact that Caleb's conquest of Hebron eventually gave rest to that particular region.

The detailed description of Judah's success, as seen in the relatively lengthy lists of cities possessed by the tribe, indicates the Bible writer's estimate of Judah's faithfulness in conquest and God's blessing upon that faithfulness. Judah's holdings are described at great length, a striking fact considering the sparse treatment given to Ephraim. Both boundary lists and town lists are given for Judah, and Judah's town lists are the most detailed of the entire book. The general historical setting implicit in the background of the present chapter is the same as that of Judges 1. But the applications differ. This chapter emphasizes Judah's faithfulness and success in gaining a great inheritance. In the Book of Judges (see Judg. 1:19), the same factual background is utilized to illustrate Israel's failure to conquer the land completely.

The opening description (**15:1–12**) tells the reader that Judah's territory goes "down to" Edom and the Wilderness of Zin, roughly south and southeast of Judah. The description of this boundary gives some support to the notion that there were Edomites to the west of the Arabah even at this early time. The southern boundary begins at the southern end of the Dead Sea (Salt Sea). It then passes southeast of Scorpion Pass and through the Wilderness of Zin until it reaches a cluster of settlements in the region of Kadesh-barnea. From there the boundary passes on to the Wadi of Egypt. The Nile River provides no reasonable continuation for this border description.

The eastern boundary, the Dead Sea, and the western boundary, the Mediterranean Sea, are briefly defined.

The northern boundary demands more detail. In rough terms, it begins at the northern tip of the Dead Sea and proceeds from Gilgal up toward Jerusalem. From Jerusalem, apparently going past the northern extent of the Valley of Rephaim, the boundary reaches the present-day Wadi Kesalon which it follows until it joins with the Wadi Sorek. The boundary then follows this stream bed through Ekron, Shikkeron, and Jabneel to the Mediterranean.

The enormous prestige of the Calebites, which is still imposing as late as the Book of Chronicles (1 Chron. 2, 4), is reflected in **15:13–19.** Only the assignment of allotments, not their ultimate disposition, is the primary topic of this section. Therefore, though Caleb's conquest is mentioned here, that conquest does not occur until after Joshua's death in the setting of Judges 1. Both Hebron and Debir are among the cities "conquered" and destroyed (but not held) in chapter 10. In trying to do justice to all the evidences we may conclude that, after Israel's devastating sweep through the south, remnants of the Anakite population reestablished themselves and had to be reconquered in this later campaign by Caleb.

The incident concerning Othniel and Aksah (vv. 16–19) reflects an incident of family history important to the family of Othniel, and the importance of water in the region.

A rough structure can be traced in the town lists of Judah (**15:20–63**). They begin with the southernmost sites (excepting those near Kadesh-barnea). Then four groups of towns in the western foothills and the Philistine plain are given. Five groups of towns in the hill country, ranging roughly from south to north, are listed. This listing continues with a cluster of desert settlements along the west coast of the Dead Sea. The section closes with the comment that Judah is not able to capture (or recapture) Jebus (v. 63).

The sites in the Negeb (vv. 21–32) are roughly clustered around Beersheba in the upper tributaries of the Wadi Besor some forty miles north of Kadesh-barnea.

The northernmost cluster of cities in the Judean Shephelah is in the vicinity of the Wadi Sorek (vv. 33–36). The cities listed in verses 42–44 come next as one moves southward through the Shephelah. These are generally in the Shephelah headwaters of the Wadi Elah. Judging from the small number, four or so, that are identifiable, the cities of verses 37–41 come next continuing southward. These three groups are possessed by Judah at a relatively early date.

By contrast, the Philistine plain (vv. 45–47), while allotted to Judah, is not actually possessed until the time of David, and then as an imperial conquest rather than as land actually settled and possessed by Israelite citizens.

The next four town lists (vv. 48–60) represent regions in the Judean hill country that range, in a very rough way, from south to north. Except for isolated centers of Amorite or Canaanite life such as Jebus (Jerusalem), this hill country generally comes under firm Israelite control and occupation. The Septuagint adds another list, omitted by the Masoretic Text, which includes Tekoa, Ephratah, Peor, Etam, Kulon, Tatam, Zobah, Karem, Sallim, Bether, and Manathah.

The allotment for Judah closes (vv. 61–62) with a list of wilderness outposts near the northwest coast of the Dead Sea. These last settlements often served as defensive outposts against attack from the Bedouin and other enemies toward the east and southeast of Judah.

In contrast to the detail given to the holdings of Judah, the descriptions of the holdings of Joseph are quite sparse, especially considering the large size and prestige that seem to mark Ephraim in this early period.

The description of the "allotment for Joseph" (**16:1–4**) actually consists of the southern boundary of the total holdings of the two Joseph tribes. It begins at the Jordan, passes westward through Jericho, runs almost directly west through Bethel and Ai, and continues westward until it meets the holdings of Dan at Gezer in the coastal plain. From Gezer, the border probably passed north and west around the allotment of Dan as it continued on to the sea.

It is not possible to discern an overall pattern in the presentation of the boundaries of Ephraim (**16:5–10**). The first two names, Ataroth Addar and Upper Beth-horon (v. 5), give a rough indication of a southern border across the central highlands. This seems to be an abbreviated, retrospective description of the border already described (cf. vv. 1–4). On the north, beginning at Michmethath, possibly located south along a ridge from Shechem, the border seems to follow that ridge north past Shechem and then southeast along the ridge just south of Wadi Faria. From this point on, the sense of the list is difficult to discern. If the list continues as a boundary list, Ephraim is cut off from the Jordan, and someone else holds land between Ephraim and the Jordan River. The line described in the text proceeds south roughly along the edge of the eastern foothills and then turns to the Jordan only at Jericho. Perhaps it was understood that Ephraim's influence extended to the Jordan, but the Jordan Valley, just north of Jericho, was too barren to be worth claiming. The description then returns to Tappuah, some distance south of Michmethath. The border proceeds from that city westward down the Wadi Kanah to the Mediterranean. In this region, Ephraim controlled cities north of this border within Manassite territory (v. 9b; cf. 17:9).

Gezer is chosen to epitomize Ephraim's failure in conquest (v. 10). In addition, Ephraim probably failed to gain control over its coastal allotments (see Judg. 1:19). Furthermore, there is reason to doubt that Ephraim was completely successful even in the hill country (cf. 17:14–16).

The relationships between the various Manassite clans can be confusing. The most significant facts follow: The six great western Manassite clans were all descendants of Gilead, who was himself a descendant of Makir, the son of Manasseh (Num. 26:28–34). The prominent east Manassite clan of Jair was descended from a daughter of Makir (1 Chron. 2:21–22). Ironically, Jair was conventionally recognized as a part of Gilead and the western Manassite clans seem to have been reckoned as part of Makir (cf. Judg. 5:14). Since all the significant clans of Manasseh were descended from Makir, it was also possible to refer to the two halves of Manasseh as two halves of Makir (Josh. 13:31), though normally the half of Mannasseh (or Makir) east of the Jordan was conventionally called "Gilead."

Some of the facts mentioned above lie behind the statements in **17:1–2.** Since all the significant Manassite clans were descended from Makir, it was possible to equate the Manassites and the Makirites (v. 1a). Since Gilead was descended from Makir, the Gileadites could be referred to as Makirites (v. 1b; cf. Josh. 13:31). The six major clans of the west Manassites are listed. With the substitution of "Iezer" for "Abiezer" and adding in Makir and Gilead, these clans are the same as those of Numbers 26:29–33. Other clans, which probably originated at a later date, are listed in 1 Chronicles 7:14–18.

A fuller account of Zelophehad's daughters (**17:3–6**) is found in Numbers 27:1–11. As in the case of Caleb (14:6–9) and the Levites (21:1–3), a specific divine promise is claimed. All three illustrate the theme of God's fulfillment of his promises. With the limited data available, many details such as the "ten tracts" (v. 5) remain unclear.

The allotment of Manasseh (**17:7–13**) is described as follows: In general, the allotment extends from the territory of Asher to Micmethath and continues southward as far as En Tappuah. Verse 9a is better translated "the boundary on the south went down the Kanah Ravine." One actually must come back slightly north to get to the Kanah Ravine from Tappuah. Dan is ignored in references to Manasseh's contiguous neighboring tribes (v. 10), perhaps because Dan never effectively occupied its allotment.

Once again, cities assigned to one tribe are located within the territory of a second tribe (cf. 16:9). Ephraim holds cities within Manasseh and Manasseh is allotted cities within the territories of Issachar and Asher. These allotments are the only comment about Manasseh's northern boundary. The most likely situation is that the allotment of Asher reached into the Valley of Jezreel from the northwest while that of Issachar extended into Jezreel from the northeast, but the string of ancient cities along the southern edge of the valley was assigned to Manasseh. In any case, the cities and the valley remain in Canaanite hands since the Israelites are unable to subdue the great valleys and the Canaanite merchant cities there. Also, it is quite unlikely that the Manassites ever thoroughly subdued the coastal region assigned to them.

The Ephraimites want more territory in keeping with their numbers and prestige, but they do not want to fight to obtain that territory (**17:14–18**). They have two alternatives: further conflict with the Perizzites and Rephaites in the hill country (v. 15) or conflict with the wealthy Canaanite cities and their chariots (v. 16). They may be contrasted with Caleb who enthusiastically undertakes conflict with the original inhabitants of the land (14:12). The applicable principle is that greater difficulty gives greater opportunity for gain and prestige if faith in God is sufficient. However, if faith is lacking, then the greater difficulty gives greater likelihood of failure. Joshua assures the Ephraimites that success is possible for them, but this success demands faith and obedience.

Chapters 18 and 19 describe the territorial allotments of what might be loosely called the "peripheral tribes" since, excepting Benjamin and Simeon, they are located, more or less, on the periphery of Israel's "heartland." In general, these allotments are characterized as follows. Their lands are, by ordinary human standards, difficult or even impossible to conquer. This is generally the case with the flat Mediterranean coastal areas, the great Canaanite valleys between Ephraim and Galilee, and perhaps parts of the Jordan Valley. The descriptions of the holdings are usually sketchy and incomplete. The tribes which inherit these allotments have great difficulty maintaining permanent tribal identity and history.

The peripheral tribes face a more difficult task and a greater risk of failure. However, in view of the provisions of the covenant, these greater difficulties also represent greater opportunities. Had these tribes been steadfast in faith and true to the covenant, God's continued faithfulness, in return, would have guaranteed full possession even of these difficult allotments.

It seems strange that another assembly is needed to allot the land (**18:1–10**), especially since it appears that all the allotting has already been accomplished in Joshua 14:2! Two interpretations are possible. First, Joshua 14:2 could be a general summary statement intended to include both the distribution described in chapters 14–17 and that of the present two chapters, however distinct the events might have been. Second, since some of the earlier allotments had not been implemented, they may have become moot; it is then fitting to resurvey and reallot the remaining land to the remaining tribes.

The transactions are conducted at Shiloh, which has already become the site of the nation's central shrine. "Under their control" (v. 1) means only that the Israelites have the potential of taking complete control of the land, not that complete control is already a reality. Joshua challenges the people to activity. He orders the sending of a survey team, the apportioning of the land, and the allotment of portions by lot. These commands are executed and the division of the land is complete.

Benjamin and Simeon are exceptions to the peripheral location of these tribes. Geographically, Benjamin is right in the heartland between Joseph and Judah. A shadow is cast by Jebusite Jerusalem eastward through Benjamite holdings. Benjamin may have been in this group for two reasons. First, the writer may have had in mind the early tragedy of the Levite's concubine (Judg. 19–20), which almost destroyed Benjamin and greatly reduced the status of that tribe. And, second, apart from the prominence of the family of Saul, Benjamin is, in fact, a minor tribe in later history.

For thoroughness, the description of Benjamin's holdings (**18:11–28**) rivals that of Judah since it includes both border lists and town lists. When the smaller size of Benjamin is taken into account, proportionally, the attention given is more nearly equal. Since Benjamin, ultimately, was part of the southern kingdom, this could be another reflection of a "southern perspective" in the Book of Joshua.

Benjamin's northern boundary (vv. 12–13) matches part of the southern boundary of Joseph (cf. 16:1–3). Verse 12 mentions Beth-aven which is not included in the earlier boundary description. Benjamin's southern border (vv. 15–19) duplicates part of the description of Judah's northern border (cf. 15:5–11) except in reverse order. "Geliloth" (v. 17) appears here in place of "Gilgal" (cf. 15:7), thus indicating that these are variants of the same name.

The cities allotted to the Benjamites include more than a fair share of cities mentioned elsewhere in Scripture. There are two groups, oriented east (vv. 21–24) and west (vv. 25–28). The second, more western group includes all the cities of the Gibeonite league. These cities, with their military strength, add to the prestige of Benjamin.

The assignment of Simeon to the territory of Judah (**19:1–9**) probably confirms a historical fact: that Simeon and Judah were already committed to a joint effort in the south (cf. Judg. 1:3). Although Simeonites generally retained their individual tribal genealogies and the great Simeonite families maintained their existence (cf. 1 Chron. 4:24–43), this arrangement did guarantee the disappearance of any cohesive, united influence by that tribe. Judah (including Simeon) and Benjamin are counted as only two tribes in the division of the Hebrew kingdom. That this same list of cities, with only minor differences, is later used by the Chronicler to describe the status of the Simeonites within Judah (1 Chron. 4:28–33) might indicate how tenaciously the Simeonite families clung to their standing within Judah.

Zebulun's inheritance consists of several cities on the northern edge of the Valley of Jezreel together with a cluster of cities further north of that valley (**19:10–16**). Two short series of names appear to be border lists: the names from Sarid west to the "ravine near Jokneam" (v. 11) and the series east (actually northeast) from Sarid to Daberath (v. 12a). These two series are most easily taken as marking the border between Zebulun and the Valley of Jezreel. The area from "Japhia" (v. 12b) to Iphtah El (v. 14) encircled a small region north of the Valley of Jezreel. The remaining names (v. 15), apparently, were significant Zebulunite settlements in this region.

This region in the hill country north of Jezreel had both advantages and disadvantages. The hill country was not as desirable to the Canaanites and other indigenous peoples as were the valleys; therefore, it was easier to seize and to hold. On the other hand, it was near the great international trade route between the Canaanite valleys of Jezreel and Beth-shean and the great Canaanite city of Hazor. Proximity to this very important line of communication naturally led to friction between the Zebulunites and their Canaanite neighbors (cf. Judg. 4; 5).

The territory of Issachar is defined by a list of cities that occupy the region between the Valley of Jezreel eastward to the Jordan River (**19:17–23**). This area is just east of the trade route between Jezreel and Hazor. The boundaries of this region can be roughly surmised from the list of cities. However, in addition to this region, Issachar may have been allotted a portion of the Valley of Jezreel itself since several of the great cities along the southern edge of the valley are described (see 17:11). The general effectiveness—or ineffectiveness—of the conquest makes it very unlikely that Issachar really implemented any such claim in the Valley of Jezreel.

On the map, Asher's inheritance looks quite imposing; it includes a significant stretch of coastline, the corresponding hill country near the coast, and, perhaps, part of the Valley of Jezreel. But, in fact, only Dan had an equally dismal future. In general, the region allotted to Asher consisted of cities in or near the coastal plain from Mount Carmel (or possibly Dor; cf. 17:11) north to Tyre (**19:24–31**). Their position placed them among the powerful, coastal Phoenician holdings. Between the pressures from the Canaanites in Jezreel and these Phoenicians, the Asherites had much to cope with. In addition to this, they were rather far removed from the main centers of Israelite power, a fact which both left them exposed on a distant border and diluted their loyalty to their nation.

The holdings of Naphtali are roughly located between those of Asher and the Jordan rift (**19:32–39**). The boundary description (vv. 33–34) is somewhat obscure. It seems to list a number of towns on the southern borders, but not in any consecutive order. Verse 33 lists locations along the southern border with Issachar, although Issachar is omitted in the list of tribes contiguous to Naphtali. Two towns—Aznoth-tabor and Hukkok—give a very approximate indication of the border with Zebulun. The borders with Asher and along the Jordan are described in these terms (v. 34b). The presence of several formidable geographic obstacles to the north—the Litani Gorge, the southern extremes of the Lebanon, and the foothills of Mount Hermon—may have marked a very natural barrier and rendered further description unnecessary. The listing of fortified cities (vv. 35–38) includes cities such as Hazor which clearly remained in Canaanite hands.

The major blessing and danger of this holding was the presence of the international trade route that passed from the northeast point of the Valley of Jezreel through the territory of Naphtali to Hazor and points beyond. For the Canaanite cities, it was unthinkable that hostile forces should be in a position to throttle traffic along this route. It is no surprise that the major combatants in Judges 4 were Hazor and the other Canaanite cities on the one hand, and Barak of Naphtali on the other.

From a human point of view, the allotment of Dan is quite discouraging (**19:40–48**). It consists of a rather small number of towns in the Shephelah, most notably Zorah and Eshtaol, and a large area along the coast which is virtually inaccessible (cf. Judg. 1:34–35). This, like the coastal plain in general, was not Israel's territory until the time of David. The Danites failed to conquer the coastal plain. In addition, the coastal Gentiles penetrated the Shephelah so that, at the time of Samson, Danite families and Gentile families were living as neighbors in Danite territory.

The section closes with the record that Joshua is given Timnath-serah (= "Timnath-heres") in Ephraim (**19:49–51**). The notice that dividing the land is completed (v. 49) is important theologically. It must be understood in terms of the ideology expressed in Joshua 23:14. God had fulfilled all his good promises in giving the land to the Israelites. True, further covenant faithfulness and obedience would be necessary for complete possession of the land, but God's part in giving the land has been accomplished.

D. The sacred inheritances (20–21). There are at least two reasons why the cities of refuge are dealt with as part of the allotment of the land. The assignment of these cities obviously involve land allotment, but, also, the issues of murder, justice regarding the murderer, and justice regarding the accidental killer revolve around the purity of the land. A killing not covered by justice pollutes the land (Num. 35:33). Thus there is an intimate relationship between provisions for the accidental killer and the status of the land.

At this point in history, the Israelites, like their neighbors in the ancient world, had no public organs for enforcing justice. Enforcement was implemented by individual force or vengeance, perhaps slightly aided by general public opinion. When the enforcement might be unjust as in the case of individual revenge against the involuntary killer, some mechanism to restrain the avenger was needed. The cities of refuge provided this mechanism (**20:1–6**). The accused fled to the city of refuge where he had a preliminary hearing at the city gate to determine if he should even be admitted to the city. This was followed by a trial before an assembly. If judged not guilty of premeditated murder, he was to be sent back to the city of refuge until the death of the high priest, after which he could safely return home.

The cities selected are reasonably dispersed and accessible (**20:7–9**). Most are historically significant and possess sacred backgrounds. The very name *Kedesh* ("holiness," v. 7) suggests that particular city's sacred character. The sacred roles of Shechem in general and of Hebron in the life of Abraham are well known. The east Jordanian cities are less well known. Ramoth-gilead (v. 8) is the most familiar of the three. The selection of these cities suggests that this chapter originated early in Israel's history when these cities were still reasonable selections for this purpose, and not at a later time when the east Jordanian holdings would have been obsolete, historical memories.

The Levites, as the Calebites and the daughters of Zelophehad earlier, request that God's promise to them be fulfilled (**21:1–3**). The Levites did not have an ordinary inheritance; the offerings of God made up their portion (13:14). They were granted urban living assignments with grazing privileges throughout the nation.

The situation of the Levites had both disadvantages and advantages. Like the Simeonites, their dispersal prevented them from developing united political influence. Theoretically they were banned from permanent ownership of agricultural land. This cut them off from the major source of prosperity, at least in early history, and forced them either to depend upon religious subsidies for part of their living or to become involved in nonagricultural means of livelihood. Their fates were tied in with those of the tribes where they lived. This was a particular disadvantage among some of the peripheral tribes whose own destinies were none too good.

On the other hand, they were left with both the freedom and the responsibility to be the dominant positive spiritual influence in the nation. The very absence of significant tribal loyalties could have strengthened their loyalty to God. Their duty as a tribe specially consecrated to mediatorial and teaching work was enhanced by scattering them throughout the nation. And they had the geographic flexibility to move without losing their tribal identity.

The general bounds of the heritages of the three great Levitical families—the Kohathites, the Gershonites, and the Merarites—are as follows (**21:4–8**). The heartland, from Judah in the south to Manasseh in the north, was allotted to the Kohathites. On the surface, this meant that the Kohathites were in the lands that offered the best prospect for long-range security and prosperity. The holdings of the Gershonites and the Merarites were in the peripheral areas. The Merarites were assigned to Reuben, Gad, and the geographically separate region of Zebulun. The Gershonites were assigned the eastern half of Manasseh and all the tribes on the northern fringe (i.e., north of western Manasseh) other than Zebulun.

The Kohathites should have shared in the relative stability and prosperity of the heartland tribes. Although the peripheral secular tribes suffered, the Gershonites and Merarites experienced a happier fate, perhaps because they had the geographic mobility to identify themselves with Judah and the Davidic line after the disruption of the kingdom. Comparison with later genealogical data (1 Chron. 6) confirms that all three of the great Levitical families maintained their existence and prestige throughout the history of the temple and the southern kingdom.

The Kohathite heritages are detailed in **21:9–26.** Thirteen cities in Judah and Benjamin were assigned to the family of Aaron. Since their service was most closely tied to the central sanctuary, this allotment was convenient both for the Shiloh location of the tabernacle and the Jerusalem location of the temple.

The remainder of the Kohathites, the nonpriestly Kohathites, were located in Ephraim, Manasseh, and Dan. Like the tribal allotments, these Levitical heritages included cities, such as Gezer, Eltekeh, and Taanach which were not controlled by Israel in this early period. The Levitical heritages, like the tribal allotments, represent what was possible through faith and obedience rather than what was actually achieved.

The Gershonites were assigned cities in eastern Manasseh, Issachar, Asher, and Naphtali (**21:27–33**). Golan (v. 27) was also a city of refuge and gave its name to the region both in ancient (cf. "Gaulan" and "Gaulanitis") and in modern times. Daberath (v. 28), here associated with Issachar, may have been a border town and thus legitimately related to both Issachar and Zebulun (cf. 19:12). The Levitical assignments in Asher were as unfavorable as those of that tribe (cf. 19:24–31). Kedesh was a city of refuge.

The Mararites were assigned holdings in Zebulun, Gad, and Reuben (**21:34–42**). The city of Jokneam, one of the Canaanite cites on the southern edge of the Valley of Jezreel, and the city of refuge, Ramoth-gilead (v. 38), were among their assignments.

Joshua **21:43–45** is of utmost importance for the theology of Joshua. God has kept his covenant; he has given the land to his people. The implicit condition for keeping the land, covenant obedience, is clearly understood though not stated. God has given the land, and the people have come to a position where complete possession is a matter of faithfulness and obedience. In the absence of faithfulness and obedience, complete possession will not become a reality until the unification of Palestine under David. The people have rest as long as they are faithful to the covenant. Their enemies cannot oppose them—as long as they are faithful to the covenant. God has kept and will continue to keep his promises, but Israel's full realization of what is promised is conditional upon the people's obedience.

III. Life in the Land (22–24)

The Book of Joshua concludes with several incidents that illustrate various aspects of life in the covenant land.

A. Covenant faithfulness (22). The first of these is the record of the divisive altar built by the east Jordanian tribesmen on their way home. The issue of a single place of national worship is important for this account. In recent years there has been a tendency to interpret the passages dealing with one place of worship as permitting more than one such place as long as each of them was a place which God had chosen (Deut. 12:4–14). However, the fact that there was only one "tent of meeting" would still permit only one legal place of sacrifice at any given time (Lev. 17:8–9).

The real genius of this account is that it takes an event whose moral status is, at best, ambiguous, and emphasizes those historical elements that make the event a statement of covenant faithfulness rather than the covenant disobedience it first appears to be.

Two significant themes are presented in **22:1–8**. First, the past faithfulness of the east Jordanian tribesmen to the covenant and to God's command is stated. The phrase *for a long time now* indicates that some time has elapsed. The events thus far are not a matter of weeks or months, but of years. And, second, they are challenged to continued obedience to the covenant.

The easterners return home with Joshua's blessing and great riches from the spoils of the conquest. Livestock was, of course, a staple in the wealth of that day. Silver and gold have always been precious. But bronze and iron are also listed as valuable spoils of war. Bronze was the major material for tools and weapons of that time.

The easterners return home. "Gilead" here seems to be a general term for all the Trans-Jordanian holdings. Apparently the term is used in different ways. On their way home, they stop at Geliloth, another name for "Gilgal" (cf. 15:7; 18:17), and build "an imposing altar" there (22:9–12). Depending upon one's general interpretation of the law of Moses, this altar violates either the demand that the nation have only one place of sacrifice or the demand that altars be built only upon God's specific command. The nation immediately mobilizes at Shiloh to deal with the offense.

The Israelites send an investigative team headed by the high priest's son and made up of one family head from each of the western tribes (**22:13–20**). The make-up of the embassy shows the importance of the participation both of the religious leadership and of the whole people in the persons of their representatives.

Initially, the embassy has no doubt that the altar is an act of rebellion. Three important points are emphasized in the dialogue about the altar. First, the comparison with the earlier immorality and idolatry involving Baal of Peor (v. 17; cf. Num. 25) shows the potential magnitude of this evil. The defilement of this sin could, like that earlier defilement, corrupt the life of the entire nation for years to come. This comparison also shows that such sin affects, not just the guilty, but the entire community as well.

Second, since the land was the most significant of the covenant blessings, the pollution of the land would be a grievous calamity (v. 19). It is not clear whether the land was seen as defiled by the illegal activity or whether the illegal altar was a misguided attempt to deal with a polluted land.

Third, the unity of the congregation comes into focus again in recalling that the sin of Achan had a damaging effect on the entire congregation (v. 20). Their sin threatens to be comparable to that of Achan in its impact on the nation. This, of course, justifies the concern and meddling of the westerners in the affairs of the eastern tribesmen. Due to the unity of the people, the other tribes would share in the dire consequences of this deed.

The eastern tribesmen clarify the issue (**22:21–29**). They appeal to God's knowledge of men's hearts and affirm that their altar is not for the offering of sacrifices. The most telling point for the truth of this assertion is that the altar was built on the Canaanite side of the Jordan (vv. 10–11).

They then present their case for the memorial altar. There was a natural boundary there which later generations might interpret as God's way of separating the easterners from orthodox worship. In that time the altar could serve as a memorial, not one commanded by God to be sure, but still a useful memorial to remind both the westerners and the easterners that they shared in the nation's centralized worship. Their closing affirmation of loyalty strengthens the notion that there was, ideally, to be only one legal shrine among the Israelites since the single authentic altar to which the easterners pledged their loyalty was the altar at the tabernacle (cf. Lev. 17:8–9).

These verses describe a constructive confrontation. The easterners were forced to sharpen and clarify their intention to remain orthodox in their worship, and the westerners were forced to affirm that they would always accept the easterners despite their geographic separation.

The response is sufficient for the matter, and the embassy rejoices that God is still present with his people (**22:30–34**). Willful sin would have broken the nation's fellowship with God. And breaking fellowship would have meant the withdrawal of God's covenant blessings. But the fact that the eastern tribesmen are not persisting in rebellion permits God's continued presence. The name assigned to the altar (v. 34) becomes, in effect, an assertion of covenant loyalty to Yahweh, and therefore an assertion of the intent to obey his covenant commands.

B. Reaffirmation of the covenant (23:1–24:27). The two remaining chapters deal mostly with covenant faithfulness and covenant renewal. The main power of the indigenous peoples has been broken. The future offers both prospects of complete victory if Israel remains faithful and prospects of humiliating failure should Israel violate the covenant.

The present chapter gives a more personal challenge from Joshua to the people and emphasizes separation from the peoples of the land and their sins. Chapter 24 is more of a formal, national occasion of covenant renewal.

Some time has passed. Joshua is old, and the nation is resting from war—but more because of Israel's failure to follow through in faith and possess their allotments than because complete victory has been achieved. Joshua gathers the people and their leaders or perhaps all the nation in the persons of their representative leaders. He first reminds them of God's deeds and faithfulness (**23:1–5**). God's past faithfulness guaranteed that the remaining unconquered regions would be conquered, but only if the people would be faithful to the covenant. The allotment of the land is an indication that God will follow through and grant complete possession of those allotments. God is willing to fight for his people in the completion of the conquest.

There are three elements in Joshua's challenge (**23:6–8**): complete, unwavering obedience to the law (v. 6); separation from the Gentile nations and their pagan ways (v. 7); and faithfulness to God, Israel's covenant lord (v. 8).

Joshua details the consequences of obedience and disobedience (**23:9–13**). Covenant faithfulness had been rewarded by God's faithfulness in driving out the nations. Covenant faithfulness is here described as "love" for God (v. 11). On the other hand, associations with the Canaanites will bring a halt to God's help in providing victory. In fact, the Canaanites themselves will become a danger to Israel and ultimately apostasy will result in the loss of the land.

Joshua closes with the sober warning that the curses of the law are just as certain as its blessings (**23:14–16**). So far, God has given Israel blessings, particularly the land. God has been completely faithful in keeping his promises. But if the Israelites are unfaithful, God will be just as faithful in executing the promised covenant curses.

In the ancient Near East, the relationships between a people and a foreign lord were partly defined as relationships between the people's leader and that lord. Therefore the death of the leader was a proper time to renew the relationship and its covenant. Deuteronomy was the renewal that marked the death of Moses. Now with the death of Joshua imminent, it is time for another renewal.

The place of Shechem in Joshua is peculiar (**24:1**). The first significant covenant renewal in Palestine took place there (8:30–34) even before the conquest had extended that far north. Now, although the central shrine is located at Shiloh—and indeed several important national convocations had gathered at Shiloh (see 18:1; 22:12)—the second great occasion of covenant renewal takes place at Shechem. Clearly there was a special affinity between the newly arrived Israelites and the region and people of Shechem.

A regular feature of the secular covenant treaty in the ancient world was the historical preamble, which stated the historical basis for the covenant. The legal legitimacy of the covenant depended upon the historical works cited in the preamble. God's historical works are here cited from four periods (**24:2–13**): the patriarchs (vv. 2–4), the exodus (vv. 5–7), the Trans-Jordanian conquest (vv. 8–10), and the Canaanite conquest (vv. 11–13). The unique feature of Israel's religion in the ancient world was that it was rooted in God's unique works in history rather than in cyclical, magical events of the calendar.

God's historical work actually began with

Abraham; earlier biblical materials are but introductory. Two of the three great blessings of the Abrahamic covenant are alluded to in this chapter. Here, the multiplication of Abraham's descendants is noted; a few verses later, the giving of the land will be described (vv. 8, 13). Even the entry into Egypt was a part of God's good purposes. Great miracles and signs were a part of God's historical works. The exodus and conquest together constitute one of the four great periods of miraculous signs in the Bible. The miracle at the Sea of Reeds was only one of many during this period. The two steps in the conquest are reviewed. These are critical since the land was the most significant of the covenant blessings as well as one of the three promises of the Abrahamic covenant. The emphasis here is on the fact that God fought for his people.

The catalog of Canaanites (v. 11) is typical. Some take the "hornet" (v. 12) to be a reference to the way in which Egyptian rule contributed to the weakness of the Canaanites. Egyptian policies weakened the Canaanites in two ways: first, Egyptian administrative policies deliberately aimed at maintaining the political fragmentation of Canaan; and second, the Egyptians naturally suppressed any movement of the Canaanite cities toward significant military strength.

The challenge in **24:14–24** is to faithfulness to God. In the preceding chapter the challenge focuses on separation from the Canaanites and obedience to the law. Here the positive side of the challenge focuses on God himself.

The challenge is that, in view of the great historical works God has done for them, they should "fear" (i.e., "be loyal devotees of") God. The contrast, then, is between God and the false gods previously worshiped by the Israelites themselves and by their enemies in the land. The thought that serving God would be undesirable (v. 15) is pure irony after all that God has done for his people. But the necessity to choose is no less real and no less ironic for Israel than for God's people today. Now, as then, one who sensitively reflects on God's works cannot do other than choose loyalty to God.

The Israelites pledge loyalty to God in view of God's great works for them. Joshua then declares the relevance of this pledge for idolatry. God is jealous and will not tolerate disloyalty in worship. Judgment will come from rebellion. The people respond that they will serve (i.e., "worship") Yahweh.

The challenge then becomes practical. After reminding the people that they themselves are the declared witnesses to the transactions of the day, Joshua challenges them to discard their idols in order to serve God. This challenge can be seen in two ways. At this point it was unlikely that the generation that had seen the judgment on Achan would have quickly fallen into widespread idolatry, so that for them this exhortation could have been a precautionary challenge. On the other hand, if converted Canaanites were in the assembly, the challenge to discard idols could have been very practical and necessary. Another positive affirmation of worship and obedience again follows.

The covenant is officially renewed, including its legal provisions (**24:25–27**). Joshua then sets up a stone memorial which will serve as a witness against Israel in case of disobedience to the covenant. This memorial could have become one of the great historical monuments of faith.

C. Three burials (24:28–33). The book concludes with three burials. These have meanings which look both to the past and to the future. First, usage of the land for burials represents possession and ownership in a special way and looks back to God's giving the land to Israel. Joseph did not want to be buried in Egypt because it was not his land. The burial of these three great figures in Canaan is a powerful sign that Canaan belonged to the Israelites and that they were there to stay. The prestige of Shechem is enhanced by Joseph's burial there.

Second, the deaths of two members of the conquest generation, Joshua (v. 29) and Eleazar (v. 32), serve to mark the end of the era of obedience to God's will and anticipates the apostasies of the Book of Judges.

SELECT BIBLIOGRAPHY

Garstang, J. *Joshua-Judges.* Reprint. Grand Rapids: Kregel, 1978.

Keil, C. F., and F. Delitzsch. *Joshua.* Old Testament Commentaries. Reprint. Grand Rapids: Associated Publishers, n.d.

Woudstra, M. H. *The Book of Joshua.* New International Commentary on the Old Testament. Grand Rapids: Eerdmans, 1981.

JUDGES

Andrew C. Bowling

INTRODUCTION

The phrase *in those days Israel had no king* (18:1; 19:1; 21:25) suggests that the writer of Judges was looking back from a time when Israel did have kings. The book's implied approval of kingship would seem to indicate a time when the monarchy was in favor. Furthermore, Judges was written while Jebusites still lived in Jerusalem (1:21; cf. also the Canaanites in Gezer, 1:29). This is usually taken as proof of a date before David captured the city. However, the decisiveness of this evidence is compromised by the fact that Jebusites continued to live in Jerusalem even after David captured it (1 Chron. 21:18). Overall, the great royal achievements of David and Solomon provide the most likely setting for the book's composition, in particular the early part of David's reign (ca. 1000 B.C.).

The human author of Judges cannot be determined. The Talmudic tradition that Samuel wrote the book is not supported by firm evidence. At best, we can only surmise that the writer was a covenant Jew with the necessary education, means, and leisure to be acquainted with the subject matter of the book.

The Book of Judges is a history of how God "raised up judges" who saved the Israelites from their enemies (2:16). The traditional meaning of the word *judge* has obscured the full scope of the office. The basic idea of "judging" is governing (NIV leading) with all its implied functions. Samuel's combined religious, administrative, executive, and judicial responsibilities best illustrate the full range of this office. Due to historical conditions, however, the military-executive function of deliverance from enemies is underscored in the Book of Judges.

In detailing the history of the judges, the book's concern is topical rather than chronological. In general, the book develops the theme of the failure of the old religious and political order under the leadership of the judges. The writer implies that this failure is due to the absence of divinely ordained kings (18:1; 19:1; 21:25). Furthermore, the specific aspects of this failure—incomplete conquest, apostasy, and societal collapse—are, by and large, issues which the Davidic monarchy would successfully deal with, at least for a time.

In fact, in view of the book's date and purpose, it is likely that many of the accounts in Judges were composed with the ideal Davidic monarch in mind. Several episodes seem to be deliberate contrasts with the life of David, especially the stories of Abimelech (chap. 9) and Jephthah (10:6–12:7). There are numerous anticipations of the functions of the Davidic monarchy, including: (1) maintaining true faith and preventing apostasy and syncretism; (2) maintaining public security; (3) establishing the unity of the people; (4) defending the land from foreign enemies; and (5) dealing with the non-Hebrew population of Palestine.

The theological foundation for the Book of Judges is, first and foremost, the three great Old Testament covenants God made with his people. The Abrahamic covenant is never specifically cited, but the emphasis upon the gift of the land (e.g., 2:1) is reminiscent of God's promise to Abraham (Gen. 15:7). There are many explicit references to the Mosaic covenant (see 2:1–2; 6:7–9; 11:15–27). The people belong to God because he delivered them from Egypt. Their acts of disobedience are violations of the Mosaic covenant. The theme of religious infidelity, as developed in Judges, recalls that same theme in the great covenant passages (e.g., Deut. 6:13–15). Finally, anticipating the role of the monarchy and probably living in David's time, the writer of Judges lays the theological groundwork for some of the basic concepts of the Davidic covenant, anticipating the tasks and character of the ideal Davidic king.

The Book of Judges deals with a time of apostasy, covenant disobedience, and religious syncretism. Even some of the great judges mix genuine faith with local, superstitious paganism. If Jephthah did, in fact, sacrifice his daughter, that act captures some of the worst features of the syncretistic religion of that time. It was a time when a tribe would risk annihilation to defend an openly homosexual community (chap. 20). It was a time when people would naively anticipate God's blessings while actively practicing idolatry (chap. 17). Yet it was also an age when God accepted whatever true faith could be found in such dismal circumstances.

OUTLINE

- I. Covenant Disobedience and Judgment (1–16)
  - A. The Incomplete Conquest (1:1–2:5)
  - B. The Pattern of Disobedience (2:6–3:6)
  - C. The Pattern Illustrated: A History of the Judges (3:7–16:31)
- II. The Collapse of Society (17–21)
  - A. The Breakdown of Religious Life: Micah's Idol (17–18)
  - B. The Breakdown of Justice and Civil Order: Civil War (19–21)

COMMENTARY

I. Covenant Disobedience and Judgment (1–16)

A. The incomplete conquest (1:1–2:5). One of the themes of the Book of Judges is that of covenant disobedience. The people of Israel had violated the covenant by failing to drive the indigenous peoples from the land. This failure led to toleration of the Canaanites, even to the extent of regularizing their status through treaties (2:2). This failure, naturally, evoked God's condemnation (2:1–5).

Before dealing with the incomplete conquest, three preliminary issues must be addressed: (1) the relationship between Judges 1 and the Book of Joshua; (2) God's intentions for the Canaanites; and (3) the chronology of Judges 1:1–2:5, Judges 2:6–16:31, and certain events in the Book of Joshua.

Judges 1 can be contrasted with the Book of Joshua from both a historical perspective and a theological perspective. Some biblical scholars see the Book of Joshua and Judges 1 as presenting totally contradictory pictures of the conquest of Canaan. Others suggest that the conquest of Canaan proceeded in two stages: (1) an initial rapid and overwhelming strike which quickly and substantially weakened Canaanite resistance; and (2) a protracted process of removing remaining Canaanite strongholds. The Book of Joshua, then, records the first stage (1–12) and some aspects of the second stage of the conquest (e.g., 15:14–19). Judges 1, assuming the successful first stage, indicates the failure of the second stage of the conquest, in which the individual tribes failed to take full possession of their specific allotments. These two conquest accounts can be taken as complementary rather than contradictory.

On the theological side, the Book of Joshua underscores God's faithfulness in "giving" the land to Abraham's descendants (23:14). In contrast, Judges 1 is a record of Israel's failure to complete the conquest, a failure stemming from disobedience and lack of faith (2:2–3).

The complete conquest did not neccessarily demand extermination of the Canaanites. As long as they were converted to Yahwism and did not preserve their Canaanite identity, there is no hint of God's disapproval (see Josh. 2). However, treaty protection for and toleration of Canaanites who maintained their pagan religion were condemned (see Josh. 9).

Concerning chronological questions, there is no need to posit discrepancies between Judges 1:1–2:5, Judges 2:6–16:31, and those passages in Joshua which deal with the allotment of the land. Since the passages in Joshua are topically distinct, there is no discrepancy if each has a different chronological tie with the death of Joshua and if their time spans overlap.

The major alleged discrepancy is that some incidents in the second phase of the conquest seem to be dated during Joshua's lifetime in the Book of Joshua, but after Joshua's death in Judges 1. However, the relevant passages from Joshua deal primarily with the allotment of the tribal inheritances and the fixing of tribal boundaries prior to Joshua's death (chaps. 14–19) and only incidentally with the disposition of those inheritances. Furthermore, some of the notices concerning the dispositions of these allotments are chronologically indefinite in respect to Joshua's death (e.g., Josh. 17:13).

Shortly after the death of Joshua, the Israelites gather, probably at Gilgal, to initiate yet another drive to complete the conquest (**1:1–2**). This is probably the renewal of an unsuccessful effort originally begun shortly after the division of the land west of the Jordan (Josh. 14). The divine oracle, likely through the Urim and Thummim, selects Judah to lead this renewed effort. God reminds the Israelites that he has given the land into Judah's hands.

Simeon goes up with Judah against the remaining Canaanites (**1:3**), resulting in the virtual disappearance of Simeon as a separate tribe. There is a significant difference in strategy between Joshua's southern campaign (Josh. 10) and this joint campaign. The earlier campaign began with an attack on cities in the Shephelah (Josh. 10:28–35), the foothills which flanked the highlands of Judah on the west. Joshua moved into the highlands (Josh. 10:36–39) only after securing his western flank. In this campaign, with the Shephelah already weakened, Judah safely moves directly south along the mountainous spine of southern Canaan, passing through Bezek, Jerusalem, Hebron, Debir, and Hormah.

At Bezek, Israel attacks the Canaanites and Perizzites,[1] dealing a fitting punishment to Adoni-Bezek (**1:4–7**). The conquest of Jerusalem (**1:8**) involves the removal of an enemy rather than occupation (cf. 1:21). The record of Judah's conquests begins with a summary of related efforts (**1:9–10**): those in the hill country are generally effective, while those in the Negeb and western foothills are not. At Hebron, the three clans of Anak—Sheshai, Ahiman, and Talmai (cf. Num. 13:22; Josh. 15:14)—are defeated. The Calebites play a key role in this conquest.

The history of the conquest of the Anakites is quite complex. Joshua, in the initial conquest, drove them completely out of the region to exile in Gaza, Gath, and Ashdod (Josh. 11:21–23). The Anakites then reestablished themselves in the region only to be driven out again

1. "Canaanite" is often a general term for all the inhabitants of Palestine (v. 3), possibly being the Hurrian counterpart to "Phoenician." Here it is contrasted with "Perizzites" and may refer only to the old Canaanitish mercantile aristocracy generally inhabiting the valleys and plains. The Perizzites are best taken as one of the Amorite groups living in the Judean highlands.

by the Calebites. Debir is also taken by the Calebites under the leadership of Othniel (**1:11–13**). Some details of Calebite family history are provided (**1:14–15**), probably due more to Calebite pride in the epic initiative of their women than to a concern with interclan struggles over water rights.

Since the Kenites are related to the Israelites, a stage of their long history in Canaan is noted (**1:16**). The conquest of Hormah and the temporary conquest of three cities later held by the Philistines complete the record of Judah's partial success (**1:17–18**).

The description of Judah's limited conquest (**1:19**) reflects the general limits of the conquests of the entire nation. The reasons for these limitations have more to do with spiritual failure than historical circumstances. The Israelites take the hill country but cannot seize the plains from the Canaanites because of their chariots.[2] A spiritually whole nation could have coped with Canaanite chariots.

While Joseph's capture of Luz (Bethel) shows a measure of faith and success, Judges **1:20–36** largely details the incomplete conquest. By documenting Israel's failure, the passage implies the greatness that might have belonged to the Israelites had they obeyed God in faith.

Manasseh fails to conquer five powerful cities (v. 27), roughly paralleling the lucrative trade route from the Mediterranean through the Valley of Jezreel into the Jordan Valley. The wealth generated from controlling this route probably helped pay for the Canaanite chariots of Hazor (chap. 4). The Ephraimites fail to destroy the Canaanites in Gezer. It is difficult to evaluate Zebulun's failure since the identities of Kitron and Nahalol are unknown. Asher fails to seize a complex of seven Phoenician cities near the coast (v. 31). Naphtali demands forced labor from two Canaanite cities, Beth Anath and Beth Shemesh, but does not destroy them.

Though Dan's allotment was to extend to the Mediterranean, "the Amorites confined the Danites to the hill country." The last verse of the chapter relates that the Amorites halt Israel's advance along a vaguely defined line in the south.

In response to Israel's covenant disobedience, the angel of the Lord[3] delivers God's condemnation at Bokim (**2:1–5**). The angel begins by reminding the Israelites of the exodus, the gift of the land, and God's faithfulness to his covenant (v. 1). He then strikes directly at the heart of Israel's disobedience—the illicit covenants which legitimized the existence of pagan religion and peoples within Israel's territory. Such covenants led to the preservation of pagan shrines and even to the adoption of Canaanite religion by the Israelites.

As a consequence, God is going to withdraw his help so that the Israelites, henceforth, will be unable to drive out their enemies (v. 3). Ironically, the incomplete conquest was both the cause and the result of God's judgment. The conquest was initially incomplete because of Israel's disobedience; with God's help withdrawn, the continued incomplete conquest is the result of God's judgment.

Following the angel's pronouncement of judgment, the people weep aloud. Bokim, meaning "weepers," may have gained its name from this occasion. Yet the Israelites' grief and repentance are not sincere enough to reverse the pattern of religious decline.

B. The pattern of disobedience (2:6–3:6). Having described the incomplete conquest, the writer of Judges now considers a new, though closely related topic: the repeated pattern of disobedience to the covenant during the period of the judges. A recurrent four-step pattern can be identified: (1) sin, (2) judgment, (3) repentance, and (4) restoration.

The immediate cause for the people's disobedience is their neglect of God's great deeds: the Israelites fail to teach these mighty acts to succeeding generations (**2:6–10**; cf. Deut. 6:20–25). Those who had seen these deeds kept the people faithful to God, but Joshua's death marks the end of the generation that heeded these works.

The fourfold pattern of disobedience is made explicit in **2:10–19**. The people's sin is described as unfaithfulness to the covenant God who brought them out of Egypt. The people practice the pagan fertility rites of Canaan, worshiping the Baals and the Ashtoreths. Judgment comes with "raiders," who reflect the international upheavals and migrations of this historical period. Israel is defeated and distressed. Repentance and restoration follow. In response to his people's cries, God raises up judges to save them.

Persistence in evil is one of the tragic facts of human depravity. Even after God's gracious forgiveness and restoration, the Israelites forget and turn back to evil. Repentance lasts only as long as the judge who delivered them from

2. "Iron chariots" were probably wooden chariots strengthened with iron instead of bronze at critical weak points. These chariots were imported—iron technology was not widespread in Canaan until after the large-scale arrival of the Philistines (ca. 1190 B.C.).

3. The angel of the Lord was a divine epiphany—likely the Old Testament manifestation of the preincarnate Christ.

oppression; then the people turn back to their evil ways.

Israel's persistent disobedience to the covenant arouses God's anger and calls forth judgment (**2:20–3:6**). Once more (cf. 2:3), God's judgment is that the Canaanites will remain in the land (2:21). Yet God will use the presence of the Canaanites for two purposes. First, the Canaanites will test the future covenant obedience of the Israelites (2:22–23; 3:4). Second, they will teach war to Israel (3:1–2). But Israel defies God's purposes by making peace with the nations that are left, intermarrying with them, and sharing in their pagan religion.

C. The pattern illustrated: a history of the judges (3:7–16:31). The Book of Judges cites six historical examples of the pattern of sin, judgment, repentance, and restoration. The first of these is the story of Othniel (**3:7–11**). Aram Naharaim has been identified as an Aramaean kingdom in northern Mesopotamia. The objection, though hardly conclusive, is that Judah was a substantial distance from Mesopotamia and there is no record of intervening Israelite areas being attacked. Therefore, some scholars see Aram Naharaim as a possible textual deviation for "Edom." (In nonvoweled Hebrew "Aram" is very similar to "Edom." Besides, Edom is more geographically appropriate.) Other less likely suggestions are that Cushan-Rishathaim was a (Neo-)Hittite ruler, a Kassite chief, or a Khapiru leader.

God, angered by the people's apostasy, brings judgment: oppression at the hands of Cushan-Rishathaim. The fact that God responds to his people may indicate that their crying out signals some measure of sincere repentance. A special enablement through the Spirit of God brings the Calebite Othniel to rescue the people. Some scholars argue that the "forty years" of peace during his leadership are best understood as a "generation."

The second historical account of Israel's apostasy is found in the story of Ehud and the Moabite alliance (**3:12–30**). Israel's sin is described merely as the fact that they "did evil" (v. 12). A Trans-Jordanian alliance, including Amalekites and Ammonites and led by Eglon of Moab, comes and attacks Israel. Jericho serves as their base of operations for eighteen years. Again, "crying out" marks the people's repentance, and intrigue against Moabite rule begins.

We should not ignore the question of rebellion against a de facto ruler. In New Testament terms, such rebellion is sin (Rom. 13:1), and God's moral principles do not change. Human government has been ordained by God. However, from the biblical perspective, the covenant nation is always a special case. Therefore, the independence of this nation is God's immediate covenant purpose, and is not dependent upon moral rules applicable to the nations in general.

Eglon is apparently the unifying factor in the alliance. Since Eglon, at least within the context of God's special covenant relationship with his people, is a recognized enemy, Ehud can justifiably assassinate him. Ehud delivers the annual tribute, possibly to Jericho, and then heads home as far as Gilgal. From there he returns to Jericho to carry out the assassination. Ehud must have previously cultivated Eglon's trust for Eglon to be willing to see him alone. Eglon's "upper room of his summer palace" (v. 20) literally means an "upper cool room." In ancient Egypt, a "cool room" was a toilet chamber. This may be the meaning here, especially since Eglon's waiting servants speak of him as "relieving himself" in an inner room of the house. Ehud assassinates Eglon and secretly escapes by means of the "porch," an architectural feature of unknown character.

Ehud flees to Seirah. "Seirah" may be the locative form of a noun meaning "forest" rather than a proper name, so that the sense of the passage might be "to the forest" (i.e., "in the hill country of Ephraim"). The death of Eglon raises the morale of the Israelites, and the Moabites and their allies west of the Jordan are killed. This results in eighty years—or two generations—of rest.

The one-verse account (**3:31**) of Shamgar's exploit (killing six hundred Philistines with an oxgoad) marks him as a mighty warrior. Both his name (from Hurrian Semiqari) and his title (son of Anath [the Canaanite war goddess]) indicate Israel's openness to foreign influences.

Judges 4–5 details the story of Deborah and the Canaanite alliance. The scope of the war with Jabin should not be minimized. There are indications that the renewed oppression was the effort of a revived northern Canaanite alliance. First, the number of chariots (nine hundred) is very large for a single city, even for a wealthy, powerful city. A mercenary chariot army was an expensive operation and normally the prerogative of great international armies. Second, the text specifically mentions "kings" as the enemy (5:19).

The pattern continues (**4:1–3**); the people sin, God gives them into the hands of Jabin of Hazor and Sisera, his general, and the people once again cry out in repentance. The rest of the chapter deals with God's deliverance and restoration.

Old Testament society was a male-oriented society. Nevertheless, within that framework, there could be great appreciation of and respect for women. In Judges **4:4–7,** a prophetess named Deborah leads Israel. The extent of her influence is striking. She lives in southern Ephraim, but exercises influence as far north as Naphtali and Zebulun. She speaks with God's voice and authority to a major military leader. At her instigation, tribes which would otherwise quickly fade into insignificance mount a major attack against the Canaanites.

At this point geography is instructive. The Israelites and the Canaanites were intermingled in Galilee and Ephraim with the Canaanites generally controlling the valleys and the Israelites the hill country. Deborah's instructions are as follows. Barak, living in Kedesh, roughly six miles north of Hazor in the hill country, is to lead ten thousand men to Mount Tabor some thirty miles south of Hazor. The region around Mount Tabor is relatively accessible to chariots, and the mere presence of ten thousand Israelites mobilized in such an area will suffice to "lure" Sisera to the region. God's sovereignty over human affairs is asserted in Deborah's promise that God will give victory.

Deborah's status is further underscored by Barak's demand that she accompany the army (**4:8–13**). In doing so, Barak forfeits part of the honor and glory of the victory. Barak sends out the call from Kedesh, apparently his hometown. Zebulun and Naphtali answer Barak's call (v. 10; cf. also 5:18). The extensive ranging of the Kenites is illustrated by Heber's move to the north (v. 11; cf. 1:16). Sisera is lured to the Kishon along with his chariots and additional infantry support troops (i.e., "all the men," v. 13).

The details of Israel's victory (**4:14–22**) are uncertain. Sisera and his army approach Mount Tabor from the west coming from Harosheth Haggoyim. As his army approaches, the Israelites charge down the slopes of Mount Tabor (v. 14), and, apparently, a sudden cloudburst immobilizes the Canaanite chariots (5:20–21). The Canaanites flee with many, if not most, heading southward toward Taanach (5:19) and then westward to Harosheth Haggoyim (4:16) being pursued and slaughtered by the Israelites during their flight. At some point, Sisera makes his way northward (4:17), followed somewhat later by Barak.

God gives the victory to Israel. "Not a man was left" (v. 16) refers to the absence of further resistance. The Kenites were neutral in the struggles of the surrounding peoples. But this time their neutrality is broken and Jael, a Kenite woman, murders Sisera as he sleeps and gains the glory for the victory. This is to be contrasted with Ehud's treachery. Ehud's treachery was directed at a recognized enemy, while Jael's treachery is directed toward a nominal "friend." In terms of basic moral principles, her treachery is questionable; but her desire to be in line with God's purposes is an act of faith. Even genuine faith is compromised by depravity.

This marks the last major Canaanite effort against Israel. Although the Canaanites would not be completely subdued until the time of David, they would never again dominate the Israelites. The importance of the victory in Israel's patriotic tradition is demonstrated by the poetic remembrance recorded in chapter 5.

Israel's victory is celebrated by the composition of a victory song, a standard literary form of the time. This is one of many passages that commemorate God's great deeds (e.g., Ps. 105).

The language, ideology, and historical setting of the poem indicate an early date roughly contemporaneous with the events it celebrates. Critical scholars often emphasize the fact that Makir and Gilead are treated as equals with the traditional tribes, allegedly indicating a date before the development of the twelve-tribe structure. However, the prominence of Makir and Gilead reflects two facts. First, these two subdivisions did, in fact, exceed some of the minor tribes in standing. Second, the events occurred during a time of such severe societal breakdown that the traditional twelve-tribe structure was losing its significance.

The poem is a typical example of ancient epic poetry. It is highly vivid and concrete, full of striking descriptions incorporated into a somewhat disjointed poetic style. This disjointedness has led to undue concern with the corruption, or even mutilation, of the text. Certainly there are difficulties and obscurities which some scholars take as indicative of textual corruption. However, most of the obscurities are well within the bounds of normal epic poetry.

The theme of godly leadership is important in this song of Deborah. The first step in deliverance demands that the leaders take the initiative, and then that the people willingly follow them (v. 2; cf. v. 9). Deborah and Barak are challenged to lead (v. 12). (Barak's timidity as a leader is tactfully disregarded.) Unknown leaders of the assembled people are mentioned (vv. 14–15). The impotence of the enemies' leaders is graphically emphasized by Sisera's death (vv. 26–27).

The meaning of the first clause of the poem (**5:2–3**) is not clear, but the interpretation in the New International Version is as good as any. The significance may be "when the leaders let their hair loose" (i.e., as an act of religious dedication in assuming leadership). If so, the opening verses draw together two themes involved in deliverance and victory: the necessity of godly leadership and praise to the Lord who is ultimately responsible for any good that happens. The world's peoples will hear God praised in the recitation of his great deeds (1 Chron. 16:9, 15–23), will so learn of God, and will then praise God themselves (1 Chron. 16:23–24, 31; Ps. 96: 7–8).

The song goes on to rehearse God's deliverance (**5:4–11**). First, the Lord appears in a powerful desert thunderstorm (vv. 4–5). In early Canaanite poetry, the thunderstorm is a regular symbol of the appearance of deity in power and majesty. God is poetically pictured, first, as coming forth from Edom, and then as "the One of Sinai." Some scholars conclude that this poem assumes that Mount Sinai is in Edom rather than in the Sinai peninsula. However, the Hebrew poet could indiscriminately mix poetic figures without regarding them as identical.

Deborah's song expresses the people's insecurity and economic instability before the deliverance. The choice of new gods (v. 8) recalls the apostasy that brought divine judgment against Israel. This results in military weakness; a clear cause-and-effect relationship between sin and political weakness is presupposed. The mention of forty thousand men does not contradict Barak's ten thousand (cf. 4:6). The text is quite indefinite concerning the occasion which involved this forty thousand. The minstrel poets (i.e., "singers") sing of the great acts of God and his warriors. In response to God's presence and the recollection of his past deeds, God's people go "down to the city gates" (i.e., mobilize against their oppressors). These verses describe a popular movement, one spurred on by the recollection of God's great deeds and the wait for a leader.

The mobilization of the people (**5:12–18**) begins with a challenge to Israel's leaders to arise willingly and to prepare for war. The content of this challenge, "take captive your captives" (KJV lead thy captivity captive), is repeated on other occasions and could receive its definition from this context. Here the phrase clearly refers to conquest over one's oppressors or enemies; and this is likely the significance that should be given to the New Testament allusion to these words (cf. Ps. 68:18; Eph. 4:8).

The tribes from which people willingly come are Ephraim, Benjamin, Makir, Zebulun, and Issachar (vv. 14–15a). The supposition that Zebulun and Naphtali were the major participants (4:6, 10; 5:18), but were assisted by the other tribes, adequately harmonizes all of the data. The mention of Ephraim's Amalekite roots (v. 14) exemplifies the fact that the chosen people were related to other peoples in the ancient world (cf. Deut. 26:5). These "roots" may have been through intermarriage, adoption of foreign clans, or close friendships. Tribal life in Israel, even kinship, was generally open to foreigners through various levels of contact.

Reuben, Gilead, Dan, and Asher (vv. 15b–17) are criticized for not responding. Judah, Simeon, and Benjamin apparently were not involved nor were they expected to be. This fact may reflect the natural tendency of the people to be segregated into northern and southern areas seen both during David's years at Hebron and in the division of the kingdom at the time of Rehoboam.

The record of Israel's victory (**5:19–23**) is terse, dramatic, and enigmatic, all typical features of epic poetry. The victory is attributed to God's miraculous works in nature. An overwhelming rain which caused the river Kishon to flood and bogged down the chariots is likely. The significance of Meroz (v. 23) is unclear. The curse warns against resisting God's purposes.

The account of Sisera's death (**5:24–27**) gives a humbling picture of the Canaanite leader's demise at the hands of a woman. The glory of God's chosen leader is contrasted with the shame of Sisera's death. The treachery of Jael is favorably described in heroic terms though it is doubtless her faith in God implied by the deed, not the treachery itself, which merits praise.

The last scene of the poem is a powerful, ironic boast of victory (**5:28–30**). The concern of Sisera's mother is described, and her wishful hopes are, by implication, contrasted with the reality known to the poet and the reader.

A number of Hebrew poems close with a postscript giving a general application of the theme (cf. Pss. 51:18–19; 107:43). The closing wish, that all God's enemies would perish in this way, transforms the poem into a statement of the nationalistic and religious hopes of Israel.

The period of peace lasts forty years, when a new threat appears. Once again events may be viewed in terms of the four-step pattern (**6:1–10**). As a result of renewed apostasy, the land is subjected to the raids of a loose collection of Bedouin peoples ("Amalekites and other eastern peoples," v. 3) better described as a horde than as an alliance. From their prominence in the account, the Midianites, led by Zebah and Zalmunna (cf. 8:6, 21), seem to play a leading role. Rather than establishing permanent settlements, they undertake annual raids of plunder, destruction, and slaughter. The weakening of the Canaanites in the north from the war with Barak (chaps. 4, 5) facilitates the Bedouin campaigns. The Canaanites, in their broad exposed valleys, probably suffered more from the invasions than did the Israelites, relatively sheltered up in the hills.

The plundering is thorough. The Israelites go into hiding during the raids in order to protect their possessions. For an invading horde to make its way across Judah all the way to Gaza drastically demonstrates the impotence of the people because of their sin. This time, the material consequences of sin are especially devastating.

The people repent and cry out to God. However, a prophet comes to remind Israel of the historical foundations of the covenant before God grants deliverance. The prophet emphasizes three points of covenant theology (cf. also 2:1–2): (1) the Israelites are God's people because he delivered them from Egypt (vv. 8–9a); (2) God has given the land to them (v. 9b); and (3) God demands religious faithfulness from his people (v. 10a). Judgment has come because God's people have not listened to (i.e., obeyed) his covenant demands (v. 10b).

Israel's deliverance and restoration begin with the appearance of the angel of the Lord (**6:11–16**). God calls Gideon, his chosen deliverer, at Ophrah, a sacred site as indicated by the presence of altars (vv. 25–26), the offering of sacrifices (vv. 20, 26), and the possible presence of a sacred tree, "the oak" (v. 11). Gideon is a Manassite from the clan of Abiezer. When the angel appears to him, Gideon is threshing his small harvest in secret to hide it from the horde. The angel tells Gideon that the Lord is with him. The title *mighty warrior* probably anticipates Gideon's future stature more than his present status. It may also be the proper title for any member of the aristocracy.

Gideon's answer (v. 13) may be taken in one of two ways. First, either in sincere misunderstanding or in a deliberate misapplication of the angel's words, Gideon applies the promised presence of God to the nation rather than to himself and asks why their fate is so dismal if God is actually with them. It is extreme presumption either to assume or to infer God's effective presence with an unfaithful, apostate nation. It is also presumptuous to ask why the people are suffering the consequences of sin when both their sin and the inevitable evil results of sin should have been very clear. Second, Gideon's words could be taken as a subtle wish that God could be present with his people despite their apostasy. This again disregards the holiness of God. Removal of sin must precede the presence of God.

Gideon also asks about the absence of wonders, the signs which demonstrate that God is able to deliver his people. Unfortunately, unfaithfulness to the covenant has kept God from repeating his great deeds. God puts his word and very person behind the coming deliverance.

Despite his protests of insignificance (v. 15), Gideon's family is quite prominent and is recognized even by their enemies (cf. 8:18–19). The immediate response to Gideon's call (cf. 6:34–35) also indicates his influence. Once again, the promise of victory is repeated.

In spite of the numerous assurances of victory (vv. 14, 16) and signs (vv. 20–21, 36–40; 7:13–15), Gideon asks for confirmation of his call (**6:17–24**). This is one of relatively few occasions in the Old Testament when miraculous fire devours a sacrifice (v. 21; cf. also 13:20); perhaps the occurrence of this sign marks the gravity of the situation. Gideon's reaction to the presence of God is instructive for an age when men have lost sight of the profound significance of God's presence: Gideon fears for his life (vv. 22–23). Gideon marks the spot as being sacred to Yahweh by building (or rebuilding) an altar. The name of the altar, "Yahweh is Peace," commemorates the "peace," "soundness," or "wholeness" which God brings to his people.

If Gideon is to deliver his people, he must initiate religious reform. God commands him to destroy his father's altar to Baal (**6:25–32**). Since "Baal" is a general title for a male deity, it is difficult to determine whether this altar honors some local fertility deity or one of the great Baals of the Canaanite religion. Some usual trappings of a Canaanite fertility shrine are mentioned.[4]

That the ritual prescriptions of the law could be properly overruled is shown when Gideon is commanded to offer a sacrifice, though he is neither a priest nor a Levite. The state of Gideon's people, perhaps of the entire nation, is revealed in this incident. Gideon's family and city are so enmeshed in religious apostasy that Gideon must destroy the altar in secret. Gideon's own father, clearly of weak character, tolerates Baalism; however, at the crucial moment he stands by his son and God's truth. Gideon receives an honorific nickname, Jerub-Baal ("Let Baal contend"), from this incident.

4. The sacred stone, either the altar itself or a sacred pillar near the altar, was devoted to the male deity. A tree or wooden pillar (carved or uncarved) represented the female deity. "Asherah" was a common noun referring to this wooden post or tree, though there was also a great goddess from Ugarit by that name.

The horde has crossed the Jordan and is camped in the Valley of Jezreel. Once Gideon, empowered by the Spirit, is ready to take the lead, the trumpet is sounded. This time, presumably due to God's working, the Israelites are ready to resist. The western tribes from Manasseh northward respond.

In contrast to the ideal Old Testament leader, many of the leaders of Judges are quite fallible. Their fallibility contrasts with God's faithfulness and grace. Gideon, in his fallibility, still needs reassurance; and God graciously grants him, not just one miraculous sign, but two (**6:36–40**).

Israel's army moves northward to the spring of Harod on the slopes of Mount Gilboa about five miles south of the enemy's camp at the foot of the hill of Moreh. The name *Jerub-Baal* is used for Gideon, thus binding his religious reform with the victory. Here just east of the Valley of Jezreel, strategic because of its easy access both to the east and to the west, the Lord has another test for Gideon. Like Chronicles, the Book of Judges has as one of its themes that nothing is accomplished by mere human ability (cf. v. 2). This theme is developed in the account of the drastic reduction in the size of Gideon's army (**7:1–8a**).

At God's command, Gideon first sends home all who are "trembling" with fear. "Gilead" here seems to be a transcription error for "Gilboa." Approximately ten thousand of an original thirty-two thousand men remain. This number is further reduced to three hundred by another test: those who lap water with their tongues "like a dog" are to be retained; those who crouch down to the water to drink are rejected. God's purpose in this is to demonstrate that victory comes by his power, not by the number of troops.

After Gideon and his men move into position near the Midianite camp, one more sign of God's presence and the coming victory is necessary for the fallible human leader (**7:8b–14**). What better sign than to have the enemy himself state the assurance of victory? The dream and explanation overheard by Gideon (vv. 13–14) are probably intended as an ironic, sarcastic barb against the Israelites. The barley loaf typifies the poor peasant, while the tent is characteristic of the Bedouin. For all practical purposes, it seemed that Israel's army had melted away so that it was about as threatening as a loaf of bread! The "friend" probably speaks in derision and contempt, but it is still the assurance Gideon needs.

The key elements in Israel's victory are surprise on the part of the Israelites and panic on the part of the Bedouin horde (**7:15–23**). Gideon returns to the camp praising God. Dividing the men into three companies, he distributes weapons: earthen jars, torches, and trumpets. The Bedouins were probably confident that there were no formidable enemies in the region; suddenly, they seem to be attacked by an overwhelming force from all sides. Add to this that there were several different peoples, marked by mutual greed, mutual distrust, and varying languages; these are the makings for a thoroughly confused, destructive panic in which the Bedouins, in the darkness of night, could easily end up fighting each other.

The path of retreat taken by the horde is uncertain. None of the names given in the text (v. 22) can be conclusively identified, but the line of retreat seems to have been southeast, skirting the territory of Ephraim (cf. v. 24), roughly toward the Wadi Jabbok and the cities of Succoth and Peniel (cf. 8:4–9). At this point, sending men ready for war back home turns out to be opportune. The newly dismissed Israelites are already armed and on the road, ready to turn around and join in the pursuit. The drastic reversal of morale changes the invaders into a demoralized mob and the Israelites into enthusiastic pursuers.

The Ephraimites join Gideon in the extended pursuit (**7:24–8:3**). Gideon asks them to seize the fords of the Jordan before the invaders are organized enough to cross the river in force. Once again the geography is obscure; Beth Barah (v. 24) is otherwise unknown. The Ephraimites seize the fords of the upper Jordan and aid in the slaughter of the Bedouin. Two princes of the Midianites, Oreb and Zeeb, fall to the Ephraimites.

Now the Ephraimites complain because they were not brought into the war from the beginning (8:1). From here on, Gideon's stature as a leader becomes obvious. Gideon's response to the Ephraimites—that they have achieved greater glory than his own clan, Abiezer—marks him as tactful and statesmanlike. The brave Ephraimites, appeased, return home rather than aiding in further pursuit.

Gideon's three hundred men constitute the backbone of the continued pursuit, though by this time they are probably joined by others. Having pursued the remnants of the horde to the vicinity of Wadi Jabbok in Trans-Jordan, Gideon asks for assistance first from Succoth and then Peniel. Both cities refuse help and belittle Gideon's victory by asking if he has already captured the enemy kings (**8:4–9**). Apparently these, and probably other cities in Trans-Jordan, wished to maintain cordial relations with the desert Bedouin. Gideon's blunt responses to their rebuffs further underscore his decisiveness and formidability.

Gideon's line of pursuit cannot be completely reconstructed from the data given (**8:10–13**). The "route of the nomads" seems to have been a wilderness trail running north and south somewhat east of Nobah and Jogbehah (v. 11). Karkor (v. 10) could have been quite distant from Nobah and Jogbehah on this route. Gideon apparently pursues the horde into the eastern deserts and ambushes them in their own territory. A major factor in such a victory would be the Bedouin confidence that no one would pursue them back into their own desert. With Zebah and Zalmunna as captives, Gideon is ready to return to Succoth and Peniel. The location of the Pass of Heres (v. 13) is not known.

Judgment on Succoth and Peniel (**8:14–17**) follows. While modern men may judge Gideon's methods as harsh, they may have been necessary in a brutal, disorderly age. Succoth is treated relatively leniently; its seventy chief elders are "threshed" (NEB v. 7) with desert thorns and briars. Threshing with thorns does not mean that they were dragged with thorns as in threshing grain; it could simply be a figure of speech for a severe flogging. Peniel is destroyed and its male inhabitants are massacred. The city may have remained in ruins until it was rebuilt by Jeroboam (1 Kings 12:25). The harshness of this judgment could indicate that Peniel had actively collaborated with the enemy.

Gideon next executes personal vengeance on Zebah and Zalmunna (**8:18–21**). Apparently these kings had killed a number of captives, "each one with the bearing of a prince," at Mount Tabor, including some of Gideon's brothers. Gideon orders his son to kill the two kings, thereby insulting them with death at the hands of a young, untried warrior. The two Midianite kings demonstrate the best, by human standards, of the Bedouin code of honor. They do not fear death; but they desire an honorable death at the hands of a proven warrior. The kings ask Gideon to kill them himself and he accommodates them.

Judges **8:22–35** details the rest of Gideon's life. Gideon rejects the offer of a hereditary kingship. This rejection is not necessarily a condemnation of the monarchy. This is a tacit condemnation of the monarchy on the wrong terms, as something offered by men rather than by God. The right monarchy is the monarchy instituted by God in his time.

Gideon, however, makes a terrible mistake. He requests a gold earring from each man's share of the booty. From this gold he makes an ephod which later becomes an object of apostate worship.[5]

Again there are forty years, or one generation, of peace. Gideon lives out his life with all the marks of success: many wives and sons, prestige, and a long life (vv. 30–32). Two other facts about his life should be noted. He is survived by a son named Abimelech (v. 31) to be dealt with in Judges 9; and immediately after his death the pattern of sin begins again (vv. 33–35). This time Gideon's own ephod contributes to the idolatrous worship. The same ties which brought Gideon into contact with his wife from Shechem may also have encouraged the syncretistic worship of Baal-Berith, the Lord of the Covenant, of Shechem.

The abortive monarchy of Abimelech is detailed in Judges 9. This chapter makes two important theological points. First, it shows the need for a divinely ordained monarchy. Without God's approval there was the danger of selfish rulers who caused, rather than prevented, disorder and bloodshed. A monarchy established in human sinfulness was merely an additional evidence of human depravity. God's monarchy, in his time and ultimately in line with his covenant, was the necessary solution to the disorders and insecurities of the time. In this light it is instructive to contrast Abimelech's human attempt to establish the monarchy with the career of David, God's ideal king. Second, the chapter illustrates the way God uses the events of history to accomplish his purposes despite the fact that men think they are in control. In this case God manipulates history to destroy Abimelech and Shechem.

The nature of the city of Shechem is important for the account. Three lines of evidence strongly indicate that Shechem was a city with a large pre-Israelite, partly Canaanite population. First, a covenant renewal ceremony took place at Shechem under peaceful circumstances before the conquest of the north (Josh. 8:30–35). Second, there is no record of the conquest of Shechem. Third, the present chapter mentions an earlier strand of population, the sons of Hamor (v. 28). These considerations strongly suggest that Shechem was inhabited by a friendly population which quickly joined the Israelites, may have participated in the earlier covenant renewal at Shechem, and sur-

5. In general an ephod was an item of clothing. The nature of an ephod made of gold is less clear. Two possibilities immediately come to mind: (1) a cloth garment heavily decorated with gold; or (2) a gold likeness of a garment. The usage of an ephod as a sacred object, even as an object of worship, could easily have developed by perverting an orthodox custom of keeping the high priest's ephod on display at the tabernacle.

vived the conquest. This chapter, then, shows the failure both of the general political order of the judges and of Abimelech in ruling a multicultural society.

Abimelech, one of Gideon's sons, conspires with the men of his mother's home city to hire assassins to murder his brothers; he then plans to seize control over part of the nation (**9:1–6**). There is a strong contrast between Abimelech, who seeks the throne by treacherous violence, and the greatest covenant king, David, who refuses to use violence against Saul to secure the throne for himself.

Abimelech carries out a shrewd plan. He allies himself with one of the stronger cities in Israel, confident that the rest of the nation will offer no significant opposition to his rule while he is allied with Shechem. He appeals to the local pride and provincial spirit of Shechem (vv. 2–3). Usually, such provincialism is antagonistic to centralized rule, but Abimelech skillfully exploits it to found his limited kingship. Even the religious authorities in Shechem give financial support to Abimelech's plot.

Abimelech's treacherous violence in murdering his brothers is a vice which the godly monarch refuses to condone. How can a kingdom founded in treacherous violence long control the very vice which brought it into existence? Beth Millo (v. 6) is probably the Tower of Shechem. Gathering for Abimelech's coronation at the pillar in Shechem suggests that the religious sanction is either that of the local deity, Baal-Berith, or possibly of an illegal, syncretistic worship of Yahweh under the same name.

Gideon's youngest son, Jotham, who managed to escape the massacre (v. 5), relates a fable which gives God's commentary on Abimelech's kingship (**9:7–21**). Abimelech's treachery will breed yet more treachery until the conspirators destroy each other. The fable itself is another expression of the widespread notion that good men have more important things to do than to seek political office. The olive, the fig, and the vine all reject kingship. It is only a worthless plant, the thornbush, that desires to rule over the trees. This, of course, is in contrast to the later, divinely ordained kings who do not seek the throne from human desire; rather God seeks them out.

It is a ludicrous notion that the great trees of the forest might find shelter in the thornbush's shadow. If, as is the case, the trees cannot seek shelter in the thornbush's shadow, then it is inevitable that fire from the thornbush will destroy the trees. In fact, during dry times, thorn thickets were a major fire hazard among trees (cf. v. 20).

The conspiracy against Abimelech (**9:22–29**) illustrates that under normal circumstances, treachery breeds more treachery. This tendency is enhanced by God's sending an evil spirit to cause enmity between the conspirators. Finally, rebellion against Abimelech arises in the very city which had made him king, though the rebellion seems to have involved other cities as well (e.g., Thebez, vv. 50–54). The details of Shechem's treachery are not given; we are told only that the Shechemites become outlaws against public order and against Abimelech. Whatever loyal following Abimelech had in Shechem (cf. Zebul, vv. 30, 38) is ineffective in preventing this disorder. Abimelech's failure to maintain control over his rebellious subjects contrasts with the ideal king's success in maintaining public order (Ps. 72:14).

Shechem turns to open rebellion when another conspirator, Gaal, repays Abimelech in kind. Like Abimelech, he appeals to factional loyalties, this time to the sons of Hamor in Shechem, for support against Abimelech. The account is so condensed that some details remain unclear.

The destruction of Shechem follows (**9:30–49**). The text deals with treacheries within treacheries. Zebul, angry at Gaal but with no positive record of loyalty to Abimelech, enters into a suicidal conspiracy with Abimelech. Two strands of the theme are identifiable: first, that treachery breeds more treachery, and second, that treachery is self-destructive.

Zebul brings about Gaal's defeat at Abimelech's hands and drives his partisans in exile from the city. However, the treachery is not yet complete. Perhaps because he realizes that Zebul is not really loyal, Abimelech captures the city by yet more trickery and destroys it. The people of the tower of Shechem take shelter in the "stronghold" of the temple of El-Berith (i.e., Baal-Berith). This may have been a large, excavated, roofed chamber. If so, they suffocate to death when Abimelech builds a huge fire over the chamber.

Abimelech's death at Thebez (**9:50–57**) completes Jotham's prediction. After the massacre at Shechem, Abimelech turns to Shechem's ally, Thebez. Abimelech, with his typical abandon and recklessness, is attacking the city's central defensive tower when a hurled millstone fatally injures him. After his armorbearer kills him to circumvent his death at a woman's hands, Abimelech's army disbands and the cycle of treachery and judgment is complete.

Judges **10:1–5** contains the record of two minor judges. The significant difference between them and the major judges is that they are not used to explicate the fourfold pattern developed in Judges. Tola is otherwise unknown although both his name and his clan name (Puah) appear elsewhere in the genealogies of Issachar (e.g., 1 Chron. 7:1). Geographic mobility is demonstrated in the fact that a judge from Issachar could live at Shamir in Ephraim—and even be buried there.

Jair of Gilead, probably named after Jair the son of Hezron (1 Chron. 2:23–24), certainly is not a minor figure, though perhaps a minor judge. His clan and territories figure prominently in other biblical contexts (see, e.g., 1 Chron. 2:23–24). His large family and stable of donkeys are signs of prestige.

Apostasy again initiates the pattern of sin, judgment, repentance, and deliverance (**10:6–9**). More details are given here than for earlier apostasies. The nations whose gods are objects of apostate worship are listed. As later events prove, a major weakness of the Israelites at this time seems to be a simple lack of will and resolve, a weakness easily attributed to spiritual failure. Predatory raids into Judah, Benjamin, and Ephraim show the extent of Ammonite power.

The description of the people's repentance (**10:10–16**) is the most detailed and complex of the book. The literary narrative presents several stages in the process. First is the initial confession (v. 10). This is followed by an ironic divine oracle of further condemnation (vv. 11–14). The oracle begins by listing past oppressors. The mention of Sidonian oppression may recall Phoenician participation in Jabin's effort against Barak (see chaps. 4, 5). Bedouin Maonites could have been part of the Midianite alliance (chaps. 6–8). The oracle rehearses the fact that God has delivered the Israelites from all their past enemies, especially when they have cried out in repentance. Despite this evidence of God's power, they have still turned to other gods, in fact, to the very gods to whom God has shown himself superior. God then challenges them, ironically, to go to those gods for deliverance.

At this point the Israelites enter into a more deeply rooted, more conscious repentance and discard these false gods. The sense of God's empathy for his people is powerfully expressed in the statement that God can "bear Israel's misery no longer" (v. 16b). Even while judging his people in holy wrath, God's compassionate sympathy for his people endures.

The Ammonite mobilization for one of their annual campaigns provides the occasion both for God's deliverance and for selecting a human agent for that deliverance (**10:17–11:11**).

At this point Jephthah the Gileadite enters the account. From the context, Jephthah's father is a contemporaneous Gilead named after the eponymous ancestor of the same name. Jephthah is an illegitimate son, and therefore excluded from officially enjoying the family status. Yet he becomes another example of the motif of the rise to prominence of the rejected, illegitimate son. Further, his career may present a deliberate literary anticipation of David in that he too attracts to himself a following of violent, reckless men (v. 3; cf. 1 Sam. 22:2).

Jephthah, who has apparently gained quite a reputation, is called back as leader. There are several stages to the negotiations. First, Jephthah is offered the temporary position of "war leader" (NIV commander, v. 6), an offer which Jephthah initially rejects, sarcastically asking why they first rejected him and now appeal to him when in trouble. Then, the Gileadite elders offer him the position of commander together with permanent tenure as "head." While the full nature of this latter office is not known, it clearly is not the kingship. Jephthah accepts their offer, but only after the Gileadites confirm the offer with a solemn oath. Mizpah, whose location is uncertain, was a recognized, if illegal, holy place for Yahweh. Clearly the Gileadites were not observing all the demands of orthodox Yahwism.

The negotiations between the leaders (**11:12–28**) illustrate the general desire of ancient rulers to demonstrate the rightness of their causes in war. For us today, it also gives a fine example of the Israelites' sense of their own history. They view the legitimacy of their case as rooted in God's historical works on their behalf. Jephthah's words also reveal popular religious attitudes of that day. There are three general arguments for Israel's legitimate claim to the region: (1) the land was taken from the Amorites; (2) God had given the land to them; and (3) three hundred years of control had removed any doubt.

Jephthah begins the negotiations with a formal request for the reason for hostilities. The Ammonites reply, probably with all the sincerity generally found in such negotiations, that the land, historically, had been theirs and that they are merely reclaiming what by right is theirs. Jephthah replies that Israel had not taken the land of the Ammonites nor of the Moabites.

In fact, God had commanded Israel not to seize the lands of the Edomites, the Moabites, or the Ammonites (Deut. 2:5, 9, 37). In obedience to God's commands, the Israelites carefully avoided entering either Edom or Moab—and though not mentioned here, Ammon as well. Then, when the Israelites encountered the Amorites, people who were not descended from Lot or Abraham, they were free to seize their lands. Therefore, Amorites, not Ammonites, had been displaced when the Israelites occupied Gilead. This contradicts the Ammonites' basis for claiming Gilead.

Jephthah's communication may provide insight into popular attitudes toward pagan deities at the time. Later pagan deities would be regarded as "nothings" having no reality or standing at all (cf. Isa. 44:15–17). But in this passage, Jephthah talks as if pagan gods have legitimate status among pagan peoples. Chemosh is to the Ammonites what God is to the Israelites.

Another possibility is that Jephthah's personal theology is monotheistic; but he makes an ironic accommodation to the false beliefs of the Ammonites. He speaks of Chemosh as being legitimate for Ammon for purposes of negotiation though he knows that Chemosh is no god.

Jephthah concludes with a warning that makes much more sense if there were a strong bond between Moabites and Ammonites at this time. He points out that Balak of Moab made no attempt to question the ownership of Gilead. Even supposing that the Moabites may have construed some historical claim, which the Ammonites had opportunely assumed, three hundred years of Moabite silence had invalidated such a claim. War is the means of committing the issue to God (or the gods) for divine adjudication.

The reason for Jephthah's "crossing" Gilead and Manasseh (**11:29**) is not clear. Commentators have indicated that, since the armies had already been mobilized (10:17), Jephthah did not have to cross these territories to mobilize the Gileadites. However, it does not contradict the evidence to see the first mobilization as the half-hearted, incomplete mobilization of a spiritually flabby, irresolute people. But now, with a determined, competent leader, the Israelites are ready to carry out a complete, effective mobilization. Jephthah crosses Manasseh and Gilead, thoroughly mobilizing their militias. Apparently Ephraim is invited to participate but ignores the offer (cf. 12:2). The forces then proceed to Mizpah of Gilead, the holy city, which is the starting point for the campaign.

Jephthah also makes a pagan vow to God (**11:30–31**). As foolish and pagan as this vow is, it may still have had some effect since God can observe a right attitude of heart even if the expression of that attitude is outrageous. Some scholars have asserted that the wording Jephthah uses could not have anticipated anything other than a human sacrifice. All the nonhuman creatures that might have met him would have been insulting sacrifices.

Few details are given, but the resolute, determined Israelites, led by the same kind of leader, inflict a disastrous defeat on the Ammonites (**11:32–33**). The ease of this victory supports the notion that Israel's greatest weakness was a simple lack of resolution.

This brings us to the troublesome question of Jephthah's daughter (**11:34–40**). It is axiomatic that God prohibited human sacrifice. However, it is conceivable that a man living in Jephthah's age, "revering" God in his own half-savage way, could commit such an atrocious act, erroneously considering it an act of reverence. This kind of ignorant tragedy would no more reflect on God's character than would any other of the many atrocities committed erroneously but sincerely by God's people. Jephthah's sacrifice would be a reflection on his primitive comprehension of Yahwism, not on Yahweh himself.

Many scholars have thought that some alternate course of action was available for Jephthah since the dedicated item was a human being. The suggestion that his daughter was dedicated to perpetual virginity has been made. This event is significant enough to warrant an annual festival of remembrance (v. 40).

Israel was perpetually caught up in a tension between forces that would peacefully unite the nation and forces that would violently fragment it. The account of the civil war with Ephraim shows violent, divisive forces at work. In this instance the Ephraimites are concerned about their imagined place of leadership among the tribes (**12:1–7**). Their prestige will be undermined if the Gileadites defeat an enemy without Ephraimite help. (The Ephraimites had been equally sensitive about Gideon's military success [8:1–3].)

The Ephraimites mobilize at Zaphon near the Jordan in west Gilead and challenge Jephthah for daring to go to war without them. Their threat to destroy Jephthah's house is probably a threat against his entire clan. Jephthah replies that Ephraim had refused to help when called upon and that he had been forced to deal with the enemy alone. Jephthah then musters Gilead in the presence of an already mobilized enemy. This task must have been much more difficult than the brief record here indicates. Jephthah then defeats the Ephraimites. Ephraim's pejorative remarks seem to motivate the Gileadites to greater efforts.

The harsh treatment of the Ephraimite fugitives at the fords of the Jordan (vv. 5–6) reflects the powerful, divisive antagonisms that sometimes existed between the various groups of Israelites. A deliberate literary anticipation of the monarchy may be found in the contrast between David's generally conciliatory policies toward fellow Israelites and Jephthah's vengeful policies. The two pronunciations of the word *shibboleth* (v. 6) illustrate the presence of dialectical variations within the Hebrew language. Perhaps the weakening of Ephraim accomplished by this war was necessary before a king from any other tribe could be accepted.

Three more minor judges now come to attention (**12:8–15**). In the popular mind of that time, Ibzan's many children and, by implication, numerous wives and concubines, reflect his greatness and prestige. Marrying his children "outside his clan" (v. 9) builds alliances that could circumvent intertribal strife like that of the Ephraimite civil war. Most dating schemes, early and late, place Ibzan in the time of the Philistines and Samson. This makes it easier to locate Ibzan in the north at the Zebulunite Bethlehem. Nothing is known about Elon (vv. 11–12) beyond the sparse data in these verses. Abdon of Ephraim again has the prestige of a large family and many consorts. The reference to the hill country of the Amalekites (v. 15) is puzzling. It would seem to refer to a region settled by Amalekite Bedouin. They may have been a part of the horde of Gideon's time which settled in Ephraim and lived peaceably with their neighbors, since there is no hint of hostility in this reference.

By the time of Samson (ca. 1075 B.C.), the Philistines had arrived in full strength and were well established on the southern coast of Palestine. Prior to the twelfth century B.C., the Israelites had dealt only with isolated trade colonies of Philistines. Over the years the Philistines had been driven from Crete by pressures from other invaders from the north. As part of the Peoples of the Sea (ca. 1200 B.C.) they had both invaded Egypt and served as mercenaries in the armies that defended Egypt. They received Egyptian permission to settle in Palestine where, by this time, they were in the process of establishing a small mercantile empire over the Israelites and other indigenous peoples. The Philistines brought to this effort a superior military organization and training as well as an advanced metals technology (1 Sam. 13:19–22). They brought the Iron Age to Palestine and gave their name to the region. This is the context in which Samson exercises his judgeship.

Of the six examples of the recurrent pattern, the Samson account is the only one that does not specifically mention the people "crying out" in repentance. The account consists of a number of miraculous events tightly structured around three periods of Samson's life: his birth, his rise to the judgeship, and his fall. The Bible credits Samson only with beginning the deliverance of Israel (13:5); his work as a deliverer was never complete. The miracles in Samson's life are difficult for many people to accept. Samson lived in an age when fabulous, miraculous events were expected. It is not strange that an omnipotent God would work miracles in such an age.

The pattern begins with sin and judgment comes through the recently arrived Philistines (**13:1**). Most scholars take this Philistine oppression as beginning concurrently with the Ammonite oppression.

The record of Samson's birth (**13:2–25**) contains several miraculous elements which serve as signs that God is working with his people. First, Samson is a miracle child. His mother is barren, and he is born only through special divine intervention. The angel of the Lord appears to Samson's mother and promises her a child. She is to drink no wine or other alcoholic drinks, and must not eat anything unclean. The first two restrictions suggest that she, like the Nazirite, has been consecrated to God. The Nazirite restrictions apply to her child as well. Samson's mother reports all this to her husband.

This report prompts her husband to request that the oracle be repeated to him as well. Manoah's request is deemed worthy. The Lord responds to Manoah, but not with instructions about how to bring up the child (Manoah's prayer). Rather, the instructions already given to the woman are simply confirmed.

Manoah asks if he might entertain the angel, and the messenger promises to wait until an offering is made to God. Manoah asks the messenger's name; the angel replies that his name is completely beyond human comprehension. Finally the offering is made and miraculously consumed by a fire from heaven; Manoah realizes that he has dealt with God himself. He falls into a panic, and tells his wife that they are doomed to die. Manoah's wife maintains a very commonsense attitude toward the whole business. God would not have done all this just to kill them! The mother of the promised deliverer shows true faith.

After his birth, his mother names the child "Samson." This name is a derivative of a Semitic word for "sun" and "sun-god." By this time, however, the name was probably religiously neutral despite its pagan origins. The chapter closes with the observation that Samson is stirred by the spirit of God (v. 25). This may refer to arousing in Samson's mind a concern for the issues that are essential to God's purposes.

As Samson reaches maturity, the deeply rooted sensuality dominating his character appears (**14:1–4**). Samson typifies the man who is clearly chosen by God and who is to be used by God, but who does not let the divine calling temper his own sensual passions. Despite that failure, the miraculous deeds associated with Samson's unfortunate marriage establish him as judge over the Israelites.

Samson wants to marry a young Philistine woman from Timnah. By this time, Philistine settlement had progressed into the western foothills (Heb. *šĕpēlāh*) almost to the edge of the mountain country of Judah. Relations between the Philistines and the Israelites were cordial enough that an intercultural marriage was possible. That social and religious barriers between Philistines and Hebrews still remained is clear from his father's reference to *uncircumcised Philistines* (v. 3). "Getting" a wife indicates that Samson, at this point, contemplates a conventional marriage in which the bride joins her husband's family.

Samson's desired marriage is "from the Lord" (v. 4), not in the sense that Samson's deeds represent God's positive, moral will. Rather, since Samson is a sensual, impious man, God uses his impiety to create an occasion against the Philistines who are ruling over Israel.

During the marriage negotiations two miraculous wonders occur (**14:5–9**). First, Samson tears a young lion apart with his bare hands while filled with God's miraculous power. We must here deal with the issue of Samson and legends. Certainly the Samson account demonstrates literary qualities of a legend. However, assuming that God really worked wonders in the life of Samson, it is not surprising that those wonders are recorded in a literary form similar to the fictional wonder stories of that time. In a setting where God can and does work miracles, this literary form in itself does not prove that the accounts are untrue.

A second miracle takes place some time later when a swarm of bees takes up residence in the lion's carcass and produces a supply of honey. Coming from a corpse, this honey would be unclean to any orthodox Israelite and especially to a Nazirite like Samson. Again, Samson shows a flagrant disregard of his spiritual calling and status.

The details of Samson's wedding feast (**14:10–20**) indicate that the bride's family rejects a conventional marriage with an Israelite in lieu of a "beena" or "sadiqa" marriage.[6] Normally, the feast would be at the groom's home with the groom's compatriots serving as his "companions." Samson's feast is at the bride's home with Philistine companions.

Samson's wedding feast catapaults him into a level of social competition clearly beyond his means. For wealthy aristocrats it is a matter of pride to risk and flaunt wealth with egotistic wagers. Early in the feast, Samson attempts to play his new social role by offering such a wager, a riddle based upon his experience with the honey in the lion's carcass (v. 14).

After trying unsuccessfully to solve the riddle for three days, the young Philistines extort the bride's help by threats of violence (v. 15). This incident demonstrates the insincerity of the cordiality and acceptance which the Philistines had shown to Samson. Samson's wife pressures him until he finally tells her the answer on the seventh day.

The conclusion of this drama is economically presented. The companions relate the solution of the riddle at the last moment (v. 18). It is obvious, even to Samson, that his wife has been disloyal. The immediate results are shocking and ominous. Samson, who cannot afford the aristocratic gamble, leaves without consummating the marriage and pays his wager by murdering thirty citizens of Ashkelon and plundering their goods. The bride's family assumes that Samson no longer wants their daughter. In order to save face, they give her to one of Samson's Philistine "friends."

Eventually Samson decides to consummate his marriage (**15:1–5**). Apparently, his marriage agreement called for a gift in return for a conjugal visit. When Samson learns that his marriage has been negated, he is furious and refuses to be appeased by the offer of the little sister as a substitute bride. Samson responds with the first of a series of violent acts of revenge. Despite Samson's unworthy motives, God uses these exchanges of violence to establish Samson as the divinely empowered leader, or judge, of the people. Samson burns the Philistine harvests by releasing foxes with torches tied to their tails among the dried fields, olive groves, and vineyards.

Conflict with the Philistines continues (**15:6–19**). The Philistine reprisal (v. 6) provokes another violent response on Samson's part, and "many" Philistines are killed (v. 8). Samson flees to Etam, south of Bethlehem, where the Philistines pursue him and negotiate with the men of

6. In such a marriage, the woman would remain with her own people and receive periodic conjugal visits from her husband. Her children would be considered part of her family.

Judah to hand Samson over to them. After Samson, bound by two new ropes, is handed over to the Philistines, God's miraculous power again comes upon him and Samson strikes down a thousand men.

Samson then creates a poetic pun (v. 16) between the similar sounding Hebrew words for "donkey" (Heb. *ḥămōr*) and "heaps" (Heb. *ḥōmer*). The location gains a new name from the incident (v. 17), one that includes the pun, "the hill of the jawbone" (Heb. *lĕḥî*) at "Lehi." One final incident occurs: the miraculous appearance of a spring which quenches Samson's thirst. As with the other signs, this miraculous event adds to Samson's prestige before his contemporaries and demonstrates to them that God is, indeed, working among his people.

These miraculous events, as contaminated with human sin as they are, establish Samson as judge. Samson judges Israel for twenty years (**15:20**). These twenty years should have been a time of deliverance. But Samson's sinful sensuality prevents him from delivering his people. Judges 16 highlights both the miraculous gifts of Samson and his final failure.

It is fair to assume that the few recorded incidents of Samson's life are typical of his general life-style. The story of Samson's visit to the prostitute at Gaza (**16:1–3**) confirms his continued sensuality. Structurally, this account is part of Samson's fall since it shows why that fall is inevitable. The prostitute was probably more like the entertaining courtesan described in Isaiah 23:15–17 than today's typical prostitute. The Philistines are delighted by the prospect of killing their enemy. The great exploit of carrying away the city gate illustrates God's grace in continuing to work through such a man as Samson. The "hill that faces Hebron" (v. 3) could have been a hill near Gaza which faced in the direction of Hebron.

Once again a relationship with a woman is crucial to Samson's career; Samson falls in love with a woman named Delilah in the Valley of Sorek (**16:4–21**). In modern terms, Samson takes Delilah as a mistress. Samson shows a lack of concern for moral principle, for public appearances, and for fraternizing with the enemy. The Philistine leaders know what kind of man they are dealing with and plot to exploit Samson's self-indulgence. Each of the five lords of the Philistines offers Delilah eleven hundred shekels of silver to betray Samson.

This account illustrates the misuse of God's miraculous signs. God's great deeds should witness to his works and character. Due to Samson's sensuality, his miraculous exploits witness only of his own seemingly magical talents rather than God's attributes. The miracles of God must be combined with godly piety before they can witness to genuine godliness. The Philistines hope to discover the secret behind Samson's great strength. Instead of a perception of God's glory, God's great signs through Samson merely stimulate an attempt to counteract a hostile magic.

Delilah sets out to earn her reward. It is difficult to comprehend Samson's naïveté and stupidity. Perhaps it is best understood as a self-imposed foolishness brought on by immorality and sensual intemperance. Willfully sinful men not only lose their insight into spiritual matters, but they may lose their insight into matters of common sense as well.

First, Delilah tries to counter Samson's strength by tying him up with seven undried thongs. With Philistine warriors waiting out of sight in the event of success, she wakes Samson up and discovers that the magic has not worked. In this and the second attempt, the special significance of something "new" may have added to Delilah's credulity. Delilah then ties Samson with new ropes, but this also fails to diminish Samson's strength. We may guess that Samson regarded these first two attempts to neutralize his strength as lover's pranks by a doting mistress.

Delilah next weaves Samson's hair into the fabric on a loom and locks it there. The traditional notion of weaving a fabric of fate together with locking in that fate might have influenced Delilah's decision to trust Samson's word.

Finally, Samson reveals the truth: his strength will disappear if his hair is cut. It is not clear that Samson really believed that this would happen. After his hair is cut, he attempts to get up and leave just as he had before. He is surprised to find that his strength is gone.

This time, Samson has gone too far in trifling with and profaning the holy things of God as they relate to his Nazirite status. Because of this irreverence, God's presence departs from Samson, and Samson's strength disappears. Delilah, though not fully understanding why, realizes better than Samson that this is decisive (v. 18).

Samson's strength departs, not because his "magical" hair has been cut, but because Samson has reached such a degree of irreverence that God can no longer work with him. God leaves him (v. 20). Samson is seized, and put in chains, and his eyes are gouged out.

While Samson is in prison, two things happen: his hair grows back and a measure of moral insight and faith comes to him. It is ironic that Samson has to be blinded before he can see spiritual issues. Separated from his sensual, debauched life-style, Samson is forced to reflect on spiritual realities. His spiritual growth is not profound; at his death his main concern is still personal revenge (v. 28) rather than God's glory. But there is sufficient spiritual growth that God's presence and power can return to Samson. Samson's hair is a fitting symbol for a small return to the proper attitudes of a Nazirite, but it is not a magical power source. The critical issue in the return of Samson's strength is the stature of his spirit, not the length of his hair.

Samson's life ends tragically (**16:22–31**). The Philistines hold a great religious festival to celebrate the victory of their god, Dagon, over Samson and, by implication, over Samson's God as well. Samson is brought out to entertain his captors; he maneuvers himself to a place between the two great pillars holding up the roof of the temple. It is to Samson's credit that, in an act of faith (Heb. 11:32), he turns to God for help. It is not to his credit that his desire in turning to God is for personal vengeance rather than God's glory. Samson dies in a spectacular way and kills many of his enemies at his death. However, his vengeance does not provide deliverance. The Israelites at the beginning of Samuel's judgeship were still firmly under Philistine control. Samson probably succeeded in bringing twenty years of partial relief from the Philistines, but he leaves his people in bondage at his death.

The Philistines permit Samson's family to come and retrieve his body for honorable burial. This graciousness may have resulted either from respect for Samson's human greatness or a superstitious desire to be rid of even the corpse of such a formidable enemy.

II. The Collapse of Society (17–21)

A. The breakdown of religious life: Micah's idol (17–18). The focus of the Book of Judges is the total collapse of Israel's society under the judges. The first sixteen chapters describe this failure in terms of covenant breaking, first in failing to complete the conquest (1:1–2:5) and second by sharing in the repeated pattern of sin, judgment, repentance, and deliverance (2:6–16:31). The third section (chaps. 17–21) presents the final result of such failure, the total collapse of society into anarchic chaos. The characteristic description of chaos is "everybody did as he saw fit" (17:6). These chapters are not appendices, but are integral to the book's purpose. However, they are not a chronological extension of the first sixteen chapters; these events actually precede most of the events of the earlier chapters. Rather, they present the logical extension or results of covenant disobedience.

Judges **17** shows the decline of religious life into complacent religious syncretism. Of course, the heart of the offense is disobedience to the Law and covenant breaking.

The story begins with Micah's response to his mother's curse concerning some stolen money. In the popular mind, the effectiveness of a curse was real and could be counteracted only by a blessing from the person who uttered the curse. The incident displays a blending of Yahwistic ideas with idolatrous superstition. Micah is superstitiously fearful of a curse, but not attuned to true godliness. His mother is marked by the same decadent syncretism; she disobeys God and makes an idol in gratitude to him. It is not clear whether the image and the idol are two distinct objects or two parts of the same object. These religious wrongs are explicitly related to the absence of a king and the resulting anarchy (v. 6).

The period's religious syncretism is even more evident in the young Levite's agreement to join in Micah's illegal, idolatrous worship (vv. 7–8). Micah's naive, complacent confidence that God will bless him because he has installed a Levite priest illustrates the most shocking feature of this time. The people have apparently lost the ability to distinguish between God's truth and pagan syncretism. There is a naive desire to "trust in" God while engaging in clear-cut covenant disobedience.

The Danite migration probably occurred quite early in the period of the judges (ca. 1360 B.C.), prior to the career of Samson. The placement of this episode near the end of Judges (chap. 18) simply reflects the topical structure of the book. The Danites failed to conquer their allotted land (1:34). The account of Samson with its record of the intermingling of Philistines and Israelites shows the precarious hold Israel later had on the territories allotted to Dan (chap. 13). Because of this failure, part of the tribe seeks to migrate to a new location.

It is possible that a variation of this story, at some time, was used to explain the origins of a well-known, illegal shrine of Dan in the north. However, in the Book of Judges, it shows how the complacent syncretism of Micah's household spread throughout an entire tribe and raised the corruption of the nation to a new level. It also places this religious syncretism in a setting of political disobedience and international disorder.

Dan's failure to conquer their allotment is, in terms of the book's ideology, a demonstration of lack of faith and covenant disobedience. Furthermore, since they are aggressively seeking other lands, not specifically assigned to them by God's covenant, their expansionistic efforts fall under God's condemnation (cf. Amos 1:13). All the Danite clans are represented in the hunt for a new location (**18:1–10**).

The Danite scouts make their way north and find themselves at Micah's house. A familiar voice catches the attention of the spies. The focus of this section is the complacent, uncritical acceptance of the idolatry and syncretism of Micah's shrine. The Danites feel no embarrassment at inquiring of Yahweh in this context of blatant disobedience to God's Law. Nor does the Levite hesitate to speak for Yahweh out of such a context.

Moving northward, the Danite scouts find a confident, apparently secure, Sidonian colony at Laish which is actually more vulnerable to attack than the Danites' southern neighbors. This colony may represent an abortive attempt at inland colonization by the coastal seafaring Phoenicians. For the most part, Phoneician colonization extended westward on the coasts of the Mediterranean. Eastern Phoenician influence was typically by political alliance rather than colonization. The time was inopportune for inland colonies; the political chaos of the age presented a threat to them as this account illustrates.

When the Danite spies return home they give their recommendations to their fellow tribesmen. This tribal conference is governed by greed and opportunism covered by a thin veneer of ignorant piety. It is easy and convenient to rationalize selfish desires by saying that the opportunity to fulfill them is God's guidance to do so.

The strength of Dan may be approximated by the number of men who move northward (**18:11–26**). Six hundred men may represent most of the strength of a weaker tribe. As the expedition moves northward, leaving their name at a site in Judah (v. 12), another opportunity presents itself. The five spies indicate that there are gods available for the seizing. The casualness of this decision to steal Micah's gods stands out. None of the religious restraints of pure Yahwism deter the Danites from their scheme. There is no feeling that a god who can be stolen is, for that reason, undesirable. The spies simply go in and steal gods for their tribe.

Micah's Levite has no moral qualms about changing his loyalties. Brute power and superstitious religious syncretism are the realities of his life. It would be more prestigious, and probably more remunerative, to serve a whole tribe even if it is a weak tribe on the move.

Micah and his neighbors arm themselves to seize back their gods. The response of the Danites amounts to blatant extortion. Once again, moral principle is irrelevant; the Danites possess the power to enforce their theft if necessary and make no attempt to be subtle in their threat to use this force. Covenant disobedience, religious syncretism, and social anarchy go hand in hand.

The Danites move northward, massacre the people of Laish, and seize their land (**18:27–31**). From this time on, Dan, as long as it existed as a recognizable tribal entity, was located in the north. The historical significance of the event is twofold: first, it accounts for the presence of the Danites in the north; and second, it accounts for the presence of a significant but illegal shrine in the north. For the theology of Judges, this account underscores the insecurity, violence, and anarchy of life lived in disobedience to God's covenant.

It is not necessary to date this episode in the second generation from Moses since the phrase *son of Gershom* (v. 30) is more likely to indicate clan membership than immediate paternity. The "captivity" (v. 30) was an early, local tragedy that probably occurred during the time of the judges.

B. The breakdown of justice and civil order: civil war (19–21). These chapters further describe the moral deterioration that accompanies covenant unfaithfulness. They also demonstrate that moral deterioration leads to political and civil disaster. The logical order between this and chapters 17–18 is significant. Chapters 17–18 relate the breakdown of religious life; chapters 19–21 show that the breakdown of religious life may bring further disastrous consequences, that the resulting immorality can threaten the very existence of a political unit. Society is a unity; its depravity cannot be contained within narrow, watertight compartments. Depravity and breakdown in one area of society, if uncorrected, will lead to deterioration and breakdown in other areas and, finally, even to the destruction of society itself.

The writer of Judges maintains that these events occurred because there were no qualified leaders to effect God's purposes. Though the judges could engineer brief periods of peace, there was no established godly leadership capable of permanently halting the evils described in these chapters. "Israel had no king" expresses both the writer's diagnosis of the disease in Israel and his indication of the cure.

Judges 19 dramatically illustrates how a series of relatively minor evils and weaknesses can contribute to a major national disaster.

The series of events begins with the unfaithfulness (some versions read "anger") of a Levite's concubine (**19:1–21**), an offense which, in isolation, would hardly cause nationwide repercussions. But, when moral offenses are widespread and casually tolerated, their consequences may become devastating.

Reconciliation is achieved after her husband visits her father's house. Then, just as the Levite is preparing to return home with his wife, a seemingly harmless weakness appears, a lack of resolve in his determination to return to the necessary business of life. There is nothing overtly sinful in this feeling; this quality can even be a virtue in fostering warm human relations. But an excessive lack of resolve, as this account shows, may prove disastrous.

The Levite, pressed by his father-in-law's good cheer, repeatedly delays his departure until he finally feels compelled to leave. By the time the journey begins, it is too late to get home. Under normal conditions, this should have been nothing more than a minor inconvenience.

It becomes necessary for the party to seek lodgings for the night. In light of later events, the Levite's refusal to seek hospitality from the Gentile Jebusites is most ironic. The party decides to seek hospitality and shelter from the Benjamites of Gibeah instead.

It is difficult to believe that the depravity of Gibeah is a complete secret. Certainly the Ephraimite host knows that something is wrong. Likely there have been hints all along; but the easy toleration of evil generally seen in these chapters causes any such hints to be disregarded. An entire community has chosen a congenial toleration of evil rather than confronting and judging it.

By this time, a series of slight failures and bad judgments have, without their knowledge, put the Levite's party in a precarious position. The first clear evidence of trouble is their slowness in finding hospitality for the night (v. 15). Finally, an Ephraimite living in Gibeah invites them in.

The full extent of the danger becomes clear when the men of the city demand the opportunity to assault the strangers homosexually. It is difficult for contemporary Westerners to understand the willingness of both the old Ephraimite and the Levite to turn their women over to the mob. The old Ephraimite, like Lot (Gen. 19:6–8), may have felt obligated to protect a guest at any cost whatsoever. However, it is difficult to identify with the Levite's callous disregard for his concubine. He sends her out to the crowd; she is brutally raped and murdered (**19:22–26**).

The Levite's shocking callousness about his concubine's fate continues into the morning. He curtly orders her to come with him, with no apparent concern about the abuse she has suffered. When he discovers that she is dead, the Levite goes home and then uses his concubine's body for a gruesome object lesson. He cuts the corpse into pieces and sends one piece to each tribe as his demand for justice (**19:27–30**). The response to this crime is typical. Men tend to disregard and tolerate evil until it becomes so blatant that it can be tolerated no further. Then they go to the opposite extreme and feel great surprise, horror, and shock at the logical consequences of the very evils they have been complacently tolerating.

All the nation—except the Benjamites—gather at Mizpah to purge the nation (**20:1–17**). The phrase *Dan to Beersheba* (v. 1) could indicate a date after the Danite migration north or it could be a later writer's expression for "all Israel" even though the events recorded predate the conditions behind that phrase. In spite of their evil and apostasy, the nation is still the covenant "people of God" (v. 2a). The number of warriors (four hundred thousand, v. 2; twenty-six thousand, v. 15) seems unreasonably high. There are three possible explanations: (1) God miraculously brought about a large population; (2) the term *thousand* (Heb. *'elef*) was not an exact arithmetic quantity; or (3) numbers, of all types of biblical data, are most liable to textual corruption. Benjamin's absence indicates its willingness to defend the sin of fellow tribesmen.

The Levite gives a straightforward account of what has happened without any evidence of personal shame. Unfortunately, his behavior seems to fit the customs of the time.

As shown by their powerful oath (v. 8; cf. 21:1), the people have passed from an easy toleration of evil to demanding judgment. They decide that God should direct the course of battle through sacred lots. But they also keep their army provisioned through prudent human efforts. An easy, nationwide toleration of evil has led the nation to the brink of civil war.

The Benjamites are faced with a difficult choice: whether to join in the moral outrage of the nation or whether to stand by their fellow tribesmen. A Westerner may have difficulty understanding the strong kinsman ties prevalent in the Near East even today. The Arab still says, "My brother and I against my cousin; my cousin and I against the stranger." The Benjamites choose tribal loyalty over moral principle and mobilize for war in defense of the men of Gibeah.

There is a significant anachronism in the

epic ideals of warfare of this time. The epic ideal was the valiant "mighty hero" who single-handedly could kill tens, even scores, of the enemy. Occasionally this ideal still worked out in practice as in Jonathan's victory at Micmash (1 Sam. 13:23–14:14). But a new age was already emerging, one in which the disciplined battle line overshadowed the individual warrior and one in which either an archer or a slinger was becoming more important tactically. The careful mention of the skill of the Benjamite slingers (v. 16) is the writer's recognition of the importance of these soldiers and their skills. The Benjamites' confidence in mobilizing against their fellow Israelites may have been based upon the thought that the nation lacked the moral conviction to fight a war over this sin.

The Israelites deserve praise for seeking God's will in conducting the war even though their efforts would be initially unsuccessful (**20:18–26**). Bethel is the site of the nation's central religious shrine (v. 27). It is a mark of grace that God's leadership is available. There is no other reason why God should have communicated with such a corrupt, apostate people.

However, God often has hard lessons for his people even after they have repented. The Israelites advance into rough country, ideal for defense and the use of missile warriors. The first day's fighting ends in a decisive defeat for Israel at the hands of the Benjamites.

The men of Israel encourage one another to continue rather than collapsing in the face of defeat. They again seek an oracle from God, and obey God's words. This obedience is severely tested by yet another defeat. The continued struggle for right seems to result only in more bitter lessons. Though there is grief and mourning, the people's resolve does not flag. They grieve but continue steadfast in their resolve to deal with the great sin.

The Israelites also continue steadfast in their desire to discern God's leading in their conduct of the political crisis. This time their faithfulness is to be rewarded with victory (**20:27–48**). The Israelites neutralize the superior battle skills of the Benjamites with clever tactics. In addition to the obvious army mobilized in battle against the Benjamite army, the Israelites set up a second picked force which is to attack the defenseless city of Gibeah from the rear and to ambush the Benjamites when they return to face this new threat.

The plan is completely successful; the Benjamites come out and appear to be victorious as before. At this point, some scholars find fault with the Hebrew account, which recapitulates a number of details. This is no more than an oddity of Hebrew prose style. The writer backs up to repeat the false retreat (v. 36b; cf. vv. 32–33a) and the ambush upon Gibeah (v. 37; cf. vv. 33b–34). The addition of a new detail, the smoke signal (v. 38), could well have justified this repetition to the Hebrew stylist. The Benjamites see the smoke, realize that disaster has come upon them, and panic.

The remaining events show the bitterness of war. This bitterness is probably due more to revenge for the losses of the earlier two battles than to zeal for righteousness. Gibeah is destroyed, and all but six hundred Benjamites are killed in the rout. The Israelites then turn back and massacre all the women, children, and men too old for war who are left in the territory of Benjamin. By this time the potential impact of sin upon the body politic is well illustrated. One of Israel's tribes is almost totally destroyed as an indirect result of an easy, congenial tolerance of sin.

Now that the Benjamites have been defeated and nearly exterminated, the Israelites have another change of heart. They had maintained an easy indulgence toward depravity, until a horrible sin shocked them into moral sensitivity. Then they turned to such a great commitment to judgment and vengeance that they had sworn that no man of Israel would let his daughter intermarry with the Benjamites. Now they regret that the Benjamites have been practically decimated (**21:1–4**). The situation is more acute since Israelite women, by oath, could not be given to the Benjamite survivors. Perhaps a prayerful release from a rash oath would have been better than the continued violence which actually occurs.

Judges 21 well expresses the nation's sense of wholeness. There were twelve tribes (actually thirteen, but with various well-known conventions to keep the official number at twelve). Something irreplaceable would have been lost if a tribe became extinct (cf. vv. 3, 6, 17). The Israelites know why the tragedy has occurred—because of sin. Their rhetorical question (v. 3) is a way of expressing grief at the course of events.

Two steps are taken to find wives for the Benjamites. The first involves a harsh reprisal against Jabesh-gilead which had failed to join the anti-Benjamite campaign (**21:5–14**). The city is massacred and approximately four hundred virgins are brought back as wives for the Benjamites. However, there are still not enough wives for all the Benjamite survivors.

The elders of the assembly address the problem of procuring two hundred additional wives. The tribal elders, obviously without the knowledge of the elders of Shiloh, decide upon the scheme recorded in Judges **21:15–24.** The remaining Benjamites kidnap wives from among the young women of Shiloh at their great annual festival. This matter is then resolved with the people of Shiloh. The Benjamites return to their territories with their new wives to rebuild their tribal life and their cities.

The Book of Judges closes with an analysis as to why these terrible events occurred: there was no king in Israel (**21:25**). There was no king to embody the concept of the ideal, godly leader. There was no king to exemplify and enforce religious loyalty to the covenant. There was no king to expedite the conversion and assimilation of the Canaanites—or the annihilation of those who resisted. There was no king to maintain public order and to prevent outrages such as the one in Gibeah. There was no king to prevent these evil trends from culminating in a murderous civil war.

Actually the consequences of the evils recorded in this book were more tragic than indicated. Even in the Old Testament, God's general purpose was to use Israel as his holy priest-nation (Exod. 19:6) to reach the entire world. Therefore, the breakdown in God's purposes recorded in this book are not merely a setback for his plans for one nation. These failures represent a setback for God's worldwide purposes for all mankind.

SELECT BIBLIOGRAPHY

Cundall, A. E. *Judges: An Introduction and Commentary*. The Tyndale Old Testament Commentaries. Downers Grove: Inter-Varsity, 1968.

Garstang, J. *Joshua-Judges*. Reprint. Grand Rapids: Kregel, 1978.

Moore, G. F. *A Critical and Exegetical Commentary on Judges*. The International Critical Commentary. Edinburgh: T. & T. Clark, 1895.

Wood, L. *A Survey of Israel's History*. Grand Rapids: Zondervan, 1970.

RUTH

R. K. Harrison

INTRODUCTION

The author of this delightful little book remains unnamed in the Scriptures, the book taking its title from one of its chief characters, a Moabite woman. The historical setting of the events described is that of the period of the judges (1:1), but this does not necessarily mean that the work was written at that time. In fact, it is much more probable that Ruth was composed in a later period, for two important reasons. First, the concluding genealogy (4:18–22) brings the narrative up to the time of David, who was obviously familiar to author and readers alike, and thus would require a date of composition in the early kingdom period at the very least. Second, the account contains some explanation of legal practices (4:1–12), required since they were already ancient. Thus it would seem that some time had elapsed between the events described and their appearance in written form.

The ancient Jews maintained that the prophet Samuel was the author of both Judges and Ruth, since they reflected the same social and historical background. This, however, seems hardly likely. Although Samuel certainly knew of David, having anointed him as Saul's successor (1 Sam. 16:1–13), he had died (1 Sam. 25:1) long before David had become well known as Israel's king. Some scholars have thought of the work as fictitious, and having had its origins in unspecified mythology. Others have suggested that Ruth is a postexilic work written to combat the rigorous mixed-marriage legislation of Ezra and Nehemiah. These views are refuted by the opening words *wayĕhî* (KJV, RV and it came to pass), which is the standard introduction to historical narrative (see Josh. 1:1; Judg. 1:1), showing that the writer wished his work to be recognized as historical. It is best, therefore, to regard the author as an anonymous scribe with outstanding literary gifts who recorded what was certainly a familiar story for the benefit of his own people, and for the blessing of those who have read the account ever since. The general literary style suggests a date in the early monarchy period, although nothing in the book points to a precise time of origin. The place where Ruth was written is also unmentioned in the book, but it was most probably composed in or near Jerusalem.

The story of Ruth's romance with Boaz must have been immensely popular, especially among Israel's women, during the lawless and morally degenerate period of the judges. Naomi, Ruth's mother-in-law, would never have tired of telling the story of how deprivation in Moab had been turned into blessing in Israel by the all-powerful Lord of the covenant. The women who were present at the time of the marriage and the subsequent birth of a cherished grandson for Naomi would also have told the story in praising the Lord for his goodness to the desolate woman. Their expectation that this heir of Boaz would rise to prominence in the nation (4:14) would itself perpetuate interest in the offspring of Obed, whose grandson was the renowned Israelite king David.

The book, therefore, comes from predominantly oral sources handed down over a few generations, with all the careful repetition of detail normally associated with the transmission of ancient Semitic pedigrees. While the atmosphere of the book is different from that of much of the Judges period, the narrative of Ruth depicts a time of peace between Moab and Israel such as that which followed the activities of Ehud (Judg. 3:12–30). The concluding genealogy, which traces Boaz's family back to Perez, one of the twin sons born to Tamar through her father-in-law Judah (Gen. 38:24–30), would have come directly from the family records of Boaz himself. The restraint and dignity of the literary style make it most unlikely that anything extraneous was added to the story, which was essentially an intimate look at life in an ordinary Israelite family. To regard the work as fiction is completely out of character with scribal activity in the ancient Near East, which was concerned with the recording of factual material as opposed to the modern type of "creative writing," which itself is seldom a pure product of the writer's imagination.

The book is striking for the way in which the principal characters exhibit an abiding faith in the Lord of Israel's covenant. They know that he is alive (3:13), and although they might be oppressed by various eventualities in life, they trust him to turn adversity into blessing. The name generally used in Ruth for God is Yahweh, which had been revealed formally to Israel at the time of the exodus, and characterized the almighty covenant God who promised to bless his chosen people as long as they honored him alone as their true and living God. At a time when her faith was enduring considerable stress, Naomi used the less personal name *Shaddai,* "Almighty" (1:20, 21), though even here she names Israel's covenant deity as the One who had directed her life. The dedication and kindness of Ruth to her bereft mother-in-law stands in sharp contrast to the attitude of Orpah, and reflects the true self-giving love of God which underlies both the Old and New Covenants.

The emphasis upon God as Israel's Redeemer is fundamentally important in the book, as indicated by over twenty occurrences of the Hebrew *gā'al,* "to redeem," in various forms. The idea was thus common in contemporary Israel, and in addition to its spiritual significance in the covenant it was a prescribed part of family law (Lev. 25:25). As Israel's Redeemer, the Lord maintained his status as One ready to protect the nation and deliver it from adversity. That was his right alone under the covenant as long as Israel walked in his ways. The compassion and rectitude of Boaz stand in this tradition, and furnish a remarkable foreshadowing of the work for human salvation achieved by his most illustrious descendant, Jesus Christ.

The motivating force of the Sinai covenant is *ḥesed,* a Hebrew term difficult to translate by one word, but which reflects the selfless compassion, kindness, and grace that is fundamental to God's nature. The concept exercises a transforming function as it possesses the individual and the community. The *ḥesed* underlying the charitable, selfless acts of Ruth and Boaz transforms Naomi's life from one of despair to a fulfilled existence of divine blessing. Similarly the Israelites were transformed from a threatened, anarchic existence in the early days of Samuel into a cohesive nation which, in the time of Solomon, enjoyed unparalleled peace, prosperity, and international supremacy. Such blessings, however, come only when the believer is consistently obedient to God's revealed will. Similarly under the New Covenant ushered in by Jesus, descendant of Boaz and David, God's gift of eternal life is realized only in the believer's experience through continuing faith and obedience.

The Book of Ruth is outstanding among the Old Testament historical narratives for its concise descriptions, development of dramatic suspense, portrayal of human-interest situations, and above all for its spiritual message of the benefits accruing to those who obey the Lord of the covenant. The work is divided symmetrically into four main sections, prefixed by an introduction and followed by a conclusion. It is thus a model of balance in the field of narrative literature.

In English Bibles Ruth occurs between Judges and Samuel. This follows the order of the Septuagint and locates it correctly with the historical books. The ancient Jewish authorities attached great importance to the book by requiring it to be read at the Feast of Weeks, when the end of the grain harvest was celebrated. The book was included in the third great division of the Hebrew canon (*Kethubim*) among the Megilloth or Scrolls. In later Jewish tradition Ruth was placed at the head of this section, preceding the Psalms.

OUTLINE

I. Introduction (1:1–5)
II. Return to Bethlehem (1:6–22)
III. Ruth Encounters Boaz (2:1–23)
IV. Ruth Visits the Threshing Floor (3:1–18)
V. Boaz Redeems and Marries Ruth (4:1–17)
VI. Concluding Genealogy (4:18–22)

COMMENTARY

I. Introduction (1:1–5)

This section introduces us to the principal characters of the story. The narrative is placed in the Judges period, possibly between 1380 and 1050 B.C., in a time of friendly relations with Moab and peace for the Israelites (cf. Judg. 3:11; 5:31). Famine had devastated southern Judah, compelling Elimelech and his family to cross the Jordan and live in the large grain-producing uplands (Heb. field) of Moab, visible to the east of the Dead Sea. It is ironic that Bethlehem ("house of bread") has an empty granary. The locating of the town "in Judah" is done to distinguish it from another, more northerly Bethlehem (see Josh. 19:15).

The name *Elimelech* is found in fourteenth-century B.C. cuneiform letters, and thus is very old. Like many other Semitic names it has the designation of Godhead in it, in this case the common term *el.* Thus the whole name could mean "God is my king." "Naomi" is also an ancient name, probably a feminine form of a fifteenth-century B.C. Canaanite word meaning "pleasant." The meanings of Mahlon and Kilion are uncertain. While ancient names generally reflected circumstances of birth or what the parents imagined their offspring were, or would become, we are far from certain of many meanings, especially of those names ending in *-yah* or *-iah.* The family is spoken of as Ephrathite, an ancient name for Bethlehem (Gen. 35:19) that carries with it here the more recent form.

Naomi's troubles begin when her husband dies. Her sons had married Moabite women named Orpah and Ruth (these names are of uncertain meaning, being Moabite). Under covenantal law the Hebrews were not prevented from intermarrying with Moabites, who were the offspring of an incestuous liaison between Lot and his elder daughter (Gen. 19:33). They were not allowed, however, to admit a Moabite to the Lord's congregation earlier than the tenth generation (Deut. 23:3–4), because the Moabites had not been hospitable to Israel as the nation came up from the wilderness preparatory to invading Canaan.

Furthermore, the Moabites had hired Balaam to curse Israel (Num. 22:4–6), and subsequently tried to destroy the holiness of the nation by introducing the Israelite soldiers to the corrupt worship of Baal of Peor (Num. 25:1–3; 31:15–16). The Israelites generally viewed the Moabites with suspicion, even when they were under firm Israelite control during the kingdom period. After a decade of marriage both Mahlon and Kilion die without leaving offspring. This eventuality desolates Naomi, who is now without any real means of support. Life for widows was precarious at best in the ancient Near East unless they were attached to some family. It is significant that the first form of social work undertaken by the primitive Christian church in Jerusalem was among needy widows (see Acts 6:1–6). Without a male provider a widow was vulnerable to exploitation of various kinds, and if she could not find a family in which to live and work she was reduced to begging, prostitution, and often death by starvation. Naomi's sole relatives in Moab are her daughters-in-law, and the future of the family unit looks bleak.

II. Return to Bethlehem (1:6–22)

A. Plans to leave Moab (1:6–7). The Book of Ruth places a characteristic emphasis upon the sovereignty of God in human life, and his gracious provision for those who love his law and trust in him completely. In the ancient world news of events was carried to a large extent by caravan traders, mariners, and other travelers. As a result, ancient peoples were usually well informed about current events (see Num. 21:1; 22:4–5), unless they lived in a remote area of a country such as Egypt. Tidings accordingly reach Moab that the famine has abated in Canaan, an eventuality that is attributed quite properly to the Lord's compassion for his people. Suddenly her homeland beckons to Naomi, and she clearly feels that she, Orpah, and Ruth will be able to partake in some way of the nation's prosperity by returning as a family. Once among her own people, Naomi and her daughters-in-law could expect to receive the humane treatment that Israelite law accorded to widows (Deut. 14:29; 16:11; etc.). Orpah and Ruth assist in the preparations for return, and obviously care for Naomi's welfare to the point of being willing to accompany her to Canaan.

B. An unselfish gesture (1:8–14). Of course, the two Moabite women were not compelled to return to Palestine with Naomi, who, seeing that they might ultimately regret leaving their homeland, offers them the option of remaining in Moab. The two women are evidently very attached to Naomi, and insist on accompanying her. However, she urges them to return home where in the Lord's mercy they might find husbands as a reward for the kindness that they had shown to Mahlon and Kilion. Though they protest, Naomi assures them that she is beyond childbearing, and thus unable to provide more sons to ensure the continuity of the line through levirate marriage (Deut. 25:5–6). Naomi is also unwilling to bring misfortune upon her daughters-in-law because she feels that her troubles have been sent by God. At this, Orpah is persuaded, and returns home.

C. Ruth returns with Naomi (1:15–22). Ruth, however, is adamant about accompanying Naomi to Bethlehem. During her life with Naomi she had forsaken the worship of the Moabite god Chemosh and had been converted to the faith of the covenant people. In a magnificent declaration of loyalty and dedication, Ruth pledges herself to Naomi's people. Her oath is sworn in the name of Israel's God, whom she accepts formally as her own.

The two women journey together to Bethlehem without incident, which itself is an indication of the Lord's protecting hand. Their arrival provokes excitement, and Naomi's old friends recognize her but apparently with some difficulty. She tells them not to call her Naomi, but Mara ("bitter") instead, because the Almighty had reversed her fortunes, changing her life from a full to an empty state. She speaks respectfully of God (Shaddai, "Almighty"), but in the characteristic Hebrew manner she regards him as the ground of all existence, whether evil or good. While she is complaining about her misfortune (Heb. the Lord has afflicted me), therefore, she should be regarded as reporting upon the trend of events, and not blaming God for disasters in the way that many Gentiles normally do.

The reader is thus left with a picture of a desolate Naomi, which stirs interest about the possibility of her renewal under a loving and provident God. Ruth is here given her formal designation as "the Moabitess," which heightens the interplay between the native Israelites and a foreign woman who would by definition be viewed with suspicion. The barley harvest was in God's mercy an excellent time to arrive in Bethlehem, because it meant employment for the womenfolk, who normally bound the cut grain into sheaves. The harvesting began in April, and was followed in May by the wheat harvest. Naomi and Ruth could not bind sheaves, not being members of a family, but were at least permitted to glean after the harvesters. Already the Lord of Israel was preparing to refill the bereft Naomi, and this prospect quickens the reader's interest accordingly.

III. Ruth Encounters Boaz (2:1–23)

A. Ruth commences work (2:1–3). Apparently the reason why Naomi chose to return to Bethlehem rather than to any other town in Judah was that her late husband had relatives there. The narrative does not mention this, however, so as not to obscure or compromise the Lord's working in the lives of Naomi and Ruth. The relative is from the family group of Elimelech, and his name is Boaz, perhaps meaning "there is strength in him." He is prominent in the town of Bethlehem, the result of his status as a landowner, since in antiquity social title was an accompaniment of holdings of land.

Ruth dutifully seeks Naomi's approval to secure gleaning work, an act which again brings Naomi fully into the process of restoration. Ruth's task is to follow the harvesters and claim as her own the barley and wheat stalks which they fail to cut down. This procedure was one way in which the Lord provided for the needs of the poor and destitute. Fields were not reaped then as thoroughly as in modern times, because landowners were instructed specifically in the Mosaic law not to reap the edges and corners (Lev. 19:9), but to harvest down the middle of the field. Even sharp flint sickles would leave some ears standing, and these, along with what was growing on the sides and corners of the field, were saved for the poor to reap and enjoy. Similarly, in the vineyards and olive groves, whatever fruit had fallen on the ground was to be left for the benefit of the oppressed and the foreigners (cf. Deut. 24:20–22). Gleaning would be arduous work because of competition among the poor for the ears of grain, which were available for those who chose to take them.

As a Moabite woman who had most probably been brought up in the eastern steppelands of her native country, Ruth would doubtless have worked among animals and crops, as the modern nomadic Bedouin women still do. Although Ruth is childless, there is no reason to think that she is not a typically hard-working, healthy, Trans-Jordanian female. The hand of God now appears evident in the story in that Ruth has been guided to a field belonging to Boaz. The Hebrew talks about Ruth's "chance" (NIV as it turned out), but Hebrew theology, which attributes everything that happens to the activity of an ever-present and all-powerful God, would have no difficulty in identifying the divine Author of such a gratifying circumstance.

B. Ruth's first encounter with Boaz (2:4–9). Barely has Ruth discovered the identity of the landowner when he arrives to supervise the harvesting. Work has already begun under the direction of a foreman, and Boaz greets the laborers with a wish for blessing that has long since passed into Jewish and Christian worship. The exchange of mutual blessings shows the friendly rapport existing between master and servants.

In this benevolent vein Boaz notices Ruth, and inquires of her family. In the ancient Near East life outside a family was impossible, and since Boaz does not recognize Ruth he is sufficiently concerned to inquire about her background. The foreman furnishes the required details, along with the fact that Ruth has requested permission to glean. The foreman himself has been keeping her under observation, and has noted the quality of her work. Even under the hot sun she takes only a brief rest interval.

Boaz speaks with affection and concern to Ruth, telling her to stay with his servant women, and to glean what they leave behind after binding the sheaves. The men are instructed not to interfere with her, and she is to have the same amenities as the workers belonging to the household.

C. Ruth's gracious acceptance of help (2:10–13). Such kindness merits humility and gratitude. Ruth adopts the position of a loyal servant to an overlord. She marvels at Boaz's beneficence, because as a stranger she has no inherent right to be gleaning, although her impoverished position certainly qualifies her for such a privilege. But Boaz has already learned of Ruth's kindness to Naomi, and he invokes blessings upon her from her newly found Lord. The "wings" of God express figuratively the ideas of protection (Exod. 19:4), the goal of the spiritual life (Isa. 40:31), healing (Mal. 4:2), and defense (Ps. 17:8). The imagery of a bird camouflaging its young with its wings as a protective measure is referred to by Christ (Matt. 23:37; Luke 13:34).

Ruth's reply shows that she is encouraged by Boaz's kindness to think that the future holds further favors, even though she is not from his household. Ruth behaves with dignity and respect to Boaz without appearing servile or ingratiating, and this seems to arouse his interest in her even further.

D. Ruth receives special favors (2:14–16). At the midday meal, consisting of roasted barley and a sauce of vinegar mixed with oil, Boaz invites Ruth to sit near him. All the harvesters seem to have eaten with Boaz, who takes special care of Ruth and gives her more of the roasted barley than she can eat. What is left is to be taken back to Naomi as her evening meal, a consideration that is doubtless observed by Boaz. The male harvesters are instructed specifically to let Ruth glean wherever she wants without any interference, and indeed to help her by leaving stalks for her to pick up. This is an additional indication of the Lord's abundant provision for the future.

E. Ruth reports to Naomi (2:17–23). Harvesters generally worked until dusk, and the servants of Boaz are no exception. His kindness to Ruth is shown in the amount of barley that she is able to collect and thresh. This latter operation consisted of beating out the ears with a stick. Ruth obtains nearly three-fifths of a bushel. Under ordinary circumstances a gleaner would have been well satisfied with about half that amount for a day's work. The divine blessings called down upon Ruth by Boaz have begun to materialize already.

On arriving home, Ruth displays her gleanings to an astonished Naomi, and also gives her the food saved from the noon meal. There can be no doubt of the genuine affection that Ruth has for her mother-in-law, even though Naomi has been in a depressed mental state for some time. When Ruth discloses the identity of her employer, Naomi's sadness lifts visibly in an exclamation of praise for God who cares for widows and needy children.

Boaz is already acting as a redeeming relative (or "kinsman-redeemer" in most modern English versions), and Naomi suddenly sees the Lord acting through a human agency to restore her fortunes and those of Ruth. She speaks of Boaz as a redeemer, and thus indicates to the reader that under the Law he has specific responsibilities toward family members such as herself and Ruth who are impoverished. Naomi's realization actually forms the turning point of the narrative, because now the provisions of the Law can be expected to take their course.

The duties which the redeeming relative was required to discharge included providing an heir to maintain the family line of a deceased brother (Deut. 25:5–10), avenging the killing of a family member (Num. 35:19–21), redeeming land sold outside the family (Lev. 25:25–28), and redeeming an impoverished relative who had been sold into slavery (Lev. 25:47–49). Up to this time Boaz has given no indication that he is related to Naomi, but concedes this subsequently (3:12).

When Ruth tells Naomi of the special consideration that Boaz has bestowed upon her, Naomi counsels her to do as she has been instructed. In this way she will not be molested sexually by some frolicking male harvester from another family group. Ruth continues working in the fields until all the wheat has been reaped in May, and must have accumulated a considerable amount of grain. Naomi would doubtless exchange some of this for other foodstuffs at the market. The Lord has indeed provided abundantly for the immediate needs of the two bereft women, who trust in his grace and mercy. This, however, is but the beginning of larger blessings for both of them.

IV. Ruth Visits the Threshing Floor (3:1–18)

A. Naomi's scheme to secure Boaz for Ruth (3:1–5). The reaping of the barley and wheat must have produced a substantial amount of grain, and for those involved would be highly gratifying. For Naomi, however, it meant that there would be no further work for Ruth until the olives and grapes were harvested. Consequently she is interested in a much more permanent situation for her daughter-in-law. Naomi is conscious of her responsibilities as a parent who, in the absence of a father, would be expected to secure an eligible husband for Ruth. Accordingly she makes plans to involve the redeeming relative in one aspect of his legal duties. The narrative makes no mention of Naomi undertaking any work in the fields, and it is possible that her physical strength was too debilitated to permit such strenuous activity. In any event, it seems highly probable from the narrative that Ruth would have summarily forbidden such work, even if Naomi had suggested it.

But now the mother-in-law becomes an agent of God's gracious provision. Toward the end of the barley harvest she speaks to Ruth about her desire to obtain a permanent home for her, since Ruth had provided so wonderfully for the impoverished Naomi. The Hebrew expresses this by the beautiful phrase *find rest* for her, with all that is involved in terms of security and comfort. Naomi is insistent that the accommodation should be ample (NIV well provided for), and there is only one person who could be relied upon to fulfill that expectation.

Two features of human psychology become evident here. The first is that the devisings of a calculating mother are formidable factors in any relationship, and cannot always be resisted successfully. The second is that men who are in love are not always articulate about their feelings, and sometimes need direct guidance in order to bring matters to a practical conclusion. Under God's approving hand Naomi determines to transform Boaz's expressed interest in Ruth into its logical fulfillment. Knowing country life and habits, she is aware that at the end of the barley harvest there would be a good deal of winnowing and heaping up of the grain into piles. Winnowing involved separating the grain from the chaff by tossing the beaten-out ears into the air and allowing wind currents to blow the chaff away. The end of harvesting was also celebrated by a feast (cf. Isa. 9:3) on the threshing floor, where the reapers often slept so as to guard the stored grain from marauders.

Naomi discovers when the feast will take place, and that Boaz will be there with the reapers. Ruth is instructed to wash and dress as a bride would and to go to the threshing floor without being seen. Although women were not encouraged to attend such feasts, prostitutes would occasionally ply their trade there. Ruth's "best clothes" would doubtless include a heavy cloak to ward off the night chill, and in which she would not be recognizable at dusk.

Naomi tells her precisely how to behave, and Ruth for her part promises implicit obedience. The excitement and apprehension in the hearts of the two women can only be imagined, as divine destiny pursues its course. The expression *uncover his feet* is a polite way of saying "expose his genitals," and has been taken by some commentators as a lewd gesture, and thus of dubious morality. In the curious mixture of sexual modesty and explicit expression found in the Scriptures, Naomi is merely providing the physical impetus necessary for Boaz to discharge his responsibilities as redeeming relative. All that Ruth is doing is lying with Boaz on the darkened threshing floor in a compromising position symbolizing marriage. With this, there could be no escape for Boaz.

B. Boaz accepts his responsibilities (3:6–14). Ruth does as she has promised Naomi, and observes where Boaz is feasting. Having feasted to his satisfaction, he retires to one end of the heap of grain and falls asleep. Ruth then uncovers him and lays down beside him. He awakens and is shocked to notice a woman beside him. In the darkness he cannot see her face, but when he asks who she is he discovers her identity. Ruth then formally requests that Boaz spread his covering over her, because he is a redeeming relative. In effect she is proposing marriage (cf. Ezek. 16:8) in a way still current in the East. The corners ("wings") of the garment remind the reader of the Lord's "wings" (2:12). Boaz must have realized suddenly that he is to become the Lord's protective agent for Ruth.

With characteristic kindness Boaz blesses Ruth instead of reprimanding her for immorality. He recalls her wonderful provision for Naomi (2:11–21), and praises her for her thoughtfulness to him. He is obviously deeply in love with Ruth, whom he addresses as "my daughter," and is flattered that she has chosen him, her evident senior, instead of flirting with the younger men. He makes a commitment to her immediately to redeem her, contingent upon the legal process. He praises her for her reputation amongst the townspeople as a noble and upright woman, thus representing her to the reader as a true counterpart to himself (2:1).

There is only one obstacle to the consummation of events, however. Boaz is not the only redeeming relative that Naomi has, for another man is even closer, and thus takes priority over Boaz. But that contingency could wait until morning. In the meantime, Ruth is instructed to stay with Boaz for the night, but she leaves discreetly before dawn so as not to compromise Boaz's character. For his part he reaffirms his determination to redeem her, taking an oath in the name of the Lord.

C. Ruth's joyful return (3:15–18). Boaz does not let Ruth return home empty-handed, but gives her six measures of unspecified weight of the winnowed barley and wraps it in a headdress or perhaps in a fold of her cloak. He is not required to do this, of course, but nevertheless he demonstrates his concern for Naomi. Boaz then returns to the town, while Ruth also goes home and is interrogated by an anxious Naomi. The generous gift of grain provides further evidence to Naomi that she is indeed being refilled. Nevertheless she counsels patience, knowing that Boaz will indeed fulfill his promise.

V. Boaz Redeems and Marries Ruth (4:1–17)

A. The redemption ceremony (4:1–10). Although Boaz is Naomi's choice as Ruth's future husband, the laws governing the redeeming relative gave the closest eligible family member the first right of levirate refusal. This contingency heightens the suspense of the narrative, because to this point there is no hint as to the outcome. The "city gate" was the open area inside the town entrance where business was generally transacted. Here Boaz could expect to meet his relative, and when he does the legal proceedings commence. As a highly respected citizen, Boaz has no difficulty securing the ten elders required for a proper legal ceremony.

The stated concern of Boaz is to redeem the land belonging to Naomi, and to give his unnamed kinsman the opportunity of purchasing it legally. The "land" had belonged to Naomi's late husband, and through Boaz she is exercising her legal right to redeem it. The kinsman-redeemer would purchase the land, thus restoring it to the family and providing a little capital for Naomi. This was a straightforward procedure, and the kinsman agrees readily to the purchase.

Had the narrative stopped here, the entire message of the story would have been frustrated and lost, for the intent of the narrator is the redemption not of property but of people. Boaz then introduces an unexpected complication to the redemption process, in which Naomi and Ruth are involved. Specifically Boaz invokes the levirate regulations (Deut. 25:5–10) by which the purchaser is required to marry the deceased relative's widow so as to maintain his line of descent. This would have threatened the relative's own line and property holdings had a son been born to him by Ruth, to say nothing of the altered state of family relations with the addition of two women to his household. By contrast with the kindly Boaz, the relative wants no responsibility for Naomi and Ruth, and accordingly withdraws from the proceedings.

The story alludes to the practice described in Deuteronomy 25:8–10, whereby the unwilling redeeming relative was humiliated by having his sandal removed. The process in Ruth is somewhat different, being apparently a later adaptation of the Deuteronomic levirate law and signifying the transfer of property, of which the sandal symbolized possession (cf. Josh. 1:3). When Boaz announces his redemption of the property and its female owners, he is testifying legally that he is assuming the heirship to Elimelech, and thus to Mahlon and Kilion also.

B. Blessings and marriage (4:11–13). Suddenly the pent-up tension disappears, and all the witnesses at the gate rejoice with Boaz. The elders call down blessings upon him and his bride, and pray that the gracious Ruth will be a mother in Israel such as Rachel and Leah were. This is indeed an optimistic expectation, since these two women as wives of Jacob built up the whole house of Israel, with the assistance of their maids Bilhah and Zilpah. Nevertheless the elders sense clearly the importance of the occasion, and recall Perez, an ancestor of Boaz, who had been born from the union of Judah and Tamar. The levirate expectation had not been fulfilled in the case of Tamar (Gen. 38:27–30), but now Boaz is entering upon a legitimate levirate marriage, approved by witnesses. It is hoped, therefore, that he will become even more notable than Perez, and in the event this is fulfilled amply.

The wedding ceremony must have been especially joyful for the entire town of Bethlehem, including the unnamed relative who had barely extricated himself from an extremely awkward situation. Hebrew weddings were notable for their festive nature, and could continue for days. But the final blessing of God is reserved for the childless Ruth, who conceives and gives birth to a son, thus fulfilling the earnest desire of all Hebrew women for male offspring. This child would continue Boaz's family line as his firstborn son.

C. Naomi is fulfilled (4:14–17). Special congratulations are appropriate for Naomi, because her restoration is now complete. The Lord has filled her life with joy, because she now has a loving family and a grandson. The women testify to God's graciousness in providing richly for the impoverished Naomi, and give outstanding praise to Ruth, who has been better to her than seven sons, the ideal of all Hebrew families. By taking the baby on her knees in the ancient Near Eastern fashion, Naomi formally adopts him as her own offspring, which the women recognize by saying, "Naomi has a son!" Obed means "serving," and the name occurs only here, in verses 21–22, 1 Chronicles 2:12, Matthew 1:5, and Luke 3:32.

VI. Concluding Genealogy (4:18–22)

Old Testament genealogies are often abbreviated and stylized, so that it should come as no surprise to see that the genealogy in Ruth contains ten names, as do the genealogies of Genesis 5:3–32 and 11:10–26. The reasons underlying the omission of names in ancient lists are unknown, but it probably turns upon the relative importance of certain individuals for the purposes of the narrative. The form of this genealogy seems ancient, and was most probably drawn upon by the compiler of Chronicles (1 Chron. 2:4–15). Elimelech's name does not occur in it because Boaz is regarded legitimately as the father of Obed. Amminadab and Nahshon are contemporary with Moses, while Salmon is also known as Salma in a number of Hebrew manuscripts.

The genealogy, paralleling the emptied Naomi's restoration, shows how the Israelites were fulfilled by the life and work of the great ruler David. The obscure Moabitess Ruth thus becomes part of the world history through the gracious plan of God for her life, and serves as a model for all time of obedience and fidelity to the Lord of the covenant. As the mother of Obed, Ruth was privileged to be included in the house of David, and thus was an ancestor of Jesus Christ, the great Son of David (Matt. 1:1), the Messiah of Israel and Redeemer of the world.

SELECT BIBLIOGRAPHY

Harrison, R. K. *Introduction to the Old Testament.* Grand Rapids: Eerdmans, 1969.

Hubbard, R. L. *The Book of Ruth.* Grand Rapids: Eerdmans, 1988.

1–2 SAMUEL

Herbert M. Wolf

INTRODUCTION

Samuel is named after the prophet Samuel, who served as the last judge and who anointed both Saul and David to be kings of Israel. Samuel ministered during the transition from the period of the judges to the time of the monarchy, and it was he who explained to the nation how the king was supposed to rule. Originally 1 and 2 Samuel were one book, but it was divided by the translators of the Greek Old Testament (Septuagint), who referred to the two books as "The First and Second Books of Kingdoms." The Latin Bible (Vulgate) called these books "First and Second Kings" and the books that followed were called "Third and Fourth Kings." Viewed together, these four books cover the entire period of the monarchy from its inception to its collapse in 586 B.C. Most modern translations follow the Hebrew custom of calling the first two books "Samuel" and the last two "Kings."

The books cover the rule of the last two judges, Eli and Samuel, and the reigns of the first two kings, Saul and David. Although the majority of the chapters deal with David and his remarkable success, the role of Samuel is also extremely important. In the early chapters of 1 Samuel we are given an account of Samuel's birth and upbringing at the tabernacle during the dark days of Eli and his wicked sons. When the Israelites are defeated by the Philistines and the ark of the covenant is captured, it seems that all is lost; but under the leadership of Samuel, Israel is able to break the Philistine yoke and enjoy a measure of peace. To Samuel's chagrin, however, the Israelites demand that he appoint a king, so they might be like all the other nations. Samuel explains the dangers of the monarchy, and urges them not to abandon the Lord. At God's direction, Samuel anoints Saul to be the first king, and Saul responds by rescuing the men of Jabesh-gilead from the Ammonites. But the new king is not so fortunate with the Philistines, who defeat him more often than not.

The last half of 1 Samuel (chaps. 15–31) contains the sad account of God's rejection of Saul, who disobeys the Lord and is to be replaced by David. Jealous of David's military success, Saul tries to kill him repeatedly and drifts further and further from God. In desperation,

Saul consults the witch of Endor before the final battle with the Philistines that ends his life.

As 2 Samuel begins, David mourns the death of Saul and Jonathan and assumes the role of leader. After a seven-year rule as king of Judah during which he wages civil war with the remnants of Saul's family, David becomes king over all Israel and establishes his capital at Jerusalem. Repulsing an attack by the Philistines, David defeats all of his enemies and expands his kingdom far beyond the borders of the Promised Land. Grateful to God, David vows to build a temple in Jerusalem but instead, God promises to "establish a house" for David (2 Sam. 7:11), giving him an unending dynasty.

In the midst of his successful reign, however, David commits adultery with Bathsheba and reaps the tragic consequences. In spite of his heartfelt repentance, the sword will strike his own family, and his sons Amnon and Absalom die violent deaths. Absalom perishes while trying to lead a revolt against his own father, and another uprising engineered by a man from the tribe of Benjamin also gives David grief.

The book ends with a four-chapter appendix dealing with a variety of topics. Chapter 22 is a psalm of praise for God's deliverance, and chapter 23 summarizes the exploits of David's mighty men. Two incidents (21:1–14; 24:1–25) are concerned with God's wrath against Israel, particularly the three-day plague that follows David's taking of a census. When David is confronted by the angel who is striking down the people (2 Sam. 24:17), he builds an altar and sacrifices to the Lord. That very place becomes the site of the temple built by Solomon years later (2 Chron. 3:1).

The message of 1 and 2 Samuel revolves around the issue of kingship and how the king of Israel is related to God as the great King. Earlier, the Lord had anticipated the desires of the nation for a king (Deut. 17:18–20). The human monarch, however, was to be subject to God and his Law (1 Sam. 10:25; 12:23). Even in the choice of a king we see how God raised up the prophet Samuel to designate Saul (1 Sam. 10:1) and then David (1 Sam. 16:13) as the chosen rulers. After David became king, God promised that David's family would remain the royal family forever, and his descendants would follow him on the throne. The relationship between God and the king would be a father-son relationship, an indication of God's full acceptance of the king (2 Sam. 7:13–14).

If David or his successors sinned, they would be subject to God's discipline, but David's dynasty would not be abolished. This was in marked contrast to Saul, whose disobedience brought about the downfall of his family (1 Sam. 15:22–23). Earlier, the family of Eli lost the high priesthood because of the wickedness of his sons (1 Sam. 2:28–30).

Most of David's life is a testimony to the way God blesses the godly. We see David's faith and courage as he defeated Goliath and repeatedly outfought the Philistines. Even though he was the youngest of Jesse's sons, he was a man after God's own heart (1 Sam. 13:14) and

God chose him to be the ruler of Israel. A remarkable confirmation of his ability is seen in the friendship that developed between David and Saul's son Jonathan. Although the two were viewed as rivals to the throne, they were deeply committed to one another and Jonathan did everything in his power to help David. After Jonathan's death, David remembered his covenant with Jonathan and took care of Jonathan's crippled son Mephibosheth (2 Sam. 9:6–7). During his years as an outcast, David developed close relationships with the men who served him, and later on, the leaders of his army gladly risked their lives for him (2 Sam. 21:15–21; 23:13–17). David—like Samuel before him—was greatly loved and his faithfulness to the Lord brought rich blessing.

God as the great King deserved the loyalty and worship of his people, and he also demonstrated his power to the nations. When the Philistines captured the ark of the covenant, they thought that their god Dagon was more powerful than the God of Israel, but they soon learned how wrong they were (1 Sam. 5:1–12). And Goliath could not defy the "Lord Almighty" in spite of his great strength, as David's stone found its mark (1 Sam. 17:45–50). After David became king, the Philistines and many other nations went down to defeat before the armies of Israel, proving that Israel's God was stronger than any other god (2 Sam. 8:6, 14).

The most important result of the establishment of kingship in Israel was the covenant which God made with David and his descendants. Like the covenants with Noah and Abraham (Gen. 9:8–17; 15:9–21), this one was an everlasting covenant, an unconditional promise made by God to David declaring that David's family would always have the right to rule over Israel (2 Sam. 23:5; Ps. 89:3–4). The term *covenant* does not occur in 2 Samuel 7, but it is clear from David's response in verses 25 and 28 that a covenant has been made.

David expressed a desire to build a temple for the Lord in order to house the ark of the covenant. God "had given him rest from all his enemies," a "rest" in fulfillment of the promise made to Moses and Joshua as the Israelites prepared to conquer the land of Canaan (Josh. 1:13). Under David and Solomon, Israel enjoyed peace and security to an unprecedented degree, allowing the nation to enjoy the fruits of centuries of toil and preparation. But God did not want David to build a house for him. Instead, the Lord announced that he would build a "house" for David, a dynasty that would last forever. David's son would succeed him as king, and in fact his house and throne would "be established forever" (2 Sam. 7:16). Overwhelmed by the announcement, David praised God for his goodness and prayed that God's name would be magnified forever (v. 26).

Although David was not allowed to build the temple, his son Solomon was given that privilege and responsibility (2 Sam. 7:13). The site for the temple was the threshing floor of Araunah the Jebusite where David encountered the angel of the Lord after a three-day plague (2 Sam. 24:16; 2 Chron. 3:1). On that hill north of Zion where David built an altar to the Lord, Solomon would later construct the temple and lead the nation in offering countless sacrifices to the God of Abraham. Centuries later Jesus Christ, a descendant of David and Solomon, would come to cleanse the temple and then give his own life as the final sacrifice for sin on Mount Calvary, only a few hundred yards from the temple mount. Raised from the dead, Jesus the Messiah is the King who will sit on David's throne to rule with justice and righteousness forever (Isa. 9:7).

Although the name *Samuel* is associated with both of these books, it is clear from the announcement of his death in 1 Samuel 25:1 that the prophet could not have written all of the material himself. According to Jewish tradition, Samuel did write the early chapters, but there is no unanimity about the rest of 1 and 2 Samuel. In 1 Chronicles 29:29, however, there is an interesting reference to "the records of Samuel the seer, the records of Nathan the prophet and the records of Gad the seer." Since 1 Chronicles also describes the reign of David and has many passages that are parallel in 2 Samuel, it is possible that the writer of Chronicles may be referring to the three main authors of 1 and 2 Samuel. Like Samuel, Nathan and Gad were prophets who were closely associated with David. Gad accompanied David during his years as a fugitive from Saul (1 Sam. 22:5), and Nathan was the one who ministered to David throughout his reign (2 Sam. 7:2; 12:1).

This theory of threefold authorship corresponds nicely to the main sections of 1 and 2 Samuel. Several scholars have noted distinct emphases in 1 Samuel 1–14, 1 Samuel 15–2 Samuel 8, and 2 Samuel 9–20. The first section describes the transition from the period of the judges to the monarchy and includes a number of stories about the ark of the covenant. In the middle section, we are told about David's rise to the throne and how his dynasty was established. The final large unit is sometimes called the "succession narrative" or "court history" of David. Linked with 1 Kings 1–2, these chapters trace the rivalry among David's sons as they vie for the right to succeed him as king. Because of its frankness and objectivity, this section has often been cited even by critical scholars as one of the earliest examples of genuine history writing.

In recent years considerable attention has been focused upon the middle section (1 Sam. 15–2 Sam. 8), partly because of its similarities to an ancient Hittite text called the "Apology of Hattusilis." Like David, King Hattusilis (1275–1250 B.C.) took over the throne under unusual circumstances and was accused of being a usurper. David was from the tribe of Judah and had to convince Saul's tribe (Benjamin) and other Israelites that he deserved to be the king. Both the Hittite text and the "Apology of David" explain in detail events that preceded the reign of the new king. David is shown to be a courageous military hero and an effective leader. Popular with all the people, David married Saul's daughter Michal and became a close friend of Saul's son Jonathan, presumed to be the crown prince. Yet even Jonathan realized that God had anointed David to be the next king, and he encouraged David at every opportunity. Meanwhile, Saul had become very jealous of David and tried to kill him. Along with this, Saul disobeyed God's commands (1 Sam. 15:17–23), was guilty of murdering the priests (1 Sam. 22:18–19), and engaged in occult practices (1 Sam. 28:6–8). Through Samuel God announced that he had rejected Saul as king; David would be the new monarch (1 Sam. 16:13). After Saul's tragic death on Mount Gilboa, the men of Judah and Israel crowned David as king and God wonderfully blessed his rule (2 Sam. 8:14). Clearly, David was not a usurper but had patiently waited for God to put him on the throne.

Even if the interpretation of this middle section as a dynastic defense, an "apology," is correct, it is still not clear if the apology was a source used by the writer of 1 and 2 Samuel or if it ever functioned independently of the other chapters. Since the Book of Jashar is mentioned as another source (2 Sam. 1:18), perhaps the author-editor who finalized 1 and 2 Samuel made use of several earlier sources.

Much of the material in 1 and 2 Samuel comes from the reign of David. Even if a later editor combined earlier materials, it is likely that the sources were left largely intact. Because of the references to "Israel and Judah" (1 Sam. 11:8; 17:52; 18:16) and to "the kings of Judah" (27:6), it appears as if the division of Solomon's kingdom into north and south had already taken place. Since Rehoboam and Jeroboam became the kings of Judah and Israel, respectively, about 930 B.C., the author may have lived shortly after this date. The opposition faced by Solomon and Rehoboam would have furnished the occasion for the vigorous defense of David's dynasty contained in these books. Since there is no reference to the fall of Samaria and the northern kingdom, we can be sure 1 and 2 Samuel were completed prior to 722 B.C.

The events described in these books cover a period of approximately 130 years, from the birth of Samuel in 1100 B.C. to the end of David's reign in 970 B.C. David reigned seven years over Judah and thirty-three years over all Israel (2 Sam. 5:4–5) from 1010–970 B.C., but the length of Saul's reign is unclear. Apparently the text of 1 Samuel 13:1 became damaged or was miscopied by scribes, because both Saul's age when he became king and the length of his reign are uncertain. Similarly, the length of Samuel's tenure as a prophet and judge can be only approximated, although from 1 Samuel 8:1, 5 we learn that Samuel was an old man when the people asked him to select a king for them.

In all likelihood, the material in 1 Samuel is arranged in chronological order, but this is not always the case in 2 Samuel. For example, the establishment of the Davidic covenant (chap. 7) may have occurred after the military victories described in chapter 8, because 7:1 says that "the LORD had given him rest from all his enemies." Likewise, the victories over the Ammonites and Arameans discussed in chapter 10 may have been an elaboration of the battles described in 8:3–12. Perhaps the lack of chronological order may be partly explained by the theory that chapters 7 and 8 conclude the "apology of David."

The final four chapters of 2 Samuel are regarded as an appendix, partly because of their uncertain chronology. The account of the Gibeonites' revenge against the family of Saul is given in chapter 21, but it probably preceded the revolt of Absalom (chaps. 15–18). In 16:7–8 a descendant of Saul named Shimei cursed David for shedding the blood of the family of Saul, and this may very well be a reference to the executions permitted by David in chapter 21. At the end of chapter 21 the author describes four battles against the Philistines which are not likely to be in chronological order.

OUTLINE

- I. A Period of Transition (1 Sam. 1–14)
  - A. Eli and Samuel (1:1–7:17)
  - B. The Early Years of Saul's Reign (8:1–14:52)
- II. David's Rise to the Throne (1 Sam. 15–2 Sam. 8)
  - A. David's Fame (15:1–17:58)
  - B. David's Struggles with Saul (18:1–27:12)
  - C. Saul's Final Battle (28:1–31:13)
  - D. David Unifies Judah and Israel (2 Sam. 1:1–5:25)
  - E. David Established as King (2 Sam. 6:1–8:18)
- III. David's Successes and Failures (2 Sam. 9–20)
  - A. David's Success (9:1–10:19)
  - B. The Turning Point (11:1–12:31)
  - C. Rebellion (13:1–20:26)
- IV. Appendix (2 Sam. 21–24)
  - A. The Gibeonites' Revenge (21:1–14)
  - B. Victories over the Philistines (21:15–22)
  - C. David's Praise (22:1–51)
  - D. David's Final Poem (23:1–7)
  - E. David's Mighty Men (23:8–39)
  - F. David's Census (24:1–25)

COMMENTARY

I. A Period of Transition (1 Sam. 1–14)

After the turbulent days of the judges, the people of Israel looked forward to better times. The economic and spiritual condition of the nation was deplorable, even though the Lord dwelled among his people and had appointed the priests to be their leaders.

A. Eli and Samuel (1:1–7:17). Samuel's importance can be seen in the lengthy account of his birth. There are no birth narratives for Saul and David, even though they are kings.

The story of Samuel's birth is a testimony to the faith of his mother, Hannah (**1:1–8**). Like Sarah and Rachel, Hannah had great difficulty becoming pregnant, and barrenness was considered to be a mark of the Lord's disfavor. To make matters worse, her husband, Elkanah, had another wife who had several children and who taunted Hannah the way Hagar scorned Sarah (Gen. 16:4). Elkanah loves Hannah dearly but cannot alleviate her grief. As in the Genesis narratives, the problems of polygamy are often devastating. Hannah's barrenness is not the result of sin, for verses 3–8 tell how she often accompanied her husband to the house of God. The yearly festival referred to in verse 3 may be the Feast of Tabernacles, celebrated at the end of the summer to commemorate God's provision for Israel in the Sinai desert after the exodus (Lev. 23:43) and to give thanks for the summer harvest. Normally a joyous occasion, for Hannah it is a reminder of her own unfruitfulness.

Though deeply discouraged, Hannah takes her problem to the Lord and to the high priest Eli at the tabernacle, which at this time was located at Shiloh, about twenty miles north of Jerusalem (**1:9–18**). In great earnestness, Hannah makes a solemn promise that if the Lord will give her a son, she will dedicate him to the Lord's work. By promising that "no razor will ever be used on his head" Hannah is in effect placing her son under the restrictions of a Nazirite vow, which also involved total abstinence from the fruit of the vine (Num. 6:1–3). Long hair was a symbol of an individual's commitment to the work of the Lord. Through her vow, Hannah voluntarily places Samuel in the same position that God had put Samson, whose mother ironically had also been sterile for years (Judg. 13:3–5). Both Samson and Samuel were to be Nazirites for life, though the vow was normally for a limited period.

Eli is watching as Hannah prays and concludes that she is drunk. Owing to the sad spiritual conditions of the time, Eli probably had to deal with drunk people coming to the sanctuary. Hannah is not "drunk on wine" but "filled with the Spirit" (Eph. 5:18). She has been "pouring out [her] soul to the LORD" (v. 15) and is completely absorbed in her anguished prayer. Rather than being a "wicked woman" she is in close touch with her God. Realizing his mistake, Eli blesses her and Hannah senses that her prayer will be answered.

When Hannah returns home to Ramah, about five miles north of Jerusalem, "the Lord remembered her," as he had remembered the barren Rachel centuries earlier (**1:19–20;** Gen. 30:22). "Remembered" does not mean that God "forgot" her but that he now intervenes in a specific way on her behalf. In due time Hannah gives birth to Samuel, whose name sounds like the Hebrew phrase *heard of God.*

After the birth of Samuel, Elkanah returns to Shiloh to offer the annual sacrifice in fulfillment of a vow he has made. Perhaps he had prayed for his flocks and crops and God had prospered him. Hannah does not accompany her husband, but nurses Samuel until he is weaned, probably at three years of age. True to her promise, she then brings him to the tabernacle and turns him over to Eli (**1:21–28**). On this occasion she also sacrifices a bull in fulfillment of her vow (Num. 15:8–10) and reminds Eli that she had prayed for a child in his hearing. It was not easy for Hannah to give up her little boy and allow him to be brought up by someone else. Eli is not a very good father (2:12), but Hannah is primarily giving Samuel to the Lord. In verse 28 the emphasis is not on the Nazirite vow (v. 11) but on the surrender of the child for a "whole life" of service. Little did Hannah realize what a significant impact her son would have as a prophet, priest, and judge during this critical period of Israel's history.

While still at the sanctuary, Hannah again prays to God, this time lifting her heart in praise for the goodness of God (**2:1–11**). She rejoices not so much in her son, Samuel, but in the Lord who gave him to her. He is the "Rock," the all-powerful God who provides security for his people. Verses 3–9 show how God humbles the proud and the rich and exalts the weak and the poor. These reversals are mentioned later by Mary in her song of praise (Luke 1:51–53), and for both Hannah and Mary it is the birth of a son that brings such great blessing. God is sovereign in the lives of all people, and his special protection rests upon his "saints." Those who are wicked and who oppose the Lord will face judgment and destruction.

In the final couplet of the song (v. 10), Hannah speaks prophetically about a coming king. By calling the king "his anointed," Hannah is the first to use the term *messiah* with reference to a ruler. Both the Hebrew word *messiah* and the Greek word *Christ* mean "anointed." Hannah's prophecy is most appropriate since her son Samuel was the one who anointed both Saul and David and figured prominently in the establishment of the monarchy.

One of the saddest episodes of this period is the disintegration of the family of Eli. The weakness and gloom of Eli contrast sharply with the faith and joy of Hannah.

If the sons of the priests are "wicked men," the condition of the nation is desperate indeed. Ironically, Eli's sons sin in the way they handle the sacrifices—the very animals brought to make atonement for sin! According to the law of Moses the priests were allowed to eat part of the meat of the sacrificial animals (except for the burnt offerings), but certain restrictions applied (Lev. 7:31–37). The fat was always considered the Lord's portion and had to be burned on the altar (Lev. 3:16). Yet Hophni and Phinehas take the meat before the fat is burned, and apparently ignore the custom of boiling the meat (v. 15). In spite of the complaints of the people, the priests refuse to change and treat "the LORD's offering with contempt" (v. 17). Such an attitude had brought death to two of Aaron's sons several centuries earlier (Lev. 10:1–3).

In sharp contrast to the sin of Eli's sons is the Lord's blessings upon Samuel and his family (**2:18–21**). Once a year Samuel's parents would visit him, and his mother would bring a robe which she had made. Apparently he wore this under the linen ephod, an apronlike garment worn by all the priests (1 Sam. 22:18). Sensing that the Lord's hand rests on Samuel,

Eli blesses his parents with the promise of additional children. Over the years three sons and two daughters are born to Hannah (2:5).

Faced by the mounting reports about the wicked deeds of his sons, Eli directly confronts them (**2:22–25**). Among other things, they are guilty of sexual immorality with women who serve at the entrance to the tabernacle. Such women are mentioned only in Exodus 38:8, but the nature of their ministry is not given. Certainly they were not supposed to function as the temple prostitutes who were present in Canaanite shrines to promote the overall fertility of the land (Num. 25:1–3). The worship of Baal with its corrupting influence was expressly forbidden (Deut. 7:3–6). Oblivious to their father's belated warnings, Eli's sons continue in their sinful ways.

For the second time in the chapter, Samuel's behavior is directly contrasted with that of Eli's sons (**2:26**). As he grows up Samuel pleases both God and men. These are words of high praise, for Jesus himself is so described at the age of twelve (Luke 2:52).

As he watches his sons, Eli knows that God's judgment will eventually come, and this is confirmed by a visit from an unnamed prophet (**2:27–36**). Called "a man of God" (9:6, 10), this prophet places part of the blame on Eli, who honors his sons more than God—perhaps by failing to oppose their sin vigorously enough.

In light of the unfaithfulness of Eli's sons, the prophet announces that disaster will strike Eli's family, and his descendants will not live out their days peacefully. Proof of this prediction would be seen when Eli's sons—Hophni and Phinehas—both die on the same day, a grim reminder of the sudden death of Aaron's sons Nadab and Abihu (Lev. 10:1–3). Instead of having choice parts of meat from the sacrifices, Eli's descendants will have to beg for "a crust of bread" (v. 36). Honor and prestige will be replaced by disgrace and poverty.

God calls Samuel (**3:1–10**). For the third time in the book, we read that Samuel ministers "before the LORD" (v. 1). He serves as a kind of apprentice priest and by now is probably about twelve years old. In this period there were very few prophets, and the Lord did not appear to many individuals. During the time of the judges the angel of the Lord appeared to Gideon and to Samson's parents (Judg. 6:11–22; 13:3–21), but these were rare occasions. Since the time of Moses, God had not spoken regularly through a prophet.

All this changes, however, as the Lord begins to speak to Samuel one night while he is sleeping in his usual place near the tabernacle. Apparently it is close to dawn, because verse 3 mentions that the golden lampstand in the Holy Place is still burning. Every evening olive oil was brought in to keep the lamps burning until morning, when the flame either grew dim or went out (Exod. 27: 20–21; 2 Chron. 13:11). The ark of the covenant was in the Holy of Holies, and it was from the ark that God used to speak with Moses (Num. 7:89). In this setting, then, it is altogether fitting for God to call a new Moses to lead his people. At first, Samuel thinks that Eli is calling him, but after Samuel makes three trips to Eli's bed, the aged priest realizes that God was calling the boy. Before this night, Samuel had not known the Lord in such a personal way but now the Lord stands there, as the angels stood before Abraham (Gen. 18:2) and Joshua (Josh. 5:12–15).

Excited about hearing God's word so directly, Samuel's heart must have sunk as he heard the message of judgment against Eli (**3:11–21**). Action that makes the ears tingle (v. 11) is nothing short of catastrophe, and destruction lay ahead for Eli's family. Eli had failed to restrain his sons, who treated the Lord with much contempt, even though he did try to warn them (2:22–25). They would never be forgiven for their stubborn rebellion regardless of the number of sacrifices they handled.

Having observed Eli's sons in action, Samuel may not have been surprised at the severity of the Lord's message, but he must have wondered what he should tell Eli. This problem is solved when Eli uses a curse formula (v. 17) to insist that Samuel tell him everything. When Samuel complies, Eli accepts God's sentence and reacts the way Hezekiah did when he learned that his descendants would be exiled to Babylon (Isa. 39:8). In an era when "everyone did as he saw fit" (Judg. 21:25), God could take appropriate measures to judge the wicked. Since Samuel's account of God's revelation is the same as the announcement given to Eli by the man of God (2:27–36), there is no doubt that God has spoken to Samuel. As time goes on, Samuel's predictions come true and all Israel recognizes that he is a genuine prophet. Chapter 3 begins with the observation that visions were given only rarely, but it ends with a reference to God's repeated revelations to Samuel. Here is a young man with a heart for God through whom the Lord will speak to his desperate people.

In fulfillment of the prophecies of chapter 3, the family of Eli suffers a devastating blow in the wake of a battle with the Philistines some years later (**4:1–11**). The conflict takes place near Aphek, a city about twenty miles west of Shiloh and somewhat north of the main Philistine territory along the Mediterranean Sea.

According to Judges 13–16, the Philistines controlled the tribe of Judah and were putting pressure on tribal regions to the north. Unlike Samson, Israel's army cannot gain the victory and in fact loses about four thousand men. Distraught, the rest of the soldiers wonder why the Lord has abandoned Israel, for they—like the surrounding nations—believe that the people with the strongest gods win the battle (1 Kings 20:23). The soldiers recall how the ark of the covenant had accompanied Israel's armies when they crossed the Jordan River and defeated the city of Jericho (Josh. 3:11, 17; 6:6, 12). The ark was God's footstool and symbolized his presence more than any other part of the tabernacle (v. 4). The men reason that the ark will guarantee victory over the Philistines. The Philistines likewise believe that the presence of the ark is a bad omen, for they have heard about the plagues with which the Lord had afflicted Egypt (v. 8).

In reality the Philistines had little to be worried about, for the mere physical presence of the ark could not compel the Lord to give Israel a victory—especially when Eli's two wicked sons, Hophni and Phinehas, had accompanied the ark to the battlefield. Their presence spells doom for Israel, and in the ensuing battle another thirty thousand men die, including Eli's two sons. The ark is captured. It is an unmitigated disaster.

Eli's family suffers disaster as well (**4:12–22**). News of Israel's defeat is brought to Shiloh by a messenger with "his clothes torn and dust on his head" (v. 12). These outward signs of grief and sorrow also mark the one who tells David about the death of Saul and Jonathan (2 Sam. 1:2). When Eli hears the commotion, he asks what has happened. According to verse 13, Eli had serious misgivings about taking the ark to battle. Old and feeble at age ninety-eight, Eli falls off his chair and breaks his neck when he hears the extent of the catastrophe, especially the news about the capture of the ark. This was worse than the report that his own two sons had been killed. Following the style of the Book of Judges, the author notes that Eli "had led Israel forty years" (v. 18). He was the only priest to serve as a judge, but his leadership had proved to be ineffective.

Death continues to stalk Eli's family when his daughter-in-law dies in childbirth after learning what has happened to her husband and father-in-law. Before succumbing she names her baby boy Ichabod, meaning "no glory," because of the capture of the ark. It is as though the cloud of glory that normally filled the Holy of Holies around the ark has left Israel. Since the Lord is "enthroned between the cherubim" above the ark (4:4), the loss of the ark symbolizes graphically his abandonment of Israel. He has refused to be manipulated by his own people.

After their triumph over Israel, the Philistines plan to celebrate their good fortune, but little do they realize the hardship in store for them.

After its capture, the ark is taken to the coastal city of Ashdod, about thirty-five miles west of Jerusalem and one of the five main centers of the Philistines (**5:1–12**). There it is placed in a temple beside the image of Dagon, a god of grain who was worshiped in many parts of the Fertile Crescent and who was the Philistines' leading deity. According to popular theology, Israel's defeat meant that Dagon was more powerful than the Lord, but after a short time the Philistines learn how wrong they are. Twice the image topples to the ground before the ark and the second time Dagon's head and hands are broken off.

Meanwhile, the hand of the Lord remains powerful and effective, affecting the people of Ashdod with tumors of some sort. The five leaders of the Philistines may have thought that the outbreak of tumors was coincidental, but when disease follows the ark to Gath, a city several miles to the east, there is no more doubt. Death comes to many and the people panic, as do the residents of Ekron, about eleven miles northeast of Ashdod. The spread of the plague confirms the original reaction of the Philistines when the ark was brought into the Israelites' camp (4:7–8). They know that Israel's God struck the Egyptians with terrible plagues, and now they are experiencing a similar plague firsthand. Instead of having a prized trophy of victory, the Philistines possess an instrument of judgment that demonstrates the power of the Lord and the corresponding weakness of Dagon.

After seven difficult months, the Philistines are ready to send the ark back to Israel (**6:1–9**). But they want to make sure they do not offend the Lord any further, so they consult with their religious leaders. The leaders urge them to send a gift with the ark to compensate for the way they have dishonored God. This guilt offering is to consist of "five gold tumors and five gold rats" (v. 4), reflecting the five main cities of the Philistines. The rats may have carried the disease as a bubonic plague. Through this offering and the return of the ark, the Philistines hope to bring an end to the plague. This seems wiser than hardening their hearts like Pharaoh and the Egyptians, who suffered through ten plagues before releasing the Hebrews (v. 6).

To carry the ark, the priests suggest that a new cart be used, one that is "ceremonially clean." The cart is to be drawn by "two cows that have calved and have never been yoked." According to Numbers 19:2, in some cases a cow could not be used in a sacrifice if it had been under a yoke. Apparently the Philistine priests correctly anticipate that the Jews will sacrifice these animals when they reach Israel. Cows that had calves normally would not leave them, let alone pull a cart for the first time and follow a road to unfamiliar territory.

When the Philistines hitch the cows to the cart and send them on their way, they realize that the hand of God has indeed brought the plague upon them. The cows head straight up the Sorek Valley to Beth-shemesh, a city of Judah close to the Philistine border. Providentially it is also a city that belongs to the priests (cf. Josh. 21:16), the ones responsible for the ark of the covenant. The people are harvesting wheat, which usually took place in May or June. When they see the ark they are overjoyed and proceed to sacrifice the cows as a burnt offering. They place the ark on a large rock, which becomes a monument to this event (v. 18).

Tragedy strikes, however, when God puts seventy men to death for looking into the ark (v. 19). According to the law of Moses, the sacred articles of the tabernacle had to be treated with great reverence. Not even the Levites could look at the holy things without risking death (cf. Num. 4:20). Since the ark was the most sacred object of all and since it was closely associated with the presence of God, access to it was even more restricted. Not even the high priest could look into the ark without great danger.

The people of Beth-shemesh wonder if anyone can stand in God's presence. This is a reminder to all of us that God requires clean hands and a pure heart (cf. Ps. 24:4). Distraught at the death of their friends, the rest of the townspeople follow the example of the Philistines and look for another city to send the ark. Kiriath-jearim, located about fifteen miles northeast of Beth-shemesh, accepts the ark and a man named Abinadab, probably a Levite, is given custody of it (7:1). The ark was probably not put back in the tabernacle because of the destruction of Shiloh by the Philistines. Although the tabernacle itself was moved in time, it did not have a more permanent home for many years.

Approximately twenty years elapse before the Israelites gain any real relief from Philistine oppression. Finally, Samuel senses that a genuine repentance is underway, so he challenges the people to get rid of their Baals and Ashtoreths (**7:2–6**). Throughout the period of the judges, Israel worshiped these deities all too frequently. Baal was the Canaanite god of rain and agriculture and, ironically, was sometimes described as the son of Dagon. The Ashtoreths were female deities such as Astarte (the Babylonian Ishtar), goddess of fertility, love, and war. As in Judges 10:16, the Israelites stop worshiping these gods and begin to serve the Lord. Samuel gathers the people of Mizpah, about 7½ miles north of Jerusalem, and true to his prophetic calling, promises to pray for them. As they fast and confess their sin, they pour out water before the Lord, perhaps symbolic of their earnestness and wholehearted commitment to God.

Believing that the Israelites have gathered at Mizpah for military reasons, the Philistines attack them (**7:7–12**). In light of their repentant attitude, the men of Israel beg Samuel to pray for them, and he does so as he sacrifices a burnt offering. True to his covenant promise, the Lord intervenes on behalf of his beleaguered people and thunders against the Philistines. Apparently the Lord sends a storm similar to the one that routed the Amorites (Josh. 10:11–12) or bogged down the chariots of Sisera (Judg. 5:20–21). Thunder, hail, and heavy rain cause panic among the Philistines and send them fleeing to the west and south. Recognizing that it is the Lord's victory, Samuel sets up a stone as a monument and calls it "Ebenezer," "stone of help," for "God is . . . an ever present help in trouble" (Ps. 46:1). This important victory may have been partially due to Samson's destruction of three thousand Philistines not many years earlier (see Judg. 16:27–30).

After this victory, the Israelites gain the upper hand over the Philistines and at least temporarily put an end to Philistine oppression. During this time of peace, Samuel travels to many towns in the tribe of Benjamin, serving as a judge and spiritual leader (**7:13–17**). Since Samuel ministers as a priest and prophet, he builds an altar to the Lord in his hometown of Ramah.

B. The early years of Saul's reign (8:1–14:52). Even though Samuel is a godly and effective judge, he is the last of the judges. Under pressure from the people, Samuel anoints Saul as the first king and ushers in a new era of Israel's history. Saul's initial years as king are promising, and it appears that the unified nation will be a powerful one.

Unlike most judges, Samuel appointed his sons to succeed him, but their dishonesty creates serious problems for both Samuel and the nation. Using the misconduct of Samuel's sons as a pretext, the elders ask Samuel to appoint a king over Israel (**8:1–9**). They want to be like all the other nations, led by a man who will command an army and protect the borders of the land. By this request the people are rejecting the leadership of Samuel, but, more importantly, they are rejecting the Lord. Earlier, Gideon had acknowledged that the Lord was Israel's King (Judg. 8:23; see Deut. 33:5), so the desire for a human monarch could easily undermine the nation's reverence for God. Dependence on a new "savior" or "deliverer" could replace trust in God himself.

To help the people see the implications of their request, Samuel tells them what it will be like to have a king (**8:10–22**). Using the policies of other Near Eastern kings as a pattern, Samuel describes how sons and daughters will be drafted into the army and how government officials will take control of fields and vineyards. In addition to the tithe required by the law of Moses, the king will demand an additional 10 percent of crops and flocks and livestock. Eventually the people will feel like the king's slaves and will cry out to God for relief, just as they cried for help during times of foreign oppression.

Ignoring the urgency of Samuel's arguments, the people remain firm in their desire for a king. Their minds are made up even though Samuel has pointed out some very real dangers. When Samuel takes their decision to the Lord, God tells him to "give them a king" (v. 22).

The Lord's choice is a man named Saul, who belongs to a prominent family from the tribe of Benjamin (**9:1–13**). He is tall—a head taller than anyone else—but he is looking for lost donkeys and not a crown when he encounters Samuel. After searching the tribal areas of Ephraim and Benjamin, Saul is ready to give up the search, but his servant suggests that they consult a highly respected man of God, perhaps in the city of Ramah. It seems strange that neither Saul nor his servant mentions Samuel by name and that neither recognizes him by sight. Perhaps they had not seen him often enough to be able to recognize him easily. Fortunately the servant has a small amount of silver to give to the prophet, for payment of some sort was customary (see 1 Kings 14:3). When the two men ask about the prophet, they are told that he is on his way to bless a sacrifice at the local high place. High places were shrines located on hills and contained, among other things, an altar. Although later writers condemned the high places, those dedicated to the worship of the Lord were apparently acceptable prior to the construction of the temple (see 2 Chron. 1:3).

Unknown to Saul, Samuel had been told by the Lord that he was to anoint a man from Benjamin as king of Israel that very day (**9:14–10:1**). The Hebrew verb *māšaḥ*, "to anoint," from which the noun *Messiah*, "anointed one," is derived, is used of a king for the second time in the book in verse 16 (see 2:10). In Exodus we are told that priests were anointed for service (29:7; 40:12–15), but from now on "the anointed one" is usually the king. Anointing indicates that a person has been set apart for a particular task and that the Lord will give him the ability to perform that task. The anointing oil is a symbol of the Holy Spirit, who empowered both Saul and David after they were anointed (see 10:6; 16:13).

Another term that can refer to a priest as well as a king is the word *leader* (v. 16). Here it refers to the one designated to be the highest official, hence the king. Later it will be used of David (13:14) and Solomon (1 Kings 1:35). Perhaps this term was chosen to represent the transition between a judge and a king, lest the king be too powerful at the outset of the monarchy.

When Saul meets Samuel, the prophet surprises him by announcing that the lost donkeys have been found and that "all the desire of Israel" is directed to Saul as the new king (v. 20). Saul protests that the tribe of Benjamin is not very prominent, although neatly situated between the powerful tribes of Judah and Ephraim. During the period of the judges, however, Benjamin was nearly wiped out in a civil war that seemed to end its influence permanently (Judg. 20:46–48). Like Gideon before him (Judg. 6:15), Saul protests that his clan is too small and insignificant to be considered for such an honor. But Samuel insists that Saul join the invited guests at the high place for a meal after the sacrifice, and Samuel reserves for Saul a choice part of the animal, the thigh. Normally the right thigh of fellowship offerings belonged to the priests (see Lev. 7:33–34), so the people realize that Saul is in line for special honor.

That night Saul stays with Samuel, no doubt wondering what will happen to him next. They probably talked about the spiritual and economic conditions of the nation and the ever-present Philistine threat. The next morning Saul and his servant prepare to leave, but Samuel sends the servant ahead while he gives Saul "a message from God" privately. Then, taking a flask of olive oil, Samuel pours it on Saul's head and anoints him king. So begins Samuel's key role as a king-maker, and Israel's monarchy is launched. A new era has begun.

Before Saul leaves, Samuel gives him some signs as further proof that God has indeed chosen him to be king (**10:2–8**). Samuel predicts the location at which Saul will meet various individuals and what they will do, once again demonstrating that he is a true prophet of the Lord (see Deut. 18:21–22). The third sign is the most significant one for it deals with Saul's empowering by the Spirit of God. A group of prophets will approach Saul playing musical instruments. While the band of prophets is prophesying, Saul will join with them and the Spirit of the Lord will come upon him in power, just as he had come upon Othniel (Judg. 3:10), Gideon (Judg. 6:34), and Jephthah (Judg. 11:29). Each of these judges had been designated as God's chosen leader in this fashion, and the same was true for both Saul and David. When God gives an individual an assignment he also supplies divine power to finish that assignment. In Saul's case he will be "changed into a different person" (v. 6), which may be an Old Testament description of conversion or a reference to the personality change that gave Saul the boldness and confidence he needed as a leader. Whatever the precise significance, Saul recognizes that God is with him to bless and strengthen him.

Even though Saul would have the authority of a king, verse 8 is a reminder that he also needed to obey the Word of God. At a forthcoming gathering at Gilgal—the sacred town near the Jordan River—Saul is instructed to wait a full week for Samuel to advise him.

The rapid fulfillment of signs leaves little doubt that God has indeed spoken through Samuel (**10:9–16**). Saul's participation in prophesying startles his friends, and they ask, "Is Saul also among the prophets?" Apparently the more exuberant prophets were looked down upon by the rest of society (see 2 Kings 9:11), and since Saul is from a prominent family, his friends do not expect him to behave in this fashion. Another possible explanation for their question is Saul's previous lack of spiritual concern. One who had shown little interest in prophets and priests would normally not enter into the prophetic spirit so fully.

By this time the curiosity of Saul's uncle has been aroused, but when he questions Saul about his visit with Samuel, he says nothing about the anointing. Saul is not about to brag about his appointment—not even to his relatives.

As rumors about Saul begin to multiply, Samuel summons the people to reveal God's choice of king (**10:17–27**). Before proceeding with the selection, however, he scolds the people for rejecting the Lord and reminds them that God is the One who rescued them from Egypt and saved them out of all their calamities. Even with a king, Israel has to remember that God is the source of their strength and salvation.

The selection of the king was probably accomplished through casting lots in conjunction with the Urim and Thummim handled by the priest (see Exod. 28:30; 1 Sam. 14:41–42). By this means the tribe of Benjamin and the clan of Matri are chosen, and finally Saul himself is singled out. Knowing that he will be selected, Saul has hidden himself among the baggage (v. 22). At this point, at least, he is humble and not at all impressed with his new importance. When he is finally presented to the people, they shout with enthusiasm, "Long live the king!" (v. 24).

To help the nation function with a new form of government, Samuel explains to the people "the regulations of the kingship" (v. 25). This written document apparently listed the duties and responsibilities of the king and probably indicated how the human king would be subservient to God as the great King. Samuel is deeply concerned that Israel's monarchy be different from that of other nations, for her success depends above all upon her relationship with God. So important is this document about kingship that Samuel deposits it "before the LORD." Centuries earlier Moses had placed the Book of the Law beside the ark of the covenant (Deut. 31:26), and the two tablets containing the Ten Commandments were placed in the ark (Exod. 25:21).

When Saul returns to his hometown of Gibeah he enjoys the support of many valiant men. The tribe of Benjamin was renowned for its excellent warriors, and now one of their number is king of the whole land. Some of the people are dubious about Saul's abilities, however, and openly withhold their support.

Before long Saul has a chance to prove himself when the Ammonites besiege the city of Jabesh-gilead, a town just east of the Jordan River, about forty miles northeast of the area of Benjamin (**11:1–5**). The Ammonites also lived in Trans-Jordan and had captured a large section of Israel's territory before Jephthah drove them out (Judg. 11:29–33). The people of Jabesh-gilead are willing to submit to the Ammonites, but not on the condition that their right eyes be gouged out (v. 2). Such treatment was given to prisoners of war to humiliate them and destroy their capacity to fight.

Since the people of Jabesh-gilead had close family ties with the tribe of Benjamin (cf. Judg. 21:12–14) and since Saul had been appointed king over all the tribes, they decide to appeal to

Saul for help. Saul hears the news when he comes in from plowing the fields, an indication that his kingly responsibilities are not yet very extensive.

For the second time, "the Spirit of God came upon him in power" (cf. 10:6, 10) as Saul, like the judges before him, goes into action against the enemy (**11:6–15**). Asserting his authority as king, Saul cuts up two oxen and sends the pieces throughout the land to indicate that death is in store for those who do not respond to the crisis. More than three hundred thousand soldiers gather, proving that the whole nation stands solidly behind Saul. Following the strategy used by Abraham and Gideon, Saul surprises the enemy in the middle of the night and thoroughly defeats them. Jabesh-gilead is saved and Saul is a hero.

On the heels of victory the people want to execute those who had opposed the selection of Saul as king, but Saul refuses to go along with the idea. This is a day to rejoice, because God has given them a great victory. Samuel suggests that everyone assemble at Gilgal, the town near the Jordan where Joshua and his army had celebrated the conquest of Canaan (Josh. 10:43). There they present fellowship offerings to thank the Lord for his goodness to the nation and to confirm Saul as king.

Like Moses and Joshua, Samuel does not relinquish his leadership without challenging the nation to be faithful to the Lord. The theme of covenant renewal that characterizes the whole Book of Deuteronomy and Joshua 24 is here emphasized once again.

Since the wickedness of Samuel's sons was a factor behind the initial request for a king (cf. 8:3–5), Samuel begins his speech with an examination of his own conduct as leader (**12:1–5**). He challenges the people to point out any instance where he has wronged anyone or used his position for financial gain. By pointing to his own clean record Samuel hopes to provide an example for Saul and future kings to follow. How important it is for leaders to be honest and fair if a nation expects to remain strong!

As Samuel seeks to establish the monarchy on a sound footing, he reminds the Israelites of the way God has provided for them in the past (**12:6–15**). When they cried for relief in Egypt, the Lord sent Moses and Aaron to deliver them from slavery. When their own sinfulness brought oppression in Canaan, God raised up judges such as Gideon, Barak, and Jephthah to rescue them from the enemy. God is faithful; he would have saved them from the recent Ammonite attack also even if no king had been appointed. Although the Lord used Saul in a remarkable way, the monarchy brings with it a new danger. Will the people put their trust in a human leader at the expense of their relationship with the Lord? Samuel warns that both the people and the king must serve and obey the Lord. The covenant structure remains the same, for the Lord demands the unwavering allegiance of all the people.

To impress upon the Israelites the evil inherent in their request for a king—and their rejection of God as King—the Lord sends thunder and rain in the dry season (**12:16–18**). The wheat harvest normally occurred in June, and it rarely rains in Israel during the summer. The people stand in awe as their forefathers did at Mount Sinai, when God revealed his power in thunder and lightning (Exod. 19:16; 20:18). God had spoken through Moses, and now he is speaking through Samuel, and the message must be taken seriously.

In 1 Samuel 7:8 the people asked Samuel to pray when the Philistines attacked. Now that God has revealed himself they ask Samuel to pray for them again (**12:19–25**). Like the generation at Mount Sinai, they are afraid they might die. Samuel assures them that the Lord will not reject them, but he urges them to "serve the LORD with all your heart" (v. 20). God has done "great things" for them (v. 24), and he will continue to work wonders on their behalf (cf. Ps. 126:2). And Samuel promises to keep praying for them and teaching them how to live. Although he is retiring as the official national leader, he continues to function as a prophet for the nation and as an advisor for the king.

After the victory over the Ammonites east of the Jordan, Saul turns his attention to the Philistines, Israel's perennial enemy along the Mediterranean coast. Undoubtedly the Philistines are worried about Israel's upstart king and want to attack him before he becomes too powerful.

Since the conquest under Joshua, the cities that were most solidly under Israel's control were located in the hill country, an area about two thousand feet above sea level that ran from north to south through much of central Palestine. Saul's capital of Gibeah was located there but this does not stop the Philistines. As chapter 13 begins, the Philistines have pushed to within five miles of the capital (**13:1–7**). Jonathan, Saul's oldest son, who is to become such a good friend of David, attacks the Philistine outpost at Geba, and this angers the Philistines. They amass a large army supported by three thousand chariots, and the Israelites withdraw to Gilgal by the Jordan. Some of Saul's soldiers hide "in caves and thickets, among the rocks, and in pits and cisterns" (v. 6). This is a foretaste of the judgment associated with the day of the Lord and is reminiscent of the dreaded Midianite invasion years earlier (cf. Judg. 6:2).

Saul starts with only a few thousand troops, but the number dwindles to six hundred while Saul delays at Gilgal. He is waiting for Samuel to come and offer sacrifices as he has promised to do (cf. 10:8). After seven days Saul violates Samuel's command by offering the sacrifices himself with the hope of gaining God's blessing upon the upcoming battle. When Samuel finally arrives, he condemns Saul's action and announces that his son will not succeed him on the throne (**13:8–15**). Instead, God will choose "a man after his own heart" to rule Israel (16:7). Saul is guilty of ignoring the Lord's command through his prophet. In subsequent years, all of Israel's kings were responsible to obey the law of Moses and the instructions of the prophets (cf. Jer. 25:4). If a king was guilty of wrongdoing, often a prophet would appear on the scene to announce God's judgment.

In spite of mounting difficulties, Saul and Jonathan return to Gibeah, only a few miles from the Philistines at Micmash. The Philistines send out raiding parties to take plunder and to demoralize the people, and Saul seems unable to stop them (**13:16–22**). One reason for Israel's predicament is a lack of weapons. According to verse 19 the Philistines had a monopoly on the production of iron and refused to share the secret. They may have learned how to smelt iron from the Hittites of Asia Minor, who used iron to great advantage prior to 1200 B.C. The Israelites have to pay the Philistines to have their farming tools sharpened, but in time of war no plowshares are beaten into swords. Only Saul and Jonathan have a sword or spear; the rest of the troops use slingshots, bows and arrows, or even oxgoads. No wonder many of Saul's men desert!

When all seems lost, Saul's son Jonathan leads a daring attack on the Philistine position north of the Micmash pass (**14:1–14**). At the time Saul is still near Gibeah, trying to take care of national business as he sits under a pomegranate tree. No one else knows that Jonathan and his armor-bearer are embarking on a dangerous mission. Even though Eli's great-grandson Ahijah is with Saul and could have been consulted (v. 3), Jonathan exercises faith in God and chooses not to ask the priest. He believes that God will intervene on behalf of his people and save them from "those uncircumcised fellows" (v. 6). Like David (17:26, 36), Jonathan believes that God can give victory even against great odds.

As Jonathan and his armor-bearer make their way across the Micmash pass, the Philistines spot them and challenge them to come up and fight. This response is a sign to Jonathan "that the LORD has given them into the hand of Israel" (v. 10), and he takes courage as Gideon did before facing the Midianites (Judg. 7:15). The Philistines mock Saul's troops for hiding in holes and refer to the Israelites as "Hebrews," a term that is sometimes used by foreigners in a disparaging way (cf. Gen. 39:17). Perhaps it was the equivalent of the term *uncircumcised* as applied to the Philistines. Clearly the Philistines expect to make short work of the two men, but convinced that God is with them, Jonathan and his armor-bearer fight valiantly and kill about twenty men. Their faith has been vindicated.

As confusion begins to grow among the Philistine forces, the Lord sends the whole army into a panic by shaking the ground (**14:15–23**). Coupled with the damage done by Jonathan and his armor-bearer, the earth tremor badly frightens the Philistines. Thinking that a large group of Israelites has followed Jonathan, they begin to flee and fight among themselves in all the confusion. It is the same sort of panic that lay behind the victory at Mizpah (7:7–12) and the defeat of the Midianites under Gideon (Judg. 7:22).

Saul's lookouts at Gibeah report the commotion to their commander, and Saul immediately consults Ahijah the priest. There is some question as to whether the ark or the ephod is used to consult the Lord (v. 18). Before receiving an answer from the Lord, however, Saul takes his men to the battle and finds the Philistines in total confusion. As word about the battle spreads, the soldiers who abandoned Saul earlier rejoin his forces to take part in the chase, just as the ranks of Gideon had swelled once the Midianites were on the run (Judg. 7:23). Since Saul had done almost nothing to bring about the defeat of the Philistines, he cannot take credit for the victory. It is the Lord who has rescued Israel. The victory leaves Israel with some security in their own heartland and keeps the Philistines at a safe distance for years to come.

As in the case of Jephthah's victory over the Ammonites in Judges 11:32–35, the celebration of the Philistines' defeat ends abruptly because of an ill-advised oath (**14:24–30**). In an apparent attempt to win the Lord's favor, Saul puts a curse on anyone who eats any food before evening. The curse shows Saul's poor judgment, because the weary troops needed to be refreshed so they could continue the pursuit of the Philistines. To make matters worse, Jonathan does not hear the curse and eats some honey along the way. He immediately receives some much-needed strength but is upset when someone tells him about his father's oath. As a direct result of Saul's curse the rest of the troops are guilty of breaking the law of Moses (**14:31–35**). They are famished after chasing the Philistines into the western foothills, so when they are finally allowed to eat, they butcher animals without properly draining the blood. By eating blood they are breaking the Lord's command (see Lev. 17:11; Deut. 12:16), because blood was normally poured out in sacrifices and was considered sacred. Saul builds his first altar at this time, perhaps to atone for the actions of his men and to express thanks to God for the great victory over the Philistines.

After the soldiers have eaten and regained some strength, Saul proposes that they continue to pursue the Philistines during the night to follow up the victory. The men agree, but when Ahijah inquires of the Lord—presumably through the Urim and Thummim—there is no answer. Saul quickly reasons that someone must have broken his oath and prays that the Lord might identify the guilty party. Using the same Urim and Thummim to cast lots, Saul and the priest discover that Jonathan is the culprit (**14:36–46**). Even though Jonathan has only "tasted a little honey" (v. 43), Saul asserts that he must die. His insistence deeply disturbs the rest of the troops, for they know that Jonathan is the one God has used to bring about this amazing victory. Why should he be put to death for being so courageous? Saul has placed "an undeserved curse" on Jonathan and it should not take effect. Ironically, it was Saul himself who had spared the lives of several Israelites after the Lord had given him victory over the Ammonites (11:13).

The complications caused by Saul's curse prevent the Israelites from taking full advantage of the disarray of the Philistines. Many of the Philistines make it safely back to their coastal cities and resume their attacks, eventually bringing about the death of Saul and the collapse of Israel (31:1–13).

The first main section of 1 and 2 Samuel ends with a summary of Saul's rule as king (**14:47–52**). Even though Saul continues to rule until the end of 1 Samuel, chapter 15 marks the transition to the rise of David to the throne.

Along with his victories over the Ammonites and Philistines, Saul enjoys some success against Moab and Edom to the east and south and the king of Zobah, a region in the Beqa'a Valley north of Israel. None of these other battles are recorded in Scripture, but chapter 15 does describe the victory over the Amalekites.

Saul's sons are listed in verse 49, although Ish-Bosheth, who succeeds him as king briefly, is not named (see 2 Sam. 2:8). Saul's two daughters, Merab and Michal, are also mentioned. Michal plays an important role as David's first wife. The key military figure is Saul's cousin, Abner, who commands the army throughout his reign.

II. David's Rise to the Throne (1 Sam. 15–2 Sam. 8)

As noted in the introduction, these chapters serve as a defense of the dynasty of David, providing a full account of David's rise to the throne and explaining why someone from the tribe of Judah replaces Saul of Benjamin. One of the key points in this "apology" is that Saul disqualifies himself as king by his actions, paving the way for the accession of David.

A. David's fame (15:1–17:58). The Old Testament contains many stories about the young and the obscure and how they become successful, but perhaps none is loved more than the story of David. Born the youngest of eight sons in the town of Bethlehem, David becomes a hero overnight and achieves a level of fame and fortune that is incredible. Musician, poet, prophet, warrior, diplomat, and statesman, David's versatility and ability have been rarely if ever matched. Before he is allowed to develop some of these gifts, however, we see him fleeing from Saul, who views him as a dangerous rival.

As in the last chapter, Saul wins an important victory but makes a serious mistake (**15:1–9**). This time the enemy is the Amalekites, a Bedouin people that treacherously attacked the Israelites after they came out of Egypt (Exod. 17:8–16). In accord with the Lord's harsh words about Amalek given to Moses, Samuel tells Saul to attack the Amalekites and "totally destroy" all their people and animals (v. 3). This technical term for complete destruction was also applied to the Canaanites when Joshua invaded the land. Because of the wickedness of the people, God decreed that everybody and everything should be wiped out (Josh. 6:17–18). No plunder of any kind could be taken.

Saul musters a sizable army and heads south to carry out his mission. Before attacking, he warns another Bedouin group, the Kenites, to move out of the area. Unlike the Amalekites, the Kenites had been friendly to Israel, and Moses had in fact married a Kenite woman. Once the Kenites leave, Saul battles the Amalekites, chasing them to the eastern border of Egypt and wiping out all of the people. But he unwisely spares the king,

Agag, and "the best of the sheep and cattle" (v. 9).

Saul's incomplete obedience creates an immediate crisis for the nation because the Lord is grieved that he has made Saul king (**15:10–21**). Samuel knows that Saul's future is bleak. Saul's sin and the sin of his soldiers have brought deep sorrow to God, and judgment is sure to follow. As he returns from the victory, Saul sets up a victory monument in his own honor that likely reveals an attitude of pride. Then he goes to Gilgal, where he had been confirmed as king years earlier (11:14–15) but where he will now lose the kingship.

When Samuel meets him, Saul greets him warmly, but Samuel immediately asks why the sheep and cattle have been spared. Saul tries to shift the blame to the soldiers claiming that the animals were saved so that they might be sacrificed to the Lord. Based on the way the troops gorged themselves in 14:32, this claim is at least questionable here, especially since both contexts refer to "pouncing on the plunder." But even if the army had a spiritual purpose in mind, Samuel asserts that it was wrong to spare the animals. Saul protests vigorously, arguing that he has in fact carried out the assigned mission.

Samuel's response to Saul gives the classic position about the relationship between sacrifice and obedience (**15:22–31**). Stated bluntly, "to obey is better than sacrifice" (v. 22). Without question, the offering of sacrifices is an integral part of worship in the Old Testament and is valued highly, but it must be linked with a heart that is right with God. A rebellious and arrogant attitude nullifies the effect of any sacrifice. Many of the prophets wrestled with this issue and asserted that a large number of sacrifices would never atone for injustice, oppression, or pride. Genuine repentance and obedience must accompany the presentation of sacrifices. Since Saul had deliberately disobeyed the Lord's command, the Lord rejects him as king.

Alarmed by the severity of Samuel's pronouncement, Saul finally admits his sin and begs forgiveness, but Samuel condemns him again and turns to leave. As he does so, Saul, who has taken hold of his robe, accidentally tears it. The action proves symbolic of the fact that the Lord has "torn the kingdom of Israel" from Saul and given it to David (v. 28). Lest there be any doubt about the certainty of God's word, Samuel reminds Saul that God "does not lie or change his mind" (v. 29). Ironically, verse 29 is an allusion to Balaam's words to the king of Moab warning him that God had fully determined to bless Israel (Num. 23:11–12). For Saul, God's Word has become a curse.

Although at first (v. 26) Samuel refuses to accompany Saul to the place of worship, he finally agrees to go with him. If he had not gone, the break between the prophet and the king would have weakened Saul's authority. The "honor" of verse 30 is probably the honor of Samuel's presence at Gilgal, where the sacrifices were offered.

Another reason why Samuel goes to Gilgal is to deal with Agag, king of the Amalekites, whom Saul had spared (**15:32–35**). Normally victory was not complete until the opposing king was killed, especially if it was a war of "total destruction" (cf. v. 3). Like Joshua, who executed the five Amorite kings (Josh. 10:26), and Gideon, who killed the two kings of Midian (Judg. 8:21), Samuel strikes down Agag. It is a strange role for the aged prophet and priest.

From this time on Samuel does not try to contact Saul, but he does mourn for the one he had anointed as king. Samuel knows what a difficult time Saul will have in his final years, out of touch with God and with his people.

In approximately 1025 B.C. the Lord tells Samuel to go to Bethlehem, a town six miles south of Jerusalem, to anoint a new king (**16:1–13**). This was the home of Ruth and Boaz, and it is one of their great-grandsons that Samuel anoints (Ruth 4:17). Samuel is afraid Saul might kill him, but the Lord shows him how to disguise the purpose of the visit by offering a sacrifice in Bethlehem. When he arrives there, the elders wonder what is wrong, but Samuel calms their fears. He has come to anoint one of their young men, not to reprove anyone of sin. When Jesse and his sons come to the sacrifice, Samuel is impressed by the oldest son, Eliab, a tall and handsome man. But the Lord reminds Samuel that he considers inner qualities of an individual rather than the outward appearance, and the one he will choose will be "a man after his own heart" (13:14). None of Jesse's seven sons present at the sacrifice is the chosen one, so Samuel insists that the youngest son be brought from tending the sheep. When David arrives, he too is handsome and fit, but, more importantly, the Lord has chosen him to shepherd the people of Israel (cf. 2 Sam. 5:2). While his brothers look on in amazement, Samuel anoints David with oil as the new king-designate. "From that day on the Spirit of the LORD came upon David in power," as he had come upon Saul at the earlier anointing (v. 13; cf. 10:6–10). Throughout the rest of his life, David enjoyed the empowering of the Spirit upon his work and ministry.

Unlike David, Saul experiences the departure of the Spirit of God and the coming into his life of an evil spirit. This evil spirit is "from the LORD" in the sense that God permits him to torment Saul and that ultimately he is under God's control (cf. 1 Kings 22:19–23; Job 1:12). Saul's jealousy and depression are made worse because of the influence of this evil spirit, and at times he drives Saul to violence (cf. 18:10–11). According to verse 23, the evil spirit affected Saul sporadically.

In an attempt to help Saul find relief from the evil spirit, Saul's attendants suggest that he secure a musician to play soothing music. Ironically, the man they recommend is none other than David, recently anointed to succeed Saul (**16:14–23**). In addition to his ability as a shepherd, David knew how to play the harp, and he had a fine personality. He also enjoyed divine favor (v. 18). If only Saul and his aides had understood to what extent the Lord was with David, they never would have invited him to come. By doing so, Saul gives valuable court training to his successor and allows him to make many friends. Saul likes David very much and asks Jesse if David might remain in his service. Although Jesse must have realized what a dangerous position David would be in if Saul ever found out about the anointing, he could also see how the Lord was preparing David for his future work.

The event that catapults David into the public eye is his astonishing victory over Goliath (**17:1–58**). As a warrior and a general he would consistently defeat the Philistines for the rest of his life.

After years of relative peace, the Philistines once again threaten the Israelites, sending their troops into the Valley of Elah, about fifteen miles west of Bethlehem. Instead of trying to engage the Israelites in battle, the Philistines send out a champion fighter named Goliath to challenge one of the Israelites to individual combat. The outcome of the battle would hinge on the struggle between the two men. This custom was known among the Greeks, and Homer's *Iliad* contains the famous account of Achilles' victory over Hector. Apparently the Hittites of Asia Minor also practiced individual combat to a limited extent. According to 2 Samuel 2:15, a later war between Israel and Judah was to be settled by a twelve-man "team," representing each side. In view of Goliath's great size and strength, it is easy to see why the Philistines were counting on him. He is over nine feet tall and his armor weighs about 125 pounds. When he hurls his challenge toward the Israelites, Saul and his men cower in fear. Their defeatist attitude is reminiscent of the fear of the ten spies who saw the tall residents of Hebron prior to the conquest (Num. 13:31–33).

As tension mounts at the battle scene, we are told that David's three oldest brothers are among Saul's troops, listening to Goliath's defiant challenge for forty days. David is back in Bethlehem taking care of the sheep, for Saul's condition had apparently improved. Anxious about his older sons, Jesse decides to send David to visit the troops and take some food to his brothers and their commander. David probably welcomed the chance to see the excitement of impending conflict and to find out why no battle had taken place yet. When he arrives at the scene, he soon discovers the problem as Goliath steps forward to shout his defiance against Israel. Once again the Israelites shrink back in fear.

Although no one has yet volunteered to fight Goliath, Saul offers substantial rewards to the man who can defeat him. Wealth and honor will be his, along with exemption from taxes for his father's family. The victor will also receive Saul's daughter in marriage, with no further brideprice expected. Normally a sizable amount of silver or valuables was paid by the groom to the family of the bride, though military exploits were sometimes substituted. Saul's offer is attractive, but who would stand a chance against the gigantic Philistine?

David is the first one to express any interest, primarily because Goliath is defying "the armies of the living God" (v. 26). Why should he be allowed to disgrace Israel day after day? Whatever his size, Goliath is only an "uncircumcised Philistine."

If Jonathan was willing to attack a whole Philistine unit, someone should have the courage to fight Goliath. As David tries to encourage the troops, he is severely reprimanded by his oldest brother Eliab. Eliab may have been jealous of David's anointing or he may have felt guilty for not volunteering to fight Goliath himself, but in any event his assessment of his brother is totally wrong. David is not trying to avoid family chores nor is his heart conceited and wicked. He is trusting the Lord and has the confidence that God will give Israel victory.

Eventually word of David's courage reaches Saul, who sends for him and learns of his willingness to fight. In view of David's age and inexperience, however, Saul at first rejects his offer. But David reminds Saul that as a shepherd he had killed a lion and a bear, both of which were far more agile than Goliath. God has saved him from wild animals and he will save him from Goliath.

Convinced of David's faith and courage, Saul gives him his blessing and tries to outfit him with armor. But David is not used to the bulky equipment and cannot wear it. Instead, he takes his shepherd's staff, his sling, and five smooth stones from the stream and heads into battle. Since most of the expert slingers were from the tribe of Benjamin, Saul is aware of the deadly effectiveness of this weapon (see Judg. 20:16; 1 Chron. 12:2).

After waiting for forty days, Goliath is disappointed and disgusted when he sees the youthful, unarmed David coming toward him. How much glory is there in killing a defenseless youth? David listens to Goliath's curses and then acknowledges that his main weapon is "the name of the LORD Almighty" (v. 45). Because of David's apparent weakness, the glory for the victory will go to the Lord, and this could be a testimony to the whole world. Like Saul's son, Jonathan, David believes that the battle is the Lord's and that victory does not depend on who has the best weapons or the most soldiers. Just as the parting of the Red Sea terrified the nations (Exod. 15:14–15), so the death of Goliath will demonstrate the power of Israel's God.

As Goliath moves in to silence his brash opponent, David slings one of the stones with unerring accuracy. It strikes the Philistine on the forehead, perhaps killing him instantly (v. 49). David then removes Goliath's sword from the scabbard and cuts off his head. Stunned by this turn of events, the Philistines flee back to their coastal cities with the Israelites in hot pursuit. As David had predicted in verse 46, many of the Philistines are killed along the way. David puts Goliath's weapons in his own tent and later dedicates the sword to the Lord, taking it to the tabernacle (21:9) as a way of acknowledging that God gave him the victory. According to verse 54, David took Goliath's head to Jerusalem. This may refer to a later time after David conquered Jerusalem (2 Sam. 5:1–9) or it may mean that a number of Israelites already lived in Jerusalem. Since Jerusalem was a major city, it would have been a logical place to display a trophy of victory.

Saul's questions about David's identity seem peculiar in light of David's earlier service as a court musician (16:18–23). Since David did not stay at the court permanently, however, it is possible that Saul had forgotten his name or at least the name of his father. Saul had promised tax exemption to the family of the one who killed Goliath (v. 25), so he has to find out the name of David's father. Perhaps Saul wanted to honor David's family in other ways as well.

B. David's struggles with Saul (18:1–27:12). In light of the beneficial results that David's triumph brings to Israel as a whole, we would expect Saul to feel deeply indebted to the young hero. Instead, he soon becomes jealous of David and treats him as a rival. Perhaps Saul suspects that David is the "neighbor" who will replace him as king.

After a brief period of promotions and honor, David becomes persona non grata in Saul's court and the king tries several methods to get rid of him. Saul's attitude is diametrically opposed to that of his son Jonathan, who does all he can to help David.

Along with the rest of the nation, Jonathan admires David greatly and comes to be his close friend (**18:1–7**). Both men are courageous warriors who depend upon the Lord for victory, and both are national heroes. Out of his love for David Jonathan makes a covenant with David and gives him clothes and weapons as a pledge of his friendship. Jonathan's sword, in particular, must have been highly treasured by David. Saul gives David additional military assignments and a high rank in the army, and David continues to be successful.

When Saul and David return home after the defeat of the Philistines, the women of the land come out to greet them with singing and dancing. This had been a custom since Miriam and the women of Israel had celebrated the victory over the Egyptians at the Red Sea (Exod. 15:20). Since David had killed Goliath, his name is included along with Saul's as the women sing their praises: "Saul has slain his thousands, and David his tens of thousands" (v. 7). The refrain must have been sung throughout the country because even the Philistines knew about it (21:11).

When Saul hears the refrain, he becomes angry, thinking David has received more credit than he has (**18:8–16**). But the number 10,000 is the normal parallel to 1000 (cf. Deut. 32:30; Pss. 91:7; 144:13), so David is not placed above Saul. Saul's growing insecurity causes him to misunderstand the poem and become jealous of David. Coupled with the influences of "an evil spirit from God" (v. 10), this jealousy drives Saul to hurl his spear at David while the young warrior is temporarily back at his musician's post. Saul misses twice, and then, frustrated, sends David back to the battlefield. He knows that the Lord is with David but somehow hopes that the Philistines might kill him. When David wins additional battles, the people love him all the more and Saul's apprehensions increase.

When David killed Goliath, he won the right to marry Saul's daughter, Merab (**18:17–30**). Saul, however, adds further military responsibility as a condition of marriage (v. 17). As the oldest daughter, Merab would give a spouse an important claim in the matter of succession to the throne. David politely refuses her hand. Perhaps he did not love her or he may have realized that Saul's offer was hypocritical. In any event, when Saul's other daughter, Michal, is offered to David, he agrees to the marriage in spite of the required brideprice. Saul hopes that one of the Philistines will kill David, but instead, David and his men double the bride-price by killing two hundred Philistines. Saul is forced to make good on his offer, so Michal becomes David's wife. Twice the text states that Michal is in love with David (vv. 20, 28), so the marriage begins on a positive note in spite of the disgruntled father-in-law. Saul's position is becoming more and more precarious while David's standing is steadily improving.

Unable to bring about David's death at the hand of the Philistines, Saul appeals to his close associates to kill David. Jonathan immediately warns David and then tries to persuade his father that David is a friend and not an enemy (**19:1–7**). After all, did not David risk his life to save Saul and Israel from the Philistine threat? Jonathan's reasoning convinces Saul, and he promises not to harm David. In fact, David is restored to Saul's service in the court.

The reconciliation does not last long, however, and it may have been David's continued success as a general that triggers a new outburst of jealousy and violence (**19:8–17**). For the third time, an evil spirit afflicts Saul, and as in 18:10, David's music does not soothe the king. Again Saul throws his spear at David, and again he misses. It is the last time that David dares to be in the presence of the deranged king.

David flees to his own home, but Michal convinces him to leave that night. Like Rahab and the two spies, Michal lets David down through a window so he can escape undetected. She then buys time for David by putting an idol in his bed. Saul's men keep the idol under surveillance for some time before realizing that they have been tricked. The presence of an idol in David's house is disturbing, but most likely Michal kept it on hand to improve her chances of becoming pregnant.

When Saul learns that Michal has helped David escape, he is upset with her. She explains that David had threatened her life unless she assisted him. Michal's actions underscore her allegiance to her husband rather than to her father.

Saul is thwarted in his attempt to capture David (**19:18–24**). David decides to take refuge with Samuel. There in Ramah, only a short distance from Saul's capital at Gibeah, David pours out his troubles to Samuel, who takes him to the nearby residence of the prophets. When Saul's men come to capture David, they surprisingly begin to prophesy as the Spirit of God comes upon them. After two more groups have the same experience, Saul himself comes and he too prophesies, much as he had done after Samuel had anointed him. This time he is an enemy of Samuel and of the new "anointed one," but nonetheless the Spirit comes upon him, almost the same way the evil spirit from the Lord came upon him. The reaction of the people is the same as in 10:11. Although the whole episode is difficult to understand, perhaps the experience of Balaam is somewhat analogous. Hired to curse the Israelites by the king of Moab, Balaam nonetheless blesses Israel several times, and once, "the Spirit of God came upon him" (Num. 24:2). Like Saul, Balaam seemed to be badly out of touch with God, but his own desires were overruled by a sovereign God.

Although Jonathan is Saul's oldest son expected to succeed him on the throne, he becomes close friends with the one Saul regards as his chief rival. Jonathan believes that God has chosen David to be the next king, and he does not allow his own ambition to oppose God's will.

Within a short period of time David's status has changed from that of a national hero to a fugitive. Disappointed and confused, David seeks out his good friend Jonathan, who can perhaps explain Saul's erratic behavior (**20:1–10**). Jonathan assures David that Saul will not harm him. But he does agree to sound out his father to ascertain his current feelings about David. The next day is the New Moon Festival, a holiday on the first of the month marked by rest and special offerings (v. 5). Verse 27 indicates that it was a two-day festival. Since David is Saul's son-in-law and has held a high position in the army, Saul evidently expected David to be present at his table. In the light of recent events, however, David does not want to be anywhere near Saul, so he gives Jonathan an excuse about an annual family sacrifice in Bethlehem. Perhaps families did assemble once a year to observe a New Moon Festival together. David seeks Jonathan's help because the two pledged loyalty to one another earlier (18:3–4).

Sensing that Saul's jealousy might make future contact with David impossible, Jonathan takes David outside for a long talk (**20:11–23**). He promises to carry out David's wishes at the festival and to let David know if he should stay or flee. But beyond that, Jonathan wants to reaffirm his covenant with David. According to verse 13, Jonathan fully expects David to be the next king, and he wants David to promise that he will be kind to Jonathan's family even after he takes the throne. Often a king from a new dynasty would put to death the descendants of the previous king. David reaffirms his oath to show "unfailing kindness" to Jonathan and his family (vv. 14–15). After he became king, David remembered his oath to Jonathan and made special provision for his crippled son Mephibosheth (2 Sam. 9:7).

All hope that Saul might be reconciled to David is soon dashed by what takes place at the New Moon Festival (**20:34–44**). Saul assumes on the first day that David has a legitimate reason to be absent, but on the second day he explodes. When Jonathan tells Saul about the sacrifices in Bethlehem, Saul realizes that he will not have another chance to kill David, so he takes out his anger on Jonathan. Saul cannot understand how Jonathan can side with David when David is the one standing between him and the throne. In utter frustration, Saul hurls his spear across the table at Jonathan. He had never been able to accept Samuel's announcement that his kingdom would not endure, and in his obsession to kill David Saul has managed to alienate his own son as well. Stubborn and unrepentant, he would destroy himself and all who are around him.

The next day Jonathan goes to the field where David is hiding to give him the prearranged signal (20:35–42). Jonathan shoots an arrow beyond the boy who is with him as a sign that David must flee. Because Jonathan knows he might be watched, they had not planned to meet and talk, but after the boy returns to town, David ignores the danger and decides that he has to say goodbye to Jonathan. The two have a tearful parting as they realize they might not see each other again. Jonathan reminds David of their sworn friendship and of the Lord's involvement in their families forever. Judging from his praise of the fallen Jonathan in 2 Samuel 1:26, David greatly valued their friendship.

The next several years David spends as a fugitive, moving from place to place trying to avoid Saul. Most of the time he stays within the borders of his own tribe of Judah, but on two occasions he lives under Philistine jurisdiction.

The first place David stops is Nob, a town just northeast of Jerusalem where the tabernacle is located (**21:1–9**). When he arrives alone, the high priest Ahimelech is startled and wonders if anything is wrong. David replies that Saul has sent him on a secret mission, and then he asks for some food. The only food available is the bread of the Presence, the loaves that were kept in the Holy Place as a symbol of God's provision. Normally this bread was eaten only by the priests (Lev. 24:9), but Ahimelech agrees to give it to David provided that he and his men are ceremonially clean. This involves in particular abstinence from sexual relations (Exod. 19:15). Jesus referred to David's action as an example of doing what was right in an emergency even though it was, strictly speaking, "unlawful" (Mark 2:25–26).

After receiving the bread, David also takes with him the sword of Goliath that he had dedicated to the Lord after his great victory. According to 22:10 and 15 Ahimelech also inquires of the Lord to give David some much needed guidance.

All of this time Ahimelech is unaware that David is fleeing from Saul, since David had lied about the purpose of his visit. This deception may have helped David obtain what he needed, but it cost the priests dearly when Saul found out what they had done for him (22:17–18).

Finding a safe hiding place in a small country is not easy, so David seeks out an area where Saul will be unlikely to follow him (**21:10–15**). It is nevertheless surprising that David goes immediately to Philistine territory and to Gath, the hometown of Goliath! He clearly hopes that no one will recognize him, but almost immediately he is identified as "the king of the land" and a hero like Saul (v. 11). In this context, "king" probably means "military leader," for in recent years David had led the army of Israel more often than Saul.

Before the Philistines learn any more about him, David pretends to be insane with the hope that they will not detain him. Achish, the king of Gath, sees his behavior and refuses to let him stay in the city. Although David later returns to Gath (27:1–2), for the time being it is too dangerous.

After his narrow escape David travels about twelve miles further inland to the cave of Adullam in the western foothills (**22:1–5**). This was close to the place where he had killed Goliath in the Valley of Elah. Word of his whereabouts reaches his family and other individuals who are in trouble with Saul's regime. About four hundred malcontents join him and are molded by David into an effective and loyal fighting force. Managing this motley crew must have been extremely difficult, but it proved to be excellent training for the task of ruling the entire land. With his four hundred men David has at least some means of receiving an income.

Since Saul would be likely to take measures against the rest of David's family, David asks the king of Moab to allow his parents to live there for a while. David's great-grandmother Ruth was a Moabitess.

At this time we are introduced to the prophet Gad, who advises David and who later wrote a history of David's reign (1 Chron. 29:29). It is Gad who gives David a choice of three options after David sinned by taking a census of the land (2 Sam. 24:11–14).

Aware that David now has a growing group of supporters, Saul is worried about a conspiracy against his life (**22:6–10**). He knows that Jonathan is a close friend of David and he is afraid that other high officials might be tempted to defect to David's side. If any are so inclined, Saul warns them that David is from the tribe of Judah and most of them are from Benjamin. Would David give them high positions and valuable property if he became king?

To prove his loyalty to Saul, Doeg the Edomite, Saul's head shepherd, reports what he had seen when David received help from Ahimelech the priest. The implication is that Ahimelech might be the next leader to join David.

Armed with this new information, Saul immediately sends for Ahimelech and the rest of the priests (**22:11–15**). He accuses Ahimelech of conspiring against him by giving valuable assistance to a traitor. Ahimelech protests that he did not realize that David was regarded as an outlaw and a fugitive. Was he not the king's own son-in-law and a respected military leader who had accomplished much for the whole nation? Besides, David told Ahimelech that he was on a secret mission for Saul (cf. 21:2).

Ahimelech's reasoning is sound, but Saul is determined to make an example out of him and all the priests (**22:16–23**). From this point on, no contact with David would be tolerated. When Saul orders the guards to kill the priests, they refuse, but Doeg the Edomite performs the execution. As an Edomite, he probably did not worship the Lord, and hence would have little regard for the priests as God's special ministers. His actions do not help relations between Edom and Israel, and David later treats the Edomites harshly (cf. 2 Sam. 8:12–14).

Not only does Saul order the death of eighty-five priests, but the whole town of Nob is put to the sword, including women and children. It is the sort of total destruction normally reserved for Israel's worst enemies. In all the confusion a son of Ahimelech named Abiathar manages to escape and reach David. When David hears about the massacre he admits that his deception had contributed heavily to the priests' deaths. Abiathar remains with David and uses the ephod with the Urim and Thummim to inquire of the Lord for David. Meanwhile Saul is left without any guidance from prophet or priest.

The general movement of David's flight is toward the south and east and the more rugged areas of Judah. With the help of local residents, Saul is able to track him closely.

Throughout his time as a fugitive David protects the cities of Judah from their enemies. Keilah was a city in the western foothills about ten miles northwest of Hebron (**23:1–6**). When the Philistines steal grain from the threshing floors, David and his men attack and drive them off. Even though David is no longer in Saul's employ, he continues to enjoy mastery over the Philistines. The victory nets David considerable booty, especially livestock (v. 5).

While David and his men stay in Keilah, Saul hears about it and prepares to besiege the city (**23:7–13**). David learns of Saul's plans and inquires of the Lord through Abiathar. In spite of all that David has done for the people of Keilah, the Lord indicates that they will hand him over to Saul. The failure to extradite a fugitive was a major cause for war in the ancient Near East, so the city fathers do not want to risk the horrors of a siege. Since David is equally unwilling to fight Saul, he and his men—six hundred by now—leave the safety of the walled city.

David heads for the Desert of Ziph south of Hebron and the Lord protects him in the hills there. One day encouragement comes through an unexpected visit from Jonathan, Saul's son (**23:14–18**). In this final meeting between the two dear friends, Jonathan assures David that he will become king and that Jonathan will serve under him. Before parting, the two reaffirm the covenant they had made.

In contrast to Jonathan the people of Ziph are anxious to help Saul capture David, so they relay David's precise location to the king (**23:19–29**). Saul thanks them and keeps up a religious front by saying 'The Lord bless you for your concern for me" (v. 21). But as in verse 7 when Saul thought that God had handed David over to him, the king is badly mistaken. God has abandoned him and is frustrating his every move. In this instance Saul and his men have David cornered in the Desert of Maon when news comes that the Philistines are attacking the land. The timing is providential, allowing David and his men to escape to the strongholds of En-gedi.

David's new hideout is an area with many caves along the high cliffs. The whole region between the Dead Sea and the hill country of Judea consisted of steep valleys and gorges cut by the streams and wadis that flowed into the Dead Sea. It was a natural area for mountain goats, but outlaws also made good use of the rugged terrain. En-gedi means "spring of the goats" because of the excellent water source located there.

When Saul returns to pursue David he happens to relieve himself in the same cave where David and his men are hiding (**24:1–7**) Apparently Saul is alone, so David's men tell him that this is the Lord's timing. If they kill Saul, the kingdom will be David's. David rejects their advice but does sneak up behind Saul and cut off a corner of his robe.

After Saul leaves the cave, David calls out to him and tells him what he has done (**24:8–15**). Holding up the piece of the robe as evidence of his mercy, David asserts that he is not trying to wrest the throne from Saul and that he is not guilty of treason. Instead, he has committed the matter to the Lord who will decide the case as a righteous Judge. Just as war was considered to be a contest between the gods of the rival nations, so this personal battle will be settled by the Lord in favor of the righteous party. According to verse 14 David is no more dangerous than a dead dog or a flea, and yet Saul is consuming time and energy in an effort to eliminate him.

Confronted by clear evidence that David has spared his life, Saul expresses remorse for seeking to kill David and admits that he has treated David badly (**24:16–22**). Echoing the words of his son Jonathan (23:17), Saul asserts that David will indeed be the next king of Israel. Saul makes David promise that as the new ruler he will not wipe out Saul's descendants. In the light of this apparent reconciliation, it appears that David's years as a fugitive might be over; but David has learned that Saul's word cannot be trusted (cf. 19:6). Subsequent events indicate that before long Saul resumes his pursuit of David.

To make matters worse for David, the prophet Samuel dies (**25:1**). The revered leader who had presided over the beginning of the monarchy and had anointed both Saul and David is gone. He had been one of the greatest figures in Israel's history, playing important spiritual and political roles in the tradition of Moses. Without him, David feels even more alone, for one of his strongest supporters has passed from the scene.

After his meeting with Saul, David continues to live in the region south of Hebron. The "Carmel" mentioned in verse 2 was near Ziph and Maon, not the Mount Carmel of Elijah near the Mediterranean Sea. While living in Carmel, David and his men work for a wealthy man named Nabal, protecting his flocks and herds (**25:2–13**). When sheep-shearing time arrives, David expects to be given meat and bread in exchange for his labors. Normally this was a time of feasting for all the family and workers. When Nabal receives David's request from the ten men he had sent, he refuses to give him anything, calling David a nobody, a deserter.

News of Nabal's insulting remarks spurs David to action. If Nabal will not pay willingly, David will take his pay by force and kill Nabal's family in the process. Bent on revenge, David sets out with four hundred men.

Nabal has an intelligent and beautiful wife named Abigail who is very different from her stingy husband (**25:14–22**). When she hears what Nabal has said to David, she follows the advice of one of the servants and takes matters into her own hands. Quickly she prepares a sizable gift of meat, bread, raisins, and figs and sends them to David. She herself mounts a donkey and heads in the same direction. As she approaches, David has just invoked a curse on himself that would take effect if he did not put to death all the males in Nabal's household (v. 22).

When Abigail begins her plea for mercy, she immediately disassociates herself from her husband (**25:23–35**). She admits that he is a scoundrel and that he deserves to die. "Nabal" means "fool," "and folly goes with him" (v. 25). It is unclear why anyone would actually name a son "Fool," unless Nabal's father was as defiant as he was. Perhaps his real name is suppressed and "Nabal" is used because of the character of the man. In spite of his wealth, no one has anything good to say about him. Abigail apologizes for Nabal's behavior and for her own ignorance of David's request.

Nine times Abigail refers to David as "my lord" or "my master," a clear indication that her opinion of David differs sharply from that of her husband (cf. vv. 10–11). In this regard, Abigail realizes that David has fought "the LORD's battles" on behalf of Israel and that he will become king. She believes that God will make "a lasting dynasty" for David because of his faithfulness, but all of his enemies will perish. With such a bright future ahead of him, David will not want to "have on his conscience the staggering burden of needless bloodshed" (v. 31). Abigail admits her husband's guilt, but taking revenge on members of his own tribe of Judah would tarnish David's image as a wise and fair leader.

David thanks Abigail for her kind words and acknowledges that the Lord has used her to keep him from avenging himself. Instead of acting like the king he is destined to be, he had almost behaved like a brigand chief.

When Abigail returns home she finds Nabal

very drunk. At sheep-shearing time drunkenness and partying were common, and Nabal has enjoyed it to the hilt. The next morning Abigail tells him about her meeting with David, and Nabal immediately suffers a stroke or perhaps a heart attack. About ten days later he dies. David correctly interprets Nabal's death as the Lord's judgment for mistreating him and probably many other people as well. (**25:36–44**). The realization that the Lord upheld his cause against Nabal gives David the confidence that God will decide the dispute with Saul in his favor also. It is a sign that none of David's enemies will stand against him.

The death of Nabal also releases Abigail from a difficult marriage and gives her the freedom to accept David's invitation to become his wife. From David's standpoint, marriage to the widow of a prominent citizen of Judah would help him politically, and a new wife is compensation for the loss of Michal, whom Saul had given to another man to weaken David's claim to the throne. David never accepts Saul's imposed divorce, however, and later takes Michal back as his wife (2 Sam. 3:13–16).

David again refuses to kill Saul (**26:1–12**). As in 24:2, Saul takes three thousand men to track David down in the Desert of Ziph, where he had narrowly escaped from Saul earlier (23:24–28). David's scouts tell him where Saul and his army are camping for the night, and David himself gets close enough to see where Saul and Abner are lying down. With characteristic boldness, David decides to pay a visit to the camp, accompanied by Abishai, his nephew who later becomes one of his top generals (2 Sam 18:2). It seems like a foolish idea, but the Lord has put Saul's army "into a deep sleep" (v. 12). David and Abishai creep right up to Saul, and Abishai sees this as a golden opportunity to get rid of Saul. But as in the cave at En-gedi (24:6), David refuses the easy way out. Besides, the death of Nabal had proved how rapidly God could strike down the enemy—without any help on David's part. So David and his nephew take Saul's water jug and spear and leave the camp.

When they reach a hill a safe distance away, David calls out loudly to Saul's cousin Abner, the army commander (**26:13–25**). He scolds Abner for failing to guard the king and points out the security breach that has occurred. Awakened by the commotion, Saul reacts to David's voice exactly as he had in 24:16: "Is that your voice, David my son?" David responds with another assertion of innocence and wonders why Saul continues to chase him. He feels like a partridge relentlessly pursued by a hunter. If God has incited Saul against him, David is willing to make things right with the Lord and bring him an offering. If other men have urged Saul to pursue David, he calls on God to judge them. David feels alienated from other Israelites and he realizes he is on the verge of being forced out of the land. If that should happen, he would be far from the sanctuary and might have to worship other gods.

As in 24:16–22, Saul seems convinced by David's arguments and especially by the spear in David's hand. The king admits he has acted like a fool and promises to leave David alone. In verse 25 Saul predicts that David "will do great things and surely triumph," implying that eventually David will be king. Saul almost sounds like Balaam who really wanted to curse Israel but wound up predicting that Israel would crush their enemies (Num. 24:17).

Sad to say, David cannot believe the conciliatory words of Saul, for the king would soon forget what he has promised. Frustrated and discouraged, David decides to find refuge in Philistine territory, where Saul will not likely venture (**27:1–12**). It is a calculated risk, because the Philistines might kill him and because the Israelites might consider him a traitor and might not ever welcome him back. On the other hand, by staying with the Philistines, David could learn valuable information about their military tactics and about iron working. He also makes friends with some of the Philistines, and after he becomes king, several contingents from Philistia serve as faithful mercenary troops under him (2 Sam. 15:18).

As he had done earlier (21:10–15), David goes to Achish of Gath and asks for asylum. This time the Philistines are not so suspicious of David, because his reputation as an outcast and an enemy of Saul is now well established. Besides, David's six hundred-man army could serve Achish as a valuable mercenary force. David is allowed to live in Ziklag, a town in southern Judah not controlled by the Philistines. While there David and his men have more freedom than they would have had in Gath.

During his time in Ziklag, David actually benefits the Israelites much more than the Philistines. Although he tells Achish that he is conducting raids against areas of Judah, instead he is attacking Israel's enemies. Joshua had not been able to conquer the land of the Geshurites in the south (Josh. 13:2), but now David soundly defeats them (v. 8). Like Saul, David also successfully fights the Amalekites. Whenever he attacks a town, he leaves no survivors to complain to the Philistines, but he does take flocks, herds, and other valuables. Achish naively thinks that David has turned against the Israelites with all his heart.

C. Saul's final battle (28:1–31:13). Throughout his reign Saul had battled the Philistines in an attempt to keep them from expanding beyond their coastal strongholds. With David's help he had won many crucial victories, but now David is on the Philistines' side, and Saul knows that the Lord has left him.

David knew that eventually he would be called on to fight against Saul (**28:1–6**). As a mercenary of Achish, he would have to join with the rest of the Philistine forces. Although it was unthinkable for David to fight against his own people, he had the Philistines convinced that he was ready and eager to fight Saul. His actual statements, however, are ambiguous and carry the strong implication that he never would fight against Israel.

The Philistines assemble their troops at Shunem, in the Valley of Jezreel near the Sea of Galilee, and the Israelites gather at Mount Gilboa toward the eastern end of the valley. Saul is terrified and turns to inquire of the Lord, but the Lord had long since broken off contact with Saul. Revelation from God normally came through dreams, prophets, or priests, but Saul had massacred the priests himself (22:18) and Samuel was dead. Apparently, Saul was not in touch with any other prophet.

Endor was a few miles north of Mount Gilboa, so Saul goes there to inquire of a medium (**28:7–14**). Since Saul himself had expelled the mediums and spiritists from the land earlier in his reign, he disguises himself and takes only two men with him. The disguise seems to work until the medium sees the spirit of Samuel coming up out of the ground, and then immediately recognizes Saul. Perhaps her clairvoyant state gave her the ability to identify Saul at this time. Her loud cry has been interpreted to mean that she was startled by the success of her effort to call up Samuel, but this is not necessarily the case. Consulting the dead is referred to in Deuteronomy 18:11 and Isaiah 8:19, and although it is strongly condemned as characteristic of the spiritual corruption of pagan nations, its effectiveness is not denied. Occult practices were to be avoided by God's people, and Saul as the divinely appointed king knew this well. In this instance it is possible that God allowed the communication from the departed Samuel to be more extensive than usual, for Saul was the king and a national crisis had arisen. Another unusual aspect of this account is the description of Samuel as "spirit" (v. 13), a word normally translated "God" or "gods." Clearly the whole episode is of supernatural origin.

While Saul lies prostrate on the ground Samuel begins to speak, complaining about being disturbed in this fashion (**24:15–19**). The grave was to be a place of rest, where the righteous "enter into peace" (Isa. 57:2). Saul explains that the situation is desperate, but he has called for Samuel with the hope that perhaps in his mercy God will once again deliver Israel against great odds. He wants a glimmer of hope, a word of encouragement from Samuel, who himself had witnessed God's miraculous intervention against the Philistines (7:10–11).

Unhappily Samuel's response is anything but encouraging and contains the same grim words he had spoken at his last meeting with Saul after the battle with the Amalekites (15:22–29). Because Saul has failed to carry out God's fierce wrath against the Amalekites, Saul has lost the right to rule and the next day he and his sons will die (vv. 18–19). Just as Eli and his sons died the same day the Philistines defeated the Israelites (4:11, 18), so Saul and his family will fall before the same enemy. In both cases, Samuel announced God's word of judgment prior to the catastrophe.

Knowing now that all hope is gone, Saul falls to the ground in despair (**28:20–25**). He is completely exhausted, because he has eaten nothing all day in preparation for his encounter with Samuel. At the urging of the woman and his men, Saul finally agrees to eat something, and the woman butchers a fattened calf. In spite of his pitiful condition Saul is still the king, and she gives him the best she has.

As the battle draws near, David and his men are lined up on the Philistine side (**29:1–11**). They are "at the rear with Achish," an indication that David wanted to stay out of the battle if possible. In the light of the way David had fought against them earlier, the other four rulers of the Philistines are nervous about his presence. They wonder if he might not rejoin the Israelite side during the battle and be reconciled to Saul. If they had known of David's close friendship with Jonathan, they would have had even more reason to be concerned. In an earlier battle, a number of renegade Israelites had switched back to their own side when the Philistines began to suffer losses (14:21).

Achish protests that he has no reason to doubt David's loyalty to his new allies, but he is clearly outvoted by the other rulers. When he breaks the news to David, David acts surprised and hurt. Clearly, however, the order saves him from the horns of a dilemma. Up to this point he had consistently refused to touch the Lord's anointed and he had secretly helped the Israelites even while in exile. He has no desire to fight the people over whom he expects to be king!

When David and his men go north with the Philistine armies, the Amalekites decide to get revenge for David's earlier attacks against them (**30:1–6**). David's city of Ziklag is burned and all of the women and children are taken captive. Not knowing if any will be recovered alive, David and his men are heartbroken. The men blame David and threaten to stone him, just as an earlier generation had grumbled menacingly against Moses (Exod. 17:4). Yet in the midst of this opposition and his own personal sorrow at the loss of his two wives, "David found strength in the LORD his God" (v. 6).

Since Abiathar the priest is there and can inquire of the Lord by means of the ephod, David finds out he can overtake the raiders (**30:7–20**). Encouraged, he and his men head to the southwest. Only four hundred men are strong enough to keep up the pursuit, for they have already covered many miles in the three-day journey back home. Fortunately they receive valuable information from an Egyptian member of the raiding party who had been abandoned after taking ill. Revived by food and drink, he reveals that the Amalekites had taken advantage of all the parties involved in the war in the north by attacking several areas belonging to Judah and the Philistines (v. 14). The amount of the plunder may have slowed them down, because David finds them celebrating enthusiastically. Apparently the Amalekites thought they were a safe distance away from any pursuers, but David soundly defeats them and recovers all of the captives and plunder. Mourning turns to joy as the men are reunited with their families. It is a great triumph, reminiscent of Abraham's recovery of the people and goods of Sodom after his daring pursuit of the four northern kings (Gen. 14:15–16).

After their return, a dispute arises over the distribution of the plunder (**30:21–31**). Should the two hundred men who could not keep up with the others receive an equal share of the goods? As a wise and fair leader David insists that all the shares be the same, for the victory was the work of the Lord and none of the men could claim credit for it. The same God who had handed over Goliath to David had handed over the Amalekites. Because the plunder is so abundant David also sends presents to the elders in a number of the towns of Judah. Those towns were mostly to the south of Hebron where David and his men had tried to hide from Saul (23:24–25) and where David had received valuable assistance. Hebron, the most important of these cities, is mentioned last. A number of these places had probably been plundered by the Amalekites and were no doubt grateful for the gift of goods and livestock.

For the first time Saul is fighting the Philistines in the Valley of Jezreel, where their chariots may have given them a decided advantage. But even more important is the fact that God has abandoned Saul, leaving the armies of Israel defenseless (**31:1–6**). As the battle rages three of Saul's sons are killed, including Jonathan, the crown prince and David's close friend. One son—called Ish-Bosheth or Esh-Baal—survives, and he will serve as king briefly. Saul's leading general, Abner, also somehow lives through the battle. Saul himself is critically wounded by the archers and asks his armor-bearer to finish him off. When the armor-bearer refuses to kill him, Saul falls on his sword and takes his own life. It is a tragic ending to a reign that had begun in such a promising fashion, only to slide steadily toward destruction.

With their leaders gone and the army in full flight, the Israelites abandon their cities and flee, allowing the Philistines to take full control of the whole region (**31:7–13**). The next day the Philistines cut off Saul's head as David had done to Goliath (cf. 17:51). Word of the Philistines' triumph is announced in their temples, giving glory to their gods. Just as David had placed Goliath's sword in the tabernacle as a trophy of victory (21:9), so Saul's armor is placed in the temple of the Ashtoreths. Saul's body is hung on the wall of the public square of Beth-shan.

When the men of Jabesh-gilead hear how Saul's body is being dishonored, they cross the Jordan, take down Saul's body and those of his sons, and return home. They remember how Saul had rescued their city from the threat of the Ammonites when he first became king. Because the bodies have been mutilated, they are cremated rather than buried, though the bones are to some extent preserved and buried. Years later, David had the remains of Saul and Jonathan transferred to the family tomb of Saul's father Kish in one of the towns of Benjamin (2 Sam. 21:11–14). To mourn the death of Saul, the people of Jabesh-gilead fast for seven days.

D. David unifies Judah and Israel (2 Sam. 1:1–5:25). When Saul died it appeared that Israel's experiment with the monarchy had been a failure. Philistine control had increased rather than decreased, and Israel was on the verge of splitting into north and south because of the dispute between Saul and David. Within seven years, however, David was able to unify the people of Judah and Israel, defeat the Philistines, and establish one of the strongest nations in the entire Near East. Israel's golden age was about to begin.

It must have been with a heavy heart that David awaited news of the battle in the north. Although an Israelite defeat would hasten David's rise to the throne, it would bring hardship and sorrow to the nation as a whole.

Three days after David's return to Ziklag, he learns the outcome of the battle (**1:1–16**). An Amalekite who had escaped from the scene describes how he had himself put Saul out of his misery. His account differs from that of 1 Samuel 31. Most likely the Amalekite claims credit for killing Saul with the hope of getting a reward from David. He undoubtedly reached Saul before the Philistines did, saw his dead body, and took the crown as booty. Having confirmed the death of Saul and Jonathan, David and his men tear their clothes as a sign of their grief. David displays no joy whatever over Saul's death and in fact orders that the Amalekite be executed because he testified that he had killed the Lord's anointed. It is ironic that an Amalekite is executed for Saul's death because Saul's downfall began with the failure to destroy the Amalekites (1 Sam. 15:18–19; 28:18). In light of David's recent conflicts with the Amalekites (1 Sam. 30), the young man's hope for a reward was slim to begin with.

David's harsh treatment of Saul's alleged murderer is an important part of David's "apology." To avoid the charge of being a usurper, David expresses displeasure with anyone who hastens the demise of Saul and his family. When Saul's son Ish-Bosheth is assassinated, David likewise orders the execution of the two assassins (4:10–12). No one in the tribe of Benjamin could say that David was supporting those who killed his political rivals.

David composes a lament in honor of Israel's fallen leaders (**1:17–27**). Known as the "lament of the bow," it may have been sung by Israel's warriors in subsequent years while they practiced their technique with the bow and arrow in the hope of avoiding defeat in battle. According to verse 18, this lament was also included in the Book of Jashar, a collection of battle accounts that was not accepted as a part of Scripture (cf. Josh. 10:12–13).

The lament begins and ends with the line "How the mighty have fallen!" as David eulogizes Saul and Jonathan and emphasizes their accomplishments. Nowhere in the poem does David mention Saul's weaknesses, failures, or jealousy; instead he links father and son as an effective team, victorious in battle and benefactors of the nation's citizens. Based on his own experience among the Philistines, David realizes how much they will celebrate the victory. Yet in verse 20 he asks that somehow the singing and dancing might be stilled, lest the people defame the Lord's reputation by concluding that he is weaker than the Philistine gods. Turning his attention to the scene of the battle in verse 21, David pronounces a curse on the mountains of Gilboa, as if the terrain itself were responsible for Israel's defeat. Without dew or rain, the soil would lie barren in sympathetic mourning over the terrible catastrophe.

Although David honors the memory of Saul in several verses, his greatest praise is reserved for his dear friend Jonathan. Jonathan had made a covenant with David linking their families forever (1 Sam. 20:14–16), but his loyalty to Saul kept him by his father's side in this final and fatal conflict. Jonathan fought hard for Israel, though he would rather have fought alongside both David and Saul. Loving David as he did, Jonathan was willing to give up his own claim to the throne in favor of David, whom he would gladly have served. What a friend, what a brother, and how deeply David feels his loss!

During Saul's reign, the people of Judah were torn between loyalty to the king and loyalty to their local hero David, whom Saul had declared an outlaw. Since David had cultivated the friendship of the elders of Judah even while allegedly an ally of the Philistines (1 Sam. 30:21), his leadership status was clearly established. Nonetheless, after Saul's death David takes nothing for granted and seeks the Lord's guidance before moving to Hebron, the most important city of Judah, centrally located in the hill country nineteen miles south of Jerusalem. There, where Abraham had lived for many years and where the patriarchs were buried, David is publicly crowned as king over Judah (**2:1–7**). He has waited about fifteen years since his private anointing by Samuel in Bethlehem (1 Sam. 16:13), but the time to rule has finally arrived.

Realizing that Saul's supporters in the north will not readily accept him as king, David seeks to establish good relations with them immediately. He demonstrates his respect for Saul by thanking the men of Jabesh-gilead for burying him. By their brave actions they have shown kindness to Saul, and David promises to treat them kindly and fairly. This message is an indirect request for them to recognize David as king, but the northern tribes refuse to acknowledge him for another seven years.

The general of Saul's army, his cousin Abner, had managed to survive the Battle of Gilboa, and he emerges as the most powerful figure of the northern tribes. Instead of unifying the nation under David, Abner decides to place Saul's remaining son, Ish-Bosheth, on the throne of Israel (**2:8–11**). His reasons for doing so are not entirely clear, but later on even Ish-Bosheth suspects that Abner wants the throne for himself (3:6–8). The name *Ish-Bosheth* means "man of shame," but this was a later development. Originally his name was "Ish- (or "Esh-) Baal," meaning "man of the Lord" (1 Chron. 8:33). "Baal" is a Hebrew word for "lord" or "master," and was sometimes used to refer to God. But because "Baal" was also the name of the main Canaanite god, any name containing "Baal" was later changed to "Bosheth" to emphasize that worshiping Baal was "a shameful thing." Jonathan's son Mephibosheth was originally named "Merib-Baal" (1 Chron. 8:34).

Abner makes Ish-Bosheth king in Mahanaim, a city in Trans-Jordan that functioned as a "capital in exile." He is called king of "all Israel" (v. 9) but it is not likely that he exercised much control over the tribal areas west of the Jordan since the Philistines occupied many cities. An additional problem is the "two-year" reign of Ish-Bosheth (v. 10), which is hard to reconcile with David's 7½-year reign over Judah (vv. 10–11). Does this mean that it took five years before all the northern tribes recognized Ish-Bosheth as king, or do the two years refer to the time when he and Abner were able to reestablish control over the area west of the Jordan?

With two kings vying for control of the land, conflict between the forces of David and Ish-Bosheth was inevitable (**2:12–17**). The first battle takes place at Gibeon, about six miles north of Jerusalem, close to Saul's former capital at Gibeah. Abner brings in troops from Trans-Jordan, while David's army is led by his nephew Joab, a loyal and effective commander to whom David becomes greatly indebted. At times he was ruthless and quick to assassinate his foes, but David seemed unable to punish him. In his opening battle, twelve men fight for each side in a kind of representative warfare related to the one-on-one combat between David and Goliath. This time the result is indecisive so a full-scale battle ensues. The civil war is underway, and David's men win handily.

As the men of Israel flee the scene, Abner is chased by Joab's brother Asahel, who is a very swift runner (**2:18–23**). Asahel knew that if he could kill Abner, Ish-Bosheth's "kingdom" might collapse completely, giving David control of the whole nation. Abner is much older and unable to outrun Asahel, but he does not want to anger Joab by killing his brother. He fears that Joab might seek revenge, although the killing took place in battle. When no other alternative remains, Abner strikes Asahel with the butt of his spear, perhaps to stop him but not kill him. The blow is a powerful one, however, and Asahel dies immediately.

After the death of their brother, Joab and Abishai keep up the chase until sunset, when Israel's resistance stiffens (**2:24–32**). Abner calls for a truce, because the terrible results of civil war are already becoming clear to him, and further fighting will only make it worse. In light of the number of fatalities, Joab agrees to the truce and the battle is finally over. Both armies march all night in order to return to their respective capitals by morning. Only nineteen of David's men have perished, compared with 360 casualties for Abner and Benjamin. This large discrepancy may be due to the decimation of Saul's army at the Battle of Gilboa, a battle in which David's men were not allowed to participate (1 Sam. 29:4).

In the years that follow, David continues to enjoy success in the conflict with Ish-Bosheth. One sign of David's increasing strength is the number of sons born to him in Hebron (**3:1–5**). Since none of the six have the same mother, we learn that David has taken four more wives. One of these—Maacah, daughter of the king of Geshur—is probably married to David for political reasons, to make an alliance with the Aramean city-state northeast of the Sea of Galilee. It is Maacah's son Absalom who kills David's firstborn, Amnon, and then leads a rebellion against his own father. While the writer of Samuel does not condemn polygamy as such, like the author of 1 Kings (11:4) he shows us the disastrous results of multiple marriages.

Apparently Ish-Bosheth resented the fact that Abner was the power behind the throne, and in his jealousy he accuses Abner of wanting to seize the throne himself (**3:6–11**). The specific issue is whether Abner has slept with Saul's concubine, because a king's concubines normally became the property of his successor. Abner reacts to the charge by ending his allegiance to Saul's family and vowing to "transfer the kingdom" to David (v. 10). In his reply Abner admits that he knows the Lord has promised the throne to David. Abner's reaction is more than Ish-Bosheth had bargained for, but he feels helpless to raise any objections.

Abner immediately opens negotiations with David to discuss the conditions under which David might become the ruler of the entire nation (**3:12–21**). David is willing to work out an agreement but only if Saul's daughter Michal is returned to him. During his years as a fugitive, Saul had forced her to divorce David, but David continued to regard her as his wife. His marriage to Saul's daughter would measurably strengthen his claim to succeed Saul as king, particularly in the eyes of the northern ten tribes.

In the decision-making process, the role of the elders is an important one. As the heads of families and tribes, the elders had a voice in the selection and retention of a king (1 Sam. 15:30; 2 Sam. 5:3; 1 Kings 12:3), though their influence decreased over the years. Knowing that many of Israel's leaders had favored David all along, Abner encourages them to support him openly. Abner pays special attention to Saul's tribe of Benjamin, who are the hardest to convince. Satisfied that the leaders of Israel would be willing to make a treaty with David, Abner personally goes to Hebron, where David prepares a feast in his honor. From all indications, David's coronation over all Israel is not far off.

There is one member of David's inner circle who is not happy about the move toward unity (**3:22–27**). David's nephew, Joab, his top military commander, tries to convince David that Abner has come as a spy and that he cannot be trusted. In all likelihood, Joab feared that if the merger took place, he might lose his job to Abner. Joab also never forgave Abner for killing his brother Asahel during the Battle of Gibeon years before (2:23). Since Abner had not traveled very far from Hebron, Joab uses an excuse to bring him back secretly and then stabs him to death. Although Joab justifies his action on the basis of blood revenge, David's reaction to Abner's death exposes Joab's treachery. Abner had killed Asahel only after repeated warnings and as a last resort to save his own life. The killing took place in the middle of a battle and was in no way premeditated murder.

When David learns what Joab has done he does everything he can to express his displeasure and to indicate that he has not been personally involved in any way (**3:28–29**). In verse 29 David places a curse upon Joab and his descendants, asking God to punish them with disease, starvation, or violent death. David himself leads the mourners and weeps at Abner's tomb, and he also composes a short lament in Abner's honor (vv. 33–34). To emphasize his sorrowful attitude even further David fasts the rest of the day.

By regarding Abner's death as a great tragedy, David convinces the nation that he is not implicated in the murder and the fragile alliance with Israel remains intact. At the same time, David probably should have taken some direct disciplinary action against Joab, who does not seem to have lost any power.

David's failure to discipline his officers and his sons constitutes one of his greatest weaknesses, and it nearly cost him the kingdom some years later. Just before he died David told Solomon to bring Joab to justice for his crimes, and shortly thereafter he was executed (1 Kings 2:5–6, 29–35).

With Abner gone Ish-Bosheth's weakness as a leader is even more evident, even to the tribe of Benjamin (**4:1–12**). Not long after Abner's death, two of Ish-Bosheth's military officers gain entrance into the king's house and stab him to death. Then they cut off his head and take it to David at Hebron, hoping to be rewarded for their action. When they arrive, the two brothers connect their assassination with the Lord's vengeance "against Saul and his offspring" (v. 8). To their surprise, David does not seem at all happy over the news of Ish-Bosheth's death and orders that the murderers themselves be put to death. Once again David claims no responsibility for the elimination of any rival—whether Saul, or Abner, or Ish-Bosheth. In each case he is angry and dismayed. The bodies of the assassins are hung near the pool in Hebron as a warning to all and as a sign that David believes in justice.

After the death of Ish-Bosheth, there is no other member of Saul's family who can be considered a serious contender for the throne. Jonathan did have a son named Mephibosheth, but he had been crippled as a child (v. 4). Years later David made sure that he was well cared for in fulfillment of his covenant with Jonathan (chap. 9).

In recognition of their need of a strong leader, all the tribes of Israel journey to the southern capital to anoint David (**5:1–5**). Many thousands of soldiers representing all of the tribes come together to make an agreement with David and to acclaim him as king. They acknowledge that the Lord has chosen him and that he has demonstrated his leadership ability over the years. Even during Saul's reign, some soldiers from the northern tribes had defected to David (1 Chron. 12:1–22), but now the entire nation rallies around him. David is almost thirty-eight years old, and he will remain king until he is seventy. In many ways these next thirty-three years are the most glorious ones in Israel's history, as David strengthens the nation and extends her borders in every direction. Before David dies Israel becomes one of the most powerful nations in the world.

David made many excellent choices during his lifetime, but none was better than his decision to make Jerusalem the capital of the united nation (**5:6–8**). According to Psalm 132:13 the Lord chose Zion for his dwelling, so David is following the Lord's leading as he sets out to capture Jerusalem. Although Jerusalem had briefly belonged to the Israelites (Judg. 1:8), they had been unable to retain control of the city, leaving the Jebusites to rule the city for centuries. At times the city was even called "Jebus" (Judg. 19:10) in honor of the residents. Some scholars connect the Jebusites with the Hurrians, a people who exercised considerable influence in Mesopotamia and Asia Minor from 1800 to 1200 B.C. "Jerusalem" probably means "city of peace" and was also known as "Salem" (Gen. 14:18). "Zion," mentioned for the first time here in verse 7, is another name for Jerusalem but its meaning is uncertain.

In David's time, Jerusalem was a hill covering about eleven acres, located on the border between Judah and Benjamin, making it an ideal neutral site for one who wanted to unite the north and the south. Jerusalem was surrounded by deep valleys on every side except the north, so it could be easily defended. According to verse 6, the Jebusites were confident that David would not be able to capture the city. Jerusalem also possessed an excellent water source, the Gihon spring in the Kidron Valley east of the city. But it may have been the "water shaft" running from the Gihon spring into the city which was used by David's men to gain entrance into Jerusalem. Led by Joab, a few men make a daring and successful attempt to enter Jerusalem and enable the whole army to capture the city. Because of his courage, Joab remains David's commander-in-chief.

David takes immediate steps to fortify his new capital (**5:9–16**). His building efforts are aided by an alliance with Hiram, king of Tyre and leader of the country of Phoenicia (Lebanon). Sending the famed cedars of Lebanon and skilled craftsmen, Hiram helps David build a palace. The Phoenicians were also excellent sailors who controlled the seas, and over the years the Israelites traded their crops for merchandise. Both sides profit from the alliance, which became even stronger during the reign of Solomon. David acknowledges that his success is due to the Lord, who is making Israel a great nation as he had promised.

After coming to Jerusalem, David takes additional wives in the tradition of oriental monarchs (3:2–5). The four sons mentioned in verse 14 are the sons of Bathsheba, his favorite wife.

As long as David was only the king of Judah, the Philistines did not seem upset by his rule. In fact, they may have considered him as a vassal king, one step removed from the role he played under Achish as a mercenary commander. But once David becomes king of all Israel, the Philistines realize that he is a threat to their control of the northern parts of Israel (**5:17–25**). So before David has a chance to get established, the Philistines launch an attack, perhaps even before David has captured Jerusalem. It seems unlikely that they would have allowed him to enjoy the safety of a fortress if they could engage him in battle in the open field.

Although David had not fought against the Philistines for several years, he has not lost his touch and once again emerges victorious. Both battles are fought west of Jerusalem and determine who will control the central hill country. After the first battle, the Philistines abandon their idols, just as the Israelites had lost the ark of the covenant in the days of Eli. In 1 Chronicles 14:12, we learn that David burns the idols, in accord with Moses' command (Deut. 7:5). The second battle begins after David hears "the sound of marching in the tops of the balsam trees" (v. 24). This is the signal that the Lord and his angels are leading the way into battle. Just as the Lord went ahead of Barak as he moved against the army of Sisera (Judg. 4:14), so he enables David to rout the Philistines and chase them back to the coastal plain. Even though David's army may have been large and well trained, he continues to trust the Lord for victory rather than his own ingenuity and skill.

E. David established as king (2 Sam. 6:1–8:18). After a long wait marked by years of valuable training, David is now the king of Israel. He is determined to serve the Lord and to encourage the people to worship the Lord wholeheartedly. Because he is a man after God's own heart, the Lord gives him and his descendants the right to rule forever and he gives David victory over all his enemies. It is not long before Israel becomes a prosperous and powerful kingdom.

The ark of the covenant represented God's presence more than any other article in the tabernacle (1 Sam. 4:4), so David wants to bring it to Jerusalem. The ark has been in Kiriath-jearim, about nine miles west of Jerusalem, since the days of Eli and Samuel, but the time had come to restore the ark to its rightful place of honor. To emphasize the importance of the ark, David and his men lead a triumphant celebration, complete with singing and dancing. It is the type of celebration that usually accompanied a military victory and is David's way of proclaiming that God deserves the glory for Israel's triumphs.

In his zeal to honor the Lord, David overlooks an important requirement, however

(**6:1–11**). According to the Law, the ark had to be carried by the Levites, but David places the ark on a new cart the way the Philistines had done (1 Sam. 6:7). When the oxen pulling the cart stumble, a man named Uzzah—at whose home the ark had been kept—reaches out to steady the ark. As he does so, he is struck dead, for not even the Levites were allowed to touch the sacred articles (Num. 4:15; 1 Sam. 6:19). At this important turning point in Israel's history, the people are reminded that God's laws are to be obeyed fully. The shocking death of Aaron's sons (Lev. 10:1–3) and of Ananias and Sapphira (Acts 5:1–11) were similar in import. David is deeply upset by the Lord's anger and leaves the ark in the house of Obed-Edom.

Three months later David is encouraged by the blessing that God has brought to the household of Obed-Edom (6:12–19). Realizing that the Lord is no longer angry, David prepares once more to bring the ark to Jerusalem. This time the ark is properly carried by Levites "with the poles on their shoulders" (1 Chron. 15:15). After they have taken six steps and are still alive, David offers sacrifices in thanksgiving. As the procession continues amid music and shouting, David deliberately dresses like one of the Levites, putting on a robe of fine linen and a linen ephod, a garment usually reserved for the priest. When his wife Michal sees him dressed in this fashion, leaping and dancing before the Lord, she is shocked.

David sets up a special tent for the ark and does not try to bring the tabernacle to Jerusalem. Instead, Moses' "tent of meeting" remains at Gibeon, about six miles northwest of Jerusalem (cf. 2 Chron. 1:3). David wants to build a permanent temple to honor the ark, as we learn in chapter 7. With the ark safely in Jerusalem, David sacrifices burnt offerings and fellowship offerings and gives gifts of food to all the people. This was also a custom at the coronation of a king and, since the ark was the footstool of God's throne, David may have been emphasizing God's role as the great King over Israel.

After such a great celebration, David must have been surprised by Michal's reaction to his activity. She apparently felt that a king should not display such enthusiasm, behaving like "any vulgar fellow" (v. 20). Perhaps she was afraid that David would be like her father Saul, whose strange episodes of prophesying bore some similarities to David's behavior (cf. 1 Sam. 19:24). In any event, as a result of Michal's anger and pride, she never has any children and has to endure the disgrace of barrenness the rest of her life.

After the Phoenicians build a palace for David out of the cedars of Lebanon, David wants to build a magnificent temple for the Lord (**7:1–7**). At first Nathan the prophet encourages him, but then the Lord reveals to Nathan that David will not be allowed to construct the temple. His job is to fight battles and to make Israel's borders secure. According to 1 Chronicles 22:8, the fact that David was a man of war who had shed much blood was one reason why he could not build the temple. His son Solomon would be "a man of peace and rest" (1 Chron. 22:9) and he would be the one to build the temple. Though disappointed, David is permitted to know the plans of the temple and he expends great effort to gather materials for the building (1 Chron. 22:14; 29:1–8). In a very real sense, the temple belonged to David almost as much as to Solomon.

In further response to David's request, the Lord reveals through Nathan that he will continue to bless David and the entire nation (**7:8–17**). God promises to make David's name great, just as he has promised to do for Abraham (Gen. 12:2). Powerful leaders will no longer oppress Israel the way Pharaoh or other wicked kings did during the period of the judges. Although Joshua helped plant the nation in the land promised to Abraham, David will plant them more firmly (v. 10).

To encourage David even further, the Lord announces that he will build a house for David. David is the first king in a dynasty that will last forever. Unlike the judges or Saul before him, David's family will continue to rule for generations. The son who will immediately succeed him (Solomon) will build the Lord's temple, and his kingdom will be powerful and secure. In addition to all this, God promises to maintain a special father-son relationship with each king, assuring him of his counsel and empowering. As the Lord's "son," however, the king has to obey his commands faithfully. If the king sins, God will punish him, but he will not take the throne away from David's family (1 Kings 11:34). Eventually a king would arise who would reign "with justice and righteousness" (Isa. 9:7) and the Spirit of the Lord would rest on him in a powerful way (Isa. 11:2). Many of the later prophecies about the Messiah draw upon this great promise to David as they prefigure the coming Ruler.

Amazed at what he has heard from Nathan, David enters the tent he has set up for the ark and worships the Lord (**7:18–29**). As he prays he addresses the Lord seven times as the "Sovereign Lord," a title that stresses God's control over the nations and his covenant relationship with Israel. It is a title frequently used in prayer. David marvels that God has made such promises to him and his family, for after all, why did he deserve such honor? Unlike Saul, who became proud in his role as king, David is not impressed with his own importance.

At the same time David acknowledges God's greatness and uniqueness and his choice of Israel to be his special people. David realizes that God's promises to him are intimately connected with the promises to the patriarchs and help to fulfill the Abrahamic covenant. Ultimately, however, God's miracles on Israel's behalf serve to bring God glory and to exalt his name. Just as God established his reputation by delivering Israel from Egypt, so her prosperity in the Promised Land will further enhance that reputation. With a grateful heart David prays that God will keep his promises, and he has the faith to believe that God will indeed bless his house forever.

The battles described in chapter 8 may have taken place over a period of years. Almost all of the nations adjacent to Israel's borders fought against David, perhaps in an attempt to keep him from becoming too powerful. But by defeating them, David became the head of a large and influential kingdom (**8:1–6**). One of his first foes was Moab, with whom he had earlier been allied (1 Sam. 22:3–4). North of Israel and northwest of Damascus lay the powerful Aramean kingdom of Zobah. Victory over Hadadezer king of Zobah gave David control of land all the way to the Euphrates River. In Genesis 15:18 Abraham had been told that eventually his descendants would extend their borders to the Euphrates, and this prophecy was fulfilled under David and Solomon. Like Joshua, David hamstrung the chariot horses he captured (Josh. 11:9), for prior to the reign of Solomon the Israelites did not use chariots in battle.

Equally impressive is David's victory over the army of Damascus. Located about sixty-five miles northeast of the Sea of Galilee, this beautiful city was an important trade center and was closely allied with Zobah. David placed garrisons in Damascus, and Israel remained in control of this Aramean stronghold until well into Solomon's reign.

As a result of his military success, David receives a large amount of plunder and tribute payments from surrounding nations (**8:7–14**). Bronze, silver, and gold begin to pile up in Jerusalem. Even friendly neighbors such as Tou, king of Hamath, send gifts of precious metal to David. In recognition of the Lord's blessing upon his rule, David dedicates many of these articles to the Lord, and later on they will be used in the construction of the temple. David's victory over the Edomites gives him control of the rich copper mines south of the Dead Sea, adding further to his wealth.

Unlike many of the later kings, David's rule is characterized by justice and righteousness, and this is part of the reason for his success (**8:15–18**). David is assisted by several able administrators, including a "recorder" and a "secretary." The former may have been the head administrator of royal affairs and the latter something like our secretary of state. Neither position is mentioned in the summary of Saul's role in 1 Samuel 14:49–52, and this difference underscores the growth of Israel as a kingdom. Zadok the priest is mentioned for the first time here (v. 17). A descendant of Eleazar son of Aaron, Zadok replaced Abiathar as the leading priest under Solomon, and his descendants held the high priesthood throughout the rest of the monarchy. Strangely, David's sons are also called "priests," though the New International Version translates the word as "royal advisers." Sometimes priests did fulfill the role of advisors (cf. 1 Kings 4:5), but other scholars feel that David and his sons may have been priests of a royal order, similar to "the order of Melchizedek" (Ps. 110:4). David did wear a linen ephod when he brought the ark to Jerusalem (6:14) and he was closely involved with the worship of the Lord throughout his reign.

III. David's Successes and Failures (2 Sam. 9–20)

Although for the most part David was a godly and effective ruler, his sin with Bathsheba was a terrible blot upon his record. In the years that followed his adultery, David faced a rebellion led by his own son Absalom and another led by a Benjamite named Sheba. Jerusalem and all Israel were shaken by these events and David struggled to maintain his throne. Because of the turmoil in his own family, the question of who would succeed him as king became an important one.

A. David's success (9:1–10:19). Early in his career David was known as a wise and fair leader (1 Sam. 30:24–25), and when he became king he continued to handle problems with great skill. His kindness to Jonathan's son Mephibosheth demonstrates his genuine compassion for others. As a military leader, David had only known victory in battle ever since his triumph over Goliath, and the Ammonites and Arameans learn about this aspect of his character the hard way.

In light of the covenant God made with David promising to show kindness to his family forever, it is fitting that David remembers the covenant he made with Jonathan. When most kings came to power they sought to eliminate any survivors of the preceding king, but not David (**9:1–5**). Bound by covenant to his best friend, Jonathan, David is loyal to his oath and eager to take care of any of Jonathan's descendants. Ziba, who had been Saul's chief steward, tells David about Mephibosheth, Jonathan's crippled son, who is living in Trans-Jordan with a wealthy man named Makir. Other descendants of Saul are still alive (cf. 21:8), but Ziba knows that David is primarily interested in Jonathan's family.

We do not know if Mephibosheth knew anything about his father's covenant with David, but he certainly did not anticipate that David would treat him so royally (**9:6–13**). Not only does David give him the income from Saul's land, but Mephibosheth is allowed to eat at David's table "like one of the king's sons" (v. 11). Ziba and his family are given the responsibility of working the land for Mephibosheth, and from 16:3–4 we learn that Ziba really wanted control of Saul's land himself. For the time being, however, Ziba seems willing to serve Mephibosheth, and, unlike others who later rebel against David, Mephibosheth remains loyal to the king the rest of his life.

In light of the frequent fighting between Israel and the Ammonites, we might well wonder why David is a friend of King Nahash (**10:1–5**). Perhaps Nahash had assisted David in some way while he was fleeing from Saul, but the old animosity is not far below the surface. David's attempt to congratulate the new king is interpreted as a spy mission, and his men are badly mistreated. In the Near East, beards were shaved only during times of personal or national catastrophe as a sign of deep mourning. By cutting off the men's garments at the buttocks, the Ammonites treat the messengers as prisoners of war. Humiliated, David's men cross the Jordan River and stay at Jericho until their beards grow back.

The Ammonites realize that David will regard their insulting behavior as an act of war, so they summon a substantial number of their Aramean allies for the upcoming battle (**10:6–19**). The small kingdoms of Beth Rehob, Maacah, and Tob lay to the east and north of the Sea of Galilee, with Zobah a little further to the north. Faced by a powerful coalition, David sends Joab to engage the enemy in battle. As the leading general, Joab himself leads the best troops against the Arameans, and he sends Abishai to fight the Ammonites at their capital city of Rabhah, about thirty miles east of Jericho. Encouraging one another in the Lord, Joab and Abishai attack, with excellent results. The Ammonites take refuge behind the walls of their capital city while the Arameans head north. Hadadezer, king of Zobah and leader of the Aramean kingdom, hires reinforcements from across the Euphrates, and David himself takes the men back across the Jordan to meet this new threat. In spite of the additional troops the Arameans fall before David, and a number of kings are forced to make peace with him. Initially, David only intended to punish the Ammonites, but when the dust settles he finds himself in control of much of the land between Israel and the Euphrates. David's power and influence are growing fast and he is now the strongest ruler between Egypt and Mesopotamia.

B. The turning point (11:1–12:31). At a time when David and his people seem to be thriving, the king commits adultery and murder. Although David repents and the Lord forgives his terrible sin, this whole episode marks a major turning point in David's rule. From now on David faces serious problems in his own family and among his own countrymen, and in the process nearly loses the throne. How could this have happened to the man after God's own heart?

Like Samson before him, David is guilty of sexual immorality with all its consequences. While committing adultery is bad enough, David compounds the problem by committing murder as well. The second crime is intended to cover up the first—but the Lord knows about both of them.

After the rainy season ended in April and May, kings customarily returned to the battlefield. David and Joab want to complete the conquest of the Ammonites, so the army is sent to put Rabbah under siege. After what Joab and his troops had done to the Arameans the previous year, the campaign against the Ammonites may not have demanded David's personal leadership, but the text strongly implies he should have been with his troops. Instead, he becomes involved with the wife of one of his soldiers, Uriah the Hittite (**11:1–5**). Although the blame for adultery is placed squarely upon David, Bathsheba apparently does not discourage the illicit relationship.

To make it appear that her husband has made her pregnant, David calls Uriah back from the battlefront under the guise of gaining information about the progress of the campaign (**11:6–13**). Uriah clearly deserves a brief rest, so David sends him home to relax with his wife. Soldier that he is, Uriah refuses to go home and enjoy himself when the rest of the army is exposed to hardship in the open field. Besides, the ark had evidently been taken from Jerusalem to the battle scene, underscoring the importance of the campaign. Since the Lord is among the troops leading them to victory, Uriah feels a deep sense of duty to be there contributing to the cause. His dedication contrasts sharply with David's self-indulgence. Sexual intercourse made a man ceremonially unclean and unfit for battle for a few days and it appears that Uriah wants to get back into action quickly.

David keeps Uriah in Jerusalem one more day, however, hoping that he will sleep with his wife. To break down Uriah's defenses, David sees to it that Uriah gets drunk, but even so he does not go home.

Frustrated by the self-discipline of Uriah, David now takes more desperate measures to cover up his sin (**11:14–27**). Using Uriah as a messenger, he sends a letter to Joab asking that Uriah be placed in a very dangerous position in the front line. With Uriah dead, David will then marry his widow and legitimize the birth of Bathsheba's child. Joab complies by sending Uriah too close to the wall of Rabbah, where he is killed by Ammonite arrows. Joab knows that this tactic is unwise, but his loyalty to David is so great that he allows Uriah and several others to be struck down. By way of contrast, David's loyalty to Uriah is nonexistent. Though Uriah is one of David's top thirty-seven soldiers (23:39) and more than willing to risk his life for David and for Israel, David mercilessly steals his wife and arranges for his death. Since only Joab suspects foul play, it looks like the perfect crime. Bathsheba mourns for her husband seven days and then slips into the royal harem. It all looks very innocent, but the Lord is displeased. In his eyes David has committed adultery and murder and in fact has broken the last five commandments in this one brief episode. The consequences will be devastating.

The same prophet who had told David about the eternal dynasty God had promised him (7:11–16) now appears to deliver a very difficult message (**12:1–12**). Although many months have passed since David's sin, he has not yet realized what he has done. Perhaps David rationalized his actions by arguing that Bathsheba was virtually a widow anyway since Uriah was such a committed soldier, and though his decision to use the Ammonites to kill Uriah must have bothered him, David reasoned that Uriah might have been killed soon in battle even without any special circumstances. Nathan's visit changes everything, as David listens to a parable and pronounces a death sentence upon himself. The ewe lamb is Bathsheba, and the poor man is Uriah. David as the reigning king is guilty of misusing the power God has given him. Because the king was regarded as the shepherd of Israel, David suddenly realizes what he has done to his flock.

After pointing out David's guilt, Nathan announces that David will be punished the same way he has sinned. Violent death will strike his own family, and in subsequent years three of his four oldest sons would die by the sword.

Confronted by the Word of God, David finally realizes the true nature of his actions (**12:13–19**). The enormity of his sin overwhelms him and he feels utterly crushed (Ps. 51). Even though his sin was to affect the lives of all who were close to him, David senses how deeply he has offended God: "Against you, you only, have I sinned" (Ps. 51:4). In his agony David cries out for mercy, because murderers and adulterers deserved the death penalty (Lev. 20:10; 24:17).

Nathan informs him that God has forgiven him and will spare his life. This is difficult to explain, but there are at least three reasons for God's mercy. First, David's repentance was heartfelt and very sincere. From Psalm 51 we learn how he poured out his soul before the Lord and how his heart was broken. Second, God had made a covenant with David and had promised him an unending dynasty (7:11–16). True to his word, God kept David on the throne and did not withdraw his love from him. Third, David's act of adultery took place within the context of polygamy, and kings in particular had many wives. Even though God had warned kings against this (Deut. 17:17), he did allow polygamy for much of the Old Testament era.

In the years to follow, however, David reaps the consequences of his sin, starting with the death of Bathsheba's baby. For seven days David prays and fasts for the sick child with the hope that in his grace, God might also spare this little one. But the child dies and David tastes the first bitter fruit of his sins.

In spite of his pain, David accepts the death of the child as the Lord's will and does not lament any more (**12:20–25**). Encouraged by the knowledge that his own sin is forgiven, David goes into the house of the Lord and worships. At this point he could begin to pick up the pieces of his shattered life.

Some time later Bathsheba has another son, whom they name Solomon, which sounds like the Hebrew word for "peace" or "well-being." He is also called Jedidiah, "loved by the Lord," an indication that God would bless him and perhaps even that God had chosen him to be the next king. "Loved" can sometimes mean "chosen" (Mal. 1:2), and David knows that God's covenant love will rest upon the son who succeeds him.

After a long delay, the writer returns to the subject of the siege of Rabbah (**12:26–31**) where David probably should have been in the first place. More than a year had gone by since Joab had begun the siege. At Joab's insistence, David participates in the final assault on the Ammonite capital and receives the honor for the victory. Of unusual interest is the seventy-five-pound gold crown taken from the king, part of the substantial plunder found in the city. Additional booty is taken from the other Ammonite cities and the captives are put to work on various building projects. Slave labor of this sort played an important role in the construction activities of many Near Eastern rulers.

C. Rebellion (13:1–20:26). Although the Lord did not forbid polygamy, the sad story recounted in **13:1–14** clearly shows why multiple marriages are unwise. Hatred and jealousy among half-brothers was a constant problem and sometimes led to murder (cf. Judg. 9:5), especially when one's own sister was violated (cf. Gen. 34). Amnon should have known that sleeping with one's half-sister was forbidden by the Law (Lev. 18:9; 20:17), but this does not deter him. Taking the advice of his cousin Jonadab, Amnon pretends to be sick and asks that Tamar might visit him. When she is alone with him in the bedroom, his long-awaited chance comes. Tamar refers immediately to the rape of Jacob's daughter Dinah by the Canaanite prince Shechem (Gen. 34:7), who was soon killed by her full brothers and whose whole city was wiped out. Tamar also reminds Amnon that his own position as heir-apparent to the throne could be placed in jeopardy by his action. Would he want to ruin his future in a few moments of passion? Besides, perhaps David will allow the two of them to get married. This last comment is probably a clever attempt to buy time rather than a serious suggestion. In spite of these cogent arguments, Amnon refuses to listen and overpowers her.

Unlike the young prince Shechem, whose love for Dinah increased after he slept with her, Amnon's love turns to hate (**13:15–22**). He had been infatuated with Tamar, not really in love with her, and he has no intention of marrying her. Humbled and now rejected, Tamar leaves in mourning, throwing ashes on her head and tearing her beautiful ornamental robe. To lose one's virginity was a terrible tragedy, and Tamar feels betrayed and humiliated.

If Amnon now hates Tamar, it is more than equaled by Absalom's hatred for Amnon. Like Dinah's full brothers, Absalom will retaliate against the guilty party. David is also deeply upset over what has happened, but, strangely, he does nothing to punish Amnon. At the very least he should have announced that Amnon's deed had disqualified him as a contender for the throne. Just as Jacob's oldest son Reuben lost the birthright by sleeping with his father's concubine (Gen. 35:22; 49:4), so Amnon had forfeited any right he had to the throne. Perhaps David is reluctant to take any action against Amnon because he himself had been guilty of adultery. David's failure to discipline Joab, Amnon, and Absalom constitutes a major character flaw and has serious repercussions.

In spite of his intense hatred for Amnon, Absalom waits two years before striking back at his half-brother (**13:23–33**). He chooses a normally festive occasion, the time of sheep shearing, to invite his brothers to visit his land in Ephraim, in the center of Israel. To make it look legitimate, he invites David to join them, but when David turns down the invitation Amnon is invited as the king's representative. Apparently none of the other brothers suspect anything either, until a somewhat drunk Amnon is struck down by Absalom's men. It is a blow aimed at David as much as at Amnon and it shocks the entire kingdom. At first there is a rumor that all the king's sons have been killed, just as Gideon's seventy sons had died at the hands of their half-brother Abimelech (Judg. 9:5). David's nephew Jonadab—who was partly responsible for the whole situation in the first place—rightly insists that only Amnon has been killed. By killing Amnon, Absalom gains revenge for the rape of Tamar and eliminates a rival for the throne. With Amnon dead, Absalom is apparently the oldest surviving son.

While the rest of David's sons flee southward toward Jerusalem, Absalom heads north toward the safety of his grandfather's kingdom of Geshur, northeast of the Sea of Galilee (**13:34–39**). David had used the same strategy himself when he sought refuge in his great-grandmother's native land of Moab. In one stroke David has lost Amnon by death and Absalom by flight. Absalom's absence allows David time to postpone a decision about how to punish him. As time passes, the king recovers from the loss of Amnon and his heart grows softer toward Absalom.

Since David had responded so well to Nathan's indirect approach in 12:1–7, Joab decides to use the same method with reference to his cousin Absalom (**14:1–11**). Apparently Joab felt that Absalom was next in line for the throne and that David really wanted to be reconciled to his son. By bringing Absalom back home, David could avoid a struggle for the throne among his heirs—or so Joab hoped. The story told by the wise woman bears some resemblance to the struggle between Amnon and Absalom, but it is disguised to the extent that David could make an objective decision before applying it to his own case. He rules in the woman's favor, probably because she claims to be a widow and because the killing was not premeditated. This seems to argue against turning the other son over to the avenger of blood.

Once David has solemnly promised to spare the guilty son from death, the wise woman of Tekoa cautiously applies the decision he has made to his own situation with Absalom (**14:12–20**). What would be accomplished by putting Absalom to death? Is not God more interested in keeping men alive than seeing them die? Her reference to the reconciliation of a "banished person" to God may be an allusion to David's own restoration after he had committed murder. Implicit in the woman's reasoning is the idea that Absalom's slaying of Amnon did have some justification. It was premeditated but to some extent excusable. As a final argument, the woman refers to David's almost superhuman ability to make just decisions, such as an angel would make. Although this may be partly flattery, David did possess excellent judgment—except when it came to those close to him. By this point in the conversation David realizes that Joab has sent the woman to him and he believes that Joab is right about Absalom.

Grateful that the king has taken his "indirect" advice, Joab goes to Geshur to bring Absalom home (**14:21–27**). When he arrives in Jerusalem, Absalom is not allowed to see David, an indication that David is still having trouble deciding whether or not to forgive him. Because of his good looks, Absalom soon becomes very popular. Like David he has the rugged appearance of a king, and before long he will try to claim that office. There is special mention of his thick hair, which serves to enhance his vigorous appearance. In the ancient world, kings and warriors were often depicted with long hair as a sign of strength and courage.

The birth of sons was also an evidence of manliness, and Absalom has three of them. Since none of the three is mentioned elsewhere they may have died very young. He also has a daughter named after her beautiful aunt, Tamar. It is likely that King Rehoboam's wife "Maacah daughter of Absalom" (2 Chron. 11:20) was Absalom's granddaughter through Tamar.

After two years in Jerusalem Absalom demands to see the king and find out what his status really is (**14:28–33**). He wants David either to punish him or forgive him and to do so openly. Since Joab was instrumental in Absalom's return to Jerusalem, he calls on his cousin for help once more. This time Joab is reluctant to even talk about the problem until Absalom sets Joab's barley field on fire. This brings Joab on the run, and a visit with the king. In their face-to-face confrontation David kisses Absalom as a sign that he is forgiven and restored to the royal family. There is no indication that Absalom has repented of Amnon's murder, so it seems that some disciplinary action was in order—perhaps a clear statement that Absalom would never be king. Although Absalom may have known that he would not be David's choice as king, public censure might have made it more difficult for Absalom to gain support for his rebellion.

For four years Absalom develops a strategy to increase his popularity and chances for the throne (**15:1–12**). Pretending to be a champion of justice, Absalom wins the hearts of the people by agreeing with their complaints against the king. Handsome and charming, he personally meets large numbers of people and assures them that he is their friend.

All this time David suspects nothing, so when Absalom asks permission to go to Hebron, David raises no objection. It sounds innocent enough, much like Samuel's announcement that he will offer a sacrifice in Bethlehem—just before he anoints a king (1 Sam. 16:2–3). Hebron was the site of the cave of Machpelah, where Abraham and Sarah were buried, so it was a popular national center. But it was also the city where David had been anointed king by both Judah and all Israel—and where Absalom had been born.

By now Absalom was probably close to thirty years old and David about sixty. Very few individuals know about Absalom's plans, not even the guests he has invited from Jerusalem. From the outset, however, Absalom enjoys the support of key individuals, especially David's top advisor, Ahithophel. With their help, the revolt has a good chance of succeeding.

Up to this point in his career David had never suffered a defeat in battle, but now he is forced to flee his beloved Jerusalem (**15:13–23**). David does not want to subject the city to the horrors of war, so he takes his men and heads east toward the Jordan River. If he stays in Jerusalem, David is not sure how much support he will have. Absalom is a popular young prince and his seizing of the throne might have been interpreted as a logical succession to his father's rule—albeit a bit early.

Accompanying David in his flight are the men who have been with him since the time he was a fugitive from Saul and several contingents of mercenary troops from Philistine territory. According to 8:18 the Kerethites and Pelethites were commanded by David's general Benaiah, and the six hundred Gittites were probably from the city of Gath, where David and his men had served earlier as mercenaries. Ironically, the foreign troops are most loyal to David, although David releases Ittai the Gittite from any additional obligation. But Ittai refuses the generous offer and pledges his loyalty to David. In the showdown against Absalom, Ittai plays a key role (18:2).

Since David had been a protector of the priests and since he had brought the ark to Jerusalem, it seemed fitting for the priests and the ark to leave the capital with David. Both Zadok and Abiathar are with him and their presence seems to insure God's blessing upon David. Yet David knows that the proximity of the priests and the ark are not necessary, and he feels strongly that the ark should remain in Jerusalem as a sign that God is the true King of Israel. Besides, if Zadok and Abiathar stay in the city they can keep David informed about Absalom's activities (**15:24–29**).

Leaving his trusted companions behind, David continues his sorrowful trek up the Mount of Olives. At the summit he meets Hushai, another of his close advisors, who has heard the news about Absalom (**15:30–37**). David asks Hushai if he is willing to return to Jerusalem and become an advisor to Absalom. In this way he might contradict the excellent advice of Ahithophel and talk Absalom into a bad decision.

To make matters more confusing, David encounters two members of the tribe of Benjamin along the way (**16:1–13**). The first is Ziba, Mephibosheth's servant, and the second is an angry relative of Saul, named Shimei.

David knew Ziba from their earlier meeting, when David asked him to work for Jonathan's son Mephibosheth (9:9–10). Now that David is headed toward Trans-Jordan, Ziba brings him some much needed supplies. The amounts of bread and raisins are identical to those given to David by Abigail at an earlier time of crisis (1 Sam. 25:18) and help Ziba accomplish his objective. Apparently Ziba does not enjoy his subservient position and so tells David that Mephibosheth is hoping to regain control of his grandfather Saul's kingdom. Since David is uncertain about the extent of the revolt, he believes the lie about Mephibosheth and gives Ziba control of Saul's estate. It is a clever move by Ziba, who personally profits from the political crisis.

On the eastern side of the Mount of Olives and still only about two miles from Jerusalem, David is confronted by Shimei, a man from the same clan as Saul's family (v. 5). Frustrated by the transfer of power from Saul to David, Shimei takes out his anger on David by cursing him and pelting him with stones. Calling David a troublemaker and a wicked man, Shimei asserts that God is punishing David for shedding the blood of the household of Saul. This may be a reference to the execution of seven of Saul's descendants because of the Gibeonite problem (21:1–9) or a more general allusion to casualties in the civil war between David and the remnants of Saul's family. By throwing stones at David, Shimei implies that David should be stoned to death for his crimes.

On the other hand, David's men feel that Shimei deserves to die for cursing the king. According to the Law, slander of this sort was akin to blaspheming God (Exod. 22:28). But David does not allow anyone to strike Shimei down, partly because he knows his own sin lies behind his troubles and he deserves harsh words. By committing the matter to God, David hopes that the Lord will turn the curse into a blessing. Although David later spares Shimei's life again (19:23), eventually Shimei is executed by Solomon (1 Kings 2:46).

When Absalom arrives in Jerusalem he is congratulated by Hushai the Arkite, the man David hopes will be able to nullify the counsel of Ahithophel. In spite of Absalom's suspicions, Hushai is able to convince him that he will serve the new king because he is David's son.

As expected Ahithophel gives Absalom some shrewd advice (**16:15–23**) recommending that he sleep with his father's concubines. Usually a king's concubines belonged to his successor, so by this action Absalom is strongly asserting his kingship. At the same time he is stating his complete contempt for his father. By sleeping with the concubines in a tent pitched on the roof, he ensures Israel knows what he is doing.

In light of the political astuteness of Ahithophel's advice, the writer of Samuel notes that consulting him was like inquiring of the Lord. Whenever David decided upon a course of action he "inquired of the LORD" (1 Sam 23:4), and he also sought the advice of Ahithophel.

Given the skill and the reputation of Ahithophel, it comes as a shock to see his advice rejected in **17:1–14.** Ahithophel recommends that Absalom pursue David immediately, before he has a chance to escape very far or to organize his forces. If he would kill David quickly, then David's supporters would likely pay allegiance to Absalom and the nation would not be divided by a long and bloody civil war. It is a good plan, but Hushai tries to buy time for David by pointing out the fallacies in

Ahithophel's suggestion. He refers to David's reputation as a fighter and warns that he will not be captured so easily. Appealing to Absalom's ego, Hushai urges him to gather a huge army and make sure that he can defeat David's men.

In accord with God's sovereign plan, Absalom chooses to follow the bad advice of Hushai and so brings ruin upon himself. God is the Lord of history and he will not allow Absalom to usurp the throne at David's expense. Through his superintendence of Absalom's decision, God answers David's prayer, and because of Ahithophel's subsequent suicide, Absalom loses the services of his top advisor permanently.

Delighted with Absalom's decision, Hushai decides that he will nonetheless take no chances and warns David to cross the Jordan River as soon as possible (**17:15–22**). If he delays and if Absalom changes his mind and begins the pursuit immediately, David will be in grave danger. Following their prearranged plan, Hushai sends word to David through the sons of Zadok and Abiathar. Unfortunately they are spotted and have to hide in a well on the eastern slope of the Mount of Olives. Taking her cue from Rahab's deception of the king of Jericho, the woman hiding the young men sends the pursuers on ahead (cf. Josh. 2:5). This enables the two messengers to avoid capture and to cover the fifteen miles between them and the Jordan River. Near the fords of the Jordan the men urge David to cross the river at once lest Absalom attack him before daybreak.

Convinced that Absalom will lose the war with David and that he and the other leading rebels will be put to death for treason, Ahithophel decides to commit suicide (**17:23–29**). It is a tragic end for one whose counsel had been sought so avidly. His death is a sign to Absalom and his followers that their cause is doomed.

Meanwhile, David heads for the city of Mahanaim, north of the Jabbok River, the same city which Ish-Bosheth had used as his capital (2:8). By now Absalom has brought a sizable army across the Jordan, led by Amasa, a cousin or half-cousin of both Joab and Absalom. Cut off from the luxury and resources of Jerusalem, David and his men receive valuable supplies from Makir and Barzillai, wealthy Israelites in Trans-Jordan. David never forgets their kindness (1 Kings 2:7). More surprising is the aid he receives from the son of the king of the Ammonites, whose brother David had defeated in battle. Apparently David had at least a few friends even in this vassal kingdom, and they come to his rescue at a critical time.

As the battle draws near David's men are commanded as usual by his nephews Joab and Abishai (10:9–10), but this time a mercenary contingent is led by Ittai from Gath (**18:1–8**). David volunteers to go with them, but is dissuaded in view of the fact that the enemy wants above all to see him dead. Besides, David is growing old and is no longer an agile fighter. As the troops march out to battle, David urges them to be gentle with Absalom. Since David and his men are outnumbered they choose the rugged terrain of "the forest of Ephraim" as the battle site. Aided by this unusual setting, David's men outmaneuver the army of Israel and kill twenty thousand men. Experienced and intensely loyal to David, his men win a decisive victory and save the throne for him.

During the course of the battle Absalom somehow becomes separated from his men, and his head—or possibly his thick hair—gets caught in a low-hanging oak tree (**18:9–18**). Unable to extricate himself, Absalom is soon at the mercy of Joab, who plunges three javelins into his heart. In spite of David's specific order not to harm Absalom, Joab knows that without Absalom the revolt will collapse. Just as Ahithophel had advised Absalom to kill only David (17:2), so Joab realizes that Absalom is the enemy's key leader. Although Joab had been instrumental in bringing Absalom back from exile (14:1–20), he now feels no pity for the handsome prince and is convinced that David will be better off without him. Absalom's body is thrown into a large pit and a pile of rocks is heaped over him. Ironically, Absalom had erected "a monument to himself" near Jerusalem because he had no surviving son to carry on his name (v. 18).

Whenever an important battle was in progress, the people who sent out the troops anxiously awaited news of the outcome. Naturally everyone hoped for good news, and the messenger was called "the one who takes the good news." Sometimes, however, the news was anything but good, such as the time Eli was told about Israel's crushing defeat (1 Sam. 4:12–17). In such cases the word *good* is dropped from the translation. As Joab prepares to dispatch a messenger, he realizes that from David's perspective the news about Absalom's death is bad (**18:19–29**). For this reason, Joab hesitates to send Ahimaaz son of Zadok, who had served as a messenger before (cf. 17:17, 21). If David saw him coming, he would anticipate good news, and Joab does not want the king to get his hopes up. So Joab sends a foreigner, a Cushite, to take the news, although a little later he allows Ahimaaz to run behind him. By taking a different route, Ahimaaz outruns the Cushite and reaches David first. He tells the king about the victory but is unaware of Absalom's fate. Judging from his questions, David seems to be more interested in Absalom's condition than the outcome of the battle.

When the Cushite arrives, he gives David the information he wants in an indirect but clear way. David is crushed and begins to mourn his son's death as few fathers ever have (**18:30–19:4**). The pain is so great that David wishes he had died instead of Absalom. Over the years the tension between father and son had been great, and David realizes that he has failed as a father in a profound way. If only he would have handled things differently this tragedy might not have happened. Although Absalom had instigated the rebellion, David forgives him and mourns his passing.

As the troops return in triumph, their shouting and celebrating are quickly stilled. Instead of congratulating his men, David continues to grieve uncontrollably over the death of Absalom.

Realizing that confusion is spreading through the army, Joab confronts David and rouses him from his despondency (**19:5–8**). In a short and sarcastic speech, Joab accuses David of ignoring the fact that his soldiers have just risked their lives to win a crucial victory and that they deserve the king's profound thanks. By behaving as if he has lost the battle, David could lose the support of the very men who are so loyal to him. Torn by conflicting emotions, David responds to Joab's plea and goes out to talk to his men.

After the rebellion collapses the people in the northern tribes blame themselves for what has happened. They reflect upon all the good things David had done for the country and decide they want him to return as king (**19:9–15**). When David hears about this sentiment, he sends word to the elders of his own tribe of Judah to see how they feel. Although the rebellion had been launched in Judah, David is willing to forgive them for their actions. In fact David even announces that he will make Absalom's general Amasa the new commander of his army. Evidently David had found out about Joab's role in the death of Absalom and decided to punish his military chief. Encouraged by David's forgiving spirit, the men of Judah enthusiastically urge him to return.

When David reaches the eastern banks of the Jordan River opposite Jericho, he is met by the man who had cursed him as he fled from Jerusalem (**19:16–23**). This time Shimei is accompanied by a thousand other Benjamites, who may have feared that Shimei's disrespect would bring David's wrath on the whole tribe. Bowing low, Shimei apologizes for his earlier behavior and begs David's forgiveness. By identifying himself with the house of Joseph—a synonym for the northern tribes—Shimei may have wanted David to recall that Joseph graciously forgave his brothers, even though they had sold him into slavery (cf. Gen 45:4–7). David's men are not impressed by Shimei's "repentance" and urge the king to execute him. But in light of the end of the civil war and David's restoration to power, this is a time for conciliatory action, not revenge. David never fully forgives Shimei, however, and on his deathbed asks Solomon to find a way to put him to death (1 Kings 2:8–9).

Another piece of unfinished business has to do with Mephibosheth, Jonathan's son, who had been accused of participating in the revolt (**19:24–30**). He had wanted to join David in exile but was left behind by his steward Ziba. Since the time David left Jerusalem, Mephibosheth has remained in an unkempt condition as a sign of deep mourning. Aware that as a descendant of Saul, he does not deserve David's favor, Mephibosheth nonetheless politely asks David to rethink his decision to give Saul's estate to Ziba. Uncertain as to who is telling the truth, David decides to divide the inheritance between Ziba and Mephibosheth.

On a more pleasant note, David says goodbye to his dear friend Barzillai, who had sustained him during the difficult days in Trans-Jordan (**19:31–39**). Although David wants him to live in Jerusalem, Barzillai declines the invitation because of his advanced age. At eighty he is too old to appreciate the finer things of life in the capital. He does agree to send Kimham (probably his son) to Jerusalem, and David is glad to oblige. The king never forgets the help Barzillai gave him, and he asks Solomon to treat his sons well even after David's death (1 Kings 2:7).

The split between David and Absalom was symptomatic of the more basic division between north and south, the ten tribes of Israel and the tribe of Judah (**19:40–43**). As the various tribes scramble to be present when David crosses the Jordan and reenters the Promised Land, some of the northern tribes have not yet arrived. Apparently the men of Israel feel that the absence of these tribes could be interpreted as lack of support for David. There remains the lingering suspicion that David is partial to his own tribe, whereas the ten tribes comprised the bulk of the nation. So, at a time when David seems to have won back the hearts of the people, serious friction develops between Judah and Israel.

In spite of their recent protestations of loyalty to David, the ten northern tribes are quick to defect under the leadership of Sheba (**20:1–7**). Using a rallying cry that would be repeated when the kingdom was divided after Solomon (1 Kings 12:16), Sheba reasserts the power the tribe of Benjamin had lost after the death of Saul. David enters Jerusalem without fanfare and tries to deal with the new crisis. But first he dismisses his ten concubines from the palace; they were linked with the first rebellion when Absalom slept with them.

True to his promise, David appoints Amasa commander over the army and orders him to take action against Sheba. When Amasa moves too slowly, David asks the veteran general Abishai to take charge, again ignoring his strongheaded nephew Joab. Yet when the troops are sent out, one contingent is "Joab's men" and before long they will be led by Joab himself. The other troops include the Kerethites and Pelethites, who had been loyal to David during Absalom's rebellion.

About six miles north of Jerusalem Amasa catches up with the army, presumably bringing additional troops (**20:8–13**). As Joab steps forward to greet him, he stabs Amasa in the stomach with a dagger, once again eliminating someone who threatens his position as commander in chief. Joab knows how deeply obligated David is to him. As in the case of Shimei, David in his dying days finally asks Solomon to punish Joab for his treachery (1 Kings 2:5–6). Although David is not shocked by what Joab has done, some of the troops are stopped in their tracks by the atrocity. After the death of Amasa, Joab takes charge of the army, placing his brother Abishai in the familiar role of second in command. By pushing himself back into the spotlight Joab appears to be selfish to the extreme, but Joab is so committed to David that he wants to make sure the revolt will not succeed. Amasa had already displayed some weakness, and Abishai had never commanded the army by himself.

Meanwhile, Sheba shows respect for David's army by retreating to Abel-beth-maacah, a city north of the Sea of Galilee (**20:14–22**). After gathering additional troops, he takes refuge inside the walls of the city. When Joab reaches Abel-beth-maacah, he surrounds the city and tries to batter down the wall. Usually this was accomplished by repeatedly hitting the wall with a large metal-tipped wooden beam. When the people inside the city see the damage that is being done, they are understandably upset. The city was known for the wisdom of its residents, so one of the wise women asks to speak to Joab. Joab explains what he wants and the woman sees to it that the head of Sheba is thrown over the wall. The refusal to extradite a political foe was a major reason for war in the ancient world, and earlier David himself had to leave a walled city to avoid being handed over to Saul (1 Sam. 23:7–13).

Without a leader the revolt collapses and the northern tribes acknowledge David as their king. They continue to serve David and his son Solomon for more than forty years until they revolt successfully under Jeroboam I about 930 B.C.

Each of the major divisions of 1 and 2 Samuel ends with a list of the officials of Saul or David (1 Sam. 14:49–52; 2 Sam. 8:15–18) and each list is slightly longer. The major change in the list in **20:23–26** is the addition of Adoniram, who "was in charge of forced labor" (v. 24). As the kingdom expanded, David employed Canaanites and prisoners of war in various building projects, and during Solomon's reign even some Israelites were used on occasion for this purpose. Adoniram continues in this position throughout Solomon's reign so he must have been appointed in the final years of David's rule. Another administrative change is the appointment of Ira the Jairite as "David's priest." His role may have been closer to that of a royal advisor.

IV. Appendix (2 Sam. 21–24)

Like the Book of Judges, 1 and 2 Samuel end with a nonchronological appendix composed of several different episodes. There are two incidents describing God's wrath against Israel (chaps. 21, 24) and several short accounts of the victories of David and his men (21:15–22; 23:8–39). Between these two clusters of heroic achievements are two poems written by David praising the Lord for his deliverance (22:1–23:7). The overall symmetry of this arrangement is represented by the *a-b-c-c-b-a* pattern.

A. The Gibeonites' revenge (21:1–14). Because of the possible reference to this chapter in 16:7–8, it is likely that the Gibeonite problem was resolved prior to the revolt of Absalom. There is no clue in 1 Samuel as to when Saul became involved with the Gibeonites.

When Joshua was conquering the Promised Land, he was tricked into making a treaty with the Gibeonites, guaranteeing that they would not be put to death (Josh. 9:15, 20). Since the city of Gibeon was located in the tribal territory of Benjamin not far from Saul's capital, at some point during his reign Saul violated this treaty by attacking and killing some of the Gibeonites. As punishment, the Lord afflicts Israel with three years of famine during David's reign (**21:1–6**).

When David discovers the reason for this famine, he confers with the Gibeonites who have survived. Since the death of the guilty could turn away God's wrath, David agrees with the Gibeonites' request that seven of Saul's male descendants be killed at Gibeah, Saul's capital. The number seven was probably chosen because it represented completeness.

As David assumes the awesome responsibility of handing over Saul's descendants, he spares Jonathan's son Mephibosheth in light of the covenant they had made. But David turns over to the Gibeonites the two sons of Saul's concubine Rizpah and the five sons born to Saul's daughter Merab (**21:7–14**). Ironically, Merab should have been David's wife as a reward for killing Goliath. The seven are put to death in April during the barley harvest, and the family of Saul is all but wiped out.

Normally the dead were buried quickly but not in the case of those whose bodies were exposed "before the Lord" to atone for sin involving the whole nation (cf. Num. 25:4). So Rizpah heroically guards the exposed bodies of her sons until the rains pour down as an indication that the drought which caused the famine is over. David then orders that the bones of the deceased be buried in the tomb of Saul's father, and he shows his respect for the whole family by transferring the remains of Saul and Jonathan from Jabesh-gilead to Benjamin.

B. Victories over the Philistines (21:15–22). Revenge is also the motive in a series of battles between the Philistines and Israelites. Ever since David's victory over Goliath, the Philistines had tried to get even, but without success. Four specific Philistine warriors are mentioned, and each of them—like Goliath—is tall and powerful. All four are "descendants of Rapha," probably a reference to the gigantic Rephaites (Deut. 2:11; Josh. 12:4).

According to verse 19 a man named Elhanan "killed Goliath the Gittite." Unless this is a different Goliath from the warrior in 1 Samuel 17, we seem to have a competing account of his death. In the parallel passage in 1 Chronicles 20:5, however, we learn that Elhanan "killed Lahmi the brother of Goliath." Apparently a scribe miscopied the name in 2 Samuel, perhaps because in Hebrew "Lahmi" looks very much like "Bethlehemite." Critics argue that Elhanan may indeed have been the man who killed Goliath and only later was the hero's status transferred to David. But the whole account of David's rise to the throne is predicated upon his ability to defeat the Philistines, and the slaying of Goliath catapulted him into the national spotlight.

C. David's praise (22:1–51). Samuel begins with Hannah's prayer of thanksgiving for the birth of Samuel (1 Sam. 2) and ends with David's song of praise for God's deliverance from his enemies. The song appears in almost identical form in Psalm 18. In both passages the hymn is introduced by the same historical heading referring to Saul and other enemies. Because of David's strong declaration of innocence (vv. 21–25), it is likely that the song was written prior to his sin with Bathsheba.

When David was fleeing from Saul he was forced to take refuge in a number of caves (**22:2–4**). These hideouts were sometimes called "strongholds," the same word applied to the Lord in verse 2 ("fortress"). David realizes that God is the true source of his security and the One whom he can call upon for help.

In words reminiscent of the experience of Jonah, David describes his difficulty as if he were drowning (**22:5–7**). The cords of death were wrapped around him like seaweed. Because of his extreme danger, death seemed close indeed. In his predicament, David called out to the Lord for help, and in his heavenly temple God heard his cry.

The next verses (**22:8–16**) describe a theophany—the coming of God to defeat his foes. The imagery is derived from God's appearance on Mount Sinai, when he descended in a thick cloud amid thunder and lightning. The earth shook as God spoke with Moses before the awe-struck Israelites (Exod. 19:16–19). So powerful was God's voice that it sounded like thunder. In Judges the Lord sent a thunderstorm to bog down the chariots of Sisera and give Israel a surprising victory (Judg. 5:4–5, 20–21). There may also be an allusion in 2 Samuel 22:16 to the demise of the Egyptians at the Red Sea, where the waters were rebuked by a strong wind (Exod. 14:21). The cherubim mentioned in verse 11 are said to be transporters of the throne of God in Ezekiel 10, and this throne symbolizes the authority of the mighty King.

Just as God had delivered his people in time past, so he reached down and rescued David from his powerful enemy (**22:17–20**). Instead of being hemmed in and confined, David was brought "into a spacious place" (v. 20) and given freedom from danger and oppression. God delighted in David because he was "a man after his own heart" (1 Sam. 13:14).

Grateful for God's intervention, David reflects upon God's goodness to those who serve him and live righteous lives (**22:21–30**). His assertion of innocence does not mean that he claims to be sinless but that he is seeking to live in accord with God's Word (v. 23). Since David was the king, he had a special obligation to set an example for the rest of the nation and lead a godly life. His realization that God brings down the proud and exalts the humble (v. 28) repeats a major theme of 1 and 2 Samuel. In his own struggle with Saul David became well aware of what pride could do to a king out of touch with God.

David also knows that God responds in kind to the attitudes and actions of man. Those who are hostile toward God will eventually find that God will be hostile toward them (Lev. 26:27–28). Those who seek first God's kingdom and his righteousness will discover that he will bless them in remarkable ways (Matt. 6:33). Because of David's faithfulness as king, God gave him military victories, fame, and fortune.

Returning to the themes introduced in verses 2–4, David now spells out in greater detail what God has done for him (**22:31–46**). With a sense of exuberance David tells how the Lord has given him strength, speed, and stability, enabling him to overwhelm the enemy. In verses 38–43 David describes the plight of his foes, who were crushed and trampled under his feet. When they cried for help the Lord did not answer; no one came to their rescue.

God delivered David from his enemies within the borders of Israel and in foreign lands. Though it had seemed that he was on the verge of dying, David had been made "the head of nations" (v. 44). As his enemies fell before him one by one, the kingdom of Israel grew into an empire stretching from Egypt to the Euphrates River. The covenant blessing promised by Moses had become a reality.

David knows that he does not deserve the credit for his success, so in the final verses of this song (**22:47–51**) he exalts "God, the Rock, my Savior!" (v. 47). Through the prophet Nathan, God had made a covenant with David, promising that his dynasty would last forever (2 Sam. 7:12–16); and David acknowledges that the Lord's "unfailing kindness" (v. 51) is a guarantee that the covenant will remain valid. Such a faithful God is One whom David wishes to praise "among the nations" (v. 50). They too can worship the sovereign Lord, for "he rules over the nations" and deserves their allegiance (Ps. 22:27–28).

D. David's final poem (23:1–7). The second song contained in the appendix is much shorter than the first and gives us the last poetic piece written by David. Many of his psalms are of course preserved in the Book of Psalms, but this brief poem is not paralleled in the Psalter. As in chapter 22, David acknowledges God's blessing upon his life and in particular refers to the way the Spirit of the Lord spoke through him (v. 2). Ever since he was anointed as king, the Spirit has rested upon him and has inspired him to write and sing the psalms loved by believers down through the centuries.

Empowered by the Lord, David had been able for the most part to rule in righteousness, bringing peace and prosperity to the whole nation. His rule was a foretaste of the unending reign of his son, the Messiah, Jesus Christ, a rule marked by perfect justice and righteousness. As his own life comes to an end, David rejoices that God has made with him "an everlasting covenant" (v. 5), assuring his descendants of continuing rule. According to verses 6–7 and Psalm 110, this would ultimately mean the destruction of wicked men when Christ places his enemies under his feet.

E. David's mighty men (23:8–39). Like any commanding general, David knew the value of faithful, dedicated followers. Without the help of skilled warriors, he could not have established a powerful kingdom. Thirty-seven of his men deserve special credit for their courage and commitment.

A group called "the Three" fought so valiantly that they are singled out above the rest (**23:8–12**). Josheb-Basshebeth killed eight hundred men at one time, an accomplishment matched only by Samson's slaying of a thousand Philistines (Judg. 15:15). In another memorable battle against the Philistines, Eleazar son of Dodai singlehandedly struck down the Philistines after the rest of the Israelites had retreated. Like Samson, he was exhausted after the conflict, but through him "the Lord brought about a great victory that day" (v. 10). The third hero, Shammah son of Agee, performed a similar exploit against the Philistines. Refusing to flee with the rest of the troops, Shammah stood his ground and successfully fought the enemy by himself.

Another story about three heroes—probably not the same three just mentioned—tells how they broke through Philistine lines to get water from the well near the gate of David's hometown of Bethlehem (**23:13–17**). The incident may have occurred while David was a fugitive from Saul or just after he had been anointed king over all Israel. When the three men brought the water to David, he refused to drink it and poured it out as an offering before the Lord. By doing this he acknowledged God's goodness in giving him followers who would risk their lives for him. Surrounded by such brave men, David would surely succeed.

Two other men performed exploits that were comparable to those of "the Three" (**23:18–23**). David's nephew Abishai had once saved his life by killing a Philistine giant who had threatened David (2 Sam. 21:16–17). Here we are told that he was also responsible for killing three hundred men in battle. Benaiah son of Jehoiada was in charge of the Kerethites and Pelethites, two valuable mercenary bands which constituted the royal bodyguard, and later Benaiah replaced Joab as commander of Solomon's army (1 Kings 2:35). On the way to becoming a leader, Benaiah had gained fame for killing two of Moab's finest soldiers and "a huge Egyptian" who was first disarmed and then killed with his own spear. In the best tradition of Samson, Benaiah also killed a lion in "a pit on a snowy day" (v. 20).

While not quite attaining the stature of the aforementioned heroes, another thirty warriors constitute an elite group of mighty men (**23:23–39**). They came from many parts of Israel, including Saul's capital city of Gibeah. Most of the individuals are otherwise unknown, except for Joab's brother Asahel, who died in the civil war against Abner (2 Sam. 2:33), Uriah the Hittite, the husband of Bathsheba, and Bathsheba's father Eliam. In the parallel passage in 1 Chronicles 11:26–47 there are an additional sixteen names, individuals who probably replaced those who were too old or who died. The figure of thirty-seven given in 2 Samuel 23:39 apparently includes "the Three," Abishai and Benaiah, and possibly Joab, the indefatigable commander of the whole army.

F. David's census (24:1–25). For the second time in the appendix David has to face the wrath of God (cf. 21:1–14), but this time he bears more of the blame. It is a hard lesson for David and his people, though the chapter ends on a note of worship that paves the way for the building of the temple.

A comparison of verse 1 with 1 Chronicles 21:1 reveals a startling difference about the identity of the one who incited David to take a census (**24:1–9**). According to Samuel it is the Lord, whereas Chronicles names Satan as the instigator. Since Satan delights in tripping up men of God, we can deduce that the Lord allowed him to lead David astray, just as God permitted Satan to afflict Job (Job 1:12). None of the actions of men and of Satan are beyond God's sovereign control. Perhaps God was angry with Israel because of the rebellions of Absalom and Sheba that enjoyed considerable popular support.

Sometimes the taking of a census was perfectly acceptable (Num. 1; 26), so David's sin must involve the motivation behind the census. In all probability David was guilty of pride as he gloried in the size of his armies and the numerous victories he had won. Backed by faithful, highly skilled troops and courageous leaders, David may have overlooked his need to trust in the Lord, the one who had given Goliath into his hands. Even Joab recognizes that it is wrong to take this census, but David insists that he go ahead with it.

For almost ten months Joab and the other commanders travel throughout Israel, starting in Trans-Jordan and then counting all the able-bodied men west of the river. The total comes to 1,300,000, including 500,000 in David's own tribe of Judah. In 1 Chronicles the figures are 200,000 lower, perhaps reflecting the omission of the standing army from the census. Actually Joab never completes the census, perhaps anticipating the Lord's response to the whole idea (1 Chron. 21:6; 27:24).

After Joab and his men return David finally realizes how wrong he has been and confesses his sin before the Lord (**24:10–14**). Earlier he had repented of his adulterous relationship with Bathsheba when the prophet Nathan had confronted him (12:13). This time the prophet Gad is sent to David, offering the king a choice of three calamities. Faced with the prospect of three years of famine, three months of military defeat, or three days of plague, David chooses the final option, believing that the Lord will somehow be merciful in spite of the plague.

True to his word the Lord strikes Israel with a plague more severe than that connected with the Baal of Peor episode (Num. 25; **24:15–17**). Seventy thousand die as the angel of the Lord moves through the land, bringing relentless judgment. When the angel comes to Jerusalem the Lord has mercy on his chosen city as David cries out on behalf of the people. Later God will spare Jerusalem again when the Assyrians close in against righteous King Hezekiah in 701 B.C. (Isa. 31:5).

As the angel with a drawn sword stands near him, David is ordered to build an altar to the Lord (**24:18–25**). The place where he sees the angel is the threshing floor of Araunah the Jebusite, located north of Jerusalem on a hill overlooking the city. Chronicles refers to this hill as Mount Moriah, and it becomes the very site on which Solomon later builds the temple (2 Chron. 3:1). When David asks Araunah for permission to buy the threshing floor, the Jebusite agrees and even offers to give it to David along with oxen and wood for the offering. But David insists on paying for it, refusing to sacrifice burnt offerings that cost him nothing. He pays fifty shekels of silver for the threshing floor and the oxen, and according to 1 Chronicles 21:25 he pays six hundred shekels of gold for the whole site. It is an expensive purchase, but what a meaningful place to build the temple, where David himself experienced both the judgment and mercy of God! In the future the temple would be a place where sin could be atoned for, bringing forgiveness and life to the sinner.

When the altar is built, David presents

burnt offerings and fellowship offerings as a symbol of his renewed commitment to the Lord. These two offerings were also presented in the midst of an earlier national calamity during the time of the judges (Judg. 20:26), and Solomon sacrificed numerous burnt offerings and fellowship offerings at the dedication of the temple. Of all the offerings to be presented at the temple, none was more significant than the ones brought by David to this hastily built altar. His sense of awe at the presence of God could only have been matched by Abraham's, who had sacrificed a ram in place of Isaac at this very site (Gen. 22:2).

Coupled with David's confession and repentance, the sacrifices make atonement for sin and God answers his prayer in behalf of the land. The plague ends as the Lord has mercy on his covenant people.

SELECT BIBLIOGRAPHY

Davis, J. J. *The Birth of a Kingdom.* Grand Rapids: Baker, 1970.

Gehrke, R. D. *1 and 2 Samuel.* St. Louis: Concordia, 1968.

Laney, J. C. *First and Second Samuel.* Chicago: Moody, 1982.

Pfeiffer, C. F. *The United Kingdom.* Grand Rapids: Baker, 1970.

1–2 KINGS

Gerard Van Groningen

INTRODUCTION

In the Hebrew Bible, there is no break between the end of 1 Kings and the beginning of 2 Kings. The division into two books was made by the men who translated the Hebrew text of the Old Testament into Greek (the Septuagint). It is thought that this division was made simply because the Greek text, which includes vowels, required more space than the Hebrew, which is written without vowels. As one finishes reading 1 Kings and proceeds to 2 Kings, there is no break in the account: 1 Kings 22:51–53 records that Ahaziah became king of Israel; 2 Kings 1:1–7 records Ahaziah's injury and Elijah's prophecy of his impending death.

In the Septuagint the books are titled "The Third and Fourth Book of Kingdoms," while the Latin Vulgate has the title "Third and Fourth Kings." The editors of these Bibles considered 1 and 2 Samuel to be the first two installments of a continuous account of all the kings, from Saul to Zedekiah.

The first book begins with David's last days, during which his oldest living son Adonijah attempts to become king. Nathan and Bathsheba urge David to announce that Solomon is to be his successor. The anointed Solomon consolidates his power and begins a glorious reign. He is given wisdom; he builds the temple and his palace; his fame spreads far and wide; his wealth increases. A tragic decline begins when he marries many foreign women and participates in their idolatry. The Lord's punishment is inevitable. The kingdom territory is reduced and is then divided into Israel and Judah.

The enmity, rivalry, and warfare between the two kingdoms lasts for years. A period of peace exists between the kingdoms during the reign of Omri and his descendants. Elijah, Elisha, and other less known prophets appear on the scene to warn the kings, to oppose idolatry, and to minister by word and deed to the people. Only a few references are made to the major and minor prophets, but these books provide the historical setting for two major and nine minor prophets.

Enmity arises again between the two nations when Jehu overthrows the reigning house of Omri, Ahab, and their descendants. This enmity lasts until the northern kingdom is destroyed and many of its people are taken captive by Assyria. The nation of Judah continues for more than one hundred years until it is destroyed and its people are taken captive by Babylon.

As the history of the united nation, the divided nations, and the remaining nation is given, their kings are discussed. Four details are usually mentioned: (1) mother; (2) age; (3) date of accession; and (4) evaluation of reign and activities. No king's life is related in detail but his work, worship, and relationship with God is evaluated by employing David and his reign and the Mosaic writings as standards for judgment.

The second book concludes with three abbreviated historical references: Judah goes into captivity. Gedaliah, who was appointed governor over devastated Judah and the few people left behind, is assassinated and his Jewish and Babylonian assistants are killed by Ishmael, a Davidic descendant. The people, because of their fear of the Babylonians, flee to Egypt. Jehoiachin, the last Davidic king to rule in Jerusalem, after spending thirty-seven years in a Babylonian prison, is released and given royal privileges.

The Book of Kings is prophetic history. This means that as spoken prophecy conveys the mind, will, and word of the Lord, so also these historical writings convey the mind, will, and word of the Lord. This is why the Book of Kings was included traditionally in the category of Former Prophets. The intent of the writer is not to give a history of the people of Israel, of their kingdoms and kings, of international relationships and involvements. Neither is it the writer's intent to present a historical account of the temple or the Israelites' worship of the Lord and their attitudes toward local deities. The intent of the inspired writer is to reveal that the sovereign Lord of heaven and earth, of all people and in a specific way of Israel, is working out his divine plan. He repeatedly refers to this revealed will and plan of the Lord as nations, kings, and people are evaluated.

Various aspects, then, of the message can be stated as follows: (1) The Lord is sovereign; he rules over all of creation, over all nations, and especially over his people. He controls their destinies; he raises up servants in Israel and among other nations to serve him as kings and instruments of judgment. He raises up prophets to speak his will to kings, kingdoms, and people of all walks of life and in varied circumstances. (2) The Lord is faithful to the promises he made to the patriarchs. He blesses his people and those who bless them; he brings a curse upon those who curse his people and upon his covenant people when they depart from the covenant life and stipulations he has laid out for them. (3) The Lord is righteous and just. He carries out his will revealed through Moses. The law of the covenant stands; by it human actions are weighed; according to its promises and threats, the Lord deals with obedient and disobedient people. Kings, prophets, priests, army leaders, yes, all people regardless of station, position, rank, and influence, stand righteously before the Lord or fall under his judgment in accordance with the covenant demands which he gave through Moses. (4) The Lord demonstrates his covenant mercies and his steadfast love as he revealed these to David when he promises that David's seed would be preserved and rule forever. The repeated refrain—according to the promises made to David—affirms these covenant prerogatives. The fact that the writer concludes Kings with the account of the release of Jehoiachin and his elevation to royal treatment is a climactic statement of this aspect of the message. (5) The Lord does his part in maintaining the integrity of the kings according to his covenant promises and laws. God raises up prophets who fearlessly stand before kings, confront them, and declare the word of the Lord to them. The people of Israel, even when divided into two nations, are blessed with the living Word of God, kept in written form and spoken by the prophets. The call to hear, remember, obey, and do the will of the Lord in all areas of covenantal living continues to be placed before the kings and their people. (6) The Lord makes provisions so Israel can worship him in beauty, holiness, and faithfulness according to his prescriptions. His call for this continued worship and his total repudiation of idol worship of any kind are held before the kings and their people. The omission of and refusal to worship bring words of warning and, at various times, the execution of judgment. In the destruction and captivity of the two nations, the veracity of the Lord's Word is demonstrated. (7) The Lord remembers his people and supplies all their needs so that they can live righteously, with love, joy, and peace, before and for him. He supplies the virtues required for daily service, the means for worship, and the opportunities to serve among the nations. He rewards obedience to his covenant demands and demonstrates mercy even when he brings devastating judgments for disobedience.

No one knows who wrote the Book of Kings. The author's name is not given, and internal evidence offers no suggestion about who that person might be. Various suggestions have been made. Early Jewish tradition held that Jeremiah was the author. Jeremiah 52 repeats 2 Kings 24:18–25:31; since there is reference to what happened during the exile, and Jeremiah lived during that time, he wrote Kings. Jeremiah, however, was taken to Egypt (Jer. 43:6). What seems more likely is that the writer of Kings and the writer of Jeremiah used the same original source. It has also been suggested that Isaiah wrote Kings, because Isaiah 36–39 and 2 Kings 18:13–20:19 recount the same events. This view is difficult to support because Isaiah lived before the exile of Judah occurred.

Critical scholars have concluded that there was a series of original writers whose writings were used by compilers and editors over a long period of time—from before the exile until almost to the end of the exile. The first compilers and editors are thought to have written in the time of Josiah, when the Book of Deuteronomy was written (not *found* as the biblical text says; 2 Kings 22:8–10). Later editors altered and added details as historical circumstances developed. Major difficulties with this position are: (1) critical scholars have serious differences among themselves about many aspects of the proposed solution; (2) there is no concrete textual evidence for this view; and (3) the critical position operates under the assumption that the compilers and editors were theologians; thus 1 and 2 Kings are considered to reflect a development in theological views and evaluations.

The writer of Kings is unknown; however, it is reasonable to assume that this anonymous writer was a contemporary of Jeremiah and Ezekiel. He had prophetic gifts and unusual abilities to consult sources, select, arrange, and formulate materials under the inspiration of the Holy Spirit (2 Tim. 3:16).

Assuming that the writer was a contemporary of Jeremiah and Ezekiel and that he was among the exiles, he was probably in Babylon. This conclusion is supported by the reference to Jehoiachin's release and elevation to royal privileges that took place in Babylon (2 Kings 25:27–30). Thus, the writer experienced many of the traumatic events that occurred during the last days of the kingdom of Judah and the initial experiences of the exiles in Babylon.

When did the writer take up his pen? The most satisfying reply to this question can be derived from Scripture. The writer mentions King Jehoiachin's release "in the thirty-seventh year" of his exile. Jehoiachin had been taken into exile during the second deportation (597–596 B.C.). So it was in 560 B.C. that Jehoiachin was released. The writer, very likely impressed by this event and moved by the Spirit of God, wrote the book to encourage his fellow exiles by setting forth the faithfulness of the sovereign, covenant Lord. This writing was completed before 538 B.C. because there is no reference to the return to Jerusalem.

What source materials, if any, did the writer of Kings have available? It could be argued that as an inspired writer, he did not need sources. Also, as an exile living far from Jerusalem, he could not acquire sources. However, the Lord moved the writer to employ sources which had evidently been gathered and taken to Babylon when Nebuchadnezzar, king of Babylon, had taken captive ten thousand men, officers, army men, craftsmen, artisans, and the royal family and servants (2 Kings 24:13–16). The writer refers to three sources by name: (1) "the book of the annals of Solomon" (1 Kings 11:41); (2) "the book of the annals of the kings of Israel" (referred to seventeen times in 1 Kings 14:19–2 Kings 15:31); and (3) "the book of the annals of the kings of Judah" (referred to fifteen times in 1 Kings 14:29–2 Kings 24:5). The existence of these sources certainly implies that each royal palace (of Solomon, of Israel, and of Judah) had record keepers, annalists, and scribes. It has also been held by biblical scholars that the writer of Kings had written accounts of the ministries of Elijah and Elisha available to him; he may also have had writings from other prophets, such as those of Isaiah and Jeremiah. There is no direct reference to these; the detailed materials concerning Elijah and Elisha included in Kings warrant the conclusion that accounts of their activities were available to the writer.

Did he copy these sources word for word or did he produce summary statements? When one compares those parts of Isaiah and Jeremiah that are also in the Book of Kings, one sees much similarity but also some differences. The inspired writer selected his materials from the sources and quoted these in a manner that suited his purposes. The writer follows a discernible pattern: the accession to the throne, the king's age, his mother's name, the time (often stated in relation to other kings' reigns), and an evaluation of each king (except Zimri). After the writer gives an account of David's last days, he selects certain facts concerning Solomon and events occurring during his reign and offers his evaluation of Solomon on the basis of these. After the kingdom is divided, the writer as a rule gives a brief account first of the kings of Israel, before the contemporary monarchy in Judah. Facts and events concerning the kings of Israel usually had some relevance for what transpired in the kingdom of Judah. It is evident that the royal line of David's house is one of the writer's chief concerns. There is general agreement among scholars who have studied Kings that the writer was a man of literary skill because of the way he organizes and formulates the materials he selects and includes his own evaluations and perspectives.

OUTLINE

I. The United Kingdom (1 Kings 1:1–11:43)
   A. David and Solomon's Co-Regency (1:1–2:12)
   B. Solomon's Reign (2:12–11:43)
II. The Divided Kingdom (1 Kings 12:1–2 Kings 17:41)
   A. Enmity (1 Kings 12:1–16:28)
   B. Peace and Friendship (1 Kings 16:29–2 Kings 9:37)
   C. Enmity (2 Kings 10:1–17:41)
III. The Kingdom of Judah (2 Kings 18:1–25:30)
   A. Hezekiah's Reign (18:1–20:21)
   B. Manasseh's Reign (21:1–18)
   C. Amon's Reign (21:19–26)
   D. Josiah's Reign (22:1–23:30)
   E. Jehoahaz's Reign (23:31–35)
   F. Jehoiakim's Reign (23:36–24:7)
   G. Jehoiachin's Reign (24:8–17)
   H. Zedekiah's Reign (24:18–25:26)
   I. Jehoiachin's Release (25:27–30)

COMMENTARY—1 KINGS

I. The United Kingdom (1 Kings 1:1–11:43)

A. David and Solomon's co-regency (1:1–2:12).[1] David's physical condition had deteriorated (**1:1–4**). After a strenuous life, he is unable to reign anymore at the age of seventy years (2 Sam. 5:4). His court advisors try to help the king demonstrate that he still has some vigor, but their advice proves useless. The beautiful young virgin, Abishag, from Shunem in the tribe of Issachar, cannot warm or arouse David though she ministers (as a nurse) to him.

Adonijah, David's oldest living son, attempts to become king (**1:5–10**). He is able to demonstrate regal power with chariots, horsemen, and runners. Joab and Abiathar, men who had been loyal servants of David (1 Sam. 22:20–22; 2 Sam. 15:35ff.; 17:15), apparently

1. It is difficult to reconcile the total number of years reported and the actual length of time between Solomon's accession to the throne and the exile. The solution to the problem is found in the co-regencies of royal fathers and their successor sons. Solomon was ruling, albeit for a short period, before David's death.

conclude that it is to be expected that the oldest son is to reign, and give Adonijah their support. That certain men on whom David had relied are not invited to the coronation feast suggests that Adonijah is unsure of their loyalty. Had they eaten with him at the feast, the king could not have them killed later. The feast, held just outside Jerusalem, has a religious character in that Adonijah sacrifices to the Lord. Adonijah follows protocol in securing the throne and gaining the people's support.

There is, however, a plan (**1:11–37**) to anoint Solomon, the son of Bathsheba (2 Sam. 12:24–25), as David's successor. Nathan the prophet assumes a leading role in giving David's throne to Solomon. Prophets often combined the message of the Lord with the actual anointing (cf. 1 Sam. 10:1; 16:12–13; 2 Kings 9:1–13). In this case Nathan seems not to have received a direct message from the Lord but he understands what is happening. Should Adonijah become king, Bathsheba, Solomon, and he too would be in extreme danger of losing their lives. Nathan's message to Bathsheba refers to an agreement that David seems to have made but of which there is no written record. There is a reference to the Lord's love for Solomon that was known to Nathan (2 Sam. 12:24–25) and may have been communicated to David. The Lord's love may have motivated David to assure Bathsheba that her son Solomon would become king. The plan of how to approach the king indicates that Nathan is well acquainted with palace politics. Bathsheba receives advice from Nathan on how to proceed.

She immediately goes to David's room where Abishag is attending him. When David asks her what she wants, she repeats what Nathan has advised her to say. She adds that all Israel is waiting for the king's decision and that if Adonijah rules she and Solomon will be considered criminals. The people probably expected an appointment rather than a democratic choice. The latter, scholars have concluded on the basis of Deuteronomy 17:15b, was the people's prerogative. Moses' instruction, however, emphasizes the Lord's choice. In the case of David's successor, the Lord's choice is made known through the prophet Nathan and David.

As arranged, Nathan comes to speak to the king. Nathan honors David by bowing to him and acknowledges his right to select a successor. If what Adonijah is doing is according to the king's decision, why have the king's advisors not been informed? Thus, Nathan presses for an immediate decision by the aged king.

David summons Bathsheba back into his room. With strength and firmness, David repeats his promise and declares that Solomon will become king that day. By this act, David carries out Nathan's prophecy (2 Sam. 7:11–16). He also demonstrates by his immediate response that he is doing what he had planned all along.

David calls for his three trusted men. Zadok, descendant of Eleazar the high priest, represents the priesthood and Levites; Nathan the prophetic order; and Benaiah, a military hero and captain of David's bodyguard, the military forces. They are ordered by David to place Solomon on the throne. Specific instructions indicate that David is alert: (1) men who served David are to accompany them; (2) the royal mule is to carry Solomon; (3) Solomon is to be brought to Gihon, the spring just east of Jerusalem; (4) Zadok and Nathan are to anoint Solomon; (5) the trumpet, announcing the event, is to be blown; (6) the proclamation, "Long live King Solomon," is to be shouted; and (7) Solomon is to be brought to the palace and placed on the throne. These instructions are supported by the king's declaration, "I have appointed him." Benaiah pronounces his blessing on this decisive action by expressing the hope that the Lord will be with and do even more for Solomon than he has done for David. David thus receives assurance that his orders will be carried out; he has the support of the military forces.

Solomon is anointed king according to David's instructions (**1:38–40**). Zadok pours the oil; by this act of anointing Solomon is designated as the chosen one, declared qualified and given authority to rule as king. The people express their support with music and a tremendous outburst of joy.

Adonijah, hearing of Solomon's anointing, realizes his mistake (**1:41–53**). The message brought by a good man, Abiathar's son, is taken seriously. This message, besides reporting what has occurred, includes the account of David receiving congratulations from his servants and David's response of gratitude to God that one of his sons is seated on the throne. David expresses this because he has witnessed the fulfillment of the Lord's promises to him (2 Sam. 7:11–16). As Adonijah's guests flee to their homes, he goes to the courtyard of the tabernacle and there pleads for mercy by taking hold of the horns of the altar, the traditional sanctuary of safety. Solomon, at Adonijah's request, spares him but puts a condition upon him, that he prove himself worthy of life. Adonijah demonstrates his surrender by bowing before the enthroned Solomon. He is told to go home; he does not receive honors as a royal older brother.

David gives a charge to Solomon when he realizes he is to die soon (**2:1–9**). Some time has elapsed since Solomon's anointing because according to 1 Chronicles 28–29 Solomon is made king a second time in the presence of all the people, and David has instructed Solomon concerning the temple.

David speaks as an understanding, spiritually discerning, loving, and responsible father. A number of observations are in order: (1) God addressed the same words to Joshua when he was about to lead Israel into the Promised Land (Josh. 1:5–7). Solomon has to exercise his ability to make good decisions and to be firm in carrying these out. Emphasis is on strength of character. (2) Solomon must show himself a man; as God's image bearer, Solomon must reflect his Creator and demonstrate his regal nature. (3) Solomon must obey the Lord, carrying out his will as prescribed in the writings of Moses (cf. Josh. 1:7–8). These writings available to Solomon (Deut. 17:18–19) included a wide variety of laws and regulations covering every aspect of life. David counsels Solomon to be a covenant man, abiding in the love/life relationship the Lord has established with his people and bringing to expression that relationship by a wholehearted obedience to the Lord in every aspect of his personal and public life. David repeats the assured covenant blessing that follows upon such obedient covenant living. (4) Solomon must watch how he lives and walk faithfully as the Lord expects, for in that way his promise that one of David's descendants will always be on the throne will be fulfilled (2 Sam. 7:12–14). David places the responsibility for the continuing privilege of his seed to occupy the throne directly upon Solomon. David recognizes the sovereign goodness of the Lord while also emphasizing the gravity of man's covenantal responsibilities.

David also counsels Solomon as an astute politician. Three men have to be considered as Solomon consolidates his throne. Joab had brought blood guilt upon the kingdom. He had slain two generals, Abner (2 Sam. 3:27) and Amasa (2 Sam. 20:10), because of jealousy and had done so in a time of peace whereas such acts could be done with impunity only in time of war. Joab took advantage of David when David was in difficult circumstances—the first time in establishing his reign over all Israel, the second time in the context of Absalom's rebellion. Joab had also defied David's royal authority and had tried to make David seem responsible for his murderous acts (2 Sam. 3:28, 37). David urges Solomon to be wise in dealing with Joab but leaves no doubt in Solomon's mind that Joab deserves the death of a criminal.

In regard to Barzillai, David counsels that in gratitude for what he had done when David was threatened by Absalom's rebellion (2 Sam. 17:27–29) David's offer to support Barzillai (2 Sam. 19:31–40) has to be continued. David urges that covenantal love be demonstrated.

Shimei, who had cursed David, had been spared when David returned from his flight (2 Sam. 16:5–13; 19:16–23). David had not considered it expedient to execute Shimei. But Shimei of Saul's tribe, Benjamin, had cursed the Lord's anointed. Though he was shown mercy initially, he had to be dealt with according to his crime. This is not to be a matter of personal revenge (of which David could have been accused) but of justice. David leaves it to Solomon whom he believes to be wise (v. 6) to decide how and when this execution is to take place.

David dies at the age of seventy years, having reigned a total of forty years (**2:10–11**; 2 Sam. 5:4–5). The phrase *rested with his fathers,* used in most instances to refer to the death of a king, expresses the concept of continuity of families which death does not interrupt. David is buried on Mount Zion; in Jesus' time his tomb was known and honored.

B. Solomon's reign (2:12–11:43). Adonijah makes a move to gain influence and power, still entertaining hopes of gaining the throne (**2:13–25**). Three facts support this: (1) He seeks the queen mother's assistance. Royal wives and mothers had an influential role in ancient kingdoms. (2) He refers to the kingdom as his; Solomon recognizes that Adonijah is pressing his rights as the oldest living son. (3) He requests to have Abishag, the last woman to have had a wife's role, though she never became David's wife or concubine (1 Kings 1:4). To ask for a king's wife was to ask for his throne because of the queen's status. Bathsheba, unaware of Adonijah's intentions, plays her role. Solomon, however, proclaims that he is king by the Lord's design and promise and has Adonijah executed.

Abiathar, who supported Adonijah, is removed from the priesthood and banished to his rural home (**2:26–27**). His life is spared because of his role in bringing in the ark to Jerusalem (1 Chron. 15:11; 27:34) and his support of David (1 Sam. 22:20–22; 23:6–9; 2 Sam. 15:32–37; 17:15). His expulsion from the priesthood fulfills the prophecy against Eli (1 Sam. 2:27–36), who was a descendant of Ithamar, Aaron's youngest son. Zadok, who becomes the sole priest (2:35), is a descendant of Eleazar, Aaron's oldest living son.

Joab provides the immediate circumstance for his own death (**2:28–35**). Upon hearing of the death of Adonijah, Joab seeks clemency as Adonijah had originally done (1 Kings 1:51–52). But Solomon heeds his father's advice. When Joab refuses to leave the altar, he is executed in that place of refuge. His crimes of bloodshed warrant this. Thus Solomon removes the curse of blood guilt that Joab, as commander of the army, had brought upon the kingdom. Retribution brings peace to the Davidic throne. Benaniah, David's chief bodyguard, becomes Solomon's commander-in-chief.

Shimei's death follows (**2:36–46**). Though David's clemency could have continued under the restrictions Solomon placed upon Shimei, he is foolish enough to ignore these. Length of time and concern for his property (slaves) were not legitimate reasons to violate the imposed restrictions. Solomon relates the defiance against David and against him; both constitute threats to the kingdom the Lord has established. Solomon expects the Lord's blessing for striking Shimei down. The death of Shimei removes the last barrier to a firm establishment of the throne given to Solomon according to the Lord's promises to David (2 Sam. 7:12–16).

Suggestions of Solomon's moral and spiritual double-mindedness are present (**3:1–3**). Solomon marries a princess from Egypt, the land of physical and spiritual bondage. He may have intended to strengthen the border between Israel and Egypt, but the marriage is contrary to Mosaic ordinances (Deut. 7:3; 17:16–17). That he brings the princess into the city before he has facilities for her adds to the problem.

Solomon's use of high places (hilltops or ridges) which Canaanites also used as fertility worship centers is contrary to Mosaic legislation (Deut. 12:1–4; allowance for places of worship other than the central place had been made [Deut. 12:5–19]). That no house of worship had yet been built is one explanation for Solomon's use of high places; the tabernacle did not fulfill the requirement of that single place.

Solomon undoubtedly is sincere in his worship (**3:4–15**). His thousand burnt offerings, offered at Gibeon where the Mosaic tabernacle is, are acceptable to the Lord. At Gibeon the Lord appears to Solomon in a dream and offers him whatever he desires. Solomon's response includes the following: (1) you made and kept covenant with my father David; (2) my father lived in that covenant with you and the riches of the covenant were his; (3) you have kept covenant by placing me on the throne of your covenant people; (4) I am not able of myself to serve as a covenantal king on a covenantal throne over a numerous elect covenantal people; (5) I, as their king and judge, need a heart that loves but also understands people and is able to discern issues of justice.

The Lord demonstrates his pleasure with Solomon's wise decision to place the people's needs before and above his own desires; in addition to the gift of wisdom, Solomon receives long life, riches, honor, and the specific covenantal blessings promised to Abraham (Gen. 12:1–3). God tells Solomon that he must demonstrate love and obedience. Solomon returns to the tent in Jerusalem, where the ark of the Lord's presence is, and sacrifices, worships, and feasts there.

Solomon gives evidence of having received the gift of wisdom (**3:16–28**). He tests the heart of a mother, even if she is a sinful woman, in regard to her concern for the life and well-being of the living child. The mother of the dead child has no maternal loving concern; her deceit and falsehood become evident. Solomon proves that he understands motherhood and that he can administer justice—giving lawful due to the one who rightly expects it. An added blessing Solomon receives is the awe and respect of the people.

Solomon organizes his administration efficiently (**4:1–19**). He appoints a group of high officials who serve him personally, in the affairs of the palace, in the temple, over the military, over district officers, and over the labor forces (cf. David's organization, 2 Sam. 8:16–18). The term *priest* in this context has a wider reference than religious cult leader. Azariah, for example, is Solomon's top counselor while Zabud serves as Solomon's personal confidential counselor. Abiathar, who had been banished from Jerusalem, likely continues to hold the office of priest but does not serve as such. The forced labor is constituted of those conscripted to work in Solomon's building projects (5:13).

Solomon appoints twelve district governors. Each man is to gather provisions for the royal house for one month in the year. Since two of Solomon's sons-in-law are listed, the list probably dates from the later part of Solomon's reign.

A brief description of the extent of Solomon's kingdom is given (**4:20–21**). To the north and east his rule extends up to the west bank of the Euphrates River. To the south, it goes to the border of Egypt, including the land of the Philistines.

The daily provisions required (**4:22–28**) are detailed briefly. It is estimated that Solomon's house included, besides his personal family, five hundred officials, servants, pensioners, and guests. Food also had to be supplied for his many horses (which he should not have had according to Deut. 17:16). The writer repeats that all Israel is secure and prosperous ("each man under his own vine and fig tree") and that the many provisions could be gathered because of the immense area these were drawn from and the kings over whom Solomon ruled.

Among his many assets, Solomon's wisdom is his greatest (**4:29–34**). Wise men were known in other countries; ancient documents of wisdom have been found by archaeologists. But Solomon's wisdom exceeds that of any and all others. Solomon has a natural propensity to wisdom (he chooses it, 3:9) but the Lord greatly enhances and enlarges it. His knowledge and wisdom range over the entire spectrum of creation, human life, and its affairs. He is given the gift of expression in sayings, poems, and music.

Solomon's kingdom exhibits fulfillment of the covenant promises made to the patriarchs and through Moses to Israel. Solomon, David's son, is of Abraham's seed; he is an ancestor and type of Jesus Christ. His kingdom is an actual fulfillment of promises and a type of the eternal kingdom of God. God did not fail his people or postpone the fulfillment of his covenant promises. The biblical account reveals, however, that Solomon, his descendants, and all Israel failed to carry out their covenant responsibilities. They failed to accept their covenant privileges. They failed to appreciate their role in working with the Lord in carrying out his covenant and kingdom plans and promises.

Solomon does fulfill his father's desires and plans by becoming a builder. His attention is directed first of all to the temple. The account deals first with Solomon's preparations (**5:1–18**). Hiram, king of Tyre, sends a congratulatory message to Solomon on his becoming king after David. The relationship between David and Hiram had been cordial; Hiram had loved David. He had supplied David with materials for his palace (2 Sam. 5:11; 2 Chron. 2:3). Solomon requests Hiram to do the same for the temple. His request includes a brief explanation. David had planned to build the temple (2 Sam. 7:1–3), but could not because of the time and energy required to establish the kingdom. This had called for much warfare and bloodshed (1 Chron. 22:6–8). In addition, the Lord had informed David that the royal house had to be established first (2 Sam. 7:11). Once Solomon was enthroned as successor to David, the Davidic house (i.e., the royal messianic house) was established. Peace had been achieved. The time and conditions for the building of the Lord's permanent residence among his people had come. Solomon therefore expresses determination to carry out David's plan and to give permanent expression to the concept of "God with us," Immanuel. So he requests cedar wood and assistance from Hiram's skilled craftsmen. Hiram responds with joy. He does not acknowledge Solomon's God as his own, but praises the "god" of Israel who has led Solomon. Hiram's agreement to send cedar and cypress and to supply assistance includes the demand for food for his royal household; thus Solomon's officers had to gather a large additional amount for years. Solomon exercises his God-given wisdom in making a treaty that establishes peace and guarantees him supplies and skilled assistance in the building of the temple.

Solomon conscripts thirty thousand laborers from Israel; these are not slaves but men who give their services as tribute (free labor). Another one hundred and fifty thousand laborers are slaves—Canaanites and other people still living in Israel (cf. 1 Kings 9:20–21; 2 Chron. 2:17–18; 8:7). These laborers are forced to do the heavy work of carrying materials and cutting stone in the mountains.

The actual building of the temple begins in Solomon's fourth year as king (**6:1–38**). This, according to the writer, is 480 years after Israel left Egypt. In verses 2–10 the writer describes the frame of the temple. It is ninety feet long, thirty feet wide, and forty-five feet high. Against the side and back walls are three stories of storerooms, each 7½ feet high. Two pillars are erected, one on each side of the large entrance to the temple. A point is made of the fact that all the timbers and blocks of stone are prepared before they are brought to Mount Moriah where the temple is built. Thus all the parts only have to be fitted together; hammers, axes, and saws are not needed; they are not seen, heard, or handled at the construction site.

While Solomon is building, the Lord assures him that he will keep his covenant made with David and Israel if Solomon continues to be a covenant-keeping king. The Lord will dwell in the midst of a faithful and obedient people.

The interior of the temple consists of cedar, cypress, and olive wood; no stone is seen (v. 18). Elaborate carvings are made in the form of gourds, open flowers, cherubim, and palms. The only metal used is gold and that for overlaying some parts. The building is divided into two sanctuaries. The inner room or sanctuary, a perfect cube, has cherubim whose wings touch either a wall or the other's wing; the ark of the Lord's presence is to be placed in it. The entrances to the inner sanctuary and to the outer sanctuary are made of olive wood decorated with gold-covered carvings. It takes seven years to construct the building. Once it is finished, the furnishings are prepared and placed (7:13–8:66).

Solomon builds the royal palace after he completes the temple (**7:1–12**). Biblical scholars are not agreed on various details. The text indicates that Solomon spent a total of twenty years on this building project, thus making Jerusalem a city of splendor. Immediately to the south of the temple, Solomon constructs a number of royal buildings. The Palace of the Forest of Lebanon, known for its many cedar pillars and beams, serves as storage building and arsenal (1 Kings 10:16–17). In front of it is the Hall of Pillars; no reference is made to its specific function. The Hall of Justice is next and between this hall and the temple Solomon builds his own palace and one for his queen, the daughter of Pharaoh. These five buildings and the temple are made of expensive materials, precious stone prepared for placement at the quarries and cedar prepared for placement before being brought to the building site. An immense courtyard is prepared, with various levels and divisions.

The temple furnishings are described in some detail (**7:13–51**). Huram (also called Huram-Abi; 2 Chron. 2:13), a skilled bronze worker, makes many items of bronze. He casts two large pillars to be placed in front of the temple, one on each side of the entrance. These are decorated with capitals at the top, a network of chains, and two hundred pomegranates. Over the top of these a work of lilies is placed.

In the courtyard, a large bronze container for water (bath) is placed on top of twelve bronze oxen. Ten smaller baths are placed on ornately made stands. Thus a large supply of water for washing the sacrificial animals, those who perform the sacrifices, and their implements is available. Huram also makes pots, shovels, and tongs needed for the altar. All this bronze work is made in the plain just west of the Jordan River.

Furnishings to be placed in the first sanctuary, the Holy Place, are made of gold (the altar, the table for bread, the ten lampstands, and all the required implements). Even the door sockets are made of gold. In addition to what he has made, Solomon brings in all the gold, silver, and containers David had prepared, gathered, and dedicated to the Lord, and stores them in the treasury (likely in part of the Palace of the Forest of Lebanon).

The significance of the temple, its ornate decorations, and golden and bronze furnishings is to express the permanence of the Lord's dwelling among his people. The temple, much more than the tabernacle, is intended to express the grandeur, splendor, majesty, glory, and wonder of the holiness of the Lord. People—finite, sinful, undeserving—are taught that their gloriously holy Lord is ready to and pleased to dwell in their midst as their covenant Lord.

Once the temple and its furnishings are completed, the ark of the Lord's covenant is brought into the temple (**8:1–13**). Solomon summons all the leaders—the seventy elders (Num. 11:24), the heads of the twelve tribes, and the chief of each Israelite family. The feast referred to is the one prescribed for the fifteenth day of the seventh month and the week following, the Feast of Tabernacles or Booths (Lev. 23:34; 1 Kings 8:65). Some scholars suggest that this event took place in the seventh year, a month before the temple was completed (1 Kings 6:38 reports that the temple was completed in the eighth month). Others suggest it was in the eighth month of the eighth year. The most likely answer is that it took place after all the buildings were completed, that is, in the eighth month of the twentieth year. This date is implied by 1 Kings 9:1, when the Lord appears to Solomon. The Tent of Meeting is not the tent David had prepared on Mount Zion (2 Sam. 6:17) but the Mosaic tabernacle which had been kept at Gibeon (2 Chron. 1:3–4). The priests come from two places, Gibeon and Mount Zion, carrying the sacred objects used in Israel's worship. Once the ark arrives, many sacrifices are made before it. It is then placed in the inner sanctuary, the Most Holy Place.

The ark is referred to as "the ark of the LORD's covenant." Moses called it "the ark of the Testimony" (Exod. 25:21; 40:20–21); it contained the tables of the law of the covenant. When the ark was carried ahead of the Israelites in the wilderness, it was referred to as "the ark of the covenant" (Num. 10:33). The ark of the Lord's covenant, testimony, and name was the ark of the Lord's presence because the Lord had said to Moses that when he stood before the ark, the Lord would meet and speak with him (Exod. 25:22). That this is the ark that Moses made is supported by the reference to the poles used to carry the ark which were never to be removed (Exod. 25:13–15) and to the tables of stone on which the Lord had written the law of his covenant.

Once the ark has been placed, and the priests have gone out, the Lord makes his presence known with the cloud of his glory which fills the temple. The cloud had represented God's presence when the tabernacle was completed (Exod. 40:34–35) and when Israel traveled in the wilderness. The cloud of glory is thick and dark, making it impossible for the priests to perform their duties in the temple. Solomon can fittingly say that the Lord said he would dwell in a dark cloud. That dark cloud has taken abode in the magnificent temple prepared for the Lord in the midst of his people.

Solomon speaks to the people gathered at the temple, blesses them, and praises the Lord (**8:14–21**). Solomon is fully aware of what the Lord has promised and done. The Lord brought Israel from Egypt; the Lord chose David to rule. David desired to build a temple, but the Lord indicated that David's son was to build the house for the Lord's Name. All this had taken place. Every promise made had been kept. The blessings for Israel that were initially given in the exodus are now fully realized with the Lord's permanent residence in the temple. The Lord has kept his covenant; the presence of the ark containing the testimony of the covenant in the temple gives full assurance of this.

Solomon, standing before the altar in the presence of the whole assembly of Israel, lifts his hands in a dedicatory prayer (**8:22–53**). Solomon expresses adoration. He acknowledges God as the only incomparable Lord in heaven and on earth and as the faithful Lord who continues to demonstrate his covenant love by fulfilling his promises to David and his seed. Solomon has built the temple; it remains for the infinite Lord, whose existence is beyond comprehension, to choose to dwell in it among a finite needy people. Submission does not exclude a bold plea that the Lord might hear his people's prayer and forgive them. Solomon intercedes on behalf of the people whom he knows to be sinners and who require the Lord's dealing with them. He prays for justice for those who wrong others; for penitent people; for people suffering due to lack of rain because of sin; for people suffering from famine, plagues, invasion, disaster, or disease; for foreigners who seek the Lord; for soldiers called to war; and for all the people as they sin and suffer the consequences. Solomon expresses a deep awareness of the need for the Lord's justice to be executed when dealing with sin. He also is deeply aware of the effectiveness of prayers requesting forgiveness and healing. Above all, he is conscious of the Lord's readiness to forgive, to be merciful, and to uphold his people whom he redeemed from Egypt. Solomon concludes his prayer in the confidence that the Lord would fulfill his word which had come through Moses.

Solomon, having concluded his prayer, pronounces a blessing upon the assembly (**8:54–61**). To bless means to pronounce that the Lord is with his people and all his virtues are at the people's service and for their benefit. Solomon praises the Lord for his readiness and ability to bring his people to the Promised Land and to give them rest, for continually being with his people, for giving his covenant law to his people and enabling them to keep it, for upholding the cause of Solomon and all the people in answer to his prayer, and for giving occasion for nations to know that Israel's God is the one, only true living God. The prayer of blessing on the people concludes with the reminder that blessings come only to those who are fully surrendered to the Lord and committed to live the covenant life.

The dedication of the temple is concluded by a service of many peace sacrifices and fellowship (**8:62–66**). The flesh of these sacrifices is used to feed the people at the feast. Because the altar, large as it is, cannot accommodate all the sacrificial animals, the space between the "sea" and the altar in front of the temple doors is consecrated as a place of sacrifice. The feast extends from one week to two; the people are then sent home but they bless the king and have joy in their hearts because of what the Lord has done through Solomon for David and all the people.

The Lord appears to Solomon a second time (**9:1–9**). This is, in a real sense, a covenant renewal. Solomon had finished building the temple and the royal buildings; he had achieved what he had set out to do. The Lord confirms that he has heard Solomon's prayer and plea. He acknowledges Solomon's placing of his Name (the ark of the testimony) in the temple. The Lord reassures Solomon that he will always be among his people. The Lord will keep the covenant. Solomon, however, has to remain faithful. As David had been a man of integrity, pure of heart, obedient, and faithful, so Solomon has to, if the royal throne is to remain established and one of David's sons is to be enthroned on it. The blessings of the covenant are assured. If, however, Solomon or his descendants are disobedient and serve other gods, the curse of the covenant will be carried out. Israel will be carried off; the temple will be rejected; the people will be ridiculed. The nations will learn what happens to an unfaithful, ungrateful, disobedient people with whom the Lord has covenanted. Solomon is reminded that the Lord is always a covenant-keeping God, that covenant blessings are bestowed or the curse of the covenant is carried out on those with whom the Lord covenants.

The unity of the Old Testament is held before the readers of the Bible in a unique manner. Solomon, and all the kings after him, those ruling over Israel as well as Judah, were to consider David as a model. David was the king after God's own heart. He had learned, loved, and lived obediently according to the will of God as revealed through Moses. David had Moses as his model. Moses, in turn, was called to carry out the promises the Lord had made to Abraham (Gen. 12; 15; 17; 22), Isaac (Gen. 26:23–24), and Jacob (Gen. 28:13–15), and to explicate the law which Abraham had kept in obedience to God (Gen. 26:5). Thus Solomon and all succeeding kings were to follow in the will and way the Lord had held before Abraham, Moses, and David. Every king was to obey Moses and be the Lord's agent in carrying out the covenant promises to Abraham.

Solomon pays Hiram for the materials he had supplied by giving him twenty towns in Galilee (**9:10–14**). This is not a wise move for at least two reasons: (1) inheritances promised to the covenant people are given to a noncovenantal king; and (2) Hiram is not pleased with the towns because he considers them inferior in value to all the wealth he has supplied Solomon. The relationship between the two countries is not improved; Hiram calls the towns the Land of Cabul, "good-for-nothing."

A review of Solomon's labor force is given (**9:15–23**). Solomon had called up Israelite men (1 Kings 5:13) for temporary duty but he forces the remnants of various Canaanite people to be slave laborers. As the Gibeonites of Joshua's day (Josh. 9), these people became wood cutters, water carriers, and other menial laborers. Israelites called into the service of the kingdom were officers, soldiers, horsemen, charioteers, government officials, and supervisors over building projects.

Solomon's Egyptian queen, who was living in the City of David, takes up residence in the palace (**9:24**) Solomon built for her. Thus he brings her to a building complex that includes the temple of the Lord.

Solomon faithfully carries out his duties in regard to the temple and its services (**9:25**). The prescribed burnt and peace offerings, indicating submission and dedication, and incense offerings, indicating prayers pleasing to the Lord, are offered regularly.

Solomon builds naval vessels at Ezion-geber (**9:26–28**), on the northern tip of the Gulf of Aqaba. Having Tyrian seamen in charge of his ships, Solomon is able to reach the southeastern coast of Africa and all of southern Asia. An immense amount of gold is brought from Ophir (the exact location of which is not known) as well as other precious materials (1 Kings 10:11–12).

The queen of Sheba visits Solomon (**10:1–13**). Sheba is believed to be the land of the Sabaeans in South Arabia. Solomon's trading activities may have brought him to her attention. She had also heard of his fame, his relationship with his Lord, and his wisdom and wealth. She has many riddles, puzzles (for which Arabs are known), and questions for Solomon who gives satisfactory replies in all instances. His fame, faith, and wisdom are confirmed. His wealth, civic organization, and services overwhelm her. Her praise of the Lord who has so richly blessed Solomon does not indicate her own faith—she does not worship at the temple. She recognizes Solomon's Lord, the blessings he provides, and the joy he gives Solomon and his people just as she would recognize her own god(s). She comes with many expensive gifts; Solomon, as per oriental custom, gives equivalent gifts—and more—in return. The queen returns to Sheba richer than she had come, satisfied that what she had heard was only part of the truth concerning Solomon and probably relieved that she had made trade agreements with Solomon to protect her own interests, threatened by Solomon's expanding commercial activities. The queen's visit is a partial fulfillment of the Lord's promises to Abraham (Gen. 12:1–3; 22:17–18; cf. also Ps. 72:8–17). Jesus refers to the queen of Sheba as an example of those who would come from afar to seek him while his own people reject him (Matt. 12:42).

Solomon's wealth continues to accumulate (**10:14–29**). His control of land and sea trade routes brings much income. Approximately twenty-five tons of gold is imported each year. The gold is used to make shields, goblets, and household articles. Silver is so common that it is considered common and cheap. His throne, attended by lions and made of ivory and gold, is incomparable. Gifts accumulate as visitors and guests come to pay respect to Solomon. He engages in horse trading with Egypt, the Hittites, and the Syrians. Having many horses and carrying on trade with Egypt is contrary to the Lord's requirements for the king (Deut. 17:16). The feeding of these horses places an added burden on the people and the officers in charge of gathering provisions. Solomon's horse trade is an evidence of lack of obedience, double-mindedness, and refusal to exercise the wisdom the Lord had given him. In many respects Solomon is a type of Christ. But his sinful human nature is also very evident.

Solomon marries seven hundred foreign princesses; God had expressly forbidden such intermarriages (**11:1–8;** Deut. 7:4; 17:17). His love for the Lord grows cold; his heart of wisdom turns from the Lord. His wives lead him to worship their gods. He departs far from the ways of David; he rejects the Lord's word which had come to him twice (1 Kings 3:14; 9:6–9). Solomon becomes a covenant breaker.

The Lord speaks to Solomon about his idolatry (**11:9–13**). The Lord is angry because of Solomon's unfaithfulness and disobedience. The consequences will be tragic; after he dies, most of the kingdom will be taken from Solomon's descendants. For David's sake (2 Sam. 7:11–17) and for the sake of the chosen city the Lord keeps his covenant; the royal house, the throne, and other blessings of the covenant continue. Because of Solomon's sins, the curse of the covenant is brought upon his descendants and the kingdom.

The Lord begins to execute his curse upon Solomon's house and kingdom by raising up three instruments of judgment (**11:14–40**). Hadad, an Edomite of royal birth, had escaped when Joab slaughtered most of the Edomite males and found asylum in Egypt. When David died, Hadad returned to Edom and becomes a source of trouble on Israel's southern border. Rezon, also an escapee, gathers a group of rebels in Syria on the northern borders of Solomon's kingdom. Jeroboam, of the tribe of Ephraim, is also raised up as an agent of judgment.

As a descendant of Ephraim, Jeroboam represents the antagonism that existed between Judah and Ephraim throughout the years. Ephraim, the youngest son of Joseph, had received the firstborn blessing from his grandfather Jacob (Gen. 48). The prophet Ahijah informs Jeroboam that the Lord is going to divide the kingdom of Solomon. By tearing his new cloak into twelve pieces, and telling Jeroboam to take ten of them, the prophet dramatically demonstrates what God is going to do. Jeroboam learns why much of the kingdom is to be torn from Solomon's house, and why part is to remain. He is explicitly told that the Lord is going to do this. Jeroboam, however, is to do his part. He is to be faithful, submissive, obedient to the Lord. Jeroboam is promised a lasting kingdom for his house if he proves to be a faithful covenant servant.

Solomon is soon aware of Jeroboam's destiny. This is made evident by his attempt to kill Jeroboam. Egypt again proves to be a haven for Solomon's enemy. The treaty between Solomon and Egypt, sealed by marriage, does not serve Solomon well in regard to his enemies but may have benefited him in his horse-trading business.

Solomon dies after reigning forty years (**11:41–43**). Annals concerning all the activities and events of his reign were kept and are available to the writer of Kings.

Solomon had brought much glory, honor, influence, and fame to the kingdom of Israel. He was in a position to bring covenantal blessings for centuries to his people, to the nations under his rule, and to other nations. His incomparable wisdom, the heritage of his father David, and the messages he received directly from the Lord, however, were not sufficient to offset his love for idolatrous women and his desire to please them. The power of Solomon's love for women ultimately proved greater than the power of his love for the Lord. He is said to have rested with his fathers and was buried in David's city.

II. The Divided Kingdom (1 Kings 12:1–2 Kings 17:41)

A. Enmity (1 Kings 12:1–16:28). Rehoboam, Solomon's son, goes to Shechem, the ancient gathering place of Israel (Josh. 24:1), to have the people make him king (**12:1–15**). Solomon had not made him co-regent; thus he is not yet king. Israel, however, has had the privilege of assenting to the anointing of their divinely appointed kings (1 Sam. 11:15, Saul at Gilgal; 2 Sam. 2:4, David over Judah; 2 Sam. 5:3, David over Israel; 1 Chron. 29:22, Solomon over Israel). Jeroboam and other leaders of the ten northern tribes tell Rehoboam that if the heavy taxes and levies Solomon had imposed on them are lightened, they will acknowledge him as king. Rehoboam requests three days for consideration. He may have been surprised by the demand. Jeroboam was probably convinced that Rehoboam would not accede; thus he would not be considered the instigator of a coup when he became king. Rejecting the advice of the elders, Rehoboam foolishly refuses to grant the request. On the advice of his peers, he threatens to impose a much greater burden and a much harsher discipline than Solomon had. The inspired writer sums up the events by pointing out that the Lord is sovereignly at work guiding the events that took place. But Rehoboam and Jeroboam, as well as the people, are responsible for their decisions and deeds.

The ten northern tribes secede from the kingdom that David and Solomon had governed (**12:16–19**). They rebel; they reject David's house from which the promised Messiah is to come. They confirm their rebellion by killing Adoniram, who is in charge of forced labor and whom Rehoboam sends as his representative. Rehoboam himself flees to Jerusalem. Only the tribe of Judah remains loyal to the house of David.

Jeroboam is made king by the northern tribes (**12:20**). Though it is not stated that the Benjamites are loyal to the house of David, they do give aid to Rehoboam and eventually become part of the nation of Judah. Many people of the tribe of Simeon do not join the rebellion either because their inheritance is within the boundaries of Judah (Josh. 19:1–9).

Rehoboam is warned by the prophet Shemaiah (**12:21–24**) not to lead the army he has gathered against the rebel tribes. The prophet declares that the division has been made by the Lord. Rehoboam and his soldiers obey the prophet. The Lord's word concerning the tragic consequences of Solomon's unfaithfulness (1 Kings 11:11) become a reality. Disobedience and unfaithfulness on the part of the leader-king brings enmity and division among the people the king was to unite in loving service to the Lord.

Jeroboam does not heed the promise and fails to fulfill the duties the Lord held before him (**12:25–33**). Jeroboam realizes the influence of temple worship in Jerusalem and fears that this will draw Israel away from him. He devises a cultus for Israel as an alternative to worshiping in Jerusalem. This cultus includes two golden calves. One is placed in Bethel, on the southern border, located en route to Jerusalem. The other is placed in the north, in Dan. In addition, Jeroboam builds shrines on high places (Canaanite worship centers), appoints unacceptable non-Levitical men to be priests, and sets a week for feasting in the eighth month (similar to the divinely appointed festive week in the seventh month). The people accept the alternative shrines, priests, feast, and the golden calves. They sin in their false worship. Jeroboam leads Israel into idolatrous worship, failing to learn from Solomon's tragic disobedience. Political expediency takes priority over obedience to the Lord, faithful worship, and the giving of thanks to the Lord for his blessings.

An anonymous prophet from Judah prophesies to Jeroboam (**13:1–9**). Jeroboam, preparing to make an offering on the altar at Bethel, hears two dire prophecies against that altar: (1) Josiah, who is to ascend Judah's throne in 641 B.C., approximately 280 years later, is to burn the bones of Jeroboam's illicit priests on it; and (2) the altar is to be split apart and its ashes poured on the ground as a sign of the Lord's repudiation of Jeroboam's sinful worship. Jeroboam, ordering the seizure of the prophet, suffers the Lord's judgment immediately. His outstretched hand is paralyzed and shriveled and the altar is split apart. Upon Jeroboam's request, the prophet intercedes for him and his hand is restored. Thus Jeroboam receives another message from the Lord who alone is sovereign and to be worshiped. Yet Jeroboam sinfully rejects the message he receives as well as its implied warnings. The prophet rejects Jeroboam's offer of hospitality because the Lord had commanded him not to eat bread or drink water or return by the way he came. He is not to be entertained by those who flagrantly violate the Lord's will and reject his promises.

An old prophet intercepts the man of God from Judah (**13:11–32**) and is instrumental in his death. The Lord's hand, however, is obvious in this tragic event. Those who, like the prophet from Judah, disobey the specific commands of the Lord can expect his judgment. The old prophet reflects the chaotic religious circumstances of Israel. He proves to be of a duplicitous mind, for after lying to the prophet and, in a real sense, leading him to his death, he agrees that the prophet from Judah had spoken the word of the Lord. Judgment is to come upon the false worship Jeroboam has instituted.

Jeroboam remains obstinate (**13:33–34**). In spite of the prophecy against his illegitimate priesthood and the death of the prophet who disobeyed a specific instruction from the Lord, Jeroboam continues to maintain a priesthood that is sacrilegious and corrupt. This is the reason the Lord rejects Jeroboam and destroys his entire family. Worship that is contrary to the Lord's expressed instructions and demands is a just reason for judgment. The deeds involved in false worship cannot be separated from wrong concepts of the Lord himself. In the same way, true worship cannot be separated from the truths God has revealed about himself.

Ahijah, the prophet who had informed Jeroboam that he was to be king, is given the opportunity by Jeroboam himself to prophesy against the king (**14:1–18**). Abijah, the king's son, becomes ill. Jeroboam's wife disguises herself at the king's command and goes with staple gifts (possibly as a payment for services) to enquire of the prophet concerning the boy's future. The Lord tells Ahijah about the queen so that he has a message prepared for her. He scolds her for her pretense. The Lord and his prophets are not to be dealt with deceitfully. She is to bring a message to Jeroboam. The Lord gave him the kingdom of Israel and commanded him to serve as David had done. Jeroboam was to have obeyed the will of the Lord, loved him with all his heart, and done only what was right and pleasing to the Lord. However, Jeroboam has done more evil than his predecessors. Every one of Jeroboam's male descendants will be cut off and brought to a most humiliating end; dogs and birds will eat their dead bodies. Abijah, the only son in whom the Lord has found anything good, will die when his mother returns and be the only one to be honorably buried. Another family will be raised up to reign in Jeroboam's stead. Israel, the nation, has become weak and frail and will lose its inheritance. The nation will go into captivity. Jeroboam is the cause of Israel's demise because he angered the Lord by introducing false worship. All that Ahijah proclaims is fulfilled. Jeroboam's son dies as soon as his mother returns to Tirzah (which had become the capital city after Peniel, 12:25) and is buried as a prince loved by the people.

Jeroboam dies after reigning twenty-two years (**14:19–20**). The writer of Kings does not repeat all of Jeroboam's activities as a military leader and royal ruler; these are recorded in the royal annals of Israel (v. 19).

Rehoboam, son of Solomon, reigns for seventeen years, from 931–913 B.C. (**14:21–31**). His mother, Naamah, was an Ammonite whom Solomon had married before he began his forty-year reign. Rehoboam reigns in the Lord's chosen city where the ark of the covenant resided, where the Name of the Lord had been placed. The Lord of heaven and earth had identified himself with Jerusalem but Rehoboam does not honor the Lord there. He engages in the detestable orgiastic rituals of the Canaanites in the shrines he builds; he sets up Asherah poles (gross female sexual godlets) and has male prostitutes function in these settings. Rehoboam reintroduces the practices for which the Canaanites had been punished. Rehoboam is humiliated by the invasion of Shishak of Egypt and his plundering of the temple. The glory of his father's reign is diminished greatly when the gold is carried off and Rehoboam and his guard use bronze shields instead of the gold shields Solomon had prepared. Rehoboam, in spite of being warned not to wage war with Jeroboam, does so throughout his reign. There is no peace for either nation; both fail miserably in being agents of covenantal blessings to other nations. Rehoboam is given a royal burial when he dies.

Abijam (also called Abijah) succeeds his father as king of Judah (**15:1–8**). His mother was a daughter of Absalom, who had sought the throne of David. Abijam follows the ways of Rehoboam instead of those of his great-grandfather David. But the Lord gives Abijam a son through whom he again strengthens his chosen city. The Lord does this in fulfillment of his promises to David. Reference to the continued warfare between Jeroboam's and Rehoboam's houses indicates that Abijam did not have a peaceful reign.

Asa, Abijam's son, becomes king in 911 B.C. and reigns forty-one years, until 870 B.C. (**15:9–24**). His mother is not mentioned, but his grandmother Maacah, daughter of Absalom and wife of Rehoboam, is. She is deposed as queen mother because she had made a repulsive Asherah pole. This dethronement is part of Asa's cleansing of the kingdom. He also removes the male prostitutes and idols his predecessors, Rehoboam and Abijam, had set up. In this reforming work he is encouraged by the prophet Azariah (2 Chron. 15:1). Asa is described as doing what is right; he follows in the ways of David and his heart is committed to the Lord. He loves the Lord, seeks to know and do the Lord's will, and trusts in the Lord to enable him to be the approved king. Asa, however, commits two errors. Politically and militarily he seeks to strengthen Judah by paying Benhadad, king of Syria, to break treaty with and fight against Israel. The king of Israel was sealing Judah's northern border, closing the trade routes that were important to Judah's economy. Benhadad agrees and gives Asa a temporary advantage in that Israel's king stops building fortifications at Ramah along Judah's northern border and fighting Judah. Asa is also able to use Israel's materials for building fortifications at Geba and Mispah on his northern border with Israel. But Syria's attack weakens Israel, which served as a buffer state for Judah against invading forces from the north. Religiously, Asa errs in that he takes dedicated temple treasures to buy Benhadad's help, thereby placing himself in debt to Syria. The treasures he takes he had placed there himself to replace what Shishak had taken. Asa is rebuked for buying Syria's aid by the prophet Hanani who reminds Asa that the Lord has given him the strength and ability to defeat the Ethiopians (2 Chron. 14:9–15; 16:7–10). Asa's cruel treatment of the prophet and other people indicates that he was angry because he had to face up to his folly.

The overall effect of Asa's many achievements written in the annals of the kings of Judah, is the purifying of the land of Judah religiously and the reestablishing of the worship of the Lord. He lays good foundations upon which his God-fearing son Jehoshaphat can build. Jehoshaphat becomes co-regent with his father, probably necessitated by Asa's disease in the later years of his life.

Nadab, Jeroboam's son, reigns for a short period (910–909 B.C.; **15:25–31**). He is a contemporary of Asa of Judah. He follows in Jeroboam's way. Nadab is killed while on a military expedition against the Philistines. The entire family of Jeroboam is thereby wiped out. The Lord, in his anger against faithless and disobedient Jeroboam, carries out his word as the prophet Ahijah had proclaimed it (1 Kings 14:11). Jeroboam's dynasty rules only twenty-four years but in that short period of time the godless way Israel was to live becomes entrenched and its inexorable movement toward demise is set in motion. Jeroboam has set up a kingdom that was in opposition to the covenant and kingdom of the Lord; it cannot succeed.

Baasha, who destroys Jeroboam's family, assumes the throne of Israel and reigns from 909–886 B.C. (15:33–16:7). He is not a religious reformer, but follows the course Jeroboam set. He carries on warfare with Judah during his reign. He was raised up by the Lord as an instrument of judgment upon Jeroboam's house but he rejects covenantal and kingdom life and service. Jehu (son of the prophet Hanani, 2 Chron. 16:7) brings the familiar message to Baasha. The Lord raised Baasha up to lead Israel. However, Baasha led the people into sinful ways. His dynasty will receive the same tragic punishment Jeroboam's did. Baasha is given the opportunity to repent, but fails to heed the word of the Lord. He dies unrepentant and his son Elah becomes king.

One of the reasons for Baasha's downfall is his destruction of Jeroboam's house. This destruction was of the Lord; Baasha was raised up to carry out the Lord's prophetic word of judgment. Baasha, however, did it as a self-seeking, self-extolling rebel. He did not do it as a willing servant of the Lord.

Elah, Baasha's son, reigns for two years (**16:8–14**). The annals of the kings of Israel record Elah's deeds and the events which transpire during his reign. Elah causes Israel to commit the sins of Jeroboam and Baasha. While Elah is drunk he is killed and his assassin wipes out the entire family of Baasha and Elah. The second dynasty to rule over Israel, for a period of twenty-five years, is totally destroyed. The people of Israel, who had rejected the Davidic house, are sheep without reliable shepherds.

Zimri, a military official over half of Elah's chariots, kills the king and takes the throne of Israel (**16:15–20**). His reign lasts only seven days. The army of Israel, fighting the Philistines where Baasha had killed Nadab (1 Kings 15:27), refuses to acknowledge Zimri and chooses Omri, commander of Israel's army, to be king. The army leaves the Philistine border and captures Tirzeh, the capital. Before Zimri can be captured he sets the palace on fire around himself and dies. Tibni is selected king by a faction in Israel (**16:21–22**), but is eliminated by Omri who proves to be stronger.

Omri reigns for twelve years (884–874 B.C.; **16:23–28**). He buys a hill from Shemer and builds his capital city, Samaria, on it. This is an excellent strategic move. Archaeological records indicate that Omri was known in other nations as a strong king and military commander. However, Omri surpasses his predecessors in committing evil; details are not mentioned except to refer to Omri's following in the way of Jeroboam. The fifth ruling house of Israel fails to lead Israel into the service of the Lord though it provides more stability.

B. Peace and friendship (1 Kings 16:29–2 Kings 9:37). During this period, lasting thirty-three years, limited friendship develops between the ruling houses of Israel and Judah. However, this does not influence Israel to adopt the way of life in Judah which is described as walking in the way of Asa and David (1 Kings 22:43). The tragic fact is that Judah is influenced by Israel's royal family.

Ahab, son of Omri, becomes king in 874 B.C. and reigns until 853 B.C. Under Ahab, Israel prospers. He builds an ivory palace and extrabiblical sources indicate that he had many stables, horses, and chariots which were sent to battle against Assyria at Qarqar. Ahab carries on profitable trade with countries to the north. Peace with Judah is also to Israel's economic advantage.

However, Ahab does more evil than any of his predecessors (**16:29–33**). He marries Jezebel, a Sidonian idol worshiper, and begins to serve Baal. He adopts Canaanite fertility rites by setting up an Asherah (a female godlet). The term *Baal* in Hebrew means owner or husband. When Ahab introduces Baal-Melqart, the owner or lord of Tyre and Sidon, into Israel he openly rejects the Lord as owner and Lord of Israel. This causes the anger of the Lord to rise to a higher degree than ever before. A reference to Hiel rebuilding Jericho, though he loses two sons doing it (**16:34**), reflects the hardened attitude of the people to the Lord under Ahab's leadership. Hiel specifically rejects what the Lord had done in giving Canaan to Israel; Jericho had been the first victory in that conquest. Hiel disregards the curse Joshua had spoken in the name of the Lord (cf. Josh. 6, esp. v. 26).

The Lord, angry as he is, does not cast off his people Israel. Rather, he raises up two prophets to address Ahab and his royal sons and to minister to the people. Elijah and Elisha are not preaching and writing prophets. They, however, do carry out a ministry that is more extensive than that of Nathan, Gad, Ahijah, Zechariah, Hanani, and Jehu whose work seems to have been directed specifically to the kings. Elijah and Elisha are much like Samuel. But they also perform miracles as signs to confirm the word that the Lord had given through Moses to Israel as well as the specific messages they have to deliver. Elijah introduces a new stage in prophetic ministry and is therefore considered a forerunner and type of John the Baptist and of Jesus Christ (cf. Mal. 4:5; Matt. 11:14; 17:3–12; Mark 6:15; 9:4; Luke 1:17; 9:8, 19; John 1:21, 25).

Elijah the Tishbite, from Jabesh-gilead, just west of the Jordan between the Sea of Galilee and the Dead Sea, is presented as if he is well known; no reference is given to his family or prophetic work (**17:1–5**). Elijah confronts Ahab and lets the king know that he, Elijah, serves the only living Lord. Elijah informs Ahab that there will be no dew or rain until he gives the word. That Elijah speaks the Lord's word is confirmed by the Lord's instruction to Elijah that he cross the Jordan and hide in the Kerith Ravine. Elijah obeys; he drinks water from a brook and is fed by ravens. Ravens are voracious eaters and robber birds. But, at the Lord's direction, these birds bring food. Elijah has direct confirmation that not Baal but the Lord is Master of creation.

Elijah, when the water in the brook dries up due to the drought, is commanded by the Lord to go to Zarephath (**17:7–24**). A certain widow, whom the Lord had commanded to feed Elijah (we are not told how the Lord did this), has only enough food for one meal. She expects that she and her son will starve to death. She, however, is obedient when Elijah tells her to prepare food for him first. This Phoenician woman, in whose land Baal was honored as the god of fertility, the sun, and the owner of all nature, learns that the Lord, whom Elijah serves, alone supplies food and drink. Elijah promises that her supplies will not run out until the rain returns.

Elijah also teaches the widow that the Lord who sustains life is the Lord of life. The widow's only son becomes ill and dies. Accordingly Elijah tells the woman, who confesses her sin, that he should be given the dead child. Why Elijah stretches over the child three times is not stated. His action is accompanied by a cry to the Lord to restore life to the boy, a cry which the Lord hears and answers. Elijah's prophetic word and work are confirmed by the Lord. Thus the Lord prepares Elijah for the strenuous task of confronting Ahab, the prophets of Baal, and Jezebel, the ardent worshiper of Baal.

The Lord sends Elijah to Ahab after three years of intense drought (**18:1–15**). Ahab, considering Elijah his enemy, has searched for Elijah in vain. Therefore, when Ahab's servant Obadiah is confronted by Elijah, he is surprised. He is also fearful for his life when he is told to get Ahab for a meeting with Elijah. Ahab, note well, is to come to Elijah. The idol worshiper has to go to face the servant of the Lord. Obadiah had proven his belief in the Lord by using his position and privilege to hide fifty of the Lord's prophets from Jezebel. Obadiah is one of the seven thousand who have not bowed to Baal. He is assured that Elijah will meet Ahab that day. The time for confrontation between the Lord and Baal, between the Lord's prophet and Baal's servant, has come. The antithesis between the kingdom of the Lord and satanic powers has to be realistically demonstrated. Elijah the prophet is called to do other than prophesy. He has to wage a spiritual battle. What should have been the task of the king, the prophet has to carry on against the king.

Obadiah leads Ahab to Elijah (**18:16–19**). Ahab immediately accuses Elijah of being the source of trouble. Elijah returns the accusation. Ahab's family has brought on the affliction by unfaithfulness and disobedience to the Lord. Elijah takes command: he orders Ahab to meet him on Mount Carmel and to have with him 450 prophets of Baal and 400 prophets of Asherah. The people are to come also to witness Elijah's confrontation with the Baal prophets (**18:20–40**).

Elijah's first challenge, once all are assembled, is to the people. Elijah picturesquely describes them as swinging back and forth, as a bird hops from twig to twig. He calls for a definite commitment: to follow God or to follow Baal. Elijah calls for full allegiance to the covenant and kingdom of the Lord. Uncertainty means lack of full allegiance to the Lord; uncertainty means an openness to an alternative contrary to the Lord. The verbal challenge does not draw a response. Elijah proceeds to an actual confrontation.

Elijah challenges the prophets of Baal by means of the sacrificial rite. He alone will face the Baal prophets. Each is to have a bull for sacrifice; each is to have an altar of wood;

neither is to have fire to light the sacrificial fire. Baal, often referred to as the god of the sun (fire, heat), is appealed to in various ways—even by self-flagellation on the part of the prophets. Elijah's ridicule drives them into a frenzy. Baal, who has all day to hear, gives no response.

Elijah then takes twelve stones and repairs the ruined altar. Jezebel may have had this altar torn down when she purged the land of worship to the Lord. Elijah digs a trench around the altar and has the entire altar, bull, and wood soaked with water three times. At the appointed time of evening sacrifice, Elijah assumes the role of a priest and calls on the Lord of the patriarchs, the God of Israel. Fire falls; everything is consumed. The people immediately acknowledge the Lord, Elijah's God and Master, to be God. They do not say "our God" but clearly indicate that they understand the Lord to be the only God, the God to be worshiped and served rather than Baal. The victory for the Lord is completed by the killing of the prophets of Baal. The people obey Elijah when he calls for their capture and death in the valley at the foot of Mount Carmel.

Elijah expects rain (**18:41–46**). He tells Ahab to have his evening meal, and the king obeys. Elijah waits for the clouds to come off the Mediterranean Sea, the source of rain for the land of Canaan. At the sight of the first cloud, he sends word to Ahab to return to his capital city. With the aid of the Spirit of the Lord, Elijah demonstrates superhuman physical strength, running ahead of Ahab's horses. The victory achieved is of the Lord. The courage, conviction, and authority that Elijah demonstrates are clear evidence to all that the Lord has directed and equipped him. The sovereign Lord of heaven and earth, of fire and rain, reveals his wrath against the adherents of the false god Baal.

Elijah flees to Mount Horeb because he is afraid for his life (**19:1–18**). Jezebel swears an oath that she will kill him just as he had destroyed her Baal prophets. Ahab, who informs her of Elijah's victory, does nothing to oppose or repress his godless wife. The victory of the Lord has not influenced him.

In his flight, Elijah stops at Beersheba (Gen. 21:14–32; 22:19; 26:33; 46:1–5), a place where the patriarchs had lived and sacrificed to the Lord. There Abraham had received the command to sacrifice Isaac. Elijah leaves his servant there and proceeds into the desert. He admits defeat in that, in his human strength, he fails as his ancestors also had in keeping Israel faithful to the Lord. An angel sent by the Lord ministers to him. The Lord watches over his servant and provides food again in an unusual manner (1 Kings 17:1–6). Elijah is commanded to go to Horeb (Sinai), where Moses had ministered. Elijah needs to be reminded that he is serving the Lord in the fellowship of the patriarchs and Moses. Their cause for the Lord is his cause. He stands and works in a line of heroes of faith and service.

The Lord himself speaks to Elijah. The question "What are you doing here?" is intended to make Elijah fully aware of who he is, where he is, why he is there, what brought him there, and that it is the Lord who is in charge of his life and work. Elijah gives a factual answer. (1) He has been zealous for the Lord; his love for the Lord had motivated him to challenge Ahab, the Baal prophets, and Jezebel. (2) Israel has rejected the covenant the Lord made with his people and their rulers; they have rejected the Lord, his name, person, promises, blessings, gift of life, and love. (3) Israel has destroyed the system of worship which the Lord commanded. (4) Israel has put the prophets to death. Those appointed to proclaim and apply the Lord's Word to life have been destroyed. The living Word is thus rejected and silenced. (5) Elijah has stood alone as a prophet and now his life is threatened. He, the last remaining spokesman, has been silenced by a threat on his life—a threat that is real and would have been carried out had he remained in the land of Israel.

The Lord's response to Elijah is similar to what Moses heard after Israel had committed spiritual fornication with the golden calf (Exod. 34:6–7). He is to position himself so that he can witness the actual presence of the Lord. Elijah, who may have expected a visible, overpowering demonstration of the Lord, as on Mount Carmel, experiences three possible manifestations: a strong wind, a rock-splitting earthquake, and a fire. But in a still small voice, in complete silence, the Lord makes Elijah aware of his presence. It is with the Word, not with power, might, or overwhelming forces, that Elijah is challenged. Elijah again states his case. He does not get an immediate reply to his problem. But he is encouraged by the Lord's presence.

Elijah is commanded to return to the land of Israel. There is work to do. The Lord has not forgotten his people or their neighbors. Elijah is to make a detour around Judah and Israel and travel three hundred miles, partially following the route Israel had taken to the Promised Land. He is to anoint Hazael king of Syria, and Jehu king of Israel; Ahab's dynasty is doomed. Hazael and Jehu are to be the Lord's agents of judgment on Ahab's house. Elisha is to be anointed as prophet; Elijah is assured his prophetic work will continue. Even in judgment, the Lord will not forget his faithful seven thousand in Israel. The Lord maintains his people—be it a remnant. To these Elijah and Elisha are to be the Lord's appointed spokesmen and agents of covenant and kingdom service.

Elijah first seeks out Elisha, who lives in Abel-Meholah near Elijah's home (**19:19–21**). Elisha is the son of a prosperous farmer; he has no fewer than twelve yoke of oxen (twenty-four). Elijah uses his prophetic robe as a means to call Elisha to the prophetic ministry. Elijah seems impatient with Elisha's desire to say farewell to his parents. Elisha obediently joins Elijah as his attendant. The Lord provides for the prophetic work that is so necessary for his covenant people.

The account of Elijah's ministry is interrupted to deal with Ahab's military problems. Benhadad, king of Syria, is an enemy of Ahab and Israel. The enmity was initiated by Judah's King Asa, who requested and paid Benhadad to attack Baasha when he was king in Israel. Ahab is given another opportunity to see the Lord's favor upon Israel and to serve him. Ahab again rejects the Lord's gracious help and message.

The king of Syria leads his army against Samaria (**20:1–12**). The exact time of this attack is not known. Benhadad evidently had succeeded in making many cities his vassals. He treats Ahab as if he were one also by demanding the gold and silver of Samaria and Ahab's choice wives (those in addition to Jezebel) and children. Ahab is prepared to grant these to Benhadad. When Benhadad informs Ahab that he will enter the palace and other officials' homes and take all their valuables, Ahab seeks the advice of the elders of the land. They tell Ahab not to listen to Benhadad and that message is sent to the Syrian king. Benhadad threatens Ahab with total destruction but Ahab responds that only men who take off their armor after they have won can boast. Ahab challenges Benhadad to carry out his threat; drunken Benhadad gives the order to attack.

An unknown prophet informs Ahab that he will be victorious (**20:13–14**). This victory will testify to Ahab that Israel's covenant God is indeed the Lord; he is present, directing and controlling the affairs and activities of Israel and their king.

Ahab defeats Benhadad (**20:15–21**). A group of young commanders march toward Benhadad's camp. They attack and kill the Syrians Benhadad has sent out to take the commanders captive. The Syrian army, with its drunken commanders, scouts, and vassal subjects flees without further fight. Ahab's army pursues and kills many Syrian soldiers and captures many supplies. Benhadad escapes.

After the Israelite victory, the prophet instructs Ahab to prepare for another attack in the coming spring (**20:22**). Ahab continues to receive reminders of the Lord's presence and concern for his people.

Benhadad meanwhile receives advice to fight Israel in the level plains instead of in the hill country surrounding Samaria (**20:23–27**). The Syrians come out with a large force; Israel's army looks like two small goat herds by comparison.

Again Ahab is instructed by the Lord's prophet to attack the Syrians (**20:28**). The Syrians are to learn that the Lord is Lord of all creation, over plains and hills and over large armies.

After a seven-day wait, Ahab defeats the Syrians as the prophet had said (**20:29–34**). Thousands of Syrians are killed in battle; others die in the city of Aphek where they took refuge. Benhadad also flees to Aphek but at the advice of his officials, he seeks mercy. The Syrians have heard that the kings of Israel are merciful. Benhadad offers Syria as a vassal state to Ahab. Ahab agrees; a treaty is made. Benhadad, whom the Lord had given to Ahab, is freed. Politically it may have been expedient to keep Syria as a buffer state to the north because of Assyria's obvious intentions to march southward at an opportune time.

A member of a group of prophets is sent by the Lord to Ahab (**20:35–43**).[2] He disguises himself and waits for the king on the road. When Ahab passes by, the prophet leads the king to condemn himself: Ahab's life will be demanded since he permitted Benhadad to live, contrary to the Lord's will. Not only Ahab, but all Israel will suffer because of Ahab's unwarranted mercy to an enemy, his refusal to heed the prophet's words, and his rejection of Israel's Lord.

Some time later Ahab covets Naboth's vineyard (**21:14**). Naboth cherishes his inheritance—and rightly so. Neither pay nor trade entices him to give away his vineyard. Ahab is sullen and angry.

Jezebel has a solution to the problem (**21:5–10**). She ridicules Ahab for not exercising his royal authority and power and then does so herself. She calls for a public trial in a religious setting. The corruption of the local government

2. Such groups of prophets had been in Israel at least from Samuel's time. Their activities included teaching and giving assistance to leading or official prophets. They also served as musicians. Religious groups other than those loyal to the Lord also had bands of prophets.

and Ahab's weakness in relation to Jezebel almost defy imagination.

A trial is held (**21:11–16**). Two scoundrels willingly perjure themselves; they say that Naboth has cursed God (it is not clear whether Baal or the Lord) and Ahab. Naboth is stoned to death. Ahab's inability to interact responsibly with his foreign wife, permitting her to usurp authority and power over the Lord's covenant people, is a grievous sin. Once Naboth is gone, Ahab readily and willingly goes to the vineyard to claim it.

Elijah is sent by the Lord to confront Ahab (**21:17–29**); his message is harsh. Ahab has murdered an innocent man and stolen his property. Ahab has sold himself to evil. As Naboth's blood was licked up by dogs, so will Ahab's; these dogs will also eat Jezebel's flesh. The entire house of Ahab is to be destroyed as Jeroboam's (1 Kings 14:10–11) and Baasha's (1 Kings 16:12–13). Ahab shows remorse and humility; there is, however, no evidence of repentance. Ahab's demonstration of humility postpones the disastrous end of his family until the following generation. The Lord in mercy and justice does not bring a disastrous death upon a humbled man.

Ahab fights his last battle against Syria and dies in that battle (**22:1–4**). Three facts establish the historical setting. First, Syria and Israel had not engaged in war for three years. Second, Ramoth-Gilead, an Israelite city on the border with Syria, is in Syrian hands. Third, Jehoshaphat, king of Judah, has traveled north to visit Ahab. No reason is given for this visit. He probably went to make a marriage alliance with Ahab (cf. 2 Chron. 17–18). Ahab, with his officials' support, plans to retake Ramoth-Gilead. Jehoshaphat, requested to aid Ahab in battle, replies that as a brother Judah will not refuse to help. It is obvious that the king of Judah wished to maintain a good relationship with Israel, but as he did this, he was yoking himself with devotees of Baal and Asherah.

Jehoshaphat demonstrates his desire to do the Lord's will (**22:5–8**). Ahab brings in four hundred of his servant prophets whom Jehoshaphat does not recognize as prophets of the Lord; they are too quick and glib to assure Ahab that the Lord will give him success. When Jehoshaphat asks for a prophet of the Lord, Ahab refers to Micaiah who, on previous occasions, had spoken against the king of Israel. Ahab does not wish to hear the word of the Lord from Micaiah; Jehoshaphat rebukes Ahab.

Micaiah is brought before Ahab and Jehoshaphat (**22:9–28**). Ahab's messenger advises Micaiah that all the other prophets have predicted victory and suggests he do likewise. Micaiah responds that he can speak only what the Lord tells him. When he stands before the kings, he initially rehearses what the other prophets have said. Ahab realizes Micaiah has not spoken the word of the Lord and calls for the truth. Micaiah complies. Israel will be scattered like sheep without a shepherd (i.e., Ahab will be gone). Though Ahab protests, Micaiah continues. The Lord has sent a lying spirit to Ahab's prophets to lure him to Ramoth-Gilead and his death. The Lord has decreed disaster for Ahab and Israel. When challenged by Zedekiah the false prophet, Micaiah declares that when the prophets go into hiding they will know he spoke the truth. Ahab responds by imprisoning Micaiah; he thus demonstrates his rejection of the counsel of the Lord.

Ahab does not heed this call to submit to the Lord; he dies in the battle against Syria (**22:29–40**). Ahab disguises himself from the Syrians. Jehoshaphat is not prudent in joining Ahab in a battle that the Lord had decreed to end disastrously and in going into battle dressed in regal attire. Jehoshaphat is spared when the Syrians learn he is not Ahab. The Lord brings death to Ahab by a random arrow. Ahab stays near his troops but bleeds to death. His troops disperse and return to their homes. Dogs lick up his blood when the chariot is washed.

Ahab had been an active king; he had political and administrative abilities; he could have been a great asset to Israel. He had many opportunities to be an agent of the Lord in building the kingdom. But like Solomon, Ahab loved a heathen wife and joined her in her devotion to Baal and Asherah. He participated in her immoral behavior. He rejected the many overtures the Lord made to him by means of the prophets Elijah and Micaiah. Ahab knew how to humble himself; however, he did not humble himself before the Lord, repent, and change his ways. He became an agent in the deterioration and destruction of the kingdom of Israel.

A brief summary of Jehoshaphat's life and work is given (**22:41–50**). As Asa, Jehoshaphat walks and serves in the ways of the Lord. He cleanses the land of the last remaining male prostitutes but does not remove the shrines as places of worship, evidently considering them acceptable for the worship of the Lord. He builds a merchant fleet as Solomon had done. His ships are destroyed and he wisely refused a second attempt with the aid of Ahaziah, Ahab's son. Jehoshaphat is at peace with Israel but has other military activities. Jehoshaphat achieves many good things for the Lord and the kingdom of Judah, recorded in the annals of the kings of Judah.

Ahaziah, Ahab's son, is king in Samaria during the time Jehoshaphat reigns in Jerusalem (**22:51–53**). Unlike his fellow king, Ahaziah is a gross idolater; he leads Israel in sinning as Jeroboam, Ahab, and Jezebel had done. He provokes the Lord, the God of Israel to anger. Yet the Lord is Israel's God and Israel is God's people. The Lord has not forsaken his covenant or his covenant people in spite of the unfaithfulness and disobedience of Israel's kings. Undoubtedly it is for the sake of the seven thousand faithful ones that the Lord maintains Israel as his people and calls upon their kings to obey and serve him.

COMMENTARY—2 KINGS

Elijah's message to Ahaziah is prefaced by a reference to Moab's rebellion (**1:1–18**). Moab had been subdued by David (2 Sam. 8:2, 12). After Solomon's death Moab became free. Omri, king of Israel, later conquered Moab. However, the Moabites gave Judah trouble in the years ahead.

Ahaziah is hurt due to a fall. He sends messengers to Ekron to procure information concerning his health from Baal-Zebub, the god of Ekron. Elijah is sent by an angel of the Lord with the message that Ahaziah will die. The prophet intercepts Ahaziah's messengers and challenges them with a question: Is it because there is no God in Israel that they are going to Ekron? The only true living God is Lord of Israel and of Ahaziah.

Ahaziah, upon hearing this message, attempts to capture Elijah. Two commanders and one hundred soldiers die in the attempt because Elijah demonstrates that he is the prophet of the Lord who had brought fire upon the altar at Carmel, he again brings fire on Ahaziah's men. This demonstration of the Lord's presence, power, and judgment does not deter Ahaziah's folly. When the third commander honors Elijah and pleads for his and his men's lives, Elijah is assured of safe conduct.

Elijah goes to Ahaziah. He rebukes him for seeking help from a false god and for rejecting the only Lord who could restore him to health. The Lord's judgment falls on Ahaziah.

The time has come for Elijah to be taken to the Lord (**2:1–18**). Elijah and Elisha are traveling from Gilgal. On their way to Bethel, Elijah tells Elisha to stay behind. Elisha refuses. At Bethel a group of prophets tells Elisha that Elijah is to be taken. Elisha will not hear of it, nor does he stay in Bethel as Elijah retraces his steps toward Jericho. Prophets at Jericho remind Elisha again of Elijah's imminent departure. Elisha again will not hear of it and will not leave Elijah as he goes toward the Jordan. Elijah, with his prophetic mantle, parts the waters of the Jordan to allow dry passage across the river. Elijah demonstrates that he is fully conscious of the power of the Lord and his control over the forces of nature—an important lesson for Elisha. When Elijah asks what Elisha desires that he should do for him, he asks for a double portion of the prophetic spirit. Elisha indicates he realizes what a tremendous task awaits him as the prophet who will succeed Elijah.

Elijah is taken up to heaven by a chariot and horses of fire—messengers sent by the Lord (cf. Ezek. 1:15, 21; Zech. 6:1–8). His valiant service in confronting the forces of evil is rewarded in a unique manner. Elisha also recognizes the struggles and battles Elijah had waged. He calls him "my father," meaning teacher and leader. He refers to him as a gallant warrior, a man with princely bearing and great power when he cries "the chariots and horsemen of Israel!" Elisha realizes that the prophetic word and work of Elijah are far more effective in the battle against evil and the forces of satanic power than swords, soldiers, horses, and chariots. Elisha's tearing of his clothes indicates his grief at the departure of Elijah, but also prepares him to take up Elijah's cloak.

Elisha begins his unique prophetic ministry immediately (**2:13–25**). His first acts are, in a sense, repetitions of what Elijah had done. Thus a direct link is established between them.

Elisha picks up Elijah's cloak and returns to the Jordan. As he strikes the water with the cloak as Elijah had done, he asks, "Where now is the Lord, the God of Elijah?" He seeks confirmation that the Lord has indeed called him to serve in Elijah's stead. The waters which had resumed flowing after Elijah and Elisha passed through part again. Elisha is prepared for the prophetic service that awaits him.

The band of fifty prophets from Jericho sees Elisha return through the Jordan and knows that the Lord has endowed him with the Spirit of prophecy. Their bowing indicates that they recognize Elisha as the prophet of the Lord and that they are to consider him as their leader, director, and master. Their request for permission to search for Elijah's body gives further evidence of their recognition of him as their superior. Elisha is not quick to agree to a search for Elijah's body; when he does consent to it, the searchers find no trace of Elijah. He has truly been taken away from the earth by the Lord. Elisha's word is again confirmed.

Elisha's first miracle on behalf of the people is the curing of the water in the well of Jericho. The people complain that the water is bad and that the land is unproductive. Elisha asks for a new bowl with salt in it. Efforts to explain the chemical changes that took place are of no help. The well, possibly an artesian well, flowed for years giving wholesome water. The Lord, through Elisha, demonstrates his sovereign rule over creation.

Elisha, having traveled from Jericho to Bethel, is greeted by a jeering group of youths who ridicule him (**2:23–25**). These youths express the general view and attitude of the older generation to the prophets of the Lord. The Lord, in response to Elisha's call, demonstrates his lordship over the animal world; he confirms Elisha as prophet; he demands acknowledgment of and respect for his servants; he condemns the ridicule of his prophets; he executes just judgment.

The writer of Kings, after introducing Elisha as the confirmed prophet of the Lord, does not present a chronological account of the prophet's ministry. Rather, he selects a number of specific deeds which Elisha performed in a period of over fifty years. However, the events relating to the kings of Israel and Judah are recorded in their historical order.

Moab revolts against Joram of Israel (**3:1–6**). Mesha, king of Moab, refuses to send thousands of lambs and wool as tribute to Israel. Joram gathers his army to put down the rebellion.

Jehoshaphat, having helped Ahab, is asked by Ahab's son for assistance (**3:7–12**). His reply is as before: kinsmen share their means and help each other. Jehoshaphat advises that Moab be attacked from the south. That would mean marching south, going around the far southern tip of the Dead Sea, and traveling through the large desert area of northwest Edom. It would also mean getting Edom's cooperation. The three armies do not find fresh water in the desert. Jehoshaphat, when he learns that Elisha is available, advises that the prophet's help be sought because the word of the Lord is with him. The three kings go to the prophet.

Elisha directs his first remarks to Joram of Israel (**3:13–19**). Why should the prophet of the Lord serve Joram when the king rejects the Lord of the prophet? Why does Joram not go to the golden calves, Baal, and Asherah for assistance? Elisha gives Joram a stinging rebuke as he reminds the king that his gods are helpless. Joram's retort is that Elisha's Lord has brought them into the desert. Elisha responds that it is only because Jehoshaphat, a servant of the Lord, is present, that he will assist the kings. A harpist is supplied at his request and while the music is played, the Lord gives his word to Elisha. The kings must dig ditches for water in the desert—where there is not a drop of water. They are to wait for the water that will come without wind and rain. The Lord will also give them Moab and they will completely defeat and ransack it.

The Moabites are defeated but not entirely destroyed (**3:20–27**). The next morning water flows through the ditches in the desert. The Moabites, fully prepared for battle, are on their southern border waiting for the armies of the three kings. The early morning sun gives a red hue to the water. It looks like blood to the Moabites, who conclude that the three armies have destroyed each other. The Moabites rush to the Israelite camp, where they are met by the Israelites and completely defeated. The land and cities of Moab are devastated. The king of Moab, seeing his defeated army and ransacked land, tries to flee; the Edomites prevent him. He then sacrifices his oldest son on the city wall to Chemosh, the Moabite god. The horror and consternation upon seeing this sacrifice causes the three armies to withdraw rather than to wipe out such evil and desecration of children. Moab is not brought under Israel's domination. Later the Moabites attack Judah and Israel (2 Kings 13:20; 24:2; 2 Chron. 20). Had Elisha's instructions been carried out, these later attacks may have been avoided.

A number of events illumine Elisha's prophetic ministry. He provides means for a widow to pay her debts (**4:1–7**). As Elijah had helped a widow (1 Kings 17:8–16) so Elisha causes the little oil the widowed mother has to increase to the extent that she has to procure more containers to hold it. Elisha tells her to sell the oil and with the receipts pay her debts and retain enough funds for herself and her sons. This prophetic ministry of Elisha demonstrates the Lord's concern for and care of oppressed widows and the fatherless.

Elisha travels to Shunem located in the tribal area of Issachar, just southwest of the sea of Galilee. He is now situated right in the heart of Israel.

A well-to-do woman invites Elisha to stop by for meals. She recognizes that he is a holy man of God (**4:8–10**). Eventually, she and her husband provide a small room for Elisha.

Elisha, wishing to demonstrate his appreciation, asks the woman what he can do for her (**4:11–17**). She is satisfied, and asks for no special favors. When she is gone, Elisha's servant reminds him that she has no children and that her husband is old. When she returns at Elisha's bidding and stands in the doorway of his room, he informs her that she will have a son within a year. The woman, not wanting to be given false hope, asks Elisha not to speak that way. She does bear a son a year later. Elisha's Lord demonstrates again that he is the Lord of life and can make barren wombs fruitful.

The boy becomes ill when visiting his father who is busy harvesting (**4:18–37**). Some commentators have suggested that the boy suffered from sunstroke; no one is sure what his ailment was. He is brought home and dies. There should be no uncertainty about the terms *died* and *death*. The distraught mother will have no one come save Elisha himself. Elisha's staff, placed on the dead child by his servant Gehazi, is ineffective. When Elisha is alone with the dead child he prays and then stretches out on the child seven times—mouth to mouth, eyes to eyes, hands to hands. The Lord restores life to the child. Elijah (1 Kings 17:19–23) and Elisha are eloquent forerunners of the ministry of Jesus Christ, who will demonstrate his power over life by restoring it to some (Luke 7:11–15; 8:41–55; John 11:38–44) and arising from the grave himself.

Elisha ministers to people suffering from hunger (**4:38–41**). A famine in Gilgal, due to an extended drought, forces people to search for food. The gourds that are collected and added to the stew are believed to have had the appearance and smell of cucumbers, but to contain an irritant poison. Elisha, using flour, ministers to the hungry prophets. The Lord of nature, who can give rain, makes the food edible and wholesome.

Elisha, a forerunner of Christ (Matt. 15:32–39; John 6:1–15), feeds one hundred men (**4:42–44**). A man gives Elisha of his firstfruits; barley is the first grain to ripen. Elisha emphasizes that the Lord said this bread would be enough for one hundred men (plus, very likely, their families). The word of the Lord is fulfilled; all eat and there is food left over.

The healing of Naaman the leper (**5:1–27**) takes place late in Elisha's ministry. Which king of Aram Naaman serves is not known; the king is successful in waging war and Naaman plays a large role in these successes. That some of these victories are over Israel is obvious because Israelites have been taken captive.

Naaman is informed of Elisha's ministry of healing by an Israelite slave girl in his home. That a young girl knew and could speak about Elisha's ministry indicates that he was well known even though the worship of the Lord was not widespread because of the people's devotion to Jeroboam's calves and Phoenician idols.

Naaman's king prepares a letter of introduction to Israel's king (most likely Jehoash). The Syrian king undoubtedly considers Elisha the healer to be a prominent person in Israel. But the king of Israel believes that Syria's king is seeking a reason to attack him; he does not give Elisha, or the life-giving, life-restoring Lord of Elisha any consideration when he protests that he, as king, does not have divine healing powers or abilities.

Elisha reminds Israel's king that the Lord has his prophet in Israel and that prophet will do in the Lord's name what the king, in his service to idols, cannot. Naaman comes with a military retinue but is met by Gehazi who tells Naaman to wash in the Jordan River seven times in order to be healed. Naaman, humiliated and in a rage, expresses his preference for the cleaner waters of the Syrian rivers. His nationalistic fervor is overcome by his servant's wise advice to do a seemingly insignificant thing. He washes; his leprosy disappears. The word of the Lord through Elisha, when obeyed, leads to healing for an unbelieving Syrian.

Naaman, returning to Elisha, offers him a gift. Elisha, by his refusal, declares that not he, but the Lord is the Healer who deserves gifts of thanks. Naaman declares his belief that the God in Israel is truly the only God in the world. He promises to sacrifice to God and to worship only him. The taking of ground from Israel is to identify with Israel and the sacrifices made on it is to identify with the sacrificial worship of the Lord in Israel. A heathen commander responds to the prophetic ministry of Elisha as Israel's leaders failed to do. Naaman's request to be understood as not worshiping Rimmon when he assists his aged master's worship of the Syrian idol is granted. Elisha's parting comment, "Go in peace," can be understood in no way other than, "serve your master, but serve the Lord with your heart, soul, strength, and mind."

Gehazi, a faithful servant to Elisha for many years, cannot control his desire for wealth. He lies to Naaman to get it; he lies to Elisha to cover up his greed. Elisha has the sad duty of rebuking Gehazi. Gehazi's punishment is severe; as a leper he has to be banished from public society as well as from the service of the Lord. He cannot minister to and assist Elisha in his prophetic work.

Elisha's ministry includes a demonstration

of the Lord's power and control over the laws of nature (**6:1–7**). The company of the prophets evidently grew so much that their gathering place becomes too small. As a new one is being prepared, a borrowed iron axhead slips off its handle and falls into the water. Elisha throws a stick in the water; the axhead floats.

Elisha plays a unique role in the war between Syria (Aram) and Israel. This event takes place early in Elisha's ministry when Joram is king in Israel, and shortly before Hazael assassinates Benhadad, king of Syria (ca. 845 B.C.).

Elisha informs the king of Israel where Benhadad has gathered his army and thus enables Israel not to be surprised and be at a military disadvantage (**6:8–10**). The Lord demonstrates to both Syria and Israel that he is Lord over military affairs.

Benhadad, angry and suspicious, is informed that Elisha has communicated all that he said, even in private, to Israel's king (**6:11–14**). He is determined to capture Elisha; he sends military forces (horses, chariots, armed men) to do so.

The Syrian forces surrounding Dothan alarm Gehazi (**6:15–23**). In response to Elisha's plea, the Lord opens the eyes of the servant to see the hills filled with horses and chariots of fire around them. When the Syrians approach Elisha, they are blinded and Elisha is able to lead them to the king of Israel in Samaria. The captive Syrians are shown mercy and hospitality at Elisha's bidding. This in turn induces Benhadad to withdraw his forces. He realizes he cannot fight victoriously against the Lord, a lesson Israel's kings never learned.

Yet Benhadad forgets his lesson; he returns to fight Israel and besieges Samaria (**6:24–29**). The siege causes a tragic famine in the city. One child is eaten, while another is hidden to keep him alive. The king of Israel is helpless as frantic, hungry women call to him for help and justice.

The king dons sackcloth to indicate his remorse because of the situation in the city. He blames Elisha for the tragedy and threatens to kill him (**6:30–33**). Elisha, also in the city of Samaria, is aware of this and tells the elders that the king, the murderer, plans to cut his head off. A messenger, to be followed by the king, is coming but is not to be allowed in the house. Elisha, under the Lord's protection and speaking for the Lord, proclaims that an abundance of food at reasonable prices will be available the next day (**7:1–2**). The king's servant doubts it; Elisha assures him he will see the food but will not have any of it.

The siege is lifted (**7:3–7**). The Lord frightens the Syrians with sounds of many military forces. The Syrians flee, leaving their provisions behind. Lepers, who lived outside the city and who had been prepared to die at the Syrians' hands rather than by starvation, discover the abandoned camp, full of food.

In the darkness of early morning, the lepers take gold, clothes, and food for themselves and then report to the gatekeepers who arouse the city. The king hesitates, fearing a trick (**7:8–13**). His officers advise sending five men on horses to investigate.

Elisha's prophecy is fulfilled (**7:14–20**). The Syrian army had fled, scattering clothing and equipment in their flight. Food in abundance is available to the people. The officer, appointed to be gatekeeper, dies under the feet of the people rushing out to get food.

The king of Israel recognizes Elisha's ministry under unique circumstances (**8:1–6**). The Shunammite woman, who gave Elisha a room and whose son was restored to life, had gone to Philistia, at Elisha's advice, because of a seven-year famine. Upon her return, she asks the king to restore her possessions (these had been taken by people who remained in the land). She makes her plea just as Gehazi is telling the king of Israel about Elisha's ministry. As he tells of the boy's restoration, the woman presents her request and confirms Gehazi's story. She has her property restored and the income from it given to her.

Elisha's ministry extends into Syria where he becomes involved in its politics (**8:7–15**). He goes to Syria to make himself available to Benhadad who is sick and to Hazael who is to become king of Syria. Elisha's words come true: (1) Benhadad does not die of sickness; he is assassinated by Hazael; (2) Hazael becomes king and experiences success at the expense of Israel. Hazael is appointed by the Lord to bring judgment on Israel.

Jehoram, son of righteous King Jehoshaphat, becomes king of Judah in 848 B.C. (**8:16–24**). He has a short but evil reign. He had married Ahab's and Jezebel's daughter, Athaliah; his father had arranged this tragic and God-dishonoring marriage. Under Jehoram Judah suffers defeat in wars with Edom and Libnah. The Lord does not reject the royal house of Judah, in spite of its following the ways of Israel's kings, because of his promise to David. At his death, Jehoram is given a royal burial.

Ahaziah, son of Jehoram, begins to reign in 841 B.C. (**8:25–29**). He too follows in Ahab's ways. He joins his cousin Joram in battle against Hazael. Joram, when wounded, returns home to recover. Ahaziah, king of Judah, goes to visit the wounded king in Jezreel. This sets the stage for Jehu to carry out the Lord's word of judgment on Ahab's family.

Elisha commands a member of the sons of the prophets to go to Ramoth-Gilead, where Israel's army is trying to prevent Hazael of Syria from retaking the city (**9:1–13**). The prophet is to take a flask of oil and look for Jehu. He must take Jehu apart from the others, pour oil on him, and tell him that the Lord has anointed him king. He must then run away immediately. After Jehu is anointed, the prophet declares that he is to destroy Ahab's house; he is to avenge the blood of all the Lord's prophets and servants shed by Jezebel; he is to deal with Jezebel so that dogs will eat her. Jehu goes to his fellow officers; in reply to their query about the prophet's (whom they called a madman) message, he informs them. They immediately proclaim Jehu king and treat him as such.

Jehu proceeds to Jezreel, where Ahab and Joram had built a second home, to assassinate Joram (**9:14–29**). Joram and Ahaziah go out to meet Jehu. Joram is killed by Jehu after he informs Joram that there can be no peace as long as Jezebel's idolatry and witchcraft fill the land. Joram's body is thrown on Naboth's property in fulfillment of the word Elijah spoke to Ahab (1 Kings 21:17–19). Ahaziah tries to flee but is wounded and dies in Megiddo. His body is buried in Jerusalem, as was appropriate for a descendant of David's house.

Jehu then goes to Jezreel to find Jezebel (**9:30–37**). Jezebel, having heard of her son's death, adorns herself and challenges Jehu as a murderer. Eunuch servants of Jezebel obey Jehu; they throw Jezebel down out of a window. She is killed, and her blood spatters on the wall and horses. Dogs eat her body, except her skull, feet, and hands. No tombstone is set up to mark her resting place or to keep her name in remembrance. The Lord's word of judgment is carried out completely.

C. Enmity (2 Kings 10:1–17:41). Jehu, as commanded by the Lord, exterminates Ahab's entire family and roots out Baal worship. He challenges the elders, guardians of Ahab's descendants, to put one of Ahab's offspring on Israel's throne (**10:1–11**). They are terrified, realizing that Jehu will destroy them along with Ahab's offspring. They obey Jehu and decapitate the seventy royal princes of Ahab's house. Jehu is able to convince the people that Israel's officials support his rebellion against Ahab's dynasty by pointing to the seventy heads he has received from Samaria. Jehu appeals to Elijah's prophecy to justify his destruction of Ahab's entire family, his close friends, religious servants, and chief officials. No one is left to challenge Jehu's rule.

Jehu also kills relatives of Ahaziah, king of Judah (**10:12–17**), who have come to greet the royal family in Jezreel. These are relatives of Ahab and Jezebel; Jehonadab, who forbade his clan to have vineyards, to drink wine, and to live in towns (Jer. 35:6–10) and a worshiper of the Lord, comes out to meet Jehu and joins him in cleansing the land. Jehu's comment concerning his zeal for the Lord must be taken in the context of his military career, his methods of deception, his desire to rule, and the true character of his reign.

Jehu deceives the prophets/priests of Baal (**10:18–29**). He calls an assembly and then offers a sacrifice as if he is one of them. Making sure no worshiper of the Lord is present, he then has his men kill all the leaders of Baal worship. He roots out Baal worship completely; he also destroys the temple built for Baal. But he follows in the ways of Jeroboam and worships the golden calves. He does not honor and worship the Lord; he does not go to the Lord's house in Jerusalem.

Jehu is commended for obeying the Lord in regard to Ahab's dynasty; he is assured that four generations of his family will reign. But, following Jeroboam, his heart is not right with the Lord (**10:30–36**). Jehu cannot serve two masters. The Lord's judgment on Jehu and Israel comes through Hazael (2 Kings 8:7–15). The entire Trans-Jordan is taken from Israel.

Athaliah, mother of Ahaziah and daughter of Ahab and Jezebel, angered by the death of her son, attempts to destroy the entire Davidic house (**11:1**). As queen mother she has power and influence and removes all opposition to her efforts to rule Judah. As Jehu destroyed Baalism and its royal supporters in Israel, so Athaliah attempts to destroy the worship of the Lord. Her satanically inspired efforts fail.

Jehosheba, sister of Ahaziah, hides Joash, the one-year-old son of Ahaziah (**11:2–8**). For six years he is kept in hiding. Jehoiada the priest makes careful plans to have Athaliah removed and Joash crowned. The military commanders and the temple guards agree to cooperate.

Jehoiada officiates at Joash's coronation (**11:9–12**). The commanders form a guard around Joash and he is then brought into public by Jehoiada. The royal crown is placed on his head; the book of the covenant is given to him; he is anointed and proclaimed king by the people. The priesthood, not the prophets, has preserved the royal house. The Lord's promises to Judah (Gen. 49:8–10) and to David (2 Sam. 7:12–14) continue to be fulfilled. Athaliah tears her robes and begins to shout about treason

(**11:13–16**). However, she has no supporters; if any had shown it, they would have been executed with her outside the temple.

Jehoiada the priest leads a covenant renewal ceremony (**11:17–21**). The king and the people promise that they will keep the Lord's covenant. The people also renew their loyalty to the Davidic house. They destroy the temple of Baal and all the idols and kill the priests of Baal. The city is peaceful and all the people rejoice.

Joash decides to repair the temple (**12:1–8**). Baal worship had been removed from Jerusalem; but the shrines on high places continued to be used as worship centers by the people. Joash orders the priests to repair the temple using funds received through a census tax, personal vows, and gifts. Twenty-three years later the priests still have not repaired the temple. They had taken these special funds for themselves. They agree not to collect any more money and that they will not repair the temple themselves.

At Joash's urging, Jehoiada has a chest with a hole in its lid placed at the entrance of the temple for people to deposit their gifts in (**12:9–12**). The gifts are collected and given to the supervisor over the repair work. This proves to be an efficient way to gather funds. The funds collected are used to pay the workmen (**12:13–16**). The men in charge of the money are honest. No funds are used for utensils, tools, or ornaments; funds for these are special gifts.

Joash empties the temple of sacred objects dedicated to the Lord (**12:17–18**). He uses these to bribe Hazael of Syria and thus spare Jerusalem an attack.

Joash is assassinated by his officials (**12:17–19**). The Chronicler notes that the men who did this carried out the last words of Jehoiada's son, who, when he reproved Joash, was slain for doing so (2 Chron. 24:20–26). Joash had reigned forty years; his son Amaziah becomes king.

Jehoahaz, son of Jehu, becomes king of Israel after Jehu's twenty-eight-year reign (**13:1–8**). Most of the time he reigns, Hazael and his son Benhadad oppress Israel and reduce Israel to a helpless vassal state. Jehoahaz implores the Lord for relief; it is given. But the Lord is not honored and worshiped by a relieved people.

Jehoash, son of Jehoahaz, becomes king of Israel in 798 and reigns until 782 B.C. (13:10–25). Jehoash does evil and follows Jeroboam's ways. He wages war against the Lord's servant Amaziah, king of Judah.

Jehoash visits Elisha when the prophet is on his death bed (**13:14–19**). Weeping, he addresses Elisha with the words Elisha had spoken as Elijah was carried to heaven (2 Kings 2:12). The king knows that Elisha is the Lord's warrior, fighting so that the Lord's covenant might be kept and that his kingdom purposes might be achieved. Elisha gives Jehoash encouragement concerning Israel's battle with the Syrians at Aphek. Jehoash is reminded that the Lord gives victory, but this victory is not to be complete because of Jehoash's unwillingness to strike the ground more than three times.

Elisha dies and is buried (**13:20–21**). But in his death he is still an agent of life. When Moabite raiders sweep through Israel, some Israelites quickly throw a corpse in Elisha's tomb. Touching Elisha's bones, the man comes to life. The Lord of life continues to speak through Elisha though the prophet is dead.

Hazael had been a sword and hammer of God (2 Kings 8:7–13) to reprove Israel (**13:22–25**). When his son, Benhadad II, becomes king of Syria, he is defeated by Jehoash, as Elisha had prophesied. Jehoash frees the Israelite towns Syrian forces had captured. The Lord is gracious; as covenant God he loves and forgives. His heart reaches out with sympathy to his people caught up in idol worship and under the rule of foreigners. The Lord cares about his people, the descendants of the patriarchs with whom he made his covenant. The Lord, a covenant-keeping God, is not merely zealous for the covenant in and of itself. His zeal and love go out to the people of the covenant first of all. He longs to bless them, to have fellowship with them, and through them to work out his sovereign will on behalf of them and all nations.

Amaziah, son of Joash, becomes king over Judah for twenty-nine years. He follows, to an extent, the ways of David (**14:1–4**); he does as his father Joash had done in his early years (2 Kings 11:1–12:21). However, syncretistic ways of worship are still not discouraged.

Amaziah executes his father's assassins (**14:5–6**) but spares the families of the men, according to Mosaic law (Deut. 24:16).

Amaziah, flushed by victory over Edom, challenges Jehoash, king of Israel, to battle (**14:8–16**). Jehoash warns Amaziah and by way of a parable points out the folly of this challenge. Amaziah is defeated; Jerusalem is invaded; the temple is plundered; people are taken hostage. Kings who were right with the Lord were not always wise rulers and military leaders.

Amaziah is assassinated (**14:19–22**) as his father had been. The reason may have been his foolish decision to fight Israel and the resulting inglorious defeat.

Jeroboam, son of Jehoash, becomes the fourth king of Jehu's house to reign over Israel (**14:23–29**). He rules for forty-one years, the first twelve years as co-regent with his father Jehoash. He is an evil king. Amos prophesies against him (1:1; 7:10). Jonah prophesies that the Trans-Jordan will be restored; Jeroboam is the Lord's servant to deliver and restore blessings to Israel. He becomes Israel's savior. He extends the kingdom of Israel. Israel flourishes culturally, economically, and militarily under Jeroboam. The tragedy of Jeroboam's life and service is that, though used of the Lord, he does not love and serve the Lord; he does not obey and serve as covenant king. The Lord, however, uses him in a mighty way to give Israel its last opportunity to continue as a covenant nation. After Jeroboam it is too late.

Azariah (also known as Uzziah) becomes king of Judah in 767 B.C. He is sixteen years old when Amaziah his father is killed and he is made king (**15:1–7**). He reigns twenty-seven years when he is smitten with leprosy (or some other skin disease). The last twenty-five years of his reign, Jotham his son is co-regent with him. Azariah serves the Lord. But he fails to purify Israel's worship or have the true character of the unique, holy, and jealous covenant Lord taught to the people. Azariah's record as a military leader, builder, and agriculturalist is preserved in the annals of the kings of Judah. The Chronicler refers to some of these, including Azariah's sin of burning incense to the Lord; it was then that he was afflicted by leprosy (2 Chron. 26:1–23).

After Jeroboam's death, five men rule Israel for a period of twenty-one years (**15:8–31**). (1) Zechariah, son of Jeroboam, reigns six months. He follows the first as well as the second Jeroboam in their evil ways. He is assassinated in front of the people. Jehu's dynasty is destroyed (2 Kings 10:30). (2) Shallum, who killed Zechariah, reigns one month and is assassinated. (3) Menahem, who killed Shallum, reigns for ten years. He is ruthless, cruel, and evil. Assyria, having become a world power, causes Menahem to pay tribute, which he raises by a heavy taxation of the wealthy. (4) Pekahiah, Menahem's son, reigns for two years. He encourages Israel to continue in Jeroboam's sins. He is assassinated. Israel as a nation is fast losing its covenantal heritage. (5) Pekah, Pekahiah's murderer, reigns twenty years. It is believed that period includes the time of Menahem and Pekahiah. Israel continues to be led away from the covenant ways of the Lord. Assyria returns to Israel, and captures Gilead east of the Jordan and the northern part of Israel west of the Sea of Galilee. Captives are taken as exiles to Assyria. Israel's end is fast approaching. Pekah is assassinated by Hoshea.

Jotham, co-regent since twenty-five years of age, begins to reign alone in 750 B.C. (**15:32–38**). He reigns sixteen years; his son Ahaz is co-regent with him during the last years of his reign. Jotham is a faithful covenant servant, though the people do not consistently follow in the Lord's ways. Jotham repairs the temple and strengthens the kingdom. But the Lord chastises the people of Judah by sending the armies of Rezin (Syria) and Pekah (Israel) against them.

Ahaz, son of Jotham, begins to reign in Judah in 732 B.C. and rules sixteen years (**16:1–19**). He rejects the covenantal way for the kingdom David had established. Ahaz reintroduces Israel's idolatry into Judah. He sacrifices his children to heathen gods and offers idolatrous sacrifices throughout the land.

The Chronicler notes that the Lord in his anger punishes Judah by leading Rezin of Syria against Judah and taking away Edomite territory (2 Chron. 28:9). Ahaz foolishly sends messengers to the king of Assyria, requesting that Tiglath-pileser save him from Syria and Israel. Ahaz empties the temple and palace to bribe Tiglath-pileser, who complies by attacking Syria, killing the king, and deporting Syrians to other lands.

Ahaz meets Tiglath-pileser in Damascus, the capital of conquered Syria. He sees a Syrian altar for idol worship there and commands Uriah the high priest to make one like it in Jerusalem. Uriah obeys this God-dishonoring and worship-defiling command. Ahaz replaces the altar in the temple courtyard with this altar. By his sacrificing on it, he desecrates the temple and the worship of the Lord. Inexplicably, Uriah the priest assists Ahaz. To please Assyria's king, Ahaz removes other sacred objects from the temple.

Ahaz dies and is buried as a Davidic king. However, he had willfully rejected the way of David and consciously defiled the worship of the Lord. His son Hezekiah would face grave difficulties because of what his father had done.

Hoshea, a contemporary of Ahaz, is Israel's last king (**17:1–2**). He is evil, but not to the extent his predecessors had been. The end of the Lord's grace and compassion has come. Ahaz of Judah had bribed Assyria's king to attack Israel. Hoshea gives the opportunity for that attack.

Shalmaneser had succeeded Tiglath-pileser as king of Assyria; Israel is a vassal state to Assyria when Hoshea becomes king; he tries to ally himself with Egypt and thus be freed from Assyria. Shalmaneser marches on Samaria and lays siege to it for three years (**17:3–6**). Hoshea is taken prisoner. Samaria is captured, and most of the people are exiled to eastern parts of the Assyrian Empire.

Israel is exiled because of sin (**17:9–23**). Israel worshiped other gods; they rejected the Lord who had brought them from Egypt and gave them the Promised Land. Israel followed other nations and willfully adopted their practices, their idols, their places of worship, and their sacrifices.

Israel had proven to be obstinate. The Lord had warned Israel through prophets to turn to him and to obey him according to the Mosaic law. Moses and the prophets were rejected. The covenant made with the patriarchs was broken. When told not to do what the nations did, Israel would not listen and became stubborn. Israel forsook all the commands of the Lord and adopted ever more sinful ways.

The Lord became very angry. He had claimed Israel as his people for centuries; he had been gracious, compassionate, and patient. The time has now come for the Lord to reject Israel and deliver his people into the hands of invaders and plunderers. It is the Lord who has exiled Israel. The prophecies of the Lord, spoken to warn Israel, are fulfilled.

Samaria, the northern part of the Promised Land, is resettled (**17:24–41**). The king of Assyria takes captured subjects and exiles them to Canaan. Thus a mixed population inhabits the land. These newcomers do not know the ways of the Lord. God sends lions among them; the terrified people complain to the king of Assyria that they are being killed because of their ignorance. The Assyrian king sends an exiled priest to Bethel to teach the newcomers how to worship the Lord. He does not teach them who the Lord is; what his moral precepts and promises are; what his covenant is. The priest teaches them the basic mechanical procedures of Mosaic worship.

As a result, syncretistic worship develops. Each exiled group holds to its national gods; the people use Israelite shrines and altars to sacrifice to their gods; they also follow the procedures the priest of Israel taught them. Syncretistic worship continues for years. Those Israelites who were not exiled, but were left behind, forget the Lord who delivered them from Egypt and made a covenant with them.

III. The Kingdom of Judah (2 Kings 18:1–25:30)

A. Hezekiah's reign (18:1–20:21). Hezekiah is a God-loving, -fearing, -trusting, -obeying, and -serving king (**18:1–8**). The writer of Kings ranks him above all other kings in doing what is right before God—just as David had done. He tears down the idol shrines, altars, and Baal and Asherah symbols. He destroys the bronze serpent Moses had made (Num. 21:4–9) because the Israelites sacrifice to it; it has become an idol. The Lord blesses and prospers Hezekiah. He is successful in his rebellion against Assyria, thus undoing what Ahaz had done to get relief from Syria and Israel.

The writer repeats (**18:9–12**) what he has already written about Hoshea and Israel (17:1–6). Two reasons can be cited for this: (1) he wishes to emphasize the contrast between the Lord's dealing with a faithful and unfaithful covenant servant; and (2) he wants to underscore the difficult circumstances in which Hezekiah reigns. The northern and eastern areas of Judah now share borders with the mighty Assyrian Empire.

Sennacherib, who succeeds Sargon as king of Assyria, invades Judah in Hezekiah's fourteenth year (701 B.C.). He captures the fortified cities of Judah (**18:13–16**). Hezekiah sends word that he has done wrong to rebel against Assyria and if the invaders withdraw he will pay what they demand. Hezekiah's faith begins to waver. The temple and the palace are stripped of gold and silver to meet the demand. Sennacherib withdraws but sends his top commander with an army to Jerusalem.

The Assyrian general, with a large army, marches up to the walls of Jerusalem (**18:17–25**); he calls for the king but Hezekiah's officials go out. Sennacherib's message to Hezekiah contains these points: (1) The king of Assyria is the great king. (What makes you think you can oppose him?) (2) The military means you talk about are nothing. (3) You may think you have an ally in Egypt to support you. Egypt is weak; depend on her and she will hurt you. (4) You cannot depend on your God because Hezekiah angered him by tearing down his places of worship. (This point indicates how little the Assyrians knew of the Lord of the covenant and his demands.) (5) Prove to me that you men of Judah can handle horses and chariots—you and I know you cannot. (6) Assyria is here because your Lord sent me here to capture you.

Hezekiah's officials ask the Assyrians to speak in Aramaic instead of in Hebrew. The common people of Jerusalem understand only Hebrew (**18:26**).

The Assyrian commander boastfully replies (**18:27–36**). The people have to know they will share in the humiliation their leaders will suffer. He shouts in Hebrew to the people: (1)

Hezekiah deceives you; he cannot deliver you from Assyria. (2) Do not trust in the Lord as Hezekiah says; the Assyrian king is the great king in the earth. (3) Surrender and come with us to another land and you will be given land, homes, food—a good life. (4) Other nations relied on their gods; Assyria captured them. Your Lord cannot deliver you either.

The Assyrian king and leaders defy the Lord; they ridicule faith in him and exalt themselves as the great power in the earth. The people on the wall do as Hezekiah had commanded. They say nothing in reply to the Assyrian's defiant boasting. Hezekiah's officials, with great sorrow, inform their king of the Assyrian's message (**18:37**). Then comes the real test for Hezekiah.

Hezekiah, in deep sorrow and humility, goes into the presence of the Lord (**19:1**). He sends his officials to the prophet Isaiah (**19:2–4**). Their message is: (1) Jerusalem and its people are without means and strength. (2) If the Lord has indeed sent the Assyrians, it is a day of distress, rebuke, and disgrace. (3) Has the Lord heard how the Assyrians ridicule him, the living God? Will he not rebuke the Assyrians? (4) Pray for the remnant that still survives.

Isaiah sends an encouraging message from the Lord to Hezekiah (**19:5–7a**). The servants of the Assyrian king speak blasphemy and God has heard it. The people must not be afraid of them. The Lord himself will turn the Assyrians back by making them believe their efforts have failed, and Sennacherib will be assassinated in his own land.

The Assyrian army leaves Jerusalem to join Sennacherib at Libnah (**19:7b–13**). Libnah was a fortified city northwest of Jerusalem in territory that had been Ephraim's. Tirhakah, king of Egypt, had decided to meet the Assyrians in battle before they invaded Egyptian territory. This draws Assyrian attention away from Hezekiah. But Sennacherib sends an insulting and God-defying message to Hezekiah: Don't let your god deceive you into thinking that I will not capture Jerusalem. As I captured others, so also Jerusalem will fall. As other kings are gone, so you will be destroyed completely.

Hezekiah again goes before the Lord (**19:14–19**). His prayer reveals his knowledge of and complete trust in the Lord. Hezekiah, a kingdom servant, prays on the basis of the Lord's revelation of himself as the Creator, Redeemer, and covenant God of and over all things.

Isaiah sends a second message to Hezekiah (**19:20–28**; cf. Isa. 37:21–35). The Lord has heard his prayer; Hezekiah has not prayed in vain. Isaiah speaks a prophetic oracle in which he predicts Sennacherib's fall. Because Sennacherib has insulted and blasphemed the holy, only, and ever-living sovereign Lord, he will be conquered and devastated.

Isaiah gives a sign to Hezekiah to assure him that the Lord's prophecy concerning Assyria is wholly reliable (**19:29–31**). The Lord will provide abundantly for his people by having the farms, vineyards, orchards, and gardens produce food, without cultivation; the second year, a natural reseeding will take place; and in the third year, cultivation will result in abundant harvests. Judah will be firmly established as a nation and Jerusalem will bring forth God's chosen people (a remnant) to serve him through the years to come.

A specific message about Sennacherib is added (**19:32–34**). He will neither attack the city nor besiege it because the Lord will defend his chosen city, Jerusalem. The Assyrians will return to their country.

Sennacherib retreats and returns to Nineveh (**19:35–37**). The angel of the Lord puts thousands of Assyrian soldiers to death. The army is decimated. At home, two of Sennacherib's sons assassinate him and flee to the northeast. A third son, Esarhaddon, becomes king.

Hezekiah suffers a severe illness fifteen years before his death (**20:1–11**). Isaiah tells the king that he will die. Hezekiah prays and weeps. Isaiah is directed by the Lord to speak again. The Lord has heard Hezekiah's prayers and seen his tears. He will heal Hezekiah and give him fifteen more years. Isaiah prescribes treatment for Hezekiah's boil. Hezekiah asks for confirmation. Given the choice, the king asks that the shadow cast by the sun on the sun dial be turned back ten degrees.

At this time Hezekiah receives visitors from Babylon (**21:9–21**). Merodach-Baladan had been king in Babylon from 721–710 B.C., after which Sargon II forced him to retreat to the south. It is believed that the emissaries were sent by the exiled king who still considered himself king of Babylon and was planning a return to his throne in defiance of Assyrian rule. Hezekiah shows the Babylonians everything he has. He is rebuked by Isaiah for this. The destruction and pillage of Jerusalem and the Babylonian exile are prophesied. Hezekiah's achievements (**20:20–21**) include building the pool and its tunnel.

B. Manasseh's reign (21:1–18). Manasseh was co-regent with Hezekiah for approximately eight years; thus he is twenty years old when he becomes king.

Manasseh is described as an exceedingly wicked king (**21:1–9**). He does not learn from his father, but reinstitutes the pagan idolatry his father had destroyed. He defiles the temple with Asherah poles and sacrifices his son in a fire. He leads the people, who willingly follow him, in the abominable practices of the heathen nations. The Mosaic law and the Davidic covenant are rejected (cf. 2 Chron. 33).

Through the prophets the Lord speaks his judgment on Manasseh, Jerusalem, and Judah (**21:10–15**). A great disaster will come upon them. As Ahab and Samaria were wiped away, so the Davidic house and Judah will be. The remnant, the few who hold to the Lord, will also be plundered and exiled. This judgment is to come because Israel (and Judah), since they left Egypt, have provoked the Lord's anger. He has been gracious and patient. Now, the rebellions and rejections call for retributive justice.

Manasseh sheds much innocent blood (**21:16–18**). The Chronicler relates that Manasseh is taken captive to Assyria with a hook in his nose. He repents, prays, and is freed to return to Jerusalem. He begins a cleansing of the city and people before he dies. But Manasseh is converted too late to influence his son Amon.

C. Amon's reign (21:19–26). Amon becomes king over Judah in 643 and reigns for parts of two years (**21:19–26**). He follows in Manasseh's preconversion ways. He is removed from the throne by assassins, who in turn are slain by the people.

D. Josiah's reign (22:1–23:30). Josiah, son of Amon, is made king at the age of eight years and reigns from 641 to 609 B.C. (22:1–23:30). Considering the ages of his sons, Jehoahaz and Jehoiakim, who succeed Josiah (2 Kings 23:31, 35), it would seem that Josiah already had two wives by the time he was fifteen years of age.

Josiah is a good king (**22:1–2**). He walks and serves as the Lord's covenant with David demanded.

Josiah is twenty-six years old when he makes a major decision: the temple is to be repaired (**22:3–7**). The high priest Hilkiah is placed in charge. A system for the collection of funds had been set up under Joash (2 Kings 12:6–12); it is now used to pay the workmen but also for the materials, wood, and stone prepared for the temple. The people in charge are trusted with the funds.

Hilkiah reports to the king's secretary that the Book of the Law has been found in the temple (**22:8–10**). Many questions have been raised about this discovery. Some say the Book of the Law was not found, but was written at that time by the priests to focus attention on the temple as the central place for worship and on the laws for worship. This concept of forging a book must be totally rejected on the basis of what the Scriptures say. It was *found.* Whether scholars say it had just been written or that it was found, all agree the Book of the Law is Deuteronomy. The high priest and priests had become derelict in their duties regarding the reading of God's covenant requirements. The book of the law the king was to have (Deut. 17:18–19) had been removed and forgotten as well. Josiah receives the discovered book when his servant reports on the distribution of the funds.

The king hears the reading of the Law (**22:11–13**). He is distressed because he learns of the great anger of the Lord against Judah's disobedience. He calls for a message from the Lord concerning this serious matter. Josiah indicates that he is a believing man; he accepts the word of the Lord. He realizes his forefathers were covenant breakers and Judah can expect the curse of the Law to be carried out on them (Deut. 28–29).

The king's servants go to Huldah, wife of a palace servant, who is a prophetess (**22:14–20**). Why Jeremiah or Zephaniah, both of whom were in Judah, are not consulted is not known. Huldah knows the law of Moses; she also speaks the Lord's word with conviction. The Lord will bring disaster upon Jerusalem, Judah, and its people because the covenant Lord has been rejected by the people of his kingdom. Josiah will not experience this curse of the covenant because he has responded from the heart with faith, humility, and sorrow.

Josiah leads in covenant renewal (**23:1–27**). He calls the leaders—elders, priests, prophets—and the people to the temple. He reads Deuteronomy publicly and then renews the covenant by responding to its stipulations. He does as Deuteronomy 6:5 demands; with heart and soul he and the people pledge to love, obey, and serve their covenant Lord.

Josiah commands the priests to cleanse the temple completely. All idols and articles used in the worship of heavenly bodies, Baal, and Asherah are burned. Josiah removes all the pagan priests from their service. The male prostitutes are also removed. Josiah keeps the covenant pledge he has made.

Josiah also removes all the priests from the towns and worship centers throughout the country. He cleanses the cities and country areas of idolatry. Josiah removes all abominations. The people of Judah had gathered an amazing collection of foreign idols, idolatrous objects, and practices. Josiah smashes and destroys everything that is not devoted to the sole worship of the Lord. Josiah even goes beyond the border of Judah to Bethel and destroys Jeroboam's altar. The king will not tolerate the people of Judah going north for idol worship.

Before he smashes the altar of Jeroboam, Josiah defiles it by burning bones of devotees of Jeroboam's system on it. This is as the unknown prophet had prophesied (1 Kings 13:1–3). He does not, however, take the bones from the grave of the prophet who had spoken against Jeroboam.

Josiah goes beyond Bethel into the country of Israel and destroys the shrines the Israelites had built for their idol worship. He has the priests serving in these shrines killed. Josiah could move in Israelite territory quite freely to do this because Assyria, which had conquered Israel a century before, was declining in power and losing control of its outlying areas, and would soon be conquered by Babylon.

Josiah next undertakes positive action. He calls for the celebration of the Passover (see Exod. 12:14; Lev. 23:4–5; Num. 28:16; Deut. 16:2–3). The Passover had not been celebrated in full accordance with Mosaic law since early days in Canaan. Even David, Solomon, and Hezekiah had not done so completely.

Josiah reads Deuteronomy 18:8–14. He removes all the mediums of the evil spirit world. He calls for the removal of all idols, fetishes, and occult objects from Judah and Jerusalem. No king, not even David, has so fully carried out the Lord's covenant requirements. Josiah loves the Lord with his whole heart, mind, and strength.

Josiah's reform, however, is too late. The past sins against the Lord have to be punished. Josiah cannot undo what his grandfather Manasseh had done. The justice of the covenant Lord has to be executed.

Josiah meets an untimely death in 609 B.C. (**23:28–30**). Egypt's king Neco marches north through Judah's and Israel's territory to go to the aid of Assyria who had lost a battle with the Babylonians. Josiah is not eager to see Assyria receive help. He tries to stop the Egyptian army and loses his life in the battle. It is a tragic end for a king who was so wholeheartedly devoted to the Lord. His death also spells the beginning of Judah's decline.

E. Jehoahaz's reign (23:31–35). Jehoahaz, son of Josiah, is made king after his father Josiah (**23:31–35**). His reign is cut short. Neco, who has returned from an unsuccessful effort in the north, imprisons Jehoahaz after a three-month reign during which Jehoahaz leads Israel back to the sins of Manasseh. Neco taxes Judah, calling for a large tribute of silver and gold. He puts the second son of Josiah, Eliakim (Jehoiakim), on Judah's throne as a vassal king. Jehoahaz, the first king, is exiled to Egypt where he dies.

F. Jehoiakim's reign (23:36–24:7). Jehoiakim is an evil king. The Babylonians, having defeated the Assyrians in 612 B.C., march south and make Judah a vassal state. In 605 B.C., Daniel and others of royal Judaic blood are taken as exiles to Babylon. The Babylonians also seize Egypt's governed territories. Other nations vex Judah as well. Jehoiakim rebels against Babylon successfully. He dies after ten years of reigning.

G. Jehoiachin's reign (24:8–17). Jehoiachin, son of Jehoiakim, becomes king in 597 B.C. (**24:8–17**). He does evil during the three months he reigns. Jehoiachin is taken prisoner to Babylon (597 B.C.). Nebuchadnezzar strips the temple of everything of value. Military personnel and skilled artisans are taken captive to Babylon. Only poor people are left behind. Jerusalem and the temple are left standing. Nebuchadnezzar places a third son of Josiah, Zedekiah, on the throne. The Davidic house is still represented on the throne of Judah.

H. Zedekiah's reign (24:18–25:26). Zedekiah rules as Nebuchadnezzar's vassal king. He reigns from 597 to 586 B.C. Zedekiah does not learn from the misfortunes of his evil predecessors. He is not affected by the anger the Lord had demonstrated against former kings (**24:18–20**). Nor has he learned that a small vassal kingdom cannot rebel successfully against a strong king and his empire.

Nebuchadnezzar responds to Zedekiah's rebellion by marching against Jerusalem in Zedekiah's ninth year. He lays siege for two years.

The famine in Jerusalem becomes severe. Zedekiah and his people break through the city wall and flee eastward down the mountainside and into the Jordan Valley. They are pursued and captured by the army of Babylon. Zedekiah and his family are separated from his army. Taken to Nebuchadnezzar, Zedekiah is forced to see his sons killed and then his eyes are gouged out. The last thing he sees is the killing of the seed of the Davidic house (**25:1–7**). The blinded Zedekiah is taken in chains to Babylon.

Jerusalem and the temple are destroyed (**25:8–17**). A commander of the imperial guard supervises the destruction of the temple, the palace, and all important buildings. The walls of Jerusalem are torn down. Many more people are deported as exiles. Anything of value is carried to Babylon.

A commander in the Babylonian guard takes most of the leaders left in Judah to Nebuchadnezzar (**25:18–21**). The chief priest and his subordinate, temple attendants, military officers, city officials, and sixty men are executed at the king's command. The royal house of David is in captivity. The land promised to Abraham is no longer Judah's or Israel's inheritance. The blessings of the covenant have been forfeited because of lack of faith, trust, obedience, and humble service.

Gedaliah, the son of a former palace official, is appointed governor by Nebuchadnezzar over Judah (**25:22–24**). He governs from Mispah, north of Jerusalem. His assistants and others who had escaped deportation are assured that in the service of Babylon, peace and well-being will be theirs. But this is not to be.

Ishmael, a descendant of the Davidic house, assassinates Gedaliah as well as the men of Judah and Babylon in Mispah with him (**25:25–26**). Fearing the wrath of the Babylonians, the few scattered people who remain in the country flee to Egypt. The prophet Jeremiah, who had witnessed all the tragedies and prophesied for more than fifty years, is forcibly taken along to Egypt (cf. Jer. 41–43).

I. Jehoiachin's release (25:27–30). At the age of fifty-five years, after thirty-seven years of imprisonment, Jehoiachin is released and treated as royalty (**25:27–30**). The Davidic house is not entirely gone. But it is impotent. The Lord would carry on his covenant plan—without Abraham's descendants as a nation, without the Promised Land, and without the house of David on the throne. But the ultimate goals of his covenant promises—a royal seed, redemption, eternal inheritance in his kingdom—were never forgotten. The Lord sovereignly executed his plan. The Christ of the Davidic house came; the redemptive work was accomplished; his people were and are being gathered in; his kingdom rule is present and his eternal kingdom will be fully established at Christ's second coming.

SELECT BIBLIOGRAPHY

Gray, J. *I and II Kings.* Philadelphia: Westminster, 1970.

Hobbs, T. B. *2 Kings.* Waco: Word, 1985.

Jones, G. H. *1 and 2 Kings.* 2 vols. Grand Rapids: Eerdmans, 1984.

Keil, C. F. *The Book of the Kings.* Grand Rapids: Eerdmans, 1950.

Patterson, R. D. *1 and 2 Kings.* Grand Rapids: Zondervan, 1988.

1–2 CHRONICLES

Andrew C. Bowling

INTRODUCTION

Chronicles is closely related to Ezra–Nehemiah in that these books share a common "priestly" perspective. Many scholars in fact postulate that these books constitute a single "Chronicler's History." However, a number of considerations raise serious doubts about the validity of this hypothesis: (1) the anonymity of the author of Chronicles as contrasted to the first-person perspective of Ezra–Nehemiah (e.g., Ezra 8:15; Neh. 1:1); (2) Chronicles' openness to foreigners as opposed to the rigid separatism of Ezra (Ezra 9:1–2); and (3) Chronicles' pervasive theme of the legitimacy of the postexilic Jewish community/faith as contrasted with the wider range of interests in Ezra–Nehemiah.

Rabbinic tradition holds that Chronicles was written by Ezra, but this assertion is not supported by decisive evidence. We can only surmise that it was written by someone sympathetic to the priestly perspective in postexilic Jewish religion.

Clear-cut evidence for the date of composition is also hard to find. Literary and linguistic features point to a date around 425 B.C. The six generations after the exile listed in 1 Chronicles 3:21 may fit before this date, though some feel that only two generations are demanded by this passage. The life-span of Jaddua the high priest (Neh. 12:11–22) is relevant to the discussion only if Ezra–Nehemiah forms a literary unit with Chronicles, and that is questionable. While the evidence is not conclusive, a date around 400 B.C. is reasonable.

The Bible identifies a number of sources for Chronicles. The canonical books of Genesis, Samuel, and Kings are frequently cited verbatim. Noncanonical sources include the Midrash (NIV annotations) of the books of kings (2 Chron. 24:27) and the memoirs of several prophets (Samuel, Nathan, Gad, Ahijah, and Iddo [1 Chron. 29:29; 2 Chron. 9:29]).

Chronicles, like most of the Old Testament, is topically arranged rather than chronologically organized. The basic theme of Chronicles is the legitimacy of the postexilic community/faith. The genealogies of the opening chapters of 1 Chronicles trace the legitimate line from creation to the community in Jerusalem. The Davidic dynasty is portrayed as the institution that founded and confirmed proper worship in the postexilic community. Three areas relating to the Davidic covenant are investigated: (1) its specific dynastic provisions; (2) moral causality in history; and (3) temple worship and ritual.

Chronicles has a distinctive interpretation of the moral character of the Davidic kings. Only the positive qualities of David and Solomon are detailed. This contrasts sharply with the approach of Samuel–Kings, which often details the sins of these two kings. However, for the remaining Davidic kings, Chronicles generally adopts a more realistic perspective. Kings who are unequivocally evil in Samuel–Kings possess some worthy attributes in Chronicles (e.g., Abijah; 2 Chron. 13); while the failures of the good kings in Samuel–Kings are more likely to be highlighted in Chronicles (e.g., 2 Chron. 20:35–37; 24:17–25).

Chronicles has a good deal of respect for foreigners. An Ishmaelite is recorded among David's in-laws (1 Chron. 2:17). Several foreigners are listed among David's mighty men (1 Chron. 11:10–47). One of the ancestors of the Jerahmeelites is an Egyptian slave who was married to one of the clan's noblewomen (1 Chron. 2:35–41). Finally, aliens are listed among those participating in Hezekiah's Passover celebration (2 Chron. 30:25).

There is a marked emphasis in Chronicles on the unity of the nation. The Chronicler regularly omits materials that might compromise the ideal of single-minded acceptance of the Davidic dynasty (1 Chron. 11:1). The entire nation brings the ark up to Jerusalem (1 Chron. 13:5); the whole nation shares in acts of worship and intercession (e.g., 2 Chron. 20:4).

Genealogies are so prominent in Chronicles that they merit a special discussion. By their very nature, genealogies describe origins, but this seldom exhausts their significance. Genealogies can also be used to describe the social structure of the nation at some point in time or to establish the legitimacy of some social unit by demonstrating its genealogical origins.

Almost all biblical genealogies take one of two forms or a combination of both. A straight linear genealogy has a single name marking each generation. It is especially well suited for tracing a line of linear descent. In the extreme, it occurs as a bare list of names (e.g., 1 Chron. 1:1–3, 24–27). The second form is a branching genealogy which shows one line breaking off into several others. Since the purpose of this form is to show the kinship of different families, it is not concerned with the times at which the various lines branched off.

Some principles for interpreting biblical genealogies follow:

1. There may be gaps in biblical genealogies.

2. The reasons for including particular names or generations might be only marginally related to communicating a chain of ancestry. For example, the typical four-step genealogy during the time of Moses generally marked major administrative divisions in the nation. Achan, for example, is identified as the son of Carmi, the son of Zimri, the son of Zerah, of the tribe of Judah (Josh. 7:1).

3. Since families might assume the name of the geographic region

in which they settled, a line of descent might be identified by a geographic name older than the supposed ancestor (cf. the usage of the ancient geographic name *Gilead* as a Hebrew clan name; 1 Chron. 2:21; 5:14).

4. Sometimes a clan, identified in one place by its patronymic founder's name, may in another place be identified by the name of a famous later leader, though, in fact, not all the members of the clan were the later figure's descendants.

5. Genealogies can be so brief and fragmentary that they are understandable only to those with prior knowledge of the facts. Like some other genres of biblical literature, such genealogies are intended, not to inform, but rather to legitimize or commemorate something already well known to the original audience.

6. Maternal ancestry is sometimes significant. For example, the family of Jair, whose male ancestry was from Judah, is reckoned as part of Manasseh by virtue of maternal descent (1 Chron. 2:23).

OUTLINE—1 CHRONICLES

I. Genealogies (1:1–9:34)
 A. The Patriarchs (1:1–2:2)
 B. The Tribe of Judah (2:3–4:23)
 C. The Eleven Tribes (4:24–8:40)
 D. Postexilic Family Heads in Jerusalem (9:1–34)
II. The Reign of David (9:35–29:30)
 A. David's Predecessor: Saul (9:35–10:14)
 B. David's Assumption of Power (11–12)
 C. David's Accomplishments (13–22)
 D. David's Legacy to Solomon (23:1–29:20)
 E. Solomon's Accession to the Throne (29:21–30)

COMMENTARY

I. Genealogies (1:1–9:34)

The purpose of 1 Chronicles 1–9 is not to provide a comprehensive "history." It is rather to define status and legitimacy by means of genealogies; history, properly so-called, does not begin until chapter 9. The Hebrews' definition of their legitimate place in the universe can be described in terms of concentric circles of relationships. The Hebrew first saw himself as a part of a tribe in a nation (chaps. 2–8). The nation, in turn, had a place among the other nations (1:24–54). These, then, had their place within mankind (1:5–23); and mankind had a link with God and eternity via the creation (1:1–4). Chronicles defines and legitimizes these concentric circles of relationships by means of genealogies. The ultimate purpose of these genealogies is to confirm the status of the Chronicler's postexilic community and faith.

A. The patriarchs (1:1–2:2). A simple list of names (**1:1–4**) establishes a legitimate line of descent from Adam to Noah, demonstrating that mankind's status comes from God's creative work.

The postflood genealogical structure of the Table of Nations (**1:5–23;** cf. Gen. 10) gives tacit legitimacy to that structure and shows the place of each nation within it. All of the nations within the horizon of the ancient Hebrews are linked to one of the three sons of Noah: Japheth, Ham, or Shem.

Two major groups of Japhethites are identified: those from the Caucasus in the north (vv. 5–6) and those from the Greek and Mediterranean area (v. 7). The general regions of the Hamites (vv. 8–16) are northeast Africa, southern Arabia, Mesopotamia, some Mediterranean regions (e.g., the Caphtorim), and the land of Canaan. Both history and the Bible agree that some of these Hamitic regions were later overshadowed or ruled by non-Hamitic peoples. For example, in Mesopotamia, Arabia, and Cush (i.e., Ethiopia) the dominant language type eventually became Semitic. Even the Bible reports that Cushite Seba and Dedan eventually were ruled by the Semitic line descended from Keturah (cf. Gen. 25:3; 1 Chron. 1:32). The Semites (vv. 17–23) were generally located in Arabia and Mesopotamia.

The descriptions of the identifiable peoples in these lists vary considerably from those provided by history, but this does not mean that the Bible is inaccurate. A nation may be described from different perspectives. For example, the ruling classes of the Amorite cities of Canaan were Semites, the people the historian prefers to call "Amorites"; and the rulers of the Hittites were Indo-European. But the same nations looked at in terms of the population type of the subject peoples could be analyzed differently; the Bible describes both the Amorite and Hittite subject classes as Hamites. Apparently contradictory descriptions may both be accurate if each is understood on its own terms.

Chronicles next addresses the place of the Hebrews among those nations of Abrahamic descent (**1:24–54**). The importance of Abraham's descendants has been obscured by two common misunderstandings. Liberal scholars demean the evidence by dismissing it as mere nationalistic legend. Conservative scholars often err by assuming that the text demands that the nations be biologically descended from Abraham. In the midst of this dispute a significant fact is completely overlooked: that a particular noble family from the ancient world, with God's blessing, extends its influence over a large number of nations.

The Abrahamic aristocracies are genealogically related to the larger world scene (vv. 24–28). Then, the following regions are identified as having Abrahamic aristocracies:

1. *The descendants of Ishmael* (29–31; cf. Gen. 25:12–15). The Ishmaelites were located in regions near Egypt (Gen. 25:18). Arab tradition and secular history indicate that the Ishmaelites then spread into north Arabia.
2. *The descendants of Keturah* (32–33; cf. Gen. 25:1–4). These people generally settled in north Arabia and on the northern shores of the Red Sea.
3. *The descendants of Esau* (34–54; cf. Gen. 36). Significant descendants of Esau are listed (vv. 34–37). Then, in recognition that the Edomite nation includes earlier, non-Abrahamic elements, descendants of the patriarch Seir are listed (vv. 38–42). The listing of the dynasties that reigned "before any Israelite king" (vv. 43–54) probably represents the later Edomite nobility made up of both Abrahamic and non-Abrahamic elements.

First Chronicles 2:1–9:34 recounts the varying fortunes of the tribes of Israel (Dan and Zebulun have so faded that they are not even mentioned). It is incorrect to attribute the fate of a particular tribe purely to circumstances. Some of the allotments from the time of the conquest posed greater difficulties than others, but the greater difficulties were matched by greater opportunities should a tribe be faithful to God's covenant demands. Jacob's sons are the legitimizing framework for the structure of the Hebrew nation (**2:1–2**).

B. The tribe of Judah (2:3–4:23). Judah clearly had a more favorable history than did any other tribe, but that fact was due more to faith and obedience than to circumstances. In particular, one of the reasons for Judah's successful history is Caleb's faith, courage, and obedience. Had Caleb been no more courageous than the Ephraimites (Josh. 17:14–16), Judah too would have collapsed in weakness and impotence.

The general structure of Judah is given in 1 Chronicles **2:3–9.** The brief mention of the sons of Zerah has two interesting features. First, individuals (wise men) rather than clans are recalled (v. 6; cf. 1 Kings 4:31). Second, Achar (meaning "trouble" or "disaster") may be a derisive nickname or pun on "Achan," another of Zerah's descendants (v. 7). The line of Hezron is represented by three great houses, Jerahmeel, Ram, and Caleb. These houses may have originated at widely varying times.

The house of Ram (**2:10–17**) is David's family, and its listing partly reflects the enormous prestige of the ruling dynasty of Judah. An Ishmaelite, Amasa's father (v. 17), a member of one of the collateral Abrahamic aristocracies, holds a respected place in this genealogy.

If the attention given to Caleb's descendants (**2:18–20**) is a guide to the facts, the family of Caleb must have grown into a large house with wide-ranging political power and influence (cf. 2:42–54; 4:13–15). For the Chronicler, Caleb may have typified the bravery, resolve, and obedience that made Judah successful and great. The present passage defines the place of Caleb within the larger Hezronite family. Caleb's son, Hur, may be the Hur of 1 Chronicles 4:1. There is no firm reason to dispute that this was the Caleb of the Book of Joshua.

The historical ties of Hezron with the Gileadites in Trans-Jordan increases that house's prestige (**2:21–24**). It was probably several generations before the conquest that a second marriage of Hezron produced Segub, the father of Jair. Then, in the conquest, Jair (or, more likely, the clan bearing his name) conquered the region known as Havvoth Jair. The striking thing is that this clan was reckoned not after its male paternity from Judah, but after Manasseh, the tribe of Segub's wife.

Both the listing in **2:25–41** and geographic notices elsewhere (1 Sam. 27:10) underscore the importance of the family of Jerahmeel. An Egyptian slave is an ancestor of some of the Jerahmeelites. Foreigners, even of humble status, could gain an honored place in Israel's social structure.

The striking fact about the next verses (**2:42–55**) is the growth in importance of the Calebites. Their influence extends even into non-Judean regions such as Zorah and Eshtaol (v. 53). This is probably because of the expanding political influence of the Calebite nobility.

If Shobal the son of Hur (v. 50) is the same person as the Shobal of 1 Chronicles 4:1, then both Hur and Shobal also represent the growing influence of the Calebites. A professional guild, a clan of scribes (v. 55), is reckoned among the Calebites. Their undefined ties with the Kenites indicate a possible foreign extraction for the Calebites.

The Chronicler's goal is to present the virtues and glories of David's reign; thus David's faults are deliberately ignored. From this perspective, the record of David's large family and many wives is intended to show the king's glory (**3:1–9**). These records also confirm the status of David's nonroyal descendants who probably constituted some of the significant, if not great, houses of Judah.

Two purposes may account for the genealogical record of the Davidic kings (**3:10–16**): first, to recognize the history of the Davidic dynasty; and, second, to establish the legitimacy of the exilic and postexilic Davidic heirs of the Chronicler's day.

The legitimacy of the Davidic line even after the exile is substantiated in **3:17–24.** During the restoration, there were hints that the house of David might again rule Israel (Zech. 4:6–7). Even into New Testament times, when the concept of the Davidic throne was taking on nonpolitical, spiritual overtones, legitimate descent from David still remained an important issue. Thus, the descent of Jesus of Nazareth was traced from David. It is not surprising, then, that the Chronicler is concerned with documenting the legitimate Davidic line right up to his own day (ca. 400 B.C.).

Other clans of Judah are documented in **4:1–23.** In comparing the five great houses in verse 1 with Numbers 26, several observations can be made. The house of Zerah is represented by Carmi. The houses of Shelah and Hamul seem to have become unimportant (but cf. vv. 21–23). Perez and Hezron are still recognized, but two more great houses, Hur and Shobal, have branched off from the Calebite family of the Hezronites (cf. 1 Chron. 2:50). This development is a further testimony to the vitality and greatness of the house of Caleb as well as the long-range impact of a godly man.

Many of the genealogies of this chapter include geographic as well as personal names. They, therefore, reflect a time when some family branches were identified by their geographic locations. Furthermore, by the time of these records, some families had become identified by their occupations (v. 14). It is possible that traditional families eventually evolved into craft guilds (v. 23).

Shelah, the son of Judah (v. 21), could be either the original Shelah of the earliest genealogical lists or a later founder of a significant family. The main argument against identifying this Shelah with the original son of Judah is the fact that, contrary to the Chronicler's usual style, he is not mentioned in the list of clans at the beginning of the chapter.

C. The eleven tribes (4:24–8:40). Since the conquest, the fortunes of Simeon had been linked to Judah. The benefit was that the good fortunes of Judah were Simeon's. The disadvantage was that Simeon's identity was lost. Individual families maintained their identity and genealogies, but the tribe's unique status disappeared.

All five of the great houses of Simeon cited in the Book of Numbers (26:12–14) seem to be listed here: Nemuel, Jamin, Jarib (= "Jakin"?), Zerah, and Shaul (**4:24–43**). Attention is centered upon the house of Shaul, which, we may surmise, was best known in the Chronicler's time through the house of Shemei (vv. 26–27), perhaps the popular designation of the house of Shaul in the Chronicler's time. The geographic affinities (vv. 28–33) and contemporaneous family heads (vv. 34–38) of the house of Shemei are listed.

Two incidents show the expansion of Simeonite holdings (and God's blessings upon the Simeonites): the conquest of a Hamite settlement by a Simeonite colony and the movement of five hundred Simeonites into Edomite territory.

The location of the east Jordanian tribes was particularly unfavorable. They were in a border area, separated from the rest of the tribes and always first to be attacked both by invaders from the northeast and by Bedouin from the deserts directly east. Their lands had been assigned more by permission than by God's directive will. By the time of the exile, the area was considerably weakened.

The Chronicler first deals with the Reubenites (**5:1–10**). In recalling Reuben's loss of the birthright (v. 1), the Chronicler reminds the reader that sin has consequences. The four major families of Reuben are the same as those listed elsewhere (Gen. 46:9; Exod. 6:14; Num. 26:5–7), but in this case, it probably does not indicate the permanence of these four houses. Rather, it indicates that the tribe has suffered so greatly that these are the only ancestral notices available. The mention of Joel (vv. 4–6), given without ancestral links, may identify the setting from which the Chronicler takes these notices. This family's genealogy is traced until the Assyrian deportation (v. 6). The geographic bounds of some of the families of Joel are defined (vv. 7–9), thus giving a brief glimpse of glory and power.

The Chronicler next turns to the Gadites (**5:11–22**). After a sketchy description of the bounds of Gadite territory, the leading men (or leading families?) of the Gadites are listed. The description of the Gadite holdings (v. 16) merits further discussion. The "Sharon" here is probably the great plateau of Gilead. The resurgence of Israel's power and influence under Joash of Israel (v. 17) doubtless caused these remnants of Israel's population to gain prominence.

The report of military victory in verse 20 is typical of Chronicles. No military explanation is given; the reason for the victory is an act of piety, a prayer. The political might of the Trans-Jordanians exceeds normal historical expectations. These numbers could be literally true and reflect God's miraculous blessing. Some suggest that the numbers are symbolic, intended to convey an impression of greatness. This view does not sufficiently acknowledge the truthfulness of God in inspiration. A third possibility is that "thousand" refers to a tribal subdivision of undefined size and not to an exact arithmetic figure. The Hebrew term used here may have several meanings in different contexts. Israel's enemies were probably north Arabian Ishmaelite tribes who were infiltrating the region.

The half-tribe of Manasseh is described next (**5:23–26**). Its bounds are from Bashan to one of the peaks of Mount Hermon. The seven heads of (presumably) the seven clans of the half-tribe are listed (v. 24). Then the Chronicler shows that impiety results in judgment. The half-tribe of Manasseh, together with the Reubenites and Gadites, were unfaithful to God; therefore, they are taken captive and are exiled to the region of Gozan.

First Chronicles 6 documents the legitimacy of the tribe of Levi. Since this tribe, especially the priests, was central to the public practice of national ritual, this extended treatment of the tribe of Levi well illustrates the ritual emphasis of Chronicles.

The legitimacy of the high priests is also based upon genealogies (**6:1–15, 49–53**). At the time of David there were two high-priestly lines: (1) one from Aaron's son, Ithamar, through Eli represented by Abiathar who officiated in Jerusalem; and (2) one from Aaron's son Eleazar, represented by Zadok who officiated in Gibeon. Abiathar lost his position by supporting Adonijah's illicit bid for the throne; and the prophecy concerning Eli's house was fulfilled (1 Sam. 2:34–36). From that point on, the line of Zadok, also descended from Aaron's son, Eleazar, was recognized as the only legitimate high-priestly line. There is no firm evidence for the notion that Zadok was adopted into Aaron's family.

First Chronicles 6:1–15 traces, and thus establishes, the legitimate high-priestly line up to the captivity. Verses 49–53 emphasize the uniqueness of the high-priestly duties by emphasizing that only the priests, and not the Levites, actually offered sacrifices. This privilege of the priests was not always honored. Retracing the genealogy from Aaron to Ahimaaz (vv. 50–53) reinforces the legitimacy of Zadok's family as opposed to the family of Abiathar. Like the high-priestly line, the legitimacy of the great Levite houses is also traced back to Levi (**6:16–30**).

The genealogies of the temple musicians are presented in **6:31–47.** The amount of space devoted to their origins, the appearance of their names among the authors of the psalms, and the prominence of their genealogies in the restoration literature underscore their importance. Part of David's significance to the Chronicler lies in the fact that he established the temple musicians as a legitimate part of temple worship. Chronicles thus legitimizes the temple singers by tracing their origins back to the time of David.

There has been speculation concerning the possibility that these musical clans were foreign guilds of musicians adopted into the tribe of Levi. However, there is no definitive evidence to support this theory.

The Chronicler's reason for including a list of Levitical holdings (**6:54–81**) is to reclaim the ancient prestige and honor of the Levites. Even if the exact geographic holdings are obsolete and unattainable, their recollection reminds the readers that the Levites and priests have historic, God-ordained privileges. There are a number of differences between this list and the corresponding list in Joshua 21. These are, most likely, instances of textual corruption.

In examining the genealogies of the remaining western tribes, once more, two features of the genealogies of Chronicles should be noted. First, they involve singling out particular historical houses for attention while disregarding others. This generally reflects the historical fading of the neglected houses and the rise to prominence of the houses singled out for further treatment. Second, the grouping together of names descended from a common ancestor does not necessarily indicate that these names represent collateral descendants from the same generation. Houses could be listed together which originated at widely varying times. First Chronicles 7 may describe the state of affairs at the time of David.

Of the four original houses of Issachar (Num. 26:23–25), only the families descended from Tola maintain their identity and prestige (**7:1–5**). Of these, five families are directly reckoned to Tola (v. 2) and five more families are reckoned to Uzzi, a son of Tolah (vv. 3–4). The picture is of two great family groups, one an offshoot of the other. The disappearance of three great ancestral houses shows the precariousness of Issachar prior to the Davidic Empire.

There is no straightforward evidence for taking the genealogies of **7:6–12** as the genealogies of Zebulun. This suggestion is based upon conjectural textual emendations. Three descendants of Benjamin—Bela, Beker, and Jediael—are listed leaving several other sons, whose lines may have fallen into relative obscurity, unmentioned (cf. Gen. 46:21; 1 Chron. 8). Jediael seems to be a new line whose origins are not spelled out. The disastrous civil war between Benjamin and the rest of the nation certainly played its part in erasing houses of that tribe. Five families are linked to Bela and perhaps two more if "Ir" in verse 12 is the same person as "Iri" in verse 7; nine are linked to Beker including two clans, Anathoth and Alemeth, apparently known by the geographic locales in which they settled; and seven families are linked to Jediael through Bilhan.

The congruence between the names in **7:13** and the earlier lists (Num. 26:48–50) does not indicate that the houses of Naphtali had survived the years intact. Rather it implies that Naphtali had so thoroughly waned that the only lists available were those from the time of Moses.

It is interesting that the term *Manasseh,* perhaps implying a higher level of legitimacy, designates that part of the tribe which settled west of the Jordan (**7:14–19**); the term *half-tribe* is used for the Manassites east of the Jordan (5:23). Since Manasseh had only one direct son (Num. 26:29), Makir, all the houses of Manasseh branch off from him. Both Makir and Gilead, in the strictest sense, had received their inheritances east of the Jordan (Josh. 17:1), but the Manassite families west of the Jordan were themselves descendants of Makir and Gilead (cf. Num. 26:28–34; Josh. 17:2). By the time of these notices only the families of Asriel (v. 14) and Shemida (v. 19), branches from Gilead, and the lines descended from Makir through Maacah (v. 16) remain important.

The sons of Hammoleketh (v. 18) may represent non-Manassite families related to Manasseh by marriage, or alternatively, they may be families descended from a Manassite daughter by a stranger and then adopted into full tribal membership.

In the Ephraimite genealogies (**7:20–29**) only Shuthelah, of the three Ephraimite families of Numbers 26:35–36, is mentioned. Two leading families are singled out, that of Shuthelah (vv. 20–21) and that of Beriah (vv. 23–27). An anecdote relates the origins of the family descended from Beriah (vv. 21–24). The "Ephraim" of this anecdote seems to be a figure from the conquest rather than the patriarch of that name. Verse 29 has two peculiarities. The cities mentioned were originally Manassite, and the inhabitants are described as "descendants of Joseph" in a passage talking about Ephraim. Perhaps this is a tactful way of hinting that Ephraim had superseded Manasseh in these cities. The list of cities also roughly approximates part of the circle of fortress cities that protected the heartland of the northern kingdom.

Of the ancestral Asherite families, only the house of Beriah is represented in these genealogies (**7:30–40**).

No other chapter in Chronicles better exemplifies the problems of the genealogical materials than chapter 8. First, Benjamin is treated a second time (cf. 7:6–12). The reason may be to highlight a royal genealogy. If this suggestion is correct, this passage is similar to chapter 3: both are royal genealogies and both are placed in fairly unpredictable locations. We would expect these materials to be part of the earlier treatment of Benjamin, just as we would expect David's royal genealogies (chap. 3) to be linked with those of the house of Ram (2:10–17). It is fair to conclude that a royal genealogy could warrant a second treatment in an unexpected location.

A second problem is the many difficulties and obscurities in the text. Like chapter 4, this chapter may have been aimed at a specialized audience that could understand fragmentary materials.

Third, there is a marked difference between the names in this chapter and those in 7:6–12. The differences may reflect the different purposes of the two passages. The earlier passage, like the rest of the tribal genealogies, represents the tribal realities of Benjamin. Assuming that the focus of this chapter is Saul, then this passage deals with families prominent because of their association with him. Or, following the hint of verse 28, this passage may represent only Benjamite families who, at some time, lived in Jerusalem near the national center of power.

More information about the houses of Benjamin is given in **8:1–28.** There are several suggestions for harmonizing verses 1 and 2 and Numbers 26:38–40. First, the present passage may give alternate names for the sons of Benjamin. Second, the families descended from those sons possibly took on the names of later, prominent members of the families, although their relative order as "sons of Benjamin" remained unchanged. Third, it is plausible, though certainly unproven, that these names were the branches of the original five houses that attached themselves to Saul. It is difficult to believe that these names could have made their way into the text if they represented obvious discrepancies.

The houses of Bela (vv. 3–5) and Ehud (vv. 6–7) are listed. Ehud is another example of a genealogy whose relationship to the larger tribal structure is completely undefined. The relationship between the houses of Ehud and Gera (v. 7) is quite obscure. Perhaps Naaman and Ahijah are Ehud families and Gera's families are Uzza and Ahihud. A group of Benjamite families, settled in Moab, is listed (vv. 8–12). Some commentators feel that a new group of families is introduced in verse 13.

Chronicles now turns to Saul's own family, the house of Jeiel (**8:29–40**). Jeiel's place in the tribe apparently is common knowledge. The family line is traced up to Saul, and then beyond Saul through a surviving line of Jonathan to a certain Ulam who attains a certain degree of fame (v. 40). It is noteworthy that Chronicles, which is highly critical of Saul's spiritual failures, nevertheless records Saul's descendants, and thus bestows a kind of legitimacy upon them. The last branch discussed, that of Eshek, is omitted in the parallel passage in 9:35–44.

D. Postexilic family heads in Jerusalem (9:1–34). This is the goal and climax of the genealogies of the previous chapters. The entire genealogical record, from creation to the postexilic community, establishes the legitimate status of that community and of its faith.

The returnees from the exile are listed in **9:1–16.** The opening theological comment relates the exile to God's covenant; the people of Judah were taken captive because of their unfaithfulness to God's covenant (v. 1b). The Chronicler then turns to the legitimizing of those who returned from exile to live in Jerusalem. Others returned, but the Chronicler is generally concerned only with those who live in the sacred religious center. Several families are listed with sufficient genealogical data to establish their legitimacy.

Not only is the status of the Jerusalem families substantiated by the genealogies, but the Levitical families' rights to their hereditary cultic positions are confirmed (**9:17–34**). The gatekeepers are highlighted; the leaders, or perhaps the heads of the leading families, are listed; their duties are linked with their historical antecedents going all the way back past David and Samuel to Phinehas.

The text then proceeds to a description of the duties of the gatekeepers. In general terms, these involved protection of the premises and management of resources. The text confirms the rights of the Levites not resident in Jerusalem to participate in ritual.

One verse (v. 33) suffices for the temple musicians. The importance of their duty is shown by their exemption from any other responsibilities. The brevity of the materials dealing with the singers is more likely due to the security of their position than the loss in transmission of part of the text.

II. The Reign of David (9:35–29:30)

Chronicles now turns to a new subject, the history of the Davidic dynasty. This history is important because of David's significant contribution to Israel's religious ritual. Saul's history is included only as a preface to the history of David.

A. David's predecessor: Saul (9:35–10:14). Chronicles records Saul's genealogy twice. The genealogy in 8:29–40 completes one of the two royal tribal genealogies of the nation. The genealogy in **9:35–44** relates the story of the king who, rejected by God, left the scene to make room for David; and even that king deserves the status provided by a legitimate genealogy.

The end of Saul's reign is detailed in **10:1–14.** The northerly location of the battle at Mount Gilboa (v. 1), is strange considering the much more southerly location of the Philistines. This may reflect the Philistines' efforts to control the lucrative trade routes through the Valley of

Jezreel. Likely, Saul's suicidal despair is another evidence of his unworthiness. Historically, this defeat was a tragic reversal of all of Saul's gains against the Philistines. One indicator of the extent of the disaster is that Israel was forced to abandon hard-won territories in the Valley of Jezreel to Philistine garrisons.

Quite naturally, the Philistines rejoice at the deaths of their enemies. They plunder the corpses and send the happy news to all their cities. Even here, in Chronicles' negative treatment of Saul, a hint of his achievements appears when the people of Jabesh-gilead, grateful for the time Saul saved them from disaster, give Saul and his sons an honorable burial.

Saul was unfaithful in consulting a medium. However, this should be understood as typical of Saul's general impiety. God's judgment came because of Saul's general impiety, not just one failure. Saul's impiety, then, provides a sharp contrast to the piety of David. David is faithful to God and is accepted by God as the covenant king. Had Saul been faithful, his might have been the covenant dynasty.

B. David's assumption of power (11–12). There are two motivating factors behind the Chronicler's extensive treatment of and appreciation for David: David's sponsorship of ritual and his identity as the ideal covenant king. The former is illustrated by such activities as: (1) the capture of the cultic capital, Jerusalem; (2) the preparations for the temple; (3) the founding of the religious bureaucracy; and (4) the founding of Israel's religious musical tradition. The omissions in Chronicles are significant. Any mention of David's sin or weakness is incidental (e.g., 1 Chron. 21), nor are we told of any failure by the people to accept David as king.

More than seven years are compressed into **11:1–3.** The seven-year civil war is ignored. David's kingship is accepted immediately. Theologically, the message is that God's people readily accept the man who is to be God's covenant king. Politically, the kingship is seen as a covenant between the king and the people. Automatic dynastic succession would come only later with the full implementation of the Davidic covenant.

For the Chronicler, Jerusalem is the greatest religious center of Israel, the place where the temple and the ark should be placed; therefore capturing Jerusalem is presented as one of David's most significant accomplishments. "Restored the rest of the city" (v. 8, NIV) is better translated as "allowed the remainder [of the population] to live." After the capture of Jerusalem (**11:4–9**), it becomes the royal residence.

The remainder of the chapter deals with the men who "gave his [David's] kingship strong support" (**11:10–47**). As their king, David shares in the glory of the exploits recorded here. The incident at Pas Dammim (vv. 12–14) is credited to Eleazar while in Samuel it is associated with Shammah (2 Sam. 23:11–12). Any alleged contradiction is resolved if both men were present at that battle. David's deep piety and respect for his men are powerfully shown in his pouring out of the water brought to him from Bethlehem (vv. 15–19).

Verses 26–47 are similar in form and content to 2 Samuel 23:24–39. An examination of the names and their geographic affinities illustrates the nationwide acceptance of the covenant king and the number of foreigners who were accepted into the nation of Israel. The inclusion of foreigners, without comment or criticism, is striking—especially coming from a people noted for their narrow, legalistic nationalism.

Theologically, chapter 12 shows the entire nation responding to God's covenant king even while he is still an exile. What better way to highlight pious loyalty to the covenant king than to show it in Benjamites of Saul's own tribe (**12:1–7**)? These troops were light auxiliaries, armed with bows and slings, though some nevertheless were among David's mighty men.

Trans-Jordanian tribesmen also join David. The exact location of the wilderness stronghold (**12:8–18**) is unclear. The reference to shield and spear (v. 8) could indicate that these were heavy infantry troops equipped to stand in the battle line. Some commentators suggest that their successful missions against certain anonymous inhabitants of the Jordan valleys may have been directed against partisans of Saul who hindered their path to David. It is equally possible that these warriors established their reputations by driving out non-Hebrew colonists from these valleys. The arrival of Benjamites and Judeans (vv. 16–17) to the stronghold gives occasion for a poetic statement of God's presence with David to give him success.

Manassites and others defect to David while he is in Philistine exile (**12:19–22**). Since the major mobilization to the north at Mount Gilboa by both Israelites and Philistines left the south exposed, David had more need for mobile auxiliaries to ward off raiding parties.

David's "great army" (v. 22) need not refer simply to the numbers of his followers. Its greatness could have been a matter of the quality of David's heroes, of the army's potentiality, or even of the numbers at the end of the whole process described in chapter 12, a process which extended to the end of the Hebron period.

Though Chronicles does not explicitly recognize the seven-year civil war, knowledge of these events is shown by acknowledgment of the period at Hebron (**12:23–40**). All the tribes send their contingents to Hebron. Historically, this probably marked the time, after the civil war, when the nation as a whole accepted God's chosen, covenant king. Chronicles portrays the acceptance of the covenant king as a joyous, festive occasion.

C. David's accomplishments (13–22). David's preparations for moving the ark (**13:1–6**) mark the first of Chronicles' many cultic interests. David gathers and consults the nation's leaders. It is significant that the Levites, with their special cultic role, are singled out as participants (v. 2). Chronicles also emphasizes the need for the proper ritual for inquiring of God (v. 3).

The Israelites attempt to move the ark in a way suitable to its great importance (**13:7–8**). The "new cart" (v. 7) recalls the idea of the firstfruits; the ark was getting the "firstfruits" of the cart's usage. There are great festivities for the occasion; but ritual prescriptions are not observed.

Tragedy occurs when Uzzah's well-intended act results in his death (**13:9–24**). In this case, Israel's ritual disobedience, in spite of good intentions and attitudes, is punished. The handling of the most sacred relic of Israel's religion demands utmost obedience.

David's political glory is evident in Jerusalem (**14:1–7**). His great palace is built with the help of Hiram of Tyre. At this point Tyre was not the Mediterranean trading giant of Ahab's or Ezekiel's time; nevertheless, the beginnings are there. This alliance provides David with a basis for wealth, prestige, and future economic growth. Thus, Hiram's friendly overtures add to the covenant king's glory.

David's palace authenticates his status. David realizes that God has exalted him (v. 2), as the covenant later will confirm (17:8). David's many wives and children add to his royal glory (v. 3).

David's victories over the Philistines enhance his standing (**14:8–17**). After his consolidation of power, the Philistines move directly against David by raiding the Valley of Rephaim near Jerusalem. David's piety is seen in his inquiring of the Lord (v. 10; very likely at the ark) and his ordering the burning of the abandoned Philistine idols (v. 12). Once more the Philistines raid the valley; once more David inquires of the Lord; and again David is victorious.

Chapters 15–17 present the religious high points of David's career: (1) bringing the ark to Jerusalem (chap. 15); (2) establishing worship in Jerusalem (chap. 16); and (3) the Davidic covenant (chap. 17).

Once his personal building projects are completed, David again determines to bring the ark to Jerusalem. A new tent is constructed in Jerusalem rather than upsetting the cult at Gibeon (16:39–40). This time the ritual instructions for moving the ark are meticulously obeyed. The Levites and priests, including both high-priestly lines, are summoned (**15:1–15**). The detailed listing of Levitical families (vv. 5–10) shows the Chronicler's typical concern for cultic detail and legitimacy of cultic personnel. David's challenge (vv. 12–13) underscores the need to observe proper ritual.

The repeated references to musicians and gatekeepers in Chronicles show their great importance to official religious ritual. Here the origins and legitimacy of these offices are linked to the authority of the Davidic dynasty (**15:16–24**). Names renowned in the history of worship appear: Asaph (v. 19), Ethan (v. 19), Obed-Edom (v. 21), and Heman (v. 19).[1]

The ark is brought safely to Jerusalem (**15:25–29**). The task is portrayed as a national effort involving king, elders, and military leaders. Sacrifices and music accompany the effort. David himself, dressed in a linen ephod, shares in the ecstatic joy of the occasion. Some, including his wife, Michal, feel that this public display is inappropriate for the king.

The new religious context created by bringing the ark to Jerusalem is important because it establishes the norms for future cultic ritual (**16:1–7**). The general setting of the ark is fixed (though it would later be moved from David's tent into Solomon's temple). David appoints some of the Levites to minister before the ark, in effect originating the cultic bureaucracy of worship in Jerusalem. Three psalmic activities are defined: (1) the recitation of memorial psalms (NIV make petition); (2) the recitation of confessionals or acknowledgments (NIV give thanks); and (3) praise. In particular, the appointment of the musicians (vv. 5–6) establishes the hereditary musical bureaucracy that would last through the Babylonian exile. Finally, the regular thanksgiving is assigned to Asaph (v. 7). The root translated "thanks" and "give thanks" actually has a broader meaning. The Hebrew root, *ydh,* also includes such meanings as "acknowledge," "confess," and "extol." Verse 7 could be better translated: "In that day, David first assigned the confession to [for]

1. Concerning the possibility that these guilds may have been of foreign origin, see the commentary for 1 Chronicles 6:31–48.

Yahweh to the responsibility of Asaph and his family."

A compendium of representative confessionals adapted from several other passages (vv. 8–22 = Ps. 105:1–15; vv. 23–33 = Ps. 96; and vv. 34–36 = Ps. 106:1, 47–48) are recorded (**16:8–36**). The opening verse (v. 8) states the theme:

> Give thanks to the LORD, call on his name;
> make known . . . what he has done.

This compendium is a public acknowledgment of God's great works. As such, it is similar to the "remembrance" psalms which are public recitations (i.e., remembrances) of God's great deeds (cf. v. 4). The compendium challenges the people to tell of God's deeds (vv. 8–9, 12, 23–24), especially of God's works of covenant faithfulness. As a result, the nations will realize God's greatness (25–27), accept him as ruler, and worship him (28–33).

Chapter 16 closes with the establishment of several other places of worship for both Jerusalem and Gibeon (**16:37–43**). Asaph and the family of Obed-Edom minister in Jerusalem. Gibeon is put into the hands of Zadok, leaving the Jerusalem shrine in the hands of Abiathar's family. The lack of explicit reference to the offering of sacrifices in Jerusalem does not prove that they did not occur. On the contrary, the many sacrifices offered after the ark was moved (16:2) would seem to indicate that the ark was treated as a place of sacrifice. This silence may indicate that neither the Chronicler nor the Holy Spirit wishes to approve publicly of that detail. The text specifically states that Gibeon was provided with regular ritual as "written in the Law." David, apparently, manages to work out an acceptable compromise between the two high-priestly lines and the two remaining holy places.

God's covenant with David (chap. 17) explicitly establishes the Davidic dynasty as the divinely approved, only legitimate dynasty over God's people. It also sets up the Davidic dynasty as the moral representative of God for assigning the judgments and blessings prescribed by the Mosaic covenant. For some 250 years God's judgment upon the king of Judah is to be God's judgment upon the nation.

The occasion of the covenant is David's desire to build the temple. David is concerned about the things of God and Nathan encourages him in his plans. However, God rejects David as the one to build the temple. Even so, he brings his covenant word to David (**17:1–15**). The project has already waited many years and can wait longer. The basis for the covenant is God's past and future works for David and for the nation. The themes presented here will recur throughout the remainder of Chronicles: (1) God will make David great (v. 8); (2) God will give security to his people in their land (vv. 9–10); and (3) God's legitimate house, the temple, will be built (v. 12).

Several provisions are specifically dynastic. God will give David a great reputation (v. 8). David's dynasty (i.e., his house) will be established forever (vv. 10–11, 14; cf. 2 Sam. 7:16). The Davidic heir will be considered the "adopted" son of God himself (v. 13; cf. Pss. 2:7–9; 89:26–27). This contrasts sharply with the extravagant claims of many pagan rulers that they were the descendants of the gods. God's covenant will remain in force forever. In fact, the authority of this covenant is still in effect in the legitimate authority of Jesus of Nazareth, David's son.

David, as we should do, approaches God in prayer, in awe of what God has done for him (**17:16–27**). He fosters no pride in his own accomplishments or greatness; his boasting is in God (vv. 16–19). David then repeats two of the great themes in Old Testament theology: (1) God's unique work in choosing a nation for his special possession; and (2) God's great signs and wonders. David accepts the covenant and desires its permanence.

God makes David great (cf. 17:8) by giving David victory everywhere he goes (18:6, 13). Some of David's conquests are listed (**18:1–13**): the Philistines, Moab, the Aramean kingdoms of Zobah and Damascus, Hamath, and Edom. These conquests show the God-given success of David's obedient covenant dynasty. David does not try to save captured horses since chariotry is not important in his army. David's general policy is to dedicate foreign tribute and spoils of war to the temple-building fund (v. 11).

It is typical of Hebrew thought that some of the content of this section, specifically the data relating to the Aramean conquests, will be covered a second time in the account of the Ammonite war (see 19:1–20:3). The duplicate record is of no significance whatsoever in determining chronology or for asserting that separate events were involved. In Hebrew thought, the same content could be routinely repeated under different topical headings.

As the ideal, covenant king, David shows the qualities of justice and righteousness in his rule (v. 14; cf. Ps. 72). Men who aid him in that just rule add their stature to David's greatness (**18:14–17**).

Most of David's campaigns add to his empire in a piecemeal way. By contrast, the Ammonite war adds more than half the empire as the result of a single, difficult, widespread struggle. Thus the Ammonite war is the most important political event of David's reign.

At the beginning of this incident we see David exercising tact and diplomacy toward a pagan king (**19:1–5**). Godliness does not preclude graciousness toward pagans either individually or nationally. In contrast, Hanun's reaction is arrogant and insulting.

For David, Hanun's insult is a just reason for war. The Ammonites agree and the first phase of the war begins (**19:6–15**). They call on other significant powers of the region—the Aramean kingdoms of Zobah and Maacah together with unnamed Arameans of Mesopotamia (Aram Naharaim)—for help. This broadens the scope of the war by bringing the two great, local powers, Israel and Zobah, into conflict. Further, this means that the consequences will involve the entire realm of Zobah.

The hired Arameans have many chariots, and this produces a classic conflict between David's well-trained heavy infantry and the combined infantry and chariotry of the Arameans. Joab divides his troops (vv. 10–11)—usually poor strategy—and defeats both the Ammonites and the Arameans. Both the victory and great reputation belong to David. A factor in David's victory is a disciplined battle line. On the other hand, a nation led by a godly, obedient king could entrust the outcome of the battle to God (v. 13).

It is apparent from the role of Shophach, Hadadezer's general, that Zobah is the major power in the continued Aramean opposition to David (**19:16–19**). Zobah appeals for more assistance from the Arameans in Mesopotamia beyond the Euphrates River. The widespread Aramean response demonstrates great fear of David's rising power. Again David's infantry triumphs over the combined forces of the enemy. The subjects of Hadadezer change their loyalty from Zobah to David, and David's empire almost doubles in size.

With the Aramean allies out of the picture, Joab deals with Rabbah (**20:1–3**). He is destructive and brutal. The land is devastated, and the surviving population is consigned to forced labor. David takes the crown of Ammon, together with a great quantity of plunder. Should we assume that David's brutality is godly? Or that brutal reprisals are in order in a brutal age? Or should we judge that not all of David's actions reflect the best of God's will?

The remainder of this chapter (**20:4–8**) deals with the deaths of Goliath's kinsmen, perhaps the last of the heroic "giants" (i.e., Rephaites) among the Philistines. The meaning of the term *Rephaite* and its derivatives is unclear. It generally refers to older inhabitants of the land known for their large size and/or military prowess. It could also be an honorific term for the oldest strata of Canaanite or Philistine military aristocracy. Theologically the message is that, even for the ancient, formidable Rephaites, death is the consequence of opposing the covenant dynasty.

The Chronicler normally does not record David's faults. David's census is mentioned only because it is part of another account, that of the acquisition of the temple site. The sinfulness of David's act is probably related to his attitude rather than inherent in the deed as such, since censuses are ordered by God elsewhere in the Bible. Perhaps the issue is David's pride in numbers which overrides his trust in God.

There is a threefold level of responsibility for the census; and, if we properly understand, there is no conflict in assuming the truth of all three levels (**21:1–3**). David can be called the responsible agent because the census was his decision. Satan is responsible because he is quite willing to incite the action though David makes the decision. God is responsible (2 Sam. 24:1) because he sovereignly permits Satan to act in a way that influences David. In terms of permissive will, God does "move" David to sin. Though the reason for the wrong is obscure, the error of the deed is clearly shown by Joab's protests (v. 3).

The census is executed (**21:4–6**). The discrepancies between the numbers recorded in Samuel (2 Sam. 24:9) and in Chronicles (v. 5) should not be shocking considering the difficulties of transmission of numbers in ancient documents. Levi's omission from the census is understandable since the people already belonged to God; but any attempt to account for the exemption of Benjamin is conjecture.

David's sin demands punishment (**21:7–17**). After judgment has begun, David acknowledges his fault. As on other occasions, David's godly character is demonstrated in his repentance. God's response through the prophet Gad (v. 9) is presented in a Hebrew prose structure which features the repetition of an account or parts of an account but in an expanded form ("expanded repetition"). The three specific choices are not given in verse 9 though we can be sure that the pious prophet did not add to or embellish God's words. The Hebrew reader would readily understand that the entire message was originally given to Gad, though the full statement of the details is not recorded until Gad speaks to David (v. 12). God sends a plague on Israel that lasts three days, and seventy thousand Israelites die. The course of the plague brings David to the threshing floor of Araunah.

This brings us to the climax of the account—David's acquisition of the site of the temple (**21:18–30**). As noted, this, not David's sin, is the real subject of the passage. The angel of the Lord orders Gad to tell David to go to Araunah's threshing floor, thus giving a divine sign of the sacredness of the site.

The easiest, though not the necessary, sense of the passage is that David personally offers sacrifices (vv. 26, 28), an illegal act for one who was not a priest. The fire from heaven is a miraculous sign that God has accepted both the sacrifice and the sacred place. Once again, mention is made of the shrine in Gibeon (v. 29) which still draws inquirers. David expressly recognizes that these divine signs designate God's choice for the location of his house (**22:1**).

David's preparation for the temple (**22:2–5**) shows that practical foresight is a virtue even in spiritual undertakings. First, David recruits foreign craftsmen for the work. At this time, the Israelites were not that far removed from the rural, somewhat crude days of Samuel and Saul, and there were few, if any, skilled artisans among them. For the kind of skills necessary for the temple—and for David's own palaces—foreign craftsmen are essential.

Second, David gathers materials for the temple, particularly stone, metals, and wood. Much of these were David's spoils of war, but there were also materials brought in by peaceful trade with allies—most notably cedar logs from Lebanon.

David himself is not allowed to build the temple because he has "shed much blood" (v. 8). A significant shift in society has occurred. David lived in an age when violent warfare was essential to the preservation of society and did not necessarily conflict with godliness. By the end of his reign, Israel was moving into a more peaceful and cultured era where the wise man and the merchant could share the warrior's prestige. The Book of Proverbs also reflects this transition (Prov. 1:10–16). The new ways demanded that a peaceful, "wise" king should build the temple.

David's heir, then, in fulfillment of the covenant, is to build the temple. David challenges Solomon, as the moral representative of the people, to be strong and courageous in keeping the law (**22:6–16**). As noted earlier, the king's faithfulness is to be the basis for judging the nation. The people's prosperity depends on the prosperity of the king who obeys the covenant, and conversely, their misery lies in the judgments upon the king who has disobeyed the covenant.

David then mentions the huge wealth he has accumulated for the temple (vv. 14–16). Though problems in textual transmission and in determining equivalences make precise estimates extremely difficult, this wealth certainly was great enough to reflect David's worldwide fame and the prosperity God had given to him.

David also challenges the leaders of the people (**22:17–19**). First, a covenant blessing is echoed in the "rest on every side" (v. 18). Second, because of that rest, the people are urged to join in giving for the temple in a truly national effort.

D. David's legacy to Solomon (23:1–29:20). Shortly before Solomon's accession to the throne (ca. 970 B.C.) David finally fixes or codifies many of the already existing religious and civil administrative arrangements. These are not primarily new institutions. Three different areas are involved: (1) the religious bureaucracy (chaps. 23–26); (2) the civil bureaucracy (chap. 27); and (3) the final plans for the temple (28:1–29:20).

We begin with an overview of the Levitical families (**23:1–6**). Levites twenty (not thirty; cf. v. 24) years old and upward are officially registered for the temple work and assigned different duties. It fits the context that the temple work is the application of already existing ritual duties to the coming temple rather than the work of building the temple. The numbers are large because different courses took turns executing the actual duties. The organization of the Levitical assignments follow the three great Levitical family groups, Gershon, Kohath, and Merari.

Gershon (**23:7–11**) is represented by two families, Ladan and Shemei, elsewhere identified as Shimei and Libni (cf. 6:17). This does not necessarily indicate that Ladan is another name for Libni, the individual. The family line or clan, not the individual, may have been identified by either name. One branch of this clan produced the families Jehiel, Zetham, and Joel. Verse 9 may present a Shimei from this family. Unless we emend the text, this man is not Shemei, the son of Gershon of verse 10. He was sufficiently well known not to demand further documentation.

Four families of Kohathites are listed (**23:12–20**). Since Moses and Aaron were descendants of Amram, son of Kohath, they are referred to here—Aaron as a special case and Moses as another founder of Kohathite families.

The brief listing of Merarite families (**23:21–23**) is supplemented by 1 Chronicles 24:27–30. The two passages taken together give an unclear picture of this clan's circumstances.

In detailing the duties of the temple (**23:24–**

32) David once again alludes to the covenant theme of rest (v. 25). The rationale for the Levites' service is that it is a substitute for carrying the tabernacle in the wanderings of the people. The Levites are to assist the priests, a duty that recognizes the greater prestige of the priesthood. They are responsible, in general, for the practical, menial tasks of the ministry. They also participate in formal worship in three ways: sharing in the confessional (NIV thanks), praising, and serving at the times of sacrifices. All of this, however, is to be carried out "under" the priests, again confirming the superior status of the priesthood. These assignments did not prevent some Levite families from being assigned to other duties.

The divisions of priests are summarized in **24:1–19.** There are two high-priestly families descended from Eleazar and Ithamar, the sons of Aaron. These are represented by two competing high-priestly lines, that of Zadok from Eleazar and that of Abiathar from Ithamar through Eli. The latter is here represented by Ahimelech, son of Abiathar, David's high priest. The conflicting high-priestly claims are both honored by having Zadok serve at Gibeon while Abiathar's family serves at David's personal shrine.

Twenty-four priestly orders, separate from the high-priestly position, are assigned here (vv. 7–18). The Chronicler's careful diligence to avoid favoritism to either of the great families highlights the delicacy of the situation. Though the line of Ithamar eventually loses any claim to the high priesthood, its claim to these other orders is a permanent, hereditary privilege.

The allotment and registering of these assignments is done under David's authority. This emphasizes the fact that the legitimate origins of these cultic assignments can be traced to David, the ideal covenant king.

The Levitical genealogies of **24:20–31** supplement those of chapter 23. They give additional data about the Kohathites (vv. 20–25; cf. 24:13–20) and the Merarites (vv. 26–30). However, the purpose in recording this additional data is difficult to discern.

Over time, the musical families listed in chapter **25** may have come to function more or less like professional guilds. Here their function is described as musical "prophesying" (v. 1), that is, serving as spokesmen for God. Combining this with other biblical data, the musical psalm singers could declare a message from God, confess God's works and character, and recite God's great works.

The list of the families assigned this duty is given. Many people are involved in the music—4000 in 1 Chronicles 23:5 and some 288 leading musicians in the present passage (v. 7). These numbers are too large to describe the descendants of Asaph, Jeduthun, and Heman. It is striking that the names of the last nine sons of Heman can be read quite easily as a psalm of praise. This could indicate either that the text is seriously corrupted from mistaking a psalm for a list of names or that Heman exercised a very subtle sense of humor in naming his sons. In considering the way Hebrew genealogies could function, it is possible that the three large groups of musical families became known by their three great representatives so that "sons of Asaph" in effect meant "members of the family group identified with its illustrious leader, Asaph." Another suggestion is that "sons" refers to intellectual sons, that is, those musicians taught by the great musicians. The first suggestion is more in keeping with general Old Testament usage.

The supervision of musical worship is described. David's musical talents well equip him for supervision. The lots for the service duties of each class are described. It is clear from the context that the families listed in verses 2–5 are intended to coincide with the duty groups of verses 9–31. To achieve this agreement the following assumptions are necessary: (1) that the name *Shimei* (v. 17) has been lost since it is not present in the earlier list; (2) that "Izri" (v. 11) is a variant of "Zeri"; (3) that "Jesarelah" (v. 14) is a variant of "Asarelah"; and (4) that "Azarel" (v. 18) is "Uzziel."

The numbers of those assigned to gatekeeping are small enough to refer to individual families (**26:1–19**). However, the total manpower allotted to "gatekeeping" is about four thousand men (1 Chron. 23:5). From this we conclude that the men listed here are the hereditary administrators of the gatekeepers while Levites from other families are assigned to work under them.

Four families are identified: Meshelemiah from the house of Asaph, Obed-Edom, Obed-Edom's son, Shemaiah, and Hosah, a Merarite. The "relatives" of verse 12 are other Levites performing functions described elsewhere. Some textual corruption may be indicated by the fact that only Shuppim of the leaders chosen by lot is not mentioned in the listings by families and that Meshelemiah appears as "Shelemiah" (cf. vv. 1, 14). Their duties include the protection of the storehouses and gates. Not enough is known about the Shalleketh Gate (v. 16) to identify it.

The Gershonite descendants of Ladan supervise the treasury for the regular offerings of the people (**26:20–28**). Each of the great Kohathite families is represented. An overlap in names with 24:20–30 may indicate that the purpose of that passage is related to the present passage. Moses' descendants were supervisors of some kind of general treasuries. The Izharites supervise the treasuries for that portion of the spoils of war dedicated to God.

Other Izharites are given administrative duties away from the temple (**26:29–32**). The judging mentioned here may have been viewed as a sacred duty since the law of Moses regulated matters of justice. That Levites, representing the central religious authority, are judging such matters rather than local tribal or village elders, is the result of David's work. In Trans-Jordan, Hebronites handled these duties. Some hint of the scope of David's bureaucracy might be seen in the number of men (approximately 2700) assigned to this duty for Trans-Jordan (v. 32). The Levites were ideal choices for administering justice for the central government since they were not distracted by conflicting tribal loyalties.

The heading of **27:1–15** seems to promise a listing of several levels of military officers; in fact, only the chief commander for each of the months is given. Perhaps this heading serves as an introduction for all of the groups of officers listed in the chapter. If so, these officers "concern[ed] the army divisions" (v. 1) in some way. Two important military innovations had been introduced. First, there is a standing army with troops on duty each month of the year; those not on duty serve as a ready reserve. This contrasts with the old citizen levy army at the beginning of Saul's reign. Second, the armies are under the control of royal officers instead of local tribal elders.

David also establishes a royal civil bureaucracy (**27:16–24**). Although these offices certainly strengthen the king's central authority, they do not completely replace the family and tribal elders. In fact, whenever David deals with "the whole assembly of Israel" (13:1–2; cf. "all Israel" in 15:3) the older system of tribal elders is an important part of the group. The older assembly of elders is the group that refuses to accept Rehoboam as king (2 Chron. 10:16).

The overseers of David's personal estates are listed next (**27:25–31**). Both Saul and David acquired large personal estates (Samuel had warned the people about privately owned royal lands and industries; 1 Sam. 8:12–14). Storehouses, farmlands, vineyards, olive groves, and herds are included in David's private holdings.

David's inner circle of officials (**27:32–34**), perhaps comparable to the cabinet of a modern political chief executive, completes the listing of David's civil bureaucracy. The officers listed are counselor, scribe, friend (perhaps modeled after an Egyptian office with a similar name), leader over the king's sons (over his household?), and commander of the royal army.

Once more Chronicles describes a united national effort. David summons all the officials of Israel. His challenge (**28:1–10**) reiterates, both for himself and the Chronicler, important covenant themes. David wished to build the temple, but God sovereignly overruled that desire because David represented an older, more violent ideal (v. 3). David again notes that God, in his own sovereign working, had made him king and established the dynasty. Solomon's succession is also attributed to God's sovereign choice. That Solomon would build the temple is part of the covenant. Solomon's kingdom has the potentiality of existing eternally.

David then closes with another challenge to faithfulness to God's covenant. Permanent possession of the "good land" (v. 8) is dependent upon keeping the laws of the covenant. Solomon's zeal in service must be complete since God knows the internal motives of the heart. The individual Davidic heir could be rejected if he disobeys God.

David now turns his plans over to Solomon (**28:11–21**). No detail is too trivial for David's concern. David attributes his planning to divine guidance (v. 19), and in recording the matter, the Chronicler confirms the inspiration and divine authority of these details. This, in effect, gives the details of the temple the same divinely ordained status as that possessed by the ritual prescriptions of Moses.

Solomon is challenged to complete these divinely ordained details. As in all other matters of covenant obedience, Solomon is to be "strong and courageous" (v. 20) in building the temple. God's faithfulness to Solomon will not fail. The national scope of the effort is again emphasized; the preparations have been made, and the officials and all the people will help Solomon in this great effort.

David describes his own gifts (**29:1–5**). Huge quantities of precious metals and building materials are involved. These goods point to the vast wealth of Solomon though David's gifts are preeminently spoils of war and tribute from subject states. Solomon's wealth, by contrast, includes more profits from peaceful trade. While there are difficulties in translating these figures into modern equivalents, by any measure they show the wealth that results when God makes his covenant king great and suggest that beauty, expense, and elegance are valid components of corporate worship.

The people follow David's example of lavish

giving (**29:6–9**). God's material blessings upon the covenant king extend also to the people.

David leads in corporate prayer by reciting a psalm (**29:10–20**). Its theme, the sovereignty of God, occurs frequently in Chronicles. Greatness, power, majesty, authority, and wealth; all these belong to God (vv. 11–12). This is the God whom David is praising and to whom David and the people give their offerings.

Having praised God with a psalm, David offers a prose commentary on the incongruity of feeble, insignificant men "giving" to an infinitely wealthy, powerful, sovereign God. The insignificance of man is stated in powerful, graphic language. David and the people are merely returning to God what is already his. David prays that deep sincerity in the people's ritual life will continue.

E. Solomon's accession to the throne (29:21–30). The acknowledgment of Solomon as king is a time of festivity and joy (**29:21–25**). The joy of being ruled by the covenant dynasty is another of Chronicles' recurrent themes. Almost as important for Chronicles is the fact that Zadok's claim to the high priesthood is confirmed. Since Solomon, at least in the beginning, is obedient to the covenant, God rewards Solomon with glory and splendor. God's blessings are for those kings who obey his covenant.

With David's death (**29:26–30**) we have reached one of the pivotal points both in world political history and in sacred history. From a political perspective, David was the man who took an insignificant, backwoods nation and built it into a powerful empire. Israel filled a power vacuum when the great powers were in eclipse. Men of that time must have asked if David's work and policies could continue after his death. Then, a pivotal point in the social development of ancient Israel can be defined. With the end of David's rule the Israelites were ready to leave behind their cultural conservatism and to enter fully into the international cultural and economic life of the ancient world. In religion and worship, the founder of the legitimate dynasty had died, but the influence of David and his legitimate heirs upon Hebrew ritual life had just begun. It is no exaggeration to say that ritual practice, as known to the Chronicler, owed more to David than to Moses.

OUTLINE—2 CHRONICLES

I. Greatness and Decline: Solomon to Abijah (1–13)
  A. Greatness: The Reign of Solomon (1–9)
  B. Decline: Rehoboam and Abijah (10–13)
II. Revival and Decline: Asa to Athaliah (14–22)
  A. Revival: Asa and Jehoshaphat (14:1–21:3)
  B. Decline: Jehoram, Ahaziah, and Athaliah (21:4–22:12)
III. Revival and Decline: Joash to Ahaz (23–28)
  A. Revival: Joash to Jotham (23–27)
  B. Decline: Ahaz (28)
IV. The Remaining Kings of Judah (29–36)
  A. The Reign of Hezekiah (29–32)
  B. The Reign of Manasseh (33:1–20)
  C. The Reign of Amon (33:21–25)
  D. The Reign of Josiah (34–35)
  E. The Last Days of Judah (36)

COMMENTARY

I. Greatness and Decline: Solomon to Abijah (1–13)

The impact of God's covenant blessings and judgments is clearly seen in the remaining history of Judah. Times of greatness come in response to and roughly coincide with the covenant obedience of the kings of Judah (David and Solomon; Jehoshaphat; and Uzziah). During the reigns of Jehoshaphat and Uzziah, the human means used by God to restore covenant blessings is the apostate northern kingdom. The wicked kings of the north bring peace and prosperity to Judah. In between these times of greatness, there are times of weakness which come in response to and roughly coincide with the covenant disobedience of the kings of Judah. The first period of decline extends to the end of the reign of Abijah.

A. Greatness: the reign of Solomon (1–9). Solomon rules from 970 to 931 B.C. World politics has not changed from the time of David. The major powers are still weak so that Israel continues to fill the power vacuum.

As the builder of the temple, Solomon is second only to David and Moses in importance to Israel's faith. Chronicles emphasizes, first, Solomon's covenant faithfulness, particularly his building of the temple, and, second, the glory with which God rewards his faithfulness.

After he is firmly established in power, Solomon leads the nation (represented by its leaders) in a ceremony at the shrine at Gibeon (**1:1–6**). The recurrent motif of a united national effort again appears. At this time Gibeon is still the great national shrine. The record in Chronicles minimizes the prestige of Gibeon by saying only as much as is necessary about the shrine: (1) the tabernacle is located there; (2) the original bronze altar is there; (3) both David and Solomon make appearances there; and (4) one of the two lines claiming the high priesthood ministers there.

That night God appears to Solomon and tells him to ask for whatever he wants. The offer that God makes to Solomon is a compliment to Solomon's character. Solomon recognizes that his standing comes from God's covenant promises (**1:7–17**). Solomon chooses wisdom (v. 10), a choice that reflects a profound transformation in society. Beginning with Solomon, the wise man could enjoy as much prestige as the violent warrior. A king could be as renowned for his wisdom as for his battlefield skills.

God's response confirms the worth of wisdom in biblical faith. Because Solomon asks for the greatest gift, wisdom, all the lesser gifts—wealth, riches, and honor—are given him as well. Some of the additional blessings with which God rewards Solomon are listed: military power, mercantile wealth, and even significant influence in the international arms trade in horses and chariots, the prestige weapon of the day.

Solomon's greatest religious contribution consists of building the temple and ratifying David's assignment of religious personnel to the temple. Temple preparations begin with registering the labor brigades (**2:1–2**). The identity in figures between these verses and verses 17 and 18 show that both are discussing the same group, the non-Hebrew or "alien" labor brigades.

The Chronicler emphasizes details relating to ritual for his record of Solomon's diplomatic negotiations with Tyre (**2:3–16**). The temple is not for God's benefit, since no temple can hold God; it is for God's people to use in ritual activities. Solomon then offers to trade wheat, barley, wine, and olive oil for lumber and technical expertise. No great, prestigious building of the ancient world was complete without cedar from Lebanon. Solomon's request for a Phoenician artisan to supervise the work on the temple recognizes Phoenician technical and artistic superiority.

Hiram's response is probably formulaic and written only out of respect to Solomon's religion, but the Chronicler uses it to reiterate God's blessing upon his people in giving them a wise, godly king. Hiram promises to send a skilled expert to supervise Solomon's craftsmen.

The building report rehearses the evidences for the sacredness of the site (**3:1–2**). The name *Moriah* recalls the divine presence with Abraham when he was sacrificing Isaac, and the text mentions the epiphany to David when the site still belonged to Araunah (1 Chron. 21:16).

The dimensions of the temple's foundations (ca. 90 × 30 ft. [v. 3]) indicate the size and, therefore, the glory of the temple (**3:3–7**). A comparison with 1 Kings 6:3 indicates that the portico was an additional 15 feet added onto the length above for a total length of 105 feet. The emphasis in verses 4b–7 is on the glorious wealth and artistic decorations of the temple. Gold overlay, intricate metal work, and precious jewels are featured. The "main hall" (v. 5) is the Holy Place. "Parvaim" (v. 6) is an unidentified geographic name.

The Holy of Holies, the "Most Holy Place," is not described in much detail (**3:8–13**). The text gives only its dimensions (30 × 30 ft.) and some description of the gold used in building it. The major emphasis here is upon the cherubim. Winged creatures were regular aspects of the glory and majesty of kings and deities in the ancient world. It is likely that the concept of glory is the main significance of the cherubim. They emphasize, by their mere presence, the glory of God.

The curtain (**3:14**) separates the Most Holy Place from less sacred areas. The two pillars (**3:15–17**) are an innovation. Their significance is the subject of much scholarly debate. Among the suggestions are that they are cosmological symbols of the pillars that hold up the sky, giant incense stands, symbols of God's presence, or dynastic symbols. The meanings of their names (Boaz, "in [his] strength"; Yakin, "he establishes") could support several different interpretations.

The temple furniture is described in chapter 4. The major items are detailed in **4:1–11a.** The bronze altar is discussed first. Compared to the temple altar, its size is striking: 30 feet in width and breadth as over against 7.5 feet for the tabernacle altar, and 15 feet high as over against 4.5 feet. It is clearly intended to accommodate many offerings simultaneously.

The dimensions of the bronze basin (15 × 45 ft.) are approximate at best. The two rows of engraved "bulls" (v. 3) just below the rim are probably a textual error for some other decoration (cf. 1 Kings 7:24). Twelve cast bulls serve as a stand for the basin. Its capacity is enormous; estimates range from 10,000 to 17,500 gallons.

There are ten basins for washing sacred implements, five on the north side of the court and five on the south. The increased demands for usage would explain the larger sizes and numbers seen thus far. The reasons for ten lampstands and ten tables for the bread of Presence (cf. 1 Chron. 28:16) in the Holy Place are not clear. The usage of these latter items is not related to the amount of traffic handled by the temple; in fact, the extra items would clutter up the simplicity of the earlier Holy Place.

The less sacred bronze work is attributed to Huram-Abi (**4:11b–18**). This list contains only objects outside the sanctuary proper. The temple's glory is reflected in their immeasurable bulk.

The more sacred and expensive gold work of the sanctuary is attributed to Solomon (**4:19–22**). Huram-Abi probably helped make these items as well, but the Chronicler may be reluctant to recognize Phoenician artistic contributions to the Holy Place.

The temple is completed in seven years (959 B.C.). Israel is at its zenith both religiously and politically. It is time to bring the remaining treasures and the ark into the temple. First David's gifts are brought to the temple treasuries (**5:1**; apparently rooms for the storage of wealth and relics belonging to the temple establishment). Then, the entire nation, through its representatives, participates in the installation of the ark in the temple (**5:2–13a**).

On the great day of atonement, the people gather to bring the ark to the temple. Though the ark is the center of attention, the Tent of Meeting together with its equipment is also brought to the new temple (v. 5). Apparently, the great shrine at Gibeon (1 Chron. 16:39) has been dismantled and the tabernacle is brought to Jerusalem at this time.

All the marks of a great religious occasion are present. Numerous sacrifices, music, and public praises herald the event. There is strict adherence to the ritual commands for the transport of the ark. The contents of the ark, the two tablets, are noted (v. 10). The container of manna and Aaron's rod are not mentioned; only the tables of the Law remain. The chant of praise (v. 13a) associates the "love" (Heb. *ḥesed;* KJV mercy) of God with the covenant.

The high point of this climactic day comes when the glory of God fills the temple (**5:13b–14**). God's glory is demonstrated in the cloud that fills the temple and the fire from heaven (7:1) which devours the dedicatory sacrifices. This recalls the glorious cloud in the original tabernacle (Exod. 40:34) and the fire from heaven which burned the dedicatory sacrifices of that time (Lev. 9:23–24).

Solomon contrasts the shining or fiery clouds that reveal God's glory and his approving presence (5:13–14; 7:1–2) with the dark clouds (Heb. *ʿărāpel*) that hide God's glory and transcendence and speak of judgment (**6:1–2**). Perhaps Solomon intends to contrast the bright clouds of glory which should fill God's dwelling-place with these concealing clouds.

Solomon's proclamation to the worshipers (**6:3–11**) links two great themes together as facets of the Davidic covenant: the holy city of Jerusalem and the holy temple building. Solomon acknowledges that God has finally chosen a permanent dwelling place for his Name. From the beginnings of the covenant, the symbol of God's presence has been portable. As one of the consequences of building a permanent dwelling for God's Name, the location of that building, Jerusalem, is now a holy city. Three great themes are united in this great effort prescribed by the Davidic covenant: the sacred dynasty, the sacred temple building, and the sacred city of Jerusalem. God's entrance is symbolized by bringing the ark into the temple.

The priests and Levites are the ritual representatives of the people before God. However, Solomon's dedicatory prayer dramatically demonstrates the king's responsibility as the people's moral representative before God. The prayer itself is one of the great theological statements of the Bible. At least two themes deserve attention: (1) the nature of God; and (2) the doctrine of forgiveness in response to penitent prayer. In addition, the prayer shows a striking openness to Gentiles.

The first attribute of God Solomon mentions is his covenant faithfulness (**6:14–17**). Once again, the covenant of love (Heb. *ḥesed*) is tied in with God's faithfulness. This faithfulness is what makes God unique.

Solomon next turns to a paradox which, in varying forms, has troubled many theologians: that between God's transcendence on the one hand and his interaction with mankind on the other (**6:18–21**). God is so great that he cannot live on earth with men. Does this mean that God is inattentive to man's prayers? Solomon prays that God will hear prayers directed toward the temple. He then catalogues those prayers which may be heard (**6:22–39**).

When a man wrongs his neighbor, God will hear and judge that man's oath. The foreign wars of Solomon and David made enslavement a reality. Yet no matter how far away such slaves are, they will never get beyond God's ear, God's forgiveness, and God's ability to restore. When natural disasters come, if God's people repent and pray, God will forgive them.

Verses 32–33 present the most striking and unexpected element of Solomon's prayer: that God should hear the prayers of the foreigner. In the Old Testament, God's clear intention was to use his chosen people as a means of blessing the Gentiles. However, God's people did not always understand his purposes. Here Solomon acknowledges that even Gentiles may pray toward God's temple and be heard.

When Israel's soldiers are involved in international efforts, far from home, God will still hear their prayers from such a distance.

Solomon's prayer even anticipates the most extreme covenant punishment, that of exile from the covenant land. In that extreme event, God's ear will still be open, a prayer of repentance will still be heard, and God will still forgive.

Solomon's poetic conclusion (**6:40–42**) reiterates his desire first, that God will hear these prayers and, second, that God will take up residence in his temple. Solomon prays that God will give salvation, joy, and kindness as promised to David in the covenant.

Solomon's prayer opens a time of festivity (**7:1–10**). God's presence in the temple is demonstrated by the miraculous fire and the glorious cloud. This produces a response of worship and confession (NIV thanks) from the people. The dedicatory festival includes the symbolic participation of the whole nation, sacrifices, music, and public confession.

Three of the four great Levitical sacrifices are mentioned (v. 7). The whole burnt offering stands for total dedication to God. The fellowship offerings symbolize communion with God and with one another. The grain offerings represent God's lordship over his people. The Hebrew word *minḥāh* (NIV grain offerings) has among its meanings the tribute given to a lord.

Several features underscore the greatness of the occasion: the large number of sacrifices, the detailed ritual description, and the full two weeks of celebration.

Somewhat later, God reappears to Solomon and confirms some significant promises (**7:11–22**). First, God assures Solomon that Jerusalem is the place he has chosen for the temple. God promises that he will respond to prayers of repentance, and will forgive the people's sin. God's Name will be in the temple forever. God's consciousness (NIV eyes) and love (NIV heart) will always be there.

The promises of the Davidic covenant are also reaffirmed. But, these promises depend upon obedience to God's law. David's dynasty will never lack for an heir. However, unfaithfulness will bring humiliation and shame to the temple. Even in view of the greatness and glory of the temple, the possibility that sin will reduce it to ruin and shame is noted. Referring to the "fathers" and to Egypt (v. 22) roots the occasion in the Abrahamic and the Mosaic covenants. The people's ultimate duty is faithfulness to their covenant God.

Chapters 8 and 9 summarize the secular accomplishments and policies of Solomon's reign. Though not the warrior that David was, Solomon is active in international military activities (**8:1–6**). He regains territories from Tyre by diplomacy. He conquers or reconquers Hamath, and apparently Tadmor as well. Solomon changes the army from a force that relies on premier infantry to a more conventional chariot force.

Fortifications and storage facilities are included in Solomon's efforts. Archaeology supports Scripture in revealing the extent of Solomon's garrison cities for his chariots. It is significant that the fortified cities mentioned here—Upper and Lower Beth Horon and Baalath (Kiriath-jearim?) (vv. 5–6)—all guarded potential invasion routes from Egypt.

Solomon conscripts "all" the remaining Canaanites into forced labor brigades (**8:7–10**). The Canaanites drafted for forced labor are probably those peoples who resisted conversion and persisted in maintaining their old Canaanite identity. Israelites are not put to forced labor levies (v. 9).

The holiness of the palace complex is emphasized in **8:11–16.** Solomon refuses to compromise the holy character of David's palace with a pagan wife. Verse 12 does not necessarily indicate that Solomon personally offers sacrifices. In respect to the temple, Solomon simply reaffirms all of the ritual practices required by both Moses and David. This includes confirming the status of the temple personnel, an important issue to the Chronicler.

Only one detail of Solomon's extensive sponsorship of international trade is mentioned here, the sea expeditions to Africa and south Arabia (**8:17–18**). Solomon apparently succeeds in making the Israelites, in alliance with the Phoenicians, the middlemen for north-south trade.

Chronicles illustrates all the facets of Solomon's glory in the queen of Sheba's visit (**9:1–12**): his wealth, his great wisdom, the luxury of his court, and his great fame. The queen declares the happiness of people ruled by an obedient covenant king who share in the covenant blessings. She also declares God's goodness in making Solomon king over the people. Like Hiram, she exchanges "gifts" with Solomon.

The Chronicler continues to describe Solomon's glory (**9:13–28**), implying that this is the way things should be when the covenant king is obedient to God. Solomon's trade wealth is described. The Chronicler details the expensive decorative armor made by Solomon. Solomon's magnificent throne shows his glory, as does his tableware.

Trade expeditions and tribute from the empire add to Solomon's wealth and glory. Horses and chariots in Solomon's army and the trade in these items enhance his military power and wealth. The empire itself is an evidence of Solomon's glory. Solomon's wisdom is renowned.

Yet God's blessings may become an oppressive burden. Solomon's wealth, power, and glory were from God; and there was the potential for even greater glory had he handled these gifts wisely. As it was, Solomon handled his power in such an oppressive way that the people asked to be released from its burden after his death (2 Chron. 10:10). After forty years of glory, mixed with failures not recorded by the Chronicler, Solomon dies. He is succeeded by his son, Rehoboam (**9:29–31**).

B. Decline: Rehoboam and Abijah (10–13). Having presented the piety and glory of Solomon, Chronicles now presents the failures of the first two kings of the southern kingdom. Their wickedness brings about a general decline in Judah's fortunes that lasts until the rule of Asa.

In Rehoboam's time (931–913 B.C.) the world political scene was changing. Shishak, founder of the twenty-second dynasty of Egypt, had reasserted Egypt's power and had already meddled in international affairs affecting Israel. Damascus, led by Rezon, had gained independence under Solomon. Other more distant "great nations" were not to trouble the Hebrews for another half a century.

The Chronicler's discussion of Solomon's reign is silent on a number of critical points. The internal tensions of the kingdom are completely ignored. Though they were tolerated because of his popularity, David's innovations often clashed with more conservative Hebrew ways. Both Absalom and Adonijah appeal to these conservative elements against David and Solomon respectively.

The people apparently feel they have a legitimate voice in the succession, forcing Rehoboam to meet with their leaders at Shechem (**10:1–5**). Jeroboam, recently returned from Egypt, is their spokesman. The people complain about the despotic, oppressive burden laid upon them by Solomon. The two counsels given to Rehoboam (**10:6–11**) reflect two opinions at court: the more conservative view which counsels moderation of despotic oppression and the new thinkers, used to luxury and power, who feel that they have a right to wield despotic authority. Rehoboam opts for his father's absolutism with the result that the northern tribes reject the Davidic dynasty and covenant (**10:12–17**). Chronicles offers yet another example of dual causality in human events. Men make choices, even free choices; but the event also is from God so that his will is accomplished. The rebellious northerners kill the king's official, and the king himself barely escapes.

The secular consequences of the rebellion are catastrophic. Israel's imperial power, fragile at best, collapses. With the disappearance of the empire, the power to dominate trade also disappears. Thus the wealth both of tribute and trade is gone, and relative poverty follows. Even native resources are weakened by internal divisions. In the balance between the two kingdoms, Judah is normally the weaker party.

The aftermath of the rebellion is described in **11:1–17.** The first event after the rebellion is Rehoboam's abortive attempt to reconquer the northern tribes. Hebrew theology, as expressed by Shemaiah (vv. 2–3), opposes civil war between the two kingdoms; besides, the division is expressly God's will. Avoidance of open war, however, does not prevent border skirmishes (see 12:15).

The treatment of Rehoboam is typical of the Chronicler's perspective; good can be seen in the bad kings, and bad in the good kings. Though he is a bad king, Chronicles still has some positive things to say about Rehoboam. For example, he rebuilds Judah's defensive fortifications. Also, priests and Levites from the northern kingdom join with Judah rather than adopt Jeroboam's false worship.

We now get a glimpse of palace politics during Rehoboam's reign (**11:18–23**). He strengthens ties within the larger family of David by marrying cousins. Perhaps the most important, and most prudent, step is his marriage with Maacah, a woman from Absalom's family (v. 20). This marriage unites, in the royal line, the two most significant branches of David, those of Solomon and Absalom. Absalom was probably Maacah's maternal grandfather (see 2 Sam. 18:18); thus there is no conflict with her being called the "daughter of Uriel" (13:1). Rehoboam's large harem and his asssignment of princes to administrative positions are typical royal policies and may even have been, in the popular perception, a manifestation of royal glory.

Chapter 12 records one of the great political events of the century, Shishak's great raid into Palestine (**12:1–12**). This event symbolizes, more than any other, the end of Hebrew political preeminence. It also marks the high point of a brief period of Egyptian resurgence. Theologically, the raid is seen as a direct consequence of Rehoboam's covenant disobedience.

The subject peoples in Shishak's army show the extent of resurgence of Egyptian power. From the Libyans in the north to the Ethiopians (i.e., Cushites) in the south, Egypt's subjects and allies are united in a powerful effort. The course of the invasion is best traced from the Egyptian record. Shishak's raid goes north into Israel and plunders both Judah and the strongpoints protecting the Negeb trade routes. The Negeb operations may have diverted the north-south trade routes back to Egyptian control. The plunder from this raid supports Shishak's governmental expenses and building operations.

For Chronicles, the important result of this raid is Rehoboam's repentance (vv. 6, 12). Because of this repentance, God does not permit Jerusalem to be destroyed though its treasures are taken to Egypt. The substitution of bronze shields for Solomon's gold shields graphically symbolizes the fading of Judah's glory.

Rehoboam is the first example in Chronicles showing that the apostasy of the king, the moral representative of the nation, brings disaster and poverty to the nation (**12:13–16**).

No great political changes occur during Abijah's rule (913–911 B.C.). Egypt is still strong, but not threatening permanent conquest. The Arameans pose the other threat.

In Abijah, the lines of Solomon and Absalom are united (**13:1–2a**) though Maacah from Absalom's family is a destructive influence (2 Chron. 15:16).

Chronicles' treatment of Abijah focuses on a single incident, a victorious battle with Israel (**13:2b–19**). In Kings this event is practically ignored and there is no mention of a great Judean victory. The Chronicler uses the story to accomplish several purposes.

Abijah's words, on the surface, seem to be godly. Yet however shallow they may have been, Abijah gives a strong statement of the divinely ordained status of the Davidic covenant (vv. 5–8). Abijah, naturally, reminds the northerners that God has established the Davidic dynasty and stresses their duty to be loyal to the Davidic heir. His challenge to faithful Jerusalem worship coincides completely with the Chronicler's interests. Abijah's challenge to the apostate Israelites could serve equally well for the Chronicler's charge to his readers.

Jeroboam is presented as the more able general and the one who deserves to win the battle. But God responds to Judah's faith, however insincere it may be, and gives the victory to Judah and Abijah. This victory is limited; Israel remains the stronger of the two kingdoms. With Abijah's death, a period of religious and secular decline ends, and a necessary revival begins.

II. Revival and Decline: Asa to Athaliah (14–22)

With Asa there begins another cycle of revival and greatness followed by sin and decline. The covenant faithfulness of the Davidic heir is the necessary prerequisite for restoration of covenant blessings.

A. Revival: Asa and Jehoshaphat (14:1–21:3). Asa (911–870 B.C.) does what is good and right before God. By this time David's empire is completely lost. Both Egypt and the Arameans are potential enemies; it will be some years before the Assyrians become a threat. Asa's reign initiates a time of religious and political revival. Religious revival is the crucial first step after which God will use the political might of the northern kings to revive political and economic prestige.

The Chronicler's treatment of Asa begins with a summary of his first ten years of peaceful rule (**14:1–6**). Asa is a good king. He removes the high places and the altars to foreign deities. He also destroys the sacred stone symbols of the Baals and the Asherah poles, the wooden symbols of female fertility deities. This gives him a claim to the covenant blessings promised by God. God immediately rewards Asa's faithfulness with a measure of peace, but the long-range covenant blessing is to be the restoration of Israel's wealth and international prestige under Ahab and Jehoshaphat.

The Chronicler uses an Egyptian invasion to illustrate the role of moral causality in history (**14:7–15**). The description of the Egyptians as Ethiopians (i.e., Cushites, v. 9) probably recalls the large number of Ethiopian mercenaries who served in the Egyptian army at this time, and the title *Ethiopian* (i.e., Cushite) for their leader may reflect only an honorific title similar to the English title *Prince of Wales*. To a military historian the three hundred Egyptian chariots (v. 9) puts the battle in historic perspective. It is a significant military effort, but not a major international war which would have involved thousands of chariots.

The Israelites win through prayer and divine intervention rather than through military preparations. The presence of a hostile population around Gerar (v. 14) may indicate that Shishak had created a small, anti-Hebrew puppet state in that region, perhaps in alliance with Bedouin herdsmen. Asa's victory probably restored the boundary to its traditional location along the "River of Egypt," the present-day Wadi el-Arish.

A second round of reforms (**15:1–19**) begins with Azariah's prophetic message. Azariah emphasizes the presence of God with his people when they search for him. This principle is illustrated by highlighting the international chaos during the time of the latter judges.

Several activities mark Asa's reforms: the suppression of idolatry; repair of the altar probably accompanied by the restoration of related rituals; renewal of the covenant between the people and God; and the deposition of the idolatrous queen mother Maacah.

This is the first covenant renewal ceremony since David's day. This renewal is identified as an act of the entire nation and as a time of great joy.

The removal of the high places is problematic; Asa is described both as removing them (14:2) and as not removing them (15:17). There were idolatrous high places and high places for illegal worship of Yahweh. It is possible that Asa removed the pagan high places but did not suppress the illegal worship of Yahweh at other high places.

Chronicles recognizes Asa's late life failures (**16:1–10**). In the sixteenth year (corrected from "thirty-sixth" in v. 1) of Asa's rule (ca. 895 B.C.) Baasha of Israel invades Judah and fortifies Ramah about five miles north of Jerusalem. Despite Judah's victory over the Egyptians, this event shows Judah's relative weakness. Asa is unable to cope with Baasha, and fails in faith. Like Ahaz a century and a half later, he voluntarily submits himself and his country to foreign lordship to gain deliverance. Judah becomes vassal to Damascus and sends the appropriate tribute partly plundered from the temple treasuries. The policy is successful: Israel is drawn away, Judah seizes large amounts of building materials, and the Arameans are unable to secure lordship over Judah. But Asa's lack of faith and his trust in human strength displease God; so Hanani the prophet condemns Asa.

There is one final failure: Asa does not seek God in his final illness. However, Asa is recognized as a good king and as a revered, respected leader.

Changes begin to take place in Jehoshaphat's (873–848 B.C.) world. The brief power of Egypt's twenty-second dynasty has passed. Already, in the last years of Asa's rule, Omri had reestablished Israel as an international power. The relationship between Judah and Israel is changing from one of confrontation to one of alliance and cooperation against the Arameans of Damascus. Also, although the Bible is silent on the subject, the Assyrian Empire has become a menace. We know from secular history that Omri's dynasty was the main force in resisting the Assyrians. The stage is being set for God to use the wicked kings of Israel as a sheltering umbrella to bring covenant blessings to the good kings of Judah.

A summary of Jehoshaphat's reign is given in **17:1–19.** Jehoshaphat continues his predecessors' policies of military preparedness. At the first, these are aimed against Israel. Jehoshaphat is obedient to the Davidic covenant and implements religious reforms. Thus he merits the blessings of the covenant. Perhaps chief among his religious policies is the renewing of the teaching of the Law. This is a step beyond Asa's religious reforms. The political resurgence begun with Omri in the north affects Judah in a practical way. Judah's share of the revived international power includes control over Philistia. In addition, new nomadic invaders, here called "Arabs" (v. 11), give allegiance to Jehoshaphat. The summary closes with further details of Jehoshaphat's revived military effort.

By this time, the cornerstone of Judah's foreign policy is the military alliance with Israel. God uses this alliance to restore the two nations to positions of wealth and international prestige. This alliance is sealed by a marriage between Ahab's daughter and Jehoshaphat's heir apparent (21:6).

But this alliance also brings Judah into closer contact with the religious apostasy of Israel. Omri had allied himself with It-Baal of Sidon and had arranged a marriage between his son, Ahab, and the Phoenician princess, Jezebel. This alliance had religious implications because Jezebel was fanatically loyal to Baal-Melqart (i.e., "Lord of the City"), the national god of the Phoenicians. Baal-Melqart's prestige was enhanced by the fact that the Phoenicians controlled some two-thirds of the seafaring trade of the Mediterranean of that day. Jehoshaphat had married his son to the worship of Baal-Melqart.

This is the setting for the joint campaign of Judah and Israel against the Arameans at Ramoth-gilead (**18:1–34**). Jehoshaphat is called upon to perform the duties of an ally. Jehoshaphat, demands, however, that they first seek the counsel of the Lord. Though Ahab has twice turned back the Assyrian armies from the region, and Jezebel represents the greatest maritime power in history to that point, Jehoshaphat repeats his request until it is honored.

By human standards the false prophets' assurances of victory (vv. 10–11) are well founded. Ahab is, apparently, superior in strength and power to the Arameans. After his ironic promise of victory, the true prophet Micaiah declares that there will be defeat. Micaiah attributes the false message of his opponents to a lying spirit sent from God himself. It is not clear whether Micaiah intends his description of the heavenly assembly (vv. 18–21) to be a literal description of a heavenly debate or if it is more like a parable suggesting that God is only indirectly responsible for the deceit.

When the battle comes, Ahab evades combat through a disguise, apparently thwarting God's purposes. However, a purely fortuitous event undoes all of Ahab's plans. An archer draws his bow, purely by chance, and hits Ahab. Ahab's steadfast military resolve is powerfully shown by the dying king standing in his chariot directing the battle until his death. From a secular, political perspective, this was the death of a great military man, but a great man who lived his life outside the will and purposes of God.

In this account the Chronicler shows God's sovereign control over Ahab and his allies. He upholds the truth of God over against the message of the false prophets. He demonstrates that even the king whose military might was exploited to bring the covenant blessings to Judah is subject to God's judgment for his wickedness.

The Lord's rebuke for Jehoshaphat's alliance with Ahab comes from Jehu, the son of Hanani (**19:1–3**). The rebuke seems harsh because, humanly speaking, this alliance is the cornerstone of Judah's renewed prosperity and power. Perhaps the word *love* (v. 2) is the key. Limited cooperation with Israel might have been acceptable, but a diplomatic marriage with Israel's idolatry is not. Or, perhaps the prophet intends to condemn any cooperation whatsoever with Ahab.

Jehoshaphat takes personal initiative in leading the countryside to revival (**19:4–11**). Jehoshaphat's royal judges either replace or supplement the courts of elders at the city gates (v. 5). He also delegates authority to Levitical judges who interpret the law of God. An increasingly centralized and mercantile society demands a greater consistency and centralization in the interpretation of laws. Jehoshaphat exhorts his officials first, to remember that they represent God, not the state (v. 6), and, second, to warn the people not to sin (v. 10).

The war with the East Jordanian alliance (**20:1–30**) provides yet another example of a military victory totally dependent upon God's miraculous intervention. This intervention is the direct result of the piety of the nation.

The identity of Jehoshaphat's enemies is unclear. The New International Version judges the geographic references to the Dead (?) Sea and to En-gedi and the ethnic associations of verse 22 as good reason to understand the "Aramaeans" (v. 2) as a textual error for "Edom." However, Ammonites, Moabites, and Edomites combined could not have raised an army as formidable as the one here. The New International Version also accepts the Septuagint reading of "Meunites" (v. 1). If correct, this establishes a link with desert Bedouin. From this we may conclude that the Moabites, Ammonites, and Edomites had enlisted the help of Bedouin Meunites for a well-planned, sudden, massive raid against Judah.

The sequel of this raid follows the usual pattern for Chronicles: the people respond with religious piety; their representatives and leaders gather to fast and pray. Jehoshaphat, as the Davidic representative of the nation, leads in prayer. He acknowledges that God is sovereign, and has given the land to his people. Therefore, they can expect God to deliver them from distress especially if they pray toward the temple. Jehoshaphat then commits the enemy to God.

The people are told not to fear or be discouraged. God will miraculously destroy the enemy; Israel will not have to fight this battle. The people respond with praise and worship focused upon God's covenant love. The enemy is destroyed by divinely aroused internal dissent and squabbling. The Hebrews collect the booty and praise God for the deliverance. That the nations should fear as a result of hearing of this great deed is standard Old Testament theology.

The end of Jehoshaphat's reign is summarized in **20:31–21:3.** Jehoshaphat is said to be a good king though he did not remove the high places (most likely illegal shrines to Yahweh). His abortive mercantile alliance with Israel for trade out of Ezion-geber is condemned, and the ships are destroyed. Jehoshaphat lived honorably and is appropriately buried in the family burial vaults (21:1). Like most of his predecessors, he had used his sons as administrative personnel in the kingdom as well as bequeathing them a certain amount of cash resources.

B. Decline: Jehoram, Ahaziah, and Athaliah

(21:4–22:12). Jehoram's succession to sole authority (848 B.C.) initiates thirteen years of completely wicked rule. The resulting period of political and economic weakness for the two kingdoms lasts much longer. Although the religious revival begins in approximately 835 B.C., the revival in secular fortunes is delayed until the rule of Jehoash of Israel (798 B.C.).

Jehoram (853–841 B.C., including co-regency) is the first king for whom the Chronicler has nothing good to say (**21:4–20**). He begins with fratricidal murder to secure his position. His marriage brings the cult of Baal-Melqart to Judah. He reestablishes the high places and leads Judah into religious unfaithfulness. Only God's loyalty to the Davidic covenant keeps Jehoram alive.

Judah's political influence completely crumbles. Edom and Libnah successfully rebel against Judah. The Philistines and the Bedouin Arab allies of the Egyptians (i.e., Cushites) in the south attack Judah with disastrous consequences, including the deaths of most of the royal males. In the north the collapse is slower; the Assyrians are kept at a distance though the balance of power between Israel and Damascus constantly shifts in favor of Damascus.

God's condemnation is stated in a letter from Elijah. Jehoram has abandoned the ways of his father and grandfather; therefore judgment will come. Jehoram dies a painful, unpleasant death.

The people make Ahaziah king (841 B.C.), an act of loyalty to the Davidic covenant (**22:1–9**). His older brothers had been killed by Bedouin raiders (v. 1; 21:17). There is poetic justice in the fact that Jehoram, who murdered all but one of another man's sons, had all but one of his sons murdered. Ahaziah follows the ways of Ahab. Particularly, he supports the worship of Baal-Melqart in Judah. He continues the political alliance with Israel.

Chronicles emphasizes God's all-pervasive sovereignty in noting that God uses Ahaziah's friendship with Joram of Israel to bring about his death. Jehu kills several members of the Judean royal family along with Joram of Israel; it is a great religious irony that the heir of the covenant dynasty dies in God's judgment on the devotees of Baal-Melqart.

The reign of Athaliah (841–835 B.C.), the queen mother of Judah and the daughter of Jezebel, is one of the two lowest points in the history of Davidic rule (**22:10–12**). Her purge of the royal family marks the third time that the royal family has been reduced to a single remaining heir. The fact that the Davidic line survives demonstrates God's covenantal faithfulness (21:7).

III. Revival and Decline: Joash to Ahaz (23–28)

A. Revival: Joash to Jotham (23–27). Religious revival begins with Joash, or perhaps better, with his great teacher, Jehoiada, the high priest. However, since the revival under Joash is, at best, halfhearted, it is not surprising that the full restoration of blessings promised by the covenant comes later, during the reigns of Amaziah and Uzziah.

Historically, Assyria had faded out of the picture due to political weakness; the Arameans had reduced the Hebrews to abject servitude. But then, when political resurgence finally comes with the rule of Joash of Israel, the combined power of the two kingdoms rivals the glory and prestige of David and Solomon.

During his reign (835–796 B.C.), Joash had to struggle with idolatry, political weakness, and religious shallowness; besides, he ruled in a discouraging time. The accounts of Joash's rule are striking for the large number of seeming contradictions between the records in Kings and Chronicles. Harmonizing these alleged discrepancies is the proper task of a longer critical commentary.

Jehoiada's wisdom is demonstrated in his careful preparations for the revolt against Athaliah (**23:1–7**). He institutes long-range, nationwide plans as well as careful, immediate plans for the revolution. The basis for the revolution is the Davidic covenant.

Jehoiada is ready to use whatever force is needed. There are times when good men should use force in accomplishing good purposes. It is unlikely that the temple weapons (v. 9) were essential for practical use as weapons. Jehoiada's preparations certainly included more extensive provision of weapons. They were probably far more important as symbols of legitimacy for the young Davidic heir.

Joash is recognized as king by a covenant between him and the people and by a coronation ceremony also involving a covenant (**23:8–21**). This second covenant was likely the king's copy of the Mosaic covenant (see Deut. 17:18). The coronation has all the trappings of a major worship occasion: musical instruments, singing, and praises.

The old order fostered by Athaliah has to be obliterated, beginning with Athaliah herself. The way Athaliah is killed shows the contempt of orthodox Yahwism for the worship of Baal-Melqart. Her death is not to pollute the temple. The covenant is renewed, though the statement of renewal is strikingly brief (v. 16). Covenant renewal demands that exclusive faithfulness to Yahweh be strongly affirmed. Baalism is purged from the city, and, presumably, proper worship in all its details is reestablished. Tracing proper worship back to both David and Moses (v. 18) shows the importance of David as a founder of ritual. Finally, the official national enthronement is carried out, and the nightmare of Athaliah is over.

In summary, the Chronicler reaffirms that Joash was a good king, but only as long as Jehoiada lived (**24:1–3**). This illustrates two emphases in Chronicles: (1) the moral inconsistency of Israel's kings; and (2) the importance, at least in this example, of the priestly contribution to the moral life of the people.

The Chronicler frankly acknowledges the king's initiative and steadfastness in the restoration of the temple (**24:4–14**). Nor does he fail to indicate the hesitant cooperation of the priests, even of Jehoiada, in implementing the king's plans. Their hesitation is understandable if, as some suggest, the king was imposing on the priesthood a burden formerly carried by the royal treasury. Finally, the king himself dictates the execution of the project, money is raised, and the work is done. Even in this time of weakness, there is sufficient money to equip the temple with gold and silver implements.

Joash's later wickedness contrasts sharply with the greatness of Jehoiada (**24:15–22**). Burial in the vicinity of the royal tombs (not necessarily in one of them) shows his stature.

Two disappointments coincide with Jehoiada's death. Then, as later under Hezekiah, Yahwistic revival and reform is sometimes a thin, orthodox veneer over a deeply rooted, popular paganism. Isaiah well describes this popular paganism and its consequences (Isa. 6:9–13). Though the people had opposed the foreign paganism of Baal-Melqart, the leaders request the revival of local paganism. The king quickly grants their wish.

Zechariah's condemnation features two basic covenant themes: (1) the duty to obey God's commands; and (2) the loss of prosperity because of unfaithfulness to the covenant. Joash's murder of the son of his benefactor shows the depravity latent even in a godly king.

The end of Joash's reign is detailed in **24:23–27.** Though the revival began with Joash, it is only partial; and it is not strange that the full return of God's blessing does not yet come. In fact, the Aramean plundering raid may mark Judah's low point in political fortunes. Damascus reaches its zenith and subdues and plunders both Israel and Judah. Joash's compromises do not make everyone happy, and he is assassinated. Perhaps the fact that the king who followed the "pagan" party in the kingdom was murdered by another party reflects the fragmented political life of a nation which had lost its moorings in the covenant and in the will of God.

Amaziah rules from 796 to 768 B.C., part of the time with Uzziah as co-regent. Despite Amaziah's failures, the political and economic resurgence, warranted by religious revival, finally comes during his reign. His rule coincides with the brilliant rebuilding of Israel's power, prestige, and wealth under the leadership of Jehoash (798–782 B.C.). Amaziah is another example of a good king whose life ends in serious failure.

Amaziah is a good king. For example, he obeys God's law in dealing with his father's assassins (**25:3–4**). Such obedience on the part of the Davidic heir normally should have gained God's covenant blessings for the nation.

Like most of the good kings of Judah, Amaziah strengthens the country's army. He adds to his mobilization of Judean manpower by recruiting mercenaries from Israel, an act which an anonymous prophet condemns (vv. 7–8). Amaziah's sin seems to be his failure to trust in God's normal provision of resources. These resources, used in a godly manner, should have been sufficient for the defense of God's covenant people. Amaziah heeds the prophet and the Israelite mercenaries are sent home though they plunder northern Judah on their way.

Amaziah's victory over Edom (**25:11–16**) reflects renewed imperialism. In the north, Jehoash of Israel is conquering the Arameans. The brutality of casting the prisoners from a cliff (the great rock at Petra, v. 12) was typical in ancient warfare. However, the amazing feature of this victory is that the man who won in the power of God goes home and worships the gods which could not bring victory to his conquered enemies. This is too strange to have been a fictional invention. Had the Chronicler been engaged in fictional creativity, he could have done better. This sin brings a prophesy of Amaziah's doom.

A minor success, isolated from fellowship with God, can lead to arrogance. Amaziah challenges the successful and competent Jehoash of Israel to battle. Jehoash's response well describes the general balance of power between the two kingdoms; Israel is almost always the stronger of the two. This event illustrates once more God's control over human events; men think they are in control, but God is working his sovereign will. The result is totally disastrous to Judah (**25:17–24**). Just as the nation shared the blessings brought by the righteousness of the Davidic king, here, the army, the holy city, and the temple all share the sinful king's humiliation.

The apostasy of the king contributes to the internal faction and intrigue that weakens Judah (**25:25–28**). Amaziah, like his father, dies at the hands of assassins. In a political situation so full of violence, the remarkable survival of the Davidic dynasty can be attributed only to God's providential care.

The reigns of Uzziah of Judah (792–740 B.C. including co-regencies; 767–750 B.C. sole rule) and Jeroboam II of Israel mark the full flowering of the resurgence of Hebrew life. The Arameans had been crushed between the Hebrews and Assyria. Assyria was once again powerful and threatening the region but, though the Bible is silent on the subject, the Hebrews were an important part of the coalition that held Assyria back. There is some evidence that, after the death of Jeroboam II, Uzziah led the anti-Assyrian alliance for one campaign. Amos, and possibly Jonah, carried out their ministries at this time.

Uzziah likely began his rule as co-regent while Amaziah was alive but disgraced by religious and political failures. Uzziah is a good king—at least during the life of his godly advisor (**26:1–5**). Like his predecessors he begins well and ends poorly, though his failure is not so grievous.

Three important features of Uzziah's military policies are evident (**26:6–15**). First, Uzziah shares with Israel in the success of renewed imperialism. In covenant theology these successes mark God's blessings upon the obedient Davidic dynasty. Judah's sphere of influence includes Philistia, the Arab Bedouin in the south, some related Meunites, and Ammon. Hebrew activities in Elath are predicated upon military successes in that area as well.

Second, Uzziah supports a program of building fortifications. Unlike earlier kings who defended the Judean heartland, Uzziah extends his fortifications and other influences to the very fringes of Judea, building defensive towers in the desert some distance from the heartland of Judah.

Third, Uzziah institutes a program of manpower development and acquisition of the most up-to-date implements of war. His efforts result in great international fame—another of the covenant blessings promised to the obedient Davidic heir (cf. 1 Chron. 17:8).

Uzziah's reign ends in tragedy (**26:16–23**). His sin was his attempt to intrude into the priest's duties (vv. 16–18). Because of his "priestly" perspective, we would expect the Chronicler to be sensitive to this fault. The consequent leprosy (v. 20) seems to have excluded Uzziah from governmental functions until his death.

Jotham (**27:1–9**) holds or shares power over Judah from 750 to 732 B.C. These were years of drastic political realignment. The two great pillars of resistance against Assyria, Jeroboam II and Uzziah, were gone; and Assyrian power would move on, almost without resistance. Though Judah held on to some regional political influence, Israel had degenerated into civil war and weakness.

Unlike his three predecessors, Jotham is a good king who does not end up badly. He retains a measure of power though the general fate of the two Hebrew kingdoms was dismal. His imperialism, though limited in scope, is still successful. He too, engages in the building of fortifications.

But there is a serious flaw in his reign. The people do not follow his lead; religious revival does not overcome widespread popular paganism. Up to this point, the general perspective of Chronicles has been that the character of the king determines the moral judgment on the people. Here we see a divergence between the king's godliness and the popular apostasy of the people, a distinction that, later, could permit anticipating judgment despite the good qualities of a good king (cf. 2 Chron. 34:37–38). We may be confident that, had both the kings and the people been faithful, God could have brought covenant blessings—power, wealth, and fame—even out of the very difficult circumstances facing Jotham's successors. But an inconsistent throne and a consistently apostate populace guarantee judgment.

B. Decline: Ahaz (28). Ahaz begins his sole rule in 732 B.C. and rules until 716 B.C. The Hebrews by this time had been reduced to complete impotence before the Assyrians. Moral decadence had so dissipated the nation's inner resources (see Isa. 5) that there was no strength left with which to resist the Assyrians.

Ahaz is a bad king (**28:1–4**). The description of his offenses is long even for a wicked king (vv. 2–4). His "Baals" were the local fertility deities of Palestine rather than Jezebel's Baal-Melqart. The depth of his apostasy is demonstrated in the sacrificing of his own sons.

When the Syro-Ephraimite war (**28:5–15**) occurs, Ahaz is co-regent and has to deal with the crisis. This war was a pivotal event in the international politics of that day. Apparently Israel and Damascus wished to revive the old Hebrew-Aramean coalition that had been so successful against the Assyrians in the past. They invaded Judah to force Judah into the coalition; but Ahaz voluntarily submitted to Assyria in order to gain help. The Edomite and Philistine invasions also seem to have occurred in this context though the Chronicler treats them as a separate topic. The war has several long-range consequences. There is a brutal devastation of the Judean countryside. The entire region becomes part of the Assyrian Empire, Judah voluntarily and Israel and Damascus by conquest. There is a devastating impact upon Hebrew religious life. Any Assyrian vassal was expected to exchange cultic symbols which, when placed in the two temples, symbolized the religious subjection of the vassal's gods to the great god Asshur.

The Chronicler's theological perspective is clear in the passage. The disaster occurs only because of sin. The solution is not human political might as Ahaz mistakenly thought in seeking Assyrian help. The proper solution is piety, expressed by repentance and prayer (see 2 Chron. 20:4–19). The impact of the northern invasion is lessened by divine intervention; the prophet Obed condemns the invaders for the extent of their brutality, and the captives are released. God controls events in bringing judgment; and he further dominates events in mitigating the horrible consequences of the judgment.

Ahaz's appeal to Assyria for help only brings more misery (**28:16–21**). "At that time" (v. 16) could be taken in the sense of "during" the time of the events just described. These events were concurrent with the events described, not subsequent to them. Other evidences of the collapse of Hebrew power are obvious.

Three elements mark the worst of Ahaz's apostasy (**28:22–25**). First, he transfers his public religious loyalties to the pagan deities of Damascus (v. 23; cf. 2 Kings 16:15). Second, the underlying popular paganism of the people seems to have burst out in the "altars at every street corner" (v. 24b). Third, the routine submission to Assyrian cult demanded of any subject of the Assyrian Empire normally involved religious compromises that symbolized the submission of the local deities to Asshur, the national deity of Assyria. Add to this the closing of the temple and we have the gloomy picture of religious life under Ahaz. With his death, Judah reaches one of its lowest points religiously and politically.

IV. The Remaining Kings of Judah (29–36)

There are no more revivals of Hebrew wealth, power, and prestige in the Old Testament period. There are brief religious revivals under Hezekiah and Josiah, but even these are, for the most part, affairs of the royal house and the religious personnel loyal to the covenant. In general, the popular paganism of the people is untouched by these reforms so that their effect is only to delay the inevitable judgment rather than to restore covenant greatness (Isa. 6:11–13).

A. The reign of Hezekiah (29–32). Hezekiah's sole rule begins in 715 B.C. and continues to 686 B.C. He is a good king and is compared with David (**29:1–2**). The cornerstone of Hezekiah's policies is his religious reforms. The amount of coverage given to them shows this period to be second in importance only to the times of David and Solomon for the Chronicler. David and Solomon established the temple ritual. However, the rituals and offices as traced through Hezekiah become the legitimate expressions of the institutions founded by David and Solomon. Legitimate ritual is given especially strong historical confirmation by the miraculous deliverance of Jerusalem under Hezekiah's rule.

Opening the temple doors provides the occasion for challenging the temple personnel to reopen and cleanse the temple (**29:3–11**). In his challenge Hezekiah acknowledges that the nation had disobeyed the covenant and neglected proper ritual. This unfaithfulness had produced the disasters suffered by the people. Hezekiah states his intention to renew the covenant. Confirming the hereditary prerogatives of the ritual personnel is a significant step in reform.

The temple is purified following Hezekiah's challenge (**29:12–19**). The status of families in the future cult is confirmed by their being listed here. All three great divisions of Levi—the Kohathites, the Merarites, and the Gershonites (v. 12)—are represented in the purifying of the temple as well as three of the families in the temple courses, those of Asaph, Heman, and Jeduthun (vv. 13–14). The specific highlighting of the Kohathite descendants of Elizaphan is probably due to the fact that their hereditary responsibility was the implements of the Holy Place and of the Holy of Holies (Num. 3:30–31).

The removal of the rubble and impurities found in the temple takes sixteen days (v. 17), partly because the whole operation has to be done with the proper religious ritual.

With the temple cleansed, it is time to restore proper ritual (**29:20–36**). The reestablishment of formal worship begins with sin offerings. Forgiveness of offenses against God is the foundational truth with which religious life must begin. The king clearly commands the priests to offer sacrifices, and does not share in this priestly ministry. Hezekiah's commands specifically authenticate musical worship.

Next are the whole burnt offerings symbolizing the total dedication of the worshiper to God. This too is accompanied by prescribed musical routines. Then a place is made for the "thank" offerings and other voluntary offerings. These are either voluntary whole burnt offerings or voluntary fellowship (KJV peace) offerings. The numbers of offerings show the importance of this occasion.

Finally, though they merit only brief mention, there are the many fellowship offerings that serve as the main basis for a great national fellowship meal. Forgiveness and dedication have restored the proper fellowship between God and his people. One other offering, though not mentioned, is clearly there. Some, if not all, fellowship offerings by prescription are accompanied by grain offerings (Lev. 7:12–13). This offering, as its Hebrew name, *minḥāh,* a word used for the tribute given to a master, might suggest, signifies God's lordship over his people.

The entire city of Jerusalem had shared in the rededication of the temple. Now it is time to bring the entire nation into the renewal of religious life by resuming the celebration of the Passover.

All Hebrews, Judah and Israel, are invited to the Passover with an emphasis upon Ephraim and Manasseh, the remnants of Israel left by the Assyrian deportations (**30:1–12**). Hezekiah and his advisors show flexibility in delaying the Passover a month so that preparations can be completed.

Several central theological motifs are recalled in Hezekiah's proclamation (vv. 6–9): the origins of the covenant in the time of the patriarchs, the restoration of fellowship with God so he could restore his presence with them, the notion that judgment comes because of covenant unfaithfulness, the single place of worship, and the concept of God's gracious restoration—even from captivity—after repentance. This last item is especially powerful to the Chronicler who is a witness to the historical fact of such a restoration.

The general response of the north is rejection and mockery of God's covenant, but a remnant chooses to share in the proper worship and to come back under the covenant. The usage of specific tribal names implies that some Hebrews in the north still retain tribal identity even after all their misfortunes. Though the south responds, the general spiritual state of Judah is not one of deep, soul-renewing revival.

Why does the general purification of Jerusalem wait until this point (**30:13–14**)? There was opportunity earlier. Perhaps the popular apostasy was so strong that the city could not be purged until nationwide support for revival had come about. This is compatible with Isaiah's description of the corruption of the people (Isa. 6:8–13).

The celebration of the Passover (**30:15–22**) emphasizes the sincerity of the religious personnel. The priests and Levites purify themselves in genuine shame, not just in ritual fulfillment. There is a sensible compromise with the requirements of legalistic ritual in allowing those who are ceremonially unclean to participate. Although Uzzah earlier died because of a ritual lapse (1 Chron. 13:10), ritual strictness is here attenuated, perhaps as a result of circumstances and sincere prayer. Once again the restoration of proper ritual is an occasion of great national joy.

What better way to show the enthusiasm of the new covenant loyalty than by the people's desire for a second week of festivity (**30:23–27**)? The fact that even "aliens" from both Israel and Judah (v. 25) join in the ritual shows a commendable openness to foreigners. This is the greatest Passover since the time of Solomon, a fact which strengthens the legitimacy of the ritual confirmed by this occasion. The final note, that "God heard," takes us back to the importance of the prayer of repentance voiced in Solomon's dedicatory prayer for the temple. In hearing, God simply does what he had promised to do according to the covenant (2 Chron. 7:14).

The Passover is followed by religious reforms in the countryside (**31:1**). However, this general destruction of idolatrous symbols is more a matter of momentum and royal initiative than a society-transforming revival. The sacred stones often represented male fertility deities, the Asherah poles represented the female fertility deities. "High places" and "altars" could have included both idolatrous installations and illegal shrines for Yahweh.

Two of the most important concerns for hereditary, cultic officials were the legitimacy of their positions and their financial support. Hezekiah's reforms touch on both (**31:2–19**). The priestly divisions and orders are reassigned so that the hereditary rights of the various priestly and Levite orders are once again confirmed.

The regular offerings for the support of the religious orders are reestablished. The king sets an example and all the people join in giving tithes. The administrative offices involved in economic administration of the temple are important for the financial support of the religious orders. The specific listing of individuals serves to fix once more the hereditary hold of their families on these offices. Hezekiah also reaffirms the distribution of resources to the religious bureaucracy throughout the entire country. In his religious reforms (**31:20–21**), Hezekiah does what is "good and right," including careful attention to ritual matters as well as moral issues. Faithfulness to the covenant demands attention to both.

After Hezekiah's reforms, Sennacherib threatens Jerusalem. Scholars argue about whether Sennacherib invaded Judah once or twice. For purposes of discussion, we will assume one invasion in 701 B.C. This invasion devastates Judah. The theological focus is the miraculous protection of Jerusalem from the mighty Assyrians. This deliverance is a powerful historical confirmation of the Chronicler's theology. The authority for cult came from Moses, David and Solomon, Hezekiah, and finally, Josiah. But the most important single historical confirmation of that authority is the miraculous deliverance of Jerusalem in Hezekiah's time. This miraculous event gives historical confirmation of the validity of the covenant city, the covenant itself, and the ritual worship based upon that covenant.

Hezekiah's preparations for war (**32:1–8**) include assuring the water supply of Jerusalem with the Siloam tunnel, repairing fortifications in Jerusalem, and organizing the people for the defense of the city. Hezekiah's affirmation that God is with Jerusalem, the covenant city, places the legitimacy of Hebrew religion on the line in the struggle with Assyria.

While besieging Lachish, Sennacherib sends an embassy to Jerusalem. This incident provides a paradigm of man's arrogant boasting of his political might contrasted with God's sovereign control over the earth (**32:9–19**). Sennacherib's officers in charge of psychological warfare present the human perspective of the Assyrian high command. They belittle faith in God's care and deliverance. As interpreted by the Assyrians, Hezekiah's removal of the illegal altars of Yahweh outside Jerusalem is an offense against the God of the Hebrews; therefore even the Hebrews' own God had requested that the Assyrians punish Hezekiah (Isa. 36:10). Thus, an act of obedience is cleverly turned into a fault by the Assyrian propagandist. According to the Assyrian, the gods of all the nations are helpless before Assyria, and Asshur, their god. This contrasts with the absolute superiority of God in the Chronicler's covenant theology. This further emphasizes the struggle between the truth of the Chronicler's faith and the might of Assyria.

The godly response is to continue to trust in the God of Jerusalem and the covenant. Considering the greatness of the issue, the record of this event is quite short (**32:20–23**). By combining biblical and secular historical evidences, we may conclude that a miraculous bubonic plague decimated the Assyrian army. Not only did Jerusalem stand, but the king of Assyria is assassinated after he reaches home, though the assassination occurs some years later. God's power and the legitimacy of Hebrew religion are completely vindicated. Just as promised in the covenant (1 Chron. 17:8), God exalts the obedient, Davidic heir.

The Chronicler presents his own theological interpretation of several other events in Hezekiah's career (**32:24–31**). Hezekiah's healing produces pride (vv. 24–26). The exact content of the pride is unclear, but repentance is necessary to delay judgment. The Chronicler emphasizes Hezekiah's rebuilding of wealth after the Assyrian invasion. It is true that God does reward Hezekiah's piety with some prosperity; but it is also true that the land has long-term scars and pockets of economic loss from that invasion. Chronicles uses the coming of the Babylonian ambassadors to illustrate that God's blessings should not lead to sinful presumption.

From a purely human perspective, Hezekiah's rule is a political and economic disaster. Even in religion, popular paganism is merely suppressed, not destroyed. However, on the other side, the deliverance of Jerusalem may have been the indispensable historical step in affirming postexilic faith.

B. The reign of Manasseh (33:1–20). Manasseh assumes sole authority in 686 B.C. and rules until 643 B.C. He witnesses the height of Assyrian power, joins Ashurbanipal of Assyria in his invasion of Egypt, and, finally, catches faint hints of the coming Assyrian collapse.

It is hard to find a religious principle which Manasseh did not violate (**33:1–9**). His religious apostasy offers something for everyone except orthodox worshipers of Yahweh. For the nonorthodox Yahwists, he allows the rebuilding of the high places. For the devotees of the ancient local fertility cults, he rebuilds the religious centers of Baal and his fertility consorts. He builds altars to the deities identified with heavenly bodies. He revives the cult of Molech, passing his own sons through the fire. This probably refers to infant sacrifice, though some have argued that it could refer to dedicating a son as a male cultic prostitute. Manasseh's participation in occultism and popular superstition raises such vices to respectability. It is most probable that the Assyrians renewed their standard demand that cultic symbols of Asshur be placed in the temple.

Manasseh's evil is distinctly linked to covenant disobedience. His images and altar pollute the place where God's Name should dwell (vv. 4, 7) and thus he forfeits God's promise that the Hebrews would not be taken from their land. If God's people are even worse than their pagan predecessors, how could they avoid judgment?

Disregarding God's warnings brings judgment. However, the prayer of repentance even of someone as wicked as Manasseh is heard just as God had promised (**33:10–18**; 2 Chron. 6:36–39). Manasseh's imprisonment and restoration are in keeping with occasional Assyrian imperial policy. Neco of Egypt also was thus imprisoned and restored. This act of mercy gained the permanent loyalty of Neco's dynasty.

Manasseh's reforms are insignificant enough that the writer of Kings completely disregards them. Probably, as Assyrian power waned in the latter part of Manasseh's rule, he did enter into a mild suppression of paganism in Jerusalem; but this had little, if any, permanent effect. It is clear from the next two chapters that the regular ritual, at best, is left in a state of "benign neglect."

C. The reign of Amon (33:21–25). Amon's rule (643–641 B.C.) is no more than an extension of his father's evil. As the spiritual life of the people declines, and the partisan strife in Jerusalem increases, assassination serves as a tool for political change.

D. The reign of Josiah (34–35). Josiah rules from 641 to 609 B.C. He witnesses and perhaps even assists in the collapse of the Assyrian state. This leaves a power vacuum in the west which both Josiah and Egypt attempt to fill. Nahum, Habakkuk, Zephaniah, and Jeremiah minister during his reign. For the Chronicler Josiah's reforms and limited success, despite his political weakness, confirm legitimate worship.

Josiah's religious policies mark him as a good king (**34:1–7**). His age at the beginning of his reforms (sixteen years [v. 3]) suggests that godly counselors influenced his work. He reverses the pagan policies of his father and grandfather. The profaning of the cultic installations by scattering their rubble over graves and by profaning the bones of their buried priests is an unusual practice.

The extension of Josiah's reforms into Israel "as far as Naphtali" (v. 6) may reflect an attempt to extend his power northward to fill the power vacuum in Palestine.

It is a measure of the ignorance of Josiah and his teachers that it takes ten years for this king, who is seeking God's will, to realize that he needs to restore the temple and its worship (**34:8–13**). In the eighteenth year of Josiah's rule, restoration of the temple and worship begins. The prominence of the Levites in this work is a small recognition of correct ritual.

In the process of restoring the temple, a copy of the law of Moses is discovered (**34:14–17**). Scholars often argue that the law had been so suppressed that everyone was completely ignorant of it. But something must have motivated the reforms that had already taken place. It is also possible that the nation had retained a general recollection of the righteousness demanded by the law. In this case, the discovery of a very old, obviously authentic copy of the covenant may have added a new authenticity and seriousness to religious concepts which, while vaguely known, needed to be taken more seriously. The king's repentance and grief upon realizing the consequences of sin (**34:18–21**) shows the Davidic heir as representing the people also in this great act of repentance.

It is striking that the Chronicler records that Josiah consults a prophet rather than any ritual means for seeking God (**34:22–28**). God's word is bleak; the people are now so corrupted that God cannot accept the king's repentance as equivalent to the people's repentance. The Davidic heir's piety only delays rather than completely averts judgment.

Once more the nation, led by the Davidic heir, experiences covenant renewal (**34:29–33**). However, as under Jotham and Hezekiah, the revival is shallow and does not change the hearts of the people. Likely, revival is only as effective as the king's power to enforce orthodox religion.

Two reforms and their accompanying Passover celebrations stand out in Chronicles, those of Hezekiah and Josiah. Both of these serve as great historical confirmations of the temple and its worship. Josiah's Passover, like Hezekiah's, is involved with restoration of proper worship (**35:1–19**). He restores the priests as prescribed by David and returns the ark to its place. Many people, including the king, contribute many sacrifices, perhaps indicating a large number of poor who could not afford their own.

The listing of the details of the Passover ritual (vv. 10–14) has at least two purposes: it emphasizes the thoroughness of Josiah's obedience to the ritual legislation, and it underscores the importance of careful ritual to the readers of Chronicles.

It is not clear what makes this Passover observance unique since the time of Samuel (v. 18). The Chronicler's own data, on the surface, indicates that Hezekiah's celebration is a bigger occasion. There had certainly been other occasions when a more populous, wealthier kingdom could have produced Passovers with more pomp and numbers.

Josiah's rule and life end with an entanglement in politics (**35:20–26**). Biblical scholars generally hold that Neco of Egypt was marching northward as a nominal ally allegedly to help the Assyrians in their last stand. No doubt, Neco also saw some possibility of enhancing his own power in Palestine. Josiah, thus, is striking a blow against the collapsing Assyrian Empire when he opposes Neco. Though Josiah loses the battle, it is possible that he delays the Egyptians long enough to do some harm to the Assyrian cause.

That Neco of Egypt speaks for God (v. 21) does not indicate that Neco wishes to honor God; he is speaking presumptuously or sarcastically. The message, nevertheless, represents what God wishes to communicate. Josiah is killed. His historical significance is shown by Jeremiah's dirge and the regular commemoration of his death (v. 25).

E. The last days of Judah (36). The years from the death of Josiah (609 B.C.) to the final deportation were bad from every perspective. Politically, the disappearance of Assyria meant that the Hebrews became a prize for the Babylonians and Egyptians. The continued military invasions, plundering, and conquests ultimately impoverished and depopulated not just Judah, but the entire region. There were no more revivals. Nor were there any more good kings.

The people's choice for king, Jehoahaz (609 B.C.), lasts only three months when Neco replaces him with his older brother, who is given the throne name Jehoiakim (609–597 B.C.). Jehoiakim represents a relatively pro-Egyptian voice. The Chronicler passes a negative judgment on him though no specific details are given.

Jehoiakim's position is hopeless. In 605 B.C. Nebuchadnezzar wins control of Palestine at the Battle of Carchemish. This leads to the first of three deportations to Babylon. Apparently Nebuchadnezzar binds Jehoiakim for captivity, but then changes his mind. The Babylonians temporarily withdraw from Palestine; but in 597, Nebuchadnezzar returns and captures Jerusalem just after the death of Jehoiakim. Jehoiachin (597 B.C.), Jehoiakim's son and successor, goes into Babylonian captivity and seems to have been regarded as the legal heir by the orthodox Hebrew cult.

Zedekiah rebels against Babylon, and his rule as well as the history of Judah ends with the capture of Jerusalem in July 586. This is the occasion of the third and last deportation.

Chronicles has nothing comparable to the great apology for the exile found in 2 Kings 17:7–23. God has repeatedly warned his people of coming judgment, but his messengers have been rejected. Therefore the brutal, unpitying judgment comes. Not even God's own temple is spared.

The Chronicler often typifies general evil by focusing on one particular evil. Here the evil of failing to observe Sabbath rests for the land is singled out (v. 21). It is representative of all the ritual and moral sins of the nation. It also provides a good transition to the postscript on restoration (cf. Jer. 29:10).

Chronicles is a book of legitimacy and failures. It states the basis for the legitimate worship of the later nation and tells why the earlier nation went into captivity. But for the Chronicler, failure and judgment are but a prelude to the restoration of his own day. Therefore, he ends his work with Cyrus's decision to restore the Hebrews to their land and to permit the reestablishment of their proper ritual worship.

SELECT BIBLIOGRAPHY

Curtis, E. L., and A. A. Madsen. *A Critical and Exegetical Commentary on the Books of Chronicles.* The International Critical Commentary. Edinburgh: T. & T. Clark, 1910.

Harrison, R. K. *Introduction to the Old Testament.* Grand Rapids: Eerdmans, 1969.

Keil, C. F. *The Books of Chronicles.* Old Testament Commentaries. Reprint. Grand Rapids: Associated Publishers, n.d.

Williamson, H. G. M. *1 and 2 Chronicles.* The New Century Bible Commentary. Grand Rapids: Eerdmans, 1982.

EZRA

Louis Goldberg

INTRODUCTION

The Book of Ezra, like Nehemiah, receives its name from its principal character. The Talmudic rabbis and Josephus considered the two books to be a single unit, following the Book of Chronicles (cf. 2 Chron. 36:22f. with Ezra 1:1ff.). Not until the time of Origen (A.D. 185–253) were the two divided into separate books, reflecting contemporary Jewish practice. Jerome (ca. A.D. 345–419) also regarded Ezra and Nehemiah as distinct books, designating Nehemiah as the book of the second Ezra. From then on, the church's common practice was to consider Ezra and Nehemiah as separate works. In the English versions, these books follow Samuel, Kings, and Chronicles.

The historical setting for Ezra (chap. 7) and Nehemiah (2:1–9; 13:6) is the reign of Artaxerxes I Longimanus (464–424 B.C.) of Persia, who knew both men personally. The use of the first-person singular pronoun in Ezra 7–10 indicates that he wrote these chapters during the reign of Artaxerxes I and also recounted the fortunes of his people from the days of Cyrus until he personally returned to Jerusalem (chaps. 1–6).

While scholars are in general agreement that Nehemiah's dates (445–433 B.C.) are fairly certain, the dating of Ezra is a problem. Many biblical critics insist that Nehemiah precedes Ezra by a generation or two. For example, Nehemiah seems to know nothing about Ezra until chapter 8. Furthermore, Nehemiah has a different attitude concerning divorce (Neh. 13:27–28; cf. Ezra 10). However, the critics' objections are really not that serious if we take the chronology of the biblical text of both Ezra and Nehemiah at face value, and refuse to take liberties with the text for which there is no warrant.

The Book of Ezra is more than a bare chronicle of how the Israelites were released from Babylon to return to their land and reestablish temple life. The theological message of the book is critical. The reason for Israel's exile to Babylon was because of its pervasive idolatrous practices, but God's purpose for his people in Babylon was to refine them, weaning them away from the horrible practice of idolatry. In due time, God permitted a remnant to return to the homeland and reestablish there an acceptable presence before him. As a result, the two remnant emigrations, under Zerubbabel and Ezra, had a decidedly different testimony than the generation which had to be forcibly exiled from Judah.

The Book of Ezra affirms that the God of Israel is the God of the entire earth. Cyrus king of Persia addresses the God of the Judeans as "the LORD, the God of heaven" (1:2). When the people of Judea describe their relationship to God, they say, "We are the servants of the God of heaven and earth" (5:11; see also 6:9–10). The Judeans understand that the Lord is their God, but when addressing a pagan ruler, they use terms he can readily understand; their Lord is therefore referred to as the God of heaven as well as the earth.

Ezra has a strong belief in God's sovereignty, claiming that the Lord, the God of heaven, is the one who moved the heart of Cyrus to issue a proclamation for the release of the people of Israel from Babylon (1:1). He also praises the Lord, the God of his fathers, who moved the heart of Artaxerxes to permit Ezra to lead a second emigration to Judea (7:27–28).

Ezra has such a strong faith in the Lord God of heaven and earth that he is too ashamed to ask Artaxerxes for a military escort to protect him and his companions from enemies on the journey, declaring that "the gracious hand of our God is on everyone who looks to him" (8:22). After all, God is the great Protector of his people who trust implicitly in him.

The Book of Ezra presents the remnant as a renewed people of God. Some fifty thousand people return to the land of Judea (2:64–67), and yet, as they compare themselves with the numbers in Israel during its prosperous days under King David, their comment is, "We are left this day as a remnant" (9:15). Nevertheless, even as Moses had promised that God could restore a remnant if the nation should ever be taken into exile (Deut. 32:23–28), the emigrants under Ezra declare that the Lord is gracious in sparing them, giving light to their eyes and relief from bondage (9:8). Furthermore, even as God promised Abraham that he would be a God to his descendants through all their generations, so the newly established remnant in the ancient homeland represents the sustained people of Israel (Gen. 17:7; chap. 2).

Prior to the exile, many families, including even some of the priests, had intermarried with peoples of pagan nations—and this was one of the reasons for the exile. Therefore, in the restoration of Judea, a remnant takes pains that only those who can prove their identity with older established faithful families will be able to be part of the restored nation or be able to minister at the altar before God. This concern is further accentuated when Ezra returns with the second emigration and finds that intermarriages have again taken place between the people of Judea and surrounding pagan peoples. No wonder he becomes so severe, rebuking the people and reminding them that in view of God's judgment by exile, this very sin of intermarriage is reprehensible (chap. 9).

The "enemies of Judah and Benjamin" (4:1) live in what was once northern Israel prior to its fall in 722 B.C. Its conqueror, Assyria, had a policy of displacing captured peoples from their own countries and replacing them with other refugees. Peoples were therefore brought from Babylon and other parts of the Middle East to replace those taken from northern Israel (2 Kings 17:24–33). The result is an intermarried group (eventually called Samaritans) who worship a synthesis of the Lord and various pagan gods. Zerubbabel rebuffs these people who have asked to help in the rebuilding of the temple, adding that only those who are truly of Judah can do so (4:2–3), thereby insisting upon the national and religious purity of Judah. On the other hand, all who renounce their pagan attachments and seek the Lord, the God of Israel, are permitted to join with the Judeans when they celebrate Passover (6:19–21).

The Book of Ezra is concerned with worship. Ezra is devoted to the study and observance of the Torah and dedicated to teaching its decrees and laws (7:10) to people eager to learn them and live as God wants (Neh. 8). They are in turn to teach this word to their children, transmitting its message as the only one worth following (Deut. 6:4–9). Furthermore, before spiritual renewal can take place, Ezra has to remind the people that the Torah forbids intermarriage.

Ezra records how the first emigrants, as soon as they arrive in Judea, become involved immediately with the erection of the altar, providing for the reestablishment of the worship of the Lord. For fifty years no sacrifices could be offered, but the older people no doubt taught the younger generation that the only place where God could meet with his people was at the proper altar in the Jerusalem temple. Therefore, at the first opportunity, a restored Judea erects its altar.

Ezra also notes, however, that work on the temple ceases for many years, first, because Judea is ordered to stop all work on it, but also because the people of Judea eventually become apathetic and live only for themselves (Hag. 1:2–7). The prophets Haggai and Zechariah encourage the people to continue with the task so that the temple is finally completed (3:11; 6:16). The very heart of the worship system of the nation is now in operation.

Possibly the three major festivals are reinstituted (Exod. 23:14–16), because mention is made of the Passover and the Feast of Unleavened Bread (6:19–22). Worship would also include the observance of the Feast of Weeks as well as Tabernacles.

Ezra's work in establishing Israel on a sure footing as a nation before God is impressive. When Ezra returns to Judea in 458 B.C., some eighty years have elapsed since the first emigration under Zerubbabel. The new generation can no longer read the Hebrew script of the Scriptures of the preexilic period. The Judeans for the most part speak Aramaic; to make it possible for the people to read the Scriptures, Ezra changes the script of the Old Testament to Aramaic. Furthermore, because most of the people speak Aramaic and no longer understand Hebrew, Ezra also provides an Aramaic interpretation so that when he is called by Nehemiah to read the Word (Neh. 8), people can understand what is being read. Ezra also trains a group of Levites who interpret alternately, first the reading of Scripture, then its interpretation (Neh. 8:7) that was transmitted orally by generations of teachers. With the training of a cadre of religious leaders as interpreters, we see possibly the inception of a group of religious leaders for the nation once Ezra passes from the scene. Finally, Ezra is possibly, according to tradition, the one who composed the genealogy of Chronicles, finished off the last verses in 2 Chronicles, and wrote the book bearing his name.

Two languages are present in the book: 4:7–6:18 and 7:12–26 are in Aramaic, while the rest is in Hebrew. Since Aramaic was the official language of the Persian Empire, then it is entirely reasonable that the passages in Aramaic represent copies of official correspondence. The portions in Hebrew would have specific relevance to the people of Judea who, while speaking Aramaic as an everyday language, would also regard Hebrew as their particular language.

The key word or expression of the book is the phrase *go up* or *went up,* while "Jerusalem" appears some forty-seven times. We would expect this emphasis in Ezra because the two emigrations of Jewish people to the land of Israel, the reestablishment of life in Jerusalem, and the rebuilding of the temple are his main subject materials.

OUTLINE

- I. First Emigration (1:1–2:70)
  - A. Cyrus's Proclamation (1:1–4)
  - B. Treasures for the Temple (1:5–11)
  - C. The Emigrants (2:1–70)
- II. Restoration of the Temple (3:1–6:22)
  - A. Rebuilding the Altar (3:1–6)
  - B. Rebuilding the Temple (3:7–13)
  - C. Opposition (4:1–5)
  - D. Later Opposition (4:6–24)
  - E. God's Encouragement (5:1–2)
  - F. Official Inquiry (5:3–17)
  - G. Completion and Dedication of the Temple (6:1–22)
- III. Second Emigration (7:1–8:36)
  - A. Ezra (7:1–10)
  - B. Official Recognition (7:11–26)
  - C. Ezra's Praise (7:27–28)
  - D. The Emigrants (8:1–14)
  - E. A Search for Levites (8:15–20)
  - F. The Journey (8:21–36)
- IV. Intermarriage (9:1–15)
- V. Confession and Separation (10:1–44)
  - A. The Confession (10:1–17)
  - B. Those Guilty of Intermarriage (10:18–44)

COMMENTARY

I. First Emigration (1:1–2:70)

Generally, the Book of Ezra has two major divisions: (1) Ezra recounts the experiences of his people from their release from Babylon in 539 B.C. by the proclamation of the Persian ruler Cyrus until the second emigration in 458

B.C.; and (2) he describes his part in the second emigration and the spiritual situation in Jerusalem and Judea. The time span of this account covers a period of some eighty-two years. Included in the first part of the book is a digression in which Ezra describes the opposition the Israelites faced over the years, from the days of Zerubbabel until his own day, mentioning also the opposition Nehemiah faced in his time (Neh. 1:3). The highlights Ezra records are the release of his fellow Judeans some eighty years prior to his day, the rebuilding and dedication of the temple, and God's protection when he and some seven thousand of his people are involved in a second emigration to Judea.

A. Cyrus's proclamation (1:1–4). The release of the Israelites from Babylon must definitely take into account Jeremiah's prophecy of exile as well as Daniel's prayer that the release should actually take place. Jeremiah had predicted that Judah would spend seventy years in Babylon (Jer. 25:10; 29:10); but after seventy years, Judah would return to their land and have a second temple.

Some may wonder how this seventy-year period is determined, inasmuch as the second temple was destroyed in 586 B.C., and Cyrus conquered Babylon in 539 B.C., issuing the proclamation for the release of Judeans in 538 B.C., a time span of only forty-eight years. There are two possibilities: (1) from the time when Judea passed under Nebuchadnezzar's control in 606/605 B.C. to when Cyrus conquered Babylon in 539 B.C., providing for some sixty-six or sixty-seven years; or (2) from the time when the first temple was destroyed in 586 B.C. to the dedication of the second temple in 516 B.C., allowing for a span of some seventy years.

The Lord stirs up the heart of Cyrus king of Persia to make a proclamation, not only for Judea, but for all of the displaced persons of the Persian Empire. The policy of the Assyrians and Babylonians had been to displace peoples, taking, for example, people of northern Israel to Assyria and then sending the peoples of these areas to the cities of northern Israel (2 Kings 17:23–25). The Persians, on the other hand, sought to keep peace within the empire and to retain the loyalty of their subjects; they returned displaced peoples to their homelands and provided money for the restoration of their temples which had been destroyed. Cyrus did not care which god the peoples worshiped; what he did want was peace and order in the empire with people praying for him and other leaders.

Among all the proclamations to displaced peoples, one also permitted the Judeans to return to Judea and Jerusalem and to rebuild their temple; they were also enjoined to pray for Cyrus in their prescribed way. One might say, therefore, that one proclamation was made to many peoples, but with appropriate blank spaces for the city of destination and the corresponding name of the god of that location.

The Persian Empire supported the various temples of their subject peoples which meant that the Judeans were also assured of enough silver and gold, livestock, and freewill offerings for their temple in Jerusalem that it could function for the good of the empire. Believers, however, realized and rejoiced that a second temple could now be built with God's approval. We can well imagine the great joy among the remnant of Judeans returning to Judea and Jerusalem because God had indeed kept his word concerning their release. Now his favor had been extended to them for the establishment of a second commonwealth.

B. Treasures for the temple (1:5–11). The remnant of Judeans stirred up by God to emigrate to their home country make preparations to return. Neighbors assist them with silver and gold, goods and livestock, and valuable gifts, in addition to freewill offerings, so as to help the emigrants on their journey as well as provide for offerings for the temple. A somewhat similar situation occurred when Israel left Egypt, at which time the Egyptians also provided silver, gold, and other gifts (Exod. 12:35–36), although in this case, the Israelites as a slave people were being reimbursed for centuries of abuse.

Cyrus also brings out the vessels and articles that Nebuchadnezzar had taken from the temple when he plundered it in 586 B.C. These articles had been taken to Babylon and stored, but now, on the occasion of the emigration, Cyrus returns them to the Judean emigrants for service once more in the newly built temple. The Persian officials count out the articles of gold and silver and one of the leaders of Judah, Sheshbazzar, the "prince of Judah," receives them.

The inventory of articles mentions some 5400 articles of gold and silver, but when the individual items are totaled in verses 9–10, the sum is only 2499. Some see a discrepancy in the total of the figures in verses 9–10 as contrasted with verse 11; therefore the Revised Standard Version uses 1 Esdras 2:13, where the total figure adds up to 5469, and the itemized figures also add up to this sum. However, with no other further evidence available, we can only surmise that the Hebrew text is accurate, and that the total figure does not include smaller articles of gold and silver not worth mentioning in the inventory in verses 9–10.

The chapter closes with the phrase *when the exiles came up from Babylon to Jerusalem*, reminding us that God is indeed faithful, working through history for the recovery of his people, and allowing them to return to their homeland. There, he graciously provides for the beginning of a second commonwealth.

C. The emigrants (2:1–70). The province mentioned in verse 1 is Judah, a small country in the midst of a vast area referred to as "beyond the River" or Trans-Euphrates. The Persian rulers regarded these territories, including Judea, as west or beyond the Euphrates River. The people Ezra mentions in his list include both leaders as well as people of the exile. Now, a repentant people, even though a small group, are emigrating to the homeland, to Jerusalem and Judah, "each to his own town."

The leaders total eleven, but Nehemiah also mentions an additional person, Nahamani (Neh. 7:7), who was omitted from the Ezra list apparently during the course of transmitting the text. Apparently, twelve individuals are chosen as a special body, representing symbolically the twelve tribes of Israel, although we have no idea of the tribal origins of these individuals.

The first leader mentioned is Zerubbabel, the grandson of King Jehoiachin. Zerubbabel is the son of Shealtiel (3:2), Jehoiachin's eldest son. However, in 1 Chronicles 3:19, Zerubbabel is mentioned as the son of Pedaiah, a younger brother of Shealtiel. Perhaps there was a levirate marriage of Pedaiah to the widow of Shealtiel so that the firstborn Zerubbabel is considered the son of Shealtiel in order to keep his name as a living testimony in Israel. This being the case, Zerubbabel is in line to sit upon the throne; but he cannot do so because a curse has been placed upon the sons of Jehoiachin whereby no descendants of this line of Solomon in the second commonwealth could refer to themselves as kings (Jer. 22:28, 30). Nevertheless, Zerubbabel is the logical choice to be the leader of the emigrants.

The second name mentioned is Jeshua, although it appears as Joshua in Haggai 2:2 and Zechariah 3:1. The root meaning of the name is "he will save," and therefore in English it is Jesus. Zerubbabel and Jeshua work closely together as the leaders of Judea, the latter representing the priesthood and the former the regal position. Later in the commonwealth, the priesthood took both functions, and near the end of the second commonwealth in the first century, we see the high priest of the Sadducees functioning as both the priestly and regal leader of the nation.

The rest of the names reflect those commonly used in Ezra's day. Though some critics mention Nehemiah as the one associated with the Book of Nehemiah, this is not necessarily the case.

The laypeople are identified by two classes (vv. 3–35): (1) the clan, the descendants of Parosh (v. 3); and (2) associated with a place, Bethlehem (v. 21). The point is that the people of Israel are attached to clans and/or places, suggesting, therefore, that no Israelite existed by himself. He was associated with a tribe and a family, living in a particular place in the homeland.

When we examine the sum total of people associated with each of the families in the Ezra list, we note the contrast in figures when comparing them with corresponding families in the Nehemiah list (Neh. 7:7–38). Sometimes there are only slight variations between the same families, while as many as half the numbers on the two lists do not agree with each other. For example, in the former category, the sons of Adonikam in the Ezra list number 666 (Ezra 2:13), while Nehemiah numbers them as 667 (Neh. 7:18). In the latter category, the sons of Azgad are listed as 1222 (Ezra 2:12), while in Nehemiah they number 2322 (Neh. 7:17). The only possible explanation is that in the process of textual transmission from copyist to copyist, numbers were changed due to error. This phenomenon occurs in other lists in the Scriptures as well. One does note, however, that there is virtual agreement in the grand total of those who returned: 42,360.

The total number of priests (vv. 36–39) is 4289, which is about one-tenth of the number of emigrants. The priests were originally organized into twenty-four groups, taking turns in their service at the sanctuary, but only four of the twenty-four are mentioned among the emigrants. The same four also occur in 10:18–22, some eighty years later in the time of Ezra. Of these four, therefore, twenty-four subgroups of priests are reconstituted, using the same names David had originally assigned (1 Chron. 24:7–18).

Only a small group of Levites (vv. 40–42) returned in the first emigration, consisting of about 8 percent of the total of the number of priests, from the figures indicated in the list. We note a distinction among the Levites: those of verse 40 assist the priests in their ministry at the altar, while other Levites, the singers and the gatekeepers, belong to special groups with specific tasks.

Another class of people established by David

and his officials to minister in the temple are the Nethinim, or, "dedicated ones" (vv. 43–54; 8:20). As temple servants, they assist both Levites and priests. Possibly, they were descendants of people conquered by David whose fathers had been converted, accepting circumcision, and therefore entered into the covenant blessings.

The descendants of Solomon's servants (vv. 55–58) are added to those listed as temple servants, and their total is 392. Solomon could have engaged captives, in addition to the Nethinim, and used them for secular tasks serving the political leadership.

Sadly, there are also Israelites, coming from specific towns in the Babylonian exile, but with no record to confirm their origin (vv. 59–60). The record of attachment to family and towns was important, demonstrating that one was a part of the family of Israel, and had a claim to specific family property. If no claims could be demonstrated by certain Judeans, at the very least they were permitted to emigrate to their homeland. Their status, however, would be the same as any other circumcised alien permitted to live among Israelites but with no claim to land divided among the tribes.

As there are Israelites who cannot produce records confirming their backgrounds, so some priests likewise are not able to do so. Moses specified that "no one except a descendant of Aaron should come to burn incense before the LORD, or he would become like Korah and his followers" (Num. 16:40), and so it is absolutely necessary for a priest to demonstrate his identity before he can minister in any way.

One of the priestly families, the sons of Hakkoz (v. 61), is finally able to demonstrate its claim some eighty years later if "Meremoth son of Uriah, the priest" (8:33) is the same as "Meremoth son of Uriah, the son of Hakkoz" (Neh. 3:4, 21). There is evidently no reason to doubt the connection. But for those who cannot demonstrate their lineage, they will be unable to serve at the altar, or even eat of the sacred food in the sanctuary area. The only possibility of lifting this restriction is if God directly intervenes through a priest ministering with the Urim and Thummim so as to confirm a priest's background. By appealing to the possibility of such revelation, there is also an admission that no direct voice of God had been heard during the exile or emigration.

The sum total of the emigrants is now provided (vv. 64–67): 42,360 Judeans, and in addition, 7337 men and maidservants, along with 200 men and women singers. The same total also appears in Nehemiah 7:66 and 1 Esdras 5:41. The only problem, however, is that as one adds up the component parts, each of the three sources has a different sum: Ezra—29,818; Nehemiah—31,089; 1 Esdras—30,143. Obviously, there have been many attempts to explain the totals. The apocryphal 1 Esdras 5:41 suggests a difference because the component parts of the list do not mention children under twelve years of age, although the grand total does include them. Other possibilities are: (1) those who belonged to the northern tribes were not counted in the component parts; or (2) women were not included; both groups, however, do appear in the final figures. None of these suggestions, however, seem to provide adequate answers, and we fall back again on the problem of textual transmission where copyists made errors in reproducing the numerical lists.

The ratio of servants to their masters or mistresses, approximately one for every six, might reflect that, after having spent so many years in exile, a certain amount of wealth had been built up; the people had worked hard and had money. Or perhaps Judeans who remained behind in Babylon also gave of their means to the emigrants who were then able to bring servants with them to Judea. The reference to singers who are not temple personnel also represents a measure of wealth.

Upon arriving in Jerusalem, the heads of the families give freewill offerings "according to their ability" to the treasury for the sacred task of rebuilding the temple (vv. 68–69). Not only do the emigrants have a genuine desire to serve the Lord and thereby undertake such a long and arduous journey back to their homeland, but they also give liberally for the reconstitution of the nation and its worship center.

The mention of the religious leaders settling into their own hometowns along with the rest of the Judeans (v. 70) must also take into account the fact that on certain occasions, the priests, Levites, singers, and gatekeepers were present as well in Jerusalem for ministry at the temple. Nehemiah later insists that more of the religious leaders settle in Jerusalem (Neh. 11:1–2), although some of them also retain houses in other towns as well.

II. Restoration of the Temple (3:1–6:22)

Before anything else can be accomplished, even the collection of materials to build the temple, the altar of burnt offering in front of the temple has to be built, enabling the people of Judea to initiate sacrifices to the Lord their God. The spiritual center of life for the nation is the altar, and is one of the places where God met with his people for their dedication (Exod. 29:42–43).

A. Rebuilding the altar (3:1–6). When the seventh month arrives, as many Judeans as possible gather in Jerusalem for the rebuilding of the altar. This month was significant because of a special blowing of trumpets (Num. 29:1) on the first day, which in time came to be known as the beginning of the civil new year. The Day of Atonement was on the tenth day (Lev. 23:26–32), and beginning on the fifteenth day and running for one week, was the Feast of Tabernacles (Lev. 23:33–43). The newly arrived emigrants could not have chosen a better time to reconstitute their life by building once again an altar to the Lord.

Along with their concern for proper worship of the Lord, the Judeans also are fearful of "the peoples around them" (v. 3), and they know they need the help of God to protect them. Despite their fear, they seek to be obedient to his Word.

Instructions for building the altar for the tabernacle were given by Moses in Exodus 27:1–8; 31:2–5; and 38:1–7; it was 7½ feet square and 4½ feet high, made of acacia wood and covered with bronze. The altar Solomon designed for the first temple was larger than the one that served the tabernacle: thirty feet square and fifteen feet high (2 Chron. 4:1). This was destroyed by the Babylonians when Jerusalem fell, but there is no doubt that the Judean leaders Zerubbabel and Jeshua have it rebuilt, in accordance with the dimensions Solomon specified and on its traditional and proper site. Many people are involved in its construction, reflecting a unified desire to serve the Lord. The first official act in reestablishing worship is to commence with the daily burnt offerings as specified by Moses (Exod. 29:38–43). Both the morning and mid-afternoon sacrifices are offered, thereby indicating that the nation once again has set itself apart to God in dedication.

No mention is made of the Day of Atonement, but no doubt this occasion is also observed in accordance with Leviticus 16. Finally, "in accordance with what is written" (v. 4) they celebrate the Feast of Tabernacles, offering appropriate sacrifices on each of the seven days. This is the holiday that marked the completion of the general harvest of the land and in subsequent years, Judeans would have opportunity to thank God for his gracious provisions.

Following the occasion of Tabernacles and the crowning day, daily worship continues; worship is now in full progress with the presentation of burnt offerings, new moon sacrifices, and sacrifices for all of the appointed feasts even though the foundation of the Lord's house is not yet completed.

B. Rebuilding the temple (3:7–13). Following the institution of worship at the altar, leaders and people now turn their attention to the rebuilding of the temple itself. Everyone donates monies to the civil and priestly authorities who then hire masons and carpenters for the building project. In addition, the leaders also collect a portion of the produce of the land, grain, wine, and oil, to pay for cedar logs from Lebanon as well as to remunerate the people of Sidon and Tyre who load this lumber on ships and transport it to Joppa. Solomon had also procured cedar wood from Lebanon, paying for it likewise with the country's produce (2 Chron. 2:10, 15–16). Monies for this entire undertaking had already been given (2:68–69), and Cyrus had also given permission for procuring the lumber and transporting it. The Hebrew meaning of "permission" also implies a grant of money from the Persian treasury to cover the expenses of building the temple.

The work is guided by both Zerubbabel and Jeshua, commencing in the second month of the second year because possibly the first month had been taken up with the observance of the Passover. All the energies of the people would have been expended on this festive occasion as they observed it as a means of thanksgiving to God that life could begin anew in a reconstituted nation.

Levites are appointed to supervise those working on the house of God. When the foundations of the temple of the Lord have been laid, the priests put on their special dress and with trumpets blowing and with the Levites of the clan of Asaph in charge of instrumental and choral music, they all stand in their appointed places and sing with all of their hearts a psalm of thanksgiving as prescribed by David, king of Israel (1 Chron. 16:34).

With the foundations now laid, there comes a mixed sound of shouts of joy as well as sounds of weeping (vv. 10–13). Why anyone would want to weep on this occasion is hard to fathom, but there are present at this time many of the older priests and Levites as well as family heads who had seen the splendid Solomonic temple at the end of the first commonwealth. By comparison, the newer temple is much more modest, and therefore the older people weep as they recall what Israel had in the past. Most of the younger generation, born in Babylon, and only hearing stories about the grandeur of the temple, now rejoice because they at last have a temple wherein they might give their offerings and worship God.

The mixed response is a very human one;

older people generally have a tendency to reminisce and talk about the "good old days," but a younger generation, with no past perspective, can only look forward, dream, and expect great things from God. There is the distinct danger that the devotion of these younger people might be dampened. The response is so mixed that Haggai addresses a defeatist attitude of the older people. The prophet assures the people that even though the second temple is not as pretentious as the first, nevertheless this will be the very temple to which the "Desired One" of all the nations will come; one day this house will be filled with his glory when the promised Messiah will arrive to fulfill all that the prophets had predicted of him. Furthermore, Zechariah also addresses this "looking-back" issue so that the people should not despise "the day of small things" (Zech. 4:10) because God is able to do *beyond* what we can even ask or think! Even as these prophets had to gently chide these questionable attitudes, so likewise today God does not want people who are constantly looking back and taking comfort in the "good old days" but rather to look to the future with hope and comfort in what he will yet do.

C. Opposition (4:1–5). As is often the case, when the work of God goes forward, his people must be ever aware that there will be opposition. Even as Satan is the great challenger of God's purposes, he will also seek to thwart the people of God on every hand and at every turn. What is mentioned in this chapter is an account of the opposition to the people of Judea, not only at the beginning of the rebuilding of the temple in 536 B.C., but also across the years to the days of Nehemiah in 445 B.C., a period of some ninety-one years.

The mention of Judah and Benjamin (4:1) refers to the territory prior to the exile where the scattered tribes of Judah, Benjamin, and Simeon (Gen. 49:7) lived. But there were also representatives of the other northern tribes along with those of Levi in the southern kingdom of Judah (2 Chron. 11:13–17), especially after the united kingdom had split. When Judea was reconstituted after the exile, it included representatives from all twelve tribes.

The clue to the identity of the enemies of Judah and Benjamin is stated by their claim: "we seek your God and have been sacrificing to him since the time of Esarhaddon king of Assyria, who brought us here" (4:2). These are the descendants of the people of the northern kingdom of Israel who, after the fall of Samaria in 722 B.C., intermarried with peoples brought from Babylon and other parts of the Middle East to settle in the north. Because of their claim of attachment to the tribes of northern Israel, they feel they have a right to take part in the rebuilding of the temple. They are not, however, telling the entire truth. These very descendants "neither worship the LORD nor adhere to the decrees and ordinances, the laws and commands that the LORD gave the descendants of Jacob" (2 Kings 17:34). They do not even begin to have a grasp of what it means to worship the true God, the Lord God of Israel. The people of Judea are now a renewed people and, consequently, there is bound to be a separation from the peoples who want to help. Zerubbabel, Jeshua, and the rest of the leaders sound harsh and bigoted when they tell the mixed breed, "you have no part with us in building a temple to our God" (v. 3). The Judean leaders do not enter into any discussion as to what the difference between their worship and of those who seek to help is. They simply state the fact that they are the ones who have been commissioned by Cyrus, king of Persia, to build the temple to the God of Israel.

One can imagine, therefore, the reaction of the peoples of what was once the northern part of Israel. Not only are they hurt, but they also become angry and vindictive. They seek to discourage the people of Judah, no doubt by means of sneers and intimidation; they threaten the Judeans with bodily harm, thereby making them fearful; and they hire counselors to raise questions as to the designs and plans of the Judeans, creating confusion among the Persian officials. The opposition becomes so fierce that work on the house of God ceases during the entire reign of Cyrus king of Persia (until 530 B.C.), during the days of his son Cambyses (530–522 B.C.), and until the days of Darius I (521 B.C.). Even though the Judeans could use their documents to demonstrate that they have official sanction to build the temple, they are, nevertheless, a very small people contrasted with the great numbers of their neighbors, and their cause becomes lost amidst the chorus of their enemies.

D. Later opposition (4:6–24). Ezra pauses at this point to reflect upon opposition against Judah across an eighty-year time span, leaving off with what occurred in the days of Zerubbabel, proceeding to the time of Xerxes, and then on to his own day, when Artaxerxes I reigns as emperor. As to why Ezra does not follow a more orderly chronological pattern in dealing with the history of Judah is characteristic of the Old Testament. For whatever purposes the biblical writer had in mind, he often followed more of a topical discussion of events and issues rather than a strict chronology. Our Western mode of thinking is chronological, but the Bible is set in a culture where a chronological as well as a topical scheme is followed. Ezra, therefore, recounts a long list of opposition to Judah to demonstrate that the work of God proceeded at times, then stopped, but then through the gracious hand of God, went forward again.

As we already saw, the work ceased during the days of Cyrus, until Haggai and Zechariah, beginning in 520 B.C., encouraged the people to finish their work, which was finally accomplished by 516 B.C. However, as the people of Jerusalem and Judea attempted to rebuild the walls of Jerusalem, they were hampered, particularly during the reign of Xerxes (Heb. Ahasuerus). Whatever reconstruction the Judeans were trying to accomplish in Jerusalem was stopped, time and again, by their enemies for thirty to fifty years after the completion of the temple. Judea had powerful enemies.

The reign of Artaxerxes forms the historical background for both Ezra and Nehemiah, appearing in Ezra 7–10 as well as in the entire Book of Nehemiah. We may find it puzzling that Artaxerxes is so prone to listen to the enemies of Judea and yet at the same time is favorable to Ezra and Nehemiah, sending them back to their homeland. What we must recognize is that while kings can make their decisions on a human level, God is in control nevertheless, and can move kings to accomplish his purposes.

At the beginning of the reign of Artaxerxes, the enemies of Judea exerted a particularly powerful influence upon the Persian government, sending an official communique to the king which charged the people of Judea with a history of rebellion and advised the Persians that if they were not careful, the Judeans would once again seek to assert their independence (4:12–16). Because this is official correspondence with the Persian government, all charges and official action by these authorities appear in Aramaic, the official language (4:8–6:18).

Obviously, the charges were intended to convince Artaxerxes that he was indeed facing serious trouble if he continued to favor the people of Judea. The complaint was all the more serious because it purported to have the support of the entire region west of the Euphrates (v. 9). Other great and honorable kings such as Ashurbanipal and his predecessors had to deport the people of Israel in order to curb and completely control their opposition (v. 10). The enemies of Judea claimed to be zealous for the king's honor! That was why they wanted to inform him that he must not continue his support of these people. Furthermore, if the honorable king had any suspicions concerning the complaint, then he should search the records himself to see whether Jerusalem had indeed been a rebellious city and to learn why it was destroyed in the past. The final point of the communique was that if Jerusalem should ever be rebuilt, then the Persian Empire was in great danger because the Judeans could foment rebellion by refusing to pay their taxes, becoming an example to others. Would the Persian emperor want that prospect?

The complaint had its desired effect. As Artaxerxes ordered the records to be searched, he found from the experiences of the Babylonians that Jerusalem was indeed a rebellious city, refusing to pay taxes. Therefore, Artaxerxes gave orders to the Judeans to stop all work on the rebuilding of the city and its wall. There is even evidence that whatever had been accomplished was burned, if we take into account the report given to Nehemiah (Neh. 1:3). It would seem that God's purposes had been thwarted, with no prospect of relief.

From here, we could quite logically turn to the Book of Nehemiah to continue with the account of the opposition against Jerusalem and Judah. Ezra, however, now returns to consider what occurred earlier in the days of Cyrus, Cambyses, and Darius.

It would appear that, at the beginning of verse 24, Ezra continues with the digression, but the latter part of the passage quite logically connects with the beginning of the reign of Darius I, king of Persia. The narrative picks up again where it left off at 4:5, the days of Zerubbabel the political leader and Jeshua the high priest. This earlier opposition continued until the second year of the reign of Darius (520 B.C.).

E. God's encouragement (5:1–2). For the first time since the days of Jeremiah, the voice of God is heard in the land of Judea. God's favor is once more upon his people, and he sends two prophets, Haggai and Zechariah, to prophesy "to the Jews in Judah and Jerusalem in the name of the God of Israel" (5:1). Their task is to break the deadlock of the opposition and to encourage the people of Judea to continue on with the task of rebuilding the temple in Jerusalem. With this unexpected but very welcome word from the Lord, Zerubbabel and Jeshua set out to complete the work on the house of the Lord.

F. Official inquiry (5:3–17). No sooner have the people of Judea set about in earnest to complete the temple when they are questioned by the Persian authorities as to who gave them permission to work. With characteristic precise investigation, they want an official explanation, including the names of the men actually working on the project. By contrast, however, God's providence works on behalf of the Judean elders and no work is stopped during the entire period of the investigation and during the time it takes to send the report to Darius and receive a reply from him.

Since this report was probably influenced by the enemies of Judea, seeking to prejudice the Persian emperor, the reporter possibly seeks to weight the argument in his favor. The account to Darius of the work in Jerusalem is that the Judeans are constructing a building with "large stones and placing the timbers in the walls" (v. 8). In fact, the investigation describes the Judeans as fiercely determined to finish their task.

The report, however, also includes a reply by Zerubbabel that his people have already lost a first temple because their fathers had sinned and angered the God of Israel. Nebuchadnezzar, king of the Babylonians, was then permitted to destroy their house of worship and that is why the people were exiled to Babylon. But, the report goes on to state that King Cyrus, no less, had given permission to rebuild the temple, and had even returned the original gold and silver articles of the first house. Furthermore, Zerubbabel points out, the new house of the Lord was to be supported by the royal treasury as well, and therefore Sheshbazzar, the governor, was determined to see the task through to completion. As the Judean leader finishes his report, he respectfully asks the king to search the archives to see if Cyrus had indeed ever issued such a decree on behalf of the Judeans.

G. Completion and dedication of the temple (6:1–22). The events in this chapter complete Ezra's consideration of the first emigration, until the time when the temple was dedicated, between 538–516 B.C.

After receiving the report by his governors from Trans-Euphrates, Darius issues an order to search the archives to see if indeed a proclamation had ever been given to the Judeans to rebuild their temple. No such order is found in Babylon, but one is located in the citadel of Ecbatana in Media, one of the provinces of Persia.

The record indeed contains information about the temple that was to be rebuilt; it was to be "ninety feet high and ninety feet wide, with three courses of large stones and one of timbers" (v. 4). Furthermore, all costs for this building were to be borne by the royal treasury. In addition, the gold and silver articles that once were in the first temple, and had been removed by Nebuchadnezzar, were to be returned to the second temple and deposited there. The search in the archives has been fruitful and the information is the answer to the officials in the area west of the Euphrates. Darius has no other recourse but to honor the proclamation made by one of his honorable predecessors. He also gives due recognition and official sanction to the efforts of the Judeans who seek to carry out what they have already been commissioned to do.

God has indeed vindicated his people and substantiated the exhortations of the prophets to continue on with the work of the temple. No one, including the enemies of Judea, can now stop the Judeans in their efforts because Darius has ordered by official proclamation that there be no interference with the work on the temple in Jerusalem. The leaders there must be left in peace. Furthermore, the instructions by Darius clearly emphasize that the expenses for building this temple are to be paid out of the royal treasury and, in addition, all that is needed in the way of animals and other articles must be provided daily without fail. The policy of the Persians was that prayer be made at all sanctuaries throughout the empire, and Jerusalem is no exception. So as to emphasize the authority of Darius, the order also includes a warning that if anyone interferes with the work in Jerusalem and causes it to cease, the offender will suffer the loss of his house and even his life.

God works through the edicts of man in order that his purposes can be accomplished. His people can now finish what was begun and they can carry on with the worship prescribed by Moses. This is not the first time God works on behalf of his people, and even from today's point of view, it will not be the last time that he will exert influence through the events of history whereby his people can do his good and acceptable and perfect will.

Once the Judeans have full approval for their work, they set about to complete the task, encouraged by the prophets Haggai and Zechariah. It is amazing to note that once the people of God set their minds and hearts to finish what has been started, the work is quickly completed. Four years after Haggai starts to encourage Judah, the temple is completed, in the sixth year of the reign of Darius, in 516 B.C. (v. 15). The work ends in great triumph, some seventy years after the destruction of the first temple in 586 B.C.

The occasion of the dedication of the house of God is a joyous one. Following the instructions provided in Leviticus 8 and 9, the temple is dedicated, the priests are consecrated and installed in their ministry at the temple, and at the official dedication, leaders and people offer 100 bulls, 200 rams, 400 male lambs, and as a sin offering for all Israel, 12 male goats, one for each of the tribes. While this may be a lavish outlay of money, it pales into insignificance when compared to what was offered when Solomon dedicated the first temple with 22,000 oxen and 120,000 sheep (1 Kings 8:63). But even though the people of Judea, at the beginning of the second commonwealth, are small in number, nevertheless their joy is no less than that at the dedication of the first temple. The proclamation of atonement through the sin offering is now possible, as well as the rest of the offerings, and the high priest can minister on behalf of the nation with the full approval of the reigning Persian authorities. The priests are installed in their divisions, and the Levites in their groups. The law of Moses is the guide for the religious leaders, indicating again that the priests are well aware of the law's directives concerning the worship of God by the nation as well as for a prescribed way to live holy before the Lord.

The temple is completed during the month of Adar, the last month on the Jewish calendar, occurring about February–March. The dedication of the temple as well as the dedication and installation of the priests would have taken place at the end of Adar, and during the first days of the first month of Nisan before the Passover on the fourteenth day of this month. The first major holiday therefore, after the dedication, is the Passover. Interestingly enough, the language reverts back to Hebrew at 6:19, which is quite appropriate for the occasion of observing a holiday that meant, and still means, so much to the people of Israel.

The people go through the process of ritual purification, separating themselves "from the unclean practices of their Gentile neighbors in order to seek the LORD, the God of Israel" (v. 21). The Passover meal is eaten, and for the following seven days, the people celebrate the Feast of Unleavened Bread, filled with joy, because the Lord has changed "the attitude of the king of Assyria, so that he assisted them in the work of the house of God, the God of Israel" (v. 22). The use of the word *Assyria* is puzzling inasmuch as the official leadership is now Persian. Perhaps the people of Judea recollect, in a historical sweep, their bitter memories of how northern Israel had been conquered by Assyria in 722 B.C., and how the southern kingdom had been taken captive and the temple destroyed in 586 B.C., but now, under the Persians, their circumstances are reversed.

III. Second Emigration (7:1–8:36)

After jumping several decades, we arrive in the days of Ezra who leads a second emigration to Judea. We will be introduced to an entirely different set of circumstances which require an entirely different kind of leader. God calls a man who is a priest, teacher, and religious leader, who completely trusts him in every situation, and who proves to be just the man the people need.

A. Ezra (7:1–10). The phrase *after these things* (v. 1) encompasses a period of fifty-eight years. These are the days of Ezra, who is introduced with a lineage that goes back to Zadok who served David as priest, and to Phinehas, the son of Eleazar, the son of Aaron the high priest. He has an impeccable record that officially establishes him as a promising religious leader.

But not only is Ezra a priest; he is also a "teacher well versed in the Law of Moses" (v. 6), and therefore a learned person with a good grasp on what Moses taught and also able to interpret and apply the Word of God. He will indeed prove to be a good teacher in Judea and thereby be the man used of God to restructure the worship of Judea, placing it on a more sure foundation.

Ezra has earned the highest respect of Artaxerxes, who in turn grants this Jewish leader everything he asks in order to emigrate with a group of other Israelites, priests, Levites, singers, gatekeepers, and temple servants. The action by the Persian king is interesting in view of the fact that the enemies of Judea had lodged such a serious complaint against Judea that official action had been taken against any reconstruction of Jerusalem and its wall and gates (4:18–22), although there was a loophole whereby the order could be reviewed (v. 21). Now, however, Ezra is honored by the Persian leader for the good of Judea.

The record provides us with a brief summary of Ezra's journey (vv. 8–9). He leaves Babylon on the first day of the first month, and arrives in Jerusalem on the first day of the fifth month (in the seventh year of Artaxerxes, 458 B.C.), a period of some four months. He testifies that God indeed had watched over him because "the gracious hand of his God was on him" (v. 9).

B. Official recognition (7:11–26). Because this is official correspondence between Artaxerxes and Ezra, the account in 7:11–26 is recorded in Aramaic. To have the official blessing of Artaxerxes is indeed an honor for Ezra, who is highly regarded for his religious knowledge and leadership.

Artaxerxes authorizes any Judeans who remain in the city and province of Babylon, if they wish to do so, to return with Ezra to Jerusalem. The Persian king is vitally interested in the religious status of his subjects, and therefore also authorizes Ezra to ascertain how the law of the God of Israel is being observed.

He has no particular interest in Jewish worship; rather, Persian policy demanded that all subjects be diligent in their worship services to pray for the welfare of the empire. Artaxerxes also provides silver and gold for the cost of the sacrifices in order that worship be maintained at the temple in Jerusalem at all times. Whatever money is left over, after providing for the sacrifices as well as all other articles, could be used for religious purposes. If anything else is required, the royal treasury will cover all costs.

Ezra is also given authority to ask for further supplies from officials west of the Euphrates, up to a specified amount, some of which is used for the journey while the rest goes for the service at the temple. What is interesting to note is that Artaxerxes does not want any wrath coming down on his realm because of any offense against the God of heaven. Everything must be done to ensure peace and tranquility within the state. So as to encourage the priests and Levites in their ministry at the temple, they are exempted from any taxes, tribute, or duty so that the religious leaders will have no cause for concern; the work at the temple must proceed without any hindrance.

Ezra also has full authority to bring charges against any who would seek to do harm to the law of the God of Israel as well as the law of the king. The Persian leader, as well as many others of the Middle East, realized that there was a distinct relationship between religious devotion and ethical behavior and obedience to the state. Everything possible must be done to ensure civil order, whether by "death, banishment, confiscation of property, or imprisonment" (v. 26).

C. Ezra's praise (7:27–28). Ezra praises the God of his fathers who has stirred up the heart of Artaxerxes to honor the Lord in Jerusalem as well as to extend favor to his servant. With this show of esteem by the Persian king, but even more, the blessing of the God of Israel upon him, Ezra now takes heart and makes preparations to lead a second emigration to Judea.

D. The emigrants (8:1–14). Ezra first mentions the leaders who will make the journey with him: Gershom, a priest of the line of Phinehas, son of Eleazar; Daniel of Ithamar; and a descendant of David, Hattush of the descendants of Shecaniah.

Other family names are approximately the same as in 2:3–15, except for Joab in verse 9. This similarity could possibly mean that the ones who had originally returned several decades before had left family members in Babylon, and now, certain members of these families prepare to return to Judea. The bulk of Judean exiles remained in Babylon, but a very strong tie will exist between them and those who return to Judea.

E. A search for Levites (8:15–20). Ezra assembles the emigrants at what could be called the "jumping-off" point near the canal that flows toward Ahavah (v. 15). After checking among the people and priests, he discovers that no Levites are present. Realizing that he cannot return to Judea without them, he summons the priests of the community in the Babylonian province as well as other learned leaders, and sends them to Iddo, the leader in Casiphia. Enough pressure is brought to bear by responsible individuals in order to find Levites who might be encouraged to leave their comfortable and established surroundings and return to Jerusalem to minister at the temple. The search is fruitful because they find a gifted Levite as well as others, along with temple servants who are willing to return to the homeland. All of these Levites and temple servants have an established recorded lineage. Ezra is pleased and ascribes the successful search for responsible leaders to the "gracious hand of our God" (v. 18).

F. The journey (8:21–36). The account of the return to Judea is interesting because it demonstrates the qualities of religious leadership which Ezra exemplifies, and also describes his complete dependence upon God who will protect him along the way.

Before Ezra sets out on his journey, he proclaims a fast whereby everyone humbles himself before God and asks him for safety. The record indicates that Ezra is too ashamed to ask the Persian authorities for a military escort, preferring instead to trust wholly in God. Later on, Nehemiah sees the situation quite differently, and does accept a military escort (Neh. 2:7–9), but we must not thereby conclude that Nehemiah has less faith than Ezra. Both were leaders in their own right, but each also had a different task to accomplish. Ezra was a religious leader, a man gifted in the exposition of the law, while Nehemiah was a political leader. Both trusted God wholly in the work, but their objectives were totally different. Both, however, were honored by God.

Ezra now delegates the responsibility of guarding the silver, gold, and other valuable articles that the king and his advisors have donated to the house of God in Jerusalem. All the monies and articles are divided among the priest-leaders who are told that they, as well as the silver and gold, are consecrated to the Lord. They are to guard the wealth carefully, realizing that they are responsible for it, and what has been given to them by Ezra must tally with what will be delivered in Jerusalem.

Ezra's leadership is tested in that he is forced to share his responsibility with others. The wealth which Ezra and the priests carry is enormous: about 25 tons of silver, 3 ¾ tons of silver articles, 3 ¾ tons of gold, 20 golden bowls weighing some 19 pounds, as well as other precious articles. The fact that Ezra refuses a military escort is eloquent testimony to his faith that God will indeed protect him, considering the fact that he and his party would certainly be likely targets for attack by bandits and robbers along the way.

The emigrants set out on the twelfth day of the first month from the Ahava canal, and Ezra is able to testify afterward that no enemies or bandits attack them on the long journey of perhaps one thousand miles. God indeed protects his people, enabling them to arrive safely in Jerusalem. After resting for some three days, the leaders gather on the fourth day and weigh out all that had been given to them in Babylon. Everything is accounted for, and what was delegated to the priests is now delivered in full at the completion of the journey.

Verses 35–36 are in the third person, which possibly adds some additional information to what Ezra has provided. The emigrants are grateful for their safe journey as well as for the privilege of a new life. Accordingly, a sin offering of twelve male goats is offered, representing all twelve tribes. In addition, twelve bulls for all Israel, ninety-six rams, and seventy-seven male lambs are offered as a burnt offering. The emigrants worship God with great devotion and are thankful to him for what he has accomplished; they also dedicate themselves to the task of serving him along with the rest of their fellow Judeans.

After caring for their worship first, they now deliver the documents with orders from Artaxerxes to the authorities west of the Euphrates, explaining to them that they should not only recognize Ezra's place as a teacher among his people, but also give further assistance to Judea and the temple. The emigrants exhibit careful attention to spiritual values. They first worship God, and then recognize their civil authorities who, in this case, have been instructed to help the people in their worship.

IV. Intermarriage (9:1–15)

One of Ezra's first official tasks is dealing with the problem of intermarriage. So grave is this sin that it calls for drastic action which may sound harsh to our modern ears; we must ever remember, however, that God had called Israel as a people who were not only to be reverent before him, but were to separate themselves from the detestable practices of pagan peoples of the Middle East.

With the arrival of Ezra, well-versed in the law and no doubt recognized for his accomplishments, the Judean leaders now have to ruefully report that a grievous sin has been committed by many of the people in their midst. The report reflects somewhat the way Moses would have written in his day; the sad account states that there are those of the people of Israel, the priests and Levites, who have intermarried with "the Canaanites, Hittites, Perizzites, Jebusites, Ammonites, Moabites, Egyptians, and Ammorites" (v. 1). These peoples existed in the days of Moses, but the point of making such a connection is the reminder that Moses had banned all marriages to pagans. The Israelites were not to mix socially or politically in any way with foreign people so as to avoid the danger of intermarriage and false worship (Deut. 7:1–4). Ezra finds that his fellow Judeans have deliberately disobeyed Moses' instructions—in fact, some of the leaders and officials of Judea have actually "led the way in this unfaithfulness" (v. 2).

Ezra's immediate response is to tear his tunic and cloak, pull hair from his head and beard, and sit down, not saying a word. Seeing a religious leader acting like this puts the fear of God in those who are sensitive to God's law. These people gather around Ezra, joining him in his grief because of such a stumblingblock to the nation. Ezra sits there until the day has passed and at the time of the evening sacrifice, he falls on his knees, with his hands spread out before the Lord, and prays on behalf of his people. In a sense, Ezra reminds the people that when any article becomes impure, it remains so until the day has passed (see Lev. 11:24). Ezra is indeed a leader who leads by a godly example.

Ezra's prayer begins on a personal note first of all, declaring that because of what has happened in Judea, he is too ashamed and disgraced to even lift up his face and pray to the Lord. Ezra feels terrible about the grievous sin of intermarriage and unless it is confessed and rectified, the rebels face the judgment of God and, in fact, the entire nation will be held accountable for the sin. Very quickly, however, Ezra changes from the personal singular to the personal plural, *our* and *we*. From now on, this servant of God will intercede for Judea, recognizing that everyone, including himself, is involved with the shame and consequences of the guilt.

Ezra goes back in his prayer to the time and the experiences which had brought judgment and destruction upon Judah, and for which the people had been "subjected to the sword and captivity, to pillage and humiliation at the hand of foreign kings" (v. 7). Ultimately, Judah suffered exile for seventy years because of their sins. Intermarriage was one of the sins because it involved adopting the pagan spouse's worship practices and the land became polluted with idolatry. But God indeed had been gracious, and Ezra mentions how he had purified a remnant and brought them back to their land, enabling them to rebuild the sanctuary and thereby giving some light to their eyes and relief from their bondage. They had been slaves, but God has shown kindness to his people through the Persian kings and they have been restored.

Ezra now becomes specific in his confession of sin. Tragically, he has to declare that everyone has ignored the commands of God proclaimed by his servants, the prophets. Ezra repeats Moses' warning that God's people are not to give their daughters to the sons of pagans or take the daughters of pagan peoples for their sons (Deut. 7:1–3), thereby keeping themselves separate.

While everyone has been disobedient and has incurred great guilt, yet Ezra also observes in his prayer that God is indeed gracious, and has punished his people less than what their sins deserve, making it possible for a remnant to live once more in the land. He asks whether Judea will indeed once more break God's commands and become involved with the grievous error of intermarriage with pagans and adopt their detestable practices. Judea is guilty and God would have every right to bring judgment upon his people and be completely righteous in his actions. Ezra offers no excuses, but confesses simply that the people of Judea have sinned, not only those who are directly involved in intermarriages, but the others as well because, by their silence, they have condoned the situation. What is interesting is that Ezra makes no request of God to forgive the nation; instead, he seems to imply that the only proper response is for all the people to confess and deal with their sin. Only as they humble themselves, exhibit broken and contrite hearts, and remove the evil among them, will God's blessing be upon them once more.

V. Confession and Separation (10:1–44)

A. The confession (10:1–17). Ezra's prayer and confession, as he weeps and throws himself down before the house of God and the altar, draws a great crowd of men, women, and children around him. They, too, begin to weep bitterly as the Spirit of God convicts them. It is not long before Shecaniah confesses to Ezra: "We have been unfaithful to our God by marrying foreign women from the peoples around us" (v. 2). But he also knows what Judea must do if there is to be any possibility for restoration. The people have to face up to their sin, break up these pagan marriages, and send away the pagan women and their children. He calls for immediate action and promises on behalf of the people who stand with him that they will support Ezra in whatever has to be done.

Once Ezra is certain that he has the support of the people, he places the leading priests, Levites, and the people under oath that they will indeed handle the matter in a way honoring to the Lord. He then continues his fast as he mourns the unfaithfulness of Judea. A proclamation is then issued throughout the nation, calling for a solemn assembly before the Lord. Anyone ignoring the summons and failing to appear in the assembly will risk forfeiture of property as well as being cut off from Judea.

The assembly takes place on the twentieth day of the ninth month, in November–December, and therefore in wintertime. To make matters worse, it is raining (v. 9) and because of the seriousness of the situation, the people are in great distress. To say the least, it is a most miserable scene. Ezra reminds the assembly that they have indeed been unfaithful in marrying pagan women and have brought guilt upon the nation. The assembly is to make confession to the Lord God and those who have transgressed must now separate themselves from their foreign wives or husbands. The Spirit of God works mightily in response to the prayer already offered and the people are in earnest to do what is right. As a result, most of the assembly cries out with a loud voice concerning the sin of intermarriage and the decision to correct it: "You are right! We must do as you say" (v. 12).

However, many of the crowd declare that the matter cannot be settled in one day or even two. Their suggestion is that the officials should act on their behalf in a responsible manner. Furthermore, spokesmen of the multitude also call upon everyone who has married a foreigner to make an appointment at a set time with the elders and judges in each of their towns so that the issue can be settled once for all. The Spirit of God has burdened the entire assembly that this action must be taken "until the fierce anger of our God in this matter is turned away from us" (v. 14). The proposal is accepted by the assembly, and Ezra then appoints family heads, one from each family division; beginning with the first day of the tenth month, they are to investigate every case. It takes some three months to accomplish this task, from the first day of the tenth month until the first day of the first month, some time during March–April.

The decision is binding and almost all who married foreigners have to divorce them and send them away. Obviously, there were some who disagreed with such a distasteful action, and the record lists four, two of whom are Meshullam, a leader who had emigrated with Ezra (8:16); and Shabbethai, a Levite, who should have known better than to oppose what the law declared wrong (v. 15).

As to what happened to the foreign spouses, we are not expressly told. We can assume that many of these pagan spouses returned to their own families. A pagan could, however, decide to renounce his idolatrous status and seek conversion within the household of Israel, in which case, he or she became a part of Israel and divorce did not have to take place. A non-Israelite with no family to which he or she could return could choose to remain within Judea, abide by its laws, and give up idolatry. Such a person would be regarded as an alien but yet be accorded the right to live within the nation.

B. Those guilty of intermarriage (10:18–44). The list begins with those of the priestly families who pledged to put away their foreign wives. For their guilt they present a ram as a guilt offering (see Lev. 5:17–19). Their intermarriages are regarded as guilt before the Lord because they have not been sensitive to the Word of God regarding wrong choices for mates. The priests are to act in a responsible manner because when they turn away from the Law, then the people will follow suit. The principle still applies today: when the pulpit goes astray, then the nation likewise will not have proper spiritual guidance and will also turn away from righteousness.

The Levites who erred are mentioned next. The same principle applies to them as with the priesthood. They, too, confess their wrongdoing along with the singers and the gatekeepers.

The list next includes those of the people of Judea who put away their wives. Nine of the thirty-three families and towns which appear in 2:3–35 are mentioned here, but there are also two who are not, the descendants of Bani (v. 34) and Binnui (v. 38).

While this was indeed a painful experience, yet Ezra's task was to be faithful to what Moses had declared on behalf of God. At this point, it would appear that Ezra withdrew from public life and opened a school to train priests and Levites in the law, making his unique contributions in establishing the worship of Judea.

SELECT BIBLIOGRAPHY

Adeney, W. F. *Ezra and Nehemiah.* Reprint. Minneapolis: Klock & Klock, 1980.

Archer, G. *A Survey of Old Testament Introduction.* Rev. ed. Chicago: Moody, 1975.

Batten, L. W. *The Books of Ezra and Nehemiah.* The International Critical Commentary. Edinburgh: T. & T. Clark, 1961.

Coggins, R. J. *The Books of Ezra and Nehemiah.* The Cambridge Bible Commentary. London: Cambridge University Press, 1976.

Harrison, R. K. *Introduction to the Old Testament.* Grand Rapids: Eerdmans, 1969.

Keil, C. F. *The Books of Ezra, Nehemiah and Esther.* Old Testament Commentaries. Grand Rapids: Eerdmans, 1950.

Kidner, D. *Ezra and Nehemiah.* The Tyndale Old Testament Commentaries. Downers Grove: Inter-Varsity, 1979.

Luck, G. *Ezra and Nehemiah.* Chicago: Moody, 1961.

NEHEMIAH

Louis Goldberg

INTRODUCTION

The name *Nehemiah* means "the Lord comforts." His father was Hacaliah (1:1) and his brother was Hanani (1:2; 7:2), who possibly lived in Judea. Nothing further is known of Nehemiah's family, not even the tribe from which he came. He was born in exile and rose to the high rank of cupbearer to Artaxerxes I Longimanus (1:11; 2:1), a position God used to accomplish his purposes for his people in far-off Judea.

The Persian Empire forms the historical background for the books of Nehemiah and Ezra. After conquering Babylon in 539 B.C., Cyrus issued a proclamation in 538 B.C. permitting all refugees to return to their homelands. The Assyrians and Babylonians had displaced conquered peoples far from their homes and then in turn took other peoples and settled them in areas which had been subdued, thereby controlling large groups of their subjects. The Persians did the opposite. In order to curry the favor of conquered peoples, they permitted refugees to return to their hometowns and to rebuild their temples, and also requested that all peoples worship and pray on behalf of the well-being of the empire. God indeed worked in history for his people so that they might return to their homeland and build a second temple in Jerusalem.

Most scholars concur that Nehemiah belongs in the historical setting of Artaxerxes I, the primary evidence being the Elephantine papyri. These are documents sent by Jewish people from Egypt (ca. 410–408 B.C.), asking the high priest in Jerusalem for funds to rebuild a temple that had been destroyed by the Egyptians. He ignores their request, however, because the only legitimate temple is in the city of Jerusalem. Because the papyri mention Johanan as high priest and Sanballat as governor, and since Johanan was a grandson of Eliashib (Neh. 3:1), Nehemiah's ministry occurred in the days of Eliashib, and he therefore lived during the time of Artaxerxes I of the mid-fifth century B.C.

Nehemiah arrived in Jerusalem in the twentieth year of Artaxerxes I (1:1; 2:1; ca. 445 B.C.). He had a twelve-year ministry among his people (445–433 B.C.) and then returned in the thirty-second year of the emperor's reign (13:6). We are not sure how long he remained there, but sometime later he returned to Jerusalem (13:6–7).

The Jewish sources indicate that Ezra is the author of the Book of Nehemiah, and since both men were contemporaries, Ezra could have written the book bearing his name and also edited Nehemiah. There have been objections to the conservative view that Nehemiah could have written the book bearing his name because of a reference to Jaddua as high priest (12:11–12). According to Josephus (*Antiquities of the Jews,* 11.7.8), there was a Jaddua who served as high priest from 351–331 B.C., and was in his last year of office when Alexander the Great conquered Jerusalem. This objection can be answered by the fact that there were probably two different men with the same name.

As with Ezra, Nehemiah is not mere narrative. Through historical events, God moves to accomplish his purposes through a man well suited for political leadership. Great theological truths motivate him, thereby providing us with major lessons for today.

Nehemiah has a very strong faith in God. He declares that, in the midst of formidable opposition, God is great and awesome (4:14) and no enemy can overcome the people of Judea. While the God of the Judeans is known to the Persians as the God of heaven, to Israel he is indeed the Lord.

God moves Artaxerxes I to release Nehemiah from his duties and send him to Jerusalem to rebuild its wall and to restructure political life in Judea. He also stirs Nehemiah's heart to reconstitute a new life for Jerusalem by repopulating it so that it would again be a city reflecting his praises. So powerful is God's presence with Nehemiah during the rebuilding of Jerusalem and Judea that no enemy can thwart his purposes for his people.

As in Ezra, there is a strong sense of the continuity of Israel as a people. Therefore, Nehemiah withstands the enemies of Judea who mock his plan to rebuild the walls of Jerusalem. His response is that "the God of heaven will give us success" (2:20), thereby reflecting how he is interested in his people and wants them to be restructured politically and have a sense of order in their society.

Not only does the Lord bless the nation materially, but when Ezra reads the law of God and has it explained to the people (chap. 8), the Spirit of the living God works mightily and brings about one of the greatest spiritual renewals in the history of Israel. As the people listen to the Word, they break down and weep bitterly. Nehemiah has to urge them not to weep, but to rejoice because the joy of the Lord is their strength (8:10). One outcome of the renewal is that the Judeans willingly pledge their allegiance to the Mosaic covenant (chap. 10). This agreement was already spelled out in Deuteronomy 28 and was to be reenacted on special occasions: when Israel entered the land (Deut. 27; Josh. 8:30–35); when a new king ascended to the throne (Deut. 17:18–20); and particularly when God graciously visited Israel in spiritual renewal (2 Chron. 34:20–32).

The sanctuary was the very heart of Israel's worship and on the occasion of the dedication of the wall of Jerusalem, Nehemiah calls upon the priests and Levites to first purify themselves, and then purify the people, the gates, and the wall (12:30). In addition, he asks for two large choirs to sing antiphonally. The occasion is moving and beautiful. As the choir sings, sacrifices are offered before the Lord; so great is the rejoicing in Jerusalem that its sound is heard from afar (12:43).

After Ezra reads the law on the occasion of the seventh month, the people also celebrate the Feast of Tabernacles, building their booths all over Jerusalem; they take their meals and rejoice in the goodness of God. The temple had been dedicated amidst a great celebration upon its completion (Ezra 6:16–22), but once more, some seventy-two years later, God visits Judea with a great spiritual renewal, and the occasion in the sanctuary area is a joyous one.

The evidence for Nehemiah as a man of prayer is encountered throughout the entire book. From the very beginning when he prays on behalf of Jerusalem and Judea until the very end when he asks God to remember him (13:31), prayer is a dominant characteristic.

Nehemiah stands firm in the face of opposition from without while the wall is being rebuilt. While he organizes the workers as an armed force against any marauders, he also calls upon God for his protection and encouragement (4:4–5; 6:14).

Furthermore, we sense the tremendous power of prayer after the renewal. The Levites pray to God, blessing his name, recounting his goodness to the nation in the past, and asking his favor upon them (9:5–37). When God works in great power among his people, they will always respond in thankfulness, gratitude, and recommitment.

We cannot overlook the emphasis on the Scriptures in the Book of Nehemiah. Ezra prepared a cadre of Levites to faithfully interpret the Scriptures, and at the completion of the wall, he comes at Nehemiah's request to read the Word to the assembled people (chap. 8). Ezra had already gone to great pains to translate the Scriptures from Hebrew to Aramaic to make it possible for people to understand the Word of God. As a result, God greatly uses the teaching of the Word in the spiritual renewal of the nation.

Nehemiah's task is to help his fellow Judeans close up the broken-down parts of the wall around Jerusalem and rebuild the gates. Furthermore, he plays a role in one of the greatest spiritual renewals in Israel's history, characterized by the teaching of the Word of God bringing conviction in the hearts of the listeners; the humbling of the people amidst mourning and weeping; the experience of great joy when many in Judea turn to God; and the response of prayer, confession, and recognition of the graciousness of God in sustaining his people.

Another unique aspect of the book is the reenactment of the Mosaic covenant, as people and leaders yield their allegiance to it. Israel is a covenant people, but God many times has to work in their hearts so as to make them yield their hearts to him and affirm his Word.

Some of the key words in the book are "wall" (and walls), used thirty-two times, and "build," appearing twenty-three times.

OUTLINE

I. A Pathetic Report (1:1–11)
  A. The Report (1:1–3)
  B. Nehemiah's Prayer (1:4–11)
II. Nehemiah's Commissioning (2:1–20)
III. Jerusalem's Wall and Gates (3:1–7:3)
  A. The Builders (3:1–32)
  B. Opposition from Without (4:1–23)
  C. Opposition from Within (5:1–19)
  D. Further Opposition from Without (6:1–14)
  E. Completion of the Wall (6:15–7:3)
IV. The Exiles (7:4–73)
V. Spiritual Renewal (8:1–10:39)
  A. The Law (8:1–9)
  B. Celebration (8:10–18)
  C. Confession (9:1–37)
  D. Covenant Renewal (9:38–10:39)
VI. Residents, Priests, and Levites (11:1–12:26)
  A. New Residents for Jerusalem (11:1–36)
  B. Priests and Levites (12:1–26)
VII. Dedication of the Wall (12:27–47)
VIII. Final Reforms (13:1–31)

COMMENTARY

I. A Pathetic Report (1:1–11)

A. The report (1:1–3). More than half of Nehemiah is a personal record, beginning when he was in the Persian citadel of Susa in the month of Kislev (November–December) in the twentieth year of the reign of Artaxerxes I (445 B.C.). Susa was the winter resort of the Persian kings.

One of Nehemiah's brothers, Hanani, comes from Judah with other men and is questioned about the status of the Judean remnant as well as the city of Jerusalem. Nehemiah is genuinely interested in what has happened to the people who had returned to Judea with Ezra twelve years previously.

The men report that the Judeans are in great trouble and disgrace because the wall of Jerusalem has been broken through in many places and the gates have been burned with fire (v. 3). Hanani is not describing what happened in the days of Nebuchadnezzar in 586 B.C. when he destroyed the first temple and left the walls of the city in ruins. Nehemiah is listening to an account of how his people have attempted to reconstitute their life in the city of Jerusalem, trying to restore its walls, but the many enemies of Judea are preventing this.

B. Nehemiah's prayer (1:4–11). The normal response would be to rush in before the king with a petition to help the Judeans but Nehemiah knows better than to act rashly. Artaxerxes had acceeded to the request by Judea's enemies to destroy what had been accomplished already, and Nehemiah realizes he has to appeal to a higher King for help. Therefore, he asks God himself to intervene on behalf of his people.

Nehemiah weeps, mourns, and fasts before the God of heaven, appealing to the "great and awesome God," but to a God who is also a God of love who remembers those who love him and obey his commands (Deut. 10:12–21). His prayer includes: (1) a *cry* for God's ears to be attentive and his eyes open to what his servant has to say on behalf of the Judeans; (2) a *confession* of sin to God in intercession for his people who have acted wickedly and are in exile as a just punishment by God for their sins; (3) a *call* upon God to remember his promise to Moses that when Israel would, in exile, confess their sins and pledge themselves to obey his word, then he would bring them back to their homeland (Deut. 32:36–43); (4) a *reminder* to God that the remnant who had returned to the land are indeed his servants whom he has redeemed; and (5) a *plea* that God's ears be attentive to the prayer of his servant as well as the prayers of all those who delight to honor his name. Nehemiah also asks God for success in the presence of Artaxerxes.

As cupbearer to Artaxerxes, Nehemiah has a high position, ministering at close range to the monarch and his family and other notables during mealtimes. God will use Nehemiah's position to help Judea. Artaxerxes will be so moved that he will give his cupbearer political power to help his people. The decrees against Judea by this very king will now be overturned. The people of Judea do not realize at this point in time that their plight is to be changed, but already the machinery is set in motion to bring them relief.

II. Nehemiah's Commissioning (2:1–20)

The time has finally arrived for which Nehemiah has been praying (**2:1–8**). He has been "waiting upon the Lord" from the month of Kislev (November–December) until Nisan (March–April), remaining persistent all the while on behalf of his people. He has also fasted and the strain is beginning to show.

The king notices a change in his cupbearer's countenance and exclaims that he must be suffering "sadness of heart" (v. 2) in that he does not appear physically ill. Nehemiah's fear at the king's observation (2:2) suggests that a servant in such a high position had to keep his personal feelings to himself or they might take away from the festivities of a banquet or the joy of a family dinner.

Nehemiah, however, takes advantage of the king's statement, realizing God's opportunity and hour have arrived; there might never be another occasion quite like this one. So he introduces the concern of his heart, first by his fervent wish that the king will enjoy long life, implying also the desire for his health and prosperity. He then explains why he is sad. The city from where his fathers originated is in ruins and the gates have been burned by fire. We may wonder why he does not mention Jerusalem by name, but the king knows very well the background of his cupbearer and to which city he is referring. Nehemiah exhibits a God-given wisdom in not asking for a change of Persian political policy toward Judea, but rather, simply tells the king how he feels about his homeland and its principal city where his fathers are buried.

Artaxerxes asks his servant what he would like to do about the matter. Before replying, Nehemiah quickly breathes a prayer to the God of heaven to guide him as he presents the plans he already has on his heart. He asks the king to send him to the "city in Judah" where his fathers are buried so that it can be rebuilt. Probably during the four long months of prayer and meditation, he already had on his mind what he would do given the opportunity.

The record mentions that the queen is sitting beside the king, suggesting that Nehemiah is present at a family dinner because queens usually did not appear at formal banquets. This also implies a personal relationship between this cupbearer and both king and queen as well as the high favor he had with them. Artaxerxes then asks how long his servant will be gone as he guides the rebuilding of the wall and repair of the gates. Nehemiah sets a time although we do not know what he suggested at this point (v. 6).

Nehemiah now details his plan. He desires letters to the governors of the Trans-Euphrates, the area west of the Euphrates including Judea, so that he might have safe conduct. In addition, he also asks for letters to the keeper of the forest for enough lumber to make beams for the gates and city wall. The qualities of Nehemiah as a leader are obvious, but God's favor also rests upon his servant, and so the king grants all of his requests. God can indeed work through men and leaders in high places in order that his purposes can be accomplished.

No details of the journey are given, but Artaxerxes provides army officers and cavalry to travel with Nehemiah. Upon arriving in Jerusalem with such a show of force and authority, he presents letters to the governors from the king, thereby establishing officially his presence in Judea to accomplish the purposes for which the king has sent him.

One can imagine the response by two of Judea's most powerful enemies, Sanballat and Tobiah the Ammonite. The Elephantine papyri later refer to Sanballat as governor of Samaria; possibly he held this post when Nehemiah arrived in Judea in 445 B.C. There is also archaeological evidence that the family of Tobiah had a long-established prominence in the city of Ammon. One can imagine how perturbed these two men were that someone had come from the Persian court to help the Judeans and thereby reverse official Persian policy.

After Nehemiah rests three days, he seeks to examine the walls and determine the plan for their reconstruction before explaining it to the officials in Jerusalem (**2:9–20**). Taking a few men with him, he goes out through the Valley Gate for a night survey. The distances are not very substantial. We cannot be sure of the wall in Jerusalem in Nehemiah's day, but on the east side of the city was the Kidron Valley and from north to south the distance was not much more than one mile; crosswise, at the widest, it could not be more than a thousand yards. As to whether Nehemiah made the entire circuit around the wall, we do not know, but the text does not exclude this possibility. After his survey, he reenters the city by the Valley Gate.

Nehemiah is now ready to present his plan for reconstructing the wall to the Judean officials. He first notes that Jerusalem is without proper protection and in disgrace because its wall has many gaps and its gates are burned. He must have gone into detail how Artaxerxes had graciously made provision for the rebuilding of the walls; but most important, he insists that God's hand is upon the project. The Judeans are convinced and, with a strong leader over them, they resolve to rebuild Jerusalem and to remove its disgrace.

Once more, the enemies of Judah are mentioned: Sanballat, Tobiah, and Geshem the Arab. They mock and ridicule the plans for the wall, but they also add a sinister note: Does Judea plan to rebel against Artaxerxes? These enemies are men of influence and power. Tobiah is also in constant communication with some of the nobles of Judah (6:17–19) and possibly Sanballat's daughter was married to one of the sons of the high priest (13:28). Their connections among the Judean leadership mean that they could work from within to delay and even stop the reconstruction effort.

With Sanballat of Samaria to the north, Tobiah of Ammon to the east, and Geshem the Arab to the southeast of Judea, the Judeans are completely surrounded by hostile peoples. None of these fears stop Nehemiah; he asserts his people's right to exist; their enemies have no share, claim, or historic right to Jerusalem. We can likewise take courage from Nehemiah's leadership and face our enemies with the same confidence and resolve he had, knowing we too can tap into the same power source.

III. Jerusalem's Wall and Gates (3:1–7:3)

The account provided of those who work on the wall is a moving description of the willingness of people to share in the work and resist opposition. We also note how a man of God successfully carries out his commission.

A. The builders (3:1–32). The roster of builders includes people of faith as well as shirkers, indicating that God knows exactly their attitudes and their labor.

Eliashib, the high priest, and his fellow priests rebuild the Sheep Gate near the northeast corner of the wall. The Sheep Gate was important because through it sheep were brought to the temple for sacrifice. From this gate, we proceed counterclockwise to the Tower of the Hundred, to the Tower of Hananel, the Fish Gate, and the next two sections. The leaders on these sections, the nobles of Tekoa, will not work (3:5), indicating that they do not really support Nehemiah's project.

Involved in the work are goldsmiths and perfume-makers (v. 8), suggesting that men of all backgrounds and trades are involved and in complete agreement with the reconstruction. Important officials, rulers of half-districts of Jerusalem, also take part in the project (vv. 9, 12). Shallum is aided by his daughters (v. 12), implying that this is a family effort. Levites are involved as well (v. 17).

The account continues, mentioning next the hill of Ophel, facing the Kidron Valley. At this point, the wall begins to ascend, leading up to the temple grounds. In this region are some of the priests, Levites, and temple servants who also work on their portion of the wall. The Horse Gate, the East Gate, and the Inspection Gate are mentioned. Finally, the account ends at the Sheep Gate. At the last section of the wall, mention again is made of goldsmiths and merchants who help in the reconstruction. Nehemiah has managed to galvanize a good cross-section of people, encouraging them in their work. The church, also comprised of various peoples in many walks of life, can be united by effective leadership to do the work of God.

B. Opposition from without (4:1–23). The record indicates some of the ways in which God's work can be thwarted and even stopped. We learn firsthand the principles Nehemiah uses to repel these attacks.

Sanballat becomes angry as the work progresses and ridicules the efforts by the Judeans, mocking and sneering at the inability of the people to do hard work (**4:1–6**). Tobiah taunts their efforts, exclaiming that if a fox climbed up on the thin walls, they would fall under its weight. These scare tactics are intended to stop all work, but Nehemiah's response is to call upon God, reminding him that his people are being despised. God takes great delight when his servants make known their requests. While Nehemiah's prayer request seems somewhat harsh, yet a leader has to be decisive. Why should he pray in this way? Because the enemies of God have insulted God's people! Likewise today, while we pray for our enemies, we also ask God's protection when they seek to harm us. And, if the attacks become vicious, we can even call upon God for our enemies to be stopped in their tracks and suffer reversals in order that his work can go on. While Nehemiah prays, his fellow Judeans continue to work on the wall until it has reached half of its required height.

When these enemies realize that ridicule does not work, they plot more trouble and even seek to fight against the people of Jerusalem (**4:7–14**). Nehemiah's response again is to pray; he also posts guards both day and night to meet any physical threat.

This psychological warfare, however, begins to have its effect on some of the Judeans; they begin to entertain misgivings. The words of the enemies are repeated ten times over, as if they have become mesmerized with them (v. 12): the enemies will soon attack and put an end to the work!

Nehemiah's response is to post guards with weapons at the weaker points of the wall and then to encourage the rest to keep on working. He tells the leaders and the people that they are not to fear because a greater Power than any human enemy will care for them.

Judea's enemies realize that their plots have again been foiled, but Nehemiah takes no chances. He divides the work force, posting half of them at significant points, equipping them with spears, shields, bows, and armor, while the rest continue on with the work (**4:15–23**). Some even handle building materials with one hand and hold weapons in the other. Nehemiah takes command over the entire work force, and has a man with a trumpet beside him so that if the enemies should mount any opposing force, the trumpet will be blown and the fighting force readied for battle.

C. Opposition from within (5:1–19). Fighting enemies from without is one thing, but to face problems from within the believing community is far worse. If Satan can bring distress and division from within, the cohesiveness of the community will be torn apart and its effectiveness to function as a unit will be destroyed.

The poor raise a great outcry against the leaders, complaining that they have had to sell their fields, vineyards, and homes in order to obtain grain for the next year's planting (**5:1–5**). Because of a famine, they have no money and as a result, many have been enslaved to the leaders. Obviously, this problem had not developed since Nehemiah arrived, but rather was one of long standing. The work in rebuilding the wall took only fifty-two days (6:15), but the history of the second commonwealth of Judea by this time already covered some ninety years, allowing ample opportunity for inequities to develop among the people.

The problem is that the civil leadership has become insensitive to the law of Moses. When families were in dire need, there were a number of ways to alleviate the situation. First, they could sell the crop value of their land to the next year of Jubilee, at which time the land reverted back to the family (Lev. 25:8–17). Second, those with means were to help the poor. If money was loaned, no interest was to be taken; neither was food to be sold for a profit (Lev. 25:35–38). Third, if a person still was in great need, he could sell himself to one with means, serving for six years. Such a servant was to be paid twice the wages of a non-Israelite and when the Israelite servant was set free, he was to be supplied liberally from the flock, threshing floor, and wine press (Deut. 16:12–15). Finally, all debts were to be canceled every seven years, a measure which was designed to aid the poor (Deut. 15:1–2). The law obviously did not try to solve the problem of poverty, but it did alleviate a great deal of need.

The description in 5:1–3 is that of a disadvantaged class which no one seems to care about. If the situation should continue, the community would be in danger of splitting apart and the work on the wall would come to a standstill.

Is it ever possible for God's leader to become angry? Jesus himself was provoked with those who had stubborn hearts and refused healing (Mark 3:5). Paul could inwardly burn about those who led others into sin (2 Cor. 11:29). Nehemiah becomes angry, but not without first thinking through the problem (**5:6–13**); he then roundly accuses the nobles and officials of accepting usury from their own poor countrymen contrary to the law. After calling a meeting of all the leaders, he asks that in view of the redemption of Judea from exile, how it is possible for poor fellow Jewish people to be sold to non-Jews and then be bought back for a profit. There is dead silence because these leaders are shamed for how they have treated the poor.

Nehemiah then appeals to the decency of these erring leaders. If he and his own men are helping people with money and grain, then they should immediately give back to the poor the fields, vineyards, olive groves, houses, and interest money. The leaders have no recourse but to follow the example of their governor, and with their admission of guilt and willingness to rectify their evil deeds, Nehemiah demands they take an oath before God to do what they have promised. If they do not keep their word to which God is a witness, then he has his ways of removing their dishonest gain. Everyone agrees, saying "Amen," and praising God that the danger from within has been averted.

What Nehemiah alluded to in his argument

against the insensitive leaders (v. 10) is now explained further (**5:14–19**). He takes no provision allotted to him and his staff by Artaxerxes. Instead, he gives it to the poor; what he and his household needs is taken from his own pocket (vv. 14, 18). His concern for the disadvantaged is an example to the rest of the leaders. Previously, the people were taxed heavily for the upkeep of their officials and their entire retinue, but Nehemiah will have no such gains for himself. He has a heart for the poor as well as a reverence for God who also cares for all such people. His final prayer, therefore, is that God should remember him for his deeds on their behalf.

D. Further opposition from without (6:1–14). The problems from within serve as an interlude to the problems the Judeans face from without. Once the former have been solved, Nehemiah turns again to deal with those enemies who persist in their opposition to the work on the wall.

When the work on the wall progresses so that not a gap is left in it, Judea's enemies now call upon Nehemiah to come down to one of the villages on the plain of Ono to discuss the project. Nehemiah correctly ascertains the treachery involved. His reply to his enemies is that the work on the walls would not stop for one minute, so it is senseless for him to travel to a distant point in order to discuss it. The enemy leaders on four occasions send the same message, but Nehemiah keeps on with his task.

Sanballat's next tactic is to send an open letter throughout the entire territory for everyone to read, accusing Nehemiah and his fellow Judeans of plotting a revolt against the Persians (**6:5–9**). The letter claims that the wall is being built to fortify the city of Jerusalem in defiance of Artaxerxes. The letter even impugns Nehemiah's intentions, saying he wants to be a king. Obviously, the letter is not true, and Nehemiah replies by declaring their charge to be nothing more than lies.

Nehemiah explains to the people of Judea that their enemies are only trying to frighten them, thinking that their work will cease, but he turns to God and prays for strength and encouragement of the rest of the people.

The final deception occurs when Nehemiah visits Shemaiah, a shut-in who suggests that both of them go inside the house of God and shut the temple doors because the former's life is in danger (**6:10–14**). His reply to Shemaiah is that as the leader of Israel, he has no reason to run and hide. He senses immediately that the message is not from God. Indeed, Shemaiah is attempting to bring Nehemiah and his leadership into complete disrepute. If the governor, a civil authority, would attempt to enter the temple itself, the priests would have every right to kill him, and, completely discredited, the work on the wall would cease. Nehemiah asks God to remember in judgment these enemies of his, Tobiah and Sanballat, as well as other false prophets, Noadiah, and the rest who have sought to frighten him.

E. Completion of the wall (6:15–7:3). In spite of opposition, the wall is finally completed in only fifty-two days. It is quite possible that the people only plugged up the gaps in the wall (assuming that the entire wall was not completely destroyed) and rebuilt the burned-down gates, and at a later time finished off the construction. Perhaps Tobiah had correctly assessed this stop-gap measure by sneering that if a fox should walk across the wall, it would collapse (4:3). But once the gaps are filled in, Jerusalem can begin to take on the semblance of a normal Middle East city. All the Judeans realize that God has helped them to complete the wall while their enemies lose their self-confidence. The people of God have withstood their enemies and accomplished what both he and Nehemiah wanted them to.

While we have already noted that some of the nobles were completely insensitive to the poor (chap. 5), we can now understand the reason for Nehemiah's problems. There are leaders in Judea under oath to Tobiah, and letters and replies go back and forth between them and one of Judea's avowed enemies. His family is even intermarried with two of these leaders, suggesting the reason why Meshullam resisted the edict for dissolving the marriages to pagans (Ezra 10:15). No wonder Tobiah and his friends could bring so much pressure against Nehemiah; but he is able to resist the intrigues and threats of physical force against him as he trusts God to bring to naught such disloyal acts.

After the work on the wall has been completed and the gates are restored, Nehemiah appoints gatekeepers, singers, and Levites to their tasks. In order to protect the wall and the gates, Nehemiah gives his brother Hanani oversight over them, issuing instructions that the gates are not to be opened until the sun is hot. No business is to be done at any other time except during the middle of the day. What is interesting is that the very Hanani who had brought the sad news to Nehemiah concerning Jerusalem (1:3) is now put in charge of the gates. Others who can be trusted are posted as guards along the wall and gates, as well as near their own houses, even though some of these houses have not yet been rebuilt.

IV. The Exiles (7:4–73)

Nehemiah now faces the critical problem of Jerusalem's defense because, although the wall is now completed, the necessary manpower to defend the city is lacking. Not only are there very few people in Jerusalem, but most of the houses have not yet been rebuilt. Nebuchadnezzar had sacked the city in 586, and the continual pressure upon the Persian kings by Judea's enemies kept to the minimum any effort at rebuilding Jerusalem. Nehemiah feels that he must revitalize the city and, led by God, he now assembles the leaders and people to take a census, thereby ascertaining how to equitably repopulate it.

Nehemiah calls for the genealogical record of the first emigration in 538 B.C. under Zerubbabel and what follows in this chapter is substantially the same list of individuals one finds in Ezra 2:1–67, although there are some notable exceptions. This is no mere recitation of names and occupations. What we must remember is that the people of Israel were a living community with a genealogical record traced back across the centuries.

Judea is one very small province amidst a vast area west of the Euphrates River including Assyria, Syria, and the area east of the Jordan River as well as southeast of the province of Judea. The Judeans who returned from exile under the proclamation of Cyrus in 538 B.C. (Ezra 1:2–4) were listed in a record to which both Ezra and Nehemiah had access and was included in the books carrying their names.

The leaders are presented first (**7:6–7**). The first mentioned is Zerubbabel, the grandson of King Jehoiachin, referred to as the son of Shealtiel (Ezra 3:2), the king's eldest son. However, 1 Chronicles 3:19 indicates that Zerubbabel was the son of Pedaiah, the younger brother of Shealtiel, implying a levirate marriage of Pedaiah to the widow of Shealtiel; the firstborn was then reckoned as a son of Shealtiel in order to keep the family name.

The prophet Jeremiah was led to place a curse on Jehoiachin so that no one of his line could ever sit upon the throne of David (Jer. 22:28–40). While Zerubbabel is recognized as a representative of the house of David and is the leader of the first emigration, yet because of the prophecy, no king of the line of Solomon reigned in Judea during the entire period of the second commonwealth (538 B.C.–A.D. 70). Instead, from the close of the Old Testament, the priests functioned as religious and political leaders for the nation. Zerubbabel, however, is recognized as the governor of Judea by the days of Haggai (Hag. 1:1).

The second person mentioned is Jeshua the high priest (Zech. 3:1), who is referred to as Joshua in both the books of Haggai (1:1) and Zechariah (3:1). Zerubbabel and Jeshua ruled together, representing both the regal and priestly ministries for the nation.

The rest of the leaders are almost the same as in Ezra 2:2 except for the different spellings. One additional name appears in the Nehemiah list, Nahamani, not present in Ezra 2:2. Perhaps what is intended is that twelve names appear among the list of leaders, representing, in a sense, the twelve tribes of Israel, although we have no idea of who belonged to which tribe.

When comparing the lists of laypeople in Nehemiah (**7:8–38**) and Ezra, there are only minor differences: (1) the omission of Magbish (Ezra 2:30) from the Nehemiah list; (2) two changes of order—Ezra 2:17, 19 are transposed in Nehemiah 7:22 and 23; and Ezra 2:33, 34 and Nehemiah 7:36, 37; and (3) Jorah in Ezra 2:18 appears in Nehemiah 7:24 as Hariph and Gibbar in Ezra 2:20 is spelled as Gibeon in Nehemiah 7:25.

The number of priests totals 4289, representing about one-tenth of the total emigrants. They were originally organized by King David into twenty-four family groups, serving according to a plan for their tour of duty (1 Chron. 24:7–19). Among the emigrants, however, only four of these family groups are mentioned (10:18–22; Ezra 2:36–39). But from these four, twenty-four divisions are again structured for their tour of duty, adopting the names already assigned by David. Some of these divisions appear as late as the first century (1 Chron. 2:10; Luke 1:5).

In the first emigration under Zerubbabel, only a small number of Levites return compared to the priests, and the former are even further subdivided into those directly assisting the priests at the altar and those serving as gatekeepers and singers. Each family of Levites has a specific function to accomplish, and they return to take up their various tasks once again (**7:43–45**).

Many of the temple servants' names (**7:46–56**) are not Hebrew. They are possibly descendants of captives David conquered who then either became aliens in Israel or converted and entered into the commonwealth of Israel. These people are assigned menial tasks at the altar, assisting the priests and Levites, and are designated Nethinim, or "dedicated ones" (Ezra 8:20). They too had been exiled to Babylon but return and look forward to service in the second temple.

Very possibly, Solomon may have pursued

the same policy as David, recruiting aliens who converted and then served in his administration (**7:57–60**).

Among this emigration are Israelites from the province of Babylon who have no record of identification as to their families or the hometowns of their families (**7:61–62**). Records were important because without them, no claims to family property could be made and in addition, doubts might be raised whether they were Israelites at all. Emigration policy permitted them to remain in Judea, but only with the status of aliens who had been circumcised and with the same rights as temple servants.

Those who claimed to be priests but had no family records to establish their identity were a special class (**7:63–65**) and it is possible that a few had even become lax in their responsibility to keep their records intact. However, the sons of Hakkoz (v. 63), some eighty years later in the days of Ezra, were able to verify their claims, if Meremoth, son of Uriah the priest (Ezra 10:33) is the same person as Meremoth son of Uriah, the son of Hakkoz (Neh. 3:4, 21). There is no reason to suspect otherwise.

Barzillai (v. 63) had evidently married into the family of Barzillai the man of Gilead who was a strong supporter of David (2 Sam. 19:32), but it is not clear whether he renounced his claim to the priesthood. At any rate, there is no further information about him. But when he, or anyone else, was not able to produce a record of identity, they were excluded from the priesthood, and Zerubbabel ordered them not to eat any sacred food of the priests. This policy was to remain in effect until there was further guidance from God, who would establish the identity of a priest through the Urim and Thummim.

The total number of emigrants—42,360—is the same as in Ezra 2:64 as well as in 1 Esdras 5:41. The problem with these totals, however, is that when one adds up the component parts, three different totals result: Ezra—29,818; Nehemiah—31,089; and 1 Esdras—30,143. Whatever argument is used in trying to reconcile the sum of component parts, there is a real problem with copyists' errors in reproducing numerical lists.

The mention of 7337 men and maidservants, about one servant per six emigrants, along with gold and silver, could very well reflect the wealth which had accumulated during the exile. From the time the first captives were taken until the return in 538 B.C., the people had sufficient funds for themselves and also shared with the emigrants returning to the homeland. The mention of men and women singers suggests the people had the means to support such pleasure and enjoyment. These singers are obviously distinct from the temple singers of verse 44.

The information regarding the gifts for the temple (**7:70–72**) is more detailed than what Ezra provides (2:68–69): (1) the governor (Nehemiah?) gives 19 pounds of gold in addition to fifty bowls and 530 garments for the priests; (2) some family heads give 375 pounds of gold and 1⅓ tons of silver; and (3) the people give 375 pounds of gold, 1¼ tons of silver, and 67 garments for the priests.

The priests, Levites, gatekeepers, and singers, along with other peoples, settle into their own towns (**7:73**), but an additional phrase in 1 Esdras 5:46, *lived in Jerusalem and its vicinity*, seems to add information to the original text. Whether it is so, we are not sure, but while the priests and Levites had their own hometowns, some could also have had homes in Jerusalem and nearby, living there during the time of their ministry and on other occasions. Certainly this could have occurred soon after the altar was erected upon the emigrants' return and also after Nehemiah's return later when the city of Jerusalem was repopulated.

V. Spiritual Renewal (8:1–10:39)

Along with the other great spiritual renewals Israel had experienced under Asa (2 Chron. 14–15), Hezekiah (2 Chron. 29–31), and Josiah (2 Chron. 34–35), the one during Nehemiah's time is also significant. What is described in chapters 8 and 9 provides an interesting study of the basis for spiritual renewal and the ingredients found there have been present in every genuine revival ever since.

A. The Law (8:1–9). Ezra is called to read the Law at the beginning of the seventh month in 445 B.C. We may only speculate what Ezra was doing after the close of his book (458 B.C.), but the suggestion has been made that when he retired from public life, he opened a school to train Levites in the Torah. He also transliterated the Old Testament into Aramaic, developed an oral interpretation of the Scriptures in Aramaic, trained Levites in learning this interpretation, and finished 2 Chronicles as well as wrote the book bearing his name. As a teacher of such accomplishment, it is no wonder Nehemiah called for him to lead in worship by reading the Law.

When the first day of the seventh month arrives, the Judeans assemble before the square at the Water Gate. This month on the Jewish calendar (September–October) was significant: the first day commemorated the special blowing of trumpets (Num. 29:1); the tenth day was the Day of Atonement; and beginning on the fifteenth day and lasting for one week was the

Feast of Tabernacles. Therefore both Nehemiah and the rest of the leaders feel it is appropriate to commemorate the completion of the wall at this time by meeting with God and giving thanks for what has been accomplished.

The reading begins on the first day after the blowing of the trumpets, and lasts from daybreak until noon. A special platform is built for the occasion and when Ezra opens the scroll, he praises the Lord, the great God, and the people respond with "Amen! Amen!" They greatly revere the Lord, bowing down and worshiping with their faces toward the ground. Then they listen carefully to the Word as it is read.

One prominent ingredient for spiritual renewal is the knowledge of and respect for the Word of God. There must be a willingness to listen to it, not glassy-eyed, but with one's whole heart, expecting God to speak with power.

A number of Levites stand with Ezra and while the Word is read, they interpret it so that the people can understand it. The Aramaic interpretation is significant, and becomes the first Targum of the portions read from the first five books of Moses. It was eventually expanded to cover the entire five books. The interpretation became an oral tradition and ever afterwards, even until the days of Jesus, whenever the Scripture was read, the interpreter stood by the side of the reader and provided the oral Aramaic interpretation.

Another ingredient of spiritual renewal is the humbling of people as the Holy Spirit works in their hearts. When the people hear the Word of God, they begin to mourn and weep because they realize how far they have fallen from its requirements. Amidst their tears, they seek to repent and make amends for their misdeeds.

B. Celebration (8:10–18). Nehemiah, while realizing the necessity of repentance and tears, wants the time to be a joyous one as well, and so he, along with Ezra and the Levites who taught the people, proclaim the day as a sacred one. The people are not to continue to mourn and weep. They must also enjoy the presence of God, eating choice food and drinking sweet drink, and sharing with those who have not prepared anything. The joy of the Lord is to be their strength (v. 10). One major consequence of renewal is the experience of joy which God provides for his people when they are obedient to his directives.

As the people gather again on the second day of the month to listen to the words of the law, they regain an appreciation for what it means to live in booths during the feast of the seventh month (Lev. 23:39–43). The festival had become only a token observance, but when the people celebrate it after renewal has come, it is like returning to the days of Joshua son of Nun (8:17). The blessings of Tabernacles, the thanksgiving to God for an abundant harvest, and the enjoyment of the last day of the feast, all have profound meaning for the people of Judea.

During this entire period, except for the Day of Atonement, the people prepare for the Feast of Tabernacles, gathering branches of olives and wild olive trees, myrtles, palms, and shade trees to build booths in the courtyards of the houses in Jerusalem, on their roofs, at various points in the courts of the house of God, and elsewhere. The occasion of observing the Feast of Booths from the fifteenth to the twenty-first and then remembering the crowning day on the twenty-second of the month (Lev. 23:39) is important, and Jewish people have ever afterward observed these festivals.

C. Confession (9:1–37). After the celebration of the Feast of Tabernacles, and possibly allowing for an additional day for rest, the people gather again to listen to the Law of God. They fast in the traditional way, wearing sackcloth and with dust on their heads, and the sign of their contrition of heart is their willingness to do what God asks of them in his Word (**9:1–3**). They separate from all foreigners, yielding themselves as an elect people who desire to serve their Lord.

For about three hours, they listen to the reading and interpretation of the Word of God. For another quarter of the day, the people confess their sins and the wickedness of their fathers in a prayer of intercession, calling with loud voices on the Lord their God.

One of the ingredients of spiritual renewal is the reestablishment of a meaningful prayer life, and after the confession of sin, the Levites lead the people in a prayer of praise and thanksgiving to the Lord who alone is from everlasting to everlasting (**9:4–37**).

As the Levites lead the Judeans in prayer, they first remember that God is indeed the Creator and all his creation worships him, but He is also the one who called Abraham from Ur of the Chaldeans to go to Canaan and there established with him a covenant which still exists. The prayer continues with a reminder of how God called Israel out of Egypt. The great miracles are recounted: the Red Sea was divided as Israel passed through and was spared; the Egyptian army was destroyed; the people were led through the desert by a pillar of cloud during the day and at night by a pillar of fire; finally, at Mount Sinai, God spoke to his people and gave them the law through his servant Moses. Their forefathers never lacked for bread and water until the day they came to the land which God had sworn to give to the descendants of Abraham.

What is interesting is how "they" and "our" intermingle. The prayer recounts how their forefathers were arrogant and stiffnecked and refused to obey God's command and how the first generation all died in the desert except for Caleb and Joshua. Even though many in Israel worshiped the image of the calf (Exod. 32), God never forgot his promise to Abraham that he would be a God to him and his descendants throughout *all* their generations. The second generation experienced God's great compassion as he cared for them, enabling them to conquer territories, defeat kings, and take the land from the Canaanites. Finally, they enjoyed all the good things of the land, eating to the full and reveling in the goodness of their God.

The prayer continues to recount the rebellion of the generations after Joshua and the elders who served him. One tribe after another became disobedient, killing the prophets and setting aside the law of God, so that he had no other recourse but to permit one enemy after another to oppress the various tribes. But God's great compassion was extended to his rebellious people, and as one tribe after another repented, the Lord sent judges who delivered them from the hand of their enemies.

Except for the spiritual high points under David, Asa, Jehoshaphat, Hezekiah, and Josiah, the spirituality of both Israel to the north and Judah to the south continued to decline and in the years just prior to the exile, the people of Judah turned from God and refused to listen to him. Finally, in accordance with the warning of the covenant (Deut. 28:64–68), Judah was taken into exile. If the people would not listen to the Lord anymore, then perhaps they would in exile. God's purposes for his people in Babylon were to bring judgment upon those caught up in idolatry, but more important, to purify a remnant so that never again would Judea be caught up in idolatry. Even though the exile brought shame and loss to his people, God's mercies were still extended to them.

Confession of sin only comes from truly repentant hearts, and this prayer emphasizes the fragile status of Judea as a people: the kings of Assyria had conquered Israel; the Babylonian kings had sacked Jerusalem, destroying the first temple; and now Judea is under the Persians. Despite all these calamities, God is merciful and the people can still worship him who is the King of kings and Lord of lords. Even though foreign kings tax and take tribute, the Judeans can enjoy a measure of religious freedom. While their fathers and they have sinned, God has been gracious to them. The prayer is transparent, not hiding anything, but it also breathes praise and worship that could only come from hearts in right relationship with God.

D. Covenant renewal (9:38–10:39). Israel was constituted as an elect people through the covenant at Sinai and some thirty-eight years later, Moses taught a second generation of Israelites the covenant, expanding further upon it. On the latter occasion, he told the Israelites that as soon as they entered the land and conquered some of it, they were to proceed to the region of Mounts Ebal and Gerizim and there reaffirm the covenant in the land. Israel was to reenact the covenant every seven years at the Feast of Tabernacles when the whole nation appeared before the Lord (Deut. 31:9–11), as well as on the occasion of a new king's accession to the throne. During the great renewals, a revived people felt the necessity to yield their lives in dedication to the Lord and the covenant.

While the term *covenant* does not occur in the text itself, the phrase *binding agreement* (**9:38**) is a reference to it, and the leaders and people seek to be obedient to what God asked them to do in the first place.

Since Nehemiah is the example par excellence, he is the first one to sign the covenant as a symbol of obedience for the nation (**10:1**).

Twenty-one names of priests follow (**10:2–8**), of which fifteen are those of families. (See chap. 12, which lists the names of the priests as emigrants, many of whom appear in this list. While Ezra is not specifically mentioned, he is a member of the family of Seraiah.)

The names of seventeen Levites follow, including families with a long record (**10:9–13**). The first three—Jeshua, Binnui, and Kadmiel—are families who came with Zerubbabel in the first emigration (12:8a; Ezra 2:40). Other individuals are more contemporary, and six of them are among those whom Ezra trained in interpreting the Law (Neh. 8:7).

Next are the leaders of the people (**10:14–27**), most of whom are family leaders. The first twenty-one names, from Parosh to Magpiash, with a few exceptions, closely follow Ezra 2:3–30 except for some minor spelling differences. Others are from families involved in the building of the wall (chaps. 3, 11, 12) while the remaining are perhaps branches of older families or may even reflect newer arrivals from the province of Babylon.

The remaining people, priests, Levites, gatekeepers, singers, temple servants, and others join the rest of the leaders in reenacting the covenant (**10:28–29**). These are not stragglers; rather, there is an established order in the community, reflecting the lists already drawn up by Ezra and Nehemiah.

As if to emphasize further the specific terms of the covenant, these are now mentioned in order (**10:30–39**).

The grave sin of intermarriage means the elect people will begin to disintegrate. To ensure the nation's sacred relation to God, there must not be intermarriages with pagan peoples.

The Law required that the Sabbath be observed, a directive that would mark Judea as a special province in an empire which had no special day set apart. The Sabbath is to be a testimony to the pagans that God requires both rest and worship on a specific day. Nor are the people to forget the sabbatical year. They are to forego any work on the land at that time as well as cancel all outstanding debts.

The people of God are not to forget the temple which is the very heart of their worship. While the cost of the temple upkeep is borne by the Persian treasury (Ezra 6:8–10), the Judeans must not become dependent on their overlords for the support of their own services. Rather, they are to give willingly the tax for temple upkeep. They are also to procure wheat for the bread of the Presence in the sanctuary and other specified grain and burnt offerings, as well as offerings for the special holy days.

The priests, Levites, and people promise they will not forget the tithes; the prescribed offering of wood at set times each year; the offering of the firstfruits of crops and fruit trees; the firstborn of sons, cattle, and flocks; and the first of ground meal, grain offerings, the fruits of the trees, and new wine and oil.

VI. Residents, Priests, and Levites (11:1–12:26)

A. New residents for Jerusalem (11:1–36). So few people live in Jerusalem that Nehemiah calls for the genealogical records in order to conduct a census, with a view to determining who would live there. The account in this chapter describes those willing to leave their lands and houses which, in some cases, represents a great sacrifice.

Because Jersualem is the capital of the country, the leaders of the nation and many of the leading priests and Levites have to be there, but it is also necessary that other citizens live in Jerusalem as well (**11:1–3**). People are given opportunity to volunteer at first; then lots are cast to provide for the prescribed number of people to be in the capital. The new citizens of Jerusalem represent a good cross-section of people from both Judah and Benjamin. The mention of Israelites (v. 3, lit. Israel), is possibly a reference to the citizens of the province of Judea.

When one compares **11:4–6** with its parallel in 1 Chronicles 9:6, one finds an additional house mentioned in the latter passage, that of Zerah, twin brother of Perez (Gen. 38:27–30). The two houses in the Nehemiah passage, Perez and Shelah, correspond to the Chronicles passage except that Shelah can also refer to Shilonites. The mention of "able men" (v. 6), describes the kind of people needed to defend Jerusalem.

When **11:7–9** is compared with its parallel in 1 Chronicles 9:7–9, the latter provides further information concerning Benjamin, and the total number (956) is slightly larger than the 928 mentioned by Nehemiah. The "chief officer" (v. 9) indicates that this particular part of the city was organized into districts with officers in charge to provide for an orderly society. Nehemiah has installed his brother Hanani, along with Hananiah, as commander of the citadel in charge of the city, but Judah possibly has a subordinate position over the second district of the city.

The information in 10:2–8 refers to families of priests but not necessarily the specific head of the family. In addition, certain favorite names were used continually. As a result, it is difficult to ascertain who various individuals are in the list of priests (**11:10–14**). All these carry on work for the temple (v. 12). The Levites and other officials are listed in **11:15–24**.

The boundaries of the province of Judea are now described (**11:25–36**). To the north is the province of Samaria while at the southeast and southern borders is Idumaea or Edom. Jerusalem and the territory to the north is in Benjamin's territory, while to the south of the city is Judah. The two tribes therefore occupy the ancient territories allotted to them while the Levites are scattered among both. However, Judeans live outside of their southern boundary, in Kiriath-arba or Hebron (v. 25) as well as in Beersheba (v. 27). Judah prior to the exile included these cities and suburbs, but this represents a case where emigrants return to the cities and villages of their ancestors, even though they are outside of Judea. No matter where they live, however, their center of life is in Jerusalem.

B. Priests and Levites (12:1–26). Twenty-two names are mentioned in **12:1–7**, and as we compare them with verses 12–21, there is to a large extent a continuity of the priestly houses.

Fifteen of those who attested the Mosaic covenant, living at the same time as Nehemiah (10:2–8), retain original family names (though with some differences in spelling). There are also six who use personal names. Originally, twenty-four divisions of priests were designated by David for ministry at the temple (1 Chron. 24:7–19), but two names are missing (12:1–7), perhaps due to a copying error. Neither is Hattush mentioned in 12:12–21. However, in later Judaism, all twenty-four names were reestablished.

The list in **12:8–9** provides additional information to Ezra 2:40–42, where Jeshua and Kadmiel of the line of Hodaviah are mentioned. Perhaps Judah (v. 8) is the same as Hodaviah (2:40; cf. 3:9, where the NIV footnote suggests the similarity).

The genealogy of the family of the high priest is mentioned (**12:10–11**), from the first emigration under Ezra to the days of Nehemiah, completing 1 Chronicles 6:3–15, which ends at the the time of the Babylonian captivity. Between Jeshua of the first emigration (538 B.C.) and Eliashib of Nehemiah's time (445 B.C.), there may have been others besides Joiakim, though it is possible that he was the only one.

The list in **12:12–21** has already been compared with the first emigration under Zerubbabel (12:1–7) and that of Nehemiah's generation (10:2–8). The priestly houses generally maintain traditional names even with the appearance of new leaders.

Once before, prior to the monarchy, events were dated in connection with who was high priest at the time. Now the same scheme is followed in the absence of kings as leaders of the nation. When Nehemiah arrived in Jerusalem, the high priest was Eliashib and his successors were Joiada, Johanan, and Jaddua; the last one ministered about 410 B.C., during the time of the Elephantine papyri. The time when the Levitical families ministered was also recorded according to which high priest was in office.

The Levitical leaders who serve as musicians (v. 24) are also mentioned in 10:9–10 and 12:8. This passage refers primarily to how the choirs are arranged, each one facing each other, singing in antiphonal arrangement.

Other Levites function as gatekeepers, guarding the storerooms at the gates and serving during the ministry of Joiakim, the high priest. A further dating refers to Nehemiah as governor and Ezra as priest and scribe.

VII. Dedication of the Wall (12:27–47)

At this point in the Book of Nehemiah, the first-person account which broke off at 7:5 resumes. Nehemiah now describes the dedication of the wall following spiritual renewal and the reenactment of the covenant. The occasion marking the completion of the wall becomes quite significant.

Elaborate preparations are made to make the dedication meaningful. Levites, particularly the families of singers, come from near and far in order to practice and prepare for a grand musical celebration. The priests and Levites purify themselves and then, through the proper offerings at the altar, they sanctify the people and the temple as well as the gates and wall.

Because the choirs are already split in two groups, they take their places at different points along the wall to sing antiphonally special music for the occasion.

The beginning point where the choirs split into two groups is at the Valley Gate, where Nehemiah first began his inspection of the wall (2:12). One choir led by Ezra the scribe proceeds on top of the wall from this gate, going southward to the Dung Gate and the Fountain Gate, continuing up the steps of the city of David, and on to the Water Gate on the east. The other choir proceeds in the opposite direction, as Nehemiah and other officials follow them, going past the Tower of the Ovens, the Gate of Ephraim, the Jeshanah Gate, the Fish Gate, the Tower of Hananel, and the Tower of the Hundred, and on to the Sheep Gate, stopping at the Gate of the Guard. As the choirs stand on top of the wall, they sing praises of thanksgiving. They also offer great quantities of sacrifices. So great is the joy of the people that their sound in Jerusalem can be heard far away.

Nehemiah continues to strengthen the order of service. His desire for his fellow Judeans is that they should live as people of God and serve him with gladness of heart. So as to properly care for worship in Jerusalem, Nehemiah places responsible men in charge of the storeroom who will arrange for the contributions, fresh fruits, and tithes, storing them in a proper manner. These are to be made available to the priests and Levites as prescribed by the law. Other servants, the singers and gatekeepers, are also to minister to the Lord, according to the commands of David and Solomon (1 Chron. 23:24–31). The point of referring to David and Asa means that the people of Judea should follow the prescribed order already established in the past.

VIII. Final Reforms (13:1–31)

On another occasion of the reading of the

Law, the people hear instructions concerning the Ammonites and Moabites (**13:1–3**; Deut. 23:3–5). Because these people in the past did not aid the Israelites when they were on the march to the Promised Land, they could never be admitted into the assembly of God (except, of course, those who truly converted and entered into the household of Israel, as did Ruth the Moabitess). The Judeans are to exclude these people in obedience to the Scriptures.

Nehemiah's tour of duty appears to have lasted for some twelve years (445–433 B.C.; 13:6) though he may have returned to report on the progress of the wall and its dedication and was then sent back. In 433 B.C., he returns to Artaxerxes I, mentioned here as the "king of Babylon," one of the titles of the Persian emperor. After some time Nehemiah returns to Jerusalem, and once more discovers that many Judeans have become complacent in their worship (13:4–31). For the effects of spiritual renewal to continue, the people of God must seek to live close to the Lord.

The account of the removal of Tobiah (**13:4–9**) is introduced by "before this," leading to a number of speculations as to what this means. It would appear that during Nehemiah's absence, Eliashib the high priest actually gave a room to Tobiah in the temple area, the very place which was to serve as a storeroom for articles for temple service. Tobiah and his family had intermarried with the leading families of Judea (6:17–19), and Eliashib made concessions to permit this Ammonite into the very temple.

Tobiah's goods are thrown out of the storeroom and these rooms are then purified and restored for storing grain offerings and incense. We can imagine how incensed Nehemiah must have been with an Ammonite living in the temple area and that some priestly families thought nothing of it! He is a good picture of One who later came into the temple, overturning the tables of the moneychangers and opening up the cages of the pigeons. He too was incensed that the original purposes of the temple had been desecrated.

The people also neglect their spiritual leaders (**13:10–14**). Nehemiah learns that the Levites have not received the portions due to them and that they and the singers have returned to their towns to till their fields for their food supply. Again, Nehemiah is angry, rebuking the leaders and high priest because the house of God has been neglected. Nehemiah has to restructure order at the temple, placing priests, scribes, and Levites in office who can be trusted to do what the law requires.

Nehemiah then turns to God in prayer. He does not seek any glory for himself for what has been accomplished but rather, seeks to serve God with his whole heart. The Lord holds in high esteem a man or woman who is loyal to him and such people are instrumental for the work of God to go forward.

After Nehemiah has rectified the situation at the temple, he widens his investigation of life in the city as well as in the countryside (**13:15–22**). To his horror, he finds some Judeans conducting business on the Sabbath. All kinds of food and goods are being brought into the city with no one apparently stopping this activity. The gatekeepers have probably been bribed to open the gates! Nehemiah rebukes the leaders for desecrating the Sabbath, reminding them that such activity was one of the reasons for the exile. If the leaders do not recognize that the Sabbath is sacred, they will have to face the wrath of God for their insensitivity to his commandments.

Nehemiah therefore gives orders that the city gates are to be shut as the sixth day draws to a close and are to remain closed until the Sabbath is over. He takes precautions to station some of his own trusted men to see that his orders are carried out. When a few actually try to test his nerve (v. 20), Nehemiah warns the Sabbath breakers of the consequences if they do not go away and take their goods with them. So as to ensure the fulfillment of his orders, he calls for faithful Levites who will not only purify themselves, but also stand guard at the gates and make sure they remain shut so the Sabbath day can be kept holy.

Once again, Nehemiah calls upon God to remember his servant and show mercy for the acts of love done in his name. Nehemiah is no weak leader, but at the same time, he has a heart that is tender toward God and his Word.

Both Ezra and Nehemiah had to face the grave problem of intermarriage. Men of Judah had intermarried with pagan women of Ashod, Ammon, and Moab and already their children knew the languages of the pagans instead of the language of Judah. While Ezra took the drastic action of calling for divorce, Nehemiah, no less explosive than Ezra, does not force the issue (**13:23–29**). Perhaps his severe response of calling curses on the offenders, pulling their hair, and making them take an oath that they will not intermarry with pagans, could have implied that the Judeans were to send away their pagan spouses. He reminds the offenders that Solomon had sinned in the same way, leading eventually to the rupture of the kingdom. Nehemiah drives away one of the sons of Joiada, son of Eliashib the high priest and son-in-law of Sanballat. Nehemiah has no other choice because intermarriages within the family of the high priest were unacceptable to God himself (Lev. 21:13–15).

Once again, Nehemiah cries out to God because of the intermarriages; the priestly office and the covenant of the priesthood and Levites has been defiled.

Nehemiah now calls for the purification of priests and Levites (**13:30–31**). What is possibly implied is the sending away of any foreign wives. Perhaps the sinful example of the high priest had spread further to other priests and therefore Nehemiah felt that the priests had to be sanctified before they could truly serve at the altar and teach the people with any kind of integrity. Nehemiah makes it possible for the Judeans once again to have trusted leaders. Nehemiah also makes provision for the contributions of wood and fresh fruits in order that the work at the temple can proceed in accordance with the law.

Nehemiah closes with a cry to God that he should remember his trusted servant (**13:31**). It is the last word we hear from Nehemiah. With Ezra, he seeks to give Israel a clarity of faith and encouragement to stand strong for God. The Book of Nehemiah is of great value for the body of Christ, for from it we can derive valuable lessons, not only for ordinary believers, but also for leaders.

SELECT BIBLIOGRAPHY

Adeney, W. F. *Ezra and Nehemiah.* Reprint. Minneapolis: Klock & Klock, 1980.

Barber, C. J. *Nehemiah and the Dynamics of Effect Leadership.* Neptune, N.J.: Loizeaux, 1976.

Batten, L. W. *The Books of Ezra and Nehemiah.* The International Critical Commentary. Edinburgh: T. & T. Clark, 1961.

Coggins, R. J. *The Books of Ezra and Nehemiah.* The Cambridge Bible Commentary. London: Cambridge University Press, 1976.

Keil, C. F. *The Books of Ezra, Nehemiah and Esther.* Old Testament Commentaries. Grand Rapids: Eerdmans, 1950.

Kidner, D. *Ezra and Nehemiah.* The Tyndale Old Testament Commentaries. Downers Grove: Inter-Varsity, 1979.

Luck, G. *Ezra and Nehemiah.* Chicago: Moody, 1961.

Slotki, J. J. *Daniel, Ezra, Nehemiah.* London: Soncino, 1966.

Turnbull, R. G. *The Book of Nehemiah.* Grand Rapids: Baker, 1968.

ESTHER

Stephen F. Noll

INTRODUCTION

"A cord of three strands is not quickly broken" (Eccles. 4:12). Like the proverbial cord, the Scripture weaves together carefully and powerfully the strands of history, art, and doctrine. The Book of Esther is a fine example of this marvelous tapestry.

The story of Esther takes place in the Persian court of the famous king Xerxes ("Ahasuerus"). An amazing sequence of events involving Haman, Esther, and Mordecai displays God's salvation of his people. While these biblical figures are not mentioned specifically in Persian annals or by the Greek historian Herodotus, it is hard to imagine how such a powerful story commemorated in such a universally accepted feast could emerge without a basis in the actual history of the Jewish people.

We do not have any direct testimony outside the Bible for Esther, Mordecai, or Haman in the time of Xerxes, although the basic story line is not implausible. The accession of a foreign-born queen, the promotion of Jews to high office, the occasional persecution of alien peoples in the pagan empires—all these events are known in other historical sources. Further, the story employs names, titles, and court practices that are generally consistent with the Persian period. On the other hand, certain details, such as the 180-day feast and the edict commanding wives to obey their husbands, would seem to serve more to dramatize the human foibles of the characters. In all of this, readers are caught up into the events as if they were there!

The Book of Esther has long been appreciated as a well-crafted work of art, as a number of its characteristics resemble those of literary works. The exotic setting in the plush Persian court strikes our fancy. The drama of the selection of the new queen has a Cinderella flavor to it. The mixture of malice and pomposity in Haman reminds us of Shakespeare's Iago. The neatly arranged series of events in which the lot is changed is an example of careful plot development. And the frequent parallels with other biblical stories (e.g., Saul and Agag, Joseph, and the Passover) are meant to resonate in the ear of the believer. Some scholars find the finale (chaps. 9–10) somewhat clumsy; this may be because the book is not merely a good story but also a recitation of salvation history.

The Book of Esther does not mention the name of God. The reason for this omission continues to baffle interpreters. It is possible that the book is meant to resemble a pagan chronicle; better, that it engages in debate the fatalistic assumptions of the pagan world in order to show that even in "secular" terms, the meaning of Jewish identity and history can be understood only in light of the sovereign God. If Haman is considered a type of the practical atheist or superstitious pagan, his comeuppance is a living reminder of an overriding justice in human affairs. For the Christian this theme is reflected in Paul's assurance that nothing "in all creation, will be able to separate us from the love of God that is in Christ Jesus our Lord" (Rom. 8:39).

The chief tenet of Judaism is the conviction that God has chosen the children of Abraham in an eternal covenant (Gen. 15). The exodus from Egypt was the classic example of God's faithfulness to Israel, his "firstborn son" (Exod. 4:22–23). The setting of the Book of Esther reflects a later period when the Jews were in exile, a "people dispersed and scattered among the peoples" (3:8). It notes the dangers of such vulnerability to persecution which has marked Jewish history down to our age. The mainstream of prophetic thought envisioned the return of Jews from exile and Zion as a future center for teaching the Word of God to the nations (Isa. 2:1–5; Jer. 23:7–8). The Book of Esther speaks for scattered Jews who see an ongoing purpose for living in the pagan world. In the providential deliverance of the Jews of the Persian Empire, the author seems to endorse the worldwide mission of the Jews to be a "light to the nations," not in the citadel of Zion but in the very capital of paganism. For the Christian such an expanded vision should lead to a thankful appreciation of the two branches of the divine covenant, the synagogue and the church, and a yearning that in Christ the Jewish people might bring blessing to the whole world.

Finally, the Book of Esther teaches how folly can endanger and how godly wisdom can produce a just and peaceful society. Haman, in his contempt for both moral and legal restraints which protect the vulnerable from a tyrant's will to power, can be seen as the father of modern totalitarianism. Esther and Mordecai, on the other hand, demonstrate their moderation, which is based in piety but is not insistent on forcing their religion on their subjects. They are by no means passive leaders, but their initiatives assume a beneficent hand guiding the course of nature and history. In this respect, they are forerunners of the Servant-Messiah who said: "Take my yoke upon you and learn from me, for I am gentle and humble in heart, and you will find rest for your souls" (Matt. 11:29).

Non-Jews may be unfamiliar with the joyous, even hilarious, character of the Purim festival. For Jews, however, it is a time to make light of what is an essentially serious theme—the preservation of the Jewish people from persecution. The feast precedes Passover by one month and points to the great events of the exodus. The central act of Purim is the reading of the *Megillah* or Esther scroll, accompanied by raucous mocking at the name of Haman and his sons and congregational recitation of the verses of redemption (8:15–16; 10:3). Parallel readings from passages about Amalek highlight the long-standing threat to Jews in every generation. The feast is also accompanied by a carnival-like atmosphere—puppet shows and comic plays, drinking contests, the burning of a Haman effigy, and election of a Purim king. Such customs are, of course, much later than the book itself, but they reflect a genuine response to the book's instruction "to observe the days as days of feasting and joy and giving presents of food to one another and gifts to the poor" (9:22).

The author of Esther is anonymous, and little can be said except that he was a Jew of the Diaspora. The book is set in the time of Xerxes I (485–465 B.C.) and could derive from any time thereafter down to the second century B.C. Its authority was still in dispute among the rabbis of the first and second centuries A.D. Nevertheless the popularity of Purim (mentioned as "Mordecai's day" in 2 Macc. 15:36) confirmed the importance of the book to the Jewish people. The book is not mentioned in the New Testament and was omitted from some early lists of Old Testament books; however, by the fourth century A.D. it was included in the canon.

OUTLINE

I. Vashti's Refusal (1:1–22)
II. Esther's Accession (2:1–18)
III. Mordecai's Service (2:19–23)
IV. Haman's Plot (3:1–15)
V. Mordecai's Request (4:1–17)
VI. Esther's Request (5:1–14)
VII. Mordecai's Reward (6:1–14)
VIII. Haman's Punishment (7:1–10)
IX. The King's Edict (8:1–17)
X. The Jews' Triumph (9:1–10:3)

COMMENTARY

I. Vashti's Refusal (1:1–22)

"I am Xerxes, the great king, king of kings, king in this great earth far and wide." This inscription is no empty boast by the Persian king known in the Bible as Ahasuerus (485–465 B.C.). Xerxes reigned over 127 provinces from his royal throne in Susa. Persia was a kingdom at rest, secure in its power. The luxuriousness of the Persian court was renowned, far surpassing that of Solomon's (Herodotus, 1.133; 1 Kings 7; cf. Eccles. 2:1–12). We today can glimpse something of the grandeur of Xerxes' court from the excavated remains of his later capital at Persepolis.

In a festive spirit, the king displays the vast wealth of his kingdom to his courtiers and provincial administrators for 180 days. Then he entertains the populace of Susa for seven more days in an enclosed garden. (The Persian word for such a pleasure park comes into English as "paradise" [cf. Eccles. 2:5]). Coupled with the king's feast is Queen Vashti's party for her maids.

The Persians were noted for their practice of making decisions while drunk (Herodotus, 1.135); in true form Xerxes, in "high spirits" (v. 10), makes an ill-considered command to bring Vashti before him. He wants to flaunt her beauty just as he had displayed the other riches of his kingdom. The arbitrary monarch is refused by an equally stubborn queen. Xerxes then displays yet another unbecoming passion—anger. This royal couple knows no mutual honor or submission; his regard for her is based on lust and hers on vanity.

Nonplussed by Vashti's refusal, the king seeks recourse through legal experts. There is a comic ring to the names of these pompous officials and to their advice. Their spokesman, Memucan, argues that domestic rebellion at court will become public information, so that women everywhere will despise their husbands. From the bureaucratic viewpoint religion and decency provide no safeguards. An irrevocable decree is required: Vashti is never again to enter the presence of Xerxes; her honor will be bestowed on someone better. This decree prepares the reader for a better queen (Esther) and a better model of mutual respect (Mordecai and Esther). The king is pleased with Memucan's advice and, godlike, commands that every man should rule over his own household.

II. Esther's Accession (2:1–18)

Later, Xerxes remembers Vashti. The Hebrew word *remember* suggests that he regretted his foolish action. Did this afterthought come immediately upon waking from his stupor, or after several years when the irrevocability of the decision had sunk in? We are not told. In any case the king needs advice on how to remedy his own folly. His courtiers, now unnamed, propose a ridiculous scheme for choosing a new queen: "let the girl who pleases the king be queen" (v. 4). Note the repetition of the words *pleasing* and *finding favor* in this chapter; these are secular synonyms for "grace," suggesting that God may work through the king's whim. A beauty contest opens the position to anyone, high or low, Persian or foreigner, whom chance and the king's fancy may settle on. Strangely enough, this whimsical plan is enforced by scrupulous regulations. Vagary has supplanted tradition and statecraft; but it is by this very means that a virtuous queen is found!

The girl who pleases the king is, of course, Esther, who is introduced in verses 5–7 along with her cousin Mordecai, a Jew living in Susa. Mordecai's forebears associate him with Saul, the king whom the Lord had chosen to be savior and ruler of Israel but who disobeyed on several occasions and was finally rejected and replaced by David. These exiles are strangers in a strange land, reflected in the heroine's double name—Hadassah (Heb. Myrtle) and Esther (Babylonian Ishtar, Star, or Myrtle)—and in Esther's orphaned state. In ancient Israel orphans were provided for by law (Exod. 22:22); Mordecai fulfills the intent of the law in a new setting.

Esther is brought to court and placed in the care of Hegai. Esther pleases Hegai, and he provides special privileges—beauty treatments and select food.

Verses 10–11 parenthetically remind us that advancement at court has not disturbed Esther's loyalty to Mordecai. The reason for Mordecai's command that she conceal her origins is not transparent but reflects the tight-lipped prudence of a good courtier (Prov. 12:23).

Verses 12–14 describe the storybooklike ritual by which the hopefuls are prepared, presented—and fail to please. Their routine transfer from one eunuch to the king to another eunuch prepares us for the climax of the chapter. Their implied profligacy and ostentation is contrasted with Esther's unadorned beauty and careful adherence to Hegai's advice. Esther wins the favor of everyone who sees her—even before the king is captivated. The bedroom scene is handled delicately: she is led to the king on a date to be remembered in the kingdom (tenth month, seventh year). He loves her; she finds favor in his sight. The disquiet caused the king and kingdom by Vashti is atoned for; the king crowns Esther. The celebration begins with a feast for Esther and the court and a royal holiday (rest) and gifts for the provinces—a foreshadowing of the Purim rites of chapter 9.

III. Mordecai's Service (2:19–23)

In a second parenthesis the author assures us that Esther's elevation in no way alters her relationship with Mordecai. Mordecai continues to wait on Esther—this time perhaps as a court official. She obeys his instructions as before, and when he reports a dangerous plot against the king to her, she informs her husband, giving credit to Mordecai. The private loyalty of Jew to Jew and guardian to daughter has public consequences, but they go, strangely, unrewarded. A record is made of the deed, however; and we know that it will pay rich dividends during a greater crisis in the kingdom (6:1–3).

IV. Haman's Plot (3:1–15)

As mysteriously as Mordecai's deed is forgotten, so Haman is promoted to a seat of honor (Heb. throne) above the king's courtiers. The impact of the attribution *Haman the Agagite* would not be lost on a Jewish audience. The Agagites were Amalekites, inveterate enemies of the Jews (Exod. 17:14; Num. 31:1–12;

1 Sam. 15). The divinely sanctioned animosity against Amalek probably explains Mordecai's refusal to obey the king's command to prostrate himself before the new vizier. It also explains Haman's uncontrollable anger and the perverse logic by which he determines to destroy not only Mordecai but all the Jews.

Haman is portrayed not only as ambitious and angry, but superstitious. We find him consulting the *pur* (Heb. lot—cf. 9:24) to settle on a date for the pogrom. This act reveals Haman's arrogance in preempting the king's decision and a kind of merciful providence in that it will be nearly a year before the plan is to be carried out.

Haman seeks to persuade the king to perform an act atypical of the Persian laissez-faire policy toward subject peoples: it is not in the king's best interest to tolerate the Jews. His case hinges on two points: (1) a certain (unnamed) people are scattered among those settled in the provinces; and (2) their customs (Heb. laws) are different from other peoples', and they do not obey the king's laws (extrapolating from Mordecai's behavior). In appealing to the king's favoritism, Haman both bribes him with an extraordinary sum and perhaps misleads him as to the true nature of the decree (the phrase *to destroy* could be misheard as *to enslave*—cf. 7:4). However unwittingly, the king irresponsibly hands over his signet ring (the symbol of his authority) to Haman. The decree itself is a model of bureaucratic efficiency and demonic brutality like that of the Nazi "final solution" to the "Jewish question." The date of 13 Adar and the theme of plundering goods will to the Jewish reader foreshadow the happy ending. Verse 15 points to the varied reactions to the decree: the king oblivious, Haman triumphant, the inhabitants of Susa bewildered.

V. Mordecai's Request (4:1–17)

If the inhabitants of Susa are confused about the import of the new law, Mordecai knows exactly what it means. With as much righteous zeal as when he refused to bow to Haman, he puts on sackcloth and ashes and goes out into the city, wailing loudly and bitterly. Mordecai's Jewishness is never in doubt; indeed all the Jews of the empire follow suit. But the distance between Mordecai and Esther is increased: he is not allowed inside the palace gates.

An intricately developed dialogue through court intermediaries ensues in which Esther is brought from ignorance to conviction. At first she learns only of Mordecai's outward humiliation and sends relief in the form of new garments. His refusal signals the seriousness of the cause of his fasting, and so she next seeks an explanation through her faithful eunuch Hathach. Mordecai presents her with concrete evidence of the threat—an exact accounting of Haman's bribe and a copy of the king's edict—and a proposal that she intercede with the king. Esther's reply informs Mordecai of the extreme danger his proposal entails. The royal law requires death for the person who approaches the king presumptuously—unless he is moved to mercy and extends his gold scepter. It has been thirty days since Esther has seen the king. For all the propitious signs of her selection as queen, Esther perceives she has fallen into disfavor and can expect no better fate than Vashti if she mocks the king and his law.

Mordecai's next message raises a new issue: Esther's reticence about her Jewishness. He counsels: "There is a time to keep silent, and a time to speak and *now is the time to speak!*" Mordecai warns her to forsake the illusion that she can hide her identity from a devil like Haman. He also conveys to her a profound confidence in the workings of providence. He understands her remarkable elevation to the throne as provision for the Jews in crisis, but he also recognizes that she may refuse the role of savior of her people. In that case, relief and deliverance for the Jews will arise from another place, whether a heavenly or an earthly kingdom.

Esther's final response conveys her acceptance of the challenge to go to the king contrary to the law. Esther now reflects Mordecai's understanding of the contingency of events. She has a plan, but the success of that plan will require courage; hence she asks the Jews of Susa to fast for her. She steps out, having counted the cost.

VI. Esther's Request (5:1–14)

On the third day, after the fast, Esther ventures to undo the curse on her people. The difficulty of this task should not be underestimated. The king and his top advisor have enacted an irrevocable decree against the Jews; by contrast the potential saviors of the Jews, Esther and Mordecai, are both outsiders to the king's counsel and favor. Esther now acts, as wise as a serpent and gentle as a dove. As we shall see, she will need a remarkable sequence of coincidences for her venture to succeed.

Vashti had refused to appear in her royal apparel out of stubbornness and vanity; now Esther, voluntarily and for the sake of others, braves the royal edict and stands in the inner court of the palace. For a fateful moment we see the two figures of the king and queen poised—he sitting, she standing (v. 1). Perhaps touched by that pristine beauty that had first won his heart, Xerxes is pleased and extends the scepter. Esther astutely sidesteps the king's exaggerated offer of half his kingdom and in return invites him and Haman to a banquet. The king responds with typical decisiveness and does what Esther asks. At the feast the king repeats his offer, and Esther prudently puts him further in her debt and under her seductive charm by a second invitation. The day's interval between the two feasts is crucial to the plot, for in that time Mordecai's deed will become known and Haman in his presumption will provide the instrument of his own destruction.

In contrast to the graceful interchange between the king and queen, we now glimpse the crude vanity of Haman. His joy over Esther's invitation is the fruit of ambition—and perhaps lust (cf. 7:8). Possessing every honor, he nevertheless is filled with rage by Mordecai's implacable resistance. His self-restraint is feigned; in fact, he cannot wait for his own decree to dispose of his enemy. At home we see Haman in all his pomposity, boasting about his wealth, sons, honors, and rank. He reports the supreme proof of his success: "I'm the only person Queen Esther invited to accompany the king to the banquet she gave." In fact we know that the queen's intentions are just the opposite of Haman's expectations.

Haman cannot enjoy any of this with Mordecai around. Just as the king depends on a circle of advisors, so Haman listens to his wife, Zeresh, and his friends. Their plan reeks of the same arrogance as Haman's in chapter 3. Haman is to build the gallows first and then *tell* the king (NIV ask is too polite) to have Mordecai hanged on it. The gallows is probably a stake for impaling; it is absurdly high and would be hard to miss on the Susa skyline. They flatter Haman into thinking that revenge will satisfy his lusts. The outcome of this plan is star-crossed: Haman will go to the dinner but he will not be happy.

VII. Mordecai's Reward (6:1–14)

While Esther is spinning her web, Haman's rapacity forces the action of the story to a crisis point in which the reader will recognize the hand of God. That night the king cannot sleep. Elsewhere in the Bible, God uses dreams to convey a message; here he uses insomnia. As the restless king is read to from the book of his own memorable deeds, he is startled to hear of the service which Mordecai performed for him. He wonders what recognition Mordecai has received. His dismay that no reward has been given coincides with Haman's overeagerness in seeking Mordecai's death.

One wonders if Haman intends to hoodwink the king again, as he had in chapter 3, by warning of an anonymous malefactor; but before he can speak, the king himself poses his own hypothetical question: "What should be done for the man the king delights to honor?" Haman's thoughts are characteristically vain, though not unreasonable given his position: *Who is there that the king would rather honor than me?* His proposal to the king borders on impudence—suggesting that the man be clothed in the king's own robe and led on the king's own horse by one of the king's most noble princes (cf. Gen. 41:42–43). The ironic twist is, of course, that the man whom the king honors is Mordecai (the king does not yet know Jews are under the ban) and the nobleman is Haman himself, forced to eulogize his enemy with his own words.

This incident does not materially alter the situation for the Jews: Mordecai returns to his post. For the man who lives by reputation, however, it is a humiliation worse than death. Haman rushes home, with his head covered in grief. His wife and friends, who had put him up to the early morning scheme, now turn on him, and she fatalistically (prophetically for the reader) observes that this event is the beginning of his downfall because Mordecai is of Jewish origin. Zeresh, like other Persians in the book, reflects a "fear of the Jews" that must be ultimately understood as an acknowledgment of the superiority of their religion.

VIII. Haman's Punishment (7:1–10)

Haman's plot against Mordecai has been temporarily foiled. Now Esther makes her move. The king is once again charmed by Esther and repeats for the third time his promise of half the kingdom. This time she is ready to challenge him, although she continues to be deferential. Her revelation is dramatic: "Grant me my life—this is my petition. And spare my people—this is my request" (v. 3). Having enticed the king to identify her interest with his own, she now identifies with a people who have been "sold for destruction and slaughter and annihilation" (v. 4). This wording may have surprised the king; indeed Esther suggests that slavery would be bearable. But the enemy in seeking death has offended the king's own interest (Esther tactfully omits mention of the king's role in the whole affair). The king is hooked: Who and where is he? Esther's answer is forthright: Haman!

The character of the king and Haman are

now put to the test. The king leaves in a rage. His disappearance adds to the dramatic tension of the story. It also threatens Esther's plan to force the king's hand. Help comes now, ironically, from an unexpected quarter—Haman himself! Haman is shocked and loses heart because he realizes that he is doomed before the king. His own superstitions may now mislead him to despair in a situation where the king might easily calm down and realize that his own self-interest is with Haman and the decree. Like the hasty fool and gutless schemer he is, the enemy of the Jews begs the Jewish queen for mercy.

As chance would have it, the king returns just as Haman is prostrating himself before or on the queen's couch. *Will he even molest the queen?* The fall from power is complete. The king's eunuch Harbona now makes the clinching revelation of Haman's treachery: he has built a gallows for Mordecai. The king is at last decisive. Haman is hanged, the principle of retribution is satisfied, and things return to normal.

IX. The King's Edict (8:1–17)

The suspense of the story was caused by Haman's vengeful plot against Mordecai and the Jews in chapter 3. Haman has now been removed from the scene, but the deadly effects of his edict remain to be undone. In both chapters the king is a passive figure; Esther and Mordecai mirror the proper concern for the well-being of the Jews and the right use of law and administration.

The chapter begins with recompense and promotion: Esther receives Haman's property and Mordecai, now that his true relationship to the queen is revealed, receives his opponent's favored office, including use of the signet ring which is essential to counteracting the anti-Jewish statute. However secure their position has become, the two new leaders know that their kinsmen in the provinces are still in mortal danger.

It falls to Esther to plead with the king. Once again he extends the gold scepter to her, and she—with all deference and coyness—argues for a new edict counteracting Haman's decree (she again omits reference to the king's role in the first law). Her clinching point is an appeal to the king's sympathy for her feelings: "How can I bear to see the destruction of my family?" While the king is moved, he does not take personal charge of the restoration. He permits Esther and Mordecai to frame another statute, warning them to be careful—no document written in his name and sealed with his ring can be revoked. As if they didn't know!

The new law is published exactly seventy days after Haman's edict, which would suggest to Jewish readers the predicted seventy years of exile (Jer. 29:10; cf. Dan. 9:2); the allusion may imply that God's new act of salvation and covenant happens to the Jews as they continue to live among the nations. No return to Israel is envisioned; indeed the good news is published throughout the empire in each provincial tongue and to the Jews dispersed in each province in their own script and language.

The wording of the edict follows closely Haman's original decree. As with God's earlier injunctions to holy war, it grants them carte blanche to wipe out any nationality or province that might attack them and their women and children (whose women and children are referred to is ambiguous) and to plunder their property. The choice of 13 Adar as the day to avenge themselves on their enemies is conditioned by Haman's earlier lot and intended to highlight the day as a new day of salvation for the people of God. The good news goes out posthaste, beginning at Susa.

Mordecai, who had earlier been paraded as king for a day in Susa, now leaves the king's presence wearing royal garments. For the remainder of the book he functions as virtual "king of the Jews." The reaction in Susa, the new "Zion" of Judaism, is a joyous celebration (cf. Isa. 51:11) and throughout the empire there is joy and gladness among the Jews. Many people of other nationalities convert because of fear of the Jews ("fear" includes an awed awareness of the Jews' favored status [cf. 6:13]). Such conversion is one more sign of the beginning of a new age of salvation.

X. The Jews' Triumph (9:1–10:3)

The narrative now has but one further event to relate: the vindication of the Jews over their enemies. Liturgical interest begins to dominate the text. The action begins exactly eleven months after Haman cast the lot. Whereas the enemies of Jews at first seemed ready to devour a totally defenseless people, now the tables are turned. Even the provincial administrators help the Jews. The Jews strike down all their enemies, the relatives and allies of Haman. Some readers may take offense at the idea of vengeance, but it is a root motive behind all justice and is given limited sanction in the Old Testament, especially when carried out for God's glory. The refusal of plunder suggests just such a holy war and may compare favorably with the exodus itself (Exod. 12:36).

After another interchange between the king and Esther, Xerxes authorizes a codicil to the edict in chapter 8, allowing the Jews in Susa an extra day of vengeance on 14 Adar and making a public example by hanging Haman's ten sons. We see then the emergence of two customs commemorating these events: rural Jews observe the feast on 14 Adar, whereas Jews in "walled cities" celebrate on 15 Adar. Just as the Sabbath reminded Israel of her deliverance from Egypt (Deut. 5:15), so the new feast is characterized as days of rest, feasting, and joy, reminding the Jewish people of the covenant promises of salvation and a peaceful kingdom (Exod. 33:14; Josh. 21:44; 2 Sam. 7:11).

The pattern of the first festival, formalized by Mordecai's decree, is to be celebrated annually, and the Jews agree to continue the celebration they had begun under the name *Purim*, which is explained in terms of the *pur* (a Persian name with a Hebrew plural ending). The name of the feast reflects the key role of chance in the deliverance, which in Hebrew wisdom thought is related to God's providence. Finally, the festival accepted by the first generation is enjoined on every generation. Purim is to be remembered by all Jews for all time and thus rivals Passover in importance.

SELECT BIBLIOGRAPHY

Clines, D. J. A. *Ezra, Nehemiah, Esther.* Grand Rapids: Eerdmans, 1984.

Baldwin, J. G. *Esther.* Downers Grove: Inter-Varsity, 1984.

Moore, C. A. *Esther.* Garden City: Doubleday, 1971.

———. *Daniel, Esther and Jeremiah: The Additions.* Garden City: Doubleday, 1977.

———, ed. *Studies in the Book of Esther.* New York: Ktav, 1982.

Berg, S. B. *The Book of Esther: Motifs, Themes and Structure.* Missoula, Mont.: Scholars Press, 1979.

The Poetic Books

The ancient Hebrews were a literate people who wrote a large amount of forceful, elegant poetry. Two-thirds of the Hebrew Bible is actually written in this manner, but this went unrecognized by early Gentile translators, who rendered much of it as prose. The Psalms, which commence the third division of the Hebrew canon, have always been regarded as poetry, although just how this style of literature was written has become clear only within recent centuries. As with poetry that follows classical models, Hebrew verse is based upon patterns of stresses, but differs by not being written in rhyme, which was apparently unknown to the Hebrews.

Poetry has advantages over prose in that, through the use of throbbing rhythms, it can convey a message with elegance, emotion, and emphasis in such a manner as to make it memorable. It is an extremely important didactic instrument, and the ancient Hebrews used it in psalms which instructed the nation in its faith and history. The poetic oracles of the prophets taught covenant theology in one form or other, and the powerful *qinah* or "dirge meter" was used to devastating effect in pronouncements of doom upon disobedient Israel. By contrast, many of the psalms were of a devotional nature, examining the relationship between God and man in the varied circumstances of life. These compositions stressed the supreme might of Israel's God, his hatred of sin, the responsibilities of the covenant relationship, and the fate of the nation if it disobeyed or rejected his will. The psalms also revealed a deity who cared greatly for his people and longed to shower his covenant love upon them.

Long after prophetic oracles had been fulfilled and the nation of Israel dispersed, the psalms continued to minister to God's ancient people. The Christian church incorporated this treasured legacy into its own worship in varying ways, and continues to rejoice in its rich spirituality.

JOB

Carl Schultz

INTRODUCTION

While the inclusion of Job in the canon has not been seriously challenged, its location within the Old Testament has been subject to debate.

In English Bibles, Job is the first of the poetic books. Since Job is primarily poetic in nature, its location here is understandable. The Book of Job is filled with poetry and recognition of this fact is critical to a correct interpretation of the book.

The location of Job in English Bibles follows the order of the Septuagint (though there are differences here depending on the Greek text) and the Latin versions where Job usually precedes Psalms and Proverbs. In the Hebrew Bible Job is located in the third section known as the Writings.

The author of the book is not identified. Neither is there consensus among ancient rabbis or modern scholars. Because of its complexity, some have suggested that it is the end result of a long and complicated literary development, perhaps involving several authors.

The identity of the author(s), however, is not critical. The writer remains anonymous but his sensitivity to suffering, his literary skills, his deep theological understanding, and his handling of opinionated people shine through the pages of Job. He was perhaps one who himself had suffered, who had been told that his suffering was due to his sins, and who had had a significant encounter with God.

From textual evidence it seems that Job possibly lived in patriarchal times. Note the following: (1) Job offers his own sacrifices (1:5) as do the patriarchs (Gen. 22:13); (2) Job's wealth is measured in terms of livestock and servants (1:3) as is Abraham's (Gen. 12:6); (3) Job's longevity (42:16) is matched only by persons in patriarchal times; (4) Job is classified by Ezekiel (Ezek. 14:14, 20) with Noah (also with Dan'el—an early heroic figure though not necessarily the Daniel of the Old Testament).

A wide range of dates has been suggested for the composition of Job, ranging from the time of Moses to the Hasmonean period. Efforts to use orthography, theological ideas, institutions, and quotations from other biblical books have not resulted in any consensus. While there is little room for dogmatism it is reasonable to conclude that this book is preexilic, possibly completed between the time of Solomon and Josiah.

The literary structure of the book is obvious. A poetic section (3:1–42:6) is flanked by prose sections—a prologue (1:1–2:13) and an epilogue (42:7–17). This structure—prose-poetry-prose (*A-B-A*)—is not an unusual one.

A careful analysis of the poetic section also reveals a symmetry. It opens with two conversations between the Lord and Satan (1:6–12; 2:1–7a), and closes with two conversations between the Lord and Job (38:1–40:5; 40:6–42:6). Following the exchanges between the Lord and Satan and the subsequent disasters which befall Job are his reactions (1:20–22; 2:9–13); following the exchanges between the Lord and Job are his responses (40:3–5; 42:1–6).

After the conversations between the Lord and Satan, the exchanges between Job and his comforters follow (3:1–37:24). They occur in three symmetrical cycles:

Participants	**Cycle 1**	**Cycle 2**	**Cycle 3**
Eliphaz	4–5	15	22
Job	6–7	16–17	23–24
Bildad	8	18	25
Job	9–10	19	26
Zophar	11	20	?
Job	12–14	21	27

These three cycles are framed by Job's opening soliloquy (3:1–26) and his closing peroration (29:1–31:40). Interestingly enough, Job begins his remarks by cursing the day of his birth (3:11) and concludes them by invoking a curse upon himself if guilty of particular sins and thus deserving of his suffering (31:1–40).

The remaining chapters (28, 32–37) are not so clearly symmetrical. Chapter 28 contains a hymn on wisdom, but it is not at all clear who utters these words. In chapters 32–37 Elihu's four speeches are found. These chapters have been viewed by some as a late addition to the book since Elihu does not figure either in the prologue or epilogue. His absence in these sections is striking but may indicate the role he plays in the book. Since he speaks following Job's final presentation (chaps. 29–31), Elihu's role may be that of adjudicator. In his review of the preceding speeches Elihu seems to assess them (32:12), thus serving as a judge. If Elihu is seen as the human adjudicator, it is fitting to regard the Lord as the divine adjudicator since he, too, assesses the presentations of the three comforters (42:7). Regardless of Elihu's role, he makes a significant contribution to the teaching of this book.

Given the literary structure of this book it is imperative that we understand the author's intent. After chronicling Job's disasters and his response to them, the writer presents the efforts of the three comforters, of Job, and of Elihu to account for Job's sufferings as well as the Lord's contribution to this troubling issue. Why does the righteous Job suffer?

Eliphaz, for instance, is quite insistent that Job is suffering because of sin. He does not believe that events take place without cause, that a man should suffer without reason. Of course there is some truth in attaching suffering to wrongdoing. A person can bring suffering on himself. But this is not the case with Job. The writer clearly establishes Job's innocence in the first two chapters. Further, at the close of the book the Lord declares that Eliphaz and his associates are wrong in their reasoning (42:7). It would thus seem that the answer to Job's suffering is not provided by the three comforters.

If the answer is not to be found in the response of any one participant, is it to be found in the collective response of all the participants? This idea of adding all the answers together has some merit. Certainly there is a degree of truth in all the responses. Further, there appear to be various reasons for human suffering. But such a position ignores the clear design of this book. The book is filled with arguments and heated exchanges. Differing views are being presented and Elihu and the Lord seem to serve as adjudicators, assessing the presentations.

Is the answer to Job's suffering in the prologue? To be sure, a profound truth is found here: Shall we accept good from God, and not trouble (2:10)? Job's rhetorical question demonstrates his unconditional commitment to God. His attitude answers the challenge of Satan: Does Job fear God for nothing (1:9)? Job's piety is completely unselfish. God's confidence in Job has been vindicated. But Job is unaware of God's confidence in him. He does not hear the divine assessment of his character. Had he known that he was being tried it would have been no test. Thus the prologue does not provide an answer to Job's suffering even though it presents some significant truth relative to disinterested religion. Further, if the answer is in the prologue, what is the purpose of the materials which follow?

Where, then, does the writer locate the answer to Job's sufferings? The answer comes only at the end of the book—after the question has been established! The answer to Job's suffering is finally to be found in the words of the Lord (38:1–42:6).

While the writer of Job must have been an Israelite, the book possesses an international quality not unlike other biblical wisdom books. Consider the following:

The site. Job, we are told, lived in Uz. This is where the action of the book occurs. While we know that Uz was in the East (1:3), this information is too general to help us. From the perspective of the Israelite writer, everything beyond the Jordan River—from Midian and Edom in the south, to Moab and Ammon directly east, to Aram in the north—would be seen as the East. From the indications in the Old Testament, this was the area subject to raids by marauding bands (1:15, 17), and well known for its sages (1 Kings 4:30).

According to the available evidence, Uz could be located either with Aram in the northeast or with Edom in the southeast. Supporting the former is the claim of Josephus that Uz was one of the four sons of Aram (*Antiquities* 1.6.4) who founded Damascus and Trachonitis (cf. Gen. 10:22–23; 1 Chron. 1:17). This is supported by Genesis 22:21, which identifies Uz as the oldest son of Abraham's brother, Nahor.

The connections of Uz with Edom are equally strong. Dishan, the Horite chief of Seir (Edom), had a son named Uz (Gen. 36:28). In Jeremiah 25:19–20, the land of Uz is associated with the land of Edom. By parallelism, Uz is identified with Edom in the Book of Lamentations (4:21).

Generally, the evidence is both too scant and diverse for a dogmatic location of Uz.

The characters. The three comforters are from outside the land of Israel, representing three different countries (2:11).

Eliphaz is identified as a Temanite. In biblical genealogies, Eliphaz is an Edomite name (Gen. 36:11, 15, 42; 1 Chron. 1:36, 53). He is identified as the firstborn of Esau and the father of Teman. Teman is one of the principal sites of Edom (Jer. 49:7; Ezek. 25:13; Amos 1:12; Obad. 8, 9). The Temanites were noted for their wisdom (Jer. 49:7; Bar. 3:22–23). Thus tradition would seem to link Eliphaz with the country of Edom.

Bildad is identified as a Shuhite. Shuah was a son of Abraham and Keturah, the brother of Midian and the uncle of Sheba and Dedan (Gen. 25:2; 1 Chron. 1:32). This connection with Sheba and Dedan makes it likely that Shuah was probably located near Edom or Arabia.

Zophar is identified as a Naamathite. While the Bible mentions a town by the name of Naamah (Josh. 15:41) in the territory of Judah, it is unlikely that this is the home of Zophar. There is no other biblical data to help us locate this city.

In contrast to the others, we know the name of Elihu's father (Barachel) and clan (Buz). Buz was Abraham's nephew (Gen. 22:20–21) and the brother of Uz (Gen. 10:22–23). This would associate him with the northeast, giving him Aramean connections. In Jeremiah (25:23), however, Buz is mentioned with Dedan and Teman, thus giving him Arabian connections.

While we have not been able to locate definitively the homes of the comforters, it seems clear that they are non-Israelites, coming from the area known as the East.

The problem. Israel certainly had no monopoly on suffering. Likewise Israel was not the only nation to respond to suffering in its literature. The wisdom literature of both Mesopotamia and Egypt is similar to Job in plot and structure.

Pattern of righteousness. Job's righteousness is not depicted in cultic and ritual terms (he did offer sacrifices [1:5] but such a practice was not restricted to Israel), which we might expect had Job been a Jew (cf. the assessment of Job's righteousness with that of the kings of Israel and Judah in 1 and 2 Kings). Instead, his righteousness is detailed in universal qualities: Job was blameless, upright, feared God (not the Lord, which would have been more Hebraic), and shunned evil (1:1).

Names of the Deity. In the Old Testament deity is designated as both *God* and *Lord.* Though these terms are used interchangeably, they are not identical in meaning; the Old Testament writers keep them distinct. Nonetheless, there is a pattern of usage. (1) When deity is associated with the nation of Israel the designation *Lord* is used; the term *God* is used in relation to non-Israelites. (2) The term *Lord* is used when the theme concerns Israel's tradition, but *God* is used when the subject matter pertains to a wider tradition. These two elements are observable in wisdom literature in particular, largely because of its international character. But our interest is in biblical wisdom literature (where, with the exception of the Book of Proverbs, the biblical writers preferred the generic terms to the national name) and with Job in particular.

The prose sections of Job, coming from the pen of an Israelite author, use both *God* and *Lord.* In the introduction to the divine speeches, the writer also uses *Lord.* But in the remaining poetic sections *Lord* appears only one time (12:9—and even here the text is uncertain since some MSS read *God*) while the Hebrew terms *God* or the *Almighty* appear frequently and regularly. The non-Israelite comforters never use the term *Lord* while the non-Israelite Job uses this term only twice. In addition to the reference above (12:9), the other occurrence is in the prologue (1:21). This employment of the term *God* rather than *Lord* demonstrates the international quality of this book.

OUTLINE

- I. Prologue (1:1–2:13)
  - A. The Hero Job (1:1–5)
  - B. The First Divine Council Meeting (1:6–12)
  - C. The First Disasters (1:13–19)
  - D. Job's Reaction (1:20–22)
  - E. The Second Divine Council Meeting (2:1–5)
  - F. Job's Illness (2:6–8)
  - G. Job's Reaction (2:9–10)
  - H. The Comforters (2:11–13)
- II. Dialogue (3:1–27:23)
  - A. Job's Opening Statement (3:1–26)
  - B. First Cycle of Speeches (4:1–14:22)
  - C. Second Cycle of Speeches (15:1–21:34)
  - D. Third Cycle of Speeches (22:1–27:23)
- III. Hymn on Wisdom (28:1–28)
- IV. Job's Peroration (29:1–31:40)
  - A. The Way It Was (29:1–25)
  - B. The Way It Is (30:1–31)
  - C. Job's Claim to Innocence (31:1–40)

V. Elihu's Speeches (32:1–37:24)
  A. Introduction (32:1–5)
  B. First Speech (32:6–33:33)
  C. Second Speech (34:1–37)
  D. Third Speech (35:1–16)
  E. Fourth Speech (36:1–37:24)
VI. The Lord's Speeches (38:1–42:6)
  A. First Speech (38:1–39:30)
  B. Second Speech (40:1–42:6)
VII. Epilogue (42:7–17)

COMMENTARY

I. Prologue (1:1–2:13)

A. The hero Job (1:1–5). The book opens with the formula *there lived a man,* which is used to introduce both parable (2 Sam. 12:1) and history (Esther 2:5). It is not surprising to find this phrase here since it is regularly used to introduce an event without any connection to what precedes it. The name *Job,* an ordinary name among western Semites in the second millennium B.C., probably means "Where is Father?"

Job is described as blameless (complete) and upright (straight). These two terms used together (cf. Pss. 25:21; 37:37; Prov. 29:10) indicate thorough rectitude. The third quality, feared God, suggests that Job is a devout man. The final quality, shunned evil, indicates a deliberate rejection of evil and thus means moral. Job's righteousness is critical to the message of the book.

The wealth of Job is described in terms of both family and property. His seven sons reflect God's blessing (Pss. 127:3–5; 128:3–4). His livestock indicates that Job is not only a nomad but also a farmer (five hundred yoke of oxen for plowing). Like Abraham (Gen. 14:14), Job has many servants.

Job's piety is demonstrated in verses 4–5. The feasts mentioned here could be either daily feasts, yearly birthday celebrations, or certain annual festivals. Fearing that his children might have sinned and cursed (lit. blessed—a euphemism used by scribes to avoid putting cursing in immediate juxtaposition with God, also used in 1:11; 2:5, 9) God in their hearts (minds), Job has them undergo purification rights and he, as the head of the family, offers sacrifices. The phrase *early in the morning* does not refer so much to time as it does to persistence.

B. The first divine council meeting (1:6–12). In the Old Testament, the Lord is portrayed as a Sovereign presiding over nameless divine beings (angels), assigning and assessing their activities (1 Kings 22:19–23; Pss. 82:1; 89:5). Among these divine beings, either as a regular attender or intruder, is Satan. The Hebrew word here means adversary or accuser. It is sometimes used of a human adversary (1 Kings 11:14, 23, 25). The presence of the Hebrew article (*the* Satan) would seem to indicate that the term here is a title rather than a proper name. True to his name, after the Lord brings up the case of Job, Satan resorts to insinuations. Satan cannot deny Job's righteousness, but counters God's claim by suggesting that Job's piety is part of a bargain: Job is devout not because he loves God but rather because he wants God's gifts. It is to his advantage to be righteous. Then Satan challenges (commands) God to extend his hand against Job and destroy all Job's possessions. Only then will the integrity of Job's piety be proven. The Lord responds by putting Job's wealth in Satan's hands. He may touch Job's possessions but not Job himself.

C. The first disasters (1:13–19). Satan is eager to carry out his assignment. A series of four disasters in rapid succession strips Job of both family and possessions. In each instance only one eyewitness escapes to tell Job the bad news, and while one messenger is speaking, the reporter of the next disaster arrives. There is clearly a progression from least to most serious since Job's children perish in the fourth disaster. The identity of the human agents is difficult. The Sabeans were either from the South Arabian kingdom of Sheba (1 Kings 10:1) or from another people closer to Israel since Sheba is associated with Dedan (Gen. 10:7; 25:3; Ezek. 38:13). The Chaldeans were not likely the people from which Nebuchadnezzar came but perhaps a marauding tribe with Aramean connections. The identity of the natural phenomena is less difficult. "Fire of God" is probably lightning; "a mighty wind" is perhaps a whirlwind.

D. Job's reaction (1:20–22). Job's response is expressed as follows: he gets up; he tears his robe (a sign of grief; Gen. 37:29; 2 Kings 19:1); he shaves his head (another act of mourning, but one forbidden by the law; Lev. 19:27–28); he falls to the ground—not in despair but in reverence; and he worships. Job's words are indeed noble. He sees only the hand of God in his tragedies; he does not curse God but renders praise. Job does not charge God with wrongdoing.

E. The second divine council meeting (2:1–5). The action again moves to the divine assembly. While Satan makes no reference to his ineffective measures against Job, the Lord underscores Job's integrity. "Without any reason" could mean without cause (cf. 22:6), or for naught (cf. 1:9), or in vain (Prov. 1:17). The last meaning would underscore the failure of Satan's efforts. The reply of Satan, "skin for skin," has been viewed as the language of barter but more likely suggests that only Job's outer skin has been touched, that only the surface (his possessions) has been scratched. Now Satan wants to get at Job himself, at "his flesh and bones." This he is permitted to do but his attack must fall short of killing Job. Of course, had Job been killed the wager could not have continued.

F. Job's illness (2:6–8). It is difficult to identify Job's illness. The same Hebrew word is used to describe one of the plagues (Exod. 9:9–11), Hezekiah's illness (2 Kings 20:7), and a disease associated with the curses of Deuteronomy (Deut. 28:27). Subsequent references in Job give us the following symptoms of this disease: inflamed eruptions (2:7); intolerable itching (2:8); disfigurement (2:12); maggots in the ulcers (7:5); terrifying dreams (7:14); running tears (16:16); fetid breath (19:17); emaciation (19:20); erosion of the bones (30:17); blackening and peeling of the skin (30:30).

Job sits "among the ashes" (at the dump outside the city). He may have been here mourning his children's deaths when he was stricken, or he may have been quarantined to this place, or he may have been here reflecting on his loss of self-respect.

G. Job's reaction (2:9–10). Job's wife asks an ambiguous question: "Are you still holding on to your integrity?" She could be challenging Job's integrity, concurring with the later assessment of the three comforters, or she could be challenging God's faithfulness, concluding that he is oblivious to Job's righteousness. Whatever the meaning of her question, her recommendation is clear: Job should kill himself. Job's characterization of his wife, "foolish woman," is not so much a reflection on her intelligence as it is on her morality and spirituality. The masculine form of this word is used to designate the fool who says that there is no God (Ps. 14:1). Job again suggests that it is appropriate to receive not only good from God but also trouble. Satan had predicted that Job would sin with his lips; yet Job does not sin in what he says.

H. The comforters (2:11–13). It must have taken his friends some time to learn of Job's tragedies and then plan and execute their visit. Their purpose in coming is to sympathize with (lit. to shake the head as an act of commiseration) and comfort him. Their difficulty in being able to recognize Job is not only due to seeing him from a distance but also because of the changes which have occurred because of his illness. They perform the ritual for the dead: weeping aloud, tearing their robes, and sprinkling dust on their heads. Assuming the customary position of mourners, they sit on the ground, overwhelmed by Job's suffering and hence speechless (cf. Ezek. 3:15).

II. Dialogue (3:1–27:23)

A. Job's opening statement (3:1–26). The place of chapter 3 in the Book of Job is debated. Some see it as a soliloquy and treat it independently from the three cycles of speeches. Others see Job as beginning and ending each cycle of speeches. However, this necessitates dividing Job's second and third speeches in the middle. For convenience, we will consider that each cycle begins with Eliphaz and ends with Job.

The Job of chapter 3 is quite different from the Job of the previous chapters. He comes dangerously close to cursing God when he curses (here the euphemism *bless* is not used) the day of his birth (cf. Jer. 20:14–18), wishing that he had never been conceived, or born, or that he might at least have been stillborn. Since this outburst follows the comforters' seven days of silence, it cannot be traced to anything they have said. Could it be that Job has lost some of his original numbness and is now seeing his suffering from a more realistic perspective?

Job not only curses the day of his birth (vv. 1–5) but also the night of his conception (vv. 6–10). He treats his birthday as if it had autonomous existence, wishing that it would be stricken from the calendar.

Since his conception did occur, Job now questions why he did not die at birth. If he had he would now be at peace in his grave. Job does not refer to heaven or hell; the afterlife is not a solution to his suffering. Such a theological concept will only be clearly developed in the New Testament. Job understands that death will bring an end to his suffering and negate the inequalities of life. Note the residents of the grave: kings and counselors of the earth (v. 14), infants (v. 16), wicked and weary (v. 17), small and great (v. 19), slave and master (v. 19). Death treats all alike.

Since he was conceived and born, Job now wishes that he could die. Life is intolerable; death is preferable. He is troubled that death is so elusive to those who long for it. Death is a time to be celebrated. But access to the grave is restricted because God has hedged man in. Job then refers to his apprehensions, perhaps both past and present. Trouble is coming. Either Job is expecting more suffering or perhaps he knows that his words have aroused his comforters and they soon will be adding theological frenzy to his woe.

B. First cycle of speeches (4:1–14:22). Job's statement at the end of chapter 3—"I have no peace, no quietness; I have no rest, but only turmoil" (v. 26)—is indeed prophetic. Up to this point the sympathy of his friends has been expressed in silence. Job breaks the silence first. The comforters quickly follow with Eliphaz, possibly the oldest of the three, speaking first.

At this point, it is imperative to keep in mind the magnitude of Job's sufferings, the theology of the comforters, and the fact that none of the participants were privy to the exchanges between the Lord and Satan in chapters 1 and 2. The issue at hand may have been an academic one to the comforters, but to Job it is an existential one. None of the participants are objective. Each one clearly speaks from his own position and prejudices.

Eliphaz, the most sympathetic of the comforters, begins hesitatingly and apologetically (**4:2–11**). He reminds Job of his past involvement with those who suffer and urges him to implement in his own experience that which he has taught others. While he will later challenge Job's integrity, he now affirms it by referring to Job's piety and blameless ways. By his question (v. 7), Eliphaz presents his theology. The innocent simply do not perish and are not destroyed. Hence Job can expect speedy intervention by God.

Eliphaz immediately brings up the issue which will ultimately result in an impasse between Job and his comforters. By his observation that those who plow evil and those who sow trouble reap it, Eliphaz interjects the cause-effect explanation that will necessitate the establishment of Job's guilt. Defense of this theological tenet will be more important than friendship. Job will become expendable. Note how differently Jesus dealt with those who suffered. Also note Jesus' denial of Eliphaz's claim: Those who perish are not necessarily more guilty than those who escape (Luke 13:1–5).

The source for Eliphaz's theological position is a dream revelation which comes to him in a deep sleep (**4:12–5:7**). That moment was so awful and he was so frightened that he was able to catch only a whisper of what was said.

After this impressive build-up one would expect a sensational revelation. Not so. Eliphaz simply hears a truism: Can a mortal be more righteous than God (v. 17)? Of course not! But Job has made no such claim.

It is difficult to know whether the revelation continues through verse 21 or whether verses 18–21 are simply Eliphaz's commentary on that revelation. Regardless, the emphasis is clear. Even angels are charged with error and God places no trust in them. How much more true this is of mortals, who live in houses of clay. Man is so fragile that he is crushed more readily than a moth.

While Eliphaz claims entitlement to his direct revelation, Job need not waste his time praying since he has automatically disqualified himself by his resentment and envy. Not even an appeal to the holy ones, to those nearest God, will avail.

Eliphaz now deduces the theological tenet most critical to his position. Man is responsible for his suffering. Hardship is not like weeds that come up of themselves but rather vegetation that has been specifically planted (v. 7).

There is a discernible change in Eliphaz's approach at this point (**5:8–27**). He now urges Job to appeal to God. In verses 9–16 Eliphaz affirms his belief in God, depicting both God's creative and redemptive acts. Job should have hope because justice will triumph.

Following his affirmation of God's creative and redemptive acts, Eliphaz depicts the happiness of the person who accepts his suffering as a discipline from God. While there is a profound truth here it is not applicable in Job's case. Job is already recognized as a pure and righteous man.

The blessings which Eliphaz projects for Job are prosperity, posterity, and longevity. He seems to have forgotten that all of Job's children are dead, unless he is anticipating the new family (42:13). While Eliphaz does not promise Job hope beyond the grave, he suggests a long and vigorous life.

Eliphaz's concluding statement is quite pompous: "We have examined this, and it is true" (v. 27). Unfortunately, his claims are not applicable to Job. Worse, he will continue to maintain these claims at Job's expense.

Job is clearly irritated by Eliphaz's speech and erupts with an emotional defense. Eliphaz may have meant his presentation to be supportive, but Job clearly does not perceive it as such.

Job defends himself (**6:2–7**). He admits that his words have been impetuous but his anguish (the same Hebrew word used by Eliphaz in 5:2, where Job is cautioned against such an attitude) and misery are heavier than the sand of the seas (i.e., immeasurable). Job traces his sufferings to God, bewildered at such treatment. It is this involvement of God that poisons his spirit. To show the absurdity of his situation Job raises two rhetorical questions (vv. 5–6). The conduct of the wild donkey (bray) and the ox (bellow) communicates a message to the sensitive husbandman. Job has a right to express himself and the comforters ought to be perceptive enough to understand him. The second question pertains to unseasoned foods which, while edible, are insipid. Job has found Eliphaz's consolations equally nauseating.

Job now breaks forth into prayer (**6:8–13**). This is significant. The comforters talk *about* God but Job talks *to* God. His request here is similar to his desire of chapter 3—to be released from his sufferings by death. Even as he wanted the protective hedge removed (3:23) so here he wants God to let loose his hand (v. 9). Job does not fear but welcomes death. He has reached the limits of his tolerance since he is flesh and not stone or bronze.

Job's assessment of his friends is extremely negative (**6:14–30**). What he expected from them was devotion (the Hebrew word here is a covenant term meaning loyalty). But instead of devotion there is betrayal. His friends have failed him like streams which gush with water in the rainy season but become bone-dry in the summer. Even as caravans hope for water only to be disappointed, so Job has been let down by his friends, who have proved to be of no help. Their failure is perhaps traceable to their being afraid because of Job's dreadful condition. Job denies that he has pressed his friends for charity or a bribe. His sarcasm is perhaps a bit premature and excessive.

Job now requests evidence that he has been wrong (the Hebrew word here implies inadvertent sin; see Lev. 4:13). He complains that Eliphaz's words have been painful and that his words, those of a despairing man, have not been taken seriously but have been treated as wind.

Job's caustic approach continues in his charge that the comforters have gambled for orphans. The relationship between Job and his friends is clearly deteriorating but he attempts to check this deterioration by begging them to change their assessment of him. He wants them to look at him. Could it be that Job wants his comforters to concentrate on him, not on their theology? Their prepackaged theological ideas simply do not fit his situation.

Job's invective (**7:1–21**) is directed against God. He has been conscripted (hard service) and employed (hired) but without the benefit of rest or wages. He receives futility and misery instead. Such is Job's assessment of his life.

Job reminds God of the brevity of his life and implores God to remember him before he goes to the grave. Considering Job's duress, we ought not be surprised by his abrupt mood swings. After begging God to remember him (v. 6), he now urges God to leave him alone and quit paying so much attention to him (vv. 11–21). Job feels hedged in like the sea. He is unable to rest because of terrifying dreams. Given this situation it is no surprise that Job despises his life and wants to die. In a possible parody of Psalm 8:4 Job wonders "What is man that you make so much of him?" (v. 17). Instead of rejoicing in God's attention Job objects to it. He would prefer that God look away from him. After all, is not his suffering due to God's close attention? Why has God made Job his target?

Does Job acknowledge sin? He may, but certainly not sins of such a magnitude to warrant his present sufferings. He is not ready to admit that his troubles have been caused by his sin. In fact, he appears insolent. Even if he has sinned he feels that he has not hurt God. Further, any sin committed would have been inadvertent. God should forgive him now before it is too late. Job, who once had his beliefs about God all in place, is now struggling in the light of his unexplained suffering.

While Eliphaz is ready to concede Job's piety, Bildad argues that if Job were innocent, God would restore him. Bildad begins abruptly, accusing Job of being a windbag. Implying that Job has wrongly charged God with injustice, Bildad insists that God consistently dispenses justice (**8:2–7**). What Job's children received, they deserved. Job himself can avoid such judgment but he must look to God (i.e., search for God rather than wait for God to search for him—7:21) and be pure and upright. If he does so, God will restore Job to his rightful place.

While the source of Eliphaz's theology is mystical (dream revelation) and empirical (I have observed, 4:8), Bildad's is traditional (former generations and fathers, **8:8–19**). He does not hesitate to cite the wisdom of the ancients. Job's brief experience needs to be augmented by the accumulated wisdom of the past. Bildad even cites an ancient proverb to make his case—papyrus and reeds will wither when deprived of water (vv. 11–12). He then employs two figures. First, the confidence (prosperity) of the wicked is as flimsy as the spider's web. Second, the apparent prosperity of the wicked is as swiftly lost as the luxuriant growth of a tree once it has been uprooted.

Bildad emphasizes the promise of restoration (**8:20–22**). By contrast with the uncertainty of the wicked is the permanence of the righteous who will experience joy and the humiliation of his enemies. The statement "God does not reject a blameless man" is similar to the charge hurled at Jesus by his mockers, "he trusts in God. Let God rescue him" (Matt. 27:43).

Job seems to ignore Bildad's presentation and returns to Eliphaz's speech in which he claimed that a man could not be righteous in God's eyes (4:17). That this is true is no surprise to Job. In a legal dispute with God man must lose since God determines all the rules and is the final arbiter. He would pose questions which man could not possibly answer. This is exactly the situation in the closing chapters of the book. Job cannot answer a single question addressed to him by God.

But not only is it a matter of God's wisdom. It is also a matter of his power (**9:2–13**). A hymn celebrating God's power is presented in verses 5–10. Job shares with his friends a recognition of God's great power. Earthquakes, eclipses, and constellations are the work of God. His actions can neither be numbered nor fathomed. While God's actions are visible, he himself remains invisible. No one can call God into account and restrain him when he chooses not to be restrained.

Job envisions a court scene in which God has been summoned to appear (**9:14–24**) but sees it as a futile effort. While God will show up, he would not reply to Job's charges. If the dragon Rahab and his cohorts cannot withstand God, how can Job? Even if he were in the right, he would not be able to answer God's charges. He would be crushed and overwhelmed. Job is simply no match for God. Once in the courtroom, Job senses the possibility of saying the wrong thing ("my mouth would condemn me; . . . it would pronounce me guilty," v. 20).

Job is so convinced of and concerned about his innocence that he is willing to go to any length to maintain it. At this point Job suggests that God is indifferent to moral considerations. Given his own condition, he has no choice but to reason this way. Yet there is a profound truth in what he says. His words ("He destroys both the blameless and the wicked") remind us of the words of Jesus ("He causes his sun to rise on the evil and the good, and sends rain on the righteous and the unrighteous," Matt. 5:45). This reasoning is critical to Job's defense. A randomness is observable in nature (v. 23) and in human courts (v. 24). Job places the responsibility squarely on God—if it is not he, then who is it?

Job has already used the shuttle to depict the sinfulness of life (7:6). Now he uses three more figures to portray the brevity of life: a runner (**9:25–31**), a light boat, and eagles. While Job wants to change his expression and smile, he dreads yet more sufferings. He is convinced that God will pronounce him guilty. Should Job wash himself, God would plunge him into a slime pit. Job has clearly reached a low point in his thinking about God.

Since God is not a man like Job, he needs someone to represent him in court, to arbitrate, to effect reconciliation (**9:32–35**). Sensing that God is both judge and prosecutor, Job recognizes the need for someone to represent him. He appeals as it were *from* God *to* God. Again, Job attributes his suffering to God.

In his appeal to God (**10:1–7**), Job concurs with the comforters that God must consider him wicked. He refers to himself as the work of God's hands and is puzzled that God smiles on the schemes of the wicked. Why does God oppress him? Since Job is convinced that he is not wicked, he does not want God to probe him as if he were.

Job appeals to three crafts to depict man's creation (**10:8–12**): (1) the common biblical figure (Jer. 18:5–12; Rom. 9:20–25) of the potter and the clay; (2) the curdling of cheese; (3) the pleating of cloth. Job notes God's providential care for him in the past.

Job does have some misgivings (**10:13–17**). He is convinced that God has a covert plan to reduce him to misery whether he is righteous or wicked. God is ready to catch Job in the act. Job suffers from shame and loss of self-respect even though he is innocent. He is assailed by new witnesses and God's forces which come against him "wave upon wave" (v. 17).

Baffled by the incongruity between the God of his past experience and the God of his present experience, Job restates his desire to die, thus returning to his soliloquy of chapter 3 (**10:18–22**). Again, he wishes that he had never been born, or that he had been stillborn, or that he had not even been conceived. He wants a respite which he feels he cannot have until God turns away from him. God has been paying too much attention to him. While not privy to the conversation between the Lord and Satan, Job is remarkably close to the truth here.

Zophar lacks the courtesy of Eliphaz. He seems to be totally devoid of sympathy. His dogmatism is apparent when he claims that Job cannot possibly know the unsearchable wisdom of God.

Zophar charges Job with using a multitude of words (**11:2–6**). No one can deny that Job has been verbose and that his language at times has been strong. (Even Job himself will subsequently recognize this when he concedes that he spoke of things he did not understand [42:3].) But Zophar fails to keep Job's words in context; they are not theoretical like Zophar's but are existential.

While Job has not actually said that his beliefs are flawless and that he is pure in God's sight, Zophar has probably correctly summarized Job's words (v. 4). He now wishes that God would accept Job's challenge to meet him so that he could show him how wrong he is. Since the divine wisdom is inscrutable, only God can reveal it. Perhaps Zophar's most cutting statement is that Job actually deserves more suffering than he has received.

Zophar again focuses on the inscrutable knowledge of God (**11:7–12**). It is beyond the range of man's mind, exceeding the four major parts of the universe: sky, underworld, land, and sea. Not only is God's wisdom beyond us, but his power is irresistible. These statements about God's wisdom and power are essentially correct but they are not properly applied to Job's situation. Further, Zophar's suggestion that Job has no more chance of receiving wisdom than a wild donkey's colt can be born a man is uncalled for.

Zophar now assumes the role of the evangelist, calling on Job to repent (**11:13–20**). He calls for Job to set his heart aright, to pray, to put away sin, and to remove evil from his home. Should he do these things, Job will not need to be ashamed, will be secure, and will be free from fear. While the importance of repentance must never be minimized, it must not be seen as a remedy for suffering. Not all suffering is traceable to sin.

The comforters have finally exasperated Job and now he responds in kind. Sarcasm is used to offset sarcasm. Job shows that he recognizes God's wisdom and power as do the comforters while disagreeing with their insistence on placing God in a straitjacket, making all of his actions predictable and conformable to moral purpose.

Job pours out his resentment against the comforters (**12:2–6**). He opens with a biting remark, charging them with the erroneous belief that they speak for everybody, that they are the only ones who matter, that they have a monopoly on wisdom. He insists that he is their equal and knows all these things as well. Job feels the ridicule of the people. While marauders are safe, the righteous and blameless experience misfortune. The comforters look down on Job, insisting that his sufferings indicate God's rejection.

In support of his position Job turns not to tradition but to empirical evidence (**12:7–12**). He suggests that animals, birds, the earth, and the fish know that there is no moral order in the world. The life and death of every creature is in the Lord's hand. It is he who arbitrarily decides the fortunes of men. An apparent aside now occurs (vv. 11–12), as Job insists that the ear has as much right to test words as the tongue tastes food. He also seems to quote a claim of the comforters, doing it with a sarcastic tone or perhaps denying the statement altogether. Even the animals of the world are more perceptive than the comforters!

In contrast to the comforters who claim that they possess wisdom Job states that only God truly possesses wisdom and power (**12:13–25**). The two must be coupled together. Job allows that God acts according to wisdom even if his acts seem to be devoid of moral purpose. First, his acts in nature are depicted, particularly his deployment of rain which will become a critical element in the speeches of the Lord. Second, his disposal of men in history is shown. Numerous examples of the negative treatment of counselors, judges, kings, priests, long-established men, advisors, elders, and nobles can be found throughout history. It is God who makes nations great and destroys them, who deprives leaders of the earth of their reason. Certainly Job's concept of God is not less but is actually greater than that of the comforters. But God's might is not the issue. The debate is over the part that moral purpose plays in his actions.

Job discounts the friendship of the comforters (**13:1–12**). He accuses them of whitewashing with lies and of being worthless physicians (v. 4). They came to minister to him but have clearly failed to do so. The only way that the comforters could display wisdom would be by their silence!

Job would prefer to argue his case with God, even though he considers God arbitrary. The comforters presume to speak for God but do so wickedly, deceitfully, and with partiality. Job warns them that they cannot deceive God as they have men. Even though Job has routinely divorced moral purpose from God's actions, here he allows for God to deal with the comforters. Job compares the words of the comforters to clay and ashes, either to stress their earthly character or to suggest their deadness and ineffectiveness.

Job is now ready to state his case in no uncertain terms (**13:13–19**). He envisions himself directly confronting God. He considers himself innocent since no godless man would dare to come before God. So confident is Job that he expects no contradiction; he *will* be vindicated. It seems that Job is not so much triumphant as he is defiant. His words are desperate. He intends to take his case all the way to God even if it means that he will be slain in the process.

Job turns aside from his friends to address God (**13:20–28**). He requests that God withdraw his hand and stop frightening Job with his terrors. While Job gives God two choices relative to the format of the encounter—summon and I will answer; let me speak and you reply—God ignores the latter and uses only the former. Job wants a list of charges against him and so requests to know his wrongs (errors), his sins (missing the mark), and his offense (rebellion). He wants to know why God hides his face and why he considers him his enemy. Job feels like a windblown leaf and dry chaff, being tossed about by God's whim. Job does not feel like the tree of Psalm 1 but rather as the chaff that the wind blows away. There is a hint here that Job believes his sufferings might be due to the sins of his youth. So meticulous is God's observation that he even notes Job's footsteps.

To depict the shortness of life Job uses two figures (**13:28–14:6**): a flower that withers and a fleeting shadow (cf. Pss. 90:6; 103:15; James 1:10). Since man is so ephemeral Job is surprised that God concentrates on him. Not only is life brief; it is also sinful. Furthermore, life is determined and man cannot exceed its set limits. Given these restraints, Job wants God to allow man to have an evening of rest to enjoy his wages as the hired man before night comes (v. 6).

Job acknowledges the finality of death (**14:7–12**). A dead man is more like a parched riverbed than a cut tree. The cut tree will sprout again but not man who dies. The drought-stricken tree will revive with the coming of the rain but not man who breathes his last and is no more. Since a dry riverbed can obviously fill up again Job must have in mind erosion, which would have prevented water from returning to the area.

After seeming to deny a resurrection, Job now longs for the afterlife and reflects upon what it might be like (**14:13–17**). Death is a temporary not a final place. God will again seek Job's fellowship as in the past. Is Job speaking about release from life (cf. 7:1) or release from death? The sealing of Job's offenses in a bag (v. 17) has been understood to mean that God is saving his sins so that they will not be forgotten or that God is covering them so that Job will not confront them again. The latter seems more likely because of the second half of verse 17.

Death destroys man's hope as erosion wears away stones and soil (**14:18–22**). Death is all-embracing. In death a person is no longer able to rejoice about his children's success or to lament their failures.

C. Second cycle of speeches (15:1–21:34). The first cycle of speeches discloses the theology of the comforters. While all three essentially agree that sin is behind Job's sufferings, each adds his own nuance. Eliphaz, seeking to be supportive, accepts the piety of Job and argues from it. Bildad contrasts the fate of Job and Job's children and warns him from it. Zophar seems to offer neither support nor warning. He uses Job's sufferings to denounce him. The comforters' speeches reveal self-righteous and patronizing attitudes. At times anger and impatience are observable. There is a minimal amount of compassion and understanding.

Job also discloses his position in the first cycle of speeches. He simply is unable to reconcile his predicament with the traditional answers being offered by the comforters. Since he will not admit sin, at least not of a magnitude to warrant his intense sufferings, he has no choice but to view God differently than do the comforters.

These positions will be maintained by the participants in the second cycle of speeches. Any change will be essentially one of attitude. While the ideas remain the same and are reinforced, their very repetition will result in a hardening of resistance to any other point of view. The relationship between Job and his friends will deteriorate. Vituperation develops. Virtually no progress will be made in seeking to resolve Job's sufferings.

Eliphaz remains the most courteous of the three comforters, but there is a clear decline in his politeness.

Eliphaz sees Job's protestation of innocence as his own condemnation (**15:2–6**). Job had feared that his mouth would condemn him in God's presence (9:20). It has already done so in Eliphaz's opinion. Job's speech was prompted by his sin and expressed in a crafty way. Calling Job a "wise man" (v. 2), Eliphaz indicates that he would have expected better arguments from him than hot air! But Job not only advances poor arguments, he also sets a poor example, thereby undermining piety.

Through several questions put to Job Eliphaz seeks to alert Job to his self-delusion (**15:7–11**). These questions reflect concerns similar to those in the questions put to Job by the Lord (chaps. 38–41). These questions pertain to his identity, origin, contacts, superiority, and age. Eliphaz seems to pull rank, claiming to be older than Job.

Eliphaz criticizes Job's self-assertion (**15:12–16**). Assessing his consolations as God's consolations "gently spoken" (v. 11), Eliphaz questions Job about his passionate and unorthodox response. Returning to an emphasis in his first speech (4:17ff.), Eliphaz lets Job know what he thinks of him by his assessment of man in general—"vile and corrupt" (v. 16).

Eliphaz dwells on his favorite theme, the fate of the wicked (**15:17–35**). He begs Job to listen to his personal observations—Eliphaz's favorite source of information (4:8). Given Edom's reputation for wisdom (Jer. 49:7), the land referred to in verse 19 is probably Edom. The prosperity of the wicked is temporary and vacuous. He lives in apprehension of certain retribution; he is haunted by fears of poverty and is not at ease. All this prevents him from truly enjoying his wealth and adds to his hostility toward God. It also makes him self-indulgent.

Mixing metaphors, Eliphaz now uses a series of figures of plant life to depict the fate of the wicked; a blasted plant (v. 30), palms (v. 32), grapes and olives that never come to maturity (v. 33). Not only is Eliphaz's tirade irrelevant and inapplicable (Job is not guilty of defiance and self-indulgence), it is also clearly incorrect. All too often the wicked do prosper and the righteous do suffer. Job knows this and the details presented by Eliphaz do nothing to change Job's mind.

Job dismisses the comforters' words (**16:2–5**). Picking up on one of Eliphaz's last words (trouble, 15:35) Job turns it back on him, calling him and his colleagues "comforters of trouble" ("miserable comforters," v. 2). He also reciprocates by charging them with windy words, suggesting that if he were in their place he could make fine (polished) speeches which would have words of comfort and relief. The shaking of the head (v. 4) normally would have been viewed as an act of derision (cf. 2 Kings 19:21; Matt. 27:39), but here is a gesture of support.

Job feels abandoned by God and man (**16:6–17**). Job blames God not only for his sufferings but also for his mistreatment by men. While Job's graphic language may suggest physical aggression, it is more likely that he is referring to verbal assault. He characterizes his opponents as evil and wicked. While these are strong words, they may be directed at the comforters who have been verbally abusing Job.

The picture presented of God in this passage is frightening. God's treatment of Job is characterized as a vicious attack. He is likened to a wild beast tearing its prey (v. 9), a traitor (v. 11), a wrestler making unexpected moves (v. 12), an archer taking target practice (v. 13), and a warrior assaulting a stronghold (v. 14). Such action has stripped Job of his family and of his health.

Job does not know how to react to God's treatment. Neither speech nor silence has helped. He has put on sackcloth as a sign of mourning and buried his brow (lit. horn—a symbol of dignity; cf. Pss. 89:17, 24; 112:9) in the dust. His eyes are inflamed and he has dark shadows around his eyes. Nevertheless, Job still maintains that his hands have been free of violence and that his prayer is pure. Prayer is unacceptable to God when one's hands are not clean (Isa. 1:15; contrast Job 11:13ff. and 31:7).

Job calls for a witness (**16:18–17:10**). Still struggling for vindication, Job wants his blood to remain exposed so that like Abel's blood (Gen. 4:10) it may cry to the Lord. He is confident that he has a witness in heaven. This witness has been identified as God, an intercessor (v. 20), arbitrator (9:33), and defender (19:25).

Job returns to the inevitability of his death. Surrounded by mockers (the comforters), he turns to God and requests a pledge from him—the very one he has accused of injustice. Job begs God to act as his guarantor, both to give a pledge and to be a pledge himself (cf. Heb. 6:13ff.). Job's frustrations are quite understandable. He wants to bring a case against God but to establish his innocence he has to turn to that very God (his plaintiff) to put up security for him. As part of his appeal, Job insists that God must not allow the comforters to triumph over him and cautions that their treachery will return upon their children. Two observations are pertinent here. First, this request can be seen as a prayer. Job, like the psalmists, offers the prayer of the innocent sufferer against his foes (cf. Pss. 30:1; 41:11; 109:6–15). Second, this request can be viewed as part of an oath, charging the comforters with malicious intent and thereby subjecting them to the very punishment which their false remarks would bring on Job (cf. Deut. 19:15–21).

Job seems overly sensitive to the fact that people conclude that he is guilty and treat him with contempt by spitting in his face. His eyesight is failing (not so much because of age as grief) and he has lost so much weight that he appears as a skeleton.

The meaning and position of verses 8–10 are much debated since they do not seem to fit into Job's speech. If they are retained here, Job finds support from upright men who are appalled at his treatment. Further, he seems resolved to maintain his ways in spite of his rejection by the comforters and his apparent rejection by God. He challenges the comforters to repeat their arguments. They will simply demonstrate once again their ignorance.

Job now concedes that his life is behind him (**17:11–16**). Included here are both his plans and his desires. The meaning of verse 12 is not clear but may again reflect Job's negative assessment of the comforters' words. Job now returns to his imminent death. He appears resigned to it. While some of the expressions here are quite morbid (corruption, worm), there may be an element of hope since Job calls the grave his home (v. 13).

Although he has nothing signficantly new to say, Bildad abruptly begins his second speech in which he graphically depicts the misery of the wicked.

Bildad rebukes Job (**18:2–4**), addressing him in the plural (Job seems to be included with the wicked). Bildad charges him with unrestrained talk, and suggests that he "wise up." Bildad then betrays his concern for his own reputation (v. 3). Obviously he is more anxious about his image than he is about Job. Job is aware of this and it only intensifies the antagonism between them. Any person who would comfort another is vulnerable and must be willing to be so. Bildad accuses Job of wanting the moral order changed to accommodate him.

The moral order which Bildad accuses Job of wishing to overturn is fixed (**18:5–21**). The fate of the wicked is certain. He will experience darkness; his lamp will be snuffed out, a certain indication of disaster. He will be caught in a trap (actually, six different terms for traps and snares are used in vv. 8–10). Terrors will pursue him and he will not be able to avoid them. The king of terrors is probably death. "Death's firstborn" (v. 13) must refer to death itself (reading death as an appositive, "the first-born, death") or to some fatal disease which is not identified. The tent of the wicked is devastated. The reference to brimstone (sulphur) is either an allusion to the destruction of Sodom and Gomorrah or to the destruction of Job's property in chapter 1. The wicked is again compared to vegetable life which withers. Finally, he will have no descendants. Is this a cruel reference to Job's deceased descendants? Men on both sides of the Jordan River will be appalled at the fate of the wicked. Bildad now concludes with the claim that his representation of the fate of the wicked is certain.

Beginning with a note of despair and impatience, Job moves to a new height of faith, a belief in his certain vindication.

Job is impatient with his comforters (**19:2–6**). Job takes the expression *how long* (v. 2) with which Bildad began his two speeches (8:2; 18:2) and turns it back on him. Job feels that he has been assaulted by words that crush rather than comfort. The statement *ten times* (v. 3) is not to be read as a precise number but as a round number, perhaps expressing Job's exasperation. Job insists that if he has erred it remains his concern alone. While initially welcoming the arrival of the comforters, Job now seems to resent their facile explanations and their insistence that they speak for God. Contrary to the comforters' conclusions, it is not his sin which has resulted in his misfortunes but rather God has acted capriciously and has put him in the wrong.

Job senses that he has been cornered by God (**19:7–12**). His cry for help is ignored and he does not receive justice. His honor (this word can mean both wealth and prestige) has been lost. In his attacks on Job, God destroys Job as a building is demolished and as a tree is uprooted (v. 10). Job employs military language (troops, siege ramp) to depict God's actions against him.

In **19:13–22** Job expresses his ostracized condition. He has been alienated and estranged from all human relationships (brothers, acquaintances, kinsmen, friends, guests, maidservants, servants, wife, and little boys). Job notes his treatment by children last. This is a violation of one of Israel's significant conventions. All his intimate friends detest him. Job implores his friends for pity and begs them to desist from slander, suggesting that they already have enough of his flesh.

Job now turns from imploring his friends for pity and looks to God for vindication (**19:23–29**). He wants a record kept of his words for future generations, written on a scroll, inscribed on leaden tablets, and engraved in rock.

Verses 25–27 are among the most difficult in the book. This becomes evident when one compares English translations and commentaries. The ancient versions also reflect uncertainty here, with differing arrangements of the verses. There is general agreement on the meaning of verse 25. Job will be vindicated. The question is: When will this vindication occur?

Job's vindication will be brought about by his Redeemer. In Israel the redeemer was usually a kinsman who was obligated to exact vengeance in a blood feud (Deut. 19:6–12; 2 Sam. 14:11), to reclaim his relative from slavery (Lev. 25:48), to regain family property (Lev. 25:25), and to marry the deceased's widow (Ruth 4:1–6). This term is often applied to the Lord as the deliverer of Israel from bondage in Egypt (Exod. 6:6; 15:13) and from Babylonian exile (Jer. 50:34). It is also used of the Lord's deliverance of a person from imminent death (Ps. 103:4; Lam. 3:58). Given Job's present situation and his rejection by the comforters, it is quite obvious why Job asserts his belief in the Redeemer. Since the word *redeem* has a commercial connotation today, the use of other translations of this Hebrew word such as defender, vindicator, avenger, or champion may be preferable. What Job needs is not so much physical help as moral vindication. He knows that since his Redeemer lives this vindication will occur even though he has been forced to wait for it.

Verse 26 has been translated in several ways. These translations fall primarily into one of two categories: *from* (perspective) *my flesh I shall see God* or *out of* (privative) *my flesh I shall see God.* If the former, then Job is referring to the theophany which he experiences in chapters 38–41. After it is over, he concludes "now my eyes have seen you" (42:5). On the other hand, if the latter translation is used, then Job seems to be anticipating an afterlife, a resurrection which will result in his meeting God. Arguments have been advanced for both of these positions. Space does not permit consideration of them here. Given Job's general attitude toward the grave, it seems wise to be hesitant to develop a doctrine of the resurrection from Job's words.

Job concludes his thoughts by expressing his exhaustion with such lofty ideas. He states that his heart faints within him. In the last two verses of this chapter, he issues a warning to the comforters who have been insisting that the trouble lies in him. Such an attitude can result in divine judgment.

Zophar explodes, perhaps bothered in particular by Job's concluding remarks in the preceding chapter. His concern is with the fate of the wicked, which is both irrelevant and cruel.

Zophar's agitation is very apparent (**20:23**). Careful reflection and less self-concern would have resulted in a more pertinent presentation. Zophar is clearly reacting to what he perceives to be Job's insults.

Zophar focuses on the fate of the wicked (**20:4–29**). He suggests that the joy of the wicked is brief, that evil has a built-in retribution, and that God will vent his burning anger against the wicked.

Zophar's emphasis on the limited prosperity of the wicked is standard fare in wisdom literature. Judgment will be not only swift but also dramatic. The children of the wicked man will be forced to give back his wealth to those from whom it had been wrongfully acquired. While all must ultimately die, the wicked will die prematurely.

Evil's built-in retribution is depicted under the image of food that tastes delicious in the mouth but turns poisonous in the stomach (vv. 12–14). So sweet is the food that the wicked hides it under his tongue; he keeps it in his mouth as long as he can but once it reaches the stomach vomiting will occur. So it is with ill-gotten riches. They will not be retained but will be lost so quickly that they will provide no enjoyment. The source of the wrongfully acquired wealth is the poor whom the wicked has oppressed and left destitute. There will be no respite for the wicked. He will continue to devour both the poor and his wealth. But at the height of his success there will be a dramatic reversal of fortune.

This retribution is the work of God. Again, as with Bildad (18:13–19), Zophar seems to have in mind the adversities that Job is suffering. Both expressions, *unfanned flame* and *gleaming point,* indicate lightning, with the latter term being used of a penetrating flashing arrow (vv. 24–25). The common witnesses of the Old Testament, the heavens and the earth, will team up to indict Job. Here Zophar may be refuting Job's claim that his innocence is supported by a witness in heaven and by the earth which will continue to cry on his behalf (16:18–21). Zophar concludes his speech with the same insensitivity and inappropriateness as he began it.

Job flatly contradicts the picture of the wicked, showing a greater sensitivity to the comforters' speeches than he has previously. Job does not seem to pray in this speech. In fact, as the dialogue continues, Job will pray less and less.

Job calls for a hearing (**21:2–6**). He feels that the comforters have not been listening carefully to him. What he wants more than anything is their undivided attention. After they have listened, they can resume their mocking. Job knows that they are preoccupied with their pet doctrines and reputations. He notes that his complaint is against God and not against them. If they will listen, they will be astonished. Job himself is terrified by his own experience.

Job's picture of the wicked (**21:7–16**) is the exact opposite of Zophar's. They grow old and increase in power. Their children thrive. Their homes are safe. They do not feel the rod of God. Their herds are fertile. Their death is peaceful. These are the wicked who deliberately reject God. Yet Job refuses to be included in their circle.

Job insists on the rarity of retribution (**21:17–26**). While Bildad argues that the light of the wicked is put out (18:5), Job questions how often this is actually the case. Verse 19 aptly summarizes the position of the comforters. Job objects to hereditary guilt even as Jeremiah (31:29), Ezekiel (18:2–3), and Jesus (John 9:1–3). The wicked ought to experience retribution themselves. However, Job argues, there is no set pattern of reward and punishment. Life is too complex for a simple formula. Dying in prosperity is no indication of a righteous person (v. 23) any more than dying in bitterness is an indication of a wicked person (v. 25). Death is a common experience of all.

Job appeals to experience (**21:27–34**). He observes that the comforters are really talking about *his* fate when they refer to the fate of the wicked (v. 27). In contrast to the much repeated claim of the comforters that the home of the wicked is destroyed, Job appeals to the testimony of world travelers. Zophar claims universal support for his teachings (20:4), but no one exposes or requites the wicked, who seem to die in peace and have their bodies carefully guarded against grave robbers. This is quite the opposite of what Bildad (18:5ff.) and Zophar (20:5ff.) claim. The wicked are buried in the valley and men follow after them. The second cycle of speeches ends with Job's assessment: the comforters' efforts are "nonsense." This is a favorite word in the Book of Ecclesiastes, where it is translated "vanity." The consolations of the comforters are hollow and empty.

D. Third cycle of speeches (22:1–27:23). The definite interchange of speeches found in cycles 1 and 2 is missing here. While Eliphaz has his turn, Bildad's presentation is abbreviated. Zophar has no assigned speech in this cycle at all.

Efforts to explain the material are as follows. Chapter 22 is credited to Eliphaz, chapter 23 to Job. While 24:1–17 is attributed to Job, verses 18–25 are credited to Zophar. Bildad is identified as the speaker in chapter 25 and 26:5–14. Job is said to be the spokesman in 26:1–4 and 27:1–10. The balance of chapter 27 (vv. 11–23) is recognized as Zophar's third speech along with 24:18–25 as noted.

If the material is accepted as it stands in the text, Job now agrees with his comforters. While it is possible that he has capitulated, it does not seem likely or consistent with the general tenor of the book. There is the possibility that Job is quoting his opponents. For instance, some translations such as the Revised Standard Version add the words *you say* at the beginning of 24:18. While these words are not found in the Hebrew text, they need to be added since the text that follows is clearly not Job's words. Either Job quotes the comforters here or is now in agreement with them.

This effort to reorder the text, however, must be tempered since the order that is found in our present text is in general agreement with a second-century B.C. version of this book found at Qumran.

While it is impossible to establish an orderly progression of thought through the exchanges of these cycles, it is possible to discern a degree of development. In the first cycle, the comforters are more general in their remarks and more open to Job's repentance. In the second cycle, they emphasize the fate of the wicked, resulting in a clash with Job who does not share their simplistic explanations. In this final cycle, the comforters openly accuse Job of wickedness, accusing him of deeds which not only Job but also the author denies. Job is clearly expendable. At all costs their theological assumptions must be proven. These men are more concerned about maintaining a position than ministering to a person.

While Eliphaz has been the most courteous of the comforters, he now resorts to blatant lies, implying that Job in his wickedness has calculated on God's indifference.

Eliphaz now insists that man's piety is of no benefit to God. God is unaffected by man's actions and hence apathetic (**22:2–3**). Not only is this concept out of keeping with the biblical portrayal of God, it is also not helpful to Eliphaz's argument. If God is indifferent to righteousness, then must he not also be equally indifferent to wickedness? If he is not concerned with reward, then is it not likely that he is unconcerned with punishment? Clearly such reasoning undermines Eliphaz's contention that God is punishing Job. Perhaps Eliphaz is countering here Job's claim that God seems indifferent to wickedness (21:23–26) by suggesting that he is indifferent to virtue, that he is impartial and fair in his treatment of all men in general and Job in particular.

Eliphaz now denies Job his attested piety. Having eliminated Job's piety as the basis for divine action, it must be his wickedness which has precipitated his suffering. Eliphaz now proceeds to specify Job's particular sins (**22:4–11**). The listed sins are those routinely associated with the rich and powerful and hence allegedly practiced by Job during his earlier successful years. Job is accused of failure to return the outer garments given by the poor as collateral. According to Exodus 22:26 and Deuteronomy 24:10–13, these garments were to be returned nightly since the nights were cold and covering was necessary. Job is then accused of withholding water from the weary and food from the hungry. Finally, Job is accused of oppressing the widow and orphan, who deserve compassion since they are the special concern of God (see Deut. 10:18; 14:29; 16:11, 14; James 1:26–27). These alleged sins have resulted in Job's entrapment. The dark and a flood of water, evidences of God's judgment, are now inappropriately applied to Job.

Eliphaz accuses Job of making God indifferent (**22:12–20**). In fact, Job's sins are traceable to his attitude toward God. While others accept the transcendence of God Job takes advantage of it, insisting that God is too remote to see and care. Such an attitude was held by wicked men of old. While there may be a reference here to the flood of Noah's time, it is possible that the reference is more general since the flood is seen elsewhere as a means of destruction (20:28; 27:20). Verse 18 seems to be a quotation of Job's words in order to refute them (cf. 21:16). Although Job denies God's judgment, the righteous see their ruin and rejoice.

Eliphaz now appeals to Job to repent. If he does so his fortune will be restored (**22:21–30**). This is essentially the same advice he offered in his first speech. While verses 24 and 25 are difficult, their admonition seems to be "love God rather than gold." Is there a suggestion here that Job's love of gold has caused his sufferings? The promise of restoration is not limited to gold. It stresses delight in the Almighty and effective prayer.

Job now seems to turn aside from his friends. He does not address them in this speech. His thoughts seem to be a kind of soliloquy, perhaps directed to God.

Job longs to find God (**23:2–7**). He admits that he is bitter but with reason since God's hand is heavy in spite of his groaning. He desires to state his case to God so that he might learn any countercharges God might introduce. While earlier he had feared that God would overwhelm him (9:34–35; 13:20–22), he now believes that he will be granted a fair hearing. Job is more confident than ever that he is upright. Since God is both his adversary and judge Job wants deliverance but above all vindication. He wants and expects acquittal from all the charges leveled against him.

No matter which direction Job goes (forward = east; backward = west; lefthand = north; righthand = south), he still cannot find God (**23:8–17**). But even though he cannot find God, God knows where to find Job for he knows the way Job takes (v. 10). This verse also seems to suggest that God knows what he is doing (lit. the way with me) and that when he is finished, Job will come forth as gold. The emphasis here is not upon purification but rather upon demonstration. Job is being tested. He is confident that he has not turned aside or departed from God's commands.

Job affirms his belief in the oneness of God (lit. he is in one) and in the sovereignty of God ("he does whatever he pleases," v. 13). He knows that whatever God's decree is relative to him it will be carried out. Understandably Job is frightened by such thoughts.

Job questions God's apparent inactivity (**24:1–17**). Observing the oppression of the poor and various crimes all around him, Job questions why God has not set times for judgment. Job, having experienced the legal procedures of his day (29:7–17), expects God to maintain justice. Not only has God failed to prevent the illicit activities of the oppressors, he has also failed to establish times when he executes justice. God appears to be either indifferent or unjust.

Job cites several wrongs perpetrated against the defenseless, wrongs that are clearly forbidden by God's law: encroachment on the lands of others; seizure of flocks; removal of the ass of the fatherless and the ox of the widow; and denial to the poor of access to public paths.

Beginning with verse 5, the emphasis now turns to a description of the plight of the victims of these wrongs. They secure their food like wild donkeys in the desert, perhaps eating the food of cattle. Job emphasizes that they glean in the vineyards of the wicked; it is the wicked who are wealthy enough to own these vineyards. Not only do the poor lack food, they also lack clothing and shelter. Their children are removed by force as payment for debts and are perhaps enslaved. In spite of their carrying sheaves and crushing olives and grapes, as slaves they remain hungry and thirsty. Although they cry out to God, he remains inactive.

Attention is now focused on people who commit crimes under the cover of darkness and escape judgment. These evildoers invert values, considering the darkness to be their morning. They believe that no one sees them. They escape judgment, contrary to Eliphaz's claim that there will be public exposure (22:19).

Job **24:18–25** is exceptionally difficult and constitutes a problem. These verses do not seem to reflect the thinking of Job, but rather the sentiments of his friends. As a result, this passage is transferred by some translators and commentaries from this chapter and assigned either to Bildad (chap. 25) or to Zophar (27:11–23), giving him a speech otherwise missing in the third cycle.

Another way these verses are handled is to consider them as Job's quotation of what his friends have said. A slight modification is to consider verses 18–20 as the quotation with verses 21–24 being Job's rejoinder. While there is little room for dogmatism here, our treatment of this section will assume that it is a citation of the friends' position.

The wicked quickly disappear as from the surface of the water. Their land is cursed so that there are no grapes to tread. Even as the snow is removed by heat and drought so the wicked are carried off by Sheol. Further, the wicked will be childless, will die, will be forgotten, and will be broken like a tree.

Once again the wicked's treatment of the helpless is mentioned. In verse 22 the performer of the action is not specified. Either it is God who responds with judgment (NIV) or the wicked who sustains himself (RSV). While allowing the wicked a sense of security, God's eyes are on their ways and he will cut them off like flowers or heads of grain.

In verse 25, Job asserts the correctness of his position and challenges anyone to refute him.

The brevity of Bildad's speech (**25:1–6**) has caused some scholars to conclude that Bildad has run out of arguments. Since the ideas of this chapter have been encountered earlier, it is indeed possible that Bildad has exhausted his arguments. This could also account for the absence of a speech by Zophar in this last cycle.

Other scholars insist that this speech is truncated and should be attached to material in chapters 26 and 27 which, while assigned to Job, is not consistent with his position. In support of this position, it must be noted that this is the only speech directed toward Job that does not begin with a personal attack.

In this speech, Bildad stresses both the power and purity of God. Shifting from the disturbing picture provided by Job in the previous chapter, Bildad concentrates on the greatness of God. His dominion—extending from this earth to the heights of heaven and to the netherworld—produces awe. Establishing order in the heights of heaven may allude to references depicting war between angels (Dan. 10:13; 10:20–11:1) or rebellion against God (Isa. 14:13–15; 24:21). The forces of God include not only angels, but also the stars (Isa. 40:26) which provide light for all.

Bildad, having established the power of God, now shifts to his purity. Compared with God's brilliance and magnificence, even the moon is not bright and the stars are not pure. This position is similar to that presented earlier by Eliphaz, who noted that God even charges his angels with error (4:18). If the angels and celestial bodies are unclean in God's eyes, how can man be pure?

The reason for such an emphasis by Bildad is obvious. He again seeks to establish Job's guilt and thereby account for his sufferings. By insisting that no mortal can ever be perfect in God's sight, Bildad removes the possibility of innocent suffering. Here he flies in the face of the prologue of the book which shows that sin is not the cause of Job's sufferings.

Bildad's description of mankind is most derogatory. Both the maggot and the worm are associated with the grave, and thus Bildad is referring here to the certainty and finality of death. Comparing man to the moon and stars, the psalmist recognizes man's littleness; but he quickly adds a significant qualification when he observes that man is made a little lower than God and is crowned with glory and honor (Ps. 8:5).

Since the pronoun *you* is singular here, Job is directing his remarks to Bildad (**26:2–4**). He is either questioning the relevance of Bildad's speech (how has it helped Job?) or the necessity of it (does God need his defense?). Job senses that Bildad has considered him powerless and feeble, without wisdom. Such a condescending attitude leads to Job's biting sarcasm. Job continues to insist that he is as well informed as his friends. He challenges any tacit claim that Bildad's words are of divine origin.

Beginning where Bildad ends, Job starts with the netherworld (vv. 5–6) and goes on to include the heavens (v. 7) and the earth (v. 10), placing all under the scrutiny and jurisdiction of God. If anything, Job's assessment of God's power (**26:5–14**) exceeds that of Bildad.

Earlier, Job had expressed the wish to be hidden from God in Sheol (14:13) but now acknowledges that Sheol is naked before God and thus open to his scrutiny. Reference to the north alludes either to the mythological mountains of the north where the gods dwelt or to the heavens. The verb *spreads out* (v. 7) is used in the Old Testament of the heavens (Ps. 104:2; Isa. 40:22; 42:5; 44:24; Jer. 10:12), never of the earth or mountains. Hence it would seem preferable to see the north here as designating the celestial region. The earth is pictured as suspended over nothing. In other Old Testament passages, it is portrayed as being supported by pillars (1 Sam. 2:8; Ps. 75:3). As in the creation account God marks a boundary between light and darkness (v. 10). Rahab (v. 12) is not to be confused with the harlot (Josh. 2:1), but is rather a mythological sea monster used as a symbol of chaos. It is not by power alone, but also by wisdom that God overcomes Rahab. The gliding serpent (v. 13) is probably a reference to leviathan, a sea monster that also represents chaos, similar in nature to Rahab. While chaos was a serious threat to the pagan gods, it is no problem at all to the Lord.

This exposure to God's activity in the netherworld, the earth, and the heavens presents us with just the outer fringe of his works. At best, it is a whisper. If we have trouble grasping a fraction of his power, Job questions how we can understand the thunder of his power—the full scope of his creative power.

The speech of chapter 27 is introduced by a totally new statement—*and Job continued his discourse.* Given this formula, it is possible that chapter 27 should be kept distinct from chapter 26. If that is the case, then chapter 26 would mark the close of the third cycle of speeches and chapter 27 would mark the beginning of Job's conclusion. However, grouping chapter 27 with chapters 29–31 is problematic because of the intervention of chapter 28, which is probably not to be assigned to Job. This new formula may simply be a late editorial addition to break up a rather lengthy discourse.

Again, we need to note that many scholars assign verses 7–23 of this chapter to Zophar as his contribution to the third cycle. For the purposes of our comments, we will accept these words as being Job's and constituting the close of the third cycle of speeches.

In **27:1–6** Job continues to assert his claim to innocence. He uses an oath, swearing by the very God who has denied him justice. As noted earlier, Job is not troubled by the paradoxical fact that he swears his innocence by the very God whom he claims has wronged him. The content of his oath is found in verse 4. He promises to speak the truth. He will never admit that the charges of the comforters are right. At all costs he will retain his integrity; his conscience does not reproach him. The maintenance of his righteousness is not so much a matter of defending his person as it is a defense of his position. He is right! The friends are wrong! As long as he lives he will maintain this.

The enemies of this section are probably the friends who have falsely accused Job. What Job says about them is not descriptive, but imprecative (**27:7–12**). Job invokes a curse upon his friends: "may my enemies be like the wicked." He, in keeping with Israelite law, calls down upon his adversaries the very punishment which would have come to him had their charges been correct. To call upon his enemies the fate of the wicked is to wish for them the worst that he possibly can. This includes premature death and unanswered prayers. There is no point in the wicked praying since God will not listen. While the wicked may be inclined to pray when distress comes upon him, he is unable to delight in the Almighty.

The comforters agree with Job that God does not hear the prayers of the wicked. Yet, while regarding Job as guilty, they urge him to pray. This is contradictory, resulting in meaningless talk. If there is no hope for the ungodly and Job is such, any call for prayer and worship is nonsense.

Job **27:13–23,** attributed to Job, is very similar to the ideas of the friends. This has resulted, as noted, in the assignment of these words to Zophar. It may be that Job utters these words to turn them back upon the friends. They do not perceive themselves as wicked, but they are because of their malicious attack on Job.

The fate described here is not so much personal as it is domestic. However many children the wicked person may have, they will fall victim to the sword and famine. (The fact that Job has lost his children does make these words seem inappropriate for him.) The widow of the wicked man is apathetic about his fate.

Moving from family to possessions, Job now indicates that the wicked person will lose wealth overnight. It will become the property of the righteous. Since the moth does not construct a dwelling, it is probably better to follow the ancient versions and compare the wicked man's house to a spider's web, suggesting its flimsiness (27:18). The same idea is emphasized by comparing his house to the temporary shelter erected at harvest time.

The wicked person will be troubled night and day. Both the flood and the east wind suggest the unpleasant and the destructive. Verse 23 is ambiguous. The subject of "claps its hands" may be God, the east wind, or men. Since the wind does not clap its hands, it seems better to render this verse as God clapping his hands, deriding the wicked, or men clapping their hands, rejoicing at the plight of the wicked. Hissing is a way of expressing horror (Jer. 49:17).

III. Hymn on Wisdom (28:1–28)

Three critical questions relative to this chapter are: Who is its spokesman? Why is it located at this juncture in the book? What is its role in the book?

While this chapter is not specifically assigned to anyone, the present arrangement of the text would suggest that the words of this chapter were spoken by Job. The previous designated spokesman was Job (chap. 26) and the next designated spokesman is also Job (chap. 29), with this chapter sandwiched between the two. However, the material of this chapter is incompatible with Job's earlier and subsequent thoughts. In fact, if this chapter is assigned to Job, then the balance of the book may be rendered unnecessary since Job has already found his answer. It seems equally unacceptable to assign this chapter to one of the comforters. The suggestion that this chapter was presented by a chorus should probably also be rejected since Job is not a drama. Given our uncertainty, perhaps it is best to attribute these words to an editor.

Why is this chapter located at this point? No certain answer can be given, but it may be a kind of interlude between the dialogue now completed and Job's peroration yet to come. Further, it serves both as a kind of summary and a word of sanity in an atmosphere that has become quite heated.

The role this chapter plays in the book is to show that man, unaided by God, can never arrive at an answer to innocent suffering. Rather than preempting the Lord, who follows, it sets the stage for his appearance. If there is to be any answer, it is to be found with the Lord.

This chapter is naturally divided into three strophes by a refrain which appears in verses 12 and 20: Where can wisdom be found? Where does understanding dwell?

The first strophe (**28:1–11**) demonstrates man's determination and ingenuity in the area of mining. Silver, gold, iron, copper, and precious stones have motivated man to develop his mining technology. Darkness, remoteness, and depth are no deterrent. While birds and animals, noted for their skill and power, cannot locate or extract ore, man can. Man cuts a shaft and digs the tunnels. From the watery depths man brings hidden things to light. However, though he can locate hidden things, he cannot find wisdom unaided.

While precious metals can be extracted from the earth, it is impossible to obtain wisdom in the land of the living, in the primeval deep, or in the netherworld (**28:12–19**). Its source is the fear of the Lord (v. 28). If wisdom could be found in the world, its price would be such that no wealth could purchase it. The precise identification of the precious stones and metals mentioned in verses 15–19 is problematic and there is simply no consensus about them among scholars. However, it is clear that these are materials of great value. Even so, they cannot equal the worth of wisdom. Not only can man not find wisdom by his ingenuity, he cannot secure it with his wealth.

Wisdom is attainable only through God (**28:20–28**). While wisdom remains hidden from the eyes of every living thing, it is observed by God who sees everything under the heavens. The evidence of God's wisdom can be found in nature. Interestingly, thunder is called the voice of the Lord (cf. Ps. 29). It will be from the storm that the Lord speaks to Job (38:1).

This chapter does not deny man's abilities. On the contrary, the picture of man in this chapter shows him to be far superior to animals which are characterized by outstanding abilities (e.g., the falcon's keen sight). It is not the intent of this chapter to belittle man. In fact, if anything there may be a tendency here to offset Bildad's negative assessment of man (25:6). However, even as Job is considered great for "fearing God" (1:1), so here man can only achieve greatness by the fear of the Lord (the only use of *ădōnāy* in the Book of Job). Only in piety is there true wisdom and an ability to put life in focus.

IV. Job's Peroration (29:1–31:40)

As Job was given the first word (chap. 3) so now he is given the last word (chaps. 29–31). Here he summarizes his position, beginning with chapter 29 where he recollects his former happy condition. In chapter 30 he speaks of his present miserable condition. Finally, in chapter 31 he uses a negative confession to establish his innocence.

A. The way it was (29:1–25). This chapter is devoted to the recollection of Job's earlier happiness (vv. 2–6), his earlier benevolence (vv. 7–17), his earlier expectation of the future (vv. 18–20), and his earlier esteem (vv. 21–35).

Job begins his recollection of the past by describing his relationship with God and his family (**29:2–6**). He notes that God watched over him. While this concept can have a negative connotation—a kind of hostile watch (10:14; 13:27; 14:16)—here it clearly has a positive thrust. The lamp and light (v. 3) suggest divine blessing and direction. Job was in his prime (v. 4, lit. autumn days), the time when a person begins to reap the benefits of his earlier efforts. He experienced the intimate friendship of God. In verse 5 Job refers to his now deceased children. Their presence with him at that time was an indication that the Almighty was still with him. Further evidence of the divine presence was the fertility of his herd and the productivity of his olive trees.

Job's relationships are not limited to God

and his family, but also include the people of the city (**29:7–17**). Job was active in the administration of justice. When he went to the gate of the city, the place of judicial proceedings and public business (Deut. 21:19; 2 Kings 7:1, 18), he was given a prominent seat. The young and the old, the chief men and the nobles paid their respects to Job when he arrived at the gate of the city. Such a claim, if false, could have easily been challenged by the protagonists. The fact that it was not indicates the reliability of Job's claim. Job's benevolence was extended to the exploited, to the handicapped, and to the stranger. Job not only rescued the victims of the wicked, he also broke the power of the wicked to harm others. Understandably, Job was commended and blessed. His clothing was a garment of righteousness (cf. Ps. 132:9; Isa. 59:17) and justice.

Given his compassion for others and his favorable circumstances, Job formerly concluded that he would live a long life, that his days would be as numerous as the grains of sand, and that he would die at home in peace (**29:18–20**). Job's earlier expectation is also reflected in his reference to a luxuriant tree (v. 19). Job expected to retain his strength until he died.

The words of **29:21–25** are so similar to those of verses 7–10 that some commentators have rearranged this chapter so that verses 21–25 come after verses 7–10. However, such a rearrangement is artificial and without support in the Hebrew text. It is best to leave these verses in their present location.

In verses 7–10 Job notes the treatment he received when he arrived at the gate; in verses 21–25 he speaks about his treatment when he spoke in judicial proceedings. Men waited expectantly for his words which, when uttered, were recognized as final. Once Job had spoken, nothing more remained to be said. As the crops needed the rains of March and April, so people waited for and drank in Job's words. Verse 24 has been understood in many ways, but the most natural meaning is that people were so thrilled to have Job smile at them that they could scarcely believe it when it happened. They eagerly desired the light of his face, recognizing its beneficence. While verse 25 is difficult, it seems to be a summary verse, listing Job's titles of honor and respect.

B. The way it is (30:1–31). In this chapter Job describes his present plight which stands in stark contrast to his former condition. Instead of being respected by the leaders of the community, he is disdained by the dregs of society. God, who watched over him for good, now attacks him. His once favorable position has been replaced by an intolerable situation.

In the previous chapter Job noted that he had the respect of the distinguished people of his community. Now he laments that he is disdained by the scum, by the rabble, by the offscourings of society (**30:1–15**). Clearly, Job's pride is hurt by such treatment. The people who mock him are younger than Job, live like animals, and are rejected by the community. The Semitic attitude toward dogs is reflected here. Perhaps the ultimate insult is paid these contemptible people when Job states that they are a base and nameless brood (v. 8).

Job is made the object of their scorn and contempt. The subject of verse 11a is uncertain, simply being identified as "he." Either God or Job's scoffers are designated by this pronoun, but there is no agreement among translators. The subject of verse 11b is clearly the scoffers. If the scoffers are made the subject of 11a, then the pronoun *he* must be seen as a collective singular. If God is the subject of 11a, then God's attack on Job is simultaneous with that of the scoffers. Job stands defenseless before the rabble. The phrase *on my right* (v. 12) suggests a court scene, but the language of verses 12–14 suggests a military assault. Job is attacked, besieged, and breached as a city. As a result, his dignity and safety disappear.

As hinted at in verse 11, Job now feels that he is the object of attack not only by men, but also by God (**30:16–23**). It is God who has afflicted him with his disease which causes great suffering during the day, but particularly at night. His pain is unceasing. God seizes Job by his clothing and throws him into the mud, humiliating him ("reduced to dust and ashes," v. 19). God not only refuses to answer Job when he cries, but turns on him ruthlessly. The figures change here. Job is not hurled to the ground, but is lifted and driven before the wind and the storm. Death is certain.

Job is terrorized by his circumstances (**30:24–31**). Although in his better days Job had expressed concern and sympathy for the afflicted, there is no one who pities him now in his desperate circumstances. While he had expected good and light, he experiences evil and darkness. The churning inside him never stops. His appearance is so repulsive that he is befriended only by wild animals. Job's skin is blackened and peeling. Festive music has now been replaced by the music of mourning.

C. Job's claim to innocence (31:1–40). Having secured no justice from God and no support from his friends, Job now asserts his ultimate claim to innocence in such a way that God is forced to act.

Job's oath of clearance removes the issue from human jurisdiction and places it in the divine court. The basic format of Job's negative confessions is: If I have done *X* (specific sin) then let *Y* (appropriate punishment) happen to me. So forceful are the *if* (protasis) clauses and so frightening are the *then* (apodosis) clauses that the latter are generally omitted. In this chapter, Job omits most of the apodosis clauses, but does retain a few (vv. 8, 10, 22, 40).

There is no agreement about the number of specific sins that Job mentions. Actually, there are sixteen concrete hypotheses of sinful acts, but since one "if" can control two or three successive clauses, the number could be higher. The list of sins mentioned is clearly not exhaustive nor is their sequence systematic. Given Job's state of mind at this point, it is not surprising that the list of these sins seems lacking in organization.

Job maintains that he is untainted by immorality (**31:1–12**). Job begins this chapter with reference to a covenant he has made with his eyes. Not only had he refrained from illicit relationships (vv. 9–12), he had also refrained from sinful desires. Concern with his eyes reminds us of Jesus' warning about the lustful look and adultery (Matt. 5:28). As Job has described his conduct in his prosperous days, he continues this strophe by indicating his expectations at that time. Job believed then, and still believes, that blessing should result from piety and thus is baffled by his present circumstances. Since God sees his ways, Job is concerned with his lot and heritage from the Almighty. God's assessment is most critical to Job.

In this next strophe (vv. 5–8), Job denies falsehood and deceit. He desires to be weighed by God on honest scales (v. 6) so as to establish that he is blameless. (Of course, Job does not know that God has already found him blameless [1:8; 2:3].) His desire for honest scales reflects his conviction that his friends have judged him falsely. False scales were soundly denounced by both prophet and sage (Prov. 11:1; 20:23; Amos 8:5). Not only did Job keep his eyes from lust but also from coveting.

Next Job denies any act of adultery (vv. 9–12). He has not violated his neighbor's wife. So certain is he of his innocence that in the apodosis he calls for his wife to be reduced to a slave and be violated by another man (v. 10). So heinous would be this sexual sin that reference is made to both human (judges) and divine (fire that burns to destruction) punishment (vv. 11–12).

Job denies that he is guilty of oppression or inhumanity toward the poor or the weak (**31:13–23**). While masters were not answerable to the law, Job knows that he is accountable to God for the treatment of his slaves. He does not treat slaves as chattels since they are creatures of God. Job's view of slaves is indeed advanced for his time and culture.

Not only the slave, but the widow, the orphan, and the poor were recipients of Job's assistance. Eliphaz had earlier claimed otherwise (22:7ff.). Here Job's disclaimer is unequivocal. While the widow, the orphan, and the poor were disenfranchised by society, they were the special concern of God. This concern is reflected in the laws of Israel and in Job's practice. He shared his bread with the hungry (v. 17) and provided clothing for the naked (vv. 19–20). This compassion had not been sporadic, but constant. The statement *from my birth I guided the widow* (v. 18) is Job's way of saying that all through his life he had helped the needy and oppressed. Job exercised his considerable influence in the court on behalf of the fatherless. The self-imprecation here calls for his arm, if raised against the poor, to fall from his shoulder (v. 22). Job again indicates that his kind actions, while not compelled by law, were prompted by the fear of God.

Job strongly denies any secret worship of gold, the sun, or the moon (**31:24–28**). Job is perhaps responding to Eliphaz, who had urged him to make the Almighty rather than gold his treasure (22:25). The reference to his hand offering a kiss of homage (v. 27) seems to suggest the throwing of kisses to the celestial bodies. This is the only Old Testament reference to such a practice. Not only does Job deny the external act, he also denies that his heart was secretly enticed. Again, Job is sensitive to the potential sinfulness of the very idea or thought. To have reverenced the sun and the moon would have resulted in his being unfaithful to God.

While the psalmists frequently express imprecatory prayers, Job states that he has kept his mouth from sin by not allowing it to invoke a curse against his enemies (**31:29–30**). Job again demonstrates the high level of his faith, anticipating the teachings of Jesus.

Job denies any miserly acts (**31:31–32**). He was generous with his food and room. Job realizes, as does the writer of Hebrews (13:2), that strangers are to be entertained.

Job also denies any hypocrisy (**31:33–34**). This may be a reference to Adam but the narrative there emphasizes that Adam hid himself, not his sin. Job did not fear to leave his house and encounter the crowd. He had nothing to hide, nothing to embarrass him.

Job now demands a hearing (**31:35–37**). He

believes that he has already been tried and found guilty, and is now receiving his punishment—without knowing what his crime is. Here he calls for an indictment in writing, a bill of particulars (v. 35). He is confident that he can respond to any such charge. He would display it conspicuously on his shoulder. He would make it a source of glory (crown) rather than a source of shame. Job is ready to defend himself before God. He would not appear as a criminal but as a prince. He is willing to attach his signature to his defense. The Hebrew word *tāw*, translated here as "signature," is the name of the last letter of the Hebrew alphabet. Job could be using the word to indicate that he has now completed his comments, or he could be underscoring his worthiness to be marked so as to be spared God's wrath (cf. Ezek. 9:4, 6; Rev. 7:1ff.); or he could simply be indicating that he is placing a mark on the document. He has now forced God to respond and respond he will (chaps. 38–41).

The land is designated as a witness (cf. Gen. 4:10; Isa. 1:2). Job is not fearful of the land's testimony. He has not seized the land of others; he has made careful payment (**31:38–40**). So confident is he of his right conduct that Job's self-imprecation calls for briers and weeds rather than wheat and barley to come up.

With this chapter, the debate ends.

V. Elihu's Speeches (32:1–37:24)

A. Introduction (32:1–5). Elihu's hesitation to speak until the three friends have nothing more to say suggests that he is the youngest participant. However, if he is functioning as an adjudicator, he would not have had occasion to speak until the dialogue was ended. His anger is mentioned four times in this section. He is angry with Job because he believes Job has claimed to be right while insisting that God is wrong. He, along with the comforters, sees Job as being righteous in his own eyes. His anger is directed against the three friends because they found no way to refute Job. Their inability to produce an answer results in Elihu's claim that God (following an ancient reading) has been declared to be in the wrong. It will now be his task (Elihu means "He is my God") to come to God's defense.

B. First speech (32:6–33:33). Elihu first introduces himself and presents his credentials (**32:6–22**). He establishes his youth and then denies that advanced years should teach wisdom, obviously rejecting the claims of Job and the three that age automatically imparts wisdom. Understanding is dependent not so much upon the age of an individual as upon the spirit of that person. Spirit is parallel here with the breath of the Almighty (v. 8). The source of both life (Gen. 2:7) and wisdom (Dan. 5:13–14) is God. While Elihu may seem to be attributing his wisdom to creation, he will subsequently refer to a dream revelation (33:15). There is a similarity here with the claim of Eliphaz (4:12ff.—note the use of spirit in v. 15). Elihu is not modest. He is anxious to tell what he knows. While the others have provided inadequate answers, Elihu's efforts will be more successful! He seems to castigate the three for giving up the discussion, apparently believing that Job could not be refuted. Job has not yet confronted him, but when he does, Elihu will use different arguments. He will be so successful that there will be no need to invoke God.

In verses 15–16 Elihu again notes that the comforters have ceased to speak. While they are silent, Elihu is full of words and *must* speak. He is like bottled-up wine in new wineskins which threaten to burst unless vented (cf. Jer. 20:9; Matt. 9:17). Elihu claims impartiality; he will not flatter. Is he suggesting that the three have been too polite and gentle? Elihu has established high expectations for his speeches, expectations which will not be realized.

While Job's friends never address him by name, Elihu does. He takes the courteous approach initially used by Eliphaz (4:2–6), but one that was quickly discarded as the discussion became more intense. Elihu assesses himself (**33:1–7**). The characteristics he assigns to himself are indeed desirable: integrity, sincerity, and humanity. But his repetitious protestations are too much. They reflect his inflated sense of self-importance and result in his being patronizing. His claim that the breath of the Almighty gives him life may indicate either his claim to humanity or to special inspiration. His assurance that Job need not be intimidated by him may be a reference to Job's earlier statement that God frightened him (9:34; 13:12).

Elihu cites Job's claim to innocence (**33:8–12**). While Job had indeed insisted on his righteousness (9:21; 10:7; 16:17; 23:10; 27:5–6; 31:1–40), he had never insisted upon sinlessness (7:21; 13:16). His contention was that his sufferings were not commensurate to his sins; he did not deserve such terrible suffering. Next Elihu cites Job's claim that God is unjust. He bluntly tells Job that he is not right.

Elihu cites another one of Job's charges—that God is silent (**33:13–28**). God responds by dreams (v. 15), by illness (v. 19), and by an angel (v. 23).

In keeping with a common Old Testament

emphasis, Elihu claims that God does communicate through dreams. Eliphaz had earlier claimed that his knowledge had come from a dream (4:13). There (4:17–21) as here (vv. 16–18), the message received was so obvious that no special revelation was necessary. No dream revelation is necessary to establish man's sinfulness or to warn against the dangers of sin!

The next vehicle of divine communication (according to Elihu) is sickness. Sickness can destroy the appetite, resulting in a weight loss so severe that bones stick out and death is imminent. In this serious condition God speaks again by the sending of an angel. The angel will deal with the cause of the illness and will serve as a mediator, interceding with God on a man's behalf. This intercession will result in healing, answered prayers, and admission to God's presence. The person healed will then testify to God's intervention and mercy. Certainly if God speaks through sickness, he has emphatically spoken to Job. At least Elihu is arguing for meaning and purpose to sickness. His remedial emphasis (still not appropriate to Job) is an improvement over the penal emphasis of the three friends.

Having identified the approaches that God uses, Elihu now urges Job to respond if he has anything to say, or to be silent and listen if he has no response (**33:29–33**). It would seem that Elihu is so impressed with his own words that he assumes that Job could not possibly have anything to say. As noted, his remedial idea is helpful, but still inappropriate. Job's sufferings are not for correction, but rather for demonstration.

C. Second speech (34:1–37). Elihu begins his second speech by appealing to the wise men. These could be the three friends, but in the light of Elihu's earlier comments (32:11–12) this does not seem likely. Perhaps there was an audience present and it was to them that Elihu appealed. Or it is possible that this apppeal is directed to the readers by the editor of Elihu's comments. Elihu is confident that men of learning will agree with him. Verse 3 is a quotation from Job (12:11). Elihu calls for a decision, a determination of the right perspective: Job's or the traditional view (**34:1–9**).

Again Elihu quotes Job (v. 5; cf. 27:2a) and summarizes his position. He believes that Job has, in effect, made God a liar. This is obviously a strong accusation, but Job has repeatedly insisted that even though he is innocent, he is being treated as if he were guilty. This insistence on his innocence is tantamount, given Elihu's theology, to making God a liar. Adapting the words of Eliphaz (15:16), Elihu accuses Job of drinking scorn like water (v. 7). He agrees with Eliphaz that Job is a threat to religious faith (15:4). While there is no support for the claim, he states that Job keeps company with evildoers. This section concludes with another alleged quotation from Job (v. 9). While Job had noted that calamity comes to the good and the bad (9:22) and that prosperity often characterizes the wicked (10:3; 21:7), he had never suggested that his integrity was worthless. Actually, Job's concern about the loss of his wealth and health is indirectly a concern that he may have lost his integrity. He values his integrity and clings to it tenaciously. He needs assurance that God recognizes his integrity. Again, it needs to be noted that Job is not aware of God's affirmation of his integrity in the prologue.

Elihu will not for a moment tolerate the suggestion that God is unjust (**34:10–15**). He insists that God gives to every person what his conduct merits. This, of course, is the basis for considering Job a sinner. Beginning with Job's present state of suffering, Elihu, as did the three friends, moves backward to identify Job's sin. Again, this ignores the emphasis of the prologue and simply continues the stalemate which eventually developed between Job and the three friends. Whatever divine justice means, it clearly does not eliminate human or satanic injustice. This section concludes with Elihu's emphasis upon God's sovereignty, stressing that God may at any time withdraw his spirit and breath, resulting obviously in death.

Elihu, after having emphasized the power of God, now seeks to temper that image by arguing that God is impartial (**34:16–20**). It does not necessarily follow that the possession of power and authority is a guarantee of justice. Indeed, one who hates justice can govern. This demonstrates Elihu's faulty reasoning. Perhaps Elihu's reasoning is more sound when he suggests that God is impartial because both princes and the poor are the work of his hands. He does not show favoritism to the mighty. Is this a reference to Job's earlier situation? It is not so much what Elihu says, as its application, that is troublesome.

Elihu next stresses the wisdom of God (**34:21–30).** To defend his impartiality and his infallibility, it is necessary to establish his omniscience. God does not need to hold a trial, as Job requests, to determine guilt. He knows all and his actions are predicated on that knowledge. God not only knows, but he also executes—he shatters (v. 24), he overthrows (v. 25), he punishes (v. 26). His resolve matches his knowledge. Elihu now seems to undermine his own position by suggesting that if he remains silent who can condemn him? (v. 29). He has just argued that God does not remain silent, but acts decisively. Further, the issue of the book is not God's failure to punish the wicked, but rather his treatment of the innocent Job. Elihu's generalizations are not particularly helpful. He fails to address Job's situation. His theological platitudes raise more questions than they answer.

While Elihu's previous comments are addressed to men of understanding (v. 10), this last section (**34:31–37**) is apparently addressed to Job. However, it is a difficult and obscure passage. Elihu argues that Job cannot dictate the terms governing God's activities. When a person admits guilt and repents, God can forgive him without Job's approval. Quite obviously Job would not disagree with this claim, but such an admission would make him vulnerable to Elihu, who insists that penitence leads to forgiveness and deliverance. The fact that Job continues to suffer, Elihu reasons, proves his impenitence and stubbornness. Not only is Job guilty of stupidity, but he speaks without knowledge and is guilty of rebellion. As with the other participants, Elihu is forced to picture Job as a vicious sinner if his theological assumptions are to stand. His wish that Job might be tested to the utmost (v. 36) reflects Elihu's insensitivity, again showing that Elihu's theological position is more important than Job. Job is clearly expendable.

D. Third speech (35:1–16). In his third speech, Elihu responds to two questions which he has heard Job ask. The first one has to do with the value of virtue (vv. 2–8), the second one with the unanswered cry of the afflicted (vv. 9–16).

Elihu returns to Job's claim that he is innocent but that such innocence is profitless (**35:2–8**). His reply is not simply directed to Job, but also to his friends. Elihu argues that human behavior does not affect God. Whether man is sinful (v. 6) or righteous (v. 7), God is neither harmed nor benefited. Man's good or evil affects only himself and other men. Elihu has both insulated and isolated God. By emphasizing God's transcendence, he has protected God from the actions of men. God is neither helped nor hurt by man. But how can Elihu so reason when he has insisted that God reacts to the sins of men by punishing and disciplining them, and to the righteousness of men by rewarding them? Even if Elihu is suggesting here that inherent in actions are beneficial or destructive forces, which do not necessitate divine response, he is still not addressing the sufferings of the innocent Job. According to this view, given Job's righteous acts, beneficial results should have followed. In essence, Elihu has sacrificed God's immanence on the altar of transcendence.

Elihu now addresses Job's earlier statement (24:12) that God ignores the cry of the oppressed for help (**35:9–16**). Elihu shifts attention from the oppression itself to the motivation and attitude of the oppressed. Instead of suffering driving the afflicted to God, they are so preoccupied with their misery that they ignore God. Here man needs to observe animals who, by instinct, turn to God. Further, the oppressed are not heard due to their arrogance. Elihu actually calls the oppressed "wicked" (v. 12). This fits in with his idea that oppression is a divine means of discipline, exercised upon those who need it. Another reason for no response is that God does not listen to an empty plea. Clearly, Elihu has placed the onus of unanswered prayers on the shoulders of the person praying. How can Job expect God to hear him since his cry is more against, rather than to, God? While verse 15 is difficult, it seems to suggest that Job is criticizing God's unresponsiveness because he does not really understand it. He fails to recognize God's long-suffering. Elihu clearly puts the blame upon Job for God's silence. While there is general truth in Elihu's arguments about unanswered prayers, there is nothing directly pertinent here to Job's condition.

E. Fourth speech (36:1–37:24). This speech, which has two distinct parts, is Elihu's most significant contribution. He moves beyond the penal concerns of the three friends and emphasizes that there is a disciplinary purpose to suffering. In the second part (36:22–37:24) Elihu emphasizes the greatness of God as seen in nature, thereby anticipating the speeches of the Lord which follow.

Elihu now softens his harsh tones and asks Job to bear with him a little longer as he addresses the discipline of suffering (**36:2–15**). He is still arrogant, however, for he claims to speak on God's behalf and to secure his knowledge from afar, obviously from God himself. He is confident that his words are not false and that he is "perfect in knowledge" (v. 4). This perfection does not pertain so much to the extent of Elihu's knowledge as it does to the accuracy of his knowledge. It is complete (the same Hebrew word as in 1:1 and 2:3, when Job is said to be blameless or complete).

There is no object to the Hebrew text for the verb *despise* (v. 5). The New International Version has supplied "men," but in keeping with the text of the Septuagint which gives the object as "innocent," as well as verse 7, which parallels this verse, perhaps the idea is that God does not despise the righteous. Contrary to Job's claim (21:7), Elihu insists that the life of the wicked is not prolonged. Neither does God take his eyes off the righteous. When affliction comes and divine assistance is delayed, there is a purpose. It is to alert the righteous to their sins and to lead them to repentance. God speaks through adversity. If the righteous learn from such discipline, prosperity and contentment will follow; but if they do not learn, they will die without knowledge. Elihu's thesis is clear: sufferings are God's discipline to teach lessons. The righteous will learn what God is teaching and will be delivered. On the other hand, the godless will harbor resentment, failing to benefit from the discipline. As a result, they will die an untimely (v. 14 in their youth) and shameful (v. 14 among male prostitutes) death.

The strophe addressed to Job (**36:16–25**) is a most difficult one. Comparing various English translations reveals a wide range of interpretations. In verse 16, the subject and the tense of the verb are uncertain. Further, the verb is generally used in a negative way to allude to evil. The New International Version designates God as the subject, makes the tense present, and gives a positive meaning (wooing) to the verb. Verse 17 seems to suggest that Job is now experiencing the judgment due the wicked. Verses 18–20 are especially challenging. Elihu may be following up his comment of verse 17, suggesting that Job ought not prevent justice by being enticed by riches, or he may be implying that Job will not succeed in bribing God with his wealth and mighty efforts. Now Elihu emphasizes the purpose of his sufferings that Job's inequity has produced and shows that God is a teacher who is above criticism. Job is wrong to criticize God. Rather, he should join with all mankind and recognize the greatness of God's work. The word *afar* (v. 25) perhaps suggests that man is not in a position to fully understand the purposes of God.

Verse 26 can be seen as a conclusion to the previous section stressing God's incomprehensibility or it can be viewed as an introduction to this new section which underscores God's power in the universe and in nature (**36:26–37:13**). Either way, this verse serves to connect these two sections.

This section begins with an emphasis on the power of God as seen in the storm. God has not only created the forces of nature, he controls them. As in the Book of Genesis, so here God dispenses the rain. The text is not clear whether the rain comes from above or below the earth. Irrespective of the location of the reservoirs, it is God who sends the rain, thereby providing food.

God directs the lightning to strike its mark while the thunder is his very voice (vv. 29, 33; cf. Ps. 29 where thunder is characterized as the voice of the Lord). The destructive qualities of the storm suggest the anger of God.

In chapter 37, there is a shift from an attitude of wonder and awe to that of expectation. As noted, the thunder is recognized as the voice of God. It is in the storm that God frequently reveals himself (Exod. 19:18ff.; Ps. 18:7–15; Nah. 1:3; Hab. 3:1ff. Zech. 9:14; John 12:29). These verses are clearly a preparation for the theophany which Job will soon experience.

Beginning with verse 6, the season of the year being described is winter. The various water forms are mentioned: snow (v. 6), rain shower (v. 6), ice (v. 10), and moisture (v. 11). The conditions are such that men stay indoors, suspending their agricultural activities; the animals hibernate. All the natural forces obey the commands of God. In these forces of nature Elihu sees God at work, punishing those who are sinful or simply doing what he chooses to do, extending his grace and his love.

Elihu anticipates the format of Job's encounter with God, directing a series of ironic questions at Job (**37:14–24**). His obvious intent is to humble Job. In sharp contrast to the winter weather (vv. 6–13), Elihu describes the comfort of summer. A mirror of cast bronze (v. 18) suggests the sky in time of drought (Deut. 28:23). Elihu indicates that, in contrast to Job, he would not choose to challenge God since such an encounter would result in destruction.

Beginning with verse 21, the storm seems to have abated. The sun is so bright that no one can look at it. Likewise God's majesty is such that it is awesome. The golden splendor out of the north (v. 22) may be a reference to the Aurora Borealis. Whatever the golden splendor is, it clearly suggests the brilliance of God.

Elihu denies that God acts unjustly. He is beyond our reach and, hence, unsearchable. Elihu considers Job to be conceited and clever. Such people God does not regard. Wisdom is found with those who fear him.

VI. The Lord's Speeches (38:1–42:6)

Appropriately, at the end of the book, the Lord appears to Job. All the protagonists have had their say, but Job still has not found his answer. Throughout the exchanges with his friends, Job had been seeking an audience with God. He had offered God two possible formats: "Summon me and I will answer, or let me speak, and you reply" (13:22). The tenor of Job's remarks would indicate that he preferred the latter. Thus the format assumed in the encounter is not what Job had anticipated.

Acting as a wisdom teacher, the Lord employs the didactic method of interrogation. His questions are concerned with nature, a common medium of instruction in wisdom literature.

There is no direct reference in the Lord's speeches to Job's suffering or alleged sinfulness. He does not seem to answer any of the questions Job directs to him. This immediately raises the question of the intent of the speeches. That the speeches help Job is clear. Something about them satisfies and rehabilitates Job, but what?

The theophany itself may rehabilitate Job. The important factor is not the verbal content of the theophany, but simply the fact that the Lord appears. This is what Job had wanted.

It has also been suggested that the speeches cause Job to realize that the world is far more complex and certainly larger than he had anticipated. Up to now he has been too preoccupied with himself. Now he sees his sufferings in the perspective of the complexity of the world and the immensity of God's task. Perspective makes the difference.

Another suggestion is that the issue addressed by the speeches is not theodicy but conduct. The concern is not with the "why" of suffering, but the "how" of suffering. The speeches present the proper conduct for the sufferer, which is humble and devout silence with trust in God.

A final suggestion is that these speeches show that God does not follow the patterns of earthly courts and administer reward and punishment in keeping with the standards of man. He chooses to give each person that which is appropriate as is demonstrated by his management of nature.

There are compelling truths in all of these positions and perhaps elements from each represent adequately the purpose of these speeches.

The speeches of the Lord are cast in the form of questions. In the first speech, the initial questions address creation. The next group of questions turns from creation to a survey of the world and its management. The second speech begins with a challenge similar to the first one. Then a series of rhetorical questions follow about behemoth and leviathan.

A. First speech (38:1–39:30). The Lord addresses Job out of a storm. It is fitting that this book which opens with a storm, resulting in the death of Job's flocks and children, should end with a storm, resulting in Job's encounter with God. The question of verse 2 is directed to Job. Job is accused of darkening (obscuring) the purposes of God by speaking out of ignorance. The instruction to gird up his loins is a call to prepare himself for a demanding encounter.

The creation of the earth is described (**38:4–7**) in terms of the erection of a building. Critical are such matters as a foundation, dimensions, footings, and the cornerstone. There was music when the foundations of the earth were set, provided by the stars and the angels.

A metaphor is again used as the Lord shifts his emphasis from land to sea (**38:8–11**). The sea is personified and its origin is likened to the birth of a child. The newborn ocean is clothed with clouds even as a baby is clothed with a swaddling band. The sea is seen as unruly and must be restrained by doors and bars which establish its limits.

The reference to the succession of night and day is not so much a reference to the creation of time as to its management (**38:12–15**): God is the Master of time. The dawn takes hold of the night which clothes the earth like a garment and renews it. In the process, the wicked, who operate during the night (24:13–17), are shaken out of the garment. Even as a seal gives shape to the clay, so the dawn permits the features of the land to stand out. The light of the wicked is darkness and they are denied that by the dawn.

God is the Master of the land and sky (**38:16–38**). Job's attention is now turned to the depths of the sea and earth. The springs of the sea were the subterranean source of the sea waters. The gates of death (v. 17) were thought to stand at the entrance to Sheol, which was supposedly located at the depths of the earth. Obviously Job has never visited these places.

Light and darkness are personified. Each has its own abode, from which it comes and to which it returns. Can Job be a guide to them? Obviously not. The sarcasm of verse 21 is most apparent. Job has been acting as if he had been born before creation and was present on the first day when God separated light from darkness.

Job earlier had the animals witness to God's injustice (12:7–9). Here God sends the rain to areas not inhabited by humans (vv. 26–27), the point being that God does care about animals, even the animals of the desert. Further, God can distribute the rain as he chooses. He is not compelled to cause it to fall in areas inhabited by humans.

Continuing his interrogation, the Lord now questions Job about the paternity of the rain and dew and the maternity of the ice and frost. The language is clearly poetic, but its intent is clear. Again Job knows little or nothing about these matters.

Job is now confronted with questions about

the constellations. The first two constellations are identified as Pleiades and Orion (v. 31). The stars of verse 32 are not easily identified (as can be seen by comparing various English translations). Reference is made to the laws which govern the movement of the celestial bodies. The last half of verse 33 is rendered to designate either God's dominion over the earth or the stars' impact upon human events.

Attention is now turned to the clouds. Job cannot control the clouds and lightning bolts. Verse 36 is difficult, but may suggest that God has given wisdom to the clouds and mists, though the translation of these two terms is much debated. The poetic language of verse 37 is beautiful, suggesting that rain results when God tips over the water jars of the heavens, causing the dust to stick together.

The questions of the Lord now shift from natural phenomena and locations to animals and birds which are more easily observable (**38:39–39:30**). Even so Job remains overwhelmed by these questions.

The first animal considered is the lion (v. 39). The lion finds food for its cubs without Job's help. It is God who provides the lion with strength and hunting skills and provides it with prey.

The raven (v. 41), sandwiched between lions and goats, seems out of place, but the idea of securing food for its young attaches it to the previous section with its concern for food for the cubs. The cry of the fledglings appears to be frantic and directed to God. Again Job is reminded of the great responsibility that confronts God. Even the raven must be cared for!

Questions are now addressed to Job relative to his knowledge of the goat's and hind's delivery. Without human assistance they breed and bring forth their young. In turn, their young learn to fend for themselves. These secrets (instincts) are neither known nor dictated by Job.

Attention is now focused on the wild ass (39:5–8). In contrast to the domesticated ass, he is free and deliberately avoids (scorns) the commotion in the town. While free, his life is not easy.

The wild ox, like the wild donkey, cannot be domesticated (v. 9). While his great strength could be used by man, there is no way to rely on him or trust him. He will not submit to a harness.

The ostrich is presented next (vv. 13–18). This passage is difficult and is omitted by the Septuagint. It has no rhetorical questions and God is addressed in the third person (v. 17) as if he were not the speaker. While noted for her speed, the ostrich is seen as a stupid parent. The intent of this passage is important. This is not a scientific treatment, but a popular one which the writer adopts to make his point. God is entitled to create the bird as he chooses. If he withholds wisdom and good sense, that is his prerogative.

There is general consensus that the section dealing with the horse (vv. 19–25) is by far the best treatment of any animal. The horse is the only domesticated animal in this series, but even so, he is difficult to control. Reference here seems to be the warhorse who is impatient to be involved in the battle. He is fearless and high-spirited.

Finally, the hawk (v. 26) and the eagle (vv. 27–30) are considered. Job is questioned relative to his knowledge of the migratory instincts of the hawk. Job neither understands nor controls this instinct. It is not by his wisdom that the hawk migrates. Further, the eagle does not receive from Job the command to soar or build his nests in inaccessible places. The eagle's keen sight is alluded to in verse 29. Verse 30, cited in Matthew 24:28 and Luke 17:37, is a proverbial saying.

The Lord concludes his first speech with a challenge to Job. Either Job must correct him or desist from criticism. Job concedes that he is unworthy to reply. Job does not suggest that he has nothing to say, but rather that he will be silent (**40:1–5**). This seems to be the meaning of "I put my hand over my mouth" (v. 5). He will continue to entertain his challenge, but simply will not express it. Job may be subdued, but not vanquished.

B. Second speech (40:1–42:6). This section seems to be more relevant to Job's concerns than the subsequent treatment of behemoth and leviathan. While Job is entitled to defend his own integrity, he does not have the right to discredit God's justice. Further, talk is cheap. The issue is ability (**40:6–14**). Does Job have an arm like God's (v. 9)? Does he have both the power and resources to run the world? If so, let him adorn himself with glory and splendor. In addition to assuming these attributes, Job would need to demonstrate his morality by exercising it. He is challenged to humble the proud and to crush the wicked. Job must show an ability to cope with evil. Here we arrive at the very heart of the book. God's way of handling evil has been challenged. Can Job do better? Is it a simple matter to deal with evil? Is not contending with evil a much more complex issue than Job realizes? If Job can handle evil, God will acknowledge his power.

"Behemoth" is the plural of the Hebrew word for beast, but the verb used with it in this passage (**40:15–24**) is third-person masculine singular. A single beast is obviously in mind, suggesting that behemoth may be a proper noun, with the plural number used to show intensity or majesty.

Some consider behemoth to be an allusion to a mythical beast. Both behemoth and leviathan appear in ancient myths and apocalyptic writings. Behemoth is the land monster of chaos, while leviathan is the sea monster of chaos. While there may be a literary allusion to the mythical beast here, it is possible that the language is poetic without being mythical; the writer could be employing poetic license. Such license has already been observed in the descriptions found earlier in these speeches. If it is a real animal, behemoth is most likely a hippopotamus. Whether a real or mythical animal, behemoth was made by God. It feeds mainly on grass and lives in the water. Reference to the Jordan (v. 23) may simply be an allusion to swift running water which does not frighten behemoth. The reference to strength also fits the hippopotamus. Ranking "first among the works of God" is probably a reference to Genesis 1:24, where the first land animal life is said to be livestock. The questions of verse 24 indicate the difficulty of capturing the hippopotamus.

Whether leviathan is real or mythical is problematic. More details are given of leviathan than any of the other creatures treated in these speeches (**41:1–34**). If a real animal is in view here, it is probably the crocodile.

Like behemoth, leviathan is difficult to catch. Fish hooks, harpoons, and spears are not particularly effective. One encounter with leviathan will be sufficient.

Leviathan is so cruel that it is unwise to rouse him. He cannot be subdued. It is even more foolish to stand against God. The import of verse 11a is not clear, but may suggest that no one can challenge God and escape unscathed. This may be a warning to Job, suggesting the insanity of his approach.

Beginning with verse 12, a detailed description of leviathan is given. Reference is made to his strength and his scales. His teeth are fearsome, his jaws designated as doors of his mouth. The reference to firebrands streaming from his mouth (v. 19) may designate the expulsion of air and water as the crocodile emerges from the water. The cruelty of the crocodile is referred to in the expression *his heart is hard as rock* (v. 24). Even the mighty are terrified and their weapons are ineffective. He leaves his imprint on the ground and his motion in water is visible. Nothing on earth is his equal.

Job, still hurting and sitting among the ashes, is now satisfied (**42:1–6**). He admits that God can do all things (v. 2), though this is not a new development. Job had never questioned the power of God, but rather his seeming indifference. His concession suggests that these speeches of the Lord stress not only the already acknowledged power of God, but also the justice of God which Job has failed to understand. Rather than indifferent, God is very much involved in the operations of an exceedingly complex universe.

Job's hope, expressed in 19:27, is now realized. He had previously heard, but now he has seen. Hearing suggests the inherited, the secondhand, the indirect. While such knowledge may suffice in prosperous times, it is not adequate for times of great stress. Seeing suggests immediate confrontation. Seeing is always more direct and intimate than hearing. Having seen God, Job can now confront his sufferings.

Acute awareness of God leads to repentance. Since Job is blameless and upright (1:1), his repentance cannot be directed at any sin which triggered his suffering. Rather, his repentance pertains to his words of haste and ignorance. His harsh words are now ended; his nagging doubts have been resolved. Job humbly worships the Lord.

VII. Epilogue (42:7–17)

Now that the trial is concluded, a verdict must be given. Job's prosperity is restored—not as a reward for his piety, but rather as an acknowledgment that the trial has ended. Job's sufferings have served their purpose and there is no longer any reason to continue them. Job had not cursed God. Satan was wrong.

As the divine adjudicator, the Lord indicates that Job has won the debate. However, such a victory must be kept in context. Certainly not all that the friends said about God was wrong, while all that Job said was right. Job's repentance makes sense only if it pertains to his words of haste and ignorance. He had said things which were wrong, but his insistence on his innocence was right. The friends were clearly wrong in ascribing his sufferings to sin. Eliphaz is singled out probably because he was the principal spokesman for the comforters.

As in the prologue, so here; Job offers a burnt offering. This time he serves as a priest for the three comforters (Elihu is not mentioned). The offering of seven bulls and seven rams is a large one. Job's priestly function is not only sacrificing, but also interceding. Ironically, the three friends must depend upon the intercession of Job, whom they had earlier deemed in need of their service and wisdom.

Significantly, after Job has prayed for others, his possessions are restored doubled (v. 10). He again is blessed with seven sons and three daughters. As he had initially hoped, he is permitted a long life and dies in peace. His friends and relatives return to him, providing him with comfort and gifts. These persons, as the active participants of the debate, were unaware of the challenge of Satan and hence also designate God as the source of Job's sufferings (v. 11).

SELECT BIBLIOGRAPHY

Archer, G. L. *The Book of Job.* Grand Rapids: Baker, 1982.
Baker, W. C. *More Than a Man Can Take.* Philadelphia: Westminster, 1966.
Eaton, J. *Job.* Sheffield: JSOT, 1985.
Ellison, H. L. *A Study of Job—From Tragedy to Triumph.* Grand Rapids: Zondervan, 1975.
Hulme, W. E. *Dialogue in Despair.* New York: Abingdon, 1968.
Job, J. *Job Speaks to Us Today.* Atlanta: John Knox, 1977.
Vawter, B. *Job and Jonah.* New York: Paulist, 1983.

PSALMS

R. E. O. White

INTRODUCTION

One of the most remarkable books to survive from antiquity, the Jewish Psalter was certainly complete by the Maccabean period (ca. 150 B.C.), yet remains the beloved hymnbook of two world religions. Its form is as varied as its content, but what has endeared the psalms to every generation, and evoked most wonder, is their immense breadth of religious experience, of pious feeling, aspiration, complaint, struggle, protest, and regret. The psalms mirror the human soul in all its vicissitudes of faith and unbelief, joy and perplexity, rebellion and submission. And they do so with utmost honesty, freedom, and boldness, as individuals or congregations confess their sins, complain of man's ill-treatment or of God's silence, call down judgment on their enemies, plead piteously for longer life, healing, deliverance, or comfort. Bitter resentment at life's unfairness, protest at God's mysterious ways, his delay in helping, his anger or his inactivity, are balanced by joyous outbursts of praise, gladness, thanksgiving, and testimony to God's faithfulness. Humor is not entirely absent, nor sexual love.

To appreciate the psalmists' experience we must share their utter realism, surprised at nothing, avoiding the temptation to soften harsh expressions into smooth platitudes which hide frequent anguish and desperate longing. Plain impatience is often expressed. "How long, Lord?" the psalmists demand, with sorely tried faith; "I waited for the Lord, why . . . ? Why, Lord?" They are prepared to argue boldly with God, even to expostulate with him. Righteous indignation is sometimes confused with outraged patriotism, self-righteousness, or personal revenge, and sometimes the psalmist's enemies are assumed to be enemies of God. A request that the wicked be caught in their own snare and suffer the agonies they inflict upon others, sometimes cloaks the genuine desire to see justice done. All the psalmists are sure that God will vindicate the right and deliver his own.

Often the "helpless poor," "the needy," are seen as the truly godly, while the prosperous and powerful are assumed to be faithless and wicked. This attitude finds some justification in postexilic conditions, when unscrupulous collaborators prospered in society, while the conscientious godly who resisted foreign influence suffered impoverishment and cruel persecution.

To appreciate the psalmists' experience we must also let each poem speak for itself, in its own terms and not in ours. Occasionally, we must be prepared for forms of worship unfamiliar to us. We must accustom ourselves to a faith that rests upon experiences (the exodus, the manifold beauties of nature) and on fundamental ideas (creation, election, national glory), very different from incarnation, Calvary, resurrection, Pentecost, and eternal redemption.

Occasionally, too, reference is made to God's primeval victory over the forces of chaos, sometimes in language recalling Babylonian creation myths. We also meet with the influential wisdom school within Judaism, for whom the fear of the Lord was the foundation of all sensible living, and the only intelligent conduct for rational beings was to be aware of one's creaturehood, and to remember one's Creator with reverence at all times.

According to tradition ascribed in part to David and in part to Hezekiah, and preserved in 1 Chronicles 15:16–24, 16:37–42, chapter 25, 2 Chronicles 29:25–30, and Ezra 3:10–11, the system of worship begun during the monarchy and developed in the second (postexilic) temple period, was elaborate, highly skilled, and well staffed. Levites played musical instruments including trumpets, harps, lyres, and bronze cymbals, assisted by "brethren of the second order." Kenaiah, a musically skilled Levite, directed the singing. Trained musicians (numbering 288) did duty by turns.

Certain names continually recur, originally of leading teachers, later of choirs or music guilds preserving their styles and methods—Heman, Asaph, Etham, Jeduthun, their "sons," and many others. We read of responsive singing by priests, people, or choirs; of much shouting; of various styles of playing. We are also aware of recurrent festivals, occasions of national penitence or thanksgiving, the dedication of the temple, the promulgation of the law, of sacrificial worship, and of the continual ministry of priests and prophets. All of this is reflected, in considerable detail, in the Psalter.

The Psalter is not one but a series of five hymnbooks (or one book with four supplements):

Book I	Pss. 1–41
Book II	Pss. 42–72
Book III	Pss. 73–89
Book IV	Pss. 90–106
Book V	Pss. 107–150

This arrangement predates the second century A.D., and explains the doxologies after each section and the duplications where "supplements" overlap (Ps. 14 = Ps. 53; 40:13–17 = Ps. 70; 57:7–11 and 60:5–12 = Ps. 108).

Thus the Psalter grew over a long period of time beginning with David. The traditional nucleus gathered around it other poems from various sources to form "collections," bearing the honored names of choirmasters, teachers, founders of the music guilds, and others.

Of the names mentioned in Chronicles, Heman is attached to Psalm 88, Ethan to Psalm 89, and Jeduthun to Psalm 39 (Pss. 62, 77 seem to indicate "Jeduthun's style"). Fifty-five psalms are headed "to/for/of" an unnamed choirmaster or director of music (the Hebrew preposition bears all three meanings), and twelve "to/for/of" Asaph. Eleven psalms are "to/for/of" the "sons of Korah," which can hardly mean poems written by a group (cf. 1 Chron. 9:19). Psalm 90 bears Moses' name. Several psalms bear double, even triple, ascriptions (Pss. 75, 84, 88, 109). For all these reasons, actual authorship cannot be determined.

The simplest explanation would be that these headings indicate collections of sacred songs, used either by these musical directors or by music guilds that perpetuated their names. Most of the seventy-three headed "to/for/of" David are probably to be understood in this way, since some contain references to the temple, to the rebuilding of Jerusalem, claims to innocence, later Aramaic words, and similar details that do not fit David's experience. This would explain why Psalm 72, "of Solomon," appears among the "prayers of David"; and why Psalms 61, 62, 109, and 139 are associated with David and others.

Evidently, around David's great reputation as poet and musician, and doubtless around some of his own compositions, a collection was made including poems by other authors of different dates, the whole bearing David's revered name. It is equally clear that some early private poems were later adapted for communal use in changed circumstances. Thus Psalm 51:16 assumes that the temple and altar are standing, whereas verses 18–19 assume the city is in ruins. Thus most psalms have two dates, that of original composition (usually unknown) and that of later incorporation into public worship. Where the date and occasion of writing are discernible or relevant, investigation may be profitable; usually it is of merely academic interest, later use and timeless meaning being more important.

Unfortunately, great caution is needed in citing these psalm headings. The Greek Psalter attributes twelve more psalms to David than the Hebrew Bible does, and others to Jeremiah, Haggai, and Zechariah. Scholars usually affirm that the headings are not original. Earnest attempts to relate certain psalms to events in David's life, or in Jewish history, are very doubtful.

Many terms used in these headings are unknown. Some almost certainly suggest well-known tunes, such as "to the tune of 'Do Not Destroy' " (Pss. 59, 75; probably a grape-treading work-song; cf. Isa. 65:8); "to the tune of 'The Lilies of the Covenant' " (Ps. 80); "to the tune of 'A Dove on Distant Oaks' " (Ps. 56), and others. Some name particular instruments or record other musical directions. The frequent *Selah* in various psalms probably indicates louder music during an interlude in singing. All such instructions vividly remind us that living people, devout and skillful, sang this praise or offered these prayers in joyful or fearful worship together. If we understood their language better, we would find their instructions no more strange than our own "diminuendo," "descant," "unison," "to Rimington," "to 'For all the Saints.' "

The Book of Psalms is written in poetry. To Western ears, the feature obviously missing from Hebrew poetry is rhyme, though there is more chiming of vowels and echoing of consonants in Hebrew poetry than can be preserved in translation. But line endings are not matched in sound, as in English hymns. Instead, Hebrew poetry rhymes *thoughts*. That is to say, an idea once stated is repeated in varying language, in a parallel phrase, or in antithesis, in alternate lines, or in reverse.

Two-line parallels:

> But his delight is in the law of the LORD,
> and on his law he meditates day and night. [Ps. 1:2]
>
> Therefore the wicked will not stand in the judgment,
> nor sinners in the assembly of the righteous. [Ps. 1:5]
>
> Why do the nations conspire
> and the peoples plot in vain? [Ps. 2:1]

Three-line parallels:

> (Blessed is the man)
> who does not walk in the counsel of the wicked
> or stand in the way of sinners
> or sit in the seat of mockers. [Ps. 1:1]
>
> O LORD, how many are my foes!
> How many rise up against me!
> Many are saying of me, "God will not deliver him." [Ps. 3:1]

In antithetic thought-rhymes, the second line states the opposite of the first:

> For the LORD watches over the way of the righteous,
> but the way of the wicked will perish. [Ps. 6:1]

Sometimes the thought "grows," or "climbs," in repetition:

> Ascribe to the LORD, O mighty ones,
> ascribe to the LORD glory and strength,
> ascribe to the LORD the glory due his name. . . . [Ps. 29:1–2a]

Sometimes the pattern is more complicated:

> To you, O LORD, I called;
> to the LORD I cried for mercy:
> What gain is there in my destruction,
> in my going down into the pit?
> Will the dust praise you?
> Will it proclaim your faithfulness?
> Hear, O LORD, and be merciful to me;
> O LORD, be my help. [Ps. 30:8–10]

Here, lines 1 and 2 are parallel; lines 7 and 8 are mutually parallel and parallel with 1 and 2. Lines 3 and 4 are parallel; lines 5 and 6 are mutually parallel and parallel with 3 and 4.

It is seriously impoverishing to read such skillful poetry as one would a prosaic sermon or dull devotional passage, unaware of the workmanship, the intentional literary art, that has fashioned each poem. There is purpose in such craftsmanship. The repetition of ideas tends to lend emphasis to important thought. Moreover, such thought patterns tend to echo in the mind like familiar music: an obscure word in one line is often clarified by its parallel. It is a great advantage that this rhyming of thought is retained in translation, where the chiming of similar-sounding line endings must be lost.

To ignore the poetic form of the psalms can also be seriously misleading. In poetry, the connection between one sentence and the next often lies in feeling, not in reasoning. In Psalm 137, for example, there is no reason whatever why singing one of the songs of Zion should make one forget Jerusalem; it should make one remember the homeland more vividly. But to sing one of the joyous, sacred songs of the great temple festivals in a land peopled with idols, surrounded by symbols of sinfulness, for the amusement of alien captors, with no thought of worship, would be prostitution of the holiest emotions. It would be to "forget" all that Jerusalem meant to pious hearts; for that, the paralysis of the tongue that sang, and of the fingers that plucked the harp, would be fitting punishment.

Songs are rarely arguments. One strong poetic image may call up another without the connection between them being logical or even coherent. "The earth give[s] way—the mountains fall into the heart of the sea—its waters roar and foam—the mountains quake—nations are in uproar—kingdoms fall—the earth melts" (Ps. 46:2–6) forms a series of pictures, not an orderly story. Prosaic, overintellectual Western minds must always beware of rationalist distortions of passionate and picturesque oriental language.

Perhaps even more important is to note the freedom with which the poet can change the speaker or the person addressed without warning. Such silent "stage directions" (more correctly, liturgical rubrics) illumine many difficult psalms, though they must not be invented without justification. Nor should they be allowed to determine the psalm's meaning; they may be assumed where the meaning itself requires them. The psalms were used in corporate worship, in both the temple and the synagogue; we must try to imagine a congregation singing, or listening to priest or choir. At the very least, it is essential to remain alert when reading Hebrew poetry, or we shall miss most of the meaning.

In translations of the psalms, footnotes frequently indicate words of uncertain meaning, or provide various renderings. Hebrew was a simple language, whose few words had to convey many nuances of meaning. Sometimes possible translations are so different that the reader wonders whether they can possibly represent the same original text.

Quite often, the text itself is doubtful. Copyists struggling with reed pens and fragile papyrus sometimes missed words or lines, misspelled words, made mistakes, or substituted known for unknown words. For this reason, footnotes often refer to ancient translations (Greek Syriac, Latin, the Dead Sea Scrolls), for evidence of what early translators thought a puzzling verse meant. Occasionally, translators offer their own corrections based on knowledge of the ways of copyists.

These linguistic and textual difficulties will not surprise us if we remember that we are reading poems composed in a strange language by an alien people, in a world vastly different from ours, between two and three thousand years ago, and copied by hand hundreds of times before being fixed in print. It would be foolish, therefore, to insist upon one translation or one version of the text, as if we possessed the poet's own copy.

It is essential to realize the immense variety of occasion and purpose that produced the psalms. In addition to diverse liturgical uses, more than thirty psalms appeal for help in trouble; almost as many offer adoration, praise, and thanksgiving; some twenty-six are concerned with religious or moral instruction and warning. Ten psalms direct attention to comfort and assurance; seven represent court scenes where men or gods are arraigned before God; five offer testimony to God's goodness. Military ventures, defeat, or victory occasion a few; storms, plague, earthquake, riot, a bumper harvest or none, social protest, argument with God, or delight in nature prompt other poems. About thirty are occupied with Israel's history, drawing varied lessons from the exodus, the settlement in Canaan, the northern kingdom's deportation, the invasion by Sennacherib, the exile to Babylon and the return, later struggles for power, postexilic religious tensions. A nation's whole story, experience, reflections, disasters, triumphs, and reactions are thus written into these poems. But if, with hardly an exception, all is viewed from a moral and religious standpoint, that is almost the *only* common feature.

Poems written for so many purposes, across eight centuries, by very different authors in widely varying circumstances, inevitably exhibit differences of spiritual insight, of theological understanding, of moral emphasis and vision. There is no set theology or ethic, because each poem expresses its own age and background.

The wonder is, not that we meet uncertainties of text, variations in translation, and differences of insight, but that across the long centuries heart speaks to heart, testimony kindles faith, their thanksgiving evokes our praise, their courage renews our confidence.

Everything in the Psalter is, of course, pre-Christian. But over the course of centuries, and in the light of later events, much in the psalms (as in the prophets) gained a different connotation, as passages came to be read not simply in their immediate historical context but against the background of the biblical story as a whole.

Most of the earliest Christians were Jews, for whom the psalms were essential to worship. It was natural for the Psalter to take its place at once in Christian praise also. By the second century, the Jewish psalms were being sung by Christians; by the fourth century, every part of Christian worship and devotional discipline was enriched by psalm singing. Few modern Christian hymnbooks are without metrical versions of the psalms, sometimes heavily disguised. This Christian "adoption" of the psalms inevitably affected their interpretation.

Along with the rest of the Old Testament, the psalms deeply influenced Christian thought. It is possible to find, already in the New

Testament, two hundred clear echoes of the Psalter, and more than two hundred fainter allusions to its language. The language of Psalms 2, 8, 16, 22, 40, 45, and 110, among others, was immediately available to express Christian thinking, both in telling the story of Jesus and in defining his person and work. In consequence, these passages came to possess a Christian meaning very different from that in the mind of the Hebrew poets.

Indeed, this process of reinterpretation was anticipated within Jewry itself, as early psalms were adapted for use in later situations, and especially as psalms celebrating the Hebrew monarchy came, when that monarchy had passed away, to be "mentally translated" into promises of the coming Messiah and his glorious reign. Christians merely continued this process of adaptation.

It is not the task of a commentary to explain what the ancient words and insights under review *came to mean* long afterward, as man's thought and experience moved forward, and God's revelation was completed in Christ and the Spirit. The psalms, as written, adapted, and preserved in the Psalter, are rooted in the experience of their authors and the history of their users. In searching for their meaning, allowance must everywhere be made for that historical context. The immediate task is to seek the original meaning, setting, and relevance of each poem, so far as possible.

Yet even considered strictly by their own light and in their own historical context, the Hebrew psalms deal with timeless and changeless truths, which the passage of the centuries can neither dim nor outrun. A wonderfully courageous and tenacious faith breathes through their complaint, protest, and regret. Only a soul utterly sure of God could argue with him as boldly as some psalmists do. God is good; God reigns; God will vindicate, judge, deliver, and forgive. The paramount quality in God's character is steadfast, covenant love, unchanging and exhaustless. Psalms 23, 46, and 73 speak serenity to souls in all ages. Psalm 51 has never been excelled, even in Christianity, as an expression of penitence. Psalms 103 and 139 enshrine the very heart of religious faith, as Psalms 100 and 150 touch the supreme heights of religious ecstasy.

That is the measure of the psalmists' achievement. In numerous directions they glimpsed final truth, and the heart of their faith was eternally valid. Their God is surely ours also, more clearly known now in Jesus Christ our Lord, but not essentially different. We have seen their Shepherd give his life for the sheep and be raised again from the dead. And the God they worshiped with such fervor and joy will make known to us, too, the path of life; will fill us, too, with the joy of his presence; and reveal to us even yet eternal pleasures at his right hand.

COMMENTARY

Book I (Pss. 1–47)

Psalm 1. Happy the man who, in choosing his friends, avoids the enticements of the wicked, the company of wrongdoers, the corrosive influence of the cynical, taking pleasure instead in every revelation of the mind and will of God, feeding his mental life on the divine Word. The life of such a man is ever fresh and fruitful, like a deep-rooted riverside tree. The wicked, on the other hand, resemble dry husks, blown about by every wind of opinion, ever open to condemnation, and ostracized by society.

This simple homily contrasting the way of the righteous, which the Lord watches over, with the way of the wicked, which ends in futility, appears in some early copies as a prologue to the whole Psalter. Fittingly so, for the deliberate choice of the way of the Lord is the necessary precondition of all true worship.

Psalm 2. A new king, upon his coronation (v. 6), is immediately faced with planned revolt by hitherto subject neighbors (v. 3). He meets their threats with courageous confidence in the supreme authority of God who made him king, and with a daring image of God amused at man's futile antics. He therefore publishes the divine decree which made him son and promised him wide and powerful sovereignty. It will be wise for hostile rulers to reverently accept the Lord's appointment. Due submission to the son will avert God's anger. Blessed are all who in similar times of danger take refuge in him.

Following the disappearance of the Jewish monarchy, this psalm lent itself, in worship, to messianic application, and later to Christian reinterpretation. Its essential truth is that, public order being God's will, civic loyalty is a religious duty.

Psalm 3. The situation behind this psalm is plain, and the poet's superb trust shines through it equally clearly. The suggestion of the heading finds some support in comparing verses 2, 5, 6 with 2 Samuel 15: 12, 13; 16:8; 17:1. The psalmist's last words reveal that more than personal issues are at stake. But even if this psalm is not one of David's, some danger such as his is in mind, and must have recurred in Israel's turbulent history, making the poem timelessly relevant. Immunity from danger is not promised, but shielding, sustaining, and ultimate deliverance. So amid enemies and perils, the psalmist sleeps soundly and rises with confident hope. That is faith.

Psalm 4. The poet is distressed because the people are dishonoring his glorious one and turning to idolatry (see NIV marg.), evidently to fertility spirits supposed to reward worshipers with grain and wine (cf. v. 7 with Hos. 2:2–8). A series of poor harvests has kindled anger against God. The psalmist argues that those who belong to God cannot change their allegiance (v. 3)—and God will answer prayer for them. Meanwhile, anger must not occasion sin; it is better not to blaspheme. Better, too, to maintain regular sacrifices and to trust in God. The poet could testify that when he was in straitened circumstances, God led him into abundance. In any case, God offers a joy and security greater than mere prosperity. With that thought, his concern falls to rest.

Psalm 5. This poem alternates neatly between (1) the poet's setting out his morning devotions like a sacrifice, pleading to be heard and waiting expectantly; (2) God's rejection of evil men (under seven descriptive terms), who may not dwell, stand, or be tolerated in his presence; (3) the poet's own admission to God's house, to pray for guidance amid enemies through the day ahead; (4) the deceitfulness and defilement of evil men, whom he prays may remain banished from God's presence; (5) the sevenfold blessings enjoyed by those who take refuge in God, love him, and do his will.

The contrast is perhaps too sharp; but the facts are as stated—the earnest are welcomed daily into God's presence, the evil self-banished from all blessing.

Psalm 6. To an almost clinical description of severe illness is here added deep fear of God's anger, a moving cry, and excessive weeping caused by foes (possibly friends like Job's, who argue that sickness proves sinfulness). The poet's appeal to God's unfailing love is reinforced by the curious argument that, after all, his death will bring God no additional praise, Sheol being beyond God's reach.

In an apparent supplementary stanza, the poet acknowledges three times that his prayer was heard. Again curiously, it is the frustration of his enemies that occupies his mind. In synagogue use of the psalm, the severe sickness and the enemies' gloating could be applied to Israel, though the psalm offers no hint of that interpretation.

Psalm 7. According to 1 Kings 8:31, the temple became a courtroom where God tried cases of alleged wrongdoing between neighbors, hearing the necessary oaths (Exod. 22:8–11) and bringing down on his own head the punishment of the guilty. This psalm so clearly recalls those passages as to provide, as part of such trial ceremonies, a chanted appeal to divine justice. The poem may well have originated in some personal experience of false accusation and acquittal. A legal process is also suggested in the oath of the accused, accepting full punishment if guilty; in the eightfold appeal to God's righteous judgment; in the warning that God will fully arm himself to execute justice, though the evildoer gives birth to (v. 14) and prepares (v. 15) his own doom; and in the thanksgiving for vindication. The poet assumes that God the Judge is just, his law being the moral order of the world.

Psalm 8. From the cradle to the stars, the name of God resounds with majesty, the glory of God shines above the heavens, the handiwork of God evokes awe. Yet, between verses 1–2 and 9 is also set the astonishing greatness of man, with a place in God's mind and heart, only a little lower than the divine nature (v. 5, paraphrasing Gen. 1:26–27), crowned with glory and honor, and ruling his fellow creatures (echoing Gen. 1:26 again). As the psalmist clearly saw, only upon the assumption of God's glory and his purposes for man, does man possess such dignity; to deny God is to degrade man.

Psalm 9. In some ancient copies, Psalms 9 and 10 appear as one. It is probably better to see Psalm 10 as completing the alphabetic form of Psalm 9. The opening praise is in response to sustained victories in which the divine judgment between nations has been manifested ("the memory of them," v. 6, implies the passage of time). This shows that Israel's God is enthroned over the world and is righteous (avenging shed blood). This again calls for praise (vv. 7–12).

Verses 13–14 appear to interrupt, though the New English Bible is smoother: "Have pity . . . look upon my affliction, thou who hast lifted me up and caught me back from the gates of death," suggesting personal wounds as yet incompletely healed. Resuming the main theme, divine justice is seen in the appropriate fate of pagan nations, and in God's remembering the oppressed. The psalmist prays that the heathen nations may always be judged and kept in their place.

Psalm 10. Verses 1–2 continue the alphabet and the prayer of 9:19–20, because God does not appear to intervene at present. Verses 12–15 also resume the alphabet and the prayer, though now the opponent is the wicked man. Verses 16–18 complete the alphabet, promising that the nations (cf. 9:20) will terrify no more, for the Lord does hear.

Into this fairly smooth acrostic a description of the evil man intrudes (vv. 3–11), provoked by the mention of him in verse 2. It is a comprehensive and perceptive portrait, analyzing the desire and pride behind his evil deeds; his mental rejection of God; his self-confidence; his ruthlessness toward the weak, the undefended villagers, the unwary (vv. 8–9 may imply slave raiding). He thinks that God does not see or care (echoing 9:19; 10:1; introducing v. 12).

If the arrangement is inexplicable, the general meaning is clear. Among nations and within (Israelite) society, the ruthless too often seem to prosper unhindered. Past victories reveal divine justice at work; the poet's prayer is that still, internationally and nationally, God will show his hand.

Psalm 11. David once felt like a hunted bird in the mountains, when fleeing from Saul (1 Sam. 18–20; 26:20). This psalm reflects such a situation—and also that of postexilic resistance to heathen influences and pressures (note that the temple is built, v. 4). It might reflect any similar situation when the wicked are aggressive, the foundations of society shaken, and the overborne heart longs to flee.

Yet the refuge of the hard-pressed is in the Lord, not in distant mountains. He observes, watches, and rewards (v. 6 recalls Sodom). Loving justice, he will reveal himself to the upright—if they stand their ground.

Psalm 12. As so often, the state of society grieves the psalmist, but here especially because "good faith" (NEB) has disappeared. Lies, flattery, and deceit abound. Men claim that they own their lips (v. 4; lit. our lips are our plowshares), and boast they can achieve anything by clever propaganda. In a largely illiterate society, the uneducated poor were preeminently vulnerable to falsehood—in business, in law courts, in employment, marriage, and personal reputation.

But the Lord sees the effect upon the defenseless, and promises protection. *His* words are refined silver (NEB purified gold). The Lord will keep his own safe, though the wicked strut arrogantly in a world of distorted values.

Psalm 13. The psalmist utters a poignant cry of spiritual desolation that is quite unexplained (v. 3 does not necessarily imply sickness). The poet is acutely aware of the loss of God's conscious favor; of ceaseless inward debate, of continual sorrow, of the gloating of opponents over his state. He also seems afraid of dying in his spiritual darkness. Many of the truly devout have known such seasons of despair and have found with the psalmist that the memory of God's past goodness and trust in his unfailing love provide the answer to such dark moods.

Psalm 14. The practical folly of a generation persuading itself to live without God produces individual and social corruption, and saps every initiative of good. The consequences are: lack of understanding; vileness and filth; futility; no worthwhile impulse. All this the Lord observes. It is even more stupid to challenge God by feasting upon and frustrating the helpless poor who are his special care. Their day will come!

Psalm 53 is a duplicate of this psalm, with verbal changes; in both verse 5 is difficult. In Psalm 53, verse 5 appears to be very different. The original text is now probably irrecoverable. Verse 7 may have been added to adapt a private poem of protest for public use, identifying the poor with oppressed Israel.

Psalm 15. The Hebrew heart longed for acceptance with God. Here, a poet sets out succinctly the conditions of that acceptance. To be welcomed by God, a worshiper must be a good man, whose conduct is blameless, right, and sincere; a good neighbor, neither doing nor saying anything harmful to others; and a good citizen, scorning those who undermine morality, upholding the godly, honoring his bond at great cost, never exploiting the poor for usury, and abhorring corruption. Such a man will dwell near God, unshaken.

Psalm 16. Measureless enrichment is to be gained by choosing to serve the true God. Some contrast is implied, with the sorrows that come to those who choose other gods; verse 3 can be read either as part of this contrast (NIV marg.; NEB the gods whom earth holds sacred are all worthless, and cursed are all who make them their delight), or as part of the blessings of true godliness (NIV text).

These are numerous. God is the source of every good, the psalmist's feast, his inheritance (recalling the original division of Canaan). Quiet counsel, gladness, even bodily relaxation, flow from his setting God before him as Lord. This confidence stretches even to (or beyond) the grave (v. 10), for already God has made known the path, the presence, and timeless pleasures.

Psalm 17. Courtroom solemnity fills this appeal for a fair hearing and for vindication. A repeated plea of "not guilty" leads to a final appeal for clemency. The poet charges his accusers with callousness, pride, and cunning, and prays that God will keep, hide, and defend him. The psalmist will be satisfied with the sight of God's face turned toward him in acquittal. "When I awake" probably means "from this dark time, when the case is over."

Psalm 18. The heading of this psalm finds support in 2 Samuel 22. Yet reference to the temple and cherubim, the use of some late terms, an idealized view of David's empire, and mention of David's descendants all betray a later date. The present psalm is thus, most probably, an old victory chant, possibly by David, adapted for later worship.

The titles for God include the frequent ox-horn metaphor, the symbol of strength, defiance, and challenge (when blown); pride (when lifted up or tossed); power and victory (when "exalted"); or dignity (when God "raises" one's horn).

Triumph had nearly cost the psalmist's life (vv. 4–6). But God came and rescued him from flood and foe, even as he did Israel at the Red Sea, in reward for faithfulness.

Resuming his acknowledgment of God's help, the poet recounts the far-reaching results of his victory. A final outburst of confidence and praise fittingly closes an anthem which must have often uplifted Jewish courage and faith.

Psalm 19. The awesome testimony of sky and sun to their Maker's glory is universal and searching. The poet lauds the amazing, unsupported "stretch" of the skies, and the glorious Mediterranean sun, emerging like a bridegroom in splendor from the (Jewish) wedding canopy; addressing himself with eagerness to his course from east to west like a champion runner.

For the poet, the moral law, equally awesome, is God's revealed will, made known in written law, instruction, precepts, commandments, inward fear, and outward decrees. Under whatever form, it is a source of life, wisdom, joy, illumination, purity, and righteousness; it is precious, sweet, and rewarding. But nothing is hid from this sun. Unwittingly or willfully, man sins, unless divine forgiveness and help keep him blameless. So the poet prays that his word, conduct, and thought might be acceptable in the sight of God who strengthens and redeems.

Psalm 20. Before battle Judah's king offers sacrifices. A prophet (or presiding priest) greets him (vv. 1–3). *Selah,* a musical pause, may indicate the moments of sacrificing. The king affirms his faith in God alone; chariots and horses, alien to Israel, are feared and distrusted (cf. Isa. 31:1). As he goes forth, encouraged, the people cry after him.

Psalm 21. After battle (see Ps. 20, which this poem repeatedly echoes) the king acknowledges the help of God in eight grateful expressions. An established crown, a preserved life, and enhanced authority are the fruits of God's gift of victory, though king and people rejoice most in the divine favor which triumph demonstrates.

The Hebrew mind read in God's present

favor the guarantee of future success; God being faithful, his promises were as good as accomplished.

Psalm 22. A threnody of unparalleled pathos here breaks suddenly into unlimited hope and promise. Forsaken, unanswered by God despite his past faithfulness, the psalmist is scorned and mocked. He remembers his infant training in the faith, but now he is the prey of brutal men. He feels the ebbing strength and numbness of approaching death; the scavenging dogs already gather, mummifiers already bind his limbs, dividing his clothes for reward. A final, despairing cry that God will come quickly (echoing v. 1) to deliver from the savagery of beastlike men breaks off sharply, with "You have heard!" The sentence is unfinished. Nothing more is heard of lament, only of public praise, vows of gratitude and almsgiving, and the remarkable promise that the ends of the earth will remember this divine intervention and turn to God, whose kingdom is over all. The prosperous living, the dead, and coming generations will all proclaim God's righteousness to peoples yet unborn.

This striking portrayal of resurrection out of near-death might find illustration, in part, in the career of Jeremiah. The only close parallel, however, is the Suffering Servant of the Lord (Isa. 52:13–53:12), who would "rise" from rejection, scourging, and death. Hence it would be easy, in later worship, to transfer the sorrow, faith, and boundless hope of this psalmist to Israel as a whole, the suffering but enduring servant of God.

Jesus awaited death with this psalm's opening words upon his lips, and the story of his death came to be told in its language, with thirteen clear echoes of its statements. His rejection, likewise, ended in resurrection.

In this psalm, therefore, we are unquestionably at the very heart of Jewish and Christian faith. Utmost faithfulness in God's service does not preclude rejection and suffering, but the ultimate outcome will be truly divine success. In this portrait, drawn by prophet and psalmist, Jesus found the prefiguring of his own experience and the program of his messiahship, to win power by sacrificial love. His so-called cry of dereliction on the cross was but the opening verse of this inexpressibly comforting psalm.

Psalm 23. The Lord is shepherd, guide, and host. As shepherd, he provides provision, refreshment, and security. One frequent use of David's sling would be to aim beyond a straying sheep, scaring it back to the flock. As guide, God assures clear leading in right paths, companionship, protection, and support. The professional guide's "name" or reputation was the traveler's only guarantee of protection and safe arrival, as it was the guide's main claim to employment. As host, God assures us of welcome at his rich table, of abundance, attendance, and unending hospitality. All this even now, while enemies surround us. The psalm's last words (Heb. for length of days) do not suggest (or deny) immortality, but that the welcome and feasting will not be withdrawn while life lasts.

Psalm 24. The question in verse 3, with verses 7–10, show this psalm's processional purpose. References to God as Creator and King, with the possible replacement of the ark within the shrine, suggest the occasion is the New Year festival. The choir (or priest) declares God's ownership of all things and people; a spokesman (or choir) asks who may enter the shrine. The answer is: the man of innocent actions, pure motives, devotion to God alone, and personal integrity. Such a man will receive what he seeks. Verse 6 may add the ground for this assurance or perhaps the assent of the worshipers.

At the shrine's doors, the challenge (v. 7) is given twice, and answered twice from within. The splendid affirmation given in reply wins admission. That the King of glory is outside is probably best understood as a reenactment (note, the "doors" by this time are "ancient") of David's bringing the ark to Jerusalem (cf. 1 Chron. 15), which provided a dramatic annual reassertion of the presence of Israel's mighty King within the shrine.

Psalm 25. Twenty-two pious thoughts, threaded upon the Hebrew alphabet, are made one poem by sustained earnestness, spiritual perception, and tenacious faith expressed throughout. "I," "we," and "my" occur thirty-five times. Verse 22 was added, outside the pattern, for public worship.

The poet pleads that God will not remember the sins that weigh upon him, threatening shame, but will remember *him* as well as the great love God has shown of old. His guilty memories, enemies, loneliness, affliction, anguish, and insecurity distress him. How the poet envies those who consistently fear the Lord!

Against this inner insufficiency the psalmist places his confidence in God's goodness, patience, and love. In God is all his hope, his trust, his gaze, his refuge. Plainly this timid soul has learned the alphabet of spiritual growth.

Psalm 26. This equivocal poem can be read as a brave profession of orthodoxy, of standing firm on level ground, by some faithful priest in days of religious compromise, when sinners are willing to be bribed into disloyalty.

It can also be read as the Old Testament equivalent to Jesus' parable of the conceited Pharisee (Luke 18:9–14), with thirteen unblushing claims to divine approval, including a challenge to God to search his heart and mind and the repeated assertion of a blameless life (vv. 11b and 12b are then merely formal, like the Pharisee's "I thank God I am not as other men").

Psalm 27. We can only guess what brought together the divergent sections of this psalm: fluctuating moods, spiritual reaction, artistic contrast, or liturgical habit (praise before prayer)?

Verses 1–6 sparkle with mounting confidence, which men, enemies, an army, and even war cannot shake. All the warrior asks is to return in peace, to end his days in worship, in the assurance that God will keep him safe, hide him, lift him high above enmity. Then he will offer sacrifice joyfully, his faith exultant.

Verses 7–14 open with a sharp cry for mercy, that God will neither turn from nor forsake his servant. The poet argues (with himself?) that God's care is more dependable than any parent's; he pleads to be led where none can lie in ambush, and to be delivered from false accusation. The Hebrew of verse 13 is urgent: "Oh! if I had not believed . . . (then it would have gone ill with me)." So in the end the poet waits for the darker experience (or mood) to pass, with his faith tenacious. True faith has both dimensions.

Psalm 28. A representative individual, presumably a king and possibly David, asks not to die, as apparently others have done (vv. 1d, 3a). Gesturing toward God's shrine, he asks for mercy. A detailed description of the wicked, who deal deceitfully with neighbors and have no respect for what God's hands have done, leads into prayer that they shall receive their deserts. It may be conjectured that plague has cost many lives, and the blame is laid on the moral deterioration of society.

With considerable relief, the king testifies that God has heard, and affirms that God will likewise be the strength of his stricken people. He prays that God will carry them, shepherdlike, forever.

Psalm 29. A mighty tempest, boiling the Mediterranean and sweeping inland across the north to Lebanon and Hermon, then turning south to swing across the moors of Kadesh, with lightning splitting the cedars, thunder shaking the wilderness, the gale twisting the oaks and stripping the forests, floods deluging the plains, makes the exulting psalmist feel that everything in the temple of nature is crying "Glory!" at such majestic power.

So he calls upon angels (lit. sons of gods or of God) and men to join in nature's worship. For the force of the storm is God's strength, the thunder is his voice, and such release of power manifests his glory. God sits as King above the storm, and all that power is available as strength for his people. The quiet, beautiful end is peace.

Psalm 30. A near-fatal illness has passed, the anticipation of enemies has been disappointed; all is well. The poet is moved to lilting praise for the swift change of God's anger to favor, from weeping to joy. It has been a salutary lesson. For he had been overconfident, feeling immovable, until God hid his face. Then he begged mercy, and argued with God that death would profit neither. God heard, turned wailing to dancing, penitence to joy, silence to song. No wonder the psalmist is grateful.

Psalm 31. Two-thirds of this poem could well be by Jeremiah (cf. vv. 7–18 with Jer. 20:7–13; vv. 6, 12, 13, 18 also echo Jeremiah). The psalmist affirms his devotion to God's service fifteen times, making only passing reference to guilt. Yet affliction, enmity, physical distress, social rejection, slander, and conspiracy beset him. He had felt like a city besieged, a lost child, and dreaded becoming ensnared and ashamed.

Why this should be is not considered. How to react is more important. The psalmist holds fast to all he has known of God (vv. 5, 7, 8, 16, 19, 21–23). Second, he takes refuge from men in God; images of safety abound (vv. 1, 2, 3, 19, 20). Third, he commits to God his inmost self, his times, his trust. The consequence: he can recommend all to remain faithful and take heart.

Psalm 32. Illness and guilt bring conviction of sin; at last, inward acknowledgment and full outward confession bring the bliss of forgiveness, a heart freed from concealment. With deepened understanding, the poet urges others to pray. Thus they will find a place of safety when floods (of sorrow?) rise, a hiding place from all harm.

A forgiven soul can best counsel others facing temptation, urging constant sensitivity toward God, that will not need the bit and bridle of discipline and punishment, but will live surrounded with salvation and the Lord's unfailing love. In such souls, sheer gladness keeps evil at bay.

Psalm 33. The psalmist calls the believer to joyful worship. Such praise is fitting:

because of God's utterly dependable character, assuring that the earth is full of his unfailing love;
because of the creative, controlling power of God's spoken word;
because history reflects God's purpose, supreme and enduring—especially his dealings with his own people;
because of God's watchful care, in danger and famine, for those who hope in him.

Brief but moving homage is then offered, perhaps (when the psalm was publicly used) by leader, congregation, and both, in turn.

Psalm 34. This poem knits together personal testimony to the benefits of living in fear of the Lord (mentioned fifteen times), and formal instruction in that fear. The testimony is personal, though not merely individual; others have known, others are invited to share, this radiant, blessed, and satisfying experience. The instruction (v. 11 is the wisdom teacher's usual address to pupils) covers careful speech, good behavior, and peaceful aims, with advice to remember that the Lord is watching, opposing evildoers, helping all who are in need or are crushed. For even the righteous meet many hardships, but the Lord limits them and delivers. In the end, the righteous will be totally vindicated.

Psalm 35. Verse 1 says it all. An individual pleads for vindication, that is, that his innocence will be publicly acknowledged. That he has supporters as well as numerous ruthless enemies suggests that he is important. Any persecuted prophet or king might compose (or later use) this eloquent self-defense. Some details suggest a postexilic leader resisting compromise with paganism. Almost every form of opposition and ill-usage is named. All is made more bitter by the poet's former friendship, sympathy, and prayers for his persecutors, and by the absence of any cause for their ill-will. The psalmist repeatedly mentions his enemies' gloating over his own stumbling, but no clue is offered as to its nature. Throughout, the oriental fear of "losing face" is clearly evident.

A sevenfold malediction (vv. 4–8) sounds revengeful, but is essentially a cry for justice, for evil to return upon the evildoers. The poet's main plea is that God will awaken, rise up, arm himself, and provide reason for those who have supported him to testify to God's righteous intervention.

Psalm 36. The Hebrew of verses 1–4 is terse and rugged, but the analysis of the wicked man's manner of life is clear. Self-flattery and moral blindness follow directly from practical atheism, with deceit and deliberate evildoing in their train.

In sharp contrast (the style becomes lyrical) the landscape of the godly life is beautiful. God's love is the sky, overarching all; God's faithfulness fills the vault of heaven, like scudding clouds; God's righteousness provides the massive mountain background; God's judgments are an unfathomable sea. Within that scenery the Lord preserves all living things, providing the shade of his care, the feast of his gifts, the river of divine delight (the Hebrew echoes Eden), the springing fountain of life; while over everything glows the daylight of divine illumination (vv. 5–9).

In such spiritual country the godly live. The poet prays that evildoers may not keep him from it; and he foresees, in that kind of world, the final downfall of all the wicked.

Psalm 37. An experienced teacher (v. 25) illustrates in alphabetical order the main principles of a God-centered life, in contrast with that of the wicked, in a period of intense persecution. He describes at length the difficulty of the present time, for the meek, the faithful, and the righteous. It is not only that evil men flourish in society, grow wealthy, corrupt justice, and seem to escape retribution. That is sufficiently unjust, so that even the godly become envious, fretting at the unfairness of life.

Moreover, the evil actively persecute the good, plotting against the righteous. It is a time when to be truly pious, strictly loyal to divine law ("righteous"), is to be in danger of physical violence, and even death. In addition, some fear of want harasses the faithful; the righteous are "the poor and needy," a fact alluded to five times (vv. 14, 16, 19, 25–26).

All these features point to the postexilic period under foreign rule, when pagan influences and laws were imposed upon Judah; when to be safe and prosperous demanded compromise and to be conscientious involved persecution and poverty. Such a background to the psalm illumines both the counsel given and the promises made, each so emphatically (the repetitions are significant).

The psalmist's counsel is practical. It is foolish to fret or grow angry; this tends only to evil. The people of God, in such a time, should steadfastly maintain their inward resources, their independence, their life-style. To do this, they should trust, and delight themselves in the Lord; commit their way to him; be still before him; wait upon him. They will be stronger if they do not seek to defend themselves, but rely upon God for vindication, upholding, provision, stronghold, refuge, and salvation. Meanwhile, they should persist in doing good, not letting external pressures change their conduct.

To encourage this intrepid attitude, the psalmist promises, not personal wealth, the redivision of landed property (as might appear), or the opportunity to gloat over suffering enemies, but what the persecuted deeply desire: the assurance that the future belongs to them. This must imply the downfall of the compromising, evil-inclined, persecuting party. They will wither, be cut off, disappear, their weapons and power broken, themselves destroyed. Collaborators with paganism have no prospect of success.

But those faithful to God will see their righteousness demonstrated, their cause vindicated. The psalmist promises that they will inherit the land and enjoy peace (vv. 11, 18, 27, 29, 34). They should leave the outcome in the hands of God, who declares, in the midst of conflict and persecution, that "there is a future for the man of peace" (v. 37).

The best antidote against fretting over the time in which God has placed us is not argument, but the firm affirmation of faith in the permanence of whatever is rooted in God.

Psalm 38. This poem is a dreadful, heart-rending description of extreme illness, probably advanced leprosy. The patient is not bedridden, but feeble, silenced, near the end, suspicious of those who would take advantage of his helplessness. The usual assumption that suffering presupposes sin reinforces his own remorse; he interprets his condition as divine rebuke. But he makes no excuses. The ground of his plea is his agony, his penitence, and his prayer to "my Savior."

Psalm 39. This psalm is possibly a funeral hymn, expressing with great honesty the difficulty of submitting to the imminent end. The sick man is aware how unguarded the words of dying men may be, how misrepresented by evil report. He had resolved that when his end approached he would be silent, but anguish and fever demand relief, and he speaks his mind to God.

His dominant feeling is of the brevity of life; all that the busiest man gathers is left to others. The dying have nothing to look for but forgiveness, relief from scorn, divine sympathy as for a passing guest or pilgrim. But the psalmist pleads for respite from God's displeasure, that some quiet pleasure may remain before the end.

Psalm 40. Can this be one poem? Verses 1–3 offer testimony to divine rescue. The slimy pit endangered many travelers; the rescue to firm footing and renewed song is vividly described. The experience behind the metaphor is not explained, but it is evidently some radical change in life-style that should persuade others to turn to God for help, and not to become proud idolaters.

For his thanksgiving, the usual four sacrifices are repudiated in favor of complete obedience from the heart, and full acknowledgment, in public assembly, of the saving goodness of God.

Tone and circumstances change abruptly in verses 11–17. Now, innumerable troubles and sins beset the psalmist, and his heart fails. He pleads that God will come quickly to save; that all who wish him ill will suffer for it; that those who seek God will rejoice. This section closes with renewed prayer that he not be forgotten but helped without delay. With small changes, verses 13–17 appear in Book II as Psalm 70, confirming the impression of a second, separable poem.

Psalm 41. Six forms of blessedness are assured (in a quotation?) to the man who is concerned for the "poor-weak-helpless" (the Hebrew term is comprehensive).

As one who (apparently) has shown such concern, the poet seizes on the fourth blessing (v. 2c), for when he was seriously ill, praying for mercy and confessing his sins, his enemies took opportunity to anticipate his death gladly, to visit him only to speak falsely, and to gather news to gossip about. Even a friend kicked back at him, like a treacherous ox. So the psalmist prays for mercy, and the opportunity to repay them (to reestablish his position?). He assures himself that the frustration of his enemies shows that God is pleased with him, will uphold him, and will grant him his presence.

Book II (Pss. 42–72)

Psalms 42–43. Theme, refrain, and style link these poems, though slight differences cast doubt upon their actual unity. The refrain crystallizes their theme—reproachful self-examination about despondency, which must pass since God is the poet's Savior.

Desolating thirst for his absent God is sharpened by taunts and by memories of former festival blessings. In 42:6–10, he is at the Upper Jordan, amid the cataracts of Hermon and Mizar, which mirror his experience. He mourns for God, feeling forgotten among enemies. In 43:1–4, the enemies are an ungodly nation, and he feels rejected; he prays for guidance back to the hill, dwelling, and altar of God, where he will praise with the harp—all suggesting Zion.

Psalm 44. This poem is beautifully planned, with a sting of protest in its tail. The approved tradition describing God's intervention at the occupation of Canaan is reverently rehearsed. The assent of the present generation to the deep faith implied is clearly affirmed. Nevertheless God has let them down, no longer accompanying the army, given them up to plunder, like a dishonest shepherd selling sheep in his care for a pittance. The disgrace hurts deeply.

Why? Israel had not forgotten God or sought another—God would have known! Yet God crushed them, made the land a wilderness, the people sheep for slaughtering.

Suddenly sweet reasonableness breaks down. "Awake, O Lord! Why do you sleep? Rouse yourself! Rise up and help." Is this the way to speak to God? The psalmist would say, "If you feel it, say it." What is deeply significant, unique to Israel, is the expectation that God will be consistent and just, and the freedom of faith to speak honestly with him.

Psalm 45. The court poet, saluting the royal groom and bride, finds the theme congenial. Flattery is laid on heavily, extolling the king's excellence, appearance, marital prowess, character, wedding array, fragrance, music, and harem. To address the king as "God" exceeds flattery.

The bride is urged to forget her past (implying that she is foreign) and to submit to the king. Within her apartment the bride is gloriously arrayed. Attended by bridesmaids, she is led in procession to the king's court. The marriage blessing promising noble posterity throughout the land refers to the royal dynasty, which (with the poet's help) will be celebrated for generations.

When later custom called every marriage pair "king and queen," the court poem became a wedding hymn, with messianic overtones.

Psalm 46. Several prophetic, or mythological, ideas are discernible (or imaginable) within this poem, but as usual the refrain (probably sung antiphonally, after v. 3 as well as vv. 7, 11) summarizes the main message. The immediate evidence that he "is with us," our fortress, is some recent victory so unexpected as to require divine intervention to explain it. Hezekiah's deliverance from Sennacherib comes readily to mind (2 Kings 18–19).

Considered alone, verses 1–3 might describe physical convulsions, but the context implies a vivid metaphor for war's upheaval. Verses 4–6 suggest the inner spiritual resources of a besieged city which knows that God has only to speak and all opposition melts. Verses 8–10 reveal the desolations which God, too, can make. So Judah should learn to "let be" and see God exalted in the earth.

Psalm 47. The Talmud claims that this is a hymn for the Feast of Tabernacles with rhythmic hand-clapping, shouts of gladness, the resounding ram's horn, and a praise chorus to mark the climax of ceremonies that celebrated the annual recognition of God as King. Verses 5–8 mark the restoration of the ark to its place in the shrine, different singers doubtless answering each other with the repeated phrases.

The abounding confidence behind such an occasion is obvious, as well as the certainty that God had created this land and people. Especially remarkable is the confident anticipation that God's universal sovereignty, of which Israel had no doubt, would be universally acknowledged, racial distinctions notwithstanding. Both of these features, together with the sheer joy that irradiates these verses, make this psalm a high point in the Old Testament.

Psalm 48. Enthusiasm and eloquence combine in a pilgrim's report on Jerusalem. The height of "the mountain city" is the first impression, especially for eyes accustomed to the plains of Galilee. But primarily, this is God's city: he is present, he defends it. God's defense of Zion is vividly recalled, because pilgrim cities need historical associations.

All previous reports on Jerusalem have been abundantly justified. The "atmosphere" of the place is unique. Within the temple, the mind fills with thoughts of God's faithful love and his righteous victories stirring all lands to praise. From the city wall, the peaceful, happy villages ("daughters") of Judah, like the capital, bask in God's protection. A final circuit of that wall, memorizing its features, brings determination to report in detail to the children back home, because this place is the very citadel of the nation's faith and of her God.

Psalm 49. Without envy or complaint, in a cool philosophic mood, a teacher of wisdom propounds a moral lesson for all concerned, namely, that the wealthy die like other men, like the beasts that perish. Great wealth makes men boastful, self-confident, ostentatious, yet no wealth can redeem a brother or oneself from death. Since even the wise die, how much more will fools who trust in their wealth leave it behind! Even the social influence which wealth bestows ends with the grave.

In contrast, the upright will win in the end. God can and will redeem the soul of the wise, and take him to himself. Essentially, the poet compares temporary and eternal values, material and spiritual blessedness, by the test of what outlives the grave.

Psalm 50. God lays a double charge against Israel before a world court, summoned before him as Judge in Zion, in the presence of heaven and earth as witnesses. The basis of the arraignment is the covenant with Israel established by sacrifice and law at Sinai. The sacrifices have been maintained, but as though putting God in debt and making God grateful, rather than in thankfulness for all that God does, and from an obligation to honor him. Similarly, the law is taught and recited, but not obeyed. Not only are the commandments broken, but the breaking is excused; people condone stealing, befriend adulterers, bear false witness even against their brothers. They have thought that God, too, condoned disobedience. Now God accuses and warns.

Psalm 51. Historical background aside, this poem is a marvelously perceptive expression of penitence. Rebelliousness, producing distorted inclination and resulting in "missing of the mark," is seen clearly as directed against God, proving his judgments right, whatever other social consequences may be involved. This manifold sinfulness is inward, a quality of personality itself from the start; it stains that inner life where God requires truth and wisdom.

So the psalmist feels deeply unclean, crushed, needing to be re-created from within. He longs that God will wash him thoroughly, will turn his face from the sin, yet neither banish him nor withdraw his Spirit, but restore his lost joy, his willingness to obey, his silenced testimony and praise.

But beyond cleansing and re-creation, the psalmist knows that more is necessary to erase the memory of iniquity and save from guilt. Here he feels helpless, as every penitent must. He is convinced that no animal sacrifice can atone. Only God's unfailing love and great compassion can avail. All the sinner can offer is a broken, contrite heart—but that God will not despise.

Psalm 52. The psalmist describes uncompromisingly the strong and wealthy who oppress others by deceitful, injurious, treacherous speech. The vulnerable have no weapons; only fear of the God of truth will restrain the practiced liar. God will vigorously bring down, snatch up, tear, and uproot these social weeds from public life.

In contrast stands the man who grows in God's presence, who trusts God's love, praises his deeds, hopes in his reputation for honesty.

The air of antagonism and of self-righteousness is probably due to the Hebrew mind avoiding abstractions like "deceitfulness" and "integrity," preferring to personalize the contrast and speak of "him who lies," "him who is honest."

Psalm 54. Under attack by ungodly men, the psalmist asks God's help. The grounds of his appeal are God's name and faithfulness, and the promise of a freewill offering (Exod. 35:29) with praise. He confidently anticipates a favorable outcome, and speaks as though it has already been granted.

The identity of these ruthless men is doubtful. Strangers (v. 3) suggests foreign invaders; "insolent ones" (RSV, NEB) suggests private enemies. The words are similar in Hebrew; possibly the psalm could be used privately with one pronunciation, publicly with the other.

Psalm 55. In anguish because of the enemy and the fear of death, the poet would gladly escape like the solitary dove to rest and shelter. The city is torn by destructive forces, violence, rioting, and falsehood; one embittering feature is the treachery of a friend and fellow worshiper, who now with smooth words hides the enmity in his heart.

The poet prays that (as at Babel, Gen. 11:9) God will confuse lying speech and frustrate the plans of the rioters. He asks that as his enemies give lodging to evil, so Sheol may give lodging to them. His regular prayers find renewed confidence. The psalmist is sure that from his throne God will see and act.

Another voice (priest? prophet?) appears to give God's answer; God will uphold the righteous and bring down the wicked. So the psalm ends in trust. The circumstances are impossible to recover, but not rare; any time of violence and treachery would find the psalm appropriate.

Psalm 56. The slightly varying refrain (vv. 4, 10–11) affirms an intention to trust in place of fear; offers praise for some word given; and declares contempt for human threats. The circumstances are familiar: attacks, slander, pride, plotting of evil men. The psalmist would have God record his lament and tears, and not let his persecutors escape. The enemies' discomfiture will be the sign that God is for him, and he will fulfill his vows of thanksgiving, aware that God has delivered him from death and stumbling to walk before him in life.

Psalm 57. The total impression is of a soul fearful and shaken but seeking reassurance by repeating familiar affirmations of faith. In verse 7 steadfastness is established, and a burst of music leads into public praise of the universal and infinite love, faithfulness, and glory of God. That the poem has suffered some manipulation is evident from the reappearance of verses 7–11 in Psalm 108:1–5.

Psalm 58. The last line of this poem contains the essence of its imaginative protest. The Hebrew *elōhîm* (v. 1) means gods, or supernatural ruling spirits of the nations, as verse 2b confirms. Here, they are challenged for not "weighing" evil seriously and justly.

Evil begins at birth, and evil men are deadly as the cobra, deaf to all appeal. The psalmist prays that they will be thwarted, like toothless lions, spilled water, blunted arrows (or, grass drying to straw in the sun); like the slug wearing away in the trail it leaves, the stillborn child, the traveler's fire scattered by wind before the cooking pot is even warm. All are figures of futility. The poet, and the righteous, long to see evil frustrated and good totally triumphant. Then men will know that this is a moral world, and that God is Judge.

Psalm 59. The poet uses the image of snarling dogs prowling the city to describe foes who lie in wait beyond the walls. The weapon of dangerous words, curses, and lies recalls the siege of Jerusalem by Assyria and the Rabshakeh's alien, offensive, demoralizing propaganda (2 Kings 18:17–19:8, 19–21). Like Hezekiah, the psalmist wants all kingdoms to know the outcome.

But similar unprovoked attacks doubtless occurred, which could be likened to pariah dogs unsatisfied by the city's rubbish. The poet urges God to arise, to look and act, scoffing back at the foe. Through the night he keeps vigil, asking that God will not destroy the enemy so swiftly that the people will forget the crisis and underrate their deliverance (v. 11). He likes to repeat, too, his confidence in God's love and strength—sufficient answer to drown the snarling of the enemy!

Psalm 60. This outspoken poem well illustrates the psalmist's forthright realism. God has been "burstingly" angry, but it is time for him to lay anger aside! The people have been through desperate times; an earthquake and serious military defeat have left the nation staggering like drunken men.

The people's world is shaken. The psalmist prays, therefore, somewhat boldly, offering no penitence, asking no mercy, for God's strong help, and quotes a familiar oracle declaring all Palestine to be God's, to divide as he will (vv. 6–7). Let God remember that the whole land is his! Let God lead Israel forth again to Edom; none other can.

Psalm 61. Five images show the poet to be "taking cover," having known God's protection hitherto and now needing it again (the rock may shade from the sun or lift above danger; the tent offers protective hospitality). The circumstances are obscure; the change from "I" to "the king" in verses 6–7 is puzzling. It is probably recalling vows and the given heritage, treasured by a king in exile, followed by his own prayer that the monarchy may endure through coming generations.

Psalm 62. In his struggle to retain his position the psalmist remains unshaken, for his soul rests in God alone, on whom his salvation and honor depend. So he cares nothing for men's opposition, whatever their rank or wealth; they are weightless breath, worth nothing in the balances. His trust is in God.

The firm foundation for this superb independence of mind is grandly uttered. God said it, others confirm it, that in God alone is power, love, justice. That is a conviction upon which any heart can rest, and on which a stable society can be built despite the plotting of evil men.

Psalm 63. Earnest longing for God passes into rich testimony. As drink to the thirsty, food to the hungry, music to the sad, cheer to the sleepless, songs in shadow, a strong arm to lean upon, and the source of all joy, God has proved to be all that the king's soul, body, lips, hands, and mouth can want. Who can say more?

One striking detail is added, however. Neither the dry, weary land, nor his bed, nor those seeking his life, are in the sanctuary. Now, far from the sanctuary, the king finds the love of God still better than life, spiritual feasting still within reach, songs on his lips, the night watches enriched with thoughts of God. Still he clings to God, and God to him. His life, wherever he goes, is filled with the goodness of God. That is a tremendous discovery. In its light the threats of men mean nothing. They will descend to Sheol, their neglected bodies unburied (the final insult). All who genuinely swear by this ever-present God will be filled with praise; those who swear falsely will be struck dumb.

Psalm 64. Someone especially vulnerable to slander (see Ps. 12) has experienced a totally unexpected, sharp, concerted, secret, and unjust attack that imperils his life (perhaps bringing capital charges; possibly involving his public life as a leader of society). The opposition is both numerous and cunning.

But God too has "arrows," and acts suddenly, though not in secret. He will expose falsehood to the scorn of all who witness the outcome. Indeed, all men will see and reflect upon God's intervention, and the righteous will rejoice. Like the psalmist, they will seek refuge from men's tongues in the God who ever defends the truth.

Psalm 65. God is known in the sanctuary. Praise, vows, prayer, confession, atonement, and an elected priesthood all comprise the good things of God's house.

God is known, too, in actions that evoke awe, hope, fear, and songs to the ends of the earth and seas, where morning dawns and evening fades. These deeds of God manifest his righteousness (in the moral order of the world), his creative power, and his victory over nature and the nations.

God is known also in his goodness as evidenced in the surrounding fields (watered, enriched, softened after summer drought, blessed with fertility), pastures, hillsides, meadows, and valleys. Such wide-ranging knowledge of God bestows blessing and kindles joy and song: truly, praise is fitting for God.

Psalm 66. The invitation to come and see is addressed to all the earth, amid calls to praise God and acknowledge his power, if only reluctantly. What the nations are to see and acknowledge is God's activity on behalf of Israel, from the exodus and the conquest of Canaan, through the discipline of succeeding generations and exile in Babylon. Truly, when surrounding peoples thought that Israel had perished, God preserved their lives. The poet is so moved by even this telescoped version of so wonderful a history, that he promises elaborate thanksgiving, the temple and sacrificial worship being fully restored.

The invitation to come and listen is addressed to Israel, to hear what God has done for the psalmist, though he is exceedingly discreet as to details. He has experienced trouble (v. 14); there has been temptation to inward, secret sin, which threatened alienation from God, now happily past. Verses 16–20 might represent Israel's testimony, if the personal pronoun were not so prominent.

More probably, the psalmist means that as in Israel's historic experience, so in his personal life, God has neither rejected prayer nor withheld his covenant love. All generations could sing that!

Psalm 67. Changes in the persons addressed (congregation, God, congregation), the refrain, and the musical pause reveal a moving liturgy of thanksgiving. Assembled after a good harvest from the whole region, the congregation gives thanks and prays for even greater blessing than fruitful fields. The leader recites verse 1. After a pause filled with music, the congregation (possibly the choir) responds (v. 2). All unite in verse 3, because surrounding peoples have shared in God's bounty. The leader emphasizes this beneficent rule of God in all the earth, followed by another pause and repeated response. The leader then explicitly acknowledges the bumper harvest, adding that "God has blessed us," to which the people respond with Israel's far-reaching hope.

Psalm 68. Notoriously difficult, this "psalm" is best understood as a liturgical script. A ceremonial procession reenacts the bringing of God's ark to Jerusalem, and proclaims God's presence and power at his chosen shrine. On the way, song and recitation recall the glorious past, challenging surrounding peoples; divine deliverance is the theme (v. 20). All celebrate Israel's glorious God.

Taking up the ark with prescribed words (Num. 10:35–36; 2 Chron. 6:41–42), and warning any who oppose, the procession sets out singing praise. The exodus journey and its blessings are remembered as they walk. The ensuing battles are recalled next, in six echoes of the oldest war-song in Israel.

As the procession comes within sight of Zion's height, the theme changes to the envy of loftier mountains at God's choice of dwelling-place, and recalls David's establishing the ark there after great victories. This memory kindles fresh praise and hope of victory.

The procession, bearing the ark and representing all Israel, moves toward the sanctuary (described as from within the shrine, vv. 24–27). The whole company bursts into fresh song, celebrating the might of God over surrounding peoples. The ceremony closes with the ark again within the temple, and a summons to all the world to worship him whose power, like the skies, overarches all and thunders through all lands, while always ensuring strength to God's own.

Psalm 69. The opening plea is elaborated in a catalog of suffering, and the water-depths-floods image recurs ten times. Scorn, shame, alienation, insult, mockery at the meeting-place and in drunken song, pain, and distress are added; many enemies seek to destroy the psalmist, for no reason but hatred. Even God does not answer. The poet is brokenhearted, helpless, uncomforted.

Yet he suffers for God's sake, in zeal for God's house for he is God's servant. But he is conscious of guilt and folly, and fears lest something in his conduct bring disgrace on others who love God. He has repented with tears and sackcloth, only to be scorned, and has been chastened by God, only to become a byword. The enigmatic end of verse 4 may be a proverb for robbing-by-slander, but it appears to be a hint of what foolishly gave ground for false (or true?) accusation. Now the psalmist can only throw himself in despair upon the goodness of God's love, pleading that God will not turn from him. But his bitterness overflows in imprecation; may his foes get as they have given. A final piteous plea echoes verse 1.

Much here might recall Jeremiah's experience but for the guilt and the imprecation. The feeling and the plea would be understood by any good man who has made a mess of his life and finds it hard to return to piety.

Two closing stanzas adapt the personal

poem to public use. Verses 30–33 identify the ill-used penitent with God's people, or with the pious remnant under foreign occupation. A promise is added of worship better than sacrifices, when God answers his people's cry. Verses 34–36 add the assurance that God will hear, and will rebuild and repopulate the empty land, which suggests a date for these verses just after the disappointing return from Babylonian exile.

Psalm 71. The poet is old, and cannot forget it, looking back upon a checkered history (v. 20). Now wicked, evil, cruel men assail him, accusing him and seeking his death. He has no explanation. In the same way, his sources of consolation keep returning to him: his former refuge in God, his lifelong hope in God, his early training, his memory of past mercies. The old man's prayers, too, are scattered through the psalm, that he might not be shamed, forsaken, or deserted, but rescued, delivered, heard, saved. And so are his affirmations of confidence, for he is sure that God will again see him through present opposition to restoration and honor. When this confidence has been proved valid, the poet promises constant praise and testimony, that a new generation may know God as he himself has known him.

This somewhat incoherent record of thoughts and aspiration (much is quoted), set down as they come to mind, is itself a symptom of age. The old man's faith, testimony, and praise shine clearly through, and these, after all, fashion the crown of old age.

Psalm 72. When political changes made this psalm inappropriate for public worship, it was preserved as a description of the reign of the Messiah. The poem is a manifesto of the ideal society ruled as God intends.

Above all, social justice will prevail, banishing the oppression, corruption, and poverty that so often disfigured absolute monarchy in the ancient Near East. Justice will confer permanence and refreshing renewal (in v. 5 the Hebrew suggests such a king would be too feared for rebellion). Foreign peoples will gladly bring tribute or gifts.

The needy, weak, oppressed, and endangered will benefit from such social compassion. The wishes, prayers, and gratitude of the people will support this ideal social order; the result will be prosperity beyond measure and universal blessedness. Although God is not mentioned after verse 1, only God can achieve so marvelous a world. This, certainly, is the Bible's vision of the future for mankind.

But whether this is the poet's original purpose is doubtful. The Messiah is nowhere here identified or described. Verses 2b, 4, 9b, 12–14 show that in the mind of the poet the ideal age has not yet arrived. It could be that the poet gives expression to the vision and hope which sustained the hearts of Israel under later foreign rulers, details of the time and the expected ruler being purposely left vague; but one would expect a more apocalyptic tone in such a "resistance" poem. More probably, what was originally a coronation ode by a court poet, writing in typically hyperbolic style to please a new king and prophesying for him an unending dynasty, was found to serve admirably this later purpose, and so was preserved.

Book III (Pss. 73–89)

Psalm 73. Self-analysis can be wonderfully healing and nurturing, given sufficient honesty. The poet recognizes that while it is good to belong to the people of God, who (it is said) rewards the innocent, yet one's own heart may still be far from him. He frankly acknowledges, too, that the cause of his slipping away is plain envy. Verses 4–14 reveal how he had dwelt upon the careless ease and prosperity, the peace and pride, of the wicked, compared with his own self-torturing conscientiousness, rewarded only by chastening.

Such contradiction of all morality oppresses the psalmist. He keeps silent, lest he injure the childlike faith of those who believe that godliness brings gain and wickedness causes ruin. At length, entering the house of God brings understanding—not a malicious anticipation of coming destruction, but a realization of the insecurity of the sinners' position compared with his own immeasurable and permanent blessings. He has been senseless and brutish not to value privileges rightly. For he possesses God's constant presence, guidance, and hope. In heaven or on earth, nothing can surpass the privilege of knowing God, his strength now, his inheritance forever.

Which would he choose: a life prosperous but far from God, or a life near to God, filled with goodness, security, and a faith worth sharing?

Psalm 74. Why? . . . How long? . . . ring through this psalm with earnestness. The situation could not be more vividly described nor the emotions it provokes more eloquently expressed. Why? raises the contradiction between Israel's election and her apparent rejection. How long? focuses upon the mockery of the foe against the name and honor of God. The poet pleads that God will remember that the people are his and urges that God take his hand from his pocket and act in his own defense, as he has done before.

The echo of the Babylonian creation myth, the absence of prophets, and the backward look in verses 1, 3, 5–8, 10, and 18, suggest that the poem originated at the deportation of the exiles to Babylon or (probably) at their sad return. Once written, the cry could be repeated often in Israel's later years.

Psalm 75. The dialogue pattern of this psalm ("we . . . you say . . . I say . . . comment . . . as for me") is difficult to recover, but clearly in verse 1 a group gives thanks for God's past actions (perhaps just recited), and then recalls (or hears a prophet declare) an oracle in God's name. A lesson is drawn from a recent earthquake, which occurred suddenly and exhibited both God's judgment and his power to hold the earth safe upon its foundations (v. 3). To the deeply shaken people the oracle continues with solemn warning against arrogance and obstinacy.

Verses 6–8 seem to be a comment on the oracle. No one from east, west, or south, no one but God, can raise or bring down man. Changing the metaphor, the comment adds that God hands to all a cup of "ordeal" to drain, though it too makes them shake and stagger, so relentless is his resistance of the proud (cf. Num. 5:11–31; Isa. 51:17; Jer. 25:15–16). The original speaker (?) resolves to keep this warning before the people, so as always to humble the wicked and exalt the righteous, as God does.

Psalm 76. It has been demonstrated dramatically that God dwells in (Jeru)Salem, because there he has rendered useless all the weapons threatening the city, unnerved and overcome invading armies, laid still horses and chariots—in short, has uttered his rebuke, his anger, and his judgments, reducing the whole land to fear and silence. No wonder God is known in Judah, his great name acknowledged in ravaged Israel. What response could be more fitting than earnest vows and votive offerings to One so deserving to be feared (so "terrible," four times in Hebrew)—even by the great ones of the earth?

Detailed comparison with Isaiah 37:9–36 leaves little doubt that, like Psalms 46 and 59, this poem expresses the astonished awe evoked by the sudden overthrow of Sennacherib's army before Jerusalem, a memorable lesson to Israel.

Psalm 77. A distressed and sleepless night of groaning and weakness, with attendant musing, brings the psalmist only doubt and questioning. No explanation is offered, though spiritual desolation, unanswered prayer, and the sense of being out of divine favor and unloved, is clearer than illness or fear of death. With considerable spiritual insight, the psalmist suggests that relief comes when the questioning spirit turns outward from its self-communing to remember the miraculous deeds of God: to the ways of God repeatedly revealed in history, in miracles, and the redemption of Israel; to the immense convulsion of nature when God passes by in a mighty tempest.

The relevance of such memories lies in knowing that God's past acts and present power both focus in the redemption of his people—of whom, doubtless, the psalmist, despite all his personal questioning, still feels himself a living part.

Psalm 78. Israel's faith was historically founded upon truth made known through events. This distinguishes revelation from philosophy. It makes the preservation of the historical tradition in the context of worship all-important. Yet history can be distorted. After seven verses claiming reverent attention to the explanation of "things from of old" (v. 2) and expounding the sacred tradition as God commanded, the poet reveals a distinct moral intention—the listeners must not imitate their fathers!

But the fathers in question turn out to be the northern kingdom, Ephraim or Israel. Of the following sixty-four verses, thirty-five condemn Israel: disloyal, faithless to God, forgetful of his deeds, constantly caviling against God's power and provision, not trusting his deliverance, provoking his anger. Punished, Israel repented briefly, with flattery and deceit, presuming upon God's patience. Not even the plagues upon Egypt warned Israel of God's might, nor did his provision win their confidence. Even when settled in Canaan, they remained as treacherous as an unseasoned bow, abandoning God's shrine at Shiloh for idols, forfeiting the ark of the covenant until God abandoned them to enemies and to war.

The northern kingdom, Joseph, was therefore utterly rejected; God chose Judah for his foremost people, Zion for his dwelling-place, David for undershepherd. And how well David had led Judah!

Up to this point in this one-sided history, the name *Israel* means the northern kingdom, as though Judah had no part in past faithlessness and guilt. Now (v. 71) Judah is the true "Israel," descended from Jacob/Israel, God's faithful inheritance. The story ends there, because its purpose is fulfilled. The poem was written to justify the rejection of Israel, now deported to Assyria, and the election of Judah as God's people henceforth. It is history told as pious and patriotic propaganda against apostasy.

Psalm 79. The background of this psalm closely resembles that of Psalm 74, but here the temple is defiled rather than destroyed, and the viewpoint is contemporary rather than retrospective. This suggests a date soon after the deportation to Babylon. In nine verses it echoes other psalms, Micah, and Jeremiah; the language of the great catastrophe had become familiar.

To leave the dead unburied (v. 2) was an outrageous insult, and left the soul restless in Sheol; this was but typical of the enemy's mockery of God's inheritance, temple, city, and servants. Behind the scorn of men is the anger of God. The poet feels it is unjust not to punish nations more wicked than Israel; like Ezekiel he thinks it unfair to punish one generation for another's sins. The admission of present guilt is quite cursory (v. 9). The people's desperation, and God's own good name, call for divine intervention to forgive, avenge, and deliver those captured and condemned. The psalmist would have God repay sevenfold the evil that men have done; then God's own people, his flock, will praise him endlessly.

Psalm 80. The refrain (possibly sung by the congregation) and its growing title for God suggesting deepening earnestness, shows this psalm to be a plea born of serious danger. God is angry with Israel's northern kingdom, led by the tribes of Ephraim and Manasseh. Her prayer goes unanswered; tears, contention, and mockery afflict her; the land is plundered by strangers and ravaged by beasts; the people perish; God has left them. The description suggests the eve of the deportation to Assyria; salvation is still possible (so the refrain), but the future is ominous.

The essence of the psalmist's prayer is that God will turn the situation to salvation. This plea is clothed in two metaphors taken from the ancient blessing pronounced upon Joseph (Gen. 49:22–24: "a fruitful vine near a spring," "his strong arms . . . limber . . . because of the Shepherd"). From God the Shepherd (v. 1) the poet pleads for shepherdlike protection. The vine (vv. 8–11) had in Solomon's day reached from the Mediterranean to the Euphrates, but now it is withering; may God remember and protect it.

Special favor appears to be asked for Benjamin in the present peril. First Kings 12:20–21 suggests that Benjamin was first counted with northern Israel at the disruption, but was eventually incorporated in Judah, and so preserved. The psalmist's prayer is not granted—except for the favor shown to Benjamin. The cup of northern Israel's iniquities was too full.

Psalm 81. However these verses came together they now summarize the ritual of the Feast of Tabernacles, recalling the exodus and the wilderness journey and adding a contemporary lesson.

A call to celebrate sounds the appropriate music and response, and cites the ordinance (in v. 5, "against Egypt," as punishing her for oppressing Israel). All being assembled, a spokesman pronounces a divine oracle. The oracle first recalls the exodus, the freeing from slavery, rescue from oppression, recognition at Sinai, testing and promise at Meribah (Num. 20:2–13), the essentials of the covenant law, and the promise of full provision ("land of milk and honey"). This event, creating the nation, the Feast of Tabernacles reexperiences, in symbols.

But (the oracle-spokesman continues) the people did not listen. They suffered in consequence. If only they would listen, now, they would be delivered from their foes, who would come cringing before God (NIV; NEB before Israel), while Israel would be nourished (as promised) on wheat and wild honey, that is, she would flourish and prosper. "If only"—for the most eager celebrants of religious festivals do not always listen to what the festival celebrates!

Psalm 82. Here also God arraigns the "rulers" of other nations before the heavenly court for injustice toward the defenseless, the weak and ignorant, in their various lands, whose lives are shadowed and whose world is insecure because their society is corrupt. Despite their exalted status, they will die like men for their abuse of power. The psalmist urges that God execute this heavenly verdict on the earth also, since all nations belong to him.

Familiar now, this magnificent vision of God's universal righteousness needed Amos (chaps. 1–2) and Isaiah (chaps. 13–23) to expound it, but even they do not rise to this imaginative height, to see Israel's God charge all other gods, before the judgment of the universe, with failing to do justly or to love mercy.

Psalm 83. Judah is besieged, in mortal danger from cunning and united foes. Verses 5–8 describe encirclement: Edomites, Ishmaelites, Hagrites, Gebal, Bedouin from the eastern and southern desert, Ammon and Amalek from the northeast, Philistia and Tyre from west and northwest, and Assyria.

For encouragement, the psalmist turns to history to recall what God formerly did against two similar conspiracies (Judg. 5:19–21, 26; 6:33; 7:25; 8:10–12). So may God do to the present invaders, making them like tumbleweed rolling before the wind, chaff in a gale, fire in a forest, boats before a tempest, covering them with shame and disgrace. Thus they may discover that Israel's Lord is God of the whole earth.

Psalm 84. Pilgrims make their way to another New Year festival, to proclaim that God, under nine glowing titles, is Creator and King, and to pray at the end of the hot dry summer for the early rain that will herald another growing season. Verses 1–4 express that deeper spiritual thirst which prompts such pilgrimage, and anticipate the beauty and joy that await the journey's end.

In verses 3–4 the poet envies the privileged who dwell within those open courts, priests, servants, the very birds who nest there. But blessed, too, are those who set their hearts on pilgrimage, already finding refreshment on their way, and increasing in strength, not weariness, as they draw near to Zion and to God.

Arriving, the pilgrim-poet prays for a hearing, pleads for favor toward the king (note the parallelism in v. 9), and expounds upon the measureless privilege of spending even one day in the temple, or on the threshold ("doorkeeper," a position of prestige, should probably be "a beggar on God's threshold," contrasted with a guest in the tents of the wicked).

Adoring testimony and a further exclamation of blessedness close a heart-warming hymn of gladness in God.

Psalm 85. The opening acknowledgment of forgiveness, together with poor harvests presupposed by verse 12, provide the clue to this poem. The situation resembles that facing the returned exiles, described by Haggai, Ezra, Nehemiah, and Zechariah. The Hebrew of verse 1—"You brought again the captivity of Jacob"—confirms this background.

That God has forgiven the sins that caused the exile is clear from the people's return home. Yet their poverty, ruined villages, untilled soil, and spoiled pastures were intensely disappointing. It appeared that God was still displeased. Hence the earnest plea in verses 4–7. After all, no people can live on forgiveness alone.

The poet then speaks as though God has answered with firm promises of peace, salvation, and glory. The closing preview of that salvation is unsurpassed—reconciliation of heaven and earth, prosperity restored, a just order stretching like a shining path before God's feet. Forgiveness is *not* all.

Psalm 86. Most verses in this psalm can be paralleled from Exodus to Jeremiah, closely enough to suggest conventional religious language. In verses 1–7, eight petitions follow rapidly, each with its attendant reason, while verse 5 almost assumes that God should forgive! Even verses 8–10, fine though the sentiments are, have an air of formal acknowledgment, rather than of excitement, conviction, or joy.

The requests in verses 11–13 are again unrelated and low-key. The brief reference to deliverance from the grave has no strong feeling of relief; some think it metaphorical. One more noticeable request is verse 11c. Not until verse 14 is any immediate circumstance or need specifically mentioned, and then only cursorily; verse 15 (= Ps. 103:8) seems only slightly connected with it.

There is, of course, nothing wrong in what is stated or requested, except that it is predictable, largely borrowed, unconnected, devoid of sustained feeling. Consequently, the final request for a sign of God's goodness (even though chiefly to disconcert his enemies) is not unexpected. "Give us a sign" is ever the prayer of hearts unable to feel God always near and everywhere.

Psalm 87. Despite uncertainties, it is plain that God founded and loves Zion, city of glorious repute (vv. 1–3; gates distinguish cities from open villages). Rahab is here Egypt; Cush, the Upper Nile; verse 4 defines Israel's political world.

Verse 7 prophesies that many will find in Jerusalem all their motivation and joy, but whether singers, musicians, or dancers are meant, translators cannot decide.

The psalmist's main thought is of great pride in claiming Zion as one's birthplace. It expresses more than national or racial identity; it defines one's religious roots (the fountains of v. 7), the deep source of life's assumptions and initiatives.

Psalm 88. This darkest corner of the Psalter is a lament of unchecked despair, so complete that ancient and modern commentators often assume it is the nation in exile speaking (of which there is no hint), or that a redeeming final passage has been lost. The psalmist pleads to be heard, morning after morning; there is no suggestion that his prayers are answered. From youth he has been close to death, friendless, with companion and lover denied (suggesting lifelong leprosy). He comes to die, full of trouble, numbered already among those likely to go soon, weakening, his eyes failing (v. 9; note darkness three times). Worst of all, it has been all God's doing (ten times; the darker side of belief in divine sovereignty). God has rejected him, hidden his face, allowed his wrath to lie heavily upon him, his terrors to surround and engulf him.

There is no escape, only the prospect of Sheol—and there, God no longer remembers, or cares, or shows wonders, love, faithfulness. So the poet truly despairs; final darkness is the sole friend left to him (v. 18b, a line as awful as Job 17:14, where the grave provides the only family; other translations variously amend the original).

Thus a man nears the grave, after a sad life

unrelieved by any gleam of testimony, gratitude, praise, or hope; without any faith in that divine love and faithfulness of which he has heard, and can speak. What could the end be, but darkness?

Psalm 89. This poet has a serious argument with God. But he begins with a splendid festal hymn celebrating God's covenant love and faithfulness. A foretaste is given of what the argument is about (God's firm covenant with David's royal house) and the hymn is resumed with a bold description of God's unrivaled supremacy among heavenly beings, especially his faithfulness. On earth, too, God has shown might, subduing primeval chaos (see Ps. 74), creating and subduing all things by his power. Again, God is worthy of all praise; his righteousness, justice, love, and faithfulness delight all who enjoy his presence. God's favor makes his people strong, giving them a King for a shield.

Then the psalmist comes to the point. He expresses in eloquent poetry the substance and nine or ten details of the prophet Nathan's vision about the Davidic dynasty (cf. 2 Sam. 7). The emphasis falls heavily on God's promises "forever."

In spite of that faithfulness, that all-subduing power, that righteous character, these oaths and promises, Judah has been rejected, the covenant renounced, the crown defiled, Jerusalem plundered, David's current descendant humiliated. All has turned sour. God has broken his sworn word.

Verse 49 is the crux. Into the mouth of the present Davidic king the poet puts the demand, "How long?" (possibly young Jehoiachin, v. 45; 2 Kings 24:8–14, last of the free Davidic kings, exiled to Babylon).

The psalmist is asking, "You promised so much; what about it, Lord?"

Book IV (Pss. 90–106)

Psalm 90. Man's life is but a journey back to dust, dawn-springing grass bleached before evening, seventy or eighty years—a mere span, a bird's flight, a soldier's brief watch, a dream, a swift-flowing stream, ending with a sigh. Nor are the swift years trouble-free; sin and divine anger add terrors; the earlier years, affliction; and age, trouble and sorrow. It is all beautifully expressed, but deeply melancholy, and if that were all, profoundly pessimistic.

But the great backdrop of man's brief life is God's eternity. Man's home in all generations, from everlasting until everlasting, is God alone. The eternal God has shaped man's existence, judges man's achievement, and teaches wisdom by which to handle life's experiences. God has pity, shows covenant love, infuses gladness and justice into life. Even the creature's frail life finds meaning, as its Creator's favor rests upon it; otherwise it is indeed nasty, brutish, and short.

But the hunger for permanence will not be stifled. There are coming generations—may they too know God's splendor. And there is the work of men's hands—may it be established for the future. The poetry cannot hide the pathos. Old Testament faith reaches forward, but awaits further revelation before the heart of man can find a satisfying hope.

Psalm 91. In this rhythmic poem, strong assurance of security is offered to any who will take shelter in God, based upon the poet's personal experience. To this, God adds a footnote. So much is clear. Thereafter two interpretations are possible.

Jewish teachers recommended this psalm for repelling demons. Verse 5 avoids naming Lilith, the night-hag with her meteoric "arrow"; verse 6, Namtar, the night-demon of plague, striking down thousands. Dangers constantly threaten, at home or abroad. This later use of the psalm at least supports the view that it was written to discourage recourse to witchcraft. Instead, it urges men to dwell in the shelter of God, "Shaddai," under the protecting shadow, the mothering wings, the strong shield of God, with angel guardians against demons. In verses 14–16 God firmly underwrites this promise of his presence and protection.

The superstitious avoidance of dread names (with, possibly, rabbinic editing) made possible the more usual interpretation of the poem as a promise of complete immunity from more familiar forms of harm, both at home and abroad. On that understanding, verses 14–16 read like afterthoughts, when the assurance given was seen to be too sweeping. Complete immunity from harm is not the experience of the godly; but ultimate protection, answered prayer, and divine protection, and that satisfies the man of faith.

Psalm 92. The psalmist enjoys worship; the music, the remembrance of God's loving faithfulness, the reminder of God's deeds in history and his handiwork in nature, make for him a great day. This may account for the later Sabbath use of this psalm. Moreover, the reading of and meditation upon the Law recalls how profound God's thoughts are. Senseless people, who never worship, do not understand how insecure their lives are. They flourish in the world, it is true, but God remains God, and his enemies will perish; all evildoers will be scattered (like chaff?).

The worshiper has been uplifted and comforted. He has seen his opponents defeated, and the righteous flourishing (vv. 12–13) like graceful palms, like strong enduring cedars, fresh and fruitful in sheltered sacred courts (cf. Ps. 52:8). So they testify, to the end, the upright ways of God.

It is just not true that only the wicked flourish; the godly, too, have a good time!

Psalm 93. Never a maritime people, the Jews found the sea mysterious and awesome. This poet has watched wave after wave lift up and pound the shore, listened to their roar and crash, pondered their immeasurable power, and thought of God.

But is that impressive seascape all that stirs the poet's mind? After the Babylonian exile (and possibly before) the myth of God's struggles with chaos, the great deep, to establish the solid earth, was certainly known (cf. Pss. 74, 89, 104). Moreover, "the Lord reigns" was the watchword of the New Year festival's acknowledgment that God is King, his holy rule unending. The psalm thus became a festival carol for New Year, rejoicing again in the sovereignty of the Lord over nature and time.

Psalm 94. An urgent call is here addressed to God to avenge his crushed people, the oppressed, the widow, the alien, and the fatherless, who suffer at the hands of proud, jubilant, arrogant evildoers. The situation resembles that faced by Amos and Micah, in which an unscrupulous ruling class oppressed the defenseless in society, those whom the prophets insisted were God's special care.

Especially arrogant is the claim that God does not notice, or heed, which is answered by a simple but effective piece of logic (vv. 8–11). The man disciplined in God's law finds relief in such a time from the confidence that God will not forsake his people, but will execute justice in the end. All the upright live by that conviction.

The poet, however, seeks allies. He has known God's help in speaking out, in standing firm. But effective social protest requires support. The usual defense of all misgovernment, the argument that in a theocracy conscience must obey the rulers appointed by God, does not hold true (v. 20). God, who has defended the poet, will yet repay the wicked for their social sins, and destroy those unworthy of the authority they wield.

Psalm 95. The admittedly diverse sections of this psalm (vv. 1–7, 8–11) unite in the solemn purpose for which the congregation comes, with shouting, music, and song, before the Lord. The supremacy of God, as the One who made and owns the heights and depths of creation, is the theme of Sabbath worship, evoking reverent adoration and the quiet confidence of a flock resting in God's care.

Remember! The fathers' hardened hearts put God to the test; their waywardness showed that they had not learned God's ways. Not for them, therefore, was the inheritance of Sabbath rest. For forty years that generation wandered in the wilderness, and never entered Canaan.

To share God's Sabbath rest, it is not enough to crowd God's house; we must today hear his voice and not harden *our* hearts.

Psalm 96. If enthusiastic repetition is the mark of joyous, exuberant worship, this psalm, shared by the congregation, must have been a thrilling anthem, a spiritual experience.

Almost every form of worship is mentioned: song, praise, credal recital, ascription of glory and honor, offering, worship, "holy array," reverent fear, and declaration. Equally comprehensive are the reasons offered: God's "salvation," glory, deeds, greatness, creative power, splendor, majesty, strength, holiness, sovereignty, and (most of all) for an unjust, often oppressive world, the promise of his righteous judgment and equity.

Finally, the excitement of worship bursts forth from the sanctuary (assumed in v. 8) to include the joyous heavens, the glad earth, the jubilant fields, the wild creatures, and the wind-blown forest, because God comes. Comment is inappropriate; the only fitting response is to join in.

Psalm 97. As in Psalms 93 and 99 the phrase *the LORD reigns* brings to mind the annual acknowledgment of God's sovereignty at the New Year festival. Any such prolonged and repeated religious occasion needs a number of hymns, similar in content and varying only in emphasis. The Psalter contains several of these. In this version, traditional language (recalling God's appearing at Sinai, with volcanic accompaniments) describes the majesty and glory of the King. The familiar contrast of the living God with idols is repeated, and the joy of Zion and her villages at God's exaltation is mentioned again.

Emphasis falls on the righteousness, justice, and judgments of God. This absolute rightness of the God of Israel is the foundation of his sovereignty (v. 2), the theme of universal proclamation (v. 6), the reason for joy (v. 8), the source of light and joy for those who are righteous (vv. 11–12). The explanation lies partly in the characterless, unpredictable inconsistency of other nations' gods; partly in the widespread injustice, oppression, and disorder of society, for which the just judgment of God offered the only restraint or hope of cure.

Psalm 98. Another version of familiar festival themes is offered: the announcement that the Lord is King, the call to praise, the great deeds of God, his special relation to Israel, the repeated call to joy, the gladness of nature, the promise of righteousness (v. 9 = Ps. 96:13), and the world's interest in God's sovereignty (seven times).

If there is a special emphasis in this briefer New Year carol, it is upon music, instrumental worship, and shouting.

Psalm 99. The opening words again recall the New Year festival. In this variation of the festal hymn, "enthroned between the cherubim" indicates the ark as God's throne within the shrine. While God's righteous rule is mentioned (as in Ps. 97), and his sovereignty over the nations (as in Ps. 98), all emphasis here falls upon God's fair dealings with Israel, in answering prayer, guiding through the wilderness, and forgiving their sin while disciplining their waywardness (or, avenging their wrongs, v. 8).

Great names are recalled as witnesses to this divine justice, which in the refrain (vv. 3b, 5c, 9c) is expressed as God's holy character. Perhaps the author was a priest, to whom holiness was as important as righteousness would be in the thought of rulers. It may be, too, that names of past leaders—Moses, Aaron, Samuel—served to remind the people each year that the sovereignty of God which they were celebrating was represented on earth by his spokesmen to the nation, and the people's representatives before him. Politicians, priests, and prophets were still the divinely ordained sources of authority within society.

Psalm 100. An excited, joyous invitation, universal in scope, is extended to shout, worship, come, know, enter, give thanks, and praise, not as a duty but because God made us, shepherds us, is good, loving, and timelessly faithful. The only adequate response is acceptance.

Psalm 101. Sixteen good resolutions, in rhythmic pattern, almost certainly constitute a formal oath of office. Verse 8 suggests a king, with Jerusalem as the venue, though every local governor could so enhance his prestige with pardonable exaggeration. The vows cover private, domestic life (promising integrity, with no "swervings"—literally—toward "worthlessness," or idolatry); personal relationships (silencing slanderers, rejecting pressure from the arrogant who threaten or patronize, banishing liars, flatterers, deceivers, and employing only trustworthy men); and the daily work of administering justice, devoted to cleansing society of evil. Each promise is directly relevant to holding public office.

The presence in the hymnbook of this official declaration of intent confirms that the vows were made in God's presence, emphasizing that integrity in civil life constituted a religious duty.

Psalm 102. A heartbroken prayer for immediate aid is prompted by desperate sickness and fear. The psalmist's few remaining days are dispersing like smoke; fever, weakness, loss of appetite, and physical wasting are made more painful by great loneliness (like that of solitude-haunting birds) and by the taunts of adversaries, who use his pitiful condition as a curse upon others. His wretchedness is further embittered by a sense of God's anger and of abandonment after former favors. He feels the end is near.

Abruptly, he turns to the state of Jerusalem. Her condition too is desperate; she too needs compassion. The time has come to rebuild Zion, whose fallen stones and dust move devout hearts to pity (following Judah's deportation to Babylon?). But God will hear the city's prayer, appear in glory, hear the groans of prisoners and the condemned. Other nations will note and fear; future generations, even peoples yet unborn, will praise God for his compassion upon Zion, when they assemble there to worship.

But the individual's distress supervenes. His strength fails, like a runner's before the race is done. He pleads for time. God, after all, endures, older than earth and heaven, outlasting all things as the wearer survives his outworn clothes. So God will be the same to the children who will follow, and to their children after them. Though the individual passes, the generations continue—with God.

Is the central paragraph an insertion into a private poem? Or does the individual's distress impersonate the nation's sad condition? It seems too poignant to be mere metaphor. Or does the dying man, in loneliness and sorrow, reach out after permanence (cf. Ps. 90), and lay hold upon God's city and timeless cause, the unforgotten record of God's deeds, the generations to come who will share the same faith, the coming recognition of God's supremacy, and God himself? All these abide.

Psalm 103. Unless the six indications of returning health in verses 1–5 are literary or coincidental, the psalmist has been seriously ill, and now recovering resolves never to forget the goodness of God. But "all his benefits" (v. 2) reaches far beyond individual experience, to the interventions of God in a moral world on behalf of the oppressed and to the revelation given to Israel through God's activity.

God's benefits reveal his character, here described in one of the greatest passages in

Scripture as compassionate, forgiving, loving, gentle. Man's life span is brief as the flower's before the hot wind from the desert; but God's encompassing love is everlasting, his justice steadfast through the generations for all who keep covenant with him.

Behind the benefits and the character stands God's kingdom. Of course everything must praise him: the powerful messengers beside his throne, the hosts of servants everywhere obeying his commands, the works he does throughout his dominions, and the poet's grateful, awestruck soul.

Psalm 104. A godly man looks at the world about him and lifts his heart in spontaneous praise, rejoicing in the evidence, and the glory, of the Lord. A somewhat conventional moral remark (v. 34) intrudes but does not spoil this most magnificent survey of the beauties, order, and wonder of nature. Reverence prohibits description of more than God's garments, dwelling, carriage, and agents, but God's presence is manifest in the teeming world he made, sustains, and superintends.

Between opening and closing worship, the poet remembers, quotes, observes, and appreciates, with unusual perceptiveness and pleasure. Everywhere is beauty, order, wisdom, life, variety, provision, satisfaction, dependence. It follows that God is everywhere.

Psalm 105. In this historical psalm, all is sunlight and success, from Abraham through Jacob in the nomadic infancy of the nation, to Egypt and Joseph; through multiplying numbers under Moses and Aaron to the plagues that made Egypt glad when they left. The journey to Canaan is swiftly recounted, with everything easy, satisfactory, miraculous. In the lands of the nations they fell heirs to what others had toiled for, and all ended happily.

The immediate purpose of this liturgical recital of the story of the nation is to stir the people once again to thanksgiving, praise, glorying in God's name; and to the living faith which still looks to this covenant-keeping God and ever seeks his face.

Psalm 106. In Psalm 78 the sins that threatened to frustrate God's purposes are all blamed on the northern tribes; here the guilt of the past is ascribed to the whole people, and to the present generation (v. 6).

Some thirty instances are given of the failures of the chosen people, introduced by a reminder of God's enduring love. Those who maintain righteousness are blessed—but few; the psalmist prays that he may share that blessedness when at last the people are saved. The faults of Israel are fully recited.

So the psalmist, with the people ("us"), prays still that God will save and shelter, even yet; that Israel may "glory in your praise" (v. 47).

Book V (Pss. 107–150)

Psalm 107. Though highly wrought, this psalm of exhortation and testimony is earnest and moving. A double refrain (vv. 6, 13, 19, 28; vv. 8, 15, 21, 31) knits together four instances of God's intervention in distressing circumstances in answer to prayer. To the first two are added reasons, to the second pair exhortations (vv. 9, 16; vv. 22, 32). The basis of testimony is not here history but present experience.

The perils of desert travel were all too familiar. In answer to prayer, the fainting wanderers are led straight home; let them be grateful to God the Provider. Criminals brought to punishment and repentance are set free by prayer; let them be grateful to God the Liberator. Those who foolishly court sickness by gluttony and sin are healed and restored through prayer; let them show gratitude by sacrifice and testimony to the God of love. Those venturing to sea in tempests are through prayer rescued and brought to safe haven; let them exalt God the Deliverer.

Some argue that the change of pattern and of theme from gratitude to reward and punishment, shows that verses 32–43 form a different poem. The poet drops the pattern, however, just where it might become tedious, to make his main point another way. God is ever working such changes, by intervention in nature and by intervention in society. The wise, observing these things and remembering the great love of God, are prayerful and grateful.

Psalm 108. The oracle of verses 6–13 is valuable in any period of defeat. The introduction of Psalm 60 being too closely identified with one historical situation, a new opening is presumably here provided from the more confident Psalm 57.

Psalm 109. As prayer can rise to intercession, so it can sink to cursing, as this poem almost does. Never used in Jewish worship in later years, but recommended as protection against enemy conspiracy, it has even been regarded as a magic spell.

Malicious speaking, accusation, lies, and cursing are mentioned thirteen times, and their effects on body and spirit vividly described. The psalmist protests his innocence and remembers his former friendship with his accusers; he longs to hear God speak, dealing faithfully with him, turning cursing to blessing. He promises to praise God, who stands at his right hand to vindicate him. But he also asks for requital, even revenge.

Psalm 110. Varied translations make interpretation of this poem tentative. An oracle is pronounced, probably at a coronation, inviting the king to take a seat beside God in triumph, sharing divine authority. Extension of rule and willing armies (important to a new king) are assured, for the king possesses "sacred majesty" and was born to such dignity.

A divine oath also confers upon the new king priesthood (Gen. 14:18, cf. 2 Sam. 6:18; 1 Kings 3:4, 15; 9:25). Through him God will execute judgment on earth.

With the cessation of the Jewish monarchy, the notion of divinely appointed kingship centered in the coming Messiah. Jesus cited the opening words of this psalm to dissociate himself from this militaristic conception.

Psalm 111. This poem enshrines the very heart of wisdom theology. Twenty-two lines, alphabetically arranged and intended for recitation in worship (v. 1), dwell upon the works of the Lord. They are worth pondering, glorious and right, memorable and compassionate, generous, powerful, faithful, enduring, and redemptive. Nature, history, and covenantal religion all witness to divine activity. Surrounded by evidence of an active God, it is the very starting point of wisdom to live in the fear of the Lord.

Psalm 112. These twenty-two alphabetic lines supplement Psalm 111 by extolling the blessedness of fearing the Lord. It is not merely sensible, but also uncommonly profitable. The full implications of such "fear" are spelled out: uprightness, righteousness, graciousness, compassion, generosity, integrity, steadfastness, benevolence. So too are its benefits. The God-fearer's children come to influence; he prospers; he is illumined (NEB he is a beacon in darkness); good befalls him; he is secure; he grows in dignity. In contrast, the wicked envies the good. His life ebbs away and all his aims are frustrated.

Psalm 113. This first of the "Hallel" group of psalms seizes upon God's dramatic reversal of human conditions, as in raising the poorest beggars to mix with princes, or bestowing home and children upon the barren woman. The immediate occasion for this observation is lost to us, though both metaphors occur (among others with similar import) in Hannah's song (1 Sam. 2:5, 8). In public worship, the change in Judah's fortunes on return from exile could well find expression in such figures of speech. This particular manifestation of the condescending graciousness of God, glorious above all nations, is the reason given for praising the name of the Lord, at all times and in all places.

Psalm 114. The whole story of the exodus and the settlement in Canaan is here told in eight lines (vv. 1–3, 8; v. 2a includes Solomon's temple). In ironic, or playful, wonder the poet asks why the landscape reacted as it did to the coming of Israel, and provides the answer: because of the presence of God at the birth of the nation. By ending with the giving of water on the way, the poet adapts his leap of delight in the great story to the festivals of Passover and Tabernacles (when this psalm was used, and the need of rain was much in mind). But so perfect a lyric needs no practical excuse; its beauty is sufficient justification.

Psalm 115. The puzzled question in verse 2 occurs six times in the Old Testament, because Israel's neighbors had visible deities. To them, Israel's worship seemed to be offered to no one. A leader asks the pagans' question (apparently), and the congregation replies that Israel's God is spiritual and sovereign, adding a familiar credal affirmation of the helplessness and dumbness of idol gods.

Moreover their worshipers will grow like them. The leader then recites good reasons why the congregation, the priesthood, and the "God-fearers" (proselytes?) should trust in the living though invisible God (vv. 9–13), the congregation responding with verses 9b, 10b, 13b. A blessing follows. The congregation replies with a solemn declaration of faith and dedication.

Psalm 116. This poem tells an intensely personal story with moving clarity. Details apart, the heartfelt thankfulness that spontaneously asks "How can I repay?" and finds answer in public acknowledgment and private vow, still awakens echoes in devout souls.

Psalm 117. The two central emphases of Israel's religious experience—God's steadfast ("covenanted") love, and his faithfulness through all vicissitudes—here constitute her witness to "all . . . nations," in a brief exhortation somewhat resembling a doxology. The words may have closed a service, or perhaps some definite section of the liturgy.

Psalm 118. As with Psalm 68, the ritual "bidding" and close of this poem, with the change of pronouns, alert us to a liturgical pattern. An individual's testimony is greeted with a corporate response; further individual testimony is again answered unitedly; a third testimony ends with a request to enter the sanctuary (v. 19), which evokes a welcome. The promised thanksgiving is then offered, and the whole company exults.

All now enter the sanctuary with prayer,

being welcomed by those already within, and the festal procession moves with song and garlands to the altar. Twists of palm, willow, and myrtle twigs, and a marshaled circle (perhaps dancing) moving round the altar, are intended, as the Mishnah describes. The "horns" here mentioned formed a small ornamental fringe. The individual who has been welcomed makes his vow, and the assembly assents, with thanksgiving.

The twisted branches, later called "Hosannas" (which means "save us"), the reference to light (v. 27), and the traditional form of welcome mark the Feast of Tabernacles, for which this was an appointed psalm. The lone figure recalling military struggle, personal chastening, and God-given triumph, is probably the king, who thus makes the festival the occasion of his own acknowledgment of God's past help, and his own rededication among his people. In all, this psalm is a most impressive assertion of the close relation between religion and good statesmanship.

Psalm 119. Twenty-two eight-line sonnets, each line beginning with the same letter and mentioning God's "word," the sonnets strictly following the Hebrew alphabet, scarcely allow freedom for feeling, poetic fancy, or congregational fervor. One can hardly imagine any worshiping assembly chanting doggedly through so many pedestrian, repetitious, and often borrowed lines, so mechanically arranged. A set exercise for a student rabbi would better explain the repetitions, quotations, and air of contrivance.

Hence, probably, arise the twenty-seven prayers to be kept upright and pure, half-revealing early emotional conflicts; twenty-four requests to be taught, given knowledge, and judgment; a youthful (and typically student) reference to knowing and understanding more than all his teachers and elders and to his choice of an (unpaid) career in divine law.

God's self-revelation is mentioned in every verse, though modern paraphrases obscure this. Association of thoughts sometimes links verses (e.g., God's inward work, vv. 33–37), but no consistent analysis or discussion is discernible. Intense love for God's every utterance is evident throughout, as is the influence of Psalm 19; the writer is indignant toward compromisers, perhaps under postexilic heathen rule.

Psalm 120. The psalmist asks what God will do to the slanderers among whom he dwells. He offers the reply that God will pierce the arrow-tongued with deadlier arrows, and cauterize scorching words with glowing charcoal.

The slanderers' antagonism wears the psalmist down. His civil greeting of "Shalom" evokes only threats. He finds refuge in prayer (v. 1), and now (apparently, from the inclusion of this psalm among "Songs of Ascents") in the congenial company of fellow pilgrims.

Psalm 121. This song is a simple but beautiful assurance of divine care (lit. keeping, six times) amid all the perils of the pilgrim journey. The very mountains to which they travel symbolize that surrounding care for those who journey where God sends. We go our own way at our own risk.

Psalm 122. The excitement of the neighbors' initial suggestion (v. 1) is recalled in the greater excitement of arriving (v. 2). The first impression for the country dweller is of enclosure by streets and walls. This is the nation's rallying-point, where scattered tribes are enclosed in the unity of one worship and one law; it is the seat of justice and government, and above all, the national shrine. Patriotism, piety, and the sense of the unity of God's people from many places, combine in prayer for the city's peace and prosperity.

Psalm 123. When the world's high and mighty ones are intolerable, it is good to look above them. Jews under arrogant Gentile rule or among proud Gentile neighbors, have suffered continual ridicule, but they look higher, as a slave to his lord, as maid to mistress, in submissive trust before One higher than all. They know that God will look down from his throne not in contempt but in mercy. That effectively cuts the world's arrogant down to size. (Only the echo of Ps. 121:1 places this among the pilgrim songs.)

Psalm 124. In four metaphors of totally unexpected escape—from monster, torrent, wild beast, and snare—the poet urges Israel to acknowledge that only the Lord, Maker of all, rescues his own from attack by furious foes. Deliverance from overwhelming invasion, exile, or from Egypt under Moses, may be in the pilgrims' minds as they "ascend" to celebrate the truth that illumines all of Israel's history: "the Lord is on our side."

Psalm 125. As towering, unshakeable Zion is almost enfolded by hills, so God's people are immovable—despite the temporary rule of the wicked, which might entice even the righteous to compromise (v. 3). This thought might often occur to those visiting Jerusalem under foreign rule. The world is moral, in spite of appearances; the Lord befriends the upright and banishes the crooked; therein lies all hope of peace under pressure.

Psalm 126. The situation here presupposed (a great deliverance needing further help to be complete) and the language of verses 1, 5–6, recall Psalm 85. When God turned the tide of

Zion's fortune by bringing Judah back from exile, she felt like those rising from nightmare with glad relief. Even Gentile onlookers saw God's hand in so wonderful a deliverance. Now, facing new trouble, the poet asks God to "turn the tide" again (v. 4), as water rises in the summer-dried wadis of the south when the rains return. The metaphor is significant, for the desperate need of the returned exiles was for renewed pasture and fields in a ruined countryside. If God will thus be gracious, then just as every sad risking of the precious seed leads in time to the joy of harvest, so another hard experience for Judah will prove to have been a sowing-time, crowned with sheaves and songs.

Psalm 127. No "house" is well built, securely guarded, or provisioned without God. Without divine favor, all human effort is "in vain . . . in vain . . . in vain."

Psalm 128. A statement that all who fear the Lord are truly blessed leads into a wish, that the hearers may know such blessing in their lives as well. This may be a benediction upon pilgrims returning "from Zion" (v. 5). The blessing is at first domestic: prosperity, a good wife, sons like olive shoots around the parent tree, and spiritual well-being. But it extends to Jerusalem, to coming generations, and to the nation.

Relating domestic, civic, and national prosperity to the "fear of the Lord" is especially characteristic of the wisdom school in later Israel but characteristic also of Hebrew religion generally.

Psalm 129. A harvest scene inspired this poem. Since the exodus (her "youth"), Israel has been "bound tightly" like sheaves, scourged like plowed soil, and harnessed like oxen, by successive enemies. Yet she has survived, and has been set free. May future enmity, likewise, come to nothing—like the rootless grass on a flat roof which never fills a mower's hand, or the bosom of a harvester's robe, and never merits the customary blessing of the passer-by. The same metaphor, used by Isaiah (37:27) of Sennacherib's invasion, may reveal this poem's historical setting.

Psalm 130. Three remarkable spiritual insights match the earnestness of the psalmist. The only basis of plea, in the matter of forgiveness, is the divine character; no excuses are appropriate. Divine forgiveness evokes reverence, fear, and awe, whereas judgment instills only dread. Nevertheless, salvation is not always instantaneous; the penitent soul must often *wait* for blessing, longingly as night watchmen wait for the dawn, holding on to the divine promise (v. 5).

The final glance beyond personal penitence to Israel's need of mercy may well be a priest's reply, pronouncing absolution, when the personal prayer became a congregational confession.

Psalm 131. Has the poet watched a mother soothe a fretful toddler, envying its contentment? Putting aside pride, curbing ambition, restraining curiosity, and not letting one's heart be troubled, are his recipe for inner serenity, such as individuals and the nation long for.

Psalm 132. Ancient terms (vv. 2, 5, 6), changing pronouns, treasured quotations, and a hint of ritual suggest ceremonial commemoration of the origin of the temple, city, and throne. Verses 1–5 recall David's (unrecorded) vow to bear "hardships" in building the temple. But verses 6–7 recount the earlier removal of the ark from Kiriath-jearim to Jerusalem. The ark sanctified the temple, and the temple hallowed the city. This recollection is set within prayers for the current Davidic king.

In verses 13–18, God's spokesman responds with full assurance that city, shrine, and monarchy will remain forever. When the monarchy ended, this profound association of community, shrine, and throne was transferred to the future as the messianic hope.

Psalm 133. Family gatherings added joy to religious festivals and to the journeys involved. The resulting overflowing affection is here likened to the fragrant oil of Aaron's priestly consecration (Exod. 29:7; 30:22–30) and to the revitalizing dew, abundant as that which fell around lofty Hermon. Even so, in shared worship divine blessing refreshes and reconsecrates the life of the godly family, and ensures its continuance through coming generations.

Psalm 134. Night services may have been held at times in the temple (1 Chron. 9:33; Isa. 30:29), but this fragment is hardly sufficient for liturgical use. As the last "song of ascents," it is more probably a brief, formal farewell from the last worshipers departing at nightfall, spoken to the temple guards, and answered with the pious wish that blessing will follow them as they return home.

Psalm 135. According to the Mishnah, with this psalm on the morning of Passover Day the congregation and ministers are called to praise the Lord, because the Lord is good and praise is pleasant (NEB praise . . . is good, honouring his name . . . is pleasant). Then the great truths of Israel's creed are recited: her election, the greatness of God, his sovereign will in nature, Israel's deliverance from Egypt into Canaan. Choral voices (apparently) then celebrate the divine renown, affirming faith in future favors. A familiar contrast between the living God and lifeless idols leads to renewed exhortation to priests and people to unite in praise.

Little here is new, but grateful hearts love to rehearse familiar truths and recall great memories.

Psalm 136. This psalm is a review of God's actions in nature and history, similar to Psalm 135, but calling for thanksgiving (rather than praise) and recited (chanted?) responsively. The familiar refrain, in which "love" means covenant, steadfast, unchanging loyalty, reiterates the central theme of Israel's faith and experience.

Psalm 137. This psalm rehearses the intensely moving memory of exile, and of the insensitive demands for merry music amid bitter humiliation. The vigorous refusal invokes a curse upon the singer's skillful hand and voice if he so forgets Jerusalem. Now back home, the poet remembers also the malicious glee of neighboring Edom at Jerusalem's destruction and the barbarities of the invasion. Shocking though verses 8–9 are, such bitter anger is the natural response to appalling cruelty, until grace refashions human nature.

Psalm 138. Prayer toward the temple (recalling 1 Kings 8:48; Dan. 6:10) and before the "gods" confirms the exilic setting of this poem, but something has happened that stirs wholehearted praise for God's faithful keeping of his word. When the event becomes known, all earthly rulers should praise the Lord's ways. The lesson of the event is the Lord's watching over the lowly, his protection of his own amid continuing trouble, and the ultimate fulfillment of his purposes. But all is not yet accomplished; hence the prayer (v. 8c). Any incomplete deliverance might prompt such a psalm, but no situation fits it better than the eve of return from Babylon, with permission granted but the journey to complete—hence the last line. God has sustained in the midst of trouble; now he is about to fulfill his promise of return. How exiled hearts would thrill with gratitude!

Psalm 139. This psalm represents the peak of the Psalter, the maturest individual faith in the Old Testament, and the clearest anticipation of the New. All the marks of intimate friendship—detailed knowledge, reading of minds, a hand on the shoulder to encourage or check—are here ascribed to God. His companionship is unbroken; even the occasional attempt to hide from God is frustrated.

Nor did this divine intimacy begin with conscious life. God himself fashioned the poet's soul, his body, and his coming days, before his birth.

Again the psalmist marvels at God's detailed, weighty, and uncountable thoughts about him. Nevertheless the psalmist cannot deny the evil in the world; he hates it wholeheartedly and wishes that God would remove it. In this instance, the poet counts God's enemies as his own. But he knows that evil can infect his own heart also, and so ends with self-searching prayer.

In its sense of the omnipresence of the divine Spirit, its delight in walking daily with God from birth to death, and its awareness of the need for inner holiness, this psalm truly stands alone.

Psalm 140. The postexilic conflict between strict and lax Jews is betrayed here by the identification of the "poor" and "needy" with the "righteous" and "upright." Hence the harsh charges of plotting, slander, violence (when argument fails), pride, and attempts to trap the pious; religious quarreling always brings out the worst in both sides. Hence, too, the prayer that the compromising "liberal" party will not succeed (vv. 8, 11) for society's sake; it is no merely personal contention. In the prayer-curse (vv. 9–11) both falling coals and the pits (of hot asphalt?) recall Sodom. Verses 12–13 breathe the only spirit in which unavoidable religious strife may be reluctantly pursued.

Psalm 141. The poet's earnest cry to be preserved from temptation is abundantly clear. He would make his private prayer as solemn as evening sacrifice in the sanctuary. Under pressure, he pleads for guarded speech, an innocent heart, strength to refuse enticements, and the hospitality of evil men. He prefers the rebuke, even the blows, of the good to the blandishments of the evil. But most of all, his refuge in a life beset by snares is in God, who will keep him secure while the wicked entangle themselves in evil.

Similarity to Psalm 140 in language and feeling suggests the same background. But here the poet admits to feeling enticed. The danger lies within himself, as well as in the social pressures of the time. This reveals shrewd self-understanding and a wise reaction.

Psalm 142. Sharpest among the sorrows of this beset soul is the sense of being abandoned. No one stands beside him in his emergency. He is faint-hearted, fearful of danger, in desperate need, pursued, in prison, and alone. So he turns passionately to God. He tries to reassure himself with familiar affirmations, and promises praise when he is set free. Most of all he longs for evidence of God's favor which will bring the righteous to his side. In God's understanding, God's deliverance, and good men's support, is all his hope.

Some have thought the psalmist's trouble was all in his mind. The author of the heading thought the poem reflected 1 Samuel 22:1–2 and chapter 24, although David's "cave" was neither a prison nor lonely. The poem could express the longing of anyone feeling wrongfully used and forsaken; its vagueness makes it universal.

Psalm 143. Two themes run through this urgent plea. The writer is pursued, crushed, "darkened," faint, dismayed, beset, in danger of death. He urges that his foes be silenced and destroyed. He is plainly hard-pressed and frightened.

But his cry is also for mercy, relying on God's faithfulness alone; he cannot face God's judgment. He seeks comfort from the past, but needs a present blessing to slake his spiritual thirst. He begs for a quick answer, an early (morning) reassurance, especially that God will not turn away. He acknowledges his need to be shown God's way, taught God's will, helped by God's Spirit to walk safely. He is, as plainly, spiritually despondent and penitent.

Psalm 144. Verses 1–4 offer praise to God, tutor in warfare, for some recent victory. Verses 5–8 adapt the traditional language of theophany, used as testimony in Psalm 18:7–16, into prayer for deliverance from lying, treacherous enemies. Verses 9–10 promise new praise (perhaps in contrast with the traditional words just used) to the Giver of victory to the Davidic dynasty. Verses 11–15 repeat most of verses 7–8 to lead into an eloquent description of peace and plenty enjoyed by the people of God.

How these four items comprise one poem is difficult to decide. Glowing praise for victory and repeated pleas for deliverance sit oddly together. Nevertheless, the conclusion stands. In war and in peace, blessed are the people whose God is the Lord.

Psalm 145. The psalmist is evidently thinking of the continuity of faith and testimony through the generations to the present (vv. 4–7)—especially of testimony to God's wide dominion (vv. 11–13), his care for all that he has made, and his compassion toward the sinful, the fallen, the bowed down, and all who cry to him for help.

This psalm appears in ancient copies with refrains for antiphonal recitation. God is here known as active, compassionate, faithful, generous, good, gracious, great, judge, king, loving, majestic, near, powerful, righteous, and watchful.

Psalm 146. This first call to praise concentrates upon what God is, as shown by his gracious activities. Its immediate occasion appears to be the failure of some prince's promise, though the cause is his unexpected death. The poet contrasts the faithfulness of God to all generations with men's impermanence. But his emphasis falls upon God's lovingkindness. The God of Jacob (= "Israel," and the distant past) and of creation (v. 6) is wonderfully described as the hope of all in need of care and protection. Confronted with such enduring goodness, what can man do but praise?

Psalm 147. This second call to praise concentrates upon what God has done and is doing. Verses 2–3 suggest as background one of the happier periods of the postexilic years. Thereafter, God's activity in nature, evoking wonder, is mingled with his activity in history, evoking gratitude, especially from his privileged people. God's understanding in nature extends to understanding men and their ways. He provides for all creatures, but delights most in men who respond in fear and trust. Hence his protection and provision for Jerusalem. His word achieves marvels in nature, yet even this is nothing compared to the words he has given to Israel. What can Israel do, but praise?

Psalm 148. The third call to praise gathers into one great choir all that God has made in heaven and on earth—and a splendid chorus of worship they offer. People, from kings to children, must join in; but above all *his* people, close to his heart.

Here is a joy in all moving, living things, as God's delightful world, that is yet totally free from nature-mysticism; for God commanded and they were created, and his decree holds all in being. In such a world, everything prompts praise.

Psalm 149. This fourth call to praise is addressed to God's own. We move out of history and nature into the assembly of the saints. All is joy, movement, and music, in honor of Israel's Maker and King, who delights in his people. Such joy will linger through the night.

But the mood abruptly changes. The song on the lips is accompanied by the sword in the hand, to inflict punishment in God's name. This is "the glory of all his saints," and we are sharply reminded that we are still in the Old Testament.

Yet the word *saints* and the use of "humble" or "meek" in parallel with "his people" (v. 4) recall the postexilic struggle of the pious against the compromisers in the days of the Maccabeans.

Psalm 150. Possibly composed to close Book V and the whole Psalter, this "Hallelujah Chorus" calls for the fifth time upon heavenly and earthly worshipers to join in praise. The precentor calls first upon strident ram's horns; then upon sweet-plucked lyres and harps to join them; then for percussive hand-drum and feet-tapping dancers. Next the larger guitars (?) and melodious flutes add to the swelling sound. Then he brings in the thin copper ("eastern-sounding") clappers, and the large metal cymbals, all sounding together. Finally, the waiting congregation gets its cue, and angels, orchestra, and congregation join in a ringing shout of praise. All the vicissitudes of experience, the changing moods of faith, are eclipsed by the goodness and greatness of God. Hallelujah! Even the Psalter can go no further.

SELECT BIBLIOGRAPHY

Anderson, A. A. *The Book of Psalms.* The New Century Bible Commentary. Grand Rapids: Eerdmans, 1981.

Eaton, J. H. *Kingship and the Psalms.* London: SCM, 1976.

Ringgren, H. *The Faith of the Psalmists.* Philadelphia: Fortress, 1963.

PROVERBS

R. K. Harrison

INTRODUCTION

The Book of Proverbs belongs to the group of Old Testament books known as the Wisdom Literature, the others being Job and Ecclesiastes. Each book deals with the theme of wisdom in a different way. The subject dominates the Book of Proverbs, the stated purpose of the book (1:2) making this aim abundantly clear. Proverbs contains considerably more teachings and sayings about wisdom than Job and Ecclesiastes combined, and thus furnishes the reader with many insights into the activities and traditions of Israel's "wise men," who composed and collected them.

The question then arises as to exactly who these sages were, and for an answer it is best to look at the ancient Near Eastern cultural background as a whole. It is important to recognize that the Hebrews and their Scriptures were part of a multilingual and multicultural environment. In earlier generations all that was thought necessary for an understanding of Scripture was a knowledge of its contents. But as a result of modern discoveries in the areas of ancient languages, cultures, social relations, religion, and so on, it has become apparent that there are many things in Scripture which need to be understood in the light of conditions obtaining in the various periods to which the narratives refer.

Thus ancient Hebrew terminology can be clarified when equivalent words or phrases can be identified in Sumerian, Babylonian, Egyptian, or Canaanite sources. The same is true for the wise men of antiquity. They were not restricted to Israel, but could be found in the royal courts and centers of learning in all the Near Eastern countries. Some of their sayings, as with the legacy of Sumerian, Babylonian, and Egyptian sages, were current before the time of Solomon. The composing and preserving of proverbs seems to have been a cultural pursuit of royal courts, scribes, and priests, as well as educated or professional people who coined proverbs out of their life's experience. Predominantly, however, the nurturing of wisdom was the function of the king and his royal court. Interestingly enough, some of this traditional lore was intended to educate successors to the throne in their future duties, or to instruct members of the court in matters of protocol.

For example, an Egyptian document written by or for a pharaoh for the benefit of his son and successor, Meri-ka-re, coming from the unsettled First Intermediate period (ca. 2280–2000 B.C.), instructed him in the principles of justice: "Do justice as long as you live on earth. . . . Beware of punishing wrongly, do not kill . . . do not trust in a long life." The preface to *The Teachings of Amenophis,* which is dated about 950 B.C. and is roughly contemporary with Solomon, commences as follows: "The beginning of instruction on how to live, guidance for well-being . . . rules for a courtier, ability to refute an accuser, and to bring back a report to one who has sent him. . . ." Sometimes the recipients were addressed familiarly as "my son," a tradition followed in Proverbs, and the general intent of the instruction was to groom a person for success in life. But some of the ancient wisdom sayings had to do with moral problems such as suffering and evil.

A Babylonian text from about 1400 B.C. asks why the righteous suffer: "In my youth I sought the will of my god. . . . My god decreed poverty instead of wealth. . . . A rogue has been promoted but I have been demoted. . . ." An unknown Egyptian writer, also from the First Intermediate period, expresses disapproval of the contemporary moral scene in dialogue form: "To whom shall I speak today? Brothers are evil . . . hearts are rapacious . . . everybody appropriates his neighbor's property . . . goodness is neglected everywhere. . . ."

Instructional writings of the wisdom variety formed part of the curriculum in Sumerian and Egyptian scribal schools, and in both cultures they go back to an early period. Since such proverbs were often composed in temple schools, or at least in an environment controlled by priests, they were an essential part of the national religious tradition, and should therefore not be considered strictly secular compositions.

Inevitably a good deal of common ground is exhibited when moral issues are being discussed, whatever the particular cultural background, if only because the fallen nature of humanity has remained constant throughout history. Consequently it should hardly be surprising that problems and issues raised in the Old Testament wisdom books are matched by similar concerns in the wisdom writings of pagan nations. Thus while the problem of the righteous sufferer is dealt with in a Babylonian composition entitled *I Will Praise the Lord of Wisdom* against a polytheistic background, the author reaches conclusions regarding obedience and trust that have elements in common with the Book of Job. The latter, however, is a far more thorough and systematic examination of the whole issue of the righteous sufferer against a background of monotheistic covenantal revelation.

One of the most outstanding wise men in Israelite history was Joseph, who as a prisoner in Egypt was promoted by God's help until he was second only to Pharaoh in importance (Gen. 41:33–44). By his divinely given gift of wisdom and insight he was able to make adequate provision for a forthcoming famine, and when he died his life was recognized by the supreme accolade of that land for a life well lived: "Joseph died, being an hundred and ten years old" (Gen. 50:26 KJV).

The first formal contact that the Israelites seem to have had with pagan wise men was just prior to the exodus, when Moses and Aaron confronted the court counselors, sorcerers, and magicians of Egypt (Exod. 7:11). At first these individuals could match the miracles of Moses and Aaron, but ultimately they reached the limits of their ability (Exod. 8:18). The tradition of wise men as advisors was initiated in Israel by Moses, who was instructed to select wise, understanding, and reputable men (Deut. 1:13) to assist him in the wilderness period. When the Israelites had occupied Canaan, they discovered that women also shared in the wisdom tradition. Thus there were "wise women" in the court of Sisera (Judg. 5:29) who were companions to his mother, but unfortunately the answers they gave to her questions were completely false, and were derided as such in Deborah's victory chant.

King David had a highly credible counselor named Ahithophel (2 Sam. 15:12), whose wisdom seemed to be of divine origin (2 Sam. 16:23). But during Absalom's revolt Joab sought the assistance of a wise woman of Tekoa (2 Sam. 16:2), while Absalom subsequently consulted Hushai (2 Sam. 16:16) and Ahithophel himself (2 Sam. 16:20). Another wise woman of this period lived at Abel (2 Sam. 20:16), and by negotiating with Joab she delivered the city from destruction. Solomon as king was the exemplar of wisdom, as his dying father David perceived (1 Kings 2:6, 9), having requested wisdom from God in a vision (1 Kings 3:9). This gift made Solomon's wisdom surpass that of all the people of Mesopotamia and Egypt combined (1 Kings 4:30). Rehoboam disregarded the advice of Solomon's senior court officials (1 Kings 12:6–9), and consequently the kingdom was divided into two unequal sections. Similar royal counselors existed in the days of Amaziah of Judah (796–768 B.C.), for on one occasion a prophet was reviled for presuming to act in that capacity (2 Chron. 25:15–16).

Isaiah was probably referring to court counselors who were trusting in Egypt rather than in God (29:14–15; 30:1–5), while Jeremiah (18:18) and Ezekiel (7:26) also seem to be describing senior court advisors. In the exilic period Daniel proved to be a second Joseph, rising by God's power to become chief of all the Babylonian sages (2:48), and ultimately one of three rulers of the kingdom (6:2). For Hosea it was divine wisdom that enabled a person not merely to know what the Lord's will was, but more particularly to follow it unswervingly (14:9). Wisdom was to be a special attribute of the messianic ruler to descend from David's line. The Spirit of the Lord would rest upon him, bestowing divine wisdom and understanding, the spirit of counsel and might, the spirit of knowledge and the fear of the Lord (Isa. 11:2). When Jesus came he proved to be the "man poor but wise" who "saved the city by his wisdom" (Eccles. 9:14), redeeming human beings from bondage to sin by his atoning death. On this redemptive basis Paul could thus describe Christ as "the power of God, and the wisdom of God" (1 Cor. 1:24 KJV).

Having now seen something of the nature and scope of wisdom in Near Eastern antiquity, it is necessary to understand the meaning of the word. The Hebrew term *ḥokmāh,* which is most commonly used for wisdom, is rather like the Greek *aretē* ("excellence," "skill") in exhibiting a range of meaning from the purely practical to the moral. The earliest Near Eastern understanding of "wisdom" was that of skill or ability in performing tasks, whether as a carpenter, shipbuilder, jeweler, or other craftsman. Subsequently it was applied to a person of administrative ability, and also to individuals such as rulers or military personnel who exhibited perception or foresight in the affairs of state. With this shift from the practical to the cerebral, the way was opened for wisdom to be regarded as a moral or spiritual quality which graced the character of the person possessing it. In Mesopotamia these sequences doubtless followed one another in rapid succession, and the same was probably true of Egypt which, though it did not have an assemblage of wisdom writings as such, still recognized a utilitarian type of school teaching text as well as the more moral ones that taught justice or truth.

The same tendency is found in the Old Testament. *Ḥokmāh* can refer equally to skill in making cloth (Exod. 35:26), the fabricating of metal or wood (Exod. 31:1–5), fighting in battle (Isa. 10:13), sailing a ship at sea (Ps. 107:27), and exercising political leadership (Deut. 34:9). At its highest metaphysical level wisdom is understood to be a divine attribute (Job 38:26). Clearly the wise persons in Israel who were mentioned previously had some form of insight or perception, whether it consisted of natural talent or the sort of revelation given by God to his servants the prophets. It certainly expressed itself in the area of administrative recommendations or decisions, although the effect of some of them, as with Ahithophel, raises questions as to the character of the "wisdom" undergirding such activities.

After the return from exile, the Judean community was established firmly on the basis of the Mosaic law as the result of the efforts of Ezra and Nehemiah. At that time it became acceptable for wisdom to be identified with the Law or Torah (lit. instruction). While it is therefore possible to entertain the idea of various meanings of the word *wisdom,* it is important to avoid the notion that such differences exhibit a uniform development of a monolinear kind, moving from the purely secular to the metaphysical. Those persons who were unwilling or unable to contemplate wisdom in a purely abstract sense were afforded the opportunity of personifying it as an entity that was established from the beginning and was in fact present when the cosmos was created (cf. Prov. 8:22–31). But such personification leads to theological difficulties for a strictly monistic covenant faith. Unless it is thought of as treating wisdom as a surrogate for God, it could be interpreted as adding another person to the Godhead, which destroys the monotheistic concept. Yet if it is actually a genuine personification, how can wisdom be considered part of the divine nature when it is being depicted as the whole?

The interpretation of wisdom as a female instructor who wanders about the city trying to attract people, presumably men, to accept her offer of health, wealth, happiness, and the like, is considerably less suspect theologically. At the least it removes any involvement with the Godhead, but it also reduces wisdom to a more pragmatic level by presenting it as the means to an end which has material as well as moral components. Precisely why this teacher is female is uncertain, aside from the feminine gender of the Hebrew word, since Israelite women did not engage in the formal instruction of adults, a tradition that was reinforced in the early church (1 Tim. 2:13). In fact the image of wisdom as a woman trying to promote her virtues is the inverse picture of a harlot peddling her favors, and perhaps this constituted the underlying subtlety of the personification.

Having examined the common word for "wisdom" to determine its meaning and usage, attention must now be devoted to understanding the concept of a proverb. The Hebrew term *māšāl* is thought to have come either from a root meaning "to rule," or one signifying an act of comparison. But at best these suggestions furnish only a general understanding of what a proverb was and how it functioned. Unfortunately *māšāl* was used in a variety of ways, and hence it could apply to a pithy utterance enshrining some aspect of experience; to a lengthy pronouncement intended as formal instruction for the hearer; to a general discourse; to a scornful remark that summed up a particular situation reasonably well.

The first of these four meanings can be illustrated by Proverbs 15:20, "A wise son brings joy to his father, but a foolish man despises his mother," or Proverbs 17:3, "The refining pot is for silver and the furnace for gold, but the LORD tests the hearts" (NKJV). In the first of these there is a decided contrast, while in the second the thought moves from practical experience to a corresponding moral or spiritual activity. The force of the saying in each case is heightened by the introduction of contrast.

The understanding of a proverb as comprising systematic instruction, with or without warnings, can be seen in Proverbs 3:1–35, where the benefits that the exercising of wisdom brings are extolled. A straightforward discourse on a topic related to wisdom is illustrated by Job 27:1–23, where Job continues his *māšāl* in the form of an address dealing with personal moral integrity. The final division, that of the sarcastic or taunting remark, occurs at intervals throughout the Old Testament, as in 1 Samuel 10:12, where Saul's ecstatic outburst was assessed by the terse question, "Is Saul also among the prophets?" Jesus anticipated his audience's criticism of his activities by quoting the proverb, "Physician, heal yourself" (Luke 4:23).

While the four varieties mentioned here give some idea of the range of meaning which *māšāl* could embrace, they do not exhaust the character of the proverb, since, for example, they do not include such mental exercises as the riddle (cf. Judg. 14:12–14). Consequently any attempt at mechanical classification of such sayings, however detailed it may be, must be regarded with caution, since ultimately the meaning of the *māšāl* can be determined only by the situation in which it is used. The Septuagint translation of Proverbs is unhelpful in understanding the nuances of *māšāl,* since it normally renders the term by *parabolē,* which actually designates only one type of wisdom material.

The great antiquity of wisdom sayings has been noted already, and would suggest that the proverb as such emerged as an early product of human interaction. The Sumerians were adept at observing behavior and crystallizing its foibles in short, telling utterances. More than a millennium later, a celebrated collection of Mesopotamian wisdom sayings known as *The Words of Ahikar* became popular throughout the Near East. It is significant for the present study because some of the sayings parallel certain parts of the canonical Proverbs. Many verses of the didactic portion of *Ahikar* commence with the phrase *my son,* familiar also in the Book of Proverbs. *Ahikar*'s wisdom is predominantly secular in tone, however, and thus lacks the theistic spirituality of the biblical book. In that respect the Egyptian wisdom writings are similar to the work of Ahikar, since they are concerned primarily with making the successful life.

The proverb probably owes its origin to an attempt to intellectualize some of the paradoxes and contradictions of human life. In that event the proverb need not have been significantly different on occasions from the humorous remark or allusion, since both come from a common ground of human interaction. It is therefore highly probable that some of the ancient proverbs were greeted with gusts of laughter or howls of derision, depending upon how aptly the essence of the situation was portrayed. If this assessment is correct, the traditional picture of solemn-faced men sitting in a group and coining proverbial sayings of somber significance may need to be revised.

In the same way it is conventional to think of proverbs having originated predominantly in court circles, but since individuals of social standing were satirized frequently in Mesopotamian proverbs, it seems likely that some of the ancient aphorisms came from the observations of people living and working outside the bureaucratic circle and represented their comments on that particular way of life. In other respects a goodly number of proverbs were based upon observed facets or patterns of nature, while others reflected the skills of specific craftsmen such as goldsmiths, silversmiths, and jewelers, who were able to furnish a moral interpretation for aspects of their crafts. Yet moral observations were available for anyone who surveyed human conduct at all carefully, as illustrated by the saying: "From evildoers come evil deeds" (1 Sam. 24:13). When David was quoting this proverb in a confrontation with Saul, he described it as a "proverb of the ancients," thereby illustrating the currency which some of these rather ordinary perceptions claimed in antiquity.

The coining of proverbs in Israel seems to have been at its height at the beginning of the Iron Age II period, that is, about 1000 B.C. When Solomon became king of Israel, neighboring nations were largely inactive, both militarily and politically. Solomon's outstanding reputation for wisdom would obviously attract people to his court besides the queen of Sheba, and it may well be that an important form of diversion in the royal circle consisted in imitating the practical wisdom of the Egyptians. If *The Teachings of Amenophis* was written about the beginning of the Nineteenth Dynasty (ca. 1300 B.C.), it would have acquired sufficient veneration to have established a pattern for such pragmatic advice, and not least because there seem to be points of contact between it and the Book of Proverbs. There is no reason to doubt that Solomon was the author of many proverbial sayings, especially those that have to do with the conduct of rich people. It seems equally probable that Solomon's counselors (cf. 1 Kings 12:6) played a part in formulating them, so that in some cases authorship would have been a conjoint effort. This would have occurred if the various sayings were constructed on the basis of one person making a statement, and another one, or perhaps several persons, suggesting either a synonymous response, which agreed with the initial proposition, or an antithetical one, which introduced contrast by presenting an opposite set of conditions. The ancient Hebrews were highly proficient in poetry, as indicated by the fact that two-thirds of the Hebrew Bible was written in poetic form. Hence Solomon and his courtiers could have exercised their minds profitably by formulating such maxims as have been preserved in the Book of Proverbs.

The literary form of the book follows to some extent that of the secular aphorisms in the Near East. The shortest proverbs consisted of one line only, and these seem generally to have been very early, such as the proverbial reference "Like Nimrod, a mighty hunter before the LORD" (Gen. 10:9), which occurs in an ancient portion of Semitic history writing. But the most common form comprises two lines and follows a pattern found in the psalms that allows the proverb to have been written according to one of three forms of literary parallelism. The first is known as synonymous parallelism, where the second line supports and emphasizes the thought of the first (cf. Prov. 6:4). The second, antithetic parallelism, brings a distinct contrast in the second line to the thought of the first, so that together they present opposite positions in the one aphorism. The second line of such a construction usually begins with "but," which introduces the contrast (cf. Prov. 10:7), and is a feature of those maxims attributed directly to Solomon. The third literary form is normally described as synthetic parallelism, in which the second line not merely reinforces the thought of the first but actually adds to its meaning and content (cf. Prov. 18:8).

There are variations and additions to these basic patterns, of course. A proverb may be expressed as a figure of speech, which conveys poetic grace and heightens the general effect. Similes are generally introduced by "like" or "as," either of which may be explicit (cf. Prov. 10:26) or implied (cf. Prov. 25:25). Direct comparison, which favors wisdom over other things in life, is used to encourage persons to follow wise ways of living (cf. Prov. 15:16). Sometimes the first part of a proverb contains a number, to be followed in the next part by the next highest integer, as with Proverbs 30:18: "There are three things that are too amazing for me, four that I do not understand." This is the so-called numerical ladder, which is seen elsewhere in Job 5:19 and Amos 1:3–2:6. The succeeding number points to the most important item on the list, which is in Proverbs 30:19, "the way of a man with a maid" (KJV). An elegant style of Hebrew poetry was introverted parallelism, in which two successive statements were repeated in reverse order, as in the Hebrew of Proverbs 3:10.

Some proverbs are strictly prohibitive in nature, corresponding to the categorical commandments of the Law (Exod. 20:13–17). Others, while emphatic, are positive in nature, urging the listener to heed instruction so as to obtain a better life (cf. Prov. 19:20); these are generally regarded as admonitions. They are different from a simple categorical prohibition in furnishing a rationale for the proposed course of action. In this manner the admonition proverbs supply a practical aspect to the theoretical concept of wisdom. Such a proverb is thus not just an attractive idea, but a form of motivation which produces positive, beneficial results in a person's life. The various proverbs coined in Israel became a fundamental part of the national literary heritage and were reflected on numerous occasions in the teachings of Jesus (cf., e.g., Matt. 7:13–14; 10:24; 12:25, 33; Mark 9:43–47). This tradition was also followed in the New Testament epistles (cf., e.g., Rom. 12:9–21; Gal. 6:7–11; Eph. 5:21–6:9; Col. 3:18–4:1; James 3:1; 4:7–10).

The Hebrew title of the book is "the proverbs of Solomon," and this was rendered in the Greek Septuagint by *Paroimiai* (Proverbs), although elsewhere in the Greek text the Hebrew *māšāl* is normally translated by *parabolē* (parable). In classical Greek *paroimia* meant a "by-word," "common saying," or "proverb," and was the preferred term used in the fourth Gospel for *parabolē* (John 10:6; 16:25, 29). The English title, "Proverbs," is an abbreviated form of the Latin *Liber Proverbiorum* (Book of Proverbs).

The books of the Hebrew Bible were divided into three sections: the Law, the Prophets, and the Writings. The Book of Psalms headed the list of the third section, and was followed usually by Job and Proverbs. But there were some canonical lists in Judaism which placed Proverbs between Psalms and Job for reasons which are not altogether clear. Any supposed difference, however, is of no practical significance, since both Proverbs and Job belong to the same class of Wisdom Literature. In English Bibles Proverbs follows Psalms and precedes Ecclesiastes, an order which is also valid since it groups certain poetical materials in a section of the Old Testament canon. Perhaps those lists which placed Proverbs ahead of Job did so in the realization that Proverbs contained more accumulated wisdom material than any other single scriptural book. In the Septuagint, Proverbs followed Psalms and preceded Ecclesiastes, the Song of Solomon, and Job.

The Book of Proverbs is a collection of sayings from different sources and periods, some of which at least must have circulated independently before being assembled in the canonical book. Headings of main sections in the text furnish the names of three authors: Solomon (1:1; 10:1), Agur (30:1), and Lemuel (31:1). Other anonymous contributors were groups of wise men whose utterances were thought worthy of inclusion along with Solomon's sayings in the completed book. The sayings attributed to these wise men occur in Proverbs 22:17–24:22 and 24:23–29. Whether they were priests or secular counselors is not indicated, but they certainly espoused the ethic and spirituality of the Sinai covenant. Some scholars would divide the sayings of King Lemuel into two groups, namely, Proverbs 31:1–9 and 31:10–31, and have regarded the latter as the work of someone other than the king himself. One reason is that the style and content of the two sections are markedly different. Furthermore, the literary style of 31:10–31 is distinctive, comprising an acrostic based on the sequence of the Hebrew alphabet. It is entirely possible that this elegant composition was the work of one of Lemuel's court officials, and was included among the sayings which the king had to learn, but without attribution to the author. While it is true that royalty have often taken credit for the talents of their subjects, there are no grounds for supposing that King Lemuel engaged in such activities. A more probable attribution of authorship is to the king's mother, whose teachings comprise the first nine verses of the chapter. But whoever the author was, the writings stand firmly in the wisdom tradition of Israel and are remarkable for the praise which they heap upon what by any standards must be considered as an outstanding wife.

Because of the diverse authorship of the component sections of Proverbs, it is difficult to date the composition precisely. Nobody knows, for example, just how ancient the proverbs presented by the wise men are. They appear to be pragmatic in nature and could well have been current for some centuries before being included in the canonical work. Equally possible is the supposition that some of them were formulated in the early monarchy period in Jerusalem.

The dating of the Solomonic material is more certain. Proverbs 10:1 makes a direct claim to the great king's authorship, and this is thoroughly consistent with the traditions of his wisdom. Solomon was credited with writing 3000 proverbs and 1005 songs (1 Kings 4:32), in addition to possessing a prodigious knowledge of Near Eastern flora and fauna. Both proverbs and songs could have been produced conjointly with his advisors as a form of diversion, but whether that was the case or not, the overall number of wise sayings in the Old Testament attributed traditionally to Solomon falls far short of the total recorded in the Book of Kings. This would indicate that the monarch's written and musical achievements encountered a significant degree of attrition after his death. Some of them may have been absorbed into the wisdom traditions of other nations, but of this there is no evidence.

Solomon's father, David, was eminent as a musician and psalmist, and a great many of his poetic compositions have survived in the canonical Book of Psalms. By contrast, only two psalms (Pss. 72; 127) carry Solomon's name in the title. The Hebrew particle often translated "of" in such titles can also mean "for" or "to," pointing to compositions written as a dedication, or attributed to the person named, or presented to him as an act of loyalty, admiration, and friendship. This fact could have some bearing on the authorship of some Davidic psalms also, especially those without historical certification in the title, and the same would apply to Solomon also. Whether this was the case or not, it is evident that the musical sweetness of Solomon was wasted on the desert air of contemporary culture.

Some scholars have questioned the attribution of Proverbs 1:1 of the first nine chapters to the great king, suggesting that it is instead a general title for the book that was provided by an editor, perhaps in the period of Hezekiah (728–687 B.C.). This distinguished ruler of Judah possessed his own collection of Solomonic proverbs, which he contributed to form part of the present book. Of Agur and Lemuel almost nothing is known. The former has been identified as a tribal chieftain of Massa in northern Arabia, an area well known in antiquity for wisdom (cf. 1 Kings 4:29–34), but this is conjectural at best. Similarly Lemuel has been supposed to be a non-Israelite sage who clearly owed his wisdom to his mother's tutelage (Prov. 31:1). The superscription to his proverbs can be interpreted to mean "Lemuel king of Massa," which at face value might imply two contributors to Israelite Wisdom Literature from the same territory. There is another consideration, however, in that the Hebrew term *maśśā'* means "oracle," and this would result in Agur and Lemuel being described respectively as "Agur the oracle" and "Lemuel the oracle." In this way they would be recognized as special recipients of wisdom and as men thereby equipped to proclaim the oracles of God.

To assign a date to the completed form of the canonical Proverbs is far from easy, since the book is a composite work. Given the great antiquity of the proverb, it does not seem unreasonable to date Proverbs reasonably close to the death of Hezekiah, in the first half of the seventh century B.C. If the title in Proverbs 1:1 was not part of the original compilation, it could conceivably have been added at that time.

Proverbs is a book which deals with the theory and practice of wisdom, which is depicted as a divine endowment characterized by insight, instruction, knowledge of divine truth, and the resolution to apply all these qualities on the basis of a shrewd and informed mind. Wisdom is God's gift (Prov. 2:6) and is fostered by a constant search for divine truth. While it is offered freely to all levels of society, it demands a firm rejection of evil (Prov. 8:13), a turning toward God in faith and reverence (Prov. 9:10), and continued obedience to its moral precepts. There is no exposition of covenant theology such as occurs in the Torah and the prophets, but monotheism and the ethic of the Sinai covenant are presupposed.

Wisdom has the effect of dividing the population into such classes as fools, lazy people, scoffers, simple-minded persons, and those who are deceived easily into following evil patterns of behavior. Wisdom is presented as a sophisticated attribute of life which enables its possessor to make a creative and successful mark on society by God's power, avoiding meantime the snares and pitfalls which beset the foolish and ignorant. God desires his priestly kingdom and holy people (Exod. 19:6) to live in discernment and prosperity, pursuing ethical and moral behavior as a consistent witness to the spiritual relationship of reverence and obedience that they enjoy with him.

The moral teachings of Proverbs are meant to relate the believer's faith successfully to life in society. Under wisdom's guidance he will follow an honest, unselfish pattern of life that will be honored by God and recognized in human society. Its reward will be a sense of security in the Lord (Prov. 29:25) and an increasing knowledge of who and what God is as the believer searches the depths of divine wisdom (cf. Prov. 2:5) and applies its teachings to social and economic concerns.

For the most part the Hebrew text has been transmitted very well. There are occasional words or phrases which appear to have suffered in the process, but this may only be the result of modern ignorance of ancient linguistic forms, literary styles and conventions, cultural attitudes, and so on. A wider knowledge of ancient Near Eastern languages and literature will help to clarify textual difficulties in Proverbs, as elsewhere in the Hebrew Bible. Many translators choose to emend the text at the first sign of difficulty, but this procedure should be avoided in general. The Septuagint translation, begun in the third century B.C., is actually more of a paraphrase than a strict translation and therefore is of limited value in attempts to restore the Hebrew text.

OUTLINE

I. Title and Prologue (1:1–7)
II. Wisdom and Some Opponents (1:8–9:18)
  A. Criminals (1:8–19)
  B. Wisdom's Call (1:20–33)
  C. Wisdom's Rewards (2:1–4:27)
  D. Adultery (5:1–23)
  E. Business and Society (6:1–19)
  F. Adultery (6:20–7:27)
  G. Wisdom Praised (8:1–36)
  H. Human Choices (9:1–18)
III. The Proverbs of Solomon (10:1–22:16)
IV. Sayings of the Wise Men (22:17–24:34)
V. Solomonic Proverbs from Hezekiah's Collection (25:1–29:27)
VI. Sayings of Agur (30:1–33)
VII. Sayings of Lemuel (31:1–9)
VIII. Postscript: The Excellent Wife (31:10–31)

COMMENTARY

I. Title and Prologue (1:1–7)

While David was Israel's preeminent psalmist, his son Solomon gave definitive stature to the nation's proverbs. If paradox is at the heart of the proverb, it is certainly afforded full expression in this corpus of wise sayings. But the *māšāl,* as observed previously, covers a wide range of forms, varying from a telling simile (10:25) to an address dealing with the character of wisdom (8:1–36). The mention of Solomon in the title recognizes him as Israel's famed progenitor of wise sayings, and this is an entirely appropriate recognition. Although some scholars have questioned whether he was the author of chapters 1–9, there can be little doubt that he was as well informed on the subject of wisdom as anyone in antiquity, and thus eminently qualified to introduce systematic teaching on this vitally important matter. Whether a later editorial addition or not, therefore, it designated accurately the character of the wisdom sayings, which may be attributed confidently to Solomon and his entourage. In the ancient world, the ruler of a city-state was the absolute owner not merely of the land, but also the property of the citizens and the people themselves. He could therefore lay legitimate claim to everyone and everything, including such intellectual property as proverbs formulated in a court environment. As a result there would be nothing exceptional in Solomon's claim to proprietorship of the whole literary corpus.

The author, having identified himself, states the purpose of the material, which is to provide instruction for successful living against a background of covenant ethics and morality (v. 1). Verses 2–3 furnish a list of synonyms for wisdom, which makes clear the scope of the term. The instruction aims at developing mental acumen in people of varying backgrounds and capabilities, and if followed promises to lead to success in business and social endeavors. Through wisdom its adherents will become discriminating in judgment and will be able to derive maximum benefit from all the traditional proverbs, figures of speech, the utterances of wise men, and certain "mind games" such as riddles. But the imbibing of wisdom is not exactly a matter of salvation by works. The process has its beginnings in the individual's commitment to God in fear and reverence. God is himself true wisdom and gives good things freely to those who ask of him (cf. Matt. 7:11). The very character of wisdom imposes limitations upon potential disciples, however. The fool (Heb. *petî*), who is gullible, naive, and deficient in moral attributes, despises wisdom (v. 7) and therefore excludes himself automatically from its benefits.

II. Wisdom and Some Opponents (1:8–9:18)

A. Criminals (1:8–19). Both parents are portrayed as instructing their children in wisdom and should be obeyed accordingly (Exod. 20:12). The teaching given here is depicted at the most personal level. The term *my son* would also apply to daughters, who were expected to grow up to become like the virtuous woman of Proverbs 31:10–31. A special warning is given about consorting with violent criminals such as terrorists, who ambush and murder innocent victims. The mention of "Sheol" or "the Pit" is a reference to the location of the dead. It seems to be a familiar description of death and is given little explanation. The criminals mentioned here include thieves as well as murderers, who pursue one of the commonest forms of lawlessness known to humanity. But wisdom teaches soberly that criminal activity brings its own just reward.

B. Wisdom's call (1:20–33). In verse 20, and also in 9:3, wisdom is a plural noun (Heb. *ḥākmôt*), thought to be either a Phoenician singular form or a plural of "majesty." Personified as a woman, wisdom appeals in all the public places of the city for self-centered, irresponsible people to begin fearing God and thus be enlightened and blessed by wisdom. She has stretched out her hands to a wayward people (cf. Isa. 65:2; Rom. 10:21), while warning them that if they spurn her she will repudiate them when they come whining to her in trouble. Even divine mercy needs human acceptance if it is to be truly redemptive, and while those who yield to wisdom's entreaties will live, the simpletons who reject her will bring about their own destruction.

C. Wisdom's rewards (2:1–4:27). There is always the possibility that a child will disobey parental instruction, but if he is seeking desperately to understand reverence for the Lord, he will find it (cf. Matt. 7:7), because the covenant Lord bestows wisdom as a precious gift. Such a search, however, is not for the mocker or the fool who asserts that there is no God (Pss. 14:1; 53:1). Those who come to God must believe that he exists, and that he rewards those who seek him diligently (Heb. 11:6). The search must be meticulous, as though one were prospecting for silver or gold, which are often difficult to locate and even harder to remove from the ore body. But when wisdom has been unearthed as though it were buried treasure, the searcher will have established for himself the validity of the truth enunciated in Proverbs, namely that "the fear of the LORD is the beginning of wisdom" (2:1–6).

Worshiping God to the exclusion of all other deities was the first commandment of the law (Exod. 20:2–3), and thus the wise Israelite gives to God the exclusive reverence, loyalty, and praise due to his name. The divine gift of wisdom is accompanied by knowledge, perception, and a sense of personal moral integrity. Furthermore, God provides protection for believers who follow the path of righteousness, equity, and justice because he takes very seriously the death of the saints (Ps. 116:15). Wisdom in the life of the believer is thus an ongoing, dynamic experience which is entirely different from a passive, intellectual assent to the existence of some mysterious quality in the Godhead which otherwise has little or no personal meaning. When the sinner comes to God in fear and reverence, he finds not merely forgiveness but a new way of life (2:7–11). Or as Paul put it, "Therefore, if anyone is in Christ, he is a new creation; the old has gone, the new has come!" (2 Cor. 5:17).

This experience of renewal affects the total personality, that is, body and soul, and is nurtured by divine wisdom so that the believer can attain maturity (cf. Matt. 5:48; Eph. 4:13). In Proverbs 2:10 the "heart" is the locale of purposiveness, intellect, and will, while the "soul" is the actual self. Wisdom and knowledge will therefore achieve in the individual's life an integration of the personality, which is the manifestation of health in its most fundamental sense.

Those people thus transformed by the renewing of their minds (cf. Rom. 12:2) will experience divine protection from evil habits and criminal persons because wisdom has taught them discretion and understanding (2:12–15). God is indeed living in them and has lavished his precious gift of wisdom upon them to safeguard their very steps. The practice of wisdom precludes association with "the unfruitful works of darkness" (Eph. 5:11 KJV), but instead it emphasizes that honesty, integrity, unselfishness, and purity will be manifested in all their social relations. They will be walking uprightly in the way of light, whereas criminals, by contrast, will be lurking on the roads under cover of darkness, seeking occasion to perpetrate their nefarious deeds.

The author now warns against the adulterous woman for the first time (2:16–22). The Hebrew speaks of her as a "strange woman" and a "foreign woman." At one time she had been a faithful adherent to the Sinai covenant, but has now forsaken her young husband and rejected the ethic of Sinai in favor of immorality. She has thus sinned on two counts and leads her victims to destruction along the same slippery slope. She encourages a direct violation of the prohibition regarding adultery (Exod. 20:14), which was intended to ensure fidelity to the marriage vows made before God and to deter the nation from indulging in the immoral sexual practices of neighboring peoples. A priestly kingdom and a holy nation was required to live in a specified ethical and moral manner so that God would be glorified in his people. To be united carnally with a harlot brings the man down to her immoral level, since, as Paul pointed out many centuries later, he becomes one body with her (1 Cor. 6:16), having in effect married her by his act. The person guided by wisdom and integrity, however, will avoid the harlot's blandishments and live to prosper in the land, whereas the wicked will be destroyed.

The teacher continues his instruction by urging his "son" to remember and apply his teachings so as to live long and prosper (3:1–2). Because the Hebrews had no direct expectation of immortality, this life was the only one that could be contemplated. The wisdom writings generally thought of life falling into three phases: (1) a period of instruction; (2) a period of testing, when the lessons learned were applied to everyday living; and (3) a period of reward, when the righteous would receive specific recompense from God while the wicked would be destroyed. Loyalty and faithfulness toward God must ornament the person who is seeking wisdom (3:3–4). To succeed, the wise person must wrap these high values metaphorically around his neck, just as was required for the covenant stipulations (Deut. 6:8). When they are in his heart, they will motivate him correctly.

Wise living demands complete and unswerving trust in the Lord (3:5), allowing his complete overlordship of the personality (3:6) and manifesting reverence for him (3:7). This will result in specific physical benefits as well as spiritual blessings. The wise person must never be selfish, but must honor God by giving back to him a token payment for what has been received (3:8–10). In an agricultural economy, firstfruits are mentioned, indicating God's prior claim on gross income. Elsewhere a specified amount had been designated as God's portion ("tithe," Deut. 12:11). If given freely, it would be returned in superabundance (3:10; cf. Mal. 3:10).

Because wisdom involves discipline, the believer will probably receive a certain amount of correction in the quest for wisdom (3:11–12). This, however, should be taken as a sign of God's love and concern for his children (cf. Heb. 12:5–6; Rev. 3:19). The end of the search for wisdom is blessedness, which involves intellectual and spiritual understanding rather than mere pleasure. The person pursuing a life governed by wisdom finds that to the promises of prosperity, longevity (3:2), and health (3:8) is added divine blessing. This great gift of grace is bestowed upon the person who delights to do the Lord's will (cf. Pss. 1:1–2; 40:8; Rom. 7:22) and proves to be more profitable than gold or silver. Wisdom is thus depicted as offering the best of all possible worlds (3:13–18). On the one hand she gives long life, and on the other she bestows riches, honor, peace, and prosperity. There is no false distinction here between spirituality and the possessing of riches. The latter is actually part of the former, being God's material reward for fidelity and obedience. To assume that the believer can be pleasing to God only when impoverished finds no support in these verses.

Following this phase of instruction comes reinforcement of the previous teaching that wisdom is the product of a close relationship with God, characterized by faith and obedience (3:21–26). This assurance relieves the believer of preoccupation with every step of the journey, for he can go forward in the assurance that God has provided for all contingencies. Trusting in God involves surrendering everything to him, in the belief that not merely is he able to save his children from their sins, but can shelter them in his protective care, thus removing the need for worry. A modern proverb crystallizes the message by saying: "If we trust, we do not worry. If we worry, we do not trust."

In terms of the believer's dealings with society, wisdom imposes certain fundamental rules for success (3:27–35). Proverbs 3:27, which is a little awkward in the Hebrew ("Do not withhold good from its owners . . .") teaches that delay in paying one's debts is both inconsiderate and unjust. The Greek version seems to imply poor people rather than business creditors, but that does not seem to be the sense of the Hebrew. A neighbor must be treated with honesty and consideration. Unnecessary argument must not be entertained, since a priestly kingdom should be peaceable. Violence must be neither admired nor emulated because it is a perversion of right. People whose lives are not governed by wisdom will be punished for their folly.

The father continues to instruct his "sons" in the rewards of wisdom. The plural form may imply the teaching of several persons at once, but it could also represent a simple error in copying. The teacher demands attention from his audience and ensures that he receives it by demonstrating his great anxiety for their moral and social behavior. His is no dry-as-dust theoretical instruction which has little relevance for the hard practicalities of everyday life, but is a vital, living body of knowledge founded on his own relationship with his father. For him to say "my son(s)," therefore, is to bring his hearers into a close personal bond which goes far beyond the usual teacher-student relationship. Because the teacher was the only son, he was cherished particularly and given the full benefit of parental instruction. The father clearly wanted his heir to be a worthy successor, and accordingly patterns his instruction positively by extolling wisdom and negatively by warning against the dangers to which life in society exposes a person (4:1–9). In summary form and in reverse order they read: "Do not forget and do not ignore: get wisdom, get insight." While verse 7 may seem unduly repetitious, it is important because it reinforces the theme of the book. Wisdom is indeed the crowning attainment of a person's life, since it adorns character and behavior alike.

To possess wisdom gives the individual promise of a long life which will be all the more successful when the precepts of wisdom are being practiced (4:10–19). The negative aspect of Solomon's instruction is expressed in terms of avoiding evil persons and their corrupting influence. To achieve this, one has to hold, retain, and cherish the instruction which wisdom supplies. The wicked persons mentioned here are not petty thieves but professional criminals whose day is not complete until they have committed some act of wrongdoing. Wickedness and violence are their meat and drink (4:17), and while the crimes are not specified they could range from simple fraud to murder. The contrast between the way of the wicked and that of the wise man is the difference between night and day. Whereas the wise person is guided to see the way clearly, the wicked individual is so morally and ethically blind that he falls over unobserved obstacles.

The final section dealing with wisdom's rewards contains another reminder about the need for constant attention to the precepts of wisdom (4:20–27). It is a common temptation for believers to imagine that they have mastered moral and spiritual principles, and therefore have little if any need for further instruction. But human memory is frail at best, and thus believers need constant reminders to feed on the Lord's Word and to hear yet again the old, old story of his redemptive love. To enable these teachings about wisdom to be remembered easily, they are related to four important areas of the body. Particular care must be taken of the *heart,* because this organ is the will (11:20; 14:13), the mind (3:3), the emotions (15:15), and in some situations the entire person (3:5). If all these facets of individuality are informed and directed by wisdom, the person will be integrated behaviorally, morally, and spiritually.

Since the *mouth* often expresses what is in the heart (cf. Luke 6:45), care must be taken with one's speech, lest a cynical, corrupt, or ill-considered pronouncement should dishonor God or bring ill-repute upon believers (cf. James 3:5–10). The *eyes* can be attracted to evil pursuits very easily, and thus are in particular need of the discipline which wisdom provides. Jesus was well aware of the potential for temptation and lust that the eyes provided and taught the serious consequences of allowing them to cause one to stumble into sin (Matt. 5:28–29). But eyes that are illumined by wisdom light up the whole body (cf. Matt. 6:22). Finally, attention must be paid to the direction which the *feet* take, since they often give practical expression to individual motivation. They must not be allowed to wander haphazardly, but must follow consistently the paths of righteousness if blessing is to result.

D. Adultery (5:1–23). This section of advice for the person attempting to live an ethical and moral life under the covenant deals with an extremely important theme: human sexuality in its normal and illicit forms. The Hebrews were somewhat ambivalent in their attitude toward sexuality, sometimes employing explicit language ("went into"), while on other occasions using euphemisms ("feet," "thigh") to describe the sex organs. In general, couples married at a young age, since the normal life expectancy was only about forty years. A woman probably had her first child while in her early teens.

A woman was under parental care until she married; thereafter she was subject to her husband. A wife who committed adultery was punished by death if caught, along with the offending man (Lev. 20:10). Aside from adultery, considerably more sexual latitude seems to have been accorded to a man, possibly because his sexual activities were restricted by the lengthy nursing period which his wife experienced after the birth of a child. Prostitutes seem to have been readily available throughout the Near East, but they were associated predominantly with pagan religions and thus were prohibited to the Israelites, whose covenantal faith could have been easily corrupted by such contacts. Men doubtless exploited female household servants sexually, sometimes with the wife's approval (Gen. 16:2–4), but the legal wife was generally considered the only one able to bear heirs for her husband. While some women were unable to secure husbands, it was the norm for a Hebrew man to marry, and those who remained bachelors diverged noticeably from this tradition. Sexual relations were meant to be confined to marriage, and a high esteem was placed upon premarital chastity.

Against this social background, the author seems to be speaking as one married man to another (vv. 15–19). There is considerable irony in the situation if Solomon is the teacher, since his rejection by God was due to his marriages to pagan women (1 Kings 11:1–11). Thus he would have been able to speak from experience, but would hardly have been able to criticize adultery and retain much credibility. There are, of course, numerous converted sinners who derive a perverse delight from regaling their audiences with tales of illegal or immoral exploits, at the same time warning them not to become involved in the same way. Solomon's position as a ruler, however, could have granted him exemption from censure, since kings were traditionally permitted to have more than one wife, especially if political benefits resulted for the nation. Even as late as New Testament times, Jewish rulers could have more than one wife, as illustrated by Herod the Great, who may have had as many as ten wives.

The immoral woman can be recognized easily as a person of beguiling speech, whose remarks appear pleasant initially ("honey . . . oil") but end in disaster when her victim has been compromised (vv. 3–4). Because she has strayed from the path of covenant morality, she is following the way to Sheol and taking her consorts with her. The teacher's warning in this matter concerns discretion, which means keeping at a distance from such a person. By having relations with a harlot a man loses chastity, dissipates his powers, perhaps opens himself to blackmail (v. 10), and possibly will die from a sexually transmitted disease (v. 11). Little notice seems to have been taken of the latter contingency in Scripture, but if the disease in Asa's "feet" was actually venereal, both the possibility and character of the ailment were recognized (2 Chron. 16:12–14). But by that time it would be too late for Solomon's pupil to indulge in self-castigation (vv. 12–14).

By contrast, the virtue of fidelity within a monogamous marriage is extolled in poetic language of exquisite beauty and delicacy. The positive values of a loving marriage relationship far outweigh the supposed delights of carnal indulgence with a harlot. Furthermore, wisdom's values receive the seal of approval from One who watches a person's ways (v. 21). Refraining from associating with harlots is a mark of discipline which the wicked lack because they have spurned wisdom. In the end, that foolish act becomes their undoing.

E. Business and society (6:1–19). The theme of prudence and discretion as attributes of wisdom is applied in a practical manner to a variety of social situations. Three forms of hazardous behavior leading to sin are described, namely, co-signing (vv. 1–5), laziness (vv. 6–11), and deception (vv. 12–19). The first instance of imprudent behavior is that of a person agreeing to assume responsibility for the debts of a neighbor. The circumstances surrounding the situation are unfortunately not clear. Under the Law, the Israelite community ideally had no poor people in it. But some persons manage their monetary resources better than others, so that however desirable the concept of fiscal equality might be, some people are always going to be poor. In ancient Israel, a person who had lent another money was forbidden to charge interest (cf. Lev. 25:36), but that is not the issue here in Proverbs.

To act as surety for a neighbor whom one may know reasonably well is on any basis a calculated risk, since the extent of the liability assumed may not be immediately clear. If the neighbor is but a casual acquaintance whose situation one does not really know, such an undertaking is either an act of sheer bravado on the part of a rich man flaunting his wealth, or an example of the worst form of fiscal stupidity.

The cases outlined do not indicate whether money has changed hands, but only that the agreement has been ratified formally, apparently by a handshake. Because the undertaking is for an unspecified length of time and the extent of the liability is unknown, a serious error consists of the absence of any collateral which might offset the assistance to some extent. All that seems to have happened is that a person of some means has pledged financial help with little or no investigation of the circumstances which required the investment in the first instance. It is possible that the predicament was sketched deliberately in a vague manner so that the hearer could react in increasing horror at a situation which must surely be the worst possible scenario for anyone involved in debt financing.

Experience teaches that the donor, who has evidently acted on a purely voluntary basis to assist a person of perhaps only casual acquaintance, is trapped in an embarrassing financial situation through his own stupidity. He is evidently the kind of fool who is soon parted from his money, and accordingly the teacher recommends that, in order to reduce the losses caused by his generosity, the surety should endeavor to extricate himself immediately from his pledge, going on hands and knees to the debtor, if necessary, and begging for release. The teacher does not guarantee, of course, that the underwriter, once released from his obligations, will not repeat the same mistake in a moment of misguided impetuosity, but it is hoped that some practical wisdom will have been gained from the experience.

The second social situation (vv. 6–11) depicts the lazy person who is making no contribution to the economy, but is apparently subsisting in some manner on the efforts of other people. In every society there are people who, although able-bodied, are unwilling to expend energy in working for a living. Such habitually indolent people are parasites on society, having no intention of doing anything other than the most minimal of duties, and at that under tremendous pressure.

The teacher suggests that he can be embarrassed into action by observing the ants at work. They do not require an overseer to direct their activities, whereas the sluggard needs continual and vociferous prodding if he is to act at all. The ant knows times and seasons, and thus is able to accumulate food in summer to last throughout the winter. The lazy person, meanwhile, is sleeping in the shade during the summer days when others are working, and suddenly discovers when it is too late that winter and starvation are upon him. They come swiftly and rapaciously like bandits, and the lazy person is left bereft. There are many ant species in the Near East, and the harvester ants in particular build their mound-nests beside places where the grain has been threshed or stored. They store grain kernels in their nests and throw the husks outside on the ground, having accumulated all they will need for the coming winter. Although described as "creatures of little strength" (Prov. 30:25), they can actually transport weights many times heavier than themselves. Only a person who is utterly devoid of wisdom can fail to learn lessons of industry, organization, and productivity by observing ants at work.

The third social cameo is that of the deceiver. He is described in the Hebrew as the "man of Belial," that is, a wicked, worthless individual. He is a troublemaker, cunning, using a variety of gestures, some possibly obscene, to promote his devious plans. But his opportunities for making mischief are suddenly terminated, and he is destroyed. In a list of social abominations, the man of discord is marked out specifically as a person hated by the Lord. Other evils include murder, lying, and false witness.

F. Adultery (6:20–7:27). Practical wisdom is again invoked as the teacher advises his "son" to gird himself with such understanding as will illumine his way. Again the concern is with the adulteress, who seems in this instance to be a neighbor's wife (6:29). Such a person is a grave threat to marital stability, and if entertained does the additional harm of supplanting wisdom in an individual's life. Verse 26 is difficult to translate, the Hebrew reading "For because of a harlot to a piece of bread . . ." which several ancient translations altered to read "for a harlot may be hired for a loaf of bread. . . ." This change is suspect if only because it seeks to draw a distinction between a cheap whore and an expensive adulteress, when in fact it is the basic immorality that is being condemned. The King James Version reads "for by means of a whorish woman a man is brought to a piece of bread . . ." and seems to capture the point at issue, which the New International Version simplifies by reading "for the prostitute reduces you to a loaf of bread."

Fornication demeans a man's character, while adultery demolishes it systematically. The penalties for holding "fire," that is, a neighbor's wife, close to one's bosom and walking upon hot coals are obvious. There is a word play on the word *feet* here, which can also mean "sexual organs," indicating that the "burning" could be the pain caused by venereal disease. Even a thief could evoke sympathy if he stole to satisfy hunger, but the man who gratifies sexual appetite through adultery is a fool. The implication of the discourse (6:34–35) is that the husband of the immoral woman has discovered the offense and is bent upon exacting revenge. His honor has been outraged, and no amount of money can compensate for the damage. In Leviticus 20:10, both the adulteress and her consort were to be executed, which served as fitting punishment for defilers of a holy community and also prevented lengthy blood-feuds.

In a renewed commendation of wisdom's virtues, the instructor urges the disciple to keep this teaching before his eyes and in his hands. The recipient of wisdom is urged to keep his gaze upon the instructor's teachings so that they are reflected continually in his eyes. This intimate relationship with wisdom will foil the alluring advances of the evil woman.

Such a protective screen is vitally important where the adulteress is bent on satisfying her desires. A lengthy eyewitness account is provided to illustrate the ease with which a foolish person can be seduced. In the first place, the young victim is walking near the prostitute's house when he should have been elsewhere. Then he is too simple to suspect anything sinister when he is accosted by the harlot, who is dressed in a way appropriate to her trade. She has been walking the streets, looking for a willing victim, and so she grabs him, kisses him, and takes him by surprise with a display of affection. Her plan is to tell him that she has discharged certain religious obligations, perhaps a peace offering (cf. Lev. 7:16–18), and is now ready to hold a party with him as the principal guest. The details indicate that the author is thoroughly familiar with the evil ways of these adulteresses (7:19), whereas the simple-minded victim is not. Thus he mentions the colored Egyptian linen bedspreads and the couch perfumed with spices. The woman purports to be alone and thus able to offer the victim uninterrupted pleasure. With these and other enticements she ensnares him, and he follows her obediently with all five senses thoroughly aroused. But because he lacks the sixth sense which wisdom bestows, he is actually going like an animal to the slaughter.

On this note the lengthy discourse on adultery terminates. Despite the prescribed penalties it must have been prevalent as a sin of the more wealthy, otherwise less emphasis would have been laid on it. Accordingly the teacher's "sons" are to beware of the possibility of temptation: keep out of the way of harm physically and emotionally and take note of the victim's awful fate. "Sheol" and the "abodes of the dead" are synonyms for death. Wisdom, by contrast, counsels a choice of life.

G. Wisdom praised (8:1–36). In this adulation of wisdom the writer does not address his audience personally, but instead personifies wisdom. In harmony with the character of wisdom established previously, her image is a consistently positive one. She is the one universal element without which everything else fails. She is not the shadowy female who frequents dark alleys in search of sexual gratification, but instead positions herself publicly beside the city gates where she can expect to attract a large audience (v. 3). Her remarks are directed particularly to those persons who are not familiar with her teachings, namely, the naive and the foolish. Wisdom personified begins by affirming her credibility (vv. 6–9), stressing that she speaks only true, noble, and righteous words. She assures her audience that even ignorant people can learn her teachings and thereby enrich their lives immeasurably. If they persist, they will discover that her rewards far exceed gold, silver, and jewels, the marketplace standard of wealth, for wisdom transcends all these prized commodities.

The Hebrew of 8:12 is rather obscure, but traditional renderings isolate three attributes of wisdom which are actually synonymous with wisdom, namely, prudence, knowledge, and discretion. The fear of the Lord induces hatred of four antagonistic influences: evil in its many manifestations, pride, arrogance, and perverse speech. These two opposite groups of qualities are set side by side so that the hearers will know what does and does not constitute wisdom. The distinctions are established: the boundaries are marked out clearly, and there can be no misunderstanding on the part of the hearers.

Wisdom reveals three more of her attributes: counsel, insight, and strength, which with other qualities are reflected in the way that rulers govern and promulgate just decrees (v. 15). It is interesting to observe that wisdom associates herself with the powerful and rich rather than with the poor. But this is consistent with other assertions that wisdom brings great wealth to those who cherish her. Such sentiments would be completely characteristic of Solomon's court, where rich and noble individuals were part of the royal entourage.

By far the most spectacular claim for wisdom is made in verses 22–31, where she claims great antiquity as the very first of God's acts of creation. Wisdom thus antedates the universe, and this theme is reiterated in beautiful poetic form. Yet this very fact calls for caution in interpreting the exuberance of the text, as well as the actual translation of verses 22, 26, and 28. In verse 22, the Hebrew verb *qānā'* was translated as "created" in the Greek Septuagint, the Jewish Targums, and the Revised Standard Version, but by "possessed" in the Latin Vulgate, the King James Version, and the 1881 Revised Version. The latter rendering seems preferable because it is illogical and inconsistent to think of the Creator either lacking or creating part of himself. Possession of some kind, however, which is the usual Old Testament usage of *qānā'* and its derivatives, is consistent with God's self-revelation. It is he who possessed the wisdom to fashion the cosmos and organize it so that its final form was "very good" (Gen. 1:31).

From this it would follow that wisdom here is a personification, that is, some abstraction depicted as being endowed with personal qualities, and not a divine hypostasis, which is an element of Godhead and a person within the divine personality. Personified wisdom does not claim to have performed any creative acts, but merely states quite properly, "I was there." The Hebrew word *'āmôn* in verse 30 was rendered "craftsman" by the Greek Septuagint, the Syriac, and Latin Vulgate translations and occurs in this sense in Jeremiah 52:15. But the Hebrew consonants can also be understood to mean "little child," and if this is the correct interpretation it diminishes the place of wisdom in creation to an unrealistic degree.

A final admonition from wisdom (vv. 32–36) is to hear rather than neglect instruction, for in so doing the obedient will find life and obtain divine favor.

H. Human choices (9:1–18). This chapter is a cleverly contrived composition of three equal sections, in which the first and last half-dozen verses describe the contrasting themes of wisdom and folly. The intervening passage contains a mixture of material relating to both positions. The chapter commences with an impressive description of the prominence of wisdom, who has established an imposing dwelling graced by seven pillars. Precisely what the latter signify has been much debated, and solutions ranging from the mythological to the merely architectural have been proposed. Some have even suggested a cosmic allusion involving planetary bodies, which is appealing to those who think that wisdom took a practical part in the work of creation.

Wisdom's abode is a mansion in which a sumptuous feast has been prepared. Meat and wine, the choice items on a banquet menu, are awaiting the guests. In the meantime wisdom has sent her attendants throughout the city to invite people to the celebration. Her particular concern is with the simple-minded, who stand to benefit most from her company. Accordingly they are offered a cordial invitation to enter her house, feast at her table, and forsake the foolishness which has characterized them hitherto.

The scene is distinctly similar to a story told by Jesus. A certain man made a great supper (Luke 14:16–24) and issued many invitations, all of which were declined. In anger the man ordered his servants to bring in the crippled, poor, and destitute, and when there was still room he instructed his servants to comb the hedges and byways to complete the number of guests. In both instances those who did not attend the feast proved themselves unworthy of the riches in store.

The second group of six verses begins by showing the dangers involved in trying to reform those who mock wisdom. But a person who follows wisdom's precepts will benefit both from admonition and further instruction. The mocker has already decided the issues and has shut his mind to anything that might upset or refute his conclusions. The wise person, however, possesses a mind that is open to improvement and thus welcomes the opportunity to learn more about wisdom. The familiar motto of Proverbs is repeated to stress the way in which wisdom is grounded in the fear and reverence of God. It cannot be acquired in any other manner, but once gained it results in insight and a long life which is healthy because wisdom has integrated the various parts of the individual into an organism that functions at the most efficient level.

The final section deals with foolishness as a characteristic of certain women. Because of translation difficulties her exact character is hard to grasp. Thus in verse 13, the King James Version reads "A foolish woman is clamorous: she is simple, and knoweth nothing." The Revised Standard Version substitutes "wanton" for "simple," and follows the Greek Septuagint in reading "knows no shame," but both involve textual changes and are thus far from assured. The New International Version rendering "she is undisciplined and without knowledge" is unfortunately equally conjectural. Whatever the Hebrew means, it does not reflect eminent qualities of character. This type of woman, probably a prostitute, appeals to the same clientele as wisdom (vv. 5, 16), but with diametrically opposite results. Whereas wisdom brings life and health, the foolish woman lures her victims to their deaths, and the instruction ends with "Sheol," the abode of the departed, an appropriate end for covenant violators who think that their illicit activities will go undetected.

III. The Proverbs of Solomon (10:1–22:16)

The character of the book changes somewhat in that Solomon's proverbs are not extended personifications of wisdom. The idealized gives way to the practical, which suggests that many of the sayings were coined in the environment of Solomon's court and were essentially practical maxims for everyday living. Much of the chapter consists of antithetic parallels, that is, short sentences linked by "but" to introduce contrast. The verse must be read as a whole to gain its full meaning. Wisdom is still commended, but on a more pragmatic level. A man will act responsibly if he has applied his wisdom practically. Since wealth comes after hard work, the wise man will not sleep at harvesttime (10:5). Paying heed to the commandments and living a life of integrity are sure indications of wisdom (10:9).

An important group of proverbs (10:11–14) has to do with the contrast between the speech of wise persons and that of fools. The wise proclaim the living truth, but the violent destroy themselves by what they say. As Jesus was to state centuries later, the mouth speaks from the abundance of the heart (Matt. 12:34; Luke 6:45). Indiscretion in speech can be extremely dangerous, and in this connection the penalties attaching to careless utterances as stated by Christ constitute a serious warning (Matt. 12:36–37). The righteous man speaks in well-chosen, eloquent phrases, and does not descend to the virulent level of an angry, aggressive person. Consequently he addresses life in a positive way, and this brings benefit to himself and others.

The second half of verse 22 presents translation problems. The King James Version reads, "and he addeth no sorrow with it," this being followed by the Revised Standard Version and most modern English versions with only slight modifications. But the Hebrew can also be rendered "hard work adds nothing to it," if "work" is regarded as the subject of the verb, which is questionable. This rendering conflicts with some other wisdom sayings which imply that riches result from industry, thrift, and hard work. Accordingly the King James reading is to be preferred and means that when God bestows upon a person the ability to become rich, the recipient recognizes the true source of his wealth as God's gift. In Hebrew thought generally the third and final phase of life, in which one receives appropriate recompense for earlier years, was expected by the upright to be one of financial gain. If riches represent divine blessing, they can be accepted joyously without any sense of guilt or embarrassment for what they actually are. If obtained by corrupt means, however, they constitute ill-gotten gains and will haunt their possessor in various ways.

Wisdom ensures the permanence of the righteous, but the ungodly perish in the storms of life because of their basic dishonesty (10:24–25). In a fallen world, the person who reverences God and lives uprightly will never be removed, and his expectation of prosperity at the end of his life will be justified.

One of the more serious social evils of the Old Testament period was the attempt by merchants to use weights that were lighter than they should have been (11:1). There was no uniform standard in antiquity for the shekel weight, and this fact alone caused considerable confusion, to say nothing of the ease with which unscrupulous merchants could defraud their customers. Some attempt was made to regulate this situation in Israel when God prescribed the sanctuary shekel as the standard weight for religious purposes. It may actually have been somewhat heavier than its business counterpart, since people were expected to give more generously to the Lord's work, but this is uncertain. The Law demanded the use of correct scales and weights (Lev. 19:35–36), because the Redeemer of Israel was not only mighty but just and delighted in honest dealings among his people.

One of wisdom's attributes is humility (11:2), a word which is rare in the Old Testament, being found elsewhere as a verb ("walk humbly," Mic. 6:8). Humility suggests that the self has become hidden in God by the operation of wisdom (cf. Col. 3:3), and in the New Testament Paul recommends humility to Christians in terms of a realistic self-appraisal before God (Rom. 12:3). The opposite of humility is pride, which in the Hebrew emphasizes "swelling up," an attribute found in people with inflated egos. They are self-assertive, arrogant, domineering, haughty, and opinionated and hold other people in contempt. But a fall normally follows pride, and with it comes disgrace.

The differences between righteous and wicked people are reexamined (11:4–23), showing that righteousness delivers one from death, whereas when the wicked die, their expectations perish with them. The practical application of righteousness brings social and spiritual blessings upon a city's inhabitants, but these benefits can be nullified if there are too few wise men to counsel the population in the practice of wisdom. A wicked person may amass wealth by deception, but will be punished and die (11:19, 21). In a pungent simile, an indiscreet woman is compared to a gold ring in the nostrils of a pig (11:22). Liberality is commended as a virtue which results in additional riches, but people are advised not to trust in wealth because they and their riches can be easily dissipated. One's trust must be in God, and then a person will possess heavenly treasure (cf. Luke 12:15, 21). Since recompense for deeds was expected to occur in a person's lifetime, how much more serious would be the fate of the sinner than that of the righteous!

The contrast between good and evil people continues in chapter 12. A good man is blessed and is established in society, and a good wife is her husband's crowning glory. But their evil counterparts are corrupt and disreputable, bringing dissension and ruin as the result of their doings. Ultimately they are overthrown, while the righteous are stabilized (12:7). Proverbs thus recognizes cycles in people's lives, as well as the kind of retribution which their deeds provoke. Applied good sense wins recognition (12:8), whereas a confused, misguided approach to life invites scorn.

A righteous farmer can be recognized by the way he treats his livestock. The Mosaic law prescribed a Sabbath rest for animals as well as people (Exod. 23:12), in the expectation that they would work all the harder on other days. Animals were not to be yoked unevenly so that the smaller would bear a heavier load, and they were allowed to nibble at the grain as they were threshing it with their hoofs (Deut. 25:4). Although animals are inferior creatures, mankind has a definite responsibility to them, based on kindness and consideration. Cruelty has no place in such a relationship and can sometimes prove fatal to the one inflicting it. The righteous person similarly uses his land wisely, as a divine gift, and is careful to observe the seasons so as to provide abundant food (12:11).

In the moral sphere the wise man will always perform good deeds, since a person's actions are characteristically rewarded in kind (12:14). Whereas fools become angry at real or imagined insults, the wise man is mature enough emotionally to let them pass without comment. When the wise person speaks his words are honest and reliable. Unlike those who wound others by callous remarks, he speaks in a soothing, reassuring manner calculated to restore confidence. He knows the permanence of truth and the joy that comes from performing good deeds. By contrast, the deceitful ways of the wicked can only result in trouble. Situations sometimes arise in life where it is necessary for the prudent man to withhold counsel or advice until a more propitious occasion arises. But under these conditions the fool would proclaim his folly to all by making hasty, injudicious remarks which antagonize rather than help (12:23). The chapter ends on the theme of avoiding evil so as not to be led astray and working diligently and honestly in the pursuit of worldly success. The overall consideration by which a wise man should be guided is the consistent pursuit of righteousness, which leads to life, whereas the way of wrongdoing ends in death.

A new section of practical material (13:1–25) opens with the contrast between a wise son who absorbs his father's teachings and a mocker who dismisses any attempt at guidance. The latter can never benefit from wisdom because he has basically dismissed its reality and thus is in the same position as one who denies God's existence (Ps. 14:1). Emphasis is laid upon the spoken word and its effects. Because of the potential for damage the wise man must be circumspect, or he may come to ruin like the fool (13:3). The Hebrew of verse 5 speaks explicitly of the wicked man as one who "causes to stink and makes ashamed." Therefore an honest person will work strenuously to avoid such a reputation and its consequences.

It is a counsel of wisdom not to take people at face value. Someone living ostentatiously may well be a poor person trying to compensate for his inferior status in life, while an impoverished-looking individual could actually be a wealthy man maintaining a low public profile to avoid unwelcome attention. Both situations are well known in the modern world. A rich man who is kidnapped can buy his release, but a poor person need not fear such an eventuality (13:7–8). Wealth that is accumulated quickly (Heb. from vanity) tends to disappear in the same fashion, as many a gambler will concede, but when built up gradually is likely to remain and increase, if only because of the skill and effort expended in amassing it. The maxim about hope (13:12) has long passed into English proverbial lore and is a warning to those making promises to ensure that their fulfillment is not unduly delayed. This is a particularly important consideration for parents to remember when dealing with children.

The dangers of despising written commandments, including those of the Mosaic law, are pointed out because they direct individuals along the way of life and bring rich rewards to the obedient. In New Testament phraseology, they were "written to teach us" (Rom. 15:4). Since Torah literally means "instruction," its lessons will be taken to heart by the wise. By its counsel the ruin which overtakes the wicked and the snares of death that entrap them will be avoided (13:14–15). But those who deny its authority and value for practical living, choosing instead to follow their own inclinations, will sooner or later find their careers in ruins. It seems that there have always been those who have felt that divine revelation was irrelevant to the hard practicalities of daily living. But wisdom shows the exact opposite to be true, for poverty and disgrace come to such people (13:18). Keeping company with wise men begets wisdom, whereas fools, individually or in groups, suffer misfortune. For one reason or other they will not attain to the traditional Hebrew ambition of leaving behind an estate, and the righteous will acquire the property subsequently. Verse 23 seems to teach that poor administrative ability can squander the best agricultural resources. The proverb about "sparing the rod" occurs elsewhere (cf. 19:18; 22:15; etc.) and is expressed in the context of loving discipline. The chapter concludes with the theme of retribution overtaking the wicked in the form of hunger, which could have been avoided if the teachings of wisdom had been heeded consistently.

Chapter 14 begins by commending a woman's wisdom as that which builds up a home and family, and this is an important recognition of the vital role that a wife can play in overall family welfare. Unfortunately not all wives are wise, and as can be expected, a foolish woman destroys rather than builds up a home. For the husband, the veneration of the Lord will guarantee a life of integrity (14:1–2). His lips will be kept from offense by wisdom, whereas the outpourings of the fool's mouth will return to harass him. A wise man finds the acquisition of knowledge easy, but he will not encounter it in the company of scoffers and fools.

Verse 10 is a caution to those counselors who, out of concern, would empathize with sufferers, warning them that they simply cannot enter realistically into another's sufferings. Each experience is an individual one, and while a counselor may recognize a general pattern, there are always details that are peculiar to the person involved. Even appearances can be deceptive, as illustrated by the old English proverb "Many a merry heart beats beneath a widow's weeds [mourning attire]."

Another caution regarding appearances has to do with the road one takes in life. Instead of working hard to learn a trade or profession or listening to older persons, many individuals try to adopt alternative, shorter ways to success. But as Jesus warned, many have thought that the broad, open road led straight to heaven, whereas it was the hidden, narrow road that actually achieved that objective (Matt. 7:14). The saying in verse 13 is a very perceptive comment upon the close psychological connection between pleasure and pain and the basic predominance of the latter in the experience of fallen humanity.

Some contrasts are noted between simple and wise persons (14:14–20). The simple are gullible, reckless, careless, foolish, and unpopular, whereas the wise are discerning, cautious, discreet, knowledgeable, and popular. The negative values result from ignoring reverence of the Lord and will bring the simple to destruction; the qualities possessed by the wise will help them to avoid the snares of death. Understanding is typical of one who is slow to become angry (Heb. of a long nose), while hasty temper (Heb. short of breath) makes fools out of people. Verse 30 is the Semitic equivalent of the Latin *mens sana in corpore sano*, "a sound mind in a healthy body." Modern studies in psychosomatic conditions have verified the accuracy of this ancient observation. Internalized negative emotions can damage bodily tissues (14:30). Many earlier teachings individualized righteousness, but the chapter ends by relating it to the community: "righteousness exalts a nation." Sin, by contrast, brings its own reproach.

A much-quoted proverb (15:1) suggests that a gentle response can defuse a potentially explosive situation. This is vastly different from unwholesome speech, which demeans and destroys a person. Wise people can expect continued prosperity, but the wicked will be beset by threats to their improperly acquired wealth as a form of divine retribution. God refuses to be appeased by sacrifices from the wicked, evidently because they have not repented, but is delighted by the prayers of the righteous. There are stern warnings from an all-seeing God about forsaking the way of wisdom. If the very depths of the abyss, symbolized by Sheol and Abaddon as the uttermost recesses of destruction and death, are exposed to the Lord, how much more evident are human motives.

Another psychosomatic observation relates the emotions to physical and mental conditions (15:13) in a way that can be substantiated by common observation. The Old Testament was consciously linking emotional states and bodily changes for many centuries before modern scientific studies documented the same phenomena. Cheerfulness of disposition, whether it is a natural inheritance or the result of personal discipline, is like being at a continuous feast. It promotes and sustains positive feelings within the individual which are shared by others in that person's company. The entire atmosphere is one of enjoyment rather than depression or sorrow. This situation is contrasted with the condition of the afflicted, whatever the nature or cause of their unfortunate state, which is described as "evil." If the affliction is a form of divine retribution for wicked behavior, the righteous person can only regard it as the outworking of a foolish philosophy. If not, it must be endured with faith and patience until God visits the individual with his blessing.

Verses 16–17 deal with the theme of poverty versus riches and stress that the most important considerations are positive emotional and spiritual values, not what is on the table. If reverence for the Lord is present, the least amount will suffice and will more than compensate for riches and their associated troubles. In the same way, a salad eaten with loving companions is preferable to roast beef in an environment of hatred.

It is interesting that poor people with spiritual qualities are contrasted with rich persons who are clearly not adherents of wisdom. Why the spiritually minded poor are not rich is unexplained, and this is curious in view of the fact that the Hebrews made no artificial distinction between divine blessing and material prosperity, as some Christians do today. Commentators have suggested that these verses teach one how to be happy though poor, or that poverty may not be such a bad experience after all. The fact is that poverty debases and demeans the human spirit, produces dissension, despair, and hopelessness, and is the cause of much disease and suffering.

The proverb in 15:20 is repeated from 10:1 without mentioning the mother's sadness. Favorite proverbs, as with familiar psalms, tend to be repeated. Speaking the right words was considered an important social asset, then as now, and was pleasing to God (15:23–26). What angered God were the unjust schemes and bribes of the wicked, from whom he separates himself. The righteous man gains a deeper understanding of wisdom, meanwhile, and learns that humility precedes honor.

The opening verses of chapter 16 deal with God's sovereignty. Human beings may propose various plans, but God disposes. If one's way is committed to the Lord, one's plans are confirmed. Everything in life has a purpose, even the wicked, who will be destroyed. Obedience to the Lord and the acquisition of wisdom please him so much that even a person's enemies are prevented from interfering with him (16:7).

Several sayings deal with wise kings who promulgate inspired decisions (16:10), hate evil intensely (16:13), delight in righteous speech, and show anger over misdemeanors (16:14). In this Solomonic wisdom, concern is expressed again for God's desire to see just balances and accurate weights used in commerce. In verse 18 pride is mentioned as preceding destruction, which has also passed into English usage as "pride goes before a fall."

Pride is regarded as an undesirable attribute, and hence a person of impoverished condition is deemed better than one dividing the spoils of battle with the proud (16:19). Wisdom is praised as the source of discernment and persuasiveness of speech, both of which result from an instructed mind. The latter was evidently valued as an esteemed gift in Solomon's court, where discussion of a wide range of topics was bound to have occurred. Pleasant, judicious speech was likened to the honeycomb, which when eaten gratified the spirit as well as the body.

Contrasted with the satisfying pursuits of the Solomonic circle are the activities of an assortment of criminals and other worthless people who plan evil: perverse individuals who spread enmity, whisperers who gossip and create trouble among friends, a violent man who embroils his neighbors in quarrels, and the sinister figure of the smirking man who winks with his eyes as he pursues his evil schemes.

This dismal category of transgressors is followed by the mention of a familiar image in Semitic life, namely an old man with grey hair (16:31). Because of the comparatively short life expectancy of most Israelites, such a person was regarded as an individual of distinction, especially if he was recognized as a wise man. He was thus accorded great respect and may have been erroneously credited with a store of wisdom.

The chapter closes with the recognition that calmness of spirit is more advantageous than being powerful, since the personality is obviously under proper control. This leads to what must have been a familiar saying, especially in priestly circles, where lots were cast when major decisions from the Lord were needed. The lots used would probably have been the Urim and Thummim, two divinatory objects of uncertain nature set in the high priest's breastplate (Exod. 28:30). The statement in Proverbs 16:33 indicates that the lot was cast in a lap, probably that of the officiating priest, and that the decision on the matter under review had come directly from God, who had influenced the material objects so that the meaning was clear. The Urim and Thummim were not used indiscriminately, but only when an urgent problem needed to be resolved.

Chapter 17 commences with an aphorism similar to those in 15:16–17, but does not involve poverty and wealth so much as quietness contrasted with strife. If one's main concern is peace of mind, little else is important. If excellent working conditions are a priority, they will take precedence over higher wages in a far less congenial environment. A wise slave is preferred to an undeserving son and heir and will even share in the inheritance. Ironically enough, this proverb was fulfilled in the lives of Solomon's son Rehoboam and his servant Jeroboam, son of Nebat (1 Kings 11:28; 12:1–24). In modern times rich persons can disinherit unworthy heirs very simply.

The analogy of crucibles for reducing gold and silver ore is used to portray the testing of human motivation by God. In each case the approved product is "yet so as by fire" (1 Cor. 3:15 KJV). Ridiculing the poor and gloating over the misfortunes of others are abhorrent to God, who may well return these insults with interest. Israelite culture valued grandchildren as the crown of the aged. This is true not merely because they represent family continuity, but also because grandparents convey a sense of family history and stability (17:6). The function of a bribe as a motivating force is noted; this practice was evidently widespread in Israel, as elsewhere.

The fool pursuing his ridiculous activities is far worse than a mother bear robbed of her cubs, who will go to extreme lengths to regain her offspring (17:12). Controlling anger was a constant concern of the ancient sages, and Solomon likened its spread to the rupturing of a dam. If the opening is blocked at the very start, no harm is done. This is true of quarreling also, which can assume dangerous proportions if unchecked.

The outrageous practice of justifying the wicked and condemning the righteous, which was prevalent then as now, is condemned as being abominable to God (17:15). Yet another practical proverb questions the wisdom of investing money to educate unworthy people when they have no desire to benefit from the process. In modern Western society, where education is very expensive, this matter is a burning issue. The question of individual "worth" has to be decided on the broad basis of potential for success. But as the proverb suggests, there comes a point where realism makes the decision. An observation on friendship stresses its component of love and remarks on the value of a brother when times are difficult (17:17). But friendship has its limits, and the concerns expressed in Proverbs 6:1–5 are recalled (17:18). Succeeding proverbs deal with exhibitionists who "make the door high," either literally in a lavish home or figuratively by boasting (17:19); people who reap what they sow (17:20); stupid sons (17:21); wicked people who accept bribes to pervert justice (17:23); the therapeutic values of a cheerful disposition (17:22); and the grief that a foolish son brings (17:25). Court aristocrats obviously coined the maxim in verse 26. They also observed that even the fool, when silent, can be mistaken for a wise man (v. 28).

A problem in Hebrew society were misfits who insisted upon boorish behavior, for which they sought excuses (Heb. desires). Modern cosmopolitan cities can testify to the reality of this situation (18:1). The fool, who may also be one of these persons, is interested solely in his own opinion (18:2). Consequently, what he has to say stirs up trouble, ruining him ultimately in the process. Neither the interests of wisdom nor society are served by partiality to wickedness or penalizing the righteous. Wisdom itself is described as a "gushing stream," which implies freshness and vitality of a kind not found in standing water (cf. Jer. 2:13).

The influence of gossip is also noted (18:8), and its attractiveness is described vividly. While it is not condemned rigorously, its association with the sinister "whisperer" (KJV talebearer) is sufficient warning for the wise person to heed (cf. Lev. 19:16). The "name of the LORD" is mentioned figuratively as a strong defensive tower, to which the righteous can withdraw confidently from any oppression (18:10). Continuing the theme of safety, a wealthy man's riches are for him a strong city. Hence he tends to trust in them, whereas righteous people believe in God for his provision. The upright need not necessarily be poor, however, since in Hebrew tradition wealth was one sign of divine blessing. But to be a believer and also possess a substantial bank balance is for most Christians the ideal way of life.

Another proverb about pride (18:12) indicates that it is at its height before calamity occurs. But if humility is the hallmark of one's character, it will be graced ultimately by honor (cf. 15:33; 16:18). Courtesy and common sense are advocated by the observation that a person who responds before the question has been asked or a statement has been made can appear stupid, especially if his premature response betrays total ignorance of the matter under discussion. Derisive laughter can then be expected as his reward. Another psychosomatic observation recognizes that the human spirit can endure sickness, but has no defense when its resistance is broken, and hence the person dies (18:14).

The question of bribery in social dealings is addressed again (18:16). By using money in this way it is possible to gain access to the highest levels of society and perhaps perform some useful service having once paid the "admission fee." In ancient as in modern times, entrance to select groups in the community required evidence of fiscal responsibility, and this could have been all that the "gift" comprised under some circumstances. The proverb does not comment upon the morality of the situation, but merely notes it as a fact of life. The moral issue would turn on the intent attaching to the gift of such money. Procedures by which justice is served (18:17–18) are followed by statements illustrating the power of speech (18:19–21, 23) and divine blessing in the person of a good wife (18:22). Verse 24 is difficult, beginning literally "a man of friends is to be shattered," that is, some friends are destructive whereas others are more permanent than blood brothers. For the Christian, the latter type of friend is Jesus (cf. John 15:13–14).

In terms of comparison, a poor honest person is better than a corrupt foolish one (19:1). Nothing is said about the financial state of the latter, but corrupt people in the language of Proverbs have generally amassed wealth improperly. Honesty is promoted as the best policy, even if it does not result in riches. To be devoid of knowledge is bad for a person (KJV soul) because it denies him the opportunity of making measured decisions, causing him possible difficulties in business and social life. To blame God for the results of one's own foolishness (19:3) is stupidity indeed, but is as common now as in the days of Solomon. Newfound friends gather around a rich person looking for favors, whereas even a poor man's brothers detest him (19:4). When a rich man distributes gifts, he has a host of admirers who are motivated simply by greed. Verse 9 repeats verse 5 regarding the punishment of false witnesses. This must have been a favorite saying and stresses the importance of the ninth commandment (Exod. 20:16). Social protocol is at issue in the following verse, which insists that fools should no more live in luxury than slaves should rule over princes. The ancient Near East was very class-conscious, and although the Israelites were supposed to live as a priestly kingdom, this egalitarian ideal was distorted considerably by the hard facts of economic life. A few wealthy people ultimately governed the affairs of the remainder, who on average were poor. In general terms, poverty rather than wealth has characterized human society.

As part of the social picture, domestic situations naturally feature in the Book of Proverbs. Morally deficient or stupid sons brought parental heartbreak, then as now (19:13), and the torture exerted by a continuously whining or nagging wife is compared picturesquely to the continuous dripping of rain. The good wife (19:14) is a gift of divine grace which cannot be inherited like property. Keeping the commandments brings life, as Jesus indicated (Matt. 19:17), but repudiating them incurs death. The "life" mentioned here involves other subsidiary commandments as well as the Decalogue, including the precepts that wisdom teaches. Because of their numbers, the poor always need consideration, and the attitude of charity toward them is described with beauty and delicacy as "lending to the Lord" (19:17), who can be expected to repay such indebtedness with interest.

Family concerns resurface in the advice to discipline a son to forestall delinquency (19:18). Yet it must be done lovingly, befitting a devoted parent, and administered to build up rather than destroy the offender. The overall purpose of this exercise is to strengthen the "son" for the future (19:20). The key words are "listen," "accept," and "gain," which is the essence of the wisdom teaching, as indeed of the Christian gospel.

Reverence for the Lord brings a quality of life that has nothing in common with the lazy person, the scorner, and the abuser of parents (19:24–26), all of whom lack understanding. The "son" must listen to all this instruction and remember it. Although perverted witnesses mock justice and the wicked thrive on their evil ways, punishment will overtake all transgressors as they reap what they have sown. The penalty, it appears, will fit the crime (19:29).

Drunkenness (20:1) was probably the greatest social problem in antiquity because of a comparative lack of nonalcoholic beverages. Wine here is distinguished from "strong drink" (Heb. *šēkār*), the latter probably being a fermented liquid. The drunkard is not in control of himself and is made to look pathetic and foolish in his inebriation. This sad situation has been repeated countless times in human history and will continue, since ethyl alcohol is the world's most widely abused drug. A royal proverb points to its court origin and promotes the image of a mighty king who controls the destinies of his subjects.

The lazy person who never has enough for the winter must have been a recurring social problem, because he is mentioned again here (20:4). Procrastination, which is a lack of discipline, lies at the root of his problems, and if the "autumn" means the "cold season" (cf. Gen. 8:22; Jer. 36:22), he would have an excellent excuse for postponing his work.

Proverbs often examines human purposiveness, and here (20:5) it is likened to deep waters. But by careful psychological counseling a wise man can draw it out where necessary, presumably by using nondirective techniques. Many physical diseases are rooted in the depths of the personality, and need to be cleansed through Christ's blood for individuals to be made whole. The question raised in verse 9 was answered centuries later when Christ the Messiah redeemed the world from sin. Commercial abuses of weights are mentioned once more (20:10) as abominations in God's sight (cf. 11:1; 16:11). Another psychological observation recognizes character and motivation in children by what they do. Since fallen humanity is dominated by sin rather than grace, some juvenile actions will necessarily be sinful, thus casting doubt on the notion of "innocent children." But for them as for adults, God has made the senses of seeing and hearing so that they can obtain wisdom. Thus when the eyes are open to opportunity, prosperity results (20:13). There is a short anecdote about a businessman who drives a hard bargain and afterward boasts about his astuteness (20:14). But if his bread has actually been gained by deceit, he will be left with a mouthful of grit (20:17).

The question of co-signers is dealt with a little differently in verse 18, where the acceptance of collateral is recommended. The penalty for disobeying the fifth commandment (Exod. 20:12) is mentioned (20:20), indicating that such repudiation of parents actually occurred. Useful advice is given about making promises and vows (20:25), advocating careful, balanced thought. Unmarried women were protected from rash undertakings (Num. 30:3–6), whereas men were not. The image of God in mankind is likened to a lamp which illumines and guides the mind of the wicked person. Two royal proverbs depict the king as punishing the wicked and upholding his throne by righteousness (20:26–28), which was true of Solomon initially. While young men glory in their physique, their grey-haired elders have earned veneration by their wisdom.

Another royal proverb commences chapter 21, comparing the king's heart to a life-giving irrigation stream, the flow of which is under the Lord's control, who bestows all life. The "heart" denotes intelligence, feeling, and will, as informed by divine wisdom. The thought of Proverbs 16:2 is recapitulated in verse 2, which has overtones of the period of the judges. Although a man may feel satisfied with his way of life, God will be the ultimate assessor. Abuse of the Hebrew sacrificial system had evidently not gone unnoticed by the sages. Along with an offering it demanded true repentance and a changed way of life. Yet the wicked continued to offer sacrifices (cf. Prov. 15:18), and therefore the prophets, following Solomonic wisdom, stressed the superior value of righteousness, mercy, covenant love, and humble obedience to God (cf. Amos 5:24; Mic. 6:6–8).

Verse 4 can be read either as "the plowing of the wicked . . ." (Heb.) or "the lamp of the wicked" (LXX). Many commentators prefer the latter, which implies that arrogance and pride illumine the wicked person's way. In any event the negative attributes mentioned are not characteristic of divine grace. In their greed, the hasty tend toward precipitate decisions, and when lying is involved the gain proves to be transient (21:5–6). The very occurrence of physical or moral violence will carry them off to requite their injustices, whereas the pure motivation of the righteous ensures their blessing (21:8). This is no idle promise, because the upright live to see the wicked destroyed.

The quarrelsome wife must have presented many problems in ancient Israel. She is introduced in Proverbs 19:3 and mentioned also in 21:19 and 25:24. Life was extremely difficult for the ancient Israelite woman, who was not always helped or provided for by her husband. Under such conditions, recriminations were bound to occur. Then as now, the difficulties could have been lessened by the community of interest that a loving husband and a devoted, excellent wife ought to have.

The gift of verse 14 proves to be a bribe and is used as a pacifier to prevent a difficult situation from becoming worse. While it might achieve its effect, it raises certain moral questions. A genuine gift could work wonders for domestic harmony, but a bribe suggests covert dealings. The mocker comes in for further criticism, being defined as a proud, arrogant person (21:24), but his punishment proves instructive for the simple-minded (21:11). Frugality, temperance (21:17), charity to the poor (21:13), and righteousness ensure life and honor, but the profligate will come to want, and the man who is too lazy to work will die from starvation (21:25).

The wicked man, described as intensely covetous (21:26; Heb. he covets covetously), sacrifices in a thoroughly hypocritical manner and puts on a bold face when conducting business dealings, but all this is to no avail. When a righteous man speaks, his credibility triumphs over the bluff, bluster, and blatant lies of the wicked (21:28). No matter how cleverly hatched a plan is, or how deviously it is executed, it will not succeed if it is not of the Lord (21:30). There may be many horses and chariots arrayed for battle, but victory comes from the Lord (cf. 1 Cor. 15:57).

Chapter 22 begins with the final group of Solomonic sayings and commends a good reputation rather than great wealth. Rich or poor, people's lives are in God's hands. Yet riches are part of God's reward to those who reverence him and follow him in humility (22:1–4). The familiar maxim of verse 6 conceals some translation problems. First, the Greek Septuagint omitted it, thus precluding any reconstruction of the Hebrew. Second, the word rendered "train" is rare and means "dedicate," while the phrase *the way he should go* is in Hebrew "on the mouth of his way." Thus the moral imperative in English ("should") is not part of the original wording. Is one therefore supposed to train a child for a predetermined position in life, instilling in him the precepts of wisdom, or to nourish him in instruction but allow him to follow the avocation best suited to his abilities? The wisdom content of the training is obviously a constant, but anything else can be debated, it would appear. Children, being human, need discipline to forsake foolishness (22:15). Generosity brings blessing (22:9), and an honest, articulate man can move in royal circles (22:11). The lazy person invents a spectacular excuse for avoiding work (22:13), and those who exploit the poor are promised deprivation (22:16).

IV. Sayings of the Wise Men (22:17–24:34)

These teachers demand attention, concentration, a retentive memory, and an ability to quote the precepts as occasion requires (22:17–18). These sayings have been compiled to encourage faith in God, to admonish, and to instruct the one seeking wisdom. The Hebrew consonants *shlshwm* admit of various renderings, including "thirty," "formerly," and "excellent." "Thirty" may be correct, since the material can be divided roughly into thirty sections, comparable to the "thirty chapters" of *The Teachings of Amenophis.* While "formerly" seems rather contrived, "excellent," that is, "noble things," is certainly characteristic of the sayings and is preferred by the King James Version and New King James Version ("pleasant thing").

The sayings begin by forbidding the exploitation of the poor and the unjust treatment of the afflicted (22:23). If this occurs, divine vengeance will fall upon their oppressors. Warnings are given about associating with angry persons in case their attitudes become infectious and lead to harm. Acting as surety for a debtor is forbidden, since one could lose everything as a result. Commitments of this kind are deemed bad business risks by these sages. The property marker was of concern throughout the ancient world, and its removal was forbidden in the Law (Deut. 19:14) and Amenophis (6:1 seq.). This prevented encroachment upon the property of others, which in the case of widows could constitute exploitation or theft (cf. 15:25). A craftsman of outstanding skill can achieve a prominence that cannot be secured by lesser persons.

Chapter 23 commences with much needed advice on table etiquette, which reflects the emphasis placed upon proper deportment at select social functions. The guest's attention must be fixed on his host, not upon the splendor of the banquet hall or the delicious array of food. This practical wisdom, which is of eminent value today, demands discipline as well as good breeding if a guest is to profit from it. The transient nature of wealth is noted, and therefore a man should not exhaust himself amassing what can disappear so easily. It is thus a counsel of wisdom to know how much wealth is enough. For the majority, unfortunately, greed dictates no limits. The wise man should not dine with a miserly (Heb. evil eye) person, nor desire to do so, because though outwardly pleasant, he is actually grudging the guest his food. Should this unfortunate situation occur, it will sicken the guest (23:6–8).

The warning against removing landmarks is repeated with a caution against trespassing and a reminder that the Lord will punish offenders. He is described as a *gā'al,* a term used of a near relative who was obliged to help a family member in need (cf. Lev. 25:25; Ruth 3:12; etc.). Discipline should not be withheld from children out of a false sense of compassion, but administered with a rod. The recipient may feel brutalized, but will live to rejoice over his deliverance from death. A wise son will delight his father, especially when he hears his pupil testifying to righteousness (23:16). The wise man will not despair at the prosperity of the wicked but will continue to reverence and obey the Lord in the expectation that God will reward him (23:17–18).

Further wise advice is directed to the widespread social problem of drunkenness. Since it was often associated with gluttony, the two are considered together. Both should be avoided by the wise man, because such indulgence can consume a person's resources (cf. Luke 15:13).

The advice offered on envy (23:17–18) is supplemented here (24:1–2) by further practical suggestions. Envious people are always planning violent acts of some sort, trying to gain an advantage over others. By avoiding such company a person escapes the effects of violence, which tend to escalate. Wisdom builds, establishes, and furnishes a house (24:3–4), whether it be a physical structure, a family (cf. 14:1), a business, or a personal reputation. Brains outrank sheer brute force because they can plan a winning strategy (24:5–6), but the fool reveals his true self by being unable to conduct proper negotiations in the city courts and councils (24:7). Evil acts begin in the mind and affect others by word and deed. This behavior is sin against God and man, and the person who repudiates this counsel is a menace to humanity. The believer needs to be strong at all times to cope with the stresses of life and to take a proper part in assuring a just social and spiritual order by fighting both oppression and stupidity. To plead ignorance of these responsibilities is no excuse, because God has a mission in society for the believer, who will be judged ultimately according to his deeds. The remarks in James 2:26 are pertinent here.

Wisdom is as palatable to the spirit as honey is to the body but carries with it a more permanent reward. The wicked are warned about the resilience of the godly, who can be defeated, trapped, exploited, and cheated frequently (Heb. seven times), yet rise again to conquer. This is reminiscent of Jesus, who suffered the apparent defeat of death only to triumph magnificently in his resurrection. It is thus not in the best interests of the wicked to harass the righteous, and the commands "do not . . . " are rather unusual in this connection. When his enemy falls, however, the godly person is forbidden to gloat over his defeat but should thank God that he is victorious over evil. God does not delight in the death of a sinner (Ezek. 33:11), but prefers him to repent and be saved, a process which produces joy in heaven (Luke 15:7, 10). The righteous should not be envious of, or irritated by, evildoers, because by continuing as such they will be destroyed.

The prosperity and stability of the state will be ensured when people reverence God and honor the ruler. The latter is the earthly representative of the former, and his authority, though derived, demands respect and obedience (cf. Rom. 13:4; 1 Pet. 2:17). Christians, therefore, have a loyalty both to God and the state, and to be good citizens must be true to each (Matt. 22:21).

Another section of sayings (24:23–34) contains more excellent advice. The authors give evidence of a well-informed life experience, and their thoughts have a timeless quality about them. The concept of balanced judgment was raised previously (cf. 17:15; 18:5) and will be mentioned again (28:21). Judging was often the responsibility of the king in his court, hence these thoughts can be assigned confidently to Solomon. A judge must hear the evidence and then be instructed by wisdom to give an impartial and fair decision, so that justice is meted out to the poor, and the wicked are punished for their crimes. Such honest, forthright behavior is like receiving a kiss from a close friend. The condemnation of false witness, forbidden by the Law (Exod. 20:6), is reiterated (24:28), but acts of revenge are prohibited, this being God's prerogative (Deut. 32:35; Rom. 12:19). A memorable description of the lazy man and his vineyard teaches that indolence and procrastination will end in ruin (24:30–34).

V. Solomonic Proverbs from Hezekiah's Collection (25:1–29:27)

This royal material also begins with sayings

about the king, who is indeed glorious if he can search out the deep things of God (25:2). The typical Near Eastern flattery used in addressing or describing royalty occurs in verse 3, which could imply great breadth of mind, but in a negative sense bewilderment at some royal decisions. The wicked are compared to the slag from an ore-refining process, which when removed reveals the precious metal. The silver thus survives, but the worthless slag is thrown away. Removing the wicked from his kingdom enables a king to rule in righteousness. This image looks forward to a future date when the King of kings will be enthroned, having judged and dispensed with the wicked (Rev. 20:11–15).

Ostentation, aggression, or forwardness do not help one's promotion in a royal court. One should be seen, not heard, and be commended by deportment and character, in which reticence and humility will be prominent. A different kind of court is described in verse 8, where litigation is the topic. A precipitate charge may not be backed by sufficient evidence, to the ultimate embarrassment of the prosecutor. Neighbors should be treated as friends, and a private, common-sense approach adopted toward disputes. Jesus advocated such an attitude in his teachings (Matt. 5:25) and clearly preferred an out-of-court settlement (Luke 12:58) to a harsh judgment which could ruin a defendant.

Elegance and succinctness of speech were prized by the ancient sages, and here an appropriate statement is likened to small golden apples clustered in a silver setting. The entire situation bespeaks understated elegance and blesses the donor as much as the recipient. Even a rebuke can be framed so beautifully and discreetly that it is accepted precisely on those grounds and is valued as though it had been made of gold. The point of this approach is that the carefully crafted utterance dignifies rather than denigrates the recipient, and it commends the wisdom of a person who can utter such complimentary or conciliatory remarks (25:11–12).

Trustworthy servants receive their share of praise (25:13–14), being likened to a refreshing cold drink on a hot day. The messenger who is faithful has demonstrated his capabilities, unlike the proud braggart who promises more than he can deliver. It is noted in passing that patience and persuasiveness will even influence the opinions of kings, who had power of life and death over their subjects. Self-discipline will counteract greed in the matter of food intake (25:16), and good manners will prevent a person from becoming a nuisance to others. The false witness is censured again (25:18), while placing trust in an unworthy person is as bad as having a toothache or a lame foot. Verse 20 may mean that the singer has a heavy heart, or that he is serenading someone in that condition. Whatever the situation, the activity is inappropriate, being likened to disrobing on a cold day, or having soda put on a wound. The contentious woman is mentioned again. The capitulation of a good person to evil is likened to a muddied spring, and the supreme value of self-control is illustrated by a negative simile (25:24–26).

The first twelve verses of chapter 26 offer various kinds of advice on dealing with fools. To honor such a person is as inappropriate as snow at harvest. The unjustified curse, presumably uttered by a fool, does no harm. The best way to treat a fool is to handle him like a potentially unruly animal and not to descend to his level by arguing. In a seeming contradiction, a fool has to be answered, presumably by the rod, so that he will recognize his own mistakes. Entrusting fools with messages or listening to them is as useless an exercise as attempting to honor them. As an employee the fool can cause serious damage and tends to return to repulsive habits. But even the fool is exceeded in stupidity by the person who possesses exaggerated self-esteem.

The lazy person's way of life is reexamined in 26:13–16, and his famous excuse for staying indoors and avoiding all danger, including that of manual work, is quoted from Proverbs 22:13. But here the treatment is as thorough as that of 24:30–34, in that it describes his behavior rather than his environment. It must be remembered that, in the early monarchy, it was possible that mountain lions could appear at Jericho or in the Hebron area. Nevertheless, the lazy man is pushing his flimsy excuse to its limits. The image of a sluggard turning in bed as a door turns on its hinges is both amusing and apposite. Each has a very limited degree of movement, and both are basically fixtures. He manages to get his hand into his dish of food by sheer gravity, but is worn out by the attempt to put it to his mouth. He fancies himself as an intellectual, however, and imagines that he can outclass all other persons. A little sidelight on the pranks played on animals is seen in verse 17. Dogs were considered fair sport, being consistently derided in Scripture, but these half-wild animals could inflict serious bites on the unwary or unfortunate provoker.

Mentally disturbed arsonists were evidently not unfamiliar in antiquity (26:18) and were deemed as dangerous as the man who played a deceptive prank on a neighbor. In the thought of Proverbs, both were grossly deficient morally. A short section (26:20–23) deals with gossip, part of which reproduces Proverbs 18:8 and indicates that the priestly community of Israel enjoyed digesting titillating items of potentially malicious conversation. While some gossip is little more than chatter about people and current events, it becomes sinister when innuendos appear to suggest a degree of impropriety in relationships. At this stage facts and truth not infrequently become casualties, and great harm can result from such malicious interchanges. The image of how something inferior can be covered up with a shiny, attractive surface is certainly apt and is matched by the "whitewashed tombs" of Christ's time (Matt. 23:27). The malicious conversationalist is a deadly menace to the community until his deceit is discovered and he is exposed publicly. But in God's providence these and other troublemakers suffer for their sins.

Another section of Hezekiah's collection (27:1–27) contains a short saying about boasting (27:1–2). This is deemed inadvisable because nobody knows the future, and thus if praise is merited it should be uttered by someone else. The Hebrews were thoroughly familiar with the disadvantages of sandy wastes and land that first had to be cleared of stones, but even they acknowledged that provocation by a fool was far more grievous. Jealousy was considered to be much more devastating than either fury or displeasure (27:4), while a love which conceals deserved rebukes is inferior to frank criticism. If, therefore, a friend inflicts some hurt through a rebuke, it is still well intentioned, whereas the deceiving affections of an enemy are highly suspect.

Another proverb touches upon the disparity between rich and poor (27:7), and shows how these two states can affect human disposition. The second part of verse 9 is obscure, the Hebrew reading literally "and the sweetness of his friend from counsel of soul." The King James Version's "so doth the sweetness of a man's friend by hearty counsel" seems to capture the sense adequately. A lengthier proverb deals with the responsibilities of friends, both inside and outside the family (27:10). This advice is very important today, where the mobility of the population can devastate friendships. A teacher is always delighted to observe progress in his students, and this encourages him to continue his work, even in the face of criticism (27:11). The next verse is almost the same as Proverbs 22:3, which emphasizes that prudent men do not confront danger deliberately, whereas the simple person does so and pays the penalty.

Verse 13 repeats the advice offered in Proverbs 20:16, namely, to obtain collateral when standing as surety, especially where foreign women are concerned. The rights of others must be respected even when acts of worship are being practiced, and this requires sound judgment (27:14). The contentious woman reappears as a cause for complaint (cf. 19:13). For reasons that are not clear, most people find a continuous dripping one of the most difficult noises to endure, and the nagging woman fits the description beautifully. Preventing her diatribes is like trying to grasp the wind or hold oil in one's hand (27:15–16).

The "sharpening" process which pits iron against iron and man against man must have been thoroughly familiar to the ancient court sages, who probably formulated many of their sayings as the result of an exchange of wits. This was important to them, because they taught that "a man's heart reflects the man" (27:19). Sheol, the abode of the dead, and Abaddon, the place of destruction, are never satisfied, and the same is true of people who are ever searching for new opportunities in society.

An agricultural section closes the chapter, and depicts the hapless fool locked into his folly (27:22), a statement of the conservation of values, namely, that one has to keep adding to them to maintain them (27:23–24), and the suggestion that what applies to livestock is equally true of education and the spiritual life. Hence the need for the Christian to study the Word consistently to repair forgetfulness and increase knowledge.

Chapter 28 deals mainly with respect for government and law. The sages observed that the wicked are always fleeing in fear, whereas the righteous walk about boldly under divine protection (cf. Ps. 23:6). What sounds like an observation on the history of the northern kingdom links a succession of rulers with social instability, the basic cause being sin. If "poor" instead of "wicked" is the preferred reading, such a person's dealings with his peers are as devastating as a harvest flood (28:3). The wicked and the good conflict because the former do not understand justice, but rich and poor alike will prosper when fearing the Lord (28:4–7). Although the Law prohibited lenders from charging interest (Exod. 22:25; Lev. 25:36–37), the practice had gained currency in the monarchy. It is not prohibited here, but God will ensure that such ill-gotten gains will somehow be returned to the poor.

Those who mislead the righteous will themselves be misled, and if a rich man is the cause, the deserving poor will discover it (28:10–11). Righteous leaders bring glory, but tyrants produce social instability (28:12) and run rampant because they lack understanding (28:15–16). Yet even they can obtain mercy by confessing their sins. Verse 17 is translated differently in a number of versions. The sense seems to be: "Do not assist anyone fleeing as a murderer, because he will seal his own fate." Therefore, nobody should interfere with the processes of justice. Integrity guarantees success and deliverance from evil, whereas the wicked dig their own graves, an assurance occurring frequently in Proverbs. Industry and diligence are commended again as a work ethic, but the pursuits of the wastrel will yield a corresponding amount of poverty. Greed for riches will also bring its own reward (28:19–20), because a man should be seeking to glorify God first (Matt. 6:33). Thus the miser comes in for special rebuke because of his preoccupation with wealth, being reminded again that his accumulated money will disappear. Once more the sages commend forthright speech rather than flattery, which may sound pleasing at the time but ultimately proves shallow (28:22–23). To steal from one's parents while denying that such action is sinful shows a grave misunderstanding of morality and the significance of close family bonds. Parents are to be honored, not robbed, even if the imposition is of the most subtle nature.

The final section of Hezekiah's collection (29:1–27) begins with the warning that the inflexibility of a stubborn will can cause the offender permanent damage. Social stability based on wisdom is emphasized again, but a ruler greedy for wealth, such as Rehoboam (1 Kings 12:10–11), brings disaster. The righteous person knows and respects the rights of the poor, whereas the wicked man does not and exploits them shamefully (29:7).

It has been observed earlier that theoretically the holy nation of Israel should be devoid of poor people, since all presumably started off in the Sinai desert basically equal. Yet while some people manage their resources, others mismanage their affairs. Because of this there could be expected to arise among the covenant people circumstances which called for understanding and assistance. A fairly common example would be that of a childless widow who found it difficult to cope with her bereavement and became destitute. In the ancient world a person survived by being a member of a family, and therefore a childless widow, capable or not, was in an extremely precarious position unless she had surviving relations who would pity her.

The Mosaic law made provision for the poor in terms of allowing them the privilege of gleaning (Lev. 19:9–10) and instituted the custom of giving the poor whatever grew by itself on land allowed to lie fallow during the sabbatical year (Exod. 23:11; Lev. 25:16). When the jubilee year came, the land reverted to its original owners, so that the poor could once again possess their ancestral inheritance (Lev. 25:25–30). The poor were also protected from usury, and limitations were imposed upon what could be retained by a creditor as a pledge (Exod. 22:25–27; Lev. 25:35–37).

In addition, the Law forbad permanent servitude unless undertaken voluntarily (Exod. 21:5–6), because it was unworthy of a nation freed from bondage by God's power. It also required those Hebrews who had committed themselves to temporary servitude to be released every seventh year and in the jubilee year (Deut. 15:12–15). The Law prescribed that portions of the tithes should be given to the poor (Deut. 14:28; 26:12–13), and that they should share fully in the celebrations at the Feast of Booths (Tabernacles), when the nation looked back to its origins. Finally, it was a rule in Israel that wages should not be accumulated, but paid daily to those able to work (Lev. 19:13) to offset the possibility of abject poverty and starvation.

There was thus enacted into Hebrew law what in modern times would be described as a welfare system. There was no need for any able-bodied person to starve, and opportunities were provided for poor people to subsist in the community without feeling guilty. Both the wise and the wicked would know about this system for dealing with poverty, but while the wise would be considerate and give assistance to the needy, the wicked would either ignore them or oppress them even further. The poor have thus always held a special place in the mind of God, and this was illustrated most fully in the incarnate Christ, who identified himself at birth with the poor, and during his ministry lived as a person who had no settled abode. It was through his poverty that the Christian has become rich (2 Cor. 8:9), a prospect that the sages of Proverbs were not able to envision.

Political agitators can cause a great deal of trouble, whatever the point at issue, and need careful handling if the turbulence is to be contained (29:8). If a wise man is so ill-advised as to argue with a fool, he cannot win because he only becomes a target for the fool's stupidity. This will often be violent in character, and will require all of the wise person's skill to avoid a serious confrontation (29:9–11). The king who heeds lies will surround himself with evil courtiers, but if he judges the poor fairly he and his house will thrive because he has cared for those least able to threaten him, thereby winning their loyalty (29:14).

With wicked people in power, crime increases, and the righteous can only hope for their overthrow. Where there is no prophetic revelation the people abandon the restraints of God's Law, and anarchy ultimately results (29:16, 18). Discipline in the sense of guidance is recommended for children for their benefit and the joy of their parents. If discipline is applied in love it will be received without resentment, and this will strengthen family bonds. A servant may need more than verbal discipline (29:19) if he listens but does not obey. Pampering a servant from childhood brings results, but the end of verse 21 is obscure and could mean "benefit" (so RSV) or "grief" (so NIV) for the master. Pride will devastate a man by humbling him, but the one who is already humble can expect God to honor him. Verse 24 is obscure but seems to mean that the thief's partner in crime fears to make any disclosure under oath for fear of reprisal, a situation which furnishes yet another glimpse of urban crime. The Lord bestows safety and justice upon the righteous, an act which causes them to detest the wicked.

VI. Sayings of Agur (30:1–33)

The author of this material and his father are unknown. "Massa" may be a place in northern Arabia (cf. Gen. 25:14), but it could also mean "oracle." If the latter, it is of a rather disconnected nature; but this is typical of much wisdom teaching. The author is a humble sage, and his sayings have an obscure beginning with an appeal to Ithiel ("God is with me"?) and Ucal ("I am consumed"?). Some scholars suggest that these are not proper names and combine them in Hebrew to read "I am weary, O God, I am weary, O God, and have become weak," but this is conjectural. Equally dubious are such translations as "I have weakened myself for God, and have fainted," and "I have labored for God and have obtained."

The style of the material has elements in common with the Book of Job, and this integrates Proverbs with the rest of the Hebrew wisdom corpus. Like Job the author is a keen observer of nature and sees the work of the mighty Creator in his surroundings. His poetic approach, however, is related to the practicalities of life, and the result is a collection of aphorisms which heightens the reader's awareness of the character of a proverb.

The author obviously exaggerates his supposed ignorance by uttering beautiful and lucid pronouncements on life, but his approach is an attempt to demonstrate his humility. It is simply a fact that the more information highly educated people have acquired, the more aware they are of the vast body of knowledge as yet unmastered. The sage's remarks, therefore, should not be taken at face value but as hyperbole. The author, like Job, seems aware that God has somehow departed from him. He claims not to have learned wisdom (30:3) and in that sense to be too stupid to be human, since even ordinary people can learn the precepts of wisdom.

If the word *massa* in the title actually means a prophetic oracle, the sage would have received it by revelation rather than intellectual reasoning, yet he states that he does not have knowledge of the Holy One. What he really seems to be implying is that he is conscious of the coarseness and narrow perspective of the human mind in all areas of life and not least in the metaphysical sphere. Reminiscences of Job 38–39 appear in the five questions of verse 4, which deal with elements of cosmic creation. The interrogation is climaxed by a demand for the name of the responsible agent. The answer is, of course, "God." Looking at the larger perspective of creation has answered the author's doubts.

The person in question is a communicating God whose every word proves to be true, and people have only to trust him to secure his mighty protection. The reference in verse 6 to "adding" is reminiscent of ancient scribal practices, where authentication that material had been copied without additions, checked, and rechecked, would often appear at the end of documents.

The sage makes his requests before he dies, asking for the removal of lies and falsity from him, and the provision of a modest supply of daily bread (30:7–8). He does not crave great riches because he has made known his humility, hence he speaks of human needs rather than wants. He is anxious to avoid excesses at his age and does not want to be sated with food, thinking that it has been acquired by purely human effort. This would deny the provident God whom he has embraced. Nor does he desire poverty, which for some would be an ideal, because he would be tempted to steal for food. In doing so he would be breaking one of God's express commandments (Exod. 20:15) and would profane God's holy name. There is a good deal of sentimental idealism associated with poverty, but the sage is a realist and recognizes that it would demean him and lead him into sin, as it has done countless others. His sense of divine reverence compels him to think of his social inferiors, hence the maxim about a servant (30:10). The one who curses could be the slandered servant or his master, but the penalty is the same.

A link is established with the next four verses (30:11–14), which begin with a collective *those*. The author records his observations without formal judgment, but the character of the deeds speaks for itself. The evil words of verse 10 are now applied by "those" to parents, in defiance of the Law (Exod. 20:12), to the self-righteous, to the self-deceivers, and to those who oppress the poor, of whom the author is marginally one. Verse 15 begins with a rare word of uncertain meaning, traditionally rendered "leech," and using the numerical ladder introduces Sheol, the infertile womb, drought-parched earth, and fire, none of which can ever be satisfied (30:15–16). The punishment for mocking parents (30:17) is not merely death but the ignominy of having one's flesh pecked and eaten by birds of prey.

The celebrated passage dealing with mysteries (30:18–19) seems to refer to individual mastery of special environments. An abhorrent fifth (30:20) is the hateful adulteress who, being satisfied, denies any wrongdoing. The numerical series continues (30:21–23) with such intolerable situations as the ambitious slave who becomes a ruler, a sated fool, a hateful woman who finally marries, and a maid who usurps her mistress's position. All these present difficulties because they are traditionally inappropriate.

Four small things (30:24–28), which exert a disproportionately large influence, are marvelous because of their special abilities. These are the ants (cf. 6:6–8), the badger, the well-organized locusts, and the insect-eating lizard which can be held in the hand. There is clearly no necessary correlation in nature between size and effectiveness, as the atom demonstrates. Another series deals with four instances of stately demeanor (30:29–31), of which only the King James Version's "grayhound" (LXX strutting rooster) presents translation difficulties. A final utterance reminds the boaster or the plotter to refrain from speaking, as a conciliatory gesture. The Revised Standard Version (30:33) shows the threefold repetition of the Hebrew verb *press*, the implication being that the more people advance their opinions, the more likely they are to provoke trouble.

VII. Sayings of Lemuel (31:1–9)

King Lemuel is just as mysterious as Agur, and while his residence could also be northern Arabia, it is unknown. If "Massa" means "oracle," the title refers to the wisdom taught by his mother, who is the real author. She asks three questions, each of which augments its precursor somewhat, and then informs her son, whom she addresses affectionately yet respectfully, about royal duties.

He is counseled to avoid squandering his energies on women (as Solomon did), and to guard against the perils of alcohol (31:3–7). Solomon's drinking habits are unknown, but Elah was killed when drunk (1 Kings 16:9–10) and Benhadad of Syria came close to meeting a similar fate (1 Kings 20:16). Lemuel's mother recommends alcohol as a remedy for depression or those at death's door, presumably because the latter have no future. Lemuel is counseled to champion the cause of the needy and desolate, who would have difficulty in obtaining a hearing, and to maintain their rights under the law (31:8–9).

VIII. Postscript: The Excellent Wife (31:10–31)

This section, which is an acrostic in Hebrew, was probably written by Lemuel's mother also, who counsels him about the qualities of an excellent wife. Kindness, resourcefulness, and versatility characterize the virtuous woman, but these attributes, desirable as they are, do not begin to exhaust her potential. In addition, she exercises the age-old role of the Hebrew matriarch in supervising closely the affairs of her entire household (31:27). This task demands energy, foresight, and careful planning, so that nobody for whom she is responsible will go hungry or lack clothing.

To meet this situation she always has available an adequate supply of whatever is needed for all those who are under her care, and with the work of her own hands she makes certain that they are fed properly and clothed appropriately (31:13–22). Yet she does not consider these duties to be demeaning but rather rejoices in them as a fulfillment of her responsibilities to her family and to society in general.

As a result of all this, her husband is the recipient of special attention and recognition when he sits with the council of elders inside the city gate (31:23). Not content with providing clothing for her own household, she also devotes her talents to making fabrics for sale to the city merchants (31:24). Nothing in the nature of guile debases her character, because she is clothed with strength, honor, and gentleness (31:25). A natural outcome of her conduct is the way in which she becomes the object of outright praise and admiration from her husband, children (31:26), and others.

It is eminently fitting that, in a book devoted to wisdom, an excellent, praiseworthy woman should have the last word.

SELECT BIBLIOGRAPHY

Crenshaw, J. *Studies in Ancient Israelite Wisdom.* New York: Ktav, 1976.

Kidner, D. *The Proverbs.* Downers Grove: Inter-Varsity, 1975.

McKane, W. *Proverbs, A New Approach.* Philadelphia: Westminster, 1970.

Whybray, R. N. *Wisdom in Proverbs.* Naperville, Ill.: A. R. Allenson, 1965.

ECCLESIASTES

Carl Schultz

INTRODUCTION

Ecclesiastes is a difficult book. One should not be misled by its title. The English title comes from the Greek word for church, but the writer, whom we will call by his given Hebrew name, Qoheleth (sometimes spelled Koheleth), is not very ecclesiastical. He not only charges "do not be overwicked" but surprisingly urges "do not be overrighteous" (7:16–17). He has been correctly viewed as an iconoclast—one who destroys the gods of wealth, power, pride, fame, even religion.

He rejects out of hand easy answers to the purpose of life, even religious answers. He warns that "the words of the wise are like goads" (12:11)—sharp pointed stakes used to prod animals. No wonder then that the reader has the impression that Qoheleth is poking him, nudging him on.

Not only Qoheleth's approach, but also the format of this book makes it difficult. Qoheleth is no systematic theologian. There are so many shifts in mood and position that the formation of the book is uncertain and much debated. Rather than the product of one mind, is this book the product of an academy of sages? It has been suggested that two, or three, or even as many as nine different minds are at work in this book. Or, is it the notebook of a man who mixes his thoughts with those of others without carefully distinguishing them? Or is it the diary of the writer, a record of his thoughts without any reference to time or setting? If this is the case, then the alleged self-corrections or the alleged self-contradictions of the book are not due to a plurality of minds, but the oscillation of a single mind grappling with the complexities of life.

But the difficulty of this book is not limited to its approach or format. There are also the conclusions at which the writer seems to arrive. "Meaningless! Meaningless! Utterly meaningless! Everything is meaningless!" (1:2). Terms such as fatalism, pessimism, skepticism, even nihilism, seem appropriate for this book—so much so that the acceptance of this book into the canon was seriously challenged by Jews and Christians alike.

There are perhaps four reasons for our fascination with this book.

First, the climate out of which it grew is present with us today, so much so that it has been called the most modern book in the Bible. Boredom, surfeit, disillusionment, and world-weariness characterize our times as they did the time of Qoheleth. Certainties and values have crumbled and new purposes to life are sought now as then.

The society which Qoheleth addressed was an earthly one—a secular one imprisoned by this world. Its view was bounded by the horizons of this world. Even its religion had become as secularized as our religion today. Such a condition accounts for the frequent reoccurrence of the phrase *under the sun*. This was the area of concern for Qoheleth's audience and he chose to meet his audience on their own ground to reveal the vanity of a self-contained world, of a purely secular order.

The society which Qoheleth addressed was also a commercial one. This follows as no surprise. Certainly Qoheleth was affluent and probably so were the people being addressed. This provides another point of contact with our time. This book is filled with commercial language, using terms such as advantage, profit, toil, occupation, position, success, money, wealth, owner, lack, and deficit. The familiar verse, "Cast your bread upon the waters, for after many days you will find it again" (11:1) suggests trade and investment. "Give portions to seven, yes to eight, for you do not know what disaster may come upon the land" (11:2) seems to suggest an uncertain future and is perhaps calling for diversification, that is, a caution against putting all our eggs in one basket. It would seem that Qoheleth is musing here upon a society dominated by commerce, an acquisitive society. He frequently seems to take aim at commonly held commercial values (e.g., 1:3; 2:11; 5:10).

Second, the questions which the book raises are the very questions we are raising. Not only are we acquisitive, we are inquisitive. Qoheleth raises questions about meaning (1:3), monotony (1:10), destiny (3:21), justice (6:8), nostalgia (7:10), and the future (8:7). It is his ability to give utterance to a deep and universal need—a need to know the meaning of life—that makes this book enduringly attractive.

It is appropriate that Ecclesiastes was one of the last books of the Old Testament written—appropriate because the writer seems to remain open in his assessment. His penetrating questions point clearly in the direction of the answer of the New Testament.

Third, the methods used by the writer to collect his data are amazingly up to date. As with all wisdom literature, of which Ecclesiastes is a vital part, there is an absence of "Thus saith the Lord." Data are gathered from observations. This is not to challenge the inspiration or authority of Qoheleth's words, but simply to recognize that revelation can reach us from the horizontal as well as the vertical. The material in this book could be called "the confessions/the reflections" of Qoheleth. Qoheleth chooses to view the world from a natural perspective ("under the sun") to meet his audience on its own ground in order to show the utter futility of a soulless and godless world.

Modern man is also a man of sight, his conclusions about life being based upon what he can see with his own eyes. But he has become so dependent upon his eyes that he is trapped. He can only perceive that which is seen. Failing to see God and to detect his purposes, modern man becomes weary and disgusted, concurring with Qoheleth's worldly finding—all is vanity.

Fourth, the conclusion that Qoheleth arrives at is the same one that man reaches today: "Vanity of vanities, all is vanity" (1:2 RSV). The Hebrew literary form *X of X* indicates the superlative and adds to the intensity of the statement (King of kings; Song of Songs; holy of holies)—not only vanity, but *utter* vanity. The phrase emphasizes not only intensity, but also comprehensiveness—*all* is vanity.

Qoheleth, in meeting man on his own ground, is devastating. He demolishes everything in sight. But there is a purpose to this approach. Qoheleth can build only after he has finished his demolition.

Both in Jewish and Christian tradition this book has been attributed to Solomon. One rabbinic source suggests that Solomon wrote Song of Songs (emphasis on love) in his youth; Proverbs (emphasis on practical living) in his maturity; and Ecclesiastes (emphasis on meaninglessness) in his old age (Midrash *Shir Hashirim* Rabbah 1:1 sec. 10). Up to the time of Luther most Christian scholars considered Solomon to be the author.

But Solomon's name never appears in the book. The reference to "son of David" (1:1) may seem to suggest Solomon, but this phrase could simply designate any later Davidic king. The phrase *king in Jerusalem* (1:1) is never used of Solomon. The use of the perfect "I *was* king" (1:12) implies that the writer is no longer king. There is no evidence that Solomon abdicated, but rather that he died a king. Thus, this phrase does not fit Solomon, but one who assumes the role of Solomon.

The author is simply identified as Qoheleth. This Hebrew word appears seven times (1:1, 2, 12; 7:27; 12:8, 9, 10) in this book, but nowhere else in the Bible. Qoheleth, a Hebrew feminine participle, comes from the Hebrew root *qhl* which means "to gather" or "to assemble." The object of this action is always people, never things. Qoheleth then is a title meaning "one who gathers persons to address and instruct them" (12:9–10; see 1 Kings 8:1, 55, where such action is assigned to Solomon). This word can appear with the article (12:8), suggesting that it is a title.

It is also possible that Qoheleth should be viewed as a name. In Hebrew, as in other languages, function can determine a person's name, although in turn, the name and function may be separated. Consider such English names as Cook, Smith, Fowler, and Penman.

If Qoheleth is a proper name, then it could simply be transliterated (see JB). Generally in English translations efforts are made to translate it: Preacher (KJV, RSV); Teacher (NIV); Speaker (NEB); Philosopher (TEV). While "Preacher" is the most popular rendition, it is not the best. The intent of this book is not sermonic, but sapiential. As such, "Teacher" is a better translation. Qoheleth then should be viewed both as a title and a name.

This raises the intriguing question of why Qoheleth assumes the role of Solomon. Clearly he wants us to think of Solomon. Solomon is, of course, the example par excellence of the futility of life. There is another reason for using Solomon's name. The writer, probably with the full knowledge of his contemporaries (Qoheleth is as artificial as the pen name John Doe, President of the United States), wants to show that what he wrote stood squarely in the tradition of Solomon's own wisdom. Solomon had encyclopedic knowledge—"a breadth of understanding as measureless as the sand on the seashore. . . . He described plant life . . . [and] also taught about animals and birds, reptiles and fish" (1 Kings 4:29–34). There is no effort at forgery here. Qoheleth never uses the name *Solomon* but rather assumes the sapiential authority of Solomon. What he wrote is what Solomon would have written.

Reference has already been made to the fact that this book is difficult—difficult because of its composition, contradictions, and conclusions. Even a casual reading of the book will reveal apparent contradictions. Qoheleth not only seems to contradict himself, he also seems to contradict the traditional views of Israel. He appears to be skeptical rather than confessional.

There have been many efforts either to deny the contradictions or to explain them. These denials or explanations are fundamental to the composition of this book.

Spiritualizing exegesis has been used by both Jews and Christians. Difficult passages are not taken in a straightforward manner, but are spiritualized, thus muting any problem. An example of this is a rabbinic tradition which suggests that wherever eating and drinking are mentioned in this book, the reference is to Torah and good deeds (*Koheleth Rabbah* 2:25).

Ecclesiastes has also been considered the product of two, or three, or as many as nine minds/sources at work. The alleged contradictions are then due to the debate of wise men or dialogues between sages with differing viewpoints. Another suggested possibility is that the original book as prepared by the sage was heterodox. In order to secure it a place in the canon a pious believer added numerous glosses that made the book orthodox. This inclination to dissect the book does not presently have general scholarly support.

Some suggest that Qoheleth put himself and his audience in the shoes of the secularists—the persons whose perspective is limited to "under the sun"—to demonstrate their inability to cope with evil and death. By assuming this role, Qoheleth is able to meet the secularists on their own turf, showing that enslavement to this world results in anxiety, wretchedness, and boredom. By shattering all earthly gods he devastates all false hopes and drives the reader to the true God. He is a kind of negative theologian, exposing the futility of life limited to "under the sun."

Closely related to this approach is the idea that Qoheleth presents ideas that he does not approve of and then refutes them. Being a teacher of wisdom, Qoheleth cites maxims to which he then reacts. Sometimes he cites contrasting positions. Since these quotations are not identified with an introductory formula or marked with quotation marks they are frequently not recognized as quotations, thus creating the impression of internal contradictions. Ecclesiastes is then a kind of notebook in which Qoheleth enters the thoughts of others and his reflection on them. This could, at least in part, explain the apparent lack of overall organization in the book.

Sometimes the alleged contradictions are traced to the difficulty of the mysteries considered in light of the complexity of Qoheleth himself. Qoheleth takes the reader on a journey through the maze of issues discussed in the book, not hesitant to reveal his doubts and perplexities in process before he arrives at his conclusion. The book is then like a diary in which the writer sets down his thoughts without indicating when or why. Even as a diary must be read with the heart as well as the head, so must Ecclesiastes. Understanding the writer and his struggles will help us to read the book sympathetically and realistically.

OUTLINE

- I. Title and Theme (1:1–11)
  - A. Title (1:1)
  - B. Theme (1:2–11)
- II. Wisdom Reflections (1:12–4:16)
  - A. The Search for Satisfaction (1:12–2:26)
  - B. A Catalog of Times (3:1–15)
  - C. A Question of Justice (3:16–22)
  - D. A Matter of Oppression (4:1–3)
  - E. A Critique of Work (4:4–12)
  - F. The Transience of Fame (4:13–16)
- III. Admonitions and Observations (5:1–12:8)
  - A. Religious Practice (5:1–7)
  - B. A Matter of Political Corruption (5:8–9)
  - C. The Vanity of Wealth (5:10–6:9)
  - D. Man's Helplessness and Ignorance (6:10–12)
  - E. "Better Than" Proverbs (7:1–14)
  - F. An Avoidance of Extremes (7:15–24)
  - G. The Search for Wisdom (7:25–8:1)
  - H. Court Protocol (8:2–8)
  - I. Failure of Retribution (8:9–17)
  - J. A Common Destiny (9:1–6)
  - K. Enjoyment of Life (9:7–10)
  - L. The Inadequacy of Wisdom (9:11–18)
  - M. Assorted Practical Sayings (10:1–20)
  - N. A Call to Action (11:1–6)
  - O. Youth and Age (11:7–12:8)
- IV. Conclusion (12:9–14)

COMMENTARY

I. Title and Theme (1:1–11)

A. Title (1:1). While the term *Qoheleth* could be a proper name, it is more likely a title, describing rather than identifying the writer. The writer, regardless of precise identity, is a researcher, editor, and teacher. Since he further identifies himself as the son of David, king in Jerusalem, and rates himself as superior to all who preceded him (1:16), the writer wants us to think of Solomon. This is a kind of dramatic impersonation, not for the purpose of literary forgery (pseudepigraphic), but for the purpose of establishing an effective atmosphere in as brief a time as possible. Qoheleth chooses to impersonate Solomon in the first two chapters to demonstrate that wisdom, works, and wealth—things in which Solomon was reputed to have excelled—are meaningless and do not lead to personal satisfaction.

B. Theme (1:2–11). Verse 2 frames the book, occurring here at the beginning of the book and at the conclusion of the book (12:8). Given this assessment of life, Qoheleth in the intervening chapters will consider how a person is to live in such a world. The Hebrew word *hăbēl* has popularly been translated as vanity. It designates that which is not substantial—a breath, a puff of wind, a vapor, an airy nothingness, a cipher. By doubling this word as the writer does he achieves the superlative as in the case of holy of holies and Song of Songs. This is vanity at its ultimate. What is pointless? Everything! By the time that we finish this book we will note that virtually nothing escapes this assessment. Everything is meaningless!

Verses 3–11 demonstrate the repetitious character both of the motions of nature and the toil of man. There is sunrise and sunset (v. 5), the shifting of the wind (v. 6), the flowing of streams (v. 7). These motions of nature are repeated over and over, resulting in endless rounds. Not only are the patterns of nature repetitive, but so are the efforts of man. There is the coming and going of generations (v. 4), the continual search for emotional and psychological satisfaction (v. 8), and the redoing of that which has already been done (v. 9). There is nothing new under the sun. This is not a commentary on scientific achievement, but rather on the human scene. The more man prides himself on development, the more he remains the same. His experiences are repeated as are the motions of nature without a sense of achievement or advancement. Not only does man become bored, but even nature becomes bored. The sun pants wearily as it makes its monotonous movement across the sky. "Gain" (v. 3) is the translation of a Hebrew word found in no other Old Testament book. It is a commercial term, suggesting surplus or profit. Qoheleth's question suggests that there is no profit from man's toil. "All things" (v. 8) is probably more correctly translated as "all words." The point of this verse is either that man's dissatisfaction is beyond words or that it is impossible for man to express in words the meaning or wearisomeness of his life.

The phrase *under the sun* appears only in this book of the Hebrew Bible. It seems to refer to the world we can observe, the place and time of the unfolding of the human drama, the immediate world of the sage. Here there can be no lasting satisfaction. The repetitious experience of nature demonstrates this. A life confined to the horizons of this world will never find satisfaction. Only hopelessness can result from the premise that life is what we see, since that which is visible is material, superficial, and frequently absurd. Nor is the answer to be found in posterity.

II. Wisdom Reflections (1:12–4:16)

A. The search for satisfaction (1:12–2:26). Assuming the guise of Solomon, Qoheleth initiates his search for meaningful living. Availing himself of Solomon's reputation for wisdom, he gives credibility to his experiment and also demonstrates that his approach to this test will be that of the sage. The use of the perfect tense, implying that Qoheleth is no longer king over Israel in Jerusalem (1:12), may have been employed to show that the conclusions reached are those fitting for the end of Solomon's life. Speaking words appropriate for Solomon, he declares that he has "grown and increased in wisdom more than anyone who has ruled over Jerusalem before me" (1:16). He is eminently able to conduct this experiment.

The nature of this experiment is revealed by the choice of verb. The Hebrew word translated "explore" (1:13) is the one used of the spies in Numbers 13:2, 16, 17 while the word translated "study" (1:13) means to penetrate to the very core of a matter. A thorough investigation of life at its apex will be made. This search will be limited to the horizontal—"all that is done under heaven."

Qoheleth reaches three conclusions. First, it is God who has appointed man to the unhappy business of the restless quest for meaning. Because this restlessness is directly traceable to

God, there is a meaning behind it. It should drive us to God, the ultimate goal of living.

Qoheleth's next conclusion is that man is frustrated by his desire for the unattainable. It is a chasing after wind (1:14, 17; cf. 2:11, 17, 26; 4:4, 6, 16; 6:9). The picture of grasping at the wind demonstrates well the utter futility of all human efforts.

The third conclusion is that there is extremely little that man can do in the light of the fixed nature of things. What is crooked has been made crooked by God (7:13). It cannot be straightened. Nor can the void be filled. There seems to be a distinction here between what was once straight but is now crooked, and that which is lacking, that which never existed. Man can analyze and assess, but he cannot alter. The sameness continues.

Given the Solomonic aura it is not surprising that the first area tested is wisdom. Wisdom here seems to be both the means employed to find purpose in the universe and the end itself. Qoheleth has not simply been an observer of, but a participant in, wisdom and knowledge. The association of madness and folly (1:17) with wisdom seems incongruous. Perhaps they should be seen as alternatives to wisdom and understanding. However, it is also possible that they are the results of Qoheleth's effort to understand wisdom. The results of applying himself was to learn that wisdom is nothing other than madness and folly. Instead of wisdom resolving his problem, it only compounds it. Profound thought results in sorrow and grief. Greater knowledge results in greater pain. One can almost hear the claim here that ignorance is bliss.

Qoheleth, by reliving the experiences of Solomon (1 Kings 10:10–27), seeks to find meaning in life. He hopes to experience (lit. to see) good (contentment, pleasure). But such is not the case. Even before he details the experiment he gives us his conclusion. Laughter (2:2; this Hebrew word often designates an entertaining and shallow joy—cf. Judg. 16:25, 27; Jer. 15:17) is foolishness. Even pleasure (this Hebrew word often suggests a thoughtful joy—cf. Num. 10:10; 2 Sam. 6:12; Ezra 3:12) achieves nothing.

Now he gives us the details of his experiment with pleasure. While still retaining his reason and hoping to find what is best for mankind, he drank wine freely. He undertook great projects. Those specified are ones for which Solomon was known. Solomon built houses (1 Kings 7:1–12; 9:1; 10:21) and planted vineyards (Song of Sol. 1:14; 8:11). Solomon is credited with a profound knowledge of trees (1 Kings 4:33). Parks suggest that the delights of paradise are at his disposal. Reservoirs were needed for irrigation purposes.

Not only great projects but also possessions were tested. Slaves were considered an indication of wealth (Gen. 14:14; Job 1:15–17). Among Solomon's daily provisions were herds and flocks (cf. 1 Kings 4:23). Solomon was known for his amassing silver and gold (cf. 2 Chron. 9:13–16, 27). Not only did Solomon have wealth common to rich people, but he also had wealth peculiar to royalty. The reference to provinces may refer either to Solomon's redistricting of Israel (1 Kings 4:7–19) or to subjugated lands that provided wealth. Professional singers of both sexes were known to be employed by kings (cf. 2 Sam. 19:35). The translation *harem* (2:8) is debated, but is very suggestive of Solomon (1 Kings 11:1–3). The statement, "I became greater" (v. 9), is also appropriate for Solomon who was said to be "greater in riches and wisdom than all the kings of the earth" (1 Kings 10:23).

In order for the test to be valid Qoheleth denied himself nothing. Every desire was gratified and every pleasure was experienced. The heart and eyes (2:10) are considered to be the locus of lust. Yet his achievements failed to satisfy. Looking back, Qoheleth is forced to conclude that he has found no ultimate meaning. Any meaning is at best temporary, limited to the moments of activity. Pleasure has proven no more satisfying than wisdom.

While wisdom is better than folly in a practical sense, there is ultimately no difference since the same fate overtakes both the wise and the foolish. The superiority of wisdom over folly is as great as the difference between light and darkness. The wise man has eyes while the fool walks in darkness. But any gain of the wise man is lost because he will experience the fate of the fool. The common fate of extinction robs life of any meaning. The last half of verse 12 is difficult. There is no basis for adding "do" or casting it in the form of a question. The apparent meaning is that Qoheleth, in his assumed role as Solomon, has so thoroughly tested wisdom and pleasure that there is no need for further experimentation.

Not only did Qoheleth hate life because of a common fate, but also he hated all things he had toiled for because they had to be left to one who comes after him. This recipient could be a wise man or a fool. He might be undeserving and unappreciative. He could conceivably destroy the efforts of his predecessor. Hence even toil is meaningless, proportionate to the effort.

Qoheleth now enlarges upon an idea he presented earlier: "I refused my heart no pleasure" (2:10b). Satisfaction is to be found in performance rather than outcome. It is not the result of eating and drinking which provides joy, but the process. An activity is not to be measured by potential gain, but by the pleasure that accompanies it—a pleasure determined by God. Verse 26 has been subject to considerable discussion, being seen by some as a later orthodox addition to offset the hedonistic implications of the previous verses and to provide a kind of security for the person whom God favors. Perhaps the emphasis should not initially be placed upon the sinner (lit. one who misses the mark) and the man who pleases God, but rather upon their focal areas. The man who pleases God desires and seeks wisdom, knowledge, happiness. On the other hand the sinner is occupied with the task of gathering and storing up wealth which he cannot keep. Anyone so preoccupied with amassing wealth that he ignores the natural enjoyment of life is identified by Qoheleth as a fool. Hence the word *sinner* here is used not so much in a moral sense as in a pragmatic sense, indicative of one who has failed to avail himself of the satisfying gifts of God because of his concentration on accumulating material wealth. Such is a chasing after wind.

B. A catalog of times (3:1–15). These verses have been variously understood. A common interpretation is that all the events of life are predetermined. These verses are not suggesting that there are proper or appropriate times for such activities, but rather that the various times and seasons of life have been set by God. Even as the monotonous movements of the sun are fixed so the events of man's life are determined. Given this fact, Qoheleth is said to despair and to protest the divine control of life. So regulated is life that the only possible response for man is one that is similar to the sun's—a response of frustration and exhaustion. Man's efforts are fruitless. Industry does not offer meaning any more than do pleasure and wisdom.

However, it is possible to view these verses as the basis of hope rather than despair. Since all has been determined by God, there is purpose and meaning in the events of life. Since there is a set time for everything, there can be a sense of security. Instead of despair, there can be delight: "He has made eveything beautiful," that is, right or proper for its time (v. 11). God has both purpose for and relationship with man. That God remains in charge of all events is a common Old Testament concept.

Time does not refer to the ticking away of a clock, but rather to occasions or happenings. The pairing of events is not unusual in the Old Testament and is a means of indicating totality and comprehensiveness. There are seven verses with four events in each. This employment of seven is also a common literary phenomenon in the Old Testament. With the exception of verse 8, there is internal parallelism. (That is, when the first line of the verse considers the favorable event first and the unfavorable event second, the second line follows that pattern. When the sequence of the first line is reversed so is the sequence of the second line.) The exception of verse 8 may be due to a desire to end on a positive note—peace rather than war.

The first pair (birth/death) sets the parameters for the events that follow. The next three sets present creative and destructive activities: plant/uproot, kill/heal, and tear down/build—set times pertain also to inanimate objects. Now follow two pairs expressing human emotions: weep/laugh and mourn/dance. If the reference to scatter/gather stones is understood to mean to have/to refrain from sex, then the next two sets have to do with human relations. The parallel to this set is to embrace/to refrain. The next two pairs deal with the disposition of possessions: search/give up, keep/throw away. The next pair (tear/mend) may suggest a time for mourning and a time for ending mourning, or possibly a time for preparing new clothes for a wedding. The last note of verse 7 has to do with speech (silent/speak). The sets of verse 8 have to do with affections and their consequences (love/hate, war/peace).

Following the listing of these twenty-eight fixed events, Qoheleth draws his conclusions. Here he again seems to alternate between two polarities. At first his assessment of this fixed situation is negative as he considers its impact on man's toil. Nothing can be achieved by seemingly wasted toil. In verse 11 he allows for a more positive evaluation. God has made everything beautiful (proper) for its time. God's actions are not simply arbitrary, but appropriate; not simply confining, but releasing; not simply disconcerting, but reassuring.

The remainder of verse 11 is one of the most difficult passages of the book to translate and interpret. At issue is the Hebrew word *ʿālam*. It has been translated ignorance, enigma, world, future, eternity. This verse portrays God as Creator, making everything beautiful and making man with a desire to know and to understand the scheme of things. But man is not in a position to view what God has done from beginning to end. He wants to comprehend God's plan in its entirety, but cannot. It remains a mystery. Man is not satisfied with experience and observation limited to the fixed and closed world. Man's desire is for eternity and he will not be satisfied with anything less. Given his limitations, however, he should find satisfaction in the activities of life: eating, drinking, and working. Joy is to be found in the doing rather than in the arriving.

In verses 14 and 15 Qoheleth returns to an earlier emphasis (1:9–11). He affirms the permanence ("will endure forever"), the completeness ("nothing can be added to it"), and the immutability ("nothing taken from it") of God's actions. The purpose behind all this is that men will revere him. The first part of verse 15 connects the present with the past; the second, the future with the past, and concludes that God causes the past to be repeated.

C. A question of justice (3:16–22). Qoheleth now struggles with the corruption of justice. Recognizing that there is a time for all events, he states that the time for justice will come (v. 17). There are present inequities (injustice and oppression) but these will yield to justice. Qoheleth does not date God's judgment, but given his emphasis upon this world it would seem appropriate to have God judicially at work now rather than relegating his activity to the future.

God's toleration of injustice has a purpose. It is to show men that they are like the animals. The presence of injustice in the world and the fact of human mortality demonstrate that we are like beasts. Perhaps in our injustice we sink to a level below the beasts.

The question about survival after death is raised. Initially Qoheleth states that in regard to death, man has no advantage over animals. Both man and animal have come from dust and to dust return. This is a clear reference to Genesis 2:7, 19 and 3:19, where reference is made to man and beast being formed out of the ground. Subsequently he suggests the possibility that the spirit of man rises upward (v. 21). Only into man's nostrils did God breathe the breath of life (Gen. 2:7). This allows for the return of man's spirit to God at death, but Qoheleth can only raise the question. He does not provide an answer.

This chapter concludes with the common theme that man is to enjoy his work. He has no knowledge of, or control over, what will happen after him. This attitude of joy is not so much resignation as it is confidence resulting from God's control of all events.

D. A matter of oppression (4:1–3). Continuing his concern with injustice, Qoheleth now considers acts of oppression. The oppressors abuse their power, exercising it against the vulnerable, who are abandoned ("they have no comforter"—repeated twice for emphasis). The oppressed are powerless. Their only response is tears. Given this situation, Qoheleth again turns to the contemplation of death as in the previous chapter when considering injustice. The dead and the unborn are more fortunate than the living, for they are spared exposure to these cruel acts of oppression.

E. A critique of work (4:4–12). In this section Qoheleth challenges some commonly held ideas about hard work. In verse 4 he refers both to the effort and to the skill involved in work. A common motive behind work which he has observed is man's desire to surpass his neighbor. It is envy of and rivalry with his neighbor that prompts man to work rather than the joy inherent in work. Any work done because of this competitive urge is meaningless.

Qoheleth now cites two contrasting proverbs about work. Verse 5 cites a popular proverb about indolence: the person who refuses to work is a fool and will destroy himself. While this may be true, Qoheleth argues that it is better to earn less (what can be held in the palm of one hand) and have tranquility, than to earn more (what can be held in both hands cupped) and experience difficult labor.

Still considering work, Qoheleth now turns to the solitary worker. In contrast to 2:18–21 where he was concerned with the worker who must leave the fruits of his labors to others, Qoheleth here addresses the situation where the laborer has neither son nor brother. This person is so obsessed with wealth that he forgoes all enjoyment, toiling endlessly without ever asking why he works so hard. His motivation is not envy but avarice. His drive for wealth has virtually dehumanized him—he is all alone. Qoheleth labels his efforts as "meaningless—a miserable business" (v. 8).

Addressing himself to the man all alone, Qoheleth speaks of the advantages of companionship. While he condemns a competitive spirit (v. 4), here he calls for a cooperative one (v. 9). Greater productivity results from working together. There are additional advantages to companionship. In traveling a companion can assist a man who falls. This perhaps refers both to a fall in a ditch and a lapse in judgment. Verse 11 may refer to the advantages of marriage or a sleeping companion in general (even an animal) who will provide warmth. Should there be an attack by an enemy one may be overpowered, but two can defend themselves. A three-ply cord is stronger than one or two plies. This movement from two to three may suggest offspring if marriage is in mind or simply allow that companionship is not restricted to two.

F. The transience of fame (4:13–16). This passage reflects the danger of isolation—a king who loses contact with his constituency. The emphasis here seems to be one of "rags to riches." It is neither possible nor necessary to know the specific person (if any) that Qoheleth has in mind, but it does not require much ingenuity to list biblical characters who fit this description: Moses, Joseph, Saul, David. The identity of the second youth is uncertain. It could be a successor to the first youth or the old king could be seen as the first, while the poor but wise youth could be the second. Assuming the latter, the young succeeds in attracting his contemporaries. But his fame is fleeting. Those who were before them (old king and wise youth) obviously did not know the youth's fame. Further, those who come after would not be interested in the success of the youth. Qoheleth has given another example of chasing after the wind.

III. Admonitions and Observations (5:1–12:8)

A. Religious practice (5:1–7). Qoheleth now addresses the matter of appropriate conduct in the presence of God. His approach understandably is not that of the priest or prophet, but that of the sage. This is critical to note since the interest of the sage was normally the secular world. Qoheleth's concern here is not so much theological as it is practical. Continuing his assessment of man, he now sees him as a worshiper. In this section there are four separate sayings.

First, he urges caution relative to the frequency of approach to the temple and the quality of that approach. While not necessarily rejecting sacrifice, he clearly declares that the primary purpose should be to listen (cf. 1 Sam. 15:22; Hos. 6:6). This Hebrew word means more than to hear. It also means to understand and to obey. The sacrifice refers to an offering which was not totally consumed on the altar but which provided a meal. Hence the objection voiced is perhaps against the festive motivation that prompted the sacrifice and the meaningless and careless performance of that sacrifice—thus, the characterization "sacrifice of fools" (v. 1). The sacrifice is legitimate; the problem is with the offerer. The last clause of verse 1 literally reads "who do not know how to do evil."

Next Qoheleth warns against impetuosity and multiplication of words during prayer. Heart and mouth are placed in a parallel arrangement, indicating that rash words originate in a hasty heart. Careful reflection should precede our speaking. That Qoheleth has prayer in mind here is shown by his locating such impetuosity in the presence of God, who in turn is located in heaven. The issue here is not spatial, but symbolic. Man must speak with caution and hesitation. While man can draw near to God, adequate awe and respect must be maintained. Locating God in heaven and man on earth cautions against arrogance and flippancy. It serves not only to impede hasty words, but also to prevent the multiplication of words. In verse 4 Qoheleth associates the speech of a fool with a dream. Just as a dream has fleeting and unrelated scenes, so the speech of a fool is hasty and incoherent. Excessive words result in folly as extreme busyness results in dreams. These cautions relative to prayer remind us of Jesus' injunction against many words in prayer (Matt. 6:7) and his call for brevity and precision in prayer as demonstrated by the model prayer (Matt. 6:9–13).

The third saying pertains to vows. This is a restatement of Deuteronomy 23:22–24. Qoheleth does not object to refraining from taking a vow. That is acceptable conduct. However, once a vow is made it must be fulfilled quickly and adequately. Otherwise one is acting like a fool and God has no pleasure in fools.

The fourth saying is a continuation of the third and perhaps should be included with it. The issue here is evasion of a pledge that was made to God through a temple priest. While the term *messenger* can indicate an angel in the Old Testament and occasionally a prophet (Hag. 1:3; Mal. 3:1), here it clearly seems to designate the priest or his emissary who has come to collect the pledge. The communicant justifies the failure to keep his pledge by suggesting that it was a mistake. Such an excuse will not prevent divine anger and judgment. Great care must be exercised lest the mouth make the flesh (the entire person) sin. Sin here refers to the consequence of sin, to guilt and punishment. While small, the mouth affects the entire life (James 3:5). Again Qoheleth draws a comparison between meaningless words and unreal dreams. His call is a classical wisdom one: stand in awe of God (v. 7). The fear of God is expressed by silence rather than by aimless chatter or deluded daydreaming.

B. A matter of political corruption (5:8–9). This passage treats again the matter of injustice (cf. 3:16–22) and oppression (cf. 4:1–3). Qoheleth's attitude toward this corruption is that of resignation. He does not campaign against it, but accepts it as inevitable. Thus his injunction, "do not be surprised at such things" (v. 8). The scenario he presents is a bureaucratic hierarchy where public office holders at various levels are preyed upon by higher ones who, in turn, are victimized by others higher still. The system is corrupt from the lowest to the highest levels. The poor are passed from official to official. A check of the various English translations will indicate the obscurity of verse 9. Its emphasis upon agriculture (sages were favorable to the agrarian way of life) with its king (sages were indeed promonarchy), may suggest that even with the existence of corruption, a bureaucratic government is essential in a settled land. Both of these verses are apparently a commentary on the political system of Qoheleth's time.

C. The vanity of wealth (5:10–6:9). The section begins with three sayings about money. Verse 10 is a proverb indicating that desire for money is insatiable. The accumulation of money (silver) and wealth (property) will never satisfy. Income suggests the yield which comes from the land, clearly a word with agricultural connotations.

The second saying notes that goods will attract hangers-on who will consume them. At best the only benefit that comes to the owner is a glance at his wealth. Much effort was involved in its accumulation but it will provide only a temporary advantage since it will soon be consumed by others.

The third saying notes that the laborer can sleep but the rich man suffers from insomnia. Preventing the rich man from sleeping is his abundance, his satiety. The primary reference here is to his overeating, although there may be a reference to sleeplessness caused by worry attributable to his wealth. The laborer is free of such stress and sleeps whether his stomach is full or empty.

In the next sections Qoheleth presents an example of what he considers a grievous evil (vv. 13–17). It is cast in the form of a case study. The details, though brief, are graphic; and while they appear to be particular, they are also universal. Accumulated wealth is hoarded and is lost, with the result that nothing is left for the son. Instead of this wealth being a source of joy, it turns out to be a source of harm. Given his parsimonious attitude the harm perhaps was the kind endemic to the miser. His misfortune is not detailed, but probably refers to a bad business venture. The final touch to this case study is the death of this man. He is unable to take any of his wealth with him. He exits life as he entered—naked (v. 16; cf. Job 1:21). He leaves no witness to his efforts. Not only the loss of his wealth, but even the accumulation of it was disappointing. He spent his days in darkness (gloom) with great frustration (troubled with cares and vexation), affliction (sickness), and anger (enraged by circumstances).

Qoheleth now presents a picture of what could have been the experience of this rich man. Since wealth must be left behind it has no ultimate significance. Rather than toil to accumulate wealth it is more appropriate to enjoy oneself—to eat and drink and find satisfaction. This suggests companionship and celebration, something the miser does not know. Most significant in this section is the mention of God (four times). In the previous section (vv. 10–17) no reference was made to God. Recognizing God and appropriating wealth and possessions as a gift of God make a significant difference. While life will not be extended he will not be occupied with the brevity of life. Rather, he will be occupied with gladness of heart, enjoying his life and wealth rather than hoarding it. It is clear that it is possible to have wealth without joy. Only when man accepts from God the mastery of wealth and the ability to rule over his wealth rather than having the wealth mastering him, will he find joy in that wealth.

Qoheleth next turns to another evil under the sun which he has observed (6:1–2). The introduction is similar to 5:13, 16 except the qualifying word, *grievous*, has been omitted. In this instance Qoheleth laments the man who not only has wealth and possessions but also position (honor), but whom God has not permitted to enjoy (lit. eat) them (cf. 2 Chron. 1:11, where these same three words are applied to Solomon).

The case now presented seems to be a new one since this person has a large family in contrast to the previous man who was childless. This man seems to have the possessions of the previous man with the additional blessings of a large family and longevity. But he, too, fails to find pleasure and contentment. The figures employed here are exaggerated for the purpose of emphasis. Even a hundred children and a lifespan of a thousand years twice over (double Methuselah's life) are meaningless if pleasure is not found and proper burial is not realized. Burial—being gathered to one's fathers—was viewed as an essential conclusion to earthly existence. Without it there was disgrace and no rest. The stillborn child—without any experience, achievement, or fame—is better off than the rich man just described. At least the stillborn has rest. The one place to which all go is Sheol.

Verses 7–9 are proverbial summaries of the futility of life. Man works to satisfy his appetite but it is never sated. Here we see the mastery of the physical. Man must work to eat to receive strength to continue to work so that he may continue to eat. His desires exceed his achievements. Verse 8 presents two questions expecting a negative answer. The wise man of the first part of the verse is perhaps synonymous with the poor man of the second part. Even though this wise man knows how to conduct himself before others, he has no advantage over a fool. While Qoheleth allows that wisdom is superior to folly (2:13), he does not conclude that the person possessing wisdom is superior to the person possessing folly. The wise man has a disproportionate amount of sorrow (1:18) and must die with the fool (2:16). What, then, are his advantages? Verse 9 emphasizes that it is better to use that which is available than to yearn for that which is beyond us.

D. Man's helplessness and ignorance (6:10–12). Here we seem to have Qoheleth's summary of what he has said to this point. While these words can be understood to be pessimistic they can be seen as realistic. Man must accept himself and the world as they are. All that exists has already been named, that is, its essence and character have been determined. To name something or someone is to give existence to and to exercise superiority over that thing or person (cf. Gen. 2:19–20; Isa. 40:26). Reinforcing this idea is the word *known.* The statement *what man is has already been known* (v. 10) indicates that his destiny has already been determined. Man is limited; he is mortal. While he may challenge God, he is not able to alter the way he and the world were made. Words cannot effect change. Increasing words does not lead to meaning and results in no advantage to man. Verse 12 presents a double issue in terms of two questions. Man not only lacks knowledge, he also lacks advisors. He knows not what to do with the present or with the future. There are no answers provided to these questions. The plans of God for man and the world are both unknowable and unchangeable.

E. "Better than" proverbs (7:1–14). Perhaps in an effort to answer the question of 6:12 Qoheleth now gives a series of "better than" proverbs—proverbs of comparative value. There are seven such proverbs (vv. 1, 2, 3, 5, 8 [twice], 11). These proverbs are grouped according to literary sameness rather than thematic sameness, although, as already noted, they perhaps address the question of what is good (compar. better) for man.

This section starts by establishing that reputation predicated on character (name) is better than perfume. There may be a pun here, playing on the Hebrew words for name (*šēm*) and oil (*šemen*). Reputation is more valuable than, and travels further than, the scent of perfume.

The second proverbial saying indicates that it is better to attend a wake than a party (v. 2). The reason is obvious. Death causes us to reflect on the transitoriness of life. The funeral, not the party, causes one to number his days and to gain a heart of wisdom (Ps. 90:12).

A similar emphasis is found in the next saying, where sorrow is seen as preferable to laughter. While sorrow saddens the countenance, it improves the mind. Frivolity characterizes the fool whose occupation (heart) is with the house of pleasure while pensiveness characterizes the wise whose occupation (heart) is with the house of mourning.

The fourth comparison (vv. 5–7) states that the rebuke of the wise man is preferable to the song of fools. This song perhaps can indicate the boisterous music of revelers or empty words of praise and flattery. There is another pun in verse 6 with a play on the Hebrew words *pot* (*sîrâ*) and *thorns* (*sirîm*). The superficiality of the laughter of fools is seen in this comparison. Thorns burn quickly and noisily and are easily extinguished. By contrast, the criticism of the wise man is beneficial because it has the potential to effect change. However, the wise man is not beyond corruption. Oppression and a bribe can convert the wise man into a fool. This is another instance of life's vanity.

The next section (vv. 8–10) has a double comparison. Even as death is preferable to birth, so the end of a matter is better than its beginning. It is only the conclusion of a matter that can be properly assessed. Hence patience (waiting for the end) is better than pride expressed prematurely. Verses 9 and 10 expand the emphasis of verse 8. Impatience can lead to anger and to preoccupation with the past. While many objections can be raised to anger, contextually the objection is that anger is often premature. One needs to wait until the end of the matter in order to register an appropriate response. Nostalgia raises the notion that the past was better. Qoheleth is not so convinced since there is nothing new. The present is duplicating the past. One must not look back (beginning), but ahead (end).

The seventh proverbial saying, while not as apparent in the English translation, is found in verses 11–12. While recognizing the value of wisdom, Qoheleth observes that it must be linked with means, as he did in the opening chapters, where he combined them in his evocation of Solomon. Not only is it possible for the fool to lose his wealth; it is also possible for the wise man to be poor. When this happens the wise man's wisdom and words will be ignored. Wisdom's benefits pertain to the present—for the living—for those who see the sun. The Hebrew word for shelter (v. 12) is the same one used in 6:12 and 8:13 where the more literal meaning *shadow* is used. Wisdom and money may provide shelter but not ultimate protection against death. Indeed wisdom has an advantage over wealth, but at best this advantage is relative. Any advantage pertains only to this life.

The last part of this section emphasizes that man cannot change the plans of God or the basic structure of the world and that God has determined the lot of man, whether weal (good times) or woe (bad times). The former should produce joy; the latter should evoke caution. It is impossible for man to know his future. He may be faced with prosperity or adversity. Consolation is to be found in the fact that God is at work even though we may not understand. The events of life must not be forced into a narrow retributive system.

F. An avoidance of extremes (7:15–24). Qoheleth continues in this section to share what he has seen. As a sage he is an observer. He has observed what would be considered anomalies: a righteous man perishing/a wicked man living long. Traditional thought stressed the theory of retribution but this has been contradicted by Qoheleth's observations. Qoheleth will go beyond even Job by urging moderation in righteousness, wisdom, and wickedness. To strive to be overrighteous and overwise could result in desolation; to be overwicked could result in premature death. The warning against being overly righteous has been understood in various ways. Some see Qoheleth as being consistently practical here; some understand the righteousness involved to be morality (overscrupulous); some, liturgical and legalistic righteousness; some, a crusading, reforming righteousness; others, self-righteousness. Verse 18 is difficult because of the identity of the one and the other. Do they refer back to the extremes of verses 16 and 17 or do they suggest general openness on any given issue? Here the fear of God results in moderation.

Verse 19 is a well-known proverb but its relationship to the previous verses is uncertain. Perhaps it is placed here to offset the previous warning against excessive wisdom. Wisdom does have a role to play. It provides more strength (protection) than can be given to a city by its ruling council.

Verse 20 is somewhat pivotal. It lends support to the call for moderation in righteousness since no man is completely righteous. On the other hand, it prepares us for that which follows in verses 21–22. The fact that no man is completely righteous should serve as an incentive for forbearance. Recognizing his own failures a man should not exact punishment of a servant who curses him. One must forgive because he himself needs forgiveness.

It is difficult to know whether to attach verses 23–24 to what has preceded or what follows. It seems that the "all this" of verse 23 refers to the previous reflections. In verse 26 Qoheleth concedes the unattainability of wisdom, thus reinforcing his warning against excessive wisdom even as in verse 20 he concedes the impossibility of absolute righteousness, thus strengthening his charge not to be excessive in righteousness. The wisdom that is far off and most profound belongs to the very mind of God. This he could never discover.

G. The search for wisdom (7:25–8:1). When Qoheleth learned that he could not achieve the ultimate meaning of wisdom, ultimate reality, he tried to understand the common and mundane experiences of life. Note how Qoheleth associates wisdom and meaning together, and stupidity, wickedness, madness, and folly together.

While Qoheleth, as other sages (Prov. 31:10–31), can be positive about women he can also be as negative as other sages. The language used here indicates that Qoheleth is expressing his personal observations from experience. Care should be exercised not to insist that his experiences are normative. Even worse than death is the woman who entraps and who clutches man. One cannot help but think of Joseph when Qoheleth affirms that the man who pleases God will escape her.

In verse 28 Qoheleth extends his assessment both to man and woman. The picture is no more encouraging. While he could not find one upright woman, his results with man were not much better—one upright man among a thousand. Righteousness is rare in both genders.

In verse 29 Qoheleth locates the blame for this perversity in mankind itself. God created mankind upright, but man has corrupted himself by his scheming.

There is nothing like a wise man. Such a man knows the meaning of things. Further, such a man is gracious and gentle.

H. Court protocol (8:2–8). Qoheleth here lends his support to the monarchy. The pupils of the sage were most likely from the upper classes and needed such practical advice. Given the capriciousness of kings, subjects should exercise discretion. If this passage seems to demand too much respect for and obedience to the king, it must be balanced with other Old Testament teaching and examples where courage and integrity rather than expediency govern response.

In verse 2 Qoheleth counsels obedience to the king. The translation "command" is perhaps too narrow since the Hebrew text has "mouth," suggesting all that the king has to say. The sage cautions against a precipitous break with the king or a spur-of-the-moment desertion of a post, no matter how distasteful the situation is. Should one find himself supporting a bad cause, he must not persist in it. The king is able to do whatever he pleases, exacting retribution. It is futile to rebel against the king since his word is supreme. Royal power cannot be challenged. Such power with its potential of abuse caused the prophets to resist the monarchy (1 Sam. 8:10–18).

Propriety should govern one's response to the king so that the proper response is given at the proper time. This seems to suggest that the king could be fickle and inconstant. The subject must be sensitive to these sudden shifts. Insensitivity here could lead to harm. Again the emphasis seems to be more on expediency than on morality. The phrase *though a man's misery weighs heavily upon him* (v. 6) has been understood in various ways. The word *misery* (lit. evil) may suggest either the pervasiveness of man's weakness or the excessiveness of man's punishment. If the former, the wise subject will know how to exploit the weakness of man to his own advantage, but if the latter, then the wise subject, already suffering at the hands of the king, will avoid any additional distress.

Qoheleth has already alluded to the unpredictability of the king, but the area of man's ignorance is not limited to the monarchy. The future is closed to man, again demonstrating his powerlessness. Verse 8 has been understood to indicate the limits even of royal power. Indeed kings are subject to death. But this verse should probably be treated more broadly and applied to the servants of the kings in particular (the ones Qoheleth has been addressing) and man in general (the all-inclusive "no man" of v. 7). Four limitations are mentioned in this verse. First, no man has power over the wind to contain it. The Hebrew word translated "wind" can also mean spirit (cf. various translations). This translation would result in a parallelism with the next line, suggesting that man cannot retain his spirit (the departure of the spirit clearly indicates death). Second, no man has power over the day of his death. Third, there is no discharge in time of war. Given the context, the war referred to is the battle with death. Here no man has immunity. Fourth, wickedness will not release those who practice it. No devious efforts, no matter how great, will prevent death. There is no way to cheat death.

I. Failure of retribution (8:9–17). A shift is now made from human impotence to human injustice. Verse 9 is pivotal, being seen both as a conclusion to the previous section and an introduction to this new section. The same Hebrew root is used in verse 8 (twice, there rendered "power") and in verse 9 (here rendered "lords"). Even though man is powerless before death he attempts to lord it over others. Such power results in harm to the person who is the recipient of this abuse.

Qoheleth now shares his reflections on the failure of the retributive process. Verse 10 is one of the most difficult verses of Ecclesiastes. According to the New International Version, this verse suggests that the wicked receive an honorable burial, being eulogized in the very city where they had done their evil acts. "The holy place" has been understood either to mean the temple or the cemetery. The ones eulogizing are perhaps the same ones who were victims of the evil deeds of the wicked. This is another instance of vanity. Delay in retribution incites wrongdoing and perhaps also accounts for toleration of other's wrongdoing.

In verses 12 and 13 Qoheleth is either protesting present injustices, affirming his faith in ultimate justice, or citing a popular position which he then proceeds to reject, giving the contradicting empirical data he has collected. Even though the evil deeds of a wicked man are many and his life is prolonged, God's patience should not be misunderstood. There is a limit to the success of the wicked, who are likened to unenduring shadows. By contrast it will ultimately be well with those who fear God. The duplication of this concept indicates its importance. The present situation, however, denies all this. The general rule just cited is all too often reversed. The righteous receive what the wicked deserve and vice versa. This just does not make sense to Qoheleth who labels it, as he frequently does, "meaningless." He does not offer a solution here but rather practical advice. He recommends joy and contentment.

While Qoheleth has been thorough in his thoughts and observations, he has not been able to penetrate through the mystery of man's life. He observes but he is not able to comprehend. Excessive claims here must be rejected. Man simply has to arrive at the place where he can live with his ignorance for he cannot discover its meaning.

J. A common destiny (9:1–6). The concerns of the previous chapter are continued here. The treatment that the righteous and the wise will receive is unknown. They and their actions are in God's hands, under his control. The emphasis here is not so much on trust as on resignation. It is not so much being under the providence of God as being under his arbitrary power. Even the righteous and the wise, who are in the best position to further the moral government of God, cannot be certain about the outcome of their lives—whether love or hate awaits them. If the terms *love* and *hate* designate the actions of God, then the righteous cannot know whether they will be accepted or rejected. Predicated on "under the sun" observations a person cannot be certain of the character of God. Since the terms *love* and *hate* are clearly human in verse 6, it is possible that here too they should be seen as human. If that is the case, then the righteous either cannot be certain of others' attitudes toward them in the future or possibly know their own attitude toward others. If love and hate are unpredictable, then it follows that all of life is equally unpredictable.

Qoheleth now addresses the commonness of destiny. While ultimately death is in view here, the opening statement—a common destiny—does not refer exclusively to death. Simply stated, Qoheleth contends that anything can happen to anyone. He shows this by presenting pairs and eliminating the distinctions between them. The righteous and the wicked are the innocent and the guilty. While the Hebrew text does not have "bad," the English versions do and it seems necessary to balance "good." The terms *clean* and *unclean* are ritual ones and refer to the pure and impure. The fourth pair has to do with those who offer the prescribed sacrifices and those who do not. Again the good are contrasted, this time with sinners (those who miss the mark). The final pair contrasts persons who swear by God's name and those who do not. All these share a common destiny. It would appear that God is disinterested in the distinctions we so carefully make. Qoheleth finds this reprehensible. The Hebrew text here suggests that this evil (no distinctions) stands out prominently amid all other evils and is the underlying cause of the evil in everything under the sun. Since death comes to all and no distinctions are made under the sun, evil thrives. Men's minds are filled with it. Linked with evil is madness, suggesting violence and corruption.

Qoheleth now focuses on death. He argues that life, even with all its frustrations, is better than death. A live dog—a despised scavenger—is better off than a dead lion, the mightiest of animals, the royal animal. Life at its very worst is preferable to death. The reason is most apparent. There is awareness in life; in death there is nothing. This verse helps to explain Israel's attitude toward the dead. No provisions were brought to the grave as was done in the surrounding cultures. The dead simply had no needs. They had no further reward since such is the result of human toil which the dead no longer perform. Further, even their memory is forgotten. Not only can they not alter their image, but their reputation is quickly forgotten after they cease to work. Not only do the dead lose their retentive faculty, they also lose their emotions and feelings—their love, hate, jealousy. The absence of such passions indicates the destructiveness of death. Death precludes any further participation in the happenings under the sun.

K. Enjoyment of life (9:7–10). Up to this point Qoheleth has been providing advice; he now assumes a sense of urgency. This is seen in his admonitions, which are expressed in the imperative. Even though his actions are in God's hands man must take the initiative and act. Qoheleth calls for joy and contentment during life because such will not be realized following death. The first two imperatives have to do with bread and wine. These are the staff and comfort of life and are frequently coupled in the Old Testament. Such action has already been determined and approved by God. Moving from food, Qoheleth calls for festive raiment. While clothing and oil would suggest comfort and feasting, such were not to be used in times of sorrow. While bread, wine, white garments, and oil can be viewed as necessities of life, they are also suggestive of celebration. The certainty of death is not to prevent the enjoyment of life.

Next Qoheleth urges fidelity in marriage. Companionship is essential in facing the frustrations of life. The joys of life are to be shared with one's wife. Further, this wife is to be loved throughout life. While we might have expected the text to read that she—the wife—is your compensation, it rather reads that it—the enjoyment of life—is your compensation.

Finally, Qoheleth urges thoroughness in our efforts. The word *hand* suggests ability, *find* suggests opportunity, and *might* suggests intensity. Now is the time for such intense activity since Sheol (the place of the dead) provides no such opportunity. There will be no doing or reckoning or knowing or understanding there. Life must be lived now to its fullest. The certainty of death must not lead to inertia. There will be ample time for that in Sheol.

L. The inadequacy of wisdom (9:11–18). The relationship between this section and the preceding one is not clear, nor is the coherence of these verses themselves. The subject connecting these verses is wisdom or folly.

Wisdom (in the practical sense of ability or skill) cannot ensure success. Qoheleth demonstrates this by considering four different areas of life: athletics, military service, industry, and economics. In none of these areas is there a guarantee of success. Man's prowess—whether speed or strength or intelligence—is not necessarily the determinant of outcomes. There are two factors beyond human control: time and chance. While these factors can be positive, the connotation here is negative: bad times and unexpected events (accidents). These are simply beyond the control of man.

To demonstrate the uncertainty man confronts, his situation is compared to unsuspecting fish and birds who are caught (v. 12). Man is no better than the animals. He is not so much the master of his fate as he is a victim of time and chance—a victim of the unexpected and the inescapable.

Another anecdote (precise incident is beyond identification) that reflects the vulnerability of wisdom is now presented. Qoheleth was greatly impressed by this event, perhaps both by the success of wisdom over power and yet the failure of the city to remember this poor man. The success of wisdom over power is graphically portrayed. The attacked city was small, its population was few, and its amateur strategist was poor but wise! The aggressor was powerful, persistent, and well equipped with weapons. Obviously the powerful king should have won, but the diplomacy of the wise man saved the city. Qoheleth concludes that wisdom is better than strength. Yet even though wisdom may be superior to power, it is not always rewarded. The poor man, rather than being immortalized, was forgotten. But not only was he forgotten, his advice was despised and unheeded, perhaps because of his humble origins. This fact has resulted in some reading verse 15 as "he might have saved," suggesting that the rejection of his advice resulted in defeat. But if he did not effect deliverance, what is the significance of his being forgotten?

Qoheleth continues his "better than" statements about wisdom (vv. 17, 18). Wisdom, even when quiet, is better than clamor or babbling, even when official. Authority is not always on the side of the wise. Is there a hint that the words of the wise man (v. 15) were not heeded? Qoheleth suggests that the pen is mightier than the sword. He closes, however, on a negative note. As effective as wisdom is, a single person—one sinner—can cancel much good. He can counterbalance or contradict the words of the wise. It is significant that the opponent of wisdom here is the sinner. Clearly there is a moral element associated with biblical wisdom.

M. Assorted practical sayings (10:1–20). This chapter is a collection of assorted maxims. These proverbs, dealing with practical virtues, have little organic connection. They are the type of sayings that would be expected from a wisdom teacher.

Verse 1 is frequently attached to the previous chapter, serving as an illustration of the damage that one sinner can do (9:18). Even as a single sinner can undo the effects of wisdom, so a small mistake can offset the fragrance of wisdom and honor. Clearly it is easier to ruin something than it is to develop it. Folly seems to enjoy an advantage over wisdom, for an abundance of wisdom can be canceled by a little folly.

Now a distinction is made between the wise and the fool relative to understanding. The terms *right* and *left* designate the skilled versus the awkward. They also designate the favorable position and the less favorable one as in the case of Jacob's blessing on Ephraim who received the right hand and Manasseh who received the left hand (Gen. 48:13). While the emphasis here is clearly practical and probably not moral, one is reminded of the location of the sheep and the goats in the judgment described by Jesus (Matt. 25:32). The thoughts of the wise will lead him to the right—to the beneficial and the valuable—while the thoughts of the fool will lead him to the left—to the less valuable and to the detrimental.

A fool could attempt to conceal his identity by remaining silent but even then he betrays himself by his general demeanor. Though transient his momentary presence is sufficient to reveal his foolishness. His lack of heart (Heb. his heart is lacking) cannot be hidden. By his outward actions, he demonstrates his inner emptiness.

Verse 4 cautions restraint. When the ruler's anger is aroused, the bureaucrat must not panic and desert his post, nor should he insist on justifying himself, but rather he should show calmness. "Great errors" (v. 4) could refer to the offenses of the subject which caused the ruler's anger or it could indicate the indignation of the ruler.

The ruler of verse 5 seems to refer again to the ruler, even though some are inclined to understand it as referring to God, thus attributing blame to God for the fools' occupying high positions while the rich occupy the low ones. If it refers to the ruler of verse 4, then one of his troublesome errors would be inequities in the structure of society. Rather than being governed by principles, this ruler makes decisions based on his whims, bringing about social changes unacceptable to the sage. Verse 7 repeats the point of verse 6. The respective positions of slaves and princes are reversed like those of the fools and the rich of verse 6. In the Old Testament horses were associated with royalty and with the rich. This inversion in society, the failure of the rich (equated with the wise by the sage) to have high position, demonstrates the limitations of wisdom.

In verses 8 and 9 four actions are mentioned which seem to have a common point. In these endeavors there is the distinct possibility of accident. These proverbs do not suggest the inevitable, but rather the possible and hence sound a realistic note of warning. Man simply does not have total control over the events of life; a positive action may have negative results. The first action refers to the digging of a pit. Frequently such an action has a sinister purpose, with the digger falling into his own hole, but here the intent does not appear to be evil. The simple truth is that anyone who digs a hole could conceivably fall into it. The second action refers to the destruction of a fence. Since snakes may be in the crevices of a fence, there is the danger of being bitten. In the process of destroying a fence, the loosened stones could cause harm to the person moving them. This is the third action. The fourth action, the felling of trees, is obviously dangerous. These four actions demonstrate that there are risks associated with any human effort.

The value of preparation is stressed in verse 10. The preparation of a tool is more critical than the metal itself. Failure to prepare—to sharpen the ax—results in the expenditure of more energy. Even as it is advantageous to prepare an ax in advance, so it is advantageous to sharpen one's skill in advance. Again the superiority of wisdom over brute strength is emphasized. The importance of preparation and timing is seen in verse 11. The snake must be charmed before it bites. Otherwise the charmer does not receive his fee; his art is useless.

Verses 12–14 address the matter of words. While a wise man's words secure favor (the Hebrew word here means "grace") for him, a fool's words will lead to his own destruction. From beginning to end there is no sense to the words of the fool. What began as foolish ends as disastrous. Not only are the words of the fool dull, they are also evil. While Qoheleth emphasizes the inability of man to predict the future, he notes that the fool is arrogant because he multiplies words. If the wise man does not know what is coming, it is presumptuous for the fool to think that he does. Restraint of speech is a characteristic of the wise (6:11) in contrast to the loquacity of the fool.

It does not take much to weary the fool. Though he neither knows nor accomplishes anything, he becomes weary. His limited knowledge and accomplishments are quite apparent since he does not even know the way to town. This indicates extreme stupidity. Although he does not know the most elementary things, the fool becomes loquacious and audacious, claiming to know the future.

While the beatitude is a common form in wisdom literature, the malediction used extensively by the prophet is seldom used by the sage. Woe is pronounced upon the land whose king is immature. The word *child* does not pertain so much to chronological age as it does to maturity. A land whose king acts childishly is in serious trouble. Equally calamitous is the situation when the princes feast (carouse) in the morning. Drinking in the morning indicates a lack of moral restraint (cf. Isa 5:11; Acts 2:15). The morning hours are to be reserved for the administration of justice (Jer. 21:12). By contrast a blessing is promised to the land whose king is born into that position. In addition to a king of noble birth a blessed land needs disciplined princes—ones who eat at the proper time and for proper reasons. Moderation is essential.

The identification of the house of verse 18 is uncertain. If continuity is maintained with the previous verse, it could designate the community but it could just as well indicate the individual since many of the proverbs are so directed. Laziness (lit. the letting down of hands—failure to keep them at work) results in deterioration. Failure to attend to the demands of life will lead to ruin.

Verse 19 may refer back to profligate princes who feast at the expense of the people of the kingdom. They squander the kingdom's resources on their feasts. However, there may be a positive emphasis here upon the utilization of the resources of life. Bread leads to laughter and wine makes life merry. This seems to be the practice of the princes of verse 17, who are sensitive to the proper time for, and a proper amount of feasting. Even money has its purpose, being necessary for life. This may be a challenge to the lazy man of verse 18 to become industrious.

Even if the leadership of the country is profligate, the critic must be careful in his disapproval. What is thought will ultimately be verbalized and what is uttered in private will be announced. The words become as a bird which is released, cannot be recalled, and will make its flight to the intended person. Or perhaps a gossip is being likened to a bird, as he moves about, disclosing what he has heard.

N. A call to action (11:1–6). Qoheleth to this point has been stressing ideas that could result in inertia. Since appropriate outcomes could not be assured, there was the danger of coasting, of drifting aimlessly. Qoheleth will not tolerate this. Here he calls for action, for boldness, for decisiveness. In spite of life's uncertainties, he calls for the exercise of faith.

The injunction to "cast your bread upon the waters" (v. 1) has been understood to encourage philanthropy, or agricultural pursuits, or sea trade. If charity, the suggestion is to be generous to a stranger who perhaps will not be seen again. This act of kindness will then be repaid at a time when the giver is in need. The reference may be to a practice found in Egypt of planting seeds in the receding Nile. Most likely, however, this verse refers to maritime trade. While there is a risk in such ventures, there is also the possibility of significant returns. Solomon was involved with sea trade, his fleet sailing once every three years (1 Kings 10:22). The word *bread* in a commercial context would suggest goods. Such a business venture demands patience and faith. Verse 2 calls for diversification. It is simply unwise "to put all one's eggs into one basket." The formula *seven, yes even to eight* (v. 2) indicates an indefinite number. Dividing one's wealth into seven or eight parts and distributing them widely will reduce the risk of total loss in case of disaster.

The intent of verses 3 and 4 is uncertain. If the previous verses are concerned with charity, then the clouds could serve as a worthy example of generosity. They pour their water upon the earth which returns it to the clouds by a natural cycle. On the other hand, the tree serves as an effective negative example. Once the tree ceases to bear fruit, it is cut down and left untended. If verse 3 is closely linked with verse 4, as it probably should be, then the intent of these verses has to do with farming which demands hard work. One cannot stand by and wait for the needed rains or favorable winds. One must not second-guess nature. Both the anticipated ("clouds pour rain") and the unexpected ("a tree falls") are beyond man's control and he must not delay his efforts, awaiting a favorable time. Man must do his part and not be immobilized by the independence of nature. He can neither predict nor manipulate nature. Nature follows her own laws. Procrastination is not the answer. Man must do his work. Again, Qoheleth urges bold action even though there are uncertainties and uncontrollable factors. The tasks of life must be done.

Not only is nature beyond man's understanding; the work of God in general is as well. Again Qoheleth emphasizes the inscrutable activity of God. Since wind is used in the previous verse, the New International Version translates this ambiguous Hebrew word as wind. Man does not know the path of the wind. This Hebrew word can also be translated "spirit," which seems to be preferable if the second line of verse 5 is considered. In this case man is ignorant both of the origin of the human spirit and the formation of a baby in its mother's womb. The ambiguity here utilized by Qoheleth is similar to that found in Ezekiel 37:1–14 and John 3:1–15. If man does not understand the mystery of human life, he will be unable to understand the work of God who is the maker of all things.

Verse 6 is a call for diligence through the employment of an illustration from farming. While there are no guarantees, the call is to action. The terms *morning* and *evening* have been understood literally and figuratively. Certain activities are seen as more appropriate for the various times of the day. However, these terms may simply be metaphorical, suggesting the entire day and the entire life. Man must make the most of the time allotted him. The days of darkness are coming; the present is to be enjoyed. Even though there are risks, indolence is not tolerated. Man must do his work no matter how great the risks for only then will he realize the possibilities of life.

O. Youth and age (11:7–12:8). In this section Qoheleth considers youth with its joys and advantages and old age with its troubles and disadvantages. The contrast here is between light and darkness. Light metaphorically refers to life; darkness refers to death. It is also clear that light refers to the pleasing and joyous moments of life (Job 30:26; Ps. 97:11; Isa. 45:7) while darkness alludes to the calamitous and vexatious moments (5:17). The statement *to see the sun* (v. 7) refers not only to living life, but to enjoying life. "Sweet" would be more appropriate to the sense of taste rather than that of sight, but the meaning here is clear—sweet is the opposite of bitter. While the length of life is beyond our control, the attitude toward life is not. Regardless of its length we are to enjoy it all. At its longest, life is brief compared to death. Hence the challenge to enjoy life. There is a sense of urgency here, perhaps coming from the mature Qoheleth as he reflects upon his life. The enjoyment of life is not to be delayed since life at best is unreliable.

The call to enjoy life continues in verse 9 where Qoheleth urges that it be done "while you are young." The source of this joy is to be the heart. The heart is recognized as the wellspring of life (Prov. 4:23), being the potential source for joy; but it is also the potential source of disobedience (Num. 15:39). Both the heart and eyes are organs of desire. If to follow the ways of the heart and whatever the eye sees suggests unrestrained living, it seems to be offset by the ideas of judgment. What is done following the heart does matter to God. The details of judgment are not given. God will call us to account whether this be a specific future judgment or daily testings brought about by the vicissitudes of life.

Verse 10 expresses in a negative way the call to a life of joy. Anything that prevents joy, whether pertaining to the heart or body, is to be avoided. "Banish anxiety" suggests peace of mind while "cast off the troubles of your body" suggests good health. Bodily discomfort should be avoided if possible. The urgency of all this is underscored in the emphasis that youth and vigor are fleeting. They will not last.

Qoheleth now turns from the potential of youth to the problems of old age. He has already cautioned the youth about the approaching days of darkness (11:8) and now presents a graphic allegory of old age. It is introduced with the call to remember, the same Hebrew word used in 11:8.

The Hebrew word translated "Creator" has been variously understood. The Hebrew word for pit is similar to this word both in form and pronunciation, and is metaphorically used to refer to the grave. Further, grave is consonant with the context here. Qoheleth has already warned the youth to remember the days of darkness (death). Also, he has already noted the value of reflection upon death.

Another alternative, again similar in spelling and sound, is the Hebrew word for well. This word is used figuratively to designate source. There is not much support for this alternative. Rabbi Akivah utilized all three of these translations in his dictum: Know your source—from where you came; your grave—where you are going; and your Creator—before whom you are destined to give an account and reckoning.

Even though elsewhere Qoheleth simply refers to deity as God, there is no reason to reject this reference to God under the designation *Creator*. Not only must the youth reckon with old age and with death, he must also reckon with God. God must be remembered in the days of youth—prior to the days of trouble, the infirmities of old age, and the time when there will be no pleasure. The call to remember is not simply an invitation to a mental act, but an invitation to commitment.

Beginning with verse 2, the frailty of old age is presented in a series of pictures. Among the pictures are the aging of the various parts of the body, the destruction of the lives of the inmates of the house by an approaching storm, or the ruin of a wealthy estate due to the failure of its guardians.

If the image of the aging of the various parts of the body is used, verse 2 describes the features of the face. Eyesight is weakened (perhaps by weeping), the sparkle of the eyes is lost, and the eyes become cloudy. Finding reference here to the forehead (sun), the eyes (light), the cheeks (moon), and the eyeballs (stars) seems a bit strained. If the fall comes, can the winter rains be far behind? This suggests the inevitability of the problems associated with old age. Old age is the winter of life.

Verse 3 is viewed by some as comparing the human body to a house in ruins. The keepers of the house are the arms, the strongmen are the legs, the grinders are the teeth, and those looking through the windows are the eyes. It is also possible to view this verse as the description of an estate in decline as the guardians (keepers, strongmen), and the slaves (grinders) grow old and few in number and the ladies of the house cease to look through the windows. The house falling into ruin is a picture of the debilitation of the body because of old age. Verse 4 continues this picture of a house in decline. The doors and the mill could refer to the failure of the digestive function. The rising up at the sound of birds suggests that old men are easily awakened.

In the first part of verse 5 the figurative is interpreted and gives way to the literal—old men are afraid of heights and of traveling. The rest of this verse is figurative, but there is no agreement on its interpretation. Almond-tree blossoms are white and perhaps indicate the white hair of the aged. The grasshopper who drags himself along may refer to the impaired mobility that characterizes the aged. Reference to the capperberry seems to suggest loss of virility. Since the old house is becoming more decrepit, the man must move on to a new home—his eternal home. The term *eternal home* refers to the grave.

In verse 6 there are four expressions, divided into two pairs, which are figures of death. The first figure is that of a lamp suspended by a cord which is cut, causing the bowl to fall and be broken. This fall obviously ruins the lamp. The second figure is the destruction of the pitcher and the apparatus associated with a well. The shattered pitcher and the broken wheel cut off water which is essential to life. There appears to be a harshness in these metaphors, a sense of finality.

In verse 7 the reversal of Genesis 2:7 is seen. Man returns to the ground from whence he came. While the body returns to dust, the spirit returns to God. Minimally, the spirit can be seen as the breath of life—the animation of the body provided by God. Note that man has no control over the departure of the spirit. God gave and he has the power to remove the spirit.

Some would like to see the spirit defined from a Christian perspective. While the body is mortal, the spirit is immortal.

The fact of death now brings Qoheleth back in verse 8 to his recurring words—everything is meaningless!

IV. Conclusion (12:9–14)

It is common in critical thought to see verse 8 as Qoheleth's conclusion. He begins and ends with this emphasis. Verses 9–14 are seen as a postscript, an assessment of Qoheleth's thought by another sage who warns the reader not to be so preoccupied with intellectual difficulties that he fails to fear God and keep his commandments. The biographical data which are added and the reference to Qoheleth in the third person are seen as supporting the involvement of another sage. While this position has merit it is also possible to view this section as a kind of summary. Throughout the book contrasting views have been presented. Here is perhaps another instance of such. While one conclusion to life might be negative it is possible to conclude that life has great meaning and importance since all will be subject to the ultimate scrutiny of God.

Not only was Qoheleth wise, he was also an effective instructor. Since he is contrasted with the people whom he taught, it is possible to view him as having some official standing as a sage, but a sage given not only to participation in the academies and with the rich, but one who was involved through his writings with the people. His preparation is indicated by three verbs: *pondered, searched out,* and *set in order.* The Hebrew word for ponder means to weigh, suggesting that Qoheleth carefully tested his proverbs. They were selected from available proverbs. Then the proverbs that were weighed and selected were arranged. This may provide some insight to the polarities in the book.

As already noted, Qoheleth was an effective instructor. He sought to express himself in words of delight (the literal meaning of "right words"), in an appropriate and pleasing style. Observe that Qoheleth's means of communication was writing. But there was more than literary elegance. What he wrote was right and true.

In verse 11 the twofold effect of wise men's words are noted. They prod and they stick in the memory. To endorse Qoheleth's editing, the ultimate source of his teaching is said to be one Shepherd. This seems to be a clear reference to God, suggesting inspiration. While the sage functions differently from the prophet, his words are no less divine. Beyond the words of one Shepherd, care is to be exercised. The reader is cautioned to take warning. This conclusion to the book is similar to that found in other books (cf. 2 Thess. 3:14; 1 Tim. 6:20–21; Rev. 22:18–19). Some have argued that this statement pertains to the whole of the Hebrew Bible even as Revelation 22:18–19 is projected beyond that book to the entire Bible by Christians.

The observations that the composing of many books has no end may refer to the wisdom literature of the surrounding countries with which Israel was well acquainted. This along with other kinds of literature was prolific. Perhaps more important than this reservation is a very practical one: much study wearies the body.

In spite of intense and broad investigations, Qoheleth has not found meaning. His experiments are done. The answer is to be found in fearing God and keeping his commandments. Here at the end of the book emphasis is put on fearing God, which is the beginning and the very essence of wisdom. Not only is worship stressed, but also conduct. True worship will result in obedience, the keeping of the commandments. Worship and conduct are the whole of man. Here the meaning is that all men in everything are to reverence God and obey his laws. Again, reference is made to judgment without any effort to locate it in time and to describe its format. Regardless, the result is clear. All men will have all their deeds assessed. Such a fact lends meaning to life.

SELECT BIBLIOGRAPHY

Bergant, D. *Job, Ecclesiastes.* Wilmington: Michael Glazier, 1982.

Bottoms, L. W. *Ecclesiastes Speaks to Us Today.* Atlanta: John Knox, 1979.

Eaton, M. A. *Ecclesiastes: An Introduction and Commentary.* Downers Grove: Inter-Varsity, 1983.

Goldberg, L. *Ecclesiastes.* Grand Rapids: Zondervan, 1983.

Kaiser, W. *Ecclesiastes: Total Life.* Chicago: Moody, 1979.

Kidner, D. *A Time to Mourn, and a Time to Dance.* Downers Grove: Inter-Varsity, 1976.

SONG OF SOLOMON

Andrew E. Hill

INTRODUCTION

The book takes its title from the superscription (1:1) and is variously labeled the Song, Songs, Song of Songs, Song of Solomon, and the Best Song. The alternative name, Canticles, is derived from the Latin Vulgate.

The Song is placed among the books of wisdom and poetry in the Septuagint and most English versions. While not wisdom literature in the strict sense, the Song shares some affinities with wisdom in that the work is associated with wise King Solomon (1 Kings 4:29–34), concerns itself with the mystery of man created male and female, and offers instruction (at least implicitly) on human behavior as it relates to sexuality and marriage. The Song is grouped first among the five festival scrolls (Megilloth) in the Hebrew canon, and in later Judaism it was designated to be read as part of the Passover celebration.

Like Psalms, Proverbs, and Lamentations, the Song is entirely poetic in literary form (with the exception of the superscription). The distinguishing feature of Hebrew poetry, and all poetry in the ancient Near East, is rhythm of sound and rhythm of thought. Rhythm of sound is the regular pattern of stressed or unstressed syllables in lines of poetry, including the repetition of sounds through alliteration and assonance. Rhythm of thought is the balancing of ideas in a structured or systematic way. The primary vehicle for conveying this thought rhythm is word parallelism, in which similar or opposite ideas are offset in the lines of poetry (e.g., earrings/strings of jewels, 1:10; mountains/hills, 2:8; opened/left, gone, 5:6). Sometimes this poetic parallelism arranges ideas synthetically or climactically in that each idea in the successive lines of the verse build on the previous one (e.g., wall/windows/lattice, 2:9).

Poetry is a language of images often given to making comparisons by utilizing simile and metaphor. This is especially true of the Song as lyrical love poetry. Frequently the Western reader finds these comparisons humorous or even uncomplimentary (e.g., "your waist is a mound of wheat," or "your nose is like the tower of Lebanon," 7:2, 4), not to mention difficult to understand. The bold language and vivid imagery of the love poetry sometimes shock and embarrass the modern reader (e.g., 7:8). In part this may be due to the idyllic overtones of the Song. Although the Song is not an idyll in the technical sense, today's technologically sophisticated audience experiences uneasiness when encountering these kinds of pastoral scenes.

Yet, the Song conforms to literary conventions of love poetry in the second millennium B.C. For example, the Egyptian love songs of the New Kingdom (ca. 1570–1085 B.C.) contain many of the same themes and employ similar figures of speech. The garden motif as erotic symbol and lyrics in praise of the rapture and mystery of human sexual love are prominent. Simile and metaphor abound, including descriptive songs that compare the physical features of the lovers to exotic flora and fauna. Songs of desire calling the partners to love, to partake of delicate foods, and to drink spiced wine to refresh "lovesickness," and even the attention to fine apparel and exquisite perfumes and ointments are commonplace in the literature. When viewed against this literary backdrop the strangeness of the Song is diminished and appreciation for its simple beauty and sensitive treatment of the subject matter is enhanced.

Specific literary forms and formal features identified in the love poetry of the Song include: descriptive songs in which each lover sketches the other in highly figurative language (4:1–7; 6:4–7; 7:1–9); self-description (1:5–7; 8:10); songs of admiration calling attention to the lover's adornment (1:9–11; 4:9–11); songs of desire characterized by an invitation to love (1:2–4; 8:1–4); and search narratives, recounting the maiden's energy and persistence in seeking her lover (3:1–4; 5:2–7).

Several more technical literary devices recognized in the Song include: oath formulas (2:7; 3:5; 5:8; 8:4); the teasing song as the lovers banter in their desire to unite (2:14–17; 5:2–7); the boasting song in which the maiden flaunts her uniqueness (6:8–10); the urgent call to love usually prefaced with an imperative verb (2:5, 17; 4:16; 7:11–13; 8:14); and the game of love comprised of the search narrative (5:2–7), an oath formula (5:8), the "teasing question" posed by the friends (6:9), the maiden's answer song (5:10–16), followed by another teasing question from the friends (6:1), and concluding with the "formula of belonging" (6:2–3).

There are as many outlines for structuring the content of the Song as methods of interpretation. While the book contains repeated phrases and lines (e.g., "how beautiful you are, my darling," 1:15, 4:1, 7; "my lover is mine," 2:16, 6:3; "who is this?" 3:6, 6:10, 8:5; "my sister, my bride," 4:9, 12, 5:1; and "daughters of Jerusalem, I charge you," 2:7, 3:5, 5:8, 8:4), only the charge to the daughters of Jerusalem in 2:7, 3:5, and 8:4 appears to serve as a refrain perhaps marking strophic structure. The speeches or direct discourse provide clues for dividing the text, yet the speakers remain largely unidentified. Speech content can aid in the identification of the speaker, but this is not conclusive. The terse language and cryptic nature of the poetry often make ascertaining the exact extent of a given speech no easy task. These efforts to assign the speeches to specific participants in the love story are complicated by the question of the exact number of characters in the story. This commentary on the Song views the poetry as a unified composition and "reweaves" the narrative along the lines of a three-character love story in a series of sequential events.

Traditional biblical scholarship has ascribed the Song of Solomon to King Solomon and dated the poetry to the late tenth century B.C.—largely on the strength of the superscription to the book (1:1). Some ancient Jewish traditions credit the work to King Hezekiah, the Judahite ruler accorded a prominent place in the preservation of the Israelite wisdom literature (Prov. 25:1; cf. 2 Chron. 32:27–29).

The problems of authorship and the date of the Song are closely related. The inconclusive nature of the book's title further complicates the matter. The Hebrew phrase *lišlōmōh* (1:1) may be understood variously as "of/to/for/about Solomon" (cf. the notations in Pss. 3:1; 4:1; 5:1; etc.). Thus this title may infer that Solomon wrote the poetry, that the poems were dedicated to him, or that they are songs composed about him.

Scholarly appeal to other criteria related to authorship proves no more useful in helping to establish the identity of the writer of the Song. Though Solomon's name occurs six times elsewhere in the book (1:5; 3:7, 9, 11; 8:11, 12), and other passages attest to his sagacity and literary skill (e.g., 1 Kings 4:29–34), these references assert nothing concerning his authorship of this poetry. Instead, they merely confirm Solomon's role as a key figure in the love story.

The exotic vocabulary (e.g., perfume, 1:12; saffron, calamus, aloes, 4:13–14) and the author's knowledge of Palestinian flora and fauna (including fifteen species of animals and twenty-one varieties of plants) might suggest Solomonic authorship (cf. 1 Kings 4:33).

As the previous discussion indicates, however, neither the Solomonic references nor the language of the poetry yields solid evidence for ascertaining the authorship of the "best of songs." Unhappily, the results are similar when these various criteria are examined and applied to the problem of dating the Song.

The presence of Aramaisms and Persian and Greek loan words has caused biblical commentators to assign dates to the book ranging from Israel's united monarchy (tenth century B.C.) to the Persian and Greek periods (ca. 500–300 B.C.).

The juxtaposition of Jerusalem and Tirzah in a poetic couplet (6:4) is often suggested as a clue to fixing the date of the Song since Tirzah was the capital city of the northern kingdom during the reigns of Baasha, Elah, Zimri, Tibni, and Omri (ca. 900–870 B.C.). Yet the city may have been used by Jeroboam I as a secondary royal residence (cf. 1 Kings 14:17) and was likely a prominent and beautiful city long before it became the capital (cf. Josh. 12:24).

Additionally, the indiscriminate mention of geographical localities found in both the northern and southern kingdoms (e.g., Jerusalem, 1:5; En Gedi, 1:14; Sharon, 2:1; Gilead, 4:1) may suggest the united monarchy when these places were part of the same political realm. The preponderance of northern and eastern cities and regions (e.g.,

Bethrabbim, Carmel, Damascus, Gilead, Hermon, Heshbon, Lebanon, Mahanaim, Sharon, Shulam, and Tirzah), however, better argues for the time of the divided monarchy and a northern provenance for the writing of the book.

One final factor influencing informed opinion on the authorship and date of the Song deserves mention. The interpretive method adopted by the individual translator/commentator in large measure determines how one outlines the text, understands the poetry with respect to the number of characters in the story and plot development, and ultimately, colors the way one arranges and evaluates the various strands of evidence bearing on the question of authorship and date.

For example, those who contend the love story is a two-character drama are likely to focus attention on the exotic vocabulary, the plethora of references to flora and fauna, and the apparent unity of geography within the poems and opt for a date in the Solomonic age, if not Solomonic authorship. By contrast, those who view the poetry depicting a love triangle with King Solomon cast as the "villain" would tender a northern kingdom provenance and an early divided kingdom date. The scholar employing the typological or cultic approach to the Song will likely emphasize the late lexical features of the text and the device of "literary-fiction" in the poetry where Solomon simply represents the "great lover" and conclude the book should be dated to the Persian period.

Although awareness of these complexities connected with authorship and date is crucial to any study of the Song, caution and restraint are clearly in order since no consensus exists even among conservative biblical scholars. However, despite this inability to firmly establish an author and date for the Song of Solomon, the lack of concrete knowledge on these two issues in no wise diminishes the beauty of the poetry or the power of its message.

Given the uncertainties associated with the superscription and the unusual nature of the book's vocabulary and style, the Song is best regarded as an anonymous composition. The weight of the literary, historical, and linguistic evidence as currently assessed points to a northern kingdom provenance and an early (preexilic) date for the writing of the book. Attempts to be more precise than this are tenuous and return relatively little benefit for the overall comprehension of the message and meaning of the love songs.

No single Old Testament book has proven more perplexing for biblical interpreters than the Song of Solomon. Centuries of careful study, analysis, and commentary by biblical scholars of various traditions and theological persuasions have produced little interpretive consensus.

First, the theme or topic of the Song has confused, shocked, and embarrassed both Jewish and Christian interpreters—so much so that the rabbis and early church fathers debated the value of the Song and its place in the Old Testament canon for generations. What merit in a book that contains no suggestion of worship, no hint of social concern, no affirmation of faith in God, indeed not even any mention of God (save the possible reference "the very flame of the LORD [NIV note] in 8:6)? What value in a book vaunting human affection, physical passion, and erotic sexual love?

Second, the nature and structure of the poetry does not lend itself to ready analysis. Aside from the ambiguous references to King Solomon, clear historical parallels or allusions are wanting. Much of the language of the book is unusual if not unique and obscure, making translation and interpretation difficult. By definition lyrical poetry is brief in length, concentrated in meaning, and often lacking smooth transitions, posing a dilemma for commentators seeking to divide the book into smaller logical units. In turn, this makes for uncertainty in identifying the number of different characters in the love story and assigning these smaller units of speech to specific individuals.

The *dramatic* approach has been part of church tradition since the third century A.D. It understands the Song as an ancient Hebrew play, based largely on the analogy of later Greek drama. The poetry is considered a dramatic script intended for royal entertainment. Speeches are assigned to the principal characters of the melodrama (whether two or three, depending on the identification of the shepherd as one in the same with the king), with the daughters of Jerusalem (or harem) represented by a female chorus. Attempts to divide the Song into acts and scenes often requires significant emendation of the text, and efforts to cast the book as Greek drama are forced and artificial.

Unlike allegory, the *typological* method recognizes the historicity of the book (whether it commemorates Solomon's marriage to Pharaoh's daughter or recounts the king's wooing of the Shulamite maiden), but subordinates the literal presentation of Old Testament history to a correspondent New Testament pattern or parallel. The traditional "type/antitype" fulfillment is God's covenant relationship to Israel for the Jewish interpreter or Christ's relationship to the church as his bride for the Christian interpreter. While the expression of love in the Song may illustrate the truth of God's relationship to his creation or his chosen people, or Christ's relationship to the church, the major failing of the typological method is the fact that the Song itself gives no hint that it is intended as typology, nor does the New Testament make any use of the Song, either by direct quotation or indirect allusion.

The *cultic* or *mythological* approach views the Song as a Hebrew adaptation of Mesopotamian fertility cult liturgy. The annual ritual was a reenactment of the ancient myth recounting the goddess Ishtar's search for her dead lover in the netherworld, finally restoring him to life through sexual union, and thus ensuring creation's continued fertility. It is assumed that the cultic associations of the Song were forgotten or consciously changed to make the book acceptable to the Israelite faith.

The *wedding cycle* approach assumes the Song is an amalgam of nuptial poems. The series of songs honoring the bride and groom were eventually formalized into a cycle of recitations that were incorporated into the wedding celebration. The Song does contain numerous parallels to ancient Jewish wedding customs and to this day is chanted or sung as an integral part of the orthodox Jewish wedding ceremony.

While the historical aspects of the book are not denied, the *didactic* view understands the poem as a vehicle for instruction and simply subordinates the circumstances surrounding the occasion of the book in favor of the moral and didactic purposes of the literature. The book is seen to present the purity and wonder of sexual love, to promote ideals of simplicity, faithfulness, and chastity, and to instruct on the virtue of human affection and the beauty and holiness of marriage.

The *allegorical* method is the oldest and most popular approach to the Song—this despite the fact that the book nowhere claims to be an allegory. Here it is important to distinguish between allegory as a literary type and allegorizing as an interpretive method. Allegory is defined as an obvious symbolic representation in literature, or simply, extended metaphor. Allegory says one thing but conveys another, deeper, hidden meaning. The allegorizing of a text occurs when the interpreter understands a given passage as allegory, even though it was not intended as such by the author. The allegorical method presupposes the Song contains no factual record; the poetry merely serves as the vehicle for some hidden spiritual truth. The allegorizing method as applied to the Song has predominantly yielded insights on the spiritual truth of God's covenant relationship to Israel for Jewish interpreters, or Christ's relationship to his church and the individual believer for Christian interpreters.

The *literal* approach takes the Song at face value and interprets the love poetry for what it appears to be—a sensual, even erotic expression of emotion and passion as two young lovers voice their desire for each other. The literal interpretive stance makes no attempt to apologize for the frankness of language or boldness of imagery in the poem by resorting to typology or allegorizing. Nor does it seek to justify the biblical treatment of the subject of human love and sexuality since God made man male and female and sanctioned their union as one flesh at creation. Whether composed by him or not, the love poetry of the Song is believed to reflect real events associated with the reign of King Solomon.

This commentary assumes a three-character love story and adopts the literal-historical approach in combination with elements of the didactic approach. The book is likely a northern kingdom satire on the reign of Solomon and his exploitation of women (ironically to his own demise), and a memorializing of the exemplary character of the Shulamite maiden who rejected the wooing of the king because of her faithfulness to her shepherd lover.

OUTLINE

I. The Shulamite Maiden (1:1–3:5)
   A. Superscription (1:1)
   B. The King and the Maiden Banter (1:2–2:2)
   C. The Maiden Seeks Her Shepherd Lover (2:3–3:5)

II. The King Woos the Shulamite Maiden (3:6–7:9)
   A. The King's First Proposal (3:6–5:8)
   B. The King's Second Proposal (5:9–7:9)
III. The Shulamite Maiden Rejects the King (7:10–8:4)
IV. The Shulamite Maiden and Her Shepherd Lover Are Reunited (8:5–14)

COMMENTARY

I. The Shulamite Maiden (1:1–3:5)

A. Superscription (1:1). The title of the book, both English and Hebrew, is taken from the first verse. Literally translated, the verse reads, "the song of songs, which is of Solomon." The expression *song of songs* is an idiom for the superlative in Hebrew, or "the best song." The word *song* is a generic term for any happy, festival song (cf. Isa. 24:9; 30:29). The possessive pronoun attributing the work to Solomon, if original, is ambiguous at best.

B. The king and the maiden banter (1:2–2:2). The opening sections of the poem find the maiden in the royal court of King Solomon, with no indication as to how she came to be there (although 6:11–12 implies she was taken from the countryside against her will). Those who espouse a three-character Song recognize 1:9–2:2 as a dialogue between the king and the maiden, but understand her speeches as projections directed to the shepherd lover she has left behind, and not direct responses to Solomon's flattery.

In the anxiety and confusion of her separation from her home in the northern hill country and her shepherd lover, the maiden recalls the tenderness of his affection and the pleasure she experienced when kissing him (**1:2–4a**). The pleasure of the lover's kiss is likened to wine, a connection well attested in ancient literature (4:10; 5:1; 7:9; Prov. 9:2, 5). More than the physical sensations of lovemaking, the maiden recalls and longs for the sense of belonging and security she enjoyed in the presence of the shepherd lover.

A pun occurs in verse 3 in that the words for perfume and name sound alike in Hebrew. The name of a person and his or her character and personality were inseparable in the ancient mind. Remembering the sweet fragrance of the shepherd's cologne causes her to glory in the strength and richness of the shepherd's character. Like the aroma of expensive ointment, the shepherd's personality attracts all the young maidens. A sense of urgency surfaces in the maiden's plea for the lover to rescue her from her plight, indicated by the use of an imperative verb ("take me away"). The maiden is not asking to be brought into the king's private chambers! Rather, she implores the shepherd to rescue her from the royal harem before Solomon violates her sexually and destroys their relationship.

The shift to the first person plural (**1:4b**) marks the end of the maiden's speech and may represent a dramatic interjection in the poem. The "we" is thought to be the women of the royal harem. Apparently they recognize the unique nature of the maiden's love for her absent shepherd and they extol her sincere affection and faithfulness. Indeed, this admixture of these qualities in the chemistry of a male-female relationship merits more praise than wine.

Perhaps the interjection of the harem women reminds the maiden of her visage in contrast to theirs (**1:5–7**). Unlike the soft and white-skinned harem women she is black or dark, yet very beautiful. Like the tents of the Trans-Jordanian nomads woven of black goat hair, the maiden has been tanned dark brown by exposure to the sun while working in her family's vineyards. The curious stares of the other women prompt self-justification. No reason is given for her brothers' anger, though they do reappear later in the poem (8:8–9). It is possible that it is no more than word play, as she has been "burned" by the sun and "burned" by the anger of her brothers. The vineyard she has neglected is her own person. The duration and intensity of her outdoor activity have interrupted or even cancelled normal hygenic and cosmetic routines. The imperative verse addressed to the absent shepherd parallels that of verse 4 and underscores the distress of the maiden's situation. If the shepherd can call to her from among all the flocks and shepherds seeking refuge from the noonday heat in the shade of rocks and trees, her search for him will be expedited.

The shift to the feminine form (**1:8**) marks a different speaker, probably the women of the royal harem. The phrase *most beautiful of women* is repeated three times in refrains by the harem women (1:8; 5:9; 6:1) and it echoes a constant theme in the poem—the flawless beauty of the maiden. Verse 8 has puzzled interpreters in that the women's instructions to follow the sheep tracks and then graze her young goats nearby in hopes of finding the shepherd seem nonsensical because they encourage the very behavior the maiden wishes to avoid.

Solomon now enters the scene and his first words are an attempt to divert the maiden's attention from the shepherd to himself through flattering speech and the presentation of costly gifts (**1:9–11**). Complimentary comparisons of women to animals are a common feature of ancient Near Eastern love poetry. In the Song the maiden is likened to a mare (1:9), dove (1:15), goats and sheep (4:1–2), and gazelle fawns (4:5), while the shepherd is compared to the gazelle or stag (2:9, 17). The maiden's rustic beauty excites interest in the king in the same way a mare might attract attention among Pharaoh's stallions. The radiance of the maiden's countenance is enhanced by her jewelry and ornamentation, an important part of female dress in the Old Testament world. The shift back to the first person plural in verse 11 may indicate that the harem women are speaking again, although this is not clear. Ornaments crafted especially for the maiden are ordered, the reference to gold and silver perhaps indicating expensive and exquisite jewelry befitting her rapturous beauty.

The juxtaposition of the "king" and "my lover" in the maiden's soliloquy (**1:12–14**) indicates they are not one in the same person. While the king entertains at a royal banquet (whether publicly or privately is unclear), the maiden's own perfume incites erotic imaginations of the shepherd lover. The intensity of her romantic response is reinforced by the mention of three separate fragrances. "Spikenard" (NEB) was an exotic and expensive ointment derived from plants native to India; myrrh is an aromatic resin manufactured from the gum of a species of tree in South Arabia. The sachet or necklace with a pouch was a common way to use myrrh as a perfume. The myrrh was mixed with a fat or oil base and placed in a hollow pod or wrapped in a cloth or leather pouch and worn as a necklace or bracelet. As body heat melted the fat the aroma of the solid stick of myrrh was released.

The king continues to laud the captivating comeliness of the maiden (**1:15**), twice repeating the word *beautiful.* The expression *your eyes are doves* is obscure. Both the maiden and shepherd are described as having "dove eyes" (1:15; 4:1; 5:12) and the dove is elsewhere one of the metaphors used of both lovers (2:14; 5:2; 6:9). The dove is a symbol of peace, purity, and tenderness in the Old Testament. The eyes are thought to reveal inner character, so "dove eyes" may suggest qualities of innocence, purity, loyalty, and fidelity evident in the lovers.

The maiden's initial response may have given Solomon false hope as she repeats his very words. However, she quickly lets it be known that her words are intended for another and that she does not belong in the presence of the king (**1:16–2:1**). The scene of her lovemaking is pastoral, in grassy fields and under spreading trees—not the palace precincts. In her modesty she compares herself to the more common wildflowers of the countryside, flowers of Sharon not far from her home in Shulam.

The king's final simile, a weak attempt to play on the maiden's words, falls on deaf ears (**2:2**). He continues to exalt her beauty above the "thorns" of his harem, oblivious to the fact that the banter has another dimension. This other dimension is intimated by the satirical repetition of "my" in the opening exchange of speeches (1:9, 13, 14, 15, 16; 2:2, 3) and demonstrated more clearly in the maiden's next discourse.

C. The maiden seeks her shepherd lover (2:3–3:5). The literary form of this pericope (**2:3–7**) is the boasting song, common in ancient love poetry. The maiden touts her lover and rejoices in the delight his lovemaking arouses in her. The cultivated fruit tree in the midst of a wild wood calls attention to the uniqueness of her lover. To "sit in his shade" (v. 3) suggests cool refreshment and the comfort and protection of the lover's physical proximity. The fruits sweet to her taste are the elements of his lovemaking. In contrast to Solomon's banquet, the maiden imagines her own wedding feast with her shepherd's pure and faithful love as her banner or emblem of betrothal (2:4; cf. Pss. 20:5; 60:4). Overcome with exhaustion in the ecstasy of lovemaking, the maiden requests refreshment with foods the ancients believed possessed powers to restore and enhance romantic energies and capabilities. These aphrodisiacs included raisins, apples, raisin cakes, pomegranates, and spiced wine (2:5; 4:13; 7:8, 12–13). The "raisin cakes" (JB, NASB) embodied considerable erotic symbolism as they were associated with the rites of the ancient fertility cults (cf. Jer. 7:18; 44:18–19).

The maiden's charge to the daughters of Jerusalem or harem women in her company is a recurring refrain in the poem (2:7; 3:5; 8:4). The refrain marks major breaks in the text of the poem and usually occurs in the context of physical intimacy. "By the gazelles and by the does of the field" is a rustic oath formula underscoring urgency and seriousness in her entreaty. Love is not to be stirred until the partners have taken full satisfaction in the intimate physical delights of each other's company.

The imperative verbs in the opening and closing verses of **2:8–13** signal an intensification of emotion in the maiden as she continues to dream about the shepherd lover left behind. The repetition of "Arise, my darling" in verses 10 and 13 is an envelope construction making this a separate stanza in the unit. Dwelling on her lover and the sweetness of his affection moves the maiden to fantasize that he has come to rescue her from the king's harem. The analogy to the wild animals of the hill country continues, perhaps a subtle foil between the freedom the "stag" enjoys and the confinement of the "doe" behind the walls, lattices, and windows of the palace complex. The stag, staring, gazing, bounding from window to window seeking a glimpse of his "doe," is the picture of both crestfallen loneliness and energetic impatience. Winter is over and the spring season has come, evidenced by the blooming flowers, nesting birds, and early fruit of the fig orchards (vv. 11–13). Love is awakened; it is now time for the lovers to be rejoined in their natural setting. The certainty of warmth and spring growth following the winter rains no doubt images the ever-budding affections of the lovers. The two-character interpretation of the poem strains at this point to make sense of the plot. If Solomon is the lover why must he come from the hills and peer through garden lattices for a glance of the maiden? If the maiden is confined in the palace precincts and Solomon and the lover are one in the same, why must she (even in a dream) steal through the streets of Jerusalem pursuing her lover?

The comparison of the maiden to a nesting rock dove (**2:14–15**) echoes 2:12 and maintains the springtime imagery of the previous section. The "dove" is a pet name for the maiden (1:15; 4:1; 5:2, 12; 6:9) and a common symbol of love and fertility in the ancient Near East. "Face" (lit. appearance) and "voice" are paired in chiasmus in verse 14 in the maiden's memory of the playfulness of their love. The meaning of verse 15 is obscure. It may be a literal reference to measures taken in the vineyards to prevent spoilage by foxes (since the maiden worked the vineyards prior to her abduction, 1:6) or it may be a symbolic statement of the blossoming love shared by the two and a veiled expression of their desire to prevent the relationship from being "ruined" by the foxes (intruders or rivals?) before it matures.

The vivid memory of the shepherd and the vibrance of the intimate moments she shared with him during the spring season(s) in the vineyards elicits an affirmation of love and loyalty from the maiden (**2:16–17**). Verse 16 is repeated in 6:3 and emphasizes the exclusiveness of their relationship. "Browsing" or "feeding" among the lilies is a metaphor for the lover's enjoyment of the maiden's physical charms (cf. 6:2). "Until the day breaks" is a poetic idiom for the dawn. The joy and pleasure of the physical intimacies shared through the night are ended at daybreak. As the sun rises and chases away the shadows of night so the shepherd lover turns and runs like a stag back into the hills. Like the dove, the gazelle or stag has connections with Mesopotamian fertility rites, being a model of sexual prowess (cf. 2:8–9).

The expression *my lover* (NIV) or *beloved* (RSV) in verse 16 is the favorite epithet of the maiden for the rustic shepherd lover. The word occurs more than thirty times in the book and elsewhere in the Old Testament the term can mean "uncle" or "kinsman" (Num. 36:11; 2 Kings 24:17; Amos 6:10) or even "lovemaking" (Prov. 7:18; Ezek. 16:8; 23:17; cf. 1:2; 4:10). In extrabiblical literature the cognate word for the Hebrew signified "darling (sexual) partner" and was employed in ancient love poetry and fertility cult liturgies with erotic connotations. The term may even be a euphemism for the breasts or genitals (cf. 7:12).

The opening line of the "search narrative" in **3:1–5** confirms that the entire section (2:3–3:5) is to be understood as the recounting of the maiden's fantasy as she pines for her absent lover. The dream or fantasy concludes dramatically with her frantic search of the city for the shepherd and the passionate reunion of the lovers in the deserted streets of Jerusalem. The plural "nights" implies that the fantasy or dream is a recurring one (NEB night after night) or that it lasts all night long (NIV). The refrain in verses 1–2 continues the pattern of repeated phrases and lines throughout the entire stanza (e.g., 2:7 and 3:5; 2:10 and 2:13) and accentuates the earnestness and persistence of the maiden's search. Soon after encountering the watchmen or night police making their rounds, the maiden locates her lover and the dream sequence ends ideally. Her second night-search fantasy has no such happy ending (5:2–8). In her joy and relief the maiden clutches her lover and refuses to release him from her embrace—almost a prophetic foreshadowing of how she intends to respond to the shepherd lover should they ever be reunited (cf. 8:1–4). The leading of the lover into her mother's house may signify the formalizing of their love relationship (i.e., parental approval and a public wedding; cf. 8:8, 13). The phrase *to the room of the one who conceived me* (v. 4b) is probably a reference to the sexual consummation of their relationship. Only then will she freely give him the "nectar of her pomegranates" and the delicacies of her love (8:2). The first stanza of the poem concludes (v. 5) with a word-for-word repetition of the charge previously made to the harem women.

II. The King Woos the Shulamite Maiden (3:6–7:9)

A. The king's first proposal (3:6–5:8). The two-character approach to the Song identifies this unit (3:6–5:8) as a segment of what was probably a longer royal nuptial song honoring the marriage of Solomon and the maiden and celebrating the consummation of their love (cf. Ps. 45). However, this understanding of the poem cannot adequately account for the maiden's second night search for her lover, nor her charge to the harem women concerning the absent lover and their response (5:8–9). The refrain in 3:5 and 8:4 is followed by the same question "Who is this coming up from the desert?" Here the question is posed by the harem women and it introduces the pericope under discussion.

The verses seem to be a lyrical flashback reminding the maiden of how she came to be a part of the royal harem. The "who" in verse 6 is probably the maiden since the accompanying demonstrative pronoun *this* is feminine singular in form. The king has returned to the royal city in all his splendor with yet another beautiful woman from the kingdom for his ever-expanding harem. (This sight was no doubt fairly common in the capital as Solomon had 140 women in the harem at the time of this episode [6:8], and a total of 1000 women populated the royal harem by the end of his reign [1 Kings 11:1–8].) The convoy of armed bodyguards suggests a tour or review of the empire, not a military campaign. The word for palanquin (JB litter; NASB traveling couch) is unique in the Old Testament and its derivation is uncertain. The Jerusalem Bible understands two different vehicles in the royal procession—the litter which transports the Shulamite maiden and the exquisitely constructed portable throne upon which Solomon is carried. The crown the king wears is not the diadem of kingship but a wedding wreath.

The king's rehearsal of the maiden's beauty and his invitations to love (**4:1–15**) comprise the longest single unit in the poem. The first half of the passage is a descriptive song with highly figurative language, and is bounded by the inclusio *How beautiful you are, my darling* (4:1, 7). The descriptive song mixes pastoral, domestic, and urban images common in ancient love poetry (e.g., myrrh, lilies, pomegranates, etc.). The language of the love poem now becomes increasingly erotic and explicit. The import of the descriptive song is the maiden's flawless beauty from head to toe (lit. eyes, v. 1 to breasts, v. 5); she mirrors the beauty, freshness, and innocence of the natural world and the strength and elegance of the manmade world. The phrases *mountain of myrrh* and *hill of incense* (v. 6) are more difficult to understand. This may be a generic allusion to all the physical charms of the maiden or another erotic figure of speech signifying the breasts or vulva. Either way the king's objective is transparent—to fully possess *all* the maiden's physical charms through intimate sexual relations. Portions of the descriptive song (vv. 1–3) are repeated later in the king's second poetic sketch of the maiden (6:5–7). The phrase *until the day breaks* also occurs in 2:17. There the Shulamite encourages the shepherd to take full satisfaction in her love all night. Here the king foists his desire for the same upon the maiden.

The two imperatives in verse 8 mark the transition from descriptive song (vv. 1–7) to a song of admiration (vv. 9–11) as Solomon continues to woo the maiden. Geographically the Shulamite has been brought to Jerusalem from her home in the northern hill country. Now the king urges that she break from her past socially and emotionally by accepting his proposal for love and marriage. She has ravished his heart with her physical beauty and sensual charm, as the admiration song calling attention to her adornment confesses. "Sister" and "brother" are titles of endearment spoken commonly between lovers in the poetry of the ancient Near East (4:9, 10, 12). "Bride" is better understood as "betrothed one," in that her relationship to Solomon has not yet been consummated sexually. The girl remains a virgin, a garden locked up and a sealed spring. The garden metaphor is also a popular motif in ancient Near Eastern love poetry. The female character is often depicted as an orchard, a garden full of choice fruit and exotic plants. The trees and plants mentioned are predominantly those associated with the accouterments of romance and lovemaking (e.g., spices, oils, perfumes, and even foods and potions considered aphrodisiacs), all serving to heighten the erotic and the sensual.

The two-character interpretation understands **4:16–5:1b** as the climax of the love poem. According to this view, the maiden has succumbed to the king's passionate wooing, willingly offering him the "fruit of her garden," and the king happily "possesses" the garden, consummating their marital relationship. This approach assumes that the imperative *awake* (4:16) in the lovers' dialogue is conjunctive, not disjunctive. Yet, in previous speeches the maiden has used the imperative verb disjunctively, indicating her address or response is intended not for the king but for another. The two-character approach also fails to adequately explain how the maiden remains a virgin (who has stored up her "delicacies" for her lover [7:12–13] and stood like "a wall" against the amorous advances of the king [8:10]) until she is reunited with her lover at the end of the poem. The maiden imagines and yearns for the breezes of fate to waft the fragrance of her love to her true lover, alluring him to deliver her from the confines of the royal harem. Interestingly enough, this very sequence of events constitutes the maiden's second night-search fantasy (5:2–8). She can only invent the absent shepherd lover's ideal response to her invitation.

The harem women may be speaking in **5:1c,** applauding the lovers' faithfulness and encouraging their continued enjoyment of the pleasures of lovemaking. The "friends" may also be guests and companions of the lovers (perhaps at a wedding feast?), advising them to take full satisfaction in the physical intimacies of the marriage bond.

That King Solomon is not the lover the maiden has invited to enter her "garden" is made clear by a second lengthy search narrative (**5:2–8**). Her wishful thinking in 4:16–5:1b becomes a reality, if only in a night vision. The one she has longed for, the one to whom she has pledged her love, stands at her very door! The shepherd identifies himself by making mention of his dew-drenched hair, hardly unusual for one who sleeps outside and tends flocks through the night; but most unusual for a king with the reputation for self-indulgent luxury.

The maiden's hesitation and excuse making delay her answering the door, turning the lover away. The reason for her behavior is unclear. Her reaction may be attributed to fear of another disappointment, fatigue, or disbelief, or perhaps even a fatalistic resignation to her present plight. Her continued shouts and frantic searching for the departed lover avail nothing, save incurring the wrath of the night watchmen who partially strip and beat her (for disturbing the peace, mistaking her for a prostitute, or for a second offense in violating the harem curfew?).

The two-character view considers this a temporary lapse in the marriage of the king and the maiden because he is late in returning home. The maiden pouts in her self-pity, lamenting the postponement of the tryst she has anticipated. When the lover finally arrives she greets him with apathy and indifference, then later regrets her action and seeks to make amends. This view not only distorts the literary intentions of the search-find motif in love poetry, but also tarnishes the idyllic love relationship portrayed everywhere else in the poem.

The charge to the harem women is a partial repetition of 2:7 and 3:5, and like 3:5 signals another major break in the poem. The maiden is either asking the women to inform her lover she is forlorn, weak, and love-sick because of his absence, or rhetorically stating she is not exhausted from lovemaking (cf. 2:5).

The cultic interpretation of the Song highlights this second night-search narrative (in combination with the occurrence of "lover" in the singular) as a vestige of Canaanite fertility cult influence in the Song. The maiden is thought to be the goddess searching for her lover, the god Dod, who died and rests in the netherworld. Upon finding him she renews him with sexual intercourse, commemorated annually in the ritualistic marriage of the king to a virgin in his harem. This approach ignores the immediate context of the lovers' dialogue, discounts the literal interpretation of the search narrative, and dismisses the other preexilic citations of the word *lover.*

B. The king's second proposal (5:9–7:9). The subsequent material introduced by **5:9** constitutes one of the more stylized sections of the poem (5:9–6:13). The highly figurative descriptive speeches are placed within the framework of a series of transitional interrogative interjections by the harem (5:9; 6:1, 10, 13). The harem women are bewildered by the maiden's behavior. Their confusion is voiced in the form of a query to the Shulamite. What is so special about her lover that she refuses the king? There is also the practical matter of seeking justification for the charge given to them earlier (5:8).

The answer to the question posed by the harem women takes the form of a descriptive song reciting the lover's good looks (**5:10–16**). Once the harem women witness his handsome features they will know why he is "better than others." The descriptive song is characterized by romantic exaggeration and several of these similes and metaphors have their antecedents in the earlier descriptive songs praising the maiden's beauty. The only thing remarkable about the passage is its subject matter, as descriptive songs about male characters in ancient love poetry are exceptional. The comeliness, strength, and splendor of his physical appearance no doubt reflect the incomparable inner qualities of character and personality the lover possesses. This man is her lover—reason enough to spurn the wooing of the king and sufficient rebuttal to the harem's interrogation.

Convinced that the maiden's lover is indeed better than others and worthy of such loyal devotion, the harem women accept the maiden's charge (**6:1**). They too will join the quest for the absent lover, if she can only provide some clue as to his whereabouts so they might commence searching.

The maiden's enigmatic response (**6:2–3**) almost defies explanation. Is she speaking literally of his vineyard or of a secluded garden haunt the lover frequented? If so, she should go there and seek him out instead of combing the city streets and enlisting the help of the harem women. Is she confined to the palace precincts? Elsewhere the garden motif has represented the physical intimacies of lovemaking. Yet, if the maiden is understood as speaking figuratively about herself the response still carries little meaning for the location of the absent lover. Perhaps the mutual pledge of loyalty (v. 3) offers a solution in that the bond of love between the two is so strong that in spite of his physical absence the lover continues to "browse among the lilies of his garden" in the mind and heart of the maiden.

If the descriptive song in 7:1–9 is ascribed to the shepherd lover then **6:4–9** is Solomon's final speech in the poem and represents his last attempt to betroth and wed the Shulamite maiden. Tirzah (the name means "beauty") was a Canaanite stronghold appropriated by Jeroboam I (ca. 930–909 B.C.; 1 Kings 14:17; 15:21, 23) as the first royal city of the northern kingdom. Later the city was fortified and refurbished as the primary residence of the Omride dynasty (ca. 885 B.C.; 1 Kings 16:8, 15, 17, 23). The "queens" and "concubines" are a reference to Solomon's harem, while the "virgins" or "maidens" are probably the countless number of women of marriageable age in the realm. The two-character interpretation of the poem argues (most unconvincingly!) that the love of the king (Solomon) and the maiden (perhaps Abishag) is pure and genuine since there are only 140 women in the royal harem at the time.

The final question posed by the harem women (**6:10**) is rhetorical in that it is not so much directed toward the maiden as it makes a statement about her unrivaled beauty. The verse may well represent part of the chorus by which the queens and concubines praise the extraordinary beauty of the maiden (6:9). The interrogative *Who is this?* is identical in form to the expression in 3:6 and also appears in 8:5. The threefold repetition of the question comprises a perfect foil summarizing the drama of the love poem:

3:6 *Who is this?* The maiden arriving in Jerusalem with Solomon, bereft of home and lover.
6:10 *Who is this?* The maiden unsurpassed in beauty, unmatched in loyal devotion, praised by the harem women.
8:5 *Who is this?* The maiden freed, reunited with her lover, and returning to her village home.

The celestial similes not only portray the radiance, brightness, and freshness of the maiden's appearance, but also celebrate her uniqueness. The sun and moon dominate the heavens without equal. The phrase *majestic as the stars in procession* (NIV) repeats the last colon of 6:4 and is better translated "terrible like an army with banners" (so JB, RSV). The image conveys the awesome splendor associated with army troops in dress parade.

The next section (**6:11–12**) is crucial to the understanding of the Song and yet verse 12 is the most difficult line of the poem to translate and interpret sensibly (see the variations in the major English versions). Literally rendered, the verse reads "I did not know, my soul, (it/he) set me in the chariot of Amminadab." The confusion results from the ambiguous syntax in the verse, especially the relationship of "my soul" to the verbs in the line. (Here the Septuagint actually changes the first verb ["know"] from first to third person and reads "my soul did not know" to solve the problem.) Is "my soul" the subject or object of "did not know" or the subject of "set me"? If the latter, then "my soul" is a figure for another person (hence "my desire," JB, NIV; "my fancy," RSV in reference to the lover). The maiden uses many terms of endearment for her lover, but "my soul" is not one of them. Perhaps the maiden here recounts her abduction by Solomon and transport to Jerusalem upon venturing into the orchard of nut trees near her home one spring.

As previously noted, imperative verbs often signal significant shifts in speech patterns or breaks in the dramatic action of the poem. This section (6:13–7:9) marks the maiden's last appearance among the harem women and records Solomon's final attempt to woo and wed the Shulamite. The women urge her to return (**6:13a**), apparently to dance. The fourfold repetition of their plea emphasizes their urgency and the seriousness of the situation (the maiden's departure from the harem?). The verse implies that the maiden has been or intends to go somewhere away from the palace confines. Presumably the shepherd has arrived to claim the maiden as his own, or she has refused to participate in the harem dance (at the wedding feast—perhaps her own?). Whatever the reason, it is the maiden's continued refusal of the king that finally induces him to release her from the harem and any betrothal obligations.

The maiden has no interest in being a court spectacle for the friends of the king. The Shulamite has no intention of submitting to inspection by the male onlookers in attendance (the verb *look* is masculine in form = "why should you men look?") This exchange (**6:13b**) contains the only Old Testament occurrence of the appellative *Shulamite.* Shulam was probably the home of the maiden. The location of the site is unknown but the village of Shunem near Mount Tabor in the region of Galilee is regarded as the most likely identification. The meaning of the last colon eludes interpreters. The phrase literally means "the dance of the two armies" (NIV Mahanaim, a proper name; JB two rows; NEB the lines). Exact meaning notwithstanding, the maiden shuns the idea of being made an exhibition at the court dance.

The answer to the maiden's question (**7:1–9**) is predictable: "dance for us because your physical beauty infatuates us." The two-character interpretation makes this another descriptive song of the maiden by the king or bridegroom. This portrait of the maiden's physical charms moves up from the feet instead of down from the head (cf. 5:1–5). The reference to the king as a third party in verse 5 has led many to assign verses 1–5 to the friends of the bridegroom or royal (male) onlookers. Prominent in the descriptive song are the graphic sketches of the distinctively sexual aspects of the maiden's anatomy (thighs, pudenda, belly, and breasts). The repetition of "how beautiful" in verse 6 (cf. 7:1) may indicate that the king or bridegroom now joins in the adoration of the maiden (recalling the ecstasy of the sexual intimacies experienced the previous night according to the two-character interpretation). The language of the passage is the most erotically explicit of the poem.

The three-character understanding of the poem views the passage as Solomon's last attempt to betroth the maiden and add her permanently to the ranks of the royal harem. The descriptive song of the bawdy onlookers (vv. 1–5) is particularly sexual in focus, lacking the sensitivity and dignity of the more euphemistic sensual symbolism encountered earlier in the poem, as well as the mutuality of the sexual experience. The "grasping" and "climbing" and the breast/genital orientation of the king's speech (vv. 6–9) invoke images of conquest, self-indulgence, lust, and self-gratification. Again, the gentleness, tenderness, willing surrender, and reciprocation in lovemaking as a shared experience by the lovers seems absent. Thus the passage provides an effective foil for the two kinds of human love, contrasting the purity and genuineness of one-to-one love with the one-to-many love found in the royal harem.

III. The Shulamite Maiden Rejects the King (7:10–8:4)

The maiden, for the final time, affirms her love for another, the shepherd lover out in the countryside. It is this concluding assertion of loyalty and faithfulness which gains the maiden's release from the claims of the king and the confines of the royal harem. Perhaps in recognition of her great virtue and unswerving loyalty the king permitted the maiden to return to her northern village. Her persistent rejection of the king's wooing and her unfading devotion to her absent lover must have won Solomon's favor as it had among the harem women. She had remained a garden locked up and a spring enclosed (4:12), a wall fortified with towers (8:10), and now her desire to freely give the love she has stored up to her shepherd lover is apparently granted (vv. 12–13). The beauty of sexual love is represented in the fertility symbols of the vineyards, pomegranates, and mandrakes ("every delicacy," v. 13). The maiden's desire to share love's intimacies with the shepherd is so overwhelming she almost wishes he were a brother so any public display of affection would not incur the contempt of the villagers.

In escorting the shepherd to her mother's home the maiden accomplishes two goals: she gains approval from her mother and the brothers of the shepherd; and she fulfills her dream of consummating their vows in the place where she had been "schooled" by her mother in the art of romance and lovemaking. "Spiced wine" and mandrake apples were renowned aphrodisiacs in Egypt and Mesopotamia. The phrase *nectar of my pomegranates* (v. 2b) has distinctly erotic connotations, with the woman's breasts being identified with pomegranates in Egyptian love poetry. The love repose the maiden imagines in 2:6 will soon be a reality, as the awakening of love fancied in 4:16 now comes to fruition. The refrain closing this major section of the poem carries the full force intended by the writer. The maiden and the shepherd have been rejoined in love.

IV. The Shulamite Maiden and Her Shepherd Lover Are Reunited (8:5–14)

Admittedly, the collage of poetic units comprising the conclusion of the Song presents numerous difficulties for the interpreter. The problem in identifying the character speaking, determining the extent of that speech, and then assigning those speech units to the appropriate characters is so acute that many commentators regard these last ten verses as a separate collection of poetic fragments appended to the Song by later scribes or editors. The dissimilarity of the material with the rest of the poem, along with the moralizing tendencies of 8:6–7 are cited as further evidence of the disjunctive nature of this section.

The interrogative *who is this* echoes 3:6 and 6:10, and as in the other two instances, the maiden is the object of the question (**8:5a**). Here it is probably the maiden's brother (or her brothers) who calls attention to the pair approaching arm in arm by questioning his companions in the field or vineyard.

The Hebrew verb forms in **8:5b–7** have masculine suffixes indicating the maiden is speaking to her lover. The apple-tree motif of 8:5b occurred previously in the context of the maiden's description of the lover and her delight in his lovemaking (2:3–6). While it is clear the maiden initiates the love-play and the passage makes reference to marital love, verse 5b has defied explanation. Perhaps the verse is an oblique statement about the cycle of love in humanity—lovemaking, conception, birth, life, and love aroused, leading to lovemaking and conception in the next generation. This then is the maiden's poetic declaration that she is fulfilling her destiny in life by her love relationship with the shepherd.

Seals (v. 6) were pieces of stone or metal inscribed with personalized markings and were tantamount to an individual's signature. The seal was an important emblem of ownership and possession in the ancient world. When stamped the impression of the seal registered the seal-bearer's claim whether in economic or legal documents, or even on private property. The maiden requests that the seal of her lover be stamped indelibly on her heart. Then he, and he alone, would have claim to the maiden's love. Why? The proverbial statements of verses 6–7 help explain the didactic purposes of the poem and serve as the climax to the foil of the maiden's one-to-one love and Solomon's one-to-many love. Genuine human love is as permanent as death and the righteous jealousy of this affection will never surrender possession of the loved one just as the grave tenaciously clings to the dead. True love burns bright and intense, a "most vehement flame" (v. 6, RSV). This phrase literally reads "flame of Yah," and has puzzled translators and interpreters. If this is a reference to Yahweh the verse implies God himself kindles the flames of human love. Finally, the flames of genuine human love are unquenchable in the face of life's surging floodtides. The worth, the value of this kind of love is beyond calculation. The wealth of a household, indeed the wealth of an empire (even Solomon's), cannot purchase the loyalty, devotion, true passion, and faithfulness of genuine human love.

The maiden's brothers recall her growth and development from their "little sister" into a mature woman ready for a life of her own (**8:8–9**). The earlier anger of the brothers (1:6) was likely their jealous protection of their sister's chastity against the designs of overzealous suitors in an attempt to prevent "premature" love until the proper time for her marriage. The phrase *on the day she is spoken for* (v. 8) infers this was the purpose of the lovers' return to her home village—the granting of approval for marriage. If she proves worthy of such a union (i.e., if she has preserved her virginity) they will dutifully provide her with the dress, ornamentation, and dowry befitting such a momentous occasion.

In reply to the conditional pledge of her brothers the maiden avows she has guarded her chastity and she remains a virgin (**8:10–12**). Despite her abduction and the wooing of Solomon she has remained a garden locked, a spring sealed, a reservoir of faithful love. Implicit in the maiden's boast of chastity is her maturing and blossoming womanhood and her readiness for wedlock ("my breasts are like towers"). "His eyes" is a reference to the shepherd lover and "bringing contentment" suggests his recognition of the rightness and the wholesomeness of their relationship.

The term *vineyard* has consistently been a metaphor for the person of the maiden (including her sexual charms). The strongest support for the three-character interpretation of the Song is found here. The maiden's "vineyard," her love and sexual delicacies, belonged to her and were hers to give. Solomon had let out his vineyard (his own person and his own sexual energies) to "tenants" (i.e., the women of the royal harem). Whether 200 women (cf. the 140 in 6:8) or the 1000 women (1 Kings 11:3), Solomon has made his choice—including the ugly consequences that surfaced later in his reign. The maiden has preserved her "vineyard" from the exploitation and corruption of harem love and now experiences the joy of freely giving it to her *one* lover.

The shepherd either addresses those who live in the maiden's village or the maiden herself (**8:13**). If the former, he is seeking public approval and support from the clan for his marriage to the maiden or else calling for shouts of celebration in response to the wedding feast. If the latter, he beckons the maiden for a song confirming her desire for him and commitment to a life of love even rivers cannot wash away (8:7).

The maiden's response (perhaps part of a nuptial song) is immediate and complete (**8:14**). Her invitation to love oft repeated will finally, joyously be realized. The maiden will pour out her love long stored, and the lovers will eat, drink, feast, and linger over love's delicacies. Love will not be aroused until its desire has been fulfilled (2:7; 3:5; 8:4). The gazelle/stag simile calls to mind an early fantasy of the maiden (2:8–13). The erotic symbolism of the poem's concluding verse is simple and appropriate. The maiden tenderly invites the shepherd to playfully, happily commune with her in all the jubilation, ecstasy, and mystery of sexual love.

SELECT BIBLIOGRAPHY

Bullock, C. H. *An Introduction to the Old Testament Poetic Books.* Chicago: Moody, 1979.

Carr, G. L. *The Song of Solomon.* Downers Grove: Inter-Varsity, 1984.

Fuerst, W. J. *The Song of Songs.* Cambridge: Cambridge University Press, 1975.

Ohlsen, W. *Perspectives on Old Testament Literature.* New York: Harcourt, Brace, Jovanovich, 1978.

Seerveld, C. *The Greatest Song.* Amsterdam: Trinity Pennyasheet Press, 1967.

The Prophetic Books

These works recorded the messages of persons inspired and called by God to minister to the spiritual condition of the covenant people. The term *prophet* comes from a Greek word, and has often been interpreted as either a "forthteller" or a "foreteller." The principal Hebrew term for "prophet" (*nabi'*), however, means "one called" to proclaim a message of divine origin. The prophets announced good and bad tidings alike, depending upon the circumstances, over a period of several centuries.

Sometimes the prophets received their messages directly from God, but on other occasions indirectly in visions. Although there were prophetesses in Israel, only men seem to have made public proclamations and had them recorded. Prophets came from various social levels. Some were of obscure origin, such as Elijah, while others were priests (Ezekiel and possibly Jeremiah). Isaiah was probably a highly placed court official in Judah, while Daniel, though not strictly a prophet in the usual sense, was a distinguished statesman of Hebrew origin in a pagan court.

The purpose of prophecy was to confront the nation with the demands of traditional covenantal faith, to condemn idolatrous practices in Israel, and to promise punishment if such behavior continued. Predictions of a Messiah and a new kingdom of righteousness are notable elements of prophecy, along with the assurance of a new covenant, the latter being established by the death of Christ. The prophets also criticized wrongdoing in contemporary society, so that in effect they served both as "forthtellers" and "foretellers." The ancient Hebrews, however, made no distinction between these two concepts.

The prophets' messages were based on a thorough knowledge of the Law, and the individuals concerned received their proclamations as part of their spiritual communion with God. Their words were recorded in somewhat different ways, but written accounts would have been made at or shortly after the time of oral delivery. Their proclamations glorified God as supreme Lord, revealed his will for the nation, and demanded a high level of dedication and spiritual living among the Israelites. Their declaration of God's redemption in history was climaxed by the work of Jesus, who came to fulfill all that the Law and the prophets had spoken concerning him. The prophetic writings are among the great spiritual treasures of the Christian church.

Old Testament Chronology
850–400 B.C.

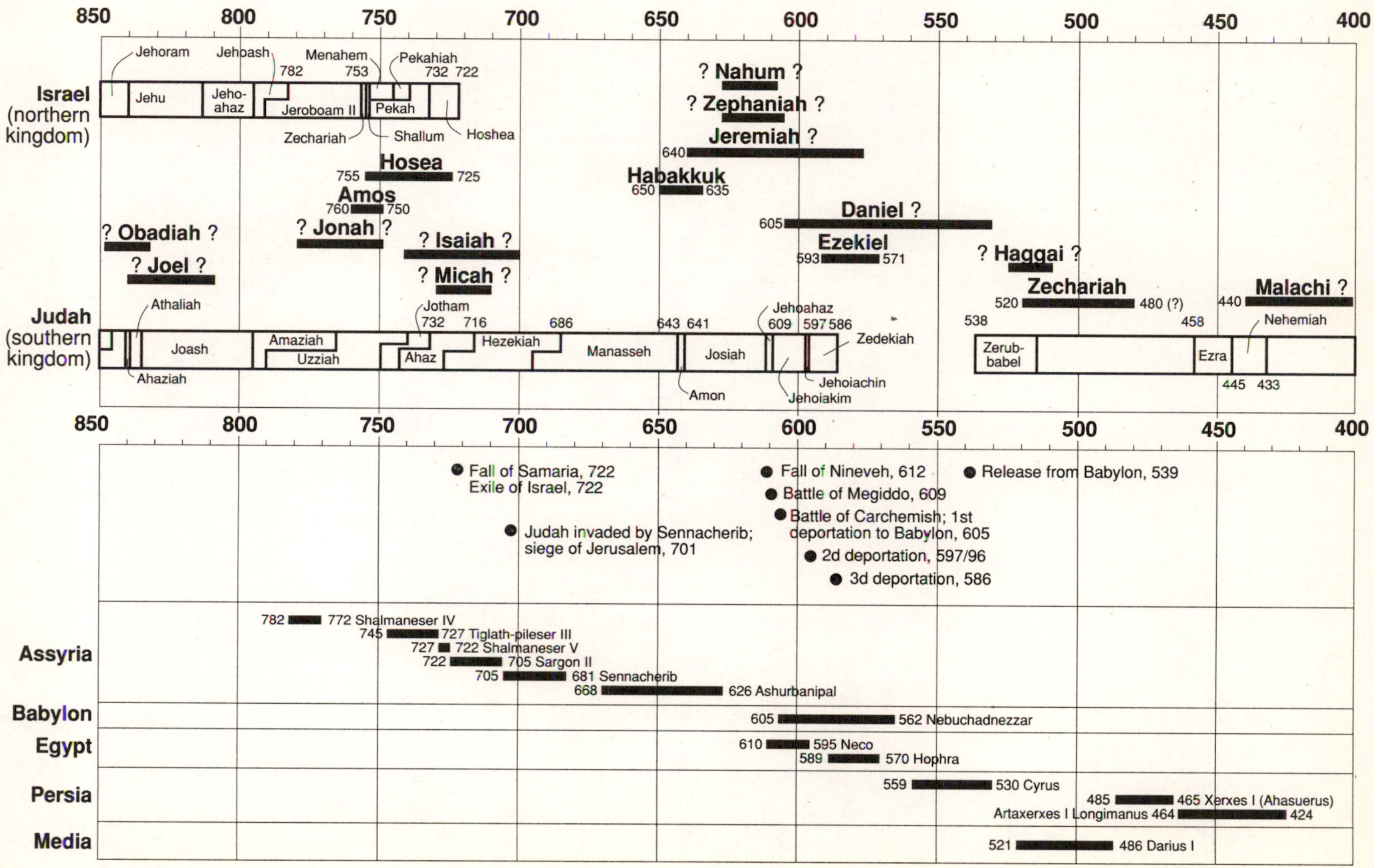

ISAIAH

Willem A. VanGemeren

INTRODUCTION

Little is known about the prophet Isaiah other than that he loved Jerusalem, freely associated with Judah's kings, was married, and had two children. The name *Isaiah* means "Yahweh is salvation." His name and the names of his sons—Shear-Jashub ("a remnant will return") and Maher-Shalal-Hash-Baz ("the booty shall very quickly be taken")—were symbolic to the nation (8:18). These three names capture the essence of the book: (1) Yahweh is the source of salvation; (2) Yahweh will spare a remnant for himself; and (3) Yahweh's judgment is certain to come.

The prophet's relationship to the royal house of David has been a subject of speculation. The prophet moved easily into and out of the palace and had access to the king. He was respected by Ahaz and Hezekiah. Though the relationship does not prove that Isaiah was of royal lineage, it is clear that he held a respected position in the court. The tradition of Isaiah's royal lineage cannot, however, be demonstrated. Isaiah was, nevertheless, very familiar with court protocol and life in Jerusalem. He was respected in the court of Jerusalem, even when he was critical of the ruling classes.

Isaiah's father, Amoz, is not to be identified with the prophet Amos who ministered a generation earlier in the northern kingdom. The spelling of these two names is different both in Hebrew and in English. Isaiah was a highly educated man who lived mainly in Jerusalem. He ministered to God's people roughly from 742 to 700 B.C. in an era of great political tumult.

What little is known about Isaiah's death is derived from extrabiblical sources. There are several traditions which, when taken together, strongly suggest that Isaiah may have suffered martyrdom under Manasseh, who succeeded Hezekiah.

Isaiah was a "son of Jerusalem." The prophecy is full of Isaiah's love and concern for the city. He believed that the city was representative of the people as a whole.

Clearly Isaiah was well acquainted with the city of Jerusalem, the temple (1:11–15), the ways of the rich, and the suffering of the poor. Because of his love for Jerusalem, he never delights in the messages of doom on the city and her inhabitants. He pictures the city as a "shelter" in a vineyard (1:8), and he gratefully speaks about God's mercy and desire to call a remnant who will return to Jerusalem after the exile and share in the joy God has prepared for the city and her population:

> But be glad and rejoice forever
> in what I will create,
> for I will create Jerusalem to be a delight
> and its people a joy. [65:18]

Even though it is nowhere clearly stated where Isaiah was born and raised, all indications point to a man who knew the city of Jerusalem, walked in it, and loved it as the city God had chosen in which to establish his name and glory.

The beginning of Isaiah's ministry can be dated by the reference to Uzziah's death in 6:1 (ca. 740 B.C.). From Uzziah's death on Judah would be cast into the midst of a stream of international developments that would leave her a vassal state of the Assyrian Empire. During his ministry, Isaiah witnessed the fall of Aram (Syria) and Israel as well as the desolation of Judah by the Assyrians. Under Uzziah, Judah had gained remarkable economic achievements (2 Chron. 26:6–15) and had made an attempt to reassert herself as a political power.

Jotham (750–732 B.C.) ruled a nation which was strong materially, but corrupt in her values and apostate in her adherence to Yahweh. The excesses of wealth and injustice in the north had been condemned by Hosea and Amos. Isaiah brought the same condemnation against the southern kingdom. Jotham died in peace, while the Assyrian fist was being raised toward Aram, Israel, and Judah. Tiglath-pileser III ("Pul" in 2 Kings 15:19) subjugated cities lying on the route from Nineveh to Damascus. When Jotham died the handwriting was on the wall.

Ahaz's role is more prominent in the Book of Isaiah. He ruled over Judah from 732 to 716 B.C. Though Ahaz was not the kind of man to seek the counsel of a prophet, God sent a word of encouragement through Isaiah (chap. 7).

Chronicles enumerates a list of objectionable practices instituted by Ahaz and explains the idolatrous practices and the reason for Ahaz's international troubles (28:2ff.). The Book of Isaiah presents Ahaz as an imprudent man in political affairs. The alliance of Rezin, king of Aram, and Pekah, king of Israel, was intended to create a buffer against the expansionist drive of Assyria. In order to accomplish this, the allied kings needed Ahaz to join their confederacy. When he refused, Rezin and Pekah marched against Ahaz, intending to dethrone him and to set up a king who would be sympathetic to their political schemings in Ahaz's place (2 Kings 16:5; Isa. 7:6). Ahaz was greatly disturbed about the Syro-Ephraimite alliance. Into this context, Isaiah brought God's Word. Isaiah challenged Ahaz not to fear their power, and instead to look to God's presence in Jerusalem as the strength of Judah. Ahaz, instead, looked for a political solution and asked Tiglath-pileser to help him (2 Kings 16:7). Tiglath-pileser of Assyria swiftly reacted to the threat on the western front. In 734 B.C. he marched through Phoenicia as far as Philistia, conquering as he went. In the following years he invaded Judah, which was reduced to a vassal state. Ahaz went to Damascus to celebrate Assyria's victories and, while there, he saw an altar, a replica of which he constructed and set up in the temple court (2 Kings 16:10–16).

Hezekiah was a godly king who sought counsel from the prophet Isaiah in times of national and personal tragedy. He ruled from 715 B.C. until his death in 686 B.C. During his rule he instituted many reforms (2 Kings 18:4, 22), including the celebration of the Passover (2 Chron. 30). He witnessed the fall of Israel, which was overrun by the Assyrians when Hoshea refused to pay tribute to Assyria. Shalmaneser IV began the campaign and his successor Sargon II destroyed Samaria and exiled her population in 722 B.C. Assyria's hegemony in the Syro-Palestinian region grew. In 711 B.C. Sargon descended on Ashdod in Philistia, because it was thought that Ashdod had conspired against Assyria (Isa. 20:1). At Sargon's death (705 B.C.), Sennacherib took over. He faced an immediate coalition of Egypt, Philistia (except for Ekron), Babylon, and Judah (2 Kings 18:7), organized by Hezekiah. The southern king had hoped that the time had come to throw off the hegemony of Assyria, and he believed that Judah had the power to lead the conspiracy. The rebellion was quick to spark the anger of Sennacherib. On his way to Judah he put down various rebellions in Mesopotamia, Phoenicia, and Philistia. His forces moved through Judah and may have taken as many as forty-six cities (some of which may be listed in Isa. 10:28–32 and Mic. 1:10–16).

Finally, Sennacherib besieged Jerusalem. Hezekiah was locked in Jerusalem, surrounded by Assyrian forces. He had prepared well for the siege, but the Assyrians had the fortitude to wait for the surrender of Jerusalem. Hezekiah had to surrender to Sennacherib and pay tribute (2 Kings 18:13–16). However, he was permitted to continue his rule. The people of Judah celebrated the miraculous deliverance from a cruel tyrant (2 Kings 19:35–36).

As far as literary style, the prophet Isaiah is a master of the Hebrew language. He knows how to express himself well and has a distinctive literary quality in his writing.

First, Isaiah uses rich vocabulary. Many of Isaiah's words are unique. They are used only once, or just a few times, in the whole Hebrew Bible. Both the extent of vocabulary and the choice of expression show Isaiah's ability in using the Hebrew language. His style is highly poetic with a variety of parallel forms.

In addition to variety in vocabulary, the book has brilliant and imaginative descriptions of war, social, and rural life. Often these descriptions come from Isaiah's familiarity with rural life, such as the parable of the vineyard (chap. 5). They are also derived from his understanding of diplomacy and warfare. Isaiah is an extremely gifted preacher who knows exactly how to use the right illustration as he is speaking and who, in his illustrations, communicates the contents of God's revelation.

Many literary devices were available to him in the Hebrew literary tradition: personifications, metaphors, similes, word plays, alliterations, songs, and satires. If one compares Isaiah with a book like 1 Samuel, both of which are inspired, the difference in style becomes apparent. Isaiah captures the imagination with the use of various images. His sentences flow one into the other. Everything is tightly knit together. The imagery demonstrates that Isaiah knew the world in which he lived.

Critical commentaries on Isaiah divide the material into three major divisions: chapters 1–39 are thought to have come from the eighth-century prophet Isaiah; chapters 40–55 from a sixth-century prophet known as the Deutero (Second) Isaiah; chapters 56–66 from a fifth-century source known as Trito (Third) Isaiah. Three arguments may be advanced in support of the unity of Isaiah.

First, Jesus and the apostles held to the unity of Isaiah. Whenever they quoted from the Book of Isaiah, whether from the beginning or the end, they always referred to the prophet Isaiah. The Gospel of John has an interesting passage that combines two quotations from Isaiah, and each comes from a different section. John comments on the unbelief of the people at Jesus' time by referring to Isaiah 53:1 and on the effect of their unbelief by appealing to Isaiah 6:12. In this instance one quotation comes from Isaiah 1–39 and another from 40–66, yet both of them are introduced as the words of Isaiah: "This was to fulfill the word of Isaiah the prophet" (John 12:38a) and "as Isaiah says elsewhere" (John 12:39b). So whether in the first or second part of Isaiah, the whole of the prophecy is seen as being the work of one author: Isaiah.

Second, many of the dissimilarities between the critical divisions of Isaiah can be explained by a change in subject matter. The first division emphasizes the coming doom of the Lord on all flesh, whereas the latter part of the Book of Isaiah brings out the comfort and consolation given to the remnant, for whom God still has a future. In fact, the second section begins with these words: " 'Comfort, comfort my people,' says your God" (40:1). The theme of comfort is characteristic of most of the chapters in the second division. Though there may be some indication of judgment, the main message is one of comfort.

Moreover, even though the emphasis in the first part is on judgment, there is also a message of restoration. A brief comparison of two sections on the restoration (35:7–10 and 43:19–21) reveals a number of common elements: water, the road, animals, and the statement that the people of God do not have to be afraid.

Third, the dissimilarities in vocabulary and theme are not as great as some people believe. Vocabulary cannot be a sole criterion for authorship; conservative scholars have explained the dissimilarity of words and style in the three sections as dissimilarities that arise from differences in theme and emphases.

The scope of the book takes us beyond Isaiah's days to the new heavens and the new earth. The prophecy spans the preexilic, exilic, and postexilic eras, the coming of the Messiah, the messianic age, the church, and the final consummation. The book unfolds God's plan for the redemption of his people. The name *Isaiah,* variously translated as "salvation is of the Lord," or "salvation of Yahweh," and even "Yahweh is salvation," unfolds the purpose of the book.

The message of the gospel is found throughout the prophecy, and as a matter of fact the prophet concludes with it.

> "As the new heavens and the new earth that I make will endure before me," declares the LORD, "so will your name and descendants endure. From one New Moon to another and from one Sabbath to another, all mankind will come and bow down before me," says the LORD. [66:22–23]

Salvation is not to be limited to Israel only, for Isaiah as the "evangelical" prophet speaks also to Gentiles.

OUTLINE

- I. Prophecies Against Judah (1:1–12:6)
  - A. Judgment and Comfort (1:1–2:5)
  - B. Judgment and Comfort (2:6–4:6)
  - C. Judgment (5:1–30)
  - D. Isaiah's Call (6:1–13)
  - E. Crisis in Perspective (7:1–8:22)
  - F. The Messiah (9:1–7)
  - G. The Wrath of God (9:8–10:34)
  - H. The Branch from Jesse (11:1–16)
  - I. Songs of Praise (12:1–6)
- II. Oracles Against the Nations (13:1–23:18)
  - A. Babylon (13:1–14:23)
  - B. Assyria (14:24–27)
  - C. Philistia (14:28–32)
  - D. Moab (15:1–16:14)
  - E. Damascus and Israel (17:1–14)
  - F. Cush (18:1–7)
  - G. Egypt (19:1–20:6)
  - H. Babylon, Edom, and Arabia (21:1–17)
  - I. Jerusalem (22:1–25)
  - J. Tyre (23:1–18)
- III. The Apocalypse of Isaiah (24:1–27:13)
  - A. God's Judgment (24:1–23)
  - B. The Redemption of God's People (25:1–26:6)
  - C. A Prayer for God's People (26:7–21)
  - D. Deliverance of Israel (27:1–13)
- IV. Oracles of Woe (28:1–33:24)
  - A. Ephraim (28:1–29)
  - B. Ariel (29:1–24)
  - C. Foreign Alliances (30:1–33)
  - D. Judgment and Hope (31:1–32:20)

E. Distress and Help (33:1–24)
V. Cataclysmic Judgment (34:1–17)
VI. The Day of God's Glory (35:1–10)
VII. Hezekiah (36:1–39:8)
A. Challenge and Deliverance (36:1–37:8)
B. Hezekiah's Illness (38:1–22)
C. Envoys from Babylon (39:1–8)
VIII. The Beginning of Restoration (40:1–48:22)
A. Prologue (40:1–11)
B. Disputations (40:12–31)
C. Deliverance (41:1–44:23)
D. Yahweh's Sovereignty (44:24–47:15)
E. Proclamation of Restoration (48:1–22)
IX. Reconciliation and Restoration (49:1–55:13)
A. The Servant of the Lord (49:1–13)
B. Zion's Surprise (49:14–21)
C. Israel's Restoration (49:22–26)
D. Sin and Obedience (50:1–9)
E. Everlasting Salvation (51:1–52:12)
F. The Suffering Servant (52:13–53:12)
G. The New Covenant (54:1–17)
H. Assurance (55:1–13)
X. The Glory and Responsibility of Zion (56:1–66:24)
A. Response to Redemption (56:1–8)
B. Unfaithful Leaders (56:9–57:2)
C. Unfaithful People (57:3–13a)
D. The Future of God's People (57:13b–21)
E. True Religion (58:1–14)
F. Responsibility (59:1–21)
G. The Glory of Zion (60:1–62:12)
H. The Day of Vengeance (63:1–6)
I. A Prayer for God's People (63:7–64:12)
J. God's Response (65:1–25)
K. Judgment and Restoration (66:1–24)

COMMENTARY

I. Prophecies Against Judah (1:1–12:6)

The first twelve chapters of Isaiah may be compared to a painting with three panels (triptych). Isaiah's call to be a prophet (chap. 6) is at the center, while the other two parts of the triptych concern judgment and hope. The first section (chaps. 1–5) is in the form of a covenantal lawsuit and the third section (chaps. 7–12) presents God's word of judgment and hope in the historical situation of the growing Assyrian Empire. A holistic approach to these chapters presents the reader with Yahweh's holiness (6:3), Isaiah's prophetic calling (6:8), the finality of God's judgment (6:11–13a), and the hope for the remnant (6:13b). Each motif is developed throughout the triptych. The prophet begins with Yahweh's charges against Judah and Jerusalem (1:2–31) and concludes with the new song of the remnant who have discovered that the Holy One of Israel is still in the midst of his people (12:6). The focus, then, of all twelve chapters is on the Holy One of Israel who cleanses Isaiah (6:7), and who, through the process of judgment, cleanses his people from all their sins and defilement (4:3–4).

A. Judgment and comfort (1:1–2:5). Isaiah calls upon "heaven and earth" to witness against God's people in language reminiscent of Moses' Song of Witness (Deut. 30:19; 32:1; cf. Mic. 6:1–2). God's people have severed their relationship with Yahweh, their Father (**1:1–4**). Though Yahweh has treated them as sons and Judah has received great benefits, the people foolishly abandon their heritage. They have become fools, who do not "know" and "do not understand" (v. 3). Their folly has led to open rebellion against their suzerain (covenant) Lord. They have forsaken their loyalty to Yahweh and replaced it with hatred and apostasy. They are not children of God but "a brood of evildoers" (v. 4). They have rejected "the Holy One of Israel," the God who not only sovereignly rules over his people but also has promised to dwell in their midst so as to sanctify them.

Yet Judah has been severely judged in order to get her attention (**1:5–9**). Her wounds symbolize the extent to which God has patiently dealt with his people. He has used wars, oppression, desolation, and famine in order to bring his people to their senses and to himself. The desolation may very well reflect the situation in 701 B.C., when Sennacherib despoiled the land, destroyed the cities, and nearly took the city of Jerusalem. Were it not for the grace of God, Judah would have been destroyed like Sodom and Gomorrah. The leaders were responsible for bringing judgment upon Judah. Clearly God did not intend to destroy her from under the face of the sun. The "daughter of Zion" (Jerusalem, remnant) is spared like "a shelter" (v. 8). The intent of God's judgment is purification, and to that end Yahweh is patient and merciful.

The leaders are corrupt like the people of Sodom and Gomorrah (**1:10–17**; Gen. 18:20). They are reminded of God's law which requires righteousness as a prerequisite for bringing offerings and sacrifices (Deut. 33:19). The prophet is not antagonistic to offerings and sacrifices, feasts and festivals, and prayer. Yet he knows that God rejects any act of worship at any time, even in the holy court of his temple, when it is little more than an empty ritual. Worship must be pure. The requirements of ritual purity must be kept and sacrifices are to be offered from a pure heart. The intensity of God's hatred of their worship affects sacrifices, convocations, and individuals. In their rebellion against God, they have maintained "religion," but in their practices they are corrupt. They cannot merit God's grace by their "pious" activities. Their "hands are full of blood" (v. 15b), because they have disregarded the rights of the needy. It is impossible to pray for relief from the enemy as long as no compassion is shown to the oppressed.

The proper response, then, to the grace of Yahweh is obedient faith (**1:18–20**). Obedient faith entails the willingness to remove and cleanse oneself from the evil of one's generation, to love one's neighbor, and to receive divine cleansing and forgiveness. True repentance results in faithful obedience, as an expression of gratitude and the willingness to let God be God. The remnant which has survived the ordeal may again be restored to enjoy God's blessings. God has graciously opened up a future for them, but for those who rebel, judgment is sure to come.

In a lament, the prophet speaks about the filth of Jerusalem (**1:21–26**). Rather than resembling pure silver in the practice of justice, righteousness, and faithfulness, the city's silver has become dross (vv. 21–22). Isaiah reflects on the era of David and Solomon as a period in which Israel was characterized by justice, righteousness, and loyalty to the Lord, because these leaders upheld God's law. But Jerusalem has become faithless, like a harlot. She is as worthless as wine diluted with water. People and leaders are all alike: each one is out for himself. Yahweh, the great and merciful King, has seen their insensitivities and will come to the defense of the poor. He will bring them through another judgment in order to remove the "foes." The "enemies" are all those who do not do his will, and it is significant that he addresses the covenant community. One is reminded of Jesus' words that whoever is not for him is against him (Matt. 12:30; Luke 11:23).

A distinction between the righteous and the wicked will certainly be made (**1:27–31**). The future belongs to the remnant which repents by *doing* righteousness, but judgment will make an end of rebels and idolators. The people as a whole are compared to the effects of a drought in which the leaves of an oak fall off and the garden is burned up (v. 30). However, the oak still stands and the garden is still there. Hard times may come upon the godly, but they will persevere. On the other hand, the wicked will be utterly consumed as by fire.

In four verses (**2:1–4**) Isaiah describes the nature of God's kingdom: its glory, its extent, and its effect. The glory of God's kingdom is so great that it will be recognized by the nations. God's kingdom will not be limited to the Jews in Jerusalem or Judea, but will extend to the nations, who will desire to be instructed by the people of God. The language is centripetal; the people are coming to one center to be instructed. The knowledge of God will be among the nations; and the nations, having been disciplined in the ways of God, will live in accordance with God's Word. The universal knowledge of God is the precondition for the rule of God to bring peace upon this earth. The promises of verse 4 are especially reassuring in an age in which nuclear warfare is always imminent. However, we must keep in mind that as long as nations make decisions for themselves without respect to God, there is little possibility for peace. The prophet envisions a time when Yahweh himself will rule the nations and will make decisions for them. Then and only then will there be a state of shalom when weaponry can be changed into implements to be used for peaceful purposes. Before this glorious vision may be realized there is one precondition: men must respond in full submission to the Lord (2:5). It is possible to be inspired by the vision of the messianic age, but inspiration should lead to obedient faith.

B. Judgment and comfort (2:6–4:6). Isaiah now focuses on how God's people have rebelled (**2:6–22**). First, he singles out their rampant materialism, idolatry, and acceptance of pagan practices. He includes all pagan cultures by referring to the superstitions from the east and west (diviners of the Philistines). Judah, though isolated geographically, has opened herself to foreign cultures. This fits the period of Uzziah when Judah made alliances with nations, so as to maintain commercial and military relations. Their strength was in negotiation, and not in Yahweh. The people possessed silver and gold, horses and chariots, and idols. Judah was no different from other nations. God's judgment would show that idols would provide no help, that gold and silver could not save his people in the hour of disaster, and that the nations would be impotent in the hour of need. God's judgment comes against any and every monument of human pride. Yahweh alone will be exalted. The "day" of God's judgment (v. 12) is a reference to an era in which God reveals his wrath. The emphasis on arrogance fits in with the imagery of the cedars of Lebanon, the oaks of Bashan, the mountains and hills, the high towers and fortified walls, and the stately ships (lit. ships of Tarshish) which sailed the seas and brought crafts and products from other nations into the finest homes of Jerusalem. All these objects symbolize human pride and autonomous accomplishments. Man will have to face God, who comes to reduce the rebellion of his subjects. Yahweh's day is the day of his self-exaltation, which excludes man and his reasons for pride.

Isaiah now charges the people with open rebellion (**3:1–15**). Their leaders are particularly responsible. He charges the leaders with irresponsibility and injustice, which have caused the poor to become poorer. This charge is to be understood also in the light of the previous charge of rebellion (2:8–9). The combination of corrupt leadership and widespread, open rebellion has resulted in social and moral upheaval. The Lord's judgment, however, will result in an even more catastrophic disruption of life in Judah. He will take away their food and water. He will remove the divinely ordained officers and instead will put over the people corrupt leaders who are immature and lacking in experience like "boys" and "children" (v. 4). They will contribute to further social and moral decay in Judah. Further, judgment comes in the form of the collapse of the economy and political structures. The ruins and the absence of qualified leaders reflect the situation in Judah after the ravages of Nebuchadnezzar (586 B.C.). Though God's judgment will result in terrible lawlessness, the righteous remnant must take heart, knowing that they will be rewarded. The Lord brings a suit against the corrupt leaders who have taken advantage of their office.

Yahweh charges the daughters of Jerusalem with pride and seduction (**3:16–4:1**). The men of Jerusalem are selfish, materialistic, and oppressive, but they have partners in their wives and lovers who have an insatiable desire to beautify themselves, enrich themselves, and compete with each other. The brief description of the "fine" women is followed by the effects of the day of Yahweh: all their "pretty" things will be removed, they will go around filled with mourning, and their men will fall in battle. Their glory will turn to shame. The severity of their loneliness is so great that these women will fight over a man, in order to remove the disgrace of their childlessness.

The prophet's theme now changes abruptly, for in **4:2–6** Isaiah speaks about the new messianic era. Human pride is gone, but this does not preclude a future for the remnant who have humbled themselves in the presence of the Lord. Isaiah develops the theme of the messianic kingdom begun in 2:1–5 by speaking about the people as "the branch of the Lord." The word *branch* is not the branch of a tree, but a new "shoot" out of the ground, and refers to the survivors of the day of judgment. "Branch" may also signify the Messiah of David, as in Jeremiah (23:5; 33:15) and Zechariah (3:8; 6:12), but the more general designation of messianic "people" fits the context best. The "fruit of the land" (v. 2) describes the blessedness of the land, as the people are restored to God's blessings.

The messianic era is here characterized as an era of restoration. The remnant, the people of God, have survived God's judgment. The day of the Lord has been a day of terror but also one of purification. The filth of corruption, the fires of rebellion, and the folly of God's people have been removed and those who are left are now described as holy and their names are recorded in the Book of Life. Having consecrated for himself a new people who will be responsive to him, God assures them of his glorious presence. The glory of the Lord, revealed to Israel in the wilderness, will protect only those who are holy and over whom his judgment has passed.

C. Judgment (5:1–30). Isaiah's poem about the vineyard (**5:1–7**) is parabolic. Isaiah may have sung it at a wine festival and surprised his listeners with the application. He sings about a "friend" (NIV loved one) who gave himself with exacting care to the preparation of a vineyard. The vineyard, however, produces only sour grapes. Isaiah asks what else this "friend" could have done for the vineyard. The rhetorical question must be answered! The prophet then explains that the vineyard represents the people of Israel and Judah, and that the Lord is the Keeper of the vineyard. He deeply cared for his people and lavished on them his grace and love, expecting justice and righteousness as the appropriate fruits. Instead of justice and righteousness, the people have responded with bloodshed, which has elicited a cry of distress from the downtrodden.

Six woes (**5:8–24**) are directly related to the parable of the vineyard. They explain the nature of oppression, bloodshed, and the cry for justice (v. 7). In these six woes Isaiah has painted for us a portrait of God's people toward the end of the eighth century. The portrait is that of a social elitism. The social elites have perverted justice, morality, religious values, and the wisdom that flows out of the fear of the Lord. In his description of the rich, Isaiah gives us a candid glimpse, not only of the Judean society of his day, but of the besetting sins of human society at any time and place. The first woe (vv. 8–10) is against economic opportunists who amass more and more material wealth. They flaunt the inalienable relationship of the people to "God's land" (Lev. 25:13–16). They accumulate houses and fields at the expense of the economically disadvantaged. Their houses will be in ruins and their vineyards and fields will not produce enough to make a living. The picture we get from these verses is one of loneliness: houses that were once full of parties will be no more. A ten-acre vineyard will only produce one bath (six gals.) of wine; a homer of seed (6.4 bus.) will yield only a little over half a bushel.

The second woe (vv. 11–17) pertains to the drunkards. They cannot wait to begin their day with a drink, and prepare banquets in order to attract others who enjoy drinking. They spend their time feasting and drinking. Isaiah does not say much about the source of the money with which their wine and strong drink are purchased, but it may be deduced from the context that the wine has been obtained with the money and labors of the poor. In their drunken stupor, they are ignorant of the ways of God. They will go into exile as fools, who did not know that the day of the Lord was coming on all. Death will inevitably overtake those who know nothing but the joys of life.

The third woe (vv. 18–19) pertains to those who corrupt justice. They have no sense of the holiness of God. They even scoff at the thought of the coming judgment.

The fourth woe (v. 20) is pronounced against those who corrupt religious values. They do not know the difference between good and evil, darkness and light, bitter and sweet. They confound their own conscience and the consciences of others. The revelation of God is no longer a light for their path because their standards have confused the clarity of God's revelation.

The fifth woe (v. 21) is to those who have exchanged the wisdom of God for the folly of man.

The sixth woe (vv. 22–23) also applies to the drunkards. Here Isaiah describes the drunkard as a man who feels strong in his drinking. He enjoys power. While he is feasting, he is getting rich at the expense of others.

While there are hints at the coming judgment of God throughout the woes, the prophet provides greater detail toward the end (**5:25–30**). Clearly social position does not deter judgment, because the ultimate polarity is between sinful men and a holy God (v. 16). When God enters into judgment he comes as the great King (Lord Almighty) and the Holy One of Israel. Because they have spurned his law and his covenant, the anger of the God of Mount Sinai will burn against his own. He will mercilessly strike his people with blow upon blow. Fierce and untiring enemies will come at God's command. With rapidity and catastrophic power they will destroy and exile God's people. The day of the Lord is not a day of restoration and light, but full of darkness, anxiety, and gloom.

D. Isaiah's call (6:1–13). The prophet dates his vision of God's glory (**6:1–4**) to the year in which King Uzziah died. Scholars have tried to understand the significance of this dating, but it is enough to recognize that this is one way of connecting chapter 6 to the context of the Syro-Ephraimite War (see 7:1). A vision of the Lord appears to the prophet. He sees Yahweh sitting on the throne, exalted in the temple. The prophet concentrates not on the throne or on the Lord seated upon it, but on "the train of the robe" as it fills the temple. The temple is filled with the glorious presence of the Lord. He touches the earth in his power and glory, and yet the earth and the earthly temple cannot contain him. The appearance of the Lord, transcendent in his majesty and yet immanent in his presence, is represented in the language of a theophany. It affects all things on earth: the doorposts and thresholds of the temple shake as in an earthquake. When the Lord appeared on Mount Sinai, his revelation was preceded by an earthquake, lightning, and darkness (Exod. 19:16). Isaiah finds himself gazing at a ceremony in which the seraphim announce the glorious presence of the Holy One of Israel. The seraphim are like men in appearance with faces and feet, but unlike men, they have six wings with which they cover themselves in the presence of the Lord. As they hover in his presence, they cry out, "Holy, holy, holy."

The holiness of the Lord is a most important doctrine in the teaching of Isaiah. Yahweh's holiness is an expression of his separateness from the corruption of his people. He is the Holy One of Israel and in this sense he is the "wholly other" One. Israel and Judah will not be able to experience the lovingkindness of the Lord until they have been cleansed and sanctified; only then can they experience the presence of the Holy One of Israel. The seraphim ascribe holiness to "the LORD Almighty" ("the LORD of Hosts"). He is the great King over "the hosts" of heaven (Deut. 4:19; 1 Kings 22:19; Isa. 40:26) and over the earth, which as part of his kingdom "is full of his glory" (v. 3b). The word *glory* is also important to the message of Isaiah. It signifies the majesty and splendor of the presence of Yahweh. Over against all the wealth of the rich and the royal courts of earthly kings is the King of glory whose judgment will reduce human kingdoms and frustrate human plans. When the King of glory establishes his kingdom and extends it from shore to shore, the fullness of his glory will become evident. The seraphim already see the whole earth full of his glory.

The impact of the vision of God's holiness, presence, and glory receives an appropriate response, as Isaiah calls out, "Woe to me!" (v. 5). The prophet fears for his life as he is particularly aware of his uncleanness—he *represents* the sinful nation (**6:5–7**). In response, one of the seraphs takes a burning coal with special tongs from the altar and touches Isaiah's mouth. The ceremony is reminiscent of the incense altar (Exod. 30:1–10), which was lit by a burning coal taken from the altar (Lev. 16:12–13). Before Isaiah is able to speak to the Lord he must be forgiven. This forgiveness is personal. Once Isaiah has been purified, he is permitted to speak in the heavenly council and receives his commissioning.

In his heavenly council Yahweh asks the question, "Who will go for us?" (v. 8). Isaiah volunteers and Yahweh immediately commissions him (**6:8–13**). The commission consists of a declaration that Isaiah's ministry is going to be hard and long. His message will prick the conscience of people, but they will harden themselves against God and his Word. Isaiah is shown the desolation of the land and the exile of the population. The emphasis is on judgment, devastation, and desolation. Yet, there is hope, for the "holy seed" will remain. Isaiah begins chapter 1 with "the brood of evildoers" (lit. seed of . . .) and concludes chapter 6 with a ray of hope ("holy seed").

The messages of the first triptych (chaps. 1–5—Judah's sin, God's judgment, the remnant, and the messianic kingdom) are not set in historical context. This changes with the historical reference to the year of Uzziah's death (6:1), and the third triptych begins with events associated with Ahaz. When Ahaz came to the throne, the Aramean (Syrian) power was about to be eclipsed. The Arameans were already feeling mounting pressure from the east as the Assyrians were moving westward. God's Word comes to Israel, Aram, Assyria, and Judah. Everything that happens on earth results from God's sovereign rule.

E. Crisis in perspective (7:1–8:22). The Arameans had made an alliance with the Israelites in order to create a united front against Assyria. In order to further their goals, they planned to dethrone Ahaz and place their own man ("the son of Tabeel," 7:6) on the throne in Jerusalem.

The prophet and his son Shear-Jashub (whose name signifies the hope that "a remnant will return") meet Ahaz at the upper pool. Ahaz is shaken by the alliance and needs counsel (**7:1–9**).

Isaiah calls on Ahaz to face the crisis from God's perspective. These two "mighty" kingdoms, Israel and Aram, are nothing more than "two smoldering stubs of firewood" (v. 4). Aram came to an end in 732 B.C. and Assyria exiled Israel in 722 B.C. The challenge (v. 9b) is a pun created by the assonance (in Hebrew) of the words *stand firm* and *stand;* the New International Version makes an attempt to reflect this.

The emphasis on God's presence in this crisis receives special significance in the naming of a child: Immanuel (**7:10–17**). Isaiah challenges Ahaz to ask for a sign, so that he might "stand firm in [his] faith" (v. 9b). The king piously refuses. Knowing that Ahaz has set his heart on a political solution, Isaiah rebukes him (v. 13). Ahaz is impatient with the solution of faith and looks toward Assyria for a novel approach. The Lord has a sign for Ahaz, the house of David, and all who would hear it. The sign is the "Immanuel" (v. 14).

Much controversy has surrounded the meaning of the sign: What is the meaning of "virgin" and who is the child? The validity of the sign lies in a miracle or event, and must be of significance to Ahaz. The birth of Christ was a miracle, but would be of little relevance to Ahaz in his time. If the sign was to strengthen the Word of God in Ahaz's time, it may have been that Isaiah spoke of a woman in the royal court or of his own wife (8:1–4, 18). The child could not be Hezekiah, however, since he was already born by this time. Though Isaiah's son is not *the* Immanuel, he is a *sign* of the Immanuel, in that Judah is spared. Through Isaiah God assures Judah that his promises to David (2 Sam. 7:11–16) will come to pass. The Lord has not abandoned the house of David! The Lord marshals the Assyrians to remedy this crisis situation.

As problematic as the interpretation of this passage is, the quotation in Matthew is authoritative. It focuses on Jesus the Messiah as *the* Immanuel, the Savior sent by the Father. Ahaz may have looked for a fulfillment and witnessed the desolation of Aram, but he did not understand the total prophetic witness.

Ahaz's policy pushes him into direct contact with Assyria (**7:18–25**). He appeals to Tiglath-pileser ("the razor hired"). Others had looked to Egypt. The clash for power in the Mediterranean Basin would result in great devastation. Assyria is God's appointed means and will "shave" Judah, that is, exact tribute (v. 20). Judah will be impoverished, and will only survive on "curds and honey" because its luxuriant vineyards and cultivated fields will become grazing land for cows and sheep.

The birth of Isaiah's second son is significant (**8:1–4**). To properly emphasize its significance he writes on a large scroll the name "quick to the plunder, swift to the spoil." This he does in the presence of two witnesses: Uriah the high priest and Zechariah. Then he has relations with his wife, "the prophetess," and out of that union a child is born. The child's name signifies judgment on Israel and Aram and a contemporary fulfillment of 7:14. Thus, the "plunder" of Damascus and Samaria will be carried off in a short time by Assyrian forces.

The people have rejected the Lord and his promises to David (symbolized by the waters of Shiloah; v. 6). They have lost heart over the Israelite-Aramean alliance, not trusting in God. Yet God is sovereign over the nations (**8:5–10**). He permits the Assyrians to "flood" the Mediterranean Basin with their forces. The "River" (v. 7) is the Euphrates River, which symbolizes Assyrian strength. It will overpower the nations, but will not destroy Judah, because of the Immanuel-presence of the Lord. The "outspread wings" are a figure of God's protection of his people (v. 8; cf. Ps. 91:4). God has set the bounds of Assyria's power.

The prophet calls on the nations to recognize that they are pawns in the hands of God. The Lord effectively works out all his plans. The nations cannot stand up against the God who has promised to protect his people! He is Immanuel! There also seems to be an eschatological dimension here, as it foreshadows the end of human resistance to God's plans. God's plan will be done on earth, as it is in heaven.

Isaiah is warned not to identify with the secular values of his contemporaries (**8:11–15**). Those who follow the Lord are not to give in to the prevailing political and economic winds of their age. As secularism and humanism grow stronger and the believing community is increasingly pressured in a world without God, Isaiah reminds us to look at the world from God's perspective: the world is under his judgment and the Lord himself should be the object of our fear. The name of the Lord is a "stone of stumbling" (vv. 14–15) to those who keep their political options open. The people do not listen to his message because they are hardened. Rather than enjoying God's protection, they plot their own course with self-reliance. He is the Lord of Hosts, and the Holy One, who offers "sanctuary" to those who fear him alone.

As the "stone" he evokes a response of either faith or rejection, causing an offense that will snare the people of Jerusalem.

Isaiah leads the godly remnant to find shelter in the Lord (**8:16–22**). The Lord has instructed Judah through Isaiah, whose teachings are consonant with the testimony and law of Moses. His teaching of judgment and hope is summarized in the names *Maher-Shalal-Hash-Baz*, *Shear-Jashub*, and *Isaiah* (v. 18).

As for the rest of the people, God's judgment will find them out if they continue to reject the prophetic call to repentance. The judgment is described as desolation, devastation, famine, and despair from which there is no escape. It is a time without hope for the future, because God appears to be at a great distance from his people. In their abandonment they will even consult the dead. Isaiah calls on them to seek the light of the Lord's testimony and law as revealed in his own message (v. 20). Otherwise, they will come to realize the futility of reliance on kings and nationhood.

F. The Messiah (9:1–7). In 733 B.C., Tiglath-pileser III besieged Damascus, invaded the region of Galilee, including Zebulun and Naphtali, and incorporated it into his kingdom (2 Kings 15:29) in fulfillment of God's Word. "Gloom" and "distress" result from oppression and separation from Yahweh's covenantal love. But the Lord will graciously turn humiliation into glory. How? By the coming of the Messiah of David (**9:1–7**). Although the northern tribes had rejected David's dynasty in favor of Jeroboam (1 Kings 12:1–20), their salvation will come from the very one whom they rejected. The new era will be characterized by great joy. The Messiah will free his people from their enemies and bring the actualization of the Davidic ideal.

The child (v. 6) is the Immanuel (7:14). He is God's gift to man's predicament. He is fully human ("child," "born," "son"), but he is also divine, with all the perfections of kingship in himself: supernatural wisdom, might, paternal beneficence, and peace. This son will reign forever in justice, righteousness, and peace. The certainty of his kingdom is guaranteed by "the zeal of the LORD" (v. 7b).

G. The wrath of God (9:8–10:34). The Lord's mercy is demonstrated in his patience with the corrupt northern kingdom. However, they are not responsive. The shadow of God's outstretched hand hangs over Samaria (9:12, 17, 21; 10:4; cf. 5:25; Amos 4:6–12). His judgment is relentless in view of the stubborn persistence of evil in Israel.

The attack of the Arameans and Philistines (ca. 737 B.C.) weakens Israel, but this military defeat is not viewed as an expression of the Lord's discipline. The leaders seize it as a political opportunity. Foolish Israel cannot see that the Lord has raised up the Assyrians to chasten her (**9:8–12**)!

This era is marked by civil wars and coups d'etat (**9:13–17**; 2 Kings 15:8–30). All classes of people ("head and tail," "branch and reed") will ultimately suffer at the hands of the Lord: young and old, rich and poor, political and religious leaders alike. All Israel is characterized by perversity ("ungodly"), evil, and impiety (NIV vileness; MT folly).

Godlessness and chaos are twins. Anarchy destroys the fiber of Israel's life like a fire (**9:20–21**). It spreads first through the underbrush and finally destroys everything. The Lord permits the anarchy but he is still in control. The destructive forces of civil war and anarchy are also described in the metaphor of a ferocious and uncontrollable appetite.

At the root of Israel's troubles is its resistance to God's just laws (**10:1–4**). Injustice prevails at the expense of the oppressed. In time, all Israel will be oppressed but there will be no help forthcoming from the Lord. His anger will see to the righteous execution of his decree against Israel.

The Lord has granted Assyria's rise to power (**10:5–19**). He permitted Assyria to enrich herself as he sent her on his holy mission to reduce those nations which had provoked his wrath. Assyria's lust for power, however, is unbridled. Assyria is a tyrant and boasts of her victories over cities and nations. The boast displays an attitude of autonomy and evidences no fear of God. Since Samaria has fallen (722 B.C.) and the Lord did not rescue it, how can Jerusalem expect to be rescued? The Assyrian advance has swept from Carchemish on the Euphrates to Jerusalem, and who can stop it? The Lord! Isaiah interrupts his sarcastic poem about Assyria's pride with a brief prose section (v. 12), containing the Lord's response to Assyria's taunt. He will punish Assyria. Assyria is nothing more than God's instrument.

The nature of the judgment is then given in poetic form (vv. 13–19) and is likened to a fire and a wasting disease. Assyria claimed that her wealth and strength came by clever strategy and irresistible power. Nations were despoiled, being impotent to resist the might of Assyria, but the God of Israel was witness, and will judge Assyria. When he is through with Assyria, her power will be at an end. Assyria's warriors will be rendered powerless by a "wasting disease" (v. 16), and Assyria's pomp will be easily reduced, even as a fire destroys a forest. Nonetheless, the Lord's "light," which assures Judah a future, will bring Assyria to an end!

The Lord's mercy is for the remnant's sake (**10:20–23**). Jerusalem was besieged in 701 B.C. and the country was desolate. Yet after the siege was lifted, even this remnant did not return to the Lord. Therefore, destruction has been decreed and will ultimately bring down both Judah and Jerusalem. Through the ministry of the prophets, a true remnant is sensitized. They will return and rely on the Lord. The expectation of repentance and restoration is symbolized in Isaiah's son, Shear-Jashub ("a remnant will return," 7:3).

The Lord who dealt graciously with his people in Egypt and rescued them from the Midianites in the days of the judges will come to the rescue of his people once more (**10:24–27**). The victory belongs to the Lord. The promise of his wrath passing from Judah to the enemy has eschatological overtones. The prophet looks forward to the period of restoration as the end of the Lord's wrath and the beginning of deliverance from the oppressors. In a real sense believers in Jesus are the remnant, who have been rescued from the wrath of God (1 Thess. 1:10), but who still await full deliverance from the enemies of God (2 Thess. 1:6–10).

The picture of the Assyrian advance is continued from verses 9–11 (**10:28–34**). The Assyrians are closing in on Jerusalem, devastating city after city. The Assyrian march need not be construed to be historical. The poetic imagery permits Isaiah to project the advance on Jerusalem from the direction of Samaria, as if it has just been conquered. The period between Samaria's fall (722 B.C.) and Jerusalem's siege (701 B.C.) is not his concern. He brings out a sense of panic. What will happen now? Will the Lord be faithful to his promise to remain with Judah? The answer is yes. God will first "lop off the boughs" by stopping Assyria's advance, and later he will cut down the might of Assyria. In less than a hundred years, Assyria will not be reckoned among the nations. God's Word is true.

H. The branch from Jesse (11:1–16). The threat to the Davidic dynasty (chap. 7) has passed. Ahaz has survived the attack and Aram and Israel have been conquered by Assyria. In chapter 9 the prophet speaks about "the son" to whom the everlasting government will be given and whose throne will be established with justice, righteousness, and peace. Isaiah again takes up the theme of the messianic rule in chapter 11.

Assyria and all world powers will fall like "lofty trees" (10:33), but the Lord will raise up his Messiah as a "shoot" (**11:1–9**). This shoot does not spring from one of the "branches" of a tree; its origin is the roots. The Messiah is a shoot from the roots of David's dynasty. The new leadership over God's people must come from David's dynasty, but it is also separate from the "old" dynastic interests. Kingship may cease in Judah, but God's promise to David will be kept. The messianic shoot does not conform to the old way. He introduces God's rule on earth, symbolized by the presence of the "Spirit of the Lord" (v. 2).

The new stage in God's kingdom will combine the old (the Davidic covenant) and the new (the era of the Spirit). The presence of God's Spirit on the Messiah will be evident in his rule of wisdom, justice, righteousness, faithfulness, and peace, complete with the absence of evil and the universal knowledge of God. The messianic era is an idealization of the period of David's and Solomon's rule over Israel. The qualities of the Messiah make him fit to protect his people. His relationship with God is beyond criticism, as he fears him and delights to do his will. He will protect the needy and execute judgment on the wicked without mercy. He favors his subjects with a rule of righteousness and faithfulness. The Messiah will establish a paradisic renewal of the earth in that his peace extends even to nature; all men will know God.

The Messiah of the root of Jesse will be a "banner for the peoples" (**11:10–16**). He gathers the scattered remnant of Israel and Judah from the nations in a "second" exodus. They will freely come from Egypt (Upper = Pathros and Lower), Cush (Nubia/Ethiopia, the Upper Nile region), Elam (east of Babylonia), Shinar (Babylonia), Hamath (region north of Damascus), and the Mediterranean coastlands. He will join together the twelve tribes and rule over a restored Israel. Nothing can stand in the way of God's purpose. He will even dry up the Red Sea ("Egyptian" sea), make the Euphrates passable, and make a highway from Assyria and Egypt to Israel. The restoration from exile will be more glorious and more extensive than the first exodus. The fulfillment of this prophecy began in the restoration from exile and extends to the fullness of time, when Christ came to gather both Jews and Gentiles into his flock (John 10:16).

I. Songs of praise (12:1–6). Two brief hymns (vv. 1, 4–6) and an oracle of promise (vv. 2–3) make a fitting conclusion to the first division of Isaiah (chaps. 1–12). The prophet renews the promise of full and free salvation and calls upon the godly to join him in confident trust in God. As the "strength" of his people Yahweh is able to accomplish all that has been predicted by Isaiah: universal peace, the presence of God, the restoration of the remnant, the Messiah's rule, and the universal knowledge and fear of God.

The hymns focus on two aspects of deliverance: God's comfort of his people (v. 1) and the proclamation of his acts of salvation to the nations (vv. 4–6). The day of judgment is against all flesh and God alone will be "exalted." The righteous have been delivered from the finality of judgment and know the Lord as the "exalted," Holy One of Israel. The era of restoration marks redemption, proclamation, rejoicing, and the renewal of God's presence among his people.

Isaiah calls upon the nations to exalt Yahweh's name because of what he does on behalf of his own. This expression of hope by God's own will result in responses of faith and praise by the nations. The expression of hope takes the form of thanks and songs of praise. Therefore, Isaiah calls upon the remnant to drown out their sorrows in songs of joy and expectation in the deliverance of the Holy One of

Israel. If God's own people can live in joyful expectation of the final redemption, the world will take notice.

The people who were restored to the land of Judah after the exile had reason to celebrate and to give thanks to God for the redemption they had experienced. The fullness of that redemption, however, was not yet theirs. The day to which the prophet refers in verse 1 extends from the restoration after the exile all the way to the return of the Lord Jesus Christ.

Chapter 12 forms a transition between chapters 1–11 (Yahweh's judgment on Judah) and chapters 13–23 (Yahweh's judgment on the world). The focus of chapter 12 grants us an insight into the plan of God by revealing that while God is angry with this world (including the Jews), he still holds out his arms to all who will exalt his name, whether they are Jews or Gentiles.

II. Oracles Against the Nations (13:1–23:18)

These messages are called "oracles." The word *oracle* (burden) is a technical term and occurs in the headings of Isaiah's speeches against each nation (13:1—Babylon; 17:1—Damascus; 19:1—Egypt; 23:1—Tyre; cf. also 21:1, 11, 13; 22:1; 30:6). Similar collections are found in Jeremiah 46–51 and Ezekiel 25–32. This collection of oracles forms the second major division of Isaiah and prepares the reader for the "Apocalypse of Isaiah" (chaps. 24–27).

A. Babylon (13:1–14:23). Isaiah views the Lord's judgment on Babylon as an expression of his rule over the earth (**13:1–16**). He commands the armed forces of the nations. "The holy ones" are the warriors mustered and consecrated for battle (v. 3). The Lord sovereignly rules over the nations, who serve him without knowledge of their being the instruments of the establishment of his kingdom. The descriptions of the ensuing battle and the day of the Lord take on universal proportions. The nations of the earth are involved. The day of the Lord as a time of great destruction on earth is near. Man is totally helpless. Heaven and earth heave when God expresses his anger with sinful man. Few survive, and even those who escape will come to a painful end.

The cosmic description of the day of the Lord is applied to Babylon's fall (**13:17–22**). As an expression of his sovereignty, God will also turn against mighty Babylon. The fall of Babylon will be great. In colorful language Isaiah portrays the devastation caused by her enemies. The enemies are the Medes (v. 17), who together with the Persians conquered Babylon under the leadership of Cyrus the Persian (539 B.C.). They will have no pity. Her doom is that of a deserted city. The desolation of Babylon is graphically portrayed by its becoming the haunt of wild animals, like Sodom and Gomorrah. This prophecy was not completely fulfilled when Cyrus entered Babylon because the transfer of power was rather quiet. It seems that the prophet extends the perimeter of application to all world kingdoms and empires. Babylon is symbolic of all evil, pride, oppression, and power which exalts itself against the Lord. This power will be broken (cf. Rev. 18:2–24). Thus Yahweh deals with any kingdom which exalts itself against him and his anointed people.

In the midst of a description of the world "in flames," Isaiah encourages God's people with a message of comfort (**14:1–4a**). When Babylon comes to its end, the Lord will restore the exiled people to the land. There is a hint of the cosmic effect of Israel's restoration in that the nations, too, will join in Israel's future either as converts (v. 1b) or as servants (v. 2). The era of restoration marks the freedom of God's people. As an expression of joy, God's people take up a dirge (a traditional funerary song) mocking the end of the oppressors. It is a taunt (v. 4)—not to be taken literally, but as a hyperbolic statement of the end of the aggressor. This explains the mythological allusions, as Isaiah portrays the end of Babylon in its own religious language.

The king of Babylon typifies world power. When the aggression of the oppressor comes to an end, the whole earth is at rest (**14:4b–8**). The nations, likened to trees, rejoice that Babylon no longer cuts down nations and kingdoms like a woodsman.

The mortality of Babylon is poetically set forth in the mythological language of Babylon's own religious conceptions (**14:9–10**). Babylon considered itself ruler over life and death. Kings, leaders, and people had died in the many campaigns and battles waged by the Babylonians. They had found rest in the netherworld. But with the end of Babylon, spirits in the netherworld stir themselves up as the king of Babylon knocks and desires to enter. There is a sudden commotion, as the news of Babylon's fall is announced. Babylon the great has fallen. It, too, is subject to powers greater than itself.

Babylon's fall is great (**14:11–15**). The king is compared to the "morning star, son of the dawn" (v. 12a). As the morning star is not the sun which distinguishes day from night, the king of Babylon is not God! However, in its drive to rule the world, Babylon's pride was unlimited (Dan. 4:30) and it acted as God on earth. In its imperial ambitions it acted no differently than the ancient people who built a city to make a name for themselves (Gen. 11:1–9). Likewise, Babylon's goal was to reach into heaven and to take the place of the Most High. But it, too, will be cast down. The greater the aspirations, the worse the fall. Isaiah uses this dramatic interlude to build up suspense. Will the spirits of the netherworld welcome the king of Babylon?

The spirits first gaze with amazement at the beggarly and weak king, covered with maggots. They respond with unbelief, mocking the mortality of Babylon. At this, they cast him out of the netherworld (**14:16–20a**). There will never be any rest for the king of Babylon and his offspring! He does not get the burial of a hero, but is like a soldier missing in action. The spirit of Babylon is doomed to roam.

God has reserved a time of judgment for all evildoers (**14:20b–21**). They may flourish and thrive, but then they are suddenly cut off. In Old Testament language the king and his sons, representative of the spirit of Babylon, will be cut off forever. Their memory will be forgotten. Thus the Lord will do to all evildoers. In the biblical conception of Babylon, as we have seen, Babylon represents the spirit of man without God, the spirit of autonomy, the spirit of secularization, and the spirit of antichrist. For God's kingdom to be established, the Lord must deal with any manifestation of evil.

The application is clear. Babylon must fall by the will of the Lord (**14:22–23**). Its judgment is sealed, and its final state is likened to a swamp, good only for animals (v. 23).

B. Assyria (14:24–27). Yahweh is angry not only with Babylon, but also with Assyria (cf. 10:5–34). Regardless of the question of which nation is guilty of the greater sin, all nations are under God's condemnation. The council of the nations will be frustrated, but his council will stand. These words are Yahweh's solemn assurance to his people that he will establish his kingdom on earth!

C. Philistia (14:28–32). The oracle against Philistia is dated by the year in which Ahaz died. The historical background is far from certain. It may be that Philistia made an effort to lead Judah, Edom, and Moab in an insurrection against Assyria (ca. 715 B.C.) which was put down by Sargon II in 711 B.C. The Philistines hoped for the end of Assyria's dominance, but Isaiah warns them that they will be put down several times (711, 701, 586 B.C.) until they are finally no more. The metaphors of the snake, viper, and a venomous serpent (v. 29) have been variously interpreted. They possibly refer to the several Assyrian and Babylonian campaigns, each one growing in severity. The word *root* (v. 29) denotes the offspring of the serpent. The Philistines are, thus, assured that the danger is far from over. Their own offspring (lit. root) will come to an end by famine and subsequently by the sword. The enemy from the north refers to Assyria and Babylonia. Philistia, the archenemy of God's people, will also come to an end. The Lord, however, has established his kingdom on earth and only the humble, who seek him, will find refuge in it. Regardless of the political changes and the message of the emissaries of the nations, God's people must seek the Lord and his kingdom.

D. Moab (15:1–16:14). The oracle concerning Moab is largely in the form of a lament and is partially repeated in Jeremiah 48:29–38. The judgment on Moab is marked by severity and utter frustration.

An enemy will come from the north and free the refugees to migrate southward along the King's Highway into Edom (**15:1–9**). Isaiah movingly and sympathetically pictures the fall of Moab's cities: Kir, Dibon, Nebo, Medeba, Heshbon, Elealeh, and Jahaz. With the fall of these cities, ranging from the far north to the south, Moab has come to an end. The refugees clutch in their hands whatever they can carry and move southward, wailing over their misfortunes. Isaiah joins in the lament, and evokes sympathy for the Moabites. They were, after all, Israel's relatives through Lot (Gen. 19:36–37) and David was a descendant of Ruth, the Moabite (Ruth 4:17). The brooks have dried up and the waters of Dimon (Dibon?) are filled with blood (vv. 6, 9). Thus, they cross the "Ravine of the Poplars" (Wadi Zered) into Edom.

From Edom (Sela; cf. 2 Kings 14:7) the Moabites send emissaries requesting asylum (**16:1–5**). They come with lambs as "tribute," thus recognizing Judah's supremacy. The prophet explains why it is important to seek sanctuary in Judah. First, oppression will cease from the world. Second, the messianic kingdom will be established, when a king will rule on David's throne with faithfulness, justice, and righteousness.

Moab is insincere in her request for sanctuary with God's people. They desire refuge from the enemy, but not in the Lord and his Messiah. The heart of pride, conceit, and empty boasts has not changed. Therefore, judgment has overtaken them. Still, Isaiah laments the fall of Moab (**16:6–12**). He grieves over the ruined vineyards, fields, and orchards. The songs of joy at harvest time have been changed into songs of mourning. The produce once exported to other nations has ceased. Moab's gods are unable to rescue her.

The date of Moab's doom is given: "within

three years" (**16:13–14**; lit. the years of a hireling). The beginning of Moab's disasters may have come in the Assyrian campaigns. Moab came to an end.

E. Damascus and Israel (17:1–14). The oracle against Damascus is brief in comparison to the other oracles. It seems that this oracle is intimately connected with the judgment of Israel and the judgment on the nations. The structure of the chapter is far from simple. After the declaration of the oracle against Damascus, the prophet three times employs the introductory formula *in that day* (vv. 4, 7, 9). The last section is introduced with the word *woe* (v. 12). On the other hand, if we look at the chapter from a literary perspective, we observe two major motifs in verses 1–3: destruction and the disappearance of glory. These motifs reoccur in verses 4–6, but in the reverse order, thus forming a chiastic structure. Verses 7 and 8 contain an invitation to repent, whereas verses 9–11 explain the reason for the destruction of the northern kingdom.

Finally, the last three verses give God's judgment on the nations who have been involved in the judgment of Israel and Damascus. The historical background of the oracle against Damascus can best be understood in the context of the Syro-Ephraimite alliance (ca. 734 B.C.). Ephraim and Damascus thought that they could free themselves from the yoke of Tiglath-pileser III. As we have seen in our analysis of chapter 7, the prophet has forewarned the nations that their alliance will not undo the Davidic dynasty in Judah nor will they succeed in destabilizing Assyria. Instead, both nations would shortly come to an end, which happened to Damascus in 732 when it was taken by Tiglath-pileser III and to Samaria in 722 when it was taken by Shalmaneser V and Sargon II.

The oracle against Damascus is addressed to the Aramean nation against which the prophet has already spoken (chaps. 7, 8). He portrays the city of Damascus in ruins and utter desolation (**17:1–3**). The flourishing city traces its ancestry back to a desert oasis. It had developed from a caravansary to a major commercial center. The judgment reverses the progress of Damascus; it will again be a place where flocks are pastured (v. 2b). Since Ephraim and Aram have consolidated their strength, both nations will come to an end and their glory will be wasted.

Israel's future is compared to a grain harvest in the Valley of Rephaim (**17:4–6**). Twice David fought there and defeated the Philistines (2 Sam. 5:17–25). The valley was important for the cultivation of grain needed for Jerusalem. The law of gleaning allowed for the poor to pick any ears of grain left after a harvest (Lev. 19:9–10; 23:22; Deut. 24:20–22). The future of Israel is likened to the scanty remains left to the poor for gleaning. Israel is also likened to the few olives left in an olive tree which has been shaken thoroughly during the harvest (v. 6).

Verses **7–8** constitute a beautiful interlude in which Isaiah describes the future conversion of the remnant. The verb for their conversion is not the usual verb ("to repent" / "to return") but rather it is "to look." The people must recognize that Yahweh is "their Maker" and "the Holy One of Israel" (v. 7). Therefore, they must refrain from looking to their illegitimate altars as the source of deliverance.

The fall of Israel results in exile so that the countryside will be characterized by depopulation (**17:9–11**). The reason for the judgment is given in verse 10. The people have forgotten the God of their salvation and their Rock who could provide a refuge. Instead of committing themselves fully to Yahweh they have given themselves to pagan nature cults. The character of these cults is not clear; they may be the cults of Adonis. It may very well be that at these sites there were also gardens symbolic of the powers of the deities. However, these people who do everything to appease the deities by cultivating the ceremonial gardens are assured that they will not be able to reap the benefits of their worship; rather, they will reap sickness and pain.

Isaiah uses alliterative devices to impress on his hearers that God's judgment will affect a great multitude of the nations (**17:12–14**). The nations are described in terms of the raging sea and "the roaring of great waters" (v. 12). It is as if the nations are going beyond the bounds set by God as they storm and foam, but God comes with a rebuke set in the language of a theophany. Yahweh's coming is associated with a wind and a whirlwind. The power of Yahweh is so great that the nations suddenly appear like chaff or tumbleweeds. Thus it will be with the nations: one moment they are terrifying but the next moment they are no more. Isaiah adds one final phrase to encourage the godly remnant that God will deal justly with those who have oppressed his own.

F. Cush (18:1–7). This chapter should be connected with chapter 17, as the Hebrew word for *woe* in verse 1 is also translated as *oh* in 17:12. It seems that chapter 18 is a more specific prophecy than the more general one to the nations in 17:12–14. As far as the time reference is concerned, it may be that the prophecy against Cush (Ethiopia) came some twenty years after the prophecy against Damascus (ca. 734 B.C.). In chapters 29–30 the prophet charges the people of Judah with independence from God and reliance on Ethiopia. In 705 B.C. Hezekiah sought an alliance with Ethiopia. This was because the Ethiopian king Shabaka controlled Upper Egypt as far as the Nile Delta. Apparently, the Ethiopians had taken Egypt (715 B.C.) and negotiated an alliance with Hezekiah. From the description of the Ethiopians it would seem that the Judeans stood in amazement of them because they were able to subdue the great power of Egypt. However, chapter 18 brings out God's judgment on this powerful people while intimating that God has a place reserved for them in his overall kingdom purposes.

The literary imagery is very artistic, creating a mental picture of this distant nation. The land of Ethiopia was known as a place from whence the locusts came; and therefore, Isaiah describes it as "the land of whirring wings" (v. 1a). The reference also depicts the Ethiopians as being able to cover and dominate an area very rapidly. The Ethiopians are also described as people who sent their ambassadors across the water by means of papyrus vessels (v. 2). The water probably is a reference to the Nile River, but it is unlikely that the papyrus vessels were used on as grand a scale as is suggested in verse 2a. If we keep in mind Isaiah's artistic purposes, however, we have before us a picture of a people who hasten to send their emissaries in light vessels to wherever their mission takes them. There is a certain ironic twist because the Lord has his own mission to the Ethiopians. He calls on his "swift messengers" to declare his word to the Ethiopians, who are further described as tall and "smooth-skinned"—an awe-inspiring people who have been able to expand their territory by trampling down their adversaries. Isaiah keeps us in suspense as to the nature of God's message, by turning his attention to the inhabitants of the world. They must wait for the "banner" to be raised and the trumpet to be blown. God also waits, withholding judgment, as he looks at the plotting of the nations. He hovers over them from his dwelling-place like the shimmering heat or an isolated cloud. Suddenly, the Lord seizes the moment and cuts down the nations like the branches of a grapevine (v. 5). He is compared to a vinedresser, who prunes the vines over the summer for cosmetic purposes and to increase the grape harvest. Once pollinated, the flower bears fruit, but the fruit takes three to four months to mature. God is likened to a farmer who, instead of waiting for the fruit to mature, comes in the heat of the summer to his vineyard and cuts off the shoots and the spreading branches, leaving these for the animals or for the birds of the air (vv. 5–6).

The people who have been so carefully described in verse 2 are described in the same way in verse 7. They are still tall and awe-inspiring; but this time they are coming not as messengers of war, but as worshipers of Yahweh. They are bringing gifts to Yahweh in Jerusalem. Instead of Judah bringing gifts to Ethiopia to placate the king and to join in her cause of rebellion against the Assyrians, the Ethiopians come to Mount Zion to placate the King of the Jews. In this way Isaiah moves from the historical circumstances and context in which the prophecy has been written to an eschatological description. The eschatological hope of the psalms is that the people of Ethiopia might also experience the salvation of the Lord and that they, too, may be inhabitants of the New Jerusalem.

G. Egypt (19:1–20:6). Yahweh comes on a cloud in judgment on Egypt, especially on her religious system (**19:1–4**). With the collapse of her religion, Egypt's social order falls apart. Egyptian will turn against Egyptian, city against city, and province against province. The hegemony of Pharaoh's rule will be impotent in the face of these forces and he must submit. The religious and political establishment thus abdicates to foreign rule and religious expressions.

In the second stanza (**19:5–10**) Isaiah portrays the end of Egypt's economy. The Nile River and its many canals form the essential system of economic support in Egypt. Because of lack of water, reeds, flax, and fish die and agriculture becomes impossible. Reeds were used for the production of papyrus, baskets, and simple artifacts. Flax was the raw product used in Egypt's extensive production of linen. Egypt exported both her papyrus and linen and was economically dependent on these products. Another basis of her economic support came from the fish industry, but that too is devastated by drought. All people will mourn over the great depression.

The third stanza (**19:11–15**) points out the folly of Egypt's counselors and princes. The intellectual elite are unable to avert the disaster. All are affected by God's judgment. The One who caused all Egypt to cry out on the night of the tenth plague (Exod. 12:29) will bring Egypt to her knees again.

In **19:16–25**, the prophet repeats the phrase *in that day* six times (vv. 16, 18, 19, 21, 23, 24). He speaks about the day in which there will be great "terror" that will overtake the Egyptians. The terror may be likened to the time when

Israel came out of Egypt after Yahweh demonstrated his power in the ten plagues.

In Egypt itself five cities will speak the language of Judah (v. 18). Because Jews settled in Egypt during the exile, Isaiah may be referring to the great Jewish centers in Migdol, Tahpanhes, Noph (Memphis), Pathros, and Alexandria. It is not clear what is meant by the "City of Destruction" (v. 18). A number of Hebrew manuscripts read "City of the Sun" and commentators identify it with Heliopolis. The Septuagint transliterates the Hebrew and suggests the reading "The City of Righteousness." The issue also remains whether one can be certain about the identification of these five cities. To a large extent, the identification rests on our knowledge of Jewish communities in Egypt. Perhaps we should see "five" as symbolic for "many."

In addition to cultural assimilation, the Egyptians will also assimilate religiously with the people of Judah. There will be an "altar" dedicated to Yahweh in the midst of Egypt and a "monument" (v. 19) as a memorial to his redemptive power. The Egyptians will come with voluntary sacrifices in order to keep the vows that they have made to Yahweh, the God of Israel. They were struck with plagues in the past, but now they will experience healing from Yahweh himself.

The last verses speak about a highway that extends from Egypt to Assyria, following the Fertile Crescent. The highway is symbolic of universal salvation, as it extends from west to east. The nations will join Israel in the worship of the Lord and they will be known as the blessed of the Lord.

The occasion of the prophecy of Egypt's fall (**20:1–6**) is the conquest of the city of Ashod by Tartan, the supreme commander of the forces of Sargon II. At this time the Lord commands Isaiah to walk about "stripped and barefoot" for three years (v. 2). The period of three years need not be exactly thirty-six months, because in oriental fashion, any portion of a year is considered a year. The behavior of the prophet has a calculated effect. The Lord requires this of his servant because it will be "a sign and a portent" against Egypt and Ethiopia to symbolize the way in which they will be carried off as exiles by the Assyrians. This prophetic word was partially fulfilled in 671 B.C., when Esarhaddon conquered Lower Egypt including the city of Memphis, and in 665 B.C. when Ashurbanipal conquered Thebes in Upper Egypt. Apparently Judah and Philistia continued to look to Egypt for help both in the rebellion of 705–701 B.C. as well as during the last days of Judah, when Zedekiah was looking for Egypt to help the weak state of Judah against the rising power of Nebuchadnezzar.

H. Babylon, Edom, and Arabia (21:1–17). These oracles are linked by the theme of the prophet's office of watchman (vv. 6, 8, 11, 12). Isaiah is waiting to see what the Lord is doing and proclaims what he sees as an oracle.

In the oracle concerning Babylon (**21:1–10**) the meaning of "desert by the Sea" (v. 1) is not exactly clear. It may possibly be the territory of Babylon north of the Persian Gulf. Isaiah compares the attack of Elam and Media on Babylon to whirlwinds coming from the desert. The prophet experiences great anguish when he understands the dire vision. He feels like a woman in labor, and like a man who staggers. Anguish and fear fill his heart and incapacitate him. He sees the prepared tables, the banquets, and the drinking of the Babylonians, but he cannot reach the officers to warn them. They are unprepared; their shields have not even been oiled for battle (v. 5). The prophet dramatizes his empathy to portray the sudden fall of Babylon. The picture fits in well with the feast of Belshazzar in Daniel 5. Though Isaiah expresses a longing for the "twilight" of deliverance from Babylon, his empathy keeps him from rejoicing. It is a day full of horror.

Next, the Lord commands him to serve as a watchman and to report on any movement. A man in a chariot gives him the awaited report: "Babylon has fallen" (v. 9; cf. Rev. 18:2). This is God's word of deliverance to his people.

The meaning of "Dumah" (**21:11–12**) is uncertain. It may be a corruption of the word *Edom*. This fits well with the reference to Seir (v. 11a), where the Edomites settled. Twice an Edomite calls upon the watchman (Isaiah) to predict the end of "the night" of distress. He responds that the morning of "hope" will come, but can say no more.

The Dedanites (**21:13–15**) were an Arabian tribe of caravaneers and traders located close to Edom. The caravaneers are not coming to Tema for commercial purposes, but to hide away in the "thickets" (desert shrubs) of Arabia as refugees from slaughter. They come south to Tema for food and water. They had encountered a strong enemy (Assyrians?) which had put them to flight with sword and bow.

The people of Kedar (**21:16–17**) were also known as caravaneers and were respected for their prowess with bows and arrows. These warlike archers were able to protect the caravans as they migrated across the Arabian desert, but they are not able to defend themselves. In a prosaic statement, the prophet concludes the oracles by saying that disaster will also come on Kedar.

I. Jerusalem (22:1–25). "The Valley of the Vision" (v. 5) is an obscure reference to Jerusalem. The context of this oracle is best set in the events of 701 B.C., when Sennacherib's seige of Jerusalem was lifted. Judah lay in ruins and Jerusalem had paid a dear price for freedom. The leaders had not been loyal and the soldiers were butchered without honor. While the people rejoice in their freedom, Isaiah is disconcerted. He must weep bitterly over what has happened to his people. The prophet speaks of another day, a day determined for the destruction of Jerusalem. The recent events, catastrophic as they were, are a picture of the Valley of Vision which God is preparing for all those who do not respond appropriately.

Isaiah looks out at "the Valley of the Vision," which was occupied shortly before by foreign troops (represented here by Elam and Kir, vv. 5–7). The ravages of war are all around. Isaiah reminds the people of their anguish and nervous industry as they set out to repair the walls with stones taken from their houses and to store water for the long siege. Yet, they had not looked to the Lord for help. They respond to crisis situations but do not respond to their sovereign God.

With the lifting of the siege, the people care even less for God. They are filled with a self-congratulatory spirit as they celebrate mock victory. The Lord will not forgive their callousness. His judgment on Jerusalem stands firm.

The arrogance of Jerusalem is symbolized in Shebna's desire for power and recognition (v. 15). The precise circumstances of Isaiah's outburst against Shebna are not stated, but he is characterized as too ambitious (v. 16). He will be disgraced and Eliakim will take over his office with suitable honor. Eliakim did succeed Shebna in office (see 36:3; 37:2), but Shebna maintained a prominent position as secretary (36:3). However, even Eliakim's position was not permanent. In a sense, Shebna and Eliakim represent the attitude of the people of Judah: arrogant and filled with selfish ambition. The fall of these men symbolizes, therefore, the ultimate fall of Jerusalem.

J. Tyre (23:1–18). The prophetic word against Tyre is singularly difficult. There are three main difficulties: the change of addressees (Sidon, vv. 2–4, 12; Tyre, vv. 1, 6–9, 15–18; Phoenicia, vv. 10–12), textual problems, and the historical fulfillment of the prophetic word. The cities of Phoenicia were subjugated by Assyria (701 B.C.), Nebuchadnezzar, and Alexander the Great (332 B.C.).

The prophet begins the oracle with an indirect reference to the ships of Tarshish, the large vessels which plied the seas (**23:1–5**). The rumor of Tyre's destruction is spread all around the Mediterranean area. From Larnaka, the port of Cyprus, to the ports around the Mediterranean, it is known that "the marketplace of the nations" (v. 3) has ceased doing business. Egypt, too, will hear. Its reaction is anguished.

The people of Tyre are called upon to flee to Tarshish on the Atlantic coast southwest of Spain (**23:6–9**). Even though the prophet may not have the exact region of Tarshish in mind, he is at least calling upon the people to flee the catastrophe that will befall Tyre. The city had enjoyed great prosperity. It was an ancient commercial center where tycoons ruled like princes. From Tyre these "princes" ruled over colonies and commercial empires. Because of its natural harbor, the history of Tyre goes back well into the third millennium B.C.

But, the exultation of Tyre has turned to lamentation. The ancient city has come to an end and the glory of Tyre has been defiled. The prophet assures the people of God that whatever happens to the great cities of Phoenicia (Tyre and Sidon) is the Lord's doing.

The people of Phoenicia can no longer depend on the trade advantages of Tyre (**23:10–14**). They will have to build up their own land. The Lord will judge Tyre, and his judgment is inescapable. The Babylonians/Assyrians (v. 13—the text is difficult) are the instruments of his judgment. The ruin of Tyre, Sidon, and Phoenicia affects all maritime trade.

Tyre is compared to an old prostitute unable to attract interest (**23:15–18**). Its abandonment will last "seventy years" (cf. Jer. 25:12; 29:10). The round number is symbolic of judgment and restoration. After a period of time the people will be restored, but they must also recognize that a portion of their income must be set apart for the Lord of Hosts (cf. 60:4–14). "Set apart" is related to the word *holy* and the prophet purposely uses this phraseology to indicate that the secular usage of the silver and the gold would be consecrated for God's kingdom purposes.

The prophecy, while it reflects historical events, has eschatological overtones. It is difficult to find a precise fulfillment for the restoration of Tyre except that in the middle of the third century Tyre again became a trading city. However, Tyre did not send a portion of its revenues to support the temple worship in Jerusalem. Tyre, representing all of the port cities and trading capitals of the world, is symbolic of God's judgment on national wealth, unless it is used for the kingdom of God.

III. The Apocalypse of Isaiah (24:1–27:13)

These four chapters are known as Isaiah's "apocalypse," because in them the prophet Isaiah introduces God's universal judgment, the renewal of the earth, the removal of death and the effects of sin, the deliverance of his people, and the victorious and universal rule of God. The chapters do not possess the usual characteristics of apocalyptic literature (visions, symbolic numbers, animals). Yet Isaiah gives a glimpse of the future deliverance of God's people and the establishment of his kingdom on earth after the judgment. The revelation is a witness to the power of Jesus Christ to keep his people, even in the face of all the turmoil they may experience on this earth. Likewise, Isaiah 24–27 stands as a witness of God's power to judge this present world order and to create a new people for himself.

A. God's judgment (24:1–23). In a couple of brief strokes Isaiah presents the extent of devastation effected by God's judgment on the earth (**24:1–13**). The whole earth lies contorted or twisted, as by an earthquake (NIV he will ruin its face, v. 1). It is nondiscriminatory and complete, in accordance with the word of the Lord. This destruction is the result of man's grievous sin against God and his covenant of preservation (Gen. 9:9–17). His curse rests on all of creation. Man has transgressed against God's holy ordinances governing the family, morality, preservation of life, and true worship. Therefore, God's judgment must come upon all men. All have sinned; all are covenant breakers without exception. Yet, God is faithful to his promises in the Noahic and Abrahamic covenants by preserving a remnant.

The earth is compared to a city after the ravages of fire, war, and earthquake. It lies in ruins. The people left in it are the survivors of the "gaiety" and "joy" of the past (v. 11), which are symbolized by wine (vv. 7, 9). The songs of the revelers have come to an abrupt end, but a new song is being raised.

The joy of the redeemed remnant (**24:14–16a**) is like that of redeemed Israel, as they joined Moses in a song celebrating the glory of Yahweh as King over his people (Exod. 15:1–18). From one end of the earth to the other, the redeemed of Israel praise the Righteous One. Jews and Gentiles together comprise the blessed remnant.

Isaiah returns again to the theme of universal judgment (**24:16b–23**). The words in verse 16b are variously translated as "woe to me," "I waste away," or "a secret to me." The prophet represents all God's children, yearning for the day of redemption, and yet fearing the momentary expression of God's great wrath on earth. It is a day full of "terror and pit and snare" (v. 17), from which no one can escape. It is likened to a violent earthquake and a universal flood and is similar to Noah's flood. All powers, spirits, demons, and forces of evil will be cast out of heaven and imprisoned in a "dungeon" (vv. 21–22; cf. 2 Pet. 2:4; Rev. 19:20–21; 20:10). Then the kingdom of God will be established with great triumph. The ultimate purpose of the judgment is that Yahweh alone may reign over this earth. The picture of Yahweh, the Lord of Hosts, reigning from Mount Zion and sharing his glory with all of his elders, is a beautiful picture which anticipates the visions of the apostle John, as he describes the glory of the Lamb on his throne, surrounded by the elders (Rev. 4:10; 5:8–14).

B. The redemption of God's people (25:1–26:6). The prophet's song of thanksgiving (**25:1–5**) celebrates God's victory over the enemies of his people as if it has already taken place. He is a refuge for his needy people in any age. Regardless of the exigencies of the present and the uncertainty of the future, the godly hold fast to their faithful God. The righteous are exhorted to look forward to the downfall of the capitals of the kingdoms of this world, namely, the centers of political and economic power, where ruthless tyrants rule. Isaiah provides a glimpse into God's perspective of history as an assurance to the godly that Yahweh protects his people regardless of the intensity of their adversities. He will bring down evil and provoke their enemies to jealousy.

The Lord invites all obedient nations (24:14–16; 25:3) together with the Jews to a banquet on Mount Zion (**25:6–8**; cf. 24:23). Yahweh himself has prepared a rich banquet of the finest food and drink in order to celebrate his goodness. Since it is the godly who have been the helpless and needy (v. 4), the eschatological banquet is described in the language of comfort and assurance. The Lord will take care of his people by providing for all their needs, a fact symbolized by the choice food and drink. He will also remove "the shroud" ("sheet") of mourning, as he deals with "death" and its causes. The heavenly Father himself will comfort his children by wiping away their tears (v. 8; cf. Rev. 7:17; 21:4). Instead of "disgrace" he will share his honor with them.

Then God's children will respond with thanksgiving and confidence in God's saving power (**25:9–10a**). True to character, Isaiah suddenly bursts out in hymns as he reflects on the great salvation and permanent establishment of God's kingdom (24:21–23; 25:6–8; 26:1–6). God's children wait for divine deliverance (NIV trusted; Heb. waited, v. 9).

Moab is symbolic of all of the nations (**25:10b–12**). This may be inferred from the connection between this section and the section that described the ruthless nations and the palaces of the strangers (vv. 1–5). Though Moab has not been Israel's greatest enemy, it too will be brought down. It will be trampled like straw being trampled down in manure (v. 10). Though her inhabitants will try to save themselves, they will fail. God has purposed to bring down Moab's pride.

The song of the redeemed (**26:1–6**) is not merely a song of thanksgiving but it is a celebration of trust in God whose "city" of salvation will be glorious (cf. Ps. 46). The godly community awaits the moment of their redemption. In this section Isaiah addresses those who trust in Yahweh. He encourages the godly to wait in hiding for a little while until the Lord completes his judgment upon the wicked.

The new song on the lips of the godly is a song of trust in the Lord, who protects his people as if they are in "a strong city" surrounded by "walls" and "ramparts" (v. 1). The inhabitants of the city of God are saved by him (v. 1a), "righteous" (v. 2a), and faithful (vv. 2–3). The humble will be raised, while the proud and the oppressors will be brought low. The "old" people had a history of faithlessness and apostasy; the inhabitants of the "strong city" must be a people of integrity and loyalty. God will reward these people with his peace.

C. A prayer for God's people (26:7–21). Isaiah further describes the nature of the people of God. He is aware that it may be a long time before God's purposes are fully realized on earth. In order to encourage the godly community to persevere in "righteousness" and "faithfulness," he offers a prayer of wisdom, confidence, and petition.

He prays that God's people may be wise (vv. 7–10). Wisdom is the mark of godliness in the Old Testament, as it expresses dependency on Yahweh and his Word. At the same time, however, it is not slavish dependency whereby the godly wait for Yahweh to approve every decision they make. They walk in accordance with his judgments ("laws," v. 8a) with a constant desire for God and with the hope that God's will be done by the nations on earth. Isaiah prays that godly wisdom may triumph over evildoers.

He also expresses confidence in the Lord, who will show his zeal for his people when he establishes peace for them. He will punish the wicked, who have no share in God's redemption, but will "enlarge" his people and extend their borders (vv. 14–15). He raises up his own people and will rule over them exclusively.

Isaiah prays that the time of distress will soon pass and that out of the suffering, the Lord may raise up a new people (vv. 16–19). God alone can initiate the era of restoration, and those who share in it will "wake up and shout for joy" (v. 19).

The Lord responds to the prayer with the assurance that he will avenge Israel's enemies because of their sins. Even though the bloodshed has seemingly been covered up, justice will prevail. The Lord will reveal everything that has been hidden. He encourages the godly to wait until his purposes for this present world have been fulfilled.

D. Deliverance of Israel (27:1–13). God will finally give a death blow to "Leviathan" (v. 1), symbolic of the rebellious heavenly host (**27:1–13**; cf. 24:21). The descriptions *gliding* and *coiling* are also used to describe Leviathan in Ugaritic (Canaanite) literature. The Old Testament uses the language of Canaanite mythology in order to express God's control over evil, chaos, and rebellion. The New Testament also employs this symbolic language (Rev. 12:7–10). Leviathan is "the master of the sea," whose punishment marks the end of rebellion in heaven and on earth.

Isaiah develops his vineyard poems (5:1–7) into an eschatological picture (**27:2–6**). Though the vineyard had been destroyed because of its utter worthlessness, God remains faithful to his people. Because the leaders were responsible for the ruined vineyard (3:14), the Lord himself assumes responsibility for its care. He watches, waters, and protects it. He will make war against anyone ("briars and thorns," v. 4) who opposes his people. He prevents those conditions which he had previously permitted to ruin the vineyard (5:6). He is not angry, but desires reconciliation with even hostile opponents.

His purpose for the vineyard is success on a grand scale. The root must be well established before the blossoms will produce their fruit in "all the world" (v. 6). The kingdom of God gradually extends, as God's new people are grafted in. These new people are expected to conform to God's justice and righteousness.

Isaiah **27:7–11** is obscure and intrusive. These verses are best regarded as a reflection on suffering. The Lord cleanses his people by exile and judgment (v. 8, NIV by warfare and exile; lit. measure by measure). They must abandon idolatry and return to the Lord. Even so, God does not kill off his people, as he did his opponents, whose "fortified city stands desolate" (v. 10a). Outside the walls, their farms are so devastated by drought that tree branches are used to kindle fires.

Nothing can hinder the return of the tribes

of Israel from Egypt and Assyria, because the Lord himself has ordained it (**27:12–13**). This is his harvest (v. 12; cf. Rev. 14:15). The "great trumpet" (ram's horn) ushers in the eschatological kingdom, when the restoration takes place. The prophet uses the language of accommodation, as he refers to the borders from the Euphrates to the Wadi of Egypt (Wadi El Arish, fifty miles southwest of Gaza), from where people will come to worship the Lord on Mount Zion. This word found partial fulfillment in the restoration from exile (539 B.C.). The New Testament extends the symbolism to God's worldwide harvest when Jesus returns (Matt. 24:31; 1 Cor. 15:52; 1 Thess. 4:16). The trumpet blast marks the end of man's rule and the introduction of the full reign of God on earth.

IV. Oracles of Woe (28:1–33:24)

The material in these chapters is loosely connected by the word *woe* (28:1; 29:1, 15; 30:1; 31:1; 33:1) and seems to date to the period of Judah's troubles with Assyria, during the reign of Hezekiah.

A. Ephraim (28:1–29). This section (**28:1–4**) comes from a time before the fall of Samaria when the enemy of Israel was already on the horizon. Assyria is likened to "a hailstorm and a destructive wind" and "a driving rain and a flooding downpour" (v. 2). The imagery of overflowing water is also found in Isaiah 8, where the prophet describes the coming judgment upon Israel and Aram. The northern kingdom is likened to a "fading flower" (v. 1) because the beautiful and fertile valleys characteristic of Ephraim would soon be overrun by Assyrian troops. The agricultural advantages of the northern kingdom were significant. It had excellent soil, large valleys, and finely terraced hills on which the people were able to farm and enjoy their olive groves. With all of the advantages of the northern kingdom the people had become independent and proud. Even as the wind and rain had given economic prosperity to the northern kingdom, God's judgment, likened to wind and rain, would destroy Ephraim. The freely given covenant blessings did not elicit an appropriate response on the part of Ephraim. The beauty of Ephraim, like a ripe fig, will be enjoyed by foreigners (v. 4).

Instead of the self-exalting pride of Ephraim the Lord will establish his glorious kingdom of justice and strength (**28:5–6**). The nobles of Ephraim cannot protect the people because of their drunken stupor, but the Lord will protect and strengthen the remnant who survive in Judah. The enemy will be stopped and kingship and theocracy will continue there by divine decree.

Yet Judah is no better than Ephraim (**28:7–13**). Even though Judah existed another 150 years after the fall of Samaria, the situation in the southern kingdom was generally no better than that in the northern kingdom. For this reason Isaiah strongly condemns Judah. In fact, his language is stronger against the southern kingdom than against the northern kingdom. He accuses Judah's leaders of drunkenness, an unteachable spirit, scoffing, and self-confidence.

Though the Lord is gracious in sparing Judah, its religious leaders are incapable of rendering decisions and of proclaiming the visions of God because of their drunken stupor. While sitting by their filth (v. 8), they mock Isaiah, speaking like a babbler who is explaining his message to babes and infants or like a kindergarten teacher who begins by teaching sounds: "*ṣaw lāṣāw ṣaw lāṣāw / qaw lāqāw qaw lāqāw*" (v. 10). By mimicking the sounds, the religious leaders express the intensity of their hatred for God's Word.

To this mockery Isaiah responds with God's word of judgment. Whereas the Lord had given the land to Israel as a place in which they might receive his blessings, foreign invaders will come and speak like babblers. The people who have rejected the warnings of approaching judgment as unintelligible and irrelevant will hear the same message from these foreign invaders. Then, however, it will be too late, because they will be taken captive. The prophets of whom Isaiah speaks are the false prophets who are called to share visions and to give judgments, but are unable because they are prostrate in their own vomit.

The leaders of God's people are unteachable, and for this reason they have little to teach others. They mock the prophet by asking the rhetorical question, "Who is it he is trying to teach?" They think he is nothing more than a repetitious school teacher.

These four characterizations (drunkenness, unteachable spirit, scoffing, and self-confidence) portray Jerusalem's leaders as completely insensitive to Yahweh's law and to the covenant. They have broken away from Yahweh and are unable to lead his people back to righteousness. Yahweh's words are directly related to the four accusations the prophet has made. First, foreign enemies will come into the country and take it. As the foreign forces will be using foreign languages (v. 11), the people themselves will feel like uncomprehending children. Whereas God had encouraged the people to find rest and repose for their souls (v. 12), they instead will be taken into exile by the enemy. In addition to this, the confidence and scoffing of the people will turn to terror. The people thought that they were invincible. They put their confidence in the security of Jerusalem, their leaders, the temple of Yahweh, and the priests. However, they will not be able to stand on the day of God's judgment because Jerusalem will be trampled down. The people themselves will go from terror by day to terror by night. That day will bring no peace or comfort. The prophet likens this to a time when the bed is too short and the blanket too small (v. 20). Isaiah further exhorts the people to cease their scoffing lest the judgment of God be intensified.

The political leaders also scoffed at the prophet. They did not believe that trust in the Lord ("a tested stone," v. 16) was the answer to Judah's political woes. Instead, they had relied on a covenant with Egypt. The prophet facetiously calls this treaty "a covenant with death" and the guaranteed protection "a lie" and "a falsehood" (**28:14–22**). They firmly believed that they had power to avert the judgment, which is likened to a flood.

Set over against the false security of political alliances is Yahweh. He is the "tested stone," "a cornerstone," who provides a solid foundation for all who trust in him (v. 16) and order their lives in accordance with his absolute standards of justice and righteousness. He, however, will not provide any refuge to those who have made foreign alliances. Death will overtake them and his judgment will be executed. Then their self-made remedies, likened to a short bed and a narrow blanket, will not work. The Lord will do a work, not to save as he did at Mount Perazim in David's day (2 Sam. 5:20–25), but to destroy. The decree has gone forth from the Lord Almighty.

The wise farmer does not plow continuously, but organizes his operation so as to have a time and place for plowing, sowing, and harvesting (**28:23–29**). Even in the process of harvesting, the farmer knows exactly which tools to use to obtain the desired harvest. So it is with God. He sovereignly and wisely administers his rule.

B. Ariel (29:1–24). The background of the prophecy against Ariel may best be found in the years preceding 701 B.C. A power struggle had taken place between Sennacherib and the eastern nations, making it possible for the western nations to rebel. During these years, Hezekiah turned to Egypt for help (30:1–2; 31:1). The political option of turning to Egypt for help was reasonable in that Sennacherib was busy on the eastern front. The alliance between Aram, Phoenicia, Judah, and Egypt made it imperative for Sennacherib to deal quickly and decisively with his eastern problems and then turn his attention to the west. During the intervening years the psychological mood in Judah was very positive because the people felt less threatened and were hoping for a strong political and economic resurgence. Yet Isaiah had already prophesied that Assyria was to be the instrument of God's judgment—even on Judah (8:7–8; 10:5).

With the possibility of an independent Judah on the horizon, the people viewed the prophet's words with skepticism. After all, it had seemed that the prophet spoke about a doom greater than could be realized. The future of Judah would be determined by the people and their political skills rather than by the Word of God.

The prophet preaches the word of the Lord in these optimistic times (**29:1–4**). He addresses Jerusalem as "Ariel." It is uncertain why he calls Jerusalem "Ariel" (Lion of God). There is no scholarly consensus on the meaning of "Ariel." Some have proposed that this may be an ancient Canaanite name for Jerusalem; others have suggested that the gates of Jerusalem may have had lions as a part of their decoration.

Isaiah first brings a woe on Jerusalem, the city where David lived and where the temple stood. In spite of its ties with the temple and David's dynasty, Yahweh plans to bring down Jerusalem. The future of Jerusalem will be filled with distress, lament, and mourning, because Yahweh has turned against the people and surrounded them like an enemy surrounds a city. Isaiah describes Jerusalem in a state of humiliation. He likens Jerusalem to a conquered city where the inhabitants are pushed down into the dust begging for mercy from their conquerors (v. 4a). Not only are there those who beg for their lives but also the dead whose voices are crying out from the dust.

Jerusalem will be covered by the multitude of her enemies, likened to fine dust or chaff (**29:5–8**). The future of Jerusalem looks bleak because Yahweh himself comes against his people who have been enjoying security and are relying on Egypt for their survival.

The devastation is compared to thunder, loud noise, winds, tempest, and fire, reminiscent of Yahweh's revelation on Mount Sinai (Exod. 19:16–19). This is a prophetic proclamation of the judgment to come on the day of the Lord.

Though Yahweh has given up Ariel to the nations, he protects the remnant of his people. The nations who rise against Judah and Jerusalem will leave empty. The prophet likens the reaction of the nations to that of a hungry or thirsty man who has dreamt that he has been satisfied, but in the morning wakens to find he has not actually eaten or drunk (vv. 7–8).

This will be the experience of any nation which fights against the people of God. They will have a measure of victory, but it will not last. Yahweh is still with his people. How comforting these words are to the people of God living at any time and in any place! Regardless of how God's people may fail, he has a plan to redeem a people for himself and will continue to work out the goals that he has decreed from eternity.

There are some who believe that the prophet's words are not meant for them, but possibly for others in another time. They are blind to the revelation of God (**29:9–14**). Isaiah likens them to those who stagger in a drunken stupor (v. 9) and to those who have fallen into a deep sleep that renders them unable to hear and respond to the warning of imminent judgment. There is a real danger in not applying the Word of God to one's own time, or in lacking interest in how the Word of God may be applied.

Assyria's siege of Jerusalem was imminent. In 701 B.C. they surrounded Jerusalem after devastating the countryside of Judah and leveling her fortified cities. It was only then that the people began to see; it was too late, however, because they had not responded appropriately to the prophetic message.

Isaiah concludes with a warning to the people at large (vv. 13–14). He again accuses them of hypocrisy (cf. chap. 1). The people come into the courts of the temple to pray and sacrifice, but their real love is not for Yahweh. Their wisdom is the wisdom of this world, and at that time the wisdom of the world dictated that Jerusalem ally herself with Egypt. The wisdom of that time perished, as subsequent events have shown. God, however, calls his people to a wisdom that comes from on high. He will stun them with his wonder in judgment and devastation. The future of the people lies, therefore, not in their own schemings and planning, nor in self-confidence, but in Yahweh himself.

The prophet renews his proclamation of "woe" on the people who plan and scheme as if Yahweh does not know or see (**29:15–24**). The people are the clay and the Lord is the Potter, but the clay is skeptical and critical of the Potter's abilities (v. 16).

Thus far Isaiah has portrayed a number of the people's reactions: apathy (vv. 9–10), disbelief in the relevance of the prophetic word for their time (vv. 11–12), formalism and hypocrisy (vv. 13–14), and dependence on man's schemings and planning apart from God (vv. 15–16). Yet however dark the day may be, God still has a message of salvation for his people. Isaiah now calls to spiritually sensitive people—those known as deaf, blind, poor, afflicted, and needy. The deaf and the blind are those who have suffered the judgment of God and respond to his revelation. The afflicted and the needy are those who have experienced God's judgment and whose hearts search for the living God. The spiritual remnant will hear the Word of God, see the salvation of the Lord, and rejoice in Yahweh himself.

The focus of this section is on the work of the Lord in history. The Holy One of Israel, who destroys cruel people and oppressors, gives cause for joy to people who have faith in him. The promise is to the "redeemed" children of Abraham, the spiritual seed of Abraham (v. 22). The promises concern the work of final restoration begun in history. The Lord will transform them into a "holy people" who will serve him from the heart.

C. Foreign alliances (30:1–33). The background of chapters 30 and 31 lies in the diplomatic mission to the Ethiopian ruler, Shabaka, who extended his rule as far as the Nile Delta. Because of the increase in Shabaka's power, the Judean aristocracy considered the possibility of an alliance between Shabaka, Hezekiah, the Philistines, and the Phoenicians against the Assyrian king, Sennacherib (705–701 B.C.).

The leadership of Judah relied on political solutions to political problems (**30:1–7**). They made every attempt to solve their problems creatively without consulting the Lord. Instead of finding "protection" and "refuge" (v. 2) in the Lord, they looked to Egypt for help against Assyria. Ultimately, however, their plan failed because Egypt used Judah to its own advantage and Judah was disgraced.

The stubbornness and folly of Judah's leaders are highlighted by the description of the desert and the caravans which traverse the desert to Egypt. Isaiah describes the desert as a place filled with anguish and loneliness. It is a desolate area as one travels from Judah through the Negeb and the Sinai to Egypt. Apparently the Via Maris, which was the usual route between Judah and Egypt, was not open because the delta was controlled by the Saite dynasty. Thus, the best road was not available for the Judean caravans, and they had to take the more difficult desert route to Egypt.

The desert is filled with dangers. The purpose of the reference to the animals is to make it clear that the people of Judah sent their emissaries through a torturous terrain filled with difficulties in order to get absolutely nowhere! The leaders of Judah go to great pains to have a caravan laden with precious objects sent to Egypt to obtain the favor of the Egyptians for their own political purposes. But Egypt is not able to help.

The last part of verse 7 is somewhat difficult as it describes the situation in Egypt. It is possible to read this as a question: "Is this the mighty one (Rahab) sitting still?" Apparently, the efforts of the Judeans to buy security would be futile because their fine treasures could not guarantee that Egypt would be in any position to help. As it turned out, the Egyptians were defeated by Sennacherib at Eltekeh. The areas of Phoenicia, Philistia, and Judah were taken, and Jerusalem was surrounded by Sennacherib in 701 B.C.

Isaiah returns to the theme of rebelliousness (**30:8–17**). Judah has been rebellious against Yahweh for some time, rejecting both his Torah and his prophet. In order to remind the future generations Isaiah is commanded to write on a tablet the testimony (or witness) of God against Israel and Judah. The language of the witness is reminiscent of Moses' Song of Witness (cf. Deut. 32) and of Joshua's stone of witness (cf. Josh. 24:26–27). The history of Israel and Judah is incriminating evidence against the people. They have been called to be Yahweh's people, but in essence they are false sons who have not responded appropriately.

Isaiah's words are a testimony to those who hate the Word of God and thereby the Holy One of Israel. God's Word becomes for them a word of judgment. If they persist in their self-reliance, they will suffer a sudden fall. They are like a wall that has been standing for a long time but already shows evidence of weakness by a protrusion. The wall may stand for many years but will suddenly cave in; so will Judah (vv. 13–14).

Israel is also like a piece of pottery. A potter's jar may be beautiful and may function very well. When shattered, however, it is of no use. One cannot even use the sherds to take coals of fire from the hearth or to dip water from a pool (v. 14).

Before destruction comes upon Judah, Isaiah calls upon the people to return to the Holy One of Israel. Salvation does not lie in heroic acts, but rather in repentance and trust in Yahweh. Faith and repentance are requisites for true salvation. Instead of turning to Yahweh, Judah has shown a history of unwillingness to return. They have responded in the opposite way by relying on horses and military power. Since they are intent on rejecting Yahweh's gracious invitation, Yahweh deals with the people accordingly. They rely on horses; in their haste they will have to flee as though they are on horses. Instead of experiencing God's blessing, whereby a thousand enemy troops are routed by one Israelite (v. 17a), they will experience the opposite—the entire nation fleeing from a handful of enemy troops (v. 17).

The grace of God is still evident in the remnant that will remain. They will be like a small military outpost—a flagstaff on a mountaintop or a banner on a hill. Few will be left, but still there will be some to whom the Lord will continue to show his grace.

The first effect of God's grace is that the sorrow of the people will be removed (**30:18–26**). Those who have been weeping and crying because of their great distress are assured that Yahweh will answer their prayers and will heal all their hurts. Yahweh comes to heal the wounds of his people and to assure their well-being—physical as well as spiritual. Another way in which Isaiah describes the grace of Yahweh upon his people is by delineating his blessings. The grace of God is free. How different is God's guidance in that he leads his people into the way that leads to blessing! Isaiah describes poetically the blessings of rain and sun. This combination makes it possible for crops to grow and produce abundantly, for animals to roam and be satisfied, and for people to have plenty of bread and water. In the land which Yahweh blesses there will no longer be any evidence of idolatry.

Isaiah returns to the theme of Yahweh's justice with respect to his enemies (**30:27–33**). The enemies of which he is speaking are the Assyrians in particular (v. 31), but Isaiah's words may be applied to all the enemies of God's people.

First, Isaiah describes the greatness of Yahweh's wrath. He comes in burning anger, symbolized by smoke and fire, in order to completely wipe out the enemy. Fire, wind, and flood (vv. 27–28, 30–31) are the prophet's favorite metaphors for the wrath of the Lord. The nations are put into a sieve and shaken back and forth so that the wicked might be removed. Isaiah also likens Yahweh's judgment to "a bit" which leads the people to their destiny (v. 28). None of the wicked will remain. The destiny of the nations is also described as the destruction of the wicked in the Valley of Topheth, south of Jerusalem (v. 33). Here, Yahweh will set up piles of wood on which the bodies of the enemies of his people will be placed, and with the breath of his mouth he will set these stacks of wood aflame.

The destruction of the wicked is cause for joy among the people of God who have been suffering under the ruthless power of their enemies. They are portrayed as singing in the night as during the days of a festival. They will be glad, and not afraid, because their faith is in the Rock of Israel (v. 29). There will be ritual rejoicing as they make music with their tambourines, lyres, and other instruments. They cannot help Yahweh in his war against the enemies; it is Yahweh's war. Instead, they must wait quietly with assurance that when Yahweh is finished with his enemies, the victory will also belong to them.

D. Judgment and hope (31:1–32:20). Isaiah charges Judah's leaders with autonomy by depending on Egypt's military superiority (**31:1–9**). In the ancient world, superiority generally belonged to those kings who had a great number of horses and chariots. In order to fight military power with military power Judah relied on the force which Egypt would be able to provide against the great power of Assyria. It became proverbial in Judah that the opposite of reliance on Yahweh was the reliance on horses and chariots (cf. Ps. 20:7).

Isaiah calls upon the people to look to the Holy One of Israel for wisdom and help. If not, his wisdom will turn against them and his hand will destroy both his enemies and all who do not lean on him. The people must remember that all who do not look to Yahweh for their protection have abandoned the Holy One of Israel who is powerful to put down human inventiveness and all the powers that oppose him.

Yahweh can protect his people! The prophet likens his ability to a lion, intent on getting his prey even when many shepherds make a loud noise to scare him off, and to fluttering birds, intent on scaring away a would-be intruder to protect their young in the nest. The Lord is strong like a lion as he destroys the enemies, and caring like a bird as he protects Judah (vv. 4–5).

In order to assure themselves of Yahweh's protection, the people must respond by willing submission and by repentance. The future belongs to those who repent by returning to the Lord in faith and turning from paganism.

Isaiah describes the effect of Yahweh's anger upon the Assyrians. They will fall by God's decree and not by the sword of man, and the young men will become forced laborers. The Lord's wrath symbolized by "fire" and "furnace" (v. 9) is in Jerusalem. He has a purpose for Jerusalem and will not permit it to fall.

The future age will be characterized by righteousness and justice (**32:1–8**). The king, leaders, and people will be concerned with the pursuit of wisdom from above. The wise man is blessed in that he represents God's blessedness, being likened to "a shelter," "a refuge," "streams of water in the desert," and shade (v. 2). No longer will God's people be characterized by deafness and blindness, but all will hear, see, and act in accordance with the Word of God. They will hasten to do his will upon the earth in contrast to the past when they hastened to do their own will. In their pursuit of godly wisdom, they will hate folly and wickedness. The wise person pursues what is noble (i.e., godly wisdom). The wise people of God will no longer take their counsel in accordance with earthly standards and be primarily concerned with earthly matters, but rather they will have new standards and concern about the things that pertain to God himself.

The "women" finding rest are characterized by having confidence in the future (**32:9–14**). These women are described as women of ease and complacency (v. 9), not wanting to be troubled. They seem to be happy with the way things are when they should be beating their breasts (v. 12), trembling (v. 11), dressed in sackcloth (v. 11), and troubled (v. 11), because of the thorns and briers which rob the land of productivity. The women of Jerusalem are sitting back in ease, while sin destroys the fruit of righteousness and bankrupts the city, leaving her abandoned and forsaken.

Isaiah now returns to the description of the era of righteousness (**32:15–20**). The only way in which folly will change to wisdom and the devastation of the land to blessedness is by a divinely ordered transformation. Restoration is the work of the Spirit, bringing about a return of the blessings of God on his people and on the earth. The creation will be renewed, wisdom enthroned, righteousness established, and peace restored to the people of God. The wise will experience the blessings of God in every area of their lives.

Reliance on Yahweh is one of the major emphases in these chapters. In response, God's people wait for the fullness of redemption. As Christians we believe the day of redemption is closer since the coming of the Lord Jesus. Yet, along with the saints of the Old Testament, we must have a real sense of hope and longing for the fullness of redemption to which the prophet bears witness.

E. Distress and help (33:1–24). God's judgment ("woe") rests on those who have enjoyed absolute power in this world (**33:1–6**). Because they have caused great devastation on this earth, they must answer to the Lord. When he comes he will sound a loud battle cry (v. 3) to avenge himself on the nations.

This judgment on the ungodly is in response to the prayer of the godly. The godly have been asking for Yahweh's grace to appear to them because they have been suffering in this world while the ruthless hordes were controlling it. Their hope has been that Yahweh's strength might be revealed to them in salvation. Yahweh comes as King (v. 5), seated on his throne of judgment to dispense justice and righteousness. The benefits of Yahweh's rule for his people are many: salvation, a firm foundation, and wisdom. The godly experience salvation and practice wisdom and knowledge in the fear ("awe") of the Lord.

Isaiah shows that the benefits of the messianic kingdom will be limited to the godly (**33:7–16**). The enemies of the kingdom from both within and without will be destroyed. For this reason, the prophet addresses the men of Ariel (v. 7). Scholars are in general agreement that the phrase *brave men* (NIV) may be understood as a reference to Ariel (cf. 29:1).

The proud cry because their plots have been frustrated. They have not been able to avert the very thing that they feared. The highways will become desolate, the judicial processes will be interrupted, and the land will be devastated by enemies.

Yahweh will arise in judgment. The works of the godless will consist of little more than "chaff" and "straw" (v. 11). All their selfish efforts within the covenant community will be burned up. Who, then, can come through the consuming fire? Only those who have walked righteously and have spoken uprightly and have hated bribery and oppression (v. 15; cf. Pss. 15; 24:3–5). The godly will receive protection and provision from the Lord.

The godly will see not only Yahweh's coming in great vengeance and fury to judge the wicked, but also the glory of Yahweh in its full and radiant beauty (**33:17–24**). The realm of Yahweh's rule will be extended, but there will be no place for the wicked in his kingdom. Zion, the city of God, will be full of peace like a river where no hostile ships can sail (v. 21).

Yahweh the majestic one will be for his people and will provide for them a river of life (v. 21; Rev. 22:1). The songs of Zion celebrate the glory, beauty, and rivers (or springs) that are to be found in the city of Zion. Yahweh will be present as the King, Judge, and Lawgiver of his people. He will rule, guide, and teach his people so they will know how to live in his presence. The new age will bring renewal and a deep awareness of forgiveness.

V. Cataclysmic Judgment (34:1–17)

Again Isaiah returns to the theme of God's anger against the world. God's judgment will effect complete destruction, leaving the world uninhabited.

In powerful language Isaiah calls upon all nations to hear the Word of God. All nations are the objects of the Lord's anger. The judgment is likened to a great slaughter or sacrifice (vv. 1–2). On earth the slain will be everywhere; corpses will stink and blood will cover the mountains. In heaven constellations will disappear.

Isaiah focuses on Edom as representative of the nations. Yahweh's judgment on Edom will be similar to what he will do to the whole world. Edom is under the "ban" of the Lord (v. 5c). The term *ban (ḥerem)* expresses Yahweh's decree to destroy a people for his own purposes. The sword will pierce Edom and fill the country with blood as though a great sacrifice has taken place. The day of God's judgment is the day of vengeance on his enemies and of the vindication ("retribution") of his people.

After people and animals are destroyed, the land itself will become worthless and desolate forever because of the brimstone and pitch that will cover it (v. 10). It will revert to a wilderness with thorns and nettles, a place fit only for animals.

All things will be subject to God's judgment. When Yahweh comes in judgment there will be no way of escaping. Yet there is the promise that those who belong to Yahweh are heirs of the new age.

VI. The Day of God's Glory (35:1–10)

This chapter forms the other side of the discussion of the day of the Lord's vengeance (34:8; 35:4). Here, the prophet portrays the glories that await the people of God. Whereas the "day of vengeance" (34:8) is characterized by the sword and desolation, the day of the Lord's deliverance is characterized by his glory and sustenance. Isaiah brings out the nature of the glorious kingdom, which will affect all creation—people as well as nature itself. Although the country has been laid desolate like the wilderness because of Yahweh's judgment, the desolation will give way to the glory of Lebanon and the majesty of Carmel and Sharon. There will be rejoicing, gladness, blossoming, and shouts of joy. The people will see the glory of their God reflected in the restoration of nature. They will also experience a sense of renewal, as he assures them that their "salvation" includes a salvation from their enemies and restoration. There is no place for fear in God's kingdom.

Restoration comes to those who are in need: the blind, the deaf, the lame, and the mute (vv. 5–6). The people who rejected God's way and suffered the consequences in judgment and alienation will again be the objects of his unmerited favor. They, like Israel of old, will see God's glory, experience his presence, protection, and guidance, and taste of his provisions in the wilderness.

The word of promise pertains to the postexilic community following the Jews' return to Palestine from Babylon and Persia. Yet the language of these verses transcends the experience of any ordinary road. The highway is characterized by two qualities: holiness and joy. Its use is limited to those who are holy and have been cleansed from defilement. The people who walk in it are described as "the redeemed" (vv. 9–10), who are in right relationship with God. The highway is the place where God brings full deliverance to his people and where he supplies their physical and spiritual needs. Hence, those who walk on the highway will be full of joy as they march toward "Zion" (v. 10). The redemption of which the prophet speaks will culminate in that day when Jesus comes to restore the present earth to himself.

VII. Hezekiah (36:1–39:8)

These chapters are virtually identical to the account recorded in 2 Kings 18:13–20:19. The historical background of chapters 36 and 37 lies in the events of 701 B.C., when the forces of Sennacherib devastated Judah and her fortified cities. Several years prior to this (705–702 B.C.), Hezekiah became sick. His illness and prayer are recorded in chapter 38, while his foolish act of revealing the royal treasures to the Babylonian envoys is found in chapter 39.

A. Challenge and deliverance (36:1–37:38). The pious response of Hezekiah to the intimidation of the Assyrian field commander is also recorded in 2 Kings 18:13, 17–19:37. Isaiah omits the account of Hezekiah's submission and payment of tribute (2 Kings 18:14–16). Apparently the canonical emphasis in Isaiah is on the Assyrian pride, the godly response of Hezekiah, and on God's miraculous deliverance.

Sennacherib's field commander accuses Hezekiah of overt rebellion by forming an alliance with Egypt (**36:1–22**). He attempts to undermine confidence in the Lord by playing down Hezekiah's reforms, threatening the people with intimidation, falsely arguing that the Lord is not able to deliver them, and by claiming that the Lord is on his side. Hezekiah's officers report the threats to Hezekiah with their clothes torn as a token of mourning. They themselves have not answered the challenges in accordance with the royal command.

The historical reconstruction of the international events that led to Jerusalem's deliverance is a complex problem. The trust of the king, Isaiah's restraint from saying "I told you so," the prayer of Hezekiah, and the word of the Lord through Isaiah reveal remarkable wisdom on the part of Hezekiah and Isaiah and the great concern of the Lord for the Davidic kingship and Jerusalem. This is fully consonant with Isaiah's emphases on Zion and God's protection of his people against foreign invaders (chaps. 28–33).

B. Hezekiah's illness (38:1–22). Hezekiah's psalm of lament and thanksgiving has no parallel in 2 Kings. The superscription *a writing* (*miktāb*, v. 9) may be a corrupt form of the musical term *miktām*, a heading found in Psalms 16; 56–60. The text of the psalm contains several serious difficulties, and is similar in content to Jonah's prayer (Jon. 2) and Job's speeches (e.g., chap. 7).

In lamenting his early death, Hezekiah compares it to pulling down a tent and to material taken off the loom before being completed (v. 12). Like a bird he made a noise in his anguish, but it seemed as if the Lord, like a lion, was intent on mauling him to pieces.

In the restoration from sickness, he experiences the joy of health and God's never-failing love. In response to God's kindness, he vows to walk humbly before God, to praise him, and to declare to the next generation the "faithfulness" of the Lord.

C. Envoys from Babylon (39:1–8). The account of the Babylonian messengers sent by Merodach-Baladan parallels that of 2 Kings 20:12–19. It functions here as a transition to the oracles of comfort (chaps. 40–48), which presuppose the exilic situation of Judah in Babylon. Because of Hezekiah's pride in his possessions, Isaiah proclaims God's judgment of exile into Babylon in another generation. Hezekiah's generation will escape that judgment, but the exile of Judah is inevitable.

VIII. The Beginning of Restoration (40:1–48:22)

A. Prologue (40:1–11). The context for reading Isaiah 40–48 is given in these verses. Isaiah affirms that the exile will end. The people of God have gone into exile because of their sins. The exile is therefore an expression of God's judgment. The exile is first a just judgment; second, it is a form of restitution for damages. Israel and Judah not only have abandoned Yahweh, but also have detracted from Yahweh's glory by giving it to idols. The exile was a time in which God's people could reflect on what they had done; this period of reflection was a way of paying the damages in order to be restored to fellowship with Yahweh. The statement "she has received from the LORD's hand double for all her sins" (v. 2) is an allusion to the Old Testament laws of restitution (Exod. 22:4, 7, 9).

At God's appointed time a proclamation of "comfort" comes to his people (**40:1–5**). Yahweh will come to help his own. In the Hebrew text the verb *comfort* is in the plural, but it is not clear who the comforters are. The prophet and those who follow him are charged with giving comfort to God's people. The message of comfort was also proclaimed by Jesus and is continued by all faithful ministers of the Word of God. The content of the message pertains to the coming era of the renewed relationship between Yahweh and his people, an era in which forgiveness is proclaimed and experienced. The fulfillment of this word takes us from the time of the restoration from exile all the way to the return of Jesus and the establishment of the new heavens and earth. It is for this reason that Isaiah 40–66 is so important for the church of Jesus Christ; we too are the beneficiaries of the fulfillment of the promises of God's Word.

The announcement of the coming salvation takes place in the desert (v. 3), representative of the experience of alienation. Where the people of God are in need of deliverance, the announcement comes to them that the Lord is coming. All of nature prepares for his theophany, so as to prepare a giant road through valleys and across mountains. The promise is given that all "mankind" (lit. flesh) will see the "glory of the LORD" (v. 5).

The prophet again hears a voice commanding him to speak of what he has seen (**40:6–8**). He explains the vision in terms of blessing and judgment. The judgment of the Lord will come upon all flesh, because they are nothing but grass and like the flowers of the field—here today and gone tomorrow. When the sovereign Lord comes in power to rule, the nations will be like nothing in his presence.

The emphasis on promise is more obvious. The "word of our God stands forever" (v. 8). This is the word of promise pertaining to the coming era of restoration. "Good tidings" must be proclaimed to Zion so that everyone may hear. The good news is focused in the presence of the Lord: "Here is your God!" (v. 9). He comes with power against the adversaries and with a reward for his own. The divine Warrior delivers and leads his own people like "lambs." What a Savior! What a gospel!

B. Disputations (40:12–31). Five questions are raised in the context of the proclamation of the establishment of Yahweh's kingship. These five questions, rhetorical to a large extent, are a literary device to remove any doubt from the minds of the godly as to the certainty of the establishment of the kingdom and to instill a sense of awe for Yahweh himself.

By means of the questions introduced by the word *who* (**40:12–17**; cf. Job 3:8–22), Isaiah affirms that Yahweh alone is the Creator-God. He needs no counselors. His sovereignty extends to all of creation, and especially over the nations, which are like a "drop" in the bucket or like a piece of "dust" on the scales (v. 15).

Yahweh is unique in that no one can compare him with anything which the human mind may imagine (**40:18–20**). He is not to be likened to idols, which are powerless and fully dependent on human craftsmanship.

The God of Israel is seated "above" the earth (**40:21–24**). He is the great King, the sovereign Judge over all the world. Yahweh himself oversees all that the nations do. At *his* time he will bring the nations to judgment. Even as grass is scorched and dried up, so Yahweh will bring the nations to nothing.

Yahweh is the Creator-God whose might is revealed in the stars of the sky (**40:25–26**). The Babylonians deified the stars and constellations, but they too are the work of the Creator-God.

The people are disheartened. They wonder whether God is truly able to establish his kingship (**40:27–31**). Yahweh may be the Creator of heaven and earth, know all of his creation by name, and hold the judges and rulers of this earth accountable for their actions, but does he still have concern for his people? The prophet affirms Yahweh's concern for their situation by focusing their attention on God's nature. He is the everlasting God, Yahweh, the covenant God, the Creator of heaven and earth. He tirelessly works out his plan of salvation for his people. Their restoration is based on his nature. He will renew the strength of his people, but this is contingent upon their willingness to submit themselves to him.

C. Deliverance (41:1–44:23). The message of the consolation (vv. 8–20) is enclosed by two arguments against the nations (vv. 1–7, 21–29). These arguments are addressed particularly to Israel to assure her that the nations are subject to God's power.

The nations are called to come before God's tribunal (**41:1–7**). He announces the imminence of the judgment being brought by Cyrus, and then asks the nations who is responsible for his success and their demise.

He answers his own question in the declaration, "I, the LORD—with the first of them and with the last—I am he" (v. 4). The nations respond foolishly to the sovereignty of Israel's God. They renew their commitment to idols. The prophet mocks those who are involved in the manufacture of idols. They take the raw materials, beat them smooth with a hammer, then solder them together. The irony employed in this passage highlights the folly of dependence on objects made by man for protection against the power of the nations and especially against the power of Yahweh, the God of Israel.

Israel will be restored to her former status because as Redeemer Yahweh will be loyal to his "servant" (**41:8–20**). Therefore, God's people need not fear the nations.

Though Israel has been guilty of many offenses and has consequently gone into exile, she is still God's servant because of Abraham and Jacob. The election and calling of God are freely given and his love extends to "the ends of the earth" (v. 9). The depth of his care and the strength of his might comfort his disheartened people. He gives strength and will remove any obstacle or opposition. He is Yahweh, the Redeemer, the Holy One of Israel. Although his people are as insignificant as "a worm" by themselves (v. 14), they will become like a "threshing sledge," pulverizing and crushing any obstacle (vv. 15–16). Their fear will turn to great joy in the Holy One of Israel.

Yahweh the Redeemer is able to meet all the needs of his people, whether spiritual or physical. Yahweh will extend his comfort to those who are poor in spirit. He will do everything in order to restore his people to himself. The verbs ("I will make . . . I will turn . . . I will put . . . I will set . . .") express some of the many ways in which Yahweh shows concrete concern for his people. He will not forsake them in their need. Instead, he will provide the thirsty with water and will change conditions so that his people will see the evidences of his love.

The argument of **41:21–29** is a continuation of the first (vv. 1–7). The deities of the nations are unable to do what God does. He can declare from the beginning what is going to happen. He can give signs. He has power over all nations. He can bring adversity as well as prosperity. By contrast, the gods of the nations are powerless. They cannot respond. Therefore, the nations must know that as long as they depend upon their gods they are actually without protection. Yahweh, the God of Israel, will raise up Cyrus. His victories are the outworking of God's plans. Cyrus will at least acknowledge the God of Israel, though not exclusively. The Lord who knows the future reveals the good news of his accomplishments in history according to his plan for his own people. The idols are mere vanity.

The identity of the servant of the Lord has long been a subject for discussion. In this context several arguments favor identifying the servant first with Israel (cf. 41:8–9), and then in a greater way with the Messiah in whom the perfection of servanthood is found. The language about the election, calling, and particular tasks of the servant fits in very well with the Old Testament language about Israel. The Servant Songs (42:1–9; 49:1–13; 50:4–9; 52:13–53:12) clearly reveal God's expectations of Israel and also how the Messiah, "the faithful" Servant-Son, alone fulfilled all God's expectations, especially in his vicarious suffering.

The servant is described as one in whom Yahweh has delight and whom he has elected (**42:1–4**). The language of election is an affirmation of the servant's continued existence and takes us back to the Abrahamic covenant, where God himself swore that he would be faithful to his covenant with Abraham's descendants.

The description of the Holy Spirit being "on" the servant is an Old Testament expression signifying a renewal of God's presence, by which God's servant is better equipped to serve him. The servant's task is to bring "justice" to the nations (vv. 1, 4), which is identical to the purpose of the coming messianic king (9:7; 11:4). "Justice" here signifies neither religious nor legal practices, but the rule of Yahweh on earth. The servant is tender, gentle, and faithful, and as such, there is a clear allusion to Jesus Christ. The nations are waiting for their inclusion in the kingdom. The ministry of the servant will last until the fullness of the kingdom has been established.

Yahweh the Creator-God has called the servant to be a light to the nations (**42:5–9**). He will make his mission a success by extending the covenant to the Gentiles. The messianic nature of Israel is to so affect the earth that all nations will be blessed through her and will join with her in expressing their faith in Yahweh.

Yahweh's jealousy for his glory assures his continued presence with his people. He will open the eyes of the blind, free the prisoners, and do whatever is necessary to establish his kingdom on earth, in fulfillment of his word to the patriarchs (Gen. 12:1–3) and through the prophets. The restoration of the Jews and the inclusion of the Gentiles express the "new age" planned and revealed beforehand.

Isaiah leads the godly community, including the Gentiles, to praise Yahweh, the victorious king (**42:10–13**; cf. 44:23; 49:13; 52:9). The nations are called upon to join together with the godly of Judah to sing "a new song" (v. 10). Two reasons for praising Yahweh are given by the prophet. First, Yahweh has created a new era. He has opened up a new perspective by redeeming his people to be "a light to the nations." Even the people in the wilderness of Kedar and in the Edomite city of Sela are invited to join in praise of the God of Israel (v. 11). His people praise him also, because the Lord rouses himself for battle like a mighty warrior (Exod. 15:3, 16). Zealous for his kingdom, he will not allow enemy nations to trample his rights.

Yahweh has been patient with the nations for a long time (**42:14–17**). Now he is ready to act on behalf of his people. When he comes, nothing can stop him. He is like a woman in labor who must give birth. He has the power to destroy and to make things desolate, yet he also has the power to redeem his people. His people are the blind who need light and guidance. Yahweh will build his kingdom while judging the nations and demolishing paganism.

Israel is a blind and deaf servant (**42:18–43:7**). Because of her unwillingness to respond to Yahweh, she was oppressed and exiled as an expression of Yahweh's anger. Israel's exile was evidence of God's rejection, but her redemption is an expression of his love.

Israel's formation was not a mistake. God elected ("created," "formed") Israel. He made them to be his people by calling them to be his. He loves his people and will do anything to redeem them. Regardless of how difficult the circumstances or how far he has to bring his people, *he is with them*. He is their God by covenant, the Holy One who has consecrated them, their Redeemer. He will give up nations such as Egypt, Cush (Ethiopia), and Seba (a region south of Ethiopia) in exchange for the remnant of his people, his "sons" and "daughters," who are called by his name (vv. 6–7). Thus, both the experience of rejection and the affirmation of redemption are the outworking of God's will, and are expressions of his fatherly concern for his children.

Over against the magnificent portrayal of the future of God's people is present reality: Israel is still blind and deaf (**43:8–13**). In spite of this condition, however, God still has a future for them. They will be witnesses to his majesty and authority over the nations. He cannot use the nations for this purpose because they have given themselves over to idolatry. God's people should know only Yahweh, having experienced his deliverance.

The phrases *I am he* (v. 10b) and *I am God* (v. 12) signify that only Yahweh, the God of Israel, is God. He is also the powerful Redeemer who has already shown his ability to his people. Yahweh as the God of his people has revealed himself by words as well as deeds so that all might know that he is the only true God.

In their need Yahweh reminds his people repeatedly that he is their Redeemer, the Holy One of Israel, "the Lord" (Yahweh), their King (**43:14–21**). In their self-doubt, they must never doubt him. The God who redeemed his people from Egypt will bring down Babylon and deliver his people from exile. The old, old story of the Passover and the miraculous journey through the Red Sea is dwarfed in comparison with the "new thing" (v. 19). This "new thing" refers to the new era of forgiveness, restoration, and God's presence. The servant of Yahweh, the people whom he has chosen, will be refreshed. The rivers of water speak not only of the spiritual refreshment but also about the manner in which Yahweh will take care of the physical needs of his people in bringing them out of exile and into the Promised Land. The very purpose of the deliverance is that the people may praise Yahweh upon experiencing the blessings of redemption and restoration.

The postexilic Jewish community enjoyed the benefits of restoration from exile, resettlement in the land of Canaan, and the physical and spiritual blessings of God's presence. This progressive restoration was intensified, however, in the coming of the Messiah who gives the water of life (John 4:14). Yet, the *final* restoration of all things will bring with it the climactic fulfillment of these words.

God's people do not deserve his love (**43:22–28**). God's people have failed to honor him as God by neglecting to present offerings and sacrifices. Yet the nature of God does not change. He is compassionate and gracious and ready to forgive his people (Exod. 34:6–7; Ps. 103:3, 11–14). Because of his unchanging love, the people are called upon to turn from their state of sin and to return to Yahweh.

From its beginnings, Israel has been a nation of sinners. Kings, priests, and "false" prophets rebelled against the Lord. Israel can in no way claim innocence in a case against God. Therefore, Israel has been destroyed and disgraced. God is vindicated in his judgment.

Regardless of Israel's past, she is still the servant of Yahweh (**44:1–5**). Her future lies in her election. Israel is transformed by God's grace into a new creation. The new nature of the people is described in a threefold way. First, the Spirit of the Lord is poured on the people (v. 3). The presence of the Spirit is an expression of God's intent to use the people as his servants and to equip them for his service. Second, the blessing of God will rest more markedly on their offspring (vv. 3–5). The very process of internal renewal affects generations to come. In contrast to the past generations of faithlessness (43:27), there will now be generations of faithful people, blessed by the Lord. Third, the covenant will be renewed not only with Israel, but also with Gentiles who will call on the Lord and join in Israel's heritage (v. 5).

The certainty of the future of God's people is guaranteed by Yahweh's kingship (**44:6–23**). He is Yahweh, King of Israel, Redeemer, and Lord of Hosts. There is no god like him, because he foretells what is to come. Since the God of Israel knows and controls the future, his people need not fear. God's purpose for them will stand; they *will* be his witnesses.

How different are idols from "the Rock" of Israel! In the form of a satire the prophet depicts the folly of idolatry. Idols are, after all, the work of man, and characterized by several human limitations. First, even the best artisans have human limitations. Second, idols are nothing more than creations fashioned by the best of human instruments. Third, idols are also limited by the materials from which they are made. They are made from wood, a material which is hardly appropriate to use in the production of a precious object. How can one distinguish which piece of wood is more appropriate for worship and which is to be used to kindle a fire? Clearly the whole idol industry is the work of humans and is characterized by the physical limitations of human weaknesses, the instruments, and the material itself. The pursuit of idolatry is irrational and leads to irrationality. Idolatrous people will not be able to respond appropriately to Yahweh because their eyes are shut and their hearts are hardened (v. 20). They are given to immorality and idolatry and have no way of turning back.

This section closes with a restatement of the uniqueness of Israel's God (vv. 21–22). The Lord has elected, called, and forgiven his people. He calls them to repent by returning to him, their Redeemer. The greatness of God's forgiveness and love is brought out in a hymn in which nature is called upon to rejoice in the outworking of God's plan of redemption. Nature itself awaits fulfillment of this plan and the revelation of the glory of the people of God.

D. Yahweh's sovereignty (44:24–47:15). Yahweh is the Redeemer and has the power to renew his people (**44:24–28**). Within Yahweh are two creative forces: the force to create (recreate) and the force to redeem. Yahweh is the Creator of the heavens and the earth. However, he also recreates everything in accordance with his purpose. This restoration ("recreation") makes the earth habitable for his people—an integral part of their redemption. Every act in the progression of redemption confirms his Word. While in exile, Israel needed the reassurance that Jerusalem would be repopulated and rebuilt and that the temple would be restored. The power of Yahweh in creation, renewal, and redemption stands in stark contrast to the impotence of the practitioners of magic and divination. Yahweh overturns the signs of the diviners and negates the wisdom of the sages. In spite of all the Babylonian claims to wisdom and magical powers, he will raise up Cyrus the Persian to initiate a new stage in the history of redemption. The postexilic era of "reconstruction" is a resumption of his redemptive activities which will culminate in the new heavens and earth and in the New Jerusalem.

Isaiah **45:1–8** develops the role of Cyrus in God's redemptive plan. Cyrus has been raised up and empowered by Yahweh to accomplish God's kingdom purposes. He has been anointed for the particular purpose of accomplishing God's work on earth. Therefore, it is even possible to call him "the anointed one," a designation generally limited to the kings of Israel and Judah.

God's purpose in raising up Cyrus is twofold. First, Cyrus will be raised up for the sake of Israel in order to be an instrument of redemption (v. 4). Second, Cyrus will cause the nations to recognize that Yahweh, the God of Israel, is the only true God. He alone has power to change light into darkness, adversity into prosperity, and vice versa (v. 7). The very designations "I am the LORD" and "I, the LORD, am doing these things" (vv. 6–7) express the authority of the God of Israel in fulfilling his covenantal obligations and general governance of the earth. This indirect encouragement to Israel is to assure those living in darkness and those experiencing adversity that Yahweh has the power to reverse their situation.

In another hymn (v. 8), the prophet rejoices in the salvation of the Lord which is expressed in a temporal extension of his righteous rule. Cyrus is the instrument, but the Lord is the Author of it all.

The nations are called upon to present their argument in the very presence of God (**45:9–13**). Since they do not have confidence in the God of Israel, they have questioned what Yahweh is doing. Yahweh is the Potter and mankind is nothing but clay in his hands. Yahweh's particular concern with the earth extends to mankind at large.

The Creator-God is the Redeemer-God who will establish righteousness on earth, beginning with the restoration from exile and the rebuilding of Judah.

The nations—represented by Egypt, Cush, and Seba (v. 14)—will seek the favor of God's people, having witnessed in the events of history that God is present with them (**45:14–17**).

It is likely that verse 15 continues their confession, as the nations have not known the God of Israel and express a desire to know the Savior of Israel. Israel's salvation is of the Lord, and is therefore lasting; idolatry brings only disgrace and ruin.

Yahweh, the Creator of heaven and earth, shows his peculiar interest in mankind by revealing that he created the earth to be inhabited (**45:18–19**). He will never destroy it. Therefore, he chose the seed of Jacob and revealed himself to them. His Word is open ("not . . . in secret"), righteous (NIV in truth), and "right" (v. 19). He has revealed his decrees, and their fulfillment confirms that he is victorious and faithful.

The survivors of God's judgment are invited to judge for themselves (**45:20–25**). Idols cannot foretell or control the future. Only Yahweh, the God of Israel, is able to execute his righteous plans for redeeming his people. The nations must turn to Yahweh and join freely in God's salvation—or else under compulsion at the great judgment of the nations.

At the final judgment of God, all nations will be "put to shame" (v. 24). "Shame" is that state in which one is without help, without escape, without God, and thus, completely disgraced. The righteous will rejoice in the victory, glory, and praise which Yahweh will extend to them. They will find that Yahweh is truly righteous in that he brings about all his promises. Not only will they rejoice in Yahweh's victories but also they will be assured that their descendants will be the beneficiaries of God's goodness.

The fall of Babylon is first portrayed by the carrying off of her gods (**46:1–13**). The exile of Babylon's gods is symbolic of God's intervention on behalf of Israel. The inability of Babylon's gods to save her stands in stark contrast to the power of Yahweh. Therefore, the prophet concludes by calling upon Israel to listen and respond to God because his salvation is near.

As their gods are being carried off, the people of Babylon make every effort to save them, but to no avail. Bel is the title given to Marduk, god of the capital city of Babylon. His title is related to the Hebrew word *Baal* ("Lord," "Master"). The god of the city of Borsippa was Nebo, Marduk's son, to whom wisdom and learning belonged. The political power represented by Bel and the wisdom represented by Nebo will be unable to deliver the idols of Babylon, much less the people.

In contrast, God has taken pains to carry and care for Israel, like a mother, and purposes to remain faithful. His signature affixed to this promise is "I am God" (v. 9).

The Babylonian gods are incapable of hearing or delivering those who depend upon them. Not so with Yahweh, who answers his people when they call on him in their distress.

Yahweh has revealed that he alone is God. As God, he is the Creator, Planner, and Executor of everything that has taken place on earth. His plan includes Cyrus, who is compared to a "bird of prey" (v. 11). Though stubborn Israel does not deserve it, God's salvation is very near. The future of God's people is based on God's full and free salvation. The Lord will be victorious ("righteous").

Babylon is portrayed as a "virgin" who will lose her genteel, cultured life (**47:1–4**). Her status will be reduced to that of a slave girl who, scantily dressed, works with the millstones and grinds flour. The virgin daughter of Babylon is symbolic of the whole empire. The judgment on Babylon is an expression of vindication of the Redeemer and Holy One of Israel who delivers his people from their oppressors.

Babylon is also portrayed as "the eternal queen" (**47:5–7**). She ruled over the nations like a queen mother, but showed no mercy to the subject nations. She showed no accountability to God as she ruled.

The fame of Babylon is a claim to autonomy, but also to deity (**47:8–11**). The language "I am" and "there is none besides me" (v. 8) is the language usually reserved for Yahweh and his claim that he alone is God.

Although the Babylonians had used all kinds of magic spells to secure their future, sudden disaster will overtake them. Though Babylon had used her wisdom to plot military strategies and avert political economic disasters, she could not match the wisdom and power of God. A disaster has been planned and there is no way that Babylon can ward off the purposes and plan of God. Whereas Babylon prided herself on her ability to predict and prevent, the God of Israel suddenly overwhelms her in his judgment.

The prophet sarcastically urges the people to devote themselves a little more to their magic and sorceries: there may still be some answers forthcoming from the established Babylonian systems of divination (**47:12–15**). However, these systems will prove ineffective against the God of Israel. The prophet goes to another area which was also well developed in Babylon: astrology. He calls upon Babylon to turn to the astrologers and the many counselors that they may be able to save Babylon from her fall. The irony is strong. The counselors and astrologers are compared to stubble which is quickly burned and of little use.

The prophet began by portraying Babylon's

gods being carried into exile (46:1–2) and concludes with the picture of the inability of her wise men, astrologers, and diviners to help the nation out of her great trouble. Her religious, political, and intellectual systems will completely break down.

Man's political, religious, and intellectual systems may work for a long time as did the system in Babylon. They may be revitalized and altered to meet changing conditions. However, any system which works for its own glory and for the autonomy of mankind, whether on a national or individual basis, cannot deliver people at a time when deliverance is most needed. By means of this solemn statement, the prophet has contrasted the failure of human systems over against a God who is able to deliver and establish his eternal kingdom.

E. Proclamation of restoration (48:1–22). Yahweh has planned everything that has happened and will happen upon this planet. However, the events themselves are directed toward the creation of a new era. Though God's people may fail, Yahweh himself remains faithful to introduce and bring in that new era. The new era is not eschatological in the sense that it is far off. Instead, like the judgment, it is always near. The restoration of the Jewish people from exile introduced this era in a grand way. Its future lies hidden in the revelation of God's name, which will be manifested in the glory, righteousness, and salvation of his people.

Though God's people claim to lean on Yahweh, swear by Yahweh, and point to Jerusalem as the holy city, they do not show their covenant relationship in their daily lives (**48:1–8**). They are faithless, without any righteous deeds, and stubborn. Though they claim to belong to Yahweh's "city," the city of the great king (v. 2), their life-style is in direct rebellion against him. Though Yahweh has revealed that all rebellious people will be exiled, they receive the good news of a "new" beginning. It is the new era in which Yahweh begins the restoration of Israel which will eventually include a recreation of the heavens and the earth. It will be a time especially characterized by fulfillment of the promises of God.

By means of repetition the prophet calls attention to the ground of salvation (**48:9–11**). He repeats the expression *for my own name's sake* three times (vv. 9, 11). The reason for the future salvation does not lie in Israel, but in God himself. For the sake of his own honor he restrains his anger. The restraint of God is a loving restraint as he does not unleash the fullness of his anger upon his people. Yahweh is intent on purifying a people unto himself through adversity.

The name *Yahweh* signifies that God keeps covenant by fulfilling all of the promises he has made (**48:12–16**). He is the first and the last (v. 12). By "the first," the prophet signifies the God who has been involved in the work of creation and with his people in exile. By "the last," Isaiah signifies the new era which is to be introduced at the fall of Babylon and the decree of Cyrus, also designated the era of "new things" (v. 6). Yahweh himself directs the history of redemption from beginning to end. He has not spoken or dealt secretly, but rather has made it clear that he has planned everything that comes to pass, including the mission of the servant (v. 16). The identity of the servant is not made clear, and opinions vary (Cyrus, the prophet, the messianic servant).

Yahweh is the Redeemer of his people, their covenant God and Teacher (**48:17–19**). The Teacher-God instructs his people that they might succeed. However, Israel has been unresponsive and, as such, has missed the fullness of the covenantal blessings. Instead of seeing their population explode to the point of being like the sand of the seashore, the number of people has been reduced. Instead of experiencing the peace that comes from Yahweh's victories over the enemies, they have been subjugated. Israel has lost God's great blessings because of its stubbornness.

The prophet calls the people to leave Babylon (**48:20–22**). The coming out of Babylon marks the beginning of the era of restoration. For that reason it is important to begin seeing that all of the blessings of restoration, beginning with the return from exile and extending to the coming of Jesus Christ, are expressions of the new covenant. Though Jesus would come more than five hundred years later, the benefits of Israel in the land are benefits based on and in anticipation of the finished work of Christ. Though in one sense they are still under the old covenant, in a greater sense they are already under the new covenant. The people respond to Yahweh and his Word. The Spirit of God is present in a greater way after the exile than before. There is a real joy among the people of God because they have experienced the return from exile as a token of God's redemption and kingship.

For this reason the people are to joyfully proclaim what God has done on their behalf. All the nations must hear that Yahweh has restored his people to be his servants. Yahweh has been faithful to his promises by providing water out of the rock for them. The God of the exodus will continue to redeem his people. However, the effect of redemption is limited to those who have the spiritual marks of Abraham.

IX. Reconciliation and Restoration (49:1–55:13)

A. The Servant of the Lord (49:1–13). These verses portray the various characteristics of the servant of God. The nations are called upon to pay attention to the servant even though he is despised by them.

The servant of God is not to be judged by his present or past status, but rather by his election (**49:1–6**). Yahweh himself has called and named his servant. The prophet intimates that there is a twofold purpose in the servant's calling. On the one hand, he is to proclaim the Word, which is likened to a "sharpened sword." On the other hand, he is to be like a "polished arrow" (v. 2). The sword speaks of the prophetic ministry in which the servant, filled by the Word of the Lord, speaks that Word which is able to penetrate the hearts and souls of people. The arrow as an instrument of warfare symbolizes God's judgment on those who do not respond. Yahweh himself will be glorified by his servant. He will continue to use his servant to speak to Israel as well as to the nations. Yahweh's Word will not return to him void and, as such, the servant is guaranteed that his prophetic mission will be successful.

The servant responds by looking at his own condition. He realizes that he has not been successful and asks why he must continue to labor. God's response is that he will shortly reward the servant with success. The tribes of Jacob will be restored as a part of God's mission that they might be a "light" to the nations.

Who is "the servant"? According to 41:8–9; 44:2; and 49:3, "the servant" is a prophetic designation for the restored people of God, Israel. Yet, according to verses 1–6 the servant has a mission to the nation and to the Gentiles. These words are applicable to the restored community of Jews in Judea and the Diaspora, but in a greater sense they apply to the mission of our Lord (see Luke 2:32; Acts 26:23). Since that time the mission of the servant has become the mission of the church, the new people of God.

The success of the servant's mission depends on Yahweh (**49:7**). He, "the Redeemer" and "the Holy One of Israel" (two times), is faithful to his election. Though the servant be ridiculed, impoverished, persecuted, and oppressed, the kingdom of God will be established on earth and all the sons of the great King will receive glory. The nations and kingdoms which are outside of the kingdom of God will be put down. This verse contains an allusion to the nature of the mission of Jesus Christ. He suffered, and through his suffering obtained glory. Jesus, after his resurrection and glorification in heaven, is the great Judge who will put down all unsubmissive nations and is the One before whom all the nations must eventually lie prostrate.

The phrase *the time of my favor* signifies the era of Yahweh's gracious acceptance of his people (**49:8–13**). It denotes an era of proclamation of freedom. It marks the renewal of the covenant and the fulfillment of God's promises. The renewal of the covenant finds expression in God's redemption, protection, provision, and guidance. He will remove obstacles and gather his people from all over the Diaspora.

The prophet then bursts out in another hymn of praise. Nature observes and participates in the care, comfort, and relief of the afflicted children of God (v. 13).

B. Zion's surprise (49:14–21). "Zion" is a metaphor for the people of God who lament, asking whether the Lord has completely forgotten them. Yahweh, like a mother, can never forget his children.

Zion is also likened to a mother bereft of her children and abandoned in the ruins. The Lord assures her that he will never forget her because she is "engraved . . . on the palms of my hands" (v. 16). The scattered will return and be so numerous that the land will be too small. The land and its cities will be restored and its enemies will be kept away. The fulfillment of these words applies to postexilic Judaism and extends until the renewal of this earth.

C. Israel's restoration (49:22–26). The nations themselves will become instruments of the redemption of God's people. They will cooperate with God's plans so that the people of God may draw comfort and not be disappointed. The Lord will bring down the nations which seek to harm his people and will not submit to him. "The Mighty One of Israel" will fight the battle for them that the nations may know that he is Yahweh, the Deliverer and Redeemer of his people.

D. Sin and obedience (50:1–9). Because of the great guilt of the people of God and their lack of responsiveness, Yahweh has justly exiled them (**50:1–3**). In the past he called them tenderly, but there was no response. He has the power to avert the exile, as seen in the plagues on Egypt, but he acts freely by deciding to let it happen. Yet even though he sent them away, he has not divorced or sold Israel to the creditors.

Who is this obedient and suffering servant (**50:4–9**)? Since his suffering is not unto death and he seems to be untouched by the rejection of man, the servant is probably the prophet himself. The prophet, in pursuit of his prophetic mission, directs himself to the people of God in the hope of being heard and understood. Instead, he is reviled. If 50:4–9 is a restatement of 49:1–6, it is also possible to identify the servant with faithful Israel as a good "disciple" of the Lord.

The servant has a mission to encourage the "weary"—the dejected Jews in exile and all who long for God's redemption. The authenticity of the message is guaranteed by the Lord himself, who teaches and opens the ear of the servant. The servant is a responsive disciple who executes and speaks whatever has been taught. Even in the face of unbelief and opposition he does not hesitate, because of his unique relationship with God and because of his conviction that the Lord will contend for him. No one can bring a charge against him. Over against the victorious outworking of God's plans are the unbelievers who will perish.

The response to the ministry of this servant may be one of faith or further obstinacy. He calls for a wise response rather than a continuation in folly and dark ways. If people continue to insist on walking by their own light, the judgment of God will overtake them and there will be no escape. These verses also form an appropriate transition from chapters 49–50 to 51:1–52:12.

E. Everlasting salvation (51:1–52:12). The theme of the restoration of the people of God is developed in nine strophes (51:1–3, 4–6, 7–8, 9–11, 12–16, 17–23; 52:1–2, 3–6, 7–12). These strophes are connected by the repetition of imperatives (*listen,* 51:1, 4, 7, 21; 52:8; *look,* 51:1–2; *awake,* 51:9, 17; 52:1; and *depart,* 52:11), promises of comfort, and references to creation and redemption.

God's words of comfort (**51:1–3**) are addressed to those who still fear the nations among whom they are dwelling. They believe but have not yet come to the point where their faith is a conquering faith. There are many lingering questions. Will Yahweh restore his people to the land? Will he multiply his people again? Will their enemies prevail once more?

The pursuit of righteousness focuses on God's ordering of all things in accord with his promises. The prophet encourages all who long for the fulfillment of God's Word by pointing to God's work in the past. He promised to multiply Abraham and Sarah's descendants and to bless them (Gen. 17:2, 5–6, 16) and so he did (51:1–2). Their solidarity with Abraham, as they come from the same "rock" and "quarry" (v. 1), should be comforting because God is the same and his promises do not change. Since the people are looking for God's grace, he will comfort Zion. The Lord will restore the land and the people, so that the work of restoration points back to the garden of Eden. His people will again experience his presence as in Eden, and will rejoice in the beginning of God's restoration.

Only the godly constitute the "new people of God," with whom he renews his covenant (**51:4–6**). They receive the words of assurance that God's rule ("the law," "my justice," v. 4) will extend beyond Israel to the nations. They will also see the light. The present heaven and earth must be made into a new creation, characterized by God's triumphant and everlasting rule. Israel and the nations join together in eager expectation of the new heaven and earth.

The comfort of God is limited to those who have appropriated for themselves the "knowledge" of his righteous rule and salvation (**51:7–8**). They do not wait passively; they are God's agents in establishing the new age. They firmly believe in God's plan for them and for the world. Yet in their weakness they need encouragement. These verses essentially repeat the words of comfort previously given: God will judge the wicked and restore all things to his divinely purposed order.

In a most urgent way, reminiscent of the psalms of lamentation (cf. Ps. 44:23), the prophet calls on the Lord to act on a scale grander than the exodus from Egypt (**51:9–11**). Then, God revealed his strong arm by redeeming his people and inflicting plagues and death on the Egyptians (Exod. 7:14–12:23). When God acts in history, the redeemed will experience his deliverance. Their sorrow and sighing will be turned into an everlasting life of great joy.

The Creator-God is the Redeemer-God. He is the Maker of heaven and earth *and* Zion. He comforts his people like no one else (**51:12–16**). His own need not be afraid of people who by their very nature are mortal. He shall free them so magnificently that the oppressors will be unable to oppose his power. He is the Lord, the great Warrior whose name is Yahweh of Hosts ("LORD Almighty," v. 15). The Word of the Lord is true and he will protect his own until he has accomplished the restoration of all things.

The prophet brings the people back to their own situation (**51:17–23**). When God's judgment came on them, there was no word of comfort. The suffering of judgment is metaphorically described as a "cup" (v. 17). The "cup" is an expression of the fullness of the anger of the Lord: "ruin and destruction, famine and sword" (v. 19). Now, he graciously rouses them from their drunken stupor. The Lord who judged them will again defend his people. He removes the cup of judgment from them. He encourages them in that their lot will fall on their oppressors.

In response to their prayer ("awake, awake"

[51:9]), the Lord calls his people to wake up from their stupor (**52:1–2**). He has sovereignly and graciously exchanged the shame of their exile and alienation for the glory of his presence. Jerusalem, the "mother-city," will again be a glorious queen. Her reproach will be removed when the ungodly desist from oppressing. Only a holy people will inhabit the holy city.

Israel's bondage in Egypt and her exile in Babylon were not due to God's inability to deliver them. He freely handed them over, and freely he will deliver them (**52:3–6**). His purpose was that they might witness that he is Yahweh, who is constant and faithful to his people.

The good news of God's kingship is freely proclaimed in Zion (**52:7–12**). The anger of God has subsided. He has cleansed his people and returns to dwell again in their midst. Only those who are "pure," untouched by the defilements of this world, may experience his presence as in the days of the exodus. However, the new exodus is unlike the exodus under Moses in two ways. First, they need not hasten (v. 12) because God will protect them. He will "bare his holy arm" so that all the nations will submit to him in fear. Second, he himself will go before them, instead of merely showing his presence symbolically in the cloud of glory or the ark of the covenant. God's people, the recipients of his fatherly comfort, will be led home triumphantly.

F. The Suffering Servant (52:13–53:12). The servant of the Lord will share the throne with God himself, as he will be "lifted up and highly exalted" (**52:13–15**). He will succeed in his mission, for which reason he is described as acting "wisely" (v. 13). He does what is right and pleases God. The Lord will raise him up to glory. The nations who marvel at his appearance, because the servant was greatly humiliated in his suffering, will witness his glory.

The kings and nations were amazed when they heard about the suffering servant and so are the godly in Israel (**53:1–3**). Therefore, the question "Who has believed?" is raised. The question is meant not only to draw attention to the servant, but also to introduce the servant as the "means" of redemption. Yahweh has chosen to reveal "his arm" through the servant. The "arm of the Lord" is a symbol of the Lord's judgment as well as of his deliverance (cf. Ps. 98:1). In this context it is the means of deliverance for those who trust in the suffering servant.

The servant was characterized by humility. He is compared to a "tender shoot" coming forth out of "dry ground" (v. 2a). He was an ordinary human being and not a king or potentate. The servant was unimpressive and readily rejected by man.

The suffering servant was one who knew sorrows and fully identified with mankind. Not only was he born with little chance of success, he was also extremely vulnerable. He lived as a man among men. This language is most applicable in understanding the nature and mission of Jesus Christ. He was born of the virgin Mary, came from Galilee, and was rejected by the religious leaders and by the people. Jesus stood out because of his wonders, but was ultimately rejected by men.

The rejection of the servant is more graphically described: he was "stricken," "smitten," and "afflicted" (**53:4–6**). He took upon himself the very curse of God. Since God's curse comes on any who break his covenant, the servant was either a great sinner or carried the sins of others. In addition to the language of the curses of the covenant he is described as one who was "pierced" ("wounded"), "crushed," and "punished" (v. 5). He suffered in order that he might bring restoration ("peace" and "healing") between God and man.

The servant suffered not for himself, but rather to bear "our sorrows," "our transgressions," and "our iniquities" (vv. 4–5). The benefits of the vicarious suffering of the servant include reconciliation to God and forgiveness. He carried the sins and guilt of the people; therefore, he was able to bring the people of God back into fellowship with their heavenly Father. All mankind has gone astray, but through the suffering of the servant there is still the possibility for peace and healing. Jesus Christ gave himself that he could be our peace and that through him we could experience healing and restoration of fellowship with the heavenly Father.

The servant himself did nothing wrong (**53:7–9**). He did no violence nor did he speak in a deceptive way. Why, then, did Yahweh lay such suffering upon him? The reason for the suffering must be found in the nature of the judgment of God. The Lord brought him through torture, judgment, death, and finally burial. In these verses Isaiah describes how the servant was oppressed and afflicted, how he did not receive a just sentence. He was put to death and buried like a criminal. Even though his suffering was unjust, the servant accepted his humiliation quietly, patiently, and obediently. He is compared to a lamb which is led to the slaughter or to a sheep when it is being sheared (v. 7). Quietly he received the judgment from God because he bore that judgment for others.

The prophet returns to the blessed effect of

the suffering of the servant (**53:10–12**). The servant's death was not in vain. He had done the Lord's will, even when he was crushed. He suffered as a human "guilt offering." The guilt offering was an expiatory offering in addition to the sin offering. The guilt offering anticipated the suffering of our Lord Jesus Christ. God has accepted the guilt offering of the suffering servant as the basis for extending the benefits of reconciliation and forgiveness. In life he identified with our toil, as a part of the human condition. He suffered as a rebel against God. The Lord rewards him with "life," "offspring" (v. 10), success, and honor. Through him many may be justified. The servant suffered on behalf of others. They share in his benefits, if they turn to him as the means of forgiveness by reconciliation with the heavenly Father.

G. The new covenant (54:1–17). The covenant people are called upon to rejoice because of the change in their condition (**54:1–10**). The sufferings of the past and present will give way to a new era. The people are compared to "a barren woman" (v. 1), a widow (v. 4), and a woman separated from her husband (v. 6).

The blessedness of the reversal from barrenness and desolation is the reward of the servant. The new age will resemble God's graciousness to Sarah, who was barren (Gen. 11:30), but who by God's promise became the mother of nations and kings (Gen. 17:16). The mother's "tent" will be full (v. 2) and the land will be repopulated.

The description of the new condition serves to encourage the people of God not to be afraid or ashamed. In the past they have been ashamed because of the disgrace which they carried. However, the Lord assures them that their shame will be removed. The hope for the future lies in the Lord himself. He will again take his people to himself, because he is their Maker and Husband. He is their great King ("the Lord of Hosts"), their Redeemer, the Holy One of Israel who desires to sanctify his people; he is God of the whole world.

This is a description of the covenant God who graciously renews the covenant with his people. He has abandoned them for a short time only to renew his love with great compassion—*forever.* The length and intensity of the love of God cannot be compared with the shortness of his wrath. The Lord assures his people by oath that he will never be angry with them again. He will never again use exile as an expression of his animosity toward his people. The certainty of the covenant lies in Yahweh himself. The Lord swears that he will never remove his covenantal blessings of peace, mercy, and kindness from his people. The ground for the restoration of the Jewish people lies in the divine oath to be gracious to all those who call upon him. This covenant blessing has been extended by Jesus Christ to all who call on him.

The prophet contrasts the situation of the desolate Jerusalem with its glorious future (**54:11–17**). It had been attacked and disgraced and received no pity or compassion. The glory of the "mother-city" will be great. She will be completely rebuilt as the "New Jerusalem."

Within the city itself the people are blessed. This blessedness is limited to those who are righteous. Their children will know the Lord and will be blessed by him. They will experience the presence and protection of God. They will not fear because Yahweh will destroy every enemy. Nothing can separate them from him. They enter into their heritage from the Lord.

After the exile the Jews experienced some of the benefits as they were restored to the land and lived in the city of Jerusalem and in Judea. Yet, the people of God are still looking forward to the revelation of their glorious city, the New Jerusalem, which will come from above. While on this earth we rejoice in the love which God has shown for his church. We rejoice in having children who know the Lord, and we rejoice in his presence and protection. However, our hope still lies in the day in which our Lord Jesus Christ will reveal his glory.

H. Assurance (55:1–13). Yahweh's invitation to the people is not an esoteric one (**55:1–5**). His call is like the cry of a vendor selling his wares in the marketplace. The Lord calls on anyone and everyone to turn to him as the one who is able to provide for their needs. The open proclamation of the Lord assures that whosoever will may come, including Gentiles. He promises to take care of *all* man's needs. The redemption is gracious and free.

The gift of God is an everlasting covenant, such as the Lord made with David (2 Sam. 7:8–16). The people of God will join with the Davidic Messiah in leading nations into the covenant fellowship. The nations will submit to the witness-bearing role of God's people.

The prophet joins the invitation of Yahweh with a call to the people to have faith in him and to openly show their faith by repentance from their evil works (**55:6–9**). There is still the possibility of reconciliation and forgiveness. Yahweh is greater than man; as such, his thoughts cannot be likened to man's thoughts. Man's thoughts are evil for evil, but Yahweh can be gracious even when he has been hurt, dishonored, and disobeyed. *Now* is the day for the people to come to Yahweh in faith. The prophet calls on the people to respond by signing the contract and seeking him in the present moment.

The certainty of free redemption and the free offer of the gospel lies in Yahweh himself (**55:10–13**). As long as the moment of grace is *here,* Yahweh's invitation will not return to him void. He has planned to call out a people to himself, and in this he will succeed. The prophet likens the power of the Word to the rain and the snow which are useful in germinating the seed and permitting it to develop. The Word of the Lord concerns the redemption and the restoration of all things.

With the postexilic developments, redemption begins. The people are called upon to depart from Babylon. The people who leave are assured that they will be restored to the land and that the land itself will be restored so that instead of briers and thorns, cypress and myrtle will grow up. Even nature joins with the people of God in the restoration and now awaits further restoration. The redemption of God's people from exile is a sign to all the godly that Yahweh is the Redeemer. He calls on his people to have faith in him for their free redemption. The One who led Israel from Egypt and provided for them in the wilderness with manna, meat, and drink again proves himself faithful by redeeming his people from Babylon. Redemption is the sign of the covenant. From the moment of the restoration from exile, all the godly are assured that the new heavens and the new earth and the New Jerusalem will be established because God is the Redeemer.

X. The Glory and Responsibility of Zion (56:1–66:24)

A. Response to redemption (56:1–8). Salvation is the act of God whereby he gathers his people, both Jews and Gentiles, and unites them with himself and with one another (**56:1–2**). To these he extends the privilege of being subjects under his righteous rule along with all its benefits.

The proper response of the people of God is that of covenant loyalty. The Lord expects his people to act like him. He expects that the people who have been justified and thereby have entered into a relationship with him will act in accordance with his own standards. There is a blessing for all who keep the covenant.

The Sabbath is singled out as the sign of the covenant and is representative of all the commandments (**56:3–8**). How one relates to the Sabbath is an indication as to how one relates to the other commandments. The Sabbath commandment, as such, is a barometer of one's spiritual condition.

The Gentile ("foreigner") as well as the eunuch show their commitment to the covenant Lord by keeping the Sabbath. In the past the eunuch could not be a part of the covenant community; there were also limitations on foreigners (Deut. 23:1–8). However, the renewed covenant is extended to those who were previously unfit.

The Lord responds to the needs of those who join his covenant. The eunuch is assured that he will have a remembrance among the people of God. His name will be remembered forever. The foreigner who has been kept away from the worship of the Lord in Jerusalem is assured that he, too, will be able to bring sacrifices and worship the Lord.

The temple will be known as the "house of prayer" for all nations (v. 7b). The prophet looks forward to the new era in which Jews and Gentiles will worship God together. Our Lord Jesus Christ brought together the two folds—the Jews and the Gentiles.

The prophet proclaims the Word of God to the people of his time and at the same time issues a warning to future generations. Since the prophet warns God's people against the dangers of apostasy, faithlessness, and formalism, the exhortation of the prophet still speaks to issues that the people of God face today.

B. Unfaithful leaders (56:9–57:2). The leaders are called "watchmen" (v. 10; cf. Isa. 52:8; Ezek. 3:17; 33:7). Leaders, whether civil or religious, were charged with responsibility for the people of God. They are likened to "mute" and greedy dogs (vv. 10–11)—irresponsible in discharging their responsibility for instructing God's people and greedy for material gain.

The struggle between righteousness and wickedness extends even to Zion. The wicked are those who enjoy the benefits of the covenant community, without committing themselves fully to God and to his righteous purposes. As long as evil is in the world, its dark power seems to overshadow the glory of Zion.

C. Unfaithful people (57:3–13a). The people of God are compared to bad "seed." They are nothing but rebels because they love idolatry in all its forms. They have given themselves over to idolatry and immorality.

Isaiah describes the extent of Judah's apostasy. Wherever they are, the people are corrupt, whether they go to the ravines (v. 6), to the hills (v. 7), stay at home (v. 8), or go to Sheol (v. 9).

The wicked will be left to themselves. The Lord has been patient in not destroying them thus far. Because they have shown no sign of repentance or fear of him, however, they will not stand in the judgment of God. They will fall with the rest of mankind.

D. The future of God's people (57:13b–21). In contrast to the greedy and idolatrous ways of the wicked, the righteous and devout, who walk uprightly and commit their way to the Lord, will have a future. What a contrast between verses 1–2 and 13b! The perishing will have a glorious future, because they have made the Lord their refuge.

The Lord himself initiates the full redemption of his children. All obstacles will be removed for his coming. He is the exalted King, "the high and lofty One," who lives "in a high and holy place" (v. 15). He reaches down to save, revive, and even to dwell with the devout, "who [are] contrite and lowly in spirit" (v. 15). The holy God will allow the humble to dwell with him on his "holy mountain."

If God were to be continually angry the righteous would also lose heart. Therefore, he revives the spirit of his people by words of comfort. He assures the humble that they will receive all that they need for this life and the life to come. In healing his people, the Lord gives them rest and consolation, guidance and protection, and joy. They will be at peace with God. The wicked are compared to a "tossing sea" (v. 20). They will never have a lasting peace.

Thus, the prophet assures the godly that the Lord is intent on providing restoration for his people, though it may take a long time. While on earth, the righteous experience some rest and peace. However, these are but tokens of the grace of God. The fullness of rest and peace will come when the Lord has fully restored the heavens and the earth and when the wicked are no more.

E. True religion (58:1–14). The prophet again calls on the people to look upon themselves in terms of their commitment. The people had their fasts and the Sabbath which were derived from the law. However, even as syncretism and paganism are abominable to God, so is religious formalism. It is not enough for people to *conform* to the law of God if in one or more ways they continue to sin against it. The prophet emphasizes true religion and the rewards of true godliness.

First, the prophet shows what true religion is not (**58:1–9a**). True religion includes obedience to the law of God and a delight in the presence of God, but when sought for a reward it degenerates into formalism or pharisaism. The love of God must show itself in love of one's neighbor. Godliness is shown not by appearing outwardly pious, but by being sensitive to the sufferings of people.

The Lord regards those who fast in humility. To fast in humility is to have regard for God and for others. This regard for others is expressed by giving people a sense of importance and freedom, by giving people food, and by speaking and acting in such a way that brings honor to the people of God. Fasting as an act of humility and contrition can only be acceptable to God if it is an expression of love for God and neighbor.

True godliness shows itself in a concern for justice and a love of the Sabbath (**58:9b–14**). Justice is God's concern, and therefore cannot be limited to the Jewish people under the Law. God is concerned with oppression, slander, and unrighteous acts. The glorious presence of God will dawn on the righteous. The godly are likened to a well-irrigated garden (v. 11b). They are God's appointed instruments of restoration. Such is the ministry of healing and reconciliation which God has given to his people—then as well as now.

The second expectation pertains to the keeping of the Sabbath. The Sabbath was a day in which the people were to give themselves to the worship of the Lord. While doing so, they were also to think about ways of enriching themselves. The prophet calls the people to look upon the Sabbath as a day that the Lord has given to them in which to rest. To rest from one's labors is, first, not to think about personal gain, and second, to do what is right. To call the day a delight is to think about ways in which other people, too, may delight in the day. The Sabbath day is most appropriate as a day in which to do works of mercy in order to give an experience of light and joy to those who are oppressed and distressed.

F. Responsibility (59:1–21). The postexilic experience was marked by disillusionment because God's promises pertaining to the new era were not completely fulfilled. The early church also had to adjust to delay (see 2 Pet. 3:3–10). Isaiah explains that the delay is not because God cannot deliver. Instead of charging God with injustice or unfairness, the community of believers must look at its own sins and shortcomings (**59:1–8**). It is guilty of murder, untruth, and injustice, and buried in all kinds of evil. Israel looks like the nations instead of God's people. The people are like mothers of evil who hatch vipers and cover sin with a veneer as thin as cobwebs.

The community lament contains a moving confession of sin and an expression of Israel's longing for the day of redemption (**59:9–15a**). It will be a day of "light" and rejoicing; darkness and mourning will be dispelled. In the confession, the community expresses sorrow for its shortcomings. The people have sinned against their neighbors. They have scorned justice, fidelity, and integrity and crushed the honest man. The dawning of God's kingdom is related to, but not dependent on, God's people ordering their lives in harmony with his purposes.

Because of the absolute bankruptcy of the people no one is able to deliver them. Only the Lord whose arm is strong to deliver can deal with his people (**59:15b–21**). The Lord is described as a warrior readying himself to aid the godly. He puts on the breastplate, representative of "righteousness," the helmet, representative of "salvation," and the garments, signifying his "vengeance" and "zeal" (v. 17; cf. Eph. 6:14–17). God is concerned about the remnant and his concern is expressed by his coming to judge the wicked, who will be punished according to their deeds. The Lord may delay his judgment, but he sees everything, including the affliction of his people and the evil done to those who call on his name.

The Redeemer God will reveal his glory to the ends of the earth, singling out Zion for his kingdom. The covenant will be renewed by the pouring of his Spirit on them and their children forever, so that all God's people will be inspired to know, do, and speak according to his Word. Paul cites these words in his argument that God will redeem apostate Israel, which has rejected the Messiah (Rom. 11:27).

G. The glory of Zion (60:1–62:12). The delay in the revelation of God's victorious kingdom concerns God's people, but God still expects them to live in accordance with his rule by practicing justice, righteousness, love, and peace. The word of the Lord (59:21) will be fulfilled.

The revelation of God to his people also extends the glory and light—characteristic of the Lord himself—to his people (**60:1–9**). They will be surrounded with glory and light so that the glory of God will be seen. The repetition of the words *light, brightness, shining,* and *glory* is to create a poetic effect.

The light in combination with "thick darkness" sets the background of a theophany. The response of the nations will be twofold. First, they will desire inclusion in the new era which will dawn on Zion (v. 3). Second, they will cooperate by contributing to the welfare of Zion (vv. 4–9). The resources of the nations will be used to "honor the Lord . . . the Holy One of Israel." Riches, herds, flocks, and ships of Tarshish will all be submitted to God.

The tribute and labor of the nations will be used to rebuild Zion as an expression of God's compassion and justice (**60:10–14**). The enemies and oppressors of Zion will receive their just deserts. The walls and gates symbolizing God's kingdom are not for protection; the gates will always be open (v. 11). The Lord will share the spoils of his victory with his people. Furthermore, he will reestablish his glorious presence in their midst. Zion will be called the "city of the Lord" and "Zion of the Holy One of Israel" (v. 14; cf. Ps. 48).

The Redeemer-God will restore the fortunes of Zion (**60:15–18**). They had been forsaken, but will become "the everlasting pride" and "the joy of all generations" (v. 15). They will know that he is their Redeemer. His governance will not only be just, but glorious as well. He will prosper his people greatly with a kingdom of peace and righteousness, in which his victorious rule brings lasting salvation and joy.

The glory of the New Jerusalem is in the experience of God's presence (**60:19–22**; cf. Rev. 21:23; 22:5). The people will all be "righteous," that is, enjoy the benefits of his kingdom: the new creation. The certainty of fulfillment is guaranteed by his signature: "I am the Lord." He will restore everything, especially the New Jerusalem.

Judah and Jerusalem have been assured that Yahweh has a plan for a remnant of the people. They will return from exile. The Lord has promised to restore heaven and earth, to restore the people to himself, and to hasten the day of redemption. The announcement of the year of the Lord's favor means that the Lord is reconciled to man and that man may obtain forgiveness from God. In chapter 61 the Lord himself, together with the prophet, confirms the eternal covenant which cannot be broken.

The person of whom the prophet speaks (61:1–7) is a servant of God. (Technically this is not a Servant Song.) The presence of the Spirit of God (v. 1a) and the anointing and proclamation suggest the purpose of the servant of God. The servant of the Lord, who has been called to proclaim the good news, can be none other than the prophet himself. He has been called to proclaim the acceptable year of the Lord to those in exile, but in a fuller sense the proclamation of the "servant" applies to the ministry of our Lord.

The messages of comfort begin with a call to proclaim loudly the good news of the Lord's forgiveness and restoration of his people. The prophetic proclamation consists particularly of the preaching of "the year of the Lord's favor" (v. 2). In the restoration from exile, the prophets were instrumental in bringing the good news to the captives. Jesus further proclaimed the good news and focused on himself as the one bringing in the era of restoration. He also promised that he would accomplish all when he returns. The year of restoration is not limited to one particular day or year, but extends from the postexilic restoration to the full restoration of heaven and earth.

The proclamation of the acceptable year of the Lord is directly connected to the proclamation of the day of vengeance. The one focuses on God's kindness to his people, whereas the other focuses on God's judgment on the wicked.

"The year of the Lord's favor" is also a prophetic reference to God's administration of grace which culminates in the restoration of all things. This restoration includes the promises of forgiveness and full fellowship with God, and the removal of physical problems, obstacles, and mourning. It is the year of Jubilee, the year of liberation (Lev. 25:10). Jesus applied this word to his healing of the blind, deaf, and lame as a token that God is concerned about our whole being, including our physical welfare.

Finally, the acceptable year of the Lord proclaims comfort to all the people of God. The prophet calls the new people of God "oaks of righteousness" and the "planting of the LORD" (v. 3). Instead of being rejected, the people of God will be accepted and prepared for a great and glorious future.

This redemption, however, is not to be limited to the eschatological future. The prophet quickly moves from the restoration of the people to the restoration of the land. God is also concerned with the ruins and assures his people that the cities will be rebuilt and that this will be funded by the wealth of the nations. The new position of the people of God is expressed by the word *priests* (v. 6). They will be priests of the living God while others take care of menial tasks.

Spiritual benefits are mixed with God's concern for physical well-being. The people have been disgraced in exile, but they are assured that they will have a double portion in the land. The Lord knows that his people have suffered double for all of their sins (40:2) and he gives back what they have missed during the exile. The purpose of the acceptable year of the Lord is to prepare the Lord's people for the fullness of redemption. While they are on earth they receive the firstfruits of redemption. The Jews after the exile experienced restoration of the cities, help from the nations, and productivity of the land. They were comforted by God's grace physically as well as spiritually. Since the coming of our Lord Jesus Christ the people of God are now made up of Gentiles as well as Jews. Our heavenly Father has assured us that he is concerned about our physical well-being. Moreover we are the recipients of the grace, comfort, and forgiveness of God. Yet this message speaks of a greater era in which our heavenly Father will restore heaven and earth through the ministry of Jesus Christ.

The new era is "forever," because the covenant is forever (**61:8–9**). God knows how his people can be unpredictable and faithless; therefore, the outworking of the covenant is not dependent on them. He is faithful. His covenant will accomplish the purpose for which he has made it: that his people may be blessed.

The glory prepared for God's people is likened to the adornments of a bride, bridegroom, and priest (**61:10–11**). She will serve the Lord in the presence of the nations as a priest, adorned with "a crown of beauty" (v. 3), anointed with "oil of gladness" (v. 3), and clothed in "a garment of praise" (v. 3). The new era of the priesthood of all believers will introduce a renewal of God's kingdom.

The prophet prays that the era of God's victorious kingship, bringing full "salvation" to his people, may come soon (**62:1–5**). Then the nations will recognize the glory of Zion, which had been trampled down by the enemies of God. The new names given are descriptive of the new era: "Hephzibah" ("my delight is in her") instead of "Deserted," and "Beulah" ("married") instead of "Desolate" (vv. 3–4). The Lord will rejoice over his people.

Out of concern for his people, the Lord has appointed watchmen (**62:6–12**). The watchmen are not needed for the protection of the city, for Yahweh makes his people secure. The watchmen pray day and night for the full restoration of the people of God. The Lord responds to the prayer by an oath of assurance that he will never again do what he has done to his people. Redemption is certain to come and the prophet calls the people to prepare themselves for the Savior's coming.

The people receive a new name. God sets them apart as a holy people and the redeemed of the Lord: "The Holy People," "The Redeemed of the LORD," "Sought After," "The City No Longer Deserted" (v. 12; see also 60:14, 18; 62:4). These names for the new people of God signify the new relationship, the glory, and the purpose of the people of God.

H. The day of vengeance (63:1–6). Since the Lord is righteous and speaks righteously, the day of vengeance is the day of redemption of God's people (v. 4). In his verdict as the great Judge, he assures the people that he truly is able to save them. Because of his righteousness, his concern for his people, and his great anger, the Lord comes to this world as the great Warrior (v. 1). The portrayal of the judgment of Edom is a picture of God's judgment on the whole earth.

The day of the vindication of the Lord is an expression of the day of the Lord. It is an eschatological event when God brings his cataclysmic judgment upon all the earth.

I. A prayer for God's people (63:7–64:12). Isaiah publicly proclaims the acts of the Lord's love (*ḥesed*) for his people, whom he adopted as his sons (**63:7–14**). He redeemed them in the expectation that they would be loyal to him. However, they were unfaithful sons and opposed his will ("grieved his Holy Spirit," v. 10).

The past era of grace and compassion is over. The godly look back over the history of redemption with a renewed longing to be included. In the past God raised up Moses, and no one could oppose his will. God showed the power of "his glorious arm" (v. 12). He brought the people through the Red Sea and safely into the Promised Land by his divine will. The past reveals that nothing stood in the way of God's will and presence.

The prophet leads God's people in a prayer for redemption (**63:15–64:12**). He grounds the petition on God's promise to establish his sanctuary as a footstool among his people (vv. 15, 18), on the father-son relationship (v. 16), and on the covenantal relationship with the tribes (vv. 17–19). Now it seems that they had never been called by his covenant name.

The prayer also focuses on the revelation of God. As the people pray that the Lord might descend to shake the mountains and show himself in his glorious fire, they call upon the Lord to come to their aid by taking vengeance on their enemies and by redeeming his faithful people. The people confess that they are not ready for him because they are sinners, unclean, hopeless, and objects of wrath. But they pray that the Lord may forgive and forget their sins. They call on the Lord as their Father and wait for his compassion. They confess his authority and their helplessness and need of forgiveness, restoration, and fellowship. They remind him that the land, the cities, Jerusalem, and the temple are in ruins.

J. God's response (65:1–25). The Lord is ready to respond in a most self-giving way (**65:1–7**). But the people are still too engrossed in sin. They show themselves to be idolaters and have little concern for spiritual purity, as they keep vigils among the graves and eat pork—against God's explicit commandment. They are like Gentiles. They respond with a self-made holiness. The Lord will respond in turn in judgment. Even as the Lord has promised not to be silent until he has accomplished the redemption of his people, so he will not be silent until the enemies of his kingdom have been put down.

God assures his own that he knows them and will separate the ungodly from the godly (**65:8–16**). On one hand, God promises his grace to the remnant. On the other, he makes it clear that his judgment will rest upon the ungodly until they are no more.

The prophet likens the covenant community to a cluster of grapes. Not all the grapes in a cluster are good; some are spoiled and others are unripe. However, some may still produce wine and obtain a "blessing" on the cluster. For the sake of the whole, God will be patient with the community; his judgment will be selective. Those who seek Yahweh will be rewarded, whereas the wicked will be judged.

The ungodly have forgotten the Lord and have given themselves over to idolatrous practices. They are unresponsive and rebellious toward him. They will mourn their disgrace, whereas the righteous will rejoice in the Lord because of the many benefits that he has extended to them. The Lord assures his own that they will be satisfied with food and drink and a new name representative of their restored status. Instead of the troubles associated with the "old era," they will experience the fullness of the restoration God has promised to all his people: the new heavens, the new earth, and the New Jerusalem.

It is tempting to think of the state of restoration (**65:17–25**) as the eschatological, everlasting state of the new heavens and the new earth. Even though the prophet portrays the blessings of the people of God in a final way, he is addressing those in exile, assuring them that they will have a future. The Lord will again rejoice in his people. Because they are blessed by the Lord their former troubles are forgotten. The "former" era is the experience of judgment and exile. The Lord will create a "new era"—"new heavens" and a "new earth" (v. 17). The new era is characterized by the joy of the people of God because Yahweh himself rejoices over his people. The sorrow of past sufferings will cease because of the comfort of the Lord. The new era is described in terms of physical health and longevity, the enjoyment of God's benefits in physical ways, answers to prayer, and peace and the absence of malice and corruption. Even their children will know the Lord and will be blessed by him.

These blessings were experienced to some extent by those who returned from exile. However, many of these blessings were only partially realized. Jesus reaffirmed that it is the Father's will to restore the heavens and the earth. He showed his concern for the physical and spiritual needs of people. Jesus has also pointed us to the great future that awaits all who have faith in him. He will bring in the new era in an even greater way. Then Christians will enjoy the fullness of God's benefits, spiritual as well as physical. As such Isaiah 65:17–25 is a continual reminder of the Christian's heritage in Jesus Christ.

K. Judgment and restoration (66:1–24). The last chapter provides a complementary answer to that of chapter 65. The Lord affirms the certainty of his judgment on idolatry and religious hypocrisy among his people and the blessings of the new age on faithful Jews and Gentiles. The extension of the new age to the Gentiles is a further development beyond chapter 65 and is in full harmony with the prophet's teaching on the universal nature of God's kingdom.

It was tempting for Old Testament believers to localize God's kingship. They knew that God ruled over the whole earth and that his throne was in heaven. They had also been taught that the earth, and especially the temple in Jerusalem, was his footstool. To approach the temple was to approach God. For that reason, it was important to approach the Lord with gifts befitting his sovereignty and royal splendor. But rather than being the place of true worship, the temple had become a place where people came to pacify their own consciences; they were trying to atone for their own misdeeds without exhibiting a spirit of true contrition. In their corruption, injustice, and hatred, they were presenting sacrifices that were offensive to him.

The prophecy of Isaiah concludes with God's concern for true worship (**66:1–6**). God desires to have fellowship with those who show sensitivity to his Word by acts of obedience, love, and justice. The love of God is evident in those who are humble and contrite in spirit. They may suffer in an unjust world, but he promises to vindicate them. On the other hand, he will avenge himself on those within the community of faith who worship in their own ways, not having a heartfelt love for God and for their brothers and sisters in the faith.

The judgment of God clearly comes against all those who have opposed his kingdom (**66:7–9**). The noise coming from the temple (vv. 5–6) is the sound of the Lord himself who has come to defend his children by bringing retribution on the wicked.

The Lord invites all to rejoice with "mother Jerusalem." Those who love her in adversity and prosperity will be rewarded with joy, fullness of life, peace, and comfort (**66:10–14**). These benefits are further guaranteed to all who love the Lord Jesus Christ.

As God's people are encouraged that the Lord is going to be with his children, he also assures the enemies that his vengeance will come upon them (**66:15–17**). His coming is depicted in prophetic imagery: fire, chariots, whirlwinds, and swords. The effect of Yahweh's judgment is that the wicked will be slain. The prophet gives the scene of God's judgment on the wicked in order to assure the ungodly who have been members of the covenant community that they too will be under God's judgment. Those who have made their own rules of sanctification and defilement will be consumed together with the wicked.

In quick strokes the prophet describes how many nations will be instrumental in bringing together the people of God (**66:18–23**). They will be instrumental in restoring the Jews to full participation in the kingdom of God. But in the very process, they too will see the glory of the Lord. The Lord himself will set a sign among the nations by sending missionaries who will proclaim the glorious acts of God. The restoration of the Jews to the land, God's continued care for the Jewish people, and God's acts of redemption (including the finished work of our Lord Jesus Christ and the work of missionaries and evangelists) will result in many nations (including the Jews) bringing sacrifices to the Lord and serving as priests and Levites in God's presence. They will gather together from festival to festival and enjoy covenant fellowship from generation to generation.

The prophet introduced the coming judgment and its effects in verses 15 and 16. He returns to this motif in the last verse of the prophecy (**66:24**) as a perpetual reminder that God's judgment on the wicked is everlasting and that those who have been condemned to separation from him in life will suffer eternal separation in death.

SELECT BIBLIOGRAPHY

Kaiser, O. *Isaiah 1–12*. The Old Testament Library. Philadelphia: Westminster, 1972.

———*Isaiah 13–39*. The Old Testament Library. Philadelphia: Westminster, 1974.

Ridderbos, J. *Isaiah*. Bible Student's Commentary. Grand Rapids: Zondervan, 1985.

Westermann, C. *Isaiah 40–66*. The Old Testament Library. Philadelphia: Westminster, 1969.

Young, E. J. *The Book of Isaiah*. 3 vols. Grand Rapids: Eerdmans, 1965–1972.

JEREMIAH

Elmer A. Martens

INTRODUCTION

The Book of Jeremiah is one of unusual intensity. The destiny of God's people was at stake. A prophet, against great odds, alerted his people to a monumental crisis. He argued persuasively, sometimes feverishly, for a specific course of action to avert the impending doom. His counsel, though given in the name of God, was rejected, and the catastrophe about which he warned, happened. Life was miserable. People were killed or deported. The people's king was tortured. Property was destroyed. The temple was burned. Their land was lost. The end of a 250-year national history had come.

That which brought on the political crisis in the land of Judah at the turn of the sixth century was a moral and religious depravity traceable to the long reign of Manasseh, Judah's most evil king (686–643 B.C.). Manasseh reintroduced Baal worship and set up altars to foreign gods in the Jerusalem temple area, not to mention other practices of the most bizarre kind (2 Kings 21:6). For offenses not nearly as gross, Israel, Judah's northern neighbor, had been invaded by the Assyrians in 722 B.C.. Its capital, Samaria, had been captured. Judah, the prophet Jeremiah warned, would face a greater tragedy.

Yet "crisis" could hardly describe Judah during Josiah's reign (641–609 B.C.). Manasseh before him had been a vassal of the Assyrians. But with Assyrian power waning, Josiah enlarged Judah's territories. Times were prosperous. It even seemed that Josiah would turn the nation to God. When the scroll, possibly Deuteronomy, was discovered in the temple in 622, he took strong measures to reform Judah's religious life (2 Kings 22–23). But the reforms turned out to be temporary. A number of prophetic oracles in the first six chapters date from Josiah's reign. They claim that the situation, for all its apparent calm, is serious.

To aggravate matters, Jehoiakim (609–597 B.C.), Josiah's son, reversed the direction set by Josiah. He, in fact, returned to pagan idols and even practiced child sacrifice. Despite wealth being drained to Egypt, to whom Judah had become a vassal, Jehoiakim built himself a showy palace. He failed to compensate the laborers, nor did he care for society's poor. He callously disregarded the God of Israel, whose message was read to him from a scroll prepared by Jeremiah. He sliced the written columns as they were read and tossed them into the fire (chap. 36).

Such brazen disregard for God propelled the people into a national crisis, both religious and political. Josiah, the highly respected king, had been killed in 609 at Megiddo in an attempt to halt the Egyptians who were moving northward to the aid of an ailing Assyria. A fast-moving Babylonian, Nabopolassar, had captured Nineveh, Assyria's capital, in 612. With a decisive victory over Egypt at the Battle of Carchemish in 605, Nebuchadnezzar, who succeeded Nabopolassar to the throne, was about to swallow the little countries of Syria-Palestine, including Judah.

He swept down the Mediterranean coast soon after 605, and in response to Jehoiakim's maneuvers, attacked Jerusalem. He took the elite of that city, including Jehoiachin, the recently inaugurated king who followed Jehoiakim, captive to Babylon. In its last two decades Judah had five different kings. With the Babylonian attack in 597, disaster had come to Judah as God's prophet had warned.

Nebuchadnezzar appointed Zedekiah to be his vassal king in Jerusalem. God's messenger threatened further disaster if king and people would not turn from their evil, their lying, their violence, their injustice, and their flirting with strange gods. Zedekiah was a vacillating king, controlled and confused by rival political parties, the strongest of which urged alliance with Egypt. At one point Zedekiah made a courageous social and religious move. He followed the Mosaic law and released the slaves—but days later he went back on his word (chap. 34). Widespread corruption reached crisis proportions. God's agent, the Babylonians, were on hand. When Zedekiah rebelled against his overlord in 589, Nebuchadnezzar laid siege and after eighteen months broke into the city. He destroyed it, including the palace and the four-hundred-year-old temple.

More persons were taken captive to Babylon. Gedaliah was appointed governor. One of his own countrymen, an Israelite, assassinated him. Fearing revenge from the Babylonians, some Jews left to settle in Egypt. Even after all this, little had been learned, so it seemed, because there too people preferred a pagan deity, the Queen of Heaven, to the worship of the God of Israel.

The story line of the book stretches from 627, the year of Jeremiah's call to be a prophet, to 562, the last chronological marker mentioned in the book's appendix. For Judah those years were the most convulsive in its history.

One of God's spokespersons during these troubled decades was Jeremiah. His contemporaries included Zephaniah, Habakkuk, Nahum, and Ezekiel. Born, it is believed, into a priestly family in 640, Jeremiah was commissioned by God in 627. As a youth, Jeremiah witnessed Josiah's reform, and was almost certainly supportive of it, though explicit endorsements are not found in the book. Most of his oracles were given during the reigns of Jehoiakim and Zedekiah. When Jerusalem fell, Jeremiah was singled out by the Babylonians for preferential treatment. Yet he chose to stay with his people, even when, against his counsel, they went to Egypt. There he died.

Jeremiah's message, largely one of warning, made him few friends. Indeed, he was pitted against kings, prophets, priests, and society at large. He reprimanded Jehoiakim for his extravagance. He prophesied woe for Jehoiachin, and urged Zedekiah to submit to the Babylonians rather than to resist them. Jeremiah charged his peers, the prophets, with complicity. He branded them liars. He railed at them for talking about peace, when God was about to inflict disaster. He wrote to the exiles, naming the prophets of whom they should beware. As for the priests, they, like the prophets, disliked him. So did the ruling officials. Jeremiah languished in a mud dungeon because of their schemes and came close to death. A sermon at the temple brought him a near-lynching by the incensed crowd. At times he was forced, along with Baruch his scribe, into hiding.

God asked him to engage in symbolic actions. Jeremiah bought a new garment, then promptly buried it in sand. He bought a jar and in an object lesson to the city elders, smashed it before their eyes. He wore an ox yoke as he laid out God's Word to dignitaries from neighboring nations, for he was a prophet not just to Israel, but to the nations.

Jeremiah was an intense man. His emotions ran deep for his people. He agonized over the messages God asked him to give. He was disgusted by the evil around him and devastated because of the lack of response. Even the joy of being God's servant vanished on occasion. He was so depressed that he cursed the day of his birth. No other prophet allows us such a deep look into his interior life.

Jeremiah was courageous, for he presented God's Word at the risk of his life. He was persevering. For more than twenty years, he called on people to repent but without result. Jeremiah was gentle, tender, and sensitive. He felt pain that God would have to mete out punishment. Uncompromisingly he delivered the unpopular but necessary warning. The Word of God was to him like a fire and like a hammer. More than 150 times one reads, "Thus says the Lord," or similar expressions.

In the New Testament period, some identified Jesus with Jeremiah (Matt. 16:14) and for good reason. Both were opposed to the religious establishment. Each preached repentance. Each warned about the fall of Jerusalem. Both had a small band of supporters. Both endured the rejection of the masses. Jesus' passion story has its counterpart in the passion narrative of Jeremiah (chaps. 26–44). According to one count, there are forty quotations and allusions from Jeremiah in the New Testament. Many are found in the Book of Revelation; the most striking is Hebrews 8, which quotes the new covenant passage in full (Jer. 31:31–34).

Simplified, one could say that Jeremiah's message for his society touched on the interplay between God, people, and land.

Between God and people there was a covenant. It consisted of a commitment for God to be God of his people and a demand for the people to be God's kind of people. Covenant was an intimate arrangement that called for loyalty from the covenant partners. It had been established at God's initiative when he called Abraham and later delivered his people from bondage into freedom. In the opening oracles, this covenant is depicted using the marriage metaphor (chaps. 2–3).

But Israel's sporadic disloyalty became chronic, and therein lay the crisis. The relationship between God and Israel was strained to the breaking point. In fact, God declared that the covenant was broken. Yet through repeated exhortation, encouragement, and warnings, God intended to salvage the covenant.

The presupposition for God's message to Judah about the covenant was also the backdrop for God's message to nations: God the Lord is the sovereign Lord. The title, *Lord of Hosts* (NIV God Almighty), though common in the Old Testament, is concentrated in Jeremiah where it appears eighty-two times. That title, with its military overtones, emphasizes God as supremely in command. As sovereign Dispatcher, it was God who sent Nebuchadnezzar, "his servant," against Jerusalem. Because God is God, idolatry is both intolerable and foolish. As supreme Creator, God is able to make his purposes stand, whether these be for Israel or for nations. With him nothing is impossible (32:17).

God delights in righteousness. Of prime value, therefore, is not human wisdom, strength, or riches, but a knowledge of God who "exercises kindness, justice and righteousness on earth, for in these I [God] delight" (9:24). His wrath is against all unrighteousness; and Judah was grossly unrighteous. For this reason, perhaps, God's wrath is a secondary theme in the book.

The shape of evil, as Jeremiah exposed it, on the part of nations, was a disregard of the sovereign God, and on the part of Israel, a rejection of the covenant God. A stinging rebuttal is addressed to all who substitute images for the sovereign God (10:1–16), or to nations who worship deities other than God, such as Chemosh, Molech, or Marduk. Besides, arrogance and ego obsession also come under the judgment of God.

In Judah an assortment of evils jeopardized the covenant relationship. Preponderant among them was injustice. The poor, the disadvantaged, the marginal people were neglected and even exploited. Violence and sexual license had become common. Lying and deceit were widespread national ailments that affected even religious persons. Prophets, for example, sanctioned the evil plans of others with their benedictions (23:14–18). Religiously the people were stiff-necked. They refused to listen to God's Word, and refused, too, to take correction.

Israel had set God aside; people were secure in the land—or so they thought. They were wrong! Covenant breaking, the severing of ties between people and God, has consequences—among them the dislocation of people from their land. Repeatedly Jeremiah warned that a northern foe would invade Judah. Havoc would come to Jerusalem. Worst of all, for those who escaped death, there would be the loss of land and an ordered life. People would be taken into exile. God's judgment on the sin of covenant disloyalty in his people affected their land. Drought came. Eventually they lost their land.

God judges all sin—also that of nations. They too would suffer loss of life and property. Empires would shatter and nations would go into exile. Removing people from their land or returning them to their land were both acts of God. The land of Israel, while geographical territory, eventually became a symbol of the good life, the life with God. Land was something like litmus paper in chemistry: it was an indicator of where one was theologically.

Loss of land was not the last word, however. The salvation word was about land too. Israel would return to its land. More than that, she would recover what was lost, and good times would come again (chaps. 30–31). Central to these good times would be a spiritual return to God. In fact, God would make a new covenant—certainly the high point in Jeremiah's message—in which people would be given a new heart and would know God immediately and intimately (31:31–34). God would save his people. The announcement of good news was sealed as was the announcement of bad news, by a symbolic action. Jeremiah bought property to show that after the exile normal routines would be resumed.

Jeremiah's message raises questions appropriate in every age. What is the nature of the relationship between God and his people? What is the shape of evil in church or society? Where and by whom is God's message freely proclaimed? When is the message of repentance appropriate? What is the word from God to modern nations on the brink of global disaster? To what extent and in what way is a believer to be involved in society, especially in its political life? To what degree is the good life "guaranteed"?

The book has several distinctive features. It is the longest, by word count, in the Bible. Several short sections are duplicated in scattered places. The book has an appendix taken largely from 2 Kings 24–25. The book as a "prophetic" book supplies an amazing amount of historical information. Similarly, there is more of a biography of the prophet, including Jeremiah's emotional pilgrimage, than in any other prophetic book. Among personal interest stories are Jeremiah's symbolic actions.

The first twenty chapters plus the first two in the "Book of Comfort" are mostly poetry. The poetry is vigorous and expressive, filled with metaphor. Metaphors such as the marriage metaphor between God and Israel are drawn from Hosea. The prose sections are much like Deuteronomy in style—a fact that has spawned numerous theories about the relationship between Deuteronomy and Jeremiah. Frequently occurring expressions are: they/you did not listen; stiff heart; the Lord of Hosts; I will be their God, they shall be my people. Much of the book is punctuated with exclamation marks.

The book appears scrambled because it is not chronologically or even topically arranged. In addition, the Greek (or Septuagint) text is one-eighth shorter and places chapters 46–51 in the middle of the book (after 25:13). Many have been the theories on how the book came to be composed. One possibility is that the scroll Jehoiakim burned was dictated a second time. Since it contained warnings, it is likely, though not stated, that part or all of chapters 1–20 were part of that scroll (see 36:32). Since Baruch was Jeremiah's scribe, and since the narratives about Jeremiah appear in the third person, it has been suggested that chapters 26–45, excluding the Book of Comfort (31–33), are his work. In summary, Jeremiah himself as "author" would be responsible for chapters 1–20 (25), 30–33, and 46–51. Baruch may have been the author-compiler of chapters 26–29 and 34–45. An editor may have added the appendix (chap. 52).

More helpful than trying to determine authorship is attention to the book as it now lies before us. Several different blocks of material can be distinguished. The warnings and threats to Judah, sermonlike, dominate chapters 1–20. Stories from Jeremiah's experience are found in chapters 21–29 and 34–45 to illustrate the wicked society. The Book of Comfort (30–33) has a tone totally different from the rest of the book. The oracles against the nations (46–51) put the reader on world stage. The book tells about the experiences of a prophet; it surveys nations. Most of all it acquaints us with God, and that with a passion!

OUTLINE

I. Jeremiah's Credentials (1:1–19)
II. Sermons Warning of Disaster (2–10)
   A. A Marriage About to Break Up (2:1–3:5)
   B. A Story of Two Sisters (3:6–4:4)
   C. Trouble from the North (4:5–6:30)
   D. Examining Public Worship (7:1–8:3)
   E. Treachery, Trouble, and Tears (8:4–10:25)
III. Stories about Wrestling with People and with God (11–20)
   A. Coping with Conspiracies (11:1–12:17)
   B. Pride Ruins Everything (13:1–27)
   C. Dealing with Drought (14:1–15:21)
   D. Much Bad News, Some Good (16:1–17:27)
   E. A Pot Marred, a Pot Smashed (18:1–19:15)
   F. Terror on Every Side (20:1–18)
IV. Challenging Kings and Prophets (21–29)
   A. Addressing Rulers and Governments (21:1–23:8)
   B. Addressing Prophets and Their Audiences (23:9–40)
   C. Divine Anger (24:1–25:38)
   D. Jeremiah Versus the People (26:1–24)
   E. Submit to Babylon's Yoke! (27:1–28:17)
   F. A Pastoral Letter (29:1–32)
V. The Book of Comfort (30–33)
   A. Coming Back to the Land (30:1–24)
   B. Coming Back to God (31:1–40)
   C. A Property Purchase (32:1–44)
   D. Things Great and Unsearchable (33:1–26)
VI. Case Studies in the Failure of Leadership (34–39)
   A. Going Back on One's Word (34:1–21)

B. Obedience (35:1–19)
C. The Burning of a Scroll (36:1–32)
D. Troubling a Prophet (37:1–38:28)
E. The Fall of Jerusalem (39:1–18)

VII. After the Catastrophe (40–45)
A. Trouble from Within (40:1–41:18)
B. Trouble in Egypt (42:1–43:13)
C. Failure to Learn from History (44:1–45:5)

VIII. Oracles about the Nations (46–51)
A. Egypt (46:1–28)
B. Philistia (47:1–7)
C. Moab (48:1–47)
D. Ammon (49:1–6)
E. Edom (49:7–22)
F. Damascus (49:23–27)
G. Kedar and Hazor (49:28–33)
H. Elam (49:34–39)
I. Babylon (50:1–51:64)

IX. The Fall of Jerusalem (52:1–34)

COMMENTARY

I. Jeremiah's Credentials (1:1–19)

The stage is set by introducing person, place, event, and historical time (**1:1–3**). The person is Jeremiah, whose name probably means "the Lord is exalted." He is of a priestly line. It is unclear whether Jeremiah came from the family of Abiathar, a priest exiled by David to Anathoth (1 Kings 2:26–27). The place is Anathoth, the modern Anata, two to three miles northeast of Jerusalem. The event is the coming of the Word of God, which means that the subsequent book has a divine quality to it.

The time frame extends from Josiah, through Jehoiakim, to Zedekiah, Judah's last king. This list omits two three-month reigns: Johoahaz (609) and Jehoiachin (598–597). Jeremiah's life coincides with the final years of Judah and its collapse. The prophet lives through Josiah's reform, Nebuchadnezzar's siege of Jerusalem in 597, the reign of the vacillating Zedekiah, and the capture and burning of Jerusalem in 587, as well as the horror of Gedaliah's assassination.

The introduction, while appropriate for the entire book, is, to be technical, limited to chapters 1–39, since Jeremiah's ministry did not conclude with Zedekiah (v. 3; cf. chaps. 40–44). Almost certainly, therefore, the book grew in stages.

The date for the prophet's call (**1:4–10**) is 627 B.C., the thirteenth year of Josiah's rule. Jeremiah is in his middle or late teens. The dialogue points to an intimacy between the Lord and Jeremiah.

God's "forming" activity recalls Genesis 2:7. "To sanctify" is to set apart, usually for some service. The word order emphasizes the unexpected: "a prophet to the nations I have appointed you." Prophet, said to mean "speaker" or even "gushing at the mouth," is more appropriately defined, according to the Hebrew root, as "one who is called." Prophetic work was exemplified by Moses (Deut. 18:18) and is depicted in Exodus 7:1.

Jeremiah registers an excuse. The word *youth* or *child* suggests inexperience and inadequacy as well as age. God identifies the given reason (inability to speak) as well as the unspoken but deeper reason (fear). The fear is met with the so-called divine assistance formula, *I am with you* (cf. vv. 8, 19; Gen. 28:15; Matt. 28:20).

The installation ceremony has a personal touch. Jeremiah's primary vocation is speaking, though he will engage in sign acts (chaps. 13, 19, 32). The gift of words recalls Moses (Deut. 18:18).

Jeremiah's ministry is to extend beyond Judah/Israel to other nations. He is called to demolish false securities (7:1–15) and to root out the cancer of idolatry and social corruption. Deconstruction precedes construction. Much of Jeremiah's message is about threat and punishment; good news, as in the Book of Comfort (30–33), is less characteristic. Excerpts of his six-part job assignment are noted in 18:7–9; 24:6; 31:28; 42:10; and 45:4.

Two objects—a flowering branch and a boiling pot—are used to further clarify the call (**1:11–16**). There is a word play between "almond" (*šāqēd*) and "watch" (*šāqad*). Almond trees are among the first to flower in spring and so become "watching trees." The word over which God is watching is the promise to Jeremiah.

The boiling pot, likely tilting northward, represents an unnamed northern army (later to be identified as Babylon; cf. chap. 39). The reason for disaster, variously nuanced throughout, is basically that the people have forsaken God. This summary accusation and the announcement of disaster foreshadow two themes that will dominate chapters 2–10.

Jeremiah's commission is restated (**1:17–19**). "To gird loins" points to promptness in obeying an order (1 Kings 18:46) and means "Get going!" Jeremiah, like Jesus, will face strenuous opposition from religious officialdom. He will be opposed by kings, by princes, by priests, and by the people. But God will make him as strong as a fortified city. To call Jeremiah a weeping prophet is not incorrect, yet the projected portrait is of a man of steel. His unbending personal courage is most impressive.

II. Sermons Warning of Disaster (2–10)

A. A marriage about to break up (2:1–3:5). The prophet's opening sermon, dated prior to Josiah's reform in 621, is direct, even abrupt. The first scene (vv. 1–3) shows God with his people who are like a new bride on a honeymoon. But almost at once there is trouble. The last scene (3:1–5) puts divorce talk squarely at the center. It is a case of a ruined marriage.

God does not want a divorce. Through these verses rings the pathos of a hurt marriage partner. The strong feelings that accompany the marriage break-up are caught in the questions God poses, the quotations from the people, and the picturesque language about wells, donkeys, camels, lions, yokes, vines, brides, and prostitutes.

Here is sweet talk about a honeymoon, nostalgic talk about good times, angry talk about people turning to Baal, and exasperated talk about guilty people who claim innocence. Evidence of the partner's neglect, her arrogance, self-sufficiency, idolatry, injustice, and physical/spiritual adultery is cited. There is no outright call to repent—as yet. Pleas for a people to reconsider are frequent.

The initial honeymoon (**2:1–3**) has been called the "seed oracle" for chapters 2–3, where the themes are expanded. The house of Jacob technically refers to all descendants of Jacob, which includes the ten tribes exiled by the Assyrians in 722 B.C., as well as the people in the southern territories of Judah and Benjamin who have, at the time of speaking (627–622), been spared an invasion.

Both partners share courtship memories of good days: the exodus and Sinai. To that covenant the people, like a bride wanting to please, responded, "We will do everything the LORD has said; we will obey" (Exod. 24:7). Devotion (*ḥēsēd*) is a strong word indicating covenant love. As the firstfruit is choice fruit, so Israel was special to God. As a protective bridegroom, God would not allow the slightest injury to be inflicted on his bride. God and Israel were intimate and close.

Then there was trouble (**2:4–8**). Neither the leaders nor the people asked for the Lord, to seek orientation. Ironically, the priests, whose major duty was to teach the law—a law which called for the worship of the Lord—did not bother about the Lord. The prophets, who were to rebuke transgressions, instead now themselves prophesied by Baal. Each group of leaders mishandled its responsibility.

Baal was the god of the Canaanites, a god of weather and fertility. Among the archaeological discoveries in the 1930s at Ugarit on the Mediterranean, are stories that depict him as young, lusty, and aggressive. But God's favors, not Baal's, made crops productive. God as partner spelled benefits. To walk after Baal was of no profit. "Worthless" is Jeremiah's customary word for idols (8:19; 10:8, 15; 16:19). Disregard for God, departure from God, and courtships with another god spelled deep trouble for the covenant.

A court lawsuit is underway (**2:9–13**). It is the Lord Yahweh versus Israel. God the Prosecutor claims that Israel's behavior is unprecedented. Were one to go west to the island of Cyprus in the Mediterranean or east to the Kedar tribes in Arabia, one could not find an example of a pagan people switching allegiance to another god. Israel's action is irrational. She has exchanged God, with his deliverance at the exodus, his law at Sinai, his care of the people in the wilderness, and his blessing of Canaan, for a god of no worth. It is a bad bargain. The move is shocking. The heavens are court witnesses.

Israel is like a man who decides to dig for water despite the artesian well on his property. Beyond the hard work of digging the cistern and lining it with plaster, he faces the problem of leaky cisterns, not to mention stale water. The unsatisfactory "cisterns" (Egypt and Assyria) are described in verses 14–19. Living (fresh) water is at hand (Isa. 55:1; John 4:1–26).

Enough has been said to dispose the court in favor of God and against Israel.

God's questions serve both to accuse and to bring his marriage partner to reconsider her ways (**2:14–19**). First, the question about status implies the answer. "No, Israel's destiny was not to be some servant or slave." Second, a question is raised about Israel's ravaged condition. Since the lion was the insignia for Assyria, that country may be in view. Noph, which is ancient Memphis, was the capital of the pyramid-building Pharaohs. Tahpahnes was a Nile Delta fortress city. Egypt had "shaved Israel's head." The expression certainly refers to a humiliation brought on by Egypt, possibly a raid into Israel's choice lands. The third question is about assigning blame. The fourth question concerns direction. Sihor is a body of water, possibly a river in the Nile Delta area of Egypt. Will Israel go for help to Egypt, which has already mistreated her? Or to Assyria, which has invaded the ten northern tribes and occupies the area just north of Jerusalem?

The summary accusation is that Israel has forsaken her covenant partner (v. 19) and that there is no reverence or appropriate fear of God. The title *Lord of Hosts* (NIV Lord Almighty) speaks of power and rulership.

God's pleas fail. Hard evidence must now be marshaled (**2:20–28**). While some Hebrew manuscripts read, "I broke your yoke," it is preferable, given the line of argument, to follow those ancient manuscripts that read, "For of old you broke your yoke" (v. 20). The yoke continues the figure of a partnership, a binding relationship. The Canaanite god Baal was worshiped on hilltops and in the shelter of large spreading trees—a practice noted in Hosea 4:13 and forbidden in Deuteronomy 12:2.

Figures of speech follow in profusion. The vine, Israel, is of a good variety. The soda and soap (mineral and vegetable alkalis) metaphor stresses the deeply ingrained nature of Israel's evil. The young camel, wobbly on its feet, illustrates how directionless Israel is as she criss-crosses her ways. The donkey at mating time illustrates the passion with which Israel pursues the Baals even in the valley, which, if the Hinnom Valley, would be the place for child sacrifice.

In sarcasm, Israel is warned in all this pursuing of other gods not to stub her toe (to use a modern idiom) or to overexert and so become thirsty. Israel, self-consciously determined to do evil, responds in fiery language. Wood posts and stone pillars were both worship objects in the Baal cult.

Courtroom language continues (**2:29–37**). God complains of breach of covenant, as exemplified by the way Israel handles correction, treats the prophets, and announces her independence: "I am free." Her deliberate "no" is incomprehensible, for God and people, like bride and wedding gown, belong together.

Four additional accusations undermine any protests of innocence: (1) Israel has sought other lovers, and in such an abandoned way as to teach the professionally wicked women, the prostitutes, a thing or two; (2) Israel is guilty of social violence by killing off innocent ones; (3) Israel is guilty of lying by claiming she has not sinned; (4) flighty behavior puts her in league, once with Egypt, next with Assyria, but not with the Lord.

God's patience is huge but not infinite. A court sentence is missing but implied in the announcement of Israel's exile from her land (v. 37), for to go with hands on one's head is to go as a captive.

Israel acts as though she can at any time sweet-talk her way back to God (**3:1–5**). Not so. The law forbade a divorced husband from returning to his former, now-married wife (Deut. 24:1–4). Israel is now "married" to Baal.

Israel has not simply been overtaken by temptation. As an Arab is ready to ambush, so Israel has deliberately planned to be promiscuous. Language of harlotry has a double meaning: physical unfaithfulness in marriage, and spiritual disloyalty to God (sacred prostitution was part of Baal worship). Israel's immature appeals to a supposedly indulgent father only add to the ugly picture of her evil.

B. A story of two sisters (3:6–4:4). Two sisters, Israel to the north and Judah to the south, are each characteristically tagged: "ever-turning" (faithless, backsliding) Israel, and "wicked" (run-away) Judah. The split of the united kingdom came after Solomon's reign. In 722 B.C. Assyria captured Samaria and occupied Israel. In Jeremiah's time Judah was still an independent nation but the Assyrian garrison was only a few miles away. God argues that Judah is more evil than Israel. For Israel, distressed because of God's punishment, there is an earnest plea to return to God. For Judah, there is a short but very stern warning (4:3–4). The passage is piled with word plays on the word *turn*, which in its various forms occurs sixteen times. The messages date early in Jeremiah's ministry during Josiah's reign, possibly between 625 and 620 B.C.

"Ever-turning" Israel is accused of harlotry (**3:6–10**). Harlotry, with its overtones of desertion from the marriage partner and illicit sex, is a graphic way of describing Israel's unfaithfulness to God. God's harsh action in divorcing Israel by sending her into exile should have been a lesson to Judah, who not only saw all that happened, but was herself severely threatened by the Assyrians (2 Kings 18–19). Stone pillars, sometimes representing the male sex organ, and trees or wood poles representing the female deities were standard Baal symbols.

Instead of making the expected judgment speech, God issues a plea for "ever-turning" Israel to turn once more, this time to him (**3:11–18**). The word play can be caught in "Come back, backsliding Israel." Verses 12–14 contain three exhortations in as many verses: return, acknowledge, return. The word *turn* is one of two words used for the idea of "repent."

The appeal is persuasive. God advances reasons for Israel to return: (1) he is merciful; (2) repentance is demanded because of the breach of covenant; (3) he is still Israel's husband; (4) good things will follow if they repent. Among these good things are return from exile, godly leaders, shepherds, prosperity, a holiness extending to the entire city of Jerusalem rather than just the ark, a transformed heart, fulfillment of an earlier promise that nations should be blessed through Israel, and a returned and unified people.

The ark was a box in which were kept the stone tables of law that symbolized the presence of God. It had been relocated during Josiah's reform into the most holy area in the temple (2 Chron. 35:3). To do away with the ark would be radical in the extreme. In the new era all of Jerusalem would contain God's presence. Also striking in these annoucements is Israel's return to the land from the exile, a subject frequent in Jeremiah (24:6; 30:1–3; 31:17; 32:37).

Further motivations are advanced for the people to return to God (**3:19–4:2**). Verse 19 is not so much a statement as it is a thought, a dream. For a moment we see inside God's mind. He schemes how he can give his people the very best. And he has pleasant thoughts of how in response Israel would in love call out "My Father" (cf. 31:9). Imagery moves between marriage and family.

The dream is shattered, yet it continues. Hypothetically, we must understand, God envisions a change, as though he hears voices calling to him from out of Israel's perversion. A dialogue between God and Israel follows. In imagination, so one must suppose, Israel does an about-turn. The people who said they wanted nothing but to go after alien gods (2:25) now declare the Lord Yahweh to be their God. A liturgy of a model repentance follows. They admit they were wrong, and that from the mountains (the place of noisy Baal worship) no help could come. The shameful gods are Baals. Here is no attempt to look good. Here is no excuse and no belittling of evil. The speech, however, is God putting words in Israel's mouth.

For this reason the divine response begins with "if" (4:1). "Ever-turning" Israel might turn, yet fail to turn to God. Turning to God demands action as well as words. Negatively it means throwing away the detestable things—all that is ungodly. Positively it means a change in behavior to just and righteous dealings. Then Israel can rightfully make promises by invoking the name of the Lord. Meeting the conditions means good things to nations who will be blessed and who will give the Lord praise; for God's eye is not on his people alone, but on other peoples as well.

After the message to Israel (3:11–4:2), Jeremiah turns to his immediate audience, the city of Jerusalem and the territory of Judah (**4:3–4**). This group will be in focus in the book until chapter 30. Israel appeared ready to change, and so the plea. But Judah is hard, and therefore a threat.

The call is for drastic action. The hard soil of stubbornness is to be broken before good seed is sown—otherwise it will still fall among thorns. In spiritual renewal one cannot shortcut repentance. The exhortation turns from agricultural symbolism to the physiological (v. 4). Circumcision for Israel was a physical sign of the covenant (Gen. 17:1–14). Since it signified a people spiritually linked with God, circumcision talk came to be associated with the heart. The circumcision of hearts refers to removing whatever spiritually obstructs (Deut. 10:16). The sense is, "Give yourself totally to God's service."

God's anger—a very frequent theme in the book—will go forth as a fire, so hot that stopping it is impossible.

C. Trouble from the north (4:5–6:30). The story now shifts from marriage language to military language. In his capacity as a watchman, Jeremiah sees a God-appointed nation from the north about to invade Palestine.

In earlier prophets a judgment speech classically included an accusation followed by an announcement. In Jeremiah both elements appear, but not in the usual order. In broad strokes, however, one can identify the sequence: announcement (4:5–31); accusation (5:1–13); announcement (6:1–9); accusation (6:1–9); accusation (6:10–20); and announcement (6:22–30). The announcement is about the invader. The accusation attacks lack of moral integrity, spiritual crustiness and social injustice, and widespread covetousness and corruption. Laced within announcements and accusations are expressions of the prophet's great sorrow, and appeals by God to a people to wash their hearts and to walk in the old paths.

Urgency is the note in **4:5–18.** Through short, commandlike calls, people are urged to leave their fields and hurry into the walled cities, Zion (Jerusalem) in particular. The destroyer from the north, frequently mentioned in subsequent chapters, is unnamed, but later identified as Babylon (27:6). The large Assyrian Empire which had dominated the Middle East for 150 years crumbled quickly after the rise of Nabopolassar, the Babylonian, in 626 B.C. This oracle is likely early in Jeremiah's ministry, before 621 or between 612 and 608.

The power of this nation is lionlike (v. 7). Before it the leaders, both political and religious, lose their courage.

Verse 10 is the first of many personal responses by the prophet. Jeremiah is markedly affected by the message he preaches. Boldly he faces God with the contradiction—as listeners would see it—between what was promised and what is. The deceit is not to be attributed to God; it is Jerusalem's wickedness that accounts for the impending disaster.

The burst of the invading nation upon the scene is graphically pictured as a windstorm of hurricane proportions. The announcement of the army's march is sounded first from Dan, Israel's northern border town, and then from Mount Ephraim, roughly in the middle of Palestine, thirty miles north of Jerusalem. Like a security force, the enemy directly surrounds Judah's cities. Nor need Judah ask, "Why?" Her rebellion has brought disaster on herself.

The upcoming invasion is not a skirmish, but an onslaught that will demolish everything (**4:19–31**). Like a photographer using a zoom lens, the prophet first gives an initial picture of the devastation of the whole earth (vv. 23–26); then a wide-angle shot of all the land (v. 27); and finally a close-up of what happens in a town (v. 29). The earth becomes chaotic, formless, and empty as before the creation (Gen. 1:2). There are four references to nonlife (earth, heaven, mountain, hill) and four mentions of life (man, birds, fruitful land, cities). Behind that army is God's wrath. God is fully committed to this action of judgment and will not be dissuaded.

This description of devastation is bracketed by expressions of pain and hurt. Jeremiah is bent over with pain as with prophetic perception he hears the war trumpet and sees the war flag. The invaders are like murderers who will strangle Judah to death.

God complains that his people are as those who have not known (i.e., experienced) him; they are unwise and undiscerning. Proof of their lack of discernment is that Judah, sitting atop a dynamite keg, misreads the situation: with trouble about to break in on her, she is primping herself with cosmetics and jewelry. She is preparing to meet her lovers, who are really her murderers.

So far statements about Judah's evil have been only sketches. Now the people (not only Jeremiah) are commanded to investigate the moral situation by means of a citywide poll (**5:1–13**) to show statistically, so to speak, that like Sodom and Gomorrah (Gen. 18:23–33) the place totally lacks persons of integrity. And worse—people are outrightly defying the Lord. The poll gives warrant for God's severe judgment.

Were there even only one who would seek after truth, God would pardon the city! "Doing justice" (NIV who deals honestly) refers to honorable and upright relationships, not only in the law court, but in every social contact or transaction. Justice is a prime requirement of God's people. Some merely mouth the words of an oath ("As the Lord lives"). Taking the oath, however, is not proof that people mean it.

Jeremiah participates in the research. The poor are not excused because they are poor, but are faulted for hard-heartedness. The "great," the leaders with every advantage, fail the test. Besides, they lead in breaking the relationship (yoke) between people and God. Deliberate defiance and covenant breaking will bring God's judgment—attack by wild animals.

God responds to the statistical research. Like a highly sexed male horse, Judah goes neighing adulterously after another man's wife (v. 8). Prosperity apparently led to luxury, which led to sexual liberties. God will judge sexual promiscuity. This people disparagingly suggest that God does not know what is going on, or if he does, he is too nice to punish! Vineyard language of pruning is figurative for enemies "pruning" Israel. In mercy God stops short of complete destruction. There is a difference between punishment and annihilation.

The people conclude that God will not punish them. To Jeremiah will be given fiery words that will devastate the people's arguments (**5:14–19**). Babylon, still unnamed, will demolish Judah's fortresses and consume stored provisions as well as current harvests. The sense of verse 16 is that their arrows are deadly. War casualties are many.

A second round of announcements and accusations begins in 5:20, in which greater stress is put on the evils that necessitate severe judgment. Specifically, Judah has spurned the Creator God and within society, including even religious life, people practice injustice (**5:20–31**).

God presents himself as the Creator, basically the God of space and time. God curbs the mighty sea. God insures regularity of seasons. Yet his people, unimpressed, have violated God's limits and have no awe before him. Irreverently, their eyes and ears are closed to God's wonders. Along with the evils of omission are evils of defiant action. In rebel spirit they have deserted their God, much to their own hurt, for the rains have ceased. Sinning people cheat themselves out of what is good.

On the human plane there are likewise sins of action and sins of neglect. Evil persons, like hunters of game, fill their traps (cages) to the limit. By their exploitive maneuvers, they exploit other people. Their riches have accumulated, due to their deceptive schemes. They are described as overstepping even the usual evils. They have neglected the defense of orphans and other marginal people who do not have access to power. God makes careful treatment of the disadvantaged a measuring stick for social righteousness (cf. Mic. 2:1–5; Isa. 3:13–15).

Corruption has penetrated even the religious arena. Prophets prophesy falsely. The priests are conniving power grabbers who use their position unethically. For these evils God would judge any other nation. And Israel is no exception.

Earlier, people hurried into the city for safety (4:5). But now the invader (compared to a nomadic shepherd whose flocks eat away the pasture) has moved southward to Benjamite territory just north of Jerusalem (**6:1–9**). Verse 2 is best taken as "I will destroy fragile Zion."

Attacks are made early in the day. The commander barks orders; the attackers are determined. The Lord, now on the side of the enemy, adds his orders to build a ramp up against the city wall (cf. Jer. 21:4). Oppression, violence, and plundering are the reasons for this turn of events. God may, if Judah does not take warning, do even worse by turning completely away and not restraining the enemy at all. The enemy will make a thorough search, like a grape gatherer reaching into the vine branches, for the last fugitive.

With language heightened in intensity, additional reasons are given for the invasion (**6:10–20**): disinterest in God's message; covetousness; corrupt religious leaders who fail to be radical but instead do easy counseling, assuring peace and well-being; callousness about evil; intentional disobedience; and rejection of God's Word. Sacrifices continue with rare incense from Sheba in Arabia and specialties possibly from India. But these are unacceptable because of Judah's moral condition.

Even so, Jeremiah gives warning; God counsels Judah to return to the older tried life-style and calls forth watchmen (prophets). The warning, however, is not heard because of stopped-up (uncircumcised) ears, nor is the counsel heeded, nor is ear given to the prophets. God's anger will therefore be unleashed. Nations are called to witness that such proceedings are just. Jeremiah's personal outrage seems to ignite God's anger, for in the interchange both become increasingly exasperated.

Throughout the larger block (4:5–6:30) more and more details about the invader from the north have been supplied. Here the army is depicted as advancing fully armed and altogether cruel and merciless (**6:21–30**). The defenders are hopelessly enfeebled. Escape routes are cut off. Jeremiah anticipates sackcloth rituals of mourning for those slain.

The foe from the north has been said to be the Scythians, but that is hardly likely since their invasion is historically questionable. Since in mythology the mountain of the north was not only the home for the gods but also the source of evil, some have advocated that Jeremiah used this myth to generate fear and foreboding. Most likely, even though the enemy remains unnamed and may initially not have been known to Jeremiah, the "northerner" was the Babylonian army.

Jeremiah is to assay the worth of metals (v. 27). Lead was added to silver ore so that when heated, it would remove alloys. Here there is ore, but not enough silver. Jeremiah's conclusion: these are (literally) "rebels of rebels." There is no true Israel. This negative judgment is elsewhere tempered with some words of hope. But now, refine as one will, there is no precious metal, only scum silver at best, and that is to be rejected. On this hopeless note ends a passage which has included strong warnings, earnest appeals for change, and dire threats.

D. Examining public worship (7:1–8:3). The basic mode of poetry in 2:1–10:25 is interrupted by a prose sermon. The sermon, a sharp attack on moral deviations and misguided doctrinal views about the temple, stirs up a vehement response, as we learn from a parallel account in 26:1–15. Attack on venerated tradition is risky business (cf. Acts 7). The sermon's subject of worship leads to some instructions designed to correct misguided worship (7:16–26) and to halt bizarre worship (7:27–8:3). The sermon is prelude to further talk about siege (8–10). Similarly, the sermon of chapters 2–3 precedes the announcement of the northern invader (4:5–6:30).

The famous temple sermon (**7:1–15**) at once identifies the points at issue: a call to reform of behavior and a challenge to belief about the temple. The first point is amplified in verses 5–7; the second in verses 8–12. A biting announcement concludes the sermon, which was preached early in the reign of Jehoiakim.

The temple gate, perhaps the so-called New Gate (26:10), from which Jeremiah spoke, belonged to the three-hundred-year-old Solomonic temple. The call to reform is given without preamble but with specifics. Practicing justice, that is, the observance of honorable relations, is a primary requirement. Specifically "doing justice" (as contrasted to the Western notion of "getting justice") means coming to the aid of those who are helpless and otherwise the victims of mistreatment, often widows, orphans, and strangers.

To shed innocent blood is to take life by violence or for unjust cause. The gift of land was outright; the enjoyment of that gift was conditional. The theme of land loss and land repossession is frequent in Jeremiah (16:13; 24:6; 32:41; 45:4).

A second consideration is a popular chant which had become a cliché: "the temple of the Lord." Its popularity arose from the teaching that God chose Zion, and by implication, the temple (Ps. 132:13–14). A century earlier, with the Assyrian threat, God had shielded and spared the city (2 Kings 19). Any threat to the city's safety was apparently shrugged off with the argument that God would protect his dwelling-place under any circumstance. A theology once valid had become stale, even false.

Jeremiah points to violations of the Ten Commandments (v. 9; Exod. 20:1–17). It is incongruous that people who steal and go after Baal, this Canaanite nature deity of weather and fertility, should claim immunity on the basis of the temple. Brashly these worshipers contend that standing in the temple, performing their worship, gives them the freedom to break the law. The temple, like a charm, has become a shelter for evildoers. Theirs is (eternal) security, so they think. But God sees not only their "holy" worship, but their unholy behavior.

The clincher in Jeremiah's sermon comes from an illustration in their history more than four hundred years earlier (vv. 12–14). Shiloh, located in Ephraimite territory some twenty miles north of Jerusalem, was the worship center when Israel entered the land (Josh. 18:1). Eli was its last priest. It was destroyed, likely by the Philistines, in 1050, according to Danish archaeologists. Samaria, capital of Israel, was taken by the Assyrians in 722. God threatens to do to Jerusalem what he did to Shiloh and Samaria. The people's worship is misguided in two ways (**7:16–26**): they offer to the Queen of Heaven (vv. 16–20); they offer to God but without moral obedience (vv. 21–26).

The Queen of Heaven (v. 18) was Ishtar, a Babylonian fertility goddess. Worship of Mesopotamian deities became popular with Manasseh (2 Kings 21:1–18; 23:4–14). Such apostate worship was anything but secret since it involved entire families. Cakes, round and flat like the moon or possibly star-shaped or even shaped like a nude woman, were offered as food to this deity. But any worship of gods other than the Lord Yahweh is a violation of the first commandment. Violations bring dire consequences.

The tone of verse 21 is sarcastic: "Very well, heap up offerings—as many as you want—and gorge yourselves." Some offerings required participants to eat meat; others, such as burnt offerings, were to be offered in their entirety. God did, of course, give commandments in the wilderness about sacrifices (Lev. 1–7).

External worship practices are empty without a devoted heart. Three factors should encourage obedience: (1) the promise of covenant, a part of God's initial design (v. 23; Exod. 6:7; the formula occurs twenty times in the Bible); (2) total well-being (v. 23b); and (3) prophets to encourage (v. 25).

Again the people are charged with failure to receive correction (**7:27–8:3**). The result is the disappearance of truth and integrity and a turning to a bizarre religion. God's punishment will be as outlandish as their practice is bizarre. Anticipating that awful death, Jeremiah is commanded to cut his hair and to cry on the bare hilltop as was customary to mark a calamity.

Vandalism in worship exists. Representations of other deities were brought into the temple reserved for the Lord Yahweh. The Valley of Hinnom, also known as Topheth, is immediately south of old Jerusalem. Topheth ("fire pit") was a worship area (high place) in this valley. Child sacrifice was introduced by Ahaz and Manasseh (2 Kings 16:3; 21:6), abolished by Josiah (2 Kings 23:4–7), but renewed by Jehoiakim.

The judgment speech of 7:32–8:3 predicts that so overwhelming will be the deaths either through plague or military slaughter, that the valley's new name will be Valley of Killing. The sacrifice area will become the cemetery. None will be left to chase off vultures who feed on corpses. Bones of past kings will be exhumed by the enemy as an insult. The astral deities, so ardently served and worshiped, will look coldly and helplessly on.

E. Treachery, trouble, and tears (8:4–10:25). "O that my eyes were a fountain of tears!" It is from such expressions in this section that Jeremiah has been called the weeping prophet. The prophet aches for his people. Trouble will be everywhere and it will be terrible. Crops will fail; fields and properties will be taken over by strangers; and the dreaded foe from the north will be on the way.

Things will never be the same. And the reason is that God's people have forsaken God's law (8:9; 9:13). Specifically, they have not repented of their evil. They speak lies, and they prefer wooden self-made idols to the living God. Desolation will come. The emotional outpourings of sorrow are a new dimension in the development of the theme of judgment.

As the book now stands this kaleidoscope of accusation, threat, and lament—mostly in poetry—follows the temple sermon, which is in prose. One can discern three rounds of presentation: 8:4–9:2; 9:3–25; 10:1–25. Three sections occur in each round:

- —the people's sins (8:4–13; 9:3–9; 10:1–16)
- —the coming trouble (8:14–17; 9:10–16; 10:17–18)
- —sorrow in the minor key (8:18–9:2; 9:17–22; 10:19–25)

Those who stumble ordinarily get up. Those who find themselves on a wrong road turn around. Not so Israel (**8:4–13**). The word *turn* occurs five times in verses 4–5. Like horses with blinders, Israel stubbornly charges ahead. Israel has less sense than birds or animals, whose instinct at least returns them to their original place or owner.

There are four other problems. (1) *Pseudo-wisdom.* Judah prides herself in the possession of the law, possibly a reference to the newly found law book (Deuteronomy?) in 621 under Josiah (2 Kings 22:1–10). "The lying pen of the scribes" (v. 8) does not refer to miscopying or questionable interpretations as much as to leaving a corrupt society unchallenged. (2) *Greed.* (3) *Lying.* Relgious leaders treat Israel's serious wounds (her crisis of wickedness) lightly. They say, "All is well." The duty of prophets was to expose evil, not to minimize it. One can be occupied with God's Word, yet have an unscriptural message. (4) *Failure to feel shame.* The prophet, in contrast to Israel, knows what time it is.

The list of harmful consequences continues (**8:14–17**). It is now the people who understand that the human evils of the enemy's advancing cavalry and poisoned water, as well as natural evils such as poisonous snakes, are God's agents. Sarcastically it is noted that people leave the fields only to die in the cities. Resistance is futile. Poisonous adders cannot be charmed; horses, like modern cruise missiles, are unstoppable.

We have here not a dispassioned onlooker but a tender care-giver torn up over the news of the coming disaster (**8:18–9:2**). Verse 18 is variously translated because of alternate readings in Hebrew and Greek texts. It is best read: "My grief is without healing."

The prophet, perhaps imaginatively, hears the cry of a now-exiled people. Plaintively they ask about God, their King. The terms *God* and *King* are in parallel (v. 19). At the same time the prophet hears God saying in effect: "I can't stand their idolatry." Listening once more, the prophet detects the hopeless cry of those in exile who approach a dreaded winter without provisions. The early harvests of grain (May–June) and the later harvests of fruits (Sept.–Oct.) are over. This agricultural allusion may be a way of saying, "We counted on help (our own or that of others) but nothing came of it."

The prophet identifies with the people ("*my* people"—found three times in three verses; 8:21–23). Since they are crushed, he is crushed. The prophet is beside himself with grief. Exhausted, he cries and wishes for his head to be a never-ending fountain so that he could cry more (9:1). On the other hand, he would like to get away from it all. The people's sins disgust him. Prophets did not stand at a distance lobbing bombshells; they were closely involved with their listeners.

Lying, only mentioned in 8:10, is now treated in full as a major problem (**9:3–9**). Deception has replaced integrity as a way of life.

The usual translation of verse 3 pictures the tongue as a bow and lies as arrows. Equally possible and more stinging (and more in line with v. 8) is the translation that makes the lies the bow and the tongue the arrow. Out of a false person come falsehoods. In any case lies have a lethal quality about them. Verse 4 has a clever turn of phrase: "Jacob" is synonymous with "deceiver"; hence, literally, every one deceives ("Jacobs") his brother.

For any other nation such flagrant violation of truth and integrity would mean God's punishment. Should Israel be spared? It is as though God throughout wrestles with the issue of what is the just and right thing to do.

The "I" of verse 10 is Jeremiah, who once more responds emotionally by weeping at the prospect of punishment (**9:10–16**). The desolation is complete. No mooing of cattle and no sound of birds is heard. All signs of life are gone (cf. 4:25). The "I" of verse 11 is God. Scattering among the Gentiles would be a fate for some; death through the sword the fate for others. The title *Lord Almighty* (NIV), that is, "Lord of Heaven's Armies," does not leave the outcome of his decision in doubt.

Such destruction calls for an explanation. In a nutshell the reasons are: faithlessness to the law (in which they boasted, 8:8); disobedience to the Lord; a godless life-style; and long-practiced idolatry of the Canaanite variety. Other reasons are given in 9:3–9.

Voices of wailing in response to the total destruction come from three quarters (**9:17–22**). First, professional women mourners, usually engaged to prompt crying at funerals and calamities, are hurriedly summoned to lament this awful disaster. Second, wailing is heard from Jerusalem itself, where plundered fugitives explain that they must vacate their dwellings and leave their land because all is ruined. Third, since in the future mourners will be in great demand, the professionals are urged to train daughters and neighbors in the art of mourning.

The epidemic is described metaphorically: "Death has climbed in through our windows" (v. 21). Alternatively, "death" may be a personification of a demonlike figure Lamastu known from Akkadian literature.

Proper boasting is described (**9:23–26**). The connection of verses 23–24 with the foregoing is not at once clear. The "wise" have been noted in verse 12 and again in verse 17. Wisdom and riches could refer to the royal life-style under Solomon. Jehoiakim gloried in riches, in contrast to his father Josiah for whom knowing God was important; "knowing God" meant caring for the disadvantaged. The Hebrew word for "know" obviously goes beyond possessing information!

Kindness or covenant love is voluntary help extended to those in need. Justice includes honorable relations in every transaction. Judged by this quality alone, the situation described in the foregoing verses is nauseating. Righteousness is that inner disposition of integrity and uprightness that issues in right action.

The nations listed (v. 26) were likely in a military alliance against Babylon. The historical situation is assumed to be 597 when Nebuchadnezzar led an attack against Jerusalem. For Israelites to hear their country named along with others must have been shocking. Yet this emphasizes that inner obedience is more crucial in God's sight than mere outward compliance.

The blistering tirade against idols (**10:1–16**) is directed against "Israel," which as an umbrella term includes both Israel and Judah. Here Judah is particularly in view. Judah is warned about the astral deities commonly worshiped in Babylon. Some scholars claim an exilic setting for the poem. Many deny its unity and that Jeremiah wrote it. The contrast between homemade idols and the living God has seldom been better drawn. With cutting sarcasm the process of shaping, stabilizing, and clothing these gods is described. The contrast between the idol and God is heightened by alternating a mocking poem with a doxology: idols (3–5); God (6–7); idols (8–9); God (10); idols (11); God (12–13); idols (14–15); God (16).

The idols are nonfunctioning, a "work of errors" (NKJV). They are an embarrassment to their makers and will be the object of divine punishment. Fear, quite inappropriate before idols, is necessary before God.

To clinch the contrast with the unnamed figurines, God is given a name: Yahweh, the Lord of Heaven's Armies, Lord Almighty. The name *Portion of Jacob* (v. 16) points to God's lively interest in people. He is also known as "King of the nations" and "King" (vv. 7, 10). From a statement about his incomparability (God is in a class by himself) and his function as Creator, the writer moves to God's crowning activity: his election and shaping of Israel to be his special people.

The crisp word about picking from the ground the fugitive's bundle announces the theme of coming trouble heard throughout these chapters (**10:17–18**). God serves notice, as to a tenant, that he will sling out (cf. the same word in Judg. 20:16) the inhabitants. There is about this a tone of a final warning.

Judah is without shelter and without family (**10:19–25**). Blame properly falls on her leaders, chiefly kings, who have failed to seek God. The destruction comes at the hand of the northerner—still unnamed but a reference to Babylon.

Instead of taking satisfaction in his announcement coming true, Jeremiah interjects, "This is my sickness and I must endure it." Jeremiah speaks again in verse 23. Given the dull-hearted leaders, he is unsure of his next step. The request to be corrected may be for himself or may be made in behalf of the people. The prayer for God's anger to fall on the Gentiles could be a quotation from the people (cf. Ps. 79:6–7). Like the prayers for vengeance (Pss. 109; 137), while not representing the New Testament ideal of loving enemies, the prayer at least turns the situation over to God instead of taking it in hand personally.

III. Stories about Wrestling with People and with God (11–20)

The preceding chapters, though grim with dark announcements and heavy accusations, have had a formal cast. Only rarely has the prophet expressed personal anguish. In chapters 11–20, however, Jeremiah as a person is much more at center stage. In these stories Jeremiah wrestles hard to persuade his audience of their serious situation. He engages in sign acts. Here also we observe a man wrestling with God as he deals with frustrations and discouragements. The so-called laments or confessions—seven of them—are unique windows into the prophet's interior life (11:20–23; 12:1–4; 15:10–11, 15–21; 17:14–18; 18:18–23; 20:7–13).

A. Coping with conspiracies (11:1–12:17). Two scenes of conspiracy dominate these two chapters. The first is a conspiracy of a covenant people against its covenant God (11:9–13). In the second conspiracy, in the private arena, plotters conspire to do away with Jeremiah (11:18–19). The double conspiracy leads to two personal encounters with God in which the prophet pours out his complaint (11:20; 12:1–4). In each case God answers, but not necessarily as Jeremiah expected (11:21–23; 12:5–17).

Covenant has been a presupposition in the foregoing chapters but it is now made explicit (**11:1–8**). Covenant is more than a contract. "Contract" suggests negotiation and terms, has generally to do with goods or services, and is task-oriented. "Covenant," while it is not without terms, is a bonding between two persons which has mutual relationships as its goal. At stake is intimacy and loyalty. The intimacy factor is pinpointed in the covenant formula: *You will be my people, and I will be your God.* The loyalty component is explicit in "Obey." The charge that Israel has not obeyed is repeated more than thirty times in chapters 7, 11, 26, 35, and 42.

"This covenant" (v. 2) may be the renewed covenant under Josiah (2 Kings 23). More likely, because the context is "forefathers" and Egypt, it is the Sinai covenant (Exod. 19–24). Since the Josianic covenant was a renewal of the earlier covenant, we may properly see in these verses Jeremiah's aggressive preaching in behalf of the reform launched by Josiah in 621 B.C.

Deliverance was the presupposition for covenant. The idiom *land flowing with milk and honey* (v. 5) suggests paradise and in Western idiom could be rendered "God's country." Set in between these grace gifts is a call to obedience. "To obey," very frequent in verses 2–8, is to comply with the will of another.

Covenant, it has been suggested, has close parallels with ancient political treaties. These treaties concluded by invoking strong curses on the party which failed to observe the treaty terms (cf. Deut. 27:15–26). God threatens to set these curses in motion. By saying "Amen" (v. 5b), Jeremiah consents to this understanding of covenant and invites his audience to stand with him on common ground.

Jeremiah **11:9–13** is in the pattern of the traditional judgment speech which begins with an accusation and ends with an announcement. The accusation becomes the reason for, and shapes the nature of, the announcement.

The accusation is conspiracy. Both Judah and Israel have conspired to return to old ways. In defiance they have gone after other gods. In political language this is an act of treason. Jeremiah puts it boldly and shockingly: (they) have broken the covenant (v. 10).

God closes the door to any change of mind by forbidding prophetic intercession (**11:14–17**). The sense of verse 15 is that Judah/Israel, God's beloved, has no business in his temple (perhaps meaning the land) because she has plotted numerous times against him. Sacrifices, which she still offers, are called "consecrated meat" to suggest her notion that only the outward matters.

Now Israel, a highly desirable and potentially productive olive tree, is hit by a lightning storm and destroyed. Covenant curses have been activated.

To pronounce the covenant broken is to stir opposition (**11:18–23**). The men of Anathoth, Jeremiah's townfolk, are almost certainly his immediate family (cf. 12:6). Embarrassed, then incensed, they eventually plot murder. People who resent a disconcerting message resort to silencing or eliminating the messenger (cf. Amos 7:12; Jesus in John 19; Stephen in Acts 7:54–59).

The episode triggers an appeal by Jeremiah to God for him to deal with the plotters. As a righteous God, he tests internal motives. "Kidneys" were thought to be the seat of emotion. The "heart" symbolized thought and will. Commendably, the prophet refrains from retaliation. His prayer is in accord with the teaching: "Vengeance is mine, I will repay says the Lord."

God's response to bring disaster on the plotting townsfolk must be seen as a miniature scene showing how God can be expected to deal with covenant partners who conspire. Verses 20–23 make up Jeremiah's first personal lament.

The second of Jeremiah's seven personal laments touches on God, the wicked, the prophet himself, and the land (**12:1–4**). Jeremiah uses court language and asks about justice, right dealing. "Righteous" is a term of relationship describing integrity and uprightness. On what grounds can God prosper evil persons? It is an old question. The wicked discount God by claiming that God will not have final jurisdiction over them.

The prophet protests innocence, a feature of other laments. Moral corruption has ecological effects, death among them (v. 4; Hos. 4:1–3).

Jeremiah **12:5–17** is a reply to the questions of verses 1–4. There are two answers. The first is to rebuke Jeremiah: "If such (little) problems upset you, how will you successfully deal with weighty issues?" The Jordan Valley has its jungles—a considerable obstacle course. Here is no offer of sympathy nor divine coddling, but a call to toughen up. Far harder to explain than the success of the wicked is God's overturning of his own people.

Verses 7–13, a second answer, give a partial response to the evil about which Jeremiah has complained. God will judge that wicked people even though it is his inheritance, his special people. Already surrounding nations have beset her, as a flock of birds is known to peck at an odd speckled bird (v. 9). Or perhaps the scene is one of a hen with hawks circling overhead. The raids of hordes, including the Moabites and Ammonites, could be in view in verse 10. Shepherds are kings commonly so-called in the Orient.

Successively God loses his vineyard, his field, in fact, his entire portion. As in the previous lament (11:20–23), Jeremiah's challenge to God's justice becomes an excuse to reiterate the now-familiar announcement of coming destruction. One clue to the question about justice lies in the future when God will punish his people.

God's justice, about which Jeremiah inquired, means that the nations who as God's agents bring desolation will themselves be judged (12:14–17). This of course raises other issues, not addressed here but elaborated elsewhere (Isa. 10:5–7). One does not harm God's possession, his people, without receiving harm in turn. But later on God will restore Moab and Ammon (48:47; 49:6). He will bless Egypt (Isa. 19:24). The agenda of justice has become the agenda of compassion. God's missionary purpose must not go unnoticed (Isa. 2:1–4; 19:16–25).

B. Pride ruins everything (13:1–27). The ruined girdle (**13:1–11**) is the first of several sign acts that are dramatized attention-getters for people who have stopped listening. Sign acts consist of a divine command, the report of compliance, and an explanation. The *'ēzôr* (loincloth, girdle) is more than a belt; it is like a short skirt that reaches down to the knees but hugs the waist.

Jeremiah's symbolic act has a double message, the first of which is the evil of pride. God detests pride (2 Chron. 32:24–26; Prov. 8:13). Arrogance, an exaggerated estimate of oneself, brings the disdain of others and accounts for the evils of verse 10. Second, the sign act pictures the way in which God would take proper pride in Israel, who like the girdle worn around the waist, would be close, as well as beautiful. That hope was dashed.

Wine at harvest was put into storage jars. Two-foot-tall clay jars held about ten gallons each. Jeremiah states the obvious (or is it a riddle?) in order to secure assent (**13:12–14**). Those drunk with actual wine or with divine intoxication (25:15) are civil and religious rulers as well as ordinary citizens. The smashing of these jars suggests the violent clash between these groups, with resulting factions. The entire social structure will disintegrate.

A discussion of pride precedes a miscellaneous collection of evils, all of which justify harsh punishment (**13:15–27**). To "give glory" (v. 16) is literally to give weight or to make God, not self, prominent. To look for light is to look for the time of salvation. The picture is one of a traveler in the mountains overtaken by nightfall. The captivity, indeed Judah's wholesale exile, is here first mentioned (v. 19), even though the northern agent (Babylon) has been announced earlier (4:6). In the invasion, the fortified cities of the Negeb in the south will be surrounded and blockaded, becoming inaccessible.

Jerusalem is addressed as a woman in verses 20–22. Those persons and countries whom Judah enlisted as allies will be appointed by the enemy to rule over them. Like civilian women in wartime, so Judah will be violated. She will be disgraced, stripped from head to toe, and exposed.

C. Dealing with drought (14:1–15:21). If past chapters have emphasized God's punishment of his people through the sword, these two deal primarily with drought. Famine pushes the people to pray, even to acknowledge their sinfulness. God refuses to help; no relief is in sight. The prophet is pained by the people's plight, and in a different way, his own. Chapter divisions obscure two symmetrical halves (14:2–16 and 14:17–15:9). In each there is a description of the famine (14:2–6; 14:17–18), a prayer (14:7–9; 19–22), and a divine response (14:10–16; 15:1–9).

The droughts (pl.) are vividly depicted in

their effect on high-ranking people, farmers, and animals (**14:1–9**). City gates, more like open areas comparable to modern malls, were places for merchandizing and legal transactions. All has come to a standstill because of the downturn in the economy. To "cover the head" (v. 3) is a cultural expression of embarrassment or frustration.

When people's livelihood is in jeopardy, they pray. There is recognition of evil (lit. crookedness, perversity), acknowledgment of their continual "turning," and their sin (lit. missing the mark). "For the sake of your name" (v. 7) refers to the name *Yahweh* which means, "I am present to save." To "bear your name" (v. 9b) is to belong to God. People chide God for being uninvolved and for failure of nerve. They seek consolation from old assurances and, in bargaining fashion, ask that God forget their sins.

The finality of God's "No!" to the people's prayer is evidenced in his forbidding prophetic intercession (**14:10–18**). All access to God such as fasting and sacrifice is barred (Isa. 58:3–11). False prophets who kept announcing good times and "true peace" were Jeremiah's constant irritation. His experience of seeing victims of sword (animals put out of misery) in the field and hunger in the city totally contradicts any optimism. The conclusion: the prophets and priests, who are called to show the way, wander aimlessly. "They do not know" (v. 18) may mean that they do not know the mind of the Lord.

Suffering, such as hunger, is not necessarily sin-related; however, this famine is a judgment (**14:19–22**). Hope for an answer lies in the Lord's name, his covenant, and his creation power. "Do not dishonor your glorious throne" (v. 21) is an appeal on the basis of the temple (cf. 17:12).

Again intercession is ruled out (**15:1–9**). Moses and Samuel, both prophets, interceded at critical times. God fulfills an earlier announcement not to hear pleas for help (11:11). Manasseh, who ruled Judah fifty years earlier, was Judah's most wicked king (v. 4; 2 Kings 21:1–8). A generation is being punished for another's sin, but also for its own sin.

By sword or other means God will annihilate the men, leaving widows. Once-proud mothers of many sons will gasp in their confused, possibly demented state. The covenant promising many descendants has been reversed.

Two laments from the prophet follow (**15:10–21**). Both are in response to the droughts and, more particularly, Jeremiah's devastating announcement that God will destroy his people.

Jeremiah claims he is not to be faulted for the nagging and the widespread antagonism against him. He would rather not have been born (v. 10). God's assurance is for his safety. Verse 12 is a reference to the strong northern killer nation who, like iron, will not be broken in his advance. While to Jeremiah the enemy will show mercy, the land generally will be plundered. People will be removed from their land. The response to the prophet's woes, instead of softening the announcement, hardens it yet more.

The lament of verses 15–18 is by one who shirks further engagement. The prayer for vengeance falls short of the Christian teaching to love enemies. "When your words came" may refer to the discovery of the scroll in the temple (2 Kings 22:13). High joy (to be called by the name of the Lord of Heaven's armies and so be on the winning side) is followed by loathsome misery, hot indignation, and isolation (Jeremiah did not marry, 16:2). Jeremiah has disgust for his enemies, difficulty stabilizing his personal life, and is disappointed in God, who has become a problem. Dry stream beds give a Palestine traveler the mirage of water.

God's answer deals with all three parts of the lament. First, Jeremiah is to turn, to repent, a word which keynoted the sermon in 3:6–4:4. The word play is represented in: "If you change your heart and come back to me, I will take you back." Second, he must not take his cue from others. Third, God recalls the promise of his presence given at the time of Jeremiah's call (1:19). The prophet who levels with God finds that God levels with him.

D. Much bad news, some good (16:1–17:27). These two chapters are a mixture. God instructs Jeremiah privately not to socialize; God speaks publicly about keeping the Sabbath. The people of God will be exiled; but there will be a restoration. A prophet turns to God in his frustration; Gentiles turn en masse to God in conversion. There are mini-essays; there are proverblike sayings. However, the theme remains unchanged: sin is pervasive and judgment will be certain and terrible.

God gives Jeremiah three commands about his social life (**16:1–13**). The reason for each command arises out of the coming disaster. First, Jeremiah is to be celibate. Having children, which was highly desirable, is forbidden him, for all existing families will disappear. Gruesome death will come to children from terrible diseases, the enemy's sword, and famine.

Second, Jeremiah must not attend funerals or extend comfort. The reason: God has withdrawn his covenant blessings of peace, covenant love, compassion, and favor. So must the prophet withdraw his involvement. "Cutting oneself" to show grief, though forbidden (Lev. 19:28; Deut. 14:1), was apparently practiced.

Third, Jeremiah is to avoid weddings and all parties as a way of announcing the end of all joyful socializing. Judah had deserted God because of the stubbornness of an evil heart (v. 12), an expression found eight times (3:17; 7:24; 9:14; 11:8; 13:10; 16:12; 18:12; 23:17). Forewarned of the reason for the disaster, Judah would be able to survive.

Placing promise oracles next to judgment oracles is not new (**16:14–18**; see Hos. 1:9–10). The oracle is repeated in 23:7–8, where it better suits the context. The idiom of verses 14–15 is not to deny the exodus event, but to emphasize that the return from exile will be even more impressive.

Verse 16 notes that fishermen with nets will catch the masses, while hunters will catch the stragglers, so that no one will escape. The language about idols is filled with disgust.

Ironically, while Judah turns from God to idols, Gentiles, world over, turn from idols to God (**16:19–21**). The vision is refreshing and overpowering (cf. 12:14–17; Isa. 2:1–4; 45:14–25; Zech. 8:20–23). Gentiles are saying about these gods what God says about them. God speaks in verse 21. He will teach the Gentiles in the sense of giving them an experience of his power.

The judgment speech in **17:1–4** consists of an accusation and an announcement. Sin written indelibly on the heart will one day be replaced by God's law written on the heart (31:33). Horns were corner projections on an altar to which the animal was tied and on which the atoning blood was put. Asherah poles were wooden carvings erected to honor the astral goddess Asherah, known in Babylon as Ishtar.

The announcement summarizes the disaster. "My mountain" (v. 3) refers to Mount Zion in Jerusalem where the temple stood. High places were hilltop areas set apart for worship of Canaanite gods. By default, the people will lose their belongings, their land, and their freedom. The "cause" is twofold: Judah's sin and God's anger.

In the parable of **17:5–8** the issue is trust, "throwing oneself forward." Jeremiah's announcements, if taken seriously, would trigger military preparations. But on a national scale confidence was not to be placed in human leadership (even a new king) or in military resources. The prospect for nations or individuals leaning on human strength is death and isolation.

In stark contrast, "blessed" or "empowered" are the God-trusting persons. "It does not fear when heat comes" (v. 8). Similar comparisons between the godly and ungodly are made in Psalm 1 and Matthew 7:13–14.

Three separate and only loosely related wisdomlike pieces are joined together (**17:9–13**). The heart, the seat of the will, is searched and explored and diagnosed as deceptive. "Deceitful" is a variant for "Jacob" (deceiver, heel-grabber). The term *incurable* (v. 9) depicts Jeremiah's despair in the human situation. The antidote is a heart transplant (31:33).

The proverb of verse 11 emphasizes both the wrongfulness of riches acquired by devious means, and the way such riches are vulnerable to attack and loss. A partridge or calling bird is said to gather the eggs of other birds and then brood on them to hatch them.

Verse 12 continues the motif of contrasts begun in verse 5. The temple is the place of God's dwelling and hence the place of safety. "Written in the dust" (v. 13) points to some disgrace or may mean "consigned to the netherworld" and thus death, quite opposite to "written in the book of life" (Exod. 32:32; Dan. 12:1).

Another lament as a personal response interrupts the attention focused on the nation (**17:14–18**). It depicts Jeremiah, however, as one who trusts the Lord. To be "saved" (v. 14) is to be brought from restrictive places to the freedom of open spaces. Jeremiah's personal request for healing and salvation arises from the mocking taunts of others. They jeeringly ask about the unfulfilled announcements of disaster—a question likely asked prior to the first Babylonian invasion of Judah in 605. Jeremiah protests innocence. Nor has he wished for the catastrophic event.

The harshness of his prayer for disaster to come on his opponents can be appreciated if his opponents are understood to be those opposing God. "Double destruction" (v. 18), it has been argued, is proportionate destruction (cf. 16:18).

The people are exhorted to observe the Sabbath (**17:19–27**; Sabbath laws are given in Exodus 20:8–11; 23:12; 34:21; Num. 15:32–36). "Be careful" is a frequent admonition in Deuteronomy. The instruction is to desist from public trading and from work generally.

Reform and renewal start with specifics. Some have suggested that of the Ten Commandments Jeremiah singled out the fourth because it was the easiest to observe; besides it was a tangible sign of the covenant (Exod. 31:16–17). As with God's instructions generally, so here, difficulty ensues for those who disregard them; blessing follows those who obey. After two three-month reigns (Jehoahaz; Jehoiachin) the promise of a stable monarchy (vv. 25–26) would be important. Political stability and religious commitment provide the setting for the good life.

Appropriate sacrifices will be brought from the whole land. Verse 26 names the regions: Benjamin, a territory adjoining Judah to the north; the Shephelah, foothills west of Jerusalem; the hill country, the range from Ephraim south; and the Negeb, in the desert south. In the gates, the very place of desecration, fiery destruction will begin should the Sabbath not be observed.

E. A pot marred, a pot smashed (18:1–19:15). These two chapters describe two sign acts. Both involve clay pots. In the first a marred pot is a prelude to a call to repentance—a call that is defiantly rejected. In the second sign act, a pot is smashed as a visual message about the coming catastrophe upon the city of Jerusalem. God's sovereignty is evident throughout.

If one includes chapter 20 one can see two symmetrical halves, the second half more elaborate and precise than the first:

1. Pottery making/smashing 18:1–10; 19:1–13
2. God shapes disaster 18:11–17; 19:14–15
3. Attack on the prophet 18:18; 20:1–16
4. A response of lament 18:19–23; 20:17–18

The sign act or symbolic action is in the traditional form: (1) an instruction; (2) report of compliance; and (3) an interpretation.

The potter's equipment consisted of two stone discs placed horizontally and joined by a vertical shaft. The lower would be spun using the feet; the other, at waist level, had on it the clay for the potter's hand to shape.

Uprooted, torn down, and destroyed, as well as build and plant recall words from Jeremiah's call which occur there, as here, in the context of nations generally (1:10; cf. 24:6).

It is not so much that God offers a second chance, but that just as the potter is in charge and decides what to do when things go other than planned, so God is in charge and at any given moment has the option of choice. In some sense at least, prophetic announcements are conditional. God is not arbitrary; repentance makes a difference.

The principle stated in verses 6–8 is next applied to Judah (**18:11–17**). Their decision to follow their own stubborn heart is confirmed by their explicit statement.

God assesses their decision as "horrible" (v. 13)—unlike the decision of other nations (2:10–11). The argument in verse 14 is that it is contrary to nature for snow to leave Lebanon. The seriousness of coming disaster is described by responses of others to it: scorn (v. 16) is hissing or whistling in unbelief. God's "face" (v. 19) is language for blessing and favor.

The decision to follow personal plans puts into effect plans to do away with the prophet (**18:18–23**). Priests, wise men, and prophets, along with kings, represent that society's leaders.

Jeremiah's prayer incorporates elements similar to those in his other laments (see 11:18–23; 12:1–4; 15:10–21; 17:14–18). There is personal petition, complaint, and a call for God to bring vengeance. Evil has been paid him for the good he has done—specifically, he has sought the well-being of those now turned against him. The question of verse 20a could also be a question asked by his persecutors who think of their actions as good.

We are shown an angry prophet. Against families (women, youths, children) Jeremiah would bring famine and sword. Even more, he prays God to forestall any atonement for their sins. Here is a lapse in prophetic intercession. Even acknowledging that Jeremiah leaves the matter in God's hands, he falls short of Jesus' response to his enemies: "Father forgive them" (Luke 23:34). One may, however, in Jeremiah's response see mirrored how God in justice might deal with those opposing him.

The terrible message of doom is first made vivid to the elders by means of a smashed pot; later the same message is announced to all the people (**19:1–15**). Egyptians wrote names of enemies on pottery jars and then smashed them, believing that such action magically triggered disaster.

F. Terror on every side (20:1–18). Here is the first one-on-one announcement of the coming catastrophe (**20:1–6**). Pashhur might well have been among the religious leaders taken by Jeremiah on a tour to see Tophet (19:1–15). Magor-Missabib (v. 3), which means "terror on every side," catches the emotional dimension of the coming disaster. The name is a reversal of Pashhur, which, though Egyptian, in Aramaic might mean "fruitful on every side." Babylon, now named for the first time in the book (v. 4), will be Pashhur's destiny, not because he arrested Jeremiah, but because he collaborated in the big lie of announcing continued safety (8:10–11). In keeping with the principle of corporate personality or social solidarity, Pashhur's household will share his fate.

The lament in **20:7–13** follows the classical lament pattern: complaint, statement of confidence, petition, and praise. Jeremiah's address to God is daring. "Deceived" (v. 7) is elsewhere rendered as "entice" or "seduce" (Exod. 22:16), but may here be used in the sense of "persuade," though with a sinister purpose (Prov. 24:28). God has victimized the prophet. Jeremiah cries out as an innocent sufferer. To shout violence is the equivalent of the modern "Emergency!"

Jeremiah's personal frustration in dealing with an irresistible urge to speak is compounded by external opposition. "Friends" (v. 10) is a tongue-in-cheek designation. His "support system" has collapsed. They mock him with the slogan of his own message, "Terror on every side."

The statement of confidence about God as warrior (v. 11) harks back to Jeremiah's call (1:8, 19). God's vengeance contrasts with the enemy's vengeance. Praise within a lament is a standard component; one-third of all the psalms are classified as laments, and all but one contain praise. In contrast to other laments, there is no recorded response from God here.

The classical statement of cursing in **20:14–18** likely describes another occasion; otherwise its link with verse 13 presents a schizophrenic prophet. Or, this may be not Jeremiah's curse, but a standard outcry made by people caught in calamity. Cursing the day of one's birth stops short of cursing God (cf. Job 3:2–10). Sodom and Gomorrah, totally destroyed, are the two cities of verse 16 (cf. Gen. 19:24–28). The speaker, in his vexation of spirit, would have preferred to be stillborn or unborn. The death wish, if it is Jeremiah's, arises not only out of personal despair, but also out of the shocking public scene.

IV. Challenging Kings and Prophets (21–29)

The preceding chapters have introduced the message of doom (2–10) and the reason for that message (11–20). Beginning with this section we are more securely locked into datable historical, though chronologically disarranged, events. We hear of kings: Josiah, Jehoiakim, Jehoiachin, Zedekiah. We meet prophets: Hananiah, Ahab, Zedekiah, Shemaiah. The leaders bear major responsibility for Judah's evil condition. Prose narrative dominates, with Jeremiah spoken of in the third person.

A. Addressing rulers and governments (21:1–23:8). The first of two delegations (**21:1–10**) from Zedekiah to Jeremiah is to be dated 588 B.C. Nebuchadnezzar, the famous ruler of Babylon (605–562), had earlier invaded Judah (597) and had appointed Zedekiah as king. Zedekiah, apparently persuaded by his advisors to invite Egypt's help, had rebelled (cf. 52:3). Now Nebuchadnezzar is back.

The delegation wonders whether God might intervene, as he had when Hezekiah was threatened by Sennacherib and the Assyrians (2 Kings 19:35–36). Pashhur (v. 1) is not to be identified with the priest of 20:1–6; he later calls for Jeremiah's death (38:1–6). Zephaniah (v. 1) is not to be confused with the priest (29:25, 29). He is a member of a later delegation (37:3–10) and appears in 2 Kings 25:18. Jeremiah as an intermediary is approached for information.

Jeremiah's answer is bad news. Judah's weapons will be turned back on themselves, possibly through Babylonian capture, or because of confusion during a rapid retreat. Judah faces a God who fights not for her, but against her. An "outstretched hand" (v. 5) is holy war language.

The fate of Zedekiah—death at the hand of Nebuchadnezzar's sword—was fulfilled (52:8–11). Jeremiah's counsel for the people to surrender peacefully to the Babylonians (also called Chaldeans) brands him a traitor.

The passage about God-pleasing government (**21:11–22:9**) is in two symmetrical parts (21:11–14 and 22:1–9):

1. instruction (21:11–12; 22:1–3)
2. announcements (21:13–14; 22:4–9)

The instruction is first to the royal dynasty generally, almost as if by way of review (21:11–12; Deut. 17:18–20; 1 Kings 3:28). Jeremiah walks downhill from the temple to the palace to address a specific ruler of David's line, possibly Zedekiah. The initial call in either case is for the king to be a guardian of justice which has been defined as "love in action" or "honorable relations." Clearly "justice" goes beyond legal court decisions, and is expressed in social concern for the oppressed and for the marginal people, those readily exploited or cheated.

The announcement in the first half (21:13–14) assumes a history of failure. God is poised to move against Jerusalem (not named, but inferred from the feminine forms; cf. v. 5). Jerusalem has valleys on three of its sides; the rocky plateau is Mount Zion. The forests refer to the pillars in the palace or to the palace itself, called "Palace of the Forest of Lebanon" (1 Kings 7:2).

The promise in the second half (22:4–9) consists of good things for the royal house or dynasty, followed by a warning.

The verdicts about Judah's kings (22:11–30) may at one time have been isolated statements. Or if Zedekiah is the king to whom 21:11–22:9 is addressed, they might have been spoken for his benefit.

Jehoahaz's failures are detailed first (**22:10–12**). The dead king (v. 10) is Josiah, Judah's king for thirty-one years who died in battle at Megiddo in 609, apparently in an attempt to halt the Egyptians. He who is exiled is Shallum, whose regal name was Jehoahaz, the fourth oldest son of Josiah (1 Chron. 3:15). He came to the throne at age twenty-three in 609 and ruled only three months. Pharaoh Neco of Egypt declared his suzerainty over Judah by taking Jehoahaz captive, first to Riblah, north of Damascus, and then to Egypt, where he died (2 Kings 23:31–34; 2 Chron. 36:1–4).

Jeremiah's sharpest and most extended critique is directed at the despot Jehoiakim, who ruled 609–597 (**22:13–23**; see 2 Kings 23:34–24:6). Midway through his eleven-year reign he became a vassal of the Babylonians. Jeremiah attacks Jehoiakim's ostentation and covetousness in connection with a new palace built, as archaeologists in the 1960s have suggested, at Ramat Rachel.

A woe statement (v. 13; cf. v. 18 where "woe" is translated "alas"), while common in Jeremiah (23:1; 48:1), is more frequent in Isaiah (5:8, 11, 18, 20, 21). Unrighteousness is lack of inner integrity, and injustice is failure to be honorable in transactions. Justice was to be a ruler's first concern (21:11; 23:5; Mic. 3:1–3). Specifically, Jehoiakim cheated his workers out of pay or resorted to forced labor. Because of the heavy tribute to Egypt he may have been unable to pay (2 Kings 23:35).

Large rooms, windows, and cedar paneling—a luxury (cf. Hag. 1:4)—and red paint signal showiness. Jehoiakim was obsessed with acquiring wealth and with shedding innocent blood. Oppression (v. 17), in its verb and noun forms, occurs more than fifty times in the Old Testament. In many contexts the term carries nuances of "force" or "violence," and sometimes misuse of power. In more than half the occurrences, the context also specifies poverty.

Jehoiakim's insensitivity to the urgency of the times is in contrast with Josiah, whose overriding concern was to do what was right and just. Concretely this meant acts of compassion and caring for the poor. Knowing (i.e., experiencing) God consists of such care giving (cf. 9:23).

People will not hold Jehoiakim, who wanted so much to be a "somebody," in regard, nor will they express loss at his death or care for his "accomplishments," his splendor. The oracle with the catchword *Lebanon* (vv. 20, 23) is directed in the feminine to Jerusalem.

The accusation is that of disobedience. Shepherds are civil rulers; "allies" refers to Egypt, Assyria, Moab, and the like who will be driven off by the wind (fulfilled in 597).

Jehoiachin, known as (Je)Coniah, was Jehoiakim's eighteen-year-old son who succeeded him and reigned for three months in 598–597 (**22:24–30**; 2 Kings 24:8–12). The signet ring (v. 24) was used to stamp official correspondence. The queen mother was Nehushta (v. 26; cf. 2 Kings 24:8). Jeremiah's prediction was fulfilled in 597 (2 Kings 24:15). The last comment about Jehoiachin is about improved conditions in exile where he died (Jer. 52:31–34).

"Pot" (v. 28) is a term for a degraded quality of jar. The address to land is likely a call for a witness (v. 29; cf. 6:19). The threefold iteration marks intensity (cf. Isa. 6:3). Jehoiachin had seven sons (1 Chron. 3:17–19), none of whom ruled. Zerubbabel, Jehoiachin's grandson, returned to Jerusalem to become governor, not king. Since Zedekiah, Judah's last king, preceded Jehoiachin in death, Jehoiachin in effect marked the end of a 350-year Davidic dynasty.

The righteous branch is celebrated in **23:1–6.** A general woe is spoken to all rulers, known in the ancient world as shepherds (cf. Ezek. 34). God notes and repays officials who have misused their office. The charge *You have scattered* refers to the scattering into exile which will be the result of sins such as child sacrifice, which kings condoned and even encouraged. "Tend" (v. 4) is used both for care giving and for supervision in the sense of paying attention. Restoration to the land of those scattered will be a chief theme of the Book of Comfort (chaps. 30–33, esp. 30:3; 31:17) and Ezekiel (11:17; 20:42; 37:21).

"Branch" is familiar language about royal family trees (Isa. 10:33–11:4) and serves as a messianic title (Isa. 4:2; Zech. 3:8; 6:12). This promise, one of the few messianic promises in Jeremiah, is echoed in 33:15–16. Justice and righteousness will be the trademark of the coming ideal king, as it was to have been of all kings. The name *Lord our Righteousness* (v. 6) memorably embodies God's concern for justice. Since the name *Yahweh Tsidqenu* is close to Zedekiah's *Tsidqi Yahu* (My justice is Yahweh), some have thought that this oracle has allusions to Judah's last king. If so, then all of Judah's last kings, beginning with Josiah, would have been named (22:10–23:6). It is better, since the oracle is in the future tense, to see in it the description of the ideal king, who from our vantage point is Jesus, the Messiah.

The oracle about a glorious return from exile (vv. 7–8) is elaborated in chapters 30–31. The exodus from Egypt was significant in shaping a people. So will the "new" exodus of the exiles, the descendants of Israel, inaugurate a new era. The "return" took place in 538 and partially fulfilled the oracle which promised more spectacular things. It has been noted that a god-sized problem was given a God-sized cure.

B. Addressing prophets and their audiences (23:9–40). The challenge to leaders continues. The address to the kings, the civil leaders (21:1–23:6), is followed by an address to the religious leaders, the prophets and priests (23:9–40). They are faulted for giving leadership in Baal worship, for personal immorality, and for being out of touch with God's message for their time. Their message is either self-originated, or comes by dreams, or is borrowed from others.

Jeremiah's denunciation of his peers is sad before it is harsh (**23:9–10**; cf. 9:1ff.). Confronting persons with their evil is difficult for a caring person. However, so strong and overpowering are God's words to him that, like a drunken man, he feels himself out of control. Since elsewhere the figure of drunkenness is used for those on whom God's wrath comes (13:13–14; 25:15–16), we perhaps should see here a man absorbing punishment intended for his colleagues.

Verse 10 depicts the results for which the prophets are held accountable. Adulterers may refer to faithless marriage partners (5:8). Like Hosea before him (Hos. 1–3), Jeremiah uses adultery to refer to faithlessness of a people with their God. Curses follow covenant breaking. The environment (land) is affected by the people's immorality (cf. Hos. 4:1–3). Drought and famine are described in chapters 14–15.

The word *godless* begins the accusation and ends the announcement against the corrupt clergy (**23:11–15**). "Godless" translates a word meaning "to pollute," "to defile," or "to profane." It means to live in opposition to all that is right. The wickedness in the temple is described elsewhere (2 Kings 16:10–14; 2 Kings 23:7; Ezek. 8:6–18). The prophet's fate is compared to walking in slippery places in the dark.

Two groups of prophets are identified, the second more evil than the first. Samaria was the capital of the ten northern tribes; it fell to the Assyrians a century earlier in 722. Baal was a Canaanite weather and fertility god. The horrible scene in Jerusalem consists of immoralities comparable to those in Sodom and Gomorrah, cities known for their thoroughgoing corruption. The charge of adultery is laid against Ahab and Zedekiah. Lying suggests that these are special "con men."

Jeremiah warns of disaster, but false prophets speak soothing platitudes of presumptuous optimism. They tell people what they want to hear. In this crisis of prophetic ministry, each side accuses the other. Bitter food and poisoned water (v. 15) are both results of army invasions. Food will be in short supply; water sources could be poisoned by the enemy.

The false prophets' messages are misleading and wrong; they are self-induced and not God-originated (**23:16–22**). The prophets give their benediction to God-despisers (v. 17). False prophets make things easy.

Prophetic ministry calls for careful listening and looking during the divine briefing session (vv. 18, 22). Verses 19–20 must be understood as the council's "decision": a whirlwind of wrath from God will crash on the heads of evildoers. Meanwhile, false prophets, altogether out of touch with the purposes of God's heart, predict peaceful times. When future judgment comes, the people will understand it clearly.

Dreams are essentially (though not completely) discounted as a vehicle of divine communication (**23:23–32**). Fascination with dreams had become a substitute for interest in God's name. Ordinary dreams, like chaff, ought by a true prophet to be distinguished from God's firelike word. Jeremiah's testimony to the burning nature of God's Word is given in 20:9. God's Word like a hammer has force and matters; dreams are inconsequential fluff. Reaching for a message to proclaim, these prophets resort to stealing a word from fellow prophets, either their contemporaries or those of an earlier time.

God is against pseudoprophets who plagiarize, misrepresent him, and wish to be sensational. Prophets are called to expose evil. Those who fail to do so do not help God's people.

In the next passage the prophet puns on a word which means either "oracle," a weighty message, or "burden," something that is physically carried. The abruptness of frequent questions in **23:33–40** gives a sense of confusion, no doubt purposely, so as to characterize the religious scene.

Jeremiah alone is depicted as having the true word from the Lord. The word is that God will abandon his people. Verses 37–38 chide the people who, it would seem, go from prophet to prophet to get new or better-sounding messages.

C. Divine anger (24:1–25:38). From concerns about kings and prophets, we move in rapid succession to the future: Judah's, Babylon's, and that of other nations. In his anger—a key theme—God consigns Judah to seventy years of desolation, Babylon to devastation, and all the nations to destruction.

Either in a vision or in actuality, Jeremiah sees two baskets of figs (**24:1–10**). These stand for two major population groups. The date is 597 B.C. Judah now has two rulers: one exiled and one reigning. With whom does the future lie? Two baskets of figs, possibly brought to the temple as a firstfruit offering (Deut. 16:9–12), evoke the Lord's answer.

In the interpretation, the future surprisingly is with the exiles, though the reason, apart from God's initiative and choice, is not given. God can plan calamity or good. The words *build, plant, tear down,* and *uproot* (v. 6) were important in Jeremiah's call (1:10). The covenant formula—*They will be my people, and I will be their God*—captures God's design for bondedness. Here spiritual restoration follows physical return to the land; elsewhere spiritual restoration seems to precede the homecoming (cf. 31:18–22).

The survivors in the homeland feel that God's future with his people will be with them. The obvious conclusion, however, is the wrong conclusion. Some Jews may have been carried to Egypt with Jehoahaz (2 Kings 23:34); others went there later (43:7). The siege of 597 had not completely fulfilled the prophecies for disaster as some may have thought. Jeremiah overturns popular beliefs.

Chronologically, **25:1–14** precedes chapter 24. The date, when allowance is made for variant practices in counting regnal reigns, can be synchronized with Daniel 1:1 to be 605 B.C. Soon after the battle of Carchemish in 605 between the Egyptians and the Babylonians (46:2), Nebuchadnezzar succeeded Nabopolassar as king. In 609 Jehoiakim followed the godly Josiah to the throne. Since Josiah's rule began in 640, the thirteenth year (v. 3) was 627/6. In much of the book Jeremiah has spoken in the first person; here (as also in 20:1–6; 21:1–10; 26:1ff.) he is referred to in the third person.

The summary of the prophet's ministry is in the form of an accusation. It emphasizes the people's failure to listen, a charge made more than thirty times in the book. "Again and again" (v. 4) translates an idiom about early rising ("persistently and without interruption"). A spiritual "turn-around" is here, as elsewhere, linked with continued occupancy in the land. Prophets reinforce the first of the Ten Commandments through their warnings (v. 6; Exod. 20:3).

The announcement (vv. 9–10) identifies the northerner with Nebuchadnezzar of Babylon for the first time. "My servant," also used to describe the prophets, is used here in the sense of "agent." Surrounding nations, such as Edom and Moab, like Judah were in Babylon's path to Egypt. "Completely destroy" (v. 9) is a chilling term from the language of holy warfare where it means "to destroy as in a sacrifice, leaving no survivor."

Social life (marriages), business (millstones), and home life (light) will cease. Seventy years, if intended literally, are best calculated from 605 (an early Babylonian attack) to 535 (the first return came in 538). Other uses of the number, including Assyrian texts, suggest this to be a symbol for indefinite time (Ps. 90:10). Babylon's guilt is pride (50:31). The punishment fits the crime.

Visionlike, the prophet sees the cup of God's wrath (**25:15–29**). It contains God's fury, which is associated with sword and destruction (vv. 16, 27; Isa. 51:17–23; cf. Lam. 4:21; Rev. 18:6). As wine intoxicates and confuses, so will nations gag on this "wine." God's people in Judah are the first to drink. The scene of destruction and the resulting aspersions cast on Judah are presumably repeated for the other nations mentioned.

The roster of nations—nations from every point on the compass—begins with Egypt in the south and ends with Babylon to the east. These two were the superpowers of that century. Foreign people in Egypt and in Arabia designate smaller, usually adjacent kingdoms and allies. Uz bordered the desert east of Jordan. The Philistine city-states lay between Judah and the Mediterranean.

Edom was to the south of Judah; Moab and Ammon were to the east. Tyre and Sidon were in the north. Dedan, Tema, and Buz were in the Arabian desert. Zimri is unknown. Sheshach (v. 26) is a code name for Babylon formed by substituting *B B L* (letters in the second and twelfth positions in the alphabet), with their counterparts when numbering the alphabet backward. Jeremiah, as foretold (1:10), is a prophet to the nations.

Jerusalem is the city that bears God's name. If God's people are not spared because of their sin, how will others, whose sin is presumably greater, fare?

The poem of **25:30–38**, a repetition and reflection of verses 15–29, begins and ends with an angry God. The poem is charged with emotion. With vigor and vehemence God moves against Judah/Israel and all mankind.

Beyond massive deaths of the "flock," the leaders, the high and mighty ones, along with their own deaths, face the dismantling of all they have known.

D. Jeremiah versus the people (26:1–24). Numerous accusations against the kings, prophets, and people in preceding chapters are confirmed in the incidents that follow. A sermon on repentance brings a near lynching (chap. 26). A yoke with its sign message of "surrender" serves to unmask a false prophet (chap. 28). A letter discloses sinister power plays (chap. 29).

It has been argued, quite plausibly, that Baruch compiled these vignettes from Jeremiah's life.

Chapter 26 supplies details surrounding the temple sermon recorded in 7:1–15. Here (**26:1–6**) the focus is on audience response. In 609, Pharaoh Neco of Egypt, who humiliated Judah to vassal status, appointed Jehoiakim king (2 Kings 23:34–35). The public address given early in his reign, likely in 609/8, appeals for general repentance (cf. 25:4–7).

Verse 3 appeals to the principle laid out in 18:7–8: God does not desire the death of the wicked (Ezek. 33:11). Shiloh (v. 6), north of Jerusalem in Ephraimite territory, was the central worship place during the time of the judges (1 Sam. 1–4). It was destroyed, likely by the Philistines, in the middle of the eleventh century, more than four hundred years before Jeremiah. The threat is both against the prized three-hundred-year-old temple and the cherished city of Jerusalem. For a nation which had just lost its revered king, Josiah, and had been subjugated by Egypt, further disaster seems intolerable.

Priests and prophets, whose livelihood depended on the temple, are enraged (**26:7–16**). Promoters of "civil religion," they fail to hear the call to repent. They interpret the threat against temple and city (both held to be divinely chosen) as blasphemy which called for the death penalty (Lev. 24:10–16; 1 Kings 21:13). Court trials were held in the city gate area. Ostensibly Jeremiah is on trial; in reality the people are on trial.

Jeremiah answers the leaders' question; he is divinely deputized. Instead of qualifying the message, he reiterates it together with another appeal. The crowd, initially on the side of the prophet, comes over to the side of the officials.

The elders invoke precedent (**26:17–24**). A century earlier, Micah, like Jeremiah, threatened destruction for both temple and city in the name of the Lord (Mic. 3:12). Hezekiah's response is recorded in 2 Kings 18:4 and 2 Chronicles 29–31. The evil which his repentance forestalled was perhaps Sennacherib's advance on Jerusalem.

Baruch, the likely compiler of this section, adds verses 20–23 to indicate the risk which Jeremiah takes. Officials then were unsympathetic to Uriah, the prophet. Elnathan, a high official, possibly Jehoiachin's father-in-law (2 Kings 24:8), later urges restraint on behalf of Jeremiah (36:25). Ahikam was of the Shaphan family, whose son later befriends Jeremiah (40:5). Ahikam was the father of Gedaliah, governor of Judah after 586. An additional indignity for Uriah was burial as a stateless citizen, likely in the Valley of Kidron (2 Kings 23:6).

E. Submit to Babylon's yoke! (27:1–28:17). The northerner, Babylon, has come! Jeremiah had preached repentance (25:5). Now he "meddles" in foreign policy and urges submission to Babylon rather than resistance or revolt. This unusual counsel, given not as a politician but as a prophet, is pressed on the visiting envoys, on Zedekiah himself, and on the priests and people. Each group is instructed to submit to Babylon; each is warned not to heed false prophets.

The sign act of a wooden yoke makes the message memorable: "Surrender to Nebuchadnezzar" (**27:1–11**). It comes early in Zedekiah's reign, likely 593. In 597 Nebuchadnezzar had appointed Zedekiah to rule (2 Kings 24:15–20). The plot by a coalition of surrounding small states, who like Judah are in Nebuchadnezzar's grip, is to revolt. The time for revolt seems auspicious since Nebuchadnezzar is attending to some revolts nearer home. Also, Pharaoh Neco of Egypt died in 594, and his successor is engaged in wars.

Envoys are on hand in Jerusalem to persuade Zedekiah or were perhaps invited by him. Jeremiah, as a prophet to the nations (1:10), gives them the Lord's word: *submit!*

The yoke is likely an ox yoke consisting of leather straps and a carrying frame. It is one of Jeremiah's several sign acts (chaps. 13, 19, 32, 43). The accompanying message is compelling.

Ancient kings surrounded themselves with prophets and soothsayers. The latter were forbidden in Israel (Lev. 19:26; Deut. 18:10–11). Prophets who give their support to the planned insurrection are branded "liars." Jeremiah fights for a hearing both inside and outside of Judah. Everywhere his unwelcome message of disaster—and now of surrender—is contested and contradicted.

The same message is given to the king and to the people—as the plurals of verse 12 indicate (**27:12–15**). False prophets, such as Hananiah, also speak in the Lord's name. To follow these prophets is to follow a lie (*šeqer*)—a much-used word in Jeremiah (thirty-seven times). It is the way of kings to meet force with force; to submit is alien strategy.

The twofold refrain continues: submit to Babylon; be warned against false prophets (**27:16–22**). The temple, in which the priests had vested interests, is prominent. Some temple articles had been carried off by Babylon in 605 (Dan. 1:2) and again in 597 (2 Kings 24:13). Optimistically, false prophets predict these will be speedily recovered. Jeremiah announces *eventual* recovery. True prophets are marked by intercession.

The year 594/3, in which there was plotting of a revolt, must be assigned to both chapters 27 and 28, if one takes "of that same year" (28:1) seriously. Hananiah, whose name means "the Lord is gracious," hailed from Gibeon, a town five miles northwest of Jerusalem (**28:1–11**). He is repeatedly called "prophet" (vv. 1, 5, 10, 12, 15, 17). Both Jeremiah and Hananiah speak in the name of the Lord Almighty. Hananiah's announcement, however, directly contradicts Jeremiah's (27:16–22). While both predict the return of temple furnishings (27:22; 28:3), it is the time of their return that is at issue: two years (so Hananiah) or seventy years (so Jeremiah—25:12; 29:10). Hananiah also announces Jehoiachin's return. The people now hear conflicting interpretations of the yoke sign act; the onus for a decision about the true prophet is on the people.

Jeremiah proposes two tests for the accuracy of a prophecy. Former prophets, given similar societal conditions, prophesied disaster. Examples would be Amos (2:4), Hosea (4:6), and Isaiah (3:13–15). The first test then is one of consistency with tradition. A second test has to do with the fulfillment of a prediction. Hananiah meets Jeremiah's symbolic action with one of his own: he breaks the yoke. In so doing he endorses the proposed revolt against Nebuchadnezzar.

Jeremiah, who clearly speaks for himself in verse 7, now speaks in the name of the Lord Almighty (**28:12–17**). Hananiah is branded a liar. A pun on the word *sent* could be rendered: "I did not send you, but now I am sending you right off the face of the earth" (vv. 15–16). Prophetic predictions to individuals, other than kings, are relatively rare. The preaching of rebellion calls for the death penalty (Deut. 13:5; 18:20). Two months later there is one less false prophet.

F. A pastoral letter (29:1–32). Jeremiah's letter to the Judean captives in Babylon advises them to adjust to the new circumstances. It warns about false prophets and manipulators.

A brief explanation of the letter is given first (**29:1–3**). A full title for God opens the letter before Jeremiah exhorts the people to work and pray (**24:4–9**). God is the ultimate agent of the exile. Jeremiah counsels the people to resume work because the exile will be long and not short as the false prophets are announcing. His advice is also intended to forestall notions the exiles might have about revolting or assisting those who do. The exiles, who live in colonies (Ezek. 3:15), seem to have considerable freedom.

Prayer to God on behalf of the city (Babylon) is essentially to pray for one's enemies. Prayer can be directed to the Lord in Babylon and not only in Jerusalem, the Lord's land. Jeremiah urges intercession and good citizenship. False prophets are active in Babylon as well as in the homeland. Their announcements and dreams are in response to people's wishful thinking. And so both people and prophets are accountable for the lies.

God has good plans (**29:10–14**). Seventy years, counting from 605, the battle of Carchemish, would extend to 535 B.C. Babylonian supremacy ended when Cyrus the Mede took Babylon in 539 B.C. Jeremiah refers to restoration to the land, a promise, even if in the distance, to encourage homesick captives. God desires to bless his people, and his plans are firm (Isa. 46:10). "Prosper" (v. 11) translates *šālōm,* a term denoting well-being, wholeness, harmony, and peace. Seeking God will be characteristic of the "new heart." "Hope and a future" is a Hebrew form that could be rendered, "a future full of hope." Along with physical restoration to the land, there will be spiritual restoration to God.

Prophets in Babylon, of whom Ahab and Zedekiah are examples, are optimistic about the rapid return to normalcy in Jerusalem. Jeremiah insists that the problems in Jerusalem have not yet peaked (**29:15–19**). Jerusalem's king, Zedekiah, like the bad figs of the vision (24:8–10), will come to grief. The reason for the disaster is that people have not listened. The exiles' failure to listen makes the good plans of verses 10–14 all the more remarkable.

The letter to the exiles continues with an exposé of two prophets, Ahab and Zedekiah, of whom nothing more is known (**29:20–23**). They operate under false pretenses without a mandate. Their fate, execution by burning, is foretold; of it there is no record. In Judah the decimation of Jerusalem would prompt curses of others; a counterpart in the exile would be the curse occasioned by the two prophets. The reason for their fate is sin in their personal life (adultery) and in their vocational life (speaking lies).

In a power maneuver calculated to diminish Jeremiah's influence, Shemaiah in Babylon by unilateral action appoints Zephaniah as priest (**29:29–34**). The priest was also head of the temple police (cf. 20:1). Shemaiah, more concerned about "political" points of view than temple service, instructs Zephaniah to arrest persons, madmen like Jeremiah, whose views differ from his own. For an unknown reason, Zephaniah discloses the contents of the letter.

The "flow" of the material is a problem.

Perhaps verse 29 is a parenthetical explanation. This would mean that Jeremiah reviewed the contents of Zephaniah's letter (vv. 25–29)—all the more likely if we omit, "This is what the Lord says" in verse 25a. Or, the rehearsal of the incident (vv. 24–29) is an insert, perhaps by Baruch, to help the reader make sense of Jeremiah's announcement about Shemaiah (vv. 31–34). Still another possibility is that verses 30–32 represent a later letter from Jeremiah, since Shemaiah in his letter refers to instructions, presumably from Jeremiah's pastoral letter.

V. The Book of Comfort (30–33)

As now arranged, the book so far has had several urgent warnings, some earnest pleas, and many dire announcements of coming disaster. By contrast, chapters 30–33 fulfill that part of Jeremiah's assignment that called for "building and planting" (1:10). Now come promises of return from exile, of a secure and stable society in the homeland, and of an intimate relationship once again of people with their God. The "book" proper is in poetry (30–31); the prose expansion (32–33) continues the theme of a bright prospect.

A. Coming back to the land (30:1–24). Generally the address is to "Israel"; other names for these people are Jacob, Rachel, and Ephraim. The specific word to Judah is short (31:23–24, 38–40). The theme of the "book" is the future (**30:1–3**).

Cries of fear describe a people in great trouble (**30:4–11**). The setting could be the Assyrian capture of Samaria in 722, the Babylonian invasion of Jerusalem in 587, or any calamity, past or future. Childbirth is a frequent illustration in Jeremiah of great distress, anxiety, and pain (4:31; 6:24; 13:21; 49:24). Verses 4–7 are the backdrop against which the following promises of comfort must be seen.

Breaking the yoke (v. 8) recalls Jeremiah's sign act. Two nations which held Israel captive were Assyria and Babylon. David their king is hardly the tenth-century monarch, but his descendants, or as the ancient Aramaic Targum paraphrases, the Messiah. "Do not fear" is salvation language. "Save," with its sense of release from confinement, is an apt term to describe freedom from exile. "I am with you" is the divine assistance formula.

Using the metaphor of injury and healing, the oracle of **30:12–17a** sets the tone for the specific announcements that will follow. The wound (v. 12; lit. brokenness) is figurative for the calamity, namely the takeover of the country by a foreign power and the removal of its population into exile. It is beyond healing in the sense that the pain of punishment for sin must be endured.

The God who has afflicted is the God who will heal. God will deal decisively with the agents of punishment. The reasons are not given here but elsewhere (cf. 46–51).

"Because you are called an outcast" (v. 17b) introduces a new oracle and a new theme: rebuilding a ruined city and living in it to the full (**30:17b–24**). The sorry plight is depicted before the promise of reversal is given. Disparaging statements by nations about God's people move him to action. "I will restore the fortunes" is now applied to buildings and to society. Laughter replaces terror and agony. Honor replaces reproach. A leader from within replaces a foreign (or like Zedekiah, a foreign-appointed) overlord.

Verses 23–24 are to be understood as a guarantee by oath of good times ahead. Good times are possible if the enemies are removed. The verses are a repeat from 23:19–20, where they are the conclusion of the heavenly council. What seems too good to be true will really happen.

B. Coming back to God (31:1–40). This chapter is striking for its news and its exuberance. The recovery of the land (chap. 30) is followed by the recovery of a relationship with God (chap. 31). God is pictured successively as father, shepherd, mother, and covenant maker. The announcement of the coming restoration is given first to the exiles (vv. 1–9), then to the nations (vv. 10–14), then to Israel (vv. 15–22).

The covenant formula (v. 1) is the basis for the great trek (vv. 7–9). A reference to distress prepares for promise. The refugees from both the Assyrian invasion of Israel in 722 and those of the Babylonian invasion of 586 survive. Only here in Jeremiah is God the subject of love.

"Again," used three times and in Hebrew each time in first position, anticipates the reconstruction process, the return of joyful times, uninterrupted economic pursuits, and vigorous religious activity. Jeremiah prays for those left alive and dispersed in various places. If people from Ephraim (a name for the northern kingdom) come to Zion (Jerusalem), it will mean a united Israel in worship.

The "land of the north" (v. 8) likely refers to the Habor River region to which the Assyrians took the northern kingdom captive. The weeping in the new exodus may be tears of reform for sin, tears of joy for deliverance, or both. God, the Father, is the initiator of the trek and its protector.

Nations, even distant islands, hear the message of Israel's regathering, of her return, and of her abundance (**31:10–14**). Such a message would reverse the slurring byword spoken by them about Israel's destroyed cities.

Laments, in one sense, stir God to action. The hope-filled future of 29:11 is now elaborated as Jeremiah describes the return of the prodigal (**31:15–22**).

Ephraim (v. 18) here designates the ten northern tribes. The pun on "turn," translated "restore," "return," "stray," intermingles turning to (or away from) God, and (re)turning to the land. Israel's repentance is like that earlier prescribed. "Beating the breast" (lit. thighs) was a gesture of great feeling, especially of remorse.

God's response is motherlike. The word *compassion* (v. 20) is a derivative from "womb." God reprimands and rebukes Israel for her sins. Still, the two, God and Ephraim, have found each other and have been reconciled.

Verses 21–22 round off a promise introduced in verses 3–6. Verse 22 has evoked much discussion. The "new thing" is puzzling. Some interpretations put forward are: (1) a role reversal such that women, rather than men, become aggressive; (2) in the poem two women—Rachel and Virgin Israel—"surround the man" Ephraim; (3) a messianic promise in which a woman (Mary) "surrounds" the God-man Jesus (so Jerome in the fourth century); (4) a proverb whose meaning is lost to us but which may describe a topsy-turvy situation; and (5) formerly God encompassed Israel; now Israel will embrace God—certainly a new thing. The last interpretation is preferred; it anticipates the new covenant of verse 31.

Jeremiah **31:23–26** focuses on Judah in contrast to Israel, the northern kingdom. "O righteous dwelling" (v. 23) refers to the temple on Mount Zion, God's dwelling. A restored people will be a worshiping people. Farmers, settled on their land, often clashed with roaming shepherds who disregarded property rights. These will now coexist peacefully. The unexpected reference to sleep may mean: "This is all too good to be true."

The concluding section is in three parts, each beginning with "days are coming" (**31:27–30**; vv. 31–37; vv. 38–40). God promises to plant or repopulate the territories that have been decimated. God watched over Jeremiah's first assignment announcing destruction; he will watch over the second one announcing recovery. The proverb about grapes and blunt teeth restates (and exaggerates) Exodus 20:5 and Numbers 14:18. Complaints that the children's miseries (the exile) were the result of the fathers' sins (Manasseh) will cease. People are individually accountable.

In the justly famous salvation oracle of **31:31–37**, an unprecedented announcement takes shape. A covenant is an arrangement of bonding between persons and differs from a contract. The old covenant from Sinai (Exod. 19:5–6) was broken and is no longer operative. A fresh arrangement, not a covenant renewal, is put into effect. It is God's prerogative and his initiative (cf. repetitions: "I will . . . " and "declares the Lord").

In Jeremiah's analysis, the heart is deceitful and stubborn (3:17; 7:24; 9:14; 11:8; 17:1, 9). God's law or teaching in the heart is the equivalent of a new heart. The objective of the Sinai covenant, "I will be their God, and they will be my people," remains. Ancient nations associated their gods with territories. The binding of a deity to a people is unique in world religions.

"Knowing God" is more explicitly "experiencing God." The new covenant marks the end of the teaching profession. The new covenant passage, the longest Scripture quoted in the New Testament (Heb. 8:7–12), is said to be fulfilled in Christ. Quite possibly, judging from verse 33, originally only Israel was in view. Later, Judah was included (v. 31). The New Testament promise includes the Gentiles.

Just as the first half of the poetic Book of Comfort ends with an oathlike statement (30:23–24), so also here (vv. 35–37). The creation is an expression of the "Lord of Hosts." The decrees (v. 36) are the laws that govern the natural elements of the universe. Israel's continuous existence as a people is guaranteed by the natural ordering of the universe.

The repeated announcement of a return of the exiles to the homeland and the rebuilding of a city climax in the specifics of **31:38–40**. The place names specify the extent of the rebuilt and enlarged Jerusalem. More important than the boundaries is the fact that the city will be "for the Lord," holy and permanent.

C. A property purchase (32:1–44). The prophet's purchase of a field becomes a sign. After the fiery destruction of Jerusalem, people will eventually return to the city. Normal commerce will resume.

The account of the purchase takes the form of a sign act (**32:1–15**; cf. 13:1ff.; 19:1ff.; 27:1ff.). The instruction is brief; so is the initial interpretation. Most attention is given to the report of compliance. A man who through poverty or debt was about to forfeit his land was to solicit a next-of-kin to buy it (Lev. 25:25–28; cf. Ruth 4:7).

The business transaction is given in detail—one of the fullest records we have on such matters. Scales were used to weigh bars or rings of silver. Seventeen shekels of silver equaled seven ounces. The two copies of the transaction, either transcribed on clay tablets, as is known from Mesopotamia, or on papyrus, as is known from Egypt, would be identical. The unsealed copy would be accessible. The sealed copy would be opened only should the unsealed copy be tampered with or lost. The accompanying divine message (v. 15) confirms the announcements of hope found elsewhere in the book, some of which undoubtedly preceded this sign act.

Apparently the purchase happens quickly and certainly without the prophet's forethought. Jeremiah is perplexed about his own action (**32:16–25**). Given the state of siege and his own prediction that Babylon would capture Jerusalem, his investment seems foolish. His prayer extols God as Creator. Recalling God's power in creation brings fresh perspective in prayer. The name *Lord of Hosts* refers to God's rule of both celestial bodies and military armies. The name, therefore, is a "bridge" between God's work in creation and in history.

In reply, the Lord addresses first the immediate circumstance of the invasion, and then elaborates on the sign act of the purchase (**32:26–35**). "Is anything too hard for me?" (v. 17) puts into question form Jeremiah's opening assertion (v. 2b). Judah's sins—the list is familiar—are said to have provoked God's anger.

Judgment, however, is not the last word (**32:36–44**). The regathering of a dispersed people and their return to the homeland are familiar themes, especially in the Book of Comfort. The everlasting covenant is called the "new covenant" in 31:31–34, where themes of a covenant people and a new heart are taken up.

God's beneficent intentions are not in doubt. Bustling commercial activity will characterize Benjamin which is adjacent to Judah in the north, the hill country farther north, and cities in the Negeb, such as Beersheba.

D. Things great and unsearchable (33:1–26). Positive announcements about a glorious future for city and people tumble over one another. Divine pardon, energetic praise songs, enterprising shepherds, established royal and priestly lines, and a united and permanent people—all are part of the kaleidoscope of future assurance. In content the chapter duplicates and slightly expands chapters 30–31.

The promise of restoration extends to both city and country (**33:1–13**). When judgment has been completed, wholeness will be God's gift. God's general stance of good will contrasts with the wrath that precipitated the destruction.

Both Judah, the southern kingdom, and Israel, the northern kingdom, are in view. God mercifully forgives sin and iniquities. The city of Jerusalem and God's people generally are intended as a prime exhibit of his goodness. God's goodness should prompt repentance. Celebrations will mark the future in stark contrast to earlier mourning. The empty land will be populated. "Will pass . . . who counts them" (v. 13) refers to the shepherd taking nightly inventory of the flock. Life will be back to its routine.

The city's safety is not separate from a spiritual realignment. "Just" describes observable behavior that is correct before God; "right" describes inner integrity. The promise to David (2 Sam. 7:13) is guaranteed by the fixed appointment of day and night. The covenant with the Levites (Num. 25:12–13; Mal. 2:5) is similarly guaranteed. The Davidic and Abrahamic covenants (2 Sam. 7:8–16; Gen. 15, 17) are the background for verse 26.

The popular opinion that "it is all over" would be understandable, even if inaccurate, following the demise of Israel in 721 and Judah in 586. The strong guarantees (vv. 25–26) essentially repeat 31:36–38, except that the continuation of the Davidic monarch is of paramount concern.

VI. Case Studies in the Failure of Leadership (34–39)

Incidents from the reigns of two kings, Jehoiakim and Zedekiah, are told here. The "actors" include Jeremiah, princes, and the Recabite family. The stories, not chronological, are prelude to the fall of Jerusalem (chap. 39). "Fire" and "burning" are key words. The stories are a forceful commentary on ungodly leadership and on spiritual rebellion. Here is the account of the total rejection of the Word of God, whether received via a scroll or from a prophet. Both ungodly leadership and spiritual rebellion are reasons for the burning destruction of chapter 39.

A. Going back on one's word (34:1–21). Chapters 34 and 35, when taken together, display a similar pattern:

Prophetic revelation formula	34:8a	35:1
Report of incident	34:8b–11	35:2–11
Prophetic revelation formula	34:12a	35:12–13a
Retelling of incident	34:12b–16	35:13b–16
General announcement	34:17–20	35:17
Particularized announcement	34:21–22	35:18–19

While the issues in the two stories are very different—national policy in the one case and diet in the other—the main idea in both is integrity in covenant keeping. The fickle King Zedekiah contrasts with the tenacious Recabites. In both, Jeremiah complains, "You have not listened [obeyed]" (34:17; 35:16).

Jeremiah's message deals with Zedekiah's personal safety (**34:1–7**; cf. 21:1–10). "Burn it down" or "burned" are prominent terms in chapters 34–38 that anticipate the burning of Jerusalem. Zedekiah's gruesome fate (v. 3) stops short of a violent death. A funeral fire, perhaps the burning of spices, indicates the citizenry's good will. The promise of verse 4 is conditional on Zedekiah's surrender to Babylon.

Persons in poverty or in a crisis of debt made themselves available as slaves. Mosaic law called for the release of slaves every seventh year (Exod. 21:1–11). The seriousness of siege apparently brings compliance with God's law, perhaps to secure God's favor. Freed slaves would defend the city better; owners need not be responsible for their provisions. When the siege slackens in the summer of 588 because the Babylonians leave to fend off the Egyptians, the king and others promptly go back on their word.

The incident inspires a sermon. Covenant making must be taken seriously. The rescinding of covenant is ultimately an offense against God, for it disregards God's stipulations. To profane or desecrate is to make commonplace, to rob something of its special character, to render something holy unholy. What if God in his covenant making waffled as did Zedekiah?

A paraphrase of the pun on freedom could read: "Since you have not freed up the slaves, I [God] am freeing you up for the sword, pestilence, and famine—and for anyone who wants you." An accompanying ritual in covenant making included a "walk" between the two halves of a slain animal (vv. 18–19; Gen. 15:9–17). The practice is known from non-Israelite writings. By this action covenant violators called on themselves the fate of the slain calf. The announced disaster is a consequence of Zedekiah's violation. He will not be exempt, even though, for the moment, he has reason for optimism. God will "turn" the Babylonians around; they will be back.

B. Obedience (35:1–19). In nonhistorical sequence, but as a contrast to chapter 34, the story of the Recabites focuses on uncompromising obedience.

The account (**35:1–11**) is from the year 601 (see v. 11). The Recabites are from the clan of the Kenites, a people who associated themselves with Israel (1 Chron. 2:55). The Recabites were a conservative, if not reactionary, group. No evaluation of the rightness or wrongness of their views is given, but their tenacity for obedience is applauded. Theirs is the prospect of a perpetual ministry.

Jeremiah's commentary on the incident (**35:12–19**) contrasts the absolute and unquestioning obedience of the Recabites to their ancestor, with Judah's disobedience to the Lord Yahweh. The people's refusal to "take lessons" (Heb. discipline or correction) is a repeated accusation (2:30; 5:3; 7:28; 17:23). An example of this refusal is given in 7:1–15. Themes about disobedience (34:17; 35:17b) and disaster (34:18–22; 35:17a) alternate in this and the preceding chapter.

C. The burning of a scroll (36:1–32). Like Zedekiah (chap. 34), Jehoiakim scorns the law of God. Incidentally, the chapter provides a glimpse into how books of the Old Testament came to be.

God commands Jeremiah to write on a scroll (**36:1–7**). His restriction (v. 5) may have resulted from his controversial temple sermon (7:1–15), or his "lecture" to the elders (19:1–20:6). Jeremiah had censured Jehoiakim for his extravagance and extortion in building a palace (22:13–23). Since the scroll was read three times in one day it may not have been that extensive. The purpose of the reading, despite the accusations and warnings, is to bring the people to a spiritual "turn-around."

The scroll is read three times: at the temple to the people, in the secretaries' room to the scribes, and at the royal winter apartment to the king and his officials (**36:8–26**). The reverence with which the scribes treat the message shows that some spiritual sensitivity remains in Judah (vv. 11–18). It also indicates the credibility of Jeremiah. The officials, however, show contempt. The hiding of Jeremiah and Baruch is well advised in view of 26:20–23. To tear their clothes (v. 24) would be a sign of self-humiliation. The report seems deliberately to contrast Jehoiakim with his father, Josiah (cf. 2 Kings 22:11–20).

Severe judgment comes on Jehoiakim, who rejects a word intended to spare him. As Jehoiakim tried to blot out God's Word, so his own house will be blotted out. His punishment—to have no descendants on the throne—contrasts with God's promise to David (2 Sam. 7:12–16). Jehoiakim's son, Jehoiachin, who ruled for three months, ends the family rule.

D. Troubling a prophet (37:1–38:28). Chapter 36 reports on efforts to do away with the Word of God by burning it. These two chapters tell of attempts to do away with the prophet. Arrested without cause, Jeremiah is held in a dungeon, put in a prison, and then thrown into a miry hole to die. Even so, he is sought out by King Zedekiah, whose city is now under siege, for some favorable word.

The pattern of organization in chapters 37–38 parallels that of chapter 36.

Introduction	36:1–4	37:1–2
Story in three movements: three readings, three interviews	36:5–26	37:3–38:13
Message to the king	36:27–31	38:14–23
Destiny (scroll, prophet)	36:32	38:24–28

A key word throughout is "burn." "Burn," used in conjunction with Jehoiakim (36:25, 27, 28, 29, 32), corresponds to "burn" used in conjunction with Nebuchadnezzar (37:8, 10; 38:17, 18, 23). The first is an internal threat; the second is an external threat. The officials, still somewhat conciliatory in chapter 36, are single-minded toward evil in chapters 37–38. Attempts to destroy the written Word (chap. 36) and the speaker of that Word (chaps. 37–38) suggest that the rejection of God's message is total. So judgment follows (chap. 39). Still God, who announced judgment already in Jehoiakim's reign (chap. 36), waits for more than a decade before bringing it.

A lull in the two-year Babylonian siege of Jerusalem prompts Zedekiah to inquire of Jeremiah (**37:1–10**). An example of his failure to pay attention to the words of the Lord (v. 1) is Zedekiah's reenslavement of freed slaves (chap. 34). Intercession is understood to belong to the prophet's ministry. Prayer could insure the Babylonians' permanent departure. Jeremiah's message is simple: the Babylonians will be back!

Jeremiah's message to surrender to Babylon (27:12) causes suspicion about his patriotism. The charge in the arrest is that Jeremiah is defecting to the enemy (v. 13). Others had already defected (38:19; 52:15).

From a vaulted cell in a dungeon at Jonathan's house, Jeremiah is summoned personally by Zedekiah for a message from the Lord.

Thanks to Zedekiah's generosity and Jeremiah's bold request, Jeremiah, though still confined, is given improved conditions. With his limited wartime ration of bread, Jeremiah suffers the effects of siege along with others. Severe famine contributes to the city's final collapse (2 Kings 25:3).

Jeremiah's pacifist position enrages the officials (**38:1–13**). Their information may have come from Pashhur, a member of an earlier delegation (21:1–10), Jehucal (37:3–9), or through personal contact. A death sentence for Jeremiah was earlier demanded by religious leaders (26:1–15). The officials are wrong in holding that Jeremiah is not seeking the good of the people. Zedekiah, like Pilate centuries later (Matt. 27:24–26), hands the prophet over to his accusers. Dissension among leaders bodes ill for any country's future.

By disposing of Jeremiah in a cistern, the officials seek his death without physically laying hands on him. It is to the credit of a foreigner, Ebed-Melech from the land of Cush, south of Egypt, that he pleads for Jeremiah to be spared. The care with which Jeremiah is taken from the dungeon suggests that he is severely emaciated. Ebed-Melech, whose name means "servant of the king," is rewarded for his trust in the Lord; his life is spared when calamity strikes (39:15–18).

Zedekiah makes a second and last attempt at an interview with Jeremiah (**38:14–27**). Some see this as another version of the earlier visit (37:17–21), but divergent details (two different dungeons; two different precipitating occasions) argue for two accounts. The place is in the temple where state officials would have little reason to go.

Jeremiah paints the consequences of a refusal to surrender (vv. 21–22). Palace women became the property of a conqueror. The city will be burned down. The king, habitually indecisive, is isolated. Jeremiah is under no obligation to disclose full information.

E. The fall of Jerusalem (39:1–18). From a narrative point of view this chapter is the climax of the book. Repeated threats have now been fulfilled. The chapter is pivotal. Chapters 34–38 provide the reasons for the catastrophe; chapters 40–44 tell of the sequel.

The siege begins in January 588, lasts some eighteen months, and ends in July 587. Zedekiah breaks faith and rebels against the Babylonians. They respond with an invasion (2 Kings 25:1–12 = Jer. 52:4–16). Babylonian officials are named, as are Judah's officials (38:1).

The king's fate accords with Jeremiah's announcements. The city is burned as so often predicted by Jeremiah. Its citizenry is exiled as foretold. The poorer class remains.

Jewish defectors or his own intelligence sources inform Nebuchadnezzar about Jeremiah. Gedaliah will shortly be appointed governor (40:7). For his deed of kindness to Jeremiah, Ebed-Melech escapes with his life. The Lord honors those who trust in him.

VII. After the Catastrophe (40–45)

The capture of Jerusalem touches off a sordid set of events. The assassination of Gedaliah leads to strife, insecurity, and fear of Nebuchadnezzar's reprisal. Consequently some trek off to

Egypt against Jeremiah's advice. There the familiar godless life-style persists; more judgment speeches follow.

A. Trouble from within (40:1–41:18). A fresh beginning quickly turns sour with the struggle by Ishmael for power over Gedaliah.

Ramah, five miles north of Jerusalem, is the dispatching point for exiles. Apparently in the confusion Jeremiah has been arrested again after being sent to Gedaliah's house (39:14). However, some hold we have here a more detailed account of the story given in 39:11–14. The witness of the commander of the guard to God's action seems unusual (but cf. Gen. 41:38; Matt. 27:54). Jeremiah chooses to stay with Gedaliah (**40:1–6**)—a patriotic gesture—even though he knows the future is with the exiles (24:4–7).

Gedaliah, of the family of Shaphan the scribe (2 Kings 22:3–14), is appointed governor (**40:7–12**). He is cordial to Jeremiah; his policy of submission to the Babylonians echoes that of the prophet. Mizpah, headquarters for the new governor, is only a short distance from Ramah, the Babylonian command post. Officers with their men in the open country, guerillalike, had fought against Babylon. Likely they wish to know whether Gedaliah will be a "nationalist" or a Babylonian puppet. Gedaliah, in urging them to help in the harvest, is essentially calling for a return to normalcy.

Terrorist tactics are detailed in **40:13–41:10**. Johanan, one of the "guerillas," emerges as spokesperson for the restless remnant. We can only guess at Baalis's motives (40:14). Did he wish for a leader in Judah sympathetic to a policy of retaliation against the Babylonians? Did he wish to forestall any consolidation of survivors? Did he have personal ambitions? Johanan's counterplan points to the way of violence that prevailed after the loss of legitimate government. If the story beginning with 39:1 is continuous, then Gedaliah, assassinated by his own countrymen, governed less than five months.

The eighty men (v. 5) come from three cities that were former worship centers. Shaved beards, torn clothes, and gashes indicate penitence and mourning. They are headed to the temple in Jerusalem, which, even if destroyed, is considered holy. They may have come to mourn its destruction.

Johanan leads a band which intercepts Ishmael at Gibeon, three miles south of Mizpah (**41:11–18**). The Ammonites, east of the Jordan, had earlier been allies with Judah against Babylon. The murder of the Babylonian-appointed governor, along with the Babylonian soldiers, would be interpreted as insubordination. Babylon could be expected to bring quick reprisals. The motley group, having decided to head for Egypt, stops near Bethlehem. From there Johanan contacts Jeremiah for advice.

B. Trouble in Egypt (42:1–43:13). A remnant group goes off to Egypt contrary to Jeremiah's advice. There, Jeremiah, who has gone with them, rebukes them for idolatry.

Johanan, active in rescuing his countrymen from Ishmael, the assassin, has brought them on their way to Egypt as far as Bethlehem. Egypt, Judah's ally against the Babylonians, is not beset by the instability which plagues the Jews. Unsure of their next move, they seek guidance from the Lord through Jeremiah, as had Zedekiah's delegation earlier (**42:1–6**; 37:3).

Divine answers to prayer do not come on demand. God's word to the inquirers is, "Stay in the land; do not go to Egypt" (**42:7–22**). God's message allays the group's fear of the Babylonians' indiscriminate reprisal for Gedaliah's murder (41:1–3). Part of the message is the divine assistance formula, *I am with you.*

Any decision to go to Egypt must calculate the consequences: death from a variety of causes—sword, famine, and plague (vv. 16–17). Verses 19–22 add Jeremiah's personal plea to the remnant not to proceed with their plans. The fatal mistake is not the request for guidance but their double talk (lit. deceive yourselves), whereby they promise to do what in their hearts they do not intend to do.

Jeremiah had accused others of lying (9:3–6); now the same charge is thrown into his face. Johanan and company go back on their word, as did Zedekiah earlier (chap. 34). They decide to go to Egypt (**43:1–7**).

The "remnant" (v. 5) refers to those in Edom, Moab, Ammon, and other nearby countries who returned when they heard Gedaliah was appointed governor. Tahpanhes was an Egyptian fortress city in the eastern delta region of the Nile, and so the first Egyptian city they would reach.

At the Lord's command, Jeremiah engages in another sign act (**43:8–13**; cf. chaps. 13, 19, 32). The image of the shepherd's cloak suggests the speed with which Nebuchadnezzar will carry off the Egyptians' wealth. The word *wrap,* it has been plausibly suggested, can mean "delouse." Nebuchadnezzar will systematically exterminate the Egyptians as so many pests. To what extent this prediction was fulfilled is not clear since records are fragmentary. One text fragment now in the British Museum tells of an attack by Nebuchadnezzar against Pharaoh Amasis (Ahmoses II) in 568–567.

C. Failure to learn from history (44:1–45:5). Jeremiah's warnings against apostasy and his messages of doom continue in Egypt. The reason is that those emigrating from Judah to Egypt reinstate idolatrous worship. They have failed to learn from history.

Another catastrophe is in the offing (**44:1–14**). Some Jews who left Judah after Nebuchadnezzar's capture of Jerusalem settled in Egypt. Their religion is anything but a pure Yahweh religion. Burning incense and worshiping other gods are violations of the first commandment. God's fierce anger is unleashed only after his repeated calls for repentance have been spurned.

By adopting the gods of Egypt, the remnant Jews jeopardize their own welfare and that of future descendants. The accusation part of the judgment speech focuses first on sins committed (vv. 8–9) and then on things left undone: self-humiliation, reverence for God, and obedience to the law (v. 10). The announcement is that only a few refugees will eventually return to the homeland. Most of the Jews who later resettle in the land are from Babylon, not Egypt.

"We will not listen" (**44:15–19**) characterizes the people's response; it was also the decision of the Jerusalemites earlier (6:17). The remnant's reading of history is that things were better presumably during Manasseh's reign (before Josiah's) when the Mother Goddess was revered. The action of the families is united and deliberate. It is widespread and in defiance of the prophet's warnings.

Jeremiah offers a different interpretation of past history than that given by the remnant (**44:20–30**). It is their sin that has brought disaster. "Go ahead then" is said in irony. This is Jeremiah's last recorded speech. It is in keeping with his initial call.

The sign (v. 29) that the threatened doom is indeed God's work would be that Pharaoh Hophra would be handed over to the enemies, as was Zedekiah.

The year of the message to Baruch (605/4) was also the year that Jeremiah reviewed his preaching (25:1–11) and prepared the scroll (chap. 36). If Baruch is the author of chapters 34–45, then he closes this section with a modest but frank note about himself.

Baruch's situation—one of sorrow, groaning, and pain—is like Jeremiah's laments. The sorrow may be the consistent message of doom, or perhaps Jehoiakim's rejection of the Word (chap. 36), or even Jeremiah's own endangered life (36:19). Even this personal oracle reaffirms God's decision to bring judgment.

VIII. Oracles about the Nations (46–51)

God, who has been named throughout as the "Lord of Hosts," will judge the nations. Egypt and Babylon were the two superpowers of that time. The other nations are for the most part geographically near to Israel. With these oracles Jeremiah fulfills in part his call to be a prophet to the nations.

A. Egypt (46:1–28). Both Egypt and Babylon were ancient empires, and both vied for the control of Palestine, Ammon, Moab, and other territories that lay between them.

Neco ruled in Egypt from 610 to 595. Carchemish, on the Euphrates, was on the east-west trade routes sixty miles west of Haran. Nebuchadnezzar's victory at Carchemish in 605 gave him access to the countries by the Mediterranean, including Judah. The long domination of Egypt over Syria-Palestine had ended.

In sarcasm Jeremiah calls on Egypt's military to prepare for battle (**46:1–12**). But at once he sees the Egyptians retreating. "Terror on every side" (v. 5) may be a call to retreat when all is in confusion.

Verses 7–10 depict Egyptian ambitions, which crest like the surging Nile River. Verse 9 may describe a commander, or even the prophet himself, urging the troops on to make their dreams come true. Mercenary soldiers would have been recruited from Cush, Put, and Lydia, regions in Africa. "That day" (v. 10) is the "day of the Lord." God will unveil his power and demonstrate his complete control by dealing decisively and in vengeance with his foes. He will sacrifice them.

The setting is the Babylonian attack on the Egyptian home front (**46:13–26**). One such attack occurred in 601; another in 568–567. Mercenary soldiers when overpowered would consider escape to their home country. Pharaoh's "lost opportunity" could be the chance to take advantage militarily of Nebuchadnezzar's return to Babylon after Carchemish.

The "one who will come," the destroyer, is an oblique reference to Nebuchadnezzar, who is a towering figure. Mount Tabor in north-central Palestine rises two thousand feet above the plain. The gadfly (v. 20) is Babylon. The mercenaries, who are her hope, will buckle under pressure. Those more numerous than the locusts (v. 23) are the Babylonians.

The prose piece (vv. 25–26) is about Upper Egypt. The clash is basically with the sun god Amon, patron deity of Thebes. Thebes, the capital of Upper Egypt, was known for its large temple. The reasons for the disaster are not given, except by inference, nor is a reason given for Egypt's promising future.

The salvation oracle of **46:27–28** is a repeat of 30:10–11. It underscores that the defeat of

Egypt will mean salvation for Israel. For most of history Israel regarded Egypt as an enemy, though there were times when Egypt was Israel's ally.

B. Philistia (47:1–7). This oracle describes the agony of coastal cities—from Sidon in the north to Gaza in the south—ruthlessly attacked by a strong power, the foe from the north, Babylon. The Philistines occupied a strip of territory along the southern Mediterranean coast.

C. Moab (48:1–47). The Moabites, descendants of Lot (Gen. 19:37), were unfriendly to Israel at the time of the exodus (Num. 22–24). In 601–600 Nebuchadnezzar sent Moabite groups to deal with Jehoiakim's revolt (2 Kings 24:2).

The language describing Moab's woes is pithy, picturesque, and liberally sprinkled with place-names. Cities will be destroyed; anguished cries will be heard everywhere. Refugees will seek escape, while Moab's god Chemosh stands by helplessly. Our knowledge of Moab's history is scant. Apparently, the Babylonians attacked both Moab and Ammon in 598 and, if Josephus is right, again in 582.

A destroyer will ruthlessly invade the land (**48:1–10**) and Moab will be broken. The destroyer (v. 8)—an enemy, not named, but presumably Nebuchadnezzar—is urged not to slacken in the massacre.

Moab was known for her vineyards. Wine on its dregs, if left too long, loses its flavor. So Moab, whose dependence for too long has been on Chemosh, has not been "poured out," but her exile will now improve her flavor (**48:11–25**). Embarrassment over the inadequacy of her god compares with Israel's embarrassment over the god Bethel, which was worshiped in Syria and, according to the records, also by the Jews in the Elephantine colony in Egypt. Yahweh, the Lord of Hosts, stands over Chemosh, Bethel, and all other gods.

It is the cup of the Lord's wrath that makes Moab drunk (**48:26–39**; cf. 25:15–21). The reasons for her destruction emerge: (1) she defied the Lord; (2) she ridiculed Israel; (3) she is extraordinarily proud. Much of the language in verses 28–32 is found in Isaiah 16:6–12.

Verse 32 is best rendered, "I will weep for you more than I wept for Jazer" (NEB). Jazer, ten miles north of Heshbon, was in Ammonite territory but then was conquered by King Mesha of Moab. Some suggest that it was the center of the Tammuz cult, a feature of which was weeping for the dead. Visually, the shaved head and beard and the gash marks tell the story of woe (v. 37).

Moab's precarious position compares to a creature about to be the victim of an eagle's swoop (**48:40–47**). So overpowering is the enemy that warriors will seem weak. Those trying to escape will be caught one way or another.

D. Ammon (49:1–6). Ammon lies in central Trans-Jordan opposite Shechem. The area was taken over by Israel after the exodus (Josh. 10:6–12:6; Num. 32:33–37) and assigned to Gad (Josh. 13:24–28). The region was lost to Israel when the Assyrian Tiglath-pileser made war against Israel (2 Kings 15:29). The Ammonites repossessed the region. Baalis, king of the Ammonites, was involved with Ishmael in the assassination of Gedaliah (40:14–41:10).

Molech (or Milcom) was the chief god of the Ammonites. At times Israel worshiped Molech and sacrificed children to him. In his name the Ammonites undertook their conquests.

God will bring the Ammonites terror because of their aggressive conquests and because of their trust in their wealth. The funeral lament or dirge (v. 3) underscores the extent of the destruction. Nebuchadnezzar destroyed Ammon in 582.

E. Edom (49:7–22). Edom, also known as Mount Seir, lies between the Dead Sea and the Gulf of Aqabah. It was inhabited by the descendants of Jacob's brother Esau (Gen. 36:1–17). Edom took advantage of Judah's plight in 586 and occupied southern Judah.

The cup (v. 12) refers to the cup of wrath which is also passed to Edom (25:17–28).

Edom, like Moab, is characterized by pride (v. 16; 48:29). The root word for pride means "high." The concept is carried forward by the "heights of the hill" and the "nest as high as the eagle's." God will choose his agent to devastate Edom.

Verse 20, with its reference to the Lord's plans and counsel, returns to the theme of wisdom in verse 7. The language about a swooping eagle—likely Nebuchadnezzar is intended—is traditional for depicting the speed and power of an attack. Other images to reinforce the theme of destruction are Sodom and Gomorrah (v. 18; cf. Gen. 19:24–25) and the lion from Jordan's thickets (v. 19).

F. Damascus (49:23–27). Damascus, north of Palestine on the Orontes River, was the capital of the Aramean state. The Babylonian king commissioned the Aramean state to deal with Jehoiakim's revolt (2 Kings 24:2–4).

Hamath and Arpad, each about one hundred miles north of Damascus, were two city-states allied with Damascus. Both lost their independence when they were overpowered by the Assyrians between 740 and 732. The acute distress, a result of the enemy attack, is the main theme of the oracle. Behind the combat stands God.

G. Kedar and Hazor (49:28–33). The Kedar were a nomadic tribal people in the Syrian-Arabian desert. Hazor is not the well-known town in Galilee, but was another Arab tribe living in the eastern desert.

The war poem contains two summons to attack (vv. 28, 33), each followed by a list of the plunder (vv. 29, 32) and the scattering of the fugitives (vv. 30, 32).

H. Elam (49:34–39). Elam, distant from Palestine, is east of Babylon and northeast of the Persian Gulf. After the overthrow of Babylon in which Elam assisted, Elam was in turn absorbed by the Persian Empire. Its connections with Judah are unclear. Were there Elamite soldiers in the Babylonian forces? Was there a hope that rulers east of Babylon would break Babylon's grip and so shorten the captivity of the exiles? If so, this oracle squelches those dreams.

Bas-reliefs from Nineveh show the Elamites as bowmen. Their skill as archers was proverbial. The announcement to Elam is more general than to Hazor. Dispersion first, then annihilation are threatened against the Elamites. Along with Moab and Ammon, Elam's fortunes will be restored.

I. Babylon (50:1–51:64). God will punish Babylon. Her gods will be discredited; her city demolished. Repeatedly other nations are summoned to arms to destroy Babylon completely. Israel is called to escape, for this is God's deliverance for her. These three themes—Babylon, the attacking foe, and Israel—like juggler's balls recur in the oracle.

The oracle is in two halves with corresponding and contrasting features in each (50:4–44; 51:1–53).[1] "I am against you" occurs in both halves (50:31; 51:25). Each half has a song about a weapon (50:35–38; 51:20–23); and in each there is a pun on Babylon (50:21; 51:41). Both halves announce Babylon's fall (50:46; 51:31). Her fall will have a far-reaching, even universal, impact (50:12). In the first half the figures of sheep, shepherd, and pasture dominate (50:6, 17, 45); in the second, harvest and drunkenness are frequent metaphors (51:7, 33, 39, 57).

The Babylonians (also called "Chaldeans") were a tribe whose leader Nabopolassar took the Assyrian capital of Nineveh in 612. Under Nebuchadnezzar they moved westward, defeated Egypt at Carchemish in 605, and swooped down on Judah in 597 en route to Egypt. Bel is an older title for Marduk (Merodach), a war-hero god and creator. He was Babylon's patron saint. A nation from the north is stereotypical language for an invader. In the earlier part of the book the northerner coming against Israel was Babylon. Now the "northerner," namely, the Medes and other allies of Cyrus (51:27–28), will invade Babylon (**50:1–3**).

In the following verses Israel is basically told to move out (**50:4–20**). In book-end fashion, Israel is the subject of verses 4–7 and 17–20; Israel's foe is the subject of verses 8–10 and 14–16; and Babylon is the subject of the middle section (vv. 11–13).

Israel's physical return will put them in choice places. Spiritually, forgiveness will be in effect; it follows Israel's return to the covenant relationship. The image of a flock continues in verse 17 with a capsule review of history: Tiglath-pileser of Assyria made war against Israel in 734; in 722 Samaria, the capital of Israel, was taken; Babylon captured Jerusalem, capital of Judah, in 586.

Israel's hope arose concretely out of a siege laid to Babylon by an alliance of peoples from the north. They would come with arrows and bows and swords. Reasons for the divine vengeance were: Babylon pillaged Judah; and she sinned against the Lord (specifically, in her pride). The city fell in October 539 when Cyrus the Persian, the commander of an alliance consisting of the Medes and other northern peoples, took the city.

Merathaim, "twofold rebellion," and *Pekod,* "punishment," are puns on Marratim, a district in southern Babylon and Puqudu, a tribe east of Babylon. God will give the command to attack. The result of the battle is that Babylon, once a hammer shattering others, is herself broken (**50:21–32**).

Another reason for destroying Babylon, in addition to her destruction of Jerusalem's temple, is pride. To defy the Lord is to treat him insolently. The titles *Holy One of Israel* (v. 29) and *Lord Almighty* (v. 30) underscore the presumption of Babylon's sin.

The Babylonian Empire will be devastated (**50:33–46**). Verse 33 echoes the theme of Israel's release as hostage from Babylon's grip. The Redeemer overpowers the opposition (as formerly in Egypt) and as an attorney, he takes over their case. His sword will cut into the political, religious, military, and economic segments of society.

The picture of a depopulated city inhabited by desert creatures is traditional (v. 39; cf. Isa. 34:13–14). Sodom and Gomorrah are the clas-

1. Kenneth T. Aitken, "The Oracles Against Babylon in Jer. 50–51: Structures and Perspectives," *Tyndale Bulletin* 35 (1984): 35–63.

sic instances of cities in ruin. The invader from the north is also standardized language. In addition to the primary foe, a distant alliance and an army of archers are arrayed against Babylon. Besides, God is the ultimate agent. Any resistance is futile.

The end has come (**51:1–19**). The destroyer includes the Medes and their allies. The theme of harvest, together with drunkenness, threads through the chapter (vv. 7, 33, 39, 57).

Figuratively speaking, the movie camera pans jerkily to Israel (her guilt is not minimized), and then to Babylon (her cup makes others drunk), and then back to Israel. Babylon's collapse is Israel's vindication. Attention then turns to the attackers who are to take weapons and move in. Finally, it is all over.

Verses 15–19 are essentially a repetition of 10:12–16. The poem gives assurance that God will carry out his purpose. The Lord's vengeance is retaliation by the highest authority, God's settling of accounts with Babylon.

Forces are marshaled against Babylon (**51:20–33**). "You are my war club" (v. 20) is God's address to the coming "destroyer," Cyrus the Persian. "Destroying mountain" (v. 25) or towering destroyer, refers to Babylon; geographically it was situated on a plain, though it boasted a temple mountain or ziggurat. Militarily, she was the greatest power in history, but her eruptive force, like an extinct volcano, will be neutralized.

Battle preparations are urged upon the alliance that will attack. Ararat, ancient Urartu, is modern Armenia. Minni refers to a territory southeast of Lake Urmia settled by hill folk. Scythians occupied the region between the Black and Caspian seas; they were the Ashkenaz. Early in the sixth century these were conquered by the Medes; together they become part of the attacking force on Babylon. The Lord's purposes will be implemented. Babylon's chief military resource, her soldiers, are incapacitated. The threshing floor (v. 33) is figurative, representing the place where God's further smashing with his war club will take place.

The next section (**51:34–53**) focuses on Babylon and Israel. Babylon has overstepped her bounds in destroying Jerusalem. Like an attorney, God takes up Israel's case (v. 36). Babylon will be reduced to rubble (v. 37).

Israel is urged to seize the moment of Babylon's confusion and make her escape (v. 45). Rumors of a Babylonian resurgence or of new leadership are not to be believed. God as scorekeeper will see that Babylon is treated as she has treated others.

The themes throughout the oracle are gathered up in its conclusion (**51:54–58**): the destroyer, the destruction, the motivation of God's retribution, drunkenness, death, and the futility of resistance. The "leveling" of the walls of Babylon is to be understood as a figure of speech for capitulation, for when the Persians attacked in 539, surrender came quickly and without a battle. In 485, however, Xerxes I laid the walls waste.

The symbolic action (**51:59–64**; cf. chaps. 13, 19, 27, and 32) is a fitting conclusion to the oracle and to the entire book, even though the action is dated 594/3.

IX. The Fall of Jerusalem (52:1–34)

Jeremiah's words end in 51:64. This account, which expands on the story in chapter 39:1–10, is mostly taken from 2 Kings 24:18–25:30. It documents the historical fulfillment of much that is prophesied in the book and so adds to the credibility of Jeremiah's words.

Nebuchadnezzar's eighteen-month siege, begun in January 588, came in response to Zedekiah's rebellion (**52:1–11**). The famine conditions are further described in Lamentations 2:20–22; 4:1–20.

In August 587 Nebuzaradan put the torch to the city (**52:12–27a**). His second assignment was to gather those destined for exile. Temple furnishings were dismantled; precious metals were salvaged.

Of the three Babylonian raids (597, 587, and 582/1) the largest number of people were deported in 597. Since 2 Kings 24:14–16 reports a total of eighteen thousand, presumably the list here (**52:27b–34**) is of men only. King Jehoiachin was in the first deportation. The sadness of the closing chapter is brightened by the glimmer of hope in Jehoiachin's improved condition. In 538 the exiles would return. It is because of Jeremiah's message that we know both the reason for the sadness and the reason for the hope.

SELECT BIBLIOGRAPHY

Blackwood, A. W., Jr. *Commentary on Jeremiah.* Waco: Word, 1977.

Bright, J. *Jeremiah.* New York: Doubleday, 1965.

Calvin, J. *Commentaries on the Book of the Prophet Jeremiah and the Lamentations.* Reprint. Grand Rapids: Eerdmans, 1948.

Feinberg, C. L. "Jeremiah." In *The Expositor's Bible Commentary,* edited by Frank E. Gaebelein, 12 vols. Grand Rapids: Zondervan, 1982.

Harrison, R. K. *Jeremiah and Lamentations.* Downers Grove: Inter-Varsity, 1973.

Holladay, W. *Jeremiah: Spokesman out of Time.* Philadelphia: Pilgrim, 1974.

Martens, E. A. *Jeremiah.* Scottdale, Pa.: Herald, 1986.

Thompson, J. A. *The Book of Jeremiah.* The New International Commentary on the Old Testament. Grand Rapids: Eerdmans, 1979.

LAMENTATIONS

Elmer A. Martens

INTRODUCTION

The circumstance that colors the Book of Lamentations is the fall of Jerusalem in 597–587 B.C. The prophet Jeremiah had foretold an invasion by an enemy from the north. The invaders would cause devastation; they were God's agents to punish Judah for its sin of breaking the covenant.

By the turn of the century (ca. 600 B.C.) the Babylonians (Jeremiah's enemy from the north) were in the region; and the power balance was decidedly shifting. In 597 they attacked Jerusalem, and Judah became a vassal state to the Babylonians. When the vassal king Zedekiah rebelled against Nebuchadnezzar, his Babylonian overlord, reprisal was immediate. Though the city maintained itself during an eighteen-month siege, Nebuchadnezzar's victory brought the burning of the city, including the Solomonic temple. The catastrophe—loss of temple, city, leadership, freedom, and land—was shocking. Many had become convinced that such a thing could never happen because Jerusalem and the temple were indestructible. This book laments the tragic collapse of a 350-year nation state and the end of an era.

The poet wrestles in anguish with the contrast between Judah's status as God's covenant partner and her present collapse. Why had it all happened? Had God turned in anger against his people? How was one to deal with this traumatic experience? What interpretation was to be put upon events of such inexpressible horror? The book is about suffering. It can be compared to some of the psalms and parts of Isaiah 40–55.

The book, totally in poetry, is distinguished by three characteristics. First, much of the poetry is in the Qinah meter, a rhythmic accent in a 3-2 pattern (the Hebrew word for "lament" is *qînâ*). Poetic lines often consist of five words with a thought break after the third word. This 3-2 pattern, while not limited to use in lament literature, is characteristic of funeral dirges, for it gives the effect of a statement which, interrupted by a sob, is concluded with a shortened phrase. Characteristically, laments begin with "how" (1:1; Jer. 48:17). Often they contrast an earlier glory with present disarray.

A classic lament is David's song of grief upon the death of Jonathan

(2 Sam. 1:19–27). Laments or funeral dirges were effectively used by the prophets in order to portray coming disaster. Two kinds of laments are found in Lamentations: the individual lament (chap. 3) and the communal lament (chaps. 1, 2, 4). The individual lament has an address to God, a complaint, a statement of confidence, a petition, and a word of praise. The communal lament has more flexibility and is designed for group use, usually in a worship setting (e.g., Pss. 44; 60; 74). It describes the distress and there is an appeal to God for help.

A second formal characteristic of the book is the acrostic pattern in which four of the five chapters are cast. In an acrostic, poetic lines or stanzas begin with the successive letters of the alphabet. In the first two chapters, each stanza of three couplets begins with the appropriate letter of the twenty-two-letter Hebrew alphabet—hence twenty-two verses. In the third poem (chap. 3) three successive lines each begin with the same alphabetical letter; the next three with the next letter; for a total of sixty-six verses. In chapter 4 the twenty-two stanzas consist of two couplets each; each stanza is in acrostic formation. The final poem is not an acrostic, but, like the Hebrew alphabet, has twenty-two lines.

The best-known acrostic in the Bible is Psalm 119, with eight verses to each of the Hebrew letters. Thirteen other acrostics have been identified.

Why follow an acrostic form when preparing a lament? It has been noted that a formal structure acts as a restraint on statements of grief which would otherwise lack orderliness. Certainly it is a demanding task to pour emotion-filled material in a recipelike form. A further reason for an acrostic would be its help in memorization. Finally, the acrostic by its form says what is to be said about suffering from A to Z.

A third characteristic, formally speaking, is that of balance. The center poem is the longest. On either side of it are two poems, each with twenty-two stanzas, though of differing length. Moreover, as has been noted, the book itself is in Qinah (3-2) pattern: three longer poems follow two shorter ones. Further, chapters 1 and 5 have a similar emphasis, an extended description of the tragic situation. Chapters 2 and 4 both deal with suffering, enemies, and God's wrath. This leaves chapter 3, an individual lament that concentrates on giving an explanation for the suffering. The effect is that the first two chapters lead up to the central chapter; more rapidly the final chapters lead away from the climax of chapter 3.

The tone of the book is one of sadness and deep sorrow. Essentially the book processes a community's grief. The poet tries to come to terms with the disaster. He does not give as a reason that the Babylonians were militarily superior. The Babylonians are not even mentioned by name. Nor does he consider that the gods of Babylon were stronger than the God of Israel.

Specifically, the book leaves no doubt that the people's sin accounts for the tragic fall of Jerusalem. Each of the five poems makes clear that the event must be seen as God's punishment for sin. The book's message, therefore, is in keeping with what the earlier prophets proclaimed: sin will bring judgment. Such a message is also in keeping with the covenant provisions which listed destruction, loss of land, and dispersion as among the covenant curses (Deut. 28:15–64).

The fuller explanation therefore—beyond the people's sin—is that God implemented the covenant curses—but not mechanically. The poem, especially in chapter 2, elaborates on God's wrath. It was God's anger against his people that precipitated such a horrendous event. That wrath is not capricious, but is expressed in the context of God's righteousness. The tension of a good God even permitting such affliction is perhaps not resolvable, but chapter 3 is a wide-ranging attempt to respond to this tension.

The book is instructive in grief processing. First, a difficult situation is not denied or minimized. The poet pours out his grief and faces the ugliness of a crushed city and ruined dreams. Second, there is catharsis in explicitly stating the situation. Not only is the grimness not denied, but it is detailed. Sin is confessed. Third, there is a wrestling over the assertion that God has brought on the disaster, and yet that comfort and help can only be in him. The book is an illustration that in times of calamity one need not sink into despair. Fourth, the poet seizes for consolation on what is known of God, his goodness and his faithfulness (3:20–23). Fifth, in prayer the entire situation is rolled over on God himself.

The author is not named but is popularly thought to be Jeremiah. Evidence for such a belief relies on Jewish and Christian tradition. Jeremiah is said to have composed complaints (2 Chron. 35:25), though these need not be the Book of Lamentations. The Greek version of the Old Testament adds to the title of the book that it is by Jeremiah. While these are important considerations, other observations lead to a different conclusion: (1) there is nothing in the Book of Jeremiah that suggests any leaning to acrostic forms; (2) the assertion that "we looked for allies" (4:17) is altogether out of character for Jeremiah, who counseled submission to Babylon and objected to Israel's alliances with foreign powers (2:18); (3) the book has about it the mood of perplexity, whereas Jeremiah was certain about the reality of the coming disaster and its reason. One cannot be certain about the author. If the author was not Jeremiah, he was nevertheless an eyewitness of the events and wrote soon after 586, probably before 570.

The acrostic form plus the symmetrical and balanced arrangement nevertheless argue for a single author. Chapter 5, once claimed by scholars to be a later addition, is more and more thought to belong integrally to the whole. While we may not know the poet's name, we are the richer for the writer's frank statement of his grief and his proclamation of the goodness of God.

Orthodox Jews read this book on the ninth of Ab to commemorate the destruction of both Solomon's temple (587 B.C.) and Herod's temple (A.D. 70). The Roman Catholic liturgy calls for a reading of the book during Holy Week. Persons and nations who fall into disastrous circumstances find a kinship here; together with the anonymous poet they can struggle through to commitment even if not always to full clarity.

OUTLINE

I. Lamenting a City in Shambles (1:1–22)
   A. A Lost Splendor (1:1–6)
   B. Enemies Mock and Gloat (1:7–11)
   C. In Search of Comforters (1:12–17)
   D. Distressed and Vengeful (1:18–22)
II. An Angry God and an Awful Tragedy (2:1–22)
   A. God's Anger Unleashed (2:1–9)
   B. Widespread Ruin (2:10–17)
   C. A Prayer of Anguish (2:18–22)
III. Processing Grief (3:1–66)
   A. Afflicted by God (3:1–18)
   B. Confidence in God (3:19–42)
   C. Beset with Problems (3:43–54)
   D. Calling on God (3:55–66)
IV. Jerusalem's Humiliation (4:1–22)
   A. Jerusalem's Faded Glory (4:1–10)
   B. Jerusalem's Dire Plight (4:11–20)
   C. A Strange Irony (4:21–22)
V. A Summarizing Prayer (5:1–22)
   A. Refugees in One's Homeland (5:1–9)
   B. "Our Heart Is Faint" (5:10–18)
   C. "Turn Us Back" (5:19–22)

COMMENTARY

I. Lamenting a City in Shambles (1:1–22)

The city is Jerusalem. The time is either post-597 or -587. In 597, provoked by Jehoiakim (609–597), Nebuchadnezzar of Babylon attacked Jerusalem, the capital of Judah. Less than ten years later Zedekiah rebelled against his overlord Nebuchadnezzar. The Babylonian king laid siege, captured, and burned the city. The acrostic poem depicts the result, notes the enemies' triumph, and acknowledges that God brought about the disaster because of Judah's sin. The absence of a comforter is a repeated note.

A. A lost splendor (1:1–6). "How" is a literary feature of a lament or dirge (cf. 2:1; 4:1, 2; Jer. 48:17). The tone is at once affectionate and sympathetic, like a pastor coming to the bereaved. The city, once prestigious, has been reduced to slave status. Jerusalem's greatness under Solomon was world-renowned (1 Kings 10). Once this city was the hub of activity; now she is a "feeder" into the Babylonian system. Her lovers, namely her allies, such as Egypt or Moab, have deserted her.

The roads to Zion are without pilgrims who would normally come to the worship feasts in Jerusalem. Religious, economic, and social life is nonexistent. The chief foe is Babylon, though ultimately the affliction is from the Lord. Jerusalem's collapse has come for moral reasons, the result of a breach of covenant (Deut. 28:15ff.), rather than chiefly because of political misjudgment or military inadequacy. Nor is it the enemies' god who has triumphed. The city is bereft of its dignity, its status, its leaders, and its allies.

B. Enemies mock and gloat (1:7–11). Now away from their home city, the citizens remember the wealth of the city—a wealth that included the temple and its prized furnishings. These the enemy, the Babylonians, had taken away (Jer. 27:19ff.; 52:17–23). Contrary to God's law, which forbade foreigners to enter the temple (Ezek. 44:9), the Babylonians, a pagan people, had defiled the temple by entering it.

The enemies taunt Jerusalem by saying that her God is unable to defend her. The city is personified. Her nakedness, the depopulation of the city, is a disgrace; her filthiness, "menstrual uncleanness," is a tell-tale evil. She lives for the moment, and does not consider her future.

C. In search of comforters (1:12–17). From a lament about Jerusalem by some onlooker, attention shifts to a lament by Jerusalem herself. Hurting people feel their hurt accentuated when others carry on as usual. She acknowledges the Lord's role in her affliction. Anger, like fire, consumes, and here consumes completely ("into my bones"). That God, like a hunter, has become Israel's adversary, is an additional disgrace. The winepress is figurative for judgment. In a trough hewn out of stone, grapes would be trampled to release the juice. Judah's dire plight is compounded by the lack of comforters.

D. Distressed and vengeful (1:18–22). In contrast to laments in other cultures, the "righteousness of God" is the setting for confession and lament here. Verses 18–20 review the main themes: Israel's sin, suffering, exile, worthless allies, and famine. Attention turns to the enemies, upon whom the poet calls down divine vengeance (vv. 21–22). Implicit is the argument that if God punishes sin, let him punish the enemy for his excesses. Such a response at least takes seriously, "Vengeance is mine, I [God] will repay" (Deut. 32:35).

II. An Angry God and an Awful Tragedy (2:1–11)

In the second poem, an acrostic like the first, the unprecedented tragedy of Jerusalem's destruction is explained as resulting from God's anger let loose against it. The tragedy is depicted; the mournful prayer of the victims is recorded.

A. God's anger unleashed (2:1–9). Once a cloud of glory filled the temple as a sign of God's favor (1 Kings 8:10). Now God's displeasure, like a dark cloud, stands over Jerusalem. God's strength is expressed anthropomorphically by the "strong arm"; his anger, by the "hot nose." Of the five different words for "anger" here, several have to do with heat and fire; they denote an intense emotional disturbance. God's anger may be viewed as the expression of his justice, for here is not an impulsive emotional outburst, but a follow-through on a threat. By his anger God protects what he loves: justice. God's anger is against evil.

The effects of God's wrathful action are pictured in different ways. Overall Israel has toppled from the splendor of her election. The ark of the covenant and even the temple are no longer important to him. Fields and fortresses, the land and its leaders have been affected by God's anger. God's destroying action has taken the lives of the choice soldiers. Not only has God removed all outside resources, but worse, he has withdrawn his own offer for help. Even worse, he has, like an enemy, turned against Israel.

Jerusalem is in view in verse 6—first the temple, then the city. With the temple, God's dwelling and the place of meeting, destroyed, the festivals are no longer feasible. Specifically, God has rejected the altar. The altar of burnt offering stood in the courtyard; the altar of incense was inside the temple. Access to the temple is no longer monitored; the pagan Babylonians raise shouts of victory where pious Jews once raised shouts of praise to God. God directs the destruction of the city's fortifications. Finally, the leadership strata—king, lawgiver, prophet—is annihilated. Tragedy occurs where there is no word from the Lord.

B. Widespread ruin (2:10–17). The remaining verses of the poem (10–22) depict the human reaction to God's destructive wrath, and thereby add further details about the ruin. Dust and sackcloth were cultural expressions of grief, as was bowing to the ground, which denoted mourning and repentance. Multiple age ranges are represented: elders, maidens, mothers, children, and infants who "cry their hearts out." The collective group speaks in verse 10; but in verse 11 an individual, an inside observer who is deeply moved, speaks. Both questions of verse 13 suggest speechlessness. "Your wound is as deep as the sea" (v. 13) conveys the notion not only that things could not be worse, but that the catastrophe has no parallel.

Prophets, had they been true prophets, might have averted the disaster, or if not, could now be comforters. But false prophets are disqualified. A true prophet's function is to expose evil in society. Jeremiah reprimanded false prophets and those who listened to them (14:14; 23:13; 27:9–10). Neither the prophets nor the "outsiders" can be comforters. Nor can God, who is the agent of the disaster. After the description of disaster (vv. 11–16) comes the interpretation (v. 17). The word decreed long ago was God's warning that such disaster would come should Judah fail to follow God (Lev. 26:14ff.; Deut. 28:15ff.).

C. A prayer of anguish (2:18–22). Judah is encouraged to meet her frustration and grief in the presence of the Lord and to pray in behalf of the children. The encouragement is addressed to the city walls which are personified (v. 18). The metaphor is apt in view of night watches maintained on the walls. In verses 20–22 the people's prayer is offered, or the poet prays in their behalf.

The appeal to the Lord is made on the basis of lack of precedent (whom have you ever treated like this?) and compassion. A report of starved women resorting to cannibalism is found in 2 Kings 6:25–29. The statement may be literal, of course, but since covenant curses projected such a situation (Deut. 28:53), reference to it could be a way of saying, "The worst has happened." Casualties of war are in the street, a war in which the Lord is the aggressor.

III. Processing Grief (3:1–66)

The form of chapter 3, while still an acrostic, is an individual lament (at least vv. 1–20), and so differs from the communal laments that precede and follow it. Chapter 3 is the middle poem, with 3:1 exactly at the center. In concept and intensity the first two chapters lead up to chapter 3 and the last two lead from it. As an individual lament it has the customary components of complaint, statement of confidence, and prayer. Although the summons to praise is absent, this individual lament can be compared with a similar genre in the psalms (e.g., Ps. 13) and Jeremiah 15:15–21. Yet the individual fades out; a group speaks in verses 40–47. Perhaps the poem was used as a responsive reading in worship. The individual lament becomes a prism through which to elaborate on the communal experience. Or the "I" may from the outset be understood as a collective pronoun.

A. Afflicted by God (3:1–18). One characteristic of a lament is the graphic depiction of the difficulty which called it forth. The ugliness of this scenario is God-caused. He (v. 1 and throughout this section), though not named until 3:18, is the Lord. The speaker is the victim of the Lord's assaults. Verse 4 suggests that the problem is illness. To physical ailment is added psychological and spiritual isolation. Access to God has been stonewalled, "blocked" with huge boulders.

Other images follow to make graphic the individual's plight: wild animals mauling their victims (vv. 10–11); a hunter in target practice (vv. 12–13); a dietician administering bitterness (lit. poison) (v. 15). Like Jeremiah, the individual is the object of ridicule. A Western idiom corresponding to verse 16 would be: "He made me eat dirt." The tension is severe. God, who might have been his hope, has become his adversary.

B. Confidence in God (3:19–42). Verses 19–20 provide a transition from the description of distress, of which God is the cause, to a statement of confidence, wherein God is the hope. Hope is implied by the lament as such, for it looks for an answer from God. Hope in individual laments is usually made explicit in the "certainty of hearing" or confidence statements.

The Lord's great love (v. 22) follows through on covenant obligations. God's compassion cannot be exhausted. His faithfulness to his covenant is unfailing. Whereas the poet had earlier given up hope (v. 18), he now determines that God will be his hope. Verses 21–26 have been called the theological high point of the book.

One of the poet's answers to suffering is to affirm God's goodness. For this reason the afflicted do well to wait even in silence. There is approval for turning over the yoke (responsibility?) to the younger generation (v. 27). However, the context supports the view that yoke deals with suffering (cf. v. 1); the lesson of trust in God, when learned early, is orientation for the remainder of one's life.

Verses 28–30 once more picture the afflicted person in order to set the stage for verses 31–33. Despite the perception that the Lord brought on the affliction, faith affirms that it is not really in God's nature to afflict. More than that, his compassion and his unfailing love override whenever God does afflict. The poet is responding to an age-old problem: How can one reconcile belief in a God of goodness and power with the reality of suffering?

Verses 34–36 are further assertions of confidence by one who is a victim of evil. A God of justice is obligated to redress evil. The Lord's power means that limits are enforced. God as the source of good and bad echoes Job 2:10. Suffering may be the result of sin (Deut. 28:15–68). It is not, however, the only reason for suffering. Still, ruthless honesty is necessary (v. 40). Genuine repentance admits wrongdoing.

C. Beset with problems (3:43–54). The poet returns to complaints but these are now of a communal nature. His complaint involves God, enemies, and personal suffering. Former themes are incorporated: covering with a cloud of anger (vv. 43–45; cf. 2:1); killing without mercy (v. 43; 2:17); inaccessibility (v. 44; 3:8); and humiliation (v. 45; 1:1, 6). Arguments for the Lord to pay attention to the situation arise from the humiliation of God's people, the suffering, and the threat of annihilation.

D. Calling on God (3:55–66). Prayers and report of prayers close the poem. Previous experiences are invoked as reason for God to hear. Or, in a more likely interpretation, so sure is the poet of God's help, that he can speak in the past tense. Legal court language pervades verses 58–59. The enemies, in their glowering mood, though unidentified, will prompt the Lord to action. The prayer for vengeance (v. 64), while in keeping with the Old Testament admonition to turn over all vengeance to God, falls far short of the New Testament exhortation to love one's enemies (Matt. 5:44).

IV. Jerusalem's Humiliation (4:1–22)

Like the three preceding poems, this poem is an acrostic. Like chapter 2, it tells of Jerusalem's faded glory and reiterates the Lord's part, though not as sharply, in bringing about the disaster. One feature of the lament is the contrast between "then," a time of glory, and "now," a time of humiliation.

A. Jerusalem's faded glory (4:1–10). "How" is the recognizable introduction to a lament (1:1). Not Jerusalem only, but the country's suffering populace is the subject. Jerusalem the golden has become very tarnished. Its pride, the sanctuary, is dismantled, and its stones are scattered about in the streets. However, with verse 2 as a clue, gold and gems may refer to the best of its citizens. The sons of Zion, either Jerusalem's citizenry generally or the temple functionaries, like currency, have become sharply devalued.

A new and ugly ethos prevails. People have become hardened, even heartless. Ostriches lay their eggs in the sand, thus putting the future of their young in jeopardy. Besides, they treat their young harshly. The rich have become poverty-stricken.

Sodom and Gomorrah are the classic symbols of catastrophe (Gen. 19:24–25, 29; Jer. 20:16; 23:14). Instead of "princes" (v. 7), the Hebrew text reads "Nazirites." The Nazirites were a group which vowed self-discipline and devotion to the Lord's service (Num. 6:1–21). Perhaps the term suggests "the elite" who are described as the picture of health, but because of famine have become scrawny and unrecognizable.

Sudden death seems preferable to slow death by famine. The reference to cannibalism, practiced by the sensitive women, may be a way of saying that the covenant curses have been implemented (Deut. 28:53). Still, famine drives people to bizarre actions and the description may well be literal (2 Kings 6:26–29).

B. Jerusalem's dire plight (4:11–20). The Lord's anger is the theme of chapter 2. The doctrine of Zion and the temple as invincible had some theological support, but was misleading in Judah's circumstance. As a fortification, Jerusalem was strategically placed with valleys on three of her sides. Her fall was due to inside weaknesses. The sins of God's people as a reason for the disaster are noted in each of the four acrostic poems (1:8; 2:14; 3:42; 4:13) and in the final chapter (5:7).

In a profound sense, the leaders' failure to be true spokespersons for God brought on the siege that resulted in the death of the "righteous" folk. These former leaders are now among the rejected. Those once honored are not shown respect.

As Sodom in its crisis had no helpers, so Judah is without assistance. Verse 17 is often cited as proof that Jeremiah is probably not the author of Lamentations. He counseled against seeking foreign aid. Verse 19, it is almost certain, describes Zedekiah's attempt to escape (2 Kings 25:4–6; Jer. 39:4–7). Hopes were pinned on the king as the Lord's anointed. But he was captured.

C. A strange irony (4:21–22). The cup (v. 21) is metaphorical language for the "wine" of God's judgment. Nations drinking this wine go into a stupor, stagger, and fall (Jer. 25:15–28). To be stripped naked is to be disgraced. Edom took advantage of the chaos left after Babylon sacked Jerusalem; Judah was left without defenses. Edom then occupied parts of Judah, a circumstance that further fueled long-standing hostility.

V. A Summarizing Prayer (5:1–22)

This poem, unlike the four before it, is not an acrostic though it has twenty-two lines, the number of letters in the Hebrew alphabet. The prayer reviews the distressing circumstances subsequent to the fall of Jerusalem and pleads for the Lord to grant restoration. In form the poem is a communal lament with an address to God, the listing of reasons for the lament, and a request to God for help.

A. Refugees in one's homeland (5:1–9). Jerusalem has been sacked and there is chaos. A large part of the tragedy is the loss of her land, her inheritance. The land was a keystone in her covenant relationship with God. Verse 3 may refer to a sense of abandonment by God, though the literal also holds true because of war casualties.

In the days of Jehoiakim (609–597), Judah was a vassal to Pharaoh Neco of Egypt. In the early decades of the sixth century she was a vassal to Assyria. Marauding bandits were a hazard after Babylon's victory.

B. "Our heart is faint" (5:10–18). Famine, sexual abuse, and violence make for very hard times. Life has taken a turn for the worse. Youth are put to hard labor. The collapse of society marks a reversal from what things had been.

C. "Turn us back" (5:19–22). The communal prayer concludes by repeating a foundation of the faith: God's everlasting rule. The plaintive questions are rhetorical (v. 20). The prayer for restoration is like Ephraim's prayer (Jer. 31:18–19). The poet accepts the fact that God punishes sin. Although the total case has been turned over to God, the closing note is sobering indeed (cf. Mal. 4:6).

SELECT BIBLIOGRAPHY

Gordis, R. *The Song of Songs and Lamentations.* New York: Ktav, 1974.

Gottwald, N. K. *Studies in the Book of Lamentations.* Chicago: A. R. Allenson, 1954.

Harrison, R. K. *Jeremiah and Lamentations.* Downers Grove: Inter-Varsity, 1973.

Hillers, D. R. *Lamentations.* The Anchor Bible. Garden City, N.Y.: Doubleday, 1972.

Kaiser, W. C. *A Biblical Approach to Personal Suffering.* Chicago: Moody, 1982.

EZEKIEL

Victor P. Hamilton

INTRODUCTION

There are not many biographical details about Ezekiel in the book that bears his name. We know that the name of his father was Buzi (1:3). This is a strange name; the only Hebrew root we know of with which that name can be connected is "shame." Buzi means literally "my shame." But what parent would name a son "my shame"? Perhaps "Buzi" is related to another Semitic root that we cannot identify.

There are no such problems with Ezekiel's own name. It means either "El/God shall strengthen" (a statement) or "May El/God strengthen" (a prayer). In fact, Ezekiel's name is exactly the same as Hezekiah's, except that God's name in "Ezekiel" is *-el,* while in "Hezekiah" it is *iah.* In the opening chapters God reveals to the prophet why his name is Ezekiel.

We may safely surmise that Ezekiel belonged to the aristocracy. It was the policy of the Babylonians, when they invaded and conquered a country, to exile only the upper levels of leadership. This would deprive subjugated peoples of effective leaders. Hegemony was maintained by silencing (and exiling as necessary) outspoken leaders of the resistance movement.

Ezekiel is unique among the prophets in that his entire ministry was conducted outside of Palestine. Every date in Ezekiel, outside of the problematical "thirtieth year" of 1:1, is dated from the year in which Judah's king Jehoiachin was carried into Babylonian captivity. The earliest date we find in Ezekiel is 593 B.C. (1:2). The latest date in the prophecy is 571 B.C. (29:17). Thus, Ezekiel's ministry spans approximately twenty-two years.

Ezekiel carries out his ministry while in captivity. He lives and preaches among his fellow exiles by the Kebar River. Ezekiel has his own parsonage ("Go, shut yourself inside *your* house," 3:24, emphasis added). On numerous occasions the elders in exile come to talk with him or watch him at his house (8:1; 14:1; 20:1; 33:21), indicating that Ezekiel more than likely was a religious leader in Jerusalem before 597 B.C. That stature he carried with him into exile.

Ezekiel was married (24:15–18), but we never hear of any children. In 4:14 he offers the protest "from my youth until now I have never eaten anything found dead." That Ezekiel would use such a phrase indicates that he is no youngster. He is definitely older than Jeremiah.

Ezekiel 1:3 and other passages identify Ezekiel as a priest as well as prophet.

The arrangement of the prophecy of Ezekiel is clear. After a brief section describing Ezekiel's call (chaps. 1–3), we find prophecies/oracles of doom and destruction against Judah/Jerusalem (chaps. 4–24). These must have been spoken prior to the fall of Jerusalem, for every date provided by these chapters is pre-587/6 B.C. (1:2—593; 8:1—592; 20:1—591; 24:1—588).

The second section comprises chapters 25–32 and is Ezekiel's prophecies/oracles to the nations. In so preaching, Ezekiel falls in the train of his prophetic successors Amos (1–2:5), Isaiah (chaps. 13–23), and Jeremiah (chaps. 46–51). The distinctive thing about Ezekiel's foreign oracles, apart from their obsession with Tyre and Egypt, is that they are more related to contemporary history than are those of Isaiah, Jeremiah, or Amos. Seven of the thirteen dates in Ezekiel are in this section (26:1—587; 29:1—587; 29:17—571; 30:20—587; 31:1—587; 32:1—585; 32:17—586). Four of these dates refer to a day and month in 587 B.C., very close to the time of Jerusalem's destruction.

The third section is prophecies/oracles of salvation directed to the exiles (chaps. 33–39). It is in this unit that Ezekiel is inspired by God to share with his exiled congregation the revivification, restoration, regeneration, and reunification of God's scattered people as they return to Israel from exile. It is Ezekiel's hearing of the fall of Jerusalem that allows him to shift from doom prophecies to hope prophecies (33:21).

The fourth section (actually part of the third) is about the rebuilding of the city of Jerusalem, and especially the reconstruction of the temple (chaps. 40–48). There have been a number of different interpretations as to how these chapters are to be understood. One view suggests that the nation of Israel will be reestablished in the messianic age along with all the accoutrements of temple and temple worship. Such interpreters still look for the building of the temple. A second line of interpretation treats chapters 40–48 symbolically and applies them to the Christian age and to the church. The first approach reads Ezekiel extremely literally, and the second reads it extremely symbolically. Perhaps between the two there is a mediating position that sees in Ezekiel a word of God to and for his people that has not yet transpired, but does not insist on the implementation of all the data from A to Z. Suffice it to say, the return and resettlement of postexilic times had virtually nothing in common with Ezekiel's vision and temple agenda. If anything, the rituals, the personnel, and laws of that community were more Moses-like than Ezekiel-like.

At three critical points Ezekiel sees the glory of God. First is his own personal experience of that glory (chap. 1), which nerves him with boldness for his own ministry. Second is his vision of the departure of that glory both from Jerusalem and from the temple (chaps. 8–11). Third is his vision of the return of the glory of God to Jerusalem and to the temple (chap. 43).

While it is the people's persistent sin that drives the Shekinah from the temple, it is not the people's return to righteousness and repentance that lures the Shekinah back. Surprisingly perhaps, a clarion call to repentance is absent in Ezekiel. The reason for the silence is that for Ezekiel the fate of Jerusalem is sealed, foreseen, and even preenacted. This explains the reason for the many occasions (chaps. 3–4; 5:1–4; 12:1–7; 12:17–20; 21:11–17; 21:18–20; 24:15–27) on which Ezekiel pantomimes Jerusalem's demise.

Ezekiel's major concern is to establish beyond a shadow of a doubt to the exiles the justice of God. What is about to happen, or already happened, to Jerusalem is not due to the whim and caprice of an unpredictable God who one day on the spot decided to withdraw his favor from his people. At the same time, preaches Ezekiel, let not those in exile be infested with false confidence. Their survival in Babylon is not evidence of superior moral quality.

The most prolific phrase in Ezekiel is *they/you shall know that I am the Lord.* The "they/you" may be the survivors left in Jerusalem, the deportees in Babylon, or the Gentiles. Ezekiel, however, generally directs this phrase to God's own people. The prophet's concern is that God's children, who are supposed to know him already, *really* know him. At one level this means that the exiles, when they see or hear about the catastrophe of 587/6 B.C., will indeed know that the Lord is a God of power who is quite capable of fulfilling his promises and threats. At a deeper level Ezekiel, through this phrase, yearns (and so does God) that a faithless and unknowing people come to covenant allegiance and consciousness of their God's lordship.

We can be grateful that the last chapter in Ezekiel is not chapter 24 or chapter 32. There is a rabbinic tradition which holds that of the three major prophets the order should be: Jeremiah, Ezekiel, Isaiah. Jeremiah was placed first because he is the prophet of destruction; Ezekiel follows because he begins with destruction but ends with comfort; Isaiah is last because he focuses entirely on comfort.

Obviously this is not an accurate summary of these three prophets. But it does indicate the major shift in Ezekiel's thought in chapters 1–32 and 33–48. One need only compare Isaiah 66 and Jeremiah 52 with the last chapter in Ezekiel to catch the startling difference in mood. Ezekiel may start in the black of night, but he ends in the glow of a morning dawn. For Ezekiel the most spectacular thing and the most precious thing is not the rebuilt city, the rebuilt temple, or even the reassembled people of God. These are good, but not the best. What makes it all so perfect is the presence of God in the midst of all this renovation: "Yahweh shammah," the Lord is there. That is the cause for Ezekiel's ecstasy.

OUTLINE

I. Prophecies of Doom and Judgment (1–24)
   A. A Vision of the Glory of God (1:1–28)
   B. Ezekiel's Call (2:1–10)

C. Exhorter, Sentry, and Arbiter (3:1–27)
D. The Siege of Jerusalem Symbolized (4:1–5:17)
E. A Further Description of Judgment (6:1–14)
F. The End of Jerusalem (7:1–27)
G. Idolatry in the Temple (8:1–18)
H. The Execution of the Idolaters (9:1–11)
I. God's Glory Leaves the Temple (10:1–22)
J. Lost and Saved (11:1–25)
K. The Exile Symbolized (12:1–28)
L. False Prophets (13:1–23)
M. Idolatry (14:1–23)
N. A Useless Vine (15:1–8)
O. A Foundling Turned Harlot (16:1–63)
P. Two Eagles and a Vine (17:1–24)
Q. Individual Responsibility (18:1–32)
R. A Dirge for Israel's Kings (19:1–14)
S. Rebelliousness (20:1–49)
T. The Sword of Judgment (21:1–32)
U. A City of Blood (22:1–31)
V. Oholah and Oholibah (23:1–48)
W. A Steaming Cauldron (24:1–27)

II. Oracles Against the Nations (25–32)
A. Ammon, Moab, Edom, Philistia (25:1–17)
B. Tyre (26:1–28:26)
C. Egypt (29:1–32:32)

III. Restoration and Renewal (33–39)
A. Accepting Responsibility (33:1–33)
B. Shepherds and Sheep (34:1–31)
C. Edom (35:1–15)
D. Restoration and Regeneration (36:1–18)
E. Resurrection and Reunification (37:1–28)
F. Gog (38:1–39:29)

IV. The New Temple (40–48)
A. The Temple Area (40:1–49)
B. The Temple Proper (41:1–26)
C. Holy Chambers (42:1–20)
D. God's Glory Returns (43:1–27)
E. Enterings and Exitings (44:1–31)
F. Division of the Land (45:1–25)
G. Worship Protocol (46:1–24)
H. The River of Life (47:1–23)
I. Division of the Land (48:1–35)

COMMENTARY

I. Prophecies of Doom and Judgment (1–24)

A. A vision of the glory of God (1:1–28). The significance of the thirtieth year (v. 1) still eludes us. All other dates in Ezekiel are based on the year of Jehoiachin's captivity. Is it the thirtieth birthday of the prophet? An ancient Jewish tradition maintains that the thirty years refer to the number of years from the time the lost book of the law was discovered by Josiah.

Ezekiel is among the exiles in Babylon, having been taken there as a captive in 597. He is situated by the Kebar River which is near the ancient city of Nippur. It is here that he sees visions of God.

What these visions consist of is spelled out in verses 4–28. To begin with, Ezekiel sees a windstorm blowing from the north. In the midst of the storm he observes a chariot that is transported by four living creatures. These animal-like beings are cherubim, as chapter 10 makes abundantly clear. Each has four faces and four wings. The four faces are those of a man, a lion, an ox, and an eagle. The lion is the king of the beasts and symbolizes courage. The ox is king of domesticated animals and symbolizes strength. The eagle is king of the birds and symbolizes speed. Man is king of the world and symbolizes intelligence. The four most lordly creatures are, however, merely the bearers of the Lord of lords.

In the Old Testament cherubim function as symbols of God's presence. For example, in the tabernacle the dwelling-place of God is in the Holy of Holies, above the mercy seat and between the cherubim. It is appropriate, and necessary, that Ezekiel receive a vision of something that symbolizes the presence of the living Lord. After all, Jerusalem will soon be destroyed and the temple will be razed. Everything looks bleak. Ezekiel is hundreds of miles from his home. Yet God is with him in Babylon too. His presence is with his people here as much as it could be anywhere else.

The second object that Ezekiel sees above the chariot is an expanse (cf. Gen. 1:6), and above that expanse a throne. The expanse is obviously the platform on which the throne sits. The throne itself is made of sapphire. Seated on the throne is a man who is fiery from the waist up and fiery from the waist down. If cherubim stand for the presence of God, so does fire. What Ezekiel is experiencing is a vision of God himself in all of his heavenly glory.

This is not just a vision of God, but a vision of God seated upon a throne. Thus in the visual symbolism we move from cherubim to throne. The first part of this vision suggests a God who is present, even in wicked Babylon. The second part of the vision suggests a God who is sovereign. He is on a throne. Certainly the prophet needs this reminder. About the only throne he can see is Nebuchadnezzar's. Has God been deposed? Is Nebuchadnezzar now in control? Indeed not. There might be an earthly throne, but beyond that there is the heavenly throne of God himself.

The third object Ezekiel sees is a rainbow in the midst of this fire. The rainbow immediately reminds us of Genesis 9, where it is a sign of the covenant that God will never again destroy the earth by a flood. So now we move from chariot to cherubim to throne to rainbow. Ezekiel is reminded not only of a God who is near and who reigns, but also of a God who is a covenant-making and covenant-keeping God. Deportation to Babylon does not mean that God has dispossessed his people or that the covenant has been abrogated.

All that Ezekiel can do is fall facedown when he beholds the glory of the Lord. He does not say a word. He simply observes. Now we shift from something Ezekiel sees (vv. 4–28b) to something he is about to hear (v. 28b).

B. Ezekiel's call (2:1–10). That Ezekiel is told to stand up on his feet indicates that he has control of himself. If a man is unconscious one cannot tell him to get up.

The Spirit addresses Ezekiel as "son of man." This title is used for the prophet about ninety times in the book, and is used of no other prophet in the Old Testament. Possibly the repetition of this title is due to the fact that Ezekiel describes visions of the divine not found in any other prophecy. Yet, Ezekiel is still only a man, nothing more.

The congregation to which Ezekiel is sent is described with two verbs: "rebelled," "been in revolt." The first verb means "to refuse allegiance to, rise up against, a sovereign." The second verb is a political term and means something like "to violate covenant duties, breach covenant relations." The congregation is further described with two adjectives: "obstinate" (lit. hard-faced) and "stubborn." The first describes the people on the outside—their passive, emotionless faces. The second describes the people on the inside—hardhearted. Obviously these are not upbeat, encouraging words for this exilic pastor. But they are accurate, and they delineate precisely the enormity of the task before the prophet. His congregation is not a promising one.

God says nothing about their response to Ezekiel. It may go either way. What God is concerned about is not the congregation's attitude, but the prophet's attitude. Ezekiel is not to base or evaluate his ministry on their reaction. He is not to be result-oriented. Rather, he is to be obedience-oriented. He is to speak God's words to them.

His congregation is compared to briers, thorns, and scorpions. Still he is not to quiver before them, or be intimidated by them. There is no record that Ezekiel, like Jeremiah, ever faced opposition, even though his flock is far from inviting, encouraging, and supportive. Chapter 2 anticipates trouble, but it never emerges. But to be forewarned is to be forearmed anyway.

One thing Ezekiel must not do is lower himself to the people's spiritual level (v. 8). His obedience must become a model and stimulus for them, rather than their disobedience becoming a model and stimulus for him. Perhaps God is saying something like: "Do not try to get out of this like Jeremiah did" (cf. Jer. 1). It is very likely that Ezekiel knew Jeremiah.

Next Ezekiel is shown a scroll that has writing on both sides. Surely that the writing is on both sides indicates that the prophet's message is all from God. God does not write on one side, and Ezekiel on the other. It is the abundance of the divine message that is stressed. In our society "to eat words" is something negative, something unpleasant. In biblical thought "to eat words" is an agreeable experience.

Written on the scroll are lament, mourning, and woe. These are three fairly synonymous terms for lamentation, and putting three of them side by side suggests comprehensiveness. Unlike Jeremiah who mingles prophecies of hope and doom, Ezekiel is all doom until chapter 33. That is the reason for the writing on this edible scroll.

C. Exhorter, sentry, and arbiter (3:1–27). Because God twice tells Ezekiel to eat the scroll (vv. 1, 3), it may be that there was some reluctance on Ezekiel's part. If so, he stands in the train of others such as Moses, Gideon, Jonah, and Jeremiah who were not initially euphoric about God's call. Only Isaiah is eager and receptive from the start (Isa. 6). It is not enough for Ezekiel to take the scroll into his mouth (v. 1); he must ingest it as well (v. 3). To his surprise the scroll tastes as sweet as honey. This simile reminds us of Psalm 19:10 and 119:103. Ezekiel may even have borrowed the analogy from Jeremiah (Jer. 15:16). To find the word of the Lord sweet means that it is inherently desirable and attractive, and has satisfactory effects.

Ezekiel is reminded that his message is not to foreigners (v. 5). This is strange, however, in that chapters 25–32 are Ezekiel's oracles to the nations. This must mean that verse 5 refers only to the first part of the prophecy (chaps. 1–24). But if God had sent Ezekiel to them, their acceptance of his message would have been speedier than his own people's acceptance of his message (v. 6b).

If his congregation is tough, God will make Ezekiel tougher (vv. 8–9). In fact, "Ezekiel" means "God will toughen."

It might sound strange that Ezekiel is told to go to his countrymen in exile in that he is already there! Ezekiel is by himself at the river (1:1). He is now told to join his community of exiles at Tel Abib ("mound of the flood"). This place was formed over years by silt thrown up by storm-floods. Ezekiel's bitterness and anger are either reflections of God's attitude toward his people, or more likely a reflection of the prophet's realization that he has to pronounce doom on those he loves.

Ezekiel is further instructed by God to be a sentry (vv. 16–21). He is to warn his people of approaching danger. Silence on the prophet's part not only dooms the congregation, but also makes the prophet himself culpable. The prophet's responsibility extends both to the wicked and to the backslidden righteous. In either case the prophet forfeits his life by neglecting his responsibility. There is nothing here for the people. This is a private communique to the prophet. So crucial is the sentry analogy that it resurfaces in chapter 33. Ezekiel has some input in the eternal destiny of the souls of men. As a matter of fact, he has much input! There is no other way for sidetracked believers to be restored to God's good graces apart from the involvement of the prophet.

In light of verses 16–21 the divine command of verse 24 is almost inexplicable: "Go, shut yourself inside your house." First he is commanded to be a sentry. Then he is ordered to confine himself to his house! And to complicate matters, God will make his tongue stick to the roof of his mouth. Ezekiel will lose his capacity for speech. How does a dumb, tongue-tied prophet under house confinement warn his people of impending danger?

To square verses 22–27 with verses 16–21 some have suggested that the dumbness did not begin after the prophet's call, but only later, and even then it was intermittent. Others suggest that by dumbness is meant that Ezekiel will be immobile. He is to keep to his house and the people are to come to him (8:1; 14:1; 20:1; 33:30–31). In verse 26 the Hebrew word translated "rebuke" in the New International Version rather means "arbitrate on behalf of, represent." Ezekiel will only represent God to the people; he cannot represent the people before God. Communication will go only one way. This explains why Ezekiel speaks only doom until the fall of Jerusalem. Standing before God on behalf of his congregation, however, will be denied him.

D. The siege of Jerusalem symbolized (4:1–5:17). It is appropriate for Ezekiel to act out his message, as he does in chapters 4 and 5. For in the last paragraph of chapter 3 we are informed that Ezekiel was not able to talk. Conversation gives way to pantomiming.

In the first act (**4:1–3**) the prophet is told to take a clay tablet and to draw a siege of Jerusalem on it, complete with siege weaponry. Then he is to place an iron pan between himself and the inscribed city. This pan acts as a wall of separation between the prophet and the brick, and symbolizes the impenetrable barrier between God and Jerusalem (cf. Isa. 59:2: "your iniquities have separated you from your God"). The brick is a symbol of what is about to happen to Jerusalem. When Jeremiah raised this subject it got him into hot water. He was labeled a heretic and anti-Zionist. Ezekiel does not provoke such sentiment, perhaps because he is hundreds of miles away.

Ezekiel's second act (**4:4–5**) is to lie on his left side for 390 days in which he bears the sin of the house of Israel. One day matches one year of sin by Israel. To what do the 390 days refer? If one adds this number to the date of Ezekiel the number goes back to approximately 1000 B.C. (598 + 390), which is roughly the time of David and Solomon. But this is the period from the days of the united kingdom to Ezekiel. The Greek Septuagint reads "190 years," and this refers no doubt to the time of the northern kingdom which began approximately 930 B.C. and lasted until 722/1 B.C. (around two hundred years). It appears, following the Hebrew text, that Ezekiel (or God) indicts the entire monarchy period of Israel (understood all-inclusively).

Also, Ezekiel is to lie on his right side for forty days in which he bears the sin of the house of Judah (**4:6–8**). While "forty days" is often used in the Old Testament, it occurs in many instances in situations involving the removal of sin, such as Noah's flood, punishment on Egypt for forty years, forty days to the overthrow of Nineveh, forty days of Lent. The forty days represent the exile of Judah that lasts about forty years (587–539 B.C.). Having said this, "their sin" in verse 4 means just that—that is, the length of Israel's iniquity—while "the sin" of verse 6 is the length of the punishment for Judah's iniquity.

Ezekiel's third act is to prepare various foods and make them into bread for himself (**4:9–17**). It is something that Ezekiel does while the siege is being enacted. The prophet's food is to consist of wheat, barley, beans, lentils, millet, and spelt. This is not designed to help Ezekiel put on weight. His daily intake of food is to be twenty shekels (eight or nine ounces). His only beverage is water and of this he is to drink only one-sixth of a hin (two or three pints). This frugal diet symbolizes the minimal amount of food the people will have access to when Jerusalem is under siege.

The mention of a barley cake (v. 12) is ominous. Barley bread was a staple of lower-income people, while wheat products were consumed by the upper classes. In this siege only food normally eaten by the poor will be available. Food, already in short supply, will also have to be rationed.

It is crucial that the people before whom Ezekiel pantomimes, and who are already in exile, know the disaster about to visit the holy city, and more importantly, why it is visiting the city. It is impossible to sin and go against the divine order without the most serious of consequences. Jerusalem is God's chosen city but if he leaves it, it becomes as vulnerable as any other city.

Ezekiel's final gesture is cutting off his hair and shaving his head (**5:1–17**). The common denominator in all these symbolic gestures is the affliction of Ezekiel: prolonged immobility, minimal food which is defiled at that. The shaving of hair has the same impact. Shaving hair may symbolize mourning, and even disgrace and humiliation (2 Sam. 10:4). In Isaiah 7:20 shaving of the legs and the beard represents the complete destruction of Sennacherib's army. Samson lost his strength when he lost his hair. Leviticus 21:5 and Ezekiel 44:20 remind us that the priests were forbidden from shaving their hair. Interestingly Ezekiel protested when he was told to eat unclean food but he does not protest when he is told to shave his beard and head, even though he is a priest.

One-third of the hair he burns with fire inside the city (the city he just drew on the tablet, not Jerusalem). One-third he strikes with the sword. One-third he scatters to the wind. Death by catastrophe, death by war, and "death" by dispersion await the rebellious house of Israel. A few in this third group will be spared, but even some of the exiled will perish.

By being set in the center of the nations Jerusalem is more visible. Hence, her conduct ought to be more commendable. Yet just the opposite has taken place. She who has God's laws is acting at a lower moral level than those who do not have God's laws (v. 7). What an indictment! The unbelievers have become a moral conscience for what is supposed to be the community of believers. Morally, God's people come in second.

Because the people have committed unprecedented evil, God is going to unleash unprecedented judgment. Since Israel has not executed his judgments, God will execute his judgment. The famine will be so extensive and intensive that society will be driven to cannibalism. Leviticus 26:29 holds out the possibility of filicidal cannibalism (fathers eating sons), but Ezekiel reverses this and sees patricidal cannibalism (sons eating fathers). Perhaps Ezekiel borrows his graphics from Jeremiah (19:9), although there is no report of cannibalism in the siege of Jerusalem. Note that Ezekiel has sons and fathers eating each other. This may be an emphasis on individual responsibility.

How God's people have defiled his sanctuary will be spelled out in chapters 8–11. Here only the accusation is made. Verse 12 spells out the destiny of the "thirds" mentioned in verse 2. There is no indication that repentance will mitigate the divine judgment. Ezekiel, therefore, makes no room for exhortation. He gives only description. Only when punishment is complete will God's anger subside.

The remainder of the chapter (vv. 14–17) essentially repeats verses 8–12. Jerusalem will be destroyed. She will become a reproach, a taunt, and a warning to the nations. How far we have come from Genesis, where God's will was that his people be a blessing to the nations! Instead, she has become a reproach to them.

God the Creator of Israel has now become her Annihilator. The iniquity of the Israelites is full, and the period of grace is ended. When God moves in judgment he does not simply rap one on the fingers. The language here is graphic, decisive, and thorough. The word pictures suggest catastrophe. And all because the chosen choose to live no longer like the chosen!

E. A further description of judgment (6:1–14). Ezekiel addresses the mountains (v. 1). Perhaps the reason Ezekiel is told to speak to the mountains is because the majority of the people lived in the highlands rather than in the valleys. Also, mountains represent majesty, safety, and security, but they will not be the salvation of the people any longer.

The high places God will destroy are not the mountains (though juxtaposition of the two is deliberate). They are sacrificial platforms on a natural height. They represent phenomena in Israel's religious praxis that originally may have been innocent and only later became blasphemous. Altars for sacrifice and altars for incense will also be destroyed, along with idols. The Hebrew word for "idols" is used thirty-nine times in Ezekiel. It may be that the Hebrew for "idols" is to be connected with another word meaning "dung pellet." The objects may be considered holy icons by the people, but they are actually nothing but excrement. There is some problem in connecting verse 5 with verse 4. If God is going to demolish their altars, how will he scatter the bones of the people around the altars? "Demolish" cannot mean "to remove," but only "to make nonfunctional."

Note that the reasons for the people's destruction are not moral (narrowly defined: e.g., for sexual sins). The people are condemned for illicit worship styles. They have introduced into their liturgical ceremonies customs unacceptable to their Lord; they have made worship an end in itself rather than a means to an end.

Some, however, will escape the sword (v. 8). This is the remnant. God judges his people, but he does not obliterate them. In captivity this remnant will remember the Lord they have grieved. God is quite certain that exile will bring the exiled to their senses. Thus we see that deportation is not a means by which God vents his rage. It is to have both a condemnatory aspect (sin has its consequences) and a salvific aspect (now they will return to me). These two thrusts must be seen in history's first deportation—the expulsion of Adam and Eve from the garden. Its purpose was to judge them and reclaim them. The God who judges is the God who weeps. The God who ostracizes reaches out to bring the lost sheep back to the fold.

Striking the hands and stamping the feet (v. 11), if they be understood with the same expressions in 25:3, 6, indicate an expression of malicious glee. To see all this happening gives to somebody (the mountains? God?) a sense of deep satisfaction.

Three scourges will visit the people: sword, famine, plague. These scourges will overrun people whether they are living in Jerusalem, near Jerusalem, or some distance from Jerusalem. Geography will neither condemn nor save a person. The situation of his heart, rather than his house, is the critical issue.

God's judgment will stretch from the desert to Diblah (v. 14). The desert is the southern wilderness. Diblah (or Riblah?) is a town situated in Hamath, a country on the northern boundary of Israel (Ezek. 47:17; see 2 Kings 23:33).

What will be accomplished by all this? *They will know I am the Lord.* This is not necessarily conversion, but it is admittance of God's power, his control of history, and his lordship over events.

F. The end of Jerusalem (7:1–27). In this chapter the prophet focuses on the termination of Jerusalem. He uses three crisp phrases to express this: the end has come (vv. 3, 6); the day has come (v. 10); the time has come (v. 12). The Hebrew word for "end" (used twice in v. 2, once in v. 3, twice in v. 6) is related to ripe summer fruit that is ready to be harvested (see Amos 8:1–3). Harvesting means cutting down and clearing the fields. That is what the Lord is about to do, but it will not be a thanksgiving harvest.

Verses 5–9 repeat verses 3–4. Each time three themes are prominent: what God is going to do ("I will . . ."); why he is going to do it ("for all your . . ."); the result ("then you will know that I am the Lord"). The botanical metaphors of verse 10 are appropriate. But what is growing is not wheat but arrogance and violence (v. 11). The phrase *the rod has budded* recalls Aaron's rod (Num. 17), but the similarity between the two stops at vocabulary. In Numbers it is of God; in Ezekiel it is of sin.

This time will be so bad that the purchaser will not be able to enjoy his acquisition for long for it soon will be captured and ransacked by the enemy. The individual who has sold something should not be sullen at its loss/departure, for he would not have been able to keep it for long anyway, in light of the approaching enemy. (This verse needs to be compared with Jer. 32 where Jeremiah purchased land right at the climax of Jerusalem's siege, and was told to do so by God.) If an individual sells his property, he will never recover that land as long as he lives (v. 13). "Recovering land" sounds like Jubilee language (Lev. 25). But there will be no more jubilee or jubilation. It is a time for war, indicated by the blowing of the trumpet, a sign of the critical nature of the times.

"Outside and inside" (v. 15) refers to those inside and outside Jerusalem. Three different types of scourges will afflict the people: a sword for outsiders, plague and famine for insiders (see 5:12; 6:12). The few who will escape will do so to the mountains, but they will moan like doves (v. 16; for refugees compared to birds in the highlands, see Ps. 11:1; Isa. 16:2; Jer. 48:28).

Further, hands will fall down in weakness. The phrase *every knee will become as weak as water* (v. 17b) actually refers to urination. So frightened are the people, that they cannot control themselves. They are like the very young or the very elderly.

Putting on sackcloth and shaving the head (v. 18) are ostensibly mourning customs—mourning because of loss and humiliation. Even those things that normally give stability to life—silver and gold—will be abandoned. In fact, it was this silver and gold that partially got the people in trouble to start with (v. 19b). Long before Paul said it, Ezekiel shows that the love of money is the root of all evil. Silver and gold led to jewelry and jewelry led to idols.

Chains are to be prepared for the exiles, or these may be chains to restrain the people from trying to leave the city.

In a time of deep crisis people will grab for anything, even a shoestring. Prophets who have visions, priests who give teachings, and elders who transmit counsel will be of no avail. Normally these are precisely the people to whom one would turn in a time of difficulty. The three groups of would-be helpers are matched by three groups of would-be victims: king, prince, and people of the land (v. 27). The latter group refers to land-owning full citizens. Those who carry influence in society, or who ought to carry influence, will not.

G. Idolatry in the temple (8:1–18). Mention was made earlier of defiling God's sanctuary with vile images (5:11). Chapters 8–11 will now spell this out in detail. The timing of this vision is specific: sixth year, sixth month, fifth day—that is, September 592. A problem of interpretation here is as follows: Is 8:1–18 a vision or does it reflect what really happened? Ezekiel is shown at least four abominations that take place inside the temple. Ezekiel sees these from hundreds of miles away in Babylon. Jeremiah, on the other hand, who is in Jerusalem around the same time, and who preaches in the temple/in front of the temple/about the temple never gives any hint of the presence of these.

The first abomination Ezekiel is shown is "the idol that provokes to jealousy" (v. 3). While idolatry abounds throughout Israel's history only one person (Manasseh) had the audacity to place an idol in the temple (see 2 Kings 21:7). Second Kings 23:6, however, tells us that Josiah (who is pre-Ezekiel) destroyed this idol. This indicates that the abominations Ezekiel sees are not necessarily current ones. He is taken on a voyage into the past. So serious is this that it drives God from his sanctuary.

The second abomination Ezekiel observes by looking through a hole in the temple's wall (v. 10). What he sees are pictures of animals scratched on the walls, recalling the zoomorphic religion of the pagans, especially the Egyptians. In front of these pictures seventy elders are standing. Seventy elders ruled in Moses' time (Num. 11:16, 24) as a representative council. This number continued on in the determination of the number of the Sanhedrin. In Ezekiel's day even the national council is corrupt. The text names one of these elders: Jaazaniah son of Shaphan (v. 11). He is from a distinguished family in the time of Josiah. Shaphan is secretary to Josiah (2 Kings 22:3). One of his sons (Ahikam) was a staunch supporter of Jeremiah (Jer. 26:24). Another son (Gedaliah) was appointed governor of Judah by Nebuchadnezzar (2 Kings 25:22). Jaazaniah is apparently the black sheep of the family. It is not clear why the people perform their acts of homage in the darkness (v. 12), if they believe the Lord has forsaken the land. It makes most sense to take darkness as part of the ritual rather than camouflage.

The third abomination Ezekiel observes is

women mourning for Tammuz (v. 14). Tammuz is the Hebrew equivalent of Sumerian "the faithful son." He was originally a human being who was later deified. That women are weeping for Tammuz reflects the pagan ceremony observing Tammuz's annual death and descent into the netherworld. Normally this ceremony took place in the fourth month (June–July), but Ezekiel sees it in the sixth month (8:1).

The fourth abomination is twenty-five men, facing the east and engaging in sun worship (v. 16). This takes place between the portico and the altar, a sacred space. Some worship the blessings God gives, rather than the God who gives the blessings.

The statement in verse 17b about putting the branch to their nose is interpreted by some as a fifth abomination, the significance of which escapes us. Note, however, that the phrase in question follows "they also fill the land with violence and provoke me to anger." Verses 1–17a deal with temple idolatries. Verse 17b deals with social idolatries. It is likely that verse 17c connects with verse 17b, and means something like "sneer at me" or "turn their noses up at me."

H. The execution of the idolaters (9:1–11). The guards of the city that Ezekiel sees are really executioners. There are six of them. Together with the man clothed in linen (a heavenly scribe), the group numbers seven, the perfect number. This is the crew God sends against the idolaters in the city of Jerusalem.

What makes their advancement necessary is the first stage of the departure of God's presence from the temple. He moves from the Holy of Holies to the threshold. The only thing that makes the temple a holy place is the presence of a holy God. When he leaves, the temple becomes like any other building. It surrenders its sanctity.

Not everybody is evil. There were seven thousand in Elijah's day who did not bow the knee to Baal. And there are those in Ezekiel's day who grieve and lament over all the detestable things (v. 4). The heavenly scribe is to put a mark on the foreheads of these faithful believers who have not compromised religious convictions. The Hebrew says: "put a *tāw* on their foreheads." *Tāw* is the last letter of the Hebrew alphabet, and in the original Hebrew script it was shaped like an *X*. We are reminded here of the mark on Cain (Gen. 4) that saved him from the wrath of his fellow man. Or one may think of the blood at the Passover on the doorposts that saved the occupants inside from the divine wrath. This concept is reflected in the seal that is placed on the forehead of the faithful in Revelation (7:3). There is also a wrong kind of a mark (Rev. 13:16–17; 14:11).

Nobody, except the godly remnant, is exempted from divine judgment. Sex makes no difference, and neither does age. The only thing that spares one is character and commitment.

Ezekiel is not beside himself with joy as he observes this going on. He intercedes for the people. The work of the prophet is to be both exhorter and intercessor. The Hebrew phrase for this second ministry is "to stand before the Lord." The prophet must be as good on his knees and his face as he is with his voice. Ezekiel has many models here. He follows Abraham who prayed that God would not destroy all Sodom and Gomorrah if he found fifty to ten righteous people in it (Gen. 18). Moses pleaded before God on behalf of the idol-making Israelites, and even put his own life on the line in their behalf (Exod. 32). Jeremiah was an intercessor extraordinary. Perhaps there are only two references to Ezekiel doing this (9:8; 11:3) for the time for hope is now gone.

God ignores, apparently, Ezekiel's question, at least directly. In God's response the phrase *the house of Israel and Judah* (v. 9) is all-inclusive. This is why God's judgment is so far-reaching—because sin is so far-reaching. It is not just Judah or Israel, but both of them.

I. God's glory leaves the temple (10:1–22). The mood of chapter 10 is, in one respect, like that of chapter 1. Ezekiel sees a vision of the divine glory. Here the prophet uses the word *cherubim* (v. 1), whereas in chapter 1 he uses "living creatures."

God speaks again to the man in linen (v. 2). In the Old Testament it is the priest who is clothed in linen (Exod. 28:39, 42). And only a priest had the prerogative to handle the holy fire of God.

The linen-dressed man in chapter 9 is a scribe. Here he takes coals from among the cherubim and strews them over the city. Here again we encounter the symbol of fire as in chapter 1. Fire means either purification/cleansing or judgment. In chapter 10 it is clearly the latter, and reference may be made to the fire that falls upon the wicked at Sodom and Gomorrah.

Again, as in 9:3, reference is made to the initial stage of the Lord's departure from his house. Understandably the cherubim are standing on the south side of the temple (v. 3), for idolatrous acts take place on the north side (8:3, 5). God removes himself as far as possible from the iniquity. The cherubim are preparing to leave, pulling the heavenly chariot, and that is why they are flapping their wings (v. 5).

One of the cherubim reaches into the fire and hands it to the linen-clad man. The reason for this is not clear; perhaps the awfulness of what he is about to do overcomes the man in linen and he needs momentary assistance.

Verses 9–14 focus on the cherubim and the wheels of the chariot. Much of the details are like those in chapter 1 except for minor differences. For instance, a cherub's face replaces a bull's face as one of the four faces. The bull was a popular feature of Canaanite religion and this might explain the substitution.

Verse 15a describes the original ascent of the cherubim, something Ezekiel refers to again in verse 19. Here (v. 15b) he identifies them as living creatures. They fly to the east gate of the temple.

Reflection upon what he sees makes Ezekiel realize that what is in front of him are cherubim (v. 20a). The cherubim's identity only gradually dawns upon him. Ezekiel is the only person in the Old Testament to see the heavenly cherubim. It is hard to describe something which one has never seen before, or maybe even ascertain what it is.

The chapter is not really about cherubim or wheels. It is primarily about the departure of God from the temple; secondarily, it is concerned with the destruction of the city. (This last topic is confined to one verse—v. 2—and even there it is just the instructions, not the implementation of those instructions.)

Anything that is holy in the Old Testament is so because of its relationship to God. Holiness is always relational, and never intrinsic—whether we are talking about people, land, days, or buildings. Without God's presence they become ordinary. The temple had been in existence for over four hundred years by Ezekiel's time. For all that, it may exist for another four hundred years, but without the divine presence it will be an empty symbol, a shell. It will be like a box, beautifully wrapped, but empty.

J. Lost and saved (11:1–25). Again Ezekiel is transported in a vision to the temple. This time he sees twenty-five men, of whom two are named: Jaazaniah and Pelatiah. It is not known whether this is the same group as that mentioned in 8:16. Certainly the Jaazaniah of chapter 11 is different than the Jaazaniah of chapter 8, for they have different fathers. This group of men is not only lost, but is leading others astray as well with ill-conceived counsel (v. 2). That misleading counsel is that the ones who remained in Jerusalem after the deportation of 598/7 B.C. are the favored ones. Jerusalem is the cooking pot and they are the choice morsels. In verse 15 these people make a similarly false claim: "this land was given to us as our possession." Both of these sentiments (vv. 3, 15b) are the diametric opposite of the truth. What they think is permanent is in fact transitory. Those who are not exiled are chaff. The exiled are redeemable. God directly repudiates their egocentrism.

While this prophecy is being given, Pelatiah suddenly dies (v. 13a), provoking a question (really, a request for mercy) to God (v. 13b). It is hard to relate the sudden death of Pelatiah to Ezekiel's blunt question, but maybe it has something to do with the meaning of "Pelatiah"—"Yah delivers, redeems."

How wrong the Jerusalemites are! In fact, God is not far away from the deportees. On the contrary, he has been a sanctuary for them even in their banishment. There is a wall around Jerusalem, but it is no wall that confines the Lord and restricts his movement. Even years of incarceration in Babylon can be as full of the glory of the Lord if he is there.

When the exiles are brought back to their homeland they will eradicate idolatry. Following what they will do (v. 18) is what God will do for them (v. 19), and again what they will do (v. 20). God will give an undivided heart (lit. one/single heart) and a new spirit. In other words, not only will there be a geographical change, but there will be a spiritual change as well, resulting in new obedience. God will transform both their outer and inner circumstances.

In chapter 10 the divine glory leaves the temple. In chapter 11 the divine glory leaves the city. The temple has been abandoned, and now the city has been abandoned. Without the presence of God both have lost the real reason for their existence. The temple is but a building and the city is but a site. It is not without significance that the vision of the divine exit follows the promise of return. Does this suggest that God is leaving to join those in exile? Interestingly, the divine glory stops above the mountain east of Jerusalem (v. 23)—the Mount of Olives. God does not depart the city in a huff or in a rage, but, to use an anthropomorphism, with tears in his eyes.

The Spirit now brings Ezekiel back to Babylonia (v. 24). This is the return portion of his visionary trip to Jerusalem. The screen has gone blank. Now it is time for Ezekiel to share the vision with his fellow exiles (v. 25). The good news he must not keep to himself.

K. The exile symbolized (12:1–28). Once again the prophet acts out his message as in chapters 4 and 5. The people living in Jerusalem are using neither their eyes nor their ears. Accordingly, Ezekiel is told to pack his belongings, to dig through the wall of his house, to place his belongings on his shoulder, and to leave with his face covered. Why not leave through the door, as one normally does? Does this show a desperate attempt to escape, or an attempt to escape clandestinely? Covering the face may refer to shame, disgrace, or grief that the would-be escapees will feel.

Ezekiel carries out this pantomime but apparently it has little effect on the people. So, to the acted word (vv. 3–8) there is added the preached word (vv. 10–16). The leader in the flight will be none other than the prince himself who leaves under cover of darkness with his face veiled. To have the prince be the first to run is like the captain of a sinking ship hitting the lifeboats first. But in his running he runs smack into God, snared by the Divine's net (v. 13). The prince, and Jonah, and Jacob are not the only ones who in their running encountered God right in the middle of their paths. This may be a specific reference to what happened to King Zedekiah (2 Kings 25:7; Jer. 39:7; 52:11). In these days of exile only a few will be spared. For the majority, however, their destiny is sealed. This is one major difference between Jeremiah's and Ezekiel's preaching. Doom is inevitable for Ezekiel. At best a nucleus will be salvaged. This is not an easy or delightful message to preach, but it falls on Ezekiel's heart and shoulders as a divine mandate.

A second act carried out by Ezekiel is trembling and shuddering as he eats (v. 18). Did he let his hands shake to feign fear? Was there something in his facial expression as he ate? This is the second act of the prophet involving something he does with food (cf. 4:9–17). The first one stressed scarcity of food. This one stresses the terror that will accompany food consumption. A mealtime, normally a relaxing, refreshing, reinvigorating time, will be shot through with panic. The people will not be able to "eat food with gladness, drink wine with a joyful heart," as Ecclesiastes 9:7 urges.

A major part of the people's problem is their spiritual insensitivity. They are addicted to a snatch-and-grab mentality, an itch for the instantaneous. Since nothing has apparently happened, they deny the validity of the Word of the Lord. The first proverb (v. 22b) emphasizes skepticism: "you prophets speak and nothing happens." This is an attitude that both Isaiah (5:19) and Jeremiah (17:15) had to face.

The second proverb (v. 27) emphasizes irrelevance and postponement: "Ezekiel is not talking to us, but to someone down the road. Therefore we do not need to take anything he says personally." The last thing the people must do is accept personal responsibility for their circumstances. Therefore, they must evade in whatever way possible hearing the Word of the Lord and responding to it. The first saying makes Ezekiel a crackpot; the second makes him a futurist. But God will have the last say.

L. False prophets (13:1–23). Ezekiel's greatest opposition is not from "overt" sinners, but from false prophets. Jeremiah, too, had an especially difficult time with them (see Jer. 23; 27–28).

The source of their prophesying is their own imagination and spirit. Their resources are all self-oriented. They are compared to jackals among ruins (v. 4). These animals have a reputation for foraging in ruins. They show up after the damage has been done to feast on leftovers. Further, the false prophets shrink from the responsibility of being repairmen—and for a reason. By their philosophy nothing is seriously wrong; so why is there any need for one to "stand in the breach"?

Compounding their guilt is their (false) claim that they are speaking the Word of the Lord. Theirs is a false hope: they expect their words to be fulfilled. The false prophets are absolutely sincere. Sincerity, however, is not synonymous with legitimacy. They are sincere, evangelistically so, but deceived.

Their message is peace when there is no peace (v. 10). What makes a false prophet false is that his analysis of society is false. This may be due to several reasons. First, he may be paid by the establishment and therefore must say nothing to anger them. Accordingly, the false prophet will be content to be *vox populi* rather than *vox dei.* Second, the false prophet may have a false view of God. God, he believes, keeps his promises to his people unconditionally and is favorably disposed to Israel. In either case, the false prophet engenders a feeling of false security among the people: "we have God on our side—always!"

The people build a flimsy wall (v. 10) to keep out the rain. What kind of insulation do the false prophets add? Whitewash! But can such a wall and such an insipid covering withstand the storm of God's wrath? The false prophets think so, for they have little room either in their theology or in their homiletics for the wrath of God. Instead of warning their people about the wrath to come, they affirm the people's sinfulness.

The second group labeled here for condemnation is women who sew magic charms on their wrists and make veils for their heads (v. 18). More than likely the reference here is to fortune-tellers. The law demanded the fastening of objects to the body. Moses told the people to "tie them [God's commandments] as symbols on your hands and bind them on your foreheads" (Deut. 6:8). But here is a prostitution of the custom. There are no copies of the Decalogue beneath these charms or veils. What these women do is ensnare people. The reference to barley and scraps of bread (v. 19) may be a reference to the remuneration the fortune-tellers receive and a pittance at that. Such gross sin for such meager wages! Or, these items may well have been used in the magical processes. Divination by wheat (aleuromancy) and divination by barley (alphitomancy) are noted in pagan literature.

God responds to these fortune-tellers as he does to the false prophets. Both groups present a false view of God. The pseudoprophets believe they have a monopoly on God's goodness and grace. The fortune-tellers believe they have access to a power other than God. God is nice, but not necessary.

M. Idolatry (14:1–23). We are not told why the elders come and sit down in front of Ezekiel. If they are anticipating a cozy fireside chat, they are about to be disappointed.

Three times God says that these elders have set up idols in their hearts and put wicked stumbling blocks before their faces (vv. 3, 4, 7). This, however, refers to more than the practice of idolatry. Perhaps the elders have just heard Ezekiel's narration of the temple idolatries that he saw in a vision (11:25). "How awful, how blasphemous," they might have said among themselves. However, in seeing the sliver in the Jerusalemite's eye they have missed the plank in the deportee's eye.

If the exiled elders were practicing idolatry, the text would say so in straightforward language. By using the description it does, the text suggests that their sin is an inner idolatry, a mental idolatry, rather than an external idolatry. Idolatry here does not mean prostration before busts of Baal or Marduk or any other god. It is a state of mind that is at cross-purposes with the will and being of God. It is out of the heart/mind that evil comes. God has a ways to go with these people if one day he is to give them "an undivided heart" (11:19). The truth is that they have a divided heart, and in such a state not even a prophet will be of assistance (vv. 4, 7, 9). God will go so far even to mislead a prophet in giving counsel. The invitation to turn away from "idolmindedness" is here (v. 6), as is the promise of positive results from repentance (v. 11).

In verses 12–20 God parades four hypothetical cases before the exiles (vv. 12–14; 15–16; 17–18; 19–20). In each God sends some kind of a scourge into a country because of the citizens' sins. Even if Noah, Daniel, and Job lived in that country, they would save only themselves, and not even their children.

This is an odd triumvirate for several reasons. For one thing Noah and Job are both Gentiles. Daniel is a Hebrew. Noah and Job lived long before Ezekiel. Daniel is a contemporary of Ezekiel. Noah and Job were married and had sons and daughters. Daniel, to the best of our knowledge, was celibate. Finally, we note that in all three references to Daniel in this chapter (and in 28:3) Daniel is actually spelled "Danel" (see NIV fn. to 14:14). For these reasons some have suggested that this is a Daniel other than Daniel the prophet.

A righteous nucleus could be the means of salvation for the unrighteous majority (Gen. 18–19). God would spare Sodom if he could find ten righteous people in it. Not here! So corrupt are these people that what was true for Sodom (the bastion of depravity) would not be true here.

God's judgment on Jerusalem will be thorough. Yet there will be some survivors, sons and daughters of those in exile who will join their parents. But when the parents see them, rather than rejoicing, they will say: "they really are that bad, aren't they!" As such, the unit addresses the issue of the justice of God. He acts thoroughly, but always fairly, objectively, and ethically.

N. A useless vine (15:1–8). The people still living in Jerusalem are compared to a vine (wild, not cultivated) which serves no function other than fuel for the fire (v. 4). No doubt the mention of an initial burning followed by a second toss into the fire has a historical referent. The first "fire" was that involved in Jehoiachin's (and Ezekiel's) exile. Some, however, came out of that first fire. Their escape will be shortlived. The second fire—Nebuchadnezzar's invasion of 587/6 B.C.—will consume them.

It is not unusual for Israel to be referred to as a vine, and even as a choice vine (Jer. 2:21). Both Isaiah (5:1–7) and Jeremiah (2:21) speak of God as a vinedresser who experiences keen disappointment over his vine's failure to bring forth good fruit.

Ezekiel goes further than either Isaiah or Jeremiah. He suggests that a vine by its very nature is useless. Uselessness, for Ezekiel, is a congenital condition. This may be compared with Jeremiah who looked at a piece of broken pottery. He observed that the potter could refashion it and restore it to its proper shape and function. Jeremiah saw that God the Potter could make something beautiful out of the people's lives. Ezekiel, on the other hand, fails to see any future for the vine. What it is, it always will be. Hence, it is good only to be tossed onto the flames. No doubt, passages like this provide a background for Jesus' statements in John 15 that every unfruitful branch, every branch that does not abide in the vine, is "picked up, thrown into the fire and burned" (John 15:6).

O. A foundling turned harlot (16:1–63). Few chapters in the Bible, and certainly none in the Old Testament, provide a more forceful illustration of the love of God than does this one. The Lord finds a female child abandoned by her parents, who are described in verse 3 as an Amorite and a Hittite. This may be understood literally on the basis of Genesis 10:15, which connects Canaanites, Hittites, and Amorites ethnographically; or it may be understood morally. This child the Lord rescues, raises, and eventually pledges his troth to in marriage. He lavishes upon her great riches.

Instead of appreciating and loving her Lord, she squanders her dowry on fornication, engages in ritual filicide with her offspring, seeks other lovers (foreign alliances), and in the process becomes worse than all other harlots.

For these sins the Lord sentences her (Jerusalem) to a bloody death. The punishment will be twofold. First, she will be stripped naked before her lovers (v. 37b). Stripping designates public exposure and degradation. Second, God will deliver her to her paramours (vv. 37–41) who will stone her and finally burn her. Foreign nations will ravage Jerusalem. As in the Book of Judges, God's form of punishment on his own is to remove his protective hedge around them and hand them over to an alien. Only then will God's wrath be assuaged.

What makes Jerusalem's promiscuity so abominable is that she is more depraved than her sisters Sodom (to the south) and Samaria (to the north). Both of these analogies would touch a raw nerve, but the one referring to "sister Sodom" would be particularly upsetting. Not only is Jerusalem the worst of the three sisters, but she has done things that make Samaria and Sodom blush! How interesting and debilitating it is when Sodomites, the epitome of iniquity, turn red when they gaze on the behavior of the citizens of the city of God!

To shame Jerusalem even further, the Lord promises the restoration of her two sinful sisters, and Jerusalem as well. God's love is not restricted to one citizenry and to one city. Jerusalem, who once could not even bring herself to say "Sodom," will now have to share the Lord's love with Sodom. After all, if Jerusalem can spread her love around in the wrong way, why cannot the Lord spread his love around in the right way?

Finally comes the announcement of unexpected grace (vv. 59–63). The Lord will remember the covenant he made with Jerusalem in her youth. Further, he will reestablish Jerusalem's hegemony over her sisters ("I will give them to you as daughters," v. 61b). God will do so because of his grace and faithfulness. Jerusalem, now shamed and contrite before the Lord, will again know him.

The movement in this chapter is from sin to judgment to restoration; from marriage to adultery to punishment to remarriage. This sequence recalls Hosea 2 and Jeremiah 2–3. This is a chapter about grace, God's grace, grace given abundantly, grace given gratuitously. By grace was Jerusalem saved, and only by grace will she be reclaimed and restored.

P. Two eagles and a vine (17:1–24). Ezekiel is instructed to tell the people an allegory (riddle) and a parable (fable). The riddle/fable is recorded in verses 1–10; verses 11–21 are the interpretation; verses 22–24 are a prophecy of restoration.

In the riddle/fable a great eagle comes to Lebanon, removes the top part of a cedar, and carries it away. He then plants the seed in fertile soil, where it turns into a vine. Then another great eagle comes to which the vine is attracted. The second eagle does nothing. He is simply there. As a result of the vine's attraction to the second eagle, the first eagle will uproot the vine, causing it to wither. An east wind will finish it off.

There is little problem in interpreting the particulars of the message. The first eagle is Nebuchadnezzar, king of Babylon. Lebanon represents Jerusalem. The top of the cedar that is removed by the eagle and carried to another soil is King Jehoiachin and his fellow exiles. The vine that grows from the cedar crown is Jehoiachin's successor Zedekiah, and the other great eagle to which the seedling is attracted is the king of Egypt, Psamtik II. The branches that stretch out to the second eagle are various parties and emissaries Zedekiah sent to Egypt to gain assistance and support in overthrowing the Babylonian presence in Israel.

For such malfeasance Zedekiah is condemned by God to execution in exile (v. 16). Pharaoh (the second eagle) will be of little help to him then. Zedekiah's sin is that he despised the oath and broke the covenant with Nebuchadnezzar. A promise should be a promise, and a commitment a commitment. Zedekiah has put a ceiling on the reliability of his word, and in the process has condemned himself.

God himself now makes an oath ("as surely as I live," v. 19). He will requite Zedekiah for his oath violation. Verses 16–18 concentrate on the human agent of retribution; verses 19–21 concentrate on the divine agent of contribution. This does not mean that Zedekiah will get burned at two levels. Rather, it indicates that God uses human channels to implement his judgment. That the explanation should focus on human and divine devastation recalls the presence of the eagle and the east wind in the riddle/parable.

The chapter climaxes with a prophecy of restoration. God himself will plant a cedar shoot on a high and lofty mountain (i.e., Jerusalem). It will provide shelter for birds. The trees of the field (v. 24a) represent the nations of the earth. They will recognize the power of Jerusalem's God.

Zedekiah is a gambler, one who attempts to play his cards as adroitly as possible. He knows how to shift gears in the game called political opportunism. Unfortunately such ambivalence extends into Zedekiah's relationship with God. His word is unpredictable. He vacillates on the truth. That is not acceptable to Nebuchadnezzar, and certainly not acceptable to the King of kings.

Q. Individual responsibility (18:1–32). Through his prophet the Lord rebuts a popular proverb that God holds the succeeding generation accountable for the sins of the previous generation (v. 2). If the children's teeth (those in exile?) are set on edge it is because they have eaten sour grapes, and not their fathers (those back in Jerusalem?).

After disposing of this misconception, Ezekiel constructs a theological/legal argument in support of the thesis of individual responsibility. To establish his case, he uses a three-generational model. The first generation is represented by the righteous father (vv. 5–9). He is characterized by no fewer than twelve virtues. The sins of which he is free are cultic, sexual, and sociomoral. To be sure, this is a representative rather than an exhaustive listing.

Verses 10–13 deal with the second generation, the son. Unlike his father, he is a renegade. He defiantly breaks the laws of the Lord. In such a case, the son will not be able to ride on the coattails of his exemplary father. Instead, he will be put to death for his transgressions.

A discussion of the third generation (vv. 14–17) is absolutely necessary. This section deals with the sinner's son (in line with the proverb of v. 3). Just as his son rejected (for the wrong reasons) his father's example, so the grandson rejects (for right reasons) his father's example. He is like his grandfather. He does not share in the guilt of his father; he is not condemned because of his father's sins. He is saved because of his own righteousness.

Ezekiel is not creating a new doctrine. Actually, he is echoing Moses who said: "Fathers shall not be put to death for their children, nor children put to death for their fathers; each is to die for his own sin" (Deut. 24:16).

In verses 21–32 the argument turns to the principle of repentance. As in verses 5–20, a series of examples is provided. The first is that of the sinner who repents and is saved (vv. 21–23). The second is that of a righteous person who sins and is condemned (vv. 24–26). The first case affirms that repentance expunges past sins; the second case affirms that reversion expunges merits. Verses 27–28 return to the emphasis of the first example (vv. 21–23), showing preoccupation with repentance rather than with backsliding. The people think God is unfair with respect to the second example (vv. 24–26), since the teaching disregards the merits of a righteous person after he sins. But no parallel critique is forthcoming vis-à-vis verses 21–23!

Verses 30–32 are a clarion call to repentance, for God takes no joy in the death of anyone. What Ezekiel is hoping to accomplish is that the people in exile will accept responsibility for their circumstances. For they are there for their own sins, not that of their parents. Because their relationship to God is not an intractable or inherited fate, however, they can return to the Lord. And that is good news.

R. A dirge for Israel's kings (19:1–14). Almost all of this chapter is poetic, and is a lament in two parts over the fall and collapse of monarchs in Judah, here styled as "princes of Israel." In the first part (vv. 2–9), reference is made to a lioness who sees two of her cubs captured and carried off. One of the cubs is taken to the land of Egypt, the other to the land of Babylon. It is more than likely that the two cubs represent Jehoahaz and Jehoiachin.

In the second part of the lament (vv. 10–14), the analogy of a lioness and her cubs is replaced by a fruitful vine with strong branches. The entire vine, though once lofty, is uprooted, tossed to the ground, and burned. The specific identification of the vine and its branches once again is not made.

By resorting to metaphors and avoiding personal names, Ezekiel wants his audience to focus on the lesson of the lament and not on "who's who" in the lament. What it teaches is clear. The chapter may well have been titled "How the Mighty Have Fallen!" Kings have become prisoners. Once-powerful individuals have now been reduced to paupers. Glory has turned into disgrace. Riches have turned into ruin. This is all consonant with Ezekiel's earlier emphases. Jerusalem, once a city of sanctity, is now in ashes (or shortly to be so), abandoned by her God. How pitiful it is to have to look back on "what was," and not be able to resurrect it!

S. Rebelliousness (20:1–49). Like chapter 16, much of chapter 20 is a survey of Israel's past. This particular review is dated to the seventh year, fifth month, tenth day (August 591). This date is all the more ominous, for it is exactly five years to the day before Nebuchadnezzar torches the Jerusalem temple (Jer. 52:12). Again the elders come to Ezekiel for a spiritual message, only to be rebuffed.

Verses 5–29 are about the detestable practices of the exiles' fathers. This section is presented in four subunits. The first is verses 5–10 and covers the fathers in Egypt. Although chosen by God, the people still rebelled and held onto their images. Only for the sake of his reputation is the Lord restrained from destroying them.

The second subunit (vv. 11–17) covers the first wilderness generation. To these God gave his decrees and laws. But rebellion, started in Egypt, persists in the wilderness. Again, for his name's sake God does not destroy them, but he disallows entry into the Promised Land. Their children will be spared.

The third subunit (vv. 18–26) covers the second wilderness generation. It is much like the preceding. Guidelines are given, but rejected. God's reputation restrains him a third time. What is novel here is the promise of exile, which is surprising given the fact that the people have not even entered the land. Also novel, and perhaps mysterious, is that God will mislead the people into sin by replacing genuine laws with statutes that are not good and laws they cannot live by (v. 25).

The fourth subunit is verses 27–29. The people have moved beyond Egypt (subunit 1) and the wilderness (subunits 2–3), and are now settled in the land of Canaan. Particularly they are charged with worshiping at high places (Barnah means "high place"). They imitate the Canaanites and other Gentile nations in their worship.

From a survey of the past Ezekiel shifts to the present, but only for three brief verses (vv. 30–32). Here he addresses his immediate audience. That generation continues in the way of its fathers, and therefore they will not get a response from God any more than their forefathers. To be informed that God is not available, that he disallows the seeking of his face, is reflective of the miserably unregenerate state of the people.

Fortunately the chapter does not conclude with a "closed" sign hung in the window of the heavenly office. What God has in mind is a new exodus, this time from Babylon. Part of this process of deliverance will consist of judgment in the desert, but only that God may purge his people and sift out those who will accept the bond of the covenant.

The return of the people to the land will produce a sense of overwhelming shame as they recall their impious behavior, and that God acted toward them not on the basis of their merit but for his name's sake. Nothing is said here about repentance. Instead God will do what he does because of his own name, because of his reputation among the nations, and because of his promise to the fathers. God's election of his people is irrevocable, their sins notwithstanding.

T. The sword of judgment (21:1–32). Ezekiel is told to set his face against Jerusalem and to preach against the sanctuary. Not only does this sharpen the focus of chapter 21, but also it indicates that the destruction of the city and temple have not yet occurred. Thus, the oracle must be prior to 587/6 B.C.

The forest fire of 20:45–49 is now replaced by a sword as the symbol of destruction. We move from a natural disaster analogy to a military analogy. In either case, the catastrophe will be far-reaching.

Admittedly, the phrase *I am going to cut off the righteous and the wicked* (v. 4) is difficult. Had not Ezekiel, just three chapters back, said the opposite? Does character count for nothing? Granted that one's righteousness cannot save another person (chap. 14), now it seems that a righteous man cannot even save himself. Unless we are prepared to say that the prophet is grossly contradicting himself, we must interpret "righteous and wicked" not as moral categories, but as a literary device whereby one expresses totality through the use of opposites (merism). Thus, "righteous and wicked" means everybody.

Ezekiel's thespian skills are called upon once again. He is to groan before the people with broken heart and bitter grief (v. 6). This acting in turn prompts inquiry by the people, and Ezekiel is only too happy to enlighten.

In verse 9 the repetition of the word *sword* is for emphasis. The sword is sharpened and burnished (v. 10), and placed by God into somebody's hand (the king of Babylon?). All power is God's power, and earthly power can terrify only as it is aroused by the wrath of God.

Ezekiel's act of striking his hands together (v. 14), in which he is followed by God (v. 17), is the triumphant gesture of the victor over the vanquished, thus making the sword oracle all that more frightening.

The last part of the chapter has an oracle

against Israel (vv. 18–27) and an oracle against the Ammonites (vv. 28–32). It begins with another action by Ezekiel. This time he is told to mark out two roads, one of which heads for Rabbah in Ammonite country, and one of which heads for Jerusalem. Both cities are capital cities.

It may seem strange that war strategies are determined through the use of magic. Nebuchadnezzar consults arrows/lots, idols, and the liver (v. 21) in order to ascertain which of the two roads to follow. (There is at best a shade of difference, if even that, between magic and religion in pagan thought.) Jerusalem, the procedures indicate, is the direction to head. This idea is as powerful—and unorthodox—as the one sounded in verse 11. Through a magical, heathen operation, legitimate divine guidance is given. Nebuchadnezzar is on the correct road.

The prince of Israel (v. 25) must be Zedekiah. He is on the verge of surrendering all the symbols of royalty. There will be no more kings after Zedekiah, "until he comes to whom it rightfully belongs" (v. 27). The messianic thrust is difficult to miss.

The chapter concludes with an oracle against the Ammonites who gloated over Jerusalem's misfortunes, and perhaps notes judgment on the Babylonians as well. The Ammonites are not to rejoice in the fall of another, and the Babylonians must recognize, that although they are a superpower, there are limits to their aggression. God's ultimate will is that the sword be sheathed.

U. A city of blood (22:1–31). There are no fewer than eight references in this chapter (vv. 2, 3, 4, 6, 9, 12, 13, 27) to Jerusalem as a city filled with those who shed blood. It is a city marked by violence and brutality, with a soaring crime rate. All this is noted to justify God's intended annihilation of the city.

There are three sections in this oracle against Jerusalem. The first (vv. 1–16) begins with a challenge from God to the prophet to accuse the city. The city is one in which reverence for life is gone, and attachment to idols has become popular. Both the shedding of blood and idolatry foster guilt. In the process, once mighty and glorious Jerusalem becomes an object of scorn and a laughingstock.

The princes of Israel are the various individuals who have reigned on the throne in Jerusalem. As a lot, they are characterized as savage barbarians. Power has become a fetish for them. It has become a license to act insanely, even against those deserving highest respect.

Nor is there any reverence for holy things, and especially Sabbaths. Sexual decency and propriety is a thing of the past. Social exploitation is rampant.

All these deviant behaviors God will punish. The discipline will take the form of dispersion (v. 15).

The second unit in this chapter is verses 17–22. A new metaphor is introduced here. Israel has become dross to her God. Dross is, of course, the worthless material removed in the smelting process. In Moses' day God described Israel as "the apple of his eye." Here is an apple become dross. Dross is like chaff—both are good for nothing.

As silver is put into the fire, so Israel will go into the fire. There is no indication from Ezekiel that Jerusalem will emerge from this smelting process as refined silver. Again we observe a "no-hope" perspective.

The third unit is verses 23–31. Here the prophet rebukes successively the land (v. 24); princes (v. 25); priests (v. 26); officials (v. 27); prophets (v. 28); and the people of the land (v. 29). These are the "heavyweights" of the community, people with political, religious, and financial muscle. Nowhere in this list does Ezekiel confront aliens, children, slaves, or widows. Three groups in the list represent laity (princes, officials, people of the land). Two represent clerics (priests, prophets). It is one thing to have the political hierarchy go askew, but when it is joined by the religious hierarchy, then all hopes for the preservation of a conscience in society are dashed. Instead of being loyal to their calling, they place popularity ahead of obedience. The authority of "thus saith the Lord" has been quietly laid to rest.

What makes this so exasperating is that God is unable to find among these groups one individual who, taking his life in his hands, will shout at the top of his lungs: "In God's name and for God's sake, stop!" What Ezekiel once said only of the prophets (13:6) he now extends to all the "who's who" in Jerusalem. To many, silence is the best policy.

V. Oholah and Oholibah (23:1–48). This lengthy chapter is about the sad history of Samaria and Jerusalem. Oholah refers to northern Samaria, and means "her tent." Oholibah refers to Jerusalem and the southern kingdom, and means "my tent in her." The second name underscores the legitimacy of the Davidic kingdom ("my tent [i.e., God's] in her"). Whether or not "tent" has anything to do with the tent as sanctuary is not clear.

The discussion accorded Oholah, the older sister, is decidedly brief (vv. 5–10). Oholibah, the younger sister, is discussed rather extensively (vv. 11–35). The two sisters are presented simultaneously in verses 36–49, and thus the chapter ends as it began (vv. 1–4).

Using the metaphor of sexual infidelity, God pictures Samaria and Judah as harlots who have abandoned their true love (the Lord) and prostituted themselves to other paramours—really "clients" rather than lovers. In the case of Samaria this involves her attraction to the Assyrians (v. 5) and to the Egyptians (v. 8). The lovers are described as finely clad warriors. As in 16:37–39, the lovers turn out to be anything but lovers. Their lust now sated, they turn against and ravage the woman. What was supposed to be a tryst turns into a tragedy.

Oholibah tops her sister by one, for she has even a third lover—Chaldeans (v. 14). What happened to her older sister fails to deter her from her own promiscuity. History as a great teacher is ignored. She even goes so far to paint pictures or sketch drawings in red of her lover-to-be (v. 14). So obsessed with lust is Oholibah that she is unable to fetch enough lovers. Pekod (v. 23) is an Aramean tribe in east Babylonia. Shoa are a nomadic group from the Syro-Arabian desert. Koa are near the Shoa. Less important than the whereabouts of these three tribes is the sound of the names, each with an *o* in the middle—not without interest in light of the two sisters whose names begin with *o*.

Oholibah's lovers will turn against her as brutally as Oholah's did. What Oholibah thinks will be her enjoyment and salvation turns out to be her destroyer. Oholibah/Judah/Jerusalem made one very grave mistake. She looked for salvation in the wrong places. Political alliances with border superpowers, she thought, would save her. How blind! Since when does Egypt, Assyria, or Chaldea offer a genuine alternative to the Lord's safekeeping of his people? Since when do God's chosen people think they will find greater satisfaction and enjoyment in the nations of the earth than in the Lord of those nations?

To be sure, this is not an innovation of Ezekiel's contemporaries. Earlier prophets (Isa. 7–8; 30–31; Jer. 2:20–25; Hos. 7:11–13; 8:9) condemned their generation for fornicating with Gentiles, for pursuing alliances with foreign nations, under the metaphor of sexual attractiveness. God's people have become the Lord's unfaithful wife. As her "husband," the Lord demands of Israel exclusive fidelity. That is what he has given her, and she needs to reciprocate. If she insists on multiple suitors, then God's only course of action will be to abandon her.

W. A steaming cauldron (24:1–27). Again the date is very precise. It is the ninth year, tenth month, tenth day (January 588 B.C.). It is the day on which Nebuchadnezzar laid siege to Jerusalem.

On this dark day the prophet is told to put a cooking pot on the fire, and place water and choice pieces of meat in it. Already in 11:3 Jerusalemites had referred to their city as a cooking pot, and to themselves as choice morsels. The pot provides protection and insulation, they think. Not only are they wrong on that count, but they are also incorrect in equating themselves with choice pieces of meat. In fact, their victims are the choice morsels (11:7).

Chapter 24 expands on chapter 11 by including the fire beneath the pot, something on which the metaphor makers of chapter 11 had not banked. The pot, far from being a shelter, will provide charring and incineration. In fact, the Lord himself will pile the wood under the cauldron. Once again, the message is sounded that those who survived the deportation of 597 B.C. are not thereby granted immunity from subsequent disaster. Their complacency is about to be shattered.

The pot is now encrusted. Its contents are no longer choice morsels of meat, but only deposit (which may be an oblique reference to rust). The uncleanness of the city has been produced by the shedding of innocent blood. In turn, this shed blood, not covered, cries out to God for vindication (cf. Gen. 4:10).

On the heels of this incident, Ezekiel is told that his wife will die (v. 16). Ezekiel is not alone in weaving his familial experiences into his prophetic message. While Jeremiah is denied the normal enjoyments of life, Ezekiel is denied the normal grieving process for his spouse (v. 17).

Understandably, Ezekiel's stoicism throughout this ordeal provokes curiosity. Is Ezekiel incapable of remorse, is he superhuman, or is he subhuman?

The death of his wife gives the prophet an opportunity to apply her actual death to Jerusalem's impending death. It would be cruel and inhumane of God to take away the prophet's wife just to provide the residents of Jerusalem with an object lesson. And it is most unlikely that that is the case. Rather, the passing of Ezekiel's wife is an opportunity for the prophet, no doubt under heavy duress already, to make his message even that more pungent.

The Jerusalem Israel loves will be taken away, and the sanctuary will be desecrated. It is difficult for the modern reader to capture the horror of that dual announcement.

Only when the siege has taken place will Ezekiel have his mouth opened. Ezekiel will have made his last dramatic presentation. The closing of Jerusalem will parallel the opening of his mouth.

II. Oracles Against the Nations (25–32)

A. Ammon, Moab, Edom, Philistia (25:1–17). Ezekiel's message is not confined to Jerusalemites or to ex-Jerusalemites now living in captivity. He turns his attention in this chapter to four bordering nations.

Ezekiel first addresses Ammon (**25:1–7**). It is not apparent in English translation, but there are three different forms of "you" in these verses. The "you" of verses 3–4 is feminine singular; the "you" of verse 5 is masculine plural; the "you" of verses 6–7 is masculine singular. Is this the prophet's way of indicting all Ammonites?

The Ammonites were descendants of Lot. The main city of their territory was Rabbah (v. 5). David annexed them during his reign (2 Sam. 12:26–31). At some subsequent point (post-Solomonic) Ammon regained her independence. Nebuchadnezzar used Ammonites to put down insurrections in Judah (2 Kings 24:2).

What Ezekiel chastises them for is their open mockery of the devastation that hit Jerusalem in 587 B.C. They clapped their hands, stamped their feet, and rejoiced—all because of what happened to the sanctuary, to the land of Israel, to the people of Judah. As a result God will now turn them over to a foreign power.

Second, Ezekiel addresses Moab (**25:8–11**). This time God speaks indirectly. To the Ammonites he said "you." About the Moabites he says "they," thus shifting from second person to third person. Moab, too, has connections with Israel, going back to the patriarchs. Their taunt is that Judah has become like all the other nations (v. 8). Moab fails to see how Judah's God is potent and able to save. Judah has fallen under Babylonian hegemony just like every other small country.

The third nation addressed is Edom (**25:12–14**), which traces its ancestry to Esau. Their sin is more venal than that of Ammon or Moab. They actually took revenge on the house of Judah and were not content with simply sneering remarks. They will be judged, from Teman to Dedan (v. 13). Teman was in the middle of Edomite territory, Dedan to the far south. Even Israel will participate in her judgment.

The fourth nation indicted is Philistia (**25:15–17**). Like the Edomites, they actively participated in Judah's and Jerusalem's demise. The Kerethites (Cretans) were a Philistine group. There is a pun in the Hebrew here. The consonants in "cut off" and "Kerethite" are the same.

All this invective against bordering nations who treated Judah with contempt, and in turn pay a price, finds its root in Genesis 12:3. We have in Ezekiel 25 an illustration of what happened to four nations who chose to be hostile toward Abraham's seed. It is a dangerous matter to touch the Lord's anointed.

B. Tyre (26:1–28:26). Ezekiel squeezes four nations into the prophecy of chapter 25. By contrast, he devotes three whole chapters (26–28) to Tyre and four (29–32) to Egypt. Perhaps Ezekiel's extended treatment of these two nations is due to the fact that only these two were in revolt against Nebuchadnezzar at the time Judah was. They survived (for a while at least), while Judah/Jerusalem did not.

The most distinctive feature of Tyre was its physical location on a rocky island just off the Phoenician coast. Its natural and artificial harbors provided her with economic advantages and military security. Josephus tells us, in substantiation of this, that Nebuchadnezzar's siege of Tyre lasted for thirteen years, and was somewhat inconclusive at that. This was a much longer period than the Babylonian siege of Jerusalem. Not until the late 300s was the city totally breached by Alexander the Great. Tyre means "rock," which is to be understood both literally and metaphorically. He who lived within Tyre had security and protection.

This particular prophecy has four sections to it. The first (**26:1–6**) identifies the sin of Tyre and the judgment to come on her. The date for this sermon, the eleventh year, first day, is 587 (or 586 if "eleventh month" is inserted). Tyre rejoices in Jerusalem's demise, as did Ammon and Moab. Her unusual name for Judah is "the gate to the nations," and indicates that Tyre views Judah as a trading rival. Now she would have the market to herself. God has something to say about this. He will bring nations against her "like the sea casting up its waves" (v. 3b). Here is the utter relentlessness of the ocean. No one wave will bring destruction, but the incessant pounding of the waves will destroy even the strongest rock. The phrase *I will scrape away her rubble* (v. 4) suggests erosion. Tyre, the protecting rock, will become Tyre the bare rock.

The second section (**26:7–14**) describes the invasion of the king from the north (Nebuchadnezzar) against Tyre. This paragraph is a particularization of verse 3. The onslaught will be against both Tyre's mainland towns and Tyre herself. Destruction, plundering, and death will be the order of the day.

So devastating is this attack that even the

neighboring princes will lament Tyre's overthrow. This is the third section of the chapter (**26:15–18**). The lament contrasts Tyre as she once was with what she now is, and speaks of the tremors her fall has occasioned. If Tyre can be subjugated, what hope is there for anybody else?

The last section (**26:19–21**) describes Tyre's eclipse; she descends to the realm of the dead.

The impossible has happened! Impregnable Tyre is not so impregnable after all. The protection she thought she had turns out to be illusory. Tyre has been "un-tyred." Before the Rock, the rock has sunk.

In chapter 26 Ezekiel uses the metaphor of an offshore rocky island to talk to/about Tyre. In **27:1–36** he shifts the metaphor and compares Tyre to a ship. The appropriateness of these two back-to-back metaphors should be obvious. What an island and a ship have in common is that both are surrounded by water.

Tyre likes what she sees when she looks at herself: "I am perfect in beauty" (v. 3). She will shortly learn that one consumed with self-congratulation and self-adulation will eventually come to naught.

This ship is a thing of beauty. Verses 4a–7 elaborate on the precious materials brought from afar for the construction of the ship. It is not just the luxuriousness of these materials. Rather, they are products that Tyre receives in trade, as the places of origin indicate. Ships are for trade, for transporting cargo from place to place. Since Tyre's wealth and status derived from trade, how right it is to refer to Tyre as a ship.

The cities surrounding Tyre provide not only materials for the ship's construction, but also personnel for her maintenance, locomotion, and defense.

In the process Tyre becomes a trading center, with representatives and merchants of all nations bringing their wares to Tyre for sale and exchange. The city rivals any modern commercial city for frenzied activity and busyness. "We will pull down our ships and build bigger ships," decide the Tyrians.

In verse 26, however, the ship Tyre leaves port and heads out into the open seas on her maiden voyage. The ship Tyre is about to become the first Titanic. The "unsinkable" ship is about to prove the experts wrong.

The chapter begins by noting that Tyre's domain is on the high seas (v. 4a). Now, Tyre will break into pieces and sink into the heart of the sea.

The source of Tyre's strength, the sea, becomes the source of her ruin. What once brought her fame now brings her infamy. The sea, once her source of power and pride, is now an instrument of the judgment of God. It is the blatant flaunting of prosperity, the "look-what-I-have-done" attitude that materialism often encourages. A gift of God, if misused and abused, can become an albatross around one's neck. That is what happened to Tyre, and to many like her. And what is left after the ship sinks?

The concern of most of chapter 28 is an individual identified in verse 2 as the ruler of Tyre, and in verse 12 as the king of Tyre. There are two clear parts to this unit. The first is verses 1–10, and is an oracle of judgment. Verses 11–19, on the other hand, are a lament.

Verses 1–10 perpetuate the maritime connections of Tyre which chapters 26 and 27 emphasize, but verses 11–19 do not. The city is ruled by a monarch who fancies himself a god. Again the point is made, as in chapters 26 and 27, that Tyre's location confers upon it an almost superhuman exemption from the vicissitudes most cities face, and draws to itself legendary wealth.

This feeling of "nobody can interfere with us" has infected the king with a noxious egocentrism. Note how pride and proud ring in verses 2b–5. Possessions have become the yardstick by which the Tyrian king measures divinity.

Ezekiel, of course, is not a publicity agent for the king. He will attempt to be a conscience to him. The prophet announces that this "god" will be toppled—in fact, executed (vv. 6–10). The king of Tyre will become a "has-been." There has never been a shortage of pretentious gods. It started with Adam and Eve. They thought they could become like God. So did the prince of Tyre, caught up in his own little empire.

Verses 11–19 continue the message against the king of Tyre, but in the form of a lament. What is extremely provocative here is Ezekiel's use of Genesis 2–3 in reference to the king of Tyre. Some commentators have suggested that verses 11–19 are indeed about Satan (Lucifer) who once walked among the angels of God, but fell from paradise because of rebellion and insubordination. More probably Ezekiel presents the king of Tyre as an Adamic figure. The Genesis 2–3 antecedents seem clear in phrases like *you were in Eden, the garden of God* (v. 13); *the day you were created* (v. 13); *a guardian cherub* (vv. 15–16); *I drove you, I expelled you* (v. 16).

This may be Ezekiel's way of saying that Tyre, like Adam, owes all of her privileges, wealth, security, and power to God. It is not the sea that has made Tyre, but the Lord of those seas. Or Ezekiel may be pointing out that those whom God once favored and blessed (Adam and this king) he may later have to punish.

In addition to Genesis analogies the reference to the various stones the king wears (v. 13) seems suspiciously close to the high priest's ephod with its rows of precious stones (Exod. 28). The king of Tyre, in this analogy, was both Adamic and priestly, and both privileges he desecrated. As a result, the king lost what he had, and became what he never need become. His attempt to become deity, although at best a charade, cost him his existence.

C. Egypt (29:1–32:32). Egypt presented the greatest threat and challenge to Babylonian expansion in the Mediterranean world. For Ezekiel and Jeremiah, however, the Babylonians were God's instrument of judgment, and accordingly they advanced a policy of nonresistance. The Egyptian attempt to throttle the Babylonian advance is the antithesis of all they preached. The people had a choice: resistance (Egypt's way with Egypt's help), or nonresistance (the prophets' way).

Verses 1–6a compare the Pharaoh (Hophra?) to the crocodile of the Nile. The king of Tyre deduced his divinity on the basis of the geography and topos of Tyre. The king of Egypt deduces his divinity on the basis of his exclusive ownership of the life-giving waters of the Nile.

God goes on a crocodile hunt. The fish that stick to his scales, as the monster is dragged from the waters, represent the citizens of Egypt. They will suffer along with their leader.

Verses 6b–9a represent the second unit, and there is a shift in addressee and metaphor. All who live in Egypt are now spoken to, and not just the Pharaoh. The Egyptians are compared to a staff of reed for the house of Israel. This is not a new metaphor but goes back to Isaiah. The Assyrian Sennacherib sneered at Hezekiah for depending on "Egypt, that splintered reed of a staff" (Isa. 36:6) in a time of crisis.

The point here is not that Egypt failed to provide sufficient support and aid to Judah in her fight against the Babylonians. Quite the opposite. Her fault is that she even encouraged Israel to look upon her as a source of confidence (v. 16). She gave every impression of collaborating with Israel in her fight for independence from Babylon, and as such pictured herself as a false hope and a false comfort. What good is it, Ezekiel protests, to offer drowning men straws? Do not try to stop or sidetrack, Ezekiel fulminates, what God has instituted.

In the third section (**29:9b–16**) there is an amazing word. God will punish Egypt for her hubris for forty years. But when the forty years are over God will bring the Egyptians back from captivity. He will return them to Pathros (v. 14), an Egyptian word meaning "land of the South." To be sure, she will not be restored to a position of international eminence, but she will be restored.

Ezekiel has no such hopeful word for any of the other nations (chaps. 25–28). Egypt is unique, then, in receiving some clemency, some ray of hope for her future.

Verses 1–16 are dated to the tenth year, tenth month, twelfth day (January 587). Verses 17–21 are dated to the twenty-seventh year, first month, first day (570 B.C.), and represent the latest prophetic oracle in Ezekiel. Here, Ezekiel is told that Nebuchadnezzar is to gain control over Egypt as compensation for his less than all-out victory over Tyre.

Judgment on Egypt means deliverance for Israel, and that is what is meant by "I will make a horn grow for the house of Israel" (v. 21). The misfortunes of one nation bespeak fortune for another. History is replete with examples.

Ezekiel predicts that a sword will come against Egypt (**30:1–19**). Egypt will take six of her supporters with her to her doom: Cush, Put, Lydia, Arabia, Libya, and the people of the covenant land. This latter expression refers to foreign mercenaries serving in the Egyptian armies. If Tyre is a ship (chap. 28), the Lord has his ship (v. 9) and he uses it to convey serious news to complacent Cush.

The general declaration of Egypt's demise (vv. 1–9) is followed by a specific announcement of how this demise will occur (vv. 10–12). Nebuchadnezzar will be the organ of God's judgment. Verse 11 describes what the Babylonian king will do; verse 12 describes what the Lord will do, for he is the real Author of judgment.

Verses 13–19 describe the execution of God's judgment on individual places in Egypt. Most of these sites are located in the Delta region of Egypt.

No explicit reason is given for the destruction of Egypt, except for the reference to "idols, images" (v. 13) or "proud strength" (v. 6). Some clue may be provided from the word *hordes* which occurs in verses 10 and 15. An alternate translation of "hordes" is "pomp." The word occurs twenty-five times in Ezekiel, and sixteen of these are in chapters 29–32.

The second section of the chapter (**30:20–26**) is dated to the eleventh year, first month, seventh day (April 587 B.C.). God has broken the arm of Pharaoh, and there will be no healing to follow. This may refer to Neco's defeat at Carchemish in 605 B.C., or to Pharaoh Hophra's frustrated attempt to deliver Jerusalem from the Babylonians (588 B.C.). God has broken the arms of the Pharaoh, but he will strengthen the arms of the king of Babylon, enabling him to brandish the sword against Egypt.

Israel expects help from Egypt, but it will be help from a wounded, disabled ally. The prospects for real assistance from such a handicapped partner are bleak.

Ezekiel is given a message by God about the Pharaoh (**31:1–19**). The king of Egypt is compared to a mighty cedar in Lebanon. It will be destroyed and cut down, and then be carried to the underworld.

Ezekiel begins by addressing the cedar directly: Who can be compared with you? But from verse 3 on the prophet shifts to the third person.

The tree is characterized by great height, lush verdure, and superb irrigation that makes it fertile. It is so verdant that it offers shelter and nesting places for the birds. It is such a refuge that even animals bring forth their young beneath its branches (v. 6b). The tree represents a sanctuary. Any within its confines are unthreatened.

It is a tree with deep roots. In fact, the tree is incomparable. Not even the trees of paradise rival it. And all this beauty and majesty is due to God.

Unfortunately, the tree's height goes to its head. Majestic stature breeds arrogance. As a result, God hands the tree over to a ruthless nation. The Babylonians are ferocious woodcutters who quickly level the tree. As a result, the tree ceases to provide shelter for birds, animals, and people. An erect tree becomes a fallen tree. All other trees are addressed with an implicit warning in verse 14. If this magnificent tree vaunted itself and perished all the same, what will happen to lesser trees (other empires) if they become enchanted with their own greatness?

The tree falls as low as the grave. It is not just toppled; it is buried.

Verse 18 returns to the second person of verse 2: Which of the trees can be compared with you? Although she is unique in stature, she is not unique in destruction. Pharaoh, however superhuman, has no immunity against collapse. He who climbs highest, when he falls, falls farthest.

The lament for Pharaoh (**32:1–16**) is dated to the twelfth year, twelfth month, first day (March 585 B.C.), after the capture and destruction of Jerusalem.

Two figures of speech in verse 2 describe the Pharaoh. He is compared to a lion and to a sea monster. God himself throws his net over the beast, rendering him immobile. Then he hurls him on the land, and leaves him as food for the birds and animals. The blood and the remains of the carcass are so great that they fill the land. This is not just hyperbole, but a way of indicating the international stature and esteem of the fallen Pharaoh.

The demise of the Pharaoh is such that it sends shockwaves into creation and the surrounding nations. It is actually the Lord who is brandishing the sword (v. 10) attributed to the king of Babylon (v. 11) and mighty men (v. 12). Even the cattle will experience the effects of the divine judgment.

The second part of the chapter (**32:17–31**) is two weeks later than verses 1–16. In one rhetorical question Ezekiel removes from anybody's imagination the thought that Egypt has special prerogatives, that she has a special corner on grace or blessing.

As Egypt enters the underworld she is spoken to by individuals already there (v. 21). Three great nations, each with a glorious past, have already been interred in the underworld: Assyria (vv. 22–23); Elam (vv. 24–25); and Meshech and Tubal (vv. 26–27—Asia Minor). The dishonorable burial these powers suffered will be Egypt's experience too.

Ezekiel next shifts to a contemporary power—Edom—and describes the nation as if she is already vanquished. In that Ezekiel does not use the phrase *spread terror* as in three preceding paragraphs (vv. 23, 24, 26), he indicates that Edom is not a superpower.

Two last groups are mentioned: princes of the north and the Sidonians. "Princes of the north" is probably a catch-all term designating other nations to the north not previously spoken about in the chapter. The "Sidonians" are the Phoenicians. They too spread terror (v. 30).

The Pharaoh will be somewhat consoled when he discovers that he is not the lone occupant of Sheol (v. 31). Misery indeed loves company! Verse 32 is a bit of a shocker. Pharaoh's capacity for belligerence was given him by the Lord. No man, however herculean, acts independently in God's world.

III. Restoration and Renewal (33–39)

A. Accepting responsibility (33:1–33). The first half of this chapter is verses 1–20. With its emphasis on Ezekiel as a watchman, the importance of one's present situation rather than the past, and individual responsibility, there are reverberations of 3:17–19 and chapter 18.

Ezekiel is told in 33:2ff. to speak to his countrymen, indicating that what follows is an object lesson about the usefulness of a sentry to the townspeople. Those who hear the sound of the trumpet but choose to ignore it, do so at their own peril. A watchman who fails to perform his duties destroys both himself and his fellow citizens.

The watchman metaphor is applied to Ezekiel in verses 7–9. Ezekiel reveals to his fellow exiles his function as a lookout in order to motivate them to repent. The townspeople's appointment of a lookout parallels God sending his prophet. There is one difference, however. The townspeople appointed a lookout to take care of their own interests. God, on the other hand, has sent a prophet to them not for his interests but in their interests.

The people's lament that they are wasting away (v.10) is countered by the claim that God takes no pleasure in the death of the wicked (v. 11). What he takes pleasure in is their turning. Repentance of the backslidden is what brings him gratification. What follows is an impassioned appeal by God. The backsliding righteous will not be saved from punishment by his past, and the repentant evildoer will not be punished because of his past. The past does not save a person; the past does not condemn a person. Where a person is today in his or her relationship with God is what counts.

The second part of the chapter (**33:21–33**) is dated to the twelfth year, tenth month, fifth day (January 586 B.C.). About six months after the destruction of Jerusalem, a fugitive informs Ezekiel of what has happened.

Once again Ezekiel addresses those who have survived the massacre of 587/6, those still living in the homeland. These survivors are impenitent and arrogant. Neither Abrahamic descent nor sheer numbers ("we are many") nor squatters' rights guarantee them possession of the land. They need to subordinate these false crutches to what will really save them, and that is full obedience to God and to his laws. Otherwise, God will turn them over to the treaty curses of sword, wild animals, and plague.

Verses 30–33 focus on Ezekiel and the exiles, whereas verses 23–29 focus on Ezekiel and the Jerusalemites. The sequel is probably deliberate. The deportees had best not say a precipitous "amen" to Ezekiel's words of verses 23–29, as if they are righteous and the survivors are wicked. Ezekiel is not a person to be listened to for an aesthetic experience. They love to listen to the prophet's words, but they do not put them into practice. They are hearers of the Word, but not doers. There are many religious platitudes in their mouths, but their hearts are greedy. As such, Ezekiel for his exilic congregation is only an entertainment piece. They want a performer, but not a prophet; a composer, but not a conscience; a musician, but not a mandate. Ezekiel, thankfully, refuses to accept the role of a religious entertainer.

B. Shepherds and sheep (34:1–31). By the phrase *shepherds of Israel* (v. 2) Ezekiel designates the leaders of the land. In the ancient Near East "shepherd" was a stock term for "king," and even gods could be so styled. Jeremiah in particular refers to the king of Judah under the rubric of "shepherd." Indeed, there are many parallels between this particular chapter in Ezekiel and Jeremiah 23:1–8, suggesting that Jeremiah 23 may have served as the stimulation for Ezekiel 34. The point made by the prophets, then, is that a society can be no better or rise no higher than its leaders.

What are the characteristics of these pseudo-shepherds? First, they are concerned only about themselves and not about their flocks. Second, they allow the weak and sickly members of their flocks to fend for themselves. Third, they brutalize their sheep. As a result of such irresponsible lapse of duties, the flock has scattered and become prey for wild animals.

The Lord's response to this is twofold. He will relieve the bad shepherds of their duties (vv. 7–9) and he himself will become the Shepherd of the sheep (vv. 10–16). Note the "I wills" in these seven verses.

Not all the problems lie with the shepherds, however. Blame is to be attached elsewhere. For that reason, in verses 17–24 Ezekiel speaks to the sheep. Among the flock are those sheep who are thoughtless, pushy, greedy, and belligerent. In such cases the Lord will render justice.

This is followed by the staggering announcement that God will raise up a future shepherd, and his name will be David (vv. 23–24). There are only two other references in the Old Testament to a post-David David (Jer. 30:9; Hos. 3:5). It may be that we should understand "my servant David will tend them/be their shepherd/be prince among them" to mean "one from the house of David" will expedite these ministries. Christians, of course, read the passage messianically, and properly so.

Verses 25–31 shift from the metaphor of sheep and shepherds to the imagery of prosperity and peace which the restored people of Israel will enjoy once they are resettled in their own land. The "I wills" of this section may be profitably compared with the "I wills" of verses 10–16. The blessings with which God will visit his people read much like the rewards promised for obedience in the old covenant (see Lev. 26:1–13; Deut. 28:1–14). They are physical, immediate, and this-worldly.

The emphasis in this chapter on good/bad shepherding surely provides a background for the New Testament's focus on the good shepherd (Luke 15:1–7; esp. John 10:1–21). Ezekiel need not fulminate against "the good shepherd who lays down his life for the sheep, who knows his sheep, who calls his sheep by name."

C. Edom (35:1–15). It may strike the reader as odd that Ezekiel would include an oracle against Edom at this point because: (1) Ezekiel has already addressed Edom (25:12–14); (2) the section of oracles to the nations is earlier (25–32); and (3) the section now under discussion (33–39) is one given over to hope and promise for Israel's future.

There is a good reason, however, for the inclusion of chapter 35 at this particular point. As we read through the chapter we discover that Edom has visions and intentions of taking over the land of Israel. The two nations/countries (v. 10) are, of course, northern Israel and Judah. Once Israel has been destroyed, a vacuum will be created, a no man's land, and Edom will be more than delighted to incorporate that acreage into her own holdings.

The concern of chapters 33–39 is the restoration of Israel to her own land. But Israel cannot return to her land if that land has been possessed by another. The function of chapter 35 is to demonstrate that no would-be usurpers of Israel's land will succeed in that enterprise. God will see to that.

Far from extending her borders by the annexation of Israel, Edom will in fact fall under divine doom. Mount Seir is the chief mountain range of the kingdom of Edom, situated to the southeast of Judah, between the southern tip of the Dead Sea and the Gulf of Aqaba. The mount stands for the kingdom. Because she delivered Israel to the sword she herself will be delivered to the sword, to bloodshed.

D. Restoration and regeneration (36:1–18). Exile is not God's last word for his people. Babylon will never become a permanent home away from home. Israel is not about to fade into the history books. It is God's intention to bring about for his elect both geographical salvation (vv. 1–15) and spiritual salvation (vv. 16–38)—in that order.

Ezekiel is told to prophesy to the mountains of Israel and to share the good news with them. This contrasts vividly with chapter 6, where Ezekiel is told to prophesy to the mountains of Israel and share with them the bad news—Israel will be scattered. The mountains, once hearers of a horror story, are now the hearers of a salvation story.

The enemies who have taunted Israel and attempted to move into her turf, especially Edom, will find themselves rebuffed. So committed is God to this, that he swears with uplifted hand (v. 7) to see that it is so. Verses 1–7 describe what God will do with Israel's enemies. Verses 8–16 describe what God is going to do with Israel. What is involved is the restoration of lushness and fertility to the land of Israel. Prosperity and fructification will return, as will people. Key phrases such as *more than before* (v. 11), *never again* (v. 12), and *no longer* (vv. 14–15) suggest a decided shift from what was to what will be, from the past to the present/future.

God was fully justified in doing what he did to Israel in exiling them (vv. 16–21). Israel's defilement is likened to the impurity incurred by a menstruating woman (v. 17b). This analogy may reflect Ezekiel's priestly background, for ritual impurity induced by menstrual blood and other bodily emissions was a special concern of the priests.

In exiling his people and in restoring them, God does what he does for the sake of his holy name. It is not primarily the people's behavior, good or bad, that determines God's action, be it in judgment or in compassion. The point Ezekiel is making here is that whatever future Israel has comes from God. Neither the people's repentance nor their facile claims on God's mercy can regain the land. God's own character and sovereign purposes will be the determining factor. God must impress upon his people that he is holy (v. 23b), and that his name is holiness (v. 23a).

God has a more profound interest than the geographical relocation of the exiles to Judah and Jerusalem. He desires for them an interior change once they are there.

It may be no accident that the last "I will" in this list is the one about the divine Spirit. Unless there is an effusion of the Spirit into one's life that provides the resources for effective implementation of God's work of grace, then growth in that grace will be most unlikely. Note that the nations confess the power of God (v. 36), not only when old towns are repopulated, but when they see those former ghost towns repopulated by people with new hearts, with new spirits, with the Spirit.

Neither postexilic nor contemporary Judaism have manifested such interest in "new covenant" living. Ezra and Nehemiah did not lead a back-to-Jeremiah/Ezekiel movement, but a back-to-Moses movement. It is the New Testament that finds its roots in prophets like Jeremiah and Ezekiel.

E. Resurrection and reunification (37:1–28). Chapter 37 divides clearly into two sections. The first (vv. 1–14) describes Ezekiel's vision of a valley full of dry bones that come to life. In the second unit (vv. 16–34) Ezekiel takes two pieces of wood, inscribed respectively with the names of the tribes of Judah and Ephraim, and brings them together, indicating the reunification of the two nations divided for hundreds of years. It is unlikely that any section of Ezekiel is as well known as verses 1–14.

One day the Spirit of the Lord transports Ezekiel to a valley full of bones, somewhere in Babylon. He is led on an inspection tour of the site by the Spirit, and given a close-up view of the horrendous extent of death.

The question put to Ezekiel—"can these bones live?"—is followed by Ezekiel's response—"O Sovereign Lord, you alone know." Some have interpreted this as an evasive reply. Ezekiel was fairly certain that the answer to the question was "no," but was reticent to be that blunt about it. Others have suggested that his answer suggests: "Lord, you know perfectly well, so why ask me?" A third suggestion is that Ezekiel's response is a sign of wonder and trust: "Lord, I may not have the answer to this question, but I trust you, and I know that you know."

In these fourteen verses the Hebrew word *rûah* occurs no fewer than ten times. In verse 1 the word refers to the Spirit of the Lord which transports and inspires Ezekiel. In verses 5, 6, 8, 9, and 10 *rûah* is rendered (in the NIV) as "breath," that is, the life-giving breath from the Lord. In verse 11 the plural of *rûah* occurs, designating the four "winds" of heaven. Finally, in verse 12 *rûah* refers to God's Spirit as the life-giving Spirit. Although the metaphor is used for the first time, this is not the first place Ezekiel has spoken of the restoration of God's people to their land.

But what will God do with his people, once restored by the divine *rûah?* Verses 15–20 mandate Ezekiel's act of symbolism with the two sticks. Verses 21–28 then interpret that act to the people. God is going to join Joseph's stick (= northern Israel) with Judah's stick (= the southern kingdom). David will be king over a united people.

The important point here is that (northern) Israel is also involved in this redemption process. In so speaking, Ezekiel is announcing the cancellation of the stigma on the schismatic northern kingdom. There is no doubt that the perspective from the days of Rehoboam/Jeroboam on is pro-Judean. This is reflected in passages of Scripture such as Psalm 78:67–72 ("he did not choose the tribe of Ephraim; but he chose the tribe of Judah").

The single kingdom that God will establish is Davidic, but not Judean, for now membership will be extended even to the "rebellious" house of Israel. All exclusivistic and chauvinistic attitudes will have to go in this marvelous work of God's redemption of his own.

To be sure, nothing approximating this sweet unification of God's people happened in postexilic days. On the contrary, feelings of acrimony were only exacerbated. Ezekiel envisions an age beyond the postexilic era, a messianic kingdom. At the practical level, the chapter speaks to the need of believers to let unity prevail over alienation.

F. Gog (38:1–39:29). Ezekiel has already devoted one section of his prophecy to oracles to the nations (chaps. 25–32). It is somewhat strange, then, that Ezekiel has two chapters (38–39) against another outsider (Gog/Magog) in the section comprising prophecies of hope and restoration. There are many instances in the prophetic books, and elsewhere, of nations invading Israel. There are very few instances of nations invading Israel after Israel is resettled in her land (Ezek. 38–39; Zech. 14).

This particular oracle is directed to Gog of the land of Magog. This is unique in that in none of the oracles of chapters 25–32 is any specific individual named. Where Ezekiel uses names they are normally metaphorical, as in Oholah/Oholibah (chap. 23). It may be that "Gog" and "Magog" are "dummy" words. Commentators have frequently connected Gog with Gyges, king of Lydia, or with Gagaia, referred to in the cuneiform tablets from Tell el-Amarna in Egypt as a king of the barbarians. Magog is mentioned in the Old Testament only in Genesis 10:2 (= 1 Chron. 1:5), where he is listed as the second son of Japheth and grandson of Noah. In Revelation 20:8 Magog is a person.

Gog is further identified as the chief prince of Meshech and Tubal (v. 2). A footnote in the New International Version notes that the phrase may be read as "Gog, prince of Rosh, Meshech, and Tubal." It is this particular rendition that has given rise to the notion, popular in some evangelical circles, that Rosh represents Russia, Meshech represents Moscow, and Tubal represents Tobolsk. Thus, it is claimed, here is an explicit prophecy in Scripture of the Soviet Union and its belligerence against Israel. This can hardly be the case. Russia may indeed turn its hostilities on Israel, but not because Ezekiel prophesied it over two thousand years ago. Meshech and Tubal, by no means well-known or easily identifiable sites, are probably east of Asia Minor.

While verses 3–9 describe Gog's preparations for invasion of Israel, the point is made that God is the stimulus behind the attack. It is he who incites the "Magogites" to invade. This is made clear by the phrases *I will turn you around, put hooks in your jaws, and bring you out* (v. 4); *you will be called to arms* (v. 8). This is much like what Isaiah said about the Assyrians and what Jeremiah said about the Babylonians. The real Mobilizer of the invasion is God! At the same time phrases like "I will put hooks in your jaw" suggest this is something Gog is impelled to do. Gog needs to be dragged into the struggle. Nothing is said about any sin in Israel that prompts the attack.

In verses 10–13 Gog shifts from being a passive instrument to a belligerent, plundering aggressor. The subject of "I will" in verses 1–9 is God. The subject of "I will" in verses 10–13 is Gog.

In verses 14–16 God is the subject again. There is no inconsistency or contradiction in this, any more than there is in the statements "God/Satan said to David, number the people" (cf. 2 Sam. 24:1 with 1 Chron. 21:1). The Bible, in explaining phenomena, often distinguishes between a primary cause and a secondary cause. Here it is not a case of God *or* Gog, but God *and* Gog. One is the primary cause of invasion; one is the secondary cause.

Nothing in chapter 38 indicates the attack takes place or has taken place. It is all future. When Gog does attack Israel he will have God to deal with. The judgment he will receive will be akin to that on Sodom and Gomorrah, or on Egypt in Moses' day. With the exception of the reference to a sword (v. 21) all of the other judgments are in nature (earthquake, plague, rain, hailstones, burning sulfur). How all these disturbances will miss Israel is not clear.

In many ways chapter 39 is like 38. For example, in chapter 38 Ezekiel is told to set his face against Gog. Here he is told to prophesy against Gog. In 38:3 and in 39:1 Gog is told that God is against him. Third, the emphasis is made that God will forcibly bring Gog against Jerusalem. Fourth, after Gog attacks Jerusalem God will bring destruction on Gog.

What is novel in chapter 39 is the description of the immediate post-Gog days in Israel. We are told that the weapons left behind by Gog and his troops will serve as fuel for the Israelites for seven years (v. 9b). This will save cutting the forest trees for firewood (v. 10). The number of slain Magogites will be staggering. It will take Israel seven months to bury the dead of the enemy; the name of the burial site is the Valley of Hamon Gog (v. 11b; "the hordes of Gog"). In assonance Valley of Hamon is very close to Valley of Hinnom (Gehennah). The Valley of Hamon is located east toward the Sea (v. 11a), probably a reference to an area east of the Dead Sea and thus outside Israelite boundaries. To make sure that not even a bone of a slain Magogite is missed, a commission is appointed to go through the land after the first seven months' work. It is important not only that the enemy be defeated, but that he be removed and interred as well. Weapons must not only be captured, but burned.

A further novel point here is the reference to the enormous feast that follows (vv. 17–20). Even the carrion birds and wild animals are invited. The menu, admittedly gruesome, lists flesh to eat and blood to drink. Such a cannibalistic metaphor is obviously just that—a metaphor. To interpret it literally would force a primitive crudity on the text. Further, we have to reconcile the burial of the enemy (vv. 11–16) with the subsequent feasting on the dead enemy (vv. 17–20). How does one eat what one has just buried? Strict chronological concerns have been subordinated to other concerns. What Ezekiel is portraying is the total annihilation of the enemy and Israel's radical elimination of them.

Note that Israel is not allowed to taunt the one who has fallen in her midst. Other nations found themselves in hot water for expressing such feelings against Israel when she was down and out. Ridicule, sarcasm, and taunting are illicit in anybody's mouth.

What is to be accomplished by this destruction of Gog? For one thing, God will display his glory among the nations. It is not his power or his wrath, but his glory he displays. If all this stops with Israel and Gog, then the ultimate purpose of it will have been missed. Israel will now know who the Lord is and the nations will know why God exiled his people. In other words, God does not overlook in his own the sins he would condemn in an outsider. The election of Israel brings not only privileges, but primarily heightened responsibilities, the subverting of which entails horrific judgment.

The climatic phrase is "I will pour out my Spirit on the house of Israel" (v. 29). Wherever the Spirit is "poured out," the possibilities for spiritual growth, stability, and influence become almost incalculable.

IV. The New Temple (40–48)

A. The temple area (40:1–49). The vision of the new temple comes to Ezekiel in the twenty-fifth year of his exile, at the beginning of the year, on the tenth of the month; this is fourteen years after the fall of Jerusalem. This is the latest date in the book except for 29:17–21. The year mentioned in verse 1 is 573 B.C. The month designated as "the beginning of the year" could be either Nisan (spring) or Tishri (fall). The "tenth day" of each month is significant. The tenth of Nisan begins Passover observance (Exod. 12:3). The tenth of Tishri is the Day of Atonement (Lev. 16:29), and it inaugurates the year of Jubilee (Lev. 25:9). Liberation, renewal, and reconciliation are the themes of these days. Is there any possible connection with Ezekiel 40:1?

For a second time Ezekiel is transported in a vision to Jerusalem. The first excursion for the prophet was to witness Jerusalem's abominations and destruction (chaps. 8–11). This trip is for the purpose of viewing Jerusalem's and the temple's restoration.

Ezekiel is set down on the temple mount. There he sees what looks like a city, which is more than likely a reference to the walled complex of the temple (v. 5). (The phrase *what looked like* recalls the prophet's vision of the heavenly chariot in chap. 1.) He then meets a man (some kind of celestial being) who will be the prophet's guide. This bronzelike man holds a measuring rod in his hand, and it measures six long cubits (ca. 10′ 3″).

The first item shown to Ezekiel is a massive perimeter wall around the entire complex, giving the impression that the temple area is not unlike a fortress. This is followed by detailed information about the measurements of the east gate into the outer court (vv. 5–16). The gate is reached, first of all, by a seven-step staircase. Adding to the impression that Ezekiel sees a fortresslike structure is the fact that once inside the gate one observes three guard rooms (NIV alcoves) flanking the passageway on each side. It is clearly stated that these rooms are for the guards.

Approximately the same information is given about the north gate (vv. 20–23) and the south gate (vv. 24–26). These three gates all open into the outer court (vv. 17–19), in which there are thirty rooms.

Next, the prophet is shown the three gates that open into the inner court (vv. 28–37). These gates are much like those of verses 5–27, except they are eight steps (not seven) higher than the outer court. The inner court is a square of one hundred cubits.

In three of the rooms off the inner court and near the gateways there are installations for the slaughtering of the burnt offerings, sin offerings, and guilt offerings.

Finally, Ezekiel is shown two rooms off the inner court that serve as priestly chambers (vv. 44–47). One group of priests has charge of the temple and one group has charge of the altar. These are described as the sons of Zadok, Levites. Again, it is guarding responsibilities that are noted, as the Hebrew expressions used here would indicate. Verses 48–49 continue the movement in this chapter from outside in, with a brief reference to the temple proper. It is reached by a stairway of ten steps (v. 49; NIV fn.).

B. The temple proper (41:1–26). Ezekiel 40:5–47 describes the temple area (outer court/inner court). Ezekiel 40:48–41:26 turns to a description of the temple building. Like Solomon's temple, it has three parts on an east-west axis: (1) the vestibule/porch (NIV portico) (40:48–49); (2) the outer sanctuary or the Holy Place (41:1–2); and (3) the inner sanctuary or the Most Holy Place (41:3–4).

Note here the increase in numbers. So far we have seen seven steps into the outer court, eight steps into the inner court, and ten steps into the temple proper. We have also witnessed the decrease in numbers. The entrance into the portico is fourteen cubits (40:48); the entrance into the Holy Place is ten cubits (41:2); the entrance into the Most Holy Place is six cubits (41:3). Each stage gets higher and higher. Each opening gets narrower and narrower.

Off three sides of the sanctuary (north, south, west) are a number of chambers (vv. 5–12). Nothing is said about the functions of these rooms, but probably they served as storerooms for equipment and furnishings, perhaps for tithes and offerings as well. Also there is an unidentified building at the back (west) of the temple (v. 12).

The temple is one hundred cubits long (41:13a), and the inner courtyard is one hundred cubits square (41:13b–14). Also the yard/building behind the temple is one hundred cubits in length (v. 15b). The symmetry of these measurements is not coincidental. Everything in the temple fits perfectly and balances the whole.

Verses 15b–26 describe the decorations and the woodwork of the temple. Impressive here are two-faced carved cherubim and palm trees. The wooden altar (v. 22) may represent either the table of showbread or the small inner altar of incense.

C. Holy chambers (42:1–20). From 40:5 through 41:26 the movement, in the description of the temple, has been from outside to inside. Now, the prophet is led back out to the outer court (v. 1), where he is shown two sets of holy chambers (rooms for the priests), one on the north side of the outer court (vv. 2–9) and one on the south side of the outer court (vv. 10–12).

Verses 13–14 inform us of the functions of these rooms. They are, first of all, a place where the priests eat the most holy offerings. Second, they are changing rooms in which the priests remove their sacred vestments before going into the outer court where the laity are. It may appear to be a contradiction that these rooms are already in the outer court (v. 1), and yet the priests must disrobe in these rooms before going into the outer court (v. 14)! The contradiction disappears if one understands these chambers to border on the inner court and to extend into the outer court, thus serving as a transition zone between the two.

Ezekiel is shown and told the external measurements of the entire temple complex (vv. 15–20). The complex is a square of five hundred cubits.

The purpose of the temple complex is to separate the holy from the common (v. 20b). Inside is holy, outside is profane. The opposite of "holy" in the Old Testament is not sinful but "common."

D. God's glory returns (43:1–27). Now outside the temple, Ezekiel is brought to the gate facing east to witness the return of the presence of God. It was through this gate that Ezekiel saw the divine glory leave the temple (10:19). God returns through the gate by which he left. When he returns to his abode, God does not tiptoe back. He returns as a King. With God's presence restored to the place of worship, religious apostasy becomes impossible. Idolatry will be a thing of the past.

That Ezekiel is to make known to the people all the data about this new temple suggests that he is another Moses (vv. 10–11). God is the Designer; Moses and Ezekiel are the transmitters of data.

The return of God's presence and God's directive to Ezekiel are followed by information about the altar in the temple (vv. 13–27).

Note the parallel here. The temple, although now finished, is not ready for service until the divine glory returns. Similarly, the altar, although completed, is not ready for use until it has been purified.

There are many notable omissions in Ezekiel's temple when it is compared with the tabernacle in the desert or Solomon's temple. Most obvious is the absence of any reference to the ark, the mercy seat, and the cherubim. The same may be said of the laver, the lampstand, and the bronze altar. The implications of these omissions are obscure.

But the altar is there, indicating that there will never be the possibility of legitimate worship without the presence of sacrifice. Two things are necessary for the "reopening" of the temple. One thing is the presence of the glory of God. Unless the Shekinah fills, the shell (i.e., building) fails. The second indispensable element is a purified altar.

E. Enterings and exitings (44:1–31). Once again Ezekiel is taken to the outer east gate which, he is told, is to be permanently locked, for that is the gate through which the Lord passed when he returned to the temple. The one exception is that the prince may use its vestibule when eating (v. 3).

Next, Ezekiel is brought to the front of the temple by way of the north gate. Again Ezekiel sees the divine glory and falls upon his face.

Ezekiel is told to look carefully, listen closely, and give attention to everything God is about to tell him (v. 5). These imperatives sound much like 40:4, except that there they refer to what God is going to "show" Ezekiel.

God begins with a rebuke aimed particularly at the laity (the rebellious house of Israel) for allowing foreigners to guard the holy things. We cannot be sure of what Ezekiel/God speaks here. In the future, these laity will be replaced by Levites. They will slaughter the people's sacrifices, something that the laity themselves are supposed to do (Lev. 1–4). It may be that in transferring the responsibility for ritual sacrifice to the Levites, God is, in effect, punishing the people by barring them from the inner gates where the sacrifice takes place.

Although the Levites are to fulfill certain functions, they are not to serve as priests. The priesthood is reserved exclusively for the descendants of Zadok (the hereditary priesthood of the Solomonic temple). They alone may enter the sanctuary.

The remainder of the chapter is devoted to the dos and don'ts of these Levite priests/sons of Zadok who serve at the altar. This includes their clerical clothing and "street" clothing (vv. 17–19); their hair-style (v. 20); their beverages (v. 21); prospective spouses (v. 22); their teaching ministry (v. 23); their judicial obligations (v. 24a); their responsibilities as guardians of holy days (v. 24b); their limitations on incurring corpse-impurity (vv. 25–27). The chapter concludes with data about the oblations to be given them by the Israelites (vv. 28–31). God is to be the only inheritance the priests have (v. 28). In serving him they find their highest fulfillment and reward. Not possessions, but obedience in ministry, crowns the life of the altar-serving priest.

We noted in our discussion of chapters 40–43 the interesting absence from Ezekiel's temple of such standard items as the ark, cherubim, lampstand, and table of showbread. We note similarly in chapter 44 the absence from this temple of any high priest. The two omissions go together, for the inner area of the temple was the particular domain of the high priest.

F. Division of the land (45:1–25). The emphasis on priests and Levites in the previous chapter continues in chapter 45. Chapter 44 focused on the priest's responsibilities. At the end of the chapter notice was made about the food supply of the priests. Chapter 45 moves from food supply to land supply. This land supply is called a sacred district.

First of all, a portion of land twenty-five thousand cubits long and twenty thousand cubits wide is to be given to the priests. In the midst of this is the sanctuary which is five hundred cubits square. There is a fifty-cubit "green belt" around this section (vv. 1–4).

Second, there is a portion for the Levites which is twenty-five thousand cubits long, and ten thousand cubits wide. Distinction is made here between the priests who minister in the sanctuary (v. 4), and the Levites who serve in the temple (v. 5).

Third is an area designated as city land (v. 6). Fourth is a reserve for the prince (future king) on the east and west sides of the sacred district and the city (vv. 7–8).

While Ezekiel is talking about the contribution and apportionment of land for the prince, he addresses a sermonette to the kings (vv. 9–12). They are to keep their hands off their subjects' holdings and are to be honest in the collection of taxes for the upkeep of the temple. Thus, the king is to be one who "has learned in whatsoever state he is to be content," and as one who is impeccable in his business affairs.

With these collected portions the king can provide what is needed for the additional offerings on the feasts, the New Moon days, and the Sabbaths. Verses 18–25 speak of the annual sacrifices. Of special import here is the sacrifice of the first day, and the seventh day of the first month. The purpose of these sacrifices is clearly for the purification of the sanctuary (v. 18b), making atonement for the temple (v. 20b). It is God's own house that is to be purged. The two annual pilgrim feasts highlighted are Passover (vv. 21–24) and Tabernacles (v. 25).

G. Worship protocol (46:1–24). Ezekiel 45:18–25 lists the occasions of the annual sacrifices; 46:1–11 notes the occasions of the repeated sacrifices (i.e., the Sabbath day and the New Moon or first day of each month). Special emphasis is placed on how the prince and the laity are to enter and exit the place of worship.

In the prince's case, he approaches (but may not enter) the inner sanctuary by way of the eastern gate, on whose threshold he worships. He is to make certain that he enters and exits by the same gate on both Sabbaths and New Moons. In the laity's case and the prince's case, they are both to exit by the opposite gate they entered on the annual festivals. Thus they must traverse the entire outer court.

That the gate is left open until evening (v. 2) probably indicates that the laity may look into the holy precinct, while they worship by the exterior entrance.

After speaking of the prince's voluntary and daily offerings, Ezekiel takes up the matter of how the prince should give gifts of land to his sons or servants, and what limitations apply when those endowments of crownland are given to servants. Gifts that the prince gives to his courtiers are to revert to the crown in the year of Jubilee.

The chapter concludes with Ezekiel being shown the temple kitchens, the place where the sacrifices are cooked or baked (vv. 19–24). There are two sets of kitchens. One is for the priests and the other is for the laity. This second set is located in the outer court. The more minor sacrifices are prepared here. Once again the gradation of holiness is prominent even where kitchens are concerned.

H. The river of life (47:1–23). In the first twelve verses of this chapter Ezekiel is shown water coming out of the temple's south side. From there it flows for four thousand cubits through a desert and eventually empties into the Dead Sea.

A celestial man leads the prophet on a tour of this river. At one thousand cubits it is ankle-deep. At another one thousand cubits it is knee-deep. At another one thousand cubits it is an unfordable river, deep enough to swim in. It is not explained how the river gets deeper as it flows further. There is no mention of any tributaries that might explain the greater depth.

What makes this river so interesting is not only its increasing depth, but the positive effects its waters have. The river desalts the Dead Sea, so the sea becomes a fisherman's paradise. Wherever the river flows and whatever it touches, the result is life.

Not only is the Dead Sea desalinized, but the desert is fructified. Fruit trees of all kinds grow on both sides of this river. The fruit from these trees provides food and healing.

What is of interest here is that the vision of this river singles out for transformation the most barren tract of land (the Arabah) and the body of water most inhospitable to life (the Dead Sea). Moreover, the water flows from a temple built on solid rock!

This is surely a picture of the power of God's presence in his temple and among his people. It affects everything for good. There can be no doubt that Jesus had this chapter in mind when he said: "Whoever believes in me, as the Scripture has said, streams of living water will flow from within him" (John 7:38). That Jesus goes on in the next verse to connect these streams of living water with the Spirit is not without significance. The supply for the water from the temple (built on rock) is supernatural. The same is true of the follower of Jesus.

The vision of the temple river is followed by an outline of the boundaries of the land (vv. 13–23). We note with interest that these boundaries do not include land west of the Jordan. This must mean that the three Trans-Jordanian tribes (Reuben, Gad, and half-Manasseh) are to be given different territories (see chap. 48). The boundaries also leave out Aramean territory to the north, once conquered by David, and Edomite territory to the south, once part of the Judahite kingdom.

Of particular import is the fact that verses 21–23 integrate the alien into the tribal structure, and allow him to share in the patrimony of Israel. Earlier biblical injunctions had insisted on the humane and moral treatment of the alien (Exod. 22:21; Lev. 19:10; Deut. 14:29; etc.), but they still kept the alien outside of the tribal structure. Ezekiel's word is more radical than even that of the Torah. All of God's children, alien and native-born, will be part of this new community.

I. Division of the land (48:1–35). With the external boundaries now in hand, Ezekiel can turn to the matter of interior boundaries: how the land is to be divided among the tribes. The order of tribal allotments is unlike anything in any previous period of Israelite history.

The sequence from north to south is: Dan, Asher, Naphtali, Manasseh, Ephraim, Reuben, Judah, priests/Levites, Benjamin, Simeon, Issachar, Zebulun, and Gad.

Tribal areas named after Jacob's sons by concubines are placed at the extremes (in the north, Dan and Naphtali by Bilhah, Asher by Zilpah; in the south, Gad by Zilpah). Tribal areas named after Jacob's sons by Leah and Rachel are placed closer to the center. Tribal areas always a part of the north are now shifted to the south: Zebulun and Issachar. Such repositioning allows the placement of the temple more perfectly in the center of the land.

Most startling is that Judah and Benjamin are reversed. It is now Judah that is north of Benjamin, and not vice versa. Is this Ezekiel's way, and God's way, of dampening sectionalism in the new order? No one tribe will be more sacrosanct than the other, or have pride of position.

Each tribal area is to be equal in size. To be sure, this is not stated explicitly, for chapter 48 provides only east-west determinants, and not north-south boundaries. It is a legitimate inference, however. If the last few verses of chapter 47 deal with inequities between native-born and aliens, chapter 48 deals with inequities between tribal giants and tribal dwarfs. For Ezekiel, all such differences will be eradicated. Strong/weak, big/small will no longer be categories of distinction.

Between the seven tribes to the north and the five to the south is a special portion (vv. 8–22). It is a strip of land twenty-five thousand cubits long and wide, and is divided into three east-west strips. The northernmost strip is for the priests (vv. 9–12); the middle strip is for the Levites (vv. 13–14). Both strips are designated holy. The lowest strip contains a centrally located city which is surrounded by grazing land and flanked by farmland. Land outside of this square is crownland.

The last topic covered in the chapter is the reference to the four sides of the city, each of which has three gates bearing the names of three of the tribes (vv. 30–35). In this system the Ephraim and Manasseh of verses 4–5 have merged into Joseph, and Levi is counted as one of the twelve tribes. Leah's six sons (or the tribes bearing their names) are positioned at the northern and southern gates.

Finally, Ezekiel concludes his prophecy by identifying the name of this twelve-gate city. It is "THE LORD IS THERE." "Jerusalem" is conspicuous by its absence. What gives the city any kind of sanctity is not tradition, but the presence of the Lord. His glory is not confined to the temple. It spills into the whole land. In Ezekiel's city and John's city (Rev. 21:12ff.) the climax is the same: God's dwelling is with men.

SELECT BIBLIOGRAPHY

Blackwood, A. W. *Ezekiel: Prophecy of Hope.* Grand Rapids: Baker, 1965.

Eichrodt, W. *Ezekiel.* Philadelphia: Westminster, 1970.

Feinberg, C. L. *The Prophecy of Ezekiel.* Chicago: Moody, 1969.

Taylor, J. B. *Ezekiel.* Downers Grove: Inter-Varsity, 1969.

Wevers, J. W. *Ezekiel.* Grand Rapids: Eerdmans, 1969.

DANIEL

Willem A. VanGemeren

INTRODUCTION

According to the claims of the book itself (9:2; 10:2), the New Testament (Matt. 24:15), and Jewish and Christian tradition, Daniel is the author of the book that bears his name. Daniel, whose name means "God is judge," was carried into captivity from Jerusalem to Babylon in the third year of Jehoiakim (1:1), which, according to the Babylonian system of reckoning, was 605 B.C. Apparently, he was of noble descent, and was selected to become the king's courtier in a foreign land. He received special training in Babylon, but was distinguished from his peers by a God-given ability to interpret dreams. Like Joseph in Egypt, God raised up Daniel to be his spokesperson in Babylon. During his captivity, Daniel served under Nebuchadnezzar, Belshazzar, and Darius the Mede. The book recounts his ministry from about 600 B.C. to 536 B.C., the third year of Cyrus the Persian. The book must have been completed after the capture of Babylon and after the first Jewish migration to Judea. It records the transfer of authority from Babylon to Persia, but is silent on Jewish affairs.

Authorship of the book has been contested since the time of Porphyry, a third-century (A.D.) philosopher. Porphyry argued that the book reflects a second-century B.C. background, recounting the actual historical circumstances of Antiochus Epiphanes. He denied the predictive element of prophecy and explained the book as a pious hoax. Unfortunately, this line of argument has had advocates throughout the history of interpretation, based on alleged historical errors, the denial of predictive prophecy, and the presence of Greek and Persian loanwords.

The Book of Daniel has two major divisions. The first six chapters consist of third-person narratives about Daniel and his friends in a foreign court. Their response to the challenges posed by a pagan culture exemplifies loyalty to the covenant; even when their lives are threatened, they persevere in the faith. These stories are intertwined with dreams and interpretations of dreams. Chapters 7–12 are comprised solely of visions and interpretations, written in the first person.

The Book of Daniel belongs to the apocalyptic genre of literature. Apocalyptic literature flourished in Judaism from 200 B.C. to A.D. 100, but its roots were already present in the Old Testament prophets. The prophets—especially Ezekiel, Zechariah, and Daniel—employ visions and symbols. This in no way compromises the reliability of the historical information found in the Book of Daniel. At the same time, we must admit the difficulty in clearly distinguishing the historical from the symbolical.

The message of Daniel focuses on the sovereignty of the Creator-Redeemer over the kingdoms of this world, the suffering and perseverance of the saints during the wars among the kingdoms of this earth, and the persecution of the saints. Difficult as it may be to fit all the pieces together, the message of Daniel, like that of Revelation, is clear and simple. It is an encouragement to persevere and to hope in the final establishment of the everlasting kingdom of God and his Messiah.

The Book of Daniel is written in both Hebrew (1:1–2:4a; 8:1–12:13) and Aramaic (2:4b–7:28). This reflects the historical situation, as Aramaic gradually became the official language of the Near East from 1000 B.C. until the time of Alexander the Great, when Greek supplanted it.

Daniel's position in the English Bible is different from that in the Hebrew Bible. In the Hebrew Bible it is placed in the third group—the Writings—after Esther and before Ezra–Nehemiah. The reason is not entirely clear. Critics have argued that the book was not written until after the prophetic era, after the second section (the Prophets) was already closed, and therefore that it could only be included in the last section of the Hebrew Bible.

Others, contending that the spirit of prophecy does not operate outside Israel, have argued that Daniel was not a prophet at all. Against this view, however, it must be noted that Ezekiel's ministry took place wholly in exile, by the Kebar River. Yet, it must be admitted that Daniel is a different kind of prophet. He does not quite fit the traditional definition.

The prophecy of Daniel consists of revelations given over a seventy-year period, while the remnant of Judah and Israel were in exile. The people felt the absence of God, having been forcibly separated from their land and having witnessed the destruction of Jerusalem, including the temple. This period of isolation forced the people to look once again to the Lord as the source of grace and favor. In this context the Lord raised up Daniel. The words of Daniel, however, were not known to the people in exile. Apparently, he had little contact with the Jewish community. Daniel's role was that of a Babylonian statesman. Only after the exile did God's people receive the record of God's revelation to Daniel, detailing the things that would happen to them over the centuries.

The Book of Daniel is a powerful witness to the certainty of the establishment of God's kingdom. Notwithstanding the symbols, numbers, and ambiguous language, the message of Daniel is clear. Thus, God's people throughout the centuries have been challenged to look beyond historical circumstances and to count on God, in whom lies the certainty of a new age. At the same time, the difficulty of interpreting Daniel functions as a sober reminder not to seize upon one given interpretation. The complexity we find in Daniel reminds us of the complexity we find in interpreting our own historical situation in light of the past and future. God holds the key to this and has given his authority to the Messiah. We do well to take our cue from Jesus, who saw in the prophecies of Daniel a progression of the acts of God and the acts of man, the intersection of the divine and the human.

OUTLINE

I. The Preparation of Daniel and His Friends (1:1–21)
  A. Background (1:1–2)
  B. Education (1:3–7)
  C. The Challenge (1:8–20)
  D. Daniel's Service (1:21)
II. Nebuchadnezzar's Dream and Daniel's Interpretation (2:1–49)
  A. The King and His Astrologers (2:1–13)
  B. The King and Daniel (2:14–19)
  C. Daniel's Praise (2:20–23)
  D. Daniel's Interpretation (2:24–45)
  E. Nebuchadnezzar's Response (2:46–49)
III. The Fiery Furnace (3:1–30)
IV. Nebuchadnezzar's Dream and Daniel's Interpretation (4:1–37)
  A. Nebuchadnezzar's Confession (4:1–3)
  B. The Dream and Its Interpretation (4:4–27)
  C. Nebuchadnezzar's Humiliation (4:28–37)
V. The Writing on the Wall (5:1–31)
VI. The Lions' Den (6:1–28)
VII. Vision of the Four Beasts (7:1–28)
  A. The Vision (7:1–14)
  B. Its Interpretation (7:15–28)
VIII. Vision of the Kingdoms (8:1–27)
  A. The Vision (8:1–12)
  B. Its Interpretation (8:15–27)
IX. Daniel's Prayer and Vision of the Seventy Weeks (9:1–27)
  A. Daniel's Prayer (9:1–19)
  B. God's Response (9:20–27)
X. Message of Encouragement (10:1–11:45)
  A. Introduction (10:1–3)
  B. The Angel (10:4–11:1)
  C. The Vision (11:2–45)
XI. Troubles and Victory (12:1–13)

COMMENTARY

I. The Preparation of Daniel and His Friends (1:1–21)

A. Background (1:1–2). Daniel was exiled in 605 B.C., the fourth year of King Jehoiakim, together with a cross-section of prominent citizens and craftsmen (Jer. 25:1; 46:2). Daniel's method of reckoning differs from that of the Palestinian system, as he writes "in the third year of the reign of Jehoiakim king of Judah, Nebuchadnezzar king of Babylon came to Jerusalem and besieged it" (1:1). It appears that this manner of reckoning is based on the Babylonian system, according to which the first year began with the New Year.

The tragedy of that hour was that "the Lord delivered" (1:2) Jehoiakim, articles from the temple, and prominent citizens into captivity. This was the beginning of the great exile of Judah, predicted by Isaiah, Micah, Zephaniah, and Habakkuk. The people had sinned and the Lord had to discipline his rebellious children.

This was the first exile; a second followed during which Ezekiel and King Jehoiachin were deported. The third exile followed the desolation of Jerusalem and the destruction of the temple (586 B.C.).

B. Education (1:3–7). Nebuchadnezzar entrusts Ashpenaz, principal of the royal academy, with the instruction of young Jewish boys in the Babylonian culture, including cuneiform, Aramaic (the official language of the Babylonian Empire), astrology, and mathematics. All students at the royal academy were required to have no physical handicap, to be attractive in appearance, to show aptitude for learning, and to be well informed, quick to understand, and qualified to serve in the king's palace (v. 4). Ashpenaz is challenged to transform the Judean youths into cultured Babylonian princes, well-versed in Babylonian culture and literature.

The royal academy is supported by the king, who supplies the students with a daily quota of food and wine (v. 5). The curriculum lasted some three years, during which time the young men were to develop into competent statesmen to be used for the advance of the Babylonian kingdom. The royal grant was to perpetuate the Babylonian system of cultural, political, social, and economic values. The education was intended to brainwash the youths and to make them useful Babylonian subjects.

The process of cultural exchange is also evident in the change of names. Daniel ("my judge is God") becomes Belteshazzar ("may Nebo [Bel or Marduk] protect his life"). The names of his friends—Hananiah ("Yahweh has been gracious"), Mishael ("who is what God is"), and Azariah ("Yahweh has helped")—are also changed. Hananiah becomes "Shadrach" ("the command of Aku" [the Sumerian moon god]), Mishael becomes Meshach ("who is what Aku is"), and Azariah becomes Abednego ("servant of Nego" or Nebo/Marduk). Though it is clear that these names are reflections of Babylonian religious symbols, the youths do not object to them. They single out the issues that are important and do not pick quarrels over any and every thing that is different.

C. The challenge (1:8–20). The issue of food and drink is highly significant to Daniel and his friends. The Lord had clearly designated certain foods as unclean (Lev. 7:22–27; 11:1–47). Moreover, the royal court was closely associated with pagan temples, as food and drink were symbolically dedicated to the gods. Daniel humbly asks for permission not to eat the royal diet. His act of faith is rewarded; the Lord is with Daniel. The court official shows favor and sympathy to Daniel, even though he fears the wrath of the king. Again Daniel responds with courtesy and understanding of the official's predicament. He requests a test period during which the power of God's presence will be made evident in the physical well-being of Daniel and his friends. This test will last ten days; the youths will eat only vegetables and drink only water. If their appearance is not affected during these ten days, it will be clear that Daniel's God is powerful in protecting his loyal servants. The Lord is with them; after ten days they look "healthier and better nourished than any of the young men who ate the royal food" (v. 15). The youths distinguish themselves not only by their food, but also by their wisdom (v. 17). The Lord prospers them, not only physically, but also in giving them favor with Ashpenaz and a special quality of wisdom. Daniel becomes prominent among his friends, as he can understand visions and interpret dreams (v. 17).

The king agrees with Ashpenaz's judgment and orders the Judean youths into his service. Nebuchadnezzar finds them to be superior to his own courtiers in "every matter of wisdom and understanding" (v. 20).

D. Daniel's service (1:21). The text briefly mentions that Daniel remains in royal service "until the first year of King Cyrus." The transfer of power from Babylon to Persia took place in 539 B.C. Daniel has to adapt to changing expectations as the political situation shifts (cf. 10:1). The Lord is with this Judean prince in a foreign court. Daniel gains prominence in Babylon's court over a period of sixty-five years!

II. Nebuchadnezzar's Dream and Daniel's Interpretation (2:1–49)

A. The king and his astrologers (2:1–13). In Nebuchadnezzar's second year (2:1; 604 B.C.), he has a dream that disturbs him greatly. He turns to the traditional wisdom of his time by calling on his sages—"the magicians, enchanters, sorcerers and astrologers" (2:2)—to tell him what his dream means. They are all too ready to please the king, and ask for the particulars of the dream. Their request is "in Aramaic" (v. 4), the official language of the Babylonian Empire. (Here begins the Aramaic section of Daniel, which continues until 7:28.)

The wise men are used to interpretation, but are unable to reconstruct the elements of the dream from nothing. The king has decided and insists repeatedly that they tell him both the dream and its interpretation (vv. 5–7). When the king refuses to change his mind, but instead grows more and more agitated, the sages argue that the giving of dreams, the reconstruction of the parts, and the interpretation belong to the gods (v. 11). What the king demands is much more than they can handle. The gravity of the situation worsens as the king grows increasingly agitated and angry with his servants. Finally, the king orders Arioch, chief of the royal guard, to have all the sages of Babylon executed as impostors. Moreover, he decrees the destruction of their houses as well.

B. The king and Daniel (2:14–19). Daniel deals tactfully with Arioch, goes to the king, and receives a delay in the execution. During this time he and his friends pray for God's mercy. They believe that only their God, "the God of heaven" (v. 18)—a reference to God's spirituality and universal rule—can help them explain the "mystery." Daniel does not return to the king until the Lord had revealed the dream and its interpretation and until he has praised his God.

C. Daniel's praise (2:20–23). Daniel praises the Lord for his "wisdom and power" (v. 20). His wisdom and power advance his purposes, as he sovereignly rules over human affairs—even over kings and nations. He bestows insight upon the wise. God's plan for the future lies hidden from man's scrutiny, but is fully known to him. This God is no other than "the God of my fathers" who is faithful to his servants in exile. Though Daniel refrains from using the divine name *Yahweh,* he intimates that the God of the fathers and the great King has a name, and that this name will endure "for ever and ever" (v. 20), even though it may seem to the Babylonians that their gods are victorious.

D. Daniel's interpretation (2:24–45). Daniel's request to be taken to Nebuchadnezzar by Arioch, the king's hatchet man, is taken seriously. It is possible that Daniel already had a reputation for integrity and for God's being with him. The manner of Daniel's speech (v. 24) shows his confidence and Arioch's quick response reveals his trust in Daniel.

In the presence of the king Daniel gives God the glory, as, together with the sages, he admits that "no wise man, enchanter, magician or diviner can explain to the king the mystery he has asked about" (v. 27). Only Daniel's God can and does reveal mysteries.

Daniel humbly admits that he is a mere instrument in God's hands and that his abilities should not be viewed as native, but have been given to him by God. Then he proceeds to explain the dream.

The king saw a colossal statue, whose parts consisted of different materials. But—to the king's amazement—he also saw a rock cut out supernaturally (v. 34). This rock struck the statue on its feet of iron and clay, smashed them, and made it appear as if the iron, the clay, the bronze, the silver and the gold were little more than "chaff on a threshing floor" (v. 35). Nothing remained of the statue! The rock became a huge mountain and filled the whole earth.

Through the dream of the image of gold, silver, bronze, iron, and feet mingled with iron and clay, the Lord reveals how one empire will succeed another empire: Babylonia, Persia, Greece, and Rome. The resulting instability of the image is represented by the mixing of iron and clay. The image will be completely shattered by the rock, depicting the establishment of God's eternal kingdom. This kingdom had been given to Israel as a theocratic nation. It was inaugurated more fully after the exile, in the coming of Christ and in the presence of the Spirit. But it will be gloriously established at the second coming of our Lord.

All sovereignty is derived from the Lord. He has given Nebuchadnezzar "dominion and power and might and glory" (v. 37). Other kingdoms will arise, each inferior to the preceding one, but whatever the name of the kingdom, its authority is derived from God. In the end, however, no kingdom will fulfill God's will on earth. Therefore, he will establish the kingdom of God, "a kingdom that will never be destroyed, nor will it be left to another people. It will crush all those kingdoms and bring them to an end, but it will itself endure forever" (v. 44).

E. Nebuchadnezzar's response (2:46–49). Nebuchadnezzar's response to the revelation signifies a recognition of (not conversion to!) Daniel's God. His confession—"surely your God is the God of gods and the Lord of kings and a revealer of mysteries" (v. 47)—while not insignificant, marks the king as a broad-minded man who willingly makes offering to any god who helps him.

Further, he gives Daniel the honor promised to any wise man who succeeded in telling the dream and in explaining it. Daniel receives a high office and many gifts. Through loyalty to the Lord, careful use of opportunity, and by choosing wisely in important issues, Daniel wins a place for himself as a counselor to the king.

III. The Fiery Furnace (3:1–30)

Soon after this experience the king has a colossal image made. It is overlaid with gold, ninety feet high, and nine feet wide. It probably was erected in honor of Nebo (or Nabu), the patron god of Nebuchadnezzar. The Valley of Dura, where the statue was set up, is unknown as a place name. It simply may have been a place designated for the occasion.

Filled with self-esteem the king demands that all his officials worship the image. He calls on the satraps, prefects, governors, advisors, treasurers, judges, magistrates, and all provincial officials to join him in dedicating the image he has set up.

The king decrees that at the signal of the music, all his subjects proclaim allegiance to him, the Babylonian kingdom, and to Nabu. Whoever disobeys will be thrown into a blazing furnace (v. 6).

However, the Jews do not submit to this decree. Daniel's friends (Shadrach, Meshach, and Abednego) are readily singled out by the royal counselors, who may still have had an axe to grind with Daniel. The astrologers piously accuse the three Jewish leaders, acknowledging their own complete devotion to the king and thereby further implicating the Jews. They rightly assert that these Jews do not serve any of the Babylonian gods. The king's anger with the three Jews is mitigated by his concern, which explains his giving them another chance.

The contest is actually between Yahweh and the god of Nebuchadnezzar. The Jews express their conviction that their God is able to deliver them. Their faith is so strong that they are determined not to submit to this act of state worship, even if the Lord does not miraculously deliver them.

So desperately does Nebuchadnezzar want his god and state to be victorious over the God of the Jews that, without any further ado, he changes his decree and requires that the oven be made "seven times" hotter. He then has some of his strongest men throw the Jews into the oven. The writer emphasizes the king's zeal, as everything moves toward the destruction of the three "radicals" from his empire. The god of Babylon must win! However, in his zeal to destroy the three Jews, his own soldiers, who throw the Jews into the fire, are killed by the blazing heat of the oven.

Nebuchadnezzar again faces the superiority of Israel's God, as he suddenly spies four men walking in the fire. The narrative portrays the transformation of a powerful and rational emperor into an irrational and overzealous monomaniac. He has to recognize that these men are "servants of the Most High God" (v. 26). He promotes Daniel's friends and promulgates a decree giving protection to Shadrach, Meshach, and Abednego.

IV. Nebuchadnezzar's Dream and Daniel's Interpretation (4:1–37)

A. Nebuchadnezzar's confession (4:1–3). Nebuchadnezzar's confession of God's sovereignty results from a series of events described in verses 4–37. The manner of expression is typical of Israelite poetry and probably reflects editorial reworking. The intent of this section of praise is to show that even a pagan king has to acknowledge that Yahweh is great, that his kingdom extends to all "peoples, nations and men of every language, who live in all the world" (v. 1), and that "his dominion endures from generation to generation" (v. 3).

B. The dream and its interpretation (4:4–27). Nebuchadnezzar had reasons to be proud. In a short time he had consolidated the power of Babylon from the Persian Gulf to the Mediterranean, and from the Amanus Mountains to the Sinai. He had spent many years on campaigns subduing and conquering. Finally he demonstrated his control in the operation of his administration, which ran smoothly by means of a tight network of officials and checks and balances. While resting at his palace, he has a dream that terrifies him. He calls on his trusted officials to interpret the dream, but this time he tells them the dream. Regardless of how hard they try, they cannot agree on a single interpretation. Then Nebuchadnezzar calls in Daniel, who is known as "the chief of the magicians" (v. 9), trusting in his God-given ability. This time Nebuchadnezzar addresses Daniel with respect: "Belteshazzar, chief of the magicians, I know that the spirit of the holy gods is in you, and no mystery is too difficult for you" (v. 9).

The king's dream is of a tree: it is enormous and strong, its top touching the sky; it is visible to the ends of the earth, with beautiful leaves and abundant fruit, providing sustenance and shelter for man and beast. Suddenly an angel decrees that this magnificent tree be cut down and its stump and roots "bound with iron and bronze" (v. 15). Further, the angel explains that the king is to behave like an animal and be driven out to live with animals for a period of "seven times" (v. 16).

The reason for the execution of this verdict lies in the fidelity of the angels to the great King and his sovereign rule over the kingdoms of this world; he does not put up with anyone who exalts himself to godhood.

Daniel's response reveals empathy for the king. When the king encourages him to explain the vision, Daniel responds graciously: "My lord, if only the dream applied to your enemies and its meaning to your adversaries!" (v. 19). Then he proceeds with the explanation. The tree symbolizes the king and his kingdom—great and strong, reaching to the sky and extending to distant parts of the earth. The messenger serves the decree of the Most High to forewarn Nebuchadnezzar that only the God of heaven "is sovereign over the kingdoms of men and gives them to anyone he wishes" (v. 25). Daniel (or Belteshazzar) is given to understand that the tree represents the pride and power of Nebuchadnezzar, which is to be cut down by divine decree until he acknowledges that God rules.

C. Nebuchadnezzar's humiliation (4:28–37). A year later the king prides himself on his accomplishments: "Is not this the great Babylon I have built as the royal residence, by my mighty power and for the glory of my majesty?" (v. 30). Babylon was indeed a magnificent city: excellent fortifications, beautiful buildings, and hanging gardens. Its magnificence had become proverbial in a short time and Nebuchadnezzar had been the driving force behind the rejuvenation of this old kingdom. He had reasons to be proud, but in his pride he overstepped the boundary.

Suddenly he hears a voice and the decree of judgment. He begins to look like an animal. He eats grass like a bull and lives outdoors. Nebuchadnezzar may well have had the disease known as boanthropy. During the time that he suffered from the disease, he was not cared for and his appearance grew wild.

Only when he recognizes God's sovereignty and dominion, is he restored to the throne. The king confesses that God's rule is far greater than his. The kingdom of God is an everlasting dominion, extends over all creation, and is absolutely sovereign. Though this public acknowledgment need not be interpreted as conversion from paganism to Yahwism, at least the king is forced to acknowledge Yahweh's sovereignty.

V. The Writing on the Wall (5:1–31)

Upon Nebuchadnezzar's death in 562, the ruling power changed hands in quick succession due to assassinations and court intrigues. Nabonidus (556–539 B.C.) witnessed the growth of Persia on the east, but was unsuccessful in restraining Cyrus. Having been defeated in the field, he retreated, leaving the defense of Babylon to his son, Belshazzar ("May Bel protect the king!"). In verse 22 Belshazzar is also known as the son of Nebuchadnezzar, which probably means in Semitic custom "descendant" or "successor to the throne."

The spirit in the city is one of confidence. The banquet of Belshazzar reveals the self-assurance of the king and his nobles, as they drink from the vessels taken from the temple in Jerusalem. He is pagan not only in his drinking, but also in his act of sacrilege, as he praises "the gods of gold and silver, of bronze, iron, wood and stone" (v. 4).

The sudden appearance of mysterious writing on the wall greatly disturbs the king and his nobles. He calls in his sages to explain the writing. No one succeeds—even with the promise of being clothed in purple, having a gold chain placed around his neck, and being made the third highest ruler in the kingdom after Nabonidus and Belshazzar. This failure disturbs the king even more.

The queen—it is uncertain whether she is the grandmother or the queen mother—remembers Daniel. She speaks highly of Daniel, as Nebuchadnezzar had done: "In the time of your father he was found to have insight and intelligence and wisdom like that of the gods" (v. 11). She quickly reminds him of Daniel's ability to interpret dreams, explain riddles, and solve difficult problems (v. 12).

Finally, Daniel is called in to interpret the enigmatic writing. The king repeats the offer of rewards and recognizes Daniel's past. But Daniel refuses the reward and freely reads and interprets the writing: *Mene, mene, tekel, parsin* ("numbered, weighed, divided"), signifying that God's judgment will shortly fall upon Babylon and that he has given the authority of Babylon over to Persia. The same God who gave dominion to Nebuchadnezzar has authority to give it to someone else. Daniel reviews some of the events that brought Nebuchadnezzar to the recognition of Daniel's God.

Belshazzar is worse than Nebuchadnezzar. Daniel presents God's case against Belshazzar: he is filled with pride; he has desecrated the temple vessels; he has rebelled against the God of heaven (vv. 22–23). Babylon's doom is sealed. Despite this oracle of doom Belshazzar keeps his promise, proclaiming Daniel to be the third highest ruler in the kingdom. The Persians invade the city that night, using the strategy of cutting off the water from the moat around Babylon. On the fifteenth of Tishri (September), 539 B.C., Babylon falls without a siege. Darius (or Gubaru) becomes governor of Babylon at the age of sixty-two.

VI. The Lions' Den (6:1–28)

Darius reorganized the former Babylonian Empire into 120 satrapies, administered by 120 satraps (v. 1). The satraps were directly accountable to the king and to one of three administrative officers, among whom Daniel also served.

Daniel, being over them all, evokes the ire

of his fellow administrators and satraps. They make every effort to find fault with him, but Daniel is blameless. So the royal administrators, prefects, satraps, advisors, and governors come to Darius and ingratiate themselves to him with the request that Darius be the sole object of veneration for thirty days upon penalty of death in the lions' den. They are successful!

They are able to trap Daniel in his habitual worship of the God of Israel. Daniel regularly and openly prayed three times a day at fixed times. Daniel knows about the edict, but relies on God to deliver him. He does not begin to pray when times are hard, but rather continues his habitual devotion to the Lord and to his temple which now lay in ruins in Jerusalem. His crime is that of "asking God for help" (v. 11). Daniel's enemies hurriedly report him to the king, demand justice from Darius, and get it. Upon learning that Daniel is the victim of their plot, Darius understands the motivation for their flattery and is greatly outraged at this miscarriage of justice. But, trapping the king by his own decree, they demand Daniel's death, reminding the governor of the supremacy of law over loyalty and feelings.

His opponents persist until Daniel is thrown into the lions' den. Darius perceives at least something of the greatness of Daniel's God. The stone and royal seal ensure that Daniel's escape from the lions' den is impossible. Yet, the king expresses hope that Daniel's God might deliver him. He spends a restless night full of anxiety. As soon as his decree permits, the king rushes to the den and with anxiety calls to see if Daniel is still alive.

Daniel speaks and gives glory to God: "My God sent his angel, and he shut the mouths of the lions. They have not hurt me, because I was found innocent in his sight. Nor have I ever done any wrong before you, O king" (v. 22). Daniel's loyalty extends to both God and the king!

Hearing Daniel's voice, the king rejoices. He has Daniel brought out of the den and examined for wounds or scratches; he discovers that the lions have been kept from devouring this servant of God. He has the schemers and their families thrown into the lions' den. They are quickly destroyed.

Further, the king decrees public recognition of Daniel's God as the God whose kingdom remains forever and whose power manifests itself in deliverance.

VII. Vision of the Four Beasts (7:1–28)

A. The vision (7:1–14). In the first year of Belshazzar (ca. 553/2 B.C.) Daniel has a vision, whose message parallels that of the first dream of Nebuchadnezzar (chap. 2). Four beasts, symbolic of the nations (cf. Ps. 65:7), come out of "the great sea." The appearance of the beasts in each vision has both familiar and unusual features.

The lion with the wings of an eagle resembles the cherub, protecting the kingship of God above the ark. As it consolidated power, Babylon came to believe that it was destined for eternity. But Babylon's power, too, is human. Its power is forcibly removed: "its wings were torn off and it was lifted from the ground so that it stood on two feet like a man, and the heart of a man was given to it" (v. 4). Though it appeared to be the kingdom of the gods, Babylon was as frail as any other human kingdom.

The bear with three ribs in its mouth represents the coalition of Media-Persia, by whose power kingdoms were crushed. The three ribs between its teeth and its readiness to eat its fill of flesh may symbolize the Persian conquest of Lydia (546 B.C.), Babylon (539 B.C.), and Egypt (525 B.C.).

The third animal, like a leopard with four wings, represents the power of Macedonia under Alexander the Great (336–323 B.C.). The four heads typify either the four kingdoms which arose from Alexander's Macedonian kingdom (Macedonia, Thrace, Egypt, and Syria) or the extent of his rule (the proverbial four corners of the world).

The fourth and most terrifying is the beast which oppresses kingdoms. It has ten horns, from which comes another horn uprooting three of the original horns. This horn looks like a human face and is full of pride. After the fall of Rome kingdoms continued to rise and fall. These kingdoms are symbolized by the ten horns. Ten is a symbol of completion and need not be limited to a future kingdom consisting of "ten" nations, which some call a revival of the Roman Empire. This kingdom is to be more powerful, extensive, despotic, and awe-inspiring than the previous kingdoms.

Suddenly there arises "another horn, a little one" (v. 8). This little horn comes naturally from the other horns, but uproots three of the first horns in the process. It has the eyes of a man and a mouth that speaks boastfully (v. 20).

Daniel momentarily interrupts the vision of the animals from the sea to reflect on the vision from heaven. The vision of the human kingdoms gives way to a vision of God ("the Ancient of Days"), enthroned on high as the great King. Daniel describes God in more detail than any of the prophets before or after him: his clothing is as white as snow; his hair is white like wool. The throne of God is flaming with fire and mobile like a chariot, with wheels that are ablaze with fire. The Lord is the great Judge who is seated to judge the kingdoms of this world. There is no escape from his judgment. A river of fire flows before him. He is the Lord of hosts with thousands upon thousands awaiting his command. The acts of men are recorded in his books.

Daniel returns to describe the acts and words of the little horn. The pride of this kingdom is self-evident by the boastful words of the horn. Despite its power and onslaught on God's kingdom, it comes to an end and is burned with fire from God's chariot. The other kingdoms, too, are stripped of their authority, though they are permitted to rule for a period of time.

The Ancient of Days gives authority over the remaining kingdoms to "one like a son of man" (v. 13), who is permitted to approach the throne of the Ancient of Days without harm. Instead, he is given authority, glory, and sovereign power and receives the worship of all peoples, nations, and men of every language. His kingdom is not temporary or subject to God's judgment, but is an everlasting dominion.

B. Its interpretation (7:15–28). The visions of the beasts from the sea and the awe-inspiring vision of the glory of God and of his Messiah overwhelm Daniel. He is at a loss to explain what he has just seen. So he asks an angel for the interpretation. The four kingdoms symbolize the kingdoms of man, which are transitory; the everlasting kingdom belongs to "the saints of the Most High" (v. 18).

Daniel presses the angel concerning the disturbing vision of the fourth beast. Before the angel can explain, Daniel catches another aspect of the little horn. Not only does he speak boastfully, but he also opposes and persecutes the saints. It appears that he is victorious over them until the Ancient of Days intervenes on their behalf and judges the horn. Then the righteous receive their reward: the kingdom.

The angel explains that the fourth beast differs from the others by the intensity of its disregard of the laws of God and man. It "will devour the whole earth" (v. 23). The ten horns symbolize the succession of power. But the little horn will wrest power from three other kings/kingdoms and will have less regard for human rights and for the law of God than his predecessors. He will wage war with God and with his saints for "a time, times and half a time" (v. 25). Then he too will be judged as he has judged others. By the power of God his power will be taken away and completely destroyed. Instead, the saints will rule with "sovereignty, power and greatness" (v. 27). The kingdom of God and of his saints will last forever.

God will finally and victoriously crush the power of the fourth empire (Rome) and all the kingdoms which arise out of it, including the king who will "speak against the Most High" and who will persecute the saints (v. 25). This "king" may rule for a definite period (three-and-a-half times), but his authority, too, will be removed. Then the everlasting kingdom of the Messiah will be established. Who is this king? Interpretations differ, depending on how one interprets the ten kings ("horns"). He may be the Antichrist or the continuity and increase of evil in the end of days. Regardless of the identification of the little horn or of the length of his rule, the Messiah will cut him off suddenly and quickly.

Daniel is not relieved by what he has seen or by the interpretation given to him. He remains greatly disturbed and keeps the matter to himself.

VIII. Vision of the Kingdoms (8:1–27)

A. The vision (8:1–12). In the third year of Belshazzar (551/0 B.C.), Daniel sees himself in a vision in Susa, the Persian capital. There he observes a ram with two long horns standing by the Ulai Canal. The ram denotes the Medo-Persian kingdom, which rapidly gained control of the kingdoms of that time. The two horns symbolize the coalition of Media and Persia, the latter being the horn that "grew up later" (v. 3). The ram pushed westward, northward, and southward, gaining greater control and augmenting its absolute power.

However, the ram's power is suddenly broken by the he-goat (Alexander the Great). The goat with a prominent horn between his eyes comes from the west, moves rapidly as if not touching the ground, and charges into the two-horned ram. The two-horned ram is powerless and easily overcome by the goat. The sovereignty of this kingdom is ended when its large horn is broken off, and in its place four prominent horns grow up toward the four winds of heaven.

Upon Alexander's death—the breaking of the large horn—the world power was divided into four kingdoms ("four prominent horns," v. 8): Macedonia, Thrace, Egypt, and Syria. One of them began as a small kingdom ("another horn"), but exalted itself against God by turning against "the Beautiful Land" (Canaan; cf. Jer. 3:19).

This prophecy alludes to the invasion of the Seleucid (Syrian) king, Antiochus IV Epiphanes, into Judah when, due to the persecution and sacrilege in the temple for more than three years (1150 days), the evening and morning sacrifices ("the 2300 evenings and mornings") ceased (v. 14). Antiochus had no regard for God, acted as "the Prince of the Host," and required the Jews to worship the images of man. The defeat of Antiochus marked "the appointed time of the end" (v. 19), that is, the end of suffering brought by this king. God miraculously gave victory to the Maccabees. This victory is still celebrated by the Jews today at Hanukkah, the Feast of the Rededication of the Temple (December 25, 165 B.C.).

B. Its interpretation (8:15–27). An angel asks Gabriel to further explain to Daniel the meaning of this vision. At the mention of Gabriel's name, Daniel falls down in worship, as Ezekiel had done at the revelation of God's glory (Ezek. 1:28; 3:23). Daniel is addressed as "son of man." Gabriel explains that the vision pertains to "the time of the end" (v. 17). Daniel is clearly in a visionary trance ("I was in a deep sleep," v. 18). The angel raises him up to his feet to make certain that Daniel will remember the import of the moment.

He explains that the two-horned ram represents the kings of Media and Persia, that the shaggy goat signifies the king of Greece, and that the large horn is the first king (i.e., Alexander the Great). Further he explains that the four horns that supplanted the broken-off horn represent four kingdoms. From one of the kingdoms, namely the Seleucid kingdom, "a stern-faced king, a master of intrigue," will arise (v. 23). This king will be powerful in his ability to destroy and especially in his persecution of "the holy people" (v. 24). This is a description of Antiochus IV Epiphanes, who was a master of deception. He opposed the principalities, the spiritual forces protecting God's interests in the nations, and even the "Prince of princes" (v. 25). Yet his fate also lay in God's hands, as he came to a sudden end. Antiochus died at Tabae (Persia) in 163 B.C. The vision of "the evenings and mornings" is the vision of the end and is to be properly sealed up "for it concerns the distant future" (v. 26).

Daniel is so exhausted from this vision that he is sick for several days. He has to excuse himself from doing the king's business. He does not understand it, but preserves these words for later generations.

IX. Daniel's Prayer and Vision of the Seventy Weeks (9:1–27)

A. Daniel's prayer (9:1–19). In the first year of Persian rule (539/8 B.C.), Darius, son of Xerxes (Heb. Ahasuerus) and a Mede by descent, became the governor of Babylon (v. 1). Daniel is drawn to meditate on the prophecy of Jeremiah, who was one of the prophets predicting the era of restoration, consisting of covenant renewal, restoration of the people to the land, and the continuous service of the priesthood in the temple (chaps. 30–34). Jeremiah had also predicted that the Babylonian kingdom was to last seventy years (Jer. 25:11–12) and that subsequently Jerusalem would be restored. Daniel longs for the era of restoration, for the establishment of the kingdom of God and of the messianic kingdom. To this end he fasts and prays for the restoration of his people to the land.

Daniel's prayer consists of confession and petition. In the confession he identifies with the history of his people, with their sin and punishment. The prayer of confession consists of a repetition of four themes: Israel's rebellious attitude to the Law and the Prophets, Yahweh's righteousness in judgment, the fulfillment of the curses, and the hope in renewal of divine mercy and grace. Daniel begins with an affirmation of God's mercy, inherent in Israel's confession of who Yahweh is: "Lord, the great and awesome God, who keeps his covenant of love with all who love him and obey his commands" (v. 4). In contrast Israel has sinned against their covenant God: "We have been wicked and have rebelled; we have turned away from your commands and laws" (v. 5). They have rejected the prophets. Therefore the Lord is righteous in his judgment. Yet, the disgrace of Israel is apparent wherever they have been scattered. Their lot has changed by their own doing, but the Lord is still the same. Israel has received the curses of the covenant (Lev. 26:33; Deut. 28:63–67). The Lord has been faithful in judgment, even in bringing about the desolation of Jerusalem. Again Daniel affirms the righteousness of Yahweh.

Daniel throws himself on the mercy of God, as he prays for the restoration of Jerusalem, the temple, and God's presence among his people.

B. God's response (9:20–27). Daniel prays from the conviction that the Lord has decreed an end to the Babylonian rule. Now that this has taken place, Daniel prays for the speedy restoration of the people, the city, Jerusalem, and the temple. He has acknowledged the sin of Israel, but trusts the Lord to be faithful to his promises.

Suddenly, the angel Gabriel appears to him in a vision. He was sent to explain God's plan as soon as Daniel had begun to pray (v. 23)! This speedy response is an expression of God's special love for Daniel.

Building on the seventy-years motif, the angel reveals that the Lord has decreed "seventy 'sevens' " (v. 24). The purpose of the "seventy 'sevens' " is to finalize judgment on sin, to atone for sin and transgression, to bring in everlasting righteousness, to fulfill all the prophetic word, and to anoint the most holy (v. 24). The exact identification of the phrase is open to interpretation. If we take it to refer to seventy periods of time, the happenings may come to the foreground, rather than the speculations on the length of time. The first period of seven "sevens" pertains to the return of the people from exile and the rebuilding of the temple and Jerusalem (ca. 536–445 B.C.). This period begins with the issuing of the decree to restore and rebuild Jerusalem, but opinions differ on when this took place: 538 B.C. (Cyrus's decree to restore the temple in Jerusalem) or 445 B.C. (Nehemiah's permission to restore the walls of Jerusalem). There is little disagreement on the identification of "the Anointed One, the ruler," with our Lord Jesus. From the decree to the coming of our Lord the progression of redemption took place: the people returned to the land, homes and cities were rebuilt, temple worship was restored, and above all the people enjoyed God's favor and covenant renewal.

A longer period of sixty-two "sevens" brings us to the crucifixion of the Messiah. The last "seven" will witness the confirmation (renewal) of the covenant by the Messiah and the desecration of the temple. Gabriel promises that "he will confirm a covenant with many for one 'seven' " (v. 27), but our problem is the identity of the "he." Some hold that the Messiah is the subject of the sentence, but others see here a reference to Titus and the Antichrist. Indeed, Titus brought an end to sacrifices and offerings and set up pagan symbols in the temple court. This is the "abomination that causes desolation" (v. 27). On the other hand, the confirmation of covenant could be a reference to the Anointed, whereas the abomination of desolation is an allusion to Titus. These events are associated with the Romans, who destroyed the city and the sanctuary. This marks the beginning of the end. It appears that the vision refers to the restoration of God's covenant in the postexilic community, the renewal of the covenant by the Messiah, and the destruction of the temple in A.D. 70. According to another view, the last "seven" pertains to the Jewish people and marks the period of great tribulation before the millennial kingdom.

It appears that the Book of Daniel, like Revelation, has in view the eternal and complete establishment of God's kingdom, the glory of the saints, and the complete subjugation of the nations of this world. The prophecy could be explained by emphasizing the numbers, but it appears that the purpose of the revelation is encouragement and comfort in the removal of sin(ners) and the completion of redemption.

X. Message of Encouragement (10:1–11:45)

A. Introduction (10:1–3). In the third year of Cyrus (536 B.C.) Daniel is standing by the bank of the Tigris, when suddenly he receives the revelation of a long period of suffering and persecution. He is so struck by the vision that he fasts and mourns for three weeks!

B. The angel (10:4–11:1). The vision comes shortly after the celebration of Passover and the Feast of Unleavened Bread. Daniel is so moved that the people around him are terrified by his appearance; they instantly flee, leaving Daniel alone.

Daniel is addressed by someone whom he describes in great detail (10:5–6). The angel has been trying to communicate with him for three weeks, but has not been able to until Michael, one of the archangels, overcomes the spiritual power (a demon) over the Persian kingdom. The angelic visitor proclaims God's peace to Daniel and encourages him with a message pertaining to the end of Persia and the beginning of the rule of Greece. The kingdom of God is not established by flesh and blood, but by spiritual powers.

Daniel's reaction to the vision is so overwhelming that the angel has to touch him three times to wake him up. His face turns pale, he feels helpless, he is speechless, he is filled with anxiety, and he is ready to die. Even when down on his hands and knees, Daniel is trembling and remains affected by the vision. The angel encourages him with the assurance that the Lord esteems his servant, wants him to know what he has planned, and strengthens him physically and spiritually. The very resistance he endured is an indication of the spiritual warfare between the powers of darkness and the kingdom of God. Since angelic beings war against powers who are not flesh and blood, how much more must the people of God suffer from the resistance of demonic powers! Though God's people may be the object of attacks, Michael will continue to protect them. The revelation comes from "the Book of Truth" (v. 21), the record of God's plan for the progression of the redemption of his people. The angel together with Michael were sent to work out the restoration of the people of God from the moment Cyrus became king over Babylon and Darius was installed as governor (11:1).

C. The vision (11:2–45). The detailed description of the interrelationship between the kings of the south and the kings of the north in Daniel

11 has long challenged biblical scholars. The angel reveals to Daniel that three more kings—Cambyses, Smerdis, and Darius Hystaspis—would rule over Persia. The fourth—Xerxes I—would try to incorporate Greece into the Persian Empire. Upon the death of Alexander the Great of Greece ("a mighty king," v. 3), his kingdom was divided into four parts: Macedonia, Thrace, Syria ("the king of the North" or the Seleucids), and Egypt ("the king of the South" or the Ptolemies). Verses 5–20 relate the rivalry and wars between the Ptolemies and Seleucids until the appearance of Antiochus Epiphanes.

The Seleucid Antiochus IV (nicknamed Ephiphanes, or "madman") is the "contemptible person" of verse 21. In his attempt to gain absolute control over Egypt, he was ruthless in his campaigns and encouraged his troops to loot and plunder. His mission against the Ptolemies also failed.

Finally, he aimed his anger at Jerusalem, the temple, and the Jewish people (vv. 30–35). He desecrated the altar in the temple, set up an image to Zeus (168 B.C.), and required the Jews to worship the gods of the Greeks. The Lord raised up "a little help" (v. 34; Judas Maccabeus). The godly Mattathias led the Jews to resist the order to sacrifice to the gods. His son Judas Maccabeus led the insurrection and succeeded by the grace of God in cleansing the temple. The rededication of the altar took place in December 165. This event forms the background of the Hanukkah ("dedication") celebration.

The power represented by Antiochus typifies the spirit of all kings who exalt themselves, doing whatever they please. The description of that king not only applies to Antiochus; it could also apply to the Antichrist, the Beast, or to the continuing opposition of evil. The difficulty lies in the nature of prophetic and apocalyptic language, which mixes historical details with a grand picture of opposition of the kingdoms of this world and the final, climactic victory of God's kingdom. This problem ("compenetration") is not unique to Daniel, but characteristic of prophetic language as a whole. The apocalyptic features add to the complexity of interpretation. In spite of the disagreements in interpretation, the outcome is sure: "he will come to his end" (v. 45). The conflicts between the kingdom of God and of this world will continue, but in the end the Lord will establish his glorious kingdom.

XI. Troubles and Victory (12:1–13)

The victory will not come without persecution and perseverance. These words encourage the godly in any age to await the kingdom of God. The saints are promised life everlasting and joy, whereas the ungodly will experience everlasting disgrace. All who die will be raised to life, but not all who are raised in the body will enjoy lives of everlasting bliss—only those whose names are recorded in the book of life. The godly respond to God and will be accounted to be wise; their wisdom is like a tree of life, as they will lead others to life, wisdom, and righteous living. Their future will be glorious, as they will share in the victory of the Lord.

During the affliction of the saints for three-and-a-half "times," Michael will protect them (v. 1). When it seems as if their strength will collapse, the kingdom will be established.

In the meantime, the visions are to be closed, so that the wise might read them and gain understanding. Revelation of the future is for encouragement and the development of hope, faith, and love, rather than for speculation. The godly will always find comfort in the revelation of God. Since the coming of our Lord, the Christian community has gained greater insights. The revelation of the Father in Jesus and the revelation of Jesus in the Apocalypse hold before us the assurance that Jesus will be victorious throughout the history of his church till his triumph over Babylon the Great and the defeat of Satan. He is the First and the Last (Rev. 1:17), who has revealed to his churches the things that will take place.

Daniel receives further assurance that these visions are true and will come to pass. He sees two witnesses on opposite banks of the river. In between the two is the angelic messenger, "the man clothed in linen," who is above the river. He swears by Yahweh's name that the fulfillment will take place "for a time, times and half a time" (v. 7; cf. 7:25). Concerned about what he has heard, Daniel asks about the outcome. He does not receive much of an answer, but the angelic messenger does assure him that through the process of perseverance the Lord will always have a faithful remnant. This remnant will endure the process during which they "will be purified, made spotless and refined" (v. 10). The wicked, however, will persevere in their evil. They will never come to understand their folly, but will be cast out of the kingdom.

The calculation of the end is enigmatic. The Lord reveals to Daniel visions of the progression of redemption until the final and victorious establishment of his kingdom. These words are to encourage godliness in the face of evil. Though the oppression and persecution may be longer (1335 days) than the seven years of Antiochus Epiphanes (1290 days), blessed is everyone who perseveres to the end.

SELECT BIBLIOGRAPHY

Aalders, G. C. *Daniel.* Korte Verklaring. Kampen: Kok, 1965.

Archer, G. L. "Daniel." In *The Expositor's Bible Commentary,* edited by Frank E. Gaebelein, 12 vols. Grand Rapids: Zondervan, 1985.

Baldwin, J. *Daniel: An Introduction and Commentary.* Downers Grove: Inter-Varsity, 1978.

Childs, B. S. *Introduction to the Old Testament as Scripture.* Philadelphia: Fortress, 1979.

Eaton, E. W. *The Book of Daniel: Introduction and Commentary.* London: SCM, 1964.

Ford, D. *Daniel.* Nashville: Southern Publishing House, 1978.

Porteous, N. W. *Daniel: A Commentary.* Philadelphia: Westminster, 1965.

Pusey, E. B. *Daniel the Prophet.* New York: Funk & Wagnalls, 1885.

Veldkamp, H. *Dreams and Dictators: On the Book of Daniel.* St. Catharines: Paideia, 1978.

Wallace, R. S. *The Lord Is King: The Message of Daniel.* Downers Grove: Inter-Varsity, 1979.

Young, E. J. *The Prophecy of Daniel.* Grand Rapids: Eerdmans, 1949.

HOSEA

G. Herbert Livingston

INTRODUCTION

The prophet Hosea lived somewhere in the north-central part of Israel during the reign of Jeroboam II of the northern kingdom and during the reigns of Uzziah, Jotham, Ahaz, and Hezekiah of the kingdom of Judah. Nothing is known of his date of birth or date of death. His father's name was Beeri. His wife's name was Gomer, and they had three children. His prophetic ministry can be roughly dated between 755 and 725 B.C. He probably lived in a small village, but near enough to a center of culture to be educated and well aware of what was going on in the kingdom.

Hosea was a skilled writer who composed chapters 1 and 3 in pain-filled prose and the remaining chapters in vigorous poetry. The prophet was a sensitive man capable of expressing deeply felt emotions in vivid phrases.

The first three chapters are family-related, with God as a dominant participant in the woes that wrenched Hosea and Gomer apart and then brought them together again. The Lord explained that what was happening in Hosea's family was a replica of the shattered relationship that existed between himself and Israel.

As a prophet, Hosea's function was to summon Israel to the bar of justice before the Lord and to prosecute them for their spiritual, moral, and political sins. Thus the main part of the book is a trilogy of lawsuits (4:1–19; 5:1–12:1; 12:2–14:9). Each lawsuit begins with an announcement in which the key words are "charge" and "judgment."

Hosea, under the guidance of his Lord, couches his messages on the covenant made at Mount Sinai in the context of a new metaphor, that of the marriage relationship. Never before had the spiritual dimensions of covenant and marriage been placed in such a parallel. Later prophets, Jesus, and the apostles were to turn to the marriage metaphor as an effective way to teach God's way to his people.

The Lord said that he was the husband of Israel as Hosea was the husband of Gomer, and the Israelites of the exodus had spiritual and moral shortcomings comparable to Gomer's moral flaws.

As time passed, the Israelites and their descendants repeatedly became entrapped by the sex worship of the Canaanites, just as Gomer was enticed into harlotry by her pagan neighbors. Generation after generation, many Israelites had felt alienation, shame, and embarrassment because of their rebellion. Surely as keenly, the children of Hosea and Gomer had suffered as deeply as their mother plunged into immorality. Hosea knew that the Lord experienced anger, frustration, and revulsion as his people turned their backs on him, emotions so much like his own as he watched his wife's unfaithfulness.

Hosea also knew that more fundamental than negative responses was the love of God, a love that would not let his people go. So Hosea, too, loved Gomer and paid a heavy price to bring her back into the family.

Hosea learned that in the pain of shattered relationships, whether covenant or marriage, there was a doubly sharp dilemma. In the hostile environment engendered by the apostasy of Israel, the Lord faced a difficult choice. Would he destroy his people as other peoples on the basis of strict justice? Or would he ignore the vagrancies of the Israelites, treating them as harmless activities because he loved them so much? He would forfeit his goal to expose the falsity of nature deities, the delusions of idolatry, the deceptions of divination and magic, the moral filth of sex worship. He would abandon his plan to redeem mankind from sin and form all people into holy and happy worshipers of the one true God.

In that same hostile environment, especially as it affected Gomer and their marriage, Hosea faced a similar dilemma. Would he take the accepted legal route of publicly divorcing Gomer, forcing her to survive as best she could among men who exploited and abused her? He would lose the only woman he ever loved, the mother of his children. Or would he ignore her involvement with other men, her adventures in the orgies of the pagan festivals, refusing to reprimand her because he loved her so much? He would forfeit trust and respect for his wife, the private intimacy of married lovers, a mother for his children, honor and status among neighbors who worshiped the Lord in spirit and in truth.

What choice would the Lord make? He chose to commission Hosea to be his spokesperson, giving the people of northern Israel one final opportunity to forsake their sin and return to the bonds of the covenant. He would warn them of the consequences of their refusal to come back to him. He would allow Assyria to destroy their nation and to take many into exile. However, he would not wholly abandon his people; he would preserve a remnant and begin forming a covenant community again. He would redeem them, bring them back to the land, and continue his plan to provide redemption for all the peoples of the world.

What choice would Hosea make? He chose to claim Gomer as his beloved wife, given to him by the Lord, the mother of three lonely and suffering children. Poor as he was, he took grain desperately needed for food and his tiny hoard of silver and bought back his wife from whomever had enslaved her. He redeemed her from a life of shame and accepted the task of loving her back into the family. He took charge of restoring her to purity and pledged his commitment to be at her side always.

The story of the Lord, Hosea, and Gomer is not a fantasy. The dynamics of this relationship took place as an aspect—a crucial aspect—of the larger historical scene.

For nearly two hundred years, Israel had been divided into two nations. During the reign of Solomon's son Rehoboam, ten tribes of Israel rebelled and became a rival political and religious power to the house of David which ruled from Jerusalem. But this new nation was confronted with the hostilities of Syria. The stress of this power struggle kept Hosea's homeland in constant turmoil. Leaders ruled with a heavy hand and often died violent deaths. To blunt the spiritual appeal of worshiping at Jerusalem, these northern kings compromised with polytheism.

During the early years of Hosea's life, Jeroboam II was the king of the northern kingdom and Uzziah (Azariah) was king of Judah. Both nations enjoyed peace and prosperity for forty years. Jeroboam II died in 753 and political turmoil immediately swept northern Israel. The religious situation was also at a low ebb, and moral standards were ignored.

To the northeast, a greedy and cruel empire, led by Tiglath-pileser III, was moving to the west and threatened to invade Palestine. The warnings and pronouncements of judgment in the Book of Hosea are based on this day of doom just waiting to happen. Hosea does not specifically refer to the fall of Samaria (722) as the event that ended the existence of the northern kingdom of Israel; hence, many scholars surmise that he died before it occurred.

The Canaanite religion came in like a flood under the sponsorship of Jezebel. The chief gods were Baal the storm god, and Asherah (Astarte) the earth goddess, the most popular of many nature deities. The worship of these two deities was believed by their devotees to ensure good crops and numerous calves and lambs. Their worshipers used magic, divination, and sex worship at shrines and festivals to insure reproductive blessings. Child sacrifices were also offered by these people in times of crisis.

It was this kind of religion that had captured the devotion of many Israelites. The Lord and Hosea condemned this religion and called their backslidden people back to the covenant faith. For the Israelites to continue following the ways of the Canaanites could only end in disaster.

OUTLINE

I. Hosea's Family/God's Family (1:1–3:5)
   - A. Superscription (1:1)
   - B. Unquestioning Submission (1:2–3)
   - C. Names with Special Meanings (1:4–11)
   - D. Children of Adultery (2:1–8)
   - E. A Decision to Punish (2:9–13)

F. A Decision to Restore (2:14–23)
G. The Cost of True Love (3:1–5)

II. The First Arraignment (4:1–19)
   A. Charges Brought Against Israel (4:1–5a)
   B. God's Response to Israel's Sins (4:5b–6)
   C. Charges Brought Against the Priests (4:7–9a)
   D. Sentence Passed on the Priests (4:9b–14)
   E. Appeal to Judah (4:15)
   F. Israel's Spiritual Condition (4:16–19)

III. The Second Arraignment (5:1–12:1)
   A. Israel Is Morally Corrupt (5:1–7:16)
   B. Israel Has Forgotten Her Maker (8:1–14)
   C. Israel Worships Idols (9:1–17)
   D. Israel Has Degenerated (10:1–15)
   E. Oh How I Love Israel (11:1–12:1)

IV. The Third Arraignment (12:2–13:16)
   A. An Impressive Heritage (12:2–14)
   B. Consequences of Deceitfulness (13:1–16)

V. The Possibility of Restoration (14:1–9)
   A. An Evangelistic Appeal (14:1–3)
   B. What the Lord Will Do for Israel (14:4–5a)
   C. Israel Will Be Much Different (14:5b–7)
   D. God Will Care for His People (14:8)
   E. The Difference Between Two Ways (14:9)

COMMENTARY

I. Hosea's Family/God's Family (1:1–3:5)

A. Superscription (1:1). This verse indicates the authoritative nature of Hosea's message: it is the word of the Lord. This word was not given "to whom it may concern," but was directed to a specific person; it came to Hosea. The word came during a defined span of Israel's history. Though Hosea served as God's messenger in the northern kingdom, the full scope of his service is placed during the reigns of Uzziah, Jotham, Ahaz, and Hezekiah, kings of Judah. Only Jeroboam is listed for northern Israel.

B. Unquestioning submission (1:2–3). Was Hosea praying when the Lord first spoke to him? Was he shocked when he realized that the Lord was commanding him to do a most unusual thing? We do not know, for clues are missing. The fact that the Lord told Hosea to marry an adulterous wife has shocked many readers. How could a holy God possibly tell one of his prophets to marry an immoral woman? The Lord commanded the priests not to marry such women; surely, the same should hold true of prophets.

Some have suggested that the story of this marriage is a parable and thus never really happened. Yet, the record is presented as an actual account of Hosea's life. Some would accept the account as fact but then maintain that God has provided a confusing example; elsewhere in Scripture we are told that man and woman should be one and faithful to each other in marriage (Gen. 2:24; Mark 10:5–9).

These views ignore the special role that the Lord assigned Hosea's marriage. Hosea was not called to model an ideal marriage in Israel; his unhappy marriage was to present to Israel a human parallel to the nation's shattered covenant relationship with God. The nation's spiritual behavior was so serious that the Lord regarded it as the vilest adultery. Hosea was a true prophet because he obeyed the Lord immediately by marrying Gomer and becoming the father of her first child.

C. Names with special meanings (1:4–11). It was a customary practice among the Hebrews to give their children names bearing special meanings. A name could express affirmation of faith in God, parental hope concerning a child, or a trait of a baby. In Hosea's family each name is given by the Lord to bear a divine message.

The first boy's name, Jezreel, literally means "God sows" but has geographical and historical significance as well. There was a royal city by this name at the western tip of Mount Gilboa and also a valley that lay to the west. Its soil has always been highly productive. Jehu, an army general, attacked the royal city soon after the death of Ahab and killed Jezebel with her pagan prophets. Jehu became king and continued to brutally destroy anyone he did not like. The boy's name symbolizes God's punishment for this horrible sin and that it will happen at the same place.

The name of the next child, a daughter, is Lo-Ruhamah. Her name signifies that the Lord is removing his mercy and love from Israel. From that time on the Lord will love and save Judah from her enemies, but not by earthly means.

The second son's name, Lo-Ammi, means "not my people" and declares to Israel that her relationship as the Lord's people has come to an end. No longer will they participate in the covenant made at Mount Sinai, except for the mercy of God. Yet in spite of Israel's sin, that mercy is still available and the possibility for a renewal of the relationship exists. As terrible as the day of Jezreel would be, the people of the two kingdoms could be reunited and ruled by one leader.

D. Children of adultery (2:1–8). In chapter 1, the Lord speaks four times to Hosea, but in chapter 2 the audience is different. One's first impression may be that Hosea is speaking to one of his sons, but the plural forms *brothers* and *sisters* suggest more than two sons and a daughter. And there are the phrases *your mother, my wife,* and *her husband,* along with the repeated use of the first-person pronoun and third-person feminine pronouns. Later in the chapter (vv. 13, 21) the speaker is clearly identified as the Lord. Throughout this chapter Hosea's family and the Lord's family are so closely paired that only the two identifying phrases tell the reader that Hosea's family is a mirror image of the Lord's covenant family.

Broken marriage and covenant relationships leave behind broken hearts. Such is the case with both Hosea and the Lord; grief lies behind almost every sentence uttered.

Probably one should think of Hosea as the one addressed in this section. Alternation of the themes of acceptance and rejection is further emphasized by the appeal that Israel reject adultery and unfaithfulness. Failure to do so will result in divine punishment, vividly expressed as being stripped bare, banished to a desert, dying of thirst, and denied divine love. The basis for such severity is Israel's adultery, which in the Book of Hosea is both moral sin and a synonym for idolatry and sex worship.

In shifting between rejecting and claiming Israel as his own, the Lord confronts Israel with a basic spiritual dilemma. She can still respond to the Lord's invitation to return to him, but she will have to reject idolatry and immorality. Not to do so will lead to disaster. The other horn of the dilemma is this: if Israel stubbornly continues her worship of idols and flatly rejects the love and mercies of the Lord, she will be divorced from the covenant bonds and exposed to a life of shame, emptiness, and finally death. The remainder of the book is devoted to making Israel aware that this choice is a viable one and that she need not be destroyed.

Whether it be Gomer or the women of Israel, all are corrupted by unfaithfulness to spouses. Whether it be Gomer's children or Israelite children, all are corrupted by the popular sex worship. They are denied the bonding love of the family circle, the model of purity essential to moral development, the respect of those who know the degrading nature of Baalism. The children are children of adultery, and their mother is deluded, thinking that having many lovers is the best way to obtain food and clothing. But the aftermath of adultery is suffering, disappointment, confusion, and a pitiable desire to return home. The wayward wife has misjudged the source of her wealth. The Israelites have not acknowledged that the basis of life is in the Lord. All that he has given has been squandered on the delusions of Baalism.

E. A decision to punish (2:9–13). The "therefore" and the repeated phrase *I will* are good clues that this section is a pronouncement of judgment on Israel. The Lord will deprive Israel of food and clothing, implying a famine, and thus make the nation incapable of caring for its people, morally bankrupt, and dispossessed of worship opportunities. The land will no longer be productive. Captivated by the enticements of Baalism, Gomer and Israel have worshiped the false god Baal, wasting their wealth. They think they are great lovers, but they have forgotten the true God.

F. A decision to restore (2:14–23). Following the pattern of interweaving judgment and promise, the Lord stresses the benefits of faithfully following his ways. He is going to allure Israel as in the exodus. She will be taken into the desert where the Lord will speak tenderly, provide vineyards, transform trouble (Achor) into a door of hope, and make them into a singing people.

The Lord will also change the way they talk. The word *Baal* (which means "my master") will be an unacceptable word; rather, the marriage word *husband* will take its place. As in the garden of Eden where Adam lived in peace with all animals, a renewal of covenant will include the beasts. It will also abolish violence, creating safety. The important feature of this covenant will be the introduction of marriage as a way to understand what covenant should mean. The Lord will betroth Israel as his eternal bride.

Well-known covenant words will designate the character of this covenant: (1) *righteousness;* (2) *justice,* which points to the Lord as the one who makes correct decisions and thus rules the relationship; (3) *love,* which is based on a Hebrew word that means the bonding of partners in loyalty and commitment; (4) *compassion,* which is a deeply felt caring for one another whatever the cost; (5) *faithfulness,* which provides a sense of firmness, of stability in the relationship; and (6) an acknowledgment of the Lord, a pledge of allegiance, which excludes any kind of relationship to pagan gods and goddesses.

In verses 21 and 22, one must work backward from the word *Jezreel,* which here is the Valley of Jezreel. Its ground will, by implication, cry out for seed, the earth will supply crops, and the skies will provide rain; but, behind it all will be the decision of God to activate the skies, the earth, and the seed into fruitfulness. In an imaginary and poetic way, Hosea declares that the valley of sin and destruction is to be the valley of joy and harvest.

The theme of sowing continues in verse 23 in an interpersonal context. Israel will be planted anew in the land where they have sinned, and the "love" that has been removed will be poured out toward them. The covenant relationship which had been broken, cutting Israel off from the status of being people of God will be mended and they will be his people again. The Israelites who had shamed themselves by worshiping Baal, will worship the Lord alone and covenant vows will bond them together.

G. The cost of true love (3:1–5). Hosea provides no clue as to when, where, or how the Lord made contact with him; he simply states that the Lord spoke to him directly. The first-person pronouns indicate that this chapter is a personal testimony. This word of the Lord is as surprising as the first (1:2). Purely on the basis of love, Hosea is to reach out to Gomer who by this time is involved with another man. She is now an adulteress which Mosaic law regarded as grounds for divorce (Deut. 24:1–4); but Hosea is to love Gomer as the Lord loves the Israelites. The people have become involved in the sex worship associated with other gods, thus spurning the Lord's love for them.

If Hosea has doubts or arguments with the Lord, they are not mentioned in the text. The important point is that he obeys and buys Gomer from someone who, seemingly, has enslaved her. He pays in silver and barley. At that time no one was making silver into coins so it was weighed out at about six ounces per shekel. Apparently, fifteen units (ca. 5.6 lbs.) is all Hosea has, so he draws from his supply of precious grain. The homer was a little over six bushels and the lethek was about three bushels.

Hosea places Gomer under strict discipline. Her activities are now to be restricted. She is to cut off all contacts with her lovers; in return Hosea will give her tender, loving care.

Verses 4–5 appear to be a message to Hosea's neighbors stressing that what has happened in his family is parallel to what will happen to God's family. Israel will be placed under the restrictions of exile. She will be separated from the control of idol-loving leaders, from polluted worship.

Nevertheless, Israel will have a future, for the Lord will care for his people. They will respond by returning, a word that often designates conversion from one faith to another—in this case, from idolatry to the Lord of the covenant.

The phrase *David their king* implies that the northern kingdom, led by kings who are not descendants of David, will cease to exist and that all Israelites will be ruled by someone from the house of David. Perhaps there is a messianic overtone here that points to Jesus Christ.

The word *trembling* (v. 5) suggests uncertainty. Because the people have sinned terribly against God, they cannot claim a right to be reinstated in the covenant relationship. They cannot demand that the Lord pour upon them his many blessings. They will be wholly dependent on his mercy.

II. The First Arraignment (4:1–19)

A. Charges brought against Israel (4:1–5a). The chapter begins by assuming that the Israelites are standing as the accused before the divine bar of justice. Hosea calls the court to order. The divine Judge, though invisible, is understood as present. The reason for the court session is given: the Lord has a charge to bring against his people in northern Israel. The King James Version translates the Hebrew word here as "controversy," which could be understood as a quarrel. To prevent this misunderstanding, recent translations have the legal term *charge.*

Immediately, the charge is brought forward; it is an accusation of spiritual and moral misconduct. The spiritual sins are unfaithfulness, lovelessness, and ignorance of God. In biblical Hebrew, "faithfulness" and "truth" are closely related words, for both denote firmness and dependability. In personal relationships, the opposite is fickleness and unreliability. This is true of Israel's spiritual condition. Likewise, love and mercy can be closely related, for either word can translate the Hebrew covenant word that denotes loyalty and exclusive devotion. The Israelites lack this quality of character. The fact that they do not acknowledge God is not simply because of ignorance; rather, they deliberately reject the Lord as ruler of persons and nation. The Israelites have violated the first two commandments.

The people's moral sins violate the third, ninth, sixth, eighth, and seventh commandments, which are regarded as bounds, that is, limits that cannot be crossed without sinning against God and other people. To break these limits is to engage in bloody violence.

The consequences of the people's sins are fatal. The land dries up and ceases to produce adequate harvests so that the people starve and animals die.

The Judge begins to speak directly to the people, warning them not to bring lawsuits against each other and comparing them to people who quarrel with priests. All are equally guilty, even prophets; they cannot walk (live) correctly but stumble along together.

B. God's response to Israel's sins (4:5b–6). The Judge begins to sentence the people; their mother, the nation, will be destroyed. But the pronouncement is not completed. The Judge pauses to give the reason: they are guilty of lack of knowledge. In the Old Testament, "knowledge" is a broad term encompassing facts, experience, skills, insight, and understanding. The Book of Hosea stresses moral sensitivity and an intimate, personal relationship with God. The people are not stupid; they are morally and spiritually dead, because they have rejected God and ignored his law. Having given a basis for his pronouncement, the Judge declares that he rejects the priests and their children.

C. Charges brought against the priests (4:7–9a). The Judge returns to supporting his decree. The priests are sinners because they have switched their allegiance to that which is disgraceful (idolatry). They should have served the true God. Serving idols led the priests to exploit their people and join with them in wickedness, again a reference to idolatry. Instead of providing a means of atonement for sins and instructing the people in the laws of holiness, the priests became one with the people in sin.

D. Sentence passed on the priests (4:9b–14). The sentence of judgment is expanded. The people are included but the emphasis is on the priests. Their appetites will be unlimited and their immorality will produce sterility. Why? They have left the Lord for prostitution and drunkenness which destroy understanding. They seek instruction from sticks thought to be gods. They are captured by the spirit of prostitution and are breaking all ties with the Lord and his covenant. They conduct their worship services at pagan shrines on hills and mountains with the result that their daughters and daughters-in-law become morally polluted. Yet, the Judge will not punish them; he will place the blame on the men who model immorality by their actions.

E. Appeal to Judah (4:15). The Lord desires that Judah keep free of the sins of Israel. He thus warns Judah to stay away from the favorite shrines: Gilgal and Beth-Aven (meaning "house of wickedness" and serving as a substitute name for Bethel, which means "house of God"). Both shrines were across the border just north of Jerusalem; there worshipers honored Baal while using the words of vows associated with worshiping the Lord.

F. Israel's spiritual condition (4:16–19). The Judge now concentrates on listing the sins of the people of Israel under the name of their dominant tribe, Ephraim. Vivid figures of speech are used. They are like stubborn heifers in contrast to gentle lambs which respond readily to their shepherd. The divine pronouncement comes to a climax with a resounding "Ephraim is joined to idols; leave him alone!" (v. 17).

The sentence is stated vividly. The people will be removed by a whirlwind and sacred sacrifices will not provide atonement, but will cover them with shame.

III. The Second Arraignment (5:1–12:1)

A. Israel is morally corrupt (5:1–7:16). The court opens with a summons to the priests, the Israelites, and the royal house to hear the judgment leveled against them (**5:1–7**). Immediately a short listing of charges is proclaimed. The accused are depicted as a snare and a net which entrapped the Lord's people at Mizpah and at Tabor. Both places had become centers of Baal worship and all its evils. These worshipers are called rebels who are guilty of killing people. The Judge declares he will place these sinners under discipline.

The Lord has a right to judge Ephraim because of his knowledge of Ephraim's sins; nothing is hidden from him. Note that Ephraim and Israel are synonymous throughout this arraignment. The leaders and common people are involved in immorality and corruption, which have robbed them of the ability to come back to God. Lust has chained will and emotion so completely that they will not acknowledge God as their master. They are arrogant yet they and Judah stumble as those too sick to walk. Sin has done this to them.

The people suppose they are taking their flocks and herds to offer sacrifices to the Lord; but they are actually going to the wrong worship centers. The Lord refuses to meet with his people at places where idols are located. Their unfaithfulness is a refusal to worship and live according to the covenant. Involvement with sex worship has produced children by women other than their wives. These children are illegitimate both physically and spiritually. The immoral activities at pagan festivals have lethal consequences; the seeds of death (perhaps venereal diseases) make the people so ill that they are unable to till their fields.

The action moves from criticism and judgment to a declaration of imminent punishment (**5:8–15**). The ancient places—Gibeah, Ramah, and Bethel—where God had been properly worshiped and now where Baal is worshiped, are to face the day of reckoning. Judah will be included as an object of divine wrath. Ephraim is being trampled but continues to go after idols. The Lord vividly depicts his judicial role as a moth and as rot (v. 12). To the natural consequences of sin will be added his own acts of punishment.

God's retribution will awaken the two Israelite nations to their desperate situation; but, instead of turning to the Lord, they turn to the king of Assyria for help. They fail to see that Assyria is their deadly enemy and not a friend.

At the moment the Lord seems to be their enemy, for like a great lion (v. 14) he is tearing the nation apart and carrying them off where no one can rescue them.

From wrath the Lord turns to a silent, pain-filled time of waiting. His eyes are still upon Israel and his heart is yearning for evidences that his people will admit their guilt and earnestly seek him. The Lord is using the misery of chastisement to make Israel aware of sin and to stir in them the desire to turn from idols to him.

Possibly the people are talking to each other in **6:1–3,** but it is more likely that Hosea is urging his neighbors to make an about-face and to return to the Lord. They will recognize that the Lord is not vicious, but filled with love. The people can have confidence that the Lord will heal their wounds. Returning to the Lord will not be wasted time; it will issue in new life.

Hosea does not have in mind the resurrection of Jesus when he utters the phrase *the third day he will restore us* (v. 2). The device of stating consecutive numbers (2 . . . 3) is fairly common in the Old Testament. In Amos 1:2–2:6 this numerical sequence seems to designate many sins, whereas in Hosea it seems to denote a quick occurrence. The new life the Lord will give will be in his presence. The withdrawal mentioned in 5:15 will be ended and the Lord will be united with his people again.

The word *admit* (v. 15) refers to a repentance that accepts the sovereignty of the Lord in all aspects of life, whether personal or national, not for a moment but as a steady intention of will and mind. God's people can depend on him as surely as they depend on the daily rising of the sun. They can expect his provision of gracious blessings that are here compared to the winter and spring rains.

Though the Lord has disciplined Israel and Judah, his love for them is depicted as a turmoil of emotion (**6:4–7:2**). Before, behind, and beyond wrath is love. He still wants to redeem them but his people's love is as vaporous as morning mist and dew.

That was the reason the Lord had so severely criticized them through his prophets and his words. That was why his judgments were as destructive as lightning. His people had been worshiping in a totally unacceptable way. Historically, sacrifices could be offered to the Lord, but not to idols. More importantly, even when offering sacrifices, the worshiper was required to possess mercy and submit to the exclusive rulership of the Lord over all of life.

The term *Adam* (v. 7) is ambiguous. Does it refer to the sin committed in the garden of Eden? Does it refer to an unknown site in Israel? Or does "Adam" designate all of mankind? Either way, the covenant has been broken and unfaithfulness to the Lord has created hostility between him and his people.

In the Old Testament, the term *Gilead* (v. 8) often refers to an area on the east side of the Jordan River between the Jabbok River on the south and the Yarmuk River on the north. Its chief city was Ramoth-gilead and we may have a shortened form of this city's name here. The city was allocated to the Levites by Joshua and was also designated as a city of refuge; hence, many priests lived there. These priests have become so heartless in their abuse of the common people that they are likened to marauders. The road to Shechem wound down the highlands and across the Jordan River, then on to the city of Shechem which was another city of refuge. At these sacred cities, the immorality of the Canaanites is being practiced, defiling Israel. And Judah is not exempt from the Lord's chastisement.

The last part of verse 11 is really a portion of the sentence which continues to the end of 7:3. This clause centers on the pain of the Lord who, seeking to restore his people, is frustrated by their persistence in sinning.

Moral and spiritual healing for Ephraim is thwarted by the sins that God brings to light. Exposure issues in covenant charges of wrongdoing. Sinners engage in abuse and exploitation without being aware that the Lord of the covenant is observing what is going on. They are engulfed in their sinning, and the Lord, with a heartache, is preparing to prosecute them.

The Lord begins the task of drawing up a list of charges against Israel (**7:3–11**). The people's allegiance is focused on the king and princes. The head of state has displaced the Lord as the ultimate authority in life. The government officials are being flattered and entertained with wicked activities and dishonesty.

The people imagine themselves as clever and skillful lovers, but in fact they are being consumed by an inner fire, their lust. So intense are their emotions that a hot oven best symbolizes their inner condition (v. 4). Usually, a baker had to stoke the fire several times while preparing dough for baking. Not so with the emotions of the Israelites! There is enough lust to keep them going in their sin.

A typical festival is taken as an example. The king and princes become drunk and join with the masses in their orgies that continue unrestrained through the night. The figure of an oven is repeated to make vivid their passionate debauchery. There is little concern that such behavior plunges their honored rulers to the depths of shame. No one prays to the one true God.

The Lord turns his focus upon the foreign policies of Israel. The nation freely consorts with polytheistic governments, offering no criticism of their immorality. Their impact on Israel softens their moral sensitivities. This condition is compared to the flat disk of dough which a baker places on the hot outer surface of the oven. If the dough is not turned over, one side is overbaked while the other side is half-baked.

Ephraim (Israel) supposes she is a clever diplomat, not realizing the larger, pagan nations are draining her dry. She thinks she is youthful and vigorous, but others see Ephraim as aging and impotent. She is arrogant, thinking herself strong and wise, but in fact Ephraim (Israel) has cut herself off from the source of true strength and refuses to admit she is wrong. She does not turn to God for authentic wisdom and power. In this regard, Ephraim is compared to a deceived and senseless dove making overtures to mighty but evil Egypt to the southwest and to Assyria to the northeast.

The simile of Israel being like a dove continues the movement of the prosecution as it shifts from indictment to a pronouncement of sentence which is characterized by the phrase *I will* (**7:12–16**). Again the sobbing of a hurting God punctuates the judicial words. God will throw out nets and capture his people as though they are birds—not to pet them but to destroy them. And while doing that he will be longing to redeem them. This is the Lord's dilemma. Not to net and punish his people for their sins would violate his own just and holy nature. To destroy his people would violate his unbounded love and at the same time wipe out his center of confrontation with polytheism. In his redemptive program, how can he destroy the people he has chosen as witnesses and examples of redemption?

Nevertheless, the Lord's people deliberately violate the covenant. They try to convince the Lord they are good people but they are speaking lies. They are given to wailing upon their beds, but they do not earnestly pray to the Lord for help. Their times of feasting are not in honor of God but of pagan gods and goddesses.

The Lord continues mixing substantiation of his sentence with a restatement of it. The people place no value on divine training and support, nor do they truly worship the Most High. They plot evil and speak insolent words against him. The faulty bow image (v. 16) indicates inability to send an arrow to its target. One concept of sin in the Hebrew language is missing the mark—being unable to line up with the will of God. The people's submission to Baalism and its immorality were factors in creating this inability. They are being held accountable and punished by being ridiculed in the land of Egypt. They will become the subject of international jokes and wisecracks.

B. Israel has forgotten her Maker (8:1–14). The Lord issues an international summons as though to servants who, collectively, are depicted as an eagle. The Assyrians are evidently meant by this metaphor, for this bird was one of their favorite symbols. This nation, centered on the upper Tigris River, was led by aggressive rulers who pushed their armies west and were poised north of the Israelites ready to swoop south. The eagle hovers over the house of Israel because of the rebellion and lawlessness of the covenant people (**8:1–6**). They are confused in their theology, worshiping Canaanite deities with the understanding this is identical with the worship of the Lord of Israel. They think they are honoring God by praying to him, though they have rejected all that is "good." In Hebrew this word has a wide range of positive meanings including top quality, beneficial, pleasant, beautiful, happy, precious, and correct. In this context, the emphasis seems to be on the latter two meanings, set within a moral and religious framework. What the Lord values most in human beings is spurned by these people. They will not believe it but they are being pursued by a deadly foe.

In Jerusalem, there was a succession of kings who descended from David. In the northern kingdom, there was a total of nineteen kings (by the end of Hosea's ministry), grouped in nine dynasties, all of which ended violently. The people seemed to support all that happened, though God was deeply grieved by the persistent idolatry that marked this two-hundred-year period.

In anguish, the Lord pleads with the Israelites to rid themselves of their false and impure gods. These idols have not been forced on the Lord's people; rather, their own craftsmen have fashioned them and set them up. The people have no excuse. Many times idols had been denounced as false. The true God is going to smash these idols, especially the calf of Samaria (v. 6). The children of Israel had been enthralled by calf worship during the exodus (Exod. 32) with bitter results. From the beginning of the northern kingdom, calf idols had been present in the shrines of Dan and Bethel (1 Kings 12:25–30). Never had this kind of worship been acceptable to the Lord. He now gives the decree: "It will be broken in pieces" (v. 6).

The divine decree then focuses on the nation which has been sowing the wind, a picturesque way of describing idolatry as unstable and having no substance (**8:7–10**). The harvest will be the whirlwind which will leave in its wake no heads on the stalks, hence, no flour for food. Even if grain survives, it will be swallowed by foreigners. Israel is the grain being swallowed up. Her worthless king is the head on the stalk; Assyria is the foreigner. Israel has become a worthless thing (v. 8). Astoundingly, Israel chases after Assyria like a lonely, wild donkey. Seeking satisfaction, Israel stupidly sells herself to other nations. The result is a divine gathering, a reference to exile, where they will suffer the devastating oppression of the Assyrian emperor.

The people of Ephraim are very religious (**8:11–14**). They build altars and offer many sin offerings. However, the way prescribed in the law of the Lord is not simply ignored, but is regarded as non-Israelite (alien). The name of the Lord is used while offering sacrifices; but the people are doing so in a way that displeases the Lord. This kind of worship is wickedness and the Lord sees it as a covenant violation.

The punishment for unacceptable worship practices will be a repeat of Israel's oppression in Egypt. Israel has forgotten God whereas the Lord remembers their sins. Strong fortresses and sumptuous palaces have been built, but they will not survive the fire of destruction.

C. Israel worships idols (9:1–17). Hosea's message begins with a warning (**9:1–4**). Israel has no basis for joyous celebrations or times of fun, though other nations may blindly pursue their carefree ways. The Lord has serious matters to settle with Israel. These people are his by covenant but they have been unfaithful to the God of the covenant by committing immoral acts with loose women, even on the threshing floors. The latter were areas of bare limestone where bundles of grain were piled and then processed in a primitive way to retrieve the seed.

The places of harvest, including the winepresses, will become silent as the crops become less and less productive. The magical rites of Baalism, whether in sex worship or sacrifice, were supposed to insure abundant harvests. However, the true Lord of the harvest will withhold crops so that food and drink will become scarce. The people will be separated from the land and exiled in Egypt and Assyria. They will be forced to eat food that is ceremonially unclean, and will be unable to offer sacrifices acceptable to the Lord. This food will become like the bread of mourners, who are unclean and cut off from worship in the temple of the Lord until the period of mourning is completed (see Num. 19:11–14). They can eat this bread but they cannot present it as an offering to the Lord.

The national calamity soon to happen will create a difficult situation for the Israelites (**9:5–9**). They might carry on their religious charade, in which verbal formulas and worship rituals are observed, but in fact they are worshiping Baal. In exile, they will have no temple, priesthood, or worship regulations available. How will they even pretend to honor the Lord, if these customs are missing?

Those who survive the holocaust will still experience abuse from neighboring nations. Perhaps Hosea uses Egypt (v. 6) as a symbol of exile, harkening back to the sojourn in Egypt prior to the exodus, whereas the immediate location of exile will be in Assyria. Exile will be disastrous, for the Israelites will lose their wealth and their productive homeland will be covered with thorns. This event will happen soon and Israel should face up to this reality.

The Israelites are apparently unable to do so because their understanding and emotions are so warped by their sins that the prophets are regarded as fools and maniacs. The people are largely unprepared for the catastrophe.

Hosea is frustrated by the obstinate attitude of his neighbors and is deeply hurt by their twisted perception of who is a true prophet. He is chaffing under the scorn of those who hear him speak. Yet he knows that the one who commissioned him to serve as messenger, God himself, is also the object of ridicule. Hosea is a watchman among God's people. The task of a watchman was to station himself atop a high wall or a hill and constantly scan the horizon for possible enemies or natural dangers and sound an alarm should such dangers be identified. Hosea, with other true prophets, has been doing his duty. He has identified the dangers and sounded the alarm. He is emotionally shaken by the response; his own people set snares for him and express deep hostility toward him, even in the place of worship.

These religious neighbors have become perverted by idolatry to the same extent as the people of Gibeah, who abused and killed the concubine of the Levite (Judg. 19). Those criminals had suffered the consequences of their act and God will hold the Israelites of Hosea's day accountable as well.

God, the divine Judge, interjects his further opinion of the present condition of his people (**9:10–13**). The Lord reminisces about ancient times when he found Israel in Egypt. Rarely does one find grapes in the desert, and just as rarely does the Lord select a people to be his servants through whom he would both challenge polytheism and create a God-fearing society. The Lord expected fruitage from these people. Such prompt results would be as welcome as the first ripe figs. But what a disappointment! As soon as the wandering Israelites came in contact with the Canaanites worshiping at Baal of Peor (Num. 25), they were captivated by the sensual orgies of the festival and were seduced by immoral activities and idol worship. The text is really quite strong; they consecrated themselves, that is, they deliberately separated themselves from the moral restraints of the law of God and converted to this idol-worshiping religion. The result was moral defilement and surrender to lust.

The Judge pronounces the sentence again. The tribe of Ephraim, as well as the other northern tribes, had participated in the exodus, in the conquest, and in the rise of Israel as a great power under David and Solomon. All glory associated with those achievements will fly away and the population will shrink. Even those children who may be born will experience sorrow and death. The ultimate judgment will be the Lord's separation from them. They had been as beautiful as Tyre, but not any more. Death awaits them.

Hosea cannot contain himself; he is as angry against his people as is the Lord, and the reader can almost hear the sobs of his short prayer (**9:14–17**). Hosea's words concur with the Lord's sentence. The Israelites must indeed be rendered sterile so childbearing is impossible.

The Lord then continues his decree that is based on past events as well as present conditions. Gilgal was the place near Bethel where the Israelites had persistently demanded a king as their leader (see 1 Sam. 8:5–22; 11:14; 12:12–24). The Lord now states that he hates them for making such a demand. He had allowed them to go ahead but strongly disapproved and is now holding them accountable for that event and its aftermath in northern Israel. The punishment is forcible removal from the Promised Land and the loss of God's love. The rebellious policies of their leaders is the cause of all the divine stripping of power and population from Ephraim. There is no way the northern nation can continue without God's presence and love being active in her midst.

Hosea affirms the Lord's decree with a tearful acknowledgment that disobedience requires that they be wanderers among the nations.

D. Israel has degenerated (10:1–15). The prophet glances at Israel's past and sees Israel as a fruitful vine busy building and decorating stone altars. He does not see a people of excellent character. Quite in contrast, they are deceitful to the core and responsible for that condition (**10:1–5**). The altars are not to aid in their worship of the Lord; they have other gods and goddesses in mind. The Lord is responding by destroying these altars.

There is a note of distress in the people's attempt to pray. The destruction they experience is blamed on an inept king whom they do not respect. In a halfhearted way, they admit they have not properly honored the Lord, but are more concerned with politics. They wanted a leader they could own as a king, but they really did not think he could solve their national problems. The prayer shows how mixed up they are spiritually.

The inner confusion of the people is evident in their words and actions. They relate to each other by making promises that they do not intend to keep, by uttering oaths (the legal kind) that they will only ignore, by making agreements and then filing lawsuits. Their interpersonal relationships are like a weed patch incapable of providing food, and in fact, succeeds only in choking out the food plants. Fellowship is an unknown reality; conflict characterizes their world.

Samaria was the capital of the northern kingdom and Beth-Aven (Bethel) was a government-supported shrine just north of the border with Judah. This shrine went back to the days of the rebellion when Jeroboam set up one shrine at Dan and another at Bethel. Both had golden calves which served as the gods of the rebellious ten tribes. The purpose of the shrines was to keep the Israelites in the north from worshiping at Jerusalem (1 Kings 12:25–33). The Bethel shrine—so important to the northern Israelites—would be demolished, causing grief for the people and their priests.

Hosea predicts that for the first time his people will know shame (**10:6–8**). The removal of the prized idol to Assyria will shatter their faith in its power to protect them. They are proud of it but its humiliation to the level of a tax payment will make their religion look foolish. The arrogant king will be taken into exile from his costly palace in Samaria and will be as helpless as a twig in a river (v. 7).

Other shrines scattered throughout the country will be torn apart and their treasures taken away. The sex worship practiced in them will be exposed as wickedness, and the gardens about them will be replaced by thistles that will even cover their altars whose fires will flare up no more. Utter despair will be mixed with shame, but their choke-filled prayers will not be to the Lord. They will plead that the mountains and hills on which they worshiped Baal might cover them.

The Lord supports the message of Hosea by restating the penalty of sin (**10:9–12**). Israel's long history of immoral activity since the incident at Gibeah (Judg. 19) will produce the same result: war. It has not occurred yet, but it will soon, for the Lord has made his judicial decision to punish. It remains only for him to decide on the moment to activate that punishment. What is ahead for Israel is exile and the reason for it is Ephraim's double sin. This expression seems to be a play on meanings, for the name *Ephraim* means doubly fruitful (Gen. 41:52).

The exile is referred to as bonds and then associated with the metaphor of Ephraim as a trained heifer subjected to a yoke (v. 11). The monotonous labor of threshing and plowing will severely limit freedom.

Plowing suggests sowing, but this time it will be used in an appeal to the wicked Israelites to begin an entirely new life-style. They may yet scatter the seeds of righteousness, which is God-directed conduct; in place of exile they may enjoy a harvest of unfailing love. This phrase appears to be a reference to the Lord's unlimited love for them. There is a basic requirement: they must rip up and discard their idolatrous fallow ground, their unproductive Baalism, and engage their whole being in seeking the Lord. The prospect is that when he responds to his repentant people, showers of blessing will fall upon them.

The divine cry of appeal changes abruptly to a cry of disappointment, for Israel has no interest in detaching herself from Baalism (**10:13–15**). The farmer metaphor is continued; Israel has sown the seeds of wickedness instead of righteousness. The reapers will gather evil and the food prepared from it will be deception. All this is being done in Israel's own strength, with their hope based on their many warriors. The strength available in the Lord is completely ignored.

The evil reaped at the harvest will be the roar of battle and the destruction of strong fortresses. It may be that Shalman (v. 15) is a shortened form of Shalmanezer, which was the name of five emperors of Assyria. The last one destroyed the nation of Israel in 722 B.C. but a battle at Beth-arbel is not mentioned elsewhere.

The final assault on Bethel will match the memorable massacre in cruelty, due to the wickedness of the city. The final blow will be the death of the last king of Israel whose name, Hoshea, is similar to the prophet's name (v. 15).

E. Oh how I love Israel (11:1–12:1). As is evident before in this book, the Lord's thoughts tend to return to the exodus when he considers his relationship with Israel (**11:1–4**). The Lord refers to this early period as the childhood of the nation and a time when he could express his love for his people. Through his servant Moses, the Lord was able to deliver Israel from Egypt and bring them as a free people to Mount Sinai. The metaphor used in this context is the father-son relationship. In the beginning sections of this book, the metaphor was the husband–wife relationship.

A jolt of pain disturbs this pleasant memory as the incidents of the golden calf (Exod. 32) and Baal of Peor (Num. 25) interject themselves. Israel had a strong stubborn streak and was easily seduced by the lewd activities of Baal worshipers.

Why could not the Israelites understand that the Lord was the one who had brought them into freedom? The stress on walking may refer to the journey from Egypt and through the desert, but it may also refer to the giving of the Ten Commandments and regulations at Mount Sinai. This is the way the Lord wanted them to walk (i.e., live morally and spiritually). However, the Lord's people were still too immature to distinguish between the will of the one true God and the practices of the Canaanites. During the wanderings, they felt the pangs of hunger and thirst and discounted God's miracles as ineffective.

The Lord tries to clarify his attitude toward Israel during that difficult journey. He had been with them as their leader and pictures himself bound to them with cords of human kindness and ties of love. His miracles are depicted as lifting a yoke as from oxen and feeding them with care (v. 4).

There is a touch of anger in the question voiced in **11:5–7.** Israel's obstinacy is still present in Hosea's day with the result that they could end up in exile and be dominated by the cruel Assyrians—all because they are too proud and self-centered to repent.

They may not be willing to face their dilemma, but its destructive horns are nearby to gore them. True, if they repented and renewed their covenant with the Lord, they would have to give up, painfully, their treasured idols and exciting sexual exploits in Baalism. They could see that horn and were repelled by it. Nevertheless, the other horn is present. If they refuse to repent, the consequences of their sins and the wrath of God will destroy them. They have blinded themselves to that reality, the reality of invasion by an army that will reduce cities, gates, and plans to ashes.

The decision of the angry God is based on the determination of his people to turn from him to idols. Due to their devotion to sin, the people's future salvation will be taken from them. Prayer, however earnest, will be of no avail. God will not listen and respond to them. They are doomed.

The Lord's decision to refuse salvation to Israel does not mean he ceases to be a loving, caring God (**11:8–11**). He is still the God of love and the judicial act of sentencing his people to destruction tears him deeply within. The four questions of verse 8 are punctuated with sobs. Admah and Zaboiim were wicked pagan cities, destroyed along with Sodom (Gen. 19). They had never had a covenant relationship with the Lord; but Israel had long been in such a relationship and therefore was special in the affections of the Lord. The turmoil this creates in God is graphically stated at the end of this verse.

Verses 10 and 11 suggest that the strong statements of verse 9 should be modified by the adverb *completely.* In his pain the Lord will continue working with Israel. The coming devastation of the nation and all its institutions will take place, but not all the people will die. In contrast to the men in battle who slaughtered the vanquished without restraint, the holy God of love will limit his wrath. He will roar like a lion and his surviving remnant will hear and with uncertainty and fear come trembling from exile like timid birds. The Promised Land will become the site of their homes again. The official will of the Almighty is clear.

Pathetically, the Israelites are totally unconcerned that their God is suffering so greatly over their coming demise as a nation. Their apathy is evident in their lies, the use of traditional worship forms and rituals. They do not intend to worship the true and Holy One, but to worship false idols. And Judah is just as bad.

The deception practiced by Israel is depicted as feeding on wind. The idols are not what the pagans claim them to be. Nevertheless, the Lord's people believe they are real and freely join in treaties and trade with nations that promote idolatry.

IV. The Third Arraignment (12:2–13:16)

This lawsuit has many of the same features as the other two. There are the list of sins committed, the references to the past, the attitude of defiance in Israel, the pronouncement of judgment. An obvious feature of this court scene is a more extended presentation of what the Lord wants to do for his surviving people, once the nation is in shambles.

A. An impressive heritage (12:2–14). Primarily this section of the lawsuit draws upon the history of the Lord's dealings with both Judah and Israel, beginning with Jacob. The charge the Lord is presenting centers on the way the existing descendants of Jacob differ from their ancestor.

Jacob had committed sins and deserved punishment but had found his way back to God. The incidents mentioned occurred at Peniel (Gen. 32:22–31) and at Bethel (Gen. 35:1–14). The point being made is that the sinner is forgiven; for God talked with Jacob there. The people of God in Hosea's day should do the same, living lives that uphold love in the inner being and justice in conduct. They should also truly worship the Lord.

In contrast to what they ought to do, Hosea's neighbors are buying and selling dishonestly, and loving every minute of it. Wealth is all-important. The basis of their boasting is that they are beyond the reach of the Law. They do not deny they are criminals; rather, they boast that they cannot get caught in sin.

Again the Lord's memory leaps back to the exodus and draws from the opening statement of the Ten Commandments that identifies him as their Deliverer (Exod. 20:2a). He then alludes to the wilderness wanderings when his people lived in tents and celebrated festivals as nomads. His memory selects another important aspect of his relationship with Israel. He had commissioned prophets as his spokespersons and revealed messages to them through visions and parables. How are the people responding to these great benefits? In Gilead, the land east of of the Jordan River, the people are not only wicked, they are worthless. What about their worship practices at Gilgal near Bethel? The altars on which the sacrifices are made will be strewn on the plowed field.

What did Jacob do when he sinned against Isaac and Esau? He fled to Aram many miles to the north in order to find safety among relatives and determined to secure a good future by working hard for a wife. The Lord reached out to help sinning Israel by sending a prophet (Moses) to deliver them from Egypt and care for them during the wanderings.

Ephraim is not as smart as the Israelites in Egypt and Jacob in Aram. They had sought help and a new future, but Ephraim is spurning offers of help. Her divine helper will become the Judge who will punish her for her sins.

B. Consequences of deceitfulness (13:1–16). The tribe of Ephraim had been a powerful influence for good in the early history of Israel (**13:1–3**). The members of this tribe were descendants of Joseph's youngest son and Jacob's favorite grandson, the one to whom he gave a special blessing (Gen. 48:20). Joshua, the assistant of Moses and later his successor, came from this tribe. He was successful in leading Israel into Canaan and dividing the land among them. Israel's first religious center was at Shiloh in the territory of Ephraim, and Samuel grew up within its borders. This was the span of time during which Ephraim was exalted.

The turning point happened when one of their number, Jeroboam, led a rebellion of ten tribes against Solomon's son Rehoboam. Jeroboam and his tribe led the others in forming a new nation; and, in an effort to sever all religious ties to the temple at Jerusalem, a shrine with an image of a calf was set up at Bethel. The supporters of Baalism took advantage of this cleavage; and, especially under the promotion of Ahab's wife, Jezebel, Ephraim was thoroughly corrupted by Baalism. This situation marks Ephraim's death (v. 1).

Ephraim's spiritual death is because of idolatry. The people expend their resources and the skills of craftsmen. The Hebrew text does not actually say that the sacrifices offered included human beings, although it is known that worshipers of Baal did sacrifice humans. The people are urged to do the absurd, to kiss the calf-idols as an expression of total submission.

The aftermath of spiritual death will be national death and this is described with vivid figures of speech. The nation, under the impact of Assyrian invasion, will be like morning mist, early dew, swirling chaff, and escaping smoke. Israel thinks she is powerful, but the Lord and his prophet know she is utterly helpless.

Again, the opening statement of the Ten Commandments is repeated (**13:4–6**). The identity of the God who delivers must be made clear to Israel. This God is the one Israel must recognize as the only God; no other god or goddess touted by any group or nation really exists. Only God is the Savior; he is the God of the Mount Sinai covenant and the wilderness wanderings. He cared for Israel by providing food and water as they traveled through the land of burning heat.

In spite of God's love and care, the newly delivered people bit the hand that fed them. Having plenty to eat did not engender a spirit of thanksgiving; it fostered pride. Full stomachs did not urge the people to worship the Lord; instead, they forgot him.

The Judge's gavel comes smashing down and his voice pronounces the judicial sentence (**13:7–13**). The Judge will pounce upon them like the lion, leopard, and bear. He will be as fierce as a mother bear robbed of her cubs. He will mangle his people terribly and devour them.

Why would he do such a horrible thing? He will do this because they have become his implacable enemies, following leaders who strut under banners of pride and imagined power. The kingdom that had been set up was a form of punishment, an expression of anger, and so will be the removal of the kingship. The Lord has kept a record in his memory of the misdeeds of Israel's kings and a day of reckoning is at hand.

The description of the judgment is set in the context of a woman's crisis at childbirth. The unborn child does not act as it ought and there is no birth. The implication is that death comes to both mother and child.

There is next a contrasting word of mercy (**13:14a**). God has anger against sin and will finally demolish it; but, more profoundly, he has mercy for people who turn from sin. At the very edge of the grave, the Lord will provide a ransom, offering freedom to anyone at his own great personal cost. The Lord will make possible liberation from death because he is the people's closest kin, their Father.

He is the Almighty who is stronger than death and the grave. As the victor, he can stand at the very brink of hell and demand proof that disease and epidemics are invincible. This divine cry of defiance is echoed in the writings of Paul. After an exposition of what the resurrection of Jesus Christ means as a redemptive act, he declares that the hope for eternal life is based on this momentous event and insures that believers, too, will be resurrected. He then brings this exposition to a climax by quoting Hosea 13:14 (1 Cor. 15:55).

The Lord knows full well that the Israelites will not accept the proffered redemption; but, the point has to be made that it is available. No doubt with reluctance, the Lord returns to his pronouncement of sentence (**13:13b–16**). For the hardened rebels, he has no compassion. This reality is in itself the ultimate judgment, for now anger will operate unhindered.

The coming invasion by Assyria is depicted as the well-known east wind. Periodically during the summer, the prevailing wind would shift to the east and sweep upon Palestine with intense heat. Such times were marked by misery and danger, especially because preservation of water and food was limited. Water supplies, like springs and brooks, will dry up as will sources of food in fields and gardens. The limited amount of food people place in storage will soon be consumed.

The basis of the judgment is clearly stated for the last time. The people of Samaria (v. 16) probably should be understood not merely as those living in and around the capital city, but all those ruled by the royal court located there. All the people in all the ten tribes of the kingdom are rebels against God and must suffer the consequences. These consequences will be horrible, for the brutal Assyrians know how to use the sword without restraint. Their procedure is not simply to defeat soldiers on the field of battle; they do this and far more. They unmercifully massacre women and children and leave ashes and ruins behind them. The sentence is proclaimed for the last time and the reality of utter destruction soon happens.

V. The Possibility of Restoration (14:1–9)

A. An evangelistic appeal (14:1–3). Hosea is not a critic in this passage; rather, he is a caring pastor urging that his suffering people pray to God for help. In the evangelistic appeals of the prophet, the word *return* is usually the first word uttered. The word means to turn around and go in the opposite direction. The people are walking the wrong way, yet they know how the Lord feels about their sin and what he will do about it. They still have a choice. They can stop, turn around, and come back to God. To do so, they will have to admit that their sins are causing their downfall. The Hebrew word for "sins" in this instance designates more than acts of sin. The word also suggests the warped, twisted condition of the inner self.

As they approach the Lord, they have to select the correct words, words that match their repentant attitude. They have to pray for forgiveness and plead for grace. They have to commit themselves to worship only the true God. What they say during worship—prayer, praise, affirmations of faith, testimonies—must be offerings.

The supplicants must renounce national dependence on idol-worshiping nations such as Assyria; they must renounce their dependence on war-horses, even to the extent of never mounting them again. The ultimate renunciation must be pagan deities and man-made images. Why must they make this radical renunciation? It is because even the most helpless persons in society, the orphans, find their help in God.

B. What the Lord will do for Israel (14:4–5a). The Lord responds with an announcement of salvation. He will change his people by healing them. This divine act will take care of the sins committed and the condition of sin within. Waywardness is a sin and marks a severance of spiritual relationship with the Lord. The Lord's work of grace is more than a Band-Aid or injection of an antibiotic. When he heals his people, his cure reaches to the core of the soul and restores spiritual health. The source and the agent of this healing is divine love which has no limits and is given freely. God's anger is not a permanent aspect of his relationship with those in spiritual need; it is quickly set aside when his people come humbly, earnestly repent, and plead for mercy.

Divine love is depicted as dew (v. 5). The emphasis here is not on its quick disappearance when the sun shines on it; rather, the stress is on its ability to give life-sustaining moisture during the rainless season of the year. Flowers like the lily respond to this moisture with beautiful blossoms. So will the Lord's people when they open themselves to his love and let it flood through their beings.

C. Israel will be much different (14:5b–7). The Lord's thoughts move to the beautiful land to the north of Palestine—Lebanon—to provide another metaphor for the life-giving qualities of his mercies. His people will be like the majestic cedar which has a strong root system. He then points to the verdant olive tree. It has its own splendor which matches the fragrance of the cedar. What a change for the people of God, the rebels who have been fighting their own Lord.

Everyday life will be different. There will be protective shade when things become too hot. Growth will be rapid like well-cared-for grain and Israel will bear fruit as abundantly as the vine covered with blossoms. The Lord's people will be the best and have the best when they dwell obediently in his presence.

D. God will care for his people (14:8). One may understand this verse in two ways. It may be understood as a statement uttered by Ephraim as a representative of all Israel. The question would evoke the answer *none,* and mean that all are renouncing any ties with idols. Most English translations follow this interpretation. The New International Version understands that the Lord is speaking (see also RSV) and it is quite possible to render the Hebrew this way.

Understanding the Lord as the speaker, one would interpret the question to infer that the Lord is not going to tolerate idolatry in Israel any more; the day of doom has come. Ephraim must sever all relationships with idols, or else.

Up until that event, the Lord's ear is listening for a prayer and his care is still available. Divine love is symbolized by the evergreen, the pine tree, which is sometimes called the cypress in Palestine. It is a durable tree, for no insect or disease will attack it. Thus the tree is a suitable token to represent the adequacy of God's love for Israel.

E. The difference between two ways (14:9). Pairs of similar words are used skillfully to summarize the essence of the covenant way and the idolatrous ways of faith and practice. In the two questions, "wise" and "discerning" are paired and "realize" with "understanding" in the affirmations. The four words combine to stress the point that the person committed to the covenant will have the capacity to look at the facts of nature and the demands of social, moral, and spiritual life and understand them. The covenant person will be blessed with the ability to weigh the several ways one may act and to make the right choice.

Such abilities are not natural to human beings; rather, they are gifts of God that come with his revelation of the rightness of his ways. The righteous person, the one who does things correctly, can only possess these abilities as he walks in the Lord's way obediently and faithfully. This is the thrust of the Book of Hosea.

Unfortunately, the Lord and his prophet had to spend most of their time making clear the truth of the last line. The rebellious cannot realize wisdom, nor discern or understand truth. The adversarial stance they take against the Lord dooms them to stumble into the destruction that devours them.

SELECT BIBLIOGRAPHY

Hubbard, D. A. *With Bands of Love: A Study of Hosea.* Grand Rapids: Eerdmans, 1967.

Logsdon, S. F. *Hosea: People Who Forgot God.* Chicago: Moody, 1959.

Robinson, H. W. *The Cross of Hosea.* Philadelphia: Westminster, 1949.

Ward, J. M. *Hosea: A Theological Commentary.* New York: Harper & Row, 1966.

Wolff, H. W. *Hosea.* Philadelphia: Fortress, 1973.

JOEL

Raymond B. Dillard

INTRODUCTION

The brief note in 1:1 that Joel was the son of Pethuel is all that is known about either father or son. Though some twelve other individuals in the Old Testament have the name *Joel*, the prophet cannot with confidence be identified with any of these persons known from other texts. Since the book concerns Judah and Jerusalem, and particularly temple worship, it is safe to infer that he was a Judean, probably a resident of Jerusalem. The author's concern with temple offerings and worship (1:9, 13–14; 2:1, 15–17, 32; 3:17–21) has led many to infer that he was a "cult prophet," that is, a prophet who was a member of the temple personnel, though not a priest. However, this concern on the part of the prophet by itself is insufficient to establish that he was connected with the temple staff.

In the history of interpretation some scholars have argued that the book is not the product of a single author, but that it grew in stages. An original prophecy or narrative from the preexilic period concerning a locust plague (1:2–2:27) was supplemented in the postexilic period by the eschatological and apocalyptic sections (2:28–3:21) concerning the day of the Lord. However, the pendulum of scholarship has in general swung away from multiple authorship and toward appreciating the unity of the composition in both style and subject matter.

The superscription to the book (1:1) does not provide any indication of date. In the absence of an explicit date a decision on this question can be reached only by evaluating other criteria such as historical allusions in the book, inferences about the social setting, the date of the language, the date of the theological concepts, and any evidence of dependence on other biblical books. While in theory these criteria should lead to an approximate date, in actual application establishing a reasonably certain date for the book has proved elusive. In the history of research individual scholars have proposed dates ranging from the late ninth century to the second century B.C., all claiming support from internal evidence.

It is clear that the book was written at a time when the temple was in operation on a regular basis (1:9, 13; 2:14, 17); this would eliminate the exilic period when the temple was destroyed as a date for the composition of Joel. Some have argued that since the entire community could be summoned to assemble at the temple (2:16), the book must have been set in the context of the small population early in the restoration period; however, comparison with Jeremiah 26 and 36 shows that such summons did not in fact realistically expect the attendance of every individual, so that some allowance must be made for hyperbole.

Some have also argued from the reference to the city wall (2:9) that Joel must have been written some time after the reconstruction of the wall under Nehemiah. However, this argument presumes either that the entire wall was destroyed before Nehemiah's time or that locusts would take the path of least resistance and enter the city only through breeches in the wall. Neither assumption is valid. The city walls were not destroyed completely (Nehemiah's work of reconstruction was completed in only fifty-two days [Neh. 6:15]); observation of locust behavior confirms that these insects readily climb obstacles rather than skirt them.

It is clear that a locust plague had recently taken place in the environs of Judah and Jerusalem (chap. 1), but there is no way to date this event. There must have been many locust outbreaks in Israel's history.

The enemies of Israel mentioned in the book include the Phoenicians, Philistines, Egypt, and Edom (3:4, 19). These were all occasional foes of Israel in the preexilic period; their relations with Judah in the postexilic period, however, are not well attested in the Bible itself. This list could, therefore, be viewed as favoring a comparatively early date. However, the Philistines, Greeks, Phoenicians, and Egyptians are all mentioned in the oracles of Zechariah (9:1–8, 13; 14:17–19) early in the postexilic period.

What is equally striking is the absence of references to the Assyrians or Babylonians, empires that dominated so much of Israel's history. Either the book was quite early (prior to a serious Assyrian threat) or comparatively late (after the Babylonians were no longer a factor). The Phoenicians could have been involved in slave trade with the Greeks (3:6) from the eighth century B.C. on (cf. Ezek. 27:13; Amos 1:9–10). The Sabeans (3:8) dominated the trade routes to the south in the late sixth and early fifth centuries before losing hegemony in the region to the Mineans. This factor may favor an early postexilic date for Joel, but is still not conclusive; the Sabeans need not have dominated these trade routes to be mentioned in connection with the slave trade.

Depending on how the Hebrew is translated, 3:1–2 may refer to the Babylonian captivity, so that Joel would then necessarily be postexilic.

It is striking that the Book of Joel shows no awareness of the northern kingdom. It is concerned exclusively with events in Judah and Jerusalem, and even calls Judah by the name *Israel* (2:27; 3:16), a practice more common after the exile when the northern kingdom had ceased to exist and Judah became the sole spiritual successor of the united Israel.

It is also striking that only the priests and elders are mentioned as leaders of the nation (1:2, 9, 13, 14; 2:16, 17). There are no references to a king, princes, or other officers, or to the Davidic succession. Though not conclusive, this would most naturally favor a postexilic date for the book. Those who favor a date in the late ninth century argue that the absence of reference to a king and the other trappings of the monarchy can be explained by the period when young Joash did not actually rule himself (2 Kings 11:21; 2 Chron. 24:1–3); this was also a period of conflict with Egypt, Edom, and the Philistines, all enemies mentioned in the book.

Though the evidence is somewhat ambiguous and can be interpreted in a variety of ways, on balance the data favors a date in the postexilic period, probably sometime in the fifth century B.C.

The fact that the Book of Joel is so difficult to date may be in keeping with another important characteristic of the book. Several of its features suggest that it represents (at least in part) a liturgy for a national lament, a service of prayer and confession seeking the mercy of God in the face of some threat. Some psalms appear to have been composed for a similar use, and a few narratives also provide examples of the practice. In times of natural or military disaster or threat, the people were often summoned to a fast at a sanctuary where they would present their complaint to God in prayer and remind him of his past mercies. If the Book of Joel was intended to serve as part of the temple liturgy, the difficulty in dating the book is more easily understood. Repeated liturgical use would call for a general composition that could be used on many different occasions, whether natural or military disaster threatened. Specific historical references would only narrow the range of events to which the text could be applied or for which it could be used in a liturgical way.

Perhaps the major issue in the interpretation of Joel pertains to the relationship between 1:2–20 and 2:1–11. Both are descriptions of a locust plague: the first concentrates on the plague's effect on the inhabitants of Judah; the second is couched in military terms and portrays an invading locust army. A number of possible interpretations have been offered:

1. Both are descriptions of the same historical event, an actual locust plague viewed from two different perspectives. The devastation caused by the locusts was of such magnitude as to be likened to the day of the Lord—it threatened the very survival of Judah.

2. After an outbreak of locusts in one year (1:2–20), the prophet anticipates a second and even worse outbreak for the following year, an outbreak so devastating as to warrant comparison with the day of the Lord (2:1–11).

3. The first section describes an actual locust invasion that had occurred only shortly before; the prophet then uses the devastation caused by these locusts to portray the danger posed by an enemy who

is ready to invade Judah. A foreign army, likened to locusts (2:1–11), is poised on the borders of the land; the Lord will punish his people once again through an alien conqueror. In effect, the prophet's message is: "The locusts were bad, but worse is coming."

4. The first section describes the devastation of a recent locust outbreak. The prophet uses this as a warning of the impending day of the Lord, the day of judgment when the Lord himself will come at the head of his army in holy war against evil. The second section is also an extended metaphor comparing an army with locusts, but the threat does not come from some particular historical enemy of Israel, but rather from the Lord's own army.

Although the fourth option is the most plausible, it is also possible that the text is deliberately, consciously ambiguous at this point. However one relates 1:2–20 and 2:1–11, the prophet goes on to offer hope for the repentant people of God in the face of the impending disaster.

OUTLINE

- I. The Locust Plague (1:2–20)
  - A. Effect and Extent of the Disaster (1:2–12)
  - B. Summons to Fasting and Prayer (1:13–14)
  - C. Complaint and Prayer (1:15–20)
- II. The Day of the Lord (2:1–17)
  - A. Cry of Alarm, Warning of Attack (2:1–2)
  - B. The Divine Army (2:3–11)
  - C. Offer of Repentance (2:12–14)
  - D. Summons to Fasting and Prayer (2:15–17)
- III. The Lord's Answer (2:18–3:21)
  - A. To the Immediate Disaster (2:18–27)
  - B. To the Impending Disaster (2:28–3:21)

COMMENTARY

I. The Locust Plague (1:2–20)

A. Effect and extent of the disaster (1:2–12). The uniqueness, magnitude, and severity of the locust invasion are described by invoking the attention of different social groups within Israel and describing the impact of the plague on their lives.

The first group called to pay attention is the most general: the people who live in the land and their leaders, the elders (1:2). The description of the damage inflicted by the locusts is also in very general terms. The observation that nothing like this has ever happened (1:2) recalls the description of the locust plague at the time of the exodus (10:6, 14; cf. Deut. 4:32–35; Lam. 1:12).

The Hebrew Old Testament uses twelve different terms for locusts and grasshoppers; four of these occur in 1:4 and 2:25. Both ancient and modern translators of the Old Testament have struggled over how to represent this diversity of terms in languages that have fewer words for this insect. Some translators and exegetes identify these terms as varying species of locusts or other insects. However, the best understanding of the four terms in this context is that they apply to successive stages in the growth of the immature insect.

The destruction of vineyards, fig trees, and fields of grain will have a literally sobering impact on those given to drink. The locust invasion means that there will be no beer or wine from this year's crop; the impact of the defoliation of vines will probably also cause a reduced harvest the following year. If disaster commonly promotes the tendency to tipple, there will be no alcohol available. Drunkenness is the only specific sin mentioned in the Book of Joel. Those whose stupor rendered them ordinarily oblivious to events around them will now forcibly be brought to their senses.

Here locusts are compared to an army; the reverse is usually the case in the Old Testament, where armies are likened to locust swarms (see Judg. 6:5; 7:12; Jer. 46:23; 51:14, 27; Nah. 3:15). The immensity of a locust swarm is also reflected in Exodus 10:4–6, 12–15; and Psalm 105:34.

The work of the teeth mentioned in verse 6 is described in verse 7. The locusts not only strip the leaves, but also chew the bark off twigs and shoots, leaving them bare and white.

In Israel when a man's family had paid the bride-price, he and the bride-to-be were betrothed. The bride-to-be was considered the man's "wife" and he her "husband" even though the marriage was yet to be consummated. The prophet calls for mourning following the locust plague like that most cruel mourning following unfulfilled love. Instead of the gaiety of a wedding and clothing for celebration, there is sackcloth and sadness.

The devastation of agriculture also has dire consequences for worship services in the temple. In addition to a lamb the morning and evening offerings required flour, oil, and wine (see Exod. 29:38–40; Num. 28:5–8)—but now the grain, wine, and oil are destroyed. These three commodities are representative of the complete range of agricultural products in Israel. Where trees grew, the Israelite farmer cut them to plant his orchards (olive oil); where brush and bramble covered the terrain, he planted his vineyards; where grasslands were found, there he planted his grain.

Like a wedding (1:8), a harvest should be a time of joy, but now "the joy of mankind is withered away" (1:12). The disaster for farmers is total—no grain to eat, none to sell, and none to plant. The two terms used in 1:11 for farmers and vine growers do not refer to independent landowners, but rather to landless tenant farm workers, among the poorest people in the land (2 Kings 25:12; Isa. 61:5; Jer. 39:10; 40:7–10; 52:16); for them the disaster is compounded yet again, for they cannot pay their overlords for the rent of the land.

All classes of society have been touched by the locusts—from the leaders (priests and elders) to the lowest (peasants and drunkards); none are exempt.

B. Summons to fasting and prayer (1:13–14). These verses border on being ritual or liturgical instructions for a lament. The priests are to wear sackcloth, pray through the night, and call a fast and a national assembly at the temple. Priests maintained a watch through the night apparently on a regular basis; in these dire straits, their numbers will necessarily increase. The rough, black sackcloth is a sharp contrast to the normally glorious garb of the priesthood (Exod. 28:39–43). The absence of any reference to the king or to royal officials is striking.

C. Complaint and prayer (1:15–20). Joel sees in the present locust plague both a manifestation of the day of the Lord, the day of God's wrath, and a harbinger of that yet greater and more dreadful day to come. In the prophetic expectation of the Old Testament the day of the Lord was the day of Yahweh's holy war against evil—particularly against the Gentile nations which had opposed or oppressed the people of God. However, the prophets were also quick to show that the day of the Lord came against *all* evil—not just evil among the Gentiles, but evil among the covenant people as well. Israel too would experience periodic judgment that anticipated that great and terrible day. As the imagery about the day of the Lord is developed in Joel, it is a day that threatens Israel. Yet it is also a day that can be escaped through repentance so that it becomes a day of blessing for God's people and judgment on their enemies.

These verses present us with interpretive difficulty: How is the locust plague related to the drought that dries up plants (1:11–12) and streams (1:20) and is like a fire (1:19)? There are at least two ways to relate the locust plague and drought: (1) Defoliation would produce great loss of ground moisture and extensive loss of topsoil, so that a drought could be the natural consequence of a severe locust outbreak. Since locusts follow global wind patterns, and the wind prevails in Israel from the southeast during the spring and summer, some hot desert winds may have contributed to the drought. (2) The drought could also be a second and separate catastrophe.

II. The Day of the Lord (2:1–17)

The prophet portrays a theophany, the approach of Yahweh with his army; the passage is an extended metaphor comparing the divine army to the locust invasion of the recent past. The locust plague was a warning about this yet greater and more dreadful day.

A. Cry of alarm, warning of attack (2:1–2). The blasting trumpet was the alarm sounded to warn of an impending attack. The Old Testament prophets played a prominent role in holy war, providing battle oracles and even instruction from the Lord for the conduct of warfare

(1 Kings 20; 22; 2 Kings 1; 3:14–19; 6:8–7:2; 13:14–20; 2 Chron. 11:1–4; 20:14–17). Here the prophet announces another battle oracle—but it is the Lord's army coming against Israel on the day of the Lord.

The locusts had darkened the skies with their swarms. But the darkness that is spreading here is the darkness attending God's presence with his army. The day of the Lord comes at dawn, just as the locusts had come from the east (Exod. 10:13).

B. The divine army (2:3–11). In these verses it is difficult to know whether locusts are being likened to an army, or an army to locusts; either the locusts are described in apocalyptic terms, or the day of the Lord is likened to a locust invasion.

The locust damage had been likened to fire (1:19), but fire is also a primary mode of theophany (Deut. 4:11; 5:22–26; Zeph. 1:18). Turning Eden/paradise to desolation or the reverse is a common theme in the prophets. Joel will return to this theme later (3:18).

The locusts are compared to horses and their droning and crackling noise is likened to the movement of chariots. They seem to progress in orderly ranks and overwhelm any obstacles.

The cosmic phenomena (vv. 10–11) that mark the day of the Lord are also attested for other theophanies. Created order is extinguished and plummets to the starless night of primeval chaos.

C. Offer of repentance (2:12–14). At the dedication of the temple Solomon had prayed that the Lord would hear the repentant prayer of his people when they assembled there in times of calamity; he prayed specifically about locust invasions (2 Chron. 6:28–31). When there was repentance, God promised that he would "heal their land" (2 Chron. 7:14). At the time of Joel we see the outworking of Solomon's prayer: God keeps his promise to hear prayer at the temple; he forgives and heals the land. The merciful, compassionate, and gracious nature of God is one of the great recurring themes of the Old Testament.

D. Summons to fasting and prayer (2:15–17). A series of liturgical instructions follows. The trumpet that sounded the alarm in the face of an impending attack (2:1) now summons the people to repentance, fasting, and prayer. No one is to be excused: not the elderly, not suckling children or their nursing mothers, not newlyweds. The recently married man could be exempted from warfare (Deut. 20:7), but not from this worship service and fast; the bride and groom must even delay the consummation of their marriage.

III. The Lord's Answer (2:18–3:21)

The prophet has presented two calamities: the recent devastation of a locust plague and the coming day of the Lord. Now he presents God's answer to both.

A. To the immediate disaster (2:18–27). The first step is the removal of the locusts; they are driven from the land. Israel's historic foes commonly came from the north. Here the locusts are identified both with those armies from the north that had terrorized Israel in the past and as a foretaste of apocalyptic judgment. If the "parched and barren land" is to the south, verse 20 mentions all four points of the compass.

Three categories had been affected by the locusts, and all three are mentioned in the healing of the land: now land, animals, and mankind can rejoice. Plants, rain, and food will be restored. Joy and gladness return where they had been wiped away.

B. To the impending disaster (2:28–3:21). The locust plague had portended a greater disaster that loomed on the horizon. The prophet describes how that day will affect Israel and the nations.

Joel **2:28–32** constitutes one of the more familiar passages of the Old Testament. It is cited by Peter on the day of Pentecost (Acts 2:17–21, 39); Paul also appeals to Joel 2:32 (Rom. 10:13).

Verses 28–29 draw on Numbers 11:24–12:8. When Joshua urged Moses to stop the prophesying of Eldad and Medad, Moses' response was: "I wish that all the LORD's people were prophets and that the LORD would put his Spirit on them" (Num. 11:29). God specified that one means of revelation would be through dreams and visions (Num. 12:6). Here Joel foresees the answer to Moses' prayer: the Spirit comes on all; all prophesy and have dreams and visions. The speech phenomena of Pentecost (Acts 2:6–13) are explained by Peter as due to the coming of the Spirit; a parallel is drawn with the speech phenomena in the wilderness (Num. 11:24–25).

Joel envisages a radical transformation in the society of ancient Israel. The radical change Joel foresees can well be illustrated by an ancient daybreak prayer uttered by the Jewish male, thanking God that he was not born a slave, a Gentile, or a woman. In contrast, Joel looks to a day when distinctions between old and young, slave and free, male and female are set aside; all equally possess the Spirit and have the gift of prophecy. There will be no more drought of the Word of God.

Though Joel limits himself to speaking of a transformation within Israelite society, he spoke better than he knew when he said that the Spirit would come on "all flesh." Ultimately the greatest distinction of all, that between Jew and Gentile, would be broken down; "all flesh" would include eventually those Gentile children of Abraham who comprise the new Israel. This passage may underlie Paul's statement in Galatians 3:28 that in Christ there is neither slave nor free, male nor female, Jew nor Gentile.

The day of the Lord is marked by the frightening signs and wonders that so often characterize a theophany. That dread day will be a day of salvation for those who call on the name of the Lord. The text carefully balances moral responsibility and the free offer of grace ("all who call") with the electing purpose of God ("whom the Lord calls").

The theme of a new exodus, when oppressors become plunder for the oppressed, is a common prophetic hope (Isa. 17:14; Jer. 30:16; Ezek. 39:10; Hab. 2:8; Zeph. 2:9; Zech. 2:8–9; 14:1–2). Those who had plundered and enslaved Israel will now meet the same fate (**3:1–16**).

The identification of the Valley of Jehoshaphat is uncertain. Since it is from his throne in Zion (3:16) that Yahweh will judge the nations, the Valley of Jehoshaphat has often been associated with the Kidron or Tyropoean valleys near the temple precincts. It is also possible that the Valley of Jehoshaphat has no real counterpart in the topography of the city, but that it is rather a feature of an apocalyptic geography of Jerusalem. Some associate it with a location near Tekoa where Jehoshaphat was victorious (2 Chron. 20). The word *Jehoshaphat* means "Yahweh judges," and it is an appropriate name for the valley where God will "enter into judgment" against the nations (3:2).

The Sabeans (3:8) occupied the southern ranges of the Arabian peninsula; the queen of Sheba had come from there to visit Solomon (2 Chron. 9). The point of the geography is clear: since Tyre and Sidon had sold slaves from Israel to the Greeks far to the northwest, now Israel will be the middleman and sell their people to the Sabeans, far to the southeast, the opposite direction.

Earlier the prophet had summoned Israel to a fast and lament (1:13–14; 2:15–17), but now it is Yahweh who issues a summons. He summons the nations to battle. This summons is not to yet another victory over Israel, but rather to defeat. The images of Isaiah 2:4 and Micah 4:3 are reversed: instruments of peace are made into implements of war. The Lord will also summon his warriors for the battle.

The word commonly translated "multitudes" (3:14) can also mean "tumult, turmoil." It refers to either the large numbers in the valley or the noise of the battle. The multitudes in the valley of decision are not there to make a decision about their own fate, but to hear the Lord's decision spoken in judgment from Zion.

The shaking of earth and sky accompanies theophanies (Judg. 5:4; Ps. 18:8) and often suggests a return to primeval chaos (Pss. 46; 77:18); but it also inaugurates the new age. When on the day of the Lord created reality trembles in the presence of an angry God and dissolves into chaos, the Lord will be a refuge for his people.

Joel **3:17** is a summary of prophetic hopes. The reference to the Lord's dwelling in the city suggests God's presence in the pillar of fire and smoke over the temple. That presence sanctifies the city so that Jerusalem becomes holy and is no longer subject to foreign invasion.

Israel's eschatological hopes are often described in terms of agricultural abundance; the future age is described as paradise/Eden restored (v. 18; Ezek. 47:7–12; Amos 9:13–15). The Eden of the future age forms an overwhelming contrast with the devastation of the recent locust plague.

The motif of the fountain flowing from the temple is also widely developed in the Old Testament. In Ezekiel's vision of the rebuilt temple, the sea becomes a life-giving river (47:1–12). Jesus identifies himself and his Spirit as the source of that life-giving stream (John 4:10–14; 7:37–39). The motif appears again as a feature of the new heavens and earth (Rev. 22:1–2). In the New Jerusalem, there is a life-giving river, but there is no sea (death). Judah will become a paradise restored; desolation like that left by the locusts will be the fate of her enemies.

SELECT BIBLIOGRAPHY

Ahlström, G. W. *Joel and the Temple Cult of Jerusalem.* Leiden: E. J. Brill, 1971.

Allen, L. C. *The Books of Joel, Obadiah, Jonah, and Micah.* Grand Rapids: Eerdmans, 1976.

Baaron, S. *The Desert Locust.* New York: Charles Scribner's Sons, 1972.

Bewer, J. A. *The Book of Joel.* The International Critical Commentary. Edinburgh: T. & T. Clark, 1911.

Kapelrud, A. S. *Joel Studies.* Uppsala: Almqvist och Wiksell, 1948.

Prinsloo, W. S. *The Theology of the Book of Joel.* Berlin: W. de Gruyter, 1985.

Weiser, A. *Die Propheten Hosea, Joel, Amos, Obadia, Jona, Micha.* Gottingen: Vandenhoeck und Ruprecht, 1979.

Wolff, H. W. *Joel and Amos.* Philadelphia: Fortress, 1977.

AMOS

R. K. Harrison

INTRODUCTION

This exemplary composition, dealing with the ethical and moral implications of the Israelite covenantal religion, has been attributed consistently through the ages to Amos of Tekoa. His name, which may mean "burden-bearer" or "burdensome," is distinctive in that it does not occur anywhere else in the Old Testament. The name is mentioned once in the New Testament (Luke 3:25), but an entirely different person is involved. Jewish tradition suggested that the name was a shortened form of Amaziah (see Amos 7:10, where the two are contrasted), or Amasiah, which itself occurs only once in the Old Testament (2 Chron. 17:16).

The prophet Amos was born in Tekoa, a village located on a hill some twenty-eight hundred feet above sea level, overlooking the wilderness of Judah. It was somewhat isolated from Jerusalem, the capital of the southern kingdom, being situated six miles south of Bethlehem. The ancient name has survived in the modern Arabic *Tequ'*, an area that is well suited to the rearing of sheep and goats. From this elevation the prophet could contemplate the significance of God's message for the nation as he looked beyond the nearby caravan trails to the desolate Judean wilderness. The wasteland would obviously serve as a reminder of his nation's future if covenantal law was continuously disobeyed.

Although Amos disclaimed any connection with prophetic guilds and was not a priest (as were Jeremiah and Ezekiel) or an aristocrat (as was Isaiah), he should not thereby be dismissed as an ignorant peasant just because he made a living from shepherding animals and from seasonal work in the fig groves. His prophecies show him to have been a thoughtful, spiritually minded person who was alarmed at the fate in store for the nation if its life did not reflect the justice and righteousness that were basic to covenantal law. Like many other Hebrews, Amos exhibited poetic gifts, and his oracles are models of articulate speech, beautifully crafted literary idioms, and a passionate concern for the nation to turn away from idolatry and worship the Lord of Sinai as Israel's one and only true God. A variety of images is used to proclaim his message, but all reflect the same insistence upon forsaking Canaanite idolatry and returning to the moral and spiritual traditions of the Sinai covenant.

It is not known if Amos heeded Amaziah's advice (7:12) and returned to the southern kingdom to live, or whether he attracted disciples as Isaiah did (Isa. 8:16; 28:9–10). There seem to be very few, if any, scribal changes in the text of the prophecy, which was handed down as a powerful indictment of national sin that influenced subsequent prophetic thought, especially that of Jeremiah. Just how long it took Amos to deliver his utterances is unknown. It is probable that, due to the urgency of the moral and religious situation in the nation, Amos's oracles were delivered within a comparatively short period of time, perhaps even in a few months, and that the various proclamations were punctuated chronologically by the brief biographic notation in Amos 7:10–17.

The superscription in Amos 1:1 furnishes an approximate date for the book. Uzziah (Azariah) reigned in Judah from about 767 B.C. to 740 B.C., while Jeroboam II was king of the northern kingdom from about 782 B.C. to 753 B.C. It would appear that Jotham was co-regent with Azariah after 750 B.C., so by comparing the concurrent reigns of Uzziah and Jeroboam II it is possible to date Amos between 760 B.C. and 750 B.C. The reference to "the earthquake" would have fixed his ministry more precisely in his time, since it was clearly a catastrophic event, still being referred to three centuries later (Zech. 14:5). It is not of any help, however, to the modern student of chronology.

This period is of great interest because it was one of peace for both the northern and southern kingdoms. The westward advance of the Assyrians had compelled Syria to withdraw from Israelite territory in order to defend its eastern positions. Syria suffered a shattering blow when Adad-Nirari III led Assyrian forces to victory in the destruction of the Syrian capital of Damascus (802 B.C.), and this removed the threat of oppression for the foreseeable future. The prospect of further Assyrian attacks diminished when Adad-Nirari experienced difficulties at home, and it was only in 745 B.C., when Tiglath-pileser III came to the throne of Assyria, that the next threat to Palestinian security arose.

During the subsequent half-century of peace, the northern kingdom attained the height of its prosperity, while the southern kingdom flourished also. The holdings of Israel and Judah corresponded to the extent of the undivided kingdom of David and Solomon. Quite possibly Amos 6:13 refers to this situation. Jeroboam II's territorial acquisitions were accompanied by a vast expansion of trade. A new mercantile class arose in Israel and amassed great wealth. A wave of materialism resulted from these exploits, and wealthy Israelites began to enjoy the same luxuries as did the upper classes in pagan nations.

The practice of depraved Canaanite religion struck a hard blow at the traditional covenantal faith of the Hebrews, and abandonment of the Hebrew faith allowed for unrestricted license and avarice. The rich oppressed the poor and deprived them of their smallholdings, contrary to Israelite tradition. For the first time in Israel's history the cities became overcrowded with dispossessed peasants looking for shelter and work. To this situation of material wealth but moral and spiritual depravity Amos was called to proclaim judgment on all who violated God's moral standards. The various oracles may well have been proclaimed independently more than once and in different places, but it is quite probable that they were assembled in their final form in Tekoa, if Amos returned there to live after his denunciations in Bethel. The date, nature, and location of his death are unknown.

The prophet's doctrine of God is rooted in the Sinaitic covenant, in which God extended his love and protection to the Israelites on condition that they obey and worship him as their only true and living God. He promised them a land in which they were to live as a holy people, based upon the high principles of covenant spirituality. When Israel invaded Canaan, the tribes were given the land by God the Owner in trust as tenants, so that they could put into practice the principles of divine holiness and social justice. An appropriate division of land was essential to the success of the latter, and the Mosaic law attempted to forestall the problems that would arise from some families or groups acquiring large amounts of wealth, thereby bringing about a corresponding impoverishment of others (Lev. 25:35–36). In particular, the Law condemned wealthy persons who exploited the poor (Exod. 22:25–27; Deut. 15:7–11) because such behavior violated the entire concept of a kingdom of priests and a holy nation (Exod. 19:6).

But as national life in Canaan developed, the large working class was exploited by a few rich landowners and an equally small middle class of merchants and traders. So depraved had life in Israel become that in Amos's day the judiciary was corrupt, and this opened the legal system to widespread exploitation by the unscrupulous rich, who would bribe judges to secure favorable court decisions. When peasants were deprived of their holdings they often went into "debt-slavery," but this was also true of those who became poor through mismanagement of resources or general economic troubles. The eighth century B.C. in Israel witnessed the growth of a great economic gap between rich and poor, and Amos addressed himself to this situation in an attempt to restore the social conditions provided by the Sinai covenant. In many cases where Amos refers to God he uses the covenant name *Yahweh*.

Amos endeavored to set the immorality and corruption of life in Israel and Judah against the exalted standards of God's holiness, purity, loving concern for others, righteousness, and justice, as exhibited in the covenant relationship. His utterances depict God as the supreme moral Ruler of the nations, not just the national deity of the Israelites. As Creator of the world and humanity he is the universal Lord of history. While he is aware that other gods exist among the pagans, he demands that his people be separate from them and worship him exclusively.

This supreme, righteous God will be swift to act in retribution when crimes are committed against humanity because he is not merely the Lord of the universe but also its righteous Judge. Such crimes are odious enough when pagan nations indulge in them, but when his covenant people are guilty of such offenses the punishments will be devastating (3:2); they are sinning against the revealed will of God. The covenant curses made so explicit in Deuteronomy 28:15–68 will come dramatically upon an apostate nation, constituting the penalty for violating the solemn covenant oath. God's punishment will thus be essentially just, because the nation has ignored warnings to repent, of which the utterances of Amos are but one example.

Many commentators have thought that Amos's denunciations leave no room for hope of restoration for the Israelites. But this position can be maintained only by excluding Amos 9:11–15 from the prophecy. The stern warnings of Amos are designed to draw the people, if possible, to the spiritual ideals of the Sinai covenant. Amos sees beyond the outward appearance of prosperity to the decayed moral core of national life, and proclaims boldly that restoration to true spiritual health can only come by the repudiation of depraved Canaanite religion, accompanied by a return in penitence to the worship of the Lord as Israel's exclusive God. Because Amos senses clearly that repentance is no part of the national disposition, the warnings of destruction by pagan nations are bound to be fulfilled.

Yet even this judgment will not eliminate the nation completely, if only because Amos intercedes for Israel. The Judge of all the earth is One of mercy and compassion as well as justice, and his greatest longing is for his people to live the ideal existence prescribed in the Law as a priestly kingdom and a holy nation, in complete subservience to his will.

The Book of Amos is one of the earliest to be produced by the "writing prophets" of Israel. The life of the nation is illustrated by graphic similes as well as imagery based upon Amos's personal observations. Though Amos is a countryman, there is nothing rustic about his literary style, which sparkles with impassioned rhetoric and yet reflects the subtleties of word play. He employs a dirgelike poetic rhythm to build up an ominous expectation of devastation for the nation, but also uses lyric language to describe the coming restoration of Israel. His poetic oracles are the equal of anything in Hebrew literature.

In the list of biblical books Amos is placed third among the Hebrew writings of the Minor Prophets, preceded by Hosea and Joel. This arrangement was known in the time of ben Sira (Ecclus. 49:10), and was also familiar to Josephus (*Contra Apion* 1.8.3). Rabbinic traditions stated that the "men of the Great Synagogue" edited (i.e., assembled) this group of prophetic writings. The Greek translation varied the order of the Hebrew Bible by placing Hosea first, followed by Amos, Micah, Joel, Obadiah, and Jonah. In the Palestinian Talmud, Amos was included with Micah among the major prophets in the sequence: Hosea, Isaiah, Amos, Micah. This order seems to reflect the fact that Amos was an outstanding figure in Hebrew literature.

OUTLINE

I. Superscription and Introduction (1:1–2)
II. Judgment upon the Nations (1:3–2:16)
III. Prophecies Against Israel (3:1–6:14)
IV. Five Visions of Judgment (7:1–9:10)
V. Promises of Restoration and Blessing (9:11–15)

COMMENTARY

I. Superscription and Introduction (1:1–2)

The author lays claim to the book by describing it as "the words of Amos," but his utterances actually have divine origin. He indicates this by saying that he "saw" them, using a word employed consistently by the prophets to denote divine revelation. He is thus verbalizing his communion with God as he proclaims his prophetic message. He is equally humble in describing himself as "one of the Tekoa shepherds."

It is interesting that Amos says nothing about his pedigree, unlike most other prophets. His desire for anonymity may be an expression of his humility, since his family would certainly have been known to the people of Tekoa. He is evidently not a resident alien, since he writes and preaches with the assurance of an Israelite born into the covenant community, one who accepts its traditions and obligations wholeheartedly.

The introduction to his message depicts God as a lion, roaring menacingly in order to give warning of an impending attack. David was familiar with such a situation (1 Sam. 17:34–36), since in his day the Zor or luxuriant floodplain of the Jordan Valley where the river entered the Dead Sea was a haunt for Asiatic lions (cf. Jer. 49:19). The lion's roaring is an indication of grave danger, since when hunting the male lion roared and thrashed around to divert attention from the actual prey, which the female lion was stalking. The nation is in infinitely greater peril than the superficial indications of prosperity might show. It is supremely ironic that Amos depicts the One who would have shepherded and nourished his obedient people as the Lion who will bring destruction upon all who reject his law. Because much has been given to Israel, much will be required by God. Since these expectations have not been fulfilled, the nation's punishment will be all the more severe.

II. Judgment upon the Nations (1:3–2:16)

In a very cleverly contrived piece of rhetoric, Amos tries to focus the attention of his hearers upon a close neighbor of the northern kingdom (**1:3–5**). Damascus, the capital of the Syrians—or more properly the Arameans (2 Sam. 8:5–6)—was located in the fertile territory between the Anti-Lebanon mountain range and the desert. It was one of some five principalities that formed ancient Syria, the borders of which were never clearly defined. By mentioning Damascus specifically, the prophet leaves no doubt that the object of divine wrath is the nation to the north of Israel that had troubled the northern kingdom for many years. But Assyria's westward expansion had drawn Syrian forces eastward, thus freeing Israel from attack. Because of all that the Hebrews had suffered from the Arameans in past days, it would be a pleasure to hear that the hated enemy is to be punished drastically.

Amos chooses the Aramean state craftily as the first object of denunciation, going far enough away from the unsuspecting Israelites and Judeans. He knows that he will gain a ready hearing from his audience by condemning the sins of their enemies. What his hearers do not know from the outset is that they too will be included in the list of offenders. Sin is universal in nature (Rom. 3:23), and over the centuries had become a far more prominent feature of Israelite life than was consistent with the ethos of the Sinai covenant. So as to heighten the drama of his denunciations, Amos uses a Semitic literary device that has been called the "numerical ladder." It begins with a given number to describe a particular circumstance, and as though that were not large enough for the purpose, this number is increased by one. Thus the expression *for three sins, even for four* really means "for their many sins."

The crime for which Damascus is condemned is a moral one. When the Syrians attacked the Gileadites repeatedly during the latter part of the eighth century B.C., they had behaved in a brutal and inhumane manner. Amos conveys the severity of it by employing a harvesting metaphor. When sheaves of grain were threshed, a mechanical device was often used where there was too much to be beaten out by hand. A rectangular sledge made of wooden planks, with pieces of stone or iron fastened to the lower surface, was weighted on top so as to press out the grain when it was dragged over the sheaves. A different form of this farm implement had low cylindrical wheels under the planking that acted like saws upon the ears of grain (Isa. 28:27; 41:15). Both types of instruments were crude and wasteful, to say the least, and when the image is applied to human beings it conveys a stunning sense of oppression, brutal punishment, and wanton devastation.

In the ancient world the treatment of the conquered was extraordinarily severe. The dead were mutilated and plundered while survivors were either murdered in some vicious manner, mutilated, or carried into captivity. Captured women were stripped naked, beaten, abused sexually, or mutilated by having breasts cut off. The victors often took malicious delight in disemboweling pregnant women in the presence of their families and others. The Mosaic law sought to modify this extreme behavior somewhat by imposing regulations ensuring the humane treatment of prisoners (e.g., Deut. 21:10–14).

Because the Arameans had acted so brutally, they are to suffer punishment. The "sending of fire" upon Damascus is the promise of a devastating attack in which the city will be burned. This prophecy was fulfilled in 732 B.C., when Damascus fell to the assault of the Assyrian Tiglath-pileser III, whose devastation of the capital marked the end of Syria as an independent nation.

It is now the Philistines' turn to hear God's condemnation (**1:6–8**). These people, different from the settlers in the Hebron area known to Abraham (Gen. 20–21), conquered Canaan about 1200 B.C. They took their name from the territory that they occupied, and formed a political unit comprising five city-states. The Philistines were a real threat to the Israelites of Joshua's day by virtue of their superior military technology. This consisted of the iron-fitted horse-drawn chariot, which unfortunately could function well only on level surfaces, and the compound Asiatic bow made partially of iron, which exhibited vastly superior firepower when compared with other bows. But even in the time of David, one of their chief adversaries, their power was waning, and the period of Amos saw a significant decline when Tiglath-pileser III conquered Gaza, one of the chief Philistine cities, in 732 B.C. The nation revived somewhat, but was conquered by Nebuchadnezzar in 597 B.C., and the people went into captivity in Babylonia with the Judeans.

Gaza had sinned by taking entire communities, not just military prisoners, into captivity. These Israelites, who may have come from undefended villages in southern Judah, were then sold to Edom as cattle would be. Ashdod, Ashkelon, and Ekron were three other members of the Philistine alliance. Ashdod was conquered by Sargon of Assyria in 711 B.C., while Ashkelon and Ekron fell under the onslaught of Sennacherib in 701 B.C. as God's punishment for trading captives as slaves. The fate of Gath, the remaining Philistine city, is not mentioned here, but it was most probably conquered by Uzziah (2 Chron. 26:6). As with Damascus, crimes against humanity bring about the downfall of Philistia, as Amos had foretold.

Phoenicia, on the northwest coast of Palestine, is the next foreign nation to receive a scathing denunciation (**1:9–10**). Phoenicia, a noted maritime nation in antiquity, had two major ports, Tyre and Sidon, which were actually semi-independent states. Between 1000 B.C. and 850 B.C. Phoenicia was at the height of prosperity, and established colonies throughout the Mediterranean.

In the seventh century B.C. Phoenician power declined through wars with Assyria. Mainland Tyre finally fell to the Babylonians in 572 B.C. after thirteen years of siege, marking the end of Phoenician existence as an independent nation. The island city of Tyre, however, was not destroyed until 332 B.C. by Alexander the Great. This was the punishment that fell upon Tyre for engaging in slave trade with the Edomites. While the identity of the "whole communities" is unknown, they were evidently Israelite, since a "treaty of brotherhood," presumably the friendly alliances under David and Solomon, had been breached. Thus infidelity and perfidy were added to offenses against human rights. In the ancient world the breaking of a covenant carried with it serious consequences. The mention of Tyre's walls probably refers to the island city, which was considered impregnable. But the Lord of all nations brought a more powerful people to execute his will upon Tyre, in accordance with Amos's predictions.

The oracle of God is now directed at the nation already named as a participant in the wholesale violation of human rights (**1:11–12**). The Edomites had Esau as their ancestor (Gen. 27:38–40; 36:1). Because of the ancient enmity between Esau and Jacob, the Edomites were generally hostile to the Israelites, and when the latter wished to traverse Edomite territory on their way to the Jordan after emerging from the wilderness, the Edomites refused them permission. David conquered Edom (2 Sam. 8:13–14), but in the later monarchy period Edom rebelled against Judah (2 Kings 8:20–22).

The crime for which Edom is to be exterminated is consistent animosity toward God's covenant people. Edomite rage will be met by God's consuming wrath. Teman, an important location in southern Edom, will be burned along with Bozrah, the royal city of the kingdom. God in his covenant love acts against the enemies of his people in anger and judgment in order to save his own. Thus in his vision of God's day of vengeance and redemption, Isaiah, a contemporary of Amos, sees the Lord coming from Bozrah in his blood-sprinkled garments, having trodden the winepress of his anger upon the Gentile nations (Isa. 63:1–6).

The Ammonites were descended from the incestuous union of Lot and his younger daughter (Gen. 19:35–38), and had a general history of strained relations with the Israelites. Amos follows the stereotyped rhetorical pattern in denouncing the Ammonites to his listeners (**1:13–15**), who doubtless receive these tidings with ill-concealed delight. All their traditional enemies are about to endure God's rigorous punishment, opening up a Solomonic prospect of Israel as supreme among her devastated enemies.

The mountainous Ammonite territory lay to the northeast of Moab, stretching from the Arnon River in the south to the Jabbok in the north. The Ammonites were an aggressive people who attacked the Israelites periodically (Judg. 3:13; 2 Chron. 20:1–23) and perpetrated the usual atrocities against their captives. Had Saul not come to the rescue of Jabesh-gilead, the Ammonites would have destroyed the place in an attempt to extend their territory (1 Sam. 11:1–11). Amos finds their militant activities particularly abhorrent, and in his prophetic oracle he describes Ammon's punishment in some detail. The capital's defensive walls will be burned, and the battle cries of the invading armies (in this case the Assyrians) will echo in the winds that fan the destroying flames. Ammon's ruler and court officials will be taken captive, thereby symbolizing the end of Ammon as an effective military force, and removing a brutal, callous people from Trans-Jordan. The God who placed his image in human beings will rise and defend them when that image is defaced by atrocities. The figure of a whirlwind shows that the devastation will be complete, a point that would not be lost on Amos's hearers.

With the denunciation of the Ammonites, the audience knows that it will soon be the turn of the Moabites to bear the sentence of punishment (**2:1–3**). Ammon and Moab were frequently paired in that order, although Moab was apparently the first child to issue from the relations between Lot and his daughters (Gen. 19:31–38). The Moabites lived on a mountainous plateau along the eastern shore of the Dead Sea, south of the Arnon River. Moabite territory terminated in the south at the Brook Zered, beyond which lay Edom. Moab had prospered because of the camel caravans which came along the King's Highway, a major trade route linking the Gulf of Aqabah with Syria.

The offense occasioning Moabite punishment arose from their cremation of a conquered Edomite ruler. This was an abhorrent act because it reduced the man's bones to a powder, thus dissipating his personality irreparably. Because of this crime (and probably with the intention of discouraging it in the future), God through his servant Amos promises a fiery devastation of Moabite fortresses. Kerioth is probably another name for Ar, the ancient Moabite capital where the chief shrine of Chemosh, the national deity of the Moabites and Ammonites, was located. The same terrifying celestial phenomena as those accompanying the destruction of Ammon are to be expected at the time that leadership is wiped out in Moab. The solemn assurance of the Lord makes this certain.

To this point the covenant people have escaped unscathed from the pronouncements of doom upon their neighbors. But now the chosen seed of Jacob is confronted with God's judgment upon their sin (**2:4–5**). Precisely the same rhetorical form as that used for their pagan contemporaries is employed to denounce them. Clearly God regards them as no better than the peoples around them. God's ideal of Israel as a priestly kingdom, manifesting religious purity and ethical holiness, has been thwarted by the incursions of pagan Canaanite idolatry into Hebrew rituals. When God looks upon his people, he can no longer see any moral or ethical difference between them and other nations which worship false gods.

The sin of the southern kingdom of Judah is particularly serious because the tribe through which the Messiah was to descend had at one time received, with other Israelites, the revelation of God at Sinai through Moses. The tribe of Judah had also promised solemn obedience to the laws of God, but over the years had failed to keep these laws, and had indeed repudiated them in spirit by becoming entangled in the idolatrous blandishments of Canaanite religion. God regards this behavior as outright rejection of his laws and of himself as the divine Lawgiver. Judah's sin is all the more serious because the tribe had once known the truth of God by special revelation, whereas the pagan nations around them, to whose depraved spiritual level the people of Judah had sunk, had never had the opportunity of such a disclosure from the God of the universe. Whatever ethical or moral standards the pagans possessed were the product of applied self-interest, and humane behavior was not conspicuous among them.

God's charge against Judah centers firmly upon the seductive powers of the false gods of Canaan. All pagan practices had been roundly condemned in the teachings of the covenant, and were prohibited to Israel because God desired his people to be morally and spiritually separated from the rest of society, living according to principles of divine holiness (Lev. 11:44). He had desired them to be weaned from the idols venerated by their ancestors, and to worship him alone. Instead they had repudiated the pledge given on Mount Sinai, and now are to suffer the same condemnation as their ungodly neighbors, whose religious traditions they have adopted. Divine fire will break out upon Judah in the manner prescribed for Syria, Gaza, Tyre, Edom, Ammon, and Moab. Jerusalem, the nation's capital, will be desolated, and the wealth and power of the nation squandered. This prophecy was fulfilled in 597, 587, and 581 B.C., when in three attacks upon Jerusalem by the Babylonians God's long-promised punishment for apostasy was meted out.

The climax of the prophetic denunciations is reached in the promise of punishment for the sins of the northern kingdom of Israel (**2:6–16**). It had been formed out of the ten tribes which had broken away from Judah's Rehoboam, son of Solomon, and was ruled by Jeroboam I, a former official in Solomon's kingdom. As a substitute for worship in the Jerusalem temple, Jeroboam introduced Egyptian bull worship at the shrines of Bethel and Dan. He appointed non-Levitical priests to officiate there, and devised a form of worship that had much in common with the Canaanite Baal religion. This deliberate act of apostasy became typical of the religion of Israel, despite the threat of divine judgment, and was flourishing in the time of Jeroboam II.

The same stern rhetorical formulation is addressed to Israel as to the other nations. Along with Judah, the inhabitants of the northern kingdom had in past generations pledged loyalty to the ideals of the Sinai covenant. But when Solomon died and the kingdom was divided, the leaders of the new nation dictated an entirely different course, involving indulgence in paganism. Thereafter the people would fall under the condemnation of Judah, because they also had once been recipients of divine revelation but had rejected it. With the repudiation of covenant ideals came an application of the principle of personal interest, resulting in the sins against God and society which Amos condemns.

The landed rich and the prosperous mercantile class found it easy to oppress the poor with the assistance of corrupt judges who could be bribed to give verdicts in court favoring the rapacious rich. The poor, who should have been under the care of the community according to the Sinaitic legislation, were deprived of their property and further oppressed by merchants who used balances that did not register the true weight of goods.

The Hebrew righteous were the innocent victims of the economic situation who simply could not meet their debts, while the needy were those who required economic help, but did not receive it. Verse 6 indicates the prevalence of "debt-slavery," in which debtors who were legally free citizens had no choice but to serve as slaves in households. Perhaps the lowest level of degradation to which Israel had sunk was the kind of human exploitation in which a father and son shared the same concubine. Such behavior was prohibited in the Law as a profanation of divine holiness.

God remonstrates with Israel by recounting his power when he delivered them from Egypt and formed them into a mighty nation, giving them their own land by destroying the Amorites (i.e., Canaanites). He also provided continuous spiritual leadership through prophets and Nazirites, the latter setting an example of dedicated, strict living (Num. 6:1–8)—but the Israelites corrupt the Nazirites and forbid the prophets to prophesy. God's chosen nation obviously does not want to see spirituality lived out before their eyes, nor to hear the message of the Law, with its insistent demand for separation to God and holiness.

The castigations of Amos are addressed to this appalling state of spiritual and social degeneration. The people will be crushed as though by the wheels of a loaded cart, and neither physical strength, military prowess, nor natural courage will avail in the day of divine judgment. The prophet thus identifies Israel's sins in terms of repudiation of the moral, ethical, and spiritual values of the covenant, and predicts annihilation as God's punishment for this iniquity.

III. Prophecies Against Israel (3:1–6:14)

Having set the stage for a thoroughgoing indictment of Israel, the prophet invites his audience to listen to what the Lord has to say to them directly (**3:1–15**). He thus differentiates between anything that might reflect his own personality and the oracles of God. What follows is not quite the same as the formal indictment (KJV controversy) of the nation such as appears in Hosea 4:1; 12:2; and Micah 6:2, but certainly has God summoning witnesses for that purpose. The "word" (v. 1), whatever its content, is from the covenant Lord, and is addressed to both Israel and Judah, described as the "family" that God had redeemed from bondage in Egypt and made his own possession. The thrust of the message is thus strictly theological, dealing with sin, apostasy, and punishment.

God had chosen the Israelites above all other peoples. They were thus unique, and destined to serve as witnesses to the existence and power of the one, true, living God. God chose the Israelites because of his absolute sovereignty and freedom, basing his election upon his love for them, as demonstrated in his varied provisions for their overall welfare. The Sinai covenant, which sealed this relationship, was a mutual agreement between God and his people.

God's chosen people, however, have repudiated separation from unholy things so essential to their election, and have participated in the sins of paganism. The Israelites think that, as God's elect people, they have all the rights and privileges of such a position with none of the responsibilities. Because the covenant is reciprocal, God insists upon his own rights, one of which is that of punishing sin and apostasy in the nation.

The covenantal concept is seen in the reference to two people walking together (v. 3). Such a close relationship can be impaired by unfavorable circumstances, in this case the blatant repudiation by Israel of the covenant's provisions. The mention of the roaring lion reminds the reader of Amos 1:2, and indicates that the prey has already been selected and is being stalked. Birds do not become prey unless the traps set for them are effective. God's roaring should serve as a warning to Israel of imminent disaster, ushered in by the nation's enemies who will execute divine vengeance upon them. The attack will be marked by the alarm trumpet blown in the city, which will settle decisively the destiny of God's disobedient people.

God has been fair in giving proper warning to and through his prophetic servants. The divine Predator has roared, and that alone ought to inspire fear in Israel.

The Israelites are hemmed in between the fortifications of Egypt on the south, which block the way to safety for refugees, and the attackers poised on the hills of Samaria to the north, who will sweep through the land, bringing destruction with them. The very buildings of Samaria that housed the luxurious items obtained by greed or robbery will be the first to feel the brunt of divine retribution. Instead of loving his neighbor as himself (Lev. 19:18), the wealthy Israelite has defrauded, depraved, and dehumanized him, resulting in the "great unrest" and the "oppression" which Amos denounces. This is a flagrant violation of the Mosaic legislation, and for that the sovereign Lord promises a devastating invasion of the country. All who desire can stand on the surrounding hills and watch divine vengeance being poured out upon Israel. The promised enemy was Assyria, which under Sargon II (ca. 722–705 B.C.) swept into the northern kingdom and captured Samaria after a three-year siege (2 Kings 17:3–6). Within three decades of the prophecy of Amos, the apostate and impenitent nation was taken captive to Assyria. Clearly the Lion's roar was far more significant than the majority of people had imagined.

The destruction is likened to the little bits of an animal left behind when a predator has finished its meal. These tattered remnants of a once-proud nation will be living proof that the mighty Lion has indeed struck, just as the remains of a sheep might be offered as evidence to an owner that a marauding animal has attacked it. All the illustrations from nature that Amos uses are thoroughly familiar to his audience.

The Egyptians and Assyrians are commanded to hear this prophecy of invasion and destruction, and to bear witness to the validity of the indictment. But whereas Amos 3:9–11 has concentrated upon the social evils perpetrated in the northern kingdom, the two concluding verses of the chapter place a theological rather than a moral emphasis upon the situation by speaking of a specific sin to be punished, namely, Israel's deliberate rejection of God's claims and rule. Bethel, one of the two places containing a golden bull, had become the northern kingdom's chief center of worship, rivaling the Solomonic temple in Jerusalem.

The "horns" or small projections at the upper corners of the altar traditionally furnished sanctuary for those clinging to them (1 Kings 1:50), but when God smites his rebellious and disobedient people even this form of refuge will be of no avail. The reference to winter and summer houses (v. 15) is apparently to the lavishly furnished homes built by the rich. To Amos, the humble peasant, such ostentation is utterly reprehensible, particularly since it has resulted from the exploitation of impoverished Israelites. Amos, however, is not condemning wealth as such, since in pursuing his work as a shepherd he was in contact with wealth every day. His concern is with the use and abuse of it. Israel's great material prosperity has been achieved largely by oppression, greed, extortion, and the violation of human rights, not by honest toil and fair treatment of those laborers who helped to make the wealth possible. It is this motivation that merits Amos's condemnation.

Amos commences his censure of Israel's unrepentant state by rebuking the elite women of Israel, to whom he attributes the cause of the corruption (**4:1–13**). These upper-class persons are likened to the cows of Bashan. Bashan was a rich, fertile tableland east of the Jordan and the Sea of Galilee, famous for its lush pastures and fine cattle. Commentators generally assume that the pampered women compelled their husbands to meet their increasingly extravagant demands by extorting the poor. These women seem to have become addicted to alcohol, with all the personal enslavement and degradation involved in its abuse. Some have also questioned whether Amos's allusion was flattering or otherwise to the Israelite women.

In pronouncing punishment upon them, Amos assures his audience that God has sworn by his holiness, that is, himself, so that there can be no doubt as to the severity and absolute nature of the penalty. The Holy One of Israel will teach his impenitent people what the rewards of unholy living comprise. Social crimes are just as serious as spiritual ones because they involve human beings created in God's image. The punishment will be drastic, being administered by the dreaded masters of the art of dehumanizing. The Israelites will be treated no better than fish by the Assyrians, who commonly carried people captive by ropes fastened to a hook pushed through the nose or lips.

Through Amos, God ridicules the pagan religiosity of the Israelites, who have confused religious rituals with true spirituality. Enthusiastic veneration of false gods is the absolute antithesis of covenantal theology. The utter perversity of Israel is shown in the nation's behavior at the shrines. For this the God of creation had punished them with famine, but to no avail. Even selective drought failed to produce repentance. The vines were infested with pests, while the figs and olives were devastated by locusts. But even these serious afflictions produced no contrition. The Israelites obviously have no sense of their sin, even though they have the absolute standard of covenant legislation against which they might evaluate their behavior. They continue to shrug off national disasters, and it never occurs to them that the plagues that formerly afflicted Egypt before the exodus are now being used to punish the people whom God had once redeemed from slavery by that very means. The Israelites are now controlled by evil forces that are so intense as to demand complete destruction, since all other attempts at containment have failed. In a dramatic climax, God demands that his people prepare to meet him in a day of judgment.

In a poetic lament (**5:1–17**), Amos bewails the nation's sad fate as if it has already occurred. Ironically the Lord's virgin nation has polluted itself by whoredom, and is thus legally destined to die. Her punishment will be decimation, and only a handful will survive the ordeal. But there is still hope, if only Israel will repudiate Canaanite idolatry and turn to God in sincere repentance. There can no longer be any consolation in idolatry, since the places of pagan worship will be destroyed. The prophet gives the people a choice between immediate repentance or imminent destruction, and again castigates them for defiling the Lord's ethical concepts of righteousness and justice by their abhorrent sexual abuses, which are listed once again. So bad has corruption become that the realistic Israelite knows well that he will receive no satisfaction in the courts, and is thus compelled to remain silent in the face of gross injustice. But when punishment comes, the powers that made the heavenly constellations will be unleashed against the hapless nation.

Amos then turns to a popular conception, the day of the Lord (**5:18–27**). Apparently the Israelites have presumed upon covenant grace to the point where they expect God to bless them, even though their conduct is in direct opposition to covenant principles. They look to God to destroy their enemies and usher in a period of peace and plenty in which they will be supreme. This is the least that they deserve, they think; after all, *they* are the Lord's chosen. The fact that they cherish this expectation despite their complete repudiation of covenant responsibilities, shows the extent of their presumption. The sheer perversity of this attitude is hard to imagine, and would in fact be unbelievable were it not so prevalent in modern Christianity. God's blessing can come in the believer's life only when that person lives according to God's rules in an attitude of complete trust and submission.

But the expected day will be one of darkness, as on the night when God passed through

Egypt in the final plague (Exod. 12:29). Israel's religiosity is abhorrent to God, because it has form but no spiritual content. Since the attitude of the worshipers is entirely wrong, the cultic rituals are meaningless. Instead of formal ceremonies, God desires the true worship of people motivated by covenant spirituality, as practiced during the wilderness period.

The lamentation in **6:1–14** seems to provide the reason for the unbelievable behavior of the Israelites in rejecting the spiritual values of the covenant. Their material prosperity and the prospect of continuing peace has brought about an inordinate pride of accomplishment and status in Israel. The Lord's covenant people, it is imagined, can do no wrong, despite their consistent repudiation of God's supreme lordship. In an attempt to induce a critical attitude, Amos bids Israel to dispel its complacency and learn from the example of Calneh, Hamath, and Gath.

Having censured the rich and complacent in Israel, the Lord now rebukes the nation for its pride, which has become its downfall. God again swears by himself, thereby making the oath and its consequences irrevocable. The reference to burning of bodies (v. 10) has been interpreted to mean "burning spices," since cremation was not usual for the Hebrews. But in emergencies such as a time of plague, it might have been advantageous to dispose of the dead in this way. In any case it will be no time to even mention the name of the avenging Lord, let alone take it in vain. The "great house" linked with the "small house" (v. 11) is a Hebrew way of describing total destruction. In verse 12, the idea of pointlessness is conveyed by two agricultural illustrations. Contrary to all expectations, Israel has accomplished the seemingly impossible by transforming justice into poison, and righteous fruit into bitterness. This demonstrates the extent to which their perversions have reached.

For its overwhelming pride and self-satisfaction, idolatrous Israel can expect to be ravaged from Lebo-hamath in northern Lebanon all the way to the Dead Sea, and thus the entire nation will be engulfed. The oppressing people will be the Assyrians.

IV. Five Visions of Judgment (7:1–9:10)

The prophet relates two experiences which the Lord "showed" him in visions, thus giving the reader some insight into the dynamics of such activity. In the first vision (**7:1–3**) it is harvest time, and the early mowings have been gathered in. Amos sees the Lord preparing devastating swarms of locusts just in time to ravage the second crop. Amos watches them strip the fields bare, and realizing that famine will result, cries out to God, begging forgiveness for the Israelites. God hears the pleas of his children; he does not intend to annihilate Israel totally. It should be noted that the appeal is between God and Amos exclusively, with no reference either to covenant mercies or national sin. The prophet's desire to preserve a remnant is implicit. Nevertheless, the vision demonstrates Amos's spiritual integrity as a godly man of effective prayer.

The second vision (**7:4–6**) still reflects the theme of judgment for sin. But this time it is punishment by fire rather than famine, and thus one that will destroy buildings and people rather than being confined to vegetable matter. The fire roars out, drying up sea and land, and once again Amos cries out in concern for Israel's survival, begging God to relent. Once again the Lord responds to the prophet's pleading, and thus shows that the complete destruction of the chosen people is not part of his plan for salvation. Instead, a remnant will survive. Nowhere in these two visions does God automatically forgive the sins of the apostate Israelites. Forgiveness can be preceded only by true confession of sin, and because the nation has no evident sense of sin it must be punished.

The third vision (**7:7–9**) shows the Lord standing beside a wall, ready to inspect it in his role as the Master Builder. He has a plumbline, and Amos is invited to identify the object. God informs Amos that he will use this to measure the Israelites, to see the extent to which they match his specifications. The vision is an ominous one for Amos, because he knows full well that the nation that had been built up in the Lord at Sinai has long since failed to conform to the Architect's plan.

God acknowledges his relationship to Israel by calling the nation "my people," but the reference is by no means one of affectionate possession. They are his in order to be subjected to rigorous scrutiny and consequent punishment for their many deviations. The plumbline is symbolic of God's revealed law, which provides a standard for both personal faith and daily life in society. The "holy nation" had been expected to set an example of upright, godly living in a pagan society, but through the ages they had become conformed to the world in which they lived. The tragedy of Israel's existence is that the nation had indulged in persistent apostasy and idolatry, despite the succession of divinely appointed prophets sent to call them back to the spiritual standards of the Sinai covenant.

The oracles and visions are interrupted at this point by the account of a confrontation between Amaziah, the chief priest of the Bethel shrine, and the prophet Amos, who must have been proclaiming his oracles in the vicinity (**7:10–17**). The historical interlude fits into the structure of the prophecy perfectly, since it deals with the implications of the third vision. Spurred by the thought of impending disaster overtaking the royal house, Amaziah sends a brief summary of Amos's prophecy to Jeroboam, implying that the visiting Judean prophet is guilty of treason. Without waiting for a response from the king, Amaziah dismisses Amos summarily, prohibiting him from uttering any more oracles in the area of Bethel, which was privileged royal and religious territory. By issuing such an edict Amaziah makes it clear that he has no formal connection whatever with the true priesthood of Israel.

This rebuke obviously requires Amos to declare his credentials for making such statements. He denies any association with a prophetic guild or group in Judah, stating that he is a humble worker with a divinely given message for the nation, which he is under obligation to proclaim.

Amos contrasts the priest's prohibition with the larger authority that he claims as a messenger of the Lord of Israel. To demonstrate this he utters an oracle prefaced by the dread statement: "This is the word of the Lord." There can be little doubt that Amaziah was expecting such a direct confrontation least of all. His authority as the royal priest of Israel is being challenged by a country shepherd who claims no allegiance to any prophetic group, but who speaks the message that God has given him. Even Amaziah is compelled to recognize the authority that Amos claims, however much he may have disliked the message of personal devastation that Amos pronounces upon his house. Degradation, death, and defilement will be the lot of Jeroboam's priest, as it will be of his royal master.

The book gives no indication as to whether Amos stayed in the region of Bethel or returned home. It is equally silent about the kind of repercussions his proclamations engendered. Nothing further is known about his life, and the tradition that he was murdered by Uzziah has no basis in fact. Equally lacking in verification is the more probable Jewish tradition that Amaziah killed Amos at the Bethel shrine.

In the fourth vision (**8:1–3**) the prophet is shown a basket of ripe fruit, and asked about its contents. In reply, God states that the time is now ripe for him to judge his wayward people Israel. The ripeness of the fruit indicates that it is the harvest season. What more appropriate occasion than this, therefore, for the heavenly Reaper to harvest the fruit of national life in Israel? When God comes to assess his people, he will find them barren and unproductive spiritually. They have deluded themselves into thinking that as long as they perform religious rituals, their God will be pacified, unaware of the fact that God sees the inner being of a person and not just the exterior. Consequently in the day of judgment there will be wailing as God discriminates against the evil and immoral Israelites in his righteous judgment. The promised day of darkness will arrive, and the sensuous pagan rituals will be stilled.

Amos summarizes yet again the gross iniquity of those who have oppressed the helpless in order to enrich themselves. The New Moon was a minor festival observed at the beginning of each month (Num. 10:10; 28:11), and the Israelites were impatient for its conclusion so that they could continue their corrupt commercial practices. The crass dishonesty that Amos describes was unfortunately common in antiquity, aided by the fact that there was no uniform system of weights.

The abhorrent, illegal acts of social oppression have made God so angry with the culprits that he swears an oath of everlasting remembrance of these crimes. For the Israelites, sin has become so routine that they are no longer aware of wrongdoing. They have been living by personal inclination, as the desert nomads did, because they are not subject to any formal laws. But the Sinai relationship ended that way of life forever. God's people are under legal obligation to keep the statutes and regulations which he had proclaimed. God's people, whether in the old or new dispensation, are always required to live by the law. Yet the slavish following of rules is not enough; the motivating forces of behavior are all-important. This includes nonbehavior also, with the result that it is just as much a sin to ignore blatant social injustice as to perpetrate it. When God swears by the "Pride of Jacob" he is swearing once more by himself. At one time he had been the nation's pride and source of rejoicing, but when the covenantal ethos was corrupted by paganism, the Israelites displayed their pride in more material concerns, contrary to the stipulations of the law. It is this transformed pride that will now destroy the Israelites.

To describe the coming catastrophe the Lord uses earthquake imagery. Disaster will pour upon the people like a Nile flood in spring, and just as certainly it will settle, having inundated the land. The coming day of the Lord is now described in all its terror. A frightening darkness will mark the beginning of sorrows, and the sordid rituals in which the Israelites had indulged so joyfully will now be occasions of piercing lament. All the signs of mourning will be present, and the tragedy of the time will be like the death of an only son, upon whom the entire family depended for its existence.

With the devastation of the land will come famine—not, however, so much in the matter of food as in the lack of communication from a God whom the people now need desperately. They will indeed be asking: "Is there any word from the LORD?" (Jer. 37:17). Such a query will be ironic from a people who for so long have rejected God's words. There is now no comforting assurance for them, even though they may traverse the land in a desperate search for it. The religious pretensions of the Israelites have been confronted finally by the appalling fact that the Lord of the universe has forsaken them. The tragedy of punishment for apostasy will be particularly serious for Israel's youth, who under any other circumstances would be the hope of the nation. They had evidently participated thoughtlessly in the pagan rituals at Bethel, and behaved frivolously as they enjoyed the orgiastic practices at the Canaanite religious festivals. But in the day of divine vengeance not even their youthful vigor will be able to save them, and they will die.

The fifth vision (**9:1–10**) depicts God having taken up his position beside the altar in Bethel, ready to supervise the destruction of the entire shrine. If the Israelites had crowded there in terror at the devastation wrought by the earthquake and famine, expecting to hear reassurances from the long-neglected covenant Lord, they are doomed to disappointment. The sentence has been pronounced upon rebel Israel, and will fall literally upon the heads of those in and around the shrine. The actual site to be destroyed is not mentioned, and the vision may well depict the collective devastation of all pagan shrines in Israel, not just that at Bethel.

All avenues of escape from divine retribution will be blocked. Wherever the fugitives might seek to hide in order to survive, the inexorable punishment meted out by God will hunt them down and destroy them. Even captivity in a foreign land will provide no real escape from the eyes of the Lord, because he will still execute them. The "serpent" (v. 3) is a sarcastic reference to pagan mythology. Amos turns pagan mythology upon those who believe it in a way that demonstrates the might and superiority of the Almighty Lord.

Since the Israelites have repudiated their spiritual uniqueness and have insisted upon being like other nations, God shows that he is the mighty God of all peoples, whose destiny he directs so as to fulfill his purposes for humanity. Israel will discover that God as Creator is perfectly free to treat all sinners on the same basis, without regard to nationality, creed, or color. Because Israel has ignored the miracle of the exodus and the birth of their nation at Sinai, they can no longer count upon God's power to work special acts of intervention for them. Instead, they will fall under the judgment of all their pagan neighbors. Divine punishment will sift them as wheat passing through a sieve, separating out the sinners in Israel and marking them for death. But even here there is a hint that some will survive God's drastic purging.

V. Promises of Restoration and Blessing (9:11–15)

In common with other Hebrew prophets, Amos concludes on a note of hope. The final verses of the book are an antithesis of the wrath and destruction characteristic of Amos's utterances. As if to offset the horror of the previous devastation, the fertility of the soil in this great period of restoration is described in terms of the garden of Eden. God's exiled people will be brought back to enjoy this prosperity, for they will have learned obedience through what they have suffered. The returned remnant will be faithful to the covenantal ideals, and the effects of former sin on the nation will be reversed by a loving, providential God.

Heaviness may have endured for a night, but joy has come in the morning. Never again will the nation be uprooted from its rightful heritage, and as an assurance the prophet closes his oracles with the solemn pronouncement that these are indeed the very words of God to his people, this time for their blessing and joy. The covenant Lord's promises are to redeem his people and bring judgment upon his enemies. These guarantees include that of a Messiah to come from David's house, who will give a totally new dimension to the concept of covenant relationship.

SELECT BIBLIOGRAPHY

Howard, J. K. *Amos among the Prophets.* Grand Rapids: Baker, 1968.

Kelley, P. H. *The Book of Amos.* Grand Rapids: Baker, 1968.

Motyer, J. A. *The Day of the Lion.* Downers Grove: Inter-Varsity, 1974.

OBADIAH

Andrew E. Hill

INTRODUCTION

This shortest book of the Old Testament is ascribed to Obadiah the prophet (1). His name means "servant (or worshiper) of Yahweh," and is one of the more common biblical names (cf. 1 Kings 18:3–16; 1 Chron. 3:21; 7:3; 8:38; 9:44; 12:9; 27:19; 2 Chron. 17:7; 34:12; Ezra 8:9; Neh. 10:5; 12:25). Aside from an unfounded tradition of the Babylonian Talmud (San. 39b) which identifies Obadiah with Ahab's steward, a devout believer in the Lord (1 Kings 18:3–16), personal information about Obadiah is completely wanting.

Obadiah's oracle has been dated variously to time periods ranging from 850 to 400 B.C. The date of the prophecy can be ascertained only by assuming that verses 11–14 refer to a specific episode in the history of Israel. The two most likely referents are the attack of Jerusalem by the Philistines and Arabs (ca. 844 B.C.; cf. 2 Kings 8:20; 2 Chron. 21:16–17) during the reign of Jehoram (853–841 B.C.), or the destruction of Jerusalem by the Babylonians in 587 B.C. (2 Kings 25:1–12; cf. Ps. 137:7–9; Ezek. 25:1–3, 12–14). Dating Obadiah shortly after the fall of Jerusalem seems to be the more likely option since the total conquest of the city described in verse 11 is best accounted for by Nebuchadnezzar's invasion, siege, and sack of the Judean capital.

The Book of Obadiah is one of several oracles against Edom (Isa. 21:11–12; 34:5–17; Jer. 49:7–22; Ezek. 25:12–14; 35:1–15; Amos 1:11–12) and its literary form is generally identified as a national oracle, much like Nahum's prophecy against Assyria (cf. also the national oracles in Isa. 13–23; Jer. 46–51; Ezek. 25–32; Amos 1:3–2:16; Zeph. 2:4–15). This anti-Edomite polemic can be traced through the Old Testament from the mixed blessing Isaac pronounced upon Esau (Gen. 27:39–40), to the exilic imprecation of Edom for its part in the overthrow of Jerusalem (Ps. 137:7), right through Malachi's affirmation of Edom's obliteration (1:2–4).

Obadiah's oracle, like those of Isaiah (1:1), Daniel (8:1), and Nahum (1:1), is a "vision" or revelation. In its broader sense the word signifies a divine communication to God's prophet or spokesman and it connotes the authority and authenticity of the prophetic message.

More specifically, the word is a technical term associated with the seeing of a vision. Its use in the Old Testament is restricted almost exclusively to the preexilic prophets and often occurs in the context of impending judgment. That Obadiah's oracle is a "vision" helps account for the terseness of language, the vivid imagery, and the certain realization of the event seen in advance as the prophet makes known Yahweh's word.

Obadiah 1b–4 and 5–6 repeat practically verbatim the words of Jeremiah 49:14–16 and 49:9–10. Naturally this raises the question of priority. Three views have emerged in the scholarly literature, one defending Obadiah's priority, one positing Jeremiah as the original source with Obadiah drawing from it, and one arguing for a no longer extant source common to both prophets. A common anti-Edomite source is the most likely explanation for the similarities between the two prophecies, with Jeremiah drawing more loosely from it and Obadiah adhering more carefully to the received tradition.

Although the literary unity of Obadiah has been challenged by critical biblical scholars, there is a basic strophic pattern in the prophecy evidencing an overarching design. The repetition of "Yahweh" at the beginning and end of verses 1–4 and 15–21 marks out clear literary units. The formulae *declares the Lord* (4, 8) and *the Lord has spoken* (18) are additional indicators of a deliberate structure.

The classic four-point outline standard in Hebrew prophetic literature (i.e., charges against specific sins; pronouncement of divine judgment; call to repentance; promises of restoration to the remnant) is evident in Obadiah, minus the call to repentance (characteristic of the anti-Edomite oracles). This basic theology is underscored by the recurrent themes of the day of the Lord, Esau/Edom, Edom's sin in relation to Judah, and the eventual reversal of the divinely appointed roles for each.

Obadiah, as Yahweh's envoy, proclaims a tripartite message to the nations. First, he condemns the pride and cruelty of the Edomites in their mistreatment of Judah during the sack of Jerusalem. This gross misconduct will not go unpunished and Edom's doom is certain (2–9).

Second, the prophet addresses the remnant of Israel, assuring them of the ultimate triumph of Yahweh and righteousness over the wickedness of all the nations in the day of the Lord (15–16). That day brings the promise of deliverance and restoration for the people of God, a theme common to the prophets.

Finally, implicit throughout this brief prophecy is Yahweh's dominion over the nations. He is the Sovereign Lord (1, NIV) who logs the iniquities of the peoples (10–14), administers divine justice (4, 8, 15), and controls the destinies of the nations.

Obadiah's oracle of divine retribution against Edom for assisting in and gloating over Judah's day of misfortune clearly teaches God's sovereignty over the nations of the earth and his justice in punishing the guilty. It also serves as a warning to the nations that they, too, are in jeopardy of having their deeds returned upon them as the day of God's wrath approaches (15–16).

More importantly for Israel, this prophetic statement of God's activity in history was designed to call to mind his covenant love for his people, thus bringing a word of encouragement for the present and a promise of hope for the future (cf. Ps. 111:2–9; Lam. 3:21–28).

OUTLINE

I. Superscription (1a)
II. Yahweh's Message Against Edom (1b–14)
  A. Edom's Judgment Pronounced and Reaffirmed (1b–9)
  B. Indictments (10–14)
III. The Day of the Lord (15–21)
  A. Universal Judgment (15–16)
  B. Zion Delivered (17–18)
  C. Yahweh's Kingdom Established (19–21)

COMMENTARY

I. Superscription (1a)

Unlike other prophetic books, Obadiah's oracle contains no information about the time or place of its origin, nor does it include any autobiographical data about the prophet. The brevity of the superscription matches the brevity of the book, perhaps to focus attention on the message rather than on the prophet himself.

The word used to describe Obadiah's prophecy ("vision") is a technical term having to do with receiving a revelatory word from God. More than mere human sight, this visionary experience is the result of divine inspiration and implies that the prophet actually saw and heard the communication from Yahweh. This gives him the insight and perception necessary to understand the unveiling of future events. The same expression occurs in Isaiah 1:1 and Nahum 1:1, and the ecstatic visionary experience which the word connotes may help account for the graphic imagery and explicit detail of the language found in these prophecies.

II. Yahweh's Message Against Edom (1b–14)

A. Edom's judgment pronounced and reaffirmed (1b–9). Edom (also called Hor, Seir, and Esau) and Israel were kin according to the ancestral traditions recorded in the Old Testament. The eponymous patriarchs of Edom and Israel were Esau and Jacob, respectively, both sons of Isaac (Gen. 25:19–34; 27:1–28:9; 32–33). The country of Edom was located in the highlands and sandstone cliffs on the southeastern edge of the Dead Sea, from the Brook Zered in the north to the Gulf of Aqaba in the south. A strong tribal organization existed in Edom from patriarchal times (Gen. 36:1–30), and the Edomites had a form of monarchy before the Israelites (Gen. 36:31–43). Edom was well established as a nation by the time of Israel's exodus from Egypt, as they denied Israel passage to the east and threatened them with a show of force (Num. 20:14–21; 21:4). Edom and Israel coexisted peacefully until the reign of Saul (1 Sam. 14:47); David defeated the Edomites at the Valley of Salt (2 Sam. 8:13–14). Judah controlled Edom as a satellite state until the time of Jehoram, when the Edomites successfully revolted and reestablished autonomous rule (2 Kings 8:20–22; cf. 1 Kings 11:14–25; 22:47). Later victories by the Judean kings Amaziah (2 Kings 14:7) and Uzziah (2 Kings 14:22) were localized and temporary at best.

As early as 597 B.C. control of the Negeb was wrested from Judah by the Babylonians (cf. 2 Kings 24:8–17) and the Edomites moved into the area to fill the vacuum. In 587 B.C. Edom not only assisted Babylon in the sack of Jerusalem, but also occupied Judean villages well into the Persian period (cf. 1 Esdras 4:50). The exact date of Edom's collapse remains imprecise and the circumstances are uncertain. By the time of Malachi's oracle (ca. 460 B.C.) the Edomite kingdom was in ruins (1:2–4). Edom apparently remained largely independent until a coalition of Arab tribes overpowered and displaced the Edomites sometime during the fifth century B.C. By 312 B.C. inscriptional evidence indicates the Nabateans had overrun the region of Edom, making Petra their capital city. Remaining Edomites either moved to Idumea or were absorbed by the Nabatean Arabs.

Obadiah's first pronouncement begins and ends with the Yahweh word formula characteristic of Hebrew prophetic speech, marking verses 1b–4 as a distinct utterance. The use of the formula at once identifies the source and authority of the prophetic word (cf. Amos 3:8; Mic. 3:8), as well as the covenantal context of the message (this divine name was revealed to Israel as part of the postexodus covenant experience constituting them as the people of God; Exod. 6:2–7; 19:1ff.). The title *Lord Yahweh* underscores God's rule over heaven, earth, and human history and is best translated "Sovereign Lord" (NIV). Fittingly, even as Judah was decimated and made a byword among the nations (Ps. 44:13–14; Lam. 2:15–16), Edom too will be reduced (i.e., "cut down to size"), made desolate, and despised by her neighbors (2). The self-deception induced by a sense of false security in the inaccessible heights of the surrounding terrain ironically will only compound the abasement Edom will experience once judgment comes. Like Assyria who said, "I am, and there is none beside me," Edom too is destined for ruin and the scoffing of passers-by (Zeph. 2:15). Like Babylon, Edom has not reckoned with God and so calamity and unforeseen catastrophe will suddenly befall her (Isa. 47:8–11).

Despite the terseness of Obadiah's language, it is rich with puns, imagery, and surprise. The word play in verse 3 is striking, in that the term for rocks (*sela'*) is akin to the name of the Edomite capital, Sela. Edom's perceived invincibility, similar to that of the soaring eagle which nests high in the crags, takes no account of the fact that even the eagle can soar and nest only at the express command of God. Edom has miscalculated her strength, foolishly forgetting God's pleasure "is not in the strength of the horse, nor his delight in the legs of a man" (Ps. 147:10–11).

Obadiah's second pronouncement (5–9) expands the message of judgment introduced in the previous section. The degree of Edom's punishment is at issue in verses 5–6. Thieves steal only what they want (or can carry), and grape pickers may overlook a few grapes. However, on the day Edom is ransacked and pillaged nothing will remain untouched by the looters. Even the most mundane of possessions will be pillaged by the ruthless invaders (cf. Jer. 49:9–10).

Interestingly, verse 6 begins with a variant form of the interrogative particle which opens the Book of Lamentations: "*How?*" The parallel to the lament over Judah is heightened by reference to the treachery of former allies (Lam. 1:2, 19). Judah had her "friends" too, but in the day of distress they were traitors and covenant breakers (Ps. 55:20; cf. Amos 1:9). Centuries before the prophets had warned of the folly of political alliances (cf. Hos. 7:8–11). Those who once shared food at a common meal (i.e., those in economic or political union with Edom) will lay a snare and entrap Edom unawares. (The last phrase of v. 7 is obscure, as the variations in the English versions attest.)

It seems best to understand the reference to wisdom or knowledge as further irony. Edom is about to be deceived—and in spite of all her wisdom. Pride distorts reality and blinds to the truth. This is why Edom is so easily deceived by treacherous allies. Edom's pride (3) carries the seeds of its own destruction in that God has purposed to bring low and to disgrace all who boast in conceit and insolence (Prov. 11:2; 16:16–18; Isa. 16:6; 25:11). Babylon was vaunted for her wisdom, yet it proved impotent in the face of destruction (Isa. 47:8–15). Edom's reputation as a depot of wisdom tradition in the ancient world was also widespread (see Jer. 49:7). Yet it too will fall. Teman was an important city in Edom and here it is used as an appellative for the whole (9). Military prowess, like wisdom, will prove useless in the day of God's wrath. Edom's defensive strategies will be confounded and her warriors routed. With the slaughter of the Edomites the jealous Lord has taken vengeance on his foes, punished the guilty, and restored faith and hope in the remnant of Judah for the fulfillment of covenant promises.

B. Indictments (10–14). The causal use of the Hebrew preposition *min* in verse 10 (NASB, NIV—because; NEB, RSV—for) marks the beginning of the second stanza in this first division of Obadiah's oracle. This section of the prophecy explains why divine judgment has been decreed by Yahweh against the Edomites. The list of charges (labeled "violence," 10) levied against Edom is made more weighty by the fact that the wrongdoing has been perpetrated by a brother against a brother (see Gen. 25:24–34; Deut. 23:7). They include: failure to ally with Judah in resisting a common foe (11); delighting in Judah's calamity with vindictiveness, haughtiness, gloating, and mockery (12); trespassing and looting the ruins of Jerusalem (13); ambushing fugitives fleeing east from the Babylonian onslaught and returning them to the enemy.

This catalog of crimes committed by the Edomites calls to mind the lawsuit oracle or judicial speech (e.g., Hos. 4:1–3; Mic. 6:1–2). Usually this prophetic speech form has three parts: the summons, the trial (with speeches by both prosecution and defense), and the sentence. The treachery and faithlessness of Edom has been so heinous that the sentence (Edom's humiliation and dissolution, 2–9, 10, 15) immediately follows the summons (1b). The trial contains only the speech by the prosecution (i.e., the indictments), and this merely to underscore Edom's guilt and the justice of the verdict—Edom's death warrant.

III. The Day of the Lord (15–21)

A. Universal judgment (15–16). These verses mark the beginning of the second principal section of Obadiah's oracle. The specific indictment of Edom now gives way to a more general statement of the universal judgment that characterizes the day of the Lord. The shift to the broader themes of judgment upon the nations and the restoration of Israel lends perspective to Obadiah's pressing concern for divine justice in view of Edom's role in Jerusalem's fall. It also bolsters future hope among the remnant of Jacob by validating the eschatological paradigm often repeated by the prophets—the final triumph of Yahweh in the world order (e.g., Isa. 24–27, 32; Jer. 29–33; Ezek. 33–34; Hos. 13–14; Amos 9).

This thematic alternation in verses 15–21 is heightened by the striking language variation in the Hebrew text, with the series of eight alephs (the letter *a* of the Hebrew alphabet) opening each of the lines in verses 12–14, abruptly interrupted by the fourfold repetition of the harsher palatal consonant *k* in verses 15–16 (in the prepositions *kî*, "for, because" and *ka'ăšer*, "just as"; cf. NASB, RSV). The emphatic position of the causal preposition *for/because* sets the tone for this segment of the prophet's message and further explains the relationship between the pointed denunciation of Edom and the more indefinite pronouncement of God's wrath against the nations.

The notion that crime punishes itself ("your deeds will return upon your own head," 15) or the principle of retribution is well founded in biblical teaching. The legislation of the Torah is rooted in the concept of lex talionis or "an eye for an eye" (Exod. 21:24–25; Lev. 24:20; Deut. 19:21), meaning punishment will be exacted in a fashion commensurate with the crime. Israel's wisdom tradition echoes this belief (Prov. 26:27; cf. Ps. 7:15–16); and even Paul acknowledges that a man reaps what he sows (Gal. 6:7–8). Judah witnessed the surety of this truth when God used Assyria to punish Samaria, crushed the Assyrian Empire by the hand of Nebuchadnezzar, and tragically, when he used this same Babylonian king to destroy Judah because of her guilt (Jer. 25:8–14). Obadiah calls the remnant of Judah to observe the final destiny of the wicked and to rest in Yahweh as their portion and strength (Ps. 73:17–19, 23–28).

"You drank on my holy hill" (16) is a cryptic expression for the cup of wrath God pours down the gullets of the nations as he defends his people Israel (Isa. 51:17–23; cf. Zech. 12:2). Ironically, the cup of wrath once tasted by Samaria is now passed on to Judah (Ezek. 23:31–34); finally, it will be drunk by the nations (16). Like the staggering drunkard falling unconscious to the ground in his own vomit, the nations will drink themselves into oblivion with the wine of God's anger (Jer. 25:27, 32–33). Edom's offense is all the more abominable because it participated in the destruction and desecration of Jerusalem, the city that bears God's name.

B. Zion delivered (17–18). The adversative conjunction *but* introducing these lines of the oracle alerts the reader to the upcoming comparison as the prophet contrasts the judgment and destruction pending for Edom (1b–14) with the future blessing and restoration of Israel (17–21). "Mount Zion" is a common reference in the prophets and the psalms to Jerusalem, the City of David (2 Sam. 5:7; 1 Kings 8:1). That Mount Zion will be "holy" (17) is an indication of the extent of Jacob's salvation and restoration and the fullness of renewed relationship with Yahweh.

The use of the word pair *Jacob/Joseph* heightens the foil between Jacob and Esau, and may be more than a poetic echo, as the use of "Joseph" elsewhere in the Old Testament suggests the larger collection of Israelite tribes (Ps. 77:15; Zech. 10:6; cf. Ezek. 37:16–19). The holiness characteristic of the restored remnant in Zion transforms Israel into an instrument of Yahweh's judgment, confirming Ezekiel's word about God's vengeance on Edom (25:14). The consuming fire of God's wrath which devoured the "stubble of wickedness" during the exodus (Exod. 15:7) and toppled the haughty Assyrians (Isa. 10:12–19; 29:5–6) is now unleashed against the Edomites. Unlike Israel, where the Lord preserved a remnant from Mount Zion, not one survivor will escape from the mountain of Esau (9, 19). The juxtaposition of Jacob and Esau (18) recalls the ancient narrative of fraternal rivalry and the prophecy Rebekah received concerning "two nations" in her womb (Gen. 25:21–27). It also lends perspective to the later declaration of Malachi, "yet have I loved Jacob, but Esau I have hated" (1:2–3). The concluding phrase *the Lord has spoken* serves as a sort of colophon, solemnizing the prophecy regarding the day of the Lord and emphasizing the certainty and finality of Esau's judgment.

C. Yahweh's kingdom established (19–21). Characteristic of prophetic literature, Obadiah's oracle concludes with the promise of restoration for the remnant of Israel. The promise of people moving to claim territories formerly occupied by enemies (19–20) enlarges the thought found in verse 17. Although the translation of verse 20a is difficult (here it seems best to read "the exiles of this army [or host], the sons of Israel, will have the Canaanites' land as far as Zarephath," following the NJB), there can be no doubt that the people referred to in verse 19 are indeed the house of Jacob. Zarephath was a town between Tyre and Sidon on the Phoenician coast and Sepharad has been identified with Sardis in Asia Minor or Hesperides near Benghazi in North Africa. Regions in the south (the Negev and Edom), the west (Shephelah and the coastal plain of Philistia), and the north and east (Zarephath, Samaria, and Gilead) will again be inhabited by the house of Jacob and Joseph. The prophet certainly intends to stir up memories of distant promises made to the Israelite forefathers concerning the land of Canaan as an inheritance, an everlasting possession (Gen. 17:1–8; Exod. 3:8; Josh. 1:1–9; 2 Sam. 7:10; cf. Deut. 1:6–8). The purpose of Obadiah's appeal to past history is to instill hope in the Babylonian exiles (and those who remained in Jerusalem as vassals to Nebuchadnezzar) by reinforcing their faith in Yahweh as a covenant-keeping God. By beginning and ending these verses (19–20) with the Israelite possession of the Negev, the prophet indicates the fall of Edom should be viewed as the trigger event setting in motion the fulfillment of all God's promises to Israel.

The culmination of Israel's restoration as predicted by Obadiah parallels the final outcome of human history, in that both consummate with the Lord's kingdom or sovereign rule in the created order (21). This theme of Yahweh's ultimate dominion over the world through Israel as his signet occurs frequently in the Old Testament as part of the messianic expectation of the day of the Lord (e.g., Ezek. 37:24–28; Dan. 2:44–45; 7:21–27; 9:24–27; Zech. 12:3f.). The ongoing contrast between the destinies of Mount Zion and the mountains of Esau now reaches its climax. Israel will be saved and restored while Edom will be judged for her crimes of injustice and oppression. The juxtaposition of the terms *deliverers* and *judge* is theologically significant given the close relationship of their meanings. The Hebrew judge was a divinely appointed savior for the people of Israel, the oppressed, and the socially disadvantaged (Judg. 3:9, 15; 2 Kings 13:5; Neh. 9:27). The Old Testament judge brought deliverance to the oppressed Israelites by renewing covenant faith (Judg. 6:19–32), establishing covenant justice in the community (Judg. 4:5), and by judging oppressor nations through military action (Judg. 3:10; 4:6–16). By raising up these deliverers in Zion God would not only accomplish the immediate goal of judging Edom's sin and avenging Israel, but also achieve his larger objective of establishing his righteous dominion on earth and executing true justice among the nations.

SELECT BIBLIOGRAPHY

Allen, L. C. *The Books of Joel, Obadiah, Jonah, and Micah.* Grand Rapids: Eerdmans, 1976.

Bullock, C. H. *An Introduction to the Old Testament Prophetic Books.* Chicago: Moody, 1986.

Craigie, P. C. *Twelve Prophets.* Vol. 1. Philadelphia: Westminster, 1984.

Laetsch, T. *The Minor Prophets.* St. Louis: Concordia, 1956.

Watts, J. D. W. *Obadiah: A Critical Exegetical Commentary.* Grand Rapids: Eerdmans, 1969.

———. *The Books of Joel, Obadiah, Jonah, Nahum, Habakkuk, and Zephaniah.* London: Cambridge University Press, 1975.

JONAH

Stephen R. Schrader

INTRODUCTION

Nowhere in the text is there any statement that Jonah himself wrote the book that bears his name, although the prayer in chapter 2 is in the first person singular. However, Jewish and Christian tradition has steadfastly maintained that Jonah himself is the author. In recent years many have held the position that the book is about Jonah rather than by him. There are several reasons why this view is held: (1) chapters 1, 3, and 4 are written in the third person; (2) there are supposedly late Aramaic and Hebrew expressions in the book; (3) the emphasis upon God's mercy toward foreign people indicates a postexilic date (much after the time of Jonah). Each of these objections has been refuted by conservative scholars.

The prophet Jonah (whose name means "dove") lived during the days of Hosea, Joel, Amos, and Obadiah. Jeroboam II (782–753 B.C.) was the king in Israel. Jonah predicted Jeroboam's restoration of Israel's border back to the glorious days of David and Solomon (2 Kings 14:25). He was the son of Amittai and came from Gath-hepher, a small village three miles northeast of Nazareth, the secluded place where Jesus grew up.

Jonah most likely preached in Nineveh during the reign of Ashur-dan III (771–754 B.C.), king of Assyria. Ashur-dan had been unsuccessful in reversing the deterioration of foreign affairs which had begun around 785 B.C. He also had to contend with plagues and internal revolt. These lean years in Assyria's history may have played a major role in the preparation of Nineveh for Jonah's ministry.

The Book of Jonah reveals the omnipotent and sovereign God: (1) he "hurls" a storm upon the sea; (2) he causes the lot to fall on Jonah; (3) he calms the storm when Jonah hits the water; (4) he prepares a large fish to swallow Jonah; (5) he causes the fish to deposit Jonah upon dry land; (6) he saves the Ninevites; (7) he prepares a vine overnight; (8) he prepares a worm to eat the vine; (9) he prepares a scorching east wind to cause Jonah discomfort.

Several lessons are evident from the Book of Jonah: (1) God has a genuine concern for the salvation of all people (4:11); (2) his plan will be accomplished in spite of human weakness and imperfection (Jonah's rebellion, disobedience, and bitter attitude); (3) he desires that his servants fully understand his plans and joyously fulfill his will for their lives (4:4–11); (4) he will discipline disobedient believers.

OUTLINE

I. Jonah Pursued (1:1–16)
 A. Jonah's Call (1:1–2)
 B. Jonah's Rejection (1:3)
 C. God's Pursuit (1:4–16)
II. Jonah Praises God (1:17–2:10)
 A. God's Deliverance (1:17)
 B. Jonah's Prayer (2:1–9)
 C. God Returns Jonah to Safety (2:10)
III. Jonah's Preaching (3:1–10)
 A. Jonah's Second Call (3:1–2)
 B. Jonah Obeys (3:3–4)
 C. The Ninevites' Response (3:5–9)
 D. God Spares Nineveh (3:10)
IV. Jonah's Pouting (4:1–11)

COMMENTARY

I. Jonah Pursued (1:1–16)

A. Jonah's call (1:1–2). God's call to Jonah is expressed in the standard Old Testament way by the phrase *the word of the* L*ORD came to Jonah.* This phrase occurs at least 390 times in the Old Testament to indicate a divine communication. It is difficult to ascertain exactly how God communicates this message to Jonah. Nonetheless, it is the Lord who gives this call. This personal name for God occurs in the Hebrew text as "Yahweh" (Exod. 3:14; 6:2). He is the one who redeemed Israel out of the house of bondage in Egypt, gave them moral standards to live by (the Ten Commandments), and then led them to the Promised Land.

God commands Jonah to "get up and go" just like he did Elijah (1 Kings 17:8) and Jeremiah (Jer. 13:6). Jonah's destination is to be the great city of Nineveh. "Great" is used six times of Nineveh or the Ninevites (1:2; 3:2, 3, 5, 7 [trans. nobles]; 4:11). It is a frequently repeated word in the book, being used fourteen times. It specifies the great area and population of Nineveh; its importance to God (3:3; 4:11—an object of God's pity); the extent of the response to Jonah's message.

The reason for denouncing Nineveh is expressed in terms that recall the divine statement in Genesis 18:20–21 concerning Sodom and Gomorrah. Zephaniah (2:13) and Nahum (3:19) also contain pronouncements of judgment against Nineveh and Assyria. Nineveh was the essence of human self-exaltation and anti-God power. It had been built by Nimrod, whose name is derived from the verb meaning "to rebel." The Assyrian king himself acknowledges that his people's ways are evil and characterized by violence (3:8). They are carefree, thinking they are invincible.

The Assyrians were well known for the brutal atrocities they inflicted on their war captives (impaling survivors on stakes in front of their towns; erecting pillars of skulls from slain warriors; nobles/chief officials hanging heads around their necks to demonstrate the power of their god Asshur). The city was known for its idolatry. Temples dedicated to the gods Nabu, Asshur, and Adad were located there. The Assyrians also worshiped Ishtar, a goddess of love and war.

B. Jonah's rejection (1:3). Jonah tries to run away from God (lit. to flee from before the face of Yahweh). Because Jonah has decided that he does not want to obey the instructions of the Lord, he immediately takes steps to avoid another audience with him. He decides to put as much distance as possible between himself and the place where the Lord has revealed his word to him. He is aware that he cannot escape God's power (1:9), but thinks that he can avoid another confrontation. Consequently, Jonah goes in the opposite direction from Nineveh—to Tarshish, possibly a port on the distant western end of the Mediterranean. Joppa was the chief Mediterranean port (modern Jaffa) serving Jerusalem in the Old Testament (2 Chron. 2:16).

C. God's pursuit (1:4–16). The author has structured this entire section in order to highlight the contrast between Jonah the disobedient man of God and the pagan sailors who faithfully worship their gods. God uses the sailors and their interrogation of Jonah to prick the prophet's conscience and to depict his insensitivity to people. The climax is reached with Jonah's confession in verse 9.

God is the principal person in the narrative, not Jonah. He takes control immediately ("Yahweh" is the last word in v. 3 and the first word in v. 4 in the Hebrew text) by sending a great wind on the sea that creates a violent storm threatening the life of the sailors. This act stresses his lordship over creation. Then he controls the lots and ultimately causes the raging sea to be calm just as Jonah hits the water.

Some interesting contrasts may be observed in these verses. Initially God sends a wind (Heb. hurls, which is translated "threw" in vv. 5 and 15 and "throw" in v. 12) and then the storm begins; whereas in verse 15 the sailors hurl/throw Jonah and the storm stops. Again, at the outset the sailors fear (lit. feared a great fear) and cry to their gods, but afterward they fear the Lord, offer sacrifices to him, and make vows.

Jonah's deep sleep in the face of the storm (v. 5b) may be contrasted with the sailors' desire to save him by bringing the ship to shore (v. 13). The captain requests that Jonah pray to his God (the true God!) so that they might not perish (v. 6a), something that should have been a vital concern to a man of God, a prophet in Israel! By contrast, in verse 14 the sailors pray to Jonah's God so that they do not perish when they throw him overboard. Central to this portion is Jonah's complacency. It is the captain who professes God's sovereign freedom to deliver them, rather than Jonah who should have known this from the very beginning. Jonah must be admonished to pray to his God that they might be delivered.

In the providence of God Jonah is singled out by the sailors. The lot falls upon Jonah. They then ask him a series of questions that prick his conscience. How amazing it is that they ask him: "What do you do?" He might have answered that he was a prophet and preached when he liked what the Lord told him to do. He identifies himself as a Hebrew and says he worships the Lord. He confesses that he is a believer in the true God. He adds that the Lord is also the God who made "the sea and the land" (v. 9). Jonah mouths this basic truth and then learns firsthand about God's power to control the sea. So often we flippantly repeat certain biblical truths about God and yet do not actually live in the light of these truths.

The sailors certainly understand the circumstances after his testimony for they become "terrified" (v. 10) and ask: "What have you done?" They seem to grasp the seriousness of Jonah's disobedience more than the prophet. It is amazing that the sailors exhibit more concern for Jonah's life than he does for the lost Ninevites.

Finally Jonah becomes very much aware that the storm is due to his sin. God has promised to discipline and chasten his wayward children (Prov. 3:11–12; Heb. 12:5–6). This is a prime example of such an instance.

When the sea becomes calm, the sailors recognize the reality and power of the living God of Israel. The calm also reveals that the storm had resulted from Jonah's disobedience and that an innocent life had not been snuffed out in casting him overboard. Their prayer has been answered and they now praise the Lord, in contrast to God's disobedient servant. In light of all the other miracles performed in the book it is not too unbelievable to think that these men became true believers in the Lord, as do the Ninevites. These men heard the testimony of a prophet of God and also saw a mighty demonstration of the power of the almighty God at work in a way that many have never been privileged to observe in any generation.

II. Jonah Praises God (1:17–2:10)

A. God's deliverance (1:17). Verse 17 actually begins chapter 2 in the Hebrew text and comprises a complete unit along with 2:1–10 in the English text. Yahweh (Israel's Redeemer) miraculously provides the means to save Jonah from drowning in the sea. The text reports that Jonah is swallowed by a "great fish." A different word is used here from that of "sea monster" or "Leviathan" (cf. Isa. 27:1). The fish was possibly a sperm whale, or perhaps a whale shark.

B. Jonah's prayer (2:1–9). The contents of chapter 2 correspond in several ways to the contents of chapter 1. Just as in chapter 1 the sailors have a crisis on the sea, pray to Yahweh, are delivered from the storm, and then sacrifice and make vows to Yahweh, so in chapter 2 the prophet has a crisis in the sea, prays to Yahweh, is delivered from drowning, and then promises to sacrifice and make good his vows to the Lord.

Jonah's prayer may be classified as a declarative psalm of praise. This type of psalm is common in the Psalter (e.g., Pss. 18; 30; 34; 40:1–12; 52; 66:13–20; 107; 116; 118; 138). God's intervention is the source of declarative praise, centering in what God has done. Normally the song was sung in the presence of the congregation on the occasion of sacrifices and other thanksgiving rituals. These actions were considered to be the payment of vows made while in distress.

Jonah's psalm is introduced by noting the place ("from inside the fish") where he voices his praise. In the psalm itself we are told he also prayed as he was about to drown (vv. 4, 7).

Jonah's beginning note of praise (v. 2) presents a summary of the psalm, including the fact of his distress, his prayer, and his subsequent deliverance. Thus, whereas in 1:6 the captain had admonished Jonah to "get up and call on your god"(!), now Jonah is forced to do so, for his own life is at stake. He calls upon Yahweh, Israel's covenant Redeemer and faithful God (note the emphasis on grace in v. 8). The word for "grave" here is Sheol. The reference to "earth beneath" and "pit" in verse 6 conveys the same concept.

Verses 3–6a provide some interesting insights into Jonah's perception of his experience. He acknowledges that God "hurled" him into the sea. The waves are also described as belonging to the Lord, thus showing that Jonah fully realizes that the sovereign God is disciplining him in this ordeal. Further, Jonah has become aware that his disobedience has cut him off from fellowship with Yahweh (cf. Ps. 31:22 for a similar expression, yet not due to the psalmist's sin). In spite of this, Jonah determines that he will turn to God for help.

Verses 5–6b vividly describe the hopelessness of the situation. Verse 5a may be translated: "the engulfing waters surrounded me even unto my throat." Throat, here, would be tantamount to "head." Jonah's life is about to be snuffed out! This is the end of his descent. Jonah's utter desperation is expressed in the word *forever,* because he expects to die.

God had "hurled" Jonah into the sea but now brings his life up from the pit. Similarly, David acknowledges: "O Lord, you brought me up from the grave; you spared me from going down into the pit" (Ps. 30:3). God is good!

Verse 7 recapitulates the previous three elements: Jonah's distress, his prayer to Yahweh, and his confidence that his prayer has been answered. Verse 8 summarizes the lesson that Jonah learns from this experience. His rebellion was in essence idolatry (cf. 1 Sam. 15:23). Thus, in a state of rebellion he had cut himself off from the grace of God.

Verse 9 contains three ideas. First, Jonah resolves to offer sacrifices to God with a "cry of praise" (trans. song of thanksgiving). We are to come into God's presence with cries of praise. Second, Jonah resolves to pay his vows. These most likely were made when he knew he was going to die. Third, "salvation comes from the Lord" (v. 9). God delivers the rebellious believer when he humbles himself and calls upon God. All of God's goodness is extended to undeserving sinners. There is only grace and forgiveness in God.

C. God returns Jonah to safety (2:10). God commands the fish and, in contrast to the rebellious prophet, it does what he orders. The fish is God's instrument of salvation for Jonah. Most likely he was deposited somewhere on the coast of Palestine near where he had started his journey.

Jonah had been inside the fish for three days and three nights (1:17). Matthew 12:39 refers to the "sign of the prophet Jonah" and stresses that "Jonah himself thus served as a 'sign' to the Ninevites, for he appeared to them as one who had been delivered from certain death. . . . [Apparently the Ninevites had learned what had happened to Jonah and how he got to their city.] As Jonah was three days and three nights in the belly of the fish, so the Son of Man . . . will be three days and three nights in the 'heart . . . of the earth.' [This is] a reference to Jesus' burial, not his descent into Hades. [Matthew attests that] Jesus' preaching will be accompanied by a deliverance like Jonah's only still greater; therefore there will be greater condemnation for those who reject the significance of Jonah's deliverance."[1]

III. Jonah's Preaching (3:1–10)

A. Jonah's second call (3:1–2). Jonah receives a "second" chance. He had repented and God had delivered him. If he is going to live, he must do what God wants him to do. He must preach the message that God gives him. And God in his goodness and mercy will allow Jonah to play a small part in the salvation of the Ninevites.

B. Jonah obeys (3:3–4). Jonah obeys (cf. 1:3), just as the wind, the sea, and the fish previously had responded to God's word. The trip would have been about five or six hundred miles in length and would have taken approximately a month by camel or donkey caravan. It may have taken up to five weeks for Jonah to reach Nineveh on foot.

1. D. A. Carson, "Matthew," in *The Expositor's Bible Commmentary*, edited by Frank E. Gaebelein, 12 vols. (Grand Rapids: Zondervan, 1984), 8:296.

Nineveh "was a very important city" (v. 3). It was important to God because these people had been created in his image and he has a "concern" for all lost people. Nineveh was also important in God's estimation because the sin of its people had become rampant and they were ripe for judgment.

The reference to three days depicts the amount of time it would take Jonah to complete his preaching assignment (cf. Neh. 2:6, where the king inquires as to Nehemiah's length of absence and not the distance of the trip in miles). Thus, it is not a reference to the circumference of the city; the diameter of the city; or the circuit of the administrative districts.

Jonah's message centers on imminent doom. Forty is the number employed in Scripture in relation to testing (cf. Gen. 7:17; Exod. 24:18; 1 Kings 19:8; Matt. 4:2). Some commentators have suggested that an earthquake, an eclipse, or a plague may have prepared the people psychologically to believe in God. It should be noted that at this time, Assyria was engaged in a life-and-death struggle with various mountain tribes. These peoples had been able to push their frontier to within less than one hundred miles of Nineveh.

C. The Ninevites' response (3:5–9). There are two strong arguments favoring the position that the Ninevites genuinely repented and became believers in the God of Israel. The first argument is the testimony of Jesus in Matthew 12:41. The second major argument involves the testimony of the Hebrew text itself. Verse 5 employs the most common construction used to express genuine belief or trust in God or his message (e.g., Exod. 14:31; Num. 14:11; 20:12; Deut. 1:32; 2 Kings 17:14; 2 Chron. 20:20). The same construction is found in Genesis 15:6 to convey Abram's continual trust in God and his word: "Abram believed the LORD, and he credited it to him as righteousness."

The "king of Nineveh" (v. 6) may actually have been a governor as the king's residence would not have been in Nineveh during Ashur-dan's reign (771–754 B.C.) but in Asshur or Calah. Nineveh did not become the capital of the Assyrian Empire until some time during the reign of Sennacherib (705–669 B.C.). The king (governor) gives royal approval and publishes a proclamation. This involves a fast, an act of humility, and an exhortation for everyone to "call urgently on God" (v. 8). The people are exhorted to turn from their evil ways and violence. The question "Who knows?" (v. 9) expresses the Ninevites' acceptance of the sovereignty of God. They are going to do what they need to do (human responsibility) and then let God be God (divine sovereignty) and put themselves at his mercy (cf. Exod. 32:30; Lam. 3:29; Amos 5:15; Zeph. 2:3 for similar expressions). The Ninevites articulate what Jonah refuses to allow in his God—God acts as it pleases him, which may or may not conform to human expectations.

D. God spares Nineveh (3:10). This is God's desire all along. When God sees that the people turn from their wicked ways, then he relents of his threat of destruction. He had spared Jonah (chap. 2); now he spares Nineveh. God in his grace allows men a chance to change their minds and actions to avert judgment.

IV. Jonah's Pouting (4:1–11)

The word *but* points up the contrast between God's compassion and Jonah's displeasure, and between God's turning from his anger and Jonah's turning to anger. The Hebrew is explicit: "But it was evil/displeasing unto Jonah, a very great evil/distress and it became hot to/for him."

In chapter 2 Jonah prayed earnestly for God's grace; here he is angry that God has extended grace to the Ninevites. In essence Jonah says: "I know that it is just like you to forgive people of their sins, so that is why I did not want to go to Nineveh in the first place!" He cites the great confessional of the nation of Israel (Exod. 34:6–7; Neh. 9:17; Pss. 86:15; 103:8; Joel 2:13) which expressed God's promise to forgive the sin of his covenant people. Jonah is, in fact, so upset about the possibility that the Ninevites might be saved that he actually asks to die.

Jonah's attitude reveals the depths of the depravity of the human heart. Deep down we cannot bear the grace of God being extended to others. This is expressed by Peter when he asked: "Lord, how many times shall I forgive my brother when he sins against me?" (Matt. 18:21) and the subsequent parable uttered by Jesus concerning the wicked servant (vv. 23–35). The master says, "I canceled all that debt of yours because you begged me to. Shouldn't you have had mercy on your fellow servant just as I had on you?" (vv. 32–33).

Yahweh (Jonah's gracious Redeemer) asks him the penetrating question: "Have you a right to be angry?" (v. 9). After Jonah makes a shelter for himself, God "provides" a vine to give shade for Jonah. Jonah is "very happy about the vine" (v. 6—in fact, the only time we are told he is happy). But then the vine is destroyed by God as he "provides" a worm to eat the vine. Then a "scorching east wind" and a blazing sun cause Jonah to again desire to die.

Zeroing in on Jonah, God asks him pointedly if he has a right to be angry about the vine. God reminds Jonah that he had been "concerned" about the vine (or "had looked upon the vine with compassion/pity")—something for which Jonah had not labored nor had he nurtured it to cause it to grow. If Jonah has become so attached to a gourd (upon which he has expended no thought, no labor, no toil, no sacrifice, no care, no planting, no watering, no tending, no pruning), then why shouldn't God be concerned about the 120,000 Ninevites who were spiritually lost?

Certainly God's Word pierces our hearts even today as it confronts us with our prejudices, selfish attitudes, and unforgiving spirits. Many of us become so concerned with our own vines that we forget the "concerns" of God, people for whom Christ died.

SELECT BIBLIOGRAPHY

Aalders, G. *The Problem of the Book of Jonah.* London: Tyndale, 1958.

Allen, L. C. *The Books of Joel, Obadiah, Jonah, and Micah.* Grand Rapids: Eerdmans, 1976.

Banks, W. L. *Jonah, the Reluctant Prophet.* Chicago: Moody, 1966.

Draper, James T. *Jonah: Living in Rebellion.* Wheaton: Tyndale, 1971.

Ellison, H. L. "Jonah." In *The Expositor's Bible Commentary,* edited by Frank E. Gaebelein, 12 vols. Grand Rapids: Zondervan, 1985.

Feinberg, C. L. *The Minor Prophets.* Chicago: Moody, 1976.

Fretheim, T. E. *The Message of Jonah.* Minneapolis: Augsburg, 1977.

Hannah, J. D. *Jonah.* The Bible Knowledge Commentary. Wheaton: Victor Books, 1985.

Keil, C. F. *Jonah.* Old Testament Commentaries. Reprint. Grand Rapids: Eerdmans, 1982.

Laetsch, T. *The Minor Prophets.* St. Louis: Concordia, 1956.

Walton, J. *Jonah.* Bible Study Commentary. Grand Rapids: Zondervan, 1982.

MICAH

Tremper Longman III

INTRODUCTION

The first verse names Micah of Moresheth as the one who received and communicated the vision concerning the future judgment and salvation of Samaria and Jerusalem. The name *Micah* is common in the Old Testament (a longer form of the name is Micaiah) and means "Who is like Yahweh?"

Moresheth was a village approximately twenty-five miles southwest of Jerusalem. The village was located on the edge of the rolling hills of the Shephelah, near the coastal plain. Scholars are not certain why Micah's parentage is not mentioned, but it may be because his family was not prominent. He is identified by means of his hometown because his ministry took place at a different city (probably Jerusalem).

Micah is mentioned in only one other place in the Old Testament (Jer. 26:17ff.). When Jehoiakim came to the throne in Judah, the priests and the false prophets tried to put Jeremiah to death. Some elders interceded for him and cited the ministry of Micah as a justification for Jeremiah's prophecy of judgment.

In the past, critical scholars have argued that the genuine oracles of Micah are restricted to the first three chapters. If one grants the possibility of predictive prophecy, however, there are no persuasive reasons for denying Micah the authorship of any part of the book.

The first verse once again is our source of information on the date of Micah's ministry. Three kings of Judah are listed to provide the period of time during which Micah preached threat and hope among the people: Jotham (750–732 B.C.), Ahaz (732–716), and Hezekiah (715–686). Of course, Micah's work may have begun toward the end of Jotham's reign and ended at the beginning of Hezekiah's, so we cannot be certain about the actual length of his ministry.

The reference to the coming judgment of Samaria (1:6) indicates that Micah's preaching began well before 722 B.C., the year in which Samaria fell to the forces of Assyria. Another oracle which may be fairly certainly dated is the lament in 1:8–16. The cities mentioned in this section coincide with the probable route of Sennacherib's army as he approached Jerusalem in 701 B.C. Of course, the reference in

Jeremiah 26:17ff. cites Micah 3:12 as an oracle delivered during the reign of Hezekiah.

A brief overview of the history of Israel and Judah that relates to the prophecy of Micah begins with the downfall of Samaria at the hands of the Assyrian army under the leadership of Shalmaneser V (722 B.C.). During the reign of Sargon II, Israel did not rebel, but upon this strong king's death and the accession of his son Sennacherib, Hezekiah joined a coalition led by a Babylonian rebel, Merodach-baladan (2 Kings 18ff.). In reaction Sennacherib threatened the independence of Jerusalem (701 B.C.), but through the ministry of Isaiah and Micah, Hezekiah repented of his sins and God spared the city. Nevertheless, it was not long after Hezekiah's death that the rulers of Judah turned against the Lord. Manasseh, his son, for instance, brought much grief to Judah. Micah's prophecy looks forward to the destruction of Judah at the hands of the Babylonians, which took place in 586 B.C., and even further ahead to the restoration from captivity (539 B.C.).

Much debate surrounds the structure of the Book of Micah. Opinions vary radically. Some argue that the book has no overall structure, but is simply a loose collection of prophetic oracles. Others identify extremely complex and sophisticated structures. A few points are certain:

1. Micah did not speak these oracles at one time. The book is best taken as an anthology of his prophetic messages over the years of his ministry.

2. Chronology is not the key to the structure of the book, though early in the book Micah does predict the capture of Samaria and Sennacherib's invasion, while at the conclusion of this book, he looks forward to the Babylonian captivity and the restoration.

3. The prophecy is roughly structured on the basis of alternating messages of threat and hope. God through his prophet disputes with his people in two rounds. The first is found in chapters 1–5. There is a harsh message of judgment (1:2–3:19—2:12–13 may be an exception), but also a note of salvation (4–5—5:10–15 may be an exception). The second round (6–7) also begins with judgment (6:1–7:7), but concludes on a profound note of hope (7:8–20).

The theology of Micah is largely concerned with divine judgment against sin. Yahweh commissioned Micah to bring this message of judgment against his people. Israel and Judah both departed from the way of the Lord and angered him by their sin. The sin is cultic (1:5–7) as well as social (2:1–2). Israel's civil (3:1–3) and religious leaders (2:6–11 [prophets]; 3:11 [priests]) have rejected the ways of God. They have a false security in the Lord.

The Lord, accordingly, presses his case against his people who have broken covenant with him. He reveals himself as a Warrior against his people (1:3–4). The Lord desires that his people love him and act justly. He calls his people back to himself.

While judgment against sin is the dominant note of the book, hope is not lacking. As early as 2:12–13, Yahweh speaks in comforting tones of salvation after judgment. The final picture of God (7:18–20) shows him to be unprecedented in grace and true to his covenant promise to Abraham. The promises to David are not dead, but will be fulfilled in the future (5:1–2).

OUTLINE

I. First Round of Judgment and Salvation (1–5)
  A. God's Judgment of Apostasy and Social Sin in Samaria and Judah (1:1–3:12)
  B. God's Word of Hope to Israel (4–5)
II. Second Round of Judgment and Salvation (6–7)
  A. God's Dispute with Israel (6:1–8)
  B. God's Reproach for Israel's Social Sins (6:9–16)
  C. The Prophet Laments Israel's Condition (7:1–7)
  D. Psalms of Hope and Praise (7:8–20)

COMMENTARY

I. First Round of Judgment and Salvation (1–5)

A. God's judgment of apostasy and social sin in Samaria and Judah (1:1–3:12). As with most other prophetic books, the Book of Micah begins with an introductory verse (**1:1**) that gives the prophet's name, the time period in which he ministers, and the object of the message that God gives him.

Micah begins with an invocation, a call to listen to the Lord. The call goes out to the whole earth and all who are in it, but the message is specifically directed toward Samaria, the capital of the northern kingdom, and briefly toward Jerusalem, the capital of the southern kingdom. Micah announces that the Lord has a case against Israel. He will witness against Israel by exposing her evil deeds (**1:2–7**).

The naming of the sin of Israel is preceded by the dramatic appearance of the Lord. He comes as a fearful Judge, a mighty Warrior (cf. the picture of God in the first part of the Book of Nahum). God comes from his dwelling-place, the temple, which is the earthly symbol of his true heavenly dwelling-place. He leaves it in order to destroy the high places. The high places refer to the places of false worship which the Israelites built for the worship of other gods.

When God appears as Judge or Warrior, nature reacts violently (cf. Nah. 1:4–5; Zech. 14:3ff.). The mountains, a well-known symbol of stability, will melt like wax before fire or water rushing down a slope (v. 4).

Verse 5 points the finger at the guilty parties. They are none other than Samaria and Jerusalem, the capital cities of the northern and southern kingdoms, respectively. Samaria was built by Omri and his son Ahab (1 Kings 16:24), a pair known for their sympathy with the Baal cult in the north. Jerusalem, the city chosen by God for his earthly dwelling-place, was time and time again perverted with the worship of false gods. Even the temple itself was polluted by the presence of pagan idols.

The accusation is followed immediately by God's judgment. Samaria will be devastated and turned into an empty field—a field with scattered rubble, which will be so empty that it will be used for agricultural purposes. Verse 7 directs God's judgment against the wicked religion that flourishes in Samaria. Deuteronomy 23:17–18 specifically prohibited both the practice (known among Israel's neighbors) of religious prostitution and the use of prostitute's wages for gifts to the temple. For breaking this law and others, Samaria will be destroyed.

The second half of chapter 1 (**1:8–16**) gives the reaction to God's announcement of judgment. The first to react is the prophet himself who is plunged into noisy mourning. His reaction reminds us of the later reaction of the author of Lamentations to the destruction of Jerusalem. Micah's mourning is not triggered by a concern for personal safety, but rather by the destruction which is coming upon God's people and the land he has given them. The prophet is distressed particularly by the danger that comes so near to Jerusalem. While it is difficult to precisely date these separate oracles of Micah, this oracle fits well with the various invasions of Samaria and Judah in the last quarter of the eighth century B.C. It specifically predicts the incursion of Sennacherib in 701 B.C. At this time, Sennacherib harassed many of the towns of Judah, but was stopped just short of taking Jerusalem.

The bulk of this section, however, predicts the reaction of a number of cities (vv. 10–15). These cities were likely the ones subdued by Sennacherib as he made his way down the coast of Palestine toward Jerusalem. They are located in the southern foothills (Shephelah) as one moves from the coast toward Jerusalem. The prophet employs word play between the names of the cities and their reactions in order to make his point.

The word play begins with a vengeance in verse 10. The word play in this instance is found in the similar sounds of the Hebrew sentence *bĕgat al-tagîdû*. On the Israelite side of the Shephelah Micah urges the opposite behavior—not the suppression but the expression of mourning. "In Beth Ophrah roll in the dust" (lit. house of dust).

The next four towns mentioned by Micah have either unknown or uncertain identifications. Nevertheless, the word plays continue. The inhabitants of Shaphir (v. 11), a name connected with a Hebrew word for "pleasant" or "beauty," will be naked and full of shame because of the coming judgment. The citizens of Zaanan (v. 11), a city name that probably comes from the Hebrew verb "to go out," will not come out, presumably due to fear of the invaders. The significance of the name *Beth Ezel* (v. 11) is not obvious to the modern interpreter. Maroth (v. 12) is a name related to the Hebrew word for "bitter." They waited for something sweet, but the bitter truth was the presence of the enemy at the very gate of the capital.

Lachish (v. 13) is a well-known city in the Shephelah and is singled out by the fact that a whole verse is given to it and by the content of that verse. The word play is based on the similarity in sound between the name *Lachish* and the Hebrew word *to the team* (*lārēkēš*). The significance of Lachish in this oracle may be seen in the accusation that they began the sin that infected Jerusalem. Nothing in the text indicates clearly what that sin was. Many have guessed from the reference to chariots that the sin was an overreliance on military armaments.

The next three city names also involve word play. Moresheth Gath (v. 14), Micah's hometown located near Lachish, has a name similar to the Hebrew word for "betrothed." The parting gifts are specifically those gifts given by a father to his daughter as she leaves his home to go to that of her husband. Micah alludes to the deportation that will follow the defeat of his hometown. The town known as Achzib (v. 14), related to the Hebrew word *lie,* will be a deception. Achzib was a city devoted to the production of materials that would bring in money for the support of the nation. It let Judah down in the moment of need. Mareshah (v. 15) sounds like the word for "conqueror." The ironic twist is that a conquerer will come against the town named "conquerer." The last city named is Adullam (v. 15), the location of the cave in which David sought refuge as he fled from Saul (2 Sam. 23:13).

The last verse in the chapter addresses all the inhabitants and tells them to cut off their hair (an ancient mourning rite), for God is about to separate them from their children through exile.

The second chapter begins with a woe oracle (**2:1–5**). The roots of the woe oracle are found in funeral laments, expressing sorrow over the loss of the deceased. The prophets, however, adapt the form to their own purposes. No sympathy may be heard in Micah's voice, rather threat of sure judgment. The use of the woe threat signifies that the object of the oracle is as good as dead.

The object of the oracle is described in general terms in verse 1 and then more specifically in verse 2. They are those who stay up at night contemplating how to work evil and then rise early to perform their wicked deeds. Their specific evil that Micah pinpoints is the amassing of real estate at the expense of other people. The landgrabbers both covet (breaking the tenth commandment) and seize (breaking the eighth commandment) land belonging to others. This sin is particularly grievous since the land was given to the Israelites by the Lord, so that each family might possess some. Thus, certain laws were in effect to protect the ownership of the land by the original recipients (Lev. 25). The story of Naboth and Ahab (1 Kings 21) provides a good historical example of this type of sin.

As happens so frequently in the prophets, the Lord chooses an appropriate punishment for these greedy and selfish men. It is tit for tat. The evil men plan iniquity; the Lord plans disaster against them. They desire status and riches at the expense of others; the result will be that men will ridicule them. Indeed, their own land will be taken away and given to others, even traitors. The reference in verse 5 may be an allusion to the future exile.

The false prophets come to the aid of the landgrabbers and confront Micah (**2:6–17**). This section is a dispute between the false prophets representing the interests of the wicked landgrabbers and, on the other hand, God and Micah.

The false prophets attack Micah's message

of doom, his message that God will punish their sin. They forbid Micah to prophesy. They do not believe that judgment is coming their way. The attitude of confidence expressed by the false prophets is similar to that found in Jeremiah 7, where the people trusted in the temple as the sign of God's presence in Jerusalem. According to the false prophets God will not do the things on which Micah is insisting. Indeed, the special word for "prophesy" in verse 6 may have a negative connotation ("rant" or "dribble").

Micah exposes the deeds of social injustice that were current during this time period. The false prophets and their clients rob the shirt off the back of defenseless travelers. They treat God's people like their enemy. They also rob women and children of their possessions and God's blessing. Women and children were the weak in Israelite society and accordingly are the object of God's special protection.

Once again exile is alluded to, this time in verse 10. God will eject the wicked from the land because through their wickedness they have made the land unclean.

The section ends on a strongly sarcastic note. The false prophets are prophets who bring only good news. Micah is no doubt extremely unpopular because of the generally negative tone of his prophecy. These people would rather hear a prophet who prophesies plenty of wine and beer.

Suddenly the prophet speaks in positive tones (**2:12–13**). This abrupt transition has caused many to question the plain meaning or originality of this short oracle. However, we know so little about the prophecy's structure or history of development that it is safest to accept the text as it is.

Micah glimpses that beyond the punishment of the exile God will once again bring his people together. The two opening phrases—*I will surely gather* and *I will surely bring together*—emphasize the certainty of the future promise.

The image used is the familiar one of the people of God as the sheep and the Lord as the Shepherd. The good Shepherd will gather the remnant into its pasture. He will once again, as at the time of the exodus, lead his people out of captivity.

The words *Then I said* remind us that Micah is being used of God to bring his judgment against the people (**3:1–4**). It also indicates that what follows in chapter 3 is a continuation of what came before, and indeed we find the same hard-hitting judgment brought against powerful oppressors that we saw in the earlier chapters.

Once again (cf. 1:2) Micah calls for attention, this time the attention of the leaders and rulers of Israel. These men are accused of gross sin and dereliction of duty. They are the ones who should know justice (perhaps judges are specifically in mind), but they do not. They have rejected the admonition which Amos (5:14) had earlier given, so that they hate good and love evil.

The image which Micah then evokes in his hearers' minds is that of a cannibal who rends the flesh of his victim, cooks it, and then has a meal. In other words, the leaders, who should be serving and protecting the people whom God has entrusted to their care, are exploiting them. They use them to their own advantage and to the people's disadvantage.

The time, however, will come when these wicked leaders will turn to the Lord. They will cry out to the Lord (the language reminds one of a similar phrase that occurs frequently in the Book of Judges). The Lord, however, will not respond to these individuals because their sin is too great.

The subject of God's judgment as spoken through the prophet Micah now switches to the prophets (**3:5–8**). In a word, they prophesy falsely and thus turn the people away from the Lord. Why do they do this? The Lord accuses them of loving payment more than himself or his people. A positive oracle may be gained from these false prophets if the pay is high enough. On the other hand, if no payment is offered, they prepare (lit. sanctify) war.

Their judgment is appropriate (introduced by "therefore"). They sinned with the gift of prophecy, so that gift will now be removed from them. There will be no visions and no divination, only darkness. No answers will be forthcoming from God.

A strong contrast exists between these false prophets and Micah. The Lord has given Micah his Spirit. He has empowered him with his message, and his message is one of judgment.

The third judgment oracle of the chapter (**3:9–12**) once again (cf. 3:1) opens with a call to the leaders and rulers to heed the word of the Lord. They are again characterized as those who are enemies of justice and right. The additional description identifies them as leaders in Jerusalem, who bring progress to that city through oppression and violence.

Verse 11 highlights and compares the sin of the leaders, priests, and prophets. Their common sin is that they perform their duty not in God's power and for God's glory, but rather for their own glory, specifically for money. Their confidence in the Lord is hollow. They trust in God's choice of Jerusalem as his place of special dwelling (that is, in the temple). If God's house is in Jerusalem, how can it be destroyed?

God himself will destroy this proud city. The destruction will be so complete that nothing will be left. Even the temple, which was the pinnacle of the hope that God's presence in Jerusalem would spare it from destruction, will be utterly destroyed and abandoned so that weeds will overgrow it.

We get a unique glimpse of the initial reaction to Micah's oracle from Jeremiah 26:18–19. The word of judgment came to Hezekiah and it reduced him to repentance, so that the "LORD relented."

B. God's word of hope to Israel (4–5). An abrupt transition from threat to promise takes place between the end of the third and the beginning of the fourth chapters. An oracle of severe judgment (3:9–12) is followed by a contrastingly glorious picture of salvation.

Micah looks beyond the immediate future of Zion's punishment to the more distant future in which Zion will be exalted (**4:1–5**). Isaiah (2:2) and Micah both speak of the day when Zion will be raised above all other mountains in preeminence. Zion's greatness has nothing to do with its present physical features (it is a relatively small mountain), but rather with God's choice of it as his place of earthly dwelling. When Zion is so exalted, it will be like a magnet for the nations. There will be a constant flow of people going to Jerusalem in order to learn God's law.

As the nations learn God's law and apply it to their lives, the world will be transformed. Warfare will be a thing of the past; nations will engage in constructive activities. Individuals will live out their lives in security and with satisfaction, reminding one of the high point of security reached during the reign of Solomon (1 Kings 4:25).

The hope is real. It will be fulfilled; God has spoken it. Indeed the prophecy began to be fulfilled with the rebuilding of the second temple. Nevertheless, complete fulfillment awaits the ushering in of the kingdom of God in its fullness (Rev. 21–22). Accordingly, the people of God must make their stand for the Lord in the present. Thus, Micah speaks for the people of God and reaffirms their commitment to trust and obey the Lord even though the nations follow their own false gods.

The opening phrase *in that day* marks the beginning of a second oracle of hope (**4:6–8**) and reminds the reader that once again Micah is focusing on the future. God will intervene and restore his people whom he has punished. They are weak because of God's punishment, but God brings strength out of weakness. The Lord will again establish his kingdom from Jerusalem. Further, the glories which Jerusalem once knew in the days of David and Solomon will be known again.

With the next oracle (**4:9–10**), Micah seems to take a giant step backward. He refers to the future Babylonian exile. This oracle is connected to the preceding one by its reference to Zion and to the next two because each of them begins (in the Hebrew) with the word *now*.

Micah begins the oracle with a satirical question—why do you cry aloud—addressed to the people. They are crying because they are under attack; they are in pain because the Babylonian army is pressing them and forcing them out of Jerusalem. They will be exiled to Babylon. Micah, however, does not stop there, but goes on to reveal that God will deliver them out of Babylon.

Many have trouble believing that Micah could speak of the Babylonian exile which was more than one hundred years after his death and the restoration which was even later. God, however, reveals himself in the Bible as sovereign over history and as one who chooses to reveal his will to his prophets.

Once again Micah reverts to the time of distress (**4:11–13**). Jerusalem is pressed by many nations. Verse 11 may be profitably compared with Psalm 2:2 and Zechariah 14:2, both of which picture the nations gathering to wage war against God's people. God is behind the enemy's action even though they are unaware of it. Verse 12 makes this clear since the prophet reveals that God is in control of the situation and gathers the enemy against his people only so he may devastate them. The enemy is gathered like sheaves that are on the threshing floor. They will soon feel the hoofs of the ox as Israel threshes them with particularly dangerous metallic hoofs. Jerusalem will, in brief, wage holy war against their enemies and accordingly devote the spoils to God who will provide the victory.

The next oracle (**5:1–6**) is similar to the previous two in that it begins with the word *now*. Further, like the others this oracle begins by describing a time of distress for Israel from which she will be delivered. This third oracle, however, reverses priorities and concentrates on the positive note of deliverance.

The first line of the oracle is extremely difficult. Some versions translate "marshal your troops, O city of troops," but it is best to read along with many commentators, "Now gash yourself, daughter of marauder!" The act of cutting oneself was a well-known expression of mourning in the nations surrounding Israel. Israel, however, was forbidden to engage in this practice (Deut. 14:1), thus giving the command a sarcastic tone.

The reason for mourning is clearly given. The Israelites are under siege and the ruler is publicly humiliated (slapped with a rod).

At this point, however, the mood of the oracle changes. Israel moves from the low point of humiliation to the high point of deliverance. That the deliverance will come from Bethlehem Ephrathah is a surprise! God uses the small and the weak of the world to accomplish his mighty purposes. Indeed, the choice of Bethlehem has further significance, in that David came from this small village (1 Sam. 16). The connection with David is explicit in the passage when Micah refers to the ancient pedigree of the coming ruler. That pedigree is Davidic and the roots of the fulfillment predicted in verse 2 may be found in the Davidic covenant (2 Sam. 7).

However, a delay is anticipated in the fulfillment of this great hope. This is expressed in the metaphor of verse 3: the one in labor (a symbol of the distress of the siege) must give birth first (the distress must first end). At that point the promised deliverer from Bethlehem will come and establish a kingdom of peace. He will shepherd his people. Kings were frequently titled "shepherd" in the ancient Near East. This metaphor points to the king, the one who guides and protects his people. The king predicted in these verses will excel at his job. In fact, he will be their peace.

The connection of the next two verses to this oracle is not certain. It may be a separate oracle. However, it does continue the theme of the security of Israel in the face of her enemies. In these two verses an Assyrian invasion is anticipated and calmly considered. The defense will be sufficient ("seven, even eight" signifies that there will be more than enough). Assyria here may stand for any potential enemy of Israel.

Of course, readers of the New Testament are aware that these verses find their fulfillment in the coming of Jesus Christ. Jesus comes out of Bethlehem (Matt. 2:6). He is the one "whose origins are of old, from ancient times." He is the son of David (Rom. 1:3), our peace (Eph. 2:14).

At this time Israel is being mocked by surrounding nations. In the future, Israel will dominate them (**5:7–9**). God is the one who will reverse the situation.

Micah expresses this thought through two metaphors or picture images. The second one is clear (v. 8). The remnant of Israel will be like a lion among the nations. The lion symbolized powerful and ruthless nations who were capable of devastating others. The first metaphor (v. 7) is less clear. Often in the Old Testament dew and showers signify blessing. Here dew is a curse. In any case, verse 9 makes it clear that the hope in this oracle focuses on future military victory over present enemies.

The last oracle of the second section (**5:10–15**) begins with the formula *in that day,* which again indicates that the prophet is looking into the future. God pronounces a series of purifying actions that he will bring against Israel. While it is true that the oracle never mentions Israel by name but rather addresses the object of the speech as "you," it is clear from the context that Israel is meant.

God informs Israel that he is going to remove the sources of wickedness and temptation from her midst. Specifically, he is going to abolish those objects that lead Israel to trust things other than himself.

First, God will destroy the confidence which Israel places in her military might. He will do this by removing horses, chariots, and fortified cities from the land. God has promised to protect obedient Israel from hostile attack and has proved through his numerous saving actions (the exodus is the most dramatic) that he could do so. Nevertheless, Israel constantly doubts his ability. She prefers to trust in military technology.

Second, God will destroy those objects by which Israel tries to manipulate the divine. These include magic and idolatry. Sorcery is a method for forcing God or gods to perform an act or reveal a message. Idolatry elevates a part of creation to the level of the Creator (Rom. 1:22–23).

The last verse shifts attention to the nations and presupposes that Israel has been purified. At the end time God's judging action will turn against the nations. This is a note of hope concerning Israel's future.

II. Second Round of Judgment and Salvation (6–7)

A. God's dispute with Israel (6:1–8). God's dispute with Israel takes the form of a legal proceeding. It is as if God has taken Israel to court. God calls on creation to serve as witness to his complaint against his people. The background of this section is found in the covenant that God established with his people. The covenant was like a treaty between God as King and Israel as his people. Before witnesses the people responded to God's gracious acts of deliverance by receiving God's law and promising to obey it (Exod. 19–24). Now that the people have broken the law repeatedly, God calls on the witnesses of the covenant to attest to their wickedness.

Israel is called to account for her actions toward God. She has turned against him. Why? Not only has he done nothing against Israel, but he has also done marvelous acts of salvation on her behalf. Specifically, God reminds the people of the exodus, Balaam's divinely inspired blessing when he was paid to curse Israel (Num. 22–24), and his bringing Israel into the Promised Land by a miraculous crossing of the Jordan.

This leads to God's instruction to Israel concerning what response he desires from them. How will the Israelites make their relationship with God right again? Micah contrasts external religious acts (sacrifices) with inward religious attitudes (justice, mercy, humility). These verses have been distorted to say that Micah and the prophets in general detested the priestly sacrificial system. Most scholars now admit that Micah was not attacking the sacrificial system itself, but the conviction that external religious acts without inward piety can establish a right relationship with God.

B. God's reproach for Israel's social sins (6:9–16). God once again pronounces judgment upon his people. Micah calls the people's attention to the Lord (Listen! [v. 9]). He adds a parenthetical comment directed to God that sounds familiar to those who know the Book of Proverbs: to fear God's name is wisdom. As the people will soon learn, the opposite holds true as well; to treat God wrongly or indifferently is foolish and extremely dangerous.

God then addresses the people of the city (most likely Jerusalem) and forcefully informs them that he is well aware of their sins. The sins that God highlights are those of social oppression. They cheat and lie in order to prosper in business. They grow rich at the expense of others.

God will not permit this state of affairs to continue, so he will punish them. The punishment, once again, focuses on the nature of their sin. They cheated in order to get rich and live a comfortable life. The Lord tells them, however, that they will be anything but comfortable. The Lord had blessed Israel with much material prosperity while they were faithful to him. At the time of the conquest, God told them that they would have cities, houses, vineyards, and olive groves which they did not build or plant (Deut. 6:10ff.). Now that they are disobedient, however, God tells them that no matter how much work they do, they will have no material prosperity.

The last verse of this section summarizes both the reason for punishment and the nature of that punishment. Israel has sinned by following after Omri and Ahab. These kings were known for their importation of the worship of Baal into the northern kingdom. Furthermore, Ahab was renowned for his own evil business practices. Since they go in the way of Ahab rather than in the way of justice, mercy, and humility, they will be destroyed.

C. The prophet laments Israel's condition (7:1–7). Micah continues with a lament. He mourns the spiritual condition of his people. This section may be profitably compared with the many laments found in the Book of Psalms. Two general types of laments are encountered in the Scriptures, individual and corporate. Though the latter are occasionally written in the first-person singular, the lament found in Micah 7 is best taken as an example of an individual lament, that is, as the prophet Micah's mournful cry.

Micah paints a dark picture of contemporary society. No one is left who desires to follow God. The only thing that the people do well is evil. Micah is exceedingly distressed and likens his own reaction to that of a man who craves grapes and figs, but arrives too late in the field to get any. In short, he is bitterly disappointed and frustrated. Even the most promising of his contemporaries are quite bad.

The sins of the people have caught up with them. Society has turned against itself; the situation has degenerated into chaos. Even the closest human relationships (wife, child, parents) are unreliable.

Micah realizes that hope is not to be found in human relationships. Hope may be found only in God, and Micah is confident in his God.

D. Psalms of hope and praise (7:8–20). The prophecy of Micah concludes with four sections united by their psalmlike style and their forward look to the time of restoration.

Micah continues to speak in the first-person singular, but now he stands for the whole nation. He envisions the time when Israel will be downtrodden and taunted by her enemies. He warns these nations not to rejoice too much, since God will deliver his people from their distress. The prophet proclaims that, though now the people of God are laid low, the Lord will bring salvation in the future.

This transformation of the Lord's attitude toward his people will come about due to the people's acknowledgment of their sin. When God reverses the fortunes of his people, he will lift them up and the taunting nations will become the object of judgment.

The prophet then addresses the people of Israel directly and informs them that the day of restoration will come. That future day will be a day in which the wall (probably of Jerusalem) will be restored. Such an allusion anticipates the future work of Nehemiah. People will then flock to Zion from such farflung and normally hostile locations as Assyria and Egypt. The context does not make it clear whether the reference is to the return of exiled Israelites to the land or the conversion of foreign peoples. In any case, Israel's blessing once again coincides with the downfall of the rest of the world.

Micah addresses his next words to the Lord and presents the needs of the people before him. He asks God to once again shepherd the people. The shepherd metaphor emphasizes God's guidance and care of his people (Ps. 23). The Lord will once again restore his love to his people and act for the deliverance of his people as in the days of old. For a third time the nations are mentioned as the objects of God's future punishment.

The prophecy concludes with a hymn that meditates on God's forgiveness and faithfulness to his people. The opening question, "Who is a God like you?" is a word play on the name *Micah* (in Hebrew Micah means "Who is like Yahweh?"). Micah is stirred to speak of God's incomparable forgiveness. He removes Israel's sin and throws it away. He does this because he is faithful to the covenant relationship which he established with Abraham.

SELECT BIBLIOGRAPHY

Allen, L. C. *The Books of Joel, Obadiah, Jonah, and Micah.* Grand Rapids: Eerdmans, 1976.

Mays, J. L. *Micah.* Philadelphia: Westminster, 1976.

Smith, R. L. *Micah-Malachi.* Word Biblical Commentary. Waco: Word, 1984.

Waltke, B. K. *Micah.* Forthcoming in the Tyndale Bible Commentary Series.

NAHUM

Hermann J. Austel

INTRODUCTION

The opening verse identifies the author as Nahum the Elkoshite. Apart from this nothing certain is known of him. Suggestions as to his birthplace are largely conjectural, and include Elkosi in Galilee, Al Qosh in Iraq, Capernaum ("Village of Nahum"), and Elcesei, a Judean village.

The three chapters can be divided into two parts. Chapter 1 describes the majesty and righteousness of God in his dealings with mankind, his kindness toward those who trust him, and his wrath toward those who reject him. Though Judah and Nineveh are clearly in view, the language is universally applicable. Chapters 2 and 3 describe the destruction of Nineveh and give the reasons for this.

The book can be dated somewhere between 663 and 612 B.C. According to 3:8 it was written after the destruction of Thebes (No Amon), which was destroyed in 663 by Ashurbanipal. The other limit is 612, the year of the fall of Nineveh. There is no objective evidence that the book is not what it claims to be: an oracle announcing the coming destruction of Nineveh.

Nahum forms a natural sequel to the Book of Jonah in that it reveals the alternative to the grace of God. In the Book of Jonah Nineveh experienced the forgiving grace of God about 150 years before the cataclysmic destruction depicted so graphically by Nahum. In his resentment toward God's pardoning of Nineveh, Jonah (4:2) quotes Exodus 34:6, one of the basic texts of the Old Testament and one frequently quoted or alluded to by Old Testament writers. It is a grand pronouncement by the Lord himself that he is a gracious and merciful and forgiving God. It is for this very reason that Jonah had initially refused to preach to Nineveh, because he understood very well that this pronouncement, seen in its context, was an assurance of forgiveness to all who would repent of their sins, and he had no desire to see Nineveh spared. The sparing of the Ninevites is an outstanding example of the extent of God's forgiving love.

Nahum, writing possibly 100 to 125 years after Jonah, at the high point of the power and arrogance of Nineveh, vividly sets forth the calamitous downfall of a later unrepentant generation. Nahum 1:3

quotes a portion of Exodus 34:6 ("slow to anger") and of Exodus 34:7 ("will not leave the guilty unpunished"). The point is clearly and unmistakably made that though God is slow to anger, punishment is certain and sure for unrepentant sinners.

In a very real sense, then, Jonah and Nahum vividly illustrate the "kindness and sternness of God" (Rom. 11:22). He extends his grace freely to repentant sinners, but judgment is certain and final for those who continue in sin and rebellion.

Another prominent theme is that of comfort. The very name of the prophet indicates this (Nahum means "comfort"). This theme is carried out in two ways:

1. In a number of specific statements (1:7, 12–13, 15; 2:2) Nahum declares that God is a refuge for those who trust him, that he will remove the yoke and shackles of bondage from Judah, that Judah will again rejoice in true peace and security, and that her splendor will be restored. These statements are gems that shine brightly in the midst of the graphic portrayal of Nineveh's sin and downfall.

2. The fact that God judges Nineveh with such finality and so irrevocably cannot but be an unspeakably great relief for those who for years had lived under the dread domination of the cruel and vindictive Assyrians. It is no great wonder that Jonah resented the sparing of Nineveh. Yet, though Jonah was not able to see the whole picture, Nahum shows us how carefully and accurately God keeps his books and how surely and with what finality he closes the account in his own time and way. Nineveh lies a desolate and unmourned ruin with no future, while Judah will prosper again.

The downfall of Assyria is a demonstration of the principle that God's enemies, no matter how powerful, will in God's own time fall. This principle is clearly stated in chapter 1, and the fact that God passes sentence on an unnamed enemy (though Nineveh is certainly in view) makes it easy to see Nineveh as an example of what will happen to all evil kingdoms. It would seem that chapter 1 is deliberately general for this very reason. While God is indeed slow to anger, he is not lacking in either power or resolve (1:2–3), and he will surely bring judgment on the sinner. Chapters 2 and 3, then, graphically portray the carrying out of God's judgment. That Assyria should fall was an incredible thought, yet God carried out his promise to the letter.

OUTLINE

I. The Zeal and Power of God (1:1–15)
   A. The Principle Underlying Divine Judgment (1:1–6)
   B. Destruction and Deliverance (1:7–2:2)
II. The Siege and Destruction of Nineveh (2:3–13)
III. The Cause and Certainty of Nineveh's Downfall (3:1–19)

COMMENTARY

I. The Zeal and Power of God (1:1–15)

A. The principle underlying divine judgment (1:1–6). The prophecy of Nahum is described as an oracle or "burden" (**1:1**). This word is regularly used of statements of a threatening nature. The fact that this prophecy is also designated as a vision points out that this is an official message from God, not spite on Nahum's part.

Though God has seemingly been overlooking Assyria's sins against him and Israel, this is not due to either weakness or lack of zeal on God's part (**1:2–3a**). The word *jealous* in Hebrew merges with "zealous." God does not treat sin lightly. Zeal is an essential part of his character. He is not only holy, but he zealously carries out the requirements of this holiness. His zeal will neither allow his people to sin with impunity nor will he allow Gentiles to sin against his people or his purpose with impunity. Unrepentant Nineveh will be punished and Israel will be saved. As an avenging God, he deals with injustice. Vengeance in the Old Testament is a juridical term and involves the righting of wrongs that have been done. Earlier Nineveh had experienced God's grace because they had repented. Now they will experience his vengeance. The outpouring of God's wrath has been delayed, not because he does not care or because he was helpless to act, but because he is slow to anger. The fact that Nineveh is not specifically mentioned in chapter 1, yet seems clearly to be in view, indicates that she serves as an example of the way God deals with his enemies in general. He will not leave the guilty unpunished. This is quoted from Exodus 34:7 and forms the necessary counterpoint to God's grace as described in Exodus 34:6. The nation or individual who rejects God's forgiving grace will of necessity experience the outpouring of his wrath. God will have the last word. A Jonah may be impatient with God for sparing a Nineveh for a time, but God's people may rest confidently in his determination and power to deal with sinners in his own time and way.

The awesome and irresistible power of God is displayed in nature (**1:3b–6**). If the most powerful forces of nature are at God's disposal to be used as his instrument of judgment, and if no area of creation is immune to the fierceness of God's wrath, how will any person or kingdom be able to withstand God's judgment? It must be carefully noted here, however, that judgment is not the only purpose of the manifestations in nature. Similar language is frequently employed to describe God's historical acts of redemptive activity in which judgment on the enemy may be involved, or simply the removal of obstacles to that redemption (cf. Pss. 18:7–19; 106:9; Isa. 50:2). The same is true of future events, both near and eschatological. All of nature is at God's command. He employs the whirlwind and the storm to accomplish his purpose of judgment. He dries up the sea and makes rivers run dry if need be to remove them as obstacles to the deliverance of his people. Bashan and Carmel as well as Lebanon were all noted for their fertility, the mighty oaks of Bashan and the beautiful cedars of Lebanon being proverbial expressions thereof. But when God chooses to pour out his wrath, even the most fertile and productive lands wither and fade. Even the solidity and the mass of the mountains and hills cannot stand before the power of God when he chooses to act. How much less can men who are themselves subject to the forces of nature and who build their kingdoms on shaky ground, hope to withstand the searing blast of the judgment of God! The fact that mountains were frequently employed in the ancient Near Eastern world as symbols for kingdoms allows the thought to move very naturally from quaking mountains to tottering kingdoms (1:5–14).

B. Destruction and deliverance (1:7–2:2). The Lord is good (**1:7–8**). This all-encompassing statement is one of the most frequently reiterated declarations about the character of God in the Old Testament. It stands in stark contrast to the fate awaiting God's enemies. To his own, God is goodness personified. Every need is met in him. He is the source of every blessing and benefit, from forgiveness for sin to abundant grace for daily needs, no matter how great the difficulty, to ultimate victory. In this context the goodness of God is specifically seen in terms of his being a refuge in times of trouble. God is the ultimate stronghold, the place of safety. When he sets out to judge, there is no place of safety or refuge for the sinner, but for those who trust in him there is peace and security (Ps. 46 is especially appropriate in this context). To trust in anything or anyone else can only bring bitter disappointment and loss. The New International Version "he cares for" (lit. knows; trans. watches over in Ps. 1:6) attempts to express that special concern that God has for his own. For God's enemy there is only the prospect of sudden and overwhelming defeat described in terms of an overwhelming flood.

Though according to historical sources there

was physical flooding of Nineveh at the time of its downfall, the force of the expression is to describe an overwhelming, crushing defeat as a huge wall of water wipes away all that lies before it. As if that sweeping defeat were not enough, God is said to pursue his foes into darkness. There is no possible escape. There is no place of refuge, no possibility of being overlooked. In the case of Nineveh, a few managed to escape when the city fell. They fled to Haran, but they were pursued there and were defeated in 609 B.C., leaving no trace of the once mighty empire.

The downfall of Nineveh is a pointer to the future. Nineveh serves as an example of the destruction that awaits the enemies of God and his people. This is indicated by the statement in 2:2 that Judah and Israel will have their splendor restored. This did not happen at the fall of Nineveh, but will happen in the day of the Lord after the enemies of God have been judged (cf. Zeph. 1:14–18; 3:8–20). The principle of Nahum 1:8 has been true throughout the ages, in Nahum's time relative to the destruction of Nineveh as the principal threat to Judah, and will in the end times be applied to the final enemies of God.

The futility of opposing God is here vividly set forth (**1:9–2:2**; cf. Isa. 8:9–10). However grand and well-conceived the plans of Nineveh and other world powers must be, they are doomed to utter failure. As with the "little horn" in Daniel 7, there may be initial success, but the outcome is sure. The opponents of God will be so thoroughly routed, they and the trouble they bring to the saints of God will not be able to rise again. Verse 10 is a notoriously difficult verse, but it is clear that it also describes the futility of opposing God. His foes will be as ineffective as the one caught in a thorn bush, as futile as one who staggers in his drunkenness. Finally, they will be consumed as though they were overdry stubble.

Though Nineveh is not specifically mentioned in verse 11 she is clearly in view. The one plotting evil may be Sennacherib (2 Kings 18–19), or this may be a collective reference to the evil kings of Nineveh. In any case, Nineveh is seen as a center of evil and rebellion against God, and as such stands in the line of world powers energized by Satan, culminating in the reign of the Antichrist.

Verses 12–13 are addressed to Judah in the form of assurance that Nineveh's yoke will be removed. These verses may well look beyond the temporary relief brought about by Nineveh's downfall to the final eschatological deliverance of the Messiah. Verse 14 predicts the utter destruction of Nineveh. It is a historical fact that after Nineveh fell, no trace was left of the power and influence of the mighty kingdom. It was as though Nineveh had never existed. Though Nineveh's kings assumed that their kingdom would stand indefinitely because of the protection of their idols, God buries Nineveh with the words *you are vile* (v. 14).

Yet there are glad words, declaring the delight with which God's messenger will be received when he comes with the joyful news that God has redeemed his people. The enemy has fallen and God alone reigns. The victory celebration gives the glory to God, who alone is worthy of praise.

Nahum 2:1–2 marks a transition and is the third in the series of contrasts in God's dealings with Nineveh and Judah. Verse 1 begins the description of the fall of Nineveh that is taken up again in verse 3. Verse 2 concludes the promises of the benefits that Israel will enjoy as a result of the defeat of her enemies. The result of the attack on Nineveh will be a scattering to the winds of her inhabitants (cf. 3:18). "Guard the fortress" are likely words of irony uttered by God in order to emphasize the futility of any kind of defense, no matter how strong. Both the destruction of Nineveh and the restoration of Israel are sure. The restoration of the splendor of Jacob like the splendor of Israel refers no doubt to God's carrying out his full purpose with regard to his people. One can only understand the reference to Israel as referring to all twelve tribes. In Nahum's time this seemed very unlikely since the northern kingdom had already been scattered throughout the Assyrian Empire for more than sixty years. But now it is Nineveh's turn to be scattered and Israel's turn to be exalted.

If the question be raised as to the fulfillment of this prophecy, it may be suggested that this is an example of what is sometimes called "telescoping," in which the ultimate fulfillment is anticipated by one or more anticipatory fulfillments. The fall of Nineveh brought relief to Judah from the Assyrian threat (partial fulfillment), yet within seven years Judah fell under Babylonian domination and within twenty-six years Jerusalem was destroyed along with the temple. Then about eighty years later, when Babylon had been defeated, there was a restoration of Judah to the land (but still under foreign domination). Yet ultimate fulfillment is to come, involving all Israel, not just Judah, and seeing the full establishment of glory in Israel, both material and spiritual. "Jacob" and "Israel" no doubt refer to the contrast between a self-seeking, conniving Jacob, a homeless wanderer desperate for God's help when he came to

Peniel (Gen. 32), and Israel, the man that God intended Jacob should become, one who would receive God's blessing, not by self-effort, but by trusting God and on God's terms. So will the nation experience the fullness of God's intended blessing.

II. The Siege and Destruction of Nineveh (2:3–13)

Nineveh had lived and prospered by the sword. It is now about to die by the sword. Nineveh is to be on the receiving end of the violence she has so freely meted out over the years (**2:3–6**). The assault on Nineveh is relentless, swift, fierce, and irresistible. Verse 3 describes the dread-inspiring appearance of the invader. The soldiers' shields are red, either from the blood of the battle or dyed red. This, along with the scarlet dress of warriors, when taken with Ezekiel 23:14, seems to indicate that red was a characteristic color of Babylonian armies at the time. The Medes, according to Xenophon, had a similar custom.

Verse 5 depicts the speed and the fury of the assault. There is no stopping the onrushing chariots. The streets and squares refer to the area outside the strongly fortified central city. The outer defenses have already been breached, and the assault on the inner city is now imminent. The subject of this verse is difficult to identify with certainty. The New International Version, with most commentators, sees this as a reference to the commander in Nineveh in his last desperate measures to shore up the defenses of the city. "Yet they stumble on their way" is taken, by this view, as pointing to the ineffectual efforts of the defenders to prepare for the final onslaught. An alternative, and probably more satisfactory view, is to see this as referring to the actions of the attackers. Nahum 3:3 explains the stumbling: the corpses of the defenders are so numerous that the attackers stumble over them in their rapid forward progress as they dash to the city wall. The protective shield (v. 5) is a shield put up for the protection of the attackers. The river gates are sluice gates used to control the flow of the Tebiltu and Khosr rivers to and through Nineveh. Apparently the gates were first shut to cut off drinking water; then when the reservoirs were full, they were opened so that the onrushing waters undermined part of the wall and even the palace, making it easier for the attackers to rout the defenders. Ancient tradition is in general accord with this. In light of this verse, 1:8 might well be a double entendre.

The city is emptied of its inhabitants by capture and by flight, and of its material wealth (**2:7–10**). God decrees that Nineveh should be plundered and destroyed. Verse 7 describes the captivity and grief of the inhabitants, verse 8 the precipitous flight of the defenders. Nineveh had been a pool or reservoir, collecting people and wealth. Now the flow is reversed, and there is no stopping the rushing outflow. The pungency of expression, the terseness of this passage graphically capture the drastic, unexpected, and rapid turn of events. That the supply of plunder is endless is echoed in the Babylonian Chronicle in its description of the sack of Nineveh: the spoil that was taken was "a quantity beyond counting."

Nineveh, similar to a lion's den, had been a place of security for its people as well as a repository filled with the plunder of conquered peoples. Now Nineveh has itself been destroyed and robbed of people and wealth. At the climax of this section comes the awful and unalterable declaration of the Lord of Hosts: "Behold, I am against you" (**2:11–13**). This expression is found twenty-eight times in the Old Testament and is used when God is set to act against a people that has steadfastly refused to submit to him. No matter how powerful or numerous or wise the nation, no matter what precautions taken, these words spell certain doom. But for those who trust God and seek refuge in him, the words of 1:7 apply. The voices of messengers, with their haughty and arrogant demands of submission and tribute, with their taunts and reproaches against God, will never again be heard. God has the last word.

III. The Cause and Certainty of Nineveh's Downfall (3:1–19)

This section, with its tense, powerful phrases, depicts Nineveh in a typical battle, overwhelming yet another hapless victim. The woe is here a divine denunciation and pronouncement of judgment (**3:1–4**). Verse 1 masterfully depicts both the character of Nineveh and the source of its prosperity and greatness. It was built on bloodshed and deceit and can only maintain itself and continue to grow by ruthlessly devouring other cities and kingdoms. Her appetite for blood and plunder is insatiable. Nineveh was a great and powerful city, proud of its achievements. But now comes God's assessment.

Nineveh no doubt would have gloried in the words of verses 1–2. Yet the "glory" of Nineveh's empire building is exposed as shameful and degrading. She herself will be shamed and degraded, and she who has victimized others will herself become a helpless victim without recourse. Though many commentators understand verses 2–3 as another description of the downfall of Nineveh in the form of an aside, it seems best to see them as a development of verse 1. The graphic, staccato phrases of verses 1–3 evoke the picture of a ruthless, grinding military machine. Nineveh's brutal subjugation and plundering of other cities is likened to the rapaciousness and greed of a harlot. Cruel, yet seductive, Assyria enslaved other nations, gaining permanent advantage for herself by offering temporary benefits to others.

Again the terrible words *I am against you* (**3:5–7**). Nineveh is now exposed to public disgrace, just as in the case of the judicial exposure of the nakedness of a harlot (Ezek. 16:37ff.; Hos. 2:3; Mic. 1:11). Nineveh is no longer the proud queen of harlots, holding the lives and destinies of nations in her capricious hands. Now she has been made a public object of scorn and contempt. There will be no sorrow at Nineveh's passing, only rejoicing.

Thebes (Heb. No Amon, "City of the God Amon"), situated about 140 miles north of modern Aswan, was one of the greatest cities of the ancient world. Often called simply "The City," some of its remains can be seen in the impressive temple ruins of Luxor and Karnak and the funeral monuments of the kings on the other side of the Nile. The rhetorical question "Are you better than Thebes?" has to do with strategic location rather than moral superiority. Ashurbanipal defeated it in 663 and dealt with it in typically cruel Assyrian fashion, pillaging it and razing it to the ground, killing numerous inhabitants and enslaving others. This defeat of Thebes came about despite its favorable location, numerous allies, and strong defenses. Just as the seemingly impossible happened to Thebes, so it will be with Nineveh (**3:8–11**). It may be "you too will become drunk" (v. 11) refers to the drunken condition of many of the defenders of Nineveh, as described by some ancient Greek historians. But the expression is more likely used figuratively, as is often the case in Scripture. As such it describes Nineveh's helplessness in the face of the attackers in terms of the reeling, tottering, and ineffectiveness associated with drunkenness. She will seek refuge, but there will be no place to go, no help.

Nineveh will be a choice object of plunder, easy to take, ripe for the plucking (**3:12–17**). There may be a subtle allusion as well to the fact that the time has come for Nineveh to be judged. Fruit or grain being ripe for the harvest is frequently used metaphorically in Scripture as pertaining to readiness for judgment (Jer. 51:33; Joel 3:13). The weakness of Nineveh is seen in terms of its defenders and fortifications. The formerly fierce and indomitable soldiers are all women. It is possible that this may allude to the effeminacy of Nineveh's officials as depicted by some Greek writers, but most likely this reflects the standard Near Eastern expression of the loss of stalwart manliness due to loss of morale (cf. Isa. 19:16; Jer. 50:37; 51:30). Because of the collapse of the courage of the defenders the gates of the land are wide open. The outer defenses, including fortified cities guarding the way to Nineveh, will fall before the enemy, leaving Nineveh isolated and without protection. An ample water supply was important in preparation for a protracted siege. Though extensive provisions had been made by Sennacherib to insure abundant water, special precautions were necessary to counteract the enemy's cutting off of the water supply to the city. Since stones were scarce in Mesopotamia, clay bricks were employed for fortifications. During siege conditions extensive repairs would be necessary to repair breaches in the walls. The ravages of fire and sword are compared to the terrible impact of a plague of grasshoppers (or locusts) on a field. Assyria had a long history of the establishment of trading stations. But they are depicted here as being not only as numerous as locusts, but as harmful to the land, plundering, then leaving without making any truly helpful contribution. The guards and officials of Nineveh are also compared to locusts: numerous, but then suddenly gone.

Nineveh fell in 612 B.C. Though Aššur-uballit II and his followers established a new capital at Haran, Assyria was already dead, the last remnant of the kingdom disappearing in 609, when Babylon forced the last holdouts to flee Haran.

Nahum closes with an epitaph for the king of Assyria (**3:18–19**). The word *shepherds* is a common Old Testament and ancient Near Eastern designation for rulers. With the demise of rulers and nobles, Nineveh's people will be scattered on the mountains, without a trace throughout the nations, without a hope of any healing, without a chance of regathering. Its passing will go unmourned. On the contrary, there will be great rejoicing by those who had felt the lash of Nineveh's endless cruelty.

The destruction of Nineveh was a major milestone in human history. With all the power and influence that Assyria wielded in its own time, nothing remained of Assyria after its fall but a bad memory. As such it serves well as an example of the lack of a future for the kingdoms of this world. By contrast, though God's people have been scattered, there is indeed a bright future as God raises up a Shepherd and regathers them to himself.

SELECT BIBLIOGRAPHY

Bennett, T. M. *The Books of Nahum and Zephaniah.* Grand Rapids: Baker, 1969.

Cathcart, K. J. *Nahum in the Light of Northwest Semitic.* Rome: Biblical Institute Press, 1973.

Feinberg, C. L. *The Minor Prophets.* Chicago: Moody, 1976.

Freeman, H. E. *An Introduction to the Old Testament Prophets.* Chicago: Moody, 1977.

Keil, C. F. *The Minor Prophets.* Vol. 2. Old Testament Commentaries. Grand Rapids: Eerdmans, 1951.

Kohlenberger, J. R., III. *Jonah-Nahum.* Chicago: Moody, 1984.

Laetsch, T. *The Minor Prophets.* St. Louis: Concordia, 1956.

Maier, W. A. *The Book of Nahum.* Grand Rapids: Baker, 1959.

Orelli, C. von. *The Twelve Minor Prophets.* Reprint. Minneapolis: Klock & Klock, 1977.

Pusey, E. B. *The Minor Prophets.* Vol. 2. Reprint. Grand Rapids: Baker, 1950.

Smith, J. M. P., et al. *Micah, Zephaniah, Nahum, Obadiah and Joel.* The International Critical Commentary. Edinburgh: T. & T. Clark, 1911.

HABAKKUK

R. D. Patterson

INTRODUCTION

Scholars largely agree that this prophecy was written by the man whose name serves as the title of the book—the prophet Habakkuk. Very little is known about Habakkuk except that he plainly calls himself a prophet (1:1) and presents for his readers an oracle or burden that the Lord has given him. The name *Habakkuk* has been associated either with a Hebrew word meaning "embrace" or with an Assyrian plant name *ḫambaququ.* Accordingly, some Bible scholars have suggested that Habakkuk was the son of the Shunammite woman to whom Elisha gave the promise "You will hold (embrace) a son" (2 Kings 4:16). Others, following the second etymology of the name, reason that Habakkuk must have lived and been educated in Nineveh before coming to Judah. Still others put forward the idea that he was Isaiah's successor by relating 2:1 with Isaiah 21:6. But none of these suggestions is certain. All that we know is that he was called of God to be a prophet to Judah and to proclaim God's revealed word. The fact that he uses certain musical terms in chapter 3 and adds a note that the psalm of that chapter is to be sung to the accompaniment of stringed instruments may also point to his having been a Levite (see 1 Chron. 25).

Evangelical commentators have suggested three different dates for Habakkuk's prophecy. Some suggest the time of Jehoiakim (609–597 B.C.), so that the conditions against which Habakkuk complains in the first chapter deal largely with the events of the first Neo-Babylonian invasion (ca. 605 B.C.; cf. 2 Kings 24:1–4; 2 Chron. 36:5–7). Others maintain that the desperate moral circumstances of chapter 1 reflect conditions that existed in Josiah's time before the copy of the Law was found (621 B.C.). Still others associate the details of Habakkuk's prophecy with the time of Judah's most wicked king, Manasseh (686–643 B.C.).

On the whole, the third position is to be preferred for the following reasons. First, the circumstances that Habakkuk decries reflect the debased spiritual atmosphere of Manasseh's day (cf. 2 Kings 21:1–16; 2 Chron. 33:1–10), a time that was so evil that God promised that he would bring a total "disaster on Jerusalem and Judah" (2 Kings

21:12). Second, the canonical position of Habakkuk between Nahum and Zephaniah, as well as the closeness of theological perspective among the three prophets would favor the earlier date. Third, it may be that both Zephaniah and Jeremiah knew and utilized Habakkuk's prophecy (cf. 1:8 with Jer. 4:13; 5:6; 2:10 with Jer. 51:58; 2:12 with Jer. 22:13–17; 2:20 with Zeph. 1:7). Finally, because Manasseh was carried into captivity in the latter part of his reign and subsequently repented and initiated several religious reforms, a date shortly before the western campaign of Ashurbanipal of Assyria cannot be far from wrong.

The occasion of this prophecy is to be sought in Habakkuk's spiritual perplexities about God's seeming indifference to great moral decay and outright spiritual apostasy. Habakkuk agonized over the immorality, inequities, and inequalities rampant in the society of his day. He could not reconcile such conditions with the presence of a holy and just God. Therefore, he took his soul-searching concerns to God himself. His prophecy describes his dialogue with God—his questions and God's assuring replies. God's answers also reveal something as to the nature of his person and work in Israel and with all men so that this short book contributes greatly to Old Testament theology.

Theologically, the Book of Habakkuk makes it clear that God is not only eternal and glorious but also sovereignly active in guiding all of earth's history to his desired end. God is revealed in his Word as a God of justice and mercy who has provided for the salvation of the man of faith and the deliverance of his people, Israel. Experientially, Habakkuk's short prophecy reminds the believer of the possibility of intimate communion with God that can overcome the deepest depression and the darkest seasons of doubt.

Structurally, the third chapter of Habakkuk's prophecy displays such stunning literary and thematic differences that critical scholars have often held it to be of independent origin. Some scholars even consider 3:16–19 to be a further independent unit.

It is evident that a basic difference in thematic emphasis exists between the first two chapters (Habakkuk's perplexities and God's answers) and chapter 3 (the prophet's prayer and praise). Further, chapter 3 includes some old epic material (vv. 3–15) that had been passed down through generations of Israelites since Moses' day. Again, these two portions evince distinct literary styles, the first two chapters being written in a familiar prophetic style that makes use of oracles, laments, and woes all in classical Hebrew, whereas the epic material of 3:3–15 is written in an older poetic style that contains some very difficult grammatical constructions and rare words. Nevertheless, the unity and single authorship of Habakkuk can be demonstrated from at least three conclusive facts. First, a common theme runs throughout the prophecy, namely, that God is sovereignly in control of the affairs of history. Second, demonstrable points of internal dependence and relation exist between the various portions, such as Habakkuk's patient waiting on the Lord (2:1–3, 20; 3:2, 16–19), his consistent portrayal of the godless (1:4, 13; 3:13), his reception of the Lord's answer to his perplexities (1:5; 2:2; 3:2, 16), and his confidence that the Lord will not utterly destroy his people (1:12; 3:1–2, 16–19). Finally, only with the closing verses of the third chapter is there a satisfactory answer to all of the prophet's uncertainties. Accordingly, the prophecy must be viewed as the product of one author, Habakkuk.

OUTLINE

I. The Prophet's Perplexities and God's Explanations (1:2–2:20)
   A. First Perplexity (1:2–4)
   B. First Explanation (1:5–11)
   C. Second Perplexity (1:12–17)
   D. Second Explanation (2:1–20)
II. The Prophet's Prayer and God's Exaltation (3:1–19)
   A. The Prophet's Prayer (3:1–2)
   B. The Prophet's Praise (3:3–15)
   C. The Prophet's Pledge (3:16–19)

COMMENTARY

I. The Prophet's Perplexities and God's Explanations (1:2–2:20)

Habakkuk introduces his prophecy by reporting that the words he will share with his readers are an oracle. The Hebrew word signifies that that which God has placed upon Habakkuk's heart, he will hereby proclaim to all. A similar superscription introduces Habakkuk's great prayer and praise in chapter 3 (v. 1).

A. First perplexity (1:2–4). Habakkuk cannot understand why God is ignoring the rampant corruption that he sees all around him in Judah. He has often cried to God in anguish but has received no answer. Because the call/answer motif is used often in the Old Testament to express intimacy of communion between God and the believer, God's failure to answer the prophet's call may indicate Habakkuk's fear that perhaps he is out of fellowship with God.

The Hebrew words for Judah's sin that Habakkuk employs in verses 2–3 involve the ideas of malicious viciousness, utter wickedness, and perversity. They depict a general condition of oppression, strife, and contention. What little justice there is, is perverted. The terrible conditions mentioned here are most applicable to the time of the wicked king Manasseh. According to 2 Kings 21:1–18 and 2 Chronicles 33:1–20, Manasseh plunged into every sort of Canaanite religious debauchery, including the worship of Baal and Asherah and the establishment of a state astral cult. Even the temple in Jerusalem was desecrated with Canaanite altars and symbols. The king himself not only practiced witchcraft but even involved his own son in the loathesome rites of infant sacrifice. Because Manasseh rejected God's rightful sovereignty over his life, it is small wonder that Judah was filled with violence and immorality. For Judah's law ultimately resided in the revealing teaching of God whose standards were to permeate every area of the believer's life. Accordingly, justice and righteousness, the twin expressions of God's legal and judicial holiness, are openly perverted.

Manasseh would not accept God's rebuke or instruction. Therefore, God brought judgment on him by allowing him to be carried off captive by the king of Assyria. This event probably is to be associated with the widespread revolts that plagued the reign of Ashurbanipal of Assyria in the mid-seventh century B.C. Although 2 Chronicles 33:12–16 reports Manasseh's repentance and subsequent restoration of true worship, it came too late to have any permanent effect on the spiritual tenor of the people of Judah. Indeed, when his son, Amon, succeeded Manasseh, he not only reintroduced all of his father's wickedness but "increased his guilt" (2 Chron. 33:23). Because Zephaniah and Jeremiah appear to have used Habakkuk's prophecy, and because the conditions described here must have occurred before Manasseh's captivity, release, and repentance, Habakkuk probably penned his prophecy about 655–650 B.C. Habakkuk cannot stand the immorality and injustice that permeate Judean society nor can he understand God's seeming disinterest.

B. First explanation (1:5–11). God's reply to Habakkuk's perplexity is puzzling. He tells Habakkuk that he will punish wicked Judah by using the Babylonians (or Chaldeans). Since the Neo-Babylonian Empire would not be a force to be reckoned with until the latter part of the seventh century B.C., such a threat seems totally unbelievable. In fact, although full judgment would not descend upon Judah and Jerusalem for more than half a century, Habakkuk is being told that those forces that will spell their doom are already being set in motion. Whether Habakkuk lived to see the rise of the Chaldeans is not known, but Manasseh's summons to Babylon would doubtless serve as a harbinger of Babylon's later dealings with the people of God. The pronoun *your* with the noun *days* is plural, and therefore does not indicate specifically Habakkuk's lifetime. The words are to be taken in a general way.

Verses 7–11 contain a description of the coming Babylonian army. God gives a detailed description of Judah's future foe so as to reinforce his dire pronouncement. They will be a formidable and fierce people who will be noted for both their cruelty and their arrogant spirit. Armed with a sizable cavalry, they will move swiftly across the land and with all the cunning of a ferocious wolf that uses the gathering twilight to attack the sheepfold.

On, on they ride, covering vast distances with the speed of a vulture set for the prey. The image changes in verse 9 to depict the band of despoilers as a desert storm. Just as the east wind (or simoom) carried in its cyclonic winds untold amounts of sand, so the Chaldeans will gather numerous prisoners.

In verse 10 the audacity and rapacity of the coming Babylonian host are underscored. A description is given of the siege methods typically used by armies in the ancient Near East in capturing a fortified city (cf. 2 Sam. 20:15; 2 Kings 19:32; Jer. 32:24; Ezek. 17:17). In verse 11 attention is turned to the Babylonians' unbridled conceit. Elated by their successes, they will throw away all sense of propriety, their reckless pride thereby sowing the seeds of their own destruction.

Thus, God's reply to Habakkuk is one of assurance. He is already dealing with Judah's sin but the full realization of his activity will come in God's own appointed time and way, however incredible his plan might seem to Habakkuk.

C. Second perplexity (1:12–17). Habakkuk has received God's answer to his questioning remarks. God is right! Habakkuk does not fully understand what God has said. He can understand Judah's coming punishment for sin, but he cannot reconcile the holiness of God with God's determination to use such a wicked people as the Babylonians to destroy the people of God. Throughout chapters 1 and 2 there is an indication not only of the prophet's perplexities with reconciling the nature of God and the circumstances of the world, but a suggestion of presumption on Habakkuk's part. His own theological system is unable to cope with life's realities so that rather than waiting patiently for God's purposes to unfold, he actually presumes to instruct God. He has charged God with negligence and indifference (1:2–4); he will now charge God with using evil to overcome evil. In so doing, he reminds God that, as far as Habakkuk can see, a holy God could not carry out such a plan.

In laying out his consternation at God's reply, Habakkuk diplomatically begins with the statement that he is sure Israel's God must do that which is right (**1:12**). He reaffirms his belief in God who is the everlasting Lord, the Holy One, Israel's Rock, and his very own God.

Having made the point of his allegiance to God, Habakkuk quickly points out the paradox that a holy God could use such a wicked nation to execute his purposes (**1:13–17**). Yes, Judah is wicked, but the same can be said to an even greater degree of the people whom God himself has just described. In making his point Habakkuk utilizes some of the same Hebrew words that are used to describe Judah's sin. Can God not see the danger of using such a treacherous and wicked nation as Babylon?

Habakkuk complains to God that his plan will render Judah and the surrounding nations as helpless as fish and sea creatures which fishermen catch with hooks, nets, or a dragnet. Unchecked by any foe, these Babylonian "fishermen" will know no god but their own nets. Although allusions have been found by some commentators to reports of the Scythian practice of sacrificing to a sword or to Alexander the Great's placing of a war machine in a Tyrian temple, the figure is probably not intended to refer to any literal sacrifice, for such is not known from the practices of the Babylonians. Simply put, the analogy is between fish (the conquered peoples), fishermen (the Babylonians), and the means of taking the fish (the mighty military forces of the Babylonians). What Habakkuk fears, then, is that the great success of the Neo-Babylonian army will cause them to have such pride that the Babylonians will live recklessly and riotously, believing only in themselves and raw power.

Habakkuk ends his second questioning on a note of lament. He wonders whether such arrogance and ferociousness, once unleashed, will go on mercilessly unchecked by any hand, including that of God. God had asked Habakkuk to "look at the nations" (v. 5); having done so and having heard God's solution to his first perplexity, Habakkuk is only more deeply dismayed.

D. Second explanation (2:1–20). Having voiced his protest against God's explanation, Habakkuk assumes the position of a prophetic watchman (cf. Isa. 21:8; Jer. 6:17; Ezek. 3:17; 33:2–3). Habakkuk will wait in earnest anticipation for what God will say in response to his latest complaint (**2:1–3**). Again the language is figurative. As a watchman stands ready at his post to receive news from afar, so Habakkuk will prepare his soul for God's message to him.

The Lord's reply is not long in coming. As a preliminary instruction, Habakkuk is told to write down God's revelation. Just as men write plainly important messages and information on tablets or inscribe them on stelae so that passersby may read them, so the Lord's prophet is to record God's Word for all to read. This is especially important since the fulfillment of the divine revelation will take some time. However, as the time approaches for its realization, it will be like a swift distance runner lunging with bursting lungs for the finish line. The Hebrew word translated here as "speaks" means literally to "blow out," "puff," or "pant." The verb is often used in contexts involving the giving of testimony (e.g., Prov. 6:19; 14:5, 25; 19:5, 9). Regardless of how slowly the fulfillment of God's Word seems to move, it will truly come in God's appointed time and that with sudden finality. Therefore, the words that Habakkuk is to record will bear witness to God's divine government truthfully: "they will not prove false." It is God who has said it! That ought to be enough for the man of faith.

God now discloses a great and hidden purpose in his ordered government (**2:4–5**). Behind the ebb and flow of earth's activities and the seemingly normal operations of human institutions, God is superintending the issues of the day. In doing so, he allows the two major classes of men, the righteous and the unrighteous, to be clearly distinguished. Despite the fact that God permits unrighteous people to thrive for a period and may even use them to execute his mysterious purposes, nonetheless the arrogance and self-will of the wicked will ultimately carry them to destruction. Habakkuk should see that the Babylonians certainly fit into this category. As so often is the case with the wicked, their success will produce an intellectual giddiness that will only be fed by the wine of their drink. The conquerors of Assyria will thus show themselves to be heedless of that which had contributed so heavily to Nineveh's downfall. The Babylonians' riotous life-style will bring about an insatiable lust for power and booty that would be as seemingly unquenchable as the thirst of death and the grave.

In clear distinction to the wicked is the righteous man, for unlike the wicked, neither power, nor greed, nor pride consumes him. Rather, "the righteous will live by his faith" (v. 4). The Hebrew noun translated "faith" here is also rendered at times "faithfulness." It is based upon a verbal root that means to "be firm," "be permanent," or "be secure," hence "be faithful." To the Hebrew mind no dichotomy existed between faith and faithfulness. The truly righteous person is the one whose faith is demonstrated in faithful deeds.

Verse 4 is cited three times in the New Testament. Paul uses it in Galatians 3:11 to demonstrate that salvation is not achieved by keeping the works of the law but is entered into only on the basis of genuine faith. In Romans 1:17, Paul emphasizes the fact that the believer's salvation, acquired by faith, must also be lived out totally in faith. The writer of Hebrews (10:35–38) points out that the sure coming of Christ for his faithful ones makes living by faith a categorical necessity.

Having made clear the reasons for his patience with men over the long course of history, God now tells Habakkuk plainly that despite the fact that he will allow the Babylonians' natural desires to be satisfied in order to bring Judah to judgment, nevertheless, the Babylonians will reap the fruit of their unrighteousness (**2:6–20**). God presents the self-destruction of the Babylonians in a series of pithy taunt songs in the mouth of those whom they had oppressed. Five woes are pronounced upon them, each consisting of three verses.

In the first woe (vv. 6–8) God declares that the Babylonians will be despoiled. As the Babylonians had plundered others, they, too, will learn what it is to be plundered. The long course of their rapacity will one day suddenly turn upon them. For all the while their accrued spoil will pile up like a debt which they owe and which will surely and suddenly be recalled.

In the second woe (vv. 9–11) God reports that the Babylonians will be dishonored. Those who build their kingdoms by unjust gain will be brought to shame. Using the riches that they had gained from the vast booty that the Babylonians had taken, Nebuchadnezzar would build up Babylon to be his own splendid city (cf. Dan. 4:29–30). Today the once mighty Babylon is but a heap of ruins whose very stones bewail its former grandeur.

In the third woe (vv. 12–14) God states that the Babylonians will be devastated. The Babylonians had built their proud city with the blood-bought booty of other nations. While they gloated over the treasure hoards that they had gathered to aggrandize their capital, little did they realize that it would all be used eventually for their enemies' siege fires. Worldly-wise Babylon stands as a representative of all nations who serve self rather than God. Surely all those who oppose him, as did Babylon, will one day be destroyed by the Lord at his coming to set up his universal and everlasting kingdom on earth.

In the fourth woe (vv. 15–17) God announces that the Babylonians will be disgraced. In these verses Babylon is likened to a man who gives his neighbors intoxicating wine in order to make sport of them by denuding them. Babylon had taken many lands and formed many alliances only to despoil its neighbors. All of this will turn back on them for the ones who had caused disgrace will in turn be disgraced. The Babylonians will drink to the full from their own stupefying wine and be exposed to open shame.

All of this is nothing less than the Lord's judgment. For the wine is said to be found in "the cup from the LORD's right hand" (v. 16). The cup is often used as a figure of that which God appoints for man, be it blessing (Pss. 16:5; 23:5; 116:13) or judgment (Ps. 75:8; Isa. 51:17, 22; Jer. 25:15–17; 49:12; 51:7; Ezek. 23:31–34; Rev. 14:10; 16:19). The right hand image is used in Scripture where distinct emphasis, honor, or definiteness of act is intended. Accordingly, Babylon's judgment is both certain and severe. Her vaunted glory will turn to disgrace. The force of the figure here yields a picture of one who is so overcome with drink that in his drunken stupor he lies naked in his own vomit.

Two further charges are laid against proud Babylon: she had greatly deforested Lebanon, whose cedars were prized in the ancient world, and had spilled the blood of man and animals alike in her insatiable thirst for world domination. Surely such violence will be repaid.

In the fifth woe (vv. 18–20) God proclaims the fact that the Babylonians will be deserted. What little spiritual consciousness the Babylonians had was largely the result of thousands of years of pagan polytheism. They had foolishly followed their idolatrous predecessors in calling god that which was the product of their own hands. Worst of all, in the hour of God's judgment, Babylon will be forsaken of her idols and perish with none to help her. Had Babylon only surrendered to the will of God rather than living for self and taking her huge booty and numberless captives, how different it all might have been. Now she must learn forcibly the full truth of the next verse.

Verse 20 stands both as a final word to the fifth woe and as a word for all men. It is better to pay homage to the One who inhabits the heavens than to trust in gods that are no gods.

II. The Prophet's Prayer and God's Exaltation (3:1–19)

A. The prophet's prayer (3:1–2). Habakkuk's prayer in this chapter is actually a prayer psalm. The Hebrew word for prayer used here designates five psalms (17; 86; 90; 102; 142) and is also used of the collected psalms of David (Ps. 72:20). Habakkuk's prayer psalm is both genuinely personal and yet designed for the sacred liturgy, as further indicated by the final footnote at the end of the chapter and the recurring use of the musical term *selah*, probably designating a musical interlude. The phrase *on shigionoth* is perhaps best understood as a song that can be set to several tunes.

Habakkuk recalls God's past mighty deeds on Israel's behalf and pleads with God that as he now brings Judah to judgment he will nonetheless deal with his people in mercy.

B. The prophet's praise (3:3–15). After laying bare his soul's concerns before God, Habakkuk turns to praise the Lord as the only one who can meet that need. In so doing, he draws upon a body of old (and exceedingly difficult) poetic material that had been handed down since the days of Moses. These epic poems told of God's deliverance of his people from Egypt, his preservation of them in their wilderness wanderings, and his triumphant leading of them into the land of promise. Actually, two poems are to be found here, the first describing God's leading of his redeemed people from the southland toward the place where they would cross the Jordan (vv. 3–7), and the second commemorating the exodus and early incidents within the Promised Land (vv. 8–15).

Habakkuk rehearses certain details concerned with the age-old account of God's deliverance of his people out of Egypt, the journey to Mount Sinai, and the movement from Sinai to the Jordan River. Habakkuk's first psalm joins the story at this latter stage. It may be that God gave to Habakkuk a vision of the things that he describes here.

The approach of God from the southland at the head of his people and in company with his heavenly train is detailed first. The two localities mentioned in verse 3 mark the Trans-Jordanian southland. Teman is the name of the southernmost of Edom's two chief cities. The name comes from a grandson of Esau (Gen. 36:11, 15, 42; Jer. 49:7, 20) whose descendants entered into the area. Paran designates not only a mountain range west and south of Edom and northeast of Mount Sinai but also a broad desert area in the Sinai peninsula. The event described here is given in similar words in Deuteronomy 33:1–2 and Judges 5:4, where the term *Seir* is used in parallelism with Mount Paran and Edom, and the importance of Mount Sinai is underscored.

Israel's God comes filling heaven and earth with his radiant glory. Far greater than the brilliance of the rising sun or the glaring blaze of the sun at midday is the glory of the omnipotent God. This theophany of God's awesome majesty was also accompanied by a manifestation of his power in plague and pestilence. It may be that these effects of God's coming are here personified as though they are part of his heavenly army. However glorious God's coming for his people might have been, it was horrible for his enemies.

The first poem closes with a further discussion of the effects of God's powerful activity. A violent shaking convulsed the earth so that the mountains tumbled downward. God's age-old paths collapsed before his power. Likewise, the inhabitants of the area were struck with terror at the presence of Israel's delivering God.

In verses 8–15 a vivid description is given of God's further victories involving his use of natural forces. Several incidents come to mind here such as the crossing of the Red Sea, the crossing of the Jordan River (Josh. 3–4), and the victories at the Wadi Kishon (Judg. 4–5) and Gibeon (Josh. 10). The whole imagery of verses 8–11 is somewhat difficult, but the point appears to be that God is the mighty Warrior who uses his celestial weapons on behalf of his earthly people.

In verses 12–14 the great victory of Israel's almighty Deliverer is portrayed. They focus upon God's redemption of his people out of Egypt at the time of the exodus. God is seen moving in great fury against the enemy, defeating him, disarming him, and destroying him with his own weapons. The poetic imagery implies that the evil leader of that enemy army was smashed with a blow to the head that crumpled him up like a heavy weight being delivered to the roof of a house and crushing it from top to bottom. Verse 14 is particularly picturesque. The enemy's self-confidence is compared to certain brigands who, confident of realizing their nefarious ends, lurk with eager anticipation in dark, secret places so as to set upon unsuspecting passersby. However, Israel's overconfident enemy will be rudely disappointed.

In all of this God's purpose is to be seen not so much in the fury of nature or in his ferocious assault against the enemy, but in his desire to save his people. The term *your anointed* (v. 13) has been taken to refer to Israel itself, Israel's Davidic king, Moses, or the Messiah. The term is not used elsewhere of Israel, however, making those interpretations that take it to refer to some individual to be more likely. Since the setting of the psalm is the exodus, David does not seem a likely choice. Hence, a reference to Moses or to the Messiah seems to be the most likely possibility.

Habakkuk brings this psalm to a stinging close with a reminder that Pharaoh's ambitions sank in the waters of the Red Sea (cf. Exod. 15:1–12). The point of the double psalm is clear. Just as God had led his people victoriously out of mighty Egypt, through the Red Sea, and on to Sinai, up from Sinai and through the wilderness, through the Jordan River and into the Promised Land, so he could and will yet lead his people in triumph over their enemies—but in his appointed time, way, and strength.

C. The prophet's pledge (3:16–19). The point of the divinely delivered psalms is not missed by the prophet. Having heard all of this (perhaps even having been shown the actual events in a supernatural vision), Habakkuk can feel his heart pounding (lit. my inward parts shook). The further description in verse 16 makes it clear that such stark terror gripped the prophet that he shook convulsively, from quivering lips to trembling legs. The questioning prophet now stands silent before the Lord of all the earth (cf. Job 42:1–6). He will no longer question God's purposes; he will merely wait quietly and patiently for those purposes to be realized. Though judgment must come because of Judah's sin, though all of Judah's produce fail, Habakkuk will trust in God. More than economic issues are in view in verse 17, for each of the commodities speaks of deep spiritual principles upon which the basic covenant between God and his people had been established.

Habakkuk's closing words are vastly different than his opening ones. In contrast to his harsh questions and accusations, the prophet now surrenders to God's purposes for Israel and the nations. Not only God's patient answers but the further revelation of God's person and power have been sufficient to humble the prophet. Habakkuk will live triumphantly and faithfully through it all. He will rest secure in the strength that God alone can supply.

SELECT BIBLIOGRAPHY

Armerding, C. E. "Nahum-Habakkuk." In *The Expositor's Bible Commentary*, edited by Frank E. Gaebelein, 12 vols. Grand Rapids: Zondervan, 1985.

Craigie, P. C. *Twelve Prophets*. 2 vols. Philadelphia: Westminster, 1984.

Hailey, H. *A Commentary on the Minor Prophets*. Grand Rapids: Baker, 1972.

Keil, C. F. *The Minor Prophets*. 2 vols. Old Testament Commentaries. Grand Rapids: Eerdmans, 1949.

Laetsch, T. *The Minor Prophets*. St. Louis: Concordia, 1956.

Pusey, E. B. *The Minor Prophets*. 2 vols. New York: Funk & Wagnalls, 1896.

ZEPHANIAH

Willem A. VanGemeren

INTRODUCTION

The name *Zephaniah* ("Yah has hidden") means "the LORD has protected." In the opening verse, his genealogy is traced back four generations to Hezekiah, the great reforming king of Judah. He was the son of Cushi and a contemporary of Josiah, the greatest reforming king (641–609 B.C.). He probably made his home in Jerusalem, as he shows familiarity with the city's religious and social life (1:4–13; 3:3–4) and physical appearance (1:10–13). His ministry may be dated to Josiah's early rule because Jerusalem is still full of idolatrous practices (1:4–6) and Nineveh is not yet destroyed (2:13). Because Josiah's reforms took place in 621 B.C., it is reasonable to assume that Zephaniah's ministry may have been a factor in the great revival that spread over Judah and extended to Samaria (2 Kings 22:3–23:25; 2 Chron. 34:3–35:19).

Zephaniah was born during the long rule of Manasseh (686–643 B.C.), the most wicked king in Judah's history. Manasseh had led Judah into an era of bloodshed, idolatry, and internationalism (2 Kings 21:1–18; 2 Chron. 33:1–20). The effects of his long reign were still felt in Jerusalem's religious and social life. The major political forces were Assyria and Babylonia.

Zephaniah lived through the transition of power from Manasseh to Josiah, who expressed a growing interest in Yahweh. Zephaniah seized the opportunity of calling on the aristocracy to join with Josiah in purging Jerusalem of idolatry, foreign customs, and political intrigues. Yahweh's anger had been aroused and the day of judgment was sure to come. But the future of God's people was conditioned on her present response to God's Word. Therefore, he encouraged the godly to pursue righteousness.

Zephaniah's message flows out of his view of God and the historical situation at hand. His view of God's attributes is simple, but majestic. God is sovereign over his creation (1:2–3), jealous of his kingship (1:18), righteous (3:5), and is the King who loves and rejoices over those who humble themselves (3:14–17).

The time of God's judgment on Judah, the surrounding nations, and the world is near. *Now* is the time to seek the Lord, before it is too late (2:2–3). The prophet calls for a response from God's people. The abiding significance of Zephaniah lies in his view of the day of the Lord. He telescopes the events that will take place from the fall of Nineveh to God's judgment of the earth. Since judgment is still impending, Zephaniah calls on all mankind, Jew and Gentile alike, to prepare for God's judgment.

The book is composed of three judgment oracles (1:2–6; 1:7–2:3; 3:6–8), one woe oracle of judgment (3:1–5), four oracles against foreign nations (2:4–15), a promise of salvation (3:9–13), and one oracle of salvation (3:14–20).

Zephaniah's language is strikingly similar to that of Amos and Hosea. His literary style has much in common with earlier prophets: a play on the names of cities (2:4–6; cf. Mic. 1:10–15), assonance (2:9), the description of the day of the Lord (1:14–16; cf. Amos 5:18), and descriptions of the judgment. His outstanding contributions are the development of the day of the Lord (1:14–16a) and the description of the leaders (3:3–4).

OUTLINE

- I. Oracles of Judgment (1:1–2:3)
  - A. Universal Judgment (1:1–3)
  - B. Judah's Idolatry (1:4–6)
  - C. The Day of the Lord (1:7–18)
  - D. The Call to Repentance (2:1–3)
- II. Oracles of Judgment Against the Nations (2:4–15)
  - A. Philistia (2:4–7)
  - B. Moab and Ammon (2:8–11)
  - C. Cush (2:12)
  - D. Assyria (2:13–15)
- III. Oracles of Judgment Against Jerusalem and the Nations (3:1–8)
- IV. Promises to Gentiles and Jews (3:9–20)

COMMENTARY

I. Oracles of Judgment (1:1–2:3)

A. Universal judgment (1:1–3). Zephaniah's first oracle proclaims God's judgment on the earth, including nature and all mankind. His message is universal, as it extends beyond a primary focus on Judah to include all nations. The devastation coming on the earth will be on a much larger scale than that of God's judgment by flood in the days of Noah (Gen. 6–8). The catastrophic language dramatically illustrates God's great anger with the earth on account of the wicked.

B. Judah's idolatry (1:4–6). Yahweh's judgment extends first to his own people (Judah) and to Jerusalem, which he has chosen for his dwelling-place. Yahweh's hand is stretched out with the intent to cut off all forms of paganism. The reason for Yahweh's anger is the lack of responsiveness shown by his own people. Idolatry is a flagrant breach of the covenant. For Zephaniah, idolatry is any expression which involves other deities, priests of non-Aaronic descent, illegitimate public and private forms of worship, double-mindedness, or apathy toward Yahweh. In Zephaniah's day idolatry was practiced even in the temple ("this place," v. 4).

God's judgment is on the foreign cults which had flourished during the days of Manasseh. Baalism remained even after Hezekiah's reforms (2 Chron. 33:3). The prediction that Baalism together with all other forms of idolatry will be destroyed was to some extent fulfilled during the reforms of Josiah (2 Kings 22:3–23:25; 2 Chron. 33:1–20) and more fully in the period of the exile, when the land was purged of all forms of idolatry. Molech (v. 5) was an Ammonite deity to whom children were sacrificed (1 Kings 11:5, 33; 2 Kings 23:10, 13; Jer.

32:35). In addition to these deities new gods had been added to the Judean pantheon, the astral deities introduced by the Assyrians, who encouraged the worship of the sun, moon, and stars (2 Kings 23:11; Jer. 19:13; 32:29; Ezek. 8:16). False worship was combined with the ministry of non-Aaronic priests ("pagan priests") and faithless priests of Aaronic descent ("idolatrous priests," v. 4).

Yahweh demands absolute loyalty from his people and he is angry because they have devoted themselves to other deities and are hypocritical and apathetic. Zephaniah condemns all who do not seek the Lord.

C. The day of the Lord (1:7–18). Three oracles of judgment on Jerusalem's political and commercial centers of power set forth the effect of the day of Yahweh's judgment on the political and economic leaders of Judah: the aristocracy, the traders, and the wealthy. Yahweh himself will see to it that the abuses of power and social callousness will get their rewards.

The prophet compares the day of Yahweh to a sacrificial feast (**1:7–9**). There are three parties: the host (Yahweh), the invited guests (enemies of Judah), and the sacrifice (Judah).

Man must be prepared for the day of the Lord. Zephaniah's admonition of silence (v. 7) is a prophetic call for men to recognize the difference between the Creator and his creatures. Man cannot justify himself before God, the Master of the universe. The designation *Sovereign LORD* (NIV; lit. Lord LORD, or Lord Yahweh) emphasizes the control of God. He who dwells in his holy place calls on mankind to be silent. The Judge of the universe has prepared a day of judgment.

Moreover, man must be prepared because the day of Yahweh is "near." From the prophet's perspective, the judgment of God hovers over mankind and may come at any time. The day of the Lord is compared to a sacrificial banquet, to which the Lord has summoned the enemies of Judah as guests and has consecrated them as his instruments of judgment. The sacrificial language is a prophetic metaphor of the day of Yahweh. The guests have been consecrated to participate as priests in the sacrifice. The sacrifice consists of the leaders of Judah: the princes, the royal household, and the courtiers. The aristocracy of Judah had adopted a pagan way of life and idolatrous practices, symbolized by their being clothed in "foreign clothes" (v. 8). The courtiers are those who "avoid stepping on the threshold" (v. 9). Several interpretations have been proposed: (1) they had accepted pagan superstitions (cf. 1 Sam. 5:1–5); (2) they were willing to please their masters (RSV who leaps over the threshold); or (3) they served idols. The charge against them is not that they "fill the temple of their gods" (NIV), but that they fill their master's house with wealth obtained by illegitimate means.

In the second strophe (**1:10–11**), the traders and financiers, whether Judean or foreign, are warned about the impending judgment and its effects on the financial center of Judah. Through the Fish Gate, situated by the north wall, the wall most vulnerable to attack, one had access to the business center of Jerusalem. The new prosperity had brought about the extension of the city beyond the old walls to include the New Quarter. But instead of traders, enemy forces will come and the merchants with all of their merchandise will be no more. Instead of the sound of barter, a cry together with noise of destruction will rise up from Jerusalem's market district. Jerusalem's center of trade, industry, and business will come to a violent end. The people are exhorted to prepare themselves by wailing in expectation of the judgment to come (cf. Isa. 13:6; Jer. 4:8; Joel 1:5; Amos 8:3).

In the third oracle (**1:12–13**), Yahweh's judgment is expressed against the wealthy, who are callous seekers of their own pleasures. Yahweh will carefully investigate and bring to judgment all of the wealthy. His searching is like that of a man tracking down an escapee with a searchlight. His object is to bring down the rule of the wealthy. The wealthy are compared to wine left on its dregs. The figure is borrowed from the wine industry, where wine was transferred from vessel to vessel to remove the dregs and yeast. Wine left on its dregs became undrinkable. Zephaniah's metaphor may also contain some irony (cf. NEB who sit in stupor over the dregs of their wine). The wealthy are so oblivious to the impending judgment that they think that God is powerless. They believe that they hold the future in their hands, and that God stands idly by. Yahweh's judgment reverses the fortunes of the wealthy. They have enriched themselves by having no regard for Yahweh, his covenant, his commandments, or their fellow citizens. Their aim is to build and to plant, but their goals will be frustrated by Yahweh's judgments.

Zephaniah's classic and moving poetic description of the day of Yahweh (**1:14–18**) is not original with him (Amos 5:18–20). Israel had expected that day to be victorious, marked by victory over enemies, with national glory resembling the era of David and Solomon. God's judgment was thought to be limited to Israel's enemies and could not conceivably affect his covenant people. Amos had to dispel that illusion. He characterized the day as a time of judgment marked by adversities, anguish, and despair, a judgment from which no one could escape. Zephaniah further develops the poetic imagery into an apocalyptic vision of the dreaded day when Yahweh comes to war against his own people.

The first strophe (vv. 14–16) emphasizes the speed with which Yahweh moves against his people. The terrible day of Yahweh is "near—near and coming quickly."

The appearance of Yahweh will resemble a theophany, such as at Mount Sinai when he made his covenant with Israel (Exod. 19:16; 20:21; Deut. 4:11). However, on the day of Yahweh there will be no revelation of his glory; no fire representative of his presence will appear. The day of the Lord instead will be a period of darkness, judgment, and alienation. Amos had explained the day of darkness as a series of catastrophes from which there would be no escape (5:19), a time marked by sheer helplessness. Zephaniah intensifies Amos's explanation by heaping up words portraying an admixture of cause (war), emotion (the cry of despair), and results (ruin). The intent of the prophet is to so affect his hearers that they will respond with dread and repent.

The prophet changes from a description of the day of Yahweh to the effects of the Lord's judgment (vv. 17–18a). Yahweh comes as a Warrior against his own people to bring distress on them, to make them feel helpless, even to bring a holocaust. The reason for the severity of his judgment is that the people have sinned against his holiness. When his holiness has been desecrated, he responds with jealous anger. The jealousy of God is that attribute which defines Yahweh as the source of all, the only one worthy of man's loyalty, worship, and obedience. He is jealous of his rights as the King of the universe. The jealousy of God is therefore not an expression of suspicion, but rather of precaution, so as not to permit his creatures to disregard his honor or to assume glory for themselves with little regard for him. The divine reaction of anger is an expression of his jealousy. His divine majesty has been wounded and demands retribution.

The prophet began his oracles with an oracle of judgment on the world, including mankind (1:2–3). He concludes by returning to the same motif (v. 18b, c). We are probably to understand "man" in the holistic sense as "all who live in the earth." In view of the nature of the anger of Yahweh, his judgment extends to all the earth; it does not differentiate between covenant people and Gentiles; it is inescapable.

D. The call to repentance (2:1–3). The shameful nation of Judah is called to prepare themselves like chaff for the judgment of God which will consume them like fire or blow them away like the wind.

Judah must do something before the terrible day of the Lord comes. The day of the Lord is not one of peace and prosperity but an expression of his wrath. The repetition of the warning gives ground to the exhortation to seek Yahweh. The godless have been accused of not seeking Yahweh (1:6) and the judgment will not pass them by. For the godly, however, the day of Yahweh is a day that should not be feared. God holds out an encouragement not for the people as a whole, but for the godly remnant, the "humble of the land" (lit. the poor of the earth). The humble are not poor with regard to material possessions, but are those who depend on God and walk in reliance on him. The pious remnant must continue to seek righteousness and humility. Election is not guaranteed by birth or by the sign of the covenant (circumcision). It is made evident by the fruits which belong to the life of faith.

II. Oracles of Judgment Against the Nations (2:4–15)

On the international scene, Judah's political future was far from secure. Judah was surrounded by enemies: Philistia to the west, Assyria to the north, and Moab, Ammon, and Edom to the east. Zephaniah expresses the sentiment of the population of Judah in his oracles of judgment against the nations. Yet he has a grander purpose in view. He speaks of the establishment of God's kingdom which the remnant of Judah and the nations will share together. The particular reference to the nations, therefore, is symbolic. On the one hand, Zephaniah refers to the nations which had a history of troubling Israel and Judah. On the other hand, the nations are symbolic of all kingdoms which oppose the rule of God. God's purpose is to establish out of the remnant of Judah and the nations a people who will submit themselves to him and worship him wherever they may be found (2:11). Since the coming of our Lord Jesus Christ, the salvation of which the prophet speaks has become more real to all who believe on his name, whether Jew or Gentile (1 Pet. 1:10–12). Zephaniah predicts that the future of the kingdom of God is dependent upon the way in which Yahweh deals with his enemies. Therefore, the salvation message is present in Zephaniah, but not with the same clarity as we find it in the New Testament. The way to read these oracles of judgment is to first focus on their historical context, then to trace the fulfillment of the oracles as they apply to the ancient nations and to any foe of the kingdom of God.

A. Philistia (2:4–7). Philistia, situated to the west of Judah, receives first mention because of its long-standing hostility. No reason for the judgment of Philistia is given, because every Judean understood why Philistia should fall. Zephaniah shows no feeling of hostility or joy in the description of the fall of the Philistines. He moves from a description of the fall of four Philistine cities to a proclamation of woe on Philistia to bring out how the Lord will bring blessing out of curse when the land of the Philistines is finally occupied by the remnant of his people. They will be the recipients of an era of peace and prosperity.

The judgment oracle against Philistia begins with a specific mention of four of the five major Philistine cities: Gaza, Ashkelon, Ashdod, and Ekron. Gath is not included in that it had already been destroyed (see 2 Chron. 26:6).

The literary imagery is filled with associations. Emphasis is on the poetic effect and words are carefully chosen to heighten the emotive impact. This is also the case in the ordering of the cities, in that Gaza and Ekron both begin with the same Hebrew consonant (*ayin*) and form an envelope around Ashkelon and Ashdod, which both begin with an *aleph*. The judgment on the cities is singularly brief.

Philistia will be subjected to two judgments: desolation of the land and removal of her population by death or exile. The term *Kerethite* (v. 5) is a reference to the Cretan origin of the Philistines and may also be an example of prophetic irony, since the word *Kerethite* is related to the verb "to cut off." God's judgment lies on Philistia. The war-loving Kerethites will be cut off so that Canaan, the land of promise, will have no reminders of Judah's long-standing enemy.

Philistia will become a place for shepherds with their flocks. After the cities have been leveled and the orchards destroyed, weeds and thistles will take over. The cultivated and inhabited land will become a place for grazing and trampling of animals.

The remnant of Judah will inhabit the coastland of the Philistines. War will be over. The incessant rivalry between Judah and Philistia, necessitated by the limited territories and adjoining boundaries, will be past. These verses picture the devastation of Philistia and an era of peace and prosperity when God's people will live in the land without fear.

God's promise ultimately pertains to the era of restoration, which includes the finding of pasture and lying down (v. 7). The verb *lie down* denotes the rest, provision, and protection Yahweh the great Shepherd gives to his people. The language of remnant, shepherding, and lying down is further developed in 3:12–13. God's people will be able to enjoy the inheritance promised to them by Yahweh himself. The promise belongs to "the remnant" (v. 7), a term designating the faithful among the covenant people who seek Yahweh. The promise of the peaceful possession of this earth belongs to the godly. The Lord will "care" for them by bestowing his divine favor upon them. The remnant receives the assurance that Yahweh has planned for the restoration of his own.

B. Moab and Ammon (2:8–11). Though the Israelites were related to the Moabites and Ammonites through Lot, a nephew of Abraham, their relations had always been bitter (cf. Num. 22:2–24:25; Deut. 23:3–6; Judg. 3:12–30; 1 Sam. 11; 2 Sam. 8:2; 10:1–19). The policy of Moab and Ammon was to ridicule Judah by scoffing at her precarious situation. When Judah needed political and military support against the Assyrians, Moab and Ammon did not come to her rescue, but were intent upon protecting their own delicate situation. Their concern for self-preservation and offensive relations with Judah are the object of the prophetic oracle of judgment. Yahweh has "heard the insults of Moab and the taunts of the Ammonites" (v. 8). Even when God's people fall short of what he expects, he remains loyal to his covenant. The taunting, laughing, reviling, threats, and insults directed against his children affect Yahweh as a Father. The oracle against Moab and Ammon assures the "remnant" of God's care. The oracle becomes a source of hope and comfort to all of God's people.

Yahweh rises on behalf of his own. He is the Lord of Hosts. As the King of the universe, he commands innumerable hosts and will protect the future of his people. He is still the God of Israel, as he has promised to the patriarchs to be the God of their children. He assures the pious community that he will be with them, regardless of how the nations may rise up against them or boast over their own advantages. The assurance is guaranteed by an oath, "as surely as I live." Yahweh swears by himself that he will come to the aid of his people.

The judgment on the nations is poetically portrayed as a repetition of God's judgment on Sodom and Gomorrah, a favorite metaphor in the prophets (Isa. 1:9–10; 3:9; 13:19; Jer. 23:14; 49:18; 50:40; Amos 4:11). It is not unlikely that the prophet plays on the sound of the words *Moab* and *Sodom, Ammon* and *Amorrah* (Heb. Gomorrah). He further explains the nature of the reversal of the fortunes of these nations.

They are likened to a plot of weeds and salt pits.

The future lies with the remnant. They are further identified as "my people." How this language must have spoken to the hearts of the godly community in exile! God's rule will be established and the righteous will inherit the earth. The Jews, upon their return from exile, did not receive the complete fulfillment of this prophetic word. Yet the people of God in any age can look forward to the time when God's judgment will come upon the kingdoms of this world, which will be overturned like Sodom and Gomorrah. Then the righteous will truly inherit the earth. The verb *inherit* signifies taking possession of the land (Exod. 23:30) as legal heirs. The enemies of God are not considered heirs of the world. In verse 10 the prophet explains why the fortunes of the nations will be reversed. They were filled with pride and insults. In their pride they mocked and taunted the people of the Lord. Because they have reviled the covenant people, they are subject to the curse: "Whoever curses you I will curse" (Gen. 12:3).

When the Lord acts on behalf of his own, he will appear as "awesome" or terrifying to the nations. Taunting will cease and their gloating words will not be heard anymore because of the presence of Yahweh, the God of Israel. The nations along with their national deities and idols will disappear from the earth. In place of paganism and idolatry the prophet looks forward to the universal worship of the Lord.

To some extent, this was fulfilled in the Judaism of the Diaspora, when Gentiles worshiped as God-fearers or proselytes in their local synagogues. Yet, Zephaniah goes beyond the expectation of the central and universal worship of Yahweh. He anticipates Jesus' teaching that acceptable worship may take place *wherever* God's people assemble and worship him in spirit and truth (John 4:23).

C. Cush (2:12). Ethiopia (Cush) had ruled Egypt as the twenty-fifth dynasty from 712 to 663 B.C. Here the prophet may be making a sarcastic reference to Egypt by calling it "Cush" even though it was no longer ruled by the Ethiopians. Still, it is not clear from the context whether he has Ethiopia or Egypt in mind.

D. Assyria (2:13–15). Relations between Assyria and Judah went back more than one hundred years prior to the time of Zephaniah. Isaiah had predicted the victory of Assyria over the eastern Mediterranean region. By Zephaniah's time, the Aramean and Israelite kingdoms had been subjugated and their populations exiled. Sennacherib had invaded Judah (701 B.C.) and Hezekiah had been forced to pay tribute. Hezekiah's son, Manasseh, spent time in Babylon as a part of a reform program to assure his loyalties to Assyria (2 Chron. 33:11). Josiah had to decide where his loyalties lay. He could avoid political problems by pleasing Assyria, which had been the dominant power for over a century. Due to the length of Assyria's rule, the extent of its military power, and its proximity to Jerusalem, Assyrian influence on Israel's politics, culture, and religion was pervasive. It was difficult for Zephaniah's contemporaries to realize how close Assyria was to its demise.

Zephaniah strongly condemns Assyria's religious influence on Jerusalem as well as its tyrannical power. Yahweh proclaims to the people of Judah that they should neither rely on the superpowers (Ethiopia [= Egypt?] and Assyria) nor be worried by the coalition of the small nations (Philistia, Moab, and Ammon). All kingdoms, whether great or small, will fall.

The oracle against Assyria is in the form of a message of doom. The great Assyrian power will come to nothing. It will be like a "desolate" place, a "desert." Assyria's power will be dried up like a brook without water.

The presence of animals (v. 14) indicates that life is possible in Assyria; its climate is not altered. Flocks, herds, and wild animals will inhabit Assyria's ruins.

The fall of Nineveh is sarcastically portrayed by a hyperbolic description of its greatness (v. 15). By exaggerating the greatness of Nineveh, its fall is heightened. Nineveh represents the Assyrian Empire. The treasures and booty from conquered nations came to Nineveh and enriched the empire. Because Nineveh had been the capital of the Assyrian Empire for more than one hundred years, its citizens imagined the empire was secure. Zephaniah speaks of the city in its fancied security. Nineveh represented a totalitarian regime where the king was called the "shepherd" of his people. He embodied the divine destiny of the empire. The unique position of the Assyrian king and the pride in their way of life was idolatrous from God's perspective. The prophet sarcastically personifies Nineveh by proclaiming its divine status. For Judah, the phrase *I am, and there is none besides me* (v. 15a) was a confession of the unique and exclusive claim of Yahweh (cf. Isa. 43:10; 44:6; 45:5, 18, 21–22; 46:9). The mood of the oracle changes rapidly. Sarcasm changes into lament (v. 15b). The end of Assyria will be celebrated by all who pass the ruins of the city. The scoffing and the shaking of the fist are expressions of hatred mixed with joy. The hatred for Nineveh will be turned to joy because she will receive her just rewards.

III. Oracles of Judgment Against Jerusalem and the Nations (3:1–8)

Though no direct reference is made to Jerusalem, it is clear that Zephaniah focuses on the capital city of Judah in chapter 3. As an insider familiar with the corrupt and tyrannical regimes of Manasseh and Jotham, Zephaniah charges Jerusalem with faithlessness. The oracle is a woe oracle of judgment. Jerusalem will fare no better than the surrounding nations. The charges are essentially three: Jerusalem is corrupt; it has forsaken Yahweh; its leaders are hopelessly evil.

Zephaniah paints a portrait of an incredibly evil city. Jerusalem is a "bloody" city where gangsters rule. Because of bloodshed, the city has become "defiled," suggesting ritual uncleanness (Ezra 2:62; Neh. 7:64; Mal. 1:7, 12).

At her very core, Jerusalem is a covenant-breaking city. Whatever one may say about her, she is not what she is supposed to be. Jerusalem is, moreover, a foolish city. She digs her own grave because she is unresponsive to the call of wisdom.

Zephaniah charges the leaders—the officials, rulers, prophets, and priests—with ruling like gangsters. The political, social, and religious climate of Jerusalem is corrupt. Their ferocious appetite for self-enrichment make the officials behave like tyrants. They are like "roaring lions" (cf. Amos 3:8). The officials thwart justice by shedding innocent blood. Human life has been reduced to a material resource for the self-satisfaction of her leaders. The judges pervert justice in their pursuit of personal happiness. They are compared to "evening wolves." The prophets are unreliable, wanton imposters. They are "arrogant" and "treacherous" (v. 4). The combination of these terms heightens the impact. The priests, though consecrated, are not able to apply God's law to their society. They profane whatever is holy. The word *sanctuary* might also be translated "sacred" or "holy things." Zephaniah does not specify whether the offensive behavior of the priests pertains only to the sanctuary or extends to all that is sacred. Profanation, nonetheless, is a disregard of God's commands.

In an indirect way Zephaniah warns Josiah not to trust the officials and religious leaders of Jerusalem. If he is to break away from the perverse pattern set by his father and grandfather, he has to be willing to forego the counsel of those in power and return to Yahweh. Yahweh's nature is radically different from that of the wicked leaders of Jerusalem. He is righteous, just, and faithful. Since he is unique in these qualities, he alone is qualified to judge his people. The generation of the exile, while fully aware of Yahweh's anger and judgment, can comfort themselves knowing that Yahweh has been faithful in his judgment and will continue to be faithful. Yahweh's intent is to remove all wickedness from *within* his people (v. 11) so that he may fully dwell in the *midst* of his people once more (vv. 15, 17).

The prophet affirms that God does no wrong. Wrong is the exact opposite of faithfulness and signifies perversity, wickedness, or lewdness. Instead, Yahweh dispenses justice. Morning by morning and day by day his justice and righteousness are evident. Yahweh the great King is here pictured dispensing justice without fail. In contrast to this righteous and just Judge are the wicked, who have no sense of shame. They will not even come to be tried by the Lord until it is too late. In the end his judgment overtakes them.

These foolish people have not seen how Yahweh had shown his righteous judgment in the past by cutting off entire nations, reducing them to wastelands. The story of the Old Testament is the story of redemption in which Yahweh interacts with mankind and judges peoples and nations in his own time. The prophet has predicted the fall of Philistia, Moab, Ammon, and Assyria. Now he calls upon his people to look at the record of the past and to learn from it.

With an apocalyptic tinge, Zephaniah portrays the judgment as lying just beyond the horizon. Yahweh will soon gather the nations together and witness against them. Because Judah is scarcely different from the nations, she too will attend the awesome judgment of the day of Yahweh. Yahweh acts as Accuser, Witness, and Judge of the nations. On the day of the Lord the future of the kingdoms of the world will be determined. Before the fullness of the era of restoration, the judgment of the Lord must purify the nations.

IV. Promises to Gentiles and Jews (3:9–20)

Yahweh's anger and love go together. On the day of Yahweh's anger, he will "purify the lips" of the peoples (**3:9–11**). This image is an expression of restoration. Zephaniah portrays the restoration as an era in which all languages are pure. The division of languages and cultural and religious differences will be over. The tower of Babel will no more be a symbol of human autonomy because the nations will serve one God. Scattered peoples will come to worship the Lord together and to present him offerings appropriate to the salvation they have experienced.

The day will be a day of grace for the nations. When God has removed autonomy, haughtiness, and wickedness, only the people of God will be left. The prophet anticipates the time when all wrongdoing and all causes for shame will be removed.

Grace is also shown to the remnant of Judah (**3:12–13**). The remnant motif was first introduced in the call to repentance (2:1–3). A glorious future belongs to those who demonstrate humility, trust in the Lord, and faithfulness. The "meek and humble" (v. 12) are not only those who survived the Babylonian holocaust but all those who have opened their eyes to the reality of man's collision course with God. God thus assures the godly of every age that he looks for those who do not depend upon themselves, that is, the poor in spirit. Those who are truly humble rely upon the Lord. True humility is an expression of the fear of the Lord. The wicked do not respond to the call of wisdom (3:2, 7). In contrast, the righteous begin with trust in the Lord and commit all their ways to him.

The practical working out of godly wisdom is the expression of faithfulness to the Lord. Faithfulness is not only an attitude but also an expression of what one says and does. The essence of Old Testament piety is found here (cf. Pss. 15:2–5; 24:3–6; Mic. 6:8). The requirement is no different since the coming of Christ.

Zephaniah celebrates the joy of redemption (**3:14–15**). The imperatives *sing, shout aloud, be glad,* and *rejoice* urgently convey the assurance that past troubles are over and that the new era of redemption has begun. The people must exult in the Lord their Redeemer. First, they are to rejoice in the great power of their King, who is able to put their enemies under his feet. Second, they must also rejoice in Yahweh's kingship. Yahweh alone has the authority to judge the nations, Judah, and Jerusalem. Third, they must rejoice because Yahweh their King is in their midst. The prophet telescopes the whole progression of God's kingdom by focusing on the eschatological state in which all adversity, enemies, and evil will be removed. Yahweh alone will be King and will reside with his people. This picture of the future is the ground of the hope of God's people throughout the ages, because it assures the saints of Yahweh's sovereignty over the earth and of his loving purposes for his children.

The "Daughter of Zion" (v. 14) is a reference to either the inhabitants of Jerusalem (cf. Mic. 4:10, 13; Zech. 9:9) or the covenant people in general (cf. Isa. 52:2; 62:11; Zech. 2:10). The song of the redeemed is not a quiet musing but a loud and jubilant shouting.

The same Lord who removes pride and wickedness (3:11b) will also remove the punishment of the people. The Lord will also deal with the enemies as the source of the troubles. He reveals himself as Yahweh, King over Israel, who voluntarily comes to live in the midst of his people. He is the Immanuel, the God who is with us. With his presence, there is no need to be afraid anymore.

The song of the redeemed is rephrased as a proclamation (**3:16–17**). Yahweh quietly rejoices over his people and the success of his plans. The ultimate assurance of the redeemed lies in Yahweh's quiet rejoicing because his plans will work out. He knows the beginning from the end.

The exhortation not to let "hands hang limp" (v. 16) is a caution to the people not to become incapacitated by fear (see Neh. 6:9; Isa. 13:7; Jer. 6:24; 50:43; Ezek. 21:7). They need not fear, because Yahweh will be with them. He is the mighty Warrior. He has planned to save his people. The act of deliverance presupposes need. Those who will receive his salvation are the humble and needy. He will rejoice over his own people. He will quiet his people with his love (v. 17).

The glorious King will preserve a people for himself (**3:18–20**). He will search out and bring together the lost and scattered. The main thrust of the section lies in the future of the redeemed. Zephaniah, by means of repetition, brings out the certainty of restoration and the glory of the people of God.

The return from exile marks in a unique way another beginning in the unfolding history of redemption. The major moments in that history include creation, dispersion, promise, a holy people, a royal nation. The restoration from exile will be a second exodus, when the promises given long ago are at last renewed.

SELECT BIBLIOGRAPHY

Bartlett, J. R. "The Moabites and Ammonites." In *Peoples of Old Testament Times,* edited by D. J. Wiseman. New York: Oxford University Press, 1973.

Childs, B. S. *Introduction to the Old Testament as Scripture.* Philadelphia: Fortress, 1979.

Smith, R. L. *Micah-Malachi.* Waco: Word, 1984.

HAGGAI

Hermann J. Austel

INTRODUCTION

The author is known simply as "the prophet Haggai." Apart from this book he is mentioned in Ezra 5:1 and 6:14. His name is usually associated with Zechariah, his contemporary. He is generally thought to be older than Zechariah because his name always appears before that of Zechariah, and because of the possible (but not necessary) inference from 2:3 that he himself might have been old enough to have seen Solomon's temple.

Soon after the first band of exiles had returned from Babylon to Jerusalem (536 B.C.), they began to rebuild the temple (Ezra 3). It was not long, however, before various hindrances and waning enthusiasm brought a halt to the project. Haggai's mission was to rekindle the faith and courage of the people so that they would complete the temple. They responded almost immediately, and four years later (516 B.C.) the temple was completed and dedicated (Ezra 6:14–15).

Haggai's message is extremely practical and down to earth: Build the temple! Several truths become clear in this book:

1. God and his work must take first place in the life of his people. Only in this way is God honored.
2. Putting personal or selfish interests ahead of God is self-defeating.
3. God showers his blessings on those who put his interests before their own.
4. The value or significance of a man's work is not to be estimated by comparing it with the work of others, but by the measure of its conformity to God's will and purpose. Zerubbabel's temple seemed insignificant compared to Solomon's. Yet in God's sight it was a valued and significant part of his overall purpose.

OUTLINE

I. First Message: A Call to Action (1:1–15)
   A. Reproach (1:1–6)
   B. Admonition (1:7–11)
   C. Response (1:12–15)

II. Second Message: A Word of Encouragement (2:1–9)
 A. The Problem (2:1–3)
 B. The Encouragement (2:4–9)
III. Third Message: Confirmation of Blessing (2:10–19)
IV. Fourth Message: The Restoration of the Davidic Kingdom (2:20–23)

COMMENTARY

I. First Message: A Call to Action (1:1–15)

Each of Haggai's messages is precisely dated, with the reign of Darius I as a reference point. The modern calendric equivalent of the first date is August 29, 520 B.C. Haggai's first message is brought on the day of the festival of the New Moon (Num. 10:10), when great numbers of worshipers had gathered in Jerusalem.

Darius here is Darius I ("the Great") who reigned 521–486 B.C. Zerubbabel is the grandson of Jehoiachin, the king of Judah who was exiled to Babylon in 597 B.C. As such he is of the royal line of David, but holds an appointed office as governor of Judea under the generally benign Persians. The other person addressed is Joshua, the high priest. Joshua was among the first group to return from Babylon along with Zerubbabel (Ezra 2:1).

A. Reproach (1:1–6). Haggai's message is brief and to the point. It is also, more importantly, from the Lord, thus urgent and authoritative. "Lord Almighty" (v. 2) is literally "Lord of Hosts." This designation for God is found frequently in the prophetic books, but is especially common in Haggai, Zechariah, and Malachi. It is a reminder of the fact that, whatever man's need, all the resources of heaven and earth are at God's command. Thus for God's people there can never be any cause to fear or hesitate when backed by God's promise. But while there is great comfort for Israel in this name, there is in it as well the reminder that God is the Lord of Israel's hosts as well. He is their commander-in-chief and they are responsible to him.

The expression *these people* (v. 2) instead of *my people* is used to draw attention to God's displeasure with Israel's spiritual apathy. Their attitude is summed up in the statement *the time has not . . . come. . . .* Haggai describes a people who have lost their vision and have come to comfortable terms with leaving God's work undone. Contributing to this attitude are the following: (1) the fierce and persistent opposition of the Samaritans and other neighbors (Ezra 4); (2) the negative and disparaging reaction of the older priests at the laying of the foundations (Ezra 3:12–13); (3) a spirit of discouragement, making the people wonder if the end product will be worth all the difficulties and dangers; (4) a lack of vital trust in God; and (5) growing indifference and lukewarmness.

God's statement in verse 4 points clearly and unequivocally to Israel's wrong sense of values, a spirit diametrically opposed to that of David (2 Sam. 7:2; Ps. 132:1–5), who felt ill at ease in a luxurious house while the ark of God had only a tent as a covering. The term *paneled houses* (v. 3) refers to the practice of laying wood paneling over the basic stone walls and indicates that the people had gone far beyond providing for their real needs and were primarily concerned with personal luxury while totally neglecting the temple.

Haggai asks the people to give careful thought to the consequences of their misplaced priorities. This same admonition is given five times in the book (1:5, 7; 2:15, 18 [twice]) and is designed to shake the people out of their complacency. By taking careful stock of their physical situation they are led to realize how far they have strayed from the path of blessing. Verse 6 graphically draws attention to the realities of the situation. Though they have not been reduced to abject poverty, the fruit of their labor falls far short of expectation. On top of that, food, clothing, and money do not provide the normally expected benefits. The people bring in less than expected, and what they do bring in does not live up to expectations. God's blessing is not there!

B. Admonition (1:7–11). As Haggai again calls on the people to consider their sin in neglecting the temple and the consequences in lost blessings, he now tells them what they must do. It is simply a matter of obeying God and starting once again to build the temple. By this act of obedience they will both please God and bring him honor.

To make sure that his hearers do not lose sight of the cause-effect relationship between their poverty and their neglect of the temple, Haggai points to the fact that their harvests have been consistently much poorer than expected and that what they do harvest does not last as it should. The reason for this is simply that each is busy with his own house (v. 9) while the house of God remains in ruins. Because of their behavior all of nature is affected, not only the three basic crops (grain, grapes, olive oil), but also the productivity of men and cattle. The productivity of the land depended very much on adequate and timely rain and dew. When God withheld this and sent drought and excessive heat, land, cattle, and men all suffered. Haggai uses an appropriate word play in stressing the reason for the drought. The temple remains a ruin (*ḥārēb*); therefore God calls for a drought (*ḥōreb*). Only as men put God first can they experience his richest blessing.

C. Response (1:12–15). Haggai's message is simple and to the point. The response of the people is likewise prompt and unequivocal. They fear the Lord because they recognize the voice of God in Haggai's words (v. 12). Then they begin to work on the house of the Lord. God's gracious working provokes both fear and obedience. As a result of their response, God can now promise renewed blessing: "I am with you" (v. 13). These gracious words are repeated in 2:4, and along with the other promises of blessing in 2:5 and 2:19, constitute a powerful source of encouragement. God's presence and enablement guarantee the successful outcome of the project, no matter how severe the opposition and various difficulties might be. There is a period of twenty-three days between Haggai's first message and the actual start of work. This time was no doubt required to organize work teams and to allow the workers to finish their harvesting activities.

II. Second Message: A Word of Encouragement (2:1–9)

A. The problem (2:1–3). Not quite a month after the work had begun (cf. 1:15), Haggai speaks again to encourage the people, assuring them that their labor is not in vain, that what they are doing is indeed meaningful and pleasing to God. The problem is addressed in verse 3: "Who of you is left who saw this house in its former glory?" Those who had seen Solomon's temple disparage the new temple now under construction. Ezra 3:10–13 recounts the laying of the foundation of the temple shortly after the return of the exiles. There was great rejoicing on this occasion by the younger people, but also loud weeping on the part of the older priests, Levites, and family heads. The reason for this weeping was that they had seen the glory of Solomon's temple and knew that the present effort would not come close by comparison. This negative attitude still has a harmful impact on the people in Haggai's time, making them wonder whether all their effort might not be in vain since the temple will be so poor by comparison to Solomon's. Their temple seems to be "like nothing" (v. 3).

B. The encouragement (2:4–9). The words *be strong* (repeated three times here) are reminiscent of God's admonition in other crucial situations (**2:4–5**). Joshua was encouraged with these words (Deut. 31:23; Josh. 1:6–9) when he faced the awesome responsibility of stepping into Moses' shoes and leading Israel in the conquest of Canaan. Again, in 1 Chronicles 22:13 and 28:20 David encourages young Solomon with respect to the great task of building the temple. When God has ordered a job to be done he always does his part. It is for his servants to be strong and work. This admonition is grounded on two promises: (1) "I am with you" (v. 4); and (2) "I will fill this house with glory" (v. 7). The first promise is a link to the past, to the covenant made at Sinai. The second is linked to the future, the glory that is yet to come. The fact that God is present with his people means that he approves of the work, and that he will support and protect them. To God's people this makes all the difference between despair and rejoicing, defeat and victory.

The first reason they should not be discouraged at what seems so feeble an attempt to restore the temple to any semblance of its former glory is that God is with them in accordance with his promise. A second reason is now added. God relates their present activity to the coming surpassing glory of the temple (**2:6–9**). It was natural for the people to make comparisons between Solomon's temple and Zerubbabel's temple. But from God's perspective these temples are both his houses. These buildings are merely visible representations of the fact that God has seen fit to dwell among his people. Their temple, though less splendid than that of Solomon, is nevertheless God's house. Since God has acknowledged it and promised his presence, there is no reason for discouragement. Furthermore, the standard of excellence is not Solomon's temple, but the future temple. Their work, though seemingly insignificant, is nevertheless a part of God's overall program of establishing his presence on earth in such a way that not only Israel but ultimately all nations will be affected.

The principle of this message serves as a powerful incentive to believers of today. As long as we are doing the work God has given us to do in accordance with his will, we are valued participants in God's great program of making his salvation known to the lost, no matter how small our part may seem to be in comparison to others.

"In a little while" (v. 6) is an expression sometimes used of eschatological events. It emphasizes imminency and perhaps the suddenness of the onset of the events described. As God has acted in mighty, earthshaking fashion in the past on behalf of his people, so will he do again. This future event is described as a shaking of "the heavens and the earth . . . and all nations" (vv. 6–7). Great upheavals, political, social, and cosmic, are in God's program. All that is false and impure, all that is in opposition to God will be removed in preparation for the establishment of his kingdom. Here, the direct result of this shaking is the filling of God's house with glory.

"The desired of all nations will come" (v. 7) has commonly been understood as a messianic reference. There are, however, compelling grammatical and contextual considerations that lead some translators and commentators to see this as a reference to the great wealth of the nations. That which they have highly treasured will be brought and will fill the temple. While other passages such as Ezekiel 43:1–5 stress the presence of the glory of God in the future temple, here its physical splendor is primarily in view.

An added encouragement is found in the words *I will grant peace* (v. 9). No more conflict, no more opposition. God will reign supreme.

III. Third Message: Confirmation of Blessing (2:10–19)

The legal question asked of the priests poses no difficulty for them. It is in two parts and makes the point that uncleanness defiles everything with which it comes into contact. The opposite is, however, not the case. If a priest were to carry a piece of consecrated meat in the folds of his robe any item of food that came into contact with that fold would not thereby become ceremonially clean (though the garment itself would be clean, according to Lev. 6:27). On the other hand, a defiled person renders unclean anything he touches. Just so has the uncleanness of Judah's disobedience in neglecting the temple vitiated everything they touch. All areas of life are affected.

The date of the message in verses 15–17 is December 18. The people have been at work on the temple project for some three months now, and there are no doubt many indications of God's gracious presence. But they have not yet experienced the abundant harvests that result from God's blessing. This is due to the fact that they are between harvests. The fields are plowed and the new seed planted in anticipation of a rich harvest, but their barns and wine vats still show the effects of their former disobedience. They contain only half of what might normally be expected.

Yet the people are to mark this day, December 18, as the beginning of a new era. The barns are still empty and the vine has not yet borne fruit. But from this day on they will begin to see the visible results of their obedience as their experienced eyes observe the beginnings of a new and abundant harvest. To a certain extent they had obeyed in faith up to this point, but from now on the words *I will bless you* will become tangible reality.

IV. Fourth Message: The Restoration of the Davidic Kingdom (2:20–23)

This is the second message on this date and is directed to Zerubbabel. The events described here are clearly eschatological. The words *I will shake* are the same as those in 2:6–7, and have reference to the great upheavals that will precede the establishment of God's kingdom. God will overturn royal thrones. The same Hebrew word is used of the destruction of Sodom and Gomorrah in such passages as Deuteronomy 29:23; Isaiah 13:19; Jeremiah 20:16; and Amos 4:11. As sudden and as final as Sodom's ruin was, so will it be with the Gentile thrones. Reformation is not in view here, but utter destruction. This is the fate of the "world powers." The overthrowing of chariots and their drivers is reminiscent of the description of the destruction of Pharaoh's army in the sea (Exod. 15:1, 5). The terror and confusion will be so great that men will fall by the sword of their brothers. Just when the might of the world powers seems to be unassailable, God will shake and overthrow them and establish his own kingdom.

Zerubbabel was in the royal line, but he never reigned as king nor were there any aspirations on Haggai's part to make him king. The context is clearly eschatological, and Haggai uses Zerubbabel, the current representative of David's royal line, to point to the Messiah. The reference to Zerubbabel as "my servant" and as the one whom God has chosen is reminiscent of the messianic "servant passages" of Isaiah 42, 49, 50, and 53. God's

Messiah will successfully accomplish the task for which he was sent. The term *signet ring* (v. 23) refers to the authority given to the Messiah. He will be God's personal representative. The designation is one of high honor and privilege. It is noteworthy that the curse on Zerubbabel's grandfather Jehoiachin (Coniah) is couched in language involving the signet ring. Though he was the signet ring on God's right hand, he was pulled off and cast to his enemies the Babylonians (Jer. 22:24). But now the Davidic line in the person of Messiah is restored to the place of authority and honor, God's signet ring. Thus the book ends on a note of encouragement. The labor of Zerubbabel is not in vain. There will be immediate blessing, but also future glory in a temple of surpassing splendor and a king who rules as God's personal representative on earth. There was every reason for Judah to be encouraged. Just so is there every reason for believers today to be encouraged in obeying and serving God.

SELECT BIBLIOGRAPHY

Alden, R. L. "Haggai." In *The Expositor's Bible Commentary*, edited by Frank E. Gaebelein, 12 vols. Grand Rapids: Zondervan, 1985.

Baldwin, J. G. *Haggai, Zechariah, Malachi*. Downers Grove: Inter-Varsity, 1972.

Feinberg, C. L. *The Minor Prophets*. Chicago: Moody, 1976.

Freeman, H. E. *An Introduction to the Old Testament Prophets*. Chicago: Moody, 1977.

Orelli, C. von. *The Twelve Minor Prophets*. Reprint. Minneapolis: Klock & Klock, 1977.

Pusey, E. B. *The Minor Prophets*. Vol. 2. Reprint. Grand Rapids: Baker, 1950.

Wolf, Herbert. *Haggai-Malachi*. Chicago: Moody, 1976.

Wolff, Richard. *The Book of Haggai*. Grand Rapids: Baker, 1967.

ZECHARIAH

Hermann J. Austel

INTRODUCTION

Zechariah was the son of Berekiah and the grandson of Iddo. The latter is named in Nehemiah 12:4, 16 as one of the heads of priestly families returning from Babylon to Judea. Thus we have in Zechariah another example (with Jeremiah and Ezekiel) of a priest serving as a prophet. He seems to have been a younger contemporary of Haggai since he is always named after the latter. Zechariah was a young man when he began his prophetic ministry (2:4).

Zechariah began his written ministry in October/November 520 B.C. Two other dates are given: February 15, 519 B.C. (1:7) and December 7, 518 B.C. (7:1). The oracles of chapters 9–14 came after the completion of the temple in 516 B.C. These last chapters are commonly held to be as late as 480 B.C., but it is difficult to be certain.

The book has three major parts. The first gives encouragement for the rebuilding of the temple. After an introductory admonition, it consists of a series of eight visions that relate the rebuilding of the temple to God's overall program for Israel. The second part deals with questions about the practice of fasting and mourning for the destruction of the temple. The third, not directly related to the temple, consists of two oracles concerning Israel and the nations.

Some scholars maintain that chapters 9–14 were composed by a different author (authors) than chapters 1–8. They commonly point to differences in subject matter, style, and vocabulary as supporting evidence. By way of brief reply it should be noted: (1) Ancient Jewish and Christian tradition supports the book's unity. (2) All existing manuscripts treat the book as a unified whole. (3) Though it is true that in part 1 the temple is of great concern and part 2 is exclusively concerned with future matters, there are numerous similarities between the two sections: the return of Israel to the land, the future unity of Judah and Israel, the coming reign of God, the necessity for repentance and cleansing, and more. (4) It would be unreasonable to demand that a writer maintain the same method of presentation throughout his work, especially when the concerns and needs of the people are different. (5) There are some unique similarities in word usage in the two sections. For example, the word usually translated "sit" or "dwell" is used several times in both parts with the meaning "be inhabited." This usage is infrequent elsewhere.

When all is considered there is no valid reason the book ought not to be considered as a unified work from the hand of Zechariah.

The scope of Zechariah's theological and eschatological vision is among the grandest in the Old Testament. Zechariah relates the past, present, and coming circumstances of Israel to God's great unfolding program for his people and to the fact that the Lord (identified with the coming King) will reign supreme over a chastened and cleansed world. Some of the dominant themes are: (1) the destruction of Gentile world power; (2) the return of Israel to the land; (3) the future unity of Judah and Israel; (4) the necessity for repentance and cleansing; (5) the coming exaltation of Jerusalem and its people; (6) the joining of saved Gentiles in worship with Israel; (7) the relationship between Israel and the Shepherd/King; (8) the certainty of the fulfillment of God's purpose.

OUTLINE

I. Call for a Return to the Lord (1:1–6)
II. The Eight Night Visions (1:7–6:8)
  A. First Vision (1:7–17)
  B. Second Vision (1:18–21)
  C. Third Vision (2:1–13)
  D. Fourth Vision (3:1–10)
  E. Fifth Vision (4:1–14)
  F. Sixth Vision (5:1–4)
  G. Seventh Vision (5:5–11)
  H. Eighth Vision (6:1–8)
III. The Crowning of Joshua (6:9–15)
IV. The Observance of Fasts (7:1–8:23)
  A. The Question (7:1–3)
  B. The Rebuke (7:4–14)
  C. The Promise (8:1–23)
V. The Coming of the Messiah (9:1–14:21)
  A. The First Coming and Rejection (9:1–11:17)
  B. The Second Coming and Reception (12:1–14:21)

COMMENTARY

I. Call for a Return to the Lord (1:1–6)

The first message of Zechariah, coming during the eighth month of Darius's second year (October–November 520 B.C.), falls between Haggai's second and third messages (2:1–9 and 2:10–19, respectively). It adds a new dimension to Haggai's message of practical obedience—that of a personal relationship to the Lord.

Zechariah's opening message establishes a fitting foundation for the rest of the book, placing the matter of the rebuilding of the temple within the framework of God's overall purpose with regard to Israel and Jerusalem. It provides solid encouragement with regard to the ultimate destiny of Jerusalem and its inhabitants. God's purpose, centered in his Messiah, is immutable. Yet this brief introduction is a solemn reminder that the enjoyment of God's blessing is dependent on one's personal response to God. There are three major points: (1) their forefathers failed to respond to God's Word—thus the tragedy of the destruction of Jerusalem and the exile. (2) God's purpose as declared in his Word is unchanging. It has been and will continue to be, fulfilled to the letter. (3) Therefore do not make the mistake your forefathers made. Turn to God with all your heart.

God was furious because of the way in which Israel's forefathers had "mocked God's messengers" and "despised his words" (2 Chron. 36:16). The inevitable result was that God's Word "overtook" them (v. 5) as a fleeing thief might be apprehended by justice in pursuit. God warns them against following the same tragic path which involved outer conformity to prescribed ritual worship, yet lacked heart response to God. God desires that they should seek him. Even though the people had been at work on the temple for several months already, they needed to be reminded that more than outward obedience was needed. The blessing of God's personal presence and fellowship is for those who seek him from the heart. Men, whether evildoers or prophets, are mortal. But God's word stands forever. Whether threat or promise, that Word will surely be fulfilled. God means what he says, and he has done exactly as he has said. This forms a warning to the current generation, lest they take God's Word lightly. It serves also as an encouragement to those who seek God: his promise will unfailingly come to pass.

II. The Eight Night Visions (1:7–6:8)

Zechariah's visions relate the rebuilding of the temple to God's overall purpose with respect to Jerusalem, giving the assurance that there is a bright future for both city and people.

A. First vision (1:7–17). The visions come three months after Zechariah's opening message and two months after Haggai's last two messages. The man riding a red horse (v. 8) is identified in verse 11 as the angel of the Lord who in turn is elsewhere identified as the second person of the Trinity. He is over the "fact-finding" patrol, receives its report, and then intercedes for Israel. He is to be distinguished from the angel who was talking with Zechariah (vv. 9, 13, 14), who appears here and in other visions as an interpreter or spokesman for God. The significance of the various colors of the horses (v. 8) is not given, though in Revelation 6 the red horse is associated with warfare and the white horse with victory. It is not until the eighth vision (6:1–8), however, that the horses go forth to battle. Here they do reconnaisance work. The report brought back (v. 11) is that the whole world is at rest and in peace. From the angel of the Lord's response, this must be taken to indicate a situation in which the Gentile nations are prospering while God's people (possibly represented by the myrtle trees in a ravine or low place, v. 8) are struggling under the dominion of foreign powers. The temple has not yet been rebuilt so that full restoration from God's anger has not yet been accomplished.

God responds with kind and comforting words through the interpreting angel. His response encourages a people whom God had seemingly forgotten. God's zeal on behalf of Jerusalem will bring about the fulfillment of his promise of verses 16 and 17. At the same time the great anger that had been directed at Israel (v. 2) is now to be directed at the nations living in self-confident and smug security. This is a common prophetic theme: the wicked, who for a time are able to run roughshod over God's people, will eventually be punished. The righteous, on the other hand, will ultimately be vindicated. The nations that were God's tools or means of chastising Israel went beyond what was called for in their treatment of Israel. They were arrogant and self-sufficient, refusing to acknowledge the handiwork of God in what was taking place. God will, however, once again deal graciously with Jerusalem: the temple and the city will be rebuilt. God's choice of Jerusalem as his dwelling-place will once again be very evident.

B. Second vision (1:18–21). This vision, along with the third, states what is implicit in 1:15. Horns in Scripture symbolize kings or kingdoms in their exercise of royal might and authority. The horns of cattle, particularly of the wild ox, were used in the ancient world as symbols of invincible strength (cf. Deut. 33:17). The horns here described are kingdoms that scattered Judah, Israel, and Jerusalem (v. 19). Judah has been at their mercy. But God raises up craftsmen who will destroy the horns and the power they have over God's people. The horns are not identified. It has been suggested that they represent Assyria, Egypt, Babylonia, and Medo-Persia. Others have suggested that they represent the totality of world powers in the four points of the compass. It is, however, difficult to avoid some connection with the fourfold succession of world empires as described in Daniel 2 and 7. Zechariah and his hearers would have been familiar with the Book of Daniel and would very probably make such a connection. Whether these horns represent Gentile world powers as a whole or whether they build upon Daniel's four kingdoms, the message is clear: these powers will be destroyed and then replaced by God's own kingdom established in Jerusalem.

C. Third vision (2:1–13). With the destruction of the world empires (four horns) described in the second vision, the stage is set for a marvelously resurgent Jerusalem. Both visions together expand upon the words of the

Lord in 1:14–16. God's zeal on behalf of Jerusalem is manifested first of all in his judging the nations that have oppressed Jerusalem (vision 2). The present vision enlarges upon the statement of 1:16 with regard to the rebuilding of Jerusalem.

The man with the measuring line (v. 1) answers to the statement in 1:16 that God will stretch out a measuring line over Jerusalem. A greatly enlarged city is in view here, grand in scope and glory since God himself is the Architect and since it will be a place fit for the presence of his glory. There will be a great influx of people, necessitating a greatly enlarged city and making defensive walls impractical. It is to be noted that this prophecy was not fulfilled in Zechariah's time. Even in the days of Nehemiah, some eighty years later, the city was largely empty and had to be filled by casting lots to determine who should be required to live in it (Neh. 7:4; 11:1–2). The complete fulfillment will not be realized until the messianic or kingdom age. The message of these visions was nonetheless an encouragement for Zerubbabel in that the work in which they were presently engaged was part of God's great program for Jerusalem and Israel.

Jerusalem will have no walls of defense but God himself will be a wall of fire around it (v. 5) and its glory within. The presence of the glory of God both guarantees the safety of Jerusalem (cf. Exod. 14:19, 20, 24, 25) and attests to the favored status of Jerusalem and the renewed fellowship of Israel wth God. In view of this gloriously rebuilt Jerusalem and God's presence within, he admonishes those who are still in Babylon to flee from there and to participate in the new life in Jerusalem. This admonition was certainly valid for those in Zechariah's time who had elected to remain in Babylon and its territories (cf. similar strong exhortations in Isa. 48:20 and Jer. 51:6–10). The fact that the same message occurs in Revelation 18:4 just before the destruction of eschatological Babylon indicates that these Old Testament admonitions point forward particularly to the latter days.

There is a threefold message implicit in these words in the light of the context: (1) It is Israel's privilege to leave Babylon. They do not *have* to remain. Therefore they should return and participate in that which God is doing in Jerusalem. (2) They are no longer to be identified with Babylon and its ways but with God and Jerusalem. (3) Babylon is doomed to terrible destruction (v. 8–9; see Jer. 51 for a graphic description of Babylon's coming downfall, with repeated admonitions to flee). Therefore Israel must not get caught up in Babylon's ways and in her fate. God is going to destroy those nations that have plundered Israel, of whom Babylon is the chief representative.

Note that the speaker in verses 8ff. is the Lord Almighty (lit. the Lord of Hosts or Armies). This can be none other than the angel of the Lord whom God sends, the Messiah himself (the "he" of v. 8 can only refer to God the Father). The Messiah, the second person of the Trinity (as so often in eschatological passages) is the agent of destruction for the enemies of God's people. The translation of the Hebrew underlying the words *after he has honored me* (v. 8) has been much debated. A translation that fits both the Hebrew and the context is "with glory He has sent Me." That is, the Messiah's mission is carried out in the presence of, or in association with, the glory of God.

The reason given here for Babylon's destruction emphasizes the special status that Israel as the apple (or pupil) of his eye has before God. This knowledge ought certainly to put fresh spirit into a people who had experienced so many setbacks. With the fall of Babylon and the Gentile nations comes the rise of Israel. When all this has taken place, there can no longer be any shadow of a doubt that God is in charge of the events which have transpired. Israel will then shout and be glad, for God will be at home in their midst. Not only Israel, but many nations will be joined with the Lord, becoming God's people and participating in the glories of the new age. Nonetheless, it will be abundantly clear that Judah is God's portion, his special people (v. 12). Jerusalem will once again be the place chosen by God for his presence on earth. It is noteworthy that in this vision, Jerusalem is the center of God's presence on earth, and those who are yet in Babylon are exhorted to leave there (and come into God's presence). Babylon and all its wickedness is destined for destruction, but Jerusalem with its redeemed inhabitants is destined for blessing.

The vision concludes with the awesome admonition, "Be still before the LORD, all mankind, because he has roused himself from his holy dwelling" (v. 13). Man has had his say long enough, with complaints against God's ways, with mockery, with threats against God and his people. But now, God comes forth to take action. Man will be utterly silenced!

D. Fourth vision (3:1–10). The first three visions had to do with God's program with regard to the establishment of Jerusalem as the center of God's glory on earth. It will be filled and overflowing with a people living in the peace and security of God's presence. Gentile dominion and oppression will have been removed. This is God's work *on behalf* of his people. In the next two visions the focus is on God's ministry *within* the people themselves. In the fourth vision he cleanses them, making them fit to enter his presence; in the fifth vision he empowers them, enabling them to do God's work.

Joshua the high priest (v. 1) here serves as the representative of Israel. His cleansing symbolizes the future cleansing of God's people. God had called Israel to be a holy nation and a kingdom of priests (Exod. 19:6), a nation that would have access to God and serve him in holiness. Here Joshua is seen standing before the angel of the Lord, ministering before God in his capacity as high priest (Deut. 10:8; Ezek. 44:15). But the place of worship, the temple, appointed by God as man's means of access to him, is here invested with the characteristics of a courtroom.

Satan stands at Joshua's right side (the place of the accuser). There is just grounds for Satan's activity. Joshua's sinful uncleanness (v. 3) renders him unfit to come into God's presence. The name *Satan* is in fact a transliteration of the Hebrew word meaning "the accuser." It describes a fundamental characteristic of this fallen angel who not only hates God, but does all in his power to keep man from fellowship with God. He may represent himself as man's friend and advocate, but his real character as opponent and accuser is here clearly seen. Job 1 and 2 record his cynical attempts to discredit Job before God and to cause Job to turn from God. As Satan hates and opposes Israel (represented by Joshua), so is he depicted in Revelation 12 as attempting to devour Israel's Messiah and as persecuting Israel.

But God himself intervenes on behalf of Joshua and his people. This speaks powerfully to the infinite grace of God, and also to his unfailing adherence to his purpose with regard to Israel. God silences Satan with a double rebuke as he also gives a twofold affirmation of support for Israel: Satan is reminded that God has chosen Jerusalem and that Joshua is a burning stick snatched from the fire. God will not be deterred from carrying through with his sovereign electing love. This has already been demonstrated in the fact that God had rescued Joshua/Israel as one takes a burning stick out of a fire. This may be a reference to God's removal of Israel from Egypt (which is several times refered to as an iron furnace; Deut. 4:20; Jer. 11:4), but it is more likely that God is here describing the rescue of the exiles from Babylon. Normally, the destruction of Jerusalem and the dispersion of its people into far-flung lands would have meant an end to the nation, as a stick would rapidly be consumed by the fire. But God intervened by snatching a remnant out, ensuring the continuance of the nation. God chose Jerusalem (and its people) and also graciously preserved them from a destruction that they richly deserved. Satan's attempts to undo Israel cannot prevail against the faithful purpose and the strong hand of God.

Verse 3 describes both Joshua's unworthiness to stand before God, and also God's cleansing of Joshua, making him fit to come into God's presence and effectively stopping Satan's objections. Note that Joshua is dressed in filthy clothes as he stands before the angel of the Lord. The high priest was required to be holy and to wear special garments when he came into God's presence. But Joshua's garments are not only dirty—they are befouled as with vomit or excrement! He is most worthy of condemnation. What Joshua/Israel cannot do for himself, God does: "See, I have taken away your sin, and I will put rich garments on you" (v. 4). With these brief words God's gracious saving activity is summarized. He replaces man's feeble and inadequate attempts to produce the kind of righteousness that will stand before God with righteousness that is perfect and adequate in every way. Thus did God graciously replace unworthy Adam's fig leaves with coats of skin (Gen. 3:7, 21; cf. also Isa. 61:10; Rev. 7:14; 22:14). The new garments are not only clean; they are rich, festal garments suitable to wear in God's presence.

Zechariah seems to be so emotionally involved in the scene before him that he anticipates what is to come next, the putting on of the turban to complete the high priest's attire. The word *turban* (v. 5) here is closely related to the high-priestly turban in the Pentateuch (which had attached to it an engraved plate with the words *holy to the Lord* on it; Exod. 28:36). It is used in only two other passages, in figurative contexts. In Job 29:14 Job describes his righteousness: "I put on righteousness as my clothing; justice was . . . my turban." In Isaiah 62:3, Israel, restored to a righteousness which is evident to all, is a "crown of splendor . . . and a royal turban" (NIV diadem) in God's hand. So here also the turban gives public testimony to Joshua's new state of righteousness before God.

In verses 6 and 7 Joshua/Israel receives a twofold charge and a threefold promise. If he will now live a life of obedience and total commitment to God, consistent with his new righteous standing, he will have the privilege of an unhindered priestly ministry. As God's representative on earth he will govern (lit. execute justice, act as judge) and have charge over the temple. He will also have totally unhindered access to God, as the angels have. Verse 8 continues to make it clear that Joshua's cleansing is representative of a spiritually restored Israel. He and his associates are symbolic of things to come. A brief but important statement follows, pointing to the One through whom Israel's cleansing and restoration will be made possible: "I am going to bring my servant, the Branch." The term *servant* is a well-established designation of the Messiah in his capacity of successfully carrying out God's program of salvation (Isa. 42:1–7; 49:1–9; 50:4–9; 52:13–53:12). The term *Branch* designates the Messiah as Lord (Isa. 4:2), King (Jer. 23:5; 33:15), and man (Zech. 6:12). As the Branch (lit. shoot from the root), the Messiah both brings about a new beginning and epitomizes the ideal that God intends for Israel. The stone of verse 9 is no doubt another reference to the Messiah (cf. Ps. 118:22 and Isa. 28:16, where he is the chief cornerstone). Joshua and Zerubbabel were engaged in rebuilding the kingdom of Israel. This chapter makes it clear that the only validity for Israel's position as a royal priestly nation is through the cleansing ministry of the Messiah, and only as Joshua's work is built upon the Stone that God has given, can there be any lasting results.

The seven eyes (v. 9) may have reference to the sevenfold spirit of God (Rev. 5:6). The seven eyes of God range throughout the earth (4:10). They symbolize God's administrative activity in the affairs of his people.

The meaning of the inscription (lit. engraving) on the stone (v. 9) is uncertain. If our identification of the stone with the Messiah (Cornerstone) is correct, then it is possible that the engraving is a special distinction placed on him by God. At any rate this engraving is related to redemption: "I will remove the sin of this land in a single day." This verse summarizes the vision.

E. Fifth vision (4:1–14). The task before Zerubbabel and his associates must have seemed insurmountable, especially in view of God's descriptions of the coming glory of Jerusalem and the temple. This fifth vision is given to show Zerubbabel that God gives divine enablement for the work that he has ordained.

The vision contains two major objects. The first is a solid gold lampstand (v. 2). The lampstand no doubt is intended to symbolize the bearing of witness or testimony. Isaiah 60:1–3 speaks of restored Israel as being a light to which the nations, in a world of darkness, will come. This will be possible because the light of God in the person of the Messiah had first come on Israel (Isa. 9:2; 60:1–2). The second thing that Zechariah sees are two olive trees (v. 3) next to the lampstand, one on either side. The fact that the olive trees supply the oil that fuels the lamps suggests that what is in view here is the source of supply for the testimony symbolized by the lamps. Zechariah's question "What are these, my Lord?" (v. 4) refers to both the lampstand and the olive trees. The answer is given him in verse 6: " 'Not by might nor by power, but by my Spirit,' says the LORD Almighty." This statement constitutes the central and key message of the chapter.

Note that these words are directed to Zerubbabel, who has been charged with the leadership in the rebuilding program. There is here both encouragement and admonition. Zerubbabel need not fear the size or difficulty of the task. God's supply of power is sufficient for any and every situation. But Zerubbabel needs to rely on God rather than personal skill, strength, or ingenuity. The word translated "might" is frequently used of armies, wealth, or influence. But God's work is accomplished by the power of his Spirit. This is symbolized by the oil of the olive trees that supplies the fuel for the lamps.

Verse 7 applies the truth of verse 6 to Zerubbabel's situation. The mighty mountain might refer to the opposition of Gentile political power, since this symbolism was common in the Near East (cf. Dan. 2:44). But it probably has reference to difficulties and obstacles of any kind, no matter how mountainous. What an encouragement and comfort to Zerubbabel, and indeed to anyone engaged in the work of God, to realize that it is by *God's* power, not by human strength, that impossibilities become actualities. No mountain is so solid and so huge that God cannot level it.

As far as the specific matter at hand, the building of the temple, it will be completed. God will bring out the capstone. This has reference to the last stone to be laid. This will be a particularly joyous occasion because of the difficulties and the length of time involved in the building. The joy will be so great that there will be spontaneous shouts of "God bless it! God bless it!" It is possible that what is intended here is a cry for God's favor to rest on the completed temple, but it is far more likely an unqualified expression of approval, such as "Wonderful!" or "Bravo! Bravo!" It is also recognition of the fact that God's favor rests on the temple and that its completion is due to the working of God's power. This is to be compared to the mixed reaction of the people when the foundation was laid (Ezra 3:10–13).

Verses 8 and 9 give specific encouragement to Zerubbabel. The task is difficult, even mountainous, yet by God's enablement he will carry it out. God finishes what he starts. Verse 10 carries on the thought that there will be joyful acknowledgment of God's hand in the temple project, even by those who had despised "the day of small things." Many had minimized the rebuilding efforts as insignificant and futile. But now this negativism will be replaced by rejoicing. The message is clear and unequivocal: God, whose omniscient interest in man's activities spans the earth, has had his watchful and approving eyes on Zerubbabel's efforts.

Verses 11–14 take up again the matter of the two olive trees. More detail is given through Zechariah's questions. In addition to the olive trees, he wants to know about the two olive branches beside the two gold pipes that pour out golden oil. This question helps us to see the connection between the trees and the lampstand. The oil flows from the trees through the branches to the pipes, and through the pipes into the lampstand, supplying fuel for the lamps. The answer to the question as to what the two branches represent is given in verse 14. Both kings and priests were anointed; and Zerubbabel, in the kingly line, and Joshua the high priest, were the current representatives of these two offices. The power and effectiveness of their ministries depended on the enabling power of the Holy Spirit. As they receive the empowering of the Spirit of God, the testimony and witness of God's people to the true God can shine brightly. The ultimate responsibility of these two officials is to serve the God of all the earth. God's lordship and sovereignty are thus affirmed, and the outworking of his program through his servants will demonstrate his absolute lordship. As most expositors recognize, there are clear messianic and eschatological implications in this chapter. In Jesus the Messiah both the kingly and priestly offices are combined.

Chapters 3 and 4 form a unit in their emphasis on the internal work of God in his people. They also form a unit in looking forward to the Messiah through whom the nation will be cleansed and restored, and through whom the kingdom and the temple of God will be rebuilt, thus reestablishing God's people as an effective light to the nations and witness to the saving power and sovereignty of God.

F. Sixth vision (5:1–4). The sixth and seventh visions have to do with God's purging the land of sin. Here are internal obstacles to the building of the kingdom. (Visions 2 and 3 deal with external obstacles.) Chapter 3 promised cleansing for a penitent and responsive people. This chapter promises judgment for impenitent lawbreakers. God is gracious and forgiving to those who repent, but there is no place in God's kingdom for those who resist his grace.

In the sixth vision Zechariah sees a flying scroll (v. 1). The significance of the scroll is given in verse 3. It is a curse that is going out over the whole land. This curse brings together all the curses of the Law. It is a flying scroll because it travels through the land seeking out unrepentant lawbreakers. Two sample transgressions are named in verses 3 and 4, thievery and swearing falsely. The first is a typical crime against one's neighbor, the other a crime against the holiness of God. No transgressor will be able to evade the curse. It will seek him out even in his house, destroying it utterly while he himself is banished. Being the seed of Abraham only in the physical sense does not qualify a man for a place in the kingdom.

G. Seventh vision (5:5–11). In the previous vision, unregenerate sinners are purged from the land. In this vision wickedness as a pervasive principle is removed from the land and taken to Babylon where it is enshrined.

The measuring basket of verse 6 is literally an ephah, a measure somewhat smaller than a bushel. The basket with the woman inside represents the iniquity of the people throughout the land. She is the personification of wickedness. The woman tries to escape, but the lid is placed firmly over the mouth of the basket. The two women of verse 9 are agents of God who whisk the basket away to the country of Babylonia. A house or temple is built for the basket and its contents, and it is placed there as an idol on a pedestal, to be worshiped by those who have rejected God. From the time of the building of its tower in defiance of God to its ultimate destruction, Babylon appears in Scripture as the center of opposition to God. This, then, is the appropriate home of wickedness. Note that in 2:6–7 God's people are urged to flee from Babylon and to return to the "holy land" where God will dwell in their midst. An appropriate exchange is taking place. All this is preliminary to the final events yet to transpire: Babylon with all its wickedness will be utterly destroyed.

H. Eighth vision (6:1–8). This vision brings to a fitting conclusion the series of night visions outlining God's program of rebuilding Jerusalem and revitalizing his people. It is clearly eschatological in scope, completing what was anticipated in the first vision. There are obvious similarities to the first vision in the presence of various colored horses being sent throughout the earth. There are some differences in the colors of the horses and in the fact that there are chariots in this last vision. But the most distinctive difference is that in the first vision the horses go out on reconnaisance, bringing back their report. In this vision the horses go out to execute judgment. In the first vision the nations live in undisturbed quietness and God is disturbed and angry with them. In this vision the nations are judged and the Spirit of God is satisfied and at rest because his purpose has been accomplished.

The vision opens with the appearance of four chariots (v. 1). From the contents of this vision it becomes apparent that these are war chariots. Horses and chariots are logical symbols for the carrying out of divine judgment in war (Jer. 46:9–10; Joel 2:4ff.; Nah. 3:1–7). These chariots come out from between two mountains of bronze. These mountains are commonly identified with Mount Zion and Mount Olivet, with the Kidron Valley in between. What is important to recognize is that they come from the presence of God himself. Bronze is often associated with divine judgment (Num. 21:9), and this accords well with the symbolism of the passage.

The fact that there are four chariots relates to the universality of the judgment. All four corners of the earth (cf. Isa. 11:12) will be affected. Horses of varying colors are harnessed to the four chariots. The colors are not identical with those of chapter 1, nor are they explained. Whatever the individual colors might signify, these horses clearly mean terrible judgment on a rebellious and God-hating world. The horses with their chariots are identified in verse 5 as the four spirits (or "winds") of heaven. These are angelic beings, agents of God's justice, carrying out his sovereign purposes. The military defeats, the toppling of kingdoms, the plagues and "natural disasters," are not happenstance; they have been ordered by a God who has long been silent, giving man every opportunity to respond and repent.

God's title, *Lord of the whole world,* will no longer be questioned. Mesopotamian kings loved this title and other similar grandiose titles. But now it will be clearly seen who is truly Lord. Note that this title is assumed by God in the last days, when he sets out to enforce his lordship (Ps. 97:5; Mic. 4:13; Zech. 4:14).

The chariot with the black horses goes toward the north country (v. 6). It is the north country again in verse 8 that is particularly singled out as the focal point of judgment. The reference is almost certainly to Babylon. Though it lay to the east of Jerusalem, the invasion route of Babylon (and Assyria) was always from the north (via the Fertile Crescent).

God's angels are eager to carry out the program of judgment, to snuff out the blasphemous and boastful rebelliousness of the nations. But all is in God's control, and judgment will take place only when he gives the command, not a moment before. If only men would realize that all their vainglorious achievements in opposition to God are due only to God's patience and tolerance! This verse makes it clear that the whole earth, not only north and south, is under judgment. Nevertheless, it is the land of the north, or Babylon, that is viewed as the center of the world's opposition to God. The speaker is the angel of the Lord, the Lord of all the earth. The judgment on Babylon, the land of the north, has given rest to God's Spirit. When God had finished creating the world, he rested (Gen. 2:3), not from weariness, but because what he had made was perfect and he was satisfied. But sin brought discord into the world and God's "rest" was disturbed. In 1:14–15, God's response to the world scene is one of strong emotion and anger. Now, with the destruction of Babylon and the enthronement of God's Messiah, all is right with the world and God's Spirit is once again at rest.

III. The Crowning of Joshua (6:9–15)

The Book of Haggai, after giving assurances of immediate blessing and of the future glory of the temple, closes with a prophecy of a victorious Messiah who will reign over Jerusalem (2:20–23). In a similar way Zechariah caps off the eight visions with a remarkable and memorable symbolic action—the crowning of Joshua as a foretoken of the Messiah. The fact of the crowning is significant in that it is a reminder that when God has dealt with Babylon and the other nations, he will establish his own man on the throne. This King will flourish and be clothed with majesty. The manner of the crowning is significant in two ways: (1) It sets forth in the clearest possible way that the Messiah will unite the two offices of king and of priest. (2) It underscores the fact that the visions involving Joshua and Zerubbabel (chaps. 3 and 4) reach out beyond these men to the Messiah himself.

In verses 10 and 11 Zechariah is instructed to take the silver and gold that had been brought as a gift from Babylon and to go to the house of Josiah. There he is to make a crown and set it on the head of Joshua. The significance of this crowning is given in verses 12ff. "Here is the man whose name is the Branch." Note that Joshua the priest is here the type of Christ, but it is the office of Zerubbabel that is primarily in view. This passage, which clearly has reference to the future, serves to illustrate the far reach of the visions in chapters 3 and 4. Zerubbabel finished the temple as promised in 4:9. But the completion of that project served as the illustration of a far greater fulfillment yet to come. The words *it is he who will build the temple* (v. 13) stress the fact that Christ the Branch and no other will accomplish this task.

It must be carefully noted here that throughout the eight visions the rebuilding of the temple is inseparably related to the restoration of Jerusalem, and to the spiritual as well as the physical restoration of Israel. This is clearly the case in this context. He who had been despised is now universally acknowledged as the King of kings. He reigns now as both King and Priest, and there will be no conflict of interests between the two offices. As King he is able to rule in righteousness without having to condemn a sinful populace, because as Priest he has cleansed them of sin and brought them into fellowship with God. The crown will be a perpetual reminder that the present temple is merely the forerunner of greater things to come. Verse 15 adds that Gentiles who are far away will come and help to build the temple. This comports with many Old Testament passages that speak of the help and wealth brought by the nations. The coming of the Messiah in the way described is certain. But each individual needs to take heed that he be included.

IV. The Observance of Fasts (7:1–8:23)

A. The question (7:1–3). About two years after the temple rebuilding had recommenced, the question arises about the necessity of continuing the annual fasts that commemorated the destruction of the temple. The delegation comes from Bethel. The word *entreat* (v. 2) indicates that these people are not merely asking for a judicial decision from the priests and prophets. They are seeking a favor from God. The fasts have obviously become wearisome to them. Except for the fast of the day of atonement, God had not prescribed fasting as an annual ritual. It was appropriate on special occasions such as when there was mourning for sin (cf. Joel 1:13–14). In the present case the fasts had become a burdensome ritual that had no spiritual meaning at all.

God does not tell them what they want to hear, but rather what they need to hear. His answer is in four parts, each introduced by the expression *and the word of the Lord came again to Zechariah.* Their question is not answered directly, but the answer in its first two parts goes right to the heart of their spiritual condition. The second two parts point to the blessings of God in a renewed Jerusalem, and to the festivals that will replace the fasts.

B. The rebuke (7:4–14). The answer, with both rebuke and promise, is extended to all the people and the priests. "Was it really for me that you fasted?" This probing question goes right to the core of their problem: self-interest. Neither their fasting after the loss of the temple nor their former feasting while the temple stood were really for God's sake. Thus God dismisses their fasts as self-serving and meaningless ritual. The prophets before the exile had also condemned the futility of ritual worship without a true change of heart. As they had ignored God's wishes in prosperous times (v. 7), so they ignore his wishes now, not mourning for their sin but for their loss.

The people are concerned about fasting—whether or not it should be continued. God's concern is that they should truly listen to him for a change. What he says in these verses he has said many times in the past. His specific admonitions all relate to the essence of the commandment to "love your neighbor as yourself." These admonitions are stressed because they are tangible and more easily demonstrated than "love God. . . ."

Israel's persistent, stubborn refusal to listen to God over a long period of time has caused God to turn a deaf ear to their entreaties and pleas for deliverance. The result is their scattering as "with a whirlwind" (v. 14). The desolation of the land is not a capricious action on God's part, but a direct result of their disobedience. Thus God redirects their question from a concern about the observance of a ritual to the true need of their lives: a heart that responds to God's call.

C. The promise (8:1–23). Chapter 7 ends with a description of the desolation of the land brought about by Israel's disobedience. Now God takes it upon himself to bring about a change despite Israel's failure. This is the outworking of God's grace and his faithfulness to his promises.

The depth of God's emotion is very evident here. In 1:14 his zeal is aroused by the sight of a Gentile world that is secure and prosperous while Israel is in distress. There his zeal brings about the destruction of the godless nations and a restored Jerusalem. Here his zeal is aroused by the words of 7:13–14, and it effects spiritual as well as physical restoration. The fact that God will dwell in Jerusalem is the supreme blessing, and if God is there, what purpose does fasting serve?

The two names given to Jerusalem are more than names. They are now for the first time accurate representations of the new character with which Jerusalem is invested, names which reflect the very presence of God. In the word translated "truth" the concept of faithfulness is present as well. A related word is used in Isaiah 1:26, where Jerusalem is called both "Faithful

City" and "City of Righteousness." This latter name is paralleled by the term *Holy Mountain* used here. What a change from its former condition! Verses 4 and 5 describe the peaceful living conditions in this city where truth, faithfulness, and holiness reign. Fear and unrest are absent. To say such a thing to Zechariah's contemporaries seemed an incredible thing (v. 6), but with God nothing is impossible.

Verse 7 describes a regathering from all countries of the world (from east to west). The conditions described in these verses were certainly not realized to any large degree in Zechariah's time (hence the statement of v. 6). As is so often the case in prophetic Scripture, Zechariah sees the return from Babylon and the limited peace of his own day as simply a foretaste and small picture of the glory to come. It becomes clear in view of this that not only is their fasting wrongly motivated, but also it keeps them looking back at past defeats instead of forward to what God will do for them. The people will be restored physically and spiritually, living in close fellowship with God under the new covenant. God has always been true, faithful, and righteous, but now under the new covenant these attributes are displayed in a new way, and he can justly receive a people whose sins have been forgiven.

Zechariah continues to encourage the people to keep building the temple. They must turn from morbid reflections on the past (fasting) to joyful anticipation of the future. Verses 10 and 11 point to an upturn in economic prosperity and in the peace and safety of the people. Verse 12 promises a remarkable fertility for the land along with ideal weather conditions. All this God will provide as an inheritance to the remnant of his people. The word *remnant* refers not only to survivors of past judgments, but to a people whose heart is right with God—a redeemed people. The wording of verse 13 (as well as vv. 20–23) makes it clear that this whole passage still awaits its ultimate fulfillment.

It was Israel's destiny according to the Abrahamic covenant, not only to receive God's blessing, but to be a channel of blessing to the world in turn. Verses 15 and 16 give added assurance that the blessings described here will indeed come true. Interestingly enough, it is the destruction of Jerusalem and the temple that provides this assurance. This is because God had repeatedly threatened this destruction. The prophetic warnings went unheeded, but God demonstrated in Jerusalem's destruction that he keeps his word. Just so is the promised restoration a certainty! They can depend on it. Whatever danger or difficulties they may encounter, God will fulfill his purpose. They may confidently rely on him. What encouragement and what hope for those who trust God!

The message of verses 16 and 17 is similar to that of 7:9 and 10, but the setting is different. In chapter 7 the admonition went unheeded, and Jerusalem was destroyed. Here Jerusalem is destined to be restored; therefore, the people should now conduct their lives in anticipation of this. Jerusalem will be called the City of Truth and Holiness. They ought now to live a life of truth and holiness.

In verses 18–23 the subject of fasting again comes to the foreground, though it has always been in view. Fasting will become passé, to be replaced by joyous festivals (v. 19) because of the rich outpouring of God's blessing on Jerusalem. The admonition to love truth and peace again urges them to let their present conduct be molded by future realities. Verses 20–22 build upon Isaiah 2:1–5 and Micah 4:1–5, in which Jerusalem is seen as the focal point of the globe because the Lord is there to give direction to all peoples of the world. He will instruct multitudes of willing hearers who have come to learn his will and to do it. He will be the arbiter between nations, and there will be no more war. In the present passage the stress lies on the urgent desire of the Gentiles to seek the Lord. Contempt for, and hatred of, Jerusalem has been replaced by the recognition that it is a place of honor, where God dwells. It will not now be a few despised people who will seek God, but "many people and powerful nations" (v. 22). The Jews also will be acknowledged to have special status with God. Taking hold of the edge of a robe is an act of supplication to a superior (cf. 1 Sam. 15:27). The testimony of God's marvelous working on behalf of Israel will not fail to have its effect on a watching world.

Chapter 7 began with men entreating God from self-centered motives. Chapter 8 ends with multitudes of Gentiles joining Israel in entreating God with honest and responsive hearts. Not only is Israel blessed, but through Israel God reaches out to bless the Gentiles as well.

V. The Coming of the Messiah (9:1–14:21)

A. The first coming and rejection (9:1–11:17). For Zechariah, the coming of the Messiah is central. This is clear in two oracles (chaps. 9–11/12–14) celebrating God's worldwide triumph through the King's advent. The salvation of Israel and God's judgment against the nations is clearly in view as well. The major thrust in both cases is the last days, often referred to elsewhere in Scripture as the day of the Lord. But there are also three major differences between the two oracles: (1) In the first, the Messiah is rejected; in the second, he is received by repentant hearts. (2) In the first, there is frequent alternation between near and far fulfillments, or telescoping, a frequent prophetic practice in which distant events are viewed from the standpoint of near events. The near and the far are often intermingled in such a way that they merge into one. The second oracle describes eschatological events almost entirely (13:7 being the exception, a "flashback" to the past, given as a reason for Israel's trials). (3) The first oracle is against the nations, the second concerns Israel (12:1). In the first, God judges the nations, but always with an eye on Israel's deliverance and blessing. In the second, God brings Israel to repentance and cleanses and protects her, while the nations are destroyed.

In the first oracle, the cities named are all north of Israel (**9:1–8**). Beginning with Hadrach and proceeding southward to Philistia, Zechariah portrays the defeat of these cities as a whirlwind military campaign. When God makes his power felt as described in these chapters, men will see that it is God's hand at work, and many will turn to him. Zechariah provides a glimpse into the future with reference to various idolatrous and unclean customs practiced by the Philistines. God will effect a cleansing and transformation of these inveterate enemies of God's people. Here is another of many Old Testament passages speaking of the conversion of Gentiles. Not only will they become part of God's people, they will even become leaders in Judah, an indication of their complete acceptance by God and people alike. In this respect they will be like the Jebusites, the original inhabitants of Jerusalem, who were not destroyed when David captured their city. Rather, they were absorbed by Judah and became part of God's people.

Jerusalem stands out by contrast to other cities because of God's special care. This fact brings about a natural telescoping into the future, when once again Jerusalem stands in contrast to other cities. It is clear that Jerusalem was to suffer defeat. Zechariah knows this (14:1–3). But when the final battle is over, when the smoke of battle has cleared and city after city lies in ruins, Jerusalem will remain and will never again be overrun by an oppressor. No longer can Jerusalem say that God has forsaken her. Rather, his eyes are on her, to protect and provide for her. The word *now* signals a change to come. This comes about through the advent of the Messiah.

Zechariah directs Zion's attention to the long-awaited King, the Savior (**9:9–10**). He is righteous, in contrast to the many wicked kings who have preceded him. There will be absolute justice in his reign. He also comes with salvation, deliverance for his people. These ideal requirements for kingship are met in Christ in a unique way. Through his substitutionary death at his first advent he provided salvation from sin and imputed righteousness to all who will receive him. As reigning King at his second advent he will redeem his people from their enemies and reign with righteousness.

The Messiah's humility stands in contrast to the pomp and arrogance usually associated with kings. He rides on a donkey instead of a horse (which is associated with warfare). He comes not as a human conqueror, but as God's Servant. The removal of various instruments of war is made possible by the Messiah's reign of righteousness and peace (cf. Isa. 2:4; 11:1–9). His presence guarantees the peace and security, not only of Jerusalem, but of all nations.

Zechariah again turns to Israel (**9:11–17**). The deliverance and blessing described in these verses is on the basis of Israel's covenant relationship with God, ratified by the blood of sacrifice. There is a place of refuge and security to which released prisoners are to go, the fortress Zion secured by God himself. The prisoners of hope are those who, though still in difficulty, hope in God and his promise. God promises to restore twice as much—doubtless the abundance which he will shower on those he has redeemed. In verse 13 Judah and Ephraim are described as God's weapons—means of defeating his enemies. The victory over Greece points to the Maccabean victories over the Greek Seleucids after Antiochus Epiphanes' oppression and his desecration of the temple.

God appears on behalf of his people and will shield them while dealing with his enemies. Israel will enjoy complete victory over their enemies and utter safety. Their boundless joy, like a cup filled to overflowing, is compared to the bowl filled with the blood of sacrifice used in the sprinkling of the altar in worship. Their joy is boundless and exuberant, but they recognize God as the Author of their deliverance and the true object of praise. Verses 16–17 summarize their newly attained state of bliss and prosperity. They will be well cared for, as precious as jewels in God's crown, shining forth with the joy and glory of their newfound prosperity and standing with God. In place of poverty and humiliation there is prosperity and glory. What a future and what a blessed hope for God's people!

Zechariah **10:1–12** begins with an invitation and continues with a promise. The intent is to cause the reader's eyes to focus on God as the Author of blessing and deliverance. There are two major aspects to the promise. First, God will shepherd his flock, replacing the false shepherds (vv. 2–3). The shepherd/flock theme is already introduced in 9:16 and forms the major theme of chapter 11, where tragically the people reject the Shepherd whom God sends for their benefit. Second, God is going to bring about change on behalf of Israel. This change is first of all an internal transformation of a weak, disoriented, captive people to brave, strong, and victorious heroes. The change is also external—deliverance from the power of the enemy.

Verse 1 forms an effective transition from the picture of a vigorous and prosperous people thriving on the produce of fertile soil to the admonition to seek the Lord who is the Author of that fertility and prosperity. It is God who sends the rain, and it is God who brings comfort and deliverance to his people. The message is clear: Seek God and trust him. He will prosper and deliver his people. By failing to heed this admonition and by trusting in deceitful idols and lying diviners, Israel has fallen on hard times. They wander like sheep without a shepherd. They have been led astray, away from God and into suffering and exile. The situation is really a hopeless one, but in verse 3 God steps in. He deals with the false shepherds and leaders who abuse their authority and strength at the expense of the weak. He has long been silent, but now he will take action against the wicked leaders and will care for his flock, providing for all their needs, physical and spiritual, delivering and protecting them from their enemies, providing them with the right leadership, and making them strong.

From the last line of verse 3 through the first line of verse 5 Zechariah describes the strength and the leadership God will provide in and for Judah. The Jewish Targums as well as many Christian expositors correctly see a reference to the Messiah here. It is of course true that Judah is seen here as the source of able, stable, and victorious leadership, but the One who exemplifies all the highest qualities of leadership is God's Shepherd, the Messiah.

The cornerstone metaphor is clearly messianic in Isaiah 28:16 and in Psalm 118:22. Not only is stability in view here, but the Cornerstone is the One on whom the whole structure of the kingdom of God is built. The tent-peg metaphor symbolizes one who is both prominent and who carries on his shoulders the affairs of state (Isa. 22:22–24). Note that he carries the royal keys as symbol of great authority. The battle-bow metaphor obviously has a military reference. It is not used specifically of the Messiah elsewhere, but it is certainly clear that he will vanquish his enemies at his second coming. "Every ruler" in this context is used simply of one who imposes his will on others (as described in v. 5). Though the whole of Judah has such power over the foe, the Messiah himself as the battle bow exacts obedience from all men. Once again Judah and the house of Joseph (i.e., Ephraim) will be united. God will restore them again as one nation and as truly God's people. This is due to God's great compassion on them. In their newly exalted state it will be as though God had never rejected them. They will live in close fellowship with a responsive God and there will be great rejoicing. God will signal for his people in the lands to which they have been exiled, will gather them in, and will multiply them in the land. Though Israel is widely scattered, their remembrance of God will not die out. They will not be a feeble nation, but strong and numerous. The great powers of the past, Assyria and Egypt, will be subdued, but God will strengthen Israel. They will be strong politically, militarily, and numerically, but most importantly, spiritually.

Chapter 10 introduced the theme of the Shepherd that God will raise up to care for his people. He will destroy the power of the enemy and deliver and restore Israel. This anticipates a time when Israel will have accepted the Shepherd and follows his leadership. This clearly points to the day of the Lord. In chapter 11 an earlier time is in view, the first advent of Messiah in which he is tragically rejected by his own people, resulting in terrible consequences.

A call to lament (**11:1–3**) proclaims the devastation of the land from Lebanon through the Jordan Valley, resulting from Israel's rejection of their Shepherd. The lament is not for a raging forest fire that devours first the cedars of Lebanon, then the pines, then sweeps down through Bashan to the Jordan Valley. The devouring fire is rather a symbol for judgment and portrays here a devastating military defeat. The cedars of Lebanon, stately trees, and oaks of Bashan are the nobles of the land, the shepherds are the leaders, and the lions are the choice men, the military leaders.

Zechariah receives a commission to be a shepherd to God's flock. He represents the good Shepherd appointed by God to care for his people (**11:4–14**). "Marked for slaughter" indicates the sorry status of this flock. Their shepherds have no care or concern for them; rather they deal ruthlessly with them, using them as objects for personal profit.

It becomes clear as the passage unfolds that the abused flock has the option of receiving or rejecting God's Shepherd. They decide to reject him. In rejecting God's Shepherd, they reject God's help and salvation. They are left to suffer helplessly at the hands of their own countrymen and under an oppressing king. This came true quite literally in the factionalism and civil strife of A.D. 70, when Rome oppressed the land and destroyed Jerusalem. God did not intervene, for they had rejected his salvation.

As Zechariah symbolically tends the flock, his care is particularly for the oppressed—those who recognize the word of the Lord being fulfilled in the coming of the Shepherd. They are a small, despised minority.

In caring for the sheep, Zechariah takes up two staffs, one called Favor, the other called Union. The first signifies the especial favor exercised by God on behalf of his people; the second signifies internal unity and cohesiveness within the nation, especially the two major factions, Judah and Israel. God's Shepherd replaces the leadership of Israel (the three shepherds, symbolic of the three offices of prophet, priest, and king). He is the perfect leader, ideal in every way. Yet the flock detests him and rejects him. Therefore he leaves them to their fate, dying and consuming one another.

The breaking of the staff called Favor (v. 10) symbolizes the revoking of the protective covenant, so that the nations would not harm Israel. Only the faithful remnant recognizes Messiah at his coming and sees in the judgment, resulting from his rejection, the fulfillment of God's Word.

The Shepherd's pay—thirty pieces (lit. shekels) of silver—was the price to be paid for a gored slave (Exod. 21:32). For God's Shepherd to be evaluated this way is a deliberate insult. God's response is throw it to the potter (v. 13), evidently an act symbolizing rejection and contempt. Note that this money is thrown to the potter in the house of the Lord. This symbolic act was fulfilled by Judas when he threw the thirty shekels into the temple and when the priests used it to buy a potter's field for the burial of the poor (Matt. 27:3–10). Verse 14 describes the breaking of the second staff Union, symbolizing the lack of internal cohesion within the nation.

Israel rejected the good Shepherd provided by God for their benefit. There were immediate consequences, but much worse will be the time when they become subject to one whose qualities are opposite to those of the good Shepherd (**11:15–17**). This is the Antichrist who will exercise terrible power during the tribulation (cf. Dan. 7; Rev. 13). He is a foolish (v. 15) and worthless (v. 17) shepherd. It will be a time of incredible hardship and suffering for Israel. But God will have the last word. The worthless shepherd will be judged.

B. The second coming and reception (12:1–14:21). As God sets out to unfold his great eschatological working in and on behalf of Israel (**12:1–9**), he reminds us that he is the Creator of heaven and earth and that he also formed man's spirit within him. Thus he has the absolute right and sovereign ability to do as he wishes. There is no power in heaven or earth that can deter him from accomplishing his purpose. Israel as a nation (not just the northern kingdom) will be restored, the nations will be judged, and God's kingdom will be established.

The expression *on* (or *in*) *that day* occurs sixteen times in the last three chapters of Zechariah. The setting is in the last days when God judges the nations, restores Israel, and establishes his kingdom on earth. The particular setting of this paragraph is the last and climactic siege of Jerusalem by the forces of Antichrist. It seems as though victory is in their grasp. But God intervenes, and it is not Jerusalem that is destroyed, but the forces of Antichrist. The cup of reeling is a frequent prophetic metaphor describing the staggering effect God's judgment will have on the nations (cf. Jer. 25:15–28). Instead of being drunk with the wine of revelry, they will drink the cup of God's wrath. The nations view Jerusalem as a cup that will make them drunk with the joy of victory, but they find that they will go away staggering in utter defeat at God's hands.

Judah and Jerusalem are separated in verses 5–7. There is clearly some rift, or at least friction, between the two. Possibly those in Jerusalem are more "orthodox," the others more secular (v. 5 might indicate this; v. 7 seems to point to a spirit of elitism on the part of those in Jerusalem). Jerusalem will be a rock, apparently easy to deal with, but by God's intervention a rock that is so heavy that the nations will injure themselves. Both the cup of reeling and the immovable stone metaphors graphically illustrate the sudden and unexpected disaster that befalls the attackers. Verse 4 makes it clear that it is God's doing that saves Jerusalem. The three elements of panic, madness, and blindness are also present in the curse pronounced upon a rebellious Israel (Deut. 28:28), but here the enemy is so afflicted. At the same time that the enemy is struck with blindness, God will guard and protect Judah. The people of Jerusalem are strong because of their God. There seems to be an acknowledgment here, not only of the power and reality of God, but also of the fact that the people of Jerusalem have trusted God. At the very least their hearts are prepared for the appearance of the Messiah, their King. The leaders of Judah, encouraged by the evidence of God's work, will overcome their enemies.

God's deliverance is twofold: he provides a shield for the people and he gives them supernatural strength so that the feeblest will be as heroic as David, and the leaders will be like God, like the angel of the Lord. The angel of the Lord (equated here as elsewhere with God) is the invincible "commander of the armies of the Lord" (Josh. 5:14). No more are God's people ready prey for their voracious enemies. God is their shield and strength. Verse 9 is a pointed summary of the whole paragraph. This eschatological attack against Jerusalem is God's means of bringing the nations to judgment. To the attackers victory seems assured (they even penetrate Jerusalem initially) and to Jerusalem it might seem hopeless, but the victory is the Lord's.

Zechariah has described a great victory won on Israel's behalf by the powerful intervention of God. Now an even greater victory is won, this time an *internal* victory over sinful and rebellious hearts (**12:10–13:1**). This victory is likewise won because of God's gracious intervention. He takes the initiative and brings about a change in heart.

The outpouring of God's Spirit, like an abundant stream of water onto arid ground, will bring about a miraculous transformation in human hearts (Isa. 32:15; 44:3; Ezek. 36:25–27; 39:29; Joel 2:28–29). Not until God does this will Israel's blindness and hardness of heart be removed, and will she acknowledge and receive her Messiah. God's Spirit of grace will convict their hearts and move them to true repentance. His Spirit of supplication will move them to cry out to God. On this great day the working of God's Spirit will cause the scales to fall from Israel's eyes and they will see the Lord Jesus as their Messiah.

Verse 10 is a remarkable verse in the information given us about the One to whom they will look. (1) Since God is speaking, the "me" to whom they look is clearly God. (2) The one they have pierced is God. This conforms to Jesus' claims to deity. (3) This passage links him with the Suffering Servant of Isaiah 53:5, who was pierced for our sins. John (19:34–37) sees the piercing of Jesus' side by the spear as a fulfillment of this verse. (4) This passage clearly anticipates a twofold advent of the Messiah: the first when he was pierced; the second when they recognized him and trusted in him. The result will be true repentance. The depth of their emotion and sense of loss because they have slain him instead of receiving him is vividly expressed. The mourning of that day is compared to the weeping of Hadad Rimmon in the plain of Megiddo. This most likely refers to the tradition of mourning for the death of Josiah in battle with Pharaoh Neco in the plains of Megiddo (2 Chron. 35:22–25). The loss of Josiah was keenly felt, particularly by the godly of the land, his death being a catastrophe. Thus the mourning of Israel described here is compared to that associated with great personal loss and terrible national catastrophe. The mourning is individualized to stress the fact that this is not a case of mass psychology or of ritual mourning. Each family and each individual, from the house of David on down, will grieve deeply for their sin.

God will respond to Israel's repentance. An abundance of forgiveness is available to them (an open fountain). There is cleansing for every sin and every uncleanness. The Hebrew word for sin describes man's missing the mark, falling short of God's requirements. Uncleanness has to do with ceremonial matters, those things that disqualify a person from coming into God's presence. After years of rejection, dispersion, and suffering, Israel now comes home, is united with her Savior, and finds glorious forgiveness and peace.

Now that Israel is in right relationship to God through Jesus Christ, there is no room in the land for false prophets or idolatry (**13:2–6**).

Idolatry had played an integral part in the sins of Israel leading to the destruction of Samaria and Jerusalem. It was not a problem as such after the exile. However, as the second coming of Christ approaches, it will once again gain increasing prominence, especially as men worship the Antichrist and demons (Isa. 2:18, 20; Matt. 24:11, 15, 23f.; 2 Thess. 2:2–4; Rev. 9:20; 13:4–15). But in the messianic kingdom the land will be purged of any form of idolatry. Christ alone will reign. The whole complex of idolatry, false prophets, and demon worship is spawned of Satan and will no longer be tolerated.

The convictions of redeemed Israel will be so firm, and their love and loyalty to Christ will be so strong that parents will even put their own children to death for the sin of telling lies in the Lord's name. False prophets will attempt to conceal their true identity by claiming to be farmers. Accused prophets will claim innocence, attributing probably self-inflicted wounds (see 1 Kings 18:28) to mistreatment at the hands of so-called "friends." The impression that Zechariah leaves is that in actual fact these prophets have been involved in idolatrous activity.

Zechariah returns to the theme of the rejected Shepherd, but now from a different perspective (**13:7–9**). In chapter 11 the flock rejected its Shepherd. Man's responsibility is stressed. Here the Shepherd is slain by God's decree. The result of the rejection of chapter 11 is that the flock becomes prey to the nations and ultimately comes under the rulership of a false and worthless shepherd. Here, the flock is dispersed: two-thirds perish while the rest is refined and restored to fellowship with God. The final resolution of the rejection of chapter 11 is seen in the repentance of 12:10 and the forgiveness of 13:1. The rejected Shepherd is ultimately embraced. The final resolution of the smiting of the Shepherd here is seen in the victorious return of the Lord and his reign over the whole earth.

The sword as the instrument of death is called on by God himself to slay his Shepherd. Though the redemptive reasons are not given here, the passage makes it clear that the rejection and slaying of the Shepherd is no accident of history. He is the One whom God has appointed for his people, the One who alone can fully provide for all the needs of the flock. The remarkable designation *the man who is close to me* (v. 7) identifies the Shepherd as both man and "colleague" or "associate" of God. When the Shepherd is struck, the sheep will be scattered. The term *little ones* emphasizes their helpless condition.

A great catastrophe is to come on Israel. The destruction of Jerusalem in A.D. 70 was but a foretaste of the tribulation to come. The third of the flock that remains God will refine and purify as silver and gold. As terrible as the coming tribulation will be, its purpose is to cleanse and to prepare Israel to receive her Messiah. This is not punitive judgment, but a means of drawing Israel back to God. As a result they will call on God's name in repentance and in trust. Their hearts will be entirely directed toward God. They have turned away from all that grieves him. God will forgive them and receive them so that he can say "they are truly my people" and they will be able to say "the Lord is our God."

Chapter 14 returns to the final siege of Jerusalem. Besides adding some particulars omitted in chapter 12, chapter 14 has a different purpose. Both chapters show that much more is at stake than the defense of Jerusalem and the destruction of the enemy. In chapter 12 the impact of Christ's coming brings God's people to repentance and faith. In chapter 14 Christ's coming is seen in its impact on the world at large, in the establishment of a worldwide kingdom where Christ alone is King. The repentance of Israel in chapter 12 is a prerequisite for her proper role in the Messiah's world kingdom.

The King's coming will be victorious (**14:1–7**). "A day of the LORD" is literally "a day *for* the Lord." God is personally interested and involved in the events and their outcome. This day begins as a day of great darkness for Jerusalem (cf. Amos 5:18–20). The attacking nations will ransack Jerusalem. This is not a hit-and-run raid. Their intent is to impose the authority of Antichrist on Jerusalem completely. The attack on Jerusalem is brought about, not by political or military considerations, but by the satanically inspired motive of crushing the last major stronghold of resistance to Antichrist. But as in the case of the crucifixion of Christ, God is in control, using the ambition and malice of men to accomplish his own ends (Acts 2:23). Initially the nations will have great success, capturing the city, ransacking the houses, raping the women. The attackers, however, will be suddenly and unexpectedly interrupted in their looting and pillaging. Just as they seem to have achieved final victory, the Lord himself will fight against them.

Some details of Christ's coming and victory are now given. His feet will stand on the Mount of Olives, the place from which the glory of God left Jerusalem before the destruction of the temple in 586 B.C. (Ezek. 11:23), and from which Christ ascended into glory (Acts 1:9–12). Here also will the glory of God (in the person of Christ) return to Jerusalem (Ezek. 43:1–4). When the Lord touches the mountain it will be split in two, forming a great valley running east to west. This is only one of a number of great supernaturally caused changes that will take place (vv. 6–10). The people of Jerusalem will flee through this valley to Azel (a place east of the Mount of Olives, but not identified to date). Then the Lord will come. There is here a brief personal testimony of Zechariah's personal identification with, and loyalty to, God in this conflict. At first there will be no light, no daytime or nighttime. Then, when evening comes, there will be light again. Evidently this describes a unique and heretofore unknown state of darkness (semidarkness?) which is neither day nor night, while God's judging activity is going on. When evening comes the heavenly sources of light will resume their normal functioning. All the universe is involved in the display of God's power, heightening the terror of that day.

The physical rejuvenation of the land due to the perennial supply of living water flowing out of Jerusalem corresponds to the spiritual blessing and revitalization that the Lord effects in the lives of his people (**14:8–11**). No more will Israel be likened to a leaking cistern (Jer. 2:13). This abundant supply of water is as regular and plentiful in the dry summer season as in the wet winter. This is no wadi (intermittent stream) but a dependable, never-failing supply of water. This also serves as a wonderfully apt picture of the unfailing mercies and blessing of God to his own.

God will be King over the whole earth. His kingship will be undisputed; it will be universally acknowledged. Furthermore, there will be one Lord, and his name will be the only name. This both recalls and expounds the great Jewish Shema (Deut. 6:4). There is no longer any question as to who is Lord, who is to be worshiped. Now not only Israel, but all the world will recognize the truth: God is sovereign; he is the Redeemer; he forgives those who repent but judges the unrepentant. Probably as a part of the same upheavals in verse 4, the land around Jerusalem will become like the Arabah, the broad depression of the Jordan Valley, while Jerusalem will be raised up as a large mesa dominating the whole area. It will be inhabited, never to be destroyed again. It will be secure and remain so.

The manner in which the LORD deals with the attackers is briefly described (**14:12–15**). The word *plague* is literally "a striking (by God)" and is used in Exodus 9:14 to describe the way God struck Egypt. Whether God will employ what is known today as some form of nuclear or biological warfare, or some supernatural means not known to man is obviously not stated. What is clear is that he makes a distinction, as he did in Egypt, between his own people and his enemies. After the nations attack each other, Judah will participate in the "mop-up" phase of the battle. They, along with the people of Jerusalem, will share in the wealth of all the surrounding nations as it is collected at Jerusalem. Now Jerusalem is not being plundered, but enriched.

The attacking armies are completely destroyed. But there will be those among the nations of the world who will repent and turn to the Lord (**14:16–19**). These will enter the millennial kingdom and will join Israel in worshiping and obeying the Lord (cf. Isa. 2:1–4; Zech. 8:20–23). They go up yearly to worship and to celebrate the Feast of Tabernacles. The celebration of this festival during the millennium will be appropriate in that (1) it follows shortly after the great day of atonement, a day of national repentance and forgiveness for sins; (2) it is a thanksgiving festival commemorating the end of centuries of homeless exile; (3) as a harvest festival it acknowledges the gracious providence of God in both the physical and the spiritual realms. The keeping of the Feast of Tabernacles and the worship of the Lord are equated in verses 17–18. Since this festival is in part an acknowledgment of God as King and as gracious Provider, to refuse to participate is to refuse to acknowledge God. The punishment fits the crime, since withholding rain results in crop failure. No amount of modern technology can counteract the withholding of God's blessing on the land.

There are several possible reasons why Egypt is singled out here: (1) It is a link to Israel's background as the land which they left to journey to the land of promise. (2) Egypt was dependent on the Nile for the fertility of its land, but God can diminish and even dry up the Nile. (3) God had once before established the fact of his lordship by bringing Egypt to her knees. He can do it again if need be.

Jerusalem will be for the first time truly a "Holy City" (**14:20–21**). In the Mosaic economy the high priest had "Holy to the Lord" inscribed on his turban (Exod. 28:36). Now, even the bells of the horses are so engraved. Ordinary cooking pots will be like the sacred bowls used for sprinkling blood on the altar. The distinction between sacred and profane is now eliminated because all of Jerusalem is truly dedicated to the Lord. The priestly calling of Israel will become actuality. The term *Canaanite* (v. 21) sometimes refers to traders or merchants (see Job 41:6; Prov. 31:24) and may refer to the fact that the need for traders (who sold holy utensils to pilgrim worshipers in the temple precincts) will no longer exist, since all that is in Jerusalem will be holy and suitable for temple worship. But more likely "Canaanites" are persons who are spiritually unclean and unfit to come into God's presence. No longer will men come unworthily before the Lord, because God will have sanctified his people, making them fit to worship him.

Thus this great prophecy concludes, with God having accomplished his intended program. Israel has been transformed into a people worthy of its calling, the Gentile world powers have been judged, and the once-rejected Messiah now reigns supreme in a world blessed by his presence.

SELECT BIBLIOGRAPHY

Archer, G. L. *A Survey of Old Testament Introduction.* Chicago: Moody, 1985.

Baldwin, J. G. *Haggai, Zechariah, Malachi.* Downers Grove: Inter-Varsity, 1972.
Barker, K. L. "Zechariah." In *The Expositor's Bible Commentary,* edited by Frank E. Gaebelein, 12 vols. Grand Rapids: Zondervan, 1985.
Baron, D. *The Visions and Prophecies of Zechariah.* London: Marshall, Morgan & Scott, 1962.
Feinberg, C. L. *The Minor Prophets.* Chicago: Moody, 1976.
Freeman, H. E. *An Introduction to the Old Testament Prophets.* Chicago: Moody, 1977.
Harrison, R. K. *Introduction to the Old Testament.* Grand Rapids: Eerdmans, 1969.
Laney, J. C. *Zechariah.* Chicago: Moody, 1984.
Pusey, E. B. *The Minor Prophets.* 2 vols. Reprint. Grand Rapids: Baker, 1950.
Unger, M. F. *Zechariah.* Grand Rapids: Zondervan, 1962.

MALACHI

Willem A. VanGemeren

INTRODUCTION

Nothing is known about Malachi, his ancestry, or his place of residence. According to the church fathers, Malachi was a Levite from the region of Zebulun. It is impossible to verify this assertion, but Malachi's concern with the corruption of worship, the glory of God, the corruption of the priesthood, and the tithe would support the priestly interests if not the background of the prophet.

He lived after the exile in a world filled with shattered hopes. Scholars are in general agreement on the postexilic date of this book, and though there is some minor disagreement, his ministry is dated around 440 B.C. This date fits the present archaeological evidence of the devastation of Edom by the Nabateans (1:3–4), the reference to the "governor" of the Persian province (1:8), the existence of the temple, and the moral and social problems portrayed in Ezra–Nehemiah.

Following Israel's return from exile, the prophetic promises were only partially fulfilled. The prophets had spoken about the renewal of the covenant, the restoration of the people to the land, the messianic kingdom of peace, the renewal of temple worship, the continuity of the priestly ministry, the rebuilding of a glorious temple, and a new era characterized by Isaiah as the New Jerusalem (65:17–25).

The religious enthusiasm characteristic of the returning exiles and the contemporaries of Haggai and Zechariah had waned. The restoration of which the prophets had spoken had not yet come. God had not "shaken" the nations and the messianic kingdom had not yet been established. The Lord had not blessed his people as he had promised. The era of fulfillment had turned into a period of waiting. While waiting, some had exchanged their beliefs for the fast life (3:5, 15), while others were cynical about the value of organized religion. A minority remained faithful regardless how bad the times were (3:16). God raised up Malachi to address the problems of cynicism, formalism, unfaithfulness, and questions about the benefits of godliness.

Malachi defends the love, honor, and justice of God. God's love is shown by his election and care for his own. God, Father of Israel and King of the universe, expects his children to respond to his love, honor, and justice.

The focus of the prophet is on the veracity of God and on man's responsibility. The Lord is faithful, even when it seems as if he does not respond. The prophecy encourages all who remain faithful to him to persevere. Malachi calls for responsibility in marriage, sacrifice, religion, social concerns, tithes, and observance of God's laws. He redefines the "godly" as those who persevere in godliness. Israel may no longer claim any automatic hold on God, but must show that they have the Spirit of God. God is faithful to his own and will richly reward his children.

Malachi is the twelfth of the Minor Prophets. The placement of the book after Zechariah may not have been out of chronological considerations, but because of the connecting phrase *An oracle: The word of the* L*ORD* (1:1), also found in Zechariah 9:1; 12:1.

OUTLINE

I. Introduction (1:1)
II. God's Love for His People (1:2–5)
III. The Honor of God (1:6–14)
IV. The Knowledge of God (2:1–9)
V. Intermarriage and Divorce (2:10–16)
VI. The Justice and Patience of God (2:17–3:6)
VII. The Tithe (3:7–12)
VIII. God's Love for the Remnant (3:13–4:3)
IX. Conclusion (4:4–6)

COMMENTARY

I. Introduction (1:1)

The Book of Malachi is an oracle, a word, from Yahweh. "Oracle" ("burden") is a technical, prophetic term for a word of judgment on both the nations and on Israel/Judah. The prophet functions as an ambassador whose duty is to proclaim the Word, no matter how burdensome the message or how unresponsive the people. The prophet is appointed by God to discharge his office and in that appointment there is a sense of urgency (cf. Jer. 20:9). He *must* proclaim the oracle, because the oracle is the word of Yahweh!

II. God's Love for His People (1:2–5)

In the first disputation, Yahweh assures his people of his love. The structure is symmetric. The cynicism of the people (v. 2) is symmetric with the expression of hope in God (v. 5b). The affirmation of God's "love" (vv. 2–3) is symmetric with an affirmation of his "greatness" (v. 5). God's past acts against Edom (v. 3) are symmetric with his promise to rid the land of all evil (v. 4). The focus of the oracle is on the demonstrations of Yahweh's love for his people, which are the very reasons why the elect in Israel should put their faith in God and praise him (**1:1–2**).

Although the postexilic Jewish community was not living in the fullness of the messianic age, they had been loved. It had been nearly a century since their return from exile and the rebuilding of the temple. The priests were again serving God in the temple. God was reconciled to his people and through the ministry of the prophets Haggai and Zechariah he had encouraged them to look forward to the messianic kingship which would bring peace, prosperity, and justice (cf. Hag. 2:20–23; Zech. 9:9; 13–14). Yet the prophetic assurance of God's love receives only a cynical response from God's people.

In response to the people's question, "How have you loved us?" Malachi turns to Israel's history. Yahweh loved Jacob more than Esau. His love is not based on Israel's righteousness (Deut. 9:4) or greatness (Deut. 7:7), but on his promise of blessing (Deut. 7:8) guaranteed by oath to Abraham, Isaac, and Jacob. Esau was bypassed. No human reasoning can fully explain God's choice. His love for Jacob was an act of love, election, and sovereignty (Rom. 9:1–29).

The people may have given Malachi a cynical look as he proclaimed God's love for them a second time. The Edomites, descendants of Esau, were supposed to have been wiped out and their territory should have been given to Israel (Amos 9:11–12; Obad. 8–10, 18–19, 21). Yet they still existed as a nation, and their territory now adjoined Judah!

God's judgment on Esau, however, is progressive, slowly moving toward completion (**1:3–4**). The Edomites had harassed the Judeans as they attempted to flee Judah and Jerusalem at the time of the fall of Jerusalem (586 B.C.). The books of Obadiah and Lamentations speak of the hatred shown by the Edomites, who did not help the people of Judah in her time of need, but instead rejoiced in her tragedy. Later, the Edomites were displaced by desert nomads who had destroyed the mountain strongholds and devastated the land, forcing them to flee into the northern Negeb. The prophetic word of God's judgment on the Edomites is confirmed by Malachi. Regardless of how long it may be, Yahweh himself will see to the end of the Edomites (v. 4).

The rejection and judgment of Edom is without mercy. God promises to harass and judge the Edomites (Idumeans) until every trace of their evil scheming and activity is removed. His anger will rest on them until their land is emptied of Edomites. Malachi encourages God's people with the promise that evil will be dealt with in the day of the Lord.

In the Old Testament, Edom represents all the enemies of God's kingdom. The prophets point beyond the Edomites to the fall of all Gentile kingdoms. Since God's judgment rests on such a small nation (Edom), how much more will it extend to all kingdoms! If the Edomites, who are related to the Israelites, will not escape the judgment of God, how will other nations avoid the day of the Lord? It is in this context that we must understand God's response to Judah. He declares that he will so execrate and destroy evil that not a trace will be left. During the time of the postexilic restoration, the Jews remained subject to a foreign nation, the Persians. In the coming centuries they would be subject to the Greeks, the Ptolemies, the Seleucids, and the Romans. The Lord here affirms that he will judge all nations which oppress his people, thus purging all wickedness from his creation. History attests to the fulfillment of this promise in that the Lord brought desolation to Edom and to the enemies of his people. The Lord's anger still rests upon wickedness and he will make an end to the rule of evil forever.

In anticipation of God's coming demonstration of his love for the elect, the people of God must now pray with hope that Yahweh be exalted beyond the territory of Israel (**1:5**). This prayer is often taken as a proclamation (NIV Great is the LORD). However, the same phrase is translated correctly in the psalms as "The LORD be exalted" (40:16; 70:4). The context is hope in the deliverance of the Lord. The eyes of faith already see his victory over the enemies of the kingdom and the full establishment of God's kingdom. The translation should be: "May Yahweh be exalted beyond the borders of Israel." The phrase *beyond the borders* has occasioned difficulty. The preposition may be translated as "over" or "beyond." In view of his universal interest (1:11, 14) and his concern that evil be removed, the reading *beyond* is preferable. Yahweh, the God of Israel, is not limited to Judah. His kingship will extend to the ends of the earth!

III. The Honor of God (1:6–14)

Even though the people are not certain of God's love (v. 2), he expects a minimal response of honor and respect. Malachi likens the situation to that of a son's respect for his father or a servant's respect for his master. The people of God, however, are so self-centered that they cannot express themselves in love and devotion toward Yahweh. He affirms that he is a Father and Master. God is not only the Father of the faithful (v. 6) but also the King whose kingdom is not limited to Jerusalem or the land of Judea. His name is feared among the nations. He is the great King.

These three grounds for honoring Yahweh (as Father, Master, and King) provide the structure of the second disputation. Malachi's argument focuses on the priests' utter disregard for the God of Israel. They, of all people, should be expected to remain faithful. The job of the priests as cultic functionaries was to please God by presenting offerings and sacrifices and in teaching the law of God. They may not have been aware of their attitudes and hidden motives. This section is a warning for Christians, particularly ministers of the Word, to be careful not to "despise" the name of God by slovenly attitudes and shoddy service.

Malachi charges the priests with profaning the glorious name of the Lord (**1:6–10**). Since God is the Father of his people and the Master of the universe, it is only fair that his servants, the priests, protect his "honor" ("glory") and give reason for the Gentiles to "respect" the God of Israel. Instead, they are irreverent and nurture a low view of God. Malachi cites their disregard of the sacrificial laws as evidence of their guilt. They show contempt for God by having no regard for the revealed priestly rules and regulations. His "table" (i.e., the tables on which the sacrifices were slaughtered; cf. Ezek. 40:39–43) is treated with contempt. In response to the twofold disputation ("How have we despised your name?" and "How have we defiled you?") Yahweh charges the priests with defiling his altar by presenting offerings that are not in accordance with the priestly regulations. According to Leviticus 22:23–27, the priests were to inspect the offerings before they were consecrated to the Lord to see whether they were ritually clean. The priests had disregarded these regulations. They sacrificed anything that was presented to the Lord in the temple, whether blind, lame, or sickly. The prophet returns to the analogy with which he began by asking whether they present sickly animals as gifts to the governor, their political "master." They must repent and ask God to restore his favor. However, if they continue their practices, the priests may as well close the temple down and extinguish the fires on the altar. The Lord looks for heartfelt honor, not mere formalism.

Certainly, Yahweh's kingship extends from east to west, because his name is great among the nations (**1:11**). Malachi concludes that this worship of God is more acceptable than worship in the Jerusalem temple. This does not mean that God is pleased with pagan sacrifices but that true worship is offered to him by Gentiles who come to him in faith (cf. Zeph. 2:11; 3:9). A note of expectation of a greater fulfillment may also be present, as his kingdom extends from "the rising to the setting of the sun," from east to west. When Jews worshiped the Lord in their various locations of the Diaspora (Persia, Babylonia, Egypt), Gentiles were drawn to his worship as God-fearers and proselytes. The prophetic word was already being fulfilled in that Gentiles were joining with the Jews in the worship of Yahweh in increasing numbers. Truly, Yahweh's name was known, and was becoming great among the nations. Thus, the prophet argues against the priests that since Yahweh's name is great among the nations, how much more should the people of Jerusalem and Judea honor their God?

The prophet moves rapidly from charges and countercharges to judgment (**1:12–14**). He charges the people with profaning the Lord and his temple. The charge is a severe one. Yet, they respond by asking what wrong they have done. They are bored with their vocation. By permitting injured, lame, and sickly animals to be brought into the temple, they demonstrate that they are more concerned about their own livelihood than about the honor of the Lord. Anyone who continues to bring sickly sacrifices, even in fulfillment of a vow, will be cursed because, regardless of the priestly attitudes, God is the great King. He will turn the priestly blessing into a curse.

IV. The Knowledge of God (2:1–9)

In the second disputation, Malachi charges the priests with not giving honor to God by offering defiled and blemished offerings and sacrifices. In this third disputation, focus shifts from their cultic function to their function as teachers of God's Word. The key word is "admonition" ("commandment," vv. 1, 4). Malachi repeats the word and purposely builds up suspense so as to stimulate the question, "What commandment has been broken which causes the Lord's curse to rest on the priests?" It is not until verse 7 that the commandment is set forth in a straightforward manner: "For the lips of a priest ought to preserve knowledge, and from his mouth men should seek instruction—because he is the messenger of the LORD Almighty."

The knowledge of God is not knowledge about God or secrets pertaining to the priesthood. "Knowledge" is the ability to *know* and the desire to *do* the will of God on earth in accordance with his commandment. Knowledge is immensely practical, because it is in essence what could be called "godliness," "wise living," or "the way to holiness" (cf. Hos. 4:1, 6). The Lord had commanded the priests not only to oversee the offerings, sacrifices, and tabernacle, but also to be the guardians of his revelation (Deut. 31:9). The priests were the teachers of the law of God. The failure of the priests before the exile had brought the judgment of God on Israel and Judah. Malachi is concerned that their present insensitivity will renew God's judgment. His prophetic denunciation is an expression of his concern for the well-being of God's people.

Yahweh will not hesitate to curse his own priests (**2:1–3**). The curses are those enumerated in Deuteronomy 28:15, 20. The curses were applicable to all of God's people, but particularly to the priests, because they had been instructed in "the commandment." The curse is explicated in a threefold formula, which is best translated as "I shall send a curse on you; and I shall curse your blessings. Indeed I shall curse them."

In verse 3, the nature of the curse is brought out more clearly. Yahweh will not limit his curse to the priests, but will extend it to their children. He will also disregard their festivals. The festivals were the occasions when the priests received food from the people, so when there was an economic depression, the priests were the first to suffer. At this time, the sacrifices being presented are unacceptable to the Lord. He puts them in the same class as dung ("offal"), which was removed from the temple to be burned. The language is strong, but so is God's feeling about the priests.

The curse stands in contrast to the covenant God made with Levi (**2:4–7**). The original covenant was made with Phinehas, the grandson of Aaron, after he demonstrated his loyalty to the Lord (Num. 25:12–13). The purpose of the covenant was not curse, but life and peace. However, "life and peace" were conditioned on the faithful performance of the priests. Malachi reminds the priests of their ancestry in order to evoke in them responsive hearts. In the early days of Israel, priests feared the Lord and respected him. They were the guardians of the law of God and did not betray Yahweh by improper speech and infidelity. Instead, they were characterized by godliness in that they walked in accordance with God's standards of fidelity, peace, and equity. When the priests were the guardians of the law, were godly, and walked in fellowship with the Lord, they were his human instruments in restoring many from evil. The priests were the theocratic officers by whom the covenantal relationship was kept alive. It is at this point that Malachi explains the original "commandment" to the priests (v. 7).

The priests of Malachi's time have gone astray (**2:8**). They have departed from "the commandment" which God originally had given to them. Therefore, the Lord has withheld the fullness of blessing and will turn the blessings of "life and peace" into a curse. The problem is with the priests, who have turned away from glorifying the Lord, led people into sin, and disregarded their duties. The lives and teaching of the priests cause people to sin against the Lord. Thus, they breach the terms of the covenant. A breach in covenant fidelity evokes God's wrath, judgment, and curse.

Malachi **2:9** is a summary of 1:6–2:8. The repetition of the word *despise* (1:6; 2:9) forms an inclusio, for Yahweh has charged the priests with despising his name. They do not honor him as a Father and King in their sacred duty as priests. Their way of life and public instruction have led the people astray. The autonomy of the priests will incur God's judgment. Rather than being sought after as "messengers" of the Lord, the priests will be despised by the people. When this happens, the people will no longer be misled. The Lord does not annul the covenant with Levi, but suspends the blessings of "life and peace." Because the priests have little regard for God's glory, he will utterly reject them—unless they learn to respond by following in the ways of the Lord and by studying the Word of God. If the priests are to avert God's curse and judgment upon them, they must return to the original commandment given to their forefathers. They may again become the "messengers" of the Lord by being the guardians of his Word, faithful in their walk with God, and teachers of his people. Then the Lord's blessings of life and peace will attend his people.

V. Intermarriage and Divorce (2:10–16)

Malachi **2:10–12** opens abruptly. Who is speaking? Who is the "Father"? It seems that the people contest something the prophet has said or it may be that the prophet is quoting a proverb. Since Malachi, by the disputation method, portrays the spirit of the people as filled with cynicism and sarcasm, it is best to take verse 10 as an argument by the people. It is filled with self-righteousness and self-justification, but hollow from Malachi's perspective. The people's argument may be restated as: "Have we not all one Father? Has not one God created us? Why should we deal treacherously with one another? Why should we profane the covenant of the fathers?" Yahweh, who sees the heart, charges that they have dealt treacherously with each other and that they have broken the covenant. They have desecrated the "holy" institution of marriage by intermarriage and divorce. God is concerned with the purity of his people. The history of Israel before the exile was marked by idolatry, syncretism, and acculturation. Intermarriage was the way in which the people of Judah and Israel had accepted the cultures and gods of the nations (Judg. 2:11–13, 19; 1 Kings 11:1–8). Malachi's concerns, together with Ezra's and Nehemiah's (Ezra 9:1–2; Neh. 13:23–24), are with the identity of God's people. When any one of God's people flouts his law and breaks the covenant, he has no right to belong to the covenant community. He is to be disciplined. No offering can help the unrepentant sinner. Whoever tears down the covenant community by intermarriage has no right to be a part of that community.

In addition to intermarriage, God is concerned with divorce (**2:13–17**). If intermarriage is an affront to God's holy presence, how much more is he concerned with marital infidelity and divorce! Even if the people were to cry, bring offerings, and implore him to answer their prayers, he will have no regard for their rituals. The anticipated response to the prophetic judgment is a quick, spirited, indignant "Why?" The question receives a twofold response.

First, Malachi removes any pretense to innocence by stating that Yahweh will appear as witness to their faithlessness, which has manifested itself in divorce. The covenant relationship is characterized by fidelity, and the absence of marital fidelity is symptomatic of a deeper spiritual problem. The people are unreliable in their relationship with their peers, wives, and God. They are religious infidels.

Second, the severity of God's judgment is due to his intense hatred of divorce. The people had argued from the mistaken theological position that, since God is the Father of all Israel, they are safe from his judgment. Malachi replies that God's true children have the Spirit of God, which is manifested in faithfulness. The fruit of the Spirit of God is love and fidelity. The central verse (v. 15), which is also one of the most difficult verses in the entire book, gives the theological ground for marital fidelity: (1) God has made "man" as one, namely male and female (Gen. 2:24); (2) man is "one," being both flesh and spirit; (3) God's purpose is to raise up godly children through holy matrimony, which is characterized by a union of flesh with flesh and spirit with spirit. Therefore, not all may claim that God is their Father. The prophet has thus introduced the importance of the "spirituality" of God and of those who worship him. Since God has made man to have a spirit, man can only relate to God in the spirit. Only those who have the Spirit are his children, and must respond by guarding their spirit. Covenant fidelity has a spiritual dimension that is expressed by marital fidelity.

VI. The Justice and Patience of God (2:17–3:6)

The fifth disputation introduces a new element. The people have already questioned God's love, majesty, and fidelity. Now they raise the issue of his justice. Yet, the argument is wearing down because they have wearied the Lord (**2:17**). They have argued that they are all right and that the fault lies with God, but now they charge God with being unfair in all his dealings with man. They think that God does not discriminate between evil and good, and that he even delights in those who do evil. Therefore, they ask, "Where is the God of justice?" The threefold charge against the Lord receives a threefold response (**3:1–6**).

First, the Lord will send his "messenger" who will prepare the way of the Lord. In Isaiah 40:3–4 the preparation of the Lord's coming is made by making ready "a way." His coming in Isaiah is to introduce judgment and to reward his children. Malachi also speaks of God's coming in judgment. In view of the prediction of Elijah's coming (4:5–6) and Jesus' identification of John the Baptist as having the spirit and power of Elijah (Luke 1:17; cf. Matt. 11:14), it seems best to identify "my messenger" with John the Baptist. His purpose was to prepare the people for the coming of the Lord. In response to the first question, Malachi has introduced the "messenger" as God's means of announcing that his judgment rests on the wicked. The evil are *not* good in God's sight!

Second, the Lord will come to the temple. "The Lord" is further described as "the messenger of the covenant." Although some interpreters distinguish "the Lord" from "the messenger," the parallel construction argues for their synonymity. "The Lord" must be Yahweh who has promised to fill the temple with his glory (Ezek. 43:1–5; Hag. 2:9). Yet he is also known as "the messenger of the covenant." A "messenger" was charged to guard Israel on the way to Canaan (Exod. 23:20–23), and it may well be that the identification of "the messenger" with "the Lord" and his people is an Old Testament revelation anticipating God's fuller revelation in Jesus the Messiah. The Father sent John the Baptist and his Son to prepare man for the great judgment. The purpose of the messenger of the covenant is to "refine" the people of God.

The coming of the Messiah is to introduce an era in which the restoration of the covenant will be ushered in in a new way. In response to the accusation that God is pleased with the wicked, Malachi has introduced the coming of the messenger of the covenant as God's means of purifying a people for himself. He compares the process of purification to the refining fire of the silversmith and the soap of a launderer. His purpose is to purge the people of God so that they will be like gold and silver.

God does not delight in evil but rather delights in "offerings in righteousness" (v. 3). These can be offered only by those who have come through the process of purification. The righteous who lived before Christ looked forward to his coming and experienced the acceptance of their offerings in faith. The reference to the past is an expression of God's covenantal fidelity. God does not change! He has always expected his children to bring him offerings in the spirit of purity and righteousness. The opponents of the prophet's message had charged that God delights in evil; the prophet responds that God does not delight in evil but rather in righteousness.

Finally, the certainty of God's response is made sure by his coming in judgment. In response to their third question, "Where is the

God of justice?" God comes in judgment. Even though this judgment may be delayed for millennia (2 Pet. 3:3–9), the judgment will certainly come on all who have broken his commandments.

Even though the commentaries and versions are not in agreement as to the extent of the argument, **3:6** could be the conclusion of 2:17–3:6. The Lord has charged his people with wearying him (2:17). They should be destroyed. Though the Lord is vexed by the words of his people, he does not change. His purposes stand. As an expression of his patience, forbearance, compassion, grace, and willingness to forgive, the Lord continues his plan of redemption. He does not yet come in judgment as an expression of grace. The people may change in that the righteous may join the wicked or may wonder whether God loves the wicked more than the righteous. The comfort of the godly is the revelation that the Lord does not change. Out of concern for his loved ones, the Lord will send the messenger and the messenger of the covenant to encourage them before his coming in judgment against all wicked.

Since the coming of John the Baptist and Jesus Christ, a portion of the prophetic word of Malachi has been fulfilled. Jesus came as the "messenger of the covenant" by whom Jews and Gentiles find entrance into the covenant, by whom God accepts our offerings, and by whose Spirit we are purified. Because of God's grace we are not consumed.

VII. The Tithe (3:7–12)

In the fifth disputation, Malachi argued that God would show his justice in judgment at his appointed time. The prophet, true to the prophetic tradition, calls for a response in preparation for the coming of the messenger and the messenger of the covenant. The appeal for a particular response links this section to the third disputation (3:10–16). In both sections, God is expecting a renewal of fidelity in marriage (2:10–16) and in worship (3:7–12). The former is representative of our love for man and the latter of our love for God.

God remains faithful to his promise that he will return to those who seek him with all their heart. Israel's history is the story of a lack of responsiveness to God and his commandments. Even after the exile they were slow to respond. They were satisfied with their lack of commitment. The prophetic countercharge is quick. Malachi singles out one example of infidelity to God: the tithe.

Israel's failure in not giving the tithe exposes their failure to show loyalty to God in worship. The people have "robbed" God. The verb signifies a taking by force what belongs to someone else. The tithe was God's divine right, specified in the Law (Lev. 27:30; Num. 18:24–28; Deut. 14:28–29). From the tithes, Levites, priests, orphans, widows, and aliens were supported. The "offerings" were the portions of sacrifices which the priests were permitted to use for food (Exod. 29:27–28; Lev. 7:32; Num. 5:9). Support for the temple personnel and social programs is failing.

Greediness is not only a mark of selfishness; it is a token of infidelity and therefore of outright disobedience. The most severe penalty for failure to conform to God's will is "curse."

Malachi has demonstrated that Yahweh is not the Father of the descendants of Abraham, but of those who have the Spirit of God. God is a good Father to responsive children. He promises to take care of their needs. The covenant King is concerned with extending his blessings to his people. For that reason, the prophet details how the Lord will grant his blessings (vv. 11–12) by taking care of all their needs, by protecting their possessions, by prospering their labor, and by keeping away the locusts. Since the people are reluctant, the prophet calls upon them to test the Lord. This challenge to the people must be related to his call for them to return. By their repentance they will express their faith and dependence upon him and will therefore be restored to covenant fellowship. The Lord promises that his blessing will rest upon his people so that they will be blessed in this life and in the life to come.

VIII. God's Love for the Remnant (3:13–4:3)

In the sixth disputation, Malachi sums up the argument of the book. In the first disputation (1:2–5), he argued that the Lord loves his people and that one day the faithful will recognize and see with their own eyes the establishment of the Lord's kingdom on earth. In the meantime, the hope of the faithful is in God, whose honor, fidelity, and justice are beyond question. The prophet sums up his argument by affirming that God will reward his loyal children who persevere to the end. This disputation is also related to the fifth (2:17–3:6), but is more direct and severe. The prophet does not give a general call for repentance. He makes it clear that many in the covenant community are too concerned with self but are incapable of establishing their own righteousness. Their feet are set on slippery paths and they will perish. On the other hand, there is always a righteous remnant which does the will of God on earth and they will receive a glorious reward.

The Lord charges the community of faith with speaking harshly against him (**3:13–14**).

They say that it is "futile" to serve God and that there is no "gain" in keeping God's commandments. The prophets had argued that it was vain to serve idols, but the people turn the argument around by claiming that allegiance to the Lord brings no benefit, no reward. The Hebrew word for reward (*beṣaʿ*) is not the usual word for reward, but signifies a bribe or a means of covering the eyes toward injustice. Malachi uses the word sarcastically to reveal that the people are asking for undeserved favors. They expect God to do "big" things for them while they get by with injustice, improper sacrifices, divorce, and withholding tithes.

The people expect their religiosity to pay big dividends. They equate faithfulness to God with "going about like mourners" (v. 14). Their hearts are not in their religion. They believe, but do not have faith. Their lack of sincerity is brought out by their observation about the "arrogant." They make the bold claim that the arrogant, who are filled with pride and live independently from the Lord, are the lucky ones. They set their own lifestyle, live practically without God, test him, and still prosper. Thus, they argue against the justice, love, and fidelity of God. The Lord has invited his own to test him and to see that he is good (v. 10b), but the people here respond skeptically and sarcastically that the arrogant put him to the test by flouting his commandments and get away with it. They have already come to the conclusion that God does not care what his children do. They have called into question God's fatherly concern for his children. God leaves their argument unanswered, shifting his attention to a group of godly people.

Within the covenant community, there is a group which has kept itself distinct from the arrogant, mockers, and cynics (**3:16–18**). They are variously called "those who feared the Lord" (v. 16, twice), "those who honored his name" (v. 16), "the righteous" (v. 17), and "those who serve God" (v. 17). The godly are thus characterized by their love for God and by their obedience to him. Malachi intends to let us into the discussions of two distinct groups. The complaints of the first group are loud and clear (vv. 14–15), but what are the godly saying? It does not seem to matter. Instead, Malachi emphasizes the various designations for the godly and by drawing our immediate attention to God's responsiveness to his children, that God knows his own. It may be that the godly pray in the spirit of Psalm 73 for God to take care of their pains, while expressing trust in him:

> Surely God is good to Israel,
> to those who are pure in heart.
> But as for me, my feet had almost slipped;
> I had nearly lost my foothold.
> For I envied the arrogant
> when I saw the prosperity of the wicked.
> [Ps. 73:1–3]

In response, their names are written in "a scroll of remembrance" (cf. Exod. 32:32–33; Pss. 69:28; 87:6; Dan. 12:1). The Lord has marked a people for himself who will accept his tender care and the rewards of their labors. The greatest reward is to be a member of his "treasured possession" (Heb. *sĕgūllâ*). The word *sĕgūllâ* is difficult to translate, since it connotes a people elected and loved by the Lord, who keep his commandments, and who make up a royal priesthood and a holy nation and who will share in a glorious future that God has prepared for his own (cf. Exod. 19:4–5; Deut. 7:6–9; 14:2; 26:17–19; Ps. 135:4). The prophet compares the Lord's care to a father's care for his son who has served him well. When the Lord shows his love for his people, then they will see the difference between the righteous and the wicked. The prophet indirectly addresses those who have argued against him, but he is directly addressing the godly community with words of comfort. They will see it with their own eyes! The day of the Lord will come upon mankind as a terrifying experience (**4:1–3**). The prophet compares it to the burning of a furnace and likens the wicked to stubble and shrubs that will be unable to stand the fire of that terrible day. They will be completely removed even as trees are destroyed by fire. Yet that day will bring its rewards for the righteous. The Lord will share with them the triumphs of his victory, expressed here metaphorically as "the sun of righteousness" and "healing in its wings."

The phrase *the sun of righteousness* is to be understood in the sense of Isaiah's prophecies. Righteousness represents the effects of God's righteousness upon this earth: victory and glory (Isa. 51:6–7; 62:1–2a). Yahweh shares his victory and glory with his people. They will experience the fullness of the restoration as a healing process. Regardless of their suffering in life, Yahweh guarantees that his victory and his restoration will be shared by his own. The light will dawn for his people in such a way that all the promises of the Law, the Prophets, our Lord, and the apostles will be fulfilled in them. That moment will mark the full establishment of his kingdom! The kingdom may come in gradually and it may not always be apparent, but it will most certainly come. This will mark a time of great rejoicing. The joy and sense of fulfillment for God's children is likened to calves which, when released from the stable, paw at the ground. The arrogant and practical atheists will be unable to resist the renewal of the strength of God's children. A separation has taken place even within the community of faith between the righteous and the self-righteous. The one group will be marked for destruction while the other will be marked as God's possession.

IX. Conclusion (4:4–6)

The conclusion to the Book of Malachi includes a final appeal to observe the law of Moses in preparation for Elijah's return, to guard their spirit, and to return to the Lord. Malachi calls on the godly to love God and to love man. He emphasizes the practice of godliness in contrast to an intellectual knowledge of the Scriptures. Our Lord taught that John the Baptist came in the spirit and power of Elijah (Matt. 11:14; cf. Mal. 3:1). The new age will be characterized by a renewal of the covenant, and the sons of the covenant will enjoy a sense of continuity with their spiritual ancestors, Abraham, Isaac, and Jacob.

SELECT BIBLIOGRAPHY

Baldwin, J. G. *Haggai, Zechariah, Malachi.* Downers Grove: Inter-Varsity, 1972.

Childs, B. S. *Introduction to the Old Testament as Scripture.* Philadelphia: Fortress, 1979.

Kaiser, W. *Malachi: God's Unchanging Love.* Grand Rapids: Baker, 1984.

Mitchell, H., et al. *A Critical and Exegetical Commentary on Haggai, Zechariah, Malachi, and Jonah.* The International Critical Commentary. Edinburgh: T. & T. Clark, 1912.

Smith, R. L. *Micah-Malachi.* Waco: Word, 1984.

Westermann, C. *Basic Forms of Prophetic Speech.* Philadelphia: Westminster, 1967.

New Testament Introduction

The New Testament is a collection of twenty-seven books that were gathered together and, in time, used alongside the Old Testament. Written in Greek during the first century A.D., the New Testament consists of five divisions: Gospels first, because they tell us of Jesus; Acts next, because it tells us of Jesus' immediate followers; Paul's letters, because he was the chief theological spokesman of the early church; general Letters; and, finally, Revelation, which is the major prophetic book of the New Testament.

Because Jesus was the full and final revelation of God, the early Christians treasured those things that were said by and about him, and as a result the books we call Gospels arose. Gospel writing began early, and apparently several such attempts were made, as Luke, who wrote one himself, says (Luke 1:1–4). The church ultimately accepted four Gospels as authoritative, no doubt because they could be traced back in some fashion to those who had actually been with Jesus. In this way the authority of Jesus was extended to those books that were written about him and which contained his remembered sayings.

Jesus' authority was conferred during his lifetime to a specially chosen group of followers (the apostles). Because they were to continue the work of Jesus after his death and resurrection, their lives, and to a certain extent their words, were recorded. The Book of Acts is a follow-up to what Jesus *began* to do and teach while he was on earth (Acts 1:1); it is a record of what Jesus *continues* to do and teach through his church, his body, guided by the Holy Spirit under the direction of the apostles.

Acts tells of how the gospel spread from Jerusalem ultimately to Rome, the center of the world at that time. It accomplishes this by concentrating primarily on the lives of two early missionaries, Peter and, especially, Paul, whose three extensive trips and final journey to Rome are described in some detail.

Paul was counted as an apostle by the church even though he was not one of the Twelve. His acceptance was based on a direct call from Jesus himself that Paul received while on the road to Damascus; the experience is described three times in the Book of Acts (9:1–6; 22:1–16; 26:12–18). Paul wrote many letters to the Gentile churches he founded; these letters were used for instruction by Paul's converts. Along with the other writings, they were collected and considered authoritative. Some scholars think that the gathering of these letters actually led to the formation of the New Testament. In any event, the growing collection was used as God's Word by the church.

The general Letters were written to Christians as a whole, rather than to individual churches or people (as were Paul's letters). Here we find the letters of Peter, James, and John. The Book of Hebrews was originally considered one of Paul's letters, but most scholars do not accept that today. So, for convenience it may be considered a general letter. These letters tell us of Christian life in the outposts of the empire. Life is depicted as difficult and challenging, but supported by the grace of God in Christ.

The Book of Revelation is in a class by itself. It is a triumphant book that promises God's presence during the present suffering of his people and the ultimate victory of God at Christ's return.

The theology of the New Testament is based on that of the Old Testament. The doctrine of a personal God, who is Creator, Sustainer, and Redeemer; the responsibility of mankind for ethical behavior; the need for redemption from sin; the ultimate triumph of good over evil—all come from the Old Testament. Yet the New Testament goes beyond the Old Testament in relating God's Word to the whole world. The New Testament goes so far as to say that the Old Testament predicted its own eclipse. So, the Old Testament is the promise of God; the New Testament is the fulfillment of that promise, realized in and through the person and work of Jesus Christ.

New Testament Chronology

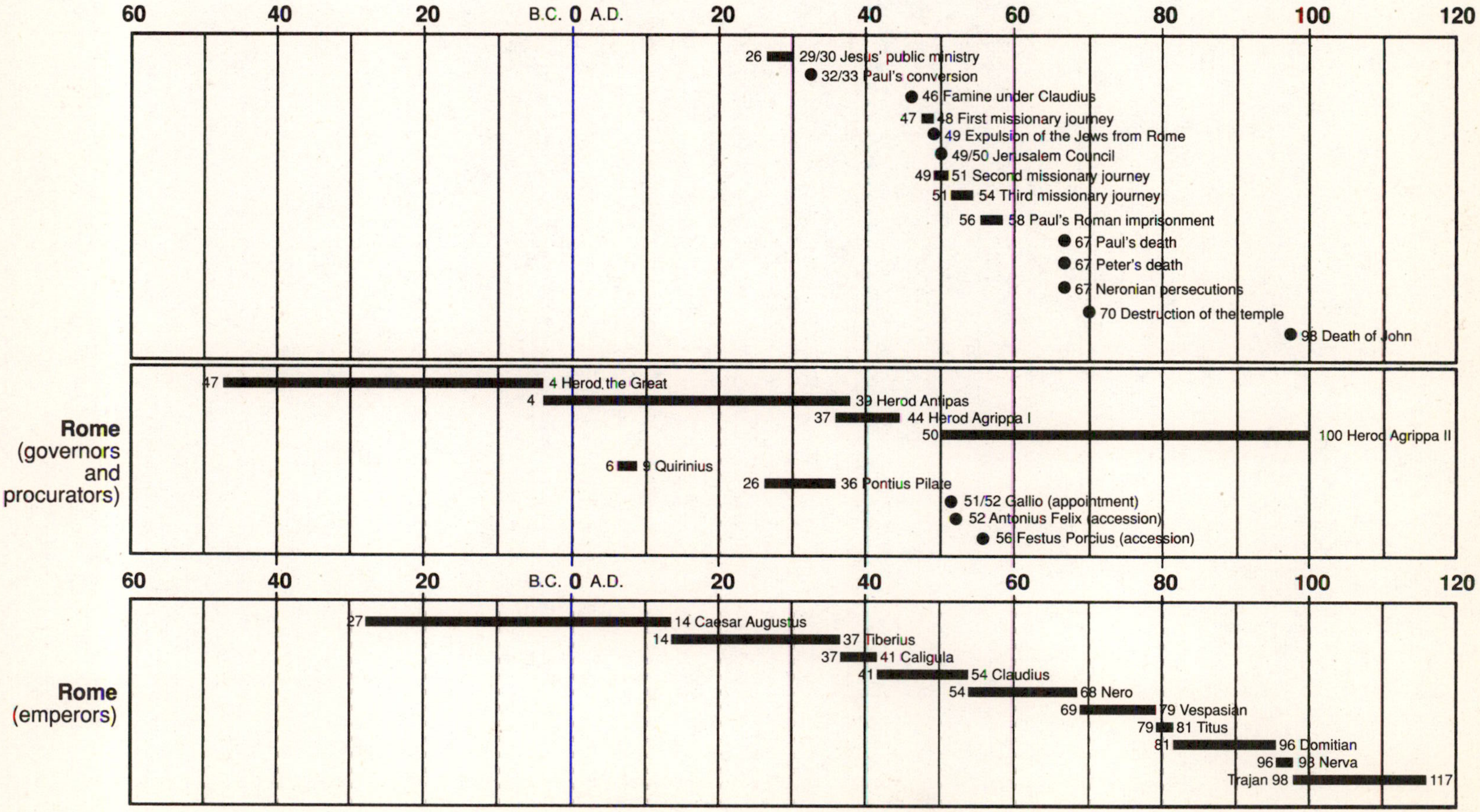

The Gospels

The New Testament properly begins with a small collection of books known as the Gospels, because they contain the essence of the Good News (that is the meaning of the word *gospel*)—the life of Jesus Christ. These books are not "lives of Jesus" or biographies in the ordinary sense because Jesus was no ordinary person. What they are designed to give us is the essence of what we need to know about Jesus as the Son of God and Savior of the world. This means that their primary focus is upon the disclosure of what his saving mission was and the facts surrounding the accomplishment of that mission, namely, his death and resurrection. The earliest form of the gospel message was that Christ died for our sins, that he was buried, that he was raised on the third day, and that he appeared to his followers (1 Cor. 15:3–8). The Gospels fill that out by adding the events surrounding his birth and early life, his teachings, his ministry of healing, his trip to Jerusalem, and the events of his last days.

From the very beginning people had a good deal of interest in Jesus' life and soon they wrote many small volumes to explain who he was. Some volumes contained authentic material; others, no doubt, were written to prove some point or other. In order to preserve the truth of what was remembered about Jesus, and under the guidance of the Holy Spirit, the four books we now have were written, gathered together by the church, and given a special place in its corporate life. There is no special reason why four were chosen; it is just that these particular books commended themselves to the earliest believers as being of supreme value and were retained as different and indispensable pictures of Jesus as God's Son and our Savior.

The shortest and earliest is Mark. It emphasizes the last week of Jesus' life, devoting six of its sixteen chapters to that. Here we see

Jesus as the divine servant of God who does his will, even unto death. Luke was probably written next. In it Jesus is presented as the ideal man, son of Adam, and the fullest embodiment of God's will for us as human beings. Matthew appeared about the same time and depicts Jesus as the new Moses, fulfiller of Israel's hopes, the true Messiah, and the light of the world. John's Gospel came last, probably in the last decade of the first century, and is a theologically oriented treatise designed to show Jesus' true nature as deity through his humanity. These four points of view combine to give us a composite picture of Jesus as God and man, Servant of God and Savior of all.

MATTHEW

J. Knox Chamblin

INTRODUCTION

Nowhere does the Gospel of Matthew clearly identify its author. Strictly speaking, the book is anonymous. Can we be more specific?

The Gospels' present titles ("according to Matthew," etc.) did not belong to the original documents. Yet they "originated no later than A.D. 140 and in all probability were handed down with the Gospel texts as early as A.D. 125."[1] The superscription may have been attached to Matthew from the earliest days of its circulation. In any case, we possess no alternative superscriptions for this document.

Eusebius (the fourth-century church historian) quotes Papias (bishop of Hierapolis, ca. A.D. 130–35): "So then Matthew recorded the oracles in the Hebrew speech, and each interpreted them to the best of his ability." Some have argued that the term *the oracles (ta logia)* denotes strictly the *sayings* of Jesus, and thus material incorporated into Matthew rather than the Gospel of Matthew itself. But a better expression for "words" or "sayings" would be *hoi logoi.* It is preferable to take *ta logia* as a reference to the entire Gospel. If the first part of the statement ("the Hebrew speech" [*Hebraidi dialektō*]) means that Matthew wrote the Gospel, how is this expression to be interpreted? It is usually taken to mean the Hebrew language. In this case either Matthew wrote a Hebrew or Aramaic Gospel which others then translated (*hērmēneusen,* rendered "interpreted") into Greek and other languages, or Papias is mistaken at this point (since our present Gospel of Matthew lacks the marks of translation into Greek). But it is more likely that Papias means the Hebrew style. The Greek *dialektos* may denote not only "language" but also "discourse, conversation; discussion, debate, argument."[2] In this case Papias uses *dialektos* as a literary rather than a linguistic term. As a description of Matthew, *dialektos* "means a Hebrew way of presenting Jesus' messiahship."[3]

Although Matthew is anonymous, it may be helpful to look at the Gospel for clues that confirm or that helped to determine the judg-

1. Ned B. Stonehouse, *Origins of the Synoptic Gospels* (Grand Rapids: Baker, 1979), 16.
2. H. G. Liddell and R. Scott, *Greek-English Lexicon* (Oxford: Clarendon, 1968), s.v. διάλεκτος, 401.
3. R. H. Gundry, *Matthew: A Commentary on His Literary and Theological Art* (Grand Rapids: Eerdmans, 1982), 620.

ment of the ancient church. One of these appears in 9:9–13. The parallels in Mark and Luke speak of "Levi"; but Matthew 9:9 employs "Matthew." If "Levi" is the man's tribal name, and "Matthew" his more personal name, and if the man in question writes Matthew, it is not surprising that he uses the personal name. (The name *Levi* never appears in Matthew.) Introducing the story of the dinner, both Mark and Luke use the phrase *his* [i.e., *Levi's*] *house*. Matthew 9:10, however, uses the phrase *in the house* (RSV and Gk.), a natural way to describe an event in one's own home. A second clue occurs in 10:2–4. All three Synoptists use the name *Matthew* in the list of the Twelve; but in Matthew alone he is also called "the tax collector" (10:3). This might serve to distinguish this Matthew from others (cf. 10:2, "James son of Zebedee"). But if this is a case of the author identifying himself, he may deliberately use the words *tax collector* to denote the life out of which Jesus called him (see comments on 9:9–13).[4] Yet a third clue occurs in 13:52. The description *teacher of the law* now embraces disciples generally (see comments on 13:51–52). But initially it was eminently suitable for Matthew individually (it is noteworthy that vv. 51–53 are peculiar to Matthew). There were religious scribes occupied with interpreting the Mosaic law (see comments on 15:1–9). But there were also secular scribes, including tax collectors. C. F. D. Moule thinks that someone other than Matthew wrote the Gospel. Yet his comments on 13:52 are suggestive: "The writer of the Gospel was himself a well-educated literate [secular] scribe. . . . But so must also have been that tax-collector who was called by Jesus to be a disciple. Is it not conceivable that the Lord really did say to that tax-collector Matthew: You have been a 'writer' . . . ; you have had plenty to do with the commercial side of just the topics alluded to in the parables [of chap. 13]—farmer's stock, fields, treasure-trove, fishing revenues; now that you have become a disciple, you can bring all this out again—but with a difference."[5]

Matthew writes to a community of Greek-speaking Jewish Christians, located in a center such as Antioch in Syria. The community is surrounded and beset by Jews hostile to Jesus and his followers. We may date the book during the 60s of the first century A.D.

We customarily speak of "the four Gospels." It is more accurate to speak of *the Gospel* according to Matthew, Mark, Luke, and John, respectively; there is only one gospel because there is only one Christ. What we have here are not four "lives of Jesus" or "biographies" (although each book contains extensive and accurate biographical material), but a new literary genre, the gospel, created under the impact of the person and work of Jesus. Matthew presents good news of salvation. And Matthew is a principal means by which Jesus' "gospel of the kingdom" is universally proclaimed (see the four instances of *euangelion:* 4:23; 9:35; 24:14; 26:13).

Matthew writes as a Jew for Jews. The book is thoroughly Jewish

4. On "Matthew" as a name conferred by Jesus (like Simon's surname *Peter*), see "Matthew," in *Harper's Bible Dictionary*, ed. Paul J. Achtemeier (San Francisco: Harper & Row, 1985), 613.

5. C. F. D. Moule, "St. Matthew's Gospel: Some Neglected Features," *Studia Evangelica* 2 (1964): 98.

in character. It is saturated with Old Testament thought and is deeply rooted in Palestinian soil. Thus the author emphasizes revelation. In Jesus of Nazareth, contends Matthew, the Old Testament reaches its appointed goal. At the beginning of Matthew, Jesus is identified as the Messiah of Israel's expectations, as "the son of David, the son of Abraham" (1:1), as the one who saves "his people from their sins" (1:21), indeed as "God with us" (1:23). In later chapters Jesus is revealed as the Son of man of Daniel 7 and the Suffering Servant of Isaiah 53 (see, e.g., 8:17; 26:64). Throughout Matthew (from 1:22–23 to 27:9–10) the events of Jesus' life are expressly represented as "fulfillments" of Old Testament prophecies. Another emphasis is that of rejection. The Jews have rejected Jesus as their Messiah, and have thus placed themselves in a most perilous position (11:20–24). A major reason for the people's repudiation of Jesus is the failure of the Jewish leadership. Matthew condemns them in the strongest language. They have not prepared the people for Jesus' coming by rightly teaching them the Old Testament; instead, they have supplanted God's Word with their own traditions (15:1–9). Nor have they provided examples that the people can afford to follow (chap. 23). Worst of all, they themselves have repudiated Jesus, have sought to turn the people against him, and were the ones chiefly responsible for condemning him to death. Finally, Matthew issues a summons. Let the Jews of Matthew's day recognize that they stand under judgment (23:33–39). Accordingly, let them repent of their sins and embrace Jesus as their Messiah before it is too late (3:7–10; 11:4–24; and the woes and warnings in chaps. 21–23), so that upon his return they may welcome him with joy (23:39).

Matthew also writes as a Christian for Christians, for a community composed chiefly of Jewish Christians. He presents Jesus as a new Moses, indeed as Yahweh incarnate, expounding his law for his people (chaps. 5–7), now newly constituted around his person under the leadership of Matthew and the other apostles. In accord with the commission of 28:20, Matthew presents to his readers everything that Jesus commanded, both for their intellectual understanding and especially for their steadfast obedience. If the Christian church is to function properly in Matthew's time and beyond, the teaching of the Messiah on a host of moral and spiritual issues must be taken with utmost seriousness. It is especially vital that church leaders follow Jesus' own example in dealing with the little ones under their care (18; 19:25–20:28).

As has been indicated, the four Evangelists have a common purpose—to tell the good news about Jesus Christ. Yet Matthew, like the other Evangelists, has his own "literary and theological art"[6] by which he makes a distinctive contribution to our knowledge of Jesus. Inevitably we shall compare Matthew to the other three documents. But let us beware, lest in doing so we lose sight of the special wonders of this book.

Matthew does not present an exhaustive account of the life and

6. Gundry, *Matthew*, 1.

ministry of Jesus. Like the other Evangelists, he is selective (cf. John 20:30–31; 21:25). For example, Matthew alone recounts the visit of the Magi (2:1–12) and the story of the temple tax (17:24–27); and while Matthew records many parables, he omits several found elsewhere (e.g., Luke 10:30–37; 15:11–32; 16:19–31). In pursuit of his purpose, in exercise of his craftsmanship, and under the guidance of the Holy Spirit, Matthew selects his material.

As an expression of his artistry, and as an aid to his purpose (especially its catechetical aspect), Matthew presents a theological textbook, a handbook for the church (both leaders and members), to instruct them concerning the person and work of Jesus, that they may grow in understanding and in holiness, and become more effective witnesses and apologists to outsiders. That these teachings may be more readily and firmly grasped, Matthew (following Jesus' own method) presents them in a highly organized and memorable way. Matthew "has more of careful design than any other of the Gospels."[7]

No one grand design is discernible; Matthew is "structurally mixed."[8] Yet three features of Matthew's literary art deserve mention. The first of these is critical junctures. The words *apo tote,* "from that time," appear at three critical points: at 4:17 (where Jesus begins his Galilean ministry), at 16:21 (where Jesus, in the wake of Peter's confession [v. 16], begins to teach his disciples about his approaching death and resurrection), and at 26:16 (where Judas's resolve completes the plot to destroy Jesus and prepares for Matthew's account of the passion itself, beginning with the Last Supper [26:17–30]).

A second feature is discourses and narratives. To facilitate learning, Matthew gathers Jesus' teachings into five major discourses (interlocked with narrative portions) in which teachings of the same kind are clustered together (chaps. 5–7, 10, 13, 18, 24–25). Observe the similarities among the five conclusions—7:28; 11:1; 13:53; 19:1; and 26:1 (with its "all," embracing all five discourses). A further feature of the discourses is Matthew's fondness for clustering materials into threes (e.g., the parables of chap. 25) and sevens (e.g., the parables of chap. 13).

A third element is an emphasis on ministry and passion. Matthew contains twenty-eight chapters. Chapters 1–2 record the coming of Jesus, chapter 3 the ministry of John the Baptist and the baptism of Jesus. In chapter 4 Jesus' public ministry begins. The focus is precisely *here;* all the years between his birth and his baptism were preparing him for this. But the public ministry is itself a preparation. Matthew, like the other Gospels, is a "Passion Narrative with a long introduction." Chapter 21 records Jesus' triumphal entry into Jerusalem. Thus the last eight chapters concentrate upon the events of Palm Sunday through Resurrection Sunday. Like every other Evangelist and indeed like every New Testament writer, Matthew considers the death and the resurrection of Jesus Christ to be the heart of the gospel.

7. Donald Guthrie, *New Testament Introduction* (Downers Grove: Inter-Varsity, 1970), 29.
8. Gundry, *Matthew,* 11.

Part of Matthew's method is to employ certain sources. As noted, the first four books of the New Testament share a common purpose. But the first three (the synoptic Gospels) share certain features with each other which they do not share with John. Much material is found in all three of these writings that is not found in John (e.g., the temptations of Jesus, the story of the rich young man). This is clear when we place the material of these three books alongside each other (whence the word *synoptic,* which means "to view together").

Scholars have long debated the exact relationship among these three documents. In speaking of "the priority of Mark," I state my view that Mark is the earliest of the synoptic Gospels, and that Matthew, in writing his Gospel, employed Mark as one of his sources.

"Q" stands for *Quelle* (Ger. source) and denotes tradition that is supplementary to the Marcan material and common to Matthew and Luke. Scholars once spoke of Q as a definite document, but it is better to speak of a Q tradition, consisting of oral and written material.

"M" denotes material found in Matthew alone (as compared to "L" material, found in Luke alone, e.g., chaps. 1–2).

Matthew has four major theological motifs; the first of these is that Jesus is the Son of God. Jesus merits this title not merely by virtue of his messianic appointment, but also—and primarily—by virtue of his *being* (see comments on 16:16). Jesus the Messiah is Yahweh incarnate, "God with us" (1:23). A second motif is the kingdom of God. In Jesus, God is invading history to inaugurate his final rule (4:23; 12:28), a rule that one day will surely be consummated (6:10) by Jesus' glorious return and the final judgment (16:27; 24:26–25:46). Yet a third motif is the salvation of God. Matthew presents Jesus as one who cares for the materially and physically needy. Yet Jesus' chief concern is man's relationship to God, not his environment. Correspondingly, his central mission is to save people from their *sins* (1:21), not from their poverty or hunger (cf. comments on 4:3–4; 5:3–10; and 25:31–46). He achieves this saving purpose by his atoning sacrifice (20:28; 26:28). A fourth and final motif is the people of God. Jesus has come to reconstitute God's covenant people around his own person and to establish "his church" (16:18), the redeemed community of the last days consisting of both Jews and Gentiles. Jesus concentrates upon "the lost sheep of Israel" during his public ministry (10:6; 15:24). But he "give[s] his life as a ransom for many" (20:28)—that is, not for Jews alone but for Gentiles too. Once this redemption has been accomplished in his death, it is ready to be announced to all the nations of the world (28:18–20).

Matthew put to good use the skills that he developed as a tax collector as he fashioned his Gospel; his gifts for detail, for precision, and for organization are now exercised for a purpose much higher than that of tax collecting (cf. Moule, as quoted above). He brings out of his storeroom old treasures (acquired as a tax collector in the service of Rome) and new (acquired as a disciple and apostle of Jesus; 13:52). Combining the two he now writes the magnificent Gospel that bears his name.

How well, how accurately, how truthfully, has Matthew recorded what Jesus said and did? Matthew is not bare history; it is *interpreted* history. But (to shift the emphasis) it is interpreted *history*. The entirety of the book is produced as a record of the life and ministry of Jesus; accordingly, Matthew has resisted the temptation to flood his book with postresurrection issues and theology. It is precisely because the whole story is historical in character that the theological interpretation of the story is true, authoritative, and trustworthy.

When speaking of Matthew's faithful recording of the *content* of what Jesus said and did, we must carefully distinguish between form and substance. Matthew is no innovator with respect to substance. As a commissioned apostle and faithful scribe, his task is to bear and to transmit the tradition concerning Jesus. But he is creative when it comes to fashioning a form in which that substance can be effectively conveyed to his audience. The first stage of this is the translation of Jesus' Aramaic into Greek. The second stage is Matthew's use of different forms from those used by the other Evangelists (e.g., he gathers Jesus' teachings into five great discourses). Yet change of form does not necessitate change of substance.

The Holy Spirit is just as truly at work in the production of Matthew as he was in Jesus' life and ministry. Just as surely as the Spirit anointed Jesus to preach, teach, and heal (4:25), he anointed Matthew for the task of selecting, recording, and arranging material from the public ministry. The form of this Gospel is just as surely the work of the Spirit as is the substance.

OUTLINE

- I. The Birth and Preparation of Jesus (1:1–4:16)
  - A. The Birth and Childhood of Jesus (1:1–2:23)
  - B. Preparation for Ministry (3:1–4:16)
- II. Jesus' Public Ministry in Galilee (4:17–16:20)
  - A. Jesus Begins His Public Ministry (4:17–25)
  - B. Jesus' Teaching on Discipleship (5:1–7:29)
  - C. Jesus' Authority Manifested (8:1–9:34)
  - D. The Disciples' Ministry (9:35–11:1)
  - E. Jesus' Ministry Receives Diverse Responses (11:2–12:50)
  - F. Jesus' Parables of the Kingdom (13:1–53)
  - G. Jesus' Teaching and Parables Receive Diverse Responses (13:54–16:20)
- III. Jesus' Private Ministry in Galilee (16:21–18:35)
  - A. Teaching on Jesus' Mission (16:21–17:27)
  - B. Teaching about Relationships among Jesus' Followers (18:1–35)
- IV. Jesus' Ministry in Judea (19:1–25:46)
  - A. Teaching on the Way to Jerusalem (19:1–20:34)
  - B. Arrival in Jerusalem (21:1–22)
  - C. Confrontations in Jerusalem (21:23–23:39)
  - D. Jesus' Teaching about the Future (24:1–25:46)
- V. Jesus' Passion and Resurrection (26:1–28:20)
  - A. Preparation for the Passion (26:1–46)
  - B. Jesus' Arrest and Trial (26:47–27:26)

C. Jesus' Crucifixion (27:27–56)
D. Jesus' Burial and Resurrection (27:57–28:20)

COMMENTARY

I. The Birth and Preparation of Jesus (1:1–4:16)

A. The birth and childhood of Jesus (1:1–2:23). The opening Greek words of verse 1, *biblos geneseōs,* introduce either "a record of the genealogy" (NIV) or "a record of the origins," found in chapters 1–2 (the Greek noun *genesis* "the birth," recurs in 1:18), not Matthew as a whole. At the same time, Matthew here introduces themes that are to be unfolded throughout his Gospel. Observe the stress on Christ, Abraham, and David (vv. 1, 17), and the structuring of the genealogy (**1:1–17**) according to these names (vv. 2–16).

Jesus is "the son of Abraham" (v. 1), in whom God fulfills his ancient promises to Jews and Gentiles (Gen. 12:1–3, etc.). He is also "the son of David" (v. 1), God's anointed King (Gk. *Christos,* vv. 1, 16, 17), heir of David's throne. Perhaps the numerical value of the Hebrew name for David, fourteen, explains the genealogy's construction (v. 17). The main reason for the differences between this genealogy and that of Luke 3:23–38 is that Matthew presents David's royal lineage through Solomon (1:6) down to Jacob and Joseph (1:16), while Luke presents Joseph's natural ancestry back to David through Heli (3:23) and Nathan (3:31).

Never abandoning his covenant with Abraham, God brings it through the centuries to its appointed fulfillment. Matthew's inclusion of women's names in a Hebrew genealogy is unusual; his choice of names is surprising. He passes over some very distinguished women (e.g., Sarah, Rebecca, Rachel) and refers instead to Tamar, Rahab, Ruth, and Bathsheba. Of these four, at least three were involved in sexual immorality, and certainly three and perhaps four were Gentiles. The promise of 1:21 offers good news to such people, including those in Old Testament times; and it embraces Gentiles as well as Jews. God restores the exiles from Babylon and keeps the royal lineage intact even when no Davidic descendants reign from Jerusalem (vv. 11–17). To raise up a new Davidic king, God unleashes his power in the womb of Mary. The fact of the virginal conception forces a grammatical change at the climax of the genealogy: "and Jacob the father of Joseph, the husband of Mary, of whom [a feminine singular pronoun] was born Jesus" (v. 16). Obvious differences separate Mary from the other women in the genealogy; yet God visits them all with saving power.

The next pericope relates the birth of Jesus Christ (**1:18–25**). Before Mary and Joseph consummated their marriage, "she was found to be with child through the Holy Spirit" (v. 18). We are told *that* this happened, not precisely *how;* clinical detail is conspicuously absent. Why did God ordain such a conception? The Savior must be both human and divine. Verse 18 calls Mary his mother; but nowhere in Matthew is Joseph called his father. The connection between the virginal conception and Jesus' identification as "the Son of *God*" (11:25–27; 16:16) should not be overlooked. The Savior's coming, like the salvation he accomplishes, takes place exclusively by the divine initiative. The Spirit that would empower Jesus for service (12:28) is active from the moment of conception to protect him from the threat of evil and the pollution of sin.

Applying Isaiah 7:14, Matthew declares Jesus to be "Immanuel—which means, 'God with us' " (1:22–23). There was *a* fulfillment of this prophecy in Isaiah's own day (probably in the birth of his son; see Isa. 8:1–18), as a sign both of judgment (for King Ahaz had refused to trust Yahweh) and of grace (Yahweh would be with his people even amidst disaster). Applied to that time, the Hebrew noun *ʿalmâ* (Isa. 7:14) means a young woman (RSV; the Hebrew for virgin is *bĕtûlâ*); and the name *Immanuel* signals God's presence without identifying the *being* of the child. With Jesus' coming (Matt. 1:22a), the cup partially filled in Isaiah's day is filled to overflowing (see Isa. 8:8; 9:1–7). Under the impact of what happened in *this* child's conception, Matthew (following the LXX) uses the Greek word *parthenos* (virgin) rather than *neanis* (young girl) in rendering Isaiah 7:14. Furthermore, "Immanuel" now bears a deeper meaning than was possible in Isaiah's day. For Jesus does more than testify to God's presence; *he himself is God*—now come personally to be with his people forever (cf. Matt. 28:20).

Greek *Iēsous* (v. 21) corresponds to the Hebrew *yĕhôšuaʿ,* which means Yahweh is salvation. Joshua served Yahweh's saving purpose, but Mary's child is the Savior himself. He is named Jesus, "because he will save his people from their sins" (v. 21). They are *his* people, and he alone has the authority to forgive their sins (9:1–8). Precluding the idea that "the Son of David" (v. 1) was to be a political or social Messiah, verse 21 defines his mission as fundamentally spiritual in character. In the phrase *they will call him Immanuel* (v. 23), "they" refers to the people whom Jesus saves. "God is with us!" exclaim his redeemed people.

Joseph was a righteous man and was therefore not willing to expose Mary to public disgrace (v. 19). In showing righteousness by an act of mercy, he becomes a model for disciples (cf. 5:6–7, 20). Moreover, Joseph is a descendant of David (vv. 6–16, 20) and Jesus' legal father (just as surely as he is not his biological father); thus he is to name the child (vv. 21, 25). Jesus is certified to be a true descendant of David. Joseph's righteousness is further evident in his obedience to God's word—as delivered both through the angel (vv. 24–25) and through the prophet (as Isaiah foretold that "the virgin . . . will give birth" [v. 23], Joseph "had no union with her until she gave birth" [v. 25]).

Next Matthew describes the visit of the Magi (**2:1–12**). Matthew calls them Magi (Gk. *magoi*, whence Lat. *magi*). They come from the east (v. lb), probably from Babylon. Later Christian tradition would call them "kings" (cf. Ps. 72:10–11; Isa. 60:3). The tradition of three kings arose from the number of gifts they presented (2:11); however, the exact number of the Magi is unknown. Verses 2 and 11 carry forward two themes from chapter 1. The Magi honor Jesus as king—as one who is already a king and not merely destined to become one. Moreover, in Matthew the very first people to worship Jesus are Gentiles (nothing is said about the homage of Jewish shepherds or of Jesus' parents). Their zeal to worship the child highlights the indifference of the Jews (none of whom join the Magi for the short trip from Jerusalem to Bethlehem) and the hostility of Herod.

The Magi's visit is prompted by a star (Gk. *astēr*, v. 2), variously identified as a comet, a supernova, a planetary conjunction, or a unique supernatural phenomenon. The Magi's language ("*his* star," v. 2) strongly suggests that they have studied the Scriptures as well as the heavens. Was not a star to herald Israel's king, and were not the Gentiles to come to his light to pay him homage (Num. 24:17–18; Isa. 60:3)?

Micah 5:2 (quoted in 2:6) reveals the place and the purpose of Messiah's coming. Judah's humiliation (Mic. 5:1) will end; for the Davidic dynasty will be restored under a ruler who is coming forth (as had David) from Bethlehem (5:2) by a means reminiscent of Isaiah 7:14 (Mic. 5:3a). Unlike the corrupt leaders of Micah's day, this king will rule in Yahweh's name and reestablish justice and peace—for Gentiles as well as Jews (Mic. 5:4; cf. 4:1–5). All these prophecies find fulfillment in Jesus, the virgin-born royal descendant of David (Matt. 1). In place of "Bethlehem . . . , *though* you are small" (Mic. 5:2), Matthew has "But you, Bethlehem, . . . are *by no means* least" (2:6a). Between Micah and Matthew stands the actual birth of Jesus in Bethlehem (v. 1), by virtue of which the lowly town is exalted.

Now Jesus is threatened by Herod as was Moses by Pharaoh; as Moses is saved for his appointed task, so is Jesus. As Egypt once provided relief from famine for Jacob and his sons, she now offers protection to Jesus and his parents (**2:13–23**). Hosea 11:1 (quoted in Matt. 2:15) is realized in two stages (as was Isa. 7:14). Israel's deliverance from Egypt anticipates the greater saving work of Jesus (Matt. 1:21). Moreover, Jesus is God's "son" in a deeper sense than were the Israelites. They were the redeemed; he is God the Son, the Redeemer himself.

The quotation of Jeremiah 31:15 in Matthew 2:18 is most appropriate. Rachel's burial was associated with both Ramah and Bethlehem (Gen. 35:16–20). Bethlehem's grief over the murdered infants mirrors Rachel's anguish over her exiled children. But as Jeremiah promises renewal (31:16–17), so does Matthew. The Babylonian exile, which concludes the second segment of the genealogy (Matt. 1:11), appeared to crush all hopes attached to David. But the exile also marks the beginning of the final segment of the genealogy (1:12), which ends with Messiah's coming. God saves this child from slaughter so that he might reverse the fortunes of God's people, turn sorrow into joy, and usher in the new covenant promised in Jeremiah 31:31–34 (cf. Matt. 26:28).

In verses 19–23 no single Old Testament passage is in view (v. 23, "prophet*s*"). In keeping with prophecy (Isa. 49:7; 53:2–3), Messiah's town is despised (he is "the Nazarene," not "the Bethlehemite"). Greek *nazōraios* (perhaps recalling Heb. *nēṣer*, "branch," of Isa. 11:1) provides a fitting conclusion to a birth narrative that began by identifying Jesus as "the son of David" (1:1), but now ends by expressing his humble and lowly origin.

B. Preparation for ministry (3:1–4:16). This section begins with the ministry of John the Baptist (**3:1–12**). Here the accent falls on John's preaching (vv. 1–3), which in turn explains his baptism (v. 11). His clothing recalls Elijah (v. 4; 2 Kings 1:8), as does his preaching, especially to the authorities, both secular (as Elijah opposed Ahab, John opposes Herod) and religious (as Elijah opposed the prophets of Baal, John opposes the Pharisees and Sadducees). As John heralds the day of Yahweh (vv. 2–3), Jesus identifies him as the coming Elijah (11:10–14; Mal. 3:1; 4:5–6). Yet John, far from identifying himself as Elijah (cf. John 1:21), focuses on the One who comes after him (Matt. 3:11); he himself is but "a voice . . . calling in the desert" (v. 3, quoting Isa. 40:3).

In verse 2 the phrase *the kingdom of heaven* (= "kingdom of *God*," Mark 1:15) respects Jewish sensibilities and stresses "the majesty of God's universal dominion"[9] (cf. 6:9; 11:25). The Greek word for "kingdom," *basileia*, points fundamentally to God's *rule*, not to the realm over which he rules. John speaks of the dawn of the last days. God is about to inaugurate his kingdom and establish his final rule; then his will will indeed be done on earth as in heaven (6:10). Such a prospect demands the right response (v. 2a). True repentance entails a change of *mind* (the literal meaning of the Greek word for repentance, *metanoia*), a change of *heart* (which means confessing one's sins, vv. 6, 11), and a change of *life* (which demonstrates the genuineness of these inner changes, vv. 8–10). While the Pharisees and Sadducees probably received baptism (vv. 7, 11), it is very doubtful that they had truly repented. John uses the strongest language (v. 7) to jar them out of their false sense of personal and national security (v. 9).

Verses 11–12 depict "the coming one" as human (he wears sandals, v. 11). But he is a man in whom God is uniquely at work (it is for *Yahweh's* coming that John prepares, v. 3). He is Israel's Lord ("*his* threshing floor . . . *his* barn," v. 12 [italics added]). Whatever John's exact beliefs, Matthew presents Jesus as God incarnate. His mission is to baptize Israel "with the Holy Spirit and with fire" (v. 11), that is, to purify the nation of sin and to prepare it to meet the holy God. He is like a farmer harvesting his crops (v. 12). Those who heed John's message will be like gathered wheat; the others will be destroyed like chaff. As with the sign of Isaiah 7, John's Messiah brings both judgment and grace.

Now Matthew focuses upon John's encounter with Jesus at the Jordan (**3:13–17**). Knowing Jesus to be the Coming One, John shrinks from the thought of his receiving "a baptism of repentance" (v. 11). *He*, not Jesus, needs such cleansing (v. 14). But Jesus is insistent (v. 15), because he desires to identify in the closest way with sinners (1:21). (Yet Jesus is not said to confess sins; cf. v. 6.) The words *to fulfill all righteousness* (v. 15) mean that Jesus, with John's cooperation, is to do all that is *right* for the completion of his mission. The nature of the baptism and the subsequent words from heaven show that the "right" will entail Jesus' bearing the iniquities of the ungodly (Isa. 53:11b). The baptism anticipates the cross.

As significant as the baptism are the results of the baptism itself. All members of the Trinity participate (cf. 28:19). Like the mission of the dove after the flood, the descent of the Spirit (v. 16) signals that God's kingdom banishes chaos and brings peace. Moreover, the power by which Jesus was conceived (1:18) now equips him for ministry (cf. 4:1; 12:28). Quoting his own Word (v. 17; cf. Ps. 2:7; Isa. 42:1), the Father declares his Son to be a servant-king who wins his subjects' allegiance by giving himself for them. The Father is well pleased with the Son, because of their fellowship within the Godhead and because Jesus has just shown his willingness to identify with sinners and to suffer for them (cf. 20:28).

The temptation of Jesus follows in **4:1–11.** Jesus' fast of forty days and forty nights (v. 2) in the Judean desert (cf. 3:1) recalls Israel's forty years in the wilderness, and especially Moses' fasts of forty days and forty nights on behalf of faithless Israel (see Exod. 34:28; Deut. 9:9, 18).

The Spirit leads Jesus into the desert and the devil tempts him (v. 1) for the purpose of testing his commitment to sonship and to mission as defined at the Jordan (3:17). The reality and severity of the tests must not be minimized. By relying on the Father and the Spirit, Jesus is *able not to sin*, able to resist and to conquer the devil. Unlike God's son Israel, this Son remains faithful in the desert.

In the first temptation (vv. 3–4) the devil, far from questioning Jesus' sonship, capitalizes upon it: "*Since* [a better translation than "if"] you are the Son of God" (v. 3). He seeks to draw Jesus away from submission to the Father into an independent, self-serving use of his status. Moreover, in tempting Jesus to satisfy physical cravings, he recommends a mission more concerned with social reform than with spiritual upheaval (1:21). In quoting Deuteronomy 8:3, Jesus affirms his dependence on the Father, who has not yet ordered an end to the fast. He shows his reliance on God's Word by quoting the Scriptures, as he will do in response to each temptation. In each case he quotes from Deuteronomy (a book associated with Israel's wilderness wanderings). Here he reaffirms that his mission is primarily spiritual in character. Mere social reformation would rob man of his most desperate need—to receive God's Word and to be rightly related to him. (The word

9. Ibid., 43.

alone in v. 4 is crucial; later chapters of Matthew show Jesus' compassion for the physically and materially needy.)

In the second temptation (vv. 5–7) the devil says in effect: Since you are God's Son, give the Father an opportunity to honor his promise (Ps. 91:11–12) and prove his love (Matt. 3:17). The choice of "the highest point of the temple" (450 feet above the Kidron Valley) urges a public display of messiahship. Satan urges Jesus to leave the Servant's lowly path and to use his divine power to gain popular acclaim—which would merge easily with popular ideas about the Davidic Messiah. Jesus responds that he who really trusts the Father ("the Lord your God," v. 7) will trust—not test—his Word.

In the third temptation (vv. 8–10) the devil depicts himself as a king with vast holdings (vv. 8–9) and asks accordingly that Jesus pay him homage—for which he shall grant the desired *end* (rule over "all the kingdoms of the world"; cf. 4:17) without the costly *means* (3:15–17). But Jesus recognizes that worship should not be divided between God and Satan (God *alone* is worthy of worship), and indeed *cannot* (How could one's ultimate allegiance be divided?). In obedience to the Father, Jesus will gain the world's kingdoms not by worshiping Satan but by wresting them from his grasp (12:22–29; 28:18).

Jesus not merely resists but conquers the tempter; in obedience to Jesus' command, the devil departs (vv. 10–11). The Son who refused to break his long fast by the wrong means (vv. 2–3) now receives provisions (v. 11). The bond between Father and Son is confirmed (the devil could not sever it), and the Son is ready for his appointed mission.

Jesus not merely "returned" (NIV) but "withdrew" (RSV) to Galilee (**4:12–16**), a haven (as in 2:22) from hostile Judea (v. 11a). Fulfilling Isaiah 9:1–2 requires both being in "Galilee of the Gentiles" and living "by the lake" (vv. 13, 15). Jesus' move to Capernaum visibly declares a saving purpose: upon unenlightened Gentiles the light has dawned (v. 16)!

II. Jesus' Public Ministry in Galilee (4:17–16:20)

A. Jesus begins his public ministry (4:17–25). Verse 17 summarizes Jesus' preaching and also signals a new phase in his ministry. He continues with the calling of the disciples (**4:17–22**). The call of the four is noteworthy, because all are later numbered among the Twelve (10:2–4), three are to enjoy a special closeness to Jesus (17:1), and one is prominent in the crucial episode at Caesarea Philippi (16:13–20). As God's appointed King, Jesus issues a sovereign command: "Come, follow me" (v. 19). A disciple is not first a learner (though Gk. *mathētēs*, disciple, literally means one who learns), but a follower. Jesus calls first for a commitment to his person, which in turn entails obedience to his teaching (11:29). The men's response is immediate and decisive (vv. 20, 22). Jesus' words *fishers of men* are inspired by the men's occupation (v. 18b) and by his announcement of the kingdom (v. 17). As he proclaims good news (v. 23), these "fish" are not being snared by the coming wrath (3:7; Jer. 16:16) but are drawn from darkness into light and from death into life (4:16).

Jesus' opening declaration (v. 17) is identical to John's (3:2). But the kingdom that John *heralded*, Jesus actually *inaugurates* (**4:23–25**; cf. 12:28); so the noun *gospel* (Gk. *euangelion*) is reserved for Jesus' preaching (v. 23). Instruction (v. 23) gives insight and direction to those who respond to the preaching (5:2). The aspect of Jesus' healing ministry is greatly emphasized (vv. 23b–24). Observe the accent in Matthew 5–7 on preaching and teaching, and in Matthew 8–9 on healing. Jesus' outreach attains great breadth, both geographical and ethnic (vv. 23–25).

B. Jesus' teaching on discipleship (5:1–7:29). Jesus ascends the mountainside above Capernaum (v. 1; cf. 4:13) to address both disciples (5:2) and crowd (7:29a; RSV he taught *them*). As he teaches the disciples, Jesus calls the crowd to discipleship. Moreover, as Moses received the law on Sinai, Jesus ascends the mountain to expound God's Torah. He sits down (v. 1) as though taking Moses' seat (23:2). But this teacher is also "God with us": as his Word once prepared Israel for life in the land, it now equips citizens of the kingdom.

In the Beatitudes (**5:1–12**) Jesus is pronouncing blessings, not issuing orders; he begins not with law but with *gospel* (v. 3; cf. Luke 4:18). The Beatitudes in turn provide the essential basis for Jesus' words about law keeping (5:17–48).

Poverty of spirit (v. 3) has causes besides disease and poverty (vv. 4–10). It is chiefly an awareness of sin that makes such people wretched, which in turn drives them to God (NEB How blest are those who know their need of God) and rids them of pretense (v. 8). Grieved as they are (v. 4) by injustice, national apostasy, and personal sin, they long "to see right prevail" (v. 6, NEB) and "to do what is right" (NEB marg.). Precisely as those who seek to obey God, they depend on his mercy and righteousness (vv. 7–10). As the "meek" (v. 5), they implore God to vanquish evil, vindicate the faithful, and restore justice to the land.

The passive verbs in verses 4, 6, 7, and 9

point to God's initiative and activity. It is not poverty of spirit that makes one "blessed," but God's approval (from which arises human happiness). Moreover, salvation is not a reward for human achievement (even acts of justice and mercy) but the gift of a sovereign God. The kingdom's consummation awaits the future: note verses 4–9 ("they will be"), 11 (ongoing persecution), and 12 ("reward in heaven"). But the coming reversal has *already* begun with Jesus' inauguration of the kingdom. Those united to the Son of God are already "sons of God" (v. 9); their sins have already been forgiven (v. 3; cf. 9:2). The Beatitudes, like the rest of the sermon, are addressed to the crowd (only vv. 11–12 are directed specifically to disciples). Jesus invites the needy within the crowd (those who suffer in the ways described here) to come to him. Because grace makes the offer, it is perilous to reject it (11:20–24).

Jesus speaks not of what disciples ought to become, but of what they already *are* (vv. 13–14)—namely, those who evidence the qualities celebrated in the Beatitudes. In salt and light (**5:13–16**), nature and function are one. As salt, disciples are a preservative to impede the spread of evil in society. As light, they bear a positive witness to that society. If what the disciples really *are* is clearly to be seen, nonbelievers will glorify the heavenly Father by becoming his children.

Next Matthew addresses the subject of Jesus and the Law (**5:17–20**). Jesus has not come to abolish the Law (v. 17) or even to remove its smallest part (v. 18). At the same time he expounds the Law in the light of the dawning kingdom (4:17). As "fulfill" (Gk. *plēroō*, v. 17) applies to both Law and Prophets, it means not merely that Jesus fulfills certain prophecies or that he keeps certain laws. Rather in this context it means "fill up": far from abolishing the Old Testament, Jesus brings it to completion (cf. v. 17 in NEB) by ushering in the kingdom of God. The age of "the Law and the Prophets" prepared for, and is now superseded by, the age of Messiah (11:12–13).

The dawn of the last days does not eliminate the need for law keeping. The Law remains in force "until everything is accomplished" (v. 18)—that is, until the kingdom is consummated. Jesus censures the religious leaders, not for taking the Law too seriously but for failing to take it seriously enough (cf. 23:3, 23); the disciples' righteousness must surpass theirs (v. 20), as verses 21–48 will make plain. Verse 19 applies especially to disciples; as those who have experienced radical grace (vv. 3–12), they are ready for radical obedience.

The following long passage (**5:21–48**) consists of six sections addressing various topics: (1) murder (5:21–26); (2) adultery (5:27–30); (3) divorce (5:31–32); (4) oaths (5:33–37); (5) vengeance (5:38–42); and (6) love for enemies (5:43–48). Each of these sets God's Word to ancient Israel over against Jesus' own authoritative pronouncement, "But I tell you . . . " (vv. 22, 28, 32, 34, 39, 44). A closer study of these sections reveals three main points.

First, since the Law has an internal dimension, the Law must not be externalized. Both murder and anger break the sixth commandment (vv. 21–22; 15:19a). Both adultery and lustful desires violate the seventh commandment; breaking the seventh begins with breaking the tenth (Exod. 20:17; Matt. 15:19). If one resolves in his heart to obey God, oaths are not necessary—only a simple "yes" or "no" (v. 37).

Second, the Law must not be circumvented. The Law was abused to the point that one might secure the required divorce certificate (5:31) even for an alleged "indecency" too trivial to have been addressed in Deuteronomy 24:1 (cf. Matt. 19:1–12). An oath (5:33; cf. Num. 30:2) was not binding (some argued) so long as one avoided the name of God and did not swear to a false proposition. But one does not escape God by such rationalizing for he is Lord of heaven and earth (Matt. 5:34b, 35a)—as is the Messiah-King (v. 35b).

Third, since the Law has ongoing demands, it must not be discarded. Far from making law keeping obsolete, the dawn of the end calls for more radical obedience than ever (cf. 5:17–20). So intense is the fellowship of the kingdom that one who verbally abuses another is worthy of death (v. 22) and must be reconciled to his offended brother if God is to accept his worship (vv. 23–24). Swift action is needed before judgment falls (v. 22) and before the breach becomes irreparable (vv. 25–26). To take 5:29–30 literally might actually reduce their force (even a one-eyed person can be lustful!). The severity of the language in verses 29–30 teaches that one must do nothing to offend the church's Lord, and do everything in light of the coming judgment (7:24–27). Jesus totally excludes the grounds for divorce assumed from Deuteronomy 24:1; for disciples, marital unfaithfulness is the only legitimate ground for divorce and remarriage. In regard to the matter of vengeance, the original law (see Exod. 21:24) was given to curb vengeance (*only* one eye for one eye). Instead of reiterating the existing law, Jesus says, "Turn to him the other also" (v. 39). This response, together with the generosity commanded in verses 40–42, witnesses to the kingdom's radical grace. Verse 43a quotes the

Old Testament law (Lev. 19:18), and verse 43b the inference from it. Disciples' love, like the heavenly Father's, must be "perfect" (v. 48), that is, all-inclusive (cf. NEB). As God's common grace is showered upon both the evil and the good (v. 45), so disciples' love is to extend not just to those who love them (v. 46), nor just to fellow Christians (v. 47), but to enemies and nonbelievers as well (cf. Matt. 22:39; Luke 6:36).

Almsgiving, prayer, and fasting (the "acts of righteousness" of v. 1) were the "three pillars" of Jewish piety (**6:1–18**). The issue for Jesus is not whether one does them (each section begins, "*When* you . . . ") but *how* and *why* (with v. 1, cf. 5:16). The hypocrite is motivated by pride, the desire to be above others; so he has no room for God (to the person bent on being supreme, no one is so threatening as God). He appears to serve God but really serves himself. Jesus' followers are to be moved instead by love for God (vv. 4, 8, 18).

Giving to the needy (v. 3) is to be neither ostentatious (let it be done inconspicuously, with the right hand only) nor self-conscious (let not the self know what the self is doing).

The answer to pride and phoniness is solitude ("you" in v. 6 is singular) and attentiveness to God (the words *pray to the Father* have no counterpart in v. 5). The Father's reward to those who seek his approval rather than men's (v. 5) is a deepened communion with himself. The pagan "babbler" (v. 7a) uses "many words" (v. 7b) because he is bewildered (Have I found the right god?), anxious (Does he know my needs?), and manipulative (How long will it take to wear him down?). But disciples address the *one* true God (they need not search for a listener), the omniscient God (he already knows their needs, v. 8), the omnipotent God (who cannot be manipulated), and their loving Father (who need not be manipulated, v. 9; 7:7–11). There is no contradiction between the Father's *knowing* (v. 8) and the disciples' *asking* (vv. 9–13; 7:7); prayer makes the children dependent on God and grateful to him.

Unlike the pagan's prayer, the Lord's Prayer is pointed and concise. Even in private (v. 6) the disciple stands within a community ("*our* Father"). The relationship is intimate ("Father") but not unduly familiar ("in heaven" acknowledges the Father's majesty). God will receive the glory due his name (v. 9b) when his final rule is established (v. 10a) and his will is universally obeyed (v. 10b). He who prays this way commits himself to personal obedience ("let *my* conduct honor your name; your will be done, by *me,* now"), for the advance of God's rule (v. 33) in his own life and society. The child trusts the Father to provide his daily material and physical needs (v. 11), to pardon his sins (v. 12; but this is inseparable from his own willingness to forgive, vv. 14–15), and to protect him in danger (v. 13, one request stated negatively and positively: "Let us not succumb to the temptations of the Evil One, but on the contrary [Gk. *alla*], rescue us from his mighty power" [author's paraphrase]).

The disciple must not draw attention to himself (vv. 16–18); still, his very fasting should be festive (v. 17) to celebrate the dawn of the kingdom (4:17, 23).

Next Jesus discusses the subject of one's attitude toward material possessions (**6:19–24**). Verse 19 denies the permanence of earthly things, not their reality or value (cf. vv. 11, 31–32). But by contrast, heavenly treasures can be neither stolen nor destroyed (v. 20). For heaven is where God dwells (vv. 9–10); it is *he* who makes heaven secure. One stores up heavenly treasure by knowing God (v. 6) and advancing his rule (v. 33). As the functioning of the body depends on good eyesight, so living in the world demands the right perception of reality (vv. 22–23), which means seeing everything under God's sovereignty (v. 24) and in light of eternity (vv. 19–21). The Greek verb behind *serve* (v. 24) is *douleuō* ("be enslaved to"). While a servant may serve more than one master, a slave *cannot* (note the verbs in v. 24); divided allegiance between God and money is impossible. Yet slavery to God brings perfect freedom, as the following verses show.

The next section describes living without anxiety (**6:25–34**), that is, the practical effects of obeying the teaching of verses 1–24 (note the "therefore" in v. 25a).

God's slave has but one task—to obey him (v. 24); he depends on the Master to provide his needs (vv. 31–33). As one who has no rights, the slave joyously receives food and clothing and all the wonders of the natural world, as gifts from a Lord who is also his Father (vv. 26–33). Freed from bondage to money, he is able to enjoy the things that money can buy. Not so the slave of money: given the elusiveness and the vulnerability of his treasures, he is perpetually anxious (vv. 19–21, 31–32). He who rejects the true God for a false one (v. 24) loses this world as well as the next.

He who offers the prayer of verse 10 in true faith (cf. v. 30b) need not fret about tomorrow (v. 34). For he trusts a heavenly Father (vv. 9, 32) who is both able (because he is sovereign) and willing (because he is loving) to provide his children's daily needs.

Now Jesus addresses the subject of one's attitude toward others and God (**7:1–12**). He initially broaches the topic of judging others. Some judging is sinful while other is righteous. With sinful judgment the judge is a hypocrite (v. 5): he appears to be righteous but is really unrighteous. Although probably guilty of the very sins he condemns (cf. Rom. 2:17–24), he is blind to his own sin and preoccupied with the brother's. Such self-righteousness, says Jesus, is the worst sin of all (see Luke 18:9); compared to others it is as a "plank" to a "speck of sawdust" (v. 3). The judge has used the right standard (the law) and has exposed real sin. Let him understand, however, that in the final judgment God will employ that very standard to bring his own sin to light (v. 2).

Righteous judgment differs from that above. Once the judge is aware of his own sin (v. 5a) and of the judgment that awaits it (v. 2), he can understand his brother's sin and help him deal with it (v. 5b). Despite the warnings of verses 1–5, there is a place for judging the spiritual condition of others (v. 6; cf. v. 15). The "dogs" and "pigs" are unbelievers who repeatedly hear Jesus' teaching, yet persist in rejecting and attacking it.

Verse 12 is linked to verses 7–11 by the word *so* (NIV). The Father's answers to prayer offer disciples an example (let them show the same generosity to others) and an assurance (God will supply the love needed in these relationships). Certain rabbis stated the golden rule negatively ("Do not do . . . what you would not have them do"). But positive acts of love (v. 12) more effectively combat a judgmental spirit (vv. 1–5). Moreover, this love shows no respect of persons; verse 12 does not speak exclusively of "brothers," as did verses 3–5. Jesus now concludes the exposition begun at 5:17, which rested in turn upon the gracious indicatives of 5:1–16. Verse 12 summarizes all that he has taught about human relationships.

The next pericope is intended to evoke a response to Jesus (**7:13–29**). Living lawlessly seems far more attractive (v. 13) than the rigorous law keeping that Jesus demands (v. 14). But the former leads to death, the latter to life (cf. Ps. 1). Jesus addresses persons who have heard his teachings (cf. vv. 24, 26), are aware of the options, and must now choose one gate or the other. We should not conclude that the number of the saved is relatively small, without also taking account of other passages (e.g., Luke 16:16; Rev. 7:9).

Then Jesus warns against false prophets (vv. 15–23). The false prophets popularize the broad road by advocating a lawless way of life. They are easily recognized, for what they *do* reveals what they *are* (vv. 15–20), and what they *do* contradicts what they *say* (vv. 21–23). In verse 23b "evildoers" (lit. workers of lawlessness) shows that the antinomian does not really live without law; he chooses his own law instead of God's.

In the story of wise and foolish builders (vv. 24–27) the foundation represents Jesus' teaching. Both sets of people (represented by the two builders) have heard the teaching; both will experience the same kinds of difficulties. What distinguishes the two is that only the first does what Jesus has taught. Building on this foundation means both hearing *and* obeying Jesus' teaching. A lawless life-style rests on a foundation which is *no* foundation (v. 25b has no parallel in v. 27), and thus has neither basis for living nor protection against destruction.

Verses 28–29 indicate that Jesus' authority comes from his person and from his fidelity to the Old Testament, as distinct from rabbinic traditions. Still, Jesus calls not just for amazement (v. 28) but for allegiance (vv. 24–27).

C. Jesus' authority manifested (8:1–9:34). Matthew 5–7 stresses Jesus' authority as a teacher, Matthew 8–9 his authority as a miracle worker.

This section begins with Jesus' cleansing of a leper (**8:1–4**). Leprosy (v. 2) was one of "various diseases affecting the skin" (NIV marg.; cf. Lev. 13), probably excluding Hansen's disease. The Law offered no remedy; one's only hope lay in the intervention of God. In saying that Jesus can heal him if he so wills (v. 2), the man expresses confidence that God's power is at work in Jesus. Jesus' touch (which according to the Law would have defiled him) cleanses the unclean; his word banishes the uncleanness (v. 3)! The command to silence (v. 4) discourages false messianic ideas (cf. 4:3–7).

Jesus has now descended the mountainside (8:1) and reentered Capernaum where he is met by a centurion (**8:5–13**). His servant's paralysis may be the effect of demonic oppression (v. 6). To translate verse 7 as a question ("Shall I go and heal him?") rather than as a statement (so NIV) accords better with Jesus' present mission and provides a closer parallel to the similar account of 15:21–28.

Himself a mediator of imperial authority (v. 9), the centurion perceives that Jesus likewise both receives and exercises authority—the very authority of God. Such is Jesus' authority that his mere word can heal (v. 8b), as confirmed in verse 13. The words of verse 8a ("I do not deserve") may reflect sensitivity to Jewish scruples, but they arise chiefly from the centurion's awareness of Jesus' divine authority. As one who recognizes both his unworthiness and his need, the centurion embodies the qualities celebrated in the Beatitudes (5:3–5). Jesus is astonished to find such faith in a Gentile (v. 10)—faith both intellectual (he recognizes Jesus' authority) and practical (he applies that insight to the problem at hand).

Verses 11–13 emphasize the salvation of the Gentiles. The "many" Gentiles (v. 11) to be won by the apostolic preaching (28:19) take the place of Jews who reject Jesus as Messiah. While the judgment is not absolute (the patriarchs and the apostles were Jews), it is catastrophic (v. 12). Jesus' healing of the servant (v. 13) anticipates the mission to Gentiles. His doing so at a distance accords with his present focus on Israel (15:24).

In **8:14–17** Jesus continues his healing ministry. By his touch Jesus expels a fever (v. 15), and by his word he drives out demons (v. 16; cf. v. 3). In verse 17 Matthew does not restrict the prophecy of Isaiah to purely spiritual maladies. Yet the One who carries infirmities (Isa. 53:4) bears iniquities too (53:5–6); Jesus' healing of diseases cannot be separated from his forgiveness of sins (9:1–8) or from the death that secures forgiveness (26:28).

With perhaps only a small group of followers, Jesus retreats to the other side of the lake where he teaches on the cost of discipleship (**8:18–22**). The teacher of the law (v. 19) and the man of verse 21 ("another disciple") were disciples in the sense that they followed Jesus about and attended to his teaching, as distinct from those committed to his lordship. Jesus clearly indicates that his followers are sure to be deprived, that is, to be despised and rejected by men (v. 20). He draws the title *Son of man* from Daniel 7, where this figure both receives the worship due God alone (Dan. 7:13–14) and identifies with the lowly, oppressed people of God (Dan. 7:14, 18). Isaiah 53 and Daniel 7 together elucidate Jesus' concept of messiahship.

The request of the second disciple (vv. 21–22) seems quite legitimate (Exod. 20:12; Deut. 27:16). Probably the father has already died. Jesus' severe language matches the absoluteness of his claims. That he is more demanding than Elijah (1 Kings 19:19–21) is not surprising, given the finality and the urgency of the hour (Matt. 4:17). Neither man's response is recorded, but the issue is clear—following Jesus supersedes all other commitments.

In Matthew **8:23–27** Jesus demonstrates his authority over the sea. The One deprived of the provisions of the natural world (v. 20) is here revealed as nature's Lord. He who has mastered human afflictions now causes the elements to obey him (v. 27). Unlike the disciples, he is not in the least threatened by the storm. Why should he fear what he controls? The disciples shout, "Lord, save us!" (v. 25). Matthew again identifies Jesus as Yahweh, who now (v. 26) as before (cf. Pss. 65:5–7; 89:9; 107:23–32) stills the raging sea. The disciples are indeed men (Gk. *anthrōpoi*, v. 27a). But it is no mere man who rules the waves; he is "God with us" (1:23).

In **8:28–34** Jesus demonstrates his authority over the demons. Jesus enters Gentile territory (v. 28), as the pigs' presence confirms! Matthew mentions two demoniacs (v. 28), while the other Synoptists report only one (Mark 5:2; Luke 8:27). Though the demons recognize Jesus as the One destined to destroy them (v. 29b), they use his name—Son of God—without acknowledging his authority (cf. Exod. 20:7). At Jesus' command the demons abandon the men and enter the pigs. The drowning of the pigs (v. 32) foreshadows the demons' destruction at the end of history. Leaving aside the socioeconomic question raised by the loss of two thousand pigs (Mark 5:13), Matthew highlights the conflict between Jesus and the demons, Jesus' mastery over them, and the effect of his victory on the witnesses (vv. 33–34).

In **9:1–8** Jesus demonstrates his authority over sin. Responding to their faith (i.e., that of the paralytic and of those who brought him), Jesus declares that the man's sins are forgiven (v. 2). The passive voice in verse 2 witnesses to God's activity. Correctly perceiving Jesus' meaning, the scribes accuse him of blasphemy; for he—a mere man—presumes to act as God. The Jews of that day expected forgiveness in the messianic age but did not expect Messiah himself to forgive sins or to be divine.[10]

Convinced that Jesus' claim to deity is fraudulent (vv. 2–3), the scribes suspect that he speaks of sins instead of paralysis to avoid exposure (vv. 4–5). It is far easier for human beings to speak of forgiving sins than of curing disease (v. 5). The former is unobservable and unprovable; but if the pronouncement of a cure is not visibly confirmed, the alleged healer is exposed as a phony. Yet forgiving sins is the far greater need, so this is what Jesus first addresses (v. 2), while embracing the lesser need in the process (vv. 6–7). He is the heavenly Son of man (Dan. 7) now come to exercise his authority on earth (v. 6). By healing the paralysis (the culture of Jesus' day often drew a causal link between sin and sickness), Jesus further manifests his divine authority.

Jews despised tax collectors for collaboration with Gentiles and for dishonesty. The placement of Matthew's call (**9:9–13**) directly after Jesus has declared his right to forgive sins (vv. 1–8) and directly before the dinner for tax

10. Ibid., 163.

collectors and sinners (vv. 10–13) identifies Matthew as a sinner to whom Jesus offers forgiveness. As in 4:19, Jesus calls first for allegiance to his person (v. 9b). Confirming the genuineness of his own commitment (v. 9b), Matthew invites into his home—and into Jesus' company—those with whom he is well acquainted and who, like him, need God's forgiveness. "Sinners" (vv. 10–11) is a technical term embracing "those who live a flagrantly immoral life" and "those who follow a dishonourable vocation or one which inclines them strongly to dishonesty."[11]

The Pharisees were offended by Jesus' intimate socializing with tax collectors and sinners (v. 11; the question is more an accusation than an inquiry). Those who react this way, says Jesus, only imagine themselves to be healthy and righteous (vv. 12–13). For the truly healthy are sick persons whom God has healed; and the really righteous are those whose unrighteousness God has forgiven and who remain aware of their spiritual poverty (5:3). In turn, that kind of person is the one who treats others mercifully (1:19; 5:7) and who desires for others to receive saving grace. The opposite reaction (v. 11) shows that one has never really understood forgiveness (cf. 18:21–35). By acknowledging his sin and receiving other sinners, Matthew is an example for the Pharisees!

The religiously unclean and socially disreputable are the very ones Jesus came to save (v. 13). The Pharisees insist that sinners become righteous to gain acceptance; Jesus insists that they be accepted as sinners. Thus he obeys Hosea 6:6—"I desire mercy." Only when the Pharisees perceive their own sinfulness will they receive Jesus' gospel of grace and rejoice over his love for society's outcasts.

In **9:14–17** Jesus is questioned about fasting. The Pharisees might fast twice a week (Luke 18:12), far more than the Law required; John's disciples followed their master's practice (Matt. 11:18). Messiah's coming to inaugurate the kingdom calls for rejoicing, not for mourning (v. 15)! But when he is snatched away (v. 15b; cf. 16:21), fasting will be appropriate. Only when he returns will their joy be complete and their fast made obsolete. Just as the actions of verses 16–17 would ruin instead of preserve, so Jesus teaches that fasting must not be abolished but safeguarded. Yet even this practice must reflect the joy of the dawning kingdom (cf. 6:16–18).

In **9:18–26** Jesus raises a dead girl and heals a sick woman.

The girl's father (v. 18; more fully identified in Luke 8:41) believes that Jesus' mere touch will raise the dead (v. 18b, a striking statement, in that Matthew previously records no such miracle), which is exactly what happens (v. 25)! Jesus does not deny the reality of death but expresses confidence in his power to awaken the girl from death (v. 24a).

The woman's malady (v. 20) would have defiled others (Lev. 15:19–33), which helps to explain why she seeks to touch Jesus unobtrusively. She recognizes Jesus' extraordinary authority ("If I only touch . . . ," v. 21). Again the healing is effected by Jesus' mighty words (v. 22); the woman's faith is the instrument, not the cause, of healing. Far from being defiled by the unclean, Jesus cleanses the defiled (cf. 8:2–4).

In **9:27–34** Jesus heals the blind and the dumb. As in verse 22, Jesus responds to faith (v. 28) with his healing touch and word (vv. 29–30). Verses 32–33 say nothing about faith. By all indications Jesus acts here in sheer grace—not to answer faith but to *evoke* it (cf. v. 33b). Having concluded this series of miracle stories, Matthew records contrasting responses. The crowd is amazed (v. 33); but the Pharisees ascribe Jesus' authority to Satan (v. 34), a foretaste of 12:22–32.

D. The disciples' ministry (9:35–11:1). Matthew **9:35–38** serves as a summary of Jesus' ministry thus far and introduces the ministry of the disciples (chap. 10). Verse 35 repeats 4:23, recalls the content of chapters 5–9, and anticipates the mission of chapter 10.

The prayer of verse 38 is founded on 6:9–10. Far from making the outcome dependent on man, prayer is a means commanded by the Lord of the harvest (v. 38) for achieving his saving purpose. The commissioning of chapter 10 is both a response to the prayer of 9:38 and an expression of the compassionate heart and the sovereign will of Jesus (vv. 36–38).

The appointment of the Twelve is recorded in **10:1–4.** For the first time Matthew refers to twelve disciples (v. 1)—those whom Jesus chose from a larger company (Luke 6:13) for special instruction. This number was deliberately chosen; it recalled the twelve tribes of Israel and signaled that Jesus had come to reconstitute the people of God. Significantly, Jesus does not make himself one of the Twelve (cf. 16:18; 23:8–10).

The Twelve are listed in six pairs (vv. 2–4; cf. Mark 6:7, "two by two"). The first two pairs include Peter, James, and John, the "inner

11. K. H. Rengstorf, "hamartōlos, anamartētos," in *Theological Dictionary of the New Testament,* ed. Gerhard Kittel, Gerhard Friedrich, and Geoffrey W. Bromiley, trans. Geoffrey W. Bromiley, 10 vols. (Grand Rapids: Eerdmans, 1964–1976), 1:327.

three" (17:1). Peter's name is placed first (v. 2); 16:13–20 explains why. Only in Matthew's list is Matthew called the tax collector—the author's witness to the life out of which Jesus called him. If the second Simon (v. 4) belonged to the Zealot party (as is probable), his association with Matthew witnesses to the remarkable breadth of Jesus' choice. Judas Iscariot is placed last (v. 4b).

These disciples (v. 1) are further identified as the twelve apostles (v. 2). Apostleship is the appointed goal of discipleship; thus Jesus authorizes them (v. 1) to go forth (Gk. *apostellō,* v. 5) to gather his harvest (9:38).

The apostles' immediate mission is the concern of **10:5–16.** For now the disciples are to avoid Gentiles and Samaritans (v. 5) and to concentrate on Jews (v. 6). The Samaritans and Gentiles will be evangelized later (10:18; 28:19; Acts 1:8). As an extension of Jesus' own ministry (v. 40), the apostles are to preach the nearness of the kingdom and to do works of healing (vv. 1, 7–8). They become channels of grace (v. 8) to those in great need ("lost sheep," v. 6). The instructions of verses 9–10 lighten the travelers' load and make them dependent on others' hospitality. The gift of peace, that is, salvation (v. 13), is for those who welcome both the apostles and their message (v. 14). Shaking the dust off one's feet (v. 14b) signals deliverance to divine judgment. Verse 15 (cf. 11:20–24) shows how perilous it is to reject the ultimate outpouring of God's grace in Jesus. Like sheep among wolves (v. 16a) the disciples must be shrewd, lest innocence become naivete (v. 16). Their shrewdness is not sinful, for (unlike Satan's, Gen. 3:1) it is under Jesus' authority and combined with innocence.

The nature of the broader mission is dealt with in **10:17–42.** Let missionaries be on their guard (v. 17), for they are sure to be hated, betrayed, and persecuted (vv. 17–22)—like Jesus (vv. 24–25).

Persecution will not impede but promote the witness. Verse 18 speaks of actions aimed at winning Gentile rulers and their subjects to faith (cf. Acts). Moreover, perils are no excuse for evading responsibility. That one is to speak is not in doubt (v. 27). Exactly *what* or *how* to speak in an extremity, the Spirit can be trusted to supply (vv. 19–20).

The deliverance of Jesus' servants is assured (v. 22b). They will not exhaust their places of refuge before the Son of man comes (v. 23b), that is, before his return (v. 22 speaks of him who endures "to the *end*"; cf. 16:27) to achieve his people's final deliverance. Verses 28–30 offer assurance that God will allow nothing to prevent the completion of the missionaries' task, and that those who suffer death for their witness will nonetheless be saved. Given the promise of salvation, Jesus urges his followers to endure to the end (v. 22) and to broaden their witness (v. 23). One might naively wish to stay in one place despite persecution, whereas shrewdness would call for "fleeing to another" (v. 23a) in order both to preserve and to extend the witness (cf. Acts 8:1). This readiness for flight rests on the certainty that the Son of man will allow nothing to halt the mission to Jews until his return.

God will surely judge those who falsely accuse the ambassadors; and his is the crucial judgment (v. 28). This process has indeed begun. Men are already being divided according to their response to Jesus (vv. 32–33); the comprehensive "whoever" embraces both bearers and hearers of the message, both the disciples and the crowd. That division inevitably causes conflicts between the two companies of people (vv. 34–38). Amidst those conflicts, let the certainty of judgment cause Christians to fear God (v. 28) and obey their commission.

He who welcomes Christ's messengers (whether apostles, prophets, or disciples, vv. 40–42) will be rewarded with eternal life (v. 39). To be worthy of that reward, one must take up his cross and follow Jesus (v. 38), that is, be utterly abandoned to Jesus. Like a condemned criminal he abdicates all personal rights (v. 39). If need be, he is willing to die for Jesus. But he does not use martyrdom as an excuse to evade responsibility. His is a *living* sacrifice (Rom. 12:1), a daily Via Dolorosa (Luke 9:23) of service and suffering (Matt. 20:26–28). The one thing harder than dying for Jesus is living for him.

E. Jesus' ministry receives diverse responses (11:2–12:50). Matthew **11:1–19** focuses on John the Baptist. John is troubled not by what Jesus *is* doing (v. 2), but by what he is *not* doing. If Jesus is indeed Messiah, where is the sweeping judgment that John predicted (3:7–12), and why is the forerunner allowed to languish in prison? Jesus reiterates what John already knows (v. 2; v. 5 summarizes the miracles recorded in chaps. 8–9). Those very works have unleashed a process of judgment (vv. 20–24); salvation depends on receiving God's grace as manifested in Jesus (v. 6).

As John's attire is shabby compared to Herod's finery (v. 8; cf. 3:4), so his fearless preaching accentuates the king's vacillating weakness (14:3–9), and it is Herod, not John, who sways like a reed (v. 7)! John is also "more than a prophet" (v. 9); for unlike the Old Testament prophets, he stands on the border of the new age to announce the dawn of the kingdom

(3:2) and to serve as Messiah's immediate forerunner (3:11). Malachi 3:1 originally read, "*I* will send . . . before *me*" (emphasis added), which Matthew now quotes (v. 10) in light of the incarnation: "*I* [God the Father] will send . . . ahead of *you* [God the Son]" (emphasis added). According to the noblest criteria for judging human beings, no one is greater than John; but what matters supremely is membership in the kingdom of God (v. 11). The meanest citizen of this kingdom is greater than the greatest of the former era—not because of superior merit (which he may lack completely), but simply because he is a citizen of *God's* kingdom. Considering oneself "the least" (v. 11b) is the very attitude required for entry into this kingdom. Far from being excluded, John is the sort of person to whom the kingdom belongs (5:3–10). He is humble (3:11); he longs to see right prevail (3:7–10); as the coming Elijah (11:14), he preaches repentance and salvation (Luke 1:17, 76–79); and he is persecuted for righteousness' sake (Matt. 5:10; 14:1–12).

Ever since John began to preach (cf. 3:2), God's kingdom has been "forcefully advancing" (v. 12a, NIV). This rendering agrees with the dominant usage of the Greek verb *biazomai;* if the verb is translated "suffer violence" (RSV), verse 12a is synonymous with 12b. The "forceful men" (v. 12b, NIV, for Gk. *biastai*) act with evil intent. The context speaks of John's imprisonment and of "this generation's" rejection of both John and Jesus (vv. 16–19). Verse 12 declares that while the kingdom is indeed forcefully advancing, it has not yet swept away all opposition as John had envisaged (cf. v. 3; 6:10). On the contrary the kingdom's enemies are intensifying their opposition, as following chapters will show.

Jesus likens his generation to a group of fussy children (vv. 16–17). The dirge recalls John's preaching of judgment and austere life-style, the mourning his call to repentance (3:2). The playing of the flute stands for Jesus' proclamation of the gospel, the dancing the joy that his message brings. But in fact "this generation" rejects both John *and* Jesus (vv. 18–19a). Wisdom, God's appointed way, is honored and demonstrated in the life-styles of both John and Jesus. Despite the great differences in their behavior, each was faithful to God's appointed task. He who abstains (v. 18) longs for the kingdom to come; he who feasts (v. 19) celebrates its arrival.

Jesus ushers in the day of grace. By refusing to repent and actively opposing the kingdom's advance (vv. 12–19), the towns in which Jesus preached (**11:20–24**) reject the ultimate revelation of God's saving power. This places them under more severe judgment than the most iniquitous Old Testament cities (11:22–24; cf. 10:15), not least because, given the same revelation, *they* would have repented (v. 21)!

In **11:25–30** the revelation of the mutual relationship between the Father and the Son is instructive for the disciples' response to Jesus. Jesus addresses God as both Father and Lord (vv. 25–26). The uniqueness and intimacy of Jesus' sonship (3:17) does not diminish but heightens his awareness of the Father's sublime majesty. Disciples' prayers too must reflect this dual recognition (6:9).

The Father, who alone knows the Son, graciously chooses to reveal that knowledge to men (vv. 26–27), that is, to grant them personal union with the Son (cf. John 6:37–45). Rightly understanding Jesus' works (vv. 20–24) requires insight from the Father (v. 25b). The Son, who alone knows the Father (v. 27b), chooses to reveal that knowledge to human beings (v. 27c), that is, to make them God's children with the right to call him Father (6:9). Jesus invites people to come to him that he might teach them about the Father (vv. 27–29). Thus "gentle and humble in heart" (v. 29) describes both Jesus *and* the Father: "Like Father, like Son."

God reveals truth about himself to the teachable ("little children") but withholds it from the intellectually proud and autonomous ("wise and learned," v. 25b). The latter will gain the true wisdom—the knowledge of God—only by ceasing to rely on their unaided reason (1 Cor. 3:18) and by humbly opening their minds and hearts to God's revelation.

One must find rest in Jesus himself (v. 28) before attempting to obey the law as Jesus expounds it ("Take my yoke upon you," v. 29). Otherwise law keeping becomes a terrible bondage. Many whom Jesus addresses are weary and burdened precisely because of their efforts to keep the Law (cf. Acts 15:10). Jesus grants rest to his people by giving them his law (vv. 28–29)! In fact, the subject of the very next passage is that God revealed the fourth commandment to grant rest (the meaning of the word *sabbath*). Jesus' yoke is easy (for "his commands are not burdensome" [1 John 5:3]), and his burden is light (v. 30; unlike others, he helps his followers bear the load; see 23:4).

In **12:1–14** the Pharisees object to Jesus' attitude about the Sabbath. The disciples pluck the grain to satisfy their hunger (v. 1). The Pharisees object (v. 2) not to the action as such (cf. Deut. 23:25) but to their doing it on the Sabbath (they considered it "harvesting," which Exod. 34:21 prohibited).

The story of 1 Samuel 21:1–6 shows the superiority of the moral law over the ceremonial law. David and the disciples honor the sixth commandment (which calls for sustaining human life) by satisfying their hunger (Matt. 12:1, 3). Changing the bread on the Sabbath (Lev. 24:8; 1 Sam. 21:6b) broke the fourth commandment; but the priests were innocent, because the Law sanctioned their actions (Matt. 12:5). Hosea 6:6a (quoted in Matt. 12:7; cf. 9:13) teaches that mercy surpasses sacrifice without excluding it (cf. 1 Sam. 15:22). Moreover, in quoting this verse Jesus indicts the Pharisees for divorcing religious ritual from a right relationship to God. Had the Pharisees been rightly related to God (through the right understanding of the Old Testament), they would have recognized and received Jesus as "God with us."

The temple is greater than the Sabbath, for in the Old Testament the priestly requirements overrode the Sabbath law (v. 5). But "something greater" than the temple is here (v. 6), meaning "some*one* greater"—Jesus himself (cf. NIV). He who is greater than the temple is greater than the Sabbath as well; indeed he is "*Lord* of the Sabbath" (v. 8). He therefore has the right to expound the Sabbath law in light of his person (he is Yahweh, the giver of the Law) and his mission.

In declaring his disciples innocent (v. 7), Jesus abrogates the Sabbath ceremonial law (cf. 15:1–20). On the other hand, in declaring himself "Lord of the Sabbath" Jesus affirms the ongoing validity of the fourth commandment (Exod. 20:8–11; Matt. 5:17–20). The very abrogation of the ceremonial law focuses attention more directly on the foundational commandment. The Sabbath remains one of God's choicest gifts. His people's grateful response is directed both to God (praise and worship) and to human beings (beneficent actions bringing blessing both to oneself, v. 1, and to others, v. 12). Precisely *how* one keeps the Sabbath will be governed by love for God and neighbor (22:34–40).

In verse 14 the Pharisees object not to healing itself, but to doing it on the Sabbath (except where life is in danger; cf. Luke 13:14). Jesus again argues from the lesser to the greater (Matt. 12:12a). Indeed, as Jews viewed the kingdom of God as the Sabbath age (the Sabbath would crown history as it crowned creation), it was especially appropriate for Jesus to heal on the Sabbath. The healing declares and celebrates the dawn of the end. Where Jesus restores (v. 13), the Pharisees plot to destroy (v. 14).

In **12:15–21** Jesus, the servant of God, responds to opposition. By withdrawing (v. 15), Jesus exemplifies the teaching of 10:23; he avoids destruction before the appointed time, and he extends his mission (to Gentiles, vv. 18, 21). The quotation of Isaiah 42:1–4 recalls Matthew 3:17, underscores 8:17, explains 12:16 (Jesus rejects false messianic notions), and expounds true messiahship. Messiah's lowliness accounts for his authority (v. 18); his gentleness (vv. 19–20b) is the path to his triumph (v. 20c).

Matthew **12:22–37** records Jesus' response to the Pharisees' accusations of collusion with the devil. In accord with the authority evidenced in chapters 8–9, Jesus heals all aspects of the man's affliction (v. 22). Seeking to dispel whatever faith may be reflected in the crowd's response (v. 23), the Pharisees accuse Jesus of driving out demons "by Beelzebub, the prince of demons" (v. 24). The Greek *Beelzeboul* possibly means "lord of the dwelling" (cf. v. 27; 10:25). The charge arises from the Pharisees' belief that Jesus is undermining the Law.

The accusation is foolish for three reasons. First, division as described in verse 25 does occur (with predictable results), but Satan is too cunning and powerful a king to permit it. Second, the Pharisees believe that God *does* grant exorcising power; they will thus be judged (v. 27b) for "hypocritical inconsistency."[12] Third, Jesus in fact casts out demons (as his opponents recognize, v. 24). Once the Pharisees' irrational explanation is abandoned, the only other one is that Jesus expels demons "by the Spirit of God." And since Jesus does so, "the kingdom of God has come upon you" (v. 28b). His exorcising activity, while resembling that of others, is unique. In him—and him alone—God acts to establish his final rule, which entails crushing Satan's empire. Far from operating in Satan's power, Jesus assaults Satan (not just his underlings, as did other exorcists), binds him, and frees his victims (v. 29).

If, having once rejected Jesus and his message, one believes his witness and acknowledges his lordship, that very blasphemy will be forgiven. For Jesus came to save the worst of sinners (9:13). Blasphemy against the Spirit means viewing the Spirit's power as Satan's power (vv. 24, 28). These blasphemers (unlike those of v. 32a) speak "not out of ignorance or unbelief, but out of a 'conscious disputing of the indisputable.' "[13] Does the very absurdity of

12. Gundry, *Matthew*, 235.

13. D. A. Carson, "Matthew," in *The Expositor's Bible Commentary*, ed. Frank E. Gaebelein, 12 vols. (Grand Rapids: Zondervan, 1979–), 291, quoting G. C. Berkouwer, *Sin* (Grand Rapids: Eerdmans, 1971), 340.

the Pharisees' charge (v. 24) expose their awareness that they are questioning the unquestionable? Such willful resistance to God's truth will never be forgiven (v. 32b).

The blasphemer against the Spirit is without hope. But let those against Jesus (v. 32a) beware, lest persistent unbelief should spell their damnation (11:20–24). One is given time to ponder the claims of Jesus; but in the end neutrality is impossible (10:32–33).

As the condition of a tree may be judged by its fruit (cf. 7:17–20), so Jesus assesses his antagonists' innermost character by what they say about him (v. 24). However worthless or insignificant words may seem to be, they are in fact an accurate index to the state of a person's heart (vv. 33–35). One will be judged by his words precisely because they reveal what he is (vv. 36–37).

Jesus' verdict to this generation is given in **12:38–50.** The opposition asks for a sign which is not subject to the charge of verse 24; which must therefore come from a source other than Jesus; and which must clearly originate with God (cf. 16:1–4).

The sign of Jonah (vv. 39–40) is the burial and resurrection of Jesus. "Jesus stayed in the realm of the dead parts of three twenty-four-hour periods. . . . But the reference to three days and three nights comes out of Jonah 2:1 rather than from the story of Jesus and causes no problem in view of the Jewish method of reckoning part of a twenty-four-hour day for the whole."[14] Jesus indeed speaks of a sign from God (cf. v. 38); but his resurrection is mentioned implicitly, not explicitly (cf. 16:21, addressed to disciples). Moreover, according to the New Testament no one witnessed the resurrection itself, only appearances of the risen Jesus. While the resurrection was to be a stupendous miracle, one that only God could achieve, even it would not exclude the need for faith. Access to the resurrection would depend on a believing response to its proclamation.

Verses 41–42 emphasize the primacy of preaching. This was true in Old Testament times: the Ninevites repented at Jonah's preaching (v. 41), without the slightest knowledge of his sojourn in the fish; and the Queen of the South came to listen to Solomon (v. 42), who was no miracle worker. Likewise in Jesus' ministry the mighty works (including the exorcisms) are intelligible only in relation to his proclamation of the kingdom (4:17, 23; 11:2–6; note the preaching of 12:28–29). In the last judgment those Old Testament listeners will stand to accuse Jesus' contemporaries (vv. 41–42). For Jonah's and Solomon's authority was preparatory and derived; Jesus' is final and inherent (cf. 9:6). Thus his hearers will incur the greater judgment (cf. 11:20–24).

Verses 43–45 indicate the peril of a partial response. Jesus' miracles must not be dissociated from his person and his preaching. Exorcism alone does not save a person. "A new master must reign there, the word of Jesus must be its rule of life, and the joy of the Kingdom of God must pervade it."[15]

Verses 46–50 offer a dramatic portrayal of Jesus' true family. Jesus is not severing ties with his family but declaring in the starkest terms that the kingdom of heaven is greater than the strongest earthly ties (10:37–38), and that the citizens of the kingdom are a genuine family consisting of those who do the Father's will.

F. Jesus' parables of the kingdom (13:1–53). Here, in the third of the five discourses, and in keeping with his pedagogical design, Matthew gathers together seven parables. Jesus elucidates spiritual truth (concerning the purpose and effect of his mission) by a series of seven pictures.

The first parable (**13:1–23**) introduces and stands over against the other six. These six share the common opening, "the kingdom of heaven is like. . . ." The next three parables (vv. 24–35) are addressed to the crowd; Jesus reserves his explanation of the second parable for his disciples (vv. 36–43; cf. v. 11). Parables five through seven (vv. 44–50) are addressed to disciples exclusively. Parables two through seven consist of three pairs, namely two and seven, three and four, and five and six. We consider the parables according to this structure.

In the parable of the sower (13:3–9, 18–23) nothing is said about plowing; the emphasis falls on the condition of the soil and its effect on the seed. The four kinds of soil (vv. 3–9) depict different responses to Jesus' preaching (vv. 18–23).

1. The resistant response (vv. 4, 19). The soil along the path is hard, so the seed cannot penetrate the surface and is soon devoured by birds. This depicts the religious leadership's unyielding opposition to Jesus' teaching.

2. The shallow response (vv. 5–6, 20–21). As the roots cannot penetrate the limestone that lies beneath the thin layer of topsoil, the plant withers under the heat of the sun. This describes nominal disciples (cf. 8:18–22) who fall away when discipleship becomes costly (cf. 10:16–39).

14. Gundry, *Matthew*, 244.

15. J. Jeremias, *The Parables of Jesus* (London: SCM Press, 1963), 198.

3. The distracted response (vv. 7, 22). The murderous thorns (v. 7) illustrate the power of money and earthly treasures (v. 22) to prevent undivided loyalty to Christ (cf. 6:19–34; 19:16–22).

4. The productive response (vv. 8, 23). Amidst the loss there is an abundant harvest; despite all obstacles the message of the kingdom achieves its purpose. This soil alone illustrates what it means to be Jesus' true disciple. That a person has really understood and received the gospel of the kingdom will be evident in the way he or she lives (v. 23; cf. 7:16–21).

The purpose of the parables is cited in 13:10–17. The disciples and the crowd are distinguished (v. 10; cf. vv. 2–3). The disciples have responded favorably to Jesus' proclamation of the kingdom and are committed to his lordship. Members of the crowd have heard the proclamation but apparently have not responded favorably to it; they still stand outside the circle of true disciples.

The parable of the sower describes various responses, not to the parables but to "the message about the kingdom" (v. 19). Understanding the parables of the kingdom depends on prior acceptance of the gospel of the kingdom (4:17, 23). Given the disciples' response to the gospel, Jesus now grants deeper understanding (vv. 11–12, 16–17). He not only tells them parables, but he also explains them. The parables elucidate and enlarge upon the truth they already possess.

Given the crowd's rejection of earlier truth, the parables, far from granting deeper insight, actually obscure the truth they have already received and thus become a means of judgment for their having rejected the message of the kingdom (v. 12b). As verse 13 makes clear, Jesus speaks to the crowd in parables *because* they do not see (what he has already told them), not *in order that* they may not see (what he is now telling them). The quotation (vv. 14–15) from Isaiah 6:9–10 describes their condition prior to Jesus' teaching them parables, not as the result of the parables. Until they rightly respond to the light they have already received, Jesus will not give them more light; rather, he will take away the light that they have received. Might not this frightful word of judgment be God's means for moving the crowds from their stupor (v. 15) toward repentance and faith?

Normally servants would sow the seed. Here in the parable of the weeds (**13:24–30**) the owner himself does so (v. 27); for he represents Jesus (v. 37)—the One who proclaims the kingdom. His mission embraces "the world" (v. 38), that is, the Gentile nations (28:19). The church is a mixed company, consisting of true and false believers (tares are sown among the wheat, v. 25). The enemy is the devil (v. 39). "The appearance of some tares would not have surprised the slaves. Their surprise therefore implies a large number due to deliberate sowing."[16] The roots of the tares have become intertwined with those of the wheat (v. 29); Satan opposes God by infiltrating his church (cf. 16:18 in this light). At the judgment men's true condition is brought to light, and genuine believers are separated from the spurious (vv. 39–43). In the meantime, church leaders must avoid hasty judgments (v. 29; cf. 7:1–5; 18:15–20).

The parable of the net (**13:47–50**) depicts the kingdom's spread throughout the world, represents the church as a mixed company (v. 47b), and emphasizes the separation at the end (which brings to light present conditions).

As the tiny mustard seed is buried in the field, and as the leaven is hidden in the dough (**13:31–33**), so the kingdom has small, inauspicious beginnings. But, says Jesus, the kingdom presently hidden is nonetheless really present. The powers of the kingdom are already at work (11:4–6; 12:28). Just as power is released in the seed and in the yeast at the very moment they are hidden away, so the powers of the kingdom are being unleashed here and now, in the very time of its small beginning. And just as the full-grown mustard tree is potentially present in the seed, so the kingdom presently revealed is the kingdom that will one day be fully revealed.

The parables of the mustard seed and the yeast are both parables of growth. The powers released now do not abate until their purpose is achieved. Out of a relatively small seed emerges the full-grown mustard tree (8–12 ft. tall). As the yeast exerts its energy until it permeates the whole batch of dough, so the kingdom will grow until it reaches the ends of the earth.

Like Asaph (Ps. 78:2, quoted in v. 35), Jesus addresses "parables" to Israel and brings to light "things hidden" since the creation (**13:34–35**). The Old Testament prepares for his coming; his ministry fulfills the Old Testament (5:17–48; 11:12–13). As Asaph stands *within* the Old Testament period and Jesus *beyond* it, the teaching of the latter represents fulfillment in a way that the former could not (v. 35a). Jesus "unites in himself streams of revelation from the old covenant that had not been so clearly united before"[17] (cf., e.g., Jesus' use of Isa. 53 and Dan. 7).

For those with eyes to see and ears to hear

16. Gundry, *Matthew*, 264.
17. Carson, "Matthew," 322.

(vv. 9, 16), things formerly mysterious are now being explained, things formerly hidden are now being revealed. Enlightenment is presently withheld from the crowd. But once they rightly respond to the light they have received, further light upon the truth will be granted. Those "things hidden since the creation" are *potentially* intelligible to them too.

The parables of the hidden treasure and the pearl (**13:44–46**) together depict the kingdom as a value different from others (one man's possessions, the other's merchandise), and far greater, so that obtaining this treasure is worth abandoning all else (cf. 6:33; 10:34–39; 13:18–23; 19:29).

The Christian scribe (**13:51–53**) refers initially to Matthew himself. By extension it also refers generally to true disciples who can now produce treasures old (what they knew before Jesus' teaching) and new (what they know since Jesus has told and explained the parables).

G. Jesus' teaching and parables receive diverse responses (13:54–16:20). The Nazarenes' bewilderment (**13:54–58**) recalls the crowd's lack of understanding (vv. 11–17). As persons impressed by Jesus' wisdom and miraculous powers (v. 54), but who persist in asking about their source and in taking offense at him (vv. 54–57), they recall the Pharisees' stance (12:24). Thus Jesus withholds blessing (v. 58).

In **14:1–12** Herod Antipas wrongly identifies Jesus with John the Baptist. Herod's misinterpretation of Jesus (vv. 1–2) and indifference to learning more recalls the crowd's response (13:11–17).

Matthew accentuates the confrontation, and the stark differences, between Herod and John. John's bravery (in speaking out against Herod's liaison with Herodias, vv. 3–4, in full knowledge of the risks involved) highlights Herod's cowardice. Wanting to kill John because of his preaching, he nonetheless refrains because he fears the people (v. 5). Pressured by Herodias and fearing what his dinner guests will think (v. 9), he reverses his decision and has John killed.

As the Nazarenes rejected Jesus' preaching (13:57), so Herod silences John by imprisoning him. As Herod tried to murder the infant Jesus (2:1–18), his son Herod Antipas imprisons and eventually kills John. By withdrawal Jesus escapes the enemy for the moment (vv. 12–13). But in time he too will die at the hands of the kingdom's enemies (11:12; 17:12–13).

The feeding of the five thousand (**14:13–21**) demonstrates Jesus' provision for the crowds. First he heals them; verse 14 implies a large number of healings. Then he feeds them (vv. 19–21; bread and fish were the basic diet of the poor; cf. 7:9–10). But Jesus is not heralding a messianic ministry primarily concerned with the relief of material needs. This would represent a change from the path chosen during his temptation (4:3–4). The present situation is extraordinary; the people could buy food if given the opportunity (v. 15).

Given the accent in Matthew 13 upon the obtuseness of the crowds and the consequent judgment, the twofold provision of healing and feeding is quite remarkable. Despite his stern words, Jesus shows compassion (v. 14), knowing the people's need for direction, protection (9:36), and rest (11:28). He makes the disciples agents of his blessing to the crowd. The smallness and seeming inadequacy of their resources magnifies the powers that Jesus releases in the miracle of multiplication (vv. 17–19).

Given the predictable impact of such a miracle upon the crowd in the face of popular messianic expectation (see John 6:14–15), Jesus acts at considerable risk. Why then does he do it? Such an act in such a place (v. 15) recalls Yahweh's miraculous provision of manna in the wilderness and declares Jesus to be Yahweh incarnate. Moreover, Jesus accomplishes this miracle, and Matthew records it, with a view to the Last Supper, especially Jesus' interpretation of the bread (26:26). Jesus acts in the hope that those with eyes to see and minds to understand will in time view the present event in the light of his atoning sacrifice (cf. John 6:51–58).

In the preceding story Jesus demonstrated his mastery of nature by multiplying food; in **14:22–36** he does so by walking on the water. In the face of the disciples' fear, Jesus' words in verse 27 perhaps refer to his deity (Gk. *egō eimi*, "I am"; cf. Yahweh's words in Exod. 3:11–15; Isa. 43:10). Recognizing who he is, the disciples offer him their worship (v. 33).

That Peter is among those who worship Jesus (v. 33) suggests that he uses the address *Lord* in the deepest sense (vv. 28, 30). Peter's walking on the water—thus obeying Jesus, drawing on his power, and following his example—provides a model of faith for Christians. Overcome by fear and doubt, he begins to sink, showing "little faith" (v. 31). Here too he illustrates what happens when fear replaces faith in the sovereign Lord. Verses 34–36 further demonstrate Jesus' divine authority: the sick are healed merely by touching him.

In **15:1–9** the Pharisees and teachers of the law confront Jesus with the question of defilement (vv. 1–2). In Jesus' day the scribes were "men learned in the Torah," "rabbis," "ordained theologians," "teachers of the law" (NIV)—only one of whose tasks was the "inscribing" of sacred texts. Some such theologians aligned with the Sadducees, but the great majority supported the Pharisees. The name *Pharisees* means *the separate ones* (Heb. *pĕrûšîm*); they were organized into tightly knit, closed communities devoted to keeping the Law. As such, they distinguished themselves from the *ʿam hāʾāreṣ*, "people of the land" (cf. John 7:49). Still, unlike the Sadducees (who associated with the upper classes), they appealed to common folk. Most of the Pharisees were themselves laymen without social distinction. As such, they depended upon the scribes—or ordained clergy—within the party to provide theological direction and spiritual leadership (as a congregation today depends upon its minister).

The oral law—no less than the written law of the Old Testament—was considered by its bearers (v. 1) to be divine revelation binding upon Israel. Whereas the written law prescribed the ceremonial washing for priests alone (Exod. 30:17–21), the oral law made it obligatory for all Jews (v. 2).

In response to his questioners, Jesus quotes the fifth commandment (v. 4a; Exod. 20:12). Referring then to its application, Jesus quotes again from the written law (Exod. 21:17), rather than from the oral law. Then he exposes a threefold opposition to God's command. (1) The tradition of verses 5–6a, far from being or applying God's command, seeks to destroy it (vv. 3, 6). (2) The corban (Heb. *qorbān*, offering; Gk. *korban* [Mark 7:11]) tradition ostensibly honors the first commandment above the fifth but actually encourages human selfishness. By declaring his property corban, one was neither required to give it to the temple nor prevented from using it himself; but he did thereby keep it from his parents. Thus this tradition "puts casuistry above love"[18]—love both for one's closest neighbors (his parents) and for God (whose commandment is being rejected; cf. 22:37–40). (3) The main objects of Jesus' judgment are not those who employ the tradition but those who have devised and promoted it, namely, the "Pharisees and teachers of the law" (v. 1). In verses 3–6, what "*you* say" opposes what "*God* said." The rabbis actually instruct the son *not* to honor his father (v. 6a) and bind him instead to their tradition. Not content to supplement revelation with tradition, or even to elevate tradition above revelation, the rabbis seek to supplant the revelation with the tradition.

The appearance ("these people honor me with their lips," v. 8a) contradicts the reality ("their hearts are far from me," v. 8b). Behind the hypocrisy is pride: a teacher determined to enthrone himself in place of God *must* replace his Word with "rules taught by men" (v. 9b). In quoting Isaiah 29:13, Jesus appeals to divine revelation in the face of human tradition; he also associates Israel's teachers not with the prophet of judgment but with the objects of judgment!

Having pronounced judgment upon the Pharisees and teachers of the law, Jesus turns to the crowd and the disciples (**15:10–20**). Though still addressing the crowd in parables and reserving explanations for disciples (vv. 15–20), Jesus holds out hope for the crowd (v. 10). Not so for the Pharisees. It is not that they understand less than the crowd, but that they have rejected understanding. A parable might offend a member of the crowd because its meaning is obscure; the parable of verse 12 scandalizes the Pharisees because its meaning is clear. Such is the hardness of their opposition, and such is their blasphemy, that they stand under irreversible judgment (vv. 13–14).

The laws in Leviticus 11 concerning unclean animals served a twofold purpose: (1) the distinction between clean and unclean animals reminded Israel that God had set her apart from other nations to be his holy people (Exod. 19:5; Deut. 7:6); (2) these ceremonial laws pointed to a moral order. "Only the normal members of each sphere of creation, e.g., fishes with fins, counted as clean. This definition, which identified 'perfect' members of the animal kingdom with purity, was a reminder that God looked for moral perfection in his people. Carrion-eating birds and carnivorous animals were unclean because they also typified a man's sinful, destructive, and murderous instincts."[19]

Verse 11a points to the principle of a moral order. Real uncleanness lies not in food that passes through the body (v. 17), but in those qualities that dwell in the heart (vv. 18–19). Ceremonial laws find their justification in relation to moral laws; otherwise they lose their significance and become empty rituals. Having quoted the fifth commandment (v. 4), Jesus proceeds to refer to the next four commandments in order (v. 19). He focuses upon the second table of the Law, that is, upon attitudes and actions affecting personal relationships. Jesus does not attack ritual as such. Rather he points up the threefold danger of severing ceremonial law from moral law, of striving for ritual cleanness rather than for moral purity,

18. J. Jeremias, *New Testament Theology* (New York: Charles Scribner's Sons, 1971), 210.

19. Gordon J. Wenham, *The Book of Leviticus* (Grand Rapids: Eerdmans, 1979), 184.

and of allowing ritual correctness to conceal great moral evil (as in the corban tradition). Jesus concentrates upon the heart (vv. 18–19), upon what a person is, which inevitably expresses itself in what he says (v. 18), does (v. 19), and values (v. 3). With the dawn of the kingdom, the Old Testament distinction between Israel and other nations becomes obsolete. Jesus reconstitutes the people of God around himself—a people inclusive of Gentiles as well as Jews. Therefore the distinctions in Leviticus 11 no longer serve a redemptive purpose. "The distinction between clean and unclean foods is as obsolete as the distinction between Jew and Gentile."[20] (Cf. Mark 7:19; Acts 10:11–16, 28; Gal. 2:11–14.)

Jesus now enters Gentile territory (v. 21) and encounters a Canaanite woman (**15:21–28**). Both Jesus (by his choice of itinerary) and Matthew (by his arrangement of material) deliberately and visibly underscore the lesson of verses 10–20.

The woman's faith is evident in her appeal (v. 22). She acknowledges Jesus' messianic status and his ability to cure her daughter. Faith is further evident in her persistence. Nothing dissuades her, neither her knowledge that Jesus is the Jewish Messiah (v. 22), nor his initial silence (v. 23a), nor the disciples' efforts to get rid of her (v. 23b), nor Jesus' statement of purpose (v. 24), nor the maxim that underscores the statement (v. 26), nor the cumulative effect of those things. The effect of this manifold opposition is to celebrate her persistence (crowned by her witty retort [v. 27] to Jesus' maxim), and to give great force to Jesus' climactic utterance (v. 28).

By healing the daughter, Jesus reveals himself as the Gentiles' Savior. Here, as in 8:5–13, he heals at a distance (in keeping with his present mission to Israel, v. 24). Perhaps Jesus deliberately chose a maxim about food (v. 26) to make a connection between the healing of a Gentile and the abolishing of unclean foods (vv. 10–20).

Jesus now leaves one Gentile territory (v. 21) for another (v. 29a; the people praise "the God of Israel," v. 31; cf. 4:12–16). Verse 29b recalls 5:1–2; as Jesus exercised his authority there by teaching Jews, here he does so by healing and feeding Gentiles (**15:29–39**). A comparison with 14:13–21 reveals many similarities; the most notable difference is that the compassion shown there to Jews (14:14) is shown here to Gentiles (15:32). All the lessons of the earlier passage now apply to them.

Matthew now returns the reader to further disputes between Jesus and the religious leaders (**16:1–12**). The Pharisees and Sadducees together confront Jesus (v. 1; cf. 3:7). Their intention is hostile (the same verb, *test*, is used of Satan in 4:1). The signs of verse 3 are Jesus' mighty works, which occasioned his earlier conflict with Pharisees (12:22–42). The Jewish leaders' obtuseness contrasts sharply with the Gentiles' responsiveness (15:21–31). As in 15:8–9, Jesus' departure (v. 4) signals abandonment.

Jesus twice warns disciples against the yeast, that is, the teaching of the Pharisees and Sadducees (vv. 6, 11–12). Given the substantial doctrinal differences between the Pharisees and Sadducees, their close association in this passage is striking. For all their differences, the Pharisees and Sadducees are united in their human-centeredness. On the one hand, this expresses itself in the Pharisees' adherence to human traditions (15:1–9), their prideful hypocrisy (6:1–18), and their domination of others (23:4), and, on the other hand, in the Sadducees' protection of their status, wealth, and power. Far from reflecting a God-centered faith, the request for a sign (v. 1) is yet another attempt to resist Jesus, the incarnate God, and to perpetuate a human-centered mentality, whether the more religious form of the Pharisees, or the more secular form of the Sadducees.

The human-centered mentality presently threatens the disciples. Their worry over food betrays lack of trust (v. 8) in a loving Father's care (cf. 6:25–34) as expressed in the feeding of the multitudes (vv. 9–10). In the face of the appeal of the human-centered teaching, Jesus urges his followers to risk being utterly God-centered—the only remedy for anxiety.

Jesus knows that by this stage of his ministry both the people generally and the disciples will have drawn conclusions about him, and that these conclusions will differ markedly from each other. Jesus will again serve the crowds (17:14–18; 19:2) and debate the authorities (21:23–27; 22:15–32). Nonetheless the next passage (**16:13–20**) represents a turning point in his ministry; henceforth, he will concentrate increasingly upon instructing his disciples, to prepare them for what lies ahead (16:21–18:35).

In verses 13–14 Jesus inquires about the beliefs of the crowd, not the religious leaders (whose judgments would be far more negative than those expressed here). All the ascriptions of verse 14 express great respect for Jesus, yet none is an adequate response to what his ministry sets forth about his person and work.

In verses 15–16 Jesus now inquires about the beliefs of his disciples. The "you" in verse 15 is

20. Ibid.

plural (indicating that Peter answers as the disciples' representative) and emphatic (contrasting the disciples' judgment to the crowd's). Within Matthew's account of Jesus' ministry, Peter's response—"You are the Christ"—is the first direct affirmation of his messiahship. These words must be closely joined to the rest of the confession. It is not sufficient to call Jesus Messiah, if by that one means merely that he is the Son of David (cf. 15:22). For Jesus is the Son of God not merely by virtue of his messianic office, but also, and primarily, by virtue of his being. Anticipated in 14:33, Peter's confession affirms Messiah's deity.

As in the Beatitudes, Jesus has the right—as God the Son—to pronounce a person "blessed" (v. 17). The blessing in this case is the disclosure of verse 16; a comparison with 11:25–27 makes it clear that God the Father has revealed to Peter the truth about God the Son.

By the words *this rock* Jesus means not himself, nor his teaching, nor God the Father, nor Peter's confession, but Peter himself. The phrase is immediately preceded by a direct and emphatic reference to Peter. As Jesus identifies himself as the builder, the rock on which he builds is most naturally understood as someone (or something) other than Jesus himself. The demonstrative *this,* whether denoting what is physically close to Jesus or what is literarily close in Matthew, more naturally refers to Peter (v. 18) than to the more remote confession (v. 16). The link between the clauses of verse 18 is made yet stronger by the play on words, "You are Peter (Gk. *Petros*), and on this rock (Gk. *petra*) I will build my church." As an apostle, Peter utters the confession of verse 16; as a confessor he receives the designation *this rock* from Jesus. Moreover, while Jesus here addresses Peter individually ("you" in vv. 18–19 is always singular), he addresses him as representative of all the apostles (the authority granted Peter in v. 19 is bestowed on all the disciples in 18:18).

In verse 18b Jesus, not Peter, dominates the passage. It is he whom Peter confesses. It is he who utters the words of verses 17–19; whatever Simon is to be and to do is the effect of Jesus' authoritative declaration about him. The church belongs to Jesus, not to Peter. Jesus, not Peter, builds the church and protects it from destruction. Far from being a builder, Peter belongs to the building; he is *Petros,* a foundation stone in the edifice, a position he shares with other apostles (Eph. 2:19–21; Rev. 21:14).

Jesus does not deny the reality of the church in the Old Testament (v. 18b; cf. Acts 7:38); but he has come to reconstitute the people of God around his person. His church will commence (note the future tense "will build") in the wake of his death and exaltation (cf. Acts 1–2).[21]

"The gates of Hades" (v. 18b) will not conquer the church. This means that Satan and the demons under his control will never prevail against the church, but will on the contrary be vanquished by the church's Lord (cf. 12:25–29); and that the gates of the realm of death "will never close on the new community so that it is irretrievably extinguished"[22]—for Jesus will defeat death (Rev. 1:18). Moreover, Jesus conquers Satan and death by building his church. The church does more than withstand assaults from evil powers; it advances against them, which is why those powers so vehemently oppose the church and its leaders.

In verse 19, as in 7:21, God's kingdom is depicted as a realm to be entered; using the keys means having authority to permit or to prohibit entry. In accord with rabbinic usage, *binding* means prohibiting entry into the kingdom to those who reject the apostolic witness, and *loosing* means granting entry to those who accept the witness (cf. John 20:23; Acts 2:38–41). What the apostles bind and loose on earth ratifies the prior decision in heaven ("whatever you shall bind . . . *shall have been bound* in heaven," v. 19, NASB [emphasis added]). At least a measure of what God has already determined, he has revealed (cf. vv. 16–17). It is that revealed truth (whether the indicative of the gospel or the imperative of the commands) that enables Peter and the other apostles to make judgments (of "binding" or "loosing") concerning persons both within (18:18) and beyond (16:19) the church.

The New Testament does not support the ideas that Peter was the first bishop of Rome and that the apostolic succession is realized in the papacy. The true apostolic succession lies in the faithful transmission of the apostolic gospel. By this means Jesus builds his church (Acts 2:41–42; 6:2–4). The keys of the kingdom are still employed by church leaders committed to biblical truth and who on that basis make judgments about persons both beyond and within the church.

21. On the relation between the kingdom that Jesus comes to inaugurate, and the church that he comes to build, see George E. Ladd, "Kingdom of Christ, God, Heaven," in *Evangelical Dictionary of Theology,* ed. Walter A. Elwell (Grand Rapids: Baker, 1984), 611.

22. F. F. Bruce, *Matthew,* Scripture Union (Grand Rapids: Eerdmans, 1970), 55.

III. Jesus' Private Ministry in Galilee (16:21–18:35)

A. Teaching on Jesus' mission (16:21–17:27). For the first time in Matthew, Jesus foretells his death (**16:21–23**). One reason for the disclosure is the nearness of the event. Another is that in the wake of Peter's confession, Jesus wants to forestall false messianic ideas. Having just pronounced Peter blessed for his confession (v. 17), Jesus immediately warns his disciples to tell no one that he is the Christ (v. 20). Just how urgently the disciples needed both the warning (v. 20) and the disclosure (v. 21) is clear from Peter's response (v. 22) and from Jesus' counterresponse (v. 23). Having just received revelation from God the Father, Peter now (however unwittingly) rejects revelation from God the Son, heeds instead the voice of Satan, and confronts Jesus with the same temptation he faced in the wilderness (4:1–11).

Peter's response to the prediction of verse 21 shows that the prospect of Jesus' suffering was not acceptable even to those who believed him to be the Messiah. "Almost certainly the Jews of Jesus' day did not think that the Messiah would suffer."[23] And not only must Messiah suffer, but all who would follow him must willingly take the same path (**16:24–28**).

Jesus must suffer (v. 21), because the Father has so ordained (3:15) and because the Scriptures have so foretold (Luke 24:25–27). More precisely, the Scriptures prophesied the suffering of the Son of man (cf. Mark 9:12). The passage from which Jesus draws the title *Son of man* (see Dan. 7) makes no explicit reference to his suffering; yet Jesus, who has both unequalled wisdom to understand the Old Testament and unique authority to interpret it, identifies the Son of man of Daniel 7 with the Suffering Servant of Isaiah 53.

By crucifying Jesus, his enemies will unknowingly serve God's purpose. For the cross is the very place of redemption and forgiveness (20:28; 26:28). The Father vindicates the suffering Son of man by raising him from the dead (v. 21). That triumph is completed at his return (v. 27). As in Daniel 7:13–14, the Son of man is revealed as divine (the angels are *his*, not just his Father's, v. 27). He will come to reward each person for what he has done—the chief deed being one's response to the claims of Jesus (cf. vv. 24–26). The "coming" of verse 28 is not the parousia itself, but anticipations of it in various events which occur by virtue of Jesus' resurrection (v. 21) and as manifestations of his resurrection power—the coming of the Spirit, the Gentile mission, and the growth of the church.

The transfiguration of Jesus follows next in **17:1–13.** The mountain (v. 1) is usually identified as Hermon or Tabor. A more likely suggestion is Mount Meron, which is rather high (3963 feet), is located roughly between Caesarea Philippi and Capernaum (v. 24), and could easily be reached within a week. The anonymity of the mountain discourages readers from venerating a place rather than Christ himself.

Both Moses and Elijah met with God on Sinai (or Horeb—Exod. 34:1–28; 1 Kings 19:9–14). Glory enveloped Sinai for six days before God spoke to Moses from the cloud (Exod. 24:16; Matt. 17:1, 5). The shining of Jesus' face (v. 2) recalls Exodus 34:29–30 where Moses' "face was radiant" from speaking with Yahweh.

Interrupting Peter's offer (v. 4b) and underscoring Peter's confession (16:16), God speaks of Jesus exclusively and declares him to be his only Son (v. 5; cf. 3:17). The command of verse 5b (cf. Deut. 18:15) immediately concerns the teaching of 16:21–28 (cf. 2 Pet. 1:16–18).

Jesus' glory is not shared with Moses and Elijah (vv. 2–3). Moreover, it recalls not only Moses, but also Yahweh on the mountain. Whereas Moses' glory was reflected, Jesus' is inherent—Yahweh's own glory. Moses, Elijah, and the disciples are with Jesus as Moses was with Yahweh. But now "God with us" bridges the gap between the Father and the frail human beings trembling before his majesty. He comes to touch and speak to them, and dispel their fears (vv. 7–8).

In verse 9 Jesus foretells his resurrection, which means that he expects to die (16:21). But, the disciples reason (v. 10), if Elijah first comes to "restore all things" (v. 11; cf. Mal. 4:5–6), why should Messiah have to die? Because, says Jesus (vv. 11–12), the restoration takes place by unexpected means—the deaths of John and Jesus. Salvation is accomplished by Jesus' suffering (v. 12b; 20:28). John's most powerful witness to Messiah is his suffering and death. Far from forestalling Jesus' death, Elijah actually foreshadows it. Jesus is not glorified *without* suffering, but *through* suffering.

In **17:14–23** the healing of the epileptic boy also focuses on the disciples' unbelief. The child's epilepsy (cf. Mark 9:18) is caused by a demon bent on destroying him (vv. 15b, 18). The transfiguration does not crown Jesus' victory over Satan but introduces the final conflict. As before, the demon is banished and the person healed by Jesus' mighty word (v. 18).

Jesus attributes the disciples' inability to unbelief (vv. 16–17, 20). Having authority to cast out demons (10:1) does not make them

23. Gundry, *Matthew*, 338.

autonomous or automatic dispensers of healing power. Continued effectiveness demands ongoing dependence on God. The presence of faith matters more than its size (v. 20b); the disciples' "so little faith" (v. 20a) is really "no faith" (v. 17a).

The prophecy of verses 22–23 (which presupposes 16:21 and is thus more succinct) speaks of Jesus' being handed over to men; since the subject is unnamed, Jesus probably has in view both his enemies' malevolent design (16:21) and his Father's saving purpose (cf. Isa. 53:6, 12; Rom. 8:32). The disciples are again reminded that glory awaits suffering (cf. v. 12). Far from invalidating the promise of verse 20, Jesus' approaching death is the gateway to resurrection power (v. 23b).

The temple tax (**17:24–27**) in the amount of two drachmas was an annual levy on Jewish males between the ages of twenty and fifty for the support of the temple (cf. Exod. 30:11–16). A four-drachma coin (Gk. *statēr*) therefore sufficed to pay the tax for two (see v. 27).

The issue in verse 25 is different from that of 22:15–22. Jesus simply draws Peter's attention to the fact that kings do not collect taxes from their own sons but from the citizenry (v. 26). As both Jesus and Peter are royal sons (v. 26) of the heavenly King whose earthly habitation is the temple (cf. 23:21), they are exempt from the tax. Yet Jesus, while not obliged to pay the tax, freely does so to avoid giving offense (v. 27). "He who submits to the payment of tax is nonetheless the master of all things."[24]

B. Teaching about relationships among Jesus' followers (18:1–35). The teaching of 17:25–27 prompts the question of verse 1, which Jesus answers in the ensuing discourse, the fourth of five in Matthew. The subject concerns relationships and attitudes within the church.

The subject of **18:1–5** is true greatness. Jesus addresses disciples (v. 1), that is, the church (v. 17); verse 3 is not an appeal to nondisciples, but a solemn warning to professing disciples. As in 11:25–30, Jesus calls them to humility (v. 4). By presenting a little child (v. 2), a person of little value in Jewish society, he asks them to become the lowliest of the lowly. This will in turn affect the way they view other people. Verse 5 especially enjoins church leaders to deal gently with the little children under their care.

Jesus speaks of the peril of offenses in **18:6–9.** He speaks chiefly of dangers from within the church. Let members beware lest they be victims (v. 6) or agents (vv. 8–9) of sin. The inevitability of such offenses does not lessen the guilt of the offenders (v. 7). Better for a teacher to drown (and escape damnation) than to lead others into error, an offense worthy of damnation (v. 6; cf. 7:15–23). Unless leaders themselves are humble (vv. 3–4), they cannot help those under their care (v. 5; cf. 1 Pet. 5:2–3).

The Father's love for his children is discussed in **18:10–14.** God is the guardian of the "poor in spirit" within the church; their angels' task is to invoke his protection (vv. 10–11). The parable (vv. 12–14) depicts the Father's gracious initiative in response to angels' intercession for his children. The sheep of Luke 15:4 is a nonbeliever whom the Father saves, but that of Matthew is a church member who has drifted into sin and whom the Father seeks to restore. The situation is extremely grave; restoration is no certainty (v. 13a, "and *if* he finds it"; cf. Luke 15:5, "and *when* . . ." [emphasis added]). It is urgent that believers be arms of God's love to the erring.

Jesus' next topic in this section is the erring brother (**18:15–20**). The sin is committed by one Christian against another (vv. 15, 21). In the church's intense fellowship, such sin is perilous indeed, regardless of its exact nature (v. 18a). Whereas in 5:23–24 Jesus instructed the offending brother, here he speaks of the offended party's responsibility. A fourfold response is prescribed (vv. 15–17). The church (Gk. *ekklēsia*) of verse 17 is the local manifestation of the church universal (16:18); excommunication is only a last resort. Applying this passage requires attention also to 7:1–5 and 1 Corinthians 5. Verse 18 belongs with verses 15–17. The repentant brother is loosed from his sin, whereas the unrepentant is still bound to his. The church's decision is based upon God's judgment and revelation (as in 16:19). Verses 19–20 are integral to the section beginning in verse 15. They witness to the need for corporate prayer in face of the problem: the "two or three" of verses 19–20 are the very persons of verse 16. As verses 19–20 presuppose the Lord's Prayer, those who pray are expected to be both forgiving toward the erring brother (6:12; cf. 18:21–35) and vigilant, lest they be snared by the very sin they are seeking to combat (6:13). They pray for love for the brother, for his repentance and restoration; and they pray for wisdom to make the right judgments (cf. v. 18).

The subject of radical forgiveness (**18:21–22**) follows next. Peter's question in verse 21 is prompted by Jesus' teaching in verses 15–20. Peter is to be credited for his willingness to forgive, to do so repeatedly, and to do so (it is implied) as many as seven times (the rabbinic

24. D. Hill, *The Gospel of Matthew*, New Century Bible Commentary (Greenwood, S.C.: Attic, 1972), 272.

consensus was that a brother might be forgiven for a repeated sin up to three times).

Jesus does more than forbid vengeance; he transposes a cry of revenge (see Gen. 4:15, 23–24) into a call for forgiveness. Whether he says "seventy-seven times" (NIV) or "seventy times seven" (NIV marg.), his words reject a calculating, quantitative approach to forgiveness. Love within the church "is expressed by an indefatigable capacity to forgive the brethren."[25] The ensuing parable illustrates the lesson (note "therefore," v. 23).

In the parable of the unforgiving slave (**18:23–35**) the first slave owes the king ten thousand talents (v. 24), that is, several million dollars. Given the enormity of his debt, the slave's promise to repay everything is absurd (v. 26). The king does not merely postpone or reduce the debt—he cancels it. The second slave owes the first only a hundred denarii, that is, a few dollars; yet the latter responds in utter ruthlessness (vv. 28–30).

In response to the first debtor's hardness and ingratitude for the mercy shown him (v. 33), the king has him imprisoned for the rest of his life (the debt could not be repaid in the best of circumstances, how much less from prison).

The king is God the Father (v. 35a). As the hugeness of the first debt illustrates the enormity of sin, so its cancellation celebrates God's amazing grace. Like the slave, disciples are debtors (6:12) who deserve punishment, who cannot prevent it by their own actions, and who must therefore depend utterly upon God's grace—a vital truth, given Jesus' demand for radical obedience to the law. Christians obey the law not to earn God's forgiveness but to express gratitude for his forgiveness.

The burden of the parable is the effect of that experience upon Christian relationships (v. 35; cf. v. 21). Failure to forgive fellow believers (none of whose debts to each other could compare with those incalculable debts that God has cancelled) shows that one has never really understood God's forgiveness. The judgment threatening such a person is just as real and final (v. 34) as that which threatens the offender (cf. vv. 14–20)—strong incentive for offering genuine, not just apparent, forgiveness (v. 35b).

IV. Jesus' Ministry in Judea (19:1–25:46)

A. Teaching on the way to Jerusalem (19:1–20:34). Jesus begins his last journey to Judea (v. 1). While concentrating on the disciples (chap. 18), he still cares for the crowd (v. 2).

In **19:1–12** Jesus answers the question of divorce. The Pharisees test Jesus (v. 3; cf. 16:1) by drawing him into debate over Deuteronomy 24:1 (cf. v. 7) to gain further proof that he opposes Moses and therefore God. Also, as Jesus has entered Herod's domain (Perea, v. 1; cf. 14:1), they hope his answer will underscore John's preaching on divorce (14:4), arouse Herod's fury, and rid them of a dangerous enemy. Jesus declares (vv. 4–6) that based on God's revelation there is *no* valid reason for divorce (cf. v. 3); such action is *always* unlawful, for it severs the marital bond that God established (Gen. 2:24). Why then the later ruling? ask the Pharisees (v. 7). How can divorce be both unlawful (Gen. 2:24) and lawful (Deut. 24:1)?

Viewing Deuteronomy 24 in the context of the old covenant, Jesus agrees with the Pharisees' application. The husband was not required to divorce his wife (so Jesus says "permitted"); but if he did, the certificate was obligatory (so the Pharisees, who, unlike Jesus, mention the certificate, rightly say "command," v. 7). But Jesus is more concerned with explanation. Deuteronomy 24:1–4 was given to curb "hardness of heart," that is, resistance to God.

The fall (Gen. 3) explains men's hardness of heart toward God and each other; separated from God, Adam and Eve became alienated from one another. As in verses 4–6, Jesus goes back to Genesis 1–2. Before the fall "hardness of heart" did not exist, and thus no divorce and no need for the ruling of Deuteronomy 24. Now, with the dawn of the kingdom, paradise is to be restored. Jesus summons disciples to honor the unity and inviolability of marriage (Gen. 2:24).

Jesus maintains (v. 9) that a divorcing husband who "leaves" his wife and "cleaves" to a second woman (Gen. 2:24) commits adultery against his first wife. The lone exception, and the only lawful reason for terminating a marriage, is *porneia*—a Greek term embracing adultery, homosexuality, and bestiality. Verse 9 does not contradict verses 4–6. For if *porneia* has occurred, the marital bond is already severed; the divorce does not cause the rift but witnesses to an existing rift. In this case the remarriage of the innocent party is not adulterous.

Knowing their own fallenness, the disciples shrink from the call to permanent and binding marriage (vv. 4–9). They reason that "it is better not to marry" (v. 10) than to enter into a union where the obligations are so strict and the risks of sin so high. The *word* (Gk. *logos*) of verse 11a is not the statement of verse 10 but the teaching (NIV) of verses 4–9. Verse 11b speaks of disciples whom God calls to marriage on the terms of Genesis 1–2, whom he empow-

25. Jeremias, *New Testament Theology*, 221.

ers for the task, and who are therefore able (v. 12c) to accept the stricture of verse 9. But if God wills marriage for some, he commands others to obey him by abstaining from marriage (v. 12). Eunuchs once excluded from the assembly (Deut. 23:1), Jesus now welcomes (v. 12)—further evidence of the dawning grace (cf. Acts 8:26–40).

Jesus' teaching on marriage is followed by teaching on children (**19:13–15**) and money (19:16–26), three subjects vitally related to each other (cf. Eph. 5:21–6:9). Little children (including infants; see Mark 10:16a; Luke 18:15) are brought for Jesus' blessing (v. 13a). The disciples rebuke them (v. 13b), that is, the children (v. 14a), not their parents; in stark contrast, Jesus receives them. In 18:2–5 he used a child to model discipleship; here he blesses the children themselves (otherwise the act of v. 15a, which has no counterpart in chap. 18, is misleading). The words *such as these* (v. 14b) indicate not a comparison but a group, namely, that of verse 14a (note the connecting "for"). God welcomes children themselves into his kingdom and invites them to call him Father.

In **19:16–22** Jesus meets the rich young man. How can I gain eternal life? (i.e., enter God's kingdom, v. 24) is the man's question (v. 16). Jesus replies, "Why do you ask me about what is good?" (cf. Mark 10:18, "Why do you call me good?"). Jesus wants the man to think of God and his commandments—which does not require turning away from Jesus (see v. 21). To know God's goodness is to love him; and to love him is to obey his commands (cf. John 14:15).

In answer to the question of verse 18, Jesus stresses love of neighbor by referring to Exodus 20:12–16 and Leviticus 19:18. The claim of verse 20 reveals the man's ignorance (v. 22 shows that he has not loved others as himself), his zeal (the question of v. 16 must have arisen from a desire to do works beyond those required by the Law), and his anxiety (he fears that his good works will be inadequate for inheriting eternal life).

For the man to be perfect (Gk. *teleios,* complete), he must both correct and supplement his way of life. The command concerning possessions and the poor will reveal the man's true attitude toward God (6:19–24) and his neighbor. Having first directed attention to God and his commandments (v. 17), Jesus now commands the man to follow *him.* Obeying God, and being perfect, means submitting to the lordship of Jesus (7:13–27). Jesus exposes the inadequacy of the man's commitment to God. But the moment of judgment is a moment of grace, for Jesus invites him into discipleship. That alone will end his false striving and nagging anxiety (6:25–34; 11:28–30).

Confronted with the choice, the man renews his allegiance to money (v. 22). Perhaps he is sad because somehow he cannot serve both God and money (6:24). By his decision he robs himself both of enjoying present wealth (6:19–34) and of obtaining true riches (v. 30; 13:44–46).

As the man's struggle demonstrates (v. 22), money has such power over its slaves that they cannot free themselves (**19:23–26**). The disciples reason (v. 25) that if the rich—whose wealth signals God's favor—are hardly saved, is there hope for anyone? Verse 26 both confirms that anyone (not just the rich) can become money's slave, and declares that God alone can rescue from that bondage.

The focus of **19:27–30** is on the riches of the kingdom. At the kingdom's consummation, the existing order will be overturned, present sacrifices rewarded, and the kingdom's blessings fully realized for Jesus' followers (vv. 27–30; cf. 5:3–10; 6:10). In that day the apostles will share in Jesus' glorious reign by governing the twelve tribes of Israel (v. 28), that is, the church (16:18) or saved Israelites (elect Israel from within ethnic Israel; cf. Rom. 9–11).

Tempering the teaching on rewards in verses 27–30 is the parable of the generous owner (**20:1–16**). All workers, including those hired for just one hour, receive a full day's wage. Responding to the protests of the first group, the owner explains that he treated them with justice (v. 13), and the last group with generosity (v. 15). The owner represents God; the story celebrates his incalculable goodness to his children. Just as surely as they do not deserve it, he has the right to freely bestow it (vv. 14–15). "God's love cannot be portioned out in quantities nicely adjusted to the merits of individuals. There is such a thing as the twelfth part of a denar. . . . But there is no such thing as a twelfth part of the love of God."[26]

Jesus spoke in 16:21 and 17:22–23 of his coming suffering at the hands of the Jews; here he mentions Gentiles as agents of the Jews' evil purpose. This third prediction of the passion and triumph (**20:17–19**) provides a foil to the petty ambitions of the disciples (vv. 20–24), anticipates the climactic verse 28, and reminds readers at what great personal cost God bestows grace upon his people (cf. vv. 14–15).

The request of the mother of Zebedee's sons (**20:20–28**) arises from the promise of 19:28; James and John seek the thrones immediately

26. T. W. Manson, *The Sayings of Jesus* (London: SCM Press, 1975), 220.

flanking Jesus' own. That the request comes from this source may be attributed to the closeness of these men to Jesus (cf. 17:1) and to family ties—if in fact the wife of Zebedee was the sister of Mary the mother of Jesus (cf. John 19:25). Jesus calls the request ignorant (v. 22a) for the following reasons.

The cup represents Jesus' death (vv. 18–19), and, since he is the sin-bearer (1:21), his experience of God's wrath (cf. 26:39). So the sons' boast of verse 22b, however sincere, is very naive. Even if the sons of Zebedee now (after the three predictions) accept the inevitability of Jesus' death, they barely understand its meaning (cf. 20:28; 26:26–28). Had they perceived that Jesus was to bear iniquities and suffer the divine wrath, would they have declared themselves able to drink his cup? Jesus' prophecy (v. 23a) is fulfilled in James' martyrdom (Acts 12:2) and John's persecution (Rev. 1:9).

The Father has indeed reserved these two thrones for chosen apostles. To judge from the immediate context, the seats belong to those who identify most closely with Jesus' service and suffering (v. 28), and who therefore are the least ambitious and the least calculating. They will be astounded to learn that they have been given the seats of honor (cf. 25:37–39); they would willingly take those furthest from him. Those most like Jesus will be seated closest to him.

The ambition of James and John arouses the indignation—and proud, competitive spirit—of the other ten disciples (v. 24). A crucial choice must now be made. On the one hand, the Twelve may use power as do the Gentile rulers—to dominate people (v. 25). The rulers' power serves their pride; by asserting power they keep their subjects beneath them. On the other hand, the disciples may choose to serve people in order to release power. The apostles are endowed with the stupendous authority of Jesus himself (10:1; cf. 28:18–20). Yet as those enslaved to Jesus the Lord, they have no right to use power to dominate others or to advance themselves. On the contrary, their slavery to Jesus manifests itself as slavery to other people (vv. 26–27), which proves to be the very means by which God releases true power. Disciples' greatness lies not *beyond* but precisely *in* service.

Jesus embodies the teaching of verses 26–27, supremely in his atoning death. His death is redemptive. Jesus liberates from the bondage and guilt of sin, at great cost to himself. He dies for many. "Many" alludes to Isaiah 53:11, 12 (Heb. *rabbîm*) and expresses the breadth of Jesus' salvation: he dies not just for the few—Israel—but for the many—all nations. Before the gospel of liberation from sin is taken to the Gentiles, the Savior must liberate them. The work of salvation precedes the news of salvation. Finally, Jesus dies as the substitute. As the sin-bearer (1:21) he dies in the place of the many.

In Matthew the healing of two blind men (**20:29–34**) occurs as Jesus leaves Jericho (the old city, seventeen miles northeast of Jerusalem). This passage recalls 9:27–31. But here Jesus issues no command to silence (this near to the cross there is less need to protect against false messianism). Nor does this passage emphasize faith (cf. 9:28–29). Rather, in keeping with verse 28, the stress falls on Jesus as the compassionate Servant (v. 34). Jesus uses his great power to heal others, not to save himself.

B. Arrival in Jerusalem (21:1–22). In the triumphal entry (**21:1–11**) Jesus fulfills and enacts Zechariah 9. His commands are exactly obeyed (vv. 6–7). A king marching to war would choose a horse; but the lowly donkey (and the especially lowly colt) was the eminently right choice for a king on a mission of peace. Jesus commands that the mother also be brought, in keeping with the prophecy (Zech. 9:9) and the colt's youth (Mark 11:2). He mounts the colt where he sits on garments. Because Israel is rejecting Jesus, Matthew omits the words *righteous and having salvation* (Zech. 9:9). For the same reason, he replaces Zechariah 9:9a ("Rejoice greatly, O Daughter of Zion!") with Isaiah 62:11b ("Say to the Daughter of Zion")—"an evangelistic challenge to unconverted Israel."[27]

In verse 9 the crowd acclaims Jesus with words from Psalm 118:25–26 (one of the Hallel psalms associated with Passover). The garments signal Jesus' royalty (Matt. 21:8). The branches recall Psalm 118:27, "With boughs in hand." The crowd rightly hails Jesus as "the Son of David . . . who comes in the name of the Lord" (Matt. 21:9; cf. 1:1; 11:3). Yet Messiah is more than a prophet (v. 14; cf. 16:14) coming in Yahweh's name; he is also Yahweh himself (16:16). Moreover, God has come to give his final answer to the cry, "Hosanna" ("Save now!"). Jesus enters Jerusalem to "save his people from their sins" (1:21) by dying for them (20:28).

Now it is Sunday, the tenth of Nisan, four days before the preparations for the Passover meal. The Law required that Passover be celebrated in Jerusalem, that every Jewish male participate annually in the festival, and that each worshiper offer animal sacrifice (Deut.

27. Gundry, *Matthew,* 408.

16:1–8, 16–17). These stipulations Jesus obeys; yet he offers not an animal but himself—the final Passover sacrifice (20:28; 26:17–30).

Now it is Monday, the eleventh of Nisan, when Jesus enters the temple (**21:12–17**). The merchants bought the requisites for sacrifice and then sold them to worshipers. Traveling from afar, most worshipers brought no offerings with them. The money changers replaced the prevalent Roman currency with Tyrian, the closest equivalent to the old Hebrew coinage. (The reason for the stipulation was thus not that Roman coins bore offensive engravings such as the emperor's image, for Tyrian coins bore heathen symbols too.)

Despite Jesus' tribal origin (Judah, not Levi, 1:1–17), Jesus has authority to take the action of verse 12. He is "greater than the temple" (12:6); he enters *his* temple (cf. v. 13, "My house").

Jesus calls them robbers (v. 13b, quoting Jer. 7:11)—both the merchants (for their exorbitant prices) and the money changers (for their exorbitant rates of exchange); among the sins indicted in Jeremiah 7 are oppression and stealing (vv. 6, 9). As Yahweh comes to his temple to purify the priesthood (Mal. 3:3–4), Jesus tacitly judges the priests for tolerating corrupt commerce. The men in question are also robbers by their very presence, for they usurp the place that God ordained as a house of prayer (v. 13a, quoting Isa. 56:7). Furthermore, Jesus expels the tradesmen because they operate in the Court of the Gentiles. The temple was to be "a house of prayer for all nations" (Isa. 56:7); yet the one place reserved for Gentiles was being taken from them.

Jesus' actions against favoritism are seen in verses 14–17 in which he reverses 2 Samuel 5:8. By healing the blind and the lame right within the temple, Jesus defies the Jews' assertion that the blind and lame should be barred from God's house (2 Sam. 5:8b RSV). In verses 15–16 Jesus receives the children, again in the face of indignation (cf. 19:13–15). The children's praise, he declares (quoting Ps. 8), is rightly ascribed to *him* (cf. Ps. 8:1, 9) and is the means appointed for silencing his enemies' unbelief (v. 15a; cf. Ps. 8:2). He then abandons his antagonists (v. 17; cf. 16:4). His need for lodging is provided in Bethany, in the home of Lazarus (cf. John 12:1–2).

In **21:18–22** Jesus uses a withering fig tree to teach an important lesson. "Because it was not the season for figs" (Mark 11:13), Jesus expected *not* to find fruit. His act is terribly shocking. Jesus wants the act to unsettle his disciples. This is a visible parable meant to jolt witnesses into an awareness of reality (see also Luke 13:6–9). Israel is the tree in question (cf. Jer. 8:13; Mic. 7:1–6). As Jesus—"God with us"—curses the tree so that it immediately withers, never to bear fruit again, so God is about to answer Israel's unfruitfulness (Matt. 3:10) and unbelief with sudden and irretrievable catastrophe (cf. 24:15–21; and the parables of 21:28–22:14).

To believe (vv. 21–22) is to depend on God (he, not faith, is sovereign) and his Word. Verse 22 must be qualified by the petition of Matthew 6:10 (cf. 1 John 5:14–15).

C. Confrontations in Jerusalem (21:23–23:39). The question of Jesus' authority is the next subject (**21:23–27**). "These things" (v. 24) are Jesus' teaching (v. 23), his miracles (v. 14), and especially his cleansing of the temple (vv. 12–13). In verses 24–25 Jesus makes explicit the basic question (Is one's authority human or divine?) and implies that John's authority has the same source as his.

The questioners' cowardice (v. 26) conceals their unbelief (v. 25), which in turn reveals their blindness to the divine authority behind both John and Jesus (cf. 11:16–19). For Jesus to say that God authorized him would not bring the questioners to faith. Still, that is just what they want Jesus to say, so that they might expose the absurdity of his claim. Instead it is they who are exposed.

The parable of the two sons (**21:28–32**) is the first of three parables in which Jesus continues the controversies with the religious leaders. The father (v. 30) represents God who sent John to show Israel how to enter the kingdom (v. 31; cf. vv. 24–27; 3:2). As the father asks both sons to work in his vineyard, John's message was for both Israel's leaders ("John came to you," v. 32a; cf. v. 23) and the whole populace, including its most disreputable members (v. 32b). "Like the first son, the publicans and prostitutes repented at the preaching of John the Baptist after exhibiting carelessness toward the law. Like the other son, the Jewish leaders refused John's message despite their claimed allegiance to the law."[28] The leaders stand doubly condemned; for they resist grace as evidenced both in John's preaching and in the lives of his audience. Responses to John and Jesus are inextricably bound together, as verses 23–27 demonstrate and as verses 33–46 will further demonstrate (cf. Luke 7:18–50).

The parable of the tenants (**21:33–46**) continues Jesus' polemic against the Jewish leaders. The landowner is Yahweh, the vineyard Israel (cf. Isa. 5:1–7), and the tenants the people, especially their leaders. The two groups of

28. Ibid., 424.

servants stand for the earlier and later Old Testament prophets, respectively. The son and heir is Jesus the Son of God, who inherits and rules over God's kingdom.

The tenants' treatment of the servants illustrates Israel's response to Yahweh's prophets before the coming of Jesus, as amply documented in the Old Testament (cf. 23:30–37). The tenants kill the son because they know who he is. Verse 39 reflects the fact that Jesus is killed outside the walls of Jerusalem (27:31–32).

Recently acclaimed in verse 9 as the Coming One of Psalm 118:26, Jesus now identifies himself in verse 42 as the rejected and newly vindicated stone of Psalm 118:22–23. He whom Israel rejects, Yahweh makes the very "capstone" (Matt. 21:42 NIV) of the building. As in the parable, it is Israel's rejection of God's Son that chiefly accounts for God's judgment (vv. 40–44)—a judgment culminating in the destruction of Jerusalem in A.D. 70 (cf. 22:7). The Stone is not only exalted, but also—for that very reason—dangerous (v. 44; cf. Isa. 8:14). The coming judgment will crush this vaunted human kingdom (ruled by the Pharisees' religious humanism and the Sadducees' secular humanism), and erect on its ashes the kingdom of God under Messiah's rule (Dan. 2:34–35, 44–45). The new tenants (vv. 41, 43) and the building of which Jesus is the capstone (v. 42) represent the church (16:18)—the New Israel consisting of Jews and Gentiles.

The parable of the wedding banquet (**22:1–14**) is the third parable of judgment (note its affinities with the previous two, 21:28–46). These parables, together with the controversies of 22:15–46, prepare for the woes of chapter 23.

The king in this parable is God the Father; the king's son is Jesus (cf. 21:37). The Father honors the Son for his redemptive work. "The marriage feast . . . is a figure for the Messianic age with all its joys."[29]

Verses 3–6 illustrate God's call to Israel through Old Testament prophets, and John and Jesus, and Israel's repudiation of the call. Verse 7 depicts the coming destruction of Jerusalem (cf. 21:41). Verses 9–10 (where streets become country roads) illustrate the coming mission to Gentiles; as in 28:19, the call is all-inclusive (v. 9, "anyone," and v. 10, "all the people").

The wedding hall filled with guests (v. 10a) represents the church, although it is a mixed company—both good and bad are present (v. 10; cf. 13:36–43, 47–50). The true disciple, unlike the false, obeys Jesus' teaching. The wedding clothes (vv. 11–12) represent disciples' good deeds—the proof, not the cause, of their salvation (7:13–29). Verse 14b speaks not of predestination but of God's judgment upon human responses to Jesus (the "for" of v. 14 provides a link to vv. 11–13). God rejects those who reject Jesus—whether they be nondisciples (like those who refuse the invitation) or false disciples (like the man without the proper garment). Verses 11–13 prefigure the final judgment, when everyone—disciples included—will be rewarded "according to what he has done" (16:27).

The next pericope (**22:15–22**) raises the question of paying taxes to Caesar, one of the hottest issues of the day. As Herod Antipas governed under Roman rule, the Herodians favored paying the tax. Like the people in general, the Pharisees paid the tax but found it economically burdensome and politically odious. If Jesus favors the tax, the Pharisees gain a means of arousing the populace against him; if he opposes it, the Herodians might charge him with treason against Rome. So, it seems, Jesus is trapped (v. 15).

Bearing as it does Caesar's portrait (a bust of Tiberius) and inscription (which ascribed divinity to the emperor), the coin belongs to Caesar; so it is right that it be given to him (v. 21). The plural "things that are Caesar's" (v. 21 RSV) embraces all the ruler's lawful requirements. If one is to submit to the civil authority without succumbing to statism and emperor worship, he must be enslaved to the one true God (cf. 6:24). By setting God over against Caesar, Jesus tacitly protests against the coin's blasphemous inscription. Only by worshiping God alone can one obey Caesar without becoming his slave. Normally, the Christian obeys God by obeying the civil authority (Rom. 13:1–7); if need be, he obeys God rather than men (Acts 5:29). Jesus' answer amazes his interrogators (v. 22); he has proven himself to be just what they had insincerely affirmed him to be (v. 16)! Their trap having failed (except to ensnare themselves), they depart (but see Luke 23:2).

The next paragraph involves a question about the resurrection (**22:23–33**). The far-fetched case (vv. 25–28) serves the Sadducees' apologetic purpose; the Mosaic teaching in question is Deuteronomy 25:5–10. But Jesus' response exposes a twofold error.

Verses 25–28 imply that resurrection life (if there were such) would restore present conditions. Jesus echoes the Old Testament's teaching about the resurrection itself. But concerning the nature of the resurrected state, he reveals new truth (v. 30): present conditions are not to be merely resumed but surpassed.

29. Manson, *The Sayings of Jesus*, 225.

The resurrected will be like angels, in that they will become immortal (cf. 1 Cor. 15:53–54) and will therefore no longer need to marry or to bear offspring. This does not mean that present marriages will be annulled. Yet they are not simply resumed but incorporated into a higher order. In that day marriages will evidence far greater freedom and intimacy than is now possible. Then the woman and those seven husbands can love one another without favoritism, exploitation, or jealousy. The question of verse 28 will have become irrelevant.

The Sadducees' denial of the resurrection betrays a more fundamental error. Thus, rather than citing prooftexts for personal resurrection (e.g., Job 19:25–27; Dan. 12:2), Jesus quotes a passage about the covenant (Exod. 3:6). At the heart of the covenant is the promise of the closest relationship between Yahweh and his people (Jer. 31:33; Matt. 1:23; 28:20). While relatively few and late, Old Testament promises of personal resurrection arise directly out of what the Bible reveals from the very beginning about God. It is inconceivable that the God who uttered the promises of Genesis 12:1–3 would ever break that covenant, or that he would allow death to sever that bond. In identifying himself to Moses as God of the patriarchs, Yahweh affirms that they cannot be finally dead. On the contrary, they will participate in the life of the kingdom together with all the people of God (Matt. 8:11). With Jesus' own resurrection (Matt. 28), the logic of the covenant becomes plainer (cf. Acts 2:24; Rom. 8:31–39), and the hope of the covenant stronger (1 Cor. 15).

Now the Pharisees attempt to trip up Jesus in a discussion concerning the great commandments (**22:34–40**). They renew their opposition to Jesus (vv. 34–35), although he has affirmed their view of resurrection and offered a brilliant argument in its favor. Their agreement with Jesus on a theological particular does not mitigate their determination to destroy him.

If there was in fact one "greatest commandment," it was vital that "an expert in the law" should know it. An evil design lies behind the question; but the man himself comes to view Jesus more sympathetically than those who sent him (cf. Mark 12:28).

Jesus responds (vv. 37–40) by quoting Deuteronomy 6:5 and Leviticus 19:18 (v. 39), and in this order, Jesus teaches that one's supreme calling is to love God (v. 38); that one must first love God if he is to love his neighbor; and that one shows how well he loves God by the way he treats his neighbor. Israel's love is to be directed wholly and exclusively to Yahweh (Deut. 6:4), not shared with false gods (Deut. 4:15–31). That love finds expression in consistent obedience to Yahweh's commands, as now set forth by Jesus (cf. Luke 6:46; John 14:15). Israel loves Yahweh in response to his saving acts (Deut. 1–3), a gratitude now intensified by virtue of Jesus' work (1 John 4:19). Deuteronomy 6:5 does not describe separate compartments of the self, but emphasizes that a person must love God with his whole being, with every capacity at his command. Leviticus 19 commands not that Israelites love themselves, but that they love others as they in fact love themselves; the whole focus is on the other party. As is clear from the echo of Leviticus 19:18 in 19:34, the love shown to fellow Israelites must embrace the resident alien as well. We show love for God by showing love for neighbor (cf. Luke 2:41–52)—starting with fellow Christians (John 13:34–35), including those of other ethnic groups (Gal. 3:28; Eph. 3:6). The entire Old Testament is based upon and gives guidance for obeying these two commandments (v. 40).

Now Jesus poses a question to the Pharisees, asking them about the sonship of Messiah (**22:41–46**). Jesus is truly the son of David (1:1–17), but not merely so. For he is preeminently the Son of God (16:16) and thus David's Lord. As Jesus now reveals, the Old Testament itself (Ps. 110) witnesses to Messiah's deity, to both the distinction of person and the identity of being between God the Father ("the LORD") and God the Son ("my Lord"). The Pharisees do not acknowledge Jesus' messiahship, much less his deity. Only a person who recognizes Jesus as both God and man could understand and answer the question of verse 45. Having been repeatedly defeated in debate (v. 46), Jesus' enemies now have but one course of action (26:3–4).

Matthew 23 climaxes the section beginning at 21:23 and includes the five debates (21:23–27; 22:15–46) and the three parables of judgment (21:28–22:14).

Jesus begins this chapter by describing the failure of the Jewish religious leaders (**23:1–36**). Verses 2–7, 25–36 describe their hypocrisy. Their practice contradicts their teaching. Insofar as they represent Moses, they are to be obeyed (vv. 2–3a). Yet what they demand of others, they do not demand of themselves (vv. 3b–4a). How could they care about the pressures that the others feel (v. 4b; cf. 11:28–30)? Their piety conceals their wickedness. By wearing large phylacteries (in literal fulfillment of Deut. 6:8) and tassels (as prescribed in Num. 15:38–39), and by seeking places and titles of honor (Matt. 23:5–7), they both express and mask their pride. Their ritual purity both contradicts and conceals hearts defiled and defiling (vv. 25–28). Even as they pay homage to Old Testament saints (vv. 29–30), they betray their descent from those who killed the prophets (v. 31) by attacking Jesus and his followers (v. 34; cf. 10:16–23). Verse 35 encompasses the whole Hebrew canon, from righteous Abel (Gen. 4:8) to Zechariah (2 Chron. 24:20–22), the first and last martyrs of the Old Testament.

Verses 13–24 describe their blindness. They vehemently oppose Jesus and his message, and seek to discredit him in the minds of the crowd. Jesus does not censure their missionary zeal but their effect on converts. Not merely is the convert kept from the true gospel, but he becomes so zealous for his teachers' doctrine (cf. 15:1–9) that he outdoes them in promoting it—making him twice as fit for hell as they.

The leaders are blind to reality (vv. 16–22). ". . . A creditor cannot place a lien on the Temple or the altar. The Temple and the altar provide no surety, therefore, and make oaths taken in their name meaningless. But a creditor might well claim the gold dedicated by his debtor to the Temple or the gift offered by his debtor on the altar."[30] Arguing from the lesser to the greater, Jesus reverses that position. The temple makes the gold sacred, and the altar the gift (vv. 17, 19); so swearing by temple or altar is a genuine oath, and a more meaningful one than swearing by gold or gift. Not only is the reasoning of verse 16 invalid, but the whole view is flawed, for it takes no account of God—who gives the temple and its contents their meaning (v. 21). Such fine distinctions (vv. 16, 18) offer no escape from the responsibility of oath-keeping or from accountability to God (cf. 5:33–37).

The leaders are also blind to fundamentals (vv. 23–24). Besides the grain, new wine, and oil (Deut. 14:23), the Pharisees tithed garden herbs in accord with their view of Leviticus 27:30. Jesus validates this practice (v. 23b). The weightier matters are not the more difficult but the more important ones (thus NIV)—justice, mercy, and faithfulness. Jesus echoes Old Testament prophecy (Mic. 6:8; Zech. 7:9) and teaches (as in 22:37–40) that one shows love for God by loving his neighbor. In the age of Moses, there was no contradiction between tithing (even the strict kind of v. 23) and being just, merciful, and faithful; indeed tithing afforded a superb means of showing faithfulness to God and generosity to others. But severed from the theology and morality expressed in the Law's weightier matters, tithing lost its raison d'être. The offenders' preoccupation with tithing blinds them (v. 24a) to the need for the other and becomes a substitute for it. Having carefully strained out a much smaller unclean gnat, they swallow a camel—a much larger unclean animal (Lev. 11:4, 20–23)!

Jesus now turns his comments to the judgment upon Jerusalem (**23:37–39**). Doom is about to befall Israel. Such will be God's response to the nation's accumulated sins, and her repeated and consistent rejection of his servants and his Word—culminating now in her repudiation of his Son and his people (vv. 34, 37). Jesus calls the temple "your house" (v. 38), because it is now to be abandoned by God (cf. 24:1–2; Ezek. 8–11). Yet even amidst the prophecy of certain doom, there is hope. The "woes" are not irreversible sentences of condemnation, but anguished warnings of judgment calling the leaders to repentance and faith before it is too late (cf. 3:7–10). Moreover, beyond the judgment that is to befall the present generation, there is hope for Israel. The mission to Jews is to continue until Jesus returns (10:23). The judgment that climaxes in the destruction of Jerusalem (A.D. 70) is itself meant to awaken Israel to the enormity of her sin and to bring her to repentance and faith. Thus stirred into spiritual awareness, Israel will be ready to welcome Jesus upon his return, and to utter Psalm 118:26 with far greater meaning than was the case at his triumphal entry (v. 39; cf. 21:9).

By denouncing the way of the teachers of the law and the Pharisees, Jesus holds up for his disciples a model to be avoided. He also presents to them a model to be followed.

The Jewish leaders are human-centered (15:1–9) and self-centered (23:5–7). By contrast, disciples are to focus on God the Father (v. 9) and God the Son (vv. 8, 10). The prohibitions of verses 8–10 strongly affirm the Father's sovereignty and the Son's lordship over the whole church, leaders included. Verse 10 does not exclude teachers from the church (cf. 28:20; Eph. 4:11), but it does warn them against lording it over those under their care (Matt. 18) and against trying to use authority independently of Jesus' lordship over them.

A God-centered outlook is the surest way to combat pride and hypocrisy, and to cultivate humility (cf. 6:5–6). Unlike the hypocrite, the humble person is marked by integrity (the external expresses rather than obscures the internal; cf. v. 26; 15:10–20), and loyalty to God (he is numbered among God's servants rather than God's enemies). It is this very person whom God exalts (v. 12, where the passives denote divine activity)—the person least intent upon being exalted.

The humble person is ready for service (v.

30. Gundry, *Matthew*, 463.

11). For he is not concerned about his status, not always thinking about moving as quickly as possible beyond the service into the position of master, and not concerned to change from being the least to being the greatest, which is why Jesus acclaims him the greatest. The greatness lies precisely in the service (cf. 20:20–28).

D. Jesus' teaching about the future (24:1–25:46). In Matthew **24:1–3** Jesus predicts the destruction of the temple. Having abandoned the temple (v. 1; cf. 23:38–39) and foretold its utter destruction (v. 2), Jesus takes his seat upon the Mount of Olives opposite the temple—an indication that the ensuing discourse, the last of the five, is delivered by One with supreme authority (cf. 5:1; 24:35).

The disciples' question in verse 3 prompts Jesus' teaching about the future destruction (**24:4–25**). It must be emphasized that the disciples' question makes the closest connection between the destruction of the temple and the end of history, and that Jesus' discourse responds directly to this question. Messianic pretenders will gain a huge following by claiming to represent or even to be Jesus (v. 5), by imitating his miracles (v. 24), and by sanctioning lawlessness (vv. 11–12). So powerful will be the deception that some will renounce the faith (v. 10), and even the elect will nearly succumb (v. 24). The safeguard is adherence to Jesus' teachings (v. 25; cf. Rev. 13:11). Second Thessalonians 2:1–12 describes the last and worst of the many antichrists (1 John 2:18) at work throughout the period.

The threat and the actual outbreak of war will mark the whole period (vv. 6–7). But let disciples not be alarmed: such conflicts are inevitable until God's rule is fully established (v. 6); and the Lord of the harvest will allow nothing to thwart his global mission (v. 14). And let disciples beware lest such conditions become an excuse for evading their prime responsibility of preaching the gospel to the nations, including those at war. At the end, such war will be intensified, and earthly struggles will culminate in the last battle between Christ and Satan (2 Thess. 2:8; Rev. 19:11–20:10).

The famines result from natural disasters and from widespread warfare (v. 7; on the worsening of such conditions as the end approaches, see Rev. 6–16). In the larger biblical picture, such upheavals become instrumental in the establishing of the new heavens and the new earth (2 Pet. 3:3–13).

Christians will experience the sufferings of men in general, but many other sufferings too because of their allegiance to Jesus (v. 9b). The very nations they evangelize (v. 14) will turn against them (v. 9). In face of the twofold threat from persecution and false teaching (vv. 10–12), Jesus challenges disciples to stand firm in the hope of the end (vv. 13–14).

The gospel is God's appointed means for calling his elect from the nations (vv. 14, 31)—a purpose aided, not thwarted, by persecution (vv. 9–14; cf. 10:17–20). Only when this purpose is accomplished shall the end come.

The Israel of Jesus' generation (Gk. *genea,* 23:36; cf. 24:34) is destined for catastrophe culminating in the Romans' destruction of Jerusalem and the temple in A.D. 70 (cf. 23:33–38).

The unparalleled terrors of the war with Rome call for the swiftest flight possible (vv. 16–20). Worst of all, the temple itself, "the holy place," will be desecrated, in fulfillment of prophecy (v. 15; cf. Dan. 9:27; 11:31)—as indeed happened when Roman soldiers "brought their legionary standards into the sacred precincts, set them up opposite the eastern gate, and offered sacrifice to them."[31]

By heeding Jesus' warnings, the disciples have hope of escape (v. 25). Moreover, while this is to be the worst disaster ever to befall Israel, it is limited in scope and will have a definite end. Once it is over, history will continue (v. 21b; cf. Luke 21:20–24). The events of verses 15–21 are catastrophic but not apocalyptic. The warnings of verses 16–20 would make no difference amidst the cosmic upheaval associated with the end of history.

The deceivers' "great signs and miracles" (v. 24) are paltry when compared to the apocalyptic signs of the coming of the Son of man (**24:26–31**). Unlike the localized appearances adduced by the false teachers (v. 26), the glorious advent of the Son of man will be universal in scope (v. 27) and effect (vv. 30, 31).

The Son of man is both human and divine (as in Dan. 7:13–14 and elsewhere in Matthew); no wonder he comes "with power and great glory" (v. 30). The Son's glory is the Father's glory (16:27). The clouds reflect his splendor, and the angels (v. 31; 16:27) swell the triumph of his train.

"The distress of those days" (v. 29), that is, the manifold tribulation of the time between the advents (vv. 4–28), will be curtailed for the sake of Christ's elect (v. 22), now to be gathered to him from all the nations (v. 31). For true disciples the judgment according to works (16:27) means their final commendation (Matt. 25; 1 Cor. 4:5). The glory of the Son of man and the prospect of standing before his throne of judgment (cf. 25:31) fill the nations with dread (v. 30). The Judge will discover the wicked as

31. F. F. Bruce, *Israel and the Nations* (London: Paternoster, 1963), 224.

surely as vultures find a carcass (v. 28). For nondisciples and false disciples the judgment of works spells condemnation (7:21–23).

In verses 32–35 Jesus returns to the subject of verses 15–21, tribulation and consummation (**24:32–36**), to events which are relatively *near,* which are to occur before the end of the present generation (Gk. *genea,* v. 34); hence the phrase *all these things* (vv. 33, 34). The unfolding of these events signals that "it [Jerusalem's destruction] is near, right at the door" (v. 33). (If, with NIV marg., we read "he" instead of "it," then the verse more closely echoes 16:28.) As in 21:18–19, the fig tree illustrates the impending destruction (v. 32).

In verse 36 Jesus refers to the subject of verses 26–31, to the relatively distant event of his return; so he speaks of "that day or hour." But which day or hour is not disclosed, lest disciples neglect present responsibilities. The call to vigilance (vv. 37–51) flows directly out of verse 36.

While distinguishable, the near and distant events are inseparable. However long the time between them, they are conceptually bound together in the closest way. The distresses of verses 15–21 may be expected to recur during the intense tribulation immediately before Jesus' return (cf. vv. 4–14, 22–29a). As "the abomination of desolation" in A.D. 70 is anticipated in Antiochus Epiphanes (168 B.C.), so the event of A.D. 70 in turn anticipates a yet more horrible abomination associated with the last and worst embodiment of antichrist (2 Thess. 2:4).

The implications of these things for the present (**24:37–51**) includes a need for watchfulness and faithfulness. Noah's contemporaries were overtaken (v. 39) because they spurned Noah's witness—both visible (the ark) and verbal (2 Pet. 2:5). Likewise those who reject Jesus are totally unprepared for the future. For the disciples, however, given the truth that Jesus has disclosed to them (v. 3), there will be no excuse for their being surprised by the impending events of verses 15–21 or the more distant ones of verses 26–31. The uncertainty of the hour of Jesus' return (v. 36) calls for constant vigilance. Since it might happen at any time, one must be watchful at every time (vv. 42–44; cf. 1 Thess. 5:1–11).

Jesus combats potential carelessness and overconfidence among his followers by holding before them the prospect of judgment. Disciples too shall be judged (16:27). Verses 40–41 illustrate both the suddenness of final judgment, and the separation incurred by it. Whether one is "taken" into judgment (v. 39) or into salvation (v. 31), the central truth is the division that will certainly occur depending on one's relationship to Jesus (cf. 10:34–39; 13:24–50). Verses 45–51 are addressed to all disciples, but especially church leaders (v. 45). Leaders who gently and respectfully nurture those under their care will be given greater responsibility (vv. 46–47; cf. 19:28–30; 25:19–23). But the one who abuses or neglects the "little ones" under his care (cf. Matt. 18) exposes himself to the very judgment in store for the hypocrites (vv. 48–51; cf. chap. 23).

The parable of the ten virgins (**25:1–13**), together with the two that follow, flows out of 24:36–51 (the fifth discourse includes chaps. 24–25). All three parables depict the crisis precipitated by Jesus' return.

At the end of betrothal it was customary for the bridegroom to lead his friends to the bride's home, thence to escort her and her friends (the virgins) to his home for the wedding festival (cf. 22:1–14). The lamps are actually torches—long sticks wrapped with rags soaked in olive oil and set afire for the bridal procession. At news of the bridegroom's approach, all ten virgins pour oil on their torches (v. 7); but only five have reserve jars of oil (vv. 3–4) needed later in the festivities. Were they to share their oil (vv. 8–9), there would soon be no torches at all. For their negligence the foolish virgins are banned from the banquet (vv. 11–12).

The five foolish virgins represent false disciples, the five wise ones true disciples (cf. 24:45–49). The bridegroom represents Jesus Christ (cf. 9:15), the sudden coming (v. 6) the unpredictable day and hour of Jesus' return (v. 13; 24:36). When he comes he will surely judge church members for their works (16:27) and separate true disciples from false (25:10–12; cf. 7:21–23; 24:40–41). The foolish virgins' lack of oil corresponds to the wedding guest's lack of the proper garment (22:11); in each case the absence of evidential works of righteousness is in view. In verse 13 Jesus reiterates 24:42 and thus links the parable to the admonitions at the end of chapter 24; because the exact time of Christ's return is unknown, constant watchfulness is required. He calls for habitual obedience, for a life of good works, as distinct from a desperate attempt at the very end to make up for years of neglect and disobedience.

The parable of the talents (**25:14–30**) exhibits a close connection with the preceding parable; the opening of verse 14 is merely transitional, suggesting that the introduction of verse 1 covers this parable too.

A talent may have been equal to six thousand denarii (a denarius equalled one day's wage for a laborer). The smaller mina might be "laid away in a piece of cloth" (Luke 19:20), but the larger and much more valuable talent had to be buried (Matt. 25:18, 25). Both the servants and the money entrusted to them belong to the master (vv. 25, 27). By the same token, whatever profit they make (vv. 16–17) is his. The third slave rightly perceives the state of affairs (vv. 24, 26). Reasoning that the master will take all the gains and deal harshly with him for any losses, he decides that the best response is no response (vv. 18, 24–25). The story records nothing of the other slaves' reasoning, only their obedience to the master's command.

Like the master, Jesus is "going on a journey" (v. 14). During his absence he requires obedience to his commands. For one day he will return to judge his people for what they have done during his absence (v. 19). Investing talents does not mean developing one's natural skills but seizing opportunities to do good works for the sake of the Master (5:14–16). Like the master, Jesus requires that each disciple be productive "according to his ability" (v. 15; cf. 13:8, 23; 2 Cor. 8:12).

The response of the first two slaves illustrates exactly what Jesus seeks from disciples—unquestioning and fruitful obedience. The third slave correctly perceives his obligation, but quite incorrectly appraises his master's character. Very significantly, the master's words do not echo the slave's evaluation of him as a hard man (vv. 24, 26). Viewing the master as he does, he cannot act in love but only in fear (v. 25).

The master remains the master, the slaves remain slaves. But now the master is seen to be one who treats his slaves benevolently. They are allowed to keep all the money—both the original talents and those they have gained (v. 28). Beyond the blessings gained from their obedience, Christians are granted heaven, where God honors their service by granting them yet more service (vv. 21, 23). The citizens of heaven are not inactive (such boredom is reserved for hell), but more active than ever: herein lies their share in their Master's happiness. Matters are just the opposite for the third slave. The tragic irony is that he experiences just what he feared—the master's wrath. Even partial obedience would have been better than sheer disobedience (v. 27). Having neglected opportunity, he is now deprived of opportunity. The judgment upon him (v. 30) is again a solemn warning to disciples to demonstrate the authenticity of their profession by steadfast obedience (cf. vv. 11–13; 22:11–14).

The parable of the sheep and the goats (**25:31–46**) continues the theme of judgment displayed in chapters 23–25. A comparison of Jesus' usage of brother (Gk. *adelphos*) elsewhere in Matthew (esp. 12:46–50; 23:8; 28:8–20) indicates that here he is speaking (vv. 40, 45) not of the poor and oppressed generally, but specifically of his disciples.

The nations are distinguished from the brothers (v. 40) and are judged according to the way they have treated the brothers. A comparison with 10:40–42 reveals that they respond to the brothers in their capacity as Jesus' representatives. The sheep are those who receive the gospel of the kingdom and its bearers and the goats are those who reject them. The brothers experience the deprivations reflected in 25:35–36 because of their allegiance to Jesus (cf. 5:10–12; 10:16–23; 24:9–14).

Like the two preceding parables, and those of 13:24–30, 36–43, 47–50, this one depicts the division of the last judgment (v. 32). Palestinian shepherds commonly herded sheep and goats together but separated them at day's end (sheep, with their heavy wool, needed less shelter than goats). As animals of greater value and of lighter color, the sheep represent the redeemed.

Those from among the nations who receive Jesus' emissaries will surely be rewarded with salvation (25:34; cf. 10:41–42). That the kingdom is "prepared . . . since the creation" underscores the certainty of the reward and offers hope amidst present trials. Those who fail to minister to Jesus' followers, and thereby demonstrate their hostility or indifference toward the message they bear and the Christ they represent, will suffer eternal loss (25:41–46).

Jesus' compassion for the materially and physically needy is everywhere evident. Yet his chief concern is man's relationship to God, not his environment; and his singular mission is to save from sins (1:21), not from poverty or hunger (cf. comments on 4:2–4; 5:3–10). This mission and responses to it are in view as Jesus concludes this final discourse (chaps. 23–25).

V. Jesus' Passion and Resurrection (26:1–28:20)

A. Preparation for the passion (26:1–46). This last major section begins with a plot against Jesus (**26:1–5**). The chief priests and the elders of the people (v. 3; cf. 21:23) "were based in Jerusalem and come to the fore in the passion narrative. Up to this point, the far-flung scribes and Pharisees have occupied center stage as Jesus' antagonists."[32] As though in obedience to the pronouncement of verse 2, the enemies now gather to plot Jesus' arrest and execution (v. 3). Some of them feared that Jesus' popular support would cause a riot if the arrest were

32. Gundry, *Matthew*, 518.

attempted during a public gathering (v. 5; cf. Luke 22:6); thus it occurs in the middle of the night (vv. 47–56).

Before Judas's betrayal of Jesus, however, Jesus is anointed by a woman at Bethany (**26:6–13**). The woman's extravagance (v. 7) springs from love—a contrast to the Jews' equally extravagant action (vv. 3–5) motivated by hate. She pours out her wealth for Jesus; money turns Judas against him (v. 15; see also John 12:5–6). The disciples interpret the prodigality of her love as a colossal waste (Matt. 26:8–9).

Whether or not the woman is thinking of Jesus' burial, he interprets her action this way (v. 12; cf. John 19:39–40), thus underscoring the prophecy of verse 2. While Jesus remains (v. 11b), no expression of genuine love for him could possibly be excessive. Far from being a cynical admission of the inevitability of poverty, verse 11a tacitly instructs disciples to offer help (cf. Mark 14:7). Once Jesus has departed, Christians show love for him by loving their neighbors, including the poorest; conversely, it is questionable how far a person who does not love God can love his neighbor (cf. Matt. 22:37–40).

In the next pericope (**26:14–16**) Judas agrees to betray Jesus. Judas was a slave of money, which prevented him from being a slave of Jesus, God incarnate (6:24). Judas asks, "What are you willing to give me if I hand him over to you?" (v. 15). While other motives may be at work, the powerful effect of money on its slaves should not be underestimated.

Thirty silver coins (v. 15) was no small sum. The demand of thirty shekels to compensate for a slave's death (Exod. 21:32) demonstrated the great value of human life. Judas's compensation is considerable, which caters well to his greed. At the same time, the amount is paltry indeed. In Zechariah 11:12 (alluded to in Matt. 26:15) it signals Israel's contempt for Yahweh and his prophet. The language of Zechariah 11:13 (cf. Matt. 27:9) is ironic. For a mere thirty pieces of silver Judas willingly betrays Yahweh's prophet—more than that, Yahweh himself!

As the words *from then on* introduced Jesus' Galilean ministry (4:17) and his prophecies about his death and resurrection (16:21), here in 26:16 they introduce the passion narrative proper. The agreement with Judas is the last ingredient needed for the success of the plot.

The Last Supper (**26:17–30**) now follows. According to Matthew's chronological reckoning, Jesus eats the Passover; however, John 18:28 says that Jesus was on trial when the Passover was yet to be eaten. Probably Matthew and John reflect two different calendars that were in use during this period.

The words of verses 24–25 are spoken and Judas departs (cf. John 13:26–30) before the main meal begins (Matt. 26:26)—and before Jesus' words of institution (vv. 26–28). Thus Judas is excluded from the promised salvation (cf. v. 24).

The bread is broken that it might be given (v. 26). As a Passover victim (1 Cor. 5:7), Jesus' body must not be broken (John 19:36). The atoning blood is provided not by the sinner but by the Savior; so it has been from the beginning (Gen. 22:8, 13; Lev. 17:11). God the Son pours out his own blood (Matt. 26:28) to save his people from their sins (1:21).

Jesus' death inaugurates a new covenant (v. 28; 1 Cor. 11:25), for here sins are actually forgiven (Matt. 1:21; cf. Jer. 31:31–34; Rom. 3:25–26). How reassuring to the reader of Matthew! "Despite his stressing obedience to Jesus' commands, Matthew bases forgiveness on the pouring out of Jesus' blood. Therefore obedience is evidential of true discipleship, not meritorious of forgiveness."[33] Moreover, Jesus dies for "the many"—not just for Jews but for Gentiles too (v. 28; 20:28). Such is the efficacy of his blood and the lavishness of his gift.

The hymn mentioned in verse 30 would have come from the Hallel psalms (Pss. 114–118). The last of the four Passover cups is omitted—to be reserved for the celebration of God's final victory (v. 29; cf. 8:11).

In **26:31–35** Jesus predicts Peter's denial. In Zechariah 13:7 Yahweh calls for the slaying of his appointed shepherd. In Matthew the imperative becomes an indicative, "I will strike" (v. 31); Yahweh personally delivers the blow. To say that Jesus is murdered by his enemies (v. 4) does not fully explain the event. He is also handed over to death by God's set purpose (Acts 2:23). Not only does God use Jesus' enemies, but the Son becomes the personal object of the Father's wrath (Isa. 53:4, 10).

The smiting of Jesus means the scattering of his flock (v. 31; cf. v. 56), which makes them more vulnerable to attack. Fear and pride beset all the disciples (vv. 31, 35). But as the "first among equals" Peter is especially vulnerable. He acclaims himself as the one who can be counted on to stand by Jesus to the end (v. 33); yet he is the very one who will deny Jesus (v. 34; cf. Prov. 16:18). Jesus remains faithful: even as he predicts his followers' falling away, he foretells their restoration by his gracious initiative (Matt. 26:32; cf. 28:16–20; Luke 22:31–32).

After this Jesus retreats with his disciples to

33. Ibid., 528.

Gethsemane (**26:36–46**), where he prays to his Father before his arrest. Verses 37–38 speak of an anguish so deep as to threaten Jesus' life before he ever reaches the cross. Over against Peter's threefold denial (v. 34) stand Jesus' three petitions. Peter's confidence (v. 35) needs no prayer; Jesus' anxiety drives him to prayer.

The prospect of the cup (cf. 20:22–23) and abandonment by the Father (27:46) explains Jesus' agony. Far from meekly resigning himself to the inevitable, God the Son pleads with God the Father to alter his plan. Yet the Son does not pit his will against the Father's. By an act of his will he submits to the Father. The submitting (v. 39b) does not substitute for, but results from, the striving (v. 39a).

In the first petition (v. 39) the conditional clause is positive; in verses 42 and 44 it is negative, expressive of Jesus' growing awareness that the cup will not be taken away until he has emptied it.

In his supreme agony, Jesus longs for support from the three men who, for all their blindness and self-centeredness, have become his dearest friends (vv. 37, 38). In verse 41 he warns them lest, amidst the approaching trial, they should be ensnared by the Evil One and prove disloyal to Messiah (cf. 6:13). Given the boasts of Peter (26:33–35) and the sons of Zebedee (20:22), the warning is noteworthy.

B. Jesus' arrest and trial (26:47–27:26). Far from catching Jesus off guard, the betrayal and arrest (**26:47–56**) fulfills his prophecy (17:22; 20:18). Judas calls Jesus rabbi; never in Matthew does Judas address him as Lord (contrast 26:22 with 26:25). The kiss (v. 49) is both hypocritical (the outward action contradicts the inner reality) and treacherous (a mark of friendship delivers the friend over to death, v. 48; cf. Luke 22:48). Jesus calls Judas a friend (v. 50), "an open-hearted but not intimate greeting."[34] If verse 50a is a command (NIV), it shows that even the arrest is under Jesus' authority. If it is a question (NIV marg.), Jesus confronts Judas with the enormity of his deed.

The disciple apparently intends to kill the high priest's servant (v. 51; cf. John 18:10). Jesus' response (v. 52) accords with his teaching (5:9, 38–42). His refusal to call upon a power easily able to prevent the arrest (v. 53) confirms his resolve to obey the Father and fulfill the Scripture (vv. 54, 56). Rejecting the way of rebellion (v. 55a), Jesus exercises power in teaching (v. 55b; cf. 7:28–29). Moreover, Jesus here deliberately turns himself over to his enemies both human and spiritual, allows their malice to envelop him, and by that very means conquers them (see comments on 20:24–28; 21:8–11). Jesus shows his power by standing his ground and submitting to the arrest. The disciples' flight (v. 56) is both the result of their having exerted spurious power (v. 51), and the proof that they lack genuine power.

Following the arrest Jesus is taken before the Sanhedrin and submits to a Jewish "trial" (**26:57–68**). Witnesses for the defense are conspicuously absent. The prejudice of verse 59 is quite predictable, for the men who are to judge Jesus' case are the very ones who plotted to kill him (v. 4) and who planned his arrest (v. 57)! The court assembled, "not with the intention of reaching a just verdict, but with a firm resolve to convict Jesus of a capital crime."[35] In pursuit of this goal, the religious leaders violate the ninth commandment (Exod. 20:16).[36]

The search for false evidence at first proves futile (vv. 59–60a); for conflicting testimonies are given (Mark 14:56–59) and agreement of at least two witnesses was required in capital cases (Deut. 17:6). So, despite the explosive charge of verse 61, more evidence is needed to secure conviction.

The adjuration in verse 63b is intended to settle the issue. By "the Son of God," the high priest means the Messiah, a human being appointed as God's earthly vicegerent (cf. Ps. 2:7; John 1:49). "If Jesus refuses to answer [as in v. 63a], he breaks a legally imposed oath. If he denies he is the Messiah, the crisis is over—but so is his influence. If he affirms it, then, given the commitments of the court, Jesus must be false. After all, how could the true Messiah allow himself to be imprisoned and put in jeopardy?"[37]

In verse 64a "Yes, it is as you say" is "affirmative in content, and reluctant or circumlocutory in formulation,"[38] for Jesus knows that he is Messiah, but also that Caiaphas's understanding of messiahship is inadequate.

In verse 64b the title *Son of man* denotes a heavenly figure who receives the worship due God alone (Dan. 7:13–14); like the title *Son of God* (16:16), it affirms Jesus' deity. His exaltation to God's right hand signals (1) the reversal of the verdict about to be issued (the One whom men condemn, God vindicates), and (2) his own right to execute judgment upon all

34. Carson, "Matthew," 547.

35. W. Lane, *Gospel According to Mark* (Grand Rapids: Eerdmans, 1974), 533.

36. On the question of the illegality of this meeting's time (the middle of the night) and place (the high priest's palace), see Hill, *Matthew*, 345, and Carson, "Matthew," 549–51.

37. Carson, "Matthew," 554.

38. D. Catchpole, "The Answer of Jesus to Caiaphas (Matt. xxvi.64)," *New Testament Studies* 17 (1971): 226.

men, including the ones who now condemn him (both "yous" of v. 64b are plural; cf. 22:44; 25:31–32)—as will happen when he returns "on the clouds of heaven" (cf. 16:27; 24:30).

Jesus' twin "blasphemy" (v. 65) is his acceptance of the title *Messiah* and his claim to deity. The former would have been enough to convict him of a capital offense; however, besides answering Caiaphas's question (v. 64a), Jesus tells him more than he expected to hear (v. 64b). Caiaphas rightly interprets the words about the Son of man as a claim to deity; thus his shocked response (v. 65a). The case against Jesus is now far stronger than could have been anticipated.

No more witnesses are needed (v. 65). Jesus is judged worthy of death (v. 66), a decision confirmed in 27:1. The indignities of verses 67–68 prove to the assailants that Jesus is a pretender (a true Messiah would not tolerate this and could identify his tormentors even while blindfolded; see Mark 14:65; Luke 22:64); in fact they prove that he is Yahweh's Servant (Isa. 50:6; 53:7).

The placement of Peter's denial (**26:69–75**) between Jesus' appearances before the Sanhedrin and Pilate respectively places Jesus' chief apostle—the very one who earlier confessed him (16:16)—among the witnesses for the prosecution! The denial exactly fulfills the prophecy (v. 34).

The suicide of Judas (**27:3–10**) expresses Judas's final, horrified realization of his bondage to money. Under its mastery, he has betrayed an innocent person—indeed the supremely Innocent One. The authorities are even more guilty. Like Judas, they hand Jesus over to death (v. 1); unlike him, they refuse to acknowledge the enormity of their deed (v. 4).

In the face of the judgment against Jesus (v. 1), verse 6 (cf. Deut. 23:18) appallingly illustrates Jewish scrupulousness (cf. 23:23–24). In verses 9–10 Matthew artfully weaves together three Old Testament passages: (1) Zechariah 11:12–13 (thirty pieces of silver thrown "into the house of the LORD to the potter"); (2) Jeremiah 32:6–9 (a purchased field); and (3) Jeremiah 19:1–11 (hence the naming of this prophet in Matt. 27:9), which speaks of a potter and the Potsherd Gate, of elders and priests (cf. Matt. 27:1), of Jerusalem's being filled with innocent blood, and of a burial site. Both Zechariah and Jeremiah speak of judgment. In Zechariah 11 the exchange of money expresses Judah's rejection of Yahweh and his judgment on her. In Jeremiah 19 the shedding of innocent blood precipitates judgment, the severity of which is preserved in the cemetery's name (Jer. 19:6, 11). "Matthew sees in Jeremiah 19 and Zechariah 11 . . . a pattern of apostasy and rejection that must find its ultimate fulfillment in the rejection of Jesus, who was cheaply valued, rejected by the Jews, and whose betrayal money was put to a purpose that pointed to the destruction of the nation."[39]

The Jews sentenced Jesus to death (v. 1); but Romans alone could execute the sentence (John 18:31), so now Jesus appears before Pilate (**27:11–26**). A charge of blasphemy (Matt. 26:65) would carry no weight with Pilate, so the Jews accuse Jesus of claiming to be the king of the Jews (vv. 11–12)—a threat to Caesar (Luke 23:2). As in Matthew 26:63, Jesus makes no reply to these charges (v. 14). He answers Pilate as he had Caiaphas, "Yes, it is as you say" (v. 11; cf. 26:64). Jesus is indeed the king of the Jews (2:2), but not in the sense alleged by his accusers or conceived by Pilate. In the end, pressure from the crowd forces Pilate to condemn Jesus. The charge against him is neither substantiated by the crowd (they show that Jesus lacks support for an uprising) nor accepted by Pilate (v. 23; Luke 23:14). By insisting on Jesus' death, the people fall under judgment and indeed invoke judgment on themselves (v. 25). Ironically, the man released poses a serious threat to political stability (v. 26a; Mark 15:7). A flogging before crucifixion was customary (v. 26b).

C. Jesus' crucifixion (27:27–56). The mocking of Jesus (**27:27–31**) begins this particular section. He is surrounded by a cohort of Roman soldiers (a company of up to six hundred men) who mock his claim to be king (vv. 28–29). A soldier's scarlet cloak suggests the imperial purple (v. 28). The spikes of the thorns may have turned outward in imitation of the radiate crowns of the time, rather than inward for the infliction of pain.[40] A royal scepter (v. 29) completes the picture. As the passage offers a grotesque parody of the truth about Jesus, it also shows how sinners respond to true kingship. The soldiers behave this way because to their mind Jesus is not a king. According to Matthew, it is *because* this is Yahweh, the Holy One of Israel, that he receives such treatment.

Now Matthew (**27:32–44**) gruesomely presents the crucifixion of Jesus. The victim had to carry the crossbeam (cf. John 19:17), which at the scene of execution would be attached to an upright post. Weakened by physical abuse (vv. 26–30), Jesus requires assistance (cf. Mark 15:21).

In verse 33 the word *Golgotha* means

39. Carson, "Matthew," 566.
40. Gundry, *Matthew*, 567.

"skull"; the Latin counterpart is *calva,* hence Calvary. The site lay just outside the north wall of the city. The use of the place (for executions) better explains the name than its alleged shape.

Myrrh (Mark 15:23) gives wine a bitter taste (hence Matthew's "gall," v. 34), so Jesus refuses it. The offer is an act not of compassion but of ridicule (cf. Ps. 69:20–21). Jesus is stripped of his personal possessions (v. 35), in accord with custom and in fulfillment of Psalm 22:18 (cf. NIV marg.). The mockery of Matthew 26:67–68 and 27:28–31 now intensifies. Jesus is taunted from every side—by onlookers (vv. 39–40), by the Jewish authorities (vv. 41–43), and by the robbers crucified with him (v. 44), as Satan makes a final attempt to turn Jesus from his appointed path (cf. 4:1–11). Indeed the mockery itself speaks deep truth (v. 42); it is through Jesus' very refusal to save himself that his kingly rule and saving power find their highest expression (26:28; John 12:32).

Following the death of Jesus (**27:45–50**) darkness covers "all the land" (v. 45), signaling God's judgment on Israel for her rejection of Messiah (see Amos 8:9–10), the cosmic phenomena associated with the end (Matt. 24:29; Acts 2:20), and God's judgment upon the sin-bearer. Out of this darkness Jesus utters the cry of dereliction.

This is the moment Jesus dreaded (26:37–39)—abandonment by the One with whom he had enjoyed the deepest communion (11:25–27), even in Gethsemane ("Abba," Mark 14:36). This dereliction is the inevitable consequence of his "becoming sin" (1:21; cf. Isa. 53:4–10; 2 Cor. 5:21). And once he is deserted by the Father, there is no hope of rescue by Elijah (v. 49) or anyone else. Even at this moment Jesus clings to God. In the words of Psalm 22:1, he directly addresses "*my* God" and cries "Why have *you* forsaken me?" As in Gethsemane, Jesus' striving with God yields peace with God (see Luke 23:46).

Even death itself (v. 50) is under Jesus' sovereign control: "he gave up his spirit" (cf. John 10:17–18).

Various immediate effects occur after Jesus' death (**27:51–56**). Verse 51 cites the tearing of the curtain in the temple. This curtain divided the Holy Place from the Most Holy Place (Exod. 26:31–35; Heb. 10:19–22). God now severs it completely. Jesus' death provides for the forgiveness of the sins of his people (26:28), giving them access into God's holy presence. Moreover, Jesus' death makes Old Testament ceremonial practices obsolete (Heb. 9:1–14; 10:1–18). The temple is to be destroyed (24:2), both as judgment upon Israel and as visible confirmation that the temple ritual is no longer needed.

The opening of the tombs (vv. 51b–53) also occurs. Since *he* is the firstfruits (1 Cor. 15:20–23), the saints are raised *after* Jesus' resurrection. (NIV begins a new sentence with "the tombs"; but it may just as easily begin with "and the bodies," v. 52b. Verse 53 is best rendered, "and coming out of the tombs after his resurrection they went . . . ," RSV.)

Apocalyptic signs are associated with both Jesus' death (vv. 45, 51–52) and his resurrection (28:2–3). The phenomena of verses 51–52 closely join these two events, in that they occur at Jesus' death but help to bring about occurrences after his resurrection. Death and resurrection are also inseparable for believers. By virtue of Jesus' atoning sacrifice, the Old Testament saints (the "many holy people," v. 52) are saved from the consequences of their sins and gain the right to resurrection life. Fullness of fellowship (as promised by the rending of the veil) cannot be enjoyed in a bodiless state. The saints must be reintegrated by the reunion of body and soul in the resurrection. That the resurrected state promises deeper fellowship not only with God but with human beings as well (cf. 22:23–32) is suggested by the saints' going into the holy city (not the heavenly but the earthly Jerusalem; cf. 4:5) and appearing to many (v. 53b).

The centurion (v. 54) represents the soldiers under his command (cf. Mark 15:39). If he speaks as a pagan, he seems to consider Jesus a divine man or deified hero—"*a* son of God" (NIV marg.). If his words reflect Jewish influence, he may be affirming that Jesus is the king of the Jews (v. 37), the Davidic Messiah, "*the* Son of God" (NIV). The centurion speaks greater truth than he knows. The crucified is no divinized man, and he is not merely David's human descendant. He is David's Lord (22:41–46), and he is the Son of the living God (16:16). Ironically, a Gentile declares truth about Jesus, and in the very terms which led the Jews to condemn him (26:63–64).

Mary, the mother of James and Joseph, is Jesus' mother (vv. 55–56; 13:55; John 19:25). By inference Salome is the mother of Zebedee's sons (Mark 15:40), Mary's sister (John 19:25; cf. Matt. 20:20), and Jesus' aunt. The presence of women at the cross accentuates the absence of male disciples, who are last mentioned in 26:56 (when they flee) and do not reappear until 28:16. The women's distance (v. 55a) shows female reticence in a male-dominated culture.

D. Jesus' burial and resurrection (27:57–28:20). Joseph makes arrangements for the burial of Jesus (**27:57–61**). Joseph was an upright, respected, and wealthy member of the Sanhedrin who dissented from the judgment against Jesus and became his disciple (v. 57; Mark 15:43; Luke 23:50–51). Arimathea is probably Ramathaim (1 Sam. 1:1).

By Jewish law, Jesus' body could not remain on the cross overnight (Deut. 21:22–23), particularly when the next day was a Sabbath (v. 62; Mark 15:42). Yet the Romans "let bodies of crucified criminals hang in full view till they rotted away. If they were buried at all, it was only by express permission of the imperial magistrate. Such permission was usually granted to friends and relatives of the deceased who made application, but never in the case of high treason."[41] Pilate's contravention of this law (v. 58) suggests that he believed in Jesus' innocence. For more information about the preparation of the body (v. 59a) see John 19:39–40.

Tombs cut out of rock had recesses and shelves for the corpses (cf. Isa. 22:16). The placing of Jesus in the rich man's own grave (v. 60) fulfills Isaiah 53:9 and witnesses to Joseph's devotion: "if Jesus was buried as a criminal, then the Law forbade the owner of the tomb to use it again."[42] The Church of the Holy Sepulchre is probably built on the site of this tomb, a site that lay outside the city wall in Jesus' day. The burial chamber was "sealed with a cut, disk-shaped stone that rolled in a slot cut into the rock. The slot was on an incline, making the grave easy to seal but difficult to open."[43]

Matthew relates the guarding of the tomb in **27:62–66.** The next day (v. 62) is Saturday (cf. 28:1). The third day (v. 64) may then be (1) the third day following Jesus' death, or Sunday (Friday being the first day on an inclusive reckoning), or (2) the third day following the authorities' request, or Monday, in which case Jesus' enemies determine to cover the whole of the third day following the crucifixion ("After three days" [v. 63] means "up to and including the third day"). If the words of verse 64 conceal the fear that Jesus might indeed fulfill his prophecy (v. 63), then the request for a guard is the most futile of gestures. Those who accuse Jesus of a double deception (the first being his claim to messiahship and to deity) are in fact the deceivers (28:11–15). Pilate grants the request, on the understanding that the guards will be Jews, not Romans (v. 65a). This explains their reporting to the chief priests (28:11) rather than to Pilate.

41. Carson, "Matthew," 584.
42. Hill, *Matthew*, 357.
43. Carson, "Matthew," 584.

News of the resurrection (**28:1–10**) comes early on Sunday morning when the two Marys come to the tomb (28:1; cf. Mark 16:1–2) to continue their vigil (cf. Matt. 27:56, 61). The angel removes the stone (as no man could do). It is he, not the earthquake, that terrifies the guards (v. 4); such are his power and presence (vv. 2–3). The women do not arrive until after the angel's descent, the earthquake, and the flight of the guards (v. 11).

The New Testament nowhere records Jesus' actual resurrection, but witnesses instead to an accomplished fact. The stone is removed (v. 2)—not to let Jesus out, but to let his followers in—so they can see that he is gone (v. 6). The angel (v. 7) echoes Jesus' own prophecy (26:32). "Going ahead" here means not "lead" but "precede" (cf. vv. 7b, 10). By his gracious initiative, Jesus is restoring the fellowship broken by the disciples' flight in 26:56.

In verses 8–10 the women's joy, expressed in their running, shows that they believe the angel's words even before Jesus confronts them. Though he does not identify himself, the women recognize him (v. 9). While his resurrected body is a transformed body, it is Jesus who is raised—the very one they had known before (v. 6). The clasping of Jesus' feet (v. 9) confirms that his risen body is substantial (cf. John 20:17); the women's worship witnesses to his deity. That Jesus now repeats the angel's instructions (v. 10) demonstrates the great importance of the meeting in Galilee. Jesus refers not to disciples (as had the angel, v. 7) but to brothers (cf. 12:49–50; 25:40), underscoring his desire to restore broken fellowship.

The guards' report (**28:11–15**) to the chief priests (v. 11) mirrors the women's witness to the disciples. Verse 13 indicates that the guards found the tomb to be empty before they fled the scene. This, together with the fact that no disciples came to the tomb until after the guards' departure, demonstrates both the authorities' steadfast refusal to believe the truth even in the face of overwhelming evidence and the enormity of their fraud. The very attempt to bribe the witnesses (v. 12) testifies to their impotence in the face of irresistible reality. The spread of the lie (v. 15) is countered by the spread of truth (v. 19).

The author concludes his Gospel with the great commission (**28:16–20**). For both Jesus and Matthew, the choice of meeting place (v. 16) serves a threefold purpose. In Matthew the mountain is a place of divine revelation (cf. 5:1; 15:29; 17:1); and in Matthew's Gospel this is the risen Lord's first manifestation to his apostles. As Jesus' ministry began in "Galilee of the Gentiles" (4:15), so here he issues his commission to "make disciples of all nations." As Jesus' first great commandments (chaps. 5–7) were delivered from a mountain in Galilee (perhaps this very one), it is appropriate that the commission to impart to Gentiles everything that he has commanded should be issued in such a place.

Like the women (v. 9), the disciples respond by worshiping Jesus (v. 17). Matthew thus climaxes a theme developed throughout his Gospel—the deity of Jesus. Only Yahweh is entitled to worship. Just as the Magi had worshiped the newborn baby (2:2, 11), so now the disciples adore the newly risen Jesus. Matthew adds that "some doubted" (v. 17), but he does not elaborate.[44]

Jesus' authority (v. 18) provides the basis for the commission (note the "therefore" of v. 19). God the Father (the subject of the passive phrase *has been given*) now wills that Jesus' existent authority (7:29; 8:9) be exercised universally. Having refused the devil's offer of all the kingdoms of the world (4:8–10), Jesus now receives them from the Father—and the dominion of heaven besides!

The commission to go to "all nations" (v. 19) climaxes another Matthean theme—the salvation of the Gentiles. At the heart of Jesus' commission is the imperative to make disciples. Jesus explains what it means to make disciples by the two participles which follow—baptizing and teaching. Discipleship entails both becoming a Christian (being baptized) and being a Christian (obeying Jesus' teaching). Baptism in the name of the Trinity (v. 19) and in the name of Jesus (Acts 8:16) are complementary; neither is an exclusive formula.

In verse 20 the statement *I am with you* forms an inclusion with *Immanuel* in 1:23. The risen Lord who stands over the disciples (v. 18) also stands with them as they embark upon this all-important mission.

44. Ibid., 593–94.

SELECT BIBLIOGRAPHY

Bruce, F. F. *Matthew*. Grand Rapids: Eerdmans, 1970.

Carson, D. A. "Matthew." In *The Expositor's Bible Commentary*, edited by Frank E. Gaebelein, 12 vols. Grand Rapids: Zondervan, 1985.

France, R. T. *Matthew*. Tyndale New Testament Commentaries. Leicester and Grand Rapids: Inter-Varsity and Eerdmans, 1985.

Gundry, R. H. *Matthew: A Commentary on His Literary and Theological Art*. Grand Rapids: Eerdmans, 1982.

Hill, D. *The Gospel of Matthew*. New Century Bible Commentary. Greenwood, S.C.: Attic, 1972.

Mounce, R. H. *Matthew*. A Good News Commentary. San Francisco: Harper & Row, 1985.

MARK

Royce Gordon Gruenler

INTRODUCTION

The Gospel of Mark, which is the shortest of the four Gospels, begins and ends abruptly. This abruptness, together with its quick pace characterized by the connector word *immediately* (Gk. *euthus*) between scenes of action, suggests a story about Jesus that is adapted for a specific audience and setting, very likely a tense situation of persecution and suffering where the slower pace and more expansive style of the other Gospels are inappropriate. It must not be assumed, however, from its relative brevity and lack of a birth story at its opening and resurrection appearances at its closing that this Gospel is doctrinally simpler. It is popular in critical circles to infer that Mark is the earliest of the Gospels because it lacks the theological developments and ornamentations of later Christian communities represented by Matthew, Luke, and John. However, this reflects a theological bias not in keeping with the high Christology of the Gospel. The hypothesis that Mark is chronologically the earliest of the Gospels may be supported on other grounds, however, though there is less evidence for thinking so than was formerly the case, and in any event the current discussion on the chronology of the Gospels is in a state of flux.

An analysis of the internal style of Mark suggests a strong tone of irony through which the author involves his readers in the action-filled ministry of Jesus as Son of God and Son of man who invades the demonic realm and meets intensely hostile resistance, requiring the utmost commitment on behalf of himself and his disciples in the redemptive task he has inaugurated. They must be willing to share the cup of suffering that he is to drink on the cross, although only he can drink it for their salvation. The irony of the Marcan story is that Jesus wars against demonic powers with unlikely and unexpected force, yet finds his disciples unwilling or unable to understand what the inauguration of the reign of God in his person really signifies.

The Gospel opens dramatically with "the beginning of the gospel about Jesus Christ, the Son of God" (1:1), the good news Jesus himself is soon proclaiming personally in Galilee after only fifteen introductory verses, as he launches faithfully into the field of battle to grapple with the demonic forces that hold humanity captive. In ironic contrast the Gospel ends on an unresolved note (assuming that the original ending is 16:8), as the women, having received the good news of Jesus' resurrection from the angel at the empty tomb, are enervated by trembling bewilderment and are fearful to say anything to anyone. It is as though Mark stops his film of Jesus' ministry at just this crucial moment and freezes his readers' attention on a single frame that graphically describes how fear may overwhelm faith and cause it to abandon joyful, confident proclamation of God's salvation in the crucified and risen Jesus.

Of course Mark knows the sequel to that momentary and frightening loss of faith through fear, and so do his readers, but they need to have their attention riveted to the disabling effect of disbelief as the familiar story is told again. We may assume that Mark is writing to Gentile Christians who are suffering persecution and, like the women in the original story, are threatened by enervating fear and need to be shocked into decisive action. What if they *never* had said anything? In this regard Mark's ending resembles the inconclusive Book of Jonah, which also highlights the importance of boldly proclaiming God's redeeming grace, yet ends unresolved (as far as Jonah's response and the response of the reader are concerned). God's missionary question is addressed to both: "Should I not be concerned about that great city?" (Jon. 4:11). The Gospel of Mark, like the action-filled and challenging Book of Jonah (and the similarly inconclusive and challenging parable of the elder son in Luke 15:25–32), ends unresolved because Mark intends to challenge his readers to make a total and uncompromised decision to proclaim Christ to an otherwise lost and sinful world, regardless of fearful and threatening circumstances and the pain of sharing Christ's cup of suffering.

If what has been said about Mark's intent has any merit, then he has fashioned his Gospel by design and not of necessity. He has not told us all he knows about Jesus but has deliberately chosen those words and works that serve his literary and theological purpose and his ironic probing style designed to exhort his Christian readers to action. Mark has selected a basic core of material from a wide range of earlier oral and written traditions: (1) the church's preaching (evangelistic, kerygmatic material with emphasis on the passion story, going back to Peter's original proclamation at Pentecost); (2) catechetical instruction for new converts, emphasizing the sayings and works of Jesus; (3) forms of expression used in worship; and (4) focus on Old Testament images and prophecy, particularly the exodus and wilderness themes, fulfilled in Jesus' ministry. Since Matthew and Luke would also have had access to this large and wider pool of early church traditions—much of which would have been in written form from earliest times because of the wide geographical expansion of the church after Pentecost and the inability of eyewitness apostles to be everywhere at once—there is no need to argue that Mark must have been the source of the core material to which they added other traditions. It is quite possible that the synoptic Gospels were written independently and concurrently (the fertile decade of the 50s, when Paul was writing his epistles, might be a likely period for their composition). Similarities between Matthew, Mark, and Luke would then be traceable to their common written sources and not to any extensive linear dependence of one upon the other. This theory of concurrent development would help account for the Gospel writers' differences in style and would allow for their having used alternate and parallel sayings of Jesus as he proclaimed common themes in various forms during his extended itinerant ministry. These variations would all be part of the pool of written and oral sources from which the Gospel writers drew (Matthew and John would also draw upon their eyewitness knowledge of Jesus' ministry).

A widely accepted alternative to the theory of concurrent development is the hypothesis that Mark was the first Gospel to be written, just prior to the destruction of the temple in A.D. 70, and that Matthew and Luke used Mark as their core in the 80s, in addition to a common oral source of Jesus' sayings (Q) and other sources distinctive to each. As this is the most widely held solution to the Synoptic Problem, it has much to commend it and can be made to work in comparing parallel passages. It exacts a penalty, however. No eyewitnesses of the ministry of Jesus would have written any of the Gospels in their final form, for Mark and Luke were not eyewitnesses in any case, and Matthew and John (the latter located in the 90s) would be anonymous, representing later reflections and redactions of the church. It also assumes a linear evolution of theology in the Gospels, beginning with the shorter and more original Mark, followed by Matthew using Mark, then Luke using Mark and possibly Matthew, with John entirely independent and latest of all.

Accordingly, it is argued, differences in wording between synoptic parallel passages that seem to describe the same subject or event in Jesus' ministry came about by the editorializing of the Gospel writers who may also have functioned as Christian "prophets," claiming new revelations from the risen Christ as he spoke to new church situations. These new sayings were then placed on the lips of the historical Jesus for homiletical effect. Thus, only a close study of the redaction process itself can identify the genuinely historical words and works of Jesus in the wider settings of the Gospels. The Gospels, created by a growing and diverse church in the second half of the first century, are in reality historical novels to be read as complex intermixtures of historical fact and pious Christian imagination. Such is the view that has gained wide popularity in contemporary critical circles and is illustrated by a present-day project among a representative group of critical scholars to produce a polychrome version of the Gospels, indicating the genuine (red), questionable (pink), almost surely not genuine (gray), and definitely not genuine (black) sayings attributed to Jesus in the Gospels.

Such radical redactional views suffer, however, from (1) a lack of credible scientific controls that would determine accurately and without prejudice how one distinguishes between genuine and nongenuine sayings of Jesus; (2) almost invariably a low Christology that discounts the Gospel testimony that Jesus was conscious of his messianic mission and asserted the claim to speak in the place of God; (3) a low level of confidence in the reliability of the Gospel writers to report and interpret the facts about Jesus accurately; and (4) a general dismissal of the plenary inspiration of Scripture. These critical presuppositions do not allow the interpreter to appreciate the supernatural genre of the Gospel story or to enter fully into the dynamic mission of Jesus who invades the demonic realm and brings salvation as Suffering Servant, Son of God, and Son of man. Christological views on the nature of Jesus' person and what he was capable of doing largely determine how the grammatical and historical tools of interpretation are to be used.

For these reasons, other factors being more or less equal, it is probably wiser to leave open the question of the origin and order of the Gospels. However, we should not see them appearing so late in time that eyewitness reliability lies in the shadowy past; there are good reasons for holding to the view that all the Gospels were written before A.D. 70.

None, including John, claims the cataclysmic and enormously important event of the temple's destruction (signifying the end of the sacrificial system) to be the fulfillment of Jesus' prophecies, as would be the case if the temple were in ruins when the Gospels were composed. (Matt. 24, Mark 13, Luke 21, and John 2:19–22 are genuine prophecies of a general nature, couched in the graphic Old Testament language of the capture of Jerusalem in 586 B.C. and lacking the precise detail and theological application that would attend later interpretation after the event.) The Acts of the Apostles does not mention the deaths of Peter and Paul (or the outcome of Paul's trial), the Neronian persecutions of the mid-60s, or the destruction of the temple. One simply has to conclude that Acts was finished shortly after Paul's arrival in Rome and should accordingly be dated about 62 or 63. But the Gospel of Luke precedes Acts, and if Luke depended on Mark then Mark cannot be as late as 68, but must have been composed no later than the early 60s. In that case, if Matthew depended on Mark, the Gospel can be dated as early as, if not earlier than, Luke and need not be thrust forward into the shadowy depository of the 80s. Furthermore, there is no reason why Mark could not have been written even earlier. Although tradition suggests that Mark's Gospel reflects the preaching material of Peter (according to Papias, A.D. 60–130) as well as a Roman setting (cf. 1 Pet. 5:13 where "Babylon" may = Rome), Eusebius, the later church historian, dates the visit of Peter to Rome early in the reign of the emperor Claudius (A.D. 41–54). Hence Mark could have been written, at least in its earliest form, as early as 45.

In that case, Matthew and Luke could be dated in the 50s if they used Mark, and even earlier if written independently. But if Matthew was written first, as the church traditionally held until modern times, with Luke following, Mark could conceivably be a simplified conflation or combination of Matthew and Luke and might have been written as late as 68. Yet none of these hypotheses works very well when carefully examined, and one must be cautious in considering claims for the "assured results" of critical study.

Obviously there is common material that Matthew/Mark/Luke share (the triple tradition) and that Matthew/Luke share (the double tradition), plus material peculiar to each. All one needs to say at the present stage of Gospel origins research is that Matthew/Mark/Luke share at various levels core material that is already part of the church's tradition in the 40s and which goes back to eyewitness accounts of the words and acts of Jesus. They are writing in different geographical centers and addressing different audiences and contexts but are making use of overlapping traditions. Perhaps the best hypothesis is to concede the complexity of the matter and date conservatively, allowing for the completion of the synoptic Gospels concurrently in the 50s or early 60s, with the beloved disciple, an eyewitness of the ministry of Jesus, writing shortly thereafter his complementary Gospel of John.

Each of the four Gospels is distinctive and complements the other three, affording a four-dimensional portrait of Jesus and his ministry. Mark limits himself to describing the kerygmatic activity of Jesus, unlike the other Gospels which begin with descriptions of Jesus' prehistory (birth or preexistence) and conclude with his posthistory (resurrection appearances). Mark 1:1 is an important clue to Mark's thematic limitation and points to the fact that he is a pedagogue par excellence who is producing a short, pithy, but intense manual for missionary work as well as for teaching and Christian instruction that calls for absolute commitment to Christ and to preaching his gospel, no matter what the cost may be in suffering. In order to appreciate Mark's distinctive opening thematic statement it is helpful to contrast the starting points of the four Gospels.

Mark opens with "the beginning of the gospel about Jesus Christ" (1:1 = Jesus the servant preacher); Matthew with Jesus' origin in Abraham by way of David (1:1–17 = Jesus, Prophet, Priest, and King); Luke with Jesus' origin in Adam (3:23–38 = Jesus the new Adam, Savior of the whole world); and John with Jesus' origin in the pretemporal divine family (1:1–18 = Jesus, God incarnate in human flesh). Each Gospel, depending on its special focus, expresses its thematic program by tracing the origin of Christ's ministry from different points in history.

In selecting and arranging his material, Mark dramatically highlights major episodes in Jesus' ministry that prove him to be the great servant preacher who announces the good news of God's saving reign. In Jesus' own person the reign of God is embodied and is now invading the demonic realm that enslaves and enervates by sin, fear, unbelief, disease, and demon possession. Though Mark limits his material quantitatively, he boldly includes extensive detail from his eyewitness sources when it qualitatively enhances Jesus' disclosure of himself as bearer of good news to those lost in the hostile wilderness (1:14–8:30) and in the hostile city (8:31–15:47). The setting of the

Gospel is a battleground in which Jesus is engaged in warfare against satanic iniquity wherever it rears its head, whether in debilitating disease or ossified religion. The fast-moving pace of the Gospel heightens the urgency of the battle and the call for decision. Jesus is the herald, bearer, and embodiment of "the gospel" (Gk. *euangelion* = "good news," 1:1, 14, 15; 8:35; 13:10).

OUTLINE

I. Thematic Prologue: The Gospel of Jesus Christ, Son of God (1:1–15)
   A. The Beginning of the Gospel (1:1)
   B. John the Baptist's Preaching in the Wilderness (1:2–8)
   C. Jesus' Baptism (1:9–11)
   D. Jesus' Temptation in the Wilderness (1:12–13)
   E. The Beginning of Jesus' Proclamation (1:14–15)
II. Jesus Invades Wilderness and City with Good News (1:16–8:26)
   A. Jesus' Inaugural Ministry in Galilee (1:16–3:6)
   B. Jesus' Itinerant Ministry in Galilee (3:7–6:29)
   C. Jesus' Withdrawal to the Wilderness Beyond Galilee (6:30–7:23)
   D. The Gentile Mission (7:24–8:10)
   E. Questions Concerning Signs and Seeing (8:11–26)
III. Jesus Invades the Hostile City of Jerusalem (8:27–15:47)
   A. The Journey to Jerusalem (8:27–10:52)
   B. Jesus Confronts Jerusalem (11:1–13:37)
   C. Jerusalem Opposes Jesus (14:1–15:47)
IV. Unfinished Epilogue (16:1–8)

COMMENTARY

I. Thematic Prologue: The Gospel of Jesus Christ, Son of God (1:1–15)

A. The beginning of the gospel (1:1). Mark's opening thematic statement should be translated "the gospel *of* Jesus Christ," that is, the good news which Jesus himself personifies and proclaims as the incarnate Son of God; only derivatively is it "the gospel *about* Jesus Christ" (NIV), which is the church's, and Mark's, proclamation of the gospel that originates with Jesus. Mark's entire Gospel focuses on the person of Jesus, the "Son of God," and the way he expresses through his intention, words, and deeds the good news of salvation. Mark's is not an abstract Gospel; his emphasis on the speaking and acting Jesus keeps his story vital, active, and Christ-centered. The three points of Jesus' proclamation (*kerygma*) in verse 15 are all (as the reader of the Gospel soon discovers) related to Jesus himself: (1) the "time" that has come is the messianic time announced by the Old Testament prophets and now inaugurated first by John the Baptist (1:2–9) and then by Jesus (1:10–15); (2) the nearness of the "kingdom of God" is actually the saving reign of God that is present in the unfolding ministry of Jesus himself; (3) the call to "repent and believe the good news" is Jesus' invitation to make a decisive commitment to himself as the one standing in the very place of God. Each of these three points is faithfully repeated in the kerygma of the early church (e.g., Acts 2:14–41).

B. John the Baptist's preaching in the wilderness (1:2–8). The "joyful tidings" of 1:1 (Gk. *euangelion* = evangel) was a term used in Roman times to honor the birth of the emperor Augustus, and a Roman audience (the likely recipients of this Gospel) would understand the significance of such words as applied to Jesus. But where the pagan world looked backward, Mark emphasizes the prophetic prelude to Jesus' coming, first in a blend of three Old Testament prophecies relating to the wilderness (Exod. 23:20; Isa. 40:3; Mal. 3:1; "in Isaiah the prophet" is a shorthand citation); second, in the inaugural fulfillment of those prophecies through the wilderness figure of John the Baptist, who calls the people to return to the wilderness and to repent of their sins. In the imagery of Hosea

(2:14–23), this is God's promised betrothal of his bride in the desert that inaugurates a new age. John's ministry prepares God's people for renewed sonship and the coming wedding of heaven and earth which Jesus the bridegroom soon announces is now in progress (Mark 2:18–20). John's powerful preaching draws great numbers from Jerusalem and the Judean countryside who repent and are baptized in the Jordan River, bringing together both wilderness and city themes that are the setting for Jesus' invasion of a hostile world in need of salvation.

By compressing his materials, Mark highlights the primary ministry of the Baptist—his preparation for the Messiah. John defers to the one to come as more powerful, more worthy (John cannot even unloose the Master's sandals), and superior in ministry, for the Baptist's is only a preparatory water baptism of repentance (the negative prelude to something more positive), whereas the baptism of the one to come is with the Holy Spirit, the positive implications of which are to be seen in Jesus' parallel prophecy in Acts 1:5, 8, and its fulfillment on the day of Pentecost. John the Baptist proves himself to be a true servant by his faithful ministry and words of deference, as Jesus later attests (9:11–13, 35).

C. Jesus' baptism (1:9–11). Jesus appears for the first time in the narrative in verse 9 and proves himself to be the greatest of all by becoming servant of all (cf. 8:35). Mark succinctly describes how the baton of servanthood passes from John to Jesus. In submitting to the baptism of repentance for the remission of sins Jesus identifies with sinners and becomes their substitute representative, symbolically undergoing the washing of water on their behalf in prophetic anticipation of his baptism in death by which the sins of the race are atoned (cf. 2 Cor. 5:21).

Jesus passes the first of two tests before his major ministry is inaugurated, winning the approval of the Father and the Spirit. The Father loves the Son and is well pleased with him, while the Spirit adds to the Father's vocal approval a visual approbation in descending like a dove upon the Son, thereby anointing him for ministry. Mark's dramatic description of the heavens "torn open" portrays an awesome theophany that causes nature to tremble (cf. Exod. 19:10–19; Isa. 64:1–3). The violence of hostile nature under satanic control is about to be subdued and conquered by the greater power of the God who created it, but it will take a divine act of creative violence to reclaim a lost kingdom, and this Jesus will proceed to do throughout his ministry as he invades the hostile powers of fallen nature. Mark provides a brief glimpse of the tremendous conflict of competing powers that is about to break forth.

D. Jesus' temptation in the wilderness (1:12–13). While John the Baptist preaches repentance in the wilderness in a preparatory way (1:2–6), it is God who takes the initiative in approving and empowering the Son's invasion of enemy-occupied territory, first in the wilderness, then in village, town, and city. All these worldly territories rightfully belong to God, but Jesus now undergoes a second test—the temptation of Satan, the usurper of the kingdoms of the world. The timing of the invasion belongs to God as Jesus the Son is sent into the wilderness by the Spirit to be tested for forty days, a biblical number that connotes a period of testing preceding a salvation assault against hostile forces (cf. Noah, Gen. 7:17; 8:6; Moses, Exod. 24:18; Elijah, 1 Kings 19:8). Mark's account is so brief as to suggest that his readers already know the details of the story, a further reason for supposing that Mark may be contemporary with or even later than Matthew and Luke, but certainly not the earliest simply because it is so brief. Mark's purpose in 1:12–13 is to contrast in a single stroke Spirit/desert, Jesus/Satan, angels/wild animals to underscore the truth that Jesus the Son of God represents heaven's power unleashed against the hostile, wild, and destructive forces of Satan. He thus assures his readers, themselves arrayed against hostile forces, that Jesus represents ultimate victory, analogous to the temporary victories of those pivotal Old Testament figures who preceded him. This triumphal theme carries over into 1:14–15 with Jesus' confident proclamation of the new time that has broken into history in his person. Satan has not yet been totally routed, however, for the struggle will continue to the cross and, indeed, beyond until the end time. This creates for Jesus' followers a season of extreme tension and paradox of testing until the strong man, mortally wounded by the work of Christ, will be finally and totally destroyed, together with his evil minions and the wild beasts (Isa. 35:9; Ezek. 34:25). The eschatological drama fought out in the wilderness between Jesus the Son and Satan the strong man has been compared to the invasion of D-Day, with the final defeat likened to V-Day. Between the first and last battles Jesus and his followers move with urgent decisiveness to capitalize on the imminent collapse of Satan's tyrannical and counterfeit kingdom.

E. The beginning of Jesus' proclamation (1:14–15). The beginning of Jesus' proclamation of the good news parallels the overall theme of 1:1, "the beginning of the gospel about Jesus Christ, the Son of God." The decisive time is now manifest in the reign of God inaugurated in the person and ministry of Jesus. It is only proper to translate the verb *ēngiken* in verse 15 as "is upon you" or "is so near as to be present" (rather than simply "is near," NIV) in view of Jesus' immediate manifestation of the present power of the kingdom in proclamation, healing, and exorcism; his binding of Satan the strong man and the invasion of his house (3:23–27); and the stronger verb for "has come" (*ephthasen*) in Matthew 12:28 (cf. Luke 11:20), "But if I drive out demons by the Spirit of God, then the kingdom of God has come upon you." All the evidence of the Gospels points to the inauguration of the reign of God in Jesus' ministry, its power being manifest by his followers until the end of the age when it will be fully realized (cf. Matt. 8:11; 20:21). The kingdom of God is present, is in process of realization, is yet to come, and accordingly calls for the immediate response of repentance and belief.

II. Jesus Invades Wilderness and City with Good News (1:16–8:26)

A. Jesus' inaugural ministry in Galilee (1:16–3:6). As John's ministry phases out and Jesus' itinerant ministry begins, his threefold proclamation (**1:15**) soon gives evidence of his intention to form a cadre of followers who will participate in his redemptive reign. The kingdom of God is primarily the salvific reign of God embodied in Jesus the Son, and secondarily the realm of believers who are progressively drawn into the redemptive mission.

Jesus inaugurates a community by first calling Simon and his brother Andrew in an acted parable that signals the missionary thrust of his ministry (**1:16–20**). Deliberately choosing ordinary Galilean fishermen as his disciples, Jesus heightens the physical model of fishing to infinite proportions (as later he uses other analogies in his teaching), calling them to the urgent task of fishing for men. It is a situation of disclosure/commitment that calls for immediate decision, and both respond "at once," as do James and John whom he also calls "without delay." Mark's narrative moves quickly and is charged with urgent expectancy, anticipating the call of the Twelve in 3:13–19, their mission in 6:7–13, and the unresolved ending of the Gospel that confronts the reader with a challenge to overcome enervating fear by decisive action. Attending this note of urgency throughout the Gospel is a tacit awareness that one must wait patiently and faithfully upon the Lord's timing and his divine call. How long Jesus may have been nurturing this small circle of followers we do not know, but when the actual call came they were ready.

Hardly a dozen verses intervene between Jesus' confrontation with Satan in the wilderness and his confrontation with an evil spirit in Capernaum (**1:21–28**). His teaching in the synagogue is conducted with amazing authority, in contrast to the theoretical reflections and debates of the teachers of the law, and is attested by a work of exorcism that signals the warfare that has begun between the Son of God and Satan. The evil spirit knows who Jesus is and voices alarm at the imminent destruction of the kingdom of evil. Jesus enjoins the evil spirit to silence as he casts him out because the time of the full revelation of the Holy One of God has not yet come (a silence motif that is repeated frequently in the Gospel [e.g., 1:34, 43–44a; 3:12; 4:11–12, 34; 5:43] and reflects Jesus' sense of divine timing; there is accordingly nothing to be said for the critical view that Mark has added the silence theme). The people of Capernaum are so amazed that they spread the news over the whole region of Galilee.

The little portrait in **1:29–31** describes the first of a series of healings that demonstrate the presence of the reign of God in Jesus' ministry. It possesses the quality of naturalness and personal intimacy that characterizes Jesus' compassion for the sick. Details are sparse; nothing is said about Peter's wife, but attention is riveted on his mother-in-law who is incapacitated in bed with a fever. She is restored instantaneously as Jesus places himself at her disposal. She then places herself at the disposal of Jesus and the disciples and begins to minister to them, a typical and proper response that would not be lost upon Mark's Christian readers.

The healing of Peter's mother-in-law evidently took place on the Sabbath (a controversial matter that Jesus will soon address in his controversy with the teachers of the law). In obedience to the Sabbath law, however, the families and friends of the sick and demon-possessed bring them after sunset when the Sabbath has ended (**1:32–34**). The crowd is enormous, as Mark intimates by the descriptive words *all* and *the whole town,* a fact that underscores the problem of Jesus' proper ministry. He is constantly in danger of being misconstrued in the image of Asclepius, the mythical Hellenistic god of healing whose adherents were widespread throughout the Mediterranean world. The people perceive him as a miracle worker when it is his intention to proclaim the saving reign of God that brings deeper healing than the physical alone. Jesus demands that the demons he exorcises not bear witness to his credentials as Son of God, for his proclamation is couched in terms of the joyful tidings of grace and salvation. Only derivatively (to those who reject his offer of grace) does his kerygma imply the fear of awesome judgment to come, a fear with which the demons are singularly consumed. Theirs is an ironic and negative witness only; they cannot be proper witnesses to the truth since they are enemies of God.

Mark **1:35–39** represents a small unit of transition, moving from Capernaum to the wilderness and back to city areas. Jesus first retreats to a place of solitude that images the wilderness (lit. a wilderness place) in order to pray, having been tested by the demanding crowds who want only external healing (cf. the other two solitary crisis prayers of Jesus [6:46; 14:32–42]). It is only through communion with the Father that Jesus is ministered to by angels as he was at the temptation, for his success as a healer among the crowds must be seen as a continuation of the temptation of Satan in the wilderness and a diversion from his redemptive mission. Miracles of healing and exorcism necessarily accompany the inbreaking of the saving reign of God but are on the lower levels of healing, the healing of spirit and heart through repentance and belief being the highest. Even Simon and his companions misconstrue Jesus' deeper intention as they seek him out and address him with a reproachful call to return to the clamoring throngs in Capernaum. Jesus does not accede to their demand but changes his field of mission away from Capernaum to the villages of Galilee, preaching in the synagogues. Jesus now invades the wilderness of the city with glad tidings of salvation and exorcisms of demons as evidence that he is binding the strong man Satan throughout Galilee and releasing his prisoners from spiritual bondage. No healings are mentioned in the summary statement of 1:39, suggesting perhaps that, like Jesus himself, Mark is concerned that his readers not misconstrue Jesus as a mere miracle worker. In all the miracles of healing that follow in the Gospel, Mark gives careful attention to their integral connection with faith and salvation, though the masses and even the disciples still misunderstand the deeper dimensions of the kingdom Jesus is bringing in his person and ministry.

This interpretation is supported by Mark's account of the leper's healing (**1:40–45**). On the one hand, Jesus responds voluntarily to the leper's challenge and is filled with compassion at the ravages exacted by the demonic realm on the leper who must suffer social ostracism because of his uncleanness (Lev. 13:45–46). After healing him, Jesus sternly warns the leper not to tell anyone of his healing but to follow Mosaic ritual prescribed for lepers (Lev. 14:2–31) and to present himself to the priests as a testimony. We are not told whether the man fulfilled the ritual requirements Jesus prescribed, but Mark makes much of his disobedient response to Jesus' injunction to silence, the result being that Jesus' ministry in the city regions is seriously curtailed and the misconception further spread abroad that he is some sort of wonder-working god-man. Jesus now has no privacy even in the lonely places to which he has retreated. Not only his immediate followers (1:36) but also the masses who clamor for physical healing (1:45) come to him. Jesus determinedly and angrily resists his success as a popular and spectacular miracle worker and views the superficial response of the populace as a continued temptation of Satan to divert and misconstrue the true intent of his ministry.

A crisis now ensues which Jesus precipitates by his determination to confront fundamental misinterpretations of his ministry head on (2:1–3:6). The conflict with Satan now moves openly from wilderness to city as Jesus invades the domain of religious misinterpretation. Irony abounds in each of the five confrontations Mark has chosen to illustrate the level of opposition Jesus encounters and his adamant and authoritative invasion of this hostile religious territory. Each episode illustrates how Jesus early on lifts his conflict with demonic forces to the higher level of cognitive theological controversy, using physical acts of healing and unorthodox feasting and eating as acted parables of the inbreaking kingdom of God.

The crowds press upon Jesus once again as a determined party of friends come bearing a paralytic to be healed (**2:1–12**; probably at the home of Peter and Andrew [cf. 1:29]). Observing their faith, Jesus proceeds to couple his healing of the man with forgiveness of his sins. Jesus reclaims the Old Testament teaching that forgiveness and healing are interrelated (Ps. 103:3; Isa. 19:22; Jer. 3:22; Hos. 4:1–4), a truth he directs to the crowd that demands healing without the price of repentance. The claim to forgive sins, however, is intended not only to restore the sick paralytic to total spiritual and physical health, but to challenge the religious authorities to make a decision concerning Jesus' claim to stand in the very place of God himself as the one who alone has authority to forgive sins. The charge that Jesus is blaspheming is their reply to what is ironically a true theological statement. They understand Jesus' syllogism: (1) only God can forgive sins; (2) I am forgiving sins; (3) therefore, I am claiming to stand in the very place of God and to exercise his authority.

This is the central christological issue Jesus forces his audience to decide upon throughout his ministry, and it continues to be the major focus of the controversy of the early church with Judaism at the time of Mark's writing. His use of the enigmatic title *Son of man* ("But that you may know that the Son of Man has authority on earth to forgive sins" [2:10]) is purposely employed, like the similar kingdom of God metaphor, both to reveal and to veil the truth. A number of interpreters, including some very conservative ones, feel that the appearance of the title *Son of man* in 2:10 and 28 is awkward so early in Jesus' ministry, since it is not used again until the crucial disclosure to his disciples at Caesarea Philippi that he is the Messiah (8:29), after which it appears a dozen times; therefore Mark must be addressing his own readers and interpolating "Son of Man" into the text of 2:10 and 28. However, the title *Son of man* is precisely suited for Jesus' purposes at this early stage, being derived from Daniel 7:13ff. which describes both a solitary figure who receives the kingdom from the Ancient of Days and the saints of the Most High who also receive the kingdom. Jesus employs the enigmatic title *Son of man* in a way that is virtually identical to his use of "the kingdom of God," for both center upon the figure who personifies each concept, namely Jesus himself, while simultaneously embracing the faithful who represent the community he is drawing around himself and with whom he is progressively sharing the responsibilities of proclamation, healing, and exorcism. Jesus uses "Son of man" in three principal ways in the Gospels: (1) as a substitute for the personal pronoun *I;* (2) as a reference to his role as Suffering Servant; and (3) as a reference to the eschatological Judge who is to come at the end of the age. In this context it functions as both a surrogate for "I" and as a declaration that the eschatological Judge has already come; accordingly, the title carries important theological significance as Jesus claims authority to forgive sins and to heal not only physical illness but also the sinful soul, which is his higher mission. With some topical variations in arrangement, Matthew, Mark, and Luke locate the incident in the early stage of Jesus' ministry, and all agree with their source or sources that Jesus used the title *Son of man* on this occasion.

Jesus' call to Levi (Matthew; Matt. 9:9; 10:3) and his table fellowship with despised tax collectors and sinners at Levi's house (**2:13–17**) is another acted parable that theologically parallels the healing of the paralytic and precipitates a further critical question from the teachers of the law. They are correct in charging that Jesus is eating with sinners, but they miss the point that he has come in order to heal sinners, a fact disguised in his spoken parable that the healthy do not need a doctor (ironically they are most in need of one), for he has come to call not the righteous (or those who think they are) but sinners. By his acted and spoken proclamation Jesus announces that the healing physician has come, inaugurating the new age of salvation and calling for decisive action on the part of his audience.

Jesus faces a third question from his critics because his followers are not keeping the fasts observed by John's disciples and the disciples of the Pharisees (**2:18–22**). His reply, which is parallel to the first two incidents, is couched in the metaphor of a bridegroom and his guests who cannot fast as long as they have him with them. Jesus proclaims in veiled language that he is the promised bridegroom (cf. Hos. 2:14–23) and that the joyful wedding of God and his people is now going on. Eschatology is now in the process of being realized because Jesus is standing in the place of God and is marrying his people by announcing the present reality of promised salvation. The mourning of repentance and fasting has had and will again have its rightful place; it has appropriately preceded Jesus in the preparatory ministry of John the Baptist, and Jesus prophesies that fasting will again endure for a "day" when he dies and as the bridegroom is briefly taken from them. But now, and following his death, joyful celebration is and will be the order of the new time Jesus has inaugurated. (Cf. the first miracle John has selected to highlight, the wedding at Cana [John 2:1–11], which also has striking christological significance and occurs early in Jesus' ministry.) For this reason the new age needs a new wineskin to contain the new wine; the old is too weak and too brittle to accommodate the new salvation, freedom, and joy that Jesus is bringing.

Jesus now evokes more intense opposition from the religious authorities who take umbrage at his approval of his disciples picking heads of grain to eat on the Sabbath (**2:23–28**). Jewish law forbade reaping on the Sabbath (one of thirty-nine works forbidden on the Sabbath), but Jesus replies by citing two higher levels of authority than Pharisaic tradition. First, in the time of Abiathar who later became high priest (the likely meaning of the reference), David and his companions ate the consecrated bread in the house of God when they were hungry (1 Sam. 21:1–6) and were not condemned for it, though they had technically broken the law. Their need invoked a higher law and a special dispensation that took precedence over ritual law. Second, by analogy, but in an even greater sense, the source of the law itself, the Son of man, has given permission to his followers to pluck grain on the Sabbath, for he is Lord of the Sabbath and restores its true intent as a day designed to benefit, not deprive man of well-being and health. The Pharisees have skewed God's intent for the Sabbath and turned it into an excuse by which they try to justify themselves as righteous by works of the law.

Mark selects a fifth incident to further illustrate the increasing hostility of Jesus' adversaries and their desire to find occasion to accuse him (**3:1–6**). The setting is again the Sabbath and now the synagogue itself, in which Jesus has to decide whether to heal a man with a shriveled hand or to keep the law by not performing a work of healing on the Sabbath. Jesus succinctly poses the question that characterizes his entire ministry: should one do good or do evil, save life or kill? A decision must be made. The lines are drawn as Jesus chooses the former and heals the man, while the Pharisees choose the latter and, forming an uneasy alliance with their erstwhile enemies the Herodians, begin to plot how they might kill Jesus. Mark concludes his sample of five typical questions and answers from Jesus' early ministry on a note of supreme irony.

B. Jesus' itinerant ministry in Galilee (3:7–6:29). Mark has described the hostility Jesus incurs from religious authorities in the city; he now describes how Jesus returns to the wilderness (represented by the Sea of Galilee) only to encounter once again Satan's temptation from the common people who press upon him for spectacular miracles (**3:7–12**). No matter where he goes he struggles against opposition; in the city it is direct and hostile, in the wilderness it is subtle and enticing. The large crowds who seek him out as they come to him from every area and his request for a small boat to keep the people from crowding him suggest his frustration with success on the superficial level and his continued rejection of the temptation to be a spectacular Messiah. He does indeed heal many, for his embodiment of the reign of God necessarily brings healing in the physical realm; yet even his exorcisms and the accompanying testimony of the evil spirits that he is the Son of God are not exploited as one would expect of a wonder worker. Rather, Jesus commands silence of the spirits not only because they are unfit messengers of his gospel of grace but because their use of his proper title is a ploy to gain mastery over him (cf. 1:34).

Jesus' withdrawal to a mountainside with his core of followers (**3:13–19**) suggests three motifs. First, his sovereign choice of "those he wanted" attests Jesus' conscious design and control of his ministry and its progressive unfolding as he patiently works out the implications of the presence of the kingdom. Second, Jesus shares in an initiatory way with his disciples the presence of the kingdom, for they are to be sent out to preach and to have authority to drive out demons. Third, the wilderness is seen to be the setting for the disciples' testing and training, recapitulating Jesus' own wilderness experience and the wilderness experience of Old Testament Israel, the number twelve designating the new Israel that Jesus is calling into being. Jesus' patient training of the Twelve is to continue and will await his proper timing, for they are not sent out until 6:7ff. The variety of names and types is arresting and typical of the divine irony and "roundness" of the God who surprises: four fishermen, a tax collector, a Zealot, five unknowns, and a betrayer, all laypeople. This is the new community in embryo.

From the wilderness we are transported back to the city (Peter and Andrew's house in Capernaum, most likely) with its crowds and opposition from two quarters, one unexpected (his own family), the other the teachers of the law. Jesus responds to those who oppose him, giving further teaching about the true family of God (3:20–35).

Jesus' family in Nazareth has been informed about his exhaustion from dealing with the crowds, and they are concerned about his well-being and distressed that people are pressing upon him so that he is not even able to eat (**3:20–21**). This alone would not account for their urgency, however, in deciding to travel thirty miles to take charge of him and declaring that he is "out of his mind." Jesus is behaving oddly according to their expectations and is not only doing but saying strange things. They consider him on the verge of a mental breakdown and are ready to take him back to Nazareth for rest and recuperation. Well-intentioned, their concern arises from a misunderstanding (similar to that of the scribes) of his mission.

While his family is journeying Jesus undergoes a further test from the scribes who accuse him of being in league with Beelzebub, the prince of demons (**3:22–30**)—an ironic charge since Jesus' major mission is to invade the house of Satan and free his prisoners. Jesus' reply is couched in a pithy parable that announces exactly that point: he is engaged in entering the strong man's house, binding up the strong man, and carrying off his possessions. The saying is clear to one who sees, for

Jesus is proclaiming that in his ministry the kingdom of God is battling against the kingdom of Satan in spiritual warfare and claiming authority over enemy-occupied space. Satan is now being bound and Jesus (together with his disciples, who will soon share in the power of the kingdom) is about to rob his house. This is an important saying of realized or inaugurated eschatology to which Matthew and Luke lend further emphasis by quoting an additional saying from the larger context of Jesus' discourse: "But if I drive out demons by the Spirit of God, then the kingdom of God has come upon you" (Matt. 12:28; cf. Luke 11:20). Jesus is driving out demons by the Spirit of God. Accordingly, the kingdom of God has emphatically come in Jesus' ministry. That is the deeper spiritual fact his family fails to comprehend, and it is the truth that the teachers of the law reject by blaspheming the work of the Holy Spirit and calling it the work of Beelzebub, thereby committing the unpardonable sin.

Jesus opposes the scribes with strong language, for they as guardians of Scripture should know better. They must figure out the parable and discern that Jesus' true family is to be found among those who are bound and held captive by subtleties and legalisms. Jesus' remonstrance to his family, when they arrive and ask for him in the midst of the crowd, is gentler and instructive of the higher family made up of those about him who do God's will (**3:31–35**). This higher family of God, the new community of Jesus' followers, takes precedence over the ordinary family and brings it into conflict when the doing of God's will is in question (cf. 10:28–30; Luke 2:49–50; Matt. 10:34–36/Luke 12:51–53). Jesus is gathering together his larger family and resists the temptation to forsake the new community when circles of religious tradition and his immediate family pressure him to capitulate to their narrower and more comfortable vision of family and ministry.

The setting now changes from city to lake, where the crowds continue to press upon Jesus, so much so that he is forced to teach them from a boat as they gather at the water's edge (4:1–34). He resists their emotional clamor for physical healing and teaches them instead. The significance of this section on the parables cannot be overestimated, for Mark states that Jesus "did not say anything to them without using a parable" (4:34), implying a more extensive teaching available in the tradition than he has selected for his readers from his sources. Aside from 7:1–22; 13:1–37; and the present parables unit, Mark has chosen to give little of Jesus' extensive teaching because his immediate purpose is to present Jesus in situations of quick and decisive action. The sustained teaching on the parables affords important insight into the ironic mode of Jesus' proclamation, for on the one hand, he employs simple illustrations drawn from ordinary life to "throw alongside of" (the literal meaning of "parable") the spiritual reality of God's saving reign that is present in his person; on the other hand, he purposely uses the parables to becloud the minds of the proud and resistant. The parables both disclose a mystery and are mysterious, depending on one's willingness and ability to perceive spiritual things (a gift, as Mark indicates, that in the ultimate sense is sovereignly given by God). They describe a disclosure/commitment situation in which the Son of God/Son of man announces the presence of the reign of God and calls for decisive commitment in light of that fact.

In the parable of the sower (**4:1–20**), the principal motif is that divine grace is present in the word Jesus is sowing. In spite of losses, it will spring up among the faithful and produce a bountiful harvest of thirty-, sixty-, even a hundredfold. Jesus' proclamation always centers upon the present reality of the reign of God and the possibility of salvation. But a corollary theme accompanies it: the call for commitment that must be made in light of this disclosure. Jesus' description of the kinds of soil that receive the seed-word reveals his realistic and prophetic insight into the psychological realm of will and choice that Satan seeks to control.

In order to understand Jesus' explanation of his purpose in speaking in parables (4:11–12) it is important to understand that the "secret" (Gk. *mystērion*) of the kingdom of God is a personal knowledge of Jesus Christ, Son of God, Son of man, whose entire life is a self-disclosure in parables, but who is a riddle-parable to those who resist in unbelief ("those on the outside"). Two factors work simultaneously in Jesus' explanation: the sovereign gift of insight bestowed by God's absolute, elective grace (the secret "has been given" to you) and the human factor of personal decision and commitment. Jesus' citation of Isaiah 6:9–10 illustrates the point. From one angle, God's call to Isaiah seems to entail the foregone conclusion that the prophet's message will result inevitably in the hardening of his people because God has predestined it to be so. And as a matter of fact, that is precisely what happened historically: the message fell largely on deaf ears, though a remnant received it. From the angle of human responsibility and decision, the Isaiah passage is filled with irony, for the very people to whom he is to proclaim his message have (in the larger context of Isa. 1–5) been worshiping idols that have eyes that do not see and ears that do not hear, and have refused to turn and be forgiven. Isaiah's message will only confirm them in their rebellion, as Jesus' message serves to confirm the rebellious in their rejection of him. The clause *otherwise they might turn and be forgiven!* is extremely ironic, for they have no intention of turning and being forgiven, and are therefore responsible for their unbelief.

But there will be a remnant, and "the holy seed will be the stump in the land" (Isa. 6:13). Jesus is the holy seed from whose stump springs forth the new community of believers, the remnant core of disciples who are being given the gift of discernment to recognize Jesus for who he truly is. Their discernment does not come all at once but only as Jesus progressively discloses himself and his mission. Thus, having said that "the secret of the kingdom of God has been given to you" (the gift of insight bestowed by God's absolute, elective grace [4:11]), Jesus chides them for their obtuseness: "How then will you understand any parable?" (their responsibility to be open to him [4:13]). Later, when the full light dawns on Pentecost the disciples see with clearer eyes the implications of Jesus' mysterious parabolic language which is even now in the process of being unveiled to them at this early stage.

Jesus again highlights the two factors of divine timing and human responsibility in the image of the lamp and the measure (**4:21–25**), two aphorisms Jesus probably repeated often in various forms along with his other teaching, in varied settings, and on different occasions. Jesus proclaims his presence as the lamp ("the lamp comes"; NIV paraphrases), which though now hidden and concealed is to be disclosed and brought out into the open. "If anyone has ears to hear" is a call for discernment on the part of the hearer to understand Jesus' secret. Jesus then exhorts the hearer to consider carefully what is heard, namely, that as one measures it will be measured out to him, and he who has will be given more, while he who has not will have nothing, meaning that now is the moment when true perception and decisive commitment to accept Jesus' message is imperative. The kingdom of God is present in the person of Jesus and must be appropriated or lost.

Jesus' parable of the growing seed (**4:26–29**) describes the growth of the reign of God by his sovereign initiative and power as it matures to the inevitable harvest of the eschatological future (which will also bring judgment; cf. Joel 3:13). What begins inauspiciously and secretly ends gloriously with the ripened grain and the putting in of the sickle at the end of the age. All the more reason, Jesus implies, to make a decisive commitment to him in light of what is now taking place.

In the parable of the mustard seed (**4:30–34**) Jesus emphasizes not so much the mysterious growth of the reign of God, as in the previous simile, but the common theme of small beginnings and big endings. Taking the smallest seed familiar to his audience, the tiny mustard seed proverbial in Jewish tradition, Jesus heightens the familiar to dynamic proportions to describe the humble beginnings of his ministry and the mighty conclusion that is coming. This is a prophetic parable; from tiny seed to huge tree-shrub, the reign of God is first veiled in Jesus' tiny beginnings, then gloriously manifest in the fruition of his work at the end of the age. Again, the parable implies a call for discernment and commitment in view of what is happening before the eyes of his audience.

The summary verses (33–34) describe Jesus' manner of teaching and point up the dual nature of the parables which he uses both as enlightening illustrations ("as much as they could understand") and as veiled references to his intention that requires further explanation given only to his inner circle ("But when he was alone with his own disciples, he explained everything").

In 4:35–5:43 Mark selects four episodes that are typical of Jesus' acts against the hostile forces of Satan. These powerful invasions complement the parables that describe Jesus' dynamic proclamation of the kingdom's planting in his ministry. Taken together, the two sections describe the range of Jesus' ministry in word and work.

Wherever Jesus goes hostile forces wait to test and tempt him—even in the natural world (**4:35–41**). From the press of the crowds who see him as a spectacular Messiah he withdraws offshore to teach them (4:1). At evening Jesus leaves the crowd again "just as he was" without getting out of the boat and sails toward the other side of the lake. Jesus is evidently exhausted, for we find him "in the stern, sleeping on a cushion" (v. 38, a small detail from an eyewitness, probably Peter). No sooner has he fallen asleep than hostile powers whip up a furious squall that threatens to swamp the boat and terrorizes the disciples, who rudely interrupt Jesus' sleep with an ironic question, "Teacher, don't you care if we drown?" The irony lies in the fact that he, more than any other, cares whether they perish in a sense far more ultimate than the immediate threat to their lives. Nonetheless, Jesus rises to answer their request, attesting his power over nature as he recapitulates the deliverance of Israel in the exodus and the crossing of the Red Sea to subdue the wilderness powers. The disciples have not yet discerned the true nature of Jesus the Son of God or sufficiently believed in him (they are not ready to be sent out with divine power until 6:7). Jesus rebukes them as he rebukes the wind and waves, challenging their terror before natural forces with an even greater terror, the terror of their not yet having the faith he expects of them, and of even failing to recognize him. "Who is this?" is their terrified response to his miracle.

This is an important episode that sheds light on the ironic theme of Mark's Gospel by which he rebukes those, as did Jesus, who are enervated by fear and self-concern when the Son of God is standing by their side and calling them to faith. Like Jesus, Mark calls for fearless trust in the Lord in spite of terrorizing circumstances, for by his powerful presence Jesus "rebukes and silences" demons both in persons and in the hostile wilderness (the same two verbs are used in 1:25 and 4:39). (For other rebukes of his disciples see 7:18; 8:17–18, 21, 32–33; 9:19, 33–37; 10:13–14, 35–45; 14:30, 37–38.)

Jesus' onslaught against demonic distortion and destruction of what was originally created to be beautiful and covenantal (the image of God in man) is dramatically described in the account of the Gerasene demoniac (**5:1–20**). Jesus and the disciples sail to the eastern shore of the lake to the predominantly Gentile territory of the Decapolis. Jesus is there confronted by a man who has been totally alienated from family, community, and even himself, and wanders tormented night and day among the tombs, crying out and cutting himself with stones. (Matt. 8:28 indicates that there were actually two demoniacs; Mark and Luke select only one in order to focus the story.) Not even chains and irons can subdue his demonic destructiveness. Mark graphically describes (from Peter's eyewitness account) a scene of total desolation and loss of the divine image in the man. It is this demonic realm that Jesus invades yet again as he parries the attempt of the demon to get control of him by using his divine name, for the demon recognizes Jesus as the Son of the Most High God who threatens his existence. When Jesus exorcises the evil spirit, the demon's shriek reveals the terror of impending judgment under which the demonic realm lies (cf. Jude 6; Rev. 20:10). The demon's warped plea for exemption from torture when it is itself the source of torture is heavy with irony. The demonic possession of the man is so complete that Jesus' conversation is at first deflected to addressing the demon, for the man's personality has been totally eclipsed; but Jesus has already taught (3:27) that one cannot enter a strong man's house and carry off his possessions unless he first ties up the strong man: "Then he can rob his house."

Jesus now proceeds to rob Satan's house. Gaining control of the evil spirit's name (which is fittingly "Legion" for the many demons that actually inhabit the man) Jesus accedes to Legion's plea to be sent into the herd of swine. This is not a favor but an acted parable that will dramatically demonstrate two facts: (1) the aim of the demonic realm is to totally destroy its hosts; (2) the material cost of bringing the possessed back to life and fellowship summons the townspeople to decision: will they rejoice in the man's healing in spite of the cost, or will they resent Jesus' expensive exorcism and reject him for economic reasons? By his request Legion seeks to embarrass Jesus in front of the townspeople and destroy his further witness in that region. Jesus uses the occasion to challenge the Gentiles of the region with a call to commitment, but they reject him and ask him to leave even though they have seen a man restored to wholeness, sitting quietly, dressed, and in his right mind. From the negative side the key to the story lies in the last clause of 5:15, "and they were afraid" (Gk. *ephobēthēsan*), for to show fear (phobia) before the claims and healings of Jesus is to reject him (so the disciples [4:41] and the women [16:8], where the same verb is used). The healed man, however, represents the positive response; though he begs to go with Jesus, he is sent to witness to his family of the Lord's mercy and begins to tell in the Gentile Decapolis how much Jesus has done for him. (Jesus does not yet permit open witness in his own country because the miracle-conscious crowds misconstrue his intent and are therefore a political danger as well as a spiritual hindrance.)

There now follow two stories that pick up this theme of faith in Jesus and provide contrast to the enervating fear of both disciples and Gerasene townspeople in the first two episodes.

In the first two episodes only one person, the healed demoniac, expresses faith in Jesus, while both disciples and Gentile townspeople fail the test. Now two Jewish individuals, a man and a woman, display the faith requisite for true healing. As a result, two women are healed, the one a mature woman who cannot contain her menstruation, the other a young girl of twelve who is about to begin her menstruation and enter into womanhood (**5:21–43**). Jesus invades the domain of demonic destruction and restores both women as he had the Gerasene demoniac, who together represent ritual uncleanness (graves, blood, and death). In each case Jesus ravages the domain of death and releases the goods held captive by the strong man Satan.

The healings of the two women are set one within the other, the composite story opening with a description of the large crowd that again presses upon Jesus. Accordingly, this crowd forms a contrasting backdrop for the singular and desperate Jairus who comes pleading for help from Jesus. His daughter is about to enter into womanhood and is dying. Though he is one of the rulers of the synagogue and therefore a layperson of some repute, Jairus nonetheless finds no power to heal in his position of authority and therefore humbly evinces the faith Jesus expects—recognition of Jesus' divine authority. Jairus's faith in Jesus' power to heal is exemplary, whereupon Jesus without a word places himself at the disposal of the distraught father and goes with him to lay his hands upon his little daughter.

Again Mark notes the large crowd that presses around Jesus as they move along, and again he uses it as a backdrop to the singular action of the woman who knows she will be healed if only she can touch Jesus' cloak. Her faith, like Jairus's, is also exemplary, for she realizes that she will get no further help from doctors and comes desperately to Jesus. Both Jairus and the woman come to Jesus in humility born of desperation and of faith, the requisite and exemplary commitment Jesus expects as the proper response to his self-disclosure. The woman is immediately healed of her bleeding and freed from her suffering, though there were others who must have been touching Jesus in the press, an inference attested by the disciples' somewhat snappish reply to Jesus' question, "Who touched my clothes?" (v. 30), for Jesus realized that power had gone out from him. Irony abounds, for the healing power of the reign of God embodied in Jesus operates at a deep level of faith that is not perceived on the surface; all one sees is the pressing crowd, when in reality a miraculous exchange has taken place between two persons. The woman, with understandable fear and trembling (but not enervating fear and trembling—a point Mark is subtly making), falls at Jesus' feet (the proper posture of addressing Jesus; so Jairus in v. 22) and tells him the whole truth, again the proper attitude before Jesus who speaks and does the truth. Jesus' response is peculiarly like a father's as, standing in the place of God, he calls her "daughter" and acknowledges that her faith has healed (lit. saved) her, implying not only her physical healing but her spiritual salvation as well. This is attested by his valediction, "Go in peace," the traditional "shalom" implying complete reconciliation with God, and the final word of permanent well-being, "Be freed from your suffering." In view of the fact that her affliction had ceremonially prevented her from social contact with others, her healing has wider implications of restoration to fellowship in the larger family of God; she is now a member and a "daughter."

The delay caused by healing the woman occasions the news that Jairus's daughter has meanwhile died and the despairing opinion that Jesus' presence is no longer needed. (Cf. Jesus' deliberate delay in healing Lazarus [John 11:6] and the mystery of divine timing that provides occasion for an acted parable of resurrection.) Jesus ignores the passive resignation of the messengers from Jairus's house and proceeds to assault the realm of death and the unbelief that accompanies this ultimate threat to family, fellowship, and well-being. That the child is really dead is evidenced by the crying and loud wailing of the professional mourners gathered at the home, whom Jesus literally "casts out" (Gk. *ekbalōn,* v. 40) as an acted parable of resistance to Satan's claim over the child. He does this when they derisively laugh at his declaration that she is not dead but asleep. Jesus is not going to allow death to claim the child, and any opposition to his power over death is to be cast out like the demons (cf. the verb *cast out* in Matt. 12:28/Luke 11:20; the messianic kingdom present in Jesus brings healing by expulsion of the demonic realm).

Jesus permits only the innermost circle of disciples and family to witness the great miracle as he touches the ceremonially unclean girl and commands her to arise from the dead. He addresses her ironically as "little girl," for at age twelve she is about to become an adult of marriageable age. The young girl now restored and walking around brings astonishment to all. Jesus gives strict orders that the five (now become six) tell no one about this (meaning the details; the girl will soon appear outside), for he refuses to play the role of the wonder worker and gain acclaim from the crowds who lack proper faith; he reveals the secret of his messiahship only to those whom he chooses, but for the rest his works, like his words, are in perplexing parables. Finally, Jesus asks that the girl be given something to eat, a further insight into his sensitivity to her needs and recognition that she has been restored to normalcy. In the larger sense, Jesus' work is an acted parable that looks ahead to the time when death will be finally overcome and the raised fed everlastingly.

The faith of Jairus and the woman with the hemorrhage, expressed against great odds, has been vindicated. Mark's audience will not miss the point in their own circumstances.

Jesus' return to his hometown of Nazareth stands in contrast to the two healings (**6:1–6a**). While it witnesses the usual recognition that Jesus does indeed speak wisdom and perform miracles, it occasions derogatory questioning and hostile rejection. The townspeople are acquainted with Jesus' family and his trade and cannot believe that God would work in anyone so common and well known. To them, Jesus is an imposter; the implication is that his wisdom and power are derived from Satan, a common reaction to Jesus' claims that arises in the context of synagogue, temple, and established religious tradition, for Mark heightens the irony by recording that this rejection takes place on the Sabbath as Jesus teaches in the synagogue. In response Jesus refers to himself as a prophet without honor in his hometown, a common adage that he fashions into a prophecy of his coming rejection by Israel. The people of Nazareth, together with his own family (3:20–21, 31–35), reject his claims to messiahship because they cannot quite believe that someone so close to them and so well known could be God's anointed. Jesus is amazed at their lack of faith and "could not do" (i.e., would not do under such circumstances) any miracles there (except for a few small healings) because of their unreceptivity and unbelief, for faith in Jesus is prerequisite to true spiritual healing, and miracles of sheer wonder-working power only harden the unbelieving heart. While this brief episode is an acted parable of the judgment that accompanies the inauguration of the reign of God in the new age and provides a negative contrast to the faith of Jairus and the woman in 5:21–43, Jesus' word of judgment does not preclude the possibility of a change of heart should faith replace doubt. Later his mother, James, and Jude are numbered among the faithful. There is a lesson in this for Mark's readers: while unbelief and rejection will be the response of many to the gospel, they are to commit themselves to the Lord with decisive belief and faith.

Verse 6b may go with 6a, in which case Jesus' third journey through the Galilean towns (see 1:14, 39) is a result of his rejection at Nazareth. More likely, it may introduce a new stage in the inauguration of the reign of God as Jesus now includes his disciples in the threefold invasion of the demonic realm through proclamation, exorcism, and healing (**6:6b–13**). Following the rejection at Nazareth, Jesus' sending out the Twelve affords ironic contrast as he gives his disciples authority over evil spirits and ravages Satan's domain. Mark reports that they drove out many demons and healed many people, and implies (in the context of vv. 12–13) that many also repented. Two important facts surface in this account of the disciples' mission. First, Jesus intimates by his act of commissioning that the kingdom of God and the Son of man not only symbolize the centrality of his person in the inbreaking of the new age of salvation, but contain a societal element as well, namely, the family of disciples he has been training for this moment. The disciples are now empowered to participate in the threefold ministry of Jesus and to join him in the invasion of the satanic kingdom to release the strong man's goods. Second, the disciples are sent out two by two to fulfill the Mosaic requirement for truthful witness ("on the testimony of two or three witnesses" [Deut. 17:6; cf. Num. 35:30]), for Jesus' invasion is an assault of truth against the falsehood of Satan that destroys fellowship and life. The disciples are to take nothing but the power he gives them. (Mark's inclusion of staff and sandals—cf. Matt. 10:9f.; Luke 9:3—may reflect either Jesus' recapitulation of Exodus 12:11 or Mark's adaptation of traveling light in the Roman idiom, probably the latter.) The disciples are to symbolize in both honoring hospitality shown them and shaking the dust off their feet the reality of the kingdom's presence which brings salvation or judgment, depending on its reception. By the sifting of dust those who reject Jesus and his disciples are themselves rejected. In light of 6:12–13, Jesus' rejection at Nazareth (6:3–6) is both ironic and ominous. The rejection of Jesus and his predecessor John the Baptist is also ironic and ominous for those of high rank, as Mark is about to show.

Mark now describes how news of the powerful ministry of Jesus troubles the conscience of the tetrarch Herod Antipas (whom Mark derisively calls "king," 6:14; **6:14–29**). While the people are not sure who Jesus is—Elijah, or one of the prophets, or John the Baptist raised from the dead—Herod is sure it is the John he beheaded, and his conscience troubles him. The tragic story of the adulterous Herod and Herodias illustrates the cost of true and fearless discipleship: John the Baptist is beheaded for courageously proclaiming the truth about Herod's marriage, and his death prefigures the death of Jesus who is to die for telling the truth to a rebellious generation. The story also implies the horrendous consequences of rejecting God's anointed prophets. In placing the Herod story immediately after the mission of the disciples who preach repentance, drive out demons, and heal the sick, but shake the dust of judgment against the deaf who will not listen, Mark skillfully portrays the ironic consequences of failure to listen to God's word of truth. Herod had defiantly built his capital Tiberias on an ancient cemetery and offended his Jewish subjects; he had married his divorced niece whose husband was still living, contrary to Jewish law (Lev. 18:16); and he had made rash promises in the setting of a lewd banquet and chose to defer to those he deemed to be more important than John. The head of John on a platter (6:27–28) illustrates ironically the cost of discipleship in the face of wicked opposition. That would not be lost on Mark's Roman readers, nor would they miss the irony of Herod's overweening pride that later moved him to request kingship from Augustus, which led to his dismissal and exile in A.D. 39.

C. Jesus' withdrawal to the wilderness beyond Galilee (6:30–7:23). The kingdom of God has been inaugurated in Jesus' ministry and brings either salvation or judgment, depending on the decision of the hearer. Jesus' disciples, like John, are called to place themselves at the disposal of the lost. They may, like John and like Jesus, give up their lives in witnessing to the truth, but the final vindication is a banquet of fulfillment and life, not a banquet of separation and death. Like the two banquets of the faithful and the unfaithful in Revelation 19:9, 17–21, the second of which has been paralleled in the previous account (for the reader knows the end to which Herod and Herodias came), Mark's narrative now contrasts the miraculous meal in the wilderness (**6:30–44**) that anticipates Jesus' own death and the marriage supper of the Lamb.

The disciples are now functional "apostles," as Mark calls them in 6:30, and they return to report to Jesus all they have done and taught. The fact that they report what they have "done and taught" indicates their participation in the twofold nature of Jesus' work-and-words mission, for they have preached, healed, and cast out evil spirits. Theirs is a report of success, not of disappointment. (In Luke's account of the success of the larger circle of seventy-two [10:17–18], Jesus describes a vision in which he sees "Satan fall like lightning from heaven," a result of the assault on Satan's kingdom by Jesus and his disciples.) The healing activity of the disciples is attested by the throngs who are coming and going and do not even give them time to eat. This gives Jesus occasion to withdraw with his disciples to "a solitary place" for rest (6:32), a recapitulation of the exodus and wilderness rest of Moses and Joshua, and the rest anticipated by the prophets (cf. Jer. 31:2). But the crowds get there ahead of them and, like sheep without a shepherd, evoke the compassion of Jesus, who proceeds to teach them and then to feed them.

There is irony in the contrast of Jesus' banquet with Herod's, for Jesus' meal is simple yet gives life and satisfaction, while Herod's is sumptuous but brings death and emptiness. There is irony also in the inability of the disciples to satisfy the hungry crowd and to think in other than human terms when Jesus asks them to provide food, when they had just returned from a mission of miraculous healings and exorcisms. They do not yet understand the full scope of the inaugurated reign of Jesus and that the invasion of Satan's realm is only the beginning of the new exodus of the new Israel that brings promised rest and food along the way to the Promised Land. Because the disciples share the powers of the kingdom, they should be able to feed the hungry in Jesus' name; but they are not yet ready.

Jesus takes the crisis in hand and performs an acted parable of feeding like the shepherd of Psalm 23 and Ezekiel 34:23–31 who safely tends and feeds his sheep in the wilderness and keeps them from fear and famine. By multiplying the five loaves and two fish, Jesus the shepherd provides for his sheep, thereby transforming the wilderness into a place of rest and nourishing manna (cf. Isa. 25:6–9) for the people of the new exodus, who are seated upon the green grass (even the grass of early spring participates in the symbolism of promise, a small but not insignificant detail of the eyewitness).

Jesus' prayer of thanks as he looks up to heaven before he breaks the loaves and gives them to his disciples to set before the people indicates not only his faithfulness to Jewish form in giving thanks before meals, but attests his awareness that what he does he does as the faithful Son, not as a wonder worker who seeks adulation and profit from the crowds. The acted parable of feeding the multitude is performed to satisfy their immediate physical needs, but on a deeper level it is intended to reveal to the disciples that Jesus is Lord of the messianic meal, for it is they who have seen the miracle, distributed the food, observed that all have eaten and are satisfied, and gathered twelve basketfuls of broken pieces of bread and fish. The deeper spiritual dimensions of the miracle are to be spiritually discerned and illustrate Jesus' words, "Blessed are those who hunger and thirst for righteousness, for they will be filled" (Matt. 5:6). There is no indication that the disciples understand the inner meaning of what Jesus has done, even less so the crowd of people, who according to John (6:14–

15) misconstrue the miracle and threaten to make him king by force, causing Jesus instead to withdraw to a mountain by himself. Later the followers of Jesus will see that in this acted parable he anticipates the final meal of his death and resurrection by which he becomes food for eternal life, not just for a day.

Before he withdraws to the mountainside to pray, Jesus sends his disciples off by boat to Bethsaida while he dismisses the crowd. A crisis is in the wind as satanic forces maneuver to deflect Jesus' messianic ministry. Jesus again tests the faith of his disciples and demonstrates his power over the hostile wind through a miracle on the lake (**6:45–52**; cf. 4:35–41). The scene needs to be understood against the backdrop of demonic resistance to Jesus and his vulnerable disciples with whom he is beginning to share the powers of the invading reign of God. For Mark's readers the contrary wind is a challenge to faith in their own situation of testing. It is night, and Jesus is alone praying (cf. 1:35–39; 14:35–42), while his disciples are being assaulted by the hostile wind on the lake. They always seem to be in trouble when they are apart from Jesus. Jesus reminds them dramatically of their responsibility to take courage and not fear (6:49–50), and then manifests his absolute power as the sovereign "It is I" (Gk. *egō eimi*) who speaks and acts out his sovereign self-revelation (cf. Exod. 3:14; 33:19, 22; 1 Kings 19:11; Job 9:8, 11; Isa. 41:4–16). It is against this Old Testament background that Jesus works his miracle of theophany. He does not actually intend to pass the disciples by (v. 48), but seems from their perspective to be doing so (cf. their similar lack of understanding of the situation in 4:38). When Jesus joins them in the boat, the wind dies down. The lesson of the theophany is disclosed in Mark's summary comment (v. 52). The disciples have not understood about the loaves because their hearts are hardened and they have failed to discern who Jesus truly is. Ironically, though they have been empowered to participate in the mission of Jesus and have already proclaimed repentance, healed the sick, and exorcised demons, they have only begun to penetrate the mystery of Jesus. The irony is that their reaction places them in the company of Jesus' opponents (cf. 3:5; 10:5). Thus faith in Jesus' authority over hostile powers as the Lord of creation is absolutely necessary if those powers are to be overcome.

Mark continues to give the reader a sense of the quick movement and intensity of Jesus' ministry as he describes how the pressure is constantly on Jesus. He has confronted the faithlessness of his disciples; now the crowds come from everywhere in the region carrying their sick to the miracle worker. The healings in Gennesaret (**6:53–56**) summarize Jesus' healing activity before his departure to Tyre (7:24), and afford an ironic contrast to the lack of faith on the part of the disciples just preceding and the stubborn opposition of the religious leaders that immediately follows. Though there is no mention of preaching or exorcisms, the people evince a faith similar to the woman with the hemorrhage as they beg to touch even the edge of his cloak (v. 56; cf. 5:25–34). Their faith is primitive but genuine, and Jesus rewards their belief with healing.

In contrast to the simple faith of those who are considered unclean because they are sick, but are healed by Jesus because their faith proceeds from proper intention within, the Pharisees and teachers of the law evidence improper intention within and preoccupation with external rituals that deceives them into thinking that righteousness consists in outer observance. The conflict described by Mark in **7:1–23** is not initiated by Jesus but by the religious leaders who are offended by the disciples' apparent lack of concern for cleansing rituals. The authorities seem oblivious to Jesus' cleansing of the inner realm of human intention where sin and hypocrisy or true righteousness originate. As ever (so Matt. 5–7, esp. 5:20, "unless your righteousness surpasses that of the Pharisees and the teachers of the law, you will certainly not enter the kingdom of heaven"), Jesus drives the debate inward to the personal realm of choice and intention, angrily excoriating the religious leaders for locating religion in the outer realm of impersonal and abstract legalisms, most of them man-made traditions that set aside the commands of God. Jesus assumes authority over the Pharisees and legal experts by approving Isaiah's condemnation of his own people for the same sin of offering lips for heart, and so worshiping God in vain (vv. 6–8; Isa. 29:13). Moving away from the impersonal abstractions of Pharisaic oral law to personal intention and the well-being of the human heart, Jesus cites a typical example of the Pharisees' hypocrisy and roundly condemns their crafty observance of external law while inwardly depriving mother and father of rightful benefit by the ancient rite of Corban, an offering made to God (vv. 9–13; cf. Lev. 2:1, 4, 12–13). Ironically, in thinking that such outer observance is true worship, the Pharisees practice the art of self-deception and radically misconstrue the intent of true worship, which comes from a humble heart.

This occasions further teaching on the without and the within. Jesus declares to the crowd and privately to his disciples that it is not external things that defile a person, but what proceeds from the heart. This teaching is absolutely basic to Jesus' mission (and later to the mission of the church, as Mark intimates in his parenthetical remark [v. 19b]; cf. Peter's vision [Acts 10:9–11:18]), for he deliberately ministers to the ritually unclean, both Jew and Gentile, who come to him in simple faith for healing and wholeness. That the evils listed in verses 21–22 come from inside the self, not outside, and are intentional "thoughts" rather than external rituals, means that the human heart itself is corrupted and is in need of radical redemption. Jesus does not lessen the law but heightens its demands by locating it in the heart where decisions originate and where personal responsibility for outer speech and actions resides. Implicit in his exchange with the Pharisees and teachers of the law is Jesus' insistence that healing and salvation must come from an inner faith that humbly and voluntarily submits to his messianic authority.

D. The Gentile mission (7:24–8:10). Typically, Mark shows how Jesus illustrates his teaching with appropriate action. Two healings of outcasts and a second feeding of the crowds in outcast territory highlight the centrality of faith from the heart that welcomes even Gentiles into the kingdom. The religion of the Pharisees has no message of hope for the outcast, but keeps its distance from their defiling sickness and sin. Jesus shows the invalidity of Pharisaic oral law by venturing again into mixed Gentile-Jewish territory where, ironically, truer faith will be found than among the teachers of the law. Jesus gives further evidence that the reign of God in his person is invading the hostile realm of Satan which keeps human prisoners bound in sickness and want until Jesus comes to release them. The change of venue some twenty miles north to Phoenician Tyre was likely occasioned by the need for rest on the part of Jesus and his disciples (cf. 6:53–56), but he turns it into an acted parable of the Gentile mission.

Jesus' response to the Syrophoenician mother's appeal on behalf of her demon-possessed daughter (**7:24–30**) is ironic and should be read as a test of her faith as well as illustrative of the divine priority in the plan of salvation ("first for the Jew, then for the Gentile" [Rom. 1:16]). Jesus' ministry is directed primarily to the Jews, but his occasional incursions into Gentile territory attest his intention that all who show faith in him, whether Jew or Gentile, will receive salvation. Unlike the Pharisees in the preceding story, the woman responds with wit and tenacity to Jesus' ironic parody of Jewish exclusivism (they considered themselves privileged children by heredity and self-righteous ritual, and Gentiles and Jews who made themselves like Gentiles no better than dogs). The woman humbly swallows her pride and opens her heart to receive Jesus' grace at whatever the price, as her primary concern is her daughter's well-being. But she also wittily picks up Jesus' own witty and gracious challenge to imaginative faith when she makes a turn on the traditional and pejorative Gentile "dogs" and calls them diminutive "little household pets" (Gk. *kynarioi,* v. 27) that eat the children's crumbs under the table. Opening the door just a crack by not employing the image of yard or stray dogs (Jesus would be speaking Greek to the woman), she opens the door wide and not only accepts his veiled invitation to eat the children's crumbs but insists on eating them now, while the favored members of the household are eating from the table, thus challenging Jesus' "First let the children eat all they want" (v. 27). He appreciates the bold and humorous turn that reveals the humility and faith of a heart that reads his own heart of compassion, for he is indeed offering salvation and healing both to Jew and Gentile in the present moment. He declares her daughter cleansed of the demon. Declaring it done is as good as done, and the woman returns home to find her child healed and the demon gone. Ironically, the unclean Gentile girl is cleansed of the unclean demon (7:30) by her mother's decisive and intercessory faith in Jesus, but the clean Pharisees remain unclean because their evils come from unrepentant and unbelieving hearts that reject Jesus (7:15, 23).

The second miracle in this contrastive unit on the Gentile mission (**7:31–37**) concerns a man of the Gentile Decapolis territory who has lost the ability to hear and to speak. Again it is intercessory faith that brings healing, as the man's friends beg Jesus to lay his hand upon him. The healing is performed, again, apart from the crowds who see Jesus only as divine wonder worker, but also to give personal attention to the man, for Jesus is healing on a level deep with redemptive significance, as the parallel with Isaiah 35:5–6 suggests. Jesus puts his fingers in the man's ears, and spits and touches the man's tongue—acted parables of what are about to become normal functions of restored fellowship. Jesus opens the man's ears and mouth with a word, *Ephphatha!* (v. 34; in this setting Jesus speaks Aramaic), dramatically opening what Satan has closed. Again Jesus enjoins silence in order to avoid misunderstanding and possible political consequences that might subvert his journey to the cross; nonetheless, the crowd's "He has done everything well" (v. 37), though it lacks depth of understanding, is a fitting doxology at this stage that echoes the "very good" of Genesis 1:31. Jesus continues to inaugurate the time of the new creation that unstops the ear that it may hear and releases the mute tongue to shout for joy (Isa. 35:5–6).

During his itinerant ministry of some three years Jesus would have repeated common teachings and miracles many times, with variations adapted for different audiences and settings. Given the length of his ministry, the dullness of hearing not only of the crowds but also of the disciples, and the constant spiritual and physical needs of those held prisoner by demonic powers, it is not surprising to find Jesus repeating miracles like the feeding of the masses who come to him in the wilderness. This time the setting is in the mixed Gentile-Jewish area of the Decapolis and is an acted parable of the Gentile mission that prefigures the mixed nature of the church (**8:1–10**). Mark selectively replicates the parallelisms in Jesus' ministry, as a close study of 6:31–7:37 and 8:1–30 suggests. It is, accordingly, not necessary to take the view of more radical interpreters who see the feeding of the four thousand as a theological reshaping of the earlier story. The disciples remain dull in understanding (and continue so until the resurrection), and Jesus remonstrates with them, referring to the earlier feeding (8:17–21).

Jesus is moved by compassion for the hungry crowd that has been with him three days and is near to collapse. He is intent on feeding them (8:2–3), whereas his compassion for the crowd in 6:34 is to teach them because they are like sheep without a shepherd. There, the disciples are concerned about the hungry and present the problem to Jesus; here, Jesus is concerned for the hungry and presents the problem to the disciples. Jesus uses each occasion to challenge his disciples to grasp the fact that his feeding of the hungry is not only a clue to his person but to their own mission as well. The original significance of the seven loaves and a few small fish, compared with the five loaves and two fish of 6:38, and the four thousand compared with the five thousand of 6:44, eludes us, but it is clear to Mark that they indicate two events as well as the fact that Jesus demonstrates again the nature of his ministry that has small beginnings and big endings. In this larger sense Jesus' intention is to act out parables of well-being that signal the inauguration of the age of salvation where the hungry are fed at the banquet of the Lord (Ps. 23; Ezek. 34:25–31). There is plenty of manna for all in this new exodus (cf. Exod. 16:31–35; John 6:48–51; Rev. 2:17); seven large baskets (*spyridas,* v. 8; cf. Paul's basket, Acts 9:25) of broken fragments are left over, symbolizing the munificence of the Lord's banquet.

Mark records that Jesus, having sent the people away, leaves the Decapolis and returns with his disciples to the western side of the lake and to Galilee (Dalmanutha may have been Magadan or Magdala; cf. Matt. 15:39).

E. Questions concerning signs and seeing (8:11–26). Back in Jewish territory, Jesus is confronted by the stubbornly unbelieving religious authorities who tempt him to produce divine signs to authenticate his (in their eyes) ambiguous words and works (**8:11–21**; cf. Moses and the wilderness generation, Deut. 32:5–20). Jesus views this request as an extension of Satan's temptation to yield to the unbelieving heart by serving up sensational signs and becoming a spectacular messiah. Jesus' sigh in 8:12 is one of anger and exasperation at their unbelief (cf. the entirely different sigh of compassion in 7:34), for they have been witnessing the mighty works that have accompanied his proclamation of good news, but assign them to the demonic realm. Jesus knows that no sign or mighty work will convince them as long as their hearts are unbelieving (had he granted a sign they would have invoked Deut. 13:1–5; in fact, at the cross they carry out the condemnation). The issue at hand is Jesus' authority, which they reject. Therefore, the unbelieving generation they represent will receive no more than the sufficient evidence Jesus is presenting. Faith perceives it, unbelief rejects it.

Jesus leaves them (v. 13) in a prophetic act of judgment and crosses again to the other side with his disciples, taking the occasion of their asking for food to draw out a response of faith both the Pharisees and Herod have failed to show. He warns them of the yeast of the Pharisees and of Herod, yeast being the evil disposition to demand signs before acting on the prophet's proclamation. But the disciples fail to understand that Jesus is the "one loaf they had with them in the boat" (v. 14; did Mark intend this ironic pun?), and go on superficially discussing their lack of bread and who might be responsible for failing to bring it. Jesus tries to get them to see with their eyes, hear with their ears, and understand with their hearts (v. 17; cf. 4:11–12) the deeper meaning of the feedings of the five thousand and the four thousand, when, as they correctly recall, they picked up twelve and seven baskets of pieces. There is a note of disappointment in Jesus' concluding question, "Do you still not understand?" (v. 21), that implies their failure to see the feedings as acted parables pointing to his own person as the sufficient bread of life.

Mark's quick and condensed account brings Jesus and his disciples to the northeastern shore of the lake, where the reader is confronted by another ironic contrast (**8:22–26**): the disciples see physically, but not spiritually; the blind man cannot see physically but sees spiritually because he has faith in Jesus. His spiritual sight leads to physical sight, as Jesus makes him whole.

The gradual healing of the blind man seems at first odd, as Jesus' healings are usually instantaneous. It is of course Jesus' sovereign choice to heal according to his own timing, but a better explanation is that Jesus intends this healing as an acted parable primarily for his disciples (it can be assumed that he takes at least some of the disciples with him outside the village where the healing occurs, as was the case with the healing of Jairus's daughter [5:37]). In the previous episode Jesus asks the disciples, "Do you still not see or understand?" (8:17), and in the episode immediately following Jesus asks the disciples who they think he is, and Peter is given to see that he is the Christ (8:29). Similarly, the blind man is like the disciples; at first he sees only dimly, then when Jesus again puts his hands on the man's eyes he sees everything clearly. The disciples still have much to learn about Jesus after the disclosure at Caesarea Philippi, but the difference between Jesus' self-disclosure to his disciples before the healing of the blind man and afterward at Caesarea Philippi is as great as the two seeings of the blind man who is healed in stages. Very likely Jesus intends this episode to be an acted parable in a double sense, not only to the man himself, but to the disciples whose spiritual eyesight is being healed only gradually. Mark accordingly includes it here as a miracle of transition that leads from the "Do you still not see or understand?" to Peter's confession of messiahship, followed by Jesus' prophecy of his coming death and resurrection. (Cf. the earlier parallel healing of the deaf and mute man [7:31–36] and the Old Testament image of the restoration of sight [Ps. 146:8; Isa. 29:18; 35:5]). The masses are not yet ready to see everything clearly, hence the warning to the restored man not to "go into the village" (v. 26) and the private disclosure of messiahship and the suffering servant at Caesarea Philippi (vv. 27–33).

The healing of the blind man and his seeing "everything clearly" brings the first half of Mark's Gospel to a high point of expectancy and prepares the disciples and the reader for the second stage of Jesus' ministry where he now clearly and miraculously discloses his suffering-servant messiahship to his disciples and sets his eyes toward the invasion of the hostile city of Jerusalem.

III. Jesus Invades the Hostile City of Jerusalem (8:27–15:47)

Jesus and his disciples travel north to the villages around Caesarea Philippi where revelations and prophecies are given to the disciples about his coming redemptive passion. They then make the long journey south to Jerusalem where the final drama of salvation will be acted out. Everything in this section anticipates the invasion of Jerusalem, the center most hostile to Jesus and the citadel that ironically symbolizes the seat of demonic power that in the name of religion keeps his people imprisoned. It is not without significance that Jesus begins his journey from Caesarea Philippi, an area that was familiar with the Greek god Pan and the lordship of Caesar, and was the residence of Herod Philip, as though symbolically he is announcing to those who have eyes to see (certainly Mark's Christian readers) that he is claiming his lordship over both pagan and Jewish powers that lay rival claim to the world.

A. The journey to Jerusalem (8:27–10:52). This narrative unit is devoted to (1) Jesus' messianic prophecies as suffering servant; (2) his glory as beloved Son of God; (3) his exhortations to radical discipleship; and (4) exorcisms that evidence his continued invasion of satanic territory. This unit ends, as does the previous section, with the healing of a blind man (cf. 8:22–26 and 10:46–52), by which Jesus acts out in an appropriate miracle the light he is bringing into darkness.

The parallels between the story of the blind man healed at Bethsaida (8:22–26) and the Caesarea Philippi confession (**8:27–30**) are too striking to be missed: (1) setting: Bethsaida/Caesarea Philippi, verse 22 = 27; (2) partial sight: people like trees/Jesus only a prophet, verse 24 = 28; (3) sight restored: everything clearly/You are the Christ, verse 25 = 29; (4) secrecy motif: Don't go into the village/not to tell anyone, verse 26 = 30.

Jesus has been widely misunderstood up to this point, being generally taken by the masses to be John the Baptist brought back to life, or Elijah, or one of the prophets (or a wonder-working god-man in the Hellenistic fashion of the day), while the religious authorities consider him demonic. That Jesus is more than an ordinary prophet will be dramatically and visually substantiated in the transfiguration (9:2–9), but is now articulated by Peter, who speaks for the disciples when he replies to Jesus' question, "You are the Christ," the Messiah, the

Anointed One. The disciples understand clearly that Jesus is the Messiah, but they do not understand his interpretation of messiahship, which involves suffering and dying for their sins, and rising again, as Jesus' later rebuke of Peter (v. 33) and the disciples' political misconception of messiahship (Acts 1:6–7) indicate. Though Peter's confession is a sovereign gift of light, it is no more the full light of seeing than the sight of the man of Bethsaida who is restored to human sight but not to full spiritual seeing. Peter confesses the Jewish political expectations of his day, understanding the Messiah as the future anointed ruler from David's line (cf. 2 Sam. 7:14–16; Isa. 55:3–5; Jer. 23:5). Peter's confession is correct but narrow. Jesus' command of silence is perhaps to be interpreted in this sense, for the next scene discloses that Peter's understanding of messiahship is close to that of the demons. The point of contention, and the central issue of Jesus' evangelical mission, is the necessity of his dying and rising again.

Some critics have denied Jesus' use of the Son of man as a personal title, his messianic self-consciousness, and his ability to prophesy his death and resurrection in **8:31–33;** 9:31; and 10:33–34. It is said that prophecies of the future are not possible and that these were written after Jesus' death and placed on his lips by his followers. Such an interpretation is controlled by modern naturalistic presuppositions foreign to the intent of Mark, who gives evidence of a high Christology in his reportage, witnessing to the supernatural nature of Jesus' ministry consistently throughout the Gospel and his self-consciousness that as Son of God and Son of man he is engaged in a spiritual battle to the death to release Satan's prisoners.

Where Jesus speaks in a veiled and parabolic manner of his death in 2:20, here he speaks openly ("plainly," v. 32) to his disciples about the nature of his messiahship, affording the key to the messianic secret that has been kept from the crowds who, in their clamor to understand him only as a wonder-working figure, actually threaten and subvert his intention of accomplishing the truly saving work, namely, going to the cross, dying, and rising again. Jesus tells his disciples that he must suffer, be rejected, be killed, and rise again. He consciously and freely makes this decision, placing himself at the disposal of those he is to save by his death and consciously intending the fulfillment of Isaiah 53:1–12. If he gave in to the temptation to show only his glory and miraculous power and allowed the crowds their adulation and the demons their howling, he would gain only a temporary victory but lose the real battle to Satan.

In his prophecy, Jesus uses "Son of Man" both as a substitute for *I* and as a title that denotes his suffering ministry as Messiah.[1] In addition, Jesus intends a veiled reference (which the disciples would later understand) to Daniel 7:13ff., where the Son of man is a single individual who is given authority, glory, sovereign power, and an everlasting kingdom by the Ancient of Days (Dan. 7:13–14), while the saints of the Most High also receive the kingdom (Dan. 7:18, 21, 27). Jesus' use of the title *Son of man* accordingly suggests that he identifies himself as the central figure who gathers around him a society of the saints who will participate in his reign. Hence, Son of man is both an individual and a corporate title, the social implications of which will become clearer in Jesus' radical call to humility and suffering discipleship in 8:34–38; 9:33–37; and 10:38–45. It is Jesus' prophecy that he will "rise again" that fulfills Hosea 6:1–2 ("on the third day he will restore us") and envisions the corporate consolation of Israel that is anticipated by the community he is calling around him.

But the suffering aspect of messiahship Peter refuses to accept as he rebukes Jesus. Jewish expectations of Messiah simply did not include the aspect of suffering servant. A double irony follows. First, Jesus rebukes Peter and identifies the source of his denial of the Messiah's suffering as satanic, not divine (v. 33). Even a disciple can act as the voice of Satan (v. 32), having just acted as the voice of God (v. 29). Jesus' rebuke is not intended to reject Peter but to call him and the disciples to loyal commitment to his self-disclosure of his messiahship and his right to define the nature of Messiah and the plan of salvation. The second irony follows: Jesus now calls his disciples and the larger crowd (for the invitation and conditions are for all believers) to accept suffering as the way of true servanthood. Peter had rejected it for Jesus; Jesus accepts it for himself and challenges Peter and the others to accept it for themselves.

The theme of total loyalty to the Son of man (**8:34–9:1**) may be from a longer discourse on the occasion (each subunit seems to be an abstract of a longer call to commitment), but its concentrated effect is striking, as Jesus focuses his call to allegiance upon himself and calls for utter disposability on his behalf, even to the point of employing (ironically and prophetically) the image of his disciples carrying a cross-

1. For a discussion of these two uses and a third, the future return of the Son of man, see R. G. Gruenler, "Son of Man" in the *Evangelical Dictionary of Theology*, ed. Walter A. Elwell (Grand Rapids: Baker, 1984).

beam on the way to crucifixion, a common sight in the Roman world of his day. The saying is prophetic because Jesus himself will go before them as cross-bearer in the ultimate sense, and will become their exemplar. The saying is ironic, because Jesus not only corrects Peter's denial of suffering messiahship, but also makes suffering, self-denial, and cross-bearing a necessary way for Peter and the disciples as well, if they want to please their Lord and save their souls. There follows the paradox that there is no other way to save one's life but to lose it for Jesus and the gospel (v. 35), just as there is no exchange a man can make for his life from the goods of this world (vv. 36–37, a reflection of Ps. 49:7–9).

Therefore, everything hangs on present faithfulness to the Son of man (v. 38) who is none other than Jesus himself (v. 35), for he will return in glory as Judge to condemn those who have been ashamed of him and have failed to follow him with utter faithfulness—even unto death. Jesus' gospel brings grace, but at the price of radical faith and trust in him. His gospel brings judgment as well to an "adulterous and sinful generation" (v. 38) that is ashamed of him and rebels against him (sin, adultery, and rebellion are also major judgmental themes of the Old Testament prophetic message that lie side by side with the offer of grace: e.g., Isa. 1:18–31; Jer. 23:5–24; Ezek. 16:1–63; Hos. 2:1–23).

The coming of the Son of man "in his Father's glory" (8:38) is a clue to 9:1, which describes the coming of the kingdom of God with power in the lifetime of the disciples. Therefore, 9:1 does not begin an entirely new subject but serves as the climax of 8:34–38 and as a transition to the transfiguration (9:2–8). Jesus gives assurance to his disciples that some of them will presently see evidence of the Son of man's glory and the power of the kingdom of God. These images are interchangeable in two respects: (1) Jesus personifies both the Son of man and the reign of God; and (2) Jesus includes his disciples corporately in the community and ministry implicit in both. (Cf. the close relationship of Son of man, kingdom, and saints in Dan. 7:13–27, and the interchangeability of the terms *Son of man* and *kingdom* in Matthew's account [16:28].) Already the disciples have seen (if not understood) the power of the reign of God in Jesus' ministry and have themselves shared in its power as they have preached, healed, and exorcised demons in his name. But Jesus is prophesying an imminent event that will further disclose his glory and power. The miraculous transfiguration of Jesus on the mountain in the presence of Peter, James, and John qualifies as a fulfillment of Jesus' prophecy, especially in view of Peter's eyewitness account (2 Pet. 1:16–18) that links power, parousia (coming), and glory with the transfiguration. (A further fulfillment is the resurrection of Jesus "who through the Spirit of holiness was declared with power to be the Son of God by his resurrection from the dead" [Rom. 1:4].)

Parallel to Peter's inspired confession at Caesarea Philippi (8:29) is the highest and most direct revelation from God himself, who identifies Jesus in a miraculous theophany (**9:2–8**): "This is my Son, whom I love. Listen to him." This disclosure of the real identity of Jesus also parallels the baptism (1:9–11), where God approves of the Son at the inauguration of his mission. The transfiguration, however, signals a new stage of Jesus' mission that has begun at Caesarea Philippi and reveals the paradox of the glorious suffering-servant messiahship of Jesus the Son. Peter, as spokesman for the disciples, comes off badly again, as he does at Caesarea Philippi (8:31–33), because he does not fathom the uniqueness of Jesus Son of man and Son of God who is greater than Elijah and Moses. Jesus is not just another prophet through whom God communicates the arrival of the promised Sabbath rest without any need for redemptive suffering. Jesus' words of prophecy about his suffering ministry must be attended to: "Listen to him!" the Father commands the disciples (v. 7; cf. Deut. 18:15).

The Old Testament parallels are significant. "After six days" (v. 2) reflects the six days God's glory cloud covered Mount Sinai before he called to Moses (Exod. 24:15–16); and Moses and Elijah received visions of God's glory on his holy mountain (Exod. 24; 1 Kings 19). But neither Moses nor Elijah was glorified or named Son. The glory on the mount of transfiguration is a prophetic glimpse of Jesus' final glory as the Son who is about to begin his descent from this high mountain (possibly Mount Hermon) to die and rise again as Suffering Servant in the hostile city of Jerusalem. Jesus has been revealed as the true tabernacle of glory to whom the Father defers. Moses and Elijah have, significantly, suddenly disappeared, and the disciples no longer see anyone with them except Jesus (v. 8). He is the one they are to listen to.

At Caesarea Philippi Jesus warns the disciples not to tell anyone about him (8:30), and now again as they descend from the mountain he gives them orders to be silent about what they have seen until the Son of man has risen from the dead (v. 9). Keeping the messianic secret is important to Jesus because the crowds are politically volatile and ready to hail him king, especially if the disciples spread the news about his transfiguration (there is no exegetical basis for arguing, as Wrede did, that the later church created the messianic secret to explain why Jesus' people did not accept him). The disciples still do not understand the redemptive goal of his ministry, though later they will, and Mark's readers will realize that these words are meant for them as well and be encouraged to take heart that a vision of the glorious conclusion of the redemptive drama is revealed on the mountain to those who have eyes to see and will respond to Jesus in faith.

As the transfiguration affirms the divine status of Jesus and parallels Peter's confession of messiahship at Caesarea Philippi, so the sequel to the transfiguration (**9:9–13**) is parallel to Jesus' prophecy of his suffering messiahship (8:31–33). Suffering, death, and rising from the dead are central themes in both settings, and if the suffering of the Son of man perplexes them so does his rising from the dead (vv. 9–10). Afraid to ask him they turn to the question of Elijah's "resurrection," since he has just been with them on the mount and is said by the teachers of the law to be coming in advance of the Messiah who will bring the "great and dreadful day of the LORD" and the time of repentance (Mal. 4:5–6). But Elijah has not yet appeared to prepare the people, so how can Jesus be the Messiah? Jesus replies that the teachers of the law are correct about Elijah, that he does come first to restore all things; but what about the biblical prophecy concerning the Suffering Servant? (Verse 12 most likely refers to Isa. 52:13–53:12.) And what about John the Baptist? Indeed, in him Elijah has already come (v. 13) and has suffered at the hands of Herod and Herodias as the Old Testament Elijah suffered under Ahab and Jezebel ("just as it is written about him"; cf. 1 Kings 19:1–2). The first and second Elijahs suffered in prophetic ministry, and so must the Son of man, even more so, to complete the work of redemption from hostile powers.

From the mountaintop of theophany and glory Jesus descends with the three disciples to the valley of unbelief to find the remaining nine disciples and the scribes arguing over the disciples' inability to exorcise a demon from an epileptic boy (**9:14–29**). Though Peter has previously been given divine utterance to confess Jesus as the Messiah (8:29), he fails to understand the true identity of Jesus on the mount. Though the disciples have been given the power to exorcise demons (6:7), they lack faith to heal the boy. The entire assemblage of people—disciples, Pharisees, and clamoring crowd—fails to grasp that Jesus is Son of God and Son of man who has come to invade and defeat the demonic kingdom whose devastating effects on a human being Mark so carefully describes (the demon robs, seizes, throws, and convulses the boy, forcing him to foam, gnash, and become rigid). The boy has suffered since childhood (vv. 21–22) and has been threatened with destruction and forcibly removed from full fellowship with family and community. Jesus angrily and impatiently castigates the disciples, the religious authorities, and the crowd as an "unbelieving generation" and asks that the boy be brought to him (v. 19). Only the boy's father shows the necessary attitude of belief, though he recognizes his weakness and asks Jesus to overcome his unbelief (v. 24). Apparently Jesus is alone with the father and son, for the crowd comes running to the scene. Jesus answers the father's prayer and casts out the evil spirit. The terrible effects of demon possession are further described by Mark as the spirit shrieks, convulses the boy, and leaves him for dead as it departs. Jesus' final work is to raise the boy from death to life and to restore him to wholeness and fellowship ("and he stood up," v. 27). The lesson of this story both for the disciples and for Mark's readers is that belief undergirded by prayer is requisite in the battle against Satan for the release of the prisoners bound up in his house. The boy's father, seemingly insignificant in the crowd of disciples, scribes, and people, puts the faithless generation to shame with his belief and prayer: "I do believe; help me overcome my unbelief!" Trust in Jesus is all that is needed, and this is what the disciples lack (vv. 28–29). "Everything," says Jesus (v. 23), "is possible for him who believes."

The journey south toward Jerusalem continues as Jesus passes through Galilee, privately teaching his disciples and repeating his prediction that as Son of man he will be betrayed and killed, but will rise again after three days (**9:30–32**; cf. 8:29–31). But the disciples still do not understand and are afraid to ask him about it (v. 32). They continue to fail the test of faith and are fearful of inquiring further into the meaning of his prophecy about suffering messiahship, disobeying the Father's command on the mount to "listen to him" (9:7).

The disciples do not hesitate to argue among themselves on the way, however, as becomes clear from Jesus' question when they arrive in Capernaum. They have been debating about who is greatest, engendered perhaps by the special privilege afforded Peter, James, and John on the mount (**9:33–37**). The altercation is heavy with irony, for he who is truly greatest is Jesus himself who has already given two prophetic clues about his suffering-servant messiahship (8:31–32; 9:30–31) and has received the Father's loving approval of his sonship and ministry on the mount of transfiguration (9:7). Jesus is the living embodiment of greatness because he has made himself last by becoming servant of all (the implication of v. 35), and he calls his disciples to do likewise. Humility, not pride, is the mark of the person who wants to be first, evidenced in the willingness to be at the disposal of others. The humbling effect of Jesus' teaching is illustrated by his acted parable of taking a little child in his arms and exhorting his disciples to become servants of "little children" (the helpless of this world), and by doing so welcoming Jesus and the Father who has sent him (vv. 36–37).

The inability of the disciples to cast out the demon from the epileptic boy (9:18) does not dampen their jealous protection of the rite and their refusal to allow an unnamed man not of their circle to exorcise in Jesus' name (**9:38–42**). Jesus' previous word on welcoming others (9:37) may have triggered an interruption on John's part as to their Lord's view on this person to whom they had just refused a welcome. Jesus' rebuke of his disciples follows in the same vein as before: they are too proud of themselves and think that somehow authority lies with the inner circle: "He was not one of us," John argues, though he was "driving out demons in your name" (v. 38). But, replies Jesus, if he is performing miracles in my name then he is one of us (vv. 39–40; cf. Matt. 12:30). It is not their names collectively but Jesus' personal name that is crucial, and what counts is not privileged status (membership in the circle of the Twelve or special status as the inner three) but powerful results in invading Satan's territory, and in this the outsider has surpassed the disciples themselves. They need to take note of the man's willingness to place himself at the disposal of the possessed, a principle illustrated in verse 41. Any gift extended in Jesus' name, whether a spectacular gift like the casting out of a demon or a simple cup of water, is a gift offered to Christ himself. Verse 42 brings the thought of disposability on behalf of others full circle back to the thought of verse 37. The man the disciples condemn has welcomed others as a servant and therefore has welcomed Jesus and the Father, whereas the implication of Jesus' warning in verse 42 is that the disciples, by their denial of the man's Christ-centered hospitality, are playing the devil's role (like Peter in 8:33 who denies Jesus' suffering servanthood) and are in danger of preventing him from serving in Jesus' name (and thereby sinning). This is ironic, for the disciples are in danger of perishing, like a person thrown into the sea with a weight (the Romans actually inflicted this punishment on Zealot insurrectionists), if they persist in their selfish preoccupation with greatness and privilege rather than servanthood in Jesus' name (the unified theme of 9:33–42).

This leads Jesus to prod his disciples to utter faithfulness and disposability in his name that they may escape the hellish consequences of anything less (**9:43–50**). If they have tempted the man of 9:38 to sin by denying him his ministry in Christ's name, they are themselves being tempted by their selfish attitude and need a stern warning to put off anything that causes them to sin by preventing them from acting in Jesus' name. Denial of self (8:34), possessions (10:21), family (10:28–29), or hand, foot, or eye (9:43–47) for the sake of Jesus and the gospel is required if any of them hinders the disciple from participating in life with God (= the kingdom of God, v. 47) and the mission of freeing others from the minions of Satan so that they may also enjoy that life. The disciples, therefore, must flee the eternal and unquenchable fire of hell (v. 48) that comes of selfishness and allow themselves to be salted with the fire of suffering as servants in the name of Christ (the theme of 9:33–50; cf. the baptism "with the Holy Spirit and with fire" [Matt. 3:11] and offerings with salt and fire [Exod. 30:35; Lev. 2:13; Ezek. 43:24]). The salt of verse 50 is the life-giving salt of sacrificial service for the world, which the disciples are in danger of losing because of their pride and desire for status (cf. Matt. 5:13). Jesus exhorts them to have the salt of servanthood in themselves, not to criticize those outside their circle who have it more than they, and to be at peace with all who minister in Christ's name. Thus the controversy of verses 33ff. will be resolved by their becoming more like Jesus and, ironically, like the man himself (v. 38) who is actually doing what they should be able to do if they are truly disciples who name the name of Christ.

Jesus continues his inexorable journey south to the hostile city of Jerusalem. He now crosses from Galilee through Samaria into Judea, then east across the Jordan into Perea, the territory of Herod Antipas (v. 1). By highlighting incidents along the way, Mark describes how fidelity to Jesus and his mission of suffering servanthood, with which the Galilean ministry concludes (9:33–50), continues to be the principal theme. The issue in **10:1–12** revolves around pure intention, personal decision, and fidelity. Attitudinal problems arise with opponents and disciples who contrast starkly with Jesus' purity of heart as suffering servant. The hostile Pharisees try to get Jesus into trouble (perhaps with Herod Antipas and Herodias as he is now in their territory; cf. 6:17–18) on the subject of divorce. The exchange is charged with irony, for the deeper significance of the debate is not remote and technical but related to the absolute fidelity Jesus has been talking about with his disciples and which he will continue to find missing in those who ought, of all the representatives of Israel, to prove themselves the faithful bride of Yahweh in this eschatological age (cf. Hos. 2). They prove to be interested only in exception clauses as they maliciously contrive to put Jesus away, first by testing, later by killing him who comes as bridegroom to call Israel to remarriage (Mark 2:19–20).

Jesus stands in the very place of God as he goes back beyond Moses' concession to human weakness (v. 5; Deut. 24:1–4) to God's original intention for the indissoluble union of male and female in marriage (vv. 6–9). He cuts across Shammai's strict interpretation of Moses (no divorce except for the wife's infidelity) and Hillel's liberal rendering (divorce of the wife by the husband for any reason) to the deeper and more primordial ground of marriage—mutual fidelity between husband and wife. Breaking the covenant bond of trust on either side is adultery and cannot be sanctioned (vv. 6–12). The declaration is not abstract but directly related to Jesus' faithfulness to his bride: she must now respond in reciprocal fidelity or be separated by her own infidelity. This is the challenge Jesus lays down to both Pharisees and disciples. The setting in Perea is significant: as Herod and Herodias commit adultery on the physical and spiritual levels and kill the only prophet who could save them, so the Pharisees commit adultery by deserting the only bridegroom who can save them, Jesus the Messiah.

From marriage Mark goes to the example of children in his selection of incidents in Jesus' southward journey toward Jerusalem (**10:13–16**). The theme continues to be the attitude of servanthood and disposability. Again the disciples come in for criticism when they show the same insensitivity as with the man in 9:38. Children are simply not important enough to be a part of their privileged circle or to occupy Jesus' time; hence they rebuke those who bring children to him to be blessed. Indignantly Jesus remonstrates with them, and with great irony not only rebukes them for not welcoming children into his presence, but also demands that the disciples become little children themselves if they want to enter the realm of God and participate in his reign. Not pride but unself-conscious and grateful receptivity is the required attitude of the faithful disciple who accepts Jesus' gift of blessing and assumes the trusting position of a child cradled in his arms (v. 16). Membership in the kingdom is a gift to be received and a gift to be shared.

The privileged possession of wealth now becomes the focus of Jesus' message concerning the proper attitude for entrance into the kingdom of God and eternal life. From the larger context of the incident Matthew (19:16–30) and Mark (**10:17–31**) abstract complementary details about what is essential for someone to inherit eternal life. Mark captures the irony of the rich man's addressing Jesus as "good teacher" on his knees (v. 17), when he has no understanding of what the word *good* denotes in Jesus' servanthood vocabulary and has no intention of giving up his goods to become good. Jesus' reply, "No one is good—except God alone" (v. 18), is not an admission that he is not good, for he soon makes the demand that if the man really wants treasure in heaven he must follow Jesus' definition of what is good, namely, sell everything he has and give to the poor, and come and follow Jesus as a disciple (v. 21; cf. v. 29). Rather, the reply is touched with irony, for the man is self-righteous (vv. 19–20) and blinded by his wealth. Even though Jesus loves him (v. 21) he decides against Jesus and goes away sad (v. 22).

In his follow-up discourse to his disciples (vv. 23–31), Jesus heightens the paradox of absolute belief in him and the gospel as the condition of entering the kingdom of God and inheriting real riches in both this life and the life to come. Only by laying aside trust in human achievement and coming to Jesus in belief and following him (v. 21) can one thread a huge camel through the tiny eye of a needle and enter the kingdom. It is impossible except by the miracle of divine grace (vv. 24–27), for what is humanly impossible is possible with God. Only by offering everything to Jesus—even one's earthly family (v. 29)—and participating in his suffering ministry can the disciples possess God's kingdom (v. 30). Jesus asks nothing that he himself is not willing to do, for he has left the security of his earthly family to gather in the new family of lost souls (3:31–35); so must they, if they wish to be first rather than last (10:31), for the rich man, though first in worldly eyes, will be last in the age to come because he is unwilling to give himself away to Jesus and those whom Jesus has come to call home.

During his journey to Jerusalem from Caesarea Philippi Jesus has presented himself as the exemplar of suffering servanthood and has called for radical participation in his mission. Antithetic contrasts of belief and unbelief pile one upon the other, and appear again as Jesus approaches Jerusalem. In the third prophecy of his coming death and resurrection (**10:32–34**) Jesus draws upon Psalm 22:6–8 and Isaiah 50:6 and evinces his full consciousness of what he is doing. By contrast, the disciples once again fail to comprehend the great moment that is about to occur because they remain self-serving, as the next unit (**10:35–45**) makes all too clear.

Mark is the master of irony, not because he creates it (the historical characters in the story do that) but because he is able to select from events those contrastive attitudes that place in sharp relief the difference between Jesus' utter hospitality toward the lost of the world and others' selfish desire for special privilege. The request of James and John to sit at Jesus' right and left in his glory reveals incredible impudence on their part, at the expense of the other disciples, not to mention the lost for whom Jesus is about to die. Jesus immediately turns their request around to the cup of suffering he is to drink and to his baptism of death (cf. Luke 12:50), inviting them to defer questions of glory and status to the more important attitude of suffering with him in drinking his cup and being baptized with his baptism (vv. 38–40). Actually, the cup Jesus will drink on the cross is the cup of God's wrath against human sin (Ps. 75:8; Isa. 51:17–23; Jer. 25:15–28; Ezek. 23:31–34) as he becomes a ransom for many (v. 45; Isa. 53); theirs will be the cup of suffering and persecution as they witness to Jesus' saving work (Acts 12:2; Col. 1:24; 1 Pet. 4:13). The attitude required is the same: loving disposability on behalf of others.[2] Discipleship does not afford opportunity for flaunting authority but for greater responsibility in servanthood (vv. 41–45). This is the irony and paradox of Jesus' own ministry, and that of his disciples, if they truly respond to his challenge.

Again Mark contrasts the disciples who see physically and ought to see spiritually with the blind beggar Bartimaeus (**10:46–52**) who has no physical sight yet sees spiritually because he believes in Jesus. As Jesus is leaving Jericho, he passes Bartimaeus. When he hears that it is Jesus, he shouts, "Jesus, Son of David, have mercy on me" (v. 47; his use of the messianic title *Son of David* suggests that he has been given divine utterance, like Peter at Caesarea Philippi [8:29], as Jesus now stands on the threshold of his final messianic work). Because Bartimaeus evidences proper faith and trust, Jesus asks him what he wants (v. 51); the answer is a simple, "I want to see," which can be taken in both a physical and spiritual sense, for Bartimaeus is spiritually perceptive and proves to be a faithful follower. Jesus honors his request (the last healing miracle he performs in Mark), whereas the request of James and John for glory and status is not honored. The difference in result is due not only to faith, for the two disciples believe Jesus has the power to grant them such a privilege, but faith born of a servant attitude that Jesus divines in Bartimaeus and not in James or John. Mark records that after Jesus pronounces healing ("Go, your faith has healed you") Bartimaeus, immediately upon receiving his sight, follows Jesus along the road (v. 52). The disciples would not have missed the irony in retrospect, nor would Mark's readers.

B. Jesus confronts Jerusalem (11:1–13:37). Jesus' plan to enter the hostile city of Jerusalem has been in focus since Peter's confession at Caesarea Philippi (8:27ff.). Now the final act begins as Jesus carries his warfare against the demonic realm into the capital city itself, the seat of enemy-occupied territory where religion and temple that should have prepared for his coming have defaulted to the enemy and will become the instruments of his death. Here again the irony of appearance and reality are highlighted by Mark, as Jesus fearlessly confronts the city by acting out two dramatic scenes (the triumphal entry and the cleansing of the temple) that betoken the tragedy of a people and a city that will not accept his true suffering kingship on their behalf. The reader should note again how Jesus uses a sense of space in his ministry (sea, city, mountains, wilderness, east, west, north, south) and now a spatial centering on Jerusalem by way of Bethphage and Bethany at the Mount of Olives. Jesus is claiming that space now demonically occupied is properly his, but the space (with its imprisoned occupants) can be won back only by allowing the enemy an apparent victory, which turns out, ironically, to be the means of the enemy's defeat and the release of his captives. It may be significant that in healing blind Bartimaeus and claiming him as a follower Jesus performs a symbolic act that guarantees his final occupation of Jerusalem, for now the blind see and are no longer obstacles to the taking of the city, as was the case with King David (2 Sam. 5:6–8); and so Jesus fulfills Isaiah 29:18–19, "the eyes of the blind will see."

The moment for the actual invasion of Jeru-

2. For a fuller treatment of this theme in Jesus' ministry, see Royce Gordon Gruenler, *The Trinity in the Gospel of John: A Thematic Commentary on the Fourth Gospel* (Grand Rapids: Baker, 1986).

salem has arrived (**11:1–11**). Jesus sends two of his disciples to procure the young colt of a donkey "which no one has ever ridden" (the messianic mount [Gen. 49:11; Zech. 9:9]; being unridden, the colt was consecrated to God [cf. Deut. 21:3; 1 Sam. 6:7]). Messianic symbolism abounds as Jesus enigmatically unveils his messiahship in fulfillment of Zechariah 9:9, allowing the people to carpet the way and chant the great Hallel psalm (118:25–26) in welcoming him into the city with popular messianic hope (vv. 9–10; cf. 2 Sam. 7:11–14). Yet there remains a veil over the triumphal entry, for what seems to swell in triumph disperses in foreboding dusk with Jesus surveying the temple area at the end of the day and returning to Bethany with the Twelve (v. 11). Quietly, however, Jesus has laid claim to the precinct of the temple in fulfillment of Malachi 3:1 and will now begin to disclose how he will judge, cleanse, and occupy the sacred space. The following two acted parables unveil what is in store.

The coming of Jesus the Messiah inaugurates the time of happiness and feasting (2:18–19) but also the time of judgment and destruction (3:23–30). Jesus' shocking destruction of the fig tree (**11:12–14**) is an acted parable that prophesies what is in store for a people who have proved faithless and whose temple, the very symbol of their faithless religiosity, will be destroyed along with the city of Jerusalem (a prophecy fulfilled in A.D. 70). Jesus prophetically fulfills Isaiah 34:4; Jeremiah 8:13; 29:17; Hosea 2:12; 9:10, 16; and Micah 7:1–6, which liken Israel's faithlessness to a fig tree gone bad and about to be destroyed. The fig tree has put forth leaves but has no fruit. Similarly, the evidence of true discipleship to Jesus the Messiah is the bearing of the fruit of faithfulness and righteousness. The refusal to participate and bear fruit is a denial of the dynamic reign of God that is producing food for the harvest (cf. 4:2–29).

Jesus' second act of violence is an acted parable that accompanies the withering of the fig tree (**11:15–19**). By his violent expulsion of the merchants from the Court of the Gentiles Jesus anticipates the terrible consequences of turning God's space into a place for traffic in human guilt. Jesus fulfills the prophecies of Jeremiah 7:1–15; 26:1–15; and Malachi 3:1–5; but especially Isaiah 56:1–8, which invites the foreigner to God's holy mountain and to his house of prayer. Jesus symbolically casts out the self-serving who would hinder his mission to the outcast by transforming sacred space into a den of robbers. He is gathering all the faithful, making space for the Gentiles at the redemptive feast of the Passover during which he will himself become the final sacrificial lamb and the new temple in whom all may gather to worship. His action amazes the crowd, but neither they nor the chief priests and teachers of the law divine the inner meaning of the symbolic cleansing; the latter out of fear seek a way to kill him (v. 18). Thus Mark ends his brief account on a note of irony, for the plot to kill Jesus will providentially open the temple space to the Gentiles in an unimaginable way and bring about the destruction of the old order with its earthly temple.

The next day the disciples see that the fig tree Jesus cursed has withered from the roots, and Peter points the fact out to Jesus (**11:20–25**). This is significant for two reasons: (1) it suggests that Mark's account has as one of its chief sources the eyewitness experience of Peter (cf. 14:72); and (2) it symbolizes the awesome judgment that the Son of God as representative of the divine community is to bring upon a disobedient nation (cf. 13:2; Ps. 90:5–9; Hos. 9:16–17; Joel 1:12). The transition to verses 22–25 seems abrupt, however, as though Jesus disregards Peter's remark and takes up another subject. Since the sayings in this unit occur in various contexts in the synoptic Gospels (e.g., Matt. 6:13–14; 7:7; 17:20; 18:19; Luke 11:9; 17:6) some commentators believe Mark has inserted them at this point. However, Jesus would have spoken about faith in this manner numerous times during his itinerant ministry, and Mark would also have seen some essential connection between the theme of judgment and faith to arrange his material this way. Jesus has acted out two parables of terrible impending judgment of unbelief—the withering of the fig tree and the cleansing of the temple; now, in response to Peter's remark, he turns to the vital component in the eschatological drama that is inexorably coming to pass, namely, faith in God. This Israel does not have, but the disciples can and must have faith if they are to participate as victors in the coming destruction of the enemy-occupied land which will split at the Mount of Olives when the terrible day comes that precedes the kingly reign of the Lord over the whole earth (so Zech. 14:1–11). Jesus urges his disciples to pray with the faith expressed in Isaiah 65:24 and participate with him in the new exodus, and so avoid the coming destruction of Jerusalem and the faithless land. But they must humbly seek forgiveness and harbor no resentment (v. 25), as Israel has not done in the presence of Jesus the Son, if they are to stand in the Father's righteousness through this cataclysmic time.

Irony plays a large role in the juxtaposition of a number of encounters with Jesus' opponents (11:27–12:37) and the preceding teaching on faith in view of impending destruction. (Cf. this section on questioning in Jerusalem with the similar questioning in Galilee [2:1–3:6].) As though on cue the adversaries of Jesus appear one after another and unwittingly validate his scathing denunciation of their hypocrisy and refusal to accept him as the authoritative voice of the Father. Within the precincts of the temple space he claims a right to occupy, Jesus challenges the highest court of Jewish authority, the Sanhedrin, comprised of chief priests, the teachers of the law, and the elders (v. 27).

The first question in this unit sets the tone of the combined attack on Jesus by the religious authorities (**11:27–33**). When they question his credentials to speak and act as he has he turns the question around and places their authority in jeopardy by asking an embarrassing question about John the Baptist: was his baptism from heaven or was he a false prophet? They decide not to answer because they are caught in their hypocrisy. Secretly they never recognized John, but they fear losing the support of the masses who believe he was a true prophet. Jesus refuses to defend his credentials before those whose hearts are false and who play a deceptive language game with human souls, hence the irony of his reply: if they do not know who John was, Jesus will not tell them who he is (v. 33). He implies that their unbelief keeps them from recognizing the authority of John and himself (this in contrast to real faith that will, ironically, realize the judgment of such hypocrites and unbelievers [11:12–25]).

In the parable of the rebellious tenants (**12:1–12**) Jesus builds upon the imagery of Isaiah 5:1–7, the Song of the Vineyard, which portrays the coming destruction of those who fail to bear fruit for God. In Jesus' adaptation God is the owner of Israel the vineyard, the Jewish leaders are the tenants, the servants are the prophets, and Jesus is the only son and heir. The parable is a scathing denunciation of their rejection of God's prophets in the Old Testament and now their final rejection of God's Son who stands before them, calling them to account as tenants to produce fruit worthy of their hire. Thus without claiming his messiahship directly, Jesus asserts his authority over against their own and describes with prophetic irony the great reversal that is coming: they will kill the Son and be killed in turn (vv. 7–8). Jesus heightens the irony by referring to Psalm 118:22–23, a prophecy about himself, where the stone (Jesus) that the builders (his opponents) rejected has marvelously been made the capstone by the Lord himself (12:10–11; cf. Acts 4:11; 1 Pet. 2:7). All this assumes, of course, that Jesus is conscious of being the Messiah and is able to prophesy what is in the process of happening and will eventuate in his death and vindication. Commentators who dismiss Jesus' messianic consciousness and the prophetic unity of Scripture interpret 12:1–11 as a "prophecy after the fact," created by the church after Jesus' death, but Mark intends his readers to understand that the account is factual as he describes the reaction of Jesus' opponents who realize the parable was spoken against them and look for a way to arrest him, but are afraid of the crowd (v. 12; cf. 11:18, 32). Jesus uses this parable to expand upon the theme of the withered fig tree (11:12–14, 20–25) and to hold the leaders of Israel accountable.

A larger range of religious authority is arrayed against Jesus as the politically compromising Herodians join forces with their erstwhile enemies the Pharisees in a ploy to trap Jesus on political and theological grounds (**12:13–17**). Again, irony prevails in this hypocritical alliance where language is used deceptively to entrap Jesus, who personifies purity of speech and intention. The denarius portrayed Caesar as worthy of divine honor. Jesus amazes his attackers by recognizing, in his reply "Give to Caesar what is Caesar's and to God what is God's" (v. 17), that one has obligations to the state (cf. Rom. 13:1–7; 1 Tim. 2:1–6; Titus 3:1–2; 1 Pet. 2:13–17) and obligations that belong to God alone. Jesus impresses his adversaries by making an authoritative and valid broad statement about the relationship of religion and state, while throwing the question back at them. Fundamental differences lie in its application; Jesus therefore highlights their fractious differences (Zealots refuse to pay the tax; Pharisees resent paying it; Herodians gladly pay it). Jesus refuses to be a political messiah, in the sense either of liberation theology with its aim of violent overthrow or of uncritical compliance with the state. God is sovereign over political structure, underwriting its positive amenities but refusing to be identified with its idolatries.

Little is known about the Sadducees, Jesus' opponents in **12:18–27**, but Mark makes clear that their denial of the resurrection (v. 18) is countermanded by Jesus as a misinterpretation of Scripture (vv. 24–27). Again Jesus shows himself to be the authoritative interpreter of God's Word, in contrast to these wealthy aristocrats whose vested interest in Jerusalem is to be destroyed in the debacle of A.D. 70, after which they are heard of no more. Using the brother-in-law (levirate) rule of Deuteronomy 25:5–6 where a man was duty-bound to protect the widow of his deceased brother and give seed to his line if he died without children, they stoop to ridicule the doctrine of the resurrection by wearing out a hypothetical widow with a serial line of seven husbands, all of whom die, and who cannot all have her as wife in the hereafter; ipso facto, they reason, there can be no resurrection. It is a ridiculous argument but probably one the Sadducees used to mock the Pharisees who believed in the resurrection. Jesus' reply is incisive on two levels. First, he accuses them of playing language games and of misinterpreting Scripture, misconstruing the power of God who not only raises the dead but raises them to a life unimaginably greater than this one, where marriage no longer obtains and the risen praise God as do the angels. Furthermore, in the Pentateuch itself (the only Scripture they recognize) God assures Moses that he is, not was, the God of the patriarchs (Exod. 3:6), attesting his faithfulness as the God of the living who has redeemed and protects the fathers with eternal life. Thus Jesus bests yet another group of religious authorities as he invades their space and authoritatively claims it, accusing them of being "badly mistaken" (v. 27). One can appreciate the irony of Jesus exposing their errant interpretation of God's Word, for not only will they miss the resurrection unto life but they will lose everything they hold idolatrously dear in the withering destruction of Jerusalem Jesus foretells. Theirs is the God of the dead; Jesus proclaims the God of the living.

Impressed by Jesus' answer, one of the teachers of the law asks him which he would weight as heaviest of the 613 commandments (**12:28–34**). (It was a common practice among the rabbis to try to establish the core requirements of their works righteousness.) Matthew 22:34 says that he comes on behalf of the Pharisees, but the irony of Mark's longer account suggests the vulnerability of the man in one-to-one conversation with Jesus. He comes with a question that is not an obvious trap, and Jesus responds by leading him away from legal questions to the heart of the messianic kingdom that is now present. The greatest commandment, says Jesus, is to listen to God ("Hear, O Israel") and to love him with one's whole being (Deut. 6:4–5); the second is to love one's neighbor, and the third, included in the second, is to love one's neighbor as oneself (Lev. 19:18). Not legalism but an attitude of love vertically, laterally, and inwardly (in that order) sums up the intent of the law, an authoritative declaration with which the man not only agrees but expresses in the spirit of 1 Samuel 15:22; Hosea 6:6; Amos 5:21–24; and Micah 6:6–8, and by so doing positions himself not far from the kingdom of God (v. 34). But he must now come to see that love of God and neighbor does not obviate the need for sacrifice, for Jesus is about to become the one great sacrifice; legalistic sacrifice without the intent of three-dimensional love is empty and hypocritical.

An ironic transition has taken place in this episode: Jesus has with authority answered his opponents' earlier question, "By what authority are you doing these things?" (11:28), and now assumes authority to ask the questions himself (12:35–37; 13:2; 14:6, 37–41, 48). His religious opponents no longer dare to ask him any more questions (12:34). In a great ironical turn he has occupied their authoritative space in the temple courts and claimed it.

Assuming his jurisdiction of authority in the temple Jesus asks and answers his own question, put to the teachers of the law, regarding the sense in which the Messiah is the son of David (**12:35–37**). In Old Testament prophecy the Messiah is to be from the family of David (Isa. 9:2–7; 11:1–9; Jer. 23:5–6; 30:9; 33:15, 17, 22; Ezek. 34:23–24; 37:24; Hos. 3:5; Amos 9:11), but if David ("speaking by the Holy Spirit" in Ps. 110:1) can describe a heavenly enthronement conversation between "the Lord" and "my Lord," is not the Messiah greater than David, though descended from him? The irony is that while the experts cannot answer the apparent contradiction, Jesus himself as the Son of God as well as the son of David is the living answer to the riddle. For those with eyes to see, Jesus speaks with divine authority ("the Lord," "my Lord," "the Holy Spirit," v. 36) and not only enigmatically discloses his divine and human origins but also prophesies through the words of the psalm his coming resurrection and exaltation to the right hand of the Father. Jesus' messianic kingdom therefore supersedes David's political domain and the nationalistic expectations of his opponents. His warfare probes deeper into the domain of the dark demonic powers that occupy the space of human beings and of nations; hence his goal as Messiah is to put his enemies underfoot (v. 36). With this veiled affirmation of his messiahship Jesus reaches the high point of authority in his debate with the interpreters of Scripture, placing them under his feet as he assumes in his own person the authority and space of Old Testament religion symbolized by the temple. Though they do not understand the deeper implication of what Jesus is doing, the crowd nevertheless listens to him with delight because of his authority over the scribes (v. 37b).

The debate between Jesus and the religious authorities (11:27–12:37) is summed up in a final antithetic contrast of attitudes (**12:38–44**) that captures the irony of a situation where the supposed protectors of religious truth have defaulted in self-centeredness, while an unexpected widow is exalted in her selfless generosity. Ironically Jesus honors her giving attitude, which reflects his own gracious disposability, and excoriates the teachers of the law for their hypocrisy and promises them severe punishment.

The scribes were venerated by the people as the representatives of the oracles of God and should have been singularly intent on giving praise to God alone. But Jesus observes that their positions of authority have seduced them from servanthood to egocentric ostentation in dress and desire for public recognition. As the embodiment of truth and wholeness in intent, speech, and acts, Jesus exposes their hypocrisy in making showy and lengthy prayers while devouring widows' houses (the teachers of the law were dependent on gifts and could abuse the patronage of widows). His exposure of their unworthiness begins and ends with strong words of condemnation: "Watch out for the teachers of the law" (v. 38); "Such men will be punished most severely" (v. 40). With this negative word Jesus concludes his public ministry. But he has further words to say to his disciples that expand upon his condemnation of Israel's leaders, first in the offering of the widow (12:41–44), followed by awesome oracles about the destruction of the temple and coming judgment (chap. 13).

In contrast to the hypocrisy and avarice of the teachers of the law, Jesus calls attention to an impoverished widow in the Court of the Women where the temple treasury was situated and to which both women and men came to present their gifts of money. It is not the rich and their large gifts that impress Jesus but the quality of sacrifice evidenced by a poor widow who gives only two tiny copper coins worth less than a penny. The irony is striking. While widows are the vulnerable objects of religious avarice in verse 40, one of their number now becomes a model of true servanthood exemplified by Jesus himself and receives his highest praise: out of her poverty she puts in everything she has, so great is her love of God. Jesus leaves his disciples and Mark his readers to conclude that in the Lord's eyes she is truly rich, though outwardly, like Jesus, she is poor, while the rich, though outwardly wealthy, are inwardly impoverished. Because the temple and its guardians have succumbed to the temptation of outward wealth and have transferred their loyalty from sacrificial worship and ministry to the time and space of material possessions, their time and space will be destroyed by the righteous judgment of God.

Mark 13 continues to focus on Jesus' confrontation with the hostile city of Jerusalem. In his invasion of enemy-occupied territory Jesus claims the sacred space that rightfully belongs to God and draws it into himself. He becomes the temple personified and calls the faithful remnant of Israel to himself. Accordingly, the withered fig tree dramatically anticipates the coming destruction of misappropriated material space with its wicked inhabitants who have proved unfaithful to God. Now that Jesus has taken the space into himself, he can specify in prophetic speech what the withered fig tree symbolizes visually, namely, the destruction of the physical temple with its desecrated space (13:1–2) and the destruction of carnal time that places its hopes in materialism and nationalism in rejection of Jesus' suffering messianic time (13:3–37). Jesus first describes the coming destruction of demonically occupied space (the stones of the temple will be thrown down). He then describes the coming suffering of his disciples as they invade demonically occupied time, a mission that demands their utter faithfulness and vigilance. However, the Son of man will come in the clouds to gather his elect from the ends of the earth to the ends of the heavens, and will claim final authority over his created time and space.

This chapter contains the longest sustained teaching of Jesus in the Gospel and has occasioned widely varied commentary. Some see it as a compilation of sayings from Jesus interspersed with commentary from the situation faced by the Marcan community, but it is best viewed as Mark's condensation of Jesus' longer teaching on the inaugurated events of the new age that lead up to the end. (Similarity of basic material, with variations in detail, attest the view that Matthew, Mark, and Luke are highlighting various aspects of Jesus' eschatological teaching.) Following the biblical pattern of repeating a theme from a number of complementary perspectives (technically termed *recapitulation;* cf. the parallels in Dan. 2, 7, 8[3] and in Rev. 1–11, 12–22), Mark faithfully represents Jesus' style of recapitulating the present age from the destruction of the temple space to the second coming of the Son of man at the end of the age. Each time Jesus prophesies of coming events leading up to the end, with exhortations to watchfulness and vigilance. The Olivet Discourse therefore may be viewed as four

3. See the *NIV Study Bible,* 1311.

parallel panoramas of the interval of the church age: (1) first view, verses 1–13; (2) second view, verses 14–27; (3) third view, verses 28–33; (4) fourth view, verses 34–37.

The basic prophecy is found in verses **1–13.** Jesus prophesies the temple's material destruction (he has already destroyed it spiritually by reappropriating its symbolism and authority), in ironic contrast to the disciples' glowing admiration of its "massive stones" and "magnificent buildings" (vv. 1–2). In answer to the disciples' question when these things will happen Jesus emphasizes a distinctive characteristic of biblical prophecy, namely, that the prophetic "when" is described only in large brushstrokes, while prominent emphasis is given to how the believer is to bear witness in the midst of wars, earthquakes, famines, and persecutions. Jesus interprets eschatology as a time of testing and opportunity for mission and ethics: "watch out" for deceivers (v. 5); "be on your guard" (v. 9); "do not worry beforehand about what to say" (v. 11); "he who stands firm to the end will be saved" (v. 13). The birthing of the messianic age will bring terrible sufferings (cf. Jer. 22:23; Mic. 4:9–10; Rom. 8:18–25), but more important is the interval for mission that comes before the end, for "the gospel must first be preached to all nations" (v. 10). This will be accomplished through the power of the Holy Spirit who will give the disciples utterance to proclaim the gospel under the most adverse circumstances (v. 11; cf. Jer 1:9; Acts 6:10). As Jesus has remained faithful, so he calls upon his disciples to remain faithful, for "he who stands firm to the end will be saved" (v. 13). The "end" (Gk. *telos*) refers primarily to the end of the persevering believer's life (cf. John 13:1) but may also be taken to designate the close of the age that will test the mettle of faith, since the age in one sense is closed for each individual with his last breath. While Jesus has presented a general overview of what is coming, his emphasis is not on eschatological signs (cf. v. 4) but on ethics (implicitly his own exemplary model) as he exhorts his disciples to place themselves at the disposal of the world in faithful witness to the gospel.

More prophetic words (**13:14–27**) about the inaugurated age now parallel the first description. In this recapitulation the biblical image of the abomination of desolation opens the scene, while the coming of the Son of man to gather his elect closes it; in between are exhortations summed up in verse 23, "So be on your guard." The "abomination that causes desolation" (or "the appalling sacrilege," v. 14) should be understood in light of Daniel 9:27; 11:31; and 12:11 (cf. Matt. 24:15; 2 Thess. 2:3–10) as the desecrating desolation of the sacred space of the temple that occurred under Antiochus IV Epiphanes in 168 B.C. This desolation will occur again under the Romans in A.D. 70, and will continue to identify the blasphemous pride, idolatry, and oppression of the satanic Antichrist in the interval up to and including the end of the age.[4] Unparalleled suffering, distress, and deception will mark the age (vv. 15–20), but Jesus warns his followers not to believe those who falsely claim to be the Christ but to be on their guard (vv. 21–23). "Following that distress" (lit. tribulation, Gk. *thlipsis,* v. 24) there will be cosmic disturbances in fulfillment of Old Testament prophecy (vv. 24–25; Isa. 13:10; 34:4) and the Son of man will be seen "coming in clouds with great power and glory," with his angels gathering his elect (vv. 26–27). The accent is on greatness ("with great power and glory" [v. 26]; "with power and great glory" [Matt. 24:30; Luke 21:27]). Jesus' exhortation to "be on your guard" is strong encouragement for his followers in light of his promised victory and vindication that will accompany his parousia (triumphant coming) at the end of the age (cf. Dan. 12:1–3).

Jesus now employs an illustration from the fig tree (**13:28–33**) to describe the inaugurated age from beginning to end. In this brief recapitulation of the interval between his first and second comings he again emphasizes the certainty yet the indefinite time of the day of the Lord, hence the supreme importance of ethical faithfulness rather than eschatological curiosity: "Be on guard! Be alert!" (v. 33). The stages of the fig tree "as its twigs get tender and its leaves come out" symbolize the approaching harvest when the ripe figs will be gathered (v. 28); just so, when Jesus' followers see "these things" happening (v. 29; cf. vv. 4, 23; i.e., the things described in 13:2–23), they will know that the end is near. Verse 30 may best be translated, "I tell you the truth, this generation will certainly not pass away until all these things *begin to take place*" (emphasis added). Jesus has already set the final age in motion by claiming the temple space for himself and in effect destroying the faithless fig tree and temple inwardly and symbolically, anticipating the external destruction of unfaithful Israel and the physical temple soon to follow. Jesus is not mistaken, as his authoritative "I tell you the truth" (v. 30) and "my words will never pass away" (v. 31) attest; his generation is already beginning to see these signs come to pass and will imminently see them unfold. The

4. See Desmond Ford, *The Abomination of Desolation in Biblical Eschatology* (Lanham, Md.: University Press of America, 1979).

final "day or hour" (v. 32) is purposely kept hidden by the Father. (Is Jesus being ironic in saying he does not know and by purposely refusing to divulge eschatological detail? Cf. the similar attitude of the risen Christ [Acts 1:6–7].) In brief compass Jesus has moved from the destruction of the temple by the Romans (v. 30) to the second coming of the Son of man at the end of the age (v. 32). What is of utmost importance is that his followers are to be faithful and vigilant, on guard and alert.

Using yet another illustration (**13:34–37**) Jesus describes the interval of the present age between his first and second comings in terms of a man who goes on a journey and leaves his servants in charge of his house. If they are faithful, they will do their assigned tasks and watch for his return. In this final unit Jesus has virtually transposed eschatology to ethics, for it is not important to know why the owner of the house has gone away or when he will come back, but only to trust him and be found faithful when he does return. Jesus transposes the "when" and the "what" of verse 4 to "watch" (vv. 34, 35, 37), a theme that permeates the Olivet Discourse (vv. 5, 9, 13, 21, 23, 33). The motif of the faithful and trusting heart is central in the Gospel and receives increasing emphasis in 8:27–16:7. It is ironic, in light of the fact that Jesus' earlier discourse has been with the male authorities of the law and now with his male disciples, that two women frame the Olivet Discourse on either side: the faithful widow in the temple (12:41–44) and the faithful woman in Simon the leper's house at Bethany (14:1–9).

C. Jerusalem opposes Jesus (14:1–15:47). Mark further unveils the irony of conflict with the chief priests and the teachers of the law by describing, immediately after Jesus' urgent call for faithful vigilance (chap. 13), their sly and murderous vigilance as they lie in wait to arrest him and kill him (**14:1–2**). Jesus has spoken of ultimate and eschatological time that will decide the state of the elect and the fate of the nation. They had been plotting Jesus' murder for some time (3:6; 11:18; 12:12). The irony is further heightened by the setting of Passover and the Feast of Unleavened Bread, the sacred time in which the urgent exodus from slavery to freedom will be reenacted in the eating of unleavened bread and the sprinkling of the blood of the lamb that saves the believer from the righteous wrath that God is about to visit upon his enemies (Exod. 12:1–14). The huge crowds that will gather for the sacred reenactment of the exodus pose a threat to their strategem, however, for they may get caught up in mob violence; they will bide and calculate their time (v. 2). Hence, the major themes of the passion narrative are compressed into these two opening verses.

Following the alternation between the motifs of faithfulness and rejection that have characterized Jesus' ministry from the beginning, but now especially in the vicinity of Jerusalem in the last days, Mark places the anointing of Jesus by the faithful woman at Bethany (**14:3–9**) next to his rejection by the plotting authorities. Moreover, within the story of the anointing itself there is further irony; some of those present indignantly reject (vv. 4–5) the woman's symbolic act of anointing Jesus for his burial (vv. 3, 6–9). The woman is likely Mary, the sister of Martha and Lazarus, and the incident the same as that reported in John 12:1–8 (the story in Luke 7:36–50 is a different occasion). John places the anointing before the entry into Jerusalem and carefully dates it "six days before the Passover"; accordingly, Mark has provided his readers a flashback and placed the story here for dramatic and ironic effect. (It should be noted that the sequence of events in the reportage of the passion narrative by the four Gospel writers often depends on the specific ironic or theological point they choose to make under the guiding presence of the Holy Spirit.) The irony of the anointing of Jesus follows the same pattern as the irony of his contest with the religious authorities: they defend religious tradition and oppose Jesus, while Jesus actually personifies and fulfills Old Testament tradition and they oppose it. Here those who oppose the woman (John identifies one of them as Judas Iscariot), being superficially concerned for the poor and the apparent waste of expensive perfume, are seen to be unconcerned for the poorest and the most righteous of all, namely, Jesus who is about to suffer and triumph over his enemies (cf. Ps. 41). While they claim to be concerned about the poor, it is the woman who shows the most kindness to Jesus in his hour of greatest poverty, prophetically anticipating his cross and burial. Jesus' word of commendation that her act will be remembered "wherever the gospel is preached throughout the world" (v. 9) evidences his consciousness of an interval of evangelization between his death and return at the end of the age.

The irony continues as Mark contrasts the treachery of a member of the inner circle of disciples with faithful Mary at Bethany (**14:10–11**). Mark succinctly describes two diametrically opposed responses to Jesus: one of belief and love, and one of unbelief and hate. In the first there is mutual honor, as Mary honors Jesus and he in turn honors her; in the second there is mutual dishonor, as Judas betrays

Jesus to those who are also betraying him, and all are dishonored by Jesus. There is also irony in Mark's brief note that the chief priests "were delighted" (their only joy in Jesus is a demonic delight in his death), and that Judas "watched for an opportunity" to betray him (a demonic watchfulness contrasted with the messianic watchfulness of 13:37).

It is around the table that the last events of Jesus' ministry in Jerusalem take place (14:12–26). At Bethany in Simon's home he reclines at table where Mary anoints him for burial (14:3), and now he will recline at table for the last time with his disciples to reenact the exodus in the Passover meal.

Jesus typologically fulfills the significance of the first exodus by superimposing upon it his own exodus that is symbolized by the preparation of the Passover lamb by his disciples (**14:12–16**; the time would be Thursday, 14 Nisan; John 18:28 likely refers to the continuing feast, the *chagigah,* not to the Passover meal itself which would have been eaten after nightfall Thursday evening, 15 Nisan; John 19:14 refers to Friday of Passover week, and John 19:31 to Saturday of Passover week). It is the last Passover lamb Jesus will eat before he becomes the Lamb sacrificed once for all (cf. Heb. 7:27; 9:26–28; 10:10). Jesus is about to take the Old Testament time and space of Passover into himself and personify its deepest meaning on the cross. The irony of the last Passover meal is the invisible process within the visible by which the old is transposed into the new.

The Passover meal had to be eaten after sundown, which signaled the beginning of 15 Nisan, and within the walls of Jerusalem. With food and wine symbolic of the original exodus Jesus solemnly announces that one of the twelve disciples at the meal will betray him (**14:17–21**). Of all the sins he decries, Jesus most vehemently opposes the hypocrisy of those whose speech and acts belie their intention. In contrast to Jesus' integrity as a friend, Judas deceives and betrays his close friend Jesus (cf. Ps. 41:9). By his treacherous unbelief he brings upon himself the ultimate condemnation from the friend who would have saved him. With irony Mark records that while Jesus affirms his faithful course as the Son of man who "will go just as it is written about him" (the Suffering Servant of Isa. 53), he condemns the betrayer who would have been better off never to have been born (v. 21). The Marcan theme of faithfulness and integrity of belief is again highlighted, for personal responsibility is crucial in the unfolding of the absolute plan of God.

During the complex paschal meal that is filled with exodus themes (**14:22–26**), Jesus takes the bread, gives thanks, breaks it, and gives it to his disciples to eat, identifying it with his own person ("this is my body," v. 22). Again, Jesus is taking Old Testament space and time into himself and is personifying the new exodus that anticipates the cross. But he is also sharing that space and time with his disciples as he invites them to participate in his presence as Son of man. Similarly, at the close of the meal, he takes the cup (the third cup of the Passover meal) and after giving thanks and offering it to them identifies the wine as "my blood of the covenant which is poured out for many" (v. 24; cf. Exod. 24:8; Isa. 53:12; Jer. 31:31–33). By this identification Jesus embodies the redemptive and homecoming themes of the Old Testament, promising a new drinking of the festal cup in the final homecoming of the redeemed community when the now inaugurated kingdom of God is completed (v. 25). The meal comes to a close with the singing of the victorious Hallel psalms 115–118 (esp. Ps. 118:14–17) before they depart to the Mount of Olives (v. 26).

On the way to the Mount of Olives Jesus prophesies that all the disciples will fail him and will be scattered like sheep when he, the shepherd, is struck (**14:27–31**); but this will be a temporary and refining defection (so the context of Zech. 13:7–9), not like the fatal denial of Judas, for Jesus promises that after he has risen he will go ahead of them into Galilee (v. 28). Peter not only rejects Jesus' first prophecy but his prediction that that very night the disciple will disown him three times. There is irony in the failure of Peter and the disciples to understand what is entailed in the suffering to come (cf. 8:31; 14:50), and irony in the vehemence of Peter's denial here and in 14:71. What is occurring is a narrowing down of the remnant of Israel to Jesus himself, as even the innermost core of followers defect at the striking of the shepherd, who alone is faithful and worthy to bear the righteous wrath of God upon human sin.

The narrowing down of the suffering role to Jesus alone continues when he selects only Peter, James, and John to accompany him to Gethsemane (**14:32–42**), where he begins to be "deeply distressed and troubled" and "overwhelmed with sorrow to the point of death" (vv. 33–34). Repeating to the three disciples the imperative of his Olivet Discourse, "watch" (Gk. *grēgoreite,* v. 34; 13:37), he falls to the ground praying that he might escape the hour of suffering when he should drink the cup of divine wrath (the terrible consequences of which are described in Jer. 25:15–38; 49:12; cf.

Ps. 75:8). The final satanic attempt to divert Jesus from the cross parallels the initial temptation in the wilderness (1:12–13). There is a distinct pattern at the beginning and close of Jesus' ministry: (1) baptism in water and first approval of the Son (1:9–11); (2) first temptation in the wilderness (1:12–13); (3) last temptation in the garden of Gethsemane (14:32–42, esp. 36a); (4) final approval of the Son that he be baptized by death (14:36b). In the presence of the Father (*Abba* is an Aramaic word that means "father" in an intimate sense) Jesus echoes the temptation of the tempter who would misconstrue the intent and timing of Scripture that the "cup of staggering" already has been or could at this point be taken away (Isa. 51:22). But the strong voice of the Son responds in faithfulness, and he conquers satanic time and space in obedience to the will of the Father. The crisis of wills on which pivots the destiny of the human race is tilted inexorably and irreversibly toward the cross.

Jesus has faced the crisis alone, for the last of his disciples have fallen asleep (v. 37) and will fail to keep the vigil of watchfulness he again enjoins upon them (once more, "watch," *grēgoreite*, v. 38). Three times he prays faithfully, three times he finds them sleeping, three times Peter will deny him. The hour has come for the Son of man to be betrayed into the hands of sinners (v. 41). The demonic opposition of Jerusalem now confronts him in force, led by the betrayer (v. 42).

There is irony in Judas's betrayal of Jesus (**14:43–52**), for his greeting ("Rabbi!" ["my master"]) and his kiss (the symbol of a disciple's respect for his rabbi) are transposed into their opposite, exposing a contemptuous and demonic destruction of language and friendship. The betrayal is devious and sly (cf. 14:1–2, 10–11) and is accomplished in the darkness of night in a garden outside the city, in contrast to Jesus' bold and open confrontation in the temple courts by day (v. 49). Jesus repudiates two forms of violence: the first an attempt by one of his disciples (Peter, John 18:10) to fight by the sword and begin an armed rebellion, the second the threat of the formidable crowd sent by the chief priests, the teachers of the law, and the elders who accompany Judas and are armed with swords and clubs (vv. 42, 48). There is more irony than meets the eye in Jesus' disavowal of the sword, for by his claim that "the Scripture must be fulfilled" (the way of the Suffering Servant, Isa. 53:12; the struck shepherd, Zech. 13:7; cf. Mark 14:27) he has lost not only the support of the religious authorities and their armed crowd, but of his disciples as well, all of whom view their ultimate salvation as God's promised restoration of Davidic nationalism by the power of the sword. Jesus is totally deserted, even by his disciples (as well as [?] by the eyewitness Mark [vv. 51–52; cf. Amos 2:16]).

Jesus now stands totally alone on trial, first, before the power of religious authority (**14:53–65**), then before the power of the state (chap. 15). The combined forces of the hostile city of Jerusalem conspire to destroy him, but Jesus defiantly stands his ground, having already taken their authority into himself as Son of man and Son of God, and sets his course to fulfill Scripture by permitting them to condemn him to death. Mark purposely parallels Jesus' faithful stand as friend of sinners with Peter's sinful denial of friendship. Mark's readers would appreciate the irony of Jesus standing before the court of the hostile Sanhedrin within and Peter warming himself at the courtyard fire outside (vv. 53–54, a contrast that will be further developed in the next scene [vv. 66–72]). The irony of the court scene itself is startling as the chief priest (Caiaphas) and the whole Sanhedrin look for evidence to put Jesus to death but cannot find any (v. 55), and are able to produce only bumbling witnesses who voice an element of truth about Jesus' prophecy of the temple's destruction but cannot agree on their testimony, making the trial a travesty of justice (vv. 56–59; cf. Deut. 17:6; 19:15).

Jesus' silence repudiates their abuse of language and unscriptural procedure and is broken only when the high priest asks the ultimate and essential question, "Are you the Christ, the Son of the Blessed One?" (v. 61), to which Jesus replies with his authoritative "I am" and a declaration of coequality with the Mighty One, as Son of man who will come visibly on the clouds of heaven (v. 62; cf. Ps. 110:1; Dan. 7:13). This brings the scene to its high point of irony, for by his bold and unveiled self-identification as Messiah, Son of the Blessed One, the "I am" and Son of man who is coequal with the Mighty One, Jesus focuses Old Testament theology upon himself and invites the charge of blasphemy from the unbelieving high priest (vv. 63–64). The irony could not be greater, for the reader knows that the high priest and the Sanhedrin unwittingly (cf. 1 Cor. 2:8) condemn as worthy of death the One who is in reality the source of their vocation as guardians of the faith. Instead of joyfully welcoming Jesus, they regale him with insults and condemnation. In the supreme moment of revelation when their Lord appears suddenly, they have failed to be watchful and have fallen asleep (13:34–37).

Mark now picks up the parallel account

about Peter (from v. 54) and underscores the irony of the situation. Peter is outside swearing false witness and denying his relationship with Jesus in order to save his own skin, while Jesus is inside bearing true testimony, about to pay the price of faithful friendship by sacrificing his life for sinners like Peter (**14:66–72**). Though Peter denies Jesus, Jesus does not deny Peter (cf. 16:7). The crowing of the rooster punctuates Peter's denial as Jesus had predicted (14:30), and the spokesman for the disciples who had himself been like the cock in his prideful self-sufficiency (14:29, 31) breaks down and weeps at what he has done. The contrast between Jesus and Peter in two parallel courtrooms within sight of each other and at the same moment of truth renders a warning to Mark's readers that at whatever the cost they must bear true witness to the One who ultimately matters, or there will be bitter weeping.

Marcan irony continues in the account of Jesus' trial before the state (**15:1–15**). Where the Jewish Sanhedrin condemns Jesus for blasphemy because he claims too much and fails to fulfill their expectations of a political Messiah, the Roman state condemns him for high treason because it misconstrues his announcement of the kingdom as a claim to political kingship. Both powers condemn him as the Messiah. There is further irony in the fact that the Sanhedrin, while rejecting Jesus for blasphemy and failure to be their political king, bind Jesus over to Pilate on the dishonest and hypocritical charge that Jesus is a political pretender, which they know to be false. Thus the cost of getting rid of Jesus is a travesty of justice that denies Old Testament jurisprudence. For his part as representative of the state, Pilate makes a travesty of justice in order to protect his own interests, knowing that the religious authorities have handed Jesus over out of envy (v. 10) and that Jesus is innocent (v. 14) and wanting to satisfy the crowd (v. 15). Surrounded by the breakdown of language and law, Jesus answers only Pilate's straightforward question (parallel to that of Caiaphas, 14:61), "Are you the king of the Jews?" "Yes, it is as you say" (15:2; John 18:33–38 gives a fuller account of Jesus' answer). In both religious and civil courts marred by illegal intentions and procedures, Jesus gives simple and true testimony to his identity, but refuses to enter into debate where justice cannot be realized, fulfilling the role of the Suffering Servant by his silence (Isa. 53:7). Pilate further flouts the law and increases the irony of the mock trial by releasing a known political insurgent and murderer, Barabbas, ordering Jesus, whom he knows to be innocent, to be flogged and delivered up to be crucified (v. 15; cf. Isa. 53:10–12).

In his descent to the cross Jesus is subject to a succession of mockeries, from the highest tribunal of Jewish faith, to the civil court of Pilate, and now to a perverted soldiery who abuse Jesus in a sadistic masquerade of kingship, heaping insults on the One who has claimed in the two highest courts of the land to be Son of God and king of the Jews (**15:16–20**). Mark's description of royal trappings and greetings that have been grotesquely and demonically vulgarized adds to the irony of Jesus' royal stature and his willingness to undergo such suffering for the salvation of the lost (Isa. 53:3–4, 10–12). In their own suffering and persecution Mark's readers are exhorted by the exemplary faithfulness of Jesus in his hour of indescribable agony.

Jesus' suffering is described with great succinctness and restraint, particularly the crucifixion (**15:21–32**), but Mark never omits the note of irony by which the perceptive reader of the Gospel is invited to contrast what is going on in the world of outer appearances and what is actually going on in the real world that only the eyes of faith can penetrate. This ironic contrast has been seen in Mark's character studies of people who respond to Jesus in belief or unbelief. Only the barest of details are given of the scene on Golgotha: Jesus' refusal to drink a narcotic potion to ease his pain; his crucifixion (only four words, "And they crucified him," that compress the excruciating agony reserved for the basest of criminals); the casting of lots for his clothes; the enigmatic sign upon the cross ("The King of the Jews"); the indignity of crucifixion between two criminals. All is told with restraint.

What fascinates Mark, and is needful for his audience to hear for their own benefit, is the regaling of Jesus by unbelievers at the supreme moment of salvation in human history (vv. 29–32). Passers-by taunt Jesus as a false prophet and shake their heads at his prophecy of the temple's destruction and resurrection in three days, not knowing that the prediction is now in the process of being fulfilled in Jesus' own person (he has become the true temple, having appropriated its space into himself); he will also come down from the cross and save himself, but not according to their timing or before he has completed his work of saving others (vv. 29–30). The chief priests and the teachers of the law make a final accusation, taunting in the same way as the others (vv. 21–32) and mocking Jesus for not being able to save himself. Ironically, these religious leaders voice for the final time the demonic temptation to escape the cross: if he is truly the Christ and the king of Israel he will come down from the cross "that we may see and believe." The coupling of "seeing" and "believing" is significant in Mark's Gospel, for without belief the inner significance of Jesus' death on the cross cannot be seen. Mark's use of irony in juxtaposing seeing and believing is important, for at the end of his Gospel the young man at the tomb will invite the vigilant women to examine the empty tomb (16:6) and bear witness to the disciples and Peter that Jesus will see them in Galilee, as he promised (v. 7). They need to believe in order to see; and there the Gospel ends. Will they believe and see, or will they be enervated by unbelief? The religious authorities at the foot of the cross do not believe in Jesus and therefore do not see who he is or what he is bringing to pass. In order to see and understand they must first believe.

In the Gospel of Mark Jesus' death (**15:33–41**) is seen to recapitulate and fulfill the themes of Passover and the exodus. The plague of darkness that fell upon Egypt before the Passover (Exod. 10:21–22) falls over the land of Judah as Jesus becomes the final Passover and substitutionary curse (v. 33; cf. Gal. 3:13). Nature participates in the prelude to Jesus' cry of dereliction as he bears in himself the holy wrath of God on behalf of sinners: "My God, my God, why have you forsaken me?" (v. 34). In this moment of deepest irony the One who alone lived in perfect fellowship with God is alienated from God and dies with a loud cry (v. 37). His final cry is not only a cry of dereliction but also a cry of victory: "It is finished" (John 19:30; cf. Luke 23:46; and the alternating despair and victory of Ps. 22). Because Jesus has taken the space of the temple into the true temple of his own person, the physical demolition of the old temple begins at his death with the tearing of the temple curtain, a sign that the rejection of Jesus as Messiah by the religious leaders will lead inexorably to the total demolition of the house of sacrifice (v. 38; 13:2; 14:58; 15:29). The inner curtain separating the Holy Place from the Holy of Holies is signified (cf. Heb. 9:8–14; 10:19–20) and would likely have been reported by priests later converted to Christian faith.

The two men who appear before and after Jesus' death (vv. 36, 39) frame with further irony two alternatives for Mark's readers. The first man, probably not a soldier but one of the Jewish bystanders who thinks he recognizes in Jesus' "Eloi, Eloi" (v. 34) a call for Elijah, represents the unbelieving nation. The second man, with Jesus' redeeming work accomplished and access into the Most Holy Place open, stands as an unlikely witness to faith. The Gentile Roman centurion, upon hearing Jesus' cry and beholding how he has breathed his last (the note of triumph in Jesus' death must have carried convincing authority), professes belief in Jesus as the Son of God (v. 39).

From the time of Jesus' entry into Jerusalem to his crucifixion, Mark mentions only two people who evidence faith Jesus deems worthy of praise, and both are women: the poor widow in the temple (12:41–44), and the woman at Bethany who anoints Jesus (14:3–9). Now a third, a Gentile centurion, is mentioned (15:39); and at a distance from the cross there are others, again women (vv. 40–41), some of whom have been healed by Jesus and who have been faithful in supporting him out of their own means (cf. Luke 8:1–3). A few are specifically mentioned by Mark and are eyewitnesses to what happened at the cross (Mary Magdalene, Mary the mother of James and Joses, and Salome, v. 40). It is important to note that with the exception of Joseph of Arimathea (vv. 42–46), no men of Israel are commended either by Jesus or Mark (the Jewish leaders have opposed Jesus; the disciples have all fled). Yet the same three women (Mary Magdalene, Mary the mother of James and Joses, and Salome), who are honored as those who cared for Jesus' needs in Galilee (vv. 40–41) and are favored with the first disclosure of the empty tomb (16:1–7), are the very ones who are enervated by fear at the end of the Gospel (16:8). The role of faithful servanthood and the constant threat of fear are significant issues for Mark as he addresses his Christian readers in their own setting of suffering and testing.

The single man of Jewish faith Mark commends in his account (John includes Nicodemus [19:38–42]) is Joseph of Arimathea, a prominent member of the Sanhedrin who has faithfully awaited the kingdom of God (v. 43; Luke adds that he was a good and upright man who had not consented to the decision and action of the Council [23:50–51]). He boldly, and at considerable risk to his reputation, requests the body of Jesus from Pilate in order to give Jesus an honorable burial before the onset of the Sabbath at sundown (**15:42–47**). His request affords Mark opportunity to record (from Joseph's eyewitness account) that Pilate summoned the centurion who oversaw Jesus' crucifixion and gave testimony that Jesus was surely the Son of God (v. 39), to give further testimony that Jesus was truly dead (vv. 44–45). Pilate's action to release the body to Joseph confirms Mark's account of the trial (15:1–15). Pilate never considered Jesus guilty of high treason (those so guilty were not permitted burial) but had acquiesced to his crucifixion only to satisfy the crowd. Joseph's piety in preparing the body for burial, placing it in the tomb, and sealing the entrance with a stone simply adds to the irony of the story. For Joseph, as for the women who witness the burial (v. 47), it is a pathetic closure on their messianic expectations. Jesus is dead and buried. Hostile Jerusalem has conquered Christ; the strong man Satan has reclaimed his space. Or so it seems.

IV. Unfinished Epilogue (16:1–8)

Two facts need to be noted in order to appreciate Mark's irony at the close of his Gospel. First, Mark does not tell the story on the women; they tell it on themselves, for the two Marys and Salome are the original witnesses who come to the tomb early on Sunday morning to pay their last respects to Jesus and find, instead of a sealed tomb, an open chamber and an angelic messenger within who announces that the crucified Jesus has risen, and that they are to go and tell his disciples and Peter that Jesus will meet them in Galilee (vv. 1–7). Like Peter, who later told Mark many embarrassing stories about himself that are recorded in the Gospel for the edification of the church, the women later relate their experience at the tomb and their initial failure to act because of their fear and bewilderment (v. 8). Second, the irony of the incident is heightened by the fact that in Jewish culture the testimony of women was disregarded as worthless (Mishnah, *Rosh Ha-Shanah* 1.8). Yet these women, who were among the most faithful of Jesus' followers, were providentially honored to be witnesses to the disciples themselves of Jesus' victorious resurrection. But even they, the most faithful and honored of Jesus' followers, failed to rise obediently to the command of the angel to "go and tell," but fled from the tomb and "said nothing to anyone, because they were afraid." As abruptly as the Gospel begins with the confident declaration, "The beginning of the gospel about Jesus Christ, the Son of God" (1:1), and the sudden appearance of John the Baptist "preaching a baptism of repentance for the forgiveness of sins" (vv. 2–4), Mark abruptly ends his Gospel on a downbeat of silence and fear, the last words being "for they were afraid."

Why? It is not because Mark and his readers do not know that the women finally came to their senses and spread the news of Jesus' resurrection. Mark ends his account where he does in order to catch his readers at a crucial moment of decision in the lives of these three women divinely chosen to be witnesses to history's greatest event, and upon whom rests the responsibility to begin the proclamation of the gospel about Jesus Christ, the Son of God. Mark freezes the frame on their enervating fear; and thus, like the unresolved ending of Jonah (4:10–11; what did Jonah do?) and the parable of the elder son (Luke 15:31–32; what did he decide?), Mark presents his readers with a final challenge—and from an oblique and discomforting angle.

With what may be a final ironic turn in which he exposes his own embarrassment before the perceptive reader, Mark contrasts the radiant, faithful, and angelic witness of the "young man" at the tomb who is dressed in a white robe (16:5) with the "young man" in the garden who forsook Jesus and fled naked, leaving his white linen garment behind (14:51–52). But the last impression is left by the faithful women who at this crucial moment are frozen by fear: "What then, reader, will *you* do in your time of testing when you are called to bear witness to the crucified and risen Jesus?" they seem to ask.[5]

SELECT BIBLIOGRAPHY

Anderson, H. *The Gospel of Mark.* Grand Rapids: Eerdmans, 1981.

Best, E. *Following Jesus: Discipleship in the Gospel of Mark.* Sheffield: JSOT, 1981.

Cranfield, C. E. B. *The Gospel According to St. Mark.* New York: Cambridge University Press, 1959.

Martin, R. P. *Mark.* Atlanta: John Knox, 1981.

Stonehouse, N. B. *The Witness of Matthew and Mark to Christ.* Grand Rapids: Eerdmans, 1958.

5. The last twelve verses (16:9–20) are appended to the NIV text, prefaced by an explanation that "the most reliable manuscripts and other ancient witnesses" do not include them.

LUKE

Thomas R. Schreiner

INTRODUCTION

Nowhere in the Gospel of Luke does the author reveal his identity. To ascertain the author of the Gospel, therefore, one should first of all examine the internal evidence of the Gospel to find clues about its authorship. Unfortunately, the Gospel does not supply the reader with much information. We do learn, however, that the author was not an eyewitness (Luke 1:2), and thus anyone who observed Jesus in his public ministry can be eliminated. Furthermore, the writer of Luke clearly was intelligent and well educated, for he displays an ability to write in excellent Greek and is well acquainted with the Old Testament.

Also, scholars almost universally agree that the author of the Gospel of Luke is the same person as the author of the Acts of the Apostles for the following reasons: (1) Both books are dedicated to the same person—Theophilus (Luke 1:3; Acts 1:1). (2) The author refers to "my former book," and says that the "former book" contains "all that Jesus began to do and to teach" (Acts 1:1). This former book refers most naturally to the Gospel of Luke. (3) Lastly, many of the themes with which Luke ends his Gospel (Luke 24:36–53) are picked up again in Acts 1:1–11, which suggests that the same author is continuing his former work, briefly tying together the two works so that the reader of Acts can pick up where the Gospel left off.

Clearly, then, the same author wrote both Luke and Acts. But Acts, unfortunately, is also anonymous. Are there any hints in Acts about the identity of the author? The chief clue is found in the "we sections" of Acts (Acts 16:10–17; 20:5–15; 21:1–18; 27:1–28:16). The careful reader notices that the author speaks of Paul and his companions as "they" (e.g., Acts 16:7–8), and then he suddenly starts using the first person plural "we" (Acts 16:10–13, 16). The author probably begins to use "we" because he is now participating in the Pauline mission. Indeed, in these sections he may be referring to a diary which he kept of these events. By comparing these "we sections" with the rest of the book the reader can begin to eliminate certain names from authorship (cf. Acts 20:4). Although other solutions are possible (e.g., that the author was Titus), it is most likely that the author of the Gospel was Paul's traveling companion—Saint Luke.

Luke is mentioned three times in Paul's letters. In Colossians 4:14 he is called "our dear friend Luke, the doctor." In Philemon 24 he is mentioned as one of Paul's fellow workers. In 2 Timothy 4:11 Paul says that "only Luke is with me." This reference to Luke's loyalty is especially poignant because the context of 2 Timothy 4 reveals that Paul is about to be executed by the Romans, and many of Paul's companions abandoned him in such a perilous situation. If Philemon and Colossians were written by Paul from Rome (and this theory is still the most probable), then the references to Luke in these letters fit with Acts 27:1–28:16 where the author of Acts accompanies Paul to Rome.

W. K. Hobart argued that Lucan authorship was supported by Luke's precise use of medical terminology, showing that the author was a physician (Col. 4:14). But H. J. Cadbury carefully tested Hobart's thesis and demonstrated that Luke's alleged medical terminology is often found in Greek writers who were not physicians; therefore, one should not claim that the language used in Luke–Acts clearly indicates that a physician wrote it. On the other hand, Cadbury's study does not preclude Lucan authorship; it simply shows that one cannot argue for Lucan authorship from medical terminology. Colossians 4:14 also implies that Luke was a Gentile and not a Jew. In Colossians 4:10–11 Paul names Aristarchus, Mark, and Jesus Justus and says that they are his only companions among the circumcision, meaning presumably that they are his only Jewish companions. Then in Colossians 4:12–14 Paul names Epaphras, Luke, and Demas and says that they send their greetings. If the three listed in Colossians 4:10–11 are the only Jews with Paul, then the obvious conclusion is that Luke was a Gentile.

Even though the internal evidence may point to Lucan authorship, decisive evidence is lacking. But it is significant that the early tradition of the church is unanimous in positing Lucan authorship. For example, the early title of the Gospel—"Gospel according to Luke"—is attached to our earliest manuscript of the Gospel in the late second century A.D. Irenaeus, the Muratorian Canon, and an ancient prologue to the Gospel (all written near the end of the second century A.D.) also assert Lucan authorship. Tertullian, writing early in the third century A.D., also held to Lucan authorship. Some scholars tend to doubt the tradition of the early church on these matters, and certainly the early church fathers were not infallible. Nevertheless, the ancient tradition is a serious witness; and since the Fathers were closer to the events than we are, they should not be forsaken unless there is compelling evidence for doing so. Furthermore, those who doubt Lucan authorship do not adequately explain why the early church would attribute the work to Luke. After all, Luke is not a notable figure in the New Testament itself. The most probable reason for the tradition of Lucan authorship is that this tradition is accurate.

Scholars often question Lucan authorship because Luke's picture of Paul seems to contradict Paul's self-portrait in his letters. But the difference in the portrait of Paul is probably due to two different perspectives. Inevitably, there will be differences between the way a person describes himself and the way an outsider views that person. In addition, it is also claimed that Luke's writing is subapostolic; an imminent parousia has been abandoned, and the church has become an institution which grants salvation. The objection regarding the parousia is too simplistic. A careful reading of the Gospel accounts shows that there are three different types of sayings about the end: some stress the imminence of the end (Mark 13:30 par.), others a period of delay (Matt. 25:14–30), and others uncertainty regarding the end (Mark 13:32–37 par.). The Gospel of Luke displays the same tension (cf., e.g., 21:9 and 21:33), and thus is in accord with the other Gospel accounts. The notion that the church has been institutionalized is also oversimplified, for it is obvious that any new movement must have some organization. The question is whether the Lucan organization is as advanced as the church of the second century A.D. Even a cursory reading of the Ignatian letters shows that there are major differences, for there is no monarchial episcopate in Luke. Neither of these objections, then, is decisive.

The date and destination of the Gospel of Luke are also shrouded in uncertainty. Indeed, the problem is particularly knotty because the date of Luke usually depends on the dates of Mark and Acts (most scholars still hold to Marcan priority). Two basic theories rule the field of scholarship today: Luke was written in either the 80s or the 60s. Those who favor a date in the 80s maintain that Luke was written after Mark, and the latter was not written until ca. A.D. 65–70. In addition, some scholars claim that Luke was probably written after the destruction of the temple in A.D. 70. Others think Luke was written in the early 60s because Acts ends (28:30–31) with Paul under house arrest, and no information is given on the outcome of his trial. According to this theory, such an abrupt ending in Acts shows that Luke finished Acts before Paul's case was resolved. In this instance Acts would be dated between A.D. 61–63. Since Luke was written before Acts, then the Gospel would be placed in the early 60s or late 50s. The same scholars would argue that the Gospel of Mark was written in the 50s. Other scholars date Luke between A.D. 65–70, arguing that it was probably written before the destruction of Jerusalem in A.D. 70. Certainty is impossible on such difficult matters, but a date before the destruction of Jerusalem in A.D. 70. seems probable.

Where was Luke when he wrote the Gospel? Early traditions suggest Achaia, Boeotia, or Rome. The latter is especially attractive because of the tradition that Mark wrote his Gospel in Rome; however, no one really knows where Luke was, but the matter is not crucial in the interpretation of the Gospel.

Almost all scholars agree that Luke wrote to Gentile Christians. The dedication of the two volumes to a person who has a Greek name (Theophilus), the excellent Greek of the prologue (Luke 1:1–4), the interest in Gentiles, and the elimination of certain Jewish customs and debates (e.g., the controversy on cleanness in Mark 7:1–23), and the substitution of Greek terms for Jewish terms all suggest a Gentile audience.

That Luke used sources is immediately evident from the prologue of the Gospel (Luke 1:1–4). He indicates that many others have written accounts of the Gospel traditions, and that these traditions have been handed down to the church. Luke specifically states that he "carefully investigated everything from the beginning" (Luke 1:3), showing that he thoroughly sifted through the information that was available to him. What were the actual sources that Luke used? This is a matter of speculation, of course, and so dogmatism is excluded.

Most New Testament scholars still agree that Luke used the Gospel of Mark when he composed his Gospel (although this theory is contested rather strongly by a significant number of scholars). The reason for this is that a substantial portion of Mark's Gospel, often including the exact words from Mark, is used in Luke's Gospel. Of course, the argument as it is stated above could support Lucan priority, but for a variety of complex reasons such a view is unlikely.

Also, both Luke and Matthew probably used a common source that was either a written document or consisted of oral tradition. This material is designated "Q" (from Ger. *Quelle,* source). Unfortunately, Q has not survived and possibly never even existed in written form. Approximately 230 verses appear in both Matthew and Luke but not in Mark's Gospel. A common source is probable since the wording of this common tradition that Luke and Matthew share is remarkably similar, and sometimes is exactly the same. But if the wording is so similar, then perhaps Luke borrowed it directly from Matthew (very few scholars think Matthew borrowed from Luke). This is improbable, however, because Luke uses the same sayings that Matthew does and places them in completely different contexts. It is highly unlikely that the same sayings would be transposed by Luke, or that Luke would break up Matthew's tightly organized Sermon on the Mount (Matt. 5–7). Thus, the idea that Luke and Matthew both used and adapted a common source, without directly depending on the other's Gospel, is the most compelling.

Lastly, any material in Luke's Gospel that is not dependent on Mark or "Q" is usually labeled "L." This is simply a convenient way of indicating that Luke had other sources of information. It is impossible to know how many.

We should also not rule out that Luke may have received information from Mary the mother of Jesus, the disciples of John the Baptist, Manaen (an early disciple; cf. Acts 13:1), Cleopas (Luke 24:18), and others. Many New Testament scholars would doubt that Luke depended on any of these persons. But it is quite probable that Luke would have spoken to living persons about what they had heard and seen of Jesus when he came into contact with them. Any twentieth-century researcher would have done the same, and in the ancient world such a procedure would have been prized just as highly, as the early church father Papias in the second century made clear.

Some scholars debate how Luke composed his Gospel. One theory is that Luke first composed the whole Gospel, so-called proto-Luke, from Q and L material. Later he came upon the Gospel of Mark (possibly when he arrived in Rome) and inserted the Marcan portions into his narrative. The arguments for such a theory are quite complex, and of course, such a view is highly hypothetical.

Some scholars have maintained that Luke's use of his sources shows that his writing lacks historical reliability, and that he was writing to edify the church and to propound his own theology and not to transmit what really happened. First, we should note that such a position contravenes Luke's own statement of his purpose in the prologue of the Gospel (Luke 1:1–4) where he indicates that accuracy in the work is one of his concerns. Second, it is methodologically flawed to pit edification and theology against history. All history writing is interpretive to some degree because the writer must select which themes he will emphasize. Clearly, Luke does have a distinctive theology, but it is not logically necessary to conclude that such interpretive selection and presentation by an author obviates historical reliability. The same point applies to edification; that is, what really happened could be edifying. Third, Luke's use of the Gospel of Mark also shows that he was interested in historical accuracy. For example, the sayings of Jesus that are shared by Luke and Mark usually have only minor differences. The modern reader needs to remember that the ancient writer was not always interested in exactly what was said. Luke would naturally be content at times to paraphrase Jesus' words and actions. Such a paraphrase would be inaccurate only if it deceived a person about what actually happened. Luke was not recording on tape the words of Jesus, but neither was he freely inventing them; he clearly felt free to record in his own style what happened. Lastly, when Luke's account does differ from the other Synoptics, we need to recall that none of the accounts claims to be exhaustive. Thus, one should not demand that any Gospel writer tell the whole story. All our questions about historicity will never be answered when reading the Gospels. But humility and the inspiration of Scripture suggest that we should give the writer the benefit of doubt.

When studying Luke's theology one must remember that he did not simply write a Gospel but that he also wrote the Book of Acts. Both works must be taken into account in formulating a Lucan theology.

It is evident from the writing of both the Gospel and Acts that Luke is interested in the continuing history of the church. The prologue to the Gospel (Luke 1:1–4) clearly shows that Luke was interested in historical accuracy. More than any other Gospel writer Luke explains the relationship between the events he narrates and Roman and Palestinian history. Of course, Luke was not a disinterested historian; he wrote these books because he saw this period of history as the decisive inbreaking of God's salvation.

It is not surprising, therefore, that Luke is usually described as a theologian of salvation history. Luke sees what is happening in the ministry of Jesus and the ministry of the early church as the fulfillment of God's plan and purpose. This saving plan comes to realization as people experience salvation.

Luke also emphasizes that this salvation is for all people, even for the people considered to be outcasts or socially marginal. Thus, Jesus proclaims his saving message to tax collectors, sinners, the poor, women, and children. This theme continues in Acts where the early church slowly grasps that God wants the gospel message to be proclaimed to both Samaritans and Gentiles. Jews and Gentiles are equal members in God's new community.

The power of the Spirit and the importance of prayer are also prominent themes in Lucan theology. In the Gospel of Luke Jesus conducts his ministry in the power of the Spirit. His messianic work can be accomplished only because "the Spirit of the Lord is on me" (Luke 4:18). After Jesus' resurrection and exaltation he becomes the dispenser of the Spirit (Acts 2:32–33), and pours the Spirit upon his disciples. Then his disciples proclaim the gospel of salvation to the ends of the earth by the power of the Spirit. Prayer also plays a vital role in Jesus' ministry. Luke emphasizes repeatedly that Jesus prayed before making important decisions or at key points in his ministry. The disciples in Acts follow the pattern of their master by continuing in prayer.

Luke also focuses on the importance of discipleship. Some of Jesus' strongest statements on the commitment that is demanded of those who would follow Jesus are found in this Gospel (Luke 9:57–62; 14:25–35). Also, Luke stresses in uncompromising terms the dangers of materialism. The love of riches ousts one's love for God, which is why Luke thinks it is a blessing to be poor, for the poor are dependent upon God (cf. Luke 6:20–26). In Acts Luke portrays the ideal of Christian community (Acts 2:42–47; 4:32–37).

Unlike Paul, Luke does not fully explain the meaning of Christ's death on the cross. Luke views the death of Jesus as the fulfillment of God's plan (Luke 24:44), and he even connects the possibility of forgiveness with the death of Jesus (Luke 24:46–47). What Luke does not do, however, is attempt to explain the relationship between Jesus' death and the forgiveness of sins.

The salvation that Luke centers on is available through Jesus of Nazareth. The significance of Jesus becomes apparent when one examines the titles which Luke ascribes to him. Jesus is Messiah, Lord, the Son of God, the Son of man, Savior, Servant, King, Prophet, and the Son of David.

OUTLINE

I. Prologue: A Reliable Account of Salvation History (1:1–4)
II. Preparation for Jesus' Ministry (1:5–4:13)
  A. Two Births Predicted (1:5–56)
  B. Two Sons Born (1:57–2:52)
  C. The Baptist's Ministry: Preparation for the Lord (3:1–20)
  D. Jesus: Endowed by the Spirit for Ministry (3:21–4:13)

III. Jesus Proclaims Salvation in Galilee by the Power of the Spirit (4:14–9:50)
  A. Proclamation of Good News in Galilee (4:14–5:16)
  B. Conflict with the Pharisees (5:17–6:11)
  C. Good News for the Poor (6:12–8:3)
  D. Revelation and Obedience (8:4–21)
  E. The Revelation of Jesus' Identity (8:22–9:50)
IV. Galilee to Jerusalem: Discipleship (9:51–19:27)
  A. The Journey Begins (9:51–13:21)
  B. The Journey Continues (13:22–17:10)
  C. The Last Leg of the Journey (17:11–19:27)
V. Arrival at Destiny: Death and Resurrection in Jerusalem (19:28–24:53)
  A. Entrance into Jerusalem (19:28–48)
  B. Controversy Between Jesus and Leaders Heightens (20:1–21:4)
  C. Apocalyptic Discourse (21:5–38)
  D. Passover Events (22:1–38)
  E. Arrest and Trial (22:39–23:25)
  F. Crucifixion and Burial (23:26–23:56a)
  G. Resurrection: Scripture Fulfilled (23:56b–24:53)

COMMENTARY

I. Prologue: A Reliable Account of Salvation History (1:1–4)

Luke's introduction is distinctive among the Gospels because it is written in excellent classical Greek, showing that Luke is consciously writing a literary work. Many have preceded Luke in composing gospels, relying on the oral testimony of eyewitnesses who handed down the tradition. Luke has also decided to compose a Gospel; one cannot demonstrate from the text that he has decided to do this because he thought the previous gospels were inadequate or inferior. Indeed, verse 2 implies that Luke trusted the reliability of the previous accounts. Luke then displays his credentials for writing a Gospel. His investigation was comprehensive ("from the beginning"), accurate ("carefully"), and well organized ("orderly"). The word *orderly* does not necessarily imply that Luke is writing in strict chronological order, but only that the Gospel itself is organized in a literary way. The work is dedicated to Theophilus, although a wider readership is clearly expected. Theophilus cannot be identified with certainty. Some think he may have been a Roman official, but the words *most excellent* may simply suggest that he was a member of the higher class in Roman society. The purpose of the work is related in verse 4. Luke is writing so that Theophilus will be convinced of the reliability ("certainty") of the matters in which he has been instructed. The reference to eyewitness testimony and the careful nature of Luke's research (vv. 2–3) support the claim of reliability. Luke, however, was not simply writing a historical treatise; he was writing about the events of salvation history, about the events that "have been fulfilled" (v. 1) through the person of Christ. Luke was not a dispassionate historian but neither was he an inferior historian. He writes history from an interpretive standpoint, showing that God's saving purposes have been fulfilled in Christ.

II. Preparation for Jesus' Ministry (1:5–4:13)

A. Two births predicted (1:5–56). In the first part of this section of the Gospel, Luke describes the prediction of the birth of John the Baptist (**1:5–25**). In verses 5–7 Luke sets the background before writing of Zechariah's vision. The Herod who is mentioned is Herod the Great (cf. Matt. 2:1–19), who ruled over Palestine from 37 to 4 B.C. Zechariah and Elizabeth were both from priestly stock, and Zechariah was from the "division of Abijah." The priestly tribe of Levi was divided into twenty-four divisions, and the division of Abijah was the eighth of the twenty-four (1 Chron. 24:7–18). Each division served in the temple at Jerusalem two weeks every year. To be childless was considered a great reproach among the Jews (cf. 1:25; Gen. 30:23; 1 Sam. 1:5–6), but verse 6 clearly shows that the failure to have children was not due to sin.

Zechariah was chosen by lot to offer incense in the temple (v. 9). The number of men in the priestly ranks was so large that no person was permitted to offer incense more than once in his lifetime. In accordance with Exodus 30:7–8, incense was offered twice a day, both in the morning and evening. The parallels with Daniel 9 suggest that the vision occurred in the evening. The word used for *temple* (Gk. *naos*) in this context refers to the Holy Place since only the high priest could enter the Holy of Holies (cf. Heb. 9:6–7). The sudden appearance of the angel Gabriel (v. 19) arouses fear in Zechariah. The content of Zechariah's prayer (v. 13) is problematic. Was Zechariah praying for a son (vv. 6–7) or was he praying for Israel's redemption? Perhaps he was praying for both since John's birth relates to both of these concerns. John's abstinence from alcohol reminds one of the Nazirites (Num. 6:3; Judg. 13:4). The filling of the Holy Spirit (v. 15) in Luke is usually related to prophetic activity, indicating that John is a prophet. Verses 16–17 reveal John's function: to prepare the people for the Lord's advent. He will fulfill the role of Elijah as was predicted in Malachi 3:1 and 4:5. Zechariah is probably punished for his doubt—clear Old Testament precedents show that children were born to childless couples (Gen. 16–21; Judg. 13; 1 Sam. 1). In addition, Zechariah's dumbness (vv. 21–22) functioned to show the people that he had seen a vision.

The announcement of Jesus' birth (**1:26–38**) has many similarities to the previous story, but the significance and superiority of Jesus' birth are heightened because he will be born of a virgin (not just barren parents) and will sit on David's throne (unlike John, who will prepare the way of the Lord). The emphasis on Davidic sonship is first implied in verse 27, for by adoption Jesus became Joseph's son. Verses 32–33 plainly show that Jesus will be the promised Messiah from the line of David (cf. 2 Sam. 7:9–16). The text, of course, goes a step further: Jesus is not just the Son of David but also the Son of God (v. 35; cf. v. 32). In Luke "Son of God" does not yet clearly refer to Christ's metaphysical oneness with the Father, but his unique relation to Yahweh.

Mary's favored status (v. 28) does not imply any intrinsic worthiness; it merely means that she has been a recipient of God's gracious activity. Nevertheless, Mary's obedience and faith (v. 38; cf. v. 45) are clearly a model for Luke's community.

Mary's question in verse 34 has engendered much controversy. Since she was engaged to Joseph why does she even ask this question (the verbs in v. 31 are future)? Some scholars have said that Mary had made a vow of perpetual virginity, but this is contradicted by her engagement to Joseph. Others claim that Mary knew from Isaiah 7:14 that the Messiah would be born of a virgin, and she was protesting because she was already engaged. But it is unlikely that Mary understood Isaiah 7:14 to refer to a virgin birth, and Luke never uses the passage. Still others take this to be a Lucan literary device. In other words, Mary never spoke these words, but the question advances the narrative to the great announcement; however, this solution impugns Luke's historical reliability. It is most likely that Mary understood the angel to be saying that the conception would be imminent, and Mary's marriage was still not consummated.

Naturally, the historicity of the virgin birth has been questioned. Some scholars have said that the story was borrowed from the pagan world where heroes were born from the union of gods and human women. These accounts, however, are different from the Lucan and Matthean accounts, for nothing in the latter texts suggests that actual intercourse took place between God and Mary. The words *come upon* and *overshadow* in verse 35 do not imply sexual relations, and Luke here describes with great delicacy an incomprehensible event. Others have questioned the veracity of the accounts because of the silence of the rest of the New Testament. The rest of the New Testament, however, does not contradict the present account.[1]

The text of **1:39–56** can easily be divided into two sections: (1) Elizabeth pronounces a blessing on Mary as the mother of the Lord (vv. 39–45); (2) Mary breaks forth in praise to God for his mighty works (vv. 46–56). The blessing of Elizabeth ties the narrative together; now the mothers of the two sons meet, and even in the womb John begins his ministry. In addition, Elizabeth's words in verse 43 confirm the promise that was made to Mary. Mary is blessed (v. 42) not because she is incomparably holy but because she is the mother of the Lord and because she believes that the divine promise will be fulfilled (v. 45). So once again Mary becomes a model for the Lucan community (cf. v. 38). The content of Mary's song is rather surprising, for only in verse 48 does Mary dwell on the personal benefits of being the mother of the Lord. The song stresses the exaltation of the humble, the humiliation of God's enemies (especially the proud and rich), and the fulfillment of God's promises to Abraham. The song is typically Jewish (cf. particularly 1 Sam. 2:1–10, which contains numerous parallels). It clearly lacks a Christian flavor for it offers

1. For a detailed discussion, see J. Gresham Machen, *The Virgin Birth of Christ* (Grand Rapids: Eerdmans, 1958).

representative Jewish description of the work of God in punishing evildoers and rewarding the righteous.

B. Two sons born (1:57–2:52). The account of John's birth (**1:57–66**) continues the parallelism between John and Jesus which is characteristic of the Lucan infancy narrative, although Jesus' birth is described in more detail (cf. 2:1–20). Circumcision on the eighth day (v. 59) was in obedience to the Old Testament law (Lev. 12:3), indicating that John was incorporated into the covenant (Gen. 17:9–14). The controversy over the naming of the child is curious because this is the only early passage that indicates that a child was named at his circumcision. In the Old Testament a child was named at birth. Moreover, there is no clear evidence that the naming of a child after his father was common or expected, although the naming of a child after his grandfather was common. The name John means "God is gracious."

The text implies that Zechariah was deaf as well as dumb (v. 62), and presumably he had communicated previously in writing to Elizabeth what the name of the child should be (v. 60). The main function of the story is to show that the Lord's hand was with John (v. 66). This is communicated to the reader and the original participants in the events in two ways: (1) Elizabeth had conceived and given birth to a child long after her childbearing days were over; (2) Zechariah was suddenly given the ability to speak again after being deaf and dumb for a period of time.

Structurally, Zechariah's hymn (**1:67–80**) can be divided into two parts. In the first part of the hymn Zechariah praises God for the redemption he has accomplished through the house of David (vv. 68–75). In the second part of the hymn he focuses on the role of John (vv. 76–79). Like the Magnificat, this hymn is full of Old Testament allusions, and the marginal references to the Old Testament should be consulted. Luke makes an editorial comment before the opening of the hymn (v. 67), explaining that Zechariah's hymn was prophetic and Spirit-inspired. In addition, the hymn also answers the question in verse 66 about the role of John in salvation history.

Zechariah begins the hymn by praising God for his deliverance (v. 68). The word *horn* (v. 69) means strength, alluding to the horns of animals. This is a very common Old Testament expression (Deut. 33:17). The salvation which God has accomplished is a fulfillment of the prophecies made to David (vv. 69–70). Clearly, Zechariah is thinking of God's promise to David that an heir would always sit on the throne (2 Sam. 7:12–16), and thus he is thinking of Mary's promised son. This may seem strange because John has just been born and Zechariah is praising God for Jesus. But we have already seen in Luke 1:11–17 that John's birth is linked with the fulfillment of God's saving purposes. The fulfillment of God's covenant (v. 72) to Abraham (v. 73) is also the object of Zechariah's praise. With the birth of John and the promised birth of Jesus, Zechariah sees the fulfillment of all the Old Testament promises. Zechariah conceives of this fulfillment in nationalistic terms; the Jews will be rescued from the onslaughts of all enemy forces so that they will be able to serve God in peace and harmony (vv. 71, 74–75).

In verses 76–77 Zechariah turns his attention to the role of John. He will be a prophet (cf. Isa. 40:3; Mal. 3:1) and will prepare the way for the Lord. Here the "Lord" is probably not a reference to God but to Jesus. John's ministry will be a spiritual one, for the people will learn the saving message that consists of the forgiveness of their sins (cf. Jer. 31:31–34). The last two verses (vv. 78–79) are particularly difficult. The salvation which John proclaims is due to the tender mercy of our God, and that same mercy also explains the advent of the rising sun. The words *rising sun* (Gk. *anatolē*) may also be translated as "root" or "branch." In either case it probably expresses a messianic title (cf. Num. 24:17; Mal. 4:2 on rising sun, and Isa. 11:1; Jer. 23:5; Zech. 3:8 and 6:12 on root or branch). The Messiah will illumine those in darkness and bring in peace.

Luke's interest in history becomes evident as he dates the birth of Jesus (**2:1–52**) in relationship to world history. Augustus (v. 1) was officially the Roman emperor from 27 B.C. to A.D. 14, and under his reign the Roman world experienced unparalleled peace and prosperity. During the reign of Augustus censuses were conducted for the purposes of taxation. The main purpose of this incident is to show that Jesus was born in the town of David, which was Bethlehem (v. 4; cf. Mic. 5:2; Matt. 2:4–6). Thus, God in his sovereignty used the decree of Augustus to accomplish his purposes (cf. Isa. 45:1ff.). Verse 5 seems to indicate that Mary was now married to Joseph, although the marriage had not yet been consummated. The wrapping of Jesus in strips of cloth (v. 7) was the usual way mothers took care of their children (cf. Ezek. 16:4). A second-century tradition places Jesus' birth in a cave, but there is no compelling evidence for that here. Jesus was born in a manger, that is, a place where domesticated animals were fed. The inn in verse 7 was probably a public place where a number of travelers would spend the night under one roof.

Possibly the manger was located under the open sky or in a barn somewhere. The text says nothing about other animals being present.

The historical accuracy of Luke's description of the census is plagued by various problems, the most serious being the date of Quirinius's governorship. Quirinius began his governorship of Syria in A.D. 6, and this is obviously too late to accord with the date of Jesus' birth, for Jesus was born before the death of Herod the Great who died in 4 B.C. Scholars have suggested various solutions to solve the problem, but we will mention only two. (1) Quirinius conducted several military operations in the eastern part of the empire, and he may have had extraordinary authority to order a census during the governorship of Saturninus (9–6 B.C.). (2) Perhaps the census began during the reign of Herod the Great and was not finished until the governorship of Quirinius. No easy resolution of this problem is available, and we must be content with some uncertainty.

The shepherds were not selected for the visitation (**2:8–20**) because they were sinners or poor but because of their lowly status. The shepherds would take turns watching the flock at night to guard against wolves and thieves. The text does not indicate the time of year, although December would be an unusual time of year to be outside at night. The shepherds are told that the good news is for all the people (v. 10), and by this Luke is probably indicating the inclusion of the Gentiles. The significance of the birth is plainly revealed to the shepherds as Jesus is called Savior (Deliverer), Christ (Messiah), and Lord (v. 11). The meaning of the last line of the angel's hymn in verse 14 has been construed in different ways. The translation of the New International Version is correct: "Glory to God in the highest, and on earth peace to men on whom his favor rests." The notion that God's peace extends to "men of good will" is a serious distortion of the doctrine of grace, and the King James Version rendering ("good will toward men") is based on an inferior text.

The story shows the spontaneous obedience of the shepherds (v. 15), the amazement of those who heard the report of the shepherds (vv. 17–18), and Mary's careful reflection over the events that were occurring (19). The reference to Mary in verse 19 may indicate that she was the source of Luke's information for this story.

The theme that ties together **2:21–40** is the fulfillment of the law, that is, the fulfillment of Scripture. Jesus is circumcised in accord with the Old Testament law (Lev. 12:3), Mary is purified (vv. 22–24; cf. Lev. 12:4–8), and both Simeon and Anna prophesy, indicating that God is fulfilling his covenant promises. In verse 39 Luke reiterates the major theme of this section by noting that "Joseph and Mary had done everything required by the Law of the Lord." The parallelism between John the Baptist and Jesus continues, but the superiority of Jesus is again emphasized. At John's circumcision and naming many wondered about the role the child was going to fill (Luke 1:65–66). The greater significance of Jesus is indicated by the startling prophetic revelations in the temple concerning his ministry.

Luke has compressed together several themes in verses 22–24 and they need to be distinguished. (1) The purification of Mary was stipulated by Leviticus 12:1–8. A woman was considered to be unclean after the birth of a boy for forty days, and when her purification was finished she was to offer sacrifices for cleansing. Mary and Joseph offered either a pair of doves or two young pigeons (v. 24; cf. Lev. 12:8) because they could not afford to offer a lamb. (2) The Old Testament also required that the firstborn child should be redeemed by a payment of five shekels (Exod. 13:13; Num. 18:15–16). Such a "redemption" reflects the Old Testament tradition that the firstborn belongs to Yahweh. Luke does not say that the payment was made, perhaps because he has combined this theme with the next one. (3) Interestingly, Luke combines the "redemption of the firstborn" with the presentation of Jesus to the Lord (vv. 22–23). Nowhere does the Old Testament require such a presentation, and the presentation of Jesus reminds one of Hannah's presentation of Samuel (1 Sam. 1:22–24, 28). Perhaps Luke's amalgamation of these three themes explains why he speaks of "their purification" in verse 22 because according to the Old Testament law only Mary needed to be purified.

The Spirit had already revealed to Simeon that he would not die before he would see the Messiah of the Lord (v. 26). "He was waiting for the consolation of Israel" (v. 25), and this means that he was waiting for God to fulfill his covenant promises to Israel. The coming of the Spirit on a person in Luke (v. 25) usually indicates prophetic activity, and thus it is not surprising that Simeon prophesies. Simeon is ready to die because he has seen God's salvation (vv. 29–30); the word *salvation* is just another way of describing Christ in this context. When Simeon speaks of "all people" (v. 31), it is clear that Gentiles are included, which verse 32 makes clear (cf. Isa. 49:6). The reference to the child's father and mother (v. 33) does not contradict the virgin birth because Joseph adopted Jesus into his family. After his positive oracle Simeon turns to a more ominous matter. Jesus will "cause the falling and rising of many in Israel" (v. 34). Either two different groups are being described here—one group will rise and one group will fall—or more probably Luke is referring to one group. Those who embrace the message of Jesus will fall before they rise. In other words, identification with Jesus will bring persecution. Such hostility to Jesus will reveal the thoughts of the heart (v. 35), that is, it will reveal that some are opposed to Jesus. Simeon, then, adds that Mary herself will experience anguish from the rejection which Jesus will encounter. Like Simeon, Anna proclaims redemption for Jerusalem (vv. 36–38; here "Jerusalem" refers to Israel as a whole), linking that redemption with Jesus. One should not read the saying about her never leaving the temple too literally. Perhaps she resided in one of the many rooms adjacent to the temple.

In **2:41–52** Luke discusses the account of the young boy Jesus at the temple. According to the Old Testament all Jewish males were required to go to Jerusalem for the great festival of Passover (Exod. 23:14–17; Deut. 16:16). By New Testament times women also attended. Jesus would have been expected to fulfill this requirement after he reached the age of thirteen. It is not entirely surprising that Jesus' parents did not know that he was still in Jerusalem. It was common for pilgrims to travel in large caravans (v. 44), and they could have easily concluded that Jesus was with relatives or friends. The account of Jesus' discussion with the religious leaders (vv. 46–47) does not imply that he was teaching them; rather, it implies that his knowledge of the Torah was penetrating and thorough. Joseph and Mary found Jesus after three days (v. 46): the first day they departed for home, the second day they returned to Jerusalem, and on the third day they found him. Jesus' answer (v. 49) to his parents' question strikes the modern reader as odd, but Luke is not interested in the psychological dynamics of the story. The point of Jesus' answer is that obedience to his Father takes precedence over obedience to his parents. Thus, the center of the story is christological—Jesus is no ordinary son. Jesus' parents are perplexed (v. 50), and Luke wants the reader to be perplexed as well, for no one can completely fathom who Jesus is. The story ends (vv. 51–52) with Jesus returning home; he submits himself to his parents and grows in grace and wisdom.

C. The Baptist's ministry: Preparation for the Lord (3:1–20). The historical introduction in 3:1 signifies the real beginning of the gospel story (cf. Acts 10:37). Luke is the only Gospel writer who clearly sets the events into the context of world history. Tiberius's reign extended from A.D. 14 to 37. The reference to Tiberius's fifteenth year (v. 1) is not definitive because there were different ways of calculating chronology in the ancient world. Most scholars agree that the date is A.D. 28/29. Pontius Pilate ruled as the governor of Judea (the correct technical term is prefect) from A.D. 26 to 36. Herod the tetrarch of Galilee is not Herod the Great but Herod Antipas who reigned over Galilee and Perea from 4 B.C. to A.D. 39. Antipas was the son of Herod the Great and is the Herod referred to in the rest of the Gospel. Philip is also a son of Herod the Great and reigned from 4 B.C. to A.D. 34. Very little is known about Lysanias. Only one person could be high priest at a time in Israel (v. 2). Annas functioned as high priest from A.D. 6 to 15, and Caiaphas was high priest from A.D. 18 to 36. Luke does not distinguish between Annas and Caiaphas because the latter was the son-in-law of Annas and because Annas continued to exercise great power during the high priesthood of Caiaphas. The event which Luke is placing into its historical context is the beginning of John the Baptist's ministry. John's ministry was conducted in the desert (v. 2) near the Jordan River. He preached "a baptism for repentance for the forgiveness of sins" (v. 3). This was not merely ritual washing, but involved a definite break with sin. Luke sees John's ministry as a fulfillment of Isaiah 40:3–5. John was the transitional prophet between the old and new era (cf. Luke 16:16), and he was preparing all people for God's salvation.

Verses 7–18 can be divided into three subsections: John preaches on (1) eschatology (vv. 7–9), (2) ethics (vv. 10–14), and (3) the Messiah (vv. 15–17). In verses 7–9 John warns that baptism without a change of life-style is worthless. Neither can the Jews rely on their heritage, for being a child of Abraham does not matter if one does not partake of the character of Abraham. John's ominous reference to "the coming wrath" confirms these warnings, for the ax of judgment is all ready to fall. What is the "good fruit" (v. 9) one should produce before judgment falls? In verses 10–14 Luke gives us a sample of John's ethical teaching. John does not call people to imitate his ascetic life-style, nor does he upset the existing social order, for he does not ask tax collectors or soldiers to leave their present jobs. Instead, he counsels those who are in these professions to be honest and content with their wages. The soldiers that are described here are probably not Romans but the soldiers of Herod. The common people are counseled to share their food and clothing with others (v. 10). John's preaching on imminent judgment and his powerful ethical message stimulate the people to consider whether or not he is the Messiah (v. 15). John clearly shows that he is not the Messiah for the following reasons: (1) one is coming who is "more powerful" (v. 16) than John; (2) John is not even worthy to untie the thongs of his sandals, a task that was usually performed by non-Jewish slaves in Palestine; (3) John's baptism is only in water, but the coming one "will baptize . . . with the Holy Spirit and with fire." Luke is thinking of the coming of the Spirit at Pentecost (Acts 2:1–4), and the reference to fire may refer either to the refining of the righteous, or to judgment on the recalcitrant (v. 17). Since Luke wants to focus on Jesus, he completes the story of the Baptist's ministry here and briefly relates the story of his imprisonment. Luke will return to the Baptist again for other reasons (cf. 7:18–35; 16:16).

D. Jesus: Endowed by the Spirit for ministry (3:21–4:13). Luke is not as interested in the actual baptism of Jesus (**3:21–22**) as he is in the events which accompany it. The descent of the Spirit indicates that Jesus is being anointed for his ministry (cf. Acts 10:37–38). The descent of the dove in bodily form, the opening of heaven, and the voice from God point to the solemnity of the occasion and the reality of the Spirit's descent. It is characteristic of Luke to mention that Jesus was praying. The words of the heavenly voice contain allusions to Psalm 2:7; Isaiah 42:1; and Genesis 22:2, indicating that Jesus is God's Son and Servant. This passage is not teaching that Jesus was adopted as God's Son, for Luke 1:35 shows that Luke considered Jesus to be God's Son from the beginning.

The inclusion of the genealogy of Jesus (**3:23–38**) here is explained by Luke's desire to give Jesus' ancestry before the onset of his ministry. In addition, there seems to be a link between 3:22 and 3:38, for Luke's genealogy is distinctive in that it ends not with a human being but with God. Obviously, the genealogy is not attempting to prove that Jesus was the Son of God in a physical sense, but Luke is making a literary and theological point in placing God at the very end of the genealogy. Indeed, the very first verse of the genealogy urges the reader to ask about the identity of Jesus' father since Joseph is not really his father (v. 23). The genealogy does not contradict the virgin birth as verse 23 makes clear. Some scholars have expressed concern because of the differences between the genealogies of Matthew and Luke (cf. Matt. 1:1–17). For example, Matthew gives the names in forward order—from Abraham to Jesus—while Luke gives the names in reverse order—from Jesus to God. A number of problems could be listed, but the most serious are: (1) Joseph's father is Heli in Luke (v. 23) and Jacob in Matthew (Matt. 1:16); (2) in Luke Jesus' descent from David is traced through Nathan (Nathan the son of David not Nathan the prophet; cf. 2 Sam. 5:14), but in Matthew Jesus' descent from David is traced through Solomon (Matt. 1:6); (3) Luke's list is considerably longer between David and Jesus. One common solution has been that Luke is giving the genealogy from Mary, but this cannot be supported from the text of Luke. A more credible solution is that Matthew is giving the royal line of David (i.e., the legal heirs to the throne), and Luke is giving the actual family line of Joseph.

The last event before Jesus' public ministry begins is his temptation in the wilderness (**4:1–13**). Two themes tie this section together. (1) Jesus by the power of the Spirit overcomes the devil by citing the Word of God. (2) The devil is challenging Jesus' filial obedience as God's Son (vv. 3, 9). Jesus shows before his ministry begins that his trust and obedience are in his Father. Matthew and Luke have a different order in recording the temptations; the second and third temptations are reversed in Matthew. Most scholars agree that Matthew retains the original order, and Luke uses a different order for theological reasons.

Luke emphasizes that Jesus was full of the Spirit and led by the Spirit (v. 1), implying that Jesus conquers the devil by the power of the Spirit. The devil attempts to seduce Jesus from obedience to his Father with three different temptations. In the first temptation (vv. 3–4) the devil tries to convince Jesus to use his status as God's Son to satisfy his own physical desires, instead of trusting in the Father to provide his needs. Jesus' answer (from Deut. 8:3) implies that the satisfaction of physical desires cannot take precedence over faithful obedience. In the second temptation (vv. 5–7) the devil promises Jesus authority over all the kingdoms of the world if Jesus will consent to worship him. Jesus' answer (from Deut. 6:13) is that worship and service belong to God alone, and thus it is unthinkable for him to worship the devil in order to gain earthly power and glory. Lastly (vv. 9–11), the devil brings Jesus to the pinnacle of the temple and, while arguing from Scripture (Ps. 91:11–12) that the angels would protect Jesus, suggests that he should leap. Jesus does not reject the devil's scriptural argument (God does protect the godly), but he does refuse to perform such a whimsical act because that would involve testing God (see Deut. 6:16). Jesus is certainly referring to his Father rather than himself when he says, "Do not put the Lord your God to the test" (Luke 4:12).

III. Jesus Proclaims Salvation in Galilee by the Power of the Spirit (4:14–9:50)

A. Proclamation of good news in Galilee (4:14–5:16). Jesus' public ministry in Luke begins at **4:14–15.** Luke emphasizes that Jesus was controlled by the Spirit, for he returned from his temptation "in the power of the Spirit" (v. 14). The scene is being set for Jesus' homecoming in the following pericope. Evidently his teaching in the synagogues was wildly admired, and thus his popularity was spreading.

In **4:16–30** Luke has probably changed the chronology of Jesus' rejection at Nazareth and moved it up to the beginning of his Gospel because of its programmatic character (cf. Mark 6:1–6; Matt. 13:53–58). Jesus returns to his hometown of Nazareth and participates in a synagogue service. This is the oldest extant account of a synagogue service. Usually such a service included hymns, prayers, a reading from the Torah, a reading from the Prophets, and a sermon. The readings from the Torah may have been prescribed by a lectionary, but the prophetic readings were not set at this time, and so Jesus himself probably chose the passage from Isaiah. The quotation in verses 18–19 from Isaiah 61:1–2 also includes a phrase from Isaiah 58:6. Jesus draws attention to several things by using this passage from Isaiah: (1) The prophecy of Isaiah has now ("today") been fulfilled (v. 21); (2) the fulfillment is Jesus himself; he is the one whom the Spirit has anointed. The reference to Isaiah 61 and the use of the word *anointed* suggest that Jesus is referring to himself as the Messiah and Servant of Yahweh; (3) Jesus' ministry is directed to those in need—the poor, the prisoners, the blind, and the oppressed (vv. 18–19). In Luke these terms refer primarily to spiritual need, although a literal meaning is not excluded. Significantly Jesus does not continue reading Isaiah, for it also speaks of the day of God's vengeance. The point is that Jesus' ministry was one of good news and grace (vv. 18–19). Initially Jesus' gracious words impress the crowd, but they take offense when they reflect on Jesus' heritage; he was merely Joseph's son (v. 22). Jesus responds with the principle that "no prophet is accepted in his home town" (v. 24). He then gives two examples from the Old Testament to illustrate his point (1 Kings 17:8–16; 2 Kings 5:1–14). Both Elijah and Elisha, who were also prophets, did not aid people from Israel but "Gentiles." Jesus implies, of course, that the Gentiles were more open to their prophetic ministry than the Jews. This incenses the people and they try to kill Jesus, but Jesus "walked right through the crowd" (v. 30). In this account Jesus reveals his messianic mission of grace and mercy. Nevertheless, the Jews reject him, and Jesus implies that the Good News will then be proclaimed to the Gentiles (cf. Acts 13:44–48; 28:23–28).

Four different events are combined together here to underline the authority of Jesus (**4:31–41**). (1) Jesus' teaching in Capernaum astonishes the populace because of its authority (vv. 31–32). (2) Jesus also manifests his authority over demons by expelling the demon from a man in the synagogue (vv. 33–37). Many people today discount the reality of the demonic and claim that what we have here is some form of mental illness; however, Jesus never discounted the reality of the demonic world, and oftentimes the rejection of the demonic is due to a rationalistic worldview that rejects any belief in the supernatural realm. One should not rule out that, in some instances, a relationship exists between demonic possession and mental illness. (3) Jesus also reveals his authority over illness by healing Peter's mother-in-law of a fever (vv. 38–39). (4) In the last scene (vv. 42–44) numerous people come to Jesus, and he heals them of illness and demon possession. The distinction that is drawn between those who were ill and those who were demonized indicates that Luke did not think that all who were sick were controlled by demons. They came to Jesus at sunset because that is when the Sabbath ended, and people could then carry the sick. These stories also function christologically. The demons recognize Jesus as "the Holy One of God" (v. 34), "the Son of God," and "the Christ" (v. 41). Jesus does not silence the demons because their words are false, neither does he silence them because he does not want demons to proclaim to others who he is. If that was his purpose it clearly did not work! Rather, the demons were trying to exercise control over Jesus by revealing his status; Jesus silences them and thereby reveals his superiority over them.

In **4:42–44** we see that Jesus' popularity continues to grow (cf. v. 37); however, Jesus does not take his directions from the populace but from his Father. He has been sent to "preach the good news of the kingdom of God" (v. 43) throughout Palestine. The kingdom of God is central in Jesus' teaching, and it is probably best defined as the dynamic rule of God. In this chapter God's rule is effective in the teaching of Jesus and his miraculous works. The reference to Judea (v. 44) seems strange (some MSS try to resolve the problem by substituting Galilee), but the word here refers to all of Palestine and includes Galilee.

The story of the disciples' call (the focus is on Peter) is placed later in Luke (**5:1–11**) than in Mark (cf. Mark 1:16–20). In contrast to Mark's account, Luke helps explain why the disciples followed Jesus, for they had already seen his miracles (Luke 4:38–39) and had heard his word. "Gennesaret" (v. 1) is an alternative name for Galilee. Peter's query about letting down the nets (vv. 4–5) is understandable because the best fishing in deep water was done at night, and during the day they fished in shallow water. Nevertheless, Peter respects Jesus enough (cf. "Master" in v. 5) to do what he says. The tremendous quantity of the fish staggers Peter, and he is profoundly struck by his unworthiness (v. 8). Luke adds that the incident had the same impact on Peter's partners, including James and John (vv. 9–10). Drawing an analogy from Simon's occupation, Jesus says that "from now on you will catch men" (v. 10). The word for *catch* (Gk. *zōgreō*) includes the idea of catching them alive. The story closes with the disciples leaving everything and following Jesus (v. 11).

The story of the cleansing of the leper (**5:12–16**) precedes the controversy stories (5:17–6:11) because Luke is showing that Jesus was obedient to the Mosaic law. In accordance with the law he commands the man healed of leprosy to report to the priest (Lev. 14:1–32). The word *leprosy* in the Bible refers to various kinds of inflammatory skin diseases, and not necessarily to Hansen's disease. Jesus shows his compassion by touching one who was considered unclean. The account also reflects Jesus' rising popularity, although he frequently spends time in communion with his Father (vv. 15–16).

B. Conflict with the Pharisees (5:17–6:11). The next five stories belong together since in each of them the Pharisees question (hence "conflict stories"), and he responds by defending the legitimacy of his behavior. The climax comes in 6:11 where Jesus' opponents move against him.

The drama of the episode is apparent from Luke's introduction. Pharisees from every area of Palestine were present to investigate Jesus' teaching (v. 17). The Pharisees were a popular religious party that emphasized obedience to both the written law and the unwritten law. The teachers of the law (or scribes) could come from any branch of the Jewish religion, but in this context they are probably Pharisees as well. Letting the paralytic down through a tiled roof (v. 19) does not contradict Mark 2:4, for tiled roofs existed in Palestine at this date and Mark does not say what the roof was made of. Responding to the faith of the paralytic's helpers, Jesus penetrated to his deepest problem (the text does not say the illness was due to sin, although such a view is possible) and pronounced a verdict of forgiveness (v. 20). The Pharisees conclude that such a statement is blasphemous because only God has the prerogative to forgive sin (v. 21). A prophet could also forgive sin in God's name (2 Sam. 12:13), but Jesus' answer in verse 24 implies that on his own authority he was pronouncing forgiveness. Perceptively reading his opponents' thoughts, Jesus responds by arguing that the visible act of healing will function as proof that he can forgive sins. The performance of the miracle stuns the onlookers and spontaneous praise is given to God (vv. 25–26). In addition to forgiving sins, Jesus also claims to be the "Son of Man" (v. 24). The Son of man in Jewish thought is a heavenly figure who will pronounce judgment on the last day (Dan. 7:13–22; Luke 9:26; 12:8).

Jesus' second controversy with the Pharisees stems from his call of Levi (**5:27–32**). Levi is a model of discipleship because he "left everything and followed him [Jesus]" (v. 27). But Levi was also a tax collector, and they were despised in Jewish society because they used the tax system to line their own pockets. Moreover, the occupation made one ritually unclean. Thus, the Pharisees and the scribes, who emphasized segregation from anything that would make one unclean, were surprised when Jesus went to a banquet attended by tax collectors and sinners (v. 30). Some have asked how Levi could throw a great banquet if he had left everything (vv. 28–29). One should not take the phrase *left everything* too literally; it is simply a way of saying that Levi left his old occupation and transferred his allegiance to Jesus. In this context "sinners" would refer to others who were ritually unclean. By eating with these people, Jesus himself would contract uncleanness. He defends his association with sinners by enunciating the principle that the doctor comes to aid the sick, not the healthy (v. 31). In verse 32 Jesus explains the meaning of his illustration; his ministry was not for the righteous but for sinners. Here the "healthy" and "righteous" refer to the Pharisees. The story does not teach that the Pharisees were actually righteous, only that they presumed they were righteous. Jesus came to call those who were aware of their spiritual need.

Fasting was practiced on the Day of Atonement by the Jews. The Pharisees fasted twice a week on Mondays and Thursdays, and apparently the disciples of the Baptist also fasted. Since fasting is a sign of one's religious devotion, Jesus is questioned because his disciples eat and drink (v. 33). Jesus replies that fasting is as incomprehensible for his disciples as it would be for wedding guests to fast when the bridegroom is with them (v. 34). Jesus clearly identifies himself as the bridegroom, insisting that his presence is a call for festivity. Fasting will commence when the bridegroom is absent, an allusion to Jesus' separation from his disciples at his death (v. 35). Jesus does not reject fasting altogether (cf. Matt. 6:16–18; Luke 4:2; 22:16, 18); however, the early church did not regularly practice fasting, but reserved it for special occasions (see Acts 13:1–4; 14:23; cf. 9:9). Jesus then tells two parables that illustrate the incompatibility between Judaism and the new community. One cannot combine the new garment of the gospel with the old garment of Judaism. Any attempt to patch up the old garment will result in the tearing of the new one, and the new will not match with the old anyway (v. 36). Jesus puts the same point another way. The new wine of the gospel cannot be poured into the old wineskins of Judaism. Such an attempt would ruin both the new wine and the old wineskins. New wine continues to ferment and expand, bursting old wineskins which are weakened by use (v. 37). Jesus' point is that his gospel cannot be combined with the legalism of Judaism; it is new, fresh, and spontaneous (v. 38). However, Jesus recognizes (v. 39) that most people find it difficult to embrace something that is new; they prefer their old comfortable ways.

In the first (**6:1–5**) of the Sabbath controversies the Pharisees accuse Jesus of doing that which is not lawful "on the Sabbath" (v. 2). The law permitted the plucking of grain while walking through a field (Deut. 23:25), but the Pharisees prohibited such on the Sabbath because harvesting constituted work. Jesus responds to this criticism by recalling how David and his companions ate the "bread of the Presence" (1 Sam. 21:6), even though only priests were permitted to eat this bread (Lev. 24:5–9). Jesus' point is that the technical requirements of the law were legitimately broken by David when human need was present. The Pharisees may have been thinking, "But you are not David." Accordingly Jesus argues that he is greater than David, for as "the Son of Man" he is "Lord of the Sabbath." So Jesus authorizes the behavior of his disciples in this situation, and thus the first Sabbath controversy ends with Jesus making a bold statement about his person and authority.

The atmosphere in the second incident (**6:6–11**) is tense, for the Pharisees were looking for evidence so that they could charge Jesus with disobedience to the law. Jesus confronts the issue openly and calls the man with the shriveled hand to come forward, asking all who were present about the real purpose for the Sabbath. Jesus' rhetorical question (v. 9) and action of healing (v. 10) show that doing good on the Sabbath is a positive duty. In other words, the failure to perform good deeds on the Sabbath is evil. Mark tells us that the religious leaders responded by plotting to kill Jesus (Mark 3:6), whereas Luke tells us of their fury and their uncertainty about what to do with him (v. 11). In any case, the series of conflicts between Jesus and the Pharisees (Luke 5:17–6:11) ends with the latter being the implacable foes of Jesus.

C. Good news for the poor (6:12–8:3). This section contrasts directly to the previous one. The religious leaders are rejecting Jesus, and he responds by choosing a faithful remnant (**6:12–16**) who will be responsible for communicating his message to others. The significance of the selection is indicated by verse 12; Jesus spent an entire night in prayer before choosing the Twelve. Some scholars have contested that Jesus would have called the Twelve (whom he chose out from his many disciples) "apostles" (v. 13), but some Palestinian evidence indicates that the Jews used a related term to designate emissaries sent to represent them. Simon Peter (v. 14) heads up every list of the apostles in the New Testament. Bartholomew is sometimes equated with Nathanael (John 1:44–51). Matthew and Levi (Luke 5:27) are the same person (v. 15). In New Testament times a person commonly had more than one name. The Zealots (v. 15) were members of a nationalistic religious party in Israel that led the revolt against Rome. Judas son of James (v. 16) should be identified with Thaddaeus in Mark's list (Mark 3:18; cf. John 14:22). The meaning of *Iscariot* is disputed. Probably it means "a man from Kerioth," a city which was in southern Judea (Josh. 15:25). It may also mean "assassin" or "liar." In any case, Judas's name evokes the memory of his betrayal.

The description of the geographical setting (**6:17–19**) of the Sermon on the Plain (v. 17) does not necessarily contradict Matthew (Matt. 5:1), for Jesus could have delivered the sermon on a level place in the mountains. Luke prepares the reader for the sermon by noting that a vast array of people had gathered specifically to listen to Jesus (v. 18). Jesus also healed many of those who were gathered to hear him.

The Sermon on the Plain (**6:17–49**) is considerably shorter than Matthew's Sermon on the Mount (cf. Matt. 5–7). The relationship between the two accounts is complex; one can probably explain some of the differences by the editorial work of the Evangelists. Jesus opens the sermon by drawing radical contrasts between two kinds of people. Those who are poor, hungry, weeping, and hated are blessed. Although this happiness is a present experience ("yours is the kingdom," v. 20), it is primarily a future blessing: "you will be satisfied . . . you will laugh" (v. 21), "your reward [is] in heaven" (v. 23). Jesus does not say that God automatically blesses if one is poor, hungry, and sad. It should be noted that Jesus is speaking to disciples (v. 20) who fall into these categories. Verse 22 makes it plain that being hated by men does not in and of itself bring a reward; the person who is rewarded is the one who is hated because of his allegiance to "the Son of Man." Clearly, then, these verses should be understood spiritually; Jesus is speaking to his disciples whose longings and desires will not be fulfilled in this world. This does not mean that the literal meaning of the words should be excluded, but one should not simplistically conclude that all the poor and the hungry of the world are blessed. Jesus is not teaching the virtues of poverty as such; he is saying that the poor, hungry, sad, and persecuted are blessed if they have given their allegiance to the Son of man. The "woes" in verses 24–26 are directed toward the rich, the well fed, the happy, and the popular. Jesus' point is that these people derive all of their satisfaction from this world. They feel no need of God, nor do they look forward to his future kingdom. This world is their heaven. Jesus pronounces a woe on such self-satisfied, prosperous, and smug people because a day is coming when fortunes will be reversed.

In the first part of the next section (**6:27–36**) Jesus describes the nature or position of people who are his disciples (vv. 20–26). In the rest of the sermon he focuses on the way disciples should live. Jesus begins with the radical message that disciples should love their enemies. The enemies who are in view are clearly those who persecute disciples (vv. 28–29). The word *love* is a slippery one, and it is usually understood in modern culture as a warm feeling; Jesus, however, understands love for enemies primarily in terms of actions: do good to them (vv. 27, 32–33, 35), bless and pray for them (v. 28), and lend to them (vv. 34–35). Jesus gives two examples of the nature of this love; it is nonretaliatory (v. 29) and generous (v. 30). The cloak would be one's outer garment and the tunic the garment that is worn next to the skin. In verses 29–30 Jesus does not suggest the capricious and arbitrary sharing of possessions with lazy people; rather, he emphasizes the spirit by which disciples should live—a revengeful, demanding, and grasping spirit is forbidden (cf. v. 31). Lastly, disciples should show a higher quality of love than sinners (v. 32). The love of nonbelievers for one another is based on mutuality and repayment, but the love which marks the "sons of the Most High" (v. 35) gives without expecting anything in return. Such unselfish love will be rewarded at the end, and disciples will be imitating their Father who is merciful and kind to all (vv. 35–36).

In the next section (**6:37–45**) Jesus addresses the theme of judging others. In verses 37–38 he forbids censorious and condemning judgment. Those who treat others with mercy will be treated mercifully by God (the text is not saying that God will not judge believers at all, but that he will judge with mercy if one shows mercy). The picture of forgiveness in verse 38 is of a measuring jar in which the corn is pressed down so that it will hold more, shaken together so that every crack is filled, and poured over the top so that it overflows. Just as God has generously given to his own, so the disciple should give an overflowing amount to others. In verses 39–45 Jesus gives three exhortations. (1) The proverb on the blind man (v. 39) is explained in the next verse (v. 40). A student cannot surpass his teacher but will end up being just like him. This probably means that the disciples need to be careful how they teach others, for false teaching has potentially disastrous consequences. (2) The point of the humorous illustration of the speck and the log (vv. 41–42) is that the former person thinks he is superior to the latter and fails to see his own inadequacy and blindness. As in verses 37–38 Jesus attacks those who smugly and censoriously condemn others. Not judging others does not mean that one does not evaluate and use discrimination; Jesus is speaking against a superior and self-righteous attitude, not against careful evaluation. One who is humbly aware of his own sin can help in removing the speck from another person's eye (v. 42; cf. Gal. 6:1). (3) Verses 43–45 are a call to self-examination. Good conduct issues from a good heart, and evil conduct springs from an evil one. The behavior of a person is not an accident; it is a revelation of the innermost motives of the heart (v. 45).

The sermon's call to obedience follows in **6:46–49.** Hearing Jesus' words without obeying them is like building a house with no foundation. On the day of judgment that person will experience destruction. The person who hears and obeys the words of Jesus is compared to one who builds his house on a secure foundation; the day of judgment holds no fear for the wise builder.

The events in this section of the Gospel (**7:1–8:3**) show that even though the religious leaders were rejecting Jesus' ministry, the members of society who were poor and looked down upon, namely, Gentiles and women, were receptive.

In Matthew 8:5–13 Jesus talks personally to the centurion, whereas in Luke **7:1–10** he speaks only to intermediaries. Matthew has probably abbreviated the account. In John the story of the healing of an official's son (John 4:46–53) is a different incident. The central point of this story is not the healing of the servant, but the faith of the centurion (v. 9). The centurion was probably a member of Herod Antipas's army since the Romans were not in Galilee before A.D. 44. From Jesus' statement in verse 9 it is also evident that the centurion was a Gentile; he thus becomes a symbol of Gentile belief in Jesus, a remarkable contrast to Israel's unbelief. The humility of the centurion is also apparent. The Jewish elders (community leaders in Capernaum) believe that he "deserves" (v. 4) Jesus' help. But the centurion considers himself undeserving and unworthy (vv. 6–7). The centurion undoubtedly knew that a Jew would become "unclean" if he entered a Gentile's house.

Jesus' compassion on a widow (**7:11–17**) further illustrates his concern for the poor. By losing her only son (v. 12) she would be deprived of her last means of support. The town of Nain was approximately six miles south of Nazareth. Not only is Jesus able to heal someone who is near death (v. 1), but he is able to resuscitate the dead by pronouncing the word, which provides the basis for his reply to John the Baptist (v. 22). The resuscitation of the son of a widow undoubtedly reminded the people of Elijah (1 Kings 17:17–24; cf. also 2 Kings 4:18–37), which explains why the people immediately conclude that Jesus is "a great prophet" (Luke 7:16). Perhaps Luke expected his readers to think of the prophet of Deuteronomy 18:15–20 as well.

The next section (**7:18–35**) can be subdivided into three smaller pericopes: (1) the Baptist's doubts about Jesus (7:18–23); (2) the role of John the Baptist (7:24–30); and (3) the fickleness of the religious leaders (7:31–35). While in prison (cf. Matt. 11:2–19) it was not surprising that John began to have doubts about whether Jesus was the "coming one" (this phrase seems to be John's way of referring to the Messiah; cf. Luke 3:16). Moreover, the judging aspect of Jesus' ministry was strangely lacking (cf. Luke 3:17). Jesus replies to the query of John's disciples by pointing to the wonders and signs which he has performed (vv. 21–22). These miracles were particularly significant because in the Old Testament they point to the arrival of the era of salvation, the coming age when God would fulfill his promises (cf. Isa. 29:18–19; 35:5–6; 61:1). Jesus is indicating to John, then, that he is fulfilling the Old Testament Scriptures, albeit in a surprising way, which is why he ends this incident by pronouncing a blessing on one who does not stumble over the nature of his messianic ministry (v. 23). The text does not tell us how John responded (although Jesus' commendation implies that he responded positively); instead, Jesus launches into a discussion on John's role in salvation history. He was not fickle nor did he dress luxuriously (vv. 24–25); his role was prophetic. But, Jesus adds, he was "more than a prophet" (v. 26), for he had the task of preparing the way for the Messiah (cf. Mal. 3:1). John's distinctive role made him the greatest of all the Old Testament saints (greatness is being described here in terms of function not of essence). Nevertheless, because John did not actually participate in the era of salvation, anyone who is a member of the kingdom "is greater than he" (v. 28; greater again in function, not in essence). Luke adds in a parenthetical remark that "all the people" glorified God because Jesus' words were a vindication of John's ministry (v. 29). On the other hand, by rejecting John's baptism the Pharisees failed to see that John and Jesus were the agents of God's saving purposes. The Pharisees' rejection of God's purpose (v. 30) leads nicely into the topic of the fickleness of the present generation. Jesus compares the religious leaders to sulking children, for they think something demonic distinguishes the asceticism of John the Baptist, and something wild and unruly underscores Jesus' eating and drinking, not to mention his association with the lower class. Jesus' exaggerated description of John and himself makes the point that nothing will satisfy these people, and yet God's wisdom (v. 35), that is, his plan, is demonstrated to be right "by all her children" (viz., by those who have responded positively to the message of John and Jesus [cf. vv. 29–30]).

The story of the forgiveness of a sinful woman (**7:36–50**) has sometimes been identified with the account in Mark 14:3–9 (pars.), but it is clearly a different story. The link with the preceding context is the accusation that is leveled against Jesus in Luke 7:34. Jesus may have been invited to Simon's home after a synagogue service. No doubt Simon respected Jesus since he gives him the honorable title *teacher* (v. 40; teacher = rabbi). Uninvited guests at a banquet in the Palestinian world were not an unusual feature, although the presence of a sinner (v. 39; she was probably a prostitute) may have sparked some surprise. Those enjoying the banquet reclined with their feet extended behind them, resting their head on the left hand and eating with the right. The woman enters behind Jesus and spontaneously begins to weep (v. 38), because of either repentance or joy. Perhaps the two were commingled. When she sees that Jesus' feet are getting wet she unlooses her hair (something a respectable woman would not do), drying his feet with her hair. She proceeds to kiss his feet and anoint them with expensive perfume (v. 38). Observing the activity, Simon concludes that Jesus cannot be a prophet (v. 39) because a prophet would know what kind of woman this was. Moreover, a prophet would prevent a sinner from touching him because touching a sinful person would make Jesus ritually unclean. (Thus the story has a twofold theme, revolving around the status of the woman and the status of Jesus.) Jesus responds to Simon's silent protest by telling him the parable of the two debtors (vv. 41–42). The point of the parable is plain—the one who is forgiven the larger amount will respond with more love and gratitude. A denarius was worth approximately a day's wages. Simon's reply (v. 43) simply reflects a careful rabbinic answer. Jesus, then, applies the parable to the treatment that he has received from Simon and the woman (vv. 44–47). Jesus does not criticize Simon for being inhospitable, for these courtesies were not necessarily an expected part of ordinary hospitality. Jesus' point is not that Simon was rude but that the woman showed "extraordinary" love. One would greet "friends" by kissing them on the head, but the woman kissed Jesus on the feet (v. 46). On a special occasion one might put inexpensive oil on a guest's head, but the woman poured expensive perfume on Jesus' feet (v. 46). Verse 47 has been incorrectly interpreted at times to mean that the woman was forgiven *because* of her love for Jesus. But the point of the entire story is that her love is the *result* of her forgiveness. That love and gratitude flow from forgiveness is clearly the point of the parable (vv. 41–42), and the woman's actions of love toward Jesus stem from her experience of a forgiveness that has already been received. In verse 48 Jesus simply confirms the forgiveness of the woman. Indeed, verse 50 clearly shows that it is *faith* that has *saved* the woman. The phrase "he who has been forgiven little loves little" (v. 47) should not be taken too woodenly. In the application of the parable it applies to Simon and has an ironic twist. The meaning is not that righteous people cannot love much because they do not need much forgiveness (an argument for sinning more so that forgiveness can be deeper; cf. Rom. 6:1ff.). Rather, people who assume they are righteous will never experience much love for Jesus since they are so unaware of their sinfulness.

Luke summarizes Jesus' preaching ministry about the kingdom of God in **8:1–3**, noting that he visited a number of towns. Contrary to Jewish custom Jesus had women followers, and they supported him financially (v. 3). These women are carefully distinguished from the twelve apostles. There is no evidence that Mary Magdalene was the woman in the prior story. The number *seven* indicates the severity of Mary's state. The Herod mentioned here is Antipas (v. 3).

D. Revelation and obedience (8:4–21). One of Jesus' distinctives was teaching in parables, and some of the most memorable of Jesus' parables occur in Luke. Jesus addressed the parable of the sower (Luke **8:4–15**; but cf. Mark 4:1–20; Matt. 13:1–23) to the crowd which was gathering (Luke 8:4–8), but he did not explain its significance to them. The sowing of seed on all kinds of soil would not be unusual in Palestine because plowing would follow sowing. In verse 8 he challenges his hearers to penetrate to the true meaning of the parable. The disciples are perplexed about the parable and inquire about its meaning (v. 9). Jesus responds in a difficult saying by explaining the rationale behind parables (v. 10). God reveals the secrets of the kingdom (the plans of God that were previously hidden but have now been made known) to the disciples, but the meaning of the parables is obscure to outsiders so that even though they hear the words they will not understand their true meaning (cf. Isa. 6:9). Jesus' hard words here cannot be applied to all the parables, for some of the parables were clearly understood even by Jesus' opponents (cf. Luke 10:25–37). Perhaps the obscurity of the parables is operative in those who have already responded negatively to Jesus' message. Jesus explains the meaning of the parable in verses 11–15. Some scholars have doubted whether Jesus would have allegorized the parables, but there is no a priori reason to exclude allegory. The modern reader should not press the allegory beyond the limits that are indicated by the biblical writer. The different kinds of soils represent various ways of responding to the proclaimed Word of God. Luke emphasizes that those who bring forth good fruit must persevere (v. 15). The problem with those who are compared to the rocky soil is that they cannot endure persecution (v. 13), and those who are compared to the thorny soil are squelched by the delights and worries of life (v. 14). Thus the parable seems to have a twofold lesson: (1) those who hear the proclaimed Word need to persevere in obedience; (2) those who proclaim the Word must realize that not everyone will respond positively. Why is this a "secret of the kingdom" (v. 10)? Perhaps because the Jews never conceived of the kingdom message having such limited success; they expected it to come in apocalyptic power and to rout their enemies.

In **8:16–18** we have three different sayings of Jesus that are combined together. The main point is revealed in verse 18: "consider carefully how you listen." In other words, this paragraph resembles the preceding one; Jesus stresses the need for faithful obedience to the preached Word. The significance of putting one's lamp on the stand (v. 16) is probably that the hearers must bear fruit in their listening, for a day will come when what they hear will not be secret any longer; it will shine for all to see. The last part of verse 18 supports our interpretation of verse 10 above. Receptive and obedient listening will lead to increased understanding, but rejection of the truth will lead to increased incomprehension of the Word of God.

The next paragraph (**8:19–21**) fits nicely with the emphasis on obedience to the Word of God that was stressed in the preceding parables. The arrival of Jesus' mother and brothers becomes an object lesson for the crowd; the true mother and brothers of Jesus are those who listen to and obey the Word of God. Luke does not imply any criticism of Jesus' family members here. The brothers of Jesus are most likely the natural children of Mary and Joseph. Joseph's absence is probably due to his death.

E. The revelation of Jesus' identity (8:22–9:50). Next Luke relates three miraculous works of Jesus, and the reader sees that Jesus has power over nature, demons, disease, and death (8:22–56). Hills and gorges surround the Sea of Galilee and sudden windstorms would sweep down onto the lake. Fearing imminent death by drowning, the disciples aroused Jesus and implored his aid. At Jesus' command the storm ceased and calm returned. Immediately Jesus communicates the lesson for the disciples: "Where is your faith?" (v. 25). Their confidence should have been in Jesus and his saving power. Then the disciples pose a question: Who is this one who has such astounding power over nature? Slowly the disciples begin to reflect on the identity of Jesus. The story ends this way because Luke wants the reader to contemplate the same question.

Jesus traveled to the other side of the lake which was largely Gentile territory. The precise location of the encounter with the Gerasene demoniac (**8:26–39**) is no longer certain, and the textual tradition reflects this uncertainty. Luke's description of the demonized man shows the severity of his condition (vv. 27–29). Jesus discovers that the man's malady is due to many demons (v. 30). The demons beg Jesus not to send them into "the Abyss"; the abyss would be the realm of the underworld where some demons were confined (Rev. 9:1–11). The sending of the demons into the pigs seems strange, and many have questioned the wisdom of such an activity. Some have rightly pointed out that pigs were unclean animals for the Jews, but this is not a satisfactory explanation for Jesus' activity since he was in Gentile territory. Perhaps the point of the story is that one man's deliverance is worth the destruction of many pigs. The neighboring townspeople arrive and are seized with fear, requesting Jesus to leave their region (v. 37). The theme of Jesus' rejection continues. But Jesus bids the the man who was delivered to proclaim his word in that region, showing that his healing was designed to lead to mission.

The next two stories are deliberately interwoven; Luke begins with the request of Jairus for his dying daughter, inserts the story of the bleeding woman, and then returns to the story of Jairus (**8:40–56**). The ruler of a synagogue (v. 41) arranged synagogue services. The accomplishment of Jairus's request is delayed by the throng that surrounded Jesus and is then interrupted by the woman who "touched the edge of his cloak" (probably his tassel; cf. Num. 15:38–39). This woman had been hemorrhaging for twelve years, and such bleeding would make her ritually unclean (Lev. 15:25–30). Luke tones down Mark's remark on how her many doctors had only made her condition worse (Mark 5:26), probably because of his profession. The woman's actions could be viewed as superstitious, but Jesus was aware that healing power had gone forth from him, and he explains that her deliverance was not due to superstition but saving faith (vv. 46–48). While Jesus was healing the woman, the daughter of Jairus had died. The friends of Jairus thought that any further activity was futile (v. 49) and they ridiculed Jesus' naivete (v. 53). But Jesus' words to Jairus were: "Don't be afraid; just believe, and she will be healed" (v. 50). Thus, we see that the resuscitation of Jairus's daughter fits with the prior story; in both instances Jesus responds to faith. Jesus manifests his power over disease and death. And his power over demons and nature as well

(8:22–39) causes the reader to reflect on Jesus' identity.

In the next episode (**9:1–9**) Jesus sends the disciples out to communicate the message of the kingdom of God (v. 1). The kingdom message includes both the proclamation of good news and apostolic power over disease and demons (vv. 1–2). Jesus forbids the Twelve from bringing extensive provisions for the journey; he wants them to rely upon God for sustenance. The disciples are to be content with the house that receives them (v. 4), but if the people reject the message the disciples are to shake the dust of the town off their feet, which symbolizes that the town was unclean and that they were severing fellowship with it. The preaching of Jesus and his followers came to the attention of Herod Antipas (v. 7). The key question Luke wants the reader to ask is, Who is this Jesus? By recording the current speculation on the identity of Jesus (Is he John the Baptist, Elijah, or one of the prophets?), and by placing the question on the lips of an important person like Herod, Luke brings the question of Jesus' identity to the center of attention.

The apostles returned from their mission, withdrawing with Jesus to the area around Bethsaida for some rest; however, the multitudes learned of Jesus' destination and followed him. The feeding of the five thousand (**9:10–17**) is probably an object lesson for the disciples. They did not have the resources to feed the multitudes, but by depending upon God they would have more than enough to satisfy the crowds. The story also continues to raise the question, Who is this? Peter answers that query in the next pericope (9:18–20). The account is suggestive, however, of Jesus' messiahship. He is the new Moses who gives manna from heaven (Exod. 16; Num. 11; cf. 2 Kings 4:42–44). The story may also evoke images of the messianic feast of the last days (Isa. 25:6–8). There is no compelling reason to doubt the historicity of the episode.

The preceding narratives have raised the question, Who is this? Now Peter gives the decisive answer: you are the Messiah (**9:18–20**). The disciples see more clearly than those who identify Jesus with Elijah, John the Baptist, or one of the prophets. Of the Synoptists only Luke tells us that Jesus was praying (v. 18).

Peter understood that Jesus was the Messiah, but the disciples also needed to grasp what kind of Messiah he would be (**9:21–27**). He did not fit the popular conception of a Messiah who would triumph over Israel's enemies by using military power. He would suffer and die before he was vindicated by the resurrection (v. 22). Jesus uses the title *Son of man*. According to Daniel 7:9–22 the Son of man was a heavenly figure who would participate in the judgment on the last day; however, Jesus pours new content into the title by claiming that the Son of man must also suffer. Thus, Jesus links together the Son of man and the Suffering Servant (Isa. 52:13–53:12). Jesus' destiny is closely associated with the responsibility of his disciples. His disciples must be prepared to suffer and to lose their life in this world for Jesus' sake. They will show that they are ashamed of Jesus and his words if they do not participate in his sufferings. If, however, the disciples share in Jesus' rejection they will end up saving their very selves. The last verse (v. 27) is difficult. It may mean that the disciples experience the kingdom in the events of the resurrection and Pentecost, or that the transfiguration itself is a manifestation of the kingdom.

The episode of the transfiguration (**9:28–36**) is closely connected with the preceding one ("about eight days after," v. 28; Mark 9:2 has "after six days"; the point is that it was about one week later). As Jesus prayed his face and clothes became gloriously radiant. Luke characteristically mentions that Jesus prayed before an important event. Moses and Elijah appeared and discussed with Jesus his departure (Gk. *exodos*) in Jerusalem. According to Jewish tradition Moses and Elijah were expected to return before the advent of the kingdom. The reference to Jesus' "exodus" shows that his passion is primarily in view (cf. 9:22), although the resurrection may also be implied. The story also focuses on who Jesus is. Peter suggests building three booths for the great men who are present. But Peter misses the significance of the event. The point is that Jesus is superior to Moses and Elijah. The story ends with Jesus alone, and Elijah and Moses are gone. In addition, the voice from the cloud (the cloud represents God's presence) says to listen to Jesus, stressing again that Jesus is God's final and definitive revelation. The scene is similar to Jesus' baptism (3:21–22), for Jesus is again called God's chosen Son. The purpose of the story is to confirm Jesus' sonship and glory. The disciples think that Jesus' passion rules out his glory, but actually the passion is the route to glory.

The juxtaposition of **9:37–43a** with the transfiguration is striking because after his glorious manifestation Jesus encounters the unbelief and frailty of human beings (v. 41). The father of a demonized boy is close to despair because no one can help his son. Luke's description emphasizes the severity of the boy's condition. The goal of the story, then, is to show that only Jesus can help him, and the crowd responds by remarking on God's greatness as manifested through Jesus.

People were marveling about Jesus' works (cf. the preceding exorcism), but Jesus says to the disciples that they should be focusing on his future suffering rather than his miracles (**9:43b–50**). Luke notes that the disciples could not comprehend what Jesus was saying (v. 45). Perhaps the next two stories provide the reason for their incomprehension. The disciples could not understand Jesus' suffering because they were consumed by rivalry and competition (vv. 46–48); however, Jesus says that true greatness comes when disciples forget about being great. Children were considered to be insignificant in ancient society. Nevertheless, a great person treats children with respect and consideration, showing by such actions that he is not using his "kindness" to advance himself, and also showing that he has received the Father. John also recalls how the disciples tried to prevent a man from expelling demons in Jesus' name since he did not become one of his disciples (vv. 49–50). Jesus replies that if a person is not against him, then he is on his side. This last saying seems to contradict 11:23, but the sayings are proverbial and not contradictory since they are in completely different contexts.

IV. Galilee to Jerusalem: Discipleship (9:51–19:27)

A clear break occurs in the text here, indicating a major division in the Gospel. Luke departs from using Mark as a source and does not recount a story from Mark until 18:15. Luke uses the motif of a travel narrative, but the reader should understand it primarily as a literary technique. As a travel narrative it gives very few details about where the events are taking place. Jesus is en route to Jerusalem so that he can fulfill the things which have been written about him. On the way he teaches his followers about discipleship.

A. The journey begins (9:51–13:21). The first account in this section reminds us that the passion of Jesus lay ahead. The resolution of Jesus to go to Jerusalem is related to his suffering and death, and the hostility of the Samaritans foreshadows what he will experience in Jerusalem. (The Samaritans and Jews were enemies with a long history of hatred.) The phrase *taken up to heaven* (v. 51) clearly refers to Jesus' ascension, but it probably also refers to all that will happen in Jerusalem, including Jesus' death, resurrection, and ascension. The refusal of the Samaritans to welcome Jesus provokes James and John to ask Jesus if he wants them to send fire on the Samaritans (like Elijah did in the Old Testament; 2 Kings 1:10, 12). Jesus rebukes his disciples, which shows them that nonretaliation is a better way and gives them a pattern to follow when they encounter opposition. The words of Jesus in verses 55–56 are not in the earliest manuscripts.

Jesus' encounter with three would-be followers indicates the stringency of discipleship (**9:57–62**). The first man is enthusiastic and pledges to follow Jesus anywhere (v. 57). But Jesus responds by underlining the cost to following him (v. 58). Even animals have a place to sleep, but Jesus experiences homelessness and rejection as the preceding episode with the Samaritans shows. Jesus invites the second man to follow him (v. 59). This man responds with a reasonable request. He wants to go home and bury his father first. In Judaism burial of dead relatives was a duty, and it was even considered more important than studying the law. Even priests were permitted to bury their relatives (Lev. 21:1–3); therefore, Jesus' answer is startling. He overturns social conventions, insisting that the kingdom of God has priority over family loyalties. When Jesus says let the dead bury their own dead, he means leave the task of burying the "physically dead" to those who are "spiritually dead." Lastly, a man promises to follow Jesus after saying farewell to his family (v. 61). Again, this is a reasonable request; Elijah let Elisha say farewell to his family before the latter followed the former (1 Kings 19:19–21). Nevertheless, Jesus' call is more radical. No one can plow effectively if one looks back, for the furrow will be crooked and the wooden plow tip might break. So too, no one can follow Jesus without making him the absolute and exclusive center of life.

Luke alone tells us that besides sending out the Twelve (Luke 9:1–6) Jesus also sent out the seventy(-two; **10:1–24**). (The textual evidence is divided so that it is impossible to say whether Jesus sent out seventy or seventy-two.) The disciples are like innocent lambs being sent out into a world full of hostility; yet workers are needed for the harvest (vv. 2–3). The instructions that are given to the seventy (-two) are very similar to the instructions that Jesus gave to the Twelve (cf. Luke 9:1–6). The urgency of the task is underlined. There is no time for the long greetings that are characteristic of oriental culture (v. 4). Financial support should come from the town in which the disciples reside, but they should be content with the food and shelter they receive from their hosts, instead of looking for a house that provides for them in a more luxurious way (vv. 4, 7–8). The greeting "peace to this house" (v. 5) is not just a way of saying hello; it refers to the peace of salvation that Jesus is bringing. The "man of peace" is one who is willing to receive the saving message (v. 6). The disciples are to proclaim the presence of the kingdom, and the sign of its presence is their healing ministry (v. 9). Those who reject the message of the kingdom are to be warned of their solemn fate (vv. 10–12).

The warning of judgment reminds Jesus of the rejection he experienced in Galilee. Even though they saw his miracles they refused to submit themselves to the kingdom message; therefore, they will certainly be judged. Jesus is not saying that Tyre and Sidon will not be judged; only that the judgment of the Galilean cities will be more severe because they had more evidence. Verse 16 shows that those who reject the message of the seventy(-two) are just as culpable as those who rejected Jesus, for those who reject Jesus' messengers reject Jesus and the Father.

The disciples return (**10:17–20**) with joy because they did not anticipate being able to expel demons (cf. 9:10). When Jesus says that he saw Satan fall from heaven (v. 18), he is not speaking of Satan's prehistoric fall, nor is he referring to a vision he had during the disciples' ministry, nor is he predicting Satan's future fall. He is merely describing in symbolic terms the impact of the disciples' ministry. The kingdom of God was making inroads on Satan's domain. The disciples were sharing in Jesus' authority over all forms of evil and destruction. "Snakes and scorpions" (v. 19) do not refer to demonic powers, but symbolize all kinds of evil (cf. Deut. 8:15); however, Jesus cautions that the disciples are not to become enamored with the sensational. The crucial thing is not the expulsion of demons and power over evil, but the assurance of having one's name written in God's book.

The joy of the disciples after returning from their mission stimulates Jesus to express his praise to the Father (**10:21–24**). The Father has not revealed the gospel of the kingdom ("these things," v. 21) to the wise and learned, probably because they were impressed with their own wisdom. But to the humble and childlike he has opened up the secrets of the kingdom. Jesus emphasizes that this was in accord with God's sovereign plan and gracious will (v. 21). In verse 22 we have one of the most important verses in the synoptic Gospels on the mutual relationship between the Father and the Son. Some scholars have questioned the authenticity of the verse, but the Jewish character of the saying shows its authenticity. When Jesus states that the Father has handed "all things" over to him, he means that the Father has given the Son authority to reveal the knowledge of the Father and Son to others. Then Jesus indicates that the Father and Son possess a mutual and exclusive knowledge of one another. The centrality and uniqueness of the Son is affirmed because no one can know the Father apart from the Son's permission. Jesus' words show that the knowledge of God is a gift bestowed from above, and thus it follows that the disciples are privileged to see the revelation of the Father in the Son. Many Old Testament persons wanted to see this capstone of God's self-revelation, but it was not part of God's gracious purpose (v. 24).

In the parable of the good Samaritan (**10:25–37**) the lawyer wants to involve Jesus in a theological argument over what was necessary for eternal life (v. 25). Instead of answering the question, Jesus directly asks the lawyer for his point of view. The lawyer responds by citing Deuteronomy 6:5 and Leviticus 19:18; eternal life is inherited when one loves God with the totality of one's being and one's neighbor as oneself. Jesus agrees with this response (cf. Mark 12:28–33), but forces the discussion into the practical realm by saying, "Do this and you will live" (v. 28). Some have thought that Jesus was speaking only hypothetically here because this answer would contradict salvation by faith. This is incorrect, for true faith always manifests itself in works (cf. James 2:14–26). The lawyer's attempt at self-justification (v. 29) probably stems from his realization that he is not fulfilling the twofold commandment, and his question leads into Jesus' parable. The road from Jerusalem to Jericho was seventeen miles long and a traveler would descend 3300 feet. Jericho lies 770 feet below sea level. Lonely roads were a prime place for robbers to strike (v. 30). Both a priest and a Levite passed by when they saw the wounded man (vv. 31–32). The priest would probably be returning from his time of service in the Jerusalem temple. Levites aided priests in the temple by carrying out minor duties related to the temple and its cult. The priest and Levite may have avoided the man because they thought he was dead, and they did not want to become ritually unclean. More probably, they were fearful of the robbers attacking them also. Jesus surprises his listeners by saying that a Samaritan helped the wounded man, for Samaritans were implacable enemies of the Jews (cf. Luke 9:51–56; John 4:9). It is interesting that Jesus does not say in the parable that Jews ought to love all people, even Samaritans. Instead, he does a more shocking thing. He uses the "unclean" Samaritan as an example of what neighborly love is. The Samaritan demonstrated his love in a practical way (vv. 34–35). In the ancient world oil and wine were commonly used to soften wounds and as an antiseptic. Jesus exposes the real issue in this parable (v. 36). Who is my neighbor? is not his question, but rather, Am I a neighbor? The lawyer asked a calculating question (v. 29), designed to exclude some from love's grasp. Jesus' story shows that love does not have any calculable limits. It may be significant that the lawyer does not say "the Samaritan" (v. 37).

The next story (**10:38–42**) may have occurred at some other time, and Luke may have inserted it here for topical reasons. Luke probably omitted the name of the village ("Bethany," John 11:1, 18; 12:1) because it was near Jerusalem, and Jesus does not arrive in Jerusalem for some time. Martha complains to Jesus about Mary's failure to help with the meal preparations. In fact, Martha seems to be blaming Jesus ("Lord, don't you care," v. 40) since Mary was not helping because she was listening to Jesus teach. The point of the story is not that a life of contemplation is better than a life of service. Rather, Jesus gently chides Martha because her preparations were too elaborate; she was distracted "by all the preparations" (v. 40; lit. "much service"), and she was "worried and upset about many things" (v. 41). Jesus says that "only one thing is needed," meaning that only one dish is needed. But this one thing also stands for the better part which Mary has chosen, namely, listening to the Word of God. The implication is that Martha, if she kept the preparations simple, could also listen to Jesus. The story is significant because Jesus, in contrast to most Jewish teachers of the day, encouraged learning among women. Sitting at a teacher's feet (v. 39) is the usual posture of a student, indicating that Mary was one of his pupils.

Next Jesus offers teaching on prayer (**11:1–13**). Prayer is an important part of Luke's Gospel, and Jesus' example of prayer and John's instructions on prayer stimulate the disciples to ask for help in praying (v. 1). The Lucan form of the Lord's Prayer is shorter than the Matthean form. The differences between the two accounts may be due to editorial modification of the prayer by the different Evangelists, or it is possible that Jesus taught the prayer on more than one occasion. The word *Father* comes from the Aramaic *Abba*. Abba emphasizes the warm and intimate relationship that exists between the believer and God. Two requests follow that center on God's purposes. "Hallowed be your name" means that disciples are to pray that God's name (i.e., his person and character) is honored, exalted, and revered. "Your kingdom come" is a request that God will bring his rule to fruition, that he will bring in the days of messianic blessing and joy. The last three petitions in the prayer focus on human needs. First, the request for daily bread certainly refers to physical bread, although many commentators also see a reference to "spiritual" bread. The word *daily* is difficult. It could refer to (1) necessary bread, (2) daily bread (so NIV), or (3) bread for tomorrow. Second, the prayer contains a plea for forgiveness since believers manifest God's forgiveness to others. Third, believers should pray that God will shield them from all temptation that would lead them into sin. Then in a story about a person requesting provisions from a friend at midnight, Jesus proceeds to tell a parable about prayer (vv. 5–8). The arrival of a friend at night would not be unusual in the Middle East because it would be too hot to travel by day. Moreover, no host would fail to offer food to a guest. The "friend" inside is reluctant to get up because he would awake all his children, probably because he lived in a one-room house. Nevertheless, the persistence of the friend outside persuades the other to get up and supply his needs. Some have argued that the friend inside responds not because of the other's persistence, but because of his fear of being embarrassed, for the next day everyone would learn of his lack of hospitality (the word *persistence* can be translated "shamelessness"). However, such an interpretation fails because in verses 9–10 the lesson of persistence is drawn from the parable. That does not mean that one needs to be persistent because God is reluctant to give. The point of the parable is not that God, like the person in the house, must be persuaded to give. Just the opposite. One needs to be persistent because God longs to give good gifts to his children, and he is sure to answer (see vv. 11–13). Clearly, God is much more generous than any human father. A water snake in Palestine could be mistaken for a fish, and a scorpion could roll up to resemble an egg (vv. 11–12).

Many people concluded that Jesus' miracles demonstrated that he was from God (cf. 7:16), but an alternate explanation soon arose (**11:14–26**). Perhaps his ability to exorcise demons stems from his alignment with Beelzebub (another name for Satan). A more convincing sign is requested to prove his authenticity (vv. 15–16); however, Jesus shows that the accusation of demonic collusion is senseless. If Jesus expels demons with satanic power, then Satan is contributing to his own demise (vv. 17–18). If Jesus' adversaries claim that he exorcises demons with satanic power, then it logically follows that exorcisms performed by their colleagues are accomplished by Satan as well (v. 19). Instead, the exorcism of demons is a sign of God's power, an indication of the presence of the kingdom (v. 20). Indeed, Jesus' exorcisms show that he has defeated the strong man (Satan) and that is why Jesus can plunder Satan's possessions (i.e., free those who are captive to Satan [vv. 21–22]). Opposition to Jesus on this issue, then, is an indication that one has joined the adversary (v. 23). In verses 24–26 Jesus warns of the danger of a demon evacuating a person when nothing positive takes its place. Such a person opens himself up to demonic possession that is even worse than the former state. It is not enough to expel demons if there is no acceptance of Jesus' kingdom message. An exorcist may make matters worse if he expels demons but does not fill the gap by taking sides with Jesus (cf. v. 23).

If we relate the next incident (**11:27–28**) to the preceding episode, Jesus is saying that his critics should focus on obedience instead of doubting his mighty works. A woman in the crowd, feeling rather sentimental, uses a Jewish expression which means "how happy is the mother of such a son" (v. 27). Jesus does not reject such an affirmation, but he points to something more fundamental. True happiness comes from hearing and obeying God's Word (v. 28).

The narrative here picks up the demand for a sign (**11:29–32**) from verse 16. Evidently, people wanted a sign that was more convincing and definitive than exorcisms; however, Jesus says that the demand for a sign is wicked, for obedience to God's Word is the real issue. The only sign that will be given to the people is the sign of Jonah. Some relate this to the preaching of Jonah, but the primary reference is probably to Jonah's deliverance from the whale, and thus we have an allusion to Jesus' resurrection (cf. Matt. 12:40). Both the Queen of Sheba, who came to test the wisdom of Solomon (1 Kings 10:1–10), and the men of Nineveh, who responded to the preaching of Jonah, will pronounce a sentence of guilty on the Jews of Jesus' day. After all, Jesus is greater than Solomon and Jonah, and this should be sufficient evidence to his contemporaries.

The paragraph in **11:33–36** is difficult. In this context the light which shines for all to see is Jesus and his message about the kingdom (v. 33). Also, the eye functions as a lamp because it is the organ by which light enters the body; however, if one's eyes are unhealthy, then light cannot enter (v. 34). The point is that those who are in darkness have refused to be illumined by Jesus. They may think they are illuminated by light, but actually they are in darkness because they have rejected the path of obedience (v. 35). Only those who have responded obediently to Jesus' message will be fully illumined with light (v. 36).

In **11:37–54** Jesus wages a full-scale attack on the practices of Pharisees and their scribes. A Pharisee was surprised that Jesus did not ritually wash himself before eating (v. 38). The Old Testament did not require this ritual washing, but the Pharisees practiced it because of the defilement one would contract from Gentiles and unclean people. The Pharisees overly concerned themselves with outward matters of cleanliness, failing to see the importance of cleansing from inward sin, especially greed (vv. 39–40). By giving alms from the heart to the poor the Pharisees would be moving in the right direction. By cleansing the inside they would be cleansing the outside as well. Jesus then exposes the faults of the Pharisees in three woes. (1) They major on the minutiae of religion, such as tithing every plant in one's garden, but forget about what is really important, namely, justice and love of God (v. 42). Tithing should not be eliminated, but it should be placed in its proper perspective, for the Pharisees tithed even more than the Old Testament required. (2) The Pharisees were enamored with the glowing reputation they gained from being religious (v. 43). (3) Indeed, they resembled "unmarked graves." Walking over an unmarked grave would defile a person in Jewish culture. The point is that even though the wickedness of the Pharisees is not apparent or observable, it is defiling and contaminating (v. 44). An objection from a scribe leads to three woes being pronounced against them also (v. 45). (1) The lawyers with their many regulations made the practice of religion so burdensome and tiring, yet they are not willing to help those they burden (v. 46). (2) In an ironical statement (vv. 47–48) Jesus says that by building the tombs of the prophets the lawyers show their sympathy with those who killed them. They wanted to keep them in the grave! The lawyers' sympathy with those who killed the prophets of old is clear because they will kill the prophets and apostles who are now God's spokesmen (vv. 49–51). (3) Lastly, the interpretation of Scripture practiced by the lawyers blocked ordinary people from receiving knowledge about God and prevented them from entering the kingdom (v. 52). After such a blistering attack it is not surprising that the Pharisees begin to plot against Jesus (vv. 53–54).

The next verses (**12:1–3**) follow naturally from the preceding discourse in which Jesus criticizes Pharisaic religion. Here he warns his disciples to be on guard against "the yeast of the Pharisees, which is hypocrisy" (v. 1). Such hypocrisy cannot be hidden forever; at the end it will be revealed for all to see (vv. 2–3). Verses 2–3 also blend in with the following exhortation (vv. 4–12) to the disciples. The disciples should not deny Jesus because ultimately such a denial will be broadcast for all to see.

The disciples are encouraged to persevere under persecution (**12:4–12**) for the following reasons: (1) Those who buckle under persecution are afraid because of the pain and deprivation of physical death. Such fear needs to be conquered because bodily pain is all that their adversaries can inflict (v. 4). (2) On the other hand God should be feared because he can cast a person into hell. A healthy fear of punishment will encourage the disciples to endure persecution (v. 5). (3) From a proper fear of destruction the text moves to a fear that is to be avoided. Under persecution one may fear that God has forgotten him. But this is not the case. God even remembers sparrows which are sold for less than a cent (v. 6). In fact, every hair on a person's head is "numbered" by God (v. 7). God remembers and cares for the person who is suffering persecution; God has not forgotten. (4) Verses 8–9 bring out what is implicit in verse 5. What should people fear when being persecuted? They should fear denying Christ, for such denial will mean that such a person is "disowned" by God. The person who confesses Christ publicly, however, will be rewarded. (5) Verse 10 is a qualification of verses 8–9. What really constitutes a denial of the Son? Apparently, forgiveness is possible if one "speaks a word against the Son of Man," but blasphemy "against the Holy Spirit will not be forgiven." What is the sin that will not bring forgiveness? Probably a persistent and stubborn refusal to submit to the gospel. It is not an occasional denial of Christ (as Peter did), but it is the hardness of heart which refuses to repent and turns completely against the witness of the Spirit. (6) Lastly, Jesus promises that when disciples are persecuted the Spirit will give them wisdom to defend themselves (vv. 11–12).

The section on possessions (**12:13–34**) can be divided into three subsections: (1) warning against greed (vv. 13–15); (2) parable of the rich fool (vv. 16–21); (3) worry over possessions (vv. 22–34). In the first paragraph (vv. 13–15) a man wants Jesus to arbitrate in an inheritance dispute between his brother and himself. This would be typical work for a rabbi. But Jesus refuses, insisting that this is not his role. In verse 15 he warns of the root problem: greed. A greedy person thinks that the good life is found in things, but this is a distorted perspective (v. 15). This discussion leads Jesus to relate the parable of the rich fool (vv. 16–21). The problem with the rich fool was not that he had bumper crops, or that he decided to build more storage space (vv. 16–18). The problem was that he invested his entire life in his possessions (cf. v. 15). He drew all his security from his material goods (v. 19), and failed to reckon with God. He was living as if he would never die and had forgotten the importance of spiritual riches (vv. 20–21). Such a shortsighted investment in temporal things is foolishness indeed. In the last section Jesus gives his disciples the proper perspective on riches (vv. 22–34). Believers should avoid anxiety about food and clothing, for true life does not consist in material possessions (cf. vv. 15, 21). And if God cares for ravens and adorns flowers with such beauty, then he will provide the fundamental physical needs of believers (vv. 24, 27–28). Jesus is not suggesting here that work is unnecessary; we need to remember that the problem being addressed here is worry, not laziness. Worry is also senseless because it does not accomplish anything (vv. 25–26). No one can live even a day longer by worrying. The root problem with worry is lack of faith (v. 29). It is understandable that pagans are consumed with the desire for security, but believers need to remember that the Father knows what they need (v. 30). If believers make the kingdom their consuming passion, then God will take care of other needs (v. 31). Disciples, then, are not to fear but to trust God (v. 32). They will not draw their security from possessions, and so they will be free to give their possessions to others. If their treasure (or security) is money, then that will be their consuming passion. Making money one's treasure is the path to insecurity, however, because it is always subject to the vicissitudes of life (v. 33).

From the proper attitude toward money Luke now speaks of the way disciples should view the interval between Jesus' ascension and return (**12:35–48**). The parable of a master returning from a wedding party (vv. 35–38) shows that while the master is absent his servants should be ready and watching for his return, even if he comes at a time that is later than they expect. (The Jews split the night into three watches, so the second or third watch would be very late.) Girding up the loins (v. 35) was necessary in Palestine because men wore long flowing robes that needed to be tied up with a belt when one wanted to run or engage in serious work. Verse 37 envisions a reversal of roles that was unheard of in Palestine. If the servants are faithful, then the master will serve them. The parable of the alert house owner (vv. 39–40) demonstrates that the disciples cannot predict with certainty when the Son of man will come; therefore, they must always be ready. Peter inquires about whether Jesus is speaking specifically to the apostles/disciples or to all people (v. 41). Jesus does not answer the question directly, although he implies that he is referring only to the apostles/disciples because they possess authority over the other servants (v. 42). In this third parable Jesus focuses on the responsibility of managers to take care of their servants (vv. 43–46). He warns that the delay of the master should not lead to the abuse of the servants by the manager. Irresponsible behavior will be punished and responsible behavior will be rewarded; however, punishment will be based on the degree of knowledge. All punishment will not be equal because those who are entrusted with more responsibility and knowledge will pay a greater penalty (vv. 47–48). The central thrust of this section is that the daily obedience of the disciple shows that he is ready for the return of Jesus; disobedience will be punished and obedience will be rewarded.

The relationship of the next paragraph (**12:49–53**) to the preceding one may be the thought of judgment. The fire that Jesus wants to be "kindled" (v. 49) is the fire of judgment that discriminates between the unrighteous and righteous. It probably does not refer to the Holy Spirit here (but cf. Luke 3:16). The purifying fire is also related to Jesus' imminent baptism (v. 50). The baptism that Jesus must undergo is not a literal baptism; rather, it is a metaphor of some overwhelming catastrophe—clearly his death on the cross. The arrival of Jesus did bring peace on earth (Luke 2:14), but the fire of judgment also means the separation and division of families. That division stems from one's stance toward Jesus (cf. Mic. 7:6).

Discerning the signs of the times is the subject in **12:54–59.** The purifying fire of God's judgment is imminent (v. 49). Jesus warns his listeners that they need to see the urgency of the present time, because the eschatological crisis is at hand. His listeners are adept at detecting forecasts of coming weather (vv. 54–55), but they fail to see the forecast of the coming crisis that is implicit in Jesus' ministry (v. 56). Jesus uses an illustration to convey the same point in another way (vv. 57–59). If a person were going to court, knowing he could lose the case and spend some time in jail (v. 59), then he would certainly try to reconcile with his adversary on the way to the courthouse. So too, a person who is under the threat of judgment should reconcile with God while there is still time.

In **13:1–9** the necessity of repentance before the coming judgment continues as Luke's theme. Pilate, probably at Passover, had some Galileans slaughtered while they were preparing their sacrifices (v. 1). Apparently, those who told Jesus about this incident thought that the Galileans were executed because of sin (v. 2). Jesus does not focus on the sin of the Galileans; instead, he uses the occasion to warn everyone that they too will perish without repentance. Jesus seizes on another example to make the same point (vv. 4–5). The tower of Siloam was probably part of the old wall in Jerusalem, near the juncture of the south and east walls. The accidental death of the eighteen was not due to any exceptional personal sin. (Jesus does not deny that the Galileans and those who died at Siloam were sinners; he denies that the manner of their death was due to any exceptional sin.) In the parable of the fig tree (vv. 6–9) the necessity of repentance before the crisis of the final judgment is underlined again. Executions and accidental deaths are not definitive signs of God's judgment (vv. 1–5); but if an individual is not bearing fruit, then judgment is certain. God, however, patiently waits for fruit to appear, giving people every possible chance to produce fruit. Nevertheless, people cannot put off the day of judgment forever, idly thinking that it will never come (vv. 8–9).

In the next pericope (**13:10–17**) we see the saving power of Jesus at work. Still, the synagogue ruler maintains that healing on the Sabbath is wrong. God made weekdays for work, never intending that work be done on the Sabbath (v. 14). Using a typical rabbinic method of arguing from the lesser to the greater, Jesus accuses those who hold this position of hypocrisy. If one cares for the physical needs of animals on the Sabbath, then it follows that one *should* care for the physical needs of people (v. 15). Indeed, the Sabbath is a particularly appropriate day to frustrate the work of Satan (v. 16). Such actions and words silenced his opponents and delighted his supporters.

The parables of the mustard seed and the leaven (**13:18–21**) teach the same lesson. The rule of God has manifested itself in Jesus' ministry. The liberation of the crippled woman from Satan is one example (cf. 13:10–17). However, the kingdom has not been ushered in with apocalyptic power. It seems small and powerless—like the proverbially small mustard seed and the leaven hidden in flour. Nevertheless, the eventual spread of the kingdom is sure. As a mustard seed grows into a tree, and as yeast spreads through dough, so too the kingdom of God will rule over all. Some have said that "leaven" here represents evil, but such an interpretation overlooks the context of the parable in Luke.

B. The journey continues (13:22–17:10). The "travel" note in verse 22 (cf. 17:11) suggests a major break here in the text. Luke introduces more instructions for disciples, focusing on the salvation which is available for the humble (13:22–15:32). But the divisions of the text are rather difficult at this point and somewhat arbitrary.

A question about the number of people who will be saved (v. 23) becomes the occasion for Jesus' instructions (**13:22–30**). Jesus does not answer the question directly (v. 24). Instead, he focuses on the necessity to expend every effort ("strive") to enter the door of salvation. The urgency of decision is also underlined because the day is coming when it will be too late to enter; the door will be closed (vv. 24–25). Those who are outside will object that they knew Jesus, that they even feasted with him and enjoyed his teaching (v. 26). But such an association with Jesus is superficial; he recognizes and admits entry only to those who obeyed his message (v. 27). Those who are excluded will feel remorse ("weeping") and fierce anger ("gnashing of teeth") because they will not be able to participate in the great eschatological banquet (cf. Isa. 25:6–8; Rev. 19:9). Indeed, the great saints of old will feast with the Gentiles in the kingdom, a warning to the Jews of Jesus' day that the roles of Jews and Gentiles can be reversed (vv. 28–30).

Some Pharisees then tell Jesus to leave Galilee or Perea (Herod's realm) because Herod wants to kill him (cf. 23:7–12). There is not enough evidence to show whether these Pharisees were friends or foes of Jesus. Jesus, however, is not impressed with Herod's threats. He compares Herod to a cunning fox, saying that in the days ahead he will continue to carry out his ministry (v. 32). Nevertheless, Jesus will be leaving Herod's realm and will arrive in Jerusalem, not because he is afraid of Herod, but because as a prophet he must "reach [his] goal" and die in Jerusalem (vv. 32–33). The temporal references in verses 32–33 should not be taken literally; they are simply a way of describing a period of time before the end (the end is "the third day"). The reference to Jesus' destination in Jerusalem reminds him that the city has rejected his message, as it has rejected the message of prophets in former times (v. 34; it also implies that Jesus has spent some time in Jerusalem). Such a rejection fills Jesus with anguish (v. 34). But Jerusalem's rejection also spells her future judgment; her house will be left desolate (v. 35). Here "house" refers to either the city as a whole or the temple. Jerusalem will not see her Messiah again until the second advent when her faith will be renewed (v. 35; cf. Rom. 11:26). Others think this last phrase means Jerusalem will not see Jesus again until he comes as her judge.

All of the episodes in chapter 14 through verse 24 take place at a banquet in a prominent Pharisee's home (v. 1). The precise nature of the Pharisee's position is uncertain. The first episode is another controversy story on the Sabbath (**14:1–6**; cf. 6:1–11; 13:10–17). Hostility was continuing to build against Jesus because of his healings on the Sabbath, and he was being watched suspiciously on this occasion (v. 1). "Dropsy" (v. 2) involves swelling due to excess fluids building up in tissues and cavities. Jesus forthrightly challenges the Pharisees on the legitimacy of healing on the Sabbath; their silence indicates that they could not refute him (vv. 3–4). Jesus justifies his healing by referring to the practice of rescuing one's son or ox from a well on the Sabbath (v. 5). Some manuscripts read "donkey" instead of "son," but the latter is a superior reading. The Pharisees were apparently more humane than the Qumran community, for the latter did not even allow rescuing a beast on the Sabbath. "Let no beast be helped to give birth on the Sabbath day; and if it fall into a cistern or into a pit, let it not be lifted out on the Sabbath" (CD 11:13–14). Jesus' actions were such that no criticism could be voiced (v. 6).

Observing that people were clamoring for the places of status at the banquet, Jesus makes some remarks on humility (**14:7–14**) to the guests (vv. 8–11) and to the host (vv. 12–14). Luke says that Jesus told a parable (v. 7); however, the word *parable* can have various meanings, and here refers to the "wisdom sayings" that Jesus utters. Jesus' advice in verses 8–10 could be understood as a sly way to get ahead. People who claim the reputable places at banquets end up being publicly humiliated when they are asked to take a lower seat. So if you really want to get ahead pretend to be insignificant and take the lowest seat. The host will notice your humility and advance you to a higher seat, indicating your intrinsic superiority. But verse 11 shows that Jesus did not have such a cunning program in mind, for such clever and false self-humiliation is still diseased with the root problem of trying to advance oneself above others. Those who try to advance themselves in a clever or a blatant way will be humbled, but those who are genuinely humble before God will be exalted by him. Jesus' words to the host in verses 12–14 can be easily misunderstood as well. He is not saying that one should never invite friends over for dinner. The problem he is addressing is the expectation of recompense, that is, the calculating spirit that does good so that more benefits will accrue to oneself. He uses the vivid (and serious) example of inviting the handicapped because such an invitation shows that one is not controlled by a spirit of repayment. Jesus promises a reward at the resurrection for those who live in such an unselfish manner. It would be a grotesque error if one were to conclude that one should treat the handicapped with kindness *so that* one could receive a reward. That is the same calculating, selfish spirit which Jesus is criticizing. Rather, those who do not live in such a calculating way will paradoxically receive a reward. The rewards come to those who are not living for them.

The reference to "the resurrection of the righteous" (v. 14) leads one guest into a reverie on the blessing of being part of the eschatological banquet (v. 15). Jesus responds by telling the parable of the great banquet (**14:15–24**), puncturing the man's sentimentality and bringing him back to reality. The kingdom of God is like a banquet, but the people invited make excuses so that they do not have to participate. The excuses (vv. 18–20) given show that these are people for whom material goods and family take priority. Their rejection at this point is extremely rude because they had already accepted the initial invitation (vv. 16–17). Jesus is probably referring to the religious leaders here; we need to remember that he was eating in a Pharisee's house (v. 1). The master responds by inviting those of the lower class (referring to tax collectors and sinners, lower-class Jews) from the town in verse 21. Luke's concern for the poor and handicapped (cf. v. 13) continues. Even after those from the lower class are brought to the banquet there is still room for more, so the master sends his servant to the countryside so that his "house will be full" (v. 23). This seems to be a clear reference to the Gentile mission. The phrase *make them come in* does not imply that some will enter the kingdom against their will. In Palestine people politely refused an invitation until they were persuaded to accept (cf. Gen. 19:3). The point of the parable is that people may talk sentimentally about the blessings of the kingdom (v. 15), but in reality many do not want to accept the invitation. Those who refuse the invitation will never enter the kingdom (v. 24).

The scene changes. Jesus is no longer in the Pharisee's house, but now a large crowd is following him (v. 25). Jesus challenges the crowd to think carefully about the radical commitment that he demands (**14:25–35**). Jesus invites all to follow him (cf. vv. 15–24). Yet, following him is not easy but requires ruthless self-denial. The call to hate one's family members is startling (v. 26). Obviously, Jesus is not speaking of "psychological hatred" (cf. 6:27–28). The use of hyperbolic language indicates that no one can take precedence over Jesus. One must renounce "even his own life" and be willing to follow Jesus in the way of death (vv. 26–27). Those who are not willing to follow Jesus in such a radical way cannot be his disciples. Two illustrations are given to show the need for counting the cost before embarking on the road to discipleship. Someone building a tower (vv. 28–30) would surely calculate the cost of the project before starting. A half-finished building would be the object of ridicule. So too, no king would plan to wage war against an enemy without considering beforehand the possibilities of victory (vv. 31–32). The application from the two illustrations is drawn in verse 33. Before one embarks on the road to discipleship one needs to recognize from the beginning that Jesus demands total and complete commitment. Only those who have such a radical commitment can be Jesus' disciples. The illustration of the salt makes a similar point (vv. 34–35). A disciple who is not salty is one who ceases to be radically committed. Such disciples are "good for nothing."

The setting for all of the "lost" parables in chapter 15 is the Pharisaic complaint that Jesus was associating and eating with tax collectors and sinners (**15:1–2**). By eating with defiled people Jesus himself would contract uncleanness. Thus, these parables all emerged from a controversial setting and need to be interpreted as parables in which Jesus defends his ministry to the "lost." Three different parables with the same basic theme are included here, the last one being the most detailed.

Jesus' association with sinners is justified because God is like a shepherd who searches diligently for any lost sheep (**15:3–7**). The retrieval of the lost sheep brings joy to God ("heaven" [v. 7] is another way of referring to God; cf. Matt. 18:14). Verse 7 adds a point that is not contained in the parable (cf. vv. 4–6), namely, that God's joy comes from the repentance of the lost. The statement about the "ninety-nine righteous persons who do not need to repent" is probably an ironical poke at the Pharisees; Jesus is not saying that some do not need repentance, only that some do not know they need repentance (cf. the lost son in 15:11–32). The parable is not intending to teach that the ninety-nine other sheep were abandoned in the wilderness (v. 4).

The parable of the lost coin (**15:8–10**) makes the same point as the former parable. A shepherd with one hundred sheep was fairly well off, but a woman who lost one coin and searched for it was probably poor. It is often said that the lost coin was part of her dowry, yet there is no evidence in the text for this. If a woman searches carefully for one lost coin and exults over finding it, then it stands to reason that God will search diligently for those who are lost, rejoicing greatly over their repentance (v. 7). A lamp would be needed during the day in a peasant's house that had no windows (v. 8).

Many themes are intertwined in the parable of the lost son (**15:11–32**), and one could easily label it a parable of the father's love, but the theme of being "lost" is consistent with the two former parables. Without doubt this is one of the most compelling and memorable stories ever told. It was not uncommon for a father to divide the estate before his death. Immediately the younger son cashed in his assets (he would receive one-third of the property since he was the younger son). He went abroad and lived wildly, ending up bankrupt. When a famine struck, he desperately needed work and was hired to feed pigs, a shocking job for any Jew since pigs were unclean animals. Nevertheless, his degradation was not yet complete. He was so hungry that he longed to eat the food which these unclean animals were eating. Such debasement stimulated him to reconsider and change his life. The depth of his repentance was profound, for he no longer felt worthy to be called his father's son; however, the father's love was spontaneous. Before hearing of any confession of guilt he ran to embrace his son while the latter was still far away. The son confessed his inadequacy, but the father did not let him finish the previous soliloquy ("make me like one of your hired men" [v. 21] is not in the best MSS). Instead, he treats him like an honored guest, adorning him with the best robe, putting a ring on his finger, and giving him sandals (slaves did not wear sandals). Indeed, he starts a celebration by having the fattened calf prepared (v. 23). Meat was not often eaten in Palestinian culture, so this surely indicated a festive occasion. The occasion of the celebration was the return to life of the lost son. The story could easily end here, but the elder son (who is often forgotten in popular renditions of the story) now returns home. The older son is hurt by the special treatment that the younger son received and refuses to participate in the party. Displaying his love, the father entreats him to come in. But the elder son is scandalized by what he considers to be favoritism for his younger brother. A young goat (v. 29) would not be near the value of a fattened calf. Indeed, he cannot even acknowledge that the younger son is his brother; instead he says "this son of yours" (v. 30). The father, however, continues to plead with his older son, noting that the entire remaining inheritance now belongs to him, and reminding him of the closeness of their relationship ("you are always with me," v. 31). The father says that the celebration was a necessity because of the return to life of the lost younger son (v. 32). Notice that the father reminds the older brother of his relationship to his kin by saying "this brother of yours" (v. 32). The parable ends up in the air. Will the older son enter the party?

Jesus is defending his association with tax collectors and sinners. The festive eating with them is a necessity, for it symbolizes God's joy over their repentance. And his acceptance of them indicates his forgiving grace. Like the older son, the Pharisees are invited to enter the party as well. This clearly indicates Jesus' heart toward the Pharisees, for often it is portrayed only in negative terms. The parable, then, is a beautiful description of the forgiving love of God, grace, and the joys of repentance. The parable does not teach that the atonement is necessary, for one cannot expect a parable's teaching to be exhaustive.

The parable of the dishonest steward (**16:1–13**) is one of the most difficult to interpret in Luke. Where does the parable end? Does it end with verse 7, 8a, 8, or 9? Is the master in verse 8 Jesus or the master of the steward in the parable? Why does the master praise the dishonest manager (v. 8)? And what is the message of the parable for the church? Before we begin to answer these questions a few preliminary matters need attention. The manager was not merely an ordinary household servant, but an estate manager, the agent of his master. He probably handled all the economic affairs of the master. He is charged with dishonesty (v. 1), and the charge must be true because no self-defense is attempted (v. 3). The master fires the manager and asks for a final accounting sheet so that his successor can conduct business (v. 2). The manager realizes his predicament. He is a white-collar worker and so he cannot handle manual labor. Also, it would be a blow to his pride to beg. By lowering the bills of the debtors he will win their friendship, insuring a future place for himself (vv. 4–7). We cannot interpret this parable any further until we answer some of the previous questions. First, it is probable that the parable ends at 8a. Second, the "master" referred to in verse 8 is not Jesus, but the master of the steward. Identifying the master as Jesus is problematic because then the parable ends suddenly and unexpectedly without any indication of how the master responded to the manager's dishonesty. The comment in verse 8b is probably from Jesus because it seems clear that a religious application is now being drawn from the story. Thus the parable ends in the middle of verse 8, closing with a comment from the manager's master. Third, almost all scholars agree that the master was not praising the dishonesty of the manager. Praise for dishonesty is inexplicable. Some scholars argue that the master was praising the manager because when the manager reduced the debts he was only eliminating the interest from the debts. According to the Old Testament the taking of interest was forbidden, but in this case the manager exacted interest so that he could line his own pockets. On this interpretation the master did not praise the manager for his dishonesty; instead, he commended the manager for renouncing the illegal practice of charging interest. This interpretation is attractive because it removes the problem of the master commending his steward for dishonesty, but it is not the most obvious meaning of the text. There is no indication in the text at all that the manager has decided not to charge "interest." And the interest in verse 6 is improbably high—100 percent! Moreover, the master in verse 8 praises his dishonest employee, showing no indication that he had just done something that was righteous. If the above analysis is correct, why did the master praise his manager? Not because of the employee's illegal and immoral behavior (although he did act immorally), but because he did something that was clever and prudent. The lesson that Jesus draws from the parable, then, involves both comparison and contrast—use money wisely and prudentially as the steward did, but do not use it dishonestly as he did (cf. vv. 10–12). When Jesus refers to "unrighteous mammon" (so AV; rightly translated "worldly wealth," NIV [vv. 9, 11]), he is not saying that money is intrinsically evil, only that it is easily abused and used for evil. The lessons Jesus draws from this parable are as follows: (1) Use your money for kingdom purposes so that in the eschaton your use of wealth will indicate that you are worthy of entering into heaven (v. 9). This is not salvation *by* works, but salvation *with* works. (2) If one is faithful in handling a small amount of money, one will be faithful with large amounts (v. 10). (3) One who cannot be trusted with money cannot be trusted with spiritual riches (v. 11). (4) One who cannot handle his own affairs will not be called on to manage the affairs of another (v. 12). In verse 13 Jesus penetrates to the root; no one can give exclusive service to both God *and* money.

Clearly, the reproof of the greedy Pharisees (**16:14–15**) continues to focus on money, but it takes the discussion in a new direction. Apparently, the Pharisees were ridiculing Jesus because they imagined some compatibility between serving God and money. Jesus replies that their attempt at self-defense is hollow because God penetrates to the true state of their hearts. An attempt to appear pious before people without reality before God is detestable to God.

It is hard to see how the statements on the law (**16:16–18**) in this paragraph relate to the preceding paragraph. In verse 16 discontinuity is drawn between the period of the law and the period of the kingdom. The "Law and the Prophets" refers here to the Old Testament Scriptures. Whether John the Baptist is to be included in the former or the latter is disputed. The main point of the text is that with Jesus the proclamation of the kingdom has arrived. What Luke means by "everyone is forcing [Gk. *biazetai*] his way into it" is problematic. It could mean (1) everyone is urgently invited to enter into the kingdom, or (2) everyone is trying hard to enter into the kingdom, or (3) everyone uses violence against the kingdom. The first view has the most to commend it, for the latter two have difficulty explaining the inclusion of the word *everyone*. Verse 16 emphasizes the discontinuity between the law and the kingdom, but verse 17 qualifies that statement. Actually, the preaching of the kingdom does not invalidate a single part of the Old Testament law. The "stroke" here refers to the marks that distinguish Hebrew letters from one another. It is not referring to ornamental crowns which are found in some manuscripts of the Torah, for the latter are not found in first-century manuscripts. Obviously, Jesus is not saying that the entire Old Testament law is still literally in force; this is a hyperbolic way of saying that the Old Testament law as it has been interpreted by Jesus is permanently valid. Verse 18 illustrates the principle of verse 17. The Old Testament nowhere forbids divorce altogether, but Jesus interprets the Old Testament in such a way that divorce is completely forbidden. Any marriage involving divorced persons constitutes adultery.

At this point the chapter returns to the theme of the proper use of riches (**16:19–31**). Verses 19–26 teach that there will be a reversal of fortunes after death. The rich man lived in great luxury during his life, but he was apparently unconcerned about the plight of the poor. Lazarus was abandoned at his gate, diseased, and hungry. Dogs, which were considered to be unclean and a nuisance, licked the sores on his body. He was even denied the pleasure of eating the leftovers from the rich man's table; however, when the two men died their roles were reversed. Lazarus went to Abraham's bosom (v. 22), perhaps another way of describing the messianic banquet. This expression occurs only here in the Bible. The rich man went to Hades (v. 23). *Hadēs* is the Greek translation of the Hebrew word *sheol* and usually indicates the realm of the dead. Here it clearly refers to a place of torment. Possibly this parable is teaching that *Sheol* is divided into two realms, one of blessing and one of punishment. But the parable should not be pressed too hard for such information since this is not the main point of the story. As Lazarus desired the crumbs from the rich man's table, now the rich man wants just a drop of water from Lazarus (v. 24). But he is denied. A chasm exists between Lazarus and the rich man, and now the rich man is reaping what he sowed. There is a clear message to Christian disciples here; they need to use their money prudently and generously in order to enter eternal dwellings (cf. 16:9). In verses 27–31 the parable takes on a different tack. The rich man realizes that it is too late for him, so he entreats Abraham to send Lazarus to warn his brothers of their imminent doom (vv. 27–28). (One should not use this detail of a parable to probe the self-consciousness of those who are being punished.) Abraham dismisses the suggestion because the brothers already have "Moses and the Prophets" (v. 29). This also suggests that the message of Jesus does not invalidate Old Testament revelation (cf. 16:17). The rich man, however, protests that the Scriptures are not enough. They need the definitive proof that a resurrection would provide (v. 30). Abraham retorts that this is incorrect. Those who do not put credence in the Scriptures will not be persuaded by a resurrection. Certainly Jesus' resurrection was in Luke's mind when he wrote this. The point of the last part of the parable is clear. No miracle can convince anyone of the credibility of the kingdom message. The Scriptures are sufficient for salvation, and those who reject their message will rationalize miraculous phenomena as well.

Four sets of sayings are combined here (**17:1–10**) which have no obvious relationship to one another except that each one is about discipleship. (1) Jesus warns the disciples about the danger of causing others to stumble in their faith (vv. 1–3a). It would be better if a person were dead than that he would lead another into sin. (2) From the subject of leading others into sin Jesus moves to the topic of forgiving those who fall into sin (vv. 3b–4). No matter how many times a person sins, if he repents after being confronted, then he should be forgiven. The number seven here should not be taken literally; it symbolizes limitless forgiveness. (3) Perhaps the extent of forgiveness that is required of disciples leads them to say, "Increase our faith" (v. 5); however, Jesus says that the problem is not the quantity of their faith but the reality of it. A small amount of faith can accomplish great things (v. 6). (4) Lastly, obedient disciples cannot claim any reward, or regard themselves as doing anything particularly notable (vv. 7–10). In the secular world a master expects the servant to serve the master before taking care of his own needs. The central point of the parable is not that God is ungrateful for the obedience of disciples because he expects such service anyway (v. 9). Rather, the point is that disciples cannot boast before God about their service.

C. The last leg of the journey (17:11–19:27). Another travel note in 17:11 indicates a break in the narrative. The setting is Jesus traveling "along the border between Samaria and Galilee." The major thrust of the cleansing of the ten lepers (**17:11–19**) is that only one returned and praised God. Moreover, this one person was a foreigner—a Samaritan. By focusing on a Samaritan Luke is stressing the universality of the gospel message. Verse 19 implies that he has received more than just physical healing.

The connection of the paragraph on the coming of the kingdom (**17:20–37**) with the former paragraph is not obvious. Some have suggested that both the nine lepers and the Pharisees fail to see the presence of the kingdom in Jesus. The Pharisees want to know when the kingdom will arrive (v. 20). Jesus replies that the coming of the kingdom cannot be calculated by observing signs. And in one sense the kingdom is present *now*—it is *within you* (v. 21). This last comment does not mean that the kingdom was internally present in the Pharisees; rather, it means that the kingdom has arrived in the person and ministry of Jesus. Jesus' words to the Pharisees on the arrival of the kingdom lead into a discourse for the disciples on the coming of the Son of man (vv. 22–37). Jesus begins by emphasizing that his followers will long to see the days of his future messianic reign (v. 22), but such anticipation should not blind their critical faculties (v. 23). They should not be misled by those who claim to know where he is, for his coming will be as sudden and obvious as lightning which flashes in the sky (v. 24). Furthermore, before any of this can happen the Son of man must suffer death (v. 25). Jesus compares the day of his coming to the days of Noah and Lot (vv. 26–30). Life was progressing in an ordinary way when the destruction of the flood and the destruction of Sodom and Gomorrah occurred.

There was no warning that an apocalyptic judgment was evident. All indications were that life was going on as usual. So too, the coming of the Son of man will be without warning. No apocalyptic signs will clearly herald his appearance. The instructions in verses 31–33 must be metaphorical rather than literal. Verse 33 supplies a hint as to the meaning of the metaphor. Jesus is saying that one should not become attached to material possessions so that one is not ready for his arrival. The one who tries to preserve his life in this world will lose it in the next. Disciples must stay faithful to their master while waiting. Verses 34–35 show that the Son of man will come suddenly and unexpectedly. People will be involved in the ordinary activities of sleeping and eating. However, there will be a separation among people who work closely together. "One who will be taken" could mean one who was taken for judgment or taken away from judgment. The latter is probable, for God took away Noah and Lot so that they would escape the judgment. Those who are left will face the full fury of the judgment. The disciples' question in verse 37 is strange. It probably indicates that they have not understood Jesus' discourse, for Jesus has already said (v. 23) that this kind of question is irrelevant. Jesus answers that his coming will be as obvious and as unmistakable as the arrival of vultures over a corpse. No one will doubt what is happening.

The previous pericope focused on the unexpected coming of the Son of man. In the parable of the unjust judge (**18:1–8**) the necessity of persistent prayer and faith until the parousia is underlined. Luke begins by giving the reader an editorial comment on the meaning of the parable (v. 1). The difficulties of life may tempt one to give up on prayer, but one should continue in prayer until the end. The parable proper follows (vv. 2–5). The unscrupulous judge cared nothing about justice for the widow. Widows were helpless and weak members of society, having virtually no recourse to overcome oppression and exploitation. Even though the widow was at a disadvantage she used her strongest weapon: persistence. She "kept coming" (v. 3) so that the judge reconsidered his habitual refusals (v. 4). He was tired of her "bothering" him, and was afraid she would "wear [him] out" (v. 5). This last phrase literally means "give a black eye to." But the judge was not worried about a physical assault, nor was he worried about his reputation (he did not care what men thought [vv. 2, 4]); he was tired of the bother. What is the meaning of the parable? Jesus asks his listeners to consider its meaning (v. 6). Obviously, it is not saying that God is like the unjust judge and that one has to bother him so that he will answer our requests even though he does not want to help us. Instead, it draws a contrast between God and the judge. Unlike the judge, God will quickly grant justice to those who call to him for it (vv. 7–8); however, there is a point of tension in the parable. If justice is received so quickly, why would anyone give up in prayer (v. 1)? And why would anyone lose faith before the Son of man comes (v. 8)? Perhaps the vindication will not seem to be quick at all for people on earth, but will be agonizingly slow—so slow that they may give up on prayer, concluding that God is not just, that he does not punish the wicked and vindicate those who long for justice. The parable promises that God will answer, despite how long it may seem to take. The human being may be asking, Can God be trusted to vindicate the elect? But the parable ends on a different note. No one can question God's faithfulness; the only question is whether human beings will be faithful to the end (v. 8).

Again it is hard to detect the relationship between the parable of the Pharisee and tax collector (**18:9–14**) and the preceding parable. Perhaps this parable illustrates the kind of faith (cf. v. 8) that God desires. Luke again begins the parable by making an editorial comment (v. 9). This parable is addressed to the self-confident and self-righteous—those who looked down on others with contemptuous disdain. Confident of his moral superiority, the Pharisee approaches the temple to pray. He praises God that he is not like other sinners, and then lauds his own religious devotion. By fasting twice a week and tithing he would be going beyond the requirement of the Old Testament law. On the other hand, the tax collector (see 5:27–32) is deeply conscious of his own unworthiness. He stands far away, fearing even to raise his eyes. All he can ask for is mercy since he knows he is undeserving of God's forgiveness. Jesus concludes by saying that the tax collector, rather than the Pharisee, was justified in God's eyes. Here Luke is indicating that the Pauline doctrine of justification by faith apart from works has its roots in the teaching of Jesus. Verse 14b also teaches Christian humility. The beauty and power of this parable are inescapable. Modern-day readers identify with the tax collector, but in the process we have unconsciously uttered the prayer, "Thank God I am not like that Pharisee," showing that the heart of the Pharisee lives in all of us.

The disciples were reproving those who were bringing children to Jesus, perhaps because they considered it to be a waste of time;

however, Jesus compares the inhabitants of the kingdom to children (**18:15–17**), probably referring to the openness, spontaneity, and freshness of children. Indeed, all those who enter the kingdom need to become like children in exercising childlike humility. Like the prior pericope, this one emphasizes that it is the humble who will be exalted.

A rich ruler inquires about the pathway to eternal life (**18:18–30**); however, Jesus immediately questions the ruler about calling him good, stressing that only God is good. Jesus is not admitting sinfulness here, nor is he leading the ruler to the realization of his divinity. He is directing attention away from himself to God, reminding the ruler that all goodness comes from him. The five commandments cited focus on those that deal with social relationships (v. 20). He is implying, of course, that eternal life comes from obedience to the law. There is no reason to doubt the truthfulness of the ruler's assertion of obedience to the law; Jesus does not accuse him of blatant hypocrisy. Instead, he probes deeper. The ruler has placed one thing above God, namely, his riches. If he really desires eternal life he must sell all and follow Jesus. Obedience to the law does not merely consist in the ability to refrain from certain sins; it means that one has placed God above everything else in one's life. Jesus has also removed any sense of respectability the ruler could derive from his obedience (cf. 18:11–12). The ruler's wealth prevented him from following Jesus, and Jesus responded by stressing how difficult it is for the rich to enter heaven. The picture of a camel going through the eye of a needle does not refer to a gate called by that name (no such gate has ever been found!), nor is the textual reading "rope" better than "camel" (v. 25). Jesus drew a vivid and humorous picture of that which is impossible. The hearers are perplexed about Jesus' statement. If rich people cannot be saved (for they were highly respected), then who could be saved (v. 26)? Jesus replies that humanly it is impossible for anyone to be saved, showing that his picture in verse 25 is supposed to convey an impossibility. Salvation is possible only with God. In verses 28–30 Jesus does not criticize Peter for asking about future rewards; instead, he promises that they will be significant for those who have left everything to follow him. The leaving of a wife (v. 29) should probably be understood as a renunciation of the privilege of marriage for the sake of the kingdom.

The third passion prediction (**18:31–34**) comes on the heels of the promise of rewards. There will be rewards, but the path to rewards is suffering. This passion prediction is distinctive because it stresses the fulfillment of Scripture, the role of the Gentiles, and the incomprehension of the disciples. We should not fail to see that the prediction of the resurrection is contained here as well.

Mark says that the healing of the blind man (**18:35–43**) occurred while Jesus was leaving Jericho (Mark 10:46–52). Some have said that Mark was referring to the old town and Luke the Herodian town. However, there is no extant evidence that the old town was called Jericho in the first century A.D. Jericho was near to the city of Jesus' destination, namely, Jerusalem. Despite being discouraged by the crowd, the blind man hails Jesus as the Son of David, referring to his messianic status as he begs him for help. The implication seems to be that the blind man is one of his disciples since he puts his faith in Jesus and follows him. Is the recovery of sight of the blind man contrasted with the failure of the Twelve to see (cf. 18:34)?

The episode with Zacchaeus (**19:1–10**) is notable because it contains many of the main themes of Luke's Gospel. A chief tax collector (v. 2) was probably the head of a group of tax collectors. The grumbling starts again when Jesus decides to lodge at another tax collector's house (cf. 5:27–32); however, Zacchaeus vindicates Jesus' decision by demonstrating the reality of his repentance. Half of what he owns he will give to the poor, and he will make fourfold restitution to those who have been cheated (v. 8). The present tense of the verbs "give" and "pay back" should be understood as futuristic presents. Some scholars claim that Zacchaeus is not repenting of sin here, but is defending himself. He has always (present tense) given half of his goods to the poor and repaid those who have been cheated. Such a view is incorrect for it does not explain the word *today* in verse 9. Zacchaeus reformed his life the day he met Jesus. Observing what has happened Jesus says that "salvation has come to this house" (v. 9). Salvation is a major Lucan theme, perhaps the central one in the book. We also see Luke's concern for the poor in this story; however, we should not fail to observe that here we have a rich man who is saved (cf. 18:18–30). The salvation of the rich is possible with God, for "the Son of Man came to seek and to save what was lost" (v. 10), both the rich and the poor, the clean and the unclean, the despised and the respectable.

The parable of the ten pounds (**19:11–27**) is similar to the parable of talents in Matthew 25:14–30, but there is no agreement on the literary relationship between the two parables. In Luke the context of the parable was the expectation that the consummation of the kingdom was imminent (v. 11). Luke has already taught that the kingdom is present in Jesus' ministry (11:20), but even though Jesus inaugurated the kingdom he has not completed it. Since he was "near Jerusalem" some thought that the completion of God's kingdom purposes was at hand. The parable implies an interval of time before the kingdom is consummated. The nobleman went on a distant journey (v. 12). Typically, Jesus is not interested in speculating on the date of the kingdom's consummation; he focuses on the need for responsible work by his servants. In the parable each of the ten servants is given one mina, which probably equalled about three months' wages. Each servant is expected to make a profit in the master's absence. The message to the disciples is that they are expected to bear fruit in the interval of time between Jesus' ascension and return. When the nobleman returns he settles account. Seven of the ten servants fall out of the picture, and the master reckons with only three. The first two invested the money responsibly and were rewarded lavishly by the master (vv. 15–19). The point is that God graciously rewards his servants with far more than they deserve. The focus, however, is on the third servant (vv. 20–24). He did not invest his money, and accuses the master of being cruel and exploitative. Perhaps he feared that if he made a profit the master would take it, and if he lost the money the master would demand repayment. The master retorts that the standard of judgment would be the servant's own words. If he is so harsh and exploitative, then obviously he will harshly judge someone who did nothing. The point of the parable is not that God is harsh and cruel, but that he will judge those who waste the resources that he has given to them. The bystanders object to the transfer of the third servant's mina to the first servant, but the transfer intentionally teaches God's sovereign graciousness. The rewards are based not on merit but on grace. Another theme is woven into the parable. The citizens of the country do not want the nobleman to assume rule over them (v. 14). When he gains the kingship, he executes those who resisted his rule (v. 27). This clearly refers to the Jews who have rejected Jesus as their king. Their rejection of Jesus will ultimately lead to judgment. This theme is appropriate in Luke's Gospel because the final rejection of Jesus is on the horizon.

V. Arrival at Destiny: Death and Resurrection in Jerusalem (19:28–24:53)

A. Entrance into Jerusalem (19:28–48). The long journey to Jerusalem is over (cf. 9:51). Jesus finally arrives in Jerusalem (**19:28–40**) and the culmination of his lifework is at hand. Verse 28 depicts Jesus traveling ahead of the disciples, which underlines his determination to go to Jerusalem. Perhaps the acquisition of the colt (vv. 29–34) was a matter that Jesus arranged beforehand. Jesus climbs upon the colt and his entry in Jerusalem is acclaimed in messianic terms. The riding of the colt may symbolize the humility of his entrance. The Pharisees object to the enthusiastic words of the crowd, but Jesus replies that if they are silent the stones will take up the shout.

The sight of Jerusalem moves Jesus to tears (**19:41–44**), not because of his own fate but the fate of the city. They had not recognized that in his person they had been visited by God, that the prospect of peace with God was being offered. Now it is too late. Judgment will come and the city will be destroyed because they rejected God's messenger.

Luke's description of the cleansing of the temple (**19:45–48**) is brief and to the point. Obviously Jesus thinks that the commercial activity that was going on in the temple was obscuring its function as a house of prayer. The cleansing would have occurred in the court of the Gentiles, not in the inner precincts. A cleansing of the temple was expected in the last times (Mal. 3:1), and it may have symbolized the future judgment of Jerusalem. Luke does not give any hint that a deeper significance lay in the cleansing. The cleansed temple does not become the location of Jesus' teaching, and it probably solidified the opposition to Jesus, convincing the leaders that it was time to do away with Jesus. Nevertheless, the popularity of Jesus frustrated the desire of the leadership.

B. Controversy between Jesus and leaders heightens (20:1–21:4). The conflict between Jesus and the religious leaders intensifies, and the debates in this chapter reflect the heightening tensions. An official group of religious leaders, probably commissioned by the Sanhedrin, approach Jesus and ask about the source of his authority (**20:1–8**). "These things" (v. 2) seems to refer to the teaching of Jesus, but it certainly includes the bold action of cleansing the temple. Jesus does not answer the question directly; instead, he poses a question about the legitimacy of the Baptist's ministry (vv. 3–4). This is not an attempt to escape from the controversy, nor is it a debating trick. It was the Baptist who proclaimed the coming of Jesus and baptized him. Before Jesus discusses his own status he needs to know what their estimation is of the message of his forerunner. After all, the answer to their question is in John's preaching: Jesus derives his authority from God. The authorities, however, claim ignorance (vv. 5–7), fearing a rebuke from Jesus on the one hand and a violent reaction from the crowd on the other. Jesus responds by not giving a direct answer to their question (v. 8), although the answer is really implied. Jesus leaves his listeners to draw their own conclusion.

Absentee landlords who rented out their land to tenant farmers were common in Palestine. In the parable of the wicked tenant farmers (**20:9–19**) the obvious allegorical features are sometimes held to be a creation of the early church, but there is no reason why Jesus could not have used an allegory. The end of the parable (v. 19) tells us that the parable was directed against the religious leaders. They had been given the responsibility to tend the vineyard (probably symbolizing Israel; cf. Isa. 5:1–7). When the owner of the vineyard desired to collect some of the fruit, he sent messengers (perhaps representing the prophets). In each case the messengers were wounded and ousted. The repetition of the same pattern three times is for rhetorical purposes. It builds the narrative to a climax. The owner of the vineyard is perplexed. The sending of his son will probably command their respect. Of course, the son here is Jesus, and instead of rejecting him the religious leaders put him to death, thinking they would inherit the vineyard. Commentators debate whether the thinking of the tenants on inheriting the vineyard was reasonable (vv. 14–15). Possibly some tenants did revolt against owners and try to take possession of the property. But this is certainly not the point of the parable. Here the action is irrational, for the owner of the vineyard will come and execute the tenant farmers, and give the vineyard to others. The kingdom of God will be taken from the religious leaders and be given to the remnant of believers in Israel and to the Gentiles. The people's response—"May this never be!" (v. 16)—is an expression of horror. It was unthinkable that any tenant farmers would act like this! Jesus, however, solemnly assures them that this is precisely what the Scriptures foretold (Ps. 118:22). The builders (the religious leaders) have rejected the stone (Jesus), which "has become the capstone" (v. 17). "Cornerstone" may be the preferred translation instead of "capstone" (see NIV note). This is not a decorative stone, but a stone placed at the corner of the building to bear the stress and weight of the two walls. Thus, it is *the* crucial stone in the building. Verse 18 expresses two thoughts: (1) those who stumble (probably in unbelief) over that stone will themselves be broken; (2) if the stone falls in judgment on anyone that person will be pulverized. This parable of judgment only provoked the leaders' desire to do away with Jesus, but his popularity with the people held firm (v. 19).

The former parable increased the opposition to Jesus, but since the religious leaders could not yet arrest him, they tried to entrap him. Their praise for Jesus' integrity was lavish, but insincere and hypocritical. Paying taxes to Caesar (**20:20–26**) was a volatile issue in Palestine in the first century. Some Jews thought that the payment of such a tax necessarily involved compromise of their religion. Moreover, the image of the emperor on the coin was thought to be a violation of the second commandment. The questioners were probably hoping that Jesus would either disavow paying taxes and incur trouble with Pilate, or that he would advocate complete submission to the government and alienate patriots. By calling for a denarius (v. 24) Jesus shows that even pious Jews possessed coins with Caesar's image, clearly showing their submission to his jurisdiction. The first part of Jesus' answer (v. 25) acknowledges the legitimacy of submission to Roman power insofar as that power is acting lawfully. But that is not the whole story. One is to give to God what belongs to him, and obviously his jurisdiction is total. Thus, Jesus is not setting up two separate realms, for the authority of God takes precedence over the state (cf. Acts 5:29). However, one should obey the earthly ruler as one who is delegated by God to enforce justice (cf. Rom. 13:1–7). Jesus' answer was so impressive that it silenced his adversaries.

A deft answer has been given to a controversial political question. Now Jesus is faced with a question about the resurrection from the Sadducees (**20:27–40**). The Sadducees were an aristocratic group who were the most powerful political faction in Palestine. They rejected both the oral tradition of the law to which the Pharisees adhered and belief in the resurrection or angels (cf. Acts 23:8). They relied only on the Old Testament Scriptures for their theology, focusing especially on the Torah. In this episode they try to show that the doctrine of the resurrection is ridiculous. Referring to the custom of levirate marriage (a man marries his deceased brother's wife who is childless to raise up children for his brother), they imply that a future resurrection is out of the question. If a wife had seven such husbands, to which husband would she be married in the resurrection? Jesus' answer has two parts. (1) The Sadducees fail to see the discontinuity between this age and the age to come. Marriage and procreation are a vital part of earthly life to preserve the human race, but in the coming kingdom there will be no institution of marriage. People will be like angels. This does not necessarily mean that sexual differences will be obliterated, nor does it mean that human beings and angels will be exactly alike. It means that human beings will be like angels in at least one way—neither group will marry. (2) What Jesus has said weakens the Sadducean objection. But now he moves to the Scriptures to demonstrate his case. If Exodus 3:6 says that God is the God of Abraham, Isaac, and Jacob, then the patriarchs must continue to live. Some have said that this example does not prove the resurrection, but only the immortality of the soul. Others have tried to argue that Jesus is speaking here only of a future resurrection, but this is not supported by verse 38. Jesus' argument seems to be this: the immortality of Abraham et al. is a guarantee of the future resurrection. Jesus' answer impressed some teachers, probably Pharisees who disagreed with the Sadducees (v. 39). His prowess in answering questions again silenced his opponents.

Now Jesus shows his superior understanding by posing a question that the religious leaders cannot answer (**20:41–44**). Quoting a messianic psalm (Ps. 110:1), he asks how the Messiah can be both the Son of David and the Lord of David. Jesus is not denying that the Messiah was to be David's son. Instead, he is implying that there is a mysterious way in which the Messiah was both David's son and Lord. A resolution of the paradox is not given here, although the reader of Luke's Gospel knows that Jesus is both the Son of David and the Son of God (cf. 1:32, 35).

The theology of the religious leaders has just been criticized. Now Jesus upbraids the religious practice of the scribes (**20:45–47**). They perform their religious duties for show and to garner respect from men, but at the same time they defraud widows of their money. Severe judgment will fall on such pretentious religiosity. We should not conclude that all scribes were hypocrites; Jesus merely focuses on the danger of religiosity (cf. 11:37–52).

The widow's sacrificial gift (**21:1–4**) is a remarkable contrast to the pretentious religion of the scribes—who exploit widows (20:45–47)! Others were giving substantial gifts to the temple, but the text suggests that the gifts were insignificant because they put no strain on the givers' budgets. On the other hand, the widow's gift was notable because of the extreme sacrifice it entailed, even though the amount of money was negligible.

C. Apocalyptic discourse (21:5–38). The temple that elicited the admiration of his disciples was beautiful indeed. Herod the Great began to refurbish it in 20/19 B.C. and the work was not completed until A.D. 63. Jesus, however, predicts that the temple will be completely demolished (**21:5–6**). The Romans fulfilled this prophecy in A.D. 70. Some scholars have maintained that this saying was attributed to Jesus after the event occurred, but such a view reflects a bias against predictive prophecy.

Jesus now warns his disciples against eschatological enthusiasm and braces them for future persecution (**21:7–19**). The question of the disciples in verse 7 clearly refers to the date of the fall of Jerusalem, but it also seems to involve the date of the end of this age. The fall of Jerusalem becomes a type of the end times. (Luke has distinguished more clearly than Matthew [Matt. 24] and Mark [Mark 13] the events that will take place in Jerusalem from the events of the end.) Jesus' answer clearly indicates that the question in verse 7 relates to the last times. He warns his disciples not to be deceived because many will claim to be the Messiah or declare that the end has come. The arrival of the end cannot be calculated from wars, insurrections, famines, earthquakes, and disease (vv. 9–11). These events will occur before the end, and they may even signal the imminence of the end, but no certain calculation can be drawn from them. The disciples ought not to think the end will deliver them from suffering because persecution will precede the end (v. 12). They will be prosecuted by civil and religious authorities. But their defense will produce an opportunity to testify about the gospel, and they will receive the necessary words with which to defend themselves. The persecution may be bitter, perhaps even involving betrayal by family members and death. They must steel themselves to face implacable hostility (v. 17). To say "not a hair of your head will perish" (v. 18) seems to contradict verse 16 where Jesus asserts that some will be put to death. The saying in verse 18 probably means that one will be spiritually preserved from any harm, since physical death does not damage one's essential self. All of this is encouragement to stand firm and persevere because such perseverance is necessary for salvation (v. 19). Again, this is not salvation by works. Such perseverance gives evidence of the genuineness of one's salvation.

In the next pericope Jesus specifically answers the question about the destruction of Jerusalem (**21:20–24**). One will know that Jerusalem's time of destruction has arrived when foreign armies surround it. This encirclement is a signal, not of the need for heroism, but the need to flee. God's avenging wrath will be poured out on the city, bringing distress to the entire populace. "The times of the Gentiles" (v. 24) refers not to the Gentile mission but to Gentile authority over Jerusalem. Josephus's

Jewish War contains a graphic commentary on the Roman conquest of Jerusalem in A.D. 70.

From the destruction of Jerusalem Luke moves to the coming of the Son of man (**21:25–28**). Luke does not specify the temporal relationship between these events, but the former clearly functions as a correspondence of the latter. The emphasis on signs in this paragraph is in tension with Luke's claim elsewhere that no signs will precede the end (cf. 17:20–25). This is probably Luke's paradoxical way of saying that the end is not calculable, and yet certain signs precede it. The signs picture in dramatic terms the breakup of the natural world order, and the resulting terror and fear which seize the human race. The Son of man will return during these troubled times. The message for believers is: When the world begins to convulse, take hope! Your redemption is imminent.

The parable of the fig tree (**21:29–33**) is easy to comprehend. Just as the appearance of leaves on a tree shows that summer is near, so too the signs previously described indicate that the coming of the Son of man is near. The assertion that "this generation will certainly not pass away" (v. 32) is difficult. It could refer to (1) the generation in which Jesus was living, (2) the Jewish race, (3) the human race, or (4) the end-time generation. It probably refers both to (1) and (4), for Jesus' generation experienced the razing of Jerusalem, and Jerusalem's destruction becomes a type of the end. In typical Jewish fashion Jesus combines in this discourse information about the destruction of Jerusalem and the end of the world.

The arrival of the Son of man and the destruction of Jerusalem have a practical message for disciples. They should constantly be vigilant (**21:34–36**), not forgetting in the interval their purpose for living. The end will come suddenly, and the entire earth will be affected. When Jesus says pray to escape what will happen (v. 36), he does not mean that people should pray that they will not be on earth. Rather, he means that they should pray that they will not face the terrible judgment of God. By following the path of obedience they will receive a favorable verdict from God and stand before the Son of man with joy.

The verses on Jesus' ministry in Jerusalem (**21:37–38**) are not part of the apocalyptic discourse. Jesus continued his teaching ministry up until the end, and his popularity with the people continued.

D. Passover events (22:1–38). The Feast of Unleavened Bread was held during Nisan 15–21, and the Passover on the fourteenth and fifteenth days of the same month (March/April in our reckoning). Because the two feasts were so close together, Luke did not differentiate clearly between them. Members of the Sanhedrin ("chief priests and teachers of the law") wanted to arrest Jesus, but they were afraid of a popular uprising among the people, for Jesus was greatly admired (cf. 19:28–40; 21:38). Judas Iscariot's decision to betray Jesus (**22:1–6**) was the crucial break that the religious leaders needed. He discussed the matter and made plans with the chief priests and the temple police. The only explanation Luke gives for Judas's disloyalty is the work of Satan (cf. John 13:2, 27), and perhaps the desire for money (v. 5). No crowd could be present when the transaction was carried out because the arrest of Jesus could have fomented a revolt among the people (v. 6).

The next paragraph concerns the Passover preparations (**22:7–13**). All the synoptic Gospels agree that Jesus ate a Passover meal with his disciples. The lambs would have been slain in the afternoon on the fourteenth day of Nisan, and the meal would be celebrated that evening (v. 7). The evening would start a new day according to the Jewish reckoning. John dates the meal before the Passover (John 13:1; 18:28; 19:14), placing Jesus' death on the fourteenth of Nisan, the day the lambs were sacrificed. The problem of the difference between John and the Synoptics is complex and cannot be treated adequately here. Some have argued that the Synoptic writers used the sectarian calendar from the Essenes, which would explain the variance in dating. It has also been suggested that the meal in the Synoptics is not actually the Passover, but a Passover type of meal. The account here suggests that Jesus secretly prearranged the location of the meal, probably so that Judas could not betray him before the celebration of the feast. "A man carrying a jar of water" (v. 10) would be notable, for this was usually done by a woman.

A Passover meal (**22:14–23**) usually had the following order: (1) preliminary events—a blessing was said, then the first cup of wine and a dish of herbs were served; (2) the Passover liturgy was recited, the second cup was drunk, and a part of the Hallel (Pss. 113–118) was sung; (3) the meal was celebrated, a blessing was pronounced over the unleavened bread, the lamb was eaten with the unleavened bread and bitter herbs, and the third cup was drunk after the meal; (4) the rest of the Hallel psalms were sung. (There is disagreement over whether there was a fourth cup.)

Jesus expresses his intense desire to partake of the Passover with the disciples (v. 15). Some scholars have said that Jesus abstained from the meal, but the most natural meaning of verse 15 is that Jesus did eat the Passover with the disciples. This Passover meal, however, is the last one Jesus will eat with his disciples. But the meal also takes on eschatological significance. Jesus will celebrate the Passover with the disciples again during the messianic banquet (vv. 16, 18). The first cup (v. 17) is either the first or second cup of the Passover service. The Passover in the Old Testament represents the liberation of Israel from Egypt, but Jesus now begins to reinterpret the Passover. The bread which he breaks symbolizes his broken body, that is, it represents his sacrificial death which was vicarious in nature (v. 19). The cup in verse 20 would be the third cup after the main meal. This cup represents the new covenant (Jer. 31:31f.), and the wine represents his blood that establishes the new agreement and is poured out in a sacrificial way for others. Some manuscripts omit Luke 22:19b–20, but most scholars now agree that these verses should be included. Jesus continues his words, predicting that one of those eating with him would betray him (v. 21). The fact that one of Jesus' closest associates, who even shared the Passover with him, would act with treachery is intended to evoke horror from the reader. Nevertheless, this betrayal accords with the divine plan.

The predicted betrayal caused the disciples to question who might be responsible (v. 23). But the conversation quickly turned to which disciple was the greatest (**22:24–30**), for if one could be in the lowest position of a traitor, then presumably there must be some kind of rank. Jesus confronts the competitive spirit of his disciples, contrasting the secular meaning of greatness with his own perspective. Gentiles use power to dominate others and to acquire a reputation for themselves. The new community, however, should not be characterized by a quest for power or greatness, for true greatness consists in serving. Jesus uses his position not to demand service but to give service and aid to others. Nevertheless, the disciples will be rewarded for their service and endurance with Jesus in his trials (v. 28). They will share with Jesus in the messianic banquet and the kingdom, having a responsibility to judge Israel.

In **22:31–34** Jesus foretells Peter's denial and restoration. Even though the disciples will eventually inherit the kingdom, their faith will be tested. In verse 31 the plural "you" (Gk. *hymas*) refers to all the disciples, and the sifting would involve the separation of the wheat from the chaff; that is, Satan wants to test the disciples so that they fall from the faith. Jesus directs the rest of his words to Peter. The test of fidelity will be severe, and Simon will even deny Jesus despite his protestations to the contrary (vv. 33–34). Nevertheless, Jesus' prayer for Peter will be efficacious. His faith will not permanently fail, and after his restoration he is to fortify the faith of the other disciples.

In this perplexing paragraph regarding the two swords (**22:35–38**) the nature of the testing that the disciples and Jesus will face is now explained more fully. On their previous mission the disciples lacked nothing, presumably because their needs were met by others. But now the time of opposition has set in. Jesus' words on acquiring a sword (v. 36) should not be interpreted literally; they are a sign of the conflict and opposition which the disciples will face. Indeed, Jesus himself will be considered to be a criminal (cf. 23:32–33), fulfilling Isaiah 53:12. The disciples mistakenly interpret Jesus' words on swords literally. Jesus rebukes their incomprehension (cf. 22:49–51) by saying, "That is enough" (v. 38).

E. Arrest and trial (22:39–23:25). After the meal ended, Jesus and the disciples went to the Garden of Gethsemane at the foot of the Mount of Olives (v. 39). The theme of testing continues from the preceding paragraphs. The account begins and ends with Jesus exhorting his disciples to pray that they will not enter into temptation (**22:39–46**). Jesus functions as the model. He naturally felt a revulsion about his destiny, entreating his Father to take the cup away from him. But through prayer he overcomes the test, remaining faithful and fixed on his Father's will. The disciples function as a foil. They do not pray but sink into sleep at the hour of testing. Verses 43–44 are textually uncertain; although they may not be original, they may contain ancient and probably authentic tradition.

The text now moves to Jesus' betrayal and arrest (**22:47–53**). Judas betrays Jesus with a mark of friendship and affection, revealing the nadir of his degradation (vv. 47–48). Still misunderstanding Jesus' words about swords (22:36–38), the disciples think that now is the time to put them to use. One disciple (Peter, according to John 18:10) severed the right ear of the high priest's servant. Jesus, however, rebukes his disciples for resorting to violence (v. 51; cf. 22:38), and compassionately heals the servant's ear, demonstrating that even during his suffering his work was one of healing and restoration. Jesus then addresses his captors with irony. Did they think he was leading a violent revolution? Is that why they have equipped themselves with such weapons? And why did they not arrest him in public? Clearly, their actions show that they are aligned with the powers of darkness.

Jesus is brought to the high priest's house. Mark tells us that Jesus was examined that night (cf. Mark 14:53–65), but Luke omits the nighttime meeting and tells us only about the examination the next morning. Peter's testing now becomes a reality (**22:54–62**). Just as Jesus predicted, Peter denies him three times, displaying a lack of courage even before a servant girl. The process of restoration begins with a poignant look from Jesus. Peter's remorse naturally must precede any restoration when he must turn and strengthen his brothers (22:32).

Those who were guarding Jesus (nothing is said about Roman soldiers) ridiculed him (**22:63–65**). This is part of the humiliation that Jesus predicted that he would undergo.

Jesus' trial begins with an interrogation before the Sanhedrin (**22:66–71**). This council, which functioned as the official court of the Jews, met to examine Jesus. They immediately address him with their central concern (v. 67): Does he claim to be the Christ? Jesus, however, refuses to answer the question, maintaining that it would be useless to give an answer to such an audience, presumably because they understand the Messiah in a way different than Jesus. Nevertheless, Jesus proceeds to conflate Daniel 7:13 and Psalm 110:1, claiming that as the Son of man he will sit (probably as judge) at God's right hand (v. 69). Jesus' answer provokes the Sanhedrin to ask whether he considers himself to be the Son of God (v. 70). Son of God should not be equated with Messiah (cf. 1:32–35), but goes beyond it, suggesting an intimate and unparalleled relationship with God. Jesus' answer is again rather mysterious and guarded. The New International Version unfortunately renders the answer as the clear affirmative, "you are right in saying that I am." But the Greek text merely says, "you say that I am." The answer is a kind of guarded affirmation, suggesting that Jesus would rather explain the same reality a different way. Nevertheless, the council concludes that the evidence is substantial enough to convict him (v. 71).

The repudiation of Jesus by the religious leaders becomes official as they now accuse him before the Roman prefect Pontius Pilate (**23:1–7**). Pilate's normal residence was the city of Caesarea (cf. Acts 23:23), yet he came to Jerusalem for Passover. The charges against Jesus are political (v. 2), but the only one that seems to arouse Pilate's interest is the idea that Jesus might be "the king of the Jews" (v. 3). Jesus replies to Pilate's question with another ambiguous answer; the Greek literally says, "you say," which is probably a qualified yes. The major point Luke wants to make is that Pilate is convinced of Jesus' innocence (v. 4). When Pilate learns that Jesus hails from Galilee he sends him to Herod Antipas since the latter had jurisdiction over Galilee. The reason Pilate sent Jesus to Herod may have been to satisfy the latter's curiosity, or he may have wanted to learn more about the case from someone who was familiar with the Jews, or perhaps he wanted to get rid of the case.

Now Jesus appears before Herod (**23:8–12**), who was thrilled about seeing Jesus, apparently expecting some kind of miracle show or at least an interesting theological discussion. But Jesus continues to show that he is in command of the situation by refusing to speak with Herod. Herod becomes disgusted with Jesus, joining his soldiers in ridiculing and mocking him. Why did Herod and Pilate become friends on this day (v. 12)? Perhaps because they experienced a kinship in their reaction to Jesus. Both of them lacked the courage to set free a man who was clearly innocent; like Pilate, Herod sees no evidence of wrongdoing. Thereby Herod becomes the second witness of Jesus' innocence (cf. Deut. 19:15).

Luke continues to emphasize the innocence of Jesus. After Jesus returns from meeting with Herod, Pilate sums up the situation and sentences Jesus (**23:13–25**). Neither Pilate nor Herod has found Jesus to be guilty of any crime (v. 15), but a flogging will be administered, probably to warn him not to run afoul of the authorities again (v. 16). The crowd, however, pressures Pilate to release Barabbas, who was a murderer and a terrorist, rather than Jesus. Indeed, they now specify that crucifixion should be the means of Jesus' death (v. 21). Pilate continues to protest that Jesus is innocent, but his good intentions collapse under the fire of the crowd. His cowardice and feebleness lead him to submit to the crowd's will. Thus, an innocent person is put up for execution while a guilty murderer is released.

F. Crucifixion and burial (23:26–23:56a). By custom the victim carried his own cross, so probably Simon was pressed into service because Jesus was breaking down under the weight of the cross. Some women who were present began to weep for Jesus. Jesus warns that their tears should be reserved for their own fate. The judgment on Jerusalem will be so horrible that the unhappy state of barrenness will be preferred (cf. Luke 1:25). People will call to the mountains and hills to shield them from the impending judgment. Verse 31 probably is saying that if the judgment is severe on the innocent Jesus, then it will be incredibly harsh for guilty Jerusalem.

The prophecy that Jesus would be "numbered with the transgressors" (22:37) finds its fulfillment here as Jesus is crucified between two criminals (**23:32–43**). Jesus' words of forgiveness (v. 34) are textually uncertain, although internal evidence suggests they should be included. Even though Jesus is treated as a criminal and is subjected to the humiliation of being stripped (v. 34), he responds with forgiveness. The misunderstanding of Jesus' messiahship is revealed by the threefold mocking (vv. 34–39). The religious leaders, Roman soldiers, and one of the criminals ridicule Jesus, asserting that if he were really the Messiah and the king of the Jews he would extricate himself from death. They fail to see that Jesus is accomplishing salvation by his death. The other criminal (vv. 40–43), however, recognizes that Jesus is innocent, imploring him to remember him when he begins his reign. Jesus' answer goes beyond the man's request, for "today" the man will be with Jesus in the bliss of paradise.

In **23:44–49** Jesus expires, prompting the centurion to proclaim his innocence. The sixth to the ninth hour would be from 12 noon to 3 P.M. The darkness that covered the land could not have been caused by an eclipse, for during Passover there was a full moon. Some have speculated that the darkness was due to a sirocco stirring up the dust, but no clear scientific explanation is available to explain the phenomenon. The darkness suggests an ominous future for Jerusalem, while the splitting of the veil between the Holy of Holies and the Holy Place suggests that free access to God has been accomplished. Placing his confidence in his Father until the end, Jesus serenely commits himself to his Father's care. The centurion underlines the Lucan theme that Jesus was innocent, while the onlookers display their regret for what happened by beating their breasts. The regret here should probably not be understood as repentance. Other followers of Jesus observed what happened from a distance.

Joseph, a member of the Sanhedrin, did not agree with the verdict against Jesus, and was obviously an admirer of Jesus. He saw to it that Jesus received an honorable burial (**23:50–56a**), and that he was not thrown into a common grave with criminals. Instead, he was placed in a new tomb which had never been used before. The day of preparation before the Sabbath would be Friday. The women did not have time to anoint Jesus in the proper manner before the Sabbath so they noted where the tomb was and prepared the spices before the Sabbath began, waiting for the Sabbath to end before returning to the tomb.

G. Resurrection: Scripture fulfilled (23:56b–24:53). On Sunday, "the first day of the week," an unspecified number of women returned to the tomb to anoint Jesus' body (**23:56b–24:12**). Luke does not tell us that they worried about removing the stone (cf. Mark 16:3), yet when they arrived the stone was rolled away and Jesus' body was no longer in the tomb. Instead, they saw two angels, dressed in dazzling apparel, who announced to them that Jesus had risen from the dead. Luke calls the angels "men" (v. 5), not because he did not know they were angels (see 24:23), but because angels in the Bible always appear as men (cf. also Acts 10:3, 30). Mark refers to only one angel (Mark 16:5). This does not contradict Luke's account unless one assumes that Mark's narrative is an exhaustive account, for nowhere does Mark say there was *only* one angel. The angels remind the women that Jesus' death and resurrection were predicted by Jesus himself, stressing that these events were in accord with the divine plan. Women, then, receive the news of the resurrection first, even though they were not considered to be credible witnesses by Jewish society. Notice that Luke says nothing about an appearance of Jesus here; the tomb is empty and angels claim he was risen. The women report the news to the apostles, yet the apostles view these tales as "nonsense." Peter, however, is stimulated to investigate further. He sees the linen that was used to wrap Jesus' body lying on the ground, and leaves the scene mystified (v. 12; cf. John 20:3–9). There are many difficult problems in harmonizing the different resurrection accounts, but such a harmonization is not impossible.[2]

The first resurrection appearance recorded in Luke's Gospel is found here (**24:13–35**). Two people were traveling to Emmaus from Jerusalem. The distance of sixty stadia is about seven miles. As they traveled they were discussing the events of the previous day, and Jesus caught up with them as they journeyed. They could not recognize Jesus, not because he looked different, but because in God's sovereignty they were prevented from identifying him. When Jesus inquires about the topic of their conversation, Cleopas (cf. John 19:25, which may refer to the same person; the identity of Cleopas's partner is unknown, but perhaps it was his wife) responds by identifying Jesus as a prophet through whom God had worked in a mighty way. Nevertheless, he had been executed by the religious leaders, indicating that he could not be the Messiah (v. 21). To make matters worse, some women were saying that this Jesus was alive. They were right that the tomb was empty, but such a report could not be believed because no one had seen

2. See John Wenham, *Easter Enigma: Are the Resurrection Accounts in Conflict?* (Grand Rapids: Zondervan, 1984).

Jesus. The "unknown" Jesus counters the belief of these two by pointing to the Scriptures. The Old Testament Scriptures clearly teach that the Messiah must suffer before he enters into glory. For the texts that Jesus used, one should probably refer to the speeches in the Book of Acts (Acts 2:14–39; 3:12–26; 13:16–41). Jesus is persuaded by the two to spend the evening with them, and in a scene that recalls the Last Supper they recognize him as he breaks bread and gives thanks. On the other hand, these two people were probably not present at the Last Supper, and thus they may simply be recalling being with Jesus on other occasions when he gave thanks. Jesus immediately vanished, and they decided to return to Jerusalem and tell the others the good news. But when they arrived the Eleven spoke first, informing them that the Lord had arisen and had "appeared to Simon" (v. 34). Then the two companions related the story of their encounter with Jesus (v. 35).

During this animated exchange about Jesus' resurrection, Jesus himself appeared to the disciples (**24:36–43**), pronouncing the message of peace (cf. 2:14). The disciples were taken aback, thinking that they were seeing a spirit. Some scholars have argued that this is improbable since they were just discussing the reality of the resurrection, but such a response is psychologically probable when an unexpected visitor suddenly appears in a room. Jesus counters their doubts with hard evidence. Do they think he is only a spirit, a hallucination, a mirage, or a vision? He encourages them to observe closely his hands and feet (vv. 39–40), presumably because of the nail prints which were in them (cf. John 20:24–28). Technically speaking, the nails were put through the wrists, but a reference to the hands would include the wrists as well. If observation of Jesus' body is not enough, then they should touch him as well, for no spirit has flesh and bones. Lastly, Jesus proves the reality of his resurrection by eating some fish before his disciples, for no spirit could do that. It is important to realize that Jesus' body was not simply resuscitated. A resuscitated body is simply a return of the old body to physical life, but such a body must die again (cf. the resurrection of Lazarus in John 11). Jesus' body was a resurrected body, a glorious body that had embarked on a new level of existence. It was still a physical body, but a transformed and empowered physical body.

The end of Luke's Gospel does not clearly indicate that a forty-day interval separated Jesus' resurrection and ascension; instead, the end of Luke seems to put the resurrection and ascension on the same day. A reading of Acts 1:1–11 shows that Luke compresses the account in his Gospel, probably intending to give a summary of what Jesus taught in the forty-day interval. Again, Acts 1:1–11 provides a parallel but supplemental account. Here (**24:44–49**) Jesus emphasizes that the Old Testament Scriptures needed to find their fulfillment in his ministry. The threefold division that Jesus refers to in verse 44 refers to the division of the Hebrew canon into the Torah, Prophets, and Writings. Indeed, the Scriptures even predict (cf. Isa. 2:1–4; 49:6) that the message of forgiveness will be proclaimed to all nations "beginning at Jerusalem" (v. 47). Here we have a foretaste of the message of Acts. Jesus' disciples will be the agents of this message since they are witnesses of the saving events (v. 48). Nevertheless, they must abide in Jerusalem until they are empowered from above, a clear reference to the Holy Spirit (cf. Acts 1:8). Jesus, who is the bearer of the Spirit in Luke, will become the dispenser of the Spirit to his disciples.

The ascension (**24:50–53**) occurs in Bethany (v. 50). This does not contradict Acts 1:12, which assigns the location to the Mount of Olives, because Bethany was located at the foot of that mountain. At the time of his departure Jesus gives his disciples a priestly blessing (cf. Num. 6:24–26). The ascension is described in spatial terms (v. 51), which has sometimes been a stumbling block to those who are part of the scientific age. But what other way would Jesus use to communicate to his disciples that he would no longer be appearing to them? Clearly, one does not have to argue that heaven is "up there" to see that the act was an effective way of demonstrating that the resurrection appearances were at an end. Acts also informs us that Jesus must be exalted before the Spirit can descend (Acts 2:33). The exaltation of Jesus leads the disciples (for the first time in Luke!) to worship Jesus. They now recognize that he is truly the Son of God (cf. 1:35). Verse 53 should not be interpreted woodenly; the disciples were not in the temple every minute. The main point of the verse is the last phrase; they were "praising God" for the salvation that Jesus had accomplished. This is a fitting response for the believer today as well.

SELECT BIBLIOGRAPHY

Ellis, E. *The Gospel of Luke.* Grand Rapids: Eerdmans, 1981.

Fitzmyer, J. A. *The Gospel According to Luke.* 2 vols. Garden City, N.Y.: Doubleday, 1981–1985.

Marshall, I. H. *The Gospel of Luke: A Commentary on the Greek Text.* Grand Rapids: Eerdmans, 1978.

Morris, L. *The Gospel According to St. Luke: An Introduction and Commentary.* Grand Rapids: Eerdmans, 1974.

JOHN

Gary M. Burge

INTRODUCTION

Few books of the Bible have influenced the life and thought of Christendom as has the fourth Gospel. Its readers have always noted its profundity and literary energy. Here Christians have discovered a portrait of Christ that has been deeply satisfying. We are intrigued to witness how John joins intimacy of expression with penetrating insight. Scholars have poured so much energy into unraveling the Gospel's many enigmas that the flood of academic articles and books shows no sign of abating. Yet the Gospel seems to evade our grasp and as a result has become an inexhaustible subject of interest.

Until the eighteenth century, the fourth Gospel was held to be the most accurate and valuable Gospel. But the rise of biblical criticism eclipsed John's prominence. Critics noted its differences from the synoptic Gospels (Matthew, Mark, Luke). Lengthy discourses replaced parables and pithy sayings. John's language and theology seemed to indicate that here the story of Jesus had been refashioned for the Greek world. The result: the fourth Gospel could no longer be viewed as contributing reliably to the history of Jesus' life. Critics looked upon its early apostolic origin with grave doubt.

Today scholars hold a variety of opinions concerning this Gospel. Textual, grammatical, historical, and theological issues are constantly being weighed. And there are few "agreed" results. This alone should caution us when yet another interpretative theory is ushered into view. But at least one trend can be charted in this mass of literature. Since the 1950s a fresh appreciation for John has become almost universal. While John does diverge from the synoptic Gospels, still, its independent narratives are to be valued. For instance, only John records Jesus' dialogue with Nicodemus, but this single witness in no way implies that the incident never happened. More importantly, John's cultural orientation is now viewed as heavily dependent on the Palestinian Judaism of Jesus' day. In other words, John's thought world does not have to be Greek. For example, important Jewish scrolls discovered near Israel's Dead Sea (Qumran) have proven that Judaism in Jesus' day was using language similar to that of the fourth Gospel. Even archaeological finds have substantiated some of the specific narratives of the Gospel which formerly had weathered heavy criticism (e.g., the pool with five porticoes in 5:2).

This "new look" has reopened a number of old questions. If John's frame of reference is Jewish, then the Gospel's date *may* be early. And if it is early, it *may* have originated with the circle of apostles—even John the son of Zebedee. Now the possibility of apostolic authority behind the Gospel is a legitimate defensible alternative. Johannine study has indeed come full circle.

Above all, this new outlook on John demands that the exegete seriously employ the Old Testament and all available Jewish materials. No longer will it suffice to interpret, for example, the miracle at Cana (2:1–11) in terms of the Hellenistic god Dionysus of Thrace who also supposedly changed water into wine. On the contrary, John's *primary* reference is to Jesus' messianic announcement (using Old Testament and synoptic imagery). This will be the approach used in this commentary. The message of the fourth Gospel is clothed with allusions and metaphors that spring from first-century Judaism. Granted, this Judaism was complex and well acquainted with Greek influences, but still, the Gospel's text is elucidated best when seen as firmly rooted in the Old Testament and Palestinian Judaism.

The fourth Gospel provides no explicit internal evidence concerning its author. "John" is nowhere identified as such. But this silence is not unusual and is a feature found in the Synoptics as well. The fourth Gospel may, however, provide us with clues concealed in the enigmatic figure of the "beloved disciple." This title occurs in six passages in John (13:23; 19:26; 20:2; 21:7, 20). John 21:24 describes the beloved disciple as the one "who testifies to these things and who wrote them down." Therefore the origin of the Gospel must in some way be connected to this person. The Gospel of John may be a record of his eyewitness account of Jesus' life.

But who is this disciple? First, some have suggested that he is an idealized literary figure: the ideal Christian disciple. To a degree this is true (he is faithful and intimate in his knowledge of Jesus). But this hardly excludes the possibility of a genuine historical person. Second, Lazarus has sometimes been nominated. Lazarus is the only male figure said to be loved by Jesus (11:3, 5, 36). Further, the beloved disciple texts occur only after Lazarus is introduced in chapter 11. But this solution is unlikely. Why would Lazarus's name be mentioned in chapters 11 and 12 but then left shrouded in subsequent accounts? Third, we know that a man named John Mark was a part of the early church (Acts 12:12) and that he was associated with Peter. If Mark was related to the Levite Barnabas (Col. 4:10), this may also explain how the beloved disciple knows the high priest in John 18:15. On the other hand, a strong patristic tradition maintains that Mark wrote the second Gospel—and besides, the beloved disciple was certainly one of the Twelve (13:23) and John Mark was not.

The best solution is the traditional one: John the son of Zebedee (Mark 3:17; Acts 1:13). This man was one of the Twelve and along with James and Peter formed an inner circle around Jesus. This is the origin of his eyewitness testimony and penetrating insight. In the Synoptics John appears with Peter more than with any other and in Acts they are companions in Jerusalem (Acts 3–4) as well as in Samaria (Acts 8:14). This dovetails with the Peter/John connection in the fourth Gospel. Raymond Brown has offered a novel theory to buttress this.[1] He suggests that John and Jesus may have been cousins (through their mothers). This explains two things. In John 19:25 Jesus entrusts Mary to John due to a natural family relation (she may have been John's aunt). And in 18:15f. John was known by the high priest through Mary's priestly relatives (Luke 1:5, 36).

Patristic evidence seems to confirm this conclusion. Writing at about A.D. 200, Irenaeus says that the beloved disciple was John, the disciple of Jesus, and that John originated the Gospel at Ephesus. Irenaeus even writes that when he was young, he knew another teacher, Polycarp, bishop of Smyrna (ca. 69–155), who claimed to have been tutored by John himself. The church historian Eusebius (ca. 300) records this John/Polycarp/Irenaeus connection in the same way. Further, Polycrates, bishop of Ephesus (189–198), refers to John's association with the Gospel in his letter to Victor the bishop of Rome. It is also confirmed by Clement of Alexandria (ca. 200) and the Latin Muratorian Canon (180–200).

Criticisms of this conclusion are commonplace and we would do well to consider the most important ones. (1) Earlier in this century critics regularly pointed to John's inaccurate geographical details. They affirmed that this could hardly come from an eyewitness writer. But subsequent historical and archaeological study have if anything shown John's reliability. (2) Could a fisherman-turned-apostle have penned a work of such subtlety and insight? Could a Galilean such as this be acquainted with Greek thought? Of course. Recent study of Palestinian Judaism has shown a remarkable degree of Greek cultural penetration at all levels of society. And while the New Testament does affirm that John the apostle was a "commoner" (Acts 4:13), we still are unwise to predict what John could or could not accomplish. Furthermore this fails to consider that the final edition of the Gospel may have been edited by John's disciples, an amanuensis (professional scribe), or John's community. (3) Finally, some lodge the complaint that John was not readily accepted in the early church. This is true. But we have to reckon with two facts. First, our evidence for John's neglect is not as weighty as it seems. Important early writers may not quote John or allude to him; but to note what a patristic writer *fails* to say is an argument from silence. Second, John found wide acceptance in heretical Gnostic circles. This has been confirmed recently by the Gnostic documents found at Nag Hammadi where in the *Gospel of Truth* Johannine themes abound. The unorthodox on the fringes of the Greek church embraced John and provided the earliest widely known commentaries (Valentinus, Heracleon). Therefore, the church

1. Raymond E. Brown, *The Gospel According to John,* 2 vols. (New York: Doubleday, 1966, 1970), 1:xcvii; 2:905f.

was cautious in its use of the Gospel because of its dangerous abuse elsewhere.

All that we have been saying about the new appreciation for the Jewishness of the fourth Gospel and the fact that John the son of Zebedee stands behind the Gospel's authority implies some conclusion about its date. The sources of John must be early and have their roots in first-generation Christianity. But fixing a certain date for the publication of the Gospel is difficult because objective data are slim. The latest possible date is A.D. 150. Not only do patristic references, allusions in apocryphal gospels (Gospel of Peter), and Nag Hammadi point to this, but recently in Egypt two papyrus fragments of John (Rylands Papyrus 457; Egerton Papyrus 2) have been dated at about A.D. 150. Allowing time for John to circulate, the Gospel could not have been completed long after 125.

The earliest possible date for the Gospel is more difficult. If John knows and employs the Synoptics (and this is disputed) then A.D. 70 or 80 is appropriate. In John 9:22; 12:42; and 16:2 we read about Jewish believers being excommunicated from the synagogues. In A.D. 85 the rabbis of Palestine instituted such expulsions for Christians (e.g., Rabbi Gamaliel II). Therefore we find a remarkable consensus of scholarly opinion that John was published somewhere between 80 and 100. Irenaeus says that the apostle lived to a great age—until the reign of Trajan (98–117). And Jerome, writing much later (ca. 375), argued that John died "in the sixty-eighth year" after Jesus' death: hence, about A.D. 98.

On the other hand, an earlier date may be within reach. Current research has challenged John's "dependence" on the Synoptics (esp. Mark and Luke). If anything, John may know presynoptic traditions. Above all, the way in which John describes the topography of Jerusalem, his knowledge of the geographical and political divisions in Judaism, and his use of metaphors all point to a date approximating that of the synoptic writers. The great watershed date of A.D. 70 (when Jerusalem was destroyed by Rome) is critical: John presupposes a Judaism before this war. And with his critical disposition toward the temple (John 2:13ff.; 4:21ff.) and severe conflicts with Jewish leaders (cf. chaps. 5, 8, 10) we are surprised to find no reference to this catastrophic event. To paraphrase C. H. Dodd, much in John is barely intelligible outside of the context of pre-70 Judaism.

To sum up, the traditions about Jesus which John preserves most likely stem from the earliest apostolic period: perhaps A.D. 60–65. But the final edition of the Gospel may have been published later. John and/or his disciples may have edited the work, making additions and sharpening its message for later Christianity.

Tradition tells us that the place of writing was Ephesus and no decisive reasons have been raised against it. There may even be biblical support for it. The fourth Gospel entertains a polemic aimed at followers of John the Baptist (see 1:19–28, 35–42; 3:22–36; 10:40–42). Elsewhere in the Book of Acts we learn about Paul encountering followers of John the Baptist with deficient beliefs. Surprisingly, they too are located in Ephesus.

The interpretation of any biblical book is strengthened when we understand the deeper motives and concerns which have led the author to write. John's vigor and concentration reveal a remarkable intensity of purpose. It is as if a powerful truth had broken upon him and he was compelled to express it. To a greater extent than the Synoptics, each section of the fourth Gospel contributes to a central theme: the appearance of the Son of God in human history. John explores two facets of this appearing: its revelation and its redemption.

John 1:5 underscores this revelation: "The light shines in the darkness and the darkness has not overcome it." Dualistic language describes this harsh invasion of the world by God. Offending every modern sensibility, John writes that in Christ we behold the glory of God—even though he has appeared in flesh. But this offense is an ancient one, too. The darkness assails the light but cannot vanquish it. The world is in permanent enmity with the Son. But even though Jesus is persecuted, tried, and crucified, still, John affirms that the light is not extinguished.

But the gift of Christ is not simply his revelation of the Father (14:9). John's second message concerns redemption: "In him was life and the life was the light of men" (1:4). There is hope for us in the world. The message of this invasion of history is also a message of sacrifice and redemption. Those who embrace this revelation, who identify with the light, and who have faith shall gain eternal life. The life of the Son is poured out in sacrifice thereby creating the community of the redeemed (John 17:6ff., 20–26). They bear Christ's Spirit which sustains them because the hatred once extended toward the Son is now extended to them (15:12ff.).

Thus John's purpose in writing is to explain this revelation and redemption and to explicate its possibilities. In John 20:31 the author makes clear this aim: "But these are written that you may believe that Jesus is the Christ, the Son of God, and that by believing you might have life in his name." Here several major themes converge: belief, acknowledgment of Jesus' sonship, and the promise of life. But even here the mystery of John confronts us. A textual variant in the Greek word *believe* places the meaning of the verse in doubt. One reading implies that John is evangelistic ("that you *might come to believe*"); the other implies encouragement ("that you *might continue believing*"). This latter reading has the best support and more helpfully explains the character of John. It is written for Christians who, already knowing the rudiments of Christ's life and Christian truth, now wish to go further. Not only is there an uncompromising maturity in this Gospel, but also its narratives imply that it was written to address certain practical circumstances in the church. Some would say that John is engaged in a polemic—asserting Christian truth amidst unsympathetic forces. On the other hand, John's purpose also includes the clarification of Christian doctrines at an early stage of church development.

John's Gospel reflects Jewish concerns. The conflict between Jesus and the Pharisees that we meet in the Synoptics is given marked attention in John. A brief perusal of John 8:31–59 or 10:19–39 makes this clear. There is a sustained attack on the religious position of Judaism. For instance, "the Jews" virtually becomes a technical term in John for those who reject Jesus. In 9:22 the parents of the blind man who are Jewish fear "the Jews." But this is not all. The messiahship of Jesus and his relationship to the festivals and institutions of Judaism are both emphasized.

What does this mean? Each Gospel was written not only to record the history of Jesus, but also to address particular circumstances in the life of its first readers. Here the Christians of John's church may have needed encouragement due to persecution and hostilities. So John buttresses Christian claims against Jewish unbelief. The historic fact of Jewish unbelief in Jesus' day is joined with Jewish opposition in John's day.

John's Gospel also reflects Christian concerns. At the time the Gospel was published the early Christian church had grown and diversified considerably. Therefore it is no surprise to find that John has included historic materials relevant to Christian needs in his generation. It would be a mistake, however, to think that any of these needs became the controlling force in John's literary design. On the contrary, they serve as subthemes that run through the Gospel and clarify John's situation. Scholars have identified an extensive list of topics, but we shall note in passing only four prominent motifs:

1. The significance of John the Baptist. Did the Baptist himself have followers who failed or refused to follow Jesus? Luke 3:15 and Acts 19:1–7 imply this while later writings confirm it (see the Latin Pseudo-Clementine Recognitions). The fourth Gospel takes pains to affirm that the Baptist was *not* the Messiah (John 1:20; 3:28), that he was *not* the light (1:8f.), and that Jesus is superior (1:30; 3:29f.; 10:41). We even witness disciples of John the Baptist becoming Jesus' first converts (1:35–42). Matthew, Mark, and Luke have no parallel motif.

2. The place of sacramentalism. John has a "sacramental" view of history inasmuch as the incarnation of Christ for him means the genuine appearance of God in history. Worship can affirm such genuine appearances when worship symbols (baptism, the Lord's Supper) take on the real properties of that which they depict. Hence they are called sacraments. Scholars have identified a unique Johannine interest in the Christian sacraments, but there is little agreement about John's intention. Some note an absence of interest (e.g., the Lord's Supper is omitted) while others see allusions everywhere (baptism: John 3, 5, 9; Eucharist: John 2, 6; both: 19:34). It seems best to conclude that John's principal message about each is corrective (see 3:1–21; 6:52–65): without the Spirit these expressions of worship become powerless rituals void of their original purpose.

3. Our future hope: eschatology. Many early Christians longed for the second coming of Christ and anticipated an imminent end to his-

tory. This explains the cherished sayings of Jesus about this in the Synoptics where this future expectation is described (see Mark 13; Matt. 24; Luke 21). How did they cope when this hope was frustrated (cf. 2 Pet. 3:1–12)? John does not record Jesus' synoptic eschatological discourses. He still maintains the future hope (5:25ff.; 1 John 2:28) but introduces a fresh emphasis: the longed-for presence of Jesus is mediated to us now in the Spirit. In the upper room Jesus' announcement of the Spirit takes on eschatological tones (see 14:18–23). That is, in one vital way that we often overlook, Jesus *has* come back and is already with us in the Spirit. In technical terms, John emphasizes a *realized eschatology* in contrast to the apocalyptic hope of the Synoptics.

4. Christology. Irenaeus, the second-century church father, wrote that the Gospel of John was penned to refute the Gnostic heretic Cerinthus. While this is not likely, nevertheless, Irenaeus correctly observed that John's presentation of Christ was carefully considered. Questions about Jesus' nature, origin, and relation to the Father are examined in a fashion unparalleled by the Synoptics. For instance, John affirms the oneness of Jesus and the Father (10:30; 14:9–10), their distinction (14:28; 17:1–5), and unity of purpose (5:17f.; 8:42). It is not surprising that in the formation of trinitarian doctrine, John's Gospel played a notable role (cf. Tertullian, *Against Praxeas*). This was particularly true at the Council of Nicea (325) when Arius denied the eternal nature of the Son. In later Arian debates, Athanasius was heavily dependent on the fourth Gospel and found in the Johannine prologue's title *Logos* a most serviceable tool depicting the person of Christ (*On the Incarnation of the Word of God*).

John claims full divinity for Jesus. If anyone were inclined toward adoptionism (that Jesus was a divinely inspired man), John's Gospel gives an unrelenting argument to the contrary. On the other hand, the Greek world was comfortable with divinities and, if anything, hesitated to affirm Jesus' full humanity (docetism). Here John contends that Jesus is truly human, truly flesh (1:14; cf. 20:27). The brilliance and abiding value of John is that it strikes a middle path between both of these concerns. Jesus was eternally divine and fully incarnate; fully God and fully human.

But scholars have been quick to point out that this "balanced Christology" seems artificial. If one removes the prologue (1:1–18) the balance is tipped and, in the words of some, John becomes a "naive docetist."[2] But this seems unfairly harsh.[3] One solution has been to view John as having stages of development; the prologue may have been added to the Gospel at a later stage when the Epistles of John were published. The battle cry of 1 John is certainly against docetism (1 John 4:1–3) and, if the high Christology of the fourth Gospel had been fueling heretical docetic beliefs, then the addition of the hymnic prologue would give the needed balance.

Nevertheless, it is vital to say that the humanity of Christ is intrin-

2. E. Käsemann, *The Testament of Jesus* (Philadelphia: Fortress, 1968).

3. L. Morris, "The Jesus of St. John," in *Unity and Diversity in New Testament Theology* (Grand Rapids: Eerdmans, 1978), 37–53.

sic to the whole of the Gospel of John. "John portrays Jesus in a two-fold light without reflection or speculation. He is equal to God; he is indeed God in the flesh; yet he is fully human."[4] This affirmation alone has rendered John valuable to the church and its creeds.

OUTLINE

I. The Prologue (1:1–18)
II. The Book of Signs (1:19–12:50)
- A. The Testimony of John the Baptist (1:19–51)
- B. Jesus and the Institutions of Judaism (2:1–4:54)
- C. Jesus and the Festivals of Judaism (5:1–10:42)
- D. Foreshadowings of Death and Resurrection (11:1–12:50)

III. The Book of Glory (13:1–20:31)
- A. The Passover Meal (13:1–30)
- B. The Farewell Discourse (13:31–17:26)
- C. The Passion (18:1–19:42)
- D. The Resurrection (20:1–29)
- E. Conclusion (20:30–31)

IV. Epilogue (21:1–25)
- A. The Miracle of One Hundred Fifty-three Fish (21:1–14)
- B. Jesus and Peter (21:15–23)
- C. Appendix (21:24–25)

COMMENTARY

I. The Prologue (1:1–18)

One reason why the Gospel of John was symbolized in the ancient church by the eagle is due to the lofty heights attained by its prologue. With skill and delicacy John handles issues of profound importance. It comes as no surprise, then, that this prologue has been foundational to the classic Christian formulation of the doctrine of Christ. Here divinity and humanity, preexistence and incarnation, revelation and sacrifice are each discussed with deceptive simplicity. This prologue may well have been an ancient Christian hymn. We know of other extant hymns, especially in Paul's writings, and here too is an artful flowing of language and theology.

The initial allusion to Genesis 1 cannot be missed (John 1:1). John begins by introducing Jesus as the Word (Gk. *logos*). Here he builds on much contemporary Jewish thought where the Word of God took on personal creative attributes (Gen. 1; Ps. 33:6, 9). In the New Testament period it was personified (Wisd. of Sol. 7:24–26; 18:15–16) and known by some (e.g., Philo) as the immanent power of God creatively at work in the world. John identifies Jesus Christ as this Word. And as such John can attribute to him various divine functions such as creation (vv. 3, 10) and the giving of life (v. 4).

But John goes further. He is ready to infer some personal identity between the Logos and God. "And the Word *was* God" (v. 1). Attempts to detract from this literal translation for grammatical reasons (e.g., "the word was a god," or "divine," etc.) run aground when we consider the number of other times such a divine ascription is given to Jesus: he employs the divine Old Testament title I AM (8:24, 28, 58, etc.); he is one with God (10:30); and he is even addressed by Thomas in the Gospel's final scene as "my Lord and my God" (20:28).

The entry of the Logos into the world (the incarnation) is described as light shining in darkness (v. 5). Even though John the Baptist's testimony was clear (vv. 6–9), still Jesus experienced rejection (vv. 10–11). But there is more. The darkness is hostile. There is enmity. John 1:5 says that the "darkness has not overcome [the light]." The Greek term *katalambanō*, translated "overcome" (RSV; cf. NIV understood), means "seize with hostile intent" (cf. 8:3, 4; Mark 9:18). The hostility of the darkness points to the cross. But as the Book of Glory (13:1–

4. G. E. Ladd, *A Theology of the New Testament* (Grand Rapids: Eerdmans, 1974), 252.

20:31) shows, the power of darkness will not prevail.

John indicates, however, that the light has its followers; Jesus has his disciples (vv. 12, 13). Even though his own people—adherents to Judaism—spurned his message, those who did receive him obtained power to become God's children. Verses 12–13 anticipate the story of Nicodemus (3:1–21), in which this rebirth is explored. A careful reading of 1 John shows that "child of God," "rebirth," and "born of God" were commonplace names describing Johannine disciples (1 John 3:2, 9; 4:4, 7, 12–13). In other words there will be a powerful transformation of those who embrace this light. In the upper room Jesus will draw out the implications: this power will come about through the Spirit who will quicken each believer (14:15–31).

The prologue's finale is found in verses 14–18. John sums up in fresh language what has already been said. Now the abstract thought of light and darkness gives way to concrete Old Testament images. John 1:14 is one of the most important verses in the Bible. The Word did not just appear to be human; *the Word became flesh.* This assertion stunned the Greek mind for whom the separation of the divine spirit and the mundane world (Gr. *sarx,* flesh) was an axiom of belief. But the second phrase is equally stunning for the Jew. This Word dwelt (*skēnoō*) among us and revealed his glory (*doxa*). John uses Old Testament terms of the dwelling (lit. tabernacling) of God with his people. The tabernacle (cf. Exod. 25:8–9; Zech. 2:10) was the dwelling-place of God. Now *Jesus* is the locus of God's dwelling. Hence, the glory of God, once restricted to the tabernacle (Exod. 40:34), is now visible in Christ. The Old Testament contrast with Jesus is extended to Moses (John 1:17–18) while the benefits of their covenants are compared. Moses gave law; Jesus brought grace. Moses' request to see God was denied (Exod. 33:20; cf. Deut. 4:12); but Jesus has come to us from the very heart of the Father (John 1:18). The authority of his revelation is that much greater (cf. Heb. 3:1–6).

II. The Book of Signs (1:19–12:50)

The Book of Signs chronicles Jesus' public ministry within Israel. It begins with the traditional synoptic starting place (John the Baptist) and concludes with Jesus in Jerusalem at his final Passover. Throughout the narrative Jesus presents himself to Judaism through a series of miracles and compelling discourses, but in the end finds rejection. Messianic fulfillment is a prominent motif. Jesus' messiahship is shown to be the fulfillment of the principal festivals and institutions of Judaism. But since the Jews fail to grasp the message of Jesus' signs, John shows us who will: the Greeks. The book closes with Jesus' final plea to Judaism and a picture of eager Greeks imploring Philip, "Sir, we would like to see Jesus" (12:21).

A. The testimony of John the Baptist (1:19–51). The opening frame establishes two points: first, it clarifies the relation between Jesus and John the Baptist; second, it provides a study in the nature of conversion and true discipleship. It is, however, a literary unit as the sequence of days makes clear (1:29, 35, 43). In each successive day, interest shifts from John to Jesus. John's disciples even become Jesus' disciples. The section is closely tied to the unit on the Baptist in 3:22–36 where again John is demoted and Jesus is elevated. The entire section may be, as 1:19 indicates, "the testimony of John."

The Gospel assumes that we know something already about John the Baptist's ministry at the Jordan River. No introduction is given. Instead we listen as priests and Levites (specialists in ritual purification) question John about his identity and work (**1:19–28**). The Baptist makes three specific denials: he is not the Messiah (v. 20; cf. Luke 3:15). Neither is he Elijah (v. 21). Jesus elsewhere indicates that John does fulfill Elijah's spiritual role as messianic forerunner (cf. Matt. 11:14 with Mal. 4:5). Apparently John needs to deny a material identification with Elijah in order to distinguish himself further from Christ. Lastly, John is not the Prophet (v. 21). This no doubt is the messianic prophet like Moses described in Deuteronomy 18:15–18. "Prophet" will later become a title for Jesus (John 6:14; 7:40).

But if John is none of these popular eschatological figures, who is he? What is he doing? The first question (vv. 22–23) is answered from Isaiah 40:3. He is a herald, a forerunner (cf. Mark 1:1–3). The second (vv. 24–27) is also anticipatory: his water baptism will be overshadowed by the appearance of a "greater one" who will baptize in Spirit (v. 33; cf. Mark 1:7f.).

The denials of the Baptist are now complete and the way is clear for true testimony to Jesus to begin (**1:29–34**). Note that this is not a narrative of Jesus' baptism, but a testimony, an account in John's own words confessing the identity of Jesus. That Jesus is announced as "the Lamb of God" is striking (v. 29). This no doubt should be understood as the sacrificial Passover lamb of Exodus 12 (cf. Isa. 53:7). Later the Gospel will fully employ this imagery when Jesus is sacrificed on the cross at Passover (19:14, 36).

The chief announcement of John the Baptist

centers on the eminence of Jesus. Jesus is superior to John inasmuch as he "was before [him]" (v. 30; cf. 1:15). It would not be unlikely if this included the thought of Jesus' anointing with the Spirit (vv. 32–33). This was the principal event at the Jordan. John's account of this differs from the Synoptics in one respect: two times John remarks that the Spirit descended and *remained* on Jesus. This permanent anointing stands in stark contrast to the temporary anointing of the Old Testament prophets. This permanency was central to the Jewish depiction of the Messiah (Isa. 42:1; 11:2; cf. Test. Levi 18:6–7).

The testimony of John continues as he now directs his disciples to follow Jesus (**1:35–42**). This section and the next model for us the true character of discipleship. First, disciples must follow Jesus (vv. 37f., 43); they must "come and see" (vv. 39, 46), experiencing for themselves the truth of Christ. And then they must go and bring others: Andrew finds his brother Simon (v. 41) and Philip finds Nathanael (v. 45). Second, we read a roll call of titles for Jesus from 1:35–51—Lamb of God (v. 36), Rabbi (v. 38), Messiah/Christ (v. 41), Jesus of Nazareth, son of Joseph (v. 45), Son of God (v. 49), King of Israel (v. 49), and Son of man (v. 51). Disciples must know whom they follow.

In 1:35–42 John the Baptist sees Jesus and repeats the identification given at Jesus' baptism (vv. 36, 29). He then ushers his disciples into Jesus' company. The language employed here is important. The first question of the disciples, "Where are you *staying*?" (v. 38) employs a vital word for John. "Staying" or "abiding" (Gk. *menō*) appears throughout the Gospel (forty times) and describes the union of the believer with Christ. (See 8:31, 35; 14:10; 15:4ff., etc.) Hence Andrew and an unnamed disciple (John?) abide with Christ.

On day three we meet the first apostles who follow Christ. Now we learn that Jesus has other followers too who are not yet apostles and who share a similar intimate discipleship (**1:43–51**). From Perea Jesus moves to Galilee and calls more followers. Philip, a native of Bethsaida (east of Capernaum), discovers the Messiah but the focus of the narrative turns to his immediate response. He finds Nathanael and extends to him the same words used by Jesus for Andrew in 1:39, "Come and see" (v. 46). Disciples must therefore make more disciples in the manner of Jesus.

To be a disciple means coming under the authority of Jesus. In 1:42 Peter is renamed. Now in 1:47–50 Nathanael experiences Jesus' prophetic power over his life. But this power is minor in comparison to what Jesus will display. The description of Jesus in 1:51 may be based on Jacob's vision in Genesis 28:12. Jesus is the locus of God's self-revelation on earth. In this regard, this final verse reiterates the affirmation of the prologue: Jesus is the full revelation of the glory and presence of God.

B. Jesus and the institutions of Judaism (2:1–4:54). The sequence of stories which hallmark the beginning of Jesus' public ministry all share a similar theme: messianic replacement and abundance. In chapters 2–4 Jesus is compared with important institutions and, in each instance, his presence makes them obsolete. (The same will be true of 5:1–10:42. There Jesus will appear during the major Jewish festivals and demonstrate his authority.) This theme is similar to the synoptic parables of replacement: new wine breaks old wineskins and new patches cannot be affixed to old cloth (Matt. 9:16–17). So too the former institutions of Judaism cannot sustain the impact of Christ's coming.

The section has an interesting literary division. The first story is set in Cana of Galilee and so is the final miracle (the healing of the official's son). The wedding miracle is called "Jesus' first sign" (2:11) while the closing healing miracle is termed "Jesus' second sign" (4:54). These literary indicators define the limits of the section. Then in 5:1 we at once learn that Jesus is on his way to a "feast of the Jews."

We know that Jesus is already in the region of Galilee (1:43) and the best identification for Cana is Khirbet Qana, nine miles north of Nazareth. John indicates that Jesus arrives here on "the third day" (2:1). This may refer to traveling time to Cana or fit the day sequence in chapter 1. In the latter case, some believe that John is chronicling the momentous first week of Jesus (a new week of creation?). Cana is a climax of sorts: here the disciples believed in him for the first time because Jesus manifested his glory (v. 11).

Weddings (**2:1–12**) were festive events in first-century Judaism and entire communities participated. Since Galilee is Jesus' home, it is not surprising that he is in attendance. When the wine fails (v. 3) Jesus' mother draws him in. His response in verse 4 is not meant to give offense. "Woman" was a customary polite address (cf. Matt. 15:28; Luke 13:12). Jesus will use it again when he is on the cross (19:26). In verse 4 "What have you to do with me?" (RSV) is an awkward English rendering of a Semitic idiom meaning, "How can this affair concern me?"

The miraculous solution is described in some detail (vv. 6–9) and like synoptic miracle stories there is a climaxing testimony, in this case on the lips of the steward (v. 10). Six stone jars each holding twenty or thirty gallons are filled with water and this in turn supplies the wedding with an enormous quantity of wine (about 175 gallons).

Some degree of symbolism can be affirmed here without denigrating the historical character of the event. This is Jesus' first public sign and the key to interpreting it is Jesus' messianic announcement and abundance. The wedding banquet was an Old Testament symbol of the Messiah's arrival (cf. Isa. 54:4–8; 62:4–5), which Jesus often employed (Matt. 22:1–14; Mark 2:19–20). The Old Testament also described this messianic era with the image of an abundance of wine (Jer. 31:12; Hos. 14:7; Amos 9:13–14). Jewish apocalyptic taught that the wine would give its fruit 10,000 fold (2 Bar. 29:5; see also 1 Enoch 10:19). Therefore Jesus announced himself with powerful eschatological metaphors.

But for Messiah to come (and this is the unexpected news) the old institutions must pass away. Jesus enacts his first miracle on a religious device of Judaism. What were these jars? The Mishnah indicated that stone jars could be used as permanent vessels for purification (ritual washing). Jesus has transformed their contents. In the previous chapter John the Baptist had offered a ritual washing, but he announced a more powerful baptism to come (1:33). Jesus has now taken up the necessary symbols as the fulfiller of Judaism.

The story is framed by two remarkable statements: "They have no more wine" (v. 3) and "you have saved the best [wine] till now" (v. 10). This is a poignant commentary on the bankruptcy of Judaism and the arrival of Jesus. The new wine is abundantly superior to the old. But moreover, that which contained the old wine must pass away.

From here Jesus travels with his family (cf. Mark 6:3) to Capernaum, a village on the north shore of the Sea of Galilee. According to the Synoptics this was an important center of activity for Jesus in Galilee.

Pilgrimage played an important role in the life of every Jewish family. Passover was one such pilgrimage festival in which Jewish families traveled to Jerusalem for worship. Hence Jesus travels from Galilee to Judea. The story of the temple cleansing (**2:13–25**) provides us with one of the closest synoptic/Johannine parallels (cf. Matt. 21:12–13; Mark 11:15–17; Luke 19:45–46). Aside from its chronological placement (the Synoptics have it at the end of Jesus' ministry), the stories are strikingly alike. Some would urge that they narrate the same event.

Jesus is offended by two things that he witnessed. First, the selling of sacrificial animals (v. 14) was necessary for worship. However, it may be that this usually took place in the Jerusalem market area east of the city in the Kidron Valley. Obviously the high priest Caiaphas had brought the commercial enterprise into the court of the Gentiles. Second, money changers converted pagan coinage (with imperial images) for acceptable currency in order for Jewish men to pay their half-shekel annual tax (cf. Matt. 17:27). The cacophony of noise and the spirit of commercial self-interest had little to do with the purposes of the season. In response Jesus drives out these merchants with a whip (v. 15), but John rightly adds that it was simply cord, for genuine weapons were prohibited by the temple police.

Again we find here the themes of messianic announcement and replacement. In the Old Testament the prophets linked the ultimate renewal of the temple with the eschatological day of the Lord (Isa. 56:7; Mal. 3:1). Jesus' rebuke in John 2:16 reflects this and stems from Zechariah 14:21. This is why in 2:18 those who witness this demand a sign—some justification. They recognize the messianic importance of the act. But Jesus' response picks up another line of Old Testament thought: in the day of the Lord a *new* temple would be built (Ezek. 40–46; Tob. 14:5; Qumran) and this temple would be Jesus' body (John 2:21). This reiterates what we have already seen (cf. 1:14, 51), namely, that this sacred Jewish institution would find a dramatic new replacement (cf. 4:21–24).

Of course it would be difficult for the citizens of Jerusalem to understand this. The Jews think that Jesus must mean a refurbishing of Herod's temple begun in 20 B.C. (v. 20). Even the disciples' comprehension has to await the resurrection (v. 22). Nevertheless Jesus' words will be remembered, twisted, and used to condemn him at his trial (Mark 14:58).

It is interesting to compare these first two signs of Jesus in Cana and Jerusalem. In Galilee Jesus finds faith (2:11), but in Jerusalem while some believe (v. 23), the Jews there generally lack comprehension. Throughout the Gospel Jesus will find faith in Galilee and conflict in Judea. Indeed, it will be in Jerusalem where he will be killed. Verses 23–25 describe the unsatisfactory nature of the Jerusalem reception and go on to generalize about the shortcomings of man (v. 25). They also serve as a transitional section for the next chapter. Nicodemus will be one such man: he has witnessed the signs and come forward (3:2), but he fails to apprehend who Jesus is and to believe.

At first glance the section on Jesus and the new birth (3:1–36) seems to consist of two disparate parts: the dialogue with Nicodemus (vv. 1–21) and the critical comparison of Jesus and the Baptist (vv. 22–36). While numerous plausible theories have offered to relocate the latter section (generally after 1:19–34), they are difficult to support. Note, for instance, how in 3:22 Jesus moves "into the land of Judea" when he had just been in Jerusalem, a city of Judea (2:13, 23). Nevertheless a connecting thread may unite the chapter. On a literary level, Jesus now dislocates yet another office in Judaism, the rabbinate. Nicodemus's ability as a teacher is faulty (v. 10), while Jesus is addressed as "rabbi" (v. 2). On another level, the subject which the teacher Nicodemus cannot penetrate (rebirth, 3:3) is really center stage. In 1:33 we learned about a new baptism in Spirit which would come with the work of Jesus; in 3:1ff. it is explicated. If "born of water and spirit" (v. 5) does refer to baptism (Jesus' baptism; Christian baptism), then the section on the relative merits of John's baptism (3:22–36) naturally follows. It extends the discussion broached in 1:33 in that Jesus' baptizing work exceeds that of John. In 4:1–3 we even find the only New Testament reference to Jesus baptizing. And here "Jesus was gaining and baptizing more disciples than John" (4:1).

While Jesus is in Jerusalem at Passover (2:13) a Pharisee named Nicodemus comes to him at night (**3:1–21**). His approach is well intentioned, but his spiritual perception is inadequate. (It may be that "night" in v. 1 is symbolic; for Nicodemus is not "of the light"; see 1:4–5; 3:19f.; 9:4; 11:10; 13:30; etc.) He reappears in 7:50 at a Sanhedrin meeting giving advice sympathetic to Jesus' case. And in 19:39 his sympathies become explicit: he joins Joseph of Arimathea in burying and anointing the body of Christ.

This passage introduces the first major discourse so typical of Jesus' teaching in the fourth Gospel. In this and other such discourses, questions posed to Jesus enable him to transpose the topic to a higher plateau (e.g., chap. 14). Earthly understanding must give way to spiritual understanding. Here Nicodemus makes three comments (vv. 2, 4, 9) each of which Jesus greets with a response (vv. 3, 5–8, 10–15).

When Nicodemus inquires about the character of Jesus' signs, Jesus replies that rebirth is a prerequisite for seeing the kingdom of God (vv. 3, 7). Nicodemus's misunderstanding (v. 4) turns on a literal understanding of the Greek phrase *born again* (*gennēthē anōthen*). How can anyone be born twice? Yet *anōthen* can also mean "from above" (a local vs. a temporal rendering) and this is Jesus' intended meaning. Typically, the Johannine Jesus employs a play on words. *Anōthen* in John takes the local sense as is evident from its use in 3:31 (also 19:11, 23). In other words, entrants to the kingdom must be born from "above" or that place from which Jesus originates. The Christian, as it were, must become like Jesus who is "from above" (v. 31). The theological language for this is brought out in 3:5–8. This birth must consist of water (repentance, baptism, or the ministration of John) and the Spirit (the eschatological endowment brought by Jesus, 7:39; 20:22). This experience cannot be quantified but, like the wind, emerges under the power of God (v. 8).

The deficits in Nicodemus's understanding are common to those who cannot understand heavenly things (v. 12; cf. 1 Cor. 2:1–16). Before Pentecost this was true of the disciples too (cf. 2:22). But the key that will unlock the problem is the complex of events which includes Christ's death, resurrection, and ascension (vv. 13–15)—in Johannine language, Christ's glorification. It is the result of this work that will release the Spirit (7:37–39).

It is difficult to know whether 3:16–21 continues the words of Jesus or represents the comments of the evangelist (see NIV n. on v. 21). The same holds for 3:31–36. Are these the words of the Baptist or the author? Some scholars urge that a certain symmetry should be seen: Jesus' and John's statements are followed by the beloved disciple's additional remarks (3:16–21 follows vv. 1–15 as 3:31–36 follows vv. 22–30).

In 3:16–21 we learn how this gift of spiritual birth offered to Nicodemus might be appropriated. Belief in the Son gains eternal life (vv. 15, 16, 18). Disbelief gains judgment and condemnation (vv. 18, 19, 35). This sums up the world-view characteristic of John's Gospel: one is either attracted to or repulsed by the light (vv. 19–21); one either pursues truth or evil. There is no equivocation here. Yet the coming of the Son was not inspired by a desire to condemn—it stemmed from love (v. 16). But judgment was an inevitable result. Light brings exposure (v. 20): it reveals who we really are.

Is the prospect of Jesus truly better? Evidence from the New Testament and the first century indicates that John the Baptist had followers who did not go over to Jesus (cf. Acts 19:1–7). The scene now shifts to the work of the Baptist with his disciples (**3:22–36**) and it makes one point: Jesus' baptism *is* superior: "He must become greater; I must become less" (3:30).

The scene is set at the Jordan River where John is at work (vv. 22–24). A minor crisis arises when it is observed that Jesus' following is exceeding that of John (v. 26). The transition was breeding animosity. But John the Baptist responds with a series of testimonies: the providence of God determines the success of ministry (v. 27) and, as he had made clear at the outset (1:29), Jesus is the Christ and bridegroom (vv. 28–29); John is merely his advocate.

These concrete expressions (echoing the synoptic tradition) now expand into abstract statements in 3:31–36. The superiority of Jesus is grounded in his superior heritage: he is from above (v. 31). The Son has come from the Father, but the Baptist belongs to the earth. John the Baptist speaks "as one from the earth" (v. 31) but the Son utters the words of God (v. 34). Therefore there is an inestimable difference. Once more, the Spirit provides the major difference: out of his love for his Son, God has given to him "the Spirit without limit" (34f.). Jesus' possession of the Spirit supplies him with superior authority and enables him to offer new birth to men like Nicodemus.

Jesus' departure from the Jordan River is prompted by his concern that the Pharisees are viewing him as supplanting John the Baptist's ministry (4:1; cf. 3:22–36). Would the hostility toward John now be aimed at Jesus? In the Synoptics, it is John's arrest that brings Jesus into Galilee (Mark 1:14). The same is true in the fourth Gospel. Jesus avoids incrimination stemming from his association with John. To be sure, Jesus' ministry was similar to that of John: both men employed baptism (4:1–2). Even in Galilee after the death of John, Herod Antipas will fear that Jesus may be "John come back from the dead" (Mark 6:14ff.).

The usual route from the Jordan River to Galilee traversed the rift valley to Scythopolis (Beth-shean) and then went northeast into the valleys of lower Galilee. Instead, Jesus climbs into the Judean mountains and follows the ridge route north through the tribal territories of Benjamin and Ephraim, and on into Samaria (4:5–6). The precise location of the city of Sychar remains uncertain; however, it is probably Shechem (so identified by Jerome and the Syriac) inasmuch as the traditional site for Jacob's Well is 250 feet from there. Further, Shechem is on the road from Judea to Galilee.

Jesus' conversation with the woman of Samaria (**4:1–42**) is striking on several counts. First, the enmity between Jew and Samaritan is well established (see Luke 10:29–37) and stands behind the woman's words in 4:9. Moreover, few Jewish rabbis would initiate open conversations with women as Jesus does (see 4:27). Nevertheless, Jesus does so and the ensuing dialogue harmonizes with the theological developments we have seen thus far: Jesus overturns the sanctity of an important religious institution. In this case it is the sacred well of Jacob. At Cana (2:1–11), Jerusalem (3:5), the Jordan (3:22–26), and here, water serves a symbolic role depicting the older institution which needs the messianic gift of Christ. As water became wine (2:9) so now well water will be replaced by living water. John's baptism must be replaced by that of Jesus (3:30; 4:1). What is this gift that makes all else obsolete? It is the eschatological Spirit promised by Jesus (3:5). This is what will bring power to John's baptism. The same is true in Samaria. John's only other reference to living water is in 7:38–39, where it is defined as the Spirit. The Spirit is explicitly emphasized even as the dialogue develops (4:23–24).

The dialogue with the woman enjoys a literary structure much like that in chapter 3: inquiries by the woman based on a misunderstanding of Jesus' spiritual intent serve to transport the discussion to deeper levels of thought. But while Nicodemus never reenters the scene to issue his response (suggesting no faith in Jerusalem?), things are different in Samaria. We read a series of improving titles for Jesus ("Sir," vv. 11, 14; "Prophet," v. 19; "Christ," vv. 25, 29; "Savior of the world," v. 42); the woman's testimony converts many in the village (v. 39); and Jesus remains with them for two days before going north into Galilee (v. 43).

In verses 7–15 Jesus discusses living water. This section (like the next) introduces an "earthly" subject and through the questions of the woman leads to a spiritual message. Jesus' request for a drink of water is rebuffed (v. 9), but he issues a challenge to the woman: if she knew who Jesus was, she would see that he is the supplier of living water (v. 10). A second round (vv. 11–15) turns on her misunderstanding: Jesus cannot supply water because he has no access to the well. But here at last Jesus' clarification unfolds his meaning. His water ends *all* thirst and provides eternal life (v. 14). It is the Spirit. (Cf. this discourse with that on living bread in John 6:35ff.) Marvelously the woman asks to drink.

In the next section Jesus' focus is upon true worship (vv. 16–26). When the light enters the darkness of the world, it necessarily brings judgment (3:19f.). Before the gifts of God can be obtained, the soul must be cleansed of sin. Jesus probes the moral life of the woman (vv. 16–18), but she does not flee—she admits to Jesus' prophetic powers (v. 19). She chooses to remain in the light; yet now she hopes that the religious institutions of her acquaintance will free her from Jesus' scrutiny. Mount Gerizim (a mountain towering over the well) was the Samaritan holy place; Jesus is obviously a Jew who venerates Jerusalem. But Jesus dismisses these institutions too (as he dismissed the well): again the new dimension that transcends these is the Spirit (vv. 23–24). This spiritual worship is not worship in the inner aesthetic recesses of man: it is worship animated by God's own eschatological Spirit. Jesus' challenge and offer in each of these scenes is the same. Yet here we move a step further; worship must also be in "truth." It must affirm the realities of truth (Jesus is the truth, 14:6), be doctrinally informed (cf. 1 John 4:1–3), and directed toward Jesus.

Now Jesus takes up the subject of true nourishment (vv. 27–38). When the disciples return from the village (see 4:8) the woman departs in haste, leaving her jar behind (v. 28). In the light of Jesus' offer is it now obsolete? Her positive report in Shechem ("Can this be the Christ?") leads many to make their own inquiries at the well. (Note the parallel on evangelism and discipleship in 1:35ff. with Andrew and Philip.)

Not even the disciples are exempt from misunderstanding Jesus. Jesus had sent them out for food (4:8) yet now when Jesus is encouraged to eat he says that he has food enough (v. 32). The disciples' misunderstanding (v. 33) propels the discourse forward (vv. 34–38). His nourishment is found in accomplishing his urgent mission.

The woman's testimony bears fruit (vv. 39–42). And yet those who are invited to come out to see Jesus for themselves (as were Peter and Nathanael in 1:35–50) must obtain their own faith. Jesus remains in Samaria for two days and many in the village believe (v. 42).

The miracle in which the official's son is healed (**4:43–54**) brings Jesus back to Cana, the town which introduced this section of the Gospel (2:1–12). In both instances the sign of Jesus is numbered (2:11; 4:54) and his work is greeted with belief. Notice how there is a progression as Jesus moves from Jerusalem (chap. 3) to Cana (chap. 4). In Jerusalem Jesus cannot trust men (2:24) and Nicodemus comes making secretive inquiries at night (3:1f.). Then in Samaria Jesus is received eagerly (4:39–42) while in Galilee the enthusiasm for him is open (v. 45). The transition from Jerusalem to Galilee is a transition from unbelief to belief; from darkness to light. The proverb of verse 44 (used in the Synoptics to refer to Nazareth; cf. Mark 6:4) is applied here to Jerusalem, the city which kills the prophets (Luke 13:33; cf. John 4:19; 6:14).

The healing miracle finds a close parallel in the synoptic cure of the centurion's servant (Matt. 8:4–13) and the story of the Syrophoenician woman (Mark 7:24–30). Both are cures effected at a distance. In John the miracle serves to display the new life promised by Jesus in the preceding discourses (3:16; 4:14, 36). In Cana, as in Samaria, Jesus hopes to inspire belief (v. 50) and in this case, the official's son is saved (v. 51). The Johannine account underscores one feature of the miracle: Jesus' word is powerful and effectual. The very hour of healing is the hour of Jesus' utterance (v. 52). This combination of miracle and belief (vv. 50, 53) is what distinguishes the Johannine term *sign.* The powerful works of Jesus are designed to evoke a response, to reveal who Jesus is. They are signs that lead elsewhere—to faith. This is the intent of the signs in Cana, Jerusalem, Samaria, and again in Cana. This is the aim that John has even for his reader of the "Book of Signs." "Many people saw the miraculous signs he was doing and believed in his name" (2:23).

C. Jesus and the festivals of Judaism (5:1–10:42). This major section now compares Jesus with the festivals of Judaism in much the same way that the earlier unit (2:1–4:54) focused on Jewish institutions. Again, themes of messianic replacement and abundance will appear. However, now the subtleties of the comparison will become vital. In each instance, Jesus is described in the context of the festival (Sabbath, Passover, Tabernacles, Dedication) and as his discourse expands, elements from the festival will be swept up and given fresh definition. Jesus is their replacement! Or better, veiled within the liturgical and theological themes of the festival are symbols that point to Jesus, symbols whose true meanings are satisfied in Christ.

All of the Book of Signs (chaps. 1–12) might be viewed as giving the reader evidence—judicial evidence—for the truth of Christ's claims. Indeed, the word *sign* (Gk. *sēmeion*) may be a judicial term for evidence. So too we have been introduced to witnesses who substantiate Jesus' case: John the Baptist ("I have borne witness," 1:34), the Spirit (1:33; 3:32–34), and the Samaritan woman ("many believed because of the woman's testimony," 4:39). In chapter 5 Jesus will be forced to itemize his witnesses (vv. 31–40).

This forensic motif will become prominent in chapters 5–10. The trial of Jesus which actually commences in chapter 18 is begun already as interrogators in Jerusalem approach Jesus, examining his case. In virtually every chapter the "Jews" play this role. They assess Jesus' case, weigh the evidence, and make a judgment. This fascinating literary format places the reader in an interesting position. He is forced to evaluate the evidence and the testimony for himself. The first witness is John the Baptist (1:19ff.) and the section closes (10:40–42) with a final reference to the Baptist's testimony and the value of Jesus' signs. By 10:42 the majority of the witnesses, the evidence, and the signs are in. The jury (the reader) may deliberate.

Jesus and the Sabbath (**5:1–47**) receive prominent attention in the next section. A feast now prompts Jesus to return to Jerusalem (v. 1). Three pilgrimage feasts were known at this time: Passover, Pentecost, and Tabernacles, and scholars debate which could be meant here. The text is unclear, but at least it serves to introduce us to the literary motif of Jewish feasts that will follow. In this chapter the festival is the weekly Sabbath, a day of worship and rest. Jesus works a healing miracle (vv. 2–9), conflict follows (vv. 10–18), and then Jesus provides a major discourse explaining the authority of his work and his divine identity (vv. 19–47).

The location of the pool (v. 2) has had a history of controversy until archaeologists excavated it in the courtyard of St. Anne's Church in Jerusalem. The pool's name, Bethesda (see NIV n.), is still unclear since manuscripts reflect numerous readings (v. 2). John notes that various people with infirmities waited at the pool hoping to benefit from healing power associated with the site. This has led some scholars to see in the archaeological remains evidence for a healing sanctuary near the pool. Jesus, however, ignores the pool's supposed powers and with a word heals the lame man (vv. 8–9). But as with so many other healing stories in the Synoptics (cf. Mark 3:1–6), it was the Sabbath and this arouses objections among the Jewish leaders.

When the lame man carries his bed he violates a well-known Sabbath prohibition (Mish. *Shabbath* 7:2). But since he does not know Jesus (Matt. 5:11, 13) he cannot indicate to his accusers who directed him thus. This comes later in the temple (v. 14) when Jesus and the man meet again. Does 5:14 teach that there was a connection between this man's sin and his infirmity? The New Testament elsewhere avoids this conclusion (see John 9:3; Luke 13:1–5). Although a causal relationship may not necessarily exist between personal suffering and sin, sin may result in human misery and penalties (cf. Rom. 1:27).

The importance of verses 16–18 cannot be missed. For the first time we learn of the Jewish hostilities toward Jesus and the plan to kill him (v. 18). The judicial theme comes out in 5:16 in the word *persecute* (*diōkō*), the grammar of which indicates a protracted period of persecution. God and Jesus form the substance of the following discourse. Jesus justifies working on the Sabbath because of his special relation with God (v. 17): if God can work, so can Jesus. This is a dangerous defense. Could it be proven?

The subject of Jesus' divine authority (5:19–47) is one of the most exalted discourses in the Gospel. Here Jesus makes explicit claims to divinity inasmuch as he associates himself directly with God. The discourse consists of three units.

First, Jesus describes his work as continuing the work of the Father (vv. 19–30). While prohibiting human labor on the Sabbath, the rabbis agree that God sustains the natural processes of life (birth, death, rainfall, etc.). Sovereignty over life was chief among these divine tasks. Jesus justifies his labors by assuming divine prerogatives (v. 21). (Note how in John 4:46–54 Jesus gave life to a young boy.) In addition, judgment (which condemns or justifies) belonged solely to God. This authority now belongs to Jesus too (vv. 22–24) who exercises it not only in the present age (v. 24) but in the future eschatological age (vv. 25–30).

Second, Jesus buttresses his case by introducing witnesses for his defense (vv. 31–40). In Jewish law one witness (even a man witnessing of himself [vv. 30–31]) was insufficient either to condemn or confirm a charge (Deut. 17:6; Mish. *Kethuboth* 2:9). Therefore this section answers the legal complaint: four witnesses are ushered forward. John the Baptist (John 5:33–35), the mighty works or signs of Jesus (v. 36), God the Father (vv. 37–38), and the Scriptures (vv. 39–40) all substantiate Jesus' claims.

But what is the root cause of Jesus' rejection? John 5:41–43 provides an analysis and prophetic critique. The problem is not intellectual—it centers instead on inner disposition. "You do not have the love of God in your hearts" (v. 42). Jesus is angered not because they refuse to glorify him (v. 41) but because they refuse to glorify God (v. 44). The desire for human praise, affirmation, and prestige has crippled them and they cannot love God (v. 44a). Human noteworthies are esteemed (v. 43b), but the Son who bears divine credentials is rejected. The very Scripture used to condemn Jesus will soon bring the severest judgment upon its possessors (vv. 45–47).

Jesus and Passover are the focus of **6:1–71.** The scene now shifts to Galilee where in the springtime festival of Passover (v. 4) Jesus miraculously feeds a multitude of five thousand people. This is the only miracle of Jesus that appears in all four Gospels; it must have been deemed very important by the early church (Mark 6:31–44; Matt. 14:13–21; Luke 9:10–17). John's Gospel follows the synoptic account closely. But John also echoes Matthew and Mark in that the feeding miracle is followed by the story of Jesus walking on the sea (vv. 16–21; cf. Matt. 14:22–33; Mark 6:45–52).

But this is where the comparisons end. Two typically Johannine literary features which we have witnessed elsewhere stand out. First, the symbolic elements of the festival are emphasized in order to highlight their christological significance. Passover spoke of Moses who not only fed the Israelites in the wilderness (Exod. 16:4ff.) but became the ideal messianic figure in Judaism. Jesus is therefore depicted as the prophet like Moses (v. 14; cf. Deut. 18:15ff.) who exceeds the manna miracle of Moses (vv. 30–34, 48–51). Second, the Johannine discourse is the vehicle used to advance this comparison. When questioned by the Jews, Jesus presses home the spiritual meaning of this event in what may be the longest public discourse in the Gospel (vv. 25–65).

The Sea of Galilee was often called the Sea of Tiberias in honor of Herod Antipas's founding of the new provincial center of Tiberias in A.D. 26 (cf. 21:1). The Passover is probably a year after the one mentioned in 2:13. During the intervening year Mark notes that John the Baptist had been arrested and by the time of the feeding of the five thousand he had been executed (Mark 6:14ff. where the Baptist is beheaded). This lapse of time explains Jesus' growing popularity (vv. 2–3).

Jesus' charge to Philip to feed the people (v. 5) recalls the conversation of 4:31–38 in Samaria. Spiritual food is at issue. It is a test (v. 6) because Jesus needs to elevate the disciples' consciousness as to the manner of his ministry. Nevertheless, misunderstanding ensues (note the motif already in 3:4; 4:11, 33; etc.). Hence, Philip inventories their savings (eight months' wages, v. 7) and Andrew spots a boy with a few provisions (v. 9). John alone records that the boy held barley bread: it was the bread of the poor but symbolically it may recall the great Old Testament feeding miracle of Elisha (2 Kings 4:42). John also notes that it is Jesus who distributes the bread (not the disciples) and that in his prayer of blessing, rather than using the synoptic *eulogeō* (to bless), Jesus gives thanks (Gk. *eucharisteō;* cf. 1 Cor. 11:24). Is this a veiled symbol of the Eucharist or the Lord's Supper? This use of symbolism seems natural to Jesus' teaching in John and in this chapter the eucharistic application will become more explicit (vv. 52–58).

The dangers of Jesus' popularity and the perils of misunderstandings are shown in the crowd's response (v. 14). They have interpreted the sign: Jesus has enacted the "Moses miracle" of Passover. However, Jesus flees (v. 15) because the crowd wishes to force upon him a political definition of messiah ("make him king by force"). Mark records this same crisis: Jesus puts the disciples on a boat and personally disappears into the mountains (Mark 6:45–46).

The destination of the disciples was Capernaum and after they had worked against the wind for hours heading to the fishing village of Peter and Andrew (vv. 16–19), Jesus joined them—walking on the sea. The fear of the disciples indicates the miraculous and incomprehensible nature of the event. Above all, Jesus reveals himself through yet another symbolic expression, "I am" (Gk. *egō eimi*). In the Greek Old Testament the name of God revealed to Moses on Mount Sinai is *egō eimi,* or "I am" (Exod. 3:13f.). John's use of this divine Old Testament title elsewhere for Jesus (8:58; 18:6) may imply its use here. Once the company arrives in Capernaum, Galileans from the earlier site of feeding follow him there and become suspicious because Jesus was not in the boat (vv. 22, 25). Jews from Tiberias likewise search for him and come to Capernaum (v. 23). The zeal of the Galilean Jews is noteworthy (cf. 4:43–45).

In the Capernaum synagogue (v. 59) Jesus provides a full discourse explaining his person and work. Again, the discourse is propelled forward by inquiries (vv. 25, 28, 30, 34, 41, 52), and at each level the revelation of Christ deepens.

Initially the crowds merely possess the surface apprehension of the miracle (v. 25). They must go deeper and unveil the sign for the signs are revelatory. Like the woman needing water (4:7) these people need imperishable food supplying eternal life (v. 27; 4:14). For this food alone they must labor. What then is labor? Faith in Christ (v. 29). But the human impulse is to demand evidence so compelling that we *must* believe. If Jesus is making personal claims on the order of Moses, then his sign must exceed that of Moses (v. 30). In John 6:31 Jesus' response is an intricate Jewish commentary (midrash) based on one or several Old Testament texts: "He gave them bread from heaven to eat" (cf. Exod. 16:4, 15; Ps. 78:24). The true bread they seek is not dependent on Moses (or Judaism): it is whatever God rains upon humans as a gift, and which gives life (v. 33). The Jews here resemble the Samaritan woman inasmuch as they are intrigued: "Lord give us/me this bread/water" (6:34; 4:15).

The divine origin of Jesus is a favorite Johannine theme (3:13–31) and John often ironically presents it in innocent inquiries (7:28, 34–36; etc.). So too the question of 6:25 about Jesus' mysterious appearance in Capernaum goes unanswered because now a theological response is at hand. Jesus is the bread of life that has mysteriously descended (vv. 35, 38). The twin themes of hunger and thirst (cf. chaps. 4, 6) are now satisfied. Belief is still the key (v. 36; cf. v. 29); however, now a new note is struck. God is sovereign over the ministry of Jesus (v. 38) as well as its results (vv. 37, 39, 44). Those whom God calls are effectively called and securely preserved (vv. 39–40; cf. 10:14–18; 17:6). In other words the work of Jesus and the gathering of disciples are both a result of God's perfect will.

From the crowd's point of view this revelation is hard to accept and they murmur (vv. 41–43). Is Jesus not a commonplace citizen of Galilee (cf. Mark 6:1–6)? How can he descend from heaven? But Jesus knows that further explanation will not complete what is lacking. The gift of faith and the ability to apprehend who Christ really is—these are divine things (vv. 44–48). Faith is not merely rational persuasion: it includes the drawing of God (v. 44). To stay in Judaism is death (v. 49) but to consume the bread of life brings life (vv. 50–51).

But a deeper revelation is to come: the bread to be consumed is Jesus' flesh offered in sacrifice (v. 51b). Still, the discourse is urged forward through a literal misunderstanding. How can humans eat his flesh (v. 52)? The following explanation (vv. 53–58) reinforces this thought and draws on images (flesh and blood) which are sacrificial. If symbolism is still at work (as it likely is), the symbols inevitably suggest the elements of the Lord's Supper. It is not the sacrament that gives life, but rather salvation is found in the sacrifice behind it and the faith that it evokes (vv. 35, 40, 47). Outside the Eucharist an admonition to drink blood in any other Jewish setting would be incomprehensible.

But if the descent of Christ gave difficulty to the crowds (vv. 41–42), this deeper teaching causes the disciples to stumble (v. 60). They too murmur (v. 61). Jesus breaks the impasse by showing that literal flesh is not the key; rather, it is the Spirit who conveys life (v. 63). If the Eucharist is still at issue the message is clear: its physical elements "count for nothing" if the Spirit's power is not present.

But to understand this fully takes more than human minds can grasp (vv. 64, 66). Jesus repeats the exhortation given to the crowds in 6:44–47. Penetrating the mysteries of God is also a divine gift (vv. 64–65). The deeper realities offend and here some disciples draw back and abandon Christ (v. 66). But Peter knows that the greatest virtue is to continue embracing Jesus no matter where he might lead (vv. 68–70).

The third feast of Judaism to inspire Johannine interest is the autumn harvest of Tabernacles (7:1–9:41). It joined Passover and Pentecost as a pilgrimage feast and was celebrated on 15 Tishri (September/October), commemorating the end of the harvest field labor (Lev. 23:39). It also recalled Israel's wandering and life in booths (Lev. 23:42–43). Every Jewish male was obligated to attend sometime during the course of seven days of worship and sacrifice (Exod. 23:14–17; Deut. 16:16).

John's interest in Tabernacles (John 7:2, 37) is specialized and builds on the symbolic ceremonies conducted at the temple. Two ceremonies in particular frame Jesus' self-disclosure. Water and light each played a ceremonial role based on eschatological prophecies in Zechariah (see below). In this context Jesus announces that he is the source of "living water" (7:38) and that he is the "light of the world" (8:12). The discourses that follow pick up prior themes (Jesus' authority and origin) and add to the judicial evidence for Jesus' case which the "Book of Signs" has been accumulating. Just as Sabbath (chap. 5) and Passover (chap. 6) became literary springboards to reveal who Jesus is, so now Tabernacles becomes a place where Jesus unveils himself in Jewish imagery.

Jesus' reluctance to return to Judea (**7:1–13**) is understandable when we recall the events of his last visit. The subject of his death arose then (5:16) and it would arise again (7:1, 7, 19). In fact, this would be Jesus' last visit to Jerusalem and in the coming spring he would be crucified. Nevertheless his brothers (cf. 2:12) urge him to go—to make his identity plain (7:3, 4), but their intentions are not in Jesus' interest since, as John states clearly, they "did not believe in him" (v. 5).

Does Jesus deceive them when he says that he will not go to the feast (v. 8) and then he does (v. 10)? (See the NIV n.) The earliest patristic interpreters of John viewed this as a classic case of Jesus' symbolism and its attendant misunderstanding. Jesus' brothers' lack of belief does not give them divine insight; not just anyone can fully comprehend the Son (cf. 6:44). "Going up" (Gk. *anabainō*) elsewhere for Jesus means death, resurrection, and ascension (cf. 20:17). This is why Jesus' "time has not yet come" (vv. 6, 8)—Jesus is sovereign over this death and departure (so 10:17–18). He may attend the feast, but he alone will control the hour of death.

Jesus' arrival is marked by controversy (7:10–13). Judaism is divided (vv. 40–44). This echoes the synoptic picture of Jesus' final days in Jerusalem where Jesus' teachings find both a popular following and the concentrated hatred of the Jewish leadership. It is possible that the Johannine chronology gives the best picture of Jesus' final Judean visit: he came to the city in the autumn, taught in the region during the winter, and was crucified during Passover in the spring.

The now familiar form of the Johannine discourse meets us again at Tabernacles. Questions which essentially misunderstand who Jesus is provoke him to respond. Irony is John's literary device throughout. Here two Jewish objections to Jesus are central to the debate: the authority of Jesus' teaching and the nature of his origin.

Educational standards for rabbis were well established in the first century. Advanced study under a rabbinic scholar (e.g., Paul under Gamaliel) in a school was common. Jesus possessed no such credentials. In effect, the Jews wish to see these and Jesus complies: his diplomas are divine (**7:14–24**). The Synoptics attest to Jesus' uncanny sense of authority (Matt. 7:28f.). Here Jesus explains the source of that authority.

The Jewish notion of authority was specialized. No one possessed *inherent* authority; it was secondary and indirect. Authority was passed down and conferred to the rabbi through ordination. It was as if the authority of Moses was preserved through the generations. And if the chain was broken, authority might be lost. Jesus' problem was this: he was not ordained. On whose shoulders was he standing? What traditions were his? What was the source of his authority? Jesus' answer is clear: his authority stems directly from God (vv. 14–18). Jesus does answer the rabbis in their own categories: his authority was properly conferred to him—but his source of authority was unconventional, to say the least.

In particular Jesus demonstrates his authority by overturning traditional teaching on the Sabbath. Note how in 7:22 the rabbinic concept of tradition and authority is employed. Still, Jesus supplants this with his own instruction: doing good (e.g., healing [5:1–18]) is no violation of the Sabbath. Circumcision is the precedent (7:23).

In chapter 5 Jesus asserted his authority in the same way and it led to speculation about destroying him (5:15f.) on the basis of his claims about himself (5:17–18). The same responses are evidenced here (**7:25–36**). Again an ironic misunderstanding (v. 27) fuels the discourse. Popular Jewish belief held that the Messiah would be concealed until his surprise unveiling to Israel. But the crowds know Jesus' home—he is from Galilee. But this is wrong at a deeper level. Jesus comes from God (vv. 28, 29). John employs the crowd's false perception of Jesus' origin in order to explain Jesus' true origin. In response, the listeners are divided (cf. 6:66–71). Some are hostile (7:30) but others step closer toward faith (v. 31). The light either draws to itself or repels.

Once again the Jewish leadership misunderstands Jesus (vv. 32–36). Jesus is going where they cannot travel. This, of course, is his return to the Father, but they take it to mean his travel to prohibited Gentile lands (v. 35). This illustrates once more the truth that access to divine revelation rests solely in God's sovereign hand (6:44ff.).

On the last feast day, numerous ceremonies involving sacrifice and ritual water could be viewed at the temple. Reading Zechariah 9–14 the priests portrayed how in the eschaton everlasting fountains would flow from Jerusalem (Zech. 13:1; 14:8). Pitchers of water from the Gihon Spring were poured on the altar as the Hallel psalms were sung (Pss. 113–118). This was especially meaningful since at this time of year water was scarce in Israel and people feared drought.

In this setting (**7:37–39**) Jesus sweeps up this symbolism and announces that he is the source of true drink (cf. 4:10). John 7:38 has always posed difficulties for interpreters. The New International Version makes the believer the one in whom living water is flowing. But the Greek can be punctuated another way: "if anyone thirsts, let him come to me; and let him drink, who believes in me." This reading is best. It means that Jesus is the source of the eschatological Tabernacles water. Jesus is the source of the Spirit (v. 39). In 19:34 we may even have a symbol of this flowing when Jesus is glorified (v. 39b).

At the middle of the feast (v. 14) Jesus' revelation is met by a response from the people (vv. 25–31) and the Jewish leadership (vv. 32–36). On this last day the same applies: the people and the leaders are divided (**7:40–52**). Some express incipient faith (vv. 40–41, 46), others show contempt (vv. 41, 44, 47–49). In both cases the issue of Jesus' inferior Galilean origins is a problem (vv. 41–42, 52). In John 1:46 this same concern troubled Nathanael, but there was a difference. He had the courage to "come and see" Jesus for himself. This too is the counsel of Nicodemus in 7:51. A true verdict requires an assessment of the evidence—the facts. This applies to the Sanhedrin. But also in John's judicial literary format, this applies to the reader too. The "Book of Signs" is submitting evidence for our inspection.

The section about the woman caught in adultery (**7:53–8:11**) has always proved difficult. Three questions persist: (1) Is it an insertion into the text of John? Most scholars answer in the affirmative. The best Greek manuscripts do not have it and when they do it appears in a variety of places (e.g., after John 7:36; 21:25; Luke 21:38; or even Luke 24:53). It also has a style unlike that of John and it interrupts the Tabernacles story (see 8:12). If it belonged here, 7:53–8:1 would imply that Jesus was at the Sanhedrin meeting in 7:45–52! (2) Is the story authentically from Jesus? Yes it is. It is similar to synoptic stories of Jewish entrapment climaxed by Jesus' profound pronouncement (8:7). (3) Why was it located here in John? The surrounding discourse (esp. chap. 8) asserts themes which the story illustrates. Jesus judges no one (8:15) and his accusers cannot convict him of sin (8:46).[5]

But these concerns should not deter us from the power and authority of the story. The account has always been a favorite for good reason. The falsehood of the scribes and Pharisees is indicated in two ways. First, the Old Testament law on which they base their charges (v. 5) required the punishment of both parties (Lev. 20:10; Deut. 22:22). The woman's partner is absent. Was she set up? Second, Jewish law carefully stipulated what evidence needed to be in hand. No execution was possible without a solid case. Hence Sanhedrin records indicate judges who would even demand to know the color of the sheets on the bed. The law even distinguished intercourse from preliminary sexual contact. This extensive demand for evidence made adultery charges rare in Judaism since couples would naturally take precautionary measures to conceal themselves. However, the law was aware of men who, rather than divorce their wives for an illicit affair, chose to have her "set up" with witnesses for execution. (If a man thus executed his wife, he became heir to her property; but not if he divorced her.) But this self-interest was deemed morally wrong. If witnesses viewed preliminary coition they were obliged to interrupt the act and prevent the greater crime. If, as we suspect, a man has discharged his wife thus and engineered testimony ("caught in the act," v. 4) to execute her without warning her, the entire affair may appear legal but reeks of injustice. In Jesus' eyes the entire situation would have been reprehensible.

The woman is simply a pawn for the Jewish leaders who wish to play off Jesus' well-known compassion for sinners (even women sinners! cf. Luke 7:36–50) against the demands of the law. They wish to discredit Jesus (v. 6). However Jesus does not deny the woman's sin but he draws her accusers into the circle of condemnation.

John 8:12 returns to the festival setting of Tabernacles (cf. 7:2). The discourse of 7:14–39 focused on one symbolic element: the everlasting temple water of Zechariah. Now Jesus employs a second ritual theme: everlasting light (**8:12–20**). Zechariah also predicted that light would shine forth perpetually from the temple in the eschaton (Zech. 14:6–7). This too was associated with Moses and the wilderness tabernacles: Was not Israel led by a pillar of light (Exod. 13:21)? The Feast of Tabernacles was further celebrated during the autumn equinox recognizing the failing summer sun.

The light ceremonies of the temple were enjoyed by Jerusalem's pilgrims (see Mish. *Sukkah* 5:2–4). Four enormous candlesticks were lit each night illuminating the brilliant temple limestone. It is a tribute to the Jewishness of John that he records an incidental detail of importance. Just as Jesus spoke of messianic fulfillment at the height of the water ceremonies (7:37), now John says that Jesus is in the area of the temple treasury (8:20). The treasury was in the Court of the Women and this was the location of the festival lampstands! Beneath the ritual lights of Tabernacles Jesus announces "I am the light of the world."

"Light" is a frequent metaphor for Jesus in the Gospel (see 1:5; 3:19; 12:46; 1 John 1:5). As light, Jesus discloses the person of God for us; illumines life and gives us meaning and purpose; and also exposes sin, judging those who dwell in darkness. These are persistent themes in the fourth Gospel. Here the Tabernacles pilgrims recognize something authoritative in Jesus' words but demand legal substantiation (8:13–19). This question was posed in chapter 5 at another festival. In the Old Testament (Deut. 17:6) and the Mishnah (*Kethuboth* 2:9) it was held that a man could not be condemned unless two witnesses were present (cf. Matt. 18:16; 2 Cor. 13:1). This was extended to self-testimony. Now, however, Jesus does not inventory his witnesses. He has done this already (5:30–47). The most acute witness to Jesus is the Father (8:18). Jesus' self-witness is also valid because Jesus can assume the authority of the Father, namely, that of judgment (5:22;

5. For a current study on the history of the text, see G. M. Burge, "A Specific Problem in the New Testament Text and Canon: The Woman Caught in Adultery (John 7:53–8:11)," *Journal of the Evangelical Theological Society* 27 (1984): 141–48.

8:16). But since Jesus' opponents do not know the Father, they can hardly perceive the weight of his testimony.

The balance of the Tabernacles discourse now takes on the traditional format we have seen many times. Misunderstanding on the part of Jesus' questioners propels the discourse forward leading Jesus to further self-revelations. Now, however, in Jerusalem, these revelations will become more profound than anything before, and the hostilities more direct. Here (8:59) and at the next feast (Dedication, 10:31, 33) violence seems imminent. If what Jesus says is true, he must be followed or destroyed.

Where is Jesus going (**8:21–30**)? This is the second time this question has been asked (cf. 7:32–36). Earlier Jesus had volunteered no explanation. Now when his audience mistakenly thinks that he will commit suicide (v. 22) Jesus unveils something of his true origins (vv. 23–24). Jesus is returning to the place from which he originated, "from above" (v. 23; cf. 3:31). The divine implications of this are explicit in 8:24. Jesus uses the divine name (*egō eimi*) as a description of his identity. In this round (vv. 24, 28) and the next (8:58) this is the climax of Jesus' testimony. The Greek form of the Hebrew name *Yahweh* (Exod. 3:14) is applied to Christ in an absolute way. Jesus is the great I AM.

Again the crowd misunderstands. "Who are you?" (v. 25). Literally, "I am" (v. 24) requires a predicate. Still they fail to see. Jesus bears the full authority of God! But here at last Jesus indicates when they will perceive: at the cross (v. 28). This is the second passion prediction in John (elsewhere 3:14 and 12:32–34; cf. the same triple prediction in the Synoptics: Mark 8:31; 9:31; 10:33f.). The metaphoric language in all three passion sayings is critical: the cross is the *lifting up* of Jesus (not his destruction). *Lifting up* (Gk. *hypsoō*) is often used for exaltation (Acts 2:33; 5:31). His elevation on Calvary is the initial step in his departure. It is in this process that his divinity will be unmistakable. He will be exalted.

Jesus discusses Abraham's true descendants in **8:31–59.** The implications of this radical teaching are clear and controversy is sure to follow. Jesus is overturning the canons of Jewish religion in their entirety! Knowing him who bears this power and authority will bring true freedom (v. 32). But again, the Jews understand this in earthly terms: they are free since they are not slaves (v. 33). But Jesus is concerned with spiritual slavery (vv. 34–36) and this they cannot perceive.

From here Jesus is engaged in the harshest polemic in the Gospel (vv. 37–59; cf. Matt. 23). Verse 35 is key. If the Jews are not sons in God's household (as Jesus claims) two results follow: their tenure there is limited and they have another father. Being a descendant of Abraham (v. 37) and being a son (vv. 35, 38) are two different things. Jesus claims that lineage has no effect on spiritual status before God (so Paul, Rom. 2:25–29). But their desire to kill Jesus is telling: they have a spiritual father other than God (vv. 38–43). At once they see where Jesus is headed: Jewish lineage is not only at issue (v. 39) but their sonship. Jesus is challenging both. The lethal attack is launched in 8:44. The failure of Jesus' opponents to accept the truth and to hear God's Word (v. 47) has led them to desire Jesus' murder.

Jesus' spiritual critique is now turned back upon him and he is assailed with words not even found in the Synoptics (vv. 48–49). If the Jews here are children of the devil (v. 44), then Jesus is demon-possessed (7:20; 8:48). The nearest parallel to this is in Mark 3:22–27, where Jesus is said to be in league with Satan. But John 8:48 cuts deeper.

Despite this offense Jesus presses home the implications of his divine status. This will bring the final crisis. Jesus and those who believe in him are free from the threat of death (cf. 8:31–33, 51). This is astounding. Does Jesus claim to be greater than Abraham and the other Old Testament heroes who died (vv. 52–53)? If this is Jesus' claim he must be demon-possessed (v. 52). But Jesus takes up the challenge. In 8:56–58 the discourse comes to its climax: Jesus is indeed making personal divine claims vis-à-vis Abraham. Two times in this discourse we hear the refrain, "Who are you?" (v. 25), "Who do you claim to be?" (v. 53). Now the answer is given. Jesus' existence has been eternal—before Abraham—and he is the bearer of the divine name (vv. 24, 28, 58). His attackers understand him fully now and try to kill him for blasphemy, but he slips away (v. 59; cf. 7:44; 8:20).

In John **9:1–41** Jesus brings light to a blind man. Cast in the form of so many synoptic conflict stories, this narrative is closely connected with the previous chapter. We are still at the Tabernacles setting and Jesus is still affirming that he is "the light of the world" (9:5; cf. 8:12). Here the light of Jesus is parabolically viewed in the service of a blind man who gains his vision. But those who live in darkness without this light (the Jewish opponents) cannot see. In the end, the Pharisees are described as blind since they do not possess the spiritual vision or the light of Christ. It is interesting to trace the attitudes of the blind man and the

Pharisees here. The former makes three confessions of ignorance (vv. 12, 25, 36) but in the end is led to true vision and faith (vv. 34–38). The latter make numerous confident statements of knowledge (vv. 16, 24, 29) but are shown to be ignorant (v. 41). The story is symbolic then of spiritual vision and blindness complete with their attendant dispositions (cf. the similar blindness motif in Mark 8:14–30).

The healing in 9:1–34 and the one described in 5:1–18 have much in common (Sabbath, pool, interrogation, conflict). Here too the question of the origin of suffering arises (9:2; 5:14). And again, the link between sin and suffering is opaque. In this case, however, there is no link. It seems that the purpose of the infirmity was the glory of God that would follow the healing.

Healing with mud and saliva was well known among the ancients and Jesus employed it often (cf. Mark 7:33; 8:23). The focus of the healing, however, is its symbolic element: the man is told to wash in the Pool of Siloam. This was the pool at the south end of the city filled by the Gihon Spring. This pool was the source for the water ceremonies at Tabernacles. But for John something deeper is at hand. We recall that Jesus had replaced these Tabernacles waters in 7:37–39. Now the pool which is their source bears Christ's name. Siloam means *sent* (v. 7) and "the sent one" is a regular title for Jesus in the fourth Gospel (5:36–38; 8:16, 18, 26; etc.). The blind man finds his healing in Jesus both in symbol and in reality.

The judicial interest that we have witnessed thus far in the "Book of Signs" takes a fresh turn. Rather than Jesus, the healed man goes on trial. Since it was the Sabbath (v. 14) the Jewish leadership feels compelled to investigate a possible criminal violation. The interrogation has four steps as various witnesses step to center stage. In much the same way that the Samaritan woman in John 4 witnessed her faith developing through a progression of titles for Christ, so here the narrative parades Christ's names ("Jesus," v. 11; "Siloam," v. 11; "prophet," v. 17; "Christ," v. 23; "from God," v. 33; "Son of Man," v. 35; "Lord," v. 38).

Step 1 involves the interrogation of the man by his neighbors (vv. 8–12). They are witnesses to the miracle but remain incredulous. After this Pharisees take over and they examine the man and his family. Step 2 (vv. 13–17) confirms the Sabbath violation but uncovers a flaw of logic in the trial. If God listens to Jesus (e.g., he heals) how can Jesus be a Sabbath violator? Step 3 (vv. 18–23) shows how they choose to resolve the dilemma: God is consistent with his law; therefore, the miracle must be a fraud. God does not entertain sin and miracles at the same time. One element must go. But the man's parents are no use. They confirm that this is their son and that he was blind, but their fear of the authorities makes them reluctant to say more.

Step 4 is easily the most important (vv. 24–34). The man is recalled a second time in hope of finding a way to condemn Jesus' sin. The brute fact of the miracle cannot be ignored and yet even with this tangible evidence in hand the religious leaders spurn both the man and Jesus. Their allegiance is set; they are intransigent. The language of 9:28 is important. The Pharisees have polarized everyone's commitments: you cannot be a disciple of Moses and a disciple of Jesus at the same time. The chasm between church and synagogue is at hand (cf. 8:39–47).

The blind man's final defense (vv. 30–33) supports the logic both of his own case and John's case in the "Book of Signs." Are not the signs of Jesus compelling evidence? Why have these leaders rejected the man and Jesus? Because there is no acceptable excuse, the result is judgment (vv. 39, 41).

In an earlier story the lame man who was healed and who suffered abuse at the temple was found again by Jesus and encouraged (5:14). So now once this blind man is expelled from the synagogue (9:34) Jesus finds him again and commends his efforts. Since the man witnessed and accepted the signs, belief was an easy thing (v. 38). His disposition to the sign was all-important. But for the Pharisees whose minds were closed, the light could not penetrate. They became blind because they remained in the darkness (v. 39). John 8:41 suggests personal responsibility for the revelation that accrues to us. To see the signs of God and reject them is a more serious matter than never having perceived them at all.

The Festival of Dedication (10:1–39) now introduces us to the fourth festival of Judaism which Jesus attends and which, like the others, becomes a place of discourse and revelation. Unlike the other feasts, Dedication was a minor, more recent celebration. It recalled the desecration of the temple in 168 B.C. by the Greek monarch Antiochus IV Epiphanes, the corrupt priests installed by him, and the Maccabean wars which finally regained and purified the temple in 164 B.C. A moving account of this is given in 1 Maccabees 4:36–58, which is followed by Judas Maccabeus's announcement that this Dedication (Hanukkah) should be celebrated each winter on the twenty-fifth day of the Jewish month Kislev (November/December).

This Jewish background provides striking

depth to the discourse of Jesus in chapter 10. As we have suggested, Jesus has been in Jerusalem since autumn (Tabernacles, 7:2f.) and now his conflict with the Jerusalem leadership has reached a peak. Jesus will not publicly debate the Jews again after chapter 10. This final crisis tone is paralleled by the synoptic account found, for instance, in Matthew 23, where Jesus' criticisms are extremely biting. The same is found in John 10. After the conflict with the Pharisees in chapter 9, which described them as blind (9:39–41), now they are depicted as false shepherds (10:1, 10, 12–13).

Because the literary division between this festival and the previous one is less clear (cf. 5:1; 6:1; 7:1), scholars are divided on the question of where 10:1–21 should fall. Does it apply to the foregoing (the subject of 10:21 implies this) or to the material in 10:22–39? We have chosen to unify all of chapter 10 under this final feast. There is a strict change of subject at 10:1 and the second half of the chapter still presupposes the sheep metaphor (see 10:26f.). Moreover, the subject of the discourse in 10:1–21 applies directly to Dedication. The feast recalled the corrupt priests of the Greek era (viz., Jason and Menelaus) and had in Jesus' day evolved into a ceremony of priestly rededication. Synagogues read aloud Ezekiel 34 in which false priests were described as false shepherds. Therefore in a season which studied religious leadership and its historic failings, Jesus gathers up the current metaphor from Ezekiel 34 and interprets it in light of his own mission.

The metaphoric teaching of Jesus in **10:1–21** closely resembles the parables of the Synoptics. The parable is given in 10:1–5, a note of incomprehension is recorded in verse 6, and then Jesus interprets the meaning of the parable (cf. the format of Mark 4).

The parable itself discusses the legitimate leaders of the sheep. Just as with the corrupt priests of the Maccabean era, Jesus suggests that there may still be false leaders of God's people whose intentions are malevolent. Two criteria set apart fraudulent leaders. First, their entry into authority is wrong (v. 1). Sheepfolds were often protective stone fences with one access gate. If the gatekeeper (v. 3) has not ordained the shepherd's entry, he is to be feared, not followed. Here Jesus indicates that he alone has true authority because he has obtained the gatekeeper's invitation. Second, the false leader's voice cannot be recognized. The intimacy between shepherd and sheep is a well-known Palestinian phenomenon. Sheep can even bear personal names! Here Jesus shows that he alone knows and is known by the sheep. In John this is a central feature of discipleship: discerning Jesus' voice and abiding in him.

As in other discourses, the failure of the listeners to understand Jesus' meaning (v. 6) leads him to explain himself more fully (cf. 3:9ff.; 7:35ff.). Initially Jesus affirms that he is the way ("the door/gate," vv. 7, 9) through which one finds salvation or pasture. This is an advance over the parable wherein the shepherd is distinguished from the gatekeeper and the gate. Now we learn that Jesus distributes not simply access to leadership, but life itself. If the parable has allegorical elements, note that now in the interpretation Jesus assumes a new sovereignty over the fold. Has he assumed divine tasks again? The sheepfold is designed to keep out those who would harm the sheep (v. 10) and Jesus is their guardian. He refuses access to many, including those like the Pharisees. These leaders destroy, but God sent Christ so that those who believe might not be destroyed (3:16; 6:39; 17:12).

But Jesus is also the good shepherd (10:11, 14). God is often described as the shepherd of Israel (Gen. 49:24; Pss. 23; 78:52–53) and similarly, the patriarchs, Moses, and David were shepherds. Leadership in Israel meant shepherding, and thus impious Israelite kings were called false shepherds (1 Kings 22:17; Jer. 10:21; 23:1–2; Ezek. 34:1–31). In Mark's account of Jesus' miraculous feeding, Jesus is evidently using this same pastoral motif for himself (6:30–44, esp. vv. 34, 39, 40). Here in 10:11–18 the superiority of Jesus' work is given. Not only is his devotion to the sheep such that he is willing to die for them while others flee from danger (vv. 11–13, 17), but he knows them deeply—so deeply that in 10:15 an appropriate analogy for this knowledge is Jesus' relationship to his Father. As Jesus is in the Father, so the disciple is in Christ (cf. 14:20, 24).

A variety of secondary themes emerges from these teachings. Is there only one flock of Jesus? Is Judaism the limit of his care? John 10:16 indicates the contrary: "other sheep" refers to members (Gentiles?) beyond Judaism. Is the death of the shepherd something tragic—beyond his control? Not at all. His power enables him voluntarily to die and regain his life (v. 18). Elsewhere in the New Testament God raises up Jesus (Acts 2:24; Rom. 4:24; Eph. 1:20; Heb. 11:19; 1 Pet. 1:21). But in Johannine thought the Father and the Son possess the same powers (vv. 28–30). The Son controls the hour of death entirely (2:4; 7:6, 8; 8:20).

The responses to Jesus' discourses have followed a pattern which is seen again here. At Passover, Tabernacles, and now at Dedication, a division erupts among the listeners (6:41, 60; 7:25, 45; 10:19–21). There is no neutral position when faced with Christ's revelation. Either hostility (v. 20) or the seeds of faith (v. 21) will follow. Those who believe are ready to cast off the extreme charge of demon possession lodged at Tabernacles (7:20; 8:48). Jesus' teachings and miracles (esp. 9:1–7) for them are confirming evidence.

With this encounter we reach a sort of crescendo in the Gospel. The evidences accumulating in the Book of Signs will shift following this chapter. No longer will Jesus discourse with the Jewish leaders. He will later be with friends in Bethany (11:1–12:8), supportive crowds (12:12ff.), and Gentiles (12:20ff.). Then Jesus will "hide himself" from all but his personal disciples (12:36). Here in chapter 10 the height of Jesus' self-revelation is completed: his identity with the Father is now explicit (vv. 30, 33) and centered on his claim to the title *Son of God* (vv. 34–36). Similarly, the hostilities are keen: attempts are made on his life twice, but he escapes (vv. 31, 39). This narrative epitomizes Jesus' ultimate claims about himself and the fateful Jewish reaction (**10:22–39**).

The temple courtyard was surrounded by colonnaded porches that gave shelter from the weather. Solomon's Porch was on the east and since it was winter (the season of Dedication) Jesus is found there sheltered from the cold Jerusalem wind (vv. 22–23). If the judicial emphases that we are following are correct, here the christological inquiries take on new significance. The evidence has been displayed (vv. 25–26) and now Judaism aims its two charges that will reappear later at the formal trial: (1) Are you claiming to be the Christ (cf. Luke 22:67)? (2) Are you the Son of God (cf. John 19:7 and Luke 22:70)?

The way in which Jesus defends his claims and explains Jewish disbelief affirms that God is sovereign over who accepts revelation. The leaders are simply not of Jesus' fold and hence cannot hear his voice. The divine control over revelation has appeared elsewhere (6:37, 44, 65; cf. 17:6). Understanding the signs alone is a divine gift.

In 10:28–29 the sovereignty of Jesus and God over the flock is in exact parallel ("no one can snatch them out of *my/his* hand"). This operational or functional unity leads to the essential or ontological unity of 10:30: "I and the Father are one." These verses are crucial and have played a vital role in the formation of trinitarian doctrine. Christ has assumed divine prerogatives regularly and he has emphasized his oneness with the Father. Now the doctrinal point is explicit. The authority of Jesus' messiahship rests above all on his unique relation with the Father.

The Jews judge it as blasphemy (v. 31). Jesus in turn employs a defense that at first may seem peculiar to us today. He debates like a rabbi. First, he notes that the general ascription of "gods" was known in the Old Testament (Ps. 82) and used for those who were vehicles for the Word of the Lord (vv. 34–35). Is Christ not at least this? Second, Christ is more. If the first premise is correct, what do we say of him who is a unique vehicle of the Word of God—who *is* the Word (John 1:1)? Of course Psalm 82:6 does not mean that agents of God are divine, but the presence of the term *god* alone is sufficient for Jesus to make his point following rabbinic theological logic.

We have seen how in the various feasts of Sabbath, Passover, and Tabernacles messianic replacement was used to unveil Jesus' identity. Here only the most careful reader will catch the allusion. We have seen how Dedication recalled the cleansing and rededication of the temple. Here one of the chief terms from 1 Maccabees 4 is used of Christ. In John 10:36 Jesus has been "set apart" (NIV) or "consecrated" (RSV) and sent into the world. This term (Gk. *hagiazō*, to make holy) recalls the Maccabean story (1 Macc. 4:48). Jesus is the truly consecrated temple of God (cf. John 1:14; 2:21).

The final appeal of Jesus in 10:37–39 again rests on his works and their evidential value. The Jews of the Book of Signs have obtained the signs sufficient for belief. And these will point the way toward the conclusion of the unity of the Father and the Son (v. 38; cf. v. 30). But just as the former revelation of this brought hostility (vv. 30–31), so now Jesus' opponents attempt to arrest him (v. 39).

Jesus now withdraws before the crucial events of his final week (**10:40–42**). He knows the region of the Jordan and Perea well (Matt. 19:1; Mark 10:1) and this is his refuge. Soon he will climb the ascent from Jericho to Bethany and inaugurate the week of the passion.

In the literary format of John these verses indicate a major transition. Jesus has withdrawn from public purview. The public signs are over. The Book of Signs that began with John the Baptist (1:18) now anticipates its completion with a second reference to him (10:40). The fourth Evangelist even reminds us of the subject of these ten chapters. Although John worked no sign, Jesus did; and those who witnessed these and perceived their truth found faith (v. 42).

More signs await those disciples of the inner circle (chaps. 11–12) and we as readers are privileged to view these. The final plea for belief, however, will come to us at 12:44–50 when we with the rest of the disciples will have viewed sufficient signs, sufficient evidences from which to reach a verdict about Jesus.

D. Foreshadowings of death and resurrection (11:1–12:50). Considerable arguments have often been advanced suggesting that 10:40–42 was at one time the conclusion of Jesus' public ministry in John's Gospel and that at some later stage the Gospel was edited to include chapters 11 and 12. For instance, the sequence of events here (movements to Perea, Bethany, Ephraim, and back) is difficult to reconcile with the Synoptics as is the motive for Jesus' arrest (11:45–53; 12:9–11). Further, the term *the Jews* now loses its harsh polemical tone so common to John (cf. 9:22 with 11:19, 45). But despite this, traditional Johannine elements abound: the use of *egō eimi* ("I AM") in 11:25 and the literary device of misunderstanding (11:11f., 23f., 50f.). Nevertheless the Synoptics know little of Mary and Martha—much less Lazarus—and this narrative is a unique (but not inauthentic) Johannine story.

What is the purpose of chapters 11–12? While the Synoptics at this point expand on Jesus' teachings in Jerusalem during his final spring visit (cf. Matt. 21–26), John has chosen a miracle story that epitomizes Christ's mission and fate. With superb dramatic form the Lazarus story (**11:1–44**) sums up Jesus' career. It is the ultimate sign. Jesus, the source of life (10:28; 11:25), now gives life to one man. But even this ultimate revelation is condemned, leaving Jesus judged as worthy of death (11:50).

Moreover, woven into this story are hints of Jesus' own passion. He too will die and come forth. The Lord of life will lay down his life and return from the grave like Lazarus. Later in the same town of Bethany, Mary will anoint Jesus—figuratively preparing him for burial (12:3–8).

Therefore chapters 11 and 12 provide a transition preparing us for John's second book, the Book of Glory (chaps. 13–20). Jesus' signs are finished and he is advancing toward "the hour"—the hour of death, resurrection, and glory.

The village of Bethany, two miles east of Jerusalem, was the regular residence of Jesus while he was in Judea (cf. Mark 11:11; 14:3). While Lazarus is not known in the Synoptics (but see Luke 16:20), Luke does refer to the sisters Mary and Martha (Luke 10:38–42). The profile of the two sisters in Luke (the compulsive Martha; the contemplative Mary) is paralleled in John (11:20; 12:2–3).

While Jesus was in the Jordan Valley (John 10:40) his whereabouts must have been known to his friends since Mary and Martha are able to contact him. Jesus' response to Lazarus' illness (11:1–44) is similar to his explanation of the blind man's infirmity in 9:3. Sometimes crises serve divine purposes so that God may be glorified when they are resolved.

That Jesus does not respond at once (11:6) in no way disparages his love for the family (v. 5). There are problems with a return to the mountains of Judea which the apostolic party fully realizes (vv. 8, 16). Threats of death have been known for over a year (5:18; 7:25) and some have even tried to kill Jesus already (8:59; 10:31). But the Lord feels the pressing need to depart. His time is short and just as with the hours of daylight for the traveler, each hour must be used to maximum benefit (9:10; cf. 12:35–36). The spiritual light now present is even more valuable than this. Jesus is the light of the world (8:12) and while he is present and able to dispel darkness, his work must progress. The task at hand is the revival of Lazarus who is now dead (vv. 11–14; note the familiar use of misunderstanding). A paradoxical exchange is thus at hand: Jesus chooses to risk death in Judea in order to save a man from death. He indeed is the good shepherd who is willing to lay down his own life for the life of his sheep (10:15).

It is a tribute to John's interest in historical detail that he mentions how long Lazarus has been dead (vv. 17, 39) and the exact location of Bethany. Because the ancient world did not have precise methods to monitor death or coma, most rabbis held theories about the impossibility of resuscitation after three or four days of death. Our story is making one point: Lazarus was fully dead by anyone's standards and the miracle (vv. 43–44) involved resurrection, not resuscitation.

When Jesus enters the hill country it is clear that the customary mourning is under way (vv. 18–19, 31). Mark 5:38f. provides an interesting parallel. Although Martha is the first to greet Jesus on the road (vv. 20–27), Mary will come later (vv. 31–32) and John no doubt wants us to compare them. Both women express the same words, "Lord, if you had been here, my brother would not have died" (vv. 21, 32). Jesus is the Lord of life (v. 25), but the women despair. Their hope was in a healing miracle because resurrection was so far beyond their comprehension (vv. 26–27). While Mary is overcome (v. 35; cf. 12:3; Luke 10:39), Martha pursues a conversation. "Even now" in 11:22 implies faith—even now in death Jesus may be able to do something. But is the only comfort in the eschaton, the future resurrection? Ironic misunderstanding (vv. 23–24) gives the conversation its classic Johannine form and allows Jesus to elevate his meaning. The resurrection life is a present experience! Eternal life begins now for the person who trusts in Christ (vv. 25–26). The horror of death is gone (v. 26; cf. 3:16–21). When pressed Martha cannot affirm Jesus' powers to this extent (v. 26b); but still she holds on to what she does know (v. 27). Jesus is her Lord; knowledge of his powerful abilities will come with time.

One unique feature of this story is the way in which Jesus expresses his emotions over Lazarus's death (vv. 33, 35, 38; cf. Luke 19:41). He does not approach suffering and death dispassionately. He feels the pain. He knows tragedy and has feelings. In this case these emerge out of his love for his friend Lazarus (11:36).

Lazarus was buried in a typical first-century stone tomb. (Cf. Jesus' tomb, 20:1; Mark 15:46.) Since these were designed for multiple burials there would be no difficulty reopening it (v. 39) if sufficient help was available. Again we are given a second confirmation that Lazarus is dead (11:39), this time in graphic terms. But this does not deter Jesus. As his feeding miracle demonstrated that he was the bread of life (6:35), and as his healing of the blind illustrated that he was the light of the world (8:12), so now he will prove that he is the resurrection and the life (11:25).

All that Jesus does has one aim: to promote the glory of God (v. 40). His audible prayer heard here (vv. 41–42; cf. 12:27) serves this purpose. Jesus is no miracle worker with simple powerful feats at his disposal. His deeds are signs which promote belief. They reveal something of God's presence at work and they illumine Christ as God's divine agent.

Burial cloths further confirm Lazarus' death (11:44) and provide another parallel to Jesus' burial (19:39–40; 20:5–7). The unusual reference to a face cloth appears only here and in 20:7. One interesting difference, however, is that Lazarus requires aid with his bindings—Jesus' grave clothes are noticeably left behind.

As with so many other signs of Jesus, the onlookers immediately divide into two camps (e.g., 7:40–44). Here too the events at Bethany compel some to believe while others file a report with members of the Sanhedrin who determine Jesus' fate (**11:45–57**). The deliberations of the Sanhedrin, now called to a formal meeting about Jesus, typify the drift of the Jewish leadership's reaction to Christ since chapter 9: Jesus' signs seem compelling, but the practical implications of this are more than they can bear. What if the masses start to follow him? Would it not upset the fragile political equilibrium with Rome (v. 48)? Would Caesar tolerate a messiah? The Sanhedrin must choose either to follow the logic of Jesus' truth, regardless of the cost, or to retreat into the safety of their own nicely controlled religion.

Caiaphas chooses the latter (vv. 49–50)—that Jesus must die in order to save Israel's precarious freedoms, but John takes this as a prophecy which the high priest himself even misunderstands (vv. 51–53). Of course Jesus must die for the sake of the Jewish nation (and for that matter the Gentiles too, v. 52), but in a sense the Sanhedrin will never understand.

Because of the high council's resolve to kill Jesus (v. 53) he goes into seclusion in much the same way that he did after the Feast of Tabernacles (cf. 10:39–42). Ephraim's location (11:54) has proved perplexing. It may be the Old Testament village of Ophrah (Josh. 18:23) northeast of Bethel (modern et-Taiyibeh).

With the pilgrimage Feast of Passover at hand, everyone is expecting Jesus to appear. Questions are alive in both the crowds and the Sanhedrin (vv. 56–57) and for good reason. The last pilgrimage feast (Tabernacles, John 7–9) witnessed numerous conflicts with Jesus. The city was astir with anticipation (7:10–13, 25–26, 32f.). Therefore precautions are taken: if Jesus appears in the city from his wilderness retreat, his whereabouts should be reported (cf. 11:46).

Both John (**12:1–8**) and the Synoptics (Matt. 26:6–13; Mark 14:3–9) record the anointing at Bethany and since the settings are virtually identical, the narratives pose a textbook case in the difficulties of synoptic/Johannine interdependence. Added to this is a Lucan story (Luke 7:36–38) with interesting parallels to both Mark and John.

Jesus' return from the wilderness (11:54) is prompted by another Feast of Passover, one year since the last festival celebrated in Galilee (6:4). Jesus returns to Bethany where Lazarus, Mary, and Martha live and from here he will make his final visit to Jerusalem (v. 12). If the Marcan account is a true parallel then this residence is also the home of Simon the leper (Mark 14:3).

Again Mary and Martha take up their usual roles (cf. Luke 10:38–42; John 11:20): Martha busies herself with the duties of a hostess and Mary makes an unusual gesture of devotion to Jesus. Imported from North India, this perfume was precious indeed and the anointing was extravagant. A denarius was one day's wage and this was worth three hundred (Mark says more than three hundred denarii)! When Mary lets down her hair (cf. Luke 7:38) she strictly breaks Jewish convention—women never did this in public. But this is simply more extravagance, justified because no devotion to Jesus can be excessive. Jesus' defense of her in Mark 14:6 makes this abundantly clear. On the other hand, Judas is the antithesis of all this. Money was his concern since he was the treasurer (John 12:6; 13:29). But his flaw is twofold: care of the poor cannot come before undiluted worship of Christ (12:8); and when this care springs from an impure heart (v. 6) its spiritual value evaporates.

Jesus' final visit to Jerusalem is recorded in 12:9–50. Before long the presence of Jesus in Bethany becomes public knowledge and crowds arrive to see both him and Lazarus. Although the Sanhedrin desired to seize him when he appeared (11:57), the crowds may have interfered with a clean arrest (cf. Luke 19:47–48). The Johannine account introduces a new element. Lazarus's death is planned too (12:10f.) because he has become a celebrity (vv. 17–19). It is this fame, spreading from Bethany, that greets Jesus as he rides into the city from the eastern hills (**12:9–19**). The triumphal entry into Jerusalem is narrated by each of the Evangelists (Matt. 21:1–11; Mark 11:1–10; Luke 19:28–40) and John's differences stem chiefly from his abbreviated version. The crowd celebrates Jesus' arrival with festive displays and shouts. The Old Testament explanation in each account comes from Zechariah 9:9, although John amends Zechariah's "Rejoice Greatly!" to "Fear Not" (John 12:15). This may be a unique allusion to Zephaniah 3:14–17 in which the prophet dispels the fears of Israel, affirming that "the LORD is in your midst" (Zeph. 3:15). For John, Jesus' arrival is a fitting fulfillment.

The celebrations of the Jews are now echoed by an entirely unexpected interest among some Greeks in Jerusalem (**12:20–36**). This is unexpected because Greeks are Gentiles (though these may be proselytes) and unaccepted by Jews. John's irony cannot be missed: when Jesus' efforts to unveil himself to Israel have been exhausted, Greeks arrive eager to see Jesus. Jewish reluctance is exceeded by Greek zeal. Mark's Gospel follows a similar structure. In Mark the watershed is in 8:27–30 and from then on Jesus devotes himself exclusively to his disciples. But prior to this revelation at Caesarea Philippi, Jesus finds an unprecedented response among the Greeks (Mark 7:24–30; 7:31–37; 8:1–10). Once Judaism fails to embrace the signs of Christ, Gentiles are given the opportunity (Matt. 21:41–44; Luke 2:32; 4:25–27; Rom. 1:16).

Jesus' response to Andrew and Philip's report is extremely important. The "hour" which has been put off for years (cf. John 2:4; 7:6; 8:20) now has arrived (12:23). Jesus recognizes the culmination of all that he has been attempting in Judaism. The cross and death are all that remain (v. 24). But in John it is not a death of disgrace and shame; Jesus will be glorified and this will mysteriously result in great things. The same is true of his followers (vv. 23–26). Self-effacement and denial are the only pathways to finding the company of Jesus or the honor of the Father (cf. Matt. 10:37–39; Mark 8:34–38). The humanity of Jesus can be seen in how even he wrestles with this truth (John 12:27; cf. Mark 14:36). Strength is found here and later in Gethsemane when he submits himself to God's higher purposes. The glory of God is manifest when his servants persevere in temptations such as this and in ultimate trials (vv. 28–29). The cross will be the ultimate test for Jesus and here in the midst of God's glory Jesus himself will be glorified (17:1–5).

The confirming voice from heaven is received by the crowds just as the signs were received (vv. 28–30). Throughout his Gospel, John's view of revelation has taken shape: a sign from God is revelatory only when it is greeted by faith. The "Book of Signs" will only speak to those whom the Father is already giving into the Shepherd's hand (6:44–45; 10:27–29).

It is now time for Jesus to define his hour of death and glory. It too will be a sign, but how will it be received? Can the average man accept that the world's judgment will be inaugurated when one man is crucified (12:31–32)? This crowd cannot (v. 34)—but neither could the disciples at this point (Mark 8:31–33; 9:30–32; 10:32–34). But fortunately the crowd stays with Jesus; they keep inquiring. The last question posed to Jesus is in John 12:34: "Who is this Son of Man?" In the previous chapter Martha could not comprehend all that Jesus revealed (11:21–27), but still she held on to the light she possessed. When confusion and uncertainty are at hand John would not have us walk away in disbelief. Jesus now affirms the same (12:35–36). Continue to engage God! Embrace the light! Walk in it!

Jesus' disclosure of himself is finished (v. 36). He now hides himself from public view because his signs are completed and they are left for us to interpret.

John the Evangelist who has been the narrator of the story all along (2:22–25; 3:16–21, 31–36; 7:5; etc.) now sums up the meaning of Jesus' public ministry (**12:37–43**). John 12:37 makes plain what all of early Christianity was forced to acknowledge: Jesus' many signs fell on disbelief. John joins the other evangelists in drawing texts from Isaiah that must have been commonly used in the early church (Isa. 6:10; 53:1; cf. Matt. 13:14–17). Isaiah too found disbelief in Israel and attributed it to God's sovereignty over revelation. John, however, has woven this theme into the entirety of the "Book of Signs." Hence the unbelievers were unable to believe (John 12:39); God affected their perception (v. 40). John, however, does not probe the mystery of the interplay between human responsibility and divine sovereignty. In 12:41 Isaiah's words are interpreted as prophecies directed to Jesus because the glory Isaiah viewed (6:1–5) was Jesus' glory too. This closing frame in the Book of Signs repeats what we read in the prologue: Christ is the glory of the Father unveiled for human eyes (1:14).

But has no one believed the signs? Of course there are the disciples, but has not God opened the eyes and ears of some Jewish leaders? John has not neglected these: there are some who believe but they fear persecution (12:42). Nicodemus typifies these men (3:1–21; 19:39) for when he did speak up (7:50–52) he was severely rebuked. Similarly the parents of the blind man feared expulsion from the synagogue (9:22). Nevertheless, the praise of God awaits those men of prominence and esteem who ignore the cost and make their faith visible (v. 43).

The "Book of Signs" concludes with a harrowing cry from Jesus imploring Judaism to believe (**12:44–50**). It reiterates much of what has gone before. Jesus is light; he reveals God and disperses the darkness (1:9; 8:12). Above all he has not spoken on his own authority; he is God's agent in the world. Belief in Christ is belief in God. To see Christ is to see the Father (12:44–45; 14:9). Even the words of Jesus have not been his own but stem from what the Father has directed (12:49–50; 17:6–8). This truth, however, has serious implications inasmuch as there will be a divine accounting for all that Jesus has said.

The signs are complete and the Book of Signs may now close. Evidence for Jesus' case is public. The Sanhedrin has made its decision about him (11:53) but the crowd still asks, "Who is this Son of Man?" For them and for us the Book of Signs is open for examination. From John's point of view, these signs will compel us to believe.

III. The Book of Glory (13:1–20:31)

With chapter 13 we move to another major literary division in the fourth Gospel which contrasts directly with the Book of Signs (1:19–12:50). The contrast is chiefly one of perspective. In the Book of Signs, for instance, Jesus addresses a public audience. His teaching provokes a crisis of faith as some believe while others reject him. Here, on the other hand, the audience is narrowed to the circle of disciples who follow him to the cross. We noted how in chapter 12 Jesus "hid himself" (12:36) indicating an end to his public self-disclosure. Now his focus is on "his own" (13:1; 17:6–19). We could also point out that while the interest of the first half of John is on the signs of Jesus, now the Gospel will concentrate on the coming of "the hour" (12:23, 27; 13:1)—that is, the hour of his glorification (13:31–32). It is not an hour of tragedy in this Gospel but one of victory which involves Christ's passion, crucifixion, resurrection, and ascension. Just as the many signs of Jesus were accompanied by discourses (cf. John 6, the feeding miracle and the bread of life discourse) so too this last sign of death and resurrection will be interpreted by lengthy teaching in the upper room (chaps. 13–16).

Raymond Brown likes to think of the Gospel as imitating the arc of a pendulum: it begins at a high point, descends, and elevates again. The Johannine prologue reflects this too as the Word is in God's presence (1:1), experiences rejection (1:10f.), and then returns to places of glory (1:18). With the Book of Glory we are in the upward swing of the arc, the descent having been chronicled by those chapters which describe Jesus' efforts to reveal himself (chaps. 1–12). The lowest point is reached when Judaism confirms Jesus' death (11:50) and John is forced to explain Jewish disbelief (12:37–50). The highest point comes with the return from the grave of the glorified Lord. Here, echoing the prologue again, the disciples are the recipients of life-giving power (1:12f.; 20:22).

A. The Passover meal (13:1–30). The Synoptics record that during his last week of ministry, during the Passover festival, Jesus enjoyed a final meal with his disciples (Mark 14:12–25). Each synoptic writer terms this "the Passover" (Matt. 26:17; Mark 14:12; Luke 22:7–9) ordinarily served after dusk on the Jewish date of 15 Nisan. John mentions such a meal (13:2, 26) and indicates through mention of the betrayal of Judas (13:21–30) that this meal is the synoptic Passover (cf. Mark 14:17–21). However, John's date cannot be 15 Nisan (Passover) for later he will say that Jesus is crucified on 14 Nisan when the temple lambs are being slaughtered (19:14). Hence the Johannine record shows the meal to be on the Day of Preparation, one night prior to the Passover feast.

Scholars have solved this riddle in a variety of ways. The easiest and most popular solution is simply to say that one Gospel tradition or the other is incorrect. But critics can find fault with each account: Would the Sanhedrin hold a trial on a feast day as the Synoptics contend? Or has John moved the cross to 14 Nisan to develop a paschal emphasis for Jesus' death (cf. 19:32–37)? Recent studies have urged that both narratives might be accurate due to competing calendars in the first century. Hence ceremonial meals may have been sponsored on more than one night during this festival week.

The synoptic emphasis is found in the words of institution during the meal (Luke 22:14–23). While it comes as a surprise that the fourth Gospel does not record this (but see 6:52–58) we find that another event, the foot washing, is prominent (**13:1–20**). The theme of servanthood so central to the narrative, however, does appear in Luke in the upper room: the disciples' interest in greatness and authority is rebuked by Jesus as he instructs them about servanthood (Luke 22:24–27).

Foot washing was a common custom due to the wearing of sandals and the dry, dusty Palestinian roads. A good host would provide a servant who would work in this capacity, but if none were there he certainly would not take up the chore himself as Jesus does (13:4–5). That which enables Jesus to serve like this may be described in 13:3. Jesus has perfect self-esteem: he knows of God's love expressed in his origin and destiny, and therefore can relinquish human status to become a servant.

A variety of themes runs through the narrative. First, foot washing speaks of Jesus' death. Jesus' dialogue with Peter (vv. 6–11) explains that an understanding of this will come about only after Jesus' death (v. 7; cf. 2:22; 12:16) Since this washing is criterion for fellowship with Christ, Peter dare not object (vv. 7–8). Cleansing (through the cross; baptism?) speaks of cleansing from sin; hence it is not just any washing that is important: Jesus must cleanse his followers (v. 8). As in other dialogues, misunderstanding follows. Peter's zeal for Christ leads him astray: If he supplements Jesus' provision, will he have more of Christ (v. 9)? Verse 10 gives Jesus' reply, but it is difficult to interpret. The reference to bathing (which is new) is often seen as an allusion to baptism (see Gk. *louein*, Acts 22:16; 1 Cor. 6:11; Eph. 5:26; Titus 3:5; Heb. 10:22) in which case Jesus may mean that once a disciple is cleansed of sin through conversion/baptism only partial washing (confession) is needed for postbaptismal sin (cf. 1 John 1:8–2:6). This is the patristic interpretation which may be right but is now complicated by some important ancient manuscripts omitting the key phrase *except for his feet* (v. 10).

Second, impurities speak of Judas (vv. 10–11). The metaphor of cleansing and impurity shifts from Peter to the larger group of apostles at the end of 13:10 (the final "you" in v. 10 is plural). Not only is Peter partially clean, but so are the disciples (v. 11) since Judas Iscariot is among them. This will be developed at length from verses 21–30.

Third, foot washing is a symbol for mutual service (vv. 12–17). In this sense Jesus has modeled behavior he wishes his followers to emulate. If service on this order was possible for him, then it cannot be beneath us (v. 16). Here disciples are pressed beyond a mere knowledge of Jesus' will. Blessing follows faith expressed in deeds (v. 17; cf. Matt. 7:24–27). But as in John 13:10–11, when Jesus' thoughts were interrupted by the imminent betrayal of Judas, so here service on this order is not possible for anyone who is not called (cf. 6:44; 10:29). This applies to Judas in particular (13:18–19).

While the fourth Gospel does not explore the motives behind Judas' betrayal (**13:21–30**) nor the overtures of the Sanhedrin (see Matt. 26:14–16, 20–25; 27:3–10; Luke 22:3–6), it does provide us with the poignant account of the beloved disciple's inquiry. This is the first real introduction to the story of this disciple. When Jesus expresses his dismay concerning the betrayal (v. 21), the disciples examine themselves (Luke 22:23) and Peter prompts the beloved disciple (John) to ask Jesus. The disciples were reclining on a couch around a low table. John was to the right of Jesus and hence in the best position for a confidential question (vv. 25–26).

Two times in this account (13:2, 27) we learn that Satan is the true power behind Judas. It is interesting that Satan's appearances are so few in this Gospel. It contains no exorcisms and Satan's only role involves the efforts of those who are Jesus' fiercest opponents (the Jews, 8:44; Judas Iscariot, 6:70; 13:2, 27). Satan's chief work is in undermining Jesus' testimony and his glorification. No suspicions are raised when Judas departs (13:27) because he was the custodian of the group's funds (cf. 12:6) and he had tasks to do: acquire provisions for the festival and give special offerings to the poor on Passover night.

Verse 30 is a crucial verse because it marks the time after which Jesus may instruct his chosen disciples privately and fully. Judas has departed and the final sentence reads, "It was night." This motif has symbolic as well as literal value. The hour of death, pushed forward by Judas, is when the light of the world is extinguished (9:4). Darkness is the opposite of light and typifies those outside of Jesus' fold (3:19) who stumble without him (11:10). At the Gethsemane arrest Luke records Jesus speaking of this period as a time "when darkness reigns" (Luke 22:53).

B. The farewell discourse (13:31–17:26). In the upper room Jesus now turns to his faithful followers and instructs them at some length. The discourse runs from 13:31 to 16:33 without narrative interruption and then concludes with Jesus' prayer (17:1–26) which precedes the arrest (18:1–11). The literary form of this section is called the "farewell speech" and was well known in Judaism at this time. For example, one can turn to the Testaments of the Twelve Patriarchs, an intertestamental extracanonical work that records the final words of Israel's patriarchs. The Assumption of Moses (first century A.D.) does the same for Israel's prophet-leader in Trans-Jordan. Each Jewish farewell speech shows similar elements that are found in Jesus' farewell: (1) There is a plea for obedience to the Law. Thus in 13:34 and 15:12 Jesus speaks of his new commandment of love. (2) Often writings are left behind (cf. As. Moses 10:11; 4 Ezra) and in the fourth Gospel itself we have the chronicle of Jesus' life now deposited for his followers. (3) Spirit-filled representatives carry on the work just as Joshua obtains the Spirit that rested on Moses (As. Moses 10–12). Here Jesus promises the Spirit of truth (14:17), who anoints the disciples and particularly the beloved disciple for his work in the Johannine community. (4) Finally the anxiety of those left behind is relieved. So Jesus speaks of comfort, terming the Spirit "the Comforter" or "Paraclete" (Gk. *paraklētos,* 14:16, 26; 15:26; etc.).

It is evident then that Jesus recognizes the importance of this evening and is making his formal farewell. He addresses his disciples' worries in light of his imminent death and departure. But above all he holds out a promise and hope centered on the coming of the Holy Spirit—one who would guide, teach, encourage, empower, and mediate to the believer the comforting presence of Christ.

The specific subject of the Farewell Discourse is Jesus' departure to the Father (**13:31–14:3**) and here we see John's technical language being employed. "Glorification" has been used to describe both Jesus' ministry (8:54; 11:4; 12:28) and his death (7:39; 12:16, 23). Now this latter specialized usage comes in full (13:31, 32; 17:1); the cross is another time in which Jesus is glorified and in turn so is the Father (21:19). But glorification as a process is complex: it is not just Christ being lifted up on the cross; rather it is the entire passion from betrayal to empty tomb—a process that inaugurates his return to the Father. Hence 13:31 states that Jesus' glorification has *already* begun. The onset of "the hour" is behind him, his departure is under way (v. 33).

As Jesus mystified his Jewish audience at Tabernacles with this teaching (7:33–36) so now Peter is perplexed (13:36–38). He presses the question about departure and unlike the Jewish leaders in chapter 7, he knows that it may involve death (vv. 37–38; cf. 8:21–22). Nevertheless Jesus answers now in full and chapter 14 will seek to answer the question of Christ's departure, provision, and return. But Jesus is not simply intent on explaining this. In the meanwhile the character of the surviving community (the church) is important (see 13:34–35). The command of love expressed in unity and fidelity to Jesus will be taken up in chapters 15 and 17.

In early Christianity the problem of Jesus' "departure" was resolved by looking forward to his return or second coming (Gk. *parousia*). For some this was the only comfort. However, the discourse in chapter 14 is a carefully designed reassessment of this. It begins with a description of the traditional futurist hope (**14:1–3**). Jesus is preparing rooms in heaven (v. 2) and someday will return to transport his followers there (v. 3). The discourse then introduces three questioners (Thomas, v. 5; Philip, v. 8; Judas, v. 22) who ask leading questions so that Jesus' answer may be sharpened. In the end this futurist eschatology is refashioned into what is called realized eschatology. That is, hope and comfort are not in the future, but can be realized now. Thus the coming of Jesus (v. 3) shifts to the coming of the Spirit (vv. 23, 28). The rooms (Gk. *monē,* v. 2) of heavenly dwelling become rooms (*monē,* v. 23) of divine indwelling.

The sequence of exchanges has an interesting thematic development. There are four interlocking steps:

1. *Jesus:* I am *going* and coming (Gk. *erchomai,* vv. 1–4).
   Thomas: We do not know the *way* you are *going* (v. 5).
2. *Jesus:* I am the *way* to the *Father* (v. 6).
   Philip: Show us the *Father* (v. 8).
3. *Jesus:* You have seen the *Father* already. I will *manifest* him (and myself) to you (vv. 9–11).
   Judas: How will you *manifest* yourself (v. 22)?
4. *Jesus:* In the *Spirit*—by coming (Gk. *erchomai,* v. 23) to you.

For Thomas (vv. 5–7) the chief concern is whether they will accompany Jesus. Note that it is not a moral or ethical way; it is salvific.

The way to be found is the way of salvation leading to the Father (**14:4–17**). Two surprises come about: Jesus is both the means (v. 6) and the end (v. 7). There is no suspended hope because the object of their faith (the Father) is now present in Christ. In him the Father is already present (cf. 8:19; 10:30, 38).

Philip now inquires about this Father/Son relationship (14:8–11) and Jesus makes himself explicit. It is the Father himself who is present in Jesus (hence John's full divinity of Jesus) and this validates both his words and works. Whenever the Father is present he manifests himself. This pertains to Jesus' followers as well (vv. 12–14), who will be enabled to exhibit similar works. Running through these verses is a theological parallel between the Father's relation to the Son and the Spirit's relation to the disciple. As the Father abides in (Gk. *menō*, v. 10) Jesus so too the Spirit abides in (*menō*, v. 17) the believer. Thus the confidence of Christ can be ours: as the Father was committed to his Son, so Jesus through his Spirit will stand with us in every need (vv. 13–14). The point in these verses is not that every prayerful request will be granted, but that the character of Christ's relationship with God at this level may be ours. But here we must recall Jesus' consistent subordination to his Father's will (5:19, 30; 6:38; 7:16f.; 8:28f.) and his desire simply to glorify (12:28; 17:4) and please God (8:29).

The provision of Jesus that will bring about this relationship is declared to be the indwelling Spirit (vv. 15–17), who now bears two new names: the Paraclete (NIV Counselor, v. 16) and the Spirit of truth. Paraclete (Gk. *paraklētos*) is unique to John (elsewhere 14:26; 15:26; 16:7; 1 John 2:1) and expresses the Spirit's strengthening, equipping role. A *paraklētos* was a judicial advocate (cf. Matt. 10:16–20) and here Jesus says that Christians alone can enjoy his aid (John 14:17). As Jesus was alien to the world (1:10) so too his provision of the Spirit will be unknown and unrecognized. As Jesus was on trial in the world (cf. the Book of Signs), now his followers have a judicial aid to support them (15:18–27).

The continuation of Jesus' reassuring words now picks up the language of the second coming (**14:18–24**). Futurist eschatology imperceptibly blends with realized eschatology. In Judaism disciples who had lost their rabbi were often called orphans (v. 18), but this will not be the case for Jesus' followers—he will come back visibly (vv. 18–19). But what sort of return is this if the world cannot take part? Will there be no secular verification? Remarkably the description of the coming of the Paraclete in verses 15–17 parallels the coming of Jesus in verses 18–21. Note the stress on love and obedience (vv. 15, 21), the world (vv. 17, 19), personal recognition (vv. 17, 19), and indwelling (vv. 17, 20).

Judas (not Iscariot, v. 22) asks the question which brings the discourse to its climax. If the manifestation of Jesus mentioned in verse 21 is private, then it needs some explaining. Finally, Jesus says that the hope he has been describing here is not apocalyptic at all. Jesus' return can also be found in the inner experience of the Son and the Father within the believer. The room of dwelling (see 14:2) is now redefined and found in the disciple's heart (v. 23).

Jesus provides further reassurance by predicting beforehand the impending crisis (vv. 29–31) and affirming that he will indeed return (v. 28). But as we have seen, this is a redefined return. The chief attribute he desires for them is peace (similarly, Paul in Rom. 5:1; Eph. 2:17) and this will come about through the Spirit (John 14:26; cf. Eph. 2:18). On Easter day when Jesus appears to the disciples, "peace" is his first word (20:19, 21) and this is followed by their anointing with the Spirit (20:22).

This second Paraclete promise (**14:25–31**) contributes to our understanding of the roles of the Spirit (cf. 14:16). Here the emphasis is on revelation. The Paraclete will be a teacher (1 John 2:22–27) bringing back to memory the sayings of Jesus (John 14:26). Thus here is practical equipment for the church! But we also have here a confirmation of the production of the Gospel record itself. The Spirit will be a preserving, conservative force in revelation. He will not primarily be creative but will reiterate Jesus' words. Once again we see the Spirit functioning like Jesus: as Jesus was dependent on the Father (14:10) so the Spirit depends on Christ.

The vine metaphor (**15:1–17**) builds on the emphases of Jesus in chapter 14. There we saw that the answer to the disciples' anxiety concerning Jesus' death and departure is found in the Spirit. Christ in Spirit will indwell the believer. Jesus' new metaphor in chapter 15 affirms this again. The verb for indwelling (Gk. *menō*, 14:17) appears numerous times (NIV remain, 15:4, 5, 6, 7, 9, 10) but now it is viewed in terms of its results. Spiritual experiences must lead to fruit bearing in the form of new obedience and love.

The vine/vineyard metaphor is used frequently in the Old Testament. Israel is often depicted as a vine transplanted from Egypt (Ps. 80:8–11) and brought to fertile soil (Ezek. 17:1–6). Enemies may trample the vineyard (Jer. 12:10–11) but God tends it carefully and looks for fruit (Isa. 5:1–7). The vineyard may be the preeminent biblical symbol of the locus of God's activity, his nurture, and his expectations (cf. Matt. 21:33–41).

Jesus' use of the metaphor is surprising. Rather than claiming to be the vinedresser and assuming the prerogatives of God (e.g., John 5), Jesus is the vine (which formerly stood for Israel). Union with Jesus means participation in the new Israel, the people of God (cf. Paul, who uses a similar metaphor in Rom. 11:17–24). This theological notion has appeared elsewhere in John 10:7 ("I am the door of the sheep") and in 14:6 ("I am the way"). Attachment to Jesus is the only means of access into God's household. In other words Jesus marks the beginning of the new Israel.

Two themes dominate the section. First, the believer must have an inner apprehension of Christ (in Spirit, 14:23). Abiding or remaining (Gk. *menō*) in Christ is a prerequisite Christian experience. Initially, Christ dwells in us (15:4, 5) but this is no tribute to our merit, for our acceptability as vessels—our cleanliness—is his accomplishment (v. 3). Conversely, we abide in Christ (vv. 4–5) and this is the origin of fruitful living. Just as branches are barren when they are unattached to the vine (v. 4), the possibility of separation from the vine is a dreadful prospect (vv. 2, 6).

Second, there should be outer evidence of Christ's indwelling. Note how carefully the passage balances our mutual participation with God. Our effort is necessary. For instance we must devote ourselves to Jesus' words and be obedient (vv. 7, 10). But on the other hand it is also the nurture of God that causes us to flourish and glorify him (v. 8). "Apart from me you can do nothing" (v. 5b). Jesus describes God as a vinedresser who prunes with skill knowing the benefits that will accrue to the branch in later seasons.

The results of this reciprocal abiding are given in 15:7–17. (1) *Prayer with confidence.* Jesus mentions twice the certainty that comes with prayer joined to spiritual union (vv. 7, 16; cf. 14:12–14). (2) *Assurance.* We acquire confidence in Jesus' love for us because it is modeled on God's love for him (15:9–10; 17:26). Assurance is closely related to our knowledge of Christ's love (see Rom. 8:35–39). (3) *Joy.* This is not mere happiness, but a deeper tranquility that is free from worry about the affairs of living and that knows that God's purposes are good (15:11; 16:20–24; 17:13). (4) *A new community.* Throughout the discourse Jesus exhorts his followers to love one another (13:34; 15:12, 17; 17:21; see 1 John 2:7–11). As his love for us is modeled on God's divine love for him (15:9), now our love for one another should be modeled on his love and sacrifice (vv. 13, 17). Christ-like love should be the hallmark of the church (see esp. 17:20–26; 1 John).

The remarkable summary of Jesus' offer and expectations appears in 15:14–17. What especially stands out is his offer of friendship. In Christ disciples have unparalleled access to God. True friendship is always hallmarked by complete candor, honesty, and transparency between persons. Jesus has become that sort of friend because he has unveiled himself fully (v. 15). Moreover this is not a casual thing passed out indiscriminately: Christ has chosen us to be his friends (v. 16)! The indwelling of Christ and his love are thoroughly individual and personal in these chapters. But Jesus' seriousness cannot be missed. If he has offered this qualitative relationship to us, we must extend it to one another (v. 17).

Early Christianity was unanimous in its outlook on the world. Insofar as the church formed a radically new community, it experienced strife and conflict with society. Social divisions recur with marked frequency in the Book of Acts. In his letters Paul describes persecution as virtually a constituent part of the Christian experience (1 Cor. 4:11–13; 1 Thess. 2:13–16; 2 Tim. 3:10–13). This treatment was expected because the disciples of Christ had inherited the hostilities shown to their Master.

Jesus had predicted these conflicts in his final teachings (Matt. 10:17–25; 24:9–14; Mark 13:9–13) and here in the Farewell Discourse the subject is addressed in full (15:18–16:33). The conflicts are outlined but in addition the provisions of Jesus are given.

Jesus explains that the precedent for this experience is his own (15:18, 20). Christ and his followers are alien to the world's values and therefore cannot obtain its affections (**15:18–16:4a**). Jesus has selectively created a new order—"I have chosen you" (v. 19)—and this implies judgment on the old. The language here is strong: hatred will typify the division between church and world.

The world's guilt is based on its accountability before divine revelation. God in Christ has come, spoken, and acted on our behalf (vv. 22–24) and our response forms the basis of our judgment. This is a common Johannine theme. In 5:45 the disbelieving Jews will be held accountable to their own Scriptures which speak of Christ. In 9:18 the judges of the blind man will themselves be judged because they rejected the sign. And in 12:37 John connects the disbelief of the Jews with a rejection of Jesus' revelatory signs.

Nevertheless the disciples will not be alone

in these conflicts. Jesus reminds them again of the Paraclete (cf. 14:16, 26) who will be their aid. This promise dovetails with similar synoptic promises (Mark 13:11) but John has heightened the judicial setting. In the Book of Signs (John 1–12) we saw how Jesus' ministry was described in forensic terms: he was on trial before a world which was weighing the evidence (signs). Now this lifelong trial is promised for the disciples. This judicial literary metaphor explains the origin of the Spirit's new title. A paraclete is a legal assistant or advocate who aids and counsels. He substantiates our witness (another legal term) as we too are placed on trial before the world. Jesus is quite specific about the extent of these hostilities (16:1–4a) in order to equip his followers for the near future (cf. 1 Pet. 4:12). In 16:1 the Greek word behind "go astray" (NIV) is *skandalizomai,* which means to trip or stumble (a *skandalon* is a trap). In Johannine thought this term refers to anything that causes the disciple to fall away or weaken in faith (6:61; 1 John 2:10; cf. Matt. 26:31).

The further work of the Paraclete (**16:4b–33**) now receives attention. In 16:4b–15 we come to Jesus' fourth and fifth predictions (cf. 14:16, 26; 15:26). The closing subject of chapter 15 (the world) continues to be Jesus' concern. While sorrow may follow Jesus' departure (16:5–6), it is actually necessary for him to go since the coming of the Spirit is dependent on his death/glorification (cf. 7:39). In some fashion the Spirit and Jesus are mutually exclusive; or, as we shall see in chapters 19 and 20, the Spirit comes in the midst of Christ's glorification. The Spirit is Jesus' Spirit and is released in his death (cf. 19:30, 34; 20:22).

The relation between the Spirit and the world has been gradually developing. In 14:15f. we learned that the world cannot know the Spirit. In 15:26f. we see the Paraclete serving as a defense advocate before the world's hostilities. Now in 16:8–11 the Paraclete passes to the attack. This too is a judicial description for in Jewish courts accusers could themselves be accused and convicted. In verse 8 the term *convict* (Gk. *elenchō*) is legal terminology for the trial. While the symmetry of the verses is difficult, their message is clear: the Paraclete will engage the world through the mission of the church. The Spirit will substantiate the church's voice, inwardly persuading the hearts of its hearers and strengthening its witnesses.

The final Spirit saying (vv. 12–15) turns to a new subject and should be compared with 14:25–26. In this earlier passage the Spirit's work was conservative, preserving the historical sayings of Christ. Now we learn that there are things to be revealed which are yet unknown (16:12). The Spirit will be a guide into truth, especially that which pertains to future disclosures (v. 13). Thus Jesus is predicting a prophetic anointing similar to that known to Paul (1 Cor. 12:29; 14:21–23; Eph. 4:11; 1 Thess. 5:19–20). First John 2:26–27 implies that the Johannine churches used this gift as well. But note a very important limit on this "charismatic" activity: the Spirit will not diverge from the historic revelation of Jesus Christ (16:13, 14). The Johannine church understood this necessary reflex back to its original moorings. Note the number of times that John points his readers back to what we knew "from the beginning" (1 John 1:1–3).

The picture so far has developed thus: Jesus must go away, but he will return; yet this return will be realized in a significant way through the Spirit indwelling the Christian. The Spirit will instruct, defend, empower, and guide the disciple within the world. The remaining question: When will these events take place? John 16:16–33 will point to Easter.

Seven times we find a reference to "a little while" (vv. 16–19), which indicates the disciples' worry about the interval between departure and return. Their concern is understandable since in 16:10 Jesus said that they would see him no more; however, a time of "seeing him" (vv. 17, 19, 22) precedes this final removal and it is not too distant. That this refers to Easter can be seen in two ways. First, joy will hallmark their attitude (vv. 20–22, 24) and on Easter day when they see Jesus, rejoicing is their response (20:22b; Gk. *chairō*). Second, "seeing" Jesus is a part of the Easter witness. In fact Mary's exclamation in 20:18 is, "I have seen the Lord!" With this evidence it comes as no surprise to find that the coming of the Spirit, the anointing described throughout these chapters, is finally given on Easter (20:19–22).

Another advantage of this day besides joy is a deepened knowledge of God and his will (16:25–28). The era of misunderstanding will be over (see this motif in chaps. 1–12) and accurate perception will be ours (cf. 2:22; 12:16). John 16:25–28 parallels 16:12–15 inasmuch as it implies a gift of previously unknown insight into God. Hence access to the Father is direct (v. 26f.) because Jesus and the Father will be united together with us (14:9, 23; 17:21).

Proof that the disciples are not yet equipped—and need to be—can be seen in verses 29–33. They think that they understand clearly (16:25, 29) and have full belief. But this cannot be theirs until the Spirit is upon them.

In fact they will flee when the crisis of the cross is upon them (v. 32). But Jesus understands the limitations of his people; when they grieve over their flight, their recollection of these words will bring comfort (v. 33).

Having concluded his discourse Jesus now turns to prayer. Each of the synoptic Gospels records a time of prayer in the Garden of Gethsemane (Matt. 26:36–46; Mark 14:32–42; Luke 22:40–46) and no doubt John 17 should be compared with this. If John 14:31 was the terminus of the upper room teaching, then John may want us to consider this prayer to be at another location. Some think that Jesus is somewhere between the upper room and the garden (Kidron Valley, 18:1) and suggest that he is in the temple since at Passover the city gates would remain open. If this is correct (and we cannot be certain) the prayer may be one of consecration since the Greek term *hagiazō*, "to make holy" (17:17, 19), appears elsewhere only at the temple (10:36). In this sense Jesus may be preparing himself for death as a holy sacrificial victim (cf. Deut. 15:19).

Just as the farewell discourse was a well-established literary custom in Judaism, the same can be said for a prayer of departure. The departure of Moses in Deuteronomy offers a good comparison. The great prophet's final words are spoken from the plains of Moab and recorded in Deuteronomy 1–31. This is followed by two prayers (Deut. 32–33) and a closing account of Moses' death (Deut. 34). In Moses' first prayer he blesses God and then he goes on to bless Israel, interceding for them as they go out to appropriate their tribal lands. In Jesus' prayer we find the same two interests. Jesus turns from his own concerns (17:1–8) to those of the church (vv. 9–26), just like Moses. In this latter role Jesus becomes a priest interceding for his people (see Rom. 8:34; Heb. 7:25). Note how in 1 John 2:1 another Johannine teaching even depicts Christ as our Paraclete (or advocate) in heaven.

The first words of the prayer in Greek bear a significant Johannine phrase: "the hour [NIV time] has come." This hour has been anticipated from the outset (2:4; 7:30; 8:20) and is described as the time of Jesus' glorification (12:23, 27; 13:1; cf. 19:14, 27). This glorification is a process culminating in Jesus' return to the Father by way of the cross. Now Jesus prays that his glory (and the Father's) might be evident (**17:1–8**). In the Book of Signs Jesus' works manifested glory (1:14; 2:11; 11:4, 40; 12:28). But if these signs were veiled, now he asks that his last great sign would speak powerfully. Note how in 12:32 Jesus predicted the true power of the sign of the cross.

In the prologue to the Gospel we learned how the arrival of God's Son made the glory of God visible (1:14). Now Jesus mentions that this effort has been successful (17:4). Those who are chosen, who have apprehended this glory, find life (v. 3); but it is a salvation strictly mediated through the Son. The Son himself possesses glory—a glory shared with the Father—and this will be reappropriated upon Christ's return (v. 5). This thought is important and draws us into the incarnational theology of John. Coming from the Father he takes up our humanity at some expense, only to return once more to his original glory with the Father. This resembles Paul's thought in Philippians 2:5–11.

The glory of God has been visible in Christ in yet one more way. Jesus has revealed God's name (Gk. *onoma*, name; NIV you, 17:6). Paul says the same: this Christ who emptied himself is the bearer of "the name that is above every name" (Phil. 2:9f.). The name of God is a vital Old Testament concept beginning with Moses' experience on Sinai (Exod. 3:13–15; Deut. 12:5; Isa. 52:6) and Jesus has given this throughout his public ministry in the great "I AM" sayings (e.g., 8:28, 58). In the Old Testament possessing God's name is precious; it implies relationship, obedience, and knowledge. Only Christians possess God's name in this Old Testament sense (v. 6) and they alone draw the correct inference: the Son who bears this name has come from God and must be believed.

Jesus now prays exclusively for his followers (**17:9–19**) even though they have been on his mind all along (vv. 6–7). In one sense this prayer is a continuation of that prayer for glory in 17:1–5. Christ's glory is continually manifested through the lives of his people (v. 10). But this will happen only if they, like him, are holy (v. 19). Three petitions of Jesus for his people will achieve this end. (1) *Unity (vv. 11–12)*. Christ prays that the unity shared between him and the Father might be realized in the church. But note the prerequisite that will facilitate this in verse 11: "Keep them in thy name" (lit.). Christian unity stems from personal faithfulness in God's presence. Like the good shepherd of 10:7–18, Jesus has protected his sheep until now, but other provisions will soon be necessary. (2) *Joy and perseverance (vv. 13–16)*. Conflict will hallmark the life of any who simultaneously live in the world and adhere to God's Word. This was made clear in 15:18–16:4a. Jesus, however, asks not simply for spiritual protection (17:15) but for a new disposition: joy in the midst of suffering. (3) *Holiness (vv. 17–19)*. This attribute reflects the presence of Christ because he, like God, is holy (v. 19). Sanctification comes through sustained exposure to the truth found in God's Word (v. 17). It is not just a superior moral effort, but something deriving from Christ's holiness in whose presence we are to live (v. 19).

Once before Jesus hinted at the church which would grow much later. The good shepherd has "other sheep not of this fold" (10:16). Now Jesus turns directly to concerns for others who will believe as a result of his disciples' work (**17:20–26**). It is interesting that Jesus' chief concern in 17:20–23 is again for unity. The later Johannine community must have been torn by divisions if 1 John is evidence (cf. 1 John 2:7–11, 18–21). Again he asks that the Father/Son relation would be the model of this unity (John 17:21; cf. v. 11). And again it is facilitated only by a profound spiritual unity with God in Christ (vv. 21, 23). Unity is not merely a human achievement, but flows from a mature walk with Christ.

Just as we noted the importance of Jesus' final public words (12:44–50), now we read his final private teachings for his disciples before his arrest. John 17:24–26 sweeps up subjects from the entire Farewell Discourse but emphasizes one central theme: Jesus desires that he and the Father indwell the believer, conveying to him the certainty of God's love. While experiences of God's presence will be in the eschaton (v. 24), the Holy Spirit will manifest the reality of Christ in us in this present world. Jesus' final prayer asks that two things be "in us": God's love and Christ's presence. Later John will write the same thing. How do we know that we abide in him? We bear God's love (1 John 4:7, 16) and Christ's own Spirit (4:13).

C. The passion (18:1–19:42). The story of Jesus' trial, death, and resurrection provides us with an excellent opportunity to test historical tradition in the fourth Gospel since so much of John's passion narrative overlaps with the Synoptics. The New Testament scholar C. H. Dodd even began his magisterial volume with a study of this section.[6] Nevertheless the Johannine account has had to weather various criticisms. Scholars have noted how John places all guilt on the Jews while leaving Pilate innocent (in Luke, however, Pilate announces Jesus' innocence three times: see Luke 23:4, 14, 22). Further we can note how John theologically reshapes a story of agony into a story of victory and glory (note 18:36). John is no doubt emphasizing themes that are important to him when, for instance, the arresting party falls to the ground at the mention of the divine name (18:6). Yet it is not necessary to argue that John has dramatically embellished his account with no regard for history.[7] Incidental historical details abound such as the name of the high priest's slave (18:10f.), his relation to Peter's questioner in 18:26, and the type of courtyard fire (charcoal, 18:18). When added to the harmony of this account with the Synoptics, these details lend significant credibility to John's independent pericope (cf. the interrogation before Annas, 18:13ff.).

The consistent sequence of events in the passion of Jesus both here and in the Synoptics shows how this story had an ancient pre-Gospel history. It may have been the first narrative circulating among the early Christians who needed to answer the apologetic question, "If Jesus was the Messiah, why was he crucified?"

It was the custom of Jewish celebrants on Passover to spend the night after their meal in prayer and meditation. Jesus does the same, crossing the Kidron Valley east of Jerusalem and entering a garden. The place of the arrest (**18:1–11**) was familiar to all since Judas who had left during the meal (13:30) now arrives with the arresting party (18:2–3). The authorities had found exactly what they needed: a quiet place where Jesus could be arrested without public notice.

John and Matthew stress the armaments of the party and imply that they expected a fight. John 18:3, however, stands out in that it tells us that a detachment of Roman troops assisted. Rather than record Judas's identifying kiss, John writes that Jesus takes the initiative to voluntarily identify himself (vv. 4–5). His hour has come and he will instigate its advance. The emphases that follow are uniquely Johannine. When Jesus utters the divine name ("I AM," v. 5) the party falls prostrate in awe. When they recover he exchanges his life for the freedom of his followers (cf. 6:39; 17:12; and the shepherd, 10:11ff.). Peter's zeal is misguided (18:10–11) since interfering with "the hour" is just as wrong as hastening its approach (7:6–9).

Once Jesus is bound he is taken for a preliminary interrogation before Annas. Annas served as high priest from A.D. 6 to 15. Even though he is deposed now, he still retains his title due to his weighty influence. In fact all of his five sons became priests (cf. Luke 3:2; Acts 4:6). His son-in-law, Caiaphas, is featured in the synoptic trial and given only passing reference in John (11:49; 18:13–14, 24).

6. C. H. Dodd, *Historical Tradition in the Fourth Gospel* (Cambridge: Cambridge University Press, 1963).

7. F. F. Bruce, "The Trial of Jesus in the Fourth Gospel" in *Gospel Perspectives*, vol. 1, ed. R. T. France and D. Wenham (Sheffield: JSOT, 1980), 7–20.

Intertwined in the trial sequence (**18:12–27**) is the story of Peter's threefold denial (vv. 15–18, 25–27; cf. Mark 14:66–72). Jesus had predicted Peter's fear of identification in this crisis (John 13:36–38) and now it is fulfilled. John diverges, however, from the synoptic story. He records that "another disciple" (likely John) who was acquainted with the priest let Peter into the courtyard (18:15–16). It is interesting that John records the specific type of fire (v. 18). A charcoal fire (Gk. *anthrakia;* NIV fire) will appear once again in 21:9 when Jesus reunites with Peter.

The Jewish interrogation is briefly recorded in 18:19–23 but certainly extensive questioning occurred. The fourth Gospel does not record the charges and countercharges well known to us in the Synoptics. Instead (as with the arrest) Jesus initiates and provides the substance of the dialogue. It is his hour of glorification. He is in control. His chief defense is that his teachings have been public—open to the inspection of all. In other words no inquiry will uncover more than is already known. On a literary level we might say that the Book of Signs has provided exhaustive evidence for Jesus' trial. No more is required.

From the house of Caiaphas (often located on Jerusalem's western hill or "upper city") Jesus is led to the praetorium or governor's palace. It was necessary to involve the Roman authorities in capital cases since the Roman subjugation of Palestine had eliminated numerous judicial powers from the Jews (see 18:31). Since A.D. 6 Pilate was the fifth Roman governor (A.D. 26–36) to rule Judea. Based in Caesarea with numerous troops Pilate came to Jerusalem occasionally to conduct his administrative duties with the Jews. The praetorium was his residence although it is uncertain whether he chose Herod's palace in Jerusalem or the Antonia Fortress with its garrison near the temple (the traditional site since Crusader times).

The entire narrative of **18:28–19:16** bears the marks of a carefully written unit. Its dramatic suspense is second to none. Pilate moves in and out of the praetorium five times (18:29, 33, 38; 19:9, 13), establishing the innocence of Jesus and exploring his title of "king." In fact kingship weaves continuously through the story, becoming the principal theme (18:33, 36, 37, 39; 19:2–3, 12, 14–15, 19–22) until Pilate's caution turns to fear (19:8). Even when Jesus is crucified, Pilate insists on Jesus' title in death (19:19–22).

Pilate meets with the Jewish leadership outside his residence so that they might not become ritually unclean due to contact with Gentiles (18:28). The accusation that Jesus is a criminal is less clear than the synoptic charges that bring political offenses to mind (esp. Luke 23:2). Pilate is initially unmoved and prefers to leave the case in Jewish courts, but his audience reminds him of the Roman restriction prohibiting capital punishment from the Jews.

Pilate now goes inside (v. 33) to Jesus who is in custody and speaks with him. In this round Pilate's first inquiry is important: "king" was a political title that was enjoyed only by Herod the Great in Judea. Is Jesus making a political challenge with this word? Jesus accepts the title but redefines it: his kingdom is otherworldly. He is not an insurrectionist of the sort that Rome fears. Pilate feels no threat and glibly dismisses Jesus, but his closing remark ("What is truth?") shows that he cannot be one who recognizes Jesus' voice (v. 37). Soon, however, Pilate's interest will be piqued.

Jesus is innocent and this judgment is conveyed outside (v. 38b). But since Pilate's generous overture is rejected (vv. 39–40) Jesus is flogged, a severe punishment often preliminary to crucifixion. However, the mocking of the soldiers serves another purpose: this is Jesus' symbolic coronation. He is hailed "king" and so arrayed (19:2–3), but Pilate hopes that the severity of Jesus' pitiful condition and profuse bleeding will permit him to be released. Instead Pilate is met with calls for death, which would usually give a governor no hesitation. But now a new title for Jesus is offered by the crowd: Jesus claims to be the Son of God. The round closes differently than the previous one. Pilate is afraid (v. 8).

When Pilate reenters the praetorium it is evident that the glib tone of 18:38 has disappeared. "Son of God" was a metaphysical claim; it evoked a meaning not unknown among Romans. Pilate's initial question (v. 9) shows that he is probing the identity of Jesus. Like Nicodemus earlier (3:1ff.) Pilate is making a discreet inquiry. And like many who came to Jesus, he has to choose to follow the light or the darkness. Pilate's reflex to his own power (v. 10) is completely demolished when Jesus explains how the governor actually derives his power from God. Furthermore, Pilate has been the unwitting pawn of other powers, the Jews, who have instigated this trial (19:11). The round ends with Pilate's earnest desire to release Jesus (cf. Matt. 27:18–19).

As Pilate readies himself to come outside already voices meet him. But now a new threat is hurled at him and his stamina collapses (**19:12b–16**). "Friend of Caesar" (v. 12) was a technical term meaning "loyal to Caesar" and it referred to people who had distinguished themselves in imperial service. It was the guarantee of a good career. Therefore Pilate must choose between this new king and Caesar. In two discourses Jesus described the dangerous temptation to regard secular acclaim above divine approval (5:44; 12:43).

Pilate chooses the former (vv. 13–16) and goes through the motions of making a judicial edict. The "Stone Pavement" (Aram. *gabbatā'*, elevated place?) may have been a visible platform for such pronouncements. (Archaeologists claim to have found this pavement in the remains of the Antonia Fortress.) The time of this announcement, the "sixth hour" or noon, is indicated (v. 14) because of a theme that will arise during the crucifixion. The hour of Jesus' condemnation is the hour when the temple began to slaughter the ritual lambs for Passover. Jesus is one such lamb (19:31–36).

The decision between Caesar and the King Jesus weighed earlier by Pilate is decided now by the chief priests (v. 15). This is their irrevocable rejection of Christ: "We have no king but Caesar" (similarly, Matt. 27:24–25).

Each of the Gospels is content to give us a brief description of the crucifixion (**19:17–37**) thereby sparing us its gruesome details. It was despised by Jews and Romans alike and employed mainly in the provinces for slaves and criminals. Following a severe flogging with a metal- or bone-tipped whip, the victim was forced to march to the site of death carrying his crossbeam even though he was often already fatally injured. Jesus had already been scourged thus (19:1; cf. Mark 15:16–20). The Synoptics mention that Jesus' condition was so serious that he could not carry anything as he walked, but a passerby named Simon of Cyrene was forced into service (Mark 15:20f.).

Golgotha is the Aramaic word for skull or cranium (v. 17) and may derive from the shape of a hill or simply be an apt metaphor for a place of death. It was certainly outside of the city walls of Jerusalem, and if the northern courses of Herod's walls have been correctly determined then the traditional site of Jerusalem's Holy Sepulchre Church can be accepted.

The extended attention given to the title on the cross is strictly Johannine (vv. 19–22; cf. Mark 15:26). While it conveys historical information its chief importance is theological. Jesus' death has been described as his glorification (John 7:39; 13:31; etc.). It has also been called his "lifting up" (3:14; 8:28; 12:32, 34) inasmuch as he is returning to the Father and to his previous glory (17:1–5). Therefore, the cross is not a place of defeat or humiliation in Johannine thought. It is a further revelatory sign since it will evoke faith and create followers (12:32). If we keep this in mind then the place of regal language (kingship) becomes clear: Christ, already crowned (19:2), is now enthroned (vv. 19–22). The irony of the scene fits well the two-level understanding that has accompanied the signs and discourses throughout the Gospel (3:3; 4:7f.; etc.). Pilate misunderstands the truth that he so valiantly defends! Only John mentions that the title is in three languages (19:20) and this underscores his interest in those outside of Judea who are also a part of Christ's fold (cf. 10:16; 12:20; 17:20).

The Romans customarily removed and confiscated the clothing of the crucified, thereby heightening his shame and giving the soldiers some benefit for their labors. This occurs at Golgotha (19:23–24; cf. Mark 15:24). John's narrative explains that Jesus' garments were divided four ways, but he focuses on a seamless undergarment valued by the guards. Its preservation is explained from Psalm 22:18 but its symbolic meaning may lie elsewhere. The garments of the high priest included this item (Exod. 28:4; 39:27) and it may suggest some priestly symbolism for Jesus (which is a common New Testament thought; see Heb. 4:14; Rev. 1:13); but this interpretation must remain uncertain.

The presence of women at the cross is striking (19:25–27). Unlike the apostles who fled, the women would have been safe from incrimination because of ancient oriental chivalry giving them a protected status. We see that John attends as well but for one purpose: Jesus' first word from the cross makes provision for his mother's future. Mary is taken into the beloved disciple's care. A plethora of symbols is often attached to this act (e.g., does John represent the church to whom the heritage of Israel, Mary, is entrusted?) but few of these suggestions find any consensus.

The remaining activity on the cross (19:28–37) now emphasizes two dominant theological themes. First, Jesus is a Passover victim dying a sacrificial death. This motif already appeared in 19:14 (also 1:29) and again comes to mind here. Jesus' thirst (19:28) echoes Psalm 22:15, while the hyssop which satisfies his thirst reflects Exodus 12:22 and Passover symbolism. Hyssop was used with blood on Israel's doorposts in Egypt. This is a uniquely Johannine note (cf. Mark 15:36). John is also the only Evangelist who speaks of the Roman *crurifragium* or breaking of legs (19:31–37). Again this serves Passover imagery in that the Passover lamb could have no broken bones (v. 36; Exod. 12:46). Jesus was already dead (19:30) but if a man were not, a violent blow to the legs with a lance would hasten death since the body would no longer have leg support. Finally, we should refer to the blood from Jesus' side (v. 34).[8] The sacrificial blood cannot be congealed—it must be a living victim—and here John has provided proof (see Mish. *Pesahim* 5:3, 5).

Second, the hour of death ushers forward the Spirit. As Jesus discussed his departure in his Farewell Discourse (John 13:16) we saw how the Spirit was promised to replace the presence of Christ (14:16). The Spirit would turn grief to joy. Here on the cross two veiled allusions indicate the connection between the Spirit and the hour of glory. In 19:30 Jesus says, "It is finished," and bowing his head "he gave over the Spirit." The phrase is different from that in the Synoptics and is found nowhere in Greek literature for death. "Give over" (Gk. *paradidōmi*) means handing something on (1 Cor. 15:3) and here Jesus directs himself *not* to the Father but to those followers below. Hence this is a symbolic act depicting an anointing about to come (John 20:22). The blood and water—especially the water—may be symbolic. John 7:37–39 states that living waters will flow from Christ; in the immediate context (7:39) this is related to the Spirit and the hour of glorification. Thus 19:34 may fulfill 7:37–39 indicating that at the hour of death Jesus' spirit is about to be released.

Since the Passover would officially begin at dusk, Joseph from Arimathea (a village of uncertain location) and Nicodemus remove the body of Jesus so that he can be buried before the feast (**19:38–42**). Mark notes that Joseph was a member of the Sanhedrin (Mark 15:43); Matthew mentions his wealth (Matt. 27:57). Along with Nicodemus (John 3:1–15; 7:50–52) Joseph exerts his influence on Pilate to obtain Jesus' body (19:38). The myrrh and aloes (v. 39) along with linen cloths were commonly used in Jewish burials, but the amount of spices (about seventy-five pounds) seems extraordinary.

D. The resurrection (20:1–29). The final chapter of the Book of Glory concludes those elements which make up the hour of Christ's glorification. First, there is the account of the empty tomb which records the evidence of the resurrection but emphasizes above all the faith of the beloved disciple (20:1–10). Second, Matthew's story of Jesus' appearance to various women (see Matt. 28:9–10) has a parallel in the account about Mary Magdalene, a woman who dramatizes the grief of the apostolic company and their joy upon seeing Jesus again (John 20:11–18). Finally, Jesus appears to his disciples and during his visit breathes on them the Holy Spirit (19:19–29).

Mary's arrival at the empty tomb (**20:1–10**) was before morning (v. 1; on Mary see 19:25 and Luke 8:2) and although John mentions her alone the synoptic Evangelists say that she was accompanied by other women (cf. Matt. 28:1; Mark 16:1; Luke 24:10). Rolling-stone tombs were not impossible to reopen and were designed to offer future access to a tomb for secondary Jewish burial or for additional primary burials. Mary's surprise centers not so much on the fact that the stone is rolled back (for to her mind Joseph or Nicodemus might have reopened it) but on the absence of Jesus' body. The text gives no indication that she believed in his resurrection at this point (John 20:9). For her Jesus' body had simply been reburied elsewhere.

Her report to the disciples introduces a complete shift in subject (vv. 3–10). While the story provides numerous accurate details about what they viewed (vv. 5–7), the story primarily emphasizes the relation between John (the beloved disciple) and Peter. In the fourth Gospel, John always gains the upper hand. He outruns Peter to the tomb (v. 4) and looks in first. Even though Peter goes in first, John *believes* when he enters (v. 8; cf. v. 29). This theme appears elsewhere in the Gospel. At the Last Supper, for instance, Peter recognizes in John some unique access to Christ (13:23–24). In 18:15–16 the beloved disciple admits Peter to the high priest's home. And in 21:6–8 they are contrasted once again. Many scholars note that John bears the remarkable title *beloved disciple* and they conclude that to some degree the fourth Gospel venerates him as a hero. No doubt the profundity of the fourth Gospel and its penetration into the truth of Christ indicate John's depth of faith and experience to which these narratives of contrast bear witness.

The story of Mary Magdalene and Jesus (**20:11–18**) bears some resemblance to two separate synoptic narratives. Mary now witnesses two angels (v. 12) and afterward meets Jesus and seeks to embrace him (vv. 16–17). In Luke two angels appear to the women when they arrive at the tomb (Luke 24:4–9) and in Matthew we read about women seeing Jesus near the tomb and worshiping him (Matt. 28:9–10). The Johannine account, while independent of these, has clear historical moorings (note that Mary Magdalene appears in both synoptic stories, Matt. 28:1; Luke 24:10).

With the hour of glory, what message does this passage convey? Weeping (Gk. *klaiō*, 20:11, 13, 15) is a prominent theme here and has a special Johannine usage. Elsewhere it appears

8. On the medical question see F. T. Zugibe, *The Cross and the Shroud* (New York: Paragon House, 1986), 118–31.

at Lazarus's funeral (11:31, 33), which is a paradigm of Jesus' death. But, moreover, it is found in Jesus' own prediction: "I tell you the truth, you will weep and mourn" (16:20). Mary experiences the grief of being alone without Jesus. Yet in the Farewell Discourse Jesus remarked that this mourning would become rejoicing (16:22).

But what will create this joy? The answer of the earlier Farewell Discourse is now dramatized. Mary misunderstands Jesus' appearance, thinking him to be a gardener (20:14–15). But when he calls her by name she at once recognizes his voice (see 10:3, "he calls his own sheep by name"). Yet now she misunderstands the meaning of Jesus' presence. Why does Jesus forbid her embrace (20:17) when in 20:27 he will invite Thomas to touch him? Mary is trying to hold on to the joy she has found in his resurrection. In effect Jesus is saying that his permanent presence with her will be in another form. This is precisely the message of the Farewell Discourse. Jesus' "coming" will also be in the Spirit Paraclete who will indwell his followers individually (14:18–26).

The message that she is to convey (20:17) is that the final steps of departure are at hand. The ascension (NIV return; Gk. *anabainō*) can be referred to in both the perfect and the present tenses: it has begun and is still under way. And it is necessary that it continue this way, since the coming of the Spirit is directly dependent on Jesus' departure (16:7).

The story of Mary, therefore, is an interpretative vehicle that underscores the transition now under way. Jesus will not leave them as orphans (14:18) because as he moves through "the hour" he will give his Spirit. For this they must make ready. The gift of the Spirit will climax the events of "the hour."

On the evening of this Easter Sunday Jesus appears to the disciples and provides confirmation of his resurrection (v. 20). Twice he speaks of "peace" (vv. 19, 21) fulfilling that which he had promised in his farewell, "Peace I leave with you; my peace I give to you" (14:27; 16:33). "Seeing the Lord" was also a part of this promise (16:16; thus for Mary, 20:18; the disciples, 20:20, 25; and Thomas, 20:25, 29) as was rejoicing (16:20; 20:20). In other words Jesus is recalling his words from the upper room and this must necessarily include the coming of the Spirit (**20:19–29**).

That this is a definitive gift of the Spirit and no symbolic event is clear. John 7:39 is satisfied: Christ has been glorified and the gift is given. The breathing of Jesus (Gk. *emphysaō*) echoes Genesis 2:7 when God gives life to Adam. Jesus is such a creator (John 1:3) and the Spirit gives life (6:63). Thus the gift of the Spirit is Christ's re-creation. Above all Jesus has given his own breath, his own Spirit, and the personal dimensions of his indwelling are emphasized.[9]

In this hour Jesus also transfers to his disciples his own mission. He sends them forth (20:21) in the same way that the Father had commissioned him (13:16, 20; 17:18). The basis of the church's authority is that it bears the commission of Christ. Furthermore they will bear the divine Spirit insuring their success. The authority over sins (20:23) also reflects Jesus' ministry (3:19f.; 9:40f.). However, its meaning must be carefully understood. The judgment of Christ stemmed from his revelation of the light and the response of his listeners. When the light is unveiled each one brings judgment on himself depending on his response. The mission of the church is to continue the revelatory work of Christ in the world.

When Jesus met with the disciples, Thomas (11:16; 14:5; 21:2) was absent. He receives the now familiar Easter greeting (20:25) but claims that unless he can acquire this certainty himself (i.e., "see the Lord") he will not believe. On the following Sunday the group is gathered again and Jesus appears offering to Thomas that which he seeks. Thomas provides the Gospel's final response to Jesus when he offers the ultimate title of divinity and lordship to him (v. 28). Jesus' final words speak to Thomas and to the church together. While "seeing" forms the basis of the apostolic witness (Acts 1:21–22; 1 Cor. 15:3–8; 1 John 1:1–4) it cannot belong to all. Those who believe without seeing—without demanding signs (cf. John 4:48)—are more blessed still.

E. Conclusion (20:30–31). It is evident that this is a natural conclusion to the Gospel (on chap. 21, see below). The fourth Evangelist stresses the purpose of his Gospel: that we might believe (the verb has two readings which the NIV marg. notes: "to begin to believe" [aorist] and "to continue to believe" [present]; the former implies an evangelistic purpose, the latter a pastoral intent for those who already believe). The Gospel is a record of signs—of evidences—which the reader must weigh. It stems from Jesus' disciples who are trustworthy witnesses (see 19:35) and in particular from the testimony of John (21:24). Its aim is to lead

9. On the relation of this anointing with that in Acts 2 see G. Burge, *The Anointed Community: The Holy Spirit in the Johannine Tradition* (Grand Rapids: Eerdmans, 1986).

us to faith in Christ because in him alone can we find life.

IV. Epilogue (21:1–25)

The origin and place of this final chapter has perplexed many. John 20:30–31 seems to be a natural ending to the Gospel, whereas chapter 21 seems to be an appendage. In 20:29 a blessing is given on those "who have not seen" and yet believe, and here we hardly expect another visit from the resurrected Christ. It is even possible that the editors who included this chapter identify themselves in 21:24 (see below).

That John's Gospel has experienced some editorial attention need not surprise us; hints to this effect have been seen all along. We noted the prologue already (1:1–18) and the account of the adulterous woman (7:53–8:11, which also raises manuscript variant problems). Each is a narrative with its own unique history. We even noted how some scholars would reverse chapters 5 and 6 for greater sequential clarity. And finally, some have pointed to chapters 11 and 12 suggesting an expansion to the Book of Signs.

But to note such features is not to say that these additions cannot be from the pen of the fourth Evangelist. On the contrary, each narrative enjoys a striking unity with the rest of the Gospel. In chapter 21 these connections are numerous. In 21:14 the appearance of Jesus is numbered as his third, which presupposes his appearances in 20:19 and 20:26. Typical of the fourth Gospel is the John/Peter rivalry in 21:7 (cf. 13:23ff.; 20:3ff.). There is also characteristic Johannine language such as the charcoal fire in 21:9 (cf. 18:18), the word for "fish" in 21:9, 10, 13 (Gk. *opsarion*, 6:9, 11), the reference to Thomas and Nathanael in 21:2 (cf. 1:45f.; 11:16; 14:5; 20:24), the name of Simon's father in 21:15 (see 1:42), and the double use of "truly/amen" in 21:18 (see 5:19; 6:26; 8:34; etc.).

This evidence suggests that chapter 21 is authentically Johannine, but secondary to the original format of the Gospel.[10] John 21:20–23 implies that John the apostle has died and that the community he founded is wrestling with his absence. Disciples who have survived their master identify themselves in 21:24 ("we know that his testimony is true"). No doubt they collected together John's teachings—including chapter 21—and gave the Gospel its final form. This may even be the origin of other editorial "seams," the testimonials such as that in 19:35, and the special title for John the son of Zebedee, "the beloved disciple."

A. The miracle of 153 fish (21:1–14). Both Mark and Matthew record a resurrection appearance to the apostles after Easter, and Matthew specifically identifies Galilee as the place (Matt. 28:16–20; Mark 16:12–20; 14:26–28). This is also the Johannine setting. The story of the miraculous catch of fish has close parallels with another miracle (Luke 5:1–11). (Some would urge that John's story is another rendering of that in Luke, but this conclusion is not necessary.) Here Jesus repeats the earlier fishing miracle and this repetition becomes the vehicle of revelation. (The same is true of the meal in 21:9–14 as well as Peter's triple confession in 21:15–17, echoing his triple denial, 18:15ff.) Jesus takes them through the same experience twice and in this discloses his identity to them.

The Sea of Tiberias is an alternate name for the Sea of Galilee and comes from Herod Antipas's regional capital of Tiberias on the western shore. The apostles and a number of additional disciples returned to their native Galilee after Easter (cf. Matt. 28:16), some apparently assuming their former occupations. In Matthew and Mark a critical note is sounded: each mentions the disciples' lack of faith and records Jesus' call to go forth into the world (Matt. 28:17, 19; Mark 16:14, 15). Something apparently had failed in the men's resolve and conviction.

In the present story Jesus takes charge of Peter's fishing venture. Despite a night of fruitless toil (v. 3; compare the earlier miracle, Luke 5:5) they are obedient to the voice on the shore even though they do not yet recognize Jesus (21:4; cf. 20:29). Just like the earlier fishing miracle the nets are filled (21:6; Luke 5:6) and just like before, Peter responds prominently in devotion to Christ (21:7; Luke 5:8). However, the familiar superiority of the beloved disciple appears even here (cf. 13:23f.; 20:3–4, 8). He recognizes Jesus first and on his word Peter runs to the beach. It is interesting to think about the beloved disciple's response in light of this rivalry motif. He stays with the fish and brings them safely to shore.

Although Peter's despair is turned to jubilation at the size of the catch and the appearance of Jesus, the meaning of the miracle lies deeper. Johannine symbolism often produces two levels of meaning (e.g., 3:3f.; 4:7f.) and we should expect the same here. The fish and bread served by Christ recall the feeding miracle in 6:1–14. (Peter might even recall an earlier charcoal fire, 18:18.) Jesus is revealing himself by evoking memories of past activities.

10. But see S. S. Smalley, "The Sign in John 21," *New Testament Studies* 20 (1974): 275–88.

But here the recently caught fish play a central role. The beloved disciple has not neglected them (21:8) and Jesus orders Peter to bring the net finally ashore (vv. 10–11). The number of fish (153) is striking and is not an accidental note. First-century writers enjoyed cryptic devices, especially numerical values that symbolized some word or thought (e.g., 666 in Rev. 13:18). Jerome says that 153 was the ancient number of known fish species. In effect John would be saying that all people are part of the church's mission. But evidence for this interpretation is slim. Some scholars suggest mathematical sums (1 + 2 + 3 . . . + 17 = 153. And 17 = 10 + 7, two numbers of perfection).[11] But the riddle remains unsolved.

Essentially Jesus is emphasizing the mission of the disciples. When Jesus directs their work they will prosper. And the beloved disciple, indeed, has chosen the correct task: to remain with the fish so that none are lost (cf. Matt. 4:19). This is the same theme in John 21:15–19. Peter will be challenged to compare his devotion to Christ with his care for Christ's sheep.

B. Jesus and Peter (21:15–23). The exchange between Jesus and Peter is one of the most celebrated dialogues in the Bible (**21:15–17**). Its interpretation turns on our understanding of verse 15: "Do you love me more than these?" What is Jesus' comparison? ("These," Gk. *toutōn,* being any gender, has no clear antecedent.) Is Peter being asked if his love for Christ exceeds his love for fishing? This is plausible since it was Peter who instigated the trip to sea (21:3) and Jesus will challenge the apostle to recommit his efforts to ministry with the new sheep metaphor. On the other hand, "these" may refer to the other disciples. If Peter's love for Christ excels generally, then it should be followed by a coordinate care for God's flock.

Either way Jesus' challenge to Peter is that he consider carefully his love for his Lord and take up the task of shepherding. The dialogue enjoys numerous interplays of Greek synonyms: two words for love (*agapaō, phileō*), the flock (*arnia, probata*), tending/caring (*boskō, poimainō*), and know (*oida, ginōskō*). Of these pairs of synonyms, the interplay of verbs for "love" has inspired most comment. (Jesus uses *agapaō* twice and then *phileō* in the final exchange; Peter uses *phileō* throughout.) This variation is either a feature of John's Greek style—the other synonym pairs suggest this—or it bears some meaning. If the latter is true then two options are possible. Either Jesus consents to Peter's verb and we find in *phileō* an affectionate love Peter desires to express, or *agapaō* is the greater love (a sacrificial love) and Jesus is challenging the quality of Peter's affection. In this sense Peter confesses some limit to his love. Above all it must be recalled that these verbs were interchangeable in the first century and that even John himself seems to use them as synonyms (cf. 3:35 with 5:20; 13:23; 19:26; 21:7, 20). This is the most common interpretation among modern commentators.

Jesus now turns to a description of the fate of Peter and John (**21:18–23**), and especially what it will mean for Peter to "follow him" (v. 19). Peter once announced that he was willing to follow Jesus even to death (13:37). Jesus demurred, predicting Peter's denial (13:38). But now all things are changed. Jesus now predicts Peter's faithfulness even to death (v. 18) and John, for fear that we might misunderstand, provides an explanatory note (v. 19; so too 12:33). "Stretch out your hands" implies crucifixion. While we know that Peter was martyred in the 60s, Tertullian in the early third century A.D. explains that he died on a cross.

In 21:20–23 the discussion of Peter's martyrdom opens the subject of the beloved disciple's death. The nature of Jesus' comment (v. 22) and the editorial notes of the writer (v. 23) indicate that within the community of believers was a belief that John was going to survive until the second coming of Christ. But he did not. Here is evidence of the dismay that must have gripped the church during the eventual death of the apostles. Jesus' words are repeated: disciples should continue to follow and not be distracted by speculations about Christ's future will. For John's church the message is clear: John's survival may not have been Christ's will at all.

C. Appendix (21:24–25). These final notes assert the authority of the beloved disciple as a reliable eyewitness and as the originator of a trustworthy historical tradition. This same sort of confirmation is given in 19:35. From 1 John 1:1–4 we can see how John's connection with the historical events of Jesus' life was valued. Moreover, the Gospel bears eloquent testimony to the power of John's spiritual perception of Christ and this too must have been deeply respected.

The disciples of John who penned these words identify themselves in the plural "we" of 21:24. They have survived their pastor and now have collected his teachings for the church. The process must have been difficult for, as 21:25 indicates, the amount of material at their disposal was voluminous.

11. For example, C. K. Barrett, *The Gospel According to St. John,* 2d ed. (Philadelphia: Westminster, 1978), 581–82.

SELECT BIBLIOGRAPHY

Beasley-Murray, G. R. *John.* Waco: Word, 1987.

Bruce, F. F. *The Gospel of John.* Grand Rapids: Eerdmans, 1984.

Ellis, E. E. *The World of St. John.* Grand Rapids: Eerdmans, 1984.

Hunter, A. M. *According to John: The New Look on the Fourth Gospel.* Philadelphia: Westminster, 1968.

———. *The Gospel According to John.* Cambridge: Cambridge University Press, 1965.

Lindars, B. *The Gospel of John.* Grand Rapids: Eerdmans, 1972.

Meye-Thompson, Marianne. *The Humanity of Jesus in the Fourth Gospel.* Philadelphia: Fortress, 1988.

Morris, L. *The Gospel According to John.* Grand Rapids: Eerdmans, 1971.

Smalley, S. S. *John: Evangelist and Interpreter.* New York: Thomas Nelson, 1978.

Vanderlip, D. G. *Christianity According to John.* Philadelphia: Westminster, 1979.

Acts

In the New Testament the Book of Acts follows immediately after the four Gospels. In the Gospels the life of Jesus is presented, in Acts the lives of his followers. In the Gospels the one who is Savior is depicted, in Acts those who are saved. In the Gospels Jesus' teachings may be found, in Acts the teaching of the apostles. In the Gospels we have what Jesus did on earth for his church, in Acts we have what Jesus does from heaven through his church. In the Gospels we have the message reaching the borders of Israel, in Acts the message reaches to the ends of the earth.

The Gospels and the Book of Acts belong together. Combined they give us an account of Christian beginnings—Jesus and his church. Acts picks up where the Gospels leave off and carries us through those turbulent early days while Christianity was being established and believers were yet a tiny minority. But from these persecuted, beleaguered few came a power that was to conquer the world in the form of God's saving truth.

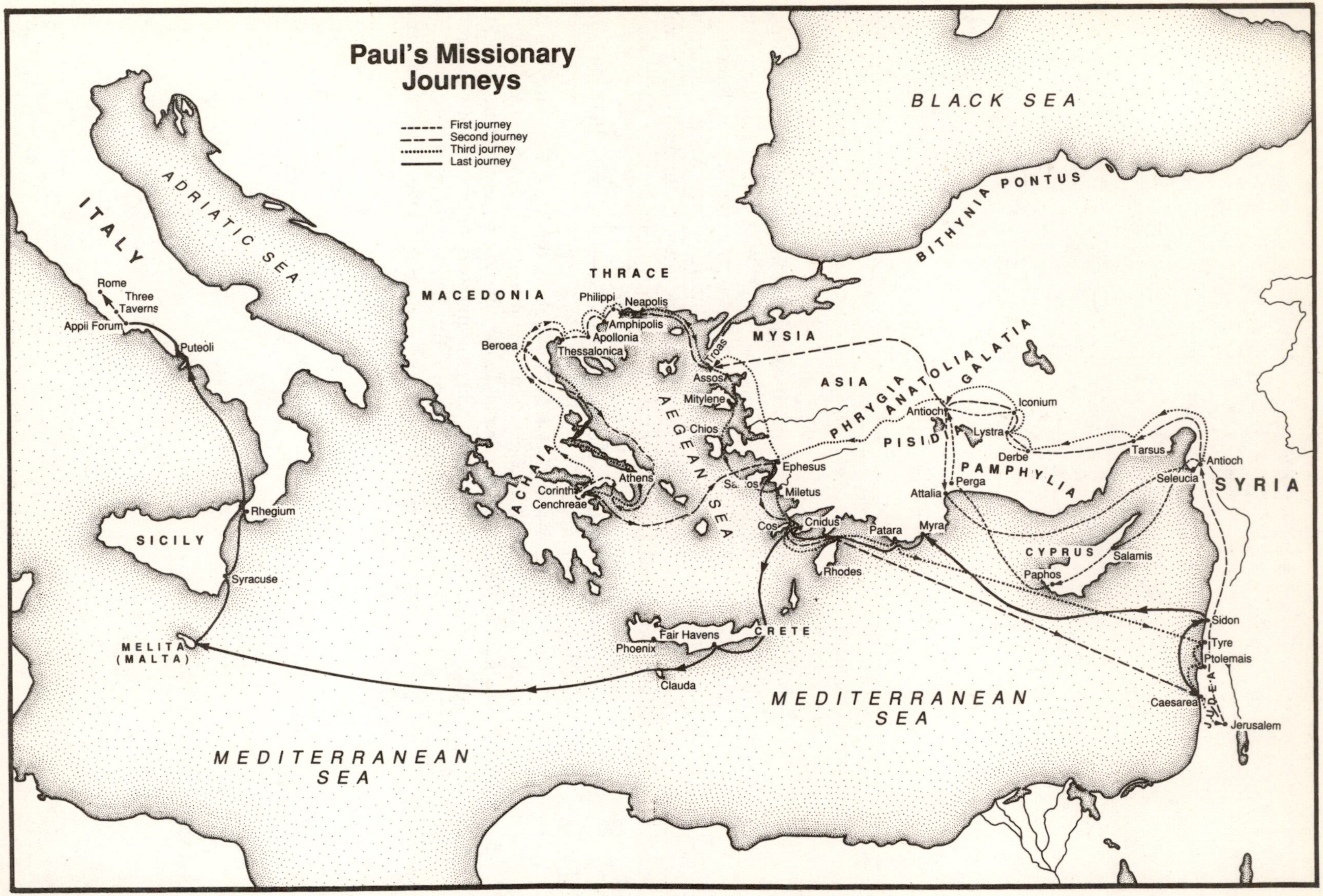
Paul's Missionary Journeys
First journey
Second journey
Third journey
Last journey
BLACK SEA
BITHYNIA
PONTUS
ITALY
ADRIATIC SEA
Rome
Three Taverns
Appii Forum
Puteoli
Rhegium
SICILY
Syracuse
MELITA (MALTA)
MACEDONIA
THRACE
Philippi
Neapolis
Amphipolis
Apollonia
Thessalonica
Beroea
ACHAIA
Athens
Corinth
Cenchreae
AEGEAN SEA
Troas
Assos
Mitylene
Chios
Samos
Ephesus
Miletus
Cos
Cnidus
Rhodes
MYSIA
ASIA
PHRYGIA
ANATOLIA
GALATIA
PISIDIA
PAMPHYLIA
Antioch
Iconium
Lystra
Derbe
Tarsus
Perga
Attalia
Patara
Myra
CYPRUS
Paphos
Salamis
Seleucia
SYRIA
Sidon
Tyre
Ptolemais
Caesarea
JUDEA
Jerusalem
CRETE
Fair Havens
Phoenix
Claudа
MEDITERRANEAN SEA
MEDITERRANEAN SEA

ACTS

William H. Baker

INTRODUCTION

The Book of Acts, like the four Gospels, does not name its author. However, the widespread belief that this book, along with the third Gospel, was composed by a man named Luke who was a companion of the apostle Paul (Col. 4:14; 2 Tim. 4:11; Philem. 24), has persisted from early times, particularly since the late second century. Both the third Gospel and Acts have prologues that tie the two together with references to a man called Theophilus and lead one to believe that they are the first and second volumes of a continuous history. The "we sections" of Acts (16:10–17; 20:5–21:18; 27:1–28:16) imply that the writer of Acts was a companion of Paul part of the time, and after one eliminates most of the people the author mentions by name in Acts, the most logical identification is Luke the physician. Thus the strong testimony of the earliest Fathers and this internal evidence, reinforced by the presence of medical language (which alone is not decisive), have led the majority of scholars, ancient and modern, to consider Luke the author.

Luke puts his narrative together from his own observations (thus the "we sections") as well as other possible eyewitness accounts, written and oral. This is implied by the statement of Luke 1:3, where the author refers to his investigations. The style and vocabulary of the speeches of Paul and Peter conform remarkably to their own writings, so that one gets the impression that someone, probably Luke in the case of a few of Paul's sermons, took careful notes during their delivery.

Acts 1:8 can be demonstrated to provide an outline of the three major parts of the entire book: the spread of the gospel witness in and around Jerusalem (1–7); its spread to Judea and Samaria (8–12); and its spread to the ends of the earth (13–28).

Acts was probably composed by Luke about A.D. 62. This conclusion is based upon several factors: its relation to the momentous destruction of Jerusalem; its relation to the death of Paul; and internal qualities that hint at the degree of historical maturity the author has toward the history he is relating.

As to the first of these factors, there is no hint in Acts of knowledge of the destruction of Jerusalem. Some scholars cite the fact that its companion, the third Gospel, refers to this event in the apocalyptic section (21:20–24), but this could be a statement of prophecy rather than history.

As to the second, Luke makes no reference to the death of Paul, which seems strange if it had occurred. These first two factors require us to place the book prior to A.D. 70 and A.D. 67, the destruction of Jerusalem and the persecutions under Nero, when Paul's death probably occurred. Other chronological factors in Acts require us to place it no earlier than A.D. 60.

As to the third factor, there is no convincing reason why Luke could not have written with the kind of judgment he has for the significance of events in the first thirty years of the church's history. There is not a trace of later, second-century interests; thus A.D. 62 is a defensible date.

As a record of the apostolic church, Acts is not quite what the modern reader might expect. Historically, the book is tantalizing in the questions it raises about events it never records. The Book of Acts is obviously highly selective in its materials. This is due to the fact that Luke is probably writing in the manner of the Greek historians Xenophon and Plutarch. What this means is that a selection of the hero's acts (*praxeis*), historical vignettes which set forth the hero's character, are his major concern. The Book of Acts, then, is not a mere chronicle of events, but a portrayal of the kinds of people and kinds of things that were taking place in the early church. This approach makes Acts a much better "handbook" for the church today.

During the first part of the nineteenth century the Book of Acts was first vigorously challenged as being historically unreliable by F. C. Baur, David F. Strauss, and others of the so-called Tübingen school of German critics. Baur's theory, for example, was that the author was trying to conciliate two opposing factions, one of legalism (Peter) and the other of Christian freedom (Paul), in the apostolic church. As a result of the alleged differences between these two, great turmoil is supposed to have existed, and the efforts to paint a picture of harmony and tranquility led the writer to make a number of historical blunders.

But the Tübingen approach was not overwhelming in its influence, and by the early twentieth century, most New Testament scholars had repudiated Baur's principles of criticism as too subjective and selective of the facts. J. B. Lightfoot, William M. Ramsay, and Adolf Harnack tended to support the historicity of Acts, and their position has dominated except in the case of such recent scholars as Ernst Haenchen, who takes a radically skeptical view of the historical reliability of Acts. To him, as with Rudolf Bultmann and Hans Conzelmann, Acts, like other ancient writings, tells us more about its author than about the events it claims to relate, because its author tries to promote his theological cause. Recently, however, the work of T. F. Glasson has shown that the ancient historians were indeed interested in what actually happened, not propaganda.

Luke seems to be setting forth a theology of world evangelization as it was practiced by a selected number of people in a limited number of places. He does this in the context of human events, crises, and character portrayals. This includes such things as how the church functions (2, 4), what the early preaching of the gospel was like (2, 17), how Paul evangelized (13) and planted churches (18), and what the roles of the Holy Spirit as well as the local church were in all of this (13).

Subsidiary ideas in Acts are such things as the cost and commitment of discipleship, the joy and excitement of serving Christ, the reaction of the pagan and Jewish worlds to Christianity, and the coping of the early church with its internal problems (for this latter idea, note particularly Acts 6 and 15).

Along with the third Gospel, the Book of Acts exhibits some of the most literary Greek in the New Testament, although it nevertheless falls into the category of *koine,* the common lingua franca of the Roman world. Some have noticed strong affinities with the Greek of the Septuagint (the Greek translation of the Old Testament).

Especially memorable are Luke's portrayals of Peter and Paul, both of which correspond well with their writings in the New Testament and give us so much insight into those writings.

OUTLINE

I. The Witness to Christ in and around Jerusalem (1:1–7:60)
- A. Introduction and Instructions (1:1–8)
- B. The Ascension (1:9–11)
- C. The Selection of Judas's Replacement (1:12–26)
- D. Pentecost: Birth of the Church (2:1–47)
- E. First Encounter of the Church with the Religious Leaders (3:1–4:35)
- F. Ananias and Sapphira: A Case of Discipline (4:36–5:16)
- G. Second Encounter of the Church with the Religious Leaders (5:17–42)
- H. The Seven Servants: An Example of Problem-Solving (6:1–7)
- I. Stephen: The First Clash with Judaism (6:8–7:60)

II. The Witness to Christ in Judea and Samaria (8:1–12:25)
- A. Saul the Persecutor and Philip the Evangelist (8:1–40)
- B. The Conversion of Saul (9:1–31)
- C. Peter's Ministry in Judea (9:32–11:18)
- D. The Antioch Church: Barnabas's Ministry (11:19–30)
- E. Peter's Miraculous Deliverance (12:1–25)

III. The Witness to Christ to the Ends of the Earth (13:1–28:31)
- A. Paul's First Missionary Journey (13:1–14:28)
- B. The Jerusalem Council: An Example of Theological Peace-Making (15:1–35)
- C. Paul's Second Missionary Journey (15:36–18:22)
- D. Paul's Third Missionary Journey (18:23–21:14)
- E. Paul's Arrest in Jerusalem and Incarceration at Caesarea (21:15–26:32)
- F. Paul's Voyage to Rome (27:1–28:10)
- G. Paul's Ministry at Rome (28:11–31)

COMMENTARY

I. The Witness to Christ in and around Jerusalem (1:1–7:60)

A. Introduction and instructions (1:1–8). Luke's reference to the former treatise and an unknown friend called Theophilus tie this book together with the third Gospel (Luke 1:1–4). Some have speculated that Theophilus may be a figurative name for all believers, since it means "lover of God," but in all likelihood he was an actual person, probably a wealthy man whom Luke wished to influence.

Luke's previous volume (or scroll) concerned "all that Jesus began to do and to teach," and with the word *began* he may imply that this second volume continues the work and teaching of Jesus Christ through his disciples, a concept consistent with Jesus' promise concerning the purpose of the coming of the Holy Spirit (John 14:16–18; 16:5–15). The first volume covered the story of Jesus through "the day he was taken up to heaven," and at that point, following Jesus' "instructions," events recorded only in Acts take place.

The proofs of Jesus' resurrection lasted for a period of forty days while he appeared to his disciples. Since Pentecost (2:1) occurred fifty days from the Sabbath of Passover week, we infer that the waiting period of 1:5 was ten days.

The disciples are forbidden to "leave Jerusalem" and instead are to "wait for the gift" of the Holy Spirit, for the very nature of their work of witnessing would unqualifiedly require his help and direction. Jesus reminds them that John the Baptist had promised the gift of the Spirit (Matt. 3:11; Mark 1:8) in which they would be baptized with the Spirit and with fire. The preposition *with* (Gk. *en*) may be translated "in" or "by," so that the whole formula would be that "Jesus will baptize you in (or by) the Holy Spirit." If 1 Corinthians 12:13 refers to the same phenomenon (the Greek is the same), then this baptism means union into one body (the church) and reception of the Spirit himself into the temples of our bodies (1 Cor. 6:19). Some charismatics believe there are two distinct baptisms; the one here exclusively for power, and the one in 1 Corinthians 12:13 primarily for union with other believers.

One of two possibilities seems plausible for the meaning of John's reference to baptism by fire: the "tongues of fire" mentioned in 2:3 or judgment by fire at the second advent. The latter idea was more likely to have occurred to John's listeners. If Luke had understood it to be fulfilled at Pentecost he probably would have included it in his quotation or reference here.

Questions concerning the restoration of the earthly "kingdom of Israel" continue to be raised by the disciples, and Jesus' answer seems to say, "This is not your concern." He discourages their speculation on "times or dates," though he does not explicitly discourage the idea of a future kingdom. Instead Jesus points them to their primary concern, to be witnesses; that is, to be those who report accurately what they have seen. Strictly speaking, these eyewitnesses would report what they had seen concerning Jesus with an emphasis (as we shall see later) on his resurrection. In due course secondary witnesses would spread the Good News.

Through the Holy Spirit the disciples will receive power to communicate. This power will make the witnesses clear and convincing and the listeners open and receptive, thus producing converts and genuine disciples (Matt. 28:19).

The scope of the witnessing is threefold: in Jerusalem, in all Judea and Samaria, and to the ends of the earth. This arrangement probably roughly corresponds geographically and culturally to one's home city (Jerusalem), nation (Judea/Samaria), and foreign lands (ends of the earth) and suggests an order of concerns. If one does not witness to Christ in his own immediate situation, he probably will not be concerned to do so elsewhere.

B. The ascension (1:9–11). With rapt attention the disciples watch as Jesus is taken up from them in a cloud. The two men, probably angelic beings (see John 20:12), explain that the ascension provides a model of sorts for the second advent, and in so doing they initiate that spirit of watchfulness that would characterize the early church as it worked and waited for its Lord to return (see 1 Thess. 1:10).

Jesus' ascension makes an indelible impression upon the disciples, giving them a renewed sense of mission to "go and make disciples of all nations" (Matt. 28:19). As he had told them, Jesus had left them, and they were soon to be comforted by the coming of the Holy Spirit, which Jesus had promised (John 16:5–16).

C. The selection of Judas's replacement (1:12–26). Luke informs us that the ascension occurred on the Mount of Olives, thus adding another detail to expectations concerning Jesus' second advent (see Zech. 14:4). From here the disciples obediently (1:4) return to Jerusalem and to the room upstairs (vv. 12–13), a reference to a specific room ("the room") which was probably well known, like the one where the Last Supper was celebrated or the one where Jesus appeared after his resurrection.

The time of waiting for the Spirit is spent in unified prayer. In such an atmosphere of unity, obedience, and prayer it is difficult to criticize, as some have, the action taken to replace Judas. The description here of Judas's death—"he fell headlong [and] burst open"—adds some details to the description of Matthew 27:5, where Judas is said to have hanged himself. The best attempt to harmonize the accounts is by assuming that Judas hanged himself and that the rope broke, causing him to fall.

Peter bases his decision to replace Judas on Psalms 69:25 and 109:8, which reflect the need to have a complete and symbolic number of leaders (twelve = twelve tribes of Israel), the view of contemporary Judaism. The church is about to be born, and its first leaders are Jews, hence, representatives of the nation, as in Revelation 21:12–14.

In characteristic Old Testament fashion the choice of God is indicated by the drawing of lots (cf. Prov. 16:33). This is the last occasion for using such a method prior to the advent of the Holy Spirit, who will give guidance via prophetic utterance and Scripture.

Two qualifications are set down for the prospective replacement. He must be one who had "been with us" and who had been a witness of the resurrection. Matthias is "added to the eleven apostles" (v. 26), a distinct group known as "the Twelve" (1 Cor. 15:5), of which later apostles like Paul were never a part. Now the stage is set for Pentecost.

D. Pentecost: Birth of the church (2:1–47). The day of Pentecost was also known as the Feast of Weeks and was commanded, along with six other holy days like Passover and the Feast of Tabernacles, in Leviticus 23:15–21. It was a festive time and tended to draw religious pilgrims from all over the world. This occasion provides a unique opportunity in which to proclaim the new message of the gospel.

Luke informs us that Pentecost began while the disciples "were all together in one place." In all likelihood, this was the same room where they were staying before (1:13). By the time the events of 2:5–12 take place, the disciples must have made their way to a large open area able to accommodate several thousand people (2:41).

One of the phenomena occurring at Pentecost (**2:2–13**) is a sound from heaven "like the blowing of a violent wind" (v. 2). This is not a literal wind, but something "as of" a wind. Apparently its purpose is to attract attention (v. 6).

Another spectacular phenomenon is the "tongues of fire that separated and came to rest on each of them" (v. 3). The precise nature of this phenomenon is not explained, but its purpose is probably to indicate the ability of every believer to witness by the power of the Spirit, since the tongues of fire rest on each one.

Not all Bible scholars would wholly agree that Pentecost was the birthday of the church. However, even those who see a strong continuity between the covenant people of Israel and the people of the "new covenant" recognize that at Pentecost a new relationship with the Holy Spirit was instituted. This new relationship occurred at the time they were filled with the Holy Spirit and was attended by notable signs (v. 4). This filling of the Spirit, mentioned again in 4:8, 31; 9:17; 13:9, is usually connected, so far as Acts is concerned, with the bold, effective proclamation of the gospel, the ability to be a witness (1:8). The question is whether this filling is the same thing as the baptism which was supposed to occur at this time (1:5), but which is not specifically referred to. That baptism did indeed occur may be inferred from Peter's retrospective remark in 11:15–17. There may be a difference between filling and baptism (though here both occur simultaneously) for three reasons. First, the phrase *baptism in the Spirit* is never again used in Acts after the second chapter. Subsequent to Acts 2 we read that someone "receives" the Spirit, or the Spirit "comes upon" someone. Second, Ephesians 5:18–21, which uses a synonym for the word *filled,* describes the filling of the Spirit as a quality of Christian life rather than a special event. Finally, 1 Corinthians 12:13 affirms that all believers *were* baptized rather than that they *need* to be baptized. It is reasonable to identify this baptism with the baptism of Acts 1:5, since the wording (*en pneumati*) is the same in both places.

The phenomenon of Pentecost that has created the most debate as to its exact nature is the speaking in other tongues. Two opinions exist about what they were: unintelligible sounds or languages not previously learned by the speaker. Those who argue in favor of the first opinion sometimes explain the words *each one heard them speaking in his own language* (v. 6) as a miracle of "translation" by the Holy Spirit in the hearing of each person in the audience. Those who take the second opinion stress that foreign languages were spoken, not only heard.

In either case the purpose for the phenomenon, which "utterly amazed" the listeners, was for a sign to the Jewish audience of the divine nature of the message being proclaimed; the

Jews had required a sign of Jesus, the basis being precedents established in such places as Exodus 4:8 and Isaiah 7:11. Paul regarded tongues as a "sign" to unbelievers (1 Cor. 14:22), and in that context he seems to mean uninterpreted tongues, such as possibly occurred at Pentecost, because interpreted tongues were for the edification of the church.

Luke gives a geographical listing of the "God-fearing Jews from every nation under heaven" (v. 5), a list puzzling in its selection of nations, ranging roughly east to west in the known world, but impressive in its breadth of representation. Some of these people are "amazed and perplexed" at the disciples (v. 12), while a few others make "fun of them" and accuse them of having "too much wine" (v. 13).

This sets the stage for Peter's sermon (**2:14–41**). He responds by explaining the meaning and significance of the phenomenon of the languages.

Denying that drunkenness is the explanation for the behavior of the disciples, Peter identifies the miraculous speech with "what was spoken by the prophet Joel" (v. 16), an endowment of the Holy Spirit and prophetic utterance. It is evident that Peter understands Joel 2:28–32 to be fulfilled by the Pentecostal phenomenon of prophetic utterance, though some scholars have explained his use of the Old Testament text as merely illustrative ("this is the kind of thing spoken by the prophet Joel"), apparently in an effort to explain why the cosmic phenomena were not also literally fulfilled at Pentecost. Others explain the "wonders in the heaven above and signs on the earth below" (v. 19) as fulfilled in some spiritual way, or by the cosmic events on the day of Christ's crucifixion, or as being yet future.

A more natural interpretation of Peter's use of Joel's prophecy is to realize that the total fulfillment was contingent on the extent to which Peter's audience responded to the gospel message. If a significant portion of the nation had repented at Pentecost, the end-time events described by Joel would have been triggered and in the course of time literally fulfilled. Similarly, Jonah's warning to Nineveh was contingent upon that city's response (Jon. 3).

The main body of Peter's sermon deals with Jesus of Nazareth. This sermon serves as a model of apostolic preaching to Jewish audiences, and modern evangelists would do well to observe its principal elements carefully as they construct their own gospel messages to people with varying religious backgrounds. Jesus' life had its significance in its "miracles, wonders and signs," devices by which God "accredited" him. Central to the message is the fact that "God raised him from the dead" (v. 24), and Peter gathers several key quotations from the Old Testament (Pss. 16:8–11; 110:1) to show its necessity. His use of these quotations is an example of the best rabbinic interpretation of his day. David by inspiration went beyond his own experience when he declared that his body would not "see decay" (v. 27); Peter applies this to David's greater son, Jesus Christ.

The resurrection is more than a victory over death in Peter's preaching. It means that Jesus is "exalted to the right hand of God" (v. 33) and thus must be confessed (Rom. 10:9) as both Lord and Christ (v. 36). The term *lord* means that Jesus has absolute authority, deity, and sovereignty. Thus this confession would lay the groundwork for the work of the Holy Spirit in sanctification by making the confessor humbly subjected to the work of God that would follow. "Messiah" is the Jewish term that stands behind the word *Christ* and means the anointed Servant of the Lord who would come to deliver his people from tyranny and sin.

The Holy Spirit now demonstrates what is meant by "power" as the people are convinced of their sin of rebellion against God by being "cut to the heart" and asking "Brothers, what shall we do?" (v. 37). Peter's response is typical of many of the messages which follow: he calls for them to "repent and be baptized" (v. 38). "Repent" here means to acknowledge their guilt in regard to the earlier accusation: "you, with the help of wicked men, put him to death." This was more than a local crime against one man; it was a symptom of universal, original sin. Repentance is, then, not an act of reformation on their part (sinners are helpless to do this), but an acknowledgment of a sin of which they could never possibly make any correction except to admit its reality.

"Be baptized . . . for the forgiveness of your sins" does not mean that forgiveness is offered on condition of water baptism, but upon both repentance and baptism. Though Peter makes no verbal reference to believing or faith, the association of repentance and faith as inseparable parts of conversion serves to make them interchangeable terms throughout Acts; that is, the presence of one implies the other (see 16:31, where only "believe" occurs without "repent"). An outward verbal confession made at the time of baptism is considered by the New Testament a necessary consequence of genuine faith (Rom. 10:9–10). To Jews, this was a humbling act, for in Judaism baptism was required only for Gentile converts making a clean break from their past.

The fulfillment of Joel's prophecy to each

person is to be realized by the gift of the Holy Spirit. With the exception of the disciples who believed in Jesus during his ministry, the Samaritan converts (8:4–15), and possibly the twelve isolated disciples of John (19:1–7), the reception of the gift of the Spirit seems to take place upon conversion (10:44–48).

With many other words Peter addresses the Pentecostal audience. This provides the clue that the messages in Acts as reported by Luke may be condensations of the originals, but nevertheless, characteristic of ancient histories, fairly close in actual wording to the originals.

Three thousand conversions imply an even larger total audience. It has been recently proven that with lack of other noises and the acoustics of some locales in Palestine, such large crowds could indeed be addressed without modern means of amplification.

In one brief paragraph, Luke gives us a summary of the activities and spirit of the early church (**2:42–47**). Verse 42 summarizes the early Christian gatherings. Four kinds of activities are enumerated; the first is the apostles' teaching, instruction based upon Old Testament Scriptures, and a growing body of new revelation (see John 14:26; 16:13). Most comprehensive of these activities is fellowship (Gk. *koinōnia*), which means sharing together in material goods as well as spiritual wealth (see 1 John). This finds expression in a temporary widespread sharing and selling of "their possessions and goods" (v. 45) to meet the enormous needs of the Pentecost pilgrims and converted widows (Acts 6). People continue to maintain private ownership, a fact implied by the meetings in their homes. Another activity is the "breaking of bread," Luke's expression for the Lord's Supper which is celebrated as they eat together their regular meals. Finally, they devote themselves to prayer (v. 42), in the Greek literally "prayers," probably implying either the several times of prayer (3:1) or, more likely, the wide participation of early believers in prayer.

In addition to the spirit of "awe" (v. 43), the general spiritual atmosphere is one of "praising God and enjoying the favor of all the people" (v. 47), the bedrock of good evangelism which gives the Lord—not the church's leaders—the basis upon which he adds "to their number daily those who [are] being saved." Believers faithfully witness; God builds the church.

E. First encounter of the church with the religious leaders (3:1–4:35). In the next section, 3:1–7:60, Luke describes a series of events that reveal the successes as well as turmoils of the early church. In doing so, he seems to set forth a statement of the church's proper relation to the world around it. On the one hand, the church must faithfully witness to Christ; on the other hand, it must resist all efforts by the world to compromise its message and moral integrity.

If the church is to witness faithfully to the world, it must give a message of courageous warning touched with compassion. Luke selects a short story of a miraculous healing in the early days of the church and the sermon that resulted to illustrate this point (**3:1–26**).

The occasion is the "time of prayer" (v. 1) at the ninth hour (3 P.M.), and the place of the miracle is "the temple gate called Beautiful" (v. 2), possibly the Nicanor Gate which led from the eastern part of the temple. A man "crippled from birth," a fact Luke notes to indicate that many could verify his infirmity (see v. 10), is approached by Peter, who "look[s] straight at him" (v. 4), perhaps discerning God's intention to heal him. The crippled man is commanded to look at Peter and John, probably to focus his attention as well as his faith on them as mediators of a far better gift than "silver or gold" (v. 6). Without any hocus-pocus Peter simply commands, "In the name of Jesus Christ of Nazareth, walk." The miracle is instantaneous and complete. The formula *in the name* is the Hebrew way of expressing the nature of a person's being, and thus releasing Jesus' power, distinct from any power of the disciples' own. This is an excellent example of the gift of healing (1 Cor. 12:9) as distinct from healing by prayer (James 5:14–15). The former is accomplished by the spoken word and serves primarily, as the sermon that follows demonstrates, to accredit God's messengers and prepare for the gospel message (see also 14:8–18).

Peter and John make their way to "Solomon's Colonnade" (v. 11), a covered portico that ran the length of the eastern side of the outer temple area and just inside the eastern wall that faces the Mount of Olives. Peter's sermon, similar to the one on Pentecost, places the primary blame for the crucifixion on the men of Israel, rather than on Pilate, who would have "let him go." The basic ingredients of the kerygma (the apostolic preaching) are here: Jesus whom they killed, the Holy and Righteous One, whom "God raised . . . from the dead." They must "repent . . . and turn to God" (v. 19). In addition to this core, Peter stresses the future restoration "promised long ago through his holy prophets" (v. 21), as well as the present spiritual blessing flowing from the covenant with Abraham upon "all peoples." The "times of refreshing" when God will "restore" (v. 21) everything is probably eschatological (in the end times), judging by the Old Testament use of the word *restore* in Jeremiah 15:19; 16:15; Ezekiel 16:53; and Hosea 11:11.

Peter's and John's first appearance before the Sanhedrin (**4:1–22**), a council of seventy men composed of scribes, priests, and various influential men plus the high priest, Caiaphas, who headed it, is instigated by one of the Judaistic parties known as the Sadducees. Led by the "captain of the temple guard," second in authority only to the high priest and guardian of the temple precincts, they arrest Peter and John and "put them in jail until the next day" (v. 3).

The Sadducees denied the concept of bodily resurrection, for this doctrine does not appear in the Pentateuch, which they considered the only bona fide Scriptures, and they were especially "disturbed" because of Peter's "proclaiming in Jesus the resurrection of the dead" (v. 2). Equally irksome to them was the fact that "many who heard the message believed" (v. 4), bringing the total number of male disciples in the early church to about five thousand.

It is a significant occasion, attended by no less than Annas, the father-in-law of Caiaphas, called high priest by Luke, because he was the real power behind the Sadducean-dominated priesthood, though several years before he had been removed from this office by the Romans (see Luke 3:2; John 18:12–24). The lead question, "By what power or what name did you do this?" (v. 7) actually reflects the prejudice that these Christians acted wholly without any divine mandate.

Peter's reply is given as he is "filled with the Holy Spirit" (v. 8), a metaphor meaning total influence and empowerment by the Holy Spirit (cf. 13:45, where being "filled with jealousy" implies one's prime motivation). There is a touch of sarcasm in his words, "we are being called to account today for an act of kindness" (v. 9), and then Peter enters into a pointed recitation of the essential message of the gospel about Jesus of Nazareth, whom they crucified but whom "God raised from the dead," and in whose name alone all must be saved.

What surprises the Sanhedrin is the "courage of Peter and John" (v. 13), Peter especially, whom they may have remembered as making himself quite scarce a few days earlier when friendship with Jesus Christ constituted a danger to his health. Furthermore, these simple Galileans were "unschooled" (in rabbinic training) and "ordinary" ("commoners"); that is, they were not trained for such erudite theological debate in which they so obviously are engaging. The only sense the Sanhedrin can make of the phenomenon is that "these men had been with Jesus," a sincere but reluctant compliment to the Lord, whose superior abilities over them they remember with jealousy.

The dilemma the Sanhedrin faces is infuriating to them. The miracle is undeniable and "there [is] nothing they [can] say" (v. 14). Although Jewish legal procedure required that on this occasion they "warn these men" (v. 17), they are nevertheless at a loss to know what to do even if the disciples should continue "to speak or teach at all in the name of Jesus" (v. 18); in other words, any action they take in the future will have no real theological basis other than their own prejudices. Peter's reply to their warning provides a model for all generations of believers faced with a choice between civil or religious tyranny and the will of God: they must obey God.

"After further threats they let them go" (v. 21), a procedure required by Jewish law under the terms of which an offender must first be warned about the consequences of his deeds and later punished if he continued in them. The fact that "all the people were praising God" because of the event makes it difficult for the Sanhedrin to know "how to punish them"—a problem similar to the one they faced with Christ.

The unity of the early church is beautifully described (**4:23–35**) in relation to the leaders' concern as they report to their own people the momentous events that have transpired. An eloquent prayer of praise, including a quotation from Psalm 2:1–2, is then offered up. This prayer focuses on the sovereign Lord whom they perceive as being truly in control of all events, especially nations, kings, and rulers who tend to oppose the Lord and his Anointed One (v. 26; Gk. *Christos* from Heb. *messiah*).

On a previous similar occasion when "Herod and Pontius Pilate met together with the Gentiles and the people of Israel" (v. 27)—a summary of all those responsible—"to conspire" against Jesus, God had done what his "power and will had decided beforehand should happen" (v. 28). This, along with the more recent experience of Peter and John, encourages these early believers "to speak [the] word with great boldness" (v. 29), which indeed they do by being "filled with the Holy Spirit" (v. 31), an expression in Acts for the influence of and ability given by the Spirit to proclaim the gospel message (see 2:4; 4:8; 9:17; 13:9).

Another quality of these early believers is their humility and sense of servanthood. This is expressed in the references to "servant." David was a servant (v. 25; Gk. *paidos,* which here applies to an honored servant); Jesus was a servant (v. 27; same word); and the disciples also are servants (v. 29; Gk. *doulos,* a more lowly servant).

The unity of the early believers is further seen in their being "one in heart and mind" (v. 32), a Hebrew idiom meaning allegiance to Christ and to one another. Also this unity appears in a form already described in 2:42–47: "they shared everything they had" (v. 32). The reference to sale of lands and houses sets the stage for the introduction of Barnabas in 4:36. Luke's apparent intention is to show that true love and faith inspire social concern, especially within the community of believers (see 1 John 3:17–18; James 2:14–17; Gal. 6:10).

F. Ananias and Sapphira: A case of discipline (4:36–5:16). Luke's picture of a courageous, unified, and loving community of believers in the early days of its Jerusalem beginnings is realistic. His brief exposé of one of the church's problems is first put into its proper setting as Luke introduces "Joseph . . . called Barnabas" (v. 36), one of those who had sold land. Barnabas's name means "Son of Encouragement," and this brief notation at this point implies that his deed is encouraging to the church. This is the first of a number of such deeds Luke intends to make reference to as he builds his characterization of Barnabas.

Evidently out of envy of the impression this act of generosity made on the church, a couple named Ananias and Sapphira attempt to gain the same prestige. Their motives are not good, and this explains why they "kept back part of the money" (5:2), desiring to make only a pretense of generosity.

The severity of the discipline may seem shocking to later generations of the church, mainly because there is a tendency to lose sight of the awfulness of any deceit which in reality means one has "lied to the Holy Spirit" (v. 3), which is, of course, to have lied to God. Such severity has not continued to be God's practice, mainly because discipline is now strictly the responsibility of the congregation, but also because a statement about its seriousness needed to be made; similarly, the death penalty which was attached to the Ten Commandments often later was replaced by a lesser sentence (Exod. 21:28–30).

The effect of the discipline is good—"great fear seized all who heard what had happened" (v. 5). A healthy church is a church where reverent fear and purity of life exist. This may have had a limiting effect upon applications for membership—professions of faith and baptisms in this case—since fear not only "seized the whole church," but also all "who heard about these events" (outsiders; v. 11).

The good effect of discipline is further seen in the vigor and success of the apostles' ministry, so that those inclined not to believe the gospel—even though they respected the believers—dare not join them, while those drawn to the gospel believe in the Lord and "[are] added to their number" (v. 14).

In fact, such remarkable blessing attaches to the apostles that extraordinary miracles of healing take place, not unlike that recorded in Mark 5:25–34 when Jesus was merely touched and healing took place. Even more remarkable is the healing due to Peter's shadow (v. 15). Jesus had promised greater things to his disciples (John 14:12).

G. Second encounter of the church with the religious leaders (5:17–42). The notoriety aroused by the miracles and conversions does not go unnoticed by the religious leaders who had given Peter and John legal notice (4:18) to cease their preaching. Luke now explains how the disciples succeed in their ministry in spite of the efforts of the Sanhedrin to silence them. Only Herod himself, in the case of James the brother of John (12:2) and Peter (12:3), attempts to deal with the disciples by incarcerating them at a later time.

It may strike the reader that in his account of the apostles' arrest and trial (**5:17–33**), Luke is making the high priest and his Sadducean associates look like fools. He depicts them as filled with jealousy, not religious zeal, and almost humorously describes their consternation when, without benefit of a prison break, the prisoners appear simply to have disappeared into thin air (vv. 19–23), leaving everyone "puzzled" (v. 24). The fact is, they *were* fools. In the face of incontestable evidence of the truthfulness of Christianity, they were willfully blind. But this is typical of unbelief where one lets his prejudices take the place of his reason.

Finding the apostles finally in the "temple courts teaching the people" (v. 25), a favorite and strategic place for evangelism, the captain and his men warily bring them without force before the Sanhedrin "to be questioned by the high priest" (v. 27).

It was probably no exaggeration that the apostles had "filled Jerusalem with [their] teaching" (v. 28). The Sanhedrin disliked also the fact that the apostles' teaching had pinned the guilt for Jesus' crucifixion primarily on them.

Again Peter repeats what he had said earlier: "We must obey God rather than men!" (v. 29). This kind of reaction must be balanced with what Peter also believed and later wrote (1 Pet. 2:13): "Submit yourselves for the Lord's sake to every authority instituted among men" (see also Rom. 13:1–6). The principle is that when a conflict between God and Caesar occurs God must be obeyed, but ordinarily one must "give to Caesar what is Caesar's, and to God what is God's" (Matt. 22:21). Nevertheless, the apostles never resisted arrest, and at least in this way submitted to authority.

Peter's calm and deliberate recitation of the gospel (vv. 30–32) causes the high priest and his associates to be furious, so that they "wanted to put them to death" (v. 33). However, divine intervention of another sort will take place to thwart what would ordinarily have occurred (**5:34–40**).

A Pharisee named Gamaliel, also a member of the Sanhedrin, intervenes at this point. Gamaliel had been the "honored" (v. 34) teacher of Saul of Tarsus (22:3) and he represents a better kind of Pharisee than those usually appearing in the Gospel records, a kind of Pharisee referred to often in the Jewish historian Josephus's *Antiquities* and parts of the Jewish Mishnah. The party called Pharisees (from the Aramaic word meaning "to separate") originated during the Maccabean times (ca. 200 B.C.) in an effort to restore the nation to observance of the law of Moses. The Pharisees' popularity among the people (though they were a minority among the Sanhedrin) and Gamaliel's personal prestige have a calming effect upon the Sanhedrin.

Two revolutionaries, Theudas and Judas, whose attempts at rebellion "came to nothing" (v. 36), illustrate Gamaliel's contention that they "leave these men alone" (v. 38) and let matters take their own course to see "if it is from God" (v. 39). The result is that they "had them flogged," a severe beating of thirty-nine stripes that served as a warning, and "let them go" (v. 40).

The references to Theudas and Judas present a historical difficulty, for Josephus places a certain Theudas at a later time (A.D. 44) and a Judas at an earlier time (A.D. 6) than would fit Luke's references. The problem may be resolved from further historical information or the simple possibility that Josephus is incorrect. Unfortunately, many modern critics seem to be prejudiced against Luke's reliability, an unwarranted attitude in light of the trend toward verification of Luke as an accurate historian.

The flogging fails to lessen the zeal of the apostles, who instead rejoice at the opportunity to suffer for the name of Jesus. It is business as usual "from house to house" as "teaching and proclaiming the good news" continue (v. 42). Luke seems to be emphasizing the boldness and freedom that resulted from their dependence upon the Holy Spirit (2:42–47; 28:31).

H. The seven servants: An example of problem-solving (6:1–7). Luke rounds out his description of the functioning of the early church with the story of how a knotty problem is solved. The growth of the church creates a problem in its social welfare.

A large group of elderly widows had believed the gospel so that the early church, like its Jewish brethren, is faced with their care (see 1 Tim. 5:3–16 for later regulations for their care). Compounding the difficulties is the fact that the "Grecian Jews" among them, probably elderly Greek-speaking widows who had lived most of their lives outside Palestine and had now returned to live out their lives in Israel, are "being overlooked" (v. 1). It appears that the Aramaic-speaking community, who had lived all their lives in Jerusalem, is reflecting some resentment toward these "outsiders." Luke admits that even Christians can have sinful carry-overs from their pre-Christian days.

This is a volatile situation. The apostles' solution to the problem is a model for future generations. Instead of trying to pin the blame on someone they take positive action by asking "all the disciples" (v. 2) to participate in a solution and a decision. This course of action was preferable, also, to the apostles' assuming further administrative duties which would force them to "neglect the ministry of the word of God." Modern leaders of the church would do well to observe such priorities and "give . . . attention to prayer and the ministry of the word" (v. 4).

What is the significance of the seven men who wait on tables (vv. 2–3)? Because the word translated "wait" (Gk. *diakonein*) is related to the word *deacon,* many have speculated that this incident is the origin of the later office of deacon (see 1 Tim. 3:8–13). If this is true, and in all likelihood it is, Luke's story provides virtually the only information we have on the function of deacons other than that which is to be inferred from the meaning of the word itself: "servant." In the New Testament, elders are exclusively invested with authority to rule (they are also called "overseers" in Titus 1:7; see also 1 Tim. 5:17, where they "direct the affairs of the church"). The leadership functions in the New Testament church, therefore, are divided into the categories of spiritual oversight for elders and support work of various kinds for which the deacons would appropriately be responsible.

The solution "pleased the whole group" (v. 5), and its success is partially guaranteed by the fact that some of these men are themselves Grecian Jews, a fact attested by their Hellenistic (Greek) names. The other guarantee of success is the fact that they are "full of the Spirit and wisdom" (v. 3), a good way to summarize leadership qualifications that one would find detailed in 1 Timothy 3 or Titus 1.

Prominent among the seven are Stephen and Philip. This is Luke's way of introducing characters who later figure significantly in his history (Stephen, Acts 7; Philip, Acts 8). He has done this already with Barnabas (4:36–37).

Luke notes the unusual fact that "a large number of priests" (v. 7) come to faith at this time. There were thousands of ordinary priests not connected with the Jerusalem aristocracy of high-priestly families who may not have been infected with the latter's prejudices. These devout men could have been attracted to Christianity.

I. Stephen: The first clash with Judaism (6:8–7:60). Stephen, who had started as an administrator of relief to poor widows, demonstrates gifts of preaching and miracle-working which soon bring him into conflict with a Hellenistic group of Jews called the Synagogue of the Freedmen. This was a group of Greek-speaking Jews who had returned to Palestine in an effort to be more faithful Jews. They were slaves who had gained their freedom, or children of such. Their fellow Hellenist, Stephen, is preaching things that they perceive to be embarrassing to them, for they desire acceptance on the part of the Jerusalem Jews who eye them with suspicion enough.

The accusations against Stephen, called "blasphemy against Moses" (v. 11) and "speaking against [the] holy place and against the law" (v. 13), probably were misrepresentations of the sort of preaching that later got the apostle Paul into trouble with Judaism, the ideas of the finality of Christ's work on the cross which abolished the effectiveness of temple sacrifices, and salvation by faith instead of works of law-keeping.

Since these legalistic Hellenists could not refute Stephen in the arena of theological debate, they try legally to silence Stephen through the Sanhedrin by bringing false witnesses to testify against him (v. 13). Their reference to Jesus of Nazareth who would destroy the temple is reminiscent of an earlier charge against Jesus himself (Mark 15:29).

Luke's description of Stephen as one whose appearance was "like the face of an angel" (v. 15) probably refers to his serenity and confidence. Perhaps such an appearance of innocence inspired the high priest's rather irenic question: "Are these charges true?" (7:1).

If Stephen is trying to gain an acquittal, the message he proclaims is the wrong way to do it, as the outcome shows (7:57–58). His approach instead is to set forth in a typical Jewish way a recital of Jewish faith by references to God's great interventions of the past. But his method is slightly oblique: he interjects throughout the story the ongoing spiritual failures (note 7:9, 25–28, 35, 39–41) leading up to the accusation that the present generation is perpetuating the same kind of spiritual blindness that characterized previous generations (7:51–53).

Stephen is also, though less obviously, dealing with three major objects of first-century Jewish faith, two of which were included in the accusation against him set forth in 6:13 ("this holy place" and "the law"): a veneration for the covenanted land (7:2–36), allegiance to the Law (7:37–43), and reverence for the temple (7:44–50). In doing so he shows that such an attitude as Jews had toward these items is actually a kind of idolatry, and, in fact, is an obstacle to their accepting the work of God done through Jesus Christ. In their worship of these gifts, they have departed from the Giver.

Stephen's accounting of the number of Jacob's family that entered Egypt is seventy-five (v. 14), which differs from the record of Genesis 46:27 of seventy. There are several minor variations between Stephen's speech and other biblical texts: precisely when Abram received his call (7:2–3; cf. Gen. 12:1); the time of Terah's death (7:4; cf. Gen. 11:26–12:4); the number of years in Egypt (7:6; cf. Exod. 12:40). As to the number seventy-five, a Genesis fragment among the Dead Sea Scrolls agrees against the Hebrew Masoretic Text, suggesting a scribal change. The other discrepancies may easily be explained as typical of the inexactitudes of current Judaism, of which Stephen's words are simply a reflection. Luke is merely recording Stephen's speech accurately, so that the Holy Spirit is not necessarily teaching historical facts in such a passage.

At the time Stephen spoke, the nation of Israel regarded their possession of the land as an end in itself, and they were blind to their true need to depend on God and cry out for spiritual redemption (**7:2–36**), a redemption which God had worked in Jesus Christ before their very eyes.

The land which the Jews cherished was indeed given them by God through Abraham (vv. 2–16). In spite of the treachery of Jacob's sons toward Joseph, God preserved them through Joseph in Egypt, a sojourn of four hundred years ending in slavery.

Stephen next recounts the story of Moses.

Once again, Israel's pattern of rejection is exposed when they did not "realize that God was using [Moses] to rescue them" (v. 25). Later their obstinacy again takes the form of rejection (v. 35). The point seems to be: they should be worshipers of God, not the land.

Stephen turns next to the giving of the Law through Moses (**7:37–43**). This event, great as it was, was not God's final word to the nation, for God would send them a prophet like Moses whom they should obey. The "fathers refused to obey" Moses (v. 39) and actually ignored the implications of God's mighty deeds. "In their hearts [they] turned back to Egypt" and the idols such as the calf which they had worshiped there, a pattern to be carried out again and again in the future and which would lead them ultimately into exile in Babylon.

Besides ordinary idolatry, Israel turned to other forms of worship. "God gave them over"—note the exact phrase in Romans 1:24, 26, and 28, as well as a similar context—"to the worship of the heavenly bodies" (v. 42). This latter reference to the stars follows the Septuagint more closely than the Masoretic Text of Amos 5:25–27. The New International Version reads, "You have lifted up the shrine of your king,/ the pedestal of your idols,/ the star of your god." In any case occultism was involved as part of their idolatry.

Next Stephen passes to the tabernacle of Testimony in the desert and then to "the house," the temple, which David desired and Solomon built (**7:44–50**). This magnificent provision for true worship nevertheless is not to be revered, Stephen implies, for the "Most High does not live in houses made by men" (v. 48). God is far too great for that.

The climax of Stephen's sermon (**7:51–53**) is one of the most severe and cutting accusations anywhere in Scripture, strongly like those of Isaiah and Jeremiah (Isa. 48:1–4; Jer. 23:9–12). He calls the Jews "stiff-necked" (v. 51), God's own characterization of the nation when it rebelled against Moses (Exod. 33:5; Deut. 9:13). They were "uncircumcised" in their hearts and ears, meaning that they were not inwardly separated and in harmony with the God of the covenant who commanded physical circumcision as a token of their allegiance. Professing believers have always fallen into the trap of hardness and outward religious observance without inner love for God.

Seldom have a group of people, religious or otherwise, reacted to an accusation with such savage fury as did the Sanhedrin (**7:54–60**). Luke says they "gnashed their teeth at [Stephen]" (v. 54). This means they ground their teeth in rage, a reaction uncommon among Westerners but which is mentioned several times in the Old Testament (Ps. 35:16; Lam. 2:16) and also in the New Testament (Matt. 8:12; 13:42; Luke 13:28, but more from remorse than anger).

In contrast to the rage of the Sanhedrin is the serenity of Stephen, who envisions Jesus standing at the right hand of God (v. 55). The majority of commentators have seen in this posture (standing, not sitting [Ps. 110:1]) a gesture of honor by the Lord toward Stephen. F. F. Bruce, in his commentary on the Book of Acts, sees also in it the act of Jesus' witnessing to his Father in response to the witness or confession of his servant, Stephen (Luke 12:8).

The stoning of Stephen is not a wholly spontaneous event. Luke mentions witnesses who "laid their clothes" at Saul's feet (v. 58), implying his instigation of this "investigation." These official listeners to Stephen's message were there to make official and legal what they fully expect to be a charge of blasphemy against him (a capital case). They were to knock the offender down and throw the first stones. The haste in which this "execution" takes place violated, most believe, what the Mishnah required, but it is likely that the Sanhedrin had already made arrangements with the Roman authorities to look the other way while they overstepped their authority.

II. The Witness to Christ in Judea and Samaria (8:1–12:25)

A. Saul the persecutor and Philip the evangelist (8:1–40). Acts **8:1–3** serves as a transition to Luke's second major division (see 1:8). Ironically, a great persecution serves as the impetus to drive disciples "throughout Judea and Samaria" (v. 1). The apostles remain behind, which fact is puzzling, for one would expect them to be prime targets of Saul. The only explanation is that they indeed were just as wanted as anyone, but courageously remained behind, perhaps hidden by some believers, in order to encourage the believers who remained. Some have speculated that greater pressure was on the Hellenistic Jews, like Philip, to leave Jerusalem.

Luke's reference to "godly men" (v. 2) is distinct from "disciples," his favorite term for all believers. It pertains to devout Jews who were sympathetic to the Christian cause (2:5), when it appears without any other reference to one's also being a disciple, as in the case of Ananias (22:12). They "mourned deeply for" Stephen, and this may imply their repentance toward conversion.

The intensity of Saul's persecution is stressed with the word *destroy* (v. 3), a similar word to that found in Galatians 1:13, where Paul reflects on the events of these early days. His putting believers in prison was more than mere incarceration; it meant that they were eventually put to death, according to Acts 22:4, and this is what Luke means by "destroy."

Luke's reference to Saul's persecution is primarily to give the background of the major advance of the gospel (**8:4–40**) into Samaria by "those who had been scattered" (v. 4; Gk. *diasparentes,* the root of the term *diaspora,* a word usually applied to the dispersion of Jews, but here applied to Christian Jews).

"Those who had been scattered preached the word wherever they went" (v. 4). This excluded the apostles (8:1) and involved mission-minded people like Philip, one of the seven servants of Acts 6, who "went down to a city in Samaria." There are two possible reasons why, throughout the Bible, one "goes down" from and "goes up" to Jerusalem. First, the Judean hills must be ascended from all directions, though Jerusalem itself is not the highest point. Second, in the ancient world one always ascends to his center of worship theologically.

Philip's message is typically accompanied by "miraculous signs" which accredit the gospel. As a result, "they all paid close attention to what he said" (v. 6). Unlike previous evangelism, Philip's ministry involves the exorcism of evil spirits. Certain areas appear to have greater infestations of demons, such as the region of Galilee during Jesus' ministry.

The Samaritans were half-Jews who had come into existence as a result of the intermarriage between peoples brought in during the deportation by the Assyrians in 722 B.C. with those that remained. Later, during the return from exile by Jews to rebuild the temple (Ezra 4:1–5), the Samaritans were refused a part in the reconstruction, and this began the long-standing animosity that is reflected in several New Testament texts (e.g., John 4:9).

It is not clear just what city is meant by "a city in Samaria," but Philip's ministry results in "great joy" (v. 8) among these previously disenfranchised people. Among those attracted is a man named Simon who practiced sorcery. Early Christian writers identify this Simon with a famous Simon Magus ("the great") who went on to become a notorious heretic, known throughout the Roman Empire. The expression *he boasted that he was someone great* and the title *Great Power* (v. 10) seem to support that identification. He is described as one who "believed and was baptized" (v. 13), but his interest appears to be an interest in the miracles rather than the gospel, like those people described in John 2:23–25.

Luke next interjects a reference to the reaction of the church in Jerusalem to the great spiritual awakening in Samaria. In order to analyze the situation and verify the reality of the faith of the Samaritans, "the apostles . . . sent Peter and John to them" (v. 14). It would be natural for the Jewish believers to be skeptical about these traditionally despised Samaritans; thus it was extremely important to determine the nature of the situation in order to preserve the unity of the early church. "The Holy Spirit had not yet come upon any of them" (v. 16), probably in order to reserve this important evidence of genuine conversion for the eyes of the two principal apostles. Peter and John verify the genuineness of the Samaritans' faith and, as an official act, place their hands on them, and the Samaritans receive the Holy Spirit (v. 17). The unique circumstances surrounding this incident and the need for verification of the Samaritans' faith make it unlikely that this reception of the Holy Spirit should be regarded as the normal way or time the Holy Spirit is to be received. The norm is implied in the conversion of Cornelius (10:44–46) and in the question of Paul to the disciples of John the Baptist (19:2), that believers receive the Spirit when they believe the gospel (see also 2:38).

Having explained how the Holy Spirit came to the Samaritans, Luke returns to the story of Simon the sorcerer (8:18–24). Evidently Simon perceived that great prestige would come to those who could confer the Holy Spirit and so he offers money to the apostles for the gift, having seen that gift conferred when the apostles laid hands on the Samaritans. This betrays his total lack of comprehension of the true significance of the gift of the Spirit, and Peter rejects his request and his money. Simon's "heart [was] not right before God" (v. 21), but the question of the genuineness of his faith must remain an enigma. The New Testament use of the word *believe* can have a range of meaning, from mental assent to certain facts (John 2:23; James 2:19) to justifying commitment (Rom. 10:9–10). At any rate, Peter's warning (vv. 21, 23) and the possibility of this man being the Simon Magus of later notoriety do not encourage one to assume that he was a true believer.

The next major incident involving Philip is recounted by Luke in Acts **8:26–40**, the evangelization on a road to Gaza—probably the southernmost, desolate ("desert") part—of an Ethiopian eunuch. The man was "an important official in charge of all the treasury of Candace, queen of the Ethiopians" (v. 27). The biblical use of the term *Ethiopian* implies that he was black (Jer. 13:23), and the term *eunuch* might be either a title given to all government officials or a reference to his being castrated.[1]

The most puzzling question is the eunuch's relationship to Judaism. He was returning from worship in Jerusalem, which suggests the possibility of his being a proselyte, a convert to Judaism. Eunuchs were forbidden by Deuteronomy 23:1 from being accepted into Judaism, but Isaiah 56:3–5 predicted that eunuchs would be accepted someday by God's graciousness. Furthermore, he was reading a scroll of the prophet Isaiah, chapter 53, a valuable possession which non-Jews were unlikely to have.

Particularly intriguing to the eunuch is the interpretation of Isaiah 53:7–8, and this becomes the springboard for Philip's gospel message. The eunuch asks if the prophet is "talking about himself or someone else" (v. 34), which reflects one of the then current explanations of the passage. His question implies a dissatisfaction with what he has heard, and Philip's application to Jesus the Messiah is far more reasonable, because it takes the words in their normal sense, an interpretive approach typical of apostolic preaching and one reason for early Christianity's impact. Jesus handled Isaiah 53 the same way (Luke 22:37 and Isa. 53:12).

Luke refers to the fact that the eunuch believed the gospel by his request for baptism. Some ancient manuscripts of Acts include a brief dialogue between Philip and the Ethiopian which is not found in the better manuscripts and which the New International Version also omits, a missing verse 37. In this dialogue Philip asks if the eunuch believes with his whole heart, and the eunuch affirms his faith in Jesus Christ as the Son of God. This verse 37 is suspect as a scribal addition that tries to put into the mouth of the eunuch an affirmation of faith that is actually sufficiently made by the eunuch's request to be baptized. In the Book of Acts the word *baptism* is probably to be read as "affirmation of faith" and always occurs immediately after one's conversion.

Luke uses the story of the Ethiopian eunuch to show how in yet another gradual step the gospel reached the world. The first step involved the Samaritans, geographically adjacent, racially close, and worshipers of One whom the Samaritans considered to be the same God, though their religious documents were limited to the books of Moses. The next step was the Ethiopian, one who was still within the Jewish religious community but racially different. In one more step the transition will be almost complete when Peter goes to the Gentile Cornelius (10).

B. The conversion of Saul (9:1–31). Luke is developing his history of early Christianity toward the evangelization of the Gentile world. At the time he wrote Acts, the question of whether evangelism should emphasize this mission to the Gentiles was a matter of controversy among Hebrew Christians, and the apostle to the Gentiles, Paul, was the storm center of the controversy (see Gal. 1–2). Therefore, Luke is offering an explanation of this strategy to his readers. He has shown how, by degrees, the Gentile mission developed from the Samaritans to the Ethiopian, and now he somewhat parenthetically explains how the man who became the leader of this mission came to faith in Christ. Luke will refer to Peter's part in the Gentile mission in Acts 10 and 11, but after a final look at Peter's exploits in Acts 12, he will focus almost exclusively on Paul for the remainder of the book.

Saul pressed his persecution with increasing fervor against the church right up to the moment of his conversion (**9:1–19**). There is no evidence that he experienced a gradual change of attitude toward Christianity. He may indeed have been impressed by Stephen's courage and eloquence (7:59–60), but that incident merely made him realize that believers in Jesus were a greater force to be reckoned with than he had first thought.

Thus Saul seems to intensify and expand his efforts by going to the high priest to ask "for letters to the synagogues in Damascus" (v. 2) which will give him authority to extradite Christians to Jerusalem.

The intensity and ferocity of Saul's hatred for this new Jewish sect probably centered in the Pharisaical view that the messianic age could come only in connection with a faithful keeping of the Law. The accusations against Stephen reveal that the believers in Jesus were perceived as enemies of the Law. Luke calls Saul's actions "murderous" (v. 1), but Saul himself would have regarded his actions as justified in light of Moses' killing of immoral Israelites at Baal of Peor (Num. 25:1–5) or Phinehas's slaying of the man and woman in Moab (Num. 25:6–15). Clearly, Saul's deeds were done out of religious zeal (Phil. 3:6).

Early Christians referred to themselves as followers of the Way, a term occurring in Acts six times including here (v. 2; 19:9, 23; 22:4; 24:14, 22). The origin of this expression is uncertain, but evidently it connotes something

1. Johannes Schneider, "eunouchos, eunouchizō," in *Theological Dictionary of the New Testament*, ed. Gerhard Kittel, Gerhard Friedrich, and Geoffrey W. Bromiley, trans. Geoffrey W. Bromiley, 10 vols. (Grand Rapids: Eerdmans, 1964–1967), 2:766.

of the idea of "the true way of God" or "the way of salvation" (cf. 16:17).

Saul's conversion occurs on the road to Damascus, one of the world's oldest cities, located in Syria. His experience involves a light from heaven which temporarily leaves him blind. This light may be the glory of Christ, usually veiled during his earthly ministry, and revealed at the transfiguration for a few brief moments (Matt. 17:1–8). Saul hears a voice from the Lord, and a brief dialogue takes place. In Acts 22:9 Luke states that Saul's companions did not hear (NIV understand) the voice, and in 26:14 he says that only Saul heard the voice, but in 9:7 he says that his companions heard the voice (Gk. *phōnē* in all of these cases). The New International Version rightly translates the word "sound" (v. 7), and this indicates the legitimate range of meaning which the word can have. In other words, everyone heard a sound, but only Saul understood the words.

Saul's answer, "Who are you, Lord?" (v. 5), in all likelihood implies recognition of the divine presence, since the words had come from heaven, but until the voice is identified as the voice of Jesus whom Saul is persecuting, there is no recognition of identity. This, along with Saul's obedience to the command to "go into the city, and . . . be told what [he] must do" (v. 6), is evidence of conversion or confessing Jesus as Lord (Rom. 10:9). Obedience results from this confession of faith and serves as evidence of the reality of Saul's faith (James 2:14).

In Damascus Saul begins his recovery from the shock of realizing that he has been persecuting the very Lord whom he thought he was serving. He also has time to begin considering the implications of the new faith which has been communicated to him in capsule form. Acts 26:15–18 expands upon the scene on the Damascus road and reveals that Saul had been given a basic outline of his new faith in Jesus of Nazareth upon which further revelation would build. This included his mission to the Gentiles, bringing of light that would free them from Satan's power, forgiveness of sins, and sanctification by faith.

The three days of waiting while still blind are brought to an end by the appearance of a "disciple named Ananias" (v. 10). Saul is staying at the "house of Judas on Straight Street" (v. 11) that runs east and west, even to this day. The Lord "in a vision" (v. 12) persuades Ananias to come, "restore [Saul's] sight," and present him to the disciples at Damascus. Saul is described as a chosen instrument to evangelize the "Gentiles and their kings" as well as "the people of Israel." Though much about Saul's conversion is typical of all believers, as a "chosen vessel" he represents those select individuals uniquely prepared for special tasks. Saul (Paul) later states that as the norm not many of Christ's followers were "wise by human standards; not many were influential; not many were of noble birth" (1 Cor. 1:26). Ananias is informed that Saul's life is to be one of suffering for the name of Christ, the lot, in fact, of "everyone who wants to live a godly life in Christ Jesus" (2 Tim. 3:12).

Ananias places "his hands on Saul" (v. 17), and "something like scales" (v. 18) fall from his eyes. "Scales" is the Greek *lepis,* a medical term of the first century which refers to a growth of skin that causes blindness. Although it is a genuine medical disorder, some see it as symbolic of Saul's conversion from darkness to light and as bearer now of that same light. In addition, some see a connection between this eye disorder and Saul's later reference to his poor eyesight (Gal. 4:15).

In addition to the restoration of his sight, Saul is apparently at this time also filled with the Holy Spirit. On this occasion there is no reference to any accompanying phenomenon such as tongues. On other occasions the reception of the Spirit serves as evidence of genuine incorporation of a convert into Christian fellowship, which might explain the delay for the benefit of Ananias's confirmation. This "filling" may not necessarily be the reception of the Holy Spirit for the first time, if filling and reception are distinct concepts. At any rate, it serves to prepare Saul for his ministry of the gospel, something that seems consistently to be involved with the filling of the Spirit. (See comments on 2:4 concerning the relationship between Spirit baptism and Spirit filling.)

Finally, Saul is baptized, and he eats. In Acts the water ritual comes as soon as possible after conversion, and it is probably safe to infer that this was performed before other disciples at Damascus, since Luke states that Saul "spent several days with the disciples."

Saul's initial preaching produces consternation among everyone who knew of his reputation (**9:20–25**). Among "the Jews living in Damascus" (v. 22) and in their synagogues, Saul's message is "powerful" (v. 22) and convincing to the effect "that Jesus is the Christ" (Messiah). Undoubtedly, Saul had much to learn, but his extensive knowledge of the Old Testament Scriptures probably came alive in their implications and prophecies of the Messiah, providing fertile sources for such evangelism. This is just the beginning!

Another pattern is begun that initially fulfilled the commission for Saul to suffer. The "Jews conspired to kill him" (v. 23), but he learns of the plot, hides himself, and eventually escapes "in a basket through an opening in the wall" (v. 25; see also 2 Cor. 11:32–33). Luke's purpose in this story is to provide clear evidence of Saul's faith and perhaps the ironical fact that the persecutor becomes the one persecuted. At least Saul could understand his pursuers' motives.

Galatians 1:15–24 presents Saul's own account of these early years and contains facts not found here in Luke's account, for each author has a different purpose in his writing. When the two versions are correlated, the order of events may likely be as follows:

1. Saul is converted (Acts 9:1–19)
2. Saul preaches in Damascus (Acts 9:20–22)
3. Saul resides in Arabia (Gal. 1:17)
4. Saul returns to Damascus (Acts 9:23–25)
5. Saul visits Jerusalem the first time, then goes on to Caesarea, Syria, and Cilicia (Acts 9:26–30; Gal. 1:18–24)

Saul's first attempt to join the disciples at Jerusalem is met with suspicion and fear (**9:26–30**). Barnabas, the "Son of Encouragement" (see 4:36), comes to his aid by giving him a proper introduction. Barnabas's confidence in the reality of Saul's conversion inspires confidence in the Jerusalem disciples, allowing him to move about freely and preach boldly. The Grecian Jews debate with him as they did with Stephen (6:8–10). History repeats itself and they try "to kill him" (v. 29). The brothers (fellow believers; v. 30) hear of it and cart him off to Tarsus, the place of his birth and principal university city of the Roman province of Cilicia. For about eleven years (A.D. 35–46), Saul drops out of the story and will not reappear until Barnabas brings him to Antioch in Syria (11:25–26). It is possible that such events as recorded in 2 Corinthians 11:23–27 and 12:1–4 took place during this period.

With Saul out of the picture as chief persecutor, the churches "throughout Judea, Galilee and Samaria" are able to enjoy relief from their hardships (**9:31**). Luke says they were "encouraged by the Holy Spirit." Generally in Scripture the Holy Spirit works through various means, most often through the medium of the spoken or written Word. In this case, his stimulation and encouragement of the proclamation of the Word and comfort between believers was probably the means by which this encouragement and growth occurred. Galilee is not mentioned elsewhere by Luke, but Jesus' extensive ministry there makes it a logical area for growth in the gospel.

C. Peter's ministry in Judea (9:32–11:18). Having introduced Saul in advance of his major exploits, as he is accustomed to do, Luke turns again to the ministry of Peter in and around Judea.

Lydda was the Old Testament city of Lod and was located twenty-five miles northwest of Jerusalem. Here Peter found and healed "Aeneas, a paralytic . . . for eight years" (**9:32–35**). Peter exercises the gift of healing (1 Cor. 12:9; see comments on Acts 3:2–10) in the dramatic, decisive words, "Jesus Christ heals you." The present tense along with the word *immediately* (v. 34) implies instant, complete activity, not a process. The fame of this incident spreads rapidly north to Sharon, a coastal plain stretching from Joppa to Mount Carmel.

Going farther west to the seacoast city of Joppa, Peter raises a disciple named Tabitha (Heb.; Gk. Dorcas, both meaning "gazelle") from the dead (**9:36–43**). The fact that she had not been fully prepared for burial and the loving ministry she had had as well as the proximity of Lydda to Joppa imply that the believers may have expected Peter to raise her from the dead.

Luke refers to widows mourning her death, indicating that Dorcas's ministry had been primarily to these destitute people, providing them with clothing.

On this occasion Peter exercises another apostolic gift described by Paul as "miraculous powers" (1 Cor. 12:10). As with Aeneas, God is more concerned with gospel proclamation than the welfare of the individual recipient of the miracle. Luke explains that the fame of the incident spread "all over Joppa, and many people believed in the Lord" (v. 42). Spiritual healing and future resurrection are far more significant to the New Testament writers than physical healing and temporary resurrection.

Luke finally inserts a transitional reference to "a tanner named Simon" (v. 43) in order to prepare for the story of Cornelius, since Peter will be at Simon's house in Joppa when he is summoned by Cornelius's servants.

Paul was called to be the apostle to the Gentiles (Gal. 2:7–10), but Peter is to make the initial step toward Gentile evangelization (**10:1–11:18**). Some scholars interpret the keys given to Peter by our Lord (Matt. 16:19) as the authority to open the door of evangelism (entrance into the kingdom) to various outsiders, starting with the Samaritans, whose salvation he confirms, and culminating with Cornelius, the first strictly Gentile convert.

Cornelius was stationed at Caesarea, a city on the Mediterranean coast, as centurion of the "Italian Regiment." During the New Testament period, Caesarea, not Jerusalem, was the actual Roman capital of Judea, perhaps because Caesarea was relatively free of political strife. A Roman centurion was literally a "captain of a hundred," but may have commanded more than that number if his regiment was up to full strength; that is, one-tenth of a legion which was officially six thousand men, making a regiment six hundred men. The Italian Regiment, or cohort, was probably an elite group of freedmen from Italy who had received citizenship.

Cornelius and his family (v. 2; lit. house) were "devout and God-fearing." This means that they were followers of the Old Testament Scriptures and worshipers of Yahweh, the God of Israel, but not necessarily proselytes who had been baptized and circumcised (see 11:3). This category of worshiper in the Jewish synagogue will appear several times in Acts as those Gentiles in the synagogues who usually respond favorably to the gospel message (13:16, 50; 16:14; 17:4, 17; 18:7; sometimes also called "worshipers").

Cornelius has a vision (v. 3) at "three in the afternoon," which literally is the ninth hour according to Jewish time, the second time of prayer during the day. The reference in verse 2 about his regularity in prayer implies that this vision took place while he was praying. The vision is of an angel of God bearing a message from God, the manner in which God often communicates in biblical times (Gk. *angelos*, messenger).

Cornelius's prayers and gifts are called a remembrance (v. 4) or memorial. Old Testament sacrifices were called this in such places as Leviticus 2:2, and subsequent to Jesus' sacrifice on the cross, a believer's prayer and service are put in the category of a memorial (Heb. 13:15–16). It simply means that Cornelius's devotion to God was acceptable and pleasing to God, and God's most valuable response was to lead him into further truth. This incident of Cornelius also illustrates the grace and sovereignty of God in salvation. Paul explains it well in Romans 10:13–15: All who call upon the name of the Lord can be saved, but knowledge of the One on whom they call must precede their calling on him, and knowledge must come by hearing about him, and hearing must come by someone preaching, and preaching cannot occur until God sends someone. Thus God sends Peter; for God has committed himself to reach all those who might call on him.

As a result of the vision, Cornelius sends men to fetch Peter where he is staying at the home of Simon the tanner in Joppa.

Coincident with Cornelius's vision is that of Peter, but the vision given to Peter has a far greater purpose than merely to tell him to whom he must go. While he is praying, Peter becomes hungry (v. 10), apparently requests food, and "while the meal [is] being prepared, [falls] into a trance." The purpose for this vision is to overcome a natural prejudice that Peter has as a devout Jew. Jewish tradition had extended the dietary regulations against "anything impure or unclean" (v. 14) to contact with Gentiles in their homes. The effect of the vision is the same as the words of Jesus in Mark 7:17–23: dietary regulations are no longer in effect; "clean" and "unclean" as categories are nullified, and thus the attitude toward Gentiles which sprang from them is also invalidated.

Typical of the way in which God impresses on people the importance or significance of something, the vision is repeated three times. Similar to this is the threefold repetition about the character of God, "holy, holy, holy" (Isa. 6:3). Nevertheless, the full implications of the vision are not clear to Peter until the Spirit tells him to go with the three men sent by Cornelius. Later, Peter indicates that he understood the message in regard to Cornelius when he realized that God "does not show favoritism" (10:34).

There are two schools of thought as to how to interpret and apply the numerous references to special guidance given by angels, the Holy Spirit, and prophecy (vv. 19–20). The modern reader is faced with decisions in which such special guidance would be quite helpful. One school of thought, a more mystical and subjective approach, is that such phenomena occur today either to the same extent as in apostolic times or to some lesser degree. In the latter case, the Holy Spirit imparts impressions to the mind, totally separate from Scripture, as to what one should do. The other school of thought considers such phenomena as found in the story of Cornelius to be peculiar to the apostolic age before the written Scriptures. Now that God's people have the Scriptures complete, the Holy Spirit inwardly illumines the mind through the medium of biblical truth as the believer seeks and prays for such guidance. This author prefers this latter interpretation of the Spirit's guidance for today.

Two days later (vv. 23–24) Peter arrives at the home of Cornelius. Impressed by the appearance earlier of the angel as the representative of God (10:31), Cornelius respectfully kneels before Peter, but Peter, afraid of any semblance of idolatry, quickly tells Cornelius to stand up.

Cornelius summons a "large gathering" (v. 27) for this occasion, apparently all Gentiles, judging by Peter's remarks (v. 28). The "law" to which Peter refers is the Talmud, but constitutes an interpretation of the dietary and ceremonial regulations of the Mosaic code. Peter, conscious of his violation of these restrictions, explains how God changed his thinking (vv. 28–29). Cornelius, in turn, explains how by vision he came to summon Peter to his home (vv. 30–33). Cornelius's receptivity, as well as that of his household and friends (see 10:44), is an ideal example of the work of the Holy Spirit in preparing peoples' hearts for evangelism. Cornelius's spiritual pilgrimage, about to be consummated, includes the essentials for anyone's comprehension and reception of the gospel: a knowledge of the nature of the biblical God (10:1–2); an understanding of man's need for the righteousness of God (implied in 10:22 in the word *righteous*); and some knowledge of Jesus Christ (implied by 10:37 in the words *you know . . . how God anointed Jesus of Nazareth*).

Peter's message (vv. 34–43) contains the basic elements of the apostolic message. In this one there is more than usual reported about the activities of Jesus before his crucifixion (vv. 37–39), things that substantiate his qualifications to be Savior. The approach here is similar to that found in the gospel according to Mark, alleged by many early Christian writers as having been influenced by Peter, if not often his very words. Also, a careful study of the Greek style reveals the kind of Greek a Jew like Peter would have spoken. Thus Luke has probably preserved Peter's actual words rather than a refined version of them. An example of Peter's style is his use of the word *tree* (v. 39) for "cross," the word Peter uses in 1 Peter 2:24 (Gk. *xulon;* NIV cross).

Peter concludes his sermon with the statement that the Lord had given the apostles a mandate to preach to the people (v. 42), meaning the Jewish people. But now, especially with Cornelius, that mandate has clearly expanded to the Gentiles, and this fact is indicated in the words *everyone who believes in him* (v. 43).

The fact that everyone would receive the forgiveness of sins is quite a sweeping statement, requiring biblical support, which possibly Peter gave from such passages as Isaiah 53:11, which indicates the Suffering Servant (Jesus) would "justify many" and "bear their iniquities."

Before Peter finished speaking, the "Holy Spirit came on all who heard the message" (v. 44). Presumably, this coincided with their believing the message and constitutes the normal time when believers receive the Holy Spirit (see 19:2). On this occasion, if not on several others, the phenomenon of speaking in tongues serves to confirm to Peter the genuineness of the event because of its similarities with Pentecost (see 11:15). This is only the second recorded occurrence of speaking in tongues, of which there are three altogether in Acts (2:4–6; this text; and 19:6). This is the first and only event where Gentiles speak in tongues in Acts, and this evidence astonishes the Jews who are present.

The full recognition of this momentous event comes when Cornelius, his friends, and his family are baptized (v. 48). Peter remains "a few days" in order to fellowship and teach them further.

Upon returning to Jerusalem, Peter predictably meets with criticism among the "circumcised believers" (Jews; 11:1–2), for he had broken the Talmudic rules against entering the house of Gentiles and eating with them (v. 3). Peter begins by explaining how God had changed his mind about "clean and unclean" matters, so that he had become willing and obedient to evangelize these Gentiles (vv. 5–14).

It is difficult for modern readers to understand the difficulty that first-century Jews had with departures from their law, whether biblical or Talmudic. Earlier, it was noted how Saul's zeal arose out of his fidelity to the Law because such fidelity was, to the Pharisees, the only grounds for God's restoring them and bringing the Messiah.

When Peter explains how the Holy Spirit had been granted to the Gentiles as it had to the Jews in the beginning (v. 15; i.e., at Pentecost), the Jewish believers "had no further objections and praised God" (v. 18). This is a marvelous change of mind on their part and must not be passed over lightly, for it shows a commendable willingness to believe the truth once it has been demonstrated. From the modern reader's point of view, their objections may seem obstinate and even asinine. Would to God that evangelicals in today's Bible-believing churches would thus respond, in spite of their prejudices, to the truth once it has been set forth!

Luke's record of the statement that "God has granted . . . repentance" (v. 18) is theologically significant. In Acts the words *repentance* and *faith* are interchangeable but not synonymous, as is made clear in 20:21. Repentance is "toward God" and involves an acknowledgment and repudiation of one's rebellion against God. Faith takes over at that point and permits God to begin the lifelong process of bringing forth the fruit of repentance (Luke 3:8). Furthermore, repentance is "granted"; God takes the initiative and brings about the circumstances which lead to repentance. To press this further and debate whether repentance comes from God or arises from within the convicted sinner is beyond the scope of this commentary.

D. The Antioch church: Barnabas's ministry (11:19–30). The Gentile mission continues to be Luke's focus as he explains how the church in Syrian Antioch came into existence. The story goes back to the persecution in connection with Stephen (v. 19; see 8:1–4) during which the disciples traveled as far north as Phoenicia, along the coast, the island of Cyprus, and eventually all the way into Syrian Antioch. Antioch in Syria was founded in 300 B.C. and lay about three hundred miles north of Jerusalem and twenty miles east of the Mediterranean. During the first century it was the third largest city in the Roman Empire (Rome and Alexandria ahead of it in that order) with half a million population. Antioch was a blend of both Western and Eastern cultures with a significant number of Jews.

The habit of these early Jewish Christian evangelists was to contact Jews only, but some Hellenistic Jews from Cyprus and Cyrene, a city on the northern coast of Africa, turned to the Greeks also, and a great number believed. Thus the first Jewish-Gentile church was founded in Antioch, a city that was eventually to become of primary importance and the launching pad of the Gentile mission under Saul (13:1–3).

The Jerusalem church hears about this novel situation and immediately dispatches a trusted Hellenistic Jew, Barnabas. Barnabas quickly sizes up the situation as definitely of God and, true to his name, "encourage[s] them" and evidently has part in further evangelism.

At this point a remarkable thing takes place. Barnabas, who might easily have taken this opportunity to extend his own ministry and further his own importance, does a most selfless but strategic thing: he goes to Tarsus and brings Saul to Antioch. The two then minister to the church and teach for a whole year. Luke then notes, as a way to characterize the importance of this ministry, that the name *Christians* (Christ-followers) is given to the disciples. The inference is that these believers, as a result of the growth and maturity they experience under Saul and Barnabas, become associated in people's thinking with Jesus Christ of Nazareth, even though originally perhaps in derision.

Also implied by this new appellation is the recognition that the disciples are more than a mere sect of Judaism. As such, they will gradually lose some status given only to legally recognized religious groups by the Roman government, something they will never fully recover until centuries later.

As a final note about the Antioch church, Luke describes its vitality in terms of its generosity. Several prophets from Jerusalem, especially one named Agabus, predict a "severe famine . . . over the entire Roman world" (v. 28). Agabus will reappear later in Luke's narrative (21:10) to issue a Spirit-inspired warning. To this present warning the Antioch believers respond by sending a gift by Barnabas and Saul, an act of unity as well as charity (v. 30).

First Corinthians 12:10, 29 and Ephesians 4:11 list prophecy as a gift of the Spirit in the early church. In the Book of Acts a prophet or prophets are referred to four times (11:27; 13:1; 15:32; 21:10), and their function seems to be similar to that of the Old Testament prophet—to bear a message or revelation from God—but their authority is not always as great as the apostles' (see, e.g., 1 Cor. 14:29, 37, 38), although some apostles, if not all, possessed the gift of prophecy themselves.

Luke gives us a vital chronological reference in dating this famine "during the reign of Claudius" (v. 28), which can be roughly dated at about A.D. 46. This date becomes a key for working out, with other information from Acts, a chronology for the life and work of the apostle Paul.

E. Peter's miraculous deliverance (12:1–25). Luke tells one further story about Peter before he turns to the exploits of Saul. His purpose is to show that, although he will focus exclusively on Saul's Gentile ministry for the remainder of the book, the Jewish mission centered in Jerusalem is of ongoing importance to God, and this is by the preservation of one of its principal leaders and removal of its principal persecutor, Herod.

When Luke uses the expression *It was about this time* (v. 1) he must be referring to the time of famine and the visit of Saul and Barnabas. Luke attaches the story of the famine visit (11:27–30) to the story of the birth of the Antioch church (11:19–26), because they are generically related. But chronologically the story of Herod's persecution and death falls between these two, for Herod died in A.D. 44 while the famine visit occurred in A.D. 46.

A fresh persecution is initiated by King Herod by the arrest of several believers. This Herod is Agrippa I who was in his middle fifties at this time and not to be confused with Agrippa II who appears in 25:13–22. Agrippa I had a policy of trying to please the Jews (v. 3), because his family was so hated by them. He held the title of king and ruled over a fairly large area from northern Palestine to Judea, all together the entire original kingdom of Herod the Great, his grandfather. He was a careful observer of Jewish law and ritual and worked his way into the affection of the Jews despite his Idumean ancestry, quite an unusual accomplishment for a Herod, even though his compliance was probably politically motivated.

Miraculous deliverances from prison are not the norm, and thus Luke includes a reference to the fact that James, the brother of John, was executed (v. 2) as a result of his imprisonment. This reference helps promote a more biblical, realistic view of divine intervention. God is not always predictable in his dealings with the righteous; he lets James die, but he intervenes for Peter. Perhaps at this time the deliverance of Peter was more crucial to the spiritual morale of the Jerusalem church.

In the case of Peter's arrest, a brief delay for the Jewish holy days intervened before his "public trial" (v. 4). Herod, on the pretext of executing him as a Jewish apostate (this was the Sanhedrin's opinion of a Christian), was also securing his position before Rome by squelching a dangerous religious radical who might incite a revolt.

Luke's reference to the prayers of the church (vv. 5, 12–17) also shows the role that prayer plays in divine intervention, and Luke apparently regards God's act as a response to this prayer. There are very few things God does apart from prayer.

Peter is heavily guarded, a note to emphasize the extraordinary nature of his deliverance. The angel awakens Peter and escorts him out of prison as chains fall off and an iron door opens "by itself" (v. 10; *automatē,* from which we get our word *automatically*). During the whole episode Peter considers himself having a vision, no doubt due to the ease with which events happen right in front of the guards who are oblivious to them all.

Left on the city street by the angel, Peter comes to full realization of what has happened and makes his way to the "house of Mary the mother of John, also called Mark" (v. 12). Thus Luke introduces another figure who will play a minor role in subsequent events (13:5, 13), John Mark.

Peter knocks on the door of "the outer entrance" (v. 13), and this reference suggests that the house was fairly large and typically had an entrance to the street, then a courtyard, and finally living quarters in the rear. Such homes were spacious enough for large gatherings and served as the assembly places for the first-century church (see Rom. 16:5).

The "servant girl named Rhoda" must have been for years the object of good-natured humor as this story was told by Christians ("And this is Rhoda; you know—the one who got so excited when she heard Peter that she forgot to let him in the house!"). We should not think ill of the congregation's reluctance to accept the fact of Peter's miraculous release. Rather than an act of unbelief, it was simply something beyond their range of expectation as to how God would deliver Peter who was, they knew, slated for a public trial, the occasion on which they probably expected God's intervention as an answer to their prayers. Besides, Rhoda's erratic behavior suggests that she might have had a reputation for unreliability ("you're out of your mind" [v. 15]). This incident may be notable for another reason, one related to our modern poorly attended prayer meetings where more than those who actually attend would surely be welcome: this is the only occasion in history in which it was easier to get out of jail than to get into a prayer meeting!

Peter motions to the disciples "to be quiet" (v. 17), because a search is surely to be made. Expecting to be hiding for a while, he gives instructions that James and others be notified. This James, the brother of Jesus and writer of the epistle of James, was rapidly becoming prominent in the Jerusalem church (see 15:12–21).

Herod in frustration puts the soldiers to death, the Roman penalty for allowing a prisoner to escape. This accounts for the great commotion (v. 18) Peter's absence created among the soldiers.

Luke concludes his story of Peter's deliverance with a postscript about Herod's ultimate fate (12:19–23). Herod leaves Jerusalem, goes to a place he preferred, Caesarea, and addresses some previously estranged subjects from Tyre and Sidon.

Normally Agrippa I conducted himself as a pious Jew, but on this occasion his true inclination lets him get carried away. The sincerity of these people who wanted desperately to placate the man who could control their food supply is doubtful, but they, in violation of the Law, attribute divinity to him. He is quite willing to accept their flattery and dies soon after by the judgment of God of a disease thought to be intestinal roundworms. Worms as much as sixteen inches long feeding on intestinal fluids can obstruct the intestines and cause great pain as well as death.

Luke notes at this point that when Barnabas and Saul complete their mission of mercy at Jerusalem, they return (v. 25) to Antioch with John Mark. He likes to make these connective, explanatory remarks in order to prepare the reader for later incidents. John Mark will accompany Barnabas, his cousin, and Saul on the first missionary journey (13:4–5).

III. The Witness to Christ to the Ends of the Earth (13:1–28:31)

The remainder and larger portion of the Book of Acts will tell the story of the Gentile mission. Further references to the Jerusalem church will be made only as they have a bearing on Gentile evangelism. For example, Acts 15 serves to clear the way of a barrier to the Gentile mission, while Acts 21–23 will take us back to Jerusalem to show how the Gentile mission made its way ultimately to Rome.

A. Paul's first missionary journey (13:1–14:28). In his account of the inception of the mission (**13:1–3**), Luke lists the primary workers at the church in Antioch and classfies them as prophets and teachers (v. 1). In the original Greek, two grammatical particles usually translated "both . . . and" appear, the "both" prior to the names of Barnabas, Simeon, and Lucius, and the "and" in connection with the names of Manaen and Saul. Thus Luke divides the names into two groups which correspond with the two classifications, prophets and teachers. This means that Barnabas, Simeon, and Lucius functioned as prophets, while Manaen and Saul functioned as teachers. The emphasis would be revelation and exhortation for the prophets and instruction and application for the teachers.

Barnabas and Saul are already familiar to us, but the others are new to the Book of Acts. Simeon called Niger bears a Latin name meaning "black" and likely was an African. It is possible that he is the same person as Simon of Cyrene who carried Jesus' cross (Luke 23:26; spelled slightly differently by Luke in this place). Lucius of Cyrene is unknown so far as we know, though some have identified him as Luke the physician, an unlikely possibility. Manaen is described as having "been brought up" with Herod, the New International Version's translation of the term *foster-brother*. This Herod would be Herod Antipas, the Herod in power during Jesus' ministry (4 B.C. to A.D. 39). What a contrast in destiny of two boys who spent their childhood together!

The reference to worshiping and fasting (v. 2) suggests that a special gathering was called for the purpose of seeking divine direction in an important decision. It is likely that out of the ministry of prophecy and teaching the believers had reached the conclusion that a mission to the yet untouched regions should be undertaken, and discovering just who should be the missionaries was the purpose of the worship and fasting. At any rate, this was indeed the outcome of this activity. Probably by a prophetic utterance—an implication of the words *the Holy Spirit said* (direct quotation)—the instructions from God come: release from ministry here in Antioch two of your leaders, Barnabas and Saul (the words *sent them off* [v. 3] mean "released").

There are some important implications to the manner in which this missionary enterprise was launched. The impulse comes ideally from within a local congregation. The "they" of verses 2 and 3 is somewhat ambiguous, but the reference to "church" in verse 1 encourages us to extend it to the whole congregation. The motivation for foreign mission candidates should be the truth of the Word of God (prophecy and teaching at this early time), not guilt or some indiscriminate exhortation that everyone should be a missionary if he can. Large-scale attempts at recruitment are not biblical. Only those chosen by God should become missionaries, for larger numbers are not necessarily the key to world evangelization. It requires only a few to plant churches and those congregations are responsible to reach their own areas, a fact that will become obvious in Saul's (Paul's) ministry.

A perplexing question for today is how, precisely, the Holy Spirit communicates his instructions. The "charismatic" answer to the question is: precisely the way he did in first-century Antioch, through vision or prophetic utterance. Such a simple answer should not be lightly dismissed, for it is possible to heap scorn on someone's claim merely because it is outside the range of our personal experience. The fact is, such an answer probably does not reflect the normal experience even of charismatic brethren today, and church history reveals that it has not been the normative experience of the evangelical, Bible-believing church since the first century either.

Whether the gift of prophecy is a valid means of such communication today really need not concern us here, for it is not clearly taught anywhere in the New Testament that this is more than an exception to the rule anyway. As the Scriptures are faithfully expounded and believers humbly seek illumination, they will receive insights. The gifts of various believers as well as believers' personal desires and aspirations will eventually lead to a growing consensus, a witness of the Spirit, and it will become obvious who should be commissioned for service.

Luke emphasizes the divine initiative of the Holy Spirit in the sending of the two missionaries, Barnabas and Saul, to Cyprus (**13:4–12**).

The role of the church is to perceive this initiative, not create it. It is true that through the teaching of the Word (13:1) and a humble, worshipful attitude (13:2) we allow the Holy Spirit to take the initiative; nevertheless, the initiative and impulse are with the Spirit.

From Seleucia (v. 4), the nearest seaport to Syrian Antioch, Barnabas and Saul sail to the island of Cyprus, the birthplace of Barnabas (4:36), very likely because of Barnabas's interests and personal relationships there. Because at this point and previously (13:2) Barnabas has been listed first in the references to him and Saul, it can be inferred that he, as senior believer, was the official leader of the mission.

At Salamis (v. 5), the principal city of the island, the missionaries preach the gospel first in the Jewish synagogues, logical places to start, since the congregations' knowledge of Old Testament truth would facilitate their understanding of the gospel. This will be Saul's procedure throughout his ministry and is his conscious strategy as stated in Romans 1:16, "First for the Jew, then for the Gentile."

At this point Luke notes somewhat incidentally that "John was with them as their helper." A "helper" is a term used of synagogue attendants who cared for the scrolls of Old Testament Scriptures and perhaps, in Mark's case, scrolls of the sayings of Jesus recorded prior to the composition of the four Gospels. The term in Luke's writings (Luke 1:2; Acts 26:16) comes to mean simply a "servant of Christ."

At Paphos, the apostles encounter a "Jewish sorcerer and false prophet named Bar-Jesus" (v. 6; "son of Jesus") as well as the provincial governor (proconsul), Sergius Paulus (v. 7). The proconsul would be responsible for examining the message of any itinerant preacher as part of his responsibility to keep peace among all religious groups. As a kind of cross-examiner in behalf of the Jewish community, Bar-Jesus "opposed them" (v. 8) and attempts to discredit the Christian message. The name *Elymas* means "sorcerer" and his practice of the same is contrary to the Law, but evidently this fact was ignored by the Jewish community whom he represents.

At this point something takes place far more significant in regard to the future than the miracle of temporary blindness inflicted on Bar-Jesus or even the conversion of Sergius Paulus, a notable Roman official. Paul takes the initiative under the control of the Holy Spirit (v. 9) and rebukes the sorcerer (vv. 10–11). So significant is the event that Luke finds this the fitting time to discontinue his use of the name *Saul* and begin to use the name *Paul* in what will be predominantly Gentile situations. This was not a new name for him, simply his Roman name given because he was a Roman citizen. This leadership initiative probably came as no surprise to Barnabas, who seems to be quite willing to let nature take its course.

The essential nature of sorcery—and of all occult practices for that matter—is suggested in Paul's words to Bar-Jesus. It is primarily demonic or satanic (v. 10) and in basic opposition to the truth. It thrives on "deceit and trickery." It perverts the "ways of the Lord," which implies that it mixes truth with error and thus makes an otherwise good thing evil.

Finally, it is important that what really impressed the proconsul was the teaching about the Lord (v. 12), not merely this miracle. This clearly confirms the secondary importance of miracles in relation to the gospel message. As a good illustration should enhance the point a speaker is making, so a miracle should advance the truth, not merely impress people by a demonstration of power. Sergius Paulus's ability to get the point certainly confirms Luke's description of him as an "intelligent man" (v. 7).

From the island of Cyprus, Paul, Barnabas, and Mark journeyed to the Galatian region (**13:13–14:28**). They "sailed to Perga in Pamphylia" (v. 13), a province on the southern coast of Asia Minor. Luke records no evangelization; merely the fact that John Mark "left them to return to Jerusalem." No reason for this departure is given, but the later strong refusal by Paul to allow Mark to accompany them on the second journey (15:37–39) implies a defect in Mark's spiritual character. At any rate, Paul and Mark were later reconciled (2 Tim. 4:11). Several speculations have been offered for this defection: Mark's disagreement about their strategy; Mark's resentment of Paul's leadership; homesickness; and Mark's inability to endure hardship.

The ministry at Pisidian Antioch, a city not to be confused with Syrian Antioch, is given extensive treatment, because it provides a pattern for Paul's methodology in both strategy and message.

It was the custom in the Jewish synagogue, after such elements as the Shema ("Hear, O Israel" [Deut. 6:4]) and the "reading from the Law and the Prophets" (v. 15), the Old Testament, that any qualified Jew in attendance would be asked to give an address. Thus Paul has an opportunity to present the gospel by invitation.

The sermon itself is preserved only in condensed form (synagogue addresses tended to last longer than two or three minutes), but this one, the sermon at Lystra (14:15–17), and the one at Athens (17:22–31) are examples of how Paul approached various kinds of audiences without altering the essential core of the gospel (*kerygma*). This audience consisted of Jews and Gentile converts to Judaism, a fairly knowledgeable group so far as the Old Testament Scriptures were concerned.

Paul begins with the redemptive history of Israel from Abraham to David, who becomes his springboard for his gospel proclamation (vv. 23–41), because Jesus is "from this man's descendants" (v. 23). Paul refers to John, who preached "repentance and baptism" and pointed to the superiority of Jesus, but of Jesus' ministry nothing is recorded, though undoubtedly it was part of the original sermon. Paul testifies to the failure of the Jerusalem Jews to recognize Jesus and to his death without just cause.

Luke records a distinctive portion of Paul's sermon following the reference to Jesus' resurrection and appearances in Jerusalem and Galilee. It provides a valuable pattern of the apostolic kerygma in which selections from Old Testament texts are used to substantiate Jesus' deity (v. 33; Ps. 2:7), his Davidic heritage (v. 34; Isa. 55:3), and his resurrection (v. 35; Ps. 16:10).

The sermon concludes with an appeal (vv. 38–41), though no explicit "invitation" is recorded. The sum of the message is that forgiveness of sins is available now to "everyone who believes" (v. 39), a justification which could not be attained by the law of Moses. Finally, Paul warns scoffers (v. 41; Hab. 1:5) in an interesting use of the prophet's words which, in their context, pertain to God's use of the Babylonians as an instrument of his judgment on Judah in 586 B.C. Applied here, the thing the congregation would not believe is God's use of a foreign power (Rome?) to judge them if they continued in rebellion against God.

One of the peculiar omissions in all of the evangelistic sermons of Acts is a theology of Jesus' death on the cross as a substitutionary sacrifice for sin, stated in Paul's kerygma in 1 Corinthians 15:3 and so thoroughly developed in his other letters (Romans, Galatians, 2 Corinthians) as well as by Peter in 1 Peter 1:18–21. The complete versions probably contained it, and it can be easily inferred from Paul's reference to the forgiveness of sins in this sermon. Both Jews and Gentiles—familiar with concepts of sacrifice, as they were in the first century—would probably have assumed this significance of Jesus' death without extensive exposition.

The principal results of the sermon are an invitation "to speak further about these things on the next Sabbath," and an apparent conversion of many Jews and Gentiles (v. 43), who go with Paul and Barnabas for further encouragement.

The second opportunity arises on the next Sabbath when most of the city comes to listen to Paul. The unbelieving Jews are aroused to jealousy, however, and another pattern is set for the rest of Paul's ministry: persecution by Jews (see 1 Thess. 2:14–16). This pattern also includes a turning away from the synagogue to a ministry exclusively to the Gentiles (vv. 46–48).

One further observation about this sermon as well as all evangelism in Acts is important: the sovereign working of the Holy Spirit permeates it all. If one stops to think about it long enough, he realizes how remarkable it is that in such a relatively brief time and with such little information many come to faith in Jesus Christ. Undoubtedly this is the result of long preparation by the Holy Spirit prior to the coming of the missionary, and goes even further back to the eternal counsels of God in which his chosen ones "were appointed for eternal life" and finally believed (v. 48) as the message was preached.

Luke offers a postscript to the Antioch ministry by describing the spreading of the gospel through the whole region (v. 49), very likely through the efforts of the new converts themselves, for Paul and Barnabas are soon "expelled . . . from [the] region," shaking "the dust from their feet in protest against them" (v. 51), a Jewish gesture of scorn commanded by Jesus himself (Matt. 10:14; Mark 6:11; Luke 9:5).

The next stop for the missionaries is Iconium (14:1), located higher on a plateau of fertile plains and forests. The pattern of Paul's strategy—going to a Jewish synagogue and suffering persecution from those Jews who failed to believe the gospel—is repeated. On this occasion the persecution is at first limited to slander, and Paul and Barnabas spend "considerable time there" in order to establish the new believers. The possible reason for this period of grace, so uncommon in the other Roman cities, is that Iconium was governed in the Greek manner by its local assembly, and the Romans did not declare this new religion illegal. Thus the people of the city are divided but no militant action is initially taken. Nevertheless, a group of Gentiles and Jews cook up a plot against the apostles and they are eventually forced to leave and go on to Lystra and Derbe (v. 6).

Lystra apparently boasted no synagogue, so Paul's approach is different. The springboard here for the gospel is the healing of a man "lame from birth" (v. 8).

The immediate consequence of the miracle is the identification of Barnabas as Zeus and Paul as Hermes. Inscriptions have been discovered at Sedasa, near Lystra, from the third century A.D. that indicate these two gods were worshiped in this region. Hermes was Zeus' son and the spokesman for the gods; thus the Lycaonians identify him with Paul. The priest of Zeus is so excited that he prepares a sacrifice. The temple was located near the city gates, and this afforded, so far as the people of Lystra were concerned, another opportunity to pay homage to their gods. The ancient writer Ovid refers to a legend in which Zeus and Hermes once came to the area disguised as mortals seeking a place to lodge. They were turned away by all except an elderly couple. In appreciation, the two gods transformed their cottage into a temple and made the couple priest and priestess. The inhospitable people of the area were destroyed.

When Paul and Barnabas finally realize what is happening they attempt to forestall the ceremony. Luke records a brief message by Paul, because it provides one of two (the other in Athens) sermons directed to pagan Gentiles. These pagans were comparatively unlearned and superstitious. Paul attempts to point them to the living God who created all things, because their concept of God was polytheistic and anthropomorphic. He further points to the fact that God had, in spite of their ignorance, provided a testimony concerning himself in the form of the good things of life. Such things would be evidences of both the goodness and the greatness of God, a message that was later to be echoed in Paul's letter to the Romans (1:18–20). In Romans 1:18–21 Paul chides mankind for substituting its idols for this testimony and accuses them of being "without excuse" (Rom. 1:20), but Luke records no such harsh rebuke at Lystra.

Jews from Antioch and Iconium stir up opposition to Paul, and they stone him, leaving him "outside the city" (v. 19) for dead. But Paul revives, returns to the city, and the next day goes on to Derbe. In his letter to the Galatians, which the majority of scholars believe is addressed to these cities of the southern part of the Roman province of Galatia, Paul refers to marks or wounds that probably resulted from this persecution (Gal. 6:17). The reference in 2 Corinthians 11:25 to a stoning is also, in all likelihood, this very occasion.

Very little is recorded by Luke about the ministry in Derbe, except that many converts were made. Paul reverses his direction after Derbe and returns to the same cities to strengthen and encourage the new disciples. An important item is included here by Luke: the appointment of elders in each church (v. 23). Presumably, sufficient time had elapsed for leadership qualities such as Paul sets forth in 1 Timothy 3:1–7 to be observed in certain men. The fact that some may have been Jews learned in the Old Testament Scriptures could partly account for this.

Three important facts should be observed regarding principles of church planting. First, Paul relatively quickly prepares these churches for independence. Second, he does not remain around long enough for them to become dependent on him, but pushes on. Third, Paul returns to his churches on all of his subsequent journeys to teach them further, but for the purpose of fostering their spiritual maturity, not to build or increase his personal following.

From the standpoint of Christian leadership, the words *committed them to the Lord, in whom they had put their trust* (v. 23), are especially significant. Paul maintained a healthy balance between concern for the churches (see 2 Cor. 11:28) and trust that God is able to keep those who are entrusted to him even in his absence. Paul recognized his responsibility, that which he was able to do, and that which only God can do. Like a wise parent he knew when to let go of his "children."

Luke traces sketchily the return to Antioch in 14:24–25. On the initial phase of the journey they had been unable to preach at Perga; now they do so.

The return to Antioch of Syria involves first the apostles' report to the church which had commissioned them (vv. 27–28). The importance of ministry to the home church cannot be overestimated. Such ministry brings the sending church into greater participation with the missionary and broadens its vision beyond its own precincts.

B. The Jerusalem council: An example of theological peace-making (15:1–35). While Paul and Barnabas ministered to the Antioch church, some men from Judea began teaching the necessity of circumcision for salvation. This is the first reference in Acts to the legalists who dogged the steps of Paul wherever he went and were dealt with specifically in his letter to the Galatians. They were Jews, and likely former members of the Pharisaical party (see 15:5) with its stress on external obedience to the Law and the traditions. With the influx of Gentiles into the church, these often well-meaning advocates of Law-keeping were concerned about the influence of pagan practices and morality corrupting the church. To their thinking, the best antidote to paganism was strict Jewish practice.

Observe, however, that Paul clearly requires

radical moral reformation (by the power of the Holy Spirit, of course) of all Gentile converts. He simply draws a line between ritual observances and moral observances and requires only the latter of Gentile believers. Why? Because of the danger of legalism that usually went with the Jewish concept of the purpose of these ritual practices. Circumcision, for example, had its purpose in its time. It was a means of helping the Jews think of themselves as different from the rest of the world, as a covenant people separated to Yahweh. Accompanied by genuine faith, the ritual accomplished its purpose; but without faith, it became a legalistic means of securing their standing before God, at least to their way of thinking. Paul repudiates legalism, because it becomes a substitute of human effort alone for the grace of God working through human efforts and leads only to failure and frustration.

It may not be fair to interpret the words *unless you are circumcised, according to the custom taught by Moses, you cannot be saved* (v. 1) as excluding faith. After all, these legalists went to Gentile converts who had already believed in Jesus; hence faith was assumed. But the difficulty was they were teaching that faith *plus* circumcision saved, not faith alone, as all the apostles taught (see 15:11). If they had merely said, "Since you have believed, it would be an appropriate sign of your faith to be circumcised," there might have been little dispute. You cannot add rituals or other deeds as requirements for salvation alongside faith without destroying the nature of grace. Indeed, grace works within the believer to produce deeds (James 2:14–26).

The matter is crucial theologically, so Paul and Barnabas are appointed to go to Jerusalem to debate the issue. In Acts 15:5 the requirement of circumcision is broadened to include the entire law of Moses. Once again, this is not an issue of the authority of the Old Testament Scriptures, but a matter of traditional customs and rituals. Many believing Jews continued, at least as long as the temple stood, to observe all the Mosaic requirements as an expression of their faith. Many godly Gentiles had also opted to follow all the Jewish customs, and this was acceptable as a matter of choice, so long as it was accompanied by faith. But making it a requirement frustrated the principle of grace.

The debate that ensues (**15:6–12**) consists of recollections of how God had worked apart from ritual requirements to save Gentiles. Peter recalls how Cornelius came into the household of faith (vv. 6–9) totally apart from ritual requirements. Putting a yoke of legalism on Gentiles, as the Jews had done to themselves in the past, is "to test God," according to Peter. This implies that God had not so employed the Law; such legalism was not his intended purpose in giving the Law, but a perversion of it. Paul elsewhere argues that the Law was given for other legitimate reasons (e.g., Gal. 3:19–25 states one of those reasons). Peter's address impresses the assembly (v. 12), and a deep silence settles over them as Barnabas and Paul continue.

Following Peter, Barnabas and Paul relate the signs and wonders God had done in their ministry to the Gentiles (v. 12). The point they probably made is the same: Gentiles, through the instrumentality of God's grace, have come to faith and salvation apart from legalistic requirements.

James, the brother of Jesus and one of the most influential of the leaders in Jerusalem (see 12:17; Gal. 2:12), seems to have the final word in the matter (**15:13–35**). The heart of his remarks is found in his conclusion that what the assembly has been hearing is in agreement with the prophets (v. 15).

The issue so far in the Jerusalem council is: Should the Gentiles become "Jews" in every respect as a requirement of salvation? James quotes Amos 9:11–12 in a way that differs from the Hebrew Masoretic Text on which our Old Testament translations are based. James appears to be quoting a variant of Amos 9:11–12 that was known in his day, which is closer to the Septuagint and almost identical to a midrash (commentary) on Amos found among the Dead Sea Scrolls. The variation of this midrash allowed James more easily to make his point, but the idea is still implicit in the Masoretic version.

The point is: someday the "tent" (v. 16) of David—the restored Israel—will be in the center of a "remnant" (v. 17) of Gentiles who will bear the Lord's name. In other words, their identity as Gentiles will remain; they will not become "Jews."

James's conclusion then is: do not "make it difficult" unnecessarily for Gentiles "who are turning to God" (v. 19); and request these Gentiles to abstain from practices that would create an unnecessary offense to their Jewish brothers. The line of reasoning here is identical to what Paul suggests to the Roman and Corinthian believers later on (Rom. 14; 1 Cor. 8–10). These items are in the category of matters of personal conscience, not moral legislation.

The items are "food polluted by idols" (v. 20; sacrifices that had been offered in pagan worship and sold in markets [1 Cor. 8:1–13]); "sexual immorality" (Gk. *porneia*, fornication; in this case the restrictive sense of marrying certain more distant relatives, since marriage to close relatives was forbidden among Gentiles as well as Jews [Lev. 18]); and "the meat of strangled animals" (because blood remained in them) and eating blood (prohibited because of its sacrificial significance [see Lev. 17:10–12]). All these matters were part of the ceremonial law which foreshadowed the death of Christ. Ceremonial law was no longer incumbent upon believers since his sacrifice, but it was important for Gentiles to observe, to maintain harmony and lack of offense between Gentile and Jew. Jews were present in every city, and thus they were present in every church.

On the basis of this conclusion by James, a letter to all the churches is drafted and Paul, Barnabas, Judas, and Silas are chosen to deliver it. The letter significantly disassociates the Jerusalem church from the legalistic teachers (v. 24), confirms the gospel of grace they had originally heard (v. 28), and sets forth the three matters of conscience as requests, not commands (v. 29).

Several principles stand out that pertain to solving the theological problems that often face us. First, an open and respectful hearing is given to all sides involved. Second, a conclusion is reached that represents a consensus, and third, a written document to the whole church is circulated to make the conclusion available to all.

The representatives return to Antioch and deliver the Jerusalem decree. Luke describes the Antioch church as "glad" (v. 31) and encouraged. Judas and Silas return to Jerusalem, and Luke later describes the letter's delivery to the churches of Galatia, and presumably Cilicia (15:23), in 16:4. For the time being, Paul and Barnabas remain in Antioch and continue their ministry (15:35).

How does the Jerusalem conference relate to the visit to Jerusalem which Paul describes in Galatians 2:1–10? The demands of brevity forbid a lengthy discussion of this puzzling question. The Galatian visit probably occurred before the Jerusalem conference, because Paul does not refer to the Jerusalem decree in Galatians, something that would have been a potent argument for him to use, and Paul states in Galatians 2:2 that he went to Jerusalem on that occasion "in response to a revelation" to compare notes with the Jerusalem leaders. The Jerusalem conference, on the other hand, was instigated by a dispute in Antioch (Acts 15:1–2).

C. Paul's second missionary journey (15:36–18:22). The apostle Paul's concern for the spiritual welfare of the churches which he had founded leads one day to his proposing to Barnabas that they "go back and visit" (15:36). But Barnabas's desire to take Mark along arouses an objection by Paul and "sharp disagreement" (15:39) results between them. Luke candidly and objectively relates the unpleasant incident, but makes no attempt to blame anyone (**15:36–41**). Since Mark and Paul were later reconciled (2 Tim. 4:11), one is inclined to side with Barnabas, who has already proven a good judge of character and potential with Paul himself. It may well be, however, that something about Mark which Luke has not recorded made him unfit for a journey such as Paul envisioned, a flaw that time and a good mentor like Barnabas would help to remove. At any rate, the result is the creation of two missions instead of only one (vv. 39–41).

One event Luke records in Paul's return to the Galatian churches (**16:1–6**) is Paul's recruitment of a young disciple named Timothy. Luke will refer to Timothy several times (17:14–15; 18:5; 19:22; 20:4) but has little to say about him later. The pastoral Letters, 1 and 2 Timothy, are addressed to him, and Paul himself reveals some pertinent facts about him. Timothy must have been converted earlier as the result of Paul's first journey to Lystra, because Paul calls him his child in the faith (1 Tim. 1:2). Paul puts him above all his other disciples as one with a genuine concern for others (Phil. 2:20). Paul left Timothy in Ephesus on one occasion to deal with "certain men" who were teaching "false doctrines" (1 Tim. 1:3), an event nowhere recorded in Acts. Conservative scholars theorize that this event took place sometime after the Acts history during a time in which Paul had been released from the Roman imprisonment recorded in Acts 28. At any rate, the event reveals the great confidence which Paul had in him.

Luke relates the fact that Paul circumcised Timothy "because of the Jews who lived in that area" (v. 3). They knew "his father was a Greek" and his "mother was a Jewess" (v. 1). This, in their eyes, still meant that he was a Jew, and the failure of his mother to circumcise him would make it difficult for him to minister to Jews, as such a fact would follow him wherever he went. Paul was not compromising principle, because this was not an issue of the requirements for salvation, but a matter of customs and culture. Paul discusses this sort of thing in 1 Corinthians 9:19–23. To a Jew, he "became like a Jew, to win the Jews" (1 Cor. 9:20).

The other matter Luke discusses in this section is Paul's return to the Galatian churches to deliver the Jerusalem decree. As a consequence of this theological victory, Luke stresses that the churches were strengthened.

Sound doctrine, not merely good technique, lies beneath all God-given church growth.

Luke says Paul and his companions traveled throughout the region of Phrygia and Galatia (v. 6). The word *region* pertains to both Phrygia and Galatia, because the article *the* is not repeated before each name. This refers to one region, not two, and most logically means the southern part of the Roman province of Galatia. This would weaken the theory, held by a few, that Paul entered the northern Galatian province and founded churches there and strengthens the opinion that the cities of the southern Galatian province, Iconium, Lystra, and Derbe, were the recipients of his letter to the Galatians.

The Holy Spirit is prominent in the turn of events in **16:7–10,** both an enlightening and a perplexing series of incidents. When Paul and his companions try to enter Asia they must have intended to take the Via Sabaste westward to the strategic city of Ephesus. But God has other plans, and Ephesus is further down the list on his agenda. Thus Luke refers to the fact that the Holy Spirit prevents it (v. 6). The group then proceeds north for a distance, but as they try to enter Bithynia (v. 7), the same thing happens. This time Luke refers to the "Spirit of Jesus" prohibiting them. This is the same Holy Spirit spoken of in such a way as to show the unity of the persons of the Trinity, a theological idea that even the earliest believers seemed to know about.

Luke does not give the precise way in which the Holy Spirit imparts his will to the apostles, but the most likely means was through the gift of prophecy possessed by Silas (15:32). What is important here is that God sometimes intervenes in man's best intentions. God often permits things to occur which are not according to his preference, but usually such things are permitted when a person is deliberately and willfully ignoring the preferences of God (see Ps. 78:17–31 for an illustration of this from Israel's history).

Having been forbidden by the Spirit to enter Bithynia, the apostles turn west and finally come to Troas (v. 8). Troas was an important port which lay at the mouth of the Dardanelles and was a strategic place between Asia Minor and Europe as well as the waterways of the Sea of Marmara, the Black Sea, and the Aegean Sea.

At Troas, "during the night," Paul receives a vision of a Macedonian "begging" him to come there to help (v. 9). This is perhaps one of the most important turning points in history, for as a result the gospel leaves the Asian world and goes to Europe. The decision to go to Macedonia does not turn automatically on the vision but on a joint decision by the apostolic group, a fact that is clear from the word *concluding* (v. 10) which is first-person plural, implying the presence of the narrator Luke as well as everyone else in the party. Paul is no autocrat but wants important decisions to be shared by the whole group.

There appears to have been an overnight stop at the island of Samothrace, and from there the group arrives at Macedonia at the port of Neapolis. The first record of evangelism involves the city of Philippi (**16:11–40**), which Luke describes as the leading city of the province of Macedonia. He also calls it a Roman colony, which means that many Roman army veterans had settled there.

There was no Jewish synagogue in Philippi, because this required, by Jewish custom, at least ten men. Only women are mentioned, and they must have been a mixture of Jewesses and Gentile converts like Lydia, who is called a worshiper of God (v. 14). Lydia was from the Asia Minor city of Thyatira (see Rev. 2:18–29) and a trader in purple cloth for which the city was famous. Like so many of the God-fearing Gentiles Paul encountered in Jewish synagogues, Lydia is receptive to the gospel. God works within her and opens her heart. Faith is a gift of God in the sense that God removes the barrier created by human rebellion so that an individual can exercise faith. She and "the members of her household" (v. 15) receive baptism, and she invites the missionaries into her home, a common expression of faith throughout the New Testament (e.g., Zacchaeus entertains Jesus [Luke 19:5]; Cornelius entertains Peter [Acts 10:48]).

During the ministry in Philippi, the missionaries encounter "a slave girl who had a spirit by which she predicted the future" (v. 16) and who had become quite profitable to her owners. The ability of evil spirits (demons) to predict the future with convincing accuracy, although they are not omniscient, is due to their ability to secure information via their vast numbers scattered throughout the world. This girl identifies Paul and his companions as servants of the Most High God who bring the message of salvation. Such endorsement was of no value to Paul, because he had no wish to be approved in this way by representatives of the Evil One, whose kingdom he sought to overthrow. Thus Paul exorcises the spirit (v. 18). The girl's enraged masters seize Paul and Silas and accuse them before the city magistrates of advocating customs unlawful to Romans (v. 21), which means that they were advocating an illegal religion (one not officially recognized by Rome).

Other townspeople "joined in the attack against Paul and Silas" (v. 22), because they, too, suffered the loss of their fortuneteller. The missionaries are "stripped and beaten" and "thrown into prison" (v. 23). Interestingly, Paul makes no appeal to his rights as a Roman citizen as he does later in Jerusalem (22:25). Instead, he is willing to suffer, perhaps sensing that a greater good will come from his imprisonment.

At midnight Paul and Silas begin worshiping God by praying and singing loudly enough for the other prisoners to hear them. An earthquake shakes the prison, opening all the doors and freeing the prisoners. The jailer, assuming the prisoners have escaped, prepares to take his life, but miraculously no one has left. His question, "what must I do to be saved?" implies that his concern has shifted from the prisoners to his spiritual condition and echoes the words (16:17) of the slave girl, whom he had probably heard about. That, along with the prayers and hymns and possibly even something of the preaching of Paul in the city, prepares him to ask the right question.

Paul's answer is terse: "Believe in the Lord Jesus, and you will be saved—you and your household" (v. 31), because he must have inferred from the jailer's question and other information that the jailer knows the other facts of the gospel and is ready to make a decision. The focus of his faith must be the lordship of Christ ("*Lord* Jesus"), essentially the requirement Peter made in Acts 2:36. This lordship is the confession of Romans 10:9—not a complete reordering of one's life, but an acknowledgment of Jesus' absolute authority granted by virtue of his resurrection and ascension. As such, it is an element of justifying faith, not sanctification which follows.

The jailer expresses his faith by washing their wounds, being baptized with his whole family, and feeding them in his house. The possibility of infant baptism seems to be ruled out in this text at least, and possibly all the other similar references by analogy; the reference to those who were baptized means believing family members.

Luke closes his story of the Philippian ministry with the amusing account of the town magistrates apparently having second thoughts about their hasty and brutal treatment—under pressure of the mob—of Paul and Silas (vv. 37–40). Paul decides, for the sake of their vindication, and because they are Roman citizens, to insist on a personal "escort" out of prison by the magistrates. This alarms the Philippian politicos and they oblige Paul by coming to the prison themselves. Paul and Silas take their good time and go to Lydia's house to encourage the believers and say a proper goodbye.

Paul and his companions reveal a tendency in their missionary strategy to go to key cities. Thus they pass through Amphipolis and Apollonia, fairly large cities, and press on to Thessalonica (**17:1–9**), the capital of the province of Macedonia, with a population of possibly two hundred thousand and an important city politically and commercially.

According to his custom Paul goes into the synagogue. Luke does not say so, but Paul probably was again invited to speak. Luke uses several words that reveal more of Paul's technique than the actual content of his message. First, he says, Paul reasons (Gk. *dialegomai*) with them from the Scriptures (v. 2). They were familiar with the Scriptures, and the term *reason* implies a conversation, or, in this case, an exchange of questions and answers, not merely a lecture. The word *explaining* (v. 3) means to appeal to reason on the basis of the facts found in Scripture, and "proving" suggests that he succeeds in identifying Jesus as the Messiah of the Old Testament, one who must both suffer and rise from the dead. The result was that some are persuaded, including Jews, God-fearing Gentiles, and prominent women. This last category pertains to women of high standing in the city, wives of principal citizens. In the New Testament, as often today, it is through the avenue of women who are spiritually inclined that the gospel first invades a home (see 1 Pet. 3:1–6).

When persecution comes from the Jews, it comes under the pretext that Christianity should be outlawed because it is contrary to Roman law and is insurrectionist. One of Paul's converts, Jason (vv. 5, 6, 7; Gk. for Joshua), who was providing housing for the missionaries, takes the brunt of the attack (vv. 6–9).

The city is thrown into such confusion that Paul and Silas are forced to leave and go on to Beroea (**17:10–15**). Their departure is so premature, so far as Paul is concerned, that he worries a great deal about the Thessalonian converts until Timothy goes to investigate and returns with a favorable report (1 Thess. 2:17–3:10). In response to this Paul writes the two Thessalonian letters from Corinth.

Luke describes the Jewish Beroeans as "more noble . . . than the Thessalonians," because they investigate from Scripture the references Paul made to Jesus (v. 11). This implies that they open-mindedly challenge what Paul said, but Paul is not offended by such inquiry, because it leads them to discover for themselves what is true. This should warm the heart of any teacher of the Bible!

Once again Paul is pursued by his Jewish antagonists from Thessalonica, and the agitation forces Paul to go on to Athens, leaving behind Silas and Timothy. Paul is the prime target, even though the work could be done by others.

Luke records no extensive mission involving all of Paul's companions at Athens. The city of the intellectuals may have been viewed in advance as unreceptive to the gospel, and the relatively meager results of Paul's message (**17:16–34**) seem to attest to this fact (v. 34). Athens had long since ceased to be significant politically, although the Romans left it free to carry on its institutions. In the first century it was the cultural and intellectual capital of the world.

What is art to travelers today was idolatry in Paul's day, and the presence everywhere of shrines to various gods "greatly distressed" this monotheistic Jew. Paul reasons in the synagogue with the Jews and their Gentile converts, but the results must have been something less than spectacular, a let-down from Beroea and Thessalonica.

Nevertheless, Luke records what may be one of the most significant of all Paul's sermons, at least so far as the intellectual pagans of today are concerned. In the marketplace Paul begins to dispute with Epicurean and Stoic philosophers, rival schools of thought. The Stoics taught that one should accept his lot in life and bravely make the most of it—individual self-sufficiency. They were pantheistic (God is everything) and viewed God as the World-soul. They were very moral and had a sense of duty, but they were very proud. The Epicureans taught that pleasure was the chief goal of life and that one should seek to avoid pain and superstitious fears. They believed in the gods but viewed them as remote from man's concerns. F. F. Bruce concludes that "post-Christian paganism has not been able to devise anything appreciably better."[2] Thus Paul's general approach is relevant today.

The philosophers take a cynical but condescending attitude toward Paul, calling him a babbler (v. 18), a term used of birds picking up seeds, used here as a term of reproach descriptive of a self-styled intellectual who picks up the ideas of others and peddles them as his own. In spite of their vaunted intelligence, some of these intellectuals seem to have misunderstood Paul's message. They interpret him as preaching foreign gods, and Luke's explanation that Paul preached about Jesus and the resurrection must mean that they confused the word *resurrection* for its Greek feminine name, Anastasia, taking it for a consort to Jesus, thus two gods.

If most of these intellectuals had really looked upon Paul as a mere babbler, they probably would not have invited him to speak before the Areopagus, a prestigious judicial body which had jurisdiction over religion and education. Luke's assessment of this forum is as disparaging as theirs is of Paul: they "spent their time doing nothing but talking about and listening to the latest ideas" (v. 21).

Taking his point of departure from his observation of a shrine to an unknown god (v. 23), Paul begins with a biblical description of God. Such anonymous altars existed in order to appease every possible local deity and secure benefits from them. Paul's observation that they were very religious is an interesting use of an ambiguous Greek term which the Athenians would have taken as a compliment and which Paul himself could have intended as a disparaging remark (like our word *superstitious*).

Paul's characterization of God touches upon the Athenians' theological misconceptions and evangelistically serves to "reprogram" them so that the gospel message can be comprehensible. First, he describes God as the Creator of the universe (v. 24). This corrects the Stoic idea that matter is eternal, as well as their pantheism, for God as Creator is distinct from the universe, not the same.

Next, Paul proclaims that God is not dependent upon his creatures for anything (v. 25), a concept that contradicts the polytheistic idea that gods are dependent on worship and service. Furthermore, he stresses the sovereignty of God: "He determined the times set for them and the exact places where they should live" (v. 26). This God has created all men from a common ancestor, and this common origin strikes at the Athenians' racist view that they had originated from the soil of their Attic homeland and were thus superior to all other men.

Paul quotes three Greek poets: Aratus (ca. 315–ca. 245 B.C.), "For we are also his offspring"; Cleanthes' (331–233 B.C.) "Hymn to Zeus" which says essentially the same thing; and Epimenides (600 B.C.), "For in thee we live and move and have our being." These words, of course, were addressed to Zeus, but they nevertheless corroborate Paul's ideas (and testify to the breadth of Paul's education).

Paul's conclusion is that the Athenians should repudiate their insufficient understanding of God and repent in preparation for the day of judgment to be rendered by the man appointed and authenticated by his resurrec-

2. F. F. Bruce, *Commentary on the Book of Acts* (Grand Rapids: Eerdmans, 1988), p. 331.

tion. This final item about the resurrection seems to arouse their derision or curiosity, and, for a few, faith. One of them, Dionysius, is himself a member of the council of the Areopagus (vv. 33–34).

The Grecian antipathy to the resurrection is toward the biblical idea of bodily resurrection, due partly to the Greek disdain for the material realm as opposed to the ideal realm. Most, except for the Epicureans, did believe in the immortality of the soul. This sort of influence can be found in the false view of the resurrection Paul addresses in his first letter to the Corinthians (15:12).

The significance of the Areopagus address for modern evangelism lies in its emphasis upon the biblical concept of God. Paganism, not unlike that in Athens, is growing in influence, so that many people in Western society entertain similar ideas. Behind the simple gospel of the death and resurrection of Jesus Christ is the assumption of the sovereign, transcendent, eternal, holy, and loving God—all ideas explicit or implicit in this sermon. Some important ideas about the nature of man—his rebellion, need to repent, and pride—also lie behind the biblical gospel, items also implicit in this sermon. No one should assume his listeners necessarily understand these things as he preaches the gospel today.

Still alone, Paul leaves Athens and goes to Corinth (**18:1–17**). In 1 Corinthians 2:3 the apostle states that he came "in weakness and fear, and with much trembling." Many commentators interpret these words as a state of depression caused by the persecution at Thessalonica and the polite contempt for his message at Athens. But Paul clearly says that his sense of weakness and fear was due to a determination that a pure and effective message empowered by the Holy Spirit would be delivered to them (1 Cor. 2:2, 4–5). Thessalonica and Athens, then, had renewed Paul's sense of humility and dependence on God. He had seen the worst that rebellious man could dispense, from overt violence to complacent scorn and indifference.

At Corinth, Paul meets a Jewish married couple, Aquila and Priscilla, with whom he has in common his trade of tentmaking. This couple will appear again in 18:18–26, and also in three of Paul's letters (Rom. 16:3; 1 Cor. 16:19; 2 Tim. 4:19 [where a shortened form of Priscilla's name, Prisca, is used; see, e.g., RSV]). Tents were made out of leather, so that the term *tentmaker* also means "leatherworker" and implies all kinds of leather goods. Allusions to this occupation of Paul's show up in several New Testament texts (Acts 20:34; 1 Cor. 9:1–18; 2 Cor. 11:7–12; 1 Thess. 2:9; 2 Thess. 3:7–10).

It appears that before the arrival of Silas and Timothy, Paul plied his trade with Aquila and Priscilla, carrying on a ministry on each Sabbath in the synagogue (v. 4). With the arrival of his two friends comes a gift of money from the Philippians (2 Cor. 11:9; Phil. 4:14–15), and this makes it possible for Paul to devote more time to gospel ministry, which also leads to a break with the Jews and an exclusively Gentile ministry in the home of Titius Justus. It is significant that in spite of the break with a majority of the Jews, their synagogue ruler, Crispus, with his entire household, believes. Paul personally baptizes Crispus (v. 8; cf. 1 Cor. 1:14).

But persecution on a scale exceeding any that Paul has yet experienced is to break out, and the Lord encourages Paul in a vision to continue the forcefulness of his preaching (v. 9). This Paul does for a year and a half.

A change of proconsuls provides an occasion for Paul's enemies to renew their attack on him by bringing him to court (v. 12). Once again, the issue is that the gospel of Jesus Christ is not merely a sect of Judaism but an entirely different and new religion without official Roman recognition (v. 13). Before Paul can make his defense, the new proconsul Gallio makes his own judgment, apparently considering Christianity to be a variation of Judaism—"it involves questions about words and names and your own law" (v. 15).

Gallio's decision probably set a precedent by tending to make Christianity legal, not only for Achaia, but all the Roman provinces that would hear about the judgment. Thus Luke's attention to the incident implies that greater freedom would be granted the Christian missionaries, at least for a while.

Paul's return to Antioch in Syria (**18:18–22**) is made in company with his friends, Priscilla and Aquila. The reversal of the names (see 18:2) may imply that Priscilla was spiritually dominant, so far as knowledge and ministry are concerned.

Paul had taken a Nazirite vow by letting his hair grow. Perhaps this had occurred in connection with his Corinthian ministry, and now the period has come to an end and God has responded to the vow by intervening in the Corinthian ministry, and Paul has cut his hair. The vow would be completed by presenting the hair in the temple at Jerusalem and offering appropriate sacrifices. This he apparently does, when he "greet[s] the church" in Jerusalem (v. 22).

Paul stops briefly at Ephesus, preaches in the synagogue, and promises to return. The response augurs well for success in that city, and Paul indeed returned to experience a fruitful ministry (19:1–41).

D. Paul's third missionary journey (18:23–21:14). "Some time" (v. 23) is spent at Antioch before Paul sets out on his third journey, once again returning through "the region of Galatia and Phrygia" to disciple further the churches he had established there.

Luke introduces a learned man (v. 24; the word can also be rendered "eloquent") named Apollos (**18:24–28**). Apollos becomes prominent later in Corinth (1 Cor. 1:12; 3:4–6, 22; 4:6; 16:12), regarded perhaps as the most effective speaker in early Christendom. Luke describes him as knowing the gospel accurately but knowing only the baptism of John (v. 25), which probably means that the Pentecost event was unknown to him. In light of the disciples (19:1) who also knew only of John's baptism, it might be that Apollos had not received the Holy Spirit either, though Luke says nothing about this.

Priscilla and Aquila take Apollos aside and fill him in on the truth "more adequately" (v. 26). This experience suggests also that he was a man of humility, willing to be taught by others of less spectacular abilities. Following this, Apollos goes to Achaia or Corinth and eventually has a flourishing ministry.

Luke returns to the travels of Paul, who has gone through the Galatian-Phrygian region on the first leg of his third journey. He probably reached Pisidian Antioch and from there "took the road through the interior"—of the province of Asia; that is, a more direct route than the ordinary trade route—"and arrived at Ephesus" (**19:1–41**).

At Ephesus Paul encounters twelve disciples. Luke's use of the term *disciples* implies that Paul recognized them somehow as believers in Jesus Christ, perhaps in a similar state of knowledge about Pentecost as Apollos (vv. 2–4). This is also implied by the rather specific nature of Paul's question about whether they had received the Holy Spirit when they believed (v. 2), the kind of question one would ask to clarify a matter after preliminary discussion. During this period of church history it was evidently possible for people who had believed in Jesus Christ to be ignorant of Pentecost and not to have been baptized in the Spirit.

It is tenuous to argue from this passage that all believers should look for a baptism in the Spirit after conversion. Paul's question implies the normal experience: believers receive the Spirit when they believe. Also, along with the belief in postconversion baptism in the Spirit is the belief that it is granted by God to those who meet the requirements of deeper commitment. The hitherto unknown information that the Holy Spirit exists does not even parallel that kind of teaching.

Luke's reason for relating this incident is probably to indicate that these twelve disciples formed the nucleus of the new church at Ephesus. The third and last reference in Acts to speaking in tongues (v. 6) occurs here and it serves as a verification of these believers' reception of the Spirit for themselves as well as Paul, due to the unusual nature of the situation.

Once again, Paul's pattern of ministry is repeated as he enters the synagogue and preaches for three months (v. 8). As elsewhere, a vocal group of Jews forces Paul to take his ministry mainly to the Gentiles, and on this occasion Paul apparently rents the "lecture hall of Tyrannus" (v. 9). Historians say that ordinarily Tyrannus would have used the hall during the morning hours and then vacated it between 11:00 A.M. and 4:00 P.M., for the purpose of the Asian equivalent of a siesta. Possibly during this period Paul used it for training his disciples.

For two years Paul teaches; the direct result is the evangelization and founding of churches in provincial Asian cities (e.g., Sardis, Laodicea, Colossae, and Thyatira—mentioned with others in Rev. 2 and 3). This illustrates again Paul's strategy of evangelizing certain principal cities and training those believers to reach out, thus multiplying his ministry, rather than going himself to one city at a time.

Paul's ministry at Ephesus is also characterized by extraordinary miracles (v. 11) similar to those experienced by Peter during his early Jerusalem ministry (see 5:15–16) when his mere shadow brought healing, and by the woman who touched Jesus' garment and was healed (Mark 5:27–31). In Paul's case, handkerchiefs ("sweat rags") and aprons (v. 12), items he had used in his leatherwork, the handkerchiefs around his head, and the aprons around his waist, bring physical healing.

In addition to healing, evil spirits leave some, and this use of the name of Jesus Christ inspires seven Jewish exorcists to try using the same name as an incantation. These Jews, by using the normally unspoken name of Yahweh, mixed magical practices with religion and enjoyed great prestige. But this time the experiment backfires, and the man with the evil spirit viciously attacks them. The spirit speaks and affirms his knowledge of Jesus and Paul, but repudiates their efforts, bringing great honor to the name of the Lord Jesus (v. 17).

This story might sound bizarre to some twentieth-century minds, at least those unfamiliar with the occult world and demonism. One lesson it teaches is that demons are real and exorcism is not to be practiced as a hobby, as the dangers are great. The name of Jesus Christ has power indeed, but only among those who are committed to the glory of God.

The incident of the seven sons of Sceva provides an occasion for a spiritual awakening primarily among those who believe (v. 18; Gk. perfect; lit. had believed); that is, those who had been Christians for a time but had either retained or fallen back into sorcery because of the great profit involved in it. This results in the burning of their occult materials, the value of which is fifty thousand drachmas, the modern equivalent being about forty-eight thousand dollars. Sometimes the effect upon one's pocketbook is a gauge of spiritual commitment! Also this teaches that one can truly acknowledge the lordship of Christ without being fully aware of all its implications.

Luke informs us at this point (19:21–22) that Paul makes a momentous decision that is to have an ongoing bearing on his future. The decision is to go to Jerusalem via Macedonia and Achaia. Ultimately, he hoped to go all the way to Rome, but little did he realize how that goal would be achieved! Two of his party, Timothy and Erastus, are sent ahead at this time. This Erastus may be the same one mentioned in Romans 16:23, the director of public works for Corinth. Paul himself stays "a little longer" in Asia.

During Paul's prolonged visit in Ephesus, the Christians' repudiation of magical arts brings about a crisis. The instigator is a silversmith named Demetrius (v. 24), a craftsman of silver idols representing Artemis (known as Diana among the Romans).

Artemis of Ephesus was more Near Eastern than Greek. Her image as the goddess of fertility was an ugly, four-breasted woman. This image was believed to have fallen from heaven, in all likelihood a meteorite that may have resembled such a creature. The temple itself was a large edifice, one of the Seven Wonders of the ancient world. It served a practical purpose also as a treasury or bank, whose deposits contained the fortunes of many throughout the world. Thus there was a mixture of religious as well as commercial reasons for the riot that ensues after Demetrius' inflammatory speech (vv. 25–27).

Paul is restrained from getting involved by his friends (vv. 30–31), and finally the crowd is quieted by an unnamed city clerk (v. 35).

Luke summarizes the European phase of Paul's journey in a brief paragraph (**20:1–6**). The purpose of this part of the journey is to encourage believers, a policy that guided Paul during the second journey as well. Reaching Greece (Corinth, presumably), he remains a brief three months due to a plot against him which presumably calculated that he would go down to Cenchrea and set sail from there as he had done previously (18:18). Instead, Paul foils the plans of his enemies and goes back the way he came through Macedonia. Some theorize that during this stay in Macedonia the gospel entered Illyricum (Rom. 15:19) either through Paul or some of his companions.

Luke makes reference to a group of men (v. 4) representing almost all the areas where the gospel had gone as accompanying Paul. The change to "we" implies that Luke himself joined the group, apparently at Philippi. The point seems to be that each area participated in the evangelistic enterprise.

After celebrating the Passover and Feast of Unleavened Bread at Philippi, Luke, Paul, Silas, and Timothy go to Troas to join the others who had gone on earlier (vv. 5–6).

All the believers at Troas (**20:7–37**) assemble on Sunday (v. 7; note what must have become at this early date a Christian practice) to break bread, Luke's expression for the Lord's Supper (see 2:42, 46). They meet together in the evening (implied by v. 8) in an upstairs room to listen to Paul's instruction. A young man named Eutychus, sitting in the window, falls asleep and tumbles to the ground. He is picked up dead (v. 9; since there were oil-burning torches—lamps, and thus a scarcity of oxygen—Paul may not be to blame). What occurs, then, when Paul says, "He's alive!" is a bona fide resurrection, one of a few of its kind in the New Testament. Perhaps equally significant is the spiritual appetite of these believers which keeps them listening to Paul all night long (v. 11), another reason for not criticizing Paul for long-windedness.

While his companions sail from Troas to Assos, Paul walks alone overland, perhaps to be alone to meditate. Joining them at Assos, he and the group sail and eventually reach Miletus where Paul, in order to save time, decides to send for the elders at Ephesus, some thirty miles inland to the northeast, in order to say farewell (v. 17).

Paul's address to the Ephesian elders is filled with references to his philosophy of ministry. The attitude which permeated his ministry is one of great humility and concern in spite of opposition. Nothing intimidated the apostle; instead he withheld nothing from them that they needed to hear. This message is summed up in two key words: repentance in relation to God—because of their rebellion

(Rom. 3:11–12); and faith in Jesus Christ as the only remedy for their condemnation (Rom. 3:21–26). Both of these elements, repentance and faith, comprise genuine conversion and must be kept in proper balance or one's response to the gospel is not complete. Neither repentance nor faith can exist biblically without the other.

Paul informs his beloved elders of a compulsion by the Spirit to go to Jerusalem, even though everywhere he has received forebodings of danger and imprisonment (v. 23). This prospect does not deter him because his life is secondary in importance to his task of proclaiming the gospel of God's grace (v. 24).

Paul's premonition that he will never again see the Ephesians is more pessimistic than the future actually turns out to be, if one assumes that after his first Roman imprisonment he was released and had the opportunity to return to Ephesus (1 Tim. 1:3). Paul refers to his gospel as "preaching the kingdom," which refutes the notion that the "gospel of grace" (v. 24) is distinct from the "gospel of the kingdom" (Matt. 24:14).

Paul refers again to the nature of his preaching as not hesitating (the word is graphic: "I have not shrunk back"—as a foolish parent might withhold necessary medicine from a child because it would be unpleasant) "to proclaim to [them] the whole will of God" (v. 27). Ministry entails as much which is unpleasant to say as what is pleasant. People must be confronted at times with truth they do not like to hear.

The function of the office of elder is suggested in two descriptive terms. The first is overseers (v. 28), which carries the idea of keeping watch, probably over matters that would arise from within, and the second is shepherds, which carries the idea of protection against false teaching that would invade from without (vv. 29–31). False teachers are called "savage wolves" (v. 29), a figure Jesus himself once used of "false prophets" (Matt. 7:15), appropriate for their selfishness and the spiritual havoc which they cause.

Finally, Paul commends the elders to God, trusting him to care for them, for Paul was expendable in the aspect of salvation called sanctification in which the believer is made holy in his life. Paul is confident that his example (vv. 33–35) will be powerful, even in his absence. Paul had not ministered for the sake of money but had worked at his occupation to support himself; this he expects of them, too, although Paul does allow for the support by the church of elders who labor full-time (1 Cor. 9:3–14). Having prayed together and said their tearful goodbyes, Paul returns with them to the ship (vv. 37–38).

Luke briefly traces the journey around the coast of Asia Minor, past the island of Cyprus, and on to Syria (**21:1–14**). The entire journey was evidently made aboard merchant vessels, which necessitated a change of boats at Patara.

At Tyre, a coastal city in the northern part of Palestine, they visit the church for a week (v. 4). These believers warn Paul through the Spirit not to go to Jerusalem.

Then again, at Caesarea, where they stay with Philip the evangelist (v. 8), Paul is graphically warned by the prophet Agabus about his impending imprisonment. It will be instigated by the Jews and carried out by the Gentiles (v. 11; see 21:27–36). Philip, one of the seven deacons of Acts 6, now has four daughters who prophesy (v. 9). In later years this family was a rich resource for knowledge of the events and people of the early years of the church, a fact handed down to us by Papias through Eusebius's church history. Undoubtedly Luke availed himself of this knowledge in composing Acts.

All the efforts by fellow believers and the prophet Agabus to prevent Paul from going to Jerusalem are well-intentioned efforts of loving people who by the Holy Spirit had received the same facts about his future as he had. But to Paul, the issue is much clearer; God was himself taking him into the jaws of the lion, as 20:22 makes clear. Thus, when Paul explains to them his perspective on the matter, they, too, acknowledge the Lord's will (v. 14).

E. Paul's arrest in Jerusalem and incarceration at Caesarea (21:15–26:32). From Caesarea Paul goes on to Jerusalem and to the home of Mnason (**21:15–26**). Paul is received warmly by the Jerusalem church and makes his report to James and the elders.

Following Paul's report (and very likely the presentation of an offering from the Gentile churches [1 Cor. 16:1–4]), the elders remind Paul of false reports about his antinomianism or efforts to turn away Jewish believers from the Law. They want Paul to make a token effort of conciliation by participating in a Nazirite vow with four men (v. 23). This ritual, for him, would involve paying their expenses as a sponsor and going with them into the temple for purification rites, and after seven days of his purification (since he had come from abroad), to be present while the four made their final offering and presentation of their hair. Since one of Paul's desires is the unity of the church, of which the offering from Macedonia, Achaia, and Asia is also a token, he agrees to do this (v.

26). Also, Paul has no scruples against performing Jewish rituals, for he himself had carried out the same kind of vow earlier (18:18).

But the whole idea fails to accomplish its purpose due to a misunderstanding on the part of some Jews from Asia who must have been among those who rejected Paul's message in Ephesus (vv. 28–29). They assume that Paul had taken Trophimus, a Gentile, into the forbidden inner precincts of the temple, an offense incurring the death penalty and backed by the Romans. The misunderstanding leads to Paul's arrest (**21:27–36**).

During the confusion and uproar the Roman garrison, stationed at the fortress of Antonia just north of and adjacent to the temple, rushes in and narrowly rescues Paul from a lynching (vv. 31–32). The commander of the soldiers arrests Paul, assuming he is a certain Egyptian who led a revolt of Assassins (Lat. *sicarii,* from *sica,* dagger; a group of men who at that time hid daggers underneath their cloaks and stealthily put certain people to death), and starts to take Paul into custody. Paul requests his permission to speak to the mob, hoping, perhaps, to salvage the situation for his original purpose (vv. 39–40).

Paul makes his defense (**21:37–22:24**) before the people in Aramaic, rather than Greek, because this is their native tongue and will help him to identify with them (v. 2; "they became very quiet"). Paul's approach is to relate his background as a Pharisee who zealously persecuted Christians (22:3–5). Paul's prestige is enhanced by the fact that he had studied under one of the greatest of the Pharisees, Gamaliel (v. 3; see comments on 5:34).

Next Paul tells how he was converted in a personal confrontation with Jesus of Nazareth (vv. 6–8) and how Ananias, "a devout observer of the law" (v. 12), met him to clarify his commission (vv. 14–16). Ananias's words reported here are much more complete than in 9:17, and here it is made clear that the bulk of Paul's commission to the Gentiles was communicated by Ananias.

The words of Ananias to Paul (22:16) need clarification. Some churchmen have extracted a concept of baptismal regeneration from the words *be baptized and wash your sins away.* A literal translation would reveal that there are two commands in the strict sense, each associated with a participle which can be taken as a command. The command *be baptized* is connected thus with the words *get up,* which are one word in Greek and a participle, while the command *wash away your sins* is connected with the participle *calling on his name.* Thus baptism does not cleanse from sin, but calling on the Lord (faith) does. To summarize by a more literal rendering: "having gotten up, be baptized; having called on the name of the Lord, be cleansed from your sins."

Paul continues his defense by attempting to explain the reason for his estrangement from orthodox Judaism. He relates a vision he had during which God warned him to leave Jerusalem, because his testimony would not be received. Paul replies that his zeal in persecuting Christians like Stephen ought to show that he is zealous for the Law, too. God's answer is, "Go; I will send you far away to the Gentiles" (v. 21).

This statement about Paul's mission to the Gentiles sends the crowd into a frenzy (vv. 22–24). Why? In effect, Paul was saying that he could go to the Gentile world and offer salvation to them totally apart from Israel's institutions; that God could be approached apart from the Law, the sacrifices, and the temple. This was, to their minds, the worst of apostasy, for they viewed the Law as a way of salvation. Paul sums up the issue succinctly in Romans 9:30–32: "the Gentiles, who did not pursue righteousness, have obtained it, a righteousness that is by faith; but Israel, who pursued a law of righteousness, has not attained it. Why not? Because they pursued it not by faith but as if it were by works." The Law was not, in itself, a way of righteousness; but if Israel had coupled its institutions with faith, it could have been a vehicle of righteousness by faith.

Such confusion has resulted from the Roman commander's attempts to clarify the issue (v. 23) that he decides to use his own methods for getting at the truth. This included flogging, and just as he is about to administer this, Paul informs him of his Roman citizenship (**22:25–29**). It was not that Paul feared the pain (he had suffered without protest at Philippi [16:22]). The kind of scourging he was facing was probably with an instrument made of leather thongs studded with pieces of metal or bone and fastened to a wooden handle. It could cripple a person for life.

Roman citizens were exempt from such torture and had the right to a trial. Upon hearing of Paul's citizenship, the centurion reports it to the commander (v. 26). The commander accepts Paul's word because a false claim of being a Roman citizen was often punishable by death. Accordingly, such papers of citizenship were kept in safe places. Paul, of course, was born a citizen, though how his Jewish family acquired this status we do not know. At any rate, this fact forces the commander to take an entirely different approach, so he decides to have Paul appear before the Jewish Supreme

Court, the Sanhedrin (v. 30), in hopes of getting at the root of the matter.

Paul's appearance before the Sanhedrin fails to clarify anything, probably to the consternation of the Roman commander (**23:1–10**). Here is a man named Paul who seems to have a knack for creating confusion. Nevertheless, each of these events is channeling Paul into a position of opportunity and advantage. If it appears that Paul keeps saying and doing the wrong things, a comprehensive look at the larger picture reveals the hand of God.

Paul's opening words, "I have fulfilled my duty to God" (23:1), so enrage the high priest Ananias, who regards him as a despicable apostate, that he orders someone to strike him on the mouth (v. 2). This Ananias, who reigned as high priest during A.D. 48–59, was known for resorting to brutality, even in such a case as this. He was also a notorious thief of temple funds, and Paul's retort, "God will strike you," was eventually carried out through the Jewish people themselves who hated him and hunted him down and killed him.

Admittedly, Paul's words reveal a loss of composure and show that in his humanity he fell short of the quiet way Jesus himself suffered insults (1 Pet. 2:23). Paul, however, quickly recognizes his error and apologizes. Perhaps his failure to recognize the high priest was due to poor eyesight; better yet, the mere appearance and disposition of this evil man were out of character with the dignity of the office of high priest. Paul describes him as a whitewashed wall, a metaphor of a crumbling wall whose defects have been covered over, an apt expression for Ananias, although Paul, who does not recognize him, is using it as a term of contempt for one whose disregard for the Law implies such a condition.

At this point, an idea occurs to Paul (v. 6). He decides to recoup whatever loss may have resulted from his outburst and take advantage of a division in the house, the fact that the Sanhedrin was composed of theological opponents, Pharisees and Sadducees (v. 7). On the surface of it, his appeal to belief in the resurrection as the root cause of his arrest seems to be far-fetched and insincere. But actually, as Paul viewed the connection between the Pharisaical doctrine of resurrection and Jesus Christ, whose gospel could be summed up in his own resurrection, the claim was quite valid.

The statement serves to divide the council (vv. 7–9), and the dispute becomes so violent (v. 10) that the commander removes Paul to the barracks out of fear for his life. While in the barracks, Paul is encouraged by the Lord (v. 11). This sort of thing had already occurred at Corinth (18:9) and will occur again during another crisis on the voyage to Rome (27:23–24). At this point he also receives assurance of a more distant goal: to go all the way to Rome.

Having failed to kill Paul in the temple precincts, more than forty men plot to ambush Paul, vowing not to eat or drink until he is dead (**23:12–22**). Paul must be moved from the barracks on the pretext of further questioning by the Sanhedrin, so the chief priests and elders join in the plot. Failure would not necessarily mean that these men would starve to death, for rabbinical law would have let them off if the task turned out to be impossible. Such a resort to violence by a religious body should not surprise us in light of Old Testament precedent which they surely claimed and which was legitimate (see comments on 9:1), but certainly not in light of the character of these particular Jews.

Nothing is known of Paul's family nor his sister and nephew who learns of the plot and warns his uncle. Paul's Roman citizenship also allowed him visitors like this, and he is able to notify the authorities (vv. 17–22). The commander wisely cautions Paul's nephew not to tell anyone about his knowledge of the plot, so that effective plans can be made to avoid the ambush.

The Roman commander, who was duty-bound to protect all citizens, musters a sizable number of men (v. 23; some have estimated half his garrison) and plans to escort Paul to Caesarea (**23:23–35**). Luke provides the text of his letter to the Roman governor, Felix (v. 26).

The letter is reminiscent of Pontius Pilate's observation of the innocence of Jesus. Paul, the commander Claudius Lysias concludes, has done nothing he can determine is worthy of punishment (v. 29).

The four hundred soldiers and spearmen accompany Paul and his two centurion captors as far as Antipatris, something of a midpoint between Jerusalem and Caesarea, because by this time any threat by the Jews planning to ambush Paul is past. The cavalry goes on with Paul to Caesarea and delivers Paul and the letter to the governor (v. 33).

When Felix learns that Paul is from the Roman province of Cilicia, he decides to handle the matter himself, as a provincial governor, since Paul was not from one of the kingdoms where the ruler would outrank him. Herod's palace (v. 35), where Paul is kept under guard, had been built by Herod the Great years before and now served as the governor's headquarters. It had facilities to retain prisoners until their cases were heard by the governor.

Luke's purpose for giving relatively greater

space to Paul's defense (**24:1–27**) before Felix appears to be to establish the fact that Christians, though charged falsely of sedition (vv. 5–8), never in fact were guilty of this (vv. 12–13), and that Jewish opposition was due to the claim that in Jesus the hope of resurrection lay (vv. 14–21).

The Jews had retained the lawyer Tertullus, who is unknown in historical records. He was evidently a Hellenistic Jew who knew his way around the Roman court system and could present the Jewish charges effectively to the Roman governor. His references to peace and reforms brought about by Felix's administration are sheer flattery, for Felix had, on the contrary, been greedy and cruel. His charges against Paul are that he was a troublemaker (v. 5) who threatened the Pax Romana (Roman peace)—Felix had executed others charged with the same crime—and that he "tried to desecrate the temple" (v. 6), also a capital crime, a reference to the allegation that he had taken a Gentile into the forbidden inner court of the temple.

Paul begins his defense with a reference to the fact that Felix had "been a judge over [the] nation" for a number of years (v. 10). This implies that, in spite of the other defects of his governorship, he was familiar enough with the religious situation in Judea to evaluate accurately his case, and thus Paul could gladly make his defense. Felix had been born a slave, set free by the mother of the emperor Claudius, promoted in Roman politics, and in A.D. 52 appointed governor of Judea. During his term insurrection and trouble had proliferated throughout Palestine. He had met them with brutality, but this approach had only created resentment and led to further trouble.

Paul flatly denies the charges and challenges his accusers to prove them (vv. 12–13), since he was not leading a revolt but privately worshiping in the temple (vv. 17–18) when he was arrested. He affirms that faith in Jesus Christ is in full accordance with the Law and the Prophets, and that he had the same hope of resurrection as his accusers (v. 15), which implies that some of the elders present were Pharisees, for Ananias, a Sadducee, would have denied the resurrection. Paul certainly considered the resurrection to be the authentic hope of Judaism. He calls attention to the fact that the Asian Jews who stirred up the first riot (21:27–29) should be present, for their accusation was a mistaken assumption which could not be proven (v. 19). He also appeals to the fact—an embarrassment to the high priest and elders—that he had not been found guilty of anything when he appeared before the Sanhedrin, except that he believed in the resurrection (v. 21).

Felix is "well acquainted with the Way" (v. 22; see comments on 9:2 for the word *Way*) and sizes up the charges fairly well: the dispute is purely religious, as were all the problems between Jews and Christians. His postponement of a decision is a delay tactic, for he already knew what Lysias the commander had to say from his letter. The best way to keep peace between Jews and Paul was to keep Paul in custody.

Drusilla (v. 24) was Felix's third wife. Felix had been attracted to her and she had broken off an earlier planned marriage in order to marry him. Out of curiosity Felix and Drusilla invite Paul to speak to them. It is easy to see why Paul's discourse on "righteousness, self-control and the judgment to come" makes Felix "afraid" (v. 25), for both he and Drusilla lived wanton lives of lust and greed. Felix continues to see Paul, not out of sincere interest, but in hope of Paul's getting restless enough to "offer him a bribe" (v. 26) to be released. Finally, the corrupt administration of Felix ends with his replacement by Porcius Festus (v. 27), and Felix lets Paul languish in prison.

Festus was welcomed by the Jewish population of Palestine and was a better administrator than most of his predecessors. In Jerusalem he hears from the elders about Paul (**25:1–12**) and unwittingly foils their scheme to ambush Paul again by preferring to have them come to Caesarea to present their case. At Caesarea Festus hears the case (vv. 6–7), and, wishing to establish good relations with the Jews, suggests that Paul go to Jerusalem to have his case tried there (v. 9). Paul repudiates the legitimacy of a Jewish court (v. 10), and sensing the inevitability of Festus's sending him there where he knew he would have no hope of clearing himself, he appeals to Caesar (v. 11).

Festus's lack of understanding of Paul's case makes him anxious for expert advice, so that when Agrippa and Bernice, his sister, arrive at Caesarea, he takes the opportunity to discuss the case with Agrippa, so that he might formulate a reasonably coherent letter to accompany Paul to Rome (see vv. 26–27).

Herod Agrippa II (A.D. 27–100), the son of Agrippa I and great-grandson of Herod the Great, was king of several combined tetrarchies to the north and "curator of the temple" in Jerusalem with power to appoint and depose the high priest and preserve its treasury and priestly vestments. He was viewed by Romans as an authority on the Jewish religion.

Upon Agrippa's arrival Festus summarizes

Paul's case and arranges for him to hear Paul (vv. 14–22). The Romans were fond of pageantry, and in this case the pomp they display is calculated to impress and intimidate Paul and make him feel inferior before his superiors. Paul appears to be something less than impressed.

Paul is aware of the expertise of Agrippa in Jewish customs and welcomes his opportunity to get a hearing (**26:2–32**). His purpose is not to answer the charges, since he had been exonerated of any capital offense (25:25), but to prove that he has not violated any tenet of Judaism. He does this by again noting that Jesus (v. 23) fulfills the belief that God raises the dead (v. 8), a tenet of Jewish faith. Paul traces his career as a persecutor (vv. 9–11), relates his conversion (vv. 12–15), and describes his commission to go to the Gentiles (vv. 16–18). He had preached "nothing beyond what the prophets and Moses said would happen" (v. 22).

Festus interrupts Paul at this point and accuses him of being insane (v. 24). Festus had politely listened to previous remarks about the resurrection, but when Paul repeats the claim of Jesus' resurrection, Festus can stand it no longer. This, to his way of thinking, is absolute nonsense. Since Paul is a learned man, he has to be insane. Festus typifies all people too committed to the natural world to leave room for the supernatural.

Paul replies that his message is "true and reasonable" (v. 25). Such a claim assumes the power of the biblical God, the testimony of Scripture, and the reports of the eyewitnesses. With this in mind, Paul appeals to Agrippa who knows these facts (vv. 26–27). Agrippa, embarrassed by this appeal to reason, tells Paul that accepting such a message requires more time (v. 28). But time is not the issue; facing the facts is. Though not converted, Agrippa is convinced of Paul's innocence (v. 32).

F. Paul's voyage to Rome (27:1–28:10). From Caesarea to Crete (**27:1–13**), Paul is under the jurisdiction of a centurion named Julius of the Imperial Regiment (v. 1), a special group of guards charged with escorting prisoners. He proves to be a humane person, allowing Paul certain privileges and saving his life.

Paul has privileges as a Roman citizen and is allowed to take Luke (inferred from the "we") and Aristarchus from Thessalonica (see Col. 4:10). At this time of year the winds are contrary for sailing (v. 4); eventually they are forced to go to a small harbor called Fair Havens on Crete.

The decision to ignore Paul's advice is fateful (vv. 9–11). This advice was sound, because the Mediterranean becomes treacherous after the middle of September, and it was already October, a fact inferred from the passing of the Day of Atonement (see 27:9).

After the ship leaves Fair Havens, a great storm arises (**27:14–44**). The efforts to secure the ship and jettison the cargo and tackle prove futile. The New International Version says they lowered the "sea anchor" (v. 17), but this word is ambiguous and may refer instead to the main yard and sail. The crew finally loses all hope, but Paul encourages them by sharing with them his experience of an angel visitation in which God promises that they will survive (v. 24).

After the storm rages for fourteen days, soundings indicate the nearness of land. Several sailors attempt to abandon the ship on the lifeboat, but Paul persuades the centurion to prevent it (vv. 31–32). Evidently, their presence would be needed to guide the ship. Paul also urges that they all break their fast and eat (vv. 33–36), possibly knowing that they will soon need all their strength. When daylight arrives, the ship runs aground on a sandbar, but all escape safely to the island (vv. 42–44).

The natives of Malta (**28:1–10**) were mostly of Phoenician extraction and were regarded by Greeks and Romans as barbarians, a more literal translation of the word *islanders,* but on this occasion prove to be quite civilized.

Although there are no vipers on Malta today, in earlier times the smaller population must have allowed some to survive. Paul's being bitten and surviving seems to have enhanced his prestige among the superstitious islanders (vv. 3–6). This, along with the healing of the father of the chief official, Publius (vv. 7–8), gives Paul the opportunity of curing many of the sick. It is not clear whether their honoring Paul (v. 10) implies their conversion to Christianity.

G. Paul's ministry at Rome (28:11–31). Luke, for the first time, mentions the name of the ship, "Twin Brothers," that carries them to Italy (v. 11; the NIV's translation, "the twin gods Castor and Pollux," is a paraphrase of the Greek word *Dioskourois,* from the Latin *Dioscuri,* "sons of Zeus," the patron gods of navigation), but it is not clear why.

The three days' stay at Syracuse may have been due to a lapse of wind. Also at Rhegium they have to wait for a south wind to get them through the strait between Sicily and Italy. At Puteoli, the principal port of southern Italy, they find some believers, and, since the centurion must have had business there, they fellowship for a week.

News of Paul's arrival somehow precedes him (vv. 14–15) and some brothers from Rome meet him halfway at the Forum of Appius. Paul thanks God, for a hazardous but promised arrival at the empire's capital has been achieved. In Rome, Paul is allowed to live by himself in rented quarters but under guard (v. 16). To call this an imprisonment is somewhat misleading.

Paul's first priority is to invite the leaders of the Jews to assemble, so that he can present his defense to them (vv. 17–20). Paul's purpose is to establish the fact that he is on the defensive and has no suit against the Jerusalem Jews. They diplomatically indicate no knowledge of his case (vv. 21–22).

On another day, Paul presents his message to them. Some "were convinced, . . . but others would not believe" (v. 24)—probably the majority, because Paul's final word to them concerns their callousness as he quotes Isaiah 6:9–10. Paul's succeeding ministry, as before, centers on the Gentiles (v. 28), and Luke tells us that for two whole years Paul ministers in Rome. This period of time probably constituted the statutory limit for Paul's accusers to state their case.

What happened after this depends on whether one accepts the authenticity of the pastoral Letters. If not, it must be presumed that Paul met martyrdom shortly after this time. If the Pastorals are authentic Pauline documents, as most evangelicals believe, the following order of events can be surmised:

1. Paul ministers in Rome and writes Ephesians, Philippians, Colossians, and Philemon.
2. The case against Paul is dismissed by default on the part of his accusers who see little to be gained by pleading a weak case in the Roman Supreme Court.
3. Paul is released about A.D. 63 and ministers further in Asia, Crete, and possibly even Spain (Rom. 15:24). At this time he writes 1 Timothy and Titus.
4. Paul is imprisoned again about A.D. 67, writes 2 Timothy, and suffers martyrdom under Nero.

SELECT BIBLIOGRAPHY

Bruce, F. F. *Commentary on the Book of Acts.* Rev. ed. Grand Rapids: Eerdmans, 1988.

Calvin, J. *Commentary Upon the Acts of the Apostles.* 2 vols. Grand Rapids: Eerdmans, 1949.

Harrison, E. F. *Acts: The Expanding Church.* Chicago: Moody, 1976.

Longenecker, R. N. "Acts of the Apostles." In *The Expositor's Bible Commentary*, edited by Frank E. Gaebelein, 12 vols. Grand Rapids: Zondervan, 1981. 9:207–573.

Marshall, I. H. *The Acts of the Apostles.* Grand Rapids: Eerdmans, 1980.

———. *Luke: Historian and Theologian.* Grand Rapids: Zondervan, 1971.

Ramsay, W. M. *St. Paul the Traveller and Roman Citizen.* Reprint. Grand Rapids: Baker, 1951.

The Epistles

The letters of the New Testament (twenty-one in all) were written by Paul, John, Peter, James, Jude, and the anonymous author of Hebrews, thought by some to be Apollos, Barnabas, or even Paul himself. They were written over a span of approximately fifty years, the bulk of them during the years of Paul's active ministry (roughly A.D. 48–65). The known writers were all close associates of Jesus, with the exception of Paul, who argues for his place among them on the basis of his intimate knowledge of Jesus, his personal encounter with the risen Christ, and the instruction he received directly from the Lord. This, he felt, qualified him to be classed as one of the apostles, equal in authority and rank to the original twelve, including Peter, James, and John, the "inner circle" of those appointed by Jesus.

These letters deal with the life of the church, usually with problems. A problem would arise, local solutions would fail, and so help would be sought from an acknowledged authority. Or perhaps one of the apostles would hear of a problem and write to correct it. Consequently the letters contain advice on difficulties in all areas of life—personal, ethical, doctrinal, liturgical, social, ecclesiastical, financial.

Because the New Testament letters were written to address specific questions, there is little if any systematic thought to be found in them. It is not that a systematic understanding did not lie behind the answers given, but the letters were not written as short treatises on systematic theology. In them we are given a glimpse of the actual lives and problems of the first Christians. We are thus able to see how they lived and are challenged to apply their insights to our own situation.

ROMANS

Royce Gordon Gruenler

INTRODUCTION

Paul's letters contain soaring theological revelations of God's nature and plan of salvation but are never written apart from his day-to-day missionary work on behalf of God's people. Each letter contains theological teaching and practical exhortations designed especially for his readers in view of their particular problems and gifts and Paul's generous desire to help them grow to greater Christian maturity. This is also true of Romans, the most systematic and sustained theological writing that has survived from his hand. An examination of 1:8–15 and 15:14–33 indicates the practical occasion of his writing (he wants to fellowship with his readers and have them speed him on to new missionary fields in Spain), while the special Jewish-Gentile teaching of chapters 9–11, together with other material in the letter, suggests that unity and mutual respect among Jewish Christians and Gentile Christians at Rome were not what they should be. Accordingly, like the other letters of Paul, Romans is both an epistle in the sense that it contains formal teaching, and a letter written for a special occasion, combining several patterns of contemporary Hellenistic writing with Paul's own distinctive epistolary style. Paul is both a systematic theologian and a missionary; hence Romans is a systematic theological treatise on central themes and a missionary document that focuses those themes on pressing and practical issues in the Roman church.

We infer from Acts 20:2–3 that Paul waited at Corinth during his third missionary journey while representatives from Macedonia and Greece brought offerings to help suffering Jewish Christians in Jerusalem (see 1 Cor. 16:1–4; 2 Cor. 8). Always the missionary of God's generous love, Paul was constantly pouring out his life and encouraging others to be at one another's disposal in imitation of Christ's generosity, even if it meant risking his life by personally returning to Jerusalem to deliver the collected love offering. He informed the Roman believers that he would not come west to see them until he had first gone east to Jerusalem to deliver the love gift from his churches (15:23–29). He appealed to them to pray that he would be protected from unbelievers in Judea and that his service to Jerusalem would be acceptable to the saints there so that by God's will he might come to the Romans with joy and be refreshed in their company (15:30–32). The successful delivery of these alms and offerings to his nation was recounted by Paul in his defense before Felix when he encountered the opposition he had anticipated (Acts 24:17). Thus the words *by God's will* (Rom. 15:32) take on ironic significance as Paul visited Rome not according to his own time or schedule as a free man but as a prisoner of Rome.

It was at Corinth that Paul had the time to compose this marvelous and intricate epistle as his third missionary journey drew to a close and for the last time he was about to set sail for Jerusalem. References in the last chapter to personal friends who were associated with Corinth indicate that city as the place of writing: "Phoebe, a servant of the church in Cenchrea" (16:1; the port of Corinth); "Timothy, my fellow worker" (16:21; cf. 2 Cor. 1:1); "Gaius, whose hospitality I . . . enjoy" (16:23; cf. 1 Cor. 1:14); "Erastus, . . . the city's director of public works" (16:23; cf. 2 Tim. 4:20). The time of writing is determined from one of the few anchor dates in New Testament chronology, the appointment of Gallio as proconsul of Achaia in A.D. 51 or 52 (he is mentioned in Acts 18:12), making by round calculation Paul's residence in Corinth the winter of A.D. 54–55 and the writing of Romans the spring of A.D. 55 (or alternatively a year later). It may be mentioned in passing that the high Christology of this epistle (e.g., 1:3; 3:21–26; 5:1–21; 6:1–11, 23; 7:25–8:39; 10:1–13; 15:1–21) and the many allusions to Jesus' teachings in the ethical exhortations of chapters 12–15 give evidence that Paul tacitly assumed the Gospel tradition as a given as he wrote to the Roman Christians, affording compelling evidence for dating the Gospels during this fertile decade of the 50s when so much early Christian thought was coming to full literary and theological expression.

Since the foregoing general remarks and the more detailed commentary that follows assume that the letter was written principally to prepare the Roman believers for Paul's imminent visit and expressed his desire to fellowship with them, enlist their support for his mission to Spain, and deal with Jewish-Gentile friction at Rome, it is important to decide whether the letter is an integral whole of sixteen chapters written by Paul at one time, or whether he originally wrote the epistle without the personal remarks of chapters 15 and 16. In spite of four points—that some manuscripts ending with chapter 14 circulated in the second and third centuries; that the epistle has several doxologies that could serve as endings (15:33; 16:24, a textually weak reading; 16:27); the positioning of 16:25–27 in some manuscripts at the end of chapter 14; and the alleged inappropriateness of the personal greetings of chapter 16, which some say would better suit a letter to the Ephesian church—the arguments in favor of the unity of the sixteen chapters are convincing. The shorter version ending at chapter 14 suggests the early influence of Marcion, who betrayed a bias against the Old Testament and would have found the preparatory work of Judaism (chap. 15) an offense. As for the argument that Paul would not have named specific persons in Rome when he had not visited there, the very opposite occurred when he wrote to churches he had founded. In those letters he gave no list of names lest he leave someone out. In Romans, he mentioned only those with whom he had worked elsewhere and who were or were about to be resident in Rome. Viewed as an integral whole of sixteen chapters, Romans can be seen as not only a great theological treatise (an epistle that sums up Paul's views on the new age that has broken in through the work of Christ), but also a genuine letter written on the occasion of his desire to fellowship with and reconcile the Roman Christians and enlist their support in his mission to Spain.

In light of what has already been said, it would appear that Paul was deeply concerned about tension between Jewish Christians and Gentile Christians within the Roman fellowship. Since Paul did not mention Peter or any other prominent apostle anywhere in the letter, had never been to Rome but wanted to preach the gospel there (1:10–15), and followed the principle not to build on another's foundation (15:20; 2 Cor. 10:16), we may safely conclude that the Roman church was begun by traveling citizens of the Roman Empire. The first of these may have been "visitors from Rome (both Jews and converts to Judaism)" (Acts 2:10–11) at Pentecost and converts to Christianity. It may also be that they were later ministered to and augmented by Christians from centers in Corinth, Ephesus, and Syrian Antioch. A report of Suetonius, a Roman historian, concerning an edict (ca. A.D. 49) of the emperor Claudius, expelling the Jews from Rome "since they were continually making disturbances fomented by Chrestus," may shed light on the Jewish-Christian question with which Paul was dealing in Romans. We may imagine that the earliest Christians in Rome were Jewish Christians who witnessed first in the synagogues in Rome. Paul addressed them throughout the letter, especially in the early sections, challenging judgmental Jewish pride (chaps. 2–4) and employing a theology of leveling so that every mouth may be stopped and the whole world, including Jews, may be held accountable to God (3:19). Later, in a more positive vein (chaps. 9–11), Paul disclosed the important role the Jewish people have in the eschatological plan of God. This appears in the context of his dealing with the equally unacceptable pride of Gentile Christians at Rome who looked down on their Jewish fellow believers because their people had as a whole rejected the gospel. So, Paul said to them, "do not be arrogant, but be afraid. For if God did not spare the natural branches, he will not spare you either" (11:20–21). The scenario may be reconstructed: Jewish Christians had been prominent at Rome from the beginning of the mission, but they suffered a serious setback in leadership when Claudius expelled them. By the time of their return Gentile leadership had become uppermost and an attitude of superiority began to assert itself against the Jewish Christians. Paul, ever alarmed by diversity that was not harmonious, received word of the situation from his friends at Rome (some of those listed in chap. 16). Since this coincided providentially with his long-standing desire to visit Rome and his hope to inaugurate a mission to Spain, he composed a brilliant argument designed to show that while Jew and Gentile have their respective roles to play in God's plan of salvation, in light of his grace "there is no difference between Jew and Gentile—the same Lord is Lord of all and richly blesses all who call on him" (10:12). Each faction was called upon to look beyond itself, to become servants of one another (12:1–15:13) and servants beyond the circle of Rome to the whole world, as Paul set an example of servanthood to Jews in Jerusalem, to Gentiles in Spain, and to both at Rome (15:14–33). This central theme of Christ-centered generosity on a practical level makes this a truly "occasional" letter, but its powerful exegetical argument, applicable to any time or place, qualifies it as a theological epistle in the true sense of the word.

The following outline highlights Paul's formal theological argument in the context of factionalism at Rome, seen through the generosity of Christ who "did not please himself" (15:3) but "has become a servant of the Jews on behalf of God's truth, to confirm the promises made to the patriarchs so that the Gentiles may glorify God for his mercy" (15:8–9). In this fundamental declaration Paul turned the Romans away from their self-centered squabbling to the motivation of Christ himself, who came as servant to redeem both Jew and Gentile according to the eschatological promises of God. Accordingly, Paul's appeal to the Romans was that they get on with the work of evangelizing the world in this new age of salvation and strive together with him in their prayers on his behalf (15:14–33) that the mission might be accomplished and the full number of Gentiles and Jews be saved and that God be glorified (11:28–36; 15:5–6). It would be accomplished only as they sought not to please themselves but to please others as servants of Christ (1:1; 15:8) and humble themselves in service as Paul had done in imitation of Christ. The way of generosity, hospitality, and disposability on behalf of others is God's way as triune family (God and Father, Lord Jesus Christ, Holy Spirit), serving in harmony for the salvation of Jew and Gentile (15:1–21). So Paul leveled the haughtiness of the factions at Rome by calling upon them to descend to humility and harmony (15:1–6) as servants, that they be filled with joy and peace and abound in hope (15:13). This motif of leveling/descent/ascent characterizes each thought unit of the epistle-letter, as the outline indicates.

OUTLINE

I. Introduction: The Generosity of Servanthood (1:1–18)
   A. The Servanthood of Paul (1:1)
   B. The Servanthood of the Triune Family (1:2–4)
   C. The Servanthood of the Saints (1:5–7)
   D. Servanthood Present and Servanthood Anticipated (1:8–15)
   E. The Gospel as Servant of God's Righteousness and Wrath (1:16–18)

II. Diagnosis: The Knowledge of God and the Sinful Fall of Humanity (1:19–3:20)
   A. The Leveling Guilt of Humanity, I (1:19–32)

B. The Leveling Guilt of Gentile and Jew (2:1–16)
C. The Leveling Guilt of the Jew (2:17–3:8)
D. The Leveling Guilt of Humanity, II (3:9–20)

III. Prognosis I: Justified by Faith in Jesus Christ (3:21–8:17)
A. The Righteousness of God Through Faith in Jesus Christ Excludes Boasting (3:21–31)
B. Abraham's Descent and Ascent in Humility and Faith (4:1–25)
C. Descent in Adam and Ascent in Christ (5:1–21)
D. Baptized into Christ from Death to Life (6:1–14)
E. No Longer Slaves of Sin but Slaves of God (6:15–23)
F. No Longer Married to the Law but Married to Christ (7:1–6)
G. Warfare Between the Spiritual and Carnal Egos (7:7–25)
H. Children of God Through the Witness of the Spirit (8:1–17)

IV. Prognosis II: Subjected to Futility, Subjected in Hope (8:18–11:36)
A. The Glorious Freedom of the Children of God (8:18–27)
B. Whom God Justified He Also Glorified (8:28–39)
C. The Mercy of God and the Riches of His Glory toward Israel and the Gentiles (9:1–33)
D. Christ Fulfills the Law for Jew and Gentile (10:1–21)
E. The Mercy and Glory of God in the Final Grafting of Jew and Gentile (11:1–36)

V. Prescription: Faithful Servants in Action (12:1–15:13)
A. In Sacrificial Worship (12:1–2)
B. In Humble Use of Gifts within the Body (12:3–8)
C. In Loving Acts of Service and Hospitality (12:9–13)
D. In Imitation of Jesus' Teaching (12:14–21)
E. In Rendering to Caesar What Is Caesar's (13:1–7)
F. In Loving One's Neighbor as Oneself (13:8–10)
G. In Living as in the Day, Not in Darkness (13:11–14)
H. In Pursuing Peace Between Weak and Strong (14:1–15:13)

VI. Conclusion (15:14–16:27)
A. Paul's Missionary Purpose and Reason for Writing Boldly (15:14–22)
B. His Missionary Agenda for Jerusalem, Rome, and Spain (15:23–33)
C. His Final Greetings, Warnings, and Doxology (16:1–27)

COMMENTARY

I. Introduction: The Generosity of Servanthood (1:1–18)

The letter as a whole is characterized by a spirit of generosity as Paul reflects the hospitality of God toward a sinful world and, close and small, focuses the power of the gospel on the Roman Christians and their need to be more generous toward one another and to others for whom Christ died. The opening words of the letter give evidence of the theme of generous servanthood in five principal ways and bring to fulfillment the motif of the servant of the Lord that in the Old Testament is applied to Moses, Joshua, David, and the prophets and denotes total ownership by and disposability to the Lord.

A. The servanthood of Paul (1:1). Though Paul places his name at the opening of the letter (not our custom but the common practice of letter writers in the first century), he hastens to qualify this position by acknowledging that Jesus Christ has pride of place in his thought and deserves immediate recognition. As his Lord takes first position within the first few words, Paul further defers to Christ by defining his disposability to him in three ways. In verse 1 parallel units of thought describe the unitary theme of being at Christ's disposal:

a servant	of Christ Jesus
called	to be an apostle
set apart	for the gospel of God

Paul's high view of the authority and inspiration of the Holy Scriptures is attested (v. 2) by the line of continuity he sees between the gospel God "promised beforehand through his prophets" in the Old Testament and the gospel Paul has been set apart to preach. God's plan of salvation is all of one piece.

B. The servanthood of the triune family (1:2–4). The key to Paul's servanthood is the astounding fact that the three persons of the triune God—Father, Son, and Spirit of holiness—cooperate as one to bring about the salvation of a fallen humanity. Paul holds (vv. 1–2) that the gospel of the Holy Scriptures (the Old Testament) and the gospel he is preaching (the New Testament in formation) speak with one voice regarding the "Son, who as to his human nature was a descendant of David" (v. 3), indicating his true incarnation and humanity and his continuity with the Old Testament royal line and God's promises regarding its future (e.g., 2 Sam. 7:12–16). As regards his present exalted status as "Jesus Christ our Lord," it was through the work of "the Spirit of holiness" that he "was declared with power to be the Son of God by his resurrection from the dead" (v. 4). The emphasis should be placed on the phrase *with power,* as it is not at the resurrection that Jesus is for the first time declared Son of God (cf. Mark 1:11; Ps. 2:7); rather, he is declared Son of God *with power.* The same expression is used in Mark 9:1; hence, Jesus' prophecy may be seen to have been fulfilled not only in the transfiguration as an anticipation of his glorification, but also in the mighty working of the Holy Spirit in the resurrection, where the reign of God comes in a new and powerful way at the climax of Jesus' saving mission. Accordingly, as the divine family is present and approving at the inauguration of the Son's ministry at his baptism with water, so here at the final baptism of Jesus in death (leading to resurrection) Father, Son, and Holy Spirit are manifest again as triune family in a powerful declaration of what the gospel means: salvation from death unto life through "Jesus Christ our Lord." This is the second instance of generous servanthood mentioned by Paul, and certainly in his mind the source from which all other generous acts proceed.

C. The servanthood of the saints (1:5–7). The third circle of generosity that evidences the theme of servanthood is described in Paul's next remark. By it he serves witness that through Christ and for his name's sake a redeemed family is being called together under the gracious apostleship of God's chosen leaders, "to call people from among all the Gentiles" (v. 5). In five verses Paul has moved from his solitary role as servant and apostle, to the hospitality of the triune family, to the growing family drawn "from among all the Gentiles." This redeemed family is called "to the obedience that comes from faith," just as Paul's mission is characterized by disposability to Christ Jesus (v. 1), and just as the work of Father, Son, and Holy Spirit (vv. 2–4) evidences in the highest sense a mutual subordination and faithfulness to one another in being at the disposal of the new human family that is coming into being. Paul makes his point as he embraces the Roman Christians as members of this redeemed family: "And you also are among those who are called to belong to Jesus Christ" (v. 6). Thus the circle of servanthood is complete when he describes them as called just as he himself is called, and claims that they "belong to Jesus Christ" as he himself is "a servant of Christ Jesus" (i.e., belonging to Christ; see v. 1). Addressing his readers by name—"to all in Rome" (v. 7)—he explains what it means to be called to belong to Jesus Christ; it means that they are "loved by God" and are "called to be saints," an invitation for them to grow into the same kind of generous servanthood to which he himself is committed. Already we may suppose that he has his agenda in mind to address their less than laudable attitudes toward one another and is working from the top down to soften their hardness, as it were, by appealing to their essential status in Christ as Jews and Gentiles and their high calling as saints, by which he has in mind their calling to faithful and holy servanthood (see the role of saints in Deut. 33:2–3; Dan. 7:22, 27). Paul sees every Christian as a servant of Christ (see 1 Cor. 7:22–23; Eph. 6:6; Rom. 12:11). The seal of approval upon the family circle is given in a blessing of "grace and peace" (v. 7) that combines both Greek and Hebrew salutations (doubly significant in this context where Paul seeks unity between Gentile and Jew) and is attested by God our Father and the Lord Jesus Christ as representative of the divine family.

D. Servanthood present and servanthood anticipated (1:8–15). Paul now reverts to his own role as servant by way of mentioning with thanks the faith of the Roman church that is being "reported all over the world" (v. 8). He bares his heart to them and claims God as witness that he prays for them "constantly," and longs to come to them (vv. 9–10). From these few words we gather something of the intense love Paul has for these unseen Christians who are part of him and he of them because of a common Lord who has created a common family of believers. Paul places himself utterly at their disposal as a faithful prayer servant "at all times," and anticipates coming to them that both he and they may be made more complete as he makes them "strong" with some spiritual gift (v. 11), and that they may be mutually encouraged by each other's faith (v. 12). Nothing in all of Paul's correspondence better illustrates the social nature of Christian fellowship and the dynamic, progressive aspect of life together in Christ. Paul includes himself in this dynamic, for he is not yet complete without them and is himself on the way to being more the faithful servant to others he has been called to be. Indeed, he wants them to know that he has "planned many times" to come to them (why he was prevented we do not know) "in order that [he] might have a harvest among [them]" (v. 13). Thus Paul expresses his disposability to the Romans in the present (he gives them constant prayerful thought) and anticipates being as fruitful among them as he has been "among the other Gentiles." Paul is a giver and is dedicated to being there for others as servant. As one who is obligated to Christ for his life and salvation he in turn feels obligated to share the good news "both to Greeks and non-Greeks, both to the wise and the foolish" (v. 14), both to Jew and Gentile (v. 16). "That is why [he was] so eager to preach the gospel also" to the believers at Rome (v. 15). The power of the gospel motivates Paul to be so hospitable a servant on God's behalf. This brings us to the fifth dimension of the central theme of generous servanthood.

E. The gospel as servant of God's righteousness and wrath (1:16–18). The gospel (the evangel or *euangelion* = beautiful news) is not an entity unto itself but is underwritten by the divine family who have made it a reality and is preached by faithful witnesses such as Paul. *Gospel* is a summary term that incorporates all the love and servanthood of those who underwrite it and verbally expresses their thought and intent in the form of factual, historical truth. It is the equivalent of the verbal expression of the personal Yahweh in Old Testament Torah which articulates his intention as the living God. In this sense Paul personifies the word *gospel* in this core text and views it as a servant because it is the very expression of the triune God and the source of all Paul's missionary activity, and it serves as a summary outline of the threefold line of argument he is about to present to the Roman Christians: "righteousness from God . . . by faith" (chaps. 1–8); "first for the Jew, then for the Gentile" (chaps. 9–11); "the righteous will live by faith" (chaps. 12–16).

Paul's claim that he is not ashamed of the gospel (v. 16) suggests that he is aware of the world's opinion of a proclamation that brings it under judgment and offers as a remedy a crucified and risen Lord who imputes righteousness to the believer. To such a perishing world the gospel is foolishness because it relies on its own wisdom which no longer knows God (Paul's argument in 1 Cor. 1:18–2:16), and the weak Christian might be ashamed of such a "foolish" gospel. But precisely because the world is fallen and without hope apart from the good news of God's gift of righteousness through Jesus Christ to those who have faith, Paul sees the gospel as the servant of God, "because it is the power of God for the salvation of everyone who believes." In 1 Corinthians 1:18–2:16 Paul similarly describes the message of the cross as power, which, while foolish to the world, is the very wisdom of God through the teaching of the Spirit. The gospel is power because it reveals the twofold nature of God's righteousness: It describes the absolutely holy nature of God, in light of which a sinful world lies rightly under his righteous wrath (1:18); but it also describes his grace in working a righteousness on behalf of an undeserving world in order to bring it back to fellowship. Thus Paul will proceed to define God's righteousness as the gracious servanthood of the divine family, stemming from its essential nature, to reconcile a hostile world. Salvation is intimately connected to reconciliation and restoration to fellowship with the divine family. The power of the gospel lies accordingly in its ability to bring together what has been torn asunder by human rebellion (described in 1:18–3:20). It must however be received by faith on the sinner's part, for God's grace does not cancel out the role of the responsible human agent (a point Paul will emphasize later as he appeals to the Romans to evidence their new righteousness in Christ through appropriate moral behavior). This synergism (working together) characterizes God's pattern and is a paradox whose two components will be held together by Paul throughout the letter. Thus the citation of Habakkuk 2:4, "The righteous will live by faith," brings together the work of God in making the sinner righteous and the believer's voluntary responsibility to persevere in faith. This is the essence of what it means to live, and it is the good news the gospel brings.

There is another side to the gospel, however, and it should not be missed as Paul moves to a description of the willful disobedience of the human race. While the gospel's primary role is to proclaim the good news of salvation ("For in the gospel a righteousness from God is revealed" [v. 17]), its proclamation is good news only to those who respond in faith; to those who do not, "the wrath of God is being revealed from heaven" (v. 18). Most commentaries and translations separate verse 18 from verse 17 by a new paragraph heading, indicating a different subject. But the parallel structure of the unit indicates that Paul views the function of the gospel as two-sided:

> "for . . . a righteousness from God
> is revealed [in it]
> . . . by faith" (v. 17)
>
> "[for] the wrath of God
> is . . . revealed from heaven
> against all the godlessness and wickedness" (v. 18)

Paul is saying that when the gospel (which is from heaven) is preached it will be good news of righteousness unto salvation for those who believe, and bad news of God's unmitigated wrath upon those who willfully reject it. Always the gospel, when faithfully proclaimed, will have this two-edged effect. The new eschatological age inaugurated by the work of Jesus Christ brings with it not only salvation by grace and faith, but also a heightened sense of the righteous wrath of God against unbelief.

II. Diagnosis: The Knowledge of God and the Sinful Fall of Humanity (1:19–3:20)

Since Paul's thought has turned to the negative effect of the gospel on a world that rejects it, he is led to portray graphically the disobedience of the human race and its fall away from servanthood to selfishness. This he does in four stages, beginning with the general, then narrowing to moralistic Gentiles and Jews, then to the Jews in particular, and finally returning to the general. His diatribe against humanity's willful rejection of God has a leveling effect, and by the time he finishes at 3:20 there is not one, Gentile or Jew, who can stand on his own righteousness. Paul not only is painting with broad theological brushstrokes but also is removing any claim on the part of the Gentile and Jewish factions at Rome that one is better than the other. In the end all are seen to be sinners in need of God's grace and equally indebted to him for salvation.

A. The leveling guilt of humanity, I (1:19–32). If 1:1–15 describes the attitude of servanthood and disposability toward others that is summarized as the power of the gospel unto salvation (vv. 16–17), the effect of rebellion and self-centeredness is revealed by the gospel as the "wrath of God . . . against all the godlessness and wickedness of men who suppress the truth by their wickedness," the summary statement of verse 18 which is followed by a description of this godlessness (humanly constructed religion) and wickedness (moral decadence). Verses 16–18 thus stand as the thematic core at the center of the positive and the negative lines of choice, one upward toward salvation and life, the other downward toward wrath and death. It is the latter that Paul now describes in some detail. But first he wants to demonstrate that God has already graciously revealed himself to humanity in nature itself so that all may be leveled to a state of responsibility before God.

God is clearly perceived, so that all are without excuse (**1:19–20**). In this powerful description of general revelation Paul removes any possibility that humankind could claim unfairness on God's part in revealing his wrath against their wickedness, as though they did not know "his eternal power and divine nature," which God "has made . . . plain to them," and which "have been clearly seen, being understood from what has been made." The signature of God is upon everything he has made and reflects his authorship. By this we may take Paul to mean that in the outer world one can see intellectually and aesthetically the symmetry of things and the wonder of ones and manys that interrelate socially, reflecting God's own oneness and manyness as triune family. Moreover, inwardly the human race has an awareness of God's glory and moral perfection through the image of God and his law that lies deep in the human heart and is perceived morally. That is why they are without excuse (lit. without apology or defense) before God. But since they try to suppress the truth (a more accurate translation) they cannot be relied upon to respond intellectually, aesthetically, or morally to God's revelation in nature that has been visible since the creation of the world. They are in rebellion against him and therefore are distorted in their perception of reality. There is no basis here for a natural theology by which an unredeemed humanity could reconcile itself to God (here Paul parts company with Stoic philosophy and Greek-influenced Jewish thought, such as the Wisdom of Solomon). On the contrary, Paul's argument is that the gospel is given by special grace to fulfill the role of reconciliation and must be accepted by faith; otherwise the gospel serves as a goad to the suppressed consciousness of humanity and reminds them of their inbuilt responsibility to God and of his rightful moral wrath against their suppression of the truth.

Fallen humanity neither glorifies nor gives thanks to God (**1:21–23**). Paul describes the fall and its aftermath as a general condition of the human race. He asserts that "their thinking became futile and their foolish hearts were darkened." This accurately describes the state of humanity from God's point of view; the primary function of persons from the beginning of their creation was to honor God and to be thankful to him, but from the fall "they neither glorified him as God nor gave thanks to him." By contrast Paul's glorification of God is evident in his letter, prominently at 11:36 and 16:27, and his attitude of thanksgiving is expressed at 1:8; 6:17; 7:25 (for a typical Old Testament example see Daniel's prayer [Dan. 2:20–23]). But with unredeemed humanity the glorification of God has been exchanged for the glorification of "images made to look like mortal man and birds and animals and reptiles," and so their claim to be wise has in reality shown them to be fools whose "thinking became futile" and whose "foolish hearts were darkened." It is important to grasp Paul's view of fallen humanity, not only because he takes such care to describe its descent into depravity (1:18–3:20) but because it is the presupposition of the passages about ascending salvation (3:20 to the end of the letter). The gospel is powerful precisely because it is able to save human beings from the inglorious exchange (v. 23), which theology terms "original sin." Dire consequences followed from the exchange of the fall.

God gave them over because they exchanged the truth for a lie (**1:24–32**). It is the irony of God's judgment that sinners receive what they seek by self-acclaimed wisdom. They seek wisdom and happiness independent of God and God gives them over to futility and frustration (see 8:20, a key verse which indicates that sinful humanity has infected all of creation with the penalty of futility); they insist on working from the bottom up (beginning with the serpent's crafty assault in Gen. 3) rather than from the top down with God's self-disclosure, so God despoils their rebellious pleasure by turning their sinful desires on the physical level to degradation. Three times in this passage Paul uses the phrase *God gave them over* (vv. 24, 26, 28), in each case indicating not God's permissiveness or withdrawal but his just punishment. In the first two instances he appropriately begins at the bottom where sin originates and describes the irony of lustful sin turned in upon itself as it insists on working outside the healthy parameters God has established for sexual relationships. According to God's irony, such sinners have "received in themselves the due penalty for their perversion" (v. 27), which is death, for those who practice homosexuality and lesbianism are a one-generation generation and cannot create an ongoing family. Similarly, working up from the physical to the rational level (vv. 28–32), Paul observes God's irony with a play on words: since they did not approve of God (*ouk edokimasan*) to have him in their knowledge, God gave them over to an unapproved mind (*adokimon noun*) (v. 28); they now approve (*syneudokousin*) only of those who sin as they do (v. 32). Paul describes in a catalogue of sins (cf. Gal. 5:19–21) how the "depraved mind" that does not "retain the knowledge of God" perpetrates every conceivable kind of attitudinal depravity and splits people apart. This is in contrast to calling them together in love and social harmony, the theme of Paul's letter. At the end of the list (v. 32) the apostle reiterates his claim of 1:20–21 that "they know God's righteous decree," indeed, they know "that those who do such things deserve death," and so they are without excuse. Yet so willful is the rebellious human heart that it is not content to sin in isolation but demands the right to carry others down in corporate sin ("they . . . also approve of those who practice them"), offering a counterfeit and deathly substitute for the genuine family that comes only from the top down by way of the gospel.

B. The leveling guilt of Gentile and Jew (2:1–16). Having described the general fallen state of humankind, Paul now turns to the moralist who looks down on those who are described in the previous section. It is difficult to determine from the text whether Paul has in mind Gentile (e.g., Stoic) as well as Jewish moralists who despise pagan behavior, or Jews only, or Jewish and Gentile Christians. In view of the fact that he addresses the Jew directly in 2:17 but speaks of Jew and Gentile in verses 9–10, and the Gentiles in verses 14–15, and the fact that he is concerned about Jewish and Gentile pride at Rome and wants to show that not superiority but servanthood is the measure of the Christian, it is perhaps best to view Paul's audience in 2:1–16 as Jewish and Gentile Christians who are guilty of judgmental pride and whom he wants to level as sinners with the rest of humankind as far as the human appetite for judging others is concerned. He is, after all, addressing the Roman Christians personally by letter. Evidence for this view is his appeal that they respond to God's kindness which "leads you toward repentance" (v. 4). Also, he argues that in "the day of God's wrath" he "will give to each person according to what he has done" (eternal life to those who do good, "wrath and anger" to those who follow evil, "first for the Jew, then for the Gentile" [vv. 7–10]), which is not in harmony with his doctrine of justification by faith in 3:21–30, unless he is addressing Christian behavior and not salvation by good works (cf. the similar forceful appeal in Heb. 10:26–39, where perseverance in faithfulness is uppermost). He refers to Gentiles, who do not by tradition have the Jewish law, who do by nature "things required by the law" (v. 14); this would necessarily suggest Gentile Christians who are able to do what the law requires only because in Christ its requirements are written on their hearts (v. 15). The point of the whole argument is focused in verse 11, "for God does not show favoritism," by which Paul is driving home (the literal meaning of the diatribe form he is using) the fact that there is no place for prideful superiority among Christians, Jewish or Gentile, a point to be further explored in 2:17–3:8. The present section is rounded off by another warning that they keep their eyes "on the day when God will judge men's secrets through Jesus Christ" (v. 16; cf. vv. 3, 5–12).

C. The leveling guilt of the Jew (2:17–3:8). Where Paul has been addressing Jew and Gentile in 2:1–16 and levels them before the God who shows no favoritism, he now concentrates his attention on Jewish pride which is in evidence at Rome. The issue will be dealt with again in the eschatological setting of chapters 9–11 when the arrogance of Gentiles toward Jewish brethren at Rome will come in for criticism. But for now the apostle wants to make the point that it will not do for the Jewish Christian to take on airs, lest he become like those whom Jesus castigated for their unmitigated hypocrisy. Indeed much of the passage reflects the teaching of Jesus on hypocrisy. Paul deliberately casts the hypercritical Jewish faction at Rome in the role of the hypercritical Jew of Jesus' ministry, asking the same rhetorical questions regarding consistency of claim and action, deed and true intention ("you, then, who teach others, do you not teach yourself?" [v. 21; cf. Matt. 23:3–4]). Paul is sharpening the point made in 2:14 by reiterating the preferable status of the Gentile Christian "who is not circumcised physically and yet obeys the law" and who will, ironically, "condemn you who, even though you have the written code and circumcision, are a lawbreaker" (v. 27). Accordingly, just as Paul declares in verses 7–11 that God shows no favoritism according to human standards but gives eternal life to Jew and Gentile who do good, so in verses 28–29 he defines the true Jew as one who is so inwardly (*en tō kryptō*; cf. the same phrase in Matt. 6:4, 6, 18, where, as here, the emphasis is on purity of intention, not outward pride and boasting), and true circumcision is "of the heart, by the Spirit, not by the written code" (v. 29). By this definition of Jew and circumcision, Jewish and Gentile believers are now on equal footing as believers, whose "praise is not from men, but from God." That is not to say that being a Jew in the traditional sense does not have some advantages, for there is a great heritage in being "entrusted with the very words of God" (3:1–2). In this section, 3:1–8, Paul digresses slightly to anticipate a later argument (chaps. 9–11) which will disclose that while Jew and Gentile have nothing to boast of, it is nevertheless true that God has a providential place for the Jews in spite of their "lack of faith," which will not "nullify God's faithfulness" (v. 3). Of course it is totally fallacious then to suggest, as some accuse Paul of arguing, "Let us do evil that good may result" (v. 8), for the whole point of this long section (2:1–3:8) has been to show that no one, whether Jew or Gentile, has a claim to superiority. All are sinners and are saved by grace alone through faith; consequently there is no justification for a bragging or condemning spirit. This leads Paul to return to his first general point and to restate it by appeal to a chain of Old Testament Scriptures.

D. The leveling guilt of humanity, II (3:9–20). Paul has made the point in 1:20 that because of God's general revelation in nature and the human heart humanity in general is without excuse, and he has just finished pointing out that both Jew and Gentile who have received special revelation also have no excuse (2:1, *anapologētos,* the same word) when they are judgmental of others yet are guilty of the same sin. As the conclusion to his argument he signs and seals this whole unit of 1:19–3:20 ("the charge that Jews and Gentiles alike are all under sin" [v. 9]) with a string of Old Testament pearls drawn mainly from the Psalms and Isaiah and parallel to the list of 1:29–32; the theme is, "There is no one righteous, not even one" (Ps. 14:1–3). Paul avers that through the law God has totally leveled humanity "so that every mouth may be silenced and the whole world held accountable to God" (v. 19). Paul is using "law" in the two senses in which he has already spoken of God's disclosure of himself, first generally in nature and the human heart (1:19–32), and more specifically to Jewish and Gentile believers (2:1–3:8). Otherwise he would not be able to say that the whole world is accountable to God. Not only is it accountable, however, but it is in a hopeless condition apart from grace, for through the general and special revelation of God as to his nature and demands upon humanity "we become conscious of sin." The law is good because it reveals God's nature and will; the fault lies with us because we "all have turned away" (v. 12). The conclusion to the entire argument is found in verse 20: "Therefore no one will be declared righteous in his sight by observing the law." This justifies the identification of the Gentiles in 2:14 (who "do by nature things required by the law") as Gentile Christians, thus making Paul's address not only applicable to all situations generally (an epistle) but also specifically (a letter) to Jewish and Gentile believers at Rome who need to be reminded that against the backdrop of the fall they can claim no special privileges against one another, no bragging (2:17, 23) or boasting (3:27). In this light 1:19–3:20, which seems to be a general digression, is actually a reminder to the Romans (as well as to all readers) that there is another side to the good news of the gospel; namely, that wherever it is preached it is a reminder that God demands perfection and will not accept compromised human works, not even of Christians who may fall back into old habits of prideful superiority, for "God does not show favoritism" (2:11). By the time Paul has concluded with 3:20 he has taken his readers to the bottom of the pit of human depravity. There is no way out and not a shred of human goodness that could form a rope or ladder of escape. God has vindicated his law but totally condemned the sinner by his rightful and righteous wrath (1:18). The effect of Paul's diatribe by the end of 3:20 is total and bleak. In the words of 8:20, by the judgment of God creation has been "subjected to frustration."

III. Prognosis I: Justified by Faith in Jesus Christ (3:21–8:17)

But, says Paul, God has not left the matter there. If he hastens to add in 8:20 that God has also "subjected it, in hope," he lays the actual groundwork for this hope in 3:21 with the deceptively little, turn-around words, "but now" (*nuni de*), probably the most important pivotal particles in Romans, for all of history and the fate of the human race hinges on what follows. In this section Paul describes how the believer moves from death to life through the work of Christ, which constitutes the first great prognosis of hope in the letter. (The second appears at 8:18.) There are eight units in this large section, each one describing a descent by faith into humility and a consequent ascent that comes by the grace of God.

A. The righteousness of God through faith in Jesus Christ excludes boasting (3:21–31). Paul attests the inspiration and unity of Scripture by witnessing to the fact that "the Law and the Prophets testify" of a "righteousness from God, apart from law," which "comes through faith in Jesus Christ to all who believe" (vv. 21–22). This righteousness of God is apart from law only in the sense that one is not hopelessly under its radical demands (as in Matt. 5:21–48), but Paul does not mean that the law is now discounted. The law reflects the righteousness of God and is personified in Jesus Christ himself who is the goal and fulfillment of the law (as we shall see in 10:4). Moreover, Paul distinctly says in 3:31 that faith does not nullify the law: "Not at all! Rather, we uphold the law." There is nothing wrong with the law, which expresses the very heart and intention of God and is an eternal given; what is wrong are the human heart and intention. Again Paul makes the point of the earlier section that "there is no difference, for all have sinned and fall short of the glory of God" (vv. 22–23). By this he is making a general statement about mankind and at the same time keeping his agenda with the Romans in the background, subtly reminding them that they, with all other believers, "are justified freely by his grace through the redemption that came by Christ Jesus" (v. 24), and that "this righteousness from God comes through faith in Jesus Christ to all who believe" (v. 22). No one, including the Roman Christians, has any cause for boasting (v. 27).

Is the phrase *dia pisteōs Iēsou Christou* (v. 22) to be translated "through faith in Jesus Christ" (so NIV, Christ is the object of the believer's faith) or "through the faith of Jesus Christ" (the believer trusts in the faith that Jesus himself had subjectively)? Although the latter has become popular with some interpreters and it can be granted that it is indeed the perfectly righteous faith of Jesus that is wholly in accord with the Father and the Spirit in the saving work of the divine family, the internal evidence counts against so translating the phrase in this passage. The same phrase (*dia pisteōs*) is used in verse 25 of "faith in his blood," which is certainly the believer's faith in the objective blood of Christ, for "God presented him as a sacrifice of atonement," an important concept (cf. Lev. 17:11) which indicates that in Jesus Christ his Son God has graciously directed against himself his own righteous wrath which the sinner deserves, and so propitiates that wrath. In verse 26 it is God "who justifies those who have faith in Jesus" (*ek pisteōs Iēsou*), and in verse 30 "there is only one God, who will justify the circumcised by faith (*ek pisteōs*) and the uncircumcised through that same faith" (*dia tēs pisteōs*). Accordingly, while the faith of Jesus is surely a tacit assumption in Paul's theology because it is the one instance in history in which the law is perfectly fulfilled, it is not the focus of attention here. Instead Paul concentrates on the fact that Jew and Gentile alike are saved not by their works but by their faith in the finished work of Christ. That is why boasting is excluded and why, paradoxically, the essential goodness of the law is established not on the principle of human effort but by the principle of faith (v. 27). Paul's explicit mention of Jews and Gentiles, circumcised and uncircumcised (vv. 29–30), as both under faith again levels all believers in this new age and renders any sense of superiority wholly unacceptable, both in a general sense throughout the church and specifically among the Christians at Rome. The principle of faith apart from any human claim of effort is so fundamental that Paul proceeds to show that this was also true of Abraham who was, ironically, the father figure through whom the Jewish/Gentile separation originated but who was first and foremost the father of all who, like him, have faith in God's unmerited grace.

B. Abraham's descent and ascent in humility and faith (4:1–25). Paul still has the matter of pride and boasting on his mind as he illustrates the previous point of justification by faith to his readers through the example of Abraham. Abraham had nothing to boast about before God because he was in fact not justified by works but "believed God, and it was credited to him as righteousness" (4:2–3). The principle by which God justifies is not in terms of a person's works, for then God would be obligated rather than giving the gift freely and undeservedly (v. 4); rather, the principle is that "to the man who does not work but trusts God who justifies the wicked, his faith is credited as righteousness" (v. 5). This was true not only of Abraham, Paul argues, but also (vv. 6–8) of that other great pivotal Old Testament figure, David, who expresses this personally in Psalm 32:1–2. Paul now moves the argument to its climax in verses 9–25 by showing that the faith principle was operative before Abraham became a bona fide Jew by circumcision, for it was under the circumstance of uncircumcision that his "faith was credited to him as righteousness," and it was only later that he received "the sign of circumcision, a seal of the righteousness that he had by faith while he was still uncircumcised" (v. 11). The argument follows the chronological order of Genesis 15:6 and 17:9–14 and carries enormous implications, for now it can be seen that Abraham is the father of all who believe, since his faith takes pride of place before circumcision and qualifies him to be called the father of all who believe, of both uncircumcised and circumcised, of Gentile and Jew (vv. 11–12, 16–17). The promise to "Abraham and his offspring" that he would be "heir of the world" was not "through law" (in the sense of having to earn the promise by fulfilling righteousness, which could only bring wrath) but "by faith" and "by grace" that it "may be guaranteed to all Abraham's offspring," as he is the father of us all, both Jews and Gentiles (vv. 13–16).

In the concluding paragraph of his argument (vv. 17c–25), Paul describes the faith of Abraham as trust in the seemingly impossible work of God "who gives life to the dead and calls things that are not as though they were." Thus he introduces the historical fact that God in his mysterious providence and testing kept Abraham and Sarah waiting for the fulfillment of the promise of a son until long after human conception and birth was a physical possibility, thereby heightening the miracle of the event and the absolute necessity of faith. It was Abraham's trust in God as true to his word in spite of appearances and the fact that he "was strengthened in his faith and gave glory to God" (v. 20, unlike the unbelievers of 1:21), "being fully persuaded that God had power to do what he had promised" (v. 21), that "was credited to him as righteousness" (v. 22), a fundamental principle that, says Paul, obtains also "for us who believe in him who raised Jesus our Lord from the dead" (v. 24). The whole matter of justification by faith is focused finally in the person of Jesus Christ and his work of descent and ascent, for "he was delivered over to death for our sins and was raised to life for our justification" (v. 25). In light of this, and the fact that Abraham anticipated the proper response to grace by his own descent in humility and his ascent in having righteousness credited to him, Paul implies that there is no ground whatever for human claims of superiority by the logic of lineage or law. Such claims are rendered null and void by the sufficient work of Christ who is the hinge of history personified and the only prognosis of hope for a fallen humanity that it can rise from death to life. This is true not only in large but also close and small at Rome where factionalism between Jew and Gentile threatens to void what Christ has done and to substitute works righteousness for justification by faith alone. Paul's gentle reminder of the basis of justification is designed to invite the readers, Jew and Gentile, to abandon boasting and to descend in faithful humility with Abraham and to ascend in oneness of faith as his offspring. (There is no inherent contradiction between Paul's use of Abraham's faith and the emphasis on Abraham's works in James 2:18–26. Each writer is looking at the same truth but from two angles: Paul from the perspective that Abraham by being first of all a person of faith is the father of Jew and Gentile believers alike, erasing any claims of superiority; James rightly pointing out from a complementary perspective that faith is evidenced in personal action. Paul would agree, and does in the practical ethical sections of this letter, but it is not the point he is making here.)

C. Descent in Adam and ascent in Christ (5:1–21). If Paul is addressing not only general and abstract theological issues (appropriate in an epistle) but also an actual situation at Rome that has occasioned his writing a letter, then it makes sense to see his appeal in 5:1 as a call to the Romans to put into practice what they already possess in principle by their professed faith in Christ. The majority of translations and commentaries render the opening words, "Therefore, since we have been justified through faith, we have peace with God through our Lord Jesus Christ" (so NIV). This is a perfectly acceptable translation and seems to make theological sense, since the reality of justification (cf. vv. 10–11) would logically entail the reality of peace, in the sense of Old Testament shalom (Gk. *eirēnē*) which signifies the removal of hostility between the believer and God. The major embarrassment to this translation is that the earliest and best Greek texts have the subjunctive *echōmen* (*let us* have) while less well attested is the reading *echomen* (we actually *do* have). If the historical context of Paul's letter is kept in mind at this point, and if it is allowed that he has been addressing the Romans personally if subtly in the previous arguments about oneness in Christ, free of boasting except in him (5:2, 11), then it makes sense to follow the stronger external textual reading. It supports what I take to be the internal situation of the letter and that Paul is appealing to the Roman Jewish and Gentile Christians to realize in actual fact and practice the peace that ought to follow as a consequence of their justification. That they do not as yet have everything as realized fact is clear from Paul's encouraging words about suffering that "produces perseverance . . . character . . . hope" by the work of the Holy Spirit by whom "God has poured out his love into our hearts" (vv. 3–5). After dwelling for a moment on humanity's prior hopeless condition and the utterly undeserved grace of God's love in the demonstrated fact that "while we were still sinners, Christ died for us" (v. 8), Paul again picks up the theme *already . . . not yet* (vv. 9–11) and makes it clear that while "we have now been justified by his blood/we were reconciled to him through the death of his Son/we have now received reconciliation," it is equally true that the eschatology of salvation is in the process of completion and has a future component. Each of the first two declarations is complemented by a future hope: "how much more shall we be saved from God's wrath through him!/how much more . . . shall we be saved through his life!" This dual aspect of salvation (the present possession and the future hope) suggests that Paul views believers as on the way, so that not only do they possess a new essence as a present reality through faith in Christ, but at every moment in this life as they move toward the future completion of their salvation they step into the next moment of decision that demands their continual faithfulness to Christ. The Roman Christians are not yet wholly reconciled and at peace with one another; hence Paul emphasizes what God in Christ did for us "when we were still powerless" (v. 6), "while we were still sinners" (v. 8), "when we were God's enemies" (v. 10). If God has been so undeservedly gracious to us while we were sinners, and promises to be faithful in completing the process of salvation ("how much more shall we be saved from God's wrath through him!" [v. 9]), can Paul's readers have any less forgiveness toward one another? This tacit appeal of 5:1–11 will be picked up in chapter 6 (which may be read with profit at this point), where the apostle deals explicitly and forthrightly with the failure of the Romans to realize in practice the fact of their new life in Christ. Paul is indeed mixing preaching with teaching.

For the moment, however, he wants to ring the changes on the theme *how much more* introduced in 5:9–10, and this he proceeds to do in verses 12–21 where the contrast of death through Adam and life through Christ is sounded in a series of parallels in ascending scales.

Paul now demonstrates in carefully orchestrated antiphonal contrasts how reality is to be understood in terms of two representative figures. The first was Adam, who by "breaking a command" (Gen. 3) brought about the intrusion of sin and death into the world. As the representative of humanity at the beginning of the race he socially incorporated every subsequent human being, so that all became sinners even though they did not commit the specific sin of Adam (v. 14) or lived "before the law was given" (the Torah; v. 13). "In this way death came to all men, because all sinned" (vv. 12–14).

The second major figure is the second Adam, "Jesus Christ" (the one to come [vv. 14–15]), who by his grace and gift generously brought not condemnation but justification and righteousness that believers might reign in life (vv. 15–17), not be reigned over by death. One should say believers because it is important not to interpret this sustained argument in a universalistic sense, as though the "how much more" implies the quantitative inclusion of every single human being, for other Scripture touching upon the importance of voluntary belief in Christ (e.g., Rom. 10:9–13) needs to interpret the sense in which Paul views Adam and Christ as representative of fallen and redeemed humanity. The meaning is qualitative, for Paul is contrasting the disobedience (v. 19) of Adam, who infects the human race with the flawed quality of his "one trespass" (his selfish and disobedient breach of fellowship) that brings death, and the obedience (v. 19) of Jesus Christ who by his "one act of righteousness" generously "infects" the new race of believers with the quality of obedient righteousness that brings eternal life (vv. 18–21). It is "those who receive God's abundant provision of grace and of the gift of righteousness" who will "reign in life through the one man, Jesus Christ" (v. 17). The "how much more" of God's grace in Christ does not obligate him to save all humanity whether by their will or against their will but emphasizes the generous consequences of Christ's utter disposability on our behalf in contrast to the ungenerous consequences of Adam's utter indisposability on behalf of his progeny. As all will not actually die as a consequence of Adam's sin since not a few receive eternal life through faith in Christ, so not all can be expected to live in Christ who willfully reject him. The number of saved is not of concern to Paul at this point but rather the extreme contrast of two ways of life personified by two fathers of two races, one disobedient and bringing loss of fellowship and death to not a few, the other obedient and bringing life and fellowship to not a few. Inserted here between the example of Abraham in chapter 4 and the practical appeal of chapter 6, the argument of chapter 5 presents Christ as the obedient Servant of the Lord (Isa. 53:11) through whom the descent of Adam into unrighteousness and death is reversed by the ascent into Christ's righteousness and life.

It is this descent/ascent motif that Paul now pursues on a personal level as he appeals to his Roman readers to realize the holy and life-giving effects of their baptism into the death of Christ Jesus and their resurrection together with him. As he brings to a close his argument concerning the two Adams and the two vectors, one leading to death, the other leading to life, Paul summarizes the theme of the passage by explaining why the law was added (by this he means the Mosaic Torah; cf. v. 13). It was added "so that the trespass might increase," that is, to intensify the sense of sin of which humanity is aware, since it has the essential law in its understanding but suppresses it (1:18–21, 25, 32), and so that it might be seen in Christ that "where sin increased, grace increased all the more" (vv. 20–21). This is the final summary of the "how much more" motif which has characterized chapter 5. Paul will now pick up the themes of descent/ascent and "all the more" of chapter 5 and, in chapter 6, after giving a silly interpretation of the latter phrase swift dismissal, will address the Roman Christians (and by way of them every reader) with a strong appeal to realize in practical fact what has been accomplished in principle through the work of Christ.

D. Baptized into Christ from death to life (6:1–14). The foolish interpretation of "all the more" is evidently, according to 3:8, a charge that some have slanderously made against Paul and his school, and he dismisses it with a word as not worthy of the Christian (vv. 1–2). Being reckoned righteous by the grace of God should not encourage sin when it is realized that the process of redemption begins by dying to sin: "We died to sin; how can we live in it any longer?" (v. 2). Addressing his Roman readers directly and personally with the familiar pronouns *we* and *you* (these are not mere rhetorical devices designed for an abstract audience), Paul lays the issue before them in strong language: "Or don't you know that [lit. Or are you ignorant of the fact that] all of us who were baptized into Christ Jesus were baptized into his death?" (v. 3). Paul's theological argument is that when believers are baptized into Christ Jesus they descend with him "into his death" (v. 3) and are "therefore buried with him" (v. 4) and have died to sin (v. 2). That is their essential status with regard to sin, and any thought that they might increase grace by sinning royally is out of the question and simply misses the point of what union with Christ means. For not only have they descended through baptism into the water, signifying death to sin through Jesus' death on the cross, and gone under the water, symbolizing burial with him, but they have been raised from the water, giving evidence that "just as Christ was raised from the dead through the glory of the Father, we too may live a new life" (v. 4). In the same manner as he rings the changes on the theme of Adam (death) and the second Adam (life) in chapter 5, Paul rings the changes on death and life in this section of chapter 6, but here he describes in more detail how Christ Jesus enters into death through his baptism on the cross in order to render death powerless, thereby reversing Adam's fall and ascending into life through his resurrection, and how, "if we have been united with him in his death, we will certainly also be united with him in his resurrection" (v. 5). We should beware of reading too much of mystical union with Christ into Paul's teaching in this verse, as the Greek suggests more the sense of "being conformed to" his death and resurrection (so Phil. 3:10), with an emphasis on what Christ has done for us by his grace, beyond some simple union with him in his descent and ascent. It is precisely because "the death he died, he died to sin once for all" (v. 10; so also Heb. 7:27; 9:12, 28; 10:10; 1 Pet. 3:18), and because our old self was crucified with him (v. 6) that Paul can appeal to his readers that they should aspire to claim the logical and ethical implications of their death and burial with Christ. Namely: "that the body of sin might be done away with, that we should no longer be slaves to sin—because anyone who has died has been freed from sin" (vv. 6–7). In these two verses is encapsulated the heart of Paul's message to the Romans as well as to the general Christian reader, and it is necessary to get the tenses correct to understand what we possess and do not yet possess as believers. Through faith in Christ and baptism in him Christians have a new essence, a new being (our language strains for adequate words) that is an accomplished fact; that is the beginning of a process which must be worked out in appropriate and holy behavior. The new essence must be seized and acted out by the believer, for there is an already and a not yet aspect to salvation, as Paul reminds the Philippians in a pregnant text that combines the two aspects of "God who works in you to will and to act according to his good purpose" and the need as responsible agents "to work out your salvation with fear and trembling" (Phil. 2:12–13). So here in Romans 6:1–14 Paul is making an impassioned plea on the basis of what Christ has done for them, and on the basis of their faith and confession to act appropriately and decisively, for they are not dead in sin but alive to God (v. 10): "count yourselves dead to sin but alive to God in Christ Jesus" (v. 11); "do not let sin reign in your mortal body" (v. 12); "do not offer the parts of your body to sin; offer yourselves to God; offer the parts of your body to him" (v. 13). These are all exhortations concerning things that need to be done to greater perfection by the Roman Christians, since in Christ believers are potentially masters over death and sin (vv. 9, 14), because they are "not under law, but under grace" (v. 14; cf. a similar exhortation in Col. 3:1–10). Of course they are still under law in the sense that it represents the immutable will of God, which all believers are expected to fulfill in holy behavior; what Paul means by not being under law but under grace is that we do not have to work from a fallen nature but by grace have been given a new nature. This matter is now addressed in the next section, 6:15–23, where the theme of the entire chapter, the call to holiness (v. 23), is heightened by the helpful analogy of two kinds of slavery. There is a paradox in all of this, however, for Paul recognizes that the old nature, though in principle put to death on the cross, lingers on in the life of the believer and can be overcome by the decisive will of the Christian who must choose to live according to the new nature, not the old. Hence Paul's continual plea throughout the chapter and the letter that his readers act responsibly.

E. No longer slaves of sin but slaves of God (6:15–23). Paul has already introduced the metaphor of slavery in verse 6 ("that we should no longer be slaves to sin") and now returns to the image to develop its two possibilities, since his assumption is that everyone is a slave through personal commitment, "whether you are slaves to sin, which leads to death, or to obedience, which leads to righteousness" (v. 16). Repeating in verse 15 the foolish suggestion from verse 1 he dismisses its logic by an appeal to his readers' past behavior, wherein they showed themselves "slaves to sin" before their conversion, but when they became Christians they "wholeheartedly obeyed the form of teaching to which [they] were entrusted" (v. 17). But having said that, Paul implies that they have slackened in their wholehearted obedience to Christ and need to be prodded to renewed faithfulness, "because you are weak in your natural selves" (lit. the weakness of your flesh [v. 19]). This is an important text, for Paul declares that the old nature described as the weakness of the flesh (flesh or *sarx* denotes the whole disobedient self) lingers on and continues to give Christians difficulty even though the new nature has been implanted by faith in Christ. Paul's is an inaugurated eschatology in which the new overlaps the old until the end of the age when the new will triumph.

Meanwhile there is inevitable tension between the authentic self and the inauthentic self, the new and the old, which requires constant vigilance and prodding. Paul is acting as a goad to the Roman Christians and reminds them of their earlier impurity and "ever-increasing wickedness" as non-Christians, while he encourages them to offer "the parts of your body [= their whole persons] to righteousness leading to holiness" (v. 19), a process that requires their utmost attention and discloses Paul's view of progressive eschatology. Their former life as "slaves to sin" reaped them no benefits but death, though they thought they were free and were indeed "free from the control of righteousness" (vv. 20–21). Paul now exhorts them to claim the basic fact that comes from faith ("But now [*nuni de;* cf. 3:21] that you have been set free from sin and have become slaves to God") and on the basis of this to reap the benefit that "leads to holiness" (or sanctification), whose end, goal, or "result is eternal life" (v. 22). Subtly but powerfully Paul summarizes his appeal in verse 23 by an ironic contrast between slavery to sin and slavery to God, for one has to work for sin and receives death as its wages, whereas God gives eternal life as a gift, made possible in Christ Jesus our Lord, who properly receives pride of place at the conclusion of the argument, for it is through his work that the believer is justified as a sheer gift of grace. Paradoxically, however, the appeal of the entire chapter is synergistic, that is, a working together of God's grace and the believer's response to grace, for holiness is a goal and a process of sanctification that justifies Paul's hortatory language to the Roman Christians here and throughout the letter. Paul views the believer as *persona viator,* a "person on the way," and in this sense underscores the existential as well as the essential nature, the becoming as well as the being, of the Christian's pilgrimage. The believer already has a new nature in Christ, but he must express this nature in decisive acts of choice and perseverance in faithfulness that confirm that fact, while the old nature lingers and must be daily repudiated as it wastes away. In another context (2 Cor. 4:16) Paul speaks of the conflict between the inner and the outer and encourages his readers not to lose heart: "Though outwardly we are wasting away, yet inwardly we are being renewed day by day." There the context is the testing of suffering while here the testing is moral choice within the life of the believer, but in both cases it is a process that, if successfully completed, leads to eternal glory and eternal life.

The question we must keep in mind as we anticipate the difficult second section of chapter 7 (vv. 7–25) is whether this moral tension between the old self and the new self is also true of the apostle Paul as he writes his letter, or whether he is an exception to this principle and to what he sees as a failure among his Roman readers. But first he wants to make the point of chapter 6 again by using another analogy, and this he proceeds to do in 7:1–6.

F. No longer married to the law but married to Christ (7:1–6). Paul is not beginning a new topic but is further illustrating the theology of 6:14, "you are not under law, but under grace." By this he does not mean that the believer is free from responsibility to fulfill the content of the law which, as we have seen, articulates God's unchangeable will for humanity. Rather, freedom from the law means no longer to be under its condemnation or obligated to undertake the impossible task of fulfilling it on our own; but Paul does expect his Christian readers to work out the spirit of the law because of what Christ has done on their behalf in bringing them from death to life (6:11–13, 19b). Hence 7:1–6 is a ringing of the changes on this fundamental theme already expressed. In 7:1–3 the metaphor of two marriages parallels the two kinds of slavery in chapter 6 and the two races in chapter 5, and repeats the theme of redemptive death that frees the believer from a previous relationship bound by law (6:3, 6, 11). In this case Paul's example is of a marriage with its obligations. At her husband's death a widow "is released from the law of marriage" (lit. she is released from the law of the husband; i.e., insofar as it binds her to her husband). The central point is the death that frees, and since Paul has already demonstrated that Christ has died once for all that we might live in him (6:8–10), it follows that we are now free to be married to Christ, and Paul makes that very point in 7:4. But as before in chapter 6 Paul moves on from the fact of dying and rising with Christ to what is now the proper fulfilling of the intent of the law, namely, "that we might bear fruit to God" (v. 4), not fruit for death as before (v. 5), "so that we serve in the new way of the Spirit, and not in the old way of the written code" (v. 6). Paul includes himself in the "we" of the exhortations. He implies that the law remains the same since it always reflects the heart of God. Our relationship to it is now to be experienced "in the new way of the Spirit," paved with hope that we can work out its holiness (cf. 6:19, 22) and not despair in "the old way of the written code" which condemned us because we were then powerless as slaves to sin. The problem has not been the law but ourselves. This point Paul will make again immediately at the beginning of the next section.

G. Warfare between the spiritual and carnal egos (7:7–25). The apostle has already had occasion to point out the goodness of the law and the fact that, in our fallen state outside of Christ, it functions negatively to condemn us (3:20; 4:15; 5:20). He repeats this theme in 7:7–11, autobiographically describing how "the very commandment that was intended to bring life actually brought death" (v. 10), not because of anything bad in the law but because of

Paul's own sinful nature that rebelled against it; hence he can state categorically, "the law is holy, and the commandment is holy, righteous and good" (v. 12). The law which is good worked death in the sinful Paul so that his "sin might become utterly sinful" (v. 13). Accordingly, there can be no ground for claiming that Paul is antagonistic toward the law, because he views it as the very expression of God's holy will for his creatures; rather, the fault lies in the sinful self.

But now the question (a difficult one) arises as to whether verses 14–25 represent Paul's description of his own continuing struggle between the two natures as he shares this fact with the struggling Roman Christians, in order to encourage them by acknowledging that even apostles feel the tension, as do all Christians; or whether he is simply using the present tense stylistically to contrast what goes on in the life of the unbeliever and what happened in his own life before he became a Christian. Interpreters of this passage are to be found on both sides. The fact that Paul switches from the past tense to the present tense in verses 14–25 would indicate that he is speaking both of himself and of all Christians when he describes the conflict of the person who now serves in the new way of the Spirit and seeks to overcome the old nature that lingers and vies egotistically with his new marriage to Christ. It is important to recall Paul's exhortations to his readers in chapter 6 (e.g., "do not let sin reign in your mortal body so that you obey its evil desires" [6:12]) and the observation that in his eschatology of the present age the Christian is "on the way" to but has not yet arrived at perfection, for Paul pleads with them to offer their lives "to righteousness leading to holiness" (6:19), as though there were lots of tough moral decisions yet to be made. Paul does not describe the unconverted as caught in intense moral struggle but rather as approving of their own and others' sin (1:32, though inwardly knowing better); the Jew is complacent (2:17, 23), as was Paul before his conversion (Phil. 3:4–6; Gal. 1:14). But could Paul possibly say as a Christian that "I am unspiritual, sold as a slave to sin" (7:14), who continues "in the sinful nature a slave to the law of sin" (7:25)? These statements seem to some interpreters to be too extreme for any Christian to assert, especially when Paul has already made so much of the Christian's freedom from sin (6:6, 14, 17–18, 22; cf. 8:2). There are, however, compelling reasons for accepting the view that Paul is here baring his heart and his personal struggle between the two natures. Several of these reasons have already been briefly mentioned.

For example, verses 14–25 are written in the present tense, affording a contrast with the past tenses of verses 7–13.

Also, Paul does not describe the unregenerate Gentile or Jew, not even himself before he came to Christ, in such terms of inner conflict; as a Christian he does however describe himself in humble terms that suggest a sense of his unworthiness (1 Cor. 15:9; Eph. 3:8; 1 Tim. 1:15, "I am the foremost of sinners," a remarkable admission, but not for the mature Christian).

Furthermore, in all of his letters Paul assumes that his Christian readers have experienced justification, yet he exhorts them to choose to live in a more holy manner, consistent with their new life in the Holy Spirit ("Since we live by the Spirit, let us keep in step with the Spirit" [Gal. 5:25]), and so here in Romans.

It is also crucial to appreciate Paul's view of eschatology (that we are between the times of Christ's first and second comings), and this necessitates a tension between the old nature that is passing away and the new nature that is being renewed every day; thus every maturing Christian experiences the kind of inner conflict between the carnal and spiritual egos that Paul describes of himself in 7:14–25. The matter is made clearer when it is realized that Paul views the Christian as a person with two Is, one false and passing away, the other true and called to faithfulness, engaged with each other in warfare. On the one hand, "I know that nothing good lives in me, that is, in my sinful nature" (v. 18, which describes the lingering inauthentic self); on the other hand, "in my inner being I delight in God's law" (v. 22, which describes the authentic self). From this wretched state of conflict there is only one who will be able to rescue Paul (note the future tense, "Who will rescue me from this body of death?" [v. 24], indicating his eschatological hope that what Christ has begun he will complete at the end of the age).

Finally, that this is the correct reading of the passage is supported by Paul's depiction in 8:22, 23, 26 of a triple groaning in the present age between the first and second comings of Christ: "the whole creation has been groaning" (v. 22); "we ourselves, who have the firstfruits of the Spirit, groan inwardly as we wait eagerly for our adoption as sons, the redemption of our bodies" (v. 23); and God groans for us through the Holy Spirit—"but the Spirit himself intercedes for us with groans that words cannot express" (v. 26). The same paradox of already/not yet obtains in respect to the Christian's status of sonship with the Father, for on the one hand Paul reminds the Romans that it is an accomplished fact: "you received the Spirit of sonship" (8:15) and "we are God's children" (8:16); but on the other hand "we wait eagerly for our adoption as sons" (8:23). This future adoption must be read, in light of the fact that we are already sons, as the completion of the redemption that has been inaugurated, and is further explained by Paul as "the redemption of our bodies" (8:23), by which he means our total selves will finally be made whole, at last totally cleansed of the residual of fleshly rebellion (7:25) that plagues Paul and every believer as long as they are in "this body of death" (v. 24) from which he prays to be rescued. Chapters 8:18–39 and 7:14–25 are of one piece, not two successive stages, and describe the groaning and tension that characterize the Christian life between the times. Understanding then Paul's realistic portrayal of the believer's groaning in this present age (a fact which every struggling Christian recognizes as all too true), and his dualism of the two Is, the carnal and spiritual egos that war against one another in the believer's life, we may appreciate the sense in which Paul, as representative of believers, can say in 7:14 that "I am unspiritual, sold as a slave to sin," yet, with the Romans, claim to have been "set free from sin" (6:18), for Paul focuses now on one and now on the other of the two Is. If there were no personal struggle in Paul then he would be an exception in the Christian community, for each of his letters deals in some aspect with the sinfulness of his Christian readers, including those in Rome. The point is, however, that believers may take heart, as Paul thankfully does in 7:25, for he is confident that he will be rescued through Jesus Christ our Lord!

H. Children of God through the witness of the Spirit (8:1–17). In typical Jewish and Hellenistic style Paul often alternates themes; he proceeds to do so in 8:1–17, a passage that corresponds to the positive appeal of 6:1–7:6, while the tension in 8:18–39 explores in a cosmic dimension the personal struggles of 7:7–25. Each section carries its predecessor on to deeper insight and appeal and combines aspects of the alternating units. So in chapter 8, after declaring the great work of the triune family as God sends his own Son (v. 3) through whom comes life according to the Spirit (v. 4), Paul makes another concerted appeal to his readers to live in accord with the new nature that has been wrought in them. This appeal parallels the call to holiness in 6:19–22. The powerful work of Christ, being sent as "Son in the likeness of sinful man to be a sin offering," by which he took on human nature while remaining himself and so "condemned sin in sinful man" (v. 3), has freed believers for a purpose expressed as a task: "in order that the righteous requirements of the law might be fully met in us" (again the law is acclaimed to be good), for we are walking in our new status not "according to the sinful nature but according to the Spirit" (v. 4). In the practical application of the work of the Son in the sanctification of believers, Father and Son defer to the Spirit (mutual deference characterizes the triune family), who properly receives focal attention in this passage. It is the indwelling Spirit who applies the perfect "sin offering" of the Son (v. 3) by engaging in the process of establishing "the righteous requirements of the law" in the believer's life, in which alone there is hope and future glory (vv. 18–39).

Paul describes this sanctifying work of the Holy Spirit in synergistic (cooperative) terms, not as something that automatically happens as a result of initial faith in Christ where the groundwork is laid; for without a voluntary desire to work out the implications of life in the Spirit the believer is choosing death, not life. This Paul makes clear in his contrast of two mindsets in verses 5–8, assuming that both are still operative in the Christian who lives between the times: those who choose to live their lives "according to the sinful nature" (or flesh) "have their minds set on what that nature desires," and choose death, are hostile to God, do not submit to God's law, and cannot please God. On the other hand, those who choose to follow through with their faith in Christ by submitting to the Spirit and "live in accordance with the Spirit have their minds set on what the Spirit desires," and choose life and peace. Pointedly challenging his readers' mindset and behavior as to whether their faith in Christ is sound, Paul views the situation conditionally. He gives the Romans the benefit of the doubt by saying, "You, however, are controlled not by the sinful nature but by the Spirit." But immediately he adds a qualifying "if": "if the Spirit of God lives in you" (v. 9); and if that is the case then "your spirit is alive because of righteousness" (v. 10), and the triune family through the "Spirit of him who raised Jesus from the dead will also give life to your mortal bodies" (v. 11; both in the processive mortification of sinfulness in the believer in this life and in the final resurrection). The conditional nature of Paul's appeal is made clearer by his reminder (tactfully and warmly made to his Roman friends as "brothers" [v. 12]) that "we have an obligation" (lit. we are debtors), not to live according to "the sinful nature" which brings death ("you will die," repeating 8:6a and

6:23a), but to live by the Spirit and to "put to death the misdeeds of the body," by which Paul clearly delineates the fact that believers who live by the Spirit have the responsibility of working out the implications of their essential status in Christ by progressively killing their old rebellious nature before it kills them. There is a warfare unto death as well as unto life going on in the Christian that Paul has already spelled out in chapters 6 and 7. Here he pleads with them again to choose life (v. 13), to be led by the Spirit of God and claim their status in God's family as sons of God (v. 14). In a word play on "spirit" Paul reminds them that "you did not receive a spirit that makes you a slave again to fear," implying that they are acting as though they might fall back again into the old nature of rebellion and fear, "but you received the Spirit of sonship," by whom we have intimate access as "God's children" into his family and may call the Father familiarly "Abba" and ourselves "heirs of God and co-heirs with Christ" (vv. 15–17a). The portrait is one of social solidarity and family relatedness through life in the Spirit. God is social as triune society and desires that his children by adoption enjoy that intimate family circle. But there is another large "if" (v. 17) that challenges Paul's readers to make their decisive choice to live as God's faithful children. Climaxing a whole list of conditional "ifs" in the passage (8:9, 10, 11, 13, 17) Paul is now about to lead his readers on to something they need to understand and practice beyond containing the inner moral warfare that besets every Christian. He lifts the question of suffering to its highest level, away from moral turpitude to suffering together with Christ as a prelude to being glorified together with him. We are, he writes, "God's children, . . . heirs of God and co-heirs with Christ," on condition that we enter into the suffering and groaning of the divine family on behalf of a world under condemnation that is in the process of being redeemed by the suffering work of Christ: "if indeed we share in his sufferings" in order that we may also share in his glory (v. 17b). This is an important transitional verse, for it introduces the reader to Paul's theology of history which is the second hinge of his eschatology, the first being Christ's work of redemption as incarnate representative of the divine family (3:21ff.), and the second (8:18ff.) the role of the children of God in his plan of redemptive suffering and glory as the plan moves inexorably to its fulfillment at the end of this age.

IV. Prognosis II: Subjected to Futility, Subjected in Hope (8:18–11:36)

A. The glorious freedom of the children of God (8:18–27). The coupling of suffering and glory within the extended family of God (8:17) allows Paul to address his Roman readers on yet a deeper level of teaching and exhortation. He shares his own groaning with them in awaiting their final adoption to God's sonship and the redemption of this flawed embodied existence between the times (8:23). He bares the sorrow and unceasing anguish of his heart over the failure of his people to accept Christ (9:1–5), laying before the Roman Christians God's scenario for the salvation of Jew and Gentile that should draw them together from their factionalism into a final doxology in praise of God's mercy (11:33–36). We note first of all that Paul accepts "present sufferings" as a fact of Christian life in this age, but that they are to be seen in perspective as a prelude to "the glory that will be revealed in us" (8:18; in us, not just "to us" as in RSV), a formidable paradox that repeats the theme of 8:17b and carries it on to explanation. In Paul's description of the actual state of things in the present age from God's point of view, creation itself is poised in "eager expectation," waiting for us, Paul says, who are the redeemed "sons of God to be revealed" (v. 19). Four points need to be noted here, the first being that in imitation of Christ's descent into suffering preceding his ascent into glorification Christians are to follow this pattern of descent in suffering and service and ascent into glory, for the way up is the way down. The path to glory is the way of disposability on behalf of Christ and the gospel (the sufferings entailed in this mission are enumerated at the end of the chapter). The second point is that Paul sees present suffering apocalyptically (the term is used twice in vv. 18–19) as a future unveiling or revelation of something glorious, and that something glorious is none other than the freedom of believers who are transformed by the grace of God, "the glorious freedom of the children of God" (v. 21). Third, this is a freedom in which creation itself will participate and "be liberated from its bondage to decay" (v. 21); for, fourth, all creation in its present unredeemed state has been "subjected to frustration [i.e., to futility, vanity, entropy, decay, death] by the will of the one who subjected it, in hope" (v. 20; i.e., by God). In this terse theology of history Paul affirms that God has of his own righteous will placed all creation, including humanity who brought about the curse, under judgment (Gen. 3:14–24; it would not have done so "by its own choice" [v. 20]). God has judged it by his righteousness and will redeem it by his grace; hence creation is also subjected in hope, for it "waits in eager expectation [lit. cranes the neck forward] for the sons of God to be revealed" (v. 19). The order of Paul's progressive eschatology is first Christ, then the children of God, then creation, with the sons of God "who have the firstfruits of the Spirit" (v. 23) in the center position, drawing creation on in the name of Christ (there are important implications in this for Christian missions and ethics). Accordingly, Paul instructs his readers to take heart because the end of all things is full of hope (vv. 20, 24, 25), even though creation has been groaning (v. 22), while we ourselves "groan inwardly as we wait eagerly for our adoption as sons" (v. 23), and "the Spirit himself intercedes for us with groans that words cannot express" (v. 26, all from the root *stenazō;* v. 26 describes the Spirit's participation in believers' weakness and suffering, not the inspired utterance of glossolalia). Because believers as the children of God may look forward to glorious and total freedom from bondage to sin and have as their helper in the present struggle the Spirit who "intercedes for the saints in accordance with God's will" (v. 27; the divine family is at the disposal of believers), they who are justified may confidently look forward to being glorified (8:30), the subject of Paul's concluding unit (8:28–39) in this concise theology of history, to which he now turns.

B. Whom God justified he also glorified (8:28–39). Paul affords his readers an eschatological panorama of redemptive history, assuring them that all that happens to them is in the sovereign hand of God who in everything "works for the good of those who love him" (v. 28), one of the great biblical texts of assurance. The apostle's teaching on God's calling, purpose, foreknowledge, and predestination (vv. 28–30) is not designed to engender controversy concerning the believer's rights to power and free will, but is set in the context of assuring his Christian readers that the sufferings and struggles they are undergoing are not absurdities that have somehow crept into the flow of things beyond God's power. They have their place in the sovereign process of salvation, as God is faithful in conforming believers "to the likeness of his Son" (v. 29; better, to the image [*tēs eikonos*] of his Son). As the Son took on "the likeness of sinful man" (see also Phil. 2:7) and became a "sin offering" (8:3) at the beginning of the redemptive process, so now, says Paul, it is the plan of God that believers be conformed to the Son's image "that he might be the firstborn among many brothers" (v. 29), bringing into being the redeemed family of God. The redemptive purposes of God are social through and through, and Paul's practical appeal to the Roman Christians is for them to realize their oneness as a family on the basis of what God has done in Christ, is doing, and will do. The final goal of redemption is the glorification of believers, a remarkable teaching that is sure to come to fulfillment because it has already been inaugurated ("those he justified he also glorified" [v. 30]), is now in process of realization ("And we, who with unveiled faces all reflect the Lord's glory, are being transformed into his likeness with ever-increasing glory, which comes from the Lord, who is the Spirit" [2 Cor. 3:18]), and will be incomparably revealed in us in the future (Rom. 8:18). Paul's appeal in 8:28–39 is optimistic in spite of suffering and is very much like his optimism in 2 Corinthians 4:17: "For our light and momentary troubles are achieving for us an eternal glory that far outweighs them all."

Consequently, Paul's readers ought to be able to withstand any suffering and any charge brought against them in the course of their mission. God is in control of things in our three dimensions of time, for God is for us, and (like Abraham, Gen. 22:12, 16; cf. Isa. 53:12) did not spare his own Son, but gave him up for us all, and together with his Son will "graciously give us all things." As God has done the difficult thing in giving his Son for sinners, how much more will he do the easier thing and graciously give us the fullness of salvation (so 5:9–10), as well as a share in all things (so also 1 Cor. 3:21–23). Paul's readers are assured that no one can condemn them, for the entire divine family works in unity on their behalf: It is God who justifies (v. 33); Christ Jesus, who died and was raised, "is at the right hand of God and is also interceding for us" (v. 34); and we have already seen that "the Spirit himself intercedes for us with groans that words cannot express" (v. 26). As the fellowship and togetherness of the redeemed society with the triune family is the hallmark of the new age that has been inaugurated by the suffering and glory of Christ, and prefigures heaven, so the hellish realm is separation from the Lord. In his concluding affirmation that in all the sufferings and testings of Christians as they witness for Christ (this is implied by the context of 8:28–39, esp. v. 36) we are more than conquerors through him who loved us (v. 37), Paul finely constructs a chiasm to assure his readers that there is nothing that can separate them from the love of Christ. In the parallel unit, "separate" (vv. 35, 39) stands at the beginning and end, then two parallel lists of threatening powers appear (vv. 35, 36; 38, 39a), and in prominent position is Christ through whom we are more than conquerors (v. 37). Believers can indeed expect trouble or tribulation (8:35) in this age, but in Christ they are saved from God's wrath (5:9) and are to look forward to fuller participation in God's glory. Paul's high Christology is attested by the fact that he refers to "the love of God that is in Christ Jesus our Lord" (v. 39; cf. the love of Christ [2 Cor. 5:14; Eph. 3:18]), while the loving unity and equality of the three persons of the triune family are further witnessed to by Romans 5:5 ("God has poured out his love into our hearts by the Holy Spirit").

Having considered the Christian's inner struggles with sin (7:7–8:16) and with the outer sufferings that come from an eschatology in progress and mission for Christ (8:17–39), Paul can turn to a large issue that has troubled him and has caused dissension at Rome: the question of the relationship of Jew and Gentile in God's plan of salvation.

C. The mercy of God and the riches of his glory toward Israel and the Gentiles (9:1–33). Great seas of ink have been spilled in the attempt to interpret this passage in view of free will and God's sovereignty, but the issue needs to be seen in the intent of the unit as a whole. Paul has been speaking of suffering both personal and corporate, both moral and eschatological, and continues the theme of suffering by baring his heart again, as he already has in context of the inner moral struggle (7:7–25). Here he cites another example of the eschatological tension that characterizes the present age in which there is not yet a resolution. He adds two more words to express his anguish over the failure of Israel to respond to the gospel: "I have great sorrow (*lypē*) and unceasing anguish (*odynē*) in my heart" (v. 2), a fact that is not merely rhetorical but actual, as he thrice "confirms it in the Holy Spirit" (v. 1). Paul is a Christian who feels deep anguish when he focuses on a problem from the human perspective (here and in 7:24), but paradoxically exhibits great optimism when the human perspective becomes peripheral and he focuses on the problem from God's point of view. Thus as he finds the ultimate answer to the moral struggle through Jesus Christ our Lord (7:25), so here he finds the ultimate solution to Jewish unbelief in the sovereign plan of God, within which there are no loose threads in the final woven tapestry. This view of God's sovereignty does not erase human responsibility, for whereas chapter 9 highlights the sovereignty of God (because Paul is focusing upon final and ultimate answers), chapter 10 highlights in a complementary way the responsibility of Jew and Gentile in regard to the preaching of the gospel (because there he is focusing on the secondary human agents by which God is carrying out his purpose). As we interpret this chapter and the whole unit comprising chapters 9–11 it will be helpful to appreciate that Paul is writing in harmony with the Old Testament view of the complementary relationship of divine sovereignty and human responsibility, alternating between them, focusing now on one, now on the other (this is technically called biblical merismus, from Gk. *meros*, a part here, a part there; Old Testament examples are Exod. 7:3–4/8:15; Isa. 45:9–13/55:1–7; Ezek. 5:1–17/18:1–32). Thus in spite of the fact that Paul is in anguish over his people's failure to accept Christ and gives evidence of his sense of disposability in his willingness to be "cursed and cut off" for their sake (vv. 2–3; knowing the impossibility of this request but expressing his compassion and sorrow in the most extreme terms), he nonetheless defends God's plan of redemption and timing as he is sovereignly working it out ("It is not as though God's word had failed" [v. 6a]). The apparent contradiction is that "my own race, the people of Israel" can claim a great heritage; here Paul gives a formidable list of advantages, including "adoption as sons," covenants, promises, and most of all (ironically, the sore point) "the human ancestry of Christ, who is God over all, forever praised!" (vv. 4–5; this last clause is correctly translated from the Gk. in the NIV and attests Paul's high Christology [cf. 14:9; Phil. 2:10]). Paul now offers to show in defense of God's word that the inner reality does not correspond one-to-one to the outer appearance, for "not all who are descended from Israel are Israel," nor are "all Abraham's children" (vv. 6–7), but there is a true Israel, an Israel within Israel, that is comprised, not of "the natural children," but of the children of the promise, and these "are God's children," and truly "Abraham's offspring" (v. 8). This is remnant theology and illustrates further the remarks made in chapter 5 concerning the "all in Adam/all in Christ" motif, where "all" does not denote every single person in a group but those to whom the description ultimately applies (not all finally die in Adam, for some come to life in Christ, and not all come to life in Christ because some reject him); so here, true Israel is made up of true believers, for as Paul has said earlier, "He is a Jew who is one inwardly, and real circumcision is a matter of the heart, spiritual and not literal" (2:29 RSV). Thus children of the promise are those whose lineage is traced by faith in God's promise, beginning with Abraham, and continuing with Isaac and Jacob (vv. 8–13). It is important to note that these three great patriarchs were persons of faith, certainly far from perfect, but men who, with their wives, trusted God's promise. God's election never contradicts the appropriate behavior of the person who receives grace, for faith in God's promise is always characteristic of the elect, as is clear in the case of Jacob who believed in the birthright promise in contrast to the legal heir, Esau, who despised it (Gen. 25:21–34; cf. Heb. 12:16–17). This needs to be remembered when we observe that Paul, though he is focusing here on God's sovereign plan of salvation and his right to be merciful in his own way and in his own time (note the significant phrase *at the appointed time,* 9:9, which is central to a theology of God's timing), purposely preempts the works of Jacob and Esau ("before the twins were born or had done anything good or bad") in order to point to the freedom and grandeur of God's mercy, "that God's purpose in election might stand, not by works but by him who calls" (vv. 11–12). Accordingly, the final solution to the meaning of history is to be found in the sovereign God in whose hand lies the hope of the future (the basis of Paul's confidence in 8:18–39), regardless of the perplexity and pain of the present (7:24; 8:23; 9:2). Without God's sovereignty there could be no prophecy and no ground of hope as expressed in 8:18–39 and 11:11–32 (the final resolution of Paul's immediate anguish), and no promise made to Rebekah, "The older will serve the younger" (9:12). God's free grace is thus independent of all human merit and is "round" in the sense that it is graciously unpredictable in human terms (though not capricious), while God's law is "square" in that it is utterly predictable in its demands, judgment, and condemnation of sinners. Thus God's words in Malachi (1:2–3) can be cited by Paul as evidence of God's free decision of grace and mercy, "Jacob I loved, but Esau I hated" (v. 13).

Paul anticipates the rejoinder that while it may be admitted that God is 50 percent gracious in loving Jacob, he is equally unjust in rejecting Esau. To the rhetorical question "Is God unjust?" he replies, "Not at all!" (v. 14), and proceeds to show in two ways that God is supremely just and merciful. As will become clear by implication before the unit of chapters 9–11 is concluded, the rejection of Esau is not everlasting but in fact is reversed by the unexpected and "round" inclusion of Gentiles (equivalent to Esau's progeny) in this new eschatological age. Immediately, however, Paul wants to deal with the larger question of what the criterion for judging God might possibly be. He rejects the Hellenistic notion, popularized by Plato in the *Euthyphro,* that God perforce must do what is right because the right is higher than he in the world of ideals. No! says Paul, and attests his continuity with Old Testament theology by quoting God's words to Moses which absolutely confirm God's right to determine what is right and merciful: "I will have mercy on whom I have mercy, and I will have compassion on whom I have compassion" (v. 15; Exod. 33:19). Hence the right is not something apart from God that he must obey; rather, everything he does is right because he is the ultimate reference of righteousness and mercy. These are absolutely determined by what he is, what he does, what he says. Human works count for nothing in establishing a right relationship with God (v. 16) and therefore cannot be turned against him to judge him and hold him responsible. God sovereignly moves in the affairs of history and its prominent figures, like Pharaoh, to "display [his] power" and "that [his] name might be proclaimed in all the earth" (v. 17). Paul anticipates a second rejoinder that it is then unfair for God to "blame us," for "who resists his will?" (v. 19). To this he continues his argument that the creature has no right "to talk back to God," to place the Creator in the dock as though he had to answer the question "Why did you make me like this?" for God is the Potter who can do with his created matter as he pleases (vv. 20–21). Again Paul shows his indebtedness to Old Testament theology and its images by referring to Jeremiah 18:6 and its metaphor of the potter and the clay (see also, e.g., Isa. 29:16; 45:9). But significantly as Jeremiah complements God's absolute sovereignty over the affairs of history ("O house of Israel, can I not do with you as this potter does?") with the promise that if a nation condemned of God "repents of its evil, then [he] will relent and not inflict on it the disaster [he] had planned" (18:8), so Paul turns the discussion from God's wrath, power, and patience concerning "the objects of his wrath—prepared for destruction" (v. 22), back to God's sovereign grace toward "the objects of his mercy" (v. 23), both Jews and Gentiles, "whom he prepared in advance in glory—even us" (vv. 23–24). Thus Paul expresses that God works mysteriously, "roundly," and wonderfully on behalf of many who formerly were objects of his wrath (the Gentiles and reprobate Israel) but repented and by faith opened themselves to his grace. Thus "prepared for destruction" does not necessarily imply an eternal reprobation, for many of "the objects of his wrath" whom he "bore with great patience" (v. 22) are in the new eschatological age that is inaugurated by the grace of Christ the very "objects of his mercy" to whom he makes "the riches of his glory known" (v. 23), "even us," says Paul, "whom he also called, not only from the Jews but also from the Gentiles" (v. 24). Hence Hosea's prophecy can be cited as brought to fulfillment in this age, for not my people become my people (vv. 25–26; i.e., the former objects of wrath have now become by the "great patience" of God the objects of his mercy, speaking generically of groups, not of specific individuals); and Isaiah's prophetic cry concerning the remnant can also be seen to have been carried out "with speed and finality" (vv. 27–28; again the sovereign and mysterious eschatological timing of God). Accordingly, the major theme of chapter 9 is the mercy of God and the riches of his glory toward Israel and the Gentiles.

Why and how God does what he does lie in the realm of mystery, and Paul does not give any philosophical explanations; he only defends God's right to be merciful in his own sovereign way and at his own time. Nor does he attempt to describe how God can be sovereignly absolute while he justly holds his creatures responsible, but such is the case and Paul concurs with the biblical tradition that both go together in mysterious merismus (now an emphasis here, now an emphasis there in Scripture, God of course receiving the greater emphasis). There is not the slightest hint in Paul of limiting God's power to underwrite human freedom, as in liberal and process forms of theology, nor does Paul even speak of genuine freedom except in Christ; but of human responsibility he says a great deal. He is about to turn from his theological explanation of why his people Israel have rejected Christ (God is patiently working out his sovereign plan of mercy through election [9:1–29]), and now takes up the complementary issue in God's plan of salvation that concerns human responsibility and response to the gospel. This he does in 9:30–33 where he briefly describes (before considering the matter in more detail in chaps. 10 and 11) the great and ironic reversal that has taken place because "Israel, who pursued a law of righteousness [good], has not attained it" because they pursued it "by works" (bad), while the "Gentiles, who did not pursue righteousness [bad], have obtained it" because they pursued it "by faith" (good; vv. 30–32). In God's mysterious and gracious timing, when "the full number of the Gentiles has come in," there will be a softening of the hardening that Israel has experienced (11:25–26), but until then Paul can only sadly observe that his people have "stumbled over the 'stumbling stone,' " meaning Christ (cf. 1 Cor. 1:23) who is the fulfillment of the law they have been pursuing (cf. 10:4), a reference to the prophetic word of Isaiah (28:16 + 8:14 LXX), a double prophecy that refers to the coming Assyrian invasion, which is the disaster resulting from Israel's failure to take refuge in God, and to the coming messianic Stone whom Israel, again lacking faith, rejects with disastrous results. But this need not be the final word, as Paul prays in the next unit.

D. Christ fulfills the law for Jew and Gentile (10:1–21). Once more Paul pours out his "heart's desire and prayer to God for the Israelites . . . that they may be saved" (10:1; cf. 9:1–3). Although "they are zealous for God," their zeal is "not based on knowledge" because they have sought to establish their own righteousness and did not submit to God's righteousness (vv. 2–3). But there is hope, for Christ has done what no human could ever do: he has himself become the goal and fulfillment of the law by perfectly keeping the law; accordingly Christ is the end of the law (not its abrogation but its completion [10:4a]). Christ personifies the purity of intention and behavior which the divine family desires for the new race of humanity described in chapter 5. It is through the perfect work of Christ in keeping the law of fellowship both vertically with the divine family and laterally with others that he is powerful to justify those who have faith, "so that there may be righteousness for everyone who believes" (10:4b).

As Paul has underscored the grace of God in the Old Testament quotations of 9:25–29 because in that section he has been dealing with the sovereign election of God, so now, since he is emphasizing human responsibility, he points to the Old Testament confirmation of the role of faith and Israel's failure in this regard by first paraphrasing Moses' dictum (Lev. 18:5) that "the man who does these things will live by them" (v. 5). Paul's reference to this Old Testament teaching is not to point to the hopelessness of the requirement but to the fact that Christ has perfectly fulfilled it (v. 5 in the Gk. continues the thought of v. 4: *for* Moses describes in this way the righteousness that is by the law; the clause should be so translated). Christ's righteousness is by works, for he is the only representative of humanity to have perfectly kept the law. Indeed, he is the law personified, for the aim of the law is perfect fellowship and sociality. The sinner by contrast (the "but" of v. 6 is significant) obtains the righteousness of the law only "by faith" in Christ who is the law, not by boasting (do not say in your heart), or storming heaven (to bring Christ down), or descending into Sheol (to bring Christ up from the dead; vv. 6–7); Paul quotes a string of Old Testament texts (Deut. 8:17; 9:4; 30:12–13) to which he gives proper christological reference. For him Christ is the living law; all human attempts at self-righteousness are arrogant invasions of the domains only Christ can enter because of his righteous works.

Human responsibility is seen to lie in oral proclamation of the gospel and faithful response to its claims as Paul cites Deuteronomy 30:14 (word, mouth, heart) and applies it to "the word of faith we are proclaiming" and the believer's confession with "mouth" that Jesus is Lord and belief in heart that God raised him from the dead, which leads to salvation (vv. 8–9). Heartfelt belief, oral confession, and trust in the Lord of salvation bring rich blessing (cf. Eph. 2:4, 7), salvation (Joel 2:32), and freedom from shame (or dismay, Isa. 28:16) for Jew and Gentile alike (vv. 10–13), for Jesus the Lord (*kyrios*, vv. 9, 12, 13, a title denoting equality with God) is the great leveler to whom alone both Jew and Gentile must come in faithful response in order to find salvation. The fact that the Old Testament is full of anticipation of the gospel of Jesus Christ to be proclaimed to all the world excites Paul to refer to Joel's prophecy about the coming day of the Lord, inaugurated by Jesus' ministry, that "Everyone who calls on the name of the Lord will be saved" (2:32). Because the theme of human responsibility has been Paul's principal focus since 9:30 he now turns to the important process of proclaiming the gospel, for God works through responsible human agents to carry out his purposes. Paul is concerned to engage and commission his readers in the urgent task of getting the gospel out that the unsaved may find salvation, for, he argues (employing a logical string of responsibilities while still exegeting Joel 2:32), Jews and Gentiles cannot call on Christ if they have not believed in him, have not heard about him, without someone preaching to them and having been commissioned and sent (vv. 14–15). In this compressed description of the mission of believers to the world and their line of responsibility, Paul encircles the community of faith and ennobles its mission by quoting from the words of Isaiah 52:7, "How beautiful are the feet of those who bring good news" (v. 15). As Paul's primary calling and motivation as a Christian is to proclaim salvation in Christ to the rebellious and unsaved, and since he makes it a central aim in his letter to the Romans to enlist their enthusiastic support in the ongoing missionary enterprise of the faith, it is especially appropriate that he identify himself and them with all who have been commissioned to proclaim the gracious word of redemption in God's salvation history.

Having made his point that sending, preaching, hearing, believing, and calling on the Lord constitute the mission of believers and the anticipated response of those who are presented with the word, Paul returns to the question of the Israelites who have had ample opportunity to hear the good news about Christ and to call upon his name but have not responded (vv. 16–21), a fact that caused Isaiah (53:1) to say of his people's rejection of the message of Christ's suffering seven hundred years in advance of the event: "Lord, who has believed our message?" (v. 16). If faith comes from hearing then Israel has had sufficient occasion to believe ("Did they not hear? Of course they did" [v. 18]), as Paul attests by referring to David's affirmation that in the order of natural revelation God has seen to it that the heavens and the skies day after day and night after night pour forth speech and knowledge about him, so that "their voice has gone out into all the earth" (Ps. 19:4; Rom. 10:18). Moses and Isaiah are now cited (vv. 19–21) to demonstrate that Israel's rejection of the gospel in the present eschatological age was anticipated by God's commissioned prophets centuries before. In his final song before Israel Moses rehearses the graciousness of God and the rebellion of his people, prophesying that God will make Israel "envious by those who are not a nation" (v. 19; Deut. 32:21); that is, the Gentiles who formerly have "no understanding" will come to understand and believe and cause Israel to become angry and envious and lead them to repentance (Paul's prophetic resolution in 11:11–12). Isaiah boldly makes the same prophecy (65:1–2) regarding the great reversal the early Christian church is witnessing (formerly Jews were accepted, Gentiles rejected; now Gentiles have been accepted, Jews rejected), combining cheek by jowl in merismus fashion the element of God's sovereign election of the Gentiles ("I was found by those who did not seek me; I revealed myself to those who did not ask for me") and the element of responsibility in regard to Israel who rebelliously reject his grace ("All day long I have held out my hands to a disobedient and obstinate people"). Though Paul seems to end this passage on a downbeat with Israel's rejection of Christ, the chapter as a whole emphasizes the positive fact that Christ fulfills the law for Jew and Gentile alike because he alone has perfectly kept the law and is, indeed, the personal embodiment of the law of social fellowship, to be received simply by faith and not rejected by obstinate claims to self-righteousness. That the Gentiles have now come to Christ in faith, while Israel has not, leads Paul to describe with broad brushstrokes the glorious resolution of the anguish he feels concerning his people, and the mysterious but wonderful plan of God to graft together Jew and Gentile at the close of the age. This prophetic vista unfolds in the next chapter.

E. The mercy and glory of God in the final grafting of Jew and Gentile (11:1–36). In 10:21 Paul has described his people in Isaianic terms as "disobedient and obstinate" while God has patiently held out his hands all day long, a portrait of God waiting upon the favorable response of Israel. Now in chapter 11 the factor of human responsibility slides into the background and becomes a tacit component of the total formula (God's sovereignty/human responsibility) as Paul focuses again on the absolute and sovereign plan of God for Israel, in answer to his third posing of the question "Did God reject his people?" (cf. 9:2–3; 10:1). As in chapters 9 and 10 Paul again answers his human anguish by viewing salvation history from God's sovereign vantage point, and from that perspective he is given to see that God has fulfilled his promises to Abraham by working through a remnant, of whom Paul is one, in company with the seven thousand faithful in the time of Elijah (1 Kgs. 19:18; vv. 2–4), and Paul's believing contemporaries ("at the present time there is a remnant chosen by grace" [v. 5]).

Pride of place is given here to God's sovereign foreknowledge (v. 2) and electing grace, not human works (v. 6), but at the same time Paul tacitly assumes that the remnant are faithful and perform works appropriate to their calling (God says of the faithful remnant in Elijah's day that they have not bowed the knee to Baal [v. 4], and Paul himself is an example of one who evidences his calling with appropriate works). Indeed, Paul undoubtedly sees in his own mission to the Gentiles a confirmation of the fact that God's elective grace toward Israel is being fulfilled. Thus in 11:1–6 the primary focus is on God's election, with a subsidiary awareness that God elects by grace not in spite of but through the response of faith; but grace comes first, not meritorious works from the human side, otherwise grace would no longer be grace (v. 6). It is important not to eliminate either component in Paul's formula, for he is working from a higher logic in which irony plays a significant role in the interweaving of sovereign election and human responsibility.

This is borne out in verses 7–10, where Paul sums up his argument that "what Israel sought so earnestly it did not obtain" by meritorious works, "but the elect did" by grace (v. 7). The concluding statement, "the others were hardened," which introduces two supportive Old Testament quotations, appears on the surface to reflect a capriciousness on God's part until one examines the contexts of the two Old Testament texts. Each of these texts expresses the frustration of God's prophets with the rebelliousness and spiritual hardness of Israel, in spite of many evidences of God's grace; they are, in other words, responsible for their hardness of heart while at the same time it can be said that God has hardened their hearts. The two are inseparable and complementary and cannot be logically reduced one to the other. In the first quotation, verse 8, which is principally from Deuteronomy 29:4 (see also Isa. 29:10), Moses addresses Israel and recounts for them the marvelous things God has done in bringing them out of Egypt and providing for their needs in the wilderness (29:2–8), obviously appealing to them to respond with thanksgiving and faithfulness. This is clear in verse 9, "Carefully follow the terms of this covenant, so that you may prosper in everything you do" (so again in vv. 10–13, 18–20, 25); all are appeals to human responsibility. It is in the course of the recounting (v. 4) that Moses observes, "The LORD has not given you a mind that understands or eyes that see or ears that hear." On this text Paul bases his paraphrase. In context Moses is focusing on Israel's responsibility and exhorting them to make the right decision, even though they give evidence of being blinded by God's decree; in context Paul is focusing on the sovereign plan of God in order to explain why Israel has rejected Christ, but his tacit assumption, in light of the passage from Deuteronomy, is that Israel is herself responsible for her blindness (so also the larger context of Isa. 29:10). Similarly Paul's second quotation, from David's psalm of lament and curse of his enemies (Ps. 69), needs to be seen in context of the entire psalm and the fact that David has cause to pray that "their table become a snare and a trap," and their eyes be darkened and "their backs be bent forever" (69:22–23; Rom. 11:9–10), in view of the fact that his enemies have chosen to heap scorn and gall on him (69:9–12, 18–21). What is significantly different in Paul's use of the quotation is that where David's imprecation against his enemies is unmitigated by grace (Ps. 69:24–25, 27–28), Paul is about to demonstrate that in God's gracious plan for Israel their backs will not be bent forever (11:10), for God is not through dealing graciously with his people; indeed, the use of the expression *to this very day* (v. 8) suggests a limit that God has set for the divine hardening (though its Old Testament usage indicates a permanent situation).

This leads Paul to ask his anguished question a fourth time, "Did they stumble so as to fall beyond recovery?" (par. to 11:1; 10:1; 9:2–3). His answer for the second time is confident and optimistic: "Not at all!" (cf. 11:1, By no means!), since he has been concentrating on God's sovereign plan as he sees it unfolding before him. Yet once again he sees that sovereign plan of God in terms of Israel's response to divine grace, for the absolute plan of God is worked out by the "transgression" of Israel so that by default salvation has come to the Gentiles, with the expected effect that it will "make Israel envious" and bring about her salvation in God's mysterious eschatological time (so vv. 25–26, all Israel will be saved). Paul sees the present "transgression" and "loss" of Israel, which brings riches to the Gentiles, in terms of the happy ending in God's sovereign plan by his divine "how much greater" (v. 12, lit. how much more; cf. 5:9, 10, 15, 17), when incomparable riches will accompany Israel's "fullness." The fullness of Israel is not precisely spelled out by Paul but is connected to the future eschatology of completion when the natural branches are "grafted into their own olive tree" and the full number of the Gentiles has come in, at which time all Israel will be saved (vv. 24–26).

In view of the final happy ending God has in store for his people Israel, Paul takes the occasion to address the Roman Gentile Christians (and Gentile readers generally), warning them against a haughtiness that snubs Israel for her present unbelief, interweaving once again God's sovereign plan of salvation with the importance of personal responsibility on the part of Gentiles and Jews. "I am talking to you Gentiles" (v. 13) introduces a string of parallel illustrations designed to impress upon them the fact that they stand indebted to the Jews, whose time of acceptance (v. 15) is coming in another of the great reversals of history; therefore Gentiles had better be careful that they not become guilty of the works arrogance that has brought about Israel's present rejection, or they also will be cut off (v. 22). By the parallel metaphors (vv. 16–24) Paul seeks to demonstrate to his Gentile readers that the beginning and the ending of Israel's long history is holy (v. 16), and therefore to be honored: the firstfruits offering of the dough is holy (cf. Lev. 19:23–25), by which he likely refers to the patriarchs (though Christ himself and the "firstfruits" of Jewish Christians like Paul may also be included in the meaning) who sanctify "the whole batch," meaning, in Paul's interpretation, repentant Israel to come; and the root is holy, pointing once again to the patriarchs to whom the promises were made (e.g., Abraham, Gen. 12:2–3), who sanctify the branches, that is, future Israel who, "if they do not persist in unbelief," will again "be grafted in" (v. 23). The metaphor of branches leads naturally in Paul's word to the Gentiles to the image of the wild olive shoot (Gentiles) that has been grafted to the "olive root" (Israel), a not altogether complimentary image for his Roman Gentile readers who are reminded, indirectly, to be thankful for their Jewish heritage since salvation comes from the Jews; Paul implies that they are not to be "arrogant" toward their Jewish fellow believers or to unbelieving Jews in general simply because the majority has been "broken off because of unbelief," but are to "be afraid" (v. 20). This complements the sense of security the believer has in knowledge of God's absolute sovereign plan with a call to decisive responsibility, on the order of Philippians 2:12–13 where sovereignty and responsibility are similarly intertwined and where the whole unit of meaning (Phil. 2:1–18) is concerned with humble service toward the other, in contrast to an arrogant spirit. So here, Paul warns his Gentile friends at Rome that if God did not spare the natural branches, "he will not spare you either" (v. 21), a strong appeal for humble faith, for God's nature is complementary in "kindness and sternness": sternness to the Jews who have rejected Christ (who fell), kindness to Gentile believers, "provided that you continue in his kindness" (another appeal to human responsibility: "Otherwise, you also will be cut off" [v. 22]). This is a severe warning that if Gentile arrogance persists they may suffer a great reversal, as have the Jews, who, "if they do not persist in unbelief [and Paul is confident they will not] will be grafted in," for "God is able" (v. 23), a combination of responsibility and sovereignty. In putting the Gentile believers in their place, Paul concludes by reminding them "how much more readily" the Jews (the natural branches) will "be grafted into their own olive tree" than, as is now the case contrary to nature, branches "cut out of an olive tree that is wild by nature" (the Gentiles; v. 24) can be grafted into a cultivated olive tree.

But Paul is not yet through dealing with Gentile Christian conceit in Rome, as he attests in the next unit (vv. 25–32) which sums up the entire argument of 9:1–11:24. That they "may not be conceited" (v. 25), he apprises them of the mystery of God's eschatological age now in process of unfolding (discernible in Old Testament prophecies but now made clear in Christ, 16:25–26; Eph. 1:9) that the hardening of Israel (combined elements of God's absolute decree and Israel's responsibility) will endure until the full number of the Gentiles "has come in"; that is, the completed number of elect from the Gentile world as a whole which will signal the end of the mission to the Gentiles, a mission that has been an act of grace on God's part and should preent the Gentile Christians at Rome from feeling superior, for the Jews' turn as God's elect is coming. In this way (and so) the completion of the remnant will take place as all the elect of Israel (all Israel; cf. 5:18; 11:32; 1 Kings 12:1; Dan. 9:11) will be saved. No temporal or quantitative signals are given by Paul as to when this is to take place or how many from Israel are to be saved; rather his point is the qualitative grace of God both to Gentiles and Jews so that the elect of each group reach their fullness in God's good time (11:25–26 = 11:12, where "fullness" is the key word). The return of Israel at the end of the age, which Paul describes as "their fullness" in 11:12, still comprises only a remnant (9:27; Isa. 10:22) of the total number over the ages; hence, "all Israel" must be construed as the full number of the elect from Israel which will be brought to completion after the full number of Gentiles has been completed, without any precise indication of the numbers involved. Paul paraphrases Isaiah 59:20–21, combined with 27:9, to indicate that the Old Testament prophecy has been set in motion in Christ (the deliverer, v. 26) who "will turn godlessness away from Jacob." Paul focuses on the aspect of God's absolute decree to bring this to pass, but he would also be subsidiarily aware of the context of Isaiah 59:20, where the focus is upon the responsible repentance of Israel ("The Redeemer will come to Zion, to those in Jacob who repent of their sins"). Hence in the larger context Paul would have in mind the return of Israel at the end of the age by the decree of God working through the responsible repentance of Israel.

In verses 28–32 Paul sums up the logically odd but true-to-life turn of events that one would not have anticipated, namely, that the favored and elect people have defaulted in faith by rejecting Christ, but God, sovereign in his ability to turn an evil into a compound good, has by this Jewish default shown mercy to the Gentiles. Yet God has not forsaken the Jews, even though they are enemies as regards Christ and Gentile salvation, but by election they are loved by God because of the promises he made to the "patriarchs," his "gifts and his call" being "irrevocable" (vv. 28–29). Accordingly, Gentile Christians need to recognize the double reversal (or double sine wave) in God's plan for the ages: they "were at one time disobedient" but have now received mercy by the disobedience of the Jews, while the Jews in turn "have now become disobedient in order that they too may now receive mercy as a result of God's mercy to you" (vv. 30–31). The parallel correspondence between verse 30 and verse 31 gives a leveling effect to Gentile and Jew respectively: "you/they; at one time/now; disobedient to God/disobedient; now/now; received mercy/receive mercy; as a result of their disobedience/as a result of God's mercy to you." This leveling prepares Paul's readers for his summary statement in 11:32 which describes God's eschatology of grace and parallels for Gentile and Jew the frustration/hope motif of 8:20; for the frustration there to which creation is subjected is here seen to lie in human disobedience to which all are bound over, while on the other hand the hope of 8:20 is here seen to lie in God's final mercy on all. ("All," in each case, is to be understood in the sense of generic groups, not every specific individual; it is more a qualitative than a quantitative term—that is, "how much more" glorious is the mercy of God than human rebellion that brings death, as we have already seen in light of Paul's use of "all" elsewhere [e.g., 5:18; so also 1 Cor. 15:22; 1 Tim. 2:4], which, when compared with the warning passages in Paul, are not to be interpreted as support for a doctrine of universalism.)

Paul has composed the large section 8:20–11:32 as an answer to the question of evil and suffering in the world and the problem of the role of God's chosen people, the Jews. In his concluding doxology he gives evidence that he has received visionary insight into the overall scheme of God's salvation, and, in view of God's mercy, can only break into a hymn of praise, the Christian's reversal of the role of unbelievers who, though from the beginning they "knew God, they neither glorified him as God nor gave thanks to him" (1:21; cf. 1 Cor. 1:20–21). So Paul comes full circle from the fall as he glorifies God and in effect thanks him for his deeply rich wisdom and knowledge (cf. 1 Cor. 1:24; Col. 2:3; Rev. 5:12) and unsearchable judgments that are beyond the ken of humans to trace out (v. 33). Insofar as Paul gives a final answer to the problems of suffering and evil and the destinies of human beings it lies here in praise of God's unfathomable mind which no one has known, for no human being has been his counselor or "has ever given to God, that God should repay him" (vv. 34–35). That is to say, as Paul does in verse 36, that the believer can give God the glory forever because God is in control of all things which are ultimately from him and through him and to him (Paul sees this as the personal activity and ultimacy of the divine family [cf. 1 Cor. 8:6; Col. 1:16–17], not as some impersonal force of nature, as in the pantheistic Stoicism of his day). Thus it is clear that Paul believes in the absolute God who controls the course of history and will faithfully bring it to an ultimate conclusion in salvation and judgment. The Amen is a fitting conclusion to a joyous doxology. The section 8:18–11:36 ends as it begins with a sharp focus on the sovereign God of history who is absolute, while the responsibility of Israel and Gentile Christians is momentarily eclipsed by such divine splendor. The sovereign God alone is at this point worthy of Paul's and his readers' attention. There should therefore be an appropriate pause after the Amen.

V. Prescription: Faithful Servants in Action (12:1–15:13)

Having given attention to the large sweep of the course of history from God's absolute vantage point, Paul now devotes a large section to prescribing the suitable response of Christians at Rome (and generally) in working out the practical implications of their calling as eschatological people in the family of God. Paul's focus now shifts to Christian responsibility, while the theme of God's sovereignty momentarily becomes subsidiary and functions as a tacit component in the subject at hand. The transitional phrase *in view of God's mercy* (12:1) links the previous section on divine sovereignty and the present unit on Christian behavior, for on this alone hangs the "therefore" of the exhortation, "I urge you, brothers."

The key to this hortatory passage is to be found in verse 2 and the phrase *but be transformed by the renewing of your mind.* It should be noted that the redemption of the believing community is in process (as is the case in chaps. 5–11), for the transformation or metamorphosis ("be transformed," *metamorphousthe*) of the mind of Paul's readers needs completion and must be evidenced in consistent Christian behavior. This implies that they are still in some sense worldly and accordingly must be exhorted not to be "schematized" (*mē suschēmatizesthe*) to this present age. The underlying assumption is that this redemptive metamorphosis of mind has been inaugurated in them by "God's mercy" (v. 1) so that they "will be able to test and approve what God's will is—his good, pleasing and perfect will." Their transformed minds will prove the will of God in eight ways.

A. In sacrificial worship (12:1–2). By "your bodies" Paul means the total self, as in Philippians 1:20 and Ephesians 5:28. The word *sōma* (body = self) also bears this connotation on occasion in the Hellenistic Greek of Paul's day. In urging his readers to "offer" their lives to God Paul exhorts them to place themselves at his disposal, for they are his property as much as were the sacrifices in Old Testament worship, and the sacrifices are to be continually repeated as living, holy, and "pleasing to God" in free and personal surrender. This constitutes spiritual worship, or better, the "logical" (*logikēn*) action of worshiping, that requires a conscious, rational, thoughtful, and intelligent offering of the self in daily sanctification that is in God's sight pleasing (cf. the word in v. 2; 14:18; 2 Cor. 5:9; Eph. 5:10; and Jesus' exemplary saying in John 8:29, "I always do what pleases him").

B. In humble use of gifts within the body (12:3–8). By the gracious work of Christ individual believers have been fashioned into an essential many-in-oneness on the analogy of the human body (v. 4, which images ultimately the one-in-manyness of the triune society of Father, Son, and Holy Spirit), so that "in Christ we who are many form one body, and each member belongs to all the others" (v. 5). This important societal theme and its implications for the harmonious interrelationship of Christians (it appears again in 1 Cor. 12:1–31 and Eph. 4:15–16) forms the basis of Paul's appeal to every one (12:4) of his Roman readers and affords a confirming clue as to the nature of the problem at Rome: "Do not think of yourself more highly than you ought" (v. 3). This accords with our interpretation of the previous chapters of the letter where friction between Jewish and Gentile Christians at Rome compels the apostle to contrast the sacrificial nature of divine grace with human pride. (The problem is not limited to the Romans but is evident in the factionalism and pride of the Corinthian church, and is evident even among the Philippians, whom Paul counsels to have the attitude of Christ Jesus and "do nothing out of selfish ambition or vain conceit" [Phil. 2:3]). Paul's argument is that God by his sovereign grace has made a varied distribution of gifts so that the many members of the one body "do not all have the same function" (v. 4). Some members do indeed have superior gifts, but the implication of the passage is that the sober judgment each should exercise "in accordance with the measure of faith God has given you" (v. 3) implies a recognition of equality in unity and that the gifts are for serving others. A servantlike attitude of disposability is what Paul is urging, in contrast to a prideful flaunting of one's superior gifts. The measure of faith would suggest a divinely given sense of propriety that whatever the gift one must use it for the good of the body, and he who is given the greater gift must be the greater servant.

As with the Corinthians, Paul now follows his teaching on divine gifting (1 Cor. 12; Rom. 12:4–8) with a passage on the proper attitude required in the expression of the gifts, namely love (1 Cor. 13; Rom. 12:9–13).

C. In loving acts of service and hospitality (12:9–13). This whole unit resonates with the theme of disposability as Paul exhorts the Romans to manifest love that is "sincere" (lit. unhypocritical), the opposite of showy and counterfeit superficiality, in serving the Lord with unflagging zeal and spiritual fervor (that comes from being "aglow with the Spirit" [v. 11 RSV]), and being "joyful" in Christian hope, patient in suffering, and "faithful in prayer" (v. 12), as they place themselves both at God's disposal and at the disposal of one another through devoted hospitality (v. 13). These identifying characteristics of Christian disposability are eminently personified in Jesus himself, whom Paul clearly has in mind as the one who gave himself for sinners and whose exemplary hospitality the Christian is to follow. That this is the case is clear as Paul continues his list of exhortations in a manner that echoes the teaching of Jesus himself in the Gospel tradition.

D. In imitation of Jesus' teaching (12:14–21). This passage images the Lord's teaching in the Sermon on the Mount and his work of redemption on the cross and gives evidence of Paul's continuity with the ministry of Jesus. Paul's counsel that his readers are to bless and not curse (v. 14) and are not to "take revenge" (v. 19) echoes Matthew 5:43–48 and the intent of the Sermon expressed in Matthew 5:20 that the believer's righteousness must surpass that of religious hypocrites. Preaching and living out the gospel do however bring God's justice along with his grace, as is indicated in Romans 1:17–18, but it is not proper for Christians to be judgmental because they are called primarily to be servants of others (including non-Christians), to rejoice with the happy and mourn with the sad, to be humble and harmonious and not to be above serving those of "low position" (vv. 15–16), and so reflect the gracious ministry of the Lord Jesus; and because they lack the proper perspective in this present age for making final judgmental pronouncements and executing divine wrath (v. 19), which only God can do. Paul does not mean that Christians are to wink at evil or not discern another's need for repentance and renewal; indeed, the apostle has been making moral judgments all along in exhorting his readers to the very kind of Christian living expressed in this chapter, and he encourages them to do the same in their relationships with others by returning good for bad and thereby searing the conscience of the offender and leading him to repentance (the likely meaning of the image of burning coals, a quotation from Prov. 25:21–22 [LXX], where the action receives a reward from the Lord; cf. 1 Thess. 5:15; 1 Pet. 3:9). Since the context of Paul's exhortation (12:17–21) indicates an absolutely upright intention in not returning evil for evil, but in doing "what is right," and living at peace with everyone as far as it is possible, it is out of the question to interpret the metaphor of burning coals as a sly way of really getting even with an enemy, for that would be to allow evil to overcome the Christian, when in fact the believer is to manifest Christ-like hospitality toward an enemy in hope that divine grace working through the believer will win him over as a friend and thereby overcome evil with good (v. 21). It must be pointed out, however, that as was the case with Jesus in his ministry, one cannot take Christian hospitality for granted, for if willfully refused it will bring the wrath of God, who "will repay" (v. 19; Deut. 32:35; cf. Lev. 19:18), for the gracious disposability of Christ and his followers does not cancel out the righteous wrath of God but offers a way by which one may escape it. Yet in keeping with Jesus' emphasis and that of Romans 1:16–17 Paul consistently urges his Christian readers to concentrate on being servants of Christ and the gospel for the salvation and welfare of others, not on standing in judgment of them. God alone has the proper perspective to do the perfectly right thing in such cases.

E. In rendering to Caesar what is Caesar's (13:1–7). This unit of instruction should be understood in the same way as the preceding instructions: Christians are not called to stand in judgment of others but as far as possible are to live in peace with everyone (12:18), and must not be found guilty of infractions of the law or insubordination to the divinely instituted order of government. Paul is focusing here on the positive side of the state, like Peter who also emphasizes the servantlike attitude of the Christian who must not misuse his Christian freedom and bring reproach upon the gospel but rather show by respectful behavior the love and brotherhood of the Christian community (1 Pet. 2:13–17). Moreover, in 1 Timothy 2:1–7 Paul requests prayers and thanksgiving for kings and those in authority that they, with others, may be saved and come to a knowledge of the truth.

Accordingly, Paul's exhortation in 13:1–7 may be seen to fall within the context of his missionary appeal in the letter. He sees the state as a gift of God's common grace to guarantee civil order and to restrain uncontrolled evil (the ruler "is God's servant to do you good" [v. 4]; cf. 2 Thess. 2:6–7, where the final eschatological eruption of rebellion by the "man of lawlessness" is being held back by "that which" and "he who" now restrains, very likely, respectively, human government and the Holy Spirit behind state structures). The Christian therefore must not be caught short by rebelling against those very governmental authorities that make it possible for the gospel to be carried throughout the empire. In the back of Paul's mind is his appreciation of Rome's legal and commercial system of roads, sea-lanes, citizenship, and common Greek language that promote the spread of Christianity and are ingredients in this right moment in history ("when the time had fully come" [Gal. 4:4]).

Elsewhere in Scripture the believer is enjoined to disobey authorities where they demand a denial of the Lord (e.g., Daniel and his three friends [Dan. 3, 6]; Peter and John [Acts 4:19–20]; and Jesus himself in his disregard for Sabbath laws and refusal to reply to official questioning [Luke 23:8–9]). Furthermore, Paul himself describes the power of the state as provisional in 1 Corinthians 6:1–6, and Revelation 13 characterizes Rome as the demonic beast from the abyss. Paul is aware of these negative and complementary aspects of human government but focuses here on the issue of respect for instituted authority as a necessary precondition for the Christian mission, centering in 13:6–7 on the dominical authority of Jesus: "Give everyone what you owe him" (Matt. 22:21), for "the authorities are God's servants" because "God is sovereign over the kingdoms of men and sets over them anyone he wishes" (Dan. 5:21; see also 2 Sam. 12:7–8; Isa. 45:1–13; Jer. 27:5–7; Dan. 2:21, 37–38; 4:17, 25, 32). It is in this sense that Paul exhorts his readers to "submit to the governing authorities" (vv. 1, 5). Insofar as human authorities are the servants of God and provide a basis for order and the mission of the church, being indirectly at the disposal of God for the carrying on of his work, Christians are to respond in cooperative servanthood. That is the meaning of submission in this unit which carries on the theme of disposability in the previous exhortations of chapter 12 and in what follows through 15:13.

F. In loving one's neighbor as oneself (13:8–10). Everything Paul has been saying reflects the teaching and person of Jesus, and this section no less so, for the declaration that "love is the fulfillment of the law" (13:10b) is parallel to 10:4, "Christ is the end [goal, fulfillment] of the law," since it is in the act of disposability on behalf of others that Christ is seen to be the personification of love and the fulfillment of the law, a theme that is implicit in Jesus' teaching (Matt. 22:39; Luke 10:27; cf. Lev. 19:18) and forms the basis of Paul's teaching here. Hence the only outstanding debt a Christian should have is "the continuing debt to love one another" (v. 8). The negative prohibitions of the law against adultery, murder, stealing, and coveting (v. 9 = the second table of the Mosaic Decalogue [Exod. 20:13–17]) are cast in a positive light by Paul's profound and simple declaration, "Love does no harm to its neighbor" (v. 10a). Where the forbidden actions destroy relations with family and neighbor, love, personified by Christ, draws the hurt and the harmed into a wider family and is constructive, not destructive, in its power. Several striking literary structures of the Greek in 13:10 capture the eye: The chiastic arrangement with *agapē* in first and last positions, and "not doing harm to neighbor" (= doing good to neighbor) positioned in the center next to its definition as "the fulfillment of the law." The absence of the first table of the law in this section and Jesus' summary of the first and greatest commandment (love of God, Exod. 20:2–11; Deut. 6:5; Matt. 22:37–38; Luke 10:27) may be explained by observing that Christ as personified love is the presupposition of this passage, as may be borne out by running in parallel the two unusually similar clauses, 13:10b and 10:4:

13:10b Therefore the fulfillment of the law is love
10:4 For the completion of the law is Christ

In this connection we should also compare the use of the terms *fulfill, goal,* and *completion* in Matthew 5:17 and 1 Timothy 1:5. Accordingly, the teaching, work, and person of Jesus continue to be tacitly present in Paul's practical prescriptions for his readers, as is the case in the next section.

G. In living as in the Day, not in darkness (13:11–14). It is conjectural to re-create the situation at Rome that Paul is addressing, but his strictures on questionable behavior (vv. 12b–13) may realistically reflect the tendencies of some in the community, particularly Gentiles, who may still be carrying on some of their old worldly patterns and not taking seriously enough the urgency of the present eschatological day that is dawning. Paul addresses them directly: "do this, wake up, clothe yourselves with the Lord Jesus Christ" (vv. 11, 14). The Romans, like other Christians, are "on the way" in bringing their behavior into conformity with their new nature in Christ and are still subject to "the desires of the sinful nature" (v. 14), as we have seen in Paul's earlier exhortations in chapters 6–8.

Again the teaching of Jesus, this time on the

urgency of decision in this last crucial eschatological hour and day, forms the background of Paul's appeal. Jesus calls for alertness and watchfulness (Matt. 25:31–46; Mark 13:33–37) and stands in the great prophetic tradition that urges vigilance and faithfulness in view of God's "round," sudden, and unexpected activity on behalf of his people and his judgment of evil (Isa. 2:12; 9:2; Dan. 8:17, 19; 11:35). Paul elsewhere urges moral faithfulness and propriety on the eschatological grounds of the imminent day of the Lord (Phil. 4:4–7; 1 Thess. 5:1–11, 23), as do other New Testament writers (Heb. 10:24–25; James 5:7–11; 1 Pet. 4:7–11). Suitable as attire and deportment for the Christian in this inaugurated day are the armor of light (v. 12), which reflects Christ who is "the light of the world" and "the light of life" (John 8:12; cf. Matt. 5:14–16; for the image of armor cf. 2 Cor. 6:7; 10:4; Eph. 6:11, 13; 1 Thess. 5:8); decent behavior (v. 13)—behaving honorably by living a Christ-like life (compare the positive meaning here of *schēma* with being "schematized" to the age [12:2]); clothing "yourselves with the Lord Jesus Christ" (v. 14). Believers have already clothed themselves with Christ by being baptized into him (Gal. 3:27), which signals their new essence in Christ; but they must express this in practice (existentially) as they stand into each new moment of decision. Thus Paul commands them not to follow the uncovenanted practices of "orgies, drunkenness, sexual immorality, debauchery, dissension, jealousy," which are destructively centered on the rebellious self. Christians must choose not to follow the urgings of their old sinful nature or essence that is doomed, but to follow Christ who has given them a new nature of hope. In so doing the transformed mind proves the will of God (12:2).

H. In pursuing peace between weak and strong (14:1–15:13). Paul continues his application of the ethic of Christ-like descent in servanthood to those believers who may be offended by the freedom of the spiritually strong. In this section (**14:1–12**) he addresses both strong and weak Christians at Rome and encourages them to agree on the essentials of faith but to consider differences regarding eating of meat and Sabbath observance (literal obedience to Old Testament legal ceremonies) as matters of individual conscience and therefore unessential to salvation (technically called *adiaphora*). This was a common problem in the churches and is referred to in Paul's correspondence to Corinth and Colossae (e.g., 1 Cor. 8:1–10:33; Col. 2:16–23; it may also secondarily reflect the religious practice of abstention popular in some philosophies and religions of the Graeco-Roman world). His advice in this passage provides further insight into the friction at Rome as he calls on the factions of freedom and formalism to respect each other in a manner consistent with the spirit of disposability that one sees in Christ himself. The key to Paul's appeal in the larger sense unit is found in 15:3, "For even Christ did not please himself." Accordingly, Christians are not to please themselves but their neighbor for his good, to "build him up" in the faith (15:1–2). The result will be a "spirit of unity" in the body of Christ where peace and joy in the Holy Spirit characterize the social nature of the church in all its variety (14:17; 15:5, 13).

In 14:1–12 Paul strongly warns against passing judgment (vv. 1, 3–4, 10–12) on one "whose faith is weak" (i.e., who lacks the maturity to distinguish between essential and nonessential matters), as long as he is fully convinced in his own mind (v. 5) and gives thanks to the Lord like the stronger believer in his own way (v. 6). The key is the lordship of Christ; Christ takes precedence over all and will do the final judging properly, as each "will give an account of himself to God" (vv. 8–12). Paul's admonition not to be judgmental applies the theme of 12:17–21 to the circle of Christian fellowship.

Paul further develops his argument on Christian freedom and nonessentials (**14:13–23**). In the Lord he is convinced that "no food is unclean in itself" (v. 14a). This is a radical teaching that characterizes the new eschatological age inaugurated in Jesus and flows from the Lord's teaching in Mark 7:1–23 that what comes from inside a person, not external things, defiles. However, if a Christian is free of deceit in holding something external to be unclean, has no doubts about it, and faithfully observes this in his personal relationship with God, "then for him it is unclean" (vv. 14b, 22–23). Therefore the stronger Christian who knows that God has declared all things clean (as Paul himself believes [vv. 14a, 20]) must not use his freedom, which allows him to eat what were formerly ceremonially unclean foods, to trip up his weaker brother who still has scruples about eating such foods. Being at the disposal of another Christian to help him or her along to maturity is more important than exercising one's "rights" as a free and mature Christian. Food (or any other item or practice in question) should not destroy the work of God (v. 20); hence Paul's plea for disposability on the part of his readers that they "make every effort to do what leads to peace and to mutual edification" (v. 19), since Christ's redemptive work is social in nature and calls for mutual hospitality and understanding.

The problem Paul is dealing with in the entire unit of 14:1–15:13 seems to be a continuation of the Jewish/Gentile question that he has tactfully and prophetically dealt with in 9:1–11:36. There we detected a certain superior attitude on the part of Gentiles over Jews that Paul warns against in view of God's inscrutable and wonderful plan of redemption which includes both at the close of the age.

Here (**15:1–13**) we see again the superior air of Gentile Christians at Rome as they flaunt their new-found freedom in Christ and look down on the ceremonial scruples of their Jewish Christian brothers and sisters. While Paul theologically sides with the Gentiles as "we who are strong" (15:1) in respect to freedom in Christ, as a Jewish Christian he is deeply aware of God's love for his patriarchal people and again places Gentile Christians in a position of dependency upon and gratitude for the Jewish heritage, reminding them that "Christ has become a servant of the Jews on behalf of God's truth, to confirm the promises made to the patriarchs so that the Gentiles may glorify God for his mercy" (15:8–9). Paul is not questioning the rightness of the Gentile Christian view on freedom in Christ, but rather their prideful attitude and unconcern for the feelings of their Jewish Christian friends at Rome.

On their part the Jewish Christians need to honor the integrity of those who do not observe dietary and Sabbath ceremonies as they do. It is a private matter of conscience. Most important is that both sides accept one another as Christ has accepted them, and so "bring praise to God" (15:7). Since the Jewish group in the church at Rome is simply trying to express its faith in worship and is not attempting to place God under obligation by ceremonial observance, the issue has none of the urgency of the Galatian situation where the latter was the goal of the Judaizers (Gal. 1:6–10; 3:1–5). Hence Paul can be gentle in his exhortation since the issue is not a fundamental one of essential doctrine.

But the problem is still serious. The irony is that those who are strong in their theoretical understanding of the freedom that comes from faith in Christ are themselves weak when it comes to having a Christ-like and loving spirit toward those brethren with whom they disagree. They are even in danger of destroying the weaker brother for whom Christ died, and that must not be allowed to happen. It should be especially true of the strong that they evidence a spirit of generosity toward the weak and be at their disposal to help them mature in faith, just as the divine family has shown redeeming hospitality to the family of believers that they "may overflow with hope by the power of the Holy Spirit" (15:5–6, 13).

VI. Conclusion (15:14–16:27)

A. Paul's missionary purpose and reason for writing boldly (15:14–22). In order to understand the historical setting of Romans it is important to take Paul's beginning (1:1–15) and concluding (15:14–33) remarks on the purpose of his mission. All of the previous comments on the contents of the letter/epistle have been informed by the apostle himself, who discloses his intention by way of a complex but thoroughly integrated missionary agenda that can be reduced to one word: servanthood. Throughout the commentary other terms (e.g., disposability, hospitality) have described this, but essentially what Paul is spelling out in 15:14–33 is already contained in 1:1 when he introduces himself as Paul, a servant. Paul's servanthood is Christ-centered and social in nature as he emulates the sociality of the divine triunity of Father, Son, and Holy Spirit (1:1–4) by embracing the Romans in the family circle of sainthood (1:5–15), encouraging them to understand the deep doctrinal truths about their salvation and unity in Christ and to realize these truths in their behavior (1:16–15:13), and finally proceeding to enlist them in prayerful support of his mission to Jerusalem with a love gift, his projected visit to them, and his preaching mission to Spain (15:23–33).

Paul has no other purpose in writing as he has to the Romans than to see that they become "an offering acceptable to God, sanctified by the Holy Spirit" (v. 16) and that they "obey God" (v. 18), by which he means not only personal and social holiness at Rome but participation in the worldwide mission of proclaiming Christ to the Gentiles, a work to which he himself is personally and totally committed. (His powerful statement in vv. 17–22 seems to claim fulfillment in his own life of Jesus' prophecy of expanding mission, beginning from Jerusalem [Acts 1:8; cf. Isa. 2:1–4; 52:15].) As a minister of Christ Jesus with a "priestly duty" (v. 16) he has not hesitated to write "quite boldly" to the Romans on some issues (v. 15), confident that their essential goodness and knowledge as believers will guarantee their competence to counsel and instruct one another "nouthetically" (*nouthetein*) on the matters about which he has written. All his doctrinal and ethical teaching in the letter now comes to one focus: To get the message out to the world. Romans is properly understood when it is seen, in light of Paul's stated intention, to be a quintessential missionary document, a fact that is borne out even more clearly in the next section.

B. His missionary agenda for Jerusalem, Rome, and Spain (15:23–33). In each of his three missions projects Paul calls upon the Romans to participate in some substantial way, assuming that his letter will have its desired effect in uniting them behind the greater missionary effort. First he discloses that in view of his completed work in the east and his long-standing desire to visit them, he hopes to have them assist him in his journey to Spain after he has enjoyed their company for a while (vv. 23–24). Before he does so, he must finish another project by taking the offering from Macedonia and Achaia to the poor among the saints in Jerusalem (vv. 25–27; note the material gratitude of Gentile toward Jew, since the former became Christians through the spiritual generosity of the latter). But this is a dangerous mission and Paul invokes the triune family in urging the believing family at Rome "to join" him in his "struggle by praying" that he may be delivered from the unbelievers in Judea and that his service to the Jerusalem family of saints may be acceptable, so that he may come to the Roman family with joy and "together with you be refreshed" (vv. 30–32). The social nature of the mission is impressive, as one individual, Paul, counts himself a member of three concentric and potential family circles (Rome, Jerusalem, Spain) which he hopes to bring to realization in person through the divine will of the first family in whose circle all believers are children. This may then be the significance of the blessing in verse 33 as Paul prays that the reconciling God of peace be with them (for the Old Testament background, see, e.g., Lev. 26:6; Num. 6:26; Isa. 26:12; and for a similar position in advance of the end of a letter, Phil. 4:9).

Of course as it turned out it was not God's will (v. 32), in the ultimate decretive sense, that all Paul's prayers were answered as he requested, for he was not rescued from unbelievers in Judea and he did not travel as he had planned to Rome, nor do we know whether he ever got to Spain. Yet Paul was used to the irony of divine working, as Romans 9–11 attests, and would not have been surprised at the unexpected "roundness" of God in sending him to Rome in a rather different way than he had planned, and indeed (as it turned out) for a wider mission in Rome itself. From the Philippians prison epistle (1:12–14) we learn about Paul's mission in Rome; Paul informs his readers of his opportunities for witness among the Roman guard and of the effect of his imprisonment ministry which has encouraged the Roman believers to be "much more bold to speak the word of God without fear." We may also assume that the love gift to the poor believers in Jerusalem was gratefully accepted; and it is possible that 1 Clement 5:7 infers a mission of the apostle to Spain, though we cannot be certain. Whatever the case, the social nature of salvation and Paul's mission are unmistakable as he claims circle after circle of present believers and potential believers for the sake of the divine family that has made the great homecoming possible. Flowing out of the past event of Christ's saving work in the cross and resurrection and sustained in the present by the power of the Holy Spirit, Paul's surging faith has a forward momentum that overflows with hope (see 15:13) in what God will do.

Accordingly, the letter fittingly ends with a personal tribute to those friends and fellow workers at Rome whom he has come to know over the years from their journeys to and fro and who have labored together with him in the mission of the gospel.

C. His final greetings, warnings, and doxology (16:1–27). It has been argued by some scholars that Romans 16 has been added to the letter and really is a fragment from another of Paul's letters to the Ephesian church, since it seems curious that Paul would greet so many people in a church he has never visited, and since a third-century manuscript closes with the doxology at 15:33. Arguments in favor of the integrity of chapter 16 are more substantial, however, as the majority of manuscript tradition contains it as well as the connective particle *de*, "and," which joins the list (**16:1–16**) naturally with the previous passage. It is not difficult to imagine these friends of Paul moving back and forth in the pulsating commercial world of Rome as fellow tentmakers in the mission of the gospel. Moreover, Paul never gives long lists of names in letters written to churches he has founded, for fear, perhaps, of leaving someone out. Here it is appropriate as a point of contact and recognition, as he already feels he knows a good deal about the church at Rome through these twenty-nine men and women whose labors for the gospel he has deeply appreciated and who have doubtless informed him of the situation at Rome, both good and bad. (The list thus becomes, indirectly, evidence of the strongest kind that Paul knows the problems at Rome intimately and is addressing them forthrightly throughout the letter, as has been assumed in the preceding comments.)

It is significant that nine of these co-laborers are women (ten, if Junia[s], v. 7, is a woman, as many believe), making one-third of the total list a tribute to women in ministry and mission of one kind or another. This invites the careful interpreter to compare other Pauline passages in which women are enjoined to silence or to primarily domestic roles that are subordinate. The evidence of this list together with the presence of women in Jesus' circles of fellowship and witness and in the Book of Acts commends careful consideration. Whatever one's conclusions may be on this difficult matter (evangelicals are divided on the issue), two issues need to be considered.

Phoebe is first in the list, all the more striking as her name indicates a Gentile believer whom the Jewish Paul commends as "our sister" in the family of God (close and small Paul puts into practice what he has been calling upon the larger Roman church to do; Phoebe may accordingly be given pride of place in the list for this reason and chosen, as is likely, to bear the letter to Rome and therefore to be received "in a way worthy of the saints" [v. 2]). She is evidently a woman of some social prominence and wealth who has been "a great help" to Paul and others, and is a deacon (*diakonon;* NIV servant) of the church at the Corinthian seaport of Cenchrea (is she only a servant or does she hold the office of deacon? See Phil. 1:1; 1 Tim. 3:11 and the alternate translation of "deaconesses" or "women helpers").

It is also worthy of note that the married couple Priscilla and Aquila (v. 3) work together as a team (her name is mentioned first, as it is also in Acts 18:18–19, 26; 2 Tim. 4:19; but not in 1 Cor. 16:19), and have "risked their lives" for Paul as servants at his disposal. The verb used of Mary's labor (v. 6, *kopiaō,* "who worked very hard for you"), is also used of those who labor in the Lord's work (e.g., 1 Cor. 4:12; 16:16; cf. 1 Tim. 5:17; and of the three women mentioned in Rom. 16:12). Some have strongly urged (see esp. C. E. B. Cranfield) that Junias (v. 7) be rendered Junia (feminine) since the gender of the Greek accusative is determined only by the accent, and there is no other occurrence of the masculine name in extant literature of the day. The conjecture would be that Andronicus and Junia were husband and wife, esteemed as "outstanding among the apostles." Whether that is true or not, the entire list of names taken together gives the reader a sense of unity in diversity within the family of believers at Rome, ranging from the privileged to those with names of slaves (Ampliatus, v. 8; Urbanus, v. 9), husbands and wives (possibly also Philologus and Julia, v. 15), women and men, Gentiles and Jews (though Gentiles predominate). The social unity and the universal acceptance of the Christians at Rome by Paul and all the churches of Christ is to be confirmed with a holy kiss (v. 16), the seal of approval typical of greeting in the East and in the churches of Paul (1 Cor. 16:20; 1 Thess. 5:26; cf. the "kiss of love" in 1 Pet. 5:14). The unity in Christ Paul has been arguing for throughout the letter is strikingly demonstrated by Paul's cohesive list of co-workers, drawn from many walks of life. It represents a cross-section of the church at large and the unifying servanthood that characterizes those who have been redeemed by the servanthood of Christ and are eager to share the good news with others.

Contrasted with these generous, hospitable people, however, is a subversive and smooth-talking group of false teachers about whom Paul now warns his Roman readers (**16:17–20**).

Earlier (1:16–18) Paul has argued that the gospel reveals not only the righteousness of God to those who respond in faith, but also the wrath of God against all who suppress the truth. It is in keeping therefore with the double effect of the gospel that Paul should follow his remarks on the gracious effects of righteousness, peace, and unity within the believing family with a warning about the "divisions" and "obstacles" that faithless deceivers create among "naive people" by "smooth talk and flattery" (vv. 17–18). Paul is confident of the obedience of his Roman friends and is "full of joy" over them, but just to make certain that they know what is at stake he appears to claim dominical warrant from Jesus and admonishes them "to be wise about what is good, and innocent about what is evil" (v. 19), a paraphrase of Matthew 10:16, "Therefore be as shrewd as snakes and as innocent as doves," a context in which Jesus is sending out his disciples "like sheep among wolves." The figure and the warning are apt, for Paul knows that the enemies of the gospel are everywhere, often posing as enlightened teachers within the church, and that some hard battles may have to be fought, as Paul well knows from personal experience, that will cause divisions within one's own household (as Jesus in the larger context of his teaching intimates [Matt. 10:32–39]). Whether there was an immediate threat from false teachers that came to Paul's attention as he was bringing his letter to conclusion can only be conjectured. More likely false teachers are a constant threat wherever he goes and simply come to mind as an antithetic contrast to peace and harmony, in the Hebraic parallelism characteristic of his thought, as happens suddenly in Philippians 3:1–2, 17–18, and again between chapters 9 and 10 of 2 Corinthians (although in the latter case he probably has received more bad news from Corinth after finishing chap. 9). Paul's reference to their serving not our Lord Christ, but their own appetites (Rom. 16:18; lit. their own belly) may refer to the "strong" who insist on eating meat even if it destroys the "weak" (14:1–15:13), to greedy exploiters (2 Cor. 11:20), to the circumcision group (Titus 1:10–11), or to abusive Gnostics who indulge the body to prove its uselessness (Phil. 3:19). In any event they fall under the general category of those who have their minds set on the desires of the sinful nature (Rom. 8:4–5).

Paul insists that the cognitive content of sound doctrinal teaching which his readers "have learned" (v. 17; both from him and his trustworthy predecessors) is what they are to hold on to. The gospel will not be kept pure and powerful by relying only on warm and emotional holy kisses, but by juxtaposing the God of peace with the God who "will soon crush Satan under your feet" (a reference to the Heb. text of Gen. 3:15; cf. Ps. 91:13; Luke 10:18–20; 2 Cor. 11:13–15). This last prophecy likely goes beyond the immediate threat of false teachers, however, as Paul envisions the full and final defeat of Satan in God's good time (soon = swiftly, surely). Accordingly, verse 20 could stand by itself (so NIV), though it is probably better to take it as a prophecy that flows confidently out of the previous warning. To the word of peace Paul adds the grace of our Lord Jesus (v. 20b), likely his subscription in his own hand. In fact, in light of the structure of 1 Corinthians 16:20–22, where the greeting with "a holy kiss" (v. 20) is followed by a curse on "anyone who does not love the Lord" and a prophecy/prayer, "Come, O Lord!" (v. 22), with the apostle saying, "I, Paul, write this greeting in my own hand" (v. 21), it is quite possible that Paul has taken pen in hand to write the whole unit of Romans 16:17–20.

Paul's final urgent warning (vv. 17–20) having been given, he resumes his list of salutations from verse 16 by conveying the greetings of his intimate associates (**16:21–23**), again impressing upon his readers the social nature of the family of God. Timothy he considers "my son whom I love, who is faithful in the Lord" (1 Cor. 4:17; cf. 2 Cor. 1:1; Phil. 2:19–24); "Lucius, Jason and Sosipater, my relatives" (or kinsmen [v. 21]) are three fellow countrymen who are with him at Corinth; Tertius, Paul's secretary or amanuensis who has written down the letter (v. 22), now includes himself in the circle; Gaius (v. 23) Paul mentions for his generous "hospitality," a distinctive mark of the Christian; Erastus, a high public official at Corinth, and Quartus, an unknown brother (v. 23), round out Paul's family of friends, all immortalized for their loyalty to the proclamation of Christ, to whom Paul now directs his final doxology (vv. 25–27; v. 24, see fn. in NIV, is not attested in the best MSS and should not be read).

The reader of this commentary is directed to discussions in more exhaustive commentaries on the history of interpretation of this concluding doxology (**16:25–27**). Suffice it to say that its content reflects the fundamental themes of Romans: "to him who is able to establish you" (v. 25) and "by the command of the eternal God" (v. 26) invoke the sovereign God who is able to work all things according to his will, a pivotal theme throughout the letter; "my gospel and the proclamation of Jesus Christ" refers the reader to the initial and central focus of 1:16; "the revelation of the mystery hidden for long ages past" carries the reader back to the mystery of 11:25; this is "now revealed and made known" through the prophetic writings (v. 26) in a way that Paul has tried to demonstrate by his use of the Old Testament and its fulfillment in Christ; to wit, "that all nations might believe and obey him," which is the disclosure of the mystery: God has included both Jew and Gentile in his redemptive grace.

That is what Romans, in a word, is all about. There is, therefore, no place for human boasting or claim of special privilege, for the divine family has paid the price for the redemption of a fallen world and grants no special favors on the basis of human heritage or works; all nations are invited to come to Christ, in whom there is no condemnation for those who believe and obey. A fitting conclusion to the letter/epistle, accordingly, is a soaring doxology: "to the only wise God be glory forever through Jesus Christ! Amen."

SELECT BIBLIOGRAPHY

Barrett, C. K. *A Commentary on the Epistle to the Romans.* New York: Harper, 1958.

Bruce, F. F. *The Epistle of Paul to the Romans.* Grand Rapids: Eerdmans, 1963.

Godet, F. *Commentary on the Epistle to the Romans.* Grand Rapids: Kregel, 1977.

Käsemann, E. *The Epistle to the Romans.* Grand Rapids: Eerdmans, 1980.

Murray, J. *The Epistle to the Romans.* 2 vols. Grand Rapids: Eerdmans, 1960, 1966.

1–2 CORINTHIANS

James A. Davis

INTRODUCTION

Among the letters of Paul, 1 and 2 Corinthians are perhaps most notable for their practical content and personal style. The first of these two features emerges as a consequence of the vital and often volatile nature of life in the church at Corinth. For it is certain that the practical questions which largely occupy the apostle in both epistles arise not at his initiative but rather at the insistence of his converts. It is in response to their circumstances and backgrounds that the practical and sometimes pointed counsel of these letters originates. The distinctly personal style of both is also largely, if not wholly, a product of the apostle's relationship to the church, and so, for that matter, are many of the stylistic peculiarities which have raised questions about the unity and integrity of 2 Corinthians. Thus it is incumbent upon the interpreter of these epistles to come to know, insofar as that is possible, the history of the circumstances which form the background to Paul's Corinthian correspondence.

The ancient history of the city of Corinth may, for the sake of convenience, be divided into four principal periods: the preclassical period (ca. 3500–1350 B.C.), the classical period (ca. 1350–338 B.C.), the Hellenistic period (338–146 B.C.), and the Roman period (146 B.C.–A.D. 395). For our purposes, we need concern ourselves with only a few of the major events in the last of these four historical periods. In 146 B.C. the ancient city of Corinth was burned to the ground by a Roman army for its participation and leadership in the rebellion of the Achaian League (a group composed of the principal city-states located in Achaia, the southern peninsula of Greece). At that time, many of the citizens of Corinth were either killed or sold into slavery, and for a century afterward the city lay derelict.

In the year 44 B.C., however, the city was refounded on the orders of Julius Caesar, who sought to redeem the strategic and economic potential of the site with a new colonial population made up of freedmen (manumitted Roman slaves), army veterans, and former residents. Because of its location, near the narrowest part of the isthmus connecting Macedonia (the northern mainland of Greece) and Achaia, and because of the hazards associated with sea travel, particularly in the winter, when the possibility of conveying cargo across the narrow isthmus must have appeared as an exceedingly attractive alternative, the city quickly regained its former prosperity, and under Augustus, in 27 B.C., it was made the capital of the senatorial province of Achaia.

Renowned for its metallurgists, who specialized in bronzework, and for its sponsorship of the biennial Isthmian games, which were second in popularity and prestige only to those of Olympia, the city rapidly attracted a variety of new residents, creating a cosmopolitan atmosphere dominated by economic stratification, cultural diversity, and religious pluralism. The reputation given to Corinth as an especially immoral place seems, however, to have been largely created by the envy of other Greek city-states, which attempted to buttress their slander by pointing to the presence of the cult of Aphrodite in Corinth as an indication of the low morals of the populace, grossly exaggerating both its size and its influence. The truth of the matter lies neither at this extreme, despite the repetition of such rumors in the literature of the time, nor at its opposite, but rather in the realization that Corinth was a large urban center, no richer or poorer in terms of morality than comparable cities either ancient or modern.

According to Acts 18:2, among the Jewish residents of Corinth in the middle of the first century A.D. were a husband and wife, Aquila, a native of Pontus (a Roman province in northeastern Asia Minor), and Priscilla (whose name suggests that she may have come from a Roman family). They had only recently come to Corinth as the result of a decree issued by the Roman emperor Claudius (A.D. 41–54) in which he expelled the Jewish population from Rome. Paul joined them shortly after his arrival in the city (Acts 18:3).

According to Orosius, a fifth-century Christian writer, the decree of Claudius was issued in the ninth year of his reign (A.D. 49). Confirmation for the issuance of the decree is provided by the first- and second-century Roman historians Suetonius and Dio Cassius, but their accounts lack any reference to the year of the decree, as do the extant works of Josephus upon which Orosius claims to depend. As a consequence, there is some debate among scholars concerning the precise date of the decree, but none with respect to the certainty of its issue.

Fortunately, Luke provides two other reference points which enable us to speak with more certainty about the chronological framework of Paul's initial ministry in Corinth. The first of these is his mention of a hearing granted by the proconsul Gallio to the Jews of Corinth in their attempt to prosecute Paul (Acts 18:12). The proconsular term of L. Junius Gallio to which Luke refers may be dated (with the help of an inscription discovered at Delphi in 1905 by the French archaeologist Emile Bourguet) as having occurred during A.D. 51–52. Thus, since Luke's account also makes reference to a period of ministry for "a year and a half" (Acts 18:11), it would appear probable that Paul's initial mission to Corinth began sometime early in A.D. 50 and finished in the latter half of A.D. 51.

Thus, in a period which in duration exceeded all of the other missions mentioned by Luke in conjunction with the apostle's second journey, the church at Corinth was brought into being by the grace of God and the labors of a man whom he had called (1 Cor. 1:1). Several further features of this founding mission should also be mentioned.

First, it is important to note that Paul's initial mission in the synagogue in Corinth seems to have lasted longer than it did in many other cities and resulted in some significant conversions within the Jewish community (e.g., of "Crispus, the synagogue ruler" [Acts 18:8; see also 1 Cor. 1:14]; "his entire household" [Acts 18:8]; and perhaps of his successor Sosthenes [Acts 18:17; cf. 1 Cor. 1:1]). Thus, from the outset there was an important and influential Jewish Christian minority within the Corinthian church.

Second, though the truth of the apostle's generalization in 1 Corinthians 1:26 must be given its full weight, the Corinthian Christian community that comprised the fruit of the Pauline mission seems, nonetheless, to have had a significant number of socially, educationally, and economically privileged members. Among them were Crispus (whose status has just been mentioned), Gaius (whose means were sufficient to provide hospitality for the whole church), and Erastus, "the city's director of public works" (Rom. 16:23), whose name has also been found on a dedicatory pavement at Corinth.

Third, partially, no doubt, as a result of the success of the initial Pauline mission, the church that the apostle left was a church accustomed to persuasive preaching, to official tolerance and relative freedom from persecution (due no doubt to the reluctance of Gallio to consider Christianity a religion separate in any significant sense from the legally sanctioned Judaism [Acts 18:15]), and to the teaching of a variety of Christian leaders (one should consider, for example, the roles that may have been played by Silas and Timothy [2 Cor. 1:19] or by Aquila and Priscilla, whom Paul names as his fellow workers [Rom. 16:3]).

The Book of Acts records in summary fashion that, following his departure from Corinth in the fall of A.D. 51, Paul returned to Antioch by way of Ephesus (where Priscilla and Aquila remained [Acts 18:26]) and Caesarea (Acts 18:18–22). However, after spending some time in Antioch, Paul decided to return to Ephesus and traveled overland back through Galatia and Phrygia, arriving in Ephesus again apparently toward the end of A.D. 52. According to Acts 19 (cf. vv. 1–10, 21–22), Paul subsequently spent more than two years in a mission to the Ephesians before deciding to return to Macedonia and Achaia to take up a collection for the church at Jerusalem. Linking this account of Paul's movements with 1 Corinthians 16:8 indicates that 1 Corinthians was written toward the end of Paul's stay in Ephesus, probably some months before Pentecost of A.D. 55.

First Corinthians itself, however, shows that there had been comparatively frequent communication between Paul and the church at Corinth for some time before its composition. From 1 Corinthians 5:9 one learns of an earlier letter from Paul to the Corinthians, from 1:11 of a report brought to Paul by members of Chloe's household, and from 16:17 of a subsequent delegation probably bearing a letter from the church that Paul had only just received. Given the regular trade between the cities of Corinth and Ephesus, such frequent contact should occasion no surprise, but it does point clearly to the fact that 1 Corinthians is itself a product, at least in part, of an ongoing dialogue between Paul and the church. The information that Paul received most recently, then, by way of a report and a letter, prompted him to write, responding in turn to both in 1:10–6:20 and 7:1–16:4, respectively.

From the report, Paul learned that the church was becoming increasingly polarized by serious divisions among its members as they attempted to locate wisdom and leadership which would enable them to develop appropriate standards for Christian conduct and spiritual maturity (1:10, 26; 2:6; 3:1–4, 18; 4:4; 5:1; 6:1). The situation, however, was further complicated by a high regard at Corinth for eloquent speech (2:1–5, 13; 4:18–20). Accordingly, differences in eloquence between teachers were apparently being taken as indicative of different degrees of inspiration, and this had led, in turn, to painful and divisive comparisons (1:12; 3:5–9, 21–23).

It is not odd, in light of this, that the Corinthians' letter should reflect their divergence of views even as they queried Paul about the propriety of marriage and divorce (7:1–40; should one state be considered more spiritual than another?), the consumption of food sacrificed to idols (8:1–11:1; should the practices of those with strong or weak consciences be followed?), the practice of authentic Christian worship (11:2–14:40; should distinctions in gender, wealth, and gifts find expression, and if so, how?), the nature of the resurrection (15:1–58; should one believe in an event which would involve the body as well as the spirit?), and the collection for God's people (16:1–4; when and how should it be gathered?).

At the time 1 Corinthians was sent, it appears to have been Paul's plan to return within the year to Corinth as his final stop on a journey through Asia Minor, Macedonia, and Achaia (1 Cor. 4:18–21; 16:5–9). Shortly after 1 Corinthians was sent, however, the apostle changed his plans and decided to make his journey to Macedonia by beginning and ending with a visit to Corinth (2 Cor. 1:15–17). Intervening events, however, made Paul modify his plans a third time following his visit to Corinth (the second visit of 2 Cor. 13:2), and on his subsequent journey through Macedonia he did not return to Corinth as he had originally promised he would (2 Cor. 1:23).

At least two of the reasons for this final change of plans become apparent in 2 Corinthians. First, Paul's second visit to Corinth was not at all as he had hoped it would be. Instead it had involved him in a number of exceedingly painful (2 Cor. 2:1) confrontations in which, according to Paul, both the Corinthians (2:2) and he himself (2:5) suffered grief. As a result, from some place along the way through Macedonia, Paul wrote a letter to pointedly express his "distress" and anguish of heart at the distance that had developed between himself and some of the Corinthians, and sent it off with Titus.

Second, upon reaching Asia at the close of his journey, Paul was beset by "hardships" and "pressure" associated with a peril so deadly that he "despaired even of life" (2 Cor. 1:8–10). In the midst of such an experience, it would have been impossible for him to return to Corinth, even if he had desired to do so. Nevertheless, having been rescued from death by God's grace, and having reached Troas once more, Paul was anxious and without peace of mind apart from news of the Corinthian response to his last letter (2 Cor. 2:13). Accordingly, he pressed on into Macedonia, hoping to meet Titus. Their meeting took place a short time later, and, as its result, Paul penned 2 Corinthians from somewhere in Macedonia (2 Cor. 7:5–7, 13–16).

Although the preceding reconstruction of events represents something of a consensus among interpreters, there is nonetheless a considerable diversity of opinion about the literary integrity of 2 Corinthians and the precise historical background which might have occasioned the composition of 2:14–7:4; 6:14–7:1; 8:1–9:15; and 10:1–13:14. Indications exist which suggest that these texts may not have been written at the same time as the rest of 2 Corinthians.

With respect to 2 Corinthians 2:14–7:4 and 8:1–9:15 the evidence is slight. For while it is true to say that 2:14–7:4 represents something of an intrusion into the narrative account which begins with 1:8–2:13 and concludes with 7:5–16, such a parenthetical and digressive intrusion is not uncharacteristic of either Paul's literary style or his Corinthian correspondence. (One may compare, for example, 1 Cor. 9:1–27 which intrudes into an apostolic reply which begins with 8:1–11 and concludes with 10:1–11:1.) Similarly, it has often been noted that there is an abrupt transition in the flow of the letter as one moves from 7:16 to 8:1 and a surprising reiteration of subject as one moves from 8:24 to 9:1. Upon further reflection, it may be seen that the abrupt transition is related to an important change of topic, and that reiteration of a principal subject, in this case the "service to the saints" (9:1), is once more a characteristic of Pauline literary style.

It is more difficult to make a definite decision about 2 Corinthians 6:14–7:1. The lack of any reference to the immediate historical situation, the logical and literary links which are apparently restored when 7:2 is read immediately after 6:13, and the concepts and vocabulary which are used in the passage argue that this text may have been a part of the letter which Paul affirms he wrote to the church prior to 1 Corinthians in order to advise them "not to associate with sexually immoral people" (1 Cor. 5:9). If that is true, then perhaps an individual, unknown to us, collected and edited Paul's Corinthian correspondence and inserted this section into 2 Corinthians. That person may have been unsure of its proper place in the sequence of Paul's letters to Corinth, or perhaps it seemed appropriate, despite its historical origins, to read this text in conjunction with the message of 2 Corinthians. On the other hand, however, it is possible that Paul may himself have felt a need at this point in the letter to remind the Corinthians of his previous counsel, and in doing so, chose to make use of thoughts and perhaps even words drawn from his memory of the earlier letter.

A decision in favor of literary integrity becomes most difficult, however, when one considers the evidence with respect to 2 Corinthians 10:1–13:14. For while earlier parts of the letter show clear signs of having been written in a conciliatory spirit, at a moment when Paul sought to commend the Corinthian Christians and gratefully acknowledge their renewed affection for him (1:7; 2:5–11; 6:11; 7:2–4, 7, 13), the spirit of 10:1–13:14 is profoundly critical, and the section contains numerous indications that these chapters were not occasioned by an effort to effect harmony between the apostle and his converts, but instead were penned by Paul in an attempt to defend his rightful apostolic authority against all those in Corinth who might attempt to deny it (10:5–8; 11:4–6, 12–16; 12:11–13; 13:1–3). Furthermore, on two occasions in the latter part of the letter (i.e., 12:14 and 13:1), Paul speaks about a third visit which he is about to make, but in the earlier portion of the letter he fails to mention it even where one would expect such a reference (i.e., 1:15–2:13). Finally, in 12:18, Paul writes as though the mission of Titus announced in 8:16–24 has already been completed.

Although it is possible, given such evidence, to propose a set of circumstances which might still enable one to maintain that 2 Corinthians 10:1–13:14 was written at the same time as 2 Corinthians 1:1–9:14, or to construct a different set of circumstances which could enable one to conceive of 2 Corinthians 10:1–13:14 as a part, if not the whole, of the letter written "out of great distress and anguish of heart and with many tears" (2:4) immediately prior to 2 Corinthians 1:1–9:14, the simplest explanation of the scriptural evidence points to the conclusion that 2 Corinthians 10:1–13:14 is a part of a letter written sometime after the composition and dispatch of 2 Corinthians 1:1–9:14. Of the letter's reception, and of the subsequent relationship between Paul and the church at Corinth, we know far less than we might like. But, comparing Romans 16:23 with Acts 20:2–3 and 1 Corinthians 1:14 we may infer that once again the letter of the apostle had a salutary effect, enabling him to make his promised third visit to Corinth, at which time he composed his letter to the Romans while residing in the house of Gaius, his convert.

OUTLINE—1 CORINTHIANS

- I. Epistolary Introduction (1:1–9)
- II. Paul's Response to Reports about the Community at Corinth (1:10–6:20)
  - A. A Report of Factions Within the Community (1:10–4:20)
  - B. A Report of Immorality, Arrogance, and Improper Judgments (5:1–6:20)
- III. Paul's Response to Questions from the Corinthians (7:1–16:4)
  - A. Questions about Marriage, Divorce, and Celibacy (7:1–40)
  - B. Questions about Food, Idolatry, and Freedom (8:1–11:1)
  - C. Questions about Worship, Gifts, and Order (11:2–14:40)
  - D. Questions about the Resurrection and Life in the Age to Come (15:1–58)
  - E. Questions about the Collection and Paul's Plans (16:1–9)
- IV. The Recommendation of Others (16:10–18)
- V. Final Greetings and Formal Closing (16:19–24)

COMMENTARY

I. Epistolary Introduction (1:1–9)

As was customary, Paul opens his letter with a greeting, or salutation (**1:1–3**). This conforms to the normal compositional pattern for personal letters written during the Graeco-Roman era.[1] A greeting of this type routinely contained the name of the sender(s) of the letter, joined on occasion by a short self-description; the name of the intended recipient(s) of the letter, again joined on occasion by some short descriptive comment; and a word of greeting.

In 1 Corinthians the senders are Paul, who describes himself as an apostle sent out by Christ Jesus and by the will of God (see also Rom. 1:1; 2 Cor. 1:1; Gal. 1:1) and Sosthenes (see Acts 18:17). The letter is addressed to the church at Corinth (that Paul addresses the church as a whole is significant; see 1:10–12).

There follows a threefold description emphasizing that the church has been set apart or sanctified to be in relationship to Christ; called within that relationship to the pursuit of holiness as saints; and united in these distinctives with all believers "in every place [who] call on the name of our Lord Jesus Christ" (v. 2 RSV).

The normal Greek word of greeting, *charein*, is, as in Paul's other letters, transformed into the Christian greeting *charis* (grace) and is joined with the Hebrew greeting *šālôm* (peace; v. 3).

Next (again, letters of this era began by showing deference to the god/gods of the sender/recipient of the letter), Paul includes a section in which he gives thanks to God for the whole of the church at Corinth (**1:4–9**). Such thanksgiving is warranted, according to Paul, first and foremost because the grace of God, his unmerited love, has been given to all of them in Christ Jesus. Furthermore, God's initial gift of grace has led to an enrichment of the community in speaking and in knowledge, which has confirmed the apostolic testimony about Christ. Thus, at present, the church does "not lack any spiritual gift" as it eagerly awaits, together with Paul, "for our Lord Jesus Christ to be revealed" at his return (v. 7).

The words that follow contain one of the strongest statements within Paul's letters of his conviction that his converts would be enabled to persevere in their faith until the time of our Lord's return. Paul bases his confidence neither on the strength of his converts' faith nor on his own ability to pastorally maintain them in the faith, but rather on the sustaining and atoning power of Christ and the faithfulness of God, both of which are constantly available to those who have been called into fellowship with the Son (vv. 8–9).

II. Paul's Response to Reports about the Community at Corinth (1:10–6:20)

A. A report of factions within the community (1:10–4:20). Having given thanks to God for those things that characterize the church as a whole, Paul now appeals to the church "so that there may be no divisions" (none having apparently taken place to this point, though the danger is clearly present), and so that they may be completely "united in mind and thought" (v. 10). Paul's appeal is more than a mere formality, as is shown by the fact that it is made "in the name of our Lord Jesus Christ," and by the following verses which demonstrate the need for the appeal by referring to a report Paul has received from members of Chloe's "household" about actual conditions at Corinth (**1:10–17**). These people, sent probably on business by Chloe (a woman of apparent importance), had brought to Paul a report of disputes that had broken out among various groups within the community (v. 11).

The disputes seem to have revolved around two interrelated issues: the search for wisdom (i.e., guidance about how one should live the Christian life after conversion; cf. the Old Testament concept of wisdom) and comparisons that were being made between teachers with respect to their ability to impart such wisdom.

Three and perhaps four groups are mentioned (v. 12). The first group has identified itself with Paul (though Paul does not reciprocate and identify himself with them, or distinguish them from the other parties). The second has aligned itself with Apollos (see Acts 18:24–19:1, which reports a visit by Apollos, a Hellenized Jewish Christian, to Corinth, and characterizes his teaching as eloquent, based upon the Old Testament Scriptures, bold, and powerful). The third group looked to Peter for leadership, or to teachers who used his name (for though it is possible that Peter himself had been at Corinth, it is not necessary to think of this as being the only way a group associated with Peter's Jewish Christian views may have come into existence at Corinth). The final slogan, "I follow Christ," has always proved difficult to interpret. Although it seems to designate a fourth group (whose apparent claim was allegiance to Christ's teaching alone), it could

1. See W. G. Doty, *Letters in Primitive Christianity* (Philadelphia: Fortress, 1973), for an excellent introduction to the pattern of Graeco-Roman letters.

denote the common claim of each of the three groups ("I am of Christ," "No, I am," etc.), or Paul's own retort to all ("You follow———, but I follow Christ").

With a series of rhetorical questions issuing out of passion and conviction Paul responds to these misplaced allegiances. Do the Corinthians really suppose that the presence of Christ is somehow divided among them? Do they really mean to suggest that their allegiance is due to someone other than the one who has been crucified for them? Have they really forgotten that they were all baptized in one name? The last question leads Paul to recall (though he admits his recollection is not complete) that he did baptize Crispus (v. 14; Acts 18:8), Gaius (v. 14; probably the Corinthian who together with Paul sends greetings in Rom. 16:23), and Stephanas (v. 16; one of the Corinthians with Paul as he was writing [1 Cor. 16:17]). But neither these nor anyone else "can say that you were baptized in my name" (v. 15).

The last verse of this section provides a bridge to the next (which criticizes the wisdom of the Corinthians and commends a different kind of wisdom [1:18–3:20]). The transition is accomplished through the denial that "words of human wisdom" have ever played a role in the preaching of the gospel. Indeed such words and wisdom are the antithesis of preaching that concentrates on the cross of Christ and its power.

Paul's criticism of the search for wisdom at Corinth (**1:18–2:5**) may be divided into three parts, in terms of its focus (1:18–25), its effects (1:26–31), and its claim to inspiration (2:1–5).

Paul begins with a corollary of the point made in the last verse. The "message of the cross" may indeed be regarded as "foolishness" rather than wisdom by those who are perishing because of their lack of perception. But for those who are being saved, the proclamation of the life, death, and resurrection of Christ with the cross as its focus is recognized as the central manifestation of God's power and wisdom (see 1:24).

The implication is that the "message of the cross" has been neglected in the Corinthians' search for wisdom in favor of a different focus. This focus Paul now begins to criticize, employing a quotation drawn from the prophetic critique of wisdom in Isaiah 29:14. In its context in the Septuagint (the Greek translation of the Old Testament which Paul often quotes), the citation promises to "hide" (see RSV) and in that sense destroy or do away with the wisdom of the wise and understanding. These words in context appear to look to a time beyond their original historical setting when the wisdom of the Old Testament Law would be superseded by God's new action among his people. That this time has come is precisely Paul's point.

The wisdom of this age/world, whether it be the wisdom of the scribal scholar or the pagan philosopher, the wisdom of the Jews (which seeks confirming signs of one's knowledge of the Law and the divine plan), or the wisdom of the Greeks (which searches for truth in the abstract; v. 22), has been superseded. It has been frustrated in its attempt to grasp the divine plan by the revelation of a new part of the wisdom of God displayed in the life, death, and resurrection of Christ, and set forth in Paul's preaching (vv. 21–22). Thus, paradoxically, while the events proclaimed in the gospel may seem to be manifestations of foolishness and weakness when evaluated with the wisdom heretofore known to Jews or Greeks, it is only through belief in the saving wisdom of such apparent foolishness and weakness that any shall be saved (vv. 21, 24–25).

In criticizing the effects of the Corinthian search for wisdom Paul next urges his readers to consider the circumstances surrounding their conversion. God's call had come not because of their possession of wisdom, influence, or noble birth. (Paul's statement implies that one effect of the search for wisdom was that some at Corinth did indeed lay claim to these attributes either literally or figuratively. Jewish wisdom writings often ascribed to the wise man all of the attributes mentioned here and others like them.) It had come, instead, on the basis of their willingness to identify with things considered foolish, weak, lowly, and despised in this world, things which characterize the life and death of "Christ Jesus, who has become for us wisdom from God" (v. 30). This took place "so that no one may boast before him" (i.e., God), but instead might "boast in the Lord" (i.e., in Christ) who is the focus of the wisdom, righteousness, holiness, and redemption that has come to us from God (vv. 29–31; cf. Jer. 9:23–24). It is illegitimate, therefore, to search for wisdom and then to use it to boast before God and distinguish ourselves at the expense of our brothers or sisters.

Finally, Paul concludes his critique of wisdom by referring to the way in which he initially "proclaimed . . . the testimony about God" (i.e., God's activity in and through Jesus Christ and him crucified) among the Corinthians. Once more a contrast is drawn, this time between the "demonstration of the Spirit's power" (v. 4) evident in Paul's preaching despite his weakness, fear, and trembling (v. 3), and eloquence, "persuasive words," and wisdom (vv. 1, 4–5). The contrast implies that those searching for wisdom at Corinth had begun to view eloquence and persuasive words as authenticating signs of divine inspiration, perhaps even judging Paul's teaching inferior on these criteria to that of others (see 1:12, 17). Paul, however, makes plain that the definitive "demonstration" (the word is a technical term used by both Jews and Greeks to denote a conclusive or compelling proof) of inspired speech lies not in its "form" but rather in its power to convince and convert (v. 5; 1 Thess. 1:5).

Having criticized the wisdom valued by some at Corinth, Paul now turns to a wisdom he can commend (**2:6–3:17**). It is a wisdom that is different in focus (2:6–9), that differently authenticates itself and its possessors (2:10–3:4), and that is different in its purpose and effect within the Christian community (3:5–17). On the basis of these contrasts Paul clearly differentiates the Christian wisdom which he commends in this section from the wisdom that he has criticized in the preceding section.

This section begins with Paul's claim to "speak a message of wisdom among the mature." But quickly and firmly he asserts that such wisdom belongs to neither this age nor the rulers of this age who, in reliance upon an obsolete understanding of God's wisdom and will, crucified the Lord of glory (vv. 6, 8).

It has long been debated whether Paul means by "rulers of this age" human religious and/or political authorities (Luke 23:35; Acts 3:17; 4:26; 13:27); supernatural demonic "powers" who are said to dominate the present world order (Eph. 3:10; 6:12); or a combination of these two groups in which the influence of demonic "powers" is judged to lie behind the actions of human authorities (Col. 2:15). In light of the fact that Paul uses the word, as here, in the plural, on only one other occasion, where it refers unambiguously to human beings (Rom. 13:3); the further fact that in the rest of the New Testament the plural likewise always refers to human "rulers"; and the final fact that this usage matches Luke's account of early Christian preaching, it seems most likely that Paul is referring to those persons in authority, both Roman and Jewish, responsible for the crucifixion.

In contrast to the wisdom which guided their actions, Paul characterizes Christian wisdom as being God's wisdom (i.e., it comes from and belongs to God). It is also secret, or mysterious in the sense that it is "a wisdom that has been hidden" in events "that God destined for our glory before time began" (v. 7). Christian wisdom may be said to find its focus in the meaning of the Christ-event as proclaimed in the gospel. Indeed, that event, properly and fully understood, points in a way that the Law alone cannot to the direction of God's plan past, present, and future, to what God has prepared for those who love him.

Over against the demonstrated ignorance of the rulers with respect to true wisdom stands Paul's assertion that "God has revealed it to us by his Spirit" (v. 10). The remainder of the section enlarges upon this remarkable claim. Verses 10b and 11 establish the Spirit of God as an adequate guide to such wisdom. For the Spirit is able to understand all of the aspects of the wise plan of God, even its deepest secrets, just as the same capacity to understand our own plans and intentions belongs only to the spirit within us. Verses 12–13 describe the process by which the Spirit's knowledge is communicated. As persons called into fellowship with God through faith in Christ, we have "received the Spirit who is from God" so that we may "understand what God has freely given us," namely, a knowledge of the divine intent, God's "thoughts" and plan for salvation, past, present, and future (v. 12). This wisdom, says Paul, is "what we speak," and even the words in which it is conveyed are a product of the Spirit's inspiration (v. 13; 2:4).

The last and largest part of this section (2:14–3:4) carefully restricts Christian wisdom to the spiritual person, for the person without the Spirit cannot understand its importance or accept its validity, because it is spiritually discerned (vv. 14–15). However, the evaluation of the spiritual person's grasp upon Christian wisdom is "not subject to any man's judgment" (v. 15). For since no one has fully known the mind of the Lord, judgment can belong only to the Lord himself (v. 16a; 4:3–4). Nonetheless, as recipients of God's Spirit, we have the assurance that we know at the very least the mind of Christ (v. 16b).

Yet even the possession of the Spirit and the mind of Christ does not necessarily assure growth in our understanding of divine wisdom, as the next four verses show. For the Corinthians are still much as they were when Paul left them, "mere infants in Christ" (3:1), unready for any wisdom that passes beyond milk (the proclamation of the gospel) to solid food (in an attempt to explore the implications of God's act in Christ for our present behavior, v. 2; cf. Heb. 5:12–14; 1 Pet. 2:2). Their "jealousy" and "quarreling" demonstrate that they are still under the influence of wisdom that is "worldly" (vv. 3–4).

Paul now uses three metaphors designed to illustrate the purpose and effects of authentic Christian wisdom. In the first (3:5–9), using a familiar Old Testament image of the community as God's field or vineyard, Paul compares his own ministry at Corinth (in which he "planted the seed" of wisdom through the proclamation of the gospel) and the ministry of Apollos (who watered it through further preaching and teaching [cf. Acts 18:27–28]) to the work of God (who made it grow). Such comparison clearly shows that "neither he who plants nor he who waters is anything" as over against "God who makes things grow" (v. 7). It also shows that "the man who plants and the man who waters have one purpose" (v. 8). They should not, therefore, be compared to one another by the community (though each "will be rewarded according to his own labor" by God's ultimate judgment). They should be regarded in the same way, as "God's fellow workers," at work side by side in God's field, or on God's building (v. 9).

This last phrase leads to the second image of the community as God's building (3:10–15). In this case, the metaphor further defines the Christian community that is growing in wisdom as one that has not only learned to value its teachers equally, but also to see clearly that there is a need for continuity between the foundational proclamation of the gospel (laid, in this case, by Paul as an "expert builder"), and the subsequent teaching of others (who seek now to build upon Paul's initial preaching; v. 10). There can be no attempt to lay a new foundation. Instead, the superstructure must always be evaluated to see if its materials conform in kind to the original foundation. For on the "day" (a reference to the Old Testament day of the Lord), the quality of every builder's work will be revealed with fire, and the builder either rewarded or singed himself with the flames that consume his work.

The final two verses (16–17) of this section reveal the reason for this severe judgment in a third vivid image. The building upon which Paul and others are at work, the church at Corinth, is God's temple (see 1 Pet. 2:5), for God's Spirit is alive in its midst. In a solemn statement of lex talionis (punishment in kind), destruction is promised to anyone who brings about the destruction of God's temple by breaking it away from its foundation.

Paul's criticism of the inadequacies of the "wisdom of this world" and his definition and commendation of the "wisdom of God" now are drawn together and the teaching applied to the tendencies of some at Corinth toward self-deception, self-centered comparisons, and self-aggrandizement.

"Do not deceive yourselves," Paul writes, and then goes on to clarify the kind of self-deception that imperils the Christians at Corinth (**3:18–20**). His concern is the possibility of self-deception with respect to wisdom because some at Corinth tend to define wisdom and designate those who are wise "by the standards of this age." In response, alluding to 1:18–31 and applying the contrast developed there between the wisdom of the world and the "foolishness" of the gospel, Paul advises anyone who is wise by such standards to throw away his "wisdom" and embrace what "the wisdom of this age" regards as "foolishness." For in reality, "the wisdom of this world [has become] foolishness in God's sight." This development, surprising as it may be to those who trust in the continuity of wisdom, is nonetheless to have been anticipated from the Old Testament Scriptures (Job 5:13; Ps. 94:11).

In **3:21–4:7** Paul turns to the situation that gave rise to his remarks on wisdom, the tendency of some at Corinth to make comparisons between their teachers, to boost their favorite above the others, and to boast of their allegiances (1:12–17). Alluding to 3:5–9, Paul again asks the Corinthians to recognize that the truth lies in precisely the opposite direction. It is not the Corinthians who "belong" to Paul, Apollos, or Cephas; rather, along with all things, life and death, the present and the future (Rom. 8:38–39), Paul, Apollos, and Cephas "belong" to them, as servants of Christ and "as those entrusted with the secret things of God" (4:1).

The mention of the word *servant* leads Paul to allude to 3:10–15, and in 4:2–5 he applies the teaching of the former passage to himself and the church at Corinth. As a teaching servant of Christ, Paul has been "given a trust" and, in order to fulfill it, "must prove faithful" (v. 2). Yet his faithfulness cannot be judged either by the Corinthians or by Paul himself, for the judgment of his faithfulness belongs to the one who gave the trust. It is the Lord, Paul writes, who judges me. It is best, therefore, for both Paul and the Corinthians to "judge nothing before the appointed time," because faithfulness to the divine trust depends as much upon "what is hidden" and imperceptible (including "the motives of men's hearts") as it does upon that which is now in the light (v. 5). Praise for Paul, Apollos, and the others who have taught the Corinthians will come not from them in the form of allegiances, but from God who will give to each one the proper amount in reward for faithfulness to the divine commission.

Paul now concludes this section in which he has dealt with the tendency of the Corinthians to make self-centered comparisons between their teachers, and in particular between Paul and Apollos, with a saying which was probably in use at Corinth (v. 6). Its reference to "what is written" is obscure, although most likely it is meant to allude to the Old Testament Scriptures, either in whole or in part. But its message is nonetheless generally clear, and the same as that of 3:5ff. The church is to learn "from us" (Paul and Apollos together) the "meaning of the saying," and apply it to their lives without taking "pride in one man over against another." Indeed pride, the desire to be different and to boast of what wisdom one has come to possess, seems to Paul to lie at the root of all of the church's present difficulties.

"Already you have all you want! Already you have become rich! You have become kings—and that without us!" (v. 8). The Corinthians in their willingness to attribute wisdom and honor to themselves and their readiness to discriminate between their teachers are acting as if the kingdom of Christ has already become complete (though whether this premise forms the actual basis for their actions or the hypothetical basis for Paul's critique is unclear). However, it has not (1 Cor. 15:23–28), and this observation, so evident in the lives of the apostles, Paul now uses ironically to negate the tendency of the Corinthians toward self-aggrandizement at the expense of others (**4:8–21**).

Along with the other apostles, Paul has been "put on display" and held up to ridicule, "like men condemned to die" who indeed were brought into the arena "at the end of the procession" (v. 9). They are viewed by those to whom they preach as a spectacle to be seen, but not taken seriously. And so together they have become fools in the eyes of the world, but fools for Christ, while the Corinthians prefer for themselves to be seen and regarded as wise. Similar contrasts are apparent between the apostles' real "weakness" and the Corinthians' self-designated "strength," or between the apostles' real "dishonor" and the Corinthians' self-conferred "honor."

In verse 11, however, ironical comparisons are dropped as Paul proceeds in his attempt to teach the Corinthians that "no servant is greater than his master, nor is a messenger greater than the one who sent him" (John 13:16). Like Christ, the apostles "go hungry and thirsty . . . [and] homeless" even now (v. 11), and in obedience to his teaching, "when we are cursed, we bless; when we are persecuted, we endure it; when we are slandered, we answer kindly" (v. 12; Matt. 5:11, 44). Thus, "to this moment," the light of the world (Matt. 5:14; John 8:12) continues to be regarded as "the scum of the earth" (v. 13).

Such words must have stung the Corinthians' pride. But in spite of this, Paul's intention is not to exalt himself or humiliate them. Rather, as one who "in Christ Jesus . . . became your father through the gospel" (v. 15), he has written in a fatherly act of compassionate correction to warn them of the dangers inherent in their self-centered attitudes, and to urge them, as his children, to grow out of their immaturity by imitating their father. In order that they might learn to imitate in the way their father intends, "I am sending to you Timothy, my son whom I love, who is faithful in the Lord." Like an older brother, he will remind his brothers and sisters of their father's "way of life in Christ Jesus" which agrees with the life-style he commends for all his children in every church that he teaches (v. 17).

Lest the Corinthians interpret this action as reluctance to confront his children, Paul writes last of his own plans. He "will come again soon, if the Lord is willing" (cf. 16:5–7 where the timing of the visit is more thoroughly thought out). And when he comes, he will not be diverted by the Corinthians' own verbal claims, but will look instead for signs of God's power evident in their midst. For the kingdom of God "is not a matter of talk but of power" (v. 20; 2:1–5). It is up to the Corinthians, therefore, to choose how they wish to see the love of their father expressed—through the corrective power of the "whip," or in a more "gentle spirit" (v. 21).

B. A report of immorality, arrogance, and improper judgments (5:1–6:20). Up to this point in the letter, Paul has dealt with a report about different allegiances resulting from a search for wisdom that has involved a considerable manifestation of pride. But Paul has also heard that Corinthian pride has expressed itself in an even more damaging way. It is actually reported that there is "sexual immorality among you, and of a kind that does not occur even among pagans." Clarification of the general term *sexual immorality* immediately follows: "A man has his father's wife." The words of the text indicate more than a single immoral act is involved. In addition, we can perhaps infer, because Paul does not speak of adultery, that the man's father is deceased; from the lack of reference to incest, that the woman is this man's stepmother; and from the failure to mention her in 5:5, that she is probably not a Christian (see also 5:12–13). Marriage or cohabitation with such a person was forbidden to Jews (Lev. 18:8; 20:11) and was also condemned by several prominent pagan moralists. Even before addressing himself to the question of proper discipline, however, Paul confronts the laissez-faire attitude of a prideful church which has failed, because of a self-centered and permissive individualism, to respond with appropriate grief and censure.

Then, counting on the Corinthians to act together with him when they "are assembled in the name of our Lord Jesus," making the word and the power of Christ manifest in the church in exactly the way that he would if physically there, Paul prescribes judgment (**5:3–5**). The man is to be handed over to Satan by expulsion from the church (cf. 5:11), which will deliver him back into the kingdom of this world which Satan rules (v. 5; Eph. 2:2). The purpose of the action is not punitive, however, but in order that "the sinful nature [i.e., that which may be presumed to have fully taken over the man's body and enslaved him in bondage for life] may be destroyed and his spirit saved on the day of the Lord" (v. 5).

Again, however, Paul's mind turns back to the church (**5:6–8**). A body of believers that could boast of its achievements and ignore its obvious failures clearly has not yet learned that "a little yeast works through the whole batch of dough." Paul employs a proverb he has used before (in Gal. 5:9), and one commonly used in Jewish circles to denote the way in which any moral evil eventually permeates its host. On this occasion, however, the proverb prompts Paul to some further analogies between the preparations for Passover (part of the ritual involved the removal of leaven from the household prior to the beginning of the festival [Exod. 12:15, 19; Deut. 16:3–4]) and Christian existence (which involves for Paul the continual call to "put off" the old sinful nature as well as to "put on" the new [Eph. 4:22–24]). In this sense Christians are indeed to "keep the Festival," to "get rid of the old yeast . . . the yeast of malice and wickedness" and to become what they "really are," a "new batch without yeast . . . the bread of sincerity and truth" (vv. 7–8). Furthermore, this must be done quickly, for the festival is already in progress: Christ, "our Passover lamb," has already been sacrificed.

In **5:9–6:11** Paul reminds the Corinthians that he has written to them before not to associate with "sexually immoral people" (5:9). His counsel, however, has been misunderstood by the church, which took it to apply to the advisability of contact with the "people of this world" (v. 10) and therefore neglected it as an impossibly rigorous and impractical standard. Adherence to such a standard would involve the Christian community's complete withdrawal from the world, and this possibility Paul does not even pause to contemplate. Rather, he writes again, more fully and clearly, what he wrote before: "you must not associate with anyone who calls himself a brother but is," as the Greek text and the specific case indicate, habitually "sexually immoral or greedy, an idolater, or a slanderer, a drunkard, or a swindler" (v. 11). And then, lest someone say that his judgment is unbalanced in its selectivity, Paul reminds his readers that his refusal "to judge those outside the church," while compelling judgment for those inside, stems from the sure promise that "God will judge those outside" and certainly impose upon them a sentence that is both harsher and more permanent (2 Thess. 1:8–9) than that which he now imposes upon his own.

However, in calling Christian brothers and sisters to judgment for their behavior, the secular law court (see 6:6) is hardly the appropriate setting. The place for such disputes, if they arise at all (6:7), should be "before the saints" (6:1). Indeed, as before, the Corinthians have acted exactly contrary to what is true, namely, that the saints will judge the world and even the angels who have fallen (see also Matt. 19:28; 25:41; 2 Pet. 2:4; Rev. 20:4). In light of their role in these ultimate judgments, they are certainly qualified to "judge" trivial cases that concern "the things of this life" (6:2–3).

That is exactly what Paul calls upon them to do in the next two verses, though his advice is full of irony. If even those of "little account" in the church are better qualified to render judgments than those outside, then surely there must be someone wise enough among the Corinthians—who value their wisdom so highly—"to judge a dispute between believers" (vv. 4–5). To fail to do so prolongs disputes and provokes lawsuits which completely defeat both the ideal of Christian community and the Christian witness. The fact that these disputes have been prolonged, however, also points to the self-centered behavior of some who refuse to be wronged in any way without rushing to their own defense and to the willingness of some Corinthians to knowingly cheat and wrong fellow believers.

Some of the Corinthians appear to have forgotten that to engage in sin routinely is to place themselves back among the "wicked" who will not inherit the kingdom of God. Paul urges them not to deceive themselves in this way. Neither those who are habitually sexually immoral (as Paul's list makes clear, the general term includes behavior other than that which has provoked judgment [5:1–13]) nor thieves (once more the list expands beyond the specific behavior condemned in 6:8) will inherit the kingdom of God. Therefore such behavior, despite its routine place in the past of some of them, must be left behind through the constant remembrance that they have been cleansed from its stain and set apart from its power to live in relationship with the God who has justified them in the name of the Lord Jesus Christ and by the Spirit.

Having made clear again the reality of standards for Christian conduct, Paul now goes on in **6:12–20** to deal with the rationalizations that had led some of the Corinthians to standards of their own: "Everything is permissible for me" (v. 12). Reasoning from the same axiomatic truths Paul reiterates in verse 11, some at Corinth had concluded that their Christian faith gave them complete freedom to set their own standards according to their individual sense of propriety. Paul does not disagree in principle, but warns them of two dangers: that they may fall into conduct that is "beneficial" neither to themselves nor to others, and that they may become "mastered" again, this time by the very patterns of behavior that marked freedom for them initially. A more specific instance of the same kind of rationalization has produced among some of the Corinthians the saying, "Food for the stomach and the stomach for food" (v. 13). Again disagreement is not to the point, as much as the remembrance that freedom to eat what one wills is an inconsequential freedom in light of the coming destruction and transformation of our bodies and therefore not one to cling to or defend at all costs.

A final rationalization, unrepeated by Paul, probably underlies the words which follow these and return us again to the subject of sexual morality. For some of the Corinthians, it followed from their freedom to eat that they were also free to indulge their sexual appetites in prostitution. For Paul, however, this action and the logical analogy that lies behind it are fundamentally wrong, because they involve the believer's body as a physical, psychological, and spiritual whole in an action that unites the Christian (whose body in this sense belongs to the Lord [v. 14] and, as such, is already "united" to Christ [vv. 15, 17; 12:27]) with the active presence and enslaving power of immorality.

From this perilous rationalization and activity Paul urges his converts to "flee." All other sins are outside of the body in that they do not involve the entire personality (v. 18). Our bodies are a temple of the Holy Spirit who dwells within each of us, and we are, as a result, no longer free to use our bodies apart from a recognition of the presence of the Spirit within us. "Bought at a price," which God did not hesitate to pay in and through his Son, we must respond in gratitude by giving "honor" to God with our whole being.

III. Paul's Response to Questions from the Corinthians (7:1–16:4)

In the first verse of chapter 7, Paul moves from reports about the church and begins to address questions posed by the Corinthians themselves in a letter, now lost, but originally perhaps carried to Paul by the three Corinthians mentioned in 16:17. The words *now for* introduce the general topic of their questions.

A. Questions about marriage, divorce, and celibacy (7:1–40). The questions to which Paul responds **(7:1–16)** can probably be inferred to have had something to do with the relative worth of marriage as compared to abstinence or celibacy. Furthermore, behind the questions probably lay the supposition that abstinence or celibacy promoted spiritual achievement.

In any case, in the first two verses Paul's words strike a balance that is characteristic of his response as a whole. "It is good for a man not to marry," but the benefit is not one that can be enjoyed apart from the constant temptations offered by a promiscuous society. As a result, it is better for each man (who has not been given the gift from God [v. 7] to resist such temptation) to have one woman as wife and each woman to have one man as husband. That the command is given reciprocally to both sexes is remarkable, as it transcends cultural norms and prepares for things to come later in the letter (11:11–12).

Moreover, within a marriage, sexual relations should not be suppressed except (Paul is making a concession, not giving a command) by "mutual consent" (again the idea of mutuality is remarkable) "and for a time" (lest prolongation lead to temptation) "so that you may devote yourselves [together] to prayer" (v. 5). For "the wife's body" no longer belongs to "her alone but also to her husband," and (most remarkably of all), neither does the husband's body "belong to him alone but also to his wife" (v. 4). Paul's desire is thus for all to be free from temptation as he is, whether through the gift of marriage or the gift of celibacy. So his counsel to the unmarried and the widows is the same. It is good for them to remain unmarried, but advisable for those to marry who might otherwise be consumed with passion.

Another set of questions concerns separation and divorce. This set relates to the preceding questions if, as is supposed, celibacy was considered preferable to marriage. For if this were so, it would give sufficient grounds for separation or divorce. For Paul, however, who relies here upon a "command" of the Lord in giving his own, this is an insufficient reason for a wife to separate from her husband or for a husband to divorce his wife. It is noteworthy that Paul addresses the woman first (perhaps this is the initial clue to a tendency among some women at Corinth toward the exercise and defense of an absolute liberty that transgressed the boundaries established for true Christian freedom [see also 11:5; 14:34]), and also that he provides as a realist and not a legalist for situations where separation still occurs (advising a woman in that case to remain unmarried or to be reconciled to her husband).

Paul's answers so far have been given to believers who are married to one another, but now he turns to the rest, and to questions (raised out of the same context of concern for a spiritual status) about mixed marriages. In doing so, Paul states openly that his instructions go beyond those of Jesus (see also v. 25). But this does not mean they lack inspiration (v. 40) or authority (1:1; 4:1). Again, the counsel is given to both the man and the woman whose spouse "is not a believer." If the unbelieving spouse is "willing" to live with the believer, they are not to seek divorce. But will such a marriage not associate the believer too closely with the influence of the world? No, responds Paul, because the unbeliever is "sanctified," set apart from the world's influence (though not completely, as are those "sanctified in Christ Jesus" [1:2; 6:11]), through the choice of constant association with a believing spouse. If this were not so, then (as some at Corinth have perhaps said) their children would be unclean. But, together with their mother and father they too are holy. On the other hand, "if the unbeliever leaves," choosing to abandon the association, then the believer is not bound to struggle to maintain the bond, because God has called us "to live in peace." There is still one other possibility, so far unmentioned, and that the best of all. Perhaps, though one cannot know, the association will serve to draw the unbeliever to faith and so to salvation.

As elsewhere in this second half of his letter, Paul's response now moves from directives (7:1–16) to a statement of principles **(7:17–27)** before turning back again to advice (7:28–40). Thus the basic conviction underlying Paul's balanced counsel (the "rule I lay down in all the churches") is now stated. Spiritual growth is not dependent on status (marital or otherwise), but on attention and obedience to God's call. Accordingly, Christians should not ordinarily seek to change their status; rather, as far as possible, they should retain the status God has assigned to them.

Paul reinforces the principle with reference to circumcision. Those who were circumcised before their call should not now seek to erase its marks, nor should those who before were uncircumcised seek its imposition (v. 18; Acts 21:17–26; Gal. 5:2). Instead, each should remain as he was. For that which served before to promote a distinction in status, knowledge, and obedience between them has now been set at nought, and both together will be enabled in Christ to know and obey God's intentions for them as they walk by the Spirit (Gal. 5:25; 1 Cor. 2:6–16).

A final illustration is of the slave and the freedman. Here, however, the analogy is incomplete, for Paul admits that the slave should use the chance to gain freedom whenever it comes. Nonetheless the main point remains intact. The distinction in status between slave and free man is irrelevant to those who belong to the Lord who makes the slave his freedman (Gal. 5:1) and the free man Christ's slave (Rom. 1:1).

All three categories now come back into the argument as the section is finished by way of summary. All, whether married or celibate, Jew or Gentile, slave or free, have been bought "at a price" and thus brought into the body of Christ where distinctions of status have no place (v. 23; 12:13; Gal. 3:28; Eph. 2:14–18; Col. 3:11). Therefore, Paul urges them not to become subject again to human standards that would make their status a basis for comparison, but to transcend them and find unity and equality in the body of Christ. The section is closed with a final repetition of the principle based upon this insight and used to formulate Paul's answers to the Corinthians' questions.

Chapter 7 began with words addressed to those contemplating marriage and questions about the value of marriage. The subsequent discussion, however, has focused primarily on related questions posed by those already married. In **7:25–40** Paul completes his answer to the questions of the unmarried and widowed.

The answer is made in light of the principles already given and reflects Paul's considered "judgment" which, though not binding as a command "from the Lord," is worthy of trust. It is based, at the same time, upon a conviction that the present unsettled state of this world reflects that the time of its existence has been shortened; it is already beginning to pass away. Therefore, it is best if the unmarried remain, like the married, as they are. This decision, however, will not be reached by all, and so, realistically, Paul adds that its opposite, a decision to marry, is no sin.

In light of the reality of the world's demise,

however, Christians should live without reference to its expectations, but rather as those who already have begun to live in God's new kingdom. Those who have wives should remember that in the kingdom the caliber of fellowship to be enjoyed between all will match that which is now the exclusive possession of husbands and wives. So marriage, in this respect, should even now cease to exist (Mark 12:25). Those who mourn should likewise recall that their mourning has already begun to call forth comfort (Matt. 5:4). And those who "are happy" in the present world should bear in mind that the age to come will reverse present fortunes (Luke 6:25b). Finally, those who buy or "use the things of the world" must realize the transitory nature of their possessions and not become engrossed in the enterprise of attainment and use (Luke 12:16–21).

A further factor must also be considered by those contemplating marriage, however, for their marriage will deservedly initiate a concern to give pleasure and comfort to the spouse in an environment constantly full of trouble, and this will be in addition to the valid concern they bear as individuals to please the Lord in response to the call to be about his business (see Mark 13:34–37; Acts 13:2; 1 Cor. 3:13; 15:58). All of this Paul would have them consider "for [their] own good" before entering into marriage. This is not said to restrict those who would marry from doing so, but written in order to remind all of the priority of devotion to the Lord.

A section of advice follows whose reference is somewhat ambiguous. In the New International Version the ambiguity gives rise to an extended footnote in which the Greek, which speaks about proper action by a man with respect to "his virgin," is interpreted with reference to a woman's father; in the text, however, the phrase is taken to refer (more probably) to her fiancé. The general point is in either case clear and largely repetitive. If a man thinks he is "acting improperly" toward a woman, or unduly prolonging a relationship without reference to her expectations, then these conditions mean marriage is his legitimate choice. But if, on the other hand, a man does not sense "compulsion," "has control over his own will" (is free from the possibility of acting simply on his own impulse), and makes a negative decision about marriage, then this man also is doing the "right thing" and choosing what to Paul is the "better" of the two alternatives (vv. 37–38).

Last comes the apostle's answer to widows who have asked about marriage. They are reminded that the unique loyalty of the marriage bond, though it is lifelong (with v. 15 as the exception, not the rule), is terminated by death. Accordingly, they are as "free to marry" as any others, or to choose not to do so, with this choice, in Paul's judgment, once again, the better.

B. Questions about food, idolatry, and freedom (8:1–11:1). A second major topic is introduced by the words *now about food sacrificed to idols* (8:1). Under this heading, as in the previous chapter, Paul treats several different though related questions. Here they concern the propriety of Christians in their own homes eating food that may have previously passed before an idol (8:4–6; 10:23–26); of Christians eating such food in the home of an unbeliever (8:7–9; 10:27–29); and of Christians accepting an invitation to dine in a pagan temple (8:10–12; 10:14–22).

It would be hard, as all these issues indicate, for any Christian at Corinth not to ask questions. Invitations to dine at a temple were, as archaeology has shown, a common social convention among everyone except slaves, and virtually all of the food sold in the marketplace would have passed through a pagan temple for symbolic purposes, or if meat for slaughter, before its sale. But the questions here appear to have been asked by some in a way that defended their own conduct and challenged Paul's (9:3) in this matter and others (9:4–6) as either too bold in its exercise of Christian and apostolic rights (9:4–12a), or too timid in its restraint (9:12b–27), and in any case inconsistent with what they had come to expect of an apostle (9:1–2). Paul's reply alternates between instructions and his own example, rather than between advice and principles.

In **8:1–13**, as in 6:12 (and perhaps in 7:1), Paul begins by giving assent to a guideline advanced by some at Corinth, in this case, the principle that possession of knowledge justifies any conduct which is consistent with it. As before, however, the guideline is quickly qualified by a reminder that knowledge can blind its possessor to its own importance and lead him in isolation from others toward a false assurance. Love, on the other hand, is a far more reliable guide, for it leads its possessor toward personal maturity in fellowship with others, and when turned toward heaven, to communion with God. Consequently, it is important both to know the truth and yet to speak it in love (Eph. 4:15).

Paul proceeds to review, for those who have need of it, the basic truths that undergird Christian monotheism. The first of these is that "an idol is nothing," having no real existence in the world except in the minds and hearts of its worshipers, who nonetheless by their ignorant devotion open themselves up to the influence of real beings with demonic power (10:14, 19–22). The second, upon which the first is founded, is that there is no God but one, who is the source of all creation, whose service is the purpose that gives life meaning, and who is the Father of the one Lord Jesus Christ, his agent in the beginning of life and in its continuation and renewal (similar ideas are expressed in Eph. 4:5–6 and Col. 1:15–16, probably a fragment from an early Christian confession).

Next, Paul reminds his readers that some among them do not yet trust the substance of this truth enough to know its power in experience beyond simple assent. Therefore they continue to have doubts about the nature of the food that they eat and the implications of doing so. Because of this, fellow believers, in their words (v. 8 probably paraphrases some of them) and actions, need to "be careful" lest the "exercise of . . . freedom" and knowledge lead them to ignore the effect of their behavior upon the faith of the weak.

Finally, Paul applies what he has said to the situation in Corinth. Some have already accepted invitations to dine in pagan temples in public view, and are in danger of leading those with a weak conscience to disregard it and act insincerely. Thus the weak, for whom Christ died, will be led to abandon action that matches their convictions, and perhaps even to depart from any attempt at morality, a path that leads to destruction (see 5:5). When this happens those who have encouraged it will be found to have sinned against both the weak and Christ who cares for even the weakest believer (Mark 9:42). Therefore Paul chooses, for himself, to restrict the actions that he might legitimately take according to the criteria of love and concern for his fellow believer.

The mention of restraint prompts Paul to recall that some at Corinth have begun to interpret his reserve as an indication that he is not free to act, as they presume an apostle would, without reference to the beliefs of others. The rhetorical questions he poses in response are not as much concerned with his defense as they are with the fact that this false supposition may cause the Corinthians to neglect his advice (**9:1–27**). So his apostolic authority must be reestablished through reference to his experience of having seen the risen Lord and to the results of his initial mission which brought the Corinthian church into existence through the preaching of the gospel. Thus, though outsiders may question his status, Paul expects his own to remember that their life in Christ is the continuing seal of its authenticity.

But does not a true apostle ask his converts to provide him with food and drink and the financial support to enable him to travel with a "believing wife" (vv. 4–5)? Do not the "other apostles and the Lord's brothers and Cephas" request such things from those whom they serve (v. 6)? Indeed they do, and so too can Paul, who now illustrates the legitimacy of this right by noting that a soldier has a recognized right to serve at the expense of others; that those who plant crops or tend livestock have a recognized right to share in the produce; and that this right of support is recognized not only in the sphere of human affairs but also in the Law of Moses, which speaks (in Deut. 25:4) about the right of an ox that treads grain to do so without a muzzle that he might eat as he works.

These last words Paul takes (employing a traditional rabbinic method; cf. Rom. 5:9–10, 15, 17) to refer just as much if not more to the reward deserved by himself and others like him (vv. 8–10). Confirmation is provided by the observation that those who have plowed or threshed the grain are also entitled to possess a "hope of sharing in the harvest." Thus Paul and the others who have "sown spiritual seed" among the Christians at Corinth are also entitled to share in the harvest of their ministry through the provision of their continuing material needs (vv. 11–12a).

But Paul has indeed, as they know, made no use of this right. Yet this is not, as his words have shown, because he is not entitled to do so. Rather, it is because he has decided to avoid any hindrance to the reception of the gospel of Christ. For despite the right of "those who preach the gospel" to "receive their living from the gospel," which is analogous to the right of those who work "in the temple" and serve at the altar to "share in what is offered on the altar" (v. 14), Paul has chosen not to make use of this or any of his rights, and he is not corresponding with the Corinthians for the purpose of requesting them. He has elected instead to make his boast in a ministry that disavows any dependence on another except the one who compels him to preach. Thus it is an almost involuntary obedience to God's call, rather than a voluntary and carefully planned decision to take up a self-supporting career, that stands behind Paul's attempt to "discharg[e] the trust committed to [him]" (v. 17; see also 4:1–2). And the reward he receives for such service is precisely the ability to make good upon the terms of his boast, to preach the gospel free of charge.

But given independence from all, Paul has freely subjugated himself again; not to their support, but to their way of life, in order to win them to faith. Though no longer bound by the notion of the Law as a covenant enabling maintenance of the righteousness necessary to fellowship with God, Paul is nonetheless willing to follow many of the customs that are indifferent to one justified by faith (see also Rom. 3:21–22; Acts 18:18; 21:26) when to do so means an opportunity to gain entrance for the gospel. Conversely, among those for whom the law was no guide, Paul is willing, to the extent permitted to him by "Christ's law" (Mark 12:28–34; Luke 10:25–37; Gal. 6:2), to loose himself from divine Law as a point of reference if this leads to the fulfillment of the gospel's objective. And so, at length, his reasons now plain, Paul repeats his readiness to abide by the standards of the weak, or even to become all things to all men if, in this way, it becomes possible for him to bring about their continuing allegiance to the saving gospel of Jesus Christ. For in the blessing of their entrance into a growing faith, Paul, as their apostle, also shares (v. 23; see also Col. 2:5).

A last illustration allows Paul to compare his restraint with that of a runner who gives up much in "strict training" to attempt to gain the winner's "crown" in "the games" (vv. 24–25). Paul does not renounce his rights to no purpose, like a half-hearted runner running aimlessly, or a casual boxer who is always beating the air. But, like the serious athlete, he beats back his physical needs until they conform with the priorities of his Christian ministry, lest after proclaiming to others Jesus' call to abandon all and follow him, Paul himself should be found seeking to retain some personal prerogative and so be "disqualified for the prize" (v. 27; see also Phil. 3:13–16).

The figure of the casual athlete allows Paul to make a transition from himself (9:1–27) to those at Corinth who have taken a casual attitude about their behavior with respect to food dedicated to idols (8:10–12). Their exercise of freedom without restraint, exemplified by a casual acceptance of invitations to dine in pagan temples, endangers themselves as well as the weak if it fails to take seriously the influence of evil behind idolatry (**10:1–22**).

The people of Israel had made similar presumptions as those who together had been under the cloud and had passed through the sea (10:1; Exod. 13:17–14:31). Indeed their experience suggests to Paul that all Israel underwent a baptism into Moses analogous to Christian baptism into Christ (12:13; Gal. 3:27). Furthermore, they all ate "spiritual food" and drank "spiritual drink" (vv. 3–4; see also Exod. 16:1–17:7; Num. 20:1–13), experiences corresponding even more closely to the Christian (John 4:10; 7:37). For the "spiritual rock," from which the drink came, continued to appear throughout their journey (according to a common Jewish understanding which interpreted Israel's repeated ability to find water in the wilderness in this way). So Paul does not hesitate even to identify this saving action with the pre-incarnate work of God in Christ. Nevertheless, these experiences did not succeed in protecting most of the people from evil or from God's judgment when they failed to take their actions seriously.

This should now serve as an example to dissuade Christians from stubbornly refusing to acknowledge and give up what is evil. The temptation (as one eats, drinks, and indulges in the "revelry" of any pagan occasion) to stubbornly ignore evil and acquiesce in an act of idolatry should be rejected (8:10–12; 10:14–22) if the Christians at Corinth are not simply to repeat in their own experience the experience of Israel (Exod. 32:6). In the same way, the temptation to "commit sexual immorality as some of them did" (Num. 25:1–9; the difference in the exact number of those who died is insignificant to the point of the argument) should also be refused. Persistence in behavior that might "test the Lord" (in his resolve either to provide or to punish) should be eschewed, as should every temptation to grumble (v. 10; Num. 16:41–50; 1 Cor. 1:11; 3:3).

Thus the past still serves to provide typical examples of divine judgment and, in this case, gives "warnings" to those who now participate in the "fulfillment" toward which all of God's action in the past was pointed (v. 11). Christians who are entrenched in the firm defense of their conduct are especially urged to be careful. Yet no temptation, even of pride and stubbornness, is theirs alone. They are involved in something that has proved itself to be common to the experience of all God's people before and since. And God can be trusted not to allow temptation to go beyond their ability to resist if they will look and not ignore the way of escape he will provide.

In this case, as Paul urges his "dear friends" to recognize, the way of escape lies in a flight from the site of idolatry (v. 14). He appeals without qualification to their ability to reason and form judgments based upon what they know, for Christians are "sensible people." Yet some of the Corinthians have failed to take account of all that needs to be considered before coming to a decision about how to respond when invited to a pagan temple. Paul has sketched out the potential implications of their conduct upon others (8:9–12); now he invites them to consider the potentially harmful effects upon themselves.

Once again the argument is by analogy. Just as the acceptance of the "cup of thanksgiving" and the "bread that we break" at the celebration of the Lord's Supper enables a corporate and real participation or communion (Gk. *koinōnia*) with Christ (v. 16; because though many are present with individual thoughts all "partake of the one loaf" and thus become one body [v. 17]), and just as the same sense of participation or communion in the sacrificial worship going on at the altar is experienced in the life of the "people of Israel" by all those who eat the sacrifices (v. 18), so the "sacrifices of pagans" (i.e., the food and drink present in a pagan temple) likewise draw all who eat or drink them into corporate communion in a sphere where demonic presence is genuine and demonic influence powerful (vv. 19–20). For despite the fact that an idol has no real or personal existence, neither the reality nor the personal character of the evil that perpetuates a false worship can ever be doubted. Thus a Christian cannot participate in a meal at a pagan temple. To do so disregards realities and the inherent contradiction of trying to drink the cup of both the Lord and the demons. Such action can only provoke the Lord to a jealous defense of his own unique right to be worshiped (Exod. 20:3; Isa. 42:8; Rom. 1:18–31) or invite the ludicrous thought that we are somehow more able in our freedom than he in his holiness.

The discussion to this point has highlighted two principles which are now summarized (**10:23–11:1**). Paul has labored thus far to show that Christian freedom is not absolute. It must be qualified through the exclusion of any attitude or action that is not "beneficial" to the development of the individual (10:1–23), or not "constructive" with respect to the growth of the community (8:1–13). Moreover, the two are tied together, because the goal for the Christian is not simply to seek one's own good, but also the "good of others" (v. 24; Phil. 2:4).

Abruptly Paul turns to those who have gone to the opposite extreme and placed more restrictions than necessary on their freedom of conscience and behavior. They should "eat anything sold in the meat market without raising questions of conscience" that are unnecessary outside the environs of a pagan temple. For beyond the confines where false worship is given and evil dwells, "the earth is the Lord's and everything in it" (v. 26; Ps. 24:1). They may also accept an invitation to a meal at the home of an unbeliever and eat whatever is "put before" them (v. 27). When they do they should not raise questions of their own conscience, although they must respond to "anyone" (a Christian or not) who feels obliged to inform them that this food is being consumed by others present in knowledge and acceptance of the fact that it has been offered in sacrifice (vv. 28–29a).

The next two questions are obviously intended to reinforce this advice, but the flow of thought is difficult. It may be, however, that the questions are intended to draw attention back to the basic advice of verse 27. If so, then the sense is that there is no need for Paul or any Christian to exercise restraint in deference to "another's conscience" unless that other person expresses his objections. For if he does not (given that our conduct should not rest on assumptions about another person's conscience), then Christians should be free to eat any meal with thankfulness and without fear of denunciation (v. 30; Gal. 2:11–16).

This action or any other, however, should be construed as an opportunity to glorify God rather than an occasion to express our freedom. And the praise of God cannot but be diminished if our action causes anyone inside or outside the church to doubt the moral integrity of the gospel. So the Corinthians should follow the example of Paul, who attempted to follow the "example of Christ" (11:1) by conforming as far as possible to different standards (9:19–23; Matt. 9:10–13; Luke 7:36–50) and neglecting the pursuit of his own good in favor of the good of many (10:24; cf. Mark 10:45) in order that they might continue in faith and so be saved.

C. Questions about worship, gifts, and order (11:2–14:40). A third topic provoking questions at Corinth concerned the proper expression and relative value of spiritual gifts, in particular the way in which certain gifts should be used in a worship service. Within this sphere of questions about worship, however, Paul takes time to deal first with two issues that have proved divisive in the worship of the church. These he has heard about, though the source of the report is not given.

The first issue is concerned with the different head coverings that appropriately distinguish women and men as they pray or prophesy in worship (**11:2–16**). The interpretation of the passage is complicated from the outset (so also to some extent is 11:17–34) by its dependence on prior teaching which Paul has given to the church but which, of course, is unknown to us. However, by beginning with "praise,"

Paul hints that the church has not departed significantly from the substance of what he has previously taught.

The discussion of the issue then begins with a call for the church to acknowledge (again or anew) that the "head of every man is Christ, and the head of the woman is man, and the head of Christ is God" (v. 3). However, the word *head* (Gk. *kephalē*), used here and repeatedly throughout this section, has various meanings. It may be used (as in 4a and 5a) to speak of a physical head. But from this literal meaning come two metaphorical ones which allow the same word to denote rule and authority (the head of the church being in authority over the body [Eph. 1:22]), or source and origin (the head of the church being the source of its existence [Col. 1:18]).

Of course, the precise meaning intended here will greatly influence the interpretation of the principle being expressed, not to mention any attempt to apply it to different, broader questions about the roles appropriate to men and women in contemporary worship. It may be helpful, therefore, to note first that either meaning enables these words to support the instructions which follow. But it is also significant to observe that the second has the advantage of according greater continuity to the section as a whole (see vv. 8–11).

If the second of the metaphorical meanings is Paul's here, then his principle will be a statement of the truth that the source of every man's existence (or perhaps "person"; the Greek can be used generically) is Christ, "through whom all things were made" (the Nicene Creed; cf. John 1:3; Col. 1:16); the source of woman's existence is "the man" (the definite article in Greek is used with the word *man,* not *woman* [see Gen. 2:22–23; 1 Tim. 2:13]); and the source of existence for the historical person of Christ is God (Gal. 4:4; Luke 2:34–35). Thus a man who prays or prophesies with his physical head covered (either, as the NIV text suggests, by some form of head covering or, as the footnote has it, with long hair) symbolically dishonors the source of his existence by obscuring that which was created in the image of God and designed to reflect that image to God's glory (v. 7; Gen. 1:26). Similarly, a woman who prays or prophesies (a practice Paul affirms apart from these comments on proper dress) with her physical head uncovered symbolically refuses to honor the source of her existence (i.e., by trying to obscure the distinctions between woman and man) and so brings dishonor upon her own head as surely as if it "were shaved." Thus if a woman refuses to "cover her head," she may as well "have her hair cut off," for the latter state is no more or less dishonoring to her than the former.

The basis for this argument is now reexpressed and supplemented (v. 9; Gen. 2:18) before Paul returns to the question of the woman's appearance. For the "reason" he has given (vv. 7–9), and because of the angels,[2] the woman who prays or prophesies must "have a sign of authority on her head." This allows her to transcend her created distinction from man (without seeking to deny it) in the expression of her gift. For both now participate in worship in a new order in Christ (12:13; 2 Cor. 5:17; Gal. 3:28; Col. 3:11). This does not mean, however, that in the Lord woman is free to disregard man, nor is man free to disregard woman. The truth is that they are dependent upon each other and both dependent upon God.

As before, the Corinthians are urged to form their own conclusions based upon Paul's presentation (v. 13). But they are reminded as they do that nature reveals this same order as surely as scriptural argument. Thus, "if anyone wants to be contentious," refusing to accept the evidence of either Scripture or nature, then Paul's practice (see also 11:1) will have to provide sufficient grounds for their conformity to these instructions.

In contrast to the previous section, Paul has no praise for what he has heard about Corinthian demeanor when they gather in worship at the Lord's Supper (**11:17–34**). Indeed, as it is, their behavior does "more harm than good." For in the midst of a celebration of unity, there are divisions among fellow believers. And while some "differences" are necessary to distinguish those who believe and act genuinely (receiving "God's approval" as a result) from those who do not, others are not, and if stubbornly or pridefully maintained they are liable to result in judgment (11:34).

The division between those who remain hungry and those who get drunk at the Lord's table is one such unnecessary and dangerous difference.[3] For when it exists, the disunity created means that "it is not the Lord's Supper" that is being eaten. Homes are settings in which one

2. The angels were present with God at creation (Job 38:4–7) and at the time the Law was given to reveal and preserve the created order (Acts 7:53; Gal. 3:19). They observe and protect that order until the time of its demise and their judgment (1 Cor. 4:9; 6:3; Rev. 7:1–2).

3. Paul's words imply that the Corinthian church celebrated the Lord's Supper at the end of a communal meal, and there is just enough evidence about the members of the church (see Gerd Theissen, *The Social Setting of Pauline Christianity: Essays on Corinth*, ed. and trans. John H. Schutz [Philadelphia: Fortress, 1982]) to suggest that the division of which Paul has heard is the product of differences in social and economic status which were a prominent feature of life in the first century.

may eat and drink freely according to his own means, but to do so in the midst of others who are hungry is to despise the new order of the church of God in which slaves and free men are united in their status in Christ (12:13; Gal. 3:28; Col. 3:11) and to humiliate Christian brothers and sisters.

Since Paul cannot praise the Corinthians for remembering what he has taught them about the Lord's Supper, he now reminds them of the words he received and "passed on" to them. (The two verbs are technical terms in Judaism for the deliberate preservation and careful transmission of a tradition as it was originally "received" from its source. Paul therefore provides what is probably the earliest account in the New Testament of this part of the tradition about Jesus' words and actions; cf. Luke 1:1–3.) Paul's testimony accords quite closely, though not exactly, with that of the Gospel records. Our Lord, on the night of his betrayal, took bread, gave thanks, broke it into pieces, and said, "This is my body, which is for you; do this in remembrance of me" (v. 24). These words, precisely in contrast to their intent, have proven to be an abiding source of division among Christians. For whatever the relationship established between the body and the bread, both are given for the benefit of all (the "you" is plural in Greek) that all may share in one body and celebrate their unity together in this memorial. In the same way, Jesus took the cup at the end of the meal and said, "This cup is the new covenant [see Jer. 31:31–34] in my blood; do this, whenever you drink it, in remembrance of me" (v. 25). Thus, whenever Christians together "eat this bread and drink this cup" (in contrast to common food and drink), they proclaim the Lord's death which is for all (2 Cor. 5:14–16), inaugurating the new age (2 Cor. 5:17; 10:11) that will be brought to its culmination when he returns.

Therefore, because of the significance invested in these elements, anyone who consumes them in a manner that is not in keeping with their purpose of uniting believers with each other and with their Lord "will be guilty of sinning against the body and blood of the Lord." He will have failed to distinguish the consumption of these elements from that of ordinary food and drink. So every person should examine his attitude toward those with whom he is about to share in this most intimate fellowship before he eats or drinks. For if the Corinthians do not sense within themselves, or within their previous behavior toward those around them, a genuine affirmation of unity, or a willingness to affirm unity, then they are failing to "recognize the body of the Lord," which is made present in order to unite and celebrate the unity of all with Christ, and they eat and drink judgment upon themselves. Furthermore (as Paul discerns from what he has heard), judgment has already begun to manifest itself in the weakness, sickness, and death of some within the church (though one should not presume that any of these symptoms is always associated with divine judgment [John 9:3]). But such signs of judgment would be unnecessary if the Corinthians would judge themselves in the manner Paul has indicated (v. 31).

The conclusion to be reached is brief. When the Corinthians gather in worship to celebrate the Lord's Supper they must "wait for each other" and come together to eat instead of going ahead as individuals with their own private provisions. If any are so hungry that they cannot wait, then they should eat at home first so as not to provoke judgment. Paul will provide more directions when he comes (v. 34).

Paul passes on now to Corinthian questions about the spiritual gifts (**12:1–14:40**), for Christians should not be "ignorant" about them (**12:1–3**). Their pagan experience should show, however, how easy it is to become carried away in ecstatic worship and "influenced" toward speech, even speech uttered falsely in the name of a dumb idol. Thus, it is important to realize that speech inspired by the Spirit of God will never produce the words *Jesus be cursed,* despite any sense of ecstasy (which, if it were false, might explain this strange utterance) or any temptation under persecution to apostasy (an alternative context in which this cry might be comprehensible). Conversely, no one can say "Jesus is Lord," producing the content of the most basic Christian confession (Phil. 2:11), without opening himself to the inspiration of the Spirit.

In this section (**12:4–31**), the major topic of discussion comes more clearly into focus. It is the relative value of the various spiritual gifts that is at issue, and probably also speculation about the degree of inspiration (or the spirit) associated with each gift. Since speech "in tongues" is mentioned repeatedly in this chapter and the next, becoming the main focus of discussion in chapter 14, it seems likely that this gift was highly regarded at Corinth, and that its recipients tended to exercise a dominant role in worship.

In response to this situation, Paul stresses first (in an early expression of trinitarian thought) that all of the "different gifts" are distributed by one Spirit just as different services are allocated by the same Lord and different "kinds of working" are enabled by the same God. Thus in the same way that services and works are performed not primarily for the benefit of the individual but for that of others, "the manifestation of the Spirit is given for the common good" (v. 7).

The list that follows is intended to be neither exhaustive nor hierarchical, but typical of the gifts that had been experienced at one time or another by Christians in Corinth (see also Rom. 12:6–8; Eph. 4:11). They include the "message of wisdom" and "message of knowledge," faith and the gifts of healing, "miraculous powers," prophecy and "the ability to distinguish between spirits" (RSV), the ability to speak in "different kinds of tongues" and the interpretation of tongues. It is then repeated that all of these are the product of the same Spirit, who distributes them not necessarily one by one, but to each person "as he determines" is best for the good of all (v. 11).

Paul now illustrates the unity (12:12–13), diversity (12:14–20), and integrity (12:21–26) produced at the Spirit's inspiration among those at Corinth who belong to the body of Christ. Though suggested by Jesus' words on the road to Damascus (Acts 9:4) and by its use in the Greek philosophical traditions of Stoicism (with which Paul shows passing familiarity elsewhere), this figure is used casually in the Pauline letters (6:15; 10:17; 11:29), with the exception of these verses.

Just as "the body is a unit though it is made up of many parts . . . so it is with Christ" (v. 12).[4] The point is analogy, not identity. Christ dwells in the church after the resurrection, but possesses his own body as well. The basis for comparison lies in the fact that all Christians, despite the inequities of their former existence, have now been brought into one body (see also Gal. 3:27–28) by a common experience of the Spirit in baptism.

This does not mean, however, that all will now be given exactly the same gifts, for a body is not constituted of a single part, but of many. Thus the diversity among the parts of the body is no cause for concern about membership or status in the body. For, in fact, "God has arranged the parts in the body" with thought for the proper place and role of each, so that there are "many parts, but one body" (v. 20).

Moreover, the unity of the body is not superficial but integral to its existence. Weaker parts of the body are indispensable, less honorable parts (i.e., those not usually receiving recognition) are given "special honor" (v. 23), and "parts that are unpresentable" accorded a modesty that witnesses to their importance. And all of this is by design (12:18). For God has now given greater honor to those members who before their incorporation into the body of Christ had little outside it, so that no cause for a division of honor, attention, status, or concern might exist within the body. Thus, if any part of the body suffers in its ability to function within the body, "every part suffers with it," and when one part is honored, all will rejoice in the recognition of its capability (v. 26).

Repeating the affirmation with which the analogy was begun, Paul now moves to his conclusion. The gifts may be differentiated, but not on the basis of supposition about the degree of inspiration. Rather, those who are given gifts are to be set in order on the basis of their ability (via God's appointment) to serve and edify the body (3:5–15). Thus apostles come first, prophets second, teachers third, then "miracle-workers," healers, helpers, administrators, and last those "speaking in different kinds of tongues" (v. 28). The point is reinforced by questions that treat the gifts in the same order. If all are not appointed and gifted to be apostles, it follows that all should not expect to receive any particular gift, including the ability to speak in tongues or interpret.

The discussion, however, is not allowed to conclude on this point. For neither the gifts nor the giver are static (12:11). Thus all may "eagerly desire" to someday sense the call and empowerment to use those gifts in service to the body that really are "greater" in the list Paul has outlined. But in the midst of this ambition (as they are encouraged to realize) they should know that these gifts are still not the "most excellent way" to serve (v. 31).

Once more Paul pauses to insert a section (**13:1–13**) that interrupts his direct reply in order to clarify the grounds upon which his response rests. He has said that the gifts are given for the "common good" (12:7), but this goal will not be reached apart from a motive to guide and direct their exercise. Thus, if I speak in the tongues of men and of angels, and love does not motivate the control of my speech, "I am only a resounding gong or a clanging cymbal" (v. 1; instruments used to produce a variety of sounds that command attention but only frustrate their audience unless accompanied by music or words that interpret their meaning). Similarly, to have "the gift of prophecy" (which conveys insight into the mysteries of God's

4. The cult of the god of healing, Asclepius, and his daughter, Hygeia, was accorded a prominent place in Corinth, and those who sought healing for a part of the body would often leave a representation of it in the Asclepion. Perhaps Paul has this in mind as he reminds his readers that the body is a unit and not simply a collection of various parts.

activity [2:7] and knowledge about God himself [8:4]) or a "faith that can move mountains" (Mark 11:23) is of no value unless these abilities are motivated by love as they are used within the body of Christ (v. 2). So also the offering of "all I possess" in sacrificial service to "the poor" or the offering of "my body to the flames" in the sacrifice of martyrdom is of no lasting benefit apart from the motivation of love (v. 3).

This love comes to expression in different ways at different times. It comes to expression through patience and kindness that elevate others. It does not express itself through the envy, boastfulness, or pride that keeps attention centered on self. On the same basis the rudeness, the pursuit of self-gain, the anger, and the vindictiveness that express themselves at the expense of others are never characteristic of love. For love cannot be identified with the enjoyment that is achieved for ourselves by such means. Its enjoyment consists in acknowledging the truth, of which our perception and interest is only a part. Such love always protects the interests of others, always trusts in their intentions, always hopes for their good, and always perseveres in its attempt to do these things.

Such love also "never fails" to express itself in the past, the present, or the future among those who belong to God. It will continue to do so even after prophecies, tongues, and knowledge cease (v. 8; there is no indication here that Paul thought any of these events likely before the time when God's kingdom is perfectly or completely manifested [13:10; 15:20–28]). For our knowledge of God and our words spoken in worship in the light of what we know (whether our knowledge is expressed in words of prophecy or in tongues) are only a part of what they should be, and when perfection in thought and expression arrives the imperfect always "disappears" (vv. 9–10).

It is this way in our own experience, for childhood speech and thought inevitably give way to different patterns in adulthood. Similarly, the "poor reflection" of anything seen in a mirror (such as those manufactured in first-century Corinth) could not be compared to the experience of seeing the same thing face to face. For now then, these analogies should caution us that our present knowledge of God (and, by implication, the worship such knowledge initiates) will change and pale when knowledge as complete as that which God has now of us becomes ours of him. In view of this three things can be trusted to "remain" unaltered by the enlargement of our knowledge: "faith, hope, and love . . . but the greatest of these is love" (v. 13).

If love motivates the exercise of the gifts, it should not be difficult, as Paul now shows (**14:1–25**), to determine which gift should be accorded priority in worship. For while all of the gifts are desirable, the "gift of prophecy" builds up or edifies the church to a greater extent than any other, and, in contrast to some at Corinth who thought otherwise, on this basis it is to be given priority over the exercise of the gift of speech in tongues. For speech in tongues is not directed in the first instance toward those present in worship but toward God. Indeed the conversation concerning divine mysteries is private to the extent that it is unintelligible to others apart from interpretation (v. 2; also v. 5). But prophecy (whether it explains the significance of God's actions and words for the present or reveals what God intends for the future) is given in language expressly to strengthen, encourage, and comfort other persons at worship. So the one who speaks in tongues edifies himself but the one who prophesies edifies the church. Therefore, the ability to speak in tongues is not to be neglected, for it has value for every one to whom the gift is given. But the exercise of prophecy in worship is preferable because it is of value not only to the individual but also to the church. This contrast holds unless the one who speaks in tongues also interprets so that the church may be made aware of the contents of an otherwise private conversation.

Several illustrations reinforce the point. If Paul were to come to the Corinthians speaking in tongues, clearly his visit would do them no good unless he also communicated in the intelligible language associated with the other speaking gifts. Similarly, the sounds produced by musical instruments must be distinct and clear if they are intended to convey a tune or a message that is understandable. Language itself furnishes a final illustration. For even languages, all of which have meaning, cannot convey their meaning so long as the hearer remains a foreigner to the language of the one who speaks.

For the reason that has now been stated and illustrated, any person who speaks in a tongue in worship should pray that he may interpret his speech to the others present. This is true even when persons pray in a tongue. For in such prayer, apart from interpretation, the individual may communicate with God in a way that brings satisfaction to the spirit without enabling the mind to comprehend its basis. However, prayer of this kind is not to be abandoned. Instead it is to be supplemented by prayer that can be understood by the mind (just as the song that springs spontaneously from our spirit is to be supplemented by that which is composed purposefully by our mind), and recognized as a form of prayer that is less desirable in corporate worship because it does not allow others to join in its praise.

The weight of Paul's own practice is now thrown behind the argument. For even though Paul himself can give thanks to God for the ability to speak in tongues, a gift he has received with greater frequency than any at Corinth, he nonetheless prefers "in the church" to speak words that are few but meaningful to all as opposed to words which may be numerous but do not promote corporate understanding or response (vv. 18–19).

The Corinthians are exhorted to have a mature evaluation of the gifts by keeping in view a passage from Isaiah (the term *Law* is used by Paul, as it was among the rabbis, to refer to any part of the Old Testament). In context (Isa. 28:11–12) these words come in response to the mocking of the form of speech used by the prophet to convey God's message. In turn Isaiah promises that since Israel will not listen to the Lord's word in their own language, they will hear the message that his judgment has come upon them spoken by men of strange tongues, and even then they will not listen readily. In this sense "tongues, then, are a sign, not for believers but for unbelievers" (v. 22), as a display of God's power sent with the intention that when they are at last understood they may also convict. Prophecy's true purpose, however, is to instruct and speedily convict those who believe in its words.

The application of this interpretative insight to the exercise of tongues and prophecy in the Corinthian worship service is made. If the church gathers and "everyone speaks in tongues," when others come in (whether they enter simply seeking an understanding of the faith or the confirmation of their disbelief) they will not readily listen to sounds they do not understand, but attribute them instead to a temporary insanity (v. 23; see also Acts 2:13–15). But if, in the same circumstances, prophecy is being exercised, then the message of conviction will be immediately understood and repentance, worship, and confession will surely follow.

The practical consequences of all of Paul's teaching in this section are now spelled out in a series of instructions (**14:26–40**). When the church gathers, "everyone" is to make the contribution that the Spirit inspires. Their ministries must be organized by their common commitment to structure the service of worship so as to promote the "strengthening of the church" (v. 26). Thus if those who have the ability to speak in tongues feel inspired to contribute they must not be allowed to dominate the service. "Two—or at the most three—should speak, one at a time," and someone should be able to interpret to all present (v. 27). If such interpretation is not made available by the Spirit, those who speak in tongues "should keep quiet" enough in the church to enable their speech to function as a private prayer (v. 28).

Prophecy likewise, despite its value, is not a gift to be exercised to excess. "Two or three prophets should speak," and then there must be time allowed for the congregation to reflect upon the significance of what it has heard (v. 29). If a prophetic insight comes to a member of the church while another person is giving a prophetic message, the latter should give way temporarily to the former. For in this way all who are inspired can "prophesy in turn" and the maximum amount of instruction and encouragement be received by the church (v. 31). Those with the gift of prophecy should not object that they cannot be interrupted, because it is within their control to remember and resume their message. In this way a peaceful order will be established that reflects God's character and brings the worship of the church at Corinth into the form which is found "in all the congregations of the saints" (v. 33; see also 4:17; 7:17; 11:16). Verse 33 then probably forms the conclusion to this paragraph rather than the introduction to the next; note the otherwise unnecessary repetition of the phrase *in the churches* in verse 34.

To explain the meaning of the next two verses and remove any tension between them and the permission given (in 11:5) to women to pray and prophesy has always proved difficult. The difficulty might conceivably be removed by the observation that some early manuscripts of 1 Corinthians place these two verses after verse 40, indicating that they may have been added later to this letter (note how the words of verse 36 follow naturally those of verse 33), placed here by someone who failed to understand the different situations addressed by the two letters, and attempted to harmonize 1 Corinthians, at least in part, with the instructions found in 1 Timothy 2. Such observation and supposition, however, cannot be substantiated by the evidence available to us.

The explanation that seems most worthy of consideration takes its clue from the evidence of verse 35. The words *if they want to inquire about something* appear to point to a certain kind of speaking that was proving itself as disruptive within Corinthian worship as the unrestrained exercise of other kinds of speech, and which was associated in this particular congregation with women. Perhaps it was simply the frustrated speech of wives whose soft-spoken questions were ignored by husbands, or the bolder speech of women who ignored their husbands entirely and interrupted to ask questions of the person who was speaking.

In any case, Paul's instruction (v. 34) is that such women "should remain silent in the churches" (the Greek words here are more accurately translated "in the meetings of the church"). "They are not allowed to speak" (in the disrespectful and disruptive way that they are doing), but "must be in submission" (to their husbands; the word *submission* is one which Paul defines for his own use in terms of respect [Eph. 5:21–33]), "as the Law says" (though there is no specific place in the Old Testament where such submission or obedience is commanded, this idea is indeed the presumption behind much of its content). Instead "they should ask" their questions of their husbands at home (either before they disrupt the speaker, or before they distract their husbands and those around them). For "it is disgraceful" (see 11:7 where the same Greek word is used of women who refuse to cover their heads as a sign of respect) "for a woman to speak [in this way] in the church" (v. 35).

The whole section is now brought to a close with two rhetorical questions, a statement of the possibilities left open by the argument, and a final exhortation. The questions are designed to deflect the Corinthian tendency toward a sense of their own inspiration and the stubbornly prideful maintenance of unhelpful and idiosyncratic customs. The statement sets forth Paul's expectation that any true "prophet" or "spiritually gifted" person will acknowledge the truth in what he has written (v. 37). If stubborn ignorance is chosen, however, then it will also be safe to ignore the claims of such an individual to be led by the Spirit. The exhortation epitomizes Paul's advice. The ability to prophesy should be sought eagerly and the ability to speak in tongues should not be forbidden. But whatever form the worship service takes as a result of adherence to these directions, "everything should be done in a fitting and orderly way" (v. 40).

D. Questions about the resurrection and life in the age to come (15:1–58). Whether this final section comes in reply to reports (15:12) or tentative questions that are just beginning to be asked (15:35), its principal purpose is clear. Paul writes to defend, to clarify, and to broaden his teaching concerning the resurrection (**15:1–11**). From the content of the statement attributed to some of the Christians at Corinth (v. 12), it seems that their attitude was being shaped by a skeptical aversion similar to that of the Athenians whose attentiveness to Paul's preaching came to an end at his mention of the "resurrection of the dead" (Acts 17:32).

If this is so then the crux of the issue was probably not a denial of the possibility of a life after death, but an opposition (which was characteristic of Greeks and, on occasion, of Jews living in a Greek environment) to the notion of a bodily resurrection and the preference for an idea of immortality of the soul. Added to this was likely a remembrance that when Paul had originally spoken about the resurrection he had done so with words about believers already being "raised with Christ" (Eph. 2:6; Col. 2:12; 3:1; in contrast, 2 Tim. 2:17–18). In response, Paul seeks to demonstrate the validity of the idea of bodily resurrection (15:1–11), its necessity (15:12–19, 29–34), its futurity (15:20–28, 51–58), and its nature (15:35–50).

Paul begins by reminding the Corinthians "of the gospel I preached to you," which they received, in which they have placed their trust, and by which they are saved if they continue to "hold firmly" to their faith in its truth. For otherwise, if initial acceptance gives way to confirmed disbelief, they will "have believed in vain" (vv. 1–2).

The content of Paul's preaching is now crystallized in a credal form that is introduced with the same technical terms for the careful transmission of tradition as were used before to demonstrate a link between Paul and others who provided sure access as witnesses to the events that are now described. The contents of this very early creed are composed from the facts of Jesus' death, interpreted (with probable reference to his teaching [Mark 10:45] and the scriptural figure of the suffering servant [Isa. 53:12]) as a death for our sins; burial (which meant he had actually died [Mark 15:44–46]); resurrection (which took place when God raised his Son in accordance with the Scriptures [Acts 2:24–32]); and appearance after death ("to Peter" [Luke 24:34]; then to the Twelve [as a group, not a number; Luke 24:36]).

The creed (whose elements are all joined to one another by the repetition of the word *that*) is now supplemented by additions. They provide evidence for an appearance of the risen Christ to more than five hundred (v. 6; otherwise unmentioned in the New Testament); to James (v. 7; accounting apparently for his conversion and rapid rise to leadership in the Jerusalem church [Mark 3:20–21; John 7:5; Acts 12:17; 15:13]); to all the apostles (an appearance distinguished here from that of v. 5; cf. Acts 1:3); and last of all (in time only, not in importance) to Paul (in an appearance so long after the others as to make Paul an apostle "abnormally born"; see also Acts 9:5).

Nonetheless, though least among the apostles and undeserving of the title because, unlike the others, he had persecuted the church of God (v. 9; Acts 9:1–2), Paul had still been called by divine grace that is "not without effect" to do the work of an apostle. In response, he had expended more effort in travel and ministry and had reaped more success (because of the "grace of God that was with me") in the founding of churches than any other (v. 10). So whether the Corinthians wish to view Paul's preaching, or those whose witness formed the tradition behind his preaching, as the source for their knowledge of Jesus' death and resurrection, it makes no difference to the content of the gospel or the substance of their faith.

Paul next points out the implications of unbelief (**15:12–19**). The Corinthians had been reminded that the resurrection lay at the heart of the gospel that had been proclaimed to them. But was it necessarily the center, or did the call to a spiritual life in union with the risen Christ demonstrate that unlike Christ, Christians were called to be those who pursued and received spiritual immortality rather than resurrection from the dead? Some such question appears to have led various persons within the church to deny any connection between the fact "that Christ has been raised from the dead" and their idea "that there is no resurrection of the dead" (in general; v. 12).

But the disjunction is a false one, for if in fact there is no such thing as a "resurrection of the righteous" (Luke 14:14; Acts 24:15), then there is no reason to believe in the anomaly of Jesus' resurrection. But if he "has not been raised," then both to preach and to believe the resurrection is "useless" (v. 14). Worse, such preaching would be tantamount to bearing "false witness" about God's actions. "For we have testified about God that he raised Christ from the dead," and that cannot be true if "the dead are not raised" (vv. 15–16). Worse still, if Christ has not been raised, then apart from God's vindication made evident by the resurrection, faith in Christ's death as the sacrifice for our sins is futile, and those who have fallen asleep or died believing in Christ as their Savior "are lost" (v. 18). Worst of all, if Christians have only a false hope in Christ for any life beyond the present, then "we are to be pitied more than all men" as self-deluded (v. 19).

In fact, however, such consequences need be explored no more as Paul gives the implications of a true understanding (**15:20–28**). "Christ has indeed been raised from the dead, the firstfruits of those who have fallen asleep" (v. 20). By the term *firstfruits,* Paul means to signify the first produce from a harvest. Such produce possessed special representative significance as a sign of what might be expected from the crop and was to be presented to God in the temple (Exod. 23:19). The thought of Christ's resurrection as a representative event triggers the comparisons that follow between Christ and Adam as representative persons. For just as death came into the world through a man whose actions were truly representative of the harvest of sin and death that has become characteristic of all who have come after him, so now the resurrection of the dead has come through a man whose destiny his progeny can also fully expect to share. For inasmuch as all who are united with Adam by birth and by sin die, all who are united with Christ by rebirth and faith will, like him, be made alive.

"But each in his own turn"; first Christ, then "those who belong to him" at his coming (v. 23; 15:52; 1 Thess. 4:14). Then "the end will come," the time when Christ hands over to the Father his kingly rule over all those who believe in him (vv. 23–24a). This will not happen, however (Ps. 110:1; Mark 12:36; Acts 2:34–35), until all of the other forces which exercise an alien power over Christ's people have been destroyed, including the last such enemy, which is death. But when all of these have been destroyed, the God who has put them all under Christ's feet (Ps. 110:1; cf. Ps. 8:6) by destroying their power must not himself be expected to subject himself to Christ. Rather, just the opposite will happen. "The Son himself will be made subject" (or perhaps, as is suggested by the Greek, he "will subject himself") to the Father who has given him his kingly authority so that God may be recognized as the true source of "all" that has happened "in all" these events (v. 28).

A series of rhetorical questions presses home the practical implications of Paul's argument (**15:29–34**). The first, however, certainly raises more questions for us than simply the one which is asked. It is surely relevant to point out that there is no value in being "baptized for the dead" if the dead are not raised (v. 29), but when and where was such a baptism practiced, and why? Paul's words most naturally suggest a baptism undertaken by Christians for Christians who died in faith without having been baptized, because of a deathbed conversion. Or perhaps they refer to some who converted and were baptized in order to be reunited with their dead Christian loved ones. In any event, Paul does not recommend the practice, but only states that it takes place.

Paul's own life is the subject of the next question. For if there is no resurrection, then to repeatedly "endanger" one's life on behalf of the gospel is foolish (v. 30). Why expend the effort that brings him unnecessarily closer to death every day? And what possible benefit could there have been in allowing himself to be put in the arena with "wild beasts" at Ephesus for the cause of Christ (an event otherwise unmentioned in the New Testament)? For if the dead are not raised then it is much more prudent to enjoy the pleasures of life for as long as possible (v. 32; Isa. 22:13).

As they reflect on their answer to these questions the Corinthians are not to be "misled" by the opinions of those outside the church, for as even the pagan playwright Menander had said, "bad company corrupts good character" (v. 33). Instead of a life lived in the sin which results from an excessive pursuit of the pleasures of the body, prompted perhaps by the notion that a spiritual union with Christ after the death of the body is assured, the Corinthians are called back from such shameful ignorance of the truth to the Christian use of right reason.

The argument could certainly have been ended at this point, but a question about the nature of the resurrection prompts further discussion (**15:35–50**). If there really is a resurrection, "How are the dead raised? With what kind of body will they come?" (v. 35). The second question explains the sense of the first. The Corinthians are not asking about the way in which God's power could make possible a resurrection, but questioning the implications of the idea. To ask the latter question, however, is foolish if the former is already answered with reference to God. The use of analogy will demonstrate this.

Paul begins with a biological analogy in common use among rabbis of the first century (John 12:24). A seed that is sown does not come to life in the form of a plant unless its first form, its bodily shell, dies. Furthermore, the form of the seed that is sown says nothing about the nature of the plant which will sprout.

The form of the seed and the plant differ because God gives the latter a bodily form according to his own plan, and that he is able to do this is demonstrated repeatedly in the present by his power to give each kind of seed its own body. Similarly, divine activity in the present also explains why "all flesh is not the same" (v. 39). But just as "earthly bodies" now manifest God's splendor differently than "heavenly bodies" (v. 40), "so will it be with the resurrection of the dead" (v. 42a).

The body which now displays God's glory is perishable. The body that will be raised will display God's glory in an imperishable form. The body whose glory is now partially obscured in the dishonor of sin and death will be raised to reflect fully and completely God's glory. The body which dies in weakness will be raised to share in the power that comes from God himself. And finally, most comprehensively, the one who dies in a "natural body" will be raised to life in a spiritual body (v. 44a; note, however, that it is still a body, which is both like and unlike ours).

Thus the plausibility of a spiritual body, and something of its nature, is demonstrated from the fact of a "natural body" (v. 44b). It may also be demonstrated from Scripture. For in the same way that Adam as a living being represents the first of his species, so Christ, the last Adam, as a spiritual being, gives life to a new race of persons whose bodily form is now represented only by his own. The point, however, is that full spiritual existence in a glorified body does not come until natural existence in a physical body is ended. But when it does, we shall share in the same kind of spiritual existence as our Lord, as surely as we now share in the same kind of physical existence as Adam. And the resemblance will extend even to our appearance.

But if the end of our natural life is a prerequisite to the transformation that allows our participation in the eternal kingdom of God, then what will happen to those who are left alive at the time of Christ's coming and this world's demise? The answer is part of the mysterious wisdom of God's plan. "We will not all sleep, but we will all be changed" (v. 51). In the same moment that the dead are raised, those who are alive will also be changed. Their perishable physical existence will be cloaked by the imperishable existence and immortality of a body transformed by God's power as surely as those who have died and been resurrected.

And so the prophetic words of Isaiah (25:8) and Hosea (13:14) will be fulfilled. For, together with those who have been resurrected, those who have not passed through death and resurrection and yet have been transformed will also be able to celebrate their victory in Christ over the sting of death (vv. 54b–55). For death's power over a sinful humanity has been destroyed by Christ, and he gives to all his own, whether living or dead, his victory over death in which they may gratefully share. Consequently, Paul encourages the Corinthians to remain true to their trust in Christ's promise to share with them his victory over death, and to devote themselves fully and without fear to the work of the Lord (v. 58).

E. Questions about the collection and Paul's plans (16:1–9). A final Corinthian question remains about "the collection for God's people" (see also Rom. 15:25–28; Gal. 2:10). From the content of Paul's reply their questions seem to have been more concerned with the nature and timing of their own participation rather than with the collection itself or the rationale behind it. The Corinthians are advised to do as Paul has already directed the "Galatian churches" (Paul's reference must be to a message sent orally or in writing, for the letter to the Galatians contains no explicit reference to the collection or directions for contributors). Each person is to save up a weekly contribution "in keeping with his income."

Paul neither specifies a level for the gift nor directs that it be collected and held by the church, but asks simply that it be set aside weekly in order that he may not have to make a special appeal and so work a special hardship upon any member of the church at the time of his arrival. When he arrives he will give those appointed by the church the appropriate letters of introduction and "send them with your gift to Jerusalem" (v. 3; Acts 20:4). Whether Paul will accompany them himself is uncertain as he writes this letter (though it seems almost certain that he did, and that the collection is the reason for a journey to Jerusalem [Acts 20–21]).

Paul now coordinates the instructions for the collection with his own plans. At this point (though as 2 Cor. 1:15–17 indicates, his plans were modified), Paul's hope is to come to Corinth after passing through Macedonia, to stay at Corinth (perhaps even for the winter), and then to continue his journey wherever that may take him. But he does not intend to begin his journey or leave Ephesus (from where this letter is written) until Pentecost; the opportunity for ministry, despite opposition, is simply too great to be abandoned any more quickly (vv. 8–9).

IV. The Recommendation of Others (16:10–18)

Paul's response to the Corinthians' questions is now concluded, but his mention of his own plans leads him to relay to his readers what news he has of other persons with whom he and his readers are acquainted. They can expect a visit by Timothy, and when he arrives they should give him no cause for fear to act and speak openly. Instead they are to overcome his fears with their acceptance of his ministry and send him back to Paul in peace. (Whether "the brothers" mentioned here are traveling with Timothy or waiting for him with Paul is uncertain.)

Next Paul writes to the Corinthians about Apollos. Paul has indeed seen him and strongly urged him to visit them again (whether on his own initiative or at the Corinthians' request is unclear). But, at least at the time Paul last saw him, "he was quite unwilling to go" and so they must not expect him until a later opportunity presents itself (whether Apollos ever returned to Corinth is not known). Perhaps, however, it is not too much to conjecture that the words of exhortation which immediately follow are meant to reflect Apollos's agreement with the substance of Paul's letter and his own greeting to the church.

Third, Paul commends to his readers those from the household of Stephanas, the first converts in Achaia. They have devoted themselves to the service of the saints, and consequently deserve the same submissive respect as others from outside the church who function as teachers and leaders or anyone else who "joins in the work, and labors at it" (v. 16).

Finally, Paul conveys to the church that Stephanas, Fortunatus, and Achaicus have arrived, and gladly commends their service in supplying him with the information that has allowed him to respond more fully to the church's needs. Such men "deserve recognition" for their ministry of keeping the apostle and the church in touch with one another (v. 18).

V. Final Greetings and Formal Closing (16:19–24)

As in the opening of this letter, Paul now reverts to the elements that were customary in the closing of a letter in his era. First are closing greetings sent by Paul and by others. The others mentioned include "the churches in the province of Asia" (among which Paul is now working), Aquila and Priscilla (who had earlier hosted Paul and worked alongside him in his initial mission in Corinth, departing and journeying with him to Ephesus where they chose to remain), "the church [at Ephesus] that meets at their house," and "all the brothers" (either the rest of the Ephesian believers or Paul's fellow workers in the Ephesian ministry—in either case the word must be understood as a generic rather than a gender-specific term). The warmth of their greeting to the Corinthians is to be conveyed symbolically with the Corinthians embracing one another in the way that these others would embrace them if they were present. Paul's final greeting in his own hand serves a double purpose: authenticating this letter as his own (Gal. 6:11; Col. 4:18; 2 Thess. 3:17) and indicating that it was probably composed, as was customary, by dictation (Rom. 16:22).

Next, again as was usual, one finds a final short message. Originating perhaps as part of an early Christian worship service (in which the response to the words found here may have been "If anyone loves the Lord, let him be blessed"), these words seem meant to remind the readers that in the end "love for the Lord" (RSV) is the paramount quality of Christian faith and as such should unite all believers. Similarly the cry "Come, O Lord" (reflecting the Aramaic expression *marana tha*) is also probably cited from the liturgical context of worship that was meant to unite all believers.

Finally, as was normal, a formal closing concludes the letter. Paul's closing ends the letter as it began—with the recognition of God's grace given in Jesus and with the conveyance of his own abiding love for all in Christ.

OUTLINE—2 CORINTHIANS

I. Epistolary Introduction (1:1–11)
II. Paul's Explanation of His Conduct in Recent Matters (1:12–2:13)
   A. The Basis for Paul's Behavior and an Appeal for Understanding (1:12–14)
   B. The Cause for Paul's Change of Plans (1:15–2:2)
   C. The Purpose of Paul's Last Letter (2:3–11)
   D. The Motive for Paul's Movement from Troas to Macedonia (2:12–13)
III. Paul's Reflection upon His Ministry (2:14–5:21)
   A. The Source and Character of Paul's Ministry (2:14–3:6a)
   B. The Message of Paul's Ministry (3:6b–4:6)
   C. The Cost of Paul's Ministry (4:7–5:10)
   D. The Perspective of Paul's Ministry (5:11–21)
IV. Paul's Appeal to the Corinthians (6:1–13:10)
   A. An Appeal for Complete Reconciliation (6:1–7:4)
   B. A New Basis for Appeal (7:5–16)
   C. An Appeal for Full Response to the Collection (8:1–9:15)
   D. An Appeal for Full Allegiance to Apostolic Authority (10:1–18)
   E. Support for the Appeal (11:1–12:13)
   F. The Conclusion of the Appeal (12:14–13:10)
V. Epistolary Conclusion (13:11–14)

I. Epistolary Introduction (1:1–11)

Paul again opens his letter with a customary greeting (see 1 Cor. 1:1–3). After naming himself as the sender of the letter, together with Timothy, he describes himself to the church in words almost identical to those used in his earlier letter. The letter's address indicates that Christians elsewhere in Achaia, probably principally at Cenchrea (Acts 18:18; Rom. 16:1) and Athens (Acts 17:34), have been affected by the recent affairs in the church (likely the largest in Achaia) at Corinth. The salutation is concluded with Paul's usual Christian greeting.

Thanksgiving typically follows greeting (see 1 Cor. 1:4–9), but Paul's thanksgiving here is not given over to God for his grace and love at work in the church. Instead, praise is given God for his comfort made manifest in a particular experience of suffering in Paul's life. The experience itself, which he compares in kind to the "suffering of Christ" as one involving distress, "hardships," "great pressure," despair, the imminence of death, and "deadly peril" (vv. 5–10), remains unmentioned (perhaps indicating that the Corinthians knew the facts well enough, including the part their own failure to honor Paul and his gospel had played in the apostle's sufferings). Paul chooses rather to extol the "Father of compassion and the God of all comfort" (v. 3) from whom he has received the strength to sustain himself in suffering.

Furthermore, precisely because of his experience, which forced him to rely exclusively upon God in a situation in which he had given himself up for dead, Paul has become uniquely equipped to minister to "those in any trouble," bringing to them the "comfort we ourselves have received from God" (v. 4). In the light of his own experience, Paul seeks to minister comfort and conciliation to the church at Corinth, and he begins by asking for their prayers.

II. Paul's Explanation of His Conduct in Recent Matters (1:12–2:13)

A. The basis for Paul's behavior and an appeal for understanding (1:12–14). Having asked for their prayers, Paul next appeals to the Corinthians in conciliation to reassess their estimation of him and his ministry. Boasting and the kind of criticism that belittles one in order to exalt another had consistently troubled the church and severely complicated its relationship with Paul (1 Cor. 3:21; 4:7; 5:6). Such boasting and criticism had also no doubt been responsible in large measure for the pain that Paul had experienced on his last visit to Corinth, pain which led him, in turn, to compose a letter that struck back severely in anguished self-defense (2 Cor. 2:1–4).

But now Paul seeks to clear away the selfish boasting of the past and to make a boast in which he invites the Corinthians to share, a boast in the Lord. In conduct, Paul has always sought to relate to the church "in the holiness and sincerity that are from God" (v. 12a). In speech and writing he has similarly shunned the attempt to present a wisdom that invites comparisons between his message and those of others in favor of a simplicity of thought and advice rooted in their common experience of "God's grace" (vv. 12b–13). It is Paul's hope, therefore, that the Corinthians will come to understand that the only boast to be made among Christians is a boast that unites them with their leaders, a mutual boast in God's holiness, sincerity, and grace at work in their lives.

B. The cause for Paul's change of plans (1:15–2:2). In 1 Corinthians 16:2–8 and at the beginning of this section (1:15–16) are found two different itineraries relating to Paul's plans to revisit the Corinthian church. However, as 2:1 indicates, neither plan was carried through. Thus, it appeared as though Paul was at best not truly concerned with his relationship to the church, and at worst a fickle person who made promises "lightly" (1:17a) and constantly went back on his word.

Once more Paul meets this obstacle to reconciliation squarely and clarifies the reasons for his conduct by relating his conduct to the conviction he shares with the Corinthians concerning God's faithfulness. Christ was preached with consistency by Paul, by Silas, and by Timothy in such a way as to emphasize that all God's promises were faithfully fulfilled in him. No matter their number, or the length of time taken in mercy to bring them to fulfillment, or the manner, expected or unexpected, of their fulfillment, the eventual fulfillment of God's promises demonstrates his glorious faithfulness. Upon this kind of faithfulness, betokened especially in the receipt of the Holy Spirit, those who are in Christ place their hope for what is yet to come.

But it is also just this kind of faithfulness that has motivated Paul to change the manner in which his plans should come to fulfillment. Out of a merciful desire not to grieve the church (2:2) Paul changed his plans; not out of a faithless, fickle sense of self-importance, but in order to work with the Corinthians rather than working purely on the basis of his own original agenda (1:24). This goal had led Paul to set aside his previous plans and to work out a different schedule for their eventual fulfillment.

C. The purpose of Paul's last letter (2:3–11). As a part of his altered agenda, Paul penned a third letter to the church (for reference to the first, see 1 Cor. 5:9; the second is our canonical 1 Cor.), the purpose of which he now seeks to explain. It was written so that on his next return to Corinth he might not "be distressed by those who ought to make me rejoice," in confidence and trust that such distress could be avoided so as to produce a joyful visit for all (v. 3). But in order to achieve its end Paul's letter had first to deal openly and honestly with the source of the problem. To write such a letter was certainly not easy, for its purpose was not simply to rebuke but to share with the church the anguish of an unrequited love.

The letter seems to have achieved its intent (v. 9), and with reconciliation now possible, Paul hastens to make sure that it is accomplished. He urges the cessation of the punishment inflicted upon the individual who had opposed his authority, causing distress both for Paul and for the church, and counsels forgiveness, granting it freely himself in concert with the rest of the church (vv. 5, 7, 10). Then, with particular pastoral sensitivity to the needs of the offender as well as those of the body and himself, Paul encourages the community not only to forgive the offender but also to comfort him and to reaffirm its love for him lest he be "overwhelmed with excessive sorrow" and the discipline that was meant to be remedial become simply retributive, thus allowing Satan yet another entrance into the situation (vv. 7–8, 11).

D. The motive for Paul's movement from Troas to Macedonia (2:12–13). In this, the final segment of Paul's explanation of his recent conduct, he seeks to acquaint the church with events in his ministry from the time of his last letter until the present moment of composition. In all probability Paul's "painful" letter had been dispatched to Corinth with Titus from Ephesus. But from there, before receiving a reply, Paul had departed to Troas. Despite the open door for the gospel of Christ that presented itself to Paul in Troas, he had been unable to feel at peace without news from Titus, and so in an attempt to meet Titus on the route of his return, he had gone on to Macedonia.

III. Paul's Reflection upon His Ministry (2:14–5:21)

A. The source and character of Paul's ministry (2:14–3:6a). Surprisingly, the conclusion to the account of Paul's anxious attempt to meet the returning Titus is not immediately related. Instead we are made to wait until 7:5 to receive the conclusion of the narrative. In the interim, we are given an opportunity to share in some of Paul's own reflections upon the nature of his ministry. The catalyst for these reflections is clearly the relationship between Paul and the church at Corinth in general, and the return of Titus to Paul with news of his recent visit to Corinth in particular. But in their breadth and scope Paul's words within this section describe, perhaps better than any other part of the Pauline correspondence, the apostle's own sense of mission and ministry.

Paul begins his reflections, accordingly, by giving thanks to God, for in its essence his apostolic ministry is simply a part of the "triumphal procession in Christ" which is directed and guided by God (2:14). The verbal imagery used here is intended to allude to a Roman triumph, a procession carefully orchestrated by a Roman military commander to display the results of a significant military victory. As a part of some of these processions fragrant spices, perfumes, and incense were used along the way, and it may be that this inspires the description of Paul's ministry as a conveyance for the aroma of Christ. The image, however, is mixed here with another drawn from the Old Testament (where a pleasing aroma is said to result from a ritual sacrifice [Lev. 1:9, 13, 17]). The aroma of Paul's ministry, as a part of the aroma of Christ, can be said to ascend to God at the same time that it diffuses itself among men and women, both those who are being saved and those who are perishing (2:15–16a; 1 Cor. 1:18).

To be the bearer of an aroma so potent as to lead to life for its recipients and death for those who reject its fragrance is a heavy responsibility. To be "equal to such a task" seems overwhelming (2:16b). But, at the same time, it is important to Paul to note that unlike many who "peddle the word of God for profit" he has made a conscientious attempt to bring himself to the task with sincerity and a sense that the proclamation of the gospel is always made before God as well as a human audience (2:17).

His words, however, in the context of the competition for ecclesiastical leadership that had been going on at Corinth (1 Cor. 1:12; 2 Cor. 10–13) needed careful clarification on two counts. First, there was the possibility that they might be read by some as a purely subjective self-commendation, and second, there was the likelihood that they might prompt an immediate comparison between Paul and others who carried formal letters of recommendation.

Paul takes up the latter point by first claiming the Corinthians themselves as the recommendation for his ministry (3:2). And unlike a letter that Paul or anyone else might write, the testimony commending the faithful work of the apostle had been permanently written by the Spirit of the living God in their lives. Then, moving back to the former point, Paul reminds his readers that his confidence is a product not of self-analysis, but of his relationship with God through Christ. Therefore, only God can give persons the competence that makes them equal to the task of functioning as ministers of a new covenant.

B. The message of Paul's ministry (3:6b–4:6). But, as is so often the case in Paul's writings, the terms that are used to conclude one argument lead inevitably to the opening of another (this is also a commonplace of Jewish literary style in general). Here the mention of a new covenant (see Jer. 31:31–34) inspires a transition in thought from discussion about the source and character of Paul's ministry to a consideration of its message. The presentation is made in terms of a comparison between the ministry which carried as its essence the written covenant "of the letter" (Exod. 24:3–8) and the ministry which proclaims the new covenant of the Spirit (the nature of the comparison suggests, as does 11:22, that the distress in the church at Corinth had come from some who pressured the whole of the church toward a strict allegiance to the law and customs of Judaism).

The comparison does not proceed, however, by way of deprecation, describing the latter ministry as glorious and the former as inglorious. Rather a comparison is made between the recognized and authentic "glory" of the former covenant (3:7, 9a, 11) and the "surpassing glory" of the latter (3:8, 9b, 10, 11b). The argument is strengthened by allusion to the account of the gift of the Law (Exod. 34:29–35). Paul provides an interpretative commentary on the meaning of this passage, inferring from the Septuagintal text that the glory which radiated from Moses' face when he brought the gift of Law down from the mount was a fading rather than a permanent possession, one which was perpetuated only by Moses' frequent reentrance into God's presence. The glory of Moses' ministry in bringing to Israel the covenant of the Law was therefore real but transitory. The glory of Christian ministry in proclaiming the new covenant is greater, for it "lasts" (3:11).

In this context of comparison Paul proceeds to set forth a contrast between the two ministries, a contrast between the effect of the "letter" and the Spirit (3:6). The contrast, however, is marked. For the letter, being lifeless, had no power to effect the way of life it commanded, and consequently it became that which "condemned" and "brought death" rather than life (3:7, 9). But the Spirit, a living and active part of God's being, has precisely that power which the Law lacked, the power which effectively "brings righteousness" (3:7; not only a knowledge of righteousness) and gives life. Thus the conclusion follows by contrast, as well as comparison, that a ministry in service of the new covenant surpasses one in service of the old.

This perspective upon the value of Christian ministry then motivates Paul to bold proclamation. He has put no veil upon his message in an attempt to shield the surpassing glory of the gospel from his fellow Jews (as had Moses, who had hidden the glow of God's glory behind a veil [Exod. 34:33–35]). Instead it was quite the other way round. If Paul's message was veiled, that was only because the Law and its traditional interpretation (given "when the old covenant is read") had veiled and dulled Jewish minds to the truth of the gospel. But, as experience had shown, whenever they turn to the Lord that veil "is taken away" (v. 16; Exod. 34:34), and it is removed (according to Paul's interpretation of Exod. 34:34) under the inspiration of the Spirit. For the Spirit brings freedom from the systematic adherence of Judaism to the Law and its traditional interpretation; the Spirit actually enables the transformation of existence that was the intention behind the letter of the Law (3:17–18).

And so, transformed "through God's mercy," Paul has been given the ministry of bearing the message which transforms its recipients. Because he has been sent from God, his proclamation can embrace neither "deception" nor the distortion of anything that God has said in the past (4:2). Thus, where it remains obscure, one may be sure that such obscurity is not a result of the proclamation, but a result of the work of the enemy, the god of this age (cf. John 12:31) who has blinded the minds of those who persist in unbelief to the light of the gospel. Neither can the proclamation promote its bearer, but only its subject, Jesus Christ, the Lord who is the very image of God (and therefore the true and second Adam, the beginning of a new creation [see 5:17]). Only through Christ can the full light of God's glory become known.

C. The cost of Paul's ministry (4:7–5:10). A change of metaphor signals the beginning of a new thought, though it is closely related to all that Paul has just said. For the light of the gospel may also be described as that which has been placed within the minds and hearts of its human bearers as a treasure placed within "jars of clay" (cf. Matt. 13:44). The power that transforms belongs to the treasure, not to its receptacle. But the receptacle, though remaining frail, is itself measurably changed by its contents.

Abandoning metaphorical language, Paul proceeds now to describe the change that has come about since the placement of the treasure within him. It is not a change in the conditions or circumstances of his life (for pressure and perplexity continue to be a part of his experience, together with persecution and physical beatings which have come more recently, since the beginning of his ministry). But instead it is a change in the attitude and fortitude of the apostle which has enabled him to bear suffering and even to triumph in the midst of it.

For the power of the treasure is clearly "revealed" through the weakness and frailty of its mortal receptacle (4:10–11). So even while death is at work upon Paul, "life is at work" through him for the "benefit" of those to whom he ministers, and this provides Paul with compensation for the cost of his ministry (vv. 12, 15). Moreover, a sure confidence provides Paul with further compensation. It is the confidence that even should death prevail, "the one who raised the Lord Jesus from the dead will also raise us with Jesus and present us with you in his presence" (v. 14). Such compensatory thoughts, kept ever more securely in view because of the inexorable renewal of his inner self, prevent Paul from despair and provide him with a new perspective upon his present afflictions.

Paul, of course, has spoken to the Corinthians before about the hope of resurrection, but now sees an opportunity to develop his thoughts further. So, in a passage that has given rise to a wealth of interpretation, Paul proceeds to reveal what he expects for himself beyond death. He employs a metaphorical description of the body as an earthly tent (5:1) in terms of his own experience (Acts 18:3) and the cultural background of his audience (the physical body having been described as a "tent" in Greek literature since the time of Plato and Pythagoras).

Paul begins by restating his confidence (built upon the experience of Christ) in the reality of the resurrection (v. 1; 4:14; 1 Cor. 15:4, 12–20). Then, taking his teaching one step beyond its formulation in 1 Corinthians 15:35–53, Paul attempts to explain more fully how our earthly tent will be transformed like that of our Lord into "an eternal house in heaven" (v. 1; cf. John 2:19–22) to become "our heavenly dwelling" (v. 4). The transformation will take place when our bodies receive a new "clothing" (v. 2; see also 1 Cor. 15:53). But rather than suggest that such a "clothing" implies the death of the mortal body and the "unclothing" of the immortal soul (a view which appears to have been favored by some at Corinth [v. 3; 1 Cor. 15:12, 35]), Paul asserts that the "clothing" process of resurrection takes place when our current "clothing" is "over-clothed" "so that what is mortal may be swallowed up by life" (v. 4). "For this very purpose" God created both the body and the soul: not for the destruction of either, but for the redemption of both. For this reason also the Spirit of the immortal God has already entered our bodies, as a "deposit guaranteeing what is to come" (v. 5).

Thus Paul is "confident," as one who lives by faith and not by sight, that when at last he leaves his home in the body, he will be transformed in a way that will allow him to be at home with the Lord. But then as now the "goal" will be the same: to give the pleasure of a returned love and service to the Lord who loved us and laid down his life for us. Against the standard of his love for us the adequacy of our response will be measured (vv. 6–10).

D. The perspective of Paul's ministry (5:11–21). With these expectations Paul's mission proceeds, and as they are known to God so now they have been made known to God's people at Corinth. In making his hopes and fears known, however, Paul is not "trying to commend" himself, but only sharing with the Corinthians in a way that will allow them to take the true measure of his apostleship in truth apart from appearances. For all that Paul has done has been in response to the compulsion of Christ's love, demonstrated in his willingness as one to die for all and representatively including all in his death (v. 14; Rom. 6:5–11; 1 Cor. 15:22; Gal. 2:20; Col. 3:3). No longer then can those who belong to Christ live for themselves; they must live instead at the direction of "him who died for them and was raised again" (v. 15).

Furthermore, if Christ has died for all, then a purely human perspective can no longer form the basis for judgments about the worth of his actions or the value in his plan of any man or woman. Anyone who is in Christ (i.e., who belongs to him through incorporation into his body) has already become a part of a new creation (i.e., a part of the transformation of human existence that has begun in Christ and will culminate in the re-creation of heaven and earth [Rom. 8:19–23; 1 Cor. 15:22; 2 Pet. 3:10, 13; Rev. 21:1]). They have passed beyond the point of living solely as a part of the old creation (though a part of that which is "old" has been left both within and without, in our bodies and our world), and have begun to live as a part of the new created order.

Moreover, the source of such new creation is God, whose work, as in the creation accounts of the Old Testament, forms the decisive beginning for it. For "God was reconciling the world to himself in Christ" (v. 19; the order of words within this Greek clause is ambiguous and has produced a variety of translations). The achievement of the work, however, depended upon Christ. For the new creation was allowed to proceed without counting the "sins" of the old only because "God made him who had no sin to be sin for us" (vv. 19, 21). And now the extension of the work rests upon those to whom has been entrusted the ministry and the message of reconciliation. For God has chosen to extend his work in Christ through "Christ's ambassadors," making his appeal through them to those who do not yet participate in the new creation to be reconciled to God (v. 20).

IV. Paul's Appeal to the Corinthians (6:1–13:10)

A. An appeal for complete reconciliation (6:1–7:4). As one of "God's fellow workers," chosen to bear the message of reconciliation, Paul now presents the Corinthians with the first in a series of appeals, urging them "not to receive God's grace" in vain (6:1). In context these words seem meant to spur the Corinthians to respond to Paul's attempt at reconciliation with the church. The citation (from Isa. 49:8) and its interpretation may then be seen as reinforcement to the appeal, entreating the church to respond without delay. Paul reminds them of what he has already written in an attempt to remove any "stumbling block" that might impede the progress of reconciliation (v. 3), and then seeks to persuade the church to look again at what he has done for them as one of the servants of God.

A statement summarizing the sufferings that have been endured by the apostle on behalf of the church now ensues.[5]

Next comes a corresponding list of Christian virtues which have marked Paul's apostolic ministry (vv. 6–7). These include "purity" (the moral uprightness which gave credence to the witness of Paul's life and mission [1 Thess. 2:10–12]), "understanding" (which balanced the apostolic commitment to holiness among believers with a godly compassion and forgiveness [Eph. 4:32; 1 Thess. 2:7]), and the "patience" and "kindness" that are associated with a "sincere love" inspired by the Holy Spirit (1 Cor. 13:4). Also mentioned among the marks of Paul's ministry are truthful speech (see also 4:2; 11:31; 13:8), the power of God (Rom. 15:19; 1 Cor. 2:4; 4:20; Eph. 3:20; Jesus' own ministry is characterized by the conjoining of proclamation and power [Luke 7:22–23]), and the weapons of righteousness (10:4; Eph. 6:14).

Then, in a series of contrasts, the paradoxical experience of the apostle is brought fully and realistically into view. In external appearance Paul's apostolic ministry may indeed at times have seemed to some, not the least of whom were Paul's opponents, to be characterized by marks of ineffectiveness and failure. But, Paul's appeal is made with the eye of faith, with a perspective that looks through appearances and perceives the realities of God's power at work in his ministry.

Having "spoken freely" in an attempt to lay his ministry open before them and make himself fully vulnerable in love and "affection," Paul brings his appeal for reconciliation to its legitimate close by entreating the Corinthians in "fair exchange" to open their hearts to his ministry (vv. 11–12). A part of such openness, however, entailed the church giving heed to his apostolic authority. Accordingly, in order to effect a full reconciliation, Paul urges the Corinthians not to "be yoked together with unbelievers" (v. 14a).

The source for such metaphorical language is undoubtedly Deuteronomy 22:10, which prohibits the yoking together of an ox and a donkey for purposes of plowing, but the precise application intended by the apostle is elusive. Clearly all association is not forbidden, and so it is probably best to understand Paul's injunction here to prohibit only those relationships in which the degree of association entails an inevitable compromise with Christian standards of conduct. The injunction is accordingly followed by a series of five rhetorical questions, all of which point to crucial differences between the believer and unbeliever. The fifth question epitomizes the distinction in terms of a contrast "between the temple of God and idols" (v. 16a), which is reminiscent of 1 Corinthians and probably represents the best clue to the apostle's intent in this passage (see 1 Cor. 8:10–11; 10:14, 19–21).

It also affords Paul the opportunity to reiterate that together Christians form the temple of the living God, a truth which has brought to fulfillment the divine vow which had been made at various points throughout the history of Israel (Exod. 25:8; 29:45; Lev. 26:11–12; 1 Kings 6:13; Jer. 32:38; Ezek. 37:27). In light of this, Paul, adapting the words of Isaiah 52:11 and Ezekiel 20:34, 41, urges the Corinthians to separate themselves from unbelievers and from practices that involve the use of "unclean things" (v. 17; his words do not refer to the separations inaugurated by Christians because of doctrinal differences). As a conclusion to this catena of scriptural citations, Paul returns to the thought with which he began and underlines his principal point in personal terms. As sons and daughters (the reference to women here is noteworthy and probably reflects a deliberate attempt to speak to a congregation in which women played an active, vital, and respected part [1 Cor. 7:3–4; 11:5]), Christians belong in association with the Lord Almighty who has promised to be a Father to each of them. Simultaneously, it is incumbent upon all who possess such promises to keep both body and spirit free from those associations which undermine their central commitment to the holiness which betokens their "reverence for God" (7:1).

Having urged upon the church actions appropriate to reconciliation, Paul concludes his appeal with a reiteration of his own readiness for reconciliation. What has been said has been to show, contrary apparently to the claims of his detractors, that no one has been wronged, corrupted, or "exploited" by Paul's ministry (v. 2). Furthermore, in making an attempt at reconciliation which urges a change in the associations of some within the church, it has not been Paul's intent to condemn. Instead, as one devoted to their service, Paul has sought to convey his confidence and pride in their ability to conform themselves to his apostolic counsel.

B. A new basis for appeal (7:5–16). In this section Paul resumes the autobiographical nar-

5. If one follows the suggestions of M. J. Harris ("2 Corinthians," in *The Expositor's Bible Commentary*, ed. Frank E. Gaebelein [Grand Rapids: Zondervan, 1976], 10:357), the nine items are a list of general, humanly inflicted, and self-imposed trials that Paul associated with his apostleship. Under the first heading come "troubles, hardships and distresses" (v. 4b); under the second, "beatings, imprisonments and riots" (v. 5a); under the third, "hard work, sleepless nights and hunger" (v. 5b).

rative which was broken off in 2:13 to allow for the inclusion of the reflective apologetic of 2:14–5:19 and the appeals for reconciliation found in 5:20–7:4. The break in the narrative may reflect Paul's desire, having heard the "comforting" news which Titus had brought back from Corinth, to convey to the church both his immediate and his considered reaction to their new attitude toward him. Furthermore, upon consideration, it may have seemed more important to present the latter before the former. In any case, the story is resumed, as it was left off, with Paul in Macedonia struggling against external adversities and inner "fears" (v. 5).

Within the context of such need and the humility imposed by it God habitually acts to comfort the downcast (Isa. 40:1; Matt. 5:4; James 4:6–10; 1 Pet. 5:5–6). In his own case, therefore, Paul interpreted the coming of Titus, and the news he brought of the Corinthians' renewed "concern" for their apostle, as a real and divinely wrought comfort (vv. 6–7). But it was not only Paul who had suffered through the events of the recent past. The church had also experienced remorse upon their receipt of his last letter. Thus, while it had not been Paul's intention to simply inflict sorrow upon those who had caused him to be sorrowful, yet in this instance, through God's working, an unintended effect led to an unexpectedly quick and thorough "repentance," leaving neither Paul nor the church with any sense of regret (vv. 9–10).

Quite to the contrary, the sorrow that had been divinely inspired had produced an eagerness within the majority at Corinth to clear themselves, and an eagerness within Paul to recognize the "innocence" which belonged to the majority of those within the church (vv. 11–13). Moreover, Titus himself had been uplifted and become enthusiastic in his "affection" for the congregation (vv. 14–15). Such an unexpectedly rich outcome from a letter sent with such hesitation was indeed an occasion for gladness and for an expression of renewed confidence in the church's ability to pay heed to future apostolic appeals.

C. An appeal for full response to the collection (8:1–9:15). Having expressed renewed confidence in the Corinthian church, Paul now proceeds to a further appeal concerning "service to the saints" (8:4). The service the apostle has in mind involves the collection of an offering intended to supply the "needs of God's people" and to be a manifest "expression of thanks to God" (9:12). There seems no doubt that this is the same gift for Jerusalem as was first mentioned in 1 Corinthians 16:3 (see also Rom. 15:26–27). Obviously, in the period between the writing of our two canonical letters, the subject had been put aside because of the strained relationship between Paul and the church. But now it recurs, for the receipt of the collection is a project in which Paul is presently engaged among the "Macedonian churches" (8:1).

Indeed it is the "rich generosity" (v. 2) of the Macedonian Christians that Paul holds up as he urges the Corinthians to become involved anew in this endeavor. The Macedonians' generous giving (**8:1–5**), however, has not sprung from human nature. It is a tangible expression of the grace of God at work in the lives of those who have given themselves to the Lord. It has originated without effort by Paul, continued despite the "most severe trial" and extreme poverty (v. 2), and produced joy among all those who have contributed "as much as they were able" (v. 3; cf. Mark 12:41–44).

It is such giving, inspired by grace, that Paul seeks from the church at Corinth (**8:6–15**), and with good reason. Titus has already been able to report that a new beginning was made during his visit. However, in order that the church might be given full opportunity to excel in "this grace of giving" (v. 7), Paul has urged Titus to return to Corinth and "bring to completion this act of grace" (v. 6). In accordance with the nature of the collection, giving is not commanded, but Paul does confess to an attempt to put the "sincerity" of the church's love for others to the test of a comparison (v. 8). To do this is only to recognize that the Corinthian church contains persons much more able to give than their Macedonian sisters and brothers. The Corinthians are urged, accordingly, to imitate Christ, who though he was rich yet agreed willingly to become poor "so that you through his poverty might become rich" (v. 9; cf. Phil. 2:5–11).

Paul is unwilling, however, to conclude his appeal apart from the provision of some specific advice with respect to response. As this is now the third time an appeal is being made to the church (1 Cor. 16:1–4; 2 Cor. 8:6), Paul's primary counsel to the church is to "finish the work," so that the "willingness" to respond which has been commendably evident from the inception of the collection may at last be matched by the "completion" of a corporate gift that is "according to [their] means" (v. 11). The principle behind Paul's advice thus becomes clear. It is the free decision to give that renders the gift acceptable. Accordingly, each person should give joyfully "according to what one has," and not attempt out of a sense of zeal or pious duty to give what one "does not have" (v. 12).

The principle is pressed home. Paul's "desire" is not to pressure the Corinthians, but instead to urge upon them a uniquely biblical notion of equality that regards the "plenty" of one as that which exists to supply the "need" of another (vv. 13–14). The idea is then illustrated, in a fashion characteristic of the Corinthian letters, by an appeal to Scripture (v. 15, based on Exod. 16:18).

Prior, however, to the use of gifts in an effort to "honor the Lord" and demonstrate an "eagerness to help" (v. 19), there remained the problem of the actual collection at Corinth. Apparently, as Paul was pondering precisely how to handle this task, the "initiative" was taken by Titus (vv. 16–17). Paul, in turn, seeks in this section to commend Titus to the church.

But Titus is not to be commended and sent on alone (**8:16–24**). So that no one may suspect Paul's motives, and in order to avoid "criticism," Titus is to be accompanied by an unnamed brother whose reputation is beyond reproach, and who has been "chosen" by the common consent of the churches (presumably all the churches associated with the collection) to "carry the offering" (vv. 18–21).

Moreover, a third brother (who is either a Corinthian or whose confidence in them derives from some other background) is also being sent in order, Paul infers, to inspire the church with his own zeal. Nonetheless, it is Titus whom Paul commends most warmly as his personal partner and fellow worker in the ministry. The other brothers come as "representatives of the churches" and as an "honor to Christ" (v. 23). It is therefore both to Paul and to the churches that the Corinthians are asked to demonstrate the "proof of [their] love" (v. 24).

Though the appeal might naturally have been concluded at the end of the previous chapter, the "eagerness" of the Corinthians "to help" (9:2) is nonetheless brought up again by Paul, suggesting that the preceding section is somewhat parenthetical. The resumption of discussion about the Corinthians' contribution to the collection, however, allows the apostle to stress to the Christians at Corinth that there is a need for their actual readiness to contribute as well as their willingness to do so (**9:1–5**), and affords him an opportunity to carry further his advice to the church about the way in which contributions should be decided upon.

Once more Paul seeks to motivate the church by referring to the initial response to his appeal. Indeed, the apostle has been using the example of their readiness as a model in urging the "Macedonians" to give to the collection (v. 2). Consequently, it is in the interest of both Paul's integrity ("that our boasting about you . . . should not prove hollow" [v. 3]) and the Corinthians' honor that all who have promised to give be urged to bring the collection of their contributions to completion, lest they be "unprepared" for the arrival of any Macedonians who might accompany Paul, and be "ashamed" at their failure (v. 4). A purpose for the parenthetical section in the previous chapter thus becomes clear. In order that the work might be finished and the contributions ready and waiting as an authentic gift, all of the brothers, including Titus, are being sent.

Paul closes his appeal (**9:6–15**) by way of reminder, either seeking to recall his own previous teaching or perhaps referring to some portion of the Gospel tradition (Luke 6:38; 19:11–27). In either case, however, the saying about sowing and reaping serves to decisively correlate giving with a Christian's financial welfare. Accordingly, each person should feel free to decide in faith on the amount of a gift. The emotion that accompanies a Christian's gift should be one of joy, rather than any sense of compulsion or reluctance.

This will be facilitated if the Corinthians will also remember that God has promised to care abundantly for their needs (Matt. 6:25–34). Thus at "all times" they may confidently step forward and contribute to every good work (v. 8). For, in accordance with the Scripture (Ps. 112:9), the person who does so will acquire an enduring sense of having done what is right. Such a person may also rest assured that God will continually and generously resupply the resources which have been expended "so that [he] can be generous on every occasion," enabling both righteousness and thanksgiving to increase (vv. 10–11).

Thus the service of giving may be seen not only as an offering to meet human "needs," but also as a way to make possible the increased worship of God. "Expressions of thanks" and "praise" will undoubtedly result, witness to the transforming power of the gospel of Christ will be eloquently and effectively rendered, and "prayers" will be offered in sincerity for the continued growth of the church in the grace that is part of God's "indescribable" gift (vv. 12–15).

D. An appeal for full allegiance to apostolic authority (10:1–18). There is a perceptible change in the tone of Paul's letter beginning at this point and continuing until its end. But the degree of difference, and the reasons for it, are very much less clear. In any event, some continuity with the previous context is afforded by the repetition of a formal appeal (**10:1–6**); in this case, the appeal concerns apostolic authority.

The appeal is sounded in the midst of apparent doubt among some at Corinth about Paul's ability to exercise apostolic authority in a clear and compelling way, especially when face to face with his audience, as over against his ability and willingness to write in a bold way from a distance. For his own part, Paul refuses, in imitation of the meekness and gentleness of Christ (see also 1 Cor. 4:12; 1 Pet. 2:23), to be moved to a demonstration of his authority simply by the challenge to do so (cf. Matt. 4:3, 6). Instead, before the necessity for authoritative action imposes itself, he chooses to beg that the challenge be withdrawn.

If it is not, then a demonstration will indeed take place. But it will not be a demonstration of Paul's deficiencies, as his opponents anticipate. It will be instead a show of the divine power which operates through the Lord's chosen apostles without regard to the criteria of authority that are recognized and accorded weight in this world (see Acts 4:13; 1 Cor. 2:1–5). For God has empowered those whom he has commissioned with weapons that "demolish arguments" about authority and "every pretension" of those who set their own perceptions about the ability to exercise power against the knowledge that comes from God (v. 5). Accordingly, should it be necessary, Paul will not hesitate to take action that will "take captive every thought to make it obedient to Christ," nor neglect the punishment due "every act of disobedience" once order and respect have been restored (vv. 5–6).

Paul's appeal has been made necessary because of the appearance of some at Corinth who have tried to dissuade the church from continuing allegiance to Paul as a primary apostolic authority (**10:7–18**). Their attempt to undermine Paul's rightful claim to authority had two thrusts.

On the one hand, they sought to belittle Paul by drawing a distinction between the frightening authority with which he gave instructions to the church when absent and his inability to manifest a similar authority through speech and the power of his person when actually present. In reply, Paul reminds his readers that as long as they look simply upon the "surface" of such an allegation it may seem to have the appearance of the truth, especially when promoted by Christians who confidently proclaim that in offering this observation their only allegiance "belongs" to Christ (v. 7). But the claim of allegiance to Christ is not an exclusive possession, and if it legitimately belongs to anyone, it certainly belongs to Paul as much as his detractors. Consequently, though the apostle will admit to a more open use of the authority that the Lord has given to him when writing, he will permit no one to think that he is embarrassed to assert such authority when seeking to build up the body of Christ with either letters or "actions" (vv. 8–11).

On the other hand, those who opposed Paul attempted to elevate their own authority by making a boast that their credentials and associations commend them as persons who enjoy a higher status than Paul in the eyes of many other churches. Paul, however, refuses to respond to the challenge of comparison directly. Instead he draws attention more subtly to the fact that the terms of measurement and comparison employed by his opponents are largely self-serving, allowing them only to "compare themselves with themselves" (v. 12). Similarly, they refuse to recognize that the limits of Paul's work and reputation are not due to any lack of eminence, but rather to the fact that he has devoted himself exclusively to the field that "God has assigned" him, including the church at Corinth (vv. 13–14).

Accordingly, because he has received his own divine commission (Acts 9:6, 15; 26:16–18; Gal. 2:11–17), Paul does not attempt to bolster his authority by "boasting" of associations between his work and that "done by others" (v. 15), as do his opponents. Instead, he simply expresses the hope that his labor in trying to build up the church at Corinth will eventually lead to the preaching of the gospel in "regions beyond" Corinth (v. 16a). For it is only through mission beyond the churches which are already established, and not through repeated incursions into territory that has already been evangelized, that the Lord's commission will be accomplished (Matt. 28:19–20; Acts 1:8). Commendation, therefore, belongs not to the "one who commends himself," but to the one who answers the call of the Lord and makes his "boast" in the divine commission (vv. 17–18).

E. Support for the appeal (11:1–12:13). Having made his appeal, countering both the criticism and the self-commendation of his opponents, Paul proceeds to support it by pointing to several subsidiary issues (in **11:1–6,** that of faithfulness to the gospel) at stake in this contest for authority. To do this, however, he must engage in the foolishness of an apology in defense of himself and his preaching. But because of his jealous love for the Corinthians, and his desire as their "father" to present the church to Christ, as a "pure virgin" bride, untainted by the errors of others, Paul is willing to make his appeal on any terms (11:2).

Paul's chief concern, however, is not his own status, but the minds of his converts (men or women) which "may somehow be led astray" by arguments about authority and deceived about truth in this matter as effectively as was Eve (v. 3; Gen. 3:1–7). The crux of his concern is the immaturity of the Corinthians' faith and their consequent childlike acceptance of those who claim authority in the name of the Lord, but whose views about Jesus, the nature of the gospel, and the experience of the Spirit are significantly different than those which were originally proclaimed at Corinth. Consequently, since the comprehension of the gospel is an issue, Paul will not permit the church to entertain even for a moment the idea that he regards himself as at all inferior to anyone whose credentials as an apostle his detractors put above his. And no one, Paul trusts, will be blinded to this by the fallacious argument that his knowledge about the faith is somehow inadequate because his self-expression is ineloquent.

Another issue in the contest for authority concerned proper apostolic practice with respect to the receipt of financial support (**11:7–15**). As was the case with the issue of faithfulness to the gospel, the Corinthians were apparently poised to accept a twisting of the truth that Paul had already taught them about the freedom of an apostle to make use or not to make use of financial support from his converts (see 1 Cor. 9:3–18). His opponents apparently charged that Paul's stance demonstrated that he had only an imperfect knowledge of the Lord's will for an apostle, and that his refusal to accept support from his converts during his initial mission at Corinth indicated lack of love for the church.

Paul, however, adamantly refuses to accept either that he has sinned against the Lord's will by "preaching the gospel . . . free of charge" (v. 7) or that his rejection of Corinthian support demonstrates any lack of love. He reminds them that he acted as he did not because of any lack of knowledge about the propriety of the principle of support (for while he was with them he was "receiving support" from "other churches"), but out of a pastoral desire not to burden his converts immediately with the necessity of his financial welfare (vv. 8–9). Thus, he vows to continue his practice of not accepting support from his converts during an initial mission and to make such a practice a part of his distinctive apostolic boast.

As for those who have come to Corinth to contest his authority to do as he has done, Paul charges that they themselves cannot make any truthful claim to be apostles. Insofar then as they have claimed apostolic authority for their mistaken teaching, they are deceitful workmen and servants of Satan, who characteristically promotes falsehood by "masquerading" as a bearer of the light of true knowledge (vv. 13–15a). If these people do not desist, "their end will be what their actions deserve" (v. 15b).

A third issue raised in the struggle for authority at Corinth involved the respective credentials of Paul and his opponents (**11:16–32**). If an inspection were made, charged Paul's detractors, then his inferiority to them, or if not to them then to those they claimed as sponsors, would be clearly seen. But contrary to his adversaries' expectations, and perhaps to those of some of the Corinthians, Paul takes up the challenge to compare his background and service with his rivals', refusing to be written off by anyone as a foolish inferior.

The real foolishness, he charges, belongs to those at Corinth who consider themselves wise enough to make decisions about the possessors of apostolic authority. In putting up with the boasting of Paul's opponents and evaluating their claim according to "the way" of "the world," they have ignored the truth that persons who resort to boasting to establish their authority are "not talking as the Lord would" (vv. 17–19). To such Corinthians also belongs (as Paul seeks to emphasize through ridicule) an illogical tolerance of teaching that aims to "enslave" or "exploit," and a ludicrous willingness to accept as an authority anyone who attempts to dominate them (v. 20). Accordingly, in words full of irony, Paul observes that with such criteria sensitivity may justly be construed as weakness, and laments his lack of strength. Nevertheless, in an attempt to redeem his own, Paul is ready to descend to whatever type of comparison they might find persuasive and to match any kind of boast.

If some Corinthians are awed by the fact that Paul's rivals are Hebrews, Israelites, or descendants of Abraham (whether there is a distinction between these terms is of little consequence), then Paul is equally entitled to such respect. If, on the other hand, the claim that has captured the Corinthians' admiration is the boast that Paul's opponents have been greater servants of Christ, then clearly the evidence should tip any scale of comparison in Paul's favor (though it is truly senseless to think of making such comparative evaluations of the Lord's servants [1 Cor. 3:5–7; 4:1–5]).

To substantiate his case, Paul now presents a summary (which goes beyond the record of Acts in completeness while demonstrating at the same time its essential trustworthiness) of his apostolic service. However, in laying claim to the title *servant of Christ*, as it has become necessary for Paul to do in the face of opposition, he sets forward for primary consideration incidents which display his moments of weakness and vulnerability rather than those that demonstrate accomplishments won as a result of his personal strengths.

In an effort to bear the gospel to the world, Paul has repeatedly suffered the lashes of the Jews, beatings inflicted by the "rods" of Gentiles (Acts 16:22), and the stones cast at him by both (Acts 14:19). He has been willing to expose himself to the physical dangers associated with travel on land and sea, and to the emotional stress of recurrent conflicts with "false brothers" (vv. 24–26). He has uncomplainingly endured countless personal deprivations including nights "without sleep," hunger and thirst, exposure to the cold without clothing, and the kind of hard labor and toil that might more naturally have been done by persons below his station in life. Finally, he has daily faced the inner "pressure of concern" for those in the churches he has left behind who have found their faith weak in moments of crisis or who have fallen away from faith and back into "sin" (vv. 27–29).

To verify his testimony, Paul takes an oath, solemnly swearing its truth in the name of the God and Father of the Lord Jesus. Then, as a last example typifying much of what he has said about facing danger, opposition, and hardship, Paul relates how he was forced to flee the city of Damascus in secret (vv. 32–33; Acts 9:23–25). It is in demonstrations of divine power at work to support him in such moments of human vulnerability that Paul urges his audience to seek confirmation of his right to be called an apostle.

A final issue, closely related to the third, apparently pertained to the ability to recount previous personal experiences of revelatory visions (**12:1–13**). Once again, though there is really nothing to be gained by an attempt to supplement the record of divine support that he has already presented, Paul consents, as before, to "go on boasting" in an attempt to win the wayward Corinthians back to his side (v. 1). But once more, he does so in a way that shows his reticence to cooperate fully in any contest of credentials proposed by his opponents, speaking modestly of his own experience as only that of a man in Christ.

Proceeding, Paul relates an experience which happened to him some fourteen years earlier (placing it in the period between his first visit to Jerusalem following his conversion and his arrival in Antioch [Acts 9:23–30; 11:19–26]). During this experience, while completely unaware of the whereabouts of his body, Paul was nonetheless brought to a form of consciousness in paradise and enabled to see and hear "things that man is not permitted to tell" (v. 4). From the point of view of Paul's opponents, it is entirely proper for "a man like that" to boast about the privilege of receiving such a vision (v. 5a). But Paul is unwilling to take this view, or to allow the Corinthians to think that this experience constitutes the real basis for his claim to be an apostle. And so he continues to present a claim that offers a clearer indication of apostolic vocation, a boast in the weakness of what he has done and said in Christ's service.

Furthermore, the Corinthians should know that following the experience of exaltation there had come still further moments of weakness as "a thorn in my flesh, a messenger of Satan, to torment me" (v. 7). Paul's picturesque description has led to a wide range of interpretations concerning the nature of his thorn, but in the end, little more can be said with certainty than what Paul, in fact, tells us; namely, that the thorn began to affect him only after his experience, that it was painful for him, and that it had enabled Satan and the thought of sin to gain entrance to his mind. Paul had "pleaded with the Lord" to remove it (v. 8). But in response, he received instead divine power which finds its perfect completion when it enables the overcoming of such weakness.

Paul's experience itself then illustrates his message to the church. The true boast of an apostle, of one sent out by the Lord on a mission (for that is what the title truly means), is that in the course of such a mission, the Lord has faithfully provided power in moments of necessity so that the apostle may claim "when I am weak, then I am strong" (v. 10). Accordingly, though he regrets having "made a fool" of himself with a different boast, Paul has shown through it that he deserves to be commended rather than written off as the inferior of his opponents or those whose apostolic authority they might claim as superior to Paul's. All the manifestations of divine power—"signs, wonders and miracles"—had been demonstrated at necessary points in the mission to Corinth along with a kind of "perseverance" that had convinced the Corinthians that these were more than the tricks of a charlatan seeking some temporary converts (v. 12). Indeed, they have received from Paul all that the other churches have except for the request that they be asked to share in the burden of his support.

F. The conclusion of the appeal (12:14–13:10). Paul concludes his appeal for Corinthian allegiance to his apostolic authority by informing the church that he is preparing to come to them a third time and urging them in advance to think over what he has said. If they do, they will surely see that his reluctance to accept their support is no more difficult to explain than the reluctance of parents to accept their children's support or to give up the privilege of spending their resources on behalf of those whom they love. It is just this kind of parental love that Paul has lavished upon the church. They can scarcely love him less for it, or for refusing for any reason to burden them with his support.

Nor can anyone seriously imagine (as Paul's sarcasm is meant to show) that he has sought to "exploit" them belatedly by sending Titus and others (including a brother known to both the Corinthians and the apostle) to visit the church on his behalf (12:17). If they admit that "Titus did not exploit" them in any way after his arrival, then neither can the apostle who sent him be justly accused of motives or actions contrary to those of his emissary (v. 18).

Paul reiterates, however, that his primary purpose is not his own defense. Instead he has written in an attempt to bring the truth, which alone can be spoken in the sight of God, plainly into view, and to strengthen its hold upon the minds of the Corinthians. The apostle's fear is that upon his return both he and his converts may find that the lies of his detractors have worked so well that neither of them will be happy to learn the truth. Indeed, for his part, Paul suspects that as a result of the work of his rivals there may already be sufficient "quarreling, jealousy, outbursts of anger, factions, slander, gossip, arrogance and disorder" at Corinth to humble the apostolic pride which he had previously taken in the origins and growth of the church, and force him to grieve over many who have "indulged" in the kinds of sin about which he had previously warned them, and who have, as a sign of disbelief in Paul's authority, made no attempt at repentance (v. 21).

However, such people have already received a warning in person and now by letter (13:2). Paul's "third visit" will be for them a time of confirmation of their sins "by the testimony of two or three witnesses" (Deut. 19:15) and fulfillment of Paul's solemn promise not to spare any of those who have sinned from the authoritative apostolic judgment and discipline that will prove that Christ is speaking "through me" (vv. 1–2). For Christ, even though he once was crucified in weakness, now lives in and through "God's power." Consequently, as the Corinthians have had occasion to learn before, he is neither weak nor powerless to deal with those who stubbornly persist in sin (vv. 3–4a). Indeed, he has given power to those who live with him, so that though they often find themselves weak in him, they may nonetheless have strength for discipline as a part of their faithful service to others in his name.

In light of this, the Corinthians are urged to sincerely examine themselves; to take a test designed to evaluate the degree to which their recent words and deeds witness to the presence of Christ as Lord within. Failure to note any degree of correlation would, of course, suggest the complete absence of faith. Much more likely is the discovery, despite Paul's prayer to the contrary, of a relative or partial lack of correspondence between faith and action, of something that is wrong, indicating the need for repentance, and a return to what is right. Paul confidently encourages his audience to apply the test to him as well as to themselves, so that they may not only reflect upon the measure of their own recent faithfulness, but also rediscover the measure of his. Yet his chief hope is not that the Corinthians "will see that we have stood the test," but rather that they will come face to face with their need for repentance (v. 7). For Paul is persuaded that neither he nor his converts will ultimately be able to continue doing anything against the truth if it is known within.

Furthermore, because his primary concern is for the Corinthians, Paul is glad to admit both his own weaknesses and their strengths. Indeed his "prayer" is not primarily for himself, but for the increasing "perfection" of his converts in actions which accord with the truth (v. 9). And the same motive explains why he writes. For Paul would rather make timely use in a letter of the authority that the Lord has given him for "building up" if the alternative is to lose communication with his converts and to be forced to use his authority belatedly for "tearing down" (v. 10 RSV).

V. Epistolary Conclusion (13:11–14)

The conclusion of the letter begins with an affectionate personal farewell, indicating that despite all that Paul has written, including some biting and pointed sarcasm, he nonetheless continues to regard his audience at Corinth with a genuine love as fellow members of the family of faith. Accordingly, as the father of their faith he continues to urge them to "aim for perfection," to "listen to [his] appeal," to "be of one mind," and to "live in peace" (v. 11b). He also encourages the Corinthians to imitate his love for them by openly manifesting a family affection for one another.

The "greetings" of the remainder of the family are conveyed and a closing prayer is added (as was also usual) for the welfare of those who would be receiving the letter. However, as might be expected, Paul's closing prayer is distinctly Christian in content and comes intriguingly close to providing an affirmation of trinitarian theology in its form as it draws the name of the Lord Jesus Christ together with that of God and the Holy Spirit in a threefold petition for the continual outpouring of the divine blessings of grace, love, and fellowship in the lives of its readers.

SELECT BIBLIOGRAPHY

Barrett, C. K. *The First Epistle to the Corinthians.* New York: Harper & Row, 1968.

———. *The Second Epistle to the Corinthians.* New York: Harper & Row, 1974.

Bruce, F. F. *I & II Corinthians.* Grand Rapids: Eerdmans, 1971.

Davis, J. A. *Wisdom and Spirit.* Lanham, Md.: University Press of America, 1984.

———. *1 Corinthians.* Waco: Word. Forthcoming.

Fee, G. D. *I Corinthians.* Grand Rapids: Eerdmans. 1987.

Furnish, V. P. *II Corinthians.* Garden City: Doubleday, 1984.

Harris, M. J. "2 Corinthians." In *The Expositor's Bible Commentary,* ed. Frank E. Gaebelein. Grand Rapids: Zondervan, 1976.

Martin, R. P. *2 Corinthians.* Waco: Word, 1985.

Murphy-O'Connor, J. *St. Paul's Corinth: Texts and Archaeology.* Wilmington, Del.: Michael Glazier, 1983.

GALATIANS

Scott E. McClelland

INTRODUCTION

Scholars have never seriously doubted that the apostle Paul was the author of the Epistle to the Galatians. The characteristic opening line which identifies his name and apostleship, the personal final greeting written in his own hand (6:11), and the characteristic theological concerns all point to the historical Paul. Only the most radical scholars of the nineteenth century attempted to undermine the universal witness of authentic authorship provided by two millennia of church tradition.

While we can assert with great certainty that the content of this epistle owes its structure to Paul, the actual mechanics of writing were, most likely, that of an amanuensis (secretary), as evidenced by the notation made as to what he personally wrote in the final words of the epistle. The majority of the epistle was likely generated through the process of dictation. The appearance of two anacoluthons (unfinished sentences) in Galatians 2:6 gives credence to this view, especially when we realize the emotional intensity of the words there.

It should also be noted that the text of this epistle appears to have been handed down with little variation. The relatively constant agreement between some of the most respected manuscripts of the New Testament gives us great assurance as to the "purity" of the text that we have received.

There are few more problematical issues for the student of the New Testament than those associated with fitting the Pauline Epistles into the historical outline supplied by the Book of Acts. Many scholars have despaired of any sort of harmonization and, consequently, have discarded Acts as unhistorical. Yet, most evangelicals retain an appreciation for the historicity of Acts; thus the harmonization problem remains an important issue to consider. Some orientation to the discussion surrounding these issues will be necessary before the reader can sufficiently weigh the evidence regarding the historical context of Galatians.

The difficulties begin even with the name of the epistle and the people Paul intends to address. The term *Galatia* referred to one of the

Roman provinces of Asia Minor (modern-day Turkey). This province cut in a north-south direction across the middle of the peninsula, encompassing a number of diverse peoples, cultures, and languages.

Beyond reference to the territory, however, the term *Galatian* could be used to designate certain groups of people within that province. These people would be the descendants of the ancient Gauls, likely a barbaric tribal group from northwestern Europe. These people settled in the northern part of the territory that would subsequently bear their name. The ancient cities of Ancyra (Ankara, the modern Turkish capital), Tavium, and Pessinus would be associated with the settled areas of the Gauls.

Thus when Paul uses the term *Galatians* (esp. in a derogatory way in Gal. 3:1), it becomes difficult to know whether he has a provincial or tribal designation in mind. Those who have attempted to answer this question opt for either the North Galatian theory or the South Galatian theory.

These theories are based on the premise that Galatians was written to one of the groups visited during one of Paul's missionary journeys recorded in Acts. The decision one makes regarding the destination of the epistle governs one's view of its date and possibly its purpose.

If one allows the possibility that Paul used the term *Galatia* to designate the Roman province, the first missionary journey would be the most likely time when he would have made initial contact with the Galatian people. The churches founded during this journey, which would be considered Galatian, would include those at Pisidian Antioch, Iconium, Lystra, and Derbe (Acts 13–14). Such a position allows for Galatians to be one of the earliest, if not the very first, of the Pauline Epistles. It does not, however, restrict the dating of this epistle from a later time as well.

The North Galatian theory, the more traditional view, is now not generally as popular as the South theory. This position is held by those scholars who find it extremely difficult to believe that Paul could refer to the church members of the south as Galatians if they were not racially associated with that tribe.

The major difficulty of holding to this position is the lack of any specific mention in Acts of Paul's travels in the northern part of the province. Paul may possibly have visited this area on one of his journeys from Antioch to Ephesus (Acts 16:6; 19:1). However, the passages in view make no mention of the founding of churches during his presumed time in these areas. This view would force the date of the writing of the epistle to a much later time period than that of the South theory.

Certainty on this issue is impossible, but there are a number of reasons to favor the South Galatian theory: (1) the churches of the south became important and strong communities in the apostolic times, though we know nothing about any northern churches; (2) two of Paul's major companions came from this area (Timothy and Gaius), and they appear to represent Galatia (1 Cor. 16) in the collection taken for Jerusalem; (3) Galatians 4:13 may well imply more than one visit by Paul to these churches, a fact verified by the Book of Acts (Acts 13–14; 16); (4) the repeated mention of Barnabas without further elaboration in Galatians seems to suppose their acquaintance with him—we know that Barnabas accompanied Paul to the churches in the south during the first missionary journey.

A further difficulty in harmonizing this epistle with the Book of Acts regards the testimony of Paul in the first two chapters of Galatians concerning his contact with Jerusalem, and, specifically, with the Jerusalem apostles. While Paul records two visits to the city after his conversion experience, Acts records three.

Most scholars agree that the reference to Paul's first postconversion visit (Gal. 1:18) is identical to the visit mentioned in Acts 9:26ff. Difficulties arise as to the alignment of the visit described in Galatians 2:1ff. with either Acts 11:30 or 15:1ff. The decision made on this issue brings with it some major implications for the determination of date, occasion, and destination of the epistle.

The proposal that Acts 11 corresponds to Galatians 2 appears most natural since the Book of Acts records one more visit than does Paul. It would seem likely, then, that Galatians was written after the second and prior to the third visit recorded in Acts.

This alignment is strengthened by the basic apologetic nature of the early chapters of Galatians. Principally the argument is that Paul, in defending his independent and equal apostolic status as compared to the Jerusalem apostles, must report on any and all interactions he has had with the church at Jerusalem.

Thus, Galatians would have been written very early in Paul's ministry, at least before the Jerusalem Council of Acts 15 (A.D. 49–50), and very close to his return from the first missionary journey (Acts 13–14). This view helps place in perspective his surprise at his readers' desertion from the gospel "so quickly" (1:6), since he would have been through the region of Galatia in the very recent past.

It seems better, however, to place Galatians after the Jerusalem Council, in which case it could still be one of Paul's earliest epistles. Commending such a date is the noticeable similarity of the style, vocabulary choice, theological development, and, importantly, the type of opposition faced by Paul in Galatians, Romans, and the Corinthian correspondence. Thus, many scholars have made a strong case that Galatians belongs to the same time frame as do these others (A.D. 54–56).

Obviously, the greatest weakness in this view is the fact that such an alignment assumes that Paul would have felt it unnecessary to mention the famine relief visit of Acts 11 in recounting his past contact with Jerusalem. Many scholars who favor the Acts 11 alignment point to this as absolutely precluding a correspondence of Galatians 2 with Acts 15. They reason that Paul would leave himself completely open to the criticism of being dishonest about his "Jerusalem connection" if he had left out any visits, and this had been discovered by his opponents.

This criticism is usually answered by pointing to the fact that

Paul's purpose in recounting his visits to Jerusalem was not to cite every visit to the city, but, rather, to indicate those occasions upon which he met with the main apostles in Jerusalem. Thus, he would not need to mention the famine relief visit of Acts 11:30 since he met with no apostles during his time there.

When all is considered, this alignment appears to have more credibility, and will be the position adopted by this author.

In the above analysis, reference was made to a group of opponents to Paul's work in Galatia. Over the years, scholars have used the term *Judaizers* to describe them. The designation refers to the view that Paul's opponents were conservative Jewish Christians who mandated that a Gentile must first obey the precepts of Judaism, especially regarding circumcision and obedience to the law of Moses, prior to being accepted as a full member of the Christian church.

The conflict which Paul had with these opponents represents a pivotal point in the history of Christianity. The outcome would determine whether the faith would retain the exclusivistic character of orthodox Judaism, or, as Jesus himself seemed to command (Matt. 28:19), would be made available to all of humankind with equal accessibility.

Both the Pauline Epistles and the Book of Acts evidence a considerable difference of opinion among the Jewish members of the early Christian movement as to how to integrate the numbers of Gentiles who seemed attracted to the faith. This difference reflected a long-standing animosity that existed between the Jewish and Gentile communities of the ancient world. The principal issue of distinction between these believers was in the area of circumcision. This rite, performed upon every male Jew shortly after birth, was seen to be both a difficult rite for adult Gentile converts to follow, as well as a culturally disdained practice in the Hellenistic world. Apparently because it was a rite which carried with it a definite measure of commitment and, usually, a permanent aspect, many Jewish members of the early church were adamant about its continued practice for all those who followed Christ. While they recognized that the message of Jesus was not universally accepted among their brethren, they did not consider the Christian movement to be outside orthodox Judaism.

Thus the Epistle to the Galatians represents the collision of those two ideologies. We gain, from the Pauline perspective, an appreciation of the issues (as well as the personalities) involved. We also gain an understanding of the viewpoint which eventually won the day and went on to characterize the Christian church.

Common to all the Pauline letters is the fact that Paul is, first and foremost, a "task theologian." His letters are primarily written to address certain concerns which were troubling the church(es) involved. Thus, we look in vain for any full systematic treatment of any theological issue. Rather, we hear Paul give only that much theological material needed to correct a crisis situation, or to maintain a church's resolve, until he can personally be on the scene.

When we look at Galatians this is quite evident, as he seems to touch upon those issues which are at stake in the Judaizer controversy, and little else. Yet what we can glean from the epistle is the overall sense of how Paul emphasized the completely new reality that was inaugurated for each believer as he or she accepted Jesus Christ as the risen Lord and Savior.

Permeating every incredulity that Paul has at the behavior of the Galatians, relative to the intruders, is the sense that they have missed the most important aspect of their life in Christ. Where formerly they were considered to be outside the realm of God's covenant promises, they have now been, through God's great initiative in Christ, fully embraced into the fullness of that covenant, far beyond even where Old Testament Judaism could take them. Rather than joining an already existing "system" of approach to God (Judaism), the Galatians had been included in the reality that Judaism had longed for: life in the Spirit. This new reality was of a nature so superior to everything that had gone before that it completely changed all social and religious categories of valuing humanity. The basis for acceptance before God was not found in ethnic, sexual, or social status, but in an individual's possession of God's Holy Spirit.

Paul's advocacy of this new reality struck at the very heart of established Judaism's exclusiveness. The law, as the guardian against man's immorality, the tutor which pointed toward the holiness of God, while revealing the imperfect state of man, had now been superseded by the appropriation of God's own Spirit into the life of each one who was found to be in Christ. Thus, rather than standing as an outsider to God's will and ways, the new reality brought mankind into an "insider" position, where the Spirit would interact directly with each person's own nature. This interaction called for no mediator or ceremonial signs of inclusion. People's response, in the light of this new reality, was to "keep in step with the Spirit," to regard all of mankind the way God does, and to continually "test" themselves as to the constancy of their walk by comparing their actions and attitudes to that of the "fruits of the Spirit" and, conversely, to the "works of the flesh." Bearing spiritual "fruit," not circumcising the flesh, had become the tangible sign of one's inclusion in the new reality of God's kingdom.

Galatians, most likely written in the same time frame as 2 Corinthians, gives further explanation to that epistle's great proclamation in 5:17: "If anyone is in Christ, he is a new creation; the old has gone, the new has come!"

OUTLINE

I. Introduction (1:1–10)
   A. Salutation (1:1–5)
   B. Occasion for Writing (1:6–9)
   C. Review of Accusations (1:10)
II. Paul and the Nature of His Apostleship (1:11–2:21)
   A. Preconversion Days (1:11–14)

B. Conversion (1:15–17)
C. First Meeting with Jerusalem Leadership (1:18–24)
D. Second Meeting with Jerusalem Leadership (2:1–10)
E. Correcting Cephas (2:11–21)
III. Treatise: The Efficacy of Grace over Law (3:1–4:7)
A. The Argument from Experience (3:1–5)
B. The Argument from Scripture (3:6–18)
C. The Purpose of the Law (3:19–25)
D. The Results of Faith (3:26–29)
E. Maturing into Sonship (4:1–7)
IV. An Appeal to the Galatians (4:8–31)
A. An Appeal to Maturity (4:8–11)
B. An Appeal to Their Personal Relationship (4:12–20)
C. An Allegorical Appeal (4:21–31)
V. Freedom in Christ (5:1–6:10)
A. Thesis (5:1)
B. Warnings and Reproof (5:2–12)
C. Proof of One's Grounding (5:13–26)
D. Practical Ethics (6:1–10)
VI. Conclusion with Personal Appeal (6:11–18)

COMMENTARY

I. Introduction (1:1–10)

A. Salutation (1:1–5). The apostle Paul followed the normal Greek letter-writing form in composing his epistles. Such a form was characterized by an introduction which cited the name of the author and the addressees. This would be followed by a greeting. These greetings could vary greatly in length, usually determined by the degree of warmth felt between the author and the recipients. We notice here, contrary to his other epistles, Paul gives only the briefest of greetings to the Galatians (v. 3). His style is proper, a bit curt, and immediately evidences a defense of his apostolic origin. Clearly, Paul perceives himself to be under attack as he writes. He wastes no time in rising to his own defense.

The attacks against him appear to revolve around the origin of his apostleship and, with it, the basis of his authority. Obviously Paul's claim to the same apostolic authority as that of the original disciples of Jesus (2:6–10; 1 Cor. 9) is one which could be verified only by himself (cf. Acts 9 for the story of his conversion). Throughout Paul's ministry, the uniqueness of his calling, with its lack of objective proofs, provided ammunition for those who disagreed with his approach (cf. 1 Cor. 5, 9; 2 Cor. 10–13; etc.).

Here in the opening words of the epistle, Paul defends the source of his apostolic calling (v. 1). The key ingredient is that his apostleship is a divinely appointed position and is in no way a product of human decision ("not from men nor by man," i.e., by human agency). Paul appears to be referring to his conversion experience, and the belief that Jesus appeared to him personally. Thus, Paul lists Christ first as the one through whom the commissioning was made, with God the Father as the ultimate source of the appointment by his action of raising Jesus from the dead (v. 1).

Though he acknowledges the greetings of others to the Galatians (v. 2), Paul seems to have little time or desire for pleasantries. His stock, but no less sincere, wish for "grace and peace" to them leads him into a further enunciation of the good news of redemption found in Christ (vv. 3–5).

In brief but effective form Paul reminds the Galatians that redemption is solely the work of God in Jesus Christ. Christ is the one who sacrificially gave himself "for our sins" (see Rom. 5:6, 8; 1 Cor. 15:3), with the result of rescuing us from "the present evil age" (v. 4). This deliverance, fully within the will of God (v. 4), does not remove the recipient from the present world. Rather, the use of the term *age* is similar to other references Paul makes to the distinction between the wickedness of the fallen world around the believer, and the newness of life afforded by the inbreaking of the rule of God into one's life by redemption (see 1 Cor. 1:20; Eph. 2:2; 6:12).

The effect of this review is to establish the ground upon which Paul will argue his grace-oriented gospel. The recognition of the completed work of God in redemption would be undermined by any claim to human activity in conjunction with it. The unusually early doxology found here (v. 5) has the effect of placing his detractors in the precarious position of lessening the glory attributable to God if they affirm any human aspect to the redemption process.

B. Occasion for writing (1:6–9). Paul moves to express condemnation for the Galatians in a paragraph that is noteworthy for its emotional intensity. He is completely astonished not only by the apparent departure of the Galatians from the core of the gospel, but also by their lack of endurance with the truth (v. 6). Such a desertion is understood not just as a differing point of view, but as a rejection of God himself ("the one who called you by the grace of Christ," v. 6)! While the use of the term *so quickly* (v. 6) may relate to Paul's recent visits there, he may also be referring to their desertion from the gospel upon its very first challenge since the establishment of their churches.

In describing the desertion, Paul uses two different terms to refer to the bogus gospel to which the Galatians were attracted. The term translated as "different" (Gk. *heteros*) (v. 6) denotes a complete difference in kind from one thing to another, rather than a difference between related things. This different, but related concept is found in the Greek term *allos,* which Paul uses immediately in verse 7 to show that the perverted gospel he describes has no relationship to the truth; it is fully of another kind and, consequently, false.

We receive our first hint that the Galatian difficulties are the results of outside agitation here (v. 7). The agitators are described as those wishing to confuse the Galatians by perverting the gospel. Paul will provide further insight into their motives later in the epistle (see 4:17; 6:12–13).

The seriousness of the situation is established by the two "curse" (Gk. *anathema*) statements (vv. 8, 9). There are few other terms which could be so reflective of the vehemence with which Paul opposes these false teachings. The use of *anathema* reflects the concept of eternal damnation (lit., it referred to the dedication of an object, usually in pagan temples, for the purpose of its destruction). Paul is not venting anger from the perspective of a wounded ego; he merely states the fact that those who are found to be advocating a false view of the work of Christ are not just mistaken, they are lost.

Quite simply, nothing, or no one, had the authority to override the truth of the gospel (including Paul himself or even angels, v. 8). Paul's concern is to place the issue of authority and the discussion of apostolic origins into a proper perspective. Ultimately it is not the preacher to whom one gives allegiance, but to that which is preached. There is only one gospel. Anything else is perverted and false.

C. Review of accusations (1:10). Because most of Paul's epistles were occasional letters (prompted in response to problems existing in the churches addressed), we are placed in a position similar to one who eavesdrops on one side of a telephone conversation. Often we must reconstruct the sense of the whole conversation with only a few clues upon which to proceed. Such is the difficulty here. Paul asks a series of rhetorical questions, each with an intended negative answer. They give us an indication of the types of accusations which were made by those who discredited his view of the gospel and/or his apostolic authority.

The Greek grammar of verse 10, with the use of the term *gar* (for) as a connective from the previous thought, indicates that Paul's questions are prompted by his previous pronouncement of *anathema.* Paul appears to be reviewing accusations, presumably from the outside agitators (v. 7), that his preaching of free grace was motivated by an attempt to win a vast following for his ministry. Those who held a view that gave an important place to a righteousness based on good works would quite understandably have believed such a "do nothing" gospel to have been formulated by a desire to be popular among the Gentiles.

Paul's previous *anathemas* (which potentially included himself in the cursing, v. 8) were designed to show that it was not popularity he sought, but faithfulness to the gospel. The final statement of the verse indicates that if pleasing men (humankind generally) was his goal, being a "servant of Christ" would not be the most logical way to proceed (v. 10). His words are reminiscent of those said by Jesus regarding the serving of two masters (see Matt. 6:24).

II. Paul and the Nature of His Apostleship (1:11–2:21)

Apparently part of the process used to sway the Galatians from Paul's influence was to cast doubt upon his credentials as an apostle. The agitators (often called Judaizers) seemed to claim for themselves a direct line of authority to someone, or some group, associated with the church in Jerusalem. While we have no way of evaluating the possibility that a countermission to Paul may have been authorized by an official(s) of that church, such a claim was apparently believed by the Galatians.

Paul's defense, then, had to center upon the only objective evidence he had: his changed life from being a persecutor of the church, to being an effective minister of the gospel. In order to reestablish his right to direct the Galatians in their spiritual affairs, Paul not only had to recount his own claim to apostleship, but he also had to establish that the apostles in Jerusalem recognized the equality of his apostolic standing with them.

A. Preconversion days (1:11–14). Similar to his denial of human agency in his apostolic calling (v. 1), Paul makes it clear that no human agency was involved in his own understanding of the gospel (vv. 11–12). This denial involves three specific areas which may have been alleged sources for the gospel Paul represented: (1) it was not "something that man made up" (by him or anyone else); (2) it was not handed down by tradition; (3) he was not instructed in it.

What Paul appears to be saying is that the ultimate triumph of Jesus as redeemer through an act of free grace (the core of the gospel as specified earlier, v. 4) came to him through the very revelation of Jesus' presence during the Damascus Road postresurrection appearance (v. 12; see Acts 9). Paul seems not to have specific declarations of doctrine in mind (see 1 Cor. 11:23ff.; 15:1–8). Rather, the reality of the victory of Jesus over death, signifying God's acceptance of his sacrifice, allowed everything Paul knew of God to fall into proper perspective. This, presumably, is what Paul means by "the gospel" in Galatians 1:11. The specifics of the history and doctrine were secondary to the reality revealed in him (v. 16) at his conversion.

Paul appeals to their own knowledge of his former superior standing in Judaism and his own attempts to "destroy" the church (vv. 13–14). As a conscientious Pharisee Paul was highly acclaimed among his peers and was able to name the revered Gamaliel as his mentor (Acts 22:3). He mentions his advancement in the "traditions of my fathers" (v. 14), which would have involved intense study of the Scriptures and the teachings of the rabbinical sages.

B. Conversion (1:15–17). What becomes clear is Paul's emphasis on the full agency of God in his conversion. Paul reflects his belief that though his change in life appeared dramatically abrupt to him and to all who heard of it, such was not the case with God, who had prepared this very step as early as his existence in his mother's womb (v. 15). Paul expresses this calling in terms reminiscent of the callings of the prophets Isaiah (Isa. 49:1) and Jeremiah (Jer. 1:5).

The revelation of God's Son *in* Paul (v. 16) had, as its purpose, the consecration of an individual to preach the gospel to the Gentiles. This is a decisive calling for Paul, one which allowed him to claim an equality of apostolic standing with the leader of the disciples, Peter, who, in Paul's view, was specifically chosen to lead the mission to the Jews (2:8). Acts 26:17 fully records God's commissioning of Paul to the Gentile mission.

His response to this dramatic change was not to seek counsel or explanation from Jerusalem or anyone else (v. 17). No such need to interpret the experience existed. Rather, Paul headed into the region of Arabia (a large kingdom similar to the area of Syria, Jordan, and Saudi Arabia today, ruled then by the Nabateans). The text does not specify what he did while in that area. The reason he mentioned it was not to explain what he did, as much as to show what he did not do (i.e., consult with Jerusalem). After a stay of some undetermined time, he returned to Damascus (v. 17) where, presumably, the incident of escape from the city took place (see details in 2 Cor. 11:30ff.).

C. First meeting with Jerusalem leadership (1:18–24). Paul's desire was to show that he did not owe allegiance to Jerusalem (and thus would not have to agree with the Judaizers who claimed to be from there). Further, he wanted to show that it was the Judaizers who would have to submit to his authority in Galatia, since he had been recognized by the major Jerusalem apostles as having leadership over the Gentile missionary enterprise. To do this he needed to show that he owed nothing to Jerusalem for the authority he had received to proclaim the gospel.

His first visit to Jerusalem is said to have occurred "after three years" (v. 18). This reference and the one in 2:1 to "fourteen years" have proved to be problematical in understanding Pauline chronology. The reference here could take either his conversion or his return to Damascus as its starting point. The reference in 2:1 may be subsequent to these three years, or could just as well refer back again to the conversion. The grammar gives us very little aid in determining these issues conclusively. In general, many scholars prefer to see Paul's conversion to be the operative point (with A.D. 32–33 as a likely date for it) and A.D. 35–36 as the date of the visit Paul mentions here. This occasion most likely aligns with the reference in Acts 9:26–30.

The three years between his conversion and the meeting of any of the Jerusalem officials emphasizes the independent nature of Paul's work. When he did go up to Jerusalem, he only had the opportunity to visit (Gk. *historēsai*, "to get to know," v. 18) with Cephas (Aramaic name for Peter—likely the term Jesus actually used for him; see Matt. 16:18) and James (vv. 18–19). The visit did not last long (fifteen days, v. 18). No time of instruction or of commissioning is implied.

In stressing that he "saw none of the other apostles—only James" (v. 19), it appears that Paul counted the "Lord's brother" (likely half-brother, the son of Joseph and Mary after the birth of Jesus) among the apostles. While some scholars have sought to deny this, it does seem that the traditional designation of only the Twelve plus Paul as apostles is far too limited.

This seems to be a crucial point for Paul. In all this time of being a Christian, his contact with the Jerusalem leadership was extremely limited. He certainly makes it clear that he and Barnabas had undertaken the ambitious first missionary journey (taking Gal. 2 = Acts 15) without being supervised in any way by Jerusalem! This display of independence so deflated the Judaizers' accusations that Paul felt compelled to offer a guarantee of its truthfulness (v. 20).

After Jerusalem it was on to the regions of Syria and Cilicia (Antioch was in Syria, Tarsus in Cilicia), with no further contact with Jerusalem, or anywhere else in Judea (v. 21). The good news about his changed life was known in Judea only by reputation (vv. 22–23). While that evoked glory to God (v. 24), it brought no formal relationship between Paul and Jerusalem. Clearly, then, Paul was not serving the leaders of Jerusalem.

D. Second meeting with Jerusalem leadership (2:1–10). The second meeting with Jerusalem is fraught with far more problems for Paul, as he attempts to indicate his degree of independence from that power base of the early church (**2:1–5**). If we are correct in assuming that this section represents the same visit as that detailed in Acts 15 (which then causes us to understand "fourteen years later" [Gal. 2:1] as referring to a time period subsequent to the "three years" of 1:18), then Paul has the task of explaining why he went to Jerusalem at all, if he did not need to appear for the purpose of defending his ministry before those who had the power to direct it.

Paul's explanation emphasizes a few points concerning his encounter with Jerusalem on that occasion. He begins, not coincidentally, with the impression that his arrival had the air of one who was the leader of a delegation from the Gentile missionary enterprise (v. 1). The mention of his fellow traveler Barnabas and the taking along of Titus (a representative of the harvest won in the Gentile lands) serve to place Paul in the position of one who arrives as an independent expert consultant on Jewish-Gentile relations. He adds that his coming also had an element of compulsion to it. His visit was initiated by revelation (v. 2). Such an inclusion further proves that his directions come from his relationship to God, and not from the authority of the Jerusalem leadership.

Paul indicates that he had his own purpose for attending the conference (v. 2). It was imperative for the leader of the Gentile mission to have the trust and support of the Jerusalem church or to face the threat of schismatic strife continually. Though the early church seemed to be learning that the same Holy Spirit was given to all individuals upon their acceptance of Christ (see Acts 10:34ff.; 11:18), the animosity characterizing Jewish-Gentile relations was not going to be eradicated easily. Paul must settle this issue early in the history of the Gentile outreach or he would face ongoing feelings of prejudice.

Thus, when Paul mentions that he submitted the content of his preaching to "those who seemed to be leaders," he is not saying that he sought their correction. Rather, he explains that they met in private in order to be sure that they could bring a united front to the conference. It is unstated if Paul knew that the Jerusalem apostles would agree with him; he describes these things from hindsight. Through everything else he had written, however, it is evident that the Jerusalem agreement was not a prerequisite to the continuance of his ministry. Disagreement on these issues, however, would certainly have led to a split and weakened church. This is likely what he had in mind when he added that he was concerned about "running in vain" (v. 2).

Paul uses the Greek term *dokeō* (lit. "the ones who seem," or "have an appearance," with the idea of holding a recognized position) in verse 2 to describe the ones to whom he submitted his preaching. Verses 6 and 9 will elaborate on the individuals he has in mind, including James, Cephas, and John.

Verses 3–5 have been difficult for interpreters to agree upon. The Greek manuscripts vary slightly, but significantly, in verse 5. The difficulties are further complicated by the awkward grammatical connections of these verses. Obviously, the emotional tone of the moment is reflected in Paul's recounting of it. Paul may have been so emotionally involved in describing the events that his secretary was hard pressed to put into written words the apostle's swift-flowing descriptions.

The most likely meaning of the text, backed by the best manuscript evidence and the context of the passage, would appear to picture a confrontation precipitated by those demanding circumcision for Gentiles, which was further complicated by the presence of Titus. Paul firmly makes it known to his readers that there was no compromise of his position, either by himself or by Titus (v. 3).

It is hard to know who the "compeller" in verse 3 was. Though Paul goes on to state that the whole matter was initiated by those he describes as "false brothers" (v. 4), most likely they would not have had the authority to compel Titus to be circumcised. It is quite possible, then, that Paul has the Jerusalem leadership in mind here. In spite of the arguments of the legalists, then, the leadership refused to compel Titus (and, by implication, any Gentile) to follow a prescription which added to the qualifications necessary for fellowship in the church beyond faith in Jesus Christ. Thus, Paul would seem to be describing, in remarkably little detail, the deliberations of the leadership on this issue. Implicitly, they are pictured as in full agreement with Paul's position.

It is interesting to notice the final remark in verse 3, "even though he was a Greek" (i.e., Gentile). Is Paul simply informing the Galatians why it was significant that Titus was under discussion for circumcision? Doubtless they were well aware of his being a Gentile. Rather, it is likely that Paul is dramatically emphasizing the new status of Gentiles in Christ. Even though Titus was among a conference full of Jews, he was treated as having a fully legitimate right to fellowship among them by virtue of his faith alone. It is likely that the Galatians were struck by this. All of those important Jewish believers, and they placed no further requirements upon Titus? Why then are these Judaizers demanding more?

As if to answer such a question, Paul momentarily interrupts his narrative of the events of the conference, digressing to the type of opponents he had encountered there (v. 4). The Galatians are to see that the ones described as "the infiltrating false brothers" who had come "to spy on the freedom we have in Christ Jesus" with the purpose "to make us slaves" (v. 4) are the same type of characters troubling them. The Greek terms for *infiltrated* (*pareisaktos;* see also 2 Pet. 2:1) and *spy* (*kataskopeō;* see 2 Kings 10:3; 1 Chron. 19:3 in the LXX) are usually found in descriptions of secret military operations designed to conduct subversive activities to undermine an enemy's defenses.[1]

Are these opponents Christians? Paul's use of "false brothers" in verse 4 and in a similar context in 2 Corinthians 11:26 suggests he is indicating that the nature of the doctrine taught by such opponents excludes their membership in the faith. This view is further enhanced by Paul's disclaimer in Galatians 2:5 that his delegation (and, possibly, he is including the Jerusalem leadership here as well) even gave a moment's hesitation on the matter "so that the truth of the gospel might remain with you." Surely the issue which plagued Jerusalem then, and was plaguing Galatia as Paul wrote, was viewed by him to be pivotal in one's inclusion or exclusion from the faith. Clearly, in Paul's view, these opponents were in danger of exclusion.

While Paul was satisfied by the decision of the Jerusalem Council, he is just as concerned to show the Galatians that the leadership in Jerusalem had made a specific point of recognizing the apostolic authority he possessed. The point is that Paul gave them no more recognition than they deserved, while they finally gave to him the recognition that he deserved (**2:6–10**).

The use of the phrase *those who seemed to be important* (v. 6) recalls for Paul's readers the individuals with whom he met prior to the confrontation with Titus (2:2). He repeats the vague reference to their authority four times (vv. 2, 6 [twice], 9). Each use of the term appears to refer to the same three leaders, James, Cephas, and John, who are also identified by the term *pillars* in verse 9.

Verse 6 has a curious mixture of Greek tenses. Paul uses the imperfect in referring to the pillars ("whatever they were"). Then he utilizes the present tense ("makes no difference") in referring to his reaction to them. It seems clear that the imperfect is referring to their reputation as being part of Jesus' inner circle. Yet Paul is making the point that no group's past performance is going to dictate the direction of his ministry.

His digression about God not showing partiality (v. 6), which reflects a Hebrew idiom of not "looking at the face" (i.e., looking upon outward appearances; Deut. 10:17; 1 Sam. 16:7; James 2:1), provides a theologically based reason for his behavior. Presumably one would expect Paul to show some deference to these men (at least to Cephas and John) since

1. See H. D. Betz, *Galatians* (Philadelphia: Fortress, 1979), 90–91, nn. 36, 307 for contemporary secular Greek usages.

they followed Jesus even before his resurrection. While such diplomatic niceties might avoid conflict, they could also be devastating, especially since, as Paul desires to show, such submission would cause him to follow men who may not be as correct as he on this important issue. When it is a question of being consistent with the gospel, or following the dictates of church politics, Paul leaves no doubt what he will follow.

Important for Paul's purposes are the results of this meeting with the "pillars." Such results are carefully discussed. While Paul is pleased that these men recognized his authority, he wants to be very sure that such a recognition does not appear as a type of commissioning. Paul arrived with the same status with which he departed; nothing was added (v. 6) to him. The real change occurs in the minds of the pillars. The results are well worth noting: (1) They recognized that Paul was entrusted by God with the Gentile missionary enterprise (v. 7). (2) The authority of Peter and Paul were equated, each in his own sphere of operation (vv. 8–9). This was as a consequence of their perception of the leading of God on the matter (v. 8), and was not simply an administrative decision. (3) They parted as equal partners in the overall enterprise of evangelization (v. 9). (4) The one additional comment made by the Jerusalem leaders, concerning sensitivity to the poor, really did not need to be stated since Paul already had that area of need in mind (v. 10). Even on this rather trivial point, Paul does not waver from his previous statement in verse 6 that the "pillars" added nothing to his ministry!

Verses 7–8 should be regarded as a type of semiquotation of an official document, or of a verbal agreement, which was reached at the council. The recognition of various spheres of responsibility are stated in terms Paul probably would not use (cf. 1:7–9; he would likely avoid any implications that two gospels were being preached). Yet the statement would be, nonetheless, sufficient for the purpose of showing his equal status with Peter. The change in Peter's name may reflect the fact that such an agreement would be framed in both Aramaic, the common language in Judea, and in Greek. In quoting the Greek for his readers, Paul utilizes the Greek translation for "Cephas," which is "Peter."

If this view is correct it may be significant that the "quotation" uses the term *apostle* (v. 8) in referring to Peter's status, but the term is not repeated in reference to Paul. There is debate as to whether the parallel construction in the Greek implies the word's presence or if it was consciously left out. It may well be that Paul assumed it and the "pillars" did not, for even with regard to the spheres of responsibility there may have been some ambiguity since we know that Peter ministered in Rome, and possibly elsewhere (Corinth? see 1 Cor. 1:12; 9:5).

E. Correcting Cephas (2:11–21). The incident related in this section (**2:11–14**) indicates that in spite of the basic agreement reached at the Jerusalem Council, certain ambiguities continued to exist. The incident at Antioch is significant for it moves us on to the next logical step in Paul's argument regarding his authority on the matters troubling the Galatians. We need to take careful note of the situation as Paul has developed it. The authorities in Jerusalem had recognized Paul's equal status relative to them, but they also acknowledged his priority over matters dealing with Gentiles.

Thus, when Paul confronts the erring Peter at Antioch, he does so in rightful exercise of his authority in that sphere. Peter was wrong in regard to his treatment of Gentile believers in Antioch. The implication is clear for the Galatians. Those who are appealing to Jerusalem as the ground for their authority should recognize that Jerusalem has relinquished its authority over such matters to Paul since, when they have dealt with the matter in the past, they have shown themselves (as represented by Peter) not to have the proper sensitivity or theological insight. All of this, of course, is Paul's own view of the matter. Unfortunately we do not have the reactions of Peter to the confrontation.

Placed as it is after the presentation of agreement on the issue of Gentile circumcision, this incident reveals what Paul believed was truly behind Jewish demands for continued segregation. For, as Paul shows, Peter theoretically agreed with the equal status of Gentiles, even to the point of eating with them (dining at the same table was a cultural sign of acceptance and fellowship). Verse 12 is skillfully constructed to indicate both reactions of Peter to his practice of having full fellowship with the Gentile believers.

The inconsistency in Peter's actions is blamed solely on the arrival of a group alternatively described as "certain men . . . from James" and as "those who belonged to the circumcision group" (lit. those out of the circumcision, v. 12). Clearly Peter gave in to the ethnic bias of the arriving Jewish contingent. It is doubtful that he actually changed his theological view as to the status of Gentiles before God. Obviously he had not fully thought through how his theology had to adjust his relations with all persons, in spite of the continued bias of some. Peter, it seems, was not alone in this problem of integrating faith with living, since even Barnabas followed his example, as well as other Jews present (v. 13).

From Paul's description of the actions of the ones who deserted the table fellowship, it is clear that he places the blame squarely on the shoulders of Peter for initiating the response. The actions of the rest of the Jews and Barnabas, described in the passive voice, indicate how Peter's action influenced their similar response. Paul describes their departure from the Gentile table fellowship with the term *hypocrisy* (Gk. *hypokrisei,* v. 13)!

Paul notes that his public rebuke ("in front of them all," v. 14) of Peter came as a consequence of Peter's action, but also appears to have been the culmination of a series of indiscretions that indicated a continuing bias against Gentiles by the Jewish members of the church (see the charge concerning his attempt to "force Gentiles to follow Jewish customs," v. 14). Paul's statement has the ring of irony. We might do well to paraphrase Paul's point: "If you, one of the sacred, live secularly, and not sacredly, how do you suppose to have the secular become sacred?" Other terms might be inserted, but the idea is clear: Jews took great advantage of their heritage, yet they still had not understood that the new covenant did not allow for any human advantage.

Paul had not confronted Peter on a trivial issue. He describes the consequences of Peter's actions as "not acting in line [Gk. *orthopodeō,* lit. walk straight] with the truth of the gospel" (v. 14). Peter's indiscretion, then, was not just a diplomatic mistake, but was related to the very heart of the Good News itself. Paul often represented the uniqueness of the gospel he preached as contained in the new reality of equal status for all persons saved by Christ (cf. 3:28; Eph. 2:11–22). One wonders, after twenty centuries, have we learned this lesson even today?

As Paul relates this story it seems that he has concluded his personal apologetic. Is Paul an apostle? Yes, the Galatians have heard his testimony of seeing Jesus personally and having his office confirmed by the Jerusalem leadership. Does he have equal authority with Jerusalem? Yes. In fact they recognized not only his equality but his primacy over matters concerning the Gentiles. Is it important that the Galatians follow him and not the Judaizers? Yes. Look what happened at Antioch. The lack of calling, knowledge, and sensitivity of the Jerusalem leadership in Gentile affairs has shown itself to be not only insulting to Gentile believers, but also inconsistent with the full truth of the gospel. The Judaizers will continue this practice.

In this section Paul has shown why the gospel is compromised through ethnic favoritism and that with his leadership the Galatians can progress in the gospel. Moving toward the Judaizers is nothing more than a giant step backward.

Many commentators have debated about where Paul ceases his address to the erring Peter (and the other Jews involved in the Antioch incident) and where he begins to address the Galatians. The present writer agrees with the New International Version, which includes **2:15–21** with the rest of Paul's Antioch address. This new section appears particularly directed to Jewish Christians, yet provides the foundation upon which Gentiles also find their place in God's family: justification by faith. It provides the groundwork for Paul's condemnation of the Galatians' attraction to adding works of law to their Christian experience.

The argument here, and in the remainder of the epistle, reminds one so much of the arguments found in Romans (esp. chaps. 3, 6–8). Such parallels have influenced many, including this writer, to view these two epistles as written at about the same time.

The context is appropriate to a Jewish audience. Paul uses terminology which reflects the universal division of the human race from a Jewish perspective: "Jews by birth" and "Gentile sinners" (v. 15). This division will be seen to have an ironic ring to it since Paul will show that the work of Christ has destroyed all previously imagined divisions among humankind (see 3:28).

Paul acknowledges his own position among the "Jews by birth," but goes on to explain that this "advantage" (see Rom. 2–3) only allowed Jews to be even more sensitive to the need for God's justification because of their own inability to perfectly follow the Torah. Paul, then, has not denied the Jewish advantage; he only shows that the advantage, in itself, is not enough to provide a right standing with God.

The key verse of the section is verse 16. We find a repetitive treatment of the doctrine of justification by faith. Paul logically progresses to the next step of a Jewish Christian's understanding. At some point in time there had to be the realization that no one, not even the Jew who attempted it, was "justified by observing the law, but by faith in Jesus Christ" (v. 16). Jewish Christianity could not exist if it were not for the recognition of these facts. It is also the foundation upon which Paul will build his argument for the equality of Jews and Gentiles in Christ (see 3:26–29; see also Rom. 3:9–18, 22–26).

Paul concludes verse 16 with a paraphrase

of Psalm 143:2 ("by observing the law no one will be justified"), giving what he sees to be a scriptural anticipation of the failure of works of the law to gain justification. Thus, both by experience and on the basis of Scripture, the act of placing one's faith in Jesus Christ has become for the Jew the only proper way to obtain justification. Paul, not incidentally, has also introduced the two categories (experience and Scripture) he will utilize in addressing the Galatians concerning their own basis of justification (3:1–18).

Verse 16 also introduces some powerful concepts. The idea of justification (Gk. *dikaiosunē*) was utilized in legal proceedings in pronouncing someone innocent of the charges brought against him. In Paul's twenty-two uses of the term in the New Testament, it has the dual effect of affirming that someone is not to be condemned (see Rom. 3:26; 8:1ff.), while it also declares that a person is viewed as righteous in God's sight (Rom. 3:24). Both benefits are appropriated through faith in Jesus Christ.

Faith (Gk. *pistis*) is used by Paul to denote the channel through which justification by Christ is obtained. It is not described as the cause of justification, only the channel by which justification is appropriated. While *pistis* itself means simply "confidence" or "trust," it always has specific content in the New Testament: confidence or trust in Christ (i.e., the sacrificial act of Christ's death on the cross; see Rom. 3:22, 26; Gal. 2:20; Phil. 3:9). This concept of faith in Christ, in Romans and Galatians especially, is contrasted with the ineffective works of law as vehicles to deliver the benefits of justification to humankind.

Law (Gk. *nomos*) here is not the villain of the story. Rather, it is a person's inappropriate use of the law that is in view. Paul, in the more elaborate argument of Romans (esp. 2:12–15; 7:7ff.), establishes the validity of the Mosaic law as a fundamental expression of the righteousness of God. Yet, too, the law displays itself as the accuser of persons (see 3:10–13) and the vehicle through which they recognize their own sin and sinful inclinations (Rom. 7:13ff.). It is the works of law that are condemned by Paul (see Gal. 3:10) as insufficient. When faith and law are opposed, Paul is indicating the difference between one's acceptance of Christ's death on his behalf, as opposed to one's determination to reject that death and seek self-justification.

For many, the problem with Paul's radical justification doctrine was in pressing fully the implication that man no longer had to work to obey the Mosaic law. If Gentiles, who have no conception of righteous living (i.e., living according to the law), accept Christ and do as they please, does that then mean "that Christ promotes sin" (v. 17; lit. Christ, servant of sin; likely a Judaizer slogan)?

Paul resoundly answers with his characteristic "Absolutely not!" (v. 17). The reason is quite clear. If the law, as a standard for making one righteous, has been supplanted, its continued use as a measurement of personal righteousness is illegitimate. Thus, if Paul (note the change from the plural "we" to the singular "I" in vv. 18ff., placing himself as representative of those following this position) were to reestablish the law's legitimacy, after it has been annulled (Gk. *kataluō;* lit. set aside; NIV destroyed, v. 18) by Christ's work, he could legitimately be viewed as a lawbreaker. But he is not doing this. Indeed, such a charge reflects a misunderstanding of the full reality of being "in Christ." Rather than just being an additional piece of the theological puzzle, faith in Christ results in an entirely new realm of being for the believer (see 2 Cor. 5:17)!

First, using a death-life scenario in verses 19–21, Paul sums up the effect of the law on his former life without Christ: "through the law I died to the law" (v. 19). The proper understanding of the function of the law is found here. It points out the rightful condemnation of man by God (see Rom. 7). This realization is the first step in one's appreciation of the work of God through Christ. Thus this death had to occur, "so that I might live for God" (v. 19).

Second, by attaching the Greek preposition *syn,* "together," to the verb *stauroō,* "crucify," Paul effectively shows that in Christ the believer was also crucified in Jesus' substitutionary death (v. 19; the KJV and RSV include this expression at the beginning of v. 20; see 5:24). Thus, Christ's experience becomes the experience of the believer when appropriated in faith. The consequent benefits of Christ's death and newness of life are also those of the believer.

Thus, the believer's new life is forever wedded to that of Christ and characterized by the nature of Christ (v. 20). Paul describes the mystical union of the believer with Christ, here and throughout the New Testament, by such expressions as "living in Christ" or "Christ living in me" (see Rom. 6:4–8; 8:2–11; 2 Cor. 5:17; Col. 2:12–14; etc.). Life in Christ is not an identification of Christ and the believer to the exclusion of the individuality of either. It is, however, the acknowledgment of the source of life, Christ the living Lord. This is, at once, the reason for and the guarantee of the believer's moral life-style. With the reality that "I no longer live, but Christ lives in me" (v. 20), the power to live righteously resides in the believer. Further, the believer is no longer motivated by an external, accusing law, but by an internal motivation to serve "the Son of God, who loved me and gave himself for me" (v. 20; the verb tense refers to the decisive act of love and sacrifice at the cross).

Concluding this section, Paul appears to reflect a charge likely used against him by the Judaizers. In viewing him as one who rejected the law of God for a form of antinomianism, they believed he had nullified the gracious acts of God in revealing himself to Israel through the law (see also Acts 21:20ff.). However, as Paul indicates, their conclusion was based upon the false assumption that righteousness comes through the vehicle of the law. In one of the most dramatic statements found in the New Testament, Paul carries their position to its logical—and devastating—conclusion: "if righteousness could be gained through the law, Christ died for nothing!" (v. 21). Allowing legalistic restrictions or ethnic differences and customs to mix with grace results in a perversion of the grace offered at the cross and mocks the very death of Christ.

The Galatians have been made to see that those Judaizers who have been attempting to institute the law into their lives are actually in danger of nullifying the cross of Christ. The so-called Jewish advantage has actually become a hindrance to the full appreciation of the new life to be found in Christ.

III. Treatise: The Efficacy of Grace over Law (3:1–4:7)

A. The argument from experience (3:1–5). The transition from a recitation of Paul's past activities to present circumstances seems abrupt, but actually it punctuates the incredible final assertion of chapter 2 which was the logical conclusion of the Judaizing "gospel": "Christ died for nothing" (2:21). Paul refers to them as "You foolish Galatians!" (v. 1) since the very idea of being attracted to a viewpoint which had, as its ultimate result, an utter rejection of the necessity of Christ's death must be ridiculed as sheer folly. In verse 1 Paul uses the Greek term *anoētos* (NIV foolish) to denote the improper thinking of those who, otherwise, should be expected to perceive things correctly. They are not incapable of proper thought. Thus, their uncharacteristic foolishness must be the result of some "magical spell" (as indicated in the sarcastic rhetorical question, "Who has bewitched you?").

Paul's outburst is related to what he had perceived to be a very successful initial ministry among them. He reminds them that "Jesus Christ was clearly portrayed as crucified" before their "very eyes" (v. 1). It is also likely that he is being quite literal here, since it was not at all unusual for those who preached religious or philosophical messages to actually act them out in dramatic forms before their audiences.

The second rhetorical question of this section is a key to understanding Paul's definition of authentic Christian experience. As to whether they had really attained the goal of being in Christ (see 2:20), Paul wants to hear from the Galatians just one thing: "Did you receive the Spirit by observing the law [lit. out of works of law], or by believing what you heard [lit. out of hearing faithfully]?"

Receiving the Spirit (i.e., the Spirit of Christ, the Holy Spirit) was the fundamental mark of authentic inclusion in the body of Christ (Rom. 8:9ff., where the following verses represent a very close parallel to Gal. 2:20). The reception of the Holy Spirit was an eschatological promise associated with the unique ministry of Jesus himself, and a fulfillment of the covenantal promises of God made throughout the Old Testament (see also Joel 2:28–32; John 1:33; Acts 2:17). Jesus encouraged his disciples to look forward to the time of reception (John 20:22), and commanded them to remain in Jerusalem until they received the Spirit (Acts 1:5). The Spirit provides the new life of the believer (Rom. 8:9; Gal. 2:20), reveals the will of God (1 Cor. 2:10), and aids in prayer (Rom. 8:26; Gal. 4:6). Thus the Spirit is a necessity for one to become, and remain, a Christian.

In many ways the rhetorical question of verse 2 highlights the problem with the Galatians and, possibly, with Christian experience itself. So many other experiences of life are progressive and gradual. Even then, only a very few ever reach the highest goal. In many ways this was the Galatian (and Judaizer) misunderstanding. Yet all may, immediately upon "believing what (they) heard," receive the very presence of the Spirit of God in their lives. While growth would still be mandated, there was no higher level left to achieve. Paul's unstated, but nevertheless implied, question throughout the remainder of the epistle is simply, "After receiving the Spirit of God, what more is there to receive? What more could you want?"

Thus Paul launches into an elaboration as to why he calls them "foolish." After receiving the goal (the Spirit) by faith, are the Galatians now going to attempt to receive it by their own effort (v. 3)? The foolishness is, of course, in the folly of embarking on an impossible course which seeks, as its goal, something they have already received!

Verse 4 appears to relate to some experiences otherwise unknown to us. Asking if they have "suffered so much for nothing" may well relate to the common opposition that believers in Christ received from their fellow countrymen, and from non-Christian Jewish zealots (cf. Paul's own persecutions during his first missionary journey, esp. in southern Galatia; see Acts 13:50; 14:5, 19). Paul's hopeful addition to this question, "if it really was for nothing," displays that under the present series of questions lies a questioner who would not even allow the possibility of failure to be the result of his work in Galatia (see 1:7).

Paul returns again to a contrast of the effectiveness of observing the law and believing what one hears (v. 5). This time the effect of such belief is the outward manifestation of miracles, a visible sign of the Spirit's reception. Repeatedly, the Book of Acts calls our attention to the fact that certain visible manifestations of the Spirit's presence were often given in order to indicate an authentic reception of the gospel in areas which were new to the message (see 8:6, 17; 10:44–46; 11:17; 19:6). Thus, when Paul asks questions (here, and v. 2) concerning the initial appearance of the Spirit in the Galatians' experience, he is reminding them of a measurable event, undeniable by anyone who had been present at that time.

B. The argument from Scripture (3:6–18). Paul links the undeniable experience of the Galatians with undeniable Scripture (**3:6–9**). Yet his turning to the example of Abraham was, most likely, not coincidental. Rather, it is probable that the Judaizing faction used Abraham as the prototypical saint of God, who received the Old Testament covenant which had circumcision as its sign. Their argument surely was that if Gentiles wished to receive the benefits of that covenant, then they also must accept its accompanying sign and legal prescriptions.

Paul's utilization of the Abraham story is basically designed to make two major points: (1) Abraham's righteous standing before God occurred prior to the institution of circumcision and the Mosaic law; (2) Abraham's righteous standing before God was made possible through a gracious declaration of God, in acceptance of Abraham's belief. Thus, the prototypical Jew is to be viewed as one who received his place in sacred history by grace through faith!

Using a quotation from Genesis 15:6 (LXX), Paul recites what he believed to be the most explicit statement concerning God's means for justifying humankind: "He believed God, and it was credited to him as righteousness" (v. 6). The faith of Abraham is interpreted to be that which operated on the premise that God was who he said he was, and was worthy of trust (see Rom. 4:17).

On the basis of the proposition in verse 6 Paul concludes that, contrary to Judaizing views, the true children of Abraham must be those who enter into peace with God in the same way as Abraham (v. 7). Abraham becomes the prime example of the effectiveness of faith since his justification occurred prior to the ceremonial rite of circumcision, and centuries before the revealing of the law (see Gal. 3:17). The old covenant, as well as the new, has faith in the promise of God as its operative element (see Rom. 4:14, 16, 18ff.). The implication for the Galatians is obvious: those who are not "those who believe" (v. 7; as opposed to the ones "observing the law," vv. 2, 5) are neither children of Abraham, nor of God!

Finishing these thoughts, Paul uses an unusual expression which personifies Scripture as being able to foresee the future when it declared, concerning Abraham, "All nations will be blessed through you" (v. 8). This quotation of the covenantal promise of Genesis 12:3 directs our attention to how closely Paul links the recorded words of Scripture with the actual words of God. God's promise to Abraham, which included a broader participation than those of his physical line, presents Paul with one of the major motivating factors to carry on with his mission to the Gentiles (Col. 1:25–27). Verse 9 summarizes the foregoing section showing that faith, not ethnic background, is man's only way to appropriate the same covenantal blessings announced to Abraham.

To show the other side of the argument, Paul conducts the Galatians on a review of Scriptures which deal specifically with the fallacy of pleasing God through legal obedience (**3:10–14**). It is interesting to consider whether this was a review for the church, or was the first time they had heard of these passages. Paul's initial missionary preaching may not have dealt extensively with Old Testament concerns, possibly because of a lack of familiarity with them among Gentiles.

It is Paul's wish to indicate that the law (the Mosaic covenant) was a unified standard, no part of which could be violated (v. 10). Thus, all men, finding themselves as violators of the law, would not be pleasing at all to God, but would be under the curse that accompanied that covenant (vv. 10–12).

Thus, contrary to Judaizing beliefs, Paul shows that Christ does not make a person able to obey the law, but accepts the curse of the Mosaic covenant (and, in effect, removes the covenant) in his own death (vv. 13–14). Such a removal of the curse opens the way for all who have been released from the demands of the old Mosaic covenant to receive the benefits of the promises for blessing which had been given in the older Abrahamic covenant (i.e., blessings which were made prior to the law and appropriated by faith, v. 14).

Now Paul attempts to show that one covenant cannot violate the provisions of a previous covenant (**3:15–18**). The New International Version's "let me take an example from everyday life" (v. 15) is a rather free rendering of the Greek "I speak as a man." Yet, the idea that Paul is drawing an illustration from human relationships is a valid description of these verses. Such agreements were made under the most sober circumstances, calling for a life-death commitment from the participants. Another agreement, made some 430 years later (v. 17), cannot alter the provisions of the covenant made earlier with Abraham.

Simply, Paul is arguing that no one acquainted with the Abrahamic covenant could mistake the Mosaic law as its fulfillment. The very terminology of the older pact, "and to your seed" (v. 16), precludes the idea that the Israelites, even if they had been capable of following the law, would have been the earlier covenant's fulfillment (this is what Paul means when he points out that a multifaceted fulfillment was never in view as would be implied if the covenant had specified "and to seeds," v. 16). The apostle is not being overly literal with the term *seed.* He only wishes to remind his readers of what they, and the Judaizers, had come to know, namely, that the Abrahamic covenant would be fulfilled by a personal deliverer, not by a legal code followed by many.

C. The purpose of the law (3:19–25). Paul characteristically argues his case with the presumed objections of a hypothetical opponent in view (see esp. Rom. 3:9, 27; 6:1, 15; 7:7; 11:1; etc.). Here he wishes not to imply that the Mosaic law was either unnecessary or without a place in salvation history. His arguments call for an understanding of the proper place of the law as a vehicle for pointing to God's grace, not as a path of righteousness in and of itself.

Verse 19 clearly points out the temporary and limited purpose of the law as an indicator of sin. Presumably, once this fact was pointed out, the need for the promised seed to come would be clear. Paul implies that once the seed had come, the need for the law would be ended.

Coming abruptly into the argument is the highly unusual expression of verse 20, which the New International Version has tried to clarify with "a mediator, however, does not represent just one party; but God is one." Historically, this has been a most perplexing verse with many different interpretations.

It appears that Paul is trying to make some distinction between the covenant of God with Abraham, and the acceptance of the law by the people of Israel through the agency of angels (Acts 7:53) and Moses. While Abraham entered into a full covenant with God, Israel simply ratified an existing legal code accepted by their representative head, Moses. Thus, the superiority of the promise over the law may be in view, as well as an additional support to verse 17 that the law had no negating effect on the promise. Further, the promised seed of verse 16, which was emphasized to be singular, may be in view here to show that only Christ, and not Moses, could be properly declared to be that "one party."

Thus, putting the law in a secondary position to the promise, and awaiting its fulfillment through that promise, the rhetorical question of verse 21 ("Is the law, therefore, opposed to the promises of God?") can be answered in the negative. Paul's commentary in this verse and the following one (v. 22) attempts to place the law in perspective as a righteous standard of God which thoroughly displays all things (Gk. *ta panta* for the entire creation) as under the power of sin.

The point of the law, then, was to prepare mankind to receive the gift of Jesus Christ, the promised seed, with an attitude of need and gratitude. Paul seals such imagery with a short discussion of the role of the law as an attendant (Gk. *paidagōgos*). But when "this faith came" (v. 23, referring specifically to faith in Jesus Christ) the need and the appropriateness of the attendant's task had ended (v. 25). The attendant's whole task was to point the way to faith in Christ (v. 24).

D. The results of faith (3:26–29). There may not be any other statements such as these in the Pauline corpus that so readily reveal the radical newness of human experience that Paul believed was a direct result of a personal encounter with Jesus Christ. In the cultural and religious context of first-century Galatia, where distinctions of national origin, gender, and economic status were the defining tools for human interaction, Paul's words here declare the inauguration of a new paradigm of human value.

Paul switches back to the second person plural from the first singular (vv. 15–25) to state his conclusion. If the Galatians are being pressured to become something more than they believe they already are, they should note with care the fact that once they have been joined to Christ (v. 26), all temporal distinctions become meaningless; all of them are already "sons of Abraham." This is where the Judaizers missed the radical nature of faith in Christ. Access to God through Christ is open to all, and once access has been appropriated, the unity of humanity that began prior to the fall is restored, with the resultant loss of fallen distinctions.

It should be noted that the main emphasis of these statements is on the reality of sonship in the covenantal family of Abraham as a result of faith in Christ. Paul's elaboration of this fact in verses 27–28 is important, but in the context of a Gentile church led to feel inferior to a Jewish experience in Christ, it is these words which make the greatest impact. Along with sonship, Paul includes the full rights of such a position by stating that Gentiles in Christ are also "heirs according to the promise" (v. 29). Such statements leave no doubt that the Judaizers' position fails to add anything to the Galatians but, in fact, would negate that which they already have received.

While much has been made of the fact that Paul uses baptismal imagery here,[2] it is too much to say with certainty that the apostle reflects an already existent wording from such a ceremony. Yet, Paul, very likely, has in mind a baptismal ceremony and the image of being "clothed" in Christ. Many early Christian baptisms utilized white robes for the participants to display the overall newness of life in Christ.

The three couplets in verse 28 may reflect an ordering by Paul devised to contradict existing prayers found in Jewish and Gentile circles which gave thanks to God for an individual's superiority over supposed inferiors.[3] In any case, Paul's elaboration on the oneness found in Christ leaves no room for those in Galatia (or for twentieth-century readers) to allow for prejudicial treatment of fellow believers in light of ethnic, economic, or gender particularities. Rather than being an exhaustive list, the apostle provides enough elaboration to show that absolutely no distinction can be carried over into the Christ experience.

We should also note, as do many, that the couplets Jew/Greek and slave/free are not exactly like male/female. While the two former couplets eradicate any distinction whatever, the latter one, linked by the conjunction *kai* (and), indicates that while the complementarity of sexual differences remains, such differences no longer represent any barriers to full participation in the newness of life found in Christ.[4]

E. Maturing into sonship (4:1–7). Paul brings together the dual images of sonship and covenantal inheritance from the previous climactic section (3:26–29) to point out an important truth in his view of salvation history. Just as the sonship of a child in a wealthy family is never in dispute, although he must await the time of his maturity to assume the control of the estate, so also the sonship of the Gentiles has never been in dispute. Though they were not God's people until the coming of Christ, it was always God's plan to include all of humankind under his grace.[5]

It is interesting that Paul's symbol of guardianship appears to be applicable to both Jews and Greeks (notice the first person plural in vv. 3, 5). All people, prior to Christ, are assessed as having been under the "basic principles" (Gk. *stoicheia*) of the world. While there has been much discussion as to what Paul includes under this term, it appears that he consigns all religious expressions (including the law!) as having been only the basic foundation of that which was to come in Christ.

Verses 4–7 show clearly the redeeming work of God in securing the sonship of mankind. In a repetition of the Greek verb *exapostellō*, God is shown to have "sent his Son" (v. 4) and "sent [his] Spirit" (v. 6). Thus, it is totally a work of God which has occurred in the fullness of time (v. 4), with the result that they are "no longer a slave, but a son" (v. 7). As if to certify the received fact of sonship, Paul describes the Spirit as crying out through the heart of redeemed man, "Abba, Father" (v. 6), which is literally the cry of a small child to his loving "Daddy."

While Paul's argumentation appears to be designed to show the Gentiles that they are positionally equal with the prejudiced Judaizers, he has, rather, shown that by the gracious work of God in Christ, they actually have received the type of intensely personal relationship that most religious Jews would never dare to assert for themselves![6]

IV. An Appeal to the Galatians (4:8–31)

A. An appeal to maturity (4:8–11). Appealing specifically to the Galatian Gentiles, Paul reminds them of their former enslavement to polytheism. He confronts them also with the inappropriateness of turning toward any other religious expressions to add to the saving work of Christ. His purpose seems to be to point out

2. Ibid., 181–85.
3. Ibid., 184 n. 26.
4. See K. R. Snodgrass, "Galatians 3:28: Conundrum or Solution?" in *Women, Authority, and the Bible* (Downers Grove: Inter-Varsity, 1984), 167ff.
5. Note the recent work on this and related subjects in F. Lyall, *Slaves, Citizens, Sons* (Grand Rapids: Zondervan, 1984).
6. See J. M. Boice, "Galatians," in *Expositor's Bible Commentary*, vol. 10 (Grand Rapids: Zondervan, 1976), 474 n. 6.

that whether they embrace Gentile religious notions or the ancient and holy traditions of Judaism, all of them are "weak and miserable principles (*stoicheia*)" (v. 9; see 4:3).

Referring to the fact that they have already begun to observe certain (presumably Jewish) regulations (v. 10), Paul asserts that such actions threaten to negate all that he had done among them (v. 11). Such actions would suggest that they have made no progress since Paul's visits. In their attempt to mature through legalism the Galatians have actually indulged in a childish flirtation with danger.

B. An appeal to their personal relationship (4:12–20). The apostle turns to offer the Galatians an objective measure by which to judge his arguments and motives. He refers back to their first meeting (v. 13; Gk. *proteron* would normally refer to the first in a series, possibly giving some weight to the South Galatia theory). His tone is now more personal (use of "brothers," v. 12, and "my children," v. 19). He calls upon them to imitate him, based upon the integrity of his former work among them (v. 12).

Because of some illness, which he does not pause to detail here (his "thorn in the flesh"?; see 2 Cor. 12:7), Paul's initial visit caused him to be obligated to the Galatians. He recalls for them their touching, sympathetic response (v. 15). He also appeals to the strong personal relationship they once had (v. 14) to press them to reject those who would attempt to drive a wedge between them and their founder (v. 17).

He applauds them for their concern to be zealous, yet immediately asks them to be very careful to judge if the object of their zeal is worthy (vv. 17–18). Referring to them as his "children" (v. 19), Paul takes the loving tack of a father who wants to encourage the first steps of his child, stumbling though they may be. His concern is not only for his readers to wish to grow, but to be capable of discerning which direction is appropriate for their growth (v. 18).

For the first time in this epistle, we get a hint of the frustration of Paul who, thinking his relationship with these churches was secure enough to withstand any adversity, now finds that he is treated with contempt. He wishes his tone could be less anxious and stern (v. 20). The fact that he has had to deal roughly with them points up the severity of the situation.

C. An allegorical appeal (4:21–31). His final appeal has perplexed many commentators. The use of the historical narrative concerning Hagar and Sarah coupled with the prophetic utterance of Isaiah (Isa. 54:1) appears to make Paul guilty of some specious scriptural interpretation. This may be an instance when our lack of specific acquaintance with all the dynamics of the Galatian situation hinders our ability to understand (possibly Paul's approach discredits interpretations offered by the Judaizers?).

The "allegory" (v. 24; NIV figuratively) stresses the main points of Paul's previous arguments, and thus stands as a good, if somewhat ironic, summation of the Judaizers' errors. Utilizing an incident revolving around Abraham (likely one of the Judaizers' favorite figures because of the institution of circumcision), Paul shows that, like the covenants of law and grace, Hagar and Sarah can be compared (Gk. *systoicheō;* lit. stand in the same line), yet have some very different characteristics:

Hagar	*Sarah*
slave woman	free woman
son, physically born	son, born according to promise
Mount Sinai (old covenant)	(new covenant?)
present Jerusalem, enslaved	Jerusalem above, free

The major difference between the two is one of kind, not circumstance. Paul appears to be relying on the Galatians' acquaintance with the historical narrative to point out the major factors in the story. One factor, which is unstated but certainly in view, is that the Hagar incident was not a necessary part of God's plan and had not been included in the promise to Abraham (see Gen. 16). So also, the covenantal promises to Abraham had not included the law (which has already been stated to be of necessity only because of man's sin; see Gal. 3:19; Rom. 5:20).

Thus, rather than being discontinuous with the promises of Abraham, the gospel of grace relates to God's best, fully aligned with such promises. As if to further enhance the point, Paul recites a prophecy of Isaiah concerning Israel's restoration from the captivity of Babylon (Isa. 54:1). While the Israelites were few in number then (as the Gentile Christians are, relative to Jewish believers, now), miraculous, God-ordained growth was promised.

Finally, then, as now, the son under slavery persecuted the son of promise (Gal. 4:29). The Judaizers are clearly portrayed as lying outside the covenantal promises of God. Sarah's statement in Genesis 21:10 conveniently allows Paul to imply that the Judaizers' position should not only be rejected, but they themselves should be cast out (v. 30), since the enslaved cannot inherit the promises with the free! Rather than being seen as second-class citizens of the Mosaic covenant, Paul indicates that the Galatian Gentile Christians have been accepted as full sons and heirs (they are Isaac, v. 28; see 3:7) of the Abrahamic covenant!

V. Freedom in Christ (5:1–6:10)

A. Thesis (5:1). Grammatically, verse 1 is related to the previous paragraph, yet it also provides both a summary and a transition point to the epistle. While the manuscript evidence varies on points of grammatical connectives, the sense of the statement is not endangered. In fact, this statement provides the thesis for Paul's insistence on the Galatians' rejection of the Judaizers.

The New International Version's rendering of the verse into two sentences appears to be quite correct (contra the KJV). The first sentence stands as the declaration of purpose for Christ's redeeming work (lit. Christ set us free to freedom), emphasizing the decisive event (note the aorist tense of the verb) which changed the believer's condition from one of slavery (under the law, and other elemental principles; see 4:3, 9) to freedom (see 2:4; John 8:32–36; Rom. 7:4, 6; 1 Cor. 9:1, 21; 11:29)!

The second part of the verse encourages the Galatians to hold to their position against those who would return them to slavery again. This encouragement will be given practical substance in verses 13–26. But Paul digresses for a moment, providing specific warnings against any Galatian hesitancy on this point (vv. 2–12).

B. Warnings and reproof (5:2–12). The digression serves to provide the last and most pointed set of warnings concerning the seriousness of the Galatians' consideration of the Judaizers' position. Beginning with an emphatically personal appeal (lit. Behold, I, Paul, say to you), he expands upon the fact that the very act of circumcision, rather than being a safeguard for those who are unsure of which position is correct, actually serves to negate the power of Christ in their lives (v. 2)! The fact that Paul seems to restate this very same proposition, in a slightly altered manner in verses 3–4, reminds us of his double curse against this teaching in 1:8–9.

The call from Paul is for them to declare their allegiance. To attempt to be justified through law is to forsake the grace offered in Christ and to forsake Christ himself (v. 4). If they are under the power of faith, then they join him (note the switch from "you" [pl.], vv. 2–4, to "we", v. 5) in awaiting the completion of the salvation begun in Christ. In this statement, one of the few about the end times, it is of crucial importance to note that the follower of the promise awaits God's declaration of righteousness (see 3:6), while the follower of law is incessantly and futilely working to keep the law (v. 4; see 3:10–12).

In summing up the ineffectiveness of the rite of circumcision, Paul needs to make the point which may well be an overriding consideration in the minds of the Judaizers and wavering Gentiles: Without circumcision, or without the legal requirements, does the Christian fall hopelessly into antinomianism? Paul assures them in verse 6 that the rite, or lack of it, guarantees nothing as to the type of life one will lead. Rather, contrary to following legal requirements, faith itself expresses a person's relationship to God through loving action. Paul will pick up on this theme in the next section of the epistle (vv. 13ff.).

An evident shift in tone takes place in verse 7 and continues throughout the rest of the epistle. As if to signal his satisfaction that his argumentation should have moved him from a defensive posture to one of resecuring his founder's status, he reflects on how the rift in their relationship could have ever taken place. The contrast now is clearly between Paul and the one (sing. in v. 10), or ones, who have been hindering the Galatians. Certainly God, "the one who calls you" (v. 8; see Rom. 8:28, 30) is not the cause of defection. Paul's expression of confidence in the Galatians arises from his knowledge of their shared faith in Christ (v. 10).

The final, somewhat inconsequential, objection to which he addresses his remarks apparently came from those opponents who knew that Paul had appeared at times to allow circumcision to coexist with his gospel of grace (v. 11). This may be a reference to his actions relative to Timothy (Acts 16:3). If so, it lends further credence to a dating for this epistle later than the Jerusalem Council (Acts 15). In any case, Paul makes it known that even his allowance of circumcision does not contradict his present position that the Judaizers are attempting to attribute to such rites (and the accompanying obligation to keep the law) something that Paul had never allowed. His action toward Timothy was one of expediency (cf. 1 Cor. 9:19–23). The Judaizers make circumcision a necessity for covenantal inclusion.

His opponents could not be serious in charging him with having preached circumcision, since they attack him so vigorously. Instead, he points to the fact that to his opponents he does not just represent an inconsistent approach to Jewish legalism. Rather, he brings to their whole system the "offense of the cross" (v. 11; Gk. *skandalon;* lit. a trap or snare) which overturns their entire man-made approach to righteousness.

Apparently the surfacing of such attacks against Paul's ministry so frustrated him that he allows a sarcastic remark to finalize his disgust with the Judaizers' preoccupation with the outward rite of circumcision (v. 12). While some commentators appear reluctant to believe Paul would utter such a condemnation, such would actually be a better fate for these opponents than the one he calls for in 1:8–9 (cf. Mark 9:43, where Jesus uses similar terminology in reference to something that is a *skandalon*).

C. Proof of one's grounding (5:13–26). The Judaizers' position has now been thoroughly analyzed and is found wanting. Paul has defended his position as an apostle and his rejection of the additional requirements of Jewish conversion for Gentiles who wanted to come into the covenantal relationship with God through faith in Christ. Yet one might ask, "What's left? If you take away law, by what standard will a person live?"

In addressing this type of question, Paul reasserts his view of the purpose of redemption in Christ (see 5:1) with the emphatic "You, my brothers, were called to be free" (v. 13). This freedom does not induce license (indulging the sinful nature, v. 13), since it is not the absence of law, but it is the culmination of the law (v. 14; see Jer. 31:31–34). Paul shows that the proper expression of the law comes from a heart full of grateful love, rather than anxious self-centeredness, and is shown through mutual service (v. 13; lit. becoming slaves to one another), and love of neighbor (**5:13–18**).

This is an especially attractive and pointed picture of the results of true freedom, since it appears to be in complete contrast to the character of their congregational relationships at that time (v. 15). Rather than being the guarantor of righteous actions among these former pagans, the inclusion of the law into their lives has only given vent to competitiveness and lack of concern for each other. You can almost hear Paul say "Precisely!" Their way shows that they use the law inappropriately, since they do not gain the results through it which all recognize to be crucial in God's righteousness (v. 14; see Lev. 19:18; Luke 10:27 and parallels).

As a counterbalance to the possibility of expressing one's "sinful nature" (v. 13) through freedom, Paul asserts that living "by the Spirit" (v. 16) will characterize true freedom. The contrast of flesh (Gk. *sarx*) and Spirit (Gk. *pneuma*) is found throughout the Pauline Epistles, as well as other parts of the New Testament. Rather than pointing to two different parts of the same individual, the terminology relates to an orientation which motivates the course of life a person will take. These two orientations conflict in the most basic sense (v. 17; see Rom. 7:15–23). Paul seems to assert that in spite of a person's will to do right (i.e., follow the law), the flesh orientation makes that will ineffective and dooms the person to failure (v. 17). This assertion reveals the utter fruitlessness of the "righteousness through law" approach.

The great emancipation for man is to be "led by the Spirit" (v. 18) which takes away his subjugation to the law, and to the sinful nature to which the law makes its appeal (see Rom. 6:11–14).

The next two sections (5:19–26) provide a practical contrast of attitudes and actions which can be a test for the Galatians' present orientation. By finding oneself on either list of vices and virtues, one could also identify whether one was led by the Spirit.

Fifteen works of the flesh are specified (**5:19–21**), with the insistence that the list is not exhaustive ("and the like," v. 21; see other lists in 1 Cor. 6:9–10; Eph. 5:5; Rev. 22:15). While they may have been grouped according to various schemes, the list includes sins that many would expect ("sexual immorality, impurity and debauchery," Gal. 5:19), and others that might be unexpected ("discord, . . . fits of rage, selfish ambition," v. 20). Some of the sins appear to relate directly to the pagan life-styles the readers once practiced ("idolatry and witchcraft; orgies," vv. 20–21), while others could even be associated with the type of "biting and devouring" (v. 15) which appeared to be a result of their new legalistic life-style ("jealousy, . . . dissensions, factions," v. 20).

Paul asserts that it does not take great spiritual insight ("the acts of the sinful nature are obvious," v. 19) to spot the inappropriateness of these activities and attitudes among believers. In fact he reminds them that he spoke to them about this before (v. 21) and told them that such acts revealed a person who would "not inherit the kingdom of God" (v. 21).

In contrast to the multiple "works" of the flesh, the singular "fruit" (likely denoting a harmonious unity) promotes a God-oriented expression of activities and attitudes that enhance one's relationship to God and fellow man. The nine attributes found here (**5:22–26**) are clearly the production of the Holy Spirit in the believer's life, and come as a composite whole, not as individual items which some have and others do not (vv. 22–23; for other lists of virtues, see 2 Cor. 6:6; Eph. 4:2; 5:9; Col. 3:12–15).

Three sets are discernible in the list. The first, "love, joy, peace" (v. 22), reflects the resultant attitude of one who has been endowed with the Spirit of the God who is identified as love (1 John 4:8), who brings complete satisfaction (John 3:29), who is declared to bring "peace on earth" (Luke 2:14), and who is identified as the "Prince of Peace" (Isa. 9:6).

The second set reflects how a Spirit-led individual will conduct interpersonal relationships ("patience, kindness, goodness," v. 22). The third set seems to focus primarily on a person's inner life when under the control of the Spirit ("faithfulness, gentleness, self-control," vv. 22–23).[7]

Paul concludes the list in verse 23 with the pronouncement, "against such things there is no law." Certainly his remarks are not just indicating that the foregoing list of "fruit" is permitted under the law. Rather, his point seems to answer those who would feel that the call to move beyond the law would leave the Galatians without any foundation upon which to measure their actions. But Paul maintains that the work of the Spirit in one's life provides an internal motivation and proper orientation to participate in the attitudes and actions that are consistent with the character of Christ. Thus, with the freedom afforded through Christ (5:1, 13), the sinful nature is crucified resulting in a new person (v. 24) who by nature *is* the righteousness demanded by the law and granted through the Spirit (see 2 Cor. 3:6).

The final exhortations of the chapter indicate that while the reality of the fruit is a gift from the Spirit, the believer's responsibility is to actively "live by the Spirit," and "keep in step with the Spirit" (Gal. 5:25).

The Christian (and Paul includes himself here) does not sit idly by with the power of the Spirit within. He is called to active participation, in accordance with the new reality of his sonship. The tension of positional and experiential reality of the new creation is evident throughout Paul's epistles (see esp. Phil. 2:12).

The final statement of the chapter may introduce the next, more practical section of exhortations. In any case, Paul's focus moves from theory (5:1, 13–25) to practice (5:26; 6:1–10). Possibly the particular statement of verse 26 is put in close proximity to the encouragement to live by the Spirit since some of the Galatians might begin to develop a new set of hierarchical stages related to their manifestation of fruit. This Paul will not allow.

D. Practical ethics (6:1–10). It is not unusual for Paul to conclude his epistles with a section on practical living, which emphasizes some of the themes he addressed in the heart of the letter (see Rom. 12:9ff.; 1 Cor. 16:13–14; 2 Cor. 13:5). It also seems to have been a pervasive problem for the gospel of grace to have the attitude of hierarchism invade the Spirit-led life (cf. Rom. 12:3ff.; 1 Cor. 1:10ff.; 2 Cor. 10:1ff., esp. v. 12). It may well be that this was the chief attraction of legalism—the opportunity to measure oneself relative to another and to appear superior to one's fellows. As Paul indicates, such an attitude is completely foreign to the gospel (Eph. 2:8–10).

In areas particularly open to the temptation of hierarchical appraisal (e.g., the awareness of another's sin, v. 1, and the awareness of another's burden, v. 2), Paul exhorts them to act as "spiritual" (v. 1, referring back to the previous chapter regarding the fruit which defines such a person). The Spirit-led individual will work toward restoration (v. 1), which has the effect of obliterating the wrong which could be used to strengthen one's claim of superiority against the erring brother.

Paul completes these exhortations with an appeal for each individual to take his own condition seriously, as one whose only concern is to test how he bears his own level of responsibility in the Lord (vv. 3–5), without falling into an attitude of conceit (v. 3). The Galatians are to see that their faithful actions in this area do fulfill a law, namely, the law of Christ (v. 3). It is interesting to note that Paul seems to regard such practical areas of personal relationships among believers as the benchmark of which type of law they follow: the one leading to works of the flesh, or the one exhibiting the fruit of the Spirit.

In the area of financial responsibility, the Galatians are also exhorted to share with those who instruct them "in the word" (v. 6). Why Paul adds this concern here is open to interpretation. He may be including a concern which related to a particular injustice done to a fellow worker. However, the following statements (vv. 7–10) seem more than coincidentally related to issues discussed in 2 Corinthians 9:6ff., where this particular sowing-reaping proverb (see Job 4:8; Hos. 8:7) is stated in a similar context. Very likely, the same Judaizing element found in Galatia was present in Corinth as well (2 Cor. 11:22–23). This group likewise denounced Paul's apostolic credentials (2 Cor. 10:2, 4, 10–15; 11:5, 7–8, 13, 15, 18ff.). Given this interpreter's position as to the dating of

7. For a full treatment of such terms, see W. Barclay, *Flesh and Spirit* (Grand Rapids: Baker, 1976), 63–127.

this epistle, it is also likely that these opponents attempted to discredit Paul's collection for the church at Jerusalem (Rom. 15:25–27; 1 Cor. 16:1–4, esp. v. 2; 2 Cor. 8–9).

Thus, the final section is provided in answer to the Judaizers' objections that participation in Paul's collection is unwise, giving a pretender the chance to defraud them (see 2 Cor. 11:8). Paul's word is to appeal to God's judgment of the matter (v. 7). Their participation is called for as a manifestation of the Spirit in their lives, an active "doing good" (v. 9), which is especially appropriate when it benefits the "family of God" (i.e., the Jerusalem church, v. 10).

VI. Conclusion with Personal Appeal (6:11–18)

Confirming the belief that most of the epistle was dictated is the notification of verse 11 that the apostle writes the remainder of the letter "with my own hand." In drawing attention to the "large letters" with which he writes, Paul may give us the final clue as to why, upon his initial visit, the Galatians were willing to tear their own eyes out for him (4:15). The "thorn in the flesh" of 2 Corinthians 12:7 and the ailment which plagued him in Galatia may well be attributed to some form of eye disease. His handwriting may have been awkward, but it authenticated his letters (see 2 Thess. 3:17, where the expression, "This is how I write," may be explained by such a theory).

Paul also takes the opportunity to personally emphasize the main point of his letter. The ones who trouble the Galatians are considered to be hypocritical opportunists, attempting to build their own misguided view of spirituality (vv. 12–13) by forcing the Galatians into a dependent relationship. The Judaizers' motivation in all this is considered to be fear—a desire not to be persecuted (v. 12), presumably by their own nonbelieving brethren (the same who have resoundly persecuted Paul!).

In ridiculing his opponents' motives, Paul sets forth his own. His only motive is found in the pivotal experience of the "cross of our Lord Jesus Christ" (v. 14). This event has caused the death of the world (v. 14; referring to the world's system, esp. with regard to values) for Paul.

As if to leave them with one final, decisive word, he declares that the rite which the Judaizers assert as being crucial becomes meaningless in relation to the gracious work of the Spirit in making a "new creation" (v. 15; see 5:6; 2 Cor. 5:17). Even the benediction, so characteristic of the final words of the Pauline Epistles, carries this message. Peace and mercy are reserved only for those who "follow this rule." Only these people can be properly identified as "*the* Israel of God" (v. 16; see Rom. 9:6; 11:7ff.; Eph. 3:6). To be admitted as a member of the old covenant people of God, one must adhere to the provisions of the new covenant which was promised as part of the old.

Paul's last words alert us to the toll such battles take on an apostle. The constant harassment concerning his apostolic credentials and the problem of legalism as an excuse for Jewish prejudice toward Gentiles are exhausting him. His authenticity is really not a matter of speculation; it is a matter of evidence, the evidence of a man scarred (Gk. *stigmata;* lit. a brand mark on an animal or slave) by a world that has persecuted him as it did his Lord. Is there really any other more convincing evidence (see 2 Cor. 11:22–30)?

The benediction is characteristic of Paul, though unusually short (see Rom. 16:25–27). Particularly poignant for this epistle is the inclusion of the title *brothers* (v. 18). He sends the letter off with a prayer that such a designation might still be appropriate.

SELECT BIBLIOGRAPHY

Barclay, W. *Flesh and Spirit.* Grand Rapids: Baker, 1976.
Betz, H. D. *Galatians.* Philadelphia: Fortress, 1979.
Boice, J. M. "Galatians," in the *Expositor's Bible Commentary.* Grand Rapids: Zondervan, 1976.
Bruce, F. F. *The Epistle to the Galatians.* Grand Rapids: Eerdmans, 1982.
Burton, E. D. *A Critical and Exegetical Commentary on the Epistle to the Galatians.* The International Critical Commentary. Edinburgh: T. & T. Clark, 1920.
Guthrie, D. *Galatians.* Greenwood, S.C.: Attic, 1977.
Lightfoot, J. B. *The Epistle of St. Paul to the Galatians.* London: Macmillan, 1866.
Ramsay, W. M. *An Historical Commentary on St. Paul's Epistle to the Galatians.* New York: G. P. Putnam's Sons, 1900.
Tenney, M. C. *Galatians: The Charter of Christian Liberty.* Grand Rapids: Eerdmans, 1950.

EPHESIANS

Richard J. Erickson

INTRODUCTION

The most crucial problem in the study of Paul's Epistle to the Ephesians is whether Paul wrote it. It claims unambiguously to come from Paul's hand, both in the very first word of the letter and in numerous other personal references. Doubts among scholars as to the literal truth of these claims have arisen due to a number of factors, however. Some of these include the author's obviously limited acquaintance with his readers, something highly puzzling if Paul is writing to his friends in Ephesus, where he spent nearly three years. Likewise, the literary relationship between this letter and that to the Colossians shows that if they were not written at the same time by the same person, then one was modeled on the other. Yet the vocabulary and style of Ephesians are considerably different from that in Colossians, suggesting that the two documents were not authored by one person. Furthermore, the teaching of Ephesians is thought to reflect situations in the early church which postdate the death of Paul by several decades in some cases (e.g., the references to "apostles and prophets" in 2:20; 3:5). All these factors add up to the possibility that Paul himself is not the author of Ephesians. Nevertheless, taken one by one, the separate pieces of evidence can be adequately explained on the assumption of Pauline authorship. It is their cumulative effect which carries the greatest weight against authenticity. Yet even the accumulation of evidence is not a watertight case, but only a case for probability, and history is replete with the improbable. Without being either dogmatic or credulous, we may still with good conscience approach Ephesians as a letter from the apostle Paul.

If Paul wrote Ephesians, it must of necessity predate his death in Rome under Nero, around A.D. 65 or 66. Assuming that the references to chains and imprisonment are to be taken literally, we should date the letter in the early 60s, probably from Rome. But to whom was it written? Clearly, Paul is not well acquainted with the intended readers (see, e.g., 1:15), which would be strange if they were Paul's congregation at Ephesus. But oddly enough, certain important and early manuscripts do not have the words *in Ephesus* (1:1), giving rise to the suspicion that the document was never meant for that congregation, but for some other that Paul had never visited. Perhaps it was a circular letter sent to a number of enclaves that may have sprung up around the vicinity of Colossae. At any rate, the real destination (if not Ephesus) and the origin of the insertion *in Ephesus* remain conjectural.

Central to the message of Ephesians is the re-creation of the human family according to God's originally intended design for it. As such, this new creation shatters the opinion long held by the Jewish community that God accepts the Jew and rejects the non-Jew. The traditionally assumed criterion of distinction between the Jew and the non-Jew is obedience to the law, but this criterion, fostering pride and pharisaism, was abolished in Christ's sacrificial death. Consequently, there remains no more hindrance to reuniting all humanity as the people of God, with Christ as the head. The fact that even within the church itself, let alone outside the church, this reunification does not seem to be fully in effect, is the result of the partial arrival of the new age of God's rule. During the interim between this new age's first inbreaking with the first coming of Christ and Pentecost, and its final consummation at the second coming of Christ, God has endowed his new family with the power of the Spirit to keep them and to enable them to live out their new life as it will be done in the future. Thus the emphasis of Ephesians is on the unity of the church in Christ through the power of the Spirit.

OUTLINE

I. Introduction (1:1–2)
II. Re-creating the Human Family: What God Has Done (1:3–3:21)
  A. Three Spiritual Blessings in Christ (1:3–14)
  B. The Importance of Knowing About It All (1:15–23)
  C. Redemption: Clearing the Ground (2:1–10)
  D. Re-creation: Removing the Barriers (2:11–22)
  E. Digression: Paul, Outsiders, and God's Glory (3:1–13)
  F. Empowerment: Realizing the Future (3:14–19)
  G. Doxology (3:20–21)
III. Re-creating the Human Family: What God Is Doing (4:1–6:20)
  A. Creating Unity: The Body Forged (4:1–16)
  B. Mind Control: The Inward Change (4:17–24)
  C. Becoming Christian: The "Little" Things (4:25–5:5)
  D. Light and Wisdom: Living Undeceived (5:6–21)
  E. The Circle of Responsibility: Mutual Submission (5:22–6:9)
  F. Making the Right Stand in the Right Strength (6:10–20)
IV. Closing Remarks (6:21–24)

COMMENTARY

I. Introduction (1:1–2)

The author identifies himself by name and calling and greets his readers in the manner usual in the Pauline Epistles, except that he is mentioned alone here, without the usual companions. The point to note is the address, *in Ephesus*, which has been dealt with above.

II. Re-creating the Human Family: What God Has Done (1:3–3:21)

A. Three spiritual blessings in Christ (1:3–14).

This opening section, which sets the agenda for the rest of the letter, is itself opened in verses 3–5. God, who in Jesus Christ originated the solution to our dilemma of sin, is blessed (thanked) for blessing us in Christ with every spiritual blessing (v. 3). The word *bless,* therefore, carries two different senses, depending on whether God or a human being (with God as object) is the subject. "In the heavenly realms" evidently implies that these blessings are secured in the very essence and character of God himself, and are not subject to the uncertainties of earthly life. This is borne out repeatedly in this very section by the emphasis on God's decision, will, and purpose.

God has made his choice before the creation of the world. We (humans? Christians?) are to be holy and unaccusable before him (v. 4). Because he loved us and simply because it pleased him to do so, he has marked us out to be his own adopted family (v. 5). The stated purpose of this sovereignly independent choice is that we might praise the glorious grace of God which he has freely given us (v. 6). This is not an indication of an egotistical God, but of one who knows better than we do that if his creatures concentrate their praise and aspirations on him, all their own creaturely potential will be realized.

Threaded throughout this tone-setting passage is the key to the entire argument of the letter: it is all done for us "through Jesus Christ," "in the One he loves," "in Christ," "in him" (vv. 3–6). The solution to the human dilemma is in Christ the Lord, whose Father is none other than the blessed God.

In Christ three spiritual blessings (vv. 7, 11, 13) have been made ours, which together amount to a whole new God-determined existence. First, we have redemption, which is made available through the payment of a price—the blood, or death, of Christ (v. 7). It consists in the forgiveness of sins, the necessary first step toward the re-creation of a truly holy, blameless family. Redemption is the foundation of God's work on behalf of humanity. Without redemption nothing else could be done. It deals effectively with the reason why the human family must indeed be re-created, namely, the sin which spoiled the original creation.

We have this redemption, this new standing with our Creator, not because of our own worthiness, but simply according to the wealth of his grace—another assurance of the security of the situation (v. 8). He has heaped grace upon us beyond measure, having (according to his own wise understanding) made known to us what he has wanted to do all along, something which gives him pleasure, something which he decided to accomplish at the proper time in Christ, namely, the "mystery of his will" (v. 9). And what is this mystery, hidden in God's will, which has been revealed to us? Nothing less than that everything in creation, heavenly and earthly, human and nonhuman, be subsumed and united in Christ—again, in Christ (v. 10).

The negative value of the first blessing is balanced by the second blessing, which indicates for what we have been redeemed. In Christ we have been appointed to participate (v. 11). The purpose of this is that we may praise God's glory and so be enabled to fulfill our proper destiny as creatures of a holy God (v. 12). What place we have been allotted has been hinted at already in verses 5 and 10, and will be detailed in 2:11–22 (just as the nature of redemption is elaborated in 2:1–10). It is a place in God's new family whose head is Christ. Again it is stressed that God himself is the author, decider, planner, and accomplisher of this; he has desired it when we did not. And desiring it, he can and will do it. Indeed, he has already done it.

To this point Paul has been speaking in the first person plural, which could mean either that he includes his readers or that he does not, contrasting them instead with some other group to which he himself belongs. This other group he has called "we, who were the first to hope in Christ" (v. 12). Now he draws the readers into the picture by centering the third blessing on them. They have heard the "word of truth," the true message, the Good News which brought them, too, into God's salvation once they had believed it (v. 13). Thus they are also "in Christ," and in him have received the third blessing—the "*seal,* the promised Holy Spirit" (v. 13). Just as Pilate sealed the tomb of Christ and thereby prohibited unauthorized tampering with it, God has set his seal upon his adopted family, proclaiming to all beings whose interference would endanger them that they belong to him and are not to be harmed. But there is more: the Spirit is a downpayment, a "deposit guaranteeing our inheritance" (v. 14; the word translated "inheritance" is related to that in v. 11 translated "chosen") while we await the full redemption of God's possession. As will be seen in 3:14–19, however, the presence of the Spirit implies more than a passive guarantee; it also means the power necessary to live out in this doomed age the ethics of the new age to come, which in Christ has already entered the scene. This new ethic, good for us and for everyone else, is rooted in the praise of the glorious Creator.

B. The importance of knowing about it al

(1:15–23). The immense significance of this threefold work of God on behalf of humanity makes it imperative that people hear about it and come to understand it. For the more they do so, the greater their ability will be to stand steady and grow in their new relationship with God and each other. Therefore ("for this reason"), Paul prays for his readers, whose faith he has heard about, that they may increase in understanding. Their two-dimensional faith is worth noting, since it capsulizes the sort of faith which the epistle promotes. It consists of faith in the Lord Jesus and love toward all the saints. In other words, it is a relationship of confidence in the work of God in Christ which itself issues in a relationship of loving concern for fellow members of the new family, no matter who they may be, acted out in attitudes and concrete deeds (v. 15). The epistle in fact readily divides in half, treating these twin aspects of the faith. That Paul never stops giving thanks for this church or praying for it is not to be taken literally. He simply means that they are now a regular concern of his; he is in fact loving them just as they love all the saints (v. 16).

The burden of his prayers for these people is that God would cause them to understand. He asks that God give them the Spirit of wisdom and revelation and enlightened hearts (v. 17). It seems unlikely that he contemplates here their need to receive the Holy Spirit, since verse 13 already declared that they do have him. What is meant rather is that they need to receive from the Spirit a revealing of the divine wisdom, the purpose of which is that they might themselves know God (or perhaps Christ). The "eyes of your heart" refers to the spirit of a person—the mind, the inner soul—in its power to grasp ideas (v. 18a). To this, God is asked to give illumination, with the implication that if he does not, it cannot be had.

Paul specifies what he wishes God to enable the Christians to understand with their enlightened hearts: (1) the hope to which they have been called; (2) the glorious abundance of his inheritance; and (3) God's more than sufficient power for those who believe (vv. 18b–19). These three concepts bear a surprising similarity to the three spiritual blessings which Paul enumerated earlier. That they are not precisely parallel may simply work to expand and unfold their significance. The prayer that these three concepts be understood better by the believers is not left without further thought; in the course of the next two chapters, and indeed over the course of the remainder of the letter, Paul himself practices his prayers by elaborating the meaning of these things.

Before beginning to do so, however, Paul makes an extremely important connection between these ethereal, abstract concepts (and blessings) on the one hand, and down-to-earth history on the other. The very same power that God has in such abundance for Christians is the power that he exercised in Christ by raising him from the dead (v. 20). It may be difficult to lay hold of the truth of one's membership in the redeemed, Spirit-sealed family of God, newly re-created on earth. Emotionally and mentally, perhaps, we are too weak to grasp these things in the onslaught of any number of reasons to doubt their reliability. However, God has anchored them in a concrete historical event—the physical resurrection of Jesus of Nazareth from the tomb. These truths, then, are no less secure and reliable than the fact that Christ is no longer dead; in fact they would not be true if that event had not occurred.

Moreover, this same exercise of power which raised Christ from the dead and secured for us our hope and inheritance has also seated Christ at the place of supreme honor in the universe, the right hand of God (v. 20). Consequently, whether viewed from below or above, Christ sits far above all competitors for power, potential or real (v. 21). Rulership and authority, power and dominion, and titles upon titles are given both in this evil age which will end and in the glorious age to come which will never end. But none of them and none of their possessors takes precedence over the Lord's Christ. The fact that some of his competitors (and all of us in our fallen natures are in that category) are permitted to compete with him and with each other is characteristic of this present age. The future age has already been initiated, however, in the life, resurrection, and exaltation of Jesus Christ, for all things have been subjected to him (v. 22, a quotation from Ps. 8:6), regardless of anyone's awareness of it. He has been made head, uniting in himself the restored universe, for the sake of the church, his body, the new, all-encompassing family of God (v. 23; see v. 10b).

C. Redemption: clearing the ground (2:1–10). Returning to the first blessing, redemption, Paul elaborates what is implied in it. Through the work of Christ, by divine fiat, God has swept clear the ground upon which he re-creates the spoiled creation.

The human predicament is described first from the Gentile perspective (2:1–2; see v. 11, and cf. v. 3, which refers to Jews). They were formerly dead, in the estimation of God, since they had led their lives in transgressions and sins. Their life-style, their code of behavior, had been determined according to this present worldly age, the selfish and competitive principle which underlies all cultures, all political and economic systems. And behind that worldly system stands the satanic "ruler of the kingdom of the air" ("air" probably referring to the presumed dwelling-place of the spirit world), who even now encourages people, both groups and individuals, in their disobedience against God.

But among such disobedient people Paul now includes—along with the Gentiles—the Jews themselves (v. 3). Jews, too, live under the influence of their fleshly, sinful human desires. Existence on earth consists of a continual struggle to satisfy the selfish demands of body and soul. Consequently, the Jew is by nature under the wrath of God, just like the rest of humanity, namely, the Gentiles.

This is no insignificant remark! First, it clearly precludes any member of humanity from supposing that he or she is not subject to judgment. All of the human race is subsumed under the headings of either Jew or Gentile, and both groups are by nature condemned. Second, this is a statement of a Jew to Gentiles, and as such it embodies, in a redeemed person, an attitude which is evidence of the newly created family of God (see vv. 11–22).

The human predicament is absolute; there is no escape. There is no way for people already condemned to avoid condemnation. Only from the outside can any effective solution come. Thus when Paul begins, "but . . . God" (v. 4), it is with just such an outside solution in mind. God's character as a boundlessly merciful God, who loves human beings with a "great love," has changed the picture. He remedied the hopeless situation in three ways with one sweeping act in Christ.

First, together with Christ, he brought these dead Jews and Gentiles back to life (the "we" in v. 5 now includes the Gentile readers). Anticipating the sum of the matter (stated in vv. 8–10), Paul asserts excitedly at this point that this salvation from death is wholly God's doing, an act of his grace (v. 5). He returns immediately to the point, however, to state the two remaining ways in which God interfered. Second, God raised us up together with Christ, and third, he seated us together with Christ in that same heavenly place of honor which he assigned to Christ himself (v. 6). In other words, just as Christ is the manifestation of God to us on earth, so Christ, as the head of his body, the church, is the manifestation of us to God. In Christ, God and humanity meet and are at peace.

God's purpose in restoring us and honoring us, in being kind to his rebellious creatures, is that he might demonstrate for all time the surpassing bounty of his forgiving grace (v. 7). The point is not that he needs the praise which would come from that demonstration, but that the creation needs to offer it.

Paul now draws the all but obvious conclusion: if we were dead and therefore helpless, and if God intervened and by his own will revived us in Christ, then it is an act of his grace alone, a gift given to us (v. 8). We receive it not by producing anything to exchange for it, but simply by succumbing to his gracious mercy, by entrusting our fate to God. In short, we are saved by faith. This free salvation has a twofold relation to human works. First, works have no part in the production of salvation. If it were otherwise, we who produced such works would lift ourselves above our proper station; we would assert our independence over against God; we would in fact destroy ourselves in our boasting (v. 9). Second, however, in the doing of good works we realize our God-intended potential. God has prepared a style of life to which we as his creatures are ideally adapted. We were made to function best and to be happiest when we live according to the way in which God originally created us to live. Such a life-style implies above all a complete dependence upon God.

Thus at the heart of redemption is a return to the pristine relationship between God and humanity: total acceptance on the part of God and total dependence on the part of humanity, all embraced in a framework of love. Upon this cleared ground, God can now re-create his family.

D. Re-creation: removing the barriers (2:11–22). One of the deepest yearnings of the human soul is to belong. We instinctively draw circles that include ourselves, giving us the coveted feeling of being a part of a group. We also need outsiders who desire to come within the circles. Yet another of the basic tendencies of the sinful human soul is to exclude. So then we draw a circle that excludes others, giving us the coveted sensation of being superior. But there can be no "inner ring," as C. S. Lewis calls it, without the despised outsiders.

The Jewish nation, God's "inner ring" in their own estimation, drew the circle at the law, epitomized in physical circumcision. Those not born into this nation, Gentiles in the flesh, were stigmatized as the "uncircumcision" as a way of self-exaltation on the part of the Jewish inner ring (v. 11). Without the despised Gentiles, the Jew would cease to be distinctive in his own eyes.

Paul reminds his Gentile readers that under such circumstances, they were without Christ (who came to us through the Jewish nation); they were permitted no part in the only known family of the true God and thus had no access to the promises which God had made to that family; in short, they were hopelessly alienated from their Creator and Savior. Ironically, the instruments through whom God had intended to show his grace to humanity had turned themselves into the chief obstacle to that goal by erecting a barrier between themselves and their mission. Based in a natural enmity toward God, the result was enmity between groups of human beings and indeed between individuals within groups (v. 12).

But the outsiders, formerly excluded and far off, have now been brought near, within the circle, by the sacrificial death of Christ (v. 13). Bringing the Gentiles "near" implies the establishment of peace, and Christ Jesus himself is the peace; the bringing near is accomplished in him. By removing the criterion of judgment, the law, he has removed the barrier separating the two groups. By tearing down the wall symbolizing and perpetuating their hostility, he has made the two into one united group (v. 14). With his physical body he did away with the barrier, the law as used by its Jewish guardians, the law understood as a list of individual commandments and ordinances which could be satisfactorily fulfilled by human effort. His death fully satisfied the law once and for all, and thereby eliminated it as a means of distinguishing between people (v. 15).

The dual purpose which Christ had in doing this was (1) to create in himself one new humanity out of the two hostile groups, making peace between them, and (2) to reconcile in this one united body both groups to God by obliterating in himself their hatred toward God and toward one another (v. 16). Thus not just Jew and Gentile, but any two (or more) persons who do not get along are deprived of all basis for castigating each other and are brought to peace both with each other and with God. It is precisely this two-directional restoration which is alluded to in 1:15.

Not to let this stupendous act of grace go unknown to those it was intended to benefit, Christ preached peace both to the outsiders and to the insiders (Isa. 52:7; 57:19). Since the ground of the insiders' security (viz., the law) had been taken away from them, they needed to have peace preached to them no less than did the outsiders (Eph. 2:17). Access to the Father, the goal of all human striving, is achieved only through Christ by the same Spirit for both Gentile and Jew. Contrary to all expectation, God views the entire race as one, and deals with it all at one time, by grace, in one Person.

In verse 19 Paul sums up: the Gentile Christians are no longer shut out from the family of God. They have been given a place within the ring. They are part of the household, part of the citizenry of God's own (holy) people; they belong. God has effected the premiere family reunion. Shifting to a metaphor, Paul describes the situation as that of the construction of a temple, a dwelling-place for God on the earth among his people. Founded upon the "apostles and prophets" (i.e., upon the promises which God has made), and with Christ himself as the cornerstone holding the whole structure together, the building grows continually as people of all kinds are added into it (vv. 20–22). This is presumably the Pauline way of describing what the Book of Revelation calls the New Jerusalem (Rev. 21:2).

On this passage the whole message of Ephesians pivots. The re-creation of the family of God upon the earth is the central purpose of Christ's coming. It is rebuilt upon the cleared ground of redeemed men, women, and children, established by divine fiat in Christ. It is brought to concrete reality in the lives of real everyday people by the power of God's Spirit working in them. This working of the Spirit's power, the third spiritual blessing, is the subject, after a digression, of the next section.

Before moving on to the digression, however, it is important to observe the implication of this passage for our own situation. Paul spoke to a group of Gentile Christians who had been made to feel unworthy and inferior by those who felt themselves religiously privileged because of their own relationship to the law. We who make up the church of Jesus Christ today must be ready to recognize ourselves in the Jew of Paul's day. Whenever we assume that our code of behavior, our manner of dress and grooming, our heritage, our habits (or lack of them), our attendance at one particular church rather than another, our work ethic, our political opinions, or any other distinction we may have over against other people—whenever we assume that one or more of such considerations have made us more acceptable than others to God, we have taken upon ourselves the role, and the condemnation (Gal. 3:10), of hypocritical, pharisaical destroyers of God's family.

E. Digression: Paul, outsiders, and God's glory (3:1–13). Paul prepares now to take up the third spiritual blessing, that of the Spirit's influence on the church. Based upon the fact of God's having made the human family new again "in heavenly places" by eliminating through Christ all cause of division, Paul begins to say that he prays for the outworking of this reality in the present, earthly life of the church through the Spirit's power (see comments below on 3:14 and following). But having mentioned the Gentile mission, for which he is suffering imprisonment, he breaks off in midsentence to explain that mission more fully.

God has given Paul a part in the administration of his grace (v. 2). Through the man Paul, God has seen fit to dispense to a particular segment of humanity the message of what has been accomplished in Jesus Christ. As stated earlier (1:9–10? Gal. 1?), God has revealed to Paul this mysterious grace which centers in Christ (Eph. 3:3). Study of that earlier communication will convince the readers of Paul's grasp of this long-hidden plan, now made known by the Spirit to (and through) God's chosen instruments, the apostles and prophets (vv. 4–5; see 2:20).

From the viewpoint of the mission to the Gentile world, the essence of the mystery is this: by virtue of Jesus Christ, the non-Jew has a place among God's people alongside the Jew, partaking in every way in the inheritance, the unity, and the covenant promises (v. 6). The astonishing thing about this (Good) News from the Jewish perspective is that there is no mention of the necessity of a proper relationship to the law for such participation. It is solely a matter of being "in Christ."

Paul was made a servant of this Good News as an undeserved honor, having been enabled, in spite of his natural human sinfulness, by the power of God (v. 7). This honor came to him who of all God's people was, in his own mind, the least (deserving?)—probably a reference to his former activity in persecuting the very people to whom he now belongs (v. 8). (But of course, on the basis of grace, what one deserves is irrelevant!) It is now his privilege to broadcast to the Gentiles the news of this inexhaustible wealth which one receives in Christ, and to make everyone possible aware that this mystery, hitherto concealed in the heart of the Creator God, is now available for all to know (v. 9).

God's purpose in revealing the mystery is that through the unlikely instrument of rebellious humanity, now transformed into his own people in the form of the church, he might make known to the whole universe his multifaceted wisdom (v. 10). This age-old, unanticipated plan he carried through in the person and work of Christ (v. 11), in whom we have the right and, by faith, full confidence for coming freely and boldly into the very presence of God (v. 12).

In view of all this and its rich benefits for the readers, Paul begs them not to be disheartened about his incarceration and other afflictions. He is, after all, a servant of the gospel (v. 7), bound to obey its purposes whatever the cost. Moreover, it is for their benefit that he is suffering in this way; it leads to their glory no less than, consequently, to God's (v. 13). Imprisonment is a small price to pay for such a prize.

F. Empowerment: realizing the future (3:14–19). Paul resumes his prayer, interrupted in verse 2, addressing the heavenly Father (v. 14) who supplies the underlying unity for the new humanity. He is the universal God of family (v. 15). Therefore, petitioning him to promote the outworking on earth of the previously described new reality is entirely proper. Accordingly Paul asks God, who has inexhaustible resources at his disposal, to provide the readers an inner strength of soul by the power of the Holy Spirit (v. 16). This is the same Spirit of the third blessing (1:13–14) and the same power which Paul connects with it later (1:19). The Spirit-provided inner power is paralleled by (or perhaps has its purpose in) the indwelling of Christ himself in the human heart which has opened up to him in trusting, dependent submission (v. 17). If there is to be an outward expression of the inward, heaven-based reality of the new humanity, it will be realized only through Christ's progressive inward control of individual Christians in their daily attitudes, decisions, and deeds, both private and communal.

Paul calls such a condition one of being "rooted and established in love" (v. 17); the church's solid foundation and nourishment for life is found nowhere else than in the indwelling Christ. The consequence and indeed the purpose of this inward work of grace is that the readers be empowered to know and experience what otherwise cannot be known or experienced, namely, the love that Christ has for them. Paul wants these Gentile Christians as well as the other members of God's family to grasp the full dimensions of this incomprehensible love (v. 18).

And here is the sum of the matter; here is the final purpose of all the foregoing purposes, the supreme goal of the family-minded God: that the readers be filled with all the fullness of God (v. 19). Redemption, re-creation, and empowerment are all aimed at one and the same object: to have again upon the earth a race of human beings who truly love both each other and their Creator. And not only so in the future "new heaven and new earth" (Rev. 21:1), but even now in this old and dying age. For in the coming of Christ and in the power of the Spirit of Christ the new age has arrived and overlaps with this age of death and sin.

It is on the basis of this profound change in the affairs of God and humanity that Paul can now in the second half of the epistle lay out a demanding ethic for the church to live by. Yet it is not so much Paul that lays it out as God, and it is not so much the church that lives by it as Christ who lives it out in the church by the Spirit's power. It is in fact what God is doing on the basis of what God has done.

G. Doxology (3:20–21). Upon the message of this threefold work of God in Christ on creation's behalf Paul now pronounces a benediction. He glorifies the God who is able to do all this, who is in fact able to do far more than we would even think of asking him to do, so small is our own vision of our need and so comprehensive and bountiful is his (v. 20). Whatever he delights to do he does according to the same power which we know is already at work within us. God's glory is to be found forever in the context of humanity: both in the church and in Jesus Christ, that form in which God himself assumed human shape (v. 21).

III. Re-creating the Human Family: What God Is Doing (4:1–6:20)

A. Creating unity: the body forged (4:1–16). Upon the firm and unchanging ground of God's completed work in Christ, Paul now urges his readers to a life together worthy of their calling (4:1). As a prisoner himself, he knows what it is to suffer the consequences of such a life and what it is he is asking his readers to risk. The *worthy* life is to be characterized by (1) humility, that proper self-estimate—both positive and negative; (2) gentleness, that genuine concern for people in their need to be loved, accepted, and treated with dignity; and (3) patience (v. 2). Patience will show itself in a loving tolerance of people (including oneself) in their weaknesses and foibles, but not in ignorance or encouragement of such shortcomings, since love seeks the best interests of others. Patience is also manifested in a strong desire to keep the unity of the Spirit in the bond of peace (v. 3). This is not the same thing as keeping the peace, which too often implies unsatisfactory (as opposed to satisfactory) compromises. To foster true unity requires endless patience as sinful personalities are brought closer to Christ and therefore to each other.

The foundation of the unity of the new family of God lies in eternally changeless facts (v. 4), all emphasizing the oneness of God, the church, and the faith. There is one body; the church is one church no matter how many local manifestations (including traditions or denominations) of it there may be. There is one Spirit of God and not a separate one for every conflicting word of prophecy that may arise. All members of the body are called to one and the same future, now already here in part. There is only one Lord, the Lord Jesus Christ (no other lord takes precedence over him, 1:20–22), one correct and approved message to be believed, and one common rite of initiation belonging to the entire church (v. 5). And it all comes back to and indeed issues from the fact that there is only one God in the universe, who has created it all and whose presence and power pervade it all (v. 6). Only on this foundation of unity, ultimately to be found in the unity of God, can the unity of the family possibly come to reality.

By the same token, the members of the body, unified in theory but fragmented by nature, could never see themselves brought to union, as God wishes them to be, without the needed tools and enablement. God has therefore given grace to them all (v. 7), to each one differently as Christ has seen fit liberally to apportion (no sense of stinginess is to be associated here with the word *apportion*). Paul quotes Psalm 68:18 to make his point; yet not only does this particular passage (and its following interpretation) seem strange to the modern reader, but Paul even substitutes the verb *gave* for the original *received* found in both the Hebrew Old Testament and its ancient Greek translation. (It has been suggested that he follows early Jewish commentators in this reading.) Taking the term *ascended* as key, Paul applies the whole passage to the ascending (at Pentecost) and descending, gift-bearing Christ (Jewish tradition applied it to Moses at Sinai), the Christ who fills the universe (vv. 9–10; 1:23).

The gifts he has given to men (v. 11) are those which promote the unity of the church (v. 13) and include apostles and prophets, those specially gifted and authoritative communicators of God's message to humanity. The category of "apostle" seems to have been temporary, while that of prophet continues in the office of preacher, God's spokesperson to particular times, cultures, and situations. Evangelists traveled from place to place with the gospel, announcing like heralds the Good News of Jesus Christ. These would be followed by pastors and teachers, or perhaps pastor-teachers, who then nurtured the flocks converted through the evangelists' message. One must not necessarily think that only one of these gifts could be found in any one given person. Some pastors, for example, could and presumably did do the work of evangelism (see 2 Tim. 4:5).

The purpose of endowing the church with

these gifts of grace is to equip the individual members for service (Eph. 4:12). No doubt we also are to understand future, potential members as among the ones who benefit from such service. The ultimate goal of this is that the church might be built up through the mutual service of the Christians, so that we all attain unity of faith and knowledge of God's Son, which will make us truly mature—by God's standard, not our own (v. 13). That standard is the fullness of Christ (see 3:19). In short the goal is that we do the same things which Christ himself would do. The corresponding immaturity to grow out of is that of being susceptible to the cunning and appeal of human opinions, especially as to the relations between God and humanity (v. 14). Instead, by living the truth in love, we are called in all things to grow into the likeness and person of Christ, who is the unifying head of the body (v. 15).

This section closes with a metaphorical model of unity. Like the human body, held together by design, the church grows through the coordinated and cooperative work of its many members, who out of love for the whole contribute their individual efforts toward the good of the whole. But the plan and the energy are drawn from the head who watches over and provides for his body. Indeed he lives his own life out through it (v. 16).

B. Mind control: the inward change (4:17–24). In 1:15–23 Paul stressed the importance of the mind's understanding the message if it is to be properly appropriated by a person. Now again, the role of the mind is described for the successful (or unsuccessful) living of a life worthy of the calling inherent in that message.

Backing his own words with the confidence that he is communicating the very counsel of the Lord, Paul urges his Gentile readers to conduct their lives no longer as their fellow unconverted Gentiles (v. 17). This unacceptable life-style is described as a progression which begins in the mind's condition. Paul portrays the Gentile (i.e., unconverted) mind as futile, vain, focused on concerns which in the end, before the throne of God, will come to nothing. A mind in such a state is one which simply does not understand what the true values and standards are; it has no light from the mind of God. In other words, where matters of everlasting consequence are concerned, such minds are full of ignorance, or worse, of hardness arising from stubborn refusal to acquiesce where the truth has been available (v. 18). (There is no need to attempt a real distinction between "heart" and "mind" or "understanding" here, as if they referred to separate compartments in a human being.) The natural result of such a state of mind is alienation from the life of God; participation in eternal life is out of the question for persons with this sort of mind.

The downward progression continues. Out of a basic need for sensitivity and tenderness, the selfishly distorted human mind turns to sensuality. A perverted mind casts over the one in favor of the other, callouses over sensitivity, and ultimately leads to outward behavior characterized by incredible inventiveness in impurity, with neither any end nor satisfaction in view.

This pagan sort of life does not reflect the Christ whom the readers have learned about (v. 20). But in saying this, Paul assumes that what they have heard and been taught about Jesus corresponds with what is actually the case (v. 21). The "truth that is in Jesus," as it touches this particular issue of inward change, is now summed up under a three-step progression. First, with respect to their previous habits of life (vv. 17–19), they are to lay aside the "old self [lit. man]" the selfish, self-centered ego which is rotting away to corruption because of its entanglement in the deceitful (futile) values of this world (v. 22). Any mind turned in upon itself eats itself alive and has no part in the life of God. The laying-off of the old, dying self is nothing less than the act of repentance, the death of the sinful nature, and must be repeated again and again throughout life whenever conviction of sin is worked by the power of the Spirit through the message.

Second, immediately upon the daily death of the old nature, the mind is made new, furnished with the light of God's mind and enabled to see as God sees and to make godly decisions (v. 23). Third, to make such decisions and actually to have Christ-like behavior, is, finally, to put on the new self, a creature not of our own making, but one designed by God according to his own taste for true righteousness and genuine dedication to the purposes of his eternal will (v. 24).

Thus the ongoing change from a godless and selfish death-bound life to a Christ-like one, filled with the eternal life of God, originates in an inward change of mind wrought by God himself as part of his bringing the new creation to present reality.

C. Becoming Christian: the "little" things (4:25–5:5). One must distinguish between becoming Christian and becoming *a* Christian, between what are commonly called sanctification and justification. The reason rests in the relation of the inward and outward changes just described (hence the "therefore" in v. 25) and will become even clearer at 5:5. It is enough to say now, however, that sanctification is a process made up of many "small" considerations.

The following instructions for being transformed outwardly into the family of God on earth seem to fall under three heads. First, believers are urged not to grieve the Holy Spirit (v. 30). To avoid this Paul commands them (quoting Zech. 8:16) to be truthful with each other, without taint of untruth (v. 25). "Neighbor" primarily applies to members of the new covenant community, but it can also extend to nonbelievers. The startlingly practical reason which is given for this is that because of our situation as fellow members of Christ's body we would be hurting ourselves by lying to each other and benefiting each other by telling the truth. The Greek version of Psalm 4:4 (LXX 4:5) is quoted now in Ephesians 5:26 (the Hebrew reads "tremble" instead of "be angry"). Anger, while useful and appropriate (indeed commanded), must be kept in its place and not permitted to brood and fester and thus gain the upper hand over the angry person (v. 27). In this it is an imitation of the anger of the God who loves the sinner while hating sin. To be otherwise is to be diabolically selfish. Any who have been accustomed to stealing should, as new creatures, do so no longer, but should use their own labor to make themselves useful (v. 28). The remarkable thing about this admonishment is the reason given for it. It is not a matter of earning one's own living, much less of getting ahead in the world. The purpose of refraining from stealing and of working with one's own hands is to provide for the needs of other people, an entirely fitting purpose for members of the new family to adopt in their work. Finally, Paul cautions the readers against obscene and worthless talk, and enjoins them instead to speak in ways which meet hurting people in their need, to speak words which ultimately encourage and strengthen the whole group (v. 29).

Attending to all these injunctions will prevent the grieving of God's Holy Spirit. This is not to be taken to mean that the Spirit becomes sad at our failings (v. 30). It simply means that an offense against any human being is an offense against the very God who created that person, against the Spirit who has been given as a seal upon the newly united humanity (1:13). Paul now sums up matters to this point, suggesting that these interpersonal problems have their root in self-centered malice and that they, like the "old nature," must be laid aside (v. 31; cf. v. 22).

Second, the readers become Christian by imitating the Godhead as children imitate their parents (5:1). Just as God has forgiven them in Christ—freely, fully, and unilaterally—they are to forgive each other (4:32). This forgiveness results from kindness and compassion for one another which enables each person to view life from the perspective of others and to understand that what may motivate another's behavior may not be all that different from what motivates his own. Imitating God in forgiveness parallels the imitation of the self-sacrificial love of Christ for us, in which we are similarly secure enough in our position and future with God, that we may lay down our own interests as an offering to God on behalf of the interests of other people (5:2). It is uncomfortably threatening to forgive without guarantee of a favorable response or to give up personal anxieties without assurance of provision. But once a person realizes that his or her ultimate worth and final provision rest with a God who has been more than favorably disposed all along, the threat evaporates (see John 13:3–5).

Third, Paul gives instructions for becoming Christian that may be classified as "appropriate conversation," both in the sense of life-style and in the usual sense of speech (Eph. 5:3). Sexually immoral behavior and any sort of impurity of life are absolutely prohibited. The same is true of greed, which perhaps is partially what is to be understood under "impurity." At any rate, whereas greed may be far less frowned upon in most congregations than sexual misbehavior is, Paul prohibits both of them. Likewise incongruous with God's new human family is any ugly coarseness in the form of foul-mouthed joking and foolish talk. Let the Christian's mouth instead be filled with the natural overflow of a thankful heart (v. 4), something which can scarcely be avoided when Christians keep in their minds the facts of what God has done for them.

Paul now warns that no one who values such sins above God's will has any part in the kingdom of Christ and God (v. 5; note that the lists in vv. 3 and 5 correspond). God's kingdom is the rule of God over whatever is part of his kingdom, and hence anyone who worships as an idolater, by giving allegiance to anything but God, cannot be under God's rule.

But this of course includes all human beings according to our old natures. The deceitfulness of the old nature must be guarded against in another way, however. Paul has been somewhat elliptical in the statement of verse 5: the impression is given that persons who commit such idolatry have no part in the kingdom because of their idolatry. The old nature seizes this idea immediately and assumes the reverse, namely, that participation in the kingdom can be experienced by avoiding idolatry and other sins, as well as by living a moral life. The situation is quite the contrary. Participation in the kingdom, in the new family of God, is a freely given gift of God's grace, bestowed upon sinners, upon those who do not deserve it. Such is the whole point of chapters 1–3. Thus 5:5 does not mean that idolatrous persons have no part in the family because of their idolatry, but that persons having no part in the family are also idolaters, and for the same reason: they have not capitulated to the grace of God in Christ, but insist on preserving the independent old nature from death in Christ. And that death of the old nature, the laying off of the old nature in repentance, is the only way in which the life of God can come to a person.

D. Light and wisdom: living undeceived (5:6–21). In spite of the renewed nature of persons who are part of the new age, the already-but-not-yet-dead old nature clings to them still, and renders them susceptible to deception and foolishness. Because of the serious dangers, outlined immediately above, which face the disobedient, the readers are warned not to let themselves be led away by worthless talk into participation in the deeds of such persons (vv. 6–7). The values and behavior of the disobedient work against the unity of the new family and therefore against the will of God, and for that reason are characterized as darkness, the opposite of the light of the Lord. Paul's readers once belonged to that realm of darkness, but no longer. Without qualification they now belong to the Lord's light (v. 8). Their conduct must produce that which corresponds to the nature of God (contrast v. 3), and a knowledge of what pleases Christ (i.e., a knowledge of how he conducted himself during his earthly ministry) is instrumental in living this way (vv. 9–10).

In addition to knowing one's status and knowing and doing what pleases the Lord, enlightened living includes a strict refusal to have any share in what does not please him. The other side of avoiding participation in evil is exposing it, both by refusing to have a part in it and, positively, by doing the deeds which Christ would do; that is, by being a light in dark places (vv. 11–12). To do so has the effect of transforming darkness into light. Hidden dark deeds are exposed for what they are by the light of Christ shining out from his followers (vv. 13–14a).

Finally, living in the light means continuously receiving the light. Quoting perhaps from an early Christian baptismal hymn, Paul states that the dispersing of darkness is an ongoing process for the believer, analogous to the resurrection from the dead (v. 14b). The death of self to one's former, sinful life gives way to a new life walking in the light of Christ.

The frame of reference shifts now from living in the light of Christ to living wisely, lifestyles which in effect amount to the same thing (v. 15). Paul enjoins careful attention to maintaining such wisdom-guided behavior because the readers, as members of God's new family in Christ, are already members and representatives of the new age to come. In the midst of the evil days of this old age, God's people are called to make use of every opportunity to act as Christ would act, to act as will be utterly natural at the consummation, though now it requires the painful, repeated death of the old nature (v. 16). Because of the urgency of the times, wise living necessitates understanding how Christ would indeed act in any given situation, for his will is that his people do as he would do (v. 17). Being unconcerned about his will in this way is foolish. The Spirit, however, implements the Christ-like behavior in the lives of the family members (v. 18).

Here four characteristics mark the Spirit-filled life. First, it brings mutual encouragement and edification by believers speaking and singing to each other the promises of God and truths of the faith as contained in Scripture and musical pieces. Second, it includes spontaneous, heart-generated musical praise to the Lord Jesus. Third, a mark of Spirit-filled living is continual thankfulness to God the Father through the relationship we have with him in Christ. Fourth, mutual submission out of reverence for Christ is a mark of the Spirit's presence in the life of the new family. The personal security to be found in Christ frees us to prefer one another in the daily affairs of living. What this means is explained in the next section using three sample situations.

It may be pointed out that these marks of the Spirit-filled life are as much the cause as the result of the fullness of the Spirit. An encouraging word from a brother or sister, a song sung in a time of discouragement, a disciplined word of thanks when the heart does not feel particularly thankful, and even acquiescence to the needs of others, can all lead to the heart's swelling with the joy of the Spirit just as much as the joy of the Spirit leads to these very same deeds.

E. The circle of responsibility: mutual submission (5:22–6:9). Mutual submission as one of the marks of being Spirit-filled is illustrated by Paul in three common areas of human experience: marital, parental, and labor relationships.

Wives are called upon to submit to the authority of their (own) husbands as they would to that of Christ, the Lord (v. 22). The chief threat in submitting to another person is the fear of being manipulated or mistreated by that person. There is no such cause for fear with Christ; his is tender guidance, not raw authority. Yet while Paul certainly does not imply that all (or any) husbands measure up to Christ in this regard, neither does he excuse wives from such submission because of the imperfection of their husbands. Whatever the hindrances, he is constantly aiming at the implementation of the sin-freed family of God. The metaphor of marriage which illustrates the relation of Christ and church becomes a two-way road, reflecting back upon that very relation of man and woman in marriage. As the church follows the leadership of its Savior, so must the wife follow her husband "in everything" (vv. 23–24). The strident protests of extreme feminism, though justified in many ways, cannot change the simple intent of this instruction. Yet much of that protest would perhaps never have arisen if teachers of the church had not stopped here, but had gone on to round out the circle of mutual responsibility by giving men their proper exhortation, which follows immediately.

Men must love their wives, regardless of any nonsubmission, in the same way as Christ loved the church when he sacrificed himself for it (v. 25). The way in which husbands submit to their wives is by dying to their own interests out of concern for the best interests of their mates (see v. 21). This is not a burdening of the wife with the decision-making responsibility, which verses 22–24 imply as the husband's, nor does it preclude the husband and wife working together in leadership, but rather it means making decisions according to her needs and her welfare, even when it means a decision she may not like.

Christ's purpose in his self-sacrifice of love was to set the church apart for himself, as the newly re-created family of God, made as clean and pure and radiant as he is himself (vv. 26–27). Cleansing and purification are bestowed by the Word of promise ritually applied to the individual believer in the water of Christian baptism. Christ's purpose, in other words, is the welfare and blossoming to full potential of the people in the new family. Similarly, a husband sacrifices his own interests for his wife's sake, not if she will start to make some self-improvements, but so she may grow toward maturity (v. 28). To love one's wife in this way is to love oneself, no less than caring for one's own body is a result of loving oneself. For, in yet another metaphor, the care we give our own bodies (e.g., grooming and feeding them) is quite the antithesis of hatred and illustrates Christ's care for the church, the members of which are members of *his* own body (v. 30).

The argument for mutual submission in the sphere of matrimony is capped in verse 31 by a quotation from Genesis 2:24 that reinforces the essential unity of mariage that takes precedence even over the relation of parent and child. Paul applies this mysterious unity metaphorically to the relation between Christ and the church (v. 32).

A second area of human experience where Spirit-filled mutual submission should express itself is that of parent-child relationships. Children are enjoined to obey their parents. Such obedience, however, is "in the Lord," subject to obedience first to Christ ("in the Lord" does not suggest that children may disobey heathen parents). The fact that such behavior is "in the Lord" makes it right (v. 1). It is also biblical for children to obey their parents. Paul quotes the Old Testament (Exod. 20:12; Deut. 5:16) to make his point, emphasizing at the same time the added promise of reward which is given along with the commandment (vv. 2–3). The promise of long and good life as the consequence of obedience is not denied by the fact that many obedient children have suffered miserably and indeed die young. It means rather that disobedience to parents is certain to bring about a troubled future.

The promise to obedient children introduces the corresponding submission demanded of parents. Since children, and especially young children, can scarcely be expected to have the sophistication necessary for recognizing the long-range benefits of present obedience, it is up to loving parents to ensure that their children learn obedience early. This is not an easy task, but its neglect is a terrible disservice to a child and will reap misery upon him or her in future years. More explicitly, parents ("fathers" is a synecdoche here) are to exercise care and effort in the training of their children (v. 4). Negatively, this implies avoidance of capricious, dictatorial, inconsistent treatment which provokes resentment in children. Positively, it means looking out for the best interests of the child, both long- and short-range, even when it means foregoing one's own comfort and convenience. In this as in all situations, the question is "What would Christ do?"

Finally, mutual submission as a mark of the Spirit is applied to the sphere of labor relations. Slaves must obey their earthly masters with the same respect and unaffected openness which they owe to Christ, who is of course their heavenly master (v. 5). In other words, a slave is to consider his or her master as if Christ himself were the person. Obedience is not to be carried out in the presence of the master while the heart harbors disobedience, but must proceed from the heart itself, so that it is exercised even in secret. This is the will of God, the God who "sees in secret" (vv. 6–7; cf. Matt. 6:6). Such heart-sprung service is enthusiastic and wholehearted, and is possible only under the influence of the Spirit. Just as husbands who love their wives do themselves a favor and just as children who learn obedience to parents decrease their chances of self-inflicted misery, so here even slaves are promised a divine reward (unspecified) for whatever good they may do (v. 8). That is the sort of master the Lord Jesus is. It is not a sign of weakness to enjoy rewards for work well done, so long as we keep in mind that our work never places God (or Christ) in our debt; his rewards are given freely out of the joy it brings him to give them.

Also, masters are to treat their slaves "in the same way," that is, they are to behave toward their slaves as if each slave were Christ himself (v. 9). A menacing attitude toward them is inappropriate since the masters are themselves slaves of Christ, and Christ is not a menacing master. In fact, Christ is master of both master and slave and makes no distinction between them for purposes of judgment or for standards of service. Thus masters will do well to remember their common lot with their slaves before God. As Christians they are members together of the new family of God.

F. Making the right stand in the right strength (6:10–20). The groundwork has been laid for God's re-creation of the human family; Christ has wrought redemption. The new family has been reestablished through God's gracious adoption of sinners as his own children. And yet while this old age of sin and death continues, the new family must struggle in battle against the powers of this age in order to live out the ethics of the new age. To this purpose, God has endowed his new family with the Spirit to seal them as his own and to enable and protect them in this war of the ages, which Paul now describes.

As members of the new family of God, believers are to find their strength and leadership for this warfare in the Lord Jesus Christ. By implication they are not to look for it in themselves, or in their spirituality or their maturity, or in education, influence, position, prestige, money, programs, personal rights, or other people. Their strength is to be found solely in Christ (v. 10). Having put on the proper armor (described in vv. 14–17), they are to fight the war against cunning and crafty satanic plots, which seek to overthrow the reestablishment of God's rule upon the earth (v. 11). Paul lists four varieties of nonhuman powers, all under the control of the devil, against which believers have their struggles. The startling thing to notice is that this struggle is ultimately *not* against "flesh and blood," that is, it is not against other human beings, but rather "rulers," "authorities," "powers of this dark world," and "spiritual forces of evil in the heavenly realms" (v. 12), all of which instigate people to practice evil. However, people through whom Satan opposes and interferes with the work of God on earth are to be compassionately loved and prayed for (Matt. 5:43–48), for it is this very tactic which works toward the defeat of satanic schemes while avoiding the struggle against "flesh and blood."

All the more reason, then, to put on the full armor of God (v. 13; most of the metaphorical images used in this passage are drawn from Isa. 11, 52, 59). Otherwise, one cannot stand firm against these deceptive onslaughts. The "day of evil" in this context does not seem to be a reference to the final day of the present evil age, but rather refers to any moment of temptation when it comes to a believer or church. One will be able to stand firm in such a time if one is properly prepared. To be prepared is to be armed first of all with the foundation of truth (v. 14). Hence, not only with God, but with other people as well, it is imperative to be truthful. Also necessary is the breastplate of righteousness, which probably refers to the Spirit-produced behavior appropriate to the new family. It is not easy to know what exactly is meant by "readiness of the gospel of peace" (as it reads literally, v. 15). Since it is associated with shoes here, it may refer to the readiness to carry the gospel to the world, or perhaps to the solid firmness upon which the Christian may stand (since the Good News of peace with God never changes).

Faith probably refers to faith in God and here it functions as a shield against the offensive attacks of the Evil One (v. 16). Finally, salvation as a protective helmet (see Isa. 59:17) and the Word (or message) of God, supplied by the Spirit, as an offensive weapon, are recommended to round out the believers' equipment (v. 17). The Word of God comes in the form of comforting reassurance to those who are filled with guilt, remorse, and terror, and it speaks condemnation and law to those who are either careless of the will of God or proud of their own perfections.

Having enlisted his readers under the right leader to fight the right war with the right equipment, Paul now tells them what the right maneuvers are (v. 18). They are to pray at all times under the direction of the Spirit (who knows what to pray for), and they are to keep themselves diligently alert in prayer and petition on behalf of other believers in the common struggle. As an example of what he means, Paul asks for their vigilant prayer on his own behalf (v. 19). He wishes for appropriate words to be given him by the Spirit so that he might openly and clearly make known the meaning of the once hidden gospel. Moreover, since his work on behalf of the gospel has landed him in jail for the time being, Paul requests prayer for boldness in the continuance of his ministry and its attendant dangers to his person (v. 20).

Thus Paul has outlined the calling which God has given to this new family in Christ as they live their new life in the midst of the old sin-bound age. They find themselves in two ages at once, already members of the new age to come, but still members of the old age of darkness.

IV. Closing Remarks (6:21–24)

But for three minor variations, the text of these two verses is identical with that at Colossians 4:7–8. Paul deputizes his fellow worker Tychicus both to deliver news of Paul's situation and to encourage the readers (vv. 21–22). He closes with a blessing of peace, love, faith, and grace, which, as he is careful to point out, originates with God and Christ and is enjoyed only by those who love the Lord Jesus (vv. 23–24).

SELECT BIBLIOGRAPHY

Bruce, F. F. *The Epistles to the Colossians, to Philemon, and to the Ephesians.* Grand Rapids: Eerdmans, 1984.

Foulkes, F. *Epistle of Paul to the Ephesians.* Grand Rapids: Eerdmans, 1963.

Houlden, J. L. *Paul's Letters from Prison.* Philadelphia: Westminster, 1970.

Mitton, C. L. *Ephesians.* Grand Rapids: Eerdmans, 1976.

Patzia, A. G. *Colossians, Philemon, Ephesians.* New York: Harper and Row, 1984.

Stott, J. R. W. *The Message of Ephesians: God's New Society.* Downers Grove: Inter-Varsity, 1979.

PHILIPPIANS

A. Boyd Luter, Jr.

INTRODUCTION

Philippi was located in Macedonia about ten miles from the Aegean Sea. It was named for Philip II of Macedon, father of Alexander the Great. After a major military victory in 42 B.C. the Romans made Philippi a privileged colony, and the names of Julius Caesar and Augustus were later added to its official title, *Colonia Iulia Augusta Philippensis.*

As the only colony in the area, it had rights such as tax exemption and legal status equivalent to the Italian cities. It was located on the Via Egnatia, the main highway from the eastern provinces to Rome, and near the famous Macedonian gold mines. These factors explain the prosperity and pride of the city of Philippi during the New Testament era.

While on his second missionary journey, Paul received his "Macedonian vision" (Acts 16:8–10). In response, he crossed the Aegean and traveled to Philippi (16:11–12). Through the apostle's ministry in that city, the gateway to Europe became the birthplace of European Christianity. Converts as diverse as Lydia and her household, a demon-possessed girl, and the Philippian jailer and his family were among the first members of the Philippian church (16:12–40), which would remain especially close to the heart of Paul (Phil. 1:7).

Only radical biblical critics have seriously questioned that the apostle Paul wrote Philippians. Internally the letter claims to have been authored by Paul (see 1:1). The theological content of the epistle, and the biographical background (see 3:4–6) and personal circumstances (e.g., 1:7, 12–26) presented fit well with what we know of Paul from other New Testament books. Externally, from the earliest church fathers on, there was overwhelming acceptance of the Pauline authorship of Philippians.

The unity of the letter has been contested more strongly. Although the Greek manuscript evidence is agreed that Philippians must be viewed as a complete whole, its unity has been questioned on other grounds. Those who hold that the epistle is two letters combined generally do so because of the use of "finally" at 3:1, followed by a sudden change of tone and subject matter at 3:2. Some believe Philippians was originally three letters, viewing 4:10–20 as a separate letter of thanks.

Such objections to the unity of Philippians can be answered, however. The meaning of "finally" in 3:1 may be transitional, as in Paul's parallel usage in 1 Thessalonians 4:1. The sudden shift at Philippians 3:2 could have been due to (1) an interval of time between writing parts of the letter, (2) an interruption (perhaps with news from Philippi), or (3) a Spirit-directed change of focus (e.g., Jude 3; see 2 Pet. 1:21). It can be safely said that both the two-letter and three-letter views are not convincing, especially since both chapter 3 (see 3:20–21) and 4:10–20 contain a number of terms and ideas used earlier in Philippians.

In general, Philippians contains the classic features of contemporary letters: (1) initial salutation, (2) body, and (3) concluding greeting. It also is like more formal epistles of the day in its inclusion of an epistolary prologue. In Philippians this initial section of thanksgiving and prayer (1:3–11) functions to introduce the central theme and anticipates the unfolding structure of the book. This is parallel to the nature of the introductory Pauline thanksgivings elsewhere.

Recently Swift[1] proposed "partnership in the gospel" (1:5 NIV) as the theme of Philippians. As will be seen in the commentary this theme is inclusive enough to clearly unify the biographical prologue (1:12–26), initial exhortation section (1:27–2:30), warnings against false teachings (3:1–4:1), latter exhortations (4:2–9), and personal epilogue (4:10–20). The entire epistle develops out of the introductory prologue (1:3–11).

The only other question regarding structure has to do with 2:5–11. Its rhythmical nature has prompted some to view it as a hymn about Christ,[2] perhaps written by Paul or borrowed from any of several suggested sources. Even if the "hymn" had a previous existence, it may well have been written by Paul, who was capable of literary heights (e.g., 1 Cor. 13), or quoted by Paul (see, e.g., 1 Tim. 3:16; Titus 1:12).

Clearly Paul wrote Philippians while imprisoned for the sake of the gospel of Christ (Phil. 1:7, 13, 19). It is not as clear where he was confined and when he wrote, although such points do not fundamentally affect the interpretation of the book. Three locations (and dates) have been proposed: (1) Ephesus (ca. A.D. 53–55); (2) Caesarea (ca. 58–59); and (3) Rome (ca. 61–62).

Various pieces of evidence must be weighed in order to decide the question of the origin of Philippians. Paul had been near death (Phil. 1:20–24), but anticipated being released soon (2:23–24). There are significant references to the "praetorian guard" (NASB, RSV; NIV palace guard) in 1:13 and "Caesar's household" in 4:22. Also, 2:25–28, for example, indicates a number of trips back and forth between Paul's location and Philippi.

The strength of an Ephesian origin is its geographical proximity to

1. Robert C. Swift, "The Theme and Structure of Philippians," *Bibliotheca Sacra* 141 (July–Sept. 1984): 234–54.

2. See R. P. Martin, *Carmen Christi: Philippians 2:5–11 in Recent Interpretation and in the Setting of Early Church Worship*, rev. ed. (Grand Rapids: Eerdmans, 1983).

Philippi. Travel from Philippi to Ephesus took about a week, but far longer to Caesarea or Rome. The difficulty with this proposal is that there is no clear record of Paul's being imprisoned in Ephesus, whether in Acts 19 or the other passages to which appeal is made (Rom. 16:4, 7; 1 Cor. 15:32; 2 Cor. 1:8–10, 11–23).

The plausibility of Caesarea as the origin of Philippians lies in offering a convincing alternative meaning for "praetorian guard" and "Caesar's household," since both appear to support Rome. It is true that Paul was imprisoned two years (Acts 24:27) in Herod's "praetorium" (NASB, RSV; NIV palace, Acts 23:35), and that "Caesar's household" may mean anyone in imperial service. However, the weakness of the view is that, while Paul's life was in danger before he arrived in Caesarea (Acts 23:12–35), there is no indication of life-threatening circumstances or imminent release while he was there. Besides, he had been told by the Lord that he "must also testify in Rome" (Acts 23:11).

Until further evidence is forthcoming, the traditional view that Paul wrote Philippians from Rome is still the best option. While it is not without difficulty, the circumstances and wording of Philippians best fit with the two-year confinement of Paul mentioned in Acts 28:30–31. Further, the early Marcionite Prologue (ca. A.D. 170) states that Philippians was sent from Rome.

Various names for Jesus Christ are used over fifty times in this brief letter. Profound awareness of the Savior saturates everything because, for Paul, "to live is Christ and to die is gain" (Phil. 1:21). The great christological passage in 2:6–11 emerges as an illustration of selfless humility for the church (2:3–5).

In keeping with Paul's constant reference to the Lord Jesus, the prevailing tone of the epistle is one of joy, from the initial thanksgiving (1:4) to the epilogue (4:10). These two emphases set the mood and provide the motivation for that which is at the theological heart of Philippians.

"Partnership in the gospel" (1:5) is both the unifying theme and theological hub of the letter. The intimate concept of partnership or fellowship (Gk. *koinōnia*) speaks of a common bond in furthering the gospel (1:5; see 4:3, 15), the church's corporate "fellowship with the Spirit" (2:1), and the need for all to be conformed to Christ's death and resurrection (3:10–11, 15).

The gospel initially brought the apostle and the church into joyful fellowship and ministry (1:5; 4:15). Now they continue to serve and extend (2:15–16) that Good News, in spite of circumstances (1:7, 12, 15, 17; 2:22). Their lives must be "worthy of the gospel of Christ" (1:27).

In Philippians faithful outreach with the gospel (1:5–6, 12–18) is emphasized more than the message of salvation through faith in Christ (3:9). The letter seeks to spur Christians to humble obedience (2:12–13) and to press forward toward maturity in Christ (3:12–15).

Even though the church is well-organized, with "overseers and deacons" (1:2), Paul is primarily concerned with it as an organism. He prayerfully seeks its united steadfastness in ministry and life-style (1:5–6, 27), its selfless humility (2:1–11), its identification with Christ (3:7–17), its serene prayerfulness (4:6–7), and its continuing generosity (4:10–20). These are the joyful, Christ-exalting ideals of this partnership in the gospel which will be perfected when Christ returns (1:6, 10; 2:16), when we will be gloriously transformed (3:20–21).

Philippians is a very personal Pauline letter. The first person is used over one hundred times, showing great rapport. It is an intensely practical epistle, filled with favorite passages of encouragement (e.g., 1:6, 21; 2:12–13; 3:20–21; 4:6–9, 13, 19). It also mentions "joy" at least sixteen times. Philippians frequently refers to Christ. His names and titles are included over fifty times. The illustration of Christ's humility in 2:6–11 is among the most profound passages in the Bible, and the key to Paul's motivation is his identification with Christ in life or death (1:20–24; 3:7–14).

OUTLINE

I. Introduction (1:1–11)
  A. Salutation (1:1–2)
  B. Prologue: Thanksgiving and Prayer (1:3–11)
II. Biographical Prologue: Paul's Present Circumstances in Serving the Gospel (1:12–26)
  A. Advance of the Gospel in Rome (1:12–18a)
  B. Outlook Toward Death and Deliverance (1:18b–26)
III. Exhortations to a Life-style Worthy of the Gospel (1:27–2:30)
  A. To Unity and Steadfastness (1:27–30)
  B. To Christ-like Humility (2:1–11)
  C. To Obedience and Blamelessness (2:12–16)
  D. As Seen in Paul, Timothy, and Epaphroditus (2:17–30)
IV. Warnings Against False Teachings Contrary to the Gospel (3:1–4:1)
  A. Stand Firm Against Self-Righteous Legalists (3:1–16)
  B. Stand Firm Against Self-Centered Libertines (3:17–4:1)
V. Further Exhortations to Application of Earlier Themes (4:2–9)
  A. To Unity in the Cause of the Gospel (4:2–3)
  B. To Joyful Peace in the Midst of Difficult Circumstances (4:4–7)
  C. To Steadfastness in Thought and Practice (4:8–9)
VI. Personal Epilogue: Paul's Gratitude for Partnership in Spreading the Gospel (4:10–20)
  A. For the Recent Gift (4:10–14)
  B. For the Previous Gifts (4:15–20)
VII. Closing Salutation (4:21–23)
  A. Greetings (4:21–22)
  B. Benediction (4:23)

COMMENTARY

I. Introduction (1:1–11)

A. Salutation (1:1–2). The initial greeting sections in all of Paul's epistles follow the pattern of ancient letters. There are three basic parts, always in the same order: (1) sender, (2) recipient, and (3) greeting. Timothy is included with Paul as sender (v. 1)—not as co-author but as trusted co-worker (2:19–23). It is striking that Paul does not refer to himself by the significant title of "apostle," but links himself with Timothy as "servants of Christ Jesus" (v. 1). Only here in the Pauline greetings does the apostle share his status (even such a lowly one) with an associate. This may have been due to Timothy's part in the founding of the Philippian church (Acts 16). It also looks ahead to the theme of humble equality (Phil. 2:3–4) and the discussion of Timothy's trip to Philippi to serve the Lord there (2:19–23).

The epistle is addressed to "all the saints . . . at Philippi" (v. 1). "Saints" is not a designation for certain superspiritual individuals. It refers to all Christians who have been "set apart" "in Christ Jesus" (v. 1). The address includes the "overseers and deacons" (v. 1), the only instance where a letter from Paul is sent to local church officials. He may be thanking the leaders for their part in a recent gift (Phil. 4:10–14), or seeking to direct their attention to responsibilities he develops later in the book (e.g., 3:2ff.).

That there were overseers (or "elders"; cf. Titus 1:5–7) and deacons in this church implies that it was a larger, more established church when Philippians was written. In the New Testament newer, smaller churches had only overseers/elders (Acts 14:23; Titus 1:5–9) while older, larger churches also had deacons (1 Tim. 3:8–13).

Paul extends his common greeting "grace and peace to you from God" (v. 2; Rom. 1:7; etc.). The initial gift of such undeserved grace is received by faith in Christ (Eph. 2:8–9), granting the spiritually dead sinner (Eph. 2:1–3) peace with God (Rom. 5:1). Other references in Philippians to grace (1:7) and peace (4:7, 9) deal with proper Christian behavior in the midst of trials and turmoil.

B. Prologue: thanksgiving and prayer (1:3–11). There is good reason to conclude that Paul is again following the literary conventions of his day in this joyous and prayerful, but carefully structured, prologue.[3] He introduces the theme of the book and related ideas that are developed throughout the epistle. These verses function as a true epistolary prologue, anticipating the thought patterns and argument of the entire letter in condensed form. In the initial thanksgiving (vv. 3–6) the theme is stated, followed by an expansion of the theme (vv. 7–8), and an application related to the theme in a prayer (vv. 9–11).

After setting an initial mood of joyous thanksgiving and prayer (vv. 3–4) that pervades the entire book (1:18–19; 2:17–18; 3:1; 4:1, 4, 6), Paul states why he is thankful for the Philippian Christians. Their "partnership [Gk. *koinōnia;* NASB participation] in the gospel" (v. 5) with the apostle since the beginning of the church in Philippi (see Acts 16:12–40) and over the ensuing years has been a great encouragement to him (Phil. 1:5). Especially meaningful were gifts the Philippians had "shared" (Gk. *ekoinōnēsen*) (4:15) with Paul in the past and most recently (4:10–20).

Having referred to their past and present faithfulness in the cause of the gospel (1:5), the apostle now looks ahead to the ultimate future event: "the day of Christ Jesus" (v. 6; see 1:10; 2:16). He is totally "confident" (v. 6, NIV, NASB; RSV sure) that the Lord will bring their "partnership in the gospel" to "completion" (v. 6) by the time the Savior comes from heaven to transform his people (3:20–21). Such an understanding of the "good work in you" (v. 6) is preferable to taking it as salvation, which is not mentioned in the context. The faithful human response of "partnership in the gospel" (v. 5) is now viewed from the perspective of the "good work" of God's sovereign oversight.

Paul expresses this same balance of human responsibility and divine sovereignty in regard to spiritual progress beyond initial salvation (2:12–13). Therefore, the above conclusion about the "good work in you" (1:6) should not be taken as bearing on the wider biblical teaching about the eternal security of the believer in Christ (John 10:28–29; Rom. 8:35–39). It is a needed clarification, however, because the rest of the letter elaborates on how to perfect their partnership in the gospel.

The next subsection (vv. 7–8) gives the basis for Paul's confidence and expresses his Christlike affection for the Philippian believers (v. 8). The word rendered "feel" (KJV think) "embraces both feeling and thought."[4] This encompassing of mind and emotions is seen repeatedly throughout the epistle (see 2:1–5; 3:15; 4:2, 10).

The reason for Paul's deep conviction (vv. 6–7a) was that the Philippians were not fair-weather friends. They stood by him in his regular ministry of defending and confirming the gospel, and now in his imprisonment (NASB, RSV; NIV chains). "Imprisonment" looks ahead to the biographical prologue (1:12–26). "Defending and confirming the gospel" likely announces the thrust of chapter 3. In verse 7 "share" (NIV; NASB, RSV, partakers; Gk. *sunkoinōnous*) looks back to *partnership* (v. 5; Gk. *koinōnia*). "God's grace" (v. 7) speaks of Paul's apostolic ministry of the gospel, which he received by God's gracious choice (Rom. 1:5; 12:3; Eph. 3:2). He viewed his readers as partners in the gospel ministry, no

3. See G. F. Hawthorne, *Philippians* (Waco: Word, 1983), 14–15.

4. Ibid., 22.

matter what the circumstances. Also, because of his identification with Christ (Phil. 3:7–11), he longed for them with the supernatural "affection of Christ Jesus" (1:8).

In Paul's prayer for the Philippians (1:9–11), we see that, although he was certain of God's work in and through them, he still interceded for them. His prayer spans all the way until the day of Christ (v. 10). His petition is for intelligent, insightful love (v. 9) for his readers. Such love produces great benefits in godly behavior. It enables the child of God to determine what is best, from the Lord's perspective (v. 10). It also motivates the believer to remain morally pure and above reproach in his life-style. Paul himself illustrates this in the biographical prologue (1:12–26). Such a discerning and blameless life will be full of "the fruit of righteousness" (v. 11; see also Gal. 5:22–23).

The prologue to Philippians (1:3–11) not only introduces the central theme (1:5) and other ideas developed later, it also challenges the reader to apply the attitudes and behavior Paul sets forth. Some of the practical lessons to be found here are: (1) the constancy and content of thankful, joyful prayer (1:3–4, 9–11); (2) the attitude of partnership in the gospel between ministers and other Christians (1:5); (3) complete confidence in God's good work in believers' lives, balanced with prayer on their behalf (1:6, 9–11); (4) the beauty of deep, God-given love between Christians; and (5) the need to pray for and increase in love, discernment, and blameless behavior (1:9–11).

II. Biographical Prologue: Paul's Present Circumstances in Serving the Gospel (1:12–26)

A. Advance of the gospel in Rome (1:12–18a). In the preceding section the apostle stated the foundational theme of Philippians: partnership in the gospel (1:5). Now he explains his present personal circumstances. It is important to understand how the two segments are related. The ideas that he expresses in this biographical prologue (1:12–26) are noted in 1:3–11. Some of the principles that Paul laid out in the prologue (1:3–11) are now seen in his own trying circumstances (1:12–26).

Paul's confinement (introduced in 1:7), contrary to what might have been expected, had not stopped the spread of the gospel. In referring to their intimate relationship as brothers in Christ (v. 12; also 3:1, 13, 17; 4:1, 8), he informs them that his imprisonment "really served to advance the gospel" (v. 12). He does not explain further "what has happened to [him]" (v. 12), but apparently the possibility of death had been before him (v. 20). What the apostle had discerned was much like the principle that Joseph had articulated to his formerly jealous brothers: "You intended to harm me, but God intended it for good" (Gen. 50:20). If anything, the providential circumstances had proven to be effective in spreading the gospel. Now Paul was "in chains for Christ" (Phil. 1:13), and not just a common criminal. We do not know if he was actually chained at this point, or whether this is a figurative way of describing confinement in his own rented quarters (Acts 28:30). We do know that in Rome there were soldiers assigned to guard him (Acts 28:16). Presumably this was the means by which the gospel spread "throughout the whole palace guard" (v. 13; NASB, RSV praetorian guard). Apparently God had opened a door for the message of the gospel (1 Cor. 16:9; Col. 4:3) so that Paul could proclaim the gospel of Jesus Christ to every guard and anyone else who came to see him (Acts 28:30–31). This unexpected opportunity for Paul the prisoner to witness to the palace guard had the unexpected effect of encouraging most of the unconfined brethren "to speak the word of God more courageously and fearlessly" (Phil. 1:14). Where the Philippians might have expected discouragement because of the apostle's bondage, there was great boldness in the spread of the gospel. If Paul could do it inside prison, they could do it outside of prison.

Unfortunately, not all of the preaching of the gospel stimulated by Paul's ministry in confinement was properly motivated. Some of the courageous believers preached out of goodwill, love, and sincerity (vv. 15–17). But others operated out of envy, rivalry, selfish ambition, and false motives (vv. 15–18). Apparently this latter group was theologically orthodox, since Paul does not dispute their message (v. 18), as he is quick to do elsewhere (Gal. 1:6–9). He even rejoices that "Christ is preached" (Phil. 1:18a) by these individuals, even though he fully realizes that they are trying to "stir up trouble" (v. 17; NASB cause me distress), perhaps by assumed competition with the apostle. What really matters to Paul is the proclamation of the true gospel, no matter how it gets out (v. 18).

B. Outlook toward death and deliverance (1:18b–26). The tone of rejoicing continues (v. 18b) as Paul thanks the Philippians for their prayers concerning his deliverance (v. 19). It is interesting to note that Paul carefully places the work of the Holy Spirit, here called "the Spirit of Jesus Christ" (v. 19; Acts 16:7; Rom. 8:9; Gal. 4:6), alongside his readers' prayers in affecting his potential deliverance (Rom. 8:26–27). At this point the deliverance spoken of could be either death (Phil. 1:20) or release from imprisonment (2:24). In the light of 1:24–25, release seems more likely. But, regardless, it was the apostle's eager expectation and hope to courageously exalt the Savior in his body (vv. 20, 22, 24), "whether by life or death" (v. 20). What would happen to Paul was entirely secondary to what testimony would be left for Christ.

At this point Paul finds himself in something of a dilemma. "Yet what shall I choose?" (v. 22) he asks. He struggles honestly and openly between the two options of life and death (v. 23). Although he has a great desire to die and enter the presence of Christ (v. 23), his concern for the welfare of the Philippians prevails (v. 24). He is persuaded that it is more important for the sake of the Philippians that he continue living in the body (vv. 22, 24). As he lives for Christ, there will be fruitful labor (vv. 21, 22), including his readers' progress and joy in the faith (v. 25). Since the apostle had said earlier that he confidently expected progress (1:6), and requested such in prayer for the Philippian Christians (1:9–11), it is obvious that he had discerned what was best (1:10). The correctness of that choice would be even more evident in the future, when Paul would be reunited with the church in Philippi (2:24). Their "joy in Christ Jesus" would "overflow" (NASB abound) at his coming (1:26).

The biographical prologue of the Epistle to the Philippians (1:12–26) takes the central theme of partnership in the gospel (1:5) and exemplifies it being worked out in very difficult circumstances in the life of Paul. Several helpful lessons to consider are: (1) God's use of negative circumstances to bring about positive ends (1:12–14); (2) the great impact of courageous witness for Christ, even in unfavorable circumstances (1:13–14); (3) the possibility of sharing the gospel of Christ with wrong motives (1:15–18); (4) the vital importance of prayer to support ministry (1:19); (5) the necessity of dependence on the power of the Holy Spirit, especially in connection with prayer (1:19); (6) Christ as the Christian's reason for living (1:20–21); and (7) the believer's eternal gain in the presence of Christ through death (1:21, 23).

The biographical prologue of Philippians (1:12–26) not only has clear conceptual links to the epistolary prologue that preceded it (1:3–11), it also looks forward to succeeding sections of the letter. Paul's example of proper partnership in the gospel (1:5), in the trying situation of his imprisonment, would serve as a challenge to his readers to live "in a manner worthy of the gospel of Christ" (1:27). His placing of the needs of other believers before his own desires looks ahead to the exhortation to humble equality (2:3–4) and the glorious illustration of the humility of Christ (2:5–11). The anticipation of his release from bondage (1:25) foreshadows the clearer mention of the apostle's intention to come to Philippi (2:24).

III. Exhortations to a Life-style Worthy of the Gospel (1:27–2:30)

A. To unity and steadfastness (1:27–30). This section marks the beginning of the actual body of the letter, which runs to 4:9. The theme of the letter (1:5) and other ideas introduced in the prologue (1:3–11) and biographical prologue (1:12–26) are further developed in this lengthy section. There are initial exhortations and illustrations relating to a life-style worthy of the gospel (1:27–2:30). The next section issues warnings against teachings contrary to the gospel (3:1–4:1). The final section of the body of Philippians gives additional exhortations related to the application of earlier themes (4:2–9).

The initial section of exhortations (1:27–2:30) contains four subsections. The first deals with steadfastness (1:27–30), the second with Christ-like humility (2:1–11), the third with obedience and blameless behavior (2:12–16), and the fourth with the godly examples of Paul, Timothy, and Epaphroditus (2:17–30). All four deal with behavior or examples "worthy of the gospel of Christ" (1:27).

In 1:27–30 conduct "worthy of the gospel" means unity among Christians (v. 27b) and steadfastness against enemies of the gospel (vv. 27c–30). Such unity will be a key focus in chapter 2, and steadfastness is expanded in chapter 3. "Conduct yourselves" (1:27) comes from the Greek word *politeuomai,* from which we derive the words *politics* and *political.* It meant to "live as a citizen," and would have special significance to the Philippians, since their city was a Roman colony. Paul later tells them that their primary "citizenship (Gk. *politeuma*) is in heaven" (3:20), strongly urging them to a worthy, godly life-style. Verse 27 recalls the central theme of 1:5, and resembles Paul's exhortation to the Ephesians to "live a life worthy of the calling you have received" (Eph. 4:1). Both exhort the Christian to live up to the high standards set by the Lord.

If his readers live out this life-style, the apostle can rest easy, whether he ever sees them again or not (v. 27). He is particularly concerned for their unity ("one spirit . . . one man," v. 27) and their steadfastness ("stand firm," v. 27). Because of his own courageous example in difficult circumstances (1:20), he can encourage them not to be "frightened in any way by those who oppose [them]" (v. 28). Such fearlessness through faith would be a sure sign that the opposition would eventually be destroyed. As a result his readers would experience God's deliverance (NIV, NASB; salvation; Gk. *sotēria;* see 2 Thess. 1:4–5), as Paul expected deliverance (Gk. *sotēria*) from his imprisonment (1:19). "Granted" (v. 29) means "given as a gift," "graced," and shows that suffering in the Christian life is not a curse, but a blessing that fosters growth (James 1:2–4; 1 Pet. 4:14). "To believe on [Christ]" and "to suffer for him" (Phil. 1:29) are two sides of the same coin of Christian living. They were simply "going through the same struggle" (Gk. *agōna*, agony) they had seen when Paul was first in Philippi (Acts 16:12–40) and "now hear" (Phil. 1:30) about from his present confinement.

B. To Christ-like humility (2:1–11). For Christians to walk "worthy of the gospel of Christ" (1:27) they must live in unity among themselves. In Philippians 2:1–11 Paul develops the idea that genuine unity is only possible where there is true humility. After listing some of the resources from the Lord for unity (2:1), he exhorts his readers to proper unity (2:2) through humility (2:3–4). The profound illustration of the humility (2:5–8) and exaltation (2:9–11) of the Lord Jesus Christ is the climax of this section.

The fourfold "if" (v. 1) assumes that each of the succeeding propositions is true, and could be translated as "since." Thus, the apostle is calling to the attention of his readers spiritual certainties to be used in the pursuit of the goal of proper Christian unity (1:27). The first is "encouragement [KJV consolation] in Christ" (NASB, RSV). To be "in Christ" is to be a new creation (2 Cor. 5:17) and to possess every spiritual blessing (Eph. 1:3), which is both an encouragement and exhortation to godly behavior. "Consolation [NIV, KJV comfort; RSV incentive] of love" probably refers to God's love in Christ for the church (John 3:16; Rom. 5:8; 8:38–39; 1 John 4:9–10). The third phrase, "fellowship with the Spirit" (see 2 Cor. 13:14), should be understood in the sense of unity and oneness (see 1 Cor. 12:13; Eph. 4:3–4), which results from the Spirit indwelling all believers, individually (1 Cor. 6:19) and corporately (1 Cor. 3:16). The last spiritual certainty mentioned is "tenderness and compassion," which Paul exemplified earlier in the letter (1:8) because of his identification with Christ (Phil. 3:7–11). In Colossians 3:12 all are commanded to exhibit these two qualities.

Because God has made these resources for unity available, Paul urges them to "make my joy complete" (Phil. 2:2) by living out such oneness. He already had much joy (1:4) because of the Philippian church, but such unity would fulfill his greatest joy on their behalf. The implication is that there was a growing problem of disunity in the church, perhaps involving Euodia and Syntyche (4:2–3). To address this problem, Paul asks for four attitudes (and corresponding actions) that apply the four spiritual realities listed in verse 1. It would be impossible for a church where Christians are "like-minded, having the same love, being one in spirit and purpose" (v. 2) to be fragmented.

While such unity does not require unthinking conformity in all details, it does necessitate mutual "humility" (v. 3). The readers must "consider others better than themselves" (NASB more important, v. 3). Surely it is "vain conceit" (v. 3) to look out merely for "your own interests" (v. 4). Christians are called to love their neighbors as themselves (Matt. 22:39). It is not a matter of superiority or comparison, but obedience (Rom. 12:10; 15:1; Gal. 5:13) and mutual submission (Eph. 5:21). What a magnetic effect the church could have if its members humbly served "the interests" of others (Phil. 2:4).

No greater example of selfless humility (vv. 3–4) could be considered than Christ Jesus. Even though his person and work are unique, his humble "attitude" (v. 5), combining proper thinking and emotion (see on 1:7), is still binding upon believers. If the Savior could give up heaven's glory to become a lowly man and suffer the ultimate humiliation of death by crucifixion (vv. 6–8) because of the divine compassion for mankind (John 3:16), Christians can also live out caring humility toward one another (Phil. 2:3–4).

It is quite possible that Philippians 2:6–11 is from an early Christian hymn (see also Eph. 5:19; Col. 3:16) written by Paul or someone else. If so, he employs it much like a preacher would use a particularly appropriate song or poem at a crucial juncture in a sermon. Whatever its original nature, and (possibly different) wording, this passage contains some of the most important teaching about Jesus Christ in all the New Testament.

The word rendered "nature" (NIV; NASB, RSV, KJV form) in verses 6 and 7 refers to "the inner, essential, and abiding nature of a person or thing."[5] The Son of God did not cease to be God when he became incarnate. Rather, he became the unique God-man, fully divine yet fully hu-

5. W. Hendriksen, *Epistle to the Philippians* (Grand Rapids: Baker, 1962), 104.

man, without any conflict between the two. As God, he did not regard his divine status and privileges in heaven before his birth "something to be grasped" (v. 6) at all costs. Rather, he willingly assumed certain self-limitations, and "made himself nothing" (NASB, RSV emptied himself) in comparison with the unlimited splendor he previously had (John 17:5). "Made himself nothing" (v. 7) translates one Greek word (*ekenōsen*) that is the basis for the much-debated doctrine of kenosis. Some have held that either Christ ceased to be God or that God changed (Heb. 13:8) when the preincarnate Son of God "emptied himself." But neither this passage nor other New Testament data support such theories.[6] His mission was to be a servant (Matt. 20:28), and he was made in the likeness of sinful human flesh (Rom. 8:3), although he was totally without sin himself (Heb. 4:15). However, such an outward appearance, like that of any other common man (Phil. 2:8; Isa. 53:2), dramatically gave way to divine glory at the Mount of Transfiguration (Mark 9:2–8). A scripturally balanced view of kenosis does not hold that Christ became less than God in taking on human flesh (John 1:14), or that the unchanging nature of God was altered, but that the God-man "humbled himself and became obedient to death" (Phil. 2:8; Heb. 5:8). This forceful lesson of ultimate humility and obedience is even more vivid when it is realized that death by crucifixion was a degrading kind of execution unworthy of a Roman citizen and cursed under the Old Testament law (Deut. 21:23; Gal. 3:13).

At this point in the illustration two radical shifts take place. The subject changes from Christ (Phil. 2:5, 6) to God the Father (vv. 9, 11). In verse 8 Christ "humbled himself," while in verse 9 "God exalted him." "Therefore" (v. 9) shows a cause-effect relationship between the self-humbling of Christ and his exaltation "to the highest place" (v. 9). Christ taught elsewhere (Matt. 20:26–27) that the way of greatness is the way of willing service, and the giving to Christ of the "name that is above every name" (v. 9) is the supreme example of that truth. "Name . . . above every name" (v. 9) may refer to the Lord (v. 11), or it may refer more generally to his office and dignity of position (Eph. 1:21; Heb. 1:4). "Every knee shall bow" (v. 10) may be an allusion to Isaiah 45:23, in which God requires "the ends of the earth" to submit fully to him. If so, this passage teaches that Christ's full authority (Matt. 28:18) and position as God will ultimately be recognized by universal worship and verbal acknowledgment. Such an admission by all creation "in heaven and on earth and under the earth" (v. 10) will resound "to the glory of God the Father" (v. 11).

C. To obedience and blamelessness (2:12–16). Using the example of Christ's humble obedience (v. 8), and reminding his "dear friends" in Philippi that they "have always obeyed" (v. 12), Paul now exhorts them to further obedience (vv. 12–14) and blameless behavior (vv. 15–16). He had witnessed such obedience during his presence in Philippi on his second and third missionary journeys (Acts 16:12–40; 20:1, 3–6). He had heard the same report in his absence through Epaphroditus (Phil. 2:25) and others. "Therefore" (v. 12) links Paul's exhortation to his readers with the preceding grand example of Christ's obedience (vv. 6–8) and its consequences (vv. 9–11).

A crucial component of being able to "work out your salvation" (v. 12) is to "do everything without complaining [NASB, RSV grumbling] or arguing" (NASB disputing, v. 14). Such practices may have been at the very heart of the problem in Philippi (4:2–3). Such patterns that promote disunity must be dealt with if the church is to be "blameless and pure" internally and "without fault" in its external witness to the world (v. 15). Although the Greek words for "blameless and pure" in 2:15 are not the same as in 1:10, the similarity in context shows that such selflessly humble behavior is in keeping with Paul's prayer for love, insight, and discernment (1:9–11). When Christians behave in this way, they "shine like stars" (v. 15; Matt. 5:14–16) in a lost and dying world. In 2:16 the Greek word rendered "hold out" (NIV) may mean "offer," speaking of proclaiming the "word of life" or "holding fast" (NASB, RSV), referring to steadfastness (looking back to 1:27 and ahead to chap. 3). Perhaps both shades of meaning are present.

As his readers pursue selfless humility (2:2–4) through this kind of obedient, blameless behavior (2:12–15), Paul will have a proper reason to "boast [NASB glory; RSV be proud] on the day of Christ" (v. 16). No one would be able to say at that point that Paul's efforts for Christ had been "for nothing" (v. 16).

D. As seen in Paul, Timothy, and Epaphroditus (2:17–30). Paul had commanded his readers to "walk worthy of the gospel" (1:27) by pursuing unity through selfless humility toward one another in the church (2:2–4), giving Jesus Christ as the classic example of such caring, humble obedience (2:5–8). After his exhortations to unity through obedience and blameless behavior (2:12–16), he concludes this first ma-

6. See S. M. Smith, "Kenosis, Kenotic Theology," in *Evangelical Dictionary of Theology*, ed. Walter A. Elwell (Grand Rapids: Baker, 1984), 600–602.

jor section of the letter (1:27–2:30) with three additional examples of those who humbly looked out for "the interests of others" (2:4): (1) himself (vv. 17–18), (2) Timothy (vv. 19–24), and (3) Epaphroditus (25–30).

It may appear presumptuous for Paul to use himself as an illustration of humility in serving others. But the facts of his living self-sacrifice (v. 17; Rom. 12:1) cannot be disputed. His reference to the Old Testament "drink offering" (Phil. 2:17) made in connection with the daily sacrifices showed that he wanted the totality of his ministry to be an aroma pleasing to God (Exod. 29:41; Num. 15:10). He was imprisoned because of the gospel of Christ, and death had been a distinct possibility (1:13–14, 20). Even with that prospect, Paul was glad and could rejoice with his readers (vv. 17–18).

The second example is that of Timothy (v. 19), who continued to have true concern for the Philippian church (v. 20). It was Paul's intention to dispatch Timothy to Philippi as soon as he knew the outcome of his present circumstances (vv. 19, 23). It is both striking and sad that Paul would say "I have no one else like him" (v. 20). Apparently those promoting their "own interests, not those of Jesus Christ" (v. 21) were even among Paul's close associates. But Paul knew he could depend on Timothy to bring back a report about the Philippian church which would encourage Paul (v. 19).

The final illustration used is Epaphroditus, who had served as a "messenger" (v. 25; Gk. *apostolos*) for the church at Philippi, who sent him to minister to Paul. Paul describes him in such glowing terms as "brother, fellow worker, and fellow soldier" (v. 25). He was to be welcomed "with great joy" and honored (v. 29) because he had sacrificed himself for "the work of Christ," almost to the point of death (vv. 27, 30). Now Epaphroditus longed to see his brethren in Philippi, and Paul was increasingly eager to send him (v. 28). Such a journey would result in gladness for the Philippian church and the lessening of Paul's sorrow (v. 28).

This section (2:17–30) concludes the first movement (1:27–2:30) of the body of Paul's letter to the Philippians (1:27–4:9). It has consisted of exhortations to a life-style "worthy of the gospel of Christ" (1:27), particularly in regard to church unity (1:27; 2:2) through humility (2:3–4) and obedient, blameless behavior (2:12–16). The matchless example of God the Son becoming a man, modeling humble obedience (2:5–11), and the additional illustrations of Paul (2:17–18), Timothy (2:19–24), and Epaphroditus (2:25–30) selflessly serving the cause of the gospel (2:22) and Christ (2:21) flesh out the description of the attitude and actions that promote the oneness of the body of Christ.

This portion also prepares for the next major section (3:1–4:1) by introducing the need for steadfastness (1:27–30; 2:16), especially against external opposition (1:28). It will be seen in the discussion of 3:17–21 that the two segments are also tied together by several of the same, or closely related, terms. Thus, any attempt to separate the two chapters based on an alleged rough transition at 3:2 must be considered extremely suspect.

Among the many applications that can be derived from the study of Philippians 1:27–2:30 are: (1) the responsibility all Christians have to live "in a manner worthy of the gospel" (1:27); (2) the need for fearless steadfastness in standing firm for the faith of the gospel (1:27–28); (3) the reality of suffering as an expected part of the Christian life (1:29–30); (4) the wonderful resources available in Christ for true Christian unity (2:1–2); (5) the necessity for selfless humility to replace selfishness and conceit among God's people (2:3–11); (6) the wisdom of trusting God's sovereign working in our midst even as we actively obey him (2:12–13); (7) the obstacle to unity in the church caused by complaining and arguing (2:14); (8) the aid to Christian testimony and outreach that blameless and pure behavior can be (2:15–16); (9) the beauty of lives totally committed to the Lord (2:17–30); and (10) the need to appreciate and honor those who give themselves in selfless sacrificial service to the Lord (2:19–30).

IV. Warnings Against False Teachings Contrary to the Gospel (3:1–4:1)

A. Stand firm against self-righteous legalists (3:1–16). In 3:1–4:1 Paul addresses two different types of false teaching that endangered the church at Philippi: legalism (3:1–16) and licentiousness (3:17–4:1).

Before turning to address the danger of Jewish legalism (3:2), Paul again sounds the note of joy (3:1). He then contrasts true Christian worship, which is internal and spiritual, with external legalism, which ultimately puts its "confidence in the flesh" (3:3). Next Paul lists the impressive credentials that were his as a Jew before coming to Christ (3:4–6). Verses 7–11 contrast the gain of identification with Christ with the spiritual loss of self-righteous legalistic confidence in the flesh. The next section (3:12–14) portrays the Christian life as a race toward a definite goal, and the last section (3:15–16) urges acceptance and application of such an outlook.

The word translated "finally" (v. 1) often

signals the concluding section of a New Testament letter (4:8; see 2 Cor. 13:11; Eph. 6:10), although this is not always the case (1 Thess. 4:1). It is possible that Paul was interrupted or had intended to end the epistle, but then decided to develop another line of thought. More likely, because of the thematic relationship between chapter 3 and what precedes it (esp. 1:27–30), "finally" should be understood as transitional (1 Thess. 4:1) meaning "furthermore" or "in addition."

The element of joy (Phil. 3:1) links up closely with previous parts of the letter (1:4, 18, 25–26; 2:17–18, 29) and others yet to come (4:4, 10). The phrase *write the same things to you again* may refer to: (1) things previously taught while in Philippi (Acts 16), (2) an unknown previous letter, or (3) instructions earlier in the epistle. Paul understood the necessity of repetition in teaching as a spiritual "safeguard" (Phil. 3:1). All three biting epithets in verse 2 describe the same opponents of the gospel (1:27–30). These Jewish legalists are called "dogs," "men who do evil," and "mutilators of the flesh" (v. 2). By sharp contrast, Paul proclaims that Christians are the true circumcision (v. 3).

Paul now challenges anyone who thinks he can equal his background and attainments as a legalistic Jew (3:9). In this enlightening autobiographical account (Acts 22:2–5; 26:2–11; Gal. 1:13–14; 1 Tim. 1:12–16), Paul details seven reasons for his former "confidence" (Phil. 3:4), his proud reliance on legalistic righteousness (v. 6). At first glance, these reasons may appear to be boastful (2 Cor. 11:17; 12:11). Yet they actually constitute a grave warning, as Paul uses the testimony of his own former life (Phil. 3:5–6) to reveal the foolhardiness of placing one's "confidence in the flesh" (vv. 3, 4) rather than Christ.

Saul (Paul's Jewish name, Acts 13:9) had been "circumcised on the eighth day" (Phil. 3:5) according to God's command to Abraham (Gen. 17:12) and the Mosaic law (Lev. 12:3). He was one "of the people of Israel" (Phil. 3:5; 2 Cor. 11:22), God's chosen nation (Rom. 3:2; 9:3–5). His lineage was proudly traced through "the tribe of Benjamin" (Phil. 3:5), and he was apparently named after Israel's first monarch, King Saul (1 Sam. 9:1–2). At the time of the disruption of the Davidic kingdom (1 Kings 12), Benjamin was the only tribe that stood with Judah (1 Kings 12:19–21), and the capital city of Jerusalem was on the border of the territory of that tribe (Josh. 18:28). The last of Paul's four advantages by birth (in the eyes of the Jewish legalist) was that he was a "Hebrew of Hebrews" (Phil. 3:5), which probably means that he "was extremely zealous for the traditions of my fathers" (Gal. 1:14) in every facet of life.

In addition to these privileges Paul mentions three more significant points. He had become a Pharisee (Phil. 3:5), a member of the strictest sect of Judaism, and had studied under Gamaliel, the great teacher of the law (Acts 22:3). In addition, Paul's Jewish zeal was so strong that he gave himself over totally to "persecuting the church" (Phil. 3:6; Acts 8:3; 9:1–2) before encountering the resurrected and glorified Christ on the Damascus Road (Acts 9:3–5). The final, climactic claim to self-righteousness that the unregenerate Saul of Tarsus could have made was in regard to his scrupulous legalistic adherence to the Jewish Torah (Phil. 3:6). From the perspective of the legalist, he was "faultless" (v. 6).

But Paul's outlook on "having a righteousness of my own that comes from the law" (v. 9) was drastically different as a Christian. Not only can self-righteous legalism be faulted (vv. 2, 6), but it is cursed by God (Gal. 3:10–12). What happened to be "profit" (NASB, RSV, KJV gain) through the eyes of the legalist must be realistically reconsidered as "loss for the sake of Christ" (Phil. 3:7). In fact, in the massive reorientation that took place in the wake of his Damascus Road conversion (Acts 9), he came to "consider everything a loss compared to the surpassing greatness of knowing Christ Jesus" (v. 8). To Paul the lost treasures of his unregenerate existence (vv. 4–6) were now seen as "rubbish" (v. 8; RSV refuse; KJV dung). His drive in life was no longer to try to earn his own righteousness by keeping the Mosaic law. Rather, it was to "gain Christ and be found in him," having "the righteousness that comes from God and is by faith" (vv. 8–9). He had finally realized the Old Testament truth that no one is righteous in and of himself (Rom. 3:10; Pss. 14:3; 53:3), and that the only hope is to be declared righteous through faith in Jesus Christ (Rom. 5:1).

In 3:10–11 "becoming like him in his death" and attaining "to the resurrection" may refer to death to the old life and sin (Rom. 6:4–11) or to deliverance through suffering in the Christian life (Phil. 1:28–30), or both.

Before proceeding any further, Paul wants it to be clearly understood that he has not experienced or received all of this (v. 12), even though he had been a believer for many years. "Made perfect" (v. 12) suggests an agent outside of Paul himself and may strike a contrast with the self-righteous, self-confident Jewish legalists (3:2). Paul knows full well that he has not arrived at the finish line of this spiritual race, and he knows what he must do as he vigorously pursues that glorious goal. "Forgetting what is behind and straining toward what is ahead" (v. 13) are both necessary in order to "win the prize" (v. 14) in a race (Paul may have in mind the Greek games). "Forgetting" cannot be loss of memory because Paul looks back at his own earlier life (vv. 4–11); instead, it means removing the obstacles of the past (vv. 4–6) that might prevent the believer from running the race of the Christian life (vv. 13–14).

Paul concludes this subsection (3:1–16) by stating that "all . . . mature" (NASB, KJV perfect) Christians "should take such a view" (v. 15), namely, that believers have not "already been made perfect" (v. 12) in this life, but must continually identify themselves with Christ (vv. 10–11) and press on without distraction in living out their commitment in faith (vv. 9, 12–14). He is confident that God will reveal to his readers any disputed point. The biggest problem to be faced, however, is not understanding, but application (v. 16). Paul knew very well the tendency Christians have not to practice what they already have in Christ.

B. Stand firm against self-centered libertines (3:17–4:1). Unfortunately, the Jewish legalists were not the only threat to the Philippian church. Much that Paul has just said (3:7–16) would also apply to the danger posed by an opposite viewpoint: pleasure-centered licentiousness. Those in the church tending to either extreme needed to follow the "example" (v. 17) of Paul and his associates. It was not at all boastful for Paul to implore his readers to do this; he could ask them to do so because he was following Christ (1 Cor. 11:1), not charting his own path. He then repeats the sad saga of these "enemies" of the gospel (v. 18) whose self-centered worldliness will be their "destruction" (v. 19). Christians, on the other hand, have a heavenly focus and await the transforming return of Christ, rather than living for bodily pleasure here and now (vv. 20–21).

Paul's readers needed to be careful not to make a mistake similar to the self-centered libertines (vv. 18–19). They must not place their trust in "earthly things" (v. 19), or even in their privileged Roman citizenship (see 1:27), which many of the Philippians would have possessed. They were not to be otherworldly, but to realize that their spiritual "citizenship is in heaven" (v. 20). Thus, Christians wait expectantly for the coming of the Savior from heaven for his own. Christ presently possesses the power and authority "to bring everything under his control" (v. 21). When he comes and exerts that matchless power it will tranform (RSV, KJV change) "our lowly bodies so that they will be like his glorious body" (v. 21). This joyous expectation reflects teaching elsewhere in the New Testament (e.g., 1 Cor. 15:43–53; 1 John 3:2–3).

There are an amazing number of clear linking concepts between Philippians 3:20–21 and the example of Christ's obedient humility and exaltation in 2:6–11. The following are obvious parallels in the Greek text: (1) Lord Jesus Christ (3:20 and 2:11); (2) "everything under his control" (3:21) and "every knee shall bow" (2:10); (3) "will transform" (3:21; Gk. *metaschēmatisei*) ("likeness" 2:7, Gk. *schēma*); (4) "lowly" (NASB humble, 3:21) and "humbled" (2:8); (5) "like" (3:21; NASB conformity with; Gk. *summorphon*) and "nature" (2:6–7; NASB form; Gk. *morphē*); (6) "glorious" (3:21 and 2:11).[7] Thus, it seems that this longed-for transformation (3:20–21) will also be the believer's exaltation (2:9–11).

In 4:1 "therefore" looks back to chapter 3, with its emphasis on steadfastness (1:27–30) in the face of false teachings contrary to the gospel. Because of his tender relationship with the Philippian church (1:7–8), seen in the piling up of affectionate terminology ("my brothers . . . whom I love and long for, my joy and crown, . . . dear friends," 4:1), Paul is as concerned that they stand firm in the Lord (1:27–30) as that they attain unity through selfless humility (2:2–4). Both prongs of his previous foundational exhortation to conduct themselves in a "manner worthy of the gospel" (1:27) were necessary. The carrying out of both ideas would cause Paul to leap with joy (2:2; 3:1; 4:1)!

Philippians 3:1–4:1 begins the second major movement of thought in the letter, and develops the theme of steadfastness originally introduced in 1:27–30. Because of this earlier mention of opponents to the gospel (1:27–30) it is not so surprising that Paul makes a sharp transition (3:1) to confront the lurking doctrinal dangers of legalism (3:2–16) and licentiousness (3:17–21), before concluding the section (4:1). His own example of putting no confidence in the flesh, but rather wholly identifying with Christ (3:4–14) is the means by which his readers can stand firm (4:1) against either menace to the gospel and Christian experience.

From this section (3:1–4:1) one may note a number of crucial applications: (1) the nature of true Christian worship—by the Spirit, glorying in Christ, putting no confidence in the flesh (3:3); (2) the need to count as loss and rubbish all religious privileges and accomplishments outside of faith in Christ (3:5–9); (3) the demands of identification with Christ in order to know the depths of Christian experience (3:10–

7. Hawthorne, *Philippians*, 169.

12); (4) the obstacle that past failures and even successes can be to progress toward the goal of Christian growth (3:4–14); (5) the reality that no believer ever arrives at perfection in this life, but must continue to grow (3:12–14); (6) the continual responsibility to apply what is learned, to practice what is known of the Lord (3:16); (7) to avoid a materialistic, worldly lifestyle (3:18–19); (8) to live expectantly, as a citizen of heaven and an ambassador for Christ, eagerly awaiting the return of Christ and the accompanying transformation of our bodies (3:20–21); and (9) the constant vigilance needed for the church to stand firm against threats to the gospel like legalism and licentiousness (3:1–4:1).

V. Further Exhortations to Application of Earlier Themes (4:2–9)

A. To unity in the cause of the gospel (4:2–3). Since Euodia and Syntyche (v. 2) are the only troublemakers mentioned by name in the letter, it seems likely that they were a large part of the problem of disunity that had emerged in the Philippian church. Paul pleads with these two women "to agree with each other" (v. 2; NASB live in harmony; KJV be of the same mind). The identity of the "loyal yokefellow" (v. 2; NASB true comrade) is not known, nor is anything else known about the Clement mentioned here (v. 3).

B. To joyful peace in the midst of difficult circumstances (4:4–7). The prevailing mood of joy has resounded through the epistle (1:4, 18, 25–26; 2:2, 17–18, 29; 3:1; 4:1). No matter how difficult it becomes to walk "worthy of the gospel of Christ" (1:27), such rejoicing is always appropriate (4:4). Perhaps the Philippian believers were downcast at the growing internal problem of disunity (chap. 2) and the external danger and pressure of the false teachings of the legalists and libertines (chap. 3). The news about Paul's imprisonment (1:12–26) and Epaphroditus's illness (2:25–30) could also cause uneasiness. Still, he repeats: "Rejoice!" (v. 4). Instead of displaying great frustration and impatience with their circumstances, the Philippians should "let [their] gentleness be evident to all" (v. 5). They could do so because "the Lord is near" (v. 5; RSV, KJV at hand; 1 Pet. 4:7; Rev. 1:3).

As important as rejoicing and gentleness are in difficult times, they are incomplete without prayer (Phil. 4:6). The readers are told not to be "anxious about anything" they are facing, but instead to direct their "requests to God" (v. 6). This anxiety does not include the proper pastoral concern that Paul speaks of in 2:20, 28 and 2 Corinthians 11:28. It may include the cares commonly faced in life (Matt. 6:25–31). But the context seems to indicate worry about opposition and suffering (Phil. 1:28–30; chap. 3) compounded by disunity in the body (1:27; chap. 2). If this is the correct understanding, then "do not be anxious about anything" (v. 6) echoes "without being frightened in any way" in 1:28. Still, constant prayer, specific petition for needs, and thanksgiving (v. 6) are not only the Lord's antidote for such anxiety but God's expressed will in all circumstances (1 Thess. 5:18).

The "peace of God" (v. 7) which replaces anxiety in the life of the prayerful believer, is impossible to experience unless one already is at "peace with God" through faith in Christ (Rom. 5:1). But it is also beyond the ability of human understanding to fully comprehend how God's peace can "guard" (garrison) the "hearts" (emotions, personality) and "minds" (thoughts) of the anxiety-ridden people (v. 7). Apparently this is another beautiful and comforting instance of God's all-powerful, sovereign care for his obedient children (also 1:5–6, 9–11; 2:12–13).

C. To steadfastness in thought and practice (4:8–9). At this point in the epistle, "finally" (v. 8) signals the conclusion of the immediate section (4:2–9) as well as the larger context which started in 1:27. This smaller portion (4:8–9) is related to the preceding promise (vv. 6–7) in that it tells what the peaceful mind, freed and guarded from anxiety, should dwell on, as well as the kind of behavior such thought patterns should produce.

In verse 8 Paul indicates what a wholesome thought life will involve. It is very doubtful that this brief catalog of general moral virtues is meant to be either an exhaustive listing or a particularly precise one. In fact, the first six listed are probably summarized by the broader categories "excellent" and "praiseworthy." Whatever the case, Paul is certain that such ethical expressions along with adherence to his teaching ("learned," "received," "heard") and example ("seen in me," v. 9; 3:17) will make a significant difference in their Christian life. Paul concludes with a promise of the presence of the "God of peace," the source of the peace that guards the emotions and minds of the Christian from circumstantial anxiety, who will be among them as they seek steadfastly to live out these godly patterns of thought and behavior.

Philippians 4:2–9 offers several principles for Christian living which can be profitably applied: (1) past faithfulness is no guarantee of present attitudes and behavior (4:2–3); (2) small numbers can cause big problems in the church (4:2–3; 2:2–4); (3) rejoicing is a necessity of Christian experience (4:4); (4) Christians have the duty of faithful forbearance in the face of frustrating circumstances (4:5); (5) thankful prayer is the correct Christian response to anxiety (4:6–7); and (6) wholesome thought patterns and the impact of mature models are building blocks of godly behavior (4:8–9).

VI. Personal Epilogue: Paul's Gratitude for Partnership in Spreading the Gospel (4:10–20)

A. For the recent gift (4:10–14). Having concluded the body of the letter (1:27–4:9), Paul now fills out in some detail what had been painted only in broad brushstrokes in the prologue (1:3–5). He thanks the Philippian church for their recent gift carried by Epaphroditus (4:10–14, 18). Then he recalls their earlier pattern of generous support for his apostolic ministry of the gospel (4:15–17), promising that their sacrificial giving will result in their own needs being met (4:19). The epilogue closes with a doxology (4:20).

The initial "but" (v. 10; NASB, KJV), sometimes deleted by other translations (e.g., NIV, RSV) indicates a return to an earlier topic that deserved fuller treatment before Paul closed the letter.[8] When Paul says "I rejoice greatly in the Lord" (v. 10), in connection with the gift Epaphroditus had brought him from his readers (vv. 10, 18), it is an echo of his introductory thankful, joyful prayer (1:3–4) concerning their mutual "partnership in the gospel" (1:5). In 2:26, 30 he had further alluded to their gifts while discussing the selfless example of Epaphroditus (2:26). Thus, the epilogue of Philippians is a highly personal note of thanks, but one that perfectly balances and completes the central theme that the epistle introduced in the prologue (1:3–11).

"At last you have renewed your concern" (v. 10) is not a rebuke. Rather, it shows that communications had resumed after a period of no contact[9] when there had been "no opportunity to show" their concern for Paul (v. 10). The Greek words translated "concern" and "concerned" (v. 10) are the final references to a proper mindset for believers, a concept found throughout the letter (1:7; 2:2, 5; 3:15, 16; 4:2). Paul hastens to add that his immediate need is not his primary focus. Through the difficult circumstances he had encountered (1:12–26; 2 Cor. 11:23–28) he had "learned the secret of being content in any and every situation" (v. 12). To the Greeks of the day, "being content" meant a serene self-sufficiency. But, for Paul, his sufficiency was centered in and drawn from Christ (v. 13). The Greek word for "to be in need" in 4:12 (NASB humble means) is not the same as that for "am in need" in 4:11. Instead, 4:12 speaks of Paul being humbled by his "circumstances" (v. 11), even as Christ humbled himself in obedience (2:8).

B. For the previous gifts (4:15–20). In his desire to make it clear that he is not minimizing the generosity of the Philippians, Paul looks beyond the more recent gift (vv. 10, 14, 18) to the other occasions on which his readers had given him financial assistance (vv. 15–16). He indicates that such gifts are spiritual investments that pay eternal dividends (v. 17), and that their needs will be met, even as they helped meet his (v. 19).

"Early days" (v. 15) looks back to the beginning of the church at Philippi (Acts 16:12–40). Paul and the Philippian Christians had possessed a vibrant partnership (1:5), which was displayed in the fact that the church had "shared" (v. 15) with Paul when he left Philippi for Thessalonica (v. 16; Acts 17:1–9) and, later, after he left Macedonia (Phil. 4:15; Acts 17:15ff.). They were the only church that had offered such assistance, and they had done it repeatedly (v. 16).

But Paul did not want his readers to misconstrue what he was saying. Instead he desired that which would be "credited" to their eternal "account" (v. 17). The language of finance and investment continues (vv. 15, 17, 18) as Paul again thanks the Philippian believers for their generosity beyond the call of duty. "Received full payment and even more" apparently means that he was "amply supplied" (v. 18) by their latest gift (2:25; 4:10, 14). This recent demonstration of kindness is described as "a fragrant offering, an acceptable sacrifice, pleasing to God" (v. 18). Since similar Old Testament phraseology is used by Paul of the atoning sacrifice of Jesus Christ in Ephesians 5:2, this is extraordinary praise of the Philippians' service on his behalf.

The epilogue (4:10–20) does not simply conclude with thanks (vv. 10, 14–17) and praise (v. 18). It also includes the beautiful promise that "God will meet all their needs" (v. 19). Even as he uses human instruments to meet such needs in many cases (2 Cor. 9:8), it is still ultimately God, the giver of "every good and perfect gift" (James 1:17), who provides for believers' "needs according to his glorious riches in Christ Jesus" (v. 19). Certainly, he should receive "glory forever and ever" (v. 20).

Several practical lessons that emerge from the epilogue (4:10–20) are: (1) the need for

8. Ibid., 196.

9. H. A. Kent, Jr., "Philippians," in the *Expositor's Bible Commentary*, ed. Frank E. Gaebelein, 12 vols. (Grand Rapids: Zondervan, 1978), 11:154.

contentment in Christ, no matter what the circumstances (4:11–13); (2) the realization that the Lord is the believer's source of strength (4:13; 2 Cor. 12:10); (3) the blessing available in supporting needy Christian ministries (4:10, 14–18); and (4) the promise that God will meet the ensuing needs of those who give such sacrificial support (4:19).

VII. Closing Salutation (4:21–23)

A. Greetings (4:21–22). The initial greeting to "all the saints in Christ Jesus" in 1:1 is repeated in 4:21. Perhaps this was done so that the "overseers and deacons" (1:1), to whom Epaphroditus would have delivered the letter (2:28), would be sure to express that wider congregational salutation. The "brothers who are with me" (4:21) are Paul's fellow workers, especially Timothy (1:1; 2:19–23). If the letter was written from Rome, as is likely, "all the saints" (4:22) are those in the church in Rome (Rom. 16:3–15), whom Paul had come to know during his confinement there (Acts 28:30). This understanding also gives the most natural meaning to the Christians "who belong to Caesar's household" (v. 22), although the phrase need not mean anything other than "imperial workers."

B. Benediction (4:23). As he began with grace (1:2), so Paul ends the Philippian epistle. This benediction is exactly the same as the one in Philemon 25, and almost identical with Galatians 6:18. "With your spirit" probably means simply "with you," and the singular "spirit" may refer either to the church collectively or individually.

SELECT BIBLIOGRAPHY

Hawthorne, G. F. *Philippians.* Waco: Word, 1983.

Hendriksen, W. *Epistle to the Philippians.* Grand Rapids: Baker, 1962.

Kent, H. A., Jr. "Philippians." In the *Expositor's Bible Commentary,* edited by Frank E. Gaebelein, 12 vols. Grand Rapids: Zondervan, 1978.

Martin, R. P. *Carmen Christi: Philippians 2:5–11 in Recent Interpretation and in the Setting of Early Christian Worship.* Rev. ed. Grand Rapids: Eerdmans, 1983.

———. *The Epistle of Paul to the Philippians.* Tyndale New Testament Commentaries. Rev. ed. Grand Rapids: Eerdmans, 1987.

———. *Philippians.* New Century Bible Commentary. Grand Rapids: Eerdmans, 1980.

Mounce, R. H. *The Epistle to the Philippians.* Chicago: Moody, 1962.

Scott, E. F., and R. R. Wicks. *The Epistle to the Philippians.* Nashville: Abingdon, 1955.

COLOSSIANS

John McRay

INTRODUCTION

The letter to the church in Colossae was probably written by Paul while he was imprisoned in Rome, in a state of house arrest, with the freedom to have people around him (Acts 28:30–31). That kind of freedom suggests the likelihood of eventual release, which is further indicated in the fact that no letters had been received from his accusers in Judea (Acts 28:21) and no one had arrived evidently to accuse him before the Roman authorities to whom he had appealed (Acts 25:11). Verses in the letter refer to his imprisonment (Col. 4:3, 10, 18). Similar references appear in Philemon (vv. 1, 9, 10, 13, 23) and Ephesians (3:1; 4:1), none of which contain any note of despair or pessimism. In Philippians, in fact, a spirit of optimism appears in his words, and despite his imprisonment (1:7, 13, 14, 17, 22) he expects to continue to live (1:25) and revisit the church in Philippi (2:24). It is only during a later imprisonment that he expects imminent death (2 Tim. 4:6–8).

New evidence found on a Jewish coin indicates a date of A.D. 56 for the accession of Festus as procurator of Judea.[1] Paul appeared before him when he arrived (Acts 25:1), appealed to Caesar, and was taken to Rome. Since he stayed in Rome two whole years (Acts 28:30), we may assign the dates A.D. 56–58 for his Roman imprisonment, and in all probability for the writing of Colossians, Philemon, Ephesians, and Philippians.

A comparison of the persons mentioned in these four prison epistles leads to the conclusion that Philemon and Colossians were written in close proximity of time and probably sent at the same time with Tychicus (Col. 4:8–9; Philem. 10–12). Tychicus was taking Onesimus back to Philemon in Colossae and would logically carry both letters with him. Paul took advantage of the opportunity to send the letters with him. He also apparently sent Ephesians with Tychicus at the same time (Eph. 6:21) since Tychicus would be sailing into Ephesus or Miletus nearby, and could drop off the letter to that church on the way. Colossae was on the opposite end of the Lycus Valley to the east. Problems of a similar nature plagued the entire valley from Ephesus to Colossae and Paul

1. J. Finegan, *Archaeology of the New Testament: The Mediterranean World of the Early Christian Apostles* (Boulder, Colo.: Westview, 1981), 14.

sent a longer, more general letter to the church in Ephesus, the capital city of the whole of Asia Minor. Here stood the Temple of Diana, one of the seven wonders of the ancient world, and from here Paul worked throughout all Asia for about three years (Acts 19:10; 20:31). Paul probably wrote Colossians first, prompted by the need to send Onesimus back and by what Epaphras had told him about the situation there (Col. 1:7). All of the churches in Colossae, Hierapolis, and Laodicea were apparently having problems (Col. 2:1; 4:13–17) due to a heresy that had developed among some Christians. They had become entangled with some kind of Jewish Hellenistic philosophy (Col. 2:8) and were trying to impose certain restrictions upon the church, such as sabbaths, festivals, and new moons (2:16), worship of angels (2:18), aescetic regulations of food and sex (2:20–23), circumcision (2:11–13; 3:11), improper teaching on the intermediary role of Christ and other angelic powers between God and man (1:15–20; 2:8, 20), and a resultant immorality (3:5ff.).

The impact of the heretical teaching must have been profound, since one of the three churches mentioned in the letter (4:13), Laodicea, is singled out for criticism in the Book of Revelation many years later (Rev. 3:14ff.). Laodicea is charged with being wretched, pitiful, poor, blind, and naked. Ephesus fares somewhat better but has left its first love and needs to repent (Rev. 2:1ff.). Hierapolis and Colossae are not included in the seven churches to which Revelation is addressed.

The letter was written to deal with a problem that was troubling churches all over the western portion of Asia Minor, from Ephesus to Colossae. The amalgamation of Jewish and Greek cultures in these churches had generated a Jewish-Hellenistic philosophy (2:8), which was essentially pagan, and which threatened to destroy the uniqueness of Jesus Christ as the Son of God, thereby undermining the very heart of Pauline preaching.

Against the intellectual fallacies promulgated in this philosophy, Paul develops a very high Christology in this letter arguing that Christ fully represents God, not only in the creation of all things (1:15–16), but also in the ongoing operation and reconciliation of the cosmos (1:17–20). The very fullness of God dwells in him (1:19); in him the whole fullness of deity dwells bodily (2:9). The Greek term *fullness,* used in these two verses, was evidently a technical term in this incipient Gnosticism (as it demonstrably was in second-century Gnosticism). It referred to a cluster of spiritual deities whose purely spiritual nature prohibited any direct involvement with human flesh. Christ, on the other hand, in whom the true "fullness" of deity dwells, has reconciled us precisely "in his body of flesh" (1:22).

These spiritual beings, whose existence and power were being proclaimed by the false teachers in Colossae, were, in Paul's view, actually demonic powers (2:8, 15, 20) who had been seeking to turn human beings away from God. Since Christ has conquered these principalities and powers by his death and resurrection (2:15), those who share this experience with him, through faith and burial in baptism (2:12), are no longer under the control of these elemental spirits (2:20).

Therefore, the Colossians should no longer be superstitiously tied to rituals of food and observances of religious holidays, which were a carryover into Colossian Christianity from the former religious profession of Jewish converts (2:16–18). They must also recognize that they are free from extreme ascetic tendencies propagated by some of these austere and rigorous teachers (2:20–23).

The implication of Christ's conquest of these spiritual beings is the same in Colossians as in Ephesians: (1) Christians are now part of a new creation, having died to all involvement with demonic powers, and should seek the things in their lives that are of a heavenly nature (2:20; 3:17; see Eph. 4:17; 5:20). (2) Being a new creature in Christ means that respect, dignity, and equality are to be extended to all—Jews, Gentiles, barbarian, Scythian, males, females, slaves, and free; and family members (husbands, wives, fathers, children, and slaves) should maintain the appropriate relationship to one another, in a spirit of mutual respect (Col. 3:11; 4:11; see Eph. 2:14–16; 5:21–29).

OUTLINE

I. Salutation (1:1–2)
   A. Sender (1:1)
   B. Addressee (1:2a)
   C. Greeting (1:2b)
II. Thanksgiving and Prayer (1:3–14)
   A. Thanksgiving for the Colossians' Love (1:3–8)
   B. Prayer for Knowledge and Godly Conduct (1:9–14)
III. Body (1:15–3:4)
   A. Christ's Work and the Reconciling of the Gentiles (1:15–23)
   B. Paul's Ministry to the Gentiles (1:24–2:5)
   C. Error and Antidote (2:6–19)
   D. New Life in Christ (2:20–3:4)
IV. Ethical Exhortations and Instructions (3:5–4:6)
   A. Put to Death What Is Earthly (3:5–11)
   B. Put on Christian Virtues (3:12–17)
   C. Relations Within Christian Households (3:18–4:1)
   D. Continue in Prayer (4:2–4)
   E. Conduct Toward Outsiders (4:5–6)
V. Closing (4:7–18)
   A. Greeting (4:7–17)
   B. Benediction (4:18)

COMMENTARY

I. Salutation (1:1–2)

A. Sender (1:1). Comparatively recent archaeological discoveries of ancient Egyptian letters, written in Greek during the New Testament period, have clearly revealed the format of a typical letter of that time. This format includes the following components: (1) salutation, consisting of the name of the author, the person or persons to whom the letter is being written, and a greeting; (2) thanksgiving, in which the author expresses thanks for whatever may be on his mind; (3) the body, containing the discussion of the major reason or reasons for which the letter was written; (4) paraenesis or ethical exhortation, containing commands, advice, and instruction; (5) and closing, which includes greetings and a benediction. Paul can now be shown to have followed that basic format with his own occasional personal changes such as adding a doxology, an exhortation to greet one another with a holy kiss, a peace wish, or some other pertinent Christian matter. It helps in interpreting the letter to understand something of its literary genre. It is not written in the format of, for example, Leviticus or Deuteronomy, but is composed as an occasional letter intended for public reading by the church in Colossae and elsewhere (4:16). The letter bears the name of the apostle Paul as its author, joined by his close associate and traveling companion Timothy, whom Paul had enlisted in his journeys from Lystra in Asia Minor (Acts 16:3). Because he has to speak authoritatively in the letter about certain departures from Christian teaching and life, he begins the letter by reminding the Colossians of his commission—it is directly by the will of God. No human being intervened in his initial call on the road to Damascus (Acts 9:22, 26) despite what some critics had tried to say (Gal. 1:12). Paul's authority was constantly challenged because he taught that Gentiles did not need to accept circumcision and keep the law of Moses to be saved as some Jewish Christians were arguing (Acts 15:1). This teaching found its way into some Gentile churches which had small Jewish minorities and caused dissension. In Colossae it had become a problem (Col. 2:10, 16).

B. Addressee (1:2a). The letter is addressed to the church in Colossae. This city was located at the eastern end of the Lycus Valley in the western part of Asia Minor (modern Turkey) in the Roman province of Asia. Colossae was located near Hierapolis (modern Pamukale) and Laodicea (4:13). Both of these ancient sites now lie in ruins, as does Colossae on a mountain high above them. Paul evidently did not establish this church and had never visited it. They apparently heard the gospel from Epaphras (1:6–7), whom Paul describes as "one of you" (4:12).

The phrase *to the holy and faithful brothers* (1:2) could be translated "to the saints and faithful brothers" since the word translated "holy" (Gk. *hagios*) is used as a noun and not an adjective in the salutations in Romans, 1 and 2 Corinthians, Ephesians, and Philippians. Sometimes Paul uses it as a technical term to refer to the minority of Jewish Christians who comprised a part of most of the congregations founded by Paul (Acts 13:42–48; 14:1; 17:4, 12). Here in Colossians Paul seems to contrast the "saints" (1:26) with the Gentiles (1:27) as he clearly does in Ephesians. In that letter he addresses the Gentiles (Eph. 2:11) and says these Gentile Christians have become "fellow citizens with the saints" (Eph. 2:19). In Ephesians 3:8 Paul refers to himself, a Jewish Christian, as "the least of all the saints" who was sent to preach to the Gentiles the unsearchable riches of Christ.

It is likely, therefore, that the first part of the salutation (*to the saints*) refers to the Jewish members of the Colossian church and the second part (*to [the] faithful brethren*) refers to Gentile members. This seems to be even more clearly the case in the salutations of 1 and 2 Corinthians. These Colossian Christians whom Paul addresses are described in the Greek text as "uncircumcised in their flesh" (2:13), a reference to their pre-Christian state as pagan Gentiles.

C. Greeting (1:2b). The greeting is consistent with the salutation. Paul modifies the customary greeting of letters in the Graeco-Roman world to suit his own Christian needs. The letters found in the ancient papyri use the greeting *chairein* ("greetings"; see Acts 15:23; 23:26) which Paul modifies to a closely related word *charis,* meaning "grace." To this Paul adds the typical Jewish greeting "peace" (*šālôm*) and thus greets a church composed of both Jews and Gentiles with a dual greeting. This is customary in most of Paul's letters.

II. Thanksgiving and Prayer (1:3–14)

A. Thanksgiving for the Colossians' love (1:3–8). In a style typical of the letters of his day, Paul now expresses thanksgiving for matters that are of special concern to him. He is particularly thankful for the love which the Colossian brothers have for "all the saints" (1:4). This phrase has caused many to deny the Pauline authorship of Ephesians because it occurs there as well (1:15), and even though Paul had only heard of the situation in Colossae, he had lived in Ephesus for about three years (Acts 20:31). The same phrase occurs also in Philemon (Philem. 5), a letter written to a Christian who apparently lived in Colossae. It would seem more likely that in all three instances Paul is not merely saying he has heard of their faith and love but rather that he has heard of their continuing faith and love "for all the saints" (i.e., Jewish Christians) who live in the midst of what must have been a predominantly Gentile Christian situation. Paul is pleased at their concern for those Jewish Christians whose heritage brought them their salvation (Rom. 11:11, 13, 17–18).

This aspect of Paul's teaching must have been proclaimed to them by Epaphras, their faithful minister and Paul's beloved fellow servant (1:7). Faith, hope, and love (1:4–5; see 1 Cor. 13:13; 1 Thess. 1:3) had been preached to them and it was bearing fruit in evangelism all over the world (Col. 1:6). Paul's world was essentially the Mediterranean and related areas and was defined in his mind in terms of kinds of people rather than geographical territory. He means that the commission to preach to "every creature" (Mark 16:16) or "all nations" (Matt. 28:18) was fulfilled in the preaching to Jews and Gentiles, who together comprise all of humankind (Rom. 1:16; Gal. 3:28; 1 Cor. 12:13). Thus he can say in Colossians 1:23 that the gospel has been preached to "every creature under heaven."

B. Prayer for knowledge and godly conduct (1:9–14). Epaphras had informed Paul and Timothy of the situation in Colossae (1:8–9) and was thus a faithful minister to Paul. Some scholars prefer the reading "your" (in reference to Epaphras) over "our" in the phrase *on our behalf* in 1:7.[2] Since the day that Paul learned of their "love in the Spirit" (v. 8), he has continued to pray for them that they will come to understand what God's will is for them (v. 9) and live a full Christian life doing works that are worthy of the Lord—works that are good (v. 10) rather than the evil ones that characterized their pagan past (v. 21).

Paul prayed that the Colossians might be strengthened by God to endure with patience and joy the hardships that confronted them so that they could share in God's redemptive purposes (vv. 11–14). The personal pronoun *you* in verse 12 contrasts the Gentile background of the Colossians with the inheritance of the Jewish saints. The meaning is that God has qualified the Colossians to share in the inheritance which he has prepared since the promise was made to Abraham (Gen. 12:3) that his seed (the Jews) would become a blessing to all nations (the Gentiles).

By their acceptance of Christ and walking worthily of him (Col. 1:10), the Gentile Colossian Christians will share this inheritance, the guarantee of which was given to them by their being sealed with the promised Holy Spirit (Eph. 1:13–14). The Gentiles also, therefore, become "honorary Jews," "seed of Abraham" or "saints." They are grafted into the Jewish trunk and are nourished by it (Rom. 11:24). God has delivered them, Jew and Gentile, out of Satan's darkness and put them into the light of his own kingdom where there is redemption, the forgiveness of their sins (Col. 1:12–14; cf. vv. 12–13 with Eph. 1:7 where Paul speaks of Jews).

III. Body (1:15–3:4)

A. Christ's work and the reconciling of the Gentiles (1:15–23). We do not know exactly what the nature of Paul's opposition is in Colossae, but its general features can be surmised even if we are only permitted to listen in to Paul's side of the conversation. Some kind of challenge to the true nature and deity of Jesus Christ had been put forward. It may have involved the worship of angels (2:18) or some other beings (1:16; 2:15, 20) who minimize if not negate the preeminence of Christ as Lord of all (1:18–19). It may have been an incipient form of a Christian heresy called Gnosticism by writers in the second century A.D. It was more a philosophy (2:8) than a religion and challenged the intellectual credibility of Christian faith, declaring that salvation was achieved by knowledge rather than faith and that the knowledge (Gk. *gnōsis*) was a gift of God to the predestined few who claimed to have it. God contacted man through divine emanations that reached from heaven to earth. These may be the object of Paul's comments in 1:15–20, where he affirms the divine nature and role of Jesus Christ. We should bear in mind, however, that the fully developed form of Gnosticism in second-century systems, such as those of Valentinius, Basilides, or Saturninus, do not likely represent the situation Paul confronted a century earlier. Instead, we may have in Colossians a reflection of a Jewish-Christian misunderstanding of the role and nature of Christ by those who desired to hold to Jewish monotheism while dealing with the implications of a divine-human redeemer and concocted a very confused philosophy which would make Jesus little more than an angel (see Heb. 1). The mention of new moons and sabbaths along with festivals suggests Jewish influence (Col. 2:16).

Although the majority of exegetes today consider Colossians 1:15–20 to be a pre-Pauline hymn that the author of Colossians reworked for his own special application, the Greek text offers clear evidence of ancient elements of poetry such as chiasmus, inclusio, alliteration, similar endings to phrases, and parallelism. Whether these were supplied by the author in formulating his teaching into a creed, however, or were taken over by him from previously existing poetry is unknown. There is no inherent reason why such exalted teaching could not have been poetically expressed by the author of Colossians, whether Paul or someone else.[3] A few rare words in these verses are not found elsewhere in Paul's writings, but there is no reason why Paul could not have used them,

2. B. Metzger, *A Textual Commentary on the Greek New Testament* (London: United Bible Societies, 1971), 619–20.

3. See Peter O'Brien, *Colossians, Philemon,* Word Biblical Commentary (Waco: Word, 1982), 32ff.

either for stylistic variation or for the specific theological needs of his subject matter.

Two major points seem to be made by Paul in dealing with the Colossian problem: (1) Christ is preeminent in relation to the entire creation (1:15) and (2) he is preeminent in relation to humanity and the church because of the resurrection from the dead (vv. 18–19). This is emphasized in both cases by referring to him as the firstborn—of creation and of the dead. The term always refers in the singular to Christ (the plural is used of other people in Heb. 11:28 and 12:23), and probably echoes Psalm 89:27, where it is used in reference to David. It indicates preeminence or sovereignty of rank as well as temporal priority in most of its uses in the Old and New Testaments. The meaning here is that Christ is unique (see Heb. 1:6) and is preeminent in all creation.

Paul also calls Christ the image (Gk. *eikōn*) of the invisible God. No one has ever seen God (John 1:18; 1 Tim. 1:17) although some have requested the privilege (John 14:8). Christ is the image of God (2 Cor. 4:4) as is man (1 Cor. 11:7). In our transformed state as Christians, as new creatures, we take on the image of God (Col. 3:10). So Christ, unlike the rest of the cosmic beings about which the Colossians were troubled (1:16), is preeminent as the firstborn and the image of God. Paul used the term *all things* (*ta panta*) to include these cosmic powers whom he calls thrones, powers, rulers, and authorities (2:15; Eph. 1:21; 3:10; 6:12). Gentile idolatry is in reality a worship of such demonic powers (1 Cor. 10:20; see Deut. 32:17; Rev. 9:20). These are designations in early Jewish and Christian documents for heavenly powers who reside in the regions between God and man (Test. of Levi 3:8). The principalities and authorities are part of the invisible world and are representatives of a collective idea—evil. They, as all of creation, were brought into existence by God in the sphere of Christ's creative activity (Col. 1:16; see John 1:3; Heb. 1:2). They were not only created in Christ, but through him and for him (Col. 1:16). Their subsequent fall and punishment is assumed in Ephesians 6:12 and repeated or paralleled in 2 Peter 2:4ff. Christ existed before all these elements of creation and indeed they even depend on him for their existence (Col. 1:17). In fact, all the fullness dwells in him (v. 19), an expression paralleling "all things" of verse 16.

Paul then asserts that Christ is the head of the body which is the church (v. 18). The Lord of all creation is also the head of his own body; the firstborn of creation is the firstborn of the dead. He was "declared with power to be the Son of God by his resurrection from the dead" (Rom. 1:4). This means that in "all things" (Col. 1:18) he has the preeminence. He is ruler of the disobedient and the obedient, the heavenly and the earthly, the world and the church, the feet and the body (see Eph. 1:22–23). Though not stated in the Greek text, the word *God* should be supplied as the subject of the verb *was pleased to dwell* (Col. 1:19) because it is required as the subject of "to reconcile" in verse 20 also. Christ is preeminent because God was pleased for the fullness of the cosmos to dwell in him and through him to reconcile all things in the cosmos. The lesson is clear: the Colossian heresy is wrong; all cosmic beings and powers are subject to Christ. He is preeminent in the heavens and on earth.

The reconciliation of which Paul speaks is that of a cosmic nature having to do with "all things" (v. 20). The assumption is that the cosmos has been disrupted since its orderly creation and needs to be reconciled with its Creator. The principalities and powers involved in this disruption have been conquered by Christ through his cross and "put in their place." They are subject to him now along with all creation. His death had cosmic implications (2:15). Peace now reigns because Christ is triumphant. The conflict manifested between him and the demons is over. He is victor (Heb. 2:14ff.).

The reconciliation spoken of in verse 20 with reference to cosmic powers is now discussed with reference to humankind. The Gentile Colossians to whom Paul writes had been alienated from God in their paganism and had been enemies of God in their minds (Rom. 12:2). Paul describes the Gentiles as people whose "thinking became futile and their foolish hearts were darkened" (Rom. 1:21). God "gave them over to a depraved mind" (Rom. 1:28). The "god of this age has blinded the minds of unbelievers, so that they cannot see the light of the gospel" (2 Cor. 4:4). They had been given to evil behavior (Col. 1:21) of the kind described at length in Romans 1:18–32 which had prompted God to "give them up" (Rom. 1:24, 26, 28). But now through Christ's physical death they have been reconciled to God (Col. 1:22), a reference perhaps to the Colossian heretics' denial of any spiritual value to the human body. Sin, they believed, was only of the mind; therefore, the body could be used purely for sensual pleasure (3:5; see 1 Cor. 6:13).

The Colossian Christians will remain in this state of reconciliation if they continue in their faith (Col. 1:23) and remain unmoved in their dedication to the gospel, which, at the time of his writing, Paul declares to have been preached to "every creature under heaven" (v. 23). For Paul this means that all of humankind, Gentiles as well as Jews, have now received the gospel. It is not a geographical reference. Paul's service as an apostle to the Gentiles has been performed (v. 23; see Eph. 3:7ff.). Yet there is much to be done and he prays that God may yet open further opportunities for him (Col. 4:3).

B. Paul's ministry to the Gentiles (1:24–2:5). Although Paul did not think of himself as a "second messiah" as some have affirmed, he does compare his work to that of Christ by asserting that he completes in his flesh "what is still lacking in regard to Christ's afflictions" (v. 24). Just as Christ was "crucified in weakness" (2 Cor. 13:4) so Paul also is suffering in carrying out the commission Christ gave him. This comparison is also made at length in Romans 15, where Paul refers to Christ as a servant (Gk. *diakonos*) to the Jews (15:8) and to himself as a priestly minister (15:16) to the Gentiles. The meaning is that Jesus went only to the Jews (Matt. 15:24) and sent the Twelve only to preach to Jews (Matt. 10:5), but Paul was commissioned at his call to preach to Gentiles now that Christ had been raised from the dead (Acts 26:17). Paul's task is to make known to Gentiles the mystery which God had for ages and generations kept hidden from the world but has now revealed to Jewish Christians (i.e., saints) like Paul (Col. 1:26). To these "saints" God has now chosen to reveal the glorious riches of this mystery (v. 27), that is, to bring in the Gentiles as "heirs together with Israel, members together of one body, and sharers together in the promise in Christ Jesus" (Eph. 3:6). They, as Gentiles, had been "excluded from citizenship in Israel" (Eph. 2:12) but now are "fellow citizens with God's people" (Eph. 2:19).

Paul labored to bring about this inclusion of the Gentiles which Christ had commissioned him to do, so that he could "present everyone perfect (Gk. *teleios*, complete) in Christ" (Col. 1:28), Gentile as well as Jew. Together they comprise the complete body of Christ (Gal. 3:26–28).

His striving to make known the gospel to Gentiles (Col. 1:27) was done with the powerful energy which God had given him (v. 29) and which he expended to the Laodiceans as well as the Colossians (2:1). Why he mentions Laodicea is not clear, but a close association among the churches of Colossae, Laodicea, and Hierapolis evidently existed. Epaphras, who was from Colossae (4:12) and who had apparently founded the church there (1:7), had also served in Laodicea and Hierapolis (4:13). This letter was to be read at Laodicea and the Colossians were to read the letter from Laodicea (4:16). Colossae was about ten miles southeast of Laodicea, which was about six miles south of Hierapolis—all situated near the Lycus River, at the east end of the valley. Paul was laboring for these and "for all the others [Gentiles] who have not seen his face" (2:1). The entire Lycus Valley was probably having trouble with this same "philosophy" (2:8), and Paul sent a similar but longer letter to Ephesus at the western end of this valley.

Paul's efforts on their behalf are for the purpose of their knowing the meaning of God's mystery about Christ (2:2). The Greek manuscripts are not clear about the relation of Christ to God in this sentence but perhaps the meaning is the same as in 1:26–27 and Ephesians 3:4ff. where it is the mystery of Christ. In both contexts the Gentiles are contrasted with the saints, probably referring to the inclusion of the former into the latter. The mystery is not the profound teaching about Christ in Colossians 1:15–20 but the fact that Gentiles are now made fellow members with the saints (Jewish Christians). The Jews are not just lights to the Gentiles (Isa. 42:6), they are now united with them in equal fellowship, and Paul is the primary apostle responsible for that achievement. Those who would impose Jewish practices of any kind upon the Colossian Gentiles, such as sabbaths, new moons, festivals (2:16), and circumcision (2:11, 13) are speaking "fine-sounding arguments" (2:4) and "hollow and deceptive philosophy" (2:8).

C. Error and antidote (2:6–19). In this paragraph Paul deals rather specifically with the content of this heresy in Colossae. Its appeal to the intellectual side of the Colossians is evident in his reference to it as "hollow and deceptive philosophy" (v. 8). False teachers were evidently promulgating a system of thought which embraced heavenly intermediaries other than Christ. Against this, Paul affirms that "in Christ all the fullness of the Deity lives in bodily form" (v. 9). He is the head over all such rule and authority (v. 10) because he disarmed the rulers and authorities (v. 15), the elemental spirits (not basic principles) of the universe (vv. 8, 20), by his death and resurrection (vv. 14–15; see Eph. 1:20–23). He has bound the strong man (Satan) and spoiled his goods (Mark 3:27). It was by his resurrection from the dead and their being united with him in it (Col. 2:12) that the Colossian Christians died to sinful living and "put off the body of flesh." Just as Jews circumcised part of the flesh, separating it from the rest of the body, so the Colossians, when they were immersed with Christ in the waters of baptism (v. 12), buried the sinful, dead body (3:5) and rose from the watery grave with a new purpose in life—to seek the things of Christ (2:20; 3:1). This is a kind of spiritual circumcision. These Gentile Christians who once lived in their trespasses and sins (Eph. 2:1) and the uncircumcision of their hearts as well as their flesh (Col. 2:13) have been circumcised with a nonphysical circumcision in their acceptance of Jesus Christ (v. 11). Thus there is no need to accept physical circumcision as some Jewish Christians were advocating. In Christ neither circumcision nor uncircumcision counts for anything, but a new creation does (Rom. 3:29–30; 4:10–12; Gal. 5:6; 6:15). After all, "a man is not a Jew if he is only one outwardly, nor is circumcision merely outward and physical. No, a man is a Jew if he is one inwardly; and circumcision is circumcision of the heart" (Rom. 2:28–29).

Not only did Christ conquer the cosmic powers by his death and resurrection and thereby become the head of all rule and authority, he also cancelled the "written code, with its regulations, that was against us" (Col. 2:14). The exact meaning of this phrase is not clear; however, in view of the underlying overtones of the letter regarding the Jewish elements of the Colossian heresy and the description of the Christian life in the immediate context in terms of circumcision of the heart, it seems best to think of this written code as the legalistic system of Jewish religion that had become oppressive due to the misuse of the law of Moses. Paul and others were "ministers of a new covenant—not of the letter [RSV written code] but of the Spirit; for the letter [written code] kills, but the Spirit gives life" (2 Cor. 3:6). In the ancient world the Greek term *cheirographon*, "written code" (Col. 2:14), referred to a handwritten certificate of indebtedness that obligated the signer. This note stood between him and the person he owed until it was paid. Paul says here that Christ "took it away" (lit. took it away from the middle).

In a clearer context in Ephesians 2:14–15, Paul spoke of the "dividing wall of hostility" between Jew and Gentile as having been destroyed. This referred to the small wall that surrounded the temple separating the Court of the Jews from that of the Gentiles. It was a "wall of hostility" with signs along it, according to the first-century Jewish historian, Josephus, "prohibiting the entrance of a foreigner [Gentile] under threat of the penalty of death" (*Antiquities* 15.417; *War* 5.193; 6.125). Two fragmentary examples of these have been found and published. In Ephesians 2:15 Paul wrote that Christ also abolished at the same time "the law with its commandments and regulations." This he did through the cross thereby making peace between Jew and Gentile and bringing the hostility to an end (Eph. 2:15–17).

Similarly, in Colossians 2:14 Paul said that Christ took the written code away that was contrary to us, nailing it to the cross. The law had become a dividing wedge between Jew and Gentile through human weakness (Rom. 8:3). Rather than being a guardian to bring the Jews to Christ (Gal. 3:24–25) it had become a barrier to keep Gentiles out. The Jews had not been "a light for the Gentiles" (Isa. 42:6). But through Christ's death, Jewish Christians no longer serve "in the old way of the written code" (Rom. 7:6) but in the "new way of the Spirit." Such a scenario best explains Colossians 2:14.

Furthermore, the subtle use of pronouns in Colossians 2:13–15 should not be lost. In verse 13 *you* Gentiles who were dead in your trespasses and the uncircumcision of your flesh, he made alive together (i.e., Jew and Gentile) with Christ, having forgiven *us* (Jew and Gentile) all *our* trespasses. He cancelled the written code, with its regulations (the law), that was against us and that stood opposed to us (the uniting of Jews and Gentiles); he took it away nailing it to the cross (vv. 14–15) and triumphed over the evil powers in the heavens that were responsible for such a misuse of the law in creating hostility between Jews and the rest of mankind. This subtle nuance of pronoun use is especially evident in Ephesians and to some extent in Galatians. The almost subconscious nature of it is what one would expect from such an ardent rabbi who had become the apostle to the Gentiles.

Next Paul encouraged the Christians of Colossae to live worthily of their conversion and let no one disqualify them from receiving the prize for running the race (vv. 16–20). This may be done by allowing those who hold the heretical philosophy at Colossae to impose upon Gentile Christians the "regulations" (v. 14) of Jewish life such as "a religious festival, a New Moon celebration or a Sabbath day" (v. 16; Deut. 5:12; Num. 10:10; 28:11–15). One need not look beyond some sort of Jewish influence for these impositions which had been combined with Hellenistic mythology and involved the worship of the elements of the universe (Gk. *stoichea;* Col. 2:8, 20). By Paul's time it was commonly believed in some Jewish circles that each of the elements had its own angel to rule over it (Jub. 2:2). Some documents refer to these as spirits which controlled the natural elements (1 Enoch 43:1–2; 80:6; 2 Enoch 4:1–2). The New Testament refers to "the angel who has power over fire" (Rev. 14:17), "the angel of water" (Rev. 16:5) and the angels who "hold back the four winds" (Rev. 7:1). The New Testament also asserts angelic mediation in the giving of the law of Moses itself (Acts 7:53; Gal. 3:19; Heb. 2:2). Those who impose circumcision upon Gentile Christians are turning back to those weak and miserable principles (i.e., *stoicheia*, "elements," Gal. 4:9) to which they were once enslaved (Gal. 4:3, 10). Some at Colossae seem to have been delighting in worship of angels (Col. 2:18) and have thus lost connection with Christ (v. 19) because he is the head of all such principalities, powers, elements, and whatever else is in the cosmos. He is head of all things.

The opponents at Colossae also advocated humility in connection with worship of angels (v. 18). This probably refers to a type of ascetic practice involving fasting and other forms of self-denial or mortification of the body (v. 21), which in the ancient world were often a prelude to receiving visions (v. 18; see the Shepherd of Hermas *Vision* 3.10.6). The way to avoid the pitfall of such erroneous worship and false humility is to remain in close relationship with Christ (Col. 2:19).

The argument that these regulations and festivals in verse 16 are just a "shadow" of the "reality . . . in Christ" (v. 17) is not only Platonic but Jewish as well. It is used by the author of Hebrews to show that the priestly sacrificial system of Israel was only a "copy and shadow" (Heb. 8:5) of the heavenly sanctuary, that is, the reality in heaven. The earthly tabernacle and temple worship was only a copy of the true one in heaven (Heb. 9:24) and the law of Moses is "only a shadow of the good things that are coming—not the realities themselves" (Heb. 10:1).

D. New life in Christ (2:20–3:4). The Colossians declared themselves dead to the influences of the elemental spirits and their intervention in the affairs of man through worship of the elements of the universe (Col. 2:20). Idolatry and the worship of heavenly bodies were laid aside when they died with Christ and were buried with him by baptism (2:12). They have put off the old pagan body through conversion to Christ and have experienced a circumcision not made with hands (2:11). It is not, therefore, consistent with such a conversion experience for them to be brought back into their sphere of control and live by their rules (v. 20) which involve certain ascetic practices: "Do not handle! Do not taste! Do not touch!" (v. 21). We have no way of knowing whether these are sexual, dietary, lustral, or social in nature; nor whether they are expressly Jewish, Hellenistic, or oriental. What is clear is that they originate in human commands and teaching and have no authority from God (v. 22). They constitute superficial piety, have no value in the restraint of sensual indulgence, and only result in harsh treatment of the body and false pride rather than in true humility. This goes beyond any notion of self-denial taught by Jesus (Luke 9:23). It is not uncommon in ancient as well as modern religions to find the erroneous principle that mortification of the body results in the purification of the soul.

If the Colossians have truly died with Christ to their old pagan ways (2:12, 20; 3:3), they have been born again as new creatures by being raised with him from their spiritual death and made alive together with him (3:1; 13; see Rom. 6:4–5). Since their minds are the primary focus of conversion (Rom. 12:2; 2 Cor. 4:4) they should concentrate on things pertaining to the kingdom of God (Col. 3:2). The kingdom belongs to the "pure in heart" (Matt. 5:8); only they will see God.

IV. Ethical Exhortations and Instructions (3:5–4:6)

A. Put to death what is earthly (3:5–11). Exhortations are customary in first-century letters, immediately following the body of the letter. At this point it is appropriate to give advice and instruction that will be helpful to the recipients of the letter. These are based on the arguments set forth by the body of the letter. Paul continues without formal break, blending his exhortations with the argumentation. The fact that he exhorts the Colossians to put to death whatever belongs to their earthly nature (3:5) clearly indicates that they have not been living consistently with the principle of a spiritual death and resurrection in their conversion as he has just argued.

Some of the kinds of sin involved in our "earthly nature" are listed by Paul, and their sexual bent (3:5) may indicate something more of the nature of the Colossian philosophy (2:8). The list is expanded, however, in 3:8ff. to include nonsexual sins as well. It was common in the Gentile world of Paul's day for religious or philosophical groups such as the Stoics to make lists of virtues and vices. These emphasize a state of mind and conduct. They do not necessarily mean that every member at Colossae, or elsewhere, was guilty of every one of these vices. These sins were indicative of an "old way of life" (3:7), characteristic of both Gentiles and Jews (Eph. 2:1, 5). But those who have "taken off [their] old self" and "have put on the new self" (Col. 3:9–10) no longer live in such sin whether they are "Greek or Jew, circumcised or uncircumcised, barbarian, Scythian, slave or free" because Christ has changed all that and is in them all (3:11).

It may only be coincidental that Paul lists five vices in 3:5 and five more in 3:8 and then five virtues in 3:12. On the other hand, he may be reacting to lists of virtues and vices drawn up by the Colossian heretics (not at all corresponding to his own). If there is Persian influence on this pre-Gnostic heresy, as some affirm, such lists of five would be understandable since they characterized Iranian thought. But this remains speculative. For whatever reasons, Paul typically makes such lists frequently and of varying lengths (see, e.g., Rom. 1:29–32; 1 Cor. 5:9–11; 6:9–10; Gal. 5:19–23; Phil. 4:8; 1 Tim. 3:1–13; Titus 1:5–9; cf. 1 Pet. 4:3).

The first group in Colossians 3:5 concerns primarily sexually related sins. The last vice of this group is covetousness or greed "which is idolatry." The word *which* is in the feminine gender in Greek and refers only to the feminine word *greed,* rather than all five of the vices. Reference to all five vices would have required a neuter gender for "which." Since greed is an insatiable desire to acquire material things, it is in reality the worship of the creation rather than the Creator (Rom. 1:25), of the earthly things rather than heavenly things (Col. 3:1–2). As O'Brien has pointed out, "Perhaps it is the more dangerous because it may assume so many respectable forms."[4] It is coupled with sexual immorality in Ephesians 5:3. Being a major cause of the exploitation of religion by false teachers (2 Pet. 2:3), a man of God, such as Paul, was always aware of its dangers (Acts 20:33; 1 Cor. 9:8–15). Those who commit these kinds of sins bring the wrath of God upon themselves (Col. 3:6).

In their former pagan life-style, the Colossians used to practice this kind of sin (v. 7) but now they are commanded to separate themselves from such conduct including even such things as improper attitudes and speech (v. 8). They have become new people in Christ, regardless of their ethnic and social status in life (v. 11) and should live in honest relations with one another.

B. Put on Christian virtues (3:12–17). Continuing his vivid use of metaphors, Paul now states that having "put off" their old self (v. 9) with its evil practices they should "put on" a new self (v. 10) which involves "putting on" virtues characterized by the five he now mentions (v. 12). Since these Gentile Christians have now joined the Jewish Christians as God's chosen people (v. 12; 1 Pet. 2:9) they should live accordingly. Paul's admonition is even more graphic as he continues the metaphor in Colossians 3:14. Over all these "garments" of compassion, kindness, humility, gentleness, and patience (v. 12) they should "put on" the cloak of love which binds all of the others together (v. 14).

The teaching of Jesus should rule in the hearts of Christian brothers, producing peace and thanksgiving. If it dwells in their hearts they will be "one body" (v. 15) and social or ethnic distinctions (v. 11) will not destroy the body of Christ. The Colossian heresy (2:8) was evidently causing great division in that church. If Christ's word dwelled in them as it should, they would be teaching and admonishing each other in their worship (3:16) and in their daily living (v. 17). The kind of music used in the early church included psalms (the Old Testament psalms), hymns (religious songs, Matt. 26:30), and spiritual songs (evidently songs sung under the impulse of the Holy Spirit, perhaps at times even in an unknown tongue, 1 Cor. 14:13–15). The scenario Paul is presenting is one of peace and happiness. Therefore, singing praise to God is the appropriate and expected response by those who have truly become "new people."

C. Relations within Christian households (3:18–4:1). At this point Paul introduces three important relationships that exist in Christian households: (1) husbands and wives, (2) parents and children, and (3) slaves and masters. Whether this sequential listing of household relations was original with Paul or adopted from Hellenistic or Hellenistic-Jewish codes is not agreed upon by scholars but is comparatively inconsequential. In any case Paul arranges his discussion so as to list in each instance the subordinate figure first (wife, child, slave, 3:18, 20, 22) with admonitions to submit to or obey their counterparts (husband, parent, master). The identical pattern appears in Ephesians with identical terminology (see Eph. 5:22; 6:1, 5). In both letters Paul immediately follows each statement of submission with a reminder of the responsibility of the second member of each pair.

In each case, he mentions the subordinate member of the relationship and then addresses the responsibility of his or her counterpart. Significantly, Paul never reverses these. Paul never says "husbands be submissive to your wives, parents obey your children, or masters obey your slaves." This kind of "reciprocity" was never intended in Ephesians 5:21, nor is it implied in Colossians. The point being made is that authority exists and should be respected. Significantly, when discussing the parent-child relationship, the father is used, not the mother, to specify the issue of authority (Eph. 6:4; Col. 3:21). In Paul's society it could not have been otherwise. The question of authoritative relationships was clear,

4. Ibid., 184.

and had to be recognized even by Christian brothers and sisters.

Society's standards were altered, not abrogated, by the church. "All who are under the yoke of slavery should consider their masters worthy of full respect . . . Those who have believing masters are not to show less respect for them because they are brothers" (1 Tim. 6:1–2). This was true even if the master was harsh (1 Pet. 2:18). Even in the church masters are never told to be submissive to their slaves. This aspect of the relationship is not reciprocal, nor is it for husbands and wives or parents and children. Relationships did not change just because of conversion. If one was converted while a slave he did not become free just because his master was a Christian (1 Cor. 7:21–22; 1 Tim. 6:2; 1 Pet. 2:18). In Corinth Paul advised that if one was converted while married, he or she did not become free of that bond (1 Cor. 7:27) and should not seek a divorce. If single, one should not try to marry (1 Cor. 7:27). This was due to a special set of circumstances there which are not revealed in the letter (1 Cor. 7:26, 29–31).

To what extent Paul's teaching is to be considered transcultural and eternal is debatable. His view of Christian slave owners (Philem. 14–16) is commonly regarded as an accommodation to the cultural situation of the time, but his teaching on the obedience of children to parents knows of no such limitation. What about the relationship of husband and wife? The question of whether husbands are to be submissive to wives as well as wives to husbands has to be answered, just as the issue of slaves and masters, from the twin perspective of the writings of Paul in context and the effect of cultural changes on the issue in different contexts. What Paul taught on the duty of Christian slaves to their masters is clear—obedience. What he might have said about it today is not at all clear. And what he said about the relation of wives to their husbands in that cultural context is also clear—they are to be in submission. What this might mean in a different cultural context is another matter.

Furthermore, there is no significant difference in the words *submit* and *obey* (Col. 3:18, 20, 22). The parallel meaning of the words and their intended implication for the first-century church are clear in 1 Peter 3:5, where it is stated that "holy women of the past who . . . were submissive (*hypotassō*) to their own husbands, like Sarah, who obeyed (*hypakouō*) Abraham and called him her master (*kurios*)." (See also 1 Pet. 3:1 where "submit" is joined with a different word for obedience, *apeitheō*.) The word *submit* (*hypotassō*) clearly means obey in Romans 8:7, as it does in Luke 2:51 where Jesus returned to Nazareth with his parents and was "obedient to them" (RSV, NIV). Paul uses parallel terms in Titus 3:1 in admonishing people "to be subject (*hypotassō*) to rulers and authorities, to be obedient (*peitharcheō*)." The generic charge to be submissive is immediately followed by the specific admonition to obedience. The object of obedience is not stated. It is a disposition of Christians, not different in kind from that of submissiveness. Another indication of the similarity of meaning in the words *submission* and *obedience* is seen in their use with "fear" or "respect" (*phobos*). In Ephesians 5 Paul admonishes wives to submit (v. 22) to their husbands and to respect (*phobeomai*, v. 33) them. Slaves are also told to "submit yourselves to your masters with all respect" (1 Pet. 2:18). Also, Colossians 3:22 instructs slaves to "obey (*hypakouō*) your earthly masters . . . with reverence (*phobeomai*) for the Lord."

Equally important is the reciprocal need for husbands, parents (especially fathers), and slave owners to be loving, right, and fair in their dealings with their counterparts (3:19, 21; 4:1). This would be especially needful in cases where the one head of the household was all of these—husband, father, and master of the household slaves. The more extensive discussion of master-slave relationships in Colossians may reflect a greater problem in that area than existed with the other two relationships discussed. This could have been prompted in part by the case of the slave Onesimus, whom Paul sent back to Colossae with Tychicus to resume his place as slave in the house of Philemon (4:7–9; see Philem.). Peter also dealt with the subject in his letter to churches in this same area of Asia Minor (1 Pet. 1:1; 2:18ff.). Both Ephesians and 1 Timothy (which was written to Ephesus apparently; 1 Tim. 1:3) contain instruction on treatment of slaves (Eph. 6:5–9; 1 Tim. 6:1–2). Ephesus was at the western end of the Lycus Valley; Colossae was at the eastern end. However, much more space is given proportionately to the husband-wife relationship than to the others in Ephesians 5:22–33, where the husband-wife relationship is treated more as an ecclesiological concern than a sociological one.

When reading Paul's letters one should keep clearly in mind that the churches to whom he writes were not functioning in the same way that churches do today. They did not own property. There were no church buildings, only occasional rentals of public buildings. Most churches met in the homes of the members.

Paul speaks of the church in Rome in this way: "Greet also the church that meets at their house" (Rom. 16:5); "Greet those in the household of Narcissus who are in the Lord" (v. 11); "Greet Philologus, Julia, . . . and all the saints with them" (v. 15). Evidently early Christians ate a common meal together (a "love feast"; Jude 12) in their homes at which time sociological concerns surfaced which were un-Christian, such as gluttony and drunkenness (1 Cor. 11:20–22), making it impossible to distinguish the Lord's Supper from their other meal (vv. 20–21). This kind of problem would have been compounded by the amalgamation of Jews, with their kosher meals (Acts 11:3), Gentiles, with their hesitancy to eat meat offered to idols (1 Cor. 8:1–13), slaves, who felt disrespectful to their masters (1 Tim. 6:2), women, wives included, who felt their freedom in Christ had made them one with their husbands so that they did not need to wear a veil (1 Cor. 11:5; Gal. 3:28), and children, who may have been dishonoring their parents (Eph. 6:1–3). With such disparate groups trying to meet in each other's homes, very serious problems were bound to occur. The Christian message that in Christ every human being is of equal importance and shares in all of God's gifts (1 Cor. 12:13), which was so central to Paul's preaching, caused immediate misunderstandings which had to be worked out. These kinds of problems prompted most of Paul's writings (see 1 Cor. 7:1). We need not look for any particular Hellenistic or Jewish background of house rules for an explanation of why these social relationships are dealt with by Paul in these very heterogeneous churches. The problems he dealt with were those that would emerge first and foremost in each new congregation. Some sort of systematic thought and presentation was needed to deal with these recurring issues, and we see this in the several lists in the New Testament dealing with submission to appropriate sociological order (Rom. 13:1–7; Eph. 5:21–6:9; Col. 3:18–4:1; 1 Tim. 2:8–15; 6:1–10; Titus 2:1–10; 3:1ff.; 1 Pet. 2:13–3:9).

Paul's teaching in these verses in Colossians seems to be that submission to appropriate authority is no problem where that authority figure is Christ-like. No one who gazes at the cross has any problem in submitting to the lordship of Jesus Christ. And no slave of Paul's day would have trouble acknowledging his master's authority when that master treated him fairly and justly, knowing that he, too, has a Master in heaven (Col. 4:1). No wife should have a problem accepting her husband as head of the house when that husband loves her as Christ loved the church, giving himself up for her (Col. 3:19; Eph. 5:25).

D. Continue in prayer (4:2–4). Paul now asks for their continuing prayers for him while he is in prison. He is there because he has proclaimed the "mystery of Christ" (v. 3). This mystery is defined as the inclusion of Gentiles into the kingdom with the status of equal members. "This mystery is that through the gospel the Gentiles are heirs together with Israel, members together of one body, and sharers together in the promise of Christ Jesus" (Eph. 3:6). Because of his preaching to Gentiles, Paul was often beaten, falsely accused of breaking Roman law, and imprisoned. While in prison he wrote Ephesians, Philippians, Colossians, and Philemon, referring in all of them to his imprisonment (Eph. 3:1; 4:1; Phil. 1:7, 13, 14, 17, 22; Col. 4:3, 10, 18; Philem. 1, 9, 10, 13, 23). The several times Paul had been imprisoned (2 Cor. 11:23) were all occasioned by the uproars created through his preaching. Paul's problems were often caused by Jews who rejected his teaching about the full acceptance of Gentiles into the church (Acts 14:2, 19; 17:5, 13; 18:5–6).

Paul asks for the Colossians to pray that "God may open a door for our message" so that he can continue to preach the "mystery of Christ" (v. 3). Even though he had now preached widely enough for "every creature under heaven" (i.e., Jew, Gentile, male, female, slave, free, etc.; see Rom. 15:19–20) to hear it he must continue to reach as many of these as possible with the message of Christ. Paul can only mean that the Gentiles have been fully accepted, without reservation or major restriction (Acts 15:19), by the Jewish church (Rom. 15:16). The skeleton is there; the body must now be fleshed out, so to speak (Eph. 4:15–16), with the conversion of as many Gentiles as possible (Rom. 11:25). He will continue, of course, in each new town to go first to the Jews and upon their rejection to preach to Gentiles (Rom. 1:16). The conversion of a "full number" of Gentiles (Rom. 11:25) will someday be instrumental in the conversion of a "full number" of Jews (Rom. 11:12, 26). Paul would not rest until he had exhausted his opportunities.

E. Conduct toward outsiders (4:5–6). The Colossians should also make the best of their opportunities (v. 5), which means they should give careful attention to their conduct in the presence of non-Christians. Their speech should be carefully controlled and used with great wisdom and love (v. 6). Paul speaks more fully of this in Ephesians 4:25, 29: "speak truthfully to [your] neighbor . . . do not let any unwholesome talk come out of your mouths, but only what is helpful for building others up according to their needs, that it may benefit those who listen." A Christian wife may even win her unbelieving husband to Christ by "the purity and reverence of [her] life" (1 Pet. 3:2). It is important for the Christian to "know how to answer everyone" (Col. 4:6). Peter writes: "Always be prepared to give an answer to everyone who asks you to give the reason for the hope that you have" (1 Pet. 3:15).

V. Closing (4:7–18)

A. Greeting (4:7–17). At this point in ancient letter writing it was customary to include greetings both from the senders and to the recipients. It appears evident in these verses in Colossians that Paul's fellow workers included both Jews and Gentiles (4:11). Tychicus is being sent to them and is probably the bearer of the letter as well as the one to Ephesus (Eph. 6:21–22). He is apparently taking the converted slave Onesimus (Col. 4:9) back to his master in Colossae (see Philem. 10). Tychicus will be passing through Ephesus on the way and probably carries all three letters (Ephesians, Colossians, and Philemon) with him. He may also be carrying the letter to Laodicea (v. 16). He himself was from this area and is called an Asian in Acts 20:4, the reference being to Asia Minor, which today is western Turkey. He is to make known Paul's current situation to those in Asia.

Onesimus is referred to as "one of you" (Col. 4:9), meaning he is a member of the church in Colossae. He is undoubtedly the same Onesimus about whom the letter to Philemon was written. This likelihood is seen in the comparatively large number of names that appear in both letters. He was a slave of Philemon who either left his master after his conversion to Christianity or was converted by Paul in Rome in circumstances not revealed in either letter. Paul considered him to be his child in the faith (Philem. 10), as he did Timothy (1 Tim. 1:2; 2 Tim. 1:2) and Titus (1:4). As a Christian, Onesimus had no right to walk away from his social responsibility, regardless of how distasteful it may have been (1 Tim. 6:1–2).

Aristarchus (Col. 4:10), in prison with Paul, was from the Macedonian city of Thessalonica (Acts 20:4). He had been with Paul in Ephesus and had been dragged into the theater there during an uprising against Paul (Acts 19:29). He accompanied Paul to Jerusalem carrying the contribution from the Gentile churches to the Jewish Christian saints in Jerusalem. Two years later he traveled with Paul to Rome (Acts 27:2), where he shared Paul's imprisonment at the time Colossians was written. We do not know the circumstances of his arrest and imprisonment. He may have voluntarily accepted imprisonment to serve Paul.

Mark, referred to in Colossians 4:10 as also sending greetings, was the cousin of Barnabas. This is undoubtedly John Mark (Acts 15:37), who lived in Jerusalem (Acts 12:12, 25) and who traveled with Paul and Barnabas on their first journey (Acts 13:4). He turned back before the journey was finished (Acts 13:13) and Paul refused to take him on the second one (Acts 15:37ff.), so he and Barnabas went to Cyprus. Evidently, by the time this letter was written, Mark had redeemed himself in the eyes of Paul, and when Paul was imprisoned again under other circumstances, he asked Timothy to bring Mark to him because "he is helpful to me in my ministry" (2 Tim. 4:11). Mark also traveled with Simon Peter (1 Pet. 5:13), translated for him what he preached (according to a second-century author named Papias), and subsequently wrote the Gospel of Mark (Eusebius *Ecclesiastical History* 3.39.14–15).

It is evident that Mark is with Paul at the time of the writing of this letter because Paul sends greetings from him to the church (Col. 4:10). Whether the instructions Colossae had received about Mark came from Paul in earlier correspondence, or from some other source such as Peter or Barnabas, is not stated (v. 10). Whether Mark ever made it to Colossae is unknown, but if he did, Paul instructed the church to receive him with Paul's full endorsement. Paul probably felt this was necessary because of Mark's former defection on Paul's first journey, a fact that undoubtedly was known among the churches in Asia.

Barnabas was a loyal traveling companion of Paul on his journeys (Acts 13:2; 15:36). Also, Barnabas had introduced him to the Christians in Jerusalem after Paul's conversion and had vouched for him at a time when every Christian in the land was afraid of him (Acts 9:26–27). Barnabas also went to Tarsus looking for Paul after Antioch experienced the conversion of large numbers of Gentiles (Acts 11:22–26). Although Barnabas's real name was Joseph, he was evidently so well loved among the apostles for his ability to exhort that they dubbed him Barnabas, which meant "son of encouragement" (Acts 4:36). He was a Levite from the island of Cyprus, off the coast of Israel (Acts 4:36) and thus was of priestly descent (Num. 2:50).

Nothing is known of the man named Jesus Justus (Col. 4:11). The name *Jesus* was not uncommon at the time (Acts 13:6) being popular among Jews because it is the Greek form of the Hebrew name *Joshua*, the hero of the conquest and successor to Moses. Justus was also a common name among Jews and proselytes (Acts 1:23; 18:7). Paul refers to the three men, Aristarchus, Mark, and Jesus Justus, as "the only Jews among my fellow workers" (Col. 4:11). The expression is literally "those of the circumcision." It is used of Jews in general in Acts 10:45 and Romans 4:12. And it has a special meaning of "Jewish or circumcision party" in Acts 11:2; Galatians 2:12; and Titus 1:10, referring to those Jewish Christians who insisted on Gentiles being circumcised according to the custom taught by Moses in order to be saved, even after they became Christians (Acts 15:2). Here in Colossians there is no reason to think that Paul is referring to the latter. These three men were the only non-Gentiles among those that Paul mentions in the closing of the letter. They would be a part of those "saints" who have been loved by the Gentile church in Colossae (1:4). In all of Paul's churches there was undoubtedly a small minority of Jewish converts who would have been rejected by their own Jewish people and neglected by the Gentile converts unless special attention was paid to them by Paul. A similar thing happened in reverse in the early days of the church in Jerusalem when it consisted predominantly of mainline Palestinian Jews (Hebraists) who neglected the widows of the Greek-cultured Diaspora Jews (Hellenists). Special arrangements were made by the apostles for this minority to be cared for by seven men who were themselves Hellenists and were selected by the people (Acts 6:1–6).

This reference to the three Jewish men among Paul's companions assumes that the others were not Jewish. Thus Luke (Col. 4:14), the author of the Gospel of Luke and the Book of Acts, was probably not a Jew. Epaphras, who founded the church at Colossae (1:7), sent greetings (see Philem. 23). He was "one of them" (Col. 4:12) and so evidently had been a part of the church there, working not only in Colossae, but also in Laodicea and Hierapolis, which were no more than twelve miles away (v. 12). That the churches had close associations is evident in the fact that Paul asks the Colossians to give his greetings to Laodicea (v. 15) and to let them read this letter (v. 16). The Colossians should also read the letter Paul sent to Laodicea (it may be assumed that the letter to Laodicea was written by Paul, though this is not explicitly stated). The reciprocity of the exchange seems to imply this, and it is unlikely that he would be charging them to read someone else's letter. One is tempted to think that this letter to Laodicea is the Ephesian letter (as did Marcion, a second-century Christian heretic). However, if the address *in Ephesus* belongs in the text of Ephesians 1:1, which it probably does, it could not be considered the Laodicean letter.

Luke and Demas are mentioned as sending greetings (v. 14). Luke is here called a physician, and as mentioned above, is likely a Gentile Christian. He may have served Paul in this capacity during his imprisonment. Both Luke and Demas are mentioned in Philemon (v. 24) and 2 Timothy (4:10–11), where "only Luke" is with Paul; Demas had forsaken him "because he loved this world" (2 Tim. 4:10) and had gone to Thessalonica at a time when Paul needed him.

The reference to Nympha (Col. 4:15) is obscure because we cannot tell from the Greek name whether the person is male or female, and the possessive pronoun in the following phrase *church in her house* is different in various Greek manuscripts of the New Testament. Many translators (NIV, RSV, NEB, JB; cf. KJV) take it as feminine in both instances. Lydia seems to have had Christians meeting in her house in Philippi (Acts 16:15, 40). Also, several house churches are mentioned in Romans 16; 1 Corinthians 16:19; and Philemon 2.

Archippus (Col. 4:17) is a common name of the time. He is mentioned in Philemon 2, which implies that he is the son of Philemon and Apphia. The ministry (*diakonia*) he is to fulfill is not necessarily that of serving as a deacon. The Greek word refers to the performing of a service, not the occupying of an office, unless its specialized use is clearly indicated in the context. Another ambiguous use of this term occurs in Romans 16:1 where it is used of Phoebe in Cenchrea. The ministry of Archippus is not revealed. Some have imagined, on the basis of Philemon 2, that his appointed task was to persuade Philemon to receive Onesimus with kindness. Others have surmised that Archippus was the actual owner of Onesimus and that Philemon was being encouraged by Paul's letter to him to persuade Archippus to be kind to Onesimus. It is best to leave the enigma unresolved since it is not capable of resolution with the information we have.

B. Benediction (4:18). Paul's personal greeting is brief, as is his benediction. His statement that he himself is writing this greeting is clear evidence that he has not written the entire letter. Paul used secretaries such as Tertius (Rom. 16:22) to write while he dictated. Evidence of this is seen in several of his letters where he refers to himself as attaching a greeting in his own hand (1 Cor. 16:21; Philem. 19), with large letters (Gal. 6:11), and mentions that it is the mark by which his letter may be identified (2 Thess. 3:17). Some scholars have suggested that it may have been an injury or deformity in Paul's hands that forced him to write sparingly and in large letters. Could this have been his "thorn in the flesh" (2 Cor. 11:7)? Or was it a problem with his eyesight? He said to the Galatians that it was through a bodily ailment, a weakness of the flesh (Gal. 4:13), that he first preached the gospel to them. Then two verses later, in Galatians 4:15, he said they would have plucked out their eyes and given them to him. Whatever the case, perhaps Paul did not write all of his letters. They may have been dictated, with perhaps some creative latitude given to the secretary in the matter of style and vocabulary, and then proofread by Paul and signed, just as is common today in professional correspondence.

SELECT BIBLIOGRAPHY

Bruce, F. F. *The Epistles to the Colossians, to Philemon, and to the Ephesians.* Grand Rapids: Eerdmans, 1984.

Martin, R. P. *Colossians and Philemon.* New Century Bible Commentary. Grand Rapids: Eerdmans, 1981.

Meyer, H. A. W. *Critical and Exegetical Handbook to the Epistles to the Philippians and Colossians and to Philemon.* Winona Lake, Ind.: Alpha, 1979.

Moule, C. F. D. *The Epistles of Paul the Apostle to the Colossians and Philemon.* Cambridge: Cambridge University Press, 1977.

O'Brien, P. *Colossians, Philemon.* Word Biblical Commentary, Waco: Word, 1982.

1–2 THESSALONIANS

David Ewert

INTRODUCTION

The city of Thessalonica (modern Salonica), named by Cassander after his wife, lay in the Roman senatorial province of Macedonia. South of Macedonia was the province of Achaia. The Via Egnatia, which ran from the Adriatic coast to the east, passed through Thessalonica. Thessalonica was situated at the head of the Thermaic Gulf, and because of trade by land and sea it became the largest and most important city of Macedonia. In 146 B.C. Thessalonica became the seat of the Roman provincial administration.

Because the city had sided with Antony and Octavian, who emerged victorious after the internal strife that followed Julius Caesar's assassination, it was given a measure of self-rule in 42 B.C., and consequently had its own magistrates (called "politarchs" in Acts 17:6). As a brisk trading center Thessalonica had attracted a great many Jews. Their synagogue became the entering wedge for the gospel, but it also became the source of fierce opposition to the apostles and to the church they established.

Early in A.D. 50, Paul, Silas, and Timothy (and possibly Luke) entered Philippi after receiving a divine call at Troas to bring the gospel to the European mainland. Here a businesswoman, Lydia, embraced the Christian faith, and her house became a base for the mission work of the apostles. In the course of their activities Paul delivered a slave girl from a spirit of divination. This enraged those who had exploited the girl and they brought false charges against Paul and Silas. As a result the two missionaries were severely beaten and imprisoned. Their miraculous release led to the conversion of the jailer and his household. The city authorities were alarmed when they discovered that they had mistreated Roman citizens without a trial, and they begged Paul and Silas to leave the city.

Leaving the infant church behind, the apostles took the Via Egnatia and, passing through Amphipolis and Apollonia, arrived in Thessalonica. Here Paul, as was his custom, participated in the services of the Jewish synagogue and argued from the Scriptures that Jesus was the Messiah (Acts 17:2, 3). Several Jewish listeners were persuaded, and one of them, Jason, opened his house to the missionaries. Other converts came from the Gentile God-fearers who attended the synagogue, including the wives of some leading citizens.

These converts from the synagogue formed the nucleus of the Thessalonian church, but an ever greater number of rank-and-file citizens "turned to God from idols to serve the living and true God" (1 Thess. 1:9).

After a stay of several weeks the preaching ministry of the apostles was rudely interrupted by a demonstration staged by a mob (Acts 17:5). Not able to apprehend the missionaries, they dragged Jason, Paul's host, together with his companions, before the politarchs and accused them of harboring seditious elements who proclaimed a rival king, Jesus (Acts 17:6–7).

The politarchs, fortunately, kept their heads and contented themselves with making Jason and the others post bond (Acts 17:9). Paul then had no option but to leave. Together with Silas he was spirited away by night and came to Beroea, which lay south of the Via Egnatia. Here again the apostles visited the synagogue and proclaimed the gospel. Again there were those, both Jews and Greeks, including a number of "prominent Greek women" (Acts 17:12), who accepted the Christian message.

When the Thessalonian Jews heard of the apostles' activity, they made their way to Beroea and stirred up the populace. Once again, for the sake of his own safety and that of his converts, Paul slipped away to Athens, accompanied by Beroean friends.

Paul felt very badly that he had been forced to leave his Thessalonian converts so abruptly. He feared they might not be able to endure the pressure of persecution, to which they were soon exposed (1 Thess. 2:14). When he could stand it no longer (1 Thess. 3:1f.), he sent Timothy back to Thessalonica to see how they were faring.

Meantime, after winning some converts in Athens, Paul moved on to Corinth, where he was joined by Silas and Timothy. Timothy (and perhaps Silas also) had been back in Thessalonica, and brought Paul the comforting news that the young church was standing firm in the faith (1 Thess. 3:6). This gave Paul new courage for his mission in Corinth (Acts 18:5).

However, Timothy's report also showed that the young church was in need of more teaching in certain areas and of encouragement in trials. Since Paul evidently could not return to Thessalonica, he wrote at least two letters to the believers in this city.

Paul's continuing relationship with the Thessalonians after he left Corinth can be traced to some extent in several other letters (see Rom. 15:26; 2 Cor. 8:1–5; 11:9). Some five years after founding the church Paul visited Macedonia (Acts 19:21; 20:1–2) on his so-called third missionary journey. And after spending the winter (A.D. 56–57) in Corinth (from where he wrote the Letter to the Romans), he returned to Macedonia (Acts 20:3). A representative of the Thessalonian church traveled with Paul, bringing famine relief to the saints in Jerusalem (Acts 20:4–6). From such references it appears that Paul's relations with the Thessalonians continued to be good and that he found in them a source of much joy.

After Paul left Thessalonica, unbelieving Jews launched a campaign to discredit both Paul and his message. Had the believers accepted the charges made against him, the effect could have been disastrous. Paul, therefore, expends a considerable effort in his first letter refuting the slanderous accusations made against him (1 Thess. 2:1–12). Moreover, both unbelieving Jews and Gentiles continued to oppose the new movement, and Paul writes to encourage and strengthen the church (1 Thess. 3:3, 7). He also instructs his readers about sexual morality (1 Thess. 4:4ff.).

Because of misunderstanding or lack of information some Thessalonians evidently believed that Christ would return any moment. As a result, some of them gave up their daily work and soon became a burden to others (1 Thess. 4:11–12). Paul had to remind them, therefore, that the time of the Lord's return is not known (1 Thess. 5:1ff.). Also, he encouraged them to respect their leaders and not to suppress the gifts of the Spirit (1 Thess. 5:13ff.).

On the whole, 1 Thessalonians is a friendly letter, full of gratitude to God for the work of grace in the lives of these recent converts to the Christian faith.

Who brought the letter to Thessalonica is not known, but it is clear from 2 Thessalonians that misunderstandings concerning the return of Christ still persisted. In fact, some appear to have believed that the day of the Lord had already come (2 Thess. 2:1ff.). Also, the problem of idleness, caused by their understanding of Christ's imminent return, had grown even worse (2 Thess. 3:6–14). In response Paul wrote the second Thessalonian letter, addressing particularly two topics: the second coming and the problem of idleness.

It has been suggested by some scholars that the Thessalonian church was divided and that 1 Thessalonians was addressed to the Gentile church and 2 Thessalonians to the Jewish church. Such a view has serious problems and has not found wide acceptance.

No serious doubts have ever been cast on the Pauline authorship of 1 Thessalonians. The style is typically Pauline and the companions of Paul mentioned are those who were with him on his second missionary journey. Also, the early canon lists (Marcion, ca. A.D. 140; Muratorian Canon, ca. A.D. 180) include this epistle. To view it as a forgery by some unknown author seems completely unwarranted.

Second Thessalonians also claims to come from Paul and has early attestation in the canon lists and the writings of the early fathers. It is sometimes argued that since 2 Thessalonians repeats things mentioned in 1 Thessalonians, another author must have written 2 Thessalonians. But it should not surprise us if there is repetition, for Paul addresses some of the same problems in both letters.

The claim that 2 Thessalonians has a different eschatology from that of 1 Thessalonians is hard to support. True, according to 1 Thessalonians, nothing seems to stand in the way of Christ's return, whereas according to 2 Thessalonians the revelation of the man of lawlessness precedes the day of the Lord. However, the two letters are not at odds, but rather supplement each other.

Granted that the tone of 1 Thessalonians appears to be friendlier than that of 2 Thessalonians, that is hardly reason to deny the Pauline authorship of the second epistle. We do best, therefore, to accept the Pauline authorship of both letters.

Paul wrote 1 Thessalonians, so it seems, shortly after Timothy came to Corinth from Thessalonica (1 Thess. 3:6). This was not long after Paul himself left Thessalonica (1 Thess. 2:17). The reference to the proconsul Gallio (Acts 18:12) helps us determine with some degree of accuracy the time of Paul's ministry in Corinth. From an inscription found at Delphi it appears that Gallio came to Corinth about A.D. 51. Paul was in Corinth for at least eighteen months (Acts 18:11), and after a period of ministry appeared in Gallio's court. It is quite possible, therefore, that Paul came to Corinth in A.D. 50 and wrote 1 Thessalonians in the early part of that year. If this is correct, then 1 Thessalonians may be the earliest extant New Testament writing, with the possible exception of Galatians.

Second Thessalonians seems to have followed shortly after the first letter and prior to Paul's visit to Thessalonica on his third missionary journey (Acts 20:1–2). Since 2 Thessalonians lists the same associates of Paul as 1 Thessalonians, it is hard to assign 2 Thessalonians to a different period.

Of course, the letters are not dated, and some scholars have suggested that what we now call 2 Thessalonians was in fact written first. However, the arguments given for such a sequence are not convincing. It appears, rather, that the problems addressed in the first letter (persecution, false understandings of the second advent, and loafing) seem to have become more acute by the time 2 Thessalonians was written.

As we turn to the interpretation of these two short epistles it should be remembered that they were written by a missionary to an infant church struggling to survive and to remain faithful to Jesus in the midst of a pagan society. These are letters born out of a deep love for the new people of God that emerged as the gospel was embraced by Jews and Gentiles in Thessalonica. Both letters were written out of pastoral concern. And the Spirit which inspired Paul to write them in the first century makes them alive and relevant for twentieth-century hearers who have an ear to hear "what the Spirit is saying to the churches."

There are four main theological themes in the Thessalonian letters. First, Paul emphasizes the *triune God.* God the Father is at work sanctifying and keeping his children; Christ holds an exalted place alongside God; the Holy Spirit empowers Christ's witness and sustains and sanctifies the church. Second, believers have been appointed to *salvation,* not to wrath. Through the hearing of the gospel and the response of faith, people are converted. Third, the Thessalonian *church* is a model for others. In spite of its suffering and weakness, it has spread the gospel. Finally, at the heart of all Christian hope is the return of Christ, the *parousia*. Although the "mystery of lawlessness" is at work and the church waits for Christ's return, the "appearing" of Christ will herald the eternal victory of God's kingdom.

OUTLINE—1 THESSALONIANS

I. The Greeting (1:1)
II. Personal Reminiscences (1:2–10)
  A. The Vitality of the Church (1:2–3)
  B. The Spiritual Roots of the Church (1:4–6)
  C. The Practical Expression of a Living Faith (1:7–10)
III. The Nature of the Apostolic Ministry (2:1–12)
  A. Patience in Suffering (2:1–2)
  B. Integrity of Motives (2:3–6)
  C. Winsome in Manner (2:7–9)
  D. Blameless in Behavior (2:10–12)
IV. The Reception of the Gospel (2:13–16)
V. Paul's Concern for the Thessalonians (2:17–3:13)
  A. Frustrated Purposes (2:17–20)
  B. Missionary Plans (3:1–5)
  C. Joyful Praise (3:6–10)
  D. Intercessory Prayer (3:11–13)
VI. Exhortation to Christian Living (4:1–12)
  A. General Guidelines (4:1–2)
  B. Morality (4:3–8)
  C. Christian Love (4:9–12)
VII. Problems Related to Christ's Coming (4:13–5:11)
  A. The State of the Dead (4:13–18)
  B. The Times and the Seasons (5:1–11)
VIII. The Internal Life of the Church (5:12–24)
  A. The Recognition of Leaders (5:12–13)
  B. Interpersonal Relations (5:14–15)
  C. The Life of Faith (5:16–18)
  D. Life in the Assembled Community (5:19–22)
  E. Paul's Second Prayer (5:23–24)
IX. Closing Comments (5:24–28)

COMMENTARY

I. The Greeting (1:1)

In Paul's day letters normally began with the name of the sender, the name of the addressee, a thanksgiving, and a greeting. Paul follows this current style of letter writing. However, as a Christian, he fills the conventional form with new meaning.

Although Paul is the actual author of this letter, he associates Silvanus and Timothy with himself in the unusually brief prescript. Silvanus (the Silas of the Book of Acts) and Timothy had shared in the evangelization of Thessalonica. Silas was a member of the Jerusalem community and a Roman citizen like Paul (Acts 15:22; 16:37). Timothy came from Lystra (Acts 16:1–3) and was the son of a Jewish mother and a Greek father. He was converted to the Christian faith when Paul and Barnabas brought the gospel to South Galatia. Both were Paul's trusted colleagues in the gospel ministry. It is a credit to Paul, the great missionary pioneer, that he surrounded himself with co-workers.

The letter is addressed "to the church of the Thessalonians." The Septuagint uses the Greek word *ekklēsia* to translate the Hebrew words designating God's people, Israel. The early Christians thought of themselves as standing in continuity with the people of God of the old covenant. At the same time they recognized that the church was a new creation, including both Jews and Gentiles. Although *ekklēsia* may embrace the whole body of Christ, here it refers to the local assembly of believers in Thessalonica.

The believers in Thessalonica are said to be "in God the Father and the Lord Jesus Christ." Without embarrassment Paul joins "God the Father" under a single preposition with "the Lord Jesus Christ." They are essentially one in the work of redemption. Although God is known as Father in the Old Testament, in the sense that he is the Creator and the one who brings Israel into being, it was through Christ's incarnation that the concept of divine fatherhood took on a depth and a meaning it did not have before (John 14:9).

For the church to be "in Christ" (or "in God") means not only that it belongs to him, but also that it stands in a special and close relationship to him. It is under his direction and care, and participates in the new life in Christ. Clearly the Christian church is quite distinct from other religious or social groupings.

The full title *Lord Jesus Christ* is in keeping with the early church's affirmation that Jesus is Lord—"a name which is above every name" (Phil. 2:9). *Kurios* is the Septuagint representation of the Hebrew tetragrammaton *Yahweh*. "Jesus is Lord" seems to have been the earliest Christian credal confession—at least in Gentile churches. For Jewish believers it was profoundly significant that Jesus of Nazareth was *Christos* (Messiah).

The two words *grace* and *peace* are found in all of Paul's letters. The normal Greek greeting was "rejoice" (*chairein;* e.g., James 1:1), and the Jewish greeting was "peace." Paul regularly uses "grace" (Gk. *charis*), which has the same root as *chairein*, and "peace," which, like grace, conveys a message of great theological import. Grace speaks of that undeserved divine love and mercy for humankind, manifested in Jesus Christ. It is the source of all spiritual blessings. "Peace," behind which stands the Hebrew *šālōm*, is the expression of God's grace in terms of salvation and wholeness.

II. Personal Reminiscences (1:2–10)

A. The vitality of the church (1:2–3). As so often in his letters, Paul begins with a thanksgiving that flows into a kind of rehearsal of the work of God in the lives of the Thessalonians (**1:2–3**). "We always thank God for all of you" may suggest that Silvanus and Timothy participated in some way in the framing of this epistle. However, the "we" may also be a literary plural, used like the singular in other letters (cf. 1 Cor. 1:4; Phil. 1:3).

To say that he "always" thanks God could mean that Paul never remembers the Thessalonians in his prayers without giving thanks to God for them. However, it could also be understood simply in the sense of "continually." Not that Paul never thought of anything else, but "continually" indicates his intense interest in his converts. It is not quite clear whether he "thanks" God for all of them or whether he "remembers" all of them in his prayers. Perhaps both! Whether he remembered their needs before God "unceasingly" (if this adverb goes with "mentioning"), or whether he mentioned their names (he must have known many of them) is not stated, but Paul singles out three things for which he constantly thanks God when he remembers the Thessalonians (v. 2): their work of faith, their labor of love, and their endurance of hope.

To "remember" the work of faith, the labor of love, and the endurance of hope means either to call these to mind or to mention them "before our God and Father." Since the trilogy, faith, hope, and love, is found repeatedly in Paul, as well as in other New Testament writers (cf. Rom. 5:2–5; 1 Cor. 13:13; Eph. 4:2–5; Heb. 6:10–12; 1 Pet. 1:3–8), we must view it as a kind of compendium of the Christian life, the quintessence of the new life in Christ. A good parallel to our text are Christ's words to the church at Ephesus: "I know your deeds, your hard work and your perseverance" (Rev. 2:2).

Paul clearly teaches that salvation is experienced by faith and not by works (Rom. 3:28). However, faith in Christ does not lead to idleness, but expresses itself in works (Gal. 5:6). Although faith has more than one meaning in the New Testament, here it refers to trust and commitment to Christ. It is the positive response of the individual to the gift of salvation that God offers in the gospel.

Salvation is by grace through faith (Eph. 2:7–8), but we are created in Christ to do good works (Eph. 2:10). The faith of the Thessalonians expressed itself in works. The word *work* (Gk. *ergon*) is in the singular here and embraces all aspects of the Christian life.

The word *labor* (Gk. *kopos*) captures the weariness and fatigue that come from exertion and hard work. Paul uses it frequently to describe his mission efforts (1 Cor. 15:10; Gal. 4:11; Phil. 2:16; 1 Thess. 2:9; 3:5).

"Love" (Gk. *agapē*) is used specifically in Christian vocabulary for God's love for humankind, displayed supremely in Jesus Christ's death and exaltation. This divine love is poured out into the hearts of Christ's followers by his Spirit (Rom. 5:5), and it leads them to arduous labor for Christ and his kingdom.

Endurance (Gk. *hupomonē*) is one of the noblest words in the New Testament. The noun occurs some thirty times. It is not blithe optimism, doggedness, or passive resignation. Rather, it is fortitude in the midst of the trials of the Christian life that springs from hope. And it is not hope in general, but hope "in our Lord Jesus Christ." Christian hope is grounded on Christ's resurrection (1 Pet. 1:3) and focuses on his return at the end of the age (1 Thess. 1:10).

The phrase *before our God and Father* should probably be read with all three: work of faith, labor of love, and endurance of hope. Not only is the Christian life lived in the awareness of our responsibility to God, but also in view of the parousia (cf. 3:13).

B. The spiritual roots of the church (1:4–6). The word *brothers* (**1:4**) is used by Paul in the ecclesiastical sense to designate believers, regardless of gender. It indicates that the church is a household, and like family members, the brothers and sisters of the *ekklēsia* are bound together intimately by a common faith and calling.

As "brothers" of the Christian community Paul's readers are "loved by God." Israel's election could be explained properly only as an act of divine love (Deut. 10:15), and so it is with the election of the New Testament believers. Election is not due to God's arbitrariness, but his infinite love (cf. Eph. 1:5).

Election (Gk. *eklogē*) took place "before the creation of the world" (Eph. 1:4), but its effects are seen in the lives of the elect (another designation for the new people of God). Election is a way of saying that God takes the initiative in salvation. It underscores the fact that salvation is entirely of God's grace. The spiritual roots of the church, then, are to be found in eternity, when God in his love and mercy chose us in Christ "to be holy and blameless in his sight" (Eph. 1:4).

From eternity we move into time, into human history: "our gospel came to you" (**1:5**). Election stems from God, but involves a human response to the call of God in the gospel.

"Our gospel" does not mean that Paul and his associates had a different gospel from that of other apostles, or that they had invented the gospel. Rather, it is the gospel which they preached in Thessalonica, which had been entrusted to them by God. Perhaps there is an added nuance in the word *our*, namely that the apostles, too, had embraced the gospel that they preached.

The word *gospel* (Gk. *euangelion*) was common enough in the Greek-speaking world. It means simply "good news" (cf. 3:6). However, the Septuagint had already used it to designate the good news of salvation in the Old Testament (Isa. 40:9; 41:27; 52:7), and that is its primary meaning in the New Testament. The dynamic character of the gospel is suggested by the verb *came*. When the good news of salvation is proclaimed, the gospel "comes" to people.

The gospel came to the Thessalonians "not simply with words, but also with power, with the Holy Spirit and with deep conviction." It did in fact come in word, but not in word alone. However eloquently the gospel is proclaimed, it is ineffective in evoking faith, unless it is empowered by the Holy Spirit. Only when the gospel is preached by "demonstration of the Spirit's power" (1 Cor. 2:4–5) does it generate true faith in its hearers. "We cannot explain the operation of the Holy Spirit which charges a bare verbal cable with high-voltage spiritual power. But we can ask what are the constituents of a good 'cable.' "[1]

A sign that the Holy Spirit confirmed the word spoken by the apostles in Thessalonica was the deep conviction, the assurance, the inward persuasion of the truth of the gospel in the hearers. However, the expression *deep conviction* could just as well refer to the preachers who proclaimed the gospel with full conviction.

Moreover, the work of the missionaries was greatly strengthened by their exemplary life: "You know how we lived among you for your sake." The gospel had entered deeply into the lives of the apostles, and their manner of life made a deep impression upon the Thessalonians. Paul and his associates had done what the Thessalonians later are asked to do: "that your daily life may win the respect of outsiders" (4:12).

The Thessalonians had "welcomed the message" as it was proclaimed by the missionaries (**1:6**). "The message" is shorthand for the Word of God, the gospel of Jesus Christ. To welcome the message is one of several ways in which to describe the positive response of people to the gospel. To welcome the message is to believe the gospel.

Having welcomed the gospel into their lives, the Thessalonians began to live in a Christian manner. "You became imitators of us and of the Lord." What they imitated in the lives of the apostles was what the apostles had learned from Christ (cf. 1 Cor. 11:1). In the early decades of Christianity, while the New Testament books were being written, believers often had little else to go by but the oral tradition and the example of the messengers of the gospel (cf. Phil. 4:9).

Details of what it meant to imitate the

1. R. A. Ward, *Commentary on 1 and 2 Thessalonians* (Waco: Word, 1973), 34.

apostles are not given, other than that they too suffered for their faith. "In spite of severe suffering, you welcomed the message with the joy given by the Holy Spirit." Our Lord, too, displayed joy in the midst of suffering (Heb. 12:2), and the Thessalonians, among other things, imitated Christ in this respect. *Thlipsis,* the Greek word for tribulation, occurs forty-five times in the New Testament. It describes the trials and tribulations of believers in the present age—sufferings endured for the sake of their faith. Such sufferings characterize the entire interim between Christ's first and second advents. "We must go through many hardships to enter the kingdom of God," was Paul's word to the oppressed followers of Jesus in South Galatia (Acts 14:22).

What strikes us as paradoxical is the frequent pairing of suffering and joy. Joy, like tribulation, has eschatological overtones. It has little to do with euphoria, but expresses rather the deep conviction that the believer's life is in God's hands. It is a joy that springs not from pleasant circumstances, but is inspired by the Holy Spirit (cf. Rom. 14:17). Joy is a fruit of the Spirit (Gal. 5:22).

C. The practical expression of a living faith (1:7–10). "And so you became a model to all the believers in Macedonia and Achaia" (**1:7**). After following the example of the apostles, the Thessalonians themselves became examples to others. *Tupos* is the Greek word meaning "model" or "pattern" (from whence comes our word *type*). The Thessalonian Christians became a prototype for other believers in Macedonia and Achaia, which together comprised the whole of Greece. The word *model* denotes not only an example which one may follow, but also a pattern which influences the one following it.

"The Lord's message rang out from you" (**1:8**). After receiving the gospel, the Thessalonians brought it to others. It was Paul's mission strategy to plant churches in the population centers and to let these churches take the good news to the surrounding districts. From Thessalonica the word of the Lord "rang out" (the Greek word *exēchetai* denotes a loud ringing sound—giving us our word *echo*). That message was still being heard when Paul wrote. In fact it had gone beyond the border of Greece. Could it be that Aquila and Priscilla had heard about the witness of the Thessalonians in Rome and told Paul about it? "Everywhere" may be a hyperbolic expression (cf. Col. 1:6), or it may refer to all the places to which Paul had traveled since leaving Thessalonica. Since rumors of the Thessalonian church and its witness had reached Corinth as well, Paul does not have to tell the Corinthians about the vibrant faith of these young Christians. It appears as if part of the message of the early missionary was a recounting of how the gospel had affected the lives of those who had embraced it.

The faith of the Thessalonians had become a topic of general conversation among the saints in the two provinces of Greece: "For they themselves report what kind of reception you gave us" (**1:9**). Paul modestly speaks of his mission in Thessalonica as an "entrance" (Gk. *eisodos*). The word does not indicate whether the visit of the missionaries was successful or not, but the context clearly indicates that the readers had gladly received them.

When the Thessalonians embraced the gospel, they "turned to God from idols to serve the living and true God." The word *converted* (Gk. *epistrephō*) literally means "to turn around." It is a metaphor for a radical change of life, and is used of the conversion of both Jews and Gentiles (e.g., Acts 3:19; 9:35; 11:21). The reference to a conversion "from idols" suggests that the majority of Paul's readers came from pagan backgrounds. Acts 17:1–9 gives the impression that most of these converts had a synagogue background, but here we see that many converts came from the Gentile world as well.

The Old Testament prophets at times compare the helpless idols with the true God (e.g., Jer. 10:3–16), and Paul seems to use that kind of language here. The Thessalonians turned from idols to serve (Gk. *douleuō* means "to be a slave") the living and true God. Since he is the only living God, he alone is the true God (Gk. *alethinos,* genuine, real), in contrast to the many false gods (1 Cor. 8:4–6). Freed from enslavement to idolatry, the Thessalonians became free to give themselves to the service of the living God.

With their conversion to God the lives of Paul's readers were given a new orientation. They now wait for God's Son from heaven (**1:10**). The Greek compound *anamenō* (to wait) is found only here in the New Testament. It means to expect, perhaps with the added notion of waiting patiently and confidently. Waiting for the parousia does not mean that believers constantly think about it; rather, their lives are shaped by this blessed hope. At the center of this hope stands the person of the Savior. They wait "for his Son from heaven." Since Christ ascended into heaven, it is expected he will return "from the heavens" (Paul uses the plural here), the dwelling-place of God.

There is good ground for this living hope: God raised Christ from the dead. With the resurrection of Jesus the Christian faith stands or falls (1 Cor. 15:14). The resurrection of Jesus vindicated his death and assures all those who believe in him of eternal life with God (1 Cor. 15:20ff.). And, as in his preaching at Athens, Paul closely connects Christ's resurrection with final judgment ("who rescues us from the coming wrath"). The coming wrath from which Christ rescues the believer is the divine judgment on the wicked at the end of the age. God's wrath is, of course, even now "revealed from heaven" against all evildoers (Rom. 1:18). In our passage, however, final judgment is meant. And with that solemn note Paul's personal reminiscences come to an end. We will, however, find references to the apostle's personal relationships with the Thessalonians throughout his two letters to them.

III. The Nature of the Apostolic Ministry (2:1–12)

A. Patience in suffering (2:1–2). Evidently slanderous rumors about Paul and his associates were making the rounds in Thessalonica and Paul defends their missionary efforts in 2:1–12. This defense gives us insight into the nature of the ministry of the gospel in the early church, and in particular, of pioneer mission work.

Paul begins by jogging the memory of his readers. "You know, brothers, that our visit to you was not a failure" (**2:1**). In 1:9, Paul's emphasis lay on their reception of the gospel; here he underscores the personal conduct of the messengers. To say that their visit to Thessalonica was not in vain (the Greek word *kenos* literally means "empty") seems like an understatement in light of the fact that a thriving church was established in a relatively short period of time.

To emphasize that the missionaries had no ulterior motives for coming to Thessalonica, Paul recalls the mistreatment they had experienced earlier at Philippi: "We had previously suffered and been insulted in Philippi" (**2:2**). The reference is to the illegal beating and imprisonment endured by Paul and Silas, about which the Thessalonians knew ("as you know"). For Roman citizens to be publicly stripped and flogged without an inquiry was an outrage, and this shameful treatment compounded the physical pain.

In spite of such abuse, however, the missionaries had the courage to come to Thessalonica with the same message, and the boldness to speak out freely. The noun *parrēsia* (Paul here uses the verb) means "freedom of speech." In the face of opposition it means to speak with courage, frankly and fearlessly. The source of this courage was not their own toughness, but rather they proclaimed the gospel boldly "with the help of our God." The gospel is here called God's gospel, which is no different from "our gospel" (1:5) or "the gospel of Christ" (3:2). Whereas the gospel is good news about God, the emphasis here seems to be rather that it comes from God; God, not man, is the source of the gospel.

Paul and his companions had preached the gospel in Thessalonica "in spite of strong opposition." The narrative of Acts 17:5–9 gives us an idea of the kind of opposition they had to face. The Greek word *agōn* (conflict, fight, race) which Paul uses here may include also the inner agony, the mental struggles, which the missionaries had to endure (cf. Col. 2:1). Had there not been a divine calling and compulsion, the apostles would certainly not have come to Thessalonica where once again they had to suffer abuse on account of the gospel.

B. Integrity of motives (2:3–6). Paul calls their preaching of the gospel an "appeal" (**2:3**). This may suggest, among other things, the spirit in which the missionaries proclaimed the good news. It was not simply a recital of theological truths, but an urgent summons to receive the message preached. Paul now defends himself and his companions against the charge that they were wrongly motivated. Their mission efforts did not spring from error. They themselves were neither deceived nor did they deceive the Thessalonians by proclaiming falsehoods.

While we have no hard evidence that the messengers of the gospel were accused of sexual irregularities, Paul seems here to repudiate the charge of moral uncleanness. Although the Greek noun *akatharsia* could refer to impure motives, its primary meaning here seems to be sexual.

Paul also denies that they came with a bag of tricks. The Greek word *dolos* (guile, cunning) originally meant bait or trap, and then took on the meaning of craft and trickery. Roving magicians, rhetoricians, and charlatans of all sorts were frequent spectacles in Paul's day, and the apostle refuses to be identified with that kind of people.

"On the contrary, we speak as men approved by God to be entrusted with the gospel" (**2:4**). Paul and his companions have been tested and approved by God (Gk. *dokimazō* has this double meaning). Having approved them, God entrusted the gospel to them. The gospel is a given; Paul did not invent it; it was entrusted to him as a stewardship (1 Cor. 9:17).

Such a trust does not allow God's servants merely to please human beings, to serve the whim and fancy of people. To be sure, Paul does try to please people (1 Cor. 10:33), but in the sense of seeking their advantage. Perhaps Paul, in his desire to become all things to others (1 Cor. 9:22), was charged with tailoring his message to his audiences. However, he insists that ultimately he seeks to please God "who tests our hearts." The idea that God searches and tests the heart is common enough in the Old Testament (cf. Ps. 139:23; Jer. 17:10). God is called the *kardiognōstēs* (Acts 1:24; 15:8), the one who examines the secret crevices of a person's life. Paul's heart, the fulcrum of life, is constantly under divine scrutiny.

Paul continues his defense by denying, once again, several wrong motives which his enemies evidently had imputed to him and his associates (**2:5–6**). As in verse 3, he lists three vices of which he could not be accused. "You know we never used flattery" (v. 5a). Flattery is not to be confused with words of affirmation. Paul himself frequently pays people compliments. Flattery, however, is basically dishonesty and is aimed at exploiting others for one's own purposes.

"Nor did we put on a mask to cover up greed" (v. 5b). Covetousness, the desire for more, is a vice which is condemned severely by the New Testament writers, including Paul. It is listed at times with the most grievous of sins (cf. Mark 7:22; 1 Cor. 6:10). Greed is a form of idolatry (Eph. 5:5). It is a craving to have more than properly belongs to a person. The apostles did not cover up avarice with pious words. They did not make use of any pretext to exploit the Thessalonians. And after calling his readers to witness ("you know," vv. 1, 5), Paul calls on God to witness the truth of what he is saying. Only God really knows the truth.

Another wrong motive repudiated by Paul is the lust for human praise. "We were not looking for praise from men, not from you or anyone else" (v. 6). If commendation came his way we may assume he accepted it graciously, but his "intention" was not self-aggrandizement. He was not looking for the applause of the Thessalonians or, for that matter, of other people.

C. Winsome in manner (2:7–9). Preachers of the gospel, Paul explains, have the right to be supported by their converts. However, Paul chose not to exercise this right (cf. 1 Cor. 9:3–18). "As apostles of Christ we could have been a burden to you" (**2:7**). Jesus had taught that a laborer deserves his pay (Luke 10:7). To be burdensome could, however, be understood in a more general sense of throwing one's weight around, giving commands, demanding respect. The word *apostles* is probably used here in a rather general and unrestricted sense of "messengers." A requirement for apostleship in the primary sense of the word was to be an eyewitness of the risen Christ (Acts 1:21–22). If the word is used in that primary sense in our text, then it would have to be limited to Paul and Silas (Acts 15:22).

Not only were the apostles careful not to place heavy burdens on their converts, but they were gentle among them. They were "like a mother caring for her little children" (v. 7b). The picture is that of a nursing mother (the Greek word *trophos* [nurse] means to feed). Paul speaks of himself as milk-feeding his converts (1 Cor. 3:1f.). The Greek word Paul uses for "caring" (*thalpō*) means basically to warm, but metaphorically it describes nurture.

Words of endearment continue to flow from Paul's pen (**2:8**). The apostles treated their converts with tender affection, with yearning love. So deep was their affection that they resolved to share their very lives with the Thessalonians. Although the sharing of one's experiences of God's grace would not be ruled out by this phrase, the basic meaning is to give of oneself in utter self-denial. Whereas the sharing of one's life (Gk. *psychē,* soul) can mean even to lay down one's life for the other, here the emphasis is on being at the disposal of someone who has become very dear. That a former Jewish rabbi should hold Gentile converts in his heart with such tender affection is in itself a miracle of grace.

Once again Paul's readers are reminded of the truthfulness of what he is saying: "Surely you remember, brothers" (**2:9**). In order not to be a burden to their converts, the apostles had worked night and day—they were constantly occupied. As a former rabbi Paul had no inhibitions about working at a trade. Manual labor was not despised in Jewish circles, as it tended to be in the Graeco-Roman world. Presumably Paul had supported himself in Thessalonica by tentmaking. How his companions supported themselves is not known. The difficulty of this kind of mission work is indicated by the alliterative phrase *toil and hardship* (Gk. *kopos kai mochthos,* toil and moil; the two words are coupled again in 2 Thess. 3:8 and 2 Cor. 11:27). "Night and day" accentuates the tiring nature of their work. Not that they worked twenty-four hours a day, but they worked both at night and by day.

This was pioneer mission work and Paul did not want to make financial demands on his converts lest the gospel fall into disrepute. He did receive some financial help from the Philippians during his ministry in Thessalonica (cf. Phil. 4:16). Through the work of their hands and with help from the Philippians, the apostles gave themselves to the proclamation of the gospel. "We preached the gospel of God to you" (v. 9b). The word *preach* (*kerysso*) means to proclaim as a herald, publicly and solemnly.

What is preached is consequently called the *kerygma* (Rom. 16:25).

D. Blameless in behavior (2:10–12). Once again Paul calls his readers and God as witnesses to the exemplary Christian life the missionaries lived when they planted the church in Thessalonica (**2:10**). Paul uses three words to describe their manner of life: holy, righteous, and blameless. As an adverb *hosiōs* (holy) is found only here in the New Testament, and it designates what is religiously and morally right. "Righteously" governs the apostles' dealings with men and women in conformity with God's law. The first two adverbs are hard to distinguish. Paul piles up adverbs to underscore the integrity with which he and his associates lived. "Blameless" describes a life without reproach. The adverb is found once again in 5:23 where, like the adjective in 3:10, it refers to blamelessness at the parousia of Jesus Christ. These three adverbs are close in meaning and are put together here for emphasis.

It was in relation to the Thessalonian believers that the apostles lived such exemplary lives. Paul was concerned about his manner of life among unbelievers (4:12), but this letter is addressed to "you who believed." Again Paul jogs their memory—"for you know" (**2:11**). From the image of motherhood (v. 7) Paul changes to that of fatherhood to express the parental care they gave to their converts ("as a father deals with his own children"). The metaphor stresses the close relationship between missionary and convert. They spoke not only to groups but paid loving attention to individuals ("each one of you").

The gospel ministry of the apostles is now broken down into several constituent parts: "encouraging, comforting and urging you to live lives worthy of God, who calls you into his kingdom and glory" (**2:12**). The translations of the Greek word *parakaleō* (encourage, exhort, appeal, comfort) are numerous, and it is at times difficult to know how to render it in a given instance. Spiritual and ethical admonition seems to be in focus here. The word is hard to distinguish from *paramutheomai* (encourage, comfort), and the two are used like a word pair (cf. 5:14; Phil. 2:1). The third verb has a more authoritative nuance than the preceding two. *Martyromai* originally meant to invoke witnesses, but here it is used in the sense of urging someone strongly (TEV kept urging). The three verbs together cover the whole range of Christian nurture.

Paul's concern was that his converts should "live lives worthy of God." That conduct should be suited to the nature of God expresses one of the deepest motives in the ethical teaching of the New Testament. In other passages Paul exhorts his readers to live lives worthy of "the saints" (Rom. 16:2), of their "calling" (Eph. 4:1), of "the gospel" (Phil. 1:27), or of "the Lord" (Col. 1:10). Christians are to reflect God's character in their daily life, just as Israel was exhorted to be holy because God is holy (Lev. 19:2).

The God of whom the Thessalonians are to be worthy keeps on calling them "into his kingdom and glory." The expression occurs again in 5:24 and, as in the passage before us, is related to the parousia. Although the word *kingdom* by itself could refer to the present reign of God (cf. 1 Cor. 4:20), when combined with "glory," it clearly has a futuristic meaning. By the Spirit believers enjoy the firstfruits of the age to come, but only when Christ returns will the glory of the future kingdom be revealed.

IV. The Reception of the Gospel (2:13–16)

The letter begins with an outburst of thanksgiving (1:2) as Paul looks back at the beginnings of the church in Thessalonica. Now once again Paul recalls the coming of the gospel to Thessalonica and breaks out in thanksgiving: "And we also thank God continually" (**2:13**). The "also" probably means no more than "we for our part." The reason for Paul's thanksgiving at this point is that the Thessalonians had received the gospel "not as the word of men, but as it actually is, the word of God."

The Greek verb *paralambanō* (receive) is used regularly for receiving a body of instruction. The Thessalonians received "the heard word from us of God"—to put it literally. The gospel is the word which the apostles preached. However, it did not come from the apostles, but from God. Before the Gospels were written, the good news was proclaimed orally, and so it was "heard," rather than "read." To hear the word, however, means also to receive it with one's heart. The Thessalonians accepted ("welcomed," as in 1:6) the gospel not merely as a human word (though it was spoken by men), but as God's Word.

The divine word which they received, albeit through human channels, continued to work in their lives ("is at work in you who believe"). The Greek verb *energeō* is used regularly in the New Testament for supernatural activity (e.g., 1 Cor. 12:6; Phil. 2:13). Where people welcome God's Word into their lives, the power of God is at work. The word of the cross is the power of God (1 Cor. 1:18).

By embracing the gospel preached by the apostles, the Thessalonians became imitators of the saints before them, who also suffered for

Christ's sake. In 1:6 the readers were commended for becoming imitators of the apostles. Now they are said to be imitators of "God's churches in Judea, which are in Christ Jesus" (**2:14**), not by choice, but by necessity. The Judean churches were persecuted by the Jewish community that saw in the Christian gospel a threat to the very essence of Judaism. Paul himself, prior to his conversion, had persecuted the Judean churches. And lest anyone should think of the churches of God in Judea as Jewish synagogues, Paul adds "in Christ Jesus." The Thessalonian church (cf. 1:1) and the Judean Christian churches are one in Christ.

The Thessalonians had suffered the same things at the hands of their countrymen as the Judean churches had endured at the hands of unbelieving Jews. Just as these Jews had made life hard for the young churches in Judea, opponents of the church in Thessalonica had oppressed the church there. Why Paul would hold up the sufferings of the churches of Judea as a model is not quite clear. Could it be that he still had vivid memories of how he had harassed these churches?

At this point Paul piles up charges against his own countrymen, the Jews (**2:15**). It is an exasperated missionary's outburst against a people (and he has only the opponents of the gospel in mind) bent on destroying God's work. The first charge he makes is that "they killed the Lord Jesus" (v. 15). Paul knows that the Romans in fact carried out the gruesome task of crucifying Christ, but he holds the Jewish rulers chiefly responsible for Christ's death (Acts 2:23, 36). The wickedness of the crime is underscored by giving Jesus the title *Lord.*

They also killed the prophets. By linking their deaths to that of Christ, Paul brings the sufferings of God's servants of old into relation with Christ's sufferings. Jesus also accused the leaders of his day of killing the prophets (Matt. 23:31ff.). Moreover, these enemies of the gospel also persecuted the apostles ("also drove us out"). The reference is specifically to the expulsion of Paul and his friends from Thessalonica (Acts 17:5–10).

Paul asserts that the Jews displease God (v. 15). "To please God" is a standard Pauline idiom for good Christian behavior (cf. 4:1). It means to live in accordance with God's will. Rather indiscriminately Paul accuses the Jews of being "hostile to all men." We must, however, read passages such as Romans 9:1–5, to feel the pain Paul carried in his heart because of the rejection of Christ by his Jewish countrymen. Wherever they could, they stopped Paul "from speaking to the Gentiles so that they may be saved" (**2:16**). Paul felt called in particular to preach the gospel to the Gentiles. It was his firm conviction that by hearing the gospel of Christ Gentiles could be saved, delivered from sin and eternal death.

By opposing God's servants and rejecting their message, "they heap up their sins to the limit." The plural *sins* suggests that one sin is being added to another until the measure is filled to the brim (cf. Gen. 15:16; Dan. 8:23). And with the measure filled up, God's wrath overtakes them: "The wrath of God has come upon them at last." God's wrath is already "revealed from heaven against all the godlessness and wickedness of men" (Rom. 1:18) though its final manifestation takes place at the parousia (2 Thess. 1:7–9). Although Paul holds out no hope to unbelieving Jewry in this passage, the many Jews who had accepted the gospel were for him the guarantee that others would come to the faith (cf. Rom. 11:25–27).

V. Paul's Concern for the Thessalonians (2:17–3:13)

A. Frustrated purposes (2:17–20). After what appears to be a digression (vv. 15–16), Paul resumes his survey of his relations with his readers: "But, brothers, when we were torn away from you for a short time (in person, not in thought), out of our intense longing we made every effort to see you" (**2:17**).

Paul wants to lay the rumor to rest that he and his friends had no intention of ever returning to Thessalonica. Quite the opposite was true, in fact. When they were driven out of the city, they felt like parents who had lost their children or like children who had lost their parents. It was their hope that they would be separated from the church only for a short time (Gk. *pros kairon hōras,* for the space of an hour). In any case the separation was "in person, not in thought." They could not be with them in body, but their thoughts were with their converts in Thessalonica. In fact, they had such a longing to see them that they made plans to return to Thessalonica.

Paul assures them that he had tried again and again to come to them, "but Satan stopped us" (**2:18**). Although Paul has used the plural throughout, he now sets himself apart from his colleagues to emphasize his personal efforts to visit the Thessalonians again. At times when Paul's plans were frustrated he attributed this to the Spirit of Jesus (Acts 16:6–7). In this instance, however, he sees no other explanation for the opposition to his work than that Satan had put up roadblocks. Just what it was that prevented him from returning to Thessalonica is not stated.

As Paul thinks of his converts, he breaks out

in a lyrical expression of friendship. "For what is our hope, our joy, or the crown in which we will glory in the presence of our Lord Jesus when he comes? Is it not you? Indeed, you are our glory and joy" (**2:19–20**). "Hope" should probably be understood in the sense of confidence—the confidence that God would complete the work he had begun in them. Also, they are the cause of the apostles' joy, in the sense that a parent might say of a child, "He is the joy of my heart." The "crown of exultation" alludes to the victory wreath (Gk. *stephanos*) given to successful athletes at the games. Paul looks forward to the parousia of the Lord Jesus, when the Thessalonian converts will be for him a kind of victory prize. They will be his "crowning glory" on that day and the source of unspeakable joy.

The noun *parousia* occurs here for the first time in this letter (v. 19). Basically it means to arrive or to be present. It has no implicit religious connotations (cf. 2 Cor. 7:6; Phil. 1:26). However, in a more technical sense it describes the arrival of royalty. An emperor's visit was called a parousia. Christians, then, transferred the latter usage to the coming of Christ at the end of the age.

B. Missionary plans (3:1–5). Because of Paul's eager desire to see the Thessalonians, and because his way back to them was blocked, he devised a plan to find out how they were getting along in their Christian life. After leaving Thessalonica the apostles established a church in Beroea and then, under pressure, Paul left for Athens. Here the separation from his Thessalonian friends became unbearable. "So when we could stand it no longer, we thought it best to be left by ourselves in Athens" (**3:1**). Where Silas was at this time is not quite clear, but evidently he, too, left Athens on a mission. Later, both Timothy and Silas rejoined Paul in Corinth (Acts 18:5). After his companions left him in Athens, Paul felt abandoned and desolate. But for the sake of the work he sent Timothy back to Thessalonica at great cost to himself.

Paul's high view of Timothy is seen in the titles he gives him. "We sent Timothy, who is our brother and God's fellow worker in spreading the gospel of Christ" (**3:2**). "Our brother" here means more than "fellow Christian." Timothy is Paul's beloved associate. He is a fellow worker in the gospel of Christ. To call someone God's fellow worker is a rather daring way of speaking. The expression could of course mean that Timothy works together with others for God, but perhaps we should understand the meaning to be that Timothy works "with God" in the gospel of Christ. In 1:5 Paul calls it "our gospel"; in 2:2 God's gospel; here "the gospel of Christ." Christ and his work of salvation make the gospel "good news."

The purpose of Timothy's mission was to strengthen and encourage the Thessalonians in their faith. Paul's readers had embraced the gospel with joy (1:6), but he was concerned that they become strong so that they would not be shaken by the trials they were asked to endure (**3:3**). He hoped they would stand firm in spite of these sufferings. "You know quite well that we were destined for them." Paul thought of suffering for Christ's sake as normal for the church. Indeed, suffering has been the story of the church from the first century till now. Not that believers have always suffered, for there have been long periods of peace as well, but there is nothing in Scripture to suggest that Christ's followers will be exempt from suffering.

Paul and his associates were realistic enough to inform their converts that the Christian way would be characterized by tribulation. "In fact, when we were with you, we kept telling you that we would be persecuted. And it turned out that way, as you well know" (**3:4**). Paul and Barnabas told their South Galatian converts that they must enter the kingdom of God "through many hardships" (Acts 14:22). To suffer because of one's faith can be a daunting thing, and so Paul sent his trusted legate, Timothy, back to Thessalonica so that he might find out about their faith (**3:5**). "Faith" is used here as a comprehensive term for the Christian life as a whole. Paul expresses apprehension over what Timothy might discover, for he knows that Satan, whom he calls "the tempter," is out to destroy God's work. To tempt can mean "to put to the test," but it can also mean "to seduce." In our text the fear is that Satan will draw the believers away from their faith on account of their afflictions. "I was afraid that in some way the tempter might have tempted you and our efforts might have been useless."

C. Joyful praise (3:6–10). Evidently Timothy got to Thessalonica and found to his pleasant surprise that the believers were standing firm in the faith. Paul meanwhile had gone to Corinth and here the good news reached him that his converts were bearing up courageously in spite of the pressures put upon them.

The report which Timothy brought is called a "gospel" (Gk. *euangelizomai,* used here in its nontheological sense). "But Timothy has just now come to us from you and has brought good news about your faith and love" (**3:6**). It appears as if Paul wrote this letter almost immediately upon the return of Timothy. He rejoices at the report about the Thessalonians' "faith and love." These two nouns are an abbreviated reference to the familiar trilogy of faith, hope, and love (cf. 1:3). The absence of the word *hope* does not necessarily suggest that this aspect of their Christian life was lacking. Their faith in God and their love for him and for others was a source of great encouragement to Paul. Not only were they making good progress in their Christian life but also they had loving memories of the apostles. The propaganda of the enemies of Paul had not had its desired effect; the believers looked back to the visit of the missionaries with joy. Whereas they might have thought of the apostles as men who had brought them no end of trouble, they longed to see them again, just as much as the apostles yearned to see the Thessalonians.

Paul was greatly encouraged by the news about the faith of the Thessalonians (**3:7**). "In all our distress and persecution" indicates that Paul carried out his mission work under great difficulties and opposition. As he faced the task of planting the gospel in the Corinthian metropolis, the good news from Thessalonica gave him a new lease on life.

"For now we really live, since you are standing firm in the Lord" (**3:8**). The verb *to live* (Gk. *zaō*) means to live the Christian life with new vigor, zest, and joy (JB "Now we can breathe again"). Paul's life is tied up with his converts so much that he suffers when they do, and he rejoices when they make progress. To stand firm in the Lord does not suggest inactivity or immobility. Rather it means to remain firm and unwavering in the face of opposition and persecution.

So thrilled is Paul at the good report by Timothy that feelings of gratitude and satisfaction well up within his heart. "How can we thank God enough for you in return for all the joy we have in the presence of our God because of you?" (**3:9**). This is a rhetorical question expressing the thought that no act of thanksgiving can equal the joy Paul experiences as he thinks of the Thessalonians. Like the psalmist he asks, "How can I repay the LORD for all his goodness to me?" (Ps. 116:12). He feels his words of thanks are inadequate in return for all the joy God has given him.

But, the apostle's joys are tempered by the recognition that his converts have not yet reached perfection, and so he lets them know how fervently he prays that God will allow him to return to them. "Night and day we pray most earnestly that we may see you again" (**3:10**). "Night and day" is an idiom for deep concern. The Greek double compound *hyperekperissou* ("most earnestly") stresses the fervency of Paul's prayer. The specific request is that they might once again see the face of their converts. Here Paul teaches us how to keep prayer vital—by being specific. However, beyond this immediate purpose, is Paul's desire to supply what is lacking in their faith. This is not a criticism of his readers, but a recognition that there is always room for growth. Also, there were areas in which Paul's converts needed further instruction. "Faith" is used here to indicate the essence of the Christian life. Since Paul could not return to Thessalonica immediately he will let his letter be a substitute for his visit. Also, he will intercede for the Thessalonians before God.

D. Intercessory prayer (3:11–13). After stating that he prays continuously and exceedingly we now have an actual prayer, such as we find occasionally in Paul's letters. He addresses "our God and Father himself and our Lord Jesus" (**3:11**). That God has revealed himself as Father in Christ is a peculiarly Christian insight. Also, it is significant theologically that Paul associates Christ with God in such a way that he is seen as sharing the prerogatives of deity. Paul's prayer to God is that he might clear the way for Paul to return to Thessalonica. The manner in which this is to happen is left to God. It appears as if this prayer was not answered for some time (cf. Acts 20:1–2).

As Paul waits for this prayer to be answered he prays for his converts: "May the Lord make your love increase and overflow for each other and for everyone else, just as ours does for you" (**3:12**). The verbs *increase* and *overflow* are practically synonymous. Paul recognizes that love is present in their lives and commends them for it (cf. 4:10). But there is no limit to growth in love "for each other" (the believers) and "for everyone else" (humankind). And Paul does not hesitate to hold up himself and his associates as examples ("just as ours does for you").

A second concern Paul expresses in his prayers is that the Thessalonians' hearts be strengthened so "that you will be blameless and holy in the presence of our God and Father when our Lord Jesus comes with all his holy ones" (**3:13**). The heart is the fulcrum of life in Hebrew psychology. People feel, think, and make decisions in their hearts. To be strengthened in heart is to be made strong in the center of personality. Growth in love is a prerequisite for becoming strong in heart. Strengthening in heart is to make the readers "blameless and holy." To be holy means to be dedicated to God and his service. Such a relationship, in turn, demands separation from all that defiles.

The process of sanctification is not complete until the believer stands in the presence of God "when our Lord Jesus comes with all his holy ones." Who the "holy ones" are is not quite clear. It appears as if Zechariah 14:5 lies behind this expression. Jesus, too, taught that he would return in the glory of the Father "with the holy angels" (Mark 8:38). However, Paul may also have had believing men and women in mind, who are called "saints" in the New Testament. Perhaps we should allow for both meanings, since both angels and saints will participate in Christ's parousia.

VI. Exhortation to Christian Living (4:1–12)

A. General guidelines (4:1–2). The word *finally* with which this section begins does not mean Paul is rounding off his letter. It is used, rather, to indicate a transition—"as for the rest." Up to this point the letter has been intensely personal. From here on Paul turns to exhortation and instruction.

Although Paul speaks with authority, he addresses his readers as "brothers." This tender appeal is made with the consciousness that he is speaking in Christ's name ("in the Lord Jesus"; **4:1**).

The object of Paul's instruction is to remind his readers that believers are under obligation to please God. To please God is a comprehensive way of thinking that one lives in accordance with God's will. Very tactfully Paul commends his readers for already doing what he exhorts them to do: "as in fact you are living." Paul is not unmindful of the progress of his readers, but growth in the Christian life is unlimited, and so he urges the Thessalonians to "do so more and more." Paul does not tell them specifically how to do so for at this point he is suggesting guidelines for all of life. He will get very specific in a moment.

Once again Paul refreshes the memories of his readers. "You know what instructions we gave you by the authority of the Lord Jesus" (**4:2**). What Paul is asking of them in his letter is not really new, for he had instructed them at the time of their conversion on how the Christian life was to be lived. These rules of conduct were not given to them as esoteric ideals which they could take or leave; they were given "by the authority of the Lord Jesus." These instructions were not meant to put external strictures on their converts, but were designed to help them develop Christ-like characters.

B. Morality (4:3–8). From the general guideline, that Christians must seek to please God in all areas of life, Paul becomes specific. The first area of concern is relations with the opposite sex. "It is God's will that you should be sanctified: that you should avoid sexual immorality" (**4:4**). To please God is to do his will; and his will is the sanctification of the believer.

Sanctification demands that Christians abstain from sexual immorality. The Greek noun *porneia* means illicit sexual relations of any kind, although originally it meant primarily traffic with harlots. Sexual union within marriage was sanctified by the gospel, but outside of marriage it was forbidden. In this respect the gospel took a firm stand in opposition to the mores of Graeco-Roman society. We need not infer that members of the Thessalonian church indulged in sexual vice. Warnings such as Paul gives here are meant to prevent such sins. Those members who came from the synagogue knew from Old Testament teaching that God frowned on fornication. Others who had come out of paganism needed to develop a conscience against illicit sexual activity.

A second area of concern to Paul is the marriage relationship (if we are correct in our understanding of the text). Literally verse 4 reads: "That each of you learn to acquire his vessel in sanctification and honor." The first question is whether *skeuos* (vessel) refers to a person's body or to his wife. Our bodies are called "earthen vessels" (2 Cor. 4:7), but no New Testament passage specifically calls a man's wife his vessel.

The Greek verb *ktaomai* (to obtain possession, to acquire) would seem to favor the view that "vessel" refers to a person's wife. A Christian must acquire a wife in an honorable manner, "not in passionate lust like the heathen, who do not know God" (**4:5**). If *skeuos* means "body" then the verb suggests that believers must gain mastery over their bodies. Scholars are divided at this point and consequently the English versions vary too. Either way, whether the text refers to finding a marriage partner and living with her, or whether the reference is to self-control, believers are to live their lives in "a way that is holy and honorable."

Such a life stands in vivid contrast to that of pagans who are dominated by lustful passion and self-indulgence. Such behavior arises out of ignorance of God (cf. Ps. 79:6; Jer. 10:25). Not that the heathen do not know that there is a God, but they do not acknowledge him in their lives, and so their ignorance is culpable (Rom. 1:21–25).

A third area of ethical concern is that members of the church do not take unfair advantage of each other. "And that in this matter no one should wrong his brother or take advantage of him" (**4:6a**). What does Paul mean by "matter" (Gk. *pragma*)? Some have understood it as a legal matter (cf. 1 Cor. 6:1ff.). Others have suggested that Paul has business matters in mind. The word *this* seems to have demonstrative force and so we do best to understand *pragma* as referring to the matter under discussion, namely, sexual morality. It would be highly reprehensible to cross a forbidden ethical boundary, and to overreach and to defraud one's brother. Illicit sexual acts are always an injustice committed against another person. Adultery is a violation of the marriage relationship. Promiscuity robs the other person of that virginity which he or she ought to bring to marriage. Although sexual transgression is wrong when an unbeliever is involved, the word *brother* in our text is probably to be understood in the sense of "Christian."

Having expressed concern about three areas of Christian ethics, Paul now gives three reasons why he takes these matters so seriously. First, "the Lord will punish men for all such sins" (**4:6b**). By the "Lord" Paul probably means Jesus. However, Jesus is never put over against God. As God, so also Jesus is "an avenger" of the evils just mentioned. Divine vengeance must not be understood as personal vindictiveness, but as the response of a holy God to evil. Whether Paul thought of vengeance in the present or at the coming parousia, is not clear. Christ will inflict vengeance on all evildoers at the parousia (2 Thess. 1:8); however, his judgments often begin here in life. Such a warning should not surprise Paul's readers, since such ethical teachings formed part of the oral instruction given to all of his converts ("as we have already told you and warned you").

Another reason they must take these ethical instructions seriously is the fact that "God did not call us to be impure, but to live a holy life" (**4:7**). Sanctification is part of a Christian's calling. The call of God comes to us in the gospel and those who receive the gospel are "the called." And they are then in turn "called to be holy" (1 Cor. 1:2), and not called "for uncleanness." Whoever hears God's call to salvation, also hears his call to a life of holiness.

A third motive for living a holy life is the fact that at conversion God's Holy Spirit is given to the believer. And so "he who rejects this instruction does not reject man but God, who gives you his Holy Spirit" (**4:8**). Although Paul is but a human being, he is God's messenger through whom God speaks. Therefore, to reject Paul's instructions really means to reject God's Word. What makes such an attitude even more reprehensible is the fact that God "gives you his Holy Spirit." The gift of the Holy Spirit (and the position of the adjective *holy* underscores the fact) calls for holy living.

C. Christian love (4:9–12). "Now about brotherly love we do not need to write to you, for you yourselves have been taught by God to love each other" (**4:9**). Sometimes the Greek introductory formula *peri de* (but concerning) introduces a reply to a question and so it has been suggested that Paul is answering a question asked by the Thessalonians in a letter they had sent with Timothy. This is not likely, however, since the exhortation to love is found rather frequently in Paul's writings. Only here and in Romans 12:10 does Paul use the compound *philadelphia* (brotherly love). The family solidarity of the early church made such terms as "brother," "brotherhood," and "brotherly love" popular among believers.

Paul does not really find it necessary to write to the Thessalonians about brotherly love, since they have been taught by God to love one another. This is the only place in the New Testament where the compound *theodidaktoi* ("God-taught") is found, although John 6:45 has *didaktoi theou* in a quote from Isaiah 54:13. The meaning may be that the Old Testament already taught people to love one another (cf. Lev. 19:18). This command was reaffirmed by Jesus (cf. John 13:34). Love is also a fruit of the Spirit (Gal. 5:22), and believers know intuitively that they should love one another.

But, not only have Paul's readers been taught to love, they are in fact practicing *philadelphia.* "And in fact, you do love all the brothers throughout Macedonia" (**4:10**). Paul has a sharp eye for what is commendable and where he can he pays his readers compliments. Just how they had demonstrated their brotherly love is not stated, but Christian love always finds ways of expressing itself. However, brotherly love is subject to infinite growth and development and so Paul exhorts them to abound in love even more. "Yet we urge you, brothers, to do so more and more." Their love is to increase in depth, sincerity, and quality. In any case, they are to do better than they are doing.

It appears that undue eschatological excitement had created problems for the Thessalonians, and this had evidently led to some violations of brotherly love. And so Paul's exhortation is, "Make it your ambition to live a quiet life, to mind your own business and to work with your hands, just as we told you" (**4:11**). "Be ambitious to be quiet" is a paradox. *Philotimeomai* is the Greek word for eager striving (lit. love for honor). "To be quiet" is not a command to silence, but is a warning against fanaticism, against "advent fever," against the temptation of becoming busybodies (cf. 2 Thess. 3:11).

The best way to remain calm is to go about one's daily tasks. Evidently some Thessalonians, caught up in the excitement of Christ's imminent return, had stopped working and were now making a nuisance of themselves.

This was a violation of brotherly love. Although believers are to be concerned about other Christians, there is also a place for "minding one's own business." Closely joined to this is the command to work with one's hands. In this respect the missionaries themselves had set a good example (cf. 2:9). The typical Greek attitude was that slaves did the manual labor. However, the apostles had instructed their converts differently by word of mouth, and Paul now underscores in writing the need for industrious habits.

Paul's overarching concern in giving these instructions is that the Christian faith not be brought into disrepute: "so that your daily life may win the respect of outsiders and so that you will not be dependent on anybody" (**4:12**). Paul wants his readers to live a life that wins the respect of "outsiders." "Outsiders" are nonmembers, people not in the church. Jews used the term for non-Jews, but in the New Testament it designates non-Christians (cf. 4:5; 1 Cor. 5:12–13). Paul knows that Christians cannot live in a manner that will endear them to outsiders. Suffering for Christ's sake at the hands of unbelievers is a mark of genuine Christianity. But believers are to live in such a fashion that they cannot be accused of wrongdoing. What attracts outsiders to the church as nothing else does is the life of believers. But what would unbelievers in Thessalonica think of church members if they neglected their daily duties and became dependent on others? They must, then, go back to work "so that you will not be dependent on anybody" (v. 12b).

VII. Problems Related to Christ's Coming (4:13–5:11)

A. The state of the dead (4:13–18). From Paul's instructions concerning the dead in Christ it appears as if the Thessalonians had been insufficiently informed or had misunderstood what Paul had told them in person. In any case, he does not want them "to be ignorant about those who fall asleep" (**4:13**).

The subject on which they need to be informed more fully is the state of the dead, "those who fall asleep." "Sleep" is a euphemism for death, found in both the Greek and the Jewish world. Christians took the idea over but with the understanding that death is a sleep from which the believer will some day awake to resurrection life.

In our text those sleeping are the Thessalonian believers who had died after Paul left. Evidently his readers were not sure of their fate, and this led to untold grief. Paul, therefore, wants to enlighten them on this problem so that they do not "grieve like the rest of men, who have no hope" (v. 13b). "The rest" are the unbelievers (cf. Eph. 2:3). All people have hopes and dreams, but those outside Christ have no hope in the sense that they do not have the hope of eternal life. To be without God is to be without hope (cf. Eph. 2:12). To die in Christ is to have the hope of the resurrection, and so believers, though they grieve when they lose loved ones, need not grieve in despair like "the rest."

This hope of the resurrection is based on the resurrection of Jesus. "We believe that Jesus died and rose again and so we believe that God will bring with Jesus those who have fallen asleep in him" (**4:14**). Christian confidence in the resurrection is not the result of speculation; it is not the product of wish-fulfillment. Rather it is based on a historical event—the resurrection of Christ. Of him it is not said that he "fell asleep," but that he died, perhaps to underscore the reality of his death.

Because the grave could not hold Christ and he rose, breaking the bonds of death, Paul assures his readers that "God will bring with Jesus those who have fallen asleep in him" (v. 14b). Christ's resurrection guarantees the resurrection of those who die in him. Paul argues this at much greater length in 1 Corinthians 15. The syntax of our text is not quite clear. Does "through Jesus" (Gk. *dia tou Iēsou*) go with "bring" or with "fallen asleep"? Will God bring the dead with him through Jesus, or are the saints laid asleep through Jesus? If the latter, then we seem to have the picture of a mother putting her child to sleep when it is tired. However, most scholars associate the prepositional phrase with "bring." But how are we to understand "bring"? Does it mean that when believers die God brings them together with Jesus? Certainly believers go to be with Christ when they die, as Paul so earnestly desired when he was in prison (cf. Phil. 1:23). Perhaps the meaning is that God brings back to life those who die in Christ prior to the parousia. It is even possible that Paul meant that God would bring back (from heaven) those who now fall asleep and go to be with Christ, or else, God will bring the deceased believers together with Jesus on the new earth (cf. Rev. 21:1–2). The text is not specific, but we can be sure that the believer who dies is asleep in Jesus, and will not be forgotten at the parousia.

That this is so, is emphasized further by a word of the Lord himself (**4:15**). Is Paul referring to an unrecorded word of Jesus, or to a word spoken by a Christian prophet, or did God give him a direct revelation? Is he simply expressing the mind of the Lord or is he alluding to some Old Testament passages on the day of the Lord? We do not really know. However, Paul is not simply expressing a personal opinion, and so his instructions must be taken seriously.

"We tell you that we who are still alive, who are left till the coming of the Lord, will certainly not precede those who have fallen asleep" (v. 15b). From the "we" it appears as if Paul expected to be alive when the parousia took place. In fact, Christians should always live as if Christ's coming is near. However, Paul was realistic enough to know that if Christ delayed his coming he would die (cf. 5:10, "whether we are awake [i.e., live] or asleep [i.e., die]"). Even if he died, however, Paul expected to be raised at Christ's coming (cf. 2 Cor. 4:14, "will also raise us with Jesus").

Those who are alive at Christ's coming will not have precedence over those who have died. It was held in Judaism that those who were alive at the end of the world would fare better than the dead.[2] Apparently some Thessalonians feared that the dead in Christ would suffer unfair disadvantages. Not so, says Paul, for when the resurrection takes place, they will be raised to life and together with the living receive bodies (1 Cor. 15:51) fit for the world to come.

With that assurance Paul now gives a thumbnail description of Christ's parousia: "For the Lord himself will come down from heaven" (**4:16**). The Lord is none other than Jesus Christ. He, not man, ushers in the great event that marks the end of this age. And he, not some deputy, will come back from heaven, the dwelling-place of God. At his ascension heavenly messengers assured his disciples that "this same Jesus, who has been taken from you into heaven, will come back in the same way you have seen him go into heaven" (Acts 1:11). Although the biblical writers do not use the language of modern astrophysics (where the question of which way is up or down may be of little consequence) their language is theologically very meaningful.

Christ's parousia will be signaled by a shouted command. This military noun (Gk. *keleusma*) may suggest that the heavenly Leader gives his armies the command to move for the final showdown with evil powers (cf. Rev. 19, where Christ leads the armies of heaven). Or, the shouted command may be a signal for the dead to rise (cf. John 5:25). Who the archangel is whose voice will be heard at Christ's coming is not stated. But just as the angelic world participated in Christ's first coming (Luke 2:8–14), so it will attend his second advent.

The reference to "the trumpet call of God" has a rich Old Testament background. At Sinai the trumpets blew and Moses led the people out of the camp to meet God (Exod. 19:17). Similarly at the parousia the trumpet will sound and God's people will go out to meet the Lord. In the Old Testament, the trumpet also came to be connected with the day of the Lord (cf. Joel 2:1, 15; Zech. 9:14). Jesus said that when the Son of man would come again, God would send his angels with a loud trumpet to "gather the elect" (Matt. 24:31). In our passage, too, the archangel and the trumpet stand in proximity and may in fact express the same summons.

According to 1 Corinthians 15:52 the dead rise "at the last trumpet." Similarly in our text the trumpet blows and the dead in Christ rise. Those who are "in Christ" in life, are "in Christ" also when they die. The fellowship with Christ established by faith is not broken by death. "The dead in Christ will rise first," that is, they will have precedence over the living saints, and will not be at a disadvantage.

"After that, we who are still alive and are left will be caught up with them in the clouds to meet the Lord in the air" (**4:17**). The believers living at the time of Christ's return will be snatched away together with the resurrected saints. The verb meaning to catch up (Gk. *harpazō*) was rendered in the Latin Vulgate as *rapiemur* and so the parousia is sometimes called the "rapture."

All the saints will be caught up "in the clouds." Clouds are a regular feature of the revelation of God in his glory. The cloud enveloped Sinai when God made the covenant with Israel (Exod. 19:16). When God made himself known in the tabernacle (Exod. 40:34) or in the temple (1 Kings 8:10–11), it was a cloud. Also, Daniel sees one like the Son of man coming in "the clouds of heaven" (Dan. 7:13). The day of the Lord is a day of clouds (Ezek. 30:3; Joel 2:2). So our Lord returns in clouds. Clouds speak of both hiddenness and revelation.

The resurrected saints and the transformed believers who are alive at Christ's coming (1 Cor. 15:50–52 speaks of their transformation) are caught up in the clouds "to meet the Lord in the air." When a dignitary paid a visit (a parousia) to a city, leading citizens would go out to meet him and to escort him into their town. This reception of the royal visitor was called an *apantēsis*. In our text the saints welcome their Lord "in the air." "Air" is used here, it seems, much like the "clouds." Sometimes, however, the air was viewed as the abode of

2. I. H. Marshall, *I and II Thessalonians* (Grand Rapids: Eerdmans, 1983), 127.

evil spirits (cf. Eph. 2:2). If that is meant, then Paul is saying that Christ's final triumph is celebrated on the very terrain where evil held sway for so long.

Once the saints have been united with their Lord they will never again be separated from him: "And so we will be with the Lord forever" (v. 17b). All imaginable bliss is summed up in this word of assurance. With such words Paul's readers can comfort one another (**4:18**). From this concluding comment it is obvious that Paul's instructions are not simply academic but are an expression of concern for his converts.

B. The times and the seasons (5:1–11). After a brief description of Christ's coming, Paul addresses the question of the time of this event. What Paul earlier called the parousia, is now called "the day of the Lord." There are, of course, many designations of Christ's second advent.

Paul does not find it necessary to add to what his readers already know about the time of the Lord's coming. "Now, brothers, about times and dates we do not need to write to you" (**5:1**). The two Greek words for time (*chronoi* and *kairoi*) appear as a doublet also in Acts 1:7. *Chronos* refers to time in its duration, while *kairos* is time in its qualitative sense; but here they are probably used pleonastically. Because the Thessalonians had been well informed on this subject ("you know very well," v. 2), Paul will spend no more time on the matter of times and seasons. Christian teachers today would do well to curb their curiosity about eschatological events not addressed in the Scriptures.

Paul's readers had been told that the day of the Lord would come "like a thief in the night" (**5:2**). The day of the Lord is an Old Testament concept for the day when God judges the wicked and vindicates the righteous. Since Jesus was confessed as Lord by the writers of the New Testament, the day of the Lord was understood as the day of Christ (Phil. 1:10). Sometimes the shorthand "the day" is found (cf. 1 Cor. 3:13; 2 Thess. 1:10). This day is already approaching—it "comes." But no one knows the time. This is vividly set forth by the simile "like a thief in the night." The point of the comparison is that a thief always comes unannounced and so the believer must always be prepared (cf. Luke 12:39). Jesus himself used this metaphor (cf. Matt. 24:42), and it is also found in Peter (2 Pet. 3:10) and in Revelation (3:3; 16:15).

"While people are saying 'Peace and safety,' destruction will come on them suddenly, as labor pains on a pregnant woman, and they will not escape" (**5:3**). Those who are unprepared for Christ's coming, the unbelievers, live in false security. Paul's language reminds us of the contemporaries of Noah (Matt. 24:37–39) and of Jeremiah (Jer. 6:14) who were deaf to the warnings of impending disaster.

Those unprepared will face sudden destruction. The inevitability of utter ruin is underscored by the imagery of a pregnant woman suddenly gripped by labor pains. Once the time has come for her child to be born, nothing can prevent it. Similarly the unbelievers will not escape (the Greek double negative, *ou me*, underscores the impossibility).

This solemn aspect of the parousia is mentioned here to alert the Thessalonians to the need for watchfulness, to which Paul now turns. His readers are emphatically contrasted with the unbelievers. "But you, brothers, are not in darkness so that this day should surprise you like a thief" (**5:4**).

To be in darkness means to be without the saving knowledge of Christ. Believers have cast off the works of darkness (cf. Rom. 13:12) and have become "light in the Lord" (Eph. 5:8). People "in darkness" will be caught unawares by the day, but believers will not be overtaken. This is because they are all "sons of the light and sons of the day" (**5:5**). To be a son of something is a common Semitic idiom meaning that a person is characterized by the thing in question. Those who come out of the darkness of sin, unbelief, and death are characterized by the light of salvation and holiness; they do not "walk in darkness" (1 John 1:5–6). Whether "sons of the day" is used synonymously here with "sons of light" is not certain. It may be that Paul has the day of the Lord in mind. Although this day has not yet arrived, believers already have a foretaste of that day in the present and so are sons of "that day." The opposites of "light" and "day" are "darkness" and "night." Those who belong to the sphere of darkness have no share in the coming day of the Lord.

Because Paul's readers belong to the day, they are now exhorted to remain awake (Gk. *grēgoreuō*, to watch, to be vigilant). "So, then, let us not be like others, who are asleep, but let us be alert and self-controlled" (**5:6**). To sleep (Gk. *katheudō*, different from *koimaō* in 4:15, 17) can mean ordinary physical sleep, the sleep of death (cf. v. 10), or spiritual and moral indifference and dullness. The latter is in focus in verse 7. The wording is reminiscent of a saying of Jesus in Matthew 24:43–44 (cf. also Luke 12:39; Mark 13:35–36). To sleep like "the rest" means to live in spiritual deadness as do the unbelievers.

A synonym for "sleep" is "drunkenness." Christians must be awake and sober. Sleep and drunkenness are associated with the night (**5:7**). Jesus warned against getting drunk and being caught unawares (Matt. 24:48–51). "But since we belong to the day," says Paul, "let us be self-controlled, putting on faith and love as a breastplate, and the hope of salvation as a helmet" (**5:8**). Paul repeats the exhortation to spiritual sobriety from verse 6, and includes himself in the plural: "Let us . . . be sober." And because believers belong to the day they must also be properly dressed (cf. Rom. 13:11–14).

The familiar triad of faith, love, and hope is seen here as appropriate armor, for the Christian warrior is opposed by evil forces (cf. Eph. 6:13–17). The breastplate of faith in Christ and love for him are part of the defensive armor the believer must constantly wear. Where trust in Christ and love for the Savior are lacking, the believer is extremely vulnerable.

The appropriate headgear for the Christian warrior is the helmet of salvation. Although we can experience salvation in the present, it remains but a foretaste of salvation yet to come. "The hope of salvation" means hope for final deliverance at the end of the age—deliverance from the wrath to come (1:10).

Lest Paul's readers should be frightened at the prospect of Christ's sudden and unannounced return, he offers them some words of assurance. "For God did not appoint us to suffer wrath but to receive salvation through our Lord Jesus Christ" (**5:9**). In their struggle against the world, the flesh, and the devil, Paul assures his readers that God's purpose for them is that they should "receive salvation."

To receive salvation does not mean that the Thessalonians do not possess salvation in the present, but salvation is viewed here from the standpoint of the future and from the perspective of human responsibility. God has not appointed them to wrath (Gk. *ethetō*, to put, place, appoint), but to experience final and ultimate salvation. And this will not happen through their own efforts but "through our Lord Jesus Christ" (v. 9b).

The basis of our salvation is the atoning death of Christ. "He died for us so that, whether we are awake or asleep, we may live together with him" (**5:10**). Although Paul does not mention the resurrection, it is implied in the title *Lord Jesus Christ*. The purpose of Christ's death is expressed in different ways (cf. Gal. 1:4, "to rescue us from the present evil age"; Rom. 14:9, "that he might be Lord both of the dead and of the living"). Here the purpose is stated thus: "so that . . . we may live together with him." This is what it means to obtain salvation: it is to lay hold of eternal life, made possible by our union with the risen Christ.

And this life in the age to come is ours "whether we are awake or asleep." To be awake here means to be alive and to sleep means to die. If, according to 4:14, Paul expects to be alive at the parousia, here he faces death. Neither death nor life can rob the believer of the salvation that is yet to be revealed and the hope of sharing eternal life with Christ.

As in 4:18, so here, Paul rounds the paragraph off with an exhortation to mutual encouragement in the light of such assurances of hope. Not only are the Thessalonians to encourage one another but they are to "build each other up" (**5:11**). To build another up is to help someone become spiritually strong. Every member of the church has a responsibility to help other members grow and become mature. And, as so often, Paul's exhortation is accompanied by a word of commendation, "just as in fact you are doing." Again we see that the advent hope is seen as an incentive to holy living and to faithfulness in duty.

VIII. The Internal Life of the Church (5:12–24)

A. The recognition of leaders (5:12–13). The blessed hope of Christ's return did not make Paul a visionary. To wait for the parousia for him meant to be about the Master's business. It meant to build the church, as Paul puts it in verse 11. However, without responsible leadership and respect for such leadership, the church will not develop very well. And so Paul asks his readers "to respect those who work hard among you, who are over you in the Lord and who admonish you" (**5:12**).

Paul describes the work of these leaders in three ways. First, they "work hard" (Gk. *kopiaō* means hard, exhausting work) among the members of the church. *Kopiaō* seems to be used quite generally here, although it may refer to laboring "in preaching and teaching" (1 Tim. 5:17).

Second, the leaders care for the members of the church. *Proistēmi* (lit. to stand before) probably does not refer so much to leading the community as to caring for it, as can be seen from some of its parallel uses (cf. 1 Tim. 3:4, 5, 12). The noun *prostatis* is used for Phoebe, who was a "great help to many people" (Rom. 16:2).

A third ministry of leaders is to admonish (Gk. *noutheteō*, to put into mind). The word is used in general for instruction or, more particularly, for correction, warning, and admonition. (See verse 14, where it is said to be the duty of all members of the church.)

The leaders of the church are to be held in high esteem "because of their work" (**5:13**). Not their social status or natural gifts but their work demands respect. Where the church's leaders exercise their ministry faithfully the members are to show their esteem for them by expressions of love. Agape indicates the manner in which the appreciation of the congregation is to be expressed.

If the ministry of church leaders is to be effective, there must be peace in the congregation. "Live in peace with each other" (v. 13b). Whether this admonition means that the Thessalonian church was troubled by dissension, is hard to say, for it is the kind of concern that Paul expresses again and again. "If you keep on biting and devouring each other, watch out or you will be destroyed by each other" (Gal. 5:15).

B. Interpersonal relationships (5:14–15). The admonition to live in peace with one another marks a transition to several more pastoral injunctions that have to do with interpersonal relationships. It is significant to note that Paul is not addressing the leaders but the members generally when he urges them to "warn those who are idle" (**5:14**). It may be that Paul had in mind those who had ceased to work because they were convinced that Christ's return was imminent. Loafers who live at the expense of others are to be corrected.

"Encourage the timid." The Greek noun *oligopsuchos* occurs only here in the New Testament and it refers to those who feel inadequate, sad, fearful, and timid. The Authorized Version of 1611 rendered it as "feeble-minded"—a translation that is entirely inappropriate today. Through persecution, perhaps, or through feelings of inadequacy of one sort or another, there were people in the church for whom life was too much. These needed to be encouraged.

"Help the weak." Who the weak are is not quite clear. At times the Greek word *antechō* is used for physical weakness, that is, sickness, but here it seems to refer to weakness in the faith (cf. Rom. 14:1) or to moral weakness in the face of sin and temptation. We should, however, not rule out other kinds of weakness, such as come from poverty and oppression. The mark of a good shepherd, according to Ezekiel 34:16, is that he cares for the weak.

"Be patient with everyone." Patience is an attribute of God (Rom. 2:4), who shows restraint in punishing the evil, and his children are to reflect this aspect of his character. Patience is also a fruit of the Spirit (Gal. 5:22), and it is one way in which Christian agape expresses itself (1 Cor. 13:4). How inclusive the command is, is not stated; the members of the church are obviously included, but surely Christian patience should extend even to unbelievers.

For good human relations to develop, Christians must overcome the temptation to seek revenge. "Make sure that nobody pays back wrong for wrong" (**5:15**). Jesus taught nonretaliation in the Sermon on the Mount (Matt. 5:44–48), and Paul follows the Lord in this respect (cf. Rom. 12:17a).

The way to overcome this evil tendency is to "be kind to each other and to everyone else" (v. 15b). One may not always feel naturally attracted to certain people, but one can still do them good. Christian love calls for this pursuit of good deeds, and not only now and then, but "always." This steadfast attempt to do good to our fellow human beings even when they harm us, must not be limited to members of the church, but extend to all.

C. The life of faith (5:16–18). Paul now gives three directives which are expressions of the divine will for the church. The first is the exhortation to be joyful always (**5:16**). In 1:6 Paul makes special note of the joy the Thessalonians experienced even in the midst of tribulation, and he attributes it to the work of the Holy Spirit. And to be sure, joy is a fruit of the Spirit (Gal. 5:22). Christian joy must not be confused with shallow feelings of happiness, for it is a joy that springs from our redemption in Christ and can be experienced even in the midst of tragedy and pain—"sorrowful, yet always rejoicing" (2 Cor. 6:10).

"Pray continually" (**5:17**). If Paul had had formal, audible prayer in mind, this imperative would have been impossible to carry out. Rather, to pray constantly means that the entire life of the believer is lived in dependence on God.

"Give thanks in all circumstances" (**5:18**). Paul is not asking his readers to thank God for tragedy and misfortune, but exhorts them to be thankful in the midst of the various and changing situations in life, be they good or bad. There are always good reasons for gratitude. In contrast to pagans whose lives are characterized by ingratitude (Rom. 1:21), God's children are to be "overflowing with thankfulness" (Col. 2:7).

"For this is God's will for you in Christ Jesus" (v. 18b). In 4:3 God's will was the sanctification of his readers; here God's will embraces the three imperatives (to rejoice, to pray, to be thankful). As members of the church who are in fellowship with Christ Jesus they are asked to do what God wants them to do in the matter of joy, prayer, and gratitude.

D. Life in the assembled community (5:19–22). There are five imperatives in this short paragraph, and they seem to be interrelated. They focus on the life of the gathered Christian community.

The first command is in the form of a prohibition: "Do not put out the Spirit's fire" (**5:19**). The verb *to quench* (Gk. *sbennumi*) is used quite literally elsewhere in the New Testament (cf. Matt. 25:8; Mark 9:48), but in our text it is used metaphorically for restricting the work of the Spirit. Since the Spirit is symbolized by fire (cf. Acts 2:3), the metaphor is quite appropriate.

In light of the next prohibition (not to despise prophecy) it appears as if the Thessalonians, in contrast to the Corinthians, were somewhat indifferent to spiritual gifts. Is Paul suggesting that the gift of tongues, for example, is also a gift of the Spirit? Or were they more interested in tongues, like the Corinthians, and less in prophecy? But Paul does not want the Spirit to be restrained or extinguished.

Second, "do not treat prophecies with contempt" (**5:20**). This prohibition, like the previous one, may suggest that both of these things were in fact happening, and Paul wants them to stop. Why the Thessalonians should have objected to prophetic utterances in the church is not clear. Had prophets made heretical pronouncements, leading to a rejection of prophecy entirely? Was it that they valued other gifts more highly? Or, had prophets called the church to obedience in such a way that the church found it hard to accept their messages? There is no evidence that some prophet had predicted a date for the parousia and that prophecy was now discredited because this prediction was not fulfilled. According to 1 Corinthians 14:3, authentic prophecy is a valuable gift and leads to "strengthening, encouragement, and comfort."

Third, "test everything" (**5:21**). Perhaps Paul's exhortation to allow the Spirit free course could be misconstrued to mean that the congregation was to accept whatever was said without discrimination. Not so, says Paul. The church is to scrutinize all manifestations of the Spirit's gifts. However, some members have the gift of discernment (the ability to distinguish between spirits [1 Cor. 12:10]) in greater measure than others. Naturally, one would expect the leaders of the church to exercise discernment in greater measure.

No criteria are given for testing prophetic utterances. However, Paul does not want the congregation to be naively credulous, but to be discerning. The fourth imperative flows out of the previous "Hold on to the good" (v. 21b). Those prophetic utterances which had the ring of truth about them and were in keeping with the apostolic tradition were to be received and then translated into everyday life.

By contrast, "avoid every kind of evil" (**5:22**). Perhaps the evil Paul has in mind here is more comprehensive than "bad" prophecy, which must be rejected. The Greek *eidōs* (appearance, form, kind, species) was understood by the translators of the Authorized Version in 1611 as something that "appeared" evil. Luther, too, rendered it as the appearance of evil (Ger. *boeser Schein*). However, that meaning does not seem to fit here. Paul wants his readers to have nothing to do with evil in any shape or form.

E. Paul's second prayer (5:23–24). Paul's prayer is addressed to "the God of peace," a title found frequently in Paul (cf. Rom. 15:33; 16:20; 2 Cor. 13:11; Phil. 4:9; 2 Thess. 3:16). "May God himself, the God of peace, sanctify you through and through" (**5:23**). The word *peace* (behind which lies the Old Testament concept of shalom) embraces all the blessings of salvation, and God is seen as the author of all of them.

The concern of Paul in 4:1–5:22 has been that the lives of his readers be sanctified more and more. It is fitting, therefore, that he should in the end pray once again for their complete sanctification (Gk. *holotelēs*, found only here in the New Testament, means "entirely," "completely"). Sanctification is a process which begins with conversion and will be completed only when "perfection comes" (1 Cor. 13:10).

To underscore his desire for the "complete" sanctification of his readers, Paul asks that God keep their "whole spirit, soul and body . . . blameless at the coming of our Lord Jesus Christ" (v. 23b). The adjective *holoklēron* (blameless) qualifies all three nouns (spirit, soul, and body) and means literally, "complete in every part." It would be unwise to take these three nouns to argue for a tripartite doctrine of human nature. The emphasis is rather on the totality of man, and the meaning is not too different from 3:13, where Paul prays that their "hearts" be established so that they might be blameless at the parousia. Then the process of sanctification will be complete. Until that day God protects, watches over, and guards his children.

Paul ends his prayer with a word of assurance. "The one who calls you is faithful and he will do it" (**5:24**). Paul has referred to God's call several times in this letter. God calls his children "into his kingdom and glory" (2:12); he calls them "to live a holy life" (4:7). In Romans 8:30 Paul explains that God will also glorify those whom he calls. And so Paul's readers can be sure that the God who initiated the work of sanctification in their lives, will also complete it (cf. Phil. 1:6).

IX. Closing Comments (5:25–28)

"Brothers, pray for us" (**5:25**). There is good reason for adding the word *also* to this request.

Paul has prayed for the Thessalonians and he now asks that they "also" pray for him. Such requests for prayer are found frequently in Paul's letters and speak of his humility and dependence on God. His high calling to be an apostle of Christ does not make him independent of the prayerful support of the churches. "Brothers" is used here in a collective way including the sisters. Whether the "us" is a literary plural or whether it includes Paul's colleagues is not quite clear.

"Greet all the brothers with a holy kiss" (**5:26**). Kissing was a common form of greeting in Paul's day. What sets this greeting apart from an ordinary kiss is that it is a "holy kiss." Believers are related to one another in Christian fellowship, and so when they greet each other, it is a "kiss of love" (1 Pet. 5:14). The kiss entered Christian liturgy and was perpetuated by the church even when such a greeting no longer fit its cultural context. The forms of greeting vary from culture to culture, but when Christians greet one another there is an added dimension: they greet each other as members of the same family. Paul's words here suggest that he wanted all the members of the church to receive a warm greeting from him.

"I charge you before the Lord to have this letter read to all the brothers" (**5:27**). From the plural Paul changes to the first person singular ("I"). This may mean that he added these final lines with his own hand. It was his custom to dictate his letters.

Paul uses strong language to underscore the importance of reading his letter to the entire congregation (Gk. *enorkizō,* to put under oath). Evidently Paul did not think his adjuration was in violation of Jesus' prohibition against making oaths (Matt. 5:34). There may have been those in the church who were staying away and Paul wants to make sure that all the members of the congregation hear his instructions as well as his assurances of love and concern.

Reading the Old Testament was an essential part of Christian worship (as it was in the synagogue). As time went on, the writings of the apostles also were read in the churches. Paul's exhortations to have his letters read when the church was gathered (cf. Col. 4:16) contributed to this practice.

It is characteristic of Paul not only to begin but also to end his letters with a prayer for grace: "The grace of our Lord Jesus Christ be with you" (**5:28**). "Grace" is a constant theme in all of Paul's writings and instead of the customary farewell he prefers to close his letter by pointing his readers to the source of all the blessings of redemption—the grace of our Lord Jesus Christ.

OUTLINE—2 THESSALONIANS

I. The Greeting (1:1–2)
II. The Judgment at Christ's Coming (1:3–12)
   A. Trials Preceding Christ's Coming (1:3–5)
   B. Retribution at the Time of Christ's Coming (1:6–10)
   C. A Prayer for the Church in Light of Christ's Coming (1:11–12)
III. Events Surrounding Christ's Coming (2:1–12)
   A. The Call for Calmness (2:1–2)
   B. The Coming Apostasy (2:3–7)
   C. Antichrist Revealed (2:8–12)
IV. Right Attitudes Encouraged (2:13–17)
   A. By Recalling the Foundations of Their Faith (2:13–14)
   B. By Exhortations to Stand Firm (2:15)
   C. By a Prayer for Spiritual Maturity (2:16–17)
V. Intercessory Prayer (3:1–5)
   A. Requests for Prayer (3:1–2)
   B. Confidence in Prayer (3:3–4)
   C. A Wish-Prayer (3:5)
VI. Instruction in Faith and Life (3:6–15)
   A. Attitude Toward the Disorderly (3:6–10)
   B. Correction of the Disorderly (3:11–13)
   C. Discipline of the Disorderly (3:14–15)
VII. Final Greetings (3:16–18)

A. The Prayer (3:16)
B. The Authentication (3:17)
C. The Benediction (3:18)

COMMENTARY

I. The Greeting (1:1–2)

As in the first letter to the Thessalonians Paul associates Timothy and Silvanus with him in the prescript. In contrast to 1 Thessalonians, however, the church addressed is said to be "in God *our* Father and the Lord Jesus Christ." God is not only "*the* Father" (1 Thess. 1:1) of our Lord, but also of all believers.

The greeting in this second letter is somewhat more extended: "Grace and peace to you from God the Father and the Lord Jesus Christ" (v. 2). This source of grace and peace is regularly indicated in Paul's letters, but is missing in 1 Thessalonians 1:1. The Greek preposition *from* is not repeated, since Paul associates Jesus with God as a single source of divine blessing. He does this without reservation since for him Jesus Christ is fully divine.

II. The Judgment at Christ's Coming (1:3–12)

A. Trials preceding Christ's coming (1:3–5). It has been suggested that this second letter is less affectionate than the first; however, in proportion to its length, Paul addresses his readers as "brothers" as often in this letter as in the previous one. They are addressed as "brothers" in his introductory thanksgiving: "We ought always to thank God for you, brothers, and rightly so" (**1:3**).

To say "we ought" does not suggest that Paul is thanking God for them grudgingly, or that he did not think there was much to be thankful for. Nor is it likely that Paul's readers had objected to his excessive commendation expressed in his first letter, and that Paul in response insists that it is quite proper ("and rightly so"). The verb *ought* simply indicates the necessity and propriety of thanking God.

Moreover, Paul has good reason for thanking God for the Thessalonians. "Your faith is growing more and more, and the love every one of you has for each other is increasing" (v. 3b). Faith and love were mentioned also in 1 Thessalonians 1:3, and while hope is missing here, the entire letter is pervaded by the hope of Christ's return. In his first letter Paul prayed that their love might increase (1 Thess. 3:10–12); now he thanks God that it has. The Greek compound verb *huperauxanō* (to grow superabundantly, exceedingly, vigorously) is found only here in the New Testament, though Paul is otherwise fond of such superlatives.

Although there were members in the Thessalonian church who created problems, they must have been in the minority, for Paul acknowledges the growing love of "all for each, and each for all."

This growth in their Christian life is going on in spite of trials and testing. "Therefore, among God's churches we boast about your perseverance and faith in all the persecutions and trials you are enduring" (**1:4**). "We ourselves boast" may suggest that it is not considered appropriate for the founders of the church to brag. However, when Paul boasts, he boasts "in the Lord," for he knows that no church is simply the result of human effort, but of God's grace. Or, it could be that the apostles wanted to add their boasting to that of others. Or, since Christian humility would prevent the Thessalonians from boasting, the apostles will boast "in the churches of God." In his first letter the churches of God "in Judea" were mentioned (1 Thess. 2:14); now Paul includes all local churches. And the "churches of God" can also be called "churches of Christ" (cf. Rom. 16:16).

Paul boasts about his readers' "perseverance and faith in all the persecutions and trials you are enduring" (v. 4b). From 1 Thessalonians 1:3 we learn that endurance (Gk. *hypomonē*) springs from hope, and since hope is missing from the familiar trilogy in verse 3, "endurance" compensates for that absence. Connected with "endurance" is "faith," which may have the meaning of faithfulness or fidelity in this context. The combination of steadfastness and faith is found in other writers as well (Heb. 6:12; 11:1; 1 Pet. 1:5–9; Rev. 13:10). In spite of their sufferings, they had remained firm in their commitment to Jesus and the gospel.

"The persecutions and trials" which the readers had to endure in the early days of the church (cf. 1 Thess. 1:6; 2:14) were continuing. However, Paul's converts were bearing up well under these troubles. The adjective *all* further indicates that their sufferings were many and varied.

These sufferings, explains Paul, are "evidence that God's judgment is right, and as a result you will be counted worthy of the kingdom of God, for which you are enduring" (**1:5**).

Just what the evidence of God's righteous judgment is, is not altogether clear. Are persecutions and trials a sign of God's righteous judgment? Or is it the fact that the Thessalonians are standing firm in these trials? Their steadfastness in suffering for Christ's cause anticipates the end of the age when God will set the records straight, justify the innocent, and condemn the wicked. For the church to be fearless in the face of opposition is a clear token that it is on the way to final deliverance, whereas for the wicked it is a sign of ultimate destruction (cf. Phil. 1:28).

The faithful who have to suffer for Christ's sake, and who remain loyal to him in spite of suffering, can anticipate a glorious future; they "will be counted worthy of the kingdom of God" (v. 5b). The kingdom of God is a present reality, inaugurated by Jesus. However, it also has a future dimension, and that aspect of the kingdom is in focus here. Entrance into the eternal kingdom cannot be earned, but after enduring tribulation and remaining true to Jesus, the Thessalonians can rest assured that God will declare them worthy of eternal life. It is for this kingdom that Paul's readers are suffering at the moment—not to gain entrance into the kingdom, but because they are already members of it.

B. Retribution at the time of Christ's coming (1:6–10). "God is just: He will pay back trouble to those who trouble you and give relief to you who are troubled, and to us as well" (**1:6–7**). There is such a thing as divine justice; it is a righteous thing for God to mete out affliction to those oppressing the Thessalonians. In the last judgment the wicked, who now oppose God and trouble his people, will be punished. Paul's language here is reminiscent of Isaiah 66:6 ("repaying his enemies all they deserve"). It is not up to believers to pay back their enemies, for God says, "It is mine to avenge; I will repay" (Rom. 12:19). God's wrath will fall upon the wicked in the end.

However, God also recompenses those who now suffer innocently for his cause (v. 7a). He promises them relief. The Greek *anesis* here refers not simply to the relaxation of persecution, but to eternal rest in the presence of God. "To us" is a tender touch, for it reminds the readers that these matters are not simply of academic interest to Paul and his co-workers. They too had their share of suffering and looked forward to the glory in the age to come. There is a fellowship of suffering that unites Paul with his readers.

And when will this reversal of roles take place? "This will happen when the Lord Jesus is revealed from heaven in blazing fire with his powerful angels" (v. 7b). "Revelation" is one of several key words used to designate Christ's second coming (cf. 1 Cor. 1:7; 1 Pet. 1:7, 13; 4:13). Christ's parousia is an unveiling, an unambiguous manifestation of Christ in all his glory, in contrast to his humility and hiddenness in his earthly life.

When Jesus is revealed from heaven, the dwelling-place of God, he will be accompanied by his powerful angels. Jesus himself had spoken of his coming, accompanied by the angels (Matt. 25:31; cf. 1 Thess. 3:13). He also spoke of the coming of the Son of man in power and glory (Mark 13:26). This revelation of Christ from heaven will be "in blazing fire." Fire is frequently used as a figure of divine judgment in both the Old Testament (cf. Isa. 66:15; Dan. 7:9) and the New Testament (cf. Matt. 25:41; 1 Cor. 3:13ff.).

It is not quite clear whether the coming of Jesus from heaven at his parousia will be in blazing fire or whether the judgment on the wicked will be in flaming fire. It all depends on how the verse is divided.

When Christ's parousia takes place, "he will punish those who do not know God and do not obey the gospel of our Lord Jesus" (**1:8**). The punishment of the wicked is here described as "giving vengeance." In Isaiah 66:15–16, Yahweh is described as coming in fire to execute vengeance (cf. also Ps. 79:6; Jer. 10:25). Vengeance must not be understood as selfish vindictiveness or revenge, but as God's righteous judgment on the wicked.

Whether Paul has two groups of people in mind ("those who do not know God" and "those who do not obey the gospel"), or whether the twofold description is synonymous, is not quite certain. It will not do to see the Gentiles as those who do not know God, and the Jews as those who do not obey the gospel. "Those who do not know God" are not people who are innocently ignorant of God, but who refuse to acknowledge him as God and are therefore culpable (cf. Rom. 1:19–25). "To know God" through personal commitment is to have eternal life (John 17:3), but to reject God is to suffer eternal ruin.

One rejects God by rejecting the gospel. Not to believe the gospel is to "disobey" it. To embrace the good news and to stake one's life on it is to "obey" the gospel. God's judgment will strike both Jews and Gentiles who refuse to accept the good news of salvation.

"They will be punished with everlasting destruction and shut out from the presence of the Lord and from the majesty of his power" (**1:9**). The gift of God to those who believe in Jesus is eternal life; eternal destruction is the portion of those who reject the gospel. "Destruction" does not mean annihilation, for that cannot be eternal, but refers to infinite and eternal suffering and pain. It means to be forever "shut out from the presence of the Lord." And to stress the tragedy of being cut off from Christ's presence forever, Paul once again, by Semitic parallelism, adds "and from the majesty of his power." The language seems to come straight from Isaiah 2:10. To be forever barred from the glory of God is to endure eternal punishment (cf. Matt. 7:23; 25:41, 46). This is the worst prospect for a human being that Paul can imagine.

However, there is a bright side to this separation between the righteous and the wicked at the parousia. When Christ comes he will be "glorified in his holy people" and "marveled at among all those who have believed" (**1:10**). Paul leaves the time of Christ's coming open, but not the fact. Christ will come, and when he does, he comes "to be glorified in his holy people." Perhaps the meaning is that Christ's glory will be reflected, mirrored in his people. If one translates the Greek preposition *en* instrumentally, Paul may be saying that Christ will be glorified (i.e., praised and honored) "by" his own. *En* could even mean "among"—Christ will be glorified in the midst of his own people.

Also, when Christ comes, he "will be marveled at among all those who have believed." God's people and all the denizens of heaven will in the end stand in amazement when they see God's saving purposes fulfilled. The community of believers is the product of God's grace, manifested in Christ, and all who belong to Christ will be overwhelmed by the wonder of it all when he is revealed from heaven.

Almost as a parenthesis Paul adds, "because you believed our testimony to you." The apostles' "testimony" was their preaching of the gospel (cf. 1 Cor. 1:6) in Thessalonica. And because the Thessalonians believed the witness of the missionaries they will be among those who will stand in wonder and amazement when Christ comes in his glory "on that day." "That day" is the day of the Lord (2:2; 1 Thess. 5:2).

C. A prayer for the church in light of Christ's coming (1:11–12). This is the first of four prayers in this second epistle, although, strictly speaking, verses 11 and 12 simply record what Paul prays for. "With this in mind, we constantly pray for you" (**1:11**). In the light of the parousia, which will bring judgment on the wicked and glory to the saints, Paul prays for the Thessalonians. The parousia is an incentive to holy living (cf. 1 Thess. 3:13), and it is Paul's prayer that God will count converts worthy of the call "into his kingdom and his glory" (1 Thess. 2:12)—a call that is heard in the gospel.

Paul "constantly" prays "that by his power he may fulfill every good purpose of yours, and every act prompted by your faith" (v. 11b). Simply put, Paul is praying that the good intentions which God puts into the minds of his readers will be carried out. Such intentions and resolves do not spring from the natural goodness of the human heart; even goodness itself is a fruit of the Spirit (Gal. 5:22). To carry out such good resolves, or to put it differently, the work of faith, one needs divine strength. Paul constantly prays that the Thessalonians may work out their faith by God's power.

The purpose of Paul's prayer ultimately is "that the name of our Lord Jesus may be glorified in you, and you in him, according to the grace of our God and the Lord Jesus Christ" (**1:12**). Christ will be glorified in the saints at the parousia (v. 10), but the saints are to glorify him also in the present, in daily life. A person's name stands for that person, particularly his or her reputation. Christ's name is glorified when his people live in such a manner that they are a credit to him. When God enables his people to carry out their good intentions, to work out their faith, Christ is honored. The addition "and you in him" is not altogether clear. Perhaps the meaning is that when the saints glorify Christ here on earth, they will also share his glory in the end.

Paul is always careful to show that all the blessings of salvation are ours through grace alone: "according to the grace of our God and the Lord Jesus Christ." God's unmerited favor has brought salvation to the Thessalonians and he will not now let them down; he will not abandon them when the last day comes. That grace in all its depth and richness comes from both the Father and the Son, is a constant refrain in the letters of Paul.

III. Events Surrounding Christ's Coming (2:1–12)

A. The call for calmness (2:1–2). In the first chapter of this letter Paul has made plain what the outcome of Christ's coming will be: the wicked will be judged and the saints will be glorified. The time of the parousia, however, is not known, as Paul had explained in his first letter (1 Thess. 5:1–2). From what Paul says in the opening verses of this chapter, there were those who had made prognostications concerning Christ's return, even to the effect that the parousia had already taken place, so it seems, and this had unsettled many of the Thessalonians.

Paul begins, therefore, with an urgent request that they remain calm (**2:1–2**). "We ask you, brothers, not to become easily unsettled or alarmed." His exhortation is affectionate ("brothers") and respectful ("we ask"). He urges them "not to be easily unsettled or alarmed." The verb is used here in the figurative sense. Paul does not want his readers to be shaken out of their wits in the matter of "the coming of our Lord Jesus Christ and our being gathered to him." Paul had already explained that all the saints would be united with Christ at his parousia (1 Thess. 4:17). Here he uses a rather novel expression, *episunagōgē* (gathering together). The only other occurrence of this noun is in Hebrews 10:25, where the word refers to the gathering of the Christian community for worship (perhaps with an eye to the parousia). The parousia, when the saints will be gathered for a meeting with their Lord, is here called the day of the Lord (v. 2). It was the hope of some prophets that scattered exiles of Israel would one day be gathered together (Isa. 52:12; Zech. 2:6), and this thought was taken over by Jesus and the early church and applied to the final gathering of the elect (Matt. 23:37; Mark 13:27; Luke 13:34).

Evidently some prophet had spoken "by the Spirit," claiming that the day of the Lord had already come. Whether this claim was made by a false prophet or whether the Thessalonians had misconstrued the utterance made by a trustworthy prophet, is not clear. Paul had earlier (1 Thess. 5:19–20) encouraged his readers to value prophecy, but also to be discriminating. In any case the church had been stirred up needlessly by such misunderstandings. Just how the spoken word (Gk. *dia logou*) is to be distinguished from prophecy (Gk. *dia pneumatos*) is not quite clear. Perhaps a sermon or a word, purporting to be the message of spiritual wisdom (1 Cor. 12:8), or any kind of utterance, is meant. Again, discrimination is called for.

Whether the phrase *supposed to have come from us* applies to "Spirit" and "word" as well as to "letter," is not certain, but very likely not. Evidently the Thessalonians had received a "Pauline" letter in which the imminence of Christ's coming had been stressed. Some concluded that the day of the Lord had already come. If "letter" is a reference to our 1 Thessalonians, as some think, then Paul is now correcting a misunderstanding of his letter. Some think the reference is to a non-Pauline epistle written in Paul's name. That Paul was concerned about forgeries of this sort may be inferred from 3:17. Be that as it may, Paul assumes no responsibility for having taught that the day of the Lord had already come.

B. The coming apostasy (2:3–7). Jesus, in his apocalyptic discourse, warned against deceivers (Mark 13:5), and Paul too is concerned that his readers not be led astray by false teachings regarding the Lord's return (**2:3**). For that reason he instructs him concerning the major developments leading up to the coming of Christ. Before the parousia takes place, Paul explains, there will come a great rebellion and the man of lawlessness will be revealed; his readers must be careful not to be deceived "in any way" (a reference perhaps to the three possibilities mentioned in v. 2).

The day of the Lord will not come "until the rebellion occurs." *Apostasia* (rebellion) can mean either a political revolt or a religious rebellion, or a combination of the two. In the Septuagint the word is used for rebellion against God (cf. Josh. 22:22; Jer. 2:19), and that is apparently the meaning here. However, we should not rule out a revolt against all civil order as part of the large-scale rebellion against God. "The thought is, we suggest, that when the moment comes for Christ to appear in glory and for all rebels against God to be unmasked and cast out, the forces of evil will arise as never before in a last desperate effort against God."[3]

Hand in hand with this massive uprising against God goes the revelation of "the man of lawlessness, the man doomed to destruction." "Man of lawlessness" is a Semitic idiom for "the lawless one" (cf. v. 8), as is the expression *son of perdition,* meaning a person destined for destruction.

Like the Lord Jesus, this man of lawlessness will also have a "revelation." This suggests that he is Christ's rival and is, in fact, the Antichrist (a term used by John in his epistles; e.g., 1 John 2:18). At the end of the age when the Son of man will be revealed in all his glory, the Antichrist will also be unmasked. His revelation will be followed by his destruction. What is said of the beast in Revelation 17:8, is said of the lawless one here: he goes to ruin, to destruction. This is the lot of all the enemies of God (1:8–9; 1 Thess. 5:3).

The activity of this wicked monster is described largely in terms taken from the Book of Daniel, where Antiochus Epiphanes' evil deeds are mentioned (Dan. 8:11–14). The Antichrist opposes God's work, and "exalts himself over everything that is called God or is worshiped" (**2:4**). The vocabulary seems to come directly from Daniel 11:36–37. Antichrist exalts himself over the true and living God as well as over

3. A. L. Moore, *I and II Thessalonians* (Greenwood, S.C.: Attic, 1969), 101.

all other gods. Moreover, he exalts himself over everything that people hold sacred. In his pride he arrogates to himself prerogatives which belong to God alone, so that he even "sets himself up in God's temple, proclaiming himself to be God" (v. 4b). The *naos* (temple) is the sanctuary proper, the holiest part of the entire temple complex. The imagery is drawn from Daniel 8, where reference is made to the desecration of the temple in Jerusalem by Antiochus Epiphanes. Similar imagery is found in Mark 13:14.

Although the Jerusalem temple still stood when Paul wrote, Jesus had predicted its total destruction. How then is this eschatological evil personage to take his seat in the holy place? Since the church is called God's temple (cf. 1 Cor. 3:16; 2 Cor. 6:16; Eph. 2:21), some think the coming lawless one will find his power base in an apostate church. However, that goes beyond what our text says. It is probably best to take "temple of God" as a metaphor, meaning that the Antichrist will usurp God's authority. And like the arrogant king of Tyre (Ezek. 28:2) the lawless one proclaims himself to be God and, by implication, demands loyalty and worship from all people. Although Antichrist has many forerunners in history, this eschatological enemy of God has not yet been revealed.

Some instructions about this eschatological revolt against God had been included in Paul's teaching while in Thessalonica. "Don't you remember that when I was with you I used to tell you these things?" (**2:5**). Apart from 3:17–18, this is the only instance in this letter where Paul uses the first person singular. He had taught the Thessalonians about the parousia, but they had not remembered that the great rebellion and the revelation of Antichrist would take place before Christ returns.

"And now you know what is holding him back, so that he may be revealed at the proper time" (**2:6**). Paul's readers knew because they had been told; we are not so fortunate and so have to make informed guesses at what it is that restrains the Antichrist from coming into the open. Implied is that God determines the time, and not the lawless one.

A number of suggestions have been made for the identification of the restraining power in **2:7**: (1) The state with its law and order is one suggestion. Paul did respect the state (Rom. 13:1–7). (2) The preaching of the gospel restrains the manifestation of evil. The "restrainer" might then be Paul, or the preachers of the gospel. We must concede that this time of grace is being extended by God (cf. 2 Pet. 3:8f.) to allow for the preaching of the gospel in the world (Mark 13:10). (3) The Holy Spirit also has been identified as "the one who now holds it back." That God's Spirit is at work in the church, as well as in the world, is clear from the New Testament. But whether Paul had this or some other power (or personage) in mind when he wrote this letter is impossible to say. What is significant for the church at all times, however, is the fact that God is in control of human history and that he has ways of keeping the titanic power of evil under control until the day when he makes an end of all resistance to his purposes.

Although it is comforting to know that evil is kept in check, Paul is realistic enough to know that "the secret power of lawlessness is already at work" (v. 7a). The Greek word *mystērion* (mystery, secret) in the New Testament means something that cannot be known except by revelation. It is a secret, concealed until God removes the veil. God's salvific purposes, which have become plain in Christ, are called "mysteries" (e.g., Eph. 1:9; 3:3, 4). "The secret power of lawlessness" is a satanic counterpart to the mystery of God's saving plans. Implied may also be the notion that unless God opens our eyes we do not see evil for what it really is.

A parallel to our text is 1 John 2:18, where the apostle predicts the coming of Antichrist and then adds that "even now many antichrists have come." So the man of lawlessness will be revealed at the parousia of the Lord Jesus, but evil powers are already at work throughout history. The present "lawlessness" foreshadows the coming of the lawless one in the end.

The last clause is elliptical: "but the one who now holds it back will continue to do so till he is taken out of the way" (v. 7b). Clearly this day of grace, in which the Spirit is at work, the gospel is proclaimed, and the church of Jesus Christ is being completed, will some day come to an end. Mercifully God restrains the sinister powers who seek to destroy his work during the interim between Christ's first and second advents. However, when the last day comes, this restraint will disappear and the lawless one will be seen for what he is.

C. Antichrist revealed (2:8–12). "And then the lawless one will be revealed, whom the Lord Jesus will overthrow with the breath of his mouth and destroy by the splendor of his coming" (**2:8**). We are encouraged to look forward to the revelation of Jesus Christ at the end of the age (cf. 1 Cor. 1:7), not to the revelation of the lawless one. Nevertheless, this evil personage will have a revelation. However, he is revealed only to be destroyed. Nothing much is said about his career or the extent of his rule; only his revelation and his end are announced.

Our Lord himself will destroy him with "the

breath of his mouth." The language here is reminiscent of Isaiah 11:4, where the coming prince of the house of David is to smite the earth with "the rod of his mouth" and destroy the wicked with "the breath of his lips." In Revelation 19 the enemies of God are destroyed by the sharp sword coming out of the mouth of the rider on the white horse.

Christ will put the Antichrist out of commission by "the splendor of his coming." The words *appearing* (Gk. *epiphaneia*) and *coming* (Gk. *parousia*) are both used to designate Christ's coming at the end of the age. *Epiphaneia* emphasizes the splendor and majesty of Christ's parousia. Antichrist, Satan's agent par excellence, will not be able to stand the dazzling presence of our Lord; he will wilt away when Christ appears in glory.

Paul does not underestimate the power of the lawless one, even though he has just spoken confidently of his end. "The coming of the lawless one will be in accordance with the work of Satan displayed in all kinds of counterfeit miracles, signs and wonders" (**2:9**). Having just mentioned our Lord's parousia (v. 8), Paul explains that this false Christ will also have a parousia. The use of the word *parousia* probably suggests a parody, a kind of caricature of Christ's second coming.

Three things are said about the parousia of the lawless one. First, Satan is behind it (v. 9a). It is "in accordance with the work of Satan." A parallel to this passage is found in Revelation 13:12, where the beast from the sea receives his power from the great red dragon, which is Satan. Antichrist receives his authority and inspiration from the devil.

Second, the power of the lawless one is displayed in "counterfeit miracles, signs and wonders" (v. 9b). *Dynamis* (power) speaks of the supernatural nature of Antichrist's work, and may be a reference to the miracles (the "all," then, would mean "all kinds" of miracles). Jesus had foreseen the coming of false messiahs and false prophets who would show signs and wonders and lead astray, if possible, even the elect (Mark. 13:22; par. Matt. 24:24). The signs and wonders performed by the lawless one are done to deceive; the signs and wonders performed by our Lord showed him to be approved by God (Acts 2:22).

Third, the powerful deeds of the lawless one deceive those who are perishing (**2:10**). His appearing at the end of the age will dazzle his followers. He will perpetuate "every sort of evil that deceives," meaning every sort of deceit that wickedness can devise. The deception of the lawless one is not defined, but in Revelation 13:13 the false prophet persuades people to worship the beast. And, as in Revelation 13:12, where the inhabitants of the earth (i.e., the wicked) are deceived, so the lawless one here "deceives those who are perishing." Those going to perdition are particularly vulnerable to his trickery. They lack discernment and are so dazzled by the powerful deeds of the lawless one that they follow him like dupes to their destruction. The destruction of the wicked is a process which begins in this life and ends in the beyond (cf. 1 Cor. 1:18).

The reason the wicked will be swept away by Antichrist's display of power is that "they refused to love the truth and so be saved" (v. 10b). The word *welcome* has been used several times (cf. 1 Thess. 1:6; 2:13) of the acceptance of the gospel by the Thessalonians. To receive the truth is to be saved. God wants all people to come to the knowledge of the truth (1 Tim. 2:4) and be saved. To reject the love of the truth means to refuse the message of the gospel. And since only those who embrace "the truth" are saved, rejection of the love of the truth leads to eternal ruin.

When people suppress the truth, God gives them up (Rom. 1:26–28). Here "God sends them a powerful delusion so that they will believe the lie" (**2:11**). God does not sit passively by. He is at work judging those who reject the gospel. Those who refuse the truth embrace the lie. To be misled by falsehood is the divine judgment incurred by those who reject God's truth. God sends them a "powerful delusion." It should, however, be added that the real author of their deception is "the god of this age," who blinds the minds of unbelievers (2 Cor. 4:4). When people reject the truth of God they "believe the lie."

Those who do not believe the truth "will be condemned" (**2:12**). The truth is the revelation of God in the gospel, and when this truth is rejected, the foundation for morality is gone. The result is that people delight in wickedness. Those who do not obey the truth, obey unrighteousness (Rom. 2:8). "To take pleasure" in something means to choose it and to approve of it. Rejection of Christ and the gospel leads to a life of sin. Such a life ends in eternal ruin.

The mystery of lawlessness is already at work. It will reach its climax when this age comes to an end and will find its ultimate expression in the lawless one, the Antichrist. However, the parousia of this evil personage will be short-lived, for our Lord will shatter his power and his reign by "the splendor of his coming" (v. 8). Those who trusted Christ by receiving the gospel will then enter into their eternal rest (1:7), but the followers of the lawless one, the unbelievers, will be condemned (v. 12).

IV. Right Attitudes Encouraged (2:13–17)

A. By recalling the foundations of their faith (2:13–14). Misunderstandings about Christ's second advent made it essential for Paul to deal with the darkness in human history. That done, he turns again to pastoral concerns—the spiritual growth of his readers. "But we" suggests a change of subject (**2:13**). From the doom of unbelievers Paul turns to the salvation of believers. He addresses them in a very affectionate manner: "brothers, loved by the Lord." The language here is similar to 1 Thessalonians 1:4, where he speaks to them as "brothers loved by God." "Lord" here probably means Jesus, rather than God. Paul ascribes to Jesus what he ascribes to God elsewhere.

"We ought always to thank God for you" is a repetition of the first clause of 1:3, with the emphatic *we* added. But whereas in 1:3 Paul feels led to thank God for the demonstration of Christian graces in the lives of his readers, here he thanks God for what he has done and is still doing in their lives.

Paul thanks God for their election: "from the beginning God chose you to be saved through the sanctifying work of the Spirit and through belief in the truth" (v. 13). Whether "from the beginning" (Gk. *ap archēs*) is the correct reading is not quite certain. There is strong manuscript evidence that we should read "firstfruits" (Gk. *aparchē*) instead. The meaning then would be that the Thessalonians are the firstfruits (a concept deeply embedded in the Old Testament cult) of a greater harvest. The context, however, seems to be against this reading.

In eternity past God in love chose the Thessalonians "to be saved." Deliverance from sin, fear, and death is experienced in the present, but it remains also a hope as long as this age lasts. The purpose of God's election is salvation. The means by which salvation is secured are twofold: "through the sanctifying work of the Spirit and through belief in the truth" (v. 13b). Sanctification is God's will (1 Thess. 4:3–8) made possible by his Spirit (par. 1 Pet. 1:2). Sanctification is a process that begins with conversion and will be completed only when Christ returns (1 Thess. 3:13; 5:23). It is a source of great comfort to believers to know that God's Spirit is at work in their lives, transforming them. Sanctification by the Spirit, however, does not rule out human responsibility. "Belief in the truth" is the language of human responsibility, but it should be remembered that without God's Spirit, faith in the gospel (i.e., the truth) is not possible either.

"He called you to this through our gospel, that you might share in the glory of our Lord Jesus Christ" (**2:14**). Salvation, sanctification, and faith are but preparatory for possessing the glory that is yet to be revealed. God's call to experience the blessings of salvation comes through the gospel. However, in this life believers never enter fully into all that Christ has procured for them, and so they look forward to the day when they will gain possession of the glory of the Lord Jesus Christ. Believers will enter Christ's glory at the parousia.

B. By exhortations to stand firm (2:15). "So then" translates a pair of inferential conjunctions in Greek. In light of the manifestation of evil prior to Christ's coming, and in light of the glory that awaits those who hear God's call to salvation, Paul calls his readers to steadfastness. "Brothers, stand firm" (v. 15a). If God's call to salvation and the sanctifying work of the Spirit underscore the divine initiative, this imperative to stand firm puts the emphasis on human response. The Thessalonians had already been exhorted to stand firm in the face of persecutions (1 Thess. 3:8); now they are urged to remain steadfast also with respect to sound doctrine.

"Hold to the teachings we passed on to you, whether by word of mouth or by letter" (v. 15b). To stand firm is to hold fast the "traditions." "Traditions" are the ethical and doctrinal teachings of Jesus and the apostles (cf. 1 Cor. 11:23). Paul's readers had been taught "the traditions" (i.e., the gospel message, including its ethical demands) by the missionaries. They had been taught orally and in writing—very likely a reference to 1 Thessalonians. There is no suggestion here that either oral or written tradition is more authoritative. "Traditions of men" can threaten a person's spiritual welfare (Mark 7:8; Col. 2:8), but the teachings of Jesus and the apostles (the traditions) are made alive from generation to generation by the Spirit of God.

C. By a prayer for spiritual maturity (2:16–17). This is the second of four short prayers in this brief epistle (1:11–12; 2:16–17; 3:5; 3:16). Paul has urged his readers to stand firm and to follow sound teachings. However, they cannot do so in their own strength, and so once again, he looks to God for help.

Paul addresses his prayer to "our Lord Jesus Christ himself and God our Father" (**2:16**). Since Christ and God are so completely united, it makes little difference if God rather than Christ is named first (see 1 Thess. 3:11). The emphatic *himself* is not uncommon in Paul's prayers (cf. 3:16; 1 Thess. 3:11; 5:23).

Paul's encouragement lies in the fact that God has lavished his love upon humankind. He "loved us and by his grace gave us eternal encouragement and good hope" (v. 16). Paul is probably referring to the incarnation and death of Christ, where God's love found its supreme expression. By God's redeeming act at Calvary he has given us "eternal encouragement." The Greek noun *paraklēsis* covers a wide area of meaning and could be translated as "encouragement," "consolation," "courage," and so forth. This *paraklēsis,* given freely by God's grace, is not only temporally unbounded, but is qualitatively different from the comfort this present age can provide.

Another gift, graciously bestowed by God upon his people, is "good hope." Our hope is good because it reaches beyond the grave; it is not rooted in the vicissitudes of this present order; it is a hope that does not disappoint (Rom. 5:5). And both "comfort" and "hope" have come to us by God's grace.

Turning now to the actual petitions, Paul prays that Jesus and God might "encourage your hearts and strengthen you in every good deed and word" (**2:17**). Paul has just assured his readers that God has given them "eternal encouragement," and now he prays that they might experience it. "Heart" stands for the inner man. Sometimes God uses people to encourage and comfort our hearts. Of Tychicus Paul says that he will "comfort their hearts" (Col. 4:8; Eph. 6:22). God is the "God of all comfort" (2 Cor. 1:3).

Paul's second wish for his readers is that God will strengthen them in every good deed and word. *Stērizō* means to support, establish, or buttress. Metaphorically it is used for "strengthening," "establishing." Paul prayed earlier (1 Thess. 3:13) that the Thessalonians be strengthened in holiness. Here he prays that they may be strengthened in every good deed and word. Believers need God's help to do good works as well as speak good words. Work and word are frequently bound together (cf. Luke 24:19; Acts 7:22), and should not be divorced in everyday life.

V. Intercessory Prayer (3:1–5)

A. Requests for prayer (3:1–2). The word *finally* here is an indication that the letter is drawing to a close. Having just prayed for his readers, Paul, in turn, asks them to pray for him. It is a sign of the apostle's humility that he would ask his converts, young in the faith, to pray for him (cf. 1 Thess. 5:25).

To make their intercession meaningful, he asks them to pray for two things in particular: First, "that the message of the Lord may spread rapidly and be honored, just as it was with you" (**3:1**). "The word of the Lord" is the gospel. It is a message about the Lord Jesus, but it also comes from him; it is his, not man's word. This word is to "run"—a metaphor taken from the stadium, although the language is found also in Psalm 147:15. When the word runs it makes progress, it spreads rapidly.

When the gospel spreads, when it is received, God's word is "honored"; it triumphs, it fulfills its purpose. Paul had good reason to hope that the gospel would triumph, for it had done so in Thessalonica ("just as it was with you").

However, Paul is realistic enough to know that the gospel often comes up against fierce opposition, and so he asks that the Thessalonians pray for his own safety: "And pray that we may be delivered from wicked and evil men, for not everyone has faith" (**3:2**). The gospel can run only when faithful messengers proclaim it. And this frequently led to violent attacks on those messengers by "wicked and evil men." The reason such people oppose the progress of the gospel is unbelief ("not everyone has faith"). Faith is for Paul the divine link between the people of God and the enemies of God. Paul himself had experienced much suffering at the hands of those who opposed the gospel, and he asks his readers to pray for his deliverance from dangerous people. Praying for the safety of Paul and his companions was tantamount to praying for the progress of the gospel.

B. Confidence in prayer (3:3–4). Paul's prayer request (vv. 1–2) leads into a confident appeal to the Lord's faithfulness. "But the Lord is faithful" (**3:3**). Not all have faith (Gk. *pistis,* v. 1), but God is faithful (Gk. *pistos,* v. 2)—a word play. To say that God is faithful means that he is credible; he is worthy of belief and trust.

Paul is confident that such a trustworthy God will strengthen his readers (as in 2:17), establishing them in the faith, and guard them from evil. This does not mean that they will have no trials or troubles, but God will shield them from "the evil one." The language is reminiscent of the petition in the Lord's Prayer, "but deliver us from the evil one" (Matt. 6:13).

Paul has confidence not only in the Lord, but also in his converts. "We have confidence in the Lord that you are doing and will continue to do the things we command" (**3:4**). Although Paul expresses enduring confidence in the Thessalonians, it is grounded, not in their strength of character but "in the Lord." The apostle trusts in the Lord that the readers are continuing and will continue to do what he commands. Not only does he expect them to observe the oral teachings they received when the missionaries visited Thessalonica, but also the written instructions given in these letters to them.

C. A wish-prayer (3:5). "May the Lord direct your hearts into God's love and Christ's perseverance" (v. 5). This is the third of four prayers in this short letter (cf. 1:11f.; 2:16f.; 3:5; 3:16). The Greek verb *kateuthunō* means to make straight or level, preparing the way, removing obstacles (cf. 1 Thess. 3:11 for the opening of the way to Thessalonica). It is not guidance Paul's readers need, but steadfastness on the path that leads to the two goals: the love of God, and the endurance of Christ.

Our love for God is a response to his love for us. It is very likely that Christ's perseverance is the endurance which he displayed when he was on earth, and which remains the model for the believer (TEV, however, has "the endurance that is given by Christ"). To take endurance in the sense of patient waiting for Christ's return does not seem to fit the context. Christ endured hostility from sinners (Heb. 12:3), and the Thessalonians must be prepared to follow in their Master's steps.

VI. Instruction in Faith and Life (3:6–15)

A. Attitude toward the disorderly (3:6–10). "In the name of the Lord Jesus Christ, we command you, brothers, to keep away from every brother who is idle and does not live according to the teaching you received from us" (**3:6**). As an apostle Paul has the authority to command. The word *command* is softened, however, by the address *brothers.* Moreover, the apostolic commands are given "in the name of the Lord Jesus Christ," and so do not come from a desire to control the church, but are given by the authority of Jesus.

Paul urges his readers to withdraw from close fellowship with those who live in "disorderly" ways. This was one of the means of disciplining faulty members in the early church. To live *ataktōs* (lit. out of step) in this context seems to mean to live a lazy life, to live in idleness, and in this way to exploit the hard work of others. Such a life is not in keeping with "the tradition" which they received from the apostles. It appears as if the admonitions in Paul's first letter (1 Thess. 4:9–12) had not had the intended effect, and so Paul has to return to this topic. Evidently Paul has in mind people who held that Christ's coming was imminent and consequently gave up their daily work. Obviously Paul is not criticizing people who are unemployed and would like to work.

In fact, that Paul has loafers in mind is made rather obvious. "For you yourselves know how you ought to follow our example. We were not idle when we were with you, nor did we eat anyone's food without paying for it" (**3:7–8**). The imitation of Paul is a recurring theme in his letters (cf. 1 Cor. 4:16; 11:1; Phil. 4:9; 1 Thess. 1:6). Paul and his associates did not live disorderly lives, and the readers ought to imitate their example.

The example Paul set before his converts is defined negatively first: they were not lazy among them, and did not eat anyone's food without paying for it. To eat someone's food gratis probably means to enjoy both board and lodging at another's expense.

Positively stated, the apostles were examples to their converts in the way they worked. "On the contrary, we worked night and day, laboring and toiling so that we would not be a burden to any of you" (v. 8b). Jesus taught that a laborer is worthy of his food (Matt. 10:10), but Paul and his companions waived this right in order not to be a burden to people. Instead, they worked incessantly ("day and night") and thereby set an example for their converts (cf. 1 Thess. 2:9, where the resaon for working is that their motives should not be misunderstood).

Paul explains that it would have been perfectly proper if they had received financial aid. "We did this, not because we do not have the right to such help, but in order to make ourselves a model for you to follow" (**3:9**). Those in the church who refused to work and became dependent on others could have claimed the example of the missionaries, had they lived at other people's expense while in Thessalonica. Fortunately, the apostles paid their own way and that should now serve as an example to their converts.

Paul repeats in writing what he and his associates had taught their converts orally: "For even when we were with you, we gave you this rule: 'If a man will not work, he shall not eat' " (**3:10**). A person who refuses to work and burdens others is not to be supported. It is not necessarily an expression of love when idlers are allowed to exploit those who labor faithfully.

B. Correction of the disorderly (3:11–13). After laying down some general guidelines, Paul speaks to the Thessalonian situation directly. "We hear that some among you are idle. They are not busy; they are busybodies" (**3:11**). Just how the rumor had come to Paul's attention is not stated, but there was enough traffic between Corinth and Thessalonica to make this kind of communication possible. The problem which Paul addresses was caused by a minority of the church ("some among you"). Certain people were living *ataktōs.* While the adverb can be understood in the wider sense of "disorderly," the participles explicating this adverb make it clear that idleness is meant: "not busy, but busybodies"—minding everyone else's business but their own. Refusing to work themselves, they meddled and interfered in other people's lives. Whereas some commentators think the

Thessalonian problem stemmed from the expectation of Christ's immediate return, others are of the opinion that the idlers had a false understanding of brotherly love, and were exploiting the generosity of their fellow believers.

For the third time in this chapter (vv. 6, 10, 12) we have the word *command.* However, it is in tandem with the verb *urge,* softening the tone of Paul's instructions. Nevertheless, Paul speaks in the name of the Lord Jesus Christ and so his counsel must be taken seriously. "Such people we command and urge in the Lord Jesus Christ to settle down and earn the bread they eat" (**3:12**). As in 1 Thessalonians 4:11, Paul urges them to lead a quiet life. To be calm and contented as they go about their daily tasks and earn their daily bread would be the antithesis of interfering in other people's affairs.

Paul now turns to the entire congregation once more: "And as for you, brothers, never tire of doing what is right" (**3:13**). The emphatic *but you* suggests a contrast with the idlers. However badly the latter behave, the church must not grow weary in well-doing (Gal. 6:9).

The verb *tire* has the primary meaning of "behaving badly," but is used in the New Testament for "tiring through discouragement" (cf. Luke 18:1; 2 Cor. 4:1; Eph. 3:13). We have a word play in Greek that could be rendered "while doing good, do not go bad." The abuse of brotherly love by idlers should not discourage the church from helping others in need.

C. Discipline of the disorderly (3:14–15). No doubt Paul hoped that the disorderly would respond positively to his instructions. However, knowing human nature, chances were that some would not. In that case, they must be disciplined. "If anyone does not obey our instruction in this letter, take special note of him. Do not associate with him, in order that he may feel ashamed" (**3:14**).

Those who reject Paul's words in this letter should be noted. That means "to mark well" (a bit like our nota bene). We have a parallel in Romans 16:17: "Watch out for those who cause divisions and put obstacles in your way. . . . Keep away from them."

The Thessalonians are to have nothing to do with the disorderly (the idlers). The verb literally means "to get mixed up with." Paul does not want his readers to have close fellowship with those whose behavior is reproachable. The same verb is used in 1 Corinthians 5:9, 11, but there the church's discipline of the man living in incest is more severe: he is to be excommunicated. Here, the offenders are to be denied close social contact (probably including social meals). The immediate purpose of withholding fellowship is to put such offenders to shame in the hope that they will repent and mend their ways and be restored to full fellowship.

When such discipline is exercised, there is the temptation to treat the offender as an enemy. Against that kind of attitude Paul cautions: "Yet do not regard him as an enemy, but warn him as a brother" (**3:15**). The person is still a member of the church, a true believer, though temporarily under discipline. The attitude of fellow believers toward those who have failed often determines whether the latter will receive correction. Offenders are to be warned. Where membership in the Christian community is taken seriously, this kind of discipline is possible and can be very effective.

VII. Final Greetings (3:16–18)

A. The prayer (3:16). As in his first letter (cf. 1 Thess. 5:23), Paul closes with a prayer: "Now may the Lord of peace himself give you peace at all times and in every way. The Lord be with all of you" (v. 16). The common address in Paul's prayers, "the God of peace," is replaced (and only here in the New Testament) by "the Lord of peace." Behind the Greek *eirēnē* (peace) lies the Hebrew *šālōm,* which has the sense of health, wholeness, and salvation, not only the absence of strife, as the Greek word suggests. "The Lord of peace" alone is able to give this kind of peace to his children "at all times and in every way."

Another wish in this parting prayer is in the form of a liturgical benediction: "The Lord be with all of you." This is the third "all" in Paul's prayer. It may be that Paul is concerned that the offenders also be embraced in his final prayer and benediction. This petition is in keeping with the promise of the risen Christ: "And surely I am with you always, to the very end of the age" (Matt. 28:20).

B. The authentication (3:17). "I, Paul, write this greeting in my own hand, which is the distinguishing mark in all my letters. This is how I write."

At this point Paul took the pen from the hand of his amanuensis to add a final personal greeting. It was not an uncommon practice in the ancient world for the one who had dictated a letter to write the last sentence or two in his own hand. That Paul dictated his letters is obvious from references such as Romans 16:22, where the amanuensis (Tertius) is, in fact, named. Here Paul alerts his readers to this practice, and this should help them distinguish genuine letters from spurious ones written in his name. It may be, too, that Paul simply wanted to stress the importance of what he had to say in his letters.

C. The benediction (3:18). This second letter ends the way the first letter did, with the exception that here another "all" is added. Although he has had some hard things to say to those who were embarrassing the church by their behavior, Paul's wish for all the members is: "The grace of our Lord Jesus Christ be with you all." What is more natural for a man upon whom God's grace had been lavished so profusely, than to express the wish before God that his readers, too, experience God's grace in all its depth and richness!

SELECT BIBLIOGRAPHY

Bruce, F. F. *I and II Thessalonians.* Waco: Word, 1982.

Frame, J. E. *A Critical and Exegetical Commentary on the Epistles of St. Paul to the Thessalonians.* The International Critical Commentary. New York: Charles Scribner's Sons, 1912.

Grayston, K. *The Letters of Paul to the Philippians and to the Thessalonians.* Cambridge: Cambridge University Press, 1967.

Harris, W. B. *I and II Thessalonians.* London: Epworth, 1968.

Hendriksen, W. *Exposition of I and II Thessalonians.* Grand Rapids: Baker, 1955.

Hiebert, D. E. *The Thessalonian Epistles.* Chicago: Moody, 1971.

Marshall, I. H. *I and II Thessalonians.* Grand Rapids: Eerdmans, 1983.

Milligan, G. *St. Paul's Epistles to the Thessalonians.* Reprint. Grand Rapids: Eerdmans, 1952.

Moore, A. L. *I and II Thessalonians.* Greenwood, S.C.: Attic, 1969.

Morris, L. *The First and Second Epistles to the Thessalonians.* Grand Rapids: Eerdmans, 1959.

Thomas, R. L. *I and II Thessalonians.* Grand Rapids: Zondervan, 1968.

Ward, R. A. *Commentary on 1 and 2 Thessalonians.* Waco: Word, 1973.

1–2 TIMOTHY/TITUS

George W. Knight III

INTRODUCTION

The letters to Timothy and Titus share a number of characteristics. In distinction from Paul's other letters they are written to apostolic assistants (Timothy and Titus) concerning the needs of the churches in which they labor and their pastoral responsibilities—hence the title *the pastoral Epistles,* or *the Pastorals.* They also seem to reflect a similar time frame (the latter period of Paul's life), concern about false teachers and the officers and organization of the church, and the intent to preserve and pass on the apostolic teaching.

The explicit self-testimony of each letter is that Paul is the author (1 Tim. 1:1; 2 Tim. 1:1; Titus 1:1). This testimony is corroborated by several other factors. The relationship between Paul and the recipients, Timothy and Titus, is known from elsewhere in the New Testament (cf., e.g., Acts 16:lff.; Gal. 2:3). A number of personal references to Paul's own life and experiences and to his relationship with Timothy and Titus are found in the letters (1 Tim. 1:2, 3, 12–16, 18–20; 3:14, 15; 4:14; 6:20; 2 Tim. 1:2–8, 13, 15; 2:1, 2; 3:10–15; 4:9–15; 19–21; Titus 1:4, 5; 3:12, 13).

Some have suggested that Paul could not and did not write these letters. One group suggests that some fragments of Paul's writings were collected and used under his name. Another group suggests that the letters in their entirety were made up by someone writing in Paul's name. An objection to these last two approaches is that such a practice seems out of accord with the assertion of authorship given. Although such a practice may have occurred in the non-Christian community, even so there is no evidence of letters being written under someone else's name. Furthermore, Paul himself warned against this (2 Thess. 2:2; cf. Gal. 6:11; 2 Thess. 3:17).

Arguments for non-Pauline authorship over against Pauline authorship may be reduced to basically three areas. First, most everyone agrees that these letters cannot be placed in the framework of the history of Acts and therefore presume Paul's release from the imprisonment of Acts 28, a further period of activity (1 Tim., Titus), and reimprisonment (2 Tim.). It is objected that this presumption has no basis in fact and is made up to validate the Pauline authorship of the

Pastorals. Others think that such passages as Acts 28 and Philippians 1:25–26 imply such a release, that the Pastorals themselves are evidence, and that several writers in the early church bear explicit witness to a release and second imprisonment.

Second, the content of these letters is said to be contrary to Pauline authorship. For example, the church's organization is said to be too advanced, the false teaching that of the second century, and the view of doctrine too orthodox and set. Furthermore, doctrines such as justification by faith, the work of the Holy Spirit, and the like are said to be missing. There may well be some progress reflected in these letters appropriate to the end of Paul's life and there may be a concern to preserve his teaching as he contemplates his death. But the characteristics are not those of the second century, as the early church historian J. N. D. Kelly has indicated, and the contents of the letters are on an appropriate continuum with Paul's earlier concerns. The different needs of the recipients and the subject matter dealt with determined in part what doctrines and phrases Paul utilized.

Finally, linguistic differences are said to be so great that the same author could not have written the Pastorals and Paul's earlier letters. These differences include more *hapaxes* (a word that occurs only once in the works of an author) per page than the earlier letters, as well as new vocabulary. There is no set standard establishing limits beyond which an author cannot go and early in this century critics pointed to great variations in Shakespeare and other writers. Several factors could account for such differences in Paul's case. Paul's vocabulary could well be enlarged with age and the contacts of various places. Since the recipients are his colleagues and the contents of the letters are somewhat different, one might expect some variance in both vocabulary and style. If his trusted companion Luke was the one who wrote the letters down for Paul, Luke's input may have affected the way in which Paul articulated these letters. No compelling reason remains to deny the self-testimony of the letters to Paul's authorship, a self-testimony also confirmed by the early church.

First and 2 Timothy and Titus presume Paul's release from his first imprisonment (Acts 28) and some period of time for the ministry referred to in them. If that imprisonment took place at the turn of or the early part of the A.D. 60s (see Acts and the prison Epistles), then 1 Timothy and Titus were most likely written in the early or mid-60s. The early church testifies that Paul was put to death by the emperor Nero, who committed suicide in June of A.D. 68. Since 2 Timothy is written with a view to Paul's death, the letter must have been written sometime during Nero's reign, that is, between A.D. 64 and 68.

First Timothy indicates that Timothy is at Ephesus (1:3) and that Paul may be in Macedonia when he writes (1:3). Presumably Timothy is still in Ephesus when he receives 2 Timothy (1:18; 4:12, 19). Paul is imprisoned again (1:8; 4:16) in Rome (1:17; 4:17) and his death is near (4:6–8, 18). The Book of Titus indicates that Titus is on Crete (1:5; cf. 1:12). All we know about Paul's whereabouts is that he is where he can send Zenas and Apollos (3:13) and that he wants Titus to meet him at Nicopolis, because he has decided to winter there.

Timothy was the son of a Jewish mother (Eunice, 2 Tim. 1:5) and a Greek father and was a native of Lystra (Acts 16:1). He was highly esteemed as a Christian disciple by believers in Lystra and Iconium (Acts 16:2). Paul took him as one of his companions (Acts 16:2) and he was set apart for this work by the laying on of hands. Timothy was included with Paul in writing to the Thessalonians (1 Thess. 1:1; 2 Thess. 1:1), the Philippians (1:1), and the Colossians (1:1). (He is also mentioned in nearly every letter of Paul's except Galatians, Ephesians, and Titus). He was with Paul on various occasions or was sent on various missions (Acts 20:4–5; 1 Cor. 4:17; 16:10–11; 2 Cor. 1:19). For such service Paul commended him most highly (1 Cor. 16:20; Phil. 2:19ff.). Finally, Timothy himself became a prisoner (Heb. 13:23).

Titus was a Greek whose acceptance as an uncircumcised Gentile Christian was defended by Paul in Jerusalem (Gal. 2:1–3). Titus served as Paul's representative in Corinth (2 Cor. 7:15; 8:23) especially in connection with the collection scheme (2 Cor. 8:6, 16) and apparently took 2 Corinthians to them (2 Cor. 8:16–17). He ministered on Crete at Paul's request and when he finished the work there, he was to join Paul in Nicopolis (Titus 3:12). Second Timothy 4:10 records his mission to Dalmatia. Eusebius (*Ecclesiastical History* 3.4.6) speaks of his return to Crete and of his being bishop there until his old age.

OUTLINE—1 TIMOTHY

I. Salutation (1:1–2)
II. Warnings Against False Teachers (1:3–7)
III. The Proper Use of the Law (1:8–11)
IV. God's Grace to Paul (1:12–17)
V. Paul's Charge to Timothy (1:18–20)
VI. Instructions Concerning Prayer (2:1–8)
VII. Instructions to Women (2:9–15)
   A. Adornment (2:9–10)
   B. Teaching and Exercising Authority (2:11–15)
VIII. Overseers and Deacons (3:1–16)
   A. Overseers (3:1–7)
   B. Deacons (3:8–13)
   C. The Basis for Conduct in God's Household (3:14–16)
IX. False Asceticism (4:1–5)
X. Ministerial Training (4:6–16)
XI. Christian Duties (5:1–6:2)
   A. Exhortation (5:1–2)
   B. Widows (5:3–16)
   C. Instructions for Elders (5:17–25)
   D. Instructions for Slaves (6:1–2)
XII. Final Indictment of False Teachers (6:3–5)
XIII. The Love of Money (6:6–10)
XIV. Final Exhortation (6:11–16)

XV. Instruction for the Rich (6:17–19)
XVI. Final Admonition (6:20–21)

COMMENTARY

I. Salutation (1:1–2)

This letter begins like other letters of the day by citing the author, the recipient, and a greeting. Paul, however, has expanded the conventional form and filled it with Christian content.

Paul, as he usually does, refers to himself as an "apostle." Thereby he designates himself as one sent with the authority and on behalf of the sender (cf. John 13:16). With only a few exceptions, Paul uses the word *apostle* to refer to one of a select inner circle of leaders personally and directly chosen by Christ Jesus, as here (cf. Gal. 1:1, 11–17), who writes as an official spokesman of Christ Jesus.

Paul not only indicates whose apostle he is but also by whose command. God has appointed Paul as Christ's apostle (Acts 22:14; 1 Tim. 2:7). The command is stated to be both that of God and of Christ.

Verse 2 indicates that Timothy is the recipient. The phrase *my true son in the faith* indicates the spiritual relationship that exists between them. Timothy is a true son even though he is half Greek, and he is such spiritually "in the faith." We cannot be sure whether Timothy was a convert of Paul's (see 1 Cor. 4:14–17) or whether the term *son* only designates Timothy's role and service as the younger one who aids one who is both older and also his spiritual nurturer and father (see Phil. 2:22).

The salutation concludes with Paul's usual, and exceedingly important, greeting. In nearly every letter he says almost exactly what he says here. The key terms are always "grace" and "peace," with "mercy" added here. The source from which they come are both God the Father and Christ Jesus the Lord.

"Grace" indicates God's favor which saves, keeps, and now instructs and enables one to live the Christian life. "Mercy" indicates God's continuing compassion which Timothy may have especially needed (cf. 2 Tim. 1:7–8). "Peace" indicates the tranquility and stability which are needed in the Christian life.

II. Warnings Against False Teachers (1:3–7)

Paul had urged Timothy to stay in Ephesus while he went on to Macedonia (the northern portion of Greece), but verse 3 indicates that Timothy is now in Ephesus. This verse further indicates what Paul had already requested of Timothy, namely, to "command certain men not to teach false doctrines any longer." The actual words that Paul uses are "other doctrines." But the translations quite appropriately render the word "false doctrines" because any teaching that is other than and thus contrary to the apostolic teaching is thereby false. The other occurrence of this word (6:3) details Paul's understanding of the word: "if anyone teaches false doctrine," he "does not agree to the sound instruction of our Lord Jesus Christ and to godly teaching."

Paul's composite picture indicates the following. The false ("other") doctrines taught by these teachers are opposed to the teachings of Christ and the apostles. They are preoccupied with Jewish myths and endless genealogies. Their teaching is meaningless talk and godless chatter. They teach an erroneous view of the moral law of God. They do not heed and obey God's law, and teach a false asceticism (not marrying, not eating certain foods).

"Myths" in the New Testament consistently means tales, legends, or fables, that is, that which is untrue and therefore false (see 1 Tim. 1:4; 4:7; 2 Tim. 4:4; Titus 1:14; 2 Pet. 1:16). Since they are called "Jewish" (in Titus 1:14), they probably refer to erroneous tales concocted about events or people from the Old Testament or Jewish extrabiblical history. Endless genealogies were possibly fabricated family histories with purported spiritual significance. These promote controversy rather than God's work.

Paul anticipates his dealing with false teaching on the law (vv. 7–11) by summarizing in verse 5 the law's true goal. Since his readers know what love Paul is talking about, he says nothing more about love itself. He does, however, indicate the three channels through which this love flows: heart, conscience, and faith. And he indicates with one-word descriptors what must be true of each.

The heart is a person's innermost being. Paul says that the heart must be pure, that is, "cleansed" (NEB a clean heart). The pure heart is the heart continually cleansed from sins by the purifying work of God.

Conscience is man's God-given ability to self-consciously evaluate the rightness or wrongness of an action because he is made in the image of God. Even though man may suppress the truth (Rom. 1:18) or damage the conscience's function, it remains an instrument by which God's standards, "the requirements of the law," are written on the hearts of men. One has a "bad" conscience when he "knows" he has done something wrong or has failed to do the right. A good conscience is the self-conscious awareness that people have who "desire to live honorably in every way" (Heb. 13:18).

The third channel is faith, trust in God and reliance upon him. This faith must be sincere. Love is channeled through those who genuinely believe that God provides by his Spirit the very love they are called to give.

Some (i.e., the false teachers) have wandered away from the concern for a cleansed heart, a good conscience, and a sincere faith and have turned to meaningless talk.

These false teachers want to be teachers of the Law. Since the usual reference to law in the New Testament and especially in Paul is the law of God and since Paul's correction of their views in verses 8–11 deals with the moral law of God and in the order found in the Ten Commandments (at least from the last third of v. 9 through v. 10), the law they want to teach is the Old Testament law of God. Yet, they do not really understand the words they are mouthing, thereby misunderstanding and misconstruing the Law itself.

III. The Proper Use of the Law (1:8–11)

Paul sets forth the proper use of the Law in opposition to the false teaching on the Law. The law in view here is the Old Testament law, especially the Ten Commandments (as the following verses would seem to indicate). Verse 8 begins with "we know." This assertion is used by Paul to affirm the common understanding of the Christian community (cf., e.g., Rom. 2:2; 3:19; 8:22, 28; 1 Cor. 8:1, 4; 2 Cor. 5:1). The Christian community knows two things, says Paul: (1) the Law is good, and (2) the Law is good, *if* a man uses it properly. If it is used improperly, that is, contrary to its intent, even though the Law is inherently good it may seem to be anything but. It is used properly (Gk. lawfully—a play on words) when it is used in the way God intended.

Verse 9 indicates the way God intended the Law to be used by relating for whom it is not made and for whom it is made. What must be known by an individual to use the Law properly is that the Law "is made not for good men but for lawbreakers and rebels." With these words we come to a crucial point in our understanding of this passage and of the purpose and significance of the Law.

Some hold that the false teachers were teaching that men needed to obey the Law to be saved (the false teachers in Galatians). Related to this view would be the understanding of the term *good men* as a designation of "justified ones." In other words, the Law was never "made" for the "justified one," that is, for the Christian. Others understand the false teachers to be teaching that the Law had a nonethical but "spiritual" significance for the Christian. On this view, the term *good men* (lit. righteous or just but translated for our understanding as "good men") refers to people in terms of their moral condition or conduct. This understanding of the term is gathered from its usage in this statement which contrasts good men with bad men; the latter are described with a number of words which are all either inherently moral designations or have a moral connotation (e.g., lawbreakers, sinful, irreligious, murderers, perjurers). Therefore the term *good men* is ethical.

Paul is hereby indicating that the false teachers should not assume that the Law was given with some extra, nonethical, "spiritual" significance for Christians who are already living good lives as lawkeepers. Paul indicates that the Law is made for man as sinner, whether actual or potential. The law's purpose is ethical and moral and not something else as the false teachers maintain.

The list of words found in verses 9 and 10 spells out in particular terms those for whom the Law is made. Although the particular significance of the terms in the first part of the list (v. 9a) may not be immediately apparent, one is struck by the fact that beginning with the reference to those who kill their parents through the reference to liars and perjurers the order of the Ten Commandments is followed. The entire list of items is made up of single words (even "father-killers" and "mother-killers"). Paul is indicating the right use of the Law by showing how the Old Testament itself applied the Ten Commandments, and he is stating these applications in the single-word terms used in the society of the Christians and the false teachers. He thereby shows that the proper use of the Law is to apply it to the moral issues of real life.

Preceding the reference to fathers and mothers (the fifth commandment), we find six terms rather than four. The first two serve as an introductory general contrast to the term *good men,* namely, lawbreakers and rebels. The first commandment is to have no other gods before God. "Ungodly" certainly could be a one-word way of saying that in the language of the day, particularly if one is designating an aggravation of that sin. If the Jews regarded the Gentiles and pagans as sinners especially because of their idolatry, then to use this term would be an appropriate one-word designation for the second commandment. The third commandment demands that God's name not be misused. Jesus said that God's name must be "hallowed," which in Greek means "to treat as holy." Those who misuse God's name could then be designated as "unholy." The fourth commandment requires the Lord's Day to be kept holy, set apart from the ordinary and profane days of the week. Those who disregard this commandment could be "profane" (NASB, the closest to the meaning of the Greek word), "worldly" (NEB), or "irreligious" (NIV).

Paul breaks off the list at this point, perhaps to indicate that this is not all there is to God's law, and then adds a general conclusion (v. 10b) which links the sound doctrine of the gospel and the Law in terms of their ethical concern. The Law is made for and given to point out the wrongness of men who sin as the list indicates. All these things are also contrary to the sound doctrine of the gospel. The Law and the teachings of the gospel are both opposed to sin and furthermore the Law is also opposed to whatever is opposed to the teachings of the gospel. Thus when one understands the teachings of the gospel, one will understand the ethical purpose of the Law. The "teaching" of the gospel is sound (cf. 1 Tim. 6:3; 2 Tim. 1:13; 4:3; Titus 1:9, 13; 2:1, 2). The word means "healthy" but is probably used by Paul in an intellectual sense to mean "correct" or "true" in opposition to another teaching. Its "truth" or "correctness" comes from its being a teaching that is "according to" (NASB) and therefore in conformity with the gospel itself, which sets forth the "glory" and "blessedness" of God.

IV. God's Grace to Paul (1:12–17)

Having mentioned the trust of the gospel (v. 11), Paul immediately indicates that his experience demonstrates that gospel. This fact is so important that he relates it twice: first in very personal terms, and then as a general truth which was applied to him.

Verse 12 indicates why Paul was entrusted with the gospel. The Lord Jesus Christ who had saved Paul gave him strength for his task and that strength made him faithful (reliable).

Paul highlights his sins. Yet as terrible as they were, Paul was shown mercy; God had compassion on him and pitied him. A true ignorance of who Jesus was kept Paul in unbelief and caused him to act out of both ignorance and unbelief. Jesus had promised that "every sin and blasphemy will be forgiven" and that "anyone who speaks a word against the Son of Man will be forgiven" (Matt. 12:31–32). So Paul was forgiven and shown mercy. God gave him newness of life, strength, and blessing (summarized in the word *grace*), so that he was brought to faith in Christ and to have the love which Christ provides.

In verse 15 we meet the first of five statements in the pastoral Letters designated by the words *a trustworthy saying* (see also 3:1; 4:9; 2 Tim. 2:11; Titus 3:8). The form and style of these statements seem to mark them as brief "creeds," "hymns," or "statements" used in worship services which had become well known to Paul and his readers.

The saying itself, "Christ Jesus came into the world to save sinners," is a compact statement of the gospel. Paul immediately applies this truth to himself. He describes himself as the "worst" (lit. the first or the foremost), because his sins directly opposed God's own Son and God's plan of salvation!

But, as verse 16 indicates, God makes Paul exhibit A of his mercy and his unlimited patience. As Paul did, so must others believe on Christ and by so doing receive eternal life. No sinner need despair.

Paul bursts into a doxology of praise in verse 17. God is the absolute Ruler of all time and ages ("the King eternal"), the one who is life himself.

V. Paul's Charge to Timothy (1:18–20)

Paul now returns to the instruction which Timothy is to follow. The instruction given is in accord with the "prophecies" (inspired utterances) given concerning Timothy's task (probably like those given concerning Paul and Silas in Acts 13:1–4). Encouraged by this reminder Timothy may then "fight the good fight." Opposition to false doctrines and false teachers is in the nature of the case good spiritual warfare. "Holding on to faith and a good conscience" is continuing to believe the truths of the gospel and to practice what the gospel requires.

By repudiating the ethical demands of the faith, however, some have been induced to abandon or to destroy their faith. Verse 20 names two. Hymenaeus is probably the same individual cited in 2 Timothy 2:17–18, where his error is specified. Whether Alexander is to be equated with the Alexander of 2 Timothy 4:14–15, is uncertain.

Paul's disciplinary action is described in terms of handing these individuals over to Satan (the only other occurrence of this phrase in the New Testament is 1 Cor. 5:5). To be put out of the church is to be put back into the "dominion of darkness" (Col. 1:13) which is "under the control of the evil one" (1 John 5:19). This jolting verdict and act should cause Paul's readers to realize how terrible their sin is. Persistent and unrepentant sin defames the name of Christ.

VI. Instructions Concerning Prayer (2:1–8)

Paul's first exhortation to the church concerns prayer. Prayers should be specific, reverently brought to God, bold, and grateful. They should be offered up "for everyone"—not every person without exception as if the entire citizenry of Ephesus is to be named one by one, but for all sorts of people without exception (NASB all men). Paul singles out one sort of prayer, namely, for civil authorities (v. 2). Paul as usual specifies the authorities his readers know (kings; see Acts 9:15), but also generalizes the principle as in Romans 13 ("all those in authority"). Prayers offered for civil authorities have both a proximate and an ultimate goal. The proximate goal is a stable life free of the disruptions and hindrances that civil strife, persecutions, and afflictions bring. The ultimate goal, for which the proximate is the setting, is godliness and holiness. Godliness is a term that Paul uses frequently to describe the Christian's piety or religion in action (see esp. 4:7–8; 6:3, 6; Titus 1:1). He wants that piety to come to full expression and to have "moral earnestness" (holiness).

Paul relates a number of reasons for such prayer. It is intrinsically good and pleases God. Since God is a Savior and wants all sorts of people to be saved, we should pray for all men. After all, God was so concerned for man that he provided that one mediator in his Son. Christ Jesus gave himself to provide the costly price (ransom) necessary to free men, and he gave his life not only for Jews or seemingly decent people but for all sorts of men. Finally, what Paul asks is in accord not only with God's actions in Christ Jesus but also with his action in appointing Paul to go to the Gentiles as a spokesman (herald), authoritative eyewitness, ambassador (apostle), and instructor (teacher). So Paul asks us to do in our prayers what God is doing in his ministry.

Christ's giving of himself was at the "proper time" (v. 6). Christ's death testifies that God was just in the past in forgiving sins and that he will be just in the future to forgive sins based on the fact of that great once-and-for-all act which bears its own testimony to this truth (Rom. 3:25–26).

Verse 8 urges those responsible for worship at home and also wherever Christians meet for worship and prayer, to lead in this activity. Paul speaks of lifting up hands in prayer not to mandate this form but to remind men of the need for their hands to be holy. Hands stand for the whole, the body, one's very life.

VII. Instructions to Women (2:9–15)

A. Adornment (2:9–10). Verses 9 and 10 urge "modesty" as the keynote for women's dress. Prostitutes and other immoral women would spend hours of time and a great deal of money to entertwine their hair with gold or pearls and to dress lavishly and lasciviously. Paul (and also Peter—1 Pet. 3:3–4) felt no need to qualify the marked contrast between material attire and the adornment of good works. What matters is a life adorned by good deeds. Three things are said: (1) be modest; (2) do not dress in the immodest styles of the day; and (3) concentrate on good deeds, "the unfading beauty of a gentle and quiet spirit, which is of great worth in God's sight" (1 Pet. 3:4).

B. Teaching and exercising authority (2:11–15). Women are part of the worshiping community and have every right to learn (v. 11). Yet this right must not be used to set aside the differing roles of men and women in the church and home. So Paul immediately adds the words *in quietness and full submission.* Submission is the concept Paul uses in describing the role relationship of a woman to her husband (see Eph. 5:22–24; Col. 3:18; Titus 2:5; see also 1 Pet. 3:1, 5, 6). Quietness is to be understood in terms of that which is not permitted, namely, to teach (v. 12), which is underscored by saying again that a woman must be silent.

Paul does not permit women to do two things in the church: to teach or to have authority over men. Paul does not forbid women to teach other women (Titus 2:4–5) or children (2 Tim. 1:5; 3:14–15). A woman must not teach a *man.* Here public teaching is in view, not personal activity (such as Priscilla and Aquila teaching Apollos [Acts 18:26]). Paul also does not permit a woman to have authority over a man. She must not exercise leadership or rule over men who are appointed by God to have that headship function in the church and home (cf. 1 Cor. 11:3, 8, 9; Eph. 5:23).

The reason for Paul's restrictions is the very order of creation of man and woman by God—namely, man first, and then woman from man. First Corinthians 11:8–9 contains Paul's fullest statement of the theological significance of this order: "For man did not come from woman, but woman from man: *neither was man created for woman, but woman for man*" (emphasis added). Blending 1 Corinthians 11 and Genesis 2 one may say that woman, equally the image of God, was created to help man and to follow his leadership, just as Christ recognizes the headship of God the Father (1 Cor. 11:3).

Paul cites the fall, where the roles were reversed, as the negative illustration of this principle. Adam definitely chose to follow his wife's leadership in their act of disobedience (cf. God's rebuke in Gen. 3:17: "Because you listened to your wife and ate from the tree . . . cursed is the ground because of you . . ."). "It was the woman who was deceived" echoes Eve's own verdict as to what happened when she exercised authority and took the position of leadership (Gen. 3:13). The simple words that she "became a sinner" (better, "fell into transgression") indicate the dire consequence of such a role reversal.

Paul notes the key role afforded to woman in Genesis 3:15: "And I will put enmity between you and the woman, and between your offspring and hers: he will crush your head, and you will strike his heel." This perspective governs verse 15 here: "But she will be saved through the childbearing—if they continue in faith, love and holiness and propriety" (my translation). The connection between Eve and women is seen in verses 13–15. Verse 13 refers to Adam and Eve. Verse 14 speaks of Adam and "the woman." Verse 15 (in the Greek) begins with a verb with a singular subject *she* (not the plural *women* as the NIV), and then changes to the plural *they* before the verb *continue*. The progression is thus: Eve–the woman–she–they. That promise made concerning "the woman," that her offspring would crush the serpent's head, was fulfilled by the birth of one child, Jesus, to one woman, Mary. Thus woman's unique role, bearing a child, was God's ordained way to bring salvation. Woman may not lead man, and Eve brought about the fall by her sinful leading, but the woman's role is still significant in God's plan, for through her the Savior was born.

Saving faith is manifested in such virtues as faith, love, and holiness. Propriety comes full circle to the concept of verse 9, reminding women that the propriety of their dress and behavior and of their relationship to the leadership of men in the church evidences their salvation.

VIII. Overseers and Deacons (3:1–16)

A. Overseers (3:1–7). The overseer (or bishop) was one of two church officers (the other is the deacon; vv. 8–13). The overseer is equated with the elder (Acts 20:17, 28; Titus 1:5, 7). Each congregation was overseen by several bishops/elders (Acts 14:23; 20:17, 28; Phil. 1:1; Titus 1:5, 7; James 5:14; 1 Pet. 5:1).

The qualifications in verses 2–7 intertwine personal self-discipline and maturity and ability to relate to and lead others. "The husband of one wife" has been variously understood. Some hold that overseers had to be married, but the singleness of Paul (1 Cor. 9:5), a fellow elder, makes this doubtful. Others think it forbids remarriage. But Scripture allows remarriage after the death of one's spouse (Rom. 7:1–3; 1 Cor 7:39). An innocent person is free to remarry when adultery breaks up a marriage (Matt. 19:9) or when deserted by an unbeliever (1 Cor. 7:15). Some think that the phrase prohibits polygamy. Yes, but is that all that Paul intends? The phrase *the wife of one husband* (5:9) does not prohibit polyandry (many husbands) since this is not in question. It refers to sexual and marital fidelity as undoubtedly the phrase in 3:2 does.

Temperance is clear-headed self-control, while "self-controlled" refers to prudent self-control. The overseer must be respected for his behavior. He must open his life to others and be able to communicate God's truth.

The overseer's leadership in the church is to be demonstrated by the effective way he cares for his family. "Keeping his children under control" (NASB) must be done in such a way that they are respectful of his authority.

A new convert should not be made an officer because he will get a "big head," and this will cause him to sin. The overseer must also have a good reputation with those in the world outside the church.

B. Deacons (3:8–13). "Deacons," the Greek word for servants, is used here to designate a special office. The term was used because it aptly described their ministry (Acts 6:1–6—they "served tables"; no teaching or oversight qualifications are required).

Paul enumerates four qualifications for deacons in verse 8. Their lives must be serious and dignified. They must not give "double talk" (NEB). They must not drink or be "greedy for money" (GNB). They must hold steadfastly to the "revealed truths" (better than NIV deep truths) of the Christian faith—that which the apostles and prophets have revealed by the Spirit—and they must be doing what they believe. There must be some way to observe what they are really like, before they are allowed to serve as deacons. They must be "beyond reproach" (NASB).

Verse 11 introduces a one-line statement about certain women. The Greek word used, *gunē*, can refer to a woman (2:9) or to a wife. Three proposals have been made for this word and this verse. Some understand both to refer to deaconesses (NIV fn.). Others understand women who have a diaconal role, perhaps who work with the deacons but are distinguished from them. Others take the word to refer to the wives of deacons (NIV text). One of the last two views is most likely correct, with the reference to wives being the most likely. Note the following: (1) The contextual use of the word *gunē* clearly means "wife" (see esp. 3:12)—the natural understanding is that it is used with the same meaning in the preceding verse. (2) The apparent "break" in thought of verse 11 can be understood if Paul does not really break his train of thought but introduces a reference to wives as introductory to or part of his description of the deacon's marriage and family (presented in the following v. 12). (3) Wives are introduced because they are expected to help their husbands in their ministry and therefore it is appropriate to recognize them and to give their qualifications. (4) Those referred to in verse 11 are compared with but also distinguished from those in view in verses 8–10 and 12–13 by the words *in the same way* (or "likewise"). (5) Those in view in verses 8–10 and 12–13 are specifically designated "deacons" but those in view in verse 11 are not, and furthermore a deacon in verse 12 is said to be the husband of one wife. (6) The qualifications for those in verse 11 are nearly identical with those in verses 8–10, but one qualification is missing which is stated for the overseer, namely, the husband (wife) of one wife (husband). This omission could be explained if it were understood that the statement about marital fidelity for the deacon/husband might presume that for his wife. (7) The objection that there is no possessive pronoun ("*their* wives") is not as forceful as it might seem because it is not necessary for a possessive pronoun to be present for the term *gunē* to mean "wives." These observations indicate why the women in verse 11 are regarded as the wives of deacons, not as deaconesses, who help their husbands carry out their office but are not regarded as deacons themselves (cf. Acts 6:3, where the "seven" chosen are required to be "men," the Greek word for males).

The qualifications for wives parallel those for deacons. Both are to be worthy of respect, both careful with their tongues, both temperate. They are to be trustworthy in everything—in obedience, conscience, and service.

There must be sexual and marital fidelity. Deacons are encouraged to labor by being reminded of the assurance this will bring them in their Christian faith and the high standing that it is accorded by Christ Jesus.

C. The basis for conduct in God's household (3:14–16). Paul writes so that Timothy will know how people ought to conduct themselves in God's household. He might be delayed and he wants them to have these instructions before he comes. The basis for their conduct must be the recognition that Christ is at work in their lives producing godliness.

"These instructions" (lit. these things) probably includes all that has gone before and likely Paul's whole letter. God's church, his saved and assembled people, must realize that all its actions are built on the foundation of God's truth and that it must also uphold that truth as a pillar. That truth, the source of Christian conduct or godliness, is the tremendous work of God's Son, Jesus Christ.

Paul presents this great truth in a short poem, probably adapted from a confession or hymn. Some maintain that this is a historical chronology, with the first line relating Christ's incarnation and the final line his ascension. But lines 4 and 5 fall logically after line 6 instead of before. The most plausible suggestion is that there are three couplets of two lines in which each couplet contains a contrast or comparison between the earthly and the heavenly in a chiastic (criss-cross) manner: (1) body/Spirit, (2) angels/nations, and (3) world/glory.

Line 1 relates Jesus' incarnation. Line 2 indicates that God's Spirit has vindicated Jesus' claim to be God's Son and man's Savior by raising him from the dead. Line 3 states that the heavenly messengers saw the resurrection. Line 4 declares that Jesus is now universally proclaimed. Line 5 indicates the response to that proclamation. Line 6 indicates how Jesus is received back in heaven (the place of glory) as the one now ruling and reigning. Lines 1 and 2 present Christ's accomplished work, lines 3 and 4 present Christ's work being made known to angels and men, and lines 5 and 6 present the response of the world and of heaven to his work.

IX. False Asceticism (4:1–5)

Paul notes that "in later times" (v. 1) some will abandon the faith. The phrase *the Spirit says* is probably used to refer to several statements made by Jesus (Matt. 24:10, 11; Mark 13:22) and Paul himself (Acts 20:28–31; cf. 2 Tim. 3:1ff.; 4:3–4) which contain this warning. To "abandon" is "to fall away from" what they had professed but really did not believe. Paul's application (vv. 2–6, esp. v. 6) shows that he understands "later times" to be this present age.

The ultimate source is demonic; the proximate source is people who are untruthful and insincere. They have so often suppressed God's truth that Paul says their consciences are seared to the point that they are insensible to the distinction between right and wrong.

Consequently, they forbid people to marry and order them to abstain from certain foods. God, however, created marriage, and these foods to be thankfully received, not rejected, by those who know the truth. To use these gifts as God intended, and to consecrate them to God, we must remember that what he creates is good (cf. Gen. 1:31) and thank him in prayer.

X. Ministerial Training (4:6–16)

The remainder of the chapter takes its point of departure from the preceding verses and indicates Timothy's responsibility to oppose error with sound teaching. To accomplish that task he himself must first be instructed in the truths of the faith and train himself to live a godly life. Then he must communicate these things to other believers and serve as their example, dependent on God's gift at work in him. Diligent progress in his own life and in his ministry to others will be the human means God uses to bring about their salvation.

A good minister must point out error but he can do so only if he himself has been nourished by the truths of the faith and has himself followed these truths.

Rather than becoming involved with asceticism and godless myths, Timothy must engage in spiritual training. "Train" in Greek means "to exercise." He is to train himself to be godly. Exercise or training is appropriating what God has given to us in Christ. Just as an athlete trains and develops the body God has given him so must the Christian train and develop what God has given him in Christ.

Paul compares and contrasts training "in godliness" with physical training. "Physical training" is a foil, serving as a contrast with godliness. Godliness has value for all things in that it "holds promise of life now and to come."

The promise of verse 8 provides the goal for the arduous labors of Christian life and ministry. We labor and strive "because" (NIV that) our expectant and patient trust is in the God who keeps this promise.

The concluding paragraph urges Timothy to instruct others and to be an example. The necessity for training in godliness must be taught and urged upon believers. Timothy must not let his youth hinder his ministry, but overcome any resistance by spiritual maturity. His example must encompass both word and deed, and display love for God and man, trust in God, and purity of life. His instruction must set the Scriptures before the people and urge response to it as he explains its meaning. He must do this in dependence on God's gift, the special work of the Spirit equipping him for ministry (see 2 Tim. 1:6–7), which the prophetic messages said God had already given him and which the laying on of the hands of the elders publicly symbolized, acknowledged, and confirmed.

In conclusion, Paul urges diligence and commitment. Only by faithfully and persistently sharing the gospel, urging others to appropriate it, and appropriating it himself will Timothy and others be saved.

XI. Christian Duties (5:1–6:2)

A. Exhortation (5:1–2). Paul emphasizes the minister's responsibility to care for people and to admonish them when they sin or are disobedient to God. Each person is to be treated as a family member. Older men and women are to be exhorted with respect, as parents. Younger men and women are to be exhorted as siblings, brothers and sisters in the faith.

B. Widows (5:3–16). The church must ascertain whether a widow really is in need. Children or grandchildren should care for their parents or grandparents and by so doing repay those parents for caring for them and also please God, putting religion into practice. A widow really in need is all alone, has no family who cares for her, and trusts God for help. A widow who lives a sinful life is spiritually dead and should not be aided by the church. Christians must care for their own widows. So important is the family to God, that to fail to provide for relatives, especially one's immediate family, is to deny one's Christianity and to act worse than unbelievers, who often realize their need to provide and do so.

Verses 9 and 10 indicate how and when the church should assume full responsibility for widows. Of course, the church does not care for widows who have families that care for them. The widow must be over sixty years old and evidence her Christianity by a godly life. The overarching concern is that she be one who has practiced all kinds of good deeds (mentioned at the beginning and end of v. 10). She should have been faithful in marriage and demonstrated concern for others: children, strangers, those in need, fellow Christians, and those in trouble. This list suggests that a widow should be qualified to offer service if and when called on by the church.

In verses 11–15, Paul indicates that younger widows should not be put on such a list and indicates why (this does not rule out temporary care). Younger widows generally want to remarry and this requires them to break their promise to Christ to serve him and the church as widows. A further reason is that there is a tendency for young widows to become idlers, gossips, and busybodies (nosing into other people's affairs where they should not be). Verse 15 may suggest that in their singleness they are drawn into sexual sin. Paul counsels younger widows to marry and to devote their energies to children and the home.

Verse 16 encourages the believer who is a woman, perhaps implying that she is single, to help widows in her family if she is able and not presume that the church should. The church must help widows really in need but must not be burdened with assuming the family's responsibility.

C. Instructions for elders (5:17–25). The elders are the overseers (3:1ff.) who are now referred to by a title implying spiritual maturity. Those who preach and teach should be given double honor. The first honor is respect, the second wages. The basis for the second honor is the principle in Scripture that applies even to animals (Deut. 25:4)—one should be compensated for his labor.

The remainder of the chapter indicates how both accusations against and sins of elders are to be dealt with. An accusation must be substantiated by witnesses (see Matt. 18:16) before it is considered. Elders must be protected from unsubstantiated accusation, but once found guilty of sin public rebuke will have the salutary effect of warning others. Paul charges Timothy to conduct such discipline without "prejudgment" and to remember that all this is done before God, Christ Jesus, and the angels.

Verses 22–25 suggest ways in which this problem may be avoided. In short, men must not be placed into office before they can be observed for problems and sins. Such care will also keep those who lay on hands from being held "responsible for" the sins of those they lay hands on. Realizing the pressure that these demands bring, Paul interjects a personal word of concern and urges a little wine for Timothy's stomach and frequent illnesses. Paul concludes his instructions for elders by noting that caution reduces the problem of sin. Some sins come to light only after a while.

D. Instructions for slaves (6:1–2). Paul gives instructions to Christian slaves in the situation in which they find themselves. He does not defend the institution (see 1 Cor. 7:21; Philem. 15–17) but gives general principles and specific instructions for living in that situation as Christians. Full respect, good service, and a proper attitude should be given to masters. Even slavery does not invalidate Paul's principles concerning work. Poor work and a poor attitude will give cause for non-Christians to speak evil of God and the teachings of Christianity.

Some Christian slaves apparently concluded that because they and their masters were brothers (spiritually equal and in the same "family") that therefore they could act in a familiar and disrespectful way. Paul argues that Christian slaves should give even better service since they serve believers whom they love.

XII. Final Indictment of False Teachers (6:3–5)

These verses reiterate and summarize Paul's indictment of the false teachers. Their teaching is different from and therefore contrary to the "sound words" which Christ had given, and to godly teaching, probably referring to that of the apostles. Such differences and opposition evidence that they are conceited and do not understand Christianity. They are preoccupied with controversies and "disputes" (NASB) which produce all kinds of jealousy, strife, and bad thoughts and actions. The ultimate explanation is that their minds have been "corrupted" and have been robbed of the truth. Their motivation is sheer profit.

XIII. The Love of Money (6:6–10)

The false teachers' motivation prompts Paul to speak of the true gain that godliness brings. True Christianity produces a proper perspective on and attitude toward life. Remembering that we came into the world with nothing and can take nothing out gives a perspective on what we need while here. We will be content with what we really need, "food and covering." People who want to get rich and make this the end of life, will be drawn into temptation and its attendant sin. The results of the pursuit of money will ultimately destroy them.

XIV. Final Exhortation (6:11–16)

Timothy, as one who belongs to God and is his servant, is to flee from such error and pursuits. He must pursue the characteristics which mark the Christian life. These are "uprightness," obedience to God's laws, reverence for God in the actions of one's life (godliness), "trust" in God (faith), love (to God and man), "perseverance," trust in God's outcome (endurance), and gentleness. Timothy needs to "to get a grip on" eternal life by pursuing the characteristics of the Christian life.

Verses 13–16 summarize and present a solemn charge to Timothy. Paul's charge is "to keep this [actually "the"] commandment without spot or blame until the appearing of our Lord Jesus Christ." The "commandment" is probably to be understood as fidelity to the Christian faith as a Christian and as a minister of the gospel. Timothy must persevere for himself but also for his hearers. The motivating factors for this charge are the judgment of God and the prospect of the return of Christ. Paul bursts forth in a doxology. God is the only Ruler of the universe and the possessor of blessedness. He alone is untouched by death and is inherently life. He is so holy that no man has or can see him. He deserves praise and "dominion" forever.

XV. Instruction for the Rich (6:17–19)

These words are an addition to those in verses 6–10. They indicate how the rich should live. First, they should not presume that they are better than others or think that their wealth gives them a basis for hope or security. Second, and most important, their hope must be in God, who himself richly provides us with everything. The controlling principle must be what God desires in our life. Third, those who are rich must involve themselves in doing good; they must be as generous in doing what God commands as they are wealthy because God has richly given to them. Fourth, they must be generous in giving to those in need. In conclusion, Paul reminds us that the proper use of wealth is the best investment one can make of money, an investment that will pay dividends in heaven (see Matt. 6:19–21). One cannot pay his way into heaven, but the proper use of wealth evidences genuine faith.

XVI. A Final Admonition (6:20–21)

Timothy is urgently called to guard what has been entrusted to his care (v. 20a; lit. keep the deposit). That "deposit" is the gospel and the apostolic teachings based on it (see 2 Tim. 1:13, 14; 2:2). Timothy must avoid opposition to apostolic teaching even though it claims, falsely so, to be real knowledge. Those who have professed that view have wandered from the faith.

"Grace be with you" is Paul's final benediction. "You" is in the plural in Greek, which implies that Paul had the church in mind when writing 1 Timothy. The key word is "grace," God's favor that will keep, instruct, and enable believers in their Christian life.

OUTLINE—2 TIMOTHY

I. Salutation (1:1–2)
II. Encouragement to Be Faithful (1:3–18)
  A. Thanksgiving for Timothy (1:3–5)
  B. An Appeal for Boldness to Endure Suffering (1:6–14)
  C. Examples of Disloyalty and Loyalty (1:15–18)
III. Be Strong and Suffer Hardship (2:1–13)
  A. The Direct Appeal to Timothy (2:1–3)
  B. The Soldier, Athlete, and Farmer Images (2:4–7)
  C. Remember Jesus Christ (2:8–10)
  D. A Hymn of Endurance in the Face of Suffering (2:11–13)
IV. What an Approved Workman Needs to Know and Do (2:14–26)
  A. Exhortation to Resist False Teachers (2:14–19)
  B. The Analogy of Household Vessels (2:20–21)
  C. Timothy's Responsibilities in the Midst of False Teaching (2:22–26)
V. The Difficult Times of the Last Days (3:1–9)
VI. Another Appeal to Timothy to Continue in the Faith (3:10–17)
VII. The Charge to Preach the Word (4:1–5)
VIII. The Final Testimony of Paul (4:6–8)
IX Personal Remarks and Instructions (4:9–18)
X. Final Greetings (4:19–22)

COMMENTARY

I. Salutation (1:1–2)

Paul, as he usually does in his letters, indicates his authority for writing by designating himself an apostle (v. 1; 1 Tim. 1:1). He also indicates both whose apostle he is and by whose will he was so appointed, and finally the perspective of his apostleship ("according to the promise of life that is in Christ Jesus"). The recipient is Timothy (v. 2), affectionately designated as his spiritual "son" (1 Tim. 1:2). The salutation ends with Paul's usual and exceedingly important Christian greeting (v. 2; 1 Tim. 1:2). "Grace" is God's enabling power, "mercy" his compassion, and "peace" his stability and tranquility. God as our spiritual Father and Christ Jesus as our Lord are the source of these necessary provisions for our daily Christian life.

II. Encouragement to Be Faithful (1:3–18)

A. Thanksgiving for Timothy (1:3–5). Paul remembers Timothy in his regular prayers ("night and day") and thanks God for him (v. 3). He interjects that he serves God "with a clear conscience," that is, with an awareness that he is seeking to be obedient (1 Tim. 1:5). His service stands in the true succession of the Old Testament ("as my forefathers did"). Paul remembers their tearful last parting and wants the "joy" of seeing Timothy again (v. 4). Paul also remembers Timothy's "sincere faith" which his "grandmother Lois" and "mother Eunice" (v. 5; Acts 16:1; 2 Tim. 3:14–15) also had and which he is persuaded is still in Timothy.

B. An appeal for boldness to endure suffering (1:6–14). Because Paul is persuaded that Timothy's faith is real, he can remind him to activate the spiritual "gift of God" for ministry which Paul knows that Timothy has. Paul was present at his ordination where that gift was both acknowledged and prayed for in a greater way by the "laying on of hands" (v. 6; 1 Tim. 4:14). The Spirit whom God has given is not characterized by "timidity" (cowardice) but rather God's Spirit is characterized by "power" which works, "love" which cares, and "self-discipline" which controls (v. 7). Because God's Spirit has been given to Timothy he can be urged to make the gift active (vv. 6–7). Because God's Spirit is not one of cowardice but of power, Paul may urge Timothy not to "be ashamed" and to join in "suffering for the gospel, by the power of God" (v. 8). He is not to be embarrassed to testify about the Lord nor about Paul who is in prison faithfully serving the Lord. The reference to God causes Paul to rehearse what God has done to save men. God delivered us from sin and called us to holiness and did this sovereignly according to his own plan and operation ("purpose and grace") and not in dependence upon our works (v. 9a).

From all eternity God purposed our salvation and set in place his gracious plan to save us in Christ Jesus (v. 9b). In history that plan is now made known in "the appearing of our Savior, Christ Jesus" (v. 10). By his suffering and death he "destroyed death" (see 1 Cor. 15:56–57; Heb. 2:14–15), and by his resurrection he brought "life and immortality" to us through the gospel message (2 Tim. 1:10). On the road to Damascus Paul was appointed to proclaim that gospel as an authoritative spokesman and to apply its truths (v. 11). Appointment to such a gospel ministry resulted in his present suffering and imprisonment (v. 12). But Paul is "not ashamed" (with the implication that Timothy should not be), because he is confident of God's ability to deliver him from death and keep his life for eternity ("for that day," v. 12).

Paul not only asks for unashamed service and suffering from Timothy but also a faithful handling and proclamation of the message of the gospel (vv. 13–14). The words which Paul preached and taught are to serve as Timothy's "pattern." Timothy has been entrusted with the message of the gospel; he must guard it as a trust and may do so faithfully when he relies on the Holy Spirit's presence and power in him (v. 14).

C. Examples of disloyalty and loyalty (1:15–18). Paul applies the foregoing to Timothy by means of two sets of examples and their obvious implications for Timothy. Paul reflects with great sadness on the opportunity a certain group had to stand by him either in Asia or in Rome (v. 15). But they all deserted him (perhaps fearful for their own lives or ashamed of his imprisonment), Phygelus and Hermogenes being examples. Timothy knows about this desertion.

Onesiphorus stands out as an example of loyalty (vv. 16–18). Paul's prayer-wish for his family implies that he is not now with them. Paul expresses thankfulness for the way Onesiphorus "often refreshed" him by his personal presence and care, and did not let Paul's chains shame him (v. 16). Even though he knew Paul was in prison and in chains, Onesiphorus continued to search for Paul until he found him (v. 17). Paul commends him to the Lord on the basis of such action and beseeches mercy in the judgment day for one who has shown mercy (v. 18a). Paul is hereby appealing to the evidence of Christ's mercy and grace in Onesiphorus's life as a basis for his being granted mercy (see Matt. 18:23–35). This verse would seem to imply that Onesiphorus is dead. Timothy is also aware of his many ways of helping Paul in Ephesus (v. 18b).

III. Be Strong and Suffer Hardship (2:1–13)

A. The direct appeal to Timothy (2:1–3). Having the negative and positive examples just given and aware that God's grace has been granted us in Christ Jesus (1:9–10), Timothy is "then" (therefore) urged to "be strong," that is, be strengthened and enabled, "in the grace that is in Christ Jesus" (2:1; Titus 2:11–12).

The truth he has heard from Paul that is attested by many other witnesses is to be passed on by Timothy to "reliable [faithful or trustworthy] men" (2 Tim. 2:2) who are also "qualified to teach others." On the basis of the principle of this passage, Christian ministers today are taught the apostolic teachings (the Bible) so that they can teach the people of God.

In particular Timothy is urged to endure hardship with Paul and others "like a good soldier of Christ Jesus" (v. 3). By the very nature of the case being a Christian in a world of sin and opposition and therefore spiritual warfare will involve "hardship" (i.e., suffering; see 3:12; 4:5; Matt. 8:10–12; Col. 1:24).

B. The soldier, athlete, and farmer images (2:4–7). Paul now illustrates what is involved in such a Christian life by appealing first to the image of the soldier (v. 4), the athlete (v. 5), and the farmer (v. 6). From the life of the soldier we learn the absolute necessity of pleasing the commanding officer and setting aside any distractions from that duty (v. 4). From the athlete we learn the necessity of competing according to the rules to win the event (v. 5). God has set the rules for this contest and it involves suffering hardship. From the farmer we learn the need for arduous labor ("hardworking") but also for appropriating for ourselves the results we are trying to bring about ("the crops," v. 6). Verse 7 urges us to "reflect on" these things and to rely on the Lord to "give insight into all this," that is, how these images instruct us about Christian life and ministry.

C. Remember Jesus Christ (2:8–10). Timothy is to "remember Jesus Christ" (v. 8a). He is to remember his life and suffering and death but especially that he was "raised from the dead" and is alive to give grace and strength. That one who so suffered and rose again was "descended from David." God's promise to David concerning his seed and the royal line was fulfilled in Jesus Christ in this way. This is the epitome of Paul's "gospel" (v. 8b); Jesus is the promised Davidic Messiah who by his death and resurrection accomplished God's plan of salvation for sinful humankind. And because Paul is faithful in proclaiming this gospel, he is suffering, even to the extent "of being chained like a criminal" in a Roman jail (v. 9a). But such suffering never chains God's Word for it cannot be fettered (v. 9b). Paul appraises his suffering as something he gladly endures for the sake of those whom God would have hear and believe and be saved (v. 10). It is all worthwhile if Paul can be the human instrument to bring about God's eternal plan for those whom he has elected. Notice how Paul correlates election by God and his own responsibility, even if it involves suffering to get out that message.

D. A hymn of endurance in the face of suffering (2:11–13). Paul concludes this section by reminding Timothy that endurance is an essential ingredient of the Christian life. He does so by relating another "trustworthy saying" (1 Tim. 1:15) known and used by the Christian community, perhaps a saying which a convert and the congregation reaffirm together in connection with the convert's baptism and reception into the church.

The saying consists of four conditional statements with the first part giving the condition and the second part giving the result. The condition (the "if" parts) speaks about the professed believer's relationship to or with Christ.

The "if" part of the first statement (v. 11) speaks of a past event ("died") in which we, in union with Christ, died to sin (Rom. 6:2–7). As a result of that death, "we will also live [here and now] with him," that is, in the power of his resurrection life (see again Rom. 6:4, 8, 11). The second "if" speaks of a present enduring, a standing up under whatever may happen (v. 10) for Christ's sake. A Christian by definition is one "who stands firm to the end" (Matt. 10:22; 24:13; Mark 13:13). The result of such endurance here and now on earth is to reign with Christ in the future (see Rev. 22:5). The third statement introduces an entirely different possibility than the first two. What if a professed believer sometime in the future should permanently "disown" (lit. deny) Christ? The result is just as necessary and automatic as were the results of the first two statements: "he [Christ] will also disown us" (v. 12). Christ has already warned us of the consequence: "whoever disowns me before men, I will disown him before my Father in heaven" (Matt. 10:33). The fourth and last statement goes with the third statement, as the second did with the first, but in this case as a balancing truth. The fourth "if" speaks of one being "faithless," like Peter who denied the Lord. Does every "denial," even when repented of, or every time when one is faithless, result in Christ disowning us? No. Christ "will remain [lit. remains] faithful" to forgive and keep us as he has promised. This result is different from the others. They have come about as necessary consequences and result from our status or actions. This result is not a necessary consequence of our faithlessness but rather of the fact that "he cannot disown [better, "deny"] himself" (v. 13). When the New Testament speaks of God as faithful, in almost every case it is in terms of fidelity to the believer and the promises God has made to him, because God is inherently faithful (1 Cor. 10:13; 2 Cor. 1:18–20; 1 Thess. 5:23, 24; 2 Thess. 3:3; Heb. 10:23; 1 Pet. 4:19; and esp. Heb. 6:17ff.).

IV. What an Approved Workman Needs to Know and to Do (2:14–26)

A. Exhortation to resist false teachers (2:14–19). Twice over Paul asserts the truth and warns against error. First, in verse 14 he urges Timothy to remind them of the truths of the preceding verses (esp. vv. 11–14)—the need for perseverance and the awful consequences of rejecting Christ. Then he warns them against "quarreling about words" (see 1 Tim. 1:6; 6:4, 5; Titus 3:9) which is not only "of no value" but also "ruins those who listen." Second, he repeats this twofold imperative, positive and negative, but this time he directs it more to Timothy than to the people (vv. 15–16). Timothy should seek God's approval and avoid the shame of being disapproved by "correctly handling the word of truth" (v. 15). The antidote to "word battles" (speculation and mere argumentation) is to correctly understand and teach the word given by God, which is itself true. Timothy is himself to "avoid godless chatter" (v. 16), talk that is empty and has no relationship to God, because it invariably leads to further ungodliness. The reason Timothy must avoid and urge his people to avoid such errors is that they spread like "gangrene"; they sweep through the church like a plague or a disease (v. 17a). Two such leaders and teachers are named (v. 17b): Hymenaeus had been disciplined by Paul (1 Tim. 1:20) but is apparently still affecting the church; Philetus is not known elsewhere in the New Testament. Their error is not that of a difference of opinion or of a mere mistake, but they "have wandered away from the truth" (v. 18a). They have done this by saying "that the resurrection has already taken place," apparently teaching that the resurrection consisted only in the believer's present spiritual relationship with Christ. For Paul this amounts to a denial of a future bodily resurrection and would be destructive of the faith of those who would believe this (v. 18b). Such a denial involves a denial of Christ's own resurrection (see 1 Cor. 15:12–20, 29–34). Over against such spreading error stands the certainty of God's knowledge and keeping power. The church considered as a house or building (v. 20) rests upon "God's solid foundation" which "stands firm" because of the two truths which the owner/architect has written and by which the house is kept and directed (v. 19). Paul then states those two truths by utilizing the concepts of Numbers 16. "The Lord knows who are his" indicates God's prior knowledge of electing love which gives security to the true believer in the midst of the spread of error. The evidence of being known by God will manifest itself by the true confessor heeding the admonition to "turn away from wickedness," just as the Israelites did from Korah, Dathan, and Abiram (Num. 16:26–27). God who knows those who are truly his keeps them from the plague of such sin by prompting them to turn from it.

B. The analogy of household vessels (2:20–21). In any large house there are vessels "for noble purposes and some for ignoble" (perhaps for garbage or excrement, v. 20). As the believer turns away from the teachings of the false teachers (1:6–19), he "cleanses himself" from corruption and sin and thereby equips himself to be "an instrument for noble purposes" (2 Tim. 2:21). In this way he will have been "made holy" (or "dedicated") and then be "useful to the Master" and also "prepared to do any good work" (v. 21). Turning from false teaching is crucial if one is to be useful and prepared.

C. Timothy's responsibilities in the midst of false teaching (2:22–26). Timothy is urged to "flee from youthful lusts" (v. 22a, NASB) because those headstrong desires either are like, or predispose one to, the foolish discussions and arguments of the false teachers. Paul urges Timothy to "pursue" the characteristics of the Christian life (v. 22b; see 1 Tim. 6:11) which he gives here with four key words: "righteousness" is conforming to God's moral law; "faith" is trust in God or faithfulness to God; "love" is the attitude and action of commitment to someone (love God with our whole being and our neighbor as ourself); and "peace" is harmonious relationship with God and men. These characteristics must be sought with God's people who strive for these "out of a pure heart." Just as Timothy was to warn the people (v. 14) so he himself is warned to reject speculations ("arguments") because of their negative results: "they produce quarrels."

"The Lord's servant must not quarrel" (v. 24a, NASB; see 1 Tim. 3:3; Titus 1:7). This does not mean that he does not oppose error (see v. 25!) but rather indicates that he must not respond with this kind of attitude but rather "be kind to everyone" (even opponents), be equipped to give an answer and able to do so ("able to teach"), and be one who is patient (v. 24b). With such positive attitudes displayed toward opponents, he can now gently "instruct" (or "correct") them (v. 25a). Paul hopes and prays that "God will grant them repentance" and lead them "to a knowledge of the truth," that is, that they will leave the error and personally embrace God's truth (v. 25b). Verse 26 reminds us that this is a spiritual struggle in which the devil has trapped them.

V. The Difficult Times of the Last Days (3:1–9)

Paul wants Timothy to know how bad these last days really are ("mark this," v. 1). To be forewarned is to be forearmed. By "last days" he means the New Testament age ushered in by Jesus Christ (Acts 2:14–17; Heb. 1:1–2).

He then describes in nineteen vivid terms the sins and sinners that will characterize this age (vv. 2–5). John Stott gives a helpful analysis.[1] Notice first the misdirected love: "lovers of themselves," "lovers of money" (v. 2), and "lovers of pleasure rather than lovers of God" (v. 4). Being self-centered they are "boastful, proud, abusive" (v. 2). The next five speak of the degeneration of family attitudes and relationships with words that depict the absence of what one would expect ("disobedient to parents . . . unforgiving," v. 2). The list widens with the next seven words indicating the terrible antisocial behavior of those who do not have "self-control" (v. 3) but are "conceited" (v. 4).

Such sinners also profess to be religious and so they are. But it is only "form"; there is no "power" because there is no reality. They have repudiated the reality. Timothy and the church are exhorted to "have nothing to do with them" (v. 5; see 1 Cor. 5:2, 11, 13).

They sought to propagate their religious views and sought to win those (women) they perceived to be vulnerable, those they knew to be guilty and readily tempted (v. 6), who liked to learn but who never reached any settled convictions (v. 7). Paul likens these false teachers to the opponents of Moses. Paul says that their minds are "depraved," so corrupted that they do not function as they should. They themselves are "rejected," not acceptable, with reference to "the faith" (v. 8). As bad as these false teachers are who oppose God's truth, they will not carry the day because finally "their folly will be clear to everyone" (v. 9).

VI. Another Appeal to Timothy to Continue in the Faith (3:10–17)

In contrast to the false teachers, Timothy has followed Paul's teaching and his way of life based on that teaching (v. 10) and seen it put to the test in actual situations (v. 11). Further, he has seen the Lord at work in rescuing Paul from "persecution" (v. 11). Persecutions of some sort or the other are to be expected by true Christians who "live a godly life in Christ Jesus" (v. 12; see Matt. 5:10–12). This may be expected because "evil men and impostors will go from bad to worse" and can deceive themselves that what they are doing is appropriate (v. 13).

Timothy, however, is urged to "continue in what [he has] learned" (v. 14a). He knows that his mother and grandmother and Paul are trustworthy and they are the ones who taught him (v. 14b). The source of that teaching has been "the holy Scriptures," whose purpose is to give the understanding that leads one to "salvation through faith in Christ Jesus" (v. 15). The reason why it is able to be the source of truth for salvation and godly living, indeed why it is altogether true, is because in its entirety it is "God-breathed" (v. 16). So we may speak of it as God's Word, for he has spoken it through writers led by his Spirit (2 Pet. 1:21). Although Paul has the Old Testament primarily if not exclusively in mind, this statement of principle applies to the New Testament as well (see 1 Cor. 2:13; Col. 4:16; 1 Thess. 5:27; 2 Pet. 3:16). The Scripture's God-breathed character also makes it "useful" for instruction ("teaching"), for refuting error ("rebuking"), for turning one's life from disobedience ("correcting"), and for directing us in godly living ("training in righteousness"). With such a God-given and profitable instrument both the Christian layman and leader ("the man of God") are "thoroughly equipped" with what they need to know and hear from God to live a godly life in every situation ("for every good work," v. 17).

VII. The Charge to Preach the Word (4:1–5)

Paul solemnly charges Timothy to "preach the Word" (vv. 1–2). The charge is given "in the presence of God" and in anticipation of the coming ("appearing") of Jesus Christ and future reign ("kingdom") when all will give an account to him, the "judge" (v. 1). The apostolic authority to charge is really the authority of God and of Christ Jesus. The charge is to authoritatively communicate God's Word. Such preaching must be urgent and persistent, suited to the needs of people ("correct, rebuke and encourage," better "exhort"), "with great patience and careful instruction." Such urgent and persistent and patient preaching is necessitated by the opposition of people to such preaching because they have made themselves and their own desires the norm for what they will hear and want to hear (v. 3). They will even desert such preaching at times (v. 4). In the midst of

1. John R. W. Stott, *Guard the Gospel* (Downers Grove: Inter-Varsity, 1973), 84–92.

such difficulties Timothy is given four commands in verse 5: (1) keep "calm and sane" (NEB); (2) be prepared to endure the difficulty of opposition; (3) keep working to evangelize; and (4) continue to do "all the duties of [his] ministry." Such opposition demands more faithfulness to reach the opponents.

VIII. The Final Testimony of Paul (4:6–8)

This testimony gives another reason for the preceding charge (note the "for"). Here Paul indicates that he expects his imprisonment to end in death (v. 18). He speaks of this end as the pouring out of a drink offering (see Num. 13:5, 7, 10) or of the loosing of a ship from its moorings (2 Tim. 4:6). In three graphic sentences he summarizes his life and ministry. He "fought the good fight" and did not surrender; he completed the race and did not stop; he "kept [guarded] the faith" and did not betray that entrusted to him either in terms of its content or the duty it required of him (v. 7). He now realizes that all of this is at an end. So he rejoices in the provision of "the crown of righteousness, which the Lord, the righteous Judge will award to [him] on that day [the judgment day]" (v. 8). Although an earthly judge may find Paul guilty, the Lord Jesus Christ will give Paul the victor's garland of righteousness which consists of Christ's own righteousness becoming Paul's own personal possession as he is fully conformed to Christ (see Phil. 3:9–12). This crown, a gift from the Lord, is for all true Christians, for "all who have longed for his appearing" (v. 8).

IX. Personal Remarks and Instructions (4:9–18)

Paul requests that Timothy come to him quickly because others have left him (v. 10). Only Luke is with him (v. 11) and he needs Mark (v. 11), his cloak, scrolls, and parchments (v. 13). Mark has now become faithful, responsible, and helpful to Paul and his ministry (Acts 13:13; 15:36–41; Col. 4:10; Philem. 24). Tychicus (Eph. 6:21–22; Col. 4:7–8), perhaps the bearer of the letter, may also be the replacement for Timothy at Ephesus, as he or Artemas had been considered for Titus on Crete (Titus 3:12). We may surmise that Paul left his cloak, scrolls, and parchments when he was arrested again, and now wants the writing materials and the cloak brought for the winter cold. Were these the Old Testament writings and also material for him to write upon? This is likely the case.

Paul warns Timothy about "Alexander the metalworker" because "he strongly opposed our message" and did Paul "a great deal of harm" (vv. 14–15). This Alexander may be either the Alexander mentioned in Acts 19:33–34 or 1 Timothy 1:19–20 (more likely), or all three references may refer to the same person. Paul says the Lord will repay him (see Pss. 28:4; 62:12).

The "first defense" (v. 16) probably refers to the first hearing in Paul's case. At that time when Paul could have expected Christian friends to support him, probably out of fear "everyone deserted" him. Like his Lord, he asks God that "it not be held against them" (see Luke 23:34; also Acts 7:60). But the Lord gave Paul strength so that he could use the occasion to proclaim the gospel even in the capital of the Roman Empire and thus many "Gentiles might hear it" (see Acts 24:1–20; 26:1–32) and even delivered him on that occasion from the one who would inflict death. Even if physical death comes upon Paul, he knows that the Lord will deliver him from this last evil deed because he will bring Paul "to his heavenly kingdom" (v. 18).

X. Final Greetings (4:19–22)

Paul concludes his letter with final greetings. First he greets old friends, Priscilla and Aquila, who worked with Paul elsewhere and hosted house churches in several places (v. 19; Acts 18:1–3, 18–26; Rom. 16:3–4; 1 Cor. 16:19). Then he greets the "household of Onesiphorus" (v. 19; 1:16–18). He mentions Erastus (the one of Rom. 16:23, or more likely of Acts 19:22?) and says he left "Trophimus sick in Miletus" (v. 20; see Acts 20:1–5; 21:27ff.; 1 Cor. 16:1–4). Picking up on verse 9, he again urges Timothy to come and now adds "before winter," lest winter make his journey on the Mediterranean impossible and also so the cloak would arrive in time (v. 21). Three of the next four persons bear Latin names and are probably local Roman Christians (v. 21).

The benediction contains two elements. The first concerns Timothy personally and asks that the Lord be constantly and personally present with him ("your spirit"; see Gal. 6:18; Phil. 4:23; Philem. 25). The second asks, as Paul always does, that the favor ("grace") of God be "with you" (pl.), that is, with all those in the church.

OUTLINE—TITUS

I. Salutation (1:1–4)
II. Qualifications for Elders (1:5–9)
III. Silencing the False Teachers (1:10–16)
IV. Instructions for Various Groups (2:1–10)
  A. Instructions for Older Men (2:1–2)
  B. Instructions for Older Women and Younger Women (2:3–5)
  C. Instructions for Young Men and Titus (2:6–8)
  D. Instructions for Slaves (2:9–10)
V. The Basis for the Instructions (2:11–15)
VI. Doing Good in Society (3:1–8)
  A. Responsibilities as Citizens (3:1–2)
  B. The Basis for the Christian's Attitude (3:3–8)
VII. Further Instructions about False Teachers (3:9–11)
VIII. Personal Instructions and Greetings (3:12–15)

COMMENTARY

I. Salutation (1:1–4)

Like other Pauline epistles this letter indicates the author (1:1–3) and the recipient (1:4a), and expresses greetings (1:4b).

Verse 1 contains the name of the author, Paul, two designations of his role, each with an indicator of relationship ("God," "Jesus Christ"), the results for which he labors ("faith . . . knowledge"), and those for whom he labors ("God's elect").

Servant means "slave" in the Greek of Paul's day. The word is also used in the Septuagint to designate the exclusive nature of man's relationship to God. "Here, as elsewhere, the distinctive thing about the concept of the *doulos* [servant] is the subordinate, obligatory and responsible nature of his service in his exclusive relation to his Lord."[1]

"Apostle" designates one who is sent with authority of and on behalf of the one who sent him, namely, Jesus Christ. The New Testament refers to that inner circle of leaders specially and directly selected and appointed by Christ (see esp. Gal. 1:11–17) with a unique function in the church (see, e.g., 1 Cor. 12:28–29; Eph. 2:20; 3:4–5) as apostles. The title *apostle* indicates the role and authority with which Paul writes Titus (Titus 1:4) and through him the members of the churches on Crete (2:2ff., 15, 3:1ff., 8, 15c).

His apostleship is "to further the faith of God's elect . . ." (RSV). The phrase *the faith of God's elect* reminds one of the statement "all who were appointed for eternal life believed" (Acts 13:48). In addition to faith Paul desired men to know the "truth" of Christianity which "leads to godliness."

Verse 2 indicates the perspective of the "faith and knowledge," namely, it is held with "the hope of eternal life." That "hope" is well founded because God who keeps his word "promised [it] before the beginning of time." Paul's own explanation of this time reference is found in 2 Timothy 1:9–11. Verse 3 makes plain that this promised eternal life comes to us by preaching, and Paul is aware that such a task was what God had commanded him to do (2 Tim. 1:11).

Paul writes to Titus (v. 4) and through him to the church (3:15). Even though Titus is an uncircumcised Greek (Gal. 2:3), Paul affirms that they are spiritually related ("my true son") and share a "common faith." Titus is the apostolic representative on the isle of Crete as verse 5 shows. As in all his letters, so here Paul gives his greetings with the key terms *grace and peace* (1 Tim. 1:2) and recognizes that the dual source of such is "God," who is their "Father" by salvation, and "Christ Jesus," who is their "Savior" (elsewhere usually "Lord").

II. Qualifications for Elders (1:5–9)

Verse 5 reminds Titus that he had been left on Crete to complete the job of organizing the churches with "elders." The churches exist but the task is "unfinished" and things must be "straightened out." This follows the pattern of Paul (see Acts 14:23). "Every town" presumes that a church exists in each. The plural "elders" indicates that in every church there should be a plurality of "elders" (see Acts 14:23; Phil. 1:1).

1. R. Tuente, *NIDNTT*, 3:596.

"Appoint" refers to the final step in the process and is used in Acts 6:3 to indicate the apostolic action (laying on of hands) after the people had elected the seven deacons (thus the NIV marg. rightly gives "ordain").

The description of the requirements of the elders are presented in verses 6–9. Verse 6 gives the general requirement, "blameless" ("above reproach"), and then singles out family life as the first area of proof (see 1 Tim. 3:2–5). The reason for these requirements is because an elder is God's steward (v. 7). Then Paul lists what an elder must not be—all having to do with the sinful assertion of self (for vv. 7–8, see 1 Tim. 3:2–3). Verse 8 indicates what the overseer must be with reference to God ("holy"), others ("upright"), and himself ("disciplined"). Finally, verse 9 indicates the commitment needed and the task to be performed.

The commitment required is that "he must hold firmly to the trustworthy message" (v. 9; 2 Tim. 2:22). Since the message is a result of the direct teaching of the apostles, the qualification *as it has been taught* reminds the elder of that truth. This appropriation of biblical truth enables him to do his job; "encourage others" (better, "exhort") means a personal and direct application of the truth in a loving manner. "Refute those who oppose it" (the sound doctrine) indicates that elders/bishops are called invariably to a confrontational ministry when necessary. To fail here is to fail where and when one is needed.

III. Silencing the False Teachers (1:10–16)

The opponents who are numerous ("many") are opposed to God's authority and to that of his leaders ("rebellious"), their talk is empty and leads others astray ("mere talkers and deceivers"), and they are primarily Jewish Christians ("especially those of the circumcision group," v. 10). The Greek word *malesta* (rendered "especially") may also mean "that is," which would indicate that not just most but *all* of the group were Jewish Christians. The demand that "they must be silenced" is necessitated by the fact that they are "ruining whole households," causing them to fall away from the Christian faith and godliness by teaching outright error ("things they ought not to teach") and doing so simply to make money off their adherents (v. 11). Paul refers to one that they (but not he) regard as a "prophet," and then cites the epigram of Epimenides of Crete (ca. 600 B.C.). That statement says that Cretans are known for untruthfulness, maliciousness, and uncontrolled greed (v. 12). Thus Paul justifies his evaluation of the false teachers from their own spokesman (v. 13a). Error so bad and with such dire results (v. 11) demands a forceful reply (v. 13), always hopeful that those influenced will repent and return to a sound faith (2 Tim. 2:25–26). The error is described (Titus 1:14) as "Jewish myths" (see 1 Tim. 1:4) and "commands of men" (RSV; see 1 Tim. 4:3–5; cf. Isa. 29:13; Matt. 15:9 par. Mark 7:7; Col. 2:22), and they who so teach as those "who reject the truth."

Verse 15 provides the basis from which one can see the error of the perspective of these man-made commandments (see 1 Tim. 4:3–5). Verse 15a says that for those who are "[morally] pure all things are [ritually or ceremonially] pure" (see 1 Tim. 4:4). Verse 15b says that for those who are morally impure ("corrupted") and unbelieving, "nothing is [ritually or ceremonially] pure" (see Hag. 2:13–14). "In fact" (v. 15c), their sin corrupts their way of looking at things ("minds") and their way of evaluating things ("conscience"). Their sinful "actions . . . deny" God and also their "claim to know him" (v. 16). Thus they themselves are regarded as impure ("detestable") by God. They are so because they are "disobedient" to God's moral law and therefore morally "unfit for doing anything good."

IV. Instructions for Various Groups (2:1–10)

A. Instructions for older men (2:1–2). In contrast to human commandments (1:14), Titus's teaching about behavior (v. 1) must be "in accord with sound doctrine" (see 1 Tim. 1:10; Titus 1:9). "Older men" must be "temperate, worthy of respect, self-controlled," and they will be such as they continue to be spiritually healthy with respect to faith, love, and endurance, that is, trusting God, loving others, and persevering (v. 2).

B. Instructions for older women and younger women (2:3–5). "Likewise" harks back to the general principle of verse 1 and may also refer to the triad of verse 2. "Reverent" indicates their respect, love, and awe of God which, on the one hand, will restrain malicious gossip and addiction to wine, and positively brings them "to teach what is good." "Then they can train the younger women" (v. 4a). The training is in that unique and important realm of the family, namely, husbands, children, and home. The older women encourage them "to love their husbands and children" (v. 4c), and to remain "pure" (v. 5a). "Busy at home" (better than KJV keeper at home) means industrious and productive home management (Prov. 31:10–31); also, they should "be kind" (v. 5b). Older women who have themselves put into practice the principle can better than any others teach how "to be subject to their husbands."

Thus compliance with these truths will prevent non-Christians from railing against the Christian message.

C. Instructions for young men and Titus (2:6–8). Instructions for young men are encapsulated in one word, *self-controlled,* for two reasons. First, the word aptly describes the Christian life and occurs for older men (v. 2), younger women (v. 5), and younger men (v. 6). Second, verses 7–8 indicate other items for younger men by saying Titus is an example for them "in everything." First "by doing what is good" (v. 7a), but also as one who demonstrates "integrity, seriousness and soundness of speech that cannot be condemned" (vv. 7–8). The result will be that opponents of Christianity will "be ashamed" in the sense that objections to Christianity from the moral perspective will be lacking (v. 8b).

D. Instructions for slaves (2:9–10). Slaves are instructed by Paul on the basis of what is an appropriate work ethic. Slavery itself does not nullify this concern; therefore, they are asked to acknowledge and follow the lead of their masters in all the things in which they are properly working. Further, they should attempt to please those served, not contradict them, and not steal from them, but be fully trustworthy so that all their conduct will commend the gospel message (vv. 9–10).

V. The Basis for the Instructions (2:11–15)

God's grace provides the basis for such instructions. It has saved, and it teaches by both telling what to do and by enabling one to act accordingly. The result is that Christians are able to say "no" (v. 12a) to sin whether it be rebellion against God ("ungodliness") or pursuit of sinful desires ("worldly passions"). God's grace enables us here and now ("in this present age") to "live self-controlled, upright, and godly lives." God's grace provides a future perspective as well. So Christians eagerly wait for "the blessed hope," "the glorious appearing of our great God and Savior, Jesus Christ." He is designated both as "Savior" and "our great God" (elsewhere in the New Testament Jesus is specifically designated as God in John 1:1; 20:28; Rom. 9.5; Heb. 1:8; 2 Pet. 1:1).

The basis for God's grace instructing and enabling us (Titus 2:11) is that Jesus Christ "gave himself for us" (v. 14) with the express purpose "to redeem us from all wickedness and to purify for himself a people that are his very own, eager to do what is good." Because of Jesus' death, believers have been and continue to be delivered from all kinds of sins and have been and continue to be transformed into the purity and likeness of Christ as a special people of the holy God. Such radical transformation is done so that they will be zealous for good deeds. This teaching is so important that Paul urges Timothy to communicate it ("teach"), to urge it ("encourage"), to "rebuke" any who resist or oppose it, to do all this authoritatively ("with all authority"), and finally to not allow any undermining of his ministry at this point (v. 15).

VI. Doing Good in Society (3:1–8)

A. Responsibilities as citizens (3:1–2). Verse 1 reminds Christians of their obligation "to be subject" to civil authorities and of their need to follow the direction of appointed civil leaders (cf. Rom. 13:1–7; 1 Pet. 2:13–17; but always under higher allegiance to God; see Acts 5:29). This includes involvement in all sorts of civil duties ("ready to do whatever is good"; see again Rom. 13:3, 6, 7). The attitude and action of Christians must not be malicious or contentious but rather gentle, humble, and fully considerate to all men (v. 2).

B. The basis for the Christian's attitude (3:3–8). The usual objection to such courtesy to non-Christians and such subjection to civil authorities is the terrible sinfulness of such people. It is then argued that a Christian cannot act that way to such repulsive and malicious people. Paul's rejoinder is to remind Christians of their own pre-Christian condition (v. 3, which was of the same character), and of God's attitude (v. 4, "kindness," "love"; v. 5, "mercy") to them at that time and the result (v. 5, "he saved us"). God's attitude to us prior to conversion must now be our attitude toward non-Christians who are now like we were. We are not saved because of anything we have or are now doing ("not because of righteous things we had done," v. 5). God effected our salvation by changing our lives through the work of the Holy Spirit (v. 5), whom Jesus Christ "poured out on us" (v. 6). Our lives were changed when we were turned into new creatures both by the new birth ("washing of rebirth") and also by the new life ("renewal") that the Holy Spirit brought and continues to bring. So by the gracious accounting of Christ's righteousness to us ("by his grace") God declares us here and now righteous ("justified") in his sight and declares us "heirs" who look forward to "eternal life" (v. 7). "This is a trustworthy saying" (v. 8; see 1 Tim. 1:15). Since we "have trusted in God" his attitude and action toward us should be the basis for our "doing what is good" (v. 8). Good works are never the basis for our salvation (v. 5) but they must always be done by those who are saved (v. 8; see Eph. 2:8–10).

VII. Further Instructions about False Teachers (3:9–11)

The various errors of the false teachers which involve among other things a misuse of the law (see 1 Tim. 1:7–11) must be avoided because they have no spiritual benefit and are even spiritually detrimental (see Titus 1:11, 14). Through a procedure like that of Matthew 18:15–18, that is, several warnings, the one who chooses to teach contrary to the apostolic teaching must be disciplined by having "nothing to do with him" (v. 10). Because he fails to heed the warnings about apostolic truth the church "may be sure that such a man is warped and sinful" and also may be sure that he has thereby condemned himself (v. 11).

VIII. Personal Instructions and Greetings (3:12–15)

Paul is going to replace Titus on Crete with someone and therefore urges him to join him in doing ministry at Nicopolis (v. 12). Nicopolis is probably the one in Epirus on the Greek mainland south of Corfu close to modern Perega. This is borne out by 2 Timothy 4:10, where it is said that Titus went to Dalmatia (i.e., Yugoslavia) just up the coast from Nicopolis. Artemas is not mentioned elsewhere in the New Testament but Tychicus is (Acts 20:4; Eph. 6:21; Col. 4:7; 2 Tim. 4:12). Zenas (not known elsewhere in the New Testament) and Apollos (Acts 18:26; 19:1; 1 Cor. 1:12; 3:4, 5, 6, 22; 4:6; 16:12) are passing through Crete (perhaps carrying the letter) as "missionaries" going to another field. The appeal for their support is noteworthy in terms of the norm or standard given. The people must "do everything" they can and they must see to it that the men "have everything they need" (Titus 3:13; see Rom. 15:24; 3 John 5–8). Such support is a prime example of "doing what is good"; it is providing for real "daily necessities" and it makes their life more productive (v. 14).

Paul sends greetings from "everyone with me" (v. 15). He greets those "who love us in the faith." He recognizes that true love is a love which holds to and prizes the apostolic faith and does not turn its back on it to follow false teaching.

He concludes, as he does in all his letters, by wishing God's enabling power ("grace") to be the present active force in their lives ("you all").

SELECT BIBLIOGRAPHY

Fee, G. D. *1 and 2 Timothy, Titus.* New York: Harper & Row, 1984.

Gromacki, R. G. *Stand True to the Charge: An Exposition of 1 Timothy.* Grand Rapids: Baker, 1972.

Guthrie, D. *The Pastoral Epistles.* Grand Rapids: Eerdmans, 1957.

Hendriksen, W. *Thessalonians, Timothy, and Titus.* Grand Rapids: Baker, 1987.

Hiebert, D. E. *Titus and Philemon.* Chicago: Moody, 1957.

Kent, H. A., Jr. *The Pastoral Epistles.* Rev. ed. Chicago: Moody, 1982.

Knight, G. W., III. *The Faithful Sayings in the Pastoral Letters.* Grand Rapids: Baker, 1979.

Moellering, H. A. *1 Timothy, 2 Timothy, Titus.* St. Louis: Concordia, 1970.

Stott, J. R. W. *Guard the Gospel.* Downers Grove: Inter-Varsity, 1973.

PHILEMON

Howard F. Vos

INTRODUCTION

This beautiful little letter to a friend is significant because it illustrates how Paul, and probably other early Christians, dealt with the problem of slavery; reveals the inner life of Paul; and presents a fine picture of the meaning of the gospel message. Contemporary exegetes no longer argue over the authenticity of this letter; it is recognized to have been written by Paul while in prison and to have been "mailed" at the same time as Ephesians and Colossians. Tychicus was the "postman" who delivered Colossians (Col. 4:7) and Ephesians (Eph. 6:21), and Onesimus (the bearer of this epistle) accompanied him (Col. 4:9). These letters could possibly have been written during the Caesarean or Ephesian imprisonment, as some assert; but the weight of evidence supports the traditional view that Paul wrote them during his Roman imprisonment. The date was probably A.D. 60 or 61.

The reason for writing seems quite clear. Onesimus, a slave of Philemon, had run away to Rome where he was converted through Paul's ministry. Paul felt an obligation to return Onesimus to his master but wanted to spare him the wrath of Philemon; so he wrote this carefully orchestrated plea for leniency and returned the runaway in the company of Tychicus. Such a plea was in order because Roman law placed no limits on how masters might treat their slaves: they might punish them, torture them, or kill them in the cruelest possible ways. This is the only one of Paul's strictly private letters to survive.

OUTLINE

I. Greeting (1–3)
II. Commendation of Philemon (4–7)
III. Intercession for Onesimus (8–22)
IV. Salutations and Benediction (23–25)

COMMENTARY

I. Greeting (1–3)

In writing a private letter to a friend and in seeking a favor, Paul appropriately omits the reference to his apostleship customary at the beginning of his other epistles. Instead, while begging mercy for one in bonds, he refers to his own bondage (v. 1; cf. vv. 9, 10, 13). In calling himself "a prisoner of Christ Jesus," Paul attests that he is in captivity for the sake of Christ and his cause. Though held prisoner by Roman officials, he knows he is actually incarcerated because of his witness for Christ. Timothy is associated with Paul in the greeting, not as a co-author, but as a companion of Paul in Rome, as one known to the recipient, and as one interested in the present case.

Philemon is unknown except from this epistle, but several things may be concluded about him. He was: (1) a Colossian (Col. 4:9); (2) led to Christ by Paul, probably in Ephesus (v. 19); (3) fairly well-to-do (implied by the generosity mentioned in vv. 5, 7 and his ownership of slaves); (4) loved by the brethren (v. 1); and (5) active in the work of the gospel (fellow worker, v. 1).

It is usually assumed that Apphia, evidently a member of Philemon's household, was his wife. If so, she would also have been wronged by Onesimus, and is now being called on to give the runaway a friendly reception. As "our sister" she would have been a Christian and therefore subject to the principles of Christian love and forgiveness that Paul is urging on Philemon. Archippus is believed to be the son of Philemon; he is a "fellow soldier," involved like Paul in contending for the cause of the gospel. Evidently he held a position of authority in the Colossian church (Col. 4:17). Paul includes in the greeting those who customarily met for worship in Philemon's house; and though the appeal being sent to Philemon is personal, pressure is put on him to grant it by including his wife, influential son, and other believers in an awareness of Paul's business.

"Grace" (the Greek greeting) stands for all the unmerited blessings that come to mankind through Jesus Christ, and "peace" (the Hebrew greeting) applies to the new relationship with God that believers have because of Christ's work on their behalf. Peace *with* God is a judicial truth; that is, by means of faith in Christ enmity with God is removed; the believer is declared righteous or justified (Rom. 5:1). The peace *of* God is experiential; as one experiences growth in the Christian life through the indwelling Spirit, he enjoys to a greater degree the peace of God (Gal. 5:22). The salutation of verse 3 is the usual Pauline greeting and appears in almost identical form or with slight variation in all his other epistles.

II. Commendation of Philemon (4–7)

"I thank my God" is the note Paul usually strikes in his epistles after the greeting (except in Gal. and 2 Cor.). This praise is not flattery and is given to God rather than to an individual, though with the individual's awareness and for his benefit. While Paul's thanksgiving must be interpreted as genuine, it should be noted that the letter-writing style of the times called for a word of thanks or appreciation at this point. Paul did not invent his epistolary style but followed the Roman form developed in the first century B.C., especially by Cicero. Thus the name of the writer appears first, then the addressee, a greeting, a word of thanks, the main body of the letter, and finally a closing benediction.

Whenever Paul prays for Philemon, he gives thanks. From this and other references in his epistles, it appears that Paul had a long prayer list (see, e.g., Eph. 1:15–16; Col. 1:9; 1 Thess. 1:2). The apostle's thanksgiving especially centers on his hearing (repeatedly) of Philemon's love and faith, evidently from Epaphras (see Col. 1:7–8; 4:12). But perhaps Onesimus too had many kind things to say about his master; in fact, Philemon's public testimony may have been an important factor in preparing the heart of Onesimus for his acceptance of Christ as Savior.

Verse 5 is somewhat ambiguous and difficult in the Greek, and there is no totally satisfactory way of rendering it. A general conclusion from biblical teaching is that faith is the root and love the fruit. Here love precedes faith, perhaps to underscore Philemon's great concern for believers. Paul refers to Philemon's love for "all the saints" and perhaps is preparing the way for an expected love for Onesimus too, now that he has become a believer. "Saints" in the New Testament refers to all who are true Christians. Literally, saints are holy or set apart—clothed in the righteousness of Christ, set apart for God's purposes in the world, called to give themselves to the highest ethical standard of life.

Paul's prayer for Philemon (v. 6) is difficult to translate from the Greek. Evidently his basic concern is that Philemon will advance in the knowledge or discernment of divine things (cf. Phil. 1:9; Eph. 1:17; Col. 1:9–10 for a contemporary and parallel concern). Presumably Paul is praying that the communication or generous sharing for Christ's sake may become effective so that he who gives for Christ's sake comes to experience a fuller knowledge of Christ. Paul is greatly encouraged because Philemon's love is so practical; Philemon has refreshed the hearts of the saints (Colossian believers) by word and deed. "Brother" here refers to Philemon, in verse 16 to Onesimus. If they are all brothers in the faith, Paul is in a strong position to make the request he is about to present to Philemon.

III. Intercession for Onesimus (8–22)

Paul now introduces the purpose for writing his letter: to restore Onesimus to Philemon's household and to secure Philemon's forgiveness for the runaway slave. The breadth of Philemon's love for the saints should now include Onesimus. Two thoughts seem to converge in verse 8. First, through union with Christ, Paul can speak as Christian to Christian with a boldness or freedom of speech based on what is right. Second, as an apostle with authority (Gal. 1:1), he has the right to charge Philemon to do what is fitting or proper.

Instead, rather than commanding, Paul issues an appeal based on love—either the love of Philemon or love as a general principle. Paul himself is described as "an old man" and a "prisoner." How these references serve as further motivation for heeding Paul's appeal takes some additional investigation. The Greek words for "ambassador" or "envoy" or "aged" are almost identical and some commentators believe that "Paul the ambassador" is intended here; as such he would have authority. If the text is to read "Paul the aged," he would still have authority because old men or elders were considered wise and thus authoritative. Paul could indeed have been considered an aged man because he was about sixty or older in a society where the normal lifespan was almost certainly under forty. And the hard life he had lived and the sufferings he had endured for the sake of the gospel had prematurely aged him. As an old man and a prisoner Paul might evoke sympathy on the part of Philemon; also it would be evident that in such a condition Paul was in no position to do much for Onesimus. Philemon would have to arrange for the young man's restitution himself.

Finally, Paul comes to the specifics: "I appeal [repeated for emphasis from v. 9] for my own son," a term of endearment applied elsewhere only to Timothy (1 Cor. 4:17; Phil. 2:22; 1 Tim. 1:2; 2 Tim. 1:2) and to Titus (Titus 1:4). "While I was in chains" may simply mean that Onesimus became a convert while Paul was a prisoner. More than that, however, Paul here suggests that Onesimus is all the more dear because he was the child of Paul's sorrows and a devoted companion when he was enduring one of the most difficult times in his life. This third clanking of Paul's chains is made to plead persuasively for Paul and Onesimus (cf. vv. 1, 9).

Having favorably disposed Philemon to his request, Paul at last reveals the name of the one about whom he is writing: Onesimus. Onesimus was a runaway Phrygian slave who had finally found his way to Rome, perhaps there to lose himself among the large number of freedmen and to live among the hundreds of thousands who eked out a living on the public dole. How he made contact with Paul is left to the imagination. Perhaps Philemon's testimony in his household had impressed Onesimus; perhaps the master had even told of his conversion through Paul's ministry. Then either in his desperation for help, or because of his need for forgiveness, Onesimus had found his way to the great apostle.

Verse 11 presents a play on the name *Onesimus,* which means "profitable." Formerly Onesimus was "useless" to Philemon as a runaway. But now, since this revolutionary change in his life as a result of his conversion, he is "useful" to both Philemon and Paul. He is presently profitable to Paul; he will be profitable to Philemon as his services are restored to his master; and Onesimus's work will be of a new and higher character (cf. Col. 3:22ff.).

That Paul sent Onesimus back to Philemon is confirmed by Colossians 4:7–9, which indicates that Onesimus accompanied this letter. Paul declares to Philemon that Onesimus is as dear to him as his inmost vitals; sending him back is like tearing out and sending his own heart.

Paul highly values the ministry of Onesimus. In fact, he is inclined to keep him in order that Onesimus might serve him on Philemon's behalf (v. 13). Paul acknowledges Philemon's great care for him and assumes that Philemon would consider any service rendered by Onesimus to have been rendered by Philemon himself. Then the apostle mentions his imprisonment for the fourth time. His chains for the sake of the gospel make the help of Onesimus more necessary. But Paul determines to do nothing that will make Philemon's kindnesses forced. Paul wants them to be spontaneous. Paul knows that Onesimus is Philemon's property and he has no choice but to send him back. Probably Paul could have kept Onesimus and have written Philemon for permission to retain him; but such would have been undue pressure and the permission would have been given under duress, not voluntarily.

In verse 15 Paul gives another reason for not keeping Onesimus. Perhaps God had allowed Onesimus to leave Philemon for a while in order that he might become a Christian, and Paul's retention of Onesimus would defeat God's purpose in that Philemon would not have him back as a Christian brother. With incredible tact, Paul does not say Onesimus ran away but that he was "separated" (in the passive voice, as if by divine providence). And the duration of his absence was only a short time (lit. an hour). His absence for a little while was to the end that Philemon should have him "back for good," permanently in this life or forever in heaven. Not only will Philemon have Onesimus back forever, but he will also enjoy a new relationship with his slave. No longer will Onesimus be merely a slave but he will be more than a slave (v. 16), a slave transformed, a beloved brother (see Col. 4:9). Some conclude that "more than a slave" implies manumission, but it need indicate only a new kind of relationship, a new kind of respect so that Onesimus might be treated as a real human being, perhaps as a hired servant rather than a slave. In a very real sense in Christ there are neither bond nor free (Col. 3:11). Onesimus is especially beloved to Paul because he is Paul's spiritual son. But he is much more valuable to Philemon as a better servant and as a Christian brother.

The grand crescendo is reached in verse 17. Paul has laid the groundwork well. Now he is ready for the punch line: If you consider me to be your partner (in the Christian faith), welcome him as you would welcome me. If Philemon rejects Onesimus it will be like rejecting Paul, his fellow worker and brother. Such would be beyond belief.

But Paul is wise enough to recognize that some hindrances could stand in the way of Onesimus's favorable reception. Chief of such difficulties is monetary loss, either because of a theft when Onesimus ran away or because of loss of his services for a period of time. Paul deals with this in verses 18–19a. "If he owes you anything" puts the matter in the hypothetical realm instead of tallying up amounts and admitting wrong; "charge it to me" is the apostle's handling of the matter. This is not an idle promise from a penniless old man, however. Paul has worked with his own hands; and he also received offerings from churches (e.g., the Philippians). It cost a lot of money to make an appeal to Caesar and to live in Rome; generous friends kept Paul's hands from being empty.

Finally, if Philemon has any misgivings about granting Paul's request, the apostle puts on some additional pressure (vv. 19b–22). First, he reminds Philemon that he owes his conversion to Paul. Since Paul had not traveled to Colossae, presumably Philemon had come to know Paul in Ephesus and was led to the Savior there. Second, Paul makes a direct and affectionate appeal of a brother to a brother. He has just reminded Philemon that he owes his salvation to Paul; now he wants to "get profit" (NIV have some benefit) from Philemon by his treatment of Onesimus. This is once again a play on the name *Onesimus,* and refers not to material advantage but to benefit from the act as a Christian act. In effect Paul is saying, "I ask for him as a favor to myself."

In verse 21 Paul expresses the conviction that Philemon will grant his wish, and that he will do even more than is requested. This does not mean that Paul expected Philemon to send Onesimus back to Rome to serve him because Paul expected to be released from prison (v. 22). Some believe it implies manumission but that is not necessarily the case. Perhaps all it means is to do more than just restoring Onesimus to his position in the household without punitive action and bestowing on him numerous benefits as a beloved brother. The ultimate pressure Paul can exert is to inform Philemon that he expects to see him soon. He is optimistic that his case will be heard at an early date and that he will be released from prison. There are hints in Scripture and indications in tradition that Paul was indeed freed from his first Roman imprisonment and permitted to conduct a fourth missionary journey. If Paul returned to Colossae, how could Philemon dare to face the apostle if he refused the plea to receive Onesimus?

The "guest room" hints of Philemon's financial status. A recognition of the affection of Philemon's household for Paul is seen in the fact that his coming visit to them is described in terms of a gracious gift to them.

IV. Salutations and Benediction (23–25)

As Paul wrote his four prison Epistles (Eph., Col., Phil., Philem.), he was not alone. Chained to a Roman soldier and maintained at his own expense (Acts 28:30), he was free to receive those who came to him and especially to enjoy the encouragement and assistance of friends and disciples. No doubt individuals came and went as circumstances dictated. Five of this group were known to Philemon and are sent greetings in this letter. They are also mentioned in Colossians 4:10–14. Epaphras is singled out as a "fellow prisoner," which probably means he so constantly attended Paul that it seemed as if he were a prisoner too. But it is also possible that he was so faithful in caring for Paul's needs that he aroused suspicion or animosity on the part of Paul's guards and that he was actually imprisoned for a while. Mark must be John Mark, the writer of the Gospel, who had left Paul's company on the first missionary journey and evidently had now been restored to fellowship with Paul (Acts 13:13; 15:36–39; 2 Tim. 4:11). Aristarchus was one of Paul's converts in Thessalonica who accompanied him on much of the third missionary journey and on the trip to Rome (Acts 20:4; 27:2). In Colossians 4:10 he is also called a "fellow prisoner." Demas later forsook Paul (2 Tim. 4:10). Luke, the author of Luke and Acts, was faithful to Paul to the end of his ministry (2 Tim. 4:11).

Paul ends the letter as he began it (v. 3), with grace extended to Philemon's entire household. They had already experienced the grace that brought them salvation; this is enabling grace for their daily walk. "Spirit" refers to the inner spiritual self.

Philemon is important as a social document because it deals so pointedly with slavery. Historically two erroneous views have developed concerning Paul's attitude toward slavery. Some have represented him as conceding the abstract rightfulness of the institution and of its divine sanction (see, e.g., Eph. 6:5; Col. 3:22–24; 4:1). Others have seen Paul as an enemy of slavery and as having a conscious intent of abolishing it. Neither seems to have been true. Paul was familiar with slavery all his life in both Hebrew and Gentile associations; the institution was universal in the Near East and in the Mediterranean world, and there is no indication that he had any thoughts of abolishing it. It is wrong to impose nineteenth- and twentieth-century ideas about slavery or politics on Paul or other leaders of the early church. What Paul addressed was regulation of existing relations. The Christian master has a duty to the slave as well as a right over him (Eph. 6:9; Col. 4:1); the Christian slave has a duty to his master as well (Eph. 6:5–6; Col. 3:22–24). But especially in the Book of Philemon the fervor of Christian love melted the fetters of slavery and counted master and slave alike as beloved brothers in the family of God.

Philemon also illustrates the gospel message. The sinner as God's property repudiates him and after wandering in sin eventually flees to Jesus, in whom he is born anew. In him he also finds an intercessor who pleads his case before God and persuades the Father to accept him. Now he is elevated to a new relationship (v. 16), even dearer to God.

SELECT BIBLIOGRAPHY

Deibler, E. C. *Philemon.* Wheaton: Victor, 1983.

Gromacki, R. G. *Stand Perfect in Wisdom: An Exposition of Colossians and Philemon.* Grand Rapids: Baker, 1981.

Hendriksen, W. *Exposition of Colossians and Philemon.* Grand Rapids: Baker, 1964.

Weed, M. R. *The Letters of Paul to the Ephesians, the Colossians, and Philemon.* Austin, Tex.: Sweet, 1971.

HEBREWS

Robert S. Rayburn

INTRODUCTION

Although the Letter to the Hebrews clearly was written to address a spiritual crisis in a specific community of Christians by one well known to them, one cannot determine with certainty the identity of the author, the specific recipients or the location of their community, or the precise date of the letter's composition.

Though the letter has been ascribed to Paul from at least the end of the second century in the Eastern church and nearly universally in Christendom from Augustine to the Reformation, the arguments against Pauline authorship now appear to be decisive. Chief among them are the following: (1) the letter is anonymous, which is uncharacteristic of Paul; (2) the style of Greek is significantly different from that of Paul's letters; (3) the statement of Hebrews 2:3 seems impossible to reconcile with Galatians 1:12; and (4) the ambiguous testimony of the early Fathers: Clement of Alexandria and Origen accepted Hebrews as Pauline but with major qualifications; Tertullian named Barnabas as the author and gave no hint of a controversy on that point—difficult to explain if the author were none other than the great apostle to the Gentiles.

The reference to Timothy (Heb. 13:23) and the ancient but inconsistent testimony to Pauline authorship have led to the widespread opinion that the author was at least a member of the Pauline circle. Origen suggested that he was a pupil of Paul who wrote what he had learned from the apostle. Others have proposed Luke either as the author or, as Clement of Alexandria supposed, the translator of Paul's Hebrew original. Most modern scholarly opinion, however, is divided between Barnabas and Apollos. Barnabas was a Hellenistic Jew, a Levite in fact, a prominent member of the apostolic circle (even called an apostle in Acts 14:14; cf. 1 Cor. 9:5–6), and has the considerable support of Tertullian's unqualified assertion that Barnabas was the author of Hebrews (*On Modesty* 20). Likewise Apollos, a highly educated Alexandrian Jew, a gifted controversialist, and a participant in the apostolic ministry (1 Cor. 1:12; 3:6), could well have written a work such as Hebrews with its sophisticated use of Scripture and its elegant Greek. If the author of Hebrews was neither of these men, he was surely like them, "a good man, full of the Holy Spirit and faith" (Acts 11:24) and "a learned man, with a thorough knowledge of the Scriptures" (Acts 18:24; cf. v. 28). Plausible arguments can be advanced in favor of either of these and some others, but presently a firm conclusion remains unobtainable.

Certainly apostolicity was a prerequisite of canonicity, but this requirement could be satisfied by authorship by a member of the apostolic circle, as in the case of Mark or Luke–Acts. In any case, canonicity does not depend upon the church's present certainty as to the authorship of a particular biblical work (e.g., Judges, Chronicles). Furthermore, the author of Hebrews would be among the first to insist that the human authorship of Scripture is of secondary importance, being only the instrumentality of its divine inspiration. As he reminds his readers (3:7; 4:7), David may have written Psalm 95, but the Holy Spirit was the primary author and the one who speaks to us in it.

The author's purpose in writing is quite clear, for he reiterates it regularly. He writes to arrest an incipient apostasy and to strengthen wavering faith. Perhaps some members of this community had already deserted the faith, turning their backs on the way of salvation and the Savior they had once acknowledged (6:4–6; 10:26–31). In any case, tempted to evade the persecution they were suffering on account of their faith and to find some way less costly than the discipleship to which Christ calls his people, many were trifling with apostasy by compromising their former beliefs (2:3, 18; 3:6, 12–15; 4:1, 11, 14; 6:4–6, 9–12; 10:19–29, 35–39; 12:1–3, 14–17, 25; 13:9, 13). With a keen appreciation of the fearful implications of such a spiritual defection, and with a deep personal interest in the outcome, the author writes this often severe, always affectionate, intensely sympathetic, and practical "word of exhortation" (13:22).

Those addressed are a community of converts from Judaism who, encountering stiff opposition from their former brethren and finding difficult the pioneering demanded of them by their new faith, were tempted to return to the comfortable security of the old ways. In recent times some scholars have maintained that the recipients of the letter were Gentiles or Christians irrespective of race and that the title *To the Hebrews* is only the by-product of a later and erroneous interpretation of the letter. However, the evidence of the epistle itself conclusively favors a Jewish Christian audience and this remains the conclusion of a majority of scholars. Admittedly, it cannot be demonstrated that the title was attached to the letter prior to the last quarter of the second century A.D., and its vagueness may appear not to comport well with a letter obviously addressed to a particular community (10:32–34; 13:18–19, 22–23) and not to Jewish Christians generally. Nevertheless, the title is very old and, so far as anyone knows, "To the Hebrews" is the only title the letter has ever had.

Further, the author throughout assumes on the part of his readers both an exact acquaintance with the Scriptures and an unshaken and unshakeable conviction of their divine authority. Of course, Gentile converts acknowledged the Old Testament as the Word of God, but if their commitment to Christianity was weakened, so too would be their confidence in the Scriptures.

Finally, and decisively, a Jewish Christian audience is demanded by the central argument of the letter, which is designed to counter the opinion that the Levitical institutions were God's definitive provision for the salvation of humankind. The argument is constructed around three contrary-to-fact conditional statements (7:11; 8:7; 10:1–2), that is, statements in which the protasis (the "if" clause) is assumed to be false. The three statements and the massive argumentation marshalled in their support presuppose a real inclination on the part of the readers to assume the contrary, namely, that perfection could be attained through the Levitical priesthood, that the covenant life of Israel was and remains the ideal, and that the sacrifices could indeed make the worshiper perfect—thus rendering Christ and his work superfluous. Such assumptions were not a temptation for Gentile believers and addressed to a Gentile audience the great argument of the letter becomes what it definitely is not, a colorless examination of largely hypothetical questions. Rather the letter is an impassioned plea to make complete and permanent the separation from Judaism (13:13).

One can possibly identify this community with some further precision. The Dead Sea Scrolls have greatly enlarged our knowledge of nonconformist Judaism in this period, that is, Judaism that was not primarily shaped by the rabbinical tradition and not represented by the Pharisees and Sadducees. Chief among representatives of such a separatist Judaism were the Essenes, whose community was located at Qumran. Among the distinctives of this sect are a number that appear to bear some relation to the argument of Hebrews. These Jews looked for the fulfillment of Jeremiah's new covenant but in the form of the restoration and purification of the Aaronic priesthood with its system of ceremonies (cf. Heb. 7:11ff.; 9:1–10); they anticipated the appearance of a great prophet, the second Moses of Deuteronomy 18:18 (1QS 9:11; 4QTest; Heb. 1:1–2) and sought to maintain a manner of life patterned after that of Israel in the wilderness (cf. Heb. 3:7–19; 4:1–11; 8:6ff.; 12:18–21); they fostered extravagant speculations concerning angels, even expecting that in the coming kingdom the archangel Michael would play a more decisive role than the Messiah (1QM 17:6–7; Heb. 1:4–2:18); they cast Melchizedek in the role of an eschatological deliverer (11QMelch; Heb. 7:1–17); and in their ritual they placed special emphasis on ceremonial washings (CD 10:10–13; 1QM 14:2–3; Heb. 6:2; 9:13). Though the evidence is by no means conclusive, a plausible case can be made for understanding Hebrews as a point-by-point refutation of the doctrines of a Jewish community of the Essene-Qumran variety, which, if correct, would indicate that the recipients of the letter were originally converts from such a nonconformist Judaism and were now inclined to return to it.

Little more than this can be said about them. They were second-generation Christians. Never having seen or heard Jesus themselves, they had been evangelized by eyewitnesses (2:3). They were presumably Hellenistic (Greek-speaking) Jews as the author cites the Greek Septuagint version of the Old Testament. They had suffered persecution but not yet martyrdom (10:32–34; 12:4). It may be that they were a distinct party or group that had separated itself from the larger believing community in their locality (10:25; 13:17, 24). Where they lived is impossible to determine. Jerusalem and Rome figure prominently in scholarly speculations, but the evidence is meager. Similarly the place of the letter's composition remains uncertain. The only evidence in the letter itself is ambiguous (13:24) and the tradition that it was written from Rome is quite late.

Clement of Rome makes use of Hebrews in his first letter, which is ordinarily dated around A.D. 95, though possibly earlier. A first-century date is further required by the facts that the recipients of the letter had learned the gospel from eyewitnesses of the Lord and that Timothy was still alive (2:3; 13:23). Other evidence supports a date of composition prior to A.D. 70. The absence of any mention of the destruction of the temple in Jerusalem furnishes a virtually unanswerable argument that the letter was written beforehand, inasmuch as mention of the demise of the temple ritual would seem so well suited to the author's purpose (8:13; 10:2). Further, the consistent use of the present tense in reference to the Levitical priesthood and ritual surely favors, though it does not demand, a date prior to the cessation of that ritual. Without knowing the location of this community of Jewish Christians it is impossible to say more than this.

The author describes his work as a "word of exhortation" (13:22), that is, a sermon, as appears from the use of the same phrase in Acts 13:15. Hebrews is a letter only secondarily, by reason of the few personal remarks at its conclusion and the fact that it was written in one place and dispatched to another. The sermonic form appears in the repeated reference to the author's speech (Heb. 2:5; 5:11; 6:9; 8:1; 9:5; 11:32); in his method, which is the citation, exposition, and application of Scripture; and in his singleness of purpose. Hebrews vies only with Galatians for the distinction of being the most single-minded work in the New Testament. It is a discourse on the absolute necessity of perseverance in the Christian faith. The arguments enlisted on behalf of this proposition are those precisely suited to allay the doubts and to unmask the errors that were undermining the faith of the author's readers. However, the letter's specific destination and pointed applications notwithstanding, Hebrews is not at all provincial or dated as might be expected of a long-ago sermon to a long-forgotten community of Christians. The danger of apostasy being always present (Matt. 24:10; 1 Cor. 10:12; 1 Tim. 4:1), Hebrews' emphatic and solemn warning is always timely. The author supports his exhortation by appeal to some of the most fundamental elements of the Good News, in particular those that have immediately to do with the nature and practicalities of the Christian's life of faith in the world. In addressing his readers' spiritual peril, he provides a scriptural elaboration of Christ's supremacy as the incarnate Son of God, his mediatorial work as intercessor, priest, and sacrifice, the nature of the Christian faith and hope, the method of God's dealing in mercy and judgment with his people, and the unity of the people of God and the gospel in the history of salvation. From these doctrines the author draws applications as profound and urgent for any believer today as for those to whom the sermon was first sent.

Like any good preacher the author never loses sight of his readers' pressing need or his own purpose. He returns to his exhortation regularly, so that what one encounters in Hebrews is a repeated alternation between scriptural or doctrinal exposition and its application to the great question of his readers' perseverance in faith (note the recurring "therefore" in 2:1; 3:1; 4:1, 11, 14; 6:1; 10:19; 12:1, 28; cf. "the point of what we are saying is this," 8:1).

Two special features of the argument, crucial to a proper interpretation of the letter, require comment. First, the author's purpose is to correct his readers' ideas, derived from the principles and forms of the Judaism whence they came, that are incompatible with true faith and participation in the salvation of God. It is imperative that this purpose be given its due in the interpretation of the letter. Too often commentators have understood the author's central argument (chaps. 3–12) to be contrasting Christianity with the provisional religion of the Mosaic administration. It is then supposed that he sustains his exhortation to persevere in the faith and to make the break with Judaism permanent by demonstrating that Judaism, embodying the temporary and imperfect economy of the Old Testament, has been superseded by and fulfilled in the religio-historical economy introduced by Christ and the apostles. Indeed, understood in this way, Hebrews is often thought to provide the New Testament's most thoroughgoing elaboration of the historical relationship between the Old Testament and the New Testament and the most complete explanation of the superiority of the latter.

But this understanding of Hebrews, though very common, is quite contrary to the author's fundamental assumptions and clear statements. His contrast is never between a supposedly inferior faith, spirituality, and system of worship that prevailed in the age before Christ and their fulfillment in the Christian era. He says nothing about the difference between the religion or spiritual privileges of believers before and after Christ. On the contrary, at every point he identifies the situation of his readers with that of the ancient people of God: the gospel preached to them was preached to Israel in the wilderness (4:2); the promise, rest, and inheritance that pious Israelites grasped from afar is nothing other than that which is set before the believers to whom he writes and which they, likewise, will obtain only in the world to come and only if they endure in faith to the end (3:4, 19; 4:1; 6:11–12; 10:35–39; 11:10, 16, 35, 39–40; 12:1; 13:14); and the danger of apostasy and the enormity of its consequences are no less now that Christ has appeared (3:12; 4:11; 6:4–6; 10:26–31, 38–39; 12:25). It is striking and very important how completely this author identifies the situation that prevailed prior to the incarnation with that of the present, and how readily he finds Christ present and active in the life of the Old Testament community (3:2–6; 11:26). The contrast the author does draw is the radical contrast between unbelief and faith, apostasy and perseverance, the forfeiture of salvation and the eternal inheritance, and the wrath of God and his forgiveness. No doubt belonging to the church in the Christian era has advantages, but the author of Hebrews does not enumerate them. Indeed, although this letter is frequently claimed to be an assertion of the supremacy of the New Testament and the obsolescence of the Old Testament, on careful examination it proves instead to be the Bible's most thorough demonstration of the unity of the covenant of grace, the church of God, and true spirituality and faith throughout all eras of the history of salvation. Crucial to the proper interpretation of the letter is how little interested this author is in distinguishing between the opportunities, privileges, responsibilities, and blessings of the saints before and after Christ and how completely he identifies them.

The failure to appreciate Hebrews' sustained emphasis on the unity of the administration of divine grace throughout the history of salvation has bedeviled the interpretation of the letter and muted its warnings. The author fashions his exhortation upon the assumption of this unity. The recognition of this is vital; otherwise it is impossible rightly to understand the severe criticism that the author levels against the Old Testament covenant and worship. An appreciation of his consistent assumption of the unity of the gospel and the life of faith before and after the incarnation opens the way to the following recognition. In his criticism the author does not have in view the Old Testament economy per se but rather that economy which eventuated when the gospel was not combined with faith, when the covenant was shorn of all but its outward forms, that is, the Old Testament economy as it was understood and practiced by the unbelieving Judaism of the author's day. This Judaism—not the true faith of the Old Testament—threatened his readers.

The great contrast drawn by this author is not between the old and new administrations or between believers before and after the incarnation, but rather between two ways of salvation, one false and one true, and between two destinies, the one obtained by those who deny the faith and the other by those who patiently endure in faith and hope. In each case the former is illustrated in the letter chiefly by unbelieving Israel, the latter by the saints of that former era. One cannot overemphasize that the author treats the Mosaic administration with its Levitical institutions under the false view of them entertained in the Judaism of that day, a Judaism that had by this time so completely lost sight of the true meaning of the covenant, priesthood, and sacrifice that it no longer had any place for a redeemer who would die for the sins of the world. In the letter's criticism of the Levitical institutions, therefore, one looks in vain for the author's admission of the proper and holy purpose of the sacrifices to signify and to confirm God's covenant, of the joy and peace which pious Israelites obtained in their evangelical use of them, and of their splendid and rightful place as an important part of covenant life. He does no justice to their rightful purpose but condemns them as utterly ineffectual to save sinners. "Weak and useless" is his scathing verdict (7:18–19). Indeed, to hear him tell it, it is hard to imagine what significant purpose was ever served by all of these carnal regulations and performances (9:9–10). The severely negative tone of his criticism of the Old Testament cultus is very impressive and it is in no way mitigated by the author's description of the shadowy, provisional character of these institutions, by any external efficacy he attributes to them, or by the fact that he declares them fulfilled in the sacrifice of Christ, for in this way he does not intend to pay tribute to the cultus but only further to demonstrate its worthlessness in comparison to the priesthood and sacrifice of Christ.

In this criticism of the Levitical institutions, then, the author places himself squarely in the tradition of the Old Testament prophets who were similarly scornful of that worship as it was practiced by a people who, without living faith in God or submission to his law, trusted instead in the efficacy of external ordinances (Isa. 1:10–20; Jer. 7:21–23; Amos 5:21–25). It is imperative to remember that almost certainly Hebrews was written when the sacrifices were still being offered and when Jewish Christians were still participating, and properly so, in the temple worship (Acts 21:20–26; cf. 1 Cor. 7:18). The author does not call for the abolition of the sacrificial ritual and the priesthood any more than the prophets before him. But like them he condemns the confidence that faithless and disobedient people are investing in mere ceremonies.

In sum, this author describes the Levitical ritual in much the same way as a preacher today might speak scornfully of the Lord's Supper to a congregation that imagines that one obtains the forgiveness of sins by the mere partaking of bread and wine. Interestingly, there is no mention of the Lord's Supper in Hebrews. The author has no intention of calling the attention of his readers, in their present state of mind, to another ceremony. Their growing confidence in externals could only too easily be transferred from the Levitical rites to those of the apostolic church—a danger to which the whole course of church history from that day to this bears sad but eloquent testimony.

Second, until relatively recent times the interpretation of Hebrews was heavily influenced by the widespread opinion that the author was a product of the Alexandrian school of biblical exegesis and, in particular, deeply indebted to Philo for his conceptual framework, his hermeneutics, and his manner of statement. The most significant consequence of this opinion was the eclipse of the eschatological perspective of the letter, a casualty of the assumption that the author shared Philo's conception of the timeless duality of the material and spiritual worlds. While there are certain affinities between Hebrews and the writings of Philo, the differences are profound and important. Recent scholarship has tended to discredit the alleged dependence upon Philo and the happy result of this has been a marked resurgence of interest in the eschatology of Hebrews. This is a great step forward, for in truth hardly any other book of the Bible more consistently throws the attention of the reader forward to the world to come.

Remarkably the author is little interested in the present fulfillment of Old Testament prophecy. Indeed, the idea of fulfillment plays almost no role in the argument. For this author the Old Testament is not a collection of prophecies now fulfilled in Christ so much as a contemporary Word of God to be heard, believed, and obeyed. Expectation *not* fulfilled rather than unfulfilled animates the letter and drives its argument. The rest of God, the eternal country and city, the resurrection, the receiving of the promise and inheritance, and even salvation itself (1:14; 9:28) were the hope of the saints of ancient days and must be no less so for every generation of believers (4:11; 10:36–37; 11:39–40; 13:14). The author's exhortation is always firmly fixed in his eschatology: the reason one must continue in the faith, holding fast to Christ, is not for fear of present consequences, but because by shrinking back one forfeits the eternal rest and exposes oneself eventually to God's fearful judgment and consuming fire. The sustained emphasis of Hebrews on the futurity of salvation is a corrective to an unbiblical preoccupation with the present benefits of faith in Christ. Further, it is a reminder that the obligations of faith and obedience will never weigh upon the church as they must until the specter of eternity is fixed before her mind's eye.

OUTLINE

I. The Superiority of the Christian Faith (1:1–10:18)
  A. Jesus Christ Superior to the Prophets (1:1–4)
  B. Jesus Christ Superior to Angels (1:5–2:18)
  C. Jesus Christ Superior to Moses (3:1–4:13)
  D. Jesus Christ Superior to Aaron (4:14–10:18)
II. Exhortations to Persevere in Christian Faith (10:19–12:29)
  A. The Danger of Apostasy (10:19–31)
  B. Encouragements to Press On (10:32–39)
  C. Faith Defined and Exemplified (11:1–40)
  D. Jesus, the Superior Example of Faith (12:1–4)
  E. The Meaning and Merit of Discipline (12:5–13)
  F. Warning Not to Turn Away from God (12:14–29)
III. Concluding Exhortations (13:1–19)
IV. Benediction and Greetings (13:20–25)

COMMENTARY

I. The Superiority of the Christian Faith (1:1–10:18)

A. Jesus Christ superior to the prophets (1:1–4). The dramatic exordium is less an introduction than a thunderous opening salvo. This written sermon goes forth precisely to arrest a waning of conviction regarding the divine supremacy of Christ and the decisiveness of his work as the redeemer of sinners (vv. 1–2). The assertion of the Son's preeminence among the prophets and the finality of his revelation is possibly intended as a corrective to the expectation of an eschatological prophet within the circle of Judaism from which these readers had come and to which they were now tempted to return. Note that no distinction is made between the message spoken formerly and "in these last days." It is not the message but the dignity of the messengers and the times and circumstances of their revelation which differ. God spoke then and now and, indeed, continues to speak through the ancient prophets as through his Son (e.g., 3:7; 10:37–38). One needs to remember that the living and active Word of God (4:13) was for this author largely what is now called the Old Testament.

"These last days" (lit. at the end of these days) is taken from the Septuagint, which literally rendered the Hebrew phrase used in the Old Testament to designate the prophetic future (cf. Gen. 49:1; Deut. 4:30; Isa. 2:2; Ezek. 38:16). "These" refers to the future days prophesied in the Old Testament, or some of those days, or the beginning of them (cf. Heb. 9:26).

In verse 3 "radiance" is indicative of the Son's sharing of the divine attributes (cf. John 1:14; 2 Cor. 4:6), and "exact representation" of the exact correspondence of his nature with the Father's (cf. Col. 1:15). "Sustaining all things" refers to his government by which he brings the course of history to its appointed end. "Sat down" signifies the completion of the atonement (10:12–14) and suggests Christ's present activity as priest (4:14–16) and king (12:2). It is self-evident that if the Son's person and work are as described, any religion that does not place them at its center, in which he is not the hope and joy of sinners and the chief object of faith and worship, stands self-condemned.

B. Jesus Christ superior to angels (1:5–2:18). The superiority of the Son to the angels is now distinctly stated and furnished with an impressive biblical demonstration (**1:5–14**). The author's evident interest in providing conclusive proof of this point surely indicates that this was a matter of dispute. Possibly his readership attributed an unwarranted eminence to angels as a consequence of their function as mediators through whom God revealed the law (2:2; cf. Acts 7:53; Gal. 3:19). If the hypothesis of their background in nonconformist Judaism be granted, they knew well an eschatology in which an angel played a more decisive role than the Messiah himself. Being Jews and Christians, their retreat from Christianity was resulting in a growing hesitance to ascribe divinity to Jesus while yet wishing to revere him, leaving him as less than God but more than man, that is, an angel. That his superior name is inherited indicates that Jesus Christ is here being considered not in his eternal and essential dignity as the Son of God but as the mediator, the "man Christ Jesus" (1 Tim. 2:5), who by his humiliation became superior to the angels (Heb. 2:9).

The fact that the author has the incarnate Son of God (v. 5) in view helps in understanding Psalm 2:7, the first of the seven citations from Scripture, which figures prominently in the New Testament as a prophecy of the incarnation, the messianic ministry, and especially the resurrection (Heb. 5:5; Mark 1:11; Luke 1:32; Acts 13:33; cf. Rom. 1:4). The eternal Son could be said to become or to "be begotten" as the Son of God only with reference to the exaltation of the human nature he took to himself when he came into the world.

The second citation (2 Sam. 7:14), God's promise to David concerning Solomon, was extended in Old Testament prophecy and became the basis of the expectation of the messianic king of Davidic descent who would usher in God's everlasting kingdom (Ps. 72; Isa. 9:7; 11:1–9; Jer. 23:5–6; Luke 1:32–33).

In verse 6 the third citation (Deut. 32:43, from the longer text of the Septuagint and DSS; cf. Ps. 97:7) verifies that when the Son of God came into the world as a man he was worshiped as divine. Perhaps the specific allusion is to Luke 2:13. "Firstborn" is another messianic title (Ps. 89:27). It suggests his consecration to God (Exod. 13:2) and his precedence as an heir. The application of this text to Christ is an instance of the attribution of the divine name *Yahweh* to Jesus.

The contrasting citations in verses 7–9 (Pss. 45:6–7; 104:4) establish that the superiority of the Son to the angels is as clear and great as that of a king to those who do his bidding, indeed, as that of God to his creatures. Psalm 45, a wedding song for an Israelite king, is properly applied to the one who establishes the reign of which the Old Testament kingship was but a foreshadowing. The ascription of this text to Christ results in one of the few places in the New Testament where Christ is directly referred to as God (cf. John 1:1; 20:28; Rom. 9:5).

In verses 10–12 the sixth citation (Ps. 102:25–27) serves to recapitulate the divine dignity of the incarnate Son of God as the Creator (v. 2) and his majesty as the eternal Yahweh. (The divine name is missing in the Hebrew text, but the Septuagint's "O Lord" may bear witness to an earlier form of the Hebrew text. In any case, Yahweh is unmistakably being addressed, as the entire psalm demonstrates.)

The final citation, which occurs in verses 13–14, is from Psalm 110 and climactically reiterates the divine honor bestowed upon Christ, the royal status he presently enjoys, and the inheritance soon to be his. On the other hand, the angels are but servants (cf. Ps. 103:20–21); some stand (Luke 1:19) but none sits in Christ's seat of honor. Their special ministry is to those who will share in Christ's inheritance. In his first mention of salvation, the author characteristically views it as yet future (2:5; 9:28).

The preceding exposition is now applied (**2:1–4**) in the first of many hortative sections that punctuate the letter and demonstrate its true purpose. The readers had no reservations concerning the legitimacy and severity of the sanctions of the Mosaic law, though it was mediated by angels (cf. Deut. 33:2 in the LXX; Acts 7:53; Gal. 3:19). How much more then ought they to fear the consequences of slighting a revelation communicated immediately by one far greater than angels, attested by eyewitnesses, and confirmed by miraculous signs of various kinds? The author is not belittling the law. It too was a revelation of God attested with marvelous signs (Heb. 12:18–27). But that only serves to heighten the sanction that attaches to the Son's own announcement of God's salvation. "Drift away" and "ignore" (vv. 1, 3) suggest less a deliberate repudiation of the faith than a squandering of salvation through an unwillingness to meet its stern requirements (3:12–13).

In the next section (**2:5–18**) the contrast between Christ and the angels continues. The assertion of the sovereignty of the Son over the world to come may be a direct rebuttal of such speculation regarding the role of angels in the coming kingdom now known to have been entertained among the Essenes. "The world to come" is the author's theme and thus may be identified with the salvation just mentioned (v. 3; cf. 9:28). Throughout Hebrews salvation is viewed in terms of its future consummation. Its present dimensions are not emphasized, since they are not immediately relevant to the author's purpose, which is to call his readers to that persevering faith which alone obtains entrance to the heavenly country (10:35–39).

The citation of Psalm 8:4–6 in verses 6–9 is introduced with an expression of striking indifference to the human authorship of Scripture. The psalm itself harks back to Genesis 1:26 and the supreme dignity bestowed upon man, God's unique image bearer and vice-regent. Elsewhere in the New Testament (Matt. 21:16; 1 Cor. 15:27; Eph. 1:22) it receives a messianic interpretation. Jesus is the perfect fulfillment of that dignity as *the* Son of man and last Adam. The incarnate Son's history has two periods: that of his humiliation and his eternal exaltation. Those in Christ recapitulate his history—they too, though lower now, will one day rule over angels (1 Cor. 6:3). Though the subjection of all things to Christ awaits the consummation, it is guaranteed by his exaltation to God's right hand, a reward for his self-sacrifice for sinners (10:13–14; 12:2; Phil. 2:6–11).

In the following paragraph (vv. 10–18) the author explains why the Son had to become a man and suffer and die as a man. As the larger subject of the comparison of the Son to angels is not forgotten (v. 16), it may be assumed that this explanation is offered in part to allay the suspicion of his readers that Jesus' reputation, on account of his humanity and humiliation at the hands of mere men, suffers in comparison to that of such purely spiritual and mighty beings.

The reason that the Son became a man and incurred such ignominy was precisely that in no other way could God save his people from their sins (v. 10; 5:8–9; 9:15). The incarnation was not a pageant but a tragic necessity, for a salvation which would meet the exigencies of sinful humans and a just God required such suffering as only a divine-human Savior could endure. The Father is identified both as the original source of salvation in Christ and the ultimate beneficiary (cf. 1 Cor. 15:24, 28; 2 Cor. 5:18–21). "Author" (Gk. *archēgos,* as in 12:2) would be better translated "pioneer" or "trailblazer," the one who opens the way that others might follow (6:20).

The sanctification which results from Christ's sacrifice is in the usage of Hebrews not the moral renewal of the believer's life which flows from and follows upon his justification (as in Paul), but rather his reconciliation to God (v. 11; 10:10, 14, 29). The oneness of Christ with the beneficiaries of his sacrifice consists not in the fact that they have the same Father (both being sons of God), but that they share a common humanity. "Is not ashamed" is an affirmation of the compassionate identification of Christ with his unworthy people which led him to empty himself. It closely approximates Paul's statement in Philippians 2:6–8.

Three citations are now adduced in demonstration of the Son's solidarity with the people of God (vv. 12–13). The first, from the unmistakably messianic Psalm 22, attests Christ's brotherhood with the redeemed. The second and third are from Isaiah 8:17–18, the prophet's cry of the heart interpreted messianically, especially on the strength of verse 14—"a stone that causes men to stumble . . . " (cf. Rom. 9:33; 1 Pet. 2:8). Jesus is so much a man that he too must trust in God and the people of God are his fellows not only as his brethren but as his offspring (cf. Isa. 53:10).

The point of Christ's sharing humanity is recapitulated and elaborated (vv. 14–15). It was necessary that the Son of God become a man, since a human death was required for the sin that separated man from God and rendered man subject to the devil. Only a man could die and only the God-man could die for the sins of the world (Gal. 4:4, 5). The breaking of the devil's grip is accomplished precisely by the breaking of the grip of sin (Eph. 2:1–5) and liberation from the fear of death is nothing else but liberation from the guilt of sin or liability to God's wrath (1 Cor. 15:54–57).

The rationale for the incarnation is developed further (vv. 16–18). Because Christ's purpose was to "help" (lit. take hold of; cf. the same word, Gk. *epilambanomai,* in 8:9) the people of God rather than angels, he had to become a man. Abraham's descendants are characteristically viewed as a spiritual rather than a racial entity—the elect of God (Rom. 9:6; 11:1–8; Gal. 3:29). There are elect angels (1 Tim. 5:21), but God's grace toward man is far more excellent than his grace to such angels as it was a far more costly and heroic work to redeem sinners than to preserve angels in their original holiness. To deliver man required that Christ become his people's high priest, to represent them in offering himself as their substitute, and in dying for them to appease God's holy wrath against their sin. The glory of Christ shines more brightly in his redeeming of one unworthy sinner than in his preserving the whole vast company of elect angels. "Make atonement for" (Gk. *hilaskomai*) is better rendered "make propitiation for," "placate" or "pacify wrath for." Propitiation is one of the main categories by which the Bible sets forth the nature and significance of Christ's sacrifice of himself for sinners (Rom. 3:24–25; 1 John 2:2). Christ's atonement is at once the gift of God's love and the requirement of his justice. Further, the experience of suffering temptation gained during his life in the world equipped him to help his people now in their temptations, an especially apposite point in this sermon to a people under temptation and one to which the author will return (4:15).

C. Jesus Christ superior to Moses (3:1–4:13). The author draws together his previous themes in a striking exhortation (3:1) which concludes the previous section and introduces the next. Their failure to give Christ the place in their minds and hearts which his divine supremacy, mediatorial work, and human sympathy deserve has led to their crisis of faith. The holy direction and management of the heart and its thoughts is fundamental to sturdy faith and holy living (Prov. 4:23; Col. 3:1–2). Only in Hebrews is Jesus called an apostle, though the fact that Jesus was sent by God to act on his behalf is commonplace in the New Testament (cf. John 5:36).

The author now compares Jesus with Moses (**3:1–6**), again perhaps to counter an unhealthy veneration of Moses at the expense of Christ in his readers' minds. At this point interpretations of the letter frequently begin to go seriously astray. Commentators often allege that these verses amount to a contrast of the inferior Mosaic order with the superior religio-historical economy introduced by Christ and his apostles. But the order of thought gives another sense altogether: there is but one house of God in which Moses served, but which Christ built, and that house includes us (v. 6). Hebrews refers repeatedly to the people of God but never in order to distinguish parts or epochs. The continuity of God's people or the church in all ages is a fundamental assumption of the author. That Christ should have built (the word employed, Gk. *kataskeuazō,* may also suggest administration) the house of God in former days is in keeping with the perspective of this author (11:26; 13:8) and of the New Testament generally (1 Cor. 3:10; Jude 5). The Son is the builder (Heb. 3:4) only as the executor of the Father's will (1:2), unless, as a number of commentators have thought, the author intends here to call Jesus God. The true superiority of Jesus to Moses will be adequately measured only in this way: Moses was never anything more than a member of the house Christ was building and a servant in that house over which Christ ruled as God's Son (vv. 5–6). Further, as a prophet, Moses pointed away from himself to Christ; his message was of salvation in Christ (cf. John 5:46; Rom. 10:6–10). Believers today belong to that house as Moses and the faithful before and after him (Heb. 11:1–40) if they hold fast to Christ and to no one and nothing else for salvation.

The warning of Hebrews 3:6 that membership in God's household is suspended upon a living and persevering faith introduces a long hortative section (**3:7–4:13**) in which the danger of apostasy and the necessity of an enduring faith are illustrated from the history of Israel. In 3:7–11 the warning of Psalm 95:7–11 is cited as the living and active Word of God (Heb. 4:12) demanding to be heard and obeyed now as then. It is introduced as the word of the Holy Spirit, though later it is ascribed to David (4:7), an example of the consistent assumption of the writers of the New Testament that what the Scripture says, God says (cf. 9:8; 10:15; Rom. 9:15, 17; Gal. 3:8). The cited portion of the psalm is an admonition not to imitate the wilderness generation in its faithlessness, only one particular instance of which is recollected in verse 8: rebellion and testing (Exod. 17:1–7; cf. Num. 20:1–13; 1 Cor. 10:1–11; Jude 5). The burden of the citation is the judgment pronounced upon unbelief in the last verse. As the argument proceeds it becomes clear that the failure to enter God's rest means nothing less than the failure to obtain eternal life, of which entrance into the Promised Land was only a figure.

The point of the citation is driven home as the author reminds his readers that in this fundamental respect nothing has changed since the wilderness (vv. 12–14): it is still possible for those numbered outwardly among the people of God to forfeit the eternal country; it still requires nothing more than spiritual neglect to harden a heart to the point that it will turn away from God; and it is still as vitally necessary that each one stand fast in faith all of his life ("as long as it is called Today," v. 13) and help one another to stand (10:23–25).

As throughout the letter, the subject is not unbelief per se but apostasy, the rejection of Christ and the faith by one who professed to believe and was considered to belong to the church of God (cf. "brothers," v. 12). The warning in no way contradicts the massive biblical witness to the security of the elect, rooted as it is in the merits of Christ and the eternal and immutable love of God (John 10:27–29; Rom. 8:28–39). But the elect are kept by the power of God through faith (1 Pet. 1:5), which faith is quickened and strengthened by warnings such as these. Further, many who claim to believe in fact do not. Some manifest the falseness of their faith by apostasy (1 John 2:19), while others remain undetected until the day of Christ (Matt. 7:21–23; 13:36–43).

For a readership that was inclined to consider the life of Israel in the wilderness as a paradigm for her own (vv. 15–19), it was particularly necessary to emphasize that it was precisely that generation, the generation lifted out of Egypt on eagles' wings, that was rejected by God for unbelief. The exhortation of 3:12–14 is thus reinforced by this explicit recollection of Israel's forfeiture of the rest of God.

That the alternatives which Israel faced in the wilderness are the same ones believers face today is demonstrated by the use of the terms *promise* (4:1; cf. 6:12; 9:15; 10:36; 11:39–40) and *gospel* (4:2; cf. also the verbal form in v. 6, *euangelizō*, "to evangelize"; cf. Rom. 10:16; Gal. 3:8) and by the striking inversion of order—not "they also," but "we also" (Heb. 4:2). This serves as an impressive verification of the author's consistent assumption that the gospel and its demands have remained unchanged from the beginning and that the spiritual world of the ancient people of God with its conditions, blessings, and powers is identical to that in which his readers now live. He commands them to take care (lit. fear) and together to take care on each other's behalf (10:24–25). Eternal salvation must never be taken for granted, but must be worked out in fear and trembling (Phil. 2:12–13), all the more as it is possible to belong to the people of God in an outward way and yet for want of a genuine and enduring faith fail to obtain eternal life. The rest which faithless Israel failed to obtain but which believers will obtain is now identified as participation in God's own rest that began after the creation of the world (vv. 3–5; Gen. 2:2–3). Israel, therefore, did not fail to obtain the rest because the rest itself was not yet available, but solely because of her unbelief. Further, Israel's forfeiture of the rest is at issue (vv. 6–8), not her failure to enter Canaan, as if the rest were one thing in the Old Testament and another today. Canaan was only a symbol of the eternal inheritance that faith obtains (cf. 11:9, 10, 13–16). Joshua brought Israel into the land and generations of Israelites had lived in the Promised Land when God issued the warning of Psalm 95. It was quite possible to inhabit Canaan and yet forfeit the rest of God.

So, the rest of God has always been available to men and remains so today. The sole question is whether a man will exercise that persevering faith which alone obtains that rest. For it is a rest which no one enters in this life, but only in the world to come when the believer has rested from his work (10:36). The author speaks of a Sabbath rest (Gk. *sabbatismos*) again to connect the rest that the believer will obtain with the rest of God (v. 4; Gen. 2:2–3). It refers not to the weekly Sabbath but to eternal salvation as different from and following upon this life of work. It should not be thought that this rest is inactivity, however, for God's rest is not (John 5:17). Again, note the author's characteristic emphasis on the futurity of salvation. The consideration of this future blessedness concludes with another summary exhortation to eschew the example of Israel, to fear the wrath of God which befell Israel, to set mind and heart on the life to come, and to strive to live by faith.

This appeal is enforced by a consideration of the character of that Word of God that confronted Israel and confronts men still today (vv. 12–13). It is the living voice of God which is never disobeyed with impunity. Here the Word is thought of as an instrument of God's judgment, discerning the secrets and motives of the heart (cf. 1 Cor. 4:5). The author's readers must not suppose that they will obtain the rest of God because they are accepted by human beings or are counted as members of the people of God. The faith required is to be exercised and will be measured in the day of Christ as much in the thoughts of the heart as in outward conformity to the will of God. The phrases *soul and spirit, joints and marrow* (v. 12) denote the inner life of man in all its aspects. The terms no more prove that man is composed of three parts (spirit, soul, and body) than Matthew 22:37 proves that he is composed of four.

D. Jesus Christ superior to Aaron (4:14–10:18). Jesus Christ's qualifications as our great High Priest are now discussed (**4:14–5:10**). The author picks up the thread of his earlier statement that Christ is the High Priest of his people (2:17–3:1) and reiterates points made previously regarding his exaltation (2:9) and his experience of the trials of human life (2:18). After the stern warnings and the threat of God's searching judgment in the previous verses, consolation and encouragement are offered to those who have discovered that the life of faith is full of painful difficulties and severe temptations. Jesus, true God and true human being, is a high priest fully willing to help, as his suffering for sinners demonstrates, and fully able to help, for he combines perfect understanding of and sympathy with the struggling believer's lot in this world of sin ("in every way," v. 15) with unlimited ability to help. He knows how to deliver the godly from temptation having been victorious himself in every moment of his sorely tested life. That he is now seated on a heavenly throne signifies both that his sacrifice for sin has been accepted by God (1:3; 10:12–14) and that his perfect sympathy as a fellow man and brother of the saints is joined with divine omnipotence. Therefore, addressing himself to Jesus, the believer should not doubt that he will receive both forgiveness for past sins and strength to bear up under present trials. "Approach" (v. 16) translates the Greek term *proserchomai,* which the Septuagint often employs for the priest's approach to God in the sacrificial ritual (e.g., Lev. 21:17, 21). The author's meaning is not that access to God (limited in the Old Testament to the priest) is now extended to all believers, for the saints of the former age also came near to God (Heb. 11:6), as the psalms and other portions of the Old Testament emphatically demonstrate (Ps. 73:28). Rather, he means that the sinner must rely upon Jesus, not upon sacrificial ritual, for mercy and grace (10:1–3).

The author now takes care to establish in the mind of his readers, steeped as they were in Levitical regulations, that Jesus is in every way qualified to be the believer's great High Priest (**5:1–10**). First, as a representative of men a priest must be a man with fellow-feeling for those he represents to God (vv. 1–3). As one who offers sacrifices for sin, he must know what it is to do battle with sin. In the Levitical ritual this was emphatically expressed in the requirement that even the high priest must offer sacrifice for his own sins (Lev. 16:6). Second, the high priest must be appointed to his office (Heb. 5:4; cf. Num. 20:23–28). Now the author demonstrates in reverse order that Jesus meets both requirements (vv. 5–6). The two citations from the Psalter, both in the form of an address by the Father to the Son, establish that Jesus has his priestly office by divine appointment. Psalm 110:4 introduces the theme to which the author will return in 6:20ff. Jesus also meets the requirement of sympathy with those he represents (vv. 7–10). It is true that he did not sin and needed no sacrifice for his own sins (v. 3) but he was tempted more severely than any other person, and only the one who resisted to the end knows the full weight of any temptation. The point made twice before (2:17–18; 4:15) is now elaborated. Christ as a man discovered what it is to cry out to God in fear and distress. The allusion to Gethsemane is unmistakable (Matt. 26:36–46). He learned to say "thy will be done" when the will of God was the way of the cross. In answer to his prayer he was enabled to bear his trial just as he will enable believers to bear theirs (4:15–16). This statement serves to demonstrate how completely and unqualifiedly the Son of God became a man like other men, though without sin. Though he was the Son of God and a sinless man, he was not exempt from the principle that it is through suffering that a person discovers the true nature and cost of obedience (vv. 8–10; 2:10). He was "a man of sorrows, and familiar with suffering" (Isa. 53:3), and it is precisely that suffering and perfect obedience in suffering which fit him for his role as Savior and High Priest. The necessity of obedience to Christ is not in contrast to the necessity of faith, for true faith and obedience are always found together, the latter the product and the sign of the former (cf. 3:18–19; 4:2, 6). The reference to Melchizedek anticipates the exposition to come in 6:20–7:28.

The exposition of Christ's high priesthood is interrupted in the interest of another exhortation to persevere in faith. This section (**5:11–6:8**) begins with a rebuke and is more severe in tone. The author intends to say more of Christ's priesthood but must first prepare the audience to listen with understanding and appreciation. Their spiritual childishness shows itself in a disposition to content themselves with their theological and spiritual status quo, apparently since by further progress they would only put greater distance between themselves and their Jewish past and sharpen the opposition they were already suffering. But such spiritual stagnation is dangerous; spiritual life is sustained by the solid food of sound doctrine and it is protected by that spiritual and ethical discernment which is the fruit of an ever-deepening knowledge and constant exercise of faith.

Though in their present state of spiritual immaturity the process of digestion will be more painful, solid food is urgently required to invigorate their flagging faith. Each of the elementary teachings (6:1–2) mentioned had a place in Judaism but had been invested with new significance in Christian preaching. These basics are not to be discarded, but neither are they sufficient. This sentence amounts to a ringing affirmation both of the obligation laid upon believers to cultivate their spiritual life and of the importance of doctrine to sanctification. Knowledge feeds faith. "Acts that lead to death" (lit. dead works) are not, as some have supposed, attempts to gain righteousness by means of works of the law or cultic performances, but simply sins in general, all evil thoughts and actions from which the conscience must be cleansed (9:14; cf. Rom. 6:21).

Though the believer is obliged to pursue maturity, God's grace and action are necessary (v. 1 reads lit. let us be carried to perfection). The New International Version omits the "for" with which verse 4 begins and which indicates that God is unwilling and will not permit in the case of apostates. Perhaps some in this community had already apostasized; others were alarmingly near to doing so, prompting the author to warn of the grim and irrevocable effects of deserting the faith.

The severity of this warning and the gravity of the situation contemplated must not be mitigated. Scripture is not silent regarding the hopeless condition of those who, having been numbered among the people of God, professed faith in Christ, received instruction in the Word of God, and experienced some measure of the blessing of the Holy Spirit's ministry and the reality of the unseen world, then deliberately repudiate Christ's lordship and salvation (cf. 10:26–27; Num. 15:30–31; Matt. 12:31–32; 1 John 5:16–17). Of course, it is imperative to maintain that, appearances notwithstanding, such people were never born again or made genuine partakers of the redemption purchased by Christ (John 6:39; 10:27–29; Rom. 9:29–30; 1 Pet. 1:3–5, 23). The brief parable in verses 7–8, similar to others in the Bible (Isa. 5:1–7; Matt. 13:1–9, 18–30, 36–43), reminds us of the impossibility to distinguish infallibly between the truly converted and the hypocrite and that spiritual fruit is the evidence of living faith. It also illustrates the righteousness of God's condemnation of those who spurn his favor.

In the next section (**6:9–20**) the author encourages his readers to press on. As a matter of fact the author has good hopes that his warnings will be taken to heart and be God's instrument to invigorate his readers' flagging faith. His confidence rests on his acquaintance with the genuinely faithful lives they had lived as Christians, especially in the early days of their faith in Jesus Christ (cf. 10:32–34). Such faith, love, and obedience, however, must continue as long as they live in the world. In exhorting his readers to imitate the faithful of the former epoch (as appears from the following verses) the author characteristically anticipates a theme he will enlarge upon subsequently (11:1–12:1).

Abraham, to whom all Jews looked as their father, is mentioned as a man of faith deserving of their emulation (vv. 13–15; cf. 2:16; 11:8–19), but the theme now is not Abraham's faith but the certainty of God's promise. Since faith must wait so long for its reward, the believer may be sorely tempted to grow weary and lose heart. The wait cannot be shortened, but hope can be revived by a reminder that hope in God will never be disappointed. Abraham had to wait many years for even the beginning of the fulfillment of the promise God made to him (Gen. 12:2; 17:5, 19, 21), but he did not wait in vain. The Lord added a solemn oath to his promise (Gen. 22:15–18) to strengthen Abraham's faith during the lengthy wait when all appearances would be contrary to God's promise.

Significantly the incident in Genesis 22 followed not only the birth of Isaac but the trial of Abraham's faith when God commanded him to offer his son as a sacrifice. In speaking of Abraham's obtaining the promise, then, the author seems to be thinking not of what Abraham obtained in this life, but of the fulfillment of the age to come (cf. Heb. 11:13–16, 39–40). The birth of Isaac and the receiving of him back from the dead (11:19) are rather a pledge of the promise that he would be a father of a great nation. As in Hebrews 3 and 4, the author assumes that the principles of life and salvation that applied in the days of Abraham and Israel are fundamentally the same as apply today. The promise was offered then as now (4:1) and is obtained by a patient and enduring faith now as then.

The oath which God swore was a condescension on his part to his people's frailty (vv. 16–

18). His word needs no confirmation (John 17:17; Titus 1:2) but man's faith is weak, the wait is long, and God takes pity on his children. Christ's exaltation to the right hand of God (1:3; 2:9; 4:14) only further confirms the certainty of the eventual fulfillment of God's promise of eternal rest for those who trust in him. These readers were no more secure than Abraham had been, resting as he did on the immutable promise of God, but they had further cause to be encouraged and less excuse for a wavering faith now that Christ had appeared and accomplished eternal redemption. "The inner sanctuary" (v. 19), a reference to the innermost chamber of the tabernacle and temple, anticipates the exposition of 9:6–14 and the contrast drawn there between the ineffectuality of the Levitical ritual and the power of Christ's sacrifice to save to the uttermost.

The author now turns to discuss Melchizedek the priest (**7:1–10**). The few details about Melchizedek (vv. 1–3) are taken from Genesis 14:18–20. In distinction to the necessity of Aaronic ancestry as a prerequisite for Levitical priestly service (Heb. 7:14) nothing is said either of Melchizedek's birth and ancestry or his death and posterity. For the author's purpose, this fact demonstrates the existence in Scripture of another order of priesthood wholly separate from the Levitical. In this, Melchizedek serves as a type or embodied prophecy of Christ's non-Levitical and eternal priesthood, which is confirmed not only directly in Psalm 110:4 (already cited in Heb. 5:6), but by his name ("king of righteousness") and his title ("king of peace"), both redolent of Christ's messianic office and dignity (v. 2; cf. Isa. 9:6; Jer. 23:6; Zech. 9:9–10).

Attention is now drawn to the fact that according to Genesis 14, Abraham, though the heir of the promise and even in his hour of triumph, clearly behaves as Melchizedek's inferior, in both paying him tithes and receiving his blessing. Abraham was under no legal obligation to pay tithes to Melchizedek as Israelites would later be required by God's law to pay a tithe to the Levitical priesthood; hence, his paying of a tithe amounted to a voluntary recognition of Melchizedek's inherent dignity as a priest of God (cf. Heb. 7:16). "Who is declared to be living" (lit. it is testified, i.e., in Scripture) looks back to verse 3 and the silence of the record regarding Melchizedek's birth and death. By the absence of this information the type is perfected and more perfectly foreshadows Christ's eternal priesthood.

With the ground thus laid, the author sets out to show that of the two priesthoods reported in the Scripture, Jesus' is superior (**7:11–28**) and the only source of salvation (5:9). Of great importance to the interpretation of Hebrews is the contrary-to-fact conditional statement in 7:11a, together with two other such statements that figure prominently as the argument unfolds (8:7; 10:2). These clearly indicate that the readers of the letter, tempted to return to the comfortable paths of their former faith and associations, were inclined to precisely the opposite conclusions, namely, that perfection *could* come through the Levitical priesthood and that the sacrifices *could* make perfect those who offered them. Further, these conditional statements demonstrate that the author is criticizing the Levitical institutions precisely for failing to provide in themselves the forgiveness of sins and the perfection of the conscience (7:18–19; 9:13–14). The fact that they were never intended to do either (cf. 10:3, the blood of bulls and goats *cannot* take away sins) is immaterial because the author is dealing with these institutions under his readers' view of them. The statements frequently encountered in commentaries to the effect that the author is contrasting the provisional and ineffectual religious forms of the Old Testament with the fulfillment enjoyed by believers of the new era utterly overturn the historical-theological perspective of Hebrews and fail to account for the letter's commonplaces: the nature and condition of salvation are not different now than formerly; the church in the new age is no less threatened by the specter of apostasy; salvation (perfection) is no more the present possession of believers now than it was of the faithful in the former epoch; and nothing is more necessary than that these readers imitate the saints of old. The contrast drawn is not between some supposed primitive and inadequate religious form with its merely provisional forgiveness and severely limited access to God and the free access and effective forms of New Testament Christianity. The contrast is rather between two ways of salvation—one by ritual performance and the other by the sacrifice of Jesus Christ. The argument that is advanced is designed to correct a misplaced confidence in rituals and to confirm the conviction that salvation is and could only be in Christ alone. The argument could be turned with equal effect upon Christian ritualism and upon the sacraments of the Christian church when they are conceived intrinsically to possess saving efficacy.

The author rejects the argument that since the inauguration of the Levitical priesthood came later, it superseded Melchizedek's order, for long after Aaron the Word of God (Ps. 110:4) speaks of another priest in the order of Melchizedek (vv. 12–17). The law was served by the priesthood that upheld it and the priesthood was, in turn, regulated by the law. But the law made no provision for a priesthood outside of the tribe of Levi, yet Jesus was of Judah. Christ's appointment as priest and all the more as an eternal priest of a wholly different order thus constitutes a superseding of the Levitical institutions and a further demonstration that they were by no means God's definitive provision for the salvation of humankind. That point is now repeated in a striking statement of the ineffectuality of that ritual. The author heaps scorn upon it precisely for its failure to bring the sinner near to God (vv. 18–19).

Though at the time of writing the temple ritual continued, the author seems to have gathered that it was near to its demise, perhaps from the fact that the burgeoning Gentile church was doing without it altogether (cf. 8:13; 9:10). But it is crucial to recognize that the Levitical cultus is being attacked for failing to provide what it was never intended to provide, a fact pious Israelites well understood (Ps. 51:16–17). It is being caricatured here because this caricature is precisely the view of these institutions seriously entertained by this readership. They viewed the ritual (or were severely tempted to view it) as a way of salvation, separated from the true covenant of God, from faith, from Christ and his work of which these rituals and institutions, like baptism and the Lord's Supper after them, were but signs and seals. In this the readers were but following in the steps of their forefathers (Ps. 50:7–15; Jer. 7:1–26). All thought of the true and evangelical significance of that priesthood and sacrifice and of the joy and spiritual benefit which was the fruit of the believer's participation in this ritual is set aside in order to pour contempt on these bare ceremonies as utterly incapable of making sinners right with God. In this, the author simply imitates the technique and the argument of the great prophets before him (Isa. 1:10–20; Amos 5:21–25; cf. 1 Cor. 10:1–5). The author's intention is certainly not to contrast believing life and experience in the Old Testament with that of the New Testament, for the exact counterpart of the sacrifice is not the priesthood and sacrifice of Christ but the Lord's Supper; and more significantly, while he states that those sacrifices could not save sinners, it is fundamental to his whole outlook and argument that sinners of the old epoch were saved just as sinners are now: by Christ, through the gospel and faith. This is underscored by his reference to the better hope. "Better" (Gk. *kreittōn*) is an important term in Hebrews and refers not to some supposed but unmentioned comparative advantage enjoyed by New Testament believers, but rather to the blessings of God's eternal salvation, grasped by faith by the saints of all ages, in comparison to the false and worldly hopes of sinful men (7:19, 22; 8:6; 9:3; 10:34; 11:16, 35, 40; 12:24).

The superiority of Christ's priesthood is further confirmed by its enactment by divine oath (vv. 20–22). Characteristically, the author anticipates the development of his argument (8:6ff.). It is noteworthy that in this first reference to the new covenant Jesus is said to be its guarantor. In keeping with the author's already well-established perspective, the new covenant, the fulfillment of subjective redemption or salvation, is not something which the faithful of the former epoch awaited in hope but which Christians today enjoy as a present possession. One does not require a guarantor for what one already has (cf. 6:17–20). The new covenant, the rest of God, the promise, even salvation itself are presented in Hebrews as different aspects of the future consummation and the fulfillment of the world to come.

Its permanence sets Christ's priesthood above the Levitical (vv. 23–25). His does not need to be replaced generation after generation, which lends a continual efficacy to all aspects of his priestly work, including his intercession (Isa. 53:12; John 17:8–9; Rom. 8:34).

Finally, Christ's priesthood excels the Levitical by reason of his personal perfection (vv. 26–28). The eternally holy Son of God lived a sinless life as a man (4:15) and advanced through suffering to the full-orbed perfection of human maturity (5:8–9). Unlike Levitical priests, then, he had no need to offer sacrifices for his own sin. His sacrifice of himself—the eternal Son of God and the true and perfectly obedient man (2:17–18)—thus has unlimited potency. Verses 26–28 serve to recapitulate the argument so far presented.

The heavenly sphere of Jesus Christ's priesthood is the subject of **8:1–6**. The intricate comparison of the two priesthoods being completed, the author advances to compare the two priestly works. The point is that Jesus' priesthood is exercised in heaven, in the very presence of God, and its effectuality is therefore neither earthly nor temporary, but spiritual and eternal (vv. 1–2; cf. 4:14). He exercises his priesthood not at some distance from God but in God's immediate presence (9:24). The point is reiterated to allay the suspicions of his Jewish readership (vv. 3–5). Although Christ is not now visible to his people as a priest, his priestly work is no less authentic inasmuch as it involves the offering of sacrifice (5:1)—that of himself, not that of the law (7:27; 9:14). The recipients of the letter are attracted to the rites of the temple, but this earthly round of ritual and its setting are but a copy of the real, heavenly sacrifice which Christ offered once-for-all and on the basis of which he now intercedes for his people. The detailed instruction God gave to Moses concerning the construction of the tabernacle (Exod. 25–40) demonstrates that the tabernacle and, by implication, the temple were not the reality but only copies of it. The author's readership is in danger of preferring the copy to the genuine article, of accepting an imitation as the true principle of salvation.

Now the author presents Jesus Christ as the guarantor of a better covenant (**8:7–13**). The argument now introduced in verse 7 parallels that of 7:11 and 10:2. Hebrews was written to a community which was inclined to regard the covenant life and experience of Israel, especially the wilderness period, as a paradigm for her own. These Jewish Christians were disposed to feel that they required nothing more than to duplicate the pattern of life with its outward forms established by their forebears. That pattern, in their minds, was the Mosaic covenant, but, in fact, they conceived of that covenant not as the proclamation of the gospel (4:1) but in legalistic and ritualistic terms. The author has already pointed out, in correcting the error of these ritualistically minded people, that the wilderness generation perished and forfeited the promise for lack of faith and thus is not at all to be emulated. In a similar way, he now argues that the very fact that another covenant was promised to replace the covenant with the fathers ipso facto demonstrates that the former covenant is obsolete and cannot serve as a paradigm for believers today (cf. another instance of this form of argument in 4:8).

But what are these two covenants? Commentaries are often singularly unhelpful at this point. It is usually asserted that the former covenant is the Mosaic administration per se and the new covenant is the superior administration introduced by Christ and the apostles. The contrast then is between a relatively inferior Old Testament revelation, faith, and spirituality and the fulfillment of the new epoch. But such an interpretation falls foul of the plain facts of the case and of the radical character of the distinction drawn between the two covenants (vv. 8–12). (1) The old covenant represents not Israel's life of faith but her culpable and damning unbelief in the gospel. The difference between the old covenant and the new is the difference between the forfeiture of salvation ("I turned away from them," v. 9) and subjective redemption ("I will be their God," v. 11), between death and eternal life. (2) The fulfillment of the promises of the better covenant is not to be found in some comparative advantage enjoyed by believers in the new epoch, but rather in the consummation. These better promises are only the ancient verities of Old Testament faith, which elsewhere in Hebrews are called "the gospel," "the inheritance," "the rest of God," "the better country," and "the better resurrection." Believers in the time before the incarnation claimed these promises from afar (11:1–38), precisely as believers must today. The popular notion that the law of God was but some external ordinance in the Old Testament but now in the new era has been inscribed upon the heart is not only generally unbiblical (Deut. 4:8–9; 6:5–6; 30:6, 14; Ps. 40:8; Prov. 3:1, 3; Isa. 51:7; Jer. 24:4–7) but wholly without support in this letter. It is very important to recognize that the author's exhortation is *never* in the form a fortiori ("if they could persevere in the old covenant, how much more ought we to do so in the new . . ."). (3) The specific promises of Jeremiah's prophecy of the new covenant are not considered by this author to have been fulfilled and cannot be so considered. Indeed, it would be highly ironic had the author understood that the expectation had now been fulfilled of a time when "no longer will a man teach his neighbor, or a man his brother, saying 'Know the Lord,' because they will all know me" (8:11) but then proceeded anyway to write Hebrews, which is nothing less than an impassioned plea to his brethren to "know the Lord" in the face of an incipient apostasy in principle no different than that of the fathers in the wilderness or of that against which Jeremiah protested. (4) Taken at face value, Jeremiah's prophecy is not a prophecy of the New Testament epoch, in which Israel's failure of faith would be repeated many times and on a far more terrible scale, but a prophecy of the final triumph of the grace of God, when the church will no more be a mixture of true and false sons or pass through periods of domination by unbelief as in the wilderness, in Jeremiah's day, and not infrequently since. The prophecy has many affinities with other prophetic texts which portray the triumph and consummation of the kingdom of God in the world (e.g., Isa. 11:6–9; 54:11–15; 59:20–21; Ezek. 16:59–63; Jer. 32:36–41; 33:14–26; Rom. 11:26–27). (5) As the argument is presented in 8:7, 13 and unfolds subsequently, the author seems interested in but two features of Jeremiah's prophecy: the covenant guaranteed by Jesus promises forgiveness and the very fact of such a promise of the new covenant constitutes a condemnation of the old. Indeed, if by "new covenant" the author means the new dispensation and by its blessings the comparative advantages believers enjoy today, he fails altogether to make that clear.

The old covenant is the broken relationship with God that resulted from Israel's response of unbelief and disobedience. Such a situation prevailed when the gospel was not combined with faith (4:2). Of course, in principle it can be repeated today; indeed, the threat of repeating a breaking of the covenant is what calls forth this letter. The old covenant is not the Mosaic administration except where that system was perverted by unbelief into an occasion of apostasy. The new covenant, contrarily, is the living relationship God creates with his people by means of his gracious and powerful working within them, calling them to faith and obedience. This covenant of grace is contemplated in Jeremiah's prophecy from the vantage point of its consummation at the end of the history of the world, but, of course, it embraces all the people of God as one (11:39–40). This covenant, which is simply the divine application of the redemption which is in Christ to those who are being saved, mediates the heavenly realities of eternal life that have always been the hope of the faithful.

The tabernacle and its ritual form the author's discussion in **9:1–10**. He continues his demonstration of the ineffectuality of the Levitical institutions to deal with sin and of his contention that forgiveness can be found only in Christ. Returning to the argument of 8:1–5, the author describes the earthly sanctuary and its furniture (vv. 1–5). He describes the tabernacle, not the similar plan of the temple, perhaps because of his readership's fascination with the wilderness period of Israel's history. The altar of incense appears to have been located in the Holy Place (Exod. 30:6; Lev. 16:12, 18) not the Most Holy Place. The wording here recalls that of 1 Kings 6:22 and perhaps is intended to suggest the intimate connection between this altar and the ark of the covenant in the priestly ritual. The activity of the priests and of the high priest on the Day of Atonement is described (vv. 6–10) but now in the present tense (contra the NIV), furnishing an argument that Hebrews was written before the destruction of the temple and the cessation of its ritual in A.D. 70 and serving as a reminder that Jewish Christians were still participating without prejudice in that ritual (Acts 21:20–26). The fact that the divinely appointed order so severely restricted access to the Most Holy Place was an enacted lesson that the true, decisive ransom, of which the Levitical sacrifices were but a figure, had not yet been paid and that those sacrifices could not remove guilt. Under discussion is the single question of what sacrifice is the basis of salvation—the Levitical sacrifice or the sacrifice of Christ. The author ought not to be understood as suggesting that believers in the former era did not have direct access to God and full forgiveness through Christ, a notion against which the whole of Scripture rises in protest (e.g., Pss. 32; 103; Mic. 7:18–19; Rom. 4:1–8) and which is particularly impossible to reconcile with the perspective of the author of Hebrews (11:4ff.). Again, he is belittling the Levitical rites under his readers' view of them, separated from Christ and from living faith, as mere externalities and, what is more, only temporary.

The next major subsection focuses upon the sufficiency of the redemption obtained by Jesus Christ (**9:11–10:18**). The imagery continues to be that of the Day of Atonement, but Christ's offering of himself is a transaction that transcends the earthly sphere and the potentialities of mere men and their rituals. Though he died on a cross near Jerusalem (13:12), his sacrifice is thought of as being offered in heaven (v. 11). Offering himself once and for all, he thus secured eternal redemption for his people (v. 12). Redemption, along with propitiation and reconciliation, is a key concept in the Bible for the representation of the character and effect of Christ's saving work. Redemption is deliverance from some bondage by the payment of a price or ransom (Exod. 6:6; 13:13–15; Lev. 25:25–27, 47–54; Mark 10:45; Rom. 3:24; Eph. 1:7). The bondage here contemplated is that of sinners to death, to the devil, and to the divine wrath; the ransom is the death of Christ in the sinner's place (Heb. 2:14–17; Gal. 3:13). Having obtained this eternal redemption, he entered heaven and sat down there to represent his people to God as their great High Priest and to await the consummation (Heb. 9:24, 28; 10:12–13).

The Levitical sacrifices and other rituals (vv. 13–14; the allusion to the ritual of sprinkling water containing the ashes of a heifer [Num. 19] could be due to the significance attached to such ceremonies of cleansing in nonconformist Judaism; cf. 1QS 2:25–3:12) did avail to remove ceremonial defilement, but the sacrifice of the incarnate Son of God, infinite in his perfection as a substitute for his guilty people (2:9–10), actually satisfied the demands of God's justice on their behalf and turned away his holy wrath from them (1:3; 2:17; 9:27, 28) and thus provided the removal of sin and guilt and established a living communion with God. "Eternal Spirit" refers either to the divine enablement of the Third Person of the Godhead by which Jesus performed his mission (Isa. 42:1; Mark 1:10) or, less probably, to his own eternal and spiritual life, by reason of which his sacrifice and priesthood are of everlasting value and effect (Heb. 7:16, 24).

The eternally effective sacrifice of himself constituted Christ the mediator, or better, guarantor of the new covenant, that is, of the eternal salvation which the gospel promises, which faith embraces, but the fulfillment of which awaits the consummation. Verse 15 is often thought to mean that Christ, by his death, retroactively satisfied for the sins of those who lived before the incarnation. That Christ's death had such a retroactive effect and was the basis of gospel forgiveness in the Old Testament is unquestionably true. But as an interpretation of the author's statement it does grave injustice to a text as programmatic in scope as John 3:16. "The sins committed under the first covenant" are not the individual transgressions committed by those who lived before the incarnation, but rather the sins connected with that covenant, that is, Israel's broken relationship with God, namely, unbelief and disobedience (4:1, 6), which are conceived to be the fundamental sins and root of every actual transgression. The proof of this is that Christ's dying for these old covenant sins guarantees the inheritance of this community of second-generation Christians (v. 14, "our consciences"). Similarly, "those who are called" can hardly be restricted, as some commentators have supposed, to saints of the pre-Christian epoch. The phrase is thoroughly comprehensive in scope and intended to include the entire company of the elect, as appears from parallel statements elsewhere ("everyone," "many sons," 2:9–10; "many," 9:28). The sins for which Christ suffered punishment in his people's place are the sins which prevented Israel (and anyone) from sharing in the eternal inheritance. By the payment of his own life, Christ has delivered those whom God is calling to salvation from the guilt and the power of unbelief and disobedience which alienate them from God.

The mention of inheritance in verse 15 perhaps prompted the author to draw an illustration in verses 16–22 from everyday life, made easier by the fact that *diathēkē,* which ordinarily means "covenant" in biblical Greek, commonly meant "last will and testament" in the Greek of the author's day. Of course, a will takes effect only after the death of the testator. The new covenant (i.e., the living relationship that God has established with the called and the promise of eternal life) is made effectual by Christ's death, a principle illustrated in the inauguration of the covenant at Sinai with blood. Several additional details not mentioned in Exodus 24:4–8 and the silence of the Pentateuch regarding any such sprinkling of the tabernacle suggest that the author was aware of sources no longer extant or drew from some authentic but now unattested tradition.

Recapitulating 7:27–28; 8:1–5; and 9:1–14, the author distinguishes the earthly ceremonies and sanctuary from the sacrifice of the Son and the spiritual and heavenly sphere of his priestly work (vv. 23–28). The principle of true salvation is not the oft-repeated Levitical rituals but the once-for-all, eternally effective self-sacrifice of Christ, sufficient to cover all the sins of all the called for all time. "End of the ages" (v. 26; NEB the climax of history) suggests that human destiny and the purpose of history pivots on this single event. As men die but once, so he who took the place of men (2:14, 17) dies but once, but with eternal effect; however, the full manifestation and development of this await Christ's return.

The Levitical sacrifices are portrayed as inadequate in **10:1–4**. They only foreshadowed the true salvation which Christ has guaranteed and will someday bring to completion. This is the third and last of the contrary-to-fact conditional statements around which the central argument of this sermon is constructed. The appeal to the repetitive character of Levitical worship and its inability to cleanse the conscience (9:13–14) indicates that the author has not deviated from his original purpose. He is determined to persuade his readers that for salvation they must trust in Christ and his sacrifice and not in the rituals of Judaism. As is often supposed, he is not comparing the Old Testament order as a more primitive state of revelation and spirituality with the Christian era. He says nothing about that, but instead compares a false theory of salvation with the fact of salvation in Christ alone. At the time Hebrews was written, a Christian might still have participated in the temple ritual (Acts 21:26), but could not think that such externalities were the substance of salvation any more than the faithful of the former epoch did (Ps. 51:16–17) or than a believer today should think of baptism or the Lord's Supper as having in themselves justifying or sanctifying efficacy. The coming of Christ is decisive to the author not because it lifts the religious experience of believers to a somewhat higher plane than that enjoyed by the saints of the former epoch, but because Christ secured the salvation that all of God's people, past, present, and future, grasp by faith in this world and will enjoy in fullness in the next (11:39–40). Believers in the former era rejoiced in the freedom from guilt that God's grace provided (Exod. 34:6–7; Pss. 32:1–2; 103:10–12; 130; Isa. 38:17; Mic. 7:18–19). For that matter, the Lord's Supper perpetually reminds the church today of her sin, for which she must constantly mourn, confess, and ask forgiveness (Matt. 5:3–6; 1 Cor. 11:27–32; 1 John 1:8–10).

Unwilling to leave a single stone unturned in his attempt to demonstrate to the satisfaction of his readers that the Levitical rituals are an insubstantial foundation upon which to rest one's hope of salvation, the author launches into another argument which adds some new points and recapitulates others (**10:5–18**).

The author understands the citation of Psalm 40:6–8 in verses 5–7 to be prophetic of Christ. The author takes the phrase *a body you prepared for me* from the Septuagint rather than the Hebrew Masoretic Text, as referring to the body the Son of God assumed at his incarnation, the human nature in which he obeyed God and died in his people's place (2:14; 5:8; cf. John 6:38; Phil. 2:7–8). The citation is perfectly suited because it compares the Levitical sacrifices unfavorably with the work of Christ.

It was a truism of the Old Testament revelation that the Levitical ritual served no good purpose without faith and obedience on the part of the worshiper (v. 8; 1 Sam. 15:22; Ps. 51:16–19; Isa. 1:11–17; Amos 5:21–24). This is the simple meaning of David's words in Psalm 40:6–8. Further, the faithful of the former era did offer such willing obedience and their sacrifices were pleasing to God (Heb. 11:4; cf. Lev. 1:9). But the author is dealing with sacrifice or, as the four different terms indicate, the whole Levitical ritual in itself, which obviously had no intrinsic power to save from sin. The individual to whom the author is addressing himself is not the person whose sacrificial worship merely gives expression to his trust in God the redeemer and to the glad consecration of his life to God, but the man who hopes that the act of sacrifice itself will cleanse him of guilt.

But Christ and his sacrifice have just that saving efficacy in themselves which the Levitical ritual lacks (vv. 9–10). The contrast drawn between the alternatives of the psalm citation is intended to nullify any idea that the sacrificial ritual could ever be the substance of salvation. This holiness or perfection has both present and future aspects (cf. v. 14; 6:1; 12:23).

The point made earlier (vv. 1–4) is recapitulated in verses 11–14. The ineffectuality of sacrifices that must be performed repeatedly is contrasted with the once-for-all sacrifice of Christ, the effectuality of which is attested by the singular honor of a place at God's right hand. The priests continue to stand (cf. Deut. 10:8; Ps. 134:1); the great High Priest has sat down, a sign both of the ultimacy of his single sacrifice for sin (1:3–4; 2:9) and of his royal dominion, now hidden but soon to be revealed (1:13; 2:7–8). It is to Christ, therefore, not to Levitical priests and rituals, that sinners must come. In nonconformist Judaism of the Essene variety, likely the form of Judaism exerting the greatest influence upon this community, there was an expectation of the restoration of the Aaronic priesthood, but it was never imagined that this would involve anything other than standing priests offering sacrifices repeatedly.

In verses 15–18 the author returns to the citation from Jeremiah 31:31–34 (cf. Heb. 8:8–12) for the dramatic conclusion to his great demonstration begun at 4:14 of the superiority of Christ's priesthood and sacrifice. The true salvation in Christ that God promises and applies to the hearts of those he calls eventuates in a full and permanent absolution. Looking to some regularly repeated sacrificial ritual as the basis of forgiveness, as his readership is tempted to do, amounts to a repudiation of the glorious gospel of salvation by the grace of God (13:9).

II. Exhortations to Persevere in Christian Faith (10:19–12:29)

A. The danger of apostasy (10:19–31). The author has completed his demonstration that salvation is to be found in Christ and is based on his sacrifice and not the Levitical rituals. Now he explicitly states and applies the purpose of that lengthy argument to the present crisis of faith in the particular community to which Hebrews is addressed. The exhortation which follows recapitulates the earlier exhortatory sections (2:1–2; 3:7–13; 4:1–11; 6:1–12) and confirms that the author has had a single purpose throughout: to reverse an incipient apostasy and to strengthen flagging faith.

First, he passes his just completed argument briefly in review (vv. 19–21). Christ's death for sin and his abiding priesthood provide free access to God (4:15–16; 6:19–20; 7:23–25; 9:8, 12–15). The "new and living way" does not suggest that believers of the former age were somehow fettered in their access to God, for neither the Old Testament nor Hebrews will tolerate the notion that those saints did not have full access to the Lord or confidence in laying claim to his forgiveness (cf. "draw near" in both v. 22 and 11:6). The old-new contrast in the Bible is absolute, not relative, and is never merely chronological. It always possesses an ethical-spiritual dimension. "Old" signifies the situation of man in sin, "new" the experience of

God's salvation (Ps. 98:1; Rom. 6:4, 6; 7:6; 1 Cor. 5:7, 8; 2 Cor. 3:6, 14; 5:17; Eph. 4:22–23; Col. 3:9, 10; Rev. 2:17; 5:9; 21:1, 5). It is not a question of varying access to God, but of access where before there was none (7:18–19). Believers of all ages have enjoyed this boldness of approach, but it has always been founded upon Christ and his sacrifice, not on external rituals. "The curtain, that is, the body" is perhaps best understood as a comparison between the curtain through which the high priest gained access to the Most Holy Place (cf. 9:3; Mark 15:38) and Christ's bodily sacrifice by which believers gain access to God.

In verses 22–25 the exhortation is fourfold. The first two reiterate the author's previous admonitions to persevere in faith with eyes fixed firmly on Christ (3:6, 14; 4:14). But such endurance requires the encouragement of others and that is given and received chiefly in the life of the congregation. That the exhortation is throughout in the first person expresses the author's personal interest in his readers, his hopes for their restoration, and his solidarity with them in the good fight of faith (cf. 6:9). (On "hearts sprinkled" [v. 22] cf. 9:13–14; Lev. 14:6–7; Ps. 51:7, 10.) "Bodies washed" is no doubt a reference to baptism but in its spiritual signification (cf. Ezek. 36:25; John 3:5; Eph. 5:26; 1 Pet. 3:21).

Exhortation is now reinforced with solemn warnings (vv. 26–31), similar to that of 6:4–8, regarding the horrifying and irremediable consequences of apostasy (cf. 2:2–3; 2 Pet. 2:20–22). "Deliberately keep on sinning" refers not to the immense sinfulness that remains in every believer's life, over which one mourns, of which one repents, and for which one turns to Christ (4:15–5:12), but to the renunciation of the faith (3:12; 6:6). If, having once become acquainted with and having laid claim to the final and perfect sacrifice of Christ, one rejects it as his hope of salvation, all hope is forever lost. The Levitical sacrifices that this readership is tempted to prefer cannot make anyone perfect, and God will not grant repentance to apostates. This striking and grim definition of apostasy is a reminder of how differently the same thing may appear to a human and to God. What the apostate defends as a calculated step to serve his best interests, God regards as contempt for his beloved Son, disdain for the terrible suffering and death he endured, and as an outrage against the Holy Spirit, impeaching his testimony to Christ's lordship (6:4; 1 John 5:6, 10). The certainty and ferocity of God's wrath toward his enemies (cf. Heb. 10:27), especially among his own highly favored people (Amos 3:2), is as unmistakable a datum of divine revelation (here Deut. 32:35–36) as his mercy toward those who repent and believe. That God is living renders his judgment inescapable by mere mortals. To this thought of God's fierce judgment the author will return in 12:18–29.

B. Encouragements to press on (10:32–39). As in 6:9–12, warning is followed by encouragement, as the author reminds his readers of their noble steadfastness in the days of their first love. They had endured public scorn, had willingly identified themselves with those already in prison for faith in Christ (and so exposed themselves to the possibility of a similar fate), and suffered the loss of their property, by looting or as a legal penalty, which happened frequently when Christians became the objects of a community's wrath. They had suffered all but martyrdom (12:4) courageously, even gladly, confident that they would reap an eternal harvest if they did not give up (Gal. 6:9; cf. Matt. 5:11–12; Acts 5:41; 1 Pet. 4:13). They must not lose heart now and have no excuse to do so (vv. 35–36). The Lord helped them before to resist the opposition which now unnerves them and will do so again. Defection now would be tantamount to Israel's irrational sin of losing confidence in the Almighty, who had lifted them out of Egypt on eagles' wings, when they were within sight of the Promised Land (4:16; Deut. 32:15; Ps. 78:9–55). The living faith which alone obtains the eternal inheritance expresses itself in a tenacity in the face of all manner of worldly opposition and temptation and the long waiting made necessary by the futurity of the consummation.

The citation of Habakkuk 2:3–4 in Hebrews 10:37–38 derives from the Septuagint, which has interpreted the original "it" (the revelation of divine judgment) as "he" (a personal deliverer), an interpretation that is ratified by the author who adds the definite article to the Septuagint's "he will surely come," yielding "he who is coming" or "the one who is coming," virtually a messianic title (cf. Matt. 11:3), though now with reference to Christ's coming again. The two lines of Habakkuk 2:4 are transposed simply to clarify the author's application of the citation to his own readership. There are but two alternatives and two destinies and the author is confident that at least most of his readers, having flirted with danger, will at last stand fast (v. 39).

C. Faith defined and exemplified (11:1–40). As a stronger faith is the need of the hour, the author sets before his readers the example of the heroes of faith (vv. 1–3). It is comforting to be reminded that the temptations one faces are neither unique nor even as severe as others have courageously endured, and the stirring examples of faith under trial will strengthen one's determination to be equally worthy of God's approval. In a statement similar to Romans 8:24–25, faith is defined as the unshakeable confidence in the reality of the yet unseen world and the certainty of God's yet unfulfilled promises. This definition of faith is illustrated by reference to the nature of creation by divine fiat.

The succession of heroes of faith begins with three antediluvians (vv. 4–7). The author does not explain in what way Abel's sacrifice was superior, but that it was due to his faith. Abel was murdered but he still speaks, crying out for the vindication that God will bring in due time (cf. 12:24; Gen. 4:10; Rev. 6:9–11). The signal honor afforded Enoch is the divine answer to his faith because he was commended as one who pleased God, which is impossible apart from faith. Noah's faith is demonstrated in the remarkable building project he undertook solely on the strength of his confidence in God's promise. Noah's faith was vindicated while the world that did not heed God's warning was destroyed (cf. 2 Pet. 3:3–7).

The next set of exemplars of faith hail from the patriarchal period (vv. 8–22). Naturally Abraham occupies the largest place in this chapter as Scripture itself singles out his faith (Gen. 15:6; Gal. 3:6–9). On the strength of God's promise alone, Abraham left his homeland for parts unknown, considered his inheritance a land that neither in his own lifetime nor in that of his son and grandson would actually belong to him (apart from a burial plot he purchased, Gen. 25:9–10), and expected God to give him a son though he was advanced in years and married to an aged and barren woman. Abraham understood both that God's promises are indefectible and that their true fulfillment would be found not in this world but in the next. He understood that God had promised him vastly more than real estate for his descendants, indeed, nothing less than an inheritance with Enoch. Abraham's obedient faith and perseverance remind us that faith must withstand not only the waiting until the promise is fulfilled, but appearances that seem directly to contradict the believer's hope. Events have so far vindicated Abraham's trust in God (v. 12). The patriarchs all died with most of God's promises to them yet unfulfilled (vv. 13–16); still they died in the sure hope of their eventual realization (cf. vv. 20–21), which further confirms the assertion of verse 10. Canaan was no more the true homeland they sought than it was the true rest of God for Israel (4:8–9). God "is not ashamed" to be called the God of Abraham, Isaac, and Jacob, that is, not of the dead but of the living who wait in hope (Matt. 22:31–32). The supreme illustration of Abraham's faith as an invincible confidence in the promise of God and in God's ability to fulfill it in defiance of appearances is his obedience in offering Isaac as a sacrifice (Heb. 11:17–18). That such indeed was Abraham's reasoning appears to be suggested in Genesis 22:5. One generation after another dies in the certainty that God's promise would not fail (Heb. 11:19–22).

The third general section of this hagiography covers the period of the exodus and the conquest of the Promised Land (vv. 23–31). Moses' faith first lived in his parents (cf. 2 Tim. 1:5). Apparently the author assumes that some divine communication was given to Moses' parents of God's purpose for their son, and their courage in the face of Pharaoh's edict (Exod. 1:22) resulted in greater security and station for their son than they had thought possible. Moses later turned his back on the exalted status he enjoyed to identify himself with the downtrodden people of God (vv. 24–26). The short-lived pleasures of the Egyptian court were not to be compared with the eternal inheritance that God bestows on those who will deny themselves to follow him. The striking reference to Moses' "disgrace for the sake of Christ" must not be minimized, as if "Christ" should be rendered "anointed one" and taken as a reference to the people of God or as if Christ is in some way to be understood as suffering in his people's suffering, which then Moses shared. The phrase is not taken from the Old Testament, it is the author's own. It agrees with his perspective that Christ was at work in the former epoch and already the object of faith (1:2; 3:2–3; 8:8; 12:2, 25; 13:8; cf. 1 Cor. 10:4; John 5:46; 8:56; Jude 5), and the parallel in 13:13 suggests that bearing disgrace for Christ's sake is something done for Christ himself. Christ was building the house in which Moses was a servant and Moses gladly bore his master's reproach in confident expectation of his eternal glory. "He left Egypt" (v. 27) probably refers to Moses' flight to Midian, which is viewed as an act of discretion, not panic (Exod. 2:14–15), and his forty-year sojourn there as a time of patient waiting for the Lord's call. Time after time Israel's deliverance was accomplished, in defiance of seemingly insurmountable obstacles, by taking God at his word and acting accordingly (vv. 28–30). The mention of a Gentile prostitute's faith and courageous action verifies that faith alone and not natural identity or personal history obtains salvation. This may also be an implied rebuke of this Jewish readership (v. 31).

Time remains for but a summary of the

remainder of the history of faith in the former epoch, from the time of the judges through the heroic resistance of the Maccabean period (vv. 32–38; cf. v. 35 with 2 Macc. 6:18–31). Some of the historical references are unmistakable ("shut the mouths of lions" [Dan. 6:22]; "quenched the fury of the flames" [Dan. 3:19–27]; "women received back their dead" [1 Kings 17:17–22; 2 Kings 4:18–37]), others less clear. The inclusion of such figures as Samson and Jephthah is a reminder that the living faith can coexist with massive imperfection. The mention of "women," "others," and "some" indicates that this faith was as much the pattern of life of many humble people as it was of the heroes of biblical history.

Verses 39–40 are frequently understood to mean that what the faithful of the former era did not receive, Christians have. Believers today live in the age of fulfillment. "Something better" (v. 40) then is taken to refer to the superior state of religious life introduced by Christ and his apostles. But such an interpretation utterly overturns the author's argument. His readers have *not* received the promise (cf. 10:36) and will not unless they persevere in faith to the end as their forefathers did. The "something better" is surely not something other than the above-mentioned "better and lasting possessions" (10:34), "better country" (11:16), and "better resurrection" (11:35), that are no more the present possession of believers today than they were of Abraham or Moses. The entire chapter has been offered as encouragement to persevere in view of the fact that God's promise remains unfulfilled, and the verses that immediately follow reiterate the same thought: one must persevere to the end if one is to receive. The thought is explicitly *not* a fortiori, as if the author were saying: "if they could endure with the promise unfulfilled, how much more we who have received it." The comparison is not between the situation of believers in the old economy and that of Christians today, but between what all believers enjoy on earth and what they will receive—after a lifetime of patient waiting—in the heavenly country. The basis of the author's exhortation is not some dissimilarity but rather the correspondence between the circumstances of believers before and after the incarnation. The object of Abraham's hope lay beyond the grave and it is no different today. Verse 40 then means simply that the consummation was delayed, the ancients had to wait patiently for it, because God intended many more to share in his salvation ("planned," lit. foreseen, in the sense of election and predestination). In the same way, believers today must wait until the whole company of the called is gathered in (cf. 9:15; Matt. 24:14).

D. Jesus, the superior example of faith (12:1–4). The author now imagines the ancient heroes of faith as a great company of spectators ready to cheer on his readers in a race the former have already completed but which the latter must yet run (vv. 1–2). The Christian athlete must divest himself of anything that will hamper him in this spiritual race, which is another way of saying that a chief principle of Christian spirituality is self-denial or self-discipline (cf. Matt. 19:27–29; 1 Cor. 9:24–27). Further, it will greatly help to avoid a harmful distraction or a loss of heart if the believer concentrates his attention on the prize he is to obtain at the end, which is Jesus himself (cf. 11:26–27; 12:24; Phil. 3:8; Col. 3:1–4). Jesus is to be looked to as the one upon whom every believer's faith "depends from start to finish" (NEB; cf. Heb. 4:14–16). But his life is also the perfect paradigm for the believer who also will find strength to endure hardship in the prospect of heavenly joy. In verses 3–4 the recipients of this written sermon are reminded that their present suffering—the opposition they are encountering on account of their faith in Christ—is not to be compared with what Christ endured for them, nor even with the trials of many of their spiritual forebears (11:37), and thus provides no excuse for their present faintheartedness.

E. The meaning and merit of discipline (12:5–13). The testing of their faith is intended by the Lord to benefit them and indicates his love for them. Any true father disciplines his children, corrects them when they err, and cultivates their maturity by requiring the endurance of adversity. In this Christians are only following in their Master's footsteps (5:8). Though painful at the time, the heavenly Father's discipline will yield its perfect fruit if believers humbly submit to it as from the Lord, trusting him to help them endure it (1 Cor. 10:13; James 1:2–4). In the confidence that such trials inevitably and necessarily litter the straight and narrow road that leads to life, the readers must press on (vv. 12–13; cf. Isa. 35:3–4 and Prov. 4:25–27, the language of which the author borrows).

F. Warning not to turn away from God (12:14–29). Each person must study holiness as the gospel requires and help others to do the same, taking special care to nip sin in the bud when it arises within the community (vv. 14–17; cf. Deut. 29:18; 1 Cor. 5:6). Esau exemplifies the person who exchanges the unseen and future inheritance for the sensible and immediate pleasures of this world and, consequently, "misses the grace of God," that is, squanders irrevocably the blessing which was in one's grasp (cf. Heb. 6:4–6; 10:26–31). Esau's tears showed remorse for the consequences of his folly, not godly sorrow that brings true repentance (cf. Gen. 27:34–40).

Verses 18–21 are commonly understood as setting forth a contrast: the old revelation and dispensation is earthly, menacing, and morbid in its concentration on law and judgment, while the new is spiritual, heavenly, and happy. But these verses present Israel not as a paradigm of Old Testament spirituality but of unbelief that leads to death in any epoch. That Israel "begged that no further word be spoken to them" was, in the judgment of this author, a culpable act of rebellion against God. Moreover, after all that has already been said of the unbelief of the wilderness generation (3:7–4:5), it is surely unlikely that here it is held up as exemplifying godly fear. The author correctly understands Israel's request (cf. Deut. 5:23–29), though not in itself sinful, as neither genuine nor indicative of future commitments. Further, as the citation of Deuteronomy 9:19 confirms, Moses' fear was not of the awesome manifestations of the divine holiness—he had already walked into that fire and gloom to the top of the mountain—but of the prospect of divine judgment against the people for the sin with the golden calf. These verses, then, depict the terror of the apostate face to face with the wrath of God, a terror no less the destiny of those who forsake the Lord today (Heb. 12:25, 29; see also 10:27, 30–31).

Contrarily, the author is confident of better things concerning his readers, the things which are obtained by a living faith (vv. 22–24). The thought is similar to that of 6:9–10 and 10:39. He is persuaded that his readers are genuinely converted (the probable meaning of Gk. *proserchomai*, "you have come"; cf. 11:6) and thus that their situation is different from Israel's in the same way it is unlike Esau's. This confidence is the basis of his appeal to them to persevere. Of course, the blessings enumerated are not peculiar to the new epoch; they are the better things of the heavenly country that believers have always grasped from afar by faith (11:10, 13–16, 26–27) and must so grasp by faith today. Hebrews was written to warn this community of believers that it would, like Israel, forfeit these very blessings if it chose to mimic Israel's apostasy. "Church of the firstborn" (v. 23) refers to the privileged station of the saints as set apart to God (Exod. 4:22; 13:2) and heirs of all things, the very privileges that Esau squandered (Heb. 12:16–17).

The admonition in verses 25–27 reiterates 3:7–12 and 4:1–2. The readers must not imitate faithless Israel in the wilderness. The threat of divine judgment is no less serious today. In view of the connection of thought between verses 24 and 25 ("that speaks . . . who speaks"), it is reasonable to assume that Jesus is to be understood as the one who thundered his law at Sinai and who utters the promise of Haggai 2:6. Believers have not yet taken possession of the better things, but soon they will and that forever (vv. 28–29). That prospect ought to awaken them to glad thanksgiving and to a new determination to work out their salvation in fear and trembling so as not to be found at last among those who miss the grace of God (12:15) and instead must face God's wrath. The warning reiterates Deuteronomy 4:23–24 and indicates that the Word of God is no less menacing to the unbeliever and the disobedient today than it was in Moses' day.

III. Concluding Exhortations (13:1–19)

In what amounts to a postscript to his sermon the author takes care to specify particular ways in which this true and living faith expresses and evidences itself. As elsewhere in the Bible, the believer is not left to work out the ethical implications of faith in Christ; the particular obedience required is carefully defined. Pride of place goes to brotherly love (vv. 1–3), a costly virtue at which these believers had already distinguished themselves, especially in regard to prisoners (6:10; 10:33–34). Abraham is again invoked as an example, this time of hospitality (Gen. 18:1–16; cf. 1 Pet. 4:9) and of the blessing that attends the gracious host. Christian sympathy and fellow-feeling (cf. Rom. 14:15; 1 Cor. 12:26) will not be satisfied with the simpler forms of charity, but will extend itself to those who cannot be brought into the home (Matt. 25:35–36).

Sexual impurity and the love of money (Heb. 13:4–6) are linked elsewhere (1 Cor. 6:9–10; Eph. 5:6) as sins of dissatisfaction with God's provision and thus sins of unbelief, as the citations from Deuteronomy 31:6 and Psalm 118:6–7 demonstrate. Neither the Lord's threatened judgment of the worldly nor his promise to provide adequately for his children is taken seriously. For both sins the antidote is contentment and fulfillment in what God has given (Prov. 5:15–20; 1 Tim. 6:6–11, 17, 19).

The leaders mentioned in Hebrews 13:7 are not, as in verses 17 and 24, the present elders but those who previously evangelized this community (2:3), provided its initial instruction in the Christian life, and marvelously adorned their doctrine by the holiness of their lives (cf. Titus 2:10). As valuable as the examples of heroic faith from the distant past may be (Heb. 11:4–38), there is yet more reason to imitate the sturdy faith of those one has known in the flesh and to whom one is greatly indebted. Whether "outcome" suggests martyrdom or, as is probable, simply the righteous character of their lives, they are apparently now numbered among the "spirits of righteous men made perfect" (12:23) and thus serve as examples of those who have persevered to the end.

Amidst all the uncertainties of life in this world, the character and word of Jesus Christ stand firm (v. 8; see also 1:12; 7:24–25; 10:23). He who sustained the faith of the saints of old (11:26) and of their former leaders just mentioned, will not forsake them.

In verse 9 the author returns one last time to the great interest of his letter: to warn his readers of the fatal error of pursuing a compromise with Judaism. Since salvation is by grace through faith in Christ, putting confidence once again in the saving virtue of ceremonial regulations regarding food and drink would amount to a repudiation of the gospel (9:9–10; cf. 1 Cor. 8:8). The argument is in principle very similar to Paul's protestation against the inroads of ritualistic legalism in the churches of Galatia and Colossae (Gal. 4:8–11; Col. 2:13–23).

The reference in verses 10–11 is again to the ritual of the Day of Atonement, which included the sin offering, the flesh of which the priests were not permitted to eat (Lev. 4:11–12; 16:15–27). The author has already demonstrated that this ritual typified the sacrifice of Christ (Heb. 9:6–12, 23–28). The superiority of the antitype is demonstrated in the fact that the believer has an altar—the sacrifice or sin offering of Christ, from which he is welcome always to partake (cf. John 6:53–56; 1 Cor. 5:7–8; 10:16). No doubt the readership is being swayed by the charge that Christianity suffers by comparison with Judaism for want of an altar. The church throughout the ages has never been immune from the temptation to gather confidence from the outward trappings of religion: altars, buildings, and impressive rites. The author's rejoinder is that the church's invisible altar is the reality of which the ceremonies of Judaism are but pale imitations (Heb. 8:1–5), and the church's food is the eternal and spiritual benefits of the Son of God's once-for-all sacrifice of himself for sin, for which beef or lamb, however impressively and ceremonially prepared, is no substitute.

The author notes a further parallel between type and antitype (vv. 12–14): the carcasses of the sin offerings were burned outside the camp while Jesus was crucified outside the city of Jerusalem. The significance of the latter fact seems chiefly to lie in its suggestion that Judaism as a whole had rejected Jesus. As once before in Israel's history, when God left the camp of Israel after her sin with the golden calf and took up station outside the camp (Exod. 33:7–11), Christ's sacrifice of himself outside the gate represented divine judgment upon the people's unbelief. To make peace with the Judaism that rejected Christ would be to make common cause with God's enemies whom he has demonstrated to be objects of his wrath. Instead, they must make the break with that apostate people and their strange teachings of salvation through the blood and the flesh of bulls and goats. These remarks would be particularly apposite directed to a community influenced by a form of Judaism like that given expression at Qumran, where great care was taken to organize the sect as a reproduction of the camp of Israel in the wilderness.

No doubt such a separation will be intensely painful for these believers, all the more because they will be marked by their former brethren with the stigma of a betrayal of the ancient faith. But loyalty to Christ demands it and the prospect of the eternal city should lessen the sting of the severing of earthly associations. In any case, such a pilgrimage from the comfortable scenes of the past to the heavenly country would be a living up to their spiritual heritage as the descendants of Abraham and Moses (11:8–10, 25–27). Those who call Jesus Lord are the true Israel (Rom. 9:1–9; Phil. 3:3).

They may no longer have animal sacrifices to offer to God, but there are yet more acceptable sacrifices than these: worship and good works (Heb. 13:15–16). The superiority of such sacrifices of the heart was a truism of the Old Testament (1 Sam. 15:22; Pss. 50:13–14; 51:17; Hos. 14:2) reiterated in the New Testament (Rom. 12:1; Phil. 4:18; 1 Pet. 2:10).

It is likely that this group of Jewish Christians had been, by reason of their drift back toward Judaism, estranged from the larger Christian community. Perhaps en masse they had begun to separate themselves (Heb. 10:25) and in other ways make life difficult for the elders. In any case, the author expresses confidence that the present leadership would, if able to exercise its authority, steer his readers in the right direction. Texts such as Hebrews 13:17 provide a needed corrective to democratic or, worse, anarchic tendencies in the church. The church is a kingdom ruled by a king who exercises his dominion through officers (Matt. 16:18–19; 1 Thess. 5:12–13). This sacred authority should be prevented from degenerating into an authoritarianism by the genuine interest in the well-being of the people of God required of elders and by the prospect of accounting for their ministry at the judgment seat of Christ (cf. James 3:1). The spiritual prosperity of the church and the honor of Christ are best served when elders fulfill their stewardship in love and truth and when the saints submit to them as to the Lord.

Like Paul, the author writes his stern and no doubt painful admonition with a clear conscience and with the humble recognition that he needs God's grace and help fully as much as those to whom he writes (Heb. 13:18–19; cf. 2 Cor. 1:10–14). No doubt he wishes to assess the situation in person and to deal with it in a more thorough fashion than he can in a written sermon, brief as it is (v. 22). Evidently he has had a close association with these believers previously, has been separated from them for some time, and, though willing, has been prevented for some reason from returning to them.

IV. Benediction and Greetings (13:20–25)

The beautiful benediction in verses 20–21 forms an exquisite conclusion to the entire work, especially in its concentration on the centrality of Christ in God's grand program of restoring sinners to himself and to a life pleasing to him.

The personal notes in verses 23–24 do little more than tantalize. Nothing else is known of Timothy's imprisonment and further references are hopelessly speculative. "Those from Italy" is ambiguous and could suggest either that the author is writing from Italy or that he is writing from some other place to a community of believers in Italy and naturally includes the greetings of expatriate Italian believers who are with him.

The salutation (v. 25) is profound in its simplicity (cf. Titus 3:15) and expresses both the author's desire for and his confident expectation of the Lord's restoring his readers to their once sturdy faith in Christ Jesus.

SELECT BIBLIOGRAPHY

Bruce, F. F. *The Epistle to the Hebrews.* Grand Rapids: Eerdmans, 1964.

Guthrie, D. *The Letter to the Hebrews.* Leicester and Grand Rapids: Inter-Varsity and Eerdmans, 1983.

Hagner, D. A. *Hebrews.* San Francisco: Harper & Row, 1983.

Hughes, P. E. *A Commentary on the Epistle to the Hebrews.* Grand Rapids: Eerdmans, 1977.

Moffat, J. *A Critical and Exegetical Commentary on the Epistle to the Hebrews.* Edinburgh: T. & T. Clark, 1924.

Montefiore, H. *The Epistle to the Hebrews.* London: Allenson, 1964.

Vos, G. *The Teaching of the Epistle to the Hebrews.* Nutley, N.J.: Presbyterian & Reformed, 1974.

JAMES

Douglas Moo

INTRODUCTION

The writer of the letter identifies himself simply as "James, a servant of God and of the Lord Jesus Christ" (1:1). Who is this James? Of the four men with this name mentioned in the New Testament, only two are significant enough to have identified themselves as simply as does the author of this letter: James, the son of Zebedee, who was one of the twelve apostles (Mark 1:19); and James, "the Lord's brother" (Gal. 1:19), who became early on the leader of the Jerusalem church (cf. Acts 15:13; 21:18; Gal. 2:9). Although a few scholars have thought that the son of Zebedee could be the author, his early martyrdom (A.D. 44; cf. Acts 12:2) probably removes him from consideration. Still others think that the good, almost literary Greek of the letter, along with the way the author handles the topic of justification (2:14–26), makes it likely that someone toward the end of the first century wrote the letter and ascribed it to James. But this theory is unnecessary and calls into question the honesty of the writer. There is every reason to accept the widespread opinion of the early church that James, the brother of the Lord, wrote this letter.

Although this view is contested, it is probable that James was a younger brother of Jesus, born to Joseph and Mary after the birth of Jesus. Not a believer during Jesus' earthly ministry (cf. John 7:5), James was probably converted as a result of a post-resurrection appearance (1 Cor. 15:7). His wise leadership of the Jewish Christian church, along with his piety and respect for ancestral traditions, earned him the title *the Just* in both Jewish and Christian history.

James is classed among the general Epistles of the New Testament, those letters that are not addressed to specific churches (e.g., 1 Corinthians) or individuals (e.g., 1 Timothy). But this does not mean that James had no definite readers in mind as he wrote. The letter is addressed to "the twelve tribes scattered among the nations" (1:1). From its original application, the phrase *twelve tribes* came to designate the complete regathering of God's people that would take place in the messianic age (cf. Isa. 49:6; Ezek. 47:13). James, then, uses this title to remind his readers that they belong to that new creation, the church, that God has brought into being on the basis of faith in his Son (cf. Matt. 16:18). These "twelve tribes" have been "scattered" or "dispersed" among the nations. What is meant by this? In one sense, all God's people, as aliens and exiles, living apart from our true heavenly home, have been "scattered" in this world (cf. 1 Pet. 1:1). But the word *scatter,* and its noun form, "those scattered" or "dispersion," was often used to designate Jews living outside Palestine. It may be that James uses the word with this more specific meaning. Suggestive here is the reference in Acts 11:19 to those early Jewish Christians in Jerusalem who were forced to flee the city because of persecution and engaged in evangelism among Jews "as far as Phoenicia, Cyprus and Antioch." Could this not furnish a plausible background for the circumstances of the letter of James? Forced to live away from their home church, these scattered parishioners required exhortation and advice on issues they were facing. What is more natural than that their spiritual guide send them a pastoral letter?

If this reconstruction of the circumstances of the letter is accepted, it would make James probably the earliest New Testament book to be written—sometime in the middle 40s of the first century. Also suggestive of an early date are the reference to the synagogue as the place of meeting (2:2) and the fact that the sharp debates over the place of the Law in Christianity, so prevalent from the latter 40s on, are not reflected in the letter. The way in which James deals with justification in 2:14–26 also fits nicely into this early time period: James's teaching implies that he has heard of Paul's slogan *justification by faith* but that he has no first-hand knowledge of what Paul really meant by it. Such a situation would exist only before the Jerusalem council of A.D. 48 or 49 (see Acts 15).

We understand James, then, to be a letter of pastoral encouragement and exhortation written to Jewish Christians living outside Palestine in the middle 40s of the first century.

As a pastoral letter, James reads like a sermon, or a series of sermonettes. The purpose of these homilies is almost always to command and exhort: it is indicative of the tone of the letter that James has a greater frequency of imperative verbs than any other New Testament book.

James has structured his series of sermonic exhortations loosely. The letter may be divided into five major sections (see the outline), but there is no clear logical progression from one section to another, and even within the sections James often jumps quickly and without explanation from one aspect of his topic to another.

Another interesting feature of the letter is James's habit of borrowing from other sources. Most prominent among these is the teaching of Jesus. Not only does James come close to quoting Jesus on one occasion (5:12; cf. Matt. 5:34–37), but also he infuses his letter with themes, images, and emphases characteristic of Jesus. Other books with which James has much in common are 1 Peter in the New Testament, Proverbs in the Old Testament, Philo, Ecclesiasticus, and the Testaments of the Twelve Patriarchs among Jewish literature, and the early Christian books Hermas and 1 Clement. The parallels between James and these other sources do not, except in the case of the teaching of Jesus, suggest that James has borrowed directly from them. Rather it would seem that some of the themes and language found in these books were known to James and he used them to make his own points.

James, it is sometimes said, has no theology. If by this it is meant that James does not present a systematic exposition of the faith or that his main intention is not to teach theology, then the statement is true enough. But in another sense, it is misleading. James approaches the practical issues he deals with from a profound knowledge of who God is and what he has done in Christ—theology indeed! And James also makes an important contribution to our understanding of several theological issues. Among these is theology proper—the doctrine of God. James emphasizes God's generous nature (1:5, 17), his total separation from evil (1:13), his jealousy (4:5), and his grace (4:6). Eschatology receives attention in 5:1–11, where James sounds the characteristic New Testament note of fulfillment without consummation: the "last days" have come and we must now live in that knowledge (5:3, 5), yet we also wait for that day when our Savior and Judge will appear in glory (5:7–11). Prominent in James also is the problem of poverty and wealth. Most of James's readers are poor, and they need to be encouraged to find solace in their spiritual wealth (1:9) and to be reminded that God will judge their wicked rich oppressors (5:1–6).

Of greatest interest theologically is undoubtedly James's teaching on justification in 2:14–26—teaching that many think to be in conflict with Paul. Does not Paul stress that "a man is justified by faith apart from observing the law" (Rom. 3:28)? How, then, can James assert that "a person is justified by what he does and not by faith alone" (2:24)? A careful study of the way in which James and Paul use the crucial word *justify* will show that the conflict is only apparent. While Paul uses the word to designate the person's initial acceptance before God, James uses it of the believer's final vindication before God in the judgment. Thus Paul emphasizes, combating Jewish legalism, that a person can "get right" with God only through faith in Jesus Christ. James, criticizing Christians who were neglecting to live out their faith, reminds them that God does take works into account when we stand before him in the judgment.

It is, of course, this plea for working faith, for a belief that is so deep and vital that it *has* to spill over into all our lives, that characterizes the message of James. He encourages his readers, both in the first and the twentieth centuries, to live out their faith, to abandon any spiritual double-mindedness, to press on to full Christian maturity. John Wesley's description in "A Plain Account of Christian Perfection" captures perfectly the goal which James encourages us to pursue: "In one view it is purity of intention, dedicating all the life to God. It is the giving God all our heart; it is one desire and design ruling all our tempers. It is the devoting, not a part, but all our soul, body, and substance to God."

OUTLINE

I. Address and Greeting (1:1)
II. Trials and Temptation (1:2–18)
  A. Overcoming Trials (1:2–12)
  B. The Source of Temptation (1:13–18)
III. Putting the Word into Practice (1:19–2:26)
  A. Anger and the Tongue (1:19–20)
  B. "Be Doers of the Word" (1:21–27)
  C. The Sin of Favoritism (2:1–13)
  D. True Christian Faith Seen in Its Works (2:14–26)
IV. Worldliness in the Church (3:1–4:12)
  A. The Taming of the Tongue (3:1–12)
  B. Peaceable Relations among Christians (3:13–4:3)
  C. A Call for Repentance (4:4–10)
  D. Arrogance and the Critical Tongue (4:11–12)
V. Looking at Life from a Christian Perspective (4:13–5:11)
  A. Recognizing Who We Are before God (4:13–17)
  B. The Dangers of Wealth (5:1–6)
  C. Waiting on the Lord (5:7–11)
VI. Concluding Exhortations (5:12–20)
  A. Oaths (5:12)
  B. Prayer (5:13–18)
  C. Being Our Brother's Keeper (5:19–20)

COMMENTARY

I. Address and Greeting (1:1)

Although James could claim to be a brother of the Lord and a leader in the early Jerusalem church, he is content to call himself a "servant." Indeed, like Moses (Deut. 34:5) and David (Ezek. 37:24) before him, James recognizes that there is no higher honor than being called to serve the living God. James's readers are also honored to belong to the people of God of the last day—"the twelve tribes." As I suggested in the introduction, these readers are probably Jewish Christians who had to flee from Jerusalem and take up new lives in lands outside Palestine.

II. Trials and Temptation (1:2–18)

A. Overcoming trials (1:2–12). As James's readers establish themselves in their new surroundings, they have to face many trials. Poverty and persecution appear to have been the biggest trials faced by these early Christians, but James has in mind all kinds of difficulties that can pose threats to our faith in God—sickness, the death of loved ones, a rebellious child, a hated job. Whatever the trial, James commands Christians to rejoice (1:2). How is this possible? By recognizing that God can use these problems and tribulations to produce Christians who are "mature and complete" (v. 4). Trials, which test us as fire refines ore (see also 1 Pet. 1:7), lead to a more settled, stable Christian character; and as we continue taking a Christian viewpoint on trials, this perseverance will be able to finish its work of producing strong, mature, unshakable believers. Right at the beginning of his letter, James sounds a note that he will repeat throughout the letter in different ways: Christians must take a distinctively Christian perspective on life.

James sometimes links his topics by repeating a word: here he joins verses 4 and 5 with the verb *lack.* A more substantive link may also exist, however. Wisdom may be that quality that is needed if the believer is to face trials in the appropriate Christian manner. Wisdom in the Bible is a practical, down-to-earth virtue that provides its possessor with insight into the will and ways of God. Like the Book of Proverbs, James emphasizes that wisdom can be gained only by asking God. And as an encouragement to ask, James reminds us that God gives "simply," "with a single, unwavering intent" (probably the meaning of the Greek word here) and without holding our past failures against us (v. 5). But not every asking, even if imploring and sincere, receives an answer from God. We must ask in faith, without doubting. In an expressive image, James compares the doubter to the constantly varied surface of the sea—forever in motion, never stable, up one day, down the next (v. 6). Such a person is literally, James says, "double-souled"—divided at the very root of his being, a spiritual schizophrenic. He must not expect that God will respond to his prayers (vv. 7–8). What James criticizes in these verses is not the person who has occasional doubts about his or her faith, or lapses into sin now and again—few indeed would ever have prayers answered were that the case! Rather, James castigates the person who is basically insincere in seeking for things like wisdom from God; the person who is seeking to serve two different masters at the same time (see Matt. 6:24; James 4:4).

The discussion of poverty and wealth in verses 9–11 may be connected to verses 2–4 (poverty as one of the most difficult of trials) or to verses 5–8 (wealth has great potential for dividing our loyalties). James contrasts two people in these verses: the poor Christian (v. 9) and "the one who is rich" (vv. 10–11). This latter phrase is ambiguous. If James has in mind a rich non-Christian, then his contrast is between the poor Christian who is to rejoice in his heavenly calling and the rich unbeliever who has nothing to boast about except his ultimate judgment for his wicked use of money. That James elsewhere uses "rich" to designate non-Christians (5:1) favors this interpretation. On the other hand, "the one who is rich" could be a Christian. In this case, James would be contrasting Christians from very different socio-economic spheres and encouraging each believer to focus not on that worldly status, but on his relationship to Christ. The poor believer should not despair at his poverty, but rejoice that he is "rich in faith and [an heir to] the kingdom" (2:5). The rich believer, on the other hand, must be careful not to take pride in his worldly possessions—for he, as a rich person, will quickly perish—but to boast in his "low position," his relationship to Jesus, "despised and rejected by men." Either interpretation makes sense of the verses, but the second alternative explains more naturally the order of the Greek words in verse 9 (where "brother" comes before "the humble one").

James concludes the opening section of the letter by returning explicitly to the theme of trials (v. 12). Remaining faithful to God during trials brings God's blessing: the reward of life eternal that God has promised to those who belong to him. The risen Jesus similarly encouraged suffering Christians: "Be faithful, even to the point of death, and I will give you the crown of life" (Rev. 2:10).

B. The source of temptation (1:13–18). The connection between James's discussion of trials in verses 2–12 and temptation in verses 13–15 is more explicit in the Greek text than in the English because a single Greek root (*peir-*) does duty for both these concepts. In meaning, however, the two are to be carefully distinguished. A trial is an outward circumstance that can pose difficulties to our faith. A temptation is the inner enticement to sin. What James is concerned about is that his readers will confuse these two and attribute temptation to God. Scripture indicates that God does "test" or put his people through trials (cf. Gen. 22:1). But, James emphatically asserts, God never tempts his people (1:13). He never entices them to sin or desires that they fail in the trials he may bring. Believers must never excuse their sin by blaming God for the temptation. Rather, James points out, the believer need look no further than within himself for the problem. It is our own "evil desire" that is the real source of temptation (v. 14). Like the bait that lures the fish and the hook that snares it, sin entices and seeks to entrap us. That James does not here mention Satan does not mean that he ignores the power of "the tempter" (see 4:7). His point here is to lay responsibility for sin clearly at the door of each individual. And, as J. A. Bengel remarks, "Even the suggestions of the devil do not occasion danger, before they are made 'our own.' "[1] Shifting his imagery, James traces the terrible process by which temptation becomes spiritual death: the impulse to sin, alive in all of us, conceives sin when we succumb to temptation; and if we do nothing to cut off the growth and maturation of sin, death is the inevitable result (v. 15).

After issuing a warning not to be deceived (v. 16), James provides a positive counterpart to verses 13–15: far from being responsible for temptation, or anything evil, God gives good gifts to his children. And that God will continue to do so can be depended upon, for he is unchangeable. Unlike the sun, moon, stars, and planets ("the heavenly lights"; cf. Ps. 136:7–9), which regularly move and change their appearance, God never changes (v. 17). As an outstanding example of God's good gifts, James cites the new, spiritual birth that Christians have experienced (v. 18). This "new birth," or regeneration, is motivated solely by the will of God; accomplished through the instrument of "the word of truth," the gospel (cf. 2 Cor. 6:7; Eph. 1:13; Col.

1. *Gnomon of the New Testament* (Edinburgh: T. & T. Clark, 1860), 5:7.

1:5; 2 Tim. 2:15), it has as its purpose the bringing into being of "firstfruits," the first harvest of the fruits produced by God's eternal plan of redemption.

III. Putting the Word into Practice (1:19–2:26)

The mention of the "word of truth" in verse 18 leads James to devote a lengthy section to a matter close to his heart—the appropriate Christian response to God's word. James stresses that the purpose of the word is to be obeyed (1:21–27); gives an example of how that word should be obeyed in practice (2:1–13); and ties that doing of the word inextricably to genuine faith (2:14–26).

A. Anger and the tongue (1:19–20). Before launching into this major topic, James interjects a warning about the misuse of the tongue—the first of several that occur in his letter (1:26; 3:1–12; 4:11–12; 5:12). James echoes a theme sounded often in Proverbs (see 10:19; 15:1; 17:27–28): the righteous person will listen well and consider carefully before he speaks, and will restrain his anger lest it lead to hasty, nasty, irretrievable words (1:19). James does not prohibit all anger, but exhorts his readers to be slow and careful about allowing anger to develop. Anger, James reminds us, "does not bring about the righteous life that God desires" (the NIV translation brings out the sense well here).

B. "Be doers of the word" (1:21–27). Many translations and commentaries take verse 21 with verses 19–20, but it really introduces the main topic of the next paragraph: the right response to God's word. James commands us to receive the word (1:21). Elsewhere in the New Testament, this expression describes conversion, but this cannot be the meaning here, since James addresses people who already are Christian. What he means is well illustrated in Jesus' parable of the sower (Mark 4:1–9): the believer has to provide the right climate for the growth of God's word in his life—he has to be fertile "soil." Thus there is need to clear out the "weeds" of moral filth and evil. James's reference to the word as being "planted in" us may allude to Jesus' parable, but probably also hints at the fulfillment of Jeremiah's famous prophecy about the new covenant, in which God promised to "put [his] law in their minds and write it on their hearts" (Jer. 31:33). Becoming more specific, James now tells us how we are to receive the word: by doing it. "Hearing" of the word is absolutely essential; but if hearing does not lead to doing, if study does not result in obedience, if attendance at worship service does not lead to a righteous life—then the Word of God has been mistreated and we are deceiving ourselves about the reality of our relationship to God (v. 22). Jesus pronounced a blessing on "those who hear the word of God and obey it" (Luke 11:28). People who hear the word without doing it are compared to a person who looks into a mirror at his face but immediately forgets what he has seen (vv. 23–24). In other words, no lasting impression is made; the Word has not really penetrated the heart and life of the person who has heard. But the person who carefully listens to God's word, and continues to put it into practice, not forgetting it—this person receives God's approval (v. 25). It will be noted that the "word" of verse 22 has become in verse 25 "the perfect law that gives freedom." This is indicative of James's holistic understanding of God's word: the "word of truth" that regenerates us is also God's law that demands our heartfelt obedience. For James this "law" clearly involves some Old Testament commands (cf. 2:10–12), but only as they have been made a part of "the royal law" that Jesus proclaimed (2:8).

James becomes more specific still. What does it mean to "do" the word? Three areas of obedience are singled out by James: personal behavior, social concern, and inner values. James again shows his concern about sins of speech by highlighting careful speech habits as an example of the religion that God accepts (v. 26). Another characteristic emphasis in James is mentioned in verse 27 for the first time: concern for the poor and needy. "Orphans and widows" became in the Old Testament a stock description of the helpless in the world. God himself is "a father to the fatherless, a defender of widows" (Ps. 68:5) and his people are to show the same concern (cf. Isa. 1:10–17). Finally, and lest obedience to the word seem entirely a matter of external behavior, James stresses the need for an inner attitude and value system distinct from that of the world in which we live.

C. The sin of favoritism (2:1–13). This section of the letter has one central purpose: to condemn any practice of favoritism in the church. "Favoritism" translates a rare word that is used by the New Testament writers to render the Old Testament Hebrew expression *receiving the face.* It connotes the treatment of any person on the basis of an external consideration—be it race, nationality, wealth, or manner of dress. Such favoritism is foreign to the nature of God (cf. Rom. 2:11) and should also be unknown among believers in Christ (2:1). James's lofty description of Jesus as the Messiah of Israel (Christ), the Lord, and the glorious one (or, less probably, "the glory," alluding to the Shekinah, the presence of God) shows just how exalted is his conception of Jesus. The illustration James uses in verses 2–3 need not refer to an actual situation, but certainly implies that this kind of behavior was a real problem. Poor people were being discriminated against; and in doing so, James says, the believers were manifesting their evil thoughts (v. 4). James's use of the word *synagogue* to describe the meeting may imply that he is thinking of a nonworship gathering of the church (perhaps for the purpose of judging between believers),[2] but it is more likely that this is a primitive Jewish Christian term for the church's gathering for worship.

James gives several reasons for his condemnation of favoritism against the poor. The first is that it stands in contradiction to God's own attitude and actions. He has chosen the poor in the world to receive the blessings of his kingdom (v. 5). Note that James does not say that God has chosen *all* the poor or *only* the poor, but that God has a special concern for the poor (Luke 6:20). That, in fact, most of the early Christians were poor (1 Cor. 1:26) is clear. The second reason James gives for condemning this favoritism has to do with the actual situation. The rich people were exploiting and persecuting the fledging church; how ironic that the church should mistreat those from whom most of them were drawn in order to curry favor with the wealthy and powerful (vv. 6–7).

The third basis on which favoritism is criticized is also the most important: it violates the "royal law" of love for the neighbor. Jesus himself cited Leviticus 19:18, along with the requirement to love God, when asked to give a summary of the law (Matt. 22:34–40), and it is probably for this reason that James calls it the *royal* law: it was highlighted by Jesus, the King, as a crucial law for the kingdom of God (cf. 2:5). Favoritism, then, by mistreating "the neighbor," involves a clear violation of the law (v. 9). Significantly, favoritism at the expense of the poor is also condemned in the context of Leviticus 19:18 (cf. v. 15). Verses 10–11 support the conclusion reached in verse 9, that those who show favoritism are convicted as lawbreakers, by arguing that the infringement of any one law incurs the penalty for the breaking of the whole law. This is so because the law is the expression of God's demand; ultimately, one either meets or fails to meet that demand—there can be no partial perfection. Therefore, James concludes, we had better speak and act with the realization that our conduct will be measured by the standard of "the law that gives freedom" (v. 12). James's Christian understanding of the law is implied here again by this description (cf. 1:25). There is law in the Christian life, but it is not identical with the Old Testament law, which itself was fulfilled by Christ (Matt. 5:17) and no longer can condemn the believer (Rom. 8:1–3). It can and will, however, judge the believer, in the sense that we will appear before Christ for an evaluation of our earthly behavior (cf. 2 Cor. 5:10). On that day, mercy will be an important evidence of the reality of our relationship to God, even as Jesus stressed in his parable of the unmerciful servant (v. 13; cf. Matt. 18:21–35).

D. True Christian faith seen in its works (2:14–26). James has firmly upheld the doing of the word as absolutely essential to valid religion. He has even warned that what we *do* will be taken into account in the judgment (2:12–13). How, one might ask, does all this square with the crucial role given to faith throughout the New Testament (and by James himself; cf. 1:6–8!)? Is James replacing faith with works? In this passage he answers that question with a decisive no by showing that true Christian faith necessarily and of its very nature produces those works pleasing to God.

In a sort of teaching style frequently used by James, he broaches the issue with a question, or, to be more precise, two questions (2:14). In the Greek, it is clear that the assumed answer to these questions is no—*this faith,* the faith this person *claims* to have, but which is without deeds, cannot save him from the judgment of God. The illustration in verses 15–16 drives home this point. What good have we done the fellow Christian who lacks the essentials of life if we simply dismiss him or her with words? Not that words are unimportant, or that there will not be occasions when words are all that we can offer. But the real test of our words is actions that back them up. Isaiah exhorted his contemporaries to put meaning into their religious rituals by sharing bread with the hungry and covering the naked (58:7–9) and Jesus promised the kingdom to those who feed and clothe "the least of these my brethren" (Matt. 25:31–46 RSV). Thus, James draws the conclusion (v. 17): faith by itself is "dead"—not just in the sense that it is not doing what it should, but that it is not even really what it claims to be.

In the ancient world, writers often used a sort of argumentative style to carry along their discussion. Paul uses it frequently in Romans, and James uses it here. He has an imaginary opponent object, "You have faith; I have deeds" (v. 18). The force of this objection has been understood in a great number of ways, but the simplest interpretation is to assume that the

2. See R. B. Ward, "Partiality in the Assembly; James 2:2–4," *Harvard Theological Review* 62 (1969): 87–97.

objector is arguing for the principle "different people, different gifts": Why cannot one believer be especially gifted with faith while another has the ability to perform good deeds? James answers this objection with a challenge (vv. 18b–19): "Give me evidence, apart from deeds, that you have faith. You can't do it, can you? But I can point to my deeds as the clear evidence of the reality of my faith. Why, faith without deeds is no better than the intellectual 'faith' of demons; they have a perfectly correct 'theology' but do not have the commitment to what they believe—their faith has affected their minds, but not their wills. So a faith without deeds is also a less than Christian faith, a bogus faith."

This "foolish man," the imaginary objector James uses to make his point, is now given evidence from the Old Testament that faith must be accompanied by works to be considered valid before God. James cites two very different people to make his point: Abraham, the honored father of the Jewish people, and Rahab, the immoral pagan. Abraham, James claims, illustrates the intimate relationship of faith and works. In going so far as to offer his son Isaac in obedience to the Lord (Gen. 22), Abraham showed that his faith was deep and strong (see also Heb. 11:17–19). His faith and his actions "were working together" in close partnership (v. 22). Indeed, it was the exercise of his faith through works that brought his faith to full maturity. But James goes even further than this. It was on the basis of his works that Abraham was "considered righteous," or "justified" (the two English words translate the same Greek root; v. 21); and although God declared Abraham righteous by faith (v. 23; cf. Gen. 15:6), this pronouncement was itself brought to its fullness of meaning (*fulfilled*) when his works completed his faith.

These statements of James about being justified by works present a problem to the person who is aware that Paul claimed that a person "is justified by faith apart from works of law" (Rom. 3:28 RSV); why, Paul even quotes Genesis 15:6 in favor of *his* point of view. To be sure, the problems being dealt with are quite different—Paul is attacking people who think that salvation can be earned; James, people who think that salvation brings no responsibility—Paul speaks of "works of law" while James says simply "works" and clearly presumes the importance of faith. But a formal contradiction still remains: Paul says "justified by faith alone"; James, "justified by faith plus works." What is vital, then, is to see that Paul and James are using the key word *justify* with different meanings. When Paul uses the word *justify*, he designates the initial acceptance of the sinner before God—the solely gracious act whereby God, the Judge of all the world, considers us "right" before him because of our identification with Christ (see Rom. 4:5). James, on the other hand, uses "justify," as was typical in Judaism, of the ultimate verdict of acquittal rendered over our lives. Jesus used the term in this way when he said, "By your words you will be acquitted, and by your words you will be condemned" (Matt. 12:37). While Paul, then, asserts that a person is initially declared righteous only through faith, James insists that our ultimate acquittal in the judgment depends on the evidence of true faith—works. And, as James makes clear, true faith will, by its very nature, produce those works that will acquit us at the judgment. So, while faith and works must be kept distinct, they must also not be separated.

In verse 24, James summarizes his position for his readers. Again, it is important to see that James's "faith alone" is far from being genuine Christian faith: this "faith alone" is mere talk without action (vv. 15–16) or head knowledge without heart knowledge (v. 19). This is *not* Christian faith. And with this Paul would have had no argument; he also stressed that it is faith "expressing itself through love" that counts (Gal. 5:6).

James's second Old Testament example is set forth in close parallelism to the first (v. 25; cf. v. 21). Rahab, too, was "considered righteous" because of her actions. On the basis of reports about the power of the Lord, she committed the fate of herself and her family to him by helping the Israelite spies (Josh. 2). In doing this, she manifested the reality of her faith (see Heb. 11:31).

The main point of the paragraph is reiterated in its concluding verse: just as a body without the invigorating spirit is dead, so faith without works is dead—barren and useless. Rather ironically, in light of his criticisms of James, Martin Luther in his preface to Romans describes this dynamic nature of Christian faith as well as anyone: "O it is a living, busy, active mighty thing, this faith. It is impossible for it not to be doing good things incessantly."

IV. Worldliness in the Church (3:1–4:12)

The heart of this section, and in many ways the heart of the whole letter, is 4:4–10, with its radical call for repentance from flirtation with the world. The worldliness plaguing the Christians to whom James writes has taken the form of a bitter jealousy and has led to quarrels

(3:13–4:3) and harmful, critical speech (3:1–12; 4:11–12).

A. The taming of the tongue (3:1–12). The concern James has already shown about sins of speech (1:19, 26) is given full exposure in this paragraph. He introduces his topic by first warning people not to be too anxious to become teachers (3:1). A particularly honored position among the Jews was occupied by the rabbi, and some of this prestige undoubtedly rubbed off on the teacher in the church. James does not want to discourage those who have the calling and the gift for teaching, but he does want to warn people about the heavy responsibility involved in teaching others about spiritual matters (see also Matt. 5:19; Acts 20:26–27). One of the reasons the teaching ministry is very difficult is that it makes use of the most dangerous, untamable member of the body: the tongue. So difficult is the tongue to control and subordinate to godly purposes that James calls the person "perfect" who is able to subdue it (v. 2).

The power of the tongue may seem to be out of proportion to its size. But James reminds us with two pointed illustrations that small objects can have great power. The skillful rider uses a small piece of metal or leather to direct the motions of a powerful horse (v. 3); the pilot controls the direction and speed of a huge sailing vessel with the touch of his hand on the rudder (v. 4). So also the tongue, though a relatively small member of the body, possesses great potential for good or for evil. It can be used to encourage, evangelize, and endear; it can also be used to criticize, mock, and curse. The destructive potential of the tongue is highlighted in verses 5–6. A "spark" that sets ablaze a massive forest fire, the tongue can also set on fire "the whole course" of a person's life (James shows his broad background here again by picking up a phrase, literally "the wheel of existence," that was current in certain Greek religions). The tongue, James says, is a veritable "world of evil," the very sum and essence of the world as fallen and hostile to God, within a person's life. A power so potentially destructive of the spiritual life can only be explained as having its origin in the influence of Satan himself.

James has described the power and destructive potential of the tongue; now he reminds us how difficult it is to tame and how inconsistent is its nature. God gave to mankind dominion over the animal world at creation (Gen. 1:26; cf. Philo *On the Special Laws* 4.110–16); but dominion over the tongue has been much more difficult to attain (vv. 7–8). In stressing that "no one among men" (a literal rendering of the Greek) has been able to tame the tongue, perhaps James wants to imply that "when it is tamed we confess that this is brought about by the pity, the help, the grace of God" (Augustine *Of Nature and Grace* 15). With a further allusion to Genesis, James highlights the "doubleness" of the tongue: we bless God with it, but we also curse people "made in God's likeness" (v. 9). This inconsistency in the tongue should not be (v. 10)—any more than a single spring should pour forth good, sweet, drinkable water one day and foul, brackish water the next (v. 11). Like Jesus before him (Matt. 7:16), James uses the image of the plant that produces according to its nature to demonstrate the fundamental incompatibility of a renewed, sanctified heart pouring forth harmful, filthy, evil words (v. 12). Although James does not specify in this paragraph the particular forms of evil speech that he has in mind, he elsewhere singles out the kind of criticism of others that springs from a judgmental attitude (4:11–12). And perhaps James would include in his strictures all those manifold sins of speech that are catalogued in Proverbs: lying, gossiping, criticizing, thoughtless and careless speaking, too much speaking.

B. Peaceable relations among Christians (3:13–4:3). Although a chapter break occurs in the middle of this section, 3:13–18 and 4:1–3 are closely related. They both analyze and condemn the bickering that is apparently all too common among James's readers. The first paragraph approaches the problem by contrasting two kinds of wisdom. There is, first of all, the "wisdom" that is "earthly, unspiritual, of the devil" (v. 15). It is characterized by "bitter envy" and "selfish ambition" (v. 14). The word *envy* could also be translated "jealousy" and probably connotes here the prideful spirit of competition for favor and honor that so often disturbs our churches. "Selfish ambition" translates a single Greek word that can best be defined by noting its apparently only pre-Christian usage: Aristotle uses it to describe and condemn the selfishly motivated "party politics" in the Athens of his day (*The Politics* 5.3.1302b4; 1303a14; cf. Rom. 2:8; 2 Cor. 12:20; Gal. 5:20; Phil. 1:17; 2:3). Where these attitudes exist, "disorder" and all kinds of evil will be the result (v. 16). On the other hand, there is the wisdom from above. It is characterized not by a selfish desire to have one's own way, but by "humility" (3:13). And, like genuine faith, it manifests itself in deeds, producing a godly and loving life-style. Most of all, James suggests, true wisdom brings peace. This is the focus of the list of virtues attributed to true wisdom in verse 17. And verse 18, with its promise of "a harvest of righteousness" to those who are peacemakers, underscores the point. Jesus likewise commended the "peacemakers" and promised them that they would be called "sons of God" (Matt. 5:9). The truly wise person will not be proud, arrogant, or quarrelsome; he will be humble, unselfish, and peaceable.

Continuing his analysis of the quarrels that have broken out among his readers, James now traces the source of these bitter disputes to evil "desires." Sin, James has reminded us, comes from within, from our "own evil desire" (1:14); so, too, the specific sin of quarrelsomeness. (James's use of a different Greek word here for "desire" is probably not significant.) These desires are fighting within us, waging "war against our souls," as Peter puts it (1 Pet. 2:11), and this fighting within results in fighting without also (4:1). The precise meaning of verse 2 depends entirely on how we punctuate the verse (the earliest copies of the New Testament had no punctuation at all). The New International Version, along with the King James Version, separates the relevant words into three separate sentences:

1. You want something but do not get it.
2. You kill and covet, but you cannot have what you want.
3. You quarrel and fight.

On the other hand, the Revised Standard Version (see also NASB, NEB, TEV) presents two sentences:

1. You desire and do not have; so you kill.
2. And you covet and cannot obtain; so you fight and wage war.

Although the "and" beginning the second sentence is a bit of a problem, this second alternative should be accepted. It results in a neat parallelism, with each statement tracing an inner attitude to an outward consequence. Furthermore, this sequence fits a popular style of moral analysis in the ancient world.[3] But does James seriously mean to accuse his readers of committing murder? While it is possible that indeed he does (some of his readers may have been Jewish Zealots who believed that violence should be used to usher in the kingdom of God), it is better to think that he is pointing to the ultimate consequence of unrestrained desire. Rather than becoming frustrated through the attempt to gain things on our own, we should ask God in prayer for what we need. If we still do not find ourselves receiving what we ask for, then we should check our motives: perhaps our prayers are oriented too much around our own selfish pleasures and not enough around the will of God and the needs of others (v. 3).

C. A call for repentance (4:4–10). In a startling change of tone, James abandons his customary "my brothers" to address his readers as "you adulterous people." This change signals a shift in focus. James has been analyzing the sin of envy and its resultant quarrelsomeness; now he calls for a radical departure from that sin. In the Greek, "adulterous people" is feminine because James is making use of the Old Testament tradition according to which God's people are pictured as the "bride of the Lord" in the intimate spiritual union that he has brought into being through his electing love (see Isa. 54:1–6; Jer. 2:2; and esp. Hos. 1–3). To flirt with the world, then, is to commit spiritual adultery against the Lord (4:4). It is this background that provides the clue to the interpretation of verse 5. Many translations (NIV, KJV, NEB, TEV) take the scriptural quotation as a warning about the tendency of the human spirit to be envious. But it is better, with the New American Standard Bible, to understand James to be citing the Old Testament teaching that pictures God as jealous for his people (cf. Exod. 20:5; 34:14; Zech. 8:2): "He jealously desires the Spirit which He has made to dwell in us." Our tendency to succumb to the allure of the world (v. 4) is so serious just because our God demands that we serve him and him alone (v. 5).

But, while God's demand is all-encompassing, his grace is more than sufficient to meet the need. Proverbs 3:34 promises that grace to those who are humble (v. 6). Consequently, we need to "submit [ourselves] to God" (v. 7) and "humble [ourselves] before the Lord" (v. 10). These commands frame three pairs of imperatives in verses 7b–9. First, we are to "resist the devil" and "come near to God." Each is accompanied by a promise: the devil will flee and God will draw near to us (see also 1 Pet. 5:5–9, which has many parallels to James 4:6–10). Second, like Old Testament priests, we are to "wash [our] hands"; to seek forgiveness for, and put away from us, outward sins. And at the same time, the inner attitude must be made right—our hearts are to be purified. Third, using the language of the Old Testament prophets (see Joel 2:12), James commands us to mourn deeply and sincerely for the sin that separates us from God (v. 9). True Christian joy comes not with the ignoring of sin, but with the experience of the forgiveness of sin; and we have to see the serious effects of our sin before we can truly turn from it and find forgiveness.

3. See L. T. Johnson, "James 3:13–4:10 and the *Topos Peri Phthonou*," *Novum Testamentum* 25 (1983): 327–47.

Jesus similarly pronounced a blessing on "those who mourn" (Matt. 5:4) and warned, "Woe to you who laugh now, for you will mourn and weep" (Luke 6:25).

D. Arrogance and the critical tongue (4:11–12). In a short paragraph, James turns once again to sins of speech. He condemns "slander," a word used elsewhere in Scripture to denote rebellion against God's authority (Num. 21:5), slandering people in secret (Ps. 101:5), and bringing false accusations against people (1 Pet. 2:12; 3:16). From the stress in verse 12 on judging, it is probable that James has particularly in mind the judgmental criticism of others that was doubtless accompanying the quarrels and arguments in the church. This kind of criticism is wrong because it assumes that we are in a position to render ultimate verdicts over people: a prerogative that is God's alone (v. 12). By criticizing others, we do not fulfill the law of love of neighbor (cf. 2:8), but break it.

V. Looking at Life from a Christian Perspective (4:13–5:11)

The paragraphs in this section focus on the way we should look at ourselves (4:13–17), our material possessions (5:1–6), and our present difficulties (5:7–11) in the light of God's person and purposes.

A. Recognizing who we are before God (4:13–17). James addresses self-confident businesspeople in 4:13—whether Christian or non-Christian is unclear. These businesspeople have decided where they are going, how long they will stay, what they will do there, and even what the outcome of their efforts will be. James has nothing against making plans, but he does condemn the arrogance of those who think they can make their plans without reference to God. We must recognize that we do not control what will happen tomorrow and that our very lives are nothing more than "a mist," or smoke, that quickly vanishes (v. 14). When we recognize who we are before God, we will see the need to consider the Lord's will in everything we do. The very continuation of our lives depends on his will (v. 15). When James encourages us to *say* "if the Lord wills" he does not mean, of course, that the simple repetition of these words in our prayers takes care of the need. Rather, we are consciously to place all our plans and hopes under the lordship of Christ, recognizing that he is the one who prospers or brings to grief those plans. At heart, the sin these businesspeople are committing is the sin of arrogance; of thinking that they, rather than God, are in the driver's seat (v. 16). With a principle that has wide application, James concludes the paragraph by reminding us that sin consists not just in doing those things we should not, but also in failing to do those things that we should. Similarly, James's readers are now responsible for putting into practice the attitude he has just set forth.

B. The dangers of wealth (5:1–6). The "rich people" whom James addresses in this paragraph are clearly the wicked rich. The Old Testament often uses "poor" and "rich" almost as synonyms for the righteous and the wicked, respectively (see Prov. 10:15–16; 14:20; Ps. 37; and also the intertestamental book 1 Enoch 94–105). Jesus reflected this usage when he blessed the poor and condemned the rich (Luke 6:20, 24). Thus, while the people addressed in this passage are clearly materially wealthy, they are not condemned for their wealth per se, but for their selfish accumulation and abuse of their wealth. Why does James send a denunciation of wicked, wealthy unbelievers to Christians? John Calvin pertinently isolates two main reasons: James " . . . has a regard to the faithful, that they, hearing of the miserable end of the rich, might not envy their fortune, and also that knowing that God would be the avenger of the wrongs they suffered, they might with calm and resigned mind bear them."[4]

Weeping and wailing are typical ways of describing the reaction of evil people to the judgment of the day of the Lord (Isa. 13:6; 15:3; Amos 8:3). These rich people will suffer condemnation on that day for four specific sins. First, they have hoarded their wealth and failed to use it to help the poor (5:2–3). James pictures their wealth rotting and corroding—evidence that it has neither done them any good nor has it benefited the needy. They have failed to follow Jesus' advice: "Sell your possessions and give to the poor. Provide purses for yourselves that will not wear out, a treasure in heaven that will not be exhausted, where no thief comes near and no moth destroys" (Luke 12:33; see also, for the connection between the decay of wealth and failure to help the poor, Ecclus. 29:9–11). This selfish hoarding of wealth is all the worse in that it is being done "in the last days." The New Testament consistently portrays the "last days," the time of God's intervention to save and to judge, as having begun with the work of Christ (Acts 2:17; 2 Tim. 3:1; Heb. 1:2; 2 Pet. 3:3; Jude 18). All the more reason to use wealth in a way that will please God!

The second reason for the condemnation of

4. *Commentaries on the Catholic Epistles* (Grand Rapids: Eerdmans, 1948), 342.

these rich people is their failure to pay their laborers what is owed them (v. 4). The Old Testament made as a prominent requirement of the law the prompt payment of wages (Lev. 19:13; Deut. 24:14–24; Mal. 3:5). James assures the rich that God, "the Lord Almighty," the Judge, is well aware of their sin against those who depend on them for daily bread. A luxurious, self-indulgent life-style is the third basis for God's judgment (v. 5). Like the people of Sodom, who lived in prosperous ease while the "poor and needy" went without (Ezek. 16:49), the rich people of James's day are preparing themselves for the judgment. James uses the image of cattle being fattened for the slaughter to picture this storing up of wrath for the day of judgment. Finally, James condemns the rich for using their influential social and political positions to condemn and murder innocent men (v. 6). In the Greek, the singular "righteous man" is used and some have thought that James may be speaking of the Jews' complicity in the execution of Jesus. But it is more likely that the singular is generic and that James describes the combination of economic and religious persecution that many early Christians suffered at the hand of the upper classes. Such persecution had long been practiced in Israel (cf. Amos 2:6; 5:12; Mic. 2:2, 6–9) and was all the worse in that the innocent had little ability to resist the machinations of the rich.

C. Waiting on the Lord (5:7–11). Much as Psalm 37 both pronounces judgment on the wicked oppressors of the "poor" and godly and encourages the righteous to "be still before the LORD" while they wait for God's vindication, James 5:1–11 encourages Christians to recognize that judgment will come upon the wicked rich and to wait patiently for the day of that judgment. Christians need to exhibit the patience of the farmer as they wait for "the Lord's coming" (5:7–8). (The rains crucial to Palestinian agriculture fell in the late autumn and early spring [cf. Deut. 11:14].) This coming is "near." Some people think that James must have been wrong to think that Jesus' return could have been near; almost two thousand years have gone by since. But when the New Testament speaks of the nearness or the imminence of the Lord's return, it does not mean that it has to take place within a short period of time. What is meant is that Christ's *parousia* is the very next event in God's timetable of redemption, and that it *could* take place within a short period of time. Every generation of believers lives in the eager expectancy of that return. As we wait, and as we suffer the difficulties of economic deprivation and other trials, we must be careful not to take out our frustrations on each other by grumbling against one another (v. 9). The Lord who is coming to deliver us from sin and want is also coming to evaluate the lives of his people.

In their patient endurance of difficulties, Christians are to imitate the prophets and Job (vv. 10–11). At first glance, Job would seem to be a curious choice to hold up for imitation, for he frequently expressed his exasperation with the Lord. But what James wants us to emulate in Job is his perseverance: despite the disasters he faced, and the relentless attack of his "friends," Job kept his faith and did not abandon his trust in God. As a result, the Lord "finally brought about" the restoration of Job's fortune (Job 42:10–17).

VI. Concluding Exhortations (5:12–20)

A. Oaths (5:12). James introduces his final section with a typical literary device: "above all" (cf. 1 Pet. 4:8 and Paul's use of "finally" in this way). James's prohibition of oaths is similar, in wording and content, to Jesus' prohibition in Matthew 5:34–37. Many think that Jesus and James intended to forbid all oaths; hence some Christians will refuse to take an oath in a court of law, for instance. But it is doubtful that such a situation is envisaged. From the emphasis on telling the truth in both contexts, it is more likely that any oath that in any way compromises our absolute truthfulness is what is forbidden.

B. Prayer (5:13–18). Prayer is often mentioned in the last section of New Testament letters: James is no exception. He begins by encouraging us to pray in any circumstance we might face. When "in trouble" we should turn to God for help; when things are going well, we should turn to God with praise (5:13). In the specific trouble of illness also prayer is the main remedy. Here, however, James gives lengthier advice. He encourages the person who is sick to call for "the elders of the church"; they should come to "pray over him" and to "anoint him with oil." The elders were the spiritual leaders in individual local churches (see Acts 14:23; 20:17; 1 Tim. 5:17; Titus 1:5; 1 Pet. 5:1). That they should be called to pray specifically for one who is sick is not surprising. But why are they to anoint with oil (see also Mark 6:13)? Although some Roman Catholic theologians find the sacrament of extreme unction "promulgated" in this text (Council of Trent 15.1), there is no basis for the identification. Since oil was a well-known medicinal agent in the ancient world (see Galen, and Luke 10:34), the anointing may have a physical purpose. But it would be unusual to single out the use of oil as applicable for *any* illness and strange that the elders of the church should apply it. More likely, the anointing has a symbolic purpose. Anointing with oil is frequently mentioned in the Old Testament as a symbolic action according to which what is anointed is set apart for God's service or blessing (while the Greek word *chriō* was more often used for this, the word *aleiphō,* found here in James, also occurs [Exod. 40:15; Num. 3:3]). By anointing the sick person with oil, then, the elders are symbolically setting that person aside for the Lord's special attention as they pray. And since it is prayer to which James returns in verse 15, it is clear that it, not the anointing, is the main agent of healing. By stressing that the prayer of faith is what brings healing, James has carefully qualified the apparently absolute nature of the promise in verse 15. For only prayers that are offered in accordance with the will of God can truly be uttered in faith. When praying for the healing of a person, the elders will often not be sure whether their specific petition is in accord with God's will. As another aspect of the healing process, the sick person is also encouraged to seek forgiveness for sins (v. 15). The New Testament makes clear that some illnesses (1 Cor. 11:30), though by no means all (John 9), are the result of sin; and that sin will need to be taken care of before healing can come. While James has focused on the role of the elders in healing, he makes clear in verse 16 that all believers can be active in the ministry of healing as we confess our sins to one another and pray for one another.

As an encouragement to pray, James stresses the great effect of the prayer offered by a "righteous man" (v. 16b). By this James does not mean to confine effective prayer to a select group of "super-saints"; "righteous" designates anyone in a right relationship with God. And even Elijah is cited not because he was a prophet or because he had a special spiritual gift. He was "a man just like us," yet he was able to stop and start the rain by his prayers (vv. 17–18; cf. 1 Kings 17:1; 18:41–45).

C. Being our brother's keeper (5:19–20). In keeping with its literary, sermonic nature, the letter of James closes not with a series of greetings or personal notes, but with a call for action. James has given many commands in the course of his appeal; now he encourages every reader to intervene to help others obey these commands. When we see a brother who has "wander[ed] from the truth," we are to "bring him back" (5:19). In doing so, we will be saving that sinner from spiritual death, the ultimate destination on that road that the sinner has chosen to follow (see 1:15). He will also "cover over a multitude of sins" (cf. Prov. 10:12; 1 Pet. 4:8). It is possible that this phrase refers to the sins of the one who does the turning back—an idea which is not unbiblical. But it is more likely that this is a further description of the forgiveness of sins granted to the sinner who has turned back from his way.

SELECT BIBLIOGRAPHY

Adamson, J. B. *Commentary on the Epistle of James.* Grand Rapids: Eerdmans, 1976.

Davids, P. H. *Commentary on James.* Grand Rapids: Eerdmans, 1982.

Dibelius, M. *A Commentary on the Epistle of James.* Rev. ed. Philadelphia: Fortress, 1976.

Laws, S. *The Epistle of James.* San Francisco: Harper & Row, 1981.

Mitton, C. L. *The Epistle of James.* Grand Rapids: Eerdmans, 1966.

Moo, D. J. *The Letter of James.* Tyndale New Testament Commentaries. Leicester/Grand Rapids: Inter-Varsity/Eerdmans, 1985.

Ropes, J. H. *A Critical and Exegetical Commentary on the Epistle of St. James.* Edinburgh: T. & T. Clark, 1916.

Tasker, R. V. G. *The General Epistle of James.* Grand Rapids: Eerdmans, 1956.

1 PETER

Stephen Motyer

INTRODUCTION

Peter's first letter is a "general epistle" in that it was written not to one person or church, but to all the churches greeted in 1:1. The precise regions listed are uncertain, for the terms could refer either to the Roman provinces so named, or to the old ethnic groups and their associated areas from which the Romans adopted their official province names. But it is most likely that the names are being used in their "official" sense, so the letter was probably addressed to all the churches in the northern half of Asia Minor (modern Turkey).

It is clear that Peter's readers were facing persecution for their faith, and this has occasioned debate among scholars on several counts. By whom was this persecution instigated, and why? Was it official or unofficial? Was the persecution merely a threat, or was it already a reality? The answers to these questions are not easy to determine, but the following seems to be most likely. The persecution was probably unofficial and local, instigated by pagan neighbors of the Christian believers with the support of minor local officials. It was certainly a present reality for some (if not all) of Peter's readers. While the Roman Empire had an ambivalent attitude toward Christianity, and persecution was occasionally launched officially, this was rare compared to spasmodic local outbursts of hatred. And in this letter, the reasons given for the persecution are purely local. Peter mentions, for example, the annoyance caused by the Christians' refusal to join in riotous festivals (4:4).

Few scholars today hold that the letter was actually written by the apostle Peter, largely on the grounds of style and language. First Peter is one of the finest examples of Greek prose in the New Testament, and scholars argue that Peter, who was an "unschooled" fisherman (Acts 4:13), could not possibly have produced such a work. In addition the letter shows close affinities with Paul's writings, particularly the letter to the Romans, and this too is held to militate against Petrine authorship. Alternative suggestions are that Silas drafted it as Peter's secretary (cf. 5:12), so that the style is his but the substance Peter's, or that it was written by another individual after Peter's death and then attributed to him out of respect for his memory. Yet why should it have been impossible for Peter to write in Greek, in that he would have grown up knowing both Greek and Aramaic? And if the letter was written from Rome, as 5:13 suggests, the influence of the letter to the Romans is hardly surprising. The ascription to Peter is universal in the manuscript tradition and attested early by the church fathers. The book was probably written from Rome toward the end of his life, perhaps in A.D. 64–65, when persecution was looming or had already broken out there.

OUTLINE

- I. Suffering as a Christian (1:1–2:10)
  - A. The Hidden Inheritance, the Hidden Lord (1:1–9)
  - B. Preparation for Action (1:10–2:3)
  - C. The Hidden Spiritual House (2:4–10)
- II. At Home, But Not in This World (2:11–3:12)
  - A. The Christian's Inner Self (2:11–12)
  - B. A Life of Submission (2:13–3:7)
  - C. The Christian's Corporate Self (3:8–12)
- III. Suffering—The Road to Glory (3:13–4:19)
  - A. Suffering for Doing Good (3:13–22)
  - B. Living for God (4:1–11)
  - C. Sharing the Sufferings of Christ (4:12–19)
- IV. Final Exhortations and Greetings (5:1–14)

COMMENTARY

I. Suffering as a Christian (1:1–2:10)

A. The hidden inheritance, the hidden Lord (1:1–9). Peter begins his letter like any other in the world of his day, with a greeting, a prayer, and an expression of thanks. But his thrill at the wonderful message he has to impart is so great that, like Paul, he fills out these bare, formal "bones" with the glories of the Christian gospel.

He is not simply "Peter," but an apostle who writes with the authority of Jesus Christ himself. His recipients are not just the Christians of northern Asia Minor, but God's elect, whose earthly address is only temporary. His prayer is not the usual "peace be yours in abundance" (see Dan. 4:1), but includes "grace." Instead of the usual expression of thanks for something quite ordinary, like the good health of his recipients, Peter launches into a shout of thanks and praise to God for all the heavenly blessings he has stored up for those who are his.

The themes of this opening greeting and doxology set the tone for the whole letter. Peter brings up the three persons of the Trinity before us again in the very next section (1:10–21), and thus picks up the trinitarian blessing of verse 2. But particularly this opening section is balanced by 2:4–10, which brings to a close the first part of the letter. There Peter returns to the theme which above all thrills him here: the hidden things which are gloriously true of his readers, even if all the world should shout a different message at them. Whether they feel like it or not, they are a royal priesthood, a holy nation (2:9).

Doubtless they felt more like his description of them in his greeting: "strangers in the world," "scattered," tiny persecuted congregations spread across the huge expanse of half of modern Turkey, struggling to keep their faith alive against the pressure of a vastly pagan environment. But Peter will not let them dwell on what they look like from the world's point of view. He wants them to see how *God* looks at them. And from God's viewpoint, their scatteredness is his election. God has plucked them out of their paganism to be his own (v. 1). He has foreknown them (v. 2). Before ever they existed, the Father knew and loved them and made them his. God has sent his Spirit to sanctify them—that is, precisely to create the distinction between them and the world that causes them so much trouble, by leading them into a life of obedience to Jesus Christ, sheltered under the forgiveness won by his blood.

At the moment they are facing all kinds of trials (v. 6), and are tempted to hopelessness and despair. But here too Peter will not let them—or us—believe what the eye sees. The reality is unseen: there is an inheritance that can never perish kept in heaven for us (v. 4), as a result of Jesus' resurrection and our new birth through him (v. 3). And there is no possibility of losing it, for however weak we may feel, we are being shielded by God's power until the moment of salvation comes. Our present experiences are all preparatory, making us fit for glory. Jesus too is unseen: but even so, with our eyes fixed on hidden realities, we will love him and our hearts will thrill with a joy that surpasses language and even now partakes of the glory that is yet to be (v. 8). We already hear the strains of heavenly praise and share in heavenly joy, because we are already "receiving . . . the salvation of our souls" (v. 9), even in the midst of suffering and pain.

These inspiring opening verses contain the whole message of 1 Peter in a nutshell. The rest of the letter merely explains and applies this vision in greater and more practical detail.

B. Preparation for action (1:10–2:3). The exhortation of 1:13 provides the keynote of this section, as Peter tackles the unspoken question, "How can I have a faith like that?" He mentions faith four times in 1:3–9, and it would be very possible for an oppressed believer to feel that the faith described is too high to attain. Peter sets out in this section to show what the roots of such a faith are—and it turns out that the way we think is absolutely vital.

Peter's sudden introduction of "the prophets" (**1:10–12**) (probably shorthand for the whole Old Testament) is at first sight surprising. But there are two excellent reasons for their appearance. First, the prophets back up what Peter writes about the foreknowledge of God the Father in 1:2. God announced centuries ago his intention to save the followers of Jesus. It was in fact the Spirit of Christ who spoke in the prophets (v. 11)! Second, from the prophets we can learn the Christian faith which Peter has just so eloquently and movingly summarized. Even though they wrote long before Christ came, they realized that they were writing about a grace to be given to someone else, and eagerly sought to learn about the time and circumstances of its coming, the sufferings of the Christ, and his glories. The prophets became aware that they were writing for someone else, so that the gospel only needed to be "announced" when the time came. The prophets had already explained it.

This is tremendously important for Peter. His letter contains no fewer than twenty-five direct quotations from the Old Testament, and many allusions to it besides. It is the basis of the Christian gospel, for without it we would not understand Christ. And so, in practice, a mind properly fed by the Old Testament is the basic prerequisite for the experience of joy in suffering described in 1:3–9.

The existence of such a prophetic Word is a summons to prepare one's mind for action (**1:13–21**). The proper response to the Scriptures is to get thinking. "Be self-controlled" (v. 13) is a poor translation. The original Greek means "make sure you keep all your faculties fully operational" (lit. be sober; Peter repeats this exhortation twice [4:7; 5:8]). The mind that is girded up, redirected by the Scriptures, will begin to think in a new way.

However threatening the present, the fully girded-up mind will set its hope "perfectly" on God's grace. The redirected mind will focus on God's priority, holiness. At its heart holiness means separateness: God calls us to be different, because he is different. Peter's readers must not worry about their distinctiveness that provokes such hostility from others. It is inevitable! If we are God's, we will begin to bear his likeness in every aspect of life.

The renewed mind knows that life will end with judgment. We must therefore live each moment under the scrutiny of the Judge. We may rejoice to know God as Father, but there must also be reverent fear! Every moment matters, eternally. The thought that we are to be judged according to our work could lead to despair; but our eternal salvation is not jeopardized by our moral feebleness. It rests upon nothing that we can produce, not even upon our silver and gold (v. 18): even our best perishes before God's judgment. But our salvation rests upon "the precious blood of Christ" (v. 19), just as the blood of the Passover lamb saved the Israelites. Christ was chosen (lit. foreknown) before the foundation of the world (v. 20): it was no sudden whim on God's part which made him the sacrifice for sin. And as a result we may place sure faith and hope in God, who though our Judge is also our Savior and Father. The resurrection seals the security of those who so believe and hope. In the midst of earthly insecurity, *here* is true confidence and security!

How may we be sure of knowing joy in suffering? Peter picks up what he wrote about the prophetic Word in 1:10–12 and applies it practically: if our hearts and lives are truly being fed by the Word of God, then we will be increasingly transformed within.

The Word of God gives new life (**1:22–25**). When we obey God's truth, love will be born in us. God's Word has a vital, life-giving power because of Who it is that speaks it. Peter quotes Isaiah 40:6–8, which contrasts the permanence of God's Word with the transitory nature of all that is earthly. The Word of God "stands forever" because of the preaching of the gospel.

The Word of God nourishes new life (**2:1–3**). Every newborn infant needs a healthy appetite and proper food or it will not grow. The pure "spiritual" milk that will produce healthy Christian growth is God's own Word.

C. The hidden spiritual house (2:4–10). Peter began his letter with the themes of God's elect and his mercy (1:1, 3). He ends this first section on the same note (2:9–10). He also returns to his central theme of hiddenness, though his treatment is different here. In 1:3–9 his thought was angled entirely toward the future, to the coming inheritance and the coming Lord, both now veiled, yet objects of love and joy. But now Peter turns to the past and the present. The hidden but coming Lord was rejected by men (v. 4), who did not see the estimation placed upon him by God. In their present rejection, therefore, Peter's readers are sharing the fate of Jesus himself. He was like the stone the builders rejected (v. 7). Peter carries through his theme of God's Word by quoting three "stone" passages which were applied to Jesus from a very early date (the tradition seems, in fact, to originate with Jesus himself; Matt. 21:42): Psalm 118:22f.; Isaiah 8:14; 28:16 (cf. Rom. 9:33). A stone can look most unimpressive—but it can perform a vital function if made the cornerstone of a large building; or it can bring a person tumbling to the ground if he or she stumbles over it. Jesus has become the cornerstone of God's spiritual temple, and there are two possible responses. We can either take our own angle and position from the Cornerstone, and line ourselves up on him; or we can refuse to live by reference to him, and stumble over him instead. It is a vivid picture.

Peter urges his readers to see that they are being built in line with Christ: sharing all the angles of his life, experiencing his rejection as well as the glory. His opponents stumble fatally, but those joined to Christ are a chosen people, a royal priesthood (v. 9), contrary to all appearances. In verses 9 and 10 Peter piles up phrases from the Old Testament (Exod. 19:6; Isa. 42:12; 43:20f.; Hos. 1:10; 2:23) to show how all that is true of God's chosen covenant people is true for those who believe in Jesus, however rejected and weak they may seem.

II. At Home, But Not in This World (2:11–3:12)

In the second section of his letter Peter tackles the question that arises at the end of the first. If Christians must reckon themselves to be gloriously different from what they *appear* to be, if they must look beyond their scatteredness and suffering and see themselves as God's chosen people, then what should their attitude be toward their earthly circumstances? Peter's readers must have been tempted to respond to persecution by adopting an antiworld attitude and withdrawing as much as possible into the comforting warmth of Christian fellowship.

But Peter will not let them do this, even though he has underlined so powerfully their new and hidden status as God's people and the life and love that binds them. Withdrawal from the world is not an option for Christians. Rather, their difference must be expressed through the distinctiveness of their life *within* their earthly callings.

A. The Christian's inner self (2:11–12). In verse 11 Peter reaffirms the general attitude toward the world which ran through the first section of his letter. His readers are "aliens and strangers" in it; their home and their roots are elsewhere. It is natural therefore that he should go on to urge them to abstain from sinful (lit. fleshly) desires. This world is not our true home, and the flesh seeks to stifle the life of the Spirit within us. Though we may be citizens of another world, we still have to "live . . . among the pagans," and do so in a way which testifies clearly to the existence and power of that new world. This declaration depends not so much on word (Peter is remarkably silent about verbal witnessing), as on behavior. Non-Christians watch what we do. The word translated *see* means to watch over a period of time, implying prolonged observation. We must see to it that, even though we may be mocked (or apparently disregarded), the evidence of our lives will speak so loudly that, on the day of judgment, non-Christians will glorify God, because they will have to concede that the testimony was laid before them quite unambiguously, even if they failed to heed it. What we are on the inside (v. 11) will become obvious on the outside (v. 12).

B. A life of submission (2:13–3:7). Romans 13:1–7 is a close parallel to **2:13–17**. Paul and Peter concur that respect for and obedience to worldly authority are important, because it is an expression of *God's* authority. Peter begins and ends by mentioning the Roman emperor as the one who embodies all the different forms of secular authority under which Christians find themselves.

In theory, worldly authorities exist "to punish those who do wrong and to commend those who do right" (v. 14; cf. Rom. 13:3f.), but Peter is as aware as we are today of the possibility of corruption in high places. He even calls Rome "Babylon" in his closing greeting (5:13). Yet just as we abstain from fleshly desires and still remain committed to ordinary human society (2:11–12), so we submit to worldly authority even though it is to pass away under the judgment of God. We know that God's world is fallen, but we submit to his ordering of it, keen to testify by our lives to what is to come. Simply by doing good we might silence (lit. muzzle) people inclined to revile us (v. 15). Peter emphasizes this by the verbs he uses in verse 17. The proper attitudes are: timely respect for all men (i.e., we are to take every opportunity to show honor to our fellow men), love for fellow believers, fear of God (full devotion of heart, mind, and soul), and continuing respect for the emperor.

Peter next homes in on a group for whom a very particular application of the principle of submission to authority is necessary: slaves (**2:18–25**). Unrest among slaves was widespread at this time, and undoubtedly some Christian slaves believed that, having been "bought" by Christ, they had been set free from their earthly masters. Later on, there were actually Christian groups which encouraged slaves to run away from their masters on these very grounds. But Peter will not allow this! The same principle of nonwithdrawal from the world means that slaves must not stop being slaves, but instead become better ones—even when their masters are harsh. If they suffer, they must make sure that they suffer unjustly, because it will not do their Lord credit if they deserve the beating they get!

Then Peter attaches to this straightforward teaching a marvelous passage about the Servant Jesus (vv. 21–25). In fact, it is likely that this is an adaptation of an early Christian hymn about Christ. It suits Peter's theme beautifully as, in close dependence on Isaiah 53, it describes how Jesus, the Suffering Servant of the Lord, submitted to suffering in this world because of his obedience to his heavenly Master. Belonging to his Lord did not deliver him from suffering, but led him straight to it! And through his suffering we have found forgiveness (v. 24). To suffer, therefore, is simply to walk in his footsteps (v. 21), and we can be sure that, whatever happens, he is a caring Shepherd (v. 25).

Peter has deliberately placed this hymn in the middle of this section, so that it has a central place: Jesus is our example, not just in the way he suffered, but in his obedient submission to the powers of this world.

The zoom lens now focuses in on another, still more intimate relationship from which Christians were tempted to withdraw because of their new, otherworldly faith: marriage (**3:1–7**). Should Christian husbands or wives leave their partners if they do not share their faith? Again, some Christians answered, "Yes." But Peter insists that they should not. He devotes more space to wives (vv. 1–6), because they could more easily be made to suffer by their husbands than vice versa. He eloquently teaches that the greatest beauty is that of character, and that the loveliness of Christian character speaks far more powerfully than a hundred sermons. The word *see* in verse 2 is the same as that in 2:12, implying extended observation. The incident in mind in verse 6 is probably that of Genesis 12:11–20, where Sarah submits to some very unkind treatment by her husband, and in that context her beauty is emphasized. Abraham tries the same trick again later (Gen. 20), insisting that Sarah must show her love for him in this improper way and she again submits. (She calls him "Lord" in Gen. 18:12.) The Christian calling is patient submission to suffering within the structures of this world.

What about the Christian husband with the unbelieving wife? Verse 7 summarizes it beautifully. No separation! Even if they cannot share on the deepest spiritual level, they are still together "heirs . . . of the gracious gift of life" (i.e., ordinary human existence). The husband must show all the respect and care due to a weaker partner; and in so doing his own bond with the Lord will not be weakened.

C. The Christian's corporate self (3:8–12). "All men will know you are my disciples, if you love one another" (John 13:35): this is the principle underlying these verses, with which Peter summarizes the whole section. Christians treasure their fellowship with one another. Faced with persecution, their common joy in their Lord becomes all the more precious. But Peter wants to impress upon them that their relationship with each other is not entirely inward-looking. People will notice what they say to each other about the injustices they suffer (v. 9). Consequently, the Lord must be their model. The quotation from Psalm 34:12–16 in verses 10–12 contains the key word of this entire section: "Do good!" It also highlights the use of the tongue, just as the end of the last section did (2:9; cf. 2:1): the way we speak will reveal the shape of our whole life.

III. Suffering—The Road to Glory (3:13–4:19)

In this section Peter focuses more precisely on the subject of suffering. The last section laid down the basic principle of submission to the structures of this world. Peter now shows how suffering fits into that submission. Once again, this section begins and ends on the same note: doing good (a favorite theme of Peter's) and suffering for God's sake or for what is right.

A. Suffering for doing good (3:13–22). These verses are among the most difficult in the whole New Testament, because Peter refers to traditions and stories obviously familiar to his readers, but unfortunately not to us. Yet the overall message is clear. Peter tells us that if we are called to suffer for what is right, we must look to Jesus, who suffered for our sins and through that suffering has come to a place of supreme authority, raised over all the powers of evil that seem so overwhelming to the persecuted Asian Christians. Jesus suffered, though he was righteous, and if we will now set apart Christ as Lord in our hearts and follow in his footsteps we can be delivered from the fear of our persecutors, confident that through suffering we will share his victory. In the meantime we must bear witness to our hope, by both word and deed, remembering that our baptism was our pledge to God to live with good consciences before him.

Peter shares with Paul, and early Christians generally, the belief that authority and power in this world are earthly expressions of unseen fallen spiritual entities. Submission to secular authority as well as submission to all the constraints of earthly existence is a form of bondage to the powers of evil. Having told us to submit, Peter must touch on the spiritual implications of his teaching.

The "spirits in prison" (v. 19) are not the souls of dead human beings, but fallen angels (2 Pet. 2:4; Jude 6). According to Jewish tradition (1 Enoch 6–20), they deceived and corrupted the generation who lived before the flood, teaching them the arts of sin (see Gen. 6:1ff.). As a result they were locked up in prison at the time of the flood, "to be held for judgment" (2 Pet. 2:4). They were the counterparts of the angels, authorities, and powers (v. 22) still active today.

Jesus' preaching to these spirits was not an offer of salvation, but a proclamation of his final victory—in fact, the announcement of the judgment hanging over them. The spiritual forces behind the greatest corruption the world has ever seen have received their final condemnation at Jesus' hands! Having dealt with them, he finished his journey to heaven and took his place at God's right hand, in full authority over the powers behind the suffering experienced by Peter's readers. However much they may feel themselves to be victims, Christ is the Victor.

The refusal of the angels to submit to their Creator was matched by the mockery of Noah's contemporaries, who did not respond to God's warning of impending judgment, given by Noah's preaching (cf. 2 Pet. 2:5) and by the slow construction of the ark miles from the sea (v. 20). The water in which they died was, paradoxically, the very medium of Noah's salvation. In this respect the flood foreshadows Christian baptism, for that too pictures death but leads to life. When they were baptized, Peter's readers pledged themselves to live for God and embraced the hope of resurrection through Jesus Christ. But in so doing they actually brought suffering upon themselves, just as Noah did by his obedience to God's command to build an ark and to warn his generation. Yet in their suffering, symbolized by their baptismal "death," they follow the path already trodden by their Savior on the way to glory.

Peter thus seeks to minister to his suffering brethren in the deepest possible way: not by simply pointing them to compensation in the world to come, nor by painting vividly the judgment in store for their enemies, but by showing them that, precisely in their suffering, already pictured in the baptism which united them with Christ, they are sharing with their Lord in his victory over all the powers of evil in the universe.

B. Living for God (4:1–11). There is no break in the flow of thought at 4:1. Although Noah is not mentioned in **4:1–6**, we will best grasp Peter's meaning if we keep him in mind. For what Peter says in essence in verses 3–5 is: "You are in the same position as Noah, who refused to join in the profligate and licentious behavior of his contemporaries, even though they thought him peculiar for his refusal. Hold yourselves aloof from such practices, for God is about to act in judgment now as he did then." The striking word *flood* in verse 4—the only occasion on which this word is used with other than its literal meaning—points toward Noah. The outpourings of vice around them are horribly reminiscent of the floods of God's wrath about to break!

It is especially helpful to read verse 6 with Noah in mind. Scholars disagree here also, but it would be most perverse—and would not fit the context—to interpret verse 6 as teaching that a further chance of embracing new life is given after death. The Bible is quite clear that the books are opened and all men's accounts are settled when the tale of our earthly existence has been told (e.g., Heb. 9:27), and Peter himself says as much in 4:17–18. The best interpretation is to take verse 6 as a reference to Noah, who was revered as a "preacher of righteousness" (2 Pet. 2:5).

Peter has his readers' persecutors in mind as he writes this. They may heap abuse on the Christians (v. 4), but no one is so far gone as to be beyond the reach of God's life-giving power. Who knows what God's purpose may be in the coming judgment? Those who heard Noah preach died in the waters of the flood. But those waters symbolized baptism, because baptism is likewise about doing away with the flesh. Who knows whether their death in the flood might not have been a baptism for them, an entry into life? The same could be true for the Christians' persecutors.

The basic principle holds true for all: "he who has suffered in his body [lit. in the flesh] is done with sin" (v. 1). This was supremely true for Christ, who through death has conquered sin in all its manifestations; it is necessarily true for his followers, who through their suffering learn to dethrone evil desires and live for the will of God (v. 2); and possibly it is even true for the persecutors of the church, who might come to life through the judgment of death and must therefore be the objects of patient testimony, by word and deed.

The flood was a partial judgment, a foreshadowing of the total winding-up which is now near. If Noah prepared with such diligence for the flood, how much more should we seek to be ready for the end (**4:7–11**)? Peter outlines the vital features of a life lived with an eye to the coming judgment.

In the privacy of heart and home, Christians need minds that think straight and hearts that pray straight. In ordinary social relationships, Christians must love each other and offer hospitality. In undertaking Christian ministry, each must put into active service whatever gift God's grace has bestowed, whether it is teaching or more practical forms of service. The believer must draw upon God's resources and provision, and not for personal gain or glory. Rather, the object of life this side of the end must be the praise of God.

C. Sharing the sufferings of Christ (4:12–19). In this final subsection Peter draws the threads together. His readers must not be surprised at the painful (lit. fiery) trial they are experiencing, because suffering is not something foreign as far as Christians are concerned. Rather, it lies at the very heart of our existence! Peter gives three reasons why we should not be surprised:

First, we are participating in the sufferings of Christ (v. 13). We must expect to receive the same treatment as our Master, simply because we are his servants (John 15:20). Suffering is woven into human experience as part of a fallen creation, but Jesus has blasted a way through death to eternal life. And so we should rejoice as we participate in this great saving movement, looking ahead to glory!

Second, because Jesus is already victorious, our suffering is a foretaste of that coming glory, a blessedness that comes to us as God's Spirit rests upon us. What a revolutionary understanding!

Finally, our sufferings are the opening phase of God's winding-up operation, the beginning of his judgment. Peter deliberately calls the tribulation "judgment," partly for theological reasons (because he understands all suffering and death as part of the curse laid by God on a fallen world), but also because he will not let his readers relax their guard. Their suffering is a trial (v. 12), and they must make sure that they do not suffer deservedly (v. 15)! But if we suffer according to God's will (v. 19—i.e., with our hearts set upon God's will, even in the midst of our suffering) then God will uphold us.

IV. Final Exhortations and Greetings (5:1–14)

The final chapter begins with a resounding "therefore" which the New International Version has strangely failed to translate. This makes the connection clear: in times of suffering and trial, special responsibility rests upon the leaders of the churches to support and be shepherds of God's flock (v. 2). Peter turns to this vital practical concern to round off his letter. But in fact his concern is not just pastoral, for there remains a theological question, raised by what he has said about submission to earthly powers and Christ's victory over them, which needs to be tackled as well. If, as he has told us, we must submit to earthly authorities even though Christ has proclaimed his victory over them, if we must continue to live as loyal citizens of Babylon (v. 13) even though we know her satanic power has been broken, then what about authority structures within the church? What kinds of submission are appropriate for those who are already touched by the glory of the coming age?

Peter's pastoral concern predominates in **5:1–5**. His self-designation in verse 1 hints at this deeper concern. He is a "fellow elder"—not an exalted apostle—and with them a witness of (better, "to") Christ's sufferings. He therefore enters into all that that means, sharing those sufferings himself, and thus participating in the glory to be revealed. His readers are not alone in their suffering! Peter stands beside them.

He urges the elders to be aware of their special responsibility as shepherds. The imperative has an urgency about it—get on with the job! Then in three pairs of balancing phrases ("not . . . but," vv. 2–3) Peter tells them how they should exercise their pastoral care as far as *inner motivation* ("not because you must, but because you are willing") and *outward incentive* ("not greedy for money") are concerned.

With the last "not . . . but," Peter's second theological concern surfaces clearly. He uses here the same word that Mark records Jesus as having used when discussing this very issue with his disciples (Mark 10:42f.). Even if the church seems to possess a conventional, earthly authority structure, it actually reverses the normal pattern, modeling its vertical relationships on the Son of man who "did not come to be served, but to serve, and to give his life . . ." (Mark 10:45). This is the style of leadership that will bring the full realization of the glory known now but in part (v. 4). Peter drives this point home beautifully in verse 5 by using the single word *likewise.* He implies that the young men must be submissive to the "elders" in the same way as the elders are submissive to the young men! On both sides there is a "submission" which recognizes the distinctive gifts and ministry of the other and seeks to serve for Christ's sake. Verse 5b puts it in a nutshell: they must all tie humility around them like a robe, so that they may enjoy God's grace in all their relationships. For God himself does not "lord it" over his creatures, but by his grace reaches out to us and suffers with us, in Christ.

Peter summarizes all for which he longs for his readers (**5:6–11**). Here is the framework upon which he wants the house of our Christian life to rest.

For all that he has urged us to submit to our earthly circumstances, however trying, it is really to God himself that we submit (v. 6), in hope of his deliverance. We humble ourselves before him not as before an earthly master, awaiting instructions, but so as to feel the burden of anxiety lifted from our shoulders (v. 7).

For all that his readers are consumed with anxiety about their earthly enemies, Peter tells them that the spiritual foe is far more deadly (vv. 8–9). And we feel his pressure upon us not just through our earthly trials, but especially through the temptation not to face those trials with faith.

For all that we seek stability and strength in this life, Peter reminds us in his closing blessing (vv. 10–11) that these are things which God reserves for the age to come. After the suffering of this age, in which we already trace his grace, he will finally complete us, strengthen us, and set us on a sure foundation.

Peter associates with himself in his final greeting not just his two closest helpers, Silas and Mark, but also the whole church to which he belongs. "Babylon" (v. 19) is almost certainly a reference to Rome, which was increasingly called "Babylon" by both Jews and Christians at this time. Using this term here fits beautifully with Peter's theme. It reminds us of the true (satanic) nature of secular power. Christ, however, has conquered it. But also—and more particularly, at this point—it reminds us of the place of Israel's exile and of the fact that we too are aliens and strangers in the world. The letter thus ends on the same note with which it began, when Peter saluted his readers as God's elect, strangers in the world, scattered. For though exiles, we are yet God's chosen, his elect people, destined for glory.

SELECT BIBLIOGRAPHY

Best, E. *1 Peter.* London: Marshall, Morgan & Scott, 1971.

Cranfield, C. E. B. *The First Epistle of Peter.* London: SCM, 1950.

Grudem, W. *1 Peter.* Tyndale New Testament Commentaries. Leicester: Inter-Varsity; Grand Rapids: Eerdmans, 1988.

Kelly, J. N. D. *The Epistles of Peter and of Jude.* New York: Harper & Row, 1970.

Mounce, R. H. *A Living Hope.* Grand Rapids: Eerdmans, 1982.

Walls, A. F., and A. M. Stibbs. *1 Peter.* London: Tyndale, 1959.

2 PETER

William H. Baker

INTRODUCTION

The vast majority of contemporary scholars deny that Peter actually wrote the letter known as 2 Peter. Even among evangelicals there is a tendency to agree that Peter did not personally write the book but that it is of sufficient quality to remain in the canon of the New Testament.

Second Peter 1:1 claims explicitly that the author is Simon Peter. This claim is followed by several personal references. Second Peter 1:13–15 refers to the imminence of Peter's death. In 1:16–18 the author claims to be an "eyewitness" of the transfiguration. In 3:1 the author reminds his readers of his first letter and calls this the "second." He implies in 3:15 that he is a contemporary of Paul.

The evidence from early Christian writers that Peter wrote 2 Peter is less than that for other New Testament books, but far greater than that for any book excluded from the New Testament. The first citation by name by a church father comes from Origen at the beginning of the third century; the book appeared in papyri copies in Egypt before that. Eusebius says that Clement of Alexandria had it in his Bible at the middle of the second century, and the pseudonymous Apocalypse of Peter from about the same time also makes use of it. There are also possible traces of it in 1 Clement (A.D. 95), 2 Clement (A.D. 150?), Valentinus (A.D. 130), and Hippolytus (A.D. 180).

The canonicity of 2 Peter was contested during the third century. Jerome notes that 2 Peter was first doubted because its style differed from that of 1 Peter. Another objection was that no long line of tradition existed for its authorship. By the fourth-century councils of Hippo and Carthage it was universally regarded as canonical. What is interesting is that other works like the Epistle of Barnabas and 1 Clement were rejected because they were not apostolic in origin.

Some of the more significant arguments against Peter's authorship are as follows:

1. The language is not that of Peter. There are many words not found in 1 Peter or the rest of the New Testament. Much of the language is Hellenistic in nature, uncharacteristic of Peter. To answer

this objection, many conservatives postulate that Peter used a secretary and gave him freedom of expression. Some call attention to the similarities between 1 and 2 Peter. Others consider that 1 Peter is not a sufficient basis on which to determine Peter's style, and that subject matter affects vocabulary and style.

2. The thought patterns of 2 Peter are late first century or early second century, not middle first century when Peter lived. For example, 2 Peter shows a concern for a delay in the return of Christ (3:4). However, such concerns are reflected elsewhere in the New Testament (see, e.g., 1, 2 Thess.).

3. Second Peter refers to the "fathers" having died (3:4), a reference to the apostles, thus an anachronism betraying a later author. This term may, however, refer to the Old Testament fathers.

4. It is believed that 2 Peter borrowed from the letter of Jude (Jude 4–13, 16–18/2 Pet. 2:1–18; 3:1–3), something that an apostle of Peter's stature would not do. This could be answered by the possibility that Jude quoted Peter, or, if Peter quoted Jude, that Jude—the brother of Jesus Christ—was worthy of such an honor.

5. Second Peter is a "testament" type of literature. Written by an admirer after Peter was dead, the book was considered a valid expression of what the apostle himself would have said. The weakness in this argument is that other nonapostolic writings were rejected by the early church.

Assuming Peter's authorship of 2 Peter, 2 Peter 3:15–16 requires that a fairly large number of Paul's epistles had already been written, so that A.D. 60 would be the earliest date for its composition. If Peter was martyred around A.D. 67, then a date between these two would be necessary for the composition of 2 Peter.

If 2 Peter 3:1 refers to 1 Peter, then 2 Peter is addressed to the same audience as 1 Peter, namely, believers of both Jewish and Gentile background in Pontus, Galatia, Cappadocia, Asia, and Bithynia.

Second Peter essentially intends to alert believers to error (3:17) and to stimulate them to spiritual growth (1:3–11; 3:18). It devotes considerable attention (3:1–16) to the end times as a remedy to false teaching.

Significant also is its classic statement on the doctrine of Scripture (1:19–21), the presence of which makes one suspicious of the origin of the attacks upon the book's authenticity. In other words, Satan had good reason to attempt to destroy its credibility.

OUTLINE

I. Salutation (1:1–2)
II. Concern for Sanctification (1:3–11)
III. Confidence in the Scripture (1:12–21)
IV. Caution Toward False Teachers (2:1–22)
  A. Their Threat and Judgment (2:1–3)
  B. God's Judgment in the Past (2:4–10)

C. Their Character (2:10–16)
D. Their Empty Teaching (2:17–22)
V. Constancy in Light of the Last Days (3:1–16)
VI. Conclusion (3:17–18)

COMMENTARY

I. Salutation (1:1–2)

The author identifies himself as Simon Peter (v. 1), Simon being his Jewish name and Peter (Gk. *Petros,* rock) his Greek nickname. Peter was usually called Simon in the New Testament and occasionally Cephas, the Aramaic equivalent of Peter. It is believed by more conservative scholars that the spelling of Simon here—Symeon rather than Simon—is a mark of Peter's authentic authorship, for it appears so seldom.

Peter refers to himself as "a servant" to identify with his readers and clarify his relationship with Christ and "apostle" to designate his office as an officially appointed messenger of Jesus Christ, one with special authority.

He describes the recipients of his letter as "those . . . who have received a faith as precious as ours" (v. 1), that is, believers equal in every respect so far as faith is concerned, not inferior because they were not original disciples and eyewitnesses. The same can be said of all believers since. This faith has been granted by God's righteousness, that is, impartially to all who have believed by grace.

Finally, the apostolic benediction appears (cf. 1 Pet. 1:2). "Grace" is a typical Greek greeting; "peace" is more Hebrew in character, the former taking on a Christian character as divine provision for salvation and life, the latter pertaining to the judicial peace granted by justification (Rom. 5:1). These foundational blessings come through the knowledge of God and Jesus Christ, first perceived when one hears and believes the gospel.

II. Concern for Sanctification (1:3–11)

There cannot be sound Christian living apart from sound doctrine. Peter ties what he is about to say concerning holy, virtuous living with God's grace and peace. In other words, everything we need for life and godliness comes from the grace and peace granted by God's power. The believer shares in the divine nature via new birth by being given new desires like God's. This in turn separates him from the world—a world opposed to God's standards and ruled by evil desires that rebel against and oppose the divine will.

In light of these resources and God's purpose to deliver believers from this world, Peter advocates that believers zealously make a series of "additions" to faith (vv. 5ff.). Goodness is moral purity; knowledge is knowledge of Jesus Christ; self-control is denial of evil desires (in light of 1:4); perseverance is steadfastness in trials; godliness is love for God and his standards; brotherly kindness is doing good for fellow believers; love is doing good for all mankind and obeying God. Occurring at the very end of the list, love is the capstone of all these virtues.

Cultivation of such qualities will cause their knowledge of Christ to be productive in practical ways and prevent believers from becoming spiritually nearsighted and blind so that they forget that they are new people. By fostering these traits believers make their calling and election sure (v. 10). God, as part of his eternal plan, sovereignly brought them to faith. To make this "sure," they, by grace, produce with God's inward working the aspect of salvation known as sanctification, without which no one sees God (Heb. 12:14).

III. Confidence in the Scripture (1:12–21)

Peter is especially concerned about his readers' spiritual welfare because he knows that he is approaching the end of his life. Peter's promise that he will see to it that they remember his teaching (v. 15) is probably a reference to the Gospel of Mark, which early Christian tradition claims was sponsored by Peter himself.

Peter next shows how reliable this body of truth is. It is "eyewitness" material, not "cleverly invented stories" (v. 16). It was epitomized by the transfiguration, something that was an anchor for Peter's faith. The word of the prophets, at first only oral, was "made more certain" in the prophecy of Scripture (v. 20). It should be heeded like a light in darkness until Christ returns. "Prophecy" is a revelation from God in the broadest sense, not merely a "foretelling." "Scripture" here pertains principally to the Old Testament but extends to the New Testament in light of the context and such statements as 3:16. God brings it about, not the prophet. The Holy Spirit moves the prophet as wind propels a ship. The impulse and movement come from

God; the prophet (like a pilot) fully and consciously participates.

IV. Caution Toward False Teachers (2:1–22)

The believer meets the threat of error by recognizing false teachers and understanding their motives and methods. Times have not changed. False prophets appeared in ancient Israel, and false teachers will be present in the church also.

A. Their threat and judgment (2:1–3). False teachers infiltrate the church secretly. They make no pretensions to position or prestige at first. Working side by side with those who teach sound doctrine, they gradually introduce their destructive heresies. The noun *heresy* (Gk. *haireseis*) comes from the verb meaning "to choose" and had a derived meaning in New Testament times of one who had chosen to align himself with a particular point of view and thus become the member of a "sect" or "school." If this allegiance became too strong it proved to be destructive to the fellowship and unity of the church. Later the word *heresy* came to mean "false teaching."

These false teachers, perhaps both in their teaching and also in their presumptuous efforts to gain a following ("sect"), even deny the sovereign Lord. This probably pertains to his deity as well as his proper authority over them. The Lord, Peter says, "bought them," and this raises the question of whether these teachers were true believers who fell from the faith or mere "professors" of faith who had never been truly redeemed (the word *bought* can be rendered "redeemed"). The answer to this problem lies in determining in what sense they were "redeemed." The death of Christ potentially redeems all mankind, but only when one truly believes, is this provision applied. These teachers probably were not genuine believers. If they were, then one must face the question of whether they lost their salvation or whether they were saved in spite of what they did.

Their followers also engage in "their shameful ways," which refers usually to sexual immorality. Somehow these teachers were perverting the concept of grace by teaching that believers were forgiven but not accountable to judgment and could live sensually (see Rom. 6:1). Such conduct has brought Christianity into disrepute before non-Christians.

These false teachers are in religion for money, and exploit their followers financially. Their persuasiveness is due to stories they have made up; they use arguments and pure myths to support their teachings. Their ultimate judgment is certain.

B. God's judgment in the past (2:4–10). The Old Testament is filled with examples of the consequences of opposing God. Peter interjects a long series of clauses, each of which begins with the word *if,* and concludes (v. 9) that God indeed will deliver the godly and judge these teachers. The reference to the angels who sinned (v. 4; see Jude 6) is frequently interpreted as the story of the "sons of God" (an expression that sometimes refers to angels) in Genesis 6:1–4 (also mentioned in the apocryphal book of 1 Enoch 6:2). Others take it as a reference to the original fall of Satan and his angels. The word *hell* is the Greek Tartarus, a special place of confinement, not necessarily the eternal hell or lake of fire to which Satan and all the lost are consigned. Following the reference to angels, Peter cites those punished in the flood and Sodom and Gomorrah. Lot (v. 7) is called "a righteous man" which at first seems inappropriate considering his compromising life-style (Gen. 13). However, a proper perspective is gained by realizing that believers who compromise are nevertheless tormented within because of their regenerate desires and nature. These compromising believers will eventually be rescued from trials as was Lot, but the unrighteous are destined for punishment because they are fully given over to the desires of their sinful nature.

C. Their character (2:10–16). The most significant trait of these false teachers is their contempt for authority, which probably refers to leaders in the church. This contempt even extends to slander of celestial beings (Gk. *doxai,* glorious ones). In Jude 8, which seems to parallel this passage, these celestial beings seem to be Satan and the fallen angels, but it is difficult to determine precisely what form this slander took. The point here is that proper respect should lead one to be like the angels and to refrain from such arrogance.

The arrogance of these false teachers leads them to irrational, bold, blasphemous assertions about matters they do not understand. Like brute beasts, no one can reason with them; they function by means of passion and instinct and will perish someday after living meaningless, bestial lives.

God's retribution will reach them sooner or later. They even participate shamelessly in Christian "love feasts" (see Acts 2:46; Jude 12); like some of the Corinthians (1 Cor. 11:20), they make orgies out of them. The reference to adultery (v. 14; lit. eyes full of an adulteress) means that their teaching has deprived them of all moral restraint, and thoughts of sexual immorality constantly occupy their minds. Coupled with this is their love of money which makes them experts in "fleecing" the flock. Peter compares them in this respect with Balaam, who loved the wages of the false prophet (see Num. 22–24).

D. Their empty teaching (2:17–22). Peter uses two metaphors from nature to describe the emptiness of their teaching. Like "springs without water" (v. 17), they do not deliver in their teachings what they promise. "Mists driven by a storm" refers to the Palestinian haze that precedes dry weather and suggests the false appearance of moisture. In Scripture water is a metaphor for truth that sustains spiritual life. Their teachings, instead, appeal to sinful human nature, attracting people struggling with sinful desires by making self-indulgence appear good. The freedom they promise is really a freedom from the self-denial and self-discipline which truly set people free. This "freedom" brings them right back into the slavery of sin. Man is a "slave" either to righteousness or sin; there is no third alternative (see Rom. 6:12–18).

Peter's assessment of the condition of the teachers and their followers is reminiscent of Hebrews 6:4–6. Upon coming to Jesus Christ, they escaped the corruption of the world but through this false teaching they are again entangled. Since Peter says they are worse off at the end than they were at the beginning, these people probably never reached full, saving faith. There is a finality implied by the words *turn their backs* (v. 21) which would not be true of believers who fall into sin. True believers do not persist in sin (1 John 3:9).

V. Constancy in Light of the Last Days (3:1–16)

So far, Peter has advocated zeal in sanctification (1:3–11), confidence in Scripture (1:12–21), and wariness toward false teachers (2:1–22) as preventatives of error. Now he turns to the matter of stability in view of the future outcome of all things.

He has once before (in his first letter) stimulated his readers to wholesome thinking by trying to prepare them for suffering—the general content of 1 Peter. He wants to do the same with this letter by getting them to recall the words of both the prophets (the Old Testament) and the Lord—particularly their words concerning the end times, as the following context suggests.

The expression *last days* (v. 3) could mean the days immediately preceding the return of Jesus Christ, but it is used elsewhere (Acts 2:17; Heb. 1:2; 2 Tim. 3:1) to refer to the times that began with the first advent of Christ. Since Peter appears to be dealing with a form of skepticism that disturbed his readers, it probably pertains to the time inaugurated by Jesus' incarnation. The scoffers' skepticism is based upon their evil desires, which lead them to prefer a view of the future in which there is no divine judgment. The "coming" (Gk. *parousia;* used of the arrival of kings) which they ridicule is the return of Jesus Christ as King and Judge.

The scoffers maintain that everything in the world goes on without divine intervention. Peter refutes this skepticism by calling attention to the flood of Noah which the scoffers deliberately forget. This divine intervention into history also had its scoffers (Matt. 24:37–39). A future judgment will occur by fire in which these ungodly men will be judged.

Some of Peter's readers are also disturbed by the apparent indifference of God toward evil. Peter's advice to them is to remember that time itself does not affect God, nor can the lapse of time be construed as laxity on God's part. The reason for the delay of Christ's return is not that God is slow to keep his promise, but rather that his patience gives time for everyone to come to repentance.

The words *not wanting anyone to perish* (v. 9) have created a theological problem for some who see a possible contradiction with the idea of divine election. If God wants all to be saved, why did he not elect all? From the human perspective, there may never be a satisfying answer, assuming both of these ideas are true. Some have suggested that the solution lies in distinguishing God's "decretive" will (election) from his "desirative" will (as here). God decrees things in view of human sin (which allows men to reject salvation), while he desires things in view of his attributes of justice and goodness (which wishes all would repent). God's "desirative" will thus is not always fulfilled.

The "day of the Lord" (v. 10) is an Old Testament expression which usually refers to judgment as it does here. This "day," which is probably a period of time, comes to the world without warning ("like a thief"; cf. 1 Thess. 5:2), and the heavens and earth will be swept clear by fire to prepare for a new beginning. Those who hold to a literal earthly kingdom (premillennialists) would place the one-thousand-year reign of Christ between the day of the Lord here and the new heaven and earth of Revelation 21:1. Others, who believe the present time between the two advents of Christ is the kingdom (amillennialists), would probably equate 2 Peter 3:10–13 and Revelation 21:1.

When people realize that the things of this world are temporary, they tend to put less value upon them and more value upon living holy and godly lives, for that kind of living will speed the coming day by inspiring more and more to repent (3:9). Though the culmination of history is certain, believers participate through prayer, holy living, and evangelism in bringing it about. Peter refers to believers looking forward to the day of God, a time of destruction of the heavens by fire and of a new heaven and a new earth. Peter may be projecting the believer's hope even further into the future to the event of Revelation 21:1, because even the millennium (Rev. 20:9) is not totally without evil, but the new heaven and earth will be the home of righteousness (v. 13; cf. Rev. 21:4).

God's work of sanctification requires believers' every effort. Paul testifies in his letters of the same responsibility. Peter notes the fact that these letters contain things difficult to understand (though not impossible, as all persistent believers have learned) and that they carry the same authority as the "other Scriptures," a reference to the growing canon of the New Testament even at this early date. Those who fail to understand Paul's writings deliberately distort them.

VI. Conclusion (3:17–18)

Peter's final appeal is to what his readers already know but need to be reminded of. He has supplied them with what they need to avoid error and to remain secure. This knowledge must be incorporated into growth in the grace and knowledge of Jesus Christ.

SELECT BIBLIOGRAPHY

Bauckham, R. J. *Jude-2 Peter.* Waco: Word, 1983.

Blum, E. A. "2 Peter." In the *Expositor's Bible Commentary,* edited by Frank E. Gaebelein, 12 vols. Grand Rapids: Zondervan, 1981.

Cranfield, C. E. B. *1 and 2 Peter and Jude.* London: SCM, 1960.

Green, Michael. *The Second Epistle of Peter and the Epistle of Jude.* Grand Rapids: Eerdmans, 1968.

Reicke, B. *The Epistles of James, Peter, and Jude.* Garden City, N.Y.: Doubleday, 1964.

1–3 JOHN

James B. De Young

INTRODUCTION

None of these brief epistles specifically includes the name of its author. In 1 John the author claims to be a witness of Christ; in 2 and 3 John he identifies himself as "the elder" (presbyter). Early church fathers (e.g., Polycarp, Papias, and Irenaeus) attributed the epistles to the apostle John; Papias apparently identified John as both apostle and presbyter.

The first epistle and the Gospel of John share similar vocabulary, sentence structure, concepts (e.g., light, darkness, life, witness), and expressions (e.g., 1:2–3 and John 3:11; 1:4 and John 16:24). Similarly, the content and vocabulary of 2 and 3 John resemble that of 1 John and indicate that the same author wrote all three letters. By the fourth century their authority was unanimously recognized.

Tradition holds that the letters were written about A.D. 90–95 (after the Gospel of John had been written). First John assumes a knowledge of the Gospel, especially chapters 13–17; 2 and 3 John assume knowledge of 1 John. Tradition also holds that the letters were written in Ephesus, and that persecution of Christians may account for the lack of an author's name and specific information about the recipients.

The recipients of 1 John were probably Christian churches in Asia Minor. A local church, rather than a person, was probably the recipient of 2 John. The third epistle is addressed to Gaius; he is not to be identified with other persons of the same name who are mentioned in the New Testament.

Two purposes are reflected in the writing of 1 John. The primary purpose was to assure readers of their fellowship in Christ and eternal life and to encourage maturity. The author's other purpose was polemical: to warn against incipient heretical doctrine, which denied either the real deity or the real humanity of Christ, and heretical ethics—the idea that sin either does not exist or does not affect one's relationship to God.

As is the case with 1 John, 2 John was written to refute heretical denial of Christ's deity and humanity. In the second epistle the author also commended the faithfulness of some believers and encouraged love and truth.

In the third epistle John encouraged Gaius, censured Diotrephes' lack of love, and recommended Demetrius.

The traditional order of these three epistles was established early; it may reflect that heresy constituted a progressively serious threat to the churches.

All three epistles share some common characteristics. For example, all of them stress the concepts of truth, love, and abiding in Christ. The thought tends to be cyclical. The author relies on antithesis to emphasize his points. Often he uses profound terms, but, unlike other New Testament writers, he does not include quotations from the Old Testament.

The first epistle is somewhat general, almost like a tract, whereas the third epistle is specific and personal. The second epistle falls somewhere between the other two in its approach. And 3 John has the distinction of being the shortest letter in the New Testament. The second epistle is the next shortest, being about one papyrus sheet in length.

OUTLINE—1 JOHN

I. The Incarnation Makes Fellowship Possible (1:1–4)
  A. John Expresses the Substance of His Proclamation (1:1–2)
  B. John Expresses His Purposes for Writing (1:3–4)
II. Fellowship with God Is Based upon Truth and Love (1:5–5:17)
  A. The Apostolic Message Declares the Partners in Fellowship (1:5–2:2)
  B. Fellowship Bears Certain Distinctives (2:3–27)
  C. Fellowship Demands Certain Prerequisites (2:28–4:6)
  D. Love Leads to Fellowship (4:7–5:5)
  E. Faith Enhances Fellowship (5:6–17)
III. Fellowship Comprises Three Certainties (5:18–21)

COMMENTARY—1 JOHN

I. The Incarnation Makes Fellowship Possible (1:1–4)

The introduction to 1 John reflects the prologue of the Gospel (John 1:1–18). There is no salutation or personal reference (see also the Epistle to the Hebrews; in contrast to 2 and 3 John). The syntax is difficult—the subject and verb are in verse 3—but emphasizes the "Word of life." The preface builds suspense and leads to a climax.

A. John expresses the substance of his proclamation (1:1–2). The substance is that God has come in human flesh. The first four clauses in verse 1 lead from eternity ("the beginning"; not the beginning of the gospel) through history to the resurrection (cf. John 1:1–3; Gen. 1:1). The eternal One became man (incarnate) and was discerned by three senses (hearing, sight, touch). He was "heard" and "seen"; the verbs *looked at* and *touched* (i.e., to behold intelligently and to handle) are the climax of the verse and point to Christ's resurrection body (Luke 24:39).

The phrase *concerning the Word of life* refers either to Christ as the living Word of God (*logos;* John 1:1, 14) or to the lifegiving message. The latter, impersonal idea is preferable to the former, personal idea: *life* rather than *Word* is stressed (v. 2). It is possible, however, that both are in view. Life may be both the content of the message and the gift of the message (it is lifegiving). Verse 2 is a parenthetical comment, expanding verse 1 and clarifying the nature of the life. "Life" and "appeared" (both occur twice) are the chief concepts. "The life" may be a title for Christ as revealed, but probably refers to one aspect of his being. The incarnate Christ is the concern of experience ("seen"), witness ("testify"), and evangelism ("proclaim"). John's authority is derived from experience and from commission. He emphasizes the eternal nature of the "life" which was "with the Father"—alluding to Christ's preexistence (John 1:1). Verses 1–2 express a high view of both the deity and humanity of Christ.

B. John expresses his purposes for writing (1:3–4). As an envoy John announces that the readers may have Christian fellowship which is both "with us" (the apostles) and "with the Father and with his Son, Jesus Christ." The incarnation of the Son makes possible eternal life (v. 2) and human-divine fellowship, as well as the knowledge of God as Father (John 5:21–27; 10:36). Throughout the letter the name *Jesus* stresses his human nature; the terms *his Son* and *Christ* stress his divine nature. The parallelism ("with the Father . . . with his Son") shows Jesus Christ to be one with God. Christ is not less than man or less than God.

The ultimate purpose of proclamation ("to make our joy complete") shows John's pastoral concern (v. 4). The phrase *joy complete* (cf. Christ's promise [John 15:11; 16:24]) probably points to eternal life (v. 2) and the messianic kingdom, when such joy is realized (Ps. 16:11). This joy can flow only from fellowship (v. 3). Thus 1:1–4 unfolds the purpose of God in five stages: eternal preexistence, historical manifestation, authoritative proclamation, communal fellowship, complete joy.[1]

II. Fellowship with God Is Based upon Truth and Love (1:5–5:17)

A. The apostolic message declares the partners in fellowship (1:5–2:2). The writer's concern in the body of the letter is to give two tests for discerning who is in fellowship with God: obedience to the truth and love. Some scholars cite a third test, righteousness.[2] Here John describes the nature of the divine Partner and the moral conduct of the human partners in fellowship. Verse 5 is closely tied to the preface. The message is apostolic in authority and also divine: it is from Jesus Christ whom John had heard (1:1, 3). To declare that "God is light" means that he by nature is holy. Elsewhere the term *light* may mean life or salvation, but here the stress is on morality (Gen. 1; Ps. 27:1; Mic. 7:8–9).[3] "Intellectually, light is truth. . . . Morally, light is purity. . . ."[4]

This section (1:5–2:2) gives the practical, ethical implications of the doctrinal declaration *God is light* (1:5). Deceivers (2:18) had heretical ideas about the natures of God and man, denying the reality of sin or at least its effects on one's relation to God. In 1:6–2:2 each verse (except 2:2) contains a conditional clause followed by an explication of consequences, either positive or negative. Three false claims (1:6, 8, 10) are answered by three contrasting genuine truths (1:7, 9; 2:1–2) giving correctives and provisions.

The first false claim (1:6) is to have fellowship with God while continuing to "walk" (live) in "darkness" (sin). This antinomianism separates ethics from faith. John's response is twofold: we lie and we do not live (practice) the truth. Truth is the revelation about God's nature as light. We contradict the truth by words and by deeds. The corrective (1:7) is to walk continuously in conformity with God's nature (truth, holiness) just as he *is* in the light. His activity is always consistent with his nature. Two results follow: fellowship with other believers (based on fellowship with the Godhead [v. 3]) and continuous cleansing—not just forgiveness—from the stain of sin by the blood of Christ. The noun *sin* (*hamartia,* missing the mark) refers to either sin we unconsciously commit while in the light or our sinful nature; blood recalls the Old Testament atoning sacrifice (Lev. 16), which was fulfilled at the cross. Both the human ("Jesus") and divine natures ("his Son") are indicated.

The second false claim (1:8) is to be without sin in our nature. This is a worse error than the first, since it denies the very fact of having sin (see John 9:41; 15:22). The consequences are worse: we practice self-deception and the truth with its moral quality is not even in us. The first error concerns one's living; this concerns one's being. The corrective (1:9) is to continually confess sins when they are known. We acknowledge being sinners in both nature and practice. The provision is twofold: forgiveness of (release from) the debt of sins and cleansing from the stain of all unrighteousness (5:17). This God will do because he is "faithful" (to his promise to forgive [the new covenant; Jer. 31:31–34; Heb. 8:8–13]) and "just or righteous" (because Christ satisfied God's justice in his death for sins). Confession (and forsaking

1. J. R. W. Stott, *The Letters of John,* rev. ed. (Leicester: Inter-Varsity; Grand Rapids: Eerdmans, 1988), 63–71.

2. Robert Law, *The Tests of Life: A Study of the First Epistle of St. John,* 3d ed. (1914; reprint ed., Grand Rapids: Baker, 1968).

3. F. F. Bruce, *The Epistles of John* (Old Tappan, N.J.: Revell, 1970), 41.

4. Stott, *The Letters of John,* 76; B. F. Westcott, *The Epistles of St. John. The Greek Text with Notes,* 4th ed. (Abingdon, Berkshire: Marcham Manor; Grand Rapids: Eerdmans, 1966), 16; Stephen S. Smalley, *1, 2, 3 John* (Waco: Word, 1984), 20.

[Prov. 28:13; James 5:16]) is an obligation; John is commanding the readers to confess sins.[5]

The third false claim (1:10) is to be without sin in conduct. This is the worst error: claiming to be incapable of doing sinful acts. The two consequences are the most serious: we make God a liar (no longer light, v. 5) and his word (truth) is not in us. This claim attacks God's nature and revelation, because his word declares sin to be universal and present (Ps. 14:3; Isa. 53:6; 64:6). The corrective (2:1–2) is that one must not commit sin; to emphasize that point is one of the chief purposes for writing. "Dear children" is terminology unique to John (2:12, 28; 3:7, 18; 4:4; 5:21; cf. John 13:33), expressing John's concern and oversight. He commands his readers to renounce sinful acts or a lax attitude toward sin. Yet if one sins, the divine provision is twofold. First, Jesus Christ is our intercessor or advocate (again, the terminology is unique to John: see John 14:16, 26; 15:26; 16:7, which refer to the Holy Spirit). As the righteous (2:29; 3:7) God-man he pleads the legal case of the unrighteous before God as the Father (not Judge). Second, Christ is himself the "atoning sacrifice" sufficient for sins for all time for all men. The description *atoning sacrifice* means a propitiatory offering: Christ satisfies God's wrath against sin (4:10). He is not simply the expiation (RSV) given by God to annul the guilt of sin. His death is applied only to all who ask for salvation (i.e., believe).

B. Fellowship bears certain distinctives (2:3–27). John proceeds from general truths about fellowship to its particular, practical distinctives. The rest of 1 John develops, in recurring cycles, the tests of fellowship (abiding in truth/belief; showing love). In **2:3–11** the phrase *the one who says (*NASB*)* introduces three tests to prove the reality of fellowship (vv. 4, 6, 9): knowing God, abiding in him, and being in the light. In each case John gives the summary of genuine experience (vv. 3, 5b, 8b), then the false claim coupled with the reality (vv. 4, 6, 9), and finally the application (vv. 5a, 7–8a, 10–11).

The first test is obedience. Fellowship means personal knowledge (experience) of God with results affecting one's conduct. The test of such experience is obedience: "if we obey." "Commands" (vv. 3–4) are probably to be equated with "truth" (v. 4) and "his Word" (v. 5). They are called new and old (vv. 7–8), and are defined as belief and love (3:22–24). The first false claim (v. 4) is to have personal acquaintance with God (or Christ?), yet deny it by continual disobedience of his commands. A person who makes such a claim is a liar, devoid of truth. The one in fellowship not only obeys his word, but also God's love (4:12; or, his love for God) is truly made complete—stands perfect—in him (1:10). Love is moral obedience, an exercise of will, not sentimentality.

The second test (vv. 5b–8) concerns fellowship, which is defined as being "in him"; that is, in Christ (rather than the Father; cf. v. 6). Throughout 2:3ff., "this One" (*autos*) and "that One" (*ekeinos*) seem to refer to Christ. The second claim (v. 6) is to "abide" (NIV live) in him. John does not explicitly state the form a false claim might take, but points out the positive obligation to righteous conduct (to "walk as Jesus did"). To abide (remain or live, NIV) in God (2:6, 24, 27, 28; 3:6, 24; 4:13, 15, 16) is to experience intimate, personal fellowship. Conformity to Christ's conduct means conformity to his commands (v. 7). One command encapsulates all the rest. It is not something new from John but old, possessed from "the beginning"—the point of conversion (probably not the beginning of the gospel, or eternity past). The command is to love (John 13:34; 15:12, 17; 1 John 3:23–24; 2 John 4–6). Yet the old is also new. The newness, "its truth," is true in Christ, whose self-sacrifice gave new meaning and depth to love, and in believers. They follow his example and are experiencing the dawning of a new, messianic era, awaiting his second coming. The old age of darkness is disappearing (v. 17). Christ is already the true (real, genuine) light (Isa. 9:2; Matt. 4:16; Luke 1:79; John 3:19; 8:12).

The third test is love for one's Christian brother (vv. 9–11). To claim to be in the light (1:5–7; i.e., in fellowship) while hating one's brother means that one is still in the darkness. A genuine believer is right with both God and man. Positive and negative principles (vv. 10–11) reinforce the illustration. He who continues to love both abides in the light (1:5–7) and advances the light. He causes no one else to sin, nor does he himself sin. But he who continues to hate produces an opposite state and outcome. Hatred breeds spiritual disaster: he walks in darkness and loses his way (John 12:35) because of spiritual blindness (Isa. 6:10; John 12:40). John's cyclical thought leads in verses 3–11 from "commands" to "love," "command," "light," "love," and "light."

Commendation and assurance (vv. **12–14**) precede exhortation (vv. 15–27). This poetic section has six sentences with the verb *write*, the group addressed, and the reason for commendation (in the perfect tense, stressing ongoing, lasting results). Each group is twice ad-

5. I. H. Marshall, *The Epistles of John* (Grand Rapids: Eerdmans, 1978), 113.

dressed; the designations *dear children* may refer to physical age, church officers (elders and deacons), or the whole congregation, but the terms of commendation seem to indicate that stages of spiritual maturity are meant. The "dear children" are babes in Christ. They have a genuine relationship because their sins are forgiven (1:9–2:2) on account of the name of Christ (3:23; 5:13; 3 John 7), the basis of forgiveness (Heb. 8:8–13). The "fathers" are spiritually mature. They have come to and retain personal experiential knowledge (2:3) of the Father (rather than Christ, although both may be meant). The "young men" are growing. Their conquest of "the evil one" (Satan embodying evil) continues. The meaning probably is that they are victorious over heresy (4:4).

In verse 14 the children are said to have come to a personal knowledge of the Father. This knowledge, like forgiveness, is basic to Christianity, yet the comment shows an advance from the description in verse 13. Fathers are described as they were in verse 13. The young men not only have conquered Satan (v. 13) but also are spiritually strong and (i.e., because) God's word abides within. Therefore they conquer Satan.

Exhortation (vv. **15–27**) is needed since experience (vv. 12–14) is not perfect. Doctrine gives place to ethical demands. Note the three contrasts (love of the world/Father; from the world/Father; world passes away/Christian abides forever). Love may be both withheld (vv. 9–11) and misplaced (2 John 10). The Christian must not love (the first direct command in the letter [2:24, 27, 28; 3:7; 4:1 (two times); 5:21]) the evil system opposed to God and consisting of worldly things. This is selfish love (contrast John 3:16) having as its goal participation in the world of evil. Two reasons support the command. First, love for the Father (or, the Father's love) and love for the world are mutually exclusive (vv. 15–16; Matt. 6:24; Luke 16:13; James 4:13–15).

The things in the world are threefold (v. 16). Lust of the flesh is sinful desire or cravings arising from fallen human nature. Lust of the eyes is sinful desire that is triggered by the things a person sees. The pride of life is arrogance, a boastfulness produced by a false estimate of external circumstances and possessions (cf. 3:17; Luke 12:15). It also may be defined as boasting about externals, or may include both ideas: "pride in one's life style."[6] Note the trilogy of the world, the flesh, and the devil. The second reason (v. 17) not to love the world is that it and lust for (or, belonging to) it are transitory (vv. 8–9), whereas the Christian abides forever (1 Cor. 7:31; 2 Cor. 4:18; 2 Pet. 3:7–13; Rev. 21). As the Father and Son are eternal, so is the life of each one in Christ (John 8:35; 12:34–36; 15:4, 16).

Verses 18–27 concern keeping the faith. The concept of abiding recurs, while the infidelity of false teachers is shown by four traits. First, they depart from the circle of believers (vv. 18–19). Because believers are maturing (vv. 12–14), they can discern the true message from falsehood. The "last hour" of the messianic last days (Heb. 1:1–2) before Christ returns (3:2) has arrived. The period will culminate in the coming of the Antichrist; many forerunners have arrived already (v. 22; 4:3; 2 John 7; cf. Dan. 9:24–27; 11:31–47; 12; 2 Thess. 2; Rev. 13:17; 19:19–20). These human teachers (v. 27; 2 John 9–10), false prophets (4:1; Mark 13:22), oppose Christ by deceptive teaching about his nature. The deliberate defection or secession of all of them from the body of genuine Christians ("from us"; perhaps the apostles) was used by God for the purpose of uncovering their false character. Second, the false teachers lack knowledge of the truth. In contrast, all believers have factual knowledge and therefore can discern the truth (v. 21). The "anointing" probably is receiving the Holy Spirit (Isa. 61:1; Acts 10:38; 2 Cor. 1:21–22), rather than a reference to the word or truth of God, the gospel; however, it may refer to both the word and the Spirit. The Spirit is from the "Holy One" (probably Christ, rather than the Father [vv. 27–28; John 6:69]) and illumines understanding of "the truth" (the gospel, vv. 21, 27; 3:24; 4:13; 5:6) for all Christians, not just a few initiated into secret knowledge. John writes not to impart the truth but to assure or confirm that his readers already know factually both the content of truth (1:8; 2:4) and its self-consistent character. Lies do not come from the truth. Third, false teachers deny the incarnation of deity (vv. 22–23). The truth is that Christ is both fully God and fully man. Other liars exist (1:6; 2:4), but the liar par excellence (spirit of Antichrist; 4:3; 2 John 7) is he who denies that Jesus is the Christ, Son of the Father, deity in human flesh (4:2–3). It is not simply a denial that Jesus is the Messiah of the Old Testament. By denying the Son one denies the Father also, for they are one (John 10:30; 14:6, 9; 2 John 3, 9). Also such a one does not possess the Father. To acknowledge the Son is to possess the Father, to have fellowship with him. Fourth, the false teachers do not abide in the Father and the Son (vv. 24–25). John commands the readers to let the gospel, heard historically from the beginning, constantly

6. Smalley, *1, 2, 3 John*, 85.

abide in them, as the anointing does. The result will be a mutual abiding: the gospel in them and they in both the Son and the Father. Hence both the anointing and the historical gospel are safeguards from error. This relationship has no end; Christ promised eternal life (John 4:14; 5:24; 6:40, 63, 68; 7:37–39; 10:10, 28; 11:25–26; 17:2–3). Heretics lose both life and the Father.

Verses 26–27 summarize the preceding section (vv. 18–25) and make a transition to John's expansion on the theme of fellowship. The antichrists are those who are attempting (so far unsuccessfully) to lead believers astray. They emulate the great deceiver, Satan (see, e.g., John 8:44; Rev. 12:9; 20:3, 8, 10). The anointing, the Holy Spirit, was received at the moment of conversion. Believers need no one but him to teach them. His teaching is constant and comprehensive (John 14:26; 16:13), accords with reality, and is not counterfeit. John commands, as the Spirit does, that believers must abide in Christ. Here mutual abiding means the Spirit in them, and they in the Son.

C. Fellowship demands certain prerequisites (2:28–4:6). This passage, the third major section of the body of the letter, concerns three requirements for fellowship: righteousness, love, and faith. The phrase *and now* marks an advance in thought from commendation to exhortation. John repeats the command for his "dear children" to abide, since such a continual relationship is a requirement for both correct doctrine and correct practice. The motive for abiding is Christ's second appearance (3:2), also termed a "coming" or "presence." Whenever it occurs, those who abide will have confidence and not be ashamed (**2:28–3:3**). Confidence is freedom of speech, boldness, in both prayer (3:21; 5:14) and future judgment (2:28; 4:17).

Verse 29 marks the transition to a section that focuses on the character of the coming One. If we know factually that Christ is righteous (2:1), then we know by personal experience that he who practices righteousness has been regenerated, born again, by God the Father (not Christ; John 3:3). The "children" (3:1) must show the parent's character. The content of 3:1 expands on 2:29, as 3:2 expands on 2:28. John commands his readers to consider "how great" (NIV; or, what kind of) love the Father "has lavished" (lit. given) upon them. Being called "children of God" shows just how great! This relationship is not just in name but in fact. Since mankind failed to recognize the Father incarnated in Christ, it fails to recognize his children. In 3:2 John asserts the spiritual relationship of his beloved—again he calls them "children of God." Then he relates their salvation to the inheritance at the second coming. Their future condition has not been revealed (Deut. 29:29). Yet believers know by instruction that when the Son is revealed (2:28), they will be transformed and conformed to him (1:7; Rom. 8:29; 2 Cor. 3:18; 2 Pet. 1:3–4). This results from seeing Christ as he actually is (Ps. 11:7; John 17:24; Heb. 12:14). This securely founded expectation of total transformation has practical implications now (3:3). Hope "in him" (Christ, or "on God in Christ"; not "in himself") means one does (as a fact) and should (as a duty) continuously purify himself. Christ is the pattern, but also the motivation and means for purity.

Abiding in Christ in righteousness is based upon his first appearing (**3:4–10**). He took away sins and destroyed the works of Satan. Two cycles (vv. 4–7, 8–9) give the cause (vv. 4, 8a), the purpose (vv. 5, 8b), and the logical result (vv. 6, 9) of his appearing. The essential nature of sin is defined as lawlessness or active rebellion (v. 4). He who practices sin "breaks the law." The term *lawlessness* may be a technical one that refers to the satanic lawlessness under Antichrist before Christ's return (Matt. 24:11–12; 2 Thess. 2:3).

Christians should not be rebellious; they know from their instruction in the gospel that Christ was revealed in history (1:2). His purpose was to remove sins (John 1:29) by his sacrificial death (2:2; 4:10). Yet he is eternally sinless by nature (2:29; 3:3, 7). The consequences (3:6) follow logically: Everyone who intimately abides in Christ (2:6) does not practice sin; everyone who sins has neither spiritually seen nor personally come to know him. Such a person cannot be living in Christ, for sin and Christ are incompatible. Compassionately John commands that his children not be deceived in either ethics or doctrine (3:7; 2:22–23). The one who does righteousness—that is, acts rightly—is righteous in character. "Doing is the test of Being."[7] The righteous Christ is again the pattern (3:3). The contrast (v. 8) is that he who does sin has his origin in and belongs to the devil (his pattern). The devil not only tempted man to sin (Gen. 3), but sins continuously since the initial rebellion against God. The Son of God (the first use of the full title) became incarnate to destroy Satan's works in every realm, including men's sins. This is the second purpose of his coming (3:5). Yet victory is fully achieved only in the future; sin is still present (1:8, 10; Heb. 2:14). Verse 9 advances the argument beyond verse 6: the Christian, reborn, not only does not practice sin

7. Law, *The Tests of Life,* 220.

but also cannot continue to sin. The reason is that "God's seed" remains in him. This means either that God's offspring live in him, or that a divine seed (God's nature) indwells the Christian. The latter is the better view. "Seed" could mean the new nature (the best interpretation), life, the Word of God or the gospel, the Holy Spirit, or Christ. If it is the Spirit and/or the Word, it is the same as the anointing (2:20, 27).

How can John say that the Christian *cannot* sin when elsewhere he teaches the possibility and confession of sin by Christians (1:7–2:2; 3:3; 5:16–17)? Various answers are possible:

1. The grammar means that believers cannot habitually sin.
2. The reference is to deliberate and conscious, not involuntary, sins; or mortal, but not venial, sin.
3. The old nature can sin, but not the new nature.
4. The ideal is to not sin.
5. It is a summons to live sinlessly, reflecting a potential to live in a spiritual way—a future reality.
6. As long as one abides he cannot sin.
7. It is exaggeration in order to oppose morally indifferent Gnostics or to oppose the false perfectionism of Gnostics.
8. The statements are implicit commands or conditions.

View 1 seems best, with view 5 next.

Deeds reveal the children of God and those of the devil (vv. 8, 11); all humanity belongs to one or the other (John 8:42–47). The test of divine sonship is stated negatively (v. 10), but John implies that Christians must be actively righteous. The specific form of doing rightly is obeying the command to love (2:10). So in 2:28–3:10 John argues that living in sin denies the purposes of Christ's two comings.

Love is the second requirement for fellowship (**3:11–24**). Love shows that the believer obeys God (vv. 11–13) and proves that he has new life (vv. 14–15). The message from the beginning is doctrinal (1:5) and ethical—the obligation of continuous mutual love (2:7–8; 3:23). Hatred, the opposite of love, is exemplified by Cain (v. 12). Since Cain belonged to Satan he had his nature. As the devil murders (John 8:44), so evil Cain brutally murdered righteous Abel (Heb. 11:4). Cain and Abel are types of the world (and its heretics) and the Christian (vv. 13–18). Therefore Christian "brothers" (the word is used only here in 1 John) must not be surprised at the world's hatred (John 15:18–25). Ongoing love for Christian brothers provides the evidence that Christians have already made the decision to pass over from the realm of spiritual death into that of spiritual (eternal) life (John 5:24). The one who does not love abides continuously in spiritual death. Verse 15 intensifies the idea of not loving into an axiom about hating. Hatred and murder are synonymous, for he who hates his brother fits the same moral category as a murderer (as Cain). Both lack life. All hatred is potentially murderous (Matt. 5:21–22).

Love manifests itself in conduct (**3:16–18**). Christians have come to experience with lasting impact the true essence of love. It is the historical work of Christ at the cross. There he surrendered his life in self-sacrifice, not only as an example but also as a substitute for man and his sin (2:2; 4:10; John 3:16; 10:11, 15, 17; Isa. 53:10). Christians in response are morally obligated (*ought*) to imitate his example and continuously sacrifice their lives for Christian brothers (John 15:13; 3 John 11). Verse 17 extends the principle of self-sacrifice to material possessions. Having ordinary, temporal possessions obligates every Christian to help needy brothers materially. To close one's heart is to be devoid of God's love (alternatively: divine love; or, love for God). The murderer and the miser alike lack love.[8] In conclusion John exhorts his dear children to practice love in the proper manner. Mutual love must be not by word and speech but "with actions and in truth" (genuineness; James 1:22–25; 2:14–17).

For three reasons love is essential to assurance before God (**3:19–24**). First, it relieves the condemnation of the heart. Love results in assurance of being in the truth and reassurance when we are troubled by conscience. By showing love we will know experientially that we "belong to the truth" (the revelation of God in Christ) and will reassure our hearts (consciences: the moral faculty) at any point of future doubt. The translation *to set . . . at rest* (reassure, satisfy) is preferable to *persuade, appeal.* In God's presence, when judgment seems near, our accusing (condemning) heart is reassured, first, by deeds of love and, second, by God's omniscience. He, being greater than an accusing heart, knows all and will give a just verdict. This is a promise of comfort rather than indictment (cf. 1:7).

Second, love is essential because it gives confidence in prayer (vv. 21–22). An uncondemning heart assures the beloved of continuous confidence (see 2:28) before God and continuous answers whenever they pray (5:14–15). God answers because we continuously keep his commands (i.e., do his will=obedience; John 8:29; 15:10) and we continuously do "what pleases" him (=service). Obedience and ser-

8. Stott, *The Letters of John,* 144.

vice, objective reasons for answered prayer, complement a clear conscience, a subjective reason.

Third, love is essential because it fulfills God's commands (3:11–24), which have two aspects. The first, prior aspect is to place initial faith in the name of God's Son (5:13) so that we are of the truth (3:19; 2 John 4). This is to acknowledge Jesus as Christ incarnate (2:22–23) and divine Son, as the Father commanded (Matt. 17:5). The second aspect is to keep loving one another, just as God (the source of the command) commanded through Christ (John 13:34–35; 14:24). Right conduct must flow from right belief (2:3–4; Gal. 5:6, 13). Verse 24 gives a further result of keeping his commands, namely, assurance. Mutual abiding is intimate relationship with God (2:6; 3:1; 4:12–13) and Christ (2:24; cf. Ezek. 37:26–27). The test of experientially knowing God's abiding within is the presence of the Holy Spirit (the first explicit reference in this letter) given to us at conversion (4:13). Note that all the persons of the Trinity are mentioned in verses 23–24.

The believer must test the spirits (**4:1–6**), and this passage applies the theological (doctrinal) test to discern between truth and error. John commands his beloved readers to stop believing that every person is inspired by a spirit of truth (v. 1). Instead they must constantly test to determine if spirits derive from God. Testing is necessary because many false prophets (antichrists, 2:18; 4:3; 2 Pet. 1:21–2:1) departed into the evil world (2:15–19). The test that believers must apply is to examine a person's creed (4:2–3): Does the prophet confess that Jesus as Christ has become and remains incarnate (2:22)? This ongoing confession is acknowledgment not of doctrine but of Christ's identity and faith in him. Verse 3 reinforces verse 2. The false spirit is he who does not acknowledge Jesus ("as Christ . . . come in the flesh" [v. 2]). Such a person belongs not to God but to Antichrist (2:18; 2 John 7). Believers have heard and remember the warning about his coming, but he is in the evil world already (2:15ff.; 3:1, 13), inspiring false prophets (2 Thess. 2:3–8).

John tenderly assures the readers that they come from and belong to God (v. 4). They have also gained and enjoy a decisive conquest (cf. 2:13–14) over the heretics in doctrine and morality. The reason for victory is that the power of the Holy Spirit (or the Trinity?) in them is greater than Satan's power inspiring false prophets. Verses 5–6 contrast unbelievers with believers and their respective audiences. The heretics with Antichrist's spirit derive from the world and give it allegiance. Consequently, their speech is worldly (John 3:31). Thus the world embraces them and their viewpoint. The positive aspect (v. 6) refers to the test of verse 1 but enlarges it: acceptance of the truth of Christ's person is now the issue. Believers (probably apostles in particular, 1:1) derive from God. The one with ongoing personal knowledge of God "listens to" (obeys) orthodox leaders (we/us=apostles in contexts of doctrine), whereas the one not belonging to God does not pay heed to the apostles. This test distinguishes between a believer inspired by the Holy Spirit (or, the Holy Spirit himself) and a false prophet inspired by a spirit of error or deceit (i.e., the Evil One).

D. Love leads to fellowship (4:7–5:5). The exhortation to love reciprocally is repeated (4:7; 2:10; 3:11, 23), not only to emphasize but also to show progress in thought. Love must flourish because of its divine origin and nature ("from God"; **4:7–16**). Practicing love is evidence of past regeneration and present personal knowledge of God. New love is the effect of new birth. Verse 8 gives the negative of verse 7. Lacking the effect (i.e., love) shows that the cause is missing: an individual never entered into a personal relationship with God. Why? "Because God is love." Love defines his personal nature, not his action. He is not only the source of love but love itself. He is personal and living.

God's character as love is revealed (v. 9) not by abstract theological reflection, but by his work in sending the Son (implying Christ's preexistence). Christ is uniquely his "one and only Son" (one of a kind; cf. John 1:14, 18; 3:16, 18). The atoning mission of the Son has lasting effect; its purpose (or result) is that we might have eternal life by means of Christ (3:14). Verse 10 expands on the idea in verse 9. The essence of love is not man's loving God. Rather it is God's love for man expressed in the historical sending of the Son as a satisfaction offering (see 2:2) for man's sins. Man's love is always and only a response to God's love.

The beloved are obligated ("ought," v. 11) to respond to God's self-sacrificial manner of loving in Christ by loving one another reciprocally (v. 7). God's love is seen in Christian love. Verse 12 explains why John did not say that we ought to love God, in response to God's love. No one has ever seen God as he actually is (3:2). As Christ revealed God (John 1:18), our mutual love reveals God spiritually. It is evidence that he abides continually within. Indeed, his love (or, our love for him) stands completed in (or, among) us when it is reproduced in us.

Verses 13–16 reassure Christians of the meaning of faith and love by giving three evidences of mutual abiding. The first evidence is the presence of the Holy Spirit (v. 13), which God has given us. The lasting result is our assurance of personal knowledge of mutual abiding (fellowship; cf. v. 12; 3:24). The Spirit is the subjective witness (v. 13); the objective witnesses are the apostles (v. 14). The apostles have seen the historical Christ (not the invisible God, v. 12) and bear constant witness (1:1–2) to his historical mission as Savior of the world (deliverer; the term occurs only here in John's epistles). Christ's work includes incarnation, atonement, and exaltation. Note that in verses 13–14 all the persons of the Trinity are mentioned. The second evidence of mutual abiding (v. 15) is decisive acknowledgment of Jesus as the Son of God (5:5). This is how the potential salvation (v. 14) becomes effective. As 4:2 emphasizes the humanity of Christ, this verse emphasizes his deity. The third evidence of mutual abiding (v. 16) is abiding in love. Believers have come to know personally and to trust and believe with lasting results God's love for them as demonstrated in Christ's mission. The verse reiterates that not only does God love but also "God is love" (see also v. 8). Abiding in love means mutual abiding in God.

Moreover, love must be perfected (or, matured; **4:17–21**). Love stands completed by the mutual abiding (v. 16); the result (NIV so that) is that believers will have "confidence" on the day of judgment. (Another interpretation is that John means that love stands completed when one has confidence on judgment day.) This is so because in this evil world we are abiding in the Father and in his love (John 14:10–11, 20; 15:9–10; 17:21–23, 26). Now and on judgment day there is no fear because complete love "drives out" fear (v. 18). Fear of punishment and love are incompatible. Sin breeds fear; fearless love breeds confidence. Verse 19 echoes verse 10. Christians do not fear but love. Yet all our love, whether of God or of men, is only a response to his first and greater demonstration of love in Christ at the cross.

Another test of love is set forth in verse 20. The phrase *if anyone says* introduces a false claim (see also 1:6, 8, 10; 2:4, 6, 9), here to love God while hating one's brother. Such a person is a liar about love (cf. about morality, 1:6, 10; 2:4; about doctrine, 2:22; 5:10). One cannot love the invisible God (the harder thing and not easily tested) if he does not love God's visible image in a brother (the easier thing, easily tested). Verse 21 completes this section by restating the command to love both God and one's brother as a single command (Mark 12:30–31). To love God is to obey his command (3:23) to love him and others (Deut. 6:4; Lev. 19:18).

In **5:1–5** John emphasizes the place of love in fellowship. He links love to faith (5:6–17; Ps. 85:10–11) in cyclical thought. Right belief and right conduct go together (v. 1). The one who believes the truth that Jesus is the divine Messiah (2:22; 4:2, 14–15; 5:5) gives evidence that he has been regenerated. Such faith also means love for both the divine Parent and the child born from him (a universal principle). Faith, doing right (2:29; 3:9–10), and love (4:7) are evidences of birth from God. Verse 2 argues the reverse of 3:14–15, 17–19; 4:20. We know personally that we are loving God's children when we love God and practice his commands (to love and believe, 3:23). Love for God proves our love for others. Both loves are essential and interwoven. "Love for God" (v. 3) is defined as obedience: keeping his commands. The nature of his commands, though exacting, is not oppressive (Matt. 11:30). There is divine enablement (v. 4). Birth from God overcomes the evil world. The victory which overcame historically is Christ's, won at the cross (John 16:33). The believer's faith enables him to share in Christ's victory. Verse 5 restates verse 4 as a question. The one who conquers the evil world is he who believes. The victory achieved historically by Christ is constantly appropriated by keeping faith that Jesus is God's Son (2:22–23; 4:15). By faith his victory becomes ours.

E. Faith enhances fellowship (5:6–17). The object of faith is Jesus the Christ; witnesses to Christ establish his history (**5:6–9**). He came historically by the manner of (or, by the instruments of) "water and blood." These words may refer to the two ordinances of baptism and communion, the water and blood at the crucifixion (John 19:34–35), the birth and death of Christ, or the termini of Christ's ministry, his baptism and crucifixion. The last view is best and argues that Christ is both truly God and truly man. Also, the Holy Spirit witnesses to his coming, from Old Testament times until the present, in preaching and within the Christian. The Spirit is the truth (2:27; 4:2), so he is able and constrained to so witness through men (3:24; 4:13). The water, blood, and Spirit have the character of witnesses (vv. 7–8). (The longer reading of the KJV [v. 7] is probably a scribal addition to the original text.) All three witnesses are historical, but the Spirit is chief and hence mentioned first (Matt. 3:16; John 20:22). The three converge on the same point ("are in agreement"): to establish the truth that Jesus is both Messiah and Son of God. The mention of three witnesses reflects the requirements of Jewish law (Deut. 19:15; John 8:17–18).

Since we receive men's testimony, we should certainly receive God's for it is greater in significance, reliability, and consequence (v. 9). The testimony of God includes both the threefold witness (vv. 7–8), since the three derive ultimately from God, and also God's own lasting witness given in the gospel (John 1:32; 12:28; Matt. 3:17; 17:5; Heb. 2:1–4).

In **5:10–12** John describes the results of faith. To believe is to have personal faith in, and to commit oneself to, the person of the Son of God. He who so believes has the Father's witness about the Son within his heart. This is the inward (subjective) witness of the Spirit, confirming that one was right to believe in Christ, and complements the outward (objective) witness of water and blood. The reverse is sobering: if one disbelieves God's historical witness about the Son, he makes God a liar (cf. 1:10) and so forfeits further witness. The second result of believing is to possess eternal life now by possessing Christ (v. 11). God's witness is that he has given us eternal life, life of the highest quality, but the sole mediator of it is his Son (1:1–2; John 1:4, 14:6; 20:31). The relationship between the Son of God and life is absolute and exclusive. To possess him in intimate relationship means life; to lack him means spiritual death (v. 12). And life in him means victory (v. 5).

The certainties of faith mark one's fellowship (**5:13–17**). Verse 13 is transitional, as John moves from teaching to application. One of John's chief purposes for writing is to assure believers that they possess eternal life here and now (vv. 11–12). It is factual certainty (2:29; 3:14, 24) only for those who keep on believing in the name of the Son (John 1:12). John wrote his Gospel to prompt faith (20:31); the epistle leads from hearing to believing, living, and knowing.

Knowledge leads to confidence in prayer (v. 14; 3:21–22). One in active fellowship with the Father and Son has assurance (confidence, 2:28) that God always hears favorably his specific requests (John 9:31; 11:41–42). The condition is that our will submit to and coincide with his (John 14:13–14; 15:7, 16; 16:21–24, 26). Verse 15 states the assurance in prayer more generally. If we know factually that God hears (favorably, promised in v. 14) we know just as certainly that we have at hand the answers to our requests, whatever they be (Matt. 21:22; Mark 11:24; James 4:2).

The principle applies also to prayer for sinning brothers. If anyone "sees" (not suspects) a brother continuing in sin which does not lead to death, he should ask and God (not the intercessor) will give to him and all such sinners life (James 5:15, 20). Several problems arise here. It seems preferable on the basis of consistency to view the brother as a Christian, not an unbeliever (although compare 2:9, 11). The background is probably the Old Testament distinction between inadvertent sins, for which there was sacrifice, and deliberate ones, for which there was no sacrifice—only God's mercy could intervene (see Lev. 4; 5:15–19; Num. 15:27–31; Ps. 19:13). Here the sin which leads to death is not specified, but from the context would include, apparently, refusal to confess Christ and disobedience to God's commands to love and believe—all marks of an unbeliever who seeks no pardon or salvation (John 3:18–21; 8:24). For an inadvertent sin which does not lead to death (believers do sin; 1:7, 9; 2:1–2), God will give life in the sense of assuring the believer as he repents that he has eternal life (abides in the Son and in life, 2:24; 3:6; 4:13; 5:11–12). John does not say that a believer can commit a sin leading to death. It is assumed that such a sinner is an unbeliever. Also, John does not forbid intercession for such sinners; he merely abstains from commanding it (perhaps he doubts its efficacy). All wrongdoing is defined as sin to remind believers that all sin is serious and a departure from rightness (v. 17; 3:4; Rom 6:13). Yet John assures that there can be forgiveness by noting that there is sin not leading to death.

III. Fellowship Comprises Three Certainties (5:18–21)

The first of three certainties ("we know") is deliverance from sin (v. 18). Anyone born of God does not sin (3:6, 9). His regeneration affects his morality. This universal occurs because Christ (rather than the believer), born from God historically, constantly protects him (not "himself"), and Satan ("the evil one"; 2:13–14) does not harm him at any time (Matt. 6:13). Deliverance is always available in Christ.

The second certainty is divine sonship (v. 19). Christians belong to God (and are in God and Christ, v. 20). By contrast the entire evil world, opposed to God, is under constant "control of the evil one" (see also 2:13–14; John 12:31; 14:30; 16:11; 17:15). Satan cannot lay a hand on the believer (v. 18) but the world lies in his arms!

The third certainty is fellowship with the true God (v. 20). Christians have factual knowledge that is both historical (Christ "has come"; 1:2; 3:5, 8) and experimental ("has given understanding") that we might have constant personal knowledge of the true (i.e., genuine) One. Christ is the perfect Redeemer and Revealer. The object of knowledge is a divine Person, not abstract truth. Christians not only know him but also exist in both him and his Son Jesus Christ (2:5, 23–24). John describes God (perhaps Jesus Christ) as the genuine God and eternal life, so ending on the same point with which he began (1:2; 5:11–13).

John's final command (v. 21), couched in tender terms, is that his children must guard themselves (demanding personal effort; see also Jude 21, 24) from false gods (in contrast to the genuine, v. 20). These are either actual idols or things substituted for God—heresy regarding knowledge or morality and doctrine about Christ (see vv. 16–17). The absence of a farewell (cf. 2 and 3 John) is noteworthy.

OUTLINE—2 JOHN

I. The Elder Greets the Elect Lady and Her Children (1–3)
II. Abiding in the Truth Is the Basis for Walking in Love (4–11)
  A. Commendation: Walking in the Truth Keeps the Command from the Father (4)
  B. Exhortation: Walking in Love Keeps the Command from the Son (5–6)
  C. Warning: Confessing and Keeping the Truth about Christ Determine the Circle of Fellowship in Love (7–11)
III. The Truth Is the Basis of Christian Fellowship (12–13)

COMMENTARY—2 JOHN

I. The Elder Greets the Elect Lady and Her Children (1–3)

The term *elder* connotes age, specific identity, church office, and authority over a group of churches (v. 1; 3 John 1). This supports the traditional identity of the author as the apostle John. The "chosen lady" and her "children" (cf. 1 John 3:1–2, 10) are probably not individuals but a local church personified. John emphasizes that he and others who have come to know personally the truth love the readers constantly in a way that accords with the truth of the gospel.

This mutual love is practiced "because of the truth," not personal affection. Truth is objective (1 John 2:7–8; 3:11) and subjective: it abides presently with the readers and will be theirs for eternity. The Christian salutation (v. 3; 1 Tim. 1:2; 2 Tim. 1:2) includes undeserved favor or love (grace), forgiveness for the needy (mercy), and well-being (peace). The concept and form *grace* is Greek; *mercy* and *peace* are Jewish. These provisions, the elder asserts, "will be" theirs from two sources viewed as equals: their divine Father and Jesus Christ in the special relation of Son to Father. The provisions exist in the truth and love which come from God and are practiced by the Christian.

II. Abiding in the Truth Is the Basis for Walking in Love (4–11)

A. Commendation: Walking in the truth keeps the command from the Father (4). John's "great joy" was caused by his past discovery that some of the church members were continuing to obey the truth, the gospel (3 John 4), just as the Father had commanded historically through Christ to believe and to love (1 John 3:23; Matt. 17:5; John 1:32–34; 13:34–35). Many others apparently were disobedient.

B. Exhortation: Walking in love keeps the commands from the Son (5–6). Obedience proves itself in love. The phrase *and now* marks a transition from emphasis on the truth to emphasis on love. John's chief purpose for writing is to make a personal plea that the orthodox constantly and reciprocally love one another. John notes parenthetically that this does not constitute a new command from him but one possessed from the beginning of the gospel (1 John 2:7–8; 3:11; 4:7–8; 5:1–3; i.e., from Christ [John 13:34–35]), if not from creation (i.e., from God [1 John 1:1; 2:24; 3:11]). Love is not passion but willing, selfless obedience responding to God's love; faith is obedient, believing commitment to the truth of God revealed in Christ. Love to God or men means to walk according to commands; the command (embodying the many) is to walk in love (or truth, since they are closely joined). All the law is fully obeyed in love (Matt. 22:37–40; Rom. 13:8; Gal. 5:14).

C. Warning: Confessing and keeping the truth about Christ determine the circle of fellowship in love (7–11). These verses emphasize truth, as verses 5–6 do love. The occasion for the whole letter is the departure of "many" habitual "deceivers" into the evil world (v. 7; 1 John 2:18–26; 4:1–6). With missionary zeal they denied the incarnation of deity in Jesus Christ—perhaps even the permanent, everlasting union of his human and divine natures (John 6:14; 11:27). Their character embodied the spirit of the archdeceiver and Antichrist (1 John 2:18, 22; 4:3). Verses 8–9 give the first of two basic commands: the readers must practice personal vigilance (Mark 13:5). The purpose is both negative and positive: to avoid losing what they have worked for and to receive a full reward or wage for faithful service. To advance beyond (not in) the apostolic teaching about Christ (or, Christ's teaching)—as those with Gnostic tendencies claimed to do—is to fail to remain in it (v. 9; 1 John 2:23–24). The "deceivers" lost God by denying the Son who reveals him. In contrast, the one who continues to abide in the doctrine possesses an intimate relationship with both the Father and the Son (John 14:6). Verses 10–11 give the second basic command: the readers must not encourage deceivers by welcoming officially to the house church (probably not a private home) itinerant, self-appointed teachers seeking converts to their false view of Christ. Neither should they be greeted in parting. Such practice implies active participation in evil deeds of deceit.

III. The Truth Is the Basis of Christian Fellowship (12–13)

The papyrus sheet is full of ink; John deliberately decides not to write any more of the many things he could. Instead he hopes to speak personally with the believers and anticipates that complete joy in fellowship will be the result (1 John 1:4; 3 John 4). He passes on a greeting from members of a sister church whence he writes in order to convey his authority, add weight to his epistle, and encourage the readers by others' faithfulness to truth and love.

OUTLINE—3 JOHN

I. The Elder Addresses Gaius in Love (1)
II. Love Must Prevail in the Circle of the Truth (2–12)
   A. Commendation of Gaius: He Walks in the Truth and Love (2–8)
   B. Condemnation of Diotrephes: He Rejects Authority and Lacks Love (9–10)
   C. Recommendation of Demetrius: He Does Good (11–12)
III. Peace Should Prevail among Friends (13–15)

COMMENTARY—3 JOHN

I. The Elder Addresses Gaius in Love (1)

The elder (see 2 John) addresses Gaius with affection (vv. 2, 5, 11). He personally has continuing love in the truth of the gospel for Gaius (2 John 1), who perhaps is his spiritual son. The words *truth* and *love* anticipate the main message.

II. Love Must Prevail in the Circle of the Truth (2–12)

A. Commendation of Gaius: He walks in the truth and love (2–8). The wish for the reader's good health is typical of secular letters; Christian greeting is lacking (2 John 1–3). John prays that Gaius may prosper in every way—healthy in body, just as in soul. Verses 3–8 explain why John is confident of Gaius's spiritual health. Christian brothers keep coming and witnessing to Gaius's faithfulness to the truth. This accords with his constant walking in the truth. Hence doctrine and devotion, creed and conduct, are balanced. John has no greater joy than hearing that his spiritual children are so walking in the truth.

Beloved Gaius faithfully shows hospitality for Christian brothers, even though they are strangers. These itinerant preachers had witnessed to his love before John's church and then returned to Gaius. Now John requests him to send them on their way in a manner that God would approve (Matt. 10:40–42); that is, to provide supplies for their journey. They are worthy of such because they went forth as missionaries on behalf of the "Name" (of Jesus Christ, rather than of God). This was their motive. They accepted nothing from unbelievers (v. 7). Christians have an obligation to show hospitality and material help to such emissaries (1 Cor. 9:11–14). Thus Christians prove to be (already) fellow workers in the truth and in its cause. Verses 5–8 are a basis for modern missions.

B. Condemnation of Diotrephes: He rejects authority and lacks love (9–10). John's earlier official letter (not 1 or 2 John) to the church of Gaius was rejected by Diotrephes. He rejects the authority of John and the missionaries (probably the brothers [v. 3]). His motive is personal ambition—preeminence over the congregation (v. 10). Because of this, John will come and remind him of his evil ways: babbling (gossiping) with malicious words; denying hospitality to Christian brothers; preventing others from showing hospitality; expelling some from the church. This lack of love brings Diotrephes' belief into question (vv. 3, 6; 1 John 3:23; 2 John 4–5), since love and truth are inseparable. Both his motive (v. 9) and his deeds (v. 10) are evil.

C. Recommendation of Demetrius: He does good (11–12). John returns to the concepts of verses 5–8 with a command and a principle. Gaius must keep imitating not the evil example of Diotrephes, but the good example of Demetrius (v. 12). The principle is that conduct reflects spiritual standing. Practicing good shows one belongs to (is of the nature of) God. Practicing evil shows one has not seen God in the person of Christ—not in a way that affects one's life (1 John 2:21; 3:10; 4:6–8, 12; John 1:18; 14:9–12). Demetrius, probably the bearer of the letter, has been witnessed to by all Christians, the truth itself, and trustworthy John and his circle (John 15:26–27; 19:35; 21:24). Mention of three witnesses reflects the provisions of Jewish law (Deut. 19:15; 1 John 5:7–8).

III. Peace Should Prevail among Friends (13–15)

John does not desire to communicate many more things by ink and pen. Discretion calls for an urgent personal visit. To his personal wish for Gaius's peace, John adds that of Christian friends. With their greetings they add their authority to John's. He also entreats Gaius to greet loyal friends individually, thus seeking their support in correcting the problem in the church.

SELECT BIBLIOGRAPHY

Boice, J. M. *The Epistles of John.* Grand Rapids: Zondervan, 1979.

Brown, R. E. *The Epistles of John.* Garden City, N.Y.: Doubleday, 1982.

———. *The Community of the Beloved Disciple.* New York: Paulist, 1979.

Bruce, F. F. *The Epistles of John.* Old Tappan, N.J.: Revell, 1970.

Houlden, J. L. *A Commentary on the Johannine Epistles.* New York: Harper & Row, 1974.

Marshall, I. H. *The Epistles of John.* Grand Rapids: Eerdmans, 1978.

Ogilvie, L. J. *When God First Thought of You.* Waco: Word, 1978.

Stott, J. R. W. *The Letters of John.* Rev. ed. Leicester: Inter-Varsity; Grand Rapids: Eerdmans, 1988.

JUDE

William H. Baker

INTRODUCTION

The name *Jude* is actually the usual English translation of the name *Judas,* a traditional way to avoid the stigma of the name of Jesus' betrayer. There are eight men by this name in the New Testament. This Jude is referred to as "a brother of James." Only one James, the half-brother of Jesus and leader of the Jerusalem church, was prominent enough to have been referred to in such an abbreviated manner. Thus Jude was probably a half-brother of Jesus Christ. This Jude, however, is not referred to by ancient church writers.

The date of the Book of Jude depends partly on its relationship to 2 Peter. If 2 Peter was indeed written by Peter, and he indeed uses Jude, then Jude must be dated between A.D. 60 and 65. If Jude uses Peter, the possible dates could be anywhere from A.D. 65 to 80.

Jude addresses his letter to a general audience (v. 4), which suggests that he had several churches in mind. Other than that, no clue or tradition is available as to who they were. We can see from the letter itself and 2 Peter (which has close parallels) that these churches were being influenced by a group of false teachers who were exploitative promoters of unrestrained sexual immorality (v. 4).

Since the days of the early church, the Book of Jude has been criticized for quoting works claiming to be written by a famous man but recognized as forgeries (Assumption of Moses [v. 9]; Book of Enoch [vv. 13–15]), something that delayed its acceptance into the canon of Scripture. Several other New Testament writers come close to the same thing. In 1 Corinthians 10:4, Paul alludes to a Jewish midrash; the writer of Hebrews occasionally seems to be alluding to the works of Philo; and in 2 Timothy 3:8 Paul refers to a piece of Jewish *haggadah* about Jannes and Jambres. The only difference is that none of these just mentioned is pseudonymous.

To quote or allude to a work does not necessarily imply total endorsement. Does the use of these, even as illustrations, imply that the apocryphal stories were mistakenly thought to be true? When Jesus quotes such works as Jonah, evangelicals appeal to his use of it to argue for its historical factuality. Since Jude, we believe, wrote under the inspiration of the Holy Spirit, it may only be consistent to assume the historical factuality of the events to which Jude alludes, or, in the case of his quotation of Enoch, that Enoch actually said it.

Significant theological ideas in the Book of Jude are defense of the truths of the gospel; the necessity of moral purity and humility; and the perseverance of true believers, in spite of pernicious influences.

OUTLINE

I. Salutation (1–2)
II. Reason for Writing (3–4)
III. God's Judgment in the Past (5–7)
IV. Warning Against False Teachers (8–16)
V. A Call to Persevere (17–23)
VI. Doxology (24–25)

COMMENTARY

I. Salutation (1–2)

Jude refers to himself as a "servant," a term of humility and a description of his purpose in life. He identifies himself as a brother of James (probably James the half-brother of Jesus Christ; see Acts 12:17; 15:13; 21:18; 1 Cor. 15:7; Gal. 1:19; 2:9, 12). He addresses his letter to "those who have been called," a reference to their response of faith to the "call" of the gospel and their subsequent salvation.

A typical benediction follows in verse 2. Mercy is God's withholding punishment which believers deserve; peace is the harmonious relationship with God believers enjoy because of justification (Rom. 5:1); love is the ongoing provision of God for believers as his children.

II. Reason for Writing (3–4)

Jude had originally intended to write about "the salvation we share," probably an exposition of Christian truth in whole or in part. But he feels compelled because of a more immediate danger to urge his readers "to contend for the faith." The word *contend* (Gk. *epagōnizomai*) appears only here in the New Testament. It is a word from which we get our English *agonize* and was used in New Testament times of the struggle between wrestlers. The emphasis is upon great effort being expended. Presumably, "contending for the faith" involves recognition of error, clarification of truth, refutation and rebuke of false teachers, and eventual exclusion.

"The faith" to which Jude refers is the body of definable Christian truth known as "the pattern of sound teaching" in the writings of Paul (2 Tim. 1:13). This body of truth was "once for all entrusted to the saints." Christians are not continuously or periodically being given new basic truths, as the false teachers had to claim, especially when their teachings conflicted with the previous teachings of Jesus and the apostles. Even the Book of Revelation contains no additions to the faith in the strict sense. It merely expands upon the doctrine of last things found elsewhere in the Bible.

Jude explains further the reason why he decided to change his subject matter: false teachers have entered the church. The fact that such men are condemned "was written about long ago." It is not clear from the original Greek by whom or where this "writing" is. Literally the Greek reads, "who long ago were written for this judgment." The New International Version is probably correct in implying that this judgment is found in the Old Testament Scriptures, for verses 5–7 illustrate it.

Jude provides a brief summary of the false teachers' teaching at this point. First, they take "grace" as mere forgiveness, leaving believers free to follow the lusts of their fallen nature. Second, they explicitly reject Christ's deity or else live in disobedience to his moral requirements (a de facto denial).

III. God's Judgment in the Past (5–7)

The first example of past judgment comes from the account found in Numbers 14. Some people whom God blessed through his mighty works in the exodus were later destroyed because they did not believe. Since the exodus included a whole nation, among whom were both believers and unbelievers, this implies that the false teachers were unbelievers pretending to be the people of God.

The next example is that of the fallen angels. Some take this as a reference to the "sons of God" (Gen. 6:1–7) who married the "daughters of men," while others relate it to the fall of Satan and certain angels (Isa. 14:12–15; Luke 10:18; Rev. 12:7–9). In either case, they are presently imprisoned in darkness; they will eventually be judged on the "great day." Those who rebel against God are destined for judgment.

The last example, Sodom and Gomorrah, stresses God's judgment on sexual immorality and perversion (lit. lusting after different flesh, probably meaning homosexuality).

IV. Warning Against False Teachers (8–16)

Jude characterizes the false teachers as "dreamers" (v. 8), because they live in a religious world of unreality. He has deliberately selected the three examples of God's judgment in the past because the sins involved are similar—sexual immorality (and possibly also homosexuality) and rejection of authority. The rejection of authority is expressed, Jude now adds, in slander of celestial beings (see 2 Pet. 2:10). It is not clear just what this involved, but Jude illustrates his case using an example from the apocryphal book, The Assumption of Moses, on how "celestial beings"—Satan in this case—should be respected. Like false teachers of all periods of history, they "speak abusively" of things they do not understand. Jude further describes them as understanding only that which animals understand, sensual animal pleasures of instinct. When these passions are unleashed, they go out of control and the dissipations that follow destroy them.

As Jesus did to the Pharisees (see Matt. 23:13–36), Jude pronounces a "woe" (v. 11) upon these heretics. They go the way of Cain—they promote a religion of works without faith (Gen. 4:3–8; Heb. 11:4). They commit Balaam's error—they practice religion for profit (cf. Num. 25:1–9; 31:16; 2 Pet. 2:15). They are like Korah—they reject God-ordained authority (Num. 16:1–4).

Further, Jude says, they are "blemishes at your love feasts" (v. 12). This means that they unashamedly participate in the meals during which believers celebrate the Lord's Supper. They pervert the feast's true meaning and feed only themselves. Jude also calls them "clouds without rain" (cf. 2 Pet. 2:17) which soon pass by, because their teaching promises that which it cannot deliver, namely, freedom. Instead, it leads to slavery to lusts (see 2 Pet. 2:19). Jude describes them as "autumn trees, without fruit." At that time of year the fruit is gone; often, also, some of the trees are uprooted for failing to bear fruit and thus a double disappointment occurs ("twice dead"). Following this, he calls them "wild waves of the sea" (v. 13), restless and unstable. The foaming refers to the mixture of bubbles and scum and serves as a picture of the uselessness of their teaching. Last of all, Jude describes them as "wandering stars"—planets which, due to their unpredictability, offer no guidance in navigation. Thus the false teachers only lead astray spiritually, and, like the planets, are destined for blackness (hell).

Jude next quotes from another apocryphal or pseudepigraphal work (a writing whose author pretends to be someone else), the Book of Enoch, which was highly regarded by both Jews and Christians. The repetition of the term *ungodly* four times stresses rebellious, evil character. Another significant insight into these false teachers is that they complain and criticize. This sort of behavior is a prelude to their substituting in place of the truth the teachings they promote. They also promote their enterprise by boasting about themselves and ingratiating themselves to others by flattery.

V. A Call to Persevere (17–23)

Jude sums up his warning with an exhortation to be faithful. He quotes the apostles (v. 17). This quotation is not found verbatim anywhere in the New Testament or apocryphal literature and must have been preserved orally by believers, unless Jude is quoting the substance of 2 Peter 3:3. "These are the men who divide you" points to the false teachers whom he has just described, and he refers again to their natural instincts (cf. v. 10)—those sensual, physical passions which motivate them. They "do not have the Spirit," whose illuminating work is necessary for anyone to understand the things of God (1 Cor. 2:6–16).

Several exhortations follow which sum up the remedy against the influences of false teaching. First, believers must build themselves up in the faith (knowledge and application of the truth). Second, they must "pray in the Holy Spirit," according to the will of God (Rom. 8:26–27). Third, they are to keep themselves in God's love, which means to maintain a devotional life and to be obedient to the truth. God is ultimately responsible for this security (note v. 24), but believers participate in the process, which will continue until the Lord Jesus Christ brings them ultimately to eternal life.

Those attracted to false teaching should be shown mercy. Effort must be made to recover those taken in by false teaching ("snatch" them). Concerning yet others just coming under the false teachers' influence, Jude repeats the exhortation for mercy. Though they are not fully taken in, that degree of influence must be hated.

VI. Doxology (24–25)

Jude concludes his letter by praising God who is able to keep believers from falling. "Falling" in light of verses 22 and 23 pertains to those who are taken in by the false teachers, not necessarily to the point of losing salvation, since they can be recovered ("snatched from the fire"). If the believer follows the advice of verses 20–21, God can prevent such falling.

In a sort of doxological summary, Jude points out that believers should acknowledge four things about God: glory—perhaps moral excellence; majesty—awesomeness; power—sovereign ability; and authority—supremacy over all creation.

SELECT BIBLIOGRAPHY

Bauckham, R. J. *Jude-2 Peter*. Waco: Word, 1983.
Cranfield, C. E. B. *1 and 2 Peter and Jude*. London: SCM, 1960.
Kelly, J. N. D. *A Commentary on the Epistles of Peter and Jude*. New York: Harper & Row, 1969.
Reicke, B. *The Epistles of James, Peter, and Jude*. Garden City, N.Y.: Doubleday, 1964.

Revelation

The Book of Revelation concludes the writings of the New Testament. It was put at the end because it looks beyond the confines of its own place in history into the future and to what God is yet to accomplish in and for his people. The other New Testament books also have this forward look, but they arise out of a specific context. So the Gospels look backward to Israel and to Jesus as the fulfillment of Israel's hopes. They also look at Jesus' life as he lived it at that time, and the Gospel writers are careful to locate it precisely in the days of Herod or Augustus or Pontius Pilate. The Book of Acts and the Epistles tell us of church life as lived by the early believers in Rome, Greece, or Asia Minor. Sometimes they are so specific that two quarreling individuals are mentioned by name (Phil. 4:2).

The Book of Revelation stands above history as well as in it. The great central vision of chapters 4 and 5 depicts the awesome throne of God as the central focus of the universe. History is important and time flows on, but always as the outworking of the will of the One whose eyes are a flame of fire. God rules above the ages and will accomplish his purposes in this age and in the age to come.

Revelation ends with the extraordinary vision of the New Jerusalem where heaven and earth have become one and where God is all in all. This is the grand future event toward which all creation moves and which concludes the New Testament. A fitting ending indeed, and one that comforts our souls and gives us the courage to go on in our daily lives below.

REVELATION

Walter A. Elwell

INTRODUCTION

The Book of Revelation has puzzled many people throughout the history of the church. This is primarily because it is so different from the other books of the New Testament. When its distinctive features are understood, however, it becomes accessible to the average person in such a way that its value is readily acknowledged. This is not to say that everything will be understood. John and his readers may have been able to unravel his complex use of symbols, but a good bit of it is obscure to us today; however, the main points are not, and that is where we must concentrate.

Five things should be remembered regarding the book itself, if it is to be understood and appreciated correctly. First, it consists of a series of over sixty visions that John had. Visions are notoriously elusive things and are very hard to describe. They may be daytime visions, like John's; night visions, like Jacob's or Daniel's; or dreams, like Joseph's. But they all have a highly complex and symbolic nature that often defies precise description. Think of your own dreams and how hard they are to pin down. John had real visions, however. They were not figments of his imagination, but rather the medium that God used to convey some important truths to the believers of John's day. The Holy Spirit made use of John's visionary powers to produce the Book of Revelation.

Second, the images found in the Book of Revelation arose from John's total experience and were familiar to him and his readers. They might seem strange to us because they are no longer a part of our psychological makeup, but they were quite ordinary at that time. Virtually all of the symbolic representations in Revelation are found in either the Old Testament or the New Testament. Revelation contains about 350 allusions to the Old Testament alone, giving it unity from beginning to end. Most of them are taken from the books of Exodus, Psalms, Ezekiel, Daniel, Isaiah, and Zechariah. Those that are not from the Old Testament or the New Testament can be found in other apocalypses current in John's day. In order to understand these images one must become a part of John's world by studying the documents he used and by immersing oneself in John's way of looking at things. It is there that the explanations of John's symbolism are to be found, not in our own or some other day.

Third, the book is written in apocalyptic, a recognized style of literature. Apocalyptic is visionary, highly symbolic, pictoral, imprecisely organized, redundant, hortatory, and exhortative. It is written to comfort, encourage, strengthen, quiet doubts, and show God to be the ultimate victor over evil. All of these qualities characterize the Book of Revelation.[1] There are other elements as well, such as the letters found in chapters 2 and 3 and the prophetic utterances scattered throughout the book, but the basic genre is apocalyptic. When this is understood it can be treated for what it is and not as though it were something else, such as allegory, parable, or historical narrative.

Fourth, the message of the book is couched in symbolism. One is confronted with multiheaded beasts, scarlet dragons, locust armies, plagues of fire, blood, and hail, fiery horsemen, colossal figures with burning eyes and a sword for a tongue, and dissolving universes. We would be at a loss as to what all this meant were it not for the fact that most of it comes from the Old Testament, so we have a clue as to how to understand it. John was also fond of symbolic numbers, with one-third, three, four, seven, and twelve being favorites. To take one example, John uses the number seven more than fifty times in Revelation. Essentially the number seven indicates completeness, showing that all things are accomplished according to God's plan. God is in complete control and accomplishes everything completely.

Fifth, Revelation is a Christian book written for the believers of John's day by one who knew Christian theology very well. To understand the book one must also know the theology that underlay the faith of the early church.

The author of Revelation calls himself John and tells us that he has been exiled to the island of Patmos for his faith. He is a Christian brother and a companion in the suffering that is being experienced by those to whom he is writing. Attempts have been made to identify John a little more precisely. In the New Testament, the possibilities are as follows: (1) John the Baptist; (2) the son of Zebedee, the apostle; (3) the father of Peter and Andrew; and (4) John Mark. Of these, John the Baptist and the father of Peter and Andrew are most unlikely and cannot be taken seriously. John Mark is possible, but not a serious option. This leaves John the apostle, if we wish to identify the author of Revelation with a "John" who appears in the New Testament. External evidence seems to confirm this. We know that he was in Asia Minor; there are similarities between Revelation and the Gospel of John (assuming that John the apostle wrote that book); the style of Greek in Revelation points to someone whose native language was not Greek; the early church fathers identified the author of Revelation with the apostle. These facts do not prove that the apostle wrote Revelation, but they make it quite likely. If the apostle did not write

1. Paul S. Minear, *New Testament Apocalyptic* (Nashville: Abingdon, 1981); D. S. Russell, *The Method and Message of Jewish Apocalyptic* (Philadelphia: Westminster, 1964).

the book, the person who did was an astute theologian who knew Christian thought very well and was an important leader in the church of Asia Minor.

The traditional view for the date of the composition of Revelation is during the reign of the emperor Domitian (A.D. 81–96). The early church fathers affirmed this and most scholars since then have accepted this. There have been other suggestions that put the book earlier, during Nero's reign (A.D. 54–69), for example, or much later, but they have not been widely held. Domitian's reign fits well with what we find in Revelation. He abused his imperial power by demanding that he be worshiped as a deity and he viciously persecuted the church. There was a great temptation to give in to the demands of Rome because it seemed invincible. To John and the early Christians, however, Rome was the embodiment of Antichrist, if not the final one who was to come, at least its current expression. As such, Rome was anything but permanent because the blasphemies found there ensured its ultimate destruction. God would not give his glory to an emperor of Rome. For those who want precision in such matters, there is a virtual consensus that Revelation was written between A.D. 94 and 96.

The Book of Revelation touches upon most aspects of early Christian thought, and careful study will pay rich dividends to the student. John makes reference to God, Christ, the work of Christ, the Holy Spirit, the second coming, the final judgment, heaven, hell, angels, creation, mankind, sin, Satan, demons, history, prayer, worship, Christian living, the church, prophecy, the Bible, perseverance of the saints, and the profound mystery of God's eternity and its relation to time. It is not possible to go into detail on all of this, so we will highlight a few points.

Central to the book is the existence, power, sovereignty, justice, wisdom, and goodness of God. God is. He is the one who was and is and is to come, the Alpha and the Omega, the Beginning and the Ending. Nothing and no one exists who can rival him. He is the Almighty and he is in control of his universe. He sits upon the throne of glory and thunders forth his unalterable commands that must surely come to pass. When he shows himself, the heavens and the earth flee away in terror, for he alone is the almighty God. He is just and wise in his dealings with his creation. Nothing that happens in Revelation is arbitrary, but rather is based upon the eternal principles of justice, fairness, and wisdom. God is also good. He made the earth for his glory and in the end restores it to its former glory, indeed, to a glory it never dreamed of having. God's goodness extends to the believers in guiding and protecting them from eternal harm and to the evildoers in calling them to repentance.

The Book of Revelation fully acknowledges the many forms of evil that exist in the world. Sin may originate in the evil thoughts of men that issue forth in immorality, murder, greed, lust, idolatry, lying, occult practices, slave trading, theft, cowardice, and abuse of power. Sin may also derive from Satan or his evil angels, who also must be seen for what they are: sworn enemies of God and his people. But sin must also be seen as defeated and doomed to failure. Evil will not win. Although it presently seems so strong and in control, this is only an illusion. Only God rules and evil will go down into the pit to destruction.

The book abounds with references to Christ, who is both closely associated with God and equal to God. Christ is divine, is to be worshiped and praised along with God, rules alongside of him, is the vanquisher of evil, the Savior of the world, the leader of his people, the hope of the oppressed, the arbiter of our destiny, the ruler of history—the Lamb, the Lion, the King of kings. The death of Christ is the world's redemption, the life of Christ on high is the world's protection, the return of Christ is the world's consummation, the thousand-year reign of Christ is the world's benediction, and the New Jerusalem where the Lamb is the light is our eternal habitation.

The believer is the one who ultimately triumphs; he is the "one who overcomes." This is done through the power of Christ at work in his life. Believers' lives are characterized by their righteous deeds, prayer, diligence, perseverance, spiritual discernment, steadfast endurance, maturity, ability to endure affliction, faithfulness, fidelity to Christ, love, faith, service, spiritual growth, submission to God's will, strength, spiritual mindedness, patience, obedience to Christ's commands, courage, and concern for others. They refuse the overtures of evil, resist the Beast and his demands, sometimes suffer martyrdom for their faith, and in all things triumph through the blood of the Lamb.

For the believers a life of eternal glory is promised. They will be without sin, will share in Christ's glory, spend an eternity in loving service to God and Christ, have all their deepest needs met, receive a reward for their good deeds done on earth, and share in the joy of the redeemed community. The unbeliever, along with the Antichrist, the devil, his angels, and all evil, including death and hades, will be thrown into the lake of fire, which is the second death.

The purpose of Revelation is ultimately to explain to the church how God is dealing with the world. Specifically, it is to encourage the believers in a time of intense persecution; to prepare them for what is coming, both in terms of evil and the power of God to see them through it; to comfort them with the hope of heaven; to provide guidance for their daily lives; to teach them how Christian theology relates to their most pressing needs; to assure them of God's victory over Satan, the Antichrist, and evil; and to give them a vision of God and his reality. A fundamental theme that runs through Revelation is that life and history can be observed from two points of view. We may look at the problems, persecution, sufferings, evil, and distress that surround us and become discouraged; or we may look beyond that to the glorious eternal realities that also surround us—God, Christ, the saints of old, the angels, the throne of God, the music, color, sound, and beauty of heaven, the New Jerusalem with its streets of gold, and the victory already won. The choice is ours; both perspectives are true. John wants us to make the right choice, because the former is doomed to destruction and the latter is eternally in place. We must hold fast for only a short time, then it will all be ours, as it indeed already is.

It would not be possible in a short introduction such as this to summarize the many interpretive views in the history of the interpretation of the Book of Revelation. Even to classify the groupings of views would take many pages. However, recognizing the limitations imposed on such a task, we may still look at a few of the major options.

First, some views see Revelation as a book written only for John's day. These views look for explanations of the symbols in events and persons whom John knew, or knew about, and do not look beyond that time to a future period. That the visions have value for future readers is readily acknowledged, just as we may read of Jacob's vision of the ladder and profit by it, but Revelation no more refers to them *directly* than does Jacob's ladder.

Second, other views see in the book the history of the church throughout the ages. Here, John's day is also described, since John is part of church history, but all the future ages are included as well. Accordingly, events such as persecution, or individuals such as Antichrist, whenever or wherever they occur, are referred to by John's symbols. Some who hold this view see a progression in church history leading to a final climax when all the symbols will be fulfilled in one catastrophic period just prior to Christ's return. Others do not, preferring to see the unfolding of the church's history as all there is.

Third, a relatively recent view is that of dispensationalism, which arose in the nineteenth century. There are variations in it, but basically it sees something of an outline of church history only in the letters to the seven churches, with Ephesus being the church of John's day, going on to Laodicea, being the church of today. This view postulates a secret return of Christ for his church which takes place somewhere at the beginning of chapter 4, usually in verse 1. Consequently, the church is exempted from everything that takes place from chapters 4 to 19. At that point Christ and his church return to destroy the Antichrist and set up a millennial (thousand-year) kingdom on earth. Chapters 4–19 describe the "great tribulation" which lasts for seven years, although various opinions are held on the precise length of time. So, the Book of Revelation is not for the church per se, but it can still be read with profit to see what God will do for the Jewish believers who live during the future great tribulation. The church is to look for its "rapture," that is, its removal from earth, which may happen at any moment.

Fourth, still other views see the book as wholly symbolic and not referring to anything very specific. These views stress the visionary nature of John's experiences and contend that just as poetry can be used to convey truth, so can apocalyptic. Essentially, Revelation symbolizes the defeat of evil by good, or the overthrow of evil by God. Seen in this way, the book is a comfort to anyone who wants to read it, except, of course, those who choose to do evil.

All of these views have something to commend them. Certainly, the book refers to John's day and must be understood in that light; equally certainly, it can refer to any period in the history of the church. But it is also true that it has a predictive element that looks to the future, and no one can deny that its symbols are descriptive of great and timeless theological truths. One should be open to the value that exists in them all.

The view taken here is basically eclectic. The commentary attempts to see the truth that is in the symbols John used and to understand them as arising out of that historical context, although such truth is also available to Christians of all ages. It also affirms that some things in Revelation await fulfillment, specifically intense persecution prior to Christ's return, his personal return, the establishment of a millennial kingdom, a final judgment, and a new heaven and a new earth.

This is perhaps a good note on which to end, for all the views agree that when historical time ends, we shall forever be with the Lord. With that ultimate prospect before us, let us be content.

OUTLINE

I. Introductory Vision (1:1–20)
  A. Thematic Introduction and Greeting (1:1–8)
  B. Vision of Christ as Divine (1:9–16)
  C. An Abbreviated Explanation of the Vision (1:17–20)
II. Letters to the Seven Asian Churches (2:1–3:22)
  A. Letter to the Church at Ephesus (2:1–7)
  B. Letter to the Church at Smyrna (2:8–11)
  C. Letter to the Church at Pergamum (2:12–17)
  D. Letter to the Church at Thyatira (2:18–29)
  E. Letter to the Church at Sardis (3:1–6)
  F. Letter to the Church at Philadelphia (3:7–13)
  G. Letter to the Church at Laodicea (3:14–22)
III. Vision of God on His Throne (4:1–5:14)
  A. Vision of God (4:1–6a)
  B. Four Living Creatures (4:6b–11)
  C. Scroll of Destiny (5:1–5)
  D. Christ as Triumphant Lamb (5:6–10)
  E. Universal Adoration of God (5:11–14)
IV. Opening of the Seals on Destiny's Scroll (6:1–17)
  A. First Seal Opened (6:1–2)
  B. Second Seal Opened (6:3–4)
  C. Third Seal Opened (6:5–6)
  D. Fourth Seal Opened (6:7–8)
  E. Fifth Seal Opened (6:9–11)
  F. Sixth Seal Opened (6:12–17)
V. Interlude before the Seventh Seal (7:1–17)
  A. Sealing of the 144,000 of Israel (7:1–8)
  B. Vision of the Redeemed Multitude of the Earth (7:9–11)
  C. Explanation of the Multitude (7:12–17)
VI. The Seventh Seal and the Seven Trumpets (8:1–9:21)

A. Opening of the Seventh Seal and the Vision of the Censer (8:1–5)
B. Blowing of the First Four Trumpets (8:6–13)
C. Blowing of the Fifth Trumpet (9:1–12)
D. Blowing of the Sixth Trumpet (9:13–21)

VII. Interlude and the Seventh Trumpet (10:1–11:19)
A. Vision of the Mighty Angel and the Scroll (10:1–11)
B. Vision of the Two Witnesses (11:1–14)
C. Blowing of the Seventh Trumpet (11:15–19)

VIII. The Cosmic Conflict of Good and Evil (12:1–13:1a)
A. The Woman Clothed with the Sun (12:1–6)
B. War in Heaven (12:7–12)
C. Spiritual Warfare on Earth (12:13–13:1a)

IX. The Beasts, the Believers, and the Judgment of Earth (13:1b–14:20)
A. The Beast from the Sea (13:1b–10)
B. The Beast from the Earth (13:11–18)
C. The Lamb and the 144,000 (14:1–5)
D. The Announcements of the Three Flying Angels (14:6–13)
E. The Reaping of the Earth in Judgment (14:14–20)

X. The Seven Last Bowls of the Wrath of God (15:1–16:21)
A. The Song of Moses and the Lamb (15:1–4)
B. The Seven Angels with the Seven Last Plagues (15:5–8)
C. Pouring out of the Seven Bowls of the Wrath of God (16:1–21)

XI. The Fall of Rome Predicted (17:1–18:24)
A. Destruction of the Woman on the Beast (17:1–18)
B. Fall of Babylon the Great (18:1–24)

XII. The Return of Christ in Glory (19:1–21)
A. The Multitude of Heaven Rejoices (19:1–10)
B. Destruction of Evil by the Rider on the White Horse (19:11–21)

XIII. The Millennial Reign of Christ (20:1–15)
A. The Thousand-Year Reign (20:1–6)
B. Satan's Doom (20:7–10)
C. The Judgment at the Great White Throne (20:11–15)

XIV. The Eternal New Order (21:1–22:6)
A. The New Heaven and the New Earth (21:1–8)
B. The New Jerusalem, the Wife of the Lamb (21:9–27)
C. The River and the Tree of Life (22:1–6)

XV. The Promise of Jesus' Return (22:7–21)

COMMENTARY

I. Introductory Vision (1:1–20)

A. Thematic introduction and greeting (1:1–8). John begins his extraordinary book by pointing out that what follows is not his own invention, but a revelation from God about Christ to be given to God's servants by Christ. John was to make known what he saw (1:2) because therein God was making known what would be taking place very soon. This point is reemphasized in 1:19. The revelation has certainty because it is nothing less than the word of God and the testimony of Jesus Christ (1:2; see also 19:9; 21:5; 22:6). A special blessing is pronounced on the one who reads the words of this book (perhaps the preacher before his congregation) as well as the ones who hear and follow what they hear (1:3; see also 22:18–19). The form of this blessing parallels the Beatitudes (Matt. 5:3–11) and such blessings are repeated throughout the book (Rev. 14:13; 16:15; 19:9; 20:6; 22:7, 14).

The seven churches in the province of Asia (1:4) are listed (1:11) in a sequential order starting with Ephesus, going northwards and circling east, then south, ending with Laodicea. This is probably the order in which an itinerant preacher traveled.

Verses 4–5 are a standard New Testament greeting (see Gal. 1:5; 2 Thess. 1:2; 1 Tim. 1:2) that emphasizes the Trinity: Father, Spirit, Son, with the latter two inverted so that John's doxology (1:5b, 6) can be directed to the Son. The eternality of the Father is stressed by referring to him as encompassing past, present, and future. God is the one who governs all of time and eternity. The Spirit is symbolized as seven, reminiscent of the sevenfold ministry mentioned in Isaiah 11:2 (wisdom, understanding, counsel, power, knowledge, fear of the Lord, delight). The Spirit is "before his throne" (Rev. 1:4) to emphasize his proximity to deity. This symbolism is continued in 3:1; in 4:5, where the seven burning lamps before the throne are the seven spirits; and in 5:6, where the seven eyes of the Lamb are the Spirit, but further defined as having been sent out into all the earth. The death ("faithful witness"), resurrection ("firstborn from the dead"), and present rule ("ruler") of Jesus are highlighted in the last part of the trinitarian greeting (1:5).

In verses 5b–7 Jesus is singled out for praise, extolling his redemptive love, which expressed itself in his death (see Rom. 5:6; Gal. 2:20). This gives a clue to the Christian readers as to what they might expect. If God the Son shed his blood, might not they shed theirs? The believers constituted a kingdom and a priesthood to serve God. The type of rule (kingdom) and intercession (priesthood) by which the believers are to serve God are defined by the example of Christ who died. "Glory and power" (v. 6) are ascribed to Christ in the first of several doxologies (4:11; 5:12–13; 7:12; 11:17–18). Such expressions in the Scriptures are reserved for God alone. That the Son shares glory points to the essential deity of the Son. John concludes his reference to the Son by pointing to his coming again, pulling together references from Daniel 7:13 and Zechariah 12:10. Here "every eye will see him" (Rev. 1:7), rather than being limited to Israel as in Zechariah's vision. They mourn either because they foresee their coming judgment, or because they see the error of their ways and shed tears of remorse.

God, who is both the beginning and end (the first and last letters of the Greek alphabet emphasize this), ratifies that all of which John speaks will come true (v. 8). The same affirmation occurs again in 21:5–6. Jesus calls himself the Alpha and Omega as he promises his return to earth again (22:12–13).

B. Vision of Christ as divine (1:9–16). John was on the island of Patmos, no doubt an exile suffering for his witness to Christ. He was enduring hardship (v. 9) just as the members of the seven churches were enduring the hardships that John would shortly be describing in chapters 2 and 3. It was on a Sunday, perhaps during a period of worship, that John fell into a Spirit-induced ecstatic state (vv. 10–11; see also 4:2; 17:3; 21:10) and heard a trumpetlike voice that commanded him to write what he saw and send it to the seven churches of Asia (Minor). Upon turning to the voice, John saw seven golden lampstands and a human form towering above them, described in terms drawn from familiar Old Testament visions (Dan. 7:9–14; 10:4–6; Ezek. 43:2). What is significant about the description John gave of the figure is that in Daniel *two* beings are present—the Ancient of Days and the Son of man—but John blends them together into *one* figure. The Son of man and the Ancient of Days are one Being. In John's later visions he never described God as he is in himself, but did describe the Son (as here) in such a way that the Son is the outward expression of the hidden God. A similar idea is found in the prologue to John's Gospel (1:1) where the Word is with God and is God. The figure John saw was dazzling in his appearance—with his robe, golden sash, fiery eyes, burning bronze feet, flashing sword as tongue, thunderous voice, and incandescent visage. In the figure's right hand are seven stars. No doubt the extraordinary luminescence of the figure made the light of the seven candlesticks and seven stars seem dim by comparison.

C. An abbreviated explanation of the vision (1:17–20). John had seen nothing less than God himself as revealed in the person of Jesus Christ. It is no wonder that he "fell at his feet as though dead" (v. 17). The divine Christ calms John's fears with a touch of his right hand, describing himself as the ruler of human destiny, holding "the keys of death and hades" (v. 18). In describing himself as "the First and the Last" (v. 17), Christ is drawing upon Old Testament depictions of God (Isa. 41:4; 44:6; 48:12; see also Rev. 21:5 where God speaks, and 22:13 where Christ speaks again).

Verse 20 gives an explanation of the seven stars and lampstands. The seven stars are the rulers of the seven churches of Asia, either human or supernatural, and the seven lampstands are the seven churches themselves. The comfort that believers may take from this explanation is that Christ stands ("walks," 2:1) among his people, and the rulers of the churches are in his hand (2:1; 3:1). God is never far from his beleaguered and persecuted people.

II. Letters to the Seven Asian Churches (2:1–3:22)

A. Letter to the church at Ephesus (2:1–7). Each of the letters is addressed to the leader of the church, who is called an angel for some uncertain reason. In each letter a different aspect of John's vision of Christ is utilized, sometimes with a slight variation, as here, where Christ "holds" the stars and "walks" among the candlesticks, emphasizing Christ's intimate involvement in the life of his churches.

The Ephesian believers are praised for their good works, their unwearied labor, their steadfastness under persecution, their refusal to accredit false apostles, their rejection of evildoers and, in particular, their rejection of the disreputable practices of the Nicolaitans. Little is known about this group except that they were active in Ephesus and Thyatira (2:15) and that they encouraged immorality and the eating of meat sacrificed to idols. Some early church fathers say the group was founded by a man named Nicholas (hence, Nicolaitans) but this is not certain.

In spite of the good deeds of the Ephesians, they fell short with respect to love (2:4). All of their zealous activity could not make up for this fundamental lack: without love all our efforts are vain (1 Cor. 13:1–3).

The promises made at the end of each letter are to the one who triumphs (v. 7; 2:11, 17, 26; 3:5, 12, 21). Here in 2:7 the believer may eat freely from the tree of life in God's paradise. Victory is an important theme throughout the Book of Revelation. Since Christ triumphed over sin and death, we too shall triumph in the end, no matter how difficult things might be at the moment.

B. Letter to the church at Smyrna (2:8–11). To the church at Smyrna the risen Christ says, "I know . . ." (2:8–9). It is both a comfort and a warning that Christ knows all about us. The Smyrnean believers were to experience a period of brief but intense persecution (2:10). Some would be cast into prison, some would be harassed, some would suffer martyrdom, but they are not to be afraid. The devil might be against them, along with the people through whom he works, but God rules over all. This kind of suffering characterized the church for several centuries, and the promise of a crown of life to those who endured to the end was held on to by the persecuted believers. In commenting on these verses, the church father Cyprian said, "Although I know, dearest brethren, that you have frequently been admonished in my letters to manifest all care for those who with a glorious voice have confessed the Lord, and are confined in prison; yet again and again, I urge it upon you, that no consideration be wanting to them to whose glory there is nothing wanting. . . . They have persevered in their faithfulness, and steadfastness, and invincibleness, even unto death. When to the willingness and the confession of the name in prison and chains is added also the conclusion of dying, the glory of the martyr is consummated." Such was the common lot of many early believers. The crown of life (2:10) was frequently taken to be a martyr's special reward. It is interesting to note that Smyrna is the only church about which nothing negative is said.

C. Letter to the church at Pergamum (2:12–17). Pergamum (2:12) was one of the great cities of antiquity, boasting a library comparable to that of Alexandria and containing more than a million volumes. It was also a center of government and worship, with fabulous temples and worship complexes dedicated to Rome, Augustus, Zeus, Athena, Asklepios, and Dionysus. Because of the intensely pagan nature of the city John described it not as a tourist attraction, but as a center of satanic activity. This activity resulted in the death of Antipas (otherwise unknown) and the pollution of the church with teaching reminiscent of what happened in Balaam's day, which included ritual eating of meat sacrificed to idols and fornication (see Num. 25:1–3). The Nicolaitans were also active at Pergamum (Rev. 2:15) and Ephesus (2:6).

The metaphor *hidden manna* (2:17) is variously interpreted as the manna in the ark of the covenant, which tradition said was hidden by Jeremiah, or the eucharistic ceremony of the church. That it provides strength to meet our present struggles is agreed upon by all. The new name on the white stone is that of being a Christian, for whom everything was made new (new covenant [Luke 22:20; 1 Cor. 2:25; 2 Cor. 3:6; Heb. 8:8]; new commandment [John 13:34; 1 John 2:8]; new creature [2 Cor. 5:17; Gal. 6:15]; new man [Eph. 2:15; 4:24]; new heavens and a new earth [2 Pet. 3:13; Rev. 21:1]; New Jersualem [Rev. 3:12; 21:2]; all things new [2 Cor. 5:17; Rev. 21:5]). In antiquity a white stone was used as an entrance ticket, or voting piece. Here it guarantees us entrance into God's kingdom and blessing.

D. Letter to the church at Thyatira (2:18–29). Thyatira was a border city with a large military garrison, hence the strong military metaphors—Christ's eyes like "a blazing fire" (2:18); "authority over the nations" (2:26); "iron scepter" (2:27); "dash them to pieces like pottery" (2:27).

The church at Thyatira allowed itself to be deceived by a prophetess who was called (or called herself) Jezebel, bringing to mind the great conflicts of Elijah's day (1 Kings 16; 2 Kings 9). She and her followers advocated radical paganism and were warned by God to repent. If they did not, judgment awaited them, as well as those who wanted to pry into "Satan's so-called deep secrets," that is, occult practices (2:24), which were a particular temptation in antiquity and condemned by the New Testament (Gal. 5:20; Rev. 21:8; 22:15). God who knows the depths of our hearts and minds (2:23) will treat everyone with care and fairness, and the victorious believer will rule with Christ (2:26, 28).

E. Letter to the church at Sardis (3:1–6). Christ is described as the one who dispenses the Spirit of God and holds the rulers of the churches in his hand, just as he rules over the kings of the earth (1:5). In spite of the Spirit's work and Christ's protection, the church at Sardis was almost dead. Its members appeared to have life, but in reality they had almost forgotten who they were. They were counseled to go back to the beginning, review what they had learned, strengthen what little there was, repent of their errors, and hold fast what was good (3:2–3). They were especially to "wake up!" (3:2), a reminder that would be familiar to them, as the city prided itself on its invincibility, although it had fallen more than once through failure to guard itself properly.

In 3:4–5 the color white is mentioned twice, symbolizing purity and acceptance before God. This is a common metaphor in the Book of Revelation (3:18; 4:4; 6:11; 7:9, 13; 19:14). Those who overcome will be acknowledged before God and his holy angels (3:5; see also Matt. 10:32; Luke 12:8) and may be assured of participation in the kingdom: "I will not blot out his name from the book of life" (3:5). The metaphor of God's book in which are written the names of God's people is found frequently in the Bible (Exod. 32:32–33; Ps. 69:28; Dan. 12:1; Phil. 4:3; Rev. 13:8; 17:8; 20:12, 15; 21:27). Interestingly, God's book of life becomes the Lamb's book of life in Revelation.

F. Letter to the church at Philadelphia (3:7–13). In verse 7 Christ is described as the one who is holy and true (both designations of God elsewhere [1 John 2:20; 5:20]) whose words are likewise true (Rev. 19:9; 21:5; 22:6).

Isaiah saw David's key, symbolizing control of Jerusalem (v. 12), given to Eliakim (Isa. 22:22); John saw David's greater Son hold the key to the New Jerusalem, to shut and open as he will, symbolizing entrance into salvation and ministry. Philadelphia had a door of service open before it, yet little strength (Rev. 3:8).

As at Smyrna (2:9), the chief opposition was from obdurate Jews, who had turned the true worship of God into idolatry. They are liars because they deny that Jesus is the Messiah, but someday they will be made to acknowledge this and the love Christ has for his own. Why there should be such bitter resentment at Christ's love for his church is hard to fathom.

As at Smyrna (2:10), the renegade Jews are going to stir up a persecution of the believers. At Smyrna it was relatively short (ten days) but intense; here it will be more severe and far-reaching. However, the believers will be protected from its worst effects (Luke 21:12–19; 2 Pet. 2:9; Rev. 9:3–4; 12:13–16; 18:4–5).

Intense persecution will herald the return of Christ (Matt. 24:21–25; 29–31; Mark 13:19, 24–27; Luke 21:20–28), who promises speedy delivery (Rev. 22:7, 12, 20). To the one who triumphs goes eternal life with God, here symbolized as being part of God's temple (3:12). That the New Jerusalem has no temple (21:22) does not contradict this. There the Lord God Almighty and the Lamb are the temple and the believer is one with them, just as the believer is part of the building here. Paul also uses metaphors like this (1 Cor. 3:9; Eph. 2:19–22). So intimately associated is the believer with God that not only is he part of the temple, but he has God's name, the city of God's name, and Jesus' new name written on him (Rev. 3:12). This is the believer's security (see also 7:3; 9:4; 14:1; 22:4). John later saw a series of visions dealing with the New Jerusalem as the bride of the Lamb (19:7–9; 21:1–4, 9–27).

G. Letter to the church at Laodicea (3:14–22). In verse 14 Jesus describes himself as the Amen (the final word), the faithful and true witness (John 18:37; Rev. 1:5), and ruler of God's creation (John 1:3; Col. 1:15–18; Heb. 1:3). That God and Christ rule the whole of creation is important in Revelation to correct any false impression that evil is in control and might win in the end. It will not (see 5:11–13; 20:10, 14).

"I know your deeds" (3:15) are ominous words. For Ephesus (2:2) and Thyatira (2:19) this knowledge was to their advantage. For Laodicea all their misery is laid bare. They are lukewarm (3:15), proud ("I am rich," v. 17), arrogant ("I do not need a thing," v. 17), "wretched, pitiful, poor, blind and naked" (v. 17). This was hardly how they viewed themselves, but God's evaluation is not the same as ours. He is not impressed by our money, fine clothes, or status. To him all of that masks a vast spiritual misery that is so profound as to make God wish to spit them out of his mouth (v. 16).

Laodicea was known for its fine products and medicines, but Christ counsels the church to purchase articles of true worth from him (3:18). Gold symbolizes what is of true value (Matt. 6:19–21; 1 Pet. 1:7; Rev. 21:21); white clothes symbolize acceptance before God and righteousness (Rev. 2:4; 4:4; 6:11; 7:9, 13–14; 19:7–8, 14); the eye salve symbolizes spiritual sight.

Verse 19 contains hard words, perhaps, but such discipline is a blessing from God, coming as it does from his love (Deut. 8:5; Prov. 3:11, 12; 1 Cor. 11:32; Heb. 12:5–11). Verse 20 is a tragic picture—Christ must humbly seek entrance into the church he purchased with his own blood. Even though the church as a whole might be indifferent to him, individuals may respond and experience intimate fellowship with him, pictured here as a meal. Christ shares a meal with us on earth; we will share a meal with him in glory as his invited guests (19:7–9; see also Luke 22:30).

The promise of royal glory is given to those who triumph. Those who stand firm to the end will be saved (Matt. 24:13); those who stand by Christ in his trials will receive the kingdom (Luke 22:28–30); those who suffer with Christ will reign with him (2 Tim. 2:12; 1 Pet. 4:13); those who triumph will rule with Christ during the millennium (Rev. 20:4–6). Sitting on Christ's throne along with him symbolizes this regal splendor.

As with all the churches (2:7, 11, 17, 29; 3:6, 13), so here, the risen Christ admonishes the reader to pay close attention, using words from the Gospels (Matt. 11:15; 13:9, 43; Mark 4:23; Luke 14:35), which will be used later in Revelation 13:9. We should heed what the Holy Spirit says because the Spirit will teach us everything we need to know (John 14:15–18, 25), and will exercise his sevenfold ministry as promised by Isaiah (11:2).

III. Vision of God on His Throne (4:1–5:14)

A. Vision of God (4:1–6a). Throughout Revelation John commonly signals a shift in vision or focus within a vision by using the phrase *after this* (4:1) or similar words (e.g., 7:1, 9; 15:5; 18:1; 19:1). Here John is shifting from the vision of the risen Christ who walks among his churches and holds the leaders in his hand (1:12–16) and the messages that Christ had for those churches, to God himself. John saw his first vision while yet on earth where he fell before Christ's feet (1:17). In this vision John sees "a door standing open in heaven" (4:1). Because the church is on earth, John saw Christ, as ruler of the church and embodiment of God, there, but God the Father's proper place is in heaven. Jesus emphasized this by consistently referring to God as the "heavenly Father" or the "Father who is in heaven" (Matt. 5:48; 6:1, 9, 14, 26, 32, 33; 15:13; 16:17; etc.). Heaven is the dwelling-place of God.

A trumpetlike voice announced the first vision that John had (1:10) and apparently the same voice pealed forth again (4:1). The source of that voice is not identified, but it is most certainly the voice of God. John is summoned up to heaven to see "what must take place after this" (4:1). This whole scene is reminiscent of Moses' experience on Mount Sinai (Exod. 19:16–20), where God called Moses into his presence on the mountain amidst the thunder, lightning, and trumpet blast.

As before (Rev. 1:10) John is overpowered by the Holy Spirit and in that state is allowed to see spiritual, heavenly realities (4:2). It was not uncommon for prophets to speak similarly when delivering their prophetic message (Isa. 61:1; Ezek. 2:2; 3:24). The Spirit mediates God's words to men and prepares them to receive God's message; hence it is the Spirit who speaks to the churches, even though the risen Christ spoke (Rev. 2:7, 11, 17, 29; 3:6, 13, 22). The Spirit led John up to heaven just as Ezekiel (Ezek. 3:12, 14; 8:3) and Philip (Acts 8:29, 39) were lifted up by the Spirit.

In numerous places the Old Testament depicts God as seated on a throne (1 Kings 22:19; 2 Chron. 18:18; Ps. 47:8; Isa. 6:1; Ezek. 1:26–27). This is an understandable figure of speech because God is the sovereign ruler over all creation. Revelation frequently uses this metaphor (Rev. 4:9; 5:1, 7, 13; 6:16; 7:10, 15; 19:4; 21:5). John never details what the one seated on the throne looks like, but simply names him as God and paints a graphic picture of the visual and auditory impression made upon him.

In the following verses John gropes to express what he saw. The jasper stone was translucent or clear, the carnelian was blood red, the rainbow was green, and the lightning flashes were yellow-white (Rev. 4:3, 5). These dazzling colors, accompanied by the crashing thunder and cacophony of voices, must have been an overwhelming spectacle. The colors are usually taken to be symbolic descriptions of the attributes of God with white representing purity or holiness; red, judgment; and the emerald rainbow, mercy. So the visual statement says the God who sits on his throne ruling the universe is a God of holiness, justice, and mercy. The events to be described later in Revelation bear this out.

The elders wear white robes (4:4), symbolizing purity and acceptance in the presence of God (3:4, 5, 18; 6:11; 7:9; 19:14), and golden crowns, symbolizing their right to rule; harps and golden censers full of incense (5:8) represent the worship and prayers of the saints. Some scholars interpret the elders to be angelic beings, but more likely, they are representatives of all the redeemed of the earth. They are seen in constant praise and adoration of God. The seven blazing lamps (4:5) are the seven spirits that John mentioned in 1:4. The crystal sea (4:6) provided a mirrorlike reflection of the heavenly scene, adding immeasurably to its splendor. In Ezekiel's vision of the throne in heaven the crystal expanse was above the heavenly scene (Ezek. 1:22).

B. Four living creatures (4:6b–11). The creatures in 4:6 strike the modern reader as exotic in the extreme, but in John's day such images were not uncommon. John drew his description from two well-known passages in the Old Testament (Isa. 6:1–2; Ezek. 1:4–21). John's description relies more heavily on Ezekiel's vision, but lacks mention of the wheels found there and has four single creatures rather than Ezekiel's four-sided creatures. John's creatures have the six wings of Isaiah's vision rather than the four wings of Ezekiel's description. The four creatures in Revelation have the appearance of a lion, an ox, a man, and an eagle. They are covered with eyes (see also Ezek. 1:18), symbolizing their vast knowledge of all things, and they never cease ("day and night") giving praise to God in words similar to those in Isaiah 6:3. The creatures are usually understood to be supernatural beings of some angelic sort, but occasionally a commentator will see them as personifications of the attributes of God himself. In this case, they would represent the omniscience and holiness of God.

C. Scroll of destiny (5:1–5). The transcendent vision of God on his glorious throne, surrounded by representatives of redeemed humanity (the twenty-four elders) and the supernatural order (the four living creatures) now fades somewhat, and as John refocuses he centers on the right hand of the one seated on the throne and the scroll it is holding (5:1). It was sealed with seven seals and no one was found in all of the created order worthy of opening the scroll (vv. 2–3). Because the scroll represented the will of God and only one equal to God could reveal its contents, no one qualified. In the Old Testament both Ezekiel (2:9–10) and Isaiah (29:11–12) experienced their prophetic vision as a scroll, in Ezekiel's case, to be eaten (i.e., lived through) and in Isaiah's case, sealed up. The imagery of divine scrolls in the Old Testament is of two sorts, cosmic/historical and personal. The passages in Isaiah and Ezekiel show the destiny of nations, and that is apparently what John sees when the scroll is in the right hand of God. The personal dimension is expressed in Psalm 139, where God is the one who has searched us, known us, loved us, and guided us. While we were yet unborn "all the days ordained for [us] were written in your book before one of them came to be" (Ps. 139:16). Here the scroll contains God's intimate knowlege of us. The Lamb's book of life will be opened later (Rev. 20:15) and those found there will be safe from eternal fire. So the scrolls cover the destiny of nations and persons individually.

John was distressed that no one could reveal the destiny of the nations, so he wept (5:5). An elder quieted his distress by announcing the arrival of one equal to the task, the long-promised conquering Messiah of the Old Testament. The Lion of Judah/Root of David can open the book! These two images were well known in John's day, being taken from the two major divisions of the Old Testament, the Law (Gen. 49:9–10, the Lion of Judah) and the Prophets (Isa. 11:1, 10, the Root of David), and as such, summed up the teaching of the Old Testament on the Messiah. He would come now to rule with the strength of a lion and the power of a king.

D. Christ as triumphant Lamb (5:6–10). John was told to expect a royal lion with fierce strength worthy to stand next to God as his equal and take the scroll of destiny to unroll it. When he looks, he sees a lamb, and a slain one, at that (5:6). Contained in this magnificent tour de force is the heart of the Christian perception of reality and of the gospel message. To triumph means to give oneself on behalf of others. God himself is like that. Jesus the Son of God became the slain Lamb of God to become the conquering lion of David's line. To suffer and die is the way to win. The road to royal enthronement is by way of the cross.

In the complex image in 5:6 John is drawing on an earlier vision found in Zechariah 4:1–14. Zechariah's vision concerned the proper way to accomplish God's will on earth, saying it must be done not by human might or power but by the Spirit of God (Zech. 4:6). Two olive trees provide oil for a central bowl from which come seven channels that go to seven burning lamps. Zechariah says, "These seven are the eyes of the LORD, which range throughout the earth" (Zech. 4:10). In John's vision the seven eyes of God become the seven eyes of the Lamb, representing the ministry of the Holy Spirit in the world. It is of significance that God and Christ (the Lamb) are identified in this way. The Holy Spirit is sent from God and Christ. The seven horns represent either political or priestly rule. In the Book of Daniel horns represent political rule (Dan. 7:7–8, 15–27; 8:3–25) and John picks up on this in describing the evil kingdoms of this world (Rev. 12:3; 13:1; 17:3, 7, 12, 16). Horns are also part of Old Testament altars and John actually hears a voice come from the horns of the golden altar that is before the Lord, commanding the sixth angel with a trumpet (9:13–14). The seven horns on the Lamb could thus be in contrast to the ten horns of the various beasts, emphasizing the difference of rule that is exercised. The kingdoms of this world rule with iron teeth crushing the life out of the people; the kingdom of God rules with service, prayer, and self-sacrifice. When the Lamb rightfully took the scroll to reveal its contents, the creatures and the elders fell before the Lamb to worship (Rev. 5:8). This parallels the falling before the throne to worship God in the vision just preceding (4:10). Because incense was burned in the temple of old it provided the image for the fragrance of heaven (5:8). The psalmist prayed, "May my prayer be set before you like incense; may the lifting up of my hands be like the evening sacrifice" (Ps. 141:2). In the presence of God, the prayers of his people fill the heavenly courts with a blessed aroma, treasured by him and providing the atmosphere in which worship takes place and the will of God is accomplished.

In the Old Testament there is a constant reminder to sing a new song to the Lord because of all that he has done (Pss. 33:3; 96:1; 98:1; 149:1; Isa. 42:10; see also Pss. 40:3; 144:9). In Revelation 5:9–10 the words of the new song are given and it is a song of redemption and deliverance. The Lamb has redeemed humankind, from every tribe and language and people and nation, making them a kingdom (a place where God rules supreme) and priests (5:10; see also 1:6). It is the blood of the Lamb that purchased God's people (1 Pet. 1:18–19) and qualified the Lamb to open the scroll of destiny. The people of God are promised a future reign on earth (5:10), a topic taken up again in 20:1–3.

E. Universal adoration of God (5:11–14). In one of Daniel's night visions he saw God as the Ancient of Days seated upon a throne with a river of fire flowing out before him. Books were opened and "thousands upon thousands attended him; ten thousand times ten thousand stood before him" (Dan. 7:10). It was typical also during the intertestamental period (ca. 432 B.C.–A.D. 70) to describe God as surrounded by innumerable angels.

All the inhabitants of heaven—the countless angels, the twenty-four elders, and the four living creatures—break forth in thunderous praise of Christ the Lamb (5:12). In the vision John had just heard the four living creatures and the twenty-four elders sing two different doxologies, both to God the almighty Creator (4:8, 11). Here combined praise is offered to God the Redeemer. It is as slain that the Lamb receives the sevenfold adulation (power, wealth, wisdom, strength, honor, glory, and praise).

The entire created order now joins in the mighty chorus—everything in heaven, on earth, under the earth, and in the sea—in adoration of both God and the Lamb together (5:13). The concluding doxology of chapter 4 praised God as Creator and Sustainer of all things that were made. Now all creation responds with thanks to him in a glorious picture, reminiscent of Psalm 148. After this series of heavenly visions, the scene will shift to the devastations on earth. Before that happens it is therefore significant that all of creation is seen as willed by God, made by God, ruled by God, and praised by God. This is John's way of telling us that the ideal world, the world as it really is and will yet be, should never be forgotten, though our visions of glory fade and earthly chaos threatens to overwhelm us. God is still on his throne, and his created order, though now in rebellion against him, is still subject to him and in some inexplicable way doing his will, and thus offering praise to him.

IV. Opening of the Seals on Destiny's Scroll (6:1–17)

After the thunderous climax of the visions centering around God on his throne, John now sees the opening of the scroll that contains the destiny of mankind, or the unfolding of human history. The Lamb is now central in this series of visions, and for the opening of the first four seals the action follows a set pattern. After the Lamb opens a seal, one of the four living creatures bellows "Come!" and a horseman comes thundering out of heaven. The fifth seal reveals God's martyrs, awaiting their final redemption, and the sixth seal shows the end of the age as the dreaded day of the Lord arrives. The seventh seal is opened (8:1) after a brief interlude.

A. First seal opened (6:1–2). The first rider appeared on a white horse, holding a bow, wearing a crown, and going forth to conquer the world. There are basically two interpretations of this vision. First, the rider is interpreted as one of God's avenging agents, sent to devastate the earth, as are the other three riders. This would make Zechariah's two visions about horsemen the background for John's account (Zech. 1:7–17; 6:1–8). A more likely interpretation is that John sees the conquering Christ arriving to enforce the will of God upon the earth. The picture is similar to that of Revelation 19:11–16 where Christ comes on a white horse, wearing many crowns, brandishing a sword, and conquering the enemies of God. The rider on the white horse in 6:2

is the victor, a designation associated with Christ throughout the book (e.g., 5:5; 17:14).

B. Second seal opened (6:3–4). The visions of Zechariah are the backdrop for what John says here. In both of Zechariah's visions, a red horse is seen (Zech. 1:8; 6:2). This rider is to take peace from the earth and to cause mankind to slay one another, driving them to such by means of the large sword in his hand. This clearly depicts war and reminds us of Jesus' words that before the end comes there would be wars and rumors of wars (Matt. 24:6).

C. Third seal opened (6:5–6). The rider on the black horse (6:5) symbolizes famine. The scale in his hand is for weighing out the food that is bought. The prices are extortionately high—a day's wage for a quart of wheat. The relative value of wheat and barley stayed the same, however, with wheat costing three times as much. The rider is told not to damage the oil and wine, which could mean they were so valuable that they should be treated with special care, thus indicating a very severe famine; or it could mean that only the grain crops were affected by the famine (the oil and wine were untouched) which would indicate a relatively limited judgment. In the Old Testament, the olive, the grape, and the grain were the great blessings of God, providing the staples of life.

D. Fourth seal opened (6:7–8). The rider of the pale horse (6:8) is identified as Death, and Hades (the realm of the dead) followed after him, ready to swallow up Death's victims. They have power to kill with four judgments: the sword, famine, plague, and wild beasts. Although the wild beasts might seem rather out of place in this list, they actually form part of a familiar Old Testament prophetic pattern. Ezekiel speaks of the four dreadful judgments of almighty God—sword, famine, wild beasts, and plague (Ezek. 14:21; for a fuller study of this idea see Jer. 14:12; 15:3; Ezek. 5:12, 17; 33:27). Although Death and Hades are active now, their time is running out. Death will be destroyed (1 Cor. 15:26, 54; Rev. 21:4) when both Death and Hades are thrown into the lake of fire (Rev. 20:14).

E. Fifth seal opened (6:9–11). The scene now shifts from judgments on earth to an altar in heaven under which reside the restless souls of those who had been slain for their Christian witness. They cry out to God, as the holy and true One (Christ is the one who is holy and true in 3:7), to avenge their blood, and are given white robes in anticipation of their future resurrection. They are told to rest a little while longer until their number is complete. These martyrs for Christ are pictured as being "under the altar" (6:9) either because their poured-out blood was being looked upon as a sacrificial offering or because the altar symbolized security and they were safely under it in the presence of God.

F. Sixth seal opened (6:12–17). With the opening of the sixth seal cosmic catastrophe strikes, described by John in terms very familiar to his readers. It was nothing less than the dreaded "day of the Lord" predicted in the Old Testament (see Isa. 13:6, 9–10; Ezek. 32:7–8; Joel 2:10, 30–31; 3:14–15). In Revelation 6:12–14 there is a sevenfold cosmic judgment, the number seven depicting finality and completion (earth shakes, sun darkens, moon reddens, stars fall to earth, sky rips apart, mountains and islands move). These same phenomena are predicted by Jesus to accompany the end of the age and the final coming of the Son of man (Matt. 24:29–30; Mark 13:24–26; Luke 21:25–27).

What seemed so unshakable and eternal, the very heavens and earth, now give way beneath God's almighty hand, offering no place to hide and no security whatsoever. In verses 15–17 a sevenfold depiction of humanity is given, starting from the highest and going to the lowest—kings, princes, generals, the rich, the mighty, slaves, and freemen—all fleeing in terror from the face of the Lord, crying out to the mountains and rocks to protect them. Mountains have always symbolized stability and rocks unchangeability, but these afford no refuge now. It could also be noted that mankind uses rocks and mountains, and what can be found in them, such as gold or iron, to fashion safety, security, and refuge for itself in the form of idols, money, or fortresses, but it is better to be crushed outright beneath our false hopes than to fall into the hands of the living God (see Hos. 10:8).

In verse 16 the throne of God is emphasized to stress his authority. This is a common figure of speech in the Old Testament and in Revelation. "The wrath of the Lamb" (v. 16) is a striking inversion of metaphor; who can imagine a lamb being wrathful? Yet so identified is the lamb with the one on the throne that "the great day of their wrath has come" (v. 17). The will of the Father and Son is one in the salvation of the world (Rev. 7:10), but becomes one in the judgment of those who reject that salvation and trust in themselves for security. The wrath of the Lord is spoken of frequently in the Bible and the end of the age is often referred to as a day of wrath (Isa. 13:13; Jer. 50:13; Ezek. 7:7–8, 19; Hos. 5:10; Zeph. 1:14–15, 18; Zech. 7:12; John 3:36; Rom. 1:18; Eph. 5:6; Rev. 14:10, 19; 15:1, 7; 16:1, 19; 19:15).

V. Interlude before the Seventh Seal (7:1–17)

A. Sealing of the 144,000 of Israel (7:1–8). John returns in his mind's eye to the world as he knew it, before the great catastrophe he had just seen which so graphically depicted the world's end. It is still a cosmic vision but now it deals with the world's salvation, rather than its judgment. The four corners of the earth and the four winds symbolize the totality of the world in common biblical figures (Jer. 49:36; Ezek. 37:9; Dan. 7:2; Matt. 24:31), but it probably goes somewhat beyond that. Zechariah 6:1–8 records a vision of four horsemen who go out to appease God's wrath. As in Revelation 6:1–8 these horsemen were used as figures to depict the judgment of God upon the world, leading to the outpouring of his wrath in 6:12–17. Perhaps there is something of a conceptual parallel to chapter 6 here in chapter 7. In chapter 6 there are three sections: the four horsemen (6:1–8); the sealing of the martyrs (6:9–11); and the wrath of the Lamb and the One who sits on the throne (6:12–17). Paralleling this in chapter 7 we have the four angels, corners, winds (7:1–3); the sealing of 144,000 and the vision of the great multitude of the saved (7:4–11); and finally, salvation and compassion from the One who sits on the throne and from the Lamb (7:12–17). "Another angel" (7:2) is variously interpreted as a messenger of God or even Christ himself, because he commands the four angels and has the seal of God (representing God's authority) and speaks in the plural as though speaking for God—" . . . until we put a seal on the foreheads" (v. 3). The seal of God marks out God's own for protection (Ezek. 9:4; Rev. 9:4). In 21:4 the name of God himself is on their foreheads. The number 144,000 represents completeness, twelve thousand from each of the twelve tribes (v. 4). John is saying that all of those who are marked out by God are those whom God will save. Their number is complete and all of them will be protected until the end. Israel, God's people of old, is used as the descriptive vehicle by John to get his point across. Evidently he is not literally referring to the actual tribes of Israel because he does not actually list them. In fact, he leaves two of them out, while still saying all the tribes are there (vv. 4–8). John's list is unlike any other in the Bible, in that Dan and Ephraim are removed, while Joseph is retained. Possibly Dan is missing because of a theory, apparently current at that time, that the Antichrist would arise from the tribe of Dan. The shuffling around of Joseph and his sons (Ephraim and Manasseh) was not uncommon. (For a discussion of the seven qualities that characterize the 144,000, see the comments on 14:1–5.)

B. Vision of the redeemed multitude of the earth (7:9–11). There is much discussion about the relationship between this multitude and the 144,000 just mentioned, with two major views on the subject. First, some scholars hold that the 144,000 represent all the redeemed on earth and the redeemed multitude is a different group, representing only the redeemed martyrs of earth and to be identified with the group seen under the altar in 6:9–11. There they cried out "how long . . . until . . . you avenge our blood?" (6:10) and were told to wait a little longer (6:11). Here in chapter 7 they are seen as glorified. That the redeemed multitude and the martyrs are the same may be seen in that both groups wear white robes (6:11; 7:9) and both groups appear to have had violent deaths (6:11; 7:14 suggests that they were killed). Second, others see the two groups—the 144,000 and the redeemed multitude—as the same group, representing all of the saved on earth, but in two separate visions. Points in favor of this view are that the size of the group, "a great multitude that no one could count" (7:9), argues that it is not a subgroup of martyrs only, but the whole group of the saved. Also, their description as being "from every nation, tribe, people and language" (v. 9) is the same as that describing the whole people of God as praised by the twenty-four elders (5:9–10). Finally, all of God's people are given white robes, not just the martyrs (3:4–5, 18; 4:4; 19:8, 14), and the white garments represent their righteous deeds, not their martyrdom.

C. Explanation of the multitude (7:12–17). Worship is the appropriate response to God who made and rules all things (v. 12). As in 5:11–14 where all of creation responds in doxology and worship, here the angels, elders, and four living creatures worship, breaking forth into a sevenfold doxology, extolling God as worthy of and possessing praise, glory, wisdom, thanks, honor, power, and strength.

One of the elders asks John a leading question and receives a polite response from John: "Sir, you know" (v. 14). John is then told who the multitudes are—those whom Christ has redeemed from out of the great tribulation. Some view this great tribulation as an especially evil time that immediately precedes the second coming of Christ, with some restricting it to seven or even three-and-one-half years duration, while others see it as descriptive of the entire time of the church's pilgrimage, from the resurrection of Jesus to his second advent. Jesus promised that we would have trouble (KJV tribulation) in this world (John 16:33); the early believers were exhorted to comfort in tribulation (2 Cor. 1:4; 7:14; 1 Thess. 3:4); Paul describes our entrance into the kingdom of God as through many hardships (Acts 14:22); and John sees himself as a companion in the believers' tribulations (Rev. 1:9). Jesus also tells us, however, to be of good cheer because he has overcome the world (John 16:33) and that after the tribulation of these days he would return (Matt. 24:29–31; Mark 13:24–27).

In another striking paradox, the saints are described as clothed in robes made white in the blood of the Lamb (Rev. 7:14). "The Lamb . . . will be their shepherd" (v. 17) is yet another paradoxical figure—the Lamb leads the flock. In verses 15–17 a marvelous picture of heavenly glory is given. It is a place of intimate fellowship with God and Christ, under God's protection ("tent"; see Isa. 4:5–6), where there is no hunger, thirst, oppressive heat, lack of direction, or need of any kind. The Lamb shepherds us to springs of living water, reminiscent of Psalm 23. All of these figures are drawn from the Old Testament (see Isa. 25:8; 49:10; Jer. 2:13; Ezek. 34:23) and are repeated again in the Book of Revelation (21:3–4).

VI. The Seventh Seal and the Seven Trumpets (8:1–9:21)

A. Opening of the seventh seal and the vision of the censer (8:1–5). As the seventh seal is broken, an ominous silence settles in across the realms of heaven (8:1). The tumultuous noise of angels' praise, elders' songs, and living creatures' words has now ceased in anticipation of what is soon to take place. The silence is of a relatively short duration, about half an hour, during which time John waits to see what it all portends. The broken seal unfolds into a new set of visions, this time seven trumpets (8:2). Some scholars discuss whether the events depicted by the seven trumpets follow sequentially upon the six opened seals, or whether, as is more probable, they run parallel to them, so that the seals, trumpets, and bowls (to come later) are all broadly descriptive of the same period of time. Before the trumpets sound, another vision crowds in upon John's sight. An angel appears in a scene reminiscent of temple worship, with a censer to be filled with incense, lit with fire from the golden altar and hurled to the earth in the midst of shattering noise, which, presumably broke the half-hour silence (8:3–5). This is reminiscent of the scene at Mount Sinai when God spoke to Moses and the people in the midst of trumpet blasts, thunder, smoke, and fire (Exod. 19:16–19). In Revelation 5:8 the incense *is* the prayers of the saints; here in 8:3–5 the incense accompanies the prayers of the saints, but the image is still the same. It is a sacrifice of sweet smell in the courts of heaven (see Ps. 141:2). The altar is the same one the martyrs are under (6:9–11) and perhaps their cry "How long?" is the prayer that now ascends with the smoke and is cast back upon the earth as an answer, in judgment upon the evil deeds of men who murdered God's servants.

B. Blowing of the first four trumpets (8:6–13). The trumpets are divided into two groups by John. The first four are a group by themselves and the last three are further identified as the three woes. So the first four trumpets stand alone, the fifth trumpet becomes the first woe; the sixth trumpet is the second woe, and the seventh trumpet in some form or other is the third woe (see discussion on 11:15–19).

The first angel sounds his trumpet (v. 7), which results in a judgment of hail and fire that is reminiscent of the seventh plague on Egypt (Exod. 9:23–25) and answers to God's threat in Ezekiel 38:22 to judge the earth in the end times with torrents of rain, hailstones, and burning sulphur. The second angel sounds his trumpet (v. 8) and a blazing mountain cast into the sea turns it into blood, reminding one of the first plague on Egypt (Exod. 7:14–21). Here, as with all of the first four trumpets, it is a partial judgment with only a third of the creation stricken. The third angel sounds his trumpet (v. 9). The star Wormwood falls into the drinking water and makes it bitter (see Jer. 9:15). Many die in this plague. The fourth angel sounds his trumpet (v. 12) and the sun, moon, and stars are darkened, so that men must grope about in an unnatural and eerie twilight. Following this an eagle announces the next three trumpets as a triple woe upon the earth.

C. Blowing of the fifth trumpet (9:1–12). John now has a panoramic view (apparently from an earthly perspective) of what is taking place. A star falls, and as it nears the earth it gradually takes the shape of a person who has a key that unlocks the shaft of the abyss, from which Satan and his forces are released upon the earth. In 20:1–3 an angel locks Satan back into the abyss for the thousand-year reign of Christ. The satanic forces are likened to a plague of locusts (9:3), reminding one of the Book of Joel where the same imagery is used (Joel 2:1–11). This judgment will fall upon those who rejected God and not upon the natural order (Rev. 9:4). The seal of God, which is upon God's servants (7:3), protects them from the torturous sting of the satanic attack. The description of the locusts (9:7–10) is interesting. They are centaurlike creatures with lionlike features, while the iron breastplate makes them more insectlike. A peculiarity is the scorpion's tail they possess. The crowns they wear symbolize invincibility and their human features make them all the more grotesque by lifting them out of the realm of the purely animal and enduing them with fallen human intelligence. They have a leader whose name, in both Hebrew and Greek, is the Destroyer (9:11). Destruction is their ultimate goal, of course, but in this visitation they are not allowed to kill, only torment. Indeed, many suffering but unrepentant humans would like to escape the consequences of their actions in death, but are not allowed to do so (9:6). They must reap what they have sown.

D. Blowing of the sixth trumpet (9:13–21). With the blowing of the sixth trumpet a voice is heard coming from the upper part of the golden altar, which is described a little more precisely as having horns (v. 13; see also Exod. 30:1–3). That the voice comes from the altar perhaps distinguishes it from the martyrs' voices heard from beneath the altar. It is as though the martyrs cry out and the altar, in some fashion, responds. The voice commands the angels who held back the Euphrates to release it and as it rushes toward the west it becomes a vast army of two hundred million mounted soldiers (9:14–15). It is interesting to note the role played by the angels in all of this and how God accomplishes his will through them. It is also important to note that nothing happens without God's appointment; the angels act at God's command at the precise moment and the judgment is unleashed. These mounted soldiers are agents of destruction and are commanded to kill, not just torment, as was the case with the locusts. The horses are colorfully described as fiery red, dark blue, and sulfurous yellow, belching out fire, smoke, and noxious fumes (9:17). Like the locusts, they had serpents' tails, which were used with devastating effect (9:19).

This sixth trumpet, or second woe, ends with an important theological observation on John's part (9:20–21). He notes that those who were not killed in the first six plagues learned nothing from their experience. Just as in the case of Pharaoh, who continued to harden his heart as God sent the plagues upon Egypt (Exod. 7:22–23; 8:15, 32; 9:7, 34–35), so here, mankind refuses to acknowledge God as God. Their evil ways include the worship of demons, idolatry, murder, occult practices, sexual immorality, and theft. Jesus' commands to love God with all our hearts and our neighbors as ourselves (Matt. 22:37–40) are violated here by the refusal to acknowledge God in worship and obedience, and by violating our fellow human beings by murder, theft, and sexual abuse. All of this calls forth the mighty judgment of God.

VII. Interlude and the Seventh Trumpet (10:1–11:19)

A. Vision of the mighty angel and the scroll (10:1–11). With the events of the first two woes swirling around in his head, and stricken by mankind's unwillingness to accept the lessons of judgment and repent, John now lifts his eyes up from where he stands on earth and perceives a startling, colossal figure, in the form of a mighty angel (10:1). He is altogether striking and every attribute he possesses strongly suggests a divine figure, no doubt Christ himself, although not all interpreters agree on this. He descends from heaven, robed in a cloud. The Old Testament says that clouds are the chariots of God (Ps. 104:3) and Paul describes the return of Christ as "in the clouds" (1 Thess. 4:17), as does John himself (Rev. 1:7). A rainbow surrounds the angel's head, symbolizing the glory of God (Ezek. 1:25–28; Rev. 4:3). "His face was like the sun" (Rev. 10:2), reminding us of the vision of Christ earlier (1:16) and of the transfiguration of Jesus in the Gospels (Matt. 17:2). "His legs were like fiery pillars" (Rev. 10:2), which again recalls the earlier vision of Christ (1:15) as well as Daniel's vision (Dan. 10:4–6). The angel plants his feet on land and sea, showing his authority over all creation, and shouts his command with the roar of a lion. In the Old Testament God roars his commands (Hos. 11:10; Amos 3:8). Taking all of this together, it is probably best to see this mighty angel as an appearance of Christ. Another series of visions and prophecies is given to John (Rev. 10:4), but he is told not to record their message. We do not know why and nothing more is said about it. There is to be no more delay in the working out of God's purposes (10:6). God himself, the eternal One and the Creator of all things, is the guarantee of that. John's readers are reminded of God's eternal power and control of the universe to keep them from losing heart. It would be all too easy to make the mistake of thinking that evil might win. It will never happen. God is the creator and the ruler of this world and his will must certainly be accomplished. What God has planned for this world, although revealed in part through the prophets remains, ultimately, a mystery.

The voice that speaks in 10:8 is the same voice that spoke to John in 10:4. Throughout the series of visions that John received he was under orders from God and willingly submitted to what God said, just as all of God's servants are to do. In verse 9 a curious sequence, but one not without precedent, now takes place. John obeys the voice that tells him to take the scroll from the hand of the mighty angel. The scroll is unrolled, signifying that its contents have been made known and are open to view. This contrasts with the scroll in the hand of God that only Christ could open (5:2–5). Possibly the book is open here because it is in the hand of Christ and the mysteries of God are now an open secret through him. The scroll is to taste sweet in John's mouth but to be sour in his stomach. Similar to this is Ezekiel's vision of God in which Ezekiel saw a hand stretched out to him holding a scroll, containing words of lamentation, mourning, and woe. He was told to eat the scroll, which would taste sweet in his mouth, and speak the words to Israel (Ezek. 2:9–3:4). After digesting its contents John is to make this bittersweet message known worldwide, to people and rulers alike. What was this sweet/sour message to be delivered to the world that concerned the completion of the mysterious will of God? No doubt it was that we must go through many hardships to enter the kingdom of God (Acts 14:22). That is a message most sweet for believers in that we will be forever with the Lord (1 Thess. 4:17) but bitter to contemplate since it promises a martyr's death for many. The message is bitter for the world in that it prophesies its destruction and ruin, but sweet in that God, his people, his holy angels, and everything good are ultimately vindicated. Believers are to be encouraged in the midst of the present distress. God is still on his throne and will surely bring his purposes to pass.

B. Vision of the two witnesses (11:1–14). After John had ingested the little scroll containing the message of God, he is visited by another vision that tells him something of the outcome of that message. God will have his messengers preach, they will be persecuted and killed, but the message cannot be stopped. God will protect his own in the midst of the chaotic disorder, and many will turn in repentance to Christ, in spite of the supernatural opposition that confronts them.

As in the last vision, John is a participant in what takes place (11:1). In most of the other visions John only observes, occasionally asking a question or being asked to respond. John is told to measure the temple and the altar, and to measure (NIV count) the worshipers. This image derives from Old Testament prophecy where measurement was for consolidation, construction, and protection (Ezek. 40–43; Zech. 2:1–5). This tells us that access to God (temple and altar) and his worshipers is under the special protection of God himself. John is told only to measure the spiritual part of the temple precincts for protection (11:2); the outer court (Court of the Gentiles) has already been profaned, as Jesus predicted (Luke 21:24). The "holy city" (i.e., Jerusalem; see Neh. 11:1; Isa. 48:2; Matt. 4:5) will be desecrated for a limited period of time, forty-two months or 1260 days (Rev. 11:3). These numbers resemble some found in Daniel's prophecies about the end times ("time, times and half a time," Dan. 7:25; 12:7; see Rev. 12:14; Dan. 12:11–12 gives two numbers, 1290 and 1335 days). Some interpreters tie this in with Daniel's larger prophecy about the seventy weeks, and make these days part of the last week of Daniel's prophecy (Dan. 9:24–27). The point John is making concerns not so much when these things will take place, but that they are under God's control and limited by him, and during which God will be offering salvation to those who will accept it.

John depicts this prophetic work of God as two men bearing testimony (Rev. 11:3). These are described in three ways. First, he calls them "the two olive trees" (11:4). This image is taken from one of Zechariah's visions (Zech. 4:1–14). In that complex vision the two trees supply oil to a golden bowl with seven pipes leading to seven lamps that provide light in the darkness. In Zechariah's day the two "trees" were Joshua and Zerubbabel, the religious and civil leaders of that time. Second, they are called the "two lampstands that stand before the Lord of the earth" (Rev. 11:4). It is not clear where the idea of two lampstands originated; in Zechariah's vision only one lampstand is mentioned. Here the symbol no doubt relates to the two olive trees, and is intended to refer to the two witnesses. Third, John picks up a common understanding about the ministries of Elijah and Moses just before the end of the age. The two witnesses here carry out their ministry in a manner strikingly similar to them, indicating that they represent the fulfillment of that expectation (11:5–6). For example, fire comes from their mouths (see 2 Kings 1:10, 12), they stop the rain from falling (see 1 Kings 17:1), turn water into blood (see Exod. 7:20), and "strike the earth with every kind of plague," as in the days of the exodus from Egypt.

"The beast . . . from the Abyss" (Rev. 11:7) was a common expression referring to the Antichrist. Daniel had spoken of an abomination that desolates (Dan. 9:27) and Jesus had echoed this idea (Matt. 24:15). John said many antichrists are already in the world preparing the way for the ultimate Antichrist who is yet to come (1 John 4:3). The beast here represents all of this activity, but especially that of the Antichrist of the last days. The beast is allowed by

God temporarily to overcome the two witnesses by killing them, but they are brought back to life after "three and a half days" (Rev. 11:7–11). This same idea is repeated in 13:7 where the beast makes war with the saints and conquers them. In 12:11, however, it is the saints who overcome him by the blood of the Lamb and the word of God to which they bore testimony. There is a contradiction in this, but it is only apparent. The victory of the beast is temporary; the victory of God through his servants and saints is eternal. John wants us to see that though we may give our lives for our faith, we will be raised again by God and taken up into heaven to be with him (11:12). This is a permanent and eternal victory. After the beast is defeated, he is thrown into the lake of fire, never to be seen again (Rev. 20:10).

As in other instances in Revelation, the judgment of God is symbolized by a great earthquake (11:13; see 6:12; 8:5; 11:19; 16:18). Here it kills seven thousand people. Many are driven by sheer terror to acknowledge that God is Lord of all and to repent of their evil ways and confess to the truth (see Josh. 7:15; Jer. 13:16).

With the passing of the last three visions—the two hundred million mounted soldiers, the angel and the little scroll, and the two witnesses—the second woe ends (Rev. 11:14). John is told that the third woe will arrive soon.

C. Blowing of the seventh trumpet (11:15–19). The first two woes are identified directly with the blowing of the fifth and sixth trumpets, but John makes no such direct identification here. Perhaps he did not want to relate the triumphant return of Christ to the series of woes because he was stressing the positive aspects of Christ's advent. That it has negative consequences for those who have rejected God is well known to John, or John sees all that takes place in 11:15–19:21 as the third woe. In 19:11–21 the return of Christ is spoken of yet again, only in terms of utmost retribution, as the "fury of the wrath of God Almighty" (19:15). If this is so, then the third woe is devastating indeed.

In 11:15 a mighty chorus of unnamed voices in heaven summarily announces that God has finally established his rule on earth through Christ, who will reign forever. The world's kingdom is gone; Christ's kingdom has arrived. The eternal reign of God is a common theme in the Old Testament (Exod. 15:18; Ps. 10:16; Dan. 2:44; 7:27; Zech. 14:9). The triumphant cry of victory brought forth a response of worship from the personification of God's redeemed people (Rev. 11:16). It is a profound moment of thanksgiving and praise when they realize that the kingdom of Christ, the Son of God's love, has arrived, and the former things are passed away. Verse 17 describes God as the eternal, all-powerful one, who has begun his reign. For that reason the designation *who is to come* (found in 1:8; 4:8) is missing here. He is no longer the one who is to come, but the one who has arrived. In verse 18 John uses words drawn from Psalms 2:1, 5, 12 and 99:13 to depict the defeat of God's enemies. They were angry, but it availed them little. In the past God held back his wrath to give everyone an opportunity to repent, but now God's purposes are complete, so his wrath is unleashed. The feeble rage of the nations is as nothing in the face of that. The return of Christ brings with it the final judgment, the resurrection, and the rewarding of God's people. It is a time when all of the trials, sacrifices, and hardships endured for Christ will be made worth it. Then we will see that "our present sufferings are not worth comparing with the glory that will be revealed in us" (Rom. 8:18). John expands upon this theme in Revelation 21:1–7, 9–27; 22:1–6. The return of Christ will also ultimately bring the destruction of those who hated God and violated his creation. Note how evil is defined as a destructive force and that it brings destruction on itself in the end. Later, John expands upon this (see 20:11–15; 21:8).

In the Old Testament the ark of the covenant was the symbol of God's faithfulness. When it was present, the people triumphed. It is seen now (Rev. 11:19), safe within the temple of heaven, never again to be lost, and signifying forever that God will be true to his word. God's enemies will be punished, and God's servants will be rewarded, because God himself has promised it. To this all nature replies with "flashes of lightning, rumblings, peals of thunder, an earthquake and a great hailstorm" (v. 19). This typically symbolizes God's judgment in Revelation (e.g., 8:5; 16:18; see also Isa. 29:6).

VIII. The Cosmic Conflict of Good and Evil (12:1–13:1a)

A. The woman clothed with the sun (12:1–6). This is a complex vision epitomizing the gospel message and the life of the church. A divinely appointed woman gives birth to a child, the Messiah, who will rule the earth. He is taken up to heaven while the woman and her other offspring are subjected to the persecutions of the dragon. The dragon's story is also told. He started a rebellion in heaven and was cast out after a war with God's hosts—Michael and his angels. He finds himself on earth where he vents his fury upon those who are siblings of the Messiah, who has taken his place at the throne of God. In all of this God supernaturally protects his own.

The images here that describe the woman who gave birth to the Messiah are not found in the Old Testament. John chooses some astral symbolism—sun, moon, stars—to show that this event has cosmic significance (12:1). The woman represents a number of things, all blended together. She is Israel, from whom Jesus came; she is the church, as the people of God, persecuted by the dragon; she is Mary, the earthly mother of Jesus; she is woman, through whom all life comes, and generally, all the people of God. That all of this should be blended into one image is not at all unusual in apocalyptic symbolism.

To describe the dragon (12:3), John draws upon the prophecies of Daniel (Dan. 7:7, 20, 23–25). As in Daniel, the dragon represents evil political powers on earth that persecute the church, but also their cosmic, evil leader, Satan. He is described as red perhaps to symbolize his murderous character. He has ten horns to tie in the vision with Daniel's vision, and crowns upon his head to signify power to rule. Evil has power and exercises it. Here the evil is mobilized to destroy God's Savior who is to be born of the woman. Aligning themselves with Satan are a third of the heavenly hosts.

Verse 5 describes Jesus in words taken from Psalm 2:9, as is done elsewhere in Revelation (2:26–28; 19:15). The child's ascension to heaven to rule with God on the throne depicts Jesus' ascension after his death and resurrection (Luke 24:50–53; Acts 1:9–11) to the right hand of God (Acts 7:55–56; Rom. 8:34; Eph. 1:20; Col. 3:1; Heb. 1:3, 13; 1 Pet. 3:22). The people of God flee from the dragon (Rev. 12:6), but God is protecting them for the 1260 days of their persecution (see comments on 11:2).

B. War in heaven (12:7–12). Satan is furious, but unable to prevail in heaven. Evil has no place there, so he is hurled down to earth to persecute the saints. In a vision Jesus saw this as well (Luke 10:18; John 12:31). Satan's many names are given here—dragon, serpent, devil, and Satan (see comments on Rev. 20:12). His mission is to "lead the whole world astray." We must always remember that he is a liar and the source of all evil and untruth (John 8:44). He cannot be trusted or believed. Only God is true, and ultimately righteousness will triumph.

With the fact of Satan's expulsion from heaven comes the establishment of God's righteous rule (Rev. 12:10). No evil now remains to cast doubt upon God's ultimate authority. Salvation is now available to all; the power of God is manifest in the defeat of evil; the rule (kingdom) of God is established by the work of Christ and the preaching of the gospel; and the lordship (authority) of Christ is exercised as the Messiah who rules with an iron scepter. These four ideas summarize the Christian understanding of the relation of God to the world.

Satan, the accuser of the believers (12:11; see also Job 1:6–11; Zech. 3:1), has been cast down in defeat from heaven, but another defeat awaits him. The saints will also defeat him by the blood of the Lamb and the word to which they bear testimony (i.e., Christ and the gospel). Paradoxically, many will lose their lives in winning the victory. There is a paradox in this, but the death of Christ explains it. If the death of Jesus is *his* victory, and we are to be victorious in him, what matter is it that we, too, die in order to win? It was always God's way for us to find strength in weakness and life in death. The heavens rejoice to hear this, as do all the dwellers in glory (12:12). In this way perhaps the third woe is said to have arrived. Satan's fury is great because he knows the time to work his nefarious schemes is limited.

C. Spiritual warfare on earth (12:13–13:1a). The plight of the persecuted church is now depicted in a typical graphic episode. Satan is now unmasked as the power behind all persecutions of the church. Everything is done to overwhelm the believer, but God protects his own. Wings are provided for an easy flight to the place prepared for the church in the desert. She is protected "for a time, times and half a time," that is, the duration of her time of persecution (12:14). Satan tries to overwhelm the church with a flood, but the earth rallies to her support by swallowing the satanic river (12:15–16). Here even the natural order is on the side of the believer. Satan attempts to use it to his own evil ends, but as a creation of God it serves his purposes. Thwarted here, the devil goes off seeking to destroy others who are faithful to God (12:17; see also Dan. 7:7, 21; Rev. 11:7; 13:7). They are described here, as elsewhere, as those who obey God's command and hold fast to their confession of Jesus. This vision ends with the dragon gazing out over the vast sea (13:1a). One wonders what the dragon is contemplating—the shortness of time? his own furious but impotent rage? his inevitable doom?

IX. The Beasts, the Believers, and the Judgment of Earth (13:1b–14:20)

A. The beast from the sea (13:1b–10). While the dragon is contemplating, a fearsome beast arises from the sea to join forces with him. Following this a third beast, arising from the earth, joins them to produce an unholy trinity of evil in mocking emulation of the one true

God who is Father, Son, and Holy Spirit. There is a great deal of discussion as to what these two beasts represent, but in all probability the first represents the abuse of governmental power and the second, the abuse of spiritual power. While acknowledging this, some also identify the beast from the sea as the dreaded Antichrist who is to come (see 2 Thess. 2:1–12; 1 John 2:18).

John again uses the dreams of Daniel to convey his message (13:1b–2). All of Daniel 7 is the indispensable background for understanding this vision of John's. Daniel saw four beasts arise from the sea (Dan. 7:3)—the first like a lion (7:4); the second like a bear (7:5); the third like a leopard (7:6); and the fourth, a terrifying beast with ten horns (7:7–8). John combines all of this into one beast, described in the reverse order of Daniel's vision. The beast is given the authority of the dragon, suffers a near-fatal wound, but is healed (Rev. 13:3), and, with the dragon's power behind him, the beast demands and receives the worship of all the world.

Like the beast of Daniel 7:8–11, John's beast boasts its power and is allowed to rule for forty-two months, a designation of time already used by Daniel and John (Dan. 7:25; Rev. 11:2–3; 12:6, 14). As with the beast in Daniel's vision, the beast from the sea blasphemes God (Rev. 13:6; Dan. 7:25); makes war with the saints and defeats them (Rev. 13:7; Dan. 7:21–25); and is given authority over the whole earth (Rev. 13:3, 7–8; Dan. 7:23). This beast reappears in a later vision of John's (Rev. 17:3, 7–14) where an explanation is given which clearly points to the Roman Empire as being the beast. It is for this reason and because Daniel sees his visions as pointing to political rule (Dan. 7:17, 23–24) that the beast in Revelation 13:1–8 is identified with human government and its abuse by the evil forces of this world. "The book of life" (v. 8) is a phrase used to describe the roster of all the redeemed of God (Exod. 32:32; Ps. 69:28; Dan. 12:10; Phil. 4:3; Rev. 3:5; 17:8; 20:15; 21:27). The book of life belongs to Jesus Christ who is described in Old Testament sacrificial terms as the slain lamb (Isa. 53:7; John 1:29, 36; Rev. 4:6, 12). The redeemed of the earth have been bought with the precious blood of Christ, a lamb without blemish or defect (1 Pet. 1:19). The saints make their robes white in the blood of the Lamb (esp. Rev. 7:14; see also 3:5, 18; 4:4; 6:11; 7:9; 19:14). The death of Jesus for the sins of the world was not an accident or unplanned by God. It was decided before the foundation of the world (13:8; Eph. 1:4; 1 Pet. 1:20). This fact ensures for the believer that his salvation is secure, being known to God from all of eternity.

"He who has an ear, let him hear" (Rev. 13:9) is an expression used by Jesus and John to alert the hearer to pay close attention (Matt. 11:15; 13:9; Rev. 2:7, 11, 17, 29; 3:6, 13, 22). Here attention is to be given to what follows in verse 10. The fatalistically sounding words in verse 10 are not meant to discourage the believers, but to tell them that given the shortness of the time, it is better to go to jail or submit to death, rather than hold out for one's own continued earthly existence. Because heaven awaits us, earth and its freedoms can be forfeited without real loss. This is indeed "patient endurance and faithfulness on the part of the saints" (v. 10).

B. The beast from the earth (13:11–18). John's attention is now directed to a beast arising out of the ground, this time in imitation of Christ ("two horns like a lamb" [v. 11]). The disguise is not successful and John recognizes it for what it is, another beast. The words of the beast betrayed it, for it spoke like a dragon. Its function was to subvert true religion and force the world to worship the first beast (v. 12). In antiquity where kings and Roman emperors were considered divine, this temptation is both understandable and serious. The second beast copies God's ways (v. 13). Jesus worked great and miraculous signs (John 2:11, 23; 20:30); so does the beast. People are too quick to believe when they see something out of the ordinary (v. 14), forgetting that Jesus warned us that false prophets would arise who could do great signs and miracles (Matt. 24:24). Paul told us that the "lawless one" will also do them (2 Thess. 2:9–10). The second beast orders that an image of the first beast be set up and worshiped, in clear violation of God's commands (Exod. 20:3–4). As in Daniel's day (Dan. 3:5–6), those who refuse to worship political, economic, and secular power will be killed (Rev. 13:15). Just as God marked out his own by putting a seal on their foreheads (7:2–8; 9:4), so the mark of the beast is put on those who reject God (13:16; 14:9, 11; 16:2; 19:20; 20:4). But the saints of God will triumph over the beast and his image and those who have received his mark (15:2). So severe will be the pressure to forsake the worship of God that all normal activities of life will fall under state control (13:17). One's very life must be given up to survive. George Orwell's modern apocalypse *Nineteen Eighty-Four* envisages a similar situation.

In coded language John now tells us who was the embodiment of the beast in his day (Rev. 13:18). It is a man, and his number (or the number of his name [15:2]) is 666. The reference is probably to some definitive historical person, although exactly who remains uncertain, despite many attempts at identification. To whom the numbers might refer before the final advent of Christ is another matter. Virtually everyone imaginable has been suggested—the pope, Luther, Calvin, Napoleon, Kaiser Wilhelm, Hitler, Mussolini, Stalin, to name just a few. Obviously, we do not know who it will be.

C. The Lamb and the 144,000 (14:1–5). The last time John saw Jerusalem in his visions it was figuratively called Sodom and Egypt, the place where Jesus was crucified, and where the two faithful witnesses of God were murdered (11:7–8). Now a glorious transformation has taken place. Mount Zion is virtually heaven itself and the scenes of heaven and earth are blended together into one marvelous whole.

It must have been a relief for John to shift his eyes from the evil triumvirate, whose goal it was to crush the believers and to deceive everyone else, to a foreshadowing of the New Jerusalem where the saints would dwell secure (14:1). It is as though John were given two views of things. From the world's point of view, all is chaos, death, and ruin; from God's point of view, heaven, God, and the Lamb await the redeemed. As in 7:4–8, the redeemed are symbolized as the 144,000 who bear the name of Christ and have his Father's name written on their foreheads. John then hears a tremendous noise, like a vast waterfall and peal of thunder; however, it is the music of heaven. The song the harpists were singing was the song of redemption (14:3), reserved for those who had gone through the trials of life and finally reached the heavenly Zion. In the Old Testament one frequently finds reference to singing a new song to the Lord (Pss. 33:3; 40:3; 96:1; 98:1; 144:9; 149:1; Isa. 42:10) where the song represents praise for something God has done. Earlier the twenty-four elders and the four living creatures sing a new song in anticipation of what God will do (Rev. 5:9–10) and here, the 144,000 and the harpists sing the new song of salvation in thanks for what God has accomplished through Christ.

Eight characteristics are listed which describe the 144,000:

(1). They are "redeemed from the earth" (14:3), which, in a way, defines who they are. They have already been described as those who have Jesus' name and his Father's name on their foreheads (14:1).

(2). "[They] did not defile themselves with women" (14:4). This verse contains a figure drawn from the Old Testament where adultery symbolizes the worship of false gods (Deut. 31:16; Jer. 3:6–10; Ezek. 23:1–21; Hos. 1:2). The redeemed of God did not worship the beast or his image.

(3). "They kept themselves pure" (Rev. 14:4). Purity is the positive side of not committing adultery and here means to maintain one's heart aright by worship of the true God.

(4). "They follow the Lamb" (14:4). The characteristic of a Christian believer is that he does the will of Christ, not his own. He willingly follows after Christ (v. 4; see also John 10:2–18, 28–29; 1 Pet. 2:21).

(5). "They are purchased from among men" (Rev. 14:4). This is an image of redemption and the same Greek verb is translated "redeemed" (NIV) in verse 3.

(6). "[They were] offered as first fruits to God and the Lamb" (14:4). This figure is drawn from agriculture where the first crops harvested are dedicated to the Lord. The 144,000 belong especially to the Lord (Jer. 2:3; James 1:18), that is, to both God and the Lamb.

(7). "No lie was found in their mouths" (Rev. 14:5). Truth characterizes the believer who follows Christ (John 14:6). Satan is the liar (John 8:44) and unbelievers turn God's truth into a lie (Rom. 1:25). The Antichrist works counterfeit wonders (2 Thess. 2:9) in order to deceive people into believing a lie (2 Thess. 2:11). Those who follow after falsehood will not enter the New Jerusalem (Rev. 21:27; 22:15). Believers, however, are true and do not lie, that is, their profession of Christ is genuine.

(8). "They are blameless" (14:5). The early church often used this term to describe the state of those who had been redeemed by Christ (Eph. 1:4; 5:27; Phil. 1:10; 2:15; 1 Thess. 2:10; Titus 1:6, 7). Because our sins have been forgiven, no charge can be laid at our feet.

D. The announcements of the three flying angels (14:6–13). John now sees events beginning to move quickly. An angel, as a representative of God, proclaims the gospel to all those who dwell on earth. The redeemed have been described as those from every tribe, language, people, and nation (5:9), and here every nation, tribe, language, and people are reached. This is reminiscent of Jesus' words that the gospel must be preached throughout the world as a testimony to all nations before the end can come (Matt. 24:14). The angel calls for repentance in the face of the coming judgment of God (Rev. 14:7). The ground of his appeal is that God is the Creator of the universe. This was the theme of the doxology sung by the twenty-four elders as they laid their crowns before the throne of God (Rev. 5:11; see also Ps. 146:6). God as the Creator of everything is alone due worship from everything. To worship anything other than God is idolatry.

In anticipation of what will be described in detail in chapters 17 and 18, an angel announces the fall of Babylon (Rev. 14:8). Babylon was a synonym for Rome (17:5) and because Rome's fall is certain (seen as the beast from the sea [13:1–10] who supported the defeated dragon [12:7–9; 20:10]), John sees an angel announcing its doom. "The maddening wine of her adulteries" (14:8) symbolizes the false worship that Rome represented (17:2, 4; 18:3, 9). It is madness to worship anything less than God.

Following the offer of the gospel and the judgment pronounced upon Rome, a third angel makes an announcement of the judgment to fall on those who follow the beast (14:9): "He . . . will drink of the wine of God's fury" (14:10). If one drinks of the wine of idolatry, he will also drink of the wine of rejection by God. To reject God ultimately will bring rejection by him. The utter desolation that awaits those who reject life is pictured by John as a smoldering ruin (14:11). Verse 12 lists three qualities that describe the believers (saints): patient endurance, obedience, and faithfulness. In the midst of total chaos around them the believers are to stand firm (Eph. 6:10–18) and endure to the end (Matt. 24:13). That this might bring martyrdom is fully recognized, but a special blessedness attends those who give their lives for Christ (Rev. 14:13). The Spirit of God promises rest from their labors and a rich reward (see also Heb. 4:8–11).

E. The reaping of the earth in judgment (14:14–20). Picking up threads from earlier visions John sees the triumphant Christ, the "son of man" (see Dan. 7:13–14; 1 Thess. 4:16–17; Rev. 1:13–16), preparing to return in judgment (14:14). The golden crown symbolizes victory and adorns the rider of the first horse (6:1–2), while many crowns are on the head of Christ in the vision of Christ as King of kings and Lord of lords (19:11–16). The image of judgment as a harvest is common in the Bible (e.g., Jer. 51:33; Hos. 6:11; Joel 3:13; Matt. 13:30, 39; Mark 4:29) and John follows the text of Joel 3:13 rather closely as he develops his theme here. When Christ was incarnate on earth he saw the world as a harvest field of a different sort, ready to be harvested in a different way (Matt. 9:37–38; John 4:35). It was "white" unto a harvest of redemption. However, at the end of the age the earth is ripe for judgment and the day of redemption has passed. In this vision the deed is accomplished and the judgment takes place (Rev. 14:16). In simple but chilling words John states it as a matter of unimpeachable fact—the sickle has slashed through the overripe grain, fat with sin, and the earth was harvested.

John now sees a second vision of judgment, still using the theme of harvest, this time by a duo of angels, one from the temple and the other from the altar. The one from the altar is in charge of the altar's fire and has already been used to hurl fiery judgment upon the earth (8:3–5). In this vision John sees a grape harvest (14:18). The grapes are cut and thrown into the vat where the wrath of God is trampled out (14:19). This image derives from the Old Testament prophets who used the picture of the blood-red juice sluicing out of the winepress to describe the outpouring of blood in war (Isa. 63:2–6; Joel 3:13; Rev. 19:13, 15). In the Old Testament the remains of a sin offering were to be disposed of outside the camp (Lev. 4:12, 21; 9:11; 16:27) and the Book of Hebrews notes that Jesus shed his blood outside the city gate to make the people holy (Heb. 13:11–12). It is only right that judgment be pictured as outside the city as well. The blood reached to a horse's bridle for a distance of 1600 stadia, or about 180 miles. The symbolic significance of this distance is not clear. Some have suggested that 1600 (4×4×10×10) signifies complete destruction of the four corners of the earth, while others have observed that the length of the Holy Land is 1664 stadia, indicating that the entire nation was judged. Whatever it means, the picture is one of unparalleled catastrophe where the boastful arrogance of man is laid low by the omnipotent power of God.

X. The Seven Last Bowls of the Wrath of God (15:1–16:21)

A. The Song of Moses and the Lamb (15:1–4). Unannounced and with no introduction, seven angels appear (15:1). John calls it a great and marvelous sign, just as he called the woman clothed with the sun (12:1). He does not say how he knows the angels have the seven last plagues. Interestingly this scene is reenacted, somewhat differently, in the next vision (15:5–8) where the seven angels come out of the temple and are given the seven bowls of wrath. These are the last plagues because with them the end of the age arrives (see the similar statements in 10:7 and 15:8). John was not certain but what he saw looked like a perfectly undisturbed sea that reflected light upwards with a crowd of people standing around the edges (15:2). We may probably identify this sea with the glassy sea before the throne which reflected the seven burning lamps (4:5–6). The crowd is identified as those who had triumphed over the Beast, his image, and his number (666). Most probably they are the martyrs mentioned in 12:11 and 13:7–10. The martyrs are given harps with which to extol God (15:3; see 14:2–3) and they do so as did Moses following the parting of the sea (Exod. 14:29–15:18). It is called Moses' song because it models on what he sang in praise of God commemorating God's victory over the Egyptians and the gods of Egypt (Exod. 12:12), but it is, even more, the Lamb's song because it commemorates his victory over all the evil forces of the world and every form of idolatry. In the form of a loose paraphrase of what Moses sang, the song is a collection of heartfelt sentiments drawn from the Old Testament. The martyrs sing of the marvelous deeds of God (see Pss. 105:5; 111:2; 139:14). The power of God is praised as an encouragement to his people (Amos 4:13; Rev. 1:8; 4:8; 11:17; 16:7, 14; 19:6, 15; 21:22). God's justice and fidelity are praised (Deut. 32:4; Ps. 145:17; Rev. 16:5, 7; 19:2). The song continues in words closely paralleling Jeremiah 10:7 stressing the sovereign and universal rule of God over all the earth. All nations will come and worship him (Pss. 22:29; 86:9; Isa. 19:21; 66:23; Rev. 21:22–24).

B. The seven angels with the seven last plagues (15:5–8). John sees a vision of the heavenly counterpart of the earthly tabernacle (see Exod. 38:21; Num. 10:11). The last time the temple was opened to John he saw the ark of the covenant (Rev. 11:19), signifying God's faithfulness. This time it is opened, but we are not told what John saw. Rather, he focuses his attention on the seven angels with the seven plagues as they emerge wearing shining linen garments with golden sashes. The angels are assigned the task of pouring out the wrath of God from the golden bowls they were given. In the Old Testament the glory of God was symbolized by clouds of smoke (Exod. 19:18; Isa. 6:4; Ezek. 10:4). Here the smoke shows that God, in all of his power and glory, is present. The exit of the angels and the smoke of God's presence signaled that an unalterable chain of events had now been set in motion. Similar things had occurred in Israel's early history (Exod. 40:34–35; 1 Kings 8:10–11; 2 Chron. 5:13–14).

C. Pouring out of the seven bowls of the wrath of God (16:1–21). The temple is mentioned sixteen times in Revelation as a somewhat elastic but profound symbol. It is acknowledged to be God's temple (3:12; 11:1, 19) and in a sense, the very center of heaven, the place where God's redeemed people worship him day and night (7:15). The symbol enlarges to include the redeemed of God as part of that temple ("pillars" [3:12]), as though the temple would not be complete without the worshiping community being a part of it. On the other hand, God and the Lamb are the temple and no temple is needed because of that (21:22). God's will is done from out of the temple (14:15, 17; 15:6) and his faithfulness is always on display there (11:19). God's glory fills the temple (15:8) and from it God's mighty commands are uttered (16:1). The loud voice that resounds through the heavens is the voice of God himself who is now bringing history to an end with the seven last plagues upon the earth.

Perhaps it is troubling to read so much of God's wrath (16:1) in Revelation, but four things must be remembered. First, God's wrath and judgment are not arbitrary, but are always in response to man's sin. God takes no delight in the death of the wicked, but the wages of sin is death (Rom. 6:23). Second, judgment comes only after every other avenue has been exhausted. God sends blessings, prophets, warnings, preliminary testings, short-term judgments—all before the final wrath appears. An example of this in the Old Testament can be found in Amos 4:6–12. God tried everything but because Israel would not return to him, he went out to meet them—in judgment. Third, God's nature does not change in the exercise of his wrath. God is love (1 John 4:16) even when he must pass judgment upon the wayward peoples of the earth. Fourth, in all of this, ample opportunity to repent is given (see Rev. 16:9, 11; Jer. 35:17). That people did not do this is testimony to the deep-seated nature of the human predicament and our bias toward evil. But God cannot be faulted. All day long he stretches out his hand to a disobedient and obstinate people (Isa. 65:2; Rom. 10:21).

The first angel pours out his bowl (Rev. 16:2) and a plague of ugly and painful sores afflicts those who refused to worship God. Note carefully that only those people who had the mark of the beast and who had worshiped his image were stricken by the judgment. This plague parallels the sixth plague on Egypt during Moses' day (Exod. 9:9–12) and corresponds to the curse pronounced upon disobedience later (Deut. 28:35). In significant ways all seven of these bowls of wrath parallel the situation just prior to Israel's exodus from Egypt. In both places the purpose of God is to effect positive changes for good, judgment falls on the evildoers, God's people are protected from the worst of it, God's mighty power is displayed, and the rebellious refuse to listen and harden their hearts, thus bringing further judgment on themselves.

Next, the second angel pours out his bowl (Rev. 16:3) and the sea turns to blood and every living thing in it dies. This is reminiscent of the first plague upon Egypt when the Nile was turned to blood (Exod. 7:17–21). Similar judgments have already been mentioned in Revelation (8:8–9; 11:6) but there the results were partial, with only a third of the sea being affected and a third of the sea creatures dying.

Here the effects are catastrophic and total. Every living thing in the sea dies.

Next, the third angel pours out his bowl (16:4). In this vision John sees the judgment, but is also given a rationale for the judgment, as well as a heavenly ratification of it. When the bowl of wrath is poured out it strikes the rivers and springs, turning them into blood. This is a calamitous event, as no other source of drinking water exists in that part of the world, except the very occasional rains. The justice and holiness of God are extolled by the angel of the waters (16:5). Here, again, God's judgments are shown not to be arbitrary (see 16:1). God is just in doing this, and holy in all his works. The rationale for God's judgment here is retribution for the killing of the prophets and the saints of God (16:6). Isaiah prophesied that such would happen (Isa. 49:26) and Jesus pointed out that the blood of the prophets would be extracted from those responsible for their death (Luke 11:47–51).

Verse 7 is a curious statement, but could mean just what it says—the altar utters its voice in praise of God who executes true and just judgments. The altar covered the souls of the martyrs who cried out "How long?" (6:9–10) and provided the fire that was thrown on the earth in judgment, in partial response to that anguished cry (8:3–5). So now it is fitting that the altar affirm the justice and righteousness of the judgment that came. It could mean, however, that the voice was heard to be coming from the vicinity of the altar, in which case it was probably the voices of the martyrs that were heard.

In 16:8 the fourth angel pours out his bowl. In this plague the sun intensifies its heat and scorches the earth with fire. In the ninth Egyptian plague the sun is darkened and a gloomy pall falls over the face of the earth (Exod. 10:21–23), similar to the other plagues that strike the sun in Revelation (6:12; 8:12). Here the opposite happens and the sun's heat is intensified and multitudes fall from sunstroke. The sun that had been created good and was a source of life to all (indeed, falsely worshiped as a god by some pagans) now becomes a mortal enemy and a dispenser of inescapable judgment. As was the case in earlier visions (9:20–21; 11:7; 14:6–7), God offered a chance to repent but it was refused (16:9). John notes that God has "control over the plagues," a somewhat paradoxical idea. John's point, however, is not to identify God with the inherent evil in the plagues, but to show that nothing, not even plagues and evil, can operate except by God's permission. Since God is good, good ultimately will result (Rom. 8:28).

In 16:10 the fifth angel pours out his bowl. The throne of the beast and his kingdom (i.e., the source of evil's power and its exercise) was attacked and everything was plunged into darkness, as was the case in the ninth plague in Egypt (Exod. 10:21–22). The darkness carried a supernatural terror in it that intensified the agony of the already suffering people, but they continued in their evil ways and refused to repent. Evil has reached that height of madness where even a way out is rejected.

Next, the sixth angel pours out his bowl (Rev. 16:12). With the sixth bowl comes a preparation for the great day of the Lord prophesied in the Old Testament. The great river Euphrates dries up and opens the way for the armies of the east, which symbolize the enemies of God. They come with demonic power, poured forth from the mouths of the dragon, the beast, and the false prophet, working devilish miracles and deceiving the rulers of the earth. The false prophet is probably another name for the second beast. This is the first mention of him in Revelation, but he reappears later to receive his eternal judgment (19:20; 20:10).

Verse 15 portrays the unexpectedness of Christ's second coming as a thief who appears in the night (see also 3:3; 22:20). Both Paul (1 Thess. 5:2, 4) and Peter (2 Pet. 3:10) also use this figure. A special blessing is pronounced on the one who stays awake, a common expression relating to the end times (Matt. 24:42–44; 25:13; Mark 13:33–37; Luke 12:39–40; 1 Thess. 5:4–6; Rev. 3:2–3). "Keeps his clothes" (Rev. 16:15) is another figure of speech relating to the end times. To be properly clothed meant to be acceptable to the Lord (Zech. 3:3–5; Matt. 22:11–13).

The place where the battle will take place is named Armageddon (Rev. 16:16), which is a translation of a Hebrew word of uncertain derivation and meaning. The valley of Esdraelon, "by the waters of Megiddo," is where Israel won a decisive victory (Judg. 5:19). Zechariah prophesies weeping near Megiddo when the Messiah is acknowledged (Zech. 12:11). Ezekiel sees great slaughter on the mountains of the Lord in his vision of the end (Ezek. 38:8–21; 39:2, 4, 17). John synthesized this background to symbolize the place where the last great battle between good and evil would be fought. He returns to this theme in a triumphant note in 19:11–21.

Verse 17 shows the seventh angel pouring out his bowl. The seventh bowl signals the end. God's voice is heard coming from the temple (see 16:1) and directly from the throne of God itself (i.e., his seat of power and authority), saying, "It is done." Just as Jesus cried out, "It is finished" (John 19:30) when our salvation was accomplished, so God calls out, "It is done" when the end of the age arrives where salvation and judgment will be ultimately accomplished (see also 21:6). Intense noise and cosmic disorder accompany the arrival of the end (see 6:12–17 for similar events). The "great city" (16:19) is identified later with the woman riding on the scarlet beast who rules over the kings of the earth, that is, Rome (17:18; see also 18:10, 16, 19). In 11:8 the great city is Jerusalem, but there it is symbolically called Sodom and Egypt, which symbolize depravity and defeat. It is unlikely that Jerusalem is meant here in 16:19. Rome, the symbol of all evil power allied against God, is seen as judged, fallen, and in ruins. The second flying angel foretold its fall (14:8) and God gave it the cup filled with his wrath. The earth has become a shaken, reeling ruin. Nothing keeps its proper place—mountains collapse, islands scatter like leaves in the wind, hailstones the size of boulders fall. Still, in the midst of this, men continue to curse God rather than repent (16:20–21). Chapters 17 and 18 will describe Babylon's fall in detail.

XI. The Fall of Rome Predicted (17:1–18:24)

A. Destruction of the woman on the beast (17:1–18). In 14:8 "Babylon the Great" makes the nations drunk with the wine of her adulteries and falls into ruin. In 16:19 the great city collapses as God judges her. Here Babylon is the great prostitute who sits on seven hills (17:9) and is the leading city on earth (17:18). That "Babylon" should be chosen as the code name for the city of Rome is understandable, since it was the destroyer of God's people in the past. Also, Babylon of old was destroyed for its sins, thus pointing the way prophetically to the fall of the new "Babylon," drunk as it now was with the sins of the earth. Calling the city a prostitute continues the Old Testament imagery of referring to false worship as adultery. The prostitute "sits on many waters," a reference drawn from Jeremiah 51:13 which describes the earlier Babylon and predicts her ruin, just as the doom of Rome is predicted here in 17:1, 16.

John then finds himself carried away "in the Spirit" (see also 1:10; 4:2; 21:10) to the desert to watch the destruction of the prostitute unfold. There he sees a woman sitting on a scarlet beast which has seven heads and ten horns. It is covered with blasphemous names. The blasphemous names are probably a reference to the cult of Caesar that had arisen by John's time whereby the Roman emperors claimed to be divine. The description of Rome's garments indicates its royalty and opulence. Every imaginable luxury was indulged in by the insatiable appetite of Rome, as she extracted the last ounce out of her subjects (see also 18:11–17). Tyre of old was described in similar terms (Ezek. 28:13) and a similar fate was predicted and occurred to her (Ezek. 28:18–19). The golden cup in the woman's hand holds filth and abomination by which she intoxicated the rulers of the world (Rev. 14:8; 18:3). A mystery surrounds the rule of Babylon (17:5). John has the mystery partially explained to him (17:7–8) as having to do with seemingly miraculous events that surround the exercise of Rome's power. Rome's true nature is now seen. She is driven to maddened intoxication at the sight of the guiltless blood she has shed (17:6; see also 16:6; 18:24). Nero persecuted many believers. In John's day Domitian also persecuted the church. Subsequent history showed that many Roman emperors sought to exterminate the faith by ruthless persecution, as has been the practice of godless empires from that day to this and will be until the end comes (Matt. 24:9–14).

John does not understand what the extraordinary vision meant and has it explained to him (Rev. 17:7). The angel's explanation draws on the earlier vision of John, which in part was derived from the Book of Daniel. The beast is from the abyss and goes to destruction. The abyss is the dwelling-place of every evil thing (Luke 8:31) and from it ascends the destructive plague of Revelation 9:2–11, whose leader was called "the destroyer" (9:11), as well as the beast who persecutes God's prophetic servants (11:7) and carries the sin-laden prostitute. It is the same beast as the beast from the sea (13:1–10). It "once was, now is not, and will come up out of the Abyss" (17:8). Revelation 17:11 tells us this is an eighth king, part of an earlier group of seven kings, who will not prevail but is destined for destruction. According to 17:8 he "yet will come." The angel thought he was explaining the mystery, but most commentators agree that he only compounded the mystery by making it even more opaque. It is possible that the images here derive from a rumor current at that time that Nero (who was dead) had not really died, but was only apparently dead. Somehow he was being kept alive by the forces of evil and would return someday as an evil world ruler. This would make him one of the seven earlier kings, but also an eighth, that is, a new ruler in his own right and different from the seven. The precise meaning of all this is no longer clear to us, but two fundamental points stand out sharply: (1) Evil will organize itself against God and his saints, and from seeming defeat it will rise to do evil again; (2) the beast will go to his destruction—evil will not win. The Lamb will overcome the beast and his allies because he is Lord of lords and King of kings (17:14; 19:16–21). Those whose names are not written in the book of life (i.e., the unbelievers) will believe the lying wonders done by the beast (2 Thess. 2:7–10). When one refuses to believe the truth, just about any convincing or startling lie will do.

The angel continues his explanation in 17:9. The seven heads of the beast from the sea (13:1), the dragon in the heavens (12:3), and the beast that carries the woman are the seven hills of Rome. They represent the place where evil reigns. They also represent the rulers in that place of evil—"They are also seven kings" (17:9). Any attempt to identify exactly which emperors are intended is doomed to failure, because we do not have the necessary information. Some have suggested that because the Nero rumor lies behind this we ought to start there. Thus figured the five who are fallen would be Nero, Galba, Otho, Vitellum, and Vespasian. The "one [who] is" would be Titus and the one who "has not yet come" would be Domitian (17:10). Nero would then be the one "who once was, and now is not, [and] is an eighth king" (17:11). Other commentators are inclined to see kingdoms, rather than kings, and suggest that Egypt, Assyria, Babylonia, Persia, and Greece are the five that are fallen, Rome is the "sixth," extant in John's day, and the seventh will come after the fall of Rome. One cannot speak with any certainty on these things, however.

Equally unclear is who these kings are (17:12). They are yet to come, will rule for only a short time ("one hour"), will have authority, will make common cause with the beast, and will make war against the Lamb (17:12–14). Whether they are in some way to be identified with the seven kings (or kingdoms) just mentioned or are separate is not clear. Nevertheless, all of their activities will be futile because the Lamb will overcome them as King of kings and Lord of lords. This identification of the Lamb with God is the clearest possible statement of the early church's belief in the full deity of Christ (see also 1 Tim. 6:15; Titus 2:13; Rev. 19:16). The New Testament often describes Christ's servants as called (Rom. 1:6; 8:28, 30; 1 Cor. 1:24; Jude 1), the elect or chosen (Matt. 24:22, 24, 31; Mark 13:20, 22, 27; Luke 18:7; Rom. 8:33; 2 Tim. 2:10; Titus 1:1), and faithful (Eph. 1:1; Col. 1:2; Rev. 2:10, 13).

The use of "waters" in Revelation 17:15 to symbolize peoples is also found in the Old Testament (Jer. 47:1–3). Here it refers to the initial description of the woman on the beast as it was found in 17:1. In 17:16–18 the images both blend together and split apart. The woman is the city (v. 18) but so is the beast (v. 9), making the beast and the prostitute one. However, the beast, seen as the people ruled by the prostitute, can act independently, making the beast and the prostitute separate ideas. In these verses the beast (as peoples ruled) turn on the prostitute (the ruler) and tear her to pieces, smash her to ruin, devour her flesh, and burn her to ashes. There are two important points here. First, notice how evil turns upon itself and becomes self-destructive in the end. Being destructive by nature, it will destroy anything, even itself, when there is nothing else to destroy. Second, notice how evil can be used to accomplish God's purposes (17:17). God's rule stands supreme over all the acts of men and angels. Even if we intend things to be evil, God can produce good from them (Gen. 50:20; Rom. 8:28). This should be a comfort to us all. "Behind a frowning providence, God hides a smiling face," as William Cowper said. God is good, his intentions are good, his will and plans are good, and his actions are good. Evil can never stop God's good from being done, and in its own peculiar way evil only cooperates in the accomplishing of God's good will.

B. Fall of Babylon the great (18:1–24). If Ezekiel 43:1–5 forms the background of this angelic appearance, then what we have is a theophany, an appearance of God (or Christ) himself. That was the case for Ezekiel. If John does not have this in mind then an exceptional angel of extraordinary splendor and power has appeared in order to pronounce judgment on Rome. The words in Revelation 18:2 echo those of the second angel in 14:8 as it flew through the heavens. Isaiah received a vision of Babylon's fall in the Old Testament (Isa. 13:1–22) and John's words here closely parallel some of the ideas found there (see esp. Rev. 18:19–21). Jeremiah also predicted the fall of Babylon using words much like Isaiah's and John's (Jer. 50:39; 51:37). In words already spoken the sins of Rome are reiterated (Rev. 18:3; see 14:8; 17:2). John makes it clear that judgment has fallen because of the sins committed. An additional reason is given for Rome's fall—greed (18:3). The exploitation of the world's peoples to satisfy Rome's own insatiable desires, with merchants growing rich through the misery of the poor, cried out to God for judgment (see also Amos 3:13–15).

Another voice from heaven warns the believers to depart from the city in order to avoid its judgment (Rev. 18:4). Similar admonitions were given to the people in Babylon of old before its fall (Isa. 48:20; Jer. 51:6–9, 45, 50). "Her sins are piled up to heaven" (Rev. 18:5) is a metaphor used in the Old Testament of something done in excess (Jer. 51:9). The justice of God gives back to Rome what she gave to others (Rev. 18:6), and more, as was the case with Babylon of old (Jer. 50:15, 29). Rome's boast that it would rule forever and never be forsaken is shown to be as hollow as the boasts of ancient Babylon. John uses words in 18:7 taken from Isaiah 47:5–9 to emphasize this. Rome's utter ruin is described as a vast conflagration (Rev. 18:8; see also 17:6). Fire is a common metaphor for total destruction (Matt. 18:8–9; Mark 9:43–48; Luke 3:17; 2 Thess. 1:7; 2 Pet. 3:7–12; Jude 7; Rev. 20:9–10, 14–15), and is reserved for the enemies of God (Isa. 26:11). The kingdoms of this world have power and Rome ruled over them all (Rev. 17:18; 18:10), yet God is mightier still. John wants us to remember this when we are tempted to give in to the threats and intimidations of the world. In the end God will judge his enemies in the world "with everlasting destruction" (2 Thess. 1:9).

Those who shared Rome's power and wealth are appalled at her ruin, not out of sympathy but terror. Rome was their protector; if the mighty are fallen, what might happen to them? The picture painted by John is drawn from Old Testament prophecy (Ezek. 26:15–18). Rome's fall will be sudden, unexpected, and catastrophic (Rev. 18:10). No one could have predicted that such magnificence and might could collapse so utterly, but it was destined to be.

A careful study of the list of the worldwide commodities traded by Rome shows that they came from places as far away as India, China, Egypt, Arabia, and Africa (Rev. 18:11–15). No extravagances were missing. Slavery was a terrible and degrading thing in antiquity (18:13), as in any age. God alone is the creator and owner of all that is, especially human beings. That traffic should be made in human beings is unconscionable in his sight. In this regard Rome reached the limits of degradation. Such arrogance cried out for judgment and the wrath of God was poured out in double measure (18:6). The lamentation continues with an elaboration of Rome's great wealth and luxury and a second observation that she was dashed from the heights of power to the rubble of destruction in the blink of an eye (18:16–17). The dirge continues as the sea captains add their lamentations to those of the merchants (18:19). In typical ancient Near Eastern fashion they are pictured as throwing dust on their heads (Josh. 7:6; Lam. 2:10; Ezek. 27:30). It might seem inappropriate for the people of God to rejoice over Rome's fall (Rev. 18:20) but this must be seen as part of the larger picture. It is not the agony of Rome's fall that is extolled, but God who judges righteously. God is being vindicated, as are his saints. Similar rejoicing attended the fall of Babylon in the Old Testament (Jer. 51:48).

Next a mighty angel picks up a boulder and throws it into the sea to signify destruction of the city of Rome. After a long message on the fall of Babylon in his day, Jeremiah was told to take his message, tie a stone around it, and cast it into the Euphrates River (Jer. 51:63). Then he was to say, "So will Babylon sink to rise no more because of the disaster I will bring upon her. And her people will fall" (51:64). Thus ended the Babylon of old; thus will end the Roman Babylon of John's day.

In words echoing Isaiah's lament over the fallen earth (Isa. 24:6–13), John now foresees the desolations that will strike Rome where all normal human life has ceased—musicians, workmen, merchants, young married couples, millers—all are gone forever and replaced by melancholy silence. Babylon of old was renowned for its astrology and magic, which brought down the judgment of God upon it then (Nah. 3:4–5). So now the beguilement of Rome that led the nations astray brought ruin once again (Rev. 18:23), demonstrating what happens in the end to the nation that forgets God. The third angel poured out his bowl of wrath upon the earth for shedding the blood of the saints (16:6). Here Rome is used to epitomize that violence (17:6). As Babylon was called a city filled with blood, justly deserving punishment (Jer. 51:49; Nah. 3:1), so Rome, typifying such brutality, will be held accountable for all the blood shed on all the earth.

XII. The Return of Christ in Glory (19:1–21)

A. The multitude of heaven rejoices (19:1–10). John has just witnessed the destruction of the earthly center of all satanic activity, where the beast, the dragon, and the false prophet found easy access to the world. Chapters 17 and 18 summarize the downfall of evil on earth and the vindication of God. John has seen this depicted earlier with the opening of the sixth seal (6:12–17), the blowing of the seventh trumpet (11:15–18), the casting of Satan out of heaven (12:10), the harvesting of the earth (14:14–20), and the pouring out of the seventh bowl (16:17–21). Now the quintessence of evil is gone—the prostitute on the beast, Babylon the Great, drunk with the blood of the saints. In chapter 19 the last act of the historical and cosmic drama is played out yet again, for the last time, ushering in the age of gold toward which all the tear-filled eyes of all ages have looked with such eager longing. Their look was not in vain. The King of kings and Lord of lords is just over the horizon, riding on his white horse of victory ready to bring this sin-weary age to a close.

Chapter 19 begins with John hearing a vast roaring sound that crystallizes in his ear as a shout that fills the heavens, coming from the vast multitude of God's redeemed people. It is the age-old word of triumph, praise, and adoration—"Hallelujah!" It means "Praise the Lord" in Hebrew and is found throughout the Psalms (see Pss. 111:1; 112:1; 113:1, 9; 117:1; 146:1, 10; 147:1, 20; 148:1, 14; 149:1, 9; 150:1, 6). It occurs only four times in the New Testament, all in this triumphant chapter (19:1, 3, 4, 6). It is as though the note of triumph is reserved until the end when God fully exercises his rule on earth. Salvation, glory, power, and justice are ascribed to God as the essence of his rule as he deals with earth. With the judgment of the great prostitute, the day of God's vengeance has arrived. Vengeance belongs only to God (Deut. 32:35; 2 Sam. 22:47–48; Ps. 94:1; Isa. 34:8; 63:4; Jer. 46:10; 51:11; Mic. 5:15; Rom. 12:19; Heb. 10:30). He will deal with evil and the wrongdoer with justice and righteousness. Human beings could not be trusted with such an awesome responsibility. In words reminiscent of Isaiah's judgment pronounced upon Edom (Isa. 34:10), John pictures the smoke of Babylon being an everlasting reminder of the fate that awaits those who choose to rebel against God (Rev. 19:3; see also 14:11).

Now the twenty-four elders and the four living creatures join in the chorus of hallelujahs and worship God while those who reverence God are commanded to praise him (19:4–5).

In the Old Testament it was common for Israel to be spoken of as God's wife or betrothed (Isa. 54:1–6; Jer. 31:32; Ezek. 16:8; Hos. 2:16–20) and this idea was carried over into the New Testament where the church becomes the bride of Christ (Matt. 25:1–10; Mark 2:19; John 3:28–29; 2 Cor. 11:2; Eph. 5:25, 32). The wedding of the Lamb is the union of Christ with the believers in eternal love and fidelity. The image of a wedding supper (Rev. 19:9) with all of its joy, hope, and promise is a beautiful image that describes the union of Christ with his people in the glory of heaven. John continues the imagery of the marriage and pictures the bride wearing fine linen (Rev. 19:7–8). The mention of fine linen or robes occurs often in Revelation (3:5, 18; 4:4; 6:11; 7:9, 14; 19:14) and here John interprets it as meaning the righteous acts of the saints. God's people are not those who *speak* about living lives that are pleasing to him, but those who are actually *doing* it. It is not those who say "Lord, Lord" who enter the kingdom of God, but those who do God's will on earth (Matt. 7:21).

To accept the wedding invitation (Rev. 19:9) is to participate in all the future glories of heaven and share in the special beatitude pronounced upon those who come. So overwhelmed is John that he offers his heartfelt adoration to the bringer of the message. John is forbidden to do this (19:9), both here and later (22:8–9). Although the worship of angels presented a temptation to some in the early church (Col. 2:18–19), it was strictly forbidden. Christ is the head of all things, having total supremacy over the entire created order (Col. 1:15–18). John is told, "Worship God!"

B. Destruction of evil by the rider on the white horse (19:11–21). In Revelation 4:1 John saw a door open in heaven. Now he sees all of heaven open up before him, with Jesus Christ upon the white horse, surrounded by the armies of heaven, ready to crash forth and annihilate the beast, the false prophet, and all who followed after them in their evil ways. He is faithful and true in his justice and judgment (see also 3:14; 15:3; 16:7; 19:2). A picture is now drawn of the conquering Christ with imagery taken, in large part, from John's earlier vision (1:12–16). The many crowns symbolize complete rule. Christ possesses some names that are open to public understanding. Here in 19:13 he is called "the Word of God" (see also John 1:1). He is called "King of kings and Lord of lords" (19:16; see 1 Tim. 6:15). But Christ also possesses an undisclosed name, known only to him (Rev. 19:12), perhaps relating to his role as Savior. Next a sharp sword comes from his mouth (Isa. 49:2); he strikes down the earth (Isa. 11:4; 2 Thess. 2:8); he rules with an iron scepter (Ps. 2:9; Rev. 2:27; 12:5); he treads out the fury of God (Rev. 14:19–20). Then the true identity of Christ is revealed (19:16). He is nothing less than the almighty God himself who rules over all (Rev. 1:5; see comments on 19:6).

In words closely approximating Ezekiel 39:17–20, John now hears an angel call together the birds of prey to feast upon the carnage found on earth (Rev. 19:17–18). In a striking metaphor John suggests that everyone is called to take part in a supper. One may attend the wedding supper of the Lamb (19:9) where all will be joy, glory, and blessing. For those who refuse, yet another supper awaits: those who reject God will become what is eaten, and the loathsome vultures of the sky will swoop down without mercy to pick apart the rotten flesh that lies unburied on the ground. The birds of prey make no distinction—kings, generals, mighty men, slave or free—all have become food to glut their insatiable appetites (19:18).

The beast who collaborates with the kings of the earth (19:19) is the woman who was judged (17:18) and the first beast that John saw (13:1–8). It represents the godless governments of the world. The false prophet (19:20) was first mentioned in 16:13 and is probably to be identified with the second beast John saw (13:11–18) and represents apostate religion. Together they conspire to overthrow God, Christ, and his saints on earth, through the Antichrist who embodies all the evil that is in the world. The insane rebellion does not succeed. The beast and the false prophet are cast into the lake of fire in fulfillment of Daniel's words (Dan. 7:11). They will be joined by the devil, whose time of judgment has not yet arrived (Rev. 20:10), as well as all of death, hades, and those whose names are not written in the book of life (20:14–15). The remainder of the armies that rose up against God were slain by the sword of Christ's mouth. In response to the angel's call the birds of the air gather over this melancholy scene to perform the gruesome task allotted to them.

XIII. The Millennial Reign of Christ (20:1–15)

A. The thousand-year reign (20:1–6). John had just seen Christ and the armies of heaven defeat the evildoers on earth and mete out punishment to the earthly leaders of the rebellion against God, the beast and the false prophet. He now sees the source of evil, Satan himself, bound and cast into the abyss to await his final judgment. In 20:2 he is identified as the serpent (see also 12:9; Gen. 3:1–7; 2 Cor. 11:3), the dragon (see 12:7–9), the devil (see Matt. 4:1, 5, 8, 11; 13:39; 25:41; John 8:44; Acts 10:38; Heb. 2:14; 1 Pet. 5:8; Jude 9), and Satan (see Matt. 4:10; 16:23; Mark 1:13; Luke 10:18; 1 Cor. 5:5; 2 Cor. 2:11; 11:14; 2 Thess. 2:9). In Jesus' day the demons begged not to be sent back to the abyss (Luke 8:31). Also, it was a place of gloomy confinement (2 Pet. 2:4). From it came the locust plague (Rev. 9:1–3) and the beast who killed the two prophets of God (11:8). Into it Satan is thrown and bound in chains to keep him from deceiving the nations, which was his self-appointed task (12:9). He will be released for a short time before his final judgment. The imprisonment of Satan gives the earth a thousand-year period of respite from evil (20:2, 3, 5, 6, 7). There have been many views as to exactly what this means, as well as much controversy throughout the history of the church. For some, the amillennialists, the thousand years is a symbolic number representing the whole church age, from Christ's resurrection to his second advent, during which Satan's activity is restricted by the grace of God and the preaching of the gospel. Others, the premillennialists, view the thousand years as a historical period of time *following* Christ's second advent during which the prophecies in the Old Testament concerning an age of bliss (e.g., Isa. 35) will take place. All things being considered, the premillennial view seems closest to what John had in mind.

John sees a picture of judgment taking place (Rev. 20:4), but only believers are taking part. Paul speaks of this as appearing before the judgment seat of Christ (2 Cor. 5:1–10; see also Matt. 16:27; 1 Cor. 3:12–15; Eph. 6:8; Col. 3:24; Rev. 22:12). Here thrones are mentioned, indicating that many people are involved in what is taking place. Special mention is made of the martyrs for Christ ("those who have been beheaded") and of their resurrection to life. They had been steadfast unto the end, having refused to worship the beast and his image. For this they paid the ultimate price. Part of their reward was to rule with Christ for the thousand years of Satan's imprisonment. John now generalizes on the resurrection that takes place before the thousand-year reign (Rev. 20:5). He calls it the first resurrection to distinguish it from the second death, which also includes a resurrection, but that is a resurrection to damnation (20:11–15; see also John 5:28–29). Jesus called it the resurrection of the righteous (Luke 14:14), and Paul, in making his case before Felix, argued that a dual resurrection, one for the righteous and one for the wicked, was common knowledge (Acts 24:14–15). The rest of the dead (i.e., the unbelievers) were not resurrected until the thousand years were finished. A special beatitude is pronounced upon those who take part in this resurrection (Rev. 20:6). This is one of a number of such blessings found in Revelation (1:3; 14:13; 16:15; 19:9; 20:6; 22:7, 14). Their special blessing is that they are protected from the second death, they are priests of God and Christ, and they reign with Christ for the thousand years.

B. Satan's doom (20:7–10). At the end of the thousand years, Satan is given freedom to deceive the nations one last time. Such is the inexplicable and intractable nature of evil that Satan is able to draw a large number after him from everywhere, that is, "the four corners of the earth," a common expression in the Bible (see Isa. 11:12; Ezek. 7:2; Rev. 7:1). John draws upon an extensive prophecy in Ezekiel 38–39 to picture the last battle on earth (Rev. 20:8). The rebellion is short-lived. God pours down fire upon them in judgment and they are consumed as the Book of Ezekiel predicts (20:9; Ezek. 38:22; 39:6; for "fire" see comments on Rev. 18:8). Satan is now eternally disposed of, never more to deceive the nations. He joins the beast and the false prophet in the fiery judgment, where they are tormented forever (20:10; see also Isa. 27:1; 30:33; Matt. 25:41; Rev. 14:10–11; 19:20).

C. The judgment at the great white throne (20:11–15). John's vision of the throne of God is so powerful that everything else is seen to fly from the presence of the almighty God who sits in judgment. Nothing can stand in his presence. Earth and sky have fled in terror, for the day of mercy has ended. Now only the judgment of God remains. Peter pictures the coming of this day as one where the heavens will disappear with a roar, the elements melt with fire, and everything be laid bare (2 Pet. 3:10). The rest of the dead (i.e., the unbelievers) are now brought back to life (Rev. 20:12; see comments on 20:5). Two books are opened: the book of life and the book of human deeds. The unbelieving dead are judged fairly on the basis of what they have done in life. This scene recalls Daniel's vision when he saw the throne of God, as court was seated and the books were opened (Dan. 7:9–10). Jesus pictured this as the separation of sheep from goats (Matt. 25:31–46). John reiterates what he has just said, emphasizing that all the dead are included. The sea (i.e., the unknown dead), death, hades—all the places where the dead may lurk undetected are now forced to give up their woeful contents to stand before the awesome throne of God (Rev. 20:13). The lake of fire becomes the final abode of all that is evil (20:14). The devil, the beast, the false prophet, those whose names were not found written in the book of life, and now death and hades are all consigned to the flames (20:15).

XIV. The Eternal New Order (21:1–22:6)

A. The new heaven and the new earth (21:1–8). After the manifold series of visions consisting of conflict, evil, judgment, and doom, John is now given a dazzling vision of the new order of things: "a new heaven and a new earth" (21:1). The prophet Isaiah looked beyond the judgment that was to fall upon his nation of Judah to a period of restoration when the former things would no longer be remembered and all things would be made new (Isa. 65:17; 66:22). Peter looked for the day when the old order would be burned up and replaced by the new (2 Pet. 3:13). Paul looked for this as well, but saw its beginnings in the work of Christ in the church and in the life of the believer (2 Cor. 5:17). In Israel's history the sea was always considered an ominous place (Job 38:3–11; Ps. 89:9, 10; Isa. 57:20) and the Israelites, in contrast to the Greeks or the Phoenicians, were not a seafaring people. In it dwelt the great monsters of the deep (see Rev. 13:1). John earlier saw Jerusalem as Sodom and Egypt, where our Lord was crucified (11:8). Now he sees it in all its splendor (Isa. 52:1), holy and new, coming down out of heaven from God. In the Old Testament God dwelt with his people indirectly, by way of the tabernacle and temple (Exod. 25:8–9; Lev. 26:11–12), but there was always the recognition that nothing could really contain God (2 Chron. 6:18). The prophets foresaw the time when God would be directly with his people (Ezek. 37:27; 48:35; Zech. 2:10). John sees that being established with the coming of the New Jerusalem (Rev. 21:3; see also v. 22). The presence of God banishes every form of evil, sorrow, suffering, and death. The old order with all of its limitations passed away. This too was foreseen by the prophets (Isa. 25:8; 35:10; 65:18–19; see also Rev. 7:17).

The work of God is always fresh and new (Rev. 21:5). When he steps into a life he wholly transforms it. God, in his sovereignty ("seated on the throne"), affirms that what John has been told is so (see also 19:9; 22:6). Then God says, "It is done" (21:6; see also 16:17). The phrase *to him who is thirsty I will give to drink* (21:6) does not contradict 7:16 where we are told we will never thirst again. In 7:16 the eternal satisfaction is stressed; here, the process of filling is stressed. The water of life is freely given as it flows from its unceasing supply (see also 22:1–3). Jesus spoke of this water of life (John 4:10, 13–14) as eternal life; here, God promises that those who drink of it will be victorious, inherit heaven, and be a child of God (21:7). A list follows of those who are not children of God (21:8). Several lists like this which characterize unbelievers are found in the New Testament (Rom. 1:28–32; 1 Cor. 6:9–10; Gal. 5:19–21; Rev. 22:15).

B. The New Jerusalem, the wife of the Lamb (21:9–27). One of the seven angels takes John to a high mountain (see Ezek. 40:2) where he could get a better view of the Lamb's wife. He had just seen this in 21:2, but there it was as part of the larger picture, which included the whole new heaven and new earth. Here it is the Holy City alone that occupies John's attention. He is "in the spirit" as at other times (1:10; 4:2; 17:3). God's glory is essentially himself (21:11). His presence is a glorious presence that can only be described in terms of magnificence and beauty. God's glory filled Israel's tabernacle and temple and the prophets promised the coming of God's glory to earth (Isa. 60:1–2, 19; Ezek. 43:2); the glory of the Lord attended Jesus' birth (Luke 2:9); Jesus will return to earth in the glory of his Father (Matt. 24:30; 25:31; Mark 8:38) because he *is* the glory of God (John 1:14; Heb. 1:3); God's glory fills heaven (Rev. 15:8); the praises of his redeemed people center around his glory (Rev. 4:9, 11; 5:12–13; 7:12; 19:1, 7); and the New Jerusalem shines with the glory of God (21:23). John draws upon Ezekiel's description of the ideal city of Jerusalem to describe the city of God (21:12; Ezek. 48:30–35), and the twelve tribes of Israel are written on the gates as representative of God's Old Testament people. A wall surrounds the city that has "twelve foundations" (Rev. 21:14) and the names of the twelve apostles of Christ are written there as representative of God's New Testament people, symbolizing the essential unity of God's people.

The angel had a rod of gold to measure the cubelike city and it was found to be 12,000 stadia (about 1400 miles) on every side. The wall was 144 (12×12) cubits high (NIV thick), that is, about 200 feet. The number twelve is used in all of these measurements to symbolize God's historical work with his people (e.g., twelve tribes of Israel, twelve apostles, twelve gates, twelve foundations, twelve angels on the gates, etc.). The beautiful gems in verses 19–20 are mixtures of blue, yellow, and green, and many of them adorned the breastplate of the priest in the Old Testament (Exod. 39:8–14). It is as though the city is one vast place of worship, fulfilling Isaiah's prophetic words that Jerusalem would be established in righteousness and built of jewels (Isa. 54:11–14). How else could someone describe heaven pictorally, except in lavish terms of fabulous wealth, dazzling color, and indescribable beauty? God is the city's light and the Lamb is its lamp (Rev. 21:23), emphasizing the equality of Christ with the Father. This too fulfills Isaiah's words (Isa. 24:23; 60:19–20). Echoing Isaiah's prophecies again, John describes the way in which the city's splendor is acknowledged (Rev. 21:24; see Isa. 60:3, 5, 11, 20). Such divine splendor excludes anything that is unworthy (Rev. 21:27; see comments on 21:8). The unworthy are those whose names are not in the Lamb's book of life (Rev. 3:5; 13:8; 17:8; 20:12, 15).

C. The river and the tree of life (22:1–6). God had said that anyone who was thirsty could drink of the water of life. John now sees that clear water flowing down through the city, filling the great golden street (see 21:12; see also Zech. 14:8). God was as good as his word. He said the water would be there and he and the Lamb provide it, flowing directly from the throne itself, lest anyone ever doubt the sufficiency of its supply. John now sees a single tree that somehow stands on both sides of the river yielding twelve fruits, one for each month of the year, with leaves to heal the nations (Rev. 22:2). This marvelous vision is an adaptation of Ezekiel 47:1–12. Ezekiel, too, saw a river, but rushing from the temple, surrounded by a great number of trees. "Fruit trees of all kinds will grow on both banks of the river. Their leaves will not wither, nor will their fruit fail. Every month they will bear, because the water from the sanctuary flows to them. Their fruit will serve for food and their leaves for healing" (Ezek. 47:12). For John it is a single tree of life, answering to what he had spoken of earlier as being in God's regained paradise (Rev. 2:7). The original paradise was lost because of sin, and flaming angels flashed their swords to keep the first fallen humans from reaching the tree of life in the original garden of God (Gen. 3:24). Now access to the tree is freely offered to anyone who wants it. Judgment is now lifted from the earth and the ancient curse removed (Rev. 22:3; see also Gen. 3:14–19). God's presence is forever within the city and his servants dwell secure (Zech. 14:11). Verse 4 fulfills Jesus' words in Matthew 5:8 and removes another aspect of the curse whereby no one was allowed to see God's face and live (Exod. 33:20). "His name . . . on their foreheads" (Rev. 22:4) marks believers out for God's own (see also 3:12; 7:3; 9:4; 14:1) and secures their redemption. The thousand-year reign is over (20:4, 6) and now the saints will reign forever (22:5). God's reign is eternal and the saints share in that. The angel affirms that God's words are true (22:6; see also 21:5) and announces that it will all take place soon.

XV. The Promise of Jesus' Return (22:7–21)

Jesus promises that he has not left us permanently, but will soon come again (Rev. 22:7; see also vv. 12, 20). Blessing is pronounced upon the one who keeps what is written in the book. John began the Book of Revelation this way (1:3). As before (19:10), John falls down to worship the angel, but is told to worship God alone (22:8–9).

The words given to John were not considered to be hidden words, but for the immediate use of God's people (22:10; cf. Dan. 8:26). The seemingly strange words in 22:11 echo Ezekiel 3:27; Daniel 12:10; and Revelation 13:10. John recognizes a certain constancy to some things. Some people have made the decision to practice wrong and have done it repeatedly. They have chosen to put themselves out of God's reach. On the positive side, other people have chosen to practice righteousness and holiness, and in the face of every pressure to do the opposite, they continue to do what is right, even if it means losing their lives.

Again Jesus promises quick deliverance (Rev. 22:12; see vv. 7, 20) and a generous reward. God spoke the same words in 22:13 (1:8; 21:6); Jesus speaks them here (see also 1:17). This represents a clear affirmation of the full deity of Jesus (see also 19:16).

Clean robes in 22:14 represent salvation and relate to the blessings of salvation that Christ has provided by his death and resurrection. In contrast to those who are clean are those who have chosen to continue to do wrong and be vile (22:15; see v. 11). A similar list appears in 21:8.

In 22:16 Jesus identifies himself as the source of this prophecy. Using words from the Old Testament, Jesus calls himself the "Root and the Offspring of David" (Isa. 11:1, 10) and the "bright Morning Star" (Num. 24:17). The words are for the churches.

In 22:17 the Spirit and the bride call out, "Come!" The wedding has come (19:7, 9), but the church on earth has not experienced the full reality of Christ's presence. That will be true only when Christ himself comes again in glory. Consequently, the bride cries out to her bridegroom, "Come!" As in 1:3 and 22:18, the hearers of the prophecy are mentioned. This probably indicates a public reading of the book in a church meeting of John's day. The water of life is an eternal blessing found in heaven itself, but it is also available now for anyone who wishes it. As God spoke through Isaiah, "Come, all you who are thirsty, come to the waters; and you who have no money, come, buy and eat" (Isa. 55:1), so now all are invited to accept the free offer of salvation in Christ.

Because the contents of this book are from God (Rev. 1:1–3; 22:16) and because God's words are faithful and true (19:9; 21:5; 22:6), they are not to be tampered with. To add or subtract from them would be to falsify what they have to say, and God excludes liars from the kingdom of God (21:8, 27; 22:15).

In response to Christ's saying that he is coming soon, the waiting church responds, "Amen. Come, Lord Jesus" (Rev. 22:20). This was apparently a liturgical response or a salutation in the early church (see 1 Cor. 16:22).

In spite of its unconventional style and content, the book closes conventionally (22:21). It was customary to pray that the grace of Christ be with those who read the book (1 Cor. 16:23; 2 Cor. 13:14; Gal. 6:18; Eph. 6:24; Phil. 4:23; Col. 4:18; 1 Thess. 5:28; 2 Thess. 3:18; 1 Tim. 6:21).

SELECT BIBLIOGRAPHY

Beasley-Murray, G. R. *The Book of Revelation.* New Century Bible Commentary. Grand Rapids: Eerdmans, 1981.

Caird, G. B. *The Revelation of St. John the Divine.* Harper's New Testament Commentaries. New York: Harper & Row, 1966.

Guthrie, D. *The Relevance of John's Apocalypse.* Exeter: Paternoster; Grand Rapids: Eerdmans, 1987.

Hendriksen, W. *More than Conquerors.* Grand Rapids: Baker, 1939.

Ladd, G. E. *A Commentary on the Revelation of John.* Grand Rapids: Eerdmans, 1972.

Morris, L. *The Revelation of St. John.* 2d ed. Grand Rapids: Eerdmans, 1987.

Mounce, R. H. *The Book of Revelation.* The New International Commentary on the New Testament. Grand Rapids: Eerdmans, 1977.

Walvoord, J. F. *The Revelation of Jesus Christ.* Chicago: Moody, 1972.

Senior copyeditor: Linda Triemstra
Copyeditors: Maria E. denBoer and Gary L. Knapp
Proofreaders: Tim Baker, Melissa J. Bartel, Marilyn S. Brannen, Norlan De Groot, Joy DuBois, Lillian Geldersma, Marilyn Gordon, Ruth K. Gray, John Iwema, June Joling, Alyson Kieda, Dawn J. Penning, Rose A. Pruiksma, Mike Rubingh, Winona Schneider, Mary Wenger, Nancy L. Wood, Jean M. Yeagle
Designer: Daniel J. Malda
Production assistant: Lisa Ramsey-Hershberger
Artist: Louise M. Bauer
Composition: Huron Valley Graphics, Ann Arbor, Michigan
Printing and binding: Arcata Graphics—Hawkins, Mt. Carmel, Tennessee